6000 CLASSIC SERMON ILLUSTRATIONS

6000 CLASSIC SERMON ILLUSTRATIONS

An Alphabetical Collection from Leaders and Writers of the Ages

BY

ELON FOSTER

Baker Books

A Division of Baker Book House Co.
Grand Rapids, Michigan 49516

Reprinted 1993 by

Baker Book House Company

P.O. Box 6287, Grand Rapids, Michigan 49516-6287

ISBN: 0-8010-3564-3

Printed in the United States of America

Previously published as

NEW CYCLOPAEDIA OF PROSE ILLUSTRATIONS, VOL. II

6,000 WINDOWS FOR SERMONS

and

6000 SERMON ILLUSTRATIONS

PREFACE

This is the second volume in an omnibus of classic sermon illustrations. This gives access to a treasury of illustrations so complete that a minister or teacher need not look in vain for some apt illustration or quotation with which to illumine or emphasize any subject he may wish to discuss.

Here are found the choicest of illustrations from the writing of hundreds of noted preachers, religious leaders, and writers of the ages. If some of the illustrations seem unfamiliar and outdated at first glance, thoughtful consideration will generally reveal them to be illustrative of some abiding truth, and readily usable through wise adaption.

The convenient alphabetical arrangement of the illustrations by subject represents the result of much careful study. This enables you to turn to the subject as to a word in a dictionary, and find a fitting illustration with similar ease and speed. A comprehensive index will guide you to additional illustrations on the topic of your interest listed under affiliated subjects.

The more you use and study this treasury of illustrations, the richer you will discover its content to be.

The Publishers

6000 CLASSIC SERMON ILLUSTRATIONS

6276. AARON, Character of. Aaron never appears so perfect a character as Moses. He was more a man of the times, subject to passing influences and prevailing tastes. He also lacked the burning enthusiasm of his meek, yet daring brother. Nevertheless, he must have possessed rare gifts to have been chosen his companion and fellow-laborer in that wonderful deliverance of the Children of Israel from Egypt, and in conducting them forty years through the wilderness to the Promised Land. Much more must he have possessed an elevation and purity of character far above his fellows, to have been chosen as the founder of the Jewish priesthood, the first to minister at the altar, and to represent a sacerdotal dynasty more glorious and immortal than the line even of David, or any succession of kings that ever filled a throne. *Headley.*

6277. ABEL, Prominence of. Abel is celebrated as the first martyr, and the first mortal to enter heaven. His blood was the first to cry for vengence. He was the first who received assurance of the acceptance of his offering, and the first believer in an atonement by blood of whom we have any record. Christ calls him "Righteous Abel." His faith was the first voice of reconciliation, and in six thousand years it has lost none of its influence.

6278. ABILITIES, Concentration of. Go out in the spring when the sun is yet far distant, and you can scarcely feel the influence of its beams, scattered as they are over the wide face of creation; but collect those beams to a focus, and they kindle up a flame in an instant. So the man that squanders his talents and his strength in many things will fail to make an impression with either; but let him draw them to a point, let him strike at a single object, and it will yield before him. *Anon.*

6279. ABILITIES, Cultivated. After a remarkable display of eloquence, in Parliament, by the famous Edmund Burke, his brother Richard was found in deep thought by a friend, who asked him its cause. He answered, "I have been wondering how Ned has contrived to mo-

nopolize all the talents of the family; but then again I remember when we were at play he was always at work."

6280. ABILITIES, Feeble. Be not discouraged because your talents number four rather than five, or one rather than two. Not the number but the use of talents fills the world with blessing. From a single dollar actively employed princely fortunes have sprung. The feeble shout of a tiny child has saved the thundering train from wreck, and snatched a hundred souls from death. In all lands the widows' mites have filled God's treasuries. He who will do nothing until he can do a great thing, will never do anything. *Dr. Geo. H. Whitney.*

6281. ABILITIES, Hindrances. How nimbly does that little lark mount up singing towards heaven in a right line! whereas the hawk, which is stronger of body and swifter of wing, towers up by many gradual compasses to his highest pitch. That bulk of body and length of wing hinder a direct ascent, and require the help both of air and scope to advance his flight; while the small bird cuts the air without resistance, and needs no outward furtherance of her motion. It is no otherwise with the souls of men in flying up to their heaven. Some are hindered by those powers which would seem helps to their soaring up thither: great wit, deep judgment, quick apprehension, send about men with no small labor, for the recovery of their own incumbrance; while the good affections of plain and simple souls raise them up immediately to the fruition of God. Why should we be proud of that which may slacken our way to glory? Why should we be disheartened with the small measure of that, the very want whereof may facilitate our way to happiness. *Salter.*

6282. ABILITIES, Wrecked. A poor man was digging in a garden, when he picked up an ancient coin. He called to a gentleman near, showed it to him, translated the Latin inscription, and gave the history of how the Romans came into that region. The gentleman was surprised to find a farm laborer so cultivated, and thought that it must be some fault that

9

had brought him to so low a position. Upon inquiry he found he had been educated at the university, had taken a degree, had been a clergyman; but had taken to drinking, was expelled from his church, became an outcast from society, and was now earning a pitiful living, digging the garden of a peasant for two-pence an hour. Thus the most brilliant abilities and finished culture may be wrecked by immorality and intemperance.

6283. ABRAHAM, Renown of. Abraham is one of the most renowned persons the world ever saw. Besides the conspicuous place he holds in the Bible history, he is introduced into the Koran of Mohammed, and is regarded by the Arabians as the father of their nation, and by the Jews as theirs. The ancient Persians pay him the highest honor, and think he was Zoroaster, as before their great teacher. In India, too, Abraham is honored by some sects as their distinguished ancestor. The people of Egypt, Chaldea, and Damascus acknowledge their obligations to this illustrious man. But what shall we say of the blessings which he received from God? His believing posterity have been multiplied as the stars of heaven. His venerable name is invested with immortal honor in the history of the Church and of the world,—second only to Him whose name is above every name. Canaan, the Land of Promise, was given to his natural posterity for fourteen centuries, as their peculiar inheritance. And, above all, from his loins the divine Savior in due time appeared in the flesh, to ransom, by His sufferings, death, resurrection, and glory, a multitude of immortal souls, whom no man can number. *Mackenzie.*

6284. ABSENCE, Mental. Thomas Aquinas, the angelic doctor of the thirteenth century, frequently forgot himself. Once when dining with King Louis IX., after a prolonged silence, he struck the table smartly, saying, "That is an overwhelming argument against the Manacheans." His superior rebuked him, and he apologized; but the King bade him give the argument. At another time, he was explaining a treatise on the Trinity, holding a candle in his fingers as he spoke, which burned down and scorched his fingers severely before his attention was aroused. He was summoned from his room to meet the Pope's legate and the Archbishop of Capua in the cloister, but on his way fell into a reverie and forgot his errand. Coming to himself, he apologized to his visitors, blaming his feebleness of mind for so slowly solving a theological difficulty. "Isaac Newton once asked a friend to dine with him, but forgetting the appointment, ordered dinner for but one. His guest came, and supposing the plate in the dining-room was for him, ate his dinner without interrupting the philosopher, and departed. Presently, Newton came into the dining room. 'I declare,' said he, 'if it were not for the empty plate, I should say that I had not dined.'"

6285. ABSENT, Faith in the. And cannot a child believe in an absent one? Why, is there not some such conversation as this going on in many a household in our country now?—"Mamma, where is papa?" "He is a long way off, in India." "What is he doing?" "Why, he is engaged in defending the country." "Did I ever see papa?" "Oh yes, my child, you saw him, but you were too young then to know him." "And what was papa like?" "Oh, when he was here, before he went, he was a very fine man; and he is a very loving man, and loves mamma very much, and he is always writing letters to mamma." "Well, mamma, I think I love papa too; I love him with all my heart." And do you not think there would be an influence upon that dear child's mind, flowing from mamma's lips with the very name of papa? And though we have never seen thee, O blessed Jesus, yet still it is true—"In whom, though now we see Him not, yet believing, we rejoice with joy unspeakable and full of glory." 1 Pet. 1: 8. *Dr. Davis.*

6286. ABSENT-MINDEDNESS, Notion of. Rufus Choate asked a witness whom he was cross-examining—"What would be his notion of absent-mindedness." "Well," said the witness, with a strong Yankee accent, "I should say that a man who thought he'd left his watch to hum, and took it out'n 'is pocket to see if he'd time to go hum and get it, was a leetle absent-minded."

6287. ABSTEMIOUSNESS, Example of. Melancthon wondered at Luther, who being such a strong healthy man, could live with taking so little food. "I have seen him," says Melancthon, "continue four days together without eating or drinking anything at all, and many days together to content himself with a little bread and one single herring."

6288. ABSTINENCE, Contrast of. An active temperance man was assailed, in a public place, by a drunkard, with the taunt, "There goes a teetotaler!" He retorted in hearing of the crowd, "There stands a drunkard! Three years ago he had a sum of $400; now he cannot produce a penny. I know he cannot; I challenge him to do it; for if he had a penny he would be at a public-house. There stands a drunkard, and here stands a teetotaler, with a purse full of money, honestly earned and carefully kept. There stands a drunkard! Three years ago he had a watch, a coat, shoes, and decent clothes; now he has nothing but rags upon him, his watch is gone, and his shoes afford free passage to the water. There stands a drunkard; and here stands a teetotaler, with a good hat, good shoes, good clothes, and a good watch, all paid for. Yes, here stands a teetotaler! And now, my friends, which has the best of it?" The chagrined drunkard slunk away, while the crowd cheered the temperance lecturer.

6289. ABSTINENCE, Economy of. An old man in an almshouse in Bristol stated that for sixty years he spent sixpence a day in drink, but was never intoxicated. A gentleman who heard this statement was anxious to ascertain how much this sixpence a day, put by every year at five per cent. compound interest, would amount to in sixty years. Taking out his pencil he began to calculate; putting down the first year's savings (365 sixpences) £9 2s. 6d., he added the interest, 9s. 1¼d., and thus went on year by year, until he found that in the sixtieth year the sixpence a day reached the startling sum of £3,225 16s. 8d. Judge of the old man's surprise when told that had he saved his sixpence a day, and allowed it to accumulate at compound interest, he might now have been worth the above sum; so that, instead of taking refuge in an almshouse, he might have comforted himself with a house of his own, costing £700, and fifty acres of land, worth £50 per acre, and have left the same as a legacy among his children and grandchildren!   *Temperance Anecdotes.*

6290. ABSTINENCE, Example of. Bishop Asbury was a guest of a family where brandy was placed on the table, and he was invited to partake, but he declined. The lady blushed, and said, "Bishop, I believe that brandy is good in its place." "So do I," said Mr. Asbury; "if you have no objection I will put it in its place:" so he put it in the old-fashioned cupboard in the corner of the room, saying, "That is the place, and there let it stay;" and there it did stay, never to be brought on the table again.

6291. ABSTINENCE, Excuse for. On the occasion of a dinner at the Bishop of Chester's, Hannah More urged Dr. Johnson to take a little wine. He replied, "I can't drink a little, child, and, therefore, I never touch it. Abstinence is as easy to me as temperance would be difficult." Many are ruined because they are destitute of the same courage.

6292. ABSTINENCE, Greeley's. Horace Greeley was once met at a railway depot by a red-faced individual, who shook him warmly by the hand. "I don't recognize you," said Mr. Greeley. "Why, yes, you must remember how we drank brandy and water together at a certain place." This amused the bystanders, who knew Mr. Greeley's strong temperance principles. "Oh, I see," replied Mr. Greeley, "you drank the brandy, and I drank the water." Mr. Greeley once wrote an account of a wine dinner, and said that the party had indulged in Heidsick and Champagne, these both being names for the same kind of wine. His associates laughed at his mistake, which they pointed out to him. "Did I write it so?" said he, with a good-natured smile. "Well, I reckon I'm the only man in this office who could have made such a mistake."

6293. ABSTINENCE, Pledge of. "Put down my name, if you please, sir. I want to join the Cold Water Army." "Why do you wish to join it, my lad?" "Because," said he, with a very serious look, "I *do not want to be such a man as my father is.*"

6294. ABSTRACTION, Securing. It is said that Democritus voluntarily put out his own eyes with the rays from a burning glass, that his attention might not be called off from intellectual contemplations by the allurements of sense. This doubtful story illustrates the importance of protection from interruption to the student.

The mystic and recluse seek solitude that the allurements of the world may lose their power, and their spiritual meditations be undisturbed.

6295. ABSURDITY, Pagan. The Sinitæ used to keep the idols which they worshiped in their houses, and if anything befel them contrary to their desire, they scourged their idol gods for it, and sometimes cast them into the street. When their anger was over, they brought back their idols, placed offerings before them, and entreated their favor.

6296. ABSURDITY, Royal. When the bridge which Xerxes threw across the Hellespont was swept away by the tempest, he sent a challenge to the sea, and commanded his servants to throw fetters into it, to give it three hundred stripes, to burn ignominious brands into it with hot irons, saying as they administered the punishment, "O thou unruly water, thy lord hath appointed thee this punishment, for that thou hast wronged him, and he deserved it not from thee; but whether thou wilt or not, he is resolved to pass over thee."

6297. ABUSE, Brevities. Though a good man and a wise, yet he is liable to every man's abuse.— *Bp. Taylor.*——The difference between coarse and refined abuse is as the difference between being bruised by a club and wounded by a poisoned arrow. *Dr. Johnson.*

6298. ABUSE, Use and. If Christ's example be our precedent, then we may allege Scripture against depraved Scripture. For the bee may gather honey on the same stalk that the spider doth poison. And though a swashbuckler kill a man with his weapon, yet a soldier may lawfully knit a sword to his side; and though there may be piracies committed on the sea, yet may the merchants traffic; or though some surfeit by gluttony, yet may others use their temperate diet. And if the devil change himself into an angel of light, shall therefore the angels lose their light? Or shall Paul therefore deny himself to be a preacher of salvation, because the Pythonite spake it? (Acts 16:17.) Or because Caiaphas by the spirit of the devil (John 11:50) said one should die for the sins of the people, must we therefore believe it? And though (Numb. 22) an enchanter wished that his soul might die the death of the righteous, yet is it a prayer fit to be used of all Christians, though he sold his soul for gold? *Philips.*

6299. ACCEPTANCE, Divine. The Lord was many times pleased to testify his acceptance of sacrifice *visibly* by fire, as doubtless in Abel's offering, Gen. 4:4; in Aaron's first offering after the erection of the Tabernacle, Lev. 9:24; in Gideon's offering, Judges 6:21; in Manoah's, Judges 13:19, 20; in David's, 1 Chron. 21:26; in Solomon's 2 Chron. 7:1; in Elijah's, 1 Kings 18:38. The Divine acceptance is marked equally of the offerings *of the poor* and of the *rich.* See Lev. 1–4. The Levites' tithe of the tithe was to be reckoned to them "as though it were the corn of the threshing floor or the fulness of the winepress," Num. 18:26, 27. Samuel's humble offering of one "sucking lamb," 1 Sam. 7:9, was far more acceptable than vast holocausts of pride

and hypocrisy; as in gospel history, the poor widow's mite was preferred before the abundant offerings of the rich, Mark 12: 43, 44. The sacrifices are in many cases spoken of as "a sweet savor unto the Lord." See Noah's sacrifice after the flood, Gen. 8: 21; Aaron's ram and wave-offering, Exod. 29: 18, 25; the Levitical offerings, Lev. 1: 9, 13, 17; 2: 2, 9, 12. *Frankincense* mixed with the offering, or placed upon the shewbread, was probably designed as a symbol of acceptance. Fragrant in its perfume, it shadowed forth the offering of faith, perfumed with the rich incense of the Saviour's merits.
Bowes.

6300. ACCEPTANCE, Personal. A little girl was helping to nurse a sick gentleman whom she loved very much. He said to her, "Ellen, it is time I should take my medicine; measure just a tablespoonful, and put it in the wine glass." She quickly did so, and brought it to his bedside. He made no attempt to take it from her, but said, "Now, dear, will you drink it for me?" "Me drink it! What do you mean? I am sure I would in a minute if it would make you well all the same; but you know it won't do you any good unless you take it yourself." "Wont it, really?" "No, I suppose it will not." "But if you cannot take my medicine for me, I cannot take your salvation for you. You must go to Jesus, and believe in him for yourself." Each human being must seek, repent, believe and obey for himself.

6301. ACCESS, Provision for. Marcus Valerius, Roman consul, for his victories was granted a triumph, and a house was built for him on Mount Palatine. The doors of other houses at that time opened inward, but he had his constructed to open outward, to show his readiness to listen to all applicants. The gates of prayer are never closed, but stand open night and day.

6302. ACCESS TO GOD, Biblical. Even amongst men we know the difficulty there often is in obtaining access to a superior. Not only difference of rank, but insubordination and offences erect a barrier. We have three examples of this in Scripture—of a wise ruler, a kind father, a great king. *Joseph* was a wise ruler, but his brethren might not see his face, except upon the condition he imposed, Gen. 44: 23. *David* was a kind father, but he forbade Absalom from coming into the royal presence for a time, 2 Sam. 14: 24–28. *Ahasuerus* was a great king; but, according to the law of his kingdom, it was death for any one to come before the king, save those to whom the king held out the golden sceptre, Esther, 4: 11; 5, 2. Under the Law the difficulty of access to the Most High, except through the intervention of sacrifice or mediation, was continually set forth. The *guards* and barriers set around *Mount Sinai* testified of this, Exod. 19: 12, 21–25; Heb. 12: 18–21. In the *Tabernacle service*, the severe restriction laid upon the people—"the *stranger* that cometh nigh shall be put to death"—repeated in Numbers five times, 1: 51; 3: 10, 38; 16: 40; 18: 7. The *people* were not to enter the tabernacle, except as represented by the priests, nor the *priests*

to enter into the Holy of Holies; but only the high priest, and he alone, once every year, not without blood, Heb. 9: 7. The *Kohathites*, when they carried the vessels of the sanctuary in their official capacity, were not to "touch any holy thing," nor "go in to see," lest they die, Num. 4: 15–20. But UNDER THE GOSPEL, through Christ, "by a new and living way," believers have "access and confidence through faith," Heb. 10: 19–22. The *vail is rent.* "Before Christ died (says one), it was death to go within, except for the high priest, once a year. Now, since the vail has been rent, it is death to remain without." Christ is the *door* into the fold, John 10: 7, 9; the *way*, 14: 6; the *High Priest* through whom we have access, Heb. 4: 14–16; 7: 19, 25; 10: 21, 22; like the *high priest* on the day of atonement, Lev. 16 12–15; Heb. 10: 19–22. *Bowes*

6303. ACCESS TO GOD, Key of. There are many locks in my house, and all with different keys; but I have one master-key which opens all. So the Lord has many treasuries and secrets, all shut up from carnal minds with locks which they cannot open; but he who walks in fellowship with Jesus possesses the master-key which will admit him to all the blessings of the covenant; yea, to the very heart of God. Through the Well-beloved we have access to God, to heaven, to every secret of the Lord. *Spurgeon.*

6304. ACCIDENT, An Infidel's. Thomas Paine was a member of the convention which ruled Paris in the Reign of Terror. He opposed the bloody measures of the convention, and was thrown into the Luxembourg prison, where he remained till after the fall of Robespierre, a period of eleven months. Paine knew that the guillotine was doing its fatal work, and expected every day that the executioner would call for him. An official passed through the prison and placed a private mark upon the door of the cells whose inmates were doomed to death. The door of Paine's cell opened outward, and set back flat against the wall. When the minister of doom passed, he put his mark upon the door, unknown to the inmates; but it was closed at night, and thereby the sign was concealed from the executioner, and Paine's life was saved. That night one hundred and sixty-eight persons were taken out of the prison, and all but eight of them were executed the next day. Paine says this escape "has all the appearance of an accident."

6305. ACCIDENTS, Providential. What men call accident is God's own part. *P. J. Bailey.*

6306. ACCOMMODATION, Law of. Without this there can be no such thing as instruction. The teacher must lower himself to his pupils, in order to raise them to himself. So to the child the man becomes a child, and explains the truth in a form adapted to its age, by making use of its childish conceptions as a veil for it. In accordance with this principle, every revelation of God has made use of this law of accommodation, in order to present the divine to the consciousness of men in forms adapted to their respective stand-points. *Neander.*

6307. ACCOUNT, The Great. An honest New

Jersey backwoodsman went into the village to settle an account, and took his wife with him, leaving her at the church where a protracted meeting was in progress. Not finding the man, he returned to the church, where the Holy Spirit was present in convicting power. He soon felt that he had a great unsettled account with God, and nothing with which to pay it. He cried "God be merciful to me a sinner," and felt that his prayer was answered, and Christ had paid the debt.

6308. ACCURACY, Importance of. There was a young man once in the office of a western railway superintendent. He was occupying a position that four hundred boys in that city would have wished to get. It was honorable, and "it paid well," besides being in a line of promotion. How did he get it? Not by having a rich father, for he was the son of a laborer. The secret was his beautiful accuracy. He began as an errand-boy, and did his work accurately. His leisure time he used in perfecting his writing and arithmetic. After awhile he learned to telegraph. At each step his employer commended his accuracy, and relied on what he did, because he was just right. And it is thus with every occupation. The accurate boy is the favored one. Those who employ men do not wish to be on the lookout, as though they were rogues or fools. If a carpenter must stand at his journeyman's elbow to be sure that his work is right, or if a cashier must run over his bookkeeper's column, he might as well do the work himself as employ another to do it in that way; and it is very certain that the employer will get rid of such an inaccurate workman as soon as he can. *President Tuttle.*

6309. ACCUSATION, False. A widower who had one daughter, placed the child with a relative, and entered a monastery. He grieved much at the separation, and finally received permission from the abbot to bring the child to live with him. The father reclaimed the girl and disguised her sex by cutting her hair, putting on her boy's clothing, and changing her name from Marina to Marinus. They lived together till she was seventeen, when the father died. She continued to occupy his cell, conformed to all the rules of the monastery, and was much beloved, known only as brother Marinus. She had sometimes lodged at an inn at the port whither she had gone for supplies for the abbey. The inn-keeper's daughter charged her with seduction, which she was too humble to deny. When this accusation had come to the abbot, he rebuked Marinus. She answered only, "I have sinned, my father." So he drove her from the monastery. Marinus lived outside the gates for five years, with the child of the inn-keeper's daughter, which had been brought to him in charge, which seemed to all a confession of his guilt. So holy was his life that the monks pleaded for his re-admission. The abbot reluctantly granted it. Marinus and the child entered and were assigned the most menial work of the house, which was cheerfully performed. Shortly after the monk sickened and died.

The secret of her sex was discovered. Her remarkable silence under false accusation and punishment was counted great virtue, and she was given a place among the saints in the calendar. Such is the record of St. Marina, of the eighth century.

6310. ACCUSERS, The Sinner's. All the elements accuse me. The heaven says, I have given the light for thy comfort. The air says, I have given every sort of winged creature for thy pleasure. The water says, I have supplied thy table with my countless luxuries. The earth says, I have furnished thee bread and wine; but yet thou hast abused all these blessings, and perverted them to a contempt of their Creator. Therefore all our benefits cry out against me. The fire says, Let him be burned in me. The water says, Let him be drowned in me. The air says, Let him be shaken by a tempest. The earth cries, Let him be buried in me. The holy angels, whom God has sent for ministers of love, and who are to be our joyful companions in the future, accuse me. By my sins I have deprived myself of their holy ministries in this life, and the hope of their fellowship in the future. The voice of God, which is the divine law, accuses me. The law must be fulfilled, or I perish; but to fulfill the law is, for me, impossible; and to perish in eternity is intolerable. God, the most severe Judge, the powerful executor of his eternal law, accuses me. I can not deceive him, for he is omniscience itself. I can not escape him, for his omnipotence everywhere reigns. *Gerhard.*

6311. ACQUIESCENCE, Example of. Æsop's master one day gave him a bitter melon and desired him to eat it. It was nauseous to the taste, but he ate it without making a wry face. His master looked and expressed his surprise. "What," answered the servant, pleasantly, "have I received so many favors from you, and cannot I manage to eat a bitter melon without making a fuss about it?"

6312. ACQUITTAL, Final. An ancient mode of indicating approbation and acquittal is described by Ovid:—

"A custom of old, and still ordains,
Which life or death by suffrage obtains;
White stones and black within an urn are cast,—
The first absolve, but death is in the last."

This ancient custom was something like our modern balloting, or voting by white and black balls. The white stone promised by our Lord seems to mean full and complete justification at the great day, through his glorious imputed righteousness. *Bible Treasury.*

6313. ACT, Influence of a Right. A right act strikes a chord that extends through the whole universe, touches all moral intelligence, visits every world, vibrates along its whole extent and conveys its vibrations to the very bosom of God! *Binney.*

6314. ACTION, Adaptation to. Action is at once the destiny and the lot of man. All the conditions of his existence are framed upon the supposition of his activity. It is so in man's physical frame. The elastic foot is for speed;

the firm lithe limb for endurance; the arm, at once supple and sinewy, for toil; the eye and the ear are for their respective revelries in sight and sound. It is so in our mental constitution. By the active exercise of the powers which God has given us, we classify objects and understand truths; we discriminate, we invent, we analyze, we compare, we combine. It is so in our moral nature. The power by which we distinguish between right and wrong; an instinct of worship, which, however we may brutalize, we cannot wholly stifle; yearnings after a nobler life, which no debauchery can extinguish nor murder absolutely kill—these are all implanted within us by the Giver of every good and perfect gift. *Punshon.*

6315. ACTION, Brevities. Marcus Antonius' rule for his own conduct was, "Manage all your actions and thoughts as if you were just going out of the world." The end of man is an action, and not a thought, though it were the noblest.—*Carlyle.*——What I must do is all that concerns me, and not what people think.—*Emerson.*——Our actions must clothe us with an immortality loathsome or glorious. —*Colton.*——Strong reasons make strong actions.—*Shakspeare.*

6316. ACTION, Eloquent. Demosthenes being asked what was the first part of oratory, answered, "Action;" and which was the second, he replied, "Action;" and which was the third, ne still answered, "Action." Shakspeare says "Action is eloquence, and the eyes of the ignorant are more learned than their ears."

6317. ACTION, Pledge of. A young Roman nobleman of the eleventh century, just married, during the nuptial feast joined in a game of ball, and to relieve himself of his wedding ring, took it off and placed it on the finger of a statue of Venus. The game ended, he went to reclaim the ring, but found it immovable, for the stone finger clenched upon it. Ever after he heard the whisper, "Embrace me; I am Venus, whom you have wedded; I will never restore your ring." Only by calling a priest to his aid was he able to recover his ring. A first act either wrong or right commits us, and is influential in shaping our character.

6318. ACTION, Prompt. The fact is, that in order to do anything in this world worth doing, we must not stand shivering on the bank and thinking of the cold and the danger, but jump in and scramble through as well as we can. It will not do to be perpetually calculating risks, and adjusting nice chances: it did all very well before the Flood, when a man could consult his friends upon an intended publication for a hundred and fifty years, and then live to see its success for six or seven centuries afterwards; but at present a man waits, and doubts, and hesitates, and consults his brother, and his uncle, and his first cousins, and his particular friends, till one fine day he finds that he is sixty-five years of age—that he has lost so much time in consulting first cousins and particular friends that he has no more time left to follow their advice. *S. Smith.*

6319. ACTION, Reward of a Good. A correspondent of a French paper says: "Baron James de Rothschild once sat for a beggar to Ary Scheffer. While the great financier, attired in the rags of a beggar, was in his place on the estrade, I happened to enter the studio of the great artist, whose friend I had the honor to be. The Baron was so perfectly disguised that I did not recognize him, and, believing that a veritable beggar was before me, I went up to him, and slipped a louis into his hand. The pretended model took the coin and put it into his pocket. Ten years later I received at my residence an order on the office in the Rue Lafitte for 10,000 francs, inclosed in the following letter: 'Sir: You one day gave a louis to Baron Rothschild in the studio of Ary Scheffer. He has employed it, and to-day sends you the little capital with which you intrusted him, together with its interest. A good action always brings good fortune.—BARON JAMES DE ROTHSCHILD.' On receipt of this order I sought the billionaire, who proved to me from the books before him that under his management my louis had actually fructified so as to have swelled to the large sum sent me."

6320. ACTION, Rules of. The highest rule of action known to the heathen was stated by Tully, "It is the first office of justice to hurt no man, except provoked by an injury." The Christian rule is, "As ye would that men should do unto you, do ye even so unto them."

6321. ACTION, Trifling. The Emperor Caligula gathered and provisioned a great navy with which it was expected he would subjugate all Greece. He sent them to gather pebbles and cockleshells, a large store of which they secured. They failed to accomplish any worthy purpose, and Caligula made himself the laughing-stock of the world.

6322. ACTIONS, Inconsistent. A fox, hard pressed by the hounds after a long run, came up to a man who was cutting wood, and begged him to afford him some place where he might hide himself. The man showed him his own hut, and the fox creeping in, hid himself in a corner. The hunters presently came up, and asking the man whether he had seen the fox, "No," said he, but pointed with his finger to the corner. They, however, not understanding the hint, were off again immediately. When the fox perceived that they were out of sight, he was stealing off without saying a word. But the man upbraided him, saying, "Is this the way you take leave of your host, without a word of thanks for your safety?" "A pretty host!" said the fox, turning round upon him, "if your actions had been as honest as your tongue, I should not have left without bidding you farewell." *Æsop.*

6323. ACTIVITY, Christian. A female with whom I am acquainted acted upon the aggressive principle in extending religion, with great zeal and diligence; and in the course of three years she had the unspeakable pleasure of leading twelve persons into the fear of the Lord, and many of them had been living in circumstances of most revolting depravity. The same line of conduct was adopted by three young men, of most fervent and decided piety; and so successful were their efforts, that above thirty persons, of whose conversion no rational doubt could be entertained, were, in one year, led to the "sinner's Friend." I have also known classes in the Wesleyan Society to act upon this principle; and, generally speaking, they have in the course of one year doubled their numbers; and one class for a considerable time doubled its numbers every quarter, and was divided four times a year.   *Robert Young.*

6324. ACTIVITY, Future. When Prof. Hascall, founder of Madison University, was near the end of his days, he spoke of his readiness to go on to the heavenly world, but said, "I expect to be busy there. If there is nothing to do there, I choose to remain here." When Captain Thomas Sullivan, sailor preacher in Boston, was retiring slowly, step by step, from this life, he was very patient, though he suffered much. His greatest trial seemed to be that he was obliged to be doing nothing. After his hope of recovery was gone, and after he could only whisper his wishes, he said to the undersigned, "I want to be gone. My view of the future state makes me wish for deliverance from this inactivity. *I want to be at work, at work, at work.*" "His servants shall serve Him, and they shall reign forever and ever" (Rev. 22: 3).   *Watchman and Reflector.*

6325. ACTIVITY, Incentive to. When Cæsar was reading the history of Alexander the Great, his friends once found him bathing the book with tears. They asked him why he wept. His reply was, "Do you think I have not sufficient cause for concern, when Alexander at my age reigned over so many conquered countries, and I have not one glorious achievement to boast?"

6326. ACTOR, Conversion of an. Ardalis was an actor, and was called to amuse his heathen audience by burlesquing a martyrdom. His imitation of Christians before the judge drew boisterous applause from the spectators. But while this amusing farce was going on, the Holy Spirit came powerfully upon him, and changed all into sober reality. Under its influence he cried with a loud voice, "Know that I am in earnest." He was condemned to be burned A. D. 300.

6327. ADAPTATION, Divine. It is said that the Jews have a tradition that in the wanderings of the children of Israel in the wilderness during those forty years, not only "did their raiment wax not old nor their feet swell" but their garments grew with their growth, so that what fitted the little child on its leaving the land of Egypt was after forty years adapted to the figure of the full-grown man.

6328. ADAPTATION, Natural. You may think, perhaps, that it would be a matter of indifference to us whether our globe were a little larger or a little smaller than it is, since for so many years man lived upon it in total ignorance of its size. But there is a necessary proportion between the size and weight of the earth and the strength which God has given to our limbs and muscles. If, for example, we could be conveyed to the moon, and if it were like the earth in all respects except its size, we should there weigh five times less than we do upon the earth. We might bound up like grasshoppers to a great height in the air, but we should be so unsteady that the hand of a child could throw us over. And if our earth, on the contrary, was as large as the planet Jupiter, all other things remaining the same, each of us should feel as if we were forced to carry the weight of eleven persons as heavy as ourselves. The weight of a man of ten stone would be 120 stone, and none of us could walk or stand upright—scarcely even move. Ah! let us repeat what we said before, "The work of the Lord is perfect. It is always good—very good."   *Prof. L. Gaussen.*

6329. ADDER, Sting of the. A gentleman encountered an adder in the fields, and studied his snakeship as well as he could. The snake was not more than a foot long. He was timid and tried to ward off all comers by a wheezy blowing, which corresponds with the alarm of the rattle-snake. His first effort was to escape. He can not coil himself up and strike, or spring like other snakes. When pressed he will open his wide jaws and bite, and woe be to the man or beast who receives his venomous fang, for its touch is certain death. The gentleman's companion pinned the snake to the ground with a crotched stick and said, "See, I will make him bite himself, and he will die of his own venom in three seconds." Sure enough the adder struck the fangs into his own body, and in less than three seconds he was dead. Wine "biteth like a serpent, and stingeth like an adder." Its venomous bite destroys the body, and plunges the soul into eternal death.

6330. ADMONITION, Benevolence of. Private admonition is rather a proof of benevolence than of malevolence. It was the saying of Austin, when his hearers resented his frequent reproofs—"Change your conduct, and I will change my conversation."   *W. Secker.*

6331. ADMONITION, Boldness in. A very bad man had been vexatious to the parish of Bünde, and no one could restrain him. When ever he pleased, he turned his horse into his neighbors' fields of sown or standing corn; and used to brawl and bluster as he passed along, so that no one dared to approach him. Rauschenbusch determined at length seriously to take him in hand. The small stream that ran through the place separated Rauschenbusch's glebe farm from the public road, along which this fellow came blustering on his way into the town. Rauschenbusch happened just then to hear him; but being on the other side of the stream, he came to the water's edge, within sight of him, and called out, "Muth (that was his name), I am coming," and the man was immediately quiet. Rauschenbusch met him directly in the wood just by; and though no one was secure of his life in meeting him there, Rauschenbusch went resolutely up to him, took hold of him with a firm hand, and said, "All Bünde is afraid of you; but I am not afraid of the devil; and I command you to come to me to-morrow, and to let me know whether you mean to be a different man!" The fellow actually came the next morning, and Rauschenbusch set before him the authority and sacredness of the law of God, and the judgment to come; and this he did with all the seriousness of his official character, and with all the importunity of an honest heart interested in him. And though he never could regard him as a converted man, yet he succeeded so far as to bind Satan within him, so that this person was constrained to cease from annoying his fellowmen.

P. B. Power.

6332. ADMONITION, Fable of. A very skillful bowman went to the mountains in search of game. All the beasts of the forest fled at his approach. The lion alone challenged him to combat. The bowman immediately let fly an arrow, and said to the lion, "I send thee my messenger, that from him thou mayest learn what I myself will be when I assail thee." The lion, thus wounded, rushed away in great fear; and on a fox exhorting him to be of good courage, and not to run away at the first attack, replied, "You counsel me in vain, for if he sends so fearful a messenger, how shall I abide the attack of the man himself?" *Æsop.*

6333. ADMONITION, Popular. A favorite method of admonishing the great and also the public in early times was the fable or allegory. By these the hearers were first pleased, and then warned, often being made to pronounce their own sentence as in the case of Nathan's parable of the ewe lamb. Æsop gained great popularity at the court of the voluptuous Cresus, though he often spoke unpleasant truths. Even then he paid the penalty for his enforcement of minor morals with his own blood, being murdered by the Delphians. In our time he who has pursued the direct method in plain language, calling a spade a spade, and not an implement of husbandry, has been the successful reformer.

6334. ADMONITION, Resentment at. It was the saying of a heathen, though no heathenish saying, that "he who would be good must either have a faithful friend to instruct him or a watchful enemy to correct him." Should we murder a physician because he comes to cure us, or like him worse because he would make us better? Truth is not always relished where sin is nourished. Light is pleasant, yet it may be offensive to sore eyes. Honey is sweet, though it cause the wound to smart. But we must not neglect the actions of friends, for fear of drawing upon ourselves the suspicion of being enemies. Most people are like restive horses, which no sooner feel the rowel than they strike with their heels; or like bees, which no sooner are angered than they put out their stings. *W. Secker.*

6335. ADOPTION, Biblical. Luke 15: 22–24. The parable of the prodigal son serves beautifully to illustrate the dignities and privileges of the believer's adoption. It sets forth at once the grace of the Father, and the spirit and privilege of the accepted son. The kiss, the robe, the ring, the shoes, the feast, were favors not given to slaves. Among the Romans and earlier nations, slaves were not allowed to wear shoes. Among the Romans, the master's inviting a slave to sit down with him at table was in itself regarded as an act of manumission; from that time the slave was free. Gal. 4: 6. "*Abba, Father.*" A beautiful word, used in his hour of suffering by Christ himself, Mark 14: 36, and now the privilege of all God's children, Rom. 8: 15; Gal. 4: 6. It is a word which belongs to children. No slave uses such language. It shows the likeness of spirit that Christ's members have to Christ. As he used it in the garden, it expressed his tender affection, his filial confidence, his undoubting trust, his earnest prayer, his entire submission to the Father's will. "*Abba, Father,*"—the Reformer Becon translated it as equivalent to "*Dear* Father." It is a word, also, which, being given both in Hebrew and Greek, is designed by the apostle to show that, whether we be Jew or Gentile, we are placed on the same footing by the gospel of Christ's grace. *Bowes.*

6336. ADOPTION, Custom of. It is the custom in India, especially among the Mohammedans, that in default of children, and sometimes where there are lineal descendants, the master of the family adopts a slave, frequently a Haffshee Abyssinian of the darkest hue, for his heir; he educates him agreeably to his wishes, and marries him to one of his daughters. As a reward of superior merit or to suit the caprice of an arbitrary despot, this honor is also conferred on a slave recently purchased or already grown up in the family; to him he bequeaths his wealth in preference to his nephews or any collateral branches. This is a custom of great antiquity in the East, and prevalent among the most refined and civilized nations. In the earliest period of the patriarchal history we find Abraham complaining for want of children, and declaring that either Eleazer of Damascus, or one born from him in his house, was his heir, to the exclusion of Lot, his favorite nephew, and all other collateral branches of his family.

Forbes.

6337. ADOPTION, Examples of. Hosea 1: 10; Rom. 9: 25, 26. We have heard of hopeless foundlings entertained by miracle, as young Cyrus in a shepherd's house, a cottage not much above the ground—no likelihood of promotion there, yet exalted to a throne; of Moses among the bulrushes, taken up to be the son of Pharaoh's daughter; of David from the sheepfold advanced to the monarchy; but no example holds proportion to this. It is of Lo-ruhamah and Lo-ammi we speak, the bastard fruit of fornication. That these should be fetched from accursed thraldom, and estated in the glorious liberty of the sons of God, this transcends all admiration. *Thos. Adams.*

6338. ADOPTION, Knowledge of. I do not mean that God testifies this by an outward voice: no, nor always by an inward voice, although he may do this sometimes. Neither do I suppose that he always applies to the heart, though he often may, one or more texts of

Scripture. But He so works upon the soul, by His immediate influence, and by a strong though inexplicable operation, that the stormy wind and troubled waves subside, and there is a sweet calm. The heart rests as in the arms of Jesus; and the sinner is clearly satisfied that God is reconciled. *John Wesley.*

6339. ADOPTION, Human. Adoption among men is an act by which a man takes the child of another, and places it in the condition of his own child, to be in every respect from thenceforth as his own, with all the rights, and privileges, and obligations, and duties of a child. *M'Neile.*

6840. ADOPTION, Spirit in. A gentleman much perplexed on the subject of the Spirit's witness, desired me to explain it to him; and, believing that he already possessed it, I asked him to describe his views and feelings on the subject, when he said, "I certainly feel that I have experienced a great change, and can now approach God with filial confidence and love." "Then, most assuredly," said I, "you have the very thing about which you are inquiring; for, according to the Apostle, the witness of the Spirit is the power given to believers to view God in His paternal character, and to draw nigh to Him with the simplicity, confidence, and affection of children. '*Because ye are sons, God hath sent forth the Spirit of His Son into your hearts, crying, Abba, Father.*' It is the indwelling Spirit that enables us to approach God as our Father, and thus bears witness to our adoption into the Divine family." *Robert Young.*

6341. ADORNMENT, Lesson of. A minister visiting a gay person, was introduced to a room near to that in which she dressed. After waiting some hours, the lady came in and for him in tears. She inquired the reason of his weeping. He replied, "Madam, I weep on reflecting that you can spend so many hours before your glass, and in adorning your person, while I spend so few hours before my God, and in adorning my soul." The rebuke struck her conscience. She put on the ornament of a meek and quiet spirit.

6342. ADORNMENT, True. Apelles, the famous painter of Greece, having observed that one of his scholars had painted Helena set out with much gold and embroidery, said unto him, "*O adolescens, quum non possis pingere pulchram, fecisti divitem:* Alas, poor young man! when thou couldst not draw her fair, thou hast made her rich." Thus many do set a fair outside on the body, and utterly neglect the inside of the soul; pamper the body, but starve the soul; trick up the body with gold and silver, whilst the soul is naked of all grace and goodness. *Jermin.*

6343. ADORNMENTS, Protest Against. Rev. T. Collins' heart ached, when, in chain and ring, bracelet and brooch, garland and plume, he thought he saw a murderer more fatal to trees in the garden of God than is the Matador to the forestry of Brazil, insidiously twining round the Churches committed to his care. Fox, Fletcher, Wesley, Bramwell, and if any

find authority in venerable names, I may go earlier and say, Clement of Alexandria, Tertullian, and Cyprian, the martyr of Carthage, each was pained, and each, in his day, found, like Isaiah, a "burden of the Lord" against "the bravery of ornaments, the round tires like the moon, the mufflers, the mantles, the wimples, and the crisping pins." But spite of them all, Apostles and Prophets, Fathers and Martyrs, Quaker witnesses and Methodist worthies, there are still daughters of Zion that are haughty; who as the Scripture says, walk "mincing as they go." *S. Coley.*

6344. ADULATION, Penalty of. Publius Affranius was notorious for fawning around the great. When the Emperor Caligula was sick, he went to him and professed that he would willingly die if Caligula could but recover. The Emperor told him "That he did not believe him;" whereupon Publius Affranius confirmed it with an oath. Caligula soon after recovered, and caused that Publius Affranius should be slain, that he might be true to his word. Being a base flatterer, he was made to undergo in earnest that which he uttered in jest.

6345. ADVENT, Christ's Second. It is described by many figures and in many ways in the Bible. The Bridegroom going forth to meet the Bride, Matt 25: 1–13. The Master returning to distribute his awards, Luke 19: 12; Matt. 24: 43–51; 25: 14–30. The Time of Harvest, Matt. 13: 30; Rev. 14: 15; and of Vintage, Rev. 14: 17–20. The Breaking forth and dawn of day, (Cant. 2: 17; 4: 6); 2 Pet. 1: 19. The Marriage Supper of the Lamb, Matt. 22: 1–14; Rev. 19: 6–9. The Times of Refreshing, Acts 3: 19. The Times of the Restitution of all things, Acts 3: 21. The Times of Separation—when the gospel net shall be brought to shore, Matt. 13: 47–50; and the Shepherd shall divide the sheep from the goats, Matt. 25: 31–46. "The day of our Lord Jesus Christ," 1 Cor. 1: 8, spoken of emphatically as the one great day ("the day for which all other days were made"). Hence described as "that day" three times in one epistle, 2 Tim. 1: 12–18; 4: 8; see also Mark 13: 32. "That hour," Mark 13: 32; John 5: 28. The very frequent recurrence of the expression "in that day," through the prophets, may be seen by the Concordance. It constantly refers to the great and final day. As an example see Zach. 12–14, where the expression occurs fifteen times. The day of the manifestation of the Son of God, Rom. 8: 19; 2 Cor. 5: 11 (Greek), when "the Chief Shepherd shall appear," and his saints shall appear with him in glory, 1 Pet. 5: 4; Col. 3: 4. The suddenness of Christ's coming is illustrated by the lightning flash, alike sudden, terrible, irresistible, Matt. 24: 27. A snare or trap, Luke 21: 35; surprising the secure and unsuspecting. A thief in the night, Matt. 24: 43; 1 Thess, 5: 2; Rev. 16: 15. It will be unlooked for by a gay and scoffing world. "As it was in the days of Noah," and "of Lot," Luke 17: 26–30. See also Luke 18: 8; 2 Pet. 3: 3–10. Nevertheless there is a waiting for it. The whole creation is earnestly expecting the great day of liberation, (expecting, as the Greek word imports, like one stretching out the neck with longing looks), Rom. 8: 19–22. The church of Christ is waiting—groaning for complete redemption, Rom. 8: 23. The members of Christ's Church are now, and will be, "looking," "watching," "praying," "waiting" for His appearance—loving the anticipation, and hasting towards it; like the wise virgins waiting for the Bridegroom, Matt. 25: 1–13; like the wise servant waiting for the Master, Matt. 24: 45: 46; Luke 12: 35: 36; like patient laborers waiting for the earth's ripe fruits, Jas. 5: 7, 8; like those night watchers who keep their garments, and are not like watchmen sleeping at their posts, Rev. 16: 15.   *Bowes.*

6346. ADVENT, Expected. It is a very remarkable fact, that God's prophecies respecting the Advent of His Son seem to have spread athwart the whole habitable globe, and in the shape of traditional echoes to have been dispersed over all the world. The great promise of a Messiah, which was the grand truth that the Jew clung to in his most desperate fortunes, found itself translated into heathen tongues, and accepted even by heathen men. For instance, the poet Virgil dedicates a poem to Pollis, his patron, in which he says that one would soon be born into the world who, it was expected, would bring in the golden age. Suetonius, an ancient historian, states, too, what is a remarkable proof of the spread of this idea, that a certain and settled persuasion prevailed in the East, that the cities of Judea would bring forth, about this time, a person who should obtain universal empire. And Tacitus, the eloquent historian, but the very incredulous one, who called the Christian religion *execrabilis superstitio*, states that it was contained in the ancient books of the Jewish priests that the East should prevail, and that a power should proceed from Judea that should possess universal dominion. These were scattered lights that went out from Judea, their reuniting centre, and gave the heathen an anticipation and persuasion that some great and illustrious deliverer was about to be born in the world.   *Trench.*

6347. ADVENT, Faith in the. I die in the faith of the speedy accomplishment of those glorious things which are spoken concerning the city of God and of the kingdom of Christ. "Amen. Even so, Lord Jesus! Come quickly!"   *Increase Mather.*

6348. ADVENT, Glory of the. There is an account come of the arrival of King George, and a great rejoicing for it in Edinburgh. I see the fires and illuminations of that city reflected on the skies. O, how will the heavens reflect and shine with illuminations, when the King of Kings, and Lord of Lords, shall erect his tribunal in the clouds, and come in his own glory, and his Father's glory, and in the glory of the holy angels! O, what a heartsome day will that be! When Christ, who is our life, shall appear, then shall we appear with him in glory. We shall then lift up our heads

with joy, because it shall be a time of refreshing from the presence of the Lord.
Ebenezer Erskine.

6349. ADVENT, Joy at the. "I remember," says the writer of Mr. John Janeway's life, "once there was a great talk that one had foretold that doomsday should be on such a day. Although he blamed their daring folly that could pretend to know that which was hid, yet, granting their suspicion to be true,"What then?" said he; "what if the day of judgment were come, as it will most certainly come shortly? If I were sure the day of judgment were to come within an hour, I should be glad with all my heart. If, at this instant, I should hear such thunderings, and see such lightnings, as Israel did at Mount Sinai, I am persuaded my very heart would leap for joy. But this I am confident of, through infinite mercy, that the very meditation of that day hath even ravished my soul, and the thought of the certainty and nearness of it is more refreshing to me than the comforts of the whole world."

6350. ADVENT, Looking for the. I was told of a poor peasant on the Welsh mountains who, month after month, year after year, through a long period of declining life, was used every morning, as soon as he awoke, to open his casement window towards the east, and look out to see if Jesus Christ was coming. He was no calculator, or he need not have looked so long; he was no student of prophecy, or he need not have looked at all; he was ready, or he would not have been in so much haste; he was willing, or he would rather have looked another way; he loved, or it would not have been the first thought of the morning. His Master did not come, but a messenger did, to fetch the ready one home. The same preparation sufficed for both; the longing soul was satisfied with either. Often when, in the morning, the child of God awakes, weary and encumbered with the flesh, perhaps from troubled dreams, perhaps with troubled thoughts, his Father's secret comes presently across him, he looks up, if not out, to feel, if not to see, the glories of that last morning when the trumpet shall sound, and the dead shall arise indestructible; no weary limbs to bear the spirit down; no feverish dreams to haunt the vision; no dark forecasting of the day's events. or returning memory of the griefs of yesterday.   *Fry.*

6351. ADVENT, Prayers for the. The words "Come, Lord Jesus," have often been on the lips of departing believers. They were the last uttered by Burkitt. They were the closing prayer of Bishop Abbott, who died early in the seventeenth century. "It is death: It is death," exclaimed Robert Hall, "Oh, the sufferings of this body!" His wife then asked him, "But you are comfortable in your mind?" He answered, "Very comfortable," adding, "Come, Lord Jesus, come." He then hesitated, as if unable to utter the next word, and one of his daughters added, "Quickly;" whereupon her dying father gave her a look expressive of the utmost delight. Lady Colquhoun seemed to long for her release, and frequently repeated the words

"Come, Lord Jesus, come quickly." Dr. Andrew Eliot, of Boston, in his last sickness, expressed unshaken confidence in the doctrines of grace which he had preached, and would frequently breathe the ejaculation, "Come, Lord Jesus come quickly." Under similar circumstances, the Rev. Dr. Joseph Sewall was sometimes heard to say, with great pathos, "Come, Lord Jesus, come quickly." The last words of the pious Henry Holmes, of Boston, were, "Lord Jesus, come quickly." In their primary sense, as referring to Christ's personal and glorious advent, these words have often dropped from the lips and pens of earnest believers. In a somewhat desponding mood, Martin Luther broke out, "May the Lord Jesus come at once! Let Him cut the whole matter short with the Day of Judgment; for there is no amendment to be expected." The martyr Ridley wrote: "The world, without doubt—this I do believe, and therefore say it—draws towards an end. Let us with John, the servant of God, cry in our hearts unto our Saviour, Christ, 'Come, Lord Jesus, come!'" *Dr. A. C. Thompson.*

6352. ADVENT, Welcoming the. No man rightly desires Christ's coming, but he that hath assurance of benefit at His coming. To him the day of Christ is as the day of harvest to the husbandman; as the day of deliverance to the prisoner; as the day of coronation to the king; the day of wedlock to the bride; a day of triumph and exultation, a day of freedom and consolation, a day of rest and satisfaction. To them the Lord Jesus is all sweetness, as wine to the palate, and ointment to the nostrils, saith Solomon; honey in the mouth, saith St. Bernard; music in the ear, and a jubilee in the heart. Get assurance of Christ's coming, as a ransomer to redeem you, as a conqueror to subdue all your enemies under you, as a friend to comfort you, as a bridegroom to marry you, and then shall you with boldness and confidence, with joy and gladness, with vehement and holy longings, say, "Come, Lord Jesus." *Grosse.*

6353. ADVERSITY, Bearing. It helps us to bear adversity to remember that the worst of our portion is better than we deserve.

6354. ADVERSITY, Effect of. I have read of a fountain that is cold at mid-day, and warm at mid-night. Thus are saints frequently cold in the mid-day of prosperity, and warm in the mid-night of adversity. Afflictions are not a *consuming*, but a *refining* fire to the godly. They are like the thorn at the nightingale's breast, which rouses and puts her upon her delightful notes. *Secker.*

6355. ADVERSITY, Preferred. If adversity hath killed his thousands, prosperity hath killed his ten thousands; therefore adversity is to be preferred. The one deceives, the other instructs; the one miserably happy, the other happily miserable; and therefore many philosophers have voluntarily sought adversity, and so much commend it in their precepts. Demetrius, in Seneca, esteemed it a great infelicity that in his lifetime he had no misfortune. *Burton.*

6356. ADVERSITY, Virtue in. A wise and virtuous man, when in adversity, may, like a dark lantern in the night, seem dull and dark to those who are about him; but within he is full of light and brightness; and when he chooses to open the door, he can show it.
Owen Feltham.

6357. ADVICE, Answer to. A very weak and puny man advised the Spartans to engage the enemy by sea and land. Pausanius, the son of Cleombrotus, said to him, "Pray, sir, will you strip and show what a man you are who advise us to engage."

6358. ADVICE, Liberality with. There is nothing with which men are so liberal as advice. It may benefit or blight a life, and save or ruin a soul forever. Good advice is better than gold. It should be given with wisdom and received with caution.

6359. ADVICE, Post facto. A swallow's nest fell from the eaves of a farm-house, and the barn-yard poultry and the hedge birds gathered about the ruins, and went into committee on them. "I knew it was going to fall; I felt sure it must the last time I went on the roof," chirped a sparrow. "Stupid thing—building its nest up there," hissed a goose. "I could have taught her how to lay her eggs without getting smashed, if she had only come to me," quacked a duck. "And I could have taught her how to hatch them—I have had to hatch yours, Neighbor Duck," clucked a hen. "Gobble, gobble, gobble—if people choose to be fools they must take the consequences," said a strutting turkey cock, puffing out his feathers. "My friends, you are very kind to take so much interest in my affairs," twittered the poor swallow; "but if you were so sure that my house was going to fall, isn't it a pity that you did'nt tell me so a little sooner?" *Good Things.*

6360. ADVICE, Too Late. A doctor had been for some time attending upon a sick man, who, however, died under his hands. At the funeral, the doctor went about among the relations, saying, "Our poor friend, if he had only refrained from wine, and attended to his inside, and used proper means, would not have been lying there." One of the mourners answered him, "My good sir, it is of no use your saying this now; you ought to have prescribed these things when your patient was alive to take them." *Æsop.*

6361. ADVOCATE, Christ our. There is an old ploughman in the country I sometimes talk with, and he often says, though in uncouth words, some precious things. He said to me one day, "The other day, sir, the devil was tempting me, and I tried to answer him; but I found he was an old lawyer, and understood the law a great deal better than I did, so I gave over, and would not argue with him any more; so I said to him, 'What do you trouble me for?' 'Why,' said he, 'about your soul?' 'Oh!' said I, 'that is no business of mine; I have given my soul over into the hand of Christ; I have transferred everything to him; if you want an answer to your doubts and queries, you must apply to my Advocate.'" *Spurgeon.*

6362. ADVOCATE, Faith in the. The little

daughter of a great judge lay upon her death-bed, and by the short and quick gasps which proceeded from the white lips, it was evident the little life had nearly completed its earthly career. The anxious father, bending over his daughter's couch, whispered: "Nellie, are you not afraid to stand in the great tribunal, before the all-ruling God and Judge?" She answered, "No, papa! for Jesus will be my lawyer; he will argue my poor case—covering up my little sins with the mantle of mercy, and extolling my good deeds in a loud voice of praise."

6363. ADVOCATE, Faithful. A faithful advocate can never sit without clients. Nor do I believe that any man could lose by it in the end, that would not undertake a cause he knew not honest. A goldsmith may gain an estate as well as he that trades in every coarser metal. An advocate is a limb of friendship; and further than the altar he is not bound to go. And it is observed of as famous a lawyer as I think was then in the world, the Roman Cicero, that he was slain by one he had defended, when accused of the murder of his father. Certainly he that defends an injury is next to him that commits it. And this is recorded, not only as an example of ingratitude, but as a punishment for patronizing an ill cause. *Feltham.*

6364. ADVOCATE, Responsibility of an. Lord Brougham said, in his defence of Queen Caroline, before the House of Lords: "An advocate, by the sacred duty which he owes his client, knows, in the discharge of that office, but one person in the world, that client and none other. To save that client by all means—to protect that client at all hazards and costs to all others, and among others to himself—is the highest and most unquestioned of his duties."

6365. ADVOCATES, Two. When any name is proposed for canonization in the Roman Catholic Church, two advocates are appointed, one to oppose the motion and one to defend it. The one, called *Advocatus Diaboli* (the Devil's Advocate), advances all he can rummage up against the person in question; the other, called *Advocatus Dei* (God's Advocate), says all he can in support of the proposal.

6366. AFFABILITY, Examples of. Alexander found a private soldier fainting with cold, and caused him to be carried and seated in his own royal seat in his tent before the fire. The soldier, coming to himself, sprang up amazed and began to apologize. Alexander smiled upon him and said, "Knowest thou not, my soldier, that your Macedonians live after another sort under your king than the Persians do under theirs; for unto them it is death to sit in the king's chair; but unto thee it hath been life." Alfonsus, King of Aragon, meeting a muleteer whose beast was pressed into the mire by a heavy load, dismounted and helped the poor man out of his difficulty.

6367. AFFABILITY, Importance of. Nothing renders a man so amiable in the sight of others, or so happy in himself, as affability and humility. They are the criteria of true greatness, and add lustre to the most brilliant qualifications, and exaltation to the highest rank. Nor in

point of policy, are these virtues less important; for they never fail to create love and esteem, and those are ever the surest friends whom repeated civilities have made so. A vulgar and unrestrained indulgence of pride and petulance is sure to render men despised and hated by others, and uneasy to themselves.

6368. AFFECTATION, Folly of. Affectation in any part of our carriage, is lighting up a candle to our defects, and never fails to make us be taken notice of, either as wanting sense or wanting sincerity. All affectation is vain and ridiculous; it is the attempt of poverty to appear rich. *Lavater.*

6369. AFFECTATION, Vanity and. I will not call Vanity and Affectation twins, because, more properly, Vanity is the mother, and Affectation is the darling daughter; Vanity is the sin, and Affectation is the punishment; the first may be called the root of self-love, the other the fruit. Vanity is never at its full growth, till it spreadeth into Affectation; and then it is complete. *Saville.*

6370. AFFECTION, Beautiful. "What kind of a woman was your mother?" said a slave-master, to a fine African boy whom he had purchased. The boy hesitated. "Come, tell me," said the master: "What kind of a woman was she? Was she tall? Was she thin? Was she old? Was she beautiful?" The boy lifted up his glistening eyes, and in broken accents said: "How could a mother but be beautiful in the eyes of her child?"

6371. AFFECTION, Filial. When Sir Thomas More was being led forth under sentence of death, his daughter Margaret rushed through the guards, threw herself upon her venerable father's neck, and wept in woeful despair. The crowd melted into compassion at the scene. Sir Thomas said, "My dear Margaret, submit with patience; grieve no longer for me, it is the will of God." He embraced her and bade her farewell. After his execution his head was exposed upon London bridge for fourteen days according to his sentence. It was about to be cast into the Thames, when his daughter was allowed to purchase it. "She survived her father only nine years, and died in 1544, in her thirty-sixth year. In compliance with her desire, the head of her father was interred with her, in her arms, as related by some, or, according to others, deposited in a leaden box, and placed upon the coffin."

6372. AFFECTION, Instinctive. Louis XVI. took great pains to teach his son. When a boy he took him into the country, and handing him his compass directed him to try and find his way to the *chateau* in a certain direction, and he would go another. The boy got out of his way many times, and was four or five hours getting home. The king ran to meet him, and exclaimed, "I thought you were lost." "Oh! papa," said the boy, "how could I? Did not my heart incline towards you, as sure as the compass towards the north?"

6373. AFFECTION, Maternal. A few years ago, a young man started from New England for California. As he left his wife he said, as soon as he accumulated sufficient money to send for her and her boy, he would do so. He was gone a long time before he was successful, and at last a letter arrived bringing money to take them to the Pacific coast. It was a joyful day for that mother and child. They went to New York and took passage in one of the Pacific steamers, and started for San Francisco. One day a cry was raised—a cry of fire! The pumps were set to work, water was thrown on the flames, but it did not stop their progress, and the Captain saw that there was no use to try and save it. He had a magazine of powder on board. The flames were advancing toward it, and he knew as soon they should reach that, all would perish. So they took to the life-boats, the strong and active jumping in first, and there remained on deck only this poor woman and her little boy. As the last life-boat was pushing away from the ship, she pleaded and prayed to these men to take herself and her boy, but the men were obdurate. They said they dare not take any more, and but one man said, "Let us take them." and the others said, "No, we dare not." At length they determined upon taking one of them, and they communicated their resolution to the mother. She caught her boy, gave him one affectionate embrace, and dropped him into the life-boat, exclaiming, "If you live to get to your father, tell him I died in your place." They boy escaped. The life-boat rowed on. The flames gradually encircled the fatal ship. It reached the powder magazine. A terrific explosion ensued, and that devoted mother met a watery grave. She died for the child she loved, but Christ died for his enemies.

6374. AFFECTION, Paternal. A profligate son resolved to kill his father to get possession of his property. This came to the father's knowledge, and he invited his son to walk with him. They went into the dense forest, and there the father said to him: "My son, I have been told, and have no doubt of the fact, that you have formed the desperate resolution of murdering me. Notwithstanding the many just grounds of complaint which I have against you, still you are my son, and I love you still, and wish to give you a last token of my tenderness. I have led you into this forest, and to this solitary place, where none are to witness our conduct, and where none can have the smallest knowledge of your crime." Then, drawing a dagger, which had been concealed, "There, my son," said he; "there is a dagger—take your will of me—execute the cruel design which you have formed against my life—put me to death according to your resolution—I shall, at least, in dying here, save you from falling into the hands of human justice; this shall be the last evidence of my tender attachment to you; in my extreme grief, this shall be some consolation to me, that I shall save your life, whilst you deprive me of mine." The son, astonished, could not refrain from crying; threw himself at his father's feet—implored the forgiveness of his foul offence, and protested before God, that he would change his

conduct to the best and most benevolent of fathers. He kept his word—renouncing his ruinous irregularities, and causing consolation and joy somewhat proportioned to the grief and sorrows of soul which he had given to his father.

6375. AFFECTION, Promotion of. One remarkable effect of the gospel among the heathen has been the strengthening of all the natural affections. Cases in point are numerous. Mothers who had been guilty of infanticide mourn for their murdered children. The aged parents are no longer abandoned. The Christian child of heathen parents becomes solicitous for their souls. A missionary visited a woman who had been torn from her parents and sold in childhood. She became a true Christian. He found her in tears and inquired the cause. He said: "My child, what is the cause of your sorrow? Is the baby still unwell?" "No," she replied, "my baby is well." "Your mother-in-law?" I inquired. "No, no," she replied, "it is my own dear mother." Here she gave vent to her grief; and, holding out the gospel of Luke in a hand wet with tears, she exclaimed, "My mother will never see this Word; she will never hear this good news." She wept again and again, and said, "O, my mother and my friends, they live in heathen darkness; and shall they die without seeing the light which has shone on me, and without tasting that love which I have tasted?" Raising her eyes to heaven she sighed a prayer, and uttered the words again, "My mother, my mother!" She died not long after in the Christian faith, and the last words she was heard to utter were an ejaculatory prayer for her mother.

6376. AFFECTION, Proof of. In the French revolution, a young man was condemned to the guillotine, and shut up in one of the prisons. He was greatly loved by many, but there was one who loved him more than all put together. How know we this? It was his own father, and the love he bore his son was proved in this way: When the lists were called, the father, whose name was exactly the same as the son's, answered to the name, and the father rode in the gloomy tumbril out to the place of execution, and his head rolled from beneath the axe instead of his son's, a victim to mighty love. See here an image of the love of Christ to sinners; for thus Jesus died for the ungodly.   *Spurgeon.*

6377. AFFECTION, Reward of. A Roman, called Titus Manlius, was extremely ill-treated by his father, for no other reason than a defect in his speech. A tribune of the people brought an accusation against the father before the people, who hated him for his imperious conduct, and were determined to punish him with severity. The young man came one morning very early from his father's country farm, where he was forced to live in the style of a slave, and finding out the house of the tribune who had impeached his father, compelled him to swear that he would immediately drop the prosecution. Oaths being at that time held inviolable in Rome, the tribune declared before the people that he withdrew his charge against old Manlius, because his son Titus had obliged him to promise upon oath that he would carry it no farther. The people, charmed with the filial piety of Titus to an unnatural father, not only forgave the old man, but next year advanced his generous son to the supreme honors of the state. *Whitecross.*

6378. AFFECTION, Test of. A rich merchant died, leaving a large fortune. He had but one son, who had been sent when quite a lad to an uncle in India. On his way home, after an absence of some years, the young man had been shipwrecked; and though it was believed he had been saved, still no certain tidings reached his father, who, meanwhile, died rather suddenly, leaving his large fortune to the care of an old friend, with strict injunctions not to give it up to any claimant until certain conditions had been complied with. At the end of a year, a young man appeared who said he was the heir; then a second, and finally a third. The guardian, who knew that two out of the three claimants must be impostors, made use of the following stratagem: He gave each rival a bow and arrow, and desired them to use the dead man's picture as the target, and to aim at the heart. The first nearly hit the mark; the second pierced the heart; but the third claimant burst into tears, and refused to dishonor his father's memory by injuring the portrait of one whom he venerated so highly. The guardian was quite satisfied with the result of his device, and at once welcomed him as the rightful heir and his old friend's son. *Anon.*

6379. AFFECTIONS, Culture of the. It is not the method and custom of reason—in imitation either of the manner of the Thracians or of what Lycurgus ordered to be done to the vines —to destroy and tear up all the passions indifferently, good and bad, useful and hurtful together; but rather—like some kind and careful Deity who has a tender regard to the growth and improvement of fruit trees and plants—to cut away and clip off that which grows wild and rank, and to dress and manage the rest that it may serve for use and profit. *Plutarch.*

6380. AFFECTIONS, Neglect of the. It appears unaccountable that our teachers generally have directed their instructions to the head, with very little attention to the heart. From Aristotle down to Locke, books without number have been composed for cultivating and improving the understanding; but few, in proportion, for cultivating and improving the affections. *Kaimes.*

6381. AFFLICTION, Benefits of. An old Puritan said, "God's people are like birds; they sing best in cages." He said, "God's people sing best when in the deepest trouble." Said old Master Brooks, "The deeper the flood was, the higher the ark went up to heaven." So it is with the child of God: the deeper his troubles the nearer to heaven he goeth, if he lives close to his Master. Troubles are called weights;

and a weight, you know, generally cloggeth and keepeth down to the earth; but there are ways, by the use of the laws of mechanics, by which you can make a weight lift you; and so it is possible to make your troubles lift you nearer heaven instead of making them sink you. Ah! we thank our God, he has sometimes opened our mouth when we were dumb; when we were ungrateful, and did not praise him, he has opened our mouth by a trial; and though when we had a thousand mercies we did not bless him, when he sent a sharp affliction, then we began to bless him. *Spurgeon.*

6382. AFFLICTION, Burden of. Nothing can render affliction so insupportable as the load of sin. Would you then be fitted for afflictions? Be sure to get the burden of your sins laid aside, and then what affliction soever you may meet with will be very easy to you. *Bunyan.*

6383. AFFLICTION, Cure for. Crantor, a heathen, says, "To be innocent is the greatest comfort in affliction." He knew nothing of the blood of Christ, that washes whiter than snow, and prepares the dying for the enjoyments of a heaven of purity; but he saw the advantage of that condition.

6384. AFFLICTION, Design of. Rev. Richard Cecil was introduced into the chamber where the child of Thomas Williams, a very prosperous bookseller of London, lay dying. "You are a father," said the afflicted parent, "or I should not have allowed you to witness such a scene." "Thank God," fervently exclaimed the minister, comprehending at a glance the situation of his friend, "thank God, he has not forgotten you! I have been much troubled on your account, my dear sir. I have thought much about you lately. I have been much afraid for you. Things have gone on so well with you for so long a time, you have been so prosperous, that I have been almost afraid that God had forgotten you. But I said to myself, surely God will not forsake such a man as this —will not suffer him to go on in prosperity, without some check, some reverse! And I see he has not. No; God has not forgotten you."

6385. AFFLICTION, Exchanging. An English hermit was afflicted with a repulsive and painful disease from his childhood. He prayed that God, in His mercy, would exchange the torments of his malady for some lighter disease that should not make his body repulsive. Soon after he felt that he was healed, and that his disorder was entirely eradicated; but, strange to relate, another disease came upon him which tormented him incessantly, night and day, for twenty years.

6386. AFFLICTION, Figures of. It is a fact of deep significance, that of the many figures which abound in the Scriptures, those for affliction and trial are most numerous. The following are amongst the most common: Baptism (of suffering), bonds, broken, bruised, crushed, (like herbs, fruits, olives, etc.), a broken vessel, captivity and imprisonment, cross, cup, darkness, day of gloom, mourning, dove, fighting, fire, furnace, the friction of precious stones, the melting of precious metals, medicine, ploughshare, purging, pruning, rod, storm and tempest, thorns, deep waters. waves, billows, floods, rivers, valley, wormwood and gall.   *Bowes.*

6387. AFFLICTION, Frost of. There are some fruits, like the persimmon, that now seem fair and ready to eat, that are most bitter and disagreeable. But the coming frosts will somehow work to change all the acids and bitterness into a most luscious and wholesome fruit. So earthly trials work to change the sour, selfish, disagreeable spirits of some Christians into a genuine sweetness. And there are many who keep up the fair form of a Christian profession who need some like power to remove their disposition to bitterness of criticism and sourness of temper.   *A. D. Vail.*

6388. AFFLICTION, Graces from. When Munster lay sick, and his friends asked him how he did, and how he felt himself, he pointed to his sores and ulcers, whereof he was full, and said, "These are God's gems and jewels, wherewith he decketh his best friends, and to me they are more precious than all the gold and silver in the world." A soul at first conversion is but a rough cast; but God by afflictions doth square and fit and fashion it for that glory above, which doth speak them to flow from precious love; therefore the afflictions that do attend the people of God should be no bar to holiness, nor no motive to draw the soul to ways of wickedness.   *Brooks.*

6389. AFFLICTION, Happiness in. Rev. Henry Venn told his children that he would take them to one of the most interesting sights in the world. He led them to a miserable hovel, whose decayed walls and broken windows bespoke poverty and want. "Now," said he, "my dear children, can any one that lives in such a wretched place as this be happy? Yet this is not all; a poor young man lies on a miserable straw bed within, dying of a fever, and afflicted with nine painful ulcers." "Oh, how wretched!" they all exclaimed at once. Mr. Venn led them into the cottage, and, going up to the poor, dying young man, said, "Abraham Midwood, I have brought my children here to show them that people can be happy in sickness, in poverty, and in want; and now tell them if it is not so." The suffering youth immediately answered, "Oh, yes, sir; I would not change my state with the richest man on earth who had not the views which I have. Blessed be God, I have a good hope through Christ of going to heaven, where Lazarus now is. He has a great while ago forgotten all his miseries; soon I shall mine. Sir, this is nothing to bear while the presence of God cheers my soul. Indeed, I am truly happy, and I trust to be happy through all eternity; and I every hour thank God, who has given me to enjoy the riches of his goodness and his grace through Jesus Christ."

6390. AFFLICTION, Honor of. In the ancient times, a box on the ear given by a master to a slave meant liberty: little would the freedman care how hard was the blow. By a stroke from the sword the warrior was knighted by his monarch: small matter was it to the new-made

knight if the hand was heavy. When the Lord intends to lift his servants into a higher stage of spiritual life, he frequently sends them a severe trial; he makes his Jacobs to be prevailing princes, but he confers the honor after a night of wrestling, and accompanies it with a shrunken sinew. Be it so: who among us would wish to be deprived of the trials, if they are the necessary attendants of spiritual advancement?   *Spurgeon.*

6391. AFFLICTION, Improvement of. Men that are wise, as the bees draw honey from the thyme, which is a most unsavory herb, extract something that is convenient and useful from the most bitter affliction.   *Plutarch.*

6392. AFFLICTION, Intention of. In Mexico a method of separating the silver from the dross is to pulverize the ore, and spread it out on a large platform. Great numbers of mules are driven over it. Quicksilver is poured over the mud, and the trampling is continued. When the metals have thoroughly amalgamated, the mass is cast into the furnace, and the silver runs off clear from the dross. So men are broken and trampled by afflictions. The quicksilver of truth is poured over them, they are cast into the furnace of tribulation, till the precious products of faith and purity are realized.

6393. AFFLICTION, Lesson of. Lokmân, the famous Oriental philosopher, while a slave, being presented by his master with a bitter melon, immediately ate it all. "How was it possible," said his master, "for you to eat so nauseous a fruit?" Lokman replied, "I have received so many favors from you, it is no wonder I should, for once in my life, eat a bitter melon from your hand." This generous answer of the slave struck the master so forcibly, that he immediately gave him his liberty. "With such sentiments," says Bishop Horne, "should man receive his portion of suffering at the hand of God."

6394. AFFLICTION, Peace from. A fierce battle between the Medes and Lydians was brought to an end by a total eclipse of the sun. The awe which it produced was so great that both armies threw down their arms and made peace. Similar to this are the effects of afflictions, sickness, bereavement, or the dark clouds which shut out the light of prosperity. Enmities are forgotten, and peace is made with all in the presence of great afflictions.

6395. AFFLICTION, Profit of. Affliction is very useful and profitable to the godly. The prodigal son had no thought of returning to his father's house till he had been humbled by adversity. Hagar was haughty under Abraham's roof, and despised her mistress; but in the wilderness she was meek and lowly. Jonah sleeps on board ship, but in that whale's belly he watches and prays. Manasseh lived as a libertine at Jerusalem, and committed the most enormous crimes; but when he was bound in chains in the prison at Babylon, his heart was turned to seek the Lord his God. Bodily pain and disease have been instrumental in rousing many to seek Christ, when those who were in high health have given themselves no concern about him. The ground which is not rent and torn with the plough bears nothing but thistles and thorns. The vines will run wild, in process of time, if they be not pruned and trimmed. So would our wild hearts be overrun with filthy, poisonous weeds, if the true Vine-dresser did not often check their growth by crosses and sanctified troubles. "It is good for a man that he bear the yoke in his youth." Our Saviour says, "Every branch that beareth fruit He purgeth, that it may bring forth more fruit." There can be no gold or silver finely wrought without first being purified with fire, and no elegant houses built with stones till the hammers have squared and smoothed them. So we can neither become vessels of honor in the house of our Father till we are melted in the furnace of affliction, nor lively stones in the walls of New Jerusalem till the hand of the Lord has beaten off our proud excrescences and tumors with his own hammers.   *Daniel Rowlands.*

6396. AFFLICTION, Right View of. Our crosses are not made of iron, though painted sometimes with iron colors; they are formed of nothing heavier than wood. Yet they are not made of pasteboard, and will never be light in themselves, though our Lord can lighten them by his presence. The Papists foolishly worship pieces of wood supposed to be parts of the true cross; but he who has borne the really true cross and known its sanctifying power, will value every sliver of it, counting his trials to be his treasures, his afflictions argosies of wealth, and his losses his best gains.   *Spurgeon.*

6397. AFFLICTION, Sanctifying Power of. Afflictions are a crystal glass, wherein the soul hath the clearest sight of the ugly face of sin. In this glass the soul comes to see sin to be but a bitter-sweet; yea, in this glass the soul comes to see sin not only to be an evil, but to be the greatest evil in the world, to be an evil far worse than hell itself. Again, they shall contribute to the mortifying and purging away of their sins (Isa. 1:15, and 27:8, 9). Afflictions are God's furnace, by which he cleanses his people from their dross, and to make virtues shine; it is a potion to carry away ill humors, better than all the *benedictum medicamentum*, as physicians call them. Aloes kill worms; colds and frosts do destroy vermin; so do afflictions the corruptions that are in our hearts. The Jews, under all the prophets' thunderings, retained their idols; but after their Babylonish captivity, it is observed, there have been no idols found amongst them. . . . Augustine, by wandering out of his way, escaped one that lay in wait to mischief him. If afflictions did not put us out of our way, we should many times meet with some sin or other that would mischief our precious souls.   *Brooks.*

6398. AFFLICTION, Songs in. The children sometimes stretch a silver thread in the window, between the sashes, to make an Æolian harp. And while the air is calm and still, there is no music. But when the wind blows softly a faint murmur of music is heard; and the stronger the wind the louder and sweeter the melody becomes. It is so with many a human heart. The purest, sweetest, holiest joy I ever witnessed in mortal on earth was in one who for fourteen years had been sitting in her chair, unable to lift hand or foot. All these years her heart had been communing with God, and the sorrows that beat upon the chords of her soul struck out songs which might have fallen from an angel's tongue.   *J. R. Miller.*

6399. AFFLICTION, Stimulation of. There is an old story in the Greek annals of a soldier under Antigonus who had a disease about him, an extremely painful one, likely to bring him soon to the grave. Always first in the charge was this soldier, rushing into the hottest part of the fray, as the bravest of the brave. His pain prompted him to fight, that he might forget it; and he feared not death, because he knew that in any case he had not long to live. Antigonus, who greatly admired the valor of his soldier, discovering his malady, had him cured by one of the most eminent physicians of the day; but, alas! from that moment the warrior was absent from the front of the battle. He now sought his ease; for, as he remarked to his companions, he had something worth living for —health, home, family, and other comforts— and he would not risk his life now as aforetime. So, when our troubles are many we are often by grace made courageous in serving our Lord; we feel that we have nothing to live for in this world, and we are driven, by the hope of the world to come, to exhibit zeal, self-denial, and industry. But how often is it otherwise in better times! for then the joys and pleasure of this world make it hard for us to remember the world to come, and we sink into inglorious ease.   *Spurgeon.*

6400. AFFLICTION, Superior to. Anaxarchus, a heathen, being thrown into a mortar and beaten with an iron pestle, cried out, "You do but beat the vessel, the husk of Anaxarchus; you do not beat me!" Socrates said of his enemies, "They may kill me, but they cannot hurt me."

6401. AFFLICTION, Support in. If you thoroughly exhaust a vessel of the air it contains, the pressure of the air on the outside will break that vessel into (perhaps) millions of pieces; because there is not a sufficiency of air within to resist and counteract the weight of the atmosphere from without. A person who is exercised by severe affliction, and who does not experience the Divine comforts and supports in his soul, resembles the exhausted receiver above described; and it is no wonder if he yields, and is broken to shivers, under the weight of God's providential hand. But affliction, to one who is sustained by the Holy Ghost, resembles the aerial pressure on the outer surface of an un exhausted vessel. There is that within which supports it, and which preserves it from being destroyed by the incumbent pressure from without.   *Salter.*

6402. AFFLICTION, Trust in. There is a young man in New England of fine capabilities, who, for years, has been so helpless that he would starve if left alone. A friend was commiserating his condition, when, with deep earnestness he exclaimed, as he slowly raised his withered hand, "God makes no mistakes."

6403. AFFLICTION, Use of. Thorns in the field, that prevented the soldiers from using their weapons, and thorns in the flesh, that acted as Satan's messengers to buffet God's saints, will both be acknowledged as instruments used by the Sovereign Spirit in preparing a people for the Lord. Let us endeavor to be patient when thorns prick us: they are the hedges which God has planted to keep us in the way of life; they will become a wreath of victory in the great day. *Arnot.*

6404. AFFLICTIONS, Challenging. Let fire and the cross, let companies of wild beasts, let breaking of bones and tearing of members, let the shattering in pieces of the whole body and all the wicked torments of the devil come upon me; only let me enjoy Jesus Christ. *Ignatius.*

6405. AFFLICTIONS, Christians in. Stars shine brightest in the darkest night; torches are better for beating; grapes come not to the proof till they come to the press; spices smell best when bruised; young trees root the faster for shaking; gold looks brighter for scouring; juniper smells sweetest in the fire; the palm-tree proves the better for pressing; chamomile, the more you tread it, the more you spread it. Such is the condition of all God's children; they are then most triumphant when most tempted; most glorious when most afflicted; most in favor of God when least in man's own: as their conflicts, so their conquests; as their tribulations, so their triumphs; true salamanders, that live best in the furnace of persecution: so that heavy afflictions are the best benefactors to heavenly affections; and where afflictions hang heaviest, corruptions hang loosest; and grace, that is hid in nature, as sweet water in rose-leaves, is then most fragrant when the fire of affliction is put under to distil it out.
Bogatzky.

6406. AFFLICTIONS, Consolations for. In afflictions men generally draw their consolations out of books of morality, which indeed are of great use to fortify and strengthen the mind against the impressions of sorrow. Monsieur St. Evremont recommends authors who are apt to stir up mirth in the minds of the readers, and fancies Don Quixote can give more relief to a heavy heart than Plutarch or Seneca, as it is much easier to divert grief than to conquer it. I should rather have recourse to authors of a quite contrary kind, that give us instances of calamities and misfortunes, and show human nature in its greatest distresses. *Addison.*

6407. AFFLICTIONS, Different Effects of. How different are summer storms from winter ones! In winter they rush over the earth with their violence; and if any poor remnants of foliage or flowers have lingered behind, these are swept along at one gust. Nothing is left but desolation; and long after the rain has ceased, pools of water and mud bear tokens of what has been. But when the clouds have poured out their torrents in summer, when the winds have spent their fury, and the sun breaks forth

again in glory, all things seem to rise with renewed loveliness from their refreshing bath. The flowers, glistening with rainbows, smell sweeter than before; the grass seems to have gained another brighter shade of green; and the young plants which had hardly come into sight, have taken their place among their fellows in the borders, so quickly have they sprung among the showers. The air, too, which may previously have been oppressive, is become clear, and soft, and fresh. Such, too, is the difference when the storms of affliction fall on hearts unrenewed by Christian faith, and on those who abide in Christ. In the former they bring out the dreariness and desolation which may before have been unapparent. The gloom is not relieved by the prospect of any cheering ray to follow it; of any flowers or fruits to show its beneficence. But in the true Christian soul, "though weeping may endure for a night, joy cometh in the morning." A sweet smile of hope and love follows every tear; and tribulation itself is turned into the chief of blessings. *Anon.*

6408. AFFLICTIONS, Favor of. St. Theresa had a vision in which Christ said to her, "Dost thou think that merit consists in enjoying? No: but rather in working, in suffering, in loving. He is most beloved of my Father on whom He lays the heaviest crosses, if these sufferings are accepted and borne with love. By what can I better show my love for thee than by choosing for thee what I chose for myself?"

6409. AFFLICTIONS, Fitness of. The cook, by mistake, prepared a broth of wormwood for St. Francis Borgia, which he ate without a word of complaint. When the cook discovered his mistake he asked pardon of the saint. He said "I never ate anything fitter for me. May the Lord bless and reward you," said he to the cook, "you are the only person amongst all my brethren who knows what suits me best. Herein is a parable of the cup mingled by the All-father, who never makes mistakes, and which he sends to his children for their good."

6410. AFFLICTIONS, Need of. Christians have frequently more of these sufferings than others. The husbandman does not prune the bramble, but the vine. The stones designed for the temple above require more cutting and polishing than those which are for the common wall. Correction is not for strangers, but children. The Christian mourns over those infirmities which are not viewed by others as sins, such as wandering thoughts and cold affections in duty. It is said of that beautiful bird, the bird of Paradise, that if it is caught and caged, it never ceases to sigh till it is free. Just such is the Christian. Nothing will satisfy him but the glorious liberty of the sons of God. *Jay.*

6411. AFFLICTIONS, Rewards of. When the Christian's last pit is digged, when he is descended into his grave, and finished his state of sorrows and suffering, then God opens the river of abundance, the rivers of life and never-ceasing felicities. As much as moments are exceeded by eternity, and the sighing of a man by the joys of an angel, and a salutary frown by the light of God's countenance, a few groans by the infinite and eternal hallelujahs; so much are the sorrows of the saints to be undervalued, in respect of what is deposited for them in the treasures of eternity. Their sorrows can die, but so cannot their joys.... Every chain is a ray of light, and every prison is a palace, and every loss is the purchase of a kingdom, and every affront in the cause of God is an eternal honor, and every day of sorrow is a thousand years of comfort, multiplied with a never-ceasing numeration; days without night, joys without sorrow, sanctity without sin, charity without stain, possession without fear, society without envying, communication of joys without lessening: and they shall dwell in a blessed country, where an enemy never entered, and from whence a friend never went away.

Jeremy Taylor.

6412. AFFLICTIONS, Unsanctified. Trust not in any unsanctified afflictions. These cannot permanently and really change the condition of your heart. I have seen the characters of the writing remain on paper which the flames had turned into a film of buoyant coal; I have seen the thread that had been passed through the fire, retain, in its cold gray ashes, the twist which it had got in spinning; I have found every shivered splinter of the flint as hard as the unbroken stone; and let trials come, in providence, sharp as the fire, and ponderous as the crushing hammer, unless a gracious God send along with these something else, bruised, broken, bleeding, as your heart may be, its nature remains the same. *Dr. Guthrie.*

6413. AGE, Comfort in Old. A cheerful, tottering, poor old man of eighty-one said, "Thank God, I have my wits and my limbs. I never was in prison, and I am not going to hell. I am the Lord's. So while I see everybody in this busy world looking keenly, as they do, after their own, the sight helps me to believe, and I am comforted in the faith, that Jesus is looking after me, and he will take me soon."

T. Collins.

6414. AGE, Computing. An old slave who could neither read nor write, was asked how old he was. He did not know, but said he could tell how long he had been the Lord's child. He brought out a bottle into which he had dropped a pebble every Christmas since his conversion. It contained fifty-one pebbles.

6415. AGE, Deception of. It is with most men's lives, as with the sand in a deceptive hour-glass; look upon its outward appearance, and it seems far more than it is, because it rises up upon the sides, whilst the sand is empty and hollow in the middle thereof, so that when it sinks down in an instant, a quarter of an hour is gone in a moment. Thus many men are mistaken in their own account, reckoning upon threescore and ten years, the age of a man, because their bodies appear strong and lusty. Alas! their health may be hollow, there may be some inward infirmity and imperfection unknown to them, so that death may surprise them on a sudden, and they be cut down like the grass. *Anon.*

6416. AGE, Reverence for. Age naturally awakens our respect. A Greek historian tells how, in the pure and early, and most virtuous days of the republic, if an old man entered the crowded assembly, all ranks rose to give room and place to him. Age throws such a character of dignity even over inanimate objects, that the spectator regards them with a sort of awe and veneration. We have stood before the hoary and ivy-mantled ruin of a bygone age with deeper feelings of respect than ever touched us in the marbled halls, and amid the gilded grandeur of modern palaces; nor did the proudest tree which lifted its umbrageous head and towering form to the skies ever affect us with such strange emotion as an old, withered, wasted trunk that, though hollowed by time into a gnarled shell, still showed some green signs of life. *Dr. Guthrie.*

6417. AGE, Softening Effects of. Men, like peaches and pears, grow sweet a little while before they begin to decay. I don't know what it is—whether a spontaneous change, mental or bodily, or whether it is thorough experience of the thanklessness of critical honesty—but it is a fact, that most writers, except sour and unsuccessful ones, get tired of finding fault at about the time when they are beginning to grow old. As a general thing I would not give a great deal for the fair words of a critic, if he is himself an author over fifty years of age. At thirty we are all trying to cut our names in big letters upon the walls of this tenement of life; twenty years later we have carved them or shut up our jack-knives. Then we are ready to help others, and care less to hinder any, because nobody's elbows are in our way. I just now spoke of the sweetening process authors undergo. Do you know that, in the gradual passage from maturity to helplessness, the harshest characters sometimes have a period in which they are gentle and placid as young children? I have heard it said, but I cannot be sponsor for its truth, that the famous chieftain, Lochiel, was rocked in a cradle like a baby in his old age. An old man, whose studies had been of the severest scholastic kind, used to love to hear little nursery stories read over and over to him. One who saw the Duke of Wellington in his last years describes him as very gentle in his aspect and demeanor. I remember a person of singularly stern and lofty bearing, who became remarkably gracious and easy in all his ways in the latter period of his life. *Holmes.*

6418. AGE, Traits of Each. Each succeeding age and generation leaves behind it a peculiar character, which stands out in relief upon its annals, and is associated with it forever in the memory of posterity. One is signalized for the invention of gunpowder, another for that of printing; one is rendered memorable by the revival of letters, another by the reformation of religion; one is marked in history by the conquests of Napoleon, another is rendered illustrious by the discoveries of Newton. If we are asked by what characteristic the present age will be marked in future records, we answer, by the miracles which have been wrought in the subjugation of the powers of the material world to the uses of the human race. In this respect no former epoch can approach to competition with it.   *Dr. Lardner.*

6419. AGED, Conversion of the. Marcus Caius Victorius was converted from heathenism in old age. So unusual was it in those primitive times for the aged to be converted, that neither the minister nor the Church would trust him. After a long time such was the evidence of the change that they could no longer doubt. He was received with acclamations and singing of psalms, the people everywhere crying, "Marcus Caius Victorius is become a Christian."

6420. AGED, Decay of the. We have seen a sere and yellow leaf hang upon the tree all the winter through. There, tenacious of its hold, dancing and whirling in the playful wind, it appeared not beautiful or graceful, but out of place and season, and in humbling contrast with the young and green companions which budding spring had hung around it. Like that wrinkled and withered thing, some men hang on by this world. They live too long, and die too late, for themselves at least. Half dead and half alive, mind failed and memory faded, outliving their usefulness, but the melancholy wrecks of what once they were, they tax affection to conceal from strangers' eyes the ravages of time, and do for them the tender office of the ivy, when she kindly flings a green and glossy mantle over the crumbling ruin or old hollow tree.   *Guthrie.*

6421. AGED, Illusions of the. One dear old saint had become possessed by a singularly happy monomania. To her every day was Sunday. The little left of life was to be all worship. The only trouble the pleasant delusion caused was that her daughter was obliged to clean the cottage early, and on the sly; for pails, scrubbing brushes and mops seemed awful improprieties to her ever Sabbath-keeping mother. Another aged woman had gone blind; "All," said she, "around is dark. I see nothing there; but when I look right up towards heaven, for months past, I have always seen the letter W printed as if in pearls; I know what it means. I am going soon, and it means welcome."   *T. Collins.*

6422. AGED, Regard for the. It was anciently a proverb among the heathen, it is good to be an old man or woman only in Sparta. The ground of it was the strict laws among the Spartans to punish the rebellion and disobedience of children to their aged parents. And shall it not be good to be an old father and mother in this land, where the Gospel of Christ is preached?   *Flavel.*

6423. AGED, Paying Respect to the. A Russian princess of great beauty, in company with her father and a young French marquis, visited a celebrated Swiss doctor of the eighteenth century, Michael Scuppack; when the marquis began to pass one of his jokes upon the long white beard of one of the doctor's neighbors who was present. He offered to bet twelve louis' d'ors that no lady present would dare to kiss the dirty old fellow! The Russian prin-

cess ordered her attendant to bring a plate, and deposited twelve louis d'ors, and sent it to the marquis, who was too polite to decline his stake. The fair Russian then approached the peasant, saying, "Permit me, venerable father, to salute you after the manner of my country," and embracing, gave him a kiss. She then presented him the gold which was on the plate, saying, "Take this as a remembrance of me, and as a sign that the Russian girls think it their duty to honor old age."

6424. AGITATION, Use of. Dr. John Ritchie, of Scotland, replied to one who disapproved of his going up and down the country resorting to agitation. "Agitation!" said John, "what good in the world was ever done without agitation? We cannot make butter even without it!"

6425. AGREEMENTS, Legal. Persæus, being about to accommodate a friend with a sum of money, paid it publicly in the market, and made the conditions before a banker. But when his friend marveled and asked, "How now, so formally and according to law?" "Yea," quoth he, "because I would receive my money again as a friend, and not have to trouble the law to recover it." For many, out of bashfulness, not taking care to have good security at first, have been forced afterwards to break with their friends, and to have recourse to law for their money.   *Plutarch.*

6426. AGRICULTURE, Importance of. Agriculture is the foundation of manufactures, since the productions of nature are the materials of art.—*Gibbon.*——Agriculture not only gives riches to a nation, but the only riches she can call her own.   *Dr. Johnson.*

6427. AGRICULTURIST, Life of the. In a moral point of view, the life of the agriculturist is the most pure and holy of any class of men; pure, because it is the most healthful, and vice can hardly find time to contaminate it; and holy, because it brings the Deity perpetually before his view, giving him thereby the most exalted notions of supreme power, and the most fascinating and endearing view of moral benignity. The agriculturist views the Deity in His works; he contemplates the divine economy in the arrangement of the seasons; and he hails *Nature* immediately presiding over every object that strikes his eyes; he witnesses many of her great and beauteous operations, and her reproductive faculties; his heart insensibly expands, from his minute acquaintance with multifarious objects, all in themselves original whilst that degree of retirement in which he is placed from the bustling haunts of mankind, keeps alive in his breast his natural affections, unblunted by an extensive and perpetual intercourse with man in a more enlarged, and, therefore, in a more corrupt state of society.   *Lord John Russell.*

6428. AIM, Direct. Do not sow the world broadcast, but, as the Scotch would say, "Dibble it in!" Make a hole in the ground with your sharpened stick and push the seed into the earth with your heel. Let every sentence tell. Shoot with an aim. Take your arrow from your quiver, put it on the bow with your eye on the soul and on the throne, then let it go home. Do not pull it out. Let it be a distinct and felt impression. Do not talk to human beings who are asleep. I have no faith in somnambulism in the church. Let every eye be engaged as though he would look you through. Give the children something worth receiving, and send the truth home.

Dr. Ormiston.

6429. AIM, Effective. A sharp-shooter from one of the Vermont regiments in the battle of —— fired ninety-six cartridges, three-fourths of which were effective. In the random shooting of common soldiers in battle it is estimated that not more than one bullet in four thousand does execution. The teacher or Christian worker who would save souls must make some particular heart his target and aim for it:—must select the best rifle and ammunition, and if he does not hit must try again, and again, till he has smitten the mark and secured the capitulation of the soul to Christ. So of every other object desired.

6430. AIM, Execution and. A gentleman calling on Thorwaldsen, found him, as he said, in a glow, almost in a trance, of creative energy. On his inquiring what had happened, "*My friend, my dear friend,*" said the sculptor, "*I have an idea, I have a work in my head, which will be worthy to live. A lad had been sitting to me some time as a model yesterday, when I bade him rest awhile. In so doing, he threw himself into an attitude which struck me very much. 'What a beautiful statue it would make!' I said to myself; 'But what would it do for? It would do— it would do— it would do exactly for Mercury drawing his sword, just after he has played Argus to sleep.' I immediately began modeling. I worked all the evening, till at my usual hour I went to bed. But my idea would not let me rest. I was forced to get up again. I struck a light, and worked at my model for three or four hours, after which I again went to bed. But again I could not rest; again I was forced to get up, and have been working ever since. O my friend, if I can but execute my idea, it will be a glorious statue.*" And a noble statue it is; although Thorwaldsen himself did not think that the execution came up to the idea. For I have heard of a remarkable speech of his, made some years after to another friend who found him one day in low spirits. Being asked whether anything had distressed him, he answered, "*My genius is decaying.*" "*What do you mean?*" said the visitor. "*Why! here is my statue of Christ: it is the first of my works that I have ever felt satisfied with. Till now, my idea has always been been far beyond what I could execute. But it is no longer so. I shall never have a great idea again.*" The same, I believe, must have been the case with all men of true genius. While they who have nothing but talents may often be astonished at the effects they produce by putting things together, which fit more aptly than they expected, a man

of genius, who has had an idea of a whole in his mind, will feel that no outward mode of expressing that idea, whether by form or colors or words, is adequate to represent it.

Guesses of Truth.

6431. AIM, Want of. The French have recently published some statistics in regard to the recent war with Germany that are significant and instructive. They count now that during the war there came into France one million Germans, but there were only one hundred thousand Frenchmen killed; therefore, nine Germans in ten fired away for seven months and never hit any one, and the tenth fellow never fired but one effective shot. All this, too, in the age of needle-guns and most perfect military education! *W. F. Crafts.*

6432. AIR, Benefits of. While the air of the atmosphere serves as the reservoir of that mass of water from whence clouds of rain, and consequently springs and rivers, are derived, at the same time it prevents, by the effect of its pressure on their surface, the unlimited evaporation and consequent exhaustion of the ocean, and other sources from whence that mass of water is supplied. And again, while the agitation of the air contributes to the health of man, by supplying those currents which remove or prevent the accumulation of local impurities, it, at the same time, facilitates that intercourse between different nations, in which the welfare of the whole world is ultimately concerned. And lastly, while in passing from the lungs in the act of expiration, it essentially forms the voice; it at the same time removes from the system that noxious principle, the retention of which would be incompatible with life. *Professor Kidd.*

6433. ALARM, False. A shepherd boy, who tended his flock not far from a village, used to amuse himself at times in crying out, "Wolf! wolf!" Twice or thrice his trick succeeded. The whole village came running out to his assistance; when all the return they got was to be laughed at for their pains. At last one day the wolf came indeed. The boy cried out in earnest. But his neighbors, supposing him to be at his old sport, paid no heed to his cries, and the wolf devoured the sheep. So the boy learned, when it was too late, that liars are not believed even when they tell the truth.

Æsop.

6434. ALARM, A Sinner's. A preacher spoke of God's efforts to win man: first by wooing him, second by warning him. If these fail, the next voice may be that of the commissioned angel saying, "Come to judgment!" A soldier in the audience sprang to his feet in great excitement exclaiming, "Say not so—say not so —oh, stop." He had become alarmed at the prospect of meeting his own sins at the bar of the Omniscient Judge. The alarmed man explained that his mother's dying injunction was "Don't be a soldier." He disregarded her wish, and was led into gross sins. As he listened to the preacher, he heard his mother's voice saying, "Don't be a soldier." This, followed by the angel's call, "Come to judgment," so moved him that he could no longer keep silence.

6435. ALCOHOL, Effects of. It may seem strange, but it is nevertheless true, that alcohol, regularly applied to a thrifty farmer's stomach, will remove the boards from the fence, let cattle into his crops, kill his fruit trees, mortgage his farm, and sow his fields with wild oats and thistles. It will take the paint off his building, break the glass out of the windows and fill them with rags. It will take the gloss from his clothes and the polish from his manners, subdue his reason, arouse his passions, bring sorrow and disgrace upon his family, and topple him into a drunkard's grave. It will do this to the artisan and the capitalist, the matron and the maiden, as well as to the farmer; for, in its deadly emnity to the human race, alcohol is no respecter of persons.   *Temperance Worker.*

6436. ALCOHOL, Passion for. An old woman in London went into a dram-shop and called for a glass of gin, which she drank. She then drew a Bible from under her apron, saying she had no money, but would leave that in pledge, and redeem it in half an hour; she, however, never returned. A woman in Glasgow, in order to gratify her immoderate craving for ardent spirits, offered her *own child for sale as a subject for dissection.*

6437. ALLEGORIES, Advantage of. Allegories, when well chosen, are like so many tracks of light in a discourse, that make everything about them clear and beautiful.   *Addison.*

6438. ALLELUIA, Victory by. The ancient Britons, in the year 420, obtained a victory over an army of the Picts and Saxons, near Mold, in Flintshire. The Britons unarmed, having Germanus and Lupus at their head, when the Picts and Saxons came to the attack, the two commanders, Gideon-like, ordered their army to shout *Alleluia* three times over, at the sound of which the enemy, being suddenly struck with terror, ran away in the greatest confusion, and left the Britons masters of the field. A stone monument, to perpetuate the remembrance of this *Halleluiah* victory, is said to remain to this day in a field near Mold.   *Whitecross.*

6439. ALLOTMENT, God's. "Sir," said a boy, addressing a man, "do you want a boy to work for you?" "No," answered the man, "I have no such want." The boy looked disappointed,—at least the man thought so, and he asked, "Can't you succeed in getting a place?" "I have asked at a good many places," said the boy; "a woman told me you had been after a boy, but it is not so, I find." "Don't be discouraged," said the man in a friendly tone. "Oh no, sir," said the boy cheerfully, "I still hope on, because this is a very big world, and I feel certain God has something for me to do in it. I am only trying to find it." "Just so, just so," said a gentleman, who overheard the talk. "Come with me, my boy; I am in search of somebody like you." He was a doctor, and thought that a boy so anxious to find his work would be likely to do it faithfully when found. From that time the boy was in his place and his success was assured.

6440. ALLUREMENTS, Avoiding. When Araspes had commended the fair Panthea to Cyrus, as a beauty worth his admiration, he replied: "For that very reason I will not see her, lest if by thy persuasion I should see her but once, she herself might persuade me to see her often, and spend more time with her than would be for the advantage of my own affairs." So Alexander, upon like consideration, would not trust his eyes in the presence of the beautiful queen of Persia, but kept himself out of the reach of her charms, and treated only with her aged mother.
     Plutarch

6441. ALLUREMENTS, Fatal. Pliny tells us, that the mermaids delight to be in green meadows, into which they draw men by their enchanting voices; but, saith he, there always lie heaps of dead men's bones by them. A lively emblem of a bewitching world! Good had it been for many professors of religion, if they had never known what the riches, and honors, and pleasures of the world are.
     John Flavel.

6442. ALLUREMENTS, Legend of. A story of the sixteenth century relates, that Leonard, the son of a tailor of Basle, Switzerland, one day entered a deep cave with a torch in his hand. He found an enchanted land. The queen of the place was a strange creature—a woman to the waist, and a snake below. She had wonderful fascination, and was said to be beautiful. On her head she wore a crown of gold. She entreated the young man to kiss her three times, and gave him gold and silver. He did so twice, but was filled with disgust at her writhing tail, and fled without giving her the third kiss. Ever after he prowled about the mountains, seeking the cave, having a constant desire for the society of the revolting creature. It was well for him that he was early frightened. Such is the fascination of evil over the hearts of men.

6443. ALMIGHTY, Shadow of the. Isaac Toms said, "I have heard of Dryden's contentment when sitting under the statue of Shakespeare; and that Buffon, the celebrated natural historian, felt himself happy at the feet of Sir Isaac Newton; but," pointing to a picture which hung over his desk, "here you find me under the shadow of good Richard Baxter. Yet, my dear, the most desirable situation in which we can be placed, is to be under the shadow of the Almighty—under the protection of the great Redeemer."

6444. ALTAR, Christ our. This brazen altar was a type of Christ dying to make atonement for our sins. The wood had been consumed by the fire from heaven, if it had not been secured by the brass; nor could the human nature of Christ have borne the wrath of God, if it had not been supported by a divine power. Christ sanctified himself for his Church, as their altar, John 17: 19; and by his mediation sanctifies the daily services of his people, who also have a right to eat of this altar, Heb. 13: 10; for they serve at it as spiritual priests. To the horns of this altar poor sinners fly for refuge when justice pursues them, and there they are safe in virtue of the sacrifice there offered.

M. Henry.

6445. ALTAR, Safety Only at the. Certain Athenian conspirators fled for their lives into the temple of Minerva, where they were safe so long as they remained. Megacles persuaded them to stand trial, but to retain their claim to the right of asylum by tying a string to the shrine of the goddess, and holding on to it. This they attempted to do, but as they were passing the temple of the Furies the thread broke. Thereby they lost their privilege, and the crowd rushed upon them, and stoned them or cut them to pieces. Thus perish those who maintain their connection with Christ, if at all, at the greatest possible distance from him, and by the smallest thread. There is safety only in close union with him.

6446. ALTARS, Jewish. They were, the one of gold, the other brazen. The brazen one stood in the outer court of the congregation. The other, the golden one, in the holy place, where none but the priests might enter. The outer court, with its brazen altar and laver, represents the earth and the work which is done in it to God-ward. The holy place, with the golden altar for incense, shows us the heavenly places and their appointed service. On the brazen altar were offered the sacrifices of Israel. Any Israelite, if clean, might draw nigh and offer there. But priests only might approach the golden altar, and nothing came on it except the perfumed incense. The position and use of these altars, and the references to them in the New Testament, unite to point out their typical meaning; the one leading us to the service of the church as on earth, the other to their service as priests in heavenly places. As to the sprinkling of blood, I need scarcely say it always refers to atonement by sacrifice: it signifies that the thing or person sprinkled is thereby brought from a state of distance from God to a state of nearness. The sprinkling of blood upon the incense altar implied that until this act was performed the altar was unapproachable; and, consequently, that all priestly service, and, therefore, all service of all kinds was stopped between God and Israel. In like manner, the sprinkling of blood on the brazen altar implied that till this was done that altar, too, was regarded as unapproachable. In each case sin is apprehended to have interrupted communion; in the one, the communion of priests; in the other that of Israel; while the sprinkling of blood declares that communion restored through the sin-offering, on the incense altar, to the priests, on the brazen altar to Israel.   *A. Jukes.*

6447. AMBITION, Carnal. Ambition was one of the first temptations that assailed and overcame our first parents—"Ye shall be as gods." Ambition will be one of the most striking features that will mark the character of Antichrist, 2 Thess. 2: 4; Dan. 7: 25; 11: 36; Rev. 13: 5, 6. The disciples of Christ. It is surprising how repeatedly the disciples were guilty of this sin, and at times when it might have least been looked for. Luke 9: 46-48.—Just after Christ's transfiguration, which three of them had beheld, and of which the rest were most probably cognizant (as is probable from Mark 9: 15). Matt. 18: 1-6.—When the Lord a second time set a little child in the midst of them. Matt. 19: 27. —After the unadvised inquiry of Peter, not unmixed with ambition, for himself and his fellow apostles. Matt. 20: 20-28.—When James and John came, through their mother, with their bold request; and were justly reproved for their ambition and self-confidence. Luke 22: 24-2⁷ —Before, or, according to others, just after the institution of the Lord's Supper. Jotham's parable, Judges 9: 8-15.—The most aspiring are frequently the most contemptible.   *Bowes.*

6448. AMBITION, Christian. It is remarkable that the Greek word which corresponds to our word ambition occurs only three times in the New Testament. Our translators seem to have shrunk from expressing the full meaning, and render it by the three words, studying—striving —laboring. Thus St. Paul speaks of it as a holy ambition—1 Thess. 4: 11—to "study to be quiet." It might almost be rendered—to be ambitious to be unambitious. Rom. 15: 20.— To carry the gospel where no other laborer had carried it. In this he strove. He was ambitious of it. 2 Cor. 5: 9.—Whether present (in the body) or absent, to be accepted of Christ. *Bowes.*

6449. AMBITION, Conquered. Henry Martin, the saintly missionary, during his college life was very ambitious, and used every effort, never losing an hour, to gain all the honors possible for himself. He won them, but found them empty. His worldly prospects were bright, and his ambition for fame would doubtless have been realized. Grace came into his heart. He began to live for Christ, and not for self. He sacrificed self, home, friends, worldly prospects and life for the cause of the lost. He was as ambitious of his Master's honor as he had before been for himself.

6450. AMBITION, Defeat of. When Napoleon returned to his palace, immediately after his defeat at Waterloo, he continued many hours without any refreshment. One of the grooms of the chamber ventured to serve up some coffee in his cabinet by the hands of a child whom Napoleon had occasionally distinguished by his notice. The emperor sat motionless, with his hand spread over his eyes. The page stood patiently before him, gazing with infantine curiosity on the image which presented so strong a contrast to his own figure of simplicity and peace; at last the little attendant presented his tray, exclaiming, in the familiarity of an age which knows so little distinction, "Eat, sire; it will do you good." The emperor looked at him and asked, "Do you not belong to Gonesse?" (a village near Paris.) "No, sire, I come from Pierrefite." "Where your parents have a cottage and some acres of land?" "Yes, sire." "There is happiness," replied the defeated Emperor of France and King of Italy.

6451. AMBITION, Disappointed. I cannot more fitly resemble an ambitious man, than to one that should have a fancy to take a journey eastward, to the place where the sun seems in rising to touch and to be joined to the earth, in hope to arrive within reach of the same, always going forward, but not coming nearer to his desire; still progressive, never at an end, being impossible to finish it; but the further that he goes, the more earnest he is, and impatient of protraction and delays. So that I may conclude such natures to be punished with Tantalus' torture, of whom it is said, that which he desired ever seemed to be near him, yet never within his command. *Anon.*

6452. AMBITION, Dream of. Napoleon I., referring to the siege of Acre, said: "I see that this paltry town has cost me many men, and occupies much time: but things have gone too far not to risk a last effort. If we succeed, it is to be hoped we shall find in that place the treasures of the pasha, and arms for three hundred thousand men. I will raise and arm the whole of Syria, which is already greatly exasperated by the cruelty of Djezzar, for whose fall you have seen the people supplicate Heaven at every assault. I advance upon Damascus and Aleppo; I recruit my army by marching into every country where discontent prevails; I announce to the people the abolition of slavery, and of the tyrannical government of the pashas; I arrive at Constantinople with armed masses; I overturn the dominion of the Mussulman; I found in the East a new and mighty empire, which shall fix my position with posterity; and perhaps I return to Paris by Adrianople or Vienna, having annihilated the house of Austria."

6453. AMBITION. End of. Alexander, journeying through a dreary desert, came to a small rivulet. In its unruffled peacefulness it seemed to say, "This is the abode of tranquillity. Come and partake of nature's bounty!" To a contemplative mind such a scene might have suggested a thousand delightful reflections; but to Alexander, whose breast was filled with schemes of ambition and conquest, it had no charms. Onward, therefore, he marched. Overcome by fatigue and hunger, he was, however, obliged to rest. He seated himself on the banks of the river, took a draught of water, which he found very refreshing, and of a very fine flavor. He then ordered some salt fish. These he dipped in the stream, in order to take off the briny taste, and was surprised to find them emit a fine fragrance. "Surely," said he, "this river, which possesses such uncommon qualities, must flow from some rich and happy country. Let us march thither." Following the course of the river, he at length arrived at the gate of Paradise. The gates were shut. He knocked, and with his usual impetuosity demanded admittance. "Thou canst not be admitted here," exclaimed a voice within; "this gate is the Lord's." "I am the lord, the lord of the earth," rejoined the impatient chief; "I am Alexander the Conqueror! will you not admit me?" "No," was the answer, "here we know of no conquerors, save such as conquer their passions; none

but the just can enter here." Alexander attempted in vain to enter the abode of the blessed; neither entreaties nor menaces availed. Seeing all his attempts fruitless, he addressed himself to the guardian of paradise, and said: "You know I am a great king, a person who received the homage of nations. Since you will not admit me, give me at least something, that I may show an astonished and admiring world that I have been where no mortal has ever been before me." "Here, madman," said the guardian of paradise, "here is something for thee: it may cure the maladies of thy distempered soul; one glance at it may teach you more wisdom than thou hast hitherto derived from all thy former instructors. Now go thy ways." Alexander took it with avidity, and repaired to his tent. But what was his confusion and surprise to find, on examining the received present, that it was nothing but the fragment of a human skull! "And is this," exclaimed Alexander, "the mighty gift that they bestow on kings and heroes? is this the fruit of so much toil, danger, and care?" Enraged and disappointed, he threw it on the ground. "Great king," said a learned man who happened to be present, "do not despise this gift. Despicable as it appears in thine eyes, it yet possesses some extraordinary qualities, of which thou mayest soon be convinced if thou wilt order it to be weighed against gold and silver." Alexander ordered it to be done. A pair of scales were brought: the skull was placed in one, a quantity of gold in the other; when, to the astonishment of the beholders, the skull overbalanced the gold. More gold was added, still the skull preponderated. In short, the more gold there was put in the one scale, the lower sunk that which contained the skull. "Strange," exclaimed Alexander, "that so small a portion of matter should outweigh so large a mass of gold! Is there nothing that will counterpoise it?" "Yes," answered the philosophers, "a very little matter will do it." They then took some earth, covered the skull with it, when immediately down went the gold and the opposite scale ascended. "This is very extraordinary!" said Alexander, astonished: "can you explain this strange phenomenon?" "Great king," said the sages, "this fragment is the socket of a human eye, which, though small in compass, is yet unbounded in its desire. The more it has, the more it craves. Neither gold nor silver nor any other earthly possession can ever satisfy it. But when it once is laid in the grave, and covered with a little earth, there is an end to its lust and ambition." *Hurwitz.*

6454. AMBITION to be First. Cæsar was passing through a little town among the Alps attended by his officers, when one of them said he wondered whether there were any contentions for office in that place. Cæsar replied, "I had rather be the first in this town than second in Rome."

6455. AMBITION, Fruitless. Demaretus, a proud Lacedemonian, was granted the privilege of asking any favor he pleased. He asked to be escorted through Sardis, crowned as a king. One of the courtiers answered him, "Demaretus, this diadem does not carry brains along with it; nor would you be Jupiter though you should take hold of his thunder."

6456. AMBITION, Insatiable. Ambition is like the sea which swallows all the rivers and is none the fuller; or like the grave whose insatiable maw forever craves for the bodies of men. It is not like an amphora, which being full receives no more; but its fullness swells it till a still greater vacuum is formed. In all probability, Napoleon never longed for a sceptre till he had gained the bâton, nor dreamed of being emperor of Europe till he had gained the crown of France. Caligula, with the world at his feet, was mad with a longing for the moon, and could he have gained it the imperial lunatic would have coveted the sun. It is in vain to feed a fire which grows the more voracious the more it is supplied with fuel; he who lives to satisfy his ambition has before him the labor of Sisyphus, who rolled up hill an ever-rebounding stone, and the task of the daughters of Danaus, who are condemned forever to attempt to fill a bottomless vessel with buckets full of holes. Could we know the secret heart-breaks and wearinesses of ambitious men, we should need no Wolsey's voice crying, "I charge thee, fling away ambition," but we should flee from it as from the most accursed blood-sucking vampire which ever uprose from the caverns of hell.   *Spurgeon.*

6457. AMBITION, Little Field of. Seneca, after contemplating the beauty and greatness of the heavenly orbs, cast his eyes to the earth, exclaiming, "Is it this to which the great designs and vast desires of men are confined? Is it for this there is such disturbance of nations, wars, and shedding of blood? O folly, O fury of deceived men! to imagine great kingdoms in the compass of an atom, to raise armies, to divide a point of the earth with their sword! It is just as if the ants should conceive a field to be several kingdoms, and fiercely contend to enlarge their borders, and celebrate a triumph in gaining a foot of earth."

6458. AMBITION, Meanness of. Ambition, that high and glorious passion, which makes such havoc among the sons of men, arises from a proud desire of honor and distinction, and, when the splendid trappings in which it is usually caparisoned are removed, will be found to consist of the mean materials of envy, pride, and covetousness. It is described by different authors as a gallant madness, a pleasant poison, a hidden plague, a secret poison, a caustic of the soul, the moth of holiness, the mother of hypocrisy, and, by crucifying and disquieting all it takes hold of, the cause of melancholy and madness.   *Burton.*

6459. AMBITION, Political. Solon, the Athenian lawgiver, said of Pisistratus, that if he could but pluck out of his head the worm, ambition, and heal him of his greedy desire to rule, that then there could not be a man of more virtue than he.

6460. AMBITION, Tricks of. Ambition, a good enough thing within reasonable bounds, is a very Apollyon among men, when it gets the mastery over them. Have you ever seen boys climbing a greasy pole to reach a hat or a handkerchief? If so, you will have noticed that the aspiring youths for the most part adopt plans and tricks quite as slimy as the pole; one covers his hands with sand, another twists a knotted cord, and scarcely one climbs fairly, and he is the one boy whose chance is smallest. How plainly see we the politician's course in these young rascals; the Right Honorable Member for the town of Corruption vies with the equally Right Honorable Representative for the county of Bribery; the most noble Conservative place-hunter will not be outdone by the Liberal office-lover; a man must have done a world of planing and shaving, chopping and chiseling, before he can reach the Treasury Bench. Nor less so is it in the path of trade. Small dealers and great contractors eager to rise, are each in their measure to Satan what a covey of partridges are to a sportsman,—fair game if he can but reach them.   *Spurgeon.*

6461. AMBITION, Unhappiness of. Ambition is a gilded misery, a secret poison, a hidden plague, the engineer of deceit, the mother of hypocrisy, the parent of envy, the original of vices, the moth of holiness, the blinder of hearts, turning medicines into maladies, and remedies into diseases. High seats are never but uneasy, and crowns are always stuffed with thorns.

T. Brooks.

6462. AMBITION, Youthful. A renowned teacher was accosted by a new student, and the following colloquy took place. "My parents have just given me leave to study the law, which is the thing I have been wishing for all my life, and I have now come to this University on account of its great fame, and mean to spare no pains in mastering the subject." The professor said: "Well, and when you have got through your course of studies—what then?" "Then I shall take my doctor's degree." "And then?" answered the doctor. "And then," continued the youth, "I shall have a number of difficult cases to manage, which will increase my fame, and I shall gain a great reputation." "And then?" repeated the man. "Why, then, there cannot be a question, I shall be promoted to some high office or other; besides, I shall make money, and grow rich." "And then?" the holy man interposed. "And then," replied the youth, "I shall live in honor and dignity, and be able to look forward to a happy old age." "And then?" was again asked. "And then—and then," said the youth, "I shall die." Here the holy man again inquired, "And then?" The young man could answer no more, but went away sorrowful.

6463. AMENDMENT, Real. Place not thy amendment only in increasing thy devotion, but in bettering thy life. This is the damning hypocrisy of this age: that it slights all good morality, and spends its zeal in matters of ceremony, and a form of godliness without the power of it.   *Fuller.*

6464. AMERICA, Future of. Agassiz says the American Continent was the first created; it will be the last in the fulfilment of the designs of the Creator. A cosmopolitan land—cosmopolitan in the intentions of its founders, in the bloody struggle of its defenders—God has in store for you who people it the accomplishment of admirable results. Northward are the Esquimaux; southward is Africa. You summon from walled China the unmoving people to dwell amid the moving nation, the stationary to mingle with the progressive; all impelled by the breath of you, the great humanitarian people. The foundation of your people is the Bible, the book that speaks of God, the living word of Jesus Christ. In an admirable manifesto from your President there shines through his words the Christian faith. A belief in Jesus is at the root of this nation: and when I return I shall tell Europe that I have found here liberty associated with Christianity, and have been among a people who do not think that to be free they must be parted from God. *Hyacinthe.*

6465. AMEN, Legend of. One Easter Eve, St. Lietbert visited the chapel of the Holy Sepulchre in Combrai, adjoining which was a large graveyard. The moon shone over the scene. It was the night during which Christ's body lay in the tomb. St. Lietbert thought of the dead whose bones lay under the mold of the graveyard outside and under the flagstones of the church on which he stood. He poured out a solemn and earnest prayer for them, and at its end there came up a chorus of Amens from the tombs and graves.

6466. AMEN, Use of. This is a Hebrew word, properly signifying "firmness," and hence "truth," which has been adopted without alteration in various languages. In many churches of England, the word Amen is pronounced aloud by the people: this was the ancient practice of the Christian world, and St. Jerome relates that when the congregated people of Rome pronounced Amen, the sound was like a clap of thunder. They probably attributed great efficacy to the loudness of their voices, after the example of the Jews, who imagined that this word, shouted forth with great force, had power to open the gates of heaven. *J. Timbs.*

6467. AMUSEMENTS, Charm of. The ill-fated Maximilian of Mexico, a man of gentle disposition, gives his emotions on attending a bull-fight. "On entering I felt uneasy and uncomfortable, and now a mania for the bloody spectacle possessed me. I could not turn my eyes away; each moment of the fight enchained me with irresistible force. The excitement produced by the sight of danger carries every mind away along the stream of enthusiasm. I was told of a stranger who expressed himself strongly as to the barbarism of this festival. His tender feelings made him abhor what he had not seen. A friend who knew from experience the charm of this pleasure, induced him, though filled with abhorrence, to visit the Corrida. At the sight of the combat he was seized with the wild in-

toxication, and eagerly asked his friend when the next bull-fight would take place." Similar was the effect of the old gladatorial shows upon the spectators. See Vol. I., No. 195. The devotee of the theatre is similarly infatuated. Everything will be sacrificed to gratify the passion. All habitual pleasures seem to bind their votaries with chains of steel.

6468. AMUSEMENTS, Demoralizing. It is said that when Bonaparte put the Duke d'Enghien to death, all Paris felt so much horror at the event that the throne of the tyrant trembled under him. A counter revolution was expected, and would most probably have taken place, had not Bonaparte ordered a new ballet to be brought out, with the utmost splendor, at the Opera. The subject he pitched on was "Ossian, or the Bards." It is still recollected in Paris, as perhaps the grandest spectacle that had ever been exhibited there. The consequence was that the murder of the Duke d'Enghien was totally forgotten, and nothing but the new ballet was talked of. So Satan distracts the thoughts of men, drives away their moral convictions and binds their souls with the chains of pleasure for the fires of eternal wrath.

6469. AMUSEMENTS, Destructive. A troop of boys were playing at the edge of a pond, when, perceiving a number of frogs in the water, they began to pelt at them with stones. They had already killed many of the poor creatures, when one more hardy than the rest, putting his head above the water, cried out to them: "Stop your cruel sport, my lads; consider, what is play to you is death to us." *Æsop.*

6470. AMUSEMENTS, Love of. Plato and Aristotle were not always seen in their long robes, dignified and serious. No, they were good natured fellows, who enjoyed a laugh with their friends like the rest of the world, and who loved and hoped, and listened to a good story with as much zest as the least learned. None ever decry play and fun but those who are strangers to their value. The love of them is one of the signs of a great nature. All true genius is, in its very essence, a joyous faculty; "wit" originally signifies the very highest efforts of mind. It is only by looking around, as well as upwards, that a large and just conception of life is attainable, and therefore that life is truly realized. A mind charged with vitality, and sustained by trust in God, will not only look cheerfully to the goal of its pilgrimage, but have ample stores of gladness to expend upon the journey. *Grindon.*

6471. AMUSEMENTS, Need of. Though recreation, with science and literature, be the most solid and unfailing kind of play, it is not the only kind we need. With all his care, and toil, and penury of time, the man who devotes himself to learning, or science, or business, is no gainer in the end, if he do not take part sometimes in lively entertainments. For a while he may seem to suffer nothing; but the belief of his being able to dispense with such playing is only a delusion; there is a heavy reckoning going on against him, which sooner or later will have to be paid in suffering and premature exhaustion. Work and play are reciprocally advantageous. While without due play there is no effective working, on the other hand, in order to play heartily with the body, we must learn how to play heartily, in privacy, with the soul. No man thoroughly enjoys play, or knows what play really is, who cannot spend hours of solitude in comfort. *Grindon.*

6472. AMUSEMENTS, Rule for. "He that is not satisfied," says Bishop Wilson, "that plays are an unlawful diversion, let him, if he dare, offer up this prayer to God, before he goes, 'Lord, lead me not into temptation, and bless me in what I am now to be employed.'" There are many other occupations and amusements, in which the same rule will apply.

6473. ANATHEMA, Effect of the. Rev. John Flavel, at Dartmouth, England, preached from these words, "If any man love not the Lord Jesus Christ, let him be Anathema Maranatha." The discourse was unusually solemn, particularly the explanation of the words Anathema Maran-atha,—"cursed with a curse, cursed of God with a bitter and grievous curse." At the conclusion of the service, when Flavel arose to pronounce the benediction, he paused and said, "How shall I bless this whole assembly, when every person in it who loveth not the Lord Jesus Christ is Anathema Maranatha?" The solemnity of this address deeply affected the audience, and one gentleman was so overcome by his feelings that he fell senseless to the floor. In the congregation was a lad named Luke Short, then about fifteen years old, and a native of Dartmouth. Shortly after the event just narrated he entered into the seafaring line, and sailed to America, where he passed the rest of his life. Short's existence was lengthened much beyond the usual term. When a hundred years old, he had sufficient strength to work on his farm, and his mental faculties were very little impaired. Hitherto he had lived in carelessness and sin; he was now a "sinner a hundred years old," and apparently ready to "die accursed." But one day, as he sat in his field, he busied himself in reflecting on his past life. Recurring to the events of his youth, his memory fixed upon Flavel's discourse above alluded to, a considerable part of which he was able to recollect. The blessing of God accompanied his meditations; conviction was followed by repentance, and this aged sinner obtained peace.

6474. ANCESTORS, Boasting of. The man who has nothing to boast of but his illustrious ancestors is like a potato; the only good belonging to him is under ground. *Overbury.*

6475. ANCESTRY, Noble. Hermodius, the descendant of an ancient family of that name, railed at Iphicrates, the son of a shoemaker, on account of his mean birth. That famous general replied, "My nobility begins in me, but yours ends in you."

6476. ANCESTRY, Pride of. A Lydian mule, viewing his own picture in a river, and admiring the bigness and beauty of his body, raises his crest; he waxes proud, resolving to imitate the horse in his gait and running; but pre-

sently, recollecting his extraction, how his father was but an ass at best, he stops his career and checks his own haughtiness and bravery. *Æsop.*

6477. ANCESTRY, Religious. Through my ancestors, so far I can trace them, I can claim to be the seed of the righteous:—a higher honor than the "blue blood" some boast of, though why noble blood should be called "blue," which is venous and polluted blood, I have yet to learn. *Dr. Guthrie.*

6478. ANCHOR, Christ the. A dying sailor said, "I now take my cable, and fix it on my anchor, Jesus, and go through the storm."

6479. ANCHOR, Christian's. The iron anchor of the seaman is cast downwards into the deep of the sea; but the hope anchor of the Christian is thrown upward into the deep of heaven, and, passing through the super-celestial waters, finds its ground and fathoming there. *Delitzsch.*

6480. ANCHOR, Parable of the. On the margin of the ocean that surrounds and laves our island home, an object of absorbing interest may often be observed,—a ship riding at anchor near a lee shore in an angry sea. She has drifted, ere she was aware, too near a rockbound coast; the wind is blowing direct on shore; there is not room to tack; whether she should point her prow north or south, she will strike a projecting headland ere she can escape from the bay. One resource remains,—to anchor where she is till the wind change. There she lies. Stand on this height and look down upon her through the drifting spray. I scarcely know in nature a more interesting or suggestive sight. The ship is dancing on the waves; she appears to be in their power and at their mercy. Wind and water combine to make her their sport. Destruction seems near; for if the vessel's hull is dashed by these waves upon the rocks of the coast, it will be broken into a thousand pieces. But you have stood and looked on the scene a while, and the ship still holds her own. Although at first sight she seemed the helpless plaything of the elements, they have not overcome—they have not gained upon her yet. She is no nearer destruction that when you first began to gaze in anticipation of her fate. The ship seems to have no power to resist the onset of wind and wave. She yields to every blast and every billow. This moment she is tossed aloft on the crest of a wave, and the next she sinks heavily into the hollow. Now her prow goes down beneath an advancing breaker, and she is lost to view in the spray; but anon she emerges, like a sea-fowl shaking the water from her wings and rejoicing in the tumult. As she quivered and nodded giddily at each assault, you thought, when first you arrived in sight, that every moment would prove her last; but now that you have watched the conflict long, it begins to assume in your mind another aspect, and promise another end. These motions of the ship now, instead of appearing the sickly movements of the dying, seem to indicate the calm, confident perseverance of conscious strength and expected victory. Let winds and waves do their worst, that ship will meet them fearless, will hold her head to the blast, and maintain her place in defiance of their power. What is the secret of that ship's safety? No other ship is in sight to which she may cling; no pillar stands within reach to which she may be moored. The bond of her security is a line that is unseen. The ship is at anchor. The line on which she hangs does not depend on the waters, or anything that floats there; it goes through the waters, and fastens on a sure ground beyond them. The soul, considered as a passenger on the treacherous sea of Time, needs an anchor; and an anchor "sure and steadfast" is provided for the needy soul. *William Arnot.*

6481. ANCHOR, Safe. A ship was overtaken by a fearful storm in a dangerous sea. The rudder had no power to direct the course of the vessel, and the wind drove her swiftly toward a rocky shore. An anchor was thrown out to stop the ship, but it did not hold. The steersman forsook the helm and ran about crying "O God, we are all lost—have mercy upon us!" Terror reigned. At this juncture, when total wreck seemed inevitable, the crew threw out another anchor which took firm hold of a rock beneath the raging waves, and at once checked the ship. The helmsman resumed his place and cried, "Thank God, we are all safe!" The passengers and crew joined in the chorus, "Thank God! Thank God!" The ship wore round and soon sailed away. O ye voyagers on life's sea, who know yourselves to be drifting upon a lee shore, your only safety lies in fixing the anchor of your hope in the Rock of Ages.

6482. ANCHOR, The Tested. In modern practice great importance attaches to the trying of an anchor. Many ships have been lost through accident or fraud in the manufacture. The instrument had a good appearance, but there was a flaw in its heart; and when the strain came, it snapped, and all was lost. For the security of the subject, the Government has erected an apparatus for testing anchors; and the royal seal is stamped on those that have been approved. When the merchantman purchases an anchor so certified, he has confidence that it will not fail him in his need. It is interesting, and even solemn work, to test anchors, and stamp them as approved. Beware! set not the seal on one that is doubtful, for many precious lives will yet be intrusted to its keeping. He who is now the anchor of the soul within the veil, was "made perfect through suffering." *William Arnot.*

6483. ANECDOTES, Advantage of. The advantages of embodying in pictures of real life, the practical lessons of the Word of God, have long been apparent; and the writer can, to a great extent, corroborate, from his own experience, the opinion given by the late Rev. Richard Cecil, when he says that "stories fix children's attention." "The moment I begin," he adds, "to talk in anything like an abstract manner, the attention subsides. The simplest manner in the world will not make way to children's minds for abstract truths. With

stories, I find, I could rivet their attention for two or three hours." *J. G. Wilson.*

6484. ANECDOTES, How to use. To make illustrations tell it is needful to introduce them seasonably as well as sparingly, and always in subordination to the best and most important of all such matter—the facts of Holy Scripture. To repeat or read anecdotes indiscriminately, will assuredly fail of either arresting attention or conveying instruction. They must only be introduced, to illustrate some weighty point of indoctrination: to use them otherwise, would be like making "a dinner of the spices which are designed as a seasoning to the meat." *J. G. Wilson.*

6485. ANECDOTES, Pleasure from. Those to whom any anecdote is old, will not be offended if it be well applied; and those to whom it may be new, will receive the double pleasure of novelty and illustration. *Colton.*

6486. ANECDOTES, Using. Bede, Damiani, Ethelred, Thomas à Kempis, Vieyra, Segneri, Latimer, Whitefield, and many other popular preachers, were wont to tell anecdotes in their sermons, with good success. Only let them be told in the terse, lively, and pointed style which characterizes our Lord's parables, and faulty indeed must be the preacher's general diction, if they do not increase rather than diminish its vivacity and grace. *G. W. Hervey.*

6387. ANGELS, Assistance of. Mohammed claims that his first battle with infidels, and signal victory, was a miracle. He threw a handful of gravel at the enemy with an imprecation at which they were filled with fear. They saw more fighting men than Mohammed had. It is said that Gabriel came to their assistance mounted upon his horse Hiazum, and attended by three thousand angels. These did the execution, though Mohammed's men fought stoutly, and imagined that they had won the victory.

6488. ANGELS, Attendant. Timothy, a preacher of Reims, near the close of the third century, was accused as a Christian before Lompadius, the governor, condemned to be beaten, and then rubbed with quicklime and vinegar. Among the crowd looking on was Apollinaris, and he saw two angels standing by, and supporting the martyr. Angels comforted the Master in his agony in the garden, and shall they not also comfort his faithful disciples? Then Apollinaris burst through the ring into the space where the martyr stood, surrounded by the rack and a fire of coals, and fell at his feet, and said: "Good Timothy, pray for me. I saw two in shining garments comforting thee. Gladly will I also die for the name of Christ." Then he was seized, and, by the order of the governor, boiling lead was poured into his mouth to silence his tongue. On the morrow, after a night in the prison, they were led outside of the city and executed with the sword.

6489. ANGELS, Charge of. One day a little boy asked his mother to let him lead his little sister out on the green grass. She had just begun to run alone, and could not step over anything that lay in the way. His mother told him that he might lead out the little girl, but charged him not to let her fall. I found them at play, very happy, in the field. I said, "You seem to be very happy, George. Is this your sister?" "Yes, sir." "Can she walk alone?" "Yes, sir, on smooth ground." "And how did she walk over these stones which lie between us and the house?" "O, sir, mother charged me to be careful that she did not fall, and so I put my hands under her arms, and lifted her up when she came to a stone, so that she need not hit her little foot against it." "That is right, George; and I want to tell you one thing. You see now how to understand that beautiful text, 'He shall give his angels charge concerning thee; and in their hands they shall bear thee up, lest at any time thou dash thy foot against a stone.' God charges his angels to lead and lift his people over difficulties, just as you have lifted little Annie over these stones. Do you understand it now?"

Anon.

6490. ANGELS, Doctrine of. The early Christians, as well as the Jews, held this belief in angels good and bad—the good our helpers, the bad our enemies and opposers. October 2d is the festival of the Angel Guardians in the Roman Church. Alban Butler says, "That particular angels are appointed and commanded by God to guard and watch over each particular person among his servants is an article of the Catholic faith, of which no ecclesiastical writer within the pale of the church in any age ever entertained the least doubt. That every man, even among sinners and infidels, has a guardian angel, is the doctrine of the most eminent among the fathers." This explains Peter's appearance after his deliverance from prison, when some said, "It is his angel."

6491. ANGELS, Nature of. Angels are spirits immaterial and intellectual, the glorious inhabitants of those sacred palaces where there is nothing but light and immortality; no shadow of matter for tears, discontentments, griefs, and uncomfortable passions to work upon; but all joy, tranquility, and peace, even forever and forever, do dwell. *Hooker.*

6492. ANGELS, Service of. Angels have two offices, *superius canere et inferius vigilare,* "to sing above, and watch beneath." These do us many invisible offices of love. They have dear and tender regard and love for the saints. To them, God, as it were, puts forth his children to nurse, and they are tenderly careful of them whilst they live, and bring them home in their arms to their Father when they die. *John Flavel.*

6493. ANGELS, Visits of. When angels have come, they have spoken to a patriarch in the door of his tent—to a distressed husbandman threshing his wheat under an oak—to persecuted apostles in prison. But can you think of an instance of divine or angelic visitation to a king on his throne—to a noble in his palace—to a rich man surrounded with splendors—to a sage amid his books? An angel once came to a seer who was trusting to his own wisdom, and trying hard to outwit omni-

science; but it was with a drawn sword; and the far-seeing prophet or necromancer owed his salvation to an ass! An angel once came to a king on a throne; but it was to smite him with worms, so that he gave up the ghost.

Dr. Raleigh.

6494. ANGELS, Witnesses. In every apartment, in every closet, in every corner, pay a respect to your angel. Dare not do before him what you dare not do before others. Consider with how great respect, awe, and modesty, we ought to behave in the sight of the angels, lest we offend their holy eyes, and render ourselves unworthy of their company. Woe to us if they who could chase away our enemy be offended by our negligence, and deprive us of their visit. We must shun what grieves them, and practice that which gives them delight; as temperance, chastity, voluntary poverty, prayer with fervor and tears. Above all things, the angels of peace expect in us unity and peace. Should not they be most delighted with that in us which represents the form of their own holy city, that they may admire a new Jerusalem or heaven on earth? On the contrary, nothing provokes them so much as scandals and dissensions, if they discern any in us.

St. Bernard.

6495. ANGELS, Works of. A wicked angel came to Eve, in order that through her man might be separated from God. A good angel came to Mary, that through her God might be united to man. *Fulgentius.*

6496. ANGER, Beholding one's. Had I a careful and pleasant companion, that should show me my angry face in a glass, I should not at all take it ill. Some are wont to have a looking-glass held to them while they wash, though to little purpose; but to behold a man's self so unnaturally disguised and disordered, will conduce not a little to the impeachment of anger. *Plutarch.*

6497. ANGER, Benefit of. The only account we have of any good done by anger was in the case of Mucius Fortia, who from his birth had an impediment in his speech. It was with great difficulty he spoke, until being overcome with extreme passion, he was so moved, and labored with such earnestness to speak, that forever after he spoke with great freedom.

6498. ANGER, Cessation of. John, Patriarch of Alexandria, had a controversy with Nicetas, a chief man of that city, which was to be decided in a court of justice. John defended the cause of the poor, and Nicetas refused to part with his money. A private meeting was held, to see if the affair could be adjusted, but in vain; angry words prevailed, and both parties were so obstinate that they separated more offended with each other than before. When Nicetas was gone, John began to reflect on his own pertinacity, and although his cause was good, "Yet," said he, "can I think that God will be pleased with this anger and stubbornness? The night draweth on, and shall I suffer the sun to go down upon my wrath? This is impious, and opposed to the Apostle's advice." He therefore sent some friends to Nicetas, and charged them to deliver this message to him, and no more: "O sir, the sun is going down!" Nicetas was much affected, his eyes were filled with tears; he hastened to the Patriarch, and saluting him in the most gentle manner, exclaimed, "Father, I will be ruled by you in this or any other matter." They embraced each other and settled the dispute instantly.

6499. ANGER, Cure of. The celebrated preacher and theologian, Dr. Hopkins, was afflicted with a very ungovernable temper. He had a brother-in-law, a member of the legal profession, who was an infidel. This man was accustomed to say to his family, "Dr. Hopkins is, at heart, no better than I am, and I will prove it to you some day." One evening Dr. Hopkins called upon his brother-in-law to adjust some business matters in which they were mutually concerned. The infidel knowing well the weak point in the Doctor's character, set up the most unjust claims for the purpose of exciting his anger. The attempt was a success. Dr. Hopkins left the house in a rage, closing the door behind him with much violence. "There!" exclaimed the infidel to his family, "you see now the truth of what I nave told you, that Dr. Hopkins is, at heart, no better than I am; and now I have got my foot on his neck and I will keep it there." Dr. Hopkins, however, went immediately home to his closet, and spent the entire night there in prayer to God. As the morning dawned, an ineffable peace pervaded his whole being. Hastening to his brother-in-law's residence, he confessed with tears, to him and his family, the sin which he had committed in their presence, not saying one word about the graceless provocation which had occasioned the sin. As the man of God retired from the house, the infidel said within himself, "There is a spirit in my brother-in-law which I do not possess, and that spirit is undeniably divine." Thus convicted, he renounced his infidel principles, became a Christian, and ultimately a preacher of the gospel which he had once despised. Thirty years afterwards, Dr. Hopkins stated that since that memorable night no temptation or provocation that he had received had ever once stirred a motion of that evil temper within him. *Dr. A. Mahan.*

6500. ANGER, Deaths from. Matthias Corvinus, king of Hungary, inquired for some fresh figs from Italy, for a second course. Finding they were already eaten up by his courtiers, he fell into such a passion as to bring on apoplexy, from which he died the day following. Victor Pisanus, a Venetian admiral, famous for his exploits, understanding that his vice-admiral, through cowardice, had suffered ten ships of the Genoese to escape out of the Sipontine haven, went into such a passion as to bring on a fever of which he died.

6501. ANGER, Effects of. Angry and choleric men are as ungrateful and unsociable as thunder and lightning; being in themselves all storm and tempest; but quiet and easy natures are like fair weather, welcome to all. *Clarendon.*

6502. ANGER, Folly of. Sinbad the Sailor, tells of being once on an island, half-famished with hunger, while overhead hung delicious cocoa-nuts, quite out of reach. In the branches were many chattering monkeys. So the sailors threw sticks and stones at them until they grew very angry. In return they pelted their enemies with cocoa-nuts with the greatest fury. The sailors kept up the war, in high spirits, until their wants were well supplied. By yielding to anger we always give the enemy the advantage and expose our own weakness.

6503. ANGER of God. Anger, we know, is the whetstone of strength; in an equality of other terms, it will make a man prevail. Nothing is able to stand before a fire which is once enraged. Now God's displeasure is kindled, and breaketh forth into a flame, against the sins of men; like a devouring lion, or a bereaved bear, like the implacable rage of a jealous man; so doth the fire of the Lord's revenge break forth upon the enemies of His Son. Add hereunto our disposition and preparedness for the wrath of God. Strength itself may be tired out in vain upon a subject which is incapable of any injury therefrom. But if the paw of a bear meet with so thin a substance as the caul of a man's heart, how easily is it torn to pieces! Every action is then most speedily finished, when the subject on which it works is thereunto prepared. Far easier is it to make a print in wax than in an adamant; to kindle a fire in dry stubble than in green wood. Now, wicked men have fitted themselves for wrath, and are the procurers and artificers of their own destruction. They are vessels; and God is never without treasures of wrath; so that the confusion of a wicked man is but like the drawing of water out of a fountain, or the filling of a bag out of a heap of treasure. *Bishop Reynolds.*

6504. ANGER, Heathen Treatment of. To cure anger the Grecian philosophers prescribe reason, but anger dethrones reason. Fundanus, in Plutarch, says it has been quieted by sprinkling cold water on its subject. Aristotle says it is extinguished by putting one into a fright. Homer says it is dissipated by sudden surprise or joy. A scoff, a jest, a laugh frequently drove it away. Fundanus' first rule is to give it no expression by action or words. Second, see how other men disgrace themselves by anger. Third, cultivate mildness and gentleness of manner and speech, just the opposite of what is felt at such a time.

6505. ANGER Inconsistent with Devotion. EPHESIANS 4: 26. "Let not the sun go down upon your wrath," we are told was an old Jewish saying, which the Apostle appropriated and stamped with the new authority of inspiration. Its ancient meaning was, "Let not your anger last till the time of the evening sacrifice, so as to destroy its acceptableness, for no true prayer can be offered in an angry spirit." When the mind is like an angry sea, the light of truth and the reflected face of God upon it will be like the shivered glory of the sun on a million breaking waves; there can be no clear thought, no defined and settled purpose. Before any other prayer is a possibility you must say with Robert Hall, "Lamb of God, calm my perturbed spirit."   *C. Stanford.*

6506. ANGER, Nourishing. Speech endeth anger, silence nourisheth it. Much malice and grudge would be avoided, and the very poison of it drawn out, did we but give it a vent at first, by reasoning with the party that wronged us, and expostulating the injury, which most times is but a mere mistake. Now many, on the contrary, harbor this viper in their bosoms till it hath eaten to their hearts; they not only let "the sun go down," but go its whole round, upon "their wrath," (Eph. 4: 26), and cannot find time from one end of the year to the other to utter their minds, and compound their discords. Not only Abraham, but Aristippus, shall rise up in judgment against such pseudo-Christians, and condemn them. For when Æschines and he had been at long debate, and there was *I stout, and thou stout,* and neither could find in their hearts to go to other, Aristippus went at length to Æschines, and said unto him, "Shall we not agree to be friends before we make ourselves a common scorn to the whole country?" Whereunto, when Æschines answered that "he was content to be friends with all his heart," Aristippus replied, "Remember then, that although I was the elder and better, yet I first sought unto thee." "In very deed," said Æschines, "thou art a far better man than I; for I began the quarrel, and thou hast been first in making up the breach:" and thus these two became fast friends for ever. *Trapp.*

6507. ANGER, Rebukes in. As Telephus, when he could find no physician that he could confide in as his friend, thought his adversary's lance would most probably heal his wound; so he that hath no friend to give him advice and to reprove him in what he acts amiss, must bear patiently the rebukes of an enemy, and thereby learn to amend the errors of his ways; considering seriously the object which these severe censures aim at, and not what the person is who makes them. For as he who designed the death of Prometheus, the Thessalian, instead of giving the fatal blow, only lanced a swelling that he had, which did really preserve his life free from the hazard of approaching death; just so the harsh reprehensions of enemies cure some distempers of the mind that were before either unknown or neglected. though these angry speeches do originally proceed from malice and ill-will.
                                    Plutarch.

6508. ANGER Restrained. Poliok, when a boy, was exceedingly passionate. At the age of fifteen a marked change was visible in his temper. On being asked what had occasioned it, he answered: "While perusing the gospels, I was struck with the meekness and calm dignity of the Saviour under persecution, and I resolved thenceforward to command my temper; and since that time, though I may feel and express anger, nothing ever puts me into a passion."

6509. ANGER, Restraint of. Socrates was

grossly abused and kicked by a profligate young man. The philosopher's friends ran after him to punish him. He recalled them and said, "What if an ass had kicked me, would you think it handsomely done to kick him again?" From that time the young man became known by the nickname of the kicker, which so annoyed him that he hung himself. Charillus, of Sparta, said to a quarrelsome slave with whom he was very angry, "I would kill thee if I were not angry."

6510. ANGER, Ruinous. When Philip destroyed the city of Olynthus it was said, "Philip is not able to build such another city." So says Plutarch it may be said of Anger, "Thou canst overthrow, and destroy, and cut down; but to restore, to save, and to bear with, is the work of gentleness and moderation."

6511. ANGER, Subduing. A monk of an irascible disposition came to Poemen for counsel. He advised him to journey far into the desert, and wrestle with his bad temper till he conquered it, and never to return to dwell among men till he was victor. "But, my father," said the monk, "how if I were to die without sacraments in the wild wastes?" "Do you not think God would receive you, coming from the battle-field where you have been striving against your passions, even should that happen?" he answered.

6512. ANGER, Subject to. A minister of the Reformed Church, at a session of his consistory, found his plans strongly opposed by one of the elders. He became greatly exasperated, and approaching his opposer, addressed him in violent language. Another elder remonstrated: "Dominie, you should restrain your temper!" "Restrain my temper! I'd have you know, sir, that I restrain more temper in five minutes than you do in five years!" retorted the enraged clergyman.

6513. ANGER, Suppressing. The Emperor Adrian commanded his crier to silence a tumultuous mob by ordering them to hold their tongues. The crier's adroitness won the emperor's especial thanks. He held out his hand only to the people. Having thus gained their attention, he said: "The emperor requires you to be silent." It was followed by the desired quiet.

6514. ANGER, Temptation to. Euthymius related the following story to his monks. There was in Egypt a man who had a very violent temper. So he ran away from his home into a monastery, where he thought he would be free from incentives to anger. But there he was frequently irritated by the other monks, who, unintentionally, gave him annoyance. So he determined to escape wholly from the society of men, and then, said he, "I cannot give way, for I shall never be tempted." So he took with him only an earthenware bowl, out of which to drink, and he hid himself in a remote desert. Now, one day, he was fetching water from the spring, and he upset the bowl, and the water fell; then he dipped the vessel again, and as he was going, his foot tripped and again the water was spilt; he dipped it once more but his hand shook, and he overturned the basin a third time. Then, flaming into a furious passion, he dashed the bowl against a stone and shivered it to fragments. And when his anger cooled down, he looked at his shattered bowl and said, "Oh, fool that I am! how can I escape the temptation which is in my nature! If I have not men to be angry with, I rage at an earthen bowl!"

6515. ANIMALS, Controlling. A deacon, naturally a high-tempered man, was accustomed to beat his oxen over the head, as all his neighbors did. When he became a Christian, his cattle became remarkably docile. A friend inquired into the secret. "Why," said the deacon, "formerly, when my oxen were a little contrary, I flew into a passion, and beat them unmercifully. This made the matter worse. Now, when they do not behave well, I go behind the load, and sit down, and sing Old Hundred. I don't know how it is, but the psalm tune has a surprising effect on my oxen."

6516. ANIMALS, Cruelty to. One day, when Mr. Hopper saw a man beating his horse brutally, he stepped up to him and said very seriously, "Dost thou know that some people think men change into animals when they die?" The stranger's attention was arrested by such an unexpected question, and he answered that he never was acquainted with anybody who had that belief. "But some people do believe it," rejoined Friend Hopper; "and they also believe that animals may become men. Now I am thinking if thou shouldest ever be a horse, and that horse should ever be a man, with such a temper as thine, the chance is thou wilt get some cruel beatings." Having thus changed the current of his angry mood, he proceeded to expostulate with him in a friendly way; and the poor beast was reprieved, for that time at least. *Life of Isaac T. Hopper.*

6517. ANIMALS, Lesson from. A doctor found a little dog with a broken limb. He took him home, set the limb, and took such good care of him that he was soon well. The dog left his benefactor, who thought much upon the ingratitude of dogs and men. Sometime after, the doctor heard a whining outside his office-door, and opening it saw his former patient and another dog with a broken limb, which he had brought for treatment and cure. He was a true missionary.

6518. ANIMALS, Power over. The legends of the Irish saints frequently give them power over the animals. The horse of St. Finnian broke his leg, when St. Mochua summoned a stag from the forest, which he yoked to the vehicle in place of the horse. It is further related of this saint, that he was a great builder of churches. To bring together the materials for these he called twelve wild stags to his aid, who wrought as tractably as oxen. St. James of the fifth century, was with his monks, cutting and hauling timber for a church. A bear attacked and killed one of his oxen. The monks were terrified and fled, but James said, "I command thee, cruel beast, to bow thy stubborn neck to the yoke in place of the ox thou hast slain." The bear obeyed.

6519. ANIMALS, Worship of. Divine homage is paid to various kinds of animals and reptiles by the deluded natives of Western Africa, from an idea that they are possessed with the spirits of departed chiefs, relatives, or friends, by a mysterious process of transmigration. Hence, there are sacred monkeys, crocodiles, serpents, etc., which are fed and attended to with the greatest possible care. Under such kind treatment they become quite tame, and woe be to any one who dares to molest these living idols of the people. *Enc. of Missions.*

6520. ANSWER, A Thoughtless. A young consumptive was going abroad to seek relief. As he entered the depot a porter taking his luggage, said, "Where are you going?" He answered. "To hell; away with you." A minister overheard the answer and was startled. Seated near the young man in the carriage, he entered into a conversation with him, and at length said, "When do you expect to arrive at your journey's end!" He answered that he did not know, as it was beyond the sea. The minister said, "I mean the place to which you told the porter you were going, on entering the carriage." He answered, "Perhaps it may be so." "Perhaps it may, but there is a way of escape," said the minister, and he expounded to him the way of salvation as Philip did to the Eunuch. A deep impression was made. The minister saw the young man on board ship for a distant land, furnished him a Bible, and parted from him feeling that his wayside seed would bear fruit in eternity.

6521. ANSWER TO PRAYER, Exact. It was necessary that a minister should undertake a journey, for which, however, he had not a sufficiency of funds. Special prayer was made to the Lord to supply the means, and on retiring to rest at a friend's house, which was on the way, the person in question saw an envelope on his looking-glass, which on being opened was found to contain a ten-pound note, and a line saying it was for "traveling expenses." The minister's hostess said "she could not go to rest until she put it there; she felt constrained to do it." Everything which is not sinful we may bring to God; the minuteness of His love will always make Him condescend to the minuteness of our need. *Power.*

6522. ANSWER TO PRAYER, Healing in. A mother of my acquaintance had a child taken alarmingly ill. She sent for the physician. The child was in convulsions. The doctor began at once vigorously to apply the customary remedies—cold water to the head, warm applications to the feet, chafing of the hands and limbs. All was in vain. The body lost nothing of its dreadful rigidity. Death seemed close at hand, and absolutely inevitable. At length he left the child, and sat down by the window, looking out. He seemed to the agonized mother to have abandoned her darling. For herself she could do nothing but pray. And even her prayer was but an inarticulate and unvoiced cry for help. Suddenly the physician started from his seat, "Send and see if there be any jimson weed in the yard," he cried. His order was obeyed; the poisonous weed was found. The remedies were instantly changed. Enough of the seeds of this deadly weed were brought away by the medicine to have killed a man. The physician subsequently said that he thought that in that five minutes every kindred case he had ever known in a quarter century's practice passed before his mind. Among them was the one case which suggested the real but before hidden cause of the protracted and dreadful convulsions. And the child was saved.

Lyman Abbott.

6523. ANSWERS TO PRAYER, Exact. A New York City missionary advanced ten dollars to a poor family and prayed the Lord to replace it. The next day a stranger met him and handed him the exact sum. Public prayer was offered for the inmates of a State prison. Soon after a reformation began there in which one hundred and sixty-five convicts were converted. A young lady said to her host, "I don't want you to talk to me about religion. I don't want to be a Christian." That day public prayer was offered for her. The next morning she was entirely changed, and said, "Last night I resolved to give my heart to the Saviour. A change come over me as I entered my chamber which I could not account for. I believe it was in answer to prayer."

6524. ANTIPATHIES, Examples of. Germanicus could not endure the sight or voice of a cock. The whim of a certain person of noble family was, that he could not endure the gaze of an old woman. By way of a joke, he was brought into the presence of one, when he fell down and died immediately. A nun fainted away, and did not recover health for a long time, the effect of having a beetle thrown into her bosom, by some girls who knew of her weakness. A nobleman of Mantua was thrown into fits by the sight of a hedge-hog. A certain German could detect the presence of a cat in a room, even when carefully concealed, and was thrown into great suffering by it. A strong healthy man named Hasnia, brave in all other cases, was convulsed with fear as often as he saw even the smallest dog.

6525. ANTIPATHIES, Restraint of. Inveterate antipathies against particular nations or persons, and passionate attachment to others, are to be avoided. *Washington.*

6526. ANXIETY, Bane of. Anxiety is the poison of human life. It is the parent of many sins, and of more miseries. In a world where everything is doubtful, where you may be disappointed, and be blessed in disappointment— what means this restless stir and commotion of mind? Can your solicitude alter the cause or unravel the intricacy of human events? Can your curiosity pierce through the cloud which the Supreme Being hath made impenetrable to mortal eye? To provide against every important danger by the employment of the most promising means is the office of wisdom; but at this point wisdom stops. *Blair.*

6527. ANXIETY, Prevention of. We may consider the year before us a desk containing three hundred and sixty-five letters addressed to us—one for every day, announcing its trials, and prescribing its employments, with an order to open daily no letter but the letter for the day. Now, we may be strongly tempted to unseal beforehand some of the remainder. This, however, would only serve to embarrass us, while we should violate the rule which our Owner and Master has laid down for us "Take, therefore, no thought for the morrow. for the morrow shall take thought for the things of itself." *William Jay.*

6528. ANXIETY, Removal of. "Leave thy fatherless children; I will preserve them alive; and let thy widows trust in me." When I was in England I knew an eminent minister, who a few months afterward died. And for a while before he died he was troubled for fear his wife and children might come to want. He carried the burden of that fear for days. A little while before he died he was lying on his sofa, and a little bird came and pecked at the window; the bird had a worm in its mouth, and afterward it flew away. The man said to himself, "Dear me! God takes care of that bird; He feeds it, yet here am I troubled about my family!" And there and then the burden was laid on the Lord. He had been one of those liberal men, and had given his money to others all through his life. Well, when he died, the people in the town raised £5,000 for his widow. God took care of them. *D. L. Moody.*

6529. ANXIETY, Sufferings from. This fear of any future difficulties or misfortune is so natural to the mind, that were a man's sorrows and disquietudes summed up at the end of his life, it would generally be found that he had suffered more from the apprehension of such evils as never happened to him, than from those evils which had really befallen him. To this we may add, that among those evils which befall us, there are many which have been more painful to us in the prospect than by their actual pressure. *Addison.*

6530. ANXIETY, Useless. The generality of mankind create to themselves a thousand needless anxieties, by a vain search after a thing that never was, nor ever will be, found upon earth. Let us, then, sit down contented with our lot, and in the meantime be as happy as we can in a diligent preparation for what is to come. *T. Adams.*

6531. APOLOGY, Sufficient. Le Clerc was walking in the streets of Paris, and accidentally trod on the foot of a young man, who immediately raised his hand and struck him in the face. Le Clerc said, "Sir, you will be sorry for what you have done when you know that I am blind."

6532. APOSTASY, Act of. Julian was no sooner proclaimed emperor than he declared himself the restorer of the old religion, that is, of heathenism. To purge himself from the waters of Christian baptism, which he recieved ten years before, he immersed himself in a bath of bulls' blood. He sought to cleanse his hands from the touch of the bloodless emblems of the Eucharist, by holding in them the entrails of the victims offered to his gods.

6533. APOSTASY, Condemnation of. Liberatus, a physician of Carthage, suffered persecution for his faith. Being torn from his family, his wife encouraged him, saying, "Think no more of thy children. Jesus Christ will be their guardian." Both himself and wife were incarcerated, but in different prisons. Her persecutors came and told her, "Thy husband has submitted to the orders of the king; therefore do thou yield also." She demanded to see him. He was brought to her, when she condemned and reproached him for his apostasy. She was rejoiced to learn from him, that she had been deceived, and praised the Lord that he was no apostate. Our best friends approve our Christian fidelity and condemn our defections.

6534. APOSTASY, Deed of. The legend of Theophilus of Cilicia is not without its lesson. He was a priest noted for his austerity, liberality, eloquence and devotion. On the death of the bishop he was elected to fill the diocese by popular acclamation. His deep humility led him to decline the office, and another was elected. Evil-minded persons circulated slanders against him which, coming to the ears of the new bishop, without investigation he acted upon and deprived Theophilus of his offices. It would seem that he who could refuse a mitre could stand up under a slander; but he could not. He constantly meditated how to clear his character. He tried every means to refute the slanders. But slander is a hydra, and when one of its heads is cut off another will grow. In his despair and weakness he sought aid of a necromancer, who led him to meet Satan at the junction of four cross roads. He promised to clear his character and reinstate him in his offices, in consideration of which Theophilus signed a deed with a pen dipped in his own blood, giving his soul to Satan and forever abjuring Jesus Christ. The next day the bishop having discovered his mistake and the falseness of the reports, publicly reinstated Theophilus, and asked his pardon. For a few days, in the joy of vindication and the return of popular favor, all went well with him. Then the awful reality of the compact he had made with Satan come over him. He prayed, fasted, grew pale and hollow-eyed, like one doomed. At length, says the story, the Virgin appeared to him and rebuked him. He implored her pardon and intercession. She promised this, and returned to him the deed by which he made over his soul to Satan. He made public confession, and died at the expiration of three days.

6535. APOSTASY, Example of. The associations of Dr. Dodd in early life were with such men as Bishop Horn, Jones of Nayland, and other religious persons. But he became gradually drawn away from them by the allurements of the world, sought popular favor, and royal preferments, until he was a stranger to them. Meeting a lady who belonged to the relinquished party, he inquired what they thought of him. She replied, "Demas has forsaken us, having loved this present world." The reply at the time affected him, but he went on in his sins, and while endeavoring to defraud Lord Chesterfield, his former pupil, he was arrested, convicted and executed.

6536. APOSTASY, Late. Nichomachus of Troas, was arraigned before the governor, A. D., 250, for being a Christian, and given the alternative of sacrificing to Venus, or suffering. Refusing to sacrifice, he was hung up by his wrists and tortured. The flames were kindled under him. His flesh was torn with red-hot pincers and iron rakes. In great agony he cried out, "Let me down, I will sacrifice." He was instantly seized with madness, bit the earth and expired. Dyonisia, a young Christian girl in the crowd, cried out, "O wretched man, for one hour's respite to have to endure endless torment." Thereupon she was seized, and soon after beheaded. None can afford to deny Christ an hour before death. This may be that hour.

6537. APOSTASY, Memento of. In the long line of portraits of the Doges, in the palace at Venice, one space is empty, and the semblance of a black curtain remains as a melancholy record of glory forfeited. Found guilty of treason against the state, Marino Falieri was beheaded, and his image as far as possible blotted from remembrance. As we regarded the singular memorial we thought of Judas and Demas, and then, as we heard in spirit the Master's warning word, "One of you shall betray me," we asked within our soul the solemn question, "Lord, is it I?" Every one's eye rests longer upon the one dark vacancy than upon any one of the many fine portraits of the merchant monarchs; and so the apostates of the church are far more frequently the theme of the world's talk than the thousands of good men and true who adorn the doctrine of God, our Saviour, in all things. Hence the more need of care on the part of those of us whose portraits are publicly exhibited as saints, lest we should one day be painted out of the church's gallery, and our persons only remembered as having been detestable hypocrites.   *Spurgeon.*

6538. APOSTASY, Possible. One of Augustine's three wishes was, that he had seen Christ in the flesh. Flavel says, "Judas not only saw him, but dwelt with him, traveled with him, and ate and drank with him. Such was the condescension of Christ to this wretched man, that he washed his feet only a little before he betrayed him." A man might have seen Christ in person upon the earth and yet become a castaway.

6539. APOSTASY, Punishment of. Rev. John Wesley, believing in the possibility of final apostasy, warned all the members of his societies to beware of it. In his sermon on the Loss of the Soul, he relates the following. "Some years since, one who had turned back as a dog to his vomit, was struck in his mad career of sin. A friend who prayed with him said, 'Lord, have mercy on those who are just stepping out of the body, and know not who shall meet them at their entrance into the other world, an angel or a fiend.' The sick man shrieked out, with a piercing cry, 'A fiend! a fiend!' and expired. Just such an end, unless he die like an ox, may any man expect who loses his own soul." "Let him that thinketh he standeth take heed lest he fall."

6540. APOSTASY, Result of. What led to Solomon's apostasy? And what, again, was the ulterior effect of that apostasy on himself? As to the origin of his apostasy the Word of God is explicit. He did not obey his own maxim. He ceased to rejoice with the wife of his youth; and loving many strangers, they drew his heart away from God. Luxury and sinful attachments made him an idolater, and idolatry made him yet more licentious; until, in the lazy enervation and languid day-dreaming of the Sybarite, he lost the perspicacity of the sage and the prowess of the sovereign; and when he woke up from the tipsy swoon, and out of the kennel picked his tarnished diadem, he woke to find his faculties, once so clear and limpid, all perturbed, his strenuous reason paralyzed, and his healthful fancy poisoned. He woke to find the world grown hollow, and himself grown old. He woke to see the sun bedarkened in Israel's sky, and a special gloom encompassing himself. He woke to recognize a sadder sight than winter—a blasted summer. Like a deluded Samson starting from his slumber, he sought to recall that noted wisdom which had signalized his Nazarite days; but its locks were shorn; and, cross and self-disgusted, wretched and guilty, he woke up to the discovery which awaits the sated sensualist: he found that when the beast gets the better of the man, the man is abandoned by his God. Like one who falls asleep amidst the lights and music of an orchestra, and who awakes amidst empty benches and tattered programmes—like a man who falls asleep in a flower-garden, and who opens his eyes on a bald and locust-blackened wilderness—the life, the loveliness, was vanished, and all the remaining spirit of the mighty Solomon yawned forth that verdict of the tired voluptuary: "Vanity of vanities! vanity of vanities! all is vanity!" *Dr. James Hamilton.*

6541. APOSTASY, Temptation to. In the Arian persecution two brothers in the city of Tombala were hung up by their wrists with heavy weights attached to their feet. At the end of a day of intolerable agony one of them weakened and asked to be released. The other said to him, "Do not so, brother, or I will accuse thee at the judgment seat of Christ. Have we not sworn to suffer together for him?" Then the temptation was overcome. The weak brother received strength to hold out a little longer. The Vandals, enraged at their obstinacy, burned them with hot irons and gashed them with iron rakes, and sent them speedily to receive their crowns.

6542. APOSTASY, Yielding to. Sir Francis Drake was overtaken by a storm in the Thames which threatened destruction. He exclaimed, "Must I, who have escaped the rage of the ocean, be drowned in a ditch!" Will you, who have outridden many a storm, despair in sight of port? Alas, that those who have overcome in hard battles should be overcome in some slight skirmish.

6543. APOSTATE, Fate of the. A soldier who had served his country for a time in the army, by deception had his name returned on the roll as dead. He was so reported from his company to his regiment, and from his regimental headquarters to the general government. In the great records of the nation, against his name "Dead" was written. After the war was over, and peace restored, the government began to dispense its bounties and pensions to those who had fought its battles and borne its burdens. This runaway soldier, that had deserted from the service and caused a false report to be returned, appeared for a reward at the hands of government. The books were examined, the name was found, but Dead was written against it. The government settles by its official records, and in the knowledge of the government he is a dead man, and not a living claimant. In Christian warfare there is like danger. Christ has enlisted a great many soldiers that have not answered to the roll-call for years. They deserted in time of danger, and the angel scribe has written against their names—Dead. The books of the last day will show erasures as well as entries; and almost the last words of the Bible warn us of the blotting out of names from the Book of Life.
William Jones.

6544. APPETITE, Resisting. An inebriate affirmed that he could not resist his appetite for whisky. His neighbor said to him, "Suppose I should put a sufficient quantity of arsenic into your jug of rum to produce certain death by the use of a tablespoonful, and you knew it, and there was no other liquor in a hundred miles of you, how long would your jug stand by you untasted?" He saw the absurdity of his assertion, and confessed that the only thing necessary to his reform was resolution.

6545. APPEARANCE, Man's. A man's look is the work of years. It is stamped on the countenance by the events of his life; nay, more, by the hand of Nature; and it is not to be got rid of easily. There is, as it has been remarked repeatedly, something in a person's appearance, at first sight, which we do not like, and which gives it an odd tinge, but which is overlooked in a multitude of other circumstances, till the mask is thrown off, and we see this lurking character verified in the plainest manner in the sequel. We are struck at first, and by chance, with what is peculiar and characteristic; also with permanent traits and general effects. These afterwards go off in a set of unmeaning and commonplace details. This sort of *prima facie* evidence, then, shows what a man is, better than what he says or does; for it shows us the habit of his mind, which is the same under all circumstances and disguises. *Hazlitt.*

6546. APPEARANCES, Evil. There is a curious Chinese proverb which says: "In a cucumber field do not stop to tie your shoe, and under a plum tree do not stop to settle your cap or your head;" which means, if you do some one may think you are stealing the cucumbers or the plums. The Apostle says, "Abstain from all appearance of evil."

6547. APPEARANCES, Regard for. A divine of the 17th century says: "Thou must not only refuse to commit broad sins, but shun the appearance of sin also: this is to walk in the power of holiness. The dove doth not only fly from the hawk, but will not smell so much as a single feather that falls from the hawk; it should be enough to scare the holy soul from any enterprise, if it be but 'male coloratum:' we are commanded to hate the garments spotted with the flesh. A cleanly person will not only refuse to wallow in the dunghill, but is careful also that he doth not get so much as a spot on his clothes as he is eating his meat. The Christian's care should be to keep, as his conscience pure, so his name pure; which is done by avoiding all appearance of evil."

6548. APPLAUSE, Effect of. Once, when a great fire broke out at midnight, and people thought that all the inmates had been taken out, way up there in the fifth story was seen a little child crying for help. Up went a ladder, and soon a fireman was seen ascending to the spot. As he neared the second story the flames burst in fury from the windows, and the multitude almost despaired of the rescue of the child. The brave man faltered, and a comrade at the bottom cried out, "Cheer," and cheer upon cheer arose from the crowd. Up the ladder he went and saved the child because they cheered him. If you cannot go into the heat of the battle yourself; if you cannot go into the harvest field and work day after day, you can cheer those that are working for the Master. *Moody.*

6549. APPLAUSE, Self. He that talks big and arrogantly of himself, Herculanus, is universally condemned as a troublesome and ill-bred companion. Those who are crowned for mastery in the games or in the learned combats have others to celebrate their victories, that the people's ears be not grated with the harsh noises of self-applause. And Timotheus is justly censured as unskilfully and irregularly setting forth his conquest of Phrynis, when he thus proudly boasted it in writing: "Happy man wast thou, Timotheus, when the crier proclaimed, 'The Milesian Timotheus hath vanquished the son of Carbo, the soft Ionian poet.'" *Plutarch.*

6550. APPLICATIONS, Biblical. Nathan applied the parable of the ewe lamb to David, saying, "Thou art the man." 2d. Sam. 12: 7. Bowes says: "One feature is observable in our blessed Lord's teachings, his pointed questions and personal applications. "He that hath ears to hear, let him hear." "Take heed how ye hear." "Dost thou believe?" "How is it that ye have no faith?" "Where is your faith?" "Are ye also yet without understanding?" "Have ye understood all these things?" "Do ye not err?" &c. It was one of Christ's modes of teaching to turn the remarks of others into pointed and personal appeals directed to themselves;

—see Luke 8: 19–21; 11: 27, 28; 13: 1–5 23, 24.

6551. ARGUMENT, Blindness to. Robert Hall was conversing with a clergyman who had obtained a lucrative living by a change of religious opinions. Mr. Hall pressed him hard upon the subject of Church reform. The gentleman's constant answer to the argument addressed to him was, "I can't see it." "I don't see it." "I can't see that at all." At last Mr. Hall took a letter from his pocket and wrote on the back of it with his pencil, in small letters, the word "God." "Do you see that?" "Yes." He then covered it with a piece of gold. "Do you see it now?" "No." "I wish you good morning, sir," said Mr. Hall, and left him to his meditations.

6552. ARGUMENTS, Decisive. A converted infidel narrating his experience said, "I could always bear sermons, and was ball-proof to argument, but I could not resist the Christian life of my wife."

6553. ARGUMENT, Gentleness in. I walked into the village, where the boat stopped for the night, and found the worshipers of Cali by the sound of their drums and cymbals. I did not think of speaking to them on account of their being Bengalese. But being invited by the Brahmins to walk in, I entered within the railing, and asked a few questions about the idol. The Brahmin, who spoke bad Hindoo-stanee, disputed with great heat, and his tongue ran faster than I could follow; and the people, who were about one hundred, shouted applause. But I continued to ask my questions, without making any remarks upon the answers. I asked, among other things, whether what I had heard of Vishance and Brahma were true, which he confessed. I forbore to press him with the consequences, which he seemed to feel, and then I told him what was my belief. The man grew quite mild, and said it was *chula-bat* (good), and asked me seriously, at last, what I thought—"Was idol worship true or false?" I felt it a matter of thankfulness that I could make known the truth of God, though but a stammerer, and that I had declared it in the presence of the devil. And this also I learned, that the power of gentleness is irresistible. I never was more astonished than at the change in the deportment of this hot-headed Brahmin. *Henry Martyn.*

6554. ARGUMENT, Rule for. Lord Cockburn's method at the bar was,—"When I was addressing a jury, I invariably picked out the stupidest-looking fellow of the lot, and addressed myself specially to him—for this good reason: I knew that if I convinced him, I would be sure to carry all the rest!"

6555. ARK, Import of the. We have first an old world to be destroyed, with one faithful family upon it, or rather one family who are saved for the faithfulness and piety of their head, as it is said,—"Come thou, and all thy house into the ark: for thee have I seen righteous." Then we have a new world coming forth in beauty, after destruction has passed on the old; while the chosen family are brought from the one world to the other in the ark, the only place of safety. Christ is the ark, taking the chosen family from the world judgment to the new heavens and the new earth. This is clear; but look at the detail. May I not say the microscope may be used here? The ark, with all its burden, rests on the mountains of the new world, months before any portion of that new world could be seen. Christ, as our ark, has rested in resurrection, with all the redeemed family in him; for in him we are already "risen," while as yet the waters of judgments (for "now is the judgment of this world") are resting on the world.   *A. Jukes.*

6556. ARK, Import of the. The Fathers observe the allegory that Peter maketh, in comparing Noah's ark unto the church; and observe, moreover, that as the dove brought the olive-branch into the ark, in token that the deluge had ceased, and the world had become habitable again; even as the dove, that lighted upon Christ, brought the glad tidings of the gospel.   *Bp. Lake.*

6557. ARK, Refusing to Enter the. The Koran relates that Noah had a son who was numbered with the unbelievers in his father's message. Noah expostulated with him, "Embark with us, my son, and stay not with the unbelievers." He answered, "I will get on a mountain, which will secure me from the water." He refused to enter the ark, and shared the fate of the doomed race.

6558. ARK, Safety in the. There was one minute when Noah was exposed to the wrath that was to come over the whole world; but when he went through the door-way of the ark, that moment he was safe. There are many who are trying to make an ark for themselves out of their feelings, out of their own good deeds. But God has provided an ark. If Noah had had to build himself an ark when the flood came, he would have been lost like the rest. A good many of those men who perished when that flood came tried to make arks for themselves, but they all perished helplessly. They tried to make boats and rafts, and tried every way they could to save themselves, but they perished because they were not in the ark that God had appointed. So, to-day, every man and every woman must perish that is not in the ark which God has appointed for their salvation. A knowledge about the ark is not going to help you. A great many persons flatter themselves they are going to be saved because they know a great deal about Jesus Christ. But your knowledge of Him will not save you. Noah's carpenters probably knew as much about the ark as Noah did, and perhaps more. They knew that the ark was strong. They knew it was built to stand the Deluge. They knew it was made to float upon the waters. They had helped to build it. But they were just as helpless when the flood came as men who lived thousands of miles away. Men who lived right in sight of the ark, that knew all about it, perished like the rest, because they were not in the ark. I know something about the different lines of steamers, and

I have crossed the Atlantic. Here is another man that has never heard there was such a line of steamers. We both want to go to Europe. My knowledge of a line of steamers does not help me a bit if I do not take the means to go there. You may hear about Christ, but if you do not believe in Christ you cannot be saved. Your knowledge is not going to help you to your salvation. What you want to do is just to make Christ your ark, and then to step into that ark and be saved.   *Moody.*

6559. ARK, Saved by the. When I was in Manchester, in one of the inquiry meetings, I went up into the gallery to talk with a few men who were standing together, and who were inquirers of the way of life. And while they were standing in a little group around me there came up another man and got on the outside of the audience, and I thought by the expression of his face that he was skeptical. I did not think he had come to find Christ. But as I went on talking I noticed the tears trickling down his cheeks. I said, "My friend, are you anxious about your soul's salvation?" He said "Yes, very." I asked him what was the trouble, and I kept on talking to that one man, thinking that if he could understand me perhaps the others would. He said he wanted to feel right about it. I explained to him by means of an illustration, and asked him, "Do you see it?" He said "No." I used another, and asked him, "Do you see it yet?" and he said "No" again. I gave still another and still he said he did not see. I then said, "Was it Noah's feelings that saved him, or was it his ark? Was what saved Noah his righteousness? was it his life, was it his prayers, was it his tears, was it his feelings, or was it the ark?" He came immediately and grasped me by the hand, and said, "I see it now; it is all right now; I've got to go away on the next train, and I'm in a hurry, but you have made it plain to me; good bye." And he went off. I thought it was so sudden that he could not have understood it. But the next Sunday afternoon he came and tapped me on the shoulder, and smiled, and asked me if I remembered him. I said no, that I remembered his face, but could not tell who he was or where I'd seen him before. He said, "Do you remember a man that came up into the inquiry-room the other day, and you explained to him how it was Noah's ark that saved him? I did not see any illustration until you used that one, and then I saw it all." I asked him how he was, and he said he had been all right ever since, and that the ark had saved him. I afterward learned that he was one of the best business men of Manchester. His feelings did not save him. The ark saved him.   *Moody.*

6560. ARMOR, Pasteboard. Do you recollect the scene in Don Quixote in which the immortal knight put upon himself a helmet made of pasteboard? That helmet being smitten and pierced by a sword, he sewed it up again, and would not part with it, but in his insanity wore it, and felt that he had an all-sufficient helmet on his head. Are there not many Don Quixotes among men, who put on armor that looks very well till some sword or spear is thrust into it, but which then is found to be like the pasteboard helmet that went to pieces the moment it was touched? If we are to have a piety that shall sustain us in the flood and in the fire; if we are to have a faith that shall be an all-sufficient armor by day and by night, the year round, and from year to year, we must have one that is made up of something better than mere pasteboard instruction or a paper belief.   *Beecher.*

6561. ARMY, Gideon's. If we don't expect a blessing we don't get it. Look at Gideon. He had 30,000 men. God said that that was too many. They would all take their share of the glory of the victory, and there was no need of dividing it up so small. We must take our place in the dust, and give God the glory, if we want to do any good. "You've got too many," said God; "let all who are afraid step out." Twenty-two thousand stepped out! Poor Gideon! I'd like to have seen him then. His faith must have been a little shaky. It was like a meeting I once attended, when some persons went out. The others, attracted by the noise, stood up, and it looked as if all were going. "Ten thousand left," said God; "that's still too many." Then 9,700 more stepped out, leaving but 300; but they were 300 such men as Caleb and Joshua. There was no power that could stand against them. I think it was John Wesley who once said that if he had 300 believing Christians he would shake the gates of hell and set God up in the world. I believe he could have done it.   *Moody.*

6562. ARROGANCE, Growth of. Arrogance is a weed which grows upon a dunghill. It is from the rankness of the soil that she has her height and spreadings.   *Feltham.*

6563. ARROGANCE, Import of. Arrogance is the proclamation which some men make of their own littleness.

6564. ARROGANCE, Ridiculous. The petty sovereign of an insignificant tribe in North America every morning stalks out of his hovel, bids the sun good-morrow, and points out to him with his finger the course he is to take for the day. Is this arrogance more contemptible than ours when we would dictate to God the course of his providence, and summon him to our bar for his dealings with us? How ridiculous does man appear when he attempts to argue with his God!   *Spurgeon.*

6565. ARROGANCE, Selfishness of. An arrogant person, if he join in the performance of any laudable action, with men of modest natures, deals with them in the sharing of the praise, as the lion in the fable did with the other beasts, dividing the prey they had taken; who making of the whole, four parts, pleads a title to three of them at least, and if they yielded him not the fourth of their own good-will, he would be no longer friends. If he write or speak a discourse of any length, he cannot forbear but he must make known somewhat of his own custom, or humor, or life, with I was this, or did this, or like this, or thus am, or

was wont; belike supposing that all men would be glad to make him the pattern of their life and actions.   *Anon.* 1620.

6566. ARROW, A Barbed. A fast young man, with a companion, was on his way to a theatre, when a little boy handed him a letter in which was written: "Sir, remember the day of judgment is at hand." He left his company, and returning homeward entered a church. He heard the text announced, "This is the finger of God." His impression deepened, and he became a Christian.

6567. ARROW, Gospel. The chief battles fought by the English Plantagenets were with the long-bow. They would take the arrow of polished wood, and feather it with the plume of a bird, and then it would fly from the bowstring of plaited silk. The broad fields of Agincourt and Solway Moss and Neville's Cross heard the loud thrum of the archer's bowstring. Now, my Christian friends, we have a mightier weapon than that. It is the arrow of the Gospel; it is a sharp arrow; it is a straight arrow; it is feathered from the wing of the dove of God's Spirit; it flies from a bow made out of the wood of the cross. As far as I can estimate or calculate, it has brought down three hundred millions of souls. Paul knew how to bring the notch of that arrow on to the bowstring, and its whir was heard through the Corinthian theatres, and through the court-room until the knees of Felix knocked together. It was that arrow that stuck in Luther's heart when he cried out, "O my sins! O my sins!" If it strike a man in the head, it kills his skepticism; if it strike him in the heel, it will turn his step: if it strike him in the heart, he throws up his hands, as did one of old when wounded in the battle, crying, "O Galilean! thou hast conquered!"   *Talmage.*

6568. ARROW, The Pestilence God's. The Arabs thus describe the pestilence. A traveler says: "I desired to remove to a less contagious air. I received from Solyman, the emperor, this message—that the emperor wondered what I meant, in desiring to remove my habitation. Is not the pestilence God's arrow, which will always hit his mark? If God would visit me herewith, how could I avoid it? 'Is not the plague,' said he, 'in my own palace? and yet I do not think of removing.'" Another remarks: "What," say they, "is not the plague the dart of Almighty God, and can we escape the blow he levels at us? Is not his hand steady to hit the persons he aims at?"

6569. ARROWS, The Sharpest. A bowman took aim at an eagle and hit him in the heart. As the eagle turned his head in the agonies of death, he saw that the arrow was winged with his own feathers. "How much sharper," said he, "are the wounds made by weapons which we ourselves have supplied!"   *Æsop.*

6570. ART, Necessity for. In no circumstance whatever can man be comfortable without art. The butterfly is independent of art, though it is only in sunshine that it can be happy. The beasts of the field can roam about by day, and couch by night on the cold earth, without dau ger to health or sense of misfortune. But man is miserable and speedily lost so soon as he removes from the precincts of human art, without his shoes, without his clothes, without his dog and his gun, without an inn or a cottage to shelter him by night. Nature is worse to him than a stepmother—he cannot love her; she is a desolate and a howling wilderness. He is not a child of nature like a hare. She does not provide him a banquet and a bed upon every little knoll, every green spot of earth. She persecutes him to death, if he do not return to that sphere of art to which he belongs, and out of which she will show him no mercy, but be unto him a demon of despair and a hopeless perdition.   *Ruskin.*

6571. ART, Poetry of. The written poem is only poetry talking, and the statue, the picture, and the musical composition, are poetry acting. Milton and Goethe, at their desks, were not more truly poets than Phidias with his chisel, Raphael at his easel, or deaf Beethoven bending over his piano, inventing and producing strains which he himself could never hope to hear. The love of the ideal, the clinging to and striving after first principles of beauty, is ever the characteristic of the poet, and whether he speak his truth to the world through the medium of the pen, the perfect statue, or the lofty strain, he is still the sharer in the same high nature. Next to blind Milton describing Paradise, that same Beethoven composing symphonies and oratorios is one of the finest things we know. Milton saw not, and Beethoven heard not; but the sense of beauty was upon them, and they fain must speak. Arts may be learned by application—proportions and attitudes may be studied and repeated—mathematical principles may be, and have been, comprehended and adopted; but yet there has not been hewn from the marble a second Apollo, and no measuring by compasses will ever give the secret of its power. The ideal dwelt in the sculptor's mind, and his hands fashioned a statue which yet teaches it to the world.   *Ruskin.*

6572. ART, Religiousness of. It is the duty of religion not to eject, but to cherish and seek fellowship with every beautiful exhibition which delights, and every delicate art which embellishes human life. So, on the other hand, it is the duty of art not to waste its high capabilities in the imitation of what is trivial, and in the curious adornment of what has only a finite significance. The highest art is always the most religious; and the greatest artist is always a devout man. A scoffing Raphael or Michael Angelo is not conceivable. *Blackie.*

6573. ASCENSION, Christ's. Christ's offering himself on earth, answered to the killing of the sacrifice without the vail; and his entering into heaven, there to intercede, answered to the priest's going with blood and his hands full of incense within the vail. So that this is a part, yea, a special part, of Christ's priesthood; and so necessary to it, that if he had not done this, all his work on earth had been ineffectual; nor had he been a priest, that is, a complete and perfect priest, if he had remained on earth, Heb. 8 : 4; because the very design and end of shedding his blood on earth had been frustrated, which was to present it before the Lord, in heaven. So that this is the perfective part of the priesthood: he acted the first part on earth in a state of deep abasement, in the form of a servant; but he acts the second part in glory, whereto he is taken up, that he may fulfill his design in dying, and give the work of our salvation its last completing act.   *John Flavel.*

6574. ASCENSION, Fable of. The body of Romulus disappeared suddenly, and no remnant of it or of his clothing could be discovered by the most diligent search. One report is that he disappeared from the temple of Vulcan; another that he was holding an assembly outside the city when there was great darkness, fearful thunderings, and a resistless tempest, which terrified and scattered the people. When this had subsided, the people came together again, but Romulus could not be found. It was thence reported by the patricians, that Romulus had been caught up to heaven, and would be to the Romans a propitious god. Thus Romulus became one of the gods of Rome. This was confirmed by the oath of his devoted and famous friend, Julius Proclus, who swore that he met Romulus while traveling on the road, clad in the most dazzling armor. Astonished at the sight, he cried out, "For what misbehavior of ours, or by what accident, O King, hast thou so untimely left us?" He answered, "It pleased the gods, my good Proclus, that we should dwell with men for a time, and having founded a city which shall be the most powerful and glorious in the world, return to heaven, from whence we came. Farewell, then! Go, tell the Romans that by the exercise of temperance and fortitude they shall attain the highest pitch of human greatness, and I, the god Quirinus, will ever be propitious to you."

6575. ASCENSION, Need of Christ's. The Apostle makes a priest's exaltation so necessary a part of his priesthood, that without it he could not have been a priest. "If he were on earth he should not be a priest." Heb. 8 : 4; that is, if he had continued here, and had not been raised again from the dead, and taken up into glory, he could not have been a complete and perfect priest. For just as it was not enough for the sacrifice to be slain without, and his blood left there; but it must be carried within the vail, into the most holy place before the Lord, Heb. 9 : 7; so it was not sufficient that Christ shed his own blood on earth, except he carry it before the Lord into heaven, and there perform his intercession work for us.
         John Flavel.

6576. ASCETICISM, Example of. In the reign of Elizabeth there was born in London a man of the name of John Martin. In the tenth year of his age he was kidnapped by a Portuguese merchant, apparently for the purpose of preserving him in the Catholic faith; and this merchant, seven years afterwards, took him to

Brazil, where, being placed under the care of the Jesuits, he soon after became a member of that fraternity, by the name of Joam de Almeida. Anchieta was his superior, then an old man, broken down with exertion and austerities, and subject to frequent faintings. No voluptuary ever invented so many devices for pampering the senses as Joam de Almeida did for mortifying them. He looked upon his body as a rebellious slave, who, dwelling within his doors, eating at his table, and sleeping in his bed, was continually laying snares for his destruction; he, therefore, regarded it with the deepest hatred, and, as a matter of justice and self-defence, persecuted, flogged, and punished it in every imaginable way. For this purpose, he had a choice assortment of scourges, some of whip-cord, some of cat-gut, some of leathern thongs, and some of wire. He often wore an under-waistcoat of the roughest hair, having on the inside seven crosses made of iron, the surface of which was covered with sharp points, like a coarse rasp or a nutmeg-grater. It is recorded among his other "virtues," that on his journeys he put pebbles or grains of maize in his shoes. His daily course of life was regulated in conformity to a paper drawn up by himself, and consisted of abstinence, sometimes relieved by bread and water, and castigating his body with scourges. The great object of his most thankful meditations was to think that having been born in England, and in London, in "the very seat and heart of heresy," he had been led to this happy way of life. In this extraordinary course of self-torment, F. Joam de Almeida attained the great age of eighty-two.
Anon.

6577. ASCETICISM, Varieties of. Three forms of asceticism have existed in this weak world. Religious asceticism, being the refusal of pleasure and knowledge, as was supposed, for the sake of religion, seen chiefly in the middle ages. Military asceticism, being the refusal of pleasure and knowledge for the sake of power; seen chiefly in the early days of Sparta and Rome. And monetary asceticism, consisting in the refusal of pleasure and knowledge for the sake of money, seen in the present days of London and Manchester. *Ruskin.*

6578. ASP, Poison of the. The asp is extremely venomous. Describing its bite, Dioscorides says, —"The sight became dim immediately; a swelling followed, and pain was felt in the stomach, which ended in convulsions and death." Death ensues about twenty-four hours after the person has been bitten. The whole body becomes of a blackish color, and mortification speedily follows. The asp is about one foot long and two inches round; oviparous, spotted with black and white. The common people of Cyprus called it *kophe* (deaf); and in Ps. 58, 4, deafness is ascribed to the *pethen*. It is commonly believed that Cleopatra died from the bite of an asp, but the manner of her death was not certainly known; "no marks, either of violence or of the action of poison, were found upon the corpse." The story of the asp was adopted by Octavian, in whose triumph there was borne a waxen figure of Cleopatra sinking into the last sleep upon her couch, with the snake clinging to her arm.

6579. ASSOCIATES, Choice of. In all societies it is advisable to associate, if possible, with the highest; not that the highest are always the best, but because if disgusted there, we can at any time descend; but if we begin with the lowest, to ascend is impossible. In the grand theatre of human life, a box ticket takes us through the house.   *Colton.*

6580. ASSOCIATES, Damage of Bad. Not long ago a young man of Springfield had a most favorable opportunity to enter a business house at a large increase over his present salary, with a prospect of soon getting a place in the firm. His recommendations were first-class, and the officers of the institution were decidedly pleased with his appearance. They, however, made him no proposals, nor did they state their favorable impressions. A gentleman of that city was requested to ascertain where the young man spent his evenings and what class of young men were his associates. It was found that he spent several nights of the week in a billiard-room, and Sunday afternoon drove a hired span into the country, with three other young men. For this reason he failed to obtain the coveted position.

6581. ASSOCIATION with Christ. "I am not the rose," says the Eastern proverb, "but I have been with the rose, and therefore I am sweet;" and he who has the Rose of Sharon in his bosom will diffuse its fragrance.

6582. ASSOCIATION, Dangerous. A mouse in an evil day made acquaintance with a frog, and they set off on their travels together. The frog, on pretence of great affection, and of keeping his companion out of harm's way, tied the mouse's hind foot to his own hind leg, and thus they proceeded for some distance by land. Presently they came to some water, and the frog bidding the mouse have good courage began to swim across. They had scarcely, however, arrived midway, when the frog took a sudden plunge to the bottom, dragging the mouse after him. But the struggling and floundering of the mouse made so great a commotion in the water that it attracted the attention of a kite, who, pouncing down, and bearing off the mouse, carried away the frog at the same time in its train.   *Æsop.*

6583. ASSOCIATION, Effect of. Mr. Moody frequently tells the story of how he carried in his pocket a gold chain. Into the same pocket he carelessly placed a lead bullet. After several days he took out the chain, and found it covered all over with a coating of lead. The contact of the two had brightened the worthless bullet, but it had greatly tarnished the gold. So a debasing thought, an unworthy motive, a bad book, an evil companion, may tarnish the pure gold of the best and noblest character. So a man may carelessly carry in his heart some doubt or ambition that may do him greatest harm.   *A. D. Vail.*

6584. ASSOCIATION, Honorable. An English soldier, on account of merit, had been pro moted to a captaincy in the army. In my country across the ocean, unlike it is in yours, soldiers never rise except by purchase or by birth. The newly-made captain, feeling ill at ease in his new position, requested his commanding officer to restore him again to the private ranks. The officer, surmising the cause of this apparently strange request, ordered a grand review of the army, and when about to pass along in front of the long drawn up lines, he requested the captain to give him his arm, and together they walked up and down before the rank and file of soldiers as they stood upon the field. The captain was reassured. He was honored with the association of the commander himself. "Thou shalt be with *me*." *Newman Hall.*

6585. ASSOCIATIONS, Circle of. "To love the little platoon we belong to in society is the germ of all public affections." True, most true! The innocent associations of childhood, the kind mother who taught us to whisper the first faint accents of prayer, and watched with anxious face over our slumbers, the ground on which our little feet first trod, the pew in which we first sat during public worship, the school in which our first rudiments were taught, the torn Virgil, the dog-eared Horace, the friends and companions of our young days, the authors who first told us the history of our country, the songs that first made our hearts throb with noble and generous emotions, the burying-place of our fathers, the cradles of our children, are surely the first objects which nature tells us to love. Philanthropy, like charity, must begin at home. From this centre our sympathies may extend in an ever-widening circle. *Lamb.*

6586. ASSUMPTION, Danger of. A jackdaw, as vain and conceited as jackdaw could be, picked up the feathers which some peacocks had shed, stuck them amongst his own, and despising his old companions, introduced himself with the greatest assurance into a flock of those beautiful birds. They, instantly detecting the intruder, stripped him of his borrowed plumes, and falling upon him with their beaks, sent him about his business. The unlucky jackdaw, sorely punished and deeply sorrowing, betook himself to his former companions, and would have flocked with them again as if nothing had happened. But they, recollecting what airs he had given himself, drummed him out of their society, while one of those whom he had so lately despised, read him this lecture: "Had you been contented with what nature made you, you would have escaped the chastisement of your betters and also the contempt of your equals." *Æsop.*

6587. ASSUMPTION, Failure of. In the reign of Adrian, the Jews, under the lead of Benchochab, organized a powerful revolt against the Romans. This leader was one of the false Christs of whom there were many about that time. He called himself the Messiah, and from the prophecy of Moses, Num. 24—"A star shall arise out of Jacob," etc.—he took his name, which in Hebrew signifies the son of a

star. Jean Baptiste says that this impostor gained possession of fifty castles in Judea, and nine hundred and eighty towns and villages. He shut himself up in Bethoron, and endured a siege of three years and a half, making many sallies, and shedding much blood. It is said that three hundred thousand Jews were killed, besides many who perished by plague and famine. At last Adrian in person led the attack upon the city. Benchochab, the false Messiah, was slain in a sally, and Bethoron was taken. The Jews, undeceived by his death, called him Benscosba, the son of a lie, instead of Benchochab, the son of a star. He was only one of many who have imposed upon the credulity of mankind. This occurred A. D. 121. As late as 1656, James Naylor of Yorkshire, England, a leader among the Quakers, declared himself to be Christ the Saviour, and gained many followers. He made a triumphal entry into Bristol, in imitation of Christ's entry into Jerusalem; his followers crying "Hosanna" before him, and strewing flowers in his path. For this he was branded with the letter B, for Blasphemer, upon his forehead, whipped through the streets of Bristol, and imprisoned for life.

6588. ASSUMPTION, Oriental. A traveler says: That in Tartary, after the Great Cham had dined, his trumpeters sounded their trumpets before his palace gate, to give notice to all the kings of the earth that now that the Great Cham had dined, they were at liberty to go to dinner.

6589. ASSUMPTION. Oriental Proverb. "You have become proud, and conduct yourself like the upstart who must 'carry his silk umbrella to keep off the sun at midnight!'"

6590. ASSURANCE, Abiding. I was once expounding the seventh and eighth of Romans to a class of colored Bible-women, deeply experienced as to their hearts, but very ignorant, as I supposed, in their heads. After I had been talking for a little while, an old colored woman interrupted me with—"Why, honey, 'pears like you don't understand them chapters." "Why not, auntie?" I asked; "what is the matter with my explanation?" "Why, honey," she said, "you talks as if we were to live in that miserable seventh chapter, and only pay little visits to the blessed eighth!" "Well," I answered, "that is just what I do think; don't you?" "Laws, honey," she exclaimed, with a look of intense pity for my ignorance, "why, I lives in the eighth." I knew it was true, for I had often wondered at the holiness of her lowly life, and for a moment I was utterly bewildered. But then I thought, "Oh! it is because she is colored and poor, that God has given her such a grand experience, to make up." And I almost began to wish I was colored and poor, that I also might have the same experience. But, I rejoice to say to-day, that even if you are white and not poor, you yet may know what it is to abide in Christ, and to rejoice in all the blessedness of such abiding. *Mrs. H. Pearsall Smith.*

6591. ASSURANCE. Absence of. While the

heaviest strokes fall on believers, their souls are ravished with the sweetest joy and exultation. Yet 'tis not thus always with the saints; for though sin be pardoned, yet the apprehensions of guilt may remain, as old wounds, though cured, yet are felt in change of weather. When a stream is disturbed, it does not truly represent the object; when the affections are disordered, the mind does not judge aright of the Christian's state. A serpent may hiss when it has lost its sting. I doubt not but some of the saints, whom death brings safely, yet not comfortably, to heaven, have often been in anxieties to the last, till their fears were dispelled by the actual fruition of blessedness; as the sun sometimes sets in dark clouds, and rises in a glorious horizon. *Salter*.

6592. ASSURANCE, Certain. It is one thing for a man to have his salvation certain, another thing to be certain that it is certain. Even as a man fallen into a river, and like to be drowned as he is carried down with the flood, espies the bough of a tree hanging over the river, which he catcheth at and clings unto with all his might to save him, and seeing no other way of succor but that, ventures his life upon it—this man, so soon as he has fastened on this bough, is in a safe condition, though all troubles, fears, and terrors are not presently out of his mind, until he comes to himself and sees himself quite out of danger. Then he is sure he is safe; but he was safe before he was sure. Even so it is with a believer. Faith is but the espying of Christ as the only means to save, and the reaching out of the heart to lay hold on him. *Usher*.

6593. ASSURANCE, Faith and. Faith, let us remember, is the root, and assurance is the flower. Doubtless you can never have the flower without the root; but it is no less certain you may have the root and not the flower. Faith is that poor trembling woman who came behind Jesus in the press, and touched the hem of his garment, (Mark 5, 25); Assurance is Stephen standing calmly in the midst of his murderers, and saying, "I see the heavens opened, and the Son of man standing on the right hand of God"(Acts 6, 56). Faith is the penitent thief, crying, "Lord, remember me" (Luke 23, 42); Assurance is Job sitting in the dust, covered with sores, and saying, "I know that my Redeemer liveth" (Job 19, 25); "Though he slay me, yet will I trust in him" (Job 13, 15). Faith is Peter's drowning cry, as he began to sink, "Lord, save me!" (Matt. 14. 30); Assurance is that same Peter declaring before the council, in after-times, "This is the stone which was set at naught by you builders, which is become the head of the corner. Neither is there salvation in any other; for there is none other name under heaven given among men whereby we must be saved" (Acts 4, 12). Faith is the anxious, trembling voice, "Lord, I believe; help thou mine unbelief" (Mark 9, 24); Assurance is the confident challenge, "Who shall lay anything to the charge of God's elect? Who is he that condemneth?" (Rom. 8, 33, 34). Faith is Saul

praying in the house of Judas at Damascus, sorrowful, blind, and alone (Acts 9, 11); Assurance is Paul, the aged prisoner, looking calmly into the grave, and saying, "I know whom I have believed. There is a crown laid up for me" (2 Tim. 1, 12; 4, 8). Faith is life. How great the blessing! Who can tell the gulf between life and death? And yet life may be weak, sickly, unhealthy, painful, trying, anxious, worn, burdensome, joyless, smileless to the very end. Assurance is more than life. It is health, strength, power, vigor, activity, energy, manliness, beauty. *Ryle*.

6594. ASSURANCE, Firm. Philip de Mornay, Prime Minister to Henry IV. of France, a great statesman, brave officer, and exemplary Christian, being asked a little before his death, if he still retained the same assured hope of future bliss which he had so comfortably enjoyed during his illness, answered, "I am as fixed in my confidence of an assured hope of future bliss from the incontestable evidence of the Spirit of God, as ever I was of any mathematical truth from all the demonstrations of Euclid."

6595. ASSURANCE, Happiness of. This assurance is the manna in the golden pot, the white stone, the wine of Paradise which cheers the heart. How comfortable is God's smile. The sun is more refreshing when it shines out than when it is hid in a cloud. It is a prelibation and a foretaste of glory, and puts a man in heaven before his time. None can know how delicious and ravishing it is, but such as have felt it; as none can know how sweet honey is but those who have tasted it. *T. Watson*.

6596. ASSURANCE, Joy of. Bilney, who suffered martyrdom in 1531, wrote: "I met with these words of the Apostle, 'This is a faithful saying, and worthy of all acceptation, that Jesus Christ came into the world to save sinners, whereof I am the chief.' O most sweet and comfortable sentence to my soul! This one sentence, through God's instruction and inward working, did so exhilarate my heart, which before was wounded by the guilt of my sins, and almost in despair, that immediately I found marvelous comfort and quietness in my soul, so that my bruised bones did leap for joy."

6597. ASSURANCE, Question of. Spangenberg, one of the Moravian pastors in Georgia, once inquired of John Wesley, "Does the Spirit of God bear witness with your spirit that you are a child of God?" Wesley was surprised at the inquiry, and knew not how to answer it. Spangenberg then asked, "Do you know Jesus Christ?" "I know him to be the Saviour of the world," responded Wesley. "True," said the Moravian; "but do you know he has saved you?" "I hope he has died for me," rejoined Wesley. Spangenberg added, "Do you know yourself?" "I do," answered Wesley. In a subsequent notice of his answer Wesley says "I fear they were mere words." The question left him no rest till from his own experience he could say, "The Spirit answers to the blood, and tells me I am born of God."

6598. ASSURANCE, Type of. Assurance is like

the sunflower, which opens with the day and shuts with the night. It follows the motion of God's face: if that looks smilingly on the soul, it lives; if that frowns or hides itself, it dies. But faith is a plant that can grow in the shade,—a grace that can find the way to heaven in a dark night. It can walk in darkness, and yet trust in the name of the Lord.

Anon.

6599. ASSURANCE, Uncertain of. Rev. J. C. Ryle supposes two English emigrants in New Zealand or Australia. He says, "Give each of them a piece of land to clear and cultivate. Let the portions allotted to them be the same both in quantity and quality. Secure that land to them by every needful legal instrument; let it be conveyed as freehold to them and theirs forever; let the conveyance be publicly registered, and the property made sure to them by every deed and security that man's ingenuity can devise. Suppose then that one of them shall set to work to bring his land into cultivation, and labor at it day after day without intermission or cessation. Suppose in the meanwhile that the other be continually leaving his work, and going repeatedly to the public registry, to ask whether the land is really his own, whether there is not some mistake—whether, after all, there is not some flaw in the legal instrument which conveyed it to him. The one shall never doubt his title, but just work diligently on. The other shall hardly ever feel sure of his title, and spend half his time in going to Sydney or Auckland with needless inquiries about it. Which now of these two men will have made most progress in a year's time? Who will have done the most for his land, got the greatest breadth of soil under tillage, have the best crops to show, be altogether the most prosperous?"

6600. ASTRONOMY, Discoveries in. The succession of noble discoveries made by Galileo, the most splendid, probably, which it ever fell to the lot of one individual to make, in a better age would have entitled its author to the admiration and gratitude of the whole scientific world; but they were viewed at the time with suspicion and jealousy. The ability and success with which Galileo had labored to overturn the doctrines of Aristotle and the schoolmen, as well as to establish the motion of the earth, and the immobility of the sun, excited many enemies. The Romish Church itself was roused to action by reflecting that it had staked the infallibility of its judgments on the truth of the very opinions which were now in danger of being overthrown. The Dialogues of Galileo contained a full exposition of the evidence of the earth's motion, and set forth the errors of the old as well as the discoveries of the new philosophy with great force of reasoning, and with the charms of the most lively eloquence. They are written with such singular felicity, that we read them at the present day, when the truths contained in them are known and admitted, with all the delight of novelty, and feel carried back to the period when the telescope was first directed to the heavens, and

when the earth's motion, with all its train of consequences, was proved for the first time. The author of such a work could not be forgiven. Galileo, accordingly, was twice brought before the Inquisition. The first time a council of seven cardinals pronounced a sentence, which ought never to be forgotten: "That to maintain the sun to be immovable, and without local motion, in the centre of the world, is an absurd proposition, false in philosophy, heretical in religion, and contrary to the testimony of Scripture. That it is equally absurd and false in philosophy to assert that the earth is not immovable in the centre of the world and, considered theologically, equally erroneous and heretical." Galileo was threatened with imprisonment unless he would retract his opinions, and a promise was at length extorted from him that he would not teach the doctrine of the earth's motion either by speaking or writing. To this promise he did not conform. In the year 1663, Galileo, now seventy years old was again brought before the Inquisition, forced solemnly to disavow his belief in the earth's motion, and condemned to perpetual imprisonment, though the sentence was afterwards mitigated, and he was allowed to return to Florence. The sentence appears to have pressed heavily on Galileo's mind, and he never afterwards either talked or wrote upon the subject of astronomy.

Anon.

6601. ASTRONOMY, Study of. The contemplation of celestial things will make a man both speak and think more sublimely and magnificently when he descends to human affairs.

Cicero.

6602. ASYLUM, The Lunatic. I recollect, as all do, the story of the Hall of Eblis, in "bathek," and how each shape, as it lifted its hand from its breast, showed its heart, a burning coal. The real Hall of Eblis stands on yonder summit. Go there on the next visiting-day, and ask that figure crouched in the corner, huddled up like those Indian mummies and skeletons found buried in the sitting posture, to lift its hand, and look upon its heart, and behold, not fire, but ashes.

Holmes.

6603. ATHEISM, Conversion from. A Griqua, in South Africa, stated that the first thing which led him to think of religion was observing the Hottentots, who belonged to the Zak River Mission, giving thanks when eating. "I went," said he, "afterwards to that settlement, where I heard many things, but felt no interest in them. But one day, when alone in the fields, I looked very seriously at a mountain, as the work of that God of whom I had heard; then I looked to my two hands, and for the first time noticed that there was the same number of fingers on each, I asked, Why are there not five on this hand and three on that? It must be God that made them so. Then I examined my feet, and wondered to find my soles both flat; not one flat and the other round. God must have done this, said I. In this way I considered my whole body, which made a deep impression on my mind, and disposed me to hear the Word of God with more

Interest, till I was brought to believe that Jesus died for my sins." *Cyclo. of Missions.*

6604. ATHEISM, Cultivation of. When people come to me, tell me they can't believe, and ask what they shall do, I tell them to do as I once knew a man do. He went and knelt down and told God honestly he could not believe in him, and I advise them to go off alone and tell it right out to the Lord. But if you stop to ask yourselves why you don't believe in him, is there really any reason? People read infidel books and wonder why they are unbelievers. I ask why they read such books. They think they must read both sides. I say that book is a lie; how can it be one side when it is a lie? It is not one side at all. Suppose a man tells right down lies about my family, and I read them so as to hear both sides; it would not be long before some suspicion would creep into my mind. I said to a man once, "Have you got a wife?" "Yes, and a good one." I asked: "Now, what if I should come to you and cast out insinuations against her?" And he said, "Well, your life would not be safe long if you did." I told him just to treat the devil as he would treat a man who went round with such stories. We are not to blame for having doubts flitting through our minds, but for harboring them. *Moody.*

6605. ATHEISM, Father of. Three young men were executed in Edinburgh. Immediately after committing the crimes for which they suffered, one evening they heard the family with whom they lodged employed in the worship of God. This suggested the question, Whether there is a God, and a world to come? After some discussion, they came to this conclusion, "That there is no God, and no world to come!"—a conclusion, as they themselves acknowledged, to which they came on this sole ground, that they wished it to be so.

6606. ATHEISM, Inexcusable. As the Lord Verulam observes, God never wrought a miracle to convince an atheist, because his ordinary works may convince him; and unless men will be willfully and stubbornly blind, they must needs subscribe to that of St. Paul (Acts 14, 17): "God hath not left himself without witness, in that he doth good, and gives us rain from heaven, and fruitful seasons, filling our hearts with food and gladness." And (Rom. 1, 20): "The invisible things of God are clearly seen from the creation of the world, being understood by the things that are made, even his eternal power and Godhead: so that they are without excuse." When we see footsteps evidently imprinted on the earth, shall we not easily collect that certainly some one hath passed that way? When we see a stately fabric built according to all the rules of art, and adorned with all the riches and beauty that magnificence can expend about it, must we not presently conclude, that certainly there was some skillful architect that built it? Truly, every creature is *quoddam vestigium Dei:* we may observe his footsteps in it; and see how his attributes, his wisdom, his goodness, and his power have passed along that way. And

the whole world is a stately fabric; a house that God hath erected for himself : the magnificence and splendor of it are suitable to the state of the Great King : it is his palace built for the house of his kingdom and the honors of his majesty; and we may easily conclude that so excellent a structure must needs have an excellent architect, and that the builder and maker of it is God. *Bp. Hopkins.*

6607. ATHEISM, Refutation of. One dandelion seed would seem to be enough to cut up all atheism by the roots. Its finely-spread balloon with its seed hanging like a miniature car as it floats through the air is certainly a piece of mechanism perfect for the end in view.
Prof. Chadbourne.

6608. ATHEISM, Unsatisfactory. There was a celebrated poet who was an atheist, or at least professed to be so. According to him there was no God. So he held when sailing over the unruffled surface of the Ægean sea. But the scene changed; and, with the scene, his creed. The heavens began to scowl upon him; and the deep uttered an angry voice, and, as if in astonishment at this God-denying man, "lifted up his hands on high." The storm increased, till the ship became unmanageable. She drifted before the tempest. The terrible cry, "Breakers ahead !" was soon heard; and how they trembled to see death seated on the horrid reef, waiting for his prey! A few moments more, and the crash comes. They are whelmed in the devouring sea? No! They are saved by a singular providence. Like apprehended evils, which in a Christian's experience, prove to be blessings, the wave, which flung them forward on the horrid reef, came on in such mountain volume as to bear and float them over into the safety of deep and ample sea-room. But ere that happened, a companion of the atheist, who, seated on the prow, had been taking his last regretful look of heaven and earth, sea and sky, turned his eyes down upon the deck, and there, among papists who told their beads and cried to the Virgin, he saw the atheist prostrated with fear. The tempest had blown away his fine-spun speculations like so many cobwebs: and he was on his knees, imploring God for mercy. In that hour—in that terrible extremity—Nature rose in her might, asserted her supremacy, vindicated the claims of religion, smote down infidelity by a stroke, and bent the stubborn knees of atheism in lowliest prayer. *Dr. Guthrie.*

6609. ATHEIST, Challenge to an. A New England minister was in the midst of a great revival, which was boldly opposed and ridiculed by an influential physician in the place, who claimed to be an atheist. One evening in his discourse he proposed to submit the issue between himself and the infidels to the test of *experiment,* agreeing, that if any one would do as *he should direct,* and fail to find religion to be a divine reality, he would renounce the Bible and become an infidel. Then, raising his voice, and looking the troublesome doctor square in the face, he asked, "Does any gentleman accept my challenge?" Upon this the doctor stepped out into the aisle and answered, "I accept it." "Well," said the preacher, "then come forward to the altar," which he did. "Now," said the preacher, "I will state my proposition again, that there may be no misunderstanding between us." Having done so the doctor assented to it. Every thing being ready, and the thronged assembly in painful anxiety, the preacher demanded of the doctor to kneel down. He did so. "Now," said he, with awful solemnity, "Doctor, call upon God Almighty to have mercy on your soul." The doctor, looking up into his face, replied, "I don't believe there is any such being." "There," said the preacher, "he breaks the contract at the start—he was to do as *I* directed." He modified the prayer to accommodate his unbelief, saying, "Well, doctor pray this way, 'If there be a God, have mercy on my soul.'" There was no getting away from this, and the doctor commenced and proceeded with perfect deliberation until he reached the *petition*, when he cried at the top of his voice, and from the deep of his heart, "Have mercy on my soul!" and went on to pray without further direction. The explanation is, that having reached that point in utter unconcern, God sent the spirit of awakening upon him as he did upon Saul of Tarsus. Of course the experiment was a success and the renewed doctor came to know the doctrine to be of God, and to defend it. *Dr. James Porter.*

6610. ATHEIST, Confusion of an. Dr. Mackay, of Hull, said in a meeting recently, "Once a skeptic in Dr. Bonar's church said: 'Sir, I do not believe there is a God.' It was ten P.M., and no time for argument. I cast the burden on the Lord in prayer, and looked so happy, that he said, 'Are you laughing at me?' No; but I was thinking if all the grasshoppers on earth were to say there is no sun, it would not alter the matter. The Bible says, 'The fool hath said in his heart, There is no God.' 'Well, that is so,' he said. I then showed him that God calls every man who does not believe in him a liar. The man went home seeming much impressed; and when I met him some months afterwards he said, 'I found out that I was a fool and a liar, and have come to Christ.'"

6611. ATHEIST, Folly of the. He that acts wisely, and is a thoroughly prudent man, will be provided against all events, and will take care to secure the main chance, whatever happens; but the atheist, in case things should fall out contrary to his belief and expectation, hath made no provision for this case. If, contrary to his confidence, it should prove in the issue that there is a God, the man is lost and undone for ever. If the atheist, when he dies, should find that his soul remains after his body, and has only quitted its lodging, how will this man be amazed and blanked when, contrary to his expectation, he shall find himself in a new and strange place, amidst a world of spirits, entered upon an everlasting and unchangeable state! How sadly will the man be disappointed when he finds all things otherwise than he had stated and determined them in this world!

When he comes to appear before that God whom he hath denied and against whom he hath spoken as despiteful things as he could, who can imagine the pale and guilty looks of this man, and how he will shiver and tremble for the fear of the Lord, and for the glory of his majesty? How will he be surprised, with terrors on every side, to find himself thus unexpectedly and irrevocably plunged into a state of ruin and desperation! And thus things may happen for all this man's confidence now. For our belief or disbelief of a thing does not alter the nature of the thing We cannot fancy things into being, or make them vanish into nothing, by the stubborn confidence of our imaginations. Things are as sullen as we are, and will be what they are, whatever we think of them. And if there be a God, a man cannot by an obstinate disbelief of him make him cease to be, any more than a man can put out the sun by winking. *Tillotson.*

6612. ATHEIST, Reform of an. Napoleon Bonaparte put a man by the name of Charney into prison. A little flower grew within the enclosure of the prison yard; above it, on the wall, was written, "All things come by chance." But day by day, as he took his lonely walk, the flower was teaching him lessons of trust, and he made a frame to support it and a shelter to protect it from pelting rains. He felt that all things could not come by chance; there is one who made this flower so wonderfully beautiful and keeps it alive. He brushed the lying words from the wall, while his heart felt "he who made all things is God." But other blessings came to the prisoner. The Empress Josephine, hearing of Charney's love for the flower, became interested in him. She thought "a man that loves and tends a flower cannot be a bad man." She persuaded the Emperor to set him at liberty. Charney carried his flower home, and carefully tended it in his own greenhouse. It had taught him to believe in God, and had also delivered him from prison.

6613. ATONEMENT, Accepting the. When a sacrifice under the law was brought to be slain, he that brought it was to put his hand upon the head of the sacrifice, and so it was accepted for him, to make an atonement (Lev. 1, 4), not only to signify that now it was no more his but God's, the property being transferred by a kind of manumission, nor yet merely that he voluntarily gave it to the Lord as his own free act; but principally it signified the putting off his sins, and the penalty due for them, upon the head of the sacrifice; and so it implied in it an execration as if he had said, "Upon thy head be the evil." So the learned observe, the ancient Egyptians were wont expressly to imprecate when they sacrificed, "If any evil be coming upon us or upon Egypt, let it turn and rest upon his head," laying their hand, at these word's, on the sacrifice's head. And upon that ground, says Herodotus, the historian, none of them would eat of the head of any living creature. You must also lay the hand of faith upon Christ your sacrifice, not to imprecate but to apply and appropriate him to your own souls, he having been made a curse for you.

John Flavel.

6614. ATONEMENT, Applying the. Canst thou look upon Jesus as standing in thy room, to bear the wrath of God for thee, canst thou think on it and not melt? That when thou, like Isaac, wast bound to the altar, to be offered up to justice, Christ, like the ram caught in the thicket, was offered in thy room. That when thy sins had raised a fearful tempest, threatening every moment to bury thee in a sea of wrath, Jesus Christ was thrown over to appease that storm! Can thy heart dwell one hour upon such a subject as this? Canst thou, with faith, present Christ to thyself, as he was taken down from the cross, drenched in his own blood, and say, These were the wounds that he received for me; this is he that loved me, and gave himself for me; out of these wounds comes that balm that heals my soul, out of these stripes my peace? *Flavel.*

6615. ATONEMENT, Appropriating the. Now we may say, "Lord, the condemnation was thine, that the justification might be mine; the agony thine, that the victory might be mine; the pain was thine, and the ease is mine; the stripes thine, and the healing balm issuing from them mine; the vinegar and the gall were thine, that the honey and sweet might be mine; the curse was thine, that the blessing might be mine; the crown of thorns was thine, that the crown of glory might be mine; thou paidst the price, that I might enjoy the inheritance."

John Flavel.

6616. ATONEMENT by the Cross. Let us no more admire the enormous moats and bridges of Caligula across to Baiæ, or that of Trajan over the Danube (stupendous work of stone and marble) to the adverse shores, whilst our timber and our trees, making us bridges to the furthest Indies and antipodes, land us into new worlds. In a word (and to speak a bold and noble truth), trees and woods have twice saved the whole world; first by the ark, then by the cross; making full amends for the evil fruit of the tree in paradise, by that which was borne on the tree in Golgotha. *Evelyn.*

6617. ATONEMENT, Effects of the. It is said of Zeleucus, a king of the ancient Locri, that he enacted a law, the penalty of which was that the offender should lose both his eyes. One of his sons became a transgressor of that law. The father had his attachment to his son, and the law he himself had promulgated as righteous in its requirements and in its penalty. The lawgiver, it is said, ordered his son into his presence, and required that one of his eyes should be taken out; and then, in order to show mercy to his son, and at the same time maintain the penalty of the law, he sacrificed one of his own eyes as a ransom for the remaining eye of his child. The king was the lawgiver; he therefore had the power to pardon his son, without inflicting the penalty upon him, and without enduring any sacrifice himself. Every mind, therefore, would feel that it was a voluntary act on the part of the king;

and such an exhibition of justice and mercy, maintaining the law and saving his son by his own sacrifice, would impress all minds with the deepest reverence for the character of the lawgiver, and for the sacredness of the law. But another effect, deep and lasting in its character, would be produced upon the son who had transgressed the law. Every time that he looked upon his father, or remembered what he had suffered for his transgression, it would increase his love for him, increase his reverence for the law, and cause an abhorrence of his crime to rise in his soul. His feelings would be more kind towards his sire, more submissive to the law, and more averse to transgression. Now, this is precisely the effect necessary to be produced, in order that pardon may be extended to transgressors, and yet just and righteous government be maintained. *Walker.*

6618. ATONEMENT, Jewish Custom of. The following is a report made by a committee of the Church of Scotland of their observations among the Jews: "We spread our mats on the clay floor at Jassy, and attempted to sleep, but in vain. We cared less for this, however, because it was the night preceding the day of atonement, and we had thus an opportunity of seeing the curious ceremony which then takes place. On the eve of that solemn day it is the custom of the Jews to kill a cock for every man, and a hen for every woman. During the repetition of a certain form of prayer, Jews or Jewesses move the living fowl round their head three times, then they lay their hands on it, as the hands used to be laid on the sacrifices, and immediately after give it to be slaughtered. We rose before one in the morning, and saw the Jewish Shochet or 'slayer' going round to the Jewish houses, waking each family, and giving them a light from his lantern, in order that they might rise and bring out their 'Chipporah' or 'atonement,' namely, the appointed cock and hen. We walked about the streets; everywhere the sound of the imprisoned fowls was to be heard, and a light seen in all the dwellings of Israel. In two houses the fowls were already dead and plucked. In another we came to the window, and saw distinctly what was going on within. A little boy was reading the prayers and his widowed mother standing over him, with a white hen in her hands. When he came to a certain place in the prayer, the mother lifted up the struggling fowl, and waved it round her head, repeating these words, 'This be my substitute, this be my exchange; this fowl shall go to death, and I to a blessed life.' This was done three times over, and then the door of the house opened, and out ran the boy carrying the fowl to the Shochet, to be killed by him in the proper manner."

6619. ATONEMENT, Illustrating the. A deaf and dumb boy was taught by a kind friend. This kind lady could speak to him only by signs and pictures. She drew upon a paper a picture of a great crowd of people, old and young, standing near a wide, deep pit, out of which smoke and flames were issuing. She then drew the figure of One who came down from heaven, and this was to represent Jesus Christ the Son of God. She explained to the boy that when this person came, he asked God not to throw the people into the pit, if he himself agreed to be nailed to a cross for them, and how, as soon as he bowed his head on the cross and died, the pit was shut up and the people saved. The deaf and dumb boy wondered much, but he made signs that the person who died on the cross was but one, and the crowd very many. How could God be contented to take one for so many? The lady took off her gold ring and put it beside a great heap of withered leaves of flowers, and asked the boy which was the best, the one gold ring, or the many, many dry leaves. The boy clapped his hands with delight, and spelt the "One! one!" And then to show that he knew what this meant, and that Jesus was the one who was worth all the rest, he ran and got his letters, and looking up, spelt the words, "Good, good one!" He had learned that day that Jesus alone had saved the crowd of people, or sinners, and he stood wondering at his love.   *A. A. Bonar.*

6620. ATONEMENT, Pagan. There is a record of an ancient Hindoo custom, in which the offender brought a horse to a priest, and confessed his sins over the head of the animal, with certain religious rites. The horse was then turned into the wilderness and supposed to bear away the sins of the offender. This custom was similar to the scapegoat of the Israelites.

6621. ATONEMENT, Reliance on the. Thomas, Earl of Kinnoul, a short time before his death, said: "I have always considered the atonement to be characteristical of the gospel, as a system of religion. Strip it of that doctrine, and you reduce it to a scheme of morality, excellent indeed, and such as the world never saw; but to man, in the present state of his faculties, absolutely impracticable. The atonement of Christ, and the truths immediately connected with that fundamental principle, provide a remedy for all the wants and weaknesses of our nature. They who strive to remove those precious doctrines from the word of God, do an irreparable injury to the grand and beautiful system of religion which it contains, as well as to the comforts and hopes of man. For my own part, I am now an old man, and have experienced the infirmities of advanced years. Of late, in the course of severe and dangerous illness, I have been repeatedly brought to the gates of death. My time in this world cannot now be long; but, with truth I can declare that, in the midst of all my past afflictions, my heart was supported and comforted by a firm reliance upon the merits and atonement of my Saviour; and now, in the prospect of entering upon an eternal world, this is the only foundation of my confidence and hope."

6622. ATONEMENT, Voluntary. A sacrifice that struggled, and came not without force to the altar, was reckoned ominous and unlucky by the heathen; our sacrifice dedicated himself, he died out of choice, and was a free-will offering.   *John Flavel.*

6623. ATTAINMENTS No Atonement. However right our experiences or attainments or walk or service may be in their place, they are not the offering for atonement, nor can they ever be the ground of peace. And indeed, for a Christian to seek his food in these things is as though an Israelite were to take his garments to feed on. In truth the man who seeks satisfaction in his own attainments just does this: what should be his raiment, he makes his meat. The garments of the Israelite are the appointed symbol of a man's deportment and manifested character. So the New Testament interprets the type: "The fine linen is the righteousness of saints." This garment might be easily defiled. But let us suppose it clean—are garments to be fed on? The type answers at once: it is the meat of the altar, the sweet savor alone, which satisfies. Our prayers, our love, our service: these things, like the leavened cake at Pentecost, though accepted for the sake of what accompanies them, are one and all in themselves blemished.   *A. Jukes.*

6624. ATTENTION, Holding. A ship-builder was asked what he thought of Mr. Whitefield's preaching. "Think!" he replied. "I tell you, sir, that every Sunday I go to my parish church I can build a ship from stem to stern under the sermon, but were it to save my soul I could not under Mr. Whitefield's preaching lay a single plank."

6625. ATTENTION, Selfish. There was a certain brazier who had a little dog. While he hammered away at his metal, the dog slept; but whenever he sat down to his dinner the dog woke up. "Sluggard cur!" said the brazier, throwing him a bone; "you sleep through the noise of the anvil, but wake up at the first clatter of my teeth."   *Æsop.*

6626. ATTRACTION, Method of. The surest way of turning a person from one pleasure is to give him a greater pleasure on the opposite side. A weeping willow planted by a pond in a pleasure garden turns all to one side in its growth, and that the side on which the water lies. No dealing with its roots or with its branches will avail to change its attitude; but place a larger expanse of water on the opposite side, and the tree will turn spontaneously and hang the other way. So must man's heart be won.   *William Arnot.*

6627. ATTRACTIONS, Personal. King Philip so far doted on a fair Thessalian lady that she was suspected to have used some private arts of fascination towards him. Wherefore Olympias labored to get the supposed sorceress into her power. But when the queen had viewed her well, and duly examined her beauty, beheld the graces of her deportment, and considered her discourse, bespake her no less than a person of noble descent and education: "Hence, fond suspicions, hence vainer calumnies!" said she, "for I plainly find the charms which thou makest use of are in thyself."   *Plutarch.*

6628. AUSTERITY, Monkish. No more conspicuous example is found than Simeon Stylites, the pillar saint. The monks of his monastery ate once a day. He made but one meal a week, and that on Sundays. He took a rough rope of twisted palm-leaves and tied it tightly around his body underneath his clothes. It cut into his flesh and made running wounds, which become offensive and revealed his self-mortification. When cut from his body in which it had become imbedded he was left as one dead. For this he was turned out of his monastery. He passed twenty-six Lents without eating or drinking anything, according to Theodoret. He built an enclosure by piling together a few rough stones on the top of Mt. Thelonissa, and bolted his right leg to a rock with an iron chain. He passed thirty-seven years on the top of pillars; four years on one six cubits high, three years on the second twelve cubits high, ten years on a third twenty-two cubits high, twenty years on the fourth forty cubits high. His fame was very great. Throngs gathered to receive his blessing; great numbers of heathen are reported to have been converted by him. He was clad in skins and wore an iron collar. He could not lie down on the top of his pillar, and had no seat. He was known to pray as many as twelve hundred times a day. Twice daily he exhorted the people. At last he bowed himself in prayer and so remained for three days. Then, one of his disciples went up to the top of his pillar and said, "Master, arise and bless us, for the people have been waiting three days and nights for a blessing from thee." It was then discovered that he was dead. He died A. D. 460, and is enrolled in the calendar for January 5.

6629. AUTHOR, Advice to an. Samuel Foote, the comedian, was much annoyed by a pompous physician of Bath, who told him he had a mind to publish his own poems, but that he had so many irons in the fire he did not know what to do. Foote replied, "Take my advice, doctor, and put your poems where your irons are."

6630. AUTHOR, Empire of the. That man has an empire beyond that of the highest monarch that now lives. It has been said that the Queen of this great empire has a kingdom upon which the sun never sets; yet her empire, great as it is, is neither so wide nor so deep as that of the man who rules in the empire of your affections and in the kingdom of thought. *Dixon.*

6631. AUTHOR, Influence of the. An author may influence the fortunes of the world to as great an extent as a statesman or a warrior; and the deeds and performances by which this influence is created and exercised, may rank in their interest and importance with the decisions of great Congresses, or the skillful valor of a memorable field. It is certainly not too much to maintain, that the exploits of Homer, Aristotle, Dante, or Lord Bacon, were as considerable events as any that occurred at Actium, Lepanto, or Blenheim. A book may be as great a thing as a battle, and there are systems of philosophy that have produced as great revolutions as any that have disturbed even the social and political existence of our centuries.   *I. Disraeli.*

6632. AUTHORITY, Deference to. The Emperor Adrian, not content with being the first in power, was ambitious to be the first in letters, He once corrected Favorinus for employing an improper word. He submitted with patience, though he was convinced that he was correct. When his friends objected to his compliance, he answered, "Shall not I easily suffer him to be the most learned of all men who has thirty legions at his command?"

6633. AUTHORITY, Private Judgment and. True it is that differences amongst Protestants are the great boast and great strength of the Church of Rome. And just so, contests between Whigs and Tories are matter of scornful exultation, no doubt, to the Russian autocrat. He has no members of Parliament making speeches against each other: all being under one despotic monarchy. And true it is that in all questions, religious or political, where there is a right and a wrong, several different parties cannot be all right. When all are forced into agreement or outward submission, what they submit to may conceivably be right. But suppose it is not? Then all are in the wrong; and truth and right have no chance at all, to the end of time. When Bonaparte was, with his attendants, overtaken in Egypt by the tide of the Red Sea, out of sight of the shore, the whole party were in danger of being drowned; and if he had given orders to proceed in some one direction, if that had chanced not to be the right one, all must have perished. He told them each to ride in the direction he judged best; and if the water was found to deepen, to turn back; if to grow shallower, to shout out to his comrades. Thus, the one who hit on the right course saved both himself and the rest. But if some of the rest had been (as in religion, politics, and other matters) too perverse to follow the proved right course, at least some would have been saved.   *Archbp. Whately.*

6634. AUTHORSHIP, Pride of. "I am going to fly," cried the gigantic ostrich; and the whole assembly of birds gathered round in earnest expectation. "I am going to fly," he cried again; and stretching out his immense pinions he shot, like a ship with outspread sails, away over the ground, without, however, rising an inch above it. Thus it happens, when a notion of being poetical takes possession of unpoetical brains; in the opening of their monstrous odes they boast of their intention to soar over clouds and stars, but nevertheless remain constant to the dust.   *Lessing.*

6635. AUTOBIOGRAPHY, Difficulty of. It is a hard and nice subject for a man to write of himself; it grates his own heart to say anything of disparagement, and the reader's ears to hear anything of praise from him. *Cowley.*

6636. AUTUMN, Harvest of. However constant the visitations of sickness and bereavement, the fall of the year is most thickly strewn with the fall of human life. Everywhere the spirit of some sad power seems to direct the time: it hides from us the blue heavens, It makes the green wave turbid; it walks through the fields, and lays the damp ungathered harvest low; it cries out in the night wind and the shrill hail; it steals the summer bloom from the infant cheek; it makes old age shiver to the heart; it goes to the churchyard, and chooses many a grave; it flies to the bell, and enjoins it when to toll. It is God that goes his yearly round; that gathers up the appointed lives; and, even where the hour is not come, engraves by pain and poverty many a sharp and solemn lesson on the heart.

James Martineau.

6637. AUTUMN, Moral of. A moral character is attached to autumnal scenes; the leaves falling like our years, the flowers fading like our hours, the clouds fleeting like our illusions, the light diminishing like our intelligence, the sun growing colder like our affections, the rivers becoming frozen like our lives—all bear secret relations to our destinies.   *Chateaubriand.*

6638. AVARICE, Absorption of. A New Hampshire farmer, stricken with mortal illness, was advised to make any business arrangements necessary before his death. He sent his son to find a stocking filled with gold under the barn, and another in the garret. They were brought and the glittering eagles poured upon the bed within his reach. He was repeatedly reminded that haste was necessary if he had any other business. In silence he handled the gold upon which his heart was set, till death stiffened his fingers, and his sordid soul entered his Maker's presence bankrupt.

6639. AVARICE, Claim of. Some Turks freighted a ship from Alexandria for Constantinople. On the voyage a storm arose, which made it necessary to throw overboard the cargo to save the lives of the passengers who were owners of the freight. The alternative of the loss of all or of the cargo was laid before them by the captain, and they consented to the loss of their freight to save their lives. Arrived safely in Constantinople, the freighters commenced an action against the captain of the vessel for the value of the goods. The judge decided that the law required that the master should pay the true value of those goods at the moment the goods were thrown into the sea. Witnesses were required, but none could be obtained save those who had in the emergency consented to give the goods for their lives. Decision was given for the defendant. Many sacrifice in peril but recall the offering as soon as safety is gained.

6640. AVARICE, Conquering. Shortly after conversion, a chimney sweep attended a Missionary meeting. He was the possessor of one shilling and two-pence. His heart was drawn out to give, and as the collector was coming up the aisle, a question of some difficulty arose, "Which shall I give? Copper, silver; which is to go? Those poor Pagans are in awful case;—but then: a shilling is a good lump;— it is my last; and where the next is to come from I don't see. Mammon has it, on goes two-pence. The closing prayer commenced. The petitions were too big for my gift. I felt mean. So quietly going up the aisle, I stealthily dropped my shilling on the plate. Then I could say 'Amen,' as lustily as the best of them.

But, I lost my two-pence. So I learned stinginess to be a losing game. When old Satan has tempted me to it, since then I've often thrown that two-pence in his face; and I don't believe he likes it."

6641. AVARICE, Cupidity of. When Dr. Vanderkemp was in Kafirland, a Pagan Chief sent him a present of two milch cows with their calves, in a time of great drouth, to induce him to procure rain, the Pagan rain-makers having failed. The doctor refused to accept the present, and assured the chief that he could not make rain, but that he would pray to his God for it He did so, and his prayer was abundantly answered. Some English adventurers then residing there, criticised Dr. Vanderkemp's rejection of the gift, and one of them named Buys, sent to the Chief in the missionaries' name, saying the gift was not enough for the service. The present was largely increased and the covetous European appropriated it to his own use. His crime was detected and so fully exposed that the missionary influence was not injured. Buys was afterward murdered. This case parallels the account of Gehazi in cupidity.

6642. AVARICE, in Death. A minister relates that one of his parishioners, a faithful attendant upon the services of the church, and a man of considerable wealth, could never be induced to give anything to any benevolent object. On his death-bed he sent for the minister and asked him what he thought would become of him. He exhorted him to repent, and renounce the world if he would be saved. The miser gazed at his admonisher in amazement. Give up the world, his treasures, he would not. Even then, within a few moments of death, he was grasping the keys to the cabinet which contained his treasures, and held them in his hands concealed under the bed-clothes. He could not give them up, but death opened his hand. He passed into eternity clutching his keys. Such is the power of avarice, as it sometimes develops when it supplants the love of God in the professor's heart.

6643. AVARICE, Evil of. Avarice isolates man from the great universe and the holy God, deadens the sensibilities to the highest joys, and shuts the soul up in its own dark self, the victim of a thousand miserable suspicions, and the subject of attributes that every generous heart must loathe.   *Dr. Thomas.*

6644. AVARICE, Expedient of. An avaricious man will proceed to any lengths of crime that his desires may be satisfied. An instance of this is given us in the story of the death of Caius Gracchus. To any one who would bring his head a reward was offered of its weight in gold. A dastardly wretch snatched it from the hand of him who had been his executioner, that he might himself procure the prize. But before he delivered up the head it is said that he took out its brains and filled the cavity with molten lead, that when it was weighed his prize might be the larger.   *Anon.*

6645 AVARICE, Folly of. Can anything be more senselessly absurd than that, the nearer we are to our journey's end, we should still lay in more provisions for it? *Cicero.*

6646. AVARICE, Greed of. Among Mohammed's revelations was the following: "If a son of Adam had two rivers of gold he would covet yet a third; and if he had three he would covet yet a fourth."

6647. AVARICE. Growth of. An indolent Oriental, says the fable, had a nice garden of leeks, but was not satisfied, and complained of the labor required to till it. Fortune favored him with the gift of a beautiful villa and two slaves to wait on him. He was delighted, and promised to crave nothing more. Not long after he coveted a neighboring garden adorned with statues and fountains, which was given him. Then he took a great fancy to the meadow beyond; this also was granted him. Then he wanted the park adjoining on the other side, and it was bestowed on him. Then like Ahab he wanted to rob a poor man of his little vineyard which lay next to the park. Avarice is an insatiable monster; the more he is fed the more he craves.

6648. AVARICE, Influence of. A charity sermon had been preached and a collection was to follow it. The collectors stood at the doors to receive it. A man came near the collector as if considering what to do. He thrust his hand in his pocket and drew out a sixpence. He held it in his hand, looked at it, kissed it, and laid it upon the plate, saying "Farewell, I shall never see thee any more." Poor object of pity. The Lord says, "Freely ye have received, freely give." Matt. 10: 8.

6649. AVARICE, Insatiable. Hunger is allayed by eating, thirst by drinking, cold by putting on more clothing; but the desire for money is never abated by any amount of silver, gold, jewels, or estate. However great one's income the desire for money is constantly crying, "More, more." This is a disease more incurable than the leprosy.

6650. AVARICE, Madness of. The ship Britannia, which struck on the rocks off the coast of Brazil, had on board a large consignment of Spanish dollars. In the hope of saving some of them, a number of barrels were brought on deck, but the vessel was sinking so fast that the only hope for life was in taking at once to the boats. The last boat was about to push off, when a midshipman rushed back to see if any one was still on board. To his surprise, there sat a man on deck with a hatchet in his hand, with which he had broken open several of the casks, the contents of which he was now heaping up about him. "What are you doing?" shouted the youth. "Escape for your life! Don't you know the ship is fast going to pieces?" "The ship may," said the man. "I have lived a poor wretch all my life, and I am determined to die rich." His remonstrances were answered only by another flourish of the hatchet; and he was left to his fate. In a few minutes, the ship was engulfed in the waves. We count such a person a madman; but he has too many imitators. Many men seem determined to die rich at all hazards. Least of all risks do they count the chance of losing the soul in the struggle. And yet the only riches we can hug to our bosom with joy in our dying hour are the riches of grace, through faith in our only Saviour, Jesus Christ. Let us make these riches ours before the dark hour comes. *Anon.*

6651. AVARICE, Mistake of. In the ruins of Pompeii there was found a petrified woman who, instead of trying to fly from the city, had spent her time in gathering up her jewels. Multitudes are making the same mistake.

6652. AVARICE, Oriental Proverbs. "My friend, why are you so anxious after this world? How much did you bring into it? How much will you take out?" "Ah, my son! be charitable to all; recollect you brought nothing into the world, and be assured you will take nothing out." "That wretch would like to carry his money and lands into the other world." "Tamby, did you bring these fields into the world with you? No, and they will remain when you are gone." *Roberts.*

6653. AVARICE, Power of.
In Mediæval Rome, I know not where,
There stood an image with its arm in air,
And on its lifted finger, shining clear,
A golden ring with the device, "Strike here!"
Greatly the people wondered, though none guessed
The meaning that these words but half expressed,
Until a learned clerk, who at noonday
With downcast eyes was passing on his way,
Paused, and observed the spot, and marked it well,
Whereon the shadow of the finger fell;
And, coming back at midnight, delved, and found
A secret stairway leading under ground,
Down this he passed into a spacious hall,
Lit by a flaming jewel on the wall;
And opposite a brazen statue stood
With bow and shaft in threatening attitude.
Upon its forehead, like a coronet,
Were these mysterious words of menace set:
"That which I am, I am; my fatal aim
None can escape, not even yon luminous flame!"
Midway the hall was a fair table placed,
With cloth of gold, and golden cups enchased
With rubies, and the plates and knives were gold—
And gold the bread and viands manifold.
Around it, silent, motionless and sad,
Were seated gallant knights in armor clad,
And ladies beautiful with plume and zone,
But they were stone, their hearts within were stone:
And the vast hall was filled in every part
With silent crowds, stony in face and heart.

Long at the scene, bewildered and amazed,
The trembling clerk in speechless wonder gazed;
Then from the table, by his greed made bold,
He seized a goblet and a knife of gold,
And suddenly from their seats the guests upsprang,
The vaulted ceiling with loud clamors rang.
The archer sped his arrow, at their call,
Shattering the lambent jewel on the wall,
And all was dark around and overhead:—
Stark on the floor the luckless clerk lay dead!

The writer of this legend then records
Its ghostly application in these words:
The image is the Adversary old,
Whose beckoning finger points to realms of gold;
Our lusts and passions are the downward stair
That leads the soul from a diviner air;
The archer, Death; the flaming jewel, Life;
Terrestrial goods, the goblet and the knife;

The knights and ladies, all whose flesh and bone
By avarice have been hardened into stone;
The clerk, the scholar whom the love of pelf
Tempts from his books and from his nobler self.

The scholar and the world ! The endless strife,
The discord in the harmonies of life!
The love of learning, the sequestered nooks,
And all the sweet serenity of books :
The market-place, the eager love of gain,
Whose aim is vanity, and whose end is pain !
           H. W. Longfellow.

6654. AVARICE, Penalty of. In one of the houses of Pompeii the skeleton of a man was found "Who apparently for the sake of sixty coins, a small plate, and a saucepan of silver, had remained in his house till the street was already half filled with volcanic matter. He was found as if in the act of escaping from the window."

6655. AVERSIONS, A Bundle of. Some people's sensibility is a mere bundle of aversions, and you hear them display and parade it, not in recounting the things they are attached to, but in telling how many things and persons they "cannot bear."   *John Foster.*

6656. AWAKENING, Simile of. Carl Steinman, who visited Mount Hecla, Iceland, just before the last great eruption in 1845, after a repose of eighty years, narrowly escaped death by venturing into the smoking crater against the earnest entreaty of his guide. On the brink of the yawning gulf he was prostrated by a convulsion of the summit, and held there by blocks of lava upon his feet. He graphically writes : "Oh, the horrors of that awful realization ! There, over the mouth of a black and heated abyss, I was held suspended, a helpless and conscious prisoner, to be hurled downward by the next great throe of trembling Nature ! ' Help, help, help !—for the love of God, help !' I shrieked in the very agony of my despair. I had nothing to rely upon but the mercy of Heaven; and I prayed to God as I had never prayed before for a forgiveness of my sins, that they might not follow me to judgment. All at once, I heard a shout; and, looking around, I beheld, with feelings that can not be described, my faithful guide hastening down the sides of the crater to my relief. ' I warned you !' said he. ' You did !' cried I : ' but forgive me and save me; for I am perishing !' ' I will save you, or perish with you !' The earth trembled, and the rocks parted; one of them rolling down the chasm with a dull, booming sound. I sprang forward; I seized a hand of the guide ; and the next moment we had both fallen, locked in each other's arms, upon the solid earth above. I was free, but still upon the verge of the pit." We do not know of a more vivid illustration of the deepest spiritual experience in the transition of the soul from impenitence to pardon. The incautious sinner ventures among the very flames of Sinai, over the crumbling verge of eternal death. If awakened to see his guilt and peril, how consciously helpless, and how hopeless his condition so far as his *self*-reliance is concerned ! But, when the cry of distress for help goes up, lo ! Jesus, the sinner's only guide, hastens through the gloom to the very sides of the flaming pit to his relief. Soon, in rapturous embrace, the rescued soul looks back to see the danger, and hear the thunder of its unsounded horrors, with thanksgiving which shall find expression for ever upon the golden harp and in the melody of the new song.
           Am. Messenger

6657. BABEL, Tower of. According to Herodotus, the Tower of Babel, which was constructed of bricks of bitumen, was a furlong on each side at the base; and Strabo adds, a furlong in height. It consisted of eight towers built one above another, which, if proportionally high, would make the elevation exactly one mile. The ascent to the top, Rollin informs us, was by stairs winding round it on the outside; that is, there was an easy sloping ascent in the side of the outer wall, which turning by very slow degrees in a spiral line, eight times round the tower, from the bottom to the top, had the same appearance as if there had been eight towers placed upon one another. In these different stories were many large rooms with arched roofs, supported by pillars. Over the whole, on the top of the tower was an observatory, by the benefit of which the Babylonians became more expert in astronomy than all other nations.   *Whitecross.*

6658. BABY, God's Care of. An infant had been taught to say,—"God will take care of baby." It was taken sick and given up to die. Its parents were themselves recovering from sickness, and came into the apartment after the child was supposed to have taken its heavenward flight. The mother's voice recalled the child's spirit. It opened its eyes and whispered, "God will take care of baby," then closed its eyes to earth. God took the child to the heavenly mansions, and gave it the care of angels, in his own glorious palace.

6659. BABY, Remarkable Death of a. The youngest child of Rev. Dr. Olin, aged two years, was ill, but not supposed to be dangerously so. The doctor was in the room with the child when the babe suddenly called, "Papa! papa, take baby!" Dr. Olin took the child, and walked up and down the room. The child said, "Pa, kiss baby! Mamma, kiss baby !" and when this was done, looked up and exclaimed, "Now God take baby!" and immediately expired in his father's arms.

6660. BACKBITING, Excused. How like a wild beast would it glare upon us, were there lying on our conscience the "damned spot" of murder ! It would not "out." The "red cincture" *would* "clasp our wrists." But let it take the form of "evil speaking," by which a reputation is stabbed, a character murdered—and then it is only a "small sin," a be-furred, be-combed, be-scented, be-ribboned, be-lady-loved, a "little fox !"   *Grosart.*

6661. BACKBITING, Injury of. Most of you have heard of the *Freischutz*, and a very instructive opera it is, if you will only keep an eye to the allegory, instead of thinking of the story. A huntsman, to forward his own purposes, seeks the devil, and together they cast seven bullets: six of these are to strike where ever the caster wills, but the seventh is to be the devil's, and is to recoil and strike the caster, who throughout the whole piece is never certain which of them all he is putting into his rifle, and at last is struck down by his own shot. These seven bullets are evil speaking; and when we use the devil's weapons, we get the devil's wages; sooner or later we hurt ourselves by our own efforts, and what is more, injure our own cause, however good and righteous in itself that cause may be. *Newland.*

6662. BACKBITING, Silenced. Dr. Johnson silenced a notorious female backbiter, who was condemning some of her friends for painting their cheeks, by the remark that "It is a far less harmful thing for a lady to redden her own complexion than to blacken her neighbor's character."

6663. BACKSLIDER, Death of a. A society of infidels were in the practice of meeting together on Sabbath mornings, to ridicule religion, and to encourage each other in all manner of wickedness. At length they proceeded so far as to meet, by previous agreement, to burn their Bibles! They had lately initiated a young man into their awful mysteries, who had been brought up under great religious advantages, and seemed to promise well; but on this occasion he proceeded the length of his companions, threw his Bible into the flames, and promised with them never to go into a place of religious worship again. He was soon afterwards taken ill. He was visited by a serious man, who found him in the agonies of a distressed mind. He spoke to him of his past ways. The poor creature said, "It all did well enough while in health, and while I could keep off the thoughts of death;" but when the Redeemer was mentioned to him he hastily exclaimed, "What's the use of talking to me about mercy?" When urged to look to Christ, he said, "I tell you it's of no use now; 'tis too late, 'tis too late. Once I could pray, but now I can't." He frequently repeated, "I cannot pray; I will not pray." He shortly afterwards expired, uttering the most dreadful imprecations against some of his companions in iniquity who came to see him, and now and then saying, "My Bible! oh, my Bible!"

6664. BACKSLIDER, Emblem of a. Maundrell says, "In the Valley of Salt, near Gebul, there is a small precipice, occasioned by the continual taking away of salt. In this you may see how the veins of it lie. I broke a piece of it, of which the part that was exposed to the rain, sun, and air, though it had the sparks and particles of salt, had perfectly lost its savor. The innermost, which had been connected with the rock, retained its savor, as I found by proof." The truth, then, which our Lord inculcated on his first disciples, and through them upon all his disciples in after ages, was that if they, the salt of the earth, the living depositaries of true wisdom and holiness among men, lost the power and savor of vital godliness, they would not only be worthless so far as the enlightening and sanctification of others were concerned, but would also be cast out themselves. A professing Christian may have the sparks and glittering particles of true wisdom, like this savorless salt, but be without its pungency and power. *Wilson.*

6665. BACKSLIDER, Hope for a. A backslider endured great distress of mind for five years, during which he took no comfort in his food nor any pleasure in life. If he ate, it was not from any appetite, but with a view to defer his damnation, thinking within himself that he must be lost so soon as his breath was out of his body. Yet, after all this, he was set at liberty, received great consolation, and afterwards lived altogether a godly life.

6666. BACKSLIDER, Recalled. In Mariposa, Cal., there lived a large-eyed, beautiful little prattler—Mary Cannon. One evening, when all was silent, she looked up anxiously into the face of her backslidden father—who had ceased to pray in his family—and said, "Pa, is God dead?" "No, my child. Why do you ask me such a question as that?" "Why, pa, you never talk to him as you used to do." These words haunted him till he was reclaimed. He related the incident to me while I was traveling that circuit. *Life Boat.*

6667. BACKSLIDER, Reclaiming a. A young woman named Pæsea, noted for her character and piety, fell into poverty and led an abandoned life. St. John, the dwarf, was solicited by the monks of Scete to undertake her reformation. He went to her house but could not gain an entrance. At length she thought she could have no cause of regret for admitting so good a man, and opened the door to him. He sat down beside her and said, "What reason can you have to complain of Jesus, that you thus abandon him, and plunge yourself in such a deplorable abyss?" She was filled with conviction, and beholding the streaming tears of the saint, she said, "Why do you weep so bitterly?" He answered, "How can I refrain from weeping when I see Satan in possession of your heart?" She asked, "Is the gate of penitence yet open to me?" "The treasures of divine mercy are inexhaustible," he answered. "Conduct me whither you will," said she. The monk arose, saying, "Let us go." She at once left all—her house and servants and treasures,—absorbed entirely with the work of saving her soul. Her recovery was complete. She died happily not long after, at her hermitage in the wilderness.

6668. BACKSLIDER, Works of a. One mechanic was asked about another, "Is Mr. B—— a Christian?" "Well, yes," said he, "I believe he used to be, but he doesn't work much at it, of late."

6669. BACKSLIDING, Biblical. Expressed in various ways: *Sliding back,* Hos. 4: 16; Jer. 8: 5. *Going back,* Isa. 1: 4; Jer. 7: 24; 15: 6; John 6: 66, 67. *Leaving the first love,* Rev. 2: 4. *Falling from stedfastness,* 2 Pet. 3: 17. *Erring from the faith,* 1 Tim. 6: 10, 21. *Drawing back,* Heb. 10: 38. *Turning away,* Jer. 3: 19; 2 Tim. 4: 4; *aside* to crooked ways, Ps. 125: 5; 1 Tim. 5: 15; again to folly, Ps. 85: 8. *Bewitched,* as by the power of fascination, Gal. 3: 1. *Corrupted from the simplicity of Christ,* 2 Cor. 11: 3. *Tripping* or stumbling (as the word "offend" means), Jas. 3: 2; Ps. 17: 5. *Surprised* or *overtaken* in a fault, Gal. 6: 1. *Swerving*, 1 Tim. 1: 6 (the word means, like an arrow missing the mark). *Wandering*, Jer. 14: 10; like blind men, Lam. 4: 14; like lost sheep, Isa. 53: 6. *Withdrawing the shoulder* from the yoke, Zech. 7: 11 (marg). Illustrated by many figures: *A deceitful bow*, Ps. 78: 57; Hos. 7: 16. *A backsliding heifer*, Hos. 4: 16. *A treacherous wife* departing from her husband, and following after other men, Jer. 3: 2; Ezek. 16; Hos. 1—3. *A branch not abiding in the true vine*, John 15: 6. *Salt losing its savor*, Matt. 5: 13. *A lost and wandering sheep*, Jer. 50: 6; Ezek. 34: 6; 1 Pet. 2: 25. *Smoking flax*, Matt. 12: 20. *One putting his hand to the plough, and looking back*, Luke 9; 62. *A noble vine* become *degenerate*, Jer. 2: 21. *The dog turned to his vomit*, and the sow that was washed, to her wallowing in the mire, 2 Pet. 2: 22. Four books of the Bible seem especially addressed to blacksliders: *Canticles*—See chap. 3 and 5, where two periods of declension are described, with the mournful results and consequent humbling of the Bride. It is especially observable how much longer the Bride was in finding her Beloved the second time, and how much more she suffered, than at the first. *Jeremiah*—The plaintive address of the weeping prophet. . The word "backsliding" occurs most frequently in this book, of all the books of the Bible. *Hosea*—Sometimes called the Gospel of backsliders. The same argument is pursued as in Jeremiah. *Galatians*—St. Paul's address to a church noted for its fickleness, "so soon removed" (1: 6); "bewitched," "driven back" (5: 7, marg.). Note also that the Epistle to the *Hebrews* is especially aimed against apostasy. It is remarkable how many saints who are spoken of in Scripture as "*perfect*," fell into grievous sin;—Noah—Job—David—Asa—Hezekiah. How many proved *weak* in their *strongest* points: Abraham, the man of faith, in unbelief; Moses, pre-eminent for meekness, overcome by anger; Job, the pattern of patience, became impatient; Solomon, renowned for wisdom, turned to folly; John, the apostle of gentleness and love, proposed revenge; Peter, the boldest in the hour of danger, turned coward at last. *Bowes*.

6670. BACKSLIDING, Effects of. "Two years since three young Englishmen, brothers, climbed Mont Blanc to its summit without a guide. On their return over the frozen snow, tied to each other, that if one slipped the others might hold him, the foremost fell at the top of a long slope, and dragged the others down with him. They slid gently and scarcely unpleasantly at first, but with an ever-increasing speed, till suddenly they went over a precipice of twenty or thirty feet, at the foot of which one lay dead and the other two insensible." Thus the backslider frequently draws his associates with him down to ruin.

6671. BACKSLIDING, Flattery of. Backsliding is a disease that is exceedingly secret in its working. It is a flattering distemper; it works like a consumption, wherein persons often flat-

ter themselves that they are not worse but something better, and in a hopeful way of recovery, till a few days before they die.
Jonathan Edwards.

6672. BACKSLIDING, Possibility of. There are weeds in almost every soil. If you throw up the soil from ten or twenty feet deep there will be found the seeds from which they grow. Now, those seeds cannot germinate until they are put in a convenient place; then let the sun shine and the dews fall, and the weeds begin to show themselves. There may be many weeds in our nature, deep down, out of sight; but should they be thrown up by some change of circumstances, we shall find in ourselves evils we never dreamed of. Oh, let no man boast; let no man say, "I should never fall into that particular sin." How knowest thou, my brother? thou mayst never have been in that position in which such a sin would have allured you. Beware! perhaps where thou thinkest thou art iron, thou art clay; and when thou thinkest that the gates are closed with bars of brass, it may be but rotten wood. With respect to none of us, even the holiest, is there reason to trust his best faculties, his best desires, his best resolutions; we are utter weakness through and through, and to transgression prone, notwithstanding all that God's grace has done for us. The sin which is in us as a taint in our constitution, might easily break out as a loathsome distemper, spreading over the entire man from head to foot, and spoiling all the character. I pray God it never may. *Spurgeon.*

6673. BACKSLIDING, Process of. Near Mauch Chunk, Pennsylvania, you are drawn up a very steep mountain side in a railroad car, by a stationary engine, to the very summit in a few minutes. The prospect is magnificent. Now your car begins its descent by another track eighteen miles long, and after running this distance by the mere force of gravity, you find yourself at the starting point. So conversion takes a man in a moment up the heights. But he may be months or years in backsliding to the starting point. *A. D. Vail.*

6674. BACKSLIDING, Repeated. A man that had fallen time after time, came to Sisoes, the hermit, as often, and was bidden by him every time, not to be discouraged but to arise and go forward. At last the man grieved with himself, said, "My father, is there to be no end of this? How often am I to be bidden to rise after a fall?" "Ever, till death finds you fallen or struggling to rise." He was asked if one who had fallen ought to be put to penance for a whole year. "That is a very long time," said he. "Well, then, for six months?" "That too seems to me very long." "Well, then, forty days?" "That is too long." After more questions similar in kind, he answered, "I think God is so loving that one bitter pang of conscience may avail with him." It is not the length of time, but the condition of penitence which is required.

6675. BACKSLIDING, Repenting of. Bishop Jewel was suddenly presented with a declaration of adherence to Romanism by the Popish

Inquisitors. In a moment of weakness he took the pen and subscribed it, saying jocosely, "Have you a mind to see how well I can write?" He had only multiplied his enemies, for the Papists were not satisfied, and his own conscience raged against him. He fled to Germany for his life, and at Frankfort, after having preached a most penitent sermon, solemnly recanted his subscription. He bewailed his fall most bitterly with sighs and tears, and was received as a brother in Christ by the congregation.

6676. BACKSLIDING. Sadness of. It is a miserable thing to be a backslider. Of all unhappy things that can befall a man, I suppose 't is the worst. A stranded ship, a broken-winged eagle, a garden overrun with weeds, a harp without strings, a church in ruins—all these are sad sights, but a backslider is a sadder sight still.   *Ryle.*

6677. BACKSLIDING, Simile of. "There was a well near here," said a bystander, "and very good water used to come from it; but it has been filled up for a long time." "Indeed! I never knew there was a well here, much less tasted the water. How did it get filled up?" "Neglect, sir. Some rubbish got in, then part of the surrounding soil; and as it was not cleared out at once, it got worse and worse till it is as you see it—quite choked up. I wonder if there is any water at the bottom?" These last words set me thinking. I wonder if there is any water at the bottom? I thought how much this old well was like some Christians. The Lord Jesus spoke of the life he gives to the believer as "a well of water" unto him (John 4, 14); but are there not many who are supposed to be Christians in whom we do not see any water; and of whom we can say, as of this old well, "I wonder if there is any water at the bottom?"   *Anon.*

6678. BACKSLIDING, Treatment of. An anchorite said to the famous hermit Poemen, "When a brother comes to see me who is a pious man, I receive him with joy; but if one comes who has fallen away from his high profession, I shut the door in his face." "You do wrong," said Poemen; "the sick soul needs the gentle hands of the nurse and the tender care of the hospital; throw open thy door, and spread your arms to the sinner."

6679. BALANCE, Weighed in the. Dan. 5: 27: "Thou art weighed in the balances, and art found wanting." Roberts remarks that this striking form of speech is much used in the East at this day. Thus, should two men be disputing respecting the moral character of a third person, one will say, "I know the fellow well; I have weighed him, and he is found wanting." "He found wanting! you are much lighter than he." "What, miscreant! do you wish to weigh against me?" "Thou art but as one part in a thousand." "Begone, fellow, or I will soon weigh thee." "Yes, yes, there is no doubt about it; you have weighed me; I am much lighter than you." "What kind of times are these? the slaves are weighing their masters." "Yes, the low castes have become

very clever; they are weighing their superiors." "What, woman! do you call in question the authority of your husband? are you qualified to weigh him?" "The judge has been weighing the prisoners, and they are all wanting."

6680. BALLS, Opposition to. A ball was to be held at Long Branch, and it was deemed desirable to secure the patronage of a young, beautiful and accomplished lady, by securing her service as manager. A member of Congress was selected to do this. All his influence of position, flattery and argument was lost upon her. She steadily refused the proffered honor, and declined the invitation to attend the ball. "Would you be kind enough to give me your reason for refusal?" said the Congressman. "Certainly, sir; I am a Christian, and I cannot attend without violating what I consider my religious obligations." He replied, "I have heard before of religious principle, but I never saw it exemplified till now. From this hour I shall have a higher respect for Christian character." Let our fashionable professors take note of this.

6681. BANQUET, Invitation to the. It was fixed at the end of August. Ameen-ad-Dowlah, or second vizier, was to give an entertainment to the ambassador and suit; and on the day appointed as is usual in Persia, a messenger came to us about five o'clock in the evening, to bid us to the feast, in strict accordance with the scriptural narrative. The difficulty which infidels have made to the passage, of which this is the commencement, arises from the apparent harshness of asking people to an entertainment, and giving them no option; by punishing them in fact, for their refusal. Whereas, all the guests to whom, when the supper was ready, the servant was sent, had already accepted the invitation, and were therefore already pledged to appear at the feast at the hour when they might be summoned: they were not taken unprepared, and could not in consistency or decency, plead any prior engagement.   *Morier*

6682. BANQUET, An Oriental. The various items of which an Oriental banquet consists—bread, flesh, fish, fowls, melted butter, honey, and fruits—are in many places set on the table at once, in defiance of all taste. They are brought in upon trays—one, containing several dishes, being assigned to a group of two, or at most three persons, and the number and quality of the dishes being regulated according to the rank and consideration of the party seated before it. In ordinary cases four or five dishes constitute the portion allotted to a guest; but if he be a person of consequence, or to whom the host is desirous of showing more than ordinary marks of attention, other viands are successively brought in, until every vacant corner of the tray is occupied.   *Dr. Knox.*

6683. BAPTISM, Enforced. When the Jesuit missionaries were engaged in Romanizing the Huron tribe of Indians, they found them slow to accept or comprehend their teachings. They listened to their words looked at their pictures,

their altars and crucifixes, and went on in their old way. The bloody Iroquois were their hostile foes, and often burst in upon their villages to spread fire and slaughter. At such times the missionary would take a vessel of holy water and go through the streets baptizing all he met. How easy it would be if the world could be converted in this way, but it cannot.

6684. BAPTISM, Notion of. An old colored Methodist of fair repute, suddenly joined the Baptists to the surprise of his friends, who demanded an explanation. He said, "I am sick and tired of the Methodists who preach nothing but 'Work, work, work;' but the Baptists preach, 'Be dipped and be done with it.'"
         Dr. Holme.

6685. BAPTISM Not Regeneration. Nor will being baptized do you any good. Yet you hear people say, "Why, I have been baptized, and I was born again when I was baptized." They believe that because they are baptized into the church, they are baptized into the Kingdom of God. I tell you that is utterly impossible. You may be baptized into the visible church, and yet not be baptized into the Son of God. Baptism is all right in its place. God forbid that I should say anything against it. But if you put that in the place of regeneration—in the place of new birth—it is a terrible mistake. You cannot be baptized into the Kingdom of God. If I thought I could baptize men into the Kingdom of God, it would be a good deal better for me to do that than to preach. I should get a bucket of water, and go up and down the streets, and save men that way. If they would not let me do it while they were awake, I would do it while they were asleep.
         Moody.

6686. BARRENNESS, Spiritual. Illustrations of barrenness, which may aptly be used as figures of the ungodly world, or fruitless professors— alike barren of spiritual fruit unto God: *The vast wilderness*, the very symbol of drought and desolation, Deut. 8: 15; 32: 10; Jer. 2: 31; 4: 26; 12: 10. *A salt land*, Deut. 29: 23; Judges 9: 45; Jer. 17: 6. *Barren earth*, Heb. 6: 8. "*The wayside*," ground, Matt. 13: 4–19. *Eunuchs*, Isa. 56: 3. *The barren fig-tree*, Luke 13: 6–9. *Jericho*, 2 Kings 2: 19–21. *Ebal*—the mountain of the curses. The word "Ebal," according to Gesenius, means "void of leaves"—bare and blasted. *Ephraim.* Strange that one whose name means *fruitful* is spoken of as being barren of fruit to God—bringing forth fruit, but "unto himself," Hos. 10: 1! It is sad to observe how, in many cases, the guilt of barrenness is aggravated by the enjoyment of much privilege; *The barren fig-tree*, it is expressly said, was planted in "a vineyard"—a place where it had every advantage of soil and special care; and yet it remained unfruitful, Luke 13: 7! The *degenerate vine*, in like manner, was planted in "a very fruitful hill"—well cleared, and fenced, and cared for, Isa. 5: 1–7; Jer. 2: 21; and yet it brought forth no good fruit. Could a sentence pronounced against such barrenness be unjust?
         Bowes.

6687. BATTLE, Prayer before. During the awful moments of preparation for the battle of Camperdown, Admiral Duncan called all his officers upon deck, and in their presence, prostrated himself in prayer before the Lord of Hosts, committing himself and them, with the cause they maintained, to his sovereign protection, his family to his care, his soul and body to the disposal of his providence. Rising then from his knees, he gave command to make an attack, and achieved one of the most splendid victories in the annals of England.   *Whitecross.*

6688. BATTLES, Indecisive. According to a new biography of Gen. Lee, all of his plans for his raid into Pennsylvania and Maryland fell into the hands of Gen. M'Clellan by a mere accident. Hence, to Lee's surprise, he found himself met at every point by superior numbers, and he was obliged to fight the battle of Antietam under the very greatest disadvantages. Had M'Clellan's energy and courage been equal to the emergency and opportunity, he might have made Antietam the crowning victory of the war, instead of letting Lee and his army escape to recuperate for other and greater battles. God has placed in our hands the plans of Satan, and on every battle-field we are superior in numbers and position. We ought to fight on to complete victories, instead of having so many drawn battles that we must needs fight over and over again. *A. D. Vail.*

6689. BEAM, Dangerous. A monk went to his abbot, Poemen, and complained of his cell, because it was in the vicinity of another monk of whom scandalous stories were in circulation. The complainant said he supposed they were true, as another monk had told him. Poemen decried the authority for them, saying, "A monk who tells such tales has fallen from his profession, and is unworthy of belief. But if the stories be true?"—Poemen picked up a straw and then looked up at a large beam over his head. "This straw is my neighbor's sin which I trample on with scorn; that log is my sin which I rarely notice, but which may one day fall and crush me."

6690. BEATITUDES, The Eight. Those of us who have traveled in mountain countries know how one range of hills rises behind another, one ever seeming the highest, till yet a higher appears behind it; each has its own beauty, each its own peculiarity. So is it with those various kinds of lesser happiness of which I before spoke. But in mountain countries there is one range, one line of lofty summits, which always conveys a new sense of beauty, of awe, of sublimity, which nothing else can give—the range of eternal snow. High above all the rest, we see the white peaks standing out in the blue sky, catching the first rays of the rising sun, and the last rays of the sun as it departs. So is it with this range of high Christian character which our Lord has set before us in the Sermon on the Mount. High above all earthly lower happiness, the blessedness of those eight beatitudes towers into the heaven itself. They are white with the snows of eternity; they give a space, a meaning, a dignity to all the rest of the earth over which they brood.   *Stanley.*

6691. BEAUTY, Attraction of. "Fair and wise," as it was said of Aspasia Milesia. Here beauty was not ill-bestowed, as a gold ring in a swine's snout, but (as the history reports of the Lady Jane Grey), adorned with all variety of moral virtues, as a clear sky with stars, as a princely diadem with jewels. Beauty is of itself very attractive, as the poet hath it. For which cause Heraclonas, the young emperor of Constantinople, being sent into banishment, together with Martina, his mother, had his nose cut off, lest his beauty should move the people to pity.   *Trapp.*

6692. BEAUTY, Blindness to. Beauty is an all-pervading presence. It unfolds into the numberless flowers of the spring. It waves in the branches of the trees and the green blades of grass. It haunts the depths of the earth and sea, and gleams out in the hues of the shell and the precious stone. And not only these minute objects, but the ocean, the mountains, the clouds, the heavens, the stars, the rising and setting sun, all overflow with beauty. The universe is its temple; and those men who are alive to it cannot lift their eyes without feeling themselves encompassed with it on every side. Now this beauty is so precious, the enjoyments it gives are so refined and pure, so congenial to our tenderest and noblest feelings, and so akin to worship, that it is painful to think of the multitude of men as living in the midst of it, and living almost as blind to it as if, instead of this fair earth and glorious sky, they were tenants of a dungeon. An infinite joy is lost to the world by the want of culture of this spiritual endowment. Suppose I were to visit a cottage, and to see its walls lined with the choicest pictures of Raphael, and every spare nook filled with statues of the most exquisite workmanship, and that I were to learn that neither man, woman, nor child ever cast an eye at these miracles of art, how should I feel their privation! how should I want to open their eyes, and to help them to comprehend and feel the loveliness and grandeur which in vain courted their notice! But every husbandman is living in sight of the works of a diviner Artist; and how much would his existence be elevated, could he see the glory which shines forth in their forms, hues, proportions, and moral expressions!   *Channing.*

6693. BEAUTY, Examples of. Beauty is said to be nature's letter of recommendation. Its great power has been recognized in the hovel and the palace, in the forum and on the battle field. Xerxes was noted for extraordinary beauty and noble stature. Cleopatra of Egypt was endowed with resistless charms, which she had art enough to display to the best advantage. Four noble Romans, Pompey, Julius Cæsar, Augustus, and Antony, were enchained by her. Zenobia, Queen of Palmyra, was noted for her singular beauty. She had sparkling black eyes and teeth of such brilliant whiteness that they were reported to be of

pearl. Aspasia was a poor girl of elegant form; a voice like the music of the Syrens; remarkable beauty; and as good as she was beautiful. She captivated Cyrus the younger, and became his wife, and after his death married Artaxerxes. Phryne and Lais were celebrated for their beauty, with which they bewitched all Greece. Lais was drawn into the Temple of Venus by the women, and there stoned to death.

6694. BEAUTY, Key to Moral. The problem of restoring to the most original internal beauty, is solved by the redemption of the soul. The ruin or the blank that we see in nature is in our own eye. The axis of vision is not coincident with the axis of things, and so they appear not transparent, but opaque. The reason why the world lacks unity is, that man is disunited himself. A life in harmony with nature, the love of truth and virtue, will purge the eyes to understand her text, so that the world shall be to us an open book, and every form significant of its hidden life and final cause.   *Emerson.*

6695. BEAUTY, Marrying for. Olympias having heard that a young courtier had married a very beautiful lady with a bad reputation, said, "Sure, the hotspur had little brains, otherwise he would have never married with his eyes." It is an honor to any wife to be more loved for the qualities of her mind than the beauty of her person.

6696. BEAUTY, Offset to. How seldom do we see combined beauties both of body and soul upon earth. The fairest jewels are sometimes enclosed in poor unsightly cases; and many a time the loveliest face and most gracefully rounded form are the handsome setting off of a distorted soul.   *Power.*

6697. BEAUTY, Promoting. I have come to the conclusion, if man, or woman either, wishes to realize the full power of personal beauty, it must be by cherishing noble hopes and purposes; by having something to do, and something to live for, which is worthy of humanity, and which, by expanding the capacities of the soul, gives expansion and symmetry to the body which contains it. *Professor Upham.*

6698. BEGGAR, Freedom of the. The ups and downs of the world concern him no longer. He alone continueth in one stay. The price of stock or land affecteth him not. The fluctuations of agricultural or commercial prosperity touch him not, or at worst but change his customers. He is not expected to become bail or surety for any one. No man troubleth him with questioning his religion or politics. He is the only free man in the universe. He is never out of the fashion, or limpeth awkwardly behind it. He is not required to put on court mourning. He weareth all colors, fearing none. His costume hath undergone less change than the Quaker's. He is the only man in the universe who is not obliged to study appearances.   *Lamb.*

6699. BEGGARS, Accommodating the. The beggars in Japan are very honest. Dr. Prime, in his "Travels" says, "Passing through a street and seeing some forty or fifty coppers hanging on as many nails at the front of a shop (the copper coin has a hole in the center) I inquired what they were for, and was told they were placed there by the shop-keeper to save time and trouble in answering the calls of the mendicants. When one came along he simply took a copper and passed on, never abusing the charity of the shopkeeper by taking two."

6700. BEGGING, Chinese. In the streets of Peking I one day found a man in a sort of wooden sentry box; large nails had been driven into it, so that their points projected through. This prevented the man from leaning against the sides, and the only rest he had was from sitting on a board within. He was a monk, and never seemed to sleep, for he had a string with which he, night and day, sounded a large, sonorous bell every few minutes, as a sort of advertisement of his purpose. This was that the benevolent should come forward with money; each nail represented a sum. When any paid that sum his name was stuck up on a bit of paper, and the nail was pulled out, making it more comfortable for the hermit within. All the nails represented the necessary amount for the repair of a temple which was close behind. This is a common proceeding for raising the wind for such purposes. I was told that this monk had been two years shut up, and that he would likely be another year before he got out of his cocoon of nails.

W. Simpson.

6701. BEGGING, Contrast of. A young lady accepted the post of missionary collector for a certain district. In twenty-four applications twenty-three were rejected. She became disheartened and returned to her pastor to resign the position. He asked her if she had first gone to her closet, and asked God to crown her efforts with success. She confessed that she had not. He advised her to try this plan, and renew the canvass. She did so with remarkable success, this time succeeding in twenty-three applications, and failing in only one.

6702. BEGGING, Eloquent. Leitch Ritchie, traveling in Ireland, passed a painful spectacle of pallor, squalor, and raggedness. His heart smote him and, turning back, he said, "If you are in want, why don't you beg?" "Sure it's begging I am, yer honor." "You didn't say a word." "Ov course not, yer honor; but see how the skin is speakin' through the holes of me trousers, and the bones cryin' out through me skin! Look at me sunken cheeks, and the famine that's starin' in me eyes! Man alive! isn't it beggin' I am with a hundred tongues?"

6703. BEGGING, Home. A minister was about to leave his own congregation for the purpose of visiting London, on what was by no means a pleasant errand—to beg on behalf of his place of worship. Previous to his departure, he called together the principal persons connected with his charge, and said to them, "Now I shall be asked whether we have conscientiously done all that we can for the removal of the debt; what answer am I to give? Brother so-and-so, can you in conscience say that you have

given all you can?" "Why, sir," he replied, "if you come to conscience I don't know that I can." The same question he put to a second, and a third, and so on, and similar answers were returned, until the whole sum required was subscribed, and there was no longer any need for their pastor to wear out his soul in going to London on any such unpleasant excursion.

Hood.

6704. BEGGING, Oriental. A late writer from Damascus says: "A singular custom prevails here during the hours of public prayers on Sabbath mornings, and frequently during the week. It is that of the poor, diseased, lame and blind being gathered about the church doors to solicit alms. They present a very strange appearance, sitting together along the walls, or standing in groups, with the hand extended for charities, and remind one of the account given in Acts 3: 2, of the laying of the lame man at the 'gate of the Temple which is called Beautiful.' The feeble and blind are often led to these public places, and the lame sometimes literally 'carried' on the shoulders of some good Samaritan friend. A most pitiable-looking man is thus often laid near the door of our school-house, where his voice may be heard the entire day, imploring blessings upon the passers, in the hope of receiving a pittance from some of the many who throng the street. My sympathies are always excited for his helplessness and deformity, as well as for his moral pollution. Bartimæus-like, blind persons are often seen by the wayside begging, and in some instances occupying the same place from year to year."

6705. BEGGING, Professional. In Japan begging is a profession, and a certain portion of the people follow it for a living. They are organized, and sometimes there is a strife among the leaders as to who shall be elected "Chief of the Beggars." Children follow the calling of their parents, and so from father to son the race of beggars continues. They are on all the highways, and plead with the traveler to give them cash.

Dr. J. P. Newman.

6706. BEGGING, Public. While I was at Djidda, a Yemen beggar mounted the minaret daily, after mid-day prayer, and exclaimed loud enough to be heard through the whole bazar, "I ask from God fifty dollars, a suit of clothes, and a copy of the Koran; O faithful, hear me; I ask of you fifty dollars," etc. This he repeated for several weeks, when at last a Turkish pilgrim, struck by the singularity of the beggar's appeal, desired him to take thirty dollars and discontinue his cries, which reflected shame upon the charity of all the hadjis present. "No," said the beggar, "I will not take them, because I am convinced that God will send me the whole of what I beg of him so earnestly." After repeating his public supplication for some days more, the same hadji gave him the whole sum he asked for, but without being thanked. I have heard people exclaim in the mosques at Mecca, immediately after prayers, "O brethren, O faithful, hear me! I ask twenty dollars from God to pay for my passage home; twenty dollars only. You know that God is all-bountiful, and may send me a hundred dollars; but it is twenty dollars only that I ask. Remember that charity is the sure road to Paradise." There can be no doubt that this practice is sometimes attended with success. *Pilgrimages to Mecca.*

6707. BEGINNING, Delayed. It was said of Alfred De Vigny that he proposed making a great poem, and he had the capacity and genius to make it; but he spent his life in gathering materials for that poem. Sometimes his friends used to say to him, "Why don't you begin? You are getting on in life, and after awhile you will be too old to write the poem." And he would keep saying, "To-morrow I will begin." One morning the papers in Paris announced his death, his work all undone; he lay dead amid the magnificient materials he had with which to begin the poem. *Talmage.*

6708. BEGINNING, Evil. That temptation that at first is but a little cloud as big as a man's hand, may quickly overspread the whole heaven. Our engaging in sin is as the motion of a stone down, *vires acquirit eundo*, "it strengthens itself by going;" and the longer it runs the more violent. Beware of the smallest beginnings of temptation. No wise man will neglect or slight the smallest spark of fire, especially if he see it among barrels of gunpowder. You carry gunpowder about you. Oh, take heed of sparks. *John Flavel.*

6709. BEGINNING OF EVIL, Biblical. Like the *letting out of water*, Prov. 17:14. *A little leaven*, 1 Cor. 5: 6. *A root of bitterness*, Heb. 12:15. The outbreak of evil comes by looking as Eve, Achan, David, Ahaz, and listening like Eve and Rehoboam.

6710. BEGINNING, Examples of. Spencer says that the heathen began from their oracles. The style of the civil law is "*A Deo optimo maximo.*" The old Saxon laws were prefaced by the ten precepts of the Decalogue. The most eminent heathen began any work by prayer and vows to their gods. Vol. I. 4550. David sought counsel of God in all his enterprises. Let every work of the Christian be spread out before God, that his blessing may favor and crown it with success.

6711. BEGINNING, Fable of. The trees of the forest held a solemn parliament, wherein they consulted of the wrongs the axe had done them. Therefore they enacted that no tree should hereafter lend the axe wood for a handle, on pain of being cut down. The axe travels up and down the forest, begs wood of the cedar, ash, oak, elm, even of the poplar. Not one would lend him a chip. At last he desired so much as would serve him to cut down the briers and bushes, alleging that these shrubs did suck away the juice of the ground, hinder the growth, and obscure the glory of the fair and goodly trees. Hereon they were content to give him so much; but, when he had got the handle, he cut down themselves too. These be the subtle reaches of sin. Give it but a little advantage, on the fair promise to remove thy troubles, and it will cut down thy soul also.

Therefore resist beginnings. Trust it not in the least. *Adams.*

6712. BEGINNING, Faulty. Some workmen were lately building a large brick tower, which was to be carried up very high. In laying a corner, one brick, either by accident or carelessness, was set a very little out of line. The work went on without its being noticed, but as each course of bricks was kept in line with those already laid, the tower was not put up exactly straight, and the higher they built the more insecure it became. One day, when the tower had been carried up about fifty feet, there was a tremendous crash. The building had fallen, burying the men in the ruins. All the previous work was lost, the materials wasted, and, worse still, valuable lives were sacrificed, and all from *one brick laid wrong* at the start. The workman at fault in this matter little thought how much mischief he was making for the future. Do you ever think what ruin may come of *one bad habit*, one brick laid wrong, while you are now building a character for life? Remember, in youth the foundation is laid. See to it that all is kept STRAIGHT. *Teacher's Treasury.*

6713. BEGINNING, Good. When the ancients said that a work well begun was half done, they meant that we ought to take the utmost pains in every undertaking to make a good beginning. *Polybius.*

6714. BEGINNING, Prayerful. Victoria was aroused at midnight and informed that she was Queen of England. She asked her informer to pray, and they knelt down in prayer together. Thus began the prosperous reign of England's worthy queen.

6715. BEGINNING, Sin's. I have seen the little pearls of a spring sweat through the bottom of a bank, and penetrate the stubborn pavement, till it hath made it fit for the impression of a child's foot; and it was dispersed like the descending dews of a misty morning, till it had opened its way, and made a stream large enough to carry away the rains of the undermined strand, and to invade the neighboring gardens; but then the despised drops were grown into an artificial river, and an intolerable mischief. So are the first entrances of sin, stopped with the antidote of a hearty prayer, and checked into sobriety by the eye of a reverend man, or the counsel of a single sermon; but when such beginnings are neglected, and our religion hath not in it so much philosophy, as to think any thing evil so long as we can endure it, they grow up to ulcers and pestential evils; they destroy the soul by their abode, which at their first entry might have been killed by the pressure of a little finger. *Jeremy Taylor.*

6716. BEGINNING, Small. "Robin Redbreast's corn" is an expression used in Brittany to represent small beginnings crowned with large success. It refers to a tradition of St. Leonore and his monks, who had established themselves far in the wilds. They cleared a space and prepared the ground for the wheat. When all was ready it was discovered that the seed-wheat was forgotten. No supply was to be had. Then a robin redbreast visited them, having in his beak a heavy wheat ear. The monks picked it up, sowed the seed, and in autumn reaped a surprising harvest.

6717. BEGINNING, Unpromising. When the balloon first came to notice, a practicalist sneeringly asked Dr. Franklin what was the use of it. The doctor replied, "What is the use of a new-born infant? It may become a man." From small to large is nature's law.

6718. BEHAVIOR, Contrast of. How lovely, and how happy, an open and ingenuous behavior! An honest, unsuspicious heart diffuses a serenity over life like that of a fine day, when no cloud conceals the blue ether, nor a blast ruffles the stillness of the air; but a crafty and designing bosom is all tumult and darkness, and resembles a misty and disordered atmosphere in the comfortless climate of the north. The one raises the man almost to the rank of an angel of light; the other sinks him to a level with the powers of darkness. The one constitutes a terrestrial heaven in the breast; the other deforms and debases it till it becomes another hell. *Dr. Knox.*

6719. BEHAVIOR, Good. During a time of famine in France, a rich man invited twenty of the poor children in the town to his house, and said to them, "In this basket is a loaf for each one of you; take it, and come back every day at this hour till God sends us better times." The children pounced upon the basket, wrangled, and fought for the bread. Each wished to get the largest loaf, and at last went away without thanking their friend. Francesca alone, a poor but neatly-dressed girl, stood modestly apart, took the smallest loaf which was left in the basket, gracefully kissed the gentleman's hand, and went away to her home in a quiet and becoming manner. On the following day the children were equally ill-behaved, and Francesca this time received a loaf that was scarcely half the size of the others. But when she got home her sick mother cut the loaf, and there fell out of it a number of bright silver coins. The mother was alarmed, and said, "Take back the money this instant, for it has no doubt got into the bread by some mistake." Francesca carried it back, but the benevolent gentleman declined to receive it. "No, no," said he, "it was no mistake. I had the money baked in the smallest loaf simply as a reward for you, my good child. Always continue thus contented, peaceable, and unassuming. The person who prefers to remain content with the smallest loaf, rather than quarrel for the larger one, will find throughout life blessings in this course of action still more valuable than the money which was baked in your loaf of bread." *Anon.*

6720. BELIEF, Derivation of. It is said that Dr. Johnson could not find the origin of this word. It is derived from the Gothic *Be-lifian*, that by which a person lives, the theory of doctrine and morals to which he conforms his life. Without this conformity a man's acts show that his faith is mere notion or opinion, which Plato calls the "half-way house between ignorance and knowledge."

6721. BELIEVER, A Dying. As the setting of the sun appears of greater magnitude, and his beams of richer gold, than when he is in the meridian; so a dying believer is usually richer in experience, stronger in grace, and brighter in his evidences for heaven, than a living one. *Salter.*

6722. BELIEVERS, Support of. A kite soaring on high is in a situation quite foreign to its nature; as much as the soul of man is, when raised above this lower world to high and heavenly pursuits. A person at a distance sees not how it is kept in its exalted situation; he sees not the wind that blows it, nor the hand that holds it, nor the string by whose instrumentality it is held. But all of these powers are necessary to its preservation in that preternatural state. If the wind were to sink, it would fall. It has nothing whatever in itself to uphold itself: it has the same tendency to gravitate to the earth that it ever had, and, if left for a moment to itself, it would fall. Thus it is with the soul of every true believer. It has been raised by the Spirit of God to a new, a preternatural, a heavenly state; and in that state it is upheld by an invisible and almighty hand, through the medium of faith. And upheld it shall be, but not by any power in itself. If left for a moment, it would fall as much as ever. The whole strength is in God alone; and its whole security is in the unchangeableness of his nature, and in the efficacy of his grace. In a word, "it is kept by the power of God, through faith, unto salvation." *Salter.*

6723. BELLS, Influence of. The following account is given of the conversion of a hardened old woman living alone in an attic near Dr. Guthrie's church. "And how did he awaken you from your state of spiritual death?" "By Dr. Guthrie's bells," replied the old woman. "When they rang on Sundays, I used to wish they would leave off—they troubled me. They seemed calling to me, till at last I could not bear it any longer; so one day I put on my shawl and went into the church, just to get peace, as it were, from the bells." "Well, and how did you like what you heard?" "Not at all. I came home very angry with Dr. Guthrie, for, as I stood in the crowded aisle, he preached all his sermon about me, and I determined never to go and hear him again. But when the next Sunday came, the bells tormented me more than ever. I was forced to go; and again I came home feeling what a great sinner I was; and thus I continued from week to week, and then I had a dream, which cut down all my hopes. I seemed to be in a square place, where a number of flowers in pots were standing, and in the middle of them I saw Dr. Guthrie with a watering-pot. He went round and watered every plant until he came to one, which I thought meant me; and then he stood still, and said, in a solemn voice, 'It is no good watering this, for it has no roots,' and he passed me by. And when I awoke, I felt what a dreadful state I was in." And thus the arrow of conviction entered this poor sinner's heart, till he who had wounded her in love was pleased to heal her wound with the atoning blood of Jesus Christ.

6724. BENEFICENCE, Advantage of. A good man, famous for his charities, received an invitation to call at a certain place. He found it a miserable room, and on the bed lay a poor sufferer. He asked for five dollars with which to get to the country. The man said, "I have but five dollars, and that I was going to spend on my family. I will give it to you, and think the Lord will return it to me." He gave the needed money to the sufferer, and prayed, "O Lord! if it is thy will, return me the money to meet my necessities to-night!" From this place he went to a prayer-meeting, and the first man he met there handed him five dollars, saying, "You must see a great deal of suffering, and have many calls for aid. Here is a little to help you on your way." It was the exact sum he had given away, for the return of which he had prayed, and he regarded it as the direct answer to his prayer.

6725. BENEFICENCE, Appropriate. Goldsmith had studied medicine in his youth, and a poor woman, hearing of his great humanity, solicited him in a letter to send her something for her husband, who had lost his appetite, and was reduced to a most melancholy state. The good-natured poet waited on her instantly, and, after some discourse with his patient, found him sinking in sickness and poverty. The doctor told him they should hear from him in an hour, when he would send them some pills, which he believed would prove efficacious. He immediately went home and put ten guineas into a pill-box, with the following label: "These must be used as necessities require; be patient, and of good heart," and sent his servant with it to the patient, who found it contained a remedy superior to drugs and potions. *Cyc. of Anecdote.*

6726. BENEFICENCE, Call to. The whole world calls for new work and nobleness. Subdue mutiny, discord, widespread despair, by manfulness, justice, mercy, and wisdom. Chaos is dark, deep as hell; let light be, and there is instead a green flowery world. O it is great, and there is no other greatness! To make some nook of God's creation a little fruitfuller, better, more worthy of God; to make some human hearts a little wiser, manfuller, happier, more blessed, less accursed! It is work for a God! Sooty hell of mutiny, and savagery, and despair, can, by man's energy, be made a kind of heaven; cleared of its soot, of its mutiny, of its need to mutiny; the everlasting arch of heaven's azure overspanning it too, and its cunning mechanisms and tall chimney-steeples, as a birth of heaven; God and all men looking on it well pleased. *Carlyle.*

6727. BENEFICENCE, Contrast of. At the outbreak of the plague at Alexandria, the heathen forgot all natural affection, drove out their friends, cast them into the streets, and left them half dead, and their bodies unburied. But the Christians, as Dionysius says, " did not spare themselves, but mutually attending to each other, they would visit the sick without fear, and ministering to each other, for the sake of Christ, cheerfully gave up their lives with them. Many died after their care had restored others to health. Many who took the bodies of their Christian brethren in their hands and bosoms, and closed their eyes, and buried them with every mark of attention, soon followed them in death."

6728. BENEFICENCE, Example of. Lady Huntingdon lived very economically that she might have the more to give for the promotion of religion. With an income of only £1,200 a year, she maintained the college she had erected, at her sole expense; she erected chapels in most parts of the kingdom; and she supported ministers who were sent to preach in various parts of the world. A minister of the Gospel, and a person from the country, once called on her. When they came out, the countryman turned his eyes towards the house, and, after a short pause, exclaimed, " What a lesson! Can a person of her noble birth, nursed in the lap of grandeur, live in such a house, so meanly furnished—and shall I, a tradesman, be surrounded with luxury and elegance? From this moment I shall hate my house, my furniture, and myself, for spending so little for God, and so much in folly."

6729. BENEFICENCE, Haste to. A lady of New York who had adopted the rule to give a tenth of all her income in charities, found it easy to execute it with her usual profits, but on coming suddenly into possession of five thousand dollars was tempted to violate her rule. She took alarm and cried, "Quick, quick, let me appropriate the tenth before my heart grows hard." She kept her purpose, and is an example to all. Give quickly! before you lose the money, or the inclination, or death robs you of all.

6730. BENEFICENCE, Howard's Rule for. The great philanthropist kept his own rule: "That our superfluities should give way to other men's conveniences; that our conveniences give way to other men's necessities; and that even our necessities sometimes give way to other men's extremities."

6731. BENEFICENCE, Hundred-fold Reward of. St. John, the alms-giver, ordered his treasurer to give a poor nobleman fifteen pounds. The treasurer, thinking it too much, reduced it to five. Immediately after a wealthy lady sent him a draft for five hundred pounds. John expected more from her and sought an explanation. She said she had written the draft for fifteen hundred pounds, but when it came back to her the ten had disappeared from it. John concluded it was God's doing, and sent to his treasurer to ascertain how much he had given the poor nobleman. On his neglect to tell, the nobleman was sent for, when it was learned that only five pounds had been given him. "The Lord restores an hundred-fold," said John. "I knew that five pounds only could have been given when he returned me only five hundred."

6732. BENEFICENCE, Increase of. An old colored man, speaking at a missionary meeting in the West Indies, said: "My dear friends, me sall increase my subscription dis time. Last year me give one dollar; dis year me sall give four dollars: one dollar for ebery quarter of de world. No, stop! Perhaps somebody will say, 'Old Sandy no lub Africa more dan other country;' so me sall give one dollar for Europe, one dollar for Asia, one dollar for America, and two dollars for Africa. My subscription is five dollars dis year."

6733. BENEFICENCE, Ingratitude for. Stephen, King of Hungary, in the eleventh century, was celebrated for his benevolence. He considered the poor of his realm especially committed to his care. He was accessible to all ranks, listened to their complaints, but always gave the preference to the poor, considering that in serving them he served Christ. He declared himself the patron and father of all the helpless orphans and widows in his kingdom, and provided for their subsistence. He frequently disguised himself, and went out among the poor to see that his officers overlooked none. One day he laid off his royal robes, and went forth in disguise, with a king's purse, to distribute alms among the most needy. A troop of beggars set upon him, knocked him down, plucked his beard, beat him, and robbed him. He rejoiced in this treatment as being like that which his Master received. Nor did he abate his attentions or charities to the poor on this account. He was, indeed, like the Divine Master.

6734. BENEFICENCE, Instructions in. A church was much embarrassed by a debt of three thousand dollars, which successive pastors tried to raise but failed, because of the insufficient subscription of the leading rich member. A new pastor, knowing the key of the situation, took "Systematic Benificence," by Rev. J. Ashworth, to this man and secured his promise to read it. The result was that the rich man came to his pastor and said: "I feel as though I had not done all I ought to do about that church debt; if you will write a subscription paper, I will sign, and will go around with you, and I guess we can remove it from the property." The minister drew up the subscription, and he, who had on former occasions put down one hundred dollars, now subscribed one thousand. With this example twenty-five hundred was soon raised, and the rich man increased his gift to fifteen hundred dollars, the result of instruction in duty.

6735. BENEFICENCE, Patron of. St. John of Alexandria was worthy to be accounted the patron saint of charity. His whole life was one of self-denial and alms-giving. His house, food, apparel and furniture was always the plainest, that he might have the more to give. A man of wealth, learning that he had only an old tattered blanket on his bed, sent him a very fine one. He slept under it one night, and thought of some poor wretches who had no blanket. So the next day he sold it, and gave its price to them. His friend, hearing of it, bought the blanket and returned it to the alms-giver. It was again sold and again returned, John receiving quite a revenue thereby. "We shall see," he said, "who will be tired first, he of buying or I of selling the blanket."

6736. BENEFICENCE, Profit of. A poor widow having charge of a lighthouse on the southern coast of England, had resolved to devote the receipts of a certain day in the year to the missionary cause. On that day, a lady and a little girl, in deep mourning, visited the lighthouse. The lady left behind her a sovereign. The unusually large gratuity immediately caused a conflict in the breast of the poor woman, as to whether she was absolutely bound to appropriate the whole to the missionary box or not. At length she compromised by putting in half-a-crown; but conscience would not let her rest. She went to bed, but could not sleep. She rose, took back the half-crown, put in the sovereign, returned to bed, and slept comfortably. A few days afterwards, to her great surprise, she received a double letter, franked; and, on opening it, she was not more astonished than delighted, to find £20 from the lady, and £5 from the little girl. The visitors were her royal highness the Duchess of Kent, and the present English sovereign, Queen Victoria.

6737. BENEFICENCE, Posthumous. An old man, of the name of Guyot, lived and died in the town of Marseilles; he amassed a large fortune by the most laborious industry and the severest habits of abstinence and privation. The populace pursued him, whenever he appeared, with hootings and execrations. In his will there were found the following words:—"Having observed, from my infancy, that the poor of Marseilles are ill supplied with water, which can only be purchased at a great price, I have cheerfully labored the whole of my life to procure for them this great blessing; and I direct that the whole of my property shall be laid out in building an aqueduct for their use."

Thoughts on Laughter.

6738. BENEFICENCE, Return for. Tiberius II. was liberal to the poor. His wife accused him of wasting his treasures by this means. He told her that he should never want money so long as in obedience to Christ's command he supplied the necessities of the poor. Soon after this, he found a great treasure, and news was also brought him of the death of a very rich man, who had left his whole estate to him.

6739. BENEFICENCE, Reward of. A poor woman in Wales was observed, by a rich man, always to give something at the church collections. He gave her a sovereign. She said, "A sovereign? I never had so much money in all my life? what shall I do with it?" "I dare say you will find means of spending it," said he, "if your heart is devoted to the Lord's cause." Soon after this a man came round to solicit subscriptions for some benevolent object. He went to one of the elders, who gave him half-a-sovereign, and another gave him five shillings, both of which were regarded as very liberal donations. Not liking to pass by any member of the church, he asked this poor woman what she would do. "Put my name down for a sovereign." "A sovereign!" said he; "why, where did you get a sovereign?" "Oh, sir," said she, "I got it honestly; put my name down for a sovereign." She gave him the sovereign, and in about two weeks from that time she received a letter from Doctors' Commons informing her that a friend had just left her one hundred pounds.

6740. BENEFICENCE, Royal. Alexander was blamed for giving so largely to an unworthy applicant. He replied, "When I give I must remember not only his deserts but my rank, and give like Alexander." So Christ gives, not regarding our merit, but his own character.

6741. BENEFICENCE, Safety of. Two men I knew very well, some years ago, on the streets of New York, were talking about the matter of benevolence. One said to the other, "You give too much. I will wait till I get a large pile of money, and then I will give." "No," said the other, "I will give as God prospers me." Hear the sequel. The former lives in New York city to-day dollarless; the latter gathered two hundred and fifty thousand dollars. I believe that the reason why many people are kept poor is because they do not give enough. If a man gives in a right spirit to the Lord Jesus and to the church, he is ensured for time and for eternity. The bank of England is a weak institution compared with the bank that any Christian man can draw upon. The man who stands by Christ, Christ will stand by him.   *Talmage.*

6742. BENEFICENCE, Trifling. A very popular picture in England has for its subject the young Princess of Wales distributing flowers to the sick soldiers. She entered the hospital one day having in her hand a superb bouquet, the gift of Queen Victoria. As she passed along a flower fell out of it, which was seized by a soldier and kissed with delight. The Princess saw the act, and beginning at the head of the ward, distributed a bud or a flower to each invalid. The soldiers prized the gift and kept the flower to be put in their coffins. As the Princess passed out the soldiers did their best to give her a hearty cheer. This is the initial of the "Flower Charity."

6743. BENEFICENCE, True. A city mission-school superintendent, whose scholars were of the very poorest class, requested each one to bring something for the missionary collection, narrating the story of the widow and her "two mites." As a result, a great variety of articles of no value, except in the minds of the poorest, were brought. One very little girl, hardly four years old, barefooted, unwashed and unkempt, handed the superintendent a basket. "What have you here, Susie?" "Our contribution, sir; but you must not let them get out." "Is there anything alive in the basket?" "Yes, sir, I caught 'em. We've got lots of 'em at our house." "Two mice! What do you suppose we can do with mice? We are overrun with them now." Disappointed that her offering was not welcomed, she said, while the tears

filled her eyes, "If the Saviour had been here, he'd a took 'em!" "Two mice! What do you mean?" "You told us the other day that a poor woman brought two mice to Jesus, and he said it was more than any of 'em." Dear, simple child! She had followed the example of the world's most famous donor as she understood it, and her gift shall be accepted of the Master.

6744. BENEFICENCE, Unexpected. A rich English gentleman subscribed a guinea a year to the Bible Society. When the collector called for the money, the gentleman threw guinea after guinea upon the table till the collector, becoming impatient, asked him to stop. He continued till he had counted out eighty guineas. "There," cried the old man, "I promised you a subscription of a guinea a year. I am eighty years old, and there are the eighty guineas."

6745. BENEFICENCE, Voluntary. It has been frequently wished by Christians, that there were some rule laid down in the Bible, fixing the proportion of their property which they ought to contribute to religious uses. This is as if a child should go to his father, and say, "Father, how many times in the day must I come to you with some testimonial of my love? How often will it be necessary to show my affection for you?" The father would of course reply, "Just as often as your feelings prompt you, my child, and no oftener." Just so Christ says to his people, "Look at me, and see what I have done and suffered for you, and then give me just what you think I deserve. I do not wish anything forced."   *Payson.*

6746. BENEVOLENCE, Criticising. A gentleman noted for liberal gifts to the cause of Christian missions was met by a wealthy man, who censured him for such profuse giving to such a cause, where the unemployed were starving all about them. "I will give fifty pounds to the poor of —— if you will give an equal sum," said the Christian friend. "I did not mean that," replied the objector; "but," continued he, "if you must go from home, why so far? Think of the miserable poor of Ireland." "I will give fifty pounds to the poor of Ireland, if you will give the same." "I do not mean that either," was the reply. The gifts of the liberal are a censure upon the penurious, which they would fain prevent. They who give most liberally to missions are most liberal in all benevolent enterprises.

6747. BENEVOLENCE, Dubious. A common female beggar once asked alms of Dr. Goldsmith as he walked with his friend up Fleet street. He gave her a shilling. His companion, who knew something of the woman, censured the bard, adding that the shilling was much misapplied, for she would spend it in liquor. "If it makes her happy in any way," replied the doctor, "my end is answered." Being much pressed by his tailor for a bill of forty pounds, a day was fixed for payment. Goldsmith procured the money; but Mr. Glover calling on him, and relating a piteous tale of his goods being seized for rent, the thoughtless doctor gave him the whole of the money. The tailor called, and was told that if he had come a little sooner he would have received the money, but he had just parted with every shilling of it to a friend in distress, adding, "I should have been an unfeeling monster not to have relieved distress when in my power."

6748. BENEVOLENCE, Proxy. Fox, the author of the "Book of Martyrs," was once leaving the palace of Aylmer, the Bishop of London, when a company of poor people importunately begged him to relieve their wants. Fox, having no money, returned to the Bishop, and asked the loan of five pounds, which was readily granted. He immediately distributed it among the poor by whom he was surrounded. Some months afterwards, Aylmer asked Fox for the money he had borrowed. "I have laid it out for you," was the answer, "and paid it where you owed it—to the poor people who lay at your gate." Far from being offended, Aylmer thanked Fox for being his steward.

6749. BENEVOLENCE, Useless. Henry the IV. wished there was a fowl stewing in every poor man's pot throughout France, but did nothing to place the luxury in the poor man's reach. Such good wishes are popular, cheap, and useless, without such action as our ability allows, to convert the wish into fact.

6750. BENEVOLENCE, Verbal. Near Fua, on my way to Cairo, when we sailed near the shore eight or ten naked boys ran along after us, begging alms; and, before I could throw them some bread, my Reis (captain of the vessel) repeatedly called to them, "May God help you; may God help you"—a most common custom in Egypt, when a man will give nothing. I never was so much struck with this custom as now, when it brought to my recollection the practices which St. James so strikingly censures.   *Leider.*

6751. BEREAVED, Consolation for the. Bishop Heber related the following beautiful apologue to a lady, who was bitterly lamenting the death of an infant child: "A shepherd was mourning over the death of his favorite child, and in the passionate and rebellious feeling of his heart, was bitterly complaining, that what he loved most tenderly, and was in itself most lovely, had been taken from him. Suddenly, a stranger of grave and venerable appearance stood before him, and beckoned him forth into the field. It was night, and not a word was spoken till they arrived at the fold, when the stranger thus addressed him: 'When you select one of these lambs from the flock, you choose the best and most beautiful among them; why should you murmur, because I, the good shepherd of the sheep, have selected from those which you have nourished for me, the one which was most fitted for my eternal fold?' The mysterious stranger was seen no more, and the father's heart was comforted."

6752. BEREAVEMENT, Fable of. I asked Death what he had done with the beautiful flowers which he had stolen from our earthly garden, for he had done that thing to me, and I felt that I had a right to ask. He replied very calmly: "You should not say stolen, for I am not a thief. There is one that owns all the flowers upon your broad, green earth, and he has a right to transplant them when and where he pleases. He sends me to your gardens." "But why," I asked, "do you snatch them so rudely, and leave hearts all torn and bleeding?" "Alas!" replied Death, "why do not mortals let them go? Little children are the flowers of paradise; of such is the kingdom of heaven. But be the world ever so bleak and desolate, mortals would keep them here; so they bind them with chords lest they be taken away, and these chords are twined with their own heartstrings. How can I loosen the one without breaking the other?"   *Anon.*

6753. BEREAVEMENT, Heathen. Chronicles tell us, that when an express came out of the field to Xenophon, the Socratic, as he was sacrificing, which acquainted him that his son perished in the fight, he pulled the garland from his head, and inquired after what manner he fell. It being told him that he died gallantly, making a great slaughter of his enemies, after he had paused awhile to recollect his thoughts and quiet his first emotion of concern with reason, he adorned his head, finished the sacrifice, and spoke thus to the messengers: "I did not make it my request to the gods, that my son might be immortal or long-lived, for it was not manifest whether this was convenient for him or not, but that he might have integrity in his principles and be a lover of his country; and now I have my desire."

6754. BEREAVEMENT, Lessons of. Baby is now one of my lesson-books. I read a word in it for you as I was playing with her the other day. She had hid her flowers between my hands, and when she tried to open them, I kept them closed, not because I wished to deprive her of her treasures, but for the pleasure of trying her little strength; and when I yielded to it her laugh was so merry. I thought it was thus with thee, Fan. Your flowers are hid in God's hand. You have asked for them and he will not open it, but not because he means to deprive you of them, but to try your childish strength. How joyful the shout of triumph will be when he yields to it. My baby found only the broken pieces of stalk she had hidden; but you will find your broken flowers transformed into a wreath of heavenly glory.
                E. H. Birks.

6755. BEREAVEMENT, Pagan. The heathen priests in Africa make little wooden images, which they anoint and consecrate for their votaries, when bereaved of their children or friends, persuading them that they have brought back the spirits of the departed to inhabit the said wooden images. One of these is now before the writer, which was given to a poor woman who had lost her only child, and which she caressed with all parental fondness, believing that the spirit of her babe was thus restored to her, till she was brought to a saving knowledge of the truth, and taught to look to the only real source of comfort in trouble, when she gave up her idol to the missionary. It stands about nine inches high, is of a very uncomely countenance, and bears evident marks of its consecration.   *Moister.*

6756. BESETTING SIN, Emblem of. In the far East there is a beautiful flower that is very dangerous. The petals are long and stout, and they bend outward and downward, leaving a platform in the centre of the flower so large and strong that a man can stand there. We are told that the cruel natives at a certain time in the year gather around that strange flower, and they compel one of their number to mount the centre of it, and no sooner does he stand there than the petals that were bending down move up gradually until they are erect, and then they curve at the tips and bend downward and compress and contract until there is strangulation, and the man's body is left a shapeless pulp, and the cruel natives come around with their chalices and catch the running gore and drink it, and dance with infernal glee over the massacre. How like this is the flower of sin. A man likes it so much he gets into it, and says, "How beautiful; how safe." But the petals begin to rise, and keep on rising until they overspan him, and begin to compress and contract, and after a while he finds himself dying amid the redolence and the radiance, and under the crush and the strangulation he perishes, while devils damned with chalices of fire catch the running gore, dancing the saturnalia of eternal darkness.   *Talmage.*

6757. BESETTING SINS, Treachery of. For many years after its course has been changed, and the art that triumphs over nature has turned its waters into a new cut, the river needs careful watching; else, swollen by winter snows or summer flood, it bursts our barriers, and, in the pride of victory, foaming, roaring, raging along its old accustomed channels, sweeps dyke and bulwark to the sea. And when he that sitteth upon the flood, and turneth the hearts of men like the rivers of water, has sent the current of our tastes and feelings in a new direction, alas! how apt are they, especially when some sudden outburst of temptation comes sweeping down like a thunder-spout, to flow back into the old and deep-worn channels of a corrupt nature.

Dr. Guthrie.

6758. BEST, Do Thy. "When I was a little boy," said a gentleman one evening, "I paid a visit to my grandfather, a venerable old man, whose black velvet cap and tassel, blue breeches and huge silver knee-buckles, filled me with great awe. When I went to bid him good-by, he drew me between his knees, and, placing his hand on my head, said: 'Grandchild, I have one thing to say to you: will you remember it?' I stared into his face and nodded; for I was afraid to promise aloud. 'Well,' he continued, 'whatever you do, do the best you can.' This, in fact, was my grandfather's legacy to me; and it has proved better than gold."

6759. BEULAH, Description of. Now, I saw in my dream, that by this time the pilgrims were got over the Enchanted Ground, and entering into the country of Beulah (Sol. Song 2: 10, 12; Isa. 62: 4, 12), whose air was very sweet and pleasant; the way lying directly through it, they solaced themselves there for a season. Yea, here they heard continually the singing of birds, and saw every day the flowers appear in the earth, and heard the voice of the turtle in the land. In this country the sun shineth night and day; wherefore, this was beyond the Valley of the Shadow of Death, and also out of the reach of Giant Despair; neither could they from this place so much as see Doubting Castle. Here they were within sight of the city they were going to; also, here met them some of the inhabitants thereof, for in this land the shining ones commonly walked, because it was upon the borders of heaven. In this land, also, the contract between the bride and the bridegroom was renewed; yea, here, "as the bridegroom rejoiceth over the bride, so did their God rejoice over them." Here they had no want of corn and wine, for in the place they met with abundance of what they had sought for in all their pilgrimage. Here they heard voices from out of the city, loud voices, saying, "Say ye to the daughter of Zion, Behold, thy Salvation cometh! Behold, his reward is with him!"   *Bunyan.*

6760. BEULAH, Land of. After this I beheld until they were come into the land of Beulah, where the sun shineth night and day. Here, because they were weary, they betook themselves awhile to rest; and because this country was common for pilgrims, and because the orchards and vineyards that were here belonged to the King of the Celestial Country, therefore they were licensed to make bold with any of his things. But a little while soon refreshed them here; for the bells did so ring, and the trumpets continually sound so melodiously, that they could not sleep; yet they received so much refreshing as if they had slept their sleep ever so soundly. Here, also, all the noise of them that walked the streets was, "More pilgrims are come to town." And another would answer saying, "And so many were let in at the golden gates to-day." They would cry again, "There is now a legion of shining ones just come to town, by which we know that there are more pilgrims upon the road, for here they come to wait for them, and to comfort them after all their sorrow." In this land was a record kept of the names of all that had been pilgrims of old, and a history of the famous deeds they had done. It was here discoursed how to some the river had had its flowings, and what ebbings it had had while others had gone over. It has been in a manner dry for some, while it has overflowed its banks for others. In this place the children of the town would go into the King's gardens, and gather nosegays for the pilgrims, and bring them to them with much affection. Here also grew camphire, with spikenard and saffron, calamus and cinnamon, with all the trees of frankincense, myrrh, and aloes, with all chief spices. With these the pilgrims' chambers were perfumed while they stayed here, and with these are their bodies anointed to prepare them to go over the river when the time appointed was come.

Bunyan.

6761. BIBLE, Advantage of the. It is an armory of heavenly weapons, a laboratory of infallible medicines, a mine of exhaustless wealth It is a guide-book for every road, a chart for every sea, a medicine for every malady, a balm for every wound. Rob us of our Bible, and our sky has lost its sun, and in the best of other books we have naught but the glimmer of twinkling stars. It is the wealth of the poor, blessing poverty with the contentment which makes it rich. It is the shield of wealth, protecting the few that are rich against the many that are poor. It may be compared to the skies, which hold at once the most blessed and the most baneful elements—soft dews to bathe the opening rose, and bolts that rend the oak asunder. *Guthrie.*

6762. BIBLE, Analogies of the. God's Word is as full of analogies as his works. The histories, offerings, and prophecies of the Old Testament are figures of better things which have been brought to light by the gospel. The lessons of the Lord and his apostles teem with types. Almost every doctrine is given in duplicate: the spirit is provided with a body; a body clothes the spirit. Every fruitful vine has a strong elm to which it clings; every strong elm supports a fruitful vine. *Arnot.*

6763. BIBLE, Attachment to the. The poet Collins, in the latter part of his life, withdrew from his general studies, and traveled with no other book than an English New Testament, such as children carry to school. A friend was anxious to know what companion such a man of letters had chosen; the poet said, "I have only one book, and that book is the best."

6764. BIBLE, Benefit of the. A Roman Catholic priest in Belgium rebuked a young woman and her brother for reading the Bible. She replied, "A little while ago my brother was an idler, a gambler, a drunkard, and made such a noise in the house that no one could stay in it. Since he began to read the Bible, he works with industry, goes no longer to the tavern, no longer touches cards, brings home money to his poor old mother, and our life at home is quiet and delightful. How comes it, that a bad book produces such good fruits?"

6765. BIBLE, Care for the. The inhabitants of the South Sea Islands were much rejoiced when copies of the Bible were first given to them. One old native preacher held up his Bible before the whole congregation and said, "My brethren and sisters, this is my resolve; the dust shall never cover my Bible, the moth shall never eat it, the mildew shall never rot it. My light! My joy!"

6766. BIBLE, Charms of the. A little boy was born blind. An operation was performed; the light was let in slowly. When, one day, his mother led him out of doors and uncovered his eyes, and for the first time he saw the sky and earth, "Oh, mother!" he cried, "why didn't you tell me it was so beautiful?" She burst into tears, and said, "I tried to tell you, dear, but you could not understand me." So it is when we try to tell what is in the Bible. Unless the spiritual sight is opened, we cannot understand. *Anon.*

6767. BIBLE, Child's View of the. A little boy in a Sabbath-school wished to put a penny into the Missionary-box, and was asked why he wished to do so. "I want to send it to the heathen," he replied. "Do you know," it was said, "who the heathen are?" "They are folks who have not got any Bible, and live a great way off." "What is the Bible?" "The word of God." "Of what use would it be to the heathen, if they had it?" "It would tell them to love God and be good." "Where did the Bible come from?" "From heaven." "Was it written in heaven?" "No; the prophets and good men wrote it." "If good men wrote it, how then is it the word of God, and come from heaven?" "Why, the Holy Ghost told them how to write it." "Did they see the Holy Ghost, and did he speak to them?", "No; but he made them think it."

6768. BIBLE, Comfort of the. Dr. Gregory relates the case of an indigent and afflicted man whose infirmities were such that he was unable even to occupy a chair without being supported by bands and braces attached to the ceiling of his poor cottage. In this helpless condition had he been for several years, unable to move a limb, while suffering the whole time extreme bodily anguish. "As soon," says Dr. Gregory, "as I recovered a little from my surprise at beholding an object which appeared a living image of death, I asked, 'Are you left alone, my friend, in this deplorable situation?' 'No, sir,' replied he, in a tone of mild and touching resignation, while nothing but his lips and eyes moved as he spoke; 'I am not alone, for my God is with me!' On advancing, I discovered the secret of this man's unspeakable comfort: a Bible lay on his knees, open at a favorite portion of the Psalms. In this way he was enabled daily to read for himself the words of eternal life, partaking of the heavenly manna, which imparted life and strength to his soul. In the midst of pain and poverty he had learned from that blessed book in whom to believe; and as he expressed his confidence that his Father would never forsake him, his eyes sparkled with faith, which beamed in celestial radiance upon his pallid cheek."

6769. BIBLE, Companionship of the. A Scotch minister was visiting among the poor, and a hovel in which dwelt alone an aged Christian woman who was feeble and nearly blind. In her poverty and feebleness he found her very happy. "How do you manage to spend your long days here all alone?" asked the minister. "I am not alone," she said, "because Jesus is with me, and thinking about him makes the time pass pleasantly. My neighbors are kind, and when they come in to help me I love to talk to them about Jesus. But there is one hour in the day which is the most pleasant of all to me. Do you see that little window?" she asked, pointing across the room. "For about one hour every day, when it is not cloudy, the sun shines in there. Then I take my large printed Bible and sit down in the sunshine, where I can see well enough to read. And oh! sir, that is a blessed hour to me!" Her case illustrates the illumination of the spirit necessary to make the Bible good company.

6770. BIBLE, Correct Interpretation of the. The progressive elucidation of the Scriptures, whether by the expository labors of critics, the researches of travelers, or the fulfillments of prophecy, may be compared to the gradual rolling away of the morning mist from a splendid landscape. As the sun advances, the shades retire, and new and interesting features of the scenery are continually opening upon the delighted eye of the spectator; or it may be said to resemble the slow but momentous process of unfolding the ancient papyri, which the ravages of time and fire have spared among the ruins of Pompeii and Herculaneum. Here, as every successive word and letter which can be redeemed from the crisp and crumpling texture of the blackened parchment is noted down with the most scrupulous care, as forming a part of the continuous record, and going to make out its entire sense; so the sense of the sacred volume is gradually elicited, item by item, and needs only to be collected and treasured up with equal solicitude, in order to constitute a possession of infinitely more value than the choicest literary relics of antiquity. Perhaps it may be safely affirmed that the materials are at this moment in existence for the satisfactory solution of nearly every doubtful passage of holy writ; but the great desideratum is to have them brought together—to collect them from their wide dispersion over a countless multitude of writings, in various languages, which the great majority of Christians can neither procure nor understand. *Bush.*

6771. BIBLE, Criticising the. A prison visitor gave a convict a Bible. He employed himself in raising questions on difficult passages to ask the donor at every visit. Seeing that the study was of no profit to the convict the visitor said, "What would you think of a hungry man, who had not eaten a morsel of food for the last twenty-four hours, and was asked by a charitable man to come in and sit down at a richly-covered table, on which were large dishes of choice meat, and also covered ones, the contents of which the hungry man did not know. Instead of satisfying his exhausted body with the former, he raises one cover after another, and insists on finding out what these unknown dishes are composed of. In spite of all the advice of the charitable man to partake first of the more substantial dishes, he dwells with obstinate inquiry on nicer compounds, until, overcome with exhaustion, he drops down. What do you think of such a man?" "He is a fool," said the convict; "and I will be one no longer. I understand you well."

6772. BIBLE, Daily Reading. The venerable Rev. Henry Bœhm, whose death in his one hundred and first year we recorded a few weeks ago, loved his Bible to the end. It was his habit to read it through at least once every year. His friends assure us that he read the Bible through over seventy times, and that when he died the book-mark was found at the first page, showing that he had just finished the year's reading, and was preparing to begin anew. At the funeral that Bible was significantly placed upon his coffin—a touching remembrance of his great love for the book of books. *Christian Advocate.*

6773. BIBLE, Defiance of the. Walid Ebu Yazid, an Arabian infidel, treated the Koran with great contempt. Opening it at random one day his eyes fell upon the passage, "Every rebellious, perverse person shall not prosper." Thereupon he stuck it on a lance and shot it to pieces with arrows, saying, "Dost thou rebuke every rebellious, perverse person? Behold I am that rebellious, perverse person. When thou appearest before thy Lord on the day of resurrection, say, O Lord, Al Walid has torn me thus." A Mohammedan idea of the Koran was that it was an embodiment of the Divine Spirit. This case can be paralleled in the treatment of the Christian's Bible.

6774. BIBLE, Delight in the. Lady Jane Grey was a great Bible reader, and while her parents were attending the chase, she would remain at home studying its pages. Her friends were surprised, and inquired her reason for doing so. She replied, "All amusements of that description are but a shadow of the pleasure which I enjoy in reading this book."

6775. BIBLE, Devotion to the. Matthew Hale Smith, in his book, *Marvels of Prayer*, tells of a shipwreck and rescue, by Captain Judkins, and the crew of the Scotia. Among the rescued was a lad, about twelve years, who had lost everything. "Who are you, my boy?" said Captain Judkins. "I am a little Scotch boy; my father and mother are dead and I am going to America to find my uncle, who lives in Illinois." "What is this?" said the captain, as he took hold of a rope that was tied around the boy's breast. "It is a piece of cord, sir." "What is that tied under your arm?" "My mother's Bible; she told me never to lose it." "That's all you saved?" "Yes, sir." "Could'nt you have saved something else?" "Not and save that." "Didn't you expect to be lost?" "I meant, if I went down, to take my mother's Bible down with me." "All right," said the captain, "I'll take care of you." Having reached the port of New York, Captain Judkins took the boy to a Christian merchant to whom he told this story. "I'll take the lad," said the merchant, "I want no other recommendation; the boy that holds on to his mother's Bible in such perils will give a good account of himself."

6776. BIBLE, Dying for the. In the persecution of 303, special effort was made to destroy the sacred books of the Christians. All who had them or knew of them were required to bring them forth to be burned or turn informers. Many did so, and thousands of volumes of the Scriptures were destroyed. Felix, bishop of Thibara, Africa, refused to comply. He was arrested, confessed that he had the books, but would not give them up. He was treated cruelly, and finally gave his life rather than his Bible to executioners at Venosa, in Apulia.

6777. BIBLE, Effect of a. Dr. Nast once met one of his infidel fellow-Germans, who sold whisky in the day-time and played the violin at night. The Doctor gave him a Bible, and asked him to read it. The man was ashamed to be seen with such a book in his hands, so he placed it under his coat and carried it home. But when he got there he was ashamed to be seen with it, and could find no place to hide it so his family would not see it. After awhile he decided to put it down the cellar on the whisky barrel; and so he went down the cellar time after time to read his Bible, till he became deeply interested; and at length he began to pray, and God filled his soul, and he began to shout glory to God, and his wife and neighbors heard the noise in the cellar, and they ran down to see what was the matter, supposing he was drunk. And so he was, with the wine of the kingdom. He gave up drinking whisky, and continued to drink of the new wine of the kingdom.   *Good News.*

6778. BIBLE, Effect of the. When Naimbana, a black prince, arrived in England from the neighborhood of Sierra Leone, the gentleman to whose care he was entrusted took great pains to convince him that the Bible was the Word of God, and he received it as such with great reverence and simplicity. When asked what it was that satisfied him on this subject, he replied, "When I found all good men minding the Bible, and calling it the Word of God, and all bad men disregarding it, I then was sure that the Bible must be what good men call it, the Word of God."   *Moister.*

6779. BIBLE, Elevating Effect of the. Chemistry never silenced a guilty conscience. Mathematics never healed a broken heart. All the sciences in the world never smoothed down a dying pillow. No earthly philosophy ever supplied hope in death. No natural theology ever gave peace in the prospect of meeting a holy God. All these things are of the earth, earthy, and can never raise a man above the earth's level. They may enable a man to strut and fret his little season here below with a more dignified gait than his fellow-mortals, but they can never give him wings, and enable him to soar towards heaven. He that has the largest share of them will find at length that without Bible knowledge he has got no lasting possession. Death will make an end of all his attainments, and after death they will do him no good at all.   *Ryle.*

6780. BIBLE, Exalt the. A late writer says: "We cannot too much honor the Bible, whether in the pulpit, or family, or in school. It is said that at the coronation of the boy King of England, Edward VI., three swords were brought, and laid before him as emblems of his power. 'Bring another,' said he, 'I need most of all the sword of the Spirit.' The Bible was brought, and has retained its place in subsequent coronations. It is the only symbol used at the inauguration of our Republican Presidents."

6781. BIBLE, Excellence of the. When in Paris, some years ago, I received an account of a French infidel, who happened to find in a drawer of his library some stray leaves of an unknown volume. Although in the constant habit of denouncing the Bible, like most infidel writers he had never read any part of it. These fugitive leaves contained the prayer of Habakkuk (Hab. 3). Being a man of fine literary taste, he was captivated with its poetic beauty, and hastened to the club-house to announce the discovery to his associates. Of course they were anxious to know the name of the gifted author, to which inquiries the elated infidel replied, "A writer by the name of HAB-BA-KOOK, of course a Frenchman!" Judge of the infidel's surprise when informed that the passage he was so enthusiastically admiring was not produced by one of his own countrymen, nor even by one of his own class of so-called free-thinkers, but was penned by one of God's ancient prophets, and was contained in that much-despised book, the Bible. This I regard as one of the sublimest passages of inspired literature; and often have I wondered that some artist, equal to the task, has not selected the prophet and his scene of desolation as the subject of a painting.   *Daniel Webster.*

6782. BIBLE, Experience of the. A gentleman met an old Christian slave, who could neither read nor write. After starting some of the common objections of infidels against the authenticity of the Scriptures, in a way calculated to confound an ignorant man, he said to him, "When you cannot even read the Bible, nor examine the evidence for or against its truth, how can you know that it is the Word of God?" After reflecting a moment, the negro replied, "You ask me, sir, how I know that the Bible is the Word of God? I know it by its effect upon my own heart."

6783. BIBLE, Faithful to the. Euplius was arrested as a Christian in Sicily in 304. He appeared before the governor with the book of the gospels in his hand. He was told that he ought not to keep such writings contrary to the edicts of the emperors, and was asked where he kept them. He answered that he had the book about him. He was asked to read something out of it, and opening it read, "Blessed are they that are persecuted for righteousness' sake, for theirs is the kingdom of heaven," and again, "If any man will be my disciple, let him deny himself, and take up his cross and follow me." "What does that mean?" "It is the law of my Lord, which hath been delivered to me." "By whom?" "By Jesus Christ, the Son of the living God." Then the judge, Calvisianus, said, "Since his confession makes his disobedience manifest, let him be delivered to the executioners, and examined upon the rack." In the midst of painful tortures he was again questioned. He answered, "I declare again that I am a Christian, and read the Holy Scriptures." His tortures were increased and he was repeatedly urged to apostatize. At last the judge said, "Sacrifice now if you would be delivered." He answered, "I sacrifice myself to Jesus Christ my God." He endured great agony, praying and thanking God till his strength failed. Then the sentence of death by the sword was pronouuced against him, for "despising the edicts of the emperors, blaspheming the gods, and not repenting." The Gospel was hung about his neck, and a herald cried before him as he was led to execution, "Euplius, a Christian, the foe of the gods and of the emperors." The martyr, most joyful, cried continually, "Thanks be to Christ my God," till his head was cut off.

6784. BIBLE, Fear of tho. A philosopher of Florence could not be persuaded to look through one of Galileo's telescopes, lest he should see something in the heavens that would disturb him in his belief of Aristotle's philosophy. Thus it is with many: they are afraid of examining God's Word, lest they should find themselves condemned. *Buck.*

6785. BIBLE, Follow the. A boy in a printing-office received from his master a list of Scripture questions and answers to be set up and printed. In the progress of the work, he asked the foreman if he should "follow copy"—that is, set up just as it is written. "Certainly," said the foreman. "Why not?" "Because this copy is not like the Bible." "How do you know that?" "Why, I learned some of these proofs at Sunday-school, and I know that two of them are not like the Bible." "Well, then, do not follow copy, but set them up as they are in the Bible." The boy took the Bible and made it his copy, guide, and pattern. That is the true and only standard. Follow it.

6786. BIBLE, Harmony of the. As when you see wheels, shafts, pins, bands, lying apart, each finished in itself, yet each adapted to others, you know that some machine is contemplated by the founder, though you may not see how to put it together; but when you see the machine put together and in action, you perceive new fitness in every part, and the grand combination of all for one end; so in the several books of the Bible you discover an adaptation to the same end, but in the completed volume you behold the grand harmony of all the books in one object—the restoration of a sinful race to its Paradise in God! The mind that conceived such a plan, and slowly unfolding it, part by part, through the ages, brought it together finished in this book, must be divine.
Dr. J. P. Thompson.

6787. BIBLE, Ignorance of the, A Roman Catholic priest in Ireland was one day passing by some men and boys who were engaged in breaking stones for a new road. He said that the road there would be of great use; "and it is a long time," said he, "since there was a road in this place." "Not since Adam was a boy," remarked one of the men. "And when was that? Can you tell me?" said the priest. "No, sir, I cannot," replied the man. The same question was asked of several persons, and a similar reply given. At length the priest turned to a young boy, and said, "Can you tell me, my lad, when Adam was a boy?" "Sir, Adam never was a boy. God created him man, and

made him perfect also." "Are ye not ashamed," said the priest, "to be excelled by a young boy like this?" "No," answered one of them appealed to, "we are not; that boy reads the Scriptures, and has them explained to him; that is what is not done for us, and we are prevented from reading them ourselves." The priest rode away without making any reply.

6788. BIBLE, Ignorant of the. A young man was boasting of his infidelity at a camp-meeting a number of years ago, and desiring very earnestly to draw some one into a controversy. Father Gruber, an eccentric old German preacher, found his way into the presence of the young man, and said, "I understand you want to have a discussion on some of these questions." "Yes, sir," replied the young man. "Well," said Father Gruber, "it is not lawful to discuss questions of that kind on the camp-ground. Will you go outside?" And they passed out into the woods. "Now," said Father Gruber, "I am not willing to discuss with any body that does not understand the scriptures. Have you read the Bible carefully and thoroughly through?" "O yes," said the young man; "again and again. I have been in the habit of reading it from early childhood, and am perfectly familiar with it." "Well," said the old gentleman, "can you tell me where is the Epistle of Peter to Paul?" "O yes," said the young man," don't think I am such a fool as not to know that it is in the New Testament, not in the Old." "Well," said the old gentleman, "I wish you would find it." He hunted for some time, and, as you know, did not find it, as there is no such epistle. That ended the controversy. *Bp. Bowman.*

6789. BIBLE, Ignorant Criticism of. An aged clergyman was traveling in a stage coach with three young men who were amusing themselves and others by trifling conversation. One of the number suggested "he would rather believe the Koran than the Bible." The minister, on interrogating him, found that he knew nothing of either the Koran or the Bible. "Surely," said the minister," it is not too much to ask men to read what they condemn; and if you will take my advice, you will apply yourself to the prayerful study of the Word of God. You will then have no occasion to inquire which book is entitled to your belief, for you will *know* and be *assured* which is the Word of God."

6790. BIBLE, Imprinting the. You cannot read the Bible as you do other books. I visited Mr. Prang's chromo establishment in Boston and saw the process of printing a picture of some public man. The first stone made hardly an impression on the paper. The second stone showed no sign of change. The third no sign. The fifth and sixth showed only outlines of a man's head. The tenth, the man's face, chin, nose and forehead appeared. The fifteenth and twentieth looked like a dim picture. The twenty-eighth impression stood forth as natural as life. It looked as though it would speak to you. So, carefully and prayerfully read the Word of God—read the same chapter again and again—and the twenty-eighth time Christ Jesus will shine forth.　　　　　*Moody.*

6791. BIBLE, Indestructibility of the. A lady asked a laborer if he would accept a Bible. He answered, "No, and if you leave one I will throw it into the fire." She laid it on his table. He seized and threw it upon the burning coals, where all was consumed save a single leaf, which was blown out. His wife picked it up and read on it, "Heaven and earth shall pass away, but my word shall not pass away." This passage was a two-edged sword in the furious man's heart. He could not sleep and was filled with terror. He sought the donor of the burned Bible, confessed his sins, and asked for pardon from herself and from God, and found the Saviour. We may burn the sacred pages, but its truths will survive to condemn or crown us.

6792. BIBLE, Infidels and the. A member of the French Academy went to see Diderot, an able champion of infidelity, and found him explaining a chapter of the Gospel to his daughter as seriously as a Christian parent. The visitor expressed his surprise. "I understand you," said Diderot, "but, in truth, what better lesson could I give her?"

6793. BIBLE, Influence of the. Robert Aitkin, a bookseller, was called upon by a gentleman, who confessed himself to be an infidel, for Paine's "Age of Reason." Not having it, Mr. Aitkin told him he would give him a better book if he would engage to read it. He assented and evinced surprise when a Bible was put in his hand, but said his word was passed and he would keep it. After a time he returned to thank the bookseller, saying the book had made him what he was not before—a happy man.

6794. BIBLE, Inspiration of the. Mr. John Williams, the Martyr of Erromanga, gave the following account of the reasons of a few converted South Sea Islanders for their belief in the Bible. They were startled when asked, "Do you believe the Bible to be the word of God?" having never had a doubt about it. After a moment's pause, one answered, "Most certainly we do." It was asked, "Why do you believe it? Can you give any reason for believing the Bible to be the word of God?" He replied, "Why, look at the power with which it has been attended, in the utter overthrow of all that we have been addicted to from time immemorial. What else could have demolished that system of idolatry which had so long prevailed amongst us? No human arguments could have induced us to abandon that false system." This question being put to another, he replied, "I believe the Bible to be the word of God, on account of the pure system of religion which it contains. We had a system of religion before; but look how dark and black a system that was compared with the bright system of salvation revealed in the word of God! Here we learn that we are sinners; and that God gave Jesus Christ to die for us, and by that goodness salvation is given to us. Now, what but the wisdom of God could have produced such a system as this presented to us in the word of God? And this doctrine leads to purity." A third reply to this question was, "When I look at myself I find I have got hinges all over my body. I have hinges to my legs, hinges to my jaws, hinges to my feet. If I want to take hold of anything, there are hinges to my hands to do it with. If my heart thinks, and I want to speak, I have got hinges to my jaws. If I want to walk, I have hinges to my feet. Now here," continued he, "is wisdom, in adapting my body to the various functions it has to discharge. And I find that the wisdom which made the Bible, exactly fits with this wisdom which has made my body; consequently, I believe the Bible to be the word of God." Another replied, "I believe it to be the word of God, on account of the prophecies which it contains, and the fulfillment of them."

6795. BIBLE, Intention of the. "The Bible is a strange book," said an infidel objector to an aged minister. "A wonderful book," was the reply. "It has some strange characters among its saints," said the objector; "such as David and Solomon. If such men lived in our day we would say that they deserved to be sent to state prison for life." "Worse than that," replied the minister. "If they got what they deserved they would be sent to hell forever. But you probably are mistaken as to the object of the Bible. It is not meant to show how good men are, but to show how the grace of God brings salvation to the very worst of men, and makes saints out of the vilest sinners."

6796. BIBLE, Interpreters of the. A learned Oriental, having been to visit the library of a French convent, writes thus to his friend in Persia, concerning what has passed—"Father," said I to the librarian, "what are these huge volumes which fill the whole side of the library?" "These," said he, "are the interpreters of the Scriptures." "There is a prodigious number of them," replied I; "the Scriptures must have been very dark formerly, and be very clear at present. Do there remain still any doubts? Are there now any points contested?" "Are there!" answered he with surprise—"are there! There are almost as many as there are lines." "You astonish me," said I; "what then have all these authors been doing?" "These authors," returned he, "never searched the Scriptures for what ought to be believed, but for what they did believe themselves. They did not consider them as a book wherein were contained the doctrines which they ought to receive, but as a work which might be made to authorize their own ideas."

6797. BIBLE, Key to the. Let me suppose a person to have a curious cabinet, which is opened at his pleasure, and not exposed to common view. He invites all to come and see it, and offers to show it to any one who asks him. It is hid, because he keeps the key, but none can complain, because he is ready to open it whenever he is desired. Some, perhaps, disdain the offer, and say, "Why is it locked at all?" Some think it is not worth seeing, or

amuse themselves with guessing at the contents. But those who are simply desirous for themselves, leave others disputing, go according to appointment, and are gratified. These have reason to be thankful for the favor, and the others have no just cause to find fault. Thus the riches of Divine grace may be compared to a richly-furnished cabinet to which "Christ is the door." The Word of God likewise is a cabinet generally locked up, but the key of prayer will open it. The Lord invites all, but he keeps the dispensation in his own hand. They cannot see these things, except he shows them; but then he refuses none that sincerely ask him. The wise men of the world can go no further than the outside of this cabinet; they may amuse themselves and surprise others with their ingenious guesses at what is within; but a child that has seen it opened can give us satisfaction, without studying or guessing at all. If men will presume to aim at the knowledge of God, without the knowledge of Christ, who is the way and the door; if they have such a high opinion of their own wisdom and penetration as to suppose they can understand the Scriptures without the assistance of his Spirit; or, if their worldly wisdom teaches them that those things are not worth their inquiring, what wonder is it that they should continue to be hid from their eyes?
Newton.

6798. BIBLE, Love in the. A converted African went to Mr. Moffat, the missionary, and told him that his dog had torn his copy of the New Testament, and swallowed some leaves of it, and that he was grieved about it, for the dog was very valuable. "But," said the missionary, "why do you grieve so? You can get another Testament, and the leaves will not hurt the dog." "Ah!" said he, "that's what I fear. He is a good hunter, and a good watch-dog, and the New Testament is so full of gentleness and love that I am afraid he will never be of any service again!"

6799. BIBLE, Marked with the. A Scotch preacher, being inducted into a church, told the people the relation that was to be between him and them, in the following words: "Sirs, I am come to be your shepherd, and you must be my sheep, and the Bible will be my tar bottle, for I will mark you with it."

6800. BIBLE, Modern Discovery and the. Lieutenant Lynch has floated down the Jordan, and explored the Dead Sea; and his sounding-line has fetched up from the deep physical confirmation of the catastrophe which destroyed the cities of the plain. Robinson, and Wilson, and Bartlett, and Bonar, have taken pleasure in the very dust and rubbish of Zion; and they come back declaring that the Bible is written on the very face of the Holy Land. Since Laborde opened up the lost wonders of Petra, its stones have cried aloud, and many a verse of Jehovah's word stands graven there with a pen of iron in the rock forever. Skepticism was wont to sneer, and ask, Where is Nineveh, that great city of three days' journey? But since Botta and Layard have shown its sixty miles of en-

closing wall, skepticism sneers no longer. Hidden in the sands of Egypt, many of God's witnesses eluded human search till within the last few years; but now, when Bibles increase, and are running to and fro through the earth, and when fresh confirmations are timely, God gives the word, and there is a resurrection of these witnesses; and from their sphinx-guarded sepulchres old Pharaohs totter into court, and testify how true was the tale which Moses wrote three thousand years ago. "In my youth," said Caviglia, when Lord Lindsay found him in the East, "I read Jean Jacques and Diderot, and believed myself a philosopher. I came to Egypt, and the Scriptures and the Pyramids converted me." And even so, a visit to Palestine, the reading of Keith's "Fulfillment of Prophecy"—nay, the mere sight of the Assyrian antiquities, has given faith to many a doubter; just as we could scarcely imagine any one reading Dr. Stroud on the "Physical Cause of Christ's Death," or Mr. Smith on the "Shipwreck of St. Paul," without carrying away the firmest conviction of these historical facts, and, consequently, of all those vital truths which the facts by implication involve. *Dr. J. Hamilton.*

6801. BIBLE, Mohammedan. The Mohammedans believe that the Koran is eternal and uncreated, remaining, as some express it, in the very essence of God; that the first transcript has been from everlasting by God's throne, written on a table of vast bigness, called the preserved table, in which are recorded the divine decrees, past and future; that a copy from the tables, in one volume on paper, was by the ministry of the Angel Gabriel sent down to the lowest heaven in the month of Ramadân on the night of power; from whence Gabriel revealed it to Mohammed by parcels, some at Mecca, and some at Medina, at different times, during the space of twenty-three years, as the exigency of affairs required; giving him, however, the consolation to shew him the whole (which they tell us was bound in silk, and adorned with gold and precious stones of Paradise) once a year; but in the last year of his life he had the favor to see it twice. *George Sale.*

6802. BIBLE, Moral Influence of the. When I visited Mexico, a year since or so, I found this: that in various places congregations had been formed and held together that no living preacher had addressed; but the soldiers had left copies of the New Testament, the people had read them, they forsook their grosser sins, and they met together to talk and read and pray. One day I went up into a mountain or high hill-side where was a cave, a kind of amphitheatre in a fort, where the people had met by one and two hundred to avoid the persecutions of the government, and there they read the Scriptures and sang and prayed. The same thing occurs in Syria and among the Mohammedans in Arabia. Wherever God's word is circulated it stirs the hearts of the people, it prepares for public morals. Circulate that word, and you find the tone of morals immediately changed. It is God speaking to man.
Bp. Simpson.

6803. BIBLE, Need of the Whole. The Burman Missionary tells of an old and blind man, who thirty years ago came into possession, through a countryman stopping over-night at his house, of a book printed in Burmese, and containing only the Psalms and a part of the Prophets. Before he had finished the Psalms he cast away his idols and Buddhism, and believed in a living God—Creator, Preserver, and Judge of men; and from that time he has worshiped and prayed to the Eternal God. He committed many of the Psalm-prayers to memory, and daily offered them, especially the 51st. For twenty years he lived in this way before ever hearing of Christ and the atonement. Coming then from the interior to Prome, he heard of a foreign teacher residing there, and from him received a copy of the New Testament. He says that if a man should go about and attend to his business twenty years by starlight, and the sun should then rise on him in all its glory, he thinks it would produce about such a change in his eyes and vision as the Gospel of Matthew produced on his mind; that then the long night of praying to God and hoping for mercy without a mediator or an atonement came to an end, and for the past ten years his hope has been firmly fixed on Christ.

6804. BIBLE, Power of the. A missionary in France offered a Bible in an humble dwelling. The man took it, tore out a dozen pages, and with them began to light his pipe. Some years after the missionary happened in the same house. The family had just lost their son in the Crimean war, and his Bible had been sent back home. The missionary took it up, and saw that it was the very same Bible that he had left in the house, and from which the leaves had been torn. The dying soldier had written on one of the leaves of the Bible: "Rejected and scoffed at, but finally believed in and saved." The Bible may be used to light the pipe of witticism by some, but for us it is a staff in life, a pillow in death, and our joy for eternity.
Talmage.

6805. BIBLE, Practicing the. I have here a music-book, one used by singers. The object of this book is to teach and promote vocal music, and also instrumental music, to be employed in worship, commonly called sacred music. Now, how does this music-book teach music? Simply by being studied? Not at all. Suppose a person previously unacquainted with the science and art of music, who has never sung a strain, and has no ear for melody, takes this book and commits it to memory, will that make him a musician? He might almost as well swallow the book, and would derive about as much benefit from it! He must reduce the book to practice. He must make the sounds indicated, or the book is a dead letter to him. Precisely so is it with the Bible.
Dr. E. O. Haven.

6806. BIBLE, Readers of the. To some the Bible is uninteresting and unprofitable, because they read too fast. Amongst the insects which subsist on the sweet sap of flowers there are two very different classes. One is remarkable for its imposing plumage, which shows in the sunbeams like the dust of the gems; and as you watch its jaunty gyrations over the fields, and its minuet dance from flower to flower, you cannot help admiring its graceful activity, for it is plainly getting over a great deal of ground. But in the same field there is another worker, whose brown breast and business-like, straightforward flight may not have arrested your eye. His fluttering neighbor darts down here and there, and sips elegantly wherever he can find a drop of ready nectar; but this dingy plodder makes a point of alighting everywhere, and wherever he alights he either finds honey or makes it. If the flower-cup be deep, he goes down to the bottom; if its dragon-mouth be shut, he thrusts its lips asunder; and if the nectar be peculiar or recondite, he explores all about till he discovers it, and then having ascertained the knack of it, joyful as one who has found great spoil, he sings his way down into its luscious recesses. His rival of the painted velvet wing has no patience for such dull and long-winded details. But what is the end? Why, the one died last October along with the flowers; the other is warm in his hive to-night, amidst the fragrant stores which he gathered beneath the bright beams of summer. Reader, to which do you belong—the butterflies or bees?
Dr. J. Hamilton.

6807. BIBLE, Reading the. Erasmus laughs at the man who attaches a benefit to the mere possession of the Bible. He likens him to one whom he calls Cyclops, who wears in his belt on this side a goodly bottle of sack, and on the other side a richly ornamented copy of the word of God, and he says in his swaggering style, "In truth, I am as good a saint as any!" Erasmus tries to disprove this, and in his witty way, "Prithee serve thy sack bottle as thy Bible. There are many virtues in a bottle of sack; it warms you when you are cold, it gets your valor up when you are half afraid. But do not take it; never take the cork out of it, and then see what its virtues are." Of course, our friend objects. He admires the bottle of sack; but he likes it better when the cork is out, and most of all when it is against his lips, and the stream is flowing merrily. "Ay," says he, "but what do you say to this book? Begin to read and study it." "Ah," he replies, "it is all dry matter that does not concern me." "Verily," then adds the other, "I see thou art indeed a true disciple of the sack, but a false disciple of the book." There is much truth in that wit. If people carry their Bibles as Erasmus wished this man to carry his sack, they will get no good out of it. We may scatter Bibles by millions, and reduce the price to two-pence or nothing; but we have done nothing but add to men's responsibility, unless we pray earnestly that God will lead men to study it, and by his Spirit bless it to their conversion, their edification, their sanctification in righteousness.
Spurgeon.

6808. BIBLE, Reasons for Believing the. A good old Highlander gave Claudius Buchanan the following reason for believing the Bible to be from God: "I know nothing about what the learned men call the external evidences of revelation; but I will tell you why I believe it to be from God: I have a most depraved and sinful nature; and, do what I will, I find I cannot make myself holy. My friends cannot do it for me, nor do I think all the angels in heaven could. One thing alone does it—the reading and believing what I read in that blessed book: that does it. Now, as I know that God must be holy, and a lover of holiness, and as I believe that book to be the only thing in creation that produces and increases holiness, I conclude that it is from God, and that he is the author of it."

6809. BIBLE, Reposing in Death on the. Here we find that knowledge which gives a feeling of firm ground below us—firm if there be *terra firma* in the universe—and on which have reposed, in death, the wisest of mankind. Newton laid not his dying head on his "Principia," but on his Bible; Cowper, not on his "Task," but on his New Testament; Hall, not on his wide fame, but his "humble hope;" Michael Angelo, not on that pencil which alone coped with the grandeurs of the "Judgment," but on that grace which for him shore the judgment of its terrors; Coleridge, not on his limitless genius, but on "Mercy for praise, to be forgiven for fame." 　　*G. Gilfillan.*

6810. BIBLE, Respect for the. I remember years ago when a great man of this nation fell in the national capital—a man whom I admired—and I exceedingly desired to learn something of the end of that man, and especially to know if his death was happy, triumphant, and if, in all probability, he had gone to enjoy a blessed reward in the kingdom of heaven. I looked in the newspapers for a week, and at last all I could fix my hopes upon was a solitary expression like this, "He had a profound respect for the Bible!" And I said, "Is that all that can be said of that man?" Why, there is not one in this house that has not a profound respect for the Bible! Huxley has it, with all his scepticism and infidelity; and within the last few years has affirmed, as have thousands of other great men, that the Bible must be in the public schools in London, because it is the only book that gives a pure morality. He respects the Bible, and yet rejects it as the word of God—as inspired from heaven. And is that all a good man does—respects the Bible? When I go to my home, as frequently I do after weeks of labor, and see my little daughter run to meet me, do I pause and fold my hands and say, "O how I admire you, how I respect and reverence you, my child!" No, but I throw wide open my arms and say, "Come to my heart, precious one, I love you; I delight in you!"
　　　　　　　　　　　　　　Bp. Bowman.

6811. BIBLE, Resting on the. "Do you believe in Christ?" said an infidel to John Jay. "I do, and I thank God that I do;" was the statesman's noble reply. Two years before his death, when eighty-two years of age, he was down by disease, and his recovery despaired

of. When urged to tell his children on what foundation he rested his hopes, and from what source he drew his consolation, his brief reply was, "They have the book."

6812. BIBLE, Result of Searching the. A gentleman was asked what led him to embrace the Gospel, which formerly he was known to have despised. He said, "A person put into my hands Paine's 'Age of Reason.' I read it with attention, and was much struck with the strong and ridiculous representation he made of many passages in the Bible. I confess, to my shame, I had never read the Bible through; but from what I remembered to have heard at church, and accidentally on other occasions, I could not persuade myself that Paine's report was quite exact, or that the Bible was quite so absurd a book as he represented it. I resolved, therefore, that I would read the Bible regularly through, and compare the passages when I had done so, that I might give the Bible fair play. I accordingly set myself to the task, and as I advanced, I was struck with the majesty which spoke, the awfulness of the truths contained in it, and the strong evidence of its Divine origin, which increased with every page, so that I finished my inquiry with the fullest satisfaction of the truth as it is in Jesus, and my heart was penetrated with a sense of obligation I had never felt before. I resolved henceforth to take the sacred word for my guide, and to be a faithful follower of the Son of God."

6813. BIBLE, Rules for Reading the. Take one book at a time. Don't be in a hurry. Read a book over, over and over. God will give light. The sixty-six books are sixty-six battering rams for Christians to conquer Satan with. So we shall slay and conquer. Try different ways of studying the Bible till you succeed. My wife wanted me to like tomatoes. I tried them raw, with vinegar, with sugar, and cooked, but I could not eat them. At last she thought of another way, and succeeded, and I thought it the best vegetable in the world.
　　　　　　　　　　　　　　Moody.

6814. BIBLE, Romanism and the. *La Capitale,* an infidel paper of large circulation, printed at Rome, thus comments on Signor Ribbetti's Wednesday lectures: "We do not at all agree with him, that every thing in the Bible is genuine; but it must be confessed there is no weapon so terrible as the Bible for fighting the Roman Catholic priesthood. In fact it lies crushed beneath these quotations. This is not a book; it is a millstone, grinding all the Lent preachers to powder."

6815. BIBLE, Salvation in the. The life-boat may have a tasteful bend and beautiful decoration, but these are not the qualities for which I prize it; it was my salvation from the howling sea! So the interest which a regenerate soul takes in the Bible, is founded on a personal application to the heart of the saving truth which it contains. If there is no taste for this truth, there can be no relish for the Scriptures. 　　*Dr. J. W. Alexander.*

6816. BIBLE, Silent Effects of Reading the. Do not think you are getting no good from the

Bible, merely because you do not see that good day by day. The greatest effects are by no means those which make the most noise and are most easily observed. The greatest effects are often silent, quiet, and hard to detect at the time they are being produced. Think of the influence of the moon upon the earth, and of the air upon the human lungs. Remember how silently the dew falls, and how imperceptibly the grass grows. There may be far more doing than you think in your soul by your Bible-reading. *Ryle.*

6817. BIBLE, Touch-stone of the. A woman entered a book-store to purchase a psalm book, and tendered a bank note in payment. It was in the days when the variety of these was great, and Thompson's Bank-Note Detector was a necessity of every merchant. The seller took the note, and looked in the detector to see if it was genuine. It was soon ascertained to be a counterfeit. The purchaser burst out in ejaculation, "Ah, man, it win na stan a book, it win na stan a book!" To such test must all human opinions be brought. If they will not stand the Bible they are false, and anathema. *Dr. J. S. Holme.*

6818. BIBLE, Treasure hid in the. On the banks of the Wabash, the effects of a poor widow, who had been left comparatively destitute at the death of her husband, had been seized by a sheriff for debt, and were being sold at auction; and among other things an old family Bible was put up for sale. She begged the constable to spare this memento of her dear and honored parents, but he was inexorable. The good book was about going for a few shillings, when the widow suddenly snatched it, and declaring she would have some relic of those she loved, cut the thread that held the brown linen cover, with the intent of retaining it. The covers fell into her hands, and with them two flat pieces of thin dirty paper. Surprised at the circumstance, she examined them, and what was her joy and delight to find that each called for £500 on the Bank of England. On the back of one, in her mother's hand-writing, were the following words, "When sorrow overtakes you, seek your Bible." And on the other, in her father's hand, "Your Father's ears are never deaf." The sale was immediately stopped, and the family Bible given to the faithful owner.

6819. BIBLE, Treasures in the. A poor shepherd, near Yoetot, bought an old Bible in 1848. One Sunday he discovered that several of the leaves were pasted together. Having separated them, he found a bank bill for five hundred francs. Accompanying it was this will and testament: "I gathered together this money with very great difficulty; but having none as natural heirs except those who have absolutely need of nothing, I make thee whosoever shall read this Bible my heir."

6820. BIBLE, Truth of the. Lord Rochester was an avowed infidel, and a large portion of his time was spent ridiculing the Bible. He was described as a great wit, a great sinner, and a great penitent. He was converted by the Holy Spirit in the use of the word. In reading the fifty-third chapter of Isaiah, he was convinced of the truth and inspiration of the Scriptures and the divinity of Christ. He trusted in the atonement, and died in expectation of heavenly happiness.

6821. BIBLE, Unity of the. The waters of the sea have many different shades. In one place they look blue, and in another green. And yet the difference is owing to the depth or shallowness of the part we see, or to the nature of the bottom. The water in every case is the same salt sea. The breath of a man may produce different sounds, according to the character of the instrument on which he plays. The flute, the pipe, and the trumpet have each their peculiar note. And yet the breath that calls forth the notes is in each case one and the same. The light of the planets we see in heaven is very various. Mars and Saturn and Jupiter have each a peculiar color. And yet we know that the light of the sun, which each planet reflects, is in each case one and the same. Just in the same way, the books of the Old and New Testaments are all inspired truth, and yet the aspect of that truth varies according to the mind through which the Holy Ghost makes it flow. The handwriting and style of the writers differ enough to prove that each had a distinct individual being; but the Divine Guide who dictates and directs the whole is always one. All is alike inspired. Every chapter and verse and word is from God. *Ryle.*

6822. BIBLE, Unsealed. A Gottingen professor narrated the following to two gentlemen from London, in the course of their tour through Germany:—"Some years ago I was in great danger of losing my sight, which had become so bad that I could scarcely distinguish anything. The prospect of passing the last days of my life in blindness made me so melancholy that I resolved to make a tour to Bremen to recover my spirits. On this tour I came to Hanover, where some friends took me into the Duke of Cambridge's library, and showed me some Bibles, lately sent by the Bible Society in London as a present to the Duke. Wishing to try whether in my blindness I could distinguish the paper and print of those from the common ones, I took one up merely for that purpose, without the least intention of selecting any particular passage; and now see what I read." He here opened the Bible, and recited Isa. 42: 16: "'And I will bring the blind by a way that they knew not; I will lead them in paths that they have not known: I will make darkness light before them, and crooked things straight. These things will I do unto them, and not forsake them.' I read this verse, and received spiritual sight." At these words he was so much affected that the tears ran down his cheeks. "With a cheerful mind I now journeyed back to Gottingen, and my greatest desire was to possess a Bible in which this verse stood on the same page and in the same place. Shortly afterwards, I was visited by a friend from London, to whom I related the occur rence, and immediately received his promise to send me a Bible as soon as possible, which he did."

6823. BIBLE, Valuing the. King George of the Friendly Islands, a noble man, who had been converted from cannibalism, met with what to him was a great loss. On hearing of the wreck of his vessel, instead of yielding to immoderate grief, he said he was sorry to lose the schooner; "But," said he, as he held up his Testament in his hand, and looked upon the messengers with a smile, "that is only a temporal loss, and may be repaired; so long as we have the word of God we are rich indeed, and have cause to be thankful."

6824. BIBLE, Value of the. Luther entered into orders, and discovered a Bible, 1507. The ignorance of the Scriptures at that time was astonishing. Conrad of Heresbach, a grave author of that age, relates the following words from the mouth of a monk: "They have invented a new language, which they call Greek; you must be carefully on your guard against it: it is the matter of all heresy. I observe in the hands of many persons a book written in that language, and which they call the New Testament. It is a book full of daggers and poison. As to the Hebrew, my brethren, it is certain that whoever learns it becomes immediately a Jew." It was in 1507, May 2, and in Luther's twenty-fourth year, that he entered into orders, and celebrated his first mass. This date is the more remarkable, because he discovered about the same time a Latin copy of the Bible lying in the library of the monastery. He eagerly laid hold of this neglected book, and persevered in studying it with so much diligence that he was able in a short time to refer with ease and promptitude to any particular passage. In the present day, we can with difficulty conceive how a copy of the Bible could remain unnoticed by the whole of a religious fraternity, or that a person so respectably educated as Luther should be unapprised that the whole of the Scriptures was not read to the people in the public service of the Church. It was with no small surprise that he discovered that there were many passages in the New Testament that were not thus read. The most striking of these Luther committed to memory, and treasured up with equal diligence many parts of the prophetic Scriptures. What a happy contrast do these days form to those of Luther! Who is without a Bible now? If any, at least in our own country, is it not their own fault? *Buck.*

6825. BIBLE, Versions of the. Four hundred years ago, including detached portions as well as complete transcripts, the whole world did not contain more than a few thousand copies of the word of God; and, although they were rapidly multiplied by the art of printing, at the beginning of the present century it is supposed that the entire amount fell short of four millions of copies. Since then the increase is amazing. The Bible Society alone has called into existence well-nigh fifty millions of copies, in one hundred and forty-eight languages or dialects, of which one hundred and twenty-one are translations never before printed. Many of these languages were never reduced to rule, had no grammar, no lexicon, had never been seen in print, had never been written down, till Bible translators undertook the arduous task; and altogether it may be presumed that the Gospel story can now be read in the speech of three-fourths of our earth's inhabitants. *Dr. J. Hamilton.*

6826. BIBLE, Why Papists Withhold the. The true reason why the Papists forbid the Scriptures to be read is not to keep men from errors and heresies, but to keep them from discovering those which they themselves impose upon them. Such trash as they trade in would never go off their hands if they did not keep their shops thus dark; which made one of their shavelings so bitterly complain of Luther for spoiling their market, saying that but for him they might have persuaded the people of Germany to eat hay. Anything, indeed, will go down a blind man's throat. *Gurnal.*

6827. BIGOTRY, Danger of. I recollect, on one occasion, conversing with a marine, who gave me a good deal of his history. He told me that the most terrible engagement he had ever been in was one between the ship to which he belonged, and another English vessel, when, on meeting in the night, they mistook each other for a French man-of-war. Several persons were wounded, and both vessels sustained serious damage from the firing. But when the day broke, great and painful was their surprise to find the English flag hoisted from both ships, and that through mistake they had been fighting, the previous night, against their own countrymen. They approached and saluted each other, and wept bitterly together. Christians sometimes commit the same error in this present world—one denomination mistakes another for an enemy; it is night, and they cannot see to recognize one another. What will be their surprise when they see each other by the light of another world, when they meet in heaven, after having shot at one another in the mist of the present state! How will they salute each other when better known and understood, after having wounded one another in the night? But they should wait till daybreak, at any rate, that they may not be in danger, through any mistake, of shooting at their friends. *Williams.*

6828. BIGOTRY, Monstrous. For wolves to devour sheep is no wonder; but for sheep to devour one another is monstrous and astonishing. *Salter.*

6829. BIGOTS, Bondage of. Bigots are stiff, straitened, and confined; like Egyptian mummies, which are bound round with thousands of yards of ribbon. *Salter.*

6830. BIGOTS, One-sided. Bigots are like some trees that grow by the seashore, which do not spread their branches equally on all sides, but are blown away, and stand entirely one way. *Salter.*

6831. BIOGRAPHIES, Useful. Biographies of great, but especially of good men, are most instructive and useful as helps, guides, and incentives to others. Some of the best are almost equivalent to gospels—teaching high living, high thinking, and energetic action for their own and the world's good. British biography is studded over as with "patines of bright gold," with illustrious examples of the power of self-help, of patient purpose, resolute working, and steadfast integrity, issuing in the formation of truly noble and manly character; exhibiting, in language not to be misunderstood, what it is in the power of each to accomplish for himself; and illustrating the efficacy of self-respect and self-reliance in enabling men of even the humblest rank to work out for themselves an honorable competency and a solid reputation.

Smiles.

6832. BIRDS, Miracle of the. In a certain season of the year, there is a revolution in nature which certainly claims our attention. It is the time the birds lay and hatch their young. This annual miracle passes in a manner before our eyes. What little we know of the generation of birds is sufficient to prove the wisdom of the Creator, as it can neither be attributed to a blind chance nor to art assisting nature. God had the wisest reasons for ordaining that certain animals should not arrive at perfection till after they came from their mother's womb, whilst others reach their full maturity in it. And it may be allowed, that whoever does not discover the hand of God in the production of birds, will not see it anywhere; for if the profoundest wisdom is not visible in this, it will appear so in nothing. O man! spectator of the wondrous works of God, adore with me the all-wise Being. Do not disdain to seek, in apparently small objects, the impression of his goodness, his power, and his ineffable wisdom.

Sturm.

6833. BIRTHDAYS, Ancient Commemoration of. The Greeks and Romans celebrated the annual return of their birthdays with music, feasting, sports, presents, and general rejoicing.

6834. BIRTHDAYS, Deathdays. Alexander the Great died on the same day of the same month in which he was born. Julius Cæsar was born on the fifteenth of March, and was slain on the same day, though warned to beware of the Ides of March. Plato died on his birthday in the same chamber in which he was born. Philip Melancthon died on his birthday, May 13, 1560, aged sixty-three.

6835. BIRTHDAYS, Fortunate. Timoleon, the successful general, gained his greatest victories on his birthdays, and his countrymen, the Syracusans, celebrated them as national holidays. Philip of Macedon counted his birthdays as the most fortunate of his life.

6836. BIRTH, Place of. Shortly after Summerfield came to this country, the young and beautiful preacher on some public occasion met a distinguished doctor of theology, who said to him,—"Mr. Summerfield, where were you born, sir?" "I was born," said he, "in Dublin and in Liverpool." "Ah, how can that be?" inquired the doctor. The boy preacher paused a moment, and answered, "Art thou a master in Israel and understandest not these things?"

6837. BISHOP, Example of a. Several hamlets belonging to the village of Alêt, are both remote and difficult of access. A poor woman, who was exceedingly ill, desired her husband to go to the curate, and request him to come and administer the sacrament immediately. It was very late in the evening, and quite dark. As the roads were besides covered with snow and exceedingly dangerous, the curate did not like to go at such an hour. "My good friend," said he, "perhaps your wife may not be so ill as you imagine. You see the weather; besides, at this late hour consider the imminent danger of falling over the precipices. I will wait on your wife early to-morrow, but it is out of the question to-night." The poor man, almost in despair, ran to the episcopal palace, and stated his case. The bishop had gone to bed, but immediately rose, and looking out of the window and seeing that the weather was really bad, he ordered torches to be lighted, and prepared to go himself. The grand vicar, astonished, asked if he had not better order the curate to go, and do what was in fact his duty. "No," said the bishop, "not for this once; a bishop, a Christian overseer at the head of his flock, like Cæsar at the head of his legions, should, if he mean to succeed, oftener say *Venite* (come) than *Ite* (go)."

6838. BISHOP, Responsibility of a. Adelbert, who lived in the 10th century, was appointed Archbishop of Prague. He was never seen to smile after his ordination, and, being asked the reason, he replied, "It is an easy thing to wear a mitre and a cross, but an awful thing to give an account of a bishopric before the Judge of quick and dead."

6839. BLAME, Reception of. A man takes contradiction and advice much more easily than people think, only he will not bear it when violently given, even though it be well-founded. Hearts are flowers; they remain open to the softly-falling dew, but shut up in the violent downpour of rain. *Richter.*

6840. BLASPHEMY, Bold. A Florentine was to fight with a young man by the name of Forchebene, named thus because he but seldom spoke. A great company went to the place of meeting, and one of the number said to the Florentine, "God give you the victory." With blasphemy he replied, "How shall he choose but give it to me?" Forchebene, as if the minister and instrument of God, gave him a thrust in his mouth with a sword that fastened his tongue down, and he fell dead, the sword remaining in his mouth. The member that had so grievously offended was apparently doomed to endure punishment even in this world.

6841 BLASPHEMY, Prize for. Some profligate young men offered a prize to the one who should be adjudged most expert in blasphemy. A sailor won the hellish honor. After the debauch he started for home. Failing to reach it, search was made for him. His body was found. He had fallen upon a scythe and severed the main artery. He won the prize for blasphemy for time and eternity.

6842. BLASPHEMY, Punishment of. In 1812, at a public house in Rochester, England, two wicked sailors meeting at a tavern began to curse and swear, when one, in a tempest of passion, swore that he would kill the other. The landlord said to the sailor who made the threat, "What if God of a sudden should strike you dead, and sink you into hell with his curse upon you!" The sailor replied with a terrible oath, "The Almighty cannot do that—give me the tankard of beer—if God can do it, I'll go to hell before I drink it up." With an awful oath he seized the tankard, but instantly fell down and expired!

6843. BLASPHEMY, Temptation to. A young hermit came to Poemen greatly distressed by temptations to blasphemy. "Do you take pleasure in these thoughts?" asked the Abbott, "I hate and detest them," answered the hermit. "Be of good cheer," said Poemen; "if you cast them out without giving them consent, they cannot hurt though they may distress you."

6844. BLESSED, Condition of the. The condition of the blessed in a better world is not likely to be a state of mere repose—of total inactivity, in which they will be occupied in mere contemplation, without having, properly speaking, anything to do; as if "peace" and "rest" necessarily implied utter indolence. On the contrary, there seems every reason to believe that, though exempted from painful toils and distressing anxieties, as well as from every other kind of suffering—and though, in that sense, they will "rest from their labors"—yet they will still be employed in doing good offices to the children of their Heavenly Father. *Abp. Whately.*

6845. BLESSEDNESS, Discovery of. The furthest that any of the philosophers went in the discovery of blessedness, was to pronounce that no man could be called blessed before his death; not that they had found what kind of better blessedness they went to after death, but that till death they were sure every man was subject to new miseries. The Christian philosophy goes further; it shows a more perfect blessedness than they conceived for the next life, and it imparts that blessedness to this life also. *Dr. Donne.*

6846. BLESSING, Condition of. When the sun rises there is light. Why, I do not know. There might have been light without the sun, and there might have been a sun that gave no light, but God has been pleased to put these two things together—sunrise and light. So, whenever there is prayer, there is a blessing. I do not know why. There might have been prayer without a blessing, for there is in the world of wrath; and there might have been a blessing without prayer, for it often is sent to some who sought it not. But God has been pleased to make this a rule for the government of the moral and spiritual universe, that there shall be prayer first, and that then there shall be the answer to prayer. *Spurgeon.*

6847. BLESSING, A Father's. When Dr. Belfrage, of Scotland, was on his death-bed, he desired to have his infant son brought to him. The dying father placed his hands upon his son's head, and pronounced the blessing of Jacob upon him, "The God before whom my fathers did walk, the God who fed me all my life long to this day, the angel who redeemed me from all evil, bless the lad." He then gave charge that the child should be told of his blessing, and his father's earnest desire that he might become early acquainted with his father's God.

6848. BLESSING, Greatest. Coleridge, the poet, in a letter written a fortnight before his death, addressed to his god-child, says: "On the eve of my departure, I declare to you, that health is a great blessing; competence, obtained by honorable industry, a great blessing; and a great blessing it is to have kind, faithful, and loving friends and relatives; but that the greatest blessing, as it is the most ennobling of all privileges, is to be, indeed, a Christian."

6849. BLESSINGS, Balance of. Think you the sorrows of life ever outnumber its joys? Suppose that you take your pencil and open an account with God's providence, just as merchants do with their customers. On one side put down all the troubles, difficulties, sorrows, and losses of your life, and on the other all the blessings, comforts, benefits, hopes and joys. And how will the account stand? On the one side there are a few sorrows, a few losses, a few pains, a few tears, a few disappointments, a little pinching poverty, may be. On the other there are life, health, provision, sunshine, friends, the Bible, heaven, eternal life. Oh, how the column of blessings outruns the column of sorrows! *J. R. Miller.*

6850. BLESSINGS, Obstructed. When our spiritual supplies fail, the channel is sometimes at fault, and not the stream; the hindrance to their coming lies with us and not with our heavenly Father. The supply of fuel to our city in midwinter sometimes fails, not because the coal-fields are exhausted, but because the weather has frozen our rivers, detained our colliers in the Channel, and blocked up our railways. The supply of water or of gas to our houses is sometimes insufficient, not because the reservoirs are low, but because the pipes which connect our dwellings with the main service are choked up or broken. News fails to reach us, not because our correspondent has neglected to write, but because the means of transmission have been imperfect. *Samuel Martin.*

6851. BLESSINGS, Transformed. Even the best things, ill used, become evils, and contrarily, the worst things, used well, prove good. A good tongue, used to deceit; a good wit, used to defend error; a strong arm to murder; authority to oppress; a good profession to dissemble; are all evil. Even God's own word is the sword of the Spirit, which, if it kill not our vices, kills our souls. Contrariwise (as poisons are used to wholesome medicine), afflictions and sins, by a good use, prove so gainful as nothing more. Words are as they are taken, and things are as they are used. There are even cursed blessings. *Bishop Hall.*

6852. BLESSINGS, Transient. When I see leaves drop from their trees in the beginning of autumn, just such, think I, is the friendship of the world; just such are the comforts and joys of this life. While the sap of maintenance lasts, my friends will swarm in abundance, my joys and comforts will abide with me; but when the sap ceases, the spring which supplies them fails, in the winter of my need they leave me naked. And those few leaves which I see falling, remind me of the coming winds and rains, when those trees shall be wholly stripped of their leaves; and of that season, that evil day, when all that administers to the gaiety and comfort of life shall fall from under me. Happy he who has that "Friend" which, saith the Scriptures, "sticketh closer than a brother," and that peace, and those pleasures, which are at God's right hand, and which shall never fade away!   *Salter.*

6853. BLIND, Groping in Darkness. Rabbi Jose says, "All my days did I feel pain at not being able to explain it; for what difference can it be to the blind man, whether he walketh in the light or in the dark? And yet," he adds, "the sacred penman would not have put down a word unnecessarily. What then does it mean?" Still the question remained unanswered, and that to the distress of the Rabbi. But "one night," he continues, "as I was walking in the road, I met a blind man with a lighted torch in his hand. 'Son,' said I, 'why dost thou carry that torch? thou canst not see its light!' 'Friend,' replied the blind man, 'true it is I cannot see, but others can: as long as I carry this lighted torch in my hand, the sons of men see me, take compassion on me, apprise me of danger, and save me from pitfalls, from thorns and briers.'" Thus was the mind of the Rabbi greatly relieved; he felt that the apparently superfluous word was meant to predict the greatness of the calamities that were to befall the Jewish people. Even at noonday they were to grope as the blind do in darkness, without a ray of light to exhibit their distress, and to appeal to the compassion of those who pass by.
Biblical Treasury.

6854. BLIND Leading the Blind. In the schoolroom of the American mission in Cairo, I found two persons reading the Bible in Arabic. One was a little girl, and she was sightless physically; both eyes were covered. But the other was a hard-looking old Mohammedan, hired to teach her to read with her fingers. She was a Christian child; he was a heathen. There was an instance of "blind leading the blind" in exact meaning of our Lord, both ways. He could see with his eyes, but only she could see with her heart, what Jesus had written for them both. And I leave it to all thoughtful Sabbath-school boys and girls to say which of those seemed to us the worst off —which was the blindest.
Dr. C. S. Robinson.

6855. BLIND, Opening the Eyes of the. Describing the school for the blind under the care of Mr. Mott at Beirut, Mr. Macgregor says:

"Only in February last, that poor blind fellow who sits on the form there was utterly ignorant. See how his delicate fingers run over the raised types of his Bible; and he reads aloud, and blesses God in his heart for the precious news, and for those who gave him this remarkable avenue to his heart. 'Jesus Christ will be the first person I shall see,' he says; 'for my eyes will be opened in heaven.' Down in that dark room again, below the printing press of the American mission (for he needs no sunlight in his work), you will find him actually printing the Bible in raised type, letter by letter, for his sightless brethren. This is one of the most important wonders I have ever looked at." At the annual examination of this school, one of the scholars said: "I am a little blind boy. I once could see; but then I fell asleep—a long, long sleep—I thought I should never awake. And I slept till a kind gentleman, called Mr. Mott, came, and opened my eyes—not these eyes," pointing to his sightless eyeballs; "but these," lifting up his tiny fingers—"these eyes; and oh! they see such sweet words of Jesus, and how he loved the blind."

6856. BLIND, Teaching the. The Rev. T. Collins tells of a poor blind man he taught to read. While doing so one day, as sentence after sentence of sweet promise revealed itself to the scholar's touch, the man suddenly exclaimed, "O this Bible is a treasure. Thank you, sir; thank you much, and thank God more; for I can now, for myself, in these holy words, feel the way to heaven with my finger tips!"

6857. BLINDNESS Cured. The legend of St. Frodobert of the seventh century, is that he was inspired with love of God from his earliest childhood. His mother was blind. He loved her greatly, and pitied her on account of her affliction. In an outburst of affection he kissed her darkened eyes, and they were miraculously opened. Love opens the eyes of the blind.

6858. BLINDNESS, Discovery of. I was in the Eye Infirmary the other day, when a woman came in with a beautiful babe. The woman said to the doctor; "Doctor, my child has not had its eyes open for a few days, and I have come to see if there can be something done for him. I did not like to open them, for it seemed to hurt him." The doctor, thereupon, pulled down the eyelids of the child, and the child gave a loud scream of pain. But he went on and made an examination, and then, turning to the poor woman, said: "Your child is blind of that eye." He then opened the other and said, "Yes, and this one too; your child will never see again." And it seemed to burst upon the woman so suddenly and so unexpectedly, that she screamed out at the top of her voice: "Oh, will my darling child never see me again? Oh, my darling child! oh, my darling child!" She pressed the child to her bosom, and I had to weep, too. Don't you sympathize with that poor mother? Don't you suppose I sympathize with her? Yes; but if I know my heart, I would rather lose my sight—have my eyes dug out as Samson's were—than to lose my soul. What is sight to the soul? Yes, I would a thousand times rather lose my sight on earth and see God in heaven than have my light here and darkness beyond the grave. *Moody.*

6859. BLINDNESS, Double. Mr. Nathaniel Partridge, one of the ejected ministers, having once preached at St. Alban's, upon the words, Rev. 3: 18, "Anoint thine eyes with eye-salve that thou mayst see," a poor man who was as blind in mind as he was in body went afterward to his house, and asked him very gravely, "Where he might get that ointment to cure his blindness?"

6860. BLINDNESS, Gratitude for Deliverance from. A poor laborer in France, blind from his birth, was a very skillful groom. A team was driven up to the hostelry which he attended, and directions given that especial care should be taken of the horses. Late in the evening their owner went to the stables and found the faithful groom still at work upon this favorite team. He was pleased with the service, and pitied his blindness, and resolved to give him a franc on leaving. During the night he thought whether he could not do something better for the blind man. In the morning he said to him, "Step out into the sunshine. You are forty. Earlier, I could have relieved you. I can perform an operation, and the chances are even that you can see or die under my hand. Come to Paris. I will pay your expenses, and the experiment shall cost you nothing." The poor man was glad to try a possibility that he might look upon the faces of his wife and children, which he had never seen. The experiment was made with entire success. He looked upon his wife, and called his children by name. Then he turned from them to the surgeon, saying, "Let me look on my friend, the surgeon, who has opened all this beautiful world to me. He is better than wife, or children, or anything else." For his vision he owed all to him, and was grateful. How much greater debt does the sinner owe to Christ!

6861. BLINDNESS, Removal of. Not long since an oculist called in a friend to witness the removing of the bandages from the eyes of a boy upon whom he had been operating, and to whom he had restored sight. The child had been blind from infancy, and this was the first moment that he was to be allowed to use his eyes and really to see. When the bandage was taken off, and the boy saw the pictures and faces of friends, he stood in silent wonder until he heard the familiar voice of his mother calling him, "Willie, can you see?" As he rushed into her arms he said, "O, mamma, is this heaven?" Such is the joy of the soul that passes from darkness to God's marvelous light. *A. D. Vail.*

6862. BLINDNESS, Selfish. The poets feign concerning Lamia, that upon her going to bed she lays aside her eyes among the attirements of her dressing-box, and is at home for the most part blind and drowsy too, and puts on her eyes only when she goes abroad a-gadding; so it is with most men, who, through a kind of affected ignorance and artificial blindness, commonly blunder and stumble at their own thresh-old, are the greatest strangers to their own personal defects, and of all others least familiarly acquainted with their own domestic ills and follies. *Plutarch.*

6863. BLOOD, Accusing. Abel's blood, and so Christ's, cry unto God, as the hire of the laborers unjustly detained, James 5: 4; or as the whole creation, which is in bondage through our sins, is said to cry and groan in the ears of the Lord, Rom. 8: 22, not vocally but efficaciously. How sad is the case of those that have no interest in Christ's blood; but instead of pleading for them, it cries to God against them, as its despisers and abusers! Every unbeliever despises it; the apostate treads it under foot. To be guilty of a man's blood is sad; but to have the blood of Jesus accusing and crying to God against a soul, is unspeakably terrible. *John Flavel.*

6864. BLOOD, Cleansing. A poor tempted Scotchman in great distress of mind proceeded to put himself in order for church, and while washing his hands, no one by, he heard a voice say, "Cannot I in my blood as easily wash your soul as that water does your hands?" "Now, Minister," he said, in telling me this, "I do not say there was a real voice, yet I heard it distinctly, word for word, as you now hear me. I felt a load taken off my mind, and went to the table and sat under Christ's shadow with great delight." *Dr. Guthrie.*

6865. BLOOD, Purification by. A custom of purifying by blood, practiced in ancient Phrygia, is thus explained: "When a person desired to be purified, he was placed by the priests in a pit prepared for the purpose, which was covered by a platform. This platform was perforated with many small holes; then a beast for sacrifice was brought and slain on this platform, so that its blood might flow through these perforations upon the person beneath. As the blood came down upon the head, the hands, the feet, the limbs, and the whole person, he was considered purified."

6866. BLOOD, Unity of. From Peter the Hermit's time to Bonaparte's, and from his to the earliest despot after, the human race, in concert with every fiendish spirit that hated God and man, have waged a perpetual crusade against that great truth which Paul uttered on Mars hill. But did they succeed? Did the dark passions of their alienated hearts, or all their crimson issues, put out that light! Nations fell in the struggle; crowns fell like stars in the Apocalypse; but did the angel flying through the midst of heaven, with the everlasting gospel, did he suspend his flight and rest upon his folded wings? No! had we but ears to hear anything but the din of this noisy world, we might even now catch the sound of his trumpet, proclaiming as he flies—"God hath made of one blood all nations of men!" *Burritt.*

6867. BLOOD OF CHRIST, Comfort from the. The commentator Bengel, during an illness, sent for a theological student and requested him to give him a word of consolation. The youth replied, "Sir, I am but a pupil, a mere learner; I don't know what to say to a teacher like you." "What!" said Bengel, "a divinity student, and not able to communicate a word of scriptural comfort!" The student, abashed, contrived to utter the text, "The blood of Jesus Christ, the Son of God, cleanseth us from all sin." "That is the very word I want," said Bengel, "it is quite enough," and taking him affectionately by the hand, dismissed him.

6868. BLOOD OF CHRIST, Experience of the. During the war a New York minister went among the soldiers in the hospital, and preached to them the way to Christ. He found one man whose eyes were closed and who was muttering something about "blood, blood," and the old doctor thought he was thinking of the carnage of the battle-field and the blood he had seen there, and going to him, he tried to divert his mind; but the young man looked up and said, "Oh, Doctor, it was not that that I was thinking of; I was thinking how precious the blood of Christ is to me now that I am dying. It covers all my sins."

6869. BLOOD OF CHRIST, Equality of the. Just before the war came on, during the days of slavery, I was in Boston. They were very exciting times there then, and Dr. Kirk was preaching on the subject of the cross. It was during the great strife, when there was a great deal of hatred and suspicion against foreigners then in our country. It was in the time of the Know-Nothing party, and there was a great deal of feeling against the blacks, and a great deal of feeling against the Irish. Dr. Kirk said when he came up to the cross to get salvation, he found a poor black man on the right and an Irishman on the left, and the blood came trickling down from the wounded side of the Son of God and made them all brothers, and all alike, and equal. That is what the blood does. It makes us all one kindred, and brings us all into the family of God. *Moody.*

6870. BLOOD OF CHRIST, Hope in the. Rev. J. Brown, of Haddington, on his death-bed said: "The Gospel is the only source of my comfort, and every sinner is as welcome as I. How pleasant that neither great sins nor great troubles can alter these consolations. Ever since God dealt savingly with my heart I have never had any comfort in the thought that my sins were small, but in the belief that the blood of Christ cleanseth from all sin."

6871. BLOOD OF CHRIST, Legend of the. The Israelites were delivered from a cruel bondage of two centuries in a single night. On the evening before their deliverance every housekeeper was commanded to kill a kid and sprinkle the door-posts with the blood. This was to be a sign to the destroying angel to pass by. There is a legend that on that night of the Exodus a young Jewish maiden—the first-born of the family—was so troubled on her sick-bed that she could not sleep. "Father," she anxiously inquired, "are you sure that the blood is there?" He replied that he had ordered it to be sprinkled on the lintel. The restless girl would not be satisfied until her father had taken her up and carried her to the door, to see for herself; and lo! the blood was not there! The order had been neglected, and before midnight the father made haste to put on his door the sacred token of protection. The legend may be false; but it teaches a very weighty and solemn admonition to the sinful soul who may be near eternity and is not sheltered under the atonement of Christ. Christ our passover has been sacrificed for us; and just as death came to every home in Egypt on that terrible night, so death is upon every soul not sprinkled with the blood of Christ.

6872. BLOOD OF CHRIST, Meditating upon the. Five persons were studying what were the best means to mortify sin. One said, to meditate on death; the second, to meditate on judgment; the third, to meditate on the joys of heaven; the fourth, to meditate on the torment of hell; the fifth, to meditate on the blood and sufferings of Jesus Christ; and certainly the last is the choicest and strongest motive of all. If ever we would cast off our despairing thoughts, we must dwell and muse much upon, and apply this precious blood to our own souls; so shall sorrow and mourning flee away. *Brooks.*

6873. BLOOD OF CHRIST, Relying on the. An old herdsman of Dartmoor, Eng., was taken to a London hospital to die. There his grandchild used to visit and read to him. One day, she was reading to him the first chapter of the first epistle of John, when she reached the seventh verse, "And the blood of Jesus Christ, his Son, cleanseth us from all sin," the old man raised himself and stopped the little girl, saying with great earnestness: "Is that there, my dear?" "Yes, grandpa." "Then read it to me again; I never heard the like before." The little girl read again: "And the blood of Jesus Christ, his Son, cleanseth us from all sin." "You are quite sure that is there?" "Yes, quite sure." "Then take my hand and lay my finger on the passage, for I should like to feel it." So she took the old blind man's hand and placed his bony finger on the verse, when he said, "Now read it to me again." The little girl read, with her soft, sweet voice: "And the blood of Jesus Christ, his Son, cleanseth us from all sin." "You are quite sure that is there?" "Yes, quite sure." "Then if any one should ask how I died, tell them I died in the faith of these words: 'And the blood of Jesus Christ, his Son, cleanseth us from all sin.'" And with that, the old man withdrew his hand, his head fell softly back on the pillow, and he silently passed into the presence of him whose "blood cleanseth us from all sin."

6874. BOASTING, Fable of. A rushlight that had grown fat and saucy with too much grease, boasted one evening before a large company, that it shone brighter than the sun, the moon, and all the stars. At that moment, a puff of wind came and blew it out. One who lighted it again said, "Shine on, friend Rushlight, and hold your tongue; the lights of heaven are never blown out." *Æsop.*

6875. BOASTING, Folly of. Now go and brag

of thy present happiness, whosoever thou art; brag of thy temperature, of thy good parts; insult, triumph and boast: thou seest in what a brittle state thou art, how soon thou mayest be dejected, how many several ways, by bad diet, bad air, a small loss. a little sorrow or discontent, an ague, &c., how many sudden accidents may procure thy ruin, what a small tenure of happpiness thou hast in this life, how weak and silly a creature thou art. Humble thyself, therefore, under the mighty hand of God, know thyself, acknowledge thy present misery, and make right use of it. "Let him that standeth take heed lest he fall." Thou dost now flourish, and hast goods of body, mind, and fortune; but thou knowest not what storms and tempests the evening may bring with it. Be not secure, then; be sober and watch, if fortunate and rich; if sick and poor, moderate thyself. *Burton.*

6876. BOASTING Fulfilled. There was continual dissension between Nicias and Cleon, in the joint administration of the Commonwealth of Athens. Nicias was considered the most experienced and successful. The Lacedemonians were defeated by the Athenians, and four hundred Spartans fled to the island of Stagyra. The Athenians besieged them for a long time without success. Cleon declared that if he had the management of the business he would have them in his hands dead or alive within twenty days; and that if the supreme command in that expedition should be given to him alone, he would give a good account of it. He made good his boast, within the time specified; the place was seized, many of the Lacedemonians were slain, and those remaining were brought prisoners to Athens.

6877. BOASTING, Groundless. When Mendoza was ambassador in France, he often declared, "God's power is in heaven and king Philip's on earth; he can command both sea and land, with all the elements to serve him," yet that invincible monarch was overcome at last by insignificant vermin and died like Herod, eaten of worms.

6878. BOASTING, Unsafe. "Nothing," says Bishop Horne, "can be got, but much may be lost, by triumphing before a battle. When Charles V. invaded France, he lost his generals and a great part of his army by famine and disease; and returned baffled and thoroughly mortified from an enterprise which he began with such confidence of its happy issue, that he desired Paul Jovius, the historian, to make a large provision of paper sufficient to record the victories which he was going to acquire."

6879. BOASTING, Vain. Sigismund, king of Hungary, looking at his own vast army as he went out to meet Bajazet and his Turks, said proudly, "What need we fear the Turks, who need not fear the falling of the heavens, which if they should fall we are able to hold up with the points of our spears and halberts." This boaster was driven like another Xerxes to fly for his life at the battle of Nicopolis.

6880. BODY, Biblical. Man's body is compared to—*A house of clay*, "whose foundation

is in the dust," Job 4: 19;—mean and mouldering. See also 13: 12. *A curiously embroidered garment*, Ps. 139: 13–16. "Curiously wrought," like tapestry interwoven with many colored threads. "Wrought as with a needle" (Lowth); "fashioned" in the secret place, into the most beautiful fabric; every member carefully noted in God's book. *A temple*, designed to be the shrine and abode of Deity, 1 Cor. 6: 15, 19. *A tent or tabernacle*, —frail and easily overturned, in contrast to a fixed and strong *house*, 2 Cor. 5: 1. *A frail vessel*, 1 Thess. 4: 4. St. Peter's words— "the weaker vessel," 1 Pet. 3: 7, imply that both are weak. *Grass*—the *flower of the field*; the flower perhaps more delicate and beautiful than the grass, but both alike when beneath the mower's scythe. Both, left to themselves, are born to wither and pass away, Isa. 40: 6–8: 1 Pet. 1: 24. *The sheath of the spirit*, Dan. 7: 15 (marg.), the scabbard concealing the bright sword within. *Bowes.*

6881. BODY, Constituents of the. Of the sixty-two primary elements known in nature, only eighteen are found in the human body, and of these seven are metallic. Iron is found in the blood, phosphorus in the brain, limestone in the bile, lime in the bones, and dust and ashes in all. Not only these eighteen human elements, but the whole sixty-two, of which the universe is made, have their essential basis in the four substances—oxygen, hydrogen, nitrogen, carbon—representing the more familiar names of fire, water, saltpetre, and charcoal. And such is man, the lord of the earth—a spark of fire, a drop of water, a grain of gunpowder, an atom of charcoal. *Phren. Jour.*

6882. BODY, Corruptibility of the. We cannot keep our bodies long here: they are corruptible bodies, and will tumble into dust; we must part with them for awhile; and if ever we expect and desire a happy meeting again, we must use them with modesty and reverence now. *Sherlock.*

6883. BODY, Death of the. We all know that every night is the day's funeral; and what is the morning but the day's resurrection again? or like the setting of the sun at evening, which the next morning shall rise again? And we all know, that when we set or put a root into the ground, that it must lie all the winter, and appear as dead; but, in the spring-time, we hope to see it revive, and show itself by virtue of the sun. Just so will it be with us at the day of our resurrection; for it is a most certain argument, that he who can do the greater work can also do the lesser; for God, who did make the world and also man at first of nothing, can, at the day of our resurrection, make us perfect bodies again of something. *S. Smith.*

6884. BODY. Exposure of the. Our bodies only lie exposed to the necessities of the common lot of nature, which we offer as a handle to fortune; but the fort-royal is still secure, where our strength lies and our most precious things are treasured up. *Plutarch.*

6885. BODY, Mechanical Perfection of the. The human body, considered simply as an engine to be worked by a superior agent—as a system of combined and organized matter, to be actuated and controlled by a living spirit—is a most wonderful instance of creative power and plastic skill. It may be considered as a world in miniature, as an epitome of all the sciences, as an abridgment of the great book of nature. To whatever part of it we direct our attention, we discover a most remarkable exemplification of the general laws of physics. In its optics, as expressive of the functions of the eye, we have mathematics of the highest order. In the formation of the bones, and in the arrangement of its various joints and ligaments, we have the principles of mechanics most strikingly exhibited to our view. In the circulation of its fluids, the heart, the arteries, and the veins, may be regarded as an hydraulic apparatus. The process of respiration is an example of pneumatic action. In the gradual formation of its general substance—in the precipitation of the various elements which constitute its specific parts—we have chemistry in some of its finest and most beautiful combinations. Over and above all these subordinate agencies, however, there is a master principle—there is life, the grand chemist, the mighty engineer, who superintends and regulates the whole. And although he is invisible to the keenest eye, and baffles the strongest microscope, the effects which he works are too palpable to admit a rational doubt of his separate and distinct existence, and the very obscurity of his retreat tends only to raise our admiration of the power and wisdom of that Being by whom he was originally created, and by whose will he has been attached to our frame. Truly then may we say, in the view of this mysterious union of body and soul—of matter and spirit —in the present condition of our nature, that we are "fearfully and wonderfully made." This is, therefore, doubtless the just and legitimate method of studying the science of physiology—to regard it as exhibiting throughout a most remarkable illustration of the "manifold wisdom of God." So forcibly was the celebrated heathen philosopher and physician, Galen, struck with this fact, that he remarked, that if there was no other proof of it, the examination of the human eye alone would be sufficient to demonstrate the existence of a Supreme Being. *Davies.*

6886. BODY, Mind and. Body and mind must be exercised, not one, but both, and that in a mediocrity; otherwise it will cause a great inconvenience. If the body be overtired, it tires the mind. The mind oppresseth the body, as with students it oftentimes falls out, who, as Plutarch observes, have no care of the body, but compel that which is mortal to do as much as that which is immortal; that which is earthly as that which is ethereal. But as the ox, tired, told the camel, both serving one master, that refused to carry some part of his burden, before it were long he should be compelled to carry all his pack, and his skin to boot, which by and by, the ox being dead, fell out; so the body may say to the soul that will

give it no respite or remission. A little after, an ague, vertigo, or consumption seizeth on them both; all his study is omitted, and they must be compelled to be sick together. He that tenders his own good estate and health, must let them draw equal yoke both alike, that so they may happily enjoy their wished health. *Burton.*

6887. BODY, Mutiny in the. In former days, when all a man's limbs did not work together as amicably as they do now, but each had a will and way of its own, the members generally began to find fault with the belly for spending an idle luxurious life, while they were wholly occupied in laboring for its support, and ministering to its wants and pleasures; so they entered into a conspiracy to cut off its supplies for the future. The hands were no longer to carry food to the mouth, nor the mouth to receive the food, nor the teeth to chew it. They had not long persisted in this course of starving the belly into subjection, ere they all began, one by one, to fail and flag, and the whole body to pine away. Then the members were convinced that the belly also, cumbersome and useless as it seemed, had an important function of its own; that they could no more do without it than it could do without them; and that if they would have the constitution of the body in a healthy state, they must work together, each in his proper sphere, for the common good of all. *Æsop.*

6888. BODY, Misuse of the. St. Francis, of Assisi, who lived early in the thirteenth century, practiced many of the austerities common to the ascetics. He called his body "Brother Ass," as he conceived it only fit to carry burdens, be beaten, and fare poorly. Later in life his ideas became modified, and before he died he asked pardon of his own body for having treated it with too great rigor. His excuse was that he meant thereby to secure the purity of his soul. He counseled moderation, but not the luxurious indulgence of these times.

6889. BODY, Resurrection. Phil. 3: 20, 21. "The body is here called vile, or the body of our vileness." Not as God made it, but as sin hath marred it. Not absolutely, and in itself, but relatively, and in comparison with what it will be at the resurrection. Then those scattered bones and dispersed dust, like pieces of old broken, battered silver, will be new-cast, and wrought in the best and newest fashion, even like to Christ's glorious body. *John Flavel.*

6890. BODY, Resurrection of the. I have stood in a smith's forge and seen him put a rusty, cold, dull piece of iron into the fire, and, after a while, he hath taken the very same numerical individual piece of iron out of the fire, but bright, sparkling. And thus it is with our bodies: they are laid down in the grave, dead, heavy, earthly; but, at that general conflagration, this dead, heavy, earthly body shall arise living, lightsome, glorious. *Dr. Fuller.*

6891. BODY, Unity of the Organs of the. Every organ of the body is in league with every other organ. Every one of them has its own pecu liar province and vocation, but is in treaty at the same moment, offensive and defensive, with every other. Nothing is proper to any member in this unique and truly royal society that does not go forth in turn for the interest and advantage of that society. Local benefits immediately become public ones; what injures in one part is as a calamity to the whole.

Grindon.

6892. BODY, Veneration for the. What an incentive to holiness, to purity of life and conduct, lies in the fact that the body of a saint is the temple of God—a truer, nobler temple than that which Solomon dedicated by his prayer, Jesus consecrated by his presence? In popish cathedral, where the light streamed through painted windows, and the organ pealed along lofty aisles, and candles gleamed on golden cups and silver crosses, and incense floated in fragrant clouds, we have seen the blinded worshiper uncover his head, drop reverently on his knees, and raise his awe-struck eye on the imposing spectacle; we have seen him kiss the marble floor, and knew that he would sooner be smitten dead upon the floor than be guilty of defiling it. How does this devotee rebuke us! We wonder at this superstition; how may he wonder at our profanity! Can we look on the lowly veneration he expresses for an edifice which has been erected by some dead man's genius, which holds but some image of a deified virgin, or bones of a canonized saint, and which time shall one day cast to the ground and bury in the dust—can we, I say, look on that, and if sensible to rebuke, not feel reproved by the spectacle? In how much more respect, in how much holier veneration should we hold this body! The shrine of immortality, and a temple dedicated to the Son of God, it is consecrated by the presence of the Spirit—a living temple, over whose porch the eye of piety reads what the finger of inspiration has written: "If any defile the temple of God, him shall God destroy; for the temple of God is holy, which temple ye are."

Dr. Guthrie.

6893. BODY AND SOUL, Judgment of the. A dispute will arise between the soul and the body, to which of them their guilt ought to be imputed; the soul saying, "O Lord, my body I received from thee; for thou createdst me without a hand to lay hold with, a foot to walk with, an eye to see with, or an understanding to apprehend with, till I came and entered into this body; therefore punish it eternally, but deliver me." The body on the other hand will make this apology: "O Lord, thou createdst me like a stock of wood, having neither hand that I could lay hold with, nor foot that I could walk with, till this soul, like a ray of light, entered into me, and my tongue began to speak, my eye to see, and my foot to walk; therefore punish it eternally, but deliver me." But God will propound to them the following parable of the blind man and the lame man, which, as well as the preceding dispute, was borrowed by the Mohammedans from the Jews. A certain king, having a pleasant garden, in

which were ripe fruits, set two persons to keep it, one of whom was blind and the other lame; the former not being able to see the fruit, nor the latter to gather it; the lame man, however seeing the fruit, persuaded the blind man to take him upon his shoulder and by that means he easily gathered the fruit, which they divided between them. The lord of the garden coming some time after and inquiring after his fruit, each began to excuse himself. The blind man said he had no eyes to see with; and the lame man, no feet to approach the tree. But the king ordering the lame man to be set on the blind man, passed sentence on and punished them both. And in the same manner will God deal with the body and soul.

George Sale.

6894. BOLDNESS, Christian. The Emperor Otho III., visiting Rome, went also to Mt. Gargano, to see St. Nilus. He was much pleased, and exclaimed, as he saw the huts of the monks, "These men are true citizens of heaven, who live in tents as strangers on the earth." The Emperor desired Nilus to accept a present of land for his monastery, but he refused. Taking his leave, the Emperor said, "Ask what you please, as if you were my son; I will give it you with joy and pleasure." St. Nilus answered, "The only favor I ask of you is that you will save your own soul. Though an Emperor, you must die and give an account to God like other men."

6895. BOLDNESS, Clerical. Rev. Samuel Wesley, the father of John Wesley, being strongly importuned by the friends of James the Second to support the measures of the court in favor of popery, with promises of preferment, absolutely refused even to read the king's declaration; and though surrounded with courtiers, soldiers and informers, he preached a bold and pointed discourse against it from these words: "If it be so, our God whom we serve, is able to deliver us out of thy hand, O king. But if not, be it known unto thee, O king, that we will not serve thy gods, nor worship the golden image which thou hast set up. "

Whitecross.

6896. BOLDNESS, A Martyr's. St. Basil suffered martyrdom in the persecution of Julian, known as the apostate, A. D. 363. Julian had given orders for the restoration of the heathen worship. Basil was very bold in denouncing the effort, and was soon charged with stirring up the people against the established religion. Macarius, a heathen priest, drew him before the magistrate, Saturninus. Macarius said, "What meanest thou, going to and fro in the city, agitating the people against the religion established by the Emperor?" Basil answered, defiantly, "God break thy jaws, thou bond-slave of Satan! It is not I who ruin thy religion, but he who is in heaven confounds thy counsels and dissipates thy lies!" Macarius then made the charge of sedition in defiance of the Emperor. The judge asked, "Who art thou, so audacious as to do these things?" Basil replied, "The best of everything—a Christian." "Then why, if thou art a Christian, dost thou not behave as a Christian?" said the judge. Basil responded, "I do; it becomes every Christian to make bare all acts." "Why dost thou make revolt, transgress good laws, and blaspheme the Emperor?" "God is my emperor, and he will bring your established religion to naught in no time." "So the religion of the Emperor is not true?" "How can I regard that religion as true whose worship consists in men running and howling about the streets like rabid dogs with raw flesh in their mouths?" "Hang him up, and scrape him!" ordered the judge. He was suspended by his wrists and ankles, and his flesh gashed with iron rakes, he in the meantime thanking God that he was counted worthy to receive these torments. Afterwards he was cast into prison, and word of his arrest was sent to the Emperor. Every effort was made to induce him to apostatize, but he was immovable. Julian himself came to Ancyra on his way to Persia, and Basil was summoned before him. There his zeal blazed forth in indignation against the apostate. He cried, "Thou, renegade, hast abdicated the throne prepared for thee in heaven. Verily, I believe that Christ, whom thou hast adjured, will take thee and pluck thee out of thy dwelling, that thou mayest know how great is that God whom thou hast offended. Thou hast not thought of his judgments, nor venerated his altars; thou hast not kept his laws, which thou didst declare often with thy lips; wherefore, great Emperor, Christ will not remember thee, but will take from thee speedily thy earthly empire, and thy body shall be deprived of a sepulchre, and thou shalt breathe forth thy soul in greatest anguish!" At this, Julian ordered him away, and that seven thongs should be cut daily from his skin. After this had been done once, he picked up one of the strips and asked to be taken before the Emperor. This was granted, as it was thought he was ready to apostatize. When he stood before Julian, he cried, "Dumb, and deaf, and blind are thy idols, Apostate! To me to live is Christ, and to die is gain. He is my helper, in whom I trust, and for whom I suffer." He threw the strip of skin before the Emperor, exclaiming, "Here is meat for thee, Julian!" He had no words of submission, and was quickly removed. On the morrow he was cast upon a bed of red-hot iron spikes, and there prayed, saying, "Receive my spirit. Amen!" and conquered. Julian died soon after, exclaiming, "Thou hast conquered, O Galilean!"

6897. BOLDNESS, Ministerial. Oliver Millard, a popular preacher of the reign of Louis XI., attacked the vices of the court in his sermons, and did not spare even the king himself, who, taking offence at it, sent the priest word that if he did not change his tone, he would have him thrown into the Seine. "The King," replied Oliver, "is the master, to do what he pleases; but tell him that I shall reach Paradise by water sooner than he will with his post-horses." The establishment of traveling post was instituted by Louis XI. This bold answer at once amused and intimidated the king, for he let the priest continue to preach as he pleased, and what he pleased.
Cyclo. of Anecdote.

6898. BOLDNESS, Required. A boy playing in the fields got stung by a nettle. He ran home to his mother, telling her that he had but touched that nasty weed, and it had stung him. "It was your just touching it, my boy," said the mother, "that caused it to sting you; the next time you meddle with a nettle, grasp it tightly, and it will do you no hurt." *Anon.*

6899. BONDAGE, Biblical. *Slavery*, Exod. 1: 13, in Egypt, "the house of bondage," and in the iron furnace, Deut. 4: 20. In later times, like the slavery of Greece and Rome, no less severe; when the slave (often a captive taken in war) was regarded as wholly the property of his master, liable to be beaten, chained, or even killed at the master's will and pleasure. The figure is aptly applied to the cruel and relentless slavery of sin; and the word "servant" would be more forcibly translated *slave;* so cf. John 8: 34; Rom. 6: 16; Titus 3: 3, "serving divers lusts and pleasures" (the slave and drudge of many masters); 2 Pet. 2: 19, "the servants of corruption." Still worse is the case, when the sinner sells himself into slavery like Ahab, 1 Kings 21: 20; and Israel 2 Kings 17: 17; Isa. 50: 1. See also St. Paul's expression, Rom. 7: 14, "sold under sin." *Captivity*, Rom. 7: 23; Isa. 61: 1; Luke 4: 18.—Probably alluding to the ancient custom of putting out the eyes of captives, and then keeping them bound in chains with cruel rigor.—See 2 Tim. 2: 26. *Yoke*, Isa. 9: 14; Lam. 1: 14; 2 Cor. 6: 14.—Like the yoke of Israel's bondage in Egypt, under which the people were bowed and bent down, and unable to "go upright," Lev. 26: 13. THAT POOR WOMAN, bound by Satan for eighteen years, Luke 13: 11–16. THE WEARINESS and TOIL of SIN.—How hard blind sinners toil for their destruction, Isa. 67: 10; Jer. 9: 5; Hab. 2: 13. "AGAIN ENTANGLED therein and overcome," 2 Pet. 2: 20; like silly sheep, no sooner freed from the thorns and briers, than ready to wander and be caught and torn again. "TIED and BOUND with the chain of sin," Prov. 5: 22; Rom. 7: 24 (like a living man condemned to be tied to a loathsome corpse). Sin comes easily, but binds strongly. "The bond of iniquity," Acts 8: 23. THE JEWS boasted of their national liberty, as they once said to Christ, "We were never in bondage to any man," John 8: 34. It was a saying manifestly untrue: but Christ's answer is very striking— "Whoever committeth sin is the servant (slave) of sin," verse 35. *Bowes.*

6900. BOOK, A Powerful. According to a story in Sanscrit, the poet Gunadhya wrote with his own blood a massive book containing seven hundred thousand slokas. He sent the book by two pupils to the king Satavahana, who rejected it because it was written in the Pisacha dialect. The poet then ascended a mountain, lighted a great fire, read aloud his stories, and as he finished a page he cast it into the flames. As he read all the beasts of the forests gathered about him, and wept tears of delight over the tales. At that time the king fell ill, and his doctors ordered a supply of game for him, but it could not be obtained, for every creature of the forest was listening to Gunadhya. This fact was reported to the king, and he hastened to the scene and desired to buy the wonderful book. Alas! on his arrival only one of the seven hundred thousand slokas remained. This opens up a new field for disappointed authors. Let them try the effect of their productions on the beasts of the forest.

6901. BOOK OF LIFE, Enrolled in the. Some people say they can't tell down here, but must wait till they get to heaven to know whether their names are written in the Book of Life. I believe it is the privilege of every Christian to know it here. Men in China tell me that the greatest honor that can be paid them there is to write their name in one of their joss houses, in the house of Confucius. Christ says, "Rejoice that your names are written in heaven." I was coming into Liverpool one night with a party of friends, and we found the Northwestern Hotel full, and they told me it had been full for days. I said to my friends, "Let us go over to the Adelphi." "No," they said, "we have a room engaged." "Why," I said, "they told me the house had been full for days, and now you say you have got a room." They said, "We sent our names on ahead and secured a room." "How wise," thought I. Many of you are laying in wood for the bleak winter, and food and clothing. Oh, prepare for the long, bleak night that is coming! See that your names are written in heaven; send your names on ahead and secure a room. And when sure that our names are written there we should see that those of our children are. A friend said to me, "Why talk of books being kept in heaven." I said, "The Bible has a good deal to say about it." In Daniel, 12: 1, "every one was saved whose name was found written in the book." In Philippians, 4: 3, Paul speaks of those whose names were written in the book. We ought to live so that not only we but others would know our names are on the record.

Moody.

6902. BOOK OF LIFE, Example of the. In the public registers all that were born of a particular tribe were entered in the list of their respective families under that tribe. This was the book of life; and when any of these died, his name might be considered as blotted out of the list. "In China, the names of the persons who have been tried on criminal processes are written in two distinct books, which are called the book of life, and the book of death; those who have been acquitted, or who have not been capitally convicted, are written in the former; those who have been found guilty, in the latter. These two books are presented to the emperor by his ministers, who, as sovereign, has a right to erase any name from either: to place the living among the dead, that he may die: or the dead, that is, the person condemned to death, among the living, that

he may be preserved. Thus he blots out of the book of life, or the book of death, according to his sovereign pleasure, on the representation of his ministers, or the intercession of friends."

6903. BOOK OF LIFE, Legend of the. St. Julian and his wife, Basilissa, resolved to live chaste lives, as if they had not been married. Their bridal chamber became illuminated, and Jesus, standing by them, said, "Thou hast conquered, O Julian!" Then two angels, clothed in white robes, girded with golden zones, having crowns, stood beside their couch. Thereon lay a book seven times brighter than silver, wherein were various names in letters of gold. Julian read there his name and that of his wife, Basilissa. And one of four witnessing elders, who were also there, said, "In that book are written the chaste and the sober, the truthful and the merciful, the humble and the gentle, those whose love is unfeigned, bearing adversities, patient in tribulation, and those who, for the love of Jesus Christ, have given up father, and mother, and wife, and children, and lands for his sake, lest they should impede the progress of their souls to perfection, and they who have not hesitated to shed their blood for his name, in the number of whom you also have merited to be written."

6904. BOOKS, Advantages of. The writers who despise books may be original perhaps, but they may pass their lives without being original to any purpose of interest or utility. Whereas, true talent will become original in the very act of engaging itself with the ideas of others; nay, will often convert the dross of previous authors into the golden ore that shines forth to the world as its own peculiar creation. From a series of extravagant and weak Italian romances, Shakspeare took the plots, the characters, and the major part of the incidents of those dramatic works which have exalted his name, as an original writer, above that of every other in the annals of literature.

Dr. Cromwell.

6905. BOOKS, Communion of. It is chiefly through books that we enjoy intercourse with superior minds; and these invaluable means of communication are in the reach of all. In the best books great men talk to us, give us their most precious thoughts, and pour their souls into ours. God be thanked for books. They are the voices of the distant and the dead, and make us heirs of the spiritual life of past ages. Books are the true levelers. They give to all, who will faithfully use them, the society, the spiritual presence, of the best and greatest of our race. No matter how poor I am; no matter though the prosperous of my own time will not enter my obscure dwelling; if the sacred writers will enter and take up their abode under my roof; if Milton will cross my threshold to sing to me of Paradise, and Shakspeare to open to me the worlds of imagination and the workings of the human heart, and Franklin to enrich me with his practical wisdom, I shall not pine for want of intellectual companionship, and I may become a cultivated man though excluded from what is called the best society in the place where I live.

Channing.

6906. BOOKS, Destruction of Bad. A French lady who kept a book store in Paris heard Father Beauregard preach against the danger of immoral books, and was deeply convinced. She sent for the father to come and examine her stock. He rejected books to the value of 6,000 livres, and she burned them in his presence, glad to make the sacrifice.

6907. BOOKS, Devotee of. Magliabechi, the celebrated librarian of Florence, lived, ate, drank, and slept among his books; he lived in the most sequestered and philosophical manner, scarcely ever leaving the city. His house was but one continued pile of books; his lower rooms were crowded with them, not only along the wainscot, but in piles to a considerable height, and so spread on the floor that there was not the least place for sitting down, much less for walking, except a long narrow passage leading from one room to the other. The porch of his house was, in the same manner, everywhere stuffed with books, as far as the projecting awning would secure them from rain. The staircase was lined all the way up with this library furniture, as were all the upper rooms. Magliabechi generally shut himself up all the day, and opened his doors in the evening to the men of letters who came to converse with him. His attention was so absorbed with his studies that he often forgot the calls of nature. He was negligent in his person, and was usually dressed in black, with a waistcoat reaching to his knees. His cloak, which was also black, served him for a morning gown in the day and for bedclothes at night; it was generally much patched, in consequence of the holes he burnt in it. He wore a large hat and a Florentine band round his neck. On one arm he carried a pan, in which was a constant fire for warming his hands, and his clothes bore evidence of their being often too nearly connected with it. His linen he usually wore until it fell to pieces. He always slept on his books; bound volumes served him for a mattress, those in boards for a pillow, and he covered himself with such as were merely stitched, throwing his cloak over all. His sole diet was eggs, bread, and water. *Disraeli.*

6908. BOOKS, Judging. Many readers judge of the power of a book by the shock it gives their feelings, as some savage tribes determine the power of their muskets by their recoil, that being considered best which fairly prostrates the purchaser. *Longfellow.*

6909. BOOKS, Need of More. The apt reply of a distinguished scholar of our own country to a benefactor of the institution of learning with which he was connected, when an increase of the library was the subject of discussion, deserves perpetual remembrance: "We need more books," said the professor. "More books!" said the merchant; "why, have you read through all you have already?" "No, I never expect to read them all." "Why, then, do you want more?" "Pray, sir, did you ever read

your dictionary through?" "Certainly not!" "Well, a library is my dictionary."

6910. BOOKS, Repositories. Books are faithful repositories, which may be awhile neglected or forgotten, but when they are opened again, will again impart their instruction. Memory once interrupted, is not to be recalled; written learning is a fixed luminary, which after the cloud that had hidden it has passed away, is again bright in its proper station. Tradition is but a meteor, which, if it once falls, cannot be rekindled. *Johnson.*

6911. BOOKS, Society of. I no sooner come into the library but I bolt the door to me, excluding lust, ambition, avarice, and all such vices whose nurse is idleness, the mother of ignorance and melancholy. In the very lap of eternity, amongst so many divine souls, I take my seat with so lofty a spirit, and sweet content, that I pity all our great ones and rich men, that know not this happiness. *Hensius.*

6912. BOOKS, Value of. To tell a good book is not really perplexing, any more than to distinguish a wholesome food. A good book, like a great nature, opens out a fine foreground, wherever we may open it, and like the breath of a summer's morning, invites us onward. It may be known by the number of fragmentary aphoristic sayings which may be gleaned from it, full of grace and pleasing truth, as flowers on that summer morning's walk. Bacon and Shakspeare have multitudes of such sayings. The Bible has more than all other books together. Books that soon perish, die because void of them. They make the difference between books of ideas, and books of mere words. The value of a book consists not in what it will do for our amusement, but in what it will communicate. Whether dealing with fancy or with fact, all books in their kind are dictionaries, and those are the best which yield most material for reflection. It is not fine writing, as many suppose, that makes fine books. Books are fine only in so far as they flow from sound and abundant knowledge, a picturesque and unobtrusive presentation of which is their infallible characteristic. *Grindon.*

6913. BORROWING, Conditions of. If thou hast of thine own, borrow not, since thou hast no need of it; and if thou hast nothing, borrow not, because thou wilt not have any means to pay. *Plutarch.*

6914. BOTTLES, Oriental. In oriental countries skin bottles, made by extracting the flesh of an animal and leaving the skin whole, except where the head and legs were cut off, were sometimes used. To these Christ refers in speaking of new wine in old bottles (Luke 5: 37). These became worn and rotten with age, and would not stand the pressure of the fermentation of new wine. Christ taught the impracticability of mingling Christianity and Judaism by this expressive figure, also by that of mending an old garment with new cloth.

6915. BOUNTY, Divine. Perillus, a friend of Alexander, besought of him portions for his daughters. The conqueror immediately ordered fifty talents to be given him. Perillus said, "Ten talents are enough." Alexander replied, "Enough for you to receive, but not enough for me to give." God gives "exceeding abundantly above all that we can ask or think."

6916. BOUNTY, Rule for. He that spends to his proportion is as brave as a prince; and a prince exceeding that is a prodigal: there is no gallantry beyond what is fit and decent. A comely beauty is better than a painted one. Unseemly bounty is waste both of wealth and wit. *Feltham.*

6917. BOY, A Converted. I knew a boy some years ago, whose father was a miserable drunken wretch and infidel, and he would not allow a praying man under his roof, for he said a man that prayed was nothing but a black-hearted hypocrite. Somebody got hold of his little boy and got him into the Sabbath-school, and he was converted. One day afterward the old man caught him praying, and he caught him by the collar and jerked him to his feet, commanding him with oaths never to be caught doing that again or he would have to leave home forever. Twice after that he caught him in the act of praying, and the last time told him to leave his house forever. The little fellow packed up his things in a handkerchief, went down into the kitchen where his mother was and bade her good-by, then went and bade his little brother and sisters good-by, and as he passed his father on his way to the door, he reached up his arms to put them around his father's neck, and said: "Good-by father. As long as I live I will pray for you," and he went down the street, but he had not gone a great while before his father came after him and said, "If that is Christianity, I want it." And the boy went back and prayed with his father and led him to Christ. *Moody.*

6918. BOY, Heroic. A boy who had been trained by the missionaries in the Loyalty Islands, set sail in a fishing boat with three other persons. A little way out they were capsized, but clung to the keel for support. After being sixteen hours in the water they drifted ashore, upon Woody Island, where neither water nor provisions of any kind could be procured. Their long exposure and exhaustion made it necessary that something should be done at once. The boy called Billy proposed to swim to another island, three and a-half miles away. In his exhaustion it was a most hazardous enterprise. On starting he said: "Suppose me catch the land, me see you again; suppose me die, good by." He reached the island, obtained aid and rescued his companions. All were full of gratitude and praise for him. He said, "Don't think of me. Thank God; it is God who has done it."

6919. BOYS, Danger to. We once saw the sentence "Perishable, don't switch off," chalked on a car belonging to a freight train. Careless conductors sometimes leave freight cars on side tracks for a day. Here was one that could not be left even one day off the main track. It had fruit, or something else, on board, which must be gotten to market at once.

A day lost might bring the fruit in a day late. Those boys in your class are "perishable property." Don't lose your hold of them an hour. Don't "switch" them off the track by any carelessness or irregularity, or dullness or severity of yours. Hold them firmly and steadily. *J. H. Vincent.*

6920. BOYS, Dull. Sir Isaac Newton was a great dunce in his early boyhood. One day the "bright boy" of the school gave him a kick in the stomach, which caused him severe pain. The insult stung him to the quick, and he resolved to make himself felt and respected by improved scholarship. He applied himself diligently to study, and, ere long, stood in his classes above the boy who had kicked him, and ultimately became the first scholar in the school. Oliver Goldsmith was a stupid child, and the teacher who taught him the alphabet was thought to have wrought a miracle. After he had written the "Traveler," people hardly believed him to be the author. Sir Walter Scott was known at the University of Edinburgh as "the great blockhead." His intense application and industry changed the title into that of "The Wizard of the North." His teacher once said to him, "Dunce you are and dunce you shall remain," but he nobly belied the prophecy.

6921. BOYS, Use for. "Get out of my way—what are you good for?" said a cross old man to a little bright-eyed boy who happened to stand in the way. The little fellow replied: "They make men out of such things as we are."

6922. BRAVERY, Inconstant. Some are brave one day, and cowards another, as great captains have often told me, from their own experience and observation. *Temple.*

6923. BRAVERY, Influence of. Antalcides said, "The youth are the walls of Sparta, and the points of their spears its bounds." To one inquiring why the Lacedæmonians fought with such short swords, he replied, "We come up close to our enemies."

6924. BRAVERY, Patriotic. During our late war, a Christian corporal seized the flag, several bearers of which had been already shot down, saying to a comrade as he bore it to immediate death, "If I fall, tell my dear wife that I die with a good hope in Christ, and that I am glad to give my life for my country." A lieutenant-colonel, who had been overwhelmed with fear amid the perils of battle, was deeply impressed at the act, and said, "I can never forget that, and I want to become a Christian, too, for I know there is a reality in religion."

6925. BRAVERY, True. True bravery is shown by performing without witnesses what one might be capable of doing before all the world. *La Rochefoucauld.*

6926. BREAD, Cost of. Water, which is one of the great necessaries of life, may in general be gratuitously procured; but it has been well observed, that if bread, the other great necessary of human life, could be procured on terms equally cheap and easy, there would be much

more reason to fear that men would become brutes for the want of something to do, rather than philosophers from the possession of leisure.
Colton.

6927. BREAD, Fragments of. Arabs have a strong respect for wheat in any shape. If a morsel of bread falls to the ground, an Arab will gather it up with his right hand, kiss it, touch his forehead with it, and place it in a recess, or on a wall, where the fowls of the air might find it; for they say, "We must not tread under foot the gift of God." I have seen this reverence exhibited constantly by all classes of people, by masters, servants, and even by little children, Moslems, and Christians. *Domestic Life in Palestine.*

6928. BREAD, Praying for and Seeking. A sick mother and her little girl were living in a very wretched attic. It was cold and dark one morning, when the hungry child awoke, and remembered that there was no bread for breakfast. Nettie's mother had often told her that the God who feeds tiny birds will not refuse bread to a little child who asks for it. The little girl slipped quietly out of bed, that she might not awake her mother, and kneeling down by the bedside, said slowly, "Give us this day our daily bread." The bare room seemed to mock the child's prayer; but she had no sooner asked God for the bread than she determined to seek it. Wrapping her shabby cloak about her, she went down the long staircase, and through the dark alley, into the busy street. No one noticed the hungry little girl, and she was beginning to wonder where God kept his bread, when a sudden turn of the street showed her a large and well-filled baker's shop. "This," thought she, "is the place." The baker looked kindly at the little eager face that entered his shop so confidently. "I've come for it," she said. "Come for what?" "My daily bread," she said, pointing to the loaves. "I'll take two, if you please; one for mother, and one for me." "All right," said the baker, putting them into a bag, and giving them to his little customer, who started at once into the street. "Stop, you little rogue!" he said, roughly; "where is your money?" "I haven't any," she said, simply. "Haven't any!" he repeated, angrily; "you little thief, what brought you here, then?" The words frightened the child, who, bursting into tears, said, "Mother is sick, and I am so hungry. In my prayers I said, 'Give us this day our daily bread;' and then I thought God meant me to fetch it; and so I came." The baker was softened by the child's simple tale, and he sent her back to her mother with a well-filled basket. As the poor sufferer received the unexpected supply, she softly said, "The God of the fatherless answers prayer. I ought to call you 'Faith!' my child."

6929. BREAD, The Worst. Upon the question, What is the worst bread which is eaten? one answered, in respect of the coarseness thereof, "Bread made of beans." Another said, "Bread made of acorns." But the third hit the truth, and said, "Bread taken out of other men's mouths, who are the true proprietors thereof."

Such bread may be sweet in the mouth to taste, but is not wholesome in the stomach to digest.
Thos. Fuller.

6930. BREAD OF LIFE, Hunger for the. The primitive Greeks fed only upon acorns, but afterward learned the art of wheat culture and bread making. They discarded their former food, and counted it only fit for swine. When a man has once tasted the bread of life he has no more desire for the "flesh-pots of Egypt," but cries, "Lord, ever, evermore give us of this bread." It is a strange and an unnatural thing for a Christian to turn again to the "beggarly elements," the husks and vanities of the world for satisfaction. Having eaten of the fruits and bread of the kingdom of grace, it is a sad day when the hunger for them is lost. It should increase till we feast with the Master in his heavenly kingdom.

6931. BREAD UPON THE WATERS, Import of. Rice is the food most used in Egypt. Every year, when the snow melts off the mountains, the river Nile rises and overflows its banks, and covers all the country round it with water. Rain is scarcely ever seen in Egypt, and it would be a desert but for the river that waters it. The people set down stakes, every man to mark out his own land, before the waters come. When the Nile has risen, and all the land is covered with water, they go out in little boats to sow their rice by casting it on the waters. The rice sinks in the mud below, and when these waters are gone they find that it has taken root and sprouted, and it grows up and gives them a harvest. This is "Casting their bread upon the waters, and finding it after many days." *Anon.*

6932. BREVITY Advised. Talk to the point, and stop when you have reached it. The faculty some possess of making one idea cover a quire of paper, is not good for much. Be comprehensive in all you say or write. To fill a volume upon nothing is a credit to nobody; though Lord Chesterfield wrote a very clever poem upon nothing. There are men who get one idea into their heads, and but one, and they make the most of it. You can see it, and almost feel it, when in their presence. On all occasions it is produced, till it is worn as thin as charity. They remind one of a twenty-four pounder discharged at a humming bird. You hear a tremendous noise, see a volume of smoke, but you look in vain for the effects. The bird is scattered to atoms. Just so with the idea. It is enveloped in a cloud, and lost amid the rumblings of words and flourishes. Short letters, sermons, speeches, and paragraphs, are favorites with us. Commend us to the young man who wrote to his father: "Dear sir, I am going to be married;" and also to the old gentleman, who replied, "Dear son, go ahead." Such are the men for action. They do more than they say. The half is not told in their cases. They are worth their weight in gold for every purpose in life. Reader, be short; and we will be short with the advice.
John Neal.

6933. BREVITY, Example of. The Duke of

Wellington wrote to Dr. Hutton for information as the scientific acquirements of a young officer who had been under his instructions. The doctor thought he could not do less than answer the question verbally, and made an appointment accordingly. When Wellington saw him he said, "I am obliged to you, doctor, for the trouble you have taken. Is —— fit for the post?" Clearing his throat, Dr. Hutton began, "No man more so; I can—" "That's quite sufficient," said Wellington; "I know how valuable your time is; mine, just now, is equally so. I will not detain you any longer. Good morning." *Chambers' Journal.*

6934. BREVITY, Motto of. That earnest minister, Dr. Cotton Mather, had inscribed in large letters over his study door the admonition "BE SHORT." It is appropriate to preachers, prayer-leaders, teachers and public speakers. The best efforts become tiresome if protracted.

6935. BRIBERY, Influence of. The Spartans were the only people that for a while seemed to disdain the love of money; but the contagion still spreading, even they at last yielded to its allurements, and every man sought private emoluments without attending to the good of his country. "That which has been is that which shall be!" *Bp. Horne.*

6936. BRIBERY, Knavery of. A thief coming to rob a house would have stopped the barking of a dog by throwing sops to him. "Away with you!" said the dog; "I had my suspicions of you before, but this excess of civility assures me that you are a rogue." *Æsop.*

6937. BRIBERY, Proof against. Great presents were sent to Epaminondas, the celebrated Theban general by the king of Persia, which he rejected. At the same time he had but one upper garment, and had to stay in-doors when it required washing or mending. He contemned riches, and when he died, nothing was found in his house but a small iron spit; nothing in which to bury his body, and his funeral was at the public expense.

6938. BRIBERY, Resisting. A Roman was appointed judge between his son and the province of Macedonia. When all the parties had been heard, the father said, "It is evident that my son has suffered himself to be bribed, therefore I deem him unworthy of the republic and of my house, and I order him to depart from my presence." Xenocrates the philosopher stood firm against temptations and bribery. Philip of Macedon attempted to gain his confidence with money, but with no success. Alexander in this imitated his father, and sent some of his friends with fifty talents for the philosopher. They were introduced, and supped with Xenocrates. The repast was small, frugal, and elegant without ostentation. On the morrow the officers of Alexander wished to pay down the fifty talents; but the philosopher asked them whether they had not perceived from the entertainment of the preceding day that he was not in want of money. "Tell your master," said he, "to keep his money; he has more people to maintain than I have." Phocion, the Athenian, was celebrated for his virtues, private as well as public. Philip, as well as his son Alexander, attempted to bribe him, but to no purpose. Antipater, who succeeded in the government of Macedonia after the death of Alexander, also attempted to corrupt him, but with the same success as his royal predecessor; and when a friend had observed to Phocion that he could so refuse the generous offers of his patrons, yet he should consider the good of his children, and accept them for their sake, Phocion calmly replied that if his children were like him, they could maintain themselves as well as their father had done; but if they behaved otherwise, he declared that he was unwilling to leave them anything, which might either supply their extravagances or encourage their debaucheries. *Buck.*

6939. BRIBERY, Witnesses of. The following case was tried before a Cadi at Smyrna. A poor man claimed a house which a rich man had usurped. The former held his deeds and documents to prove his right; but the latter had provided a number of witnesses to invalidate his title. In order to support their evidence effectually, he presented the Cadi with a bag containing 500 ducats. When the day arrived for hearing the cause, the poor man told his story, and produced his writings, but could not support his case by witnesses; the other rested the whole case on his witnesses, and on his adversary's defect in law, who could produce none; he urged the Cadi, therefore, to give sentence in his favor. After the most pressing solicitations, the judge calmly drew out from under his sofa the bag of ducats which the rich man had given him as a bribe, saying to him very gravely, "You have been much mistaken in the suit, for if the poor man could produce no witnesses in confirmation of his right, I myself can produce at least five hundred." He then threw away the bag with reproach and indignation, and decreed the house to the poor plaintiff.

6940. BRIDE, Serving for a. It is related that a rich saddler, whose daughter was afterwards married to Dunk, the celebrated Earl of Halifax, ordered in his will that she should lose the whole of her fortune if she did not marry a saddler. The young Earl of Halifax, in order to win the bride, served an apprenticeship of seven years to a saddler, and afterwards bound himself to the rich saddler's daughter for life. *Anon.*

6941. BROKEN THINGS, The Value of. It is on crushed grain that man is fed; it is by bruised plants that he is restored to health. It was by broken pitchers that Gideon triumphed; it was from a wasted barrel and empty cruse that the prophet was sustained; it was on boards and broken pieces of the ship that Paul and his companions were saved. It was amid the fragments of broken humanity that the promise of the higher life was given; though not a bone of him was broken, yet it is by the broken life of Christ that his people shall live eternally; it was by the scattering of the Jews that the Gentiles were brought in; it was by the bruised and torn bodies of the saints that the truth was so made to triumph that it be came a saying, that "the blood of the martyrs was the seed of the church." It is by this broken box (Mark 14 : 3), that throughout the wide world it is proclaimed how blessed and glorious a thing it is to do a whole thing to Christ. When the true story of all things shall be known, then will it appear how precious in God's sight, how powerful in his hands, were many broken things. Broken earthly hopes will be found to have been necessary to the bringing of the better hope which endures forever. Broken bodily constitutions will be found to have been needful in some cases to the attainment of that land where the body shall be weary and sore no more; broken earthly fortunes, to the winning of the wealth beyond the reach of rust and moth and thief; broken earthly honor, to the being crowned with the diadem which fadeth not away.

P. B. Power.

6942. BROTHER, Betrayal of a. John Diazius, a Spaniard, became a Protestant. His brother Alphonsus Diazius, hearing of this, resolved to reclaim him to Romanism or slay him. He first approached him with affectionate and brotherly kindness, and used all his influence, but in vain. He left him in a friendly manner, and hired an assassin to whom he gave a letter of introduction to his brother. The assassin delivered it, and while the brother was reading it, he drew forth a concealed hatchet and cleft his skull. For this Alphonsus was applauded by the Papists, but his conscience smote him unendurably, and during the Council of Trent he hung himself.

6943. BROTHER, Christ our. A Glasgow boy was beguiled from home till late one dark and stormy night by his love of stories. To get home he had to pass a graveyard. "I wish I were home," he said. He was a timid little boy, and began to weep. He was afraid of the dark night and the rolling thunder, and of the graveyard. After a while he got courage to say, "Keep the door open, and cry after me till I am out of hearing, and I will not be afraid." The other boys agreed, and opened the door to let him out. But just at that moment there came another flash of lightning, and another roll of thunder, and he and they ran back and cowered beside the fire. "Come with me, some of you," he next said. "Come two of you; I am afraid to go alone." But the other boys were very little older than himself. And now they also were afraid, and they began to cry. Eight o'clock! Nine! "Oh, I wish I were at home!" Ten! and still he is afraid to go. Half-past ten! eleven! "I wish—I wish I were at home." He went to the door a third time. He still saw nothing but the black, wet night. He cried more bitterly than before. He cried as if his heart would break—"I wish—I wish—I wish I were at home!" While he was sobbing out these words he saw a star of light twinkling through the gloom. It came nearer and nearer, and grew bigger the nearer it came. Joy! It was light from his father's house! His brother, carrying a lantern, had come to fetch him home. It was as if daylight had come back again. His crying was at an end; his tears were dried up. He became bold as a lion. The fear of the graveyard went away, and he stepped out into the darkness with a smile on his face. His brother was by his side, and the light of his brother's lantern would light him home! Now Christ does for his dying brothers and sisters just what this boy's brother did for him. He comes for them, with light from their Father's house, and takes them by the hand to lead them home. *Dr. A. MacLeod.*

6944. BROTHER, Discovery of a. Bauer, who commanded the Russian cavalry in Holstein, was a soldier of fortune, whose family and country were unknown to every one. When encamped near Husum, he took a way of discovering himself as novel as it was amiable. He invited all his field officers, and some others, to dine with him, and sent his adjutant to bring a miller and his wife, who lived in the neighborhood, to the entertainment. The poor couple came, very much afraid of the summons, and quite confused when they appeared before the Muscovite General. Bauer, seeing this, bade them be quite easy, for he only intended to show them kindness, and had sent for them to dine with him that day; at the same time, he conversed familiarly with them about the country. At dinner, the General placed the miller and his wife one on each hand, and nearest to him, and paid particular attention to them. In the course of the entertainment he asked the miller many questions about his family and relations. The miller stated that he was the eldest son of his father, who left the mill he then possessed, and that he had two brothers and one sister. "Have you no other brother?" said the General. "No," replied the miller; "I had once another brother, but he went away with the soldiers when he was very young, and must have long ago been killed in the wars." The General, observing the company much surprised at his conversation with the miller, said to them, "Brother soldiers, you have always been curious to know who I was, and whence I came. I now inform you that this is the place of my nativity, and you have heard from this miller, who is my elder brother, what my family is." Then turning to the astonished miller and his wife, the General embraced them, saying that he was the brother they had supposed dead. The General then invited the whole company to meet him next day at the mill, where a plentiful entertainment was provided. *Anon.*

6945. BROTHERHOOD, Claims of. At the last meeting of the Woburn Conference, Farmer Allen, of Wakefield, related the following anecdote: "One Sunday morning, while a certain deacon was preparing for church, a wandering wayfarer, or, in modern parlance, a 'tramp,' appeared at his door, pleaded his hunger, and begged for something to eat. The deacon looked solemn, and frowningly, but reluctantly, got a loaf of bread and began to cut it, but while doing so took occasion to admonish the beggar concerning the error of his ways. After reminding him that it was the holy Sabbath that he was desecrating, he asked him if he knew how to pray? 'No,' was the reply. 'Then,' said the deacon, 'I'll teach you,' and he commenced to repeat the Lord's prayer. But just as he uttered the first words, 'Our Father,' the beggar interrupted him with the question, 'What! is he your father and mine too?' 'Yes,' the deacon replied. 'Why,' exclaimed the beggar, 'we are brothers, then, ain't we? Can't you cut that slice a little thicker?'" The convention forgot its solemnity long enough to indulge in the first and only hearty laugh on the occasion.

6946. BROTHERHOOD, Condescension of. The King of England had instructed his representative to sue for the release of certain Huguenots, who had been thrown into the Bastile for their religion. "What would your master, the King of England, say, if I sue for the release of the prisoners in Newgate?" was the French king's reply. The ambassador's reply was, "Your Majesty may have every one of them if you will claim them as your brethren." The Lord Jesus Christ makes this claim in behalf of all on the earth who receive him.

6947. BROTHERHOOD, Nature's. There is a brotherhood between us and flowers and trees, between the green things that wither, and the bright and beautiful ones that die. The dead violet is the fragrant memorial of the infant that drooped and died—the still unscattered dust of the flower that fades in June brings to our remembrance the fair form that was suddenly breathed on by some mysterious emissary, and passed away in her noon. Another falls from the tree of life like that sere leaf. In the woods in winter we cannot be long alone; visions and associations will gather around us—departed forms, and almost forgotten faces will rise like their shadows from the grave, and almost forgotten faces will come forth from the past, and bear witness to the words which, like monumental inscriptions on the pavement, the feet of traffic are continually defacing, but which the sweep of years renders again clear and legible: "All flesh is as grass; the grass withereth, and the flower fadeth." *Cumming.*

6948. BROTHERS, Love of. After the death of Darius, king of Persia, his two sons, Ariamenes and Xerxes, claimed the kingdom, the first because of his seniority, and the second because of possession, for he held the sceptre in his brother's absence after his father's death. They met as private citizens, Xerxes making presents to Ariamenes, with this address: "With these presents your brother Xerxes expresses the honor he has for you; and if by the judgment and suffrage of the Persians I be declared king, I place you next to myself." Ariamenes answered: "I accept the presents, but presume the kingdom of Persia to be my right. Yet for all my younger brethren I shall have an honor, but for Xerxes is the first place." The kingdom was adjudged to Xerxes by Artabanes to whom the question was referred. Thereupon, Ariamenes took

Xerxes by the hand and seated him on the throne, and was himself made next in the kingdom by Xerxes. With fraternal devotion Ariamenes filled his office, and was slain in the naval engagement at Salamis, contending for his brother's honor.

6949. BUILDING, Enemies of. If we would be temple builders we must have a temple builder's lot. I mean, hold a sword in one hand and a trowel in the other. Faithful Nehemiahs have many Sanballats to deal with. Building the walls of the New Jerusalem is what the profane and formalist do not approve of. Would you be a Nehemiah, and no Sanballat to oppose you? *Whitefield.*

6950. BUILDING for Eternity. Piso built a house, in the construction of which he bestowed the greatest care upon every part. Augustus Cæsar commended him, saying, "You cheer my heart, who build as if Rome would be eternal." Character requires greater care, for it shall live when Piso's house is scattered in dust and the world itself is dissolved.

6951. BUILDING Little by Little. A boy watched a large building as the workmen from day to day carried up bricks and mortar. "My son," said his father, "you seem much interested in the bricklayers. Do you think of learning the trade?" "No," he replied, "I was thinking what a little thing a brick is, and what great houses are built by laying one brick upon another." "Very true, my son; never forget it. So it is in all great works; all your learning is but one lesson added to another. If a man could walk all round the world, it would be by putting one foot before another. Your whole life will be made up of a succession of moments. Learn from this not to despise little things. Be not discouraged by great labors. They become easy if divided into parts. You could not jump over a mountain, but step by step takes you to the other side. Do not fear, therefore, to attempt great things. Always remember that the large building rose by laying one brick upon another." *Presbyterian.*

6952. BUILDING, Uncertain. In countries subject to earthquakes the houses are built low and light. This is wise where the earth itself is unstable. The lesson is for all worldly affairs. The earth is unreliable, and our structures may be overthrown at any moment. Make sure of an eternal mansion in heaven.

6953. BURDEN, Crying under the. A minister was moving his library up stairs. His little boy wanted to help him, so he gave him the biggest book he could find, and the little fellow tugged at it till he got it about half way up, and then he sat down and cried. His father found him, and just took him in his arms, big book and all, and carried him up stairs. So Christ will carry you and all your burdens. *Moody.*

6954. BURDEN, Loss of a. Now I saw in my dream that the highway up which Christian was to go was fenced on either side with a wall, and that wall was called Salvation. Up this way, therefore, did burdened Christian run, but not without great difficulty, because of the load on his back. He ran thus till he came at a place somewhat ascending; and upon that place stood a cross, and a little below, in the bottom, a sepulchre. So I saw in my dream, that just as Christian came up with the cross, his burden loosed from off his shoulders, and fell from off his back, and began to tumble; and so continued to do, till it came to the mouth of the sepulchre, where it fell in, and I saw it no more. *Bunyan.*

6955. BURIAL a Fiction. As the soul is the man, and the material body only his house while upon earth; a man is never really buried. No human being since the beginning of the world has ever yet been buried—no, not even for a few minutes, buried! How can a living soul be buried? Man is where his conscious being is, his memory, his love, his imagination; and since these cannot be put in the grave, the man is never put there. So far from being our "last home," the grave is not a home at all; for we never are laid in it, or go near it. "How shall we bury you?" said Crito to Socrates, before he drank the poison. "Just as you please," replied Socrates, "if only you can catch me!" Socrates knew better than that he should die. He saw through death as a vapor curtain through which he would burst into another life. "I shall not die; I shall never die," is what every man ought to say, and energetically to think. "I shall never die; I shall never be buried; bury me if you can catch me." *Grindon.*

6956. BURIAL, Miraculous. St. Antony visited Paul the hermit, who was very aged and very holy. He found him in his cave in the attitude of prayer with hands outspread rigid in death. He prayed, wrapped the corpse in a mantle, and was sad because he had no spade with which to dig a grave for it. Then two lions came running from the inner part of the desert, their manes tossing on their necks. They came straight to the corpse of the blessed old man, wagging their tails, and roaring with mighty growls, so that Antony understood them to lament, as best they could. Then they began to claw the ground with their paws, and, carrying out the sand eagerly, dug a place large enough to hold a man; then at once, as if begging a reward for their work, they came to Antony, drooping their necks, and licking his hands and feet. But he perceived that they prayed a blessing from him; and at once, bursting into praise of Christ, because even dumb animals felt that he was God, he said, "Lord, without whose word not a leaf of the tree drops, nor one sparrow falls to the ground, give to them as thou knowest how to give;" and sent them away. Antony then laid the body of Paul in the grave and heaped the earth upon it. This event is narrated by Jerome, and declared to be authentic.

6957. BURNT-OFFERING, Import of the. "Thou shalt love the Lord thy God with all thy heart, and with all thy soul, and with all thy mind." I cannot doubt that the type refers to this in speaking so particularly of the parts of the burnt-offering; for "the head," "the fat," "the legs," "the inwards," are all distinctly enumerated. "The head" is the well-known emblem of the thoughts; "the legs," the emblem of the walk; and "the inwards," the constant and familiar symbol of the feelings and affections of the heart. The meaning of "the fat" may not be quite so obvious, though here also Scripture helps us to the solution. It represents the energy not of one limb or faculty, but the general health and vigor of the whole. In Jesus these were all surrendered, and all without spot or blemish. Had there been but one thought in the mind of Jesus which was not perfectly given to God; had there been but one affection in the heart of Jesus which was not yielded to his Father's will; had there been but one step in the walk of Jesus which was not taken for God and not for his own pleasure; then he could not have offered himself or been accepted as "a whole burnt-offering to Jehovah." But Jesus gave up all; he reserved nothing. All was burnt, all consumed upon the altar. Such was "the whole burnt-offering"—the entire surrender of self to God in everything. *A. Jukes.*

6958. BUSINESS, Ashamed of. Never shrink from doing anything which your business calls you to. The man who is above his business, may one day find his business above him. *Samuel Drew.*

6959. BUSINESS, Failures in. There were seven thousand, seven hundred and forty failures in business during the year 1875, involving liabilities to the amount of over two hundred millions of dollars. In the five years, 1871–1875, the whole number of failures reported was twenty-five thousand, seven hundred and thirty-seven, and the liabilities of these bankruptcies were nearly eight hundred millions of dollars ($794,111,153). It is estimated that eighty-five per cent. of all who go into business, fail in the course of a few years; and that only three out of every hundred gain more than a living. Such are the uncertainties of trade, with all its opportunities, its shrewd and daring operators, its varied experience, its versatility, its capital, its enterprise, and its power over men. *Talmage.*

6960. BUSINESS, Fidelity Required in. A rich farmer in Oneida county, N. Y., where Millerism was rampant, joined the society. The believers, all of them poor, welcomed the rich convert and told him that they were in the habit of having all things in common, as the end was at hand; the Master was coming speedily. The man said he would study the Bible on that subject, pray over it, and give his decision as to surrendering his property, at the next meeting. When the time came, he reported that while dwelling on the subject and seeking divine direction, the words of the Master had been deeply impressed upon him, and he had determined to obey them: "Occupy till I come."

6961. BUSINESS, God's Care for Our. A king appointed a very busy nobleman to be his ambassador to a distant court. He declined the honor on the ground of his family and urgent business concerns at home. The king answered, "You must go; only do you mind my concerns heartily and I will take care of yours." So God says to men.

6962. BUSINESS, Honesty in. An incident is related of Mr. A. T. Stewart's first day's business. A woman came to buy calico, and a clerk told her that the colors were fast and would not wash out. Mr. Stewart indignantly remonstrated with the salesman. "What do you mean by saying what you know to be untrue? The calico will fade; she will demand her money back, and she will be right. I don't want goods represented for what they are not." "Look here, Mr. Stewart," said the clerk, "if those are going to be your principles in trade, I'm going to look for another situation. You won't last long." But Mr. Stewart did last.

6963. BUSINESS to be Honored. Every man is a debtor to his profession, from the which, as men do of course seek to receive countenance and profit, so ought they of duty to endeavor themselves, by way of amends, to be a help and ornament thereunto.   *Bacon.*

6964. BUSINESS, Laws of. The planets have a two-fold action in their orbits and on their axes, the one motion not interfering, but carried on simultaneously, and in perfect harmony with the other; so must it be that man's two-fold activities round the heavenly and the earthly centre disturb not nor jar with each other; so that man may be at once "diligent in business and fervent in spirit, serving the Lord."   *Caird.*

6965. BUSINESS a Means of Grace. Dr. Hawes, in his biography of Norman Smith, a merchant in his congregation, says he never grew in grace more readily or shone brighter as a Christian than the last six or seven years of his life, when he had the greatest amount of business on his hands. From the time when he devoted all to God and resolved to pursue his business as a part of his religion, he found no tendency in his worldly engagement to chill his piety or enchain his affections to . earth. His business became to him a means of grace, and helped him forward in the divine life, just as truly as the reading the Scriptures and prayer.

6966. BUSINESS, Prayer before. Lord Ashley, before he charged at the battle of Edge Hill, made this short prayer: "O Lord! thou knowest how busy I must be this day; if I forget thee, do not thou forget me."   *Hopkins.*

6967. BUSINESS, Qualities for. Rare almost as great poets—rarer, perhaps, than veritable saints and martyrs—are consummate men of business. A man, to be excellent in this way, must not only be variously gifted, but his gifts should be nicely proportioned to one another. He must have in a high degree that virtue which men have always found the least pleasant of virtues—prudence. His prudence, however, will not be merely of a cautious and quiescent order, but that which, being ever actively engaged, is more fitly called discretion than prudence. Such a man must have an almost ig-

nominious love of details, blended (and this is a rare combination) with a high power of imagination, enabling him to look along extended lines of possible action, and put these details in their right places. He requires a great knowledge of character, with that exquisite tact which feels unerringly the right moment when to act. A discreet rapidity must pervade all the movements of his thought and action. He must be singularly free from vanity, and is generally found to be an enthusiast, who has the art to conceal his enthusiasm.   *Helps.*

6968. BUSINESS, Rivalries of. Two merchants became active enemies through the rivalries of business. One of them was converted, and sought counsel how to treat his rival. He was advised, "When any one asks for an article you have not, recommend him to go over to your neighbor." The latter being informed who sent them by the customers, was overcome by his rival's altered conduct. A reconciliation was effected, and they became friends and Christian brothers.

6969. BUSINESS, Secular. The founder of Rome marked out that city with a plough, having a brazen ploughshare drawn by a bull and a cow yoked together. Where a gate was required the plough was lifted out and the furrow discontinued. Wherever the plough touched was sacred ground not to be passed over. The whole wall was sacred except the gateways. They made the common mistake of counting the ways of trade and commerce as unholy, and carrying no elevating ideas, such as Christianity gives, into them.

6970. BUSINESS, Success in. Isaac Rich, who left a million and three-quarters to found the Boston University of the M. E. Church, began business thus: At eighteen he went from Cape Cod to Boston with three or four dollars in his possession, and looked about for something to do, rising early, walking far, observing closely, reflecting much. Soon he had an idea; he bought three bushels of oysters, hired a wheelbarrow, found a piece of board, bought six small plates, six iron forks, a three-cent pepper-box, and one or two other things. He was at the oyster boat buying his oysters at three o'clock in the morning, wheeled them three miles, set up his board near a market, and began business. He sold out his oysters as fast as he could get them, at a good profit. He repeated this experiment morning after morning until he saved $130, with which he bought a horse and wagon, and had five cents left. "How are you going to board your horse?" asked a stable-keeper who witnessed this audacious transaction. "I am going to board him at your stable." "But you're a minor," replied this Yankee, "and, mind, I can't trust you more than a week." The next morning the lad, who had established a good credit with oyster men, bought thirteen bushels of remarkably fine oysters, which he sold in the course of the day at a profit of $17. So he was able to pay for his horse's board. And right there in the same market he continued to deal in oysters and fish for forty years, became king of that business, and ended by founding a college.   *Zion's Herald.*

6971. BUSINESS, Test of. When Professor Finney was holding meetings in the city of Edinburgh, a gentleman called upon him in great distress of mind. He had listened to Mr. Finney's sermon on the previous evening, and it had torn away his "refuge of lies." Mr. Finney pointed out to him the way of life clearly, as his only hope of salvation. The weeping man assured him that he was willing to give up all for Jesus; that he knew of nothing he would reserve. "Then let us go upon our knees and tell God of that," said Mr. Finney. So both knelt at the altar, and Mr. Finney prayed: "O Lord, this man declares that he is prepared to take thee as his God, and to cast himself upon thy care now and for ever." The man responded, "Amen," heartily. Mr. Finney continued: "O Lord, this man vows that he is ready to give his wife, family, and all their interests up to thee." Another hearty "Amen" from the man. He went on: "O Lord, he says that he is willing to give thee his business, whatever it may be, and conduct it for thy glory." The man was silent—no response. Mr. Finney was surprised at his silence, and asked, "Why do you not say 'Amen' to this?" "Because the Lord will not take my business, sir; I am in the spirit trade," he answered. Any business which cannot be consecrated to Christ and done in his name must be abandoned or heaven will be lost.

6972. BUSINESS, Useful. If a man with a scythe should mow the empty air, he would sooner be weary than he who sweats with toil in cutting the standing corn. Business is the salt of life, which not only gives a grateful smack to it, but dries up those crudities that would offend, preserves from putrefaction, and drives off all those blowing flies that would corrupt it. There are in business three things necessary,—knowledge, temper, and time. Unless a man knows what he is going about, he is liable to go astray, or to lose much time in finding out the right course. If he want temper, he will be sure not to want trouble. It must be left to judgment to discern when the season is proper.   *Feltham.*

6973. BUSINESS, Unsuccessful. The man who never failed in business cannot possibly know whether he has any "grit" in him, or is worth a button. It is the man who fails, then rises, who is really great in his way. Peter Cooper failed in making hats, failed as a cabinet-maker, locomotive builder, and grocer; but as often as he failed he "tried and tried again," until he could stand upon his feet alone, then crowned his victory by giving a million dollars to help the poor boys in times to come. Horace Greeley tried three or four lines of business before he founded the *Tribune*, and made it worth a million dollars. Patrick Henry failed at everything he undertook, until he made himself the orator of his age and nation. Stephen A. Douglas made dinner tables, and bedsteads, and bureaus, many a long year before he made himself a "giant" on the floor of Con-

gress. Abraham Lincoln failed to make both ends meet by chopping wood, failed to earn his salt in the galley slave life of a Mississippi flat-boatman; he had not even wit enough to run a grocery, and yet he made himself a grand character of the nineteenth century. General Grant failed at everything; he learned to tan hides, but could not sell leather enough to purchase a pair of breeches; a dozen years ago, "he brought up" on top of a woodpile, "teaming it" to town for forty dollars a month; and yet he is head of a great nation. The lesson for every young man is this: As long as you have the health, and have power to do, go ahead; if you fail at one thing, try another, and a third—a dozen even. Look at the spider; nineteen times it tried to throw out its web to its place of attachment, and on the twentieth succeeded. The young man who has the gift of continuance is the one whose foot will be able to breast the angry waters of human discouragement.   *Graphic.*

6974. BUSY-BODIES, Work of. It is observed of the hen that, loathing the plenty of meat that is cast before her on a clean floor, she will be scratching in a hole or spurring the dunghill in search of one single musty grain. So these over-busy people, neglecting such obvious and common things into which any man may inquire and talk of without offence, cannot be satisfied unless they rake into the private and concealed evils of every family in the neighborhood. It was smartly said by the Egyptian, who, being asked what it was he carried so closely, replied, it was therefore covered that it might be secret.   *Plutarch.*

6975. CALAMITY, Benefit of. A storm led to the discovery of the gold mines in California. A storm has driven some to the discovery of the richer mines of the love of God in Christ.

6976. CALAMITY, Sympathy for. There was an Englishman in Chicago the winter before the fire, who was much impressed with the sudden growth of the city. He went back to Manchester, where he told the people about the city only forty years old, with all its fine buildings, its colleges, its churches. It was, he thought, a most wonderful city. But no one seemed to take an interest in Chicago. "But," he says, "one day the news came flashing over the wires that Chicago was on fire. The moment the people heard about the Chicago fire they became suddenly interested about Chicago. Then every man that he had tried to tell about Chicago became suddenly interested, and they couldn't hear too much." The news came flashing over the wires that half the city was burnt. He said, "There were men there couldn't help but weep." At last the news came that 100,000 people were burned out of their houses, and were in danger of starvation unless immediate help was sent. Then these men came forward and gave their thousands. It was the calamity of Chicago that brought out the love and pity of those men. In Chicago men went to bed on Sunday night millionaires, and Monday morning all was swept away. I didn't see a man shed a tear over the loss of his property. At last the news came flashing over the wires that help was coming —that a delegation was coming from New York that was bringing clothing and food and money—and I saw men weep like little children then. It was that that touched the heart of Chicago. I never loved America so much in my life. I loved the whole world. We couldn't help but love others, because they loved us; and so it was the calamity of Adam that brought out God's love. *Moody.*

6977. CALUMNY, Allegory of. A traveler, setting out upon a long journey, was assailed on the road by curs, mastiffs, and half-grown puppies, which came out from their kennels to bark at him as he passed along. He often dismounted from his horse to drive them back with stones and sticks into their hiding-places. This operation was repeated every day, and sometimes as often as twenty times a day. The consequence was, that more than half the traveler's time was consumed in chasing these dogs and puppies. At last he was overtaken by a neighbor, who was going the same road, but who had set out a long time after him. The latter traveler was very much surprised to find the other no further on his journey, and, on hearing the reason, "Alas!" said he, "is it possible that you have lost your time and wasted your strength in this idle occupation? These same animals have beset me all along the road; but I have saved my time and my labor in taking no notice of their barking, while you have lost yours in resenting insults which did you no harm, and in chasing dogs and puppies, whose manners you can never mend." *Anon.*

6978. CALUMNY, Reproof of. Some young ladies at the house of Rev. B. Jacobs, of Cambridgeport, were one day talking about one of their female friends. As he entered the room, he heard the epithets "odd," "singular," etc., applied. He asked, and was told the name of the young lady in question, and then said, very gravely, "Yes, she is an odd young lady; she is a very odd young lady; I consider her extremely singular." He then added, very impressively, "She was never heard to speak ill of an absent friend." The rebuke was not forgotten.

6979. CALUMNY, Spread of. Calumny crosses oceans, scales mountains, and traverses deserts with greater ease than the Scythian Abaris, and, like him, rides upon a poisoned arrow. *Colton.*

6980. CALUMNY, Treatment of. Boerhave, who had many enemies, used to say that he never thought it necessary to repeat their calumnies. "They are sparks," said he, "which, if you do not blow them, will go out of themselves. The surest method against scandal is to live it down by perseverance in well doing, and by prayer to God that he would cure the distempered minds of those who traduce and injure us."

6981. CALUMNY, Voracity of. Like the tiger that seldom desists from pursuing man after having once preyed upon human flesh, the person who has once gratified his appetite with calumny, makes ever after the most agreeable feast on murdered reputation. *Goldsmith.*

6982. CALUMNY, Wise Use of. Philip of Macedon was wont to say that he was much beholden to the Athenian orators; since by the slanderous and opprobrious manner in which they spoke of him, they were the means of making him a better man, both in word and deed. "For," added he, "I every day do my best endeavor, as well by my sayings as doings, to prove them liars."

6983. CALVARY, Mount. Mount Calvary is lord of the Sacred Mountains, and by its baptism of blood and agony, its moral grandeur, and the intense glory that beams from its summit, is worthy to crown the immortal group. Its moral height no man can measure, for though its base is on the earth, its top is lost in the heaven of heavens. The angels hover around the dazzling summit, struggling in vain to scale its highest point, which has never yet been fanned by even an immortal wing. The divine eye alone embraces its length and breadth, and depth and height. Oh, what associations cluster around it! what mysteries hover there! and what revelations it makes to the awe-struck beholder! Mount Calvary! at the mention of that name the universe thrills with a new emotion, and heaven trembles with a new anthem, in which pity and exultation mingle in strange yet sweet accord! *Headley.*

6984. CALVARY, Safety on. Away on the frontier of our country, out on the prairies, where men sometimes go to hunt, or for other purposes, the grass in the dry season sometimes catches fire, and you will see the flames uprise twenty or thirty feet high, and roll over the Western desert faster than any fleet horse can run. Now, what do the men do? They know it is sure death unless they can make some escape. They would try to run away, perhaps, if they had fleet horses. But they can't; that fire goes faster than the fleetest horse can run. What do they do? Why, they just take a match, and they light the grass from it, and away it burns, and then they get into that burnt district. The fire comes on, and there they stand perfectly secure. There they stand perfectly secure—nothing to fear. Why? Because the fire has burned all there is to burn. Such a place is Mount Calvary. *Moody.*

6985. CALVINISM, Dislike of. Neither of the Wesleys were very merciful to the Calvinists; but Charles was always peculiarly severe upon them; he had a theory that Calvinism, as a matter of necessity, soured the temper just as rennet sours milk. One day he was preaching in his chapel, and had got on his favorite theme: "I never knew," he said, "such a thing as a good-tempered Calvinist; it is a contradiction in terms, a moral impossibility." A man started up at the farther end of the chapel, and putting his arms akimbo, screamed out, "You're a liar!" "Ah!" said Charles Wesley, "have I drawn out Leviathan with a hook?" *Newland.*

6986. CAPACITIES Alone Insufficient. Those who, in confidence of superior capacities or attainments, disregard the common maxims of life, should remember that nothing can atone for the want of prudence; that negligence and irregularity long continued will make knowledge useless, wit ridiculous, and genius contemptible. *Johnson.*

6987. CAPACITIES, Shameful. Antisthenes, the founder of the sect of the Cynics, when he was told that Ismenias played excellently upon the flute, answered properly enough, "Then he is good for nothing else, otherwise he would not have played so well." Such also was Philip's saying to his son, when, at a certain entertainment, he sang in a very agreeable and skillful manner, "Are you not ashamed to sing so well?" Even so, when one who professes to be of the seed royal of heaven, is able to rival the ungodly in their cunning, worldliness, merriment, scheming, or extravagance, may they not blush to possess such dangerous capacities? Heirs of heaven have something better to do than to emulate the children of darkness. *Spurgeon.*

6988. CAPACITIES, Special. I am of the opinion that every mind that comes into the world has its own specialty—is different from every other mind; that each of you brings into the world a certain bias, a disposition to attempt something of its own, something your own—an aim a little different from that of any of your companions; and that every young man and every young woman is a failure so long as each does not find what is his or her own bias; that just so long as you are influenced by those around you, so long as you are attempting to do those things which you see others do well instead of doing that thing which you can do well, you are so far wrong, so far failing of your own right mark. Everybody sees the difference in children. They very early discover their tastes. One has a taste for going abroad, another for staying at home; one for books, another for games; one wishes to hear stories, another wants to see things done; one is fond of drawing, the other cannot draw at all, but he can make a machine. This difference, as you advance, becomes more pronounced. You are more distinct in your conception of what you can do—more decided in avoiding things which you cannot and do not wish to do. Now, I conceive that success is in finding what it is that you yourself really want, and pursuing it; freeing yourself from all importunities of your friends to do something which they like, and insisting upon that thing which you like and can do. *Emerson.*

6989. CAPITAL, Defined. Capital! What is capital? Is it what a man has? Is it counted by pounds and pence, stocks and shares, by houses and lands? No! capital is not what a man has, but what a man is. Character is capital; honor is capital. *Macduff.*

6990. CAPITAL, Workingman's. The working-man's capital is health and not wealth. It does not consist in landed property, but in sinew and muscle, and if he persist in the use of intoxicating liquors, they will strike at the very root of his capital—a sound physical constitution. After this is lost, he becomes unfit

for the workshop, for no master will employ a man who wants capital. He has then to repair to the poor-house or the infirmary. *Hunter.*

6991. CAPTIVES, Deliverance of. It was my privilege to go into Richmond with General Grant's army. There are a thousand poor captives, and they are lawful captives, prisoners in Libby Prison. Talk to some of them that have been there for months, and hear them tell their story. I have wept for hours to hear them tell how they suffered, how they would not hear from their homes and their loved ones for long intervals, and how sometimes they would get messages that their loved ones would die, and they could not get home to be with them in their dying hours. Let us, for illustration, picture a scene. One beautiful day in the spring they are there in the prison. All news has been kept from them. They have not heard what has been going on around Richmond, and I can imagine one says one day, "Ah, boys, listen! I hear a band of music, and it sounds as if they were playing the old battle-cry of the Republic. It sounds as if they were playing The Star-spangled Banner! long may it wave o'er the land of the free and the home of the brave!" And the hearts of the poor fellows begin to leap for joy. "I believe Richmond is taken. I believe they are coming to deliver us!" and every man in that prison is full of joy, and by and by the sound comes nearer, and they see it is so. It is the Union army! Next the doors of the prison are unlocked; they fly wide open, and those thousand men are set free. Wasn't that good news to them? Could there have been any better news? They are out of prison, out of bondage, delivered! They can go to their wives, their children, and their homes now. Ah, my friends, you could not find happier men than those that were liberated at that time: and that is just the Gospel. Christ came to proclaim liberty to the captives. Every man has been taken captive by Satan, and Christ has come to snap his bonds. *Moody.*

6992. CAPTIVITY, Memento of. A medal was struck by Vespasian on the subjugation of the Jews; on the reverse is seen a palm-tree, and a woman sitting on the ground at the foot of it, with her head leaning on her arm, weeping; and at her feet different pieces of armor with this legend, "Judea capta" (taken). Thus was exactly fulfilled the saying of the prophet, "And she, being desolate, shall sit upon the ground."

6993. CARDS, Folly of. It is very wonderful to see persons of the best sense passing away a dozen hours together in shuffling and dividing a pack of cards, with no other conversation but what is made up of a few game-phrases, and no other ideas but those of black or red spots ranged together in different figures. Would not a man laugh to hear any one of his species complaining that life is short? *Addison.*

6994. CARDS, Ruined by. Around a centre-table, where an astral lamp was shedding its light, sat three girls, one holding in her hands a pack of cards. At the back of her chair stood a young man who for years had successfully resisted every effort made by his companions to induce him to learn the game. "Come," said she, "we want one to make out our game. Play with us once, if you never play again." Her eye, cheek, and lip conspired to form an eloquent battery, which sent forth its attack upon the fortress of good resolutions in which he had so long stood secure, until it fell like the walls of an ancient city when jarred by the battering ram. He learned the cards and played. A few weeks afterward I was passing his door at a late hour, and a candle was shedding its dim light through the window. Since that time I have looked from my chamber nearly every hour of the night, from the close of day until early morn, and seen the light faintly struggling through the curtains that screened the inmates of that room from every eye save his who seeth alike in darkness and noonday. Gambling brought with it disease, and death came just as he numbered the half of his threescore years and ten. During his last hours I was sitting by his bedside, when he fixed on me a look I shall never forget, and bade me listen to his dying word: "I might have been a different man from what I am; but it is now too late. I am convinced that there is a state of being beyond the grave; and when I think of the retribution which awaits me in another world, I feel a horror which I am unable to describe." These were among the last words he ever uttered.

Am. Messenger.

6995. CARE, Biblical. Matt. 13: 22—"The cares of this world." Anxious care divides the mind and generally takes the larger half. The figure our Lord uses is a very suggestive one; comparing care and covetousness to thorns. Thorns came in with sin, and are a fruit of the curse. They are entangling, vexing, scratching, and they choke the good seed. The man that deals with thorns must be well armed and guarded, 2 Sam. 23: 6, 7. Luke 10: 40—"Cumbered about much serving." The original signifies drawn in different ways at the same time, exactly answering to our English word "distracted." Luke 12: 29—"Neither be ye of doubtful mind." Margin, "Live not in careful suspense," tossed about as thistle-down in the air; or like a ship, the sport of the changeful tide and angry billows. Phil. 4: 6—"Be careful for nothing." Care is a Christian duty. Carefulness, in the literal meaning of our English word (fullness of care) is a sin, arguing needless perplexing and unworthy distrust, 1 Cor. 7: 32. Ps. 55: 22—"Cast thy burden upon the Lord." "Thy gift" (margin) thy allotted portion—thy care. *Roll* it, as the word is, Ps. 37: 5; Prov. 16: 3, (marg.), where the text is "Commit." 1 Pet. 5: 7, "Casting all your care upon him." Not only sorrowful care, but every anxious thought—every lawful wish—the "heaviness" that "makes the heart stoop." Cast all upon God. Jesus is the care-bearer, as well as the sin-bearer of his people, Isa. 53: 4, 5. Prov. 10: 22, "True riches,"

and "no sorrow" added. 1 Cor. 3: 21, "Things present," "things to come," "all are yours." Then what need for anxious care? *Bowes.*

6996. CARE, Divine. Two little girls were walking homeward one moonlight evening when one of them said, "Sister Annie, it don't make any difference how fast we walk, the moon keeps up with us every step of the way; it don't move at all, and yet it is always going along with us." "So it is with God; though he seems far away, he is keeping step with us always in the march of life."

6997. CARE, Personification of. Care, crossing a dangerous brook, collected a mass of the dirty slime which deformed its banks, and moulded it into the image of an earthly being, which Jupiter, on passing by soon afterwards, touched with ethereal fire and warmed into animation; but, being at a loss what name to give this new production, and disputing to whom of right it belonged, the matter was referred to the arbitrament of Saturn, who decreed that his name should be man (*Homo—ab humo*, from the dirt of which he had been made); that Care should entirely possess his mind while living; that Tellus, or the earth, should receive his body when dead; and that Jupiter should dispose of his celestial essence according to his discretion. Thus was man made the property of Care from his original formation; and Discontent, the offspring of Care, has ever since been his inseparable companion. *Hyginus.*

6998. CARE, Universal. Look into the country fields, there you see toiling at the plough and scythe; look into the waters, there you see tugging at oars and cables; look into the city, there you see a throng of cares, and hear sorrowful complaints of bad times and the decay of trade; look into studies, and there you see paleness and infirmities, and fixed eyes; look into the court, and there are defeated hopes, envyings, underminings, and tedious attendance; all things are full of labor, and labor is full of sorrow; and these two are inseparably joined with the miserable life of man.

T. Rogers.

6999. CARELESSNESS, Childish. A boy who had read Matthew and Mark in the New Testament was asked if he had read about Jesus Christ. He replied, "No, I am only as far as Luke." He was like too many, small and great, old and young, who read the Bible without attention or profit.

7000. CARELESSNESS of Christians. Alluding to the carelessness of Christians, Father Taylor, of Boston, used the figure of a mariner steering into port through a narrow, dangerous channel: "False lights here, rocks there, shifting sand banks on one side, breakers on the other; and who, instead of fixing his attention to keep the head of the vessel right, and to obey the instructions of the pilot as he sings out from the wheel, throws the pilot overboard, lashes down the helm, and walks the deck whistling, with his hands in the pockets of his jacket." Here, suiting the action to the word, he puts on the true sailor-like look of defiant jollity; changed in a moment to an expression of horror, as he added, "See! see! she drifts to destruction!"   *Mrs. Jameson.*

7001. CARELESSNESS, Consequences of. Childish imbecile carelessness is enough to render any man poor, without the aid of a single positive vice.   *Wayland.*

7002. CARELESSNESS, Destructive. Beware of carelessness; no fortune will stand it long: you are on the high road to ruin the moment you think yourself rich enough to be careless.   *S. Smith.*

7003. CARELESSNESS, Result of. Stonewall Jackson, the great general of the Confederates, lost his life through an act of gross carelessness on his own part, being shot by his own soldiers while he was returning from a reconnoitering of the Federal lines near Chancellorsville. He had given orders for a strict watch in that very direction, and to fire on any one approaching that way. His cavalry, supposing him an enemy, fired on him and his escort. They all fell, fatally wounded, but two. No worker has a charmed life, and if we violate the law we cannot hope to escape. In one sense it may be true that a "man is immortal until his work is done;" but it is equally true that when we begin to be careless we either cease to be immortal or else our work is nearly done.   *A. D. Vail.*

7004. CARES, Abusing. I met a brother who, describing a friend of his, said he was like a man who had dropped a bottle, and broken it, and put all the pieces in his bosom, where they were cutting him perpetually. I have seen persons with troubles and cares that seemed like one that had fragments of glass in his bosom, that cut him, and that cut him the more the tighter he pressed them to his heart.   *Beecher.*

7005. CARES, Transient. Quick is the succession of human events; the cares of to-day are seldom the cares of to-morrow; and when we lie down at night, we may safely say to most of our troubles, Ye have done your worst, and we shall meet no more.   *Cowper.*

7006. CARICATURE, Advantage of. The caricaturist is one of the best of historical commentators. The striking peculiarities of the age, which are often but dimly seen in the pages of history, and carefully thrown into shadow in historical pictures, are always distinctly mirrored in the sketches of caricature, which has all the truth and vividness of a reflector; with permanence instead of evanescence, in its forms and colors. It gives enduring shapes to the jests of the hour. It shows us the great men of a period as they were seen and laughed at by their contemporaries; and by enabling us to feel the emotions they inspired when alive, and enjoy the mirth their conduct or appearance suggested, lets us into the understanding of their characters, both more truly and more amusingly than biography.   *Anon.*

7007. CARICATURE, Evil of. The great moral satirist, Hogarth, was once drawing in a room where many of his friends were assembled, and among them my mother. She was then a very young woman. As she stood by Hogarth, she expressed a wish to learn to draw caricature. "Alas, young lady," said Hogarth, "it is not a faculty to be envied! Take my advice, and never draw caricature; by the long practice of it, I have lost the enjoyment of beauty. I never see a face but distorted; I never have the satisfaction to behold the human face divine." We may suppose that such language from Hogarth would come with great effect; his manner was very earnest, and the confession is well deserving of remembrance.   *Bishop Sandford.*

7008. CASTE, Barrier of. I know by experience that it is unpleasant to reside in a Metawely village. Caste is an effectual barrier against forming any intimate relations with the villagers. You never contract friendship with persons who will neither eat with, nor visit you, and into whose houses you cannot enter without contracting or imparting defilement. The law must be broken down before people thus situated can either unite in religious ceremonies or contract family alliances. The Metawelies live separate both in fact and feeling from their neighbors, hating all, hated by all. They refuse to eat with all classes except themselves; and so it was with the Jews. Even the apostles esteemed it a thing unclean to associate or eat with one of another nation.   *Thompson.*

7009. CASTE, Folly of. A Spaniard in South America, who suffered severely from the gout, refused to be cured by an Indian. "I know," said he, "that he is a famous man, and would certainly cure me; but he is an Indian, and would expect to be treated with attentions which I cannot pay to a man of color, and therefore I prefer remaining as I am."

7010. CATECHISM, Influence of the. An English Sabbath-school scholar requested his mother not to allow his brother to bring home anything that was smuggled when he went to sea. "Why do you wish that, my child?" said the mother. He answered, "Because my Catechism says it is wrong." The mother replied, "But that is only the word of man." He said, "Mother, is it the word of a man which said, 'Render unto Cæsar the things that are Cæsar's?'" This reply silenced the mother; but his father still attempting to defend the practice of smuggling, the boy said to him, "Father, whether is it worse, to rob one or to rob many?"

7011. CAUTION, Christian. He that goes too near sin to-day, may fall into it to-morrow. God has been so indulgent as to give us a latitude and liberty to exercise a pious zeal over ourselves, that we may show how much we fear to offend him: and a cautious Christian will say with St. Paul, "All things are lawful, but all things are not expedient." Prudence will not always venture to the brink of innocence.   *Boyle.*

7012. CAUTION, Excessive. The plain truth is, that many believers in the present day seem so dreadfully afraid of doing harm that they hardly ever dare to do good. There are many who are fruitful in objections, but barren in actions; rich in wet blankets, but poor in anything like Christian fire. They are like the Dutch Deputies who would never allow Marlborough to venture anything, and by their excessive caution prevented many a victory being won. *Ryle.*

7013. CEMETERIES, Origin of. Anciently none were buried in churches or church-yards; it was even unlawful to inter in cities, and the cemeteries were without the walls. Among the primitive Christians these were held in great veneration. It appears from Eusebius and Tertullian, that in the early ages they assembled for divine worship in the cemeteries. Valerian seems to have confiscated the cemeteries and other places of divine worship; but they were restored again by Gallienus. As the martyrs were buried in these places the Christians chose them for building churches on, when Constantine established their religion; and hence some derive the rule, which still obtains in the Church of Rome, never to consecrate an altar without putting under it the relics of some saint. *Buck.*

7014. CENSORIOUSNESS, Victims of. Pedley, a well-known natural simpleton, was wont to say: "God help the fool." None are more ready to pity the folly of others than those who have a small share of wit themselves. "There is no love among Christians," cries the man, who is himself destitute of true charity. "Zeal has vanished," exclaims the idle talker. "O, for more consistency," groans the hypocrite. "We want more vital godliness," protests the false pretender. As in the fable the wolf preached against sheep-stealing, so very many hunt down those sins in others which they shelter in themselves. *Spurgeon.*

7015. CENSURE, Eminence and. Censure, says an ingenious author, is the tax a man pays to the public for being eminent. It is folly for an eminent man to think of escaping it, and a weakness to be affected with it. All the illustrious persons of antiquity, and, indeed, of every age in the world, have passed through this fiery persecution. There is no defence against reproach but obscurity; it is a kind of concomitant to greatness, as satires and invectives were an essential part of a Roman triumph. *Addison.*

7016. CENSURE, Improvement of. Plato, when he was in company with any persons that were guilty of unhandsome actions, was wont thus to reflect upon himself and ask this question, "Am I of the like temper and disposition with these men?" In like manner, whosoever passes a hard censure upon another man's life should presently make use of self-examination, and inquire what his own is; by which means he will come to know what his failings are, and how to amend them. Thus the very censures and back-bitings of his enemy will redound to his advantage, although in itself this censorious humor is a very vain, empty and useless thing. On the contrary, we may reap no less advantage for our being judged and censured by our enemies. *Plutarch.*

7017. CEREMONY, Legal. Ceremony resembles that base coin which circulates through a country by the royal mandate; it serves every purpose of real money at home; but it is entirely useless if carried abroad; a person who should attempt to circulate his native trash in another country would be thought either ridiculous or culpable. He is truly well bred who knows when to value and when to despise those national peculiarities which are regarded by some with so much observance. A traveler of taste at once perceives that the wise are polite all the world over; but that fools are only polite at home. *Goldsmith.*

7018. CEREMONY, Profitless. Ceremonies do but clothe the covenant of grace. There are men who cannot see the body for the clothing, the signification of the spirit for the letter, the sword for the sheath, the kernel for the shell. They cannot see Christ but in the outward bark and rind of ritual observances and ceremonies, in the shell of them; and so they become unprofitable servants. *Preston.*

7019. CHANCE, No Such Thing as. It is strictly and philosophically true in nature and reason, that there is no such thing as chance or accident; it being evident that these words do not signify anything really existing, anything that is truly an agent or the cause of any event; but they signify merely men's ignorance of the real and immediate cause. *Dr. Adam Clarke.*

7020. CHANCE, Providence not. A sailor, on going to sea, said to his religious brother: "Tom, you talk a great deal about religion, and Providence, and if I should be wrecked, and a ship was to heave in sight and take me off, I suppose you would call it a merciful Providence. It's all very well, but I believe no such thing—these things happen, like other things, by mere chance, and you call it Providence, that's all!" He went upon his voyage, and his hypothesis was soon literally true; he was wrecked, and remained upon the wreck three days, when a ship appeared, and, seeing their signal of distress, came to their relief. He returned, and in relating it, said to his brother, "Oh, Tom, when that ship hove in sight, my words to you came in a moment into my mind—it was like a bolt of thunder: I have never got rid of it; and now I think it no more than an act of common gratitude to give myself up to God who pitied and saved me."

7021. CHANGE, Emblem of. Heraclitus says that no one can step twice into the same river, since nature, by her changes, is ever altering and transforming all things. It applies to associations, influence, thoughts and emotions.

7022. CHANGE, Love of. He that will have an oar for every man's boat, shall have none left to row his own. They, saith Melancthon, that will know *aliquid in omnibus*, shall indeed know *nihil in toto*. Their admiration or dotage of a thing is extreme for the time but it is a wonder if it outlive the age of a wonder, which is allowed but nine days. They are angry with time, and say the times are dead, because they produce no more innovations. Their inquiry of all things is not *quam* *bonum*, but *quam novum*. They are almost weary of the sun for continual shining. Continuance is a sufficient quarrel against the best things; and the manna of heaven is loathed because it is common. This is not to be always the same, but never the same; and while they would be everything they are nothing; but like the worm Pliny writes of, *multipoda*, that hath many feet, yet is of slow pace. Awhile you shall have him in England, loving the simple truth; anon in Rome, groveling before an image. Soon after he leaps to Amsterdam; and yet must he still be turning, till there be nothing left but to turn Turk.   *Adams.*

7023. CHANGE, Misconception of. An old man, observing that the ancient laws were neglected, and that new evil customs crept in, said to Agis, when he had now grown old himself, "All things here at Sparta are turned topsy-turvy." He replied, with a joke, "If it is so, it is agreeable to reason; for when I was a boy, I heard my father say all things were topsy-turvy; and he heard his father say the same; and it is no wonder if succeeding times are worse than the preceding; but it is a wonder if they happen to be better, or but just as good."   *Plutarch.*

7024. CHANGES, Bodily. Our bodies are at all times like the fire which was shown to the hero of the Pilgrim's Progress in the Interpreter's house, which had water poured on it on one side of the wall against which it blazed, and oil on the other. Here one tissue is burning like fuel, and there another is becoming the depository of combustible matter. We have, as it were, millions of microscopic wind-furnaces, converting into carbonic acid, water-vapor, and other products of combustion, all the combustible elements of the body; and millions of blast-furnaces, reducing the starch and sugar of the food, and the sulphates and phosphates of the body, into inflammable oils and other fuels, which are finally transferred to the wind-furnaces, and burned there. Burning, and, what we must call in contradistinction, unburning, thus proceed together; the flame of life, like a blowpipe flame, exhibiting an oxydizing and a reducing action, at points not far distant from each other. Such is the human body—ever changing, ever abiding—a temple always complete, and yet always under repair, a mansion which quite contents its possessor, and yet has its plans and its materials altered each moment —a machine which never stops working, and yet it is taken to pieces in the one twinkling of an eye, and put together in the other—a cloth of gold, to which the needle is ever adding on one side of a line, and from which the scissors are ever cutting away on the other. Yes. Life, like Penelope of old, is ever weaving and unweaving the same web, whilst her grim suitors, Disease and Death, watch for her halting; only, for her is no Ulysses who will one day in triumph return.   *Dr. G. Wilson.*

7025. CHARACTER, Change of. An irreligious merchant had been absent from his store for some time, and on his return noticed a marked change in one of his clerks. He said to his partner, "I do not understand what has come over George. He don't seem like the same person he did when I went away. He was always smart, but now he seems more tender, respectful, and genial. I think I should love him, if I had much to do with him." "I suppose you know what has happened to him since you have been gone?" "I don't know what you refer to." "George has become a Christian."

7026. CHARACTER, Completeness of. Whilst a man is capable of changing we may be forced to retract our opinions. He may forfeit the esteem we have conceived of him, and some time or other appear to us under a different light from what he does at present. In short, as the life of any man cannot be called happy or unhappy, so neither can it be pronounced vicious or virtuous, before the conclusion of it. It was upon this consideration that Epaminondas, being asked whether Chabrias, Iphicrates, or he himself, deserved most to be esteemed? "You must first see us die," saith he, "before that question can be answered." As there is not a more melancholy consideration to a good man than his being obnoxious to such a change, so there is nothing more glorious than to keep up a uniformity in his actions and preserve the beauty of his character to the last. *Addison.*

7627. CHARACTER, Decisive. I wish a character as decisive as that of a lion or a tiger, and an impetus towards the important objects of my choice as forcible as theirs towards prey and hostility.   *J. Foster.*

7628. CHARACTER, Desirable. "I know nothing of that man's creed," said a person of a religious tradesman with whom he dealt, "because I never asked him what he believed; but a more honorable, punctual, generous tradesman, I never met with in my life, I would as soon take his word for a thousand pounds, as I would another man's bond for a shilling. Whatever he promises he performs, and to the time also."

7629. CHARACTER, Difficulty of Changing. The good or evil propensities of one age are, with their virtues and vices, transferred to the next. 'Tis extraordinary when an evil child becomes a sober, modest youth, or a dissolute youth becomes a godly man. The seed of the hemlock may pass into another stage, and be seen to blossom into flower, but it still retains its deadly principle. Childhood is as the seed in whose virtue the tree of life is contained. The characters that are cut in the bark, when the tree grows, deeply and visibly remain. 'Tis painful as death to change a sinful life of many years, and begin a contrary course of actions. There are two great branches of folly which spring out of a vicious youth: Youth will not do what it can; and manhood afterwards cannot do what it would.   *Salter.*

7630. CHARACTER, Elements of. Character is not a massive unit; it is a fabric rather. It is an artificial whole made up of the interply of ten thousand threads. Every faculty is a spinner, spinning every day its threads, and almost every day threads of a different color; and character is made up by the weaving together of all these innumerable threads of daily life. Its strength is not merely in the strength of some simple unit, but in the strength of numerous elements. *Beecher.*

7031. CHARACTER, God's Knowledge of. As the eye of the cunning lapidary detects in the rugged pebble just digged from the mine the polished diamond that shall sparkle in the diadem of a king; or as the sculptor in the rough block of marble newly hewn from the quarry beholds the statue of perfect grace and beauty that is latent there, and waiting but the touch of his hand; so he who sees all, and the end from the beginning, sees ofttimes greater wonders than these: he sees the saint in the sinner—Paul the preacher of the faith in Saul the persecutor of the faith. *Trench.*

7032. CHARACTER, Good. A good character is a coat of triple steel, giving security to the wearer, protection to the oppressed, and inspiring the oppressor with awe. *Colton.*

7033. CHARACTER, Impressiveness of. If a sheet of paper, on which a key has been laid, be exposed for some minutes to the sunshine, and then instantaneously viewed in the dark, the key being removed, a fading spectre of the key will be visible. Let this paper be put aside for many months where nothing can disturb it, and then in darkness be laid on a plate of hot metal, the spectre of the key will again appear. In the case of bodies more highly phosphorescent than paper, the spectres of many different objects which may have been laid on in succession will, on warming, emerge in their proper order. This is equally true of our bodies and our minds. We are involved in the universal metamorphosis. Nothing leaves us wholly as it found us. Every man we meet, every book we read, every picture or landscape we see, every word or tone we hear, mingles with our being and modifies it. *Christian Treasury.*

7034. CHARACTER, Judgment of. The physician by a single symptom is able to identify the disease. A comparative physiologist from a single bone reconstructs the animal, determines its class, location and habits. So single deeds, words, sentences, associates, form a remarkably correct basis of judging character.

7035. CHARACTER, Knowledge of. As for that second-hand knowledge of men's minds, which is to be had from the relation of others, it will be sufficient to observe of it, that defects and vices are best learned from enemies—virtues and abilities from friends—manners and times from servants, and opinions and thoughts from intimate acquaintance; for popular fame is light, the judgment of superiors uncertain, before whom men walk more masked and secret. The truest character comes from domestics.
Lord Bacon.

7036. CHARACTER, Light of. Have only one chief end. The head-light on an engine is a small lamp, backed and set forth by a burnished reflector. Then it casts forth its brightness, pointing out and illumining the way for the speeding travelers. Your lamp may not be large, but if you will put behind and about it the burnished reflector of a consistent, concentrated life, it may shine forth into the darkness, guiding hurrying pilgrims safely through the night. *Dr. Fowler.*

7037. CHARACTER, Materials for. Instead of saying that man is the creature of circumstance, it would be nearer the mark to say that man is the architect of circumstance. Our strength is measured by our plastic power. From the same materials one man builds palaces, another hovels; one warehouses, another villas: bricks and mortar are mortar and bricks, until the architect can make them something else. Thus it is that in the same family, in the same circumstances, one man rears a stately edifice, whilst his brother, vacillating and incompetent, lives forever amid ruins: the block of granite which was an obstacle in the pathway of the weak, becomes a stepping-stone in the pathway of the strong. *Carlyle.*

7038. CHARACTER, Similarity of. Thomas Carlyle, once passing along the Strand, London, said he would like to stop the stream of people and ask every one his history. After a little he said, "No, I will not stop them; for if I did I should find that they were like a flock of sheep following in the track of one another."

7039. CHARACTER, Sternness of. There were many Christian men in Wittemberg who said to Martin Luther, "You don't mean that you are going to hang up those on the church door?" Said Luther: "They are true; they assail damning error; my Fatherland is bowing down to Antichrist." "Pause," said the men who would stand well with everybody. "Is not this zeal without knowledge? Think how you will scandalize the University; how you will drive off men who would follow you in a more discreet course." "Avaunt!" said the Reformer. "The people are perishing in ignorance. The crowds of the common people who come into the city to market will read these words. Yours is not discretion, but cowardice." He did the deed; and, as the result of that act, Europe received the Protestant Reformation, and the night of the Middle Ages was ended. *Guest.*

7040. CHARACTER, Successful. The great things of this world have been accomplished by individuals. Vast social reformations have originated in individual souls. Truths that now sway the world were first proclaimed by individual lips. Great thoughts that now are the axioms of humanity proceeded from the centre of individual hearts. No warlike host delivered the children of Israel from the bondage of Egypt, but one man—Moses. No senate of statesmen raised Israel to a pitch of greatness that proclaimed a theocratic nation to the world, but one man—David. No school of divines gave to England the Bible in the mother tongue, but one man—Wycliffe. No learned society discovered America, but one man—Columbus. No association of science revealed the clue to interpret the laws of the universe, but one man—Galileo. No parliament saved English liberties, but one man—Pym. No assembly of theologians wrote the book which, next to the Bible, has had the most potent influence on the English language and on English hearts, but one man—John Bunyan. No confederate nations rescued Scotland from her distracted councils, from her political and ecclesiastical enemies, but one man—Knox. No chambers of commerce taught Europe to abolish the restrictions of trade, but one man—Richard Cobden. Doubtless these men found their coadjutors; but all through the ages God has put immense honor upon individuals.   *Guest.*

7041. CHARITIES, Collecting. When Dr. Goodall was collecting for missionary purposes, he entered the counting-room of a wealthy merchant; who, as he entered the door, said abruptly, "Humph! A beggar, I suppose." "No," said Dr. Goodall, buoyantly, nothing daunted, "not a beggar, but a collector; I am informed you have some of my Lord's money in your hands, and I have come to collect a portion of the interest." "Nothing for you," was the surly reply. "Very well. I will go and tell your Master what you say. He is very patient and long-suffering," and left him. The next morning he received two hundred dollars from the merchant.

7042. CHARITIES, Deposits. A religious man says, "I took a church envelope, and opening my pocket-book I put into it some money, and placed the whole in another partition of the purse; and I thought to myself, I have as much money as before. On the following Sunday the envelope and its contents were deposited in the basket; and a voice whispered, "You have as much money as ever, but a part is in a different place."

7043. CHARITIES, Small. An English lad proposed to put a penny in the box for missions. His sister rallied him on the uselessness of so small a gift, and said, "It would never be noticed among the large sums given by others. He persisted, however, and the tellers reported a collection of £6, 5s. and 1d. The boy whispered to his sister, "Hear that; that's my penny; you said it was so little it would never be noticed, and the gentleman has told the whole congregation." The most famous gift ever made was two mites. The omniscient God is a perfect accountant.

7044. CHARITY, Apologue of. Jesus arrived one evening at the gates of a certain city, and he sent his disciples forward to prepare supper while he himself, intent on doing good, walked through the streets into the market-place. And he saw, at the corner of the market, some people gathered together looking at some object on the ground; and he drew near to see what it might be. It was a dead dog with a halter round his neck, by which he appeared to have been dragged through the dirt; and a viler, a more abject, a more unclean thing never met the eyes of man; and those who stood by looked on with abhorrence. "Faugh!" said one, stopping his nose, "it pollutes the air!" "How long," said another, "shall this foul beast offend our sight?" "Look at his torn hide," said a third, "one could not even cut a shoe out of it." "And his ears," said a fourth, "all draggled and bleeding." "No doubt," said a fifth, "he has been hanged for thieving." And Jesus heard them, and looking down compassionately on the dead creature, he said, "Pearls are not equal to the whiteness of his teeth." Then the people turned to him with amazement, and said among themselves, "Who is this? This must be Jesus of Nazareth, for only he could find something to pity and approve even in a dead dog." And, being ashamed, they bowed their heads before him, and went each on his way. *Anon.*

7045. CHARITY, Compulsory. A bishop, named Troilus, was visiting John of Alexandria, famous for his charities. The latter took his guest to visit some poor people for whom he had erected some huts. While there John said. "I see you have some money with you—many pounds, if I mistake not; distribute it among these my poor." The bishop could not refuse, so his gold was emptied into the pockets of the poor beggars. Now he had previously found an elegantly chased silver drinking-cup in town, and had set his heart upon it. The price of it was thirty pounds, and the money he had unwillingly given to the beggars he had set apart for that purchase. After parting with his money he was so chagrined and disappointed that he fell into a fever. Not seeing him for some days, John sent for him and learned of his illness. Suspecting the cause, he took thirty pounds, and going to the sick man, said, "I borrowed of you thirty pounds, the other day, for my poor; if you are so disposed, I will at once repay the sum." At once the fever vanished, and the sorely vexed bishop jumped from his bed, ready to accept the patriarch's invitation to dine with him. After dinner Bishop Troilus fell asleep and thought himself in a land of wonderful beauty, and there he beheld a mansion of unearthly glory, over the door of which was inscribed "THE ETERNAL MANSION AND PLACE OF REPOSE OF TROILUS, THE BISHOP." At this he was greatly delighted. Just then a glorious One, with many white robed attendants, came by, and when he had read the title he said, "Not so; change the inscription." Then the writing was changed by the attendants, and in its place was inscribed, "THE ETERNAL MANSION AND PLACE OF REPOSE OF JOHN, ARCHBISHOP OF ALEXANDRIA, PURCHASED FOR THIRTY POUNDS." By this it appeared that Troilus had sold his mansion as Judas sold his Master.

7046. CHARITY, Immortal. A poor widow in Christ's time entered the temple and cast into the treasury the insignificant sum of two mites, equal to four mills, or less than half a cent. It was all she possessed. It attracted the attention of Christ, who graded this trifling charity according to the divine standard, and immortalized the giver of two mites. To his disciples he said, "Verily I say unto you, that this poor widow hath cast more in than all they which have cast into the treasury; for all they did cast in of their abundance, but she of her want did cast in all that **she had**, even all her living," Mark 12: 43.

7047. CHARITY, Legend of. **Marcian**, a priest of the church of Constantinople, was on his way to participate in the dedication of the church of St. Anastasia, which he had built, when he was accosted by a very ragged and importunate beggar. He found he had no money, and quickly slipping off his tunic, gave it to the emaciated pauper. This left him without a nether garment, which he thought to conceal by drawing his priestly robes closely about him. The church was crowded; the Emperor Leo, the Empress, and many senators, being present. Marcian was called to the conspicuous service of celebrating the Holy Sacrament. Fearing exposure he began. His robes parted, and all saw beneath them a garment of burnished gold, which flashed brilliantly as he moved. When the service was ended, the patriarch, Gennadius, rebuked him for wearing a garment more splendid than the Emperor's. Marcian denied having worn such a garment. Gennadius tore open his vestments and discovered that he had on no garment save his priestly garb. So glorious is the garment of charity.

7048. CHARITY, Pagan. It is written of Plato that, when he did give to a poor profligate wretch, his friends very much wondered that Plato, the great divine philosopher, should take pity on such a wretched miscreant; but he, like himself, in such misty days as those were, answered, "I show mercy to the man, not because he is wicked, but because he is a man of my own nature." His answer was warrantable; for, if we consider our first parents, we shall find ourselves bound by the same obligation to do good unto all men. "There is neither Jew nor Greek, bond nor free, neither male nor female, in Christ Jesus." *Salter.*

7049. CHARITY, Present Duty of. Two collectors called upon a rich merchant at his office to solicit a contribution to the missionary society. Their application was received courteously, and the gentleman subscribed twenty-five dollars. Encouraged by this success, the collectors asked permission to present their book to some of the clerks in the counting-house and warehouse. Whilst thus engaged, the postman entered with letters for the merchant. Amongst other items of intelligence was information of a vessel wrecked at sea with a valuable cargo, uninsured, involving a loss of several thousand dollars. The merchant was evidently affected by the bad news he had received. but seeing the missionary collectors retiring from the premises, he called them, and said: "Gentlemen, I am sorry to trouble you, but since you left my office, I have received intelligence of the loss of one of my ships at sea, with a valuable cargo, uninsured, and I am consequently poorer by several thousand dollars than I thought I was; I must therefore ask permission to alter the figure which I wrote in your collecting book." The collectors handed their book to the merchant, when, to their utter astonishment, he altered his contribution to one hundred dollars. When they inquired if he had not made a mis-

take, he replied, "No, gentlemen, I wished to alter my contribution to a higher figure since I heard of my heavy loss, for I doubt whether I have been giving to the cause of God in time past as much as I ought to have done. At all events, I am determined to give more liberally in the future, and that without delay, lest more of my property should be swallowed up in the sea as a just punishment for my past unfaithfulness."

7050. CHARITY, Private. **Mrs.** Judson, in an account of the first Burman convert, says, " I was reading with him Christ's sermon on the mount. He was deeply impressed, and unusually solemn. 'These words,' said he, 'take hold on my very heart ; they make me tremble. Here God commands us to do everything that is good in secret, not to be seen of men. How unlike our religion is this! When Burmans make offerings at the pagodas, they make a great noise with drums and musical instruments, that others may see how good they are; but this religion makes the mind fear God; it makes it, of its own accord, fear sin.'"

7051. CHARITY, Providing for. Bishop Zosimus bade his deacon, John, give two coins to a poor man who asked an alms. He replied, "Our purse is empty." "Go and sell thy cloak and give to him that needeth," was the bishop's reply. Now John was reluctant to do this, for it was a new one, just bought. Then the bishop took off his own cloak, and handing it to him, bade him go and sell it. As the deacon returned, having executed his commission and relieved the beggar, a young man came in and gave the bishop a heavy purse of gold. He rebuked John for his little faith.

7052. CHARITY, Recompense of. During the retreat of Alfred the Great, at Athelney, in Somersetshire, after the defeat of his forces by the Danes, a beggar came to his castle there, and requested alms. When his queen informed him that they had only one small loaf remaining, which was insufficient for themselves and their friends, who were gone abroad in quest of food, though with little hopes of success, the king replied, "Give the poor Christian one half of the loaf. He who could feed the 5,000 men with five loaves and two small fishes can certainly make that half of the loaf suffice for more than our necessities." Accordingly, the poor man was relieved, and this noble act of charity was soon recompensed by a providential store of fresh provisions, with which his people returned. *Percy.*

7053. CHARITY, Restraint of. A monk asked Pambo, "How is it that the divine spirit never allows me to be charitable ?" "Don't say the divine spirit," said the abbot indignantly; "say I don't want to be charitable."

7054. CHARITY, Rewarded. It was a time of great scarcity, almost famine, and prices were so high that Falk did not know how he was to get bread for his children, when a poor boy came into the Sunday-school on crutches, and said weeping, "No one pities me. The dogs have often fallen on me and bitten me. Dear sir, for Christ's sake, **pity me,** and let me have some rest. Put me in a workshop—I will be a tailor, or anything you like. Only take me in." "Dear children," said Falk, "the times are hard, but I will send none of you away; and I will take the stranger from afar off in. And I tell you—and now think of it—blessings will flow richly in upon our house; and God, who has led Ludwig Minner over the Thuringian forest in snow and rain, has not led him in vain to us, and he will provide bread, not only for him, but for us all." And before the next Sunday a tailor had taken Minner into his workshop, and the Prince of Rudolstradt had sent a donation of five hundred crowns.

P. B. Power.

7055. CHARITY, Unequal. A poor widow lady, liberal in proportion to her means to the cause of religion, unexpectedly succeeded to a large fortune, but where she had formerly given a guinea, she now gave but a shilling. Her minister felt it his duty to expostulate with her, and remind her of her former generosity when her means were so circumscribed. "Ah! sir," she replied, "then I had the shilling means, but the guinea heart; now I have the guinea means, but only the shilling heart. Then I received from my Heavenly Father's hand, day by day, my daily bread, and I had enough and to spare; now I have to look to my ample income, but I live in constant apprehension that I may come to want!" *Moister.*

7056. CHARITY, Valuing. Melania visited Pambo, the hermit, in his wilderness, and found him platting mats. She presented him with a silver vessel of great value. The monk never looked up from his work but said, "Here, steward, take and sell it for the good of the brotherhood." Melania stood before him, expecting some attention after so liberal a gift, but Pambo took no notice of her. She said, "Do you know, father, what is the value of my present?" "He to whom it was offered needs not that you should tell him," answered the abbot. At another time a man brought him money to be distributed in alms, and directed him to "count it." Pambo replied, "God does not ask how much, but how. It is not the amount, but the will with which it is given."

7057. CHASTISEMENTS, Divine. As it concerns us to observe when the creatures become corrosives, so it does also to improve this corroding dispensation. Let it be a means to eat out the proud flesh of some sin or other, which is the procuring cause of all. The creatures frown; but doth not God frown on some sin, in their frowning? It would better become those who cry out against their superiors, to consider how the taking cold in the feet is often the cause of disorder in the head. The sins of people, wives, children, servants, are the cold vapors which cause a distemper. The headache of some above others, becomes a heartache to and from those below others. View sin, then, so as to be more abased for it, and creatures less in the way of disquiet. So the prophet teaches (Lam. 3: 40). The overtaking of sin with hue-and-cry is the best remedy under such maladies. *Crane.*

7058. CHASTISEMENTS, Reception of. On one occasion a minister found it necessary to punish his little daughter. But she climbed into his lap, and, throwing her arms around his neck, said: "Papa, I do love you." "Why do you love me, my child?" the father asked. "Because you try to make me good, papa."

7059. CHASTISEMENTS, Test of. All is well as long as the sun shines and the fair breath of heaven gently wafts us to our own purposes. But if you will try the excellency and feel the work of faith, place the man in a persecution; let him ride in a storm; let his bones be broken with sorrow, and his eyelids loosed with sickness; let his bread be dipped with tears, and all the daughters of music be brought low; let us come to sit upon the margin of our grave, and let a tyrant lean hard upon our fortunes and dwell upon our wrong; let the storm arise, and the keels toss till the cordage crack, or that all our hopes bulge under us, and descend into the hollowness of sad misfortunes.

Jeremy Taylor.

7060. CHEERFULNESS, Advantages of. Give us, O give us, the man who sings at his work! Be his occupation what it may, he is equal to any of those who follow the same pursuit in silent sullenness. He will do more in the same time —he will do it better—he will persevere longer. One is scarcely sensible of fatigue whilst he marches to music. The very stars are said to make harmony as they revolve in their spheres. Wondrous is the strength of cheerfulness, altogether past calculation its powers of endurance. Efforts, to be permanently useful, must be uniformly joyous—a spirit all sunshine—graceful from very gladness—beautiful because bright.

Carlyle.

7061. CHEERFULNESS a Blessing. Persons who are always innocently cheerful and good-humored are very useful in the world; they maintain peace and happiness, and spread a thankful temper amongst all who live around them. *Miss Tallbot.*

7062. CHEERFULNESS, Cultivate. Be cheerful, no matter what reverses obstruct your pathway, or what plagues follow in your trail to annoy you. Ask yourself what is to be gained by looking or feeling sad when troubles throng around you, or how your condition is to be alleviated by abandoning yourself to despondency? If you are a young man, nature designed you "to be of good cheer;" and should you find your road to fortune, fame, or respectability, or any other boon to which your young heart aspires, a little thorny, consider it all for the best, and that these impediments are only thrown in your way to induce greater efforts and more patient endurance on your part. Far better spend a whole life in diligent, aye, cheerful and unremitting toil, though you never attain the pinnacle of your ambitious desires, than to turn back at the first appearance of misfortune, and allow despair to unnerve your energies, or sour your naturally sweet and cheerful disposition. If you are of the softer, fairer portion of humanity, be cheerful, though we know full well that most afflictions are sweet to you when compared with disappointment and neglect; yet let hope banish despair and ill-forebodings. Be cheerful; do not brood over fond hopes unrealized, until a chain, link after link, is fastened on each thought, and wound around the heart. Nature intended you to be the fountain-spring of cheerfulness and social life, and not the traveling monument of despair and melancholy.   *Helps.*

7063. CHEERFULNESS, Effects of. The poet Carpani inquired of Haydn, how it happened that his church music was always so cheerful. The great composer replied, "I cannot make it otherwise. I write according to the thoughts I feel: when I think upon God, my heart is so full of joy that the notes dance and leap, as it were, from my pen: and since God has given me a cheerful heart, it will be pardoned me that I serve him with a cheerful spirit."

7064. CHEERFULNESS, Enforced. Emerson says: "Do not hang a dismal picture on your wall, and do not deal with sable and glooms in your conversation." Beecher follows: "Away with these fellows who go howling through life, and all the while passing for Birds of Paradise. He that cannot laugh and be gay, should look to himself. He should fast and pray until his face breaks forth into light." Talmage then takes up the strain: "Some people have an idea that they comfort the afflicted when they groan over them. Don't drive a hearse through a man's soul. When you bind up a broken bone of the soul, and you want splints, do not make them out of cast iron." Hume, the historian, said that the habit of looking at the bright side of things was better than an income of a thousand a year. It was said of Cromwell that hope shone like a fiery pillar in him when it had gone out in all others.   *S. S. Journal.*

7065. CHEERFULNESS, Habit of. When Goethe says that in every human condition foes lie in wait for us, "invincible only by cheerfulness and equanimity;" he does not mean that we can at all times be really cheerful, or at a moment's notice; but that the endeavor to look at the better side of things will produce the habit, and that this habit is the surest safeguard against the danger of sudden evils.   *Hunt.*

7066. CHEERFULNESS, Reason for. Columbanus once said, "Deicolus, why art thou always smiling?" "Because no one can take my God from me," he replied.

7067. CHEMISTRY, Utility of. The transformations of chemistry, by which we are enabled to convert the most apparently useless materials into important objects in the arts, are opening up to us every day sources of wealth and convenience of which former ages had no idea, and which have been pure gifts of science to man. Every department of art has felt their influence, and new instances are continually starting forth of the unlimited resources which this wonderful science develops in the most sterile parts of nature. Not to mention the impulse which its progress has given to a host of other sciences, which will come more particularly under consideration in another part of this discourse, what strange and unexpected results has it not brought to light in its application to some of the most common objects! Who, for instance, would have conceived that linen rags were capable of producing more than their own weight of sugar, by the simple agency of one of the cheapest and most abundant acids? that dry bones could be a magazine of nutriment, capable of preservation for years, and ready to yield up their sustenance in the form best adapted to the support of life, on the application of that powerful agent, steam, which enters so largely into all our processes, or of an acid at once cheap and durable? that sawdust itself is susceptible of conversion into a substance bearing no remote analogy to bread, and though certainly less palatable than that of flour, yet no way disagreeable, and both wholesome and digestible, as well as highly nutritive? What economy in all processes where chemical agents are employed, is introduced by the exact knowledge of the proportions in which natural elements unite, and their power of displacing each other! What perfection in all the arts where fire is employed, either in its more violent applications—as, for instance, in the smelting of metals by the introduction of well adapted fluxes, whereby we obtain the whole produce of the ore in its purest state—or in its milder forms, as in sugar refining,—the whole modern practice of which depends on a curious and delicate remark of a late eminent scientific chemist on the nice adjustment of temperature at which the crystallization of syrup takes place; and a thousand other arts which it would be tedious to enumerate!   *Herschel.*

7068. CHILD, Character in the. Little snapping-turtles snap, so the great naturalist tells us, before they are out of the egg-shell. I am satisfied that, much higher up in the scale of life, character is distinctly shown as the age of two or three months.   *Holmes.*

7069. CHILD, Death of a. A boy of only six years, who had developed remarkable musical precocity, had been for some time on exhibition in the various eastern cities as a violinist, drawing crowded houses and eliciting hearty plaudits. His manager noticed indications of exhaustion, and concluded to give him a rest, but too late. After a matinee, at which he had been greatly excited, while sleeping with his father he was heard to murmur, "Merciful God, make room for a little fellow." These were his last words; and when the lights were brought it was found he was dead.

7070. CHILD, A Heaven-bound. The train was going west, and the time was evening. At a station a little girl about eight years old came aboard, carrying a little budget under her arm. She came into the car and deliberately took a seat. She then commenced an eager scrutiny of faces; but all were strange to her. She appeared weary, and placing her budget for a pillow, she prepared to try to secure a little sleep. Soon the conductor came along collecting tickets and fare. Observing him, she asked if she might lie there. The gentlemanly conductor replied that she might, and then kindly asked for her ticket. She informed him that she had none, when the following conversation ensued. Said the conductor, "Where are you going?" she answered, "I am going to heaven." He asked again, "Who pays your fare?" She then said, "Mister, does this railroad lead to heaven, and does Jesus travel on it?" He answered, "I think not. Why did you think so?" "Why, sir, before my ma died she used to sing to me of a heavenly railroad; and you look so nice, and talk so kind, I thought this was the road. My ma used to sing of Jesus on the heavenly railroad, and that he paid the fare for everybody, and that the train stopped at every station to take people on board; but my ma don't sing to me any more. Nobody sings to me now, and I thought I would take the cars and go to ma. Mister, do you sing to your little girl about heaven, you have a little girl, haven't you?" He replied, "No, my little dear, I have no little girl now. I had one once, but she died some time ago, and went to heaven." Again she asked, "Did she go over this railroad; and are you going to see her now?" By this time every person in the coach was upon his feet, and most of them were weeping. An attempt to describe what I witnessed is almost futile. Some said, "God bless the little girl!" Hearing some person say that she was an angel, the little girl earnestly replied, "Yes, my ma used to say that I would be an angel some time." Addressing herself once more to the conductor, she asked him, "Do you love Jesus? I do, and if you love him he will let you ride to heaven on his railroad. I am going there, and I wish you would go with me. I know Jesus will let me into heaven, when I get there, and will let you in too, and everybody who will ride on his railroad—yes, all these people. Wouldn't you like to see heaven, and Jesus, and your little girl?" These words, so innocently and pathetically uttered, brought a great gush of tears from all eyes, but most profusely from the eyes of the conductor. Some who were traveling on the heavenly railroad shouted aloud for joy. She now asked the conductor, "Mister, may I lie here until we get to heaven?" He answered, "Yes, dear, yes." She then asked, "Will you wake me up then, so that I might see my ma, your little girl, and Jesus? for I do so want to see them all." The answer came in broken accents, but in words very tenderly spoken, "Yes, dear angel, yes. God bless you!" "Amen!" was sobbed by more than a score of voices. Turning her eyes again upon the conductor she interrogated him again. "What shall I tell your little girl when I see her? Shall I say to her that I saw her pa on Jesus' railroad? Shall I?" This brought a fresh flood of tears from all present, and the conductor kneeled by her side, and embracing her, wept the reply he could not utter. At this juncture the brakeman called out, "H—— s." The conductor arose, and requested him to attend to his (the conductor's) duty at the sta-

tion, for he was engaged. That was a precious place. I thank God that I was witness to this scene; but I was sorry that at this point I was obliged to leave the train.   *Ch. Expositor.*

7071. CHILD, A Martyred. The Proconsul Anulinus, of Carthage, A. D. 304, examining Felix and Victoria on the charge of being Christians, they boldly declared their observance of the Lord's day and readiness to die for Christ. He thought to prevail easily with a little boy, Hilarion by name. To the proconsul's inquiry if he had been present at the meetings of the Christians, he answered, "I am a Christian; I have been at the meeting, and it was of my own choice, not of compulsion." He then threatened him with some childish punishment. The boy only laughed at it. The proconsul then said, "I will cut off your nose and ears." Hilarion answered, "You may do it, but I am a Christian still." Then he was sentenced to be taken to the prison, hearing which, he cried, "God be thanked!" In this prison he was kept till he died of starvation, and went to heaven to receive the victor's palm.

7072. CHILDHOOD, Conversion in. What a study of the Christian life a garden is! Take the matter of transplantation. Things transplanted late, when well grown, don't do well. You take an old sinner of a tomato-plant, for instance, who has been growing rank and weak in the sinful hot-bed, and put him out in the rich but wholesome soil of the garden. He goes down like a rag-baby in a shower. I had some that blossomed in their iniquity. Changed into the garden-soil—the Christian soil, if I may say so—they wilted flat, and grew as sick as death and fever and ague. But a young plant taken early from the Sunday-school does better; and most hardy and thrifty of all are those plants that spring from the seed, and grow to maturity where they stand, never needing to be transplanted into the church. Of course, the old tomatoes revive, and go on, after a time, famously, bearing loads of fruit. But they have a hard struggle and a long one.   *Christian Union.*

7073. CHILDHOOD, Devotion in. It is of the last importance to season the passions of a child with devotion, which seldom dies in a mind that has received an early tincture of it. Though it may seem extinguished for a while by the cares of the world, the heats of youth, or the allurements of vice, it generally breaks out and discovers itself again as soon as discretion, consideration, age, or misfortunes have brought the man to himself. The fire may be covered and overlaid, but cannot be entirely quenched and smothered.   *Addison.*

7074. CHILDHOOD, Haste with. A blacksmith, when he pulled his iron out of the fire, used to call out to his son, "Quick! quick! Now or never!" By this means he taught his son to strike the iron when it was hot, well knowing that if he once let it get cold, he should not be able to form it into a shoe. Now the disposition of a young person is somewhat like the hot iron; it can be easily bent into a proper form by education; but the mind of an aged person is like cold iron, not very easily altered —indeed, if it has been altogether neglected, it is next to impossible to form it aright.

Anon.

7075. CHILDHOOD, Indulgence in. Young people who have been habitually gratified in all their desires, will not only more indulge in capricious desires, but will infallibly take it more amiss when the feelings or happiness of others require that they should be thwarted, than those who have been practically trained to the habit of subduing and restraining them, and consequently will, in general, sacrifice the happiness of others to their own selfish indulgence. To what else is the selfishness of princes and other great people to be attributed? It is in vain to think of cultivating principles of generosity and beneficence by mere exhortation and reasoning. Nothing but the practical habit of overcoming our own selfishness, and of familiarly encountering privations and discomfort on account of others, will ever enable us to do it when required. And therefore I am firmly persuaded that indulgence infallibly produces selfishness and hardness of heart, and that nothing but a pretty severe discipline and control can lay the foundation of a magnanimous character. *Lord Jeffrey.*

7076. CHILDHOOD, Memories of. The impressions of childhood are proverbially the most indelible. The mind of man is like one of those ancient manuscripts that are covered with successive layers of writing, of which the last alone is visible; but the application of a chemical test reveals all the rest. In like manner, the human mind is covered with innumerable layers of imperishable memories. We speak of forgetfulness; but, in truth, we forget nothing—at least, in the sense of its passing entirely from the mind. Thus we find in the case of very old people, that, while the events of the present make scarcely any impression at all on the memory, the reminiscences of childhood come trooping back in all the vivid freshness of youth. *Anon.*

7077. CHILDREN, Benefit of. I am fond of children. I think them the poetry of the world, the fresh flowers of our hearths and homes; little conjurors, with their "natural magic," evoking by their spells what delights and enriches all ranks, and equalizes the different classes of society. Often as they bring with them anxieties and cares, and live to occasion sorrow and grief, we should get on very badly without them. Only think, if there was never anything anywhere to be seen, but great grown-up men and women! How we should long for the sight of a little child! Every infant comes into the world like a delegated prophet, the harbinger and herald of good-tidings, whose office it is "to turn the hearts of the fathers to the children," and to draw "the disobedient to the wisdom of the just." A child softens and purifies the heart, warming and melting it by its gentle presence; it enriches the soul by new feelings, and awakens within it what is favorable to virtue. It is a beam of light, a fountain of love, a teacher whose lessons few can resist. Infants recall us from much that engenders and encourages selfishness, that freezes the affections, roughens the manners, indurates the heart: they brighten the home, deepen love, invigorate exertion, infuse courage, and vivify and sustain the charities of life. It would be a terrible world, I do think, if it was not embellished by little children! *Binney*

7078. CHILDREN, Biblical. Children are represented as "Stars," Gen. 37: 9. *Arrows* in the hands of a mighty man, Ps. 127, 4. A Chinese proverb says, "When a son is born into a family, a bow and arrow are hung up at the gate." *"Olive plants"* Ps. 128: 3, the emblem of peace, richness and prosperity. *Corner stones* polished after the similitude of a palace, Ps. 144: 12, the bonds of union and upholders of harmony. *Lambs*, John 21: 15. The Hebrew idiom for childhood is taken from *building a house*, from which the Hebrew word for son is derived, Deut. 25: 9; Ruth 4: 11. Prov. 23: 15—"My son, if thine heart be wise, mine heart shall rejoice, even mine." Swinnock says, "Lord, let thy blessing so accompany my endeavors, that all my sons may be Benaiahs (the Lord's building), then will they be all Abners (their father's light); and that all my daughters may be Bethuels (the Lord's daughters), and then will they be all Abigails (their father's joy)." *Bowes.*

7079. CHILDREN, Chance for the. A writer in a recent California paper says: It was only twenty-five years ago—1850—that the following incident occured at Downieville, in Sierra County: The country was full of men engaged in mining, and Downieville was a busy camp. There had been built for public uses a large building, sometimes used as a theatre and sometimes for the purposes of a public hall. The surrounding gulches were filled with men rude of manners, but full of tender memories, and there was then but a score of women in the county, and not a baby, so far as was generally known, in the circuit of a hundred miles. It was the Fourth of July, and Downieville celebrated. The stars and stripes floated from a peeled and lofty pine, and the chorus of the anvil had re-echoed through the hills. The house was crowded with the miners; poet, reader and orator had performed their parts, and the recently organized brass band was giving in boisterous resonance some popular national anthem, when suddenly there burst out the feeble wail of an infant—first low, then swelling out in all the defiant strength of baby lungs. The band put forth its loudest strains: the baby, excited to renewed exertion, redoubled its vigor. It was nip and tuck between band and baby. The young mother did her best to divert the child and hush him, when from the audience there uprose a brawny miner, and shaking his fist at the music, cried, "Hush that infernal band and give the baby a chance!" The band stopped its playing, and never did stalwart men listen to sweeter music than those exiles from home and women as they drank in the tones of the wailing child

There were tears in many an eye. The child was hushed upon its mother's breast, and at the word there went up three rousing cheers for the first baby of the Northern Sierras. Looking over the figures of the school census we find that there are now 280,000 children in California under fifteen years of age, and the Downieville baby is only twenty-five years old. This is a good showing for a young State. Give the babies a chance, and we can get on without any further Eastern emigration.

7080. CHILDREN, Christ and the. The Lord Jesus showed in many ways the tender care he felt for children. (1.) He took them in his arms and blessed them, Mark 10: 13–16, expressing his displeasure at the disciples who would have kept them from him. (2.) He twice made them the patterns of humility and docility, Matt. 18: 2, 3; Luke 18: 17. (3.) He spoke of them as being under the guardian care of the angels in heaven, Matt. 18: 10. (4.) He received the hosannas of the children on his entry into Jerusalem, Matt. 21: 15, 16. *Bowes.*

7081. CHILDREN, Christianity and. The Gospel alone opens its warm bosom to the young. Christianity alone is the nurse of childhood. Atheism looks on them as on a level with the brutes. Deism or skepticism leaves them to every random influence, lest they catch a bias. The Romans exposed their infants. Barbarians and ancient tribes offered them as burnt sacrifices to Moloch. Mahometanism holds mothers and infants as equally of an inferior caste. Hindooism forgets the infant she bears, and leaves it to perish on the banks of the Ganges. The Chinese are notorious as infanticides. Christianity alone contemplates them as immortal creatures, and prescribes for their tuition for heaven. And the nearer the time that the rising of the Sun of Righteousness approached, the warmer and more intense did the interest of the Church show itself in regard to the young. Moses gave directions on the subject. Joshua and Abraham commanded their households after them; David declared how the young were to purify their way; and Solomon distinctly enjoined, "Remember thy Creator in the days of thy youth;" but it was reserved for him who spake as never man spake, to press that sentence, "Suffer little children to come unto me, and forbid them not, for of such is the kingdom of heaven." The temple Juggernaut presents a grave; the mosque, contempt; infidelity, neglect for children. The bosom of the Son of God alone finds them a nursery and a home. *Salter.*

7082. CHILDREN, Controlling. In order to form the minds of children, the first thing to be done is to conquer their will. To inform the understanding is a work of time, and must, with children, proceed by slow degrees, as they are able to bear it; but the subjecting the will must be done at once, and the sooner the better; for, by neglecting timely correction, they will contract a stubbornness and obstinacy which are hardly ever conquered, and not without using such severity as would be as painful to me as the child. In the esteem of the world they pass for kind and indulgent, whom I call cruel, parents, who permit their children to get habits which they know must afterwards be broken. *Mrs. S. Wesley.*

7083. CHILDREN, Disobedient. 2 Sam. 18: 18, Absalom's pillar. Travelers say the place is taken notice of to this day; and it is common for passengers to throw a stone to this heap, with words to this purpose: "Cursed be the memory of wicked Absalom, and cursed forever be all wicked children, that rise up in rebellion against their parents." *Henry.*

7084. CHILDREN, Duties of. As letters graven in the body of a tree, they grow up with the tree, and the fruit of the tree grows up with the tree, and therefore the twigs break not with the greatness of the weight of it, because they grow up together. So plant good things in those that are young, inure them to know good things, to hate ill ways, plant in them blessed desires, and inure them to holy exercises and good duties, that good exercise may grow up with them, as the fruit with the tree. *Sibbes.*

7085. CHILDREN, Effort for the. A mother who had brought up a large family of children, all of whom had become members of the Christian fold, was asked what means she had used with so much success to win them to the cross. She replied: "I have always felt that if they were not converted before they became seven or eight years of age they would probably be lost, and when they have approached that age I have been in an agony lest they should pass it unconverted. I have gone to the Lord in my anguish, and he has not turned away my prayers, nor his mercy from me."

7086. CHILDREN, First Work of. I think a good deal of all the work done in Sabbath-school is lost, because we try to teach God's truth to children before their hearts have been given to Christ. If they can only be induced to open their hearts, their minds will be illuminated by the Divine truth. I have taught in the Sunday-school, and it was a good while before I knew this. There was a Sunday-school superintendent who got discouraged, and said he was going to give up the school. "I'll tell you what you want," said a wise brother who went to him; "seek and find Jesus yourself, and you will have the strength and see the way to carry on your work acceptably in your sight and in the sight of God." And he did find Jesus and courage. *Moody.*

7087. CHILDREN, Gospel and. Rev. John Williams had a grand celebration of his Sunday-school children at Raiatea, with six hundred dressed in European costume, in procession, carrying banners with the inscriptions, "What a blessing is the gospel!" "Had it not been for the gospel we should have been destroyed as soon as we were born." "Suffer little children to come unto me." The old people who saw them lamented that they had murdered their own children. The slaughter of infants throughout heathendom is the general practice. The gospel protects life, and cherishes the weak and helpless.

7088. CHILDREN, Imagination of. Although—like ants which throw off their wings in becoming workers—most grown people have discarded their imagination before entering on actual life, the little ones still have it; and if there are no flowers, they will quickly make them. If the surrounding atmosphere be warm and genial, wakeful life will be a ceaseless joy: invention will never be exhausted, and the materials of pastime will never be far to seek; a few corks will improvise a navy, and sticks and stones a palace.   *Dr. J. Hamilton.*

7089. CHILDREN, Love of. During a famine in Germany, a family was driven to the verge of starvation. The father proposed that one of the children should be sold and food provided for those which remained. When at last the mother consented, the question arose which of the four should be selected. The eldest, the first-born, could not be spared; the second looked like the mother, the other resembled its father, and the youngest was the child of their old age—they could spare none. Rather than part with any, they decided to perish with hunger. Yet God so loved the world that he gave his only-begotten son to die for his enemies.

7090. CHILDREN, Martyred. Bassa, a Christian mother, early instructed her three boys to love Christ. Their pagan father accused them to the prefect of Edessa, thinking that the boys would soon be induced to sacrifice to idols, and the constancy of the mother would fail. Theognis, the eldest, was hung up by the wrists and ankles, and his body raked and torn with sharp irons, but he would not give up Christ. The executioners gashed his body till he became insensible, and then cast him, mangled and dead, upon the sand. Agapius, a little boy of great beauty, was next tortured. With the shrill voice of a child, he cried, "King Christ! I will not deny thee! Dear brother, I will not deny thee, but be brave as thou wast." The executioners peeled the skin from his head to his breast, and he died. The youngest was then brought, and asked his name. He answered, "My mother calls me Pistus, and says I must be what I am called—Faithful." Without other cruelty, his head was struck off. Children can be faithful to Christ, even unto death.

7091. CHILDREN, Mother's Prayers for her. A mother whose children were remarkable examples of early piety, was asked the secret of her success. She answered, "While my children were infants on my lap, as I washed them, I raised my heart to God, that he would wash them in that blood which cleanseth from all sin; as I clothed them in the morning, I asked my Heavenly Father to clothe them with the robe of Christ's righteousness; as I provided them food, I prayed that God would feed their souls with the bread of heaven, and give them to drink of the water of life. When I have prepared them for the house of God, I have pleaded that their bodies might be fit temples for the Holy Ghost to dwell in. When they left me for the week-day school, I followed their infant footsteps with a prayer, that their path through life might be like that of the just, which shineth more and more unto the perfect day. And as I committed them to the rest of the night, the silent breathing of my soul has been, that their Heavenly Father would take them to his embrace, and fold them in his paternal arms."

7092. CHILDREN, Mourning for, Prohibited. When children die, no libations nor sacrifices are made for them, nor any other of those ceremonies which are wont to be performed for the dead. For infants have no part of earth or earthly affections. Nor do we hover or tarry about their sepulchres or monuments, or sit by when their dead bodies are exposed. The laws of our country forbid this, and teach us that it is an impious thing to lament for those whose souls pass immediately into a better and more divine state.   *Plutarch*

7093. CHILDREN, Neglect of. Socrates used to say that if he could get up to the highest place in Athens, he would lift up his voice and proclaim, "What mean ye, fellow-citizens, that ye turn every stone to scrape wealth together, and take so little care of your children, to whom, one day, ye must relinquish it all?"

7094. CHILDREN, Power of. In the early French revolution the school-boys of Bourges formed themselves into a Band of Hope. They wore a uniform, and were taught drill. On their holidays, their flag was unfurled, displaying in shining letters the sentence, "*Tremblez, Tyrans, Nous grandirons!*" (Tremble, Tyrants, we shall grow up!) Without any charge of spurious enthusiasm, we may, in imagination, hear the shouts of confidence and courage, uttered by the young Christians of the future, as they say, "Tremble, O enemy, we are growing up for God!" *S. R. Pattison.*

7095. CHILDREN, Power of. Themistocles observing his son's tyranny over his mother, said this boy had more power than all the Greeks, for the Athenians governed Greece, he the Athenians, his wife him, and his son his wife.

7096. CHILDREN, Precaution with. When we see a servant bearing a lighted torch we forbid him to carry it into places where there is straw, hay or such combustible matter, for fear when he least thinks of it a spark should fall and set fire to the whole house. Let us use the same precaution with our children, and not carry their eyes to places of frivolity and amusement. If vain and wicked persons dwell near, us let us forbid our children to look upon them, or have any conversation or commerce with them; lest some spark falling into their souls should cause a general conflagration, and an irreparable damage.   *Chrysostom.*

7097. CHILDREN, Sacrifice of. An eminent historian, speaking of that diabolical custom which so long prevailed amongst the old Carthaginians, of offering their children to a detestable idol (which was formed in such a manner, that an infant put into its hands which were stretched out to receive it, would immediately fall into a gulf of fire), adds a circumstance, which one cannot mention without horror: "The mothers, who, with their own hands, presented the little innocents, thought it an unfortunate omen that the victim should be offered weeping; and, therefore, used a great many fond artifices to divert it, that, soothed by the kisses and caresses of a parent, it might smile in that dreadful moment in which it was to be given up to the idol." Pardon me, my friends; such is your concern for the present ease and prosperity of your children, while their souls are neglected—a fond solicitude that they may pass smiling into the hands of the destroyer.   *Dr. Doddridge.*

7098. CHILDREN, Teaching. A lady had asked Rev. Mr. Simeon if we ought always to be talking about religion? "No, no!" he answered, "let your speech be seasoned with salt; seasoned with salt, madam, not a whole mouthful. Nothing produces more fatal results than 'dinning' religion into a child; the 'whole mouthful' crammed into the child's mouth being simply rejected with disgust. Though, in dealing with the children, everything should be seasoned with the salt of true religion, yet we must remember that small vessels are soon filled, and he who is 'touched with the feeling of our infirmities,' certainly meant us to be touched with the infirmities of little children."

7099. CHILDREN, Thankfulnes for. Lady Storman, mother of Lord Chief Justice Mansfield, being complimented on having the three finest sons in Scotland to be proud of, replied, "No, madam, I have much to be thankful for, but nothing to be proud of."

7100. CHILDREN, Training the. On the mantelshelf of my grandmother's best parlor, among other marvels, was an apple in a phial. It quite filled up the body of the bottle, and my wondering inquiry was, "How could it have been got into its place?" By stealth I climbed a chair to see if the bottom would unscrew, or if there had been a join in the glass throughout the length of the phial. I was satisfied by careful observation that neither of these theories could be supported, and the apple remained to me an enigma and a mystery. Walking in the garden I saw a phial placed on a tree bearing within it a tiny apple, which was growing within the crystal; now I saw it all; the apple was put into the bottle while it was little, and it grew there. Just so must we catch the little men and women who swarm our streets— we call them boys and girls—and introduce them within the influence of the church, for alas! it is hard indeed to reach them when they have ripened in carelessness and sin.
                                    Spurgeon.

7101. CHILDREN, Treatment of. Children should not be flattered, but they should be encouraged. They should not be so praised as to make them vain and proud, but they should be commended when they do well. The desire of praise should not be the principle from which they are taught to act, but they should feel that the approbation of parents is a desirable thing, and when they act so as to deserve that approbation, no injury is done them by their understanding it. He who always finds fault with a child; who is never satisfied with what he does; who scolds and frets and complains, let him do as he will, breaks his spirit, and soon destroys in the delicate texture of his soul all desire of doing well. The child in despair soon gives over every effort to please. He becomes sullen, morose, stupid, and indifferent to all the motives that can be presented to him, and becomes indifferent as to what he does—since all that he does meets with the same reception from the parent.
                                    Barnes.

7102. CHILDREN, Uncontrolled. Prof. Webster was convicted of the murder of Dr. Parkman, of Boston, on circumstantial evidence. He confessed the crime, but excused it by saying, "I am irritable and passionate; a quick-handed and brisk violence of temper have been the besetting sins of my life. I was an only child, much indulged, and have never acquired the control over my temper, as I ought to have acquired early: and the consequence is all this."

7103. CHILDREN, Usefulness of. A little boy heard a passionate drunkard swearing at his horses, and asked, "Is that the way you pray, Mr. Raney?" It was the means of the conversion of the drunkard, which brought great happiness to his family.

7104. CHILDREN Watching for us. When we leave our little children for a few days they watch impatiently for our return. They stand at the window and look down the road through which they expect us to come, and say, "Will papa and mamma never come home?" If they are on a visit and expect us to come for them, they watch and say. "O that papa and mamma would come." Many of us have children in our heavenly Father's house, who are eagerly watching for our coming. A dying child, after exhorting her friends to meet her in heaven, said, "I'll be watching for you."

7105. CHIVALRY, Knighthood of. After confession, a midnight vigil in a church, and the reception of the eucharist, the knight laid his sword on the altar, to signify his devotion to the Church and determination to lead a holy life. The sword was blessed, and girded upon the candidate, by the highest ecclesiastic present. Spurs were also bound on him, and he was smitten upon the cheek or shoulder, the last affront he was to bear unrequited. He then took an oath to protect the distressed, maintain right against might, and never by word or deed to stain his character as knight or Christian. His installation was then complete. If he violated his oath his spurs were chopped off, his sword broken, his escutcheon reversed, and some religious observances were added, during which each piece of armor was taken off, and cast from the recreant knight. To be a true knight was the highest ambition in the age of chivalry. Christianity has a long list of untitled knights.

7106. CHOICE, Christian. A legend represents that Irenæus, one of the fathers of the church, was placed between an idol and a cross and required to choose between them. To prefer the idol was to have official protection, and the honors of the prevailing heathenism conferred upon him. To prefer the cross was to renounce the world and to die for Christ. It required no time for deliberation. He chose the cross and was honored by suffering death upon it like his Divine Master, A. D. 202.

7107. CHOICE, Consider thy. Better it is, toward the right conduct of life, to consider what will be the end of a thing, than what is the beginning of it; for what promises fair at first may prove ill, and what seems at first a disadvantage, may prove very advantageous. *Wells.*

7108. CHOICE, Reasonable. A young lady, in a time of religious interest, sat down and wrote out all the reasons she could think of to help her to decide whom she would serve. She wrote, 1. "Reasons why I should serve the world." 2. "Reasons why I should serve the Lord." She was surprised that she could find no satisfactory reason for the first, and urgent ones for the last. She acted upon her reason, gave herself to God and was blest.

7109. CHOICE, Results of. A Hartford pastor exchanged with the chaplain of the Connecticut State Prison. As he arose in desk he saw among the prisoners a friend of his youth. Their eyes met, and they recognized each other. At the conclusion of the service he sought the man to learn his history. "We were boys," said the prisoner, "in the same neighborhood, we went to the same school, we sat on the same seat, and my prospects were as bright as yours. At fourteen you embraced religion; I chose the world and sin. You are now an honored minister of the gospel; and I, a wretched outcast from society, lost to hope, have been already in prison ten years, and sentenced for life."

7110. CHRIST, Abode of. Martin Luther said, "If any one knocks at the door of my breast and says, 'Who lives there?' my answer is, 'Jesus Christ lives here, not Martin Luther.'" This experience is enjoyed when the soul is united in a personal, conscious, ever-abiding union with Christ. *Dr. Foss.*

7111. CHRIST, Accessibility of. John 6: 37— "Him that cometh unto me I will in no wise cast out." Recently rendered by Matthew of Erberg, in his Italian Bible, "I will by no means thrust him out of doors." Dr. A. Clarke regards the figure, as that of a poor man in deep distress and poverty, who comes to a nobleman's house for relief; he appears at the door, and the owner receives him and relieves him. The strong negative, "I will in no wise cast him out," is equal to the affirmative—I will kindly and graciously receive him. Christ was *born at an inn*, says Bishop Hall, to prefigure his willingness to receive all comers. *The cities of refuge* were distributed over the land of Canaan, and made accessible to all, and kept with the gates open—clear types of Jesus, the strong refuge, ever ready to receive all needing shelter and protection. *Bowes.*

7112. CHRIST, Advantage of the Invisible. It is said when the Duke of Wellington, on one occasion, rode up to his retreating army, a soldier happened to see him first and cried out,

"Yonder is the Duke of Wellington; God bless him!" and the retreating army had courage to nerve itself afresh and went forward and drove the enemy. One has said that the Duke of Wellington was worth more at any time than five thousand men. So it would be if we had the Captain of our salvation in front, we would go forward. How gloriously would this church contend if Christ were visibly in front of them! But the army was sometimes without the Duke of Wellington. There was a place where he could not be. And if Christ were visibly present, he would be present at the same time, only at one church in one locality; it might be in Philadelphia, but what of the thousand other cities? But an unseen Saviour is at the head of the column everywhere. We know he is there. The Captain of our salvation is where two or three are gathered in his name to inspire; and to-day, in every city on the face of this globe, where the columns meet to march, his voice sounds "Onward!" in their ears. His very being unseen inspires hope, and strength and joy. To-day, I thank God, he is leading the hosts in Lapland, in Russia, in China, in Japan, in the torrid regions of Africa, in the islands of the sea, in the mountain-tops, and in the valleys. Oh! how many hearts feel the inspiring influence of his holy presence to-day. It is because he is invisible. "Blessed are they that have not seen and yet believe." *Bp. Simpson.*

7113. CHRIST our All. "Do you know Jesus?" The question was put to a pious young wife, who, having been suddenly stricken down by typhus fever, lay sick unto death, and unconscious of every loving friend by whom she was surrounded. Her husband, to whom she had been married but two short years, had been vainly endeavoring to obtain some sign of recognition. In the agony of his grief he said, "Surely you know me, my darling Ellen? I am Charles, your husband; don't you remember?" "No," she replied, languidly opening her dying eyes; "no, I don't know you, My husband—why—I have no husband." "But you know Jesus, do you not?" inquired a friend, who sat weeping by the bedside. This seemed to touch a chord; and, almost in the very words of good Bishop Beveridge on his death-bed, she responded, whilst the radiance of the coming glory beamed on her brow, and a bright smile played upon her lips, "Jesus—Jesus—oh yes, I do know Jesus; why, he has long been my dearest friend! know Jesus? why he is my Saviour, he is close to me now, close here, quite close. Let me clasp the hand of one who talks to me of my Friend, my Brother." After a short illness of four days, she was called home to be with Christ. *Power.*

7114. CHRIST, All-sufficiency of. The greater Cham is said to have a tree full of pearls hanging by clusters; but what is the great Cham's tree to Christ, our tree of life, who hath all variety and plenty of fruit upon him. The happinesses that come to believers by Christ are so many, that they cannot be numbered; so great, that they cannot be measured; so copi ous, that they cannot be defined; so precious, that they cannot be valued: all which speaks out the fullness and all-sufficiency of Christ.

Brooks.

7115. CHRIST, Ascension of. Biblical. The *high priest* entering the Holy of Holies once every year, on the day of Atonement, Lev. xvi.; Heb. 9: 24-26. The Holy of Holies, where the symbol of Divine glory rested, typified heaven; and within that mysterious shrine the high priest, after he had made atonement for himself, for the sanctuary, and for the people, was to enter; and, dressed in the white linen robes common to the priesthood (not in the gorgeous robe of his high priesthood), was to sprinkle with blood before the mercy-seat seven times, taking with him also a censer full of burning coals, and sweet incense, beaten small. The *ark* carried up, with pomp and rejoicing, to Mount Zion, Ps. 24; 68: 18. *Moses* going up into the mount to receive the law, Deut. 10, and *Elijah's translation to heaven*, followed by the double portion of his spirit being given to his successor, have generally been acknowledged by the church as figures of Christ's ascension. Some add *Samson's* victoriously carrying up the gates of Gaza to the top of the hill, Judges 16: 3.   *Bowes.*

7116. CHRIST, Attachment to. In the time of the Marian persecution there was a woman who, being brought before bloody Bonner, then Bishop of London, upon the trial of religion, he threatened her that he would take away her husband from her. Saith she, "Christ is my husband." "I will take away thy child." "Christ," saith she, "is better to me than ten sons." "I will strip thee," saith he, "of all thy outward comforts." "Yea, but Christ is mine," saith she; "and you cannot strip me of him." O, the assurance that Christ was hers bore up her heart and quieted her spirit, under all. "You may take away my life," saith Basil, "but you cannot take away my comfort;—my head, but not my crown: yea," said he, "had I a thousand lives, I would lay them all down for my Saviour's sake, who hath done abundantly more for me."   *Brooks.*

7117. CHRIST, Attributes of. Christ is a rare jewel, but men know not his value; a sun which ever shines, but men perceive not his brightness, nor walk in his light. He is a garden full of sweets, a hive full of honey, a sun without a spot, a star ever bright, a fountain ever full, a brook which ever flows, a rose which ever blooms, a foundation which never yields, a guide who never errs, a friend who never forsakes. No mind can fully grasp his glory; his beauty, his worth, his importance, no tongue can fully declare. He is the source of all good, the fountain of every excellency, the mirror of perfection, the light of heaven, the wonder of earth, time's master-piece, and eternity's glory; the sun of bliss, the way of life, and life's fair way. "He is altogether lovely," says the saint; a morning without clouds, a day without night, a rose without a thorn; his lips drop like the honey-comb, his eyes beam tenderness. His heart gushes love.

The Christian is fed by his hands, carried in his heart, supported by his arm, nursed in his bosom, guided by his eye, instructed by his lips, warmed by his love; his wounds are his life, his smile the light of his path, the health of his soul, his rest and heaven below.

Balfern.

7118. CHRIST, Banner of. In the times of William Wallace, a daring freebooter infected the seaports of Scotland. In approaching a port he ran up a blood-red flag, and also unfurled the pirate's signal, a death's-head and crossbones, which spread general dismay. Wallace resolved to rid the seas of this cruel scourge. He fitted out a merchantman with rich lading, as if for a cruise, but filled the space between decks with armed men. The pirate gave chase, overhauled, and expected to make the rich prize an easy prey. Wallace's men waited the signal to spring upon the boarders, which they did, captured their leader, and hung him at the yard-arm. He burned the ship, and taking its crew in chains set sail for the city of Perth, flying the captured flag of the pirate at his peak. The people saw the dreaded emblem, and rang the bells of the town to give the alarm. As he neared the dock he ran up the Scotch flag above the pirate's emblem of blood and plunder. The story soon spread through the excited city of the capture of the pirate, and William Wallace, the hero of Scotland, was hailed as his country's deliverer. Christ encountered all the foes of man and conquered. His banner is over all.

7119. CHRIST, Birth of. The death of Christ is a great mystery; but his birth is even a greater. That he should live a human life at all, is stranger than that, so living, he should die a human death. I can scarce get past his cradle in my wondering, to wonder at his cross. The infant Jesus is, in some views, a greater marvel than Jesus with the purple robe and the crown of thorns.   *Crichton.*

7120. CHRIST, Blood of, a Mystery. A reader of the Bible was assailed by an infidel with such expressions as these: "That the blood of Christ can wash away sin is foolishness; I don't understand or believe it." The Bible student remarked, "You and Paul agree exactly." "How?" "Turn to the first chapter of Corinthians and read the eighteenth verse: "For the preaching of the Cross is to them that perish foolishness; but unto us which are saved, it is the power of God."

7121. CHRIST, Blood of, Needed. A man dreamed that he died, and went up to an inclosure surrounding heaven, seeking an entrance. He found a gate on which was written, "Without holiness no man shall see the Lord!" "All right," said he; "I have that;" and he was about entering when a man touched his shoulder, saying, "Stop! you think of entering through that gate?" "Certainly," said he; "I have holiness: I am no sinner." "But do you not remember that when we were boys, and were playing together, you once cheated me out of a marble?" "Yes, I believe I do." "There is one sin, then," said the man; "and since you have committed one sin, you cannot go in at that gate." At this the moralist was much distressed. While weeping at his exclusion and disappointment, he saw another gate, over which was written, "The blood of Jesus Christ cleanseth from all sin." "Thank God for that!" he cried, and immediately renounced his own righteousness, and sought admittance through the blood of Christ.

7122. CHRIST, Blood of, Preached. I was in a city in Europe, and a young minister came to me and said, "Moody, what makes the difference between your success in preaching and mine? Either you are right and I am wrong, or I am right and you are wrong." Said I, "I don't know what the difference is, for you have heard me and I have never heard you preach. What is the difference?" Said he, "You make a good deal out of the death of Christ, and I don't make anything out of it. I don't think it has anything to do with it. I preach the life." Said I, "What do you do with this: 'He hath borne our sins in his own body on the tree'?" Said he, "I never preached that." Said I, "What do you do with this: 'He was wounded for our transgressions; he was bruised for our iniquities, and with his stripes we are healed'?" Said he, "I never preached that." "Well," said I again, "what do you do with this—without the shedding of blood there is no remission?" Said he, "I never preached that." I asked him, "What do you preach?" "Well," he says, "I preach a moral essay." Said I, "My friend, if you take the blood out of the Bible, it is all a myth to me." Said he, "I think the whole thing is a sham." "Then," said I, "I advise you to get out of the ministry very quick, I would not preach a sham. If the Bible is untrue, let us stop preaching, and come out at once like men, and fight against it if it is a sham and untrue; but if these things are true, and Jesus Christ left heaven and came into this world to shed his blood and save sinners, then let us lay hold of it and preach it, in season and out of season." In the college at Princeton this last year, when the students were ready to go forth into the world, the old man, their instructor, would stand up there and say, "Young men, make much of the blood. Young men, make much of the blood!" I have learned this, that a minister who makes much of the blood, and makes much of substitution, and holds Christ up as the sinner's only hope, God blesses his preaching. And if the Apostles didn't preach that, what did they preach? You take the great doctrine of substitution out of the preaching of Paul, Peter, John, James and Philip, and of all those holy men, and you take out all that they preached. And so, my friends, there don't seem to be one ray of hope for the man that ignores the blessed, blessed subject of the blood. "Without the shedding of blood there is no remission." *Moody.*

7123. CHRIST, Bloody Sweat of. Kannegiesser remarks, "If the mind is seized with a sudden fear of death, the sweat, owing to the excessive degree of constriction, often becomes bloody."

The eminent French historian, De Thou, mentions the case of an Italian officer who commanded at Monte-Maro, a fortress of Piedmont, during the warfare in 1552 between Henry II. of France and the Emperor Charles V. This officer having been treacherously seized by order of the hostile general, and threatened with public execution unless he surrendered the place, was so agitated at the prospect of an ignominious death, that he sweated blood from every part of his body. The same writer relates a similar occurence in the person of a young Florentine at Rome, unjustly put to death by order of Pope Sextus V., in the beginning of his reign, and concludes the narrative as follows: "When the youth was led forth to execution, he excited the commiseration of many, and, through excess of grief, was observed to shed bloody tears, and to discharge blood instead of sweat from his whole body." Medical experience does so far corroborate the testimony of the gospels, and shows that cutaneous hemorrhage is sometimes the result of intense mental agitation. The awful anguish of him who said, "My soul is exceeding sorrowful, even unto death," was sufficient cause to produce the bloody perspiration on a cold night and in the open air. *Eadie.*

7124. CHRIST, Branches of. When a small scion is grafted into a tree, a stream of sap and juice begins to flow from the stock into the branch which has been grafted in, till at length it shall blossom and bud and bring forth fruit; it partakes at once both of the root and fatness of the tree. Precisely as the sap flows from the stock into the branch which has been grafted in, so does one continued stream of fruitfulness flow from the Saviour to the souls of those who are really united to him, and who are branches abiding in him. Christ is made sanctification (1 Cor. 1: 30). *F. F. Trench.*

7125. CHRIST, Calmness of. Science tells us that underlying all the tumult and restlessness of the waves of the ocean, over which the winds trample, there is a vast stratum of altogether motionless waters, so utterly tranquil, even when through storm and gloom, "there is sorrow on the sea (Jer. 44: 23), that the tiniest and most fragile shell at the bottom is not stirred, nor in the slightest abraded by all the turmoil above. It seems to me that this remarkable fact and phenomenon may be taken as a symbol of our blessed Lord, regarded as at once "the man Christ Jesus," and very God. In his human nature there was a well of tenderness, that was easily stirred to softest tears; a delight of yearning love that was eager to flow out, and pour itself into the lowliest heart that would lay itself upon his broad bosom; a measureless amplitude of sympathy that was ever ready to bear the heaviest, yea, all the burdens of others; and, I would add, a large and generous charity, that was quick to anticipate confession and to lavish forgiveness—meeting the penitent self-accusation and request of the returning prodigal, "Make me as one of thy hired servants," with the welcome of a son. But underlying all, there was the ETERNAL CALM, unstirred, un moved, of his divinity. What I have just spoken of was as the tossings of the surface-waves, that bear the infinite depths of calm, untouched.   *Grosart.*

7126. CHRIST our Commander. A personal friend, an eye-witness of the affair, informed me that at the first battle of Fredericksburg, while the attacking army had advanced beyond the Rappahannock, each of the several divisions crossing the stream in the very face of the enemy—here dashing upon the foe, here storming a redoubt, there grappling hand in hand with the enemy—while all this was going on, on the other side of the river, upon an eminence, stood the commanding general, surrounded by orderlies ready to carry any commands that were given them. Just at his side was the telegraphic battery, with wires carried in the rear of each division wherever it went; so that the single mind and heart of Burnside gave orders to every part of the advancing army. A single mind controlled the whole movement of the beleaguering host, scattered over many miles of the river bank. You know for what purpose I mention this. Christ cannot go about as he did in Galilee and Judea; but, standing above the embattled host, he overlooks the whole field, and contemplating "the peculiar race," as they go forth to victory, he himself issues the orders, and legions of angels appear for them, and the power of his Spirit, quicker than the electric spark, marshals them on to the conflict.   *Dr. Curry.*

7127. CHRIST, Conquests of. How insipid and tame are the histories of all other conquests—of the rise and fall of all other kingdoms and empires—when compared with the grand and wonderful achievements of the "King Immortal," and the fall of death beneath his power, and the giving up of all his prey; when every victim from earth and sea, though under monuments of marble, nay, rocks of adamant, shall be restored; when he shall bring forth every particular form to be repossessed by its proper spirit, from which it has been for a season divorced! Thus will he "swallow up death in victory," and then clothe his redeemed with garments of immortality. Death shall be known and feared no more. Millions of millions shall join in everlasting praises to him whom all the redeemed will acknowledge as their Great Deliverer.   *R. Hall.*

7128. CHRIST, Crowning. After King George III. was crowned, and invested with all his royal dignity, all the peers were allowed the privilege of putting on their crowns. They looked like a company of kings, as in some sense they were. But immediately they came, one by one, and laid down their crowns at their sovereign's feet, in testimony of their having no power or authority but what they derived from him; and having each kissed his sceptre, he allowed each of them to kiss himself; upon which their crowns were restored to them, and they were all allowed to reign as subordinate kings. This could not miss bringing to mind what is recorded in the Revelation of the whole redeemed company, who are said to be kings and priests unto God, and who are to reign with Jesus Christ forever and ever; their casting down their crowns, and saying, "Thou art worthy to receive power and majesty." I thought with myself were I so happy as to make one of that innumerable company, redeemed from among men, I should not envy all the nobles in England what they are now enjoying.   *Strachan.*

7129. CHRIST, Crucifier of. Wm. Shrubsole casually took up a volume, written by Isaac Ambrose, and began to read that part of it which treats of "Looking to Jesus." He was much affected at the relation of the sufferings of Christ, and sensibly interested at the inquiry which the author makes,—Who were the persons that brought the Divine Sufferer into so much distress? "I was convinced," he said, "that I was deeply concerned in that horrid transaction; and from this time I date the Lord first penetrated my dark mind with the dawn of heavenly light and salvation."

7130. CHRIST, Crucifying. Bridaine, a French preacher, discoursing on the passion of Christ, said, "A man, accused of a crime of which he was innocent, was condemned to death by the iniquity of his judges. He was led to punishment; but no gibbet was prepared, nor was there any executioner to perform the sentence. The people, moved with compassion, hoped that the sufferer would escape death. But one man raised his voice, and said, 'I am going to prepare a gibbet, and I will be the executioner.' You groan with indignation! Well, my brethren, in each of you I behold this cruel man. There are no Jews here to-day, to crucify Jesus Christ; but you dare to rise up and say, 'I will crucify him.'" These words produced most powerful emotion, and nothing was heard but the sobs of the people.

7131. CHRIST, Divinity of. Two Socinians once called on an old member of the Society of Friends, to ask what was his opinion of the person of Christ. He replied, "The apostle says, We preach Christ crucified, unto the Jews a stumbling-block, because they expected a temporal Messiah; to the Greeks foolishness, because he was crucified as a malefactor; but unto them which are called, both Jews and Greeks, Christ the power of God, and the wisdom of God. Now, if you can separate the power of God from God, and the wisdom of God from God, I will come over to your opinions."

7132. CHRIST, Enemies of. The enemies of Christ's kingdom conceive mischief, but they bring forth nothing but vanity. They conceive chaff, and bring forth stubble. "They imagine nothing but a vain thing;" their malice is but like the fighting of briars and thorns with the fire; like the dashing of waves against a rock; like a madman shooting arrows against the sun, which at last return upon his own head, like the puffing of the fan against the corn, which driveth away nothing but the chaff; like the beating of the wind against the sail, or the foaming and raging of the waters against a mill: which by the wisdom of the artificers are all ordered unto useful and excellent ends. "And surely when the Lord shall have accomplished his work on Mount Zion, when he shall by the adversary, as by a fan, have purged away the iniquity of Jacob, and taken away sin, he will then return in peace and beauty unto his people again." Look on the preparation of some large building: in one place you shall see heaps of lime and mortar; in another, piles of timber; everywhere rude and indigested materials, and a tumultuary noise of axes and hammers; but at length the artificer sets everything in order, and raiseth up a beautiful structure: such is the proceeding of the Lord in the afflictions and visitations of his church; though the enemy intend to ruin it, yet God intends only to repair it. Thus far as "*Donec*" respects Christ's kingdom in itself. *Bp. Reynolds.*

7133. CHRIST, Exaltation of. When the Jewish rulers, who had sworn the life of Jesus away before the tribunal of the Roman governor, heard first of his resurrection, they remonstrated with the witnesses: "Ye intend to bring this man's blood upon us." The resurrection of Jesus had no other meaning to them than vengeance. They reasoned: "If he whom we slew is exalted, woe unto us!" But to these very men the apostles preached pardon. They proclaimed that Jesus is exalted for the purpose of showing mercy to his murderers. He is exalted to give, and he gives even to them. He gives to all, and upbraideth not. Now that he is exalted, and his enemies are in his power, instead of taking vengeance, he gives remission of sins. The water is exalted into the heavens in order that it may give rain upon the earth—it is exalted to give. It is drawn up, as by a resurrection; and arises pure into the heavens, that it may be in a capacity to send refreshing to the thirsty ground. In the same way he who comes as rain on the mown grass was exalted that he might give—that he might give himself, as the living water, to his own. *Arnot.*

7134. CHRIST our Example. The Gospel doth not only represent the doctrine of Christ to be believed; but also the life of Christ to be followed: nor shall any have him for their advocate and propitiation, but such as are willing to have him for their pattern and example; to copy out and imitate his humility, patience, purity, benignity, and self-resignation. None shall be benefited by his death, that are unwilling to live his life. *Dr. Worthington.*

7135. CHRIST, Excellency of. As all waters meet in the sea, and as all the lights meet in the sun, so all the perfections and excellencies of all the saints and angels meet in Christ; nay, Christ hath not only the holiness of angels, the loveliness of saints, and the treasure of heaven, but also the fullness of the Godhead—the riches of the Deity are in him: "For it hath pleased the Father that in him should all fullness dwell,"—fullness of grace, fullness of knowledge, fullness of love, fullness of glory. *Dyer.*

7136. CHRIST, Figures of. Dr. Guthrie says: "How difficult it would be to name a noble figure, a sweet simile, a tender or attractive relationship, in which Jesus is not set forth to woo a reluctant sinner and cheer a desponding saint! Am I wounded? He is balm. Am I sick? He is medicine. Am I naked? He is clothing. Am I poor? He is wealth. Am I hungry? He is bread, Am I thirsty? He is water. Am I in debt? He is a surety. Am I in darkness? He is a sun. Have I a house to build? He is a rock. Must I face that black and gathering storm? He is an anchor, sure and steadfast. Am I to be tried? He is an advocate. Is sentence passed, and am I to be condemned? He is pardon. To deck him out and set him forth, Nature culls her finest flowers, brings her choicest ornaments, and lays these treasures at his feet. The skies contribute their stars. The sea gives up its pearls. From fields, and rivers, and mountains, Earth brings the tribute of her gold, and gems, and myrrh, and frankincense, the lily of the valley, the clustered vine, and the fragrant rose of Sharon." Tertullian said, "If thou endurest wrong for Christ's sake, he is a revenger; if sorrow, he is a comforter; if sickness, he is a Physician; if loss, he is a Restorer; if life, he is a reviver."

7137. CHRIST, For the Sake of. Some years ago, in war time, a well-known judge, who had been much interested himself for the welfare of the suffering soldiers, resolved that while a certain case was pending, he would turn away all applicants for charity, that he might devote himself wholly to the duties of his profession. One day a soldier came into his office, poorly clad, his face bearing the deep lines of suffering. The judge, pretending not to notice him, continued his work. The soldier fumbled in his pockets for a long time, and then said in an uncertain, disappointed voice, as though he saw that he was unwelcome, "I did have a letter for you." The judge, acting against the prompting of a warm, generous heart, made no reply. Presently a thin trembling hand pushed a note along the desk. The judge raised his face slightly, and was about to say, "I have no time for such matters as those," when he discovered the writing was that of his own son, a soldier in the army. He took up the note. It read in substance: "Dear Father—The bearer is a soldier, discharged from the hospital. He is going home to die. Assist him in any way you can, for Charlie's sake." All the tender emotions of his soul were laid open. He said to a friend afterward, "I took the soldier to my heart, for Charlie's sake; I let him sleep in Charlie's bed. I clothed him, and supplied him with every comfort, for the sake of my own dear boy." My friends, God will never turn the needy away without a blessing, for his dear son's sake—for Jesus' sake. *Moody.*

7138. CHRIST, Freedom by. Christ's work as our substitute is shown by a story of the time of Napoleon the Great. When a draft was made for soldiers to fill the armies of the Empire, one drafted man procured a substitute to take his place in the ranks. The substitute went into the field and fell, while the drafted man remained in safety at home. After a while another draft was ordered, and the name of the same man was called again. He refused to respond, saying, "I am free. I sent a substitute into the army, and he was killed. So I am as a dead man." The case was carried into the French law-courts, and there it was decided that the man was free. The law had accepted his substitute, and it could not enforce its claims against him.

7139. CHRIST, Fullness of. We know a little of Christ our Saviour, but, oh! how small a portion have we seen of the fullness that is in him! Like the Indians, when America was first discovered, we are not aware of the amazing value of the gold and treasure in our hands. *Ryle.*

7140. CHRIST, Glory of. Cannot we imagine how the hearts of the saints will be enraptured as they see and comprehend all these wonders in their Lord? The astronomer, as he surveys the vast expanse of heaven through his telescope, has his admiration drawn out as it never could have been if he surveyed it only with the naked eye; and he who examines a flower through a microscope, rises from his steady gaze, and strong light, and high magnifying power, which has let him into nature's secrets, with an enthusiasm which otherwise he never could have felt; but neither telescope nor microscope ever admitted any philosophers into such secrets in the natural world as those to which this "I will" (John 17: 24) of Jesus shall admit his glorified people in the spiritual world. *Power.*

7141. CHRIST, the God-Man. When thou hearest of Christ, do not think him God only, or man only, but both together, For I know Christ was hungry, and I know that with five loaves he fed five thousand men, besides women and children. I know Christ was thirsty, and I know Christ turned water into wine. I know Christ was carried in a ship, and I know Christ walked on the waters. I know Christ died, and I know Christ raised the dead. I know Christ was set before Pilate, and I know Christ sits with the Father. I know Christ was worshiped by the angels, and I know Christ was stoned by the Jews. And truly, some of these I ascribe to the human, others to the divine nature; for by reason of this he is said to be both together. *St. Chrysostom.*

7142. CHRIST, Go to. I am a great lover of John Bunyan, but I do not believe him infallible; for I met with a story the other day which I think a very good one. There was a young man in Edinburgh who wished to be a missionary. He was a wise young man; he thought—"Well, if I am to be a missionary, there is no need for me to transport myself far away from home; I may as well be a missionary in Edinburgh." There's a hint to some of you ladies, who give away tracts in your district, and never give your servant Mary one. Well, this young man started, and determined to speak to the first person he met. He met one of those old fishwives: those of us who

have seen them can never forget them; they are extraordinary women indeed. So, stepping up to her, he said, "Here you are, coming with your burden on your back; let me ask you if you have got another burden, a spiritual burden?" "What!" she said; "do you mean that burden in John Bunyan's 'Pilgrim's Progress?' Because if you do, young man, I have got rid of that many years ago, before you were born. But I went a better way to work than the Pilgrim did. The Evangelist that John Bunyan talks about was one of your parsons that do not preach the gospel; for he said, 'Keep that light in thine eye, and run to the wicket-gate.' Why, man alive! that was not the place for him to run to. He should have said, 'Do you see that cross? Run there at once!' But instead of that, he sent the poor pilgrim to the wicket-gate first; and much good he got by going there!—he got tumbling into the slough, and was like to have been killed by it." "But did not you," he asked, "go through any slough of despond?" "Yes, young man, I did; but I found it a great deal easier going through with my burden off than on my back." The old woman was quite right. We must not say to the sinner, "Now sinner, if thou wilt be saved, go to the baptismal pool —go to the wicket-gate—go to the church— do this or that." No, the cross should be right in front of the wicket-gate, and we should say to the sinner, "Throw thyself there, and thou art safe. But thou art not safe till thou canst cast off thy burden, and lie at the foot of the cross, and find peace in Jesus." *Spurgeon.*

7143. CHRIST, Grace of. When Pompey's adherents deserted him, and went over to Cæsar, or were taken prisoners and brought to Cæsar, he loaded them with favors and honors. He declared that it was his highest pleasure to save his enemies who had fought against him. Such clemency and favor is that which Christ shows even to those who have opposed him most.

7144. CHRIST, the Head. Denham Smith makes this remark, "They cannot 'pluck' them out; but they think they may slip out." "Ay," says he, "but they are in his hands; and they are members of his body, and of his flesh, and of his bones." And in Freemasons' Hall, holding up his hands in the midst of a large assembly, he said, "Do you expect to see my fingers fall away? Do you expect to see them drop off! No; because they are parts of myself; and because I live, they shall live also." So Christ's members are parts of himself; and while he lives, they must live. You cannot drown a man while his head is above water; therefore, though he feel below water, he is not drowned if his head is above the stream. So you cannot destroy the church, while the head is alive. Let the head be saved, and the body is saved, if we be really, vitally, personally, and spiritually one with the Lord Jesus Christ. *Spurgeon.*

7145. CHRIST in the Heart. A stationer, being at a fair, hung out his picture of men famous in their kind; among which he had also the picture of Christ. Divers men bought, according to their several fancies. The soldier buys his Cæsar, the lawyer his Justinian, the physician his Galen, the philosopher his Aristotle, the poet his Virgil, the orator his Cicero, and the divine his Augustine—every man after the dictation of his own heart. The picture of Christ hung by still, of less price than the rest; a poor shopman that had no more money than would purchase it, bought it, saying, "Now every one hath taken away his god, let me have mine!" Thus, whilst the covetous repair to their riches, like birds to their nests; the ambitious to their honors, like butterflies to a poppy; the strong to their holds; the learned to their arts; atheists to their sensual refuges, as dogs to their kennels; and politicians to their wit, as foxes to their holes; the devout soul will have no other sanctuary, fix upon no other object, but Christ Jesus, not pictured in their chamber, but planted in the inner chamber of the heart. 　　　　*Salter.*

7146. CHRIST, Heart of. One of the versions of the tradition of the age of chivalry, says that a Scottish king, when dying, bequeathed his heart to the most trusted and beloved of his nobles, to be carried to Palestine. Enclosing the precious deposit in a golden case, and suspending it from his neck, the knight went out with his companions. He found himself, when on his way to Syria, hard pressed by the Moors of Spain. To animate himself to supernatural efforts, that he might break through his thronging foes, he snatched the charge intrusted to him from his neck, and, flinging it into the midst of his enemies, exclaimed, "Forth, Heart of Bruce! as thou wast wont, and Douglas will follow thee or die." The servant cannot go among the vile where the master's heart has not gone.

7147. CHRIST, a Hiding Place. An irreligious young man was driven by a severe rain storm to take shelter in a church. He heard a sermon, but was not impressed. The preacher went to him and said, "I am glad to see you in the house of the Lord even under these circumstances. I hope you will find as good a shelter at the last great day. Remember him who is 'a covert from the storm,' and do not neglect that shelter into which the righteous run and are safe." This apposite personal application of the event which brought him there was the means of leading him to Christ.

7148. CHRIST in History. Tacitus has actually attested the existence of Jesus Christ; the reality of such a personage; his public execution under the administration of Pontius Pilate; the temporary check which this gave to the progress of his religion; its revival a short time after his death; its progress over the land of Judea, and to Rome itself, the metropolis of the empire; all this we have in a Roman historian. 　　　　*Dr. Chalmers.*

7149. CHRIST, Humanity of. Types and figures. The *Tabernacle*, both as a whole, and in its different parts. John 1: 14—"The Word was made flesh and dwelt (literally *tabernacled*) among us." The *vail*, made of beautiful and costly work, rent at Christ's death, Heb, 10:

20; Matt. 27: 51; the shittim *wood* of the brazen altar, and of the altar of incense, etc The *Temple*—the shrine of Deity, John 2 : 19–21; Col. 2: 9. The *Twig*, or sprout, from the stem of Jesse, Isa. 11: 1. Contrast the fall of the high trees, and Lebanon destroyed (the great ones of the earth). with the rise and reign of the slender twig, 10: 33, 34. The *Tender plant*, or sucker out of the dry ground, Isa. 53: 2; see 52: 23. The *Branch*, Zech. 3: 8; 6: 12; Jer. 23: 5; Isa. 4: 2; 11: 1. The Hebrew word for branch (*neetzer*) is most probably the origin of the name of Nazareth, and helps to explain Matt. 2: 23. The *day-spring from on high*, Luke 1: 18 (marg. sunrise, or branch). *Jacob's ladder*—of which the foot was on earth, and the top reached to heaven, Gen. 28: 12; John 1: 51. 　　*Bowes.*

7150. CHRIST, Hungering for. "Blessed are they which do hunger and thirst after righteousness for they shall be filled." Bunyan calls this "a text to hang a soul upon."

7151. CHRIST, Incomprehensible. In a company of literary gentlemen, Daniel Webster was asked if he could comprehend how Jesus Christ could be both God and man. "No sir;" he replied, and added, " I should be ashamed to acknowledge him as my Saviour if I could comprehend him. If I could comprehend him he could be no greater than myself. Such is my sense of sin, and consciousness of my inability to save myself, that I feel I need a superhuman Saviour, one so great and glorious that I cannot comprehend him."

7152. CHRIST, Immortal. After Wm. Pitt had finished his education he started, according to the custom of his day, to make the tour of the continent of Europe. In a German grave-yard he found the name of one upon a monument, and following it the epitaph, "The great borrower." This man had established a great business, gained the public confidence, borrowed millions, and died bankrupt. The thought came to Pitt that he was bankrupted because death put an end to his plans. "My country," said he, "can afford to borrow, for she is immortal." Such is the story of the founder of the great British national debt. Men die, nations wane and disappear, but Jesus Christ is "the same yesterday, to-day, and forever." He can afford to wait, but "he will not fail nor be discouraged till he has brought forth judgment unto victory."

7153. CHRIST our Intercessor. Phocion plead for the most unfortunate persons, and for this some of his countrymen condemned him. He used to say that the good had no need of an advocate. A celebrated criminal was cast into prison, and begged that Phocion would come to him. His friends sought to dissuade him, but he resisted all dissuasions, saying, "Let me alone, good people; where can we rather wish to speak to Aristogiton than in a prison?" So Christ pleads for those who need him most.

7154. CHRIST, Judah's Lion. The tribe of Judah had for its emblem on its banner the figure of a lion. In their marches this tribe headed the column, and their flag first challenged the enemy. "Judah is a lion's whelp," said Jacob, Gen. 49: 9. The heroism of the tribe was well-known. From this tribe the Saviour came. He took up the banner to lead his hosts to victory. The Revelator notes his progress. "The lion of the tribe of Judah, he hath prevailed." His banner leads all, floats above all, and shall triumph over all.

7155. CHRIST, our Keep. The castles of feudalism were surrounded with walls, and moats that could be filled with water. These defences were called the keep of the castle. Whosoever would reach the castle must scale or destroy its walls and encounter the archers upon them and swim its moat. Christ is the keep or keeper of all his followers. He defends them from all assaults of hell and sin.

7156. CHRIST Knocking. The Emperor Henry IV., the mightiest sovereign of Europe, brought upon himself the anathema of Pope Hildebrand by disregarding his edicts. The Pope soon stirred up the people against him, and he was glad to seek a reconciliation. The Emperor went in person to the Pope's residence at Canosa, and stood in an outer court for three days, amid the cold of winter, barefoot, clad only in a woolen shirt, seeking absolution. Christ stands without the soul of man, asking for admission. The pope self, with an assumption greater than that of Hildebrand, refuses admittance. He has waited not days, but weeks and years, and may ere long depart forever.

7157. CHRIST, Knowledge of. Though something of Christ be unfolded in one age, and something in another, yet eternity itself cannot fully unfold him. "I see something," said Luther, "which blessed Augustine saw not; and those that come after me, will see that which I see not." It is in the studying of Christ, as in the planting of a new-discovered country; at first men sit down by the sea-side, upon the skirts and borders of the land, and there they dwell; but by degrees they search further and further into the heart of the country. Ah, the best of us are yet but upon the borders of this vast continent! *John Flavel.*

7158. CHRIST, Leaning on. Miss Fiske, of the Nestorian Mission, was at one time in feeble health, and much depressed in spirits. One hot Sabbath afternoon she sat on her mat on the chapel floor, longing for support and rest, feeling unable to maintain her trying position until the close of worship. Presently she felt a woman's form seated at her back, and heard the whisper, "Lean on me." Scarcely yielding to the request, she heard it repeated, "Lean on me." Then she divided her weight with the gentle pleader, but that did not suffice. In earnest, almost reproachful tones, the voice again urged, "If you love me, lean hard!"

7159. CHRIST, Legend of. A foolish legend says that on the arrival of the holy family with the child Jesus in Egypt, all the idols fell before him, and that Aphrodisius, then governor of Egypt, recognizing the divinity of Christ from this omen, fell down and worshiped him as his God.

7160. CHRIST Lifted up. After the battle of Pittsburg Landing and Murfreesboro, I was in a hospital at Murfreesboro. And one night, after midnight, I was woke up and told that there was a man in one of the wards who wanted to see me. I went to him, and he called me "chaplain," and said he wanted me to help him die. And I said, "I'd take you right up in my arms and carry you into the kingdom of God if I could; but I can't do it; I can't help you to die." And he said, "Who can?" I said, "The Lord Jesus Christ can—he came for that purpose." He shook his head and said, "He can't save me; I have sinned all my life." And I said, "But he came to save sinners." I thought of his mother in the North, and I knew that she was anxious that he should die right, and I thought I'd stay with him. I prayed two or three times, and repeated all the promises I could, and I knew that in a few hours he would be gone. I said I wanted to read him a conversation that Christ had with a man who was anxious about his soul. I turned to the third chapter of John. His eyes were riveted on me, and when I came to the 14th and 15th verses, he caught up the words, "As Moses lifted up the serpent in the wilderness, even so must the Son of man be lifted up; that whosoever believeth on him should not perish, but have eternal life." He stopped me and said, "Is that there?" I said, "Yes," and he asked me to read it again, and I did so. He leaned his elbows on the cot and clasped his hands together and said, "That's good; won't you read it again?" I read it the third time, and then went on with the rest of the chapter. When I finished his eyes were closed, his hands were folded, and there was a smile on his face. O! how it was lit up! What a change had come over it! I saw his lips quivering and I leaned over him and heard, in a faint whisper, "As Moses lifted up the serpent in the wilderness, so must the Son of man be lifted up, that whosoever believeth on him should not perish, but have eternal life." He opened his eyes and said, "That's enough; don't read any more." He lingered a few hours and then pillowed his head on those two verses, and then went up in one of Christ's chariots and took his seat in the kingdom of God. *Moody.*

7161. CHRIST, Longing for. "Whilst we are at home in the body, we are absent from the Lord." You have a little shadow, or emblem of this in other creatures: you see the rivers, though they glide never so sweetly betwixt the fragrant banks of the most pleasant meadows in their course and passage, yet on they go towards the sea; and if they meet with never so many rocks and hills to resist their course, they will either strive to get passage through them, or if that may not be, they will fetch a compass and creep about them, and nothing can stop them till by a central force they have finished their weary course, and poured themselves into the bosom of the ocean. Or as it is with yourselves, when abroad from your habitations and relations: this may be pleasing a little while; but if every day might be a festival, it would not long please you, because you are not at home.   *Flavel.*

7162. CHRIST, Looking to. That flower which follows the sun, doth so even in cloudy days: when it doth not shine forth, yet it follows the hidden course and motion of it. So, the soul that moves after God, keeps that course when he hides his face; is content, yea, is glad at his will in all estates, or conditions, or events.   *Leighton.*

7163. CHRIST, Love to. It is said that when Cato the younger was but a child, he was asked whom he loved most. He answered, "My brother." He was then asked whom next. He replied, "My brother." Again and again whom he loved, third, fourth and fifth, and so until the questioner was tired, and he still said "My brother." As he grew older he displayed the same disposition, and was never happier than when in his brother's company. The Christian should love Christ thus, first, last and above all others.

7164. CHRIST, Mercy of. Arnot says, "A ship has caught fire at sea. The passengers and crew, shut up in one extremity of the burning ship, strain their eyes and sweep the horizon round for sight of help. At length, and just in time, a sail appears and bears down upon them. But the stranger, fearing fire, does not venture near, but puts about her helm, and soon is out of sight. The men in the burning ship are left to their fate. How dreadful their situation, when the selfish ship saved itself from danger, and left them to sink! What heart can conceive the misery of human kind, if the Son of God had saved himself from suffering, and left a fallen world to the wrath of God!" But Christ did not save himself and let the wreck of humanity go down. He sank into the dark waves of death to rescue man.

7165. CHRIST Mighty to Save. It is possible to have both knowledge and power in vain. I know not that I can better, and I feel that I cannot more touchingly, illustrate this, than by a fact concerning that good and true soldier of Jesus Christ, Hedley Vicars. A friend of his told lately to an auditory in London that his wound was not a mortal one. It was one well known, and over which a surgeon has perfect power. And yet "he died." Why? Because, in the hurry and tumult of that terrible morning, on the gray heights of the Crimea, the regiment of Hedley Vicars was carried far from the tents that held the supplies. There was no bandage with which to tie the bleeding artery; and, ere they reached the store-tents, the Christian soldier was no more. He bled to death. "If," said his friend, with the pathos of true affection, "if there had been a bandage—if the tents of supplies had been half-a-mile nearer, Hedley Vicars might have been alive to-day." It needeth not, my friends, that I "adorn this tale" of war. I leave it alone in its beautiful simplicity. You have anticipated its application. Knowledge of the wound was of no avail: power over the wound

was of no avail. Knowledge and power, in the absence of the bandage, in the distance from the supplies, were of no avail. *Grosart.*

7166. CHRIST, Miracles of. We distinguish a two-fold object of his miracles: the first a material one—the meeting of some immediate emergency, of some want of man's earthly life which his love urged him to satisfy; the other and higher one—to point himself out to the persons whose earthly necessities were thus relieved, as the one alone capable of satisfying their higher and essential spiritual wants; to raise them from this single exhibition of his glory in the individual miracle to a vivid apprehension of the glory of his entire nature. Nay, it was to be a sign to all others that they might believe in him as the son of God.   *Neander.*

7167. CHRIST, the Mirror of Truth. There is in Rome an elegant fresco by Guido, "The Aurora." It covers a lofty ceiling. Looking up at it from the pavement your neck grows stiff, your head dizzy, and the figures indistinct. You soon turn away. The owner of the palace has placed a broad mirror near the floor. You may now sit down before it as at a table, and at your leisure look into the mirror, and enjoy the fresco that is above you. There is no more weariness, nor indistinctness, nor dizziness. So God has brought otherwise inaccessible celestial truth to our world through Jesus Christ. In him, as in a glass, we may behold the glory and truth and grace of God. He is himself "the Truth." Like the Rospiglioso mirror beneath the "Aurora," Christ reflects the excellencies of heavenly character. In all essential elements he was on earth what they are in heaven.   *S. S. Journal.*

7168. CHRIST, Need of Contact with. There are two kinds of magnets, steel magnets and soft iron magnets. The steel magnet receives its magnetism from the loadstone, and has it permanently; it can get along very well alone in a small way; it can pick up needles and do many other little things to amuse children. There is another kind of magnet which is made of soft iron, with a coil of copper wire round it. When the battery is all ready and the cups are filled with the mercury, and the connection is made with the wires, this magnet is twenty times as strong as the steel magnet. Break the circuit, and its power is all gone instantly. We are soft iron magnets; our whole power must come from the Lord Jesus Christ; but faith makes the connection, and while it holds we are safe.   *C. D. Foss.*

7169. CHRIST, None Cast Out by. The custom prevailed among the pagan Kaffirs of casting out their sick and dying friends and leaving them in some desolate place, lest their houses should be defiled with the presence of the dead. The helpless are thus left to suffer cruel agonies. A little girl who had been torn by wolves, was cast out by her parents to die. She thought of the missionary's well known kindness and resolved, "I will try to creep to his house, for he is kind and will not cast me out." Slowly she made her way to his door. He received her with great tenderness, bound up her wounds and tended her carefully till they were healed. Then he asked her if she would go back to her parents; she said, "O no, they cast me out; you took me in; I will stay with you." She went also to Christ and was received. Christ says, "He that cometh unto me I will in no wise cast out."

7170. CHRIST Not a Hard Master. I remember once a party of gentlemen speaking of this parable that I read, and asking a deaf man, "What do you think of this man's hiding his talent and about the justice of his reward?" The deaf man replied, "I don't know anything about the justice of his reward, but I know he is a liar. The Lord isn't a hard master." And so these men who bury their talents, they think the Lord is a hard master; but the men who are using their talents, they don't think the Lord is a hard master.   *Moody.*

7171. CHRIST, Painting of. John Huss, the martyr of the fifteenth century, while in his dungeon awaiting execution, dreamed that the pictures of Christ, which he had caused to be painted on the walls of his study, were obliterated by the pope. By this he was grieved. The next day he dreamed that a great number of painters were restoring the pictures of Christ in greater beauty. He saw great crowds of people admiring the portraits, and heard them say, "Now let the pope and the bishops come; they will never be able to efface them again." He was much encouraged, and told his dreams to a friend who cautioned him against trusting in them. Huss answered, "I am not a dreamer, but I hold this for certain that the image of Christ shall never be effaced. They have wished to destroy it, but it shall be painted again in the hearts of men by painters abler than myself. The nation which loves Jesus Christ will rejoice thereat, and I awakening from the dead, and rising from the grave, shall thrill with great joy." A century of persecution did indeed blot the image of Jesus from the hearts of men, and a feast was held in Rome to celebrate the complete triumph of the papacy. Then appeared Luther and many more painters, restoring the image of Christ in the hearts of multitudes.

7172. CHRIST a Physician. Christ has put himself under the name of physician, a doctor for curing diseases; and you know that applause and fame is a thing that physicians much desire. That is it that helps them to patients, and that also that will help their patients to commit themselves to their skill for cure with the more confidence and repose of spirit. And the best way for a doctor or a physician to get themselves a name is, in the first place, to take in hand and cure some such as all others have given up for lost and dead. Physicians get neither name nor fame by pricking of wheals, or picking out thistles, or by laying of plasters to the scratch of a pin; every old woman can do this. But if they would have a name and a fame, if they will have it quickly, they must, as I said, do some great and desperate cures. Let them fetch one to life that was dead; let him recover one to his wits that was mad; let them make one that was born blind to see; or let them give right wits to a fool; these are notable cures, and he that can do thus, and if he doth thus first, he shall have the name and fame he desires.
Bunyan

7173. CHRIST, Preparing the Way of. Dr. Wolf, when lecturing in Philadelphia, 1837, stated that on entering Jerusalem from the west, in the direction of Gaza, the road, for a considerable distance from Jerusalem, was so full of stones that it was impossible to ride, and those who were entering the city were obliged to dismount. When Ibrahim Pacha, son of Mohammed Ali, approached Jerusalem, a considerable number of laborers went before him, and removed the stones from the way, amidst a constant cry of "Cast up! cast up the way! Remove the stones!" And on a standard was written, "The Pacha is coming;" and everywhere the cry was heard, "The Pacha is coming! The Pacha is coming! Cast up the way! Remove the stones!" The expression indicates the removal of obstacles and difficulties, preparatory to some important manifestation, or some signal event. See also Isaiah 62: 10.
Nicholson.

7174. CHRIST, Presence of. It is said that the Macedonians had a great general named Eumenes, in whom they placed immense confidence. On one occasion, when he was very sick, they were forced to march against an opposing host without his presence at their head. Seeing the lustre of the golden armor and the beauty of the purple vests of their foes, and the immense elephants with towers upon their backs filled with armed men, they halted, declaring that they would not move a step unless their leader could direct their movements. Eumenes, hearing of their indecision, hastened with speed to the front, opened the curtains that hid him from their view, and stretched forth his hand to bid them advance. Catching the inspiration, they saluted him joyously, clanked their weapons, uttered a great shout, and went forward, thinking themselves invincible. They were defeated because he was only a man, but the presence of Christ secures victory.

7175. CHRIST, Prizing. A martyr was asked whether he did not love his wife and children, who stood by him. "Love them!" said he, "Yes; if all the world were gold and at my disposal, I would give it all for the satisfaction of living with them, though it were in prison; yet in comparison with Christ I love them not."

7176. CHRIST, Receiving. A young nobleman had been long absent from his extensive domains and numerous tenantry, till he was a stranger to them. Having returned home, he was out hunting, and wandered from his party become lost and thoroughly drenched. He sought shelter and relief in the cottages of some of his tenants, but they did not recognize him as the lord of the manor, and shut their door, in his face. Knocking at the cottage of a poor widow he heard the invitation, "Come in, thou blessed of the Lord." She gave him a suit of dry though coarse clothing, and spread before him the best fare she could provide. He went away promising to return for his own clothes. The next day he appeared with his retinue, and stopped before the poor widow's door. She discovered in the young lord her unknown guest. He thanked her for the kindness shown to a stranger, and rewarded her with a better cottage and an annuity. She gave as a reason for her hospitality the case of her own boy away at sea, who might be needing shelter, and of him who had not where to lay his head, who "came unto his own, and his own received him not."

7177. CHRIST, Reflecting. A small mirror may flood a room with dazzling light if only it confronts the sun; and a child may dwell so near to Christ that he or she may be the charm and lustre of the home.　　　　*Bolton.*

7178. CHRIST our Refuge. Along the exposed routes among the Alps places of shelter have been erected. Into these the threatened or weary traveler may enter and find protection and refreshment. The pilgrim of the desert finds stone shelters erected by beneficent hands by the wayside, in which he may hide from the resistless storm. Such is Christ to thee, O pilgrim of Life; thy shelter, thy refuge, thy rest, "the shadow of a great Rock in a weary land."

7179. CHRIST, Resurrection of. *Biblical types and Illustrations.* Isaac received back from the dead, Gen. 21: 10-14; Heb. 11: 19, "he received him in a figure" (or for a type). *Joseph* raised from the prison to the throne, Gen. 39: 20; 41: 39-45. *Jonah* restored, after three days and three nights in the whale's belly, Matt. 12: 40, *Eliakim* signifies the resurrection of the Lord, Isa. 22, 20; see ver. 21-24. *The ark* resting after the flood on Mount Ararat, on the seventeenth day of the seventh month; the very day Christ rose, as some think, Gen. 8: 4.—*Jukes on Offerings. Aaron's rod that budded,*—life springing out of death. "Just as Aaron was declared to be the man of God's choice in the matter of the priesthood, by the signs of resurrection life in his rod, which budded while all the other rods remained dead; so is Jesus declared to be the chosen one of God—his great high priest, the antitype of Aaron, by the resurrection from the dead; or, as it, might have been rendered, "from among the dead ones."—*A. L. Newton. The first-fruits* offered as a pledge of the harvest, the morrow after the passover Sabbath, Lev. 23: 9-14. See 1 Cor. 15: 20, "Christ the first-fruits." *The first-born,* having the pre-eminence—the beginning of strength and highest in rank; see Col. 1: 18. Christ "the first-born from the dead;" Rev. 1: 6, "the first-begotten of the dead." *The living bird* let loose at the cleansing of the leper, Lev. 14: 53. *The scapegoat* probably, Lev. 16. *The corn of wheat*—first dying, then rising into life, John 12: 24. *The temple destroyed* and raised, John 2: 19. The TIME of Christ's resurrection is variously counted. *The first day,* the early morning, Luke 24: 1. As we now count the

days, the resurrection of Christ was, as it were, a new starting-point of time. *The third day* from his death, according to the Hebrew mode of reckoning. "It is *ten times* expressly said that our Lord rose, or was to rise again, on the third day."　　　　*Bowes.*

7180. CHRIST, Revelation of. A Jew was attracted into the hippodrome by hearing the singing. Once and again he came, the singing and the preaching having so great an effect upon him, until he felt impelled to enter the inquiry-room. Here he was met by one who asked him what he wanted. "Oh," said he, "I am very miserable; I hear the singing and the speaking, and I don't know what to do." The Christian worker called Mr. Moody, and the poor Jew told him the same story. "Believe on the Lord Jesus Christ, and thou shalt be saved," said Mr. Moody. "Don't talk to me about Jesus Christ; I don't believe in him; I hate him." "Well, then, let us talk about the serpent that was lifted up in the wilderness; you know the people had only to look and live." And then Mr. Moody knelt down and prayed that this man might be enabled to see Jesus. Suddenly he exclaimed, "Oh! I looked first only at the serpent lifted up, but it all changed into Christ on the cross. I see only Christ on the cross." He rejoiced in Jesus his Saviour—no longer a Jew, but a trusting Christian.

7181. CHRIST, Satisfied with. An aged saint was asked what was the Gospel she believed, and how she believed it. Her simple reply was: "God is satisfied with his Son, that is the Gospel I believe; and I am satisfied with him too, that is how I believe it."

7182. CHRIST Saving. A gentleman in Philadelphia was a teacher of a class of boys on Sunday nights. He was requested to go and see one of their number who was sick. The gentleman hastened to his side, and inquired if he needed medicine or food. "No, Captain, it wasn't that I wanted ye for," replied the boy, "but I wanted to ax ye two questions. Didn't you tell us the other night as how Jesus Christ died for every fellow?" "Yes, I did, for Jesus Christ tasted death for every man." Billy, then said, "I thought so. Now I've another question. Did you tell us as how Jesus Christ saves every fellow that axes him?" "Yes, for every one that asketh receiveth." With a feeble but cheerful voice, the boy replied, "Then I know that he saves me, because I axes him." His head fell back upon his pillow of rags, and his happy spirit went to be with Jesus whom he trusted.

7183. CHRIST Scourged. Oh, until I came to read all about what Christ suffered, I never before realized what he had done for us. I never knew until I came to read all about the Roman custom of scourging what it meant by Christ being scourged for me. When I first read about that I threw myself on the floor and wept, and asked him to forgive me for not having loved him more. Let us imagine the scene where he is taken by the Roman soldiers to be scourged. The orders were to put forty stripes, one after another, upon his bared back. Sometimes it took fifteen minutes, and the man died in the process of being scourged. See him stooping while the sins of the world are laid upon him, and the whips come down upon his bare back, cutting clear through the skin and flesh to the bone. And, after they had scourged him, instead of bringing oil and pouring in into the wounds, he who came to bind up the broken heart and pour oil into its wounds—instead of doing this they dressed him up again, and some cruel wretch reached out to him a crown of thorns, which was placed upon his brow. The Queen of England wears a crown of gold, filled with diamonds and precious stones, worth $20,-000,000; but when they came to crown the Prince of Heaven, they gave him a crown of thorns and placed them upon his brow, and in his hand they put a stick for a scepter.

Moody.

7184. CHRIST, Searching for. A man who was filling his barns with grain lost a bank note of large value. He knew that it was in the barn, and resolved to find it, if he had to remove every particle of hay and grain it contained. He removed bundle after bundle, and after a long and diligent search found the note. Some time after he became anxious about his soul. His son said, "Father, if you seek Jesus as you sought after that lost bank-note, you will be sure to find him." This led his father to concentrate all his energy in his search for Christ. He prayed, read the Scriptures, used the means of grace, and soon found the Saviour he sought.

7185. CHRIST, Service for. Brutus visiting Ligarius found him ill, and said, "What, sick, Ligarius?" "No, Brutus," said he, "if thou hast any noble enterprise in hand, I am well." Should the Lord Jesus condescend to us, we should be always ready with a like answer.

7186. CHRIST, Shelter in. When I was in England I had a great curiosity to visit the Zoological Gardens, because of a story I heard concerning them. There was a man who had a little dog which he had trained to run. So one day he made a bet about his dog's running, but when the time came for the race the little dog wouldn't run at all, and the man lost all his money. This so enraged the man that he beat the dog terribly, and at last he tucked him into the lion's cage. He thought the lion would make quick work of him, but the lion lapped the dog and made a pet of him, so at last the man wanted to get his dog back, and called to him, and tried by every means to make the little dog come out of the cage, but he wouldn't come. So the man went and told a man about it, and the man told the keeper, and when the keeper came, the man said to him, "That's my dog in the cage there, and I want you to get him out for me." Then the keeper said, "How came the dog there?" And the man had to tell, and the keeper said, "If you want your dog you can take him out of the cage." He could not take him out, and there he stayed for twenty years. The only safety is to keep close to Christ. The lion of

the tribe of Judah conquered the lion of hell. Keep close to Christ. None shall pluck you out of his hand. It's no delusion! It has kept me for twenty years. If it's a delusion, it's a precious delusion.   *Moody.*

7187. CHRIST Smitten. Mr. Hanway, in his travels, has recorded this scene:—"A prisoner was brought, who had two large logs of wood fitted to the small of his leg, and riveted together; there was also a heavy triangular collar of wood about his neck. The General asked me if that man had taken my goods. I told him I did not remember to have seen him before. He was questioned some time, and at length ordered to be beaten with sticks, which was performed by two soldiers with such severity as if they meant to kill him. The soldiers were then ordered to spit in his face, an indignity of great antiquity in the East. This brought to my mind the sufferings recorded in the prophetical history of our Saviour, Isaiah 50 : 6."

7188. CHRIST, Sole Dependence in. Montmorency, Constable of France, being mortally wounded, was exhorted to die with the same courage which he had shown in his lifetime. To this he replied, "Gentlemen and fellow-soldiers, I thank you all very kindly for your anxious care and concern about me; but the man who has been enabled to endeavor to live well for four-score years past, can never need to seek now how to die well for a quarter of an hour. But observe, my having been enabled to endeavor to live well is not the ground of my dependence : no, my sole dependence is on Jesus Christ. It is by the grace of God, through him, that I now am what I am."

7189. CHRIST, Superiority of. The following is by a converted Chinaman: "A man had fallen into a deep, dark pit, and lay in its miry bottom groaning and utterly unable to move. Confucius walking by, approached the edge of the pit, and said, 'Poor fellow! I am sorry for you. Why were you such a fool as to get in here? Let me give you a piece of advice: If you get out, don't get in again.' A Buddhist priest next came by, and said, 'Poor fellow! I am very much pained to see you there. I think if you could scramble up two-thirds of the way, or even half, I could reach you and lift you up the rest.' But the man in the pit was entirely helpless and unable to rise. Next the Saviour came by, and, hearing the cries, went to the very brink of the pit, stretched down and laid hold of the poor man, brought him up and said, 'Go, and sin no more.'"

7190. CHRIST, Suffering for. We see what hazards men run to get temporary riches : to the bottom of rocks for diamonds, to the bowels of the earth for gold and silver; such affections have the saints had towards the gospel. If they must dig in mines for Christ (as it was an usual condemnation, *Christiani ad metalla*) they were most willing so to do: they had a treasure there which the emperor knew not of; they had infinite more precious wealth from thence than he. If they must fetch Christ in the fire, or wrestle for him, as for a precious prize, with the wild beasts of the earth—if they be not suffered to wear Christ, except they put off themselves—how willing, how thankful are they for so rich a bargain! "Look to your life," said the governor to St. Cyprian, that blessed martyr, "be not obstinate against your own safety, but advise well with yourself." "*Fac quod tibi præceptum est*," saith the holy man; "*in re tam justa nulla est consultatio;*" "Sir, you are my judge, you are none of my counsellor; do the office which is committed to you; in so righteous a cause there is no further need of consultation."

Bp. Reynolds.

7191. CHRIST a Teacher. The famous Ascham died 1568. The loss of a valuable instructor is a matter of great grief. Ascham had been tutor in the learned languages to Queen Elizabeth, who so much lamented his death, that she declared she would rather have lost ten thousand pounds than her tutor Ascham. Christian, rejoice! thy Great Teacher never dies; nor shall the knowledge he communicates ever be lost! Antisthenes taught rhetoric, and had among his pupils Diogenes; but when he had heard Socrates, he shut up his school, and told his pupils, "Go, seek for yourselves a master; I have found one." Thus all who are convinced of their ignorance will renounce everything that would prevent them from sitting at the feet of Christ to learn of him. Philip wrote to Aristotle thus, "I inform you I have a son: I thank the gods, not so much for making me father, as for giving me a son in an age when he can have our Aristotle for his instructor." How much more may the Christian feel grateful, not only that God has given him life and rational faculties, but that he has Christ for his teacher, for "Who teacheth like him?" *Buck.*

7192. CHRIST, Testimony to. The Council of Nice was instrumental in vindicating the divinity of Christ against Arianism, which affirmed that he was a mere creature, who once did not exist, who was made by God like other creatures, and who might have fallen into sin. Here Athanasius took his firm stand for Christ, from which neither intimidation, persecution, or banishment ever moved him. *Athanasius contra mundum* then meant Athanasius for Christ. In that council were many whose dearest friends were martyrs for Christ. Many demanded to be heard because of what they had suffered in the persecutions for him. They uncovered their bodies to show the wounds they had received for the Divine Man, whose omnipotent support they had felt in the hour of need. Others had been disfigured by having an eye plucked out, or a hand cut off, or a limb stiffened by searing the sinews of the leg, and could say, "Let these speak for Christ." The formula of faith made under this influence in 325 expresses the orthodox belief of the word, and is most explicit testimony to the divinity of Christ.

7193. CHRIST, Thanking. A gentleman in England visited a company of gypsies, and found a lad alone and in bed, evidently in the last stage of consumption. His eyes were closed, and he looked as one already dead. Very slowly in his ear he repeated the Scripture, "God so loved the world that he gave his only-begotten Son, that whosoever believeth in him should not perish, but have everlasting life." He repeated it five times without any apparent response; he did not seem to hear even with the outward ear. On hearing it the sixth time he opened his eyes and smiled, and whispered, "And I never thanked him; but nobody ever told me! I 'turn him many thanks—only a poor gypsy chap! I see! I see! I thank him kindly!" He closed his eyes with an expression of intense satisfaction. The lips moved again. He caught, "That's it." Next day he was dead, or, rather, had fallen asleep in Christ. His father said he had been very "peaceable," and had a "tidy death."

7194. CHRIST, Touching. To touch Christ's work is to touch Christ. Mark 5 : 28.

Dr. Holme.

7195. CHRIST, Trampling on. I once heard of a father who had a prodigal boy, and the boy had sent his mother down to the grave with a broken heart, and one evening the boy started out as usual to spend the night in drinking and gambling, and his old father as he was leaving said, "My son, I want to ask a favor of you to-night. You have not spent an evening with me since your mother died, and now I want you to spend this night at home. I have been very lonely since your mother died. Now won't you gratify your old father by staying at home with me?" "No," said the young man, "it is lonely here, and there is nothing to interest me, and I am going out." And the old man prayed and wept, and at last he said, "My boy, you are just killing me as you have killed your mother. These hairs are growing whiter, and you are sending me, too, to the grave." Still the boy would not stay, and the old man said, "If you are determined to go to ruin, you must go over this old body to-night. I cannot resist you. You are stronger than I, but if you go out you must go over this body." And he laid himself down before the door, and that son walked over the form of his father, trampled the love of his father under foot, and went out. And that is the way with sinners. You have got to trample the blood of God's Son under your feet if you go down to death, to make light of the blood of the innocent, to make light of the wonderful love of God. *Moody.*

7196. CHRIST, Transfiguration of. It was seemingly on the Sabbath-day ("after six days") that this grand exception to the tenor of Christ's earthly history was manifested. It was a rehearsal of his ascension. His form, which had been bent under a load of sorrow—a bend more glorious than the bend of the rainbow—now erected itself, like the palm-tree from pressure, and he became like unto "a pillar in the temple of his God." His brow expanded; its wrinkles of care fled, and the sweat-drops of his climbing toil were transmuted into sparks of glory. His eye flashed forth like the sun from behind a cloud; nay, his whole frame became transparent, as if it were one eye. The light which had long lain in it concealed, was now unveiled in full effulgence: "His face did shine as the sun." His very raiment was caught in a shower of radiance, and became "white as no fuller on earth could whiten it." And who shall describe the lustre of his streaming hair, or the eloquent silence of that smile which sate upon his lips?

"Light o'erflow'd him like a sea, and raised his shining brow,
And the voice came forth, which bade all worlds the Son of God avow."

G. Gilfillan.

7197. CHRIST, Trust in. Dr. Wayland remarked shortly before his end, "I feel that my race is nearly run. I have indeed tried to do my duty. I cannot accuse myself of having neglected any known obligation. Yet all this avails nothing. I place no dependence on anything but the righteousness and death of Jesus Christ. I have never enjoyed the raptures of faith vouchsafed to many Christians. I do not undervalue those feelings, but it has not pleased God to bestow them upon me. I have, however, a confident hope that I am accepted in the beloved."

7198. CHRIST, Trusting. There is a story of Dr. Chalmers, who went to see a Scotch woman in her time of trouble about her sin. In the north of Scotland they spend a good deal of thought in just looking at themselves, and occupying themselves with their misgivings. This Scotch woman was trying to get faith. On his way he had to cross a stream over which there was nothing but a thin plank, and he thought it looked rotten and insecure; and he went up and put his foot upon the plank doubtingly, and feared to trust his weight upon it; and the Scotch woman, watching him from the window, saw that he was afraid to venture out on the plank, and she came out and shouted, "Just trust the plank, Doctor!" And the doctor did trust the plank, and walked over the stream in safety. Afterward he was talking with the woman. She hadn't the right kind of faith, she said, and was lamenting over her lot. The Doctor to explain to her what was the trust she ought to have, at last hit upon the circumstance of his crossing the plank, and, using the woman's queer Scotch expression, said to her: "Trust Christ, cannot you?" "Oh, Doctor, is that faith?" said she; "is it just to trust him?" "That is faith," said he, "just to trust him as I trusted that plank. It carried me over, and you trust God and he will carry you over." "Oh," said she, "I can do that." That means trust the plank. Just trust it, and it won't break under you. *Moody.*

7199. CHRIST United with Man. Two friends are said to come into Vulcan's shop, and to beg a boon of him: it was granted. What was it? that he would either beat them on his anvil, or melt them in his furnace, both into one. But without fiction, here is a far greater love in Christ; for he would be melted in the furnace of wrath, and beaten on the anvil of death, to be made one with us. And to declare the exceeding love, here were not both to be beaten on the anvil, or melted in the furnace; but without us, he alone would be beaten on the anvil, he alone melted that we might be spared. *Thomas Adams.*

7200. CHRIST, Venturing on. Rev. Dr. Simpson, of Hoxton, England, spoke with disapprobation of a phrase often used by some good people, "venturing on Christ." "When I consider," said he, "the infinite dignity and all-sufficiency of Christ, I am ashamed to talk of venturing on him. Oh! had I ten thousand souls, I would, at this moment, cast them all into his hands with the utmost confidence." A few hours before his dissolution, he addressed himself to the last enemy in a strain like that of the apostle, when he exclaimed, "O death! where is thy sting?" Displaying his characteristic fervor, as though he saw the tyrant approaching, he said, "What art thou? I am not afraid of thee. Thou art a vanquished enemy through the blood of the cross."

7201. CHRIST, Visit of. How great a difference there is between the prisoner in his dungeon and the visitor that has come to see him. They are both within the walls of the dungeon: one who did not know, might suppose them under equal restraint; but one is the compassionate visitor who can use his freedom when he will, the other is fast bound there for his offences. So great is the difference between Christ, the compassionate visitor of man, and man himself, the criminal in bondage for his offence.

St. Augustine.

7202. CHRIST, Voice of. When we were in Brooklyn, I found a man in the inquiry room that was greatly troubled about his soul. He told me he had had a godly mother; that she had died and he had her picture put upon the wall, but he had been living such a miserable life he had to turn the face of that picture toward the wall; that mother's prayer haunted him so he could not sleep. That was the Son of God seeking for that young man through the picture on the wall. *Moody.*

7203. CHRIST, Volunteering for. A young man went to his mother soon after the war began with the question, "Mother, may I volunteer?" He said, "I argue the matter from four plain propositions. First, my country needs me. Second, she calls me. Third, I am able to go. Fourth, I am willing. This makes the duty very clear to me, unless you, mother, interpose a veto; and I think you are too good a patriot to do that." She gave her consent and before he went, said, "You know, my son, how much I have wished to see you a Christian. Now I want you to look at the claims of Jesus exactly as you have looked at those of your country, 'simply and honestly,' and see if those same 'four plain propositions' will not lead you into the service of heaven." "I'll think of it, mother," was his answer, and they parted. He did not forget his promise. On his first Sabbath in camp he resolutely set himself to the fulfillment of his mother's request. Remembering how he had argued duty to his country, he brought before his mind in the same manner the subject of the divine claims upon his heart and life. "Does Jesus want me? Does he call me? Am I able so to serve him? Am I willing?" With an open Bible, the first three questions were clearly and quickly answered. At the last one he hesitated. But duty seemed so clear, that he dared not falter; and, falling on his knees, he gave himself to Christ. His next letter home announced him as a Christian soldier.

7204. CHRIST, the Way. The story is told that the young Irvings trotted on the sands, called the Solway Sands, which divide England from Scotland. Often the tide rolls in before persons are aware of it, cutting off all retreat, and many have been lost thereby. The two young Irvings had strolled on the sands, and been gathering sea-weed; when, at last, on a sudden, they perceived the tide had rolled in. I conceive the boys asking, "What is the 'way' by which we can escape?" And if a man in the same position as they had pointed out a path, he could not have said, "I am the way." That would have been inconsistent. But their uncle, who happened to see them on the other side, mounted a strong horse, dashed into the midst of the stream, caught up the two boys, placed them before him on his horse, and rode swiftly to shore. I think if that uncle had said to the boys, "I am the way," it would have been quite the proper way of speaking—because in this case he did it all. So Christ could not be "the way" unless he did it all. If he pointed to a something that we could do—then he would not be "the way;" but when he does it all, then it becomes the most fitting, highest use of words to say, "I am the way." If he died to put me into a salvable state, then he is not "the way;" if he died to put me in a position where I could save myself, then he is not "the way"—but if he died to save me, and has saved me, with nothing of my own, then are those words strictly true.   *Spurgeon.*

7205. CHRIST, Will of. Men make their wills and testaments; and Christ makes his. What they bequeath, they cannot be compelled to do it. And what is bequeathed to us in this testament of Christ is altogether a free and voluntary donation. Other testators usually bequeath their estates to their wives and children, and near relations; so doth this testator: all is settled upon his spouse, the church, upon believers, his children. A stranger intermeddles not with these mercies. Men give all their goods and estate that can be conveyed to their friends that survive them. Christ giveth to his church, in the New Testament, three sorts of goods: all temporal good things, all spiritual good things, all eternal good things. No such bequests as these were ever found in the testaments of princes. All that kings and nobles settle by will upon their heirs, are naught to what Christ hath conferred in the New Testament upon his people.   *John Flavel.*

7206. CHRIST, Worthiness of. A native of India named Brindelbund, had spent sixty or seventy years in the service of Satan. He was a byraggee,—that is, one who professes to have subdued his passions, and who was, as they express it, seeking some one who is worthy. He went to Outwa, where he attended Mr. Chamberlain's preaching and instructions. "I have been," said he, "many years going from one sacred place to another, seeking some one who is worthy, and to offer my flower." The sweetest flower, they say, is the human heart; this is their figurative way of talking. "I have been seeking some one to offer my flower who is worthy; but never have I found one till now. I have heard of Jesus; I give it him." The old man was faithful to his surrender—he never took his heart from Jesus. Talking to his Hindu brethren, he would say, "And whom do you need but him whom I have found?" *Moister.*

7207. CHRISTIAN, Almost. A preacher was speaking on "the almost Christian," and it happening to be just the time that the papers were full of the massacre at Cawnpore, he described the approach of Havelock's victorious troops, he drew a graphic picture of the suspense of the English prisoners in the city, how high their hopes ran when the guns told them of the nearer approach of what they hoped would prove a rescue—how the British rested for the night within a half a mile of their prison, and entered the city in the morning, only just too late. They were almost saved. *Pilkington.*

7208. CHRISTIAN, Blessedness of the. Christ begins his gospel with a blessing. His is the word of power. For him to declare blessed is to make blessed. His blessedness is more than happiness. Christ proclaims supreme, full, felicity in the sacred number, nine, of his beatitudes, and in their application to all the issues of life and to eternity. To be a true Christian is to have all things which could be blessings to us. To it nothing can be added. How blessed the privilege.

7209. CHRISTIAN, The Cheerful. John Bunyan tells us, that as Christian was going through the valley he found it a dreadful dark place, and terrible demons and goblins were all about him, and poor Christian thought he must perish for certain; but just when his doubts were the strongest, he heard a sweet voice; he listened to it, and he heard a man in front of him singing, "Yea, when I pass through the valley of the shadow of death, I will fear no evil." Now, that man did not know who was near him, but he was unwittingly singing to cheer a man behind. Christian, when you are in trouble, sing; you do not know who is near you. Sing! perhaps you will get a good companion by it. Sing! perhaps there will be many a heart cheered by your song. There is some broken spirit, it may be, that will be bound up by your sonnets. Sing! there is some poor distressed brother, perhaps shut up in the Castle of Despair, who, like King Richard, will hear your song inside the walls, and sing to you again, and you may be the means of getting him a ransom.   *Spurgeon.*

7210. CHRISTIAN, Countersign of the. A Christian soldier said in a religious meeting, "This morning, on guard, I forgot my watchword. I was troubled; but, as I was thinking of it this thought came to me: I have another counter sign,—Christ,—and with that there is no guarded line in earth or heaven which I cannot pass. When I had thought of that a little while, my other countersign came to mind and all was right."

7211. CHRISTIAN, Detention of the. An old divine compares God's treatment of the Christian to the course of a river. Its tendency is to go straight to its master, the ocean; but God sets a hill here and a mountain there, and thus compels it to make a long journey to fertilize and beautify the earth. So the young Christian "longs to depart and be with Christ," but his course is prolonged that he may carry blessings to all the associates of his life.

7212. CHRISTIAN, Faithful. I have read of that noble servant of God, Marcus Arethusius, minister of a church in the time of Constantine, who in Constantine's time had been the cause of overthrowing an idol's temple; afterwards, when Julian came to be emperor, he would force the people of that place to build it up again. They were ready to do it, but he refused; whereupon those that were his own people, to whom he preached, took him, and stripped him of all his clothes, and abused his naked body, and gave it up to the children, to lance it with their pen-knives, and then caused him to be put in a basket, and anointed this naked body with honey, and set him in the sun, to be stung with wasps. And all this cruelty they showed because he would not do anything towards the building up of this idol temple; nay, they came to this, that if he would do but the least towards it, if he would give but a halfpenny to it, they would save him. But he refused all, though the giving of a half-penny might have saved his life; and in doing this, he did but live up to that principle that most Christians talk of, and all profess, but few come up to, viz., that we must choose rather to suffer the worst of torments that men and devils can invent and inflict, than to commit the least sin, whereby God should be dishonored, our consciences wounded, religion reproached, and our own souls endangered.   *Brooks.*

7213. CHRISTIAN, Glory of the. His glory is from within. It is a radiation. Put him where you will, he shines, and cannot but shine. God made him to shine. For instance: imprison Joseph, and he will shine out on all Egypt, cloudless as the sky where the rain never falls. Imprison Daniel, and the dazzled lions will retire to their lairs, and the king comes forth to worship at his rising, and all Babylon bless the beauty of the brighter and better day. Imprison Peter, and, with an angel for a harbinger star, he will swell his aurora from the fountains of Jordan to the walls of Beersheba, and break like the morning over mountain and sea. Imprison Paul, and there will be high noon over all the Roman Empire. Imprison John, and the Isles of the Ægean and all the coasts around will kindle with sunset visions too gorgeous to be described, but never to be forgotten—a boundless panorama of prophecy, gliding from sky to sky and enchanting the nations with openings of heaven, transits of saints and angels, and the ultimate

glory of the city and kingdom of God. Not only so; for modern times have similar examples—except examples in the church, and examples in the state. For instance, bury Luther in the depths of the Black Forest, and the "angel that dwelt in the bush" will honor him there; the trees around him will burn like shafts of ruby, and his glowing orbs will lume up again, round and clear as the light of all Europe. Thrust Bunyan into the gloom of Bedford jail—and as he leans his head on his hand, the murky horizon of Britain will flame with fiery symbols—"delectable mountains" and celestial mansions, with holy pilgrims grouped on the golden hills, and the bands of bliss, from the gates of pearl, hastening to welcome him home.   *Stockton.*

7214. CHRISTIAN, God-bearing. Saint Ignatius, Bishop of Antioch, one of the apostolic fathers, because of his sanctity received the name of Theophorus, the God-bearer. Trajan is said to have asked him why he had the surname, Theophorus? He replied, because "I bore Christ in my heart." "Dost thou mean him that was crucified?" asked the emperor, scornfully. Ignatius answered, "The very same, who, by his death, overcame sin, and enabled those who bear him in their hearts to trample under foot all the powers of the devils." Then he was ordered to be taken to Rome and given to wild beasts. A fabulous writer says that after his death the name of God was found written upon his heart in letters of gold. He suffered martyrdom A. D. 107, being devoured by wild beasts in the Amphitheatre at Rome.

7215. CHRISTIAN, Growth of the. Here, no ornament to park or garden, stands a dwarfed, stunted, bark-bound tree. How am I to develop that stem into tall and graceful beauty, to clothe with blossom these naked branches, and hang them, till they bend with clustered fruit? Change such as that is not to be effected by surface dressing, or any care bestowed on the upper soil. The remedy must go to the root. You cannot make that tree grow upwards till you break the crust below, pulverize the hard subsoil, and give the roots room and way to strike deeper down; for the deeper the root, and wider spread the filaments of its rootlets, the higher the tree lifts an umbrageous head to heaven, and throws out its hundred arms to catch in dews, rain-drops, and sun-beams, the blessings of the sky. The believer in respect of character, a tree of righteousness, of the Lord's planting; in respect of strength, a cedar of Lebanon; in respect of fruitfulness, an olive; in respect of position, a palm-tree planted in the courts of God's house; in respect of full supplies of grace, a tree by the rivers of water, which yielded its fruit in its season, and whose leaf does not wither, offers this analogy between grace and nature, that as the tree grows best skyward that grows most downward, the lower the saint descends in humility the higher he rises in holiness. The soaring corresponds to the sinking.   *Dr. Guthrie.*

7216. CHRISTIAN, Knowledge Necessary to a. A missionary says: "I used to speculate as to how much divine truth a man would have to know before he could become a Christian. India and the Teloogoos have settled it. A man must know himself a sinner, and Jesus a Saviour; that is all."

7217. CHRISTIAN, Resources of the. The minister of Frederick the Great to the court of St. James, complained to his royal master that he could not maintain the equipage which characterized the representatives of other powers. That monarch replied, "Remember that you have Frederick and his hundred thousand Prussians to attend you." How much greater dignity is his who has the omnipotent God, the omnipresent Christ, and legions of angels for his defense?

7218. CHRISTIAN, Right Kind of. An officer was accosted by a brother officer thus—"You're the right kind of Christian,—not bothering people about their souls this way." The speaker himself made no pretensions to serious godliness; and the allusion was to certain officers who had a way of speaking out very intelligibly for Christ. Our friend had himself been converted; but, up to that time, he had been too timid to utter any articulate testimony. As his visitor left him that day, he began to reason with himself—"Well, if that man thinks I am the right kind of Christian, it is time I was looking about me and considering my ways." It was a somewhat novel point of departure: but, from that hour, our friend has been another man, boldly confessing Christ and laboring to win souls. *Power.*

7219. CHRISTIAN, Royalty of a. An old African negro, who had long served the Lord, when on his death-bed was visited by his friends, who came around him lamenting that he was going to die, saying, "Poor Pompey! poor Pompey is dying." The old saint, animated with the prospect before him, said to them with much earnestness, "Don't call me poor Pompey. I king Pompey."

7220. CHRISTIAN, Shield of the. In the agonies of dissolution Epaminondas asks, "Is my shield safe? are the Thebans victorious?" Viewing his shield which was brought to him, and being informed that the Spartans were defeated, a gleam of joy prevailed for a moment over the languor of death. "Mine," said he, "is a glorious departure: I die in the arms of victory; tell me not that I am childless, for Leuctra and Mantinea (meaning his victories there) are immortal children." Thus the apostle could triumph: his shield was safe; his course finished with honor; leaving behind multitudes of spiritual children, as trophies of victory, who shall be his joy and crown of rejoicing in the day of the Lord Jesus. *Buck.*

7221. CHRISTIAN Soldier. The Christian is a member of Christ's Church militant, and his duty is ever to be fighting against sin, the world, and the devil. If you read St. Paul's description of the armor of the Christian man, you will find every place armed but one. There is a helmet for the head and greaves for the legs, and a breast-plate for the chest—but no armor for the back. His duty is to stand with his face to the foe. I well remember how in my school-boy days I was struck by the fact of the lords of Roslin all being laid in the vaults of the chapel dressed in their knightly armor. The Christian has not, it is true, to carry his warfare beyond the hour of death; but like that great Duke of Northumberland, who, when he came to die, insisted on being clothed in his armor, and, sitting on his bed, faced the last enemy lance in hand, we must, till the last breath pass from us, never cease from fighting against sin.   *J. G. Pilkington.*

7222. CHRISTIAN, Three Eyes of a. A faithful man hath three eyes: the first, of sense, common to him with brute creatures; the second, of reason, common to all men: the third, of faith, proper to his profession; whereof each looketh beyond other, and none of them meddleth with others' objects. For, neither doth the eye of sense reach to intelligible things and matters of discourse; nor the eye of reason to those things which are supernatural and spiritual; neither doth faith look down to things that may be sensibly seen.   *Bp. Hall.*

7223. CHRISTIAN, The True. He that can apprehend and consider vice with all her baits and seeming pleasures, and yet abstain, and yet distinguish, and yet prefer that which is truly better, he is the true wayfaring Christian. I cannot praise a fugitive and cloistered virtue unexercised, and unbreathed, that never sallies out and sees her adversary, but slinks out of the race where that immortal garland is to be run for, not without dust and heat.   *Milton.*

7224. CHRISTIAN, Two Worlds of the. A Christian lives in two worlds at one and the same time—the world of flesh and the world of spirit. It is possible to do both. There are certain dangerous gases, which from their weight fall to the lower part of the place where they are, making it destructive for a dog to enter, but safe for a man who holds his head erect. A Christian, as living in the world of flesh, is constantly passing through these. Let him keep his head erect in the spiritual world, and he is safe. He does this so long as the Son of God is the fountain whence he draws his inspiration, his motives, encouragement, and strength. *George Philip.*

7225. CHRISTIANITY, Active. Suppose that a recluse had been discovered living alone on the side of the Alleghany mountains, in the times of the Revolution, and one of the soldiers, speaking to General Washington of him, had said: "That man—oh, what a patriot he can be, in his cabin, meditating upon his country's glory! If he was down in the camp, amid the roar of battle, or on the tedious march, he could not be a patriot!" What do you think about that? Would you not say of a patriot on the side of a mountain, that a toadstool or a mushroom was just as good, and that the man that took the front of the conflict was the patriot? Now I aver that while it may, in the providence of God, be the duty of some men to serve God by standing still, while there may be here and there a special case in which a good Christian is made out of a man that does nothing, there are far more chances of your being a Christian if you apply your powers to the active duties of life than if you do not. It is a dastardly thing for a man to run away from life, for the sake of not. being tempted by it.   *Talmage.*

7226. CHRISTIANITY, Confidence in. Two men were fellow-travelers upon the Western frontier, one of whom took every occasion to declare Christianity a delusion, and its professors hypocrites, and declared that he always took especial care of his valuables when in their company. One night they sought shelter at the uninviting cabin of a poor settler, and were welcomed to the best the place afforded. The suspicion of the travelers became aroused; this cordiality might be intended to deceive, and the loneliness of the place seemed to invite deeds of darkness. They resolved to take special precaution against surprise to have their weapons ready, and one was to watch while the other slept. Before retiring to rest the host, an old man, took down a well-worn Bible, read a portion, then prayed, asking that the strangers might have prosperity on their journey, and when their earthly journey should end, that they might have a home in heaven. Retired to their room, the sceptic, to whom fell the first watch, instead of priming his pistols, prepared for sleep. His companion reminded him of their arrangement, and the infidel confessed that he could but feel as safe where the Bible was read and such prayers offered as they had just listened to, as at a New England fireside.

7227. CHRISTIANITY, Diffusion of. A few persons of an odious and despised country could not have filled the world with believers, had they not shown undoubted credentials from the divine person who sent them on such a message.   *Addison.*

7228. CHRISTIANITY, Early Conquests of. Arnobius, a heathen philosopher, who became a Christian, speaking of the power which the Christian faith had over the minds of men, says, "Who would not believe it, when he sees in how short a time it has conquered so great knowledge? Orators, grammarians, rhetoricians, lawyers, physicians, and philosophers, have thrown up those opinions which but a little before they held, and have embraced the doctrines of the gospel!" Tertullian says, "Though but of yesterday, yet have we filled your cities, islands, castles, corporations, councils, your armies themselves, your tribes, companies, the palace, the senate, and courts of justice; only your temples have we left you free."

7229. CHRISTIANITY, Evidence of. Dr. Cotton visited Dr. Young, author of the "Night Thoughts," about a fortnight before his last illness. The subject of conversation was "Newton on the Prophecies," when Dr. Young closed the conversation thus:—"My friend, there are three considerations upon which my faith in Christ is built, as upon a rock: The fall of man, the redemption of man, and the resurrection of man. These three cardinal articles of our re-

ligion are such as human ingenuity could never have invented; therefore they must be divine. The other argument is this: If the prophecies have been fulfilled, of which there is abundant demonstration, the scripture must be the word of God; and if the scripture is the word of God, Christianity must be true."

7230. CHRISTIANITY, Intellect and. It has been the fashion, and is now, to take it for granted that intellect has no brotherhood with Christianity, that by giving the heart to God intellect is enslaved, and all exercises of the mind are crippled. Is it so? We mourn over the fact that in many cases intellect has been given to Satan, that mental power has been perverted from the loftiest purposes, and not consecrated to purposes for which it was given. Thomas Moore stands in the foremost rank as a master of words, but some of his writings have no other purpose than putting a color upon vice. Of Percy Shelley we are ready to believe that when his body was recovered a Bible was found next his heart, and we are ready to believe, with Southey, that if he had lived longer he would have become a Christian; but we cannot forget that he had no hesitation in subscribing himself as scorning to have anything to do with religion. We acknowledge that Byron has scarcely an equal, but we cannot forget how the mighty power he possessed was debased and desecrated unto evil. We are inclined to believe that one page of his writings does more harm than all the rest put together have done good. But has intellect no brotherhood with religion? Have we no samples on the other side? We glory in the majestic verses and grand poetry of John Milton, but we glory most of all in that piety which dwelt in his heart as depicted in "Paradise Lost," yet regained. Pollock, Montgomery, Philip James Bailey are other cases in point, and with these in our mind, shall we say that intellect has no brotherhood with Christianity? Atheism and intellect have gone together; but intellect is highest when devoted to Christianity, and so long as the writings of the Prophet Isaiah remain, we shall see that the mightiest genius and the profoundest piety can go hand in hand together.   *Anon.*

7231. CHRISTIANITY, Low Standard of. The reader is probably amazed at the paucity of large stars in the firmament of heaven! Will he permit me to carry his mind a little further, and either stand astonished at or deplore with me the fact that out of the millions of Christians in the vicinity and splendor of the eternal Sun of Righteousness, how very few are found of the first order? How very few can stand examination by the test laid down in the thirteenth chapter of the First Epistle to the Corinthians! How very few love God with all their heart, soul, mind, and strength, and their neighbor as themselves! How few mature Christians are found in the church! How few are in all things living for eternity! How little light, how little heat, and how little influence and activity are to be found among them that bear the name of Christ! How few stars of the first magnitude will the Son of God have to deck the crown of his glory! Few are striving to excel in righteousness; and it seems to be a principal concern with many to find out how little grace they may have and yet get to heaven. In the fear of God I register this testimony, that I have perceived it to be the labor of many to lower the standard of Christianity, and to soften down or explain away those promises of God that himself has linked with duties; and because they know that they cannot be saved by their good works, they are contented to have no good works at all; and thus the necessity of Christian obedience and Christian holiness makes no prominent part of some modern creeds. Let all those who retain the apostolic doctrine, that the blood of Christ cleanseth from all sin in this life, press every believer to go on to perfection, and expect to be saved while here below, into the fullness of the blessing of the gospel of Jesus. *Dr. A. Clark.*

7232. CHRISTIANITY, Mission of. Christ appeared; the career of Paganism was checked, the fate of Judaism was sealed. A character and a religion were placed before the eyes of men hitherto inconceivable, in the beauty and philosophy of their nature. Unlike all other founders of a religious faith, Christ had no selfishness, no desire of dominance; and his system, unlike all other systems of worship, was bloodless, boundlessly beneficent, inexpressibly pure, and, most marvelous of all, went to break all bonds of body and soul, and to cast down every temporal and every spiritual tyranny.
William Howitt.

7233. CHRISTIANITY, Mocking. A play was arranged to be enacted in the theatre at Rome, burlesquing the Christian religion, for the entertainment of Diocletian, the Emperor. A great crowd was present. Genes, a clever mimic, had the leading part. The curtain rose, exposing Genes lying on a bed, sick and groaning. He moaned out: "I am weighed down; the burden of the past is on my conscience; my sins oppress me unendurably. Oh! that I could obtain relief—that I was light and free." "Why, how so, good fellow?" said the other actors: "if you are burdened, how can we lighten you?" "Ah! ah!" laughed the clown, "there is only one way to lighten him; we must take him to a carpenter and have him sawn and planed down." "No," said the sick man, "I wish to die a Christian; by that means only can I obtain relief." "Why, what do you want to be a Christian for?" "To fly to my God." "Call in a priest and an exorcist." In come two actors dressed in character. The priest sat down by the bed and said, "Why hast thou sent for me, my son?" "I desire the favor of Christ," replied Genes, "by which I may be born again to a new, a holier, and purer life." A great vat of water was placed on the stage, the usual formula of baptism was recited, the sick man was drawn out of bed and plunged into the water, amidst bursts of merriment from the audience, and afterwards he was clothed in white. In the next act, Roman soldiers rushed

upon the stage, seized the new convert and drew him before the stall of Diocletian to be tried and sentenced. Genes shook off his guard and sprang upon a pedestal to address the crowd. "Sire, and all you present, hear what I say. I have ever hated the Christian name, and I have exulted when I have seen Christians brought before the magistrate. My parents and kinsmen have been Christians, and from them I heard all concerning the faith, and the manner of conducting the sacraments. But all I heard I turned to mockery, and this day have used my knowledge for the purpose of a merry jest against them. But, lo! sire, as I lay on the bed the realities of sickness and approaching death stood naked before me. And all my sins from infancy rose up before me, filling a long dark void. Sire, believe me, when the water touched me and I renounced the evil one with my lips, my heart went with my words. And I saw a great light, and the darkness of sin seemed to roll away before the clear dawn of a heavenly light. And now, sire, and all you people who have been laughing so heartily, believe me when I say that I confess Christ as very God, and that he is the true light shining, the eternal truth and perfect goodness, and in him, and him only do I trust." There was an appearance of reality in the actor now. His tones, his look, his attitude, convinced all that this was was no longer burlesque. Diocletian said to Genes, "Jesting may be carried too far." He ordered him behind the scenes and that the piece should be changed. "Sire, I am in earnest," said the actor. "Then I shall be in earnest also. Ho! let him be beaten." Blows were showered upon him, and the Emperor ordered that he should be taken before the prefect. He bore torture with great fortitude, saying, "There is no king but him I have seen, whom I adore: his I am and his I shall be. Bitterly do I repent that I know him only so late." His resolution being unalterable he was slain with the sword. The Holy Spirit made the form a power unto salvation.

7234. CHRISTIANITY, Morality and. About the time that Paul wrote, describing the moral corruption which prevailed in the city of Ephesus, Pliny, one of the wisest and most refined men of his age, speaks of the same city as "one of the luminaries of Asia." The one considered her as full of light, the other looked upon her as full of darkness. Both views were true, according to the standard by which the writers formed their judgment. Pliny saw her as the seat of the highest civilization that a people without revelation had attained. But in Paul's mind their impure and immoral deeds were made manifest, the false external of this world was judged. Underneath the glare of vainglory he saw moral corruption. She was "a whited sepulchre, full of dead men's bones."
Walker.

7235. CHRISTIANITY, Nothing Better than. Lord Chesterfield, when at Brussels, was invited by Voltaire to sup with him at a house of an infidel lady. The conversation happened to turn upon the affairs of England. "I think, my lord," said Madame C., "that the Parliament of England consists of five or six hundred of the best informed, and the most sensible men in the kingdom." "True, Madame, they are generally supposed to be so." "What, then can be the reason they tolerate so great an absurdity as the Christian religion?" "I suppose, madame," replied his lordship, "it is because they have not been able to establish anything better in its stead. When they can, I do not doubt that in their wisdom they will readily adopt it."

7236. CHRISTIANITY, Objection to. Mr. Brainerd when among the Indians, at one place where there was a great number, halted, and offered to instruct them in the truths of Christianity. "Why," said one of them, "should you desire the Indians to become Christians, seeing the Christians are so much worse than the Indians? The Christians lie, steal and drink, worse than the Indians. They first taught the Indians to be drunk. They steal to that degree, that their rulers are obliged to hang them for it; and that is not enough to deter others from the practice. But none of the Indians were ever hanged for stealing: and yet they do not steal half so much. We will not consent, therefore, to become Christians, lest we should be as bad as they. We will live as our fathers lived, and go where our fathers are when we die." He did all he could to explain to them that these were not Christians in heart, and that he did not want them to become such as these, yet he could not prevail.

7237. CHRISTIANITY, Permanence of. Christianity was the temple that was to be eternal, and on it, as unconscious builders, men were laboring in all the ages from the creation. And if so long in preparation, may we not anticipate it will be a finality? About the temples built by the kings of Oriental monarchies there were other lesser fabrics; but with the kingly one alone the idea of permanence was associated. So of St. Peter's at Rome and the Cathedral at Milan. The lesser fabrics have disappeared for ever. When Christianity was completed, its lesser structures and essential scaffoldings were all removed. Priests and smoking altars suddenly and forever disappeared. The temple of Christianity alone remains. *Dr. Foss.*

7238. CHRISTIANITY, Philanthropy of. Moravian missionaries in Greenland saw little fruit of their labor the first year. Toward its close the small-pox broke out among the natives in an awful manner, and the Moravians accommodated as many of the invalids as their houses would contain, surrendering to the afflicted even their only sleeping-chambers; and though unable to make themselves distinctly understood by words, they preached effectually by their conduct. One man, who had always derided them when in health, expressed his obligation to the minister shortly before he died. 'Thou hast done for us," said he, "what our own people would not do; for thou hast fed us when we had nothing to eat; thou hast buried our dead, who would else have been consumed by the dogs, foxes, and ravens; thou hast also instructed us in the knowledge of God, and hast told us of a better life."

7239. CHRISTIANITY, Power of. Lucian and Marcian were heathen magicians of the city of Nicomedia. They were surprised to find that a simple Christian maiden could successfully resist their power. They burned their magical books, and were baptized in the name of Christ. In this name they went out to preach the Gospel to the Gentiles. In 250 they were arrested and asked why they preached Christ. Lucian answered, "Every man does well to try to draw his brother out of a dangerous error." They were cruelly racked and tortured, and reproached the judge, because when they were magicians and guilty of many crimes they were not punished, but now that they had become Christians and good citizens they were barbarously treated. They were threatened with greater torments if they would not deny Christ. Marcian answered, "We are ready to suffer, but we will not renounce the true God, lest we be cast into a fire which will never be quenched." They were then burned alive, and expired singing hymns of praise to God amid the flames.

7240. CHRISTIANITY, Rapid Progress of. The rapid progress of the gospel is recorded in the Holy Scriptures, and by profane writers. Tacitus, an historian of great reputation, and an enemy of Christianity, in giving an account of the fire which happened at Rome about thirty years after our Lord's commission to his apostles, asserts that the Emperor Nero, in order to suppress the rumors of having been himself the author of the mischief, had the Christians accused of the crime. "At first," he writes, "they were only apprehended who confessed themselves of that sect; afterwards a vast multitude were discovered by them." Pliny, the younger, also an enemy to Christianity, the Governor of Pontus and Bithynia, applied to the Emperor for directions as to his conduct towards the Christians. He wrote about eighty years after Christ's ascension. He says:— "Suspending all judicial proceedings, I have recourse to your advice; for it has appeared to me a matter highly deserving consideration, especially on account of the great number of persons who are in danger of suffering: for many, of all ages, and of every rank, of both sexes likewise, are accused and will be accused. Nor has the contagion of this superstition seized cities only, but the lesser towns also, and the open country. Nevertheless it seems to me that it may be restrained and corrected. It is certain that the temples, which were almost forsaken, are beginning to be more frequented; and the sacred solemnities, after a long intermission, are revived. Victims, likewise, are everywhere bought up; whereas, for some time, there were few to purchase them. Whence it is easy to imagine that numbers of men might be reclaimed, if pardon were granted to those that shall repent." Justin Martyr wrote about thirty years after Pliny, and one hundred and six after the ascension, and says: —"There is not a nation, either of Greek or barbarian, or any other name, even of those who wander in tribes, and live in tents, amongst whom prayers and thanksgivings are not offered to the Father and Creator of the universe, in the name of the crucified Jesus."

7241. CHRISTIANITY, Reason for Accepting. In one of the meetings held by the natives of the South Sea Islands to decide upon the adoption of the Christian religion, a noble chief arose and said: "It is my wish that the Christian religion should become universal among us. I look at the wisdom of these worshipers of Jehovah, and see how superior they are to us in every respect. Their ships are like floating houses, so that they can traverse the tempest-driven ocean for months with perfect safety; whereas, if a breeze blow upon our frail canoes, they are upset in an instant, and we are sprawling in the sea. Their persons, also, are covered from head to foot in beautiful clothes, while we wear nothing but a girdle of leaves. Their axes are so hard and sharp, that with them we can easily fell our trees and do our work; but with our stone axes we must dub, dub, dub, day after day, before we can cut down a single tree. Their knives, too, what valuable things they are! how quickly they cut up our pigs, compared with our bamboo knives! Now, I conclude that the God who has given to his white worshipers these valuable things must be wiser than our gods, for they have not given the like to us. We all want these articles, and my proposition is, that the God who gave them should be our God." This speech produced a powerful effect and the people gladly received the gospel.

7242. CHRISTIANITY, Reciprocity of. A Boston sea captain called at one of the Fiji islands. Supposing the people to be still cannibals, he armed his men for any emergency. He was greatly surprised on being accosted by the chief of the islands in English. He said, himself and people had become Christians through the labors of the missionaries. The captain become the chief's guest, and was requested to lead in family prayer. The captain said he had never prayed in his life, and could not pray. The converted chief knelt and prayed, not forgetting his white guest. Strange reciprocity! That captain found through the heathen's prayer what a Christian training had not imparted, become converted, and is now a missionary to the heathen. We help ourselves in helping others.

7243. CHRISTIANITY, Science and. A few evenings since my door-bell rang violently, and a young man, trembling in every limb, and with quivering lip, said, "Will you go and pray with a dying woman?" I said "Yes," and made all haste to the chamber of death. But how could I have gone had I been a mere preacher of science? What consolation and hope would disquisitions upon science, however elaborate and learned, have afforded that dying woman? I fancy she would have turned her pallid, ghastly face upon me in disappointment and reproach, and said, "Mock me not by reading my death-warrant. I know there is law. Law has placed me here, reduced me to a mere skeleton. Aye, it is the grasp of a broken law that wrings my soul with agony and rends it with fearful forebodings. But tell me, is there no hope? Is there no power above law, and mightier than law?" How my heart exulted that I could offer her a Saviour that was able to snatch her from the very jaws of death and bear her to the joys and blessedness of Paradise. And as I talked to her about Jesus her bosom heaved, her eyes filled with tears, her lips trembled in earnest prayer, and by faith grasping him she shouted in the swelling joy of conscious pardon and salvation, and died in the triumphs of faith. O what a difference there is between science and Christianity! *Dr. J. A. M. Chapman.*

7244. CHRISTIANITY, Security of. The real security of Christianity is to be found in its benevolent morality, in its exquisite adaptation to the human heart, in the facility with which its scheme accommodates itself to the capacity of every human intellect, in the consolation which it bears to every house of mourning, in the light with which it lightens the great mystery of the grave. *Macaulay.*

7245. CHRISTIANITY Shown. A native Christian missionary in India said: "I am, by birth, of an insignificant and contemptible caste; so low, that if a Brahmin should chance to touch me, he must go and bathe in the Ganges for the purpose of purification; and yet God has been pleased to call me, not merely to the knowledge of the Gospel, but to the high office of teaching it to others. My friends, do you know the reason of God's conduct? It is this. If God had selected one of you learned Brahmins, and made you the preacher, when you were successful in making converts, by standers would have said it was the amazing learning of the Brahmin, and his great weight of character, that were the cause; but now, when any one is converted by my instrumentality, no one thinks of ascribing any of the praise to me; and God, as is his due, has all the glory."

7246. CHRISTIANITY, Temporal Advantage of. A gentleman replied to one of Paine's tirades against religion and the Bible thus: "The Scotch are the greatest bigots about the Bible I ever met; it is their school-book, their houses and churches are furnished with Bibles, and if they travel but a few miles from home, their Bible is always their companion; yet, in no other country where I have traveled, have I seen the people so comfortable and happy. Their poor are not in such abject poverty as I have seen in other countries. By their bigoted custom of going to church on Sundays, they save the wages which they earn through the week, which, in other countries that I have visited, are generally spent by mechanics, and other young men, in taverns and frolics, on Sundays; and of all the foreigners who land on our shores, none are so much sought after for servants, and to fill places where trust is reposed, as the Scotch. You rarely find them in taverns, the watch-house, alms-house, bridewell, or prison. Now, if the Bible is so bad a book, those who use it most would be the worst of people; but the reverse is the case."

7247. CHRISTIANITY Tested. A clergyman, living in a community where scepticism and infidelity had led many astray, gave a series of discourses on the Evidences of Christianity. Of course more or less of his opposers were present, and on the last night of the series a prominent infidel came in. At the close of a very impressive meeting, the speaker said, in a spirit of tenderness, "There may be, and doubtless are some here to-night, who do not believe as I do, and who do not accept the truth of the Bible. If there are any such, or if there is one willing to come forward and test this question of such vital interest to every soul, I invite him to the platform." On the instant, the infidel referred to came forward and said, "I do not believe your doctrines; I cannot accept them." "But," said the clergyman, "you have denounced, for many years, that which you have never tested; are you willing that I, who have tried Christianity and feel its truths, shall be your teacher, and will you submit to my directions? You say that you are honest in your belief, and that in an honest spirit you will meet me." "I do thus meet you, and I will allow you to be my teacher." "Then," said he, "kneel by my side and repeat the simple words 'God be merciful to me a sinner!'" "But," was the reply, "I do not believe in your teachings." "Well, you say you are honest, and are willing to test this question; if so, you will heed my direction." The audience, in hushed expectation, heard the infidel as he sullenly kneeled, utter the words desired, with sarcastic defiance. "Again repeat those words," said his teacher in tones of utmost gentleness, and again, with a tone still more defiant, yet more subdued, the infidel repeated "God be merciful to me a sinner." Once more came the request to repeat the sentence, and before that audience, held by the power of the Holy Ghost, that petition went up in a tone of almost tenderness, certainly far different from the bravado with which it was at first repeated. A fourth time came the request, "Repeat it again;" and, with his strong frame quivering with emotion, the poor man poured out his soul's need in the prayer of the publican. At the fifth repetition, the man then and there, before the large assembly, offered up from his inmost soul the prayer which, when offered, meets with a forgiving Father's pardon. We give the simple facts, as told to us, and only ask the question of all unbelievers, "Why will you denounce a faith which you have never put to the test."

Watchman and Reflector.

7248. CHRISTIANITY, Testing. A short time since, an aged man related to me his own history, which I give, as far as I can recollect, in his own words: "I did not believe in the Bible, or in the reality of religion, at all. I consid-

ered what was called Christian experience as a delusion, the effect of excitement upon the imagination, and Christians as a set of fanatics. I had studied sceptical writers, and was confirmed in my belief that death is an eternal sleep—no heaven, no hell. And yet, at times, as the years sped on, an occasional doubt would arise. The question would force itself on me, What if these things should prove true? Then what will become of me? After suffering long from these annoying doubts and suggestions, I at last resolved to try a method which would enable me to become entirely and forever free from them. I said to myself, 'I will secretly try the very method these Christians propose. They recommend prayer and Bible reading. I will test their own appointed way myself, and if there be anything in religion I will find it; if not, my mind shall never more again be disturbed by a doubt.' Accordingly, I secured a day of solitude, a Sabbath when all the members of the family were absent at church. I knelt and prayed: 'O Lord, if thou dost exist, hear me. If there be a heaven to gain, and a hell to shun, show it to me. I have never believed it, but if all these things be true, and the Bible true, reveal it unto me, and enlighten me.' Then I searched the Bible. Commencing with the New Testament, I read continuously chapter after chapter, with intense interest and absorbed attention, ever and anon asking God to show me the truth. The more I read the stronger my interest grew, and deeper and deeper the conviction, the astounding conviction fastened upon me, that all this is true! I have lived all my life believing lies! I am a sinner! I am lost! I examined the Bible throughout. I dwelt on the creation, the fall, the coming of Christ. Deeper and deeper grew the conviction of my guilt; my anxiety became intense, and I did not attempt to conceal it. Throughout every day of that week I spent all my time in searching the word of God and in prayer, sometimes spending the whole day alone in the wood, beseeching God to have mercy on my soul. At last, one Sabbath morning, just a week from the day I set apart to 'see if these things were true,' while riding to church, Christ revealed himself to me as a Saviour—my justification. The way of salvation seemed clear and plain, and I inwardly exclaimed, 'I know that my Redeemer liveth!' My soul was filled with unspeakable joy. 'My tongue broke forth in unknown strains, and sang redeeming grace.' I had, in truth, found out by my own experience the truth and reality of religion, and I soon commenced to tell others what a wondrous Saviour I had found." *Wm. Jones.*

7249. CHRISTIANITY, Treatment of. Servile, and base, and mercenary is the notion of Christian practice among the bulk of nominal Christians. They give no more than they dare not withhold: they abstain from nothing but what they must not practice. When you state to them the doubtful quality of any action, and the consequent obligation to desist from it, they reply to you in the very spirit of Shylock "they cannot find it in the bond." In short, they know Christianity only as a system of restraint. She is despoiled of every liberal and generous principle; she is rendered almost unfit for the social intercourses of life, and is only suited to the gloomy walls of a cloister, in which they would confine her. *Wilberforce.*

7250. CHRISTIANITY, Trophies of. Ishoc el Kefroory of Syria, a magician, and a member of the Greek church, was converted to Christ by the simple reading of the Bible, before he had even seen a missionary. He burned his books of magic, abandoned his church, and was cursed by the Greek priest. The head man of his town organized persecution against him, rooted up his crops, destroyed his cattle, nearly murdered him, leaving him for dead. This treatment went on for many years, he never daring to appear out after dark, till he was greatly reduced by his losses. He never swerved from the gospel principle of rendering good for evil, and of recommending Christ. At length his persecutor required his testimony in a suit at law. He stood up and testified to the truth, which won the case for his enemy. Yusef was now effectually subdued and became the strong friend of Ishoc, sending men and material to help build a house for Christian worship. Such is the power of true Christian conduct.

7251. CHRISTIANITY, Truth of. Athenagoras, a famous Athenian philosopher in the second century, not only doubted the truth of the Christian religion, but was determined to write against it. However, upon an intimate inquiry into the facts on which it was supported, in the course of his collecting materials for his intended publication, he was convinced by the blaze of its evidence, and turned his designed invective into an elaborate apology, which is still in existence. *Whitecross.*

7252. CHRISTIANITY, Zeal for. King Olaf, a notorious freebooter, after he began to rule in Norway, exhibited great regard for the ten commandments, so that he would not even whittle on Sunday. His zeal for the extension of Christianity was irresistible. The Saga says, "If any there were who would not renounce heathen ways, he took the matter so zealously in hand that he drove some out of the country, mutilated others of hands and feet, or stabbed their eyes out; hung up some, cut down some with the sword, and let none go unpunished that would not serve God." He went thus through the whole district, sparing neither great nor small. He had with him three hundred deadly men-at-arms. He went everywhere converting the people, severely punishing those who would not listen to his word. Occasionally the farmers combined against him to save their homesteads from the flames and from plunder, and their heads and feet from being hacked off by the over-zealous missionary king. Thus was Christianity extended among the Northmen in the tenth and eleventh centuries.

7253. CHRISTIANS, Advantage of. In a letter to John Sheppard, of Frome, Lord Byron said: "Indisputably, the firm believers in the Gospel have a great advantage over all others, for this simple reason—that if true, they will have their reward hereafter: and if there be no hereafter, they can be but with the infidel in his eternal sleep: having had the assistance of an exalted hope through life, without subsequent disappointment, since, at the worst for them, 'out of nothing, nothing can arise,' not even sorrow."

7254. CHRISTIANS, Attendants of. They say in England if a man walks he must be poor, if he sometimes calls a cab he is better off, if one footman rides behind him he is rich, but if two are on the back of his carriage he must have a great inheritance. God has no poor children; they all have a great inheritance; two footmen are always behind, "Goodness and mercy shall follow me all the days of my life." Or, goodness and mercy may be called God's watchdogs, following in the rear. *Moody.*

7255. CHRISTIANS, Comfort of. "For all I have preached, or written," said Rev. James Durham, "there is but one scripture I can remember, or dare grip to; tell me if I dare lay the weight of my salvation upon it, 'Him that cometh to me, I will in no wise cast out.'" His friend replied, "You may, indeed, depend upon it, though you had a thousand salvations at hazard." Joy lighted up the soul of the dying saint as he entered into the glory of eternity.

7256. CHRISTIANS, Contempt of. When a victim was slain for sacrifice, all the parts that were not fit to be offered on the altar were swept away from the floor of the temple, and cast out as pollution, and unfit to remain in the temple. "Now," says the apostle, "we are exactly like these parts of the sacrifice, which are cut off and cast away, and treated as unfit to be either dedicated to God, or employed in the service of man." A most expressive phrase, to denote the utter contempt in which the world held the apostles. *Dr. Cumming.*

7257. CHRISTIANS, Dwarfish. There was once in London a club of small men, whose qualification for membership lay in their not exceeding five feet in height; these dwarfs held, or pretended to hold, the opinion that they were nearer the perfection of manhood than others, for they argued that primeval men had been far more gigantic than the present race, and consequently that the way of progress was to grow less and less, and that the human race as it perfected itself would become as diminutive as themselves. Such a club of Christians might be established in most cities, and without any difficulty might attain to an enormously numerous membership; for the notion is common that our dwarfish Christianity is, after all, the standard, and many even imagine that nobler Christians are enthusiasts, fanatical and hot-blooded, while they themselves are cool because they are wise and indifferent, because they are intelligent. *Spurgeon.*

7258. CHRISTIANS, Endurance of. "I rode to Nallamaram," writes a missionary from India, "and saw some people of the congregation there, together with the catechist. The clothes of one of the women were rather dirty, and I asked her about it. 'Sir,' said she, I am a poor woman, and have only this single dress.' ' Well,' I asked her, ' have you always been so poor ?' 'No,' said she ; ' I had some money and jewels, but a year ago the thieves came and robbed me of all. They told me,' she continued, '"if you will return again to heathenism, we shall restore to you everything."' ' Well,' said I, ' why did not you follow their advice ? Now you are a poor Christian.' ' Oh, sir,' she replied, 'I would rather be a poor Christian than a rich heathen. Now I can say, respecting my stolen property, The Lord gave it, and the Lord has taken it again.'"

7259. CHRISTIANS, Failures of. A minister in whom the Rev. Andrew Fuller had once placed entire confidence, and with whom he had for a long series of years been very intimate, fell into an awful public sin, and threw a blasting mildew over religion throughout an extensive community. In the very midst of the intense excitement created by the sad event, came the season for a public meeting of ministers, annually held in connection with the church. Some of the neighboring clergymen proposed the omission of the service on account of the state of the public mind, but to this arrangement Mr. Fuller very decidedly objected. The usual session was held, and Mr. Fuller appointed to preach. A vast crowd assembled, expecting of course, some allusion to his former friend; nor were they disappointed. The sermon was on the sins of professors of religion—their frequency, causes, and awful result. His feelings throughout were very tender, and many of his hearers, both clergy and laity, were during the sermon mostly in tears. He, however, restrained his emotion within bounds till he approached the close of his sermon. Then addressing the unconverted part of his audience, he besought them not to become hardened in their guilt, or neglect to secure the salvation of their souls, because some who had borne the vessel of the Lord had sinned. "I need not," he added with great tenderness of spirit, "make a more distinct reference; but oh ! remember that if I, and these my brethren in the ministry, and every other professing Christian in the world, were to make shipwreck of faith and character, and to fall into crime like poor ——, religion would still be the same grand system of truth and morality, and you would be eternally lost if you reject it. The Lord Jesus Christ is the standard of character, and not poor sinners like us." *Messenger.*

7260. CHRISTIANS God's Hidden Treasure. "Thy hidden ones," Ps. 83 : 3 ; "hidden" in respect to their safety ; "hidden" in regard to their secrecy ; "the world knoweth them not," 1 John 3 : 1 ; "as unknown and yet well known," 2 Cor. 6 : 9. Valuable things are often hidden : as in nature "full many a gem of purest ray serene," etc., like beautiful flowers behind the hedge ; like beautiful shells beneath the sea ; like beautiful diamonds beneath the earth. Men hide their valued treasures under lock and key, or in some safe hold. Eastern nations bury their treasures in the ground (Matt. 13 44). The figure brings out many truths about the "hidden ones" of Christ's kingdom. Col. 3 : 3, 4 : "Your life is hid with Christ in God. When Christ—who is our life, shall appear, then," etc. The Christian is now in one sense like the manslayer in the city of refuge, hidden in safe keeping for a time ; but the day is coming of "the manifestation of the son of God," when Christ will bring forth his own, and then shall the redeemed appear with the redeemer, and be partakers of his glory.

Bowes.

7261. CHRISTIANS God's Property. "Then shall ye be a peculiar treasure." The word peculiar, derived from Latin *peculium*, private property, has for its Hebrew equivalent *segulah*, which signifies wealth, and is used not only in the text quoted above, but also in Mal. 3 : 17, with reference to the people of God's choice ; and in the New Testament the Greek word contains the same idea of acquired property. See Acts 20 : 28 ; 1 Pet. 2 : 9, in which the pious Jew and the Christian are both God's peculiar people, for he has made them his own special property, consequently he exercises the most watchful care over them.

Biblical Treasury.

7262. CHRISTIANS, Inconsistencies of. In true kindness of heart, sweetness of temper, open-handed generosity, the common charities of life, many mere men of the world lose nothing by comparison with such professors ; and how are you to keep the world from saying, "Ah ! your man of religion is no better than others ; nay, he is sometimes worse !" With what frightful prominence does this stand out in the answer, never-to-be-forgotten answer, of an Indian chief to the missionary who urged him to become a Christian. The plumed and painted savage drew himself up in the consciousness of superior rectitude ; and with indignation quivering on his lip and flashing in his eagle eye, he replied, "Christian lie ! Christian cheat ! Christian steal !—drink !—murder ! Christian has robbed me of my lands, and slain my tribe !" adding, as he turned haughtily away, "The Devil, Christian ! I will be no Christian." Many such reflections teach us to be careful how we make a religious profession ! And having made the profession, cost what it may, by the grace of God let us live up to it, and act it out. It is better not to vow, than, having vowed, not to pay. *Dr. Guthrie.*

7263. CHRISTIANS, Making. A missionary says that he was once walking in his garden, when a poor Hindu boy, who had belonged to the mission school, came after him, and in a very gentle voice said. "If you please, sir, make me a Christian." The missionary was quite surprised at what he heard, and said to the little heathen boy, "I cannot make you a Christian, my dear child, but God can. You must ask God to forgive your sins for Jesus Christ's sake, and to send his Holy Spirit to live in your heart." Not a long time after, the same little boy came to the missionary and said, with a soft voice and a sweet smile on his face, "The Lord Jesus Christ himself has come to live in my heart." How is that?" asked the missionary. "I prayed," said the little boy, "as you told me; and I said, 'O, Lord Jesus Christ, if you please. make me a Christian.' And he was so kind as to hear me, and to come and live in my heart ever since."

7264. CHRISTIANS, Nominal. Many there are who, while they bear the name of Christians, are totally unacquainted with the power of their divine religion. But for their crimes the Gospel is in no wise answerable. Christianity is with them a geographical, not a descriptive, appellation. *Faber.*

7265. CHRISTIANS, Pagan. The Catholic missionaries, trying to convert a tribe of South American Indians, told them that their God would give them victory in battle. Thereupon they were baptized, and became Romanists. Soon after they went to try their new-found power in war against their old enemies. The result was they were badly defeated. Thereupon they threw off the religion which made large promises, but failed to perform them, and returned to their pagan gods.

7266. CHRISTIANS, Periodical. In some parts of the world there are certain boiling springs, called Geysers. Their peculiarity is, that at irregular intervals they send up spouts of boiling water, and then are silent for a considerable time. Travelers will tell you, that at the time when they are silent you will find it very difficult to believe that water would ever issue out of such an orifice at all. There was a revival some years ago, was there not? The gracious rain came down upon God's inheritance. How earnest you were!—how active! But the revival passed away, and your warmth and fervor and energy passed away with it, and those who look on you would find it very difficult to believe that you have ever been zealous in God's service at all. *Dr. Punshon.*

7267. CHRISTIANS, Rich. Often as the motley reflexes of my experiences move in long procession of manifold groups before me, the distinguished and world-renowned company of Christian mammonists appears to the eye of my imagination as a drove of camels heavily laden, yet all at full speed, and each in the confident expectation of passing through the eye of the needle, without stop or halt, both beast and baggage. *Coleridge.*

7268. CHRISTIANS, Riches of. The Emperor Decius called two Christian nobles of Corduna before him. He desired to execute them that he might obtain their wealth. He asked them where it was. They answered, "Here, these limbs are our treasures. Take them, break, spoil, hack, or burn them, that we may inherit eternal riches from our Lord." They suffered excruciating torments with unyielding consistency, and were finally beaten to death with crow-bars, and went to inherit eternal riches in glory.

7269. CHRISTIANS, Water-logged. A friend of mine said he was in Liverpool some time ago, and there was a vessel coming into the harbor. It sailed right up the Mersey under full sail, and a little while after another vessel came in towed by a tug and sunken to the level of the water. He wondered it did not sink; and he went down to the water's edge and saw that they got it into the harbor with a great deal of difficulty, and he inquired and found that it was loaded with lumber. It had such material on board that it could not sink, and it had sprung a leak and had got water-logged. My friends, I think there are a good many of God's people that have got water-logged, and it takes all the strength of the church to look after those Christians that are water-logged, and so water-logged that they cannot go forth and do good to others—help the unfortunate, and lift up the poor drunkard, because they don't know whether they are saved themselves. The fact is they are off with the world; mingling with the world; acting, speaking, as though in the world, and they don't know whether they are saved themselves. *Moody.*

7270. CHRISTIAN UNION, Symbol of. It has been a frequent and a favorite metaphor, made use of by several eminent speakers and writers on this subject, to compare the fraternal union of churches, to the union of the colors in the rainbow; and a very beautiful metaphor it is. It was not till lately that the church of Christ has been at all entitled to this comparison; for if formerly it was like one, it was so distinct in its lines of color and with edges so sharp and defined, that they seemed to be intended to cut each other through the whole span of the arch. I should not admire such a rainbow as this; neither should I be much taken with a rainbow of one color only: I am afraid we should begin to dispute as to what color this should be; and if we agreed as to that, we should not long rest satisfied with it. One party would wish to have it enlivened with a little more red; and another would have it sobered with a little more purple. For my part I am contented with the rainbow of nature, with its distinct yet commingling hues; soft, beautiful, varied one. If we could see all the churches worthy to be compared to such an appearance, we say in the language of one of the writers of the Apocrypha "When thou seest the rainbow, bless him that made it; very glorious is it to behold, and the hands of the Almighty have bended it." I have no desire that the union of the churches shall be more perfect than this, till we enter into the colorless light of eternity, and see eye to eye, and face to face. *Richard Watson.*

7271. CHURCH Above and Below. The unity of the Church on earth with the Church unseen, is the closest bond of all; hell has no power over it; sin cannot blight it; schism cannot rend it; death itself can but knit it more strongly. Nothing is changed but the relation of sight; like as when the head of a far-stretching procession, winding through a broken hollow land, hides itself in some bending vale; it is still all one; all advancing together; they that are farthest on their way are conscious of their lengthened following.

they that linger with the last are drawn forwards as it were by the attraction of the advancing multitude.   *Dr. Manning.*

7272. CHURCH an Ark. The Church has many times been compared by divines to the ark of which we read in the book of Genesis; but never was the resemblance more perfect than during that evil time when she rode alone, amidst darkness and tempest, on the deluge beneath which all the great works of ancient power and wisdom lay entombed, bearing within her that feeble germ from which a second and more glorious civilization was to spring.   *Macaulay.*

7273. CHURCH, Arms of the. The Gauls were at a disadvantage when they fought the Romans, because their swords were short, blunt, pointless weapons, and the pikes of the Triarii were long and sharp, giving their adversaries a deep and terrible thrust. Many a believer has been worsted in conflict because of the bluntness of his weapon, caused by some unholy or imprudent deed, which has given the enemy an advantage in the strife. When we use the sword of reason, or science, or expediency, instead of the two-edged sword of the Spirit, which turns every way, it is no wonder that the foe gives the Church a deadly stab and drinks up some of her richest blood.   *Anon.*

7274. CHURCH, Attendance at. Rev. Thomas Collins tells about a sick farmer, who relied much upon his punctual attendance at church. "Why," said the farmer, "if there were three absences half the parish would be asking after my health." Mr. Collins replied that "the church was a good place, and regular attendance a good thing; but church and market agree in one point; more go to each than ever do business at them. Do you always profit at church." "Not always, but church-going itself is something. My clergyman says: 'Neglecters of worship, like uncut rock in the delf, cannot be used; but worshipers, like quarried stones, lie ready at hand for the builder to place them in the wall." "Very good," said Mr. Collins, "and Christ the master builder is willing to put you in a place just now; but he himself, and he alone, must be your foundation." "Of course," was the reply, "I believe that." "A stone placed rests. Is your heart at rest? Does your faith make you happy?" asked Mr. C." "Happy! No. I am not happy. No man on earth is happy," he responded. "Nay, there I must contradict you; so resting on Jesus, I am happy, and thousands of others are so too." "Well, I expect I shall go to heaven." Mr. Collins replied, "Not unless heaven first comes to you. Does your corn ripen in the barn or on the ground? You, like it, must be ready here if you would be happy there."

7275. CHURCH, Attractions of the. There is a fable of Amphion, the son of Jupiter, which says that he moved great masses of stone, and raised the walls of Thebes, simply by making melody upon his lyre. The interpretation of the story is, that by the force of eloquence he constrained a wild, uncivilized people to unite themselves together in a league of brotherhood, and build a town strong enough to fortify themselves against their enemies. This is spiritualized in the history of the church.

7276. CHURCH, Baubles in the. When Oliver Cromwell was about to turn the members of Parliament out of their chamber, he pointed to the mace, and cried, "Take away that bauble!" When he shall come, who will effectually purge the church, he will say much the same of many ecclesiastical ornaments, now held in high repute. Gowns and altars, and banners, and painted windows, will all go at one sweep with "take away those baubles." Nor will the rhetorical embellishments and philosophies of modern pulpits be any more tenderly dealt with. "Take away this bauble" will be the signal for turning many a treasured folly into perpetual contempt.   *Spurgeon.*

7277. CHURCH, Figures of the Biblical. *Body* of Christ, Eph. 1: 23—the emblem of union and subjection—many members under one head. *Bride*, the Lamb's, spouse—wife, Rev. 19: 7; 21: 9; "my sister, my spouse," Cant. 4: 12—sister for purity, spouse for love; "a chaste virgin," 2 Cor. 11: 2. *Building of God*, 1 Cor. 3: 9; 1 Pet. 2: 5; Eph. 2: 21, 22. *Candlestick*, Rev. 1: 20; 2: 1. *City*, Heb. 12: 22; Rev. 21: 2—the emblem of order, security and harmony. *Dove*, Cant. 2: 14; 5: 2. *Family*, Eph. 3: 15—the dwelling place of order, affection and union. *Fold*, John 10: 16—the abode of peace and safety. *Flock*, 1 Pet. 5: 2. *Garden*, Cant. 4: 12; Isa. 58: 11—enclosed—fair—fragrant—fruitful. *A house*—habitation—household, Eph. 2: 19, 22. *Lily*, Cant. 2: 3. *Temple*, 1 Cor. 3: 16. *Vineyard—Husbandry*, Isa. 5: 1; 1 Cor. 3: 9. Burning bush, tabernacle, temple, apocalyptic city, New Jerusalem.
                        Bowes.

7278. CHURCH, A Bride. The journey which our divine lover took, was from heaven to earth; to win his bride, he exchanged the bosom of the eternal father to lie, a feeble infant, on a woman's breast. Son of God, he left the throne of the universe, and assumed the guise of humanity, to be cradled in a manger and murdered on a cross. In his people he found a bride deep in debt, and paid it all; under sentence of death, and died in her room; a lost creature, clad in rags, and he took of his own royal robes to cover her. To wash her, he shed his blood; to win her, he shed his tears; finding her poor and miserable and naked, he endowed her with all his goods; heir of all things, everything that he possessed as his father's son she was to enjoy and share with himself; for are not his people "heirs of God and joint heirs with Christ, if so be that we suffer with him, that we may be also glorified together."   *Guthrie.*

7279. CHURCH, Conquests of the. Plutarch says that nothing contributed more largely to the greatness and glory of Rome than the fact that when any people were conquered, instead of being destroyed, they were incorporated with her, and partook of the same privileges, and in time were allowed to share her honors. It is a parallel of the progress of the church.

7280. CHURCH, Contributing for a. A worthy Quaker who lived in a country town in England was rich and benevolent, and his means were put in frequent requisition for purposes of local charity or usefulness. The townspeople wanted to rebuild their parish church, and a committee was appointed to raise funds. It was agreed that the Quaker could not be asked to subscribe towards an object so contrary to his principles; but then, on the other hand, so true a friend to the town might take it amiss if he was not at least consulted on a matter of such general interest. So one of their number went and explained to him their project; the old church was to be removed, and such and such steps taken towards the construction of a new one. "Thee was right," said the Quaker, "in supposing that my principles would not allow me to assist in building a church. But didst thee not say something about pulling down a church? Thee may'st put my name down for a hundred pounds."
Merivale.

7281. CHURCH, Deadness in the. It was an Egyptian custom at festal banquets to introduce a corpse, and seat it at the table, to remind the guests of their mortality. Its fleshless, skinny hand rested on the board, but moved not the viands; the glassy eyeballs fixed their dead stare upon the guests, but the light of life, in which those orbs once swam, was extinguished forever. In such a presence the festivities proceeded. In such a presence proceed often the sacred festivities of Zion. I have seen a corpse at a sacramental supper, stone dead amidst the guests of Jesus. Not a tear on the cheek, nor a quiver of the lips when Jesus showed his wounds. The dull, dead, unlightened eye never sparkled, the bosom heaved not, the entombed tongue clove to the roof of its mouth, amid all the outbreak of a Saviour's love and tenderness! Alas! figures are inadequate to set forth the entire melancholy of the case.   *F. F. Trench.*

7282. CHURCH, Deliverance of the. A man, by a chain made up of several links, some of gold, others of silver, others of brass, iron, or tin, may be drawn out of a pit; so the Lord, by the concurrence of several unsubordinate things, which have no manner of dependence, or natural coincidency, amongst themselves, hath oftentimes wrought the deliverance of his Church, that it might appear to be the work of his own hand. Sometimes by ordering and arming natural causes to defend his Church, and to amaze the enemy. Thus the stars, in their courses, are said to fight against Sisera. A mighty wind from heaven, beating on their faces, discomfited them, as Josephus reports; so the Christian armies under Theodosius against Eugenius the tyrant, were defended by winds from heaven, which snatched away their weapons out of their hands; to make good that promise, "No weapon that is formed against thee shall prosper." So the Lord slew the enemies of Joshua with hail. And thus the Moabites were overthrown, by occasion of the sun shining upon the water. Sometimes by implanting fantasies and frightful apprehensions into the minds of the enemy, as into the Midianites and the Assyrians. Thus the Lord caused a voice to be heard in the Temple, before the destruction of Jerusalem, warning the faithful to go out of the city. Sometimes by stirring up and prospering weak and contemptible means, to show his glory thereby. The Medes and Persians were an effeminate and luxurious people; Cyrus a mean prince, for he was at this time emperor of the Medes or Persians, but only son-in-law to Darius or Cyaxares; and yet these are made instruments to dethrone that most valiant people, the Babylonians. As Jeremiah was drawn out of the dungeon by old rotten rags, which were thrown aside as good for nothing, so the Lord can deliver his Church by such instruments as the enemies thereof before would have looked upon with scorn, as upon lost and despicable creatures. For God, as he useth to infatuate those whom he will destroy; so he doth guide, with a spirit of wonderful wisdom, those whom he raiseth to defend his kingdom. The Babylonians were feasting, and counted their city impregnable, being fortified with walls and the great river; and God gave wisdom beyond the very conjectures of men, to attempt a business which might seem unfeasible in nature, to dry up Euphrates, and divide it unto several small branches: and so he made a way to bring his army into the city while they were feasting. the gates thereof being, in great confidence and security, left open.   *Bp. Reynolds.*

7283. CHURCH, Division in. A recent fable says: "A very hard-hearted clapper in an old church-tower professed the intensest distress because its bell was hopelessly cracked. Many people thought it a pitiable position, and wished the sad-hearted clapper a better bell. But just then the ghost of ancient Diogenes, the sage, floated in through the window, and whistled most angrily: 'Master Clapper, cease your noise, and remember, in the first place, you cracked the bell; and secondly, nobody would have known it had you not told them.' I have often observed that those who bemoan divisions in a church are they who make them; and I also observe sometimes that they who make them are most ready to publish the fact; I have observed another fact, viz., that all clappers are not of as good metal as the bells they crack."

7284. CHURCH, Diversity in the. In every corn field there are plants of sickly as well as of luxuriant appearance, supplying a fit emblem of the various characters which compose the true Church of Christ. Some indeed are stunted in their growth by various causes; others ripening in the full measure of the stature of Christ, having received a larger measure of the spirit of all grace, and engaged a more copious effusion of the beams of the Sun of Righteousness. Yet all these must be permitted to mingle together till the harvest. Each have their separate uses; and as the wise husbandman is

content and thankful if the weeds do not overpower the corn, so the wise Christian will be grateful to God that errors both in doctrine and practice are not more abounding than they are, being satisfied that in the final issue and separation of the tares from the corn there will be nothing to complain of, but, on the contrary, that the purposes of God will work their way through all human hypocrisy and weakness, so as to fulfill the truth of the gracious promise.
Salter.

7285. CHURCH, False Alarm in the. During one of the wars between Austria and France a small company of French soldiers were very near falling into the hands of a much larger company of the enemy. But the shrewdness of a bugler saved them; for he, creeping around into the rear of the Austrians, sounded on his bugle a recall. They, supposing it to be from their own side, immediately ceased the attack on the French, and turned and fled in confusion, and the enemy pursued them with great vigor. So it happens that the Church of God is turned aside from its great advantages and great work by some cowardly foe, in the name and profession of a Christian, in their midst. Such men discourage every great enterprise. They urge the Church to "conservatism." They prevent, if possible, all attack on popular sins and follies, lest some godless rich man, or some empty-headed and empty-hearted woman of fashion, be driven out of the congregation. There are a good many cowardly professors, who are ready with Satan's bugles in their hands. *A. D. Vail.*

7286. CHURCH, Foundations of the. A few years ago, in making a pedestrian excursion through the Green Mountain region, my friend and I came, one night, to the top of Mount Mansfield, and though the scene was very beautiful and the sunset very clear, that night there came on a furious storm. It seemed as if the little hotel in which we had been trying to sleep would be thrown from the mountain-top. We looked out of the little window down into the mountain-sides, and it was one vast sheet of lightning all the time. The thunders were harsh, and it seemed as if, in the violence of the storm, the mountain itself would fairly fall from its resting place. It was a fearfully stormy night. The next morning, however, we looked out of the same window. How calm and beautiful it all was! We looked down upon Lake Champlain, and the surface was just as smooth as if it had never been disturbed by the keel of a boat or a boatman's oar, and far to the north we could see the spires of Montreal standing up like silver needles in the far distance; and far across westward lay the Adirondack regions, the clouds of the night before skipping off as if ashamed that they had not done more damage; and looking eastward over the White Mountain range, the air was clear as crystal, and old Mansfield just as firm as ever. So, I thought, resting upon that firm mountain, is the Church of our Lord Jesus Christ. Scepticism may come with all the violence of its errors, temptations may assail,

the thunder and lightning of opposition may come, the furious blasts may blow, and it would seem as if the Church were trembling and falling with the violence and the shock of the great tornado; but it does stand, and will stand, because it is founded upon a rock.
Dr. J. F. Hurst.

7287. CHURCH, Frozen. Look at that frozen stream. It moves not the mill which should grind the grain. The brook, which produces verdure on its banks while running, is useless to vegetation when frozen. The noble river, which bears millions of tons of freight, and myriads of passengers on its liquid bosom, is useless to steamboat and sailing vessel when bound in chains of frost. And what can a Church do for God or for souls when frozen by formality and pride? It may glitter brightly, but its influence will not hinder sinners from going to damnation. *E. Osborn.*

7288. CHURCH, Invalids in the. I once read of a man who started with all his wealth for a fabulous country, where the people never died, and when he got there he found old great-great-great-grand people, who lived helpless, and had to be fed by their young descendants. It took one-half the population to feed the other half, and the Jew would not stay in that country It seems to take half the church to take care of the other half. *A. G. Tyng.*

7289. CHURCH, Leader of the. The army under the command of Paulus Æmilius, consisted of busy, talkative soldiers, each of them having some scheme of his own, and all being ready to advise their general. He gave them orders to the effect that each should keep his hand fit for action and his sword sharp, and leave the rest to him. Weapons of war are always prone to rust whilst soldiers debate and quarrel about plans of action. To be prepared for conflict is the duty of the Christian. But let our Leader be our only dictator, and, neither submitting plans to him, nor questioning his own plans, nor even submitting plans to ourselves, we shall be led on, under his high and sublime inspiration, to perfect victory. *Anon.*

7290. CHURCH, Materials of a. In the second century, Celsus, a celebrated adversary of Christianity, distorting our Lord's expression, complained, "Jesus Christ came into the world to make the most horrible and dreadful society; for he calls sinners, and not the righteous, so that the body he came to assemble is a body of profligates, separated from good people, among whom they before were mixed. He has rejected all the good, and collected all the bad." "True," says Origen in reply, "our Jesus came to call sinners—but to repentance. He assembled the wicked—but to convert them into new men, or rather to change them into angels. We come to him covetous, he makes us liberal; lascivious, he makes us chaste; violent, he makes us meek; impious, he makes us religious."

7291. CHURCH, Membership in the. Many years ago I was on my way to Philadelphia, to fill a situation. In the car, same seat with myself, was a veteran Massachusetts man, who inquired of me my destination, my home, occu pation, etc. Rather suddenly changing the subject, he remarked:—"And your certificates —have you any?" "Yes, sir;" and I handed him one in the handwriting of Wilbur Fisk. "Very good—very good; have you any other?" "Yes, sir;" and I handed him one made out by Dr. Holdich. "Excellent—but have you no other?" "No more, sir." "None from your preacher?" "O, yes, I have one of that sort," said I, drawing it out instantly. "Well, sir, that is what I wished to see. Now let me give you a little advice. I am an old sea captain, and have seen a good deal of society, a good deal of the world, and a good deal of the church. I have found it good policy, in coming into port, always to tie my vessel up at once, fore and aft, to the spiles on the wharf, although it may cost me something for wharfage, instead of anchoring her in the stream, and letting her swing with the tide. You understand me, I see. Hand in your certificate, then, as soon as you reach Philadelphia." *Allyn.*

7292. CHURCH Militant. There was a small band of three hundred cavalry in the Theban army who proved a great terror to any enemy with whom they were called to fight. They were companions who had bound themselves together by a vow of perpetual friendship, determining to stand together until the last drop of their blood was spilled upon the ground. They were called "The Sacred Battalion," or "The Band of Lovers," and they were bound alike by affection for the State and fidelity to each other, and thus achieved wonders. The church are bound together by more sacred ties, and her annals show equal devotion.

7293. CHURCH, A Powerless. I have seen a large mill in which there was not a moving spindle. Its walls were beautiful and strong. Its machinery was wonderful in its completeness and variety. There was nothing wanting. Yet not a hum of noise was heard in the great building. There was not a shaft, or wheel, or spindle in motion. And when I inquired the cause I found that nothing was defective in the machinery. Nothing was broken or deranged. But when I went down to the engine room I found that the fires were all out. And that was the reason why the great mill was silent, and all that splendid machinery inoperative. Unless the fires were burning under the boilers the mill was useless. So there are churches with tall spires, strong walls, cushioned pews, magnificent adornings, many members, and perfect organizations, in which there is no motion, and no sign of life. And men wonder why it is, and can find no fault in the creed, in the organization, in the preaching or in the singing. But the fault lies further down —the fires are out. *J. R. Miller.*

7294. CHURCH, A Preaching. When Dr. Lyman Beecher was laboring most successfully in the city of Boston, he was asked how it was that he was able to accomplish so much. He replied, "It is not I that do it: it is my church. I preach as hard as I can on Sabbath, and then I have four hundred members who go out and preach every day of the week."

10

7295. CHURCH, Preservation of the. Christ preserves his church as a spark in the ocean, as a flock of sheep among the wolves. That the sea should be higher than the earth, and yet not drown it, is a wonder; so that the wicked should be so much higher than the church in power, and not devour it, is because Christ hath this inscription on his vesture and on his thigh: King of kings. They say lions are *insomnes;* they have little or no sleep; it is true of the Lion of the tribe of Judah; he never slumbers, nor sleeps, but watcheth over his church to defend it (Isa. 27: 2, 3): "Sing ye unto her, a vineyard of red wine; I the Lord do keep it; lest any hurt it, I will keep it day and night." If the enemies destroy the church, it must be at a time when it is neither night nor day, for Christ keeps it day and night. Christ is said to carry his church as the eagle her young ones upon her wings (Ex. 19: 4). The arrow must first hit the eagle before it can hurt the young ones, and shoot through her wings; the enemies must first strike through Christ before they can destroy his church. Let the winds and storms be up, and the church almost covered with waves, yet Christ is the ship of the church, and so long there is no danger of shipwreck. *T. Watson.*

7296. CHURCH, Pride in a. St. Pachomius built a fine church from his own design, and under his own supervision. When completed he entered it with some of his monks, and became conscious of the swelling of his heart, with pride at the beauty of the building which he had erected. He called to his companions, "Quick, get ropes, and pull these pillars out of the perpendicular, to tease my eyes whenever I enter this house of God."

7297. CHURCH, Purpose of the. Christ is the sun; his church is the moon, to reflect upon the world the light of the "Sun of Righteousness," during his absence in the heavens. In herself she has no light at all; without her sun she has virtually no existence; severed from him, she is nothing worth. The church has nothing whatever in herself which can radiate those beams of light, and life, and love, without which all is darkness within; yea, a darkness which may be felt. No doctrine will fully enlighten the mind, but the doctrine of Christ. No truth will dissipate the error of fallen nature's teachers, but the truth as it is in Jesus. The ordained purpose of God is, that the church upon earth should not dispense the heat of her absent sun, but continually, and unto all the ends of the earth, dispense his light. For this, and this alone, was the church ordained to exist in the world; this purpose must be sadly mistaken by those who virtually substitute the church for the Saviour; who, instead of holding her up in her true character, as the faithful reflector of the Sun of Righteousness, present her before us as a self-lighting instrument. *Kidd.*

7298. CHURCH, Quiet of the. As we may say of a rock—nothing more quiet, because it is never stirred; and yet nothing more unquiet, because it is ever assaulted;—so we may say of the Church—nothing more peaceable, because it is established upon a rock; and yet nothing more unpeaceable, because that rock is in the midst of seas, winds, enemies, persecutions.

Reynolds.

7299. CHURCH, Separatists from the. One evening I went out with a shepherd to collect his sheep. After they had been gathered together, and were being driven off the moor, I observed that there were some among them who did not belong to his flock. I particularly noticed, also, that he paid no attention whatever to these wandering strangers, urged forward, though they were, by the barking dog, further and further from their rightful companions. At last, thinking I must have been mistaken in supposing they were not his, I pointed to one or two of them, and said, "Are those your sheep?" And he answered, "No." I said unto him, "Why, then, do you not separate them from the flock?" And he answered, and said, "They will find out directly they are not of us, and then they will go away of themselves." And immediately I remembered the words of John, and how he had said, "They went out from us, but they were not of us; for if they had been of us, they would no doubt have continued with us; but they went out that they might be made manifest that they were not all of us." *Anon.*

7300. CHURCH a Tree. The church is a tree. Strip off its leaves, it is still a tree. It can put forth new leaves. Rob a church of its membership, the Bible and a ministry still remain, and new members may be won. Strip off the limbs of a tree, it may put forth others. Rob a church of its ministry, it can develop another. A church may lose its sacraments, and still be a church. Load a tree with poisonous vines, smother it with unclean things, it may possibly survive. So a church may be weighted down with auricular confessions, prayers to saints, and other superstitions, and yet it is possible they may die and it yet live and grow and clothe itself with beauty. But what of a tree without sap—a church without piety? Better root it up and occupy its place with another. *Dr. E. O. Haven.*

7301. CHURCH, Victory of the. At the close of the war of 1866, the triumphant army of Prussia came to Berlin for a reception of welcome. As each regiment approached the city gate from the Thiergarten, it was halted by a choir, demanding by what right it would enter the city. The regiment replied in a song, reciting the battles it had fought, the victories it had won; then came a welcome from the choir, "Enter into the city." And so the next came up, reciting its deeds, and another, and another, each challenged and welcomed. They marched up the Linden between rows of captured cannon, with the banners they had borne and the banners they had taken, and they saluted the statue of grand old Frederick, the creator of Prussia. So, when all the fierce warfare of earth shall have been accomplished, and the kingdom of Christ assured, the phalanxes of his church shall go up to the city with songs

and tokens of victory. They shall march in together, singing hallelujahs, and shall lay their trophies at the feet of him upon whose head are many crowns—King of kings and Lord of lords. *Thompson.*

7302. CIRCUMSPECTION, Necessity for. Persons who want experience should be extremely cautious how they depart from those principles which have been received generally, because founded on solid reasons; and how they deviate from those customs which have obtained long, because in their effect they have proved good: thus circumspect should all persons be, who cannot yet have acquired much practical knowledge of the world; lest, instead of becoming what they anxiously wish to become, more beneficial to mankind than those who have preceded them, they should actually, though inadvertently, be instrumental towards occasioning some of the worst evils that can befall human society. *Bishop Huntingford.*

7303. CIRCUMSTANCES, Adjustment to. If you cannot frame your circumstances in accordance with your wishes, frame your will into harmony with your circumstances. *Epictetus.*

7304. CIRCUMSTANCES, Man the Creature of. To deny that man is, in a sense, the creature of circumstances, is equal to the denial that two and two make four; and to deny that man cannot make circumstances is equal to affirming that two and two make five. *J. Johnson.*

7305. CIRCUMSTANCES, Master of. It is a painful fact, but there is no denying it, the mass are the tools of circumstances; thistle-down on the breeze, straw on the river, their course is shaped for them by the currents and eddies of the stream of life; but only in proportion as they are things, not men and women. Man was meant to be not the slave, but the master of circumstances; and in proportion as he recovers his humanity, in every sense of the great obsolete word—in proportion as he gets back the spirit of manliness, which is self-sacrifice, affection, loyalty to an idea beyond himself, a God above himself, so far will he rise above circumstances and wield them at his will. *Kingsley.*

7306. CIRCUMSTANCES, Servants of. If a letter were to be addressed to that most influential word, circumstances, concluding thus: "I am, sir, your very obedient humble servant," the greater part of the world might subscribe it without deviating from the strictest veracity. *Horace Smith.*

7307. CITIES, Benefit of. I bless God for cities. Cities have been as lamps of life along the pathway of humanity and religion. Within them science has given birth to her noblest discoveries. Behind their walls freedom has fought her noblest battles. They have stood on the surface of the earth like great breakwaters rolling back or turning aside the swelling tide of oppression. Cities, indeed, have been the cradles of human liberty. They have been the active centres of almost all church and state reformation. Having, therefore, no sympathy with those who, regarding them as the excrescences of a tree, or the tumors of disease, would raze our cities to the ground, I bless God for cities.   *Guthrie.*

7308. CITIES, Ignorance in. In cities, people are brought up in total ignorance of, and blamable indifference for, country affairs; they can scarce distinguish flax from hemp, wheat from rye, and neither from barley: eating, drinking, and dressing, are their qualifications; pastures, copses, after-grass, inning harvest, are Gothic words to them. If to some of them you talk of weights, scales, measures, interest, and books of rates, to others of appeals, petitions, decrees, and injunctions, they will prick up their ears. They pretend to know the world, and, though it is more safe and commendable, are ignorant of Nature, her beginnings, growths, gifts, and bounties. This ignorance is often voluntary, and founded on the conceit they have of their own callings and professions.   *La Bruyère.*

7309. CITY, The Celestial. When you survey the spacious firmament, and behold it hung with such resplendent bodies, think—if the suburbs be so beautiful, what must the city be! What is the footstool he makes to the throne whereon he sits!   *W. Secker.*

7310. CITY, Sin in the. "Nine o'clock, all's well," once chanted the pacing watchman; but when he said, "All's well," the devil must have laughed in sardonic scorn: the red fires of his work were burning all over the crowded city. "Ten o'clock, and all's well;" and pious people said their prayers, and laid down to sleep; and here—and in this city alone—here two thousand dram-shops stood open, as he saw the sons of ministers and deacons, class-leaders, stewards, sons of very good people in the country turning in, well he knew for what they were in training. "Eleven o'clock, and all's well;" and yet theatres crowded with young men and women, boys and girls, lurid with the air of sin, redolent of blasphemy, the air thick with moral pollution, were in full blast; concert cellars gathered their motley crews; dance-houses rung with wassail cheer. The tempted, turned away from honest labor, sought in vain, crouched beside the wall, and an eager, hungry look was in their eyes. The devil must have laughed as he heard the drowsy watchman cry, "All's well," and saw good people sound asleep. "Twelve o'clock, and all's well." Once a year some churches hold a watch-night, and with solemn song and prayer live the old year out and the new year in. It is an event prepared for, talked of, got ready for, and remembered as an epoch. Now go out. Midnight! Hear the billiard balls as they are smitten; hark to the rattle of dice; hear the oaths and curses of men around their card table! The gambling hells keep watch-night seven times each week! Midnight! Yet through half-opened blinds streams the light of the house of the strange woman. Her doors are open, and from them there is a direct and short path to the shade of hell. On through the small hours, hot-footed, he keeps his way. Along his path is theft, and arson, and violence, ghastly murder, or outraged vir-

tue; the sin-born babe is strangled; the wandering, homeless wretch takes his plunge into eternity to escape the starvation or retribution of time!   *Christian Advocate.*

7311. CITY, Work in the. The reclaiming of men in the city is like digging out those noble monuments of the past so long buried amid the ruins of Nineveh. In excavating this vast population you have as it were laid bare the head of a huge winged bull, until you can observe that it has a human countenance and will well repay you for your toils. Are you going to congratulate yourselves that you have succeeded thus far? Why, there are the colossal feet, and the mighty wings, and all the rest of the body; all these are to be uncovered from the ruins, and the whole mass uplifted from the depth in which it lies imbedded. But, because you have done a little to bless London, and have brought a thousand, three thousand, ten thousand to hear the word of God, are you to sit down and say, "It is done." What is to be done with the rest of the three millions? Where are the other tens of thousands who are not hearing the word? Where is the great outlying mass of our leviathan city?   *Spurgeon.*

7312. CIVILITY, Neglected. An old man in the Olympic games, being desirous to see the sport, and unprovided of a seat, went about from place to place, was laughed and jeered at, but none offered him the civility; but when he came to the Spartans' quarter, all the boys, and some of the men, rose from their seats, and made him room. At this all the Greeks clapped and praised their behavior: upon which the good old man, shaking his hoary hairs, with tears in his eyes, said, "Good God! how well all the Greeks know what is good, and yet only the Lacedæmonians practice it!" And some say the same thing was done at Athens. For at the great solemnity of the Athenians, the Panatheniac festival, the Attics abused an old man, calling him as if they designed to make room for him, and when he came putting him off again; and when after this manner he had passed through almost all, he came to that quarter where the Spartan spectators sat, and all of them presently rose up and gave him place; the whole multitude, extremely taken with this action, clapped and shouted, upon which one of the Spartans said, "By heaven! these Athenians know what should be done, but are not much for doing it." A stranger being at Sparta, and observing how much the young men reverenced the old, said, "At Sparta alone it is desirable to be old."   *Plutarch.*

7313. CIVILIZATION, Current of. Civilization, like an immense stream, is carrying in its current science, power, and wealth, and any effort to oppose it must be utterly defeated.   *Chevalier.*

7314. CIVILIZATION, Future. There are half-a-dozen men, or so, who carry in their brains the *ovarium* eggs of the next generation's or century's civilizations. These eggs are not ready to be laid in the form of books as yet; some of them are hardly ready to be put into the form of talk. But as rudimentary ideas or inchoate tendencies, there they are; and these are what must form the future. *Holmes.*

7315. CIVILIZATION, Progress of. I think that the civilized world never was so happy in ancient times as it is now—relatively, I mean, compared with what civilization is now doing. If you go back two thousand years, even, you will find it to be so. Men like to praise old times. They like to praise, for instance, the good, old hearty days of England, before King Henry VIII. reigned, when there was simplicity, and when there was a rude yeomanry virtue, and when men were gay and happy. I tell you that were you to take these men up, and carry them back there, and let them sleep where men slept then, and let them eat what men ate then, and let them do what men had to do then, and take away from them what men did not have then, but do have now, you would hear the most piteous moaning and whining and complaining that ever afflicted your ears. For we have grown in the number of enjoyments, in the refinements of sensibility, in the realization of life, in all the sweet elements that go to constitute satisfaction in life. No pen can record, no tongue can tell, the growth that has been made in five hundred years. *Beecher.*

7316. CLAIMS, False. We claim things as rights, to which we have no right at all. We have no right to anything; and sometimes God teaches us this, by taking things from us. There was a sick man to whom a benevolent gentleman for a long time gave a quart of milk a day. At last the time came for him to die, and of course the gift of milk was expected to come to an end. When the poor man was gone the gentleman called upon the widow. "I must tell you, sir," said she to him, "my husband has made a will, and has left the quart of milk to his brother!" There was a beggar who had received a penny every day from a gentleman. One day the gentleman being ill did not go out; and when, the day after, he gave the usual penny, the beggar said to him, "But you owe me a penny, sir!" We smile, but we do the like ourselves. *Power.*

7317. CLEANLINESS, Advantages of. With what care and attention do the feathered race wash themselves and put their plumage in order; and how perfectly neat, clean, and elegant do they appear! Among the beasts of the field we find that those which are the most cleanly are generally the most gay and cheerful, or are distinguished by a certain air of tranquillity and contentment; and singing birds are always remarkable for the neatness of their plumage. So great is the effect of cleanliness upon man, that it extends even to his moral character. Virtue never dwelt long with filth; nor do I believe there ever was a person scrupulously attentive to cleanliness who was a consummate villain. *Rumford.*

7318. CLEANLINESS, Experiment of. When Isaac Hopper met a boy with a dirty face or hands, he would stop him, and inquire if he ever studied chemistry. The boy, with a wondering stare, would answer, "No." "Well then, I will teach thee how to perform a curious chemical experiment," said Friend Hopper. "Go home, take a piece of soap, put it in water, and rub it briskly on thy hands and face. Thou hast no idea what a beautiful froth it will make, and how much whiter thy skin will be. That's a chemical experiment: I advise thee to try it."
Life of Isaac T. Hopper.

7319. CLEMENCY, Benefit of. Alphonsus, King of Naples and Sicily, was asked why he was so favorable to all men, even to those most notoriously wicked. He answered, "Because good men are won by justice; the bad by clemency." Some of his Ministers complained to him of his lenity, which they said was more than became a Prince: "What, then!" exclaimed he; "would you have lions and tigers to reign over you? Know you not that cruelty is the attribute of wild beasts—clemency that of man?"

7320. CLEMENCY, Example of. A slave upset the boiling hot contents of a dish upon Hasan, the son of Ali, as he sat at table. He fell at his master's feet and began to repeat a passage from the Koran, "Paradise is for those who bridle their anger." Hasan replied, "I am not angry." "And for those who forgive men," continued the slave. "I forgive you," said Hasan. The slave finished the passage, saying, "For God loveth the beneficent." "Since it is so, I give you your liberty and four hundred pieces of silver," said Hasan.

7321. CLEMENCY, Noble. Louis the Twelfth the heir apparent to the throne of France, was persecuted and imprisoned by Charles the Eighth, the reigning king, the nobles and people uniting in the persecution. But Charles dying suddenly, Louis ascended the throne, much to the discomfiture of those who had been his enemies. Some sought to insinuate themselves into his good graces, while those that stood by him in adversity began to exalt themselves, and begged for the estates of their enemies. The king made this reply to those that urged their claims, "Ask something else of me, and I will show that I have respect unto your merits; but of this say no more, for the King of France doth not concern himself with the injuries of the Duke of Orleans"—his title before he came to the crown.

7322. CLERGY, Labors of the. A person expressed regret to Dr. Johnson that he had not become a clergyman, because he considered the life of a clergyman an easy and comfortable one. The Doctor made this reply: "The life of a conscientious clergyman is not easy. I have always considered a clergyman as the father of a larger family than he is able to maintain. No, sir, I do not envy a clergyman's life as an easy life, nor do I envy the clergyman who makes it an easy life."

7323. CLERGY, Office of the. Ministers of the gospel in this quarter of the globe resemble the commanders of an army stationed in a conquered country, whose inhabitants, overawed and subdued, yield a partial obedience: they have sufficient employment in attempting to conciliate the affections of the natives, and in carrying into execution the orders and regulations of their Prince; since there is much latent disaffection, though no open rebellion, a strong partiality to their former rulers, with few attempts to erect the standard of revolt.

Robert Hall.

7324. CLERGY, Snares of the. Before I parted with honest Glascott, I cautioned him much against petticoat snares. He has burnt his wings already. Sure he will not imitate a foolish gnat, and hover again about the candle! If he should fall into a sleeping lap, he will soon need a flannel night-cap and a rusty chain to fix him down like a church-Bible to the reading-desk. No trap so mischievous to the field-preacher as wedlock, and it is laid for him at every hedge-corner. Matrimony has quite maimed poor Charles (Wesley) and might have spoiled poor John (Wesley) and George (Whitefield), if a wise master had not graciously sent them a brace of ferrets. *John Berridge.*

7325. CLOSET, Communion of the. Bengel was much given to intercessory prayer. One who was anxious to find out his secret, watched him, unobserved, in his hours of retirement. "Now," said he, "I shall hear Bengel pray." The aged saint sat long comparing Scripture with Scripture, till the hour of midnight sounded. Nature seemed exhausted. He folded his arms over the open word, and looking up, gave utterance to these words: "Lord Jesus, thou knowest me; we are on the same old terms." In a few moments he was sleeping soundly.

7326. CLOSET, Importance of the. The closets of God's people are where the roots of the church grow. And if the roots be not nourished, there can be no tree with branches and fruit. In many senses the root of the plant is the most important part of it. Men do not see it. It is hidden away down under the ground. Yet in the dark it works away, and in its secret laboratory it prepares the life which goes up into the plant or tree, and manifests itself in trunk and branches, in leaves and fruits. The beautiful leaf-fabrics are woven down in the looms of that dark earth-factory. The colors that tint the flowers are prepared in that lowly work-shop. The little blocks that are piled in silence, one by one, as the fabric of the tree goes up, are hewn out in the secret quarries of the roots. He that would bless a tree must first bless its roots. So it is in the spiritual life. It is not the closet which men see It is not a man's secret, personal religious life which the world understands and praises. Yet it is in the closet that the roots of his life grow. And if the roots be not nourished, then the tree will soon die.

J. R. Miller.

7327. CLOSET, Meeting Christ in the. About the middle of the fifteenth century, in one of the retreats of his order, a pious recluse, as he used to walk with his brethren in the cloisters or in the garden, would sometimes stop and say, "Dear brethren, I must go: there is some one waiting for me in my cell." Those who heard him knew with whom he wished to commune.

This monk was Thomas á Kempis, the supposed author of that religious classic, "The Imitation of Christ."

7328. CLOSET, Secret of the. "Mother," said a girl, "I want to know the secret of your going away alone every night and morning." "Why, my child?" "Because it must be to see some one you love very much." "And what leads you to think so?" "Because I have always noticed that when you come back you appear to be more happy than usual." "Well, suppose I do go to see a friend I love very much, and that, after seeing him and conversing with him, I am more happy than before, why should you wish to know anything about it?" "Because I wish to do as you do, that I may be happy also." "Well, my child, when I leave you in the morning and evening, it is to see my blessed Saviour; I go to pray to him; I ask him for his grace to make me happy and holy; I ask him to assist me in all the duties of the day, and especially to keep me from committing any sin against him; and, above all, I ask him to have mercy on your soul, and to save you from the ruin of those who go down to hell." "Oh! that is the secret," said the child, "then I must go with you."

7329. CLOUDS, Transformation of. Did I mention to you what I thought as I saw the picture of the German painter some time ago? I could not make out what he meant by it. It was called "Cloud Land," and it seemed nothing but cloud upon cloud. As I looked I saw that every cloud turned into an angel or an angel's wing; and the whole picture, which at first seemed only a mass of gloom, looked out upon me with a hundred angels' eyes. So with all clouds, if God comes nigh to us by them; look at them and they turn into angels. They are not desirable in themselves. We foolish men would walk always in day brightness—we do not want clouds—but God knows their value, else he would never send them to us. *E. P. Hood.*

7330. CLOUDS, Vanishing. More than once we had noticed in our early mornings dull masses of cloud in the sky. As the sun got up and gathered strength, these all vanished. They did not drift away, or pass to a different region of the heavens; but they vanished on the spot, such was the absorbing power of the desert sun. Clouds that would have brought a whole day's rain in our climate disappeared. We recognized the figure in Job,—"As the cloud is consumed and vanisheth, so he that goeth down to the grave shall come up no more."

Bonar.

7331. COLD, Effect of. Very striking and curious is the story of Dr. Solander's escape, when in company with Sir Joseph Banks, among the hills of Terra del Fuego. They had walked a considerable way through swamps, when the weather became suddenly gloomy and cold, fierce blasts of wind driving the snow before it. Finding it impossible to reach the ships before night, they resolved to push on through another swamp into the shelter of a wood, where they might kindle a fire. Dr

Solander, well experienced in the effects of cold, addressed the men, and conjured them not to give way to sleepiness, but at all costs to keep in motion. "Whoever sits down," said he, "will sleep, and whoever sleeps will wake no more." Thus admonished and alarmed, they set forth once more; but in a little while the cold became so intense as to produce the most oppressive drowsiness. Dr. Solander was the first who found the inclination to sleep—against which he had warned the others so emphatically—too irresistible for him, and he insisted on being suffered to lie down. In vain Banks entreated and remonstrated; down he lay upon the snow, and it was with much difficulty that his friend kept him from sleeping. One of the black servants began to linger in the same manner. When told that if he did not go on he would inevitably be frozen to death, he answered that he desired nothing more than to lie down and die. Solander declared himself willing to go on, but said he must first take some sleep. It was impossible to carry these men, and they were therefore both suffered to lie down, and in a few minutes were in a profound sleep. Soon after some of those who had been sent forward to kindle a fire returned with the welcome news that a fire awaited them a quarter of a mile off. Banks then happily succeeded in awakening Solander, who, although he had not been asleep five minutes, had almost lost the use of his limbs, and the flesh was so shrunk that the shoes fell from his feet. He consented to go forward, with such assistance as could be given; but no attempts to rouse the black servant were successful, and he, with another black, died there.
                                        Banks.

7332. COMFORT, Abiding. I have taken much pains to know everything that was esteemed worth knowing amongst men; but with all my disquisitions and reading, nothing now remains with me to comfort me, at the close of life, but this passage of St. Paul—"It is a faithful saying, and worthy of all acceptation, that Christ Jesus came into the world to save sinners:" to this I cleave, and herein I find rest.   *Selden.*

7333. COMFORT, Greatest. Believe me, I speak it deliberately, and with full conviction, I have enjoyed many of the comforts of life, none of which I wish to esteem lightly. Often have I been charmed with the beauties of nature, and refreshed with her bountiful gifts. I have spent many an hour in sweet meditation, and in reading the most valuable productions of the wisest men. I have often been delighted with the conversation of ingenious, sensible, and exalted characters: my eyes have been powerfully attracted by the finest productions of human art, and my ears by enchanting melodies. I have found pleasure when calling into activity the powers of my own mind; when residing in my own native land, or traveling through foreign parts; when surrounded by large and splendid companies—still more, when moving in the small endearing circle of my own family; yet, to speak the truth before God, who is my judge, I must confess I know

not any joy that is so dear to me; that so fully satisfies the inmost desires of my mind; that so enlivens, refines, and elevates my whole nature, as that which I derive from religion, from faith in God: as one who not only is the parent of men, but has condescended, as a brother, to clothe himself with our nature. Nothing affords me greater delight than a solid hope that I partake of his favors, and rely on his never failing support and protection. He, who has been so often my hope, my refuge, my confidence, when I stood upon the brink of an abyss, where I could not move one step forward; he who, in answer to my prayer, has helped me when every prospect of help vanished; that God who has safely conducted me, not merely through flowery paths, but likewise across precipices and burning sands. May this God be thy God, thy refuge, thy comfort, as he has been mine.   *Lavater.*

7334. COMFORT, Personal. For the enjoyment of real personal comfort, I would rather, infinitely rather, be the occupant of the poorest hut, with its homeliest fare, in the coldest and bleakest cleft that flanks the sides of the Shihallion or Ben Nevis, than be the possessor of the stateliest palace, with its royal appurtenances, in the plains of Bengal.   *Dr. Duff.*

7335. COMFORT in Trial. In the exhaustless catalogue of heaven's mercies to mankind, the power we have of finding some germs of comfort in the hardest trials must ever occupy the foremost place; not only because it supports and upholds us when we most require to be sustained, but because in this source of consolation there is something, we have reason to believe, of the Divine Spirit; something of that goodness which detects, amidst our own evil doings, a redeeming quality; something which, even in our fallen nature, we possess in common with the angels; which had its being in the old time when they trod the earth, and lingers on it yet, in pity.   *Dickens.*

7336. COMFORTS, Carnal and Godly. Carnal comforts, like comets, appear for a time, and then vanish; when the portion of a saint, like a true star, is fixed and firm. A worldling's wealth lieth in earth, and, therefore, as wares laid in low, damp cellars, corrupts and moulders; but the godly man's treasure is in heaven, and, as commodities laid up in high rooms, continueth sound and safe. Earthly portions are often like guests which stay for a night, and away, but the saint's portion is an inhabitant that abides in the house with him forever.
                                        Swinnock.

7337. COMFORTS, Divine. In the multitude of our thoughts within us, the divine comforts do delight our souls; and it is they only that can do it. Miserable are all other comforters, and vain is all the comfort that they administer. Neither philosophic discourses, nor the common arts of diversion, music, dancing, drinking, or gaming, can afford any great or long relief to a troubled spirit: its weight will soon make way through these slight things, and indeed will never find a stay strong enough to bear it up, till it repose itself upon the divine comforts. After all experiments, its last sanctuary must be in God and religion.　　*Norris.*

7338. COMFORTS, How We Lose Our. The planet Venus teaches an important lesson to the followers of Christ, viz: that the earth was never yet known to come between her and the sun. Whence the languor, and the spiritual declensions, the darkness, and the soul distresses, of many a child of light? Come they not, very frequently, from giving way to earthly cares, earthly joys, and earthly pursuits? We let these things shut out the sun. No wonder that we move heavily, and walk in the dark, while we cultivate that " friendship with this world, which is enmity with God." But if, on the contrary, our affections are set on things above—if our treasure and our hearts are with Christ in heaven—we shall, probably, "walk in the light," and enjoy an abiding perception of interest in his precious blood which "cleanseth from all sin."　　*Salter.*

7339. COMMANDMENTS, Breach of Each of the. As David with a little stone slew Goliath, because his forehead was open, so can our enemy easily deal with us if he observe any faculty naked and neglected. The actual and total breach of any one commandment—total, I mean, when the whole heart doth it, though haply it execute not all the obliquity which the compass of the sin admits—is an implicit, habitual, interpretative, and conditional breach of all; his soul stands alike disaffected to the holiness of every commandment, and he would undoubtedly adventure on the breach of this if such exigencies and conditions as misguided him in the other should thereunto as strongly induce him. He that hath done any one of these abominations hath done all these abominations on God's account. There being then in a Christian man a suitable life and vigor of holiness in every part, and a mutual conspiring of them all in the same ways and ends, there must needs likewise be therein an excellent beauty.　　*Bp. Reynolds.*

7340. COMMANDMENTS, Breaking the Ten. Lord Eldon told Mr. Spence, the queen's counsel, that he was first brought into notice on the northern circuit by breaking the ten commandments: "I'll tell you how it was. I was counsel in a cause, the fate of which depended upon our being able to make out who was the founder of an ancient chapel in the neighborhood. I went to view it. There was nothing to be observed which gave any indication of its date or history. However, I observed that the ten commandments were written on some plaster, which, from its position, I conjectured might cover an arch. Acting on this, I bribed the clerk with five shillings to allow me to chip away part of the plaster; and after two or three attempts I found the keystone of an arch, on which were engraved the arms of an ancestor of one of the parties. This evidence decided the cause, and I ever afterwards had reason to remember, with some satisfaction, my having on that occasion broken the ten commandments."　　*Life of Lord Eldon.*

7341. COMMANDMENTS, Burden of the. The Talmud reckons the laws of Moses to be six hundred and thirteen in number; *i. e.*, the positive at two hundred and forty-eight, and negative three hundred and sixty-five. "To keep so many laws," said the Jews, "is an angel's work." Hence they had much question which was the great commandment, so that they might keep that in lieu of the whole. *Lange.*

7342. COMMANDMENTS, Disposing of the. Pericles told the ambassadors who came to him, desirous of making some changes in the Lacedemonian laws, that it was against the law to take down any of the tablets upon which a decree of the people was written. One of the ambassadors said there was no reason for taking them down, but "he could turn the other side outward—and there was no law against that." Too many treat the Commandments of God in the same way. They will not deny them altogether, but they cover them up, so that they may not be troubled by them.

7343. COMMANDMENTS, Rejecting the. An Antinomian called on Rowland Hill, to bring him to account for his too severe and legal Gospel. "Do you, sir," asked Mr. Hill, "hold the Ten Commandments to be a rule of life to Christians?" "Certainly not," replied the visitor. The minister rang the bell, and on the servant making his appearance, he quietly added, "John, show that man the door, and keep your eye upon him until he is beyond the reach of every article of wearing apparel or other property in the hall."

7344. COMMANDMENTS, Shortening the. The Abbe Boileau stated that the Jesuits had lengthened the creed and shortened the decalogue.

7345. COMMANDMENTS, Suppressed. As the second commandment so expressly forbids the use of images in the worship of God, the Roman Catholics omit it in their catechisms and books of devotion, and divide the tenth into two. The Rev. Mr. Temple, missionary at Malta, relates the following fact: "My teacher, a native of Italy, came into my room one morning, and took up a tract then lying on the table, and immediately cast his eyes upon the Ten Commandments, which I had inserted at the end. As soon as he had read the second commandment, he confessed much astonishment and asked whether this was part of the decalogue? I immediately showed him this commandment in Archbishop Martini's Italian translation of the Latin Vulgate. He could not suppress his feelings of surprise on reading this in the Italian Bible, and in a version, too, authorized by the Pope. "I have lived," said he, "fifty years; have been publicly educated in Italy; have had the command of a regiment of men, and fought in many campaigns; but, till this hour, I never knew that such a commandment as this is written in the pages of the Bible."　　*Whitecross.*

7346. COMMANDMENTS, Value of. The Queen does not make requests, does not even offer gifts; she commands those whom she favors to accept what she desires to bestow. Such is the formula which has grown into use as the most fitting medium for conveying a sovereign's gifts. The form is seemly, and the idea in which it originated is just. Yet the command of the sovereign is in its essence a bounty bestowed, is the greatest favor that a subject can receive. So when the King eternal means to confer on his child the richest privilege, he throws it into the form of a command. *Arnot.*

7347. COMMENDATION, Excessive. It is always esteemed the greatest mischief a man can do to those whom he loves, to raise men's expectation of them too high by undue and impertinent commendations. *Sprat.*

7348. COMMERCE and Christianity. Have you ever watched, in the balmy spring-time, the bee as it flits from flower to flower? and are you aware that not only is it gathering honey for its own use, but also that it conveys to the flowers that pollen or farina which causes the seed to germinate? Just so our merchants and mariners, in their eager pursuit after wealth, carry with them from shore to shore the seeds of the gospel of truth. And as we doubt not that God placed the honey in the heart of the flower for the very purpose of attracting thither the busy insect which should convey to it the seed of reproduction, so he has distributed in different regions of the world those various products—the cotton, the silk, the tea, the coffee, the indigo, the ivory, and the gold—which shall tempt the enterprising trafficker, and open the way to the missionary who shall sow the regenerating seed of life in the hearts of men.
Canon Melvill.

7349. COMMUNION, Divine. How many beautiful expressions suggest sweet thoughts as to the believer's near communion with God: *Abiding* before God. Ps. 61: 7; under the shadow of the Almighty, Ps. 91: 1; in the light, 1 John 2: 10; in the love of Jesus, John 15: 4, 10; as the branch in the vine, John 15: 4, 5; the beautiful emblems of constant nourishment, calm security, and upholding trust. *Dwelling* in the secret place of the Most High, Ps. 91: 1; in God, 1 John 4: 16; implying the ideas of refuge and rest. *Delighting in the Lord,* Ps. 37: 4; Isa. 58: 14—"If desire be love in motion, like a bird on the wing; delight may be compared to love at rest, rejoicing in its own happiness." *Drawing near,* Ps. 73: 28; as with Abraham's reverence and confidence, Gen. 18:23. *Entering into the holiest,* Heb. 10: 19. *Fellowship,* 1 Cor. 1: 9; 1 John 1: 3; symbolized by eating and drinking together, as in the ancient sacrifices, and now in the Lord's Supper. *Sitting in heavenly places* in Christ Jesus, Eph. 2: 6, our heart and hope being there already. *Bowes.*

7350. COMMUNION, Open. One of our Baptist friends, Dr. Colver, visited his son's farm in Illinois. He found the gate at the usual place in front of the house, but the fence was down all along the road. He could have entered anywhere else just as well as at the gate. To him this farm seemed like an open communion church. It has a door, but is open all around. *Dr. Holme.*

7351. COMMUNION, Renewal of. In one of the coal-pits of the north, while a considerable number of the miners were down below, the top of the pit fell in, and the shaft was completely blocked up. Those who were in the mine gathered to a spot where the last remains of air could be breathed. There they sat and sang and prayed after the lights had gone out, because the air was unable to support the flame. They were in total darkness, but a gleam of hope cheered them when one of them said he had heard that there was a connection between that pit and an old pit which had been worked years ago. He said it was a long passage through which a man might get by crawling all the way, lying flat upon the ground; he would go and see if it were passable. The passage was very long, but they crept through it, and at last they came out to light at the bottom of the other shaft, and their lives were saved. If my present way of access to Christ as a saint is blocked up by doubts and fears, if I cannot go straight up the shaft and see the light of my Father's face, there is an old working, the old-fashioned way by which sinners have gone of old, by which poor thieves go, by which harlots go. I will creep along it, lowly and humbly; I will go flat upon the ground; I will humble myself till I see my Lord, and cry, "Father, I am not worthy to be called thy son; make me as one of thy hired servants, so long as I may but dwell in thy house." In our very worst cases of despondency we may still come to Jesus as sinners. "Jesus Christ came into the world to save sinners." Call this to mind, and you may have hope. *Spurgeon.*

7352. COMMUNION, Sacramental. Especially in acts of sacramental communion with his Lord does the Christian gather up and consecrate the powers of his life-long communion with heaven. Then it is that he has most vivid impressions of the nearness of God to his soul, a most comfortable assurance of strength for his need. *Bp. Mackarness.*

7353. COMPANION, A Wise. In his company you learn how trees have tongues, sermons are found in stones, books in the running brooks, and good in everything. To him a blade of grass is a volume—a handful of simple flowers a library. A wise, communicative companion is a priceless treasure, not to be compared with rubies, precious stones, or indeed anything that this world has to offer. *J. Johnson.*

7354. COMPANIONS, Bad. A heathen named Bias was at sea with a number of wicked men, when a great storm arose, and they began to call loudly upon their gods for deliverance. Bias called out to them, "Forbear prayer, hold your tongues; I would not have the gods notice that you are here; they surely would drown us all if they should." Such is a heathen's conception of the danger of bad associations.

7355. COMPANIONS, Wicked. The impious lives of the wicked are as contagious as the most fearful plague that infects the air. When the doves of Christ lie among such pots, their yellow feathers are sullied. You may observe that in the oven the fine bread frequently hangs upon the coarse, but the coarse very seldom adheres to the fine. If you mix an equal portion of sour vinegar and sweet wine together, you will find that the vinegar will sooner sour the wine than the wine sweeten the vinegar. That is a sound body that continues healthful in a pest-house. It is a far greater wonder to see a saint maintain his purity among sinners than it is to behold a sinner becoming pure among saints. Christians are not always like fish, which retain their freshness in a salt sea; or, like the rose, which preserves its sweetness among the most noisome weeds; or, like the fire, which burns the hottest when the season is coldest. A good man was once heard to lament "that, as often as he went into the company of the wicked, he returned less a man from them than he was before he joined with them." The Lord's people, by keeping evil company, are like persons who are much exposed to the sun, insensibly tanned.   *Secker.*

7356. COMPANY, Caution Regarding. Be cautious with whom you associate, and never give your company or your confidence to persons of whose good principles you are not certain. No person that is an enemy to God can be a friend to man. He that has already proved himself ungrateful to the Author of every blessing, will not scruple, when it will serve his turn, to shake off a fellow-worm like himself. He may render you instrumental to his own purposes, but he will never benefit you. A bad man is a curse to others; as he is secretly, notwithstanding all his boasting and affected gaiety, a burden to himself. Shun him as you would a serpent in your path. Be not seduced by his rank, his wealth, his wit, or his influence. Think of him as already in the grave; think of him as standing before the everlasting God in judgment. The awful reality will instantly strip off all that is now so imposing, and present him in his true light, the object rather of your compassion, and of your prayers, than of your wonder or imitation.   *Bishop Coleridge.*

7357. COMPANY, Dangerous. Sir Peter Lely made it a rule never to look at a bad picture, having found by experience that whenever he did so, his pencil took a taint from it. "Apply this," adds Bishop Horne, "to bad books and bad company."

7358. COMPANY, How to Please. He that would please in company must be attentive to what style is the most proper. The scholastic should never be used but in a select company of learned men. The didactic should seldom be used, and then only by judicious aged persons, or those who are eminent for piety or wisdom. No style is more extensively acceptable than the narrative, because this does not carry an air of superiority over the rest of the company, and therefore is most likely to please them. For this purpose we should store our memory with short anecdotes and entertaining pieces of history. Almost every one listens with eagerness to extemporary history. Vanity often co-operates with curiosity, for he that is

a hearer in one place, wishes to qualify himself to be a principal speaker in some inferior company, and therefore more attention is given to narrations than anything else in conversation. It is true, indeed, that sallies of wit and quick replies are very pleasing in conversation, but they frequently tend to raise envy in some of the company, but the narrative way neither raises this, nor any other evil passion, but keeps all the company nearly upon an equality and if judiciously managed, will at once entertain and improve them all.   *Johnson.*

7359. COMPANY, Protection Against Bad. Rev. John Elliot was asked by a pious woman, who was vexed with a wicked husband, and bad company frequently infested her house on his account, what she should do? He answered, "Take the Holy Bible into your hand when bad company comes in, and that will soon drive them out of the house."

7360. COMPANY, Public. A religious judge, who had accepted an invitation to a public dinner, said to a scrupulous friend, "While I feel it my duty to attend on such an occasion, I certainly have as little pleasure in it as you have. But there is one way in which I find I can be present at such meetings, and yet receive no injury from them. I endeavor to conceive to myself the Lord Jesus seated on the opposite side of the table, and to think what he would wish me to do and to say, when placed in such a situation, and as long as I can keep this thought alive on my mind, I find I am free from danger."

7361. COMPANY, Rule for. Hippocratidas, a Spartan, met a youth attended by his friend, and the youth blushed deeply at the encounter. Hippocratidas said, "You should keep such company that whoever sees you, you will have no reason to change color."

7362. COMPANY, Vicious. A husbandman fixed a net in his field to catch the cranes that had come to feed on his new sown corn. When he went to examine the net, and see what cranes he had taken, a stork was found among the number. "Spare me," cried the stork, "and let me go; I am no crane. I have eaten none of your corn; I am a poor innocent stork, as you may see—the most pious and dutiful of birds. I honor and succor my father and mother. I—" But the husbandman cut him short "All this may be true enough, I dare say; but this I know, that I have caught you with those who were destroying my crops, and you must suffer with the company in which you were taken."   *Æsop.*

7363. COMPASSION, Overcome. It is said that during the first five years of his reign, the Emperor Nero was very compassionate. When the sentence of execution against a malefactor was taken to him to sign, he exclaimed, " Quam vellem me nescire literas;" (would that I could neither read nor write). Afterwards he became the personification of cruelty, torturing the innocent, and lighting his gardens in Rome with burning Christians.

7364. COMPASSION, Practical. An old soldier who had been disabled in the wars, and who had no longer any means of support, was playing his violin, one evening, on the Prater in Vienna. His dog held his hat, but no one dropped anything into it. The old man was tired and hungry; he had not the strength to play, and in despair he sat down on a stone. A passer-by noticed him, stopped, looked at him, then said: "Lend me your violin a little while." Having tuned it, he said again, "You take the money and I'll play." And he began to play. The people who stopped to stare at a gentleman playing a violin out in the street remained to listen, delighted with the strains they heard. The crowd grew larger and larger. The hat filled up fast, not only with coppers, but also with silver and even gold. The dog began to growl, the hat had never before been so heavy to hold. The old man was told to empty its contents into his pockets, which he did, and it began to fill again. After playing a national air, the gentleman handed back the violin and disappeared before he could be thanked. "Who is it?" every one asked. "It is Armand Boucher, the famous violin player," replied some one. "He has done this for charity, let us follow his example." So saying the speaker made a new collection and gave the proceeds to the astonished soldier, who, through the kindness of Boucher, was now out of want. *Anon.*

7365. COMPASSION, Self-Sacrificing. Dominic, the founder of the order of the preaching friars, appears to have been a very tender-hearted man. He met a woman who wept bitterly because her brother was enslaved among the Moors. Dominic offered himself for sale to redeem the man, and would have accomplished it, but was prevented by some of his friends. He sold his clothes and his books to procure food for the starving in a time of famine. Being remonstrated with, he said, "How can I peruse dead parchment when breathing men are perishing?" On one of his preaching excursions, the gables of a distant village came in view. He said to his companions, "Look at those roofs! What sorrows and cares, what sins and difficulties they cover! Oh! to lighten and remit some of them as we pass by." He died at Bologna in 1221, while his friars were reciting the service for a departing soul; "Come to his aid, saints of God! Come, angels of the Lord, and bear his soul into the presence of the Most High!"

7366. COMPASSION, Tears of. Josephus says that Titus Vespasian, the Roman General, wept at the overthrow of Jerusalem, and the burning of the temple, and cursed the obstinacy of the Jews, who had compelled it. Christ wept over it also in compassion.

7367. COMPETENCE, Desirable. Abundance is a trouble, want a misery, honor a burthen, baseness a scorn, advancements dangerous, disgrace odious. Only a competent estate yields the quiet of content. I will not climb, lest I fall, nor lie on the ground, lest I am trod on. I am safest while my legs bear me. A competent heat is most healthful for my body: I would desire neither to freeze nor to burn. *Warwick.*

7368. COMPETITION, Considerate. Cyrus, when a young stripling, was most worthy of admiration, who would never challenge his equals and playfellows to any exercise wherein he excelled, but to such only wherein he knew himself to be inferior; unwilling that they should fret for the loss of the prize which he was sure to win, and loath to lose what he could himself gain from the others' better skill. *Plutarch.*

7369. COMPLAINING, Habit of. Every one must see daily instances of people who complain from a mere habit of complaining.
Graves.

7370. COMPLAINING, Self. I will not be as those who spend the day in complaining of headache; and the night in drinking the wine that gives the headache. *Goethe.*

7371. COMPLAINT, Foolishness of. We do not wisely when we vent complaint and censure. Human nature is more sensible of smart in suffering than of pleasure in rejoicing, and the present endurances easily take up our thoughts. We cry out for a little pain, when we do but smile for a great deal of contentment.
Feltham.

7372. COMPLAINT, Noisy. As some oxen were dragging a wagon along a heavy road, the wheels set up a tremendous creaking. "Brute!" cried the driver to the wagon; "why do you groan, when they who are drawing all the weight are silent?" Those who cry loudest are not always the most hurt. *Æsop.*

7373. COMPLAINT, Useless. The soldiers in the late war showed remarkable fortitude. Their sufferings and privations were many and great, but they never complained. It is the study of a soldier's life to endure hardship. When asked why they never complained, one answered, "We've been where it did no good to complain." If people in the common walks of life would learn this lesson, half their ills would vanish.

7374. COMPLAISANCE, Cultivate. Complaisance, though in itself it be scarce reckoned in the number of moral virtues, is that which gives a lustre to every talent a man can be possessed of. It was Plato's advice to an unpolished writer, that he should sacrifice to the Graces. In the same manner I would advise every man of learning, who would not appear in the world a mere scholar, or philosopher, to make himself master of the social virtue which I have here mentioned. Complaisance renders a superior amiable, an equal agreeable, and an inferior acceptable. It smooths distinction, sweetens conversation, and makes every one in the company pleased with himself. It produces good nature and mutual benevolence, encourages the timorous, soothes the turbulent, humanizes the fierce, and distinguishes a society of civilized persons from a confusion of savages. *Addison.*

7375. COMPLIMENT Unscriptural. The first time Father Seraphin preached before Louis XIV., he said to this monarch, "Sire, I am not ignorant of the custom according to the prescription of which I should pay you a compliment. This I hope your Majesty will dispense with; for I have been searching for a compliment in the Scriptures, and unhappily I have not found one."

7376. COMPOSURE, Philosophic. Pyrrhon, being at sea and in great danger, by reason of a tempest that arose, took particular notice of a hog that was on board, which all the while very unconcernedly fed upon some corn which lay scattered about; he showed it to his companions, and told them that they ought to acquire by reading and philosophy such an apathy and unconcernedness in all accidents and dangers as they saw that poor creature naturally have. *Plutarch.*

7377. CONCEIT, Advantage of. Little localized powers, and little narrow streaks of specialized knowledge, are things men are very apt to be conceited about. Nature is very wise: but for this encouraging principle how many small talents and little accomplishments would be neglected! Talk about conceit as much as you like, it is to human character what salt is to the ocean; it keeps it sweet and renders it endurable. Say rather it is like the natural unguent of the seafowl's plumage, which enables him to shed the rain that falls on him and the wave in which he dips. When one has had all his conceit taken out of him, when he has lost all his illusions, his feathers will soon soak through, and he will fly no more. Conceit is just as natural a thing to human minds as a centre is to a circle. But little-minded people's thoughts move in such small circles that five minutes' conversation gives you an arc long enough to determine their whole curve. An arc in the movement of a large intellect does not differ sensibly from a straight line. *Holmes.*

7378. CONCEIT, Example of. "Is not this great Babylon that I have builded?" An old farmer walked out over his broad acres and said aloud, "Whose fine farm is this?" With great complaisance he answered himself: "Squire Doubleday's." "Whose elegant mansion is that yonder?" Stroking his breast he answered, "Squire Doubleday's." There is a Squire Doubleday in every man. *Dr. Holme.*

7379. CONCEIT, Fable of. A gnat that had been buzzing about the head of a bull, at length settling himself down upon his horn, begged his pardon for incommoding him; "but if," says he, "my weight at all inconveniences you, pray say so and I will be off in a moment." "Oh, never trouble your head about that," says the bull, "for 'tis all one to me whether you go or stay; and, to say the truth, I did not know you were there." The smaller the mind the greater the conceit. *Æsop.*

7380. CONCESSION, Duty of. A Welsh preacher stated that men's treatment of one another was inferior to that of the brutes. "Two goats," he said, "met upon a bridge so narrow that they could not pass each other. And how do you think they acted? I will tell you. One goat laid down and let the other leap over him. Ah, beloved, let us live like goats."

7381. CONCESSION, The First. A woodman came into a forest to ask the trees to give him a handle for his axe. It seemed so modest a request that the principal trees at once agreed to it, and it was settled among them that the plain homely ash should furnish what was wanted. No sooner had the woodman fitted the staff to his purpose, than he began laying about him on all sides, felling the noblest trees in the wood. The oak now seeing the whole matter too late, whispered to the cedar, "The first concession has lost all; if we had not sacrificed our humble neighbor, we might have yet stood for ages ourselves." *Æsop.*

7382. CONDEMNATION, Dying. Jeine, a chief of one of the South Sea Islands, had manifested strong opposition to the introduction of Christianity. During his last sickness he often expressed a wish that he had died ten years before. Then the influence of the Holy Spirit was at work on his heart, but he had quenched its light, increased his guilt, and was stung by an upbraiding conscience.

7383. CONDEMNATION, Freed from. A Welshman heard a woman preach. She said, "There is no condemnation to them that are in Christ Jesus." That impressed him. He said, "I could think of nothing else all night. I could not sleep. I knew nothing of Christ's atonement, and I was very unhappy in my mind. I was led to read God's Word, and at length found comfort and peace."

7384. CONDEMNATION, Record of. A book-keeper handed his employer a sheet saying, "The trial-balance." The merchant had dreaded to know the truth, but it was even worse than he feared. His frame shook and his heart fainted under the revelation. He fell into a dangerous fever and in his delirium kept repeating, "The trial-balance, the trial-balance." At length he began to mend. His mind turned from his accounts with men to his standing with God. His conscience condemned him, and declared his trial-balance with God to be in a worse case. "I know it," said he. "O, shall I be an everlasting bankrupt?" He sorrowed deeply for his sins. Christ with all his great treasure appeared for him and paid the debt. He felt himself forgiven and looked with the assurance of hope to the great reckoning day.

7385. CONDITION, Improvement of. If an excellent sculptor be employed to carve a statue, whatsoever the materials be, he may use as much skill in carving on an ordinary stone as upon the finest marble. So, whatsoever thy condition is in the world, thou mayest glorify God in it, and bring praise to his name, and show as excellent grace as in the highest condition. He that grinds at the mill may glorify God as well as he that sits upon the throne. *Dr. Bates.*

7386. CONDITION, Optional. Great numbers who quarrel with their condition, have wanted not the power, but the will, to obtain a better state. They have never contemplated the difference between good and evil sufficiently to quicken aversion or invigorate desire; they have indulged a drowsy thoughtlessness or giddy levity; have committed the balance of choice to the management of caprice; and when they have long accustomed themselves to receive all that chance offered them, without examination, lament at last that they find themselves deceived.   *Rambler.*

7387. CONDUCT, Importance of. My extreme youth when I took command of the army of Italy, made it necessary for me to evince great reserve of manners, and the utmost severity of morals. This was indispensable to enable me to sustain authority over men so greatly superior in age and experience. I pursued a line of conduct in the highest degree irreproachable and exemplary. In spotless morality I was a Cato, and must have appeared as such. I was a philosopher and a sage. My supremacy could be retained only by proving myself a better man than any other man in the army. Had I yielded to human weakness I should have lost my power.   *Napoleon I.*

7388. CONFESSING CHRIST Boldly. Auxensius was a great commander under the Emperor Lycinius. Lycinius came one day into the court of his palace, where there was a great bath, and some vines growing about it, with the image of Bacchus set up among the vines. The emperor commanded Auxensius to draw his sword and cut off a bunch of grapes, which, as soon as he had done, he ordered him to offer it at the feet of Bacchus, which was as much as to acknowledge him to be a god. Auxensius answered, "I am a Christian; I will not do it." "What! not do it at my command?" saith the emperor; "then you must quit your place." "With all my heart, sir," said the Christian soldier, and, in token of it, put off his belt, which was the same as giving up his commission, and departed rejoicing that he was enabled to withstand the temptation.   *Buck.*

7389. CONFESSING CHRIST, Difficulties of. The difficulties attending an open confession of Christ are the occasion of multitudes making shipwreck of their souls. In many hopeful characters that scripture, "the fear of man bringeth a snare," is verified. Cato and the philosophers of Rome honored the gods of their country, though unbelievers in the superstitions of their country. Plato was convinced of the unity of God, but durst not own his convictions, but said, "It was a truth, neither easy to find, nor safe to own." And even Seneca, the renowned moralist, was forced by temptation to dissemble his convictions, of whom Augustus saith, "He worshiped what himself reprehended, and did what himself reproved." And at the interruption which was given to the progress of the Reformation by the return of the Papists to power—some, as they went to mass, would exclaim, "Let us go to the common error." Thus, conviction is not conversion where there is no confession of Christ.   *Salter.*

7390. CONFESSING CHRIST Faithfully. According to tradition, a woman of ill-repute named Afra, was accused to Gaius, the judge of Rhœtia, Germany, of being a Christian. He summoned her before him and said, "Sacrifice to the gods, for it is better for thee to live than to perish by torture." She answered, "My sins suffice which I have committed in ignorance, without my adding this also, which thou commandest me to do." "Go to the capitol and sacrifice." "Christ is my capitol, whom I hold ever before my eyes; to whom I daily confess my misdeeds and offer myself as a willing sacrifice." "As I hear, thou art a courtesan. Sacrifice, then, for thou hast no part with the God of the Christians." "My Lord Jesus Christ said that he came down from heaven to save sinners." "Sacrifice, and thou wilt regain the love of thy lovers, and they will pour their money into thy lap," "I will never receive their money; what money I had I have cast away as dross!" "Thou canst be no Christian, thou who art a harlot." "My only title to the name is through the mercy of God." "How knowest thou that Christ accepts thee?" "In that he suffers me to confess him before thy judgment seat." "These are fables, mere fables; sacrifice!" "Christ is my salvation, who, hanging on the cross, promised salvation to the confessing thief." "Do not keep me so long arguing with you: sacrifice, and have done with this folly, or I will have thee tortured and burned alive." "Let the body that has sinned, suffer." Thus she passed the examination before the judge, made a glorious confession, and was condemned to be bound to a stake and burned, and quickly passed from the flames to heaven, to be confessed by Christ, before his father and the holy angels, A. D. 303.

7391. CONFESSING CHRIST, Neglect of. Christ asked the question, "Where are the nine?" You have read of the story of the cleansing of the ten lepers—you know how the God of glory had compassion upon them. His command was, "Go show yourselves to the priests;" and so they went—behold, the leprosy was all gone. It must have been a wonderful sight. They are going along the road; all at once one discovers the great change that has been wrought in him, and he stops suddenly. "Brothers, my leprosy is gone," he cries; "I am perfectly well, look." And another then sees his altered condition, and he cries out, "And I am well, too." And another, "Why, see! my fingers were nearly rotted off, and now the disease is all gone." So they all look at themselves, and the great truth bursts upon them that they have been made well. Nine of them continue on their journey, but one poor man turns back, and falls at the feet of Jesus and glorifies God. Perhaps he did not find his Lord right away; perhaps he had to search for him; but find him he did, and gave him the glory. Christ after seeing him alone at his feet out of all he had conferred the great boon upon, asked in astonishment, "Were there not ten cleansed? but where are the nine?" Well, I don't know what became of them. Perhaps they went and joined some church; at any rate, that is the last we hear of them. So the people think that if they join some church that is all that is required of them. Ha! my friends, "where are the nine?" If the Lord has cleansed you, why don't you lift up your voice in his praise, and give thanks? Why do you bury your tal ents? Why don't you confess Christ? It is sweet to Christ to have men confess him. One day he said, "Whom do men say that I am?" He wanted them to confess him. But one said, "They say thou art Elias," and another, "That thou art Jeremiah;" and another, "Thou art St. John the Baptist." But he asked, "Whom do you say that I am?"—turning to his disciples. And Peter answers, "Thou art the Son of the living God." Then our Lord exclaimed, "Blessed art thou, Simon Barjonas." Yes, he blessed him right there because he confessed him to be the Son of God. He was hungry to get some one to confess him. Then let every one take his stand on the side of the Lord; confess him here on earth, and he will confess you when you get to heaven. He will look around upon you with pride, because you stood up for him here. If you want the blessing of heaven and the peace that passeth all understanding, you must be ready and willing to confess him. Do you know how Peter fell? He fell as ten thousand people fall, because they don't confess the Son of God. *Moody.*

7392. CONFESSING CHRIST, Result of. A woman, whom I know, found peace with God in a prayer-meeting—went home and told her friends what great things the Lord had done for her. A deep impression was made upon their minds by her statements; and in less than six months, her husband, her father, her brother, her lodger, and two of her sisters were brought to the Saviour, and admitted into his church, as the result of her Christian exertions. *Robert Young.*

7393. CONFESSION, Bar of. A person whom I once knew, was roused from a habit of indolence and supineness to a serious concern for his eternal welfare. Convinced of his depraved nature and aggravated guilt, he had recourse to the Scriptures and to frequent prayer; he attended the ordinances of Christianity, and sought earnestly for an interest in Christ, but found no steadfast faith, and tasted very little comfort. At length he applied to an eminent divine, and laid open the state of his heart. Short but weighty was the answer: "I perceive, sir, the cause of all your distress: you will not come to Christ as a sinner. This mistake lies between you and the joy of religion; this detains you in the gall of bitterness, and take heed, oh take heed, lest it consign you to the bond of iniquity." This admonition never departed from the gentleman's mind, and it became the means of removing the obstacles of his peace. *Hervey.*

7394. CONFESSION, Biblical. Lev. 1:4; 16:21. The Jews say that when Aaron confessed the sins of the people, and laid his hands upon the head of the victim, he was to press with all his might. "*I have sinned.*" A confession uttered by men of all classes;—by Pharoah, the hardened rebel; by Balaam, the specious deceiver; by Achan; by Saul (three times); and by Judas, the arch traitor; as also by Job; by David; by the Prodigal. Gen. 3. Reluctance to confession began with the first sin. "They sewed fig leaves together," to hide their shame;

and, when summoned before the Lord, hid themselves amongst the trees of the garden; and then Adam blamed Eve, and Eve blamed the serpent; but there was no frank and contrite confession of their sin. Neh. 9:3. A remarkable instance of sincere and earnest confession. Having separated themselves from all strangers, and thereby given proof of their sincerity, they stood and confessed their sins "one fourth part of the whole day." Ps. 32:3–5. Stifled convictions, like all humors in the body, and unclean wounds, gender discomfort and distress; and yet sinners little think how closely confession and pardon lie together. See 2 Sam 12:13; Job 33:27, 28; 1 John 1:9; Jer. 3: 12, 13. Prov. 28:13. A house is not clean, though all the dust be swept together, if it lie still in a corner within doors, nor if there hang cobwebs about the walls, in how dark corners soever; a conscience is not clean, though the sin brought to our memory be confessed, unless it be forsaken. Dan. 9. It is observable that we have one of the fullest confessions of sin from Daniel; almost, if not the only, saint of whom we have any lengthened history which contains the record of no failing. *Judas*—an example of confession drawn forth by remorse with no prayer for pardon. *Bowes.*

7395. CONFESSION, Escape by. A certain king, named Asmodeus, established an ordinance by which every malefactor taken and brought before the judge should distinctly declare three truths against which no exception could be taken, or else be capitally condemned. If, however, he did this, his life and property should be safe. It chanced that a certain soldier transgressed the law, and fled. He hid himself in a forest, and there committed many atrocities, despoiling and slaying whomsoever he could lay his hands upon. When the judge of the district ascertained his haunt, he ordered the forest to be surrounded, and the soldier to be seized, and brought, bound, to the seat of judgment. "You know the law," said the judge. "I do," returned the other; "if I declare three unquestionable truths, I shall be free; but if not, I must die." "True," replied the judge; "take, then, advantage of the law's clemency, or undergo the punishment it awards without delay." "Cause silence to be kept," said the soldier, undauntedly. His wish being complied with, he proceeded in the following manner: "The first truth is this: I protest before ye all that from my youth up I have been a bad man." The judge, hearing this, said to the bystanders, "He says true." They answered, "Else he had not been in this situation." "Go on, then," said the judge. "What is the second truth?" "I like not," exclaimed he, "the dangerous situation in which I stand." "Certainly," said the judge, "we may credit thee. Now, then, for the third truth, and thou hast saved thy life." "Why," he replied, "if I once get out of this confounded place, I will never willingly re-enter it." "Amen," said the judge. "Thy wit hath preserved thee; go in peace." And thus he was saved. The emperor is Christ; the soldier is any sinner; the judge is a wise confessor. If the sinner confess the truth in such a manner as not even demons can object, he shall be saved—that is, if he confess and repent.

From Gesta Romanorum.

7396. CONFESSION, Feigned. A lady once went to Charles Wesley, complaining that she was the chief of sinners—the worst of transgressors—utterly lost and helpless. "I have no doubt, madame," replied he, "that you are bad enough." She instantly flew into a passion; declared that she was no worse than her neighbors, and scolded the preacher as a slanderer.

7397. CONFESSION, Hypocritical. You have heard, no doubt, of beggars who tie a leg up when they go a-begging, and then make a hideous lamentation of their lameness. Why, this is just your case, sir, when you go to church a-praying, which is begging; you tie your righteous heart up, and then make woful outcry for mercy on us miserable sinners. O, sir, these tricks may pass a while unnoticed, but Jesus Christ will apprehend such cheats at last, and give them their desert.

John Berridge.

7398. CONFESSION, Inconsistent. A Neapolitan peasant went to his priest, saying, "Father, have mercy on a miserable sinner! It is the holy season of Lent, and while I was busy at work, some whey spurting from the cheese-press flew into my mouth, and, wretched man, I swallowed it! Free my distressed conscience from its agonies by absolving me from my guilt!" "Have you no other sins to confess?" said his spiritual guide. "No, I do not know that I have committed any other." "There are," said the priest, "many robberies and murders from time to time committed on your mountains, and I have reason to believe that you are one of the persons concerned in them." "Yes," he replied, "I am, but these are never accounted as a crime; it is a thing practised by us all, and there needs no confession on that account."

7399. CONFESSION, Need of. I once saw a daughter in one of my meetings with tears trickling down her cheeks. I asked her what was the matter? Is there any one you cannot forgive? "Yes," she said, "my mother, who sits in the seat yonder. I have not spoken to her for years. We quarreled a great many years ago?" After a great struggle she went to her mother, threw her arms about her, and cried out, "Will you forgive me!" Down they went on their knees together, and confessed their sins, and were made happy in Jesus. We must confess to our friends. *Moody.*

7400. CONFESSIONAL, Philosophy of the. The confessional is a kind of insurance office, where periodical exposure of the heart to a man is the premium paid for fancied impunity in hiding that heart altogether from the deeper scrutiny of the all-seeing God. Popish transgressors have no particular delight in confession for its own sake. Confession to the priest is felt and dreaded as an evil. The devout often need spurring to make them come. And when they come, it is on the principle of sub-

mitting to the less evil in order to escape the greater. The incoming of the Heart Searcher is feared and loathed, like a deadly and contagious disease. A quack comes up, and by dint of bold profession, persuades the trembler that voluntary inoculation with the same disease in a milder form will secure exemption from the terrible reality. The guilty, although he does not like to have his conscience searched —because he does not like to have his conscience searched, submits to the searching of his conscience. The pretending penitent accepts the scrutiny by a man, in the hope of escaping thereby the scrutiny of God. The impudent empiric tells his patient that if he submit to inoculation, the small-pox will never come. Behold the confessional. *Arnot.*

7401. CONFIDENCE, Childish. A little orphan child, who was taken into a strange family, when being put to bed the first night after she was undressed, knelt down to say her evening prayers and repeated the words which her mother had taught her. Then she added a prayer of her own: "Oh God, make these people just as good to me as my dear father and mother were. Please do it, Jesus." And then, after pausing a moment, she exclaimed, "Of course, you will." That's the way: of course you will. Let us have faith, and he will grant our request. *Moody.*

7402. CONFIDENCE, Comfort of. Mr. Laurence, who was a sufferer for conscience' sake, if he would have consulted with flesh and blood, as was said of one of the martyrs, had eleven good arguments against suffering, viz: a wife and ten children. Being once asked how he meant to maintain them all, he cheerfully replied, "They must all live on Matt. 6: 34, 'Take therefore no thought for the morrow,'" &c. A gentleman said to a poor minister, "I wonder, Mr. W., how you contrive to live so comfortably; methinks, with your numerous family, you live more plentifully on the providence of God, than I can with all the benefits of my parish." *Buck.*

7403. CONFIDENCE, Experience and. Hannibal, when in exile, advised Prusias, King of Bythynia, with whom he had sought refuge, to give battle. Prusias told him that the oracle did not favor success. Hannibal, indignant, replied, "Wilt thou rather give credit to the liver of a calf than to an old and experienced commander?" The two Spains taken from the Romans, Gaul and Liguria, Cannae and Capua, all subdued; a new passage made over the Alps, and the victory at Lake Thrasimene, were all too fresh in his memory, to lead him to trust in unreliable omens, rather than his own well-tried power.

7404. CONFIDENCE, Over. They have succeeded in arousing us, and impressing on our minds the truth of the Irish maxim, "that despising is all very well in its way, but that the only safe plan after all is to thrash your enemy first, and despise him afterwards." *Newland*

7405. CONFIDENCE, Support of. A ship was once tossing on the stormy seas; the angry waves dashed over the deck, and the captain said the danger of shipwreck was great, and that they must leave the vessel for the boat. But the boat looked a tiny thing to trust to, and many stout hearts feared. One of the first who ventured into it, as it lay alongside the reeling ship, and while the billows seemed to play with it as you might play with a shuttlecock, was a pale, delicate woman, with a child in her arms and another clinging to her dress. She did not cry nor scream, but was very still, and the children were still also; indeed, the baby slept. "Are you not afraid?" said a gentlemen to the little quiet boy, who neither spoke nor sobbed. "I do not like the storm," he said, "but mother is here." "And are you not afraid?" asked the same gentleman of the child's mother. She shook her head, and pointing upward, said, "God is ruling the storm, sir, and I am not afraid, for he is my Father." The voice was scarcely to be heard amid the howling of the mighty wind and raging sea; but the gentleman was struck with the trust of the child in its mother, and the faith of the mother in God.   *S. S. Treasury.*

7406. CONFIDENCE, Three Epochs of. People have generally three epochs in their confidence in man. In the first they believe him to be everything that is good, and they are lavish with their friendship and confidence. In the next, they have had experience, which has smitten down their confidence, and they then have to be careful not to mistrust every one, and to put the worst construction upon everything. Later in life, they learn that the greater number of men have much more good in them than bad, and that, even when there is cause to blame, there is more reason to pity than condemn; and then a spirit of confidence again awakens within them.   *Miss Bremer.*

7407. CONFINEMENT, Solitary. About ten years ago, a young American from New York, Walter Hastings by name, dining in London, in company with Lord G——, expressed the opinion that solitary confinement in a dark cell was not so dreadful a punishment as had been represented. His Lordship—so goes the tale—offered Hastings £10,000 if he would undergo entire seclusion for ten years. The proposition being agreed to, a cell was fitted up in Lord G——'s town house. It was from twelve to fifteen feet square. The prisoner was to be allowed candles, a few books, writing materials, plain food, the latter served by a man who was not to be seen. In this way Hastings has been living for a decade of years, his term expiring about the first of the present month. He is now released, and has received, we suppose, his hard-earned money. He emerges from his dungeon in rather a dilapidated condition, appearing, though only thirty-five, like a man of sixty-five years of age, his frame stooping and his steps tottering, his face sallow, his hair and beard white, his voice tremulous, and speech hesitating.   *N. Y. Tribune.*

7408. CONSCIENCE, Aberrations of. The compass of a wooden ship will keep true to the pole unless there is something in the cargo to deflect it. It is found to be very difficult to make a compass that will work reliably on an iron vessel. We remember when Captain Murray of the ill-fated Atlantic showed us the compass of that luxurious steamship which was his especial pride and thought to be perfect. That compass failed to do perfect work, and the noble ship was wrecked upon the rocks because of it. The conscience is the compass by which man steers his bark. It is a defective thing. Base metal in the cargo has often destroyed its polarity and hurled its possessor upon the rocks. Perfect consciences are rare, and those so esteemed fail at the most important crisis. The compass is sometimes elevated on iron ships so as to get above disturbing influences. It is an example for us. We must get up so near God as to be above earthly allurements.

7409. CONSCIENCE, Accusing. On one occasion, when I was at sea, a young gentleman rushed from his bed, while yet asleep, to the middle of the cabin, and, pointing to the floor, exclaimed, "There's the blood! there's the blood! yes, there's the blood!" Some of us rose, and finding that he was asleep, we awoke him and got him back to his bed. In the morning, a sprightly young gentleman, who had got intimate with him, was requested to ascertain the cause of the terrifying dream. In the evening he told us that the gentleman was an officer in the army, on his way to join his regiment in Sicily; that some time ago he had shot a brother officer in a duel, and ever since he had been disturbed in his rest, appearing downcast and sad even when perfectly awake. He said it had been his custom every night to fasten his leg to the bed post, or to anything to which he could tie it, to prevent his getting out of bed; "but I found," said he, "nothing of the kind in the ship bed."   *Campbell.*

7410. CONSCIENCE, Action of. The unanswerable reasonings of Butler never reached the ear of the gray-haired pious peasant, but he needs not their powerful aid to establish his sure and certain hope of a blessed immortality. It is no induction of logic that has transfixed the heart of the victim of deep remorse, when he withers beneath an influence unseen by mortal eye, and shrinks from the anticipation of a reckoning to come. In both the evidence is within, a part of the original constitution of every rational mind, planted there by him who framed the wondrous fabric. This is the power of conscience: with an authority which no man can put away from him it pleads at once for his own future existence, and for the moral attributes of an omnipresent and ever-present Deity. In a healthy state of the moral feelings, the man recognizes its claim to supreme dominion. Amid the degradation of guilt it still raises its voice and asserts its right to govern the whole man; and though its warnings are disregarded, and its claims disallowed, it proves within his inmost soul an accuser that cannot be stilled, and an avenging spirit that never is quenched.   *Dr. Abercrombie.*

7411. CONSCIENCE, Awe of. Every man who

is about to do a wicked action should, above all things, stand in awe of himself, and dread the witness within him, who sits as a spy over all his actions, and will be sure, one day or other, to accuse him to himself, and put him on such a rack as shall make him accuse himself to others too.   *Pythagoras.*

7412. CONSCIENCE, Biblical Examples of. *Adam and Eve* smitten with shame and fear. They knew that they were naked, and hid themselves, Gen. 3: 7–10. *Esau* sold his birthright with profane indifference; yet what would he not have given years afterwards, could he have changed his father's mind? What bitter tears a few moments' pleasure cost him then! Gen. 25: 29–34; 27; Heb 12: 16, 17. *Jacob,* who obtained the birthright and the blessing by mean and ungenerous artifice, was filled with alarm when conscience awoke after twenty years. It is striking to compare Jacob's bold confidence when pursued by Laban, and charged with theft, Gen. 31: 36–42, with his fear and alarm when about to meet Esau, Gen. 32: 7, 8; 11. *Judah,* when he recognized his own signet and bracelets and staff, Gen. 38: 26. *Joseph's brethren*—A remarkable instance of the avenging power of conscience, long after the perpetration of a crime. Thirteen years after Joseph's brethren, with unpitying cruelty, plotted to take away his life, they stood before their brother; and, though by a circumstance which had no connection with their sin, conscience brought home the keen remembrance of long-forgotten guilt. Happily Joseph forgave them, and returned good for evil; but seventeen years of kindness could not drown the voice of conscience—when Jacob was dead, their fears revived again 50: 15. *Saul,* smitten by David's generous kindness—conscience rebuked the cruel king, 1 Sam. 24: 16–19; 26: 21. *Ahab*—"Hast thou found me, O mine enemy?" 1 Kings 21: 20. Why should Ahab address Elijah as an "enemy," when a short time before they had parted as friends? The very spot where they met gives the answer. It was in the vineyard of Naboth the Jezreelite, which Ahab had obtained by the murder of Naboth. *Zimri*—"Had Zimri peace, who slew his master?" 1 Kings 16: 18. Can there be peace in the breast when there is guilt on the conscience? Remember Joram's question and Jehu's answer, 2 Kings 9: 22. *Herod*—"It is John whom I beheaded: he is risen from the dead," Mark 6: 26. Herod was, Josephus says, a Sadducee (see Matt. 22: 23). Why, then, should he fear? It is a striking proof how little the sophistries of infidelity can withstand the awakening power of conscience. *Judas,* in the very moment of his success, found his bitterest remorse, Matt. 27: 3, 4; Prov. 5: 22. *Felix,* the judge, trembling before the prisoner, because he was the slave of a guilty conscience, Acts 24: 25.   *Bowes.*

7413. CONSCIENCE, Bonds of. The knot that binds me by the law of courtesy, pinches me more than that of legal constraint, and I am much more at ease when bound by a scrivener than by myself. Is it not reason that my con-

science should be much more engaged when men simply rely upon it? In a bond my faith owes nothing, because it has nothing lent it. Let them trust to the security they have taken without me; I had much rather break the walls of a prison, and the laws themselves, than my own word.   *Montaigne.*

7414. CONSCIENCE, A Condemning. If our conscience condemn us justly, our case is sad; because God knows more of us than we do of ourselves, and can charge us with many sins that conscience is not privy to.   *Gurnall.*

7415. CONSCIENCE Converted. Two infidel neighbors resided in New England. One of them heard the Gospel message, and believed unto eternal life. A short time afterwards the converted man went to the house of his infidel neighbor, and said to him, "I have come to talk to you. I have been converted." "Yes, I heard that you had been down there, and gone forward for prayers," said the sceptic with a sneer; "and I was surprised, for I had thought you were about as sensible a man as there was in town." "Well," said the Christian, "I have got a duty to do to you, and I want you to stop talking, and hear me. I have not slept much for two nights for thinking of it. I have got four sheep in my flock that belong to you. They came into my field six years ago, and I knew they had your mark on them, and I took them and marked them with my mark; and you inquired all round, and could not hear anything of them. But they are in my field with the increase of them, and now I want to settle this matter. I have laid awake nights and groaned over it, and I have come to get rid of it; and now I am at your option. I will do just what you say. If it is a few years in the State's prison, I will suffer that. If it is money or property you want, say the word. I have a good farm, and money at interest, and you can have all you ask. I want to settle this matter up, and get rid of it." The infidel was amazed. He began to tremble. "If you have got them sheep, you are welcome to them. I don't want nothing of you, if you will only go away; a man who will come to me as you have, something must have got hold of you that I don't understand! You may keep the sheep, if you will only go away." "No," said the man, "I must settle this matter up, and pay for the sheep—I shall not be satisfied without; and you must tell me how much." "Well," said the sceptic, "if you must pay for them, you may give me what the sheep were worth when they got into your field, and pay me six per cent. interest on the amount, and go off, and let me alone." The man counted out the value of the sheep, and the interest on the amount, and laid it down, and then doubled the whole.   *Anon.*

7416. CONSCIENCE Defined. Conscience is a Latin word, though with an English termination, and, according to the very notation of it, imports a double or joint knowledge; to wit, one of a divine law or rule and the other of a man's own action, and so is properly the application of a general law to a particular instance of practice. The law of God, the example, says, "Thou shalt not steal;" and the mind of man tells him that the taking of such a thing from a person lawfully possessed of it is stealing. Whereupon the conscience, joining the knowledge of both these together, pronounces in the name of God that such a particular action ought not to be done. And this is the true procedure of conscience, always supposing a law from God before it pretends to lay any obligation upon man. Conscience neither is nor ought to be its own rule. *South.*

7417. CONSCIENCE, Deflections of. A staunch Cunarder steamship left her dock in Liverpool for New York, had a fair voyage, and by the reckoning made with sextant and compass, was within two hundred miles of Nantucket shoals. Suddenly the look-out cried, "Land ho!" The engines were reversed instantly, and the ship was found to be within two lengths of the shoals, from which her Captain thought her two hundred miles distant. Nothing but timely warning by a vigilant look-out and prompt action saved the ship from fearful wreck. The cause of the alteration of the compass was sought, and found to be a single nail driven before leaving Liverpool, by the carpenter, in putting up a stove. It had done its work steadily and surely upon the needle, and nearly hurled the ship upon the rocks. Conscience is the needle. Some little secret sin is the nail. The conscience deflected from right by any sin, great or small, will surely wreck its possessor upon the rocks of eternal ruin.

7418. CONSCIENCE, Delights of. A palsy may as well shake an oak, or a fever dry up a fountain, as either of them shake, dry up, or impair the delight of conscience. For it lies within, it centres in the heart, it grows into the very substance of the soul, so that it accompanies a man to his grave, he never outlives it; and that for this cause only, because he cannot outlive himself. *South.*

7419. CONSCIENCE, Derivation of. We all know that this word comes from *con* and *scio*; but what does that "*con*" intend? "Conscience" is not merely that which I know, but that which I know with some other; for this prefix cannot, as I think, be esteemed superfluous, or taken to imply merely that which I know with or to myself. That other knower whom the word implies is God; his law making itself known and felt in the heart; and the work of conscience is the bringing of the evil of our acts and thoughts as a lesser, to be tried and measured by this as a greater—the word growing out of and declaring that awful duplicity of our moral being which arises from the presence of God in the soul—our thoughts, by the standard which that presence implies, and as the result of a comparison with it, "accusing or excusing one another." *Trench.*

7420. CONSCIENCE, Disordered. The hands of a watch or clock indicate the time, and to be true the works must be in good order and carry forward the hands just as fast as time itself goes. If it be out of order, it will stop; or if it continues to run, its index will be false and deceptive. Conscience is represented by the works of the watch, consciousness by the hands. If it is an enlightened and true con science, regulated by the word of God, the index of consciousness will be true. If it is disordered, it is altogether unreliable, and he who trusts it will make certain failure. A false watch has cost many a man delay, and often more serious consequences. A disordered conscience has prevented many from doing good and gaining heaven.

7421. CONSCIENCE, Fidelity to. The Emperor Vespasian was very anxious to get a law passed which he knew Helvidius would be sure to oppose. He sent a request to him not to attend the Senate that day. Helvidius answered, "It is certainly in the power of the Emperor to deprive me of my senatorship; but so long as I continue a member of that body, I cannot neglect my duty by absenting myself from it." "Well," says Vespasian, "I am content that you shall be there, provided you will be sure not to speak in the debates that shall arise to-day." Helvidius engaged that he would remain silent, provided his opinion was not asked. "Nay," said Vespasian, "but if you are there you must be consulted." "And if I be," replied Helvidius, "I must give my advice freely, according to what I conceive to be just and reasonable." "Do that at your peril," said Vespasian, "for be assured that if you are against what I propose, your head shall answer for it." "Sire," replied Helvidius, "did I ever tell you that I was immortal? If I consider it my duty, consistent with what I owe to the gods and to my country, to oppose your measure, no threat of personal resentment shall influence me; and if you wreak your vengeance on my head, posterity will judge between us."

7422. CONSCIENCE, Five Kinds of. There be five kinds of consciences on foot in the world; first an ignorant conscience, which neither sees nor says anything, neither beholds the sins in a soul, nor reproves them. Secondly, the flattering conscience, whose speech is worse than silence itself, which, though seeing sin, soothes the man in the committing thereof. Thirdly, the seared conscience which has neither sight, speech nor sense in men that are past feeling. Fourthly, a wounded conscience, frightened with sin. The last and best is a quiet and clear conscience, pacified in Christ Jesus. Of these the fourth is incomparably better than the three former, so that a wise man would not take a world to change with them. Yea, a wounded conscience is rather painful than sinful, an affliction, no offense, and is in the ready way, at the next remove, to be turned into a quiet conscience. *Thos. Fuller.*

7423. CONSCIENCE, Guilt of. A man of good reputation, being in great destitution, stole a lamb to keep his children from starving. When it was cooked and placed upon the table he could not ask a blessing over it as was hi wont. In great confusion he went to the owner confessed his sin and promised restitution.

7424. CONSCIENCE, Heathen. Mr. Campbell, a traveler in Africa, says, "I remember, when traveling from Lattakoo to Kurreechane, high up in the interior of South Africa, my party was joined by about forty or fifty persons from different tribes, some of them with a view of visiting friends higher up the country, and to be under the protection of our guns during the journey; others from having heard that we shot rhinoceroses, elephants, etc., for the sake of their skins, teeth, etc., but that we did not eat their carcasses—the last indulged the hope that they might eat the animals when they happened to be shot. When any of those nations, on their plundering expeditions, happened to kill, or rather murder a man, the honorable deed is recorded by a deep slash being cut on the fleshy part of their body. By these marks we knew that the major part of the new comers who have joined us were murderers. I observed some who had three, four, or five of those scars. Now these people were generally afraid to go to sleep in the night-time; but, in little parties around fires, they tried to keep up the most boisterous talk as long as they could, until break of day. One night, the wind being quite still, their noise was such that I found it impossible to sleep. I arose, and begged them to be quiet and go to sleep. 'Oh,' said they, 'there is a king to the right of us, a bad man, who has his spies; and were we to sleep he would come and murder us all.' About ten nights after they were continuing as bad as ever; I begged them now to be still, especially as they had got beyond the country of him of whom they were afraid. 'Oh! but,' said they, 'we are getting opposite to a worse king, to the left of us—Makkabba, king of the Waketsens.' How different was the case with my Hottentots, about twenty of whom traveled with me! Not any of them were murderers; every night did they sleep as sound as wolves, though they never were so far from their own country before."

7425. CONSCIENCE, Indestructibility of. Man's conscience was once the vicegerent of Deity; what conscience spoke within was just the echo of what God said without; and even now, conscience in its ruin has enough of its pristine eloquence and surviving affinity to God never to be altogether and always silent. The passions try to make conscience a sort of citizen-king, putting it up and down as they please; but it will not quietly submit; it resists the authority of the passions; it insists upon supremacy; it cannot forget its noble lineage and its erst holy function derived from God. As long as man can gratify his passions, and give an opiate to conscience, so long it will be partially quiet. But a day comes when the passions must be laid, and when every beat of the heart, like the curfew bell, will tell you that the time for extinguishing their fires is come, and then and there conscience will re-assert its lost supremacy, grasp its broken sceptre, and refusing to be put down, it will remit its true and eternal utterances; and reason of righteousness, and temperance, and judgment; and prove that man may peradventure live without religion, but die without it he rarely can. A death-bed is the hour when conscience reasserts its supremacy, however stupefied it may have been with the opium of half a century, and reminds its possessor of all behind and before. In such a case there are two resources: either the Romish priest, with a strong opiate, under which man will die deluded and deceived; or the blood of Jesus, with pardon for the sin, and therefore peace for the conscience, which is the joyful sound of forgiveness. *Dr. Cumming.*

7426. CONSCIENCE, Jesus Whispering. "What is conscience?" asked a Sunday-school teacher one day of his class. Several of the children answered, some one thing and some another, until a little timid child spoke out: "It is Jesus whispering in our hearts."

7427. CONSCIENCE, Liberty of. The clap-trap cry of those who would put down doctrine is "liberty"—liberty to think as you like, and to do as you will, to believe or not believe. There are some who say it is necessary there should be teachers in the church to instruct their hearers that black is white, alongside of those who hold by the old truth. The claim for such liberty reminds me of an occurrence some years ago in Ratcliffe Highway. A man had a menagerie of wild beasts; and the elephant, fumbling about his trunk one night, got hold of the peg which fastened up his den. So he got out, and being a member of the Liberation Society, he proceeded to let out the lions, the wolves, and the jackals. There was soon a terrible noise in the back yard; and the master, waking up, rushed in among the animals with his whip, and soon had them back to their respective quarters. But for his promptness, there might have been great mischief done to the people of London. The teachers of false doctrine are playing the part of the elephant, and the lies which they are letting loose upon society must be hunted back to their dens. There must be no liberty to pull up the buoys and to destroy the lighthouses of the Christian church. *Spurgeon.*

7428. CONSCIENCE, No Compulsion of. Certain persons attempted to persuade Stephen, King of Poland, to compel some of his subjects, who were of a different religion, to embrace his. He answered, "I am King of men, and not of consciences. The dominion of conscience belongs exclusively to God."

7429. CONSCIENCE, Obedience to. Lord Erskine, when at the bar, was remarkable for the fearlessness with which he contended against the bench. In a contest with Lord Kenyon, he explained his rule and conduct at the bar in the following terms: "It was the first command and counsel of my youth, always to do what my conscience told me to be my duty, and leave the consequences to God. I have hitherto followed it, and have no reason to complain that any obedience to it has been even a temporal sacrifice; I have found it, on the contrary, the road to prosperity and wealth, and I shall point it out as such to my children." *Percy.*

7430. CONSCIENCE, Power of. About seventeen years ago, a young man in the town of Sheffield was sent to get change at a neighboring shop for a ten-pound note, when by mistake he was paid ten guineas, which he received, and said nothing on the subject. Of late he has been converted to God, and having an uneasy conscience on account of this transaction, felt desirous of making restitution. But the person from whom he received the money being dead, he was unable for some time to obtain any information concerning the family. At length he discovered where the son resided, and having ascertained that neither of the parents were living, he sent a person to inform him of the circumstance, and to pay to him the extra ten shillings which had been received of his father at the time stated, with interest if required, adding that he could not be happy until he had paid the sum. The son expressed pleasure in witnessing such an instance of the grace of God, but said he would not take the interest, and that the ten shillings should be given to the cause of Christ. He has since presented it to the Wesleyan Missionary Society, as God's own peculiar property. I understand the same person has made restitution in several other cases of a like nature.
Wm. Dawson.

7431. CONSCIENCE, Protecting the. Every man should take heed to the way in which he treats his conscience. When we put a lighthouse on the coast, that in the night mariners may explore the dark and dreadful way of the sea, we not only swing glass around about it to protect it, but we enclose that glass itself in a net-work of iron wire, that birds may not dash it in, that summer winds may not sweep it out, and that swarms of insects may not destroy themselves and the light. For if the light in the lighthouse be put out, how great a darkness falls upon the land and upon the sea! And the mariner, waiting for the light, or seeing it not, miscalculates and perishes. A man's conscience ought to be protected from those influences that would diminish its light, or that would put it out. *Anon.*

7432. CONSCIENCE, Question of. Two learned men were conversing about what course they should pursue in reference to a matter upon which they had conscientious scruples. One of them said, "By my faith, I must live." The other replied, "I hope to live by my faith too, though I dare not swear by it." The one who determined to venture his temporal interest for conscience' sake, lived to see the other begging while he had power to contribute to his relief.

7433. CONSCIENCE, Record of. As the words that are written with the juice of a lemon cannot be read when they are written, but may be plainly and distinctly seen if you hold the paper to the fire, so the least letters in the book of our conscience, yea, the least notes and points and scratches, which neither any other nor ourselves see well now, shall easily be discerned by the fire of the last judgment.
Featley.

7434. CONSCIENCE, Rousing the. As gentle remedies are not sufficient for grievous maladies, but we must adopt those which physicians style powerful ones; for poisonous cancers prepared oils are not sufficient; we must use fire and iron; so, for certain souls, deeply rooted in vice, slight motives will not suffice, but the strong maxims of hell and eternity are necessary. These peals of thunder can arouse sinners from their profound lethargy; these bridles can rein in certain furious passions, and bring to pass that man do not plunge himself into wickedness. For this reason the Holy Spirit admonishes us always to keep our minds on the maxims of eternity, if we do not wish to fall into sin. *"Memorare novissima tua et in eternum non peccabis."* (Eccles. vii.)
Ignatius.

7435. CONSCIENCE, A Sick. Bp. Bramble, of Derry, Ireland, a persecutor of Christ's faithful ones, was smitten with sickness. Dr. Maxwell having been called, asked him what his particular complaint was. "It is my conscience," he replied. "I have no cure for that," said the doctor.

7436. CONSCIENCE, Sting of. How small things may annoy the greatest! Even a mouse troubles an elephant, a gnat a lion, a very flea may disquiet a giant. What weapon can be nearer to nothing than the sting of this wasp? Yet what a painful wound hath it given me! That scarce visible point, how it envenoms, and rankles, and swells up the flesh! The tenderness of the part adds much to the grief. If I be thus vexed with the touch of an angry fly, how shall I be able to endure the sting of a tormenting conscience? *Bishop Hall.*

7437. CONSCIENCE, Tortures of. Imagine what sharp and intolerable pains those martyrs sustained, who, as the Apostle tells us (Heb. 11, 37), were sawn asunder. Or, suppose that thou thyself wert now under the ragged teeth of a saw, drawn to and fro upon the tenderest parts of thy body: tearing thy flesh, thy nerves, and sinews; grating and jarring upon thy very bones: yet all the extremity of this is nothing to what torments the conscience feels, when God causeth his sword to enter into it, to rive it up; when he makes deep and bloody wounds in it, and instead of pouring in healing balm, with a heavy hand chafes them with fire and brimstone. *Bishop Hopkins.*

7438. CONSCIENCE, Voice of. Theodore Parker gives an incident of his own experience when he was but four years old. He went with his father to a distant part of the farm, and, in returning home alone, passed a pond hole. A rhodora in full bloom attracted his attention, and drew him to the water side. There he saw a spotted turtle sunning himself. He had never yet killed anything, but he had seen other boys, and he felt a disposition to follow their example. He raised the stick which he had in his hand, and was about to strike the turtle, when a voice within him, clear and loud, said, "It is wrong." He wondered at the new emotion, and hastened home to ask his mother what it was that had said "It is wrong." She took him up in her arms, wiped a tear from her eye, and said, "Some men call it conscience, but I prefer to call it the voice of God in the soul of man. If you listen, and obey it, then it will speak clearer and clearer, and always guide you right. But if you disobey, then it will fade out, little by little, and leave you all in the dark, and without a guide. Your life depends on your heeding that little voice." He says no event of his youth made such a lasting impression upon him.

7439. CONSCIENTIOUSNESS, Pagan. Seneca acquired great wealth as the preceptor of the Emperor Nero, but neither this nor the luxury and effeminacy of a court produced any alteration in his mode of life. He continued to the last to live abstemiously, correctly, and free from flattery and ambition. "I had rather," said he to Nero, "offend you by speaking the truth than please you by lying and flattery." When Seneca perceived that his favor was on the decline, and that his enemies were constantly reminding the emperor of the wealth which he had amassed, he offered to make a full surrender of all the gifts which had ever been conferred upon him. The tyrant not only declined the offer, but protested that his friendship for him remained the same. The continual machinations of his enemies were at length so successful that the emperor condemned him to death. Seneca received the mandate with calmness and composure, and only asked to be allowed to alter his will. The officer entrusted with the execution of the sentence refused to grant such permission. Seneca then, addressing his friends, said that "since he was not allowed to leave any other legacy, he requested they would preserve the example of his life, and exercise true fortitude."   *Anon.*

7440. CONSCIOUSNESS, Interrupted. The following case which M. Cromaz gave in to the Academy of Science, is the most extraordinary instance of interrupted consciousness I have ever heard of. "A nobleman of Lausanne, as he was giving orders to a servant, suddenly lost his speech and all his senses. Different remedies were tried without effect for six months, during all of which time he appeared to be in a deep sleep or deliquium, with various symptoms at different periods, which are particularly specified in the narrative. At last, after some chirurgical operations, at the end of six months, his speech and senses were suddenly restored. When he recovered, the servant to whom he had been giving orders when he was first seized with the distemper, happening to be in the room, he asked whether had executed his commission; not being sensible, it seems, that any interval of time, except a very short one, had elapsed during his illness. He lived ten years after, and died of another disease. I mention this, chiefly to the reader's amusement: he may consider the evidence, and believe or disbelieve as he pleases. But that consciousness may be interrupted by a total deliquium, without any change in our notions of identity, I know by my own experience. I am therefore fully persuaded that the identity of this substance, which I call my soul, may continue even when I am unconscious of it; and if for a shorter space, why not for a longer?"   *Buck.*

7441. CONSECRATION, Complete. A young Indian chief in Upper Canada, whose family were reduced almost to starvation, went out to hunt, but all game seemed to avoid him. He thought the Great Spirit must be angry with him and that he would secure his favor by an offering. So he took his blanket, laid it on a log, and said, "Here, Great Spirit, accept this blanket, and bless poor Indian, that he may find food, and that his wife and family may not starve." The offering did not suffice. A tomahawk hung in his belt. He advanced as before, and laid it upon the log, and said, "O, Great Spirit, take my tomahawk; it is all poor Indian has. He has nothing else to give; take it and bless me, and give me food for my children." But no answer came. There was his gun, his only means of obtaining game, his sole support, and hitherto his unfailing friend. How could he spare that? Must he part with that also? He paused, but pressed down by his forlorn condition, almost hopeless, he took the gun in his hand, and laid it on the log, and sobbed out, "O, Great Spirit, take my gun too! it is all poor Indian has: he has nothing more. Take it, and bless poor Indian, that his wife and children may not starve." Still the messenger of love came not. Almost brokenhearted, he started to his feet, a ray of light flashed through his mind. He would go to that rude altar again and offer himself up to the Great Spirit. So he sat down on the log with his blanket, his tomahawk, and his gun by his side, and said, "Here, Great Spirit, poor Indian has given up all that he has: he has nothing more; so take poor Indian too, and bless him, that he may find food for his famishing family, that they may not starve." In a moment a change came over him. His soul was filled with happiness such as he had never felt before. A deer came bounding towards him from the thicket; he raised his gun and secured him. Thus was his offering accepted and his prayer answered. On returning to his family the Indian told them what had happened; thinking that if he left the blanket, the tomahawk, and the gun on the log, they would be of no use to any one, he took them with him, and told the Great Spirit that he would take care of them for him, and use them subject to his will, and that henceforth he would regard himself, and all that he had, as belonging to him. Afterwards he heard the Christian missionary exhorting the people to give themselves to Christ. He related the above story of himself which helped him to give all to Christ and live for him.

7442. CONSECRATION, Covenant of. This is the marriage covenant: "Thou shalt be for me, and not for another; so will I be for thee." Hos. 3: 3. Ah, what a life is the life of a Christian! Christ all for you, and you all for him. Blessed exchange! "Soul," saith Christ, "all I have is thine." "Lord," saith the soul, "and all I have is thine." "Soul," saith

Christ, "my person is wonderful, but what I am, I am for thee; my life was spent in labor and travail, but it was for thee." "And, Lord," saith the believer, "my person is vile, and not worth thy accepting; but such as it is, it is thine; my soul, with all and every faculty; my body, and every member; my gifts, time, and all my talents, are thine."   *John Flavel.*

7443. CONSECRATION, Custom of. It was the custom of the Jews to select the tenth of their sheep after this manner: the lambs were separated from the dams, and enclosed in a sheepcote, with only one narrow way out; the dams were at the entrance. On opening the gate, the lambs hastened to join the dams; and a man placed at the entrance, with a rod dipped in ochre, touched every tenth lamb, and so marked it with his rod, saying, "Let this be holy." Hence, saith the Lord by the prophet Ezekiel, "I will cause you to pass under the rod." See Lev. 27:32; Jer. 33:13.   *Biblical Treasury.*

7444. CONSECRATION, Emblem of. Travelers have said that they have discovered gardens of Solomon, which were of old enclosed as private places wherein the king walked in solitude; and they have also found wells of a most deliciously cold water, dexterously covered, so that no person unacquainted with the stone in the wall, which either revolved or slid away with a touch, could have found the entrance to the spring. At the foot of some lofty range of mountains a reservoir received the cooling streams which flowed from melted snows; this reservoir was carefully guarded and shut out from all common entrance, in order that the king alone might enter there, and might refresh himself during the scorching heats. Such is the Christian's heart. It is a spring shut up, a fountain sealed, a garden reserved for Jesus only. O come, Great King, and enjoy thy possessions.   *Spurgeon.*

7445. CONSECRATION, Entire. Ralph Wells, at a late session of his Grace Mission Sunday-school, had on his blackboard the words: "See that Jesus gets it all." What did they mean? Little Emma, a child of the mission, brought into the school from a low dance-house, lay dying. Her parents were very poor. Left alone with her grandmother, she said, "Granny, will you bring me my purse?"—a gift from the school at the last Christmas anniversary. The little purse was brought to her, when, counting out therefrom forty-eight cents, she said, "Granny, this is my money that I have saved for Jesus to give to the mission-school; dear Granny, see that Jesus gets it all!"

7446. CONSECRATION, False. In 1478, a solemn deed was drawn up, signed, sealed, and recorded, in which Louis XI. conveyed to the Virgin Mary the whole county of Boulogne, France, but reserved to himself for his own use all the revenues thereof. He deluded himself with the idea that he had done a generous and pious thing by the Virgin, when he had done nothing. This king has a long line of followers, who professedly give all to God, but,

in reality, give him nothing. If vengeance should be executed, the fate of Ananias would fall upon many.

7447. CONSECRATION, Life of. Consecration is not wrapping one's self in a holy web in the sanctuary, and then coming forth after prayer and twilight meditation, and saying, "There, I am consecrated." Consecration is going one into the world where God Almighty is, and using every power for his glory. It is taking all advantages as trust funds—as confidential debts owed to God. It is simply dedicating one's life, in its whole flow, to God's service.   *Beecher.*

7448. CONSECRATION, Monastic. Plato, of Constantinople, was of noble family, and a great favorite with the Emperor and the members of his court. He had a large fortune and brilliant prospects opened to him. Putting aside the love of pleasure, wealth and the lure of ambition, and freeing all his slaves, he put off his worldly garments and had his flowing hair shorn off. He went to Theoctistus, the abbot of the monastery of Symbols, and offered himself, saying, "Father, I give thee all—mind, body, will; use thy servant as it pleases thee." He was accepted on these conditions. His obedience was tested in every way. He was made to grind the corn, and carry the water, and do the most menial service, in striking contrast with his former life. He did all obediently and cheerfully, and soon won promotion. He died in 794, and is enrolled among the saints of the Greek church.

7449. CONSIDERATION, Want of. A fox had fallen into a well, and had been casting about for some time how he should get out again; when at length a goat came to the place, and wanting to drink, asked Reynard whether the water was good, and if there was plenty of it. The fox, dissembling the real danger of his case, replied, "Come down, my friend; the water is so good that I cannot drink enough of it, and so abundant that it cannot be exhausted." Upon this the goat, without any more ado, leaped in; when the fox, taking advantage of his friend's horns, as nimbly leaped out, and coolly remarked to the poor deluded goat, "If you had half as much brains as you have beard, you would have looked before you leaped."   *Æsop.*

7450. CONSISTENCY, Advantage of. Some of the Romans who had fought against Hannibal fled in the time of battle. The Commonwealth refused to buy them back at the smallest price, rather allowing them to be put to death or sold as slaves. A few who escaped begged with tears and lamentations to be admitted again into the army; when the Senate decreed that the Commonwealth had no need of the service of cowards, but that if Marcellus chose to employ them it was on condition that no crowns or honorary rewards should be bestowed upon them. When the soldiers of the Cross turn cravens in the fight, they are not refused admission again into the ranks, but they fight under a disadvantage.   *Anon.*

7451. CONSISTENCY, Biblical. *Void of offence,*

Acts 24. *Becoming*, Rom. 16: 2. *Blameless and harmless*, without rebuke, unblamable, Eph. 1: 4; like Zacharias and Elizabeth, Luke 1: 6. *Honest* (estimable), Acts 6: 3. Of *good behaviour*, 1 Tim. 3: 2. *Walking worthy* of God—of the Lord—of our vocation—as children of light—walking circumspectly. Titus 2: 8. "That he that is of the contrary part may be ashamed, having no evil thing to say of you." Cf. the cautions, 1 Tim. v: 14; Rom. 14: 16, 21; 1 Pet. 2: 12, 15; 3: 16. James 1: 27. "To keep himself unspotted from the world." To walk through a polluting world without catching its pollution, like the little band of Sardian Christians, who "even in Sardis" had not defiled their garments, Rev. 3; 4. Examples—*Jehoshaphat*, 2 Chron. 17: 3, 4. *Nehemiah*, see Neh. 5: 9 –11, 14–18; 6: 3, 9, 11; 13: 11, 30. *Shadrach, Meshach, and Abed-nego*, Dan. 3: 16-18. *Daniel*, 1: 8; 6: 3, 4, 5, 10. *St. Paul*—see his constant commendation of Christian consistency in the many texts quoted above. Few men can appeal to their own personal consistency of life with the same confidence that St. Paul could. See Acts 23: 1; 24: 16; 1 Cor. 4: 16; 9: 1; 2 Tim .3: 10. *Bowes*.

7452. CONSISTENCY Demanded. Except you make religion your business, all is in vain. While you halt and halve it in religion, you come but half way to heaven. Settle it upon your hearts, that, except you are throughout religious, you are religious to no purpose. Be sure you shall never come to heaven except you seek it in God's order. It were not suitable to the wisdom of God so to undervalue Christ and his glory as to throw them away on those that account other matters better worthy their pains and care. *Alleine.*

7453. CONSISTENCY, Duty of. Honorable actions ought to succeed honorable sayings, lest they lose their reputation. *Cato the Elder.*

7454. CONSISTENCY, Final. Everywhere, in public and in private, Elias Hicks lifted up his voice against the sin of slavery. He would eat no sugar that was made by slaves, and wear no garment which he supposed to have been produced by unpaid labor. In a remarkable manner he showed the "ruling passion strong in death." A few hours before he departed from this world his friends, seeing him shiver, placed a comfortable over him. He felt of it with his feeble hands, and made a strong effort to push it away. When they again drew it up over his shoulders he manifested the same symptoms of abhorrence. One of them, who began to conjecture the cause, inquired, "Dost thou dislike it because it is cotton?" He was too far gone to speak, but he moved his head in token of assent. When they removed the article of slave produce, and substituted a woolen blanket, he remained quiet and passed away in peace. *Life of Isaac T. Hopper.*

7455. CONSOLATION, Failure of. Cicero was overwhelmed with grief at the death of his daughter Tullia, in whom his heart was bound up. He resorted to pagan philosophy for comfort. He wrote a book containing all the consolation which the religion or philosophy of his time afforded, but found no relief, and declared that his grief was incurable. His only comfort was found in a resolution to erect a monument to his daughter's memory, in the gardens of Rome.

7456. CONSOLATION, Form of. A form of consolation for the dying, said to be written by Anselm, Archbishop of Canterbury, in 1100, is as follows:—"Go to, then, as long as thou art in life—put all thy confidence in the death of Christ alone—confide in nothing else—commit thyself wholly to it—mix thyself wholly with it—roll thyself wholly on it; and if the Lord God will judge thee, say, 'Lord, I put the death of our Lord Jesus Christ between me and thy judgment, otherwise I contend not with thee;'—and if he say, 'Thou art a sinner,' reply, 'Put the death of our Lord Jesus Christ between me and my sins;'—and if he say, 'Thou hast deserved damnation,' let thine answer be, 'Lord, I spread the death of our Lord Jesus Christ between me and my demerits; I offer his merits for the merits I should have had, and have not.' If he still insist that he is angry at thee, reply again, 'Lord, I put the death of the Lord Jesus Christ between me and Thine anger.'"

7457. CONSOLATION, Heathen. Plutarch had an only daughter, Timoxena, who died at the age of two years. To her bereaved mother he wrote, "Consider that death has deprived your Timoxena only of small enjoyments. The things she knew were of but little consequence, and she could be delighted only with trifles." He saw no kind shepherd carrying the lamb in his arms, and had not faith to say, "We shall go to her." Of this lady it is said she bore herself in bereavement as becomes the wife of a philosoper, not giving way to the extravagance of grief, but arranging her house so that those who visited her found no more disorder than if nothing distressing had happened.

7458. CONSOLATION, Oriental. In an Eastern garden walked the monarch Selim. His head was bent, and his brow was troubled. He was mourning for his son, the child of his love, and the one object that had made the joy of his life. In vain the flowers, like censers filled with incense, offered him their perfume; in vain the vine wooed him to rest under the shadow of its shining leaves; in vain the rivulets to cheer him sent forth a tinkling murmur through the groves; the heart of the king was sad, and he found that love is better than wealth and dominion. Near him walked the sage, Adam Ben David, a man of reverend mien, whose long white beard covered his breast and told of years of experience and thought. As his sovereign passed him, he bowed his head and cried, "May the king live forever!" "Nay, not so," said the monarch; "for life is bitter when the sunshine of life is gone." "Is thine heart, O king, troubled for the child?" "My heart is troubled for the child, and I am filled with grief." "Yet the child is not dead—he only sleepeth." But the king was not comforted, and the tears rolled down his cheeks. Then

Adam Ben David spoke again, and said, "Seest thou, O king, yonder almond tree? It is covered with its pale pink blossoms now, but soon the flowers will fall from its branches, and thou wilt see only the green leaves. Then thou mayest say that the blossoms are dead, and that they have been in vain. But it will not be so, and when the time of harvest is come the fruit will take the place of the flowers, and thou wilt grieve no more for the blossoms of spring." "But, my child!" said the monarch. "Nothing can bring him back again." "Nay," the sage replied, "he blossomed as a flower in thy garden, O king, until thy God took him to be perfected in the garden above. Perchance had he lived with thee he would have been only a withered flower; but now will he be one of the fruits that grow upon the tree of life." Then the heart of the king was comforted.
Anon.

7459. CONSOLATION, Pagan. An African woman having lost her child by death, went to the priest with her tale of sorrow. The fetish-man asked her what she had brought him as a fee. Having given him a satisfactory present, he said, "Take courage, I will make it all right for you, and I will bring the spirit of your child back again to you." Taking one of his little wooden images, the priest performed his diabolical incantations over it, and then handed it to the deluded mother, assuring her that he had "brought the spirit of her child back again into it," and advised her to take it home and console herself with the thought that her child was still with her. She took the image, fondled it in her arms, caressed it, and carried it on her back as she had been wont to do her baby, under the conviction that his spirit animated the idol. Then she would take it down, look at it, and talk to it after this manner: "Now, my child, cannot you speak to me? Tell me what you have seen in the spirit land. I know you have come back again. Cannot you speak to me?" &c. But there was no response, and the poor distressed mother shed abundance of tears. Some time afterwards, she came under the sound of the Gospel and found true comfort in Jesus. The image she had received from the priest was brought with many others to be burned in the presence of the missionary, but it was saved from the fire to show to the friends of missions in England, as an illustration of the folly of African idolatry and superstition. *Moister.*

7460. CONSOLATION, Satisfactory. Friends visiting Mr. Venn in his last illness tried to encourage him by recalling his great labors and usefulness. He exclaimed, "Miserable comforters are ye all! I have had many to visit me, who have endeavored to comfort me by telling me what I have done. 'He hath spoiled principalities and powers; he hath made a show of them openly, triumphing over them in his cross.' This is the source of all my consolation; and not anything I have done."

7461. CONSOLATION, Source of. Our consolations come sweetest when immediately derived from the fountain-head. Springs fail; the fountain never can nor will. *Whitefield.*

7462. CONSTANCY, Example of. Arcadius suffered martyrdom for obstinate refusal to adore the gods of Rome about 260. The order of execution was that he should be slowly dismembered. His fingers were first taken off, joint by joint; then his toes; then his hands at the wrists; then his feet at the ankles. Extending his hands for amputation, he prayed, "Thy hands have made me and fashioned me; O give me understanding that I may keep thy law." At this his tongue was ordered to be cut out. He was thrown upon his back, and his legs were amputated at the knees and his arms at the elbows. What remained of these members was cut off at the thighs and the shoulders. He expired in a pool of blood, with his limbs cut in small fragments scattered about him. These were gathered up and buried by Christians, who glorified God for such an example of unyielding constancy.

7463. CONSTANCY, Loyal. King John left Hubert Burgh, Governor of Dover Castle. King Lewis, of France, invested the town, but found it a difficult thing to take. He sent for Hubert and told him he should put his brother Thomas, who was his prisoner, to death, with great torture, if he did not surrender. But this did not move him. He then offered him a large sum of money; but he refused all offers, preserving his loyalty as impregnable as his fortress.

7464. CONTEMPLATION of Death. Scarce anything is more necessary for weak and timorous believers to meditate on, than the time of their separation. Our hearts will be apt to start and boggle at the first view of death; but it is good to do by them as men use to do by young colts—ride them up to that which they fright at, and make them smell it, which is the way to cure them. "As bread," saith one, "is more necessary than other food, so the meditation of death is more necessary than many other meditations." Every time we change our habitations, we should realize therein our great change: our souls must shortly leave this, and be lodged for a longer season in another mansion. When we put off our clothes at night, we have a fit occasion to consider that we must strip nearer one of these days, and put off, not our clothes only, but the body that wears them too. *Flavel.*

7465. CONTEMPLATION of God. An artificer takes it ill if, when he hath finished some curious piece of work, and sets it forth to be seen, as Apelles was wont to do, men slight it, and take no notice of his hand work. And is there not a woe to such stupid persons as "regard not the work of the Lord, neither consider the operation of his hands?" (Isa. 5: 12.) *Asino quisquam narrabat fabulam, at ille movebat aures,* is a proverb among the Greeks. *Trapp.*

7466. CONTEMPLATION of Heaven. It was an excellent saying of Lewis Bavyer, emperor of Germany, "Such goods are worth getting and owning as will not sink or wash away if a shipwreck happen, but will wade and swim out with us." "It is recorded of Lazarus that, after his resurrection from the dead, he was never seen to laugh; his thoughts and affections were so fixed in heaven, though his body was on earth, and therefore he could not but slight temporal things, his heart being so bent and set upon eternals." Earth could but be a gloomy place to one who had spent even a few days amid the glories of Paradise. If absence from it made him sad, the thought of gaining it and enjoying its inconceivable pleasures forever, should make us glad.

7467. CONTEMPLATION, Pleasure of. There is a sweet pleasure in contemplation. All others grow flat and insipid on frequent use; and when a man hath run through a set of vanities in the declension of his age, he knows not what to do with himself, if he cannot think. *Blount.*

7468. Contemplation, Rules for. Conceive of things clearly and distinctly, in their own nature; conceive of things completely, in all their parts; conceive of things comprehensively, in all their properties and relations; conceive of things extensively, in all their kinds; conceive of things orderly, or in a proper method.
Dr. Watts.

7469. CONTENTION, Rule for. Whatever mitigates the woes or increases the happiness of others is a just criterion of goodness; and whatever injures society at large, or any individual in it, is a criterion of iniquity. One should not quarrel with a dog without a reason sufficient to vindicate him through all the courts of morality. *Goldsmith.*

7470. CONTENTION, Useless. Phocion was asked by the Senate of Athens concerning a demand which Alexander had made of them for a supply of ships. He told the senators that they should either have the sharpest swords, or remain upon good terms with those that had. It is well to count your resources and consider the result before going to battle.

7471. CONTENTMENT, Attainment of. That happy state of mind, so rarely possessed, in which we can say, "I have enough," is the highest attainment of philosophy. Happiness consists, not in possessing much, but in being content with what we possess. He who wants little always has enough.—*Zimmerman.*——They that deserve nothing should be content with anything. *Mason.*

7472. CONTENTMENT, Benefits of. An unquiet mind makes but a slow recovery. Contentment is the best food to preserve a sound man, and the best medicine to restore a sick man. It resembles the gilt on nauseous pills, which makes a man take them without tasting their bitterness. Contentment will make a cottage look as fair as a palace. He is not a poor man that hath but little, but he is a poor man that wants much. Never complain of thy hard fortune, Christian, so long as Jesus is thy friend. *Secker.*

7473. CONTENTMENT, Biblical. 1 Tim. 6: 8. "Having food and raiment, let us be therewith content." "*Food and raiment,*"—a portion enough for the exile-wanderer, Gen. 28: 20;

for the stranger, whom the Lord loves and provides for, Deut. 10: 18. As God provided for Israel in the wilderness, and they never wanted bread from heaven, and their raiment waxed not old, neither did their foot swell, for forty years, Deut. 8: 4; so let our daily bread be the ground of our contentment, as provided by him. Let us receive whatever God may send us as "food convenient," Prov. 30: 8 ("food of my allowance," marg.) Ps. 37: 16. "A little that the righteous hath." "*A little,* with the fear of the Lord," Prov. 15: 16; "even a dinner of herbs where love is," Prov. 15: 17; "a dry morsel," Prov. 17: 1; or "a handful with quietness," Eccles. 4: 6; is "better" "than the riches of many wicked," if they bring no contentment; "better than great treasure, and trouble therewith," Prov. 15: 16; "than a house full of sacrifices (good cheer, marg.) with strife," 17: 1; than "both hands full with travail and vexation of spirit," Eccles. 4: 6. "*A little.*" Our wants are really few and simple. "Man wants but little here, nor wants that little long."—(*Young.*) "Nature is content with little, grace with less, sin with nothing."—(*Watson.*) Gen. 33: 9, 11. "I have enough." So two brothers both exclaimed; and it is a strange thing in this murmuring world to find two brothers both uttering such a sentiment! But in the Hebrew there is a striking difference, not marked in our version. Esau said to Jacob, "I have enough,"—the Hebrew "rab" means *much*—"I have much;" but Jacob said, "I have enough,"—"kol"—*all—everything.* Esau had much, but Jacob had everything, because he had all in God, and God in all.—*Brooks.* Prov. 13: 15. "The righteous eateth to the satisfying of his soul." Our English word *satisfaction* well expresses true contentment, from the Latin *satis* (enough), and *facio* (to make). "So behave thyself in thy course of life as at a banquet. Take what is offered with modest thankfulness, and expect what is not yet offered with hopeful patience."—*Quarles.* "The nature of true content is to fill all the chinks of our desires, as the wax does the seal."—(*Adams.*) "I never complained of my lot," said the Persian poet, Sadi, "but once—when my feet were sore, and I had no money to buy shoes; but I met a man without a foot, and I became content with my lot when I saw him." *Bowes.*

7474. CONTENTMENT, Case of. I am a true laborer: I earn that I eat, get that I wear, owe no man hate, envy no man's happiness, glad of other men's good, content with my own harm, and the greatest of my pride is to see my ewes graze, and my lambs suck.
Shakspeare.

7475. CONTENTMENT, Christian. The Duke of Conde, when in poverty and retirement, was one day observed and pitied by a lord of Italy, who, out of tenderness, wished him to take better care of himself. The good duke answered, "Sir, be not troubled; and think not that I am ill provided of conveniences; for I send a messenger before me, who makes ready my lodgings, and takes care that I be royally entertained." The noble asked him who was his messenger? He replied, "The knowledge of myself; and the thoughts of what I deserve for my sins, which is eternal torments; and when, with this knowledge, I arrive at my lodging, how unprovided soever I find it, me-thinks it is better than I deserve; and as the sense of sin, which merits hell, sweetens present difficulties, so do the hopes of the heavenly kingdom."   *Whitecross.*

7476. CONTENTMENT, Condition of. A man that had health and riches, and several houses, all beautiful and well furnished, often troubled himself and his family by removing from one of them to another. On being asked by a friend why he removed so often from one house to another, he replied, "It was in order to find content in some of them." But his friend, knowing his temper, told him, if he would find content in any of them, he must leave himself behind.

7477. CONTENTMENT, Delusive. As for a little more money and a little more time, why it's ten to one if either one or the other would make you a whit happier. If you had more time, it would be sure to hang heavily. It is the working man is the happy man. Man was made to be active, and he is never so happy as when he is so. It is the idle man is the miser-able man. What comes of holidays, and far too often of sight-seeing, but evil? Half the harm that happens in on those days. And, as for money—don't you remember the old say-ing, "Enough is as good as a feast?" Money never made a man happy yet, nor will it. There. is nothing in its nature to produce happiness The more a man has, the more he wants. In-stead of its filling a vacuum, it makes one. If it satisfies one want, it doubles and trebles that want another way. That was a true pro-verb of the wise man, rely upon it: "Better is little with the fear of the Lord, than great treasure, and trouble therewith."   *Franklin.*

7478. CONTENTMENT, Examples of. Bishop Berke-ley, of Cloyne, was so entirely contented with his diocese, that when offered a bishopric much more lucrative than that he possessed, he de-clined it saying: "I love my neighbors, and they love me; why then should I begin, in my old days, to form new connexions, and tear my-self from those friends whose kindness is to me the greatest happiness I enjoy?" Plutarch, being asked why he resided in his native city, so obscure and so little, answered, "I stay, lest it should grow less."

7479. CONTENTMENT, Godliness with. 1 Tim. 6: 6—"Godliness with contentment is great gain." The apostle, observe, puts godliness first. Real contentment is the offspring of true godliness. "Contentment,"—literally self-suf-ficiency, rendered "sufficiency," 2 Cor. 9: 8. Godly contentment is independent of outward circumstances. It is "the bird that sings so sweetly in the breast," as Luther says. "A good man shall be satisfied from himself," Prov. 14: 14. No worldly gain can satisfy man's heart. Israel murmured as much when

they had manna as when they had not; **and** rich men as much troubled with what **they** possess as poor men for what they want. . . . But when piety cometh, content follows it. If you find small peace in the world, you shall have great peace in conscience. As Philip said, "Lord, show us the Father, and it sufficeth us."   *Adams.*

7480. CONTENTMENT, Imperfect. There is no estate of life so happy in this world as to yield a Christian the perfection of content; and yet there is no state of life so wretched in this world but a Christian must be content with it. Though I can have nothing here that may give me true content, yet I will learn to be truly contented here with what I have. What care I though I have not much; I have as much as I desire, if I have as much as I want; I have as much as the most, if I have as much as I desire.   *Warwick.*

7481. CONTENTMENT, Lesson of. Near Cato's country seat was a cottage, formerly belonging to Marius Curius, who was thrice honored with a triumph. Cato often walked thither, and reflecting on the smallness of the farm and the meanness of the dwelling, used to meditate on the peculiar virtues of the man, who, though he was the most illustrious character in Rome, had subdued the fiercest nations, and driven Pyrrhus out of Italy, cultivated this little spot of ground with his own hands, and after three triumphs retired to his own cottage. Here the ambassadors of the Samnites found him in the chimney corner dressing turnips, and offered him a large present of gold; but he absolutely refused it, remarking, "A man, who can be sat-isfied with such a supper, has no need of gold: and I think it more glorious to conquer the possessors of it, than to possess it myself." Full of these thoughts, Cato returned home; and taking a view of his own estate, his ser-vants, and his manner of life, increased his labor, and retrenched his expenses.

7482. CONTENTMENT, Measure of. Hagar said, "Give me neither poverty nor riches," and this will ever be the prayer of the wise. Our in-comes should be like our shoes: if too small, they will gall and pinch us; but if too large, they will cause us to stumble and to trip. But wealth after all is a relative thing, since he that has little and wants less is richer than he that has much but wants more. True con-tentment depends not upon what we have, but upon what we would have: a tub was large enough for Diogenes, but a world was too little for Alexander.   *Colton.*

7483. CONTENTMENT, Promotion of. One of the directions given by Plutarch for the promotion of tranquillity was, not to compare one's for-tune to those in a superior condition, but to those of inferiors. When thou art surprised into a false admiration of him who is carried in his sedan, cast thine eyes downward upon the slave who supports his luxury.

7484. CONTENTMENT, Reason for. They have always been accounted happy who had a king for their father, princes for their brothers, no-bles for their associates, and a palace for their home. How much happier is he who has God for his father, Christ for his brother, saints and angels for his associates, and heaven for his everlasting home?

7485. CONTENTMENT, Secret of. Some years ago I became acquainted with a youth who was lame from his birth—grew almost to manhood a cripple—and as his reason dawned and his observation extended, he sat by the window, propped up in his chair, and looking out upon the streets, saw the boys playing as they came and went, and said to himself, "Why has God made me thus? Why have I not feet and legs to run and jump as other boys? O God!" he said, "I am angry with you! Away with God! away with religion!" He was full of sharpness, and sourness, and complaint. His disposition was bitter, and this bitter disposition shed bitterness on all the world around. But a friend came in one day to see him, and loaned him "The Wide, Wide World." Aquilla read this book, and it opened new thoughts to him—new thoughts of God and creation and man; and, step by step, he was led along until he became a penitent, and saw himself a sinner condemned. Step by step he was led along, until Jesus was offered to him as a Saviour for condemned and penitent sinners, and his faith laid hold upon Christ. The burden of sin was removed; his heart was renewed; the love of God was shed abroad in his heart by the Holy Ghost; and now, as he looked out and saw the boys and girls skipping and hopping, he said, "All right." As he sat in his chair, day by day, and looked upon the beautiful sky and green earth, and knew himself condemned to be a cripple for life, he said, "It is all right. God has done it. My Father has done it. I love him. He loves me. He can but do all things for my good." Now, this is just the way religion works. *Dr. Ridgway.*

7486. CONTRITION, Biblical. The gracious sorrow of a penitent heart. EXPRESSED by many different terms in Scripture—" *Godly sorrow,*" 2 Cor. 7: 10, "Godly," because God is its author—object—end. It comes from God and leads to God. It has regard to God in Christ. It works "repentance unto salvation not to be repented of;" not like the "sorrow of the world," which "worketh death." "*A broken heart and contrite spirit,*" Ps. 51: 15; 34: 18 —a heart broken and melted by the Spirit's power. Our two English words form an apt illustration, "broken" and "contrite," like a stone taken from the quarry, broken by the hammer, and then ground to powder. The Hebrew word for broken, Ps. 51: 17, is that from which our word *shiver* is probably derived. *Mourning,* 2 Cor. 7: 7, as parent birds passionately cry for the loss of their young. In Zech. 12: 10, we find a figure stronger still. Ezek. 7: 16—mourning for iniquity, like the plaintive melancholy of doves of the valley. *Rending the heart,* with true deep grief, not as the Jews used often to rend their garments with sham repentance, Joel 2: 13. *Smiting upon the breast,* Luke 18: 13; upon the thigh, Jer. 31: 19. *Girded with sackcloth,* Ezek. 7:

18; Jonah 3: 8. *Afflicting the soul,* Lev. 16 29. *Humbling the heart,* Ps. 35: 13; Lam. 3: 20; 2 Kings 22: 19. *Weeping,* Jer. 50: 4 *Bemoaning,* Jer. 31: 18. *Repenting in dust and ashes,* Job. 42: 6. *Bowes.*

7487. CONTRITION, Eloquence of. When King Henry II., in the ages gone by, was provoked to take up arms against his ungrateful and rebellious son, he besieged him in one of the French towns, and the son being near to death, desired to see his father, and confess his wrong-doing; but the stern old sire refused to look the rebel in the face. The young man being sorely troubled in his conscience, said to those about him, "I am dying, take me from my bed, and let me lie in sackcloth and ashes, as token of my sorrow for my ingratitude to my father." Thus he died, and when the tidings came to the old man outside the walls, that his boy had died in ashes, repentant for his rebellion, he threw himself upon the earth, like another David, and said, "Would God I had died for him." The thought of the boy's broken heart touched the heart of the father. If ye, being evil, are overcome by your children's tears, how much more shall your Father who is in heaven find in your bemoanings and confessions an argument for the display of his pardoning love through Christ Jesus our Lord? This is the eloquence which God delights in, the broken heart and the contrite spirit. *Spurgeon.*

7488. CONTRITION, Transient. See the ice, how hard it is! But twelve o'clock comes, and there is a great heat from the sun, the ice cracks; but the sun goes down, and at night it is as hard as ever. How often is it so under the influence of instruction! A powerful appeal often produces a melting of the heart; the tears, apparently of contrition, flow; but the instruction ended, the tears are dried up, and the heart becomes as hard as ever. *Thos. Jones.*

7489. CONTROVERSY, Advantage of. Have we not a remarkable likeness between the natural body and that spiritual body the church? Poison, deadly, subtle poison, is lurking in the system. Does the heart continue to beat, do the lungs continue to play, with their ordinary calmness? Not so: nature, as we speak, exerts herself to the utmost to cast out the venom: she excites the system; she accelerates the action; and the man is in a fever. But the fever itself is no disease. Treat it so, and you miserably fail. But assist nature in her struggle, and by God's grace, you may hope to succeed. Thus, in the Church, irregularity of action is, I do not deny, the symbol of disease. There is something wrong somewhere when it occurs. But suppress it, and who may tell the consequences? The fever of controversy, and irritations, and clamor, are better than the cold of death. *Anon.*

7490. CONTROVERSY, Benefits of. You never need think you can turn over any old falsehood without a terrible squirming and scattering of the horrid little population that dwells under it. Every real thought on every real subject knocks the wind out of somebody or other. As soon as his breath comes back, he very probably begins to expend it in hard words. These are the best evidences a man can have that he said something it was time to say. Dr. Johnson was disappointed in the effect of one of his pamphlets. "I think I have not been attacked enough for it," he said; "attack is the reaction; I never think I have hit hard unless it rebounds." If a fellow attacked my opinions in print, would I reply? Not I. Do you think I don't understand what my friend the Professor long ago called the hydrostatic paradox of controversy? Don't know what that means? Well, I will tell you. You know that if you had a bent tube, one arm of which was of the size of a pipestem, and the other big enough to hold the ocean, water would stand at the same height in one as in the other. Controversy equalizes fools and wise men in the same way—and the fools know it. *Holmes.*

7491. CONTROVERSY, Damage of. I cannot but see, and that with trouble and regret, how much Christianity has in almost all times suffered by those nice and subtle, by those obstinate and passionate disputes, with which writers have even oppressed and stifled the most practical subjects; and do most earnestly desire to see the spirit of polemical divinity cast out of the Church of Christ, and that of a practical and experimental one established in the room of it. *Lucas.*

7492. CONTROVERSY, Love of. What Tully says of war may be applied to disputing—it should be always so managed as to remember that the only true end of it is peace: but generally true disputants are like true sportsmen—their whole delight is in the pursuit; and a disputant no more cares for the truth than the sportsman for the hare. *Pope.*

7493. CONVERSATION, Ability in. Burke is an extraordinary man. His stream of talk is perpetual; and he does not talk from any desire of distinction, but because his mind is full. He is the only man whose common conversation corresponds with the general fame which he has in the world. Take him up where you please, he is ready to meet you. No man of sense could meet Burke by accident under a gateway, to avoid a shower, without being convinced that he was the first man in England. If he should go into a stable, and talk a few minutes with the hostlers about horses, they would venerate him as the wisest of human beings. They would say, "We have had an extraordinary man here." *Dr. S. Johnson.*

7494. CONVERSATION, Benefit of. Conversation with men of a polite genius is another method for improving our natural taste. It is impossible for a man of the greatest parts to consider anything in its whole extent, and in all its variety of lights. Every man, besides those general observations which are to be made upon an author, forms several reflections that are peculiar to his own manner of thinking; so that conversation will naturally furnish us with hints which we did not attend to, and make us enjoy other men's parts and reflections as well as our own. *Addison.*

7495. CONVERSATION, Christian. There is so much correspondence betwixt the heart and tongue, that they will move at once. Every man, therefore, speaks of his own pleasure and care. If the heart were full of God, the tongue could not refrain to talk of him: the rareness of Christian communication argues the common poverty of grace. If Christ be not in our hearts, we are godless; if he be there without our joy, we are senseless; if we rejoice in him, and speak not of him, we are shamefully unthankful. I will think of thee always, O Lord; so it shall be my joy to speak of thee often; and if I find not opportunity, I will make it. *Bishop Hall.*

7496. CONVERSATION, Deficiency in. Some men are very entertaining for a first interview, but after that they are exhausted, and run out; on a second meeting, we shall find them very flat and monotonous; like hand organs, we have heard all their tunes. *Colton.*

7497. CONVERSATION, Faults of. One must be extremely exact, clear and perspicuous in everything one says; otherwise, instead of entertaining or informing others, one only tires and puzzles them. The voice and manner of speaking, too, are not to be neglected; some people almost shut their mouths when they speak, and mutter so, that they are not to be understood; others speak so fast and sputter that they are not to be understood neither; some always speak as loud as if they were talking to deaf people, and others so low that one cannot hear them. All these habits are awkward and disagreeable; and are to be avoided by attention; they are the distinguishing marks of the ordinary people, who have had no care taken of their education. You cannot imagine how necessary it is to mind all these little things; for I have seen many people, with great talents, ill-received, for want of having these talents too; and others well-received, only from their little talents, and who had no great ones. *Lord Chesterfield.*

7498. CONVERSATION a Fine Art. Some persons seem to think that absolute truth, in the form of rigidly-stated propositions, is all that conversation admits. This is precisely as if a musician should insist upon having nothing but perfect chords and simple melodies,—no diminished fifths, no flat sevenths, no flourishes, on any account. Now it is fair to say, that, just as music must have all these, so conversation must have its partial truths, its embellished truths, its exaggerated truths. It is in its higher forms an artistic product, and admits the ideal element as much as pictures or statues. One man who is a little too literal can spoil the talk of a whole tableful of men of *esprit*,—"Yes," you say, "but who wants to hear fanciful people's nonsense? Put the facts to it, and then see where it is!" Certainly, if a man is too fond of paradox—if he is flighty and empty—if, instead of striking those fifths and sevenths, those harmonious discords, often so much better than the twined octaves, in the music of thought,—if, instead of striking these, he jangles the chords, stick a fact into him like a stiletto. But remember that talking is one of the fine arts—the noblest, the most important, and the most difficult—and that its fluent harmonies may be spoiled by the intrusion of a single harsh note. Therefore conversation which is suggestive rather than argumentative, which lets out the most of each talker's result of thought, is commonly the pleasantest and the most profitable. *Holmes.*

7499. CONVERSATION, Habits of. Tasso's conversation was neither gay nor brilliant. Dante was either taciturn or satirical. Butler was sullen or biting. Gray seldom talked or smiled. Hogarth and Swift were very absent-minded in company. Milton was unsociable, and even irritable, when pressed into conversation. Kirwan, though copious and eloquent in public addresses, was meagre and dull in colloquial discourse. Virgil was heavy in conversation. La Fontaine appeared heavy, coarse, and stupid; he could not speak and describe what he had just seen; but then he was the model of poetry. Chaucer's silence was more agreeable than his conversation. Dryden's conversation was slow and dull, his humor saturnine and reserved. Corneille in conversation was so insipid that he never failed in wearying : he did not even speak correctly that language of which he was such a master. Ben. Johnson used to sit silent in company and suck his wine and their humors. Southey was stiff, sedate, and wrapped up in asceticism. Addison was good company with his intimate friends, but in mixed company he preserved his dignity by a stiff and reserved silence. Fox, in conversation, never flagged; his animation and variety were inexhaustible. Dr. Bentley was loquacious. Grotius was talkative. Goldsmith wrote like an angel, and talked like poor Poll. Burke was eminently entertaining, enthusiastic, and interesting in conversation. Curran was a convivial deity; he soared into every region, and was at home in all. Dr. Birch dreaded a pen as he did a torpedo; but he could talk like running water. Dr. Johnson wrote monotonously and ponderously, but in conversation his words were close and sinewy; and if his pistol missed fire, he knocked down his antagonist with the butt of it. Coleridge, in his conversation, was full of acuteness and originality. Leigh Hunt has been well termed the philosopher of hope, and likened to a pleasant stream in conversation. Carlyle doubts, objects, and constantly demurs. Fisher Ames was a powerful and effective orator, and not the less distinguished in the social circle. He possessed a fluent language, a vivid fancy, and a well-stored memory, *Chambers.*

7500. CONVERSATION. Influence of. Conversation opens our views, and gives our faculties a more vigorous play; it puts us upon turning our notions on every side, and holds them up to a light that discovers those latent flaws which would probably have lain concealed in the gloom of unagitated abstraction. *Melmoth.*

7501. CONVERSATION, Introduction of. I shall never forget the manner in which a thirsty individual once begged of me upon Clapham Common. I saw him with a very large truck in which he was carrying an extremely small parcel, and I wondered why he had not put the parcel into his pocket and left the machine at home. I said, "It looks odd to see so large a truck for such a small load." He stopped, and looking me seriously in the face, said: "Yes, sir, it is a very odd thing; but do you know I have met with an odder thing than that this very day. I've been about, working and sweating all this 'ere blessed day, and till now I haven't met a single gentleman that looked as if he'd give me a pint of beer till I saw you." I considered that turn of the conversation very neatly managed, and we, with a far better subject upon our minds, ought to be equally able to introduce the topic upon which our heart is set. *Spurgeon.*

7502. CONVERSATION, Religious. If there be a man who is about to found a new colony in Australia, and he has been reading and studying the subject, and has got the idea into his head that it would be a great and glorious thing to go and break up some new ground and form a colony, you get into a railway-carriage with him, and he will begin to talk about the weather and the crops, but in about five minutes by some sleight-of-hand he will bring you round to Australia, and tell you something about his intention of forming a colony there. Or if he be a great politician, who has discovered some wonderful truth whereby he thinks that all trade and government will be so revolutionized that every evil will be put down, if the idea hath actually entered into his soul, you may sit in a drawing-room with him, and gently, by degrees, he will bring you round to the subject of politics, and say, "Did you ever notice such and such a thing?" And out will come the favorite theory. And as certainly as religion has ever entered into a man's heart, he will not allow you to be long with him before his bringing you round to it. *Spurgeon.*

7503. CONVERSATION, Rules in. One of the best rules in conversation is, never to say a thing which any of the company can reasonably wish we had rather left unsaid : nor can there anything be well more contrary to the ends for which people meet together, than to part unsatisfied with each other or themselves. —*Swift.*——The first ingredient in conversation is truth, the next good sense, the third good humor, and the fourth wit. *Temple.*

7504. CONVERSATION, Stock. The profuse talker is of such a disposition that, if any discourse happen from which he might be able to learn something and inform his ignorance, that he refuses and rejects, nor can you hire him even to hold his tongue ; but after his rolling and restless fancy has mustered up some few obsolete and all-to-be-tattered rhapsodies to supply his vanity, out he flings them, as if he were master of all the knowledge in the world. Just like one amongst us who, having read two or three of Ephorus' books, tired all men's ears, and spoiled and broke up all the feasts and societies wherever he came, with his continual relation of the battle of Leuctra and the consequences of it; by which means he got himself a nickname, and every one called him Epaminondas. *Plutarch.*

7505. CONVERSION, Believing for. I once noticed a lady who sat down by the side of the pulpit, and every time I would look down her eyes would be riveted upon me. She looked so intent, trying to catch every word, that one day I said to her, "My friend, are you a Christian?" "Oh, no," she said, "I have been seeking Christ these three years, but cannot find him." I said, "There is some mistake about that;" and she answered, "Do you mean that I have not been seeking him?" "I know he has been looking for you for twenty years." She asked, "What am I to do, then?" "Do! Do nothing; probably that is the trouble, that you have been trying to do." "But how am I to be saved?" she asked. "You are to believe on him, and stop trying." She said, "Believe! believe! believe! I have heard that word until my head swims; everybody says it, and I am none the wiser." I said, "I will drop that word for another. The word believe is used in the New Testament, and the word trust in the Old. I will say to you, Trust the Lord now to save your soul." "If I say I will trust him, will he save me?" she asked. "If you really do trust him, he will save you." She said, "I trust the Lord to save me; now I do not feel any different"— just so in one breath. I told her, "I think you have not been looking for Christ; you have been looking for feeling. God does not tell you to feel; he tells you to trust him, and you are to let the feelings take care of themselves." "I have heard people say they felt happy when they became Christians." "Well, wait till you become a Christian, and then you may talk about a Christian's experience; you must trust the Lord that he will keep you." She sat there five minutes, and then put out her hand to me, and said, "I trust the Lord Jesus Christ to save my soul now." That was all there was to it, no praying, no weeping. The next night I was preaching she was in front of me, and I could see eternity written on her face, and the light from fields of glory in her eyes. *Moody.*

7506. CONVERSION, Biblical. It is described as a turning from sin back to God, Acts 3: 26; 1 Thess. 1: 9. A translation, Col. 1: 13. A restoration to a right mind, Ps. 19: 7. A healing, Isa. 6:•10. A resurrection and re-animation, Ezek. 37: 1–10.

7507. CONVERSION, Changed by. A young apprentice in New England was converted and applied for admission into a church. The pastor inquired of his employer to learn the genuineness of his conversion. Pointing to an iron chain hanging up in the room, "Do you see that chain?" said he. "That chain was forged for him. I was obliged to chain him to the bench by the week together, to keep him at work. He was the worst boy I had in the establishment. No punishment seemed to have any salutary influence upon him. I could not trust him out of my sight; but now, sir, he is completely changed; he has really become a lamb. He is one of my best apprentices. I would trust him with untold gold. I have no objection to his being received into communion. I wish all my boys were prepared to go with him."

7508. CONVERSION, Change of. A minister sought earnestly to reform a profligate. At length he met the rebuff, "It is all in vain, doctor, you can not get me to change my religion." "I do not want that; I wish religion to change you," replied the minister.

7509. CONVERSION, Complete. A converted Chinaman said to the missionary, "I want every person to know that I am converted all over."

7510. CONVERSION, Conquests of. I had the privilege of dedicating a beautiful country church in my State, in a neighborhood surrounded almost entirely with infidels. The preacher directed my attention to a tall, manly, vigorous man in the congregation, and said he would give me his history when the service was over. He was, it seems, a violent, passionate, close-fisted man. Not a solitary farthing could anybody get out of him for the salvation of souls or the elevation of humanity. He went to the altar a few months ago, said the minister, and gave his heart to Jesus. The infidels in the community said, "Wait a little while — touch his pocket and you will see where his religion is." "Presently," continued my friend, "I came to him with my subscription paper, and spoke of the difficulties and embarrassments under which we labored in the neighborhood for the want of a church." "Well," said the man, "let us build a house." "What will you give?" inquired the preacher. "Fifty dollars," was the prompt reply, and the minister passed through the community with the subscription paper, at the head of which was this amount, written in the gentleman's own handwriting, which surprised everybody. A few days afterward the most trying circumstance of his life occurred. His dear wife trembled for him. "O my husband!" she exclaimed, "don't go." His reply was, "I must go; my duty calls me there; I am perfectly cool and collected. I shall become excited, but I will not say a word or do a thing out of the way." He passed through the fiery ordeal without the least taint of anger upon him. The community then said, "Surely there is something in this; you have reached his pocket, you have conquered his anger, and you have subdued the man. There is power in this gospel of Christ." A few weeks after my visit there, I received the sad intelligence that that gentleman had been buried. He had gone out into the forest, and, unfortunately, a tree fell upon him and crushed him to the earth, and yet did not entirely destroy him. They carried him to the house, and sent for a physician and the minister. He calmly asked for the Bible, and read in a clear voice a chapter in John's gospel. After shutting the Bible, he closed his hands upon his breast, "and such a prayer," said my ministerial brother, "I never heard from mortal lips, for his wife, his children, for his pastor, for the church, and for his infidel friends." In a moment or two after saying Amen, he closed his eyes, and sweetly fell asleep in Jesus. The infidels said, "There is something in religion." A few weeks since I met with that good pastor again. I inquired what about his infiel neighbors, and he replied, "All of them but one are happily converted to God."   *Bishop Bowman.*

7511. CONVERSION, Cowper's. Cowper, the poet, speaking of his religious experience, says: "The happy period which was to shake off my fetters, and afford me a clear opening of the free mercy of God in Christ Jesus, was now arrived. I flung myself into a chair near the window, and seeing a Bible there, ventured once more to apply to it for comfort and instruction. The first verse I saw was the 25th of the third of Romans: 'Whom God hath set forth to be a propitiation through faith in his blood, to declare his righteousness for the remission of sins that are past, through the forbearance of God.' Immediately I received strength to believe, and the full beams of the sun of righteousness shone upon me. I saw the sufficiency of the atonement he had made, my pardon sealed in his blood, and all the fullness and completeness of his justification. In a moment I believed and received the Gospel."

7512. CONVERSION, C. Wesley's. Charles Wesley had been for years groping in spiritual darkness,

"Without one cheering beam of hope,
Or spark of glimmering day."

On a bright morning in May, 1738, he awoke, wearied and sick at heart, but in high expectation of the coming blessing. He lay on his bed "full of tossings to and fro," crying out, "O Jesus, thou hast said, 'I will come unto you;' thou hast said, 'I will send the comforter unto you;' thou hast said, 'My Father and I will come unto you, and make our abode with you.' Thou art God who canst not lie. I wholly rely upon thy promise. Accomplish it in thy time and manner." A poor woman, Mrs. Turner, heard his groaning, and, constrained by an impulse never felt before, put her head into his room and gently said, "In the name of Jesus of Nazareth, arise and believe, and thou shalt be healed of all thine infirmities." He listened, and then exclaimed, "Oh that Christ would but thus speak to me!" He inquired who it was that had whispered in his ear these life-giving words. A great struggle agitated his whole man, and in another moment he exclaimed, "I believe! I believe!" He then found redemption in the blood of the Lamb, and experienced the forgiveness of sins. The hymn he wrote to commemorate the anniversary of his spiritual birth shows the mighty change that had taken place, and is best expressed in his own language—

"O for a thousand tongues to sing!"
                              Stevens.

7513. CONVERSION, Crime and. A Jew in Paris stole a Bible for the silver clasps which bound it; them he tore off and sold. For the book itself he could get no sufficient price, and retained it. From curiosity he began to read it, became interested, then convinced of its truths, and then embraced Christianity.

7514. CONVERSION, Deliverance of. The legend says that Jerome Emiliani, while a soldier, was captured and cast into a noisome dungeon heavily chained, having his feet linked together and fastened to a stone. There he reviewed his past life, felt its evils, perceived his lost opportunities, and resolved to reform and make some amends for the evil he had done. He also made a vow to be fulfilled in case of his deliverance. Then he found the key which unlocked his fetters. A fair form stood by him and helped him to cast off his chains, opened the dungeon doors, and led him forth to freedom and safety. After this miraculous deliverance Jerome cast off the chains of his old evil habits, as he had done the fetters in the prison and lived a noble life, caring for the sick. The chain and ball which he wore are said to have been hung up in the chapel of the Virgin at Treviso, as a memorial of his deliverance. He died of the plague, caught in taking care of others, near Venice, in 1537.

7515. CONVERSION, Detained for. Rev. Dr. Cleveland related the following incident at a New York anniversary: In a revival of religion in the church of which he was pastor, he was visited one morning by a member of his church, a widow, whose only son was a sailor. With a voice trembling with emotion, she said, "Dr. Cleveland, I have called to entreat you to join me in praying that the wind may change." He looked at her in silent amazement. "Yes," she exclaimed earnestly, "my son has gone on board his vessel; they sail to-night, unless the wind changes." "Well, madam," said the Doctor, "I will pray that your son may be converted on this voyage; but to pray that God would alter the laws of the universe on his account, I fear, is presumption." "Doctor," she replied, "my heart tells me differently. God's Spirit is here. Souls are being converted here. You have a meeting this evening, and if the wind should change, John would stay and go to it; and I believe if he went, he would be converted. Now, if you cannot join me, I must pray alone, for he must stay." "I will pray for his conversion," said the Doctor. On his way to the meeting, he glanced at the weather-vane, and, to his surprise, the wind had changed, and it was blowing landward. On entering his crowded vestry, he soon observed John sitting upon the front seat. The young man seemed to drink in every word, rose to be prayed for, and attended the inquiry-meeting. When he sailed from port, the mother's prayers had been answered; he went a Christian.

7516. CONVERSION, Different Ways of. Sometimes you will have impetuous and heavy showers bursting from the angry clouds; they lash the plains and make the rivers flow; a storm brings them, and a deluge follows them. At other times, thin gentle dews are formed in the serene evening air; they steal down by slow degrees with insensible stillness; so subtle that they deceive the nicest eye, so silent that they escape the most delicate ear; and when fallen, so very light, that they neither bruise the tenderest, nor oppress the weakest flowers; a very different operation! yet each concurs in the same beneficial end, and both impart fertility to the lap of nature. So I have known some persons reclaimed from the unfruitful works of darkness, by violent and severe means. The Almighty addressed their stubborn hearts as he addressed the Israelites of Sinai, with lightning in his eyes, and thunder in his voice. The conscience, smitten with a sense of guilt and apprehension of eternal vengeance, trembled through all her powers; just as that strong mountain tottered to its centre, pangs of remorse and agonies of fear preceded their new birth. They were reduced to the last extremities, almost overwhelmed with despair, before they found rest in Jesus Christ. Others have been recovered from a vain conversation, by methods more mild and attractive. The "Father of Spirits" applied himself to their teachable minds in "a still small voice." His grace came down like the rain into a fleece of wool; or as these softening drops which now water the earth. The kingdom of God took place in their souls, without noise or observation. They passed from death unto life, from a carnal to a regenerate state, by almost imperceptible advances. The transition resembled the growth of corn: was very visible when effected, though scarcely sensible while accomplishing.   *Salter.*

7517. CONVERSION, Double. An unconverted man and his wife attended one of the services at a camp-meeting, where she was powerfully convicted, and resolved to present herself for prayers at the altar. Her husband did his utmost to dissuade her, and used his authority, saying, "Never return to my house if you go." She resolved to give all for Christ and went. The peace of God soon rested upon her. Her first exclamation was "Where is my husband?" "Here I am," said he. Deeply convicted himself by the Spirit, he yet resisted by opposing his wife. He was now weeping and crying for mercy by her side at the altar, and was saved. God gives us the friends we give up for him.

7518. CONVERSION, Dreams and. A candidate for admission to Church membership under the Rev. Rowland Hill being required to give some account of his experience, related a dream by which he had been affected and led to serious inquiry, to the hearing of sermons, etc. When he had ended, Mr. Hill said, "We do not wish to despise a good man's dreams by any means; but we will tell you what we think of the dream, after we have seen how you go on when you are awake."

7519. CONVERSION, Early. Alfred Cookman was converted at the age of ten years. His father was the pastor of the Methodist Episcopal church at Carlisle, the seat of Dickinson College. Much spiritual interest had been awakened among the students. On one occasion many of them bowed at the altar, and no little interest was naturally felt in their behalf. It was hardly possible to overestimate the amount of good that might result from the personal consecration of these educated young men to the Master's service. But in that congregation, quite overlooked, attracting only the peculiar attention of one Christian person at the time, was one little lad, not yet twelve years of age. He did not make himself conspicuous by the position he took, or by any marked demonstration of feeling on his part, but in a distant corner of the church, kneeling alone, he wept and prayed and earnestly cried, "Precious Saviour, thou art saving others, oh! wilt thou not save me?" There was one Christian man, who, amid the excitement of the hour, and the intense feeling aroused by the presence of the penitent students, saw the little fellow, and appreciated his situation. He drew near and tenderly laid his hand upon him. It was a pious elder in the Presbyterian church in Carlisle. With a warm heart and with gentle words he unfolded, to the faith of the weeping boy, the simple and wonderful plan by which God saves us, when we trust in him who died for us, as our Saviour. "I will believe," the sobbing child responded : "I do believe; I now believe that Jesus is my Saviour—that he saves me—yes, even now." And faith, in the trusting boy, brought its promised result of peace and love and joy. Many years after, as he recurred to this hour, he writes, "I love to think of it; it fills my heart unutterably full of gratitude, love and joy. 'Happy day; oh! happy day, when Jesus washed my sins away.'" *Dr. Ridgeway.*

7520. CONVERSION, Evidence of. A servant accustomed to disregard her mistress' direction to sweep under the door-mat was converted. She applied for admission to Mr. Spurgeon's church. He asked her, "Why do you think you are a Christian?" She knew nothing of doctrine, but showed the influence of religion on her heart in her answer, "Because, sir, I now always sweep under the door-mat."

7521. CONVERSION, Example of. A Boston sea-captain was an inveterate sinner. He was intemperate, passionate, profane, and violently opposed to religion. His wife was a Christian woman, and never failed to pray for him for twenty-three years, though often well-nigh disheartened by his constant and increasing wickedness. At length he forbade her attending the prayer-meetings of the church to which she belonged, of which Dr. Wm. Butler was then pastor. She laid her case anew in God's hands, and awaited the result. When the time for the next meeting came, he proposed to go in her place. She feared that he would disturb the meeting, and expected that he would make it a new subject of ridicule. He went, and, while listening to the prayers, the Holy Spirit began to open his eyes to see his own many and aggravated sins. On his return home, he had nothing to say to his wife in ridicule of the meeting, as she expected. Next day he went to his work as pilot on a ferryboat between Boston and Chelsea with a heavy heart. His burden was great, and he began to think of Christ. As he was making the last trip for the day, a great change came over him. He thought the trip but a moment, but found it had occupied the usual time. He hastened home, and told his wife to bring him the Bible. She expected only a renewal of old scenes of blasphemy. He took the book, and saying, "We must have family prayers," read a lesson, and then prayed. He gave up his drink, tobacco, and profanity, or rather his love for those sins was all taken from him. He arose the next morning at 3 o'clock, and, with a lantern in his hand, called on his next-door neighbor, a deacon, for whom he had always indulged great dislike. Half dressed, the deacon came to see what was wanted at that untimely hour. "Deacon," said he, "I have come to tell you that the Lord converted my soul yesterday." "Praise the Lord, brother!" was the answer. The rejoicing wife called on Dr. Butler to ask him to go and see her greatly-changed husband. He found him at his post joyful in his new experience, overflowing with love, and wondering at the grace of God which had found him after he had gone round the world committing the vilest sins. His was a Paul-like conversion, a miracle of grace.

7522. CONVERSION, Experience of. The reality of religious experience often finds confirmation in the fresh phrases used by new converts. An old woman, who until those days of grace, for a lifetime had neglected worship, rose up to tell how she had been "renewed in the spirit of her mind." "I feel," said she, "just as if I was somebody else." A little girl, with ecstasy in her beaming eyes, exclaimed, "O, I do like Jesus!" "Why?" "Because he likes me."   *S. Coley.*

7523. CONVERSION, An Indian's. The following is the experience of Peter Jacobs, a Chippewa Indian of Canada, as given at Exeter Hall, London, in 1843: "When I was in my heathen state, I heard a missionary speak of a beautiful heaven where nothing but joy was to be experienced, and of the awful flames of hell into which the wicked shall be cast if they do not believe on the Lord Jesus Christ. I made inquiry if there was any possibility of a Chippewa Indian getting to heaven. I was told that heaven was open to all believers in Christ Jesus. I was very glad when I understood this; I began to pray. I said, 'O Christ, have mercy upon me, poor sinner, poor Indian!' This was the beginning of my prayer and the end of my prayer. I could not pray any more, because I did not know any more English. I thought if I prayed in Chippewa, Christ would not understand me. Christ affected my heart very much. I felt just like the wounded deer. When we shoot a deer in the heart with bow and arrow, he runs away as if he was not hurt; but when he gets to the hill, he feels the pain,

and lays down on that side where the pain is most severe. Then he feels the pain on the other side, and turns over, and so he wanders about till he dies. I felt pain in this way; I felt pain in my heart, but could not get better. I went with Peter Jones to dine with a gentleman, and before dinner Peter Jones said grace in English. I thought God would understand that. But he said grace after meat in Chippewa; and I thought, if God understands your Chippewa, he will understand mine. I then went up into a stable where hay was kept, and there I prayed, 'O my heavenly Father, now have mercy upon me, for the sake of thy son Jesus Christ.' Then I prayed again, 'O Jesus, the Saviour of the world, I did not know that thou didst die for me personally. Now, O Jesus, the Saviour of the world, apply now thy precious blood to my heart, that all my sins may depart!' I wanted rest and sleep, but I could not rest. Like the wounded deer, I turned from side to side and could not rest. At last I got up at midnight and walked about my room: I made another effort to pray, and said, 'O Jesus, I will not let thee go until thou bless me;' and before break of day I found that my heavy heart was taken away, and I felt happy—I felt the joy which is unspeakable and full of glory. Then I found Jesus was sweet indeed to my soul."

7524. CONVERSION, Interest in Thy. You remember the occasion when the Lord met with thee. O, little didst thou think what a commotion was in heaven. If the queen had ordered out all her soldiers, the angels of heaven would not have stopped to notice them. If all the princes of earth had marched through the streets, with all their jewelry, and robes, and crowns, and all their regalia, their chariots, and their horsemen; if the pomp of ancient monarchs had risen from the tomb; if all the mighty of Babylon, and Tyre, and Greece had been concentrated in one great parade; yet not an angel would have stopped in his course to smile at these poor, tawdry things; but over you, the vilest of the vile, the poorest of the poor, over you angelic wings were hovering, and concerning you it was said on earth and sung in heaven, hallelujah, for a child is born to God to-day!   *Spurgeon.*

7525. CONVERSION, Joy of. We are told of some Turks, who have, upon the sight of Mahomet's tomb, put out their eyes, that they might not defile them, forsooth, with any common object, after they had been blessed with seeing one so sacred. I am sure many gracious souls there have been, who, by a prospect of heaven's glory set before the eyes of their faith, have been so ravished by the sight that they desired God even to seal up their eyes by death, with Simeon, who would not by his good will have lived a day after that blessed hour in which his eyes beheld the salvation of God.
                                       W. Gurnall.

7526. CONVERSION, Judson's. Adoniram Judson, the illustrious American missionary, was a minister's son. He was very able and very ambitious. He was early sent to college. In the class above was a young man of the name of E., brilliant, witty, and popular, but a determined deist. Between him and the minister's son there sprang up a close intimacy, which ended in the latter gradually renouncing all his early beliefs, and becoming as great a sceptic as his friend. He was only twenty years of age, and you may be sure it was a terrible distress and consternation which filled the home circle, when, during the recess, he announced that he was no longer a believer in Christianity. More than a match for his father's arguments, he steeled himself against all softer influences, and with his mind made up to enjoy life and see the world, he first joined a company of players at New York, and then set out on a solitary tour. One night he stopped at a country inn. Lighting him to his room, the landlord mentioned that he had been obliged to place him next door to a young man who was exceedingly ill, in all probability dying, but he hoped that it would occasion him no uneasiness. Judson assured him that, beyond pity for the poor sick man, he should have no feeling whatever. Still the night proved a restless one. Sounds came from the sick chamber—sometimes the movements of the watchers, sometimes the groans of the sufferer, and the young traveler could not sleep. "So close at hand, with but a thin partition between us," he thought, "there is an immortal spirit about to pass into eternity; and is he prepared?" And then he thought, "For shame of my shallow philosophy! What would E., so clear-headed and intellectual, think of this boyish weakness?" And then he tried to sleep, but still the picture of the dying man rose up to his imagination. He was a "young man," and the young student felt compelled to place himself on his neighbor's dying bed, and he could not help fancying what, in such circumstances, would be his thoughts. But the morning dawned, and in the welcome daylight his "superstitious illusions fled away." When he came down stairs, he inquired of the landlord how his fellow-lodger had passed the night. "He is dead!" was the answer. "Dead!" "Yes; he is gone, poor fellow; the doctor said he would probably not survive the night." "Do you know who he was?" "O, yes; it was a young man from Providence College, a very fine fellow; his name was E." Judson was completely stunned. Hours passed before he could quit the house; but when he did resume his journey, the words dead! lost! lost! were continually ringing in his ears. There was no need for argument. God had spoken, and from the presence of the living God the chimeras of unbelief and the pleasures of sin alike fled away. The religion of the Bible he knew to be true; and, turning his horse's head toward Plymouth, he rode slowly homeward, his plans of enjoyment all shattered, and ready to commence that rough and uninviting path which, through the death-prison at Ava and its rehearsal of martyrdom, conducted to the grave at Maulmain. *Dr. James Hamilton.*

7527. CONVERSION, Knowledge of. If (as they affirm) the change from bad to good were either so quick and sudden, as that he that was extremely vicious in the morning may become eminently virtuous at night, or that any one going to bed wicked, might chance to rise a virtuous man next morning, and, having all the former days' errors and imperfections absolutely removed out of his mind, might say to them, as it is in the poet,

Vain dreams! farewell, like spectres haste away
At the new light of virtue's glorious day;

do you think that any one in the world could be ignorant of so extraordinary a conversion, and perfectly shut his eyes upon the beams of virtue and wisdom so fully and manifestly breaking in upon his soul? In my opinion, if any person should have Cæneus's foolish wish, and be changed (as it is reported he was) from one sex to the other, it is more probable that such a one should be altogether ignorant of the metamorphosis than that any should, from a lazy, unthinking, debauched fellow, commence a wise, prudent, and valiant hero, and from a sottish bestiality advance to the perfection of divine life, and yet know nothing of the change. *Plutarch.*

7528. CONVERSION, Late. A clergyman was called in to visit a poor dying woman, who was quite ignorant of the truth. After conversing with her on the depravity of human nature and the way of salvation by Jesus Christ—that it was all of grace, and that there was no limitation as to person or state—the woman listened to every word with great attention; the tears began to trickle down her cheeks; and at last she said, "I know nothing of the man of whom you have been speaking;" immediately adding, "I was never brought up in the way of religion; never taught to know a letter of a book, nor yet attend a place of worship." The clergyman visiting her the next day began to discourse upon the suitableness, the ability, and willingness of Jesus to save perishing sinners. "And do you think, sir," said she, "he will save such a vile wretch as I am?" He observed, the promise ran thus, "Him that cometh unto me, I will in no wise cast out." Here she found a basis to rest on. Her knowledge of divine things rapidly increased; and she gave evidence of having become a Christian.

7529. CONVERSION, Liberty in. When we see a casket wrenched open, the hinges torn away, or the clasp destroyed, we mark at once the hand of the spoiler; but when we observe another casket deftly opened with a master-key, and the sparkling contents revealed, we note the hand of the owner. Conversion is not, as some suppose, a violent opening of the heart by grace, in which will, reason, and judgment are all ignored or crushed. This is too barbarous a method for him who comes not as a plunderer to his prey, but as a possessor to his treasure. In conversion, the Lord who made the human heart deals with it according to its nature and constitution. His key insinuates itself into the wards; the will is not enslaved but enfranchised; the reason is not blinded but enlightened, and the whole man is made to act with a glorious liberty which it never knew till it fell under the restraints of grace.

Spurgeon.

7530. CONVERSION, Need of. A man may beat down the bitter fruit from an evil tree until he is weary; whilst the root abides in strength and vigor, the beating down of the present fruit will not hinder it from bringing forth more. This is the folly of some men; they set themselves with all earnestness and diligence against the appearing eruption of lust, but leaving the principle and root untouched, perhaps unsearched out, they make but little or no progress in this work of mortification.

John Owen.

7531. CONVERSION, Occasion of a. Earl Fitzhardinge was led to Christ through the remark of Rev. Morton Brown, after a business call. "I hope, my Lord, you will forgive me, but I feel constrained, as a Christian minister, to observe that you yourself have a soul to be saved or lost." When the Earl became ill he sent for the faithful minister, the only man who had ever spoken to him about his soul. To whom else should he turn for help from his burden of sin? He died in Christian triumph. On his death-bed he said, "All is peace! all is right! I had always thought religion was a melancholy thing, but I now find it is the only thing worth living for. Here am I, a poor penitent sinner, clinging to the cross of Christ."

7532. CONVERSION, Opportune. At a meeting held in Edinburgh by Messrs. Moody and Sankey, a miner, in his working clothes was sitting near the front, obviously most attentive and impressed. At the close of the meeting he rose to go away; but after walking down the passage, he turned and sat down again. His friend came up to him and said, "Come awa' hame, John." "No," said he, "I came here to get good, and I have na' taken it 'a in yet." So he waited. There was more prayer and another hymn, and special conversation with himself. His heart was touched and changed; with his hard, rough grip, he shook the minister's hand, and said, "I have wondered if this might be true; now I believe it. It has brought peace to my soul. I know and trust my Saviour." On the next day while working a mass of coal or rock fell on him. The injuries were fatal. Death was close at hand. A fellow-workman approached him. "Bend down your ear to me," said the dying man, and then he added, "Oh, Andrew, I'm glad I settled it last night."

Anon.

7533. CONVERSION, Preaching and. A convert from heathenism answering a missionary's question as to the means of his conversion, said, "Master missionary, do you remember a sermon you preached here, on the glories of heaven?" "I remember it well," said the minister. "Master missionary, do you remember a sermon you preached on the terrors of hell?" "I remember it well," was the answer of the missionary. Again the convert said, "Master missionary, do you remember the sermon you preached on the words of Jesus 'I am the

way?' And so do I," said the happy Christian, "and that which you said was the means of my conversion." "My word shall not return unto me void."

7534. CONVERSION, Primitive. "The power of the Logos does not produce poets; it does not create philosophers, nor able orators; but by forming us anew, it makes mortal men immortal. It transports us from the earth beyond the limits of Olympus. Come and submit yourselves to its influence. Become as I am, for I too was as you are. This has conquered me; the divinity of the doctrine, the power of the Logos. As a master serpent-charmer lures out and frightens away the hideous reptile from his den, so the word drives the fearful passions of our sensual nature from the most secret recesses of the soul." Justin Martyr, the supposed author of the above, sought God in the study of the Stoic, Pythagorian and Platonic philosophies. At last he met a venerable Christian, who called his attention to the sacred writings and to Christ. As he read these a fire was kindled in his soul. He says, "I was once an admirer of the doctrines of Plato and heard the Christians abused; but when I saw them meet death and all that is accounted terrible among men, without dismay, I knew it impossible that they should live in sin; I despised the opinion of the multitude; I glory in being a Christian, and take every pains to prove myself worthy of my calling." He was the first of the apostolic fathers. He wore the garb of a Platonic philosopher till his death, by martyrdom, which occurred about A. D. 167.

7535. CONVERSION, Providential. In the city of Philadelphia, there was a mother that had two sons, who were breaking her heart, and she went into a little prayer-meeting and got up and presented them for prayer. They had been on a drunken spree and she knew their end would be a drunkard's grave, and she went among these Christians and said, "Won't you just cry to God for my two boys?" The next morning those two boys had made an appointment to meet each other on the corner of Market and Thirteenth streets—though not that they knew anything about our meeting—and while one of them was there at the corner, waiting for his brother to come, he followed the people who were flooding into the depot building, and the spirit of the Lord met him, and he was wounded and found his way to Christ. After his brother came he found the place too crowded to enter, so he too went curiously into another meeting and found Christ, and went home happy; and when he got home he told his mother what the Lord had done for him, and the second son came in with the same tidings. I heard one get up afterward to tell his experience in the young convert's meeting, and he had no sooner told the story than the other got up and said: "I am that brother, and there is not a happier home in Philadelphia than we have got;" and they went out bringing their friends to Christ.

Moody

7536. CONVERSION, Restraints of. The suspension of the ferocity of the savage animals during their continuance in the ark, is an apt figure of the change which takes place in sinners when they enter the true ark, the Church of Christ. It may also serve to remind us of the hypocrite's outward good behavior, though his nature is not changed.　　　　　*Salter.*

7537. CONVERSION, Seeking. A soldier sought Mr. Wm. Reynolds and said, " My friend, I want a discharge." Supposing he meant a discharge from the army, he said he was afraid that would be hard to obtain, as he appeared to be recovering. " Oh," said the soldier, " that's not what I mean; I want a discharge from the devil's army. I've been fighting and serving in the ranks for twenty-five years, and I'm tired and sick of the service. I want to leave his ranks and enlist under the banner of the cross, and fight for Jesus the balance of my life." He became " a soldier of the cross."

7538. CONVERSION, Simile of. Here is a little shoot of an apple tree, cut off from the parent stem. The gardener says it is a very valuable shoot. It is from a tree of the choicest and rarest kind. But it has been cut off and lies dying on the ground. It can never live or bear fruit there. But the gardener seeks out a thrifty tree, and grafts this shoot into it, and soon it puts forth leaves, and in due time bears fruit. So it is that men are saved. They are cut off by sin and lie dying on the earth. Then the heavenly husbandman takes them up and grafts them upon Christ, the living tree, and they live.　　　　　*J. R. Miller.*

7539. CONVERSION, A Slave's. Cambo, a negro slave, gave the following account of his conversion:—" While in my own country (Guinea), me had no knowledge of the being of a God; me thought me should die like the beasts. After me was brought to America, and sold as a slave, as me and another servant of the name of Bess was working in the field, me began to sing one of my old country songs, 'It is time to go home;' when Bess say to me, 'Cambo, why you sing so for?' Me say, 'Me no sick, me no sorry, why me no sing?' Bess say, 'You better pray to your blessed Lord and Massah, to have mercy on your soul.' Me look round, me look up, me see no one to pray to; but the words sound in my ears, 'Better pray to your Lord and Massah.' By and by me fell bad—sun shine sorry—birds sing sorry—land look sorry, but Cambo sorrier than them all. Then me cry out, 'Mercy, mercy, Lord! on poor Cambo!'—By and by water come in my eyes, and glad come in my heart. Then sun look gay—woods look gay—birds sing gay —land look gay, but poor Cambo gladder than them all. Me love my Massah some; me want to love him more."

7540. CONVERSION, Sudden. Gelasius was a comic actor in the theatre, at Heliopolis. A burlesque of Christian ordinances was one day given for the entertainment of the heathen audience. A large bath tub was placed on the stage filled with warm water. In this Gelasius was dipped by the other actor, who pronounced over him the usual formula, " I baptize thee in the name of the Father and of the Son and of the Holy Ghost." When he came forth he was arrayed in white, after the custom with the newly baptized. A great change was observed in his appearance. His jesting air was gone, and his face wore a look of deep seriousness. He announced his conversion, saying, " I am a Christian. I will die as a Christian." When they heard this, and understood that he was in earnest, the mob rushed upon the stage, seized him, dragged him forth in his white robe, and stoned him to death, A. D. 297.

7541. CONVERSIONS, Superficial. The Russians remained pagans until the tenth century. At that time they attracted the attention of several religions. An emissary of Mohammedanism visited King Vladimir, but the king did not like their prohibition of pork and wine. Next came a representative of the Pope, who spoke for his religion, but King Vladimir was not favorably impressed by it. Next came a Jew, who spoke of the one true God and his laws. The king asked for their country. The Jew explained that they had a country but their God became angry with them and drove them from it. " What," said Vladimir, " you wish to teach others—you whom God has rejected and dismissed? If God had loved you and your law he would never have scattered you abroad; do you wish that we should suffer the same?" The Greek church was represented to him by a philosopher, who showed a picture of the last judgment to the king, and so explained it as to make him exclaim, " Happy are those who are on the right; woe to the sinners who are on the left." The king then sent a deputation to inquire into the Mohammedan and Greek religions. They came back disgusted with the first, but charmed with the second. They were astonished at the richness of the church which they visited in Constantinople, then the most gorgeous in the world, and were awestruck at the ceremonies which they beheld. The white sleeves of the priests they mistook for wings. At this they said to their guides, " All that we have seen is awful and majestic; but this is supernatural. We have seen young men with wings in dazzling robes, who without touching the ground chanted in the air, Holy! holy! holy! and this is what has most surprised us!" The Greeks replied, " What! do you not know that angels come down from heaven to mingle in our services?" " You are right," said the Russians, " send us home again: we need no further proof." Upon their glowing report in favor of the Greek religion, the king resolved to adopt it. In order to get it he thought he must conquer some Christian city, which he did; reducing Cherson in 992. Thereupon he was baptized, and taking with him a Christian wife and some priests, returned to set up the new religion in his empire. He proceeded at once to destroy the idols of heathenism. He ordered the wooden image of Prun to be dragged over the hills at the tails of horses, to be scourged at the same time by mounted pursuers, and then to be cast into the Dneiper. The people seeing the helplessness of the god under this gross insult, abandoned it with contempt. He then ordered all the people of Kieff to prepare for baptism. The people utterly ignorant of the meaning of the rite flocked with their families to the river, and standing in the water up to their necks, holding their children in their arms, were baptized in crowds, without giving them individual names. This kind of conversion is easy under despotic rule, and has proved a curse and hindrance to true religion.

7542. CONVERSION, Time of. He that is locked up in a dungeon, or otherwise immured within some darksome place, can, and may, easily discover the very moment of time, when either the least beam of the sun, or glimmer of skylight, shall break in upon him; whereas, on the other side, he that is in the open air is very sensible that the day is broke, that the sun is up, but cannot make out any certain account of the springing of the one, or the rising of the other. Thus it is in the matter of our spiritual calling; it is possible that a man may know the very time and moment when the day-spring from on high did visit him, when it was the good pleasure of God to dart into his soul the grace of his blessed Spirit, as in the case of St. Paul, the good centurion, the jailer, the Jewish converts, and some others.   *Salter.*

7543. CONVERSION, Transformation of. The transformation of the natural into the spiritual man is one of the most wonderful achievements of divine grace, and this is the illustration that Taylor gives of it: "St. Jerome tells us of the custom of the Empire when a tyrant was overcome; they used to break the head of the conqueror, and so it passed wholly for the new prince. So it is in the kingdom of grace. Sin is overcome, and a new heart is put into us, so that we may serve under a new head; instantly we have a new name given us, and we are esteemed a new creation."
Papers on Preaching.

7544. CONVERSION, Unintentional. A profligate young man was passing the church of a popular preacher in Philadelphia at the time of service, when one of his companions challenged him to enter. He answered "No, I would not go into such a place if Christ himself was preaching." Some weeks after he was led by the Holy Spirit to enter the church in spite of his resolution. He was struck with awe at the solemn silence of the place, though it was much crowded. The new-comer's attention was caught by the text, "I discerned among the youths a young man void of understanding." Prov. 7: 7. His conscience was smitten by the power of truth. He saw that he was the young man described. A view of his profligate life passed before his eyes, and, for the first time, he trembled under the feeling of sin. He remained in the church till the preacher and congregation had passed out; then slowly returned to his home. He had early received infidel principles, but the Holy Spirit led him to a life of virtue and holiness.

7545. CONVERSION, Unwilling. During the progress of a revival in Kansas, the church was crowded and aisles filled with extra seats. One of these was occupied by a well-known judge. All were invited to stand up who wished to be prayed for. Some one whispered to him, "Won't you get up? We want to clear the aisle." He declined, thinking that to rise then would lead the people to think that he had decided to seek religion. The pressure was such as to force the chair from under him, and he was compelled to stand up. His tall figure was at once observed by all, and prayer was offered for him. Thus involuntarily he became the subject of prayer. Christian laborers came to encourage him and congratulate him on his stand for religion. He felt himself committed. The holy spirit said, "Why not now?" He responded, "It shall be now." He crossed the line of destiny, and stood on the salvation side, wondering at the providence and mercy of God. God saves many who never intended to seek him. They become willing in the day of his power. The judge found what he did not seek, as have thousands, who from curiosity stood by the way as Jesus passed by.

7546. CONVERT, Crisis of the. Gen. Sherman, in his "Memoirs," calls attention to a very wise observation of Gen. Grant, made to him after the close of the first day's battle of Shiloh. He said, "At the crisis of the battle it often happens that both sides seem to be defeated. The side that is able, at this point, to renew the attack, is sure to win." This was true at Fort Donelson, and Shiloh, and many great battles. And there is a grand point here for the battle of life and the victory over sin in these tactics of the enemy. We are all very weak after a hard fight, and then become easily demoralized by things we could easily meet under ordinary circumstances. Young converts are specially sensitive after these fights with Satan, and above all times they need the sympathy and encouragement of older Christians. We need after the battle to stand with our armor on. After you have gone through a great ordeal, and have preserved your integrity, then beware you do not fall before some inferior force.   *A. D. Vail.*

7547. CONVERT, Enthusiastic. While Mr. Moody was laboring in Manchester, a young man, who struggled hard to enter in at the strait gate towards the close of the meeting, passed through amid many demonstrations of sacred joy. The next day Mr. Moody referred to his case in the course of his address, and whilst he was depicting the gladness produced by his newly gotten pardon, the young man himself sprang from his seat, and with overwhelming emotion cried out in the presence of thousands, "That's me! that's me!"

7548. CONVERT, Joy Over a. Walking one day along the seashore, I saw a number of people running to the water's edge, and a boat putting off in haste. It was after a youth who, in bathing, had got out of his depth and sunk. After remaining for a quarter of an hour under water, he was taken out, and restoratives promptly applied to rekindle, if possible, the spark of life. I waited with many more at the door of the building to ascertain whether he was likely to recover. Several came out, but to tell of no hope. At length a person carried out of the house, the bearer of better tidings, "He has drawn a breath! he has drawn a breath!" The crowd caught and quickly echoed the cry. I thought of the joy that is felt in heaven when a penitent sinner is seen crying for mercy; for just as an infant begins to breathe when it enters the world, so does the sinner begin to pray when he is newly born to God. It is at that very moment that he draws his first spiritual breath. *E. Cornwall.*

7549. CONVERT, Love for a. There is a parable of much tenderness, which explains why a proselyte is dearer to the Lord than even a Levite. Such proselyte is compared to a wild goat, which, brought up in the desert, joins itself freely to the flock, and which is cherished by the shepherd with especial love; since that his flock, which from its youth he had put forth in the morning and brought back at the evening, should love him was nothing strange; but this, that the goat, brought up in deserts and mountains, should attach itself to him, demanded an especial return of affection. *R. C. Trench.*

7550. CONVERT, Mock. In a Swiss village lived a pious pastor, whose preaching was greatly blessed, many being converted under his ministry. There lived in the same place an abandoned man, who turned the most serious matters into ridicule, and made a laughing-stock of the preacher's expressions. One morning he went early to the public-house, and began to intoxicate himself with liquor, profaning the name and word of God, and ridiculing the term conversion. "Now," said he, "I myself will become a convert," turning himself from one side to the other, and dancing about the room with a variety of foolish gestures. On going out of the room he fell down stairs, broke his neck, and died.

7551. CONVERT, A Persecuted. On the morning which succeeded the memorable night of Captain Hedley Vicars' conversion, he bought a large Bible, and placed it open on the table in his sitting-room, determined that an "open Bible" for the future should be his "colors." "It was to speak for me," he said, "before I was strong enough to speak for myself." His friends came as usual to his rooms, and did not altogether fancy the new colors. One remarked that he had "turned Methodist," and with a shrug retreated. Another ventured on the bolder measure of warning him not to become a hypocrite: "Bad as you were, I never thought you would come to this, old fellow." So, for the most part, for a time, his quarters were deserted by his late companions. During six or seven months he had to encounter no slight opposition at mess, and "had hard work," as he said, "to stand his ground." But the promise did not fail—"The righteous shall hold on his way, and he that hath clean hands, shall wax stronger and stronger." *Power.*

7552. CONVERT, Whitefield's. Whitefield had just finished one of his sermons, when a man came reeling up to him and said, "How do you do, Mr. Whitefield?" Whitefield replied, "I don't know you, sir." "Don't know me! why you converted me so many years ago in such a place." "I should not wonder," replied Mr Whitefield, "you look like one of my converts, for if the Lord had converted you you would have been a sober man."

7553. CONVERTS, Romish. Concerning the Roman Catholic mission to Congo, in Western Africa, commenced as early as 1490, a traveler says: "The presentation of beads, Agne Dei, images of the Madonna and saints; the splendid processions, the rich furniture, and solemn ceremonials of the church, dazzled the eyes of the savage natives, and made them view the gospel only as a gay and pompous pageant, in which it would be an amusement to join. The sacrament of baptism, to which the Catholics attach great importance, was chiefly recommended by a part of the ritual that consisted in putting into the mouth a certain quantity of salt, which in Congo is an extremely rare and valued commodity; and the missionaries were not a little disconcerted to find that the very form by which the natives expressed the holy ordinance was 'to eat salt.' Thus an immense body of people were speedily baptized and called Christians, but without any idea of the duties and obligations which the sacred name imposes."

7554. CONVERTS, Service of. They not only lay down their arms, and fight no more against Christ, but repair to his camp, and fight for Christ with those weapons before employed against him: as it is said of Jerome, Origen, and Tertullian, that they came into Canaan laden with Egyptian gold; that is, they came into the church full of excellent learning and abilities, with which they eminently served Jesus Christ. *John Flavel.*

7555. CONVERTS, Trials of. There is an insect which is accustomed to deposit its eggs in the very core of the *plumula*, or primary shoot of wheat, so that this shoot is completely destroyed by the larvæ. Did the plant possess no means within itself, no means of repairing this injury, the whole previous labor of the husbandman would, in this case, have been in vain. But this destruction occurring in the spring of the year, when the vegetable power of the plant is in its greatest vigor, an effect is produced somewhat analogous to that of heading down a fruit tree. Shoots immediately spring up from the knots, the plant becomes more firmly rooted, and produces probably a dozen stems and ears but for the temporary mischief it might have sent forth one only. Thus may it often occur that those early trials which appear almost to destroy the faith of young believers are their best friends. *Duncan.*

7556. CONVICTION, Biblical Figures of. Is set forth by different figures and expressions: *Wakening from sleep*, 1 Cor. 15: 34; Eph 5: 14. "*Pricked in the heart*," Acts 2: 37

It is important to observe the contrast between the effects of St. Peter's sermon on the day of Pentecost, when great numbers were "pricked in their hearts," and the effect produced on two other occasions, when many were "cut to the heart," Acts 5: 33 ; 7: 54. In the former case the effect was a salutary conviction of sin, leading to immediate inquiry, "What must we do?" In the others it led only to rage against the preachers—"They took counsel to slay them;" "they gnashed on" Stephen "with their teeth." *Smiting*—As if with holy anger and penitent shame; upon the breast, like the publican, Luke 18: 13 ; and the Jews, 23: 48; or on the thigh, like Ephraim, Jer. 31: 19. David's heart smote him, 1 Sam. 24: 5 ; 2 Sam. 24: 10. *Digging deep*, Luke 6: 48. *The prodigal son.*—The beautiful parable of the prodigal son, affords an illustration of the risings of conviction in an awakened conscience. "*When he came to himself,*" Luke 15: 17. What is sin but a state of unconscious sleep and blind infatuation? Conviction is the sleeper roused to thought and terror and concern. The Acts of the Apostles might well be studied as a record of the different results of conviction. How strikingly it shows that conviction of sin is not conversion, as we see in the case of Felix trembling under Paul's preaching, 24: 25; compared with those who heard Peter preach at Pentecost, 2: 37; with Lydia, 16: 14; or with the Philippian jailer, 16: 25–34.. It is the work of the Holy Ghost, John 16: 8.

Bowes.

7557. CONVICTION, Cowper's. Cowper said, "One moment I thought myself shut out from mercy by one chapter, and the next by another. The sword of the spirit seemed to guard the tree of life from my touch, and to flame against me in every avenue by which I attempted to approach it. I particularly remember, that the parable of the barren fig-tree was to me an inconceivable source of anguish; and I applied it to myself, with a strong persuasion in my mind, that when our Saviour pronounced a curse upon it, he had me in his eye, and pointed that curse directly at me."

7558. CONVICTION, Description of. An Irish soldier, who had formerly been in the navy, was asked how he came to think of coming to Christ after so many years of careless trifling. He said, "The Lord got his grapnel-irons a hold of me; he pulled on the starboard side, and then he pulled on the larboard side, till I could not hold out any longer, and so I surrendered the ship." *Harris.*

7559. CONVICTION, Light in. "You see not the motes in the air, though numerous as the leaves of the forest, till the glowing ray reveals them to the eye. The river seems to flow stainless and clear till the wondrous microscope displays to the view a hundred loathsome creatures enclosed in every drop that glitters beneath the sun." You discover not the sin of your heart till the Holy Spirit throws its light upon it.

7560. CONVICTION, Need of. Till God show you the face of sin in the glass of the law, making the scorpions and serpents that lurk in the law and in your own consciences, come hissing about you, and smiting you with their deadly stings; till you have had some sick nights and sorrowful days for sin, you will never go up and down seeking an interest in the blood of his sacrifice with tears. But if ever this be thy condition, then wilt thou know the worth of a Saviour, then wilt thou value the blood of sprinkling. *John Flavel.*

7561. CONVICTION, Quenched. I knew a man that was once, as I thought, hopefully awakened about his condition. Yea, I knew two that were so awakened. But in course of time they began to draw back, and to incline again to their lusts. Wherefore, God gave them up to the company of three or four men, who, in less than three years, brought them round to the gallows, where they were hanged like dogs, because they refused to live like honest men. *Bunyan.*

7562. CONVICTION, Relief from. A young man, whose soul was passing through the deep waters of conviction, retired to a grove to pray. Ease from his heavy burden was all he desired, and he deliberately asked God to give him quiet by taking his Holy Spirit from him. It was a fearful prayer, but it was answered. He arose with all his burden gone. For twenty years he lived on, careless and unconcerned, and when death came to him he related this fact in his history to a friend standing beside him. "I know," he said, "that I shall soon be in hell. Nothing can save me. My doom is sealed, and yet I am quite indifferent to the future." *William Jones.*

7563. CONVICTION, Repentance and. Two brothers started to go West to seek their fortune. One had money, the other had not. When they got to the frontier the one without money murdered the other, and taking his money fled to California. Doctors took the head of the murdered man and preserved it in alcohol. No proof of the murder could be found. No one was present when the deed was done. The brother was accused, but declared his innocence. No eye was there but his and God's. He was brought before jury and judge, and declared his innocence. The dead face of his brother was brought into court. He gazed on it, he fainted, and fell to the floor, and confessed his sin. There is a time when all these unconfessed sins will come in before us, tramp, tramp, tramp, till they all come back. When a man comes and throws himself on his knees in the inquiry room, there is hope of him. *Moody.*

7564. CONVICTION, Revelations of. The law is only God's looking-glass dropped down from heaven to enable man to see himself. When a man measures himself by himself, or by his neighbor, he is all right, but when he measures himself by God he appears bad. A little while before the Chicago fire I promised one morning to take my children out riding. My boy clapped his hands and said, "Papa, won't you take me to Lincoln Park to see the bears?" I promised I would. Soon after I went out the boy teased his mother to get him ready so as not to lose any time. To please him she did so. Then he wanted to go out and play, and she let him go. He got into the dirt and got covered with it. When I drove up I refused to take him in. He asked, "Why?" I told him his face was dirty, but I couldn't get him to believe it until I took him inside and held him before a looking-glass. That stopped his mouth at once. But I didn't take the looking-glass to wash his face with. *Moody.*

7565. CONVICTION and Salvation. A poor Indian, who had been a very wicked man, but who had become pious, was desired to tell how it was that he had been led to Christ. He said, "I was in the mud, I tried to get out, and I could not. I tried the harder, and the harder I tried the faster I sunk. I found I must put forth all my strength; but I went down deeper, and deeper, and deeper. I found I was going all over in the mire; I gave the death-yell, and found myself in the arms of Jesus Christ."

7566. CONVICTION, Siege of. Psalms 110: 3. "Thy people shall be willing in the day of thy power, or of thine armies." The Lord Jesus sent forth his armies of prophets, apostles, evangelists, pastors, teachers, under the conduct of his spirit, armed with that two-edged sword, the word of God. But that is not all; he causes armies of conviction and spiritual troubles to begird and straiten them on every side, so that they know not what to do. These convictions, like a shower of arrows, strike into their consciences. By these convictions he batters down all their vain hopes, and levels them with the earth. Now all their weak pleas and defences, from the general mercy of God, the example of others prove but as paper walls. These shake their hearts, even to the very foundation, and overturn every high thought that exalts itself against the Lord. The day in which Christ summons the soul by such messengers as these, is a day of distress within; yea, such a day of trouble, that none is like it. But though it be so, yet Satan hath so deeply intrenched himself in the mind and will, that the soul yields not at the first summons, till its provisions within are spent, and all its towers of pride and walls of vain confidence be undermined by the gospel, and shaken down; and then the soul sees its need of Christ. Oh, now it would be glad of terms, any terms, if it may but save its life; let all go as prey to the conqueror. Now it sends many such messages as these to Christ, who is come now to the very gates of the soul; "Mercy, Lord, mercy; oh were I assured thou wouldst receive, spare and pardon me, I would open to thee next moment!" Thus the soul is "shut to the faith of Christ," Gal. 3: 23, reduced to the greatest strait and oss; and now the merciful king, whose only design is to conquer the heart, hangs forth the white flag of mercy before the soul, giving hope that it shall be spared, pitied and pardoned, though so long in rebellion against him, if yet it will yield itself to Christ. Now the will spontaneously receives Christ: that royal fort submits and yields; all the affections open to him. *John Flavel.*

7567. CONVICTION, Treatment of. In St. Dennis Hotel, in Broadway, New York, I was summoned to visit a sick young man, who came from Charleston with a widowed mother. I had known her there. They had been at Saratoga, and had come back to New York, and in this hotel the young man was lying to die. His mother had sent for another clergyman to visit him, and that clergyman said that the poor young man was crazy; and when I asked that religious brother, "What did you do to him?" he said, "Do? I tried to pacify him; I tried to quiet him; I said, 'We will not talk, but say a little prayer,' and I left him in peace." His mother was not satisfied, and sent for me. He lay before me, a splendid youth of nineteen, his eyes like jets of the brilliancy of a diamond. "Dr. Tyng," said the young man, "my mother has always told me that I must be converted; that I could not be saved except I was converted. I am not converted. How can I be converted? Can I be converted? O, tell me—how, how can I be converted?" I sat by the side of that youth, and told him the story of Jesus. I showed him the simplicity of the gospel plan of salvation. I bade him realize that his heavenly Father had received and accepted him in Christ when Christ willingly died to bear his load, and he was to come in the simplest faith of a little child, and rest himself gratefully, hopefully upon it. We spent an hour in conversation. Twenty-four hours after I called again. O, how changed that face! It shone like an angel's. He reached out his long, tapering hand to me with the sweetest possible smile, and said, "O, sir, I understand it! I understand it. Love for Jesus is conversion! Love for Jesus is conversion! Sir, all night I was asking Jesus to let me love him; to show me how to love him; and I feel to-day as if my whole soul was overflowing with love to Jesus. Is that conversion?" "My dear Julian, that is conversion." *Dr. S. H. Tyng.*

7568. CONVICTION, Two Voices in. A convicted German soldier said that there were two voices in him; one telling him to go on in sin and fear nothing; the other calling on him to reform, and serve Christ. So it is in conviction. St. Paul found it so. See seventh chapter of Romans. Satan pleads pleasure and self-indulgence, protests against reform, but the conscience and the Holy Spirit cry "Repent and reform." He "mounts the chariot of the sun" who obeys the good voice.

7569. CONVICTION, Unexpected. When Whitefield was preaching at Exeter, a man went with his pockets filled with stones, intending to throw them at the preacher. No sooner was the text announced, than he pulled out a stone; but God sent the word into his heart. The stone soon fell to the ground, and after the sermon the man went up to Whitefield, confessing his intention, and saying, "Sir, I came here intending to give you a broken head, but God has given me a broken heart." The man afterwards became a Christian.

7570. CORNER-STONE, Christ the. When the

temple was built, a stone, intended by the original designers for this purpose, seems to have been rejected by the builders, and cast aside as useless; but, either from necessity, or from some divine intimation, it was sought out and employed as God directed. Now, this event was a type, and its fulfillment is given by Christ himself, according to the harmonious account of three evangelists, to show that his treatment had been symbolized and predicted. Peter, in one of his addresses to the rulers, elders, and scribes, affirms: "This is the stone which was set at naught of you builders, which is become the head of the corner." Christ is thus called a corner-stone. 1. In reference to his being the foundation of the Christian faith; Eph. 2: 20. 2. In reference to the importance and conspicuousness of the place he occupies; 1 Pet. 2: 6. 3. As a projecting corner-stone is likely to be stumbled against, so it is not surprising that the doctrine of Christ, and him crucified, would prove an offence, and a stone of stumbling to unbelievers. *Biblical Treasury.*

7571. CORRECTION, Gracious Reception of. Demetrius, in a speech relating to a gift of corn to the hungry Athenians, spoke incorrectly. Some one gave him the right word, to which he responded. "For this correction I bestow upon you five thousand bushels more."

7572. CORRECTION, Severity in. Rev. Andrew Fuller, at a meeting of ministers, took occasion to correct an erroneous opinion, delivered by one of his brethren; and he laid on his censure so heavily, that Dr. Ryland called out, "Brother Fuller! brother Fuller! you can never admonish a mistaken friend, but you must take up a sledge-hammer and knock his brains out!"

7573. CORRECTION, Wisdom in. Correction is like physic, not to be given without good advice and caution; if it be too frequent, it works no more than our meat with us; some faults that are lesser, may be pardoned without danger (Eccles. 7: 21). We use a difference when we go about to hew a rugged piece of timber, and to smooth a little stick, which you can bend as you please. A fit season must be observed. Cut your trees at some time of the year, and you kill them; prune them at other times, and they thrive much the better. Horses too strait reined in, are apt to rise up with their forefeet; when they are allowed convenient liberty with their heads they go better.
Swinnock.

7574. CORRUPTION, Keeping down. My gardeners were removing a large tree which grew near a wall, and as it would weaken the wall to stub up the roots, it was agreed that the stump should remain in the ground. But how were we to prevent the stump from sprouting, and so disarranging the gravel walk. The gardener's prescription was to cover it with a layer of salt. I mused awhile, and thought that the readiest way to keep down my ever-sprouting corruptions in future would be to sow them well with the salt of grace. O Lord, help me so to do. *Spurgeon.*

7575. CORRUPTION, Natural. The corrupt heart is like an ant's nest, on which, while the stone lieth, none of them appear; but take off the stone, and stir them up but with the point of a straw, you will see what a swarm is there, and how lively they be. Just such a sight would thy heart afford thee, did the Lord but withdraw the restraint he has laid upon it, and suffer Satan to stir it up by temptation. If I wished to destroy an idol temple, I would not begin by stripping off some of its gew-gaw ornaments, but strike at once at the foundation. It is alike useless to endeavor to detach worldly men from the pleasures and vain amusements with which they glorify their idol, the world; we must overthrow the stony foundation of nature's corruption. *Salter.*

7576. CORRUPTIONS, Destruction of. When Sir Christopher Wren was engaged in demolishing the ruins of old St. Paul's in order to make room for his new cathedral, he used a battering-ram with which thirty men continued to beat upon a part of the wall for a whole day. The workmen, not discerning any immediate effect, thought this a waste of time; but Wren, who knew that the internal motion thus communicated must be operating, encouraged them to persevere. On the second day, the wall began to tremble at the top, and fell in a few hours. If our prayers and repentances do not appear to overcome our corruptions, we must continue still to use these gracious battering-rams, for in due time, by faith in Jesus Christ, the power of evil shall be overthrown. Lord, enable me to give hearty blows by the power of thy Holy Spirit until the gates of hell in my soul shall be made to totter and fall.
Spurgeon.

7577. CORRUPTIONS, Discovery of. In regard to our corruptions, we may learn something from the difference of glasses. You behold yourselves in your common looking-glasses, and see yourselves so fine that you admire your persons and dress. But when you view yourself in a microscope, how much may you behold in that fine skin to be ashamed of! What disfigurement to the eye! And instead of smoothness, irregularity, uncomeliness, and even impurity. So, if you will look upon yourself through the glass of faith, that glass would show you much of the corruption of your sinful nature still cleaving to you—your tempers crooked, your graces misshapen and deformed, and so much corruption cleaving to every action of your lives that would make you sin-sick that you have known God so long, and are like him so little. *Salter.*

7578. CORRUPTIONS, Indulgence of. The man of the world in the olden time bowed to the fallen statue of Jupiter, by way of bespeaking the favor of the god in the event of his being again lifted on his pedestal. What are those provisions for the flesh, which too many Christians so readily make, but a kind of homage to the old man whom they profess to have renounced? *Spurgeon.*

7579. COURAGE, Biblical. *A lion,* Prov. 28: 1; 2 Sam. 17: 10. *A goodly horse* in the battle, Zech. 10: 3. *A soldier,* brave and fearless. See Deut. 20; 5. *A defenced city* and *iron pillars*, and *brazen walls*, Jer 1: 18. *Setting the face* like a *lion*, 1 Chron. 12; 8. *Setting the face* like *flint*, Isa. 50: 7. *Setting the face* like *adamant*, "harder than flint," Ezek. 3: 9. "*Valiant for the truth*," Jer. 9: 3; Heb. 11: 34. "Not *ashamed*," Rom. 1: 16; 2 Tim. 1: 8; 1 Pet. 4: 16. Not *afraid*, nor *dismayed*, nor *confounded*." "In nothing *terrified*," Phil. 1: 20–28. 2 Pet. 1: 5. "Add to your faith virtue." Christian manliness or courage. Observe the connection —*courage*, the result of faith, tempered by knowledge, or moral discernment, enlightened by conscientiousness, and leading to love. 2 Tim. 1: 7. 1 Chron. 19: 13. A beautiful exemplification of the wise remark, "Duties are ours, results are God's." "Be of good courage." It is important to observe how frequently this, or some similar charge, was given to many chief ministers and leaders of the church at the *commencement* of their work; as in the case of Moses, Joshua, Solomon, Jeremiah, Ezekiel, the Apostles, the Seventy, St. Paul, &c. Like the oft repeated charge, "Be strong."   *Bowes.*

7580. COURAGE, Christian. Soon after the beginning of the reign of bloody Mary in England, an officer was sent to bring Bishop Latimer to London, of which he had notice six hours before he arrived. Instead of fleeing, he prepared for his journey to London; and, when the officer arrived, he said to him, "My friend, you are welcome. I go as willingly to London, to give an account of my faith, as ever I went to any place in the world. And I doubt not, but as the Lord made me worthy formerly to preach the Word before two excellent princes, he will now enable me to bear witness to the truth before the third, either to her eternal comfort or discomfort." As he rode on this occasion through Smithfield, he remarked "that Smithfield had groaned for him a long time."

7581. COURAGE, Fear and. At a certain engagement between the Moslems and the infidels. the latter thought the former only an insignificant handful, and Abu Jahl said, "one camel would be as much as they could all eat." After a while they seemed to see two Moslems to one of themselves. Their courage had given place to fear and changed the picture.

7582. COURAGE, Justice and. Agesilaus being asked which was the better virtue, courage or justice, said, "Courage would be good for nothing, if there were no justice; and if all men were just, there would be no need of courage."

7583. COURAGE, Martyrs'. When the executioner went behind Jerome of Prague to set fire to the pile, "Come here," said the martyr, "and kindle it before mine eyes; for if I dreaded such a sight, I should never have come to this place when I had a free opportunity to escape." The fire was kindled, and he then sang a hymn, which was soon finished by the encircling flames. Algerius, an Italian martyr, thus wrote from his prison a little before his death: "Who would believe that in this dungeon I should find a paradise so pleasant; in a place of sorrow and death, tranquillity, and hope and life; where others weep, I rejoice." Wishart, when in the fire which removed him from the world, exclaimed, "The flame doth torment my body, but no whit abates my spirits."

7584. COURAGE, Ministerial. About 1645, Dr. Harris, minister of Hanwell, England, frequently had military officers quartered at his house. A party of them indulged much in swearing. The doctor noticed this, and on the following Sabbath preached from these words· "Above all things, my brethren, swear not." This so enraged the soldiers, who judged the sermon was intended for them, that they swore they would shoot him if he preached on the subject again. He was not to be intimidated; and on the following Sabbath he preached from the same text, and inveighed in still stronger terms against the vice of profanity. As he was preaching, a soldier levelled his carbine at him, but he went on to the conclusion without the slightest hesitation.

7585. COURAGE, Rash. "A soldier in the Spartan army possessed extraordinary beauty of person, and at the same time remarkable daring of character. When called to fight he stripped off his clothes, anointed his body with oil, and, taking a spear in one hand and a sword in the other, rushed into the thick of the fight, striking down his adversaries on every hand. He returned from the battle without a single wound, marvelously preserved from danger. He was honored with a chaplet for his valor, but at the same time was fined a thousand drachmas for daring to go forth without his armor." Take to yourselves the whole armor of God, and then go forth to the battle with sin.

7586. COURAGE, Successful. "The soldiers of Sylla, when digging trenches at the order of their master, begged him to lead them against the enemy. He interpreted their request into an unwillingness to work, and, pointing to a very difficult position that required to be taken, bade them to show their valor by advancing sword in hand and seizing the post at once. The spirit of the men carried them forward, and, despite the difficulties in the way, they gained the spot." A dauntless spirit is half the battle, and often wins unexpected successes.

7587. COURAGE, Test of. A monk repeatedly besought his abbot, the wise Pachomius, to pray that he might become a martyr. The abbot reproved him, saying, "This is mere pride." Still the monk desired to be a martyr. So one day the abbot said, "Go thy way, my son; behold, now is the accepted time! behold, now is the day of salvation! nevertheless, be not high-minded, but fear!" and he sent him out to cut rushes on the banks of the Nile. There came along a band of negroes, who seized him, tied his hands behind him, and carried him away to the mountains. They placed him before a fetish, and insisted upon his adoring it. He stoutly refused. The negroes joined in their death song, and danced around him, brandishing their swords and spears. Martyr-dom lost its attractions to the monk. His courage gave way, and he fell down before the idol. After this he was permitted to return to his companions, which he did less self-confident and much ashamed.

7588. COURAGE, True. An officer rode up to a battery of cannon, who, observing another officer at his side looking pale, turned in his saddle to accost him, saying, "You are afraid!" "True," replied his comrade, "and were you as much afraid as I am you would turn tail!"

7589. COURAGE, Victorious. There is a story of a young man that came up with a little handful of men to attack a king who had a great army of 3,000 men. The young man had only 500, and the king sent a messenger to the young man, saying that he need not fear to surrender, for he would treat him mercifully. The young man called up one of his soldiers and said: "Take this dagger and drive it to your heart;" and the soldier took the dagger and drove it to his heart. And calling up another, he said to him, "Leap into yonder chasm," and the man leaped into the chasm. The young man then said to the messenger, "Go back and tell your king I have got 500 men like these. We will die, but we will never surrender. And tell your king another thing, that I will have him chained with my dog inside of half an hour." And when the king heard that, he did not dare to meet them, and his army fled before them like chaff before the wind, and within twenty-four hours he had that king chained with his dog. *Moody.*

7590. COURTESY, Examples of. During the Roman social war the commanders of the hostile armies met at a place midway between the camps. Scato, the Marsian general, asked a consul of the other side how he should address him. Sextus Pompeius, the Roman general, answered for the consul,—"As a friend by inclination; as an enemy from necessity."

7591. COURTESY, Power of. Courtesy allureth men's minds, as fair flowers do their eyes. Alexander the Great got the hearts of his foot-soldiers by calling them his fellow footmen. Aristotle, the better to insinuate into his hearers, read not to them, as other philosophers used to do, from a lofty seat or desk, but walking and talking with them familiarly, as with his friends, in Apollo's porch, he made them great philosophers. Vespasian was as highly esteemed by the people for his courtesy as Coriolanus contemned and condemned of all for his rusticity. With one churlish breath Rehoboam lost ten tribes, whom he would and might not recover with his blood. The Turks' salutation at this day is, *Salaum aleek*, Peace be to thee : the reply is *Aleek salaum*, Peace be to thee also. Charles V. was renowned for his courtesy: when he passed by John Frederick, the Elector of Saxony, he ever put off his hat and bowed to him, though he were his prisoner, and had been taken by him in battle. And when he had in his power Melancthon, Pomeran, and other divines of the reformed religion, he courteously dismissed them. As

he is the best Christian that is most humble, so is he the truest gentleman that is most courteous. Your haughty upstarts the French call gentle-villains. *Trapp.*

7592. COURTSHIP AND MARRIAGE. "Their courtship was carried on in poetry." Alas! many an enamored pair have courted in poetry, and after marriage lived in prose. *J. Foster.*

7593. COVENANT, Comfort of the. William Lyford was asked a short time before dissolution the reason of his hope for the future. Stretching forth his hand he said, "Here is the grave, the wrath of God, and devouring flame, the just punishment of sin, on the one side; and here am I, a poor sinful soul, on the other side. But this is my comfort, the covenant of grace, which is established upon so many sure promises, hath saved all. There is an act of oblivion passed in heaven; 'I will forgive their iniquities, and their sins will I remember no more!' This is the blessed privilege of all within the covenant, among whom I am one."

7594. COVENANT, Types of the. Hagar, the handmaid, and a bond-woman, stands the perfect type of the covenant of law; Sarah, the true wife, and a free-woman, the representative of the covenant of grace. The first son, Ishmael, born according to nature, a type of the Jew, who by natural birth came into covenant. The second son, Isaac, born contrary to nature, of parents who were "as good as dead," a type of the resurrection life of this dispensation, the life from above springing out of death. Gal. 4 : 21–31.   *A. Jukes.*

7595. COVETOUSNESS, Absorption of. Take the case of a strictly honest man possessed by this passion. He becomes the very type of rapacious grasping, greedy hoarding, and intolerable meanness. On a recent railroad ride, a plain, intelligent old gentleman, whom I invited to share my seat, gave me the history of such a man, a German by birth, who began his career in his adopted country penniless. He invested the first few hundred dollars he saved in a small farm in western New York. To this he added from year to year, until he became known as one of the most thrifty farmers in all the State. He shaved notes; he took advantage of his neighbors' necessities in buying and selling cattle and lands. His life was an "enormous suction" of everything within his reach. After he became a millionaire, he would mow all day at the head of his twenty men, and keep his accounts nights and Sundays. He never was known to give a dollar to any benevolent object. At last he died, "as a fool dieth," from overwork in carrying railroad ties upon his shoulders from morning to night for two weeks, in order to show a posse of men in his employ that the timbers were not too heavy for one man to handle. He left one million eight hundred thousand dollars personal property, besides his immense farms. Jeremiah must have had such a man before his eye when he wrote, "As the partridge sitteth on eggs and hatcheth them not" (the poor silly bird not knowing that they were addled from the start), "so he that getteth riches, and not by right, shall leave them in the midst of his days, and at his end shall be a fool."

President Foss.

7596. COVETOUSNESS, Baseness of. Caligula, emperor of Rome, seemed to be inflamed with the passion for touching money. He would frequently walk upon heaps of gold, and as the pieces lay spread out in a large room, he would roll himself over them naked. He forced men in their sickness to make him their heir, and if they recovered after making their wills, he poisoned them. The palace was made a common brothel that his revenues might be increased thereby.

7597. COVETOUSNESS, Biblical Emblems and Expressions of. *Wolves*—Proverbial for their rapacity and savage nature, Ezek. 22: 27. *Greedy dogs*, that can never have enough, Isa. 56: 11. *The horseleech* (or bloodsucker), Prov. 30: 15, with its two-forked tongue, which gorges blood, and having emptied itself, craves for more. *The four insatiable things:* the grave—the barren womb—the parched land—the fire, Prov. 30: 15, 16. The man "*greedy of gain*," Prov. 1: 19; 15: 27; "*hasting to be rich*," Prov. 28: 22; who "*enlargeth his desire* as hell" (or the grave); that is (insatiable) as death, that "cannot be satisfied," Hab. 2: 5; who makes "*gold his hope*," Job 31: 24; and turns "aside after lucre," 1 Sam. 8: 3; whose eye is evil, Prov. 28: 22; and whose heart "walketh after his eyes," Job 31: 7. The Greek word ordinarily used for covetousness means "a desire of having more than belongs to one."—*Parkhurst.*——The covetous man's desire is "only to have enough;" but what is enough? The pleasure of what we have, is lost by coveting more. Another Greek word is also used, which means the love of silver or money; see 2 Tim. 3: 2, where this is marked as a prominent sign of "the last days;" see Eccles. 5: 10; 1 Tim. 6: 10. Our English word *miser* is not more nearly allied in sound than it is in sense to its derivation—misery. Few sins have brought more bitter fruit than covetousness. Examples are Lot—Laban—Baalam—Achan—Saul—Ahab—Gehazi—Haman—Rich young ruler—Pharisees—Ananias and Sapphira. *Bowes.*

7598. COVETOUSNESS, Blight of. The covetous man is like the spider. He does nothing but lay his wits to catch every fly, gaping only for a booty of gain; so yet more in that whilst he makes nets for these flies, he consumeth his own bowels, so that which is his life is his death. And yet he is at least to be pitied, because he makes himself miserable; like wicked Ahab, the sight of another man's vineyard makes him sick; he wants it for himself. He hates his neighbors as bad as he is hated by them, and would sell his best friend, if he had one, for a groat. He pines his body that he may damn his soul; and whenever disappointed of his expected gain, through the accursed discontent of his mind, he would dispatch himself, but that he is loth to cast away the money on a cord. *Bp. Hall.*

7599. COVETOUSNESS, Fatal. In the siege of Cassilinum, Hannibal so reduced the citadel that there was a great famine. One soldier possessed a mouse that he might have eaten, and so appeased his cruel hunger, but he preferred selling it to a comrade for two hundred pence. He was destroyed by the famine, and did not live to enjoy his money, while if he had not sold the mouse, it is said he might have saved his own life.

7600. COVETOUSNESS, Folly of. Covetous men must be the sport of Satan, for their grasping avarice neither lets them enjoy life nor escape from the second death. They are held by their own greed as surely as beasts with cords, or fish with nets, or men with chains. They may be likened to those foolish apes which in some countries are caught by narrow-necked vessels; into these corn is placed, the creatures thrust in their hands, and when they have filled them they cannot draw out their fists unless they let go the grain; sooner than do this they submit to be captured. How much covetous men are like these beasts. *Spurgeon.*

7601. COVETOUSNESS, Fruitlessness of. Rich people who are covetous are like the cypress tree: they may appear well, but are fruitless; so rich persons have the means to be generous, yet some are not so; but they should consider they are only trustees for what they possess, and should show their wealth to be more in doing good, than merely in having it. They should not reserve their benevolence for purposes after they are dead; for those who give not till they die, show that they would not then, if they could keep it any longer. *Bp. Hall.*

7602. COVETOUSNESS, No Cure for. The great and learned Hippocrates wished a consultation of all the physicians in the world, that they might advise together upon the means how to cure covetousness. It is now above two thousand years since he had this desire. After him a thousand, and a thousand philosophers have employed their endeavors to cure this insatiable dropsy. All of them have lost their labor therein; the evil rather increases than declines under the multitude of remedies. There have been a number in former ages sick of it; and this wide hospital of the world is still as full of such patients as ever it was. *Wanley.*

7603. COVETOUSNESS, Penalty of. Marcus Crassus, a Roman, was possessor of three hundred talents, when called to be consul. By covetous practices he became owner of vast estates, kept an open feast for all Rome upon a thousand tables, and gave to every citizen corn to support him three months. Before entering upon a Parthian expedition he was worth seven thousand one hundred talents. Thirsting for gold he led his army against the Parthians, by whom he was overthrown. His head was chopped off and molten gold poured down his throat by Surinas, the Parthian General—in mockery of Crassus' unquenchable avarice.

7604. COVETOUSNESS, Punishment of. An oriental story says many years ago there lived in Egypt an old man named Amin. A time of great famine came upon the land, just as there was once in the days of Joseph. Amin had a great store of wheat in his granaries. When bread began to get scarce, his neighbors came to him to buy grain. But he refused to sell it to them. He said he was going to keep his stock till all the rest of the grain in the land was gone, because then he could get a higher price for it. Many died; and yet this selfish man kept his stores locked up. At last the starving people were ready to give him any price he asked for his grain. He took the great iron key of his vast granary. He opened the door and went in. Worms had entered the great heaps of his once beautiful grain, and destroyed it all. Hungry as the people were, they yet raised a great shout of gladness at what had happened. But such was the effect of the disappintment on the old man himself, that he fell dead at the door of his granary. His selfishness killed him.

7605. COVETOUSNESS, Rebuke of. Semiramis built a monument for herself, with this inscription: "Whatever king wants treasure, if he open this tomb he may be satisfied." Darius, therefore, opening it, found no treasure, but another inscription of this import: "If thou wert not a wicked person and of insatiable covetousness, thou wouldst not disturb the mansions of the dead."

7606. COVETOUSNESS, Snare of. Do you know how they catch monkeys in Africa? They get plenty of cocoa nuts, and scoop them out, leaving a little hole just large enough for monkey to put his paw in. Rice and dried fruit are thrust into the cocoa nut; something, at any rate, which monkeys are fond of, and they are then scattered about in the woods. Pretty soon the monkeys come out of their hiding-places and peep around. Not a person in sight. They spy, however, the cocoa nuts with their sharp, bright eyes, and having a good deal of curiosity, jump down to examine them. "Ah! ah! something good!" they chatter away. In go their paws through the hole, grabbing the rice and dried fruit. But they cannot get their paws out again. Of course they cannot while they hold on so. They are caught. Ah, monkey, you are caught! The man will capture you. You did not think, I dare say; yet this does not help you. But let go! let go! It is not too late yet! Monkey will not let go. The man will have him sure and fast.

S. S. Advocate.

7607. COWARDICE, Ashamed of. A Michigan soldier lay wounded in the hospital at Gettysburg. His regiment had been ordered to fall back, and in doing so he had been wounded in the back. To him this was a disgrace, and troubled him greatly. The chaplain reasoned with him and explained all the circumstances to his parents. With the love and tenderness that flows from a mother's heart, she wrote him that for thirty months he had been an active volunteer; now he was to be a suffering one. She prayed that God would comfort him. The father wrote, " As to David's wound in his back, it need give him no uneasiness. None who know him will suppose it to be there on account of cowardice." On a pleasant

September day David's ransomed spirit went home to be with Jesus.

7608. COWARDICE, Cause of. "I am in the habit," writes a sea-captain, "of reading the Scriptures to the crew. I have suffered much lately at sea, having been dismasted, and had all my boats washed away, a little to the westward of Cape Clear. I then had an opportunity of seeing who was trustworthy, and I found the most unprincipled men the most useless and the greatest cowards in this awful gale, and the Bible men altogether the reverse, most useful and courageous."

7609. COWARDICE, Instructive. A fawn one day said to her mother, "Mother, you are bigger than a dog, and swifter and better winded, and you have horns to defend yourself; how is it that you are so afraid of the hounds?" She smiled and said, "All this, my child, I know full well; but no sooner do I hear a dog bark, than somehow or other, my heels take me off as fast as they can carry me." *Æsop.*

7610. COWARDICE, Penalty of. It is said that a tall, stalwart Indian is often seen about the streets of Virginia City, dressed in calico, like a squaw. He is compelled by the Piutes to to wear woman's clothes for cowardice shown in battle several years since. If all of us who have been cowards in the conflicts of life were compelled to wear calico, what a terrible figure prints would reach! *Anon.*

7611. COWARDICE, Religious. A coward in the field is like the wise man's fool: his heart is at his mouth, and he doth not know what he does profess; but a coward in his faith is like a fool in his wisdom: his mouth is in his heart, and he dare not profess what he does know. I had rather not know the good I should do, than not do the good I know. It is better to be beaten with few stripes than with many. *Warwick.*

7612. CREATION, Benevolence in. We are raised by science to an understanding of the infinite wisdom and goodness which the Creator has displayed in all his works. Not a step can we take in any direction without perceiving the most extraordinary traces of design; and the skill everywhere conspicuous is calculated in so vast a proportion of instances to promote the happiness of living creatures, and especially of ourselves, that we feel no hesitation in concluding that, if we knew the whole scheme of Providence, every part would appear to be in harmony with a plan of absolute benevolence. Independently, however, of this most consoling inference, the delight is inexpressible of being able to follow the marvelous works of the Great Author of nature, and to trace the unbounded power and exquisite skill which are exhibited by the minutest as well as the mightiest parts of his system. *Brougham.*

7613. CREATION, Comfort from. When Mr. Simeon, of Cambridge, was on his dying bed, his biographer relates that, "after a short pause, he looked round with one of his bright smiles, and asked, 'What do you think especially gives me comfort at this time? The creation! Did Jehovah create the world or did I? I think he did: now if he made the world, he can sufficiently take care of me.'" Take as an illustration of the power of God as a a creator, the inconceivable velocity with which he made the heavenly bodies to move through infinite space. The velocity of a ship is from eight to twelve miles an hour; of a race-horse from twenty to thirty miles; of a bird, say from fifty to sixty miles; and of the clouds, in a violent hurricane, from eighty to one hundred miles an hour. The motion of a ball from a loaded cannon is incomparably swifter than any of the motions now stated; but of the velocity of such a body we have a less accurate idea; because, its rapidity being so great, we cannot trace it distinctly by the eye, through its whole range, from the mouth of the cannon to the object against which it is impelled. By experiments, it has been found, that its rate of motion is from 480 to 800 miles in an hour, but it is retarded every moment, by the resistance of the air and the attraction of the earth. This velocity, however, great as it is, bears no sensible proportion to the rate of motion which is found among the celestial orbs. That such enormous masses of matter should move at all, is wonderful: but when we consider the amazing velocity with which they are impelled, we are lost in astonishment. The planet Jupiter, in describing his circuit round the sun, moves at the rate of 29,000 miles an hour. The planet Venus, one of the nearest and most brilliant of the celestial bodies, and about the same size as the earth, is found to move through the spaces of the firmament at the rate of 76,000 miles an hour; and the planet Mercury, with a velocity of no less than 103,000 miles an hour, or 1,750 miles in a minute, a motion two hundred times swifter than that of a cannon ball. These velocities will appear still more astonishing, if we consider the magnitude of the bodies which are thus impelled, and the immense forces which are requisite to carry them along in their courses. However rapidly a ball flies from the mouth of a cannon, it is the flight of a body only a few inches in diameter; but one of the bodies, whose motion has been just now stated, is eighty-nine thousand miles in diameter, and would comprehend, within its vast circumference, more than a thousand globes as large as the earth! The planet Saturn, one of the slowest moving bodies of our system, a globe 900 times larger than the earth, is impelled through the regions of space at the rate of 22,000 miles an hour, carrying along with him two stupendous rings, and seven moons larger than ours, through his whole course round the central luminary. Were we placed within a thousand miles of this stupendous globe (a station which superior beings may occasionally occupy), where its hemisphere, encompassed by its magnificent rings, would fill the whole extent of our vision; the view of such a ponderous and glorious object flying with such amazing velocity before us, would infinitely exceed every idea of grandeur we can derive from terrestrial scenes, and overwhelm our powers with astonishment and awe. Under such an emotion, we could only

exclaim, "Great and marvelous are thy works, Lord God Almighty!" The ideas of strength and power implied in the impulsion of such enormous masses of matter through the illimitable tracts of space, are forced upon the mind with irresistible energy, far surpassing what any abstract propositions or reasonings can convey; and constrain us to exclaim, "Who is a strong Lord like unto thee? Thy right hand is become glorious in power! The Lord God omnipotent reigneth!" *Illustrations of Truth.*

7614. CREATION, Commanding. Such is the dependence amongst all the orders of creatures; the inanimate, the sensitive, the rational, the natural, the artificial; that the apprehension of one of them is a good step towards the understanding of the rest. And this is the highest pitch of human reason—to follow all the links of this chain till all their secrets are open to our minds, and their works advanced or imitated by our hands. This is truly to command the world; to rank all the varieties and degrees of things so orderly, one upon another, that standing on the top of them we may perfectly behold all that are below, and make them all serviceable to man's life. And to this happiness there can be nothing else added, but that we make a second advantage of this rising ground, thereby to look the nearer into heaven, an ambition which, though it was punished in the old world by a universal confusion, when it was managed with impiety and insolence, yet, when it is carried on by that humility and innocence which can never be separated from true knowledge, when it is designed not to brave the Creator of all things, but to admire him the more, must needs be the utmost perfection of human nature.   *Sprat.*

7615. CREATION, a Continual Miracle. How close does it bring the Creator to us to regard him, not so much as having made the world, as still engaged in making it; *i. e.*, by supplying the life on which its laws, and thus its being and incidents, depend. It is an ill-constructed theology which regards God as having created only in past ages. A gorgeous sunset, the leafing of a tree in the sweet spring-time, betokens the Divine hand no less palpably than did the miracles which provided the hungry multitudes of Galilee with food. "Depend upon it" (says an eloquent preacher), "it is not the want of greater miracles, but of the soul to perceive such as are allowed us still, that makes us push all the sanctities into the far spaces we cannot reach. The devout feel that wherever God's hand is, there is miracle; and it is simply an undevoutness which imagines that only where miracle is, can there be the real hand of God. He who will but discern beneath the sun, as he rises any morning, the supporting finger of the Almighty, may recover the sweet and reverent surprise with which Adam gazed on the first dawn in Paradise; and if we cannot find him there,—if we cannot find him on the margin of the sea, or in the flowers by the wayside—I do not think we should have discovered him any more on the grass of Gethsemane or Olivet. *Grindon*

7616. CREATION, Government of. The history of creation is itself the history of God's government; and nothing short of absolute idiotism, rather than mere ignorance, could believe it possible that this incalculably complicated, multifarious, and inconceivably extended universe could preserve its order without a government. *MacCulloch.*

7617. CREATION, Immensity of. About the time of the invention of the telescope, another instrument was formed, which laid open a scene no less wonderful and rewarded the inquisitive spirit of man. This was the microscope. The one led me to see a system in every star, the other leads me to see a world in every atom. The one taught me that this mighty globe, with the whole burden of its people and its countries, is but a grain of sand on the high field of immensity; the other teaches me that every grain of sand may harbor within it the tribes and the families of a busy population. The one told me of the insignificance of the world I tread upon; the other redeems it from all its insignificance, for it tells me that in the leaves of every forest, and in the flowers of every garden, and in the waters of every rivulet, there are worlds teeming with life, and numberless as are the glories of the firmament. The one has suggested to me that beyond and above all that is visible to man there may be fields of creation which sweep immensely along, and carry the impress of the Almighty's hand to the remotest scenes of the universe; the other suggests that within and beneath all that minuteness which the aided eye of man has been able to explore there may be a region of invisibles; and that, could we draw aside the mysterious curtain which shrouds it from our senses, we might see a theatre of as many wonders as astronomy has unfolded, a universe within the compass of a point so small as to elude all the powers of the microscope, but where the wonder-working God finds room for the exercise of all his attributes, where he can raise another mechanism of worlds, and fill and animate them all with the evidence of his glory. *Chalmers.*

7618. CREATION, Provisions of. The manner in which the Creator has contrived a supply for the thirst of man in sultry places is worthy of admiration. He has placed amidst the burning sands of Africa a plant whose leaf, twisted round like a cruet, is always filled with a large glassful of fresh water. The gullet of this cruet is shut by the extremity of the leaf itself, so as to prevent the water from evaporating. He has planted, in some other districts of the same country, a great tree, called by the negroes Boa, the trunk of which, of a prodigious bulk, is naturally hollowed, like a cistern. In the rainy season it receives its fill of water, which continues fresh and cool in the greatest heats, by means of the tufted foliage which crowns its summit. In some of the parched rocky islands of the West Indies there is found a tree called the Water Lianno, so full of sap, that if you cut a single branch of it, as much water is immediately discharged as a man can drink at a draught, and it is perfectly pure and limpid. *St. Pierre.*

7619. CREATOR, Evidence of a. See here, I hold a Bible in my hand, and you see the cover, the leaves, the letters, the words, but you do not see the writers or the printer, the letter-founder, the ink-maker, the paper-maker, or the binder. You never did see them, you never will see them, and yet there is not one of you who will think of disputing or denying the being of these men. I go further, I affirm that you see the very souls of these men, in seeing this book, and you feel yourselves obliged to allow that, by the contrivance, design, memory, fancy, reason, and so on. In the same manner, if you see a picture, you judge there was a painter; if you see a house, you judge there was a builder of it; and if you see a room contrived for this purpose, and another for that—a door to enter, and a window to admit light, a chimney to hold fire, you conclude that the builder was a person of skill and forecast, who formed the house with a view to the accommodation of its inhabitants. In this manner examine the world, and pity the man who, when he sees the sign of a wheatsheaf, hath sense enough to know that there is a joiner, and somewhere a painter, but who, when he sees the wheatsheaf itself, is so stupid as not to say to himself, "This had a wise and good creator." *Robert Robinson.*

7620. CREATOR, Question of the. "Who made you?" was asked of a small girl. She replied, "God made me that length," indicating with her two hands the ordinary size of a new-born infant, "and I growed the rest myself." This was before Topsy's time, and is wittier than even "'Spects I growed," and not less philosophical than Descartes' *nihil* with Leibnitz's *nisi* as its rider. *Horæ Subsecivæ.*

7621. CREATOR, Remember Thy. A missionary in South Australia gave the text, "Remember now thy Creator in the days of thy youth," to a boy who was utterly destitute of religious education or influence. The boy promised never to forget the text. Two years after the missionary learned that the boy had become a faithful Christian, and that he attributed his conversion to the stranger who had given him the text.

7622. CREDULITY, Folly of. Those people who are alarmed and perplexed at the danger of having to judge for themselves in religious matters, think to escape that danger by choosing to take some guide as an infallible one, and believe or disbelieve as he bids them. What is this but crossing the crazy bridge in a sedan-chair? In determining to believe whatever their guide affirms, they are in reality choosing to make every single exercise of faith which follows that original determination; and they are choosing to believe he is infallible into the bargain. There are at least as many chances of error as before against every single article of faith in the creed which they adopt upon their guide's authority; and there are also additional chances against that authority itself. Thus, in order to get over more safely, they put not only their own weight, but that of the sedan-chair also, upon the tottering arch. *Excelsior.*

7623. CRIME, Avenged. Crime has often been clad in royal purple, and has often trampled on innocence with impunity; but the purple has mouldered away, the crime remained a crime, and from the blood of persecuted innocence has arisen a triumphant avenger. In vain vice sharpened its murderous axe, and doomed virtue to die in the flames; though trembling cowards burnt incense before the ruthless tyrant, the sinner's pride was soon laid low, and the funeral pile of slandered innocence was changed into a throne of glory!
Zschokke.

7624. CRIME, The Bible and. A gentleman lately presented a Bible to a prisoner under sentence of death. He exclaimed, "O, sir, if I had had this book, and studied it, I should never have committed the crime of which I am convicted!"

7625. CRIME, Cause of. Sir Matthew Hale, one of the oldest Chief Justices of England, gave the following testimony against strong drink: "The places of judicature, which I have long held in this kingdom, have given an opportunity to observe the original cause of most of the enormities that have been committed for the space of twenty years, and by due observation I have found that if the murders and manslaughters, burglaries and robberies, the riots and tumults, the adulteries, fornications, rapes, and other enormities that have happened in that time, were divided in five parts, four of them have been the issues and products of excessive drinking—of tavern or ale-house drinking."

7626. CRIME, Expiating. A traveler among the Alps relates that in the midst of a strange solitude they encountered a cross. The guide said, "I myself erected this cross." "For what purpose?" inquired the traveler. "In fulfillment of a vow that I had made." "Why did you make the vow?" "I met with an accident here." "Indeed, of what nature?" "I killed a man." "You?" "Yes, sir, there," and he pointed to the cross. Upon various points of the mountain ridges he had erected twenty-nine of these crosses. The morality and religion of such a being belong to the darkest times.

7627. CRISES, Eventful. A switchman slept when he should have watched for the coming train. The consequence was a collision with frightful loss of life. A little sleep did it. A young man whose heart was tender resolved to serve Christ. His old comrades invited him to have "one more" good time with them. He yielded and began a series of dissipations which ended in his becoming a murderer and a suicide. A young man started for a place of amusement on a Sunday, and on the way was invited to attend a religious service. He accepted and became a Christian and a missionary martyr. He was the Rev. John Williams, of Raratonga. A reformed drunkard commenced to make New Year's calls, resolved to taste no liquors. The ridicule of a thoughtless young woman over-

came him. He was carried home drunk, and died a few months later cursing his tempter.

7628. CRISES, Important. There are moments that are worth more than years. We cannot help it; there is no proportion between spaces of time in importance nor in value. A strange unthought-of five minutes may contain the event of a life. And this all-important moment, disproportionate to all other moments, who can tell when it will be upon us?
Dr. Arnold.

7629. CRISES, Mementos of. When traveling among the Alps, we often saw a small black cross planted upon a rock, or on the brink of a torrent, or on the verge of the highway, to mark the spot where men have met with sudden death by accident. Solemn reminders these of our mortality! but they led our mind still further: for we said within us, if the places where men seal themselves for the second death could be thus manifestly indicated, what a scene would this world present! Here the memorial of a soul undone by yielding to a foul temptation, there a conscience seared by the rejection of a final warning, and yonder a heart forever turned into stone by resisting the last tender appeal of love. Our places of worship would scarce hold the sorrowful monuments which might be erected over spots where spirits were forever lost—spirits that date their ruin from sinning against the gospel while under the sound of it. *Spurgeon.*

7630. CRISIS, The American. These are the times that try men's souls. The summer soldier and the sunshine patriot will, in this crisis, shrink from the service of his country; but he that stands it now deserves the thanks of men and women. Tyranny, like hell, is not easily conquered; yet we have this consolation, that the harder the conflict the more glorious the triumph. What we obtain too cheap we esteem too lightly.
Thomas Paine's "Crisis," Dec., 1776.

7631. CRISIS, Life's. The minute is coming when we have crossed the line of doom. Take that pitiful steamer, the Atlantic, that was wrecked off the coast of Newfoundland three years ago this month. There it was in the fog; it had been in the fog three days, and just plying along toward the shore and toward the rocks. There was just one moment when they could have stopped and reversed their engines, and saved the steamer, and there was one moment when it was too late. There was one moment when it crossed the line, and 500 souls went down to a watery grave. There is a crisis in every man's life when he can stop. You can just stop to-night and say, "By the grace of God I will stop to-night, and I will just turn my face toward God." There isn't anything to hinder you; you can to-night just change your company; leave the world and join God's people. *Moody.*

7632. CRITICISM, Check to. A Spartan, being told that Philip had demolished the City of Olynthus, remarked, "But he cannot build another such." The critic's work is that of demolition. It is always easier to tear down than to build up. It may abate our conceit to try seriously to do as well as the one we criticise.

7633. CRITICISM, Muddy. Robert Hall did not like Dr. Gill as an author. When Mr. Christmas Evans was in Bristol he was talking to Mr. Hall about the Welsh language, which he said was very copious and expressive. "How I wish, Mr. Hall, that Dr. Gill's works had been written in Welsh!" "I wish they had, sir; I wish they had with all my heart, for then I should never have read them. They are a continent of mud, sir." *Gregory.*

7634. CRITICISM, Personification of. The malignant deity Criticism dwelt on the top of a snowy mountain in Nova Zembla: Momus found her extended in her den upon the spoils of numberless volumes half-devoured. At her right hand sat Ignorance, her father and husband, blind with age; at her left, Pride, her mother, dressing her up in the scraps of paper herself had torn. There was Opinion, her sister, light of foot, hoodwinked, and headstrong, yet giddy and perpetually turning. About her played her children, Noise and Impudence, Dullness and Vanity, Positiveness, Pedantry, and Ill-Manners. *Swift.*

7635. CRITICISM, Rule for. Apollodorus, the painter, who first invented the mixing of colors and the softening of shadows, was an Athenian. Over his works there is this inscription:

'Tis no hard thing to reprehend me;
But let the men that blame me mend me.
Plutarch.

7636. CRITICS, Qualities of. The pre-eminent quality needed to their vocation is Christian love to the neighbor. The primary office of a critic is not, as many seem to think, to detect imperfections. That is a very shallow mind which seeks to distinguish itself by facility in finding errors. The first duty of the critic is to create happiness, where it may be done faithfully, and to shrink from giving pain, where it can honestly be avoided. Steadfastly to adhere to this, the highest principle of criticism, requires, however, too noble a nature to be met with frequently. "A true critic," says Addison, "ought to dwell upon excellencies rather than defects; to discover the concealed beauties of a writer; and communicate to the world such things as are worth its observation." The rule applies universally. Rightly to comprehend and estimate things, whether in art, literature, or nature, we must train ourselves to admiration of excellence. The contrary course serves only to blind and darken, He who does not strive to rise above nature will sink below it. *Grindon.*

7637. CROSS, All-sufficiency of the. The Cross of Christ is the invincible sanctuary of the humble, and the dejection of the proud, the victory of Christ, the destruction of the devil, the confirmation of the faithful, the death of the unbeliever, the life of the just. It is the key of Paradise, the weak man's staff, the convert's convoy, the upright man's perfection, the soul and body's health, the prevention of all evil, and the procurer of all good. *Quarles*

7638. CROSS, Apparition of the. Constantine saw in mid-heaven, above the brightness of the sun at noon-day, a cross of wondrous shape, and on it read the legend, "In this sign conquer!" The army also saw it. Before the battle of the Milvian bridge, he put the cross, with the name of Christ upon it, in place of the Roman eagle on his standards. His soldiers hailed it as a symbol of divine protection and pledge of victory. This occurred in 312. When Julian the Apostate came to the throne, he caused the removal of the cross from the standards, and substituted for it the images of his heathen gods. Christian soldiers in his army often refused to bear them, and on this account suffered martyrdom. Such were Bonosus and Maximilian, who refused to carry images of Jove and Hercules on their standards, and after excruciating torture with loaded thongs, and then upon the rack, steadfastly affirmed, "We will have nothing to do with your standards loaded with idols!" Rather than handle the idols, they went to their death A. D. 363.

7639. CROSS, Bearing the. Mr. Simeon of Cambridge, conversing with Mr. Gurney, made the following remarks:—"Should you see a poor maniac knocking his head against a wall, and beating out his brains, you would not be angry with him however he might taunt you. You would pity him from your very soul; you would direct all your energies to save him from destruction! So it will be with you: the world will mock and trample on you; a man shall come, and, as it were, slap you on the face. You rub your face, and say, 'This is strange work; I like it not, sir.' Never mind, I say, this is your evidence; it turns to you for a testimony. If you were of the world, the world would love its own, but now you are not of the world, therefore the world hateth you. Many years ago, when I was an object of much contempt and derision in this university, I strolled forth one day, buffeted and afflicted, with my little Testament in my hand. I prayed earnestly to my God, that he would comfort me with some cordial from his word, and that on opening the book I might find some text which should sustain me. The first text which caught my eye was this, 'They found a man of Cyrene, Simon by name; him they compelled to bear his cross.' You know Simon is the same name as Simeon. What a world of instruction was here—what a blessed hint for my encouragement! To have the cross laid upon me, that I might bear it after Jesus—what a privilege! It was enough Now I could leap and sing for joy as one whom Jesus was honoring with a participation in his sufferings. My dear brother, we must not mind a little suffering. When I am getting through a hedge, if my head and shoulders are safely through, I can bear the pricking of my legs. Let me rejoice in the remembrance that our holy Head has surmounted all his sufferings and triumphed over death. Let us follow him patiently, we shall soon be partakers of his victory." *F. F. Trench.*

7640. CROSS, Clinging to the. A great crucifix stood up at the outskirts of Noyon, France, and there at midnight the moonlight showed a woman kneeling, with her arms thrown around the tree, and her head bent to the ground; and I could not but hope that she was a true penitent, in error, but still clinging with her heart to Christ as she clung with her arms to the cross; any way, at that midnight hour, in that lonely spot, a woman bowed by some secret grief to the earth, and seeking relief in prayer under the shadow of that lofty cross and its divine burden, was a solemn and touching sight.   *Guthrie.*

7641. CROSS, Denial and the. A good old lady said, "The reason why professing Christians cannot take up their daily cross is, because they do not deny themselves. If they would first deny themselves, then they would be ready to take up their every cross, and perform every known duty. We must attend to all our duties in the order in which they are placed in the Bible. 'If any man will come after me, let him deny himself, and take up his cross daily, and follow me.'"

7642. CROSS, Glorying in the. It is an old and useful observation, that many of the most excellent objects in the world are objects whose excellency does not appear at first view; as, on the other hand, many things of little value appear more excellent at first than a nearer view discovers them to be. There are some things we admire, because we do not know them, and the more we know them the less we admire them; there are other things we despise through ignorance, because it requires pains and applications to discover their beauty and excellence. This holds true in nothing more than in that glorious, despised object mentioned in the text, Gal. 6: 14. There is nothing the world is more divided about in its opinions than this. To the one part it is altogether contemptible; to the other, it is altogether glorious. The one part of the world wonders what attractions the other finds in it; the other part wonders how the rest of the world are so stupid as not to see them; and are amazed at the blindness of others, and their own former blindness.   *M'Laurin.*

7643. CROSS, Glory of the. Its glory produces powerful effects wherever it shines. They who behold this glory are transformed into the same image, 2 Cor. 3: 18. An Ethiopian may look long enough to the visible sun before it changes his black color; but this does it. It melts cold and frozen hearts; it breaks stony hearts; it pierces adamants; it penetrates through thick darkness. How justly it is called marvelous light! 1 Pet. 2: 9. It gives eyes to the blind to look to itself; and not only to the blind but to the dead! It is the light of life; a powerful light. Its energy is beyond the force of thunder; and it is more mild than the dew on the tender grass. It communicates a glory to all other objects, according as they have any relation to it. It adorns the universe; it gives a lustre to nature, and to Providence: it is the greatest glory of the lower world that its Creator was for a while its inhabitant. A poor landlord thinks it a lasting honor to his cottage that he has once lodged a prince or emperor: with how much more reason may our poor cottage, this earth, be proud of it, that the Lord of glory was its tenant from his birth to his death? Yea, that he rejoiced in the habitable parts of it, before it had a beginning, even from everlasting! Prov. 8: 31.   *M'Laurin.*

7644. CROSS, Index of the. It is related of the celebrated scholar, Humboldt, that when he was traveling in tropical America, going chiefly by night to avoid the heat of the day, that his superstitious guides greatly reverenced the constellation of the Southern Cross, and directed their course by it. At that time this constellation reached the mid-heavens just before the break of day, so that its passage over the meridian was an indication that morning was approaching. He says frequently, when he was following after his train, and wearied by a night-long tramp, he could hear the guides shout, "Courage, comrades, the Cross begins to bend." So may the Christian soldier hear and regard this voice in the hour of his trials. In the darkness, and the weariness of life-long labor, it is enough to know that the cross bends at the earnest pleading of faith and uplifted prayer to God. You know where your strength lies, where you may burnish your weapons, where you may, indeed, stand forth renewed perpetually in the strength of grace. The cross of Christ is with us, and the power of that cross is efficacious to save to the uttermost.   *Dr. Curry.*

7645. CROSS, The Key of Paradise. We do not sail to glory in the salt sea of our own tears, but in the red sea of a Redeemer's blood. We owe the life of our souls to the death of our Saviour. It was his going into the furnace which keeps us from the flames. Man lives by death; his natural life is preserved by the death of the creature, and his spiritual life by the death of the Redeemer.   *Secker.*

7646. CROSS, Legend of the. A procession of Christians, singing hymns, having a cross carried at their head, come to a place called Tetramphodos, where stood a statue of Venus and a marble altar. As the cross was borne along the idol fell down of itself, and was broken in pieces.

7647. CROSS, Might of the. The cross was two pieces of dead wood; and a helpless, unresisting Man was nailed to it; yet it was mightier than the world, and triumphed, and will ever triumph over it.   *Hare.*

7648. CROSS, Our Only Hope in the. On a rude cross by the side of an Italian highway is the motto *Spes unica.* The cross is the altar upon which the atonement for our sins was made.

7649. CROSS, Power of the. There is an Irish fable to the effect that Forannan, abbot of Waulsor, felt called to leave his native isle. He went to the sea shore with twelve companions, and not being able to procure a boat, they made a huge wooden cross, and casting it into the sea, and standing on it were wafted to the Flemish shore. Probably a raft of timbers laid crosswise has grown into a cross.

7650. CROSS, Refuge of the. A popular allegorical picture represents a huge cross hewn out of the rock standing upon the rugged shore of a stormy sea. A half-drowned female clings to it as her only hope, while another clutches her garments in the desperate struggle for safety. That sea is life and that cross is Christ.

7651. CROSS, Resting Upon the. Often does the wanderer, 'mid American forests, lay his head upon a rude log, while above it is the abyss of stars: so the weary, heavy-laden, dying Christian leans upon the rugged and narrow cross, but looks up the while to the beaming canopy of immortal life—to "those things which are above."   *G. Gilfillan.*

7652. CROSS, Our Sins on the. We must nail our sins to the cross of Christ, force them before the tree on which he suffered; it is such a sight as sin cannot abide. It will begin to die within a man upon the sight of Christ on the cross, for the cross of Christ accuseth sin, shames sin, and by a secret virtue feeds upon the very heart of sin. We must use sin as Christ was used when he was made sin for us; we must lift it up, and make it naked by confession of it to God; we must pierce the hands and feet, the heart of it by godly sorrow, and application of threatenings against it, and by spiritual revenge upon it.   *Byfield.*

7653. CROSS, Soldiers of the. A brave warrior of old time being delayed, prayed to the gods that the battle might not be ended before his arrival. The true soldier loves the warfare, despises its perils, and glories in its hardships. The Christian's Leader bore his own cross, and perished upon it. To follow his steps must be our pleasure.

7654. CROSS, Taking up the. The old crusaders used to wear a cross upon their shoulders. This was their badge of service. Peter the hermit tore up his gown and distributed the pieces among the enthusiastic volunteers. It was then the fashionable and honorable thing. So to-day a profession of religion and pew in some church is the passport to respectability. The cross is the ornament of pride or adornment of beauty, with no thought of its sacred import and responsibility, "a cheap substitute for a struggle never made, and a crown never striven for."

7655. CROSS, Traces of the. Thor the thunderer, the Scandinavian hero god, was always represented with a hammer in his hand. With this hammer he crushed the head of the great Midgard serpent, destroyed the giants, and restored to life the dead goats which drew his car, and consecrated the pyre of Baldur. Thor's hammer was a cross. As such it appears on old Scandinavian coins. So says Baring-Gould in his "Legends of the Cross." The sign of the cross was made by the Scandinavians, and may have been copied by the Christians from them. On the destruction of the temple of Serapium in Egypt, A. D. 389, a sign resembling the cross was found engraved upon the stones. It was interpreted to mean, "The life to come." The heathen claimed it

as a symbol of their god Serapis. Sozomen, Socrates and Rufinus relate this. Rufinus says, "The Egyptians are said to have the sign of the Lord's cross among those letters which are called sacerdotal, of which letter or figure this they say is the interpretation, 'The life to come.'" Baring-Gould says that the cross was a religious symbol to the lake-dwellers, that beneath it they laid their dead to rest, and trusted in it to guard and revive the loved ones whom they committed to the dust. Mortilett, who investigated the tombs of the lake-dwellers in Italy, concludes that the cross was a religious emblem, of frequent use, a thousand years before Christ.

7656. CROSS, Use of the. God's scholars have learned to think of the cross that it is the frame-house in the which God frameth his children like to his son Christ; the furnace that fineth God's gold; the highway to heaven; the suit and livery that God's servants are served withal; and the earnest and beginning of all consolation and glory.   *Bradford.*

7657. CROSS, Victory of the. This is the weapon that has won victories over hearts of every kind, in every quarter of the globe. Greenlanders, Africans, South-Sea Islanders, Hindoos, Chinese, all have alike felt its power. Just as that huge iron tube, which crosses the Menai Straits, is more affected and bent by half an hour's sunshine than by all the dead weight that can be placed in it, so in like manner the hearts of savages have melted before the cross when every other argument seemed to move them no more than stones. "Brethren," said a North American Indian after his conversion, "I have been a heathen; I know how heathens think. Once a preacher came and began to explain to us that there was a God; but we told him to return to the place from whence he came. Another preacher came and told us not to lie, nor steal, nor drink; but we did not heed him. At last, another came into my hut one day, and said, 'I am come to you, in the name of the Lord of heaven and earth. He sends to let you know that he will make you happy, and deliver you from misery. For this end he became man, gave his life a ransom, shed his blood for sinners.' I could not forget his words. I told them to the other Indians, and an awakening begun among us. I say, therefore, preach the sufferings and death of Christ our Saviour, if you wish your words to gain entrance among the heathens." Never did the devil triumph so thoroughly as when he persuaded the Jesuit missionaries in China to keep back the story of the cross.   *Ryle.*

7658. CROWN, Biblical. The emblem of honor—favor—royalty—perpetuity. Used frequently in the Book of Proverbs; applied to a virtuous wife—a wise man's riches—the righteous man's hoary head—the prudent man's knowledge—the old man's children's children. THE BELIEVER'S crown of grace and of glory; —a crown of *beauty*, Ezek. 16: 12. The description of the church's glory; applicable, also, in a general sense, to the honor put on every true believer. A crown of *gold*, Rev.

4 : 4; upon the twenty-four elders, who are spoken of as part of the redeemed, 5 : 8. A crown of *righteousness*, 2 Tim. 4 : 8. A crown of *life*, James 1 : 12; Rev. 2 : 10. A crown of *rejoicing*, 1 Thess. 2 : 19; Phil. 4 : 1. A crown of *glory*, 1 Pet. 5 : 4. *Bowes*.

7659. CROWN, Incorruptible. Petrarch, the celebrated poet, was crowned with laurels at Rome. The ceremony of his coronation (says Gibbon) was performed in the capital, by his friend and patron the supreme magistrate of the republic. Twelve patrician youths were arrayed in scarlet; six representatives of the most illustrious families, in green robes, with garlands of flowers, accompanied the procession. In the midst of the princes and nobles, the senator count of Anguillara, a kinsman of the Colonna, assumed his throne, and at the voice of a herald Petrarch arose. After discoursing on a text of Virgil, and thrice repeating his vows for the prosperity of Rome, he knelt before the throne, and received from the senator a laurel crown, with a more precious declaration, "This is the reward of merit." The people shouted, "Long life to the capital and the poet!" A sonnet in praise of Rome was accepted, as the effusion of genius and gratitude; and after the whole procession had visited the Vatican, the wreath was suspended before the shrine of St. Peter. In the act or diploma which was presented to Petrarch, the title and perogative of poet-laureate are received in the capital after the lapse of 1,300 years, and he receives the perpetual privilege of wearing, at his choice, a crown of laurel, ivy, or myrtle; of assuming the poetic habit, and of teaching, disputing, interpreting, and composing, in all places whatsoever; and on all subjects of literature. The grant was ratified by the authority of the senate and people; and the character of citizen was the recompense of his affection for the Roman name. They did him honor, but they did him justice. In the familiar society of Cicero and Livy he had imbibed the ideas of an ancient patriot, and his ardent fancy kindled every idea to a sentiment, and every sentiment to a passion. Petrarch, however, we are told, felt that such honors were incapable of conferring true happiness, and far exceeded his desert. "I blushed," says he, "at the applauses of the people, and the unmerited commendations with which I was overwhelmed." A sentiment becoming a man whose mind was deeply imbued with religion; who had, on another occasion, said, "Let us read the historians, the poets, and the philosophers, but let us have in our hearts the gospel of Jesus Christ: in which alone is perfect wisdom and perfect happiness." Let the Christian, from the above instance, endeavor to realize the thought of wearing a brighter crown than that of a laurel, a crown of glory that will not fade away. Let him bear in mind the goodness of him, who even now crowneth his life with loving kindness and tender mercies. *Buck*.

7660. CROWN, Reward of the. A worthy Christian woman of France was the subject of much persecution. She was imprisoned and attempts were made upon her life. Her little daughter cut out a great number of paper crosses and fastened them on to her mother's dress. Then she made a crown and placed it upon her mother's head and said "After the cross cometh the crown." It was an allegory of her mother's life here and reward in eternity.

7661. CROWNS, Distribution of. Forty brave soldiers of the Thundering Legion were called to adjure Christ or die. One of them said "Let us ask God to send us forty, to our crowns together." They were sentenced to be exposed, naked, on the ice of a lake through an extremely cold winter night. On the shore was a small building lighted and warmed, and into its comforts any one might run So cold was the night that people kept close about the fires in their houses. The heroes of Jesus Christ stood in prayer on the ice, or ran about to keep warm, encouraging each other to play the man, and resisting the charm of the warm and gleaming hut on the shore, till they fell benumbed into their last sleep. The soldier who kept the fire on the shore slept and had this vision. He stood and gazed upon the exposed confessors. Then an angel descended with a dazzling crown in his hand; he brought one, and another, and another, till the soldier perceived that he was distributing the diadems of victory to the faithful martyrs. Nine and thirty crowns were brought, but he came not again to bring the fortieth. Then he awoke and said, "What may this mean?" A movement revealed the entrance of one of the confessors who could not endure, who sought the relief of the fire. Then he who had dreamed went forth and took the place of the apostate. The cold was still resistless and the northern blast unendurable. Many of the sufferers were unconscious; others were praying, "Forty wrestlers we have entered the arena; let forty victors receive the prize." He had aroused the judge, professed that he was a Christian, received the same sentence as the others and stood among them awaiting the coming of the angel with the fortieth crown. Morning at last broke. A few survived. Their limbs were broken and all were cast into a fire and burned Such is the beautiful legend of the martyrs of the Thundering Legion, showing strength of purpose, power of grace, and the might of prayer.

7662. CROWNS, Expecting. Mr. Wardrobe was dying in the arms of a friend, and when he was informed there was no hope for him, he raised himself up, and in a rapture of joy exclaimed, "Crowns! crowns! crowns of glory shall adorn this head of mine ere long!" Rising higher, he added, "Palms! palms! palms ere long shall fill these hands of mine," and thus triumphantly he passed over the river to join the conquerors before the throne. *Whitefield*

7663. CROWNS, Jeweled. It is said that the crown of Ivan contains 841 diamonds. The crown of Peter contains 887 diamonds. The crown of England contains 1,700 diamonds. The Imperial crown of Russia contains 2,500 diamonds. The crown of France contains 5,352 diamonds. But the crown of the poorest of God's saints is one solid gem, not to be compared for beauty and value with all the diamonds in the world; for the Lord of Hosts is for a crown of glory and for a diadem of beauty to the residue of his people.

7664. CRUCIFIXION, Application of the. An irreligious German minister sat opposite a picture of Christ on the cross, under which was the inscription, "I did this for thee; what hast thou done for me?" It was fastened by the Holy Spirit upon his conscience. In his thoughts by day and dreams at night the one question was, "What hast thou done for me?" He felt the burden removed and rejoiced. He died not long after triumphing in redeeming love.

7665. CRUCIFIXION, Cruelty of. Of all the devices of a cruel imagination, crucifixion is the masterpiece. Other pains are sharper for a time, but none are at once so agonizing and so long. One aggravation, however, was wanting, which, owing to the want of knowledge in painters, is still, we believe, commonly supposed to have belonged to the punishment. The weight of the body was borne by a ledge which projected from the middle of the upright beam, and not by the hands and feet, which were probably found unequal to the strain. The frailty of man's frame comes at last to be its own defence; but enough remained to preserve the pre-eminence of torture to the cross. The process of nailing was exquisite torment, and yet worse in what ensued than in the actual infliction. The spikes rankled, the wounds inflamed, the local injury produced a general fever, the fever a most intolerable thirst; but the misery of miseries to the sufferer was, while racked with agony, to be fastened in a position which did not permit him even to writhe. Every attempt to relieve the muscles, every instinctive movement of anguish, only served to drag the lacerated flesh, and wake up new and acuter pangs; and this torture, which must have been continually aggravated until advancing death began to lay it to sleep, lasted on an average two or three days. *Fontenelle.*

7666. CRUCIFIXION, Impressing the. A little girl asked her mother, who had a withered hand, how it became so deformed. Her mother told her that her crib took fire and in rescuing her she had burned herself. "It was for you my child, that this poor hand suffered." But for this loving interposition the child would have been burned up. Then the mother told her of the exposure of her soul to sin and death and that Christ came to her rescue. She added that when we get to heaven and behold the wounds of Christ, and ask, what are these wounds? he will reply "I was wounded for your transgressions; I was bruised for your iniquities."

7667. CRUCIFIXION, Pre-eminence of the. If you have not yet found out that Christ crucified is the foundation of the whole volume, you have read your Bible hitherto to very little profit. Your religion is a heaven without a sun, an arch without a keystone, a compass without a needle, a clock without spring or weights, a lamp without oil. It will not comfort you. It will not deliver your soul from hell.   *Ryle.*

7668. CRUEL, Death of the. William the conqueror, extremely alarmed on his death-bed, entreated the clergy to intercede for him. "Laden with many and grievous sins," he exclaimed, "I tremble; and being ready to be taken soon into the terrible examination of God, I am ignorant what I should do. I have been brought up in feats of arms from my childhood; I am greatly polluted with effusion of much blood; I can by no means number the evils I have done these sixty-four years, for which I am now constrained, without stay, to render an account to the just judge."

7669. CRUELTY, Barbarous. Alexander, the Tyrant of Pherae, was noted for his savage cruelties. He buried men alive, others he dressed in skins of wild animals, and hunted them with dogs or shot them with arrows. Having summoned the friendly people of Maliboea and Scotusae to meet him in assembly, he caused his guards to surround them and slay them all with the sword. He slew his uncle Polyphron with a spear, and afterwards adorned it with garlands, and offered sacrifice to it as to a god. He ran out of the theatre during the performance of an affecting piece, lest the citizens should see him weep who had never pitied those he had slain.

7670. CRUELTY, Delight in. Mark Antony caused the heads of those he had proscribed to be brought to him while he was at table, and entertained his eyes a long while with that sad spectacle. Cicero's head being one of those that was brought to him, he ordered it to be put on the very pulpit where Cicero had made speeches against him. Agrippina, the mother of Nero, who was afterwards emperor, sent an officer to put to death Lollia Paulina, who had been her rival for the imperial dignity. When Lollia's head was brought to her, not knowing it at first, she examined it with her own hands, till she perceived some particular feature by which the lady was distinguished.   *Bib. Treasury.*

7671. CRUELTY, Domitian's. The Emperor Domitian, in the beginning of his reign, promised tranquillity to the people, but their expectations were soon disappointed. Among other cruelties, he invited his senators to a grand feast. When they arrived at the palace, they were introduced into a large gloomy hall, hung with black, and lighted with a few glimmering tapers. In the middle were placed a number of coffins, on each of which was inscribed the name of some one of the invited guests. On a sudden, a number of men burst into the room, clothed in black, with drawn swords and flaming torches, and after they had for some time terrified them, they permitted them to retire, who, no doubt, were happy to escape with their lives. Thus does the tyrant, the god of this world, often act towards men. He promises and invites them to a rich banquet, but, alas! it is only in the end to terrify and destroy them. Let us, then, watch and pray, lest he should get an advantage of us, and we fall victims to his wiles.   *Buck.*

7672. CRUELTY, Example of. Several wagoners coming from Breslau to Silesia, upon their way in the Duke of Saxony's country, perceived a stag with a man upon his back, running with all his might: coming near the wagons he suddenly fell down: the wagoners drawing nigh him, the poor man sitting upon his back made pitiful complaint, how that the day before he was by the Duke of Saxony, for killing a deer, condemned to be bound with chains upon that stag, his feet bound fast under the stag's belly with an iron chain soldered, and his hands so chained to the horns. The miserable man begged earnestly that they would shoot him, to put him out of his pain; but they durst not, fearing the duke. Whilst they were talking with him the stag got up again, and ran away with all his might. The wagoners computed that he had run in sixteen hours twenty-six Dutch miles in the least, which makes near one hundred of our English miles in a direct line. The miseries which that poor creature did and must undergo, especially if the stag killed him not in running, cannot be expressed, hardly imagined.   *Mercurius Politicus*, 1655.

7673. CRUELTY, Papal. The massacre of St. Bartholomew's was instigated by Catherine, a bigoted Catholic, who persuaded her son, Charles IX. of France, a young and vacillating prince, to exterminate the heretics in his realm. He gave the order with an oath, "*Kill all—all—all, so that not one be left to reproach me.*" At three o'clock on Sunday morning, August 24, 1572, at the pre-arranged signal of the ringing of bells, the Catholic party, with the sign of the cross in their caps, to distinguish them, began the merciless slaughter of the non-resisting Huguenots, striking down alike men, women, and children. For three days the horrid work went on. The blood of forty thousand victims of bigotry stains the page of history as the result of the king's bloody mandate.

7674. CRUELTY Requited. A gentleman had seven sons born dumb. The father was constantly sorrowing over them, and could not comprehend why God visited him so dreadfully, more than other fathers. One day he accompanied them to a neighboring farm, where an old Swiss sold refreshments. He looked with much feeling at his sons, who sat blooming and healthy round the table. The tears started in his eyes, and he exclaimed, "O God! why have I deserved this?" The old Swiss, who had overheard him, drew him on one side, and said, "I see you are downcast at the affliction of your sons; but I do not wonder at it. Do you not remember (I knew you from your youth) when a boy, how you laid snares for the birds, and when caught, tore their tongues out of their mouths, and then with malignant joy let them fly again? How often have I not warned you? Oh, the birds under the heavens, who could not praise God with their tongues, have accused you, and you shall never hear the sweet name of father from the lips of your children."   *Whitecross*

7675. CRUELTY, Retribution for. Richard I was besieging a castle with his army, when the besieged offered to surrender if he would grant them quarter. He, however, refused their request, and threatened to hang every one of them. Upon this, a certain soldier on the ramparts charged his bow with a square arrow and, praying that God would vouchsafe to direct the shot, and deliver the innocent from oppression, he discharged the shaft upon the ranks of the besiegers. The arrow struck the king himself, inflicting a wound, of which he soon afterwards died, and the objects of his vengeance were thus delivered.   *Speed.*

7676. CRUELTY, Romish. John Lambert suffered in the year 1538. No man was used at the stake with more cruelty than this holy martyr. They burnt him with a slow fire by inches; for if it kindled higher and stronger than they chose, they removed it away. When his legs were burnt off, and his thighs were mere stumps in the fire, they pitched his poor body upon pikes, and lacerated his broiling flesh with their halberts. But God was with him in the midst of the flame, and supported him in all the anguish of nature. Just before he expired, he lifted up such hands as he had, all flaming with fire, and cried out to the people with his dying voice, "None but Christ! None but Christ!" He was at last beat down into the fire, and expired.   *Whitecross.*

7677. CRUELTY, Spanish. The manner in which the remorseless Spaniards tortured their unoffending victims, natives of the West Indies, was worthy of the goodness of such a cause. They seized upon them by violence, distributed them like brutes into lots, and compelled them to dig in the mines until death, their only refuge, put a period to their sufferings. It was also a frequent practice among them, as one of their own historians informs us, to murder hundreds of these poor creatures merely to keep their hands in use. They were eager in displaying an emulation which of them could most dexterously strike off the head of a man at a blow, and wagers frequently depended upon this horrid exercise. It is impossible for words to express the indignation and disgust excited by such merciless cruelty. If any of these unhappy Indians, goaded by their sufferings and driven to despair, attempted resistance or flight, their unfeeling murderers hunted them down with dogs which were fed on their flesh. Weakness of age or helplessness of sex were equally disregarded by these monsters, and yet they had the impudence to suppose themselves religious and the favorites of heaven! Some of the most zealous of these adorers of the Holy Virgin forced their unhappy captives into the water, and after administering to them the rites of baptism, cut their throats the next moment to prevent their apostasy! Others made and kept up a vow to hang or burn thirteen every morning in honor of Christ and his twelve apostles!   *Bridges.*

7678. CULTURE, Advantages of. Culture! that

is the talismanic word. See what it did with the country-lad who brought milk into Sheffield every morning—it found him "whittling sticks," it converted him into Sir Francis Chantrey, the most eminent of English sculptors. Culture! it is your true philosopher's stone. Its magic influence will cause the clownish clod-hopper to cast his ill-manners and stultified notions as the caterpillar casts its skin, and walk forth erect in all the manly consciousness of possessed intelligence and refined amiabilities.   *J. Johnson.*

7679. CULTURE, Importance of. Lycurgus, the Lacedemonian law-giver, once took two whelps of the same litter, and ordered them to be bred in a quite different manner; whereby the one became dainty and ravenous, and the other of a good scent and skilled in hunting; which done, awhile after he took occasion thence in an assembly of the Lacedemonians to discourse in this manner: "Of great weight in the attainment of virtue, fellow-citizens, are habits, instruction, precepts, and indeed the whole manner of life—as I will presently let you see by example." And, withal, he ordered the producing those two whelps into the midst of the hall, where also there were set down before them a plate and a live hare. Whereupon, as they had been bred, the one presently flies upon the hare, and the other as greedily runs to the plate. And while the people were musing, not perfectly apprehending what he meant by producing those whelps thus, he added, "These whelps were both of one litter, but differently bred; the one, you see, has turned out a greedy cur, and the other a good hound." And this shall suffice to be spoken concerning custom and different ways of living.   *Plutarch.*

7680. CULTURE, Intellectual. A cultivated mind may be said to have infinite stores of innocent gratification. Everything may be made interesting to it by becoming a subject of thought or inquiry. Books, regarded merely as a gratification, are worth more than all the luxuries on earth. A taste for literature secures cheerful occupation for the unemployed and languid hours of life; and how many persons in these hours, for want of innocent resources, are now impelled to coarse and brutal pleasures! How many young men can be found who, unaccustomed to find a companion in a book, and strangers to intellectual activity, are almost driven, in the long dull evenings of winter, to haunts of intemperance and depraved society!   *Anon.*

7681. CULTURE, Surface. Mere surface culture is as thriftless in education as in agriculture. "Plough deep," says Cobbett, "if you want satisfactory crops:" and the remark applies to minds as well as soils. A woman who has nothing better to recommend her than the superficial graces, so assiduously taught in finishing schools, will not long retain the affection she may have had the adroitness to inspire.   *Anon.*

7682. CUMBERER, Thoughts of a. An opposer of religion went into his wood lot one Sunday morning to cut down the dead timber for fire wood. Finding a dry tree he said to himself "I will cut this down, it is dead and dry, and only fit to burn." At the same time the thought came into his mind, "The tree represents me; I am dead and dry, fit only to burn." With every blow of his axe the question echoed, "Am not I a dead tree, fit only to burn? Will not God say concerning me, 'Cut him down' for he cumbereth the ground?" Anxiety or account of his exposed condition fastened itself resistlessly upon him. He shouldered his axe and returned home, and besought God to have mercy, and found peace and hope.

7683. CUP, The Overflowing. In the East, the people frequently anoint their visitors with some very fragrant perfume. and give them a cup or a glass of some choice wine, which they are careful to fill till it runs over. The first was designed to show their love and respect; the latter to imply that while they remained there, they should have an abundance of every thing. Mr. Griffin, in his "Memoirs of Captain James Wilson," gives the following statement in the captain's own words:—"I once had this ceremony performed on myself in the house of a great and rich Indian, in the presence of a large company. The gentleman of the house poured upon my hands and arms a delightful odoriferous perfume, put a golden cup into my hands, and poured wine into it till it ran over; assuring me, at the same time, that it was a great pleasure to him to receive me, and that I should find a rich supply in his house."

7684. CUP, Tasting the. The cup-bearer of an oriental king carried the cup upon the three fingers of his left hand, and held his right over it to keep it from falling. Before giving it to the king, he poured a little of the wine into his left hand and drank it, to assure the king that it did not contain poison. To this custom may be referred the question of Christ, "Are ye able to drink of the cup that I drink of?"

7685. CURE, Divine. Just at the time the plague was raging worst, a stranger appeared and told them there was a cure. He said that there was a plant which healed this disorder, and he described it. He mentioned that it was a lowly plant, not conspicuous nor very arresting to the eye—that it had a red blossom and sweet-scented leaves, and a bruised-looking stem, and that it was evergreen. He told a number of other particulars regarding it, and as he could not tarry longer at that time, he left a paper in which, he said, they would find a full description of it, and directions how to find it. The tidings diffused considerable activity through the sickly colony. A plant of such efficacy deserved the most diligent search. Almost all agreed that it must be far away; but a discussion arose whether it lay beyond the cliffs or across the sea. Most thought the latter, and some set to work and built a ship, and when they had launched her, they named her Ecclesia, and hoisted a red-cross flag, and sent round word that the fine ship Ecclesia was about to set sail in search of the famous plant, and all who wished to escape the plague were invited to take passages in this good ship. A few others, however, thought the ship was going the wrong way, and that they would have better success by trying to get over the cliffs. This was an arduous enterprise, for the precipices were beetling, steep, and extremely high. A few attempts were made to climb by ravines and gullies, which, however, ended in walls of glassy smoothness; and after many weariful efforts, the climbers either grew dizzy and fell back, or allowed themselves to slide down again to the crumbing *debris* at the bottom. But others, more inventive, busied themselves constructing artificial wings and aërial engines of various kinds (*Imitatio Christi*, asceticism, penitential prayers, and such like), and some of them answered exceedingly well for a little, and rose so high that their neighbors really thought they would reach the top; but after reaching a certain height, whether it was owing to the weakness of the materials, or a powerful current which they always met at a certain elevation, and which by a sort of down-draught blew them back from the brow of the mountain, they uniformly found themselves again on the spot from which they first ascended. A long time had now passed on, and multitudes had died of the plague without clearer views of the specific plant, when a poor sufferer, who had already gone a fruitless expedition in the ship, and from the severity of his anguish was eager in trying every scheme, lay tossing on his bed. He got hold of a large paper roll which lay on a shelf beside him. It was very dirty, and the ink was faded, but to while away the time he began to unfold it, and found from the beginning that it was the book of the Balm of Gilead. He at once suspected that it was the book which the stranger had left so long ago, and wondered how they had suffered it to fall aside; and he had not read far when it told him that if he would only read on, it would put him on the way of finding the plant of renown. It gave a full description—many particulars of which he had never heard before,—and as he advanced in his feverish earnestness, unrolling it fold by fold, and reading rapidly as he went along, hoping that it would tell him the very spot where he should look for it, he found the plant itself! There it lay in the heart of the long-neglected volume; and Luther's eye glistened as he read, "Christ is the end of the law for righteousness to every one that believeth." "But where is Christ to be found? Must I ascend the height or descend into the deep? Must I climb those cliffs or cross that sea? Oh, no. Christ is here —nigh me—God's present gift to me conveyed in the volume of this book. I see him. I accept him. I believe." From that moment Christ was Luther's righteousness, and in the flash of sudden joy with which he discovered the Lord his righteousness, though it did not strike him at the moment, Luther's eternal life began.   *Dr. Hamilton.*

7686. CURE, The Sinner's. Suppose I am dying with consumption which I inherited from my father or mother. I did not get it by any fault of my own, by any neglect of my health; I inherited it, let us suppose. I go to my physician, and to the best physicians, and they all give me up. They say I am incurable; I must die; I have not thirty days to live. Well, a friend happens to come along and looks at me and says: "Moody, you have got the consumption." "I know it very well; I don't want any one to tell me that." "But," he says, "there is a remedy—a remedy, I tell you. Let me have your attention. I want to call your attention to it. I tell you there is a remedy." "But, sir, I don't believe it. I have tried the leading physicians in this country and in Europe, and they tell me there is no hope." "But you know me, Moody; you have known me for years." "Yes, sir." "Do you think, then, I would tell you a falsehood?" "No." "Well, ten years ago I was as far gone. I was given up by the physicians to die, but I took this medicine and it cured me. I am perfectly well—look at me." I say that it is a very strange case. "Yes, it may be strange, but it is a fact. That medicine cured me; take this medicine and it will cure you. Although it has cost me a great deal, it shall not cost you anything. Although the salvation of Jesus Christ is as free as the air, it cost God the richest jewel of heaven. He had to give his only son; give all he had; he had only one son, and he gave him. Do not make light of it, then, I beg of you." "Well," I say, "I would like to believe you, but this is contrary to my reason." Hearing this, my friend goes away and brings another friend to me, and he testifies to the same thing. He again goes away when I do not yet believe, and brings in another friend, and another, and another, and another, and they all testify to the same thing. They say they were as bad as myself; that they took the same medicine that has been offered to me, and it cured them. He then hands me the medicine. I dash it to the ground; I do not believe in its saving power; I die. The reason is, then, that I spurned the remedy. So it will not be because Adam fell, but that you spurn the remedy offered to you to save you. You will have darkness rather than light. How, then, shall you escape if ye neglect so great salvation? There is no hope for you if you neglect the remedy. It does no good to look at the wound. If we are in the camp and are bitten by the fiery serpents, it will do no good to look at the wound. Looking at a wound will never save any one. What we must do is to look at the remedy, to look away to him who hath power to save you from your sin. *Moody.*

7687. CURIOSITY, Danger of. Curiosity is the spiritual drunkenness of the soul; and look, as the drunkard will never be satisfied, be the cup never so deep, unless he see the bottom of it, so some curious Christians, whose souls are spread with the leprosy of curiosity, will never be satisfied till they come to see the bottom and the most secret reasons of all God's dealings towards them; but they are fools in folio, who affect to know more than God would have them. Did not Adam's curiosity render him and his posterity fools in folio? And what pleasure can we take to see ourselves every day fools in print? As a man by gazing and prying into the body of the sun may grow dark and dim, and see less than otherwise he might, so many by a curious prying into the secret reasons of God's dealings with them, come to grow so dark and dim, that they cannot see those plain reasons that God hath laid down in his word why he afflicts and tries the children of men. *Brooks.*

7688. CURIOSITY Defined. Curiosity is a desire to know why and how; such as is in no living creature but man: so that man is distinguished, not only by his reason, but also by this singular passion, from other animals; in whom the appetite of food, and other pleasures of sense, by predominance, take away the care of knowing causes; which is a lust of the mind, that, by a perseverance of delight in the continual and indefatigable generation of knowledge, exceedeth the short vehemence of any carnal pleasure. *Hobbes.*

7689. CURIOSITY, Scope of. What can limit the excursive flight of human curiosity? It dives into the bowels of the earth, explores the mine, and speculates on the formation of the world itself. The sea forms no obstacle to its career. It visits the equator and the poles, and circumnavigates the globe. Nor does it take a cursory flight only, which seems merely to measure space; it pauses to meditate and to inquire. There is not an animal that traverses the desert, there is not an insect that crawls on the ground, there is not a flower that blooms in the air, there is not a stone cast carelessly along our path, but it stops, and interrogates, and forces to declare its nature. You behold it scaling the heavens, measuring the magnitudes and distances of the celestial bodies, and even determining their weight. In short, every sound, every motion, every attitude attracts its attention. And shall man, while he thus casts an inquisitive eye on everything around him, be incurious only about himself? Shall the lord of the lower world busy himself in acquiring a knowledge of the properties, habits, and functions of the beasts which perish, while he is careless about the qualities of that superior mind which has elevated him to the rank of their master, and which betokens a dignity and a destination far beyond the limits of their nature? Shall he immerse himself in the contemplation of corporeal beings, and never once inquire into the operations of that finer spirit which actuates himself, and makes him to be what he is? *Young.*

7690. CURIOSITY, Ubiquitous. Aristophanes the comedian said, concerning Cleon, that "his hands were in Petolia, and his soul in Thieftown;" so the hands and feet, eyes and thoughts of inquisitive persons are straggling about in many places at once. Neither the mansions of the great nor the cottages of the poor, nor the privy chambers of princes, nor the recesses of the nuptial alcove, can escape the search of their curiosity. *Plutarch.*

7691. CURSE, A Sinner's. Two neighbors, one a professor and the other a neglector of religion, living on opposite sides of the same street, were dying at the same time. One of them said of the other, "I feel that I am dying. Thomas over the way, I hear, is going, too. They say he is going to heaven; it may be so· I know that I am going to hell. He must have known that I was perishing; but he never warned me of my danger, or told me of the way of escape. We were together almost every day, and we talked of the weather, and the markets, and politics, and a thousand other things; but he never spoke to me about my soul. His silence I regarded as the sanction of my sin. I could account for it in no other way. He may be going to heaven; but he will be followed to heaven with the curses of my lost soul!"

7692. CURSES, Biblical. *The Woes of Scripture,* Isa. 5; 28:1; 29:1; 30:1; 31:1; 33:1; Hab. 2; Matt. 23; Luke 6:24–26. Gen. 3:14–19. The first curse pronounced when our first parents fell. Deut. 11:29; 27:13. The curses pronounced from Mount Ebal. It is observed by some that, under the law, the curses were first pronounced, and afterward the blessings; whilst, when Christ came, his teaching began with blessing, Matt. 5, and ended with pronouncing woes, Matt. 23. Yet even on Mount Ebal Joshua was told to build an altar, and offer burnt offerings and peace offerings, Joshua 8:33. Numb. 5:11–31. "The bitter water that causeth the curse." Isa. 43:28. "I have given Jacob to the curse." *Jacob*—God's own long-favored people—once so blessed! Mark 11:12–14, 20, 21. The fig tree cursed; no doubt representing the curse upon the Jewish nation—one of the only two miracles of destruction our Lord is recorded to have wrought. Obs. how speedy was the curse in taking effect, and how complete, ver. 20—"In the (next) *morning* . . . they saw the fig tree dried up *from the roots.* Zech. 5:2, 3. The "flying roll" . . . "the curse that goeth forth over the face of the whole earth," &c. Difficult as it may be to fix the exact interpretation of the symbol, three things seem clearly hinted at—(1.) From its large size, it points out the vast extent of the many curses pronounced by God against sin and sinners, (2.) its "flying" may intimate that the Divine curse is continually hovering over the head of the impenitent, and may any moment fall upon them, John 3:36; (3.) that the curse of God is sure to find out every sinner, though a man may "hold himself guiltless" (see marg.), and will "enter into the house," and destroy all the comfort and credit and reliance of the transgressor. Gen. 3:14; Isa. 65:25. The serpent first and longest cursed. Gen. 3:15. We cannot fail, in thinking of the curse, to observe how, even from the first, Divine mercy was mingled with judgment. When man fell, the curse was forthwith pronounced; but it was not pronounced first upon Adam or the woman, but upon the serpent; and with the pronouncing of the first curse was mingled the announcement of the first promise. Gal. 3: 13. We cannot but observe how complete is the redemption brought in by Christ. In every point, it has been said, he met the curse. One part of the curse was death. The Redeemer died; and when, in after times, one particular kind of death was especially pronounced accursed, he died that death. The serpent was, at the first, pre-eminently cursed. He made the uplifted serpent the emblem of his own sacrifice, John 3; 14, 15. Thorns were another effect of the curse. He wore a crown of thorns, he sweat the bloody sweat. In all and every point he met the curse, and took it in our stead upon himself.   *Bowes.*

7693. CURSES, Causeless. He that is cursed without a cause, whether by furious imprecations or solemn anathemas, the curse will do him no more harm than the sparrow that flies over his head. It will fly away like the sparrow or the wild swallow, which go nobody knows where, until they return to their proper place, as the curse will return to him that uttered it.   *M. Henry.*

7694. CURSES, Divine. They are not merely imprecations, impotent and fruitless desires; they carry their effects with them and are attended with all the miseries denounced by God.   *Cruden.*

7695. CURSES, Human. These are hurled at us, either because we have done the right thing, or they are uttered without reason or feeling. There are men who are so in the habit of using profane language, that it almost flows from their lips without malice or meaning; and there are those who regard profane language as an indication of manly courage and gentlemanly bearing. Human curses are ofttimes more an honor than a disgrace. The greatest souls have always lived under the ban of their age.   *Dr. Thomas.*

7696. CURSES, Reflex. According to fable, a bee took an offering of honey to Jupiter, which so pleased him that he promised to grant the bee whatever she should ask. The bee said, "O glorious Jove, give thy servant a sting, that when any one approaches my hive to take the honey, I may kill him on the spot." Jupiter answered her, "your prayer shall not be granted in the way you wish, but the sting you ask for you shall have; and when any one comes to take away your honey, and you sting him, the wound shall be fatal, not to him, but to you, for your life shall go with your sting." So it is to this day. He that curses others curses himself.

7697. CUSTOM, Compliance with. Alcibiades, who, when he dwelt at Athens, was as arch and witty as any Athenian of them all, kept his stable of horses, played the good fellow, and was universally obliging; and yet the same man at Sparta shaved close to the skin, wore his cloak, and never bathed but in cold water. When he sojourned in Thrace, he drank and fought like a Thracian; and again, in Tissaphernes's company in Asia, he acted the part of a soft, arrogant and voluptuous Asiatic. And thus, by an easy compliance with the hu-

mors and customs of the people amongst whom he conversed, he made himself master of their affections and interests. So did not the brave Epaminondas nor Agesilaus, who, though they had to do with great variety of men and manners, and cities of vastly different politics, were still the same men, and everywhere, through the whole circle of their conversation, maintained a part and character worthy of themselves. And so was Plato the same man at Syracuse that he was in the Academy, the same in Dionysius' court that he was in Dion's.   *Plutarch.*

7698. DANCING, Demoralization of. "I was called," says a minister, "in the early part of my ministry, to stand beside the bed of a beautiful young mother whose life was fast ebbing away. Deep, hopeless anguish, was riveted on her countenance. Death was knocking for admission. I asked her if she was willing that I should pray with her. Her reply was, 'I have no objection, but prayers will be of no avail now; it is too late, too late; I must die; I am lost! lost for ever!' I prayed earnestly with her, but her hard heart was untouched; there was in it no fountain of love to its Maker; it was 'too late.' What was the cause of her cold and careless indifference? Listen, mothers, and from her who, 'being dead, yet speaketh,' learn a lesson. This lovely mother was, at a very early period of her life, deeply and seriously impressed with the importance of religion, and the arrows of conviction were fastened in her heart. 'My mother,' says she, 'sent me to the dancing school, and I danced all my convictions away.' As she lived, so did she die—without Christ in the world."

7699. DANCING, Evil Influence of. When I hear of a dancing party I feel an uneasy sensation about the throat, remembering that a far greater preacher had his head danced off in the days of our Lord. However pleasing the polkas of Herodias might be to Herod, they were death to John the Baptist. The caperings and wantonings of the ball-room are death to the solemn influences of our ministry, and many an ill-ended life first received its bent for evil amid the flippancies of gay assemblies met to trip away the hours.   *Spurgeon.*

7700. DANCING, Habit of. The city of Sybaris boasted of its prosperity and power. At one time it sent out three hundred thousand men against the Crotonians. They had taught their horses at a certain tune to rise on their hind feet and on their fore feet to keep a kind of time with the music. A minstrel who had been ill-used amongst them, fled to Crotona, and told them "If they would make him their captain he would put all the enemy's horse, their chief strength, into their hands." They agreed to the terms, and he immediately began to teach the tune to all the minstrels in the city. When the Sybarites came up to a close charge, at a signal given, the minstrels began to play, and all the horses began to dance. Thus rendered unserviceable, they became an easy prey to the enemy.

7701. DANCING, History of. Dancing is very

nearly as old as the world. The Hebrews danced when they emerged from the Red Sea, and about the golden calf, which was not their maiden effort. The young maidens of Silo were enjoying the dance in the field, when they were surprised by the youths of the tribe of Benjamin, and carried off by force, according to the counsel of the ancients of Israel; David danced before the ark; Socrates learned dancing from Aspasia; the soldiers of Crete and of Sparta went dancing into an assault, etc. But we leave this point of animated archæology to be resolved by others. Dancing probably originated in certain gestures which indicated contentment, pain, joy—just as music was born of certain analogous sounds. Plato, Socrates, Lycurgus, and others, held dancing in great veneration. We are further informed that in old Chinese books dancing and music are described as the two most important departments of public affairs. Under the Romans, however, dancing had degenerated; and we are reminded that Cicero addressed a grave reproach to the Consul Gabinus for having danced.   *Helps.*

7702. DANCING, Prohibition of. A young lady requested her father to permit her to learn to dance. He replied, "No, my child: I cannot comply with a request which may subject me to your censures at some future period." "No, father: I will never censure you for complying with my request." "Nor can I consent," replied the father, "to give you an opportunity. If you learn, I have no doubt but you will excel; and when you leave school, you may then want to go into company to exhibit your skill. If I then object to let you, as I most likely should, you would very naturally reply, 'Why, father, did you first permit me to learn, if I am not permitted to practise?'" This reply satisfied her. She afterwards adopted for the government of her own family, the rule "Never to comply with a request which may subject me to any future reflections from my children."

7703. DANCING, Proscription of. Dancing is an amusement which has been discouraged in our country by many of the best people, and not without some reason. Dancing is associated in their minds with balls; and this is one of the worst forms of social pleasure. The time consumed in preparing for a ball, the waste of thought upon it, the extravagance of dress, the late hours, the exhaustion of strength, the exposure of health, and the languor of the succeeding day,—these and other evils connected with this amusement are strong reasons for banishing it from the community. *Channing.*

7704. DANDY, Description of a. A dandy is a clothes-wearing man—a man whose trade, office, and existence consist in the wearing of clothes. Every faculty of his soul, spirit, person, and purse, is heroically consecrated to this one object—the wearing of clothes wisely and well; so that, as others dress to live, he lives to dress. He is inspired with cloth, a poet of cloth.   *Carlyle.*

7705. DANGER, Confidence in. Under the persuasion that no disaster can reach us without the permission of him who watches over us with an eye that never slumbers, and a tenderness which nothing but guilt can withdraw from us, we can face those unknown terrors from which pagan philosophy turned away dismayed; we can look forward, unmoved, into futurity, and contemplate all the possible contingencies that may befall us, with intrepidity and unconcern; with the cheerfulness of a mind at perfect ease, reposing itself in full confidence and security on the great Disposer of all human events.   *Bishop Porteus.*

7706. DANGER, Escape from. Two vessels, in a gale off the southern coast, and wrapped in the darkness of the night, were sailing toward each other. The commanders knew it not, until suddenly, from the deck of one of the ships, rang out the trumpet-shout, "Hard-a-larboard!" The officer had caught sight of the approaching craft through the gloom, when near the prow of his own. Instantly was heard in response the thrilling words, "Hard-a-larboard!" Every heart on those ships was still, as the white-robed arms of the leviathans of the sea-wave seemed to interlock in a terrific struggle, then part forever. Each swept onward toward its destined port, bearing the pale spectators of the scene. Those ships had doubtless often been in danger, but never before nor afterward was such threatened destruction warded off by a breath through the speaking-trumpet, and escaped by so small a margin of deliverance. We believe that in heaven every ransomed soul will see in the life-voyage, among many dangers encountered, some single peril of decisive interest. It may have been the avoiding of a meeting with a dangerous companion, or stopping at the entrance of a theatre, when the forces of evil were in wait for him, turning, as it were, a hairbreadth aside. because upon the inward ear fell, just in time. the warning tones of the silver trumpet, borne by them of whom it is written: "And he shall give his angels charge concerning thee, to keep thee in all thy ways, lest at any time thou dash thy foot against a stone." That escape will have a solitary importance in all the earthly past, and will send up to the throne a strain of highest thanksgiving. Such was its relation to life; to have failed of deliverance then was certain ruin forever. Some Christians can now look back upon this moment of dark and awful peril. Multitudes are daily passing safely, or making shipwreck, at such critical moments in probation.   *Messenger.*

7707. DANGER, Everywhere. A shipwrecked sailor clinging to fragments of the wreck looked down into the water and saw the sharks in great numbers waiting for their prey. Could we see how we are environed with dangers we should be appalled. By night and by day, on land and on sea, sheltered or exposed, calamities, sickness, temptation, destruction, hover near to seize us as their prey. Our safety is in our omnipresent God who has said "Thou shalt not fear."

7708. DANGER, Exposure to. When the instructed Christian sees his surroundings, he finds himself to be like a defenceless dove flying to her nest, while against her tens of thousands of arrows are leveled. The Christian life is like that dove's anxious flight, as it threads its way between the death-bearing shafts of the enemy, and by constant miracle escapes unhurt. The enlightened Christian sees himself to be like a traveler, standing on the narrow summit of a lofty ridge; on the right hand and on the left are gulfs unfathomable, yawning for his destruction; if it were not that by divine grace his feet are like hinds' feet, so that he is able to stand upon his high places, he would long ere this have fallen to his eternal destruction. *Spurgeon.*

7709. DANGER, Ignoring. Those people are in the road to ruin, who say to their ministers, as the Jews did of old to their Prophets: "Prophesy not;" or, what amounts to the same thing, "Speak unto us smooth things, prophesy deceits." I well remember having read, in an ancient author, the following remarkable and appropriate account: "News came to a certain town, once and again, that the enemy was approaching; but he did not then approach. Hereupon, in anger, the inhabitants enacted a law, that no man, on pain of death, should bring again such rumors, as the news of an enemy. Not long after, the enemy came indeed; besieged, assaulted, and sacked the town; of the ruins of which nothing remained, but this proverbial epitaph—"Here once stood a town that was destroyed by silence." *Anon.*

7710. DANGER, Insufficient Protection from. When the lofty spire of old St. Paul's was destroyed by lightning, there were many superstitious persons who were amazed beyond measure at the calamity, for in the cross there had long been deposited relics of certain saints, which were counted fully sufficient to avert all danger of tempests. With what amazement will ignorant, self-righteous sinners see their own destruction come upon them, notwithstanding all the refuges of lies in which they trusted. *Spurgeon.*

7711. DANGER, Keep Clear of. A vessel was approaching the dangerous point, Cape Hatteras. The outline of the rock coast was in view. Suddenly the order was given to tack and the vessel stood out into the broad ocean, leaving the coast far astern. "Is not the water deep enough to make a closer run to the shore?" asked a passenger, who was impatient to get a good sight of land after the three days' voyage. "Certainly," answered the captain, gazing off to the south at the signs of an approaching storm. "But why, then, did we tack here?" asked the man. "Because," replied the captain, "if in running close to the cape we had become in any way disabled, we might have drifted on the rocks and have been wrecked. A good sailor, when possible, stands out from danger." The seaman's greatest danger is when near the rock or sandy shores. He keeps out in the wide sea for safety. So it is with the Christian. Out on the sea of truth and love it is safe.

7712. DANGER, Playing with. A mother visited a menagerie with her infant in her arms. As they stood by the tiger's cage, the animal, apparently quiet, permitted the caresses of the child, and the mother, thinking it under the control of its keeper, and caged by iron bars, relaxed her vigilance, when suddenly the tiger seized the child, and in one fatal moment it became its prey. Keep away from the drinking and gambling saloon, and the house of the strange woman, or in an unexpected moment they will turn and rend you.

7713. DANGER, Protection from. "It shall not come nigh thee." The words came to our mind the other day as, sitting in the family room of a depot dwelling, a low rumble of an approaching express train suddenly fell upon the ear, growing louder and louder into a very thunder, as the huge and impetuous monster rushed by, within a few feet of our chair; the building shook as by an earthquake; the furniture rattled as if by hands. How near, and yet how secure! Guided by the firm and glistening rails, the mighty train swept on, restrained from inflicting the ruin which it was quite in its power to do. Of how many of the calamities and sorrows of this life is it true that, guided by the unerring lines of God's providence, they come very near us, and yet touch us not, because it is not his will. "A thousand shall fall at thy side, and ten thousand at thy right hand, but it shall not come nigh thee." *The Congregationalist.*

7714. DANGER, Reckless of. Some distance above the falls of Niagara is a ferry which is always considered very dangerous by the most experienced boatmen. The current may seize a boat and shoot it like an arrow down the rapids toward the great fall. A young man from foolish bravado resolved to try the ferry in his boat alone. Old boatmen warned him, but he was deaf alike to counsel and entreaty. He launched his boat, and rowed bravely, but all his efforts were powerless against the current, which swept him against the rocks above the falls. His boat was crushed, and he caught hold of a projecting rock. Report of his danger ran through the town, and the people flocked in crowds to the shore. Thousands of dollars were offered for his rescue. But it was impossible. No help could reach him. Just so soon as his strength gave out he must go over the fall. For twenty-four hours he hung upon the brink of fate, and then his strength gave way, and with an awful shriek he went over the fall and into eternity. Thus myriads are hanging on the rocks of sin. Their doom is sure and will be soon.

7715. DANGER, Shelter from. There is an ancient fable which says that the dove once made a piteous complaint to her fellow birds, that the hawk was a most cruel tyrant, and was thirsting for her blood. One counseled her to keep below—but the hawk can stoop for its prey; another advised her to soar aloft—but the hawk can mount as high as she. A third bade her hide herself in the woods, but alas! these are the hawk's own estates, where he holds his court. A fourth recommended her to keep in the town, but there man hunted her, and she feared that her eyes would be put out by the cruel falconer to make sport for the hawk. At last one told her to rest herself in the clefts of the rock, there she would be safe, violence itself could not surprise her there. The meaning is easy; reader, do not fail to catch it, and to act upon it. The dove is thy poor defenceless soul. Satan is thy cruel foe; wouldst thou not escape from him? Thy poverty cannot protect thee, for sin can stoop to the poor man's level and devour him in the cottage, and drag him to hell from a hovel. Thy riches are no security, for Satan can make these a snare to thee, and if thou shouldst mount ever so high, the bird of prey can follow thee and rend thee in pieces! The busy world with all its cares cannot shelter thee, for here it is that the great enemy is most at home; he is the prince of this world, and seizes men who find their joys therein as easily as a kite lays hold upon a sparrow. Nor can retirement secure you, for there are sins peculiar to quietude, and hell's dread vulture soars over lonely solitudes to find defenceless souls, and rend them in pieces. There is but one defence. O may you and I fly to it at once! Jesus was wounded for sin; faith in him saves at once and forever. *Spurgeon.*

7716. DANGER, Shield from. Artemon was a very skillful engineer, but of a very timorous disposition. Foolishly afraid of his own shadow he scarcely ever stirred out of his house. Two men stood over him at all times, with a brazen shield, so that nothing should fall upon him, and if necessity called him from home, he would be carried in a litter so near the ground that it would not harm him if he should fall. How happy are they who can say, "The Lord God is my sun and my shield."

7717. DANGER, Spiritual. I remember five or six years ago being in Chamounix, Switzerland, and the day before our arrival a young man and woman had arrived from London. They were making their bridal tour, and they had attempted to ascend Mont Blanc, and had got near the top when the husband said to the wife: "You had better tarry here with one of the guides. It will be too cold up there on that top cliff. I will hasten up and touch the top of the cliff, and hasten back again, and you stay here until I return," and he started. She, ambitious to follow him, started also, and putting her foot on what she supposed to be solid ice, it broke, and she fell through, hundreds and perhaps thousands of feet down, her body to be found forty years from now, when by the law of the glacier it will come out at the foot of the cliff. On the following days we stood and looked through our telescopes, and we saw the men digging in the snow and hewing amid the glaciers; but there was no hope —no hope. Oh! are there not souls here traveling on slippery places? You think that all is fair and well. You are going on, you are going up in life, but after a while you will put your foot down and it will break through into the grave, and you will be gone from your house, and gone from the church, and gone from the store, and gone from all the places which know you now, but will know you no more. Fly to the cross! Drop everything for that. You cannot afford to ruin your soul. Lose heaven and you lose all. *Talmage.*

7718. DANGER, Symbol of. A merchant was one evening celebrating the marriage of his daughter. While the guests were enjoying themselves above, he chanced to go into the basement where he met a servant carrying a candle without a candlestick. She passed on to the cellar for wood, and returning quickly without the candle, the merchant suddenly remembered that during the day several barrels of gunpowder had been placed in the cellar, one of which had been opened. Inquiring what she had done with the candle, to his amazement and horror her reply was, that not being able to carry it with the wood, she had set it in a small barrel of "black sand," in the cellar. He flew to the spot. A long, red snuff was ready to fall from the wick into the mass of powder, when, with great presence of mind, placing one hand on each side of the candle, and making his hands meet at the top over the wick, he safely removed it from the barrel. At first he smiled at his previous terror; but the reaction was so great that it was weeks before he overcame the shock which his nerves had sustained in that terrible moment. Beneath the surface of our social enjoyments are burning passions and terrible temptations which may bring terrible destruction at any moment. *Anon.*

7719. DANGER, Unlikely. You have read the reason why the Ephesians expelled the best of their citizens,—"*Nemo de nobis unus excellat, sed si quis extiterit, alio in loco et apud alios sit;*" "If any are determined to excel their neighbors, let them find another place to do it." You have read that he who conquered Hannibal saw it necessary to retire from Rome, that the merits of others might be more noticed. My authors tell me that "at all times nothing has been more dangerous among men than too illustrious a degree of merit." But, my readers, the terror of this envy must not intimidate you. I must press you to do good; and be so far from affrighted at it, you shall rather be generously delighted with the most envious deplumations. *Cotton Mather.*

7720. DANGER, Unseen. The preacher may be addressing one whose end is near and whose preparation for eternity must be crowded into a few hours or days. Could he lift the curtain and show the neglecter his true position, on the verge of the abyss of woe, while death stands by with uplifted hand to push him over the brink, he would cry out in the greatest alarm, "Save Lord, or I perish." Such a vision would extort the cry from every beholder, "Sinner, have mercy on thine own soul. O God, have mercy upon him and haste to save him."

7721. DANGER, Vows in. How much would the gods be enriched by danger, if we remembered the vows which it makes us offer! But, the danger once past, we no longer remember our promise. *Fontaine.*

7722. DANGER, Warning of. It was a custom in Pompeii to place a slave with a trusty dog to keep guard in the vestibule of the houses. Conspicuously posted were the words, "*Cave canem.*" Beware of the dog. There is many a dangerous place where no guard appears and no warning is given.

7723. DANGERS, Extremes of. Look upon any duty or grace, and you will find it lie between Scylla and Charybdis, two extremes alike dangerous. Faith, the great work of God, cuts its way between the mountain of presumption and the gulf of despair. Patience (a grace so necessary that we cannot be without it a day, except we would be all that while beside ourselves) keeps us that we fall neither into the sleepy apoplexy of a blockish stupidity, nor into a raging fit of discontent. *Gurnall.*

7724. DANGERS, Hidden. There is a mountain pass in Switzerland over which the traveler is conducted blindfold. He might lose his footing if he caught but one bewildering glimpse of the chasm below. In like manner a wise love conceals from us those circumstances that might distract our attention from the immediate line of duty, and withholds the knowledge that might occasion bewilderment and a fall. *Charles Stanford.*

7725. DANGERS, Influence of. When evil passions stir within, and evil men oppress without —when conscience accuses, and death overshadows—I am like a dove tossed with the tempest: I see an opening into the bosom of my Father—thither I fly away to be at rest. Blessed is even the storm which drives the dove to its window. Blessed, in the end, will be the miscellaneous dangers and trials of life; for they shut the pilgrim up to the refuge of his soul, and keep him cowering deep all his days, in God's loving kindness, which is better than life. *Arnot.*

7726. DANIEL, Tradition of. The marvelous gift of Daniel, by which he was able to discover the dream of Nebuchadnezzar, and to give the true interpretation thereof, won for him the name Belteshazzar. Josephus says that the king was so astonished at Daniel's revelation that he fell down on his face before him and worshiped him as a god, conferred the name of his own god, Belteshazzar, upon him, and gave command that men should sacrifice to him as a god. Because of this Daniel may have been exempted from the command to worship the image in the plain of Dura, for disobedience to which the other Hebrews were cast into the furnace. The reputation that he was a god extended among the pagans, increased by his sanctity and the marvels he wrought. He was a favorite with kings and people, appearing at the court of Nebuchadnezzar, rendering his dream of the great image; then in the palace of Belshazzar, reading the hand-writing on the wall; then he is prime minister to Darius, and endures the ordeal of the lions. Afterward he wrote his own life, the Book of Daniel.

7727. DARK AGES, Ignorance in the. In less than a century after the barbarous nations settled in their new conquests, almost all the effects of knowledge and civility, which the Romans had spread through Europe, disappeared. Not only the arts of elegance, which minister to luxury, and are supported by it, but many of the useful arts, without which life can scarcely be considered as comfortable, were neglected or lost. Literature, science, and taste, were words little in use during the ages which we are contemplating; or, if they occur at any time, eminence in them is ascribed to persons and productions so contemptible, that it appears their true import was little understood. Persons of the highest rank, and in the most eminent stations, could not read or write. Many of the clergy did not understand the breviary which they were obliged daily to recite; some of them could scarcely read it. The memory of past transactions was in a great degree lost, or preserved in annals filled with trifling events or legendary tales. *Dr. Robertson.*

7728. DARKNESS, Biblical. DARKNESS is one of the many *abstract* terms used to express the evil and effects of sin. Sin is not only dark, but darkness; not an enemy, but enmity. The expression, too, is intensified by the strongest epithets: "gross darkness"—"thick darkness" —"blackness of darkness." So we read of the actings of sin as "ways of darkness"—"works of darkness"—"deeds of darkness," &c. DARKNESS lies in the sinner's heart, Rom. 1: 21; and understanding, Eph. 4: 18. It is the element in which they live. So we read that they "walk" in darkness; they "sit;" they "abide;" they "grope;" they "stumble on the dark mountains." No wonder, when we read that they "prefer darkness to light;" they "hate;" "they rebel against the light;" "there is no light in them;" and "their punishment shall be analogous to their life"—"driven into darkness;" "cast into outer darkness" (three times referred to by St. Matthew, chap. 8: 12; 22: 13; 25: 20), where "the light of the wicked shall be put out, and the spark of his fire shall not shine," Job 18: 5, 6, 18. SATAN'S CONNECTION with darkness. Christ's kingdom is a kingdom of light. Satan's kingdom is that of darkness, Eph. 6: 12; Rev. 16: 10; Jude 6. *Bowes.*

7729. DARKNESS, Influence of. A little girl sat, at twilight, in her sick mother's room, busily thinking. All day she had been full of fun and noise, and had many times worried her poor tired mother. "Ma," said the little girl. "what do you suppose makes me get over my mischief, and begin to act good, just about this time every night?" "I do not know, dear. Can you not tell?" "Well, I guess it's because this is when the dark comes. You know I am a little afraid of that. And then, ma, I begin to think of all the naughty things I've done to grieve you, and that perhaps you might die before morning; and so I begin to act good." "O!" thought I, "how many of us wait till 'the dark comes,' in the form of sickness or sorrow, or trouble of some kind, before we 'begin to act good!' How much better to be good while we are enjoying life's bright sunshine! and then 'when the dark comes,' as it will in a measure to all, we shall be ready to meet it without fear." *Wellspring.*

7730. DARKNESS, Need of. Speaking of a Norwegian summer, the Rev. H. Macmillan says: "The long daylight is very favorable to the growth of vegetation, plants growing in the night as well as in the day in the short but ardent summer. But the stimulus of perpetual solar light is peculiarly trying to the nervous system of those who are not accustomed to it. It prevents proper repose and banishes sleep. I never felt before how needful darkness is for the welfare of our bodies and minds. I longed for night, but the farther north we went, the farther we were fleeing from it, until at last, when we reached the most northern point of our tour, the sun set for one hour and a half. Consequently, the heat of the day never cooled down, and accumulated until it became almost unendurable at last. Truly for a most wise and beneficent purpose did God make light and create darkness. 'Light is sweet, and it is a pleasant thing to the eyes to behold the sun.' But darkness is also sweet, it is the nurse of nature's kind restorer, balmy sleep, and without the tender drawing round us of its curtains the weary eyelid will not close, and the jaded nerves will not be soothed to refreshing rest. Not till the everlasting day break, and the shadows flee away, and the Lord himself shall be our light, and our God our glory, can we do without the cloud in the sunshine, the shade of sorrow in the bright light of joy, and the curtain of night for the deepening of the sleep which God gives his beloved."

7731. DARKNESS, Spiritual. We often see men whose blindness is such that they cannot behold the bright orb of day in the heavens. But because they are blind, do we doubt the existence of a sun, or do we quarrel with his beams? The fault, indeed, is not in the sun, but in the eyes of such persons, which will not permit them to admire his radiance. Thus blinded are the eyes of the soul, and our sins are those shadows which hide from us the glorious light of heaven and of celestial beauty. Oh, man, how art thou fallen by nature! How miserably abject thy condition! But if thou wilt, thou canst be healed. Go to the true physician of the soul; to him belongs a light which can dissipate the darkest shadows. Beseech him to open thine eyes, that thou mayest see. *Theophilus of Antioch.*

7732. DAUGHTER, The Conduct of a. When a young woman behaves to her parents in a manner particularly tender and respectful, I mean from principle as well as nature, there is nothing good and gentle that may not be expected from her in whatever condition she is placed. Of this I am so thoroughly persuaded, that, were I to advise any friend of mine as to his choice of a wife, I know not whether my very first counsel would not be—"Look out for one distinguished by her attention and sweetness to her parents." The fund of worth and affection, indicated by such a behavior, joined to the habits of duty and consideration thereby contracted, being transferred to the married state, will not fail to render her a mild and obliging companion. *Fordyce.*

7733. DAVID, Error Concerning. David is called "a man after God's own heart,"—not in his personal and private character, but in the policy of his public administration as the lieutenant and deputy of Jehovah. He most scrupulously observed the civil and ecclesiastical laws which Moses had promulgated, and carefully adjusted his own military government to the inspired maxims of the prophets and priests of the Most High. He staunchly maintained the knowledge and service of the living and true God against all forms of idolatry and will-worship, and assiduously labored to improve and perpetuate the ritual homage which was rendered to him. He therefore planned the building of a splendid temple for Jehovah, and consecrated the spoils of his many victories to its adornment; whilst he called into exercise his splendid gifts in poetry and music, that he might perfect "the service of song in the house of the Lord." "Those persons, therefore, who gather up the great faults and sins of David's private life—his craft and falsehood, his anger and revenge, his adultery and murder—in order to ask with derison and contempt, 'Is this man after God's own heart?' are quite beside the mark, missing altogether the spirit and intention of the passage they are so ready to pervert. When the prophet Samuel uttered that much-abused sentence (1 Sam 13: 14), it was in immediate connection with one that condemned the disobedience of Saul, and it therefore predicted a successor whose policy and administration should be in direct opposition to those of this king. It had, therefore, little to do with the private character of David, and only commended that course of public policy which maintained inviolate all the great maxims of the theocratic government." *John Blackburn.*

7734. DAVID, Excellence of. Never, among the mere sons of men, has there appeared on so prominent a stage, a character with so rich and varied gifts. Like the single heir of a number of wealthy families, he seemed to unite in himself the moral wealth of nearly all that had gone before him—the heavenly conversation of Enoch, the triumphant faith of Abraham, the meditative thoughtfulness of Isaac, the wrestling boldness of Jacob, the patient and holy endurance of Joseph—no less than his talent for administering a kingdom, the lofty patriotism of Moses—as well as his brilliant fancy, the war-like skill and energy of Joshua, the daring courage of Gideon, the holy fervor of Samuel—all met in a measure in the character of David. A great King—a great warrior—and a great religious reformer —he held at once the great sceptres that ruled the hearts of men. But there was still higher work in reserve for him. He was the great hymn-writer of the church, the framer of that grand liturgy in which the godly of all nations, and of all generations, were to pour out the feelings of their hearts to God. Yet higher still, he was a type of Christ. *Blaikie.*

7735. DAY, Accounting for a. Vespasian, the Roman emperor, throughout the whole course of his life used to call himself to account every night for the actions of the past day, and as often as he found he had passed any one day without doing some good, he entered in his diary this memorandum, *Diem perdidi*: "I have lost a day."

7736. DAY, Rules for Each. In the week days, when thou risest in the morning, consider, 1. Thou must die. 2. Thou mayst die that minute. 3. What will become of thy soul? Pray often. At night consider, 1. What sins thou hast committed. 2. How often thou hast prayed. 3. What hath thy mind been bent upon? 4. What hath been thy dealing? 5. What thy conversation? 6. If thou callest to mind the errors of the day, sleep not without a confession to God, and a hope of pardon. Thus, every morning and evening make up thy accounts with Almighty God, and thy reckoning will be the less at last. *Bunyan.*

7737. DAY OF GRACE, Neglecting the. When I think of opportunities, I think I may liken us here to-night to a number of men in the Arctic regions. They have been frozen up for a long time, and the ship is high and dry on great masses of ice. The thaw comes on; but the thaw, however, will last but for a very short time. They set their saws to work; they see a split in the ice; there is a long and very narrow lane of water. If they can get the ship along there before the water freezes it up again, they may yet reach the shores of dear old England, and be safe; but if not, they are frozen in for another winter, and very likely will be frozen in forever. Well, now, to-night it seems just so with us. It seems as if the Spirit of God had purposely brought some of you here; and I do trust he is opening, as it were, the lane of mercy for you—causing your sins for a little time to loose their frosty hold, and opening your heart a little to the genial influences of the Gospel. But, oh! if it should be frozen up again. *Spurgeon.*

7738. DAYS, Computation of. Every day is a little life; and our whole life is but a day repeated: whence it is that old Jacob numbers his life by days; and Moses desires to be taught this point of holy arithemetic, to number not his years, but his days. Those, therefore, that dare lose a day, are dangerously prodigal; those that dare misspend it, desperate. *Bishop Hall.*

7739. DEAD, Blessed. A Roman Catholic lady I was the means of bringing out of that church, told me that the words repeated by me, "Blessed are the dead which die in the Lord," kindled in her heart convictions which she could not allay, and which, on application to the priest, he could not hush. She told me that she was once supposed to be on the point of death. "I was given up as dying," she said, "and a priest was sent for, a venerable man, to administer extreme unction. He did so; I had full possession of my mind, and I asked him, 'Now, tell me, my father, am I saved? And he answered, 'I can pledge my own salvation that you will be ultimately safe.' 'Ultimately! what does it mean?' 'My child, you must pass through purgatory.' I said, 'I have had extreme unction administered. What is the nature of that purgatory through which I have to pass?' 'My child, purgatory is a place where you must endure the torments of the damned, only of shorter duration.'" Such was the comfort with which she was left to die; but this text seemed to her to annihilate purgatory. *Dr. Cumming.*

7740. DEAD, Burning the. Mr. Underhill, writing from India, says: "We went aboard at daylight on the 18th, and before night had entered the channel which leads to the Sunderbunds. From a slight accident to the paddle-box at starting, we were detained two or three hours at the dock opposite to Nimtollah Ghat. It is at this place the Hindoos burn their dead. Three fires were burning during our detention. We could easily see the whole process; both men and women were engaged in performing this last rite. Around the ghat were thousands of birds, waiting with solemn mien the departure of the attendants, to pick over and devour the charred remains. The walls and houses around were covered with vultures, and dogs prowled about to share in the horrid feast."

7741. DEAD, Fear of the. It is said of the late Dr. Arnold, that "finding one of his children had been greatly shocked and overcome by the first sight of death, he tenderly endeavored to remove the feeling which had been awakened, and, opening a Bible, pointed to the words, 'Then cometh Simon Peter following him, and went into the sepulchre, and seeth the linen clothes lie, and the napkin, that was about his head, not lying with the linen clothes, but wrapped together in a place by itself.'—'Nothing,' he said, 'to his mind afforded us such comfort, when shrinking from the outward accompaniments of death—the grave, the grave-clothes, the loneliness—as the thought that all these had been around our Lord himself—round him who died, and is now alive for evermore.'" *Stanley.*

7742. DEAD, Honors to the. Our respect for the dead, when they are just dead, is something wonderful, and the way we show it more wonderful still. We show it with black feathers and black horses; we show it with black dresses and black heraldries; we show it with costly obelisks and sculptures of sorrow, which spoil half of our beautiful cathedrals. We show it with frightful gratings and vaults, and lids of dismal stone, in the midst of the quiet grass; and last, and not least, we show it by permitting ourselves to tell any number of falsehoods we think amiable or credible in the epitaph. *Ruskin.*

7743. DEAD, Raising the. There was a dead man being carried out of the City of Nain, and there was a great company of the friends accompanying that widow to lay away her only child, her only son. He was an only son, it

says, and his mother was a widow. The father, the head of the house, had died perhaps long before, and long before that mother had watched over that husband, and at last she closed his eyes in death. It was a terrible blow, and now death had come again. You who are mothers can see how through all that sickness that mother was not willing to let the neighbors come in and watch over that boy. For weeks you can see a light burning in that little cottage in Nain. That mother has imprinted the last kiss upon that lovely cheek. Now they lay him in the coffin or upon the bier, and perhaps four men take him up just as they did the man with the palsy, and they bear him away to his resting place and there is a great multitude coming out of Nain. All Nain is moved. The widow was loved very much and there was a great multitude attending her. And now we see them as they are coming out of the gate of the city. The disciples look, and they see a great crowd coming out of Nain, and the two crowds, the two great multitudes come together, and the Son of God looks upon that scene. We read often where he looked toward heaven and sighed. He had followers on his right hand, followers on his left hand, followers behind him, and followers before him. He saw the woe and suffering in this wretched world, but he looked upon that weeping mother. Death has got its captive. And shall not the Son of God look upon that widow? He saw those tears trickling down her cheeks, and the great heart of the Son of God was moved. He would not suffer that son to pass. He commanded the young men to rest the bier. "Young man, I say unto thee, arise!" and the dead heard the voice of the Son of God and he arose. I can imagine him saying, "Blessed be God, I am alive."
Moody.

7744. DEAD, Reviving the. Thomas Fuller tells of a knight, one Gervase Scroop, who received twenty-six wounds in the battle of Edgehill, and was left for dead amid heaps of slain. The next day his son Adrian sought his corpse to give it a decent burial. When found, the body was not quite cold, and the son began to use the means for restoration, which met with entire success, and the knight lived more than ten years, a monument of his son's affection. There are many souls left as dead, among the slain, along the highways of sin, whom diligent personal effort would rescue. Surprising success often attends this work.

7745. DEAD, Unchangeable. A minister dreamed that he was walking with a companion of his boyhood, when suddenly the Day of Judgment, with all its appalling scenes, burst upon them. He turned to look for his companion, and saw him lying pale and motionless, with his tongue swollen, and hanging from his mouth, as if he had been trying to pray, but was struck into stone. He heard a voice say, "His character is adamant; he that is filthy, let him be filthy still; and he that is righteous, let him be righteous still." In much trepidation he awoke, and at the earliest possible time sought his

friend, and told him the dream. It was the means of reforming the man.

7746. DEAD, Unconsciousness of the. A young man, applying to St. Macarius for spiritual advice, directed him to go to a burying-place and upbraid the dead, and after that to go and flatter them. "Well," said Macarius, when the young man returned, "how did the dead receive thy abuse of them?" "They answered not a word," he replied. "And how did they behave when flattered?" "They took no notice of that either." "Then," replied Macarius, "Go, and learn neither to be moved with injuries nor flatteries. If you die to the world and to yourself, you will begin to live to Christ."

7747. DEAD, Yet Speaking. The sun sets behind the western hills, but the trail of light he leaves behind him guides the pilgrim to his distant home. The tree falls in the forest; but in the lapse of ages it is turned into coal, and our fires burn now the brighter because it grew and fell. The coral insect died, but the reef it raised breaks the surge on the shores of great continents, or has formed an isle in the bosom of the ocean to wave now with harvests for the good of man, and to be a gem hereafter for the diadem of the great Redeemer. We live, and we die; but the good or evil that we do lives after us, and "is not buried with our bones." *Dr. Cumming.*

7748. DEATH, Admonition of. Henry, Emperor of Germany in the tenth century, caused a paper to be placed upon the plate of one of his pets at a feast with the inscription, "Meinwerk! Meinwerk! set thy house in order, for in five days thou shalt die." The bishop was startled, left the table abruptly, hastened home, made his will, renounced his earthly goods and bade farewell to his clergy. Then wrapping himself in his shroud he laid down in his coffin to die. But death tarried and the bishop grew hungry. He arose from his coffin, and walked about in his grave clothes, searching for food. Just then King Henry with some of his nobles burst in, and, amid great laughter, congratulated the bishop on his resurrection. He discovered the joke and his wrath waxed hot. Next Sunday he excommunicated the king, and would not remove the ban till he had done penance standing with bare feet, clothed in a white sheet.

7749. DEATH, Advantage of Early. Regret is often expressed at the early death of promising young men. Such was the feeling when John Summerfield fell in the dawn of a brilliant morning. He died with all the beauty and fervor of piety fresh upon him, which might have become impaired with longer life. The Lord plucked the flower, before a leaf had faded, for the adornment of his everlasting gardens.

7750. DEATH, Alfred Cookman's. Rev. Alfred Cookman seemed to have premonitions of his approaching decease. About four weeks previously he preached his last sermon from, "We do all fade as a leaf," holding up at the same time a withered leaf. Passing out from the congregation he handed this to a brother, remarking, "I feel that the text and the preacher

are much alike. It may be my last testimony."
His final words to his mother were, "I am
more indebted for all I am to your prayers and
counsel and example than to aught beside."
To his sister he said, "If I could have life on
earth for the lifting up of my hand I would
not. If Jesus should come and ask me would
I live or die, I would say, 'Do as thou pleasest,
Lord.'" Lifting up his paralyzed hand with
the other, he said, "This is a paralyzed hand,
but it belongs to Jesus." And now the chariot seemed to have come, and his last words
were, "I am sweeping through the gates,
washed in the blood of the Lamb."

7751. DEATH, Avarice in. Mr. Watson, uncle to the late Marquis of Rockingham, a man
of immense fortune, finding himself at the point
of death, desired a friend who was present to
open him a drawer, in which was an old shirt,
that he might put it on. Being asked why he
would wish to change his linen when he was
so ill, he said, "Because I'm told that the shirt
that I die in must be the nurse's perquisite,
and that is good enough for her!" This was
as bad as the woman, who, with her last breath,
blew out an inch of candle—"Because," said
she, "I can see to die in the dark." *Hood.*

7752. DEATH, Beautiful. To me, few things
appear so beautiful as a very young child in
its shroud. The little innocent face looks so
sublimely simple and confiding among the terrors of death. Crimeless and fearless, that little mortal passed under the shadow and explored the mystery of dissolution. There is
death in its sublimest and purest image; no
hatred, no hypocrisy, no suspicion, no care for
the morrow, ever darkened that little one's
face; death has come lovingly upon it; there
is nothing cruel or harsh in its victory. The
yearnings of love, indeed, cannot be stifled;
for the prattle and smiles, and all the little
world of thoughts that were so delightful, are
gone forever. Awe, too, will overcast us in
its presence; for we are looking on death.
But we do not fear for the little lovely voy-
ager; for the child has gone, simple and trusting, into the presence of its all-wise Father,
and of such, we know, is the kingdom of
heaven. *Leigh Hunt.*

7753. DEATH, Bells Ringing at. The legend of
St. Hymelin is, that as he was dying all the
church chimes of the town began ringing sweet
music, though no man touched the bells.

7754. DEATH, Biblical Figures of. *The king of
terrors,* Job 18: 14. Sleep, Acts 7: 60. Putting off the tabernacle of the body, 2 Cor. 5:
1. *Cut down* like the grass or flower, Ps. 90:
5, 6. *Cut off like the weaver's thread,* Is. 38:
12; or *the ears of corn,* Job 24: 24. *Fleeing
as a shadow,* Job 14: 1. *Carried away as a
flood,* Ps. 90: 5. *The consuming* of snow-
water, Job 24: 9; *water spilt* upon the ground,
2 Sam. 14: 14. In some Eastern lands in ancient times they poured water into the grave
in token of man's frailty. *Departing* like a
vessel from the harbor, Phil. 1: 23. *The river
Jordan,* the entrance to the land of rest. *Sowing* like seed, 1 Cor. 15: 42–45. *Resting as in*
a tranquil bed, Is. 57: 2. *Returning to dust,*
Gen. 3: 19; Eccl. 12: 7. *Going the way whence
there is no return,* Job 16: 22. *A war* from
which there is no discharge, Eccl. 8: 8.
Bowes.

7755. DEATH, Bishop Butler's. As this great
Christian apologist lay on his death-bed, he
said to his chaplain: "I know that Jesus Christ
is a Saviour, but how am I to know that he is
a Saviour to me?" The chaplain replied, "It
is written, 'Him that cometh unto me I will in
no wise cast out.'" After musing awhile the
dying bishop said, "I have often read and
thought of that scripture, but never till this
moment did I feel its full power, and now I die
happy."

7756. DEATH, Calling for. An old man that
had traveled a long way with a huge bundle
of sticks, found himself so weary that he cast
it down, and called upon Death to deliver him
from his most miserable existence. Death
came straightway at his call, and asked him
what he wanted. "Pray, good sir," says he,
"do me but the favor to help me up with my
burden again." *Æsop.*

7757. DEATH, Certainty of. There is nothing
more certain than death, nothing more uncertain than the time of dying. I will, therefore,
be prepared for that at all times, which may
come at any time, must come at one time or
another. I shall not hasten my death by being
still ready, but sweeten it. It makes me not
die the sooner, but the better. *Warwick.*

7758. DEATH, Change in. There lies my friend.
He hastens to depart. Death is upon him.
The change has well-nigh come. How little
intervenes between his present humiliations
and his awaiting glories! I tremble to think
what in an instant he must be! How unlike
all he was! I bend over thee, and mark thy
wasted, pallid frame; I look up, and there is
ascending above me an angel's form. I stoop
to thee, and just can catch thy feeble, gasping
whisper: I listen, and there floats around me a
seraph's song. I take thy hand, tremulous and
cold: it is waving to me from yonder skies. I
wipe thy brow, damp and furrowed: it is en-
wreathed with the garland of victory. I slake
thy lip, bloodless and parched; it is drinking
the living fountains, the overflowing springs
of heaven! *R. W. Hamilton.*

7759. DEATH, a Change of Place only. Rev.
Thomas Sheppard, of Charlestown, Mass., on
the day before his death, said to Dr. Cotton
Mather, "My hopes are built on the free mercy
of God, and the rich merit of Christ; and I do
believe that if I am taken out of the world, I
shall only change my place: I shall neither
change my company nor my communion."

7760. DEATH, Cheerfulness at. One of the martyrs was asked why he was so light-hearted
when doomed to a terrible death. "Oh," said
he, "my heart is so light at my death, because
Christ's was so heavy at his."

7761. DEATH of Children. The good husbandman may pluck his roses and gather in his lilies at midsummer, and for aught I daresay in
the beginning of the first summer month; and

he may transplant young trees out of the lower ground to the higher, where they have more of the sun, and a more free air at any season of the year. What is that to you or me? The goods are his own. *Rutherford.*

7762. DEATH, Child's Ideas of. "She died," said Mary, "and was buried in the ground where the trees grow." "The cold ground?" said Kate, shuddering. "No, the warm ground," returned Mary, "where the ugly little seeds are turned into beautiful flowers, and where good people turn into angels and fly away to heaven."

7763. DEATH with Christ. "During seven weeks of his severe suffering, a fretful or murmuring expression never escaped Romaine's lips; but often would he say, 'How good is God to me! What entertainments and comforts does he give me! Oh, what a prospect of glory and immortality is before me! He is my God, through life, through death, and to eternity.' When inquiries were made how he felt, his general reply was, 'As well as I expect to be this side heaven.' To a brother minister he said: 'I do not repent of one word that I have printed or preached about Jesus, for I now feel the blessed comforts of that precious doctrine.' 'I have lived,' said he to another, 'to experience all I have spoken, and all I have written, and I bless God for it.' Afterwards he observed, 'I knew the doctrines I preached to be truths, but now I experience them to be blessings.' As he lay waiting for his dismission, the friend in whose house he was, said to him, 'I hope, sir, you now find the salvation of Jesus inestimably precious to you.' 'Yes,' he replied with a feeble voice, 'he is precious to my soul.' 'More precious than rubies,' said his friend. He caught the word and completed the Scriptural idea, 'and all that can be desired is not comparable to him.'"

7764. DEATH without Christ. A young lady who had been very near the gate of death and had bidden final farewell to her friends, as she supposed, recovered. She afterward said that she was then very happy, expected to go to heaven, and had no doubts, fears or suspicions but she should. Being asked, "On what was your hope founded?" "Founded?" she replied: "why, I had never injured any person, and I had endeavored to do all the good in my power. Was not this sufficient?" "It is a delightful reflection," said the questioner, "that you have never injured any person, and it is still more delightful to think that you have done all the good in your power; but this is a poor foundation for a sinner to rest upon. Was this the foundation of your hope?" She seemed quite astonished at the question, and eagerly inquired, "Was not this sufficient?" He did not give a direct answer; but observed, "I am very thankful that you did not die." "What! do you think that I should not have gone to heaven?" "I am sure you could not in the way you mentioned. Do you perceive that, according to your plan, you were going to heaven without Christ?—a thing which no sinner has done since Adam fell, and which no sinner will be able to do while the world stands." The conversation led to her conversion. Multitudes die having only the same groundless expectation, "as the fool dieth."

7765. DEATH, Chrysostom's. This famous preacher was exiled because of his purity of life and severity with the sins of priests and people, high or low. At Antioch his influence became so great that his enemies resolved to change the place of his exile. His guards were ordered to conduct him to a place on the Black Sea, and to make the journey as exhausting as possible. For three months, over hard roads and in severe storms, their journey lasted. He was broken down and needed rest. Stopping at the church of St. Basiliscus near Comona, he had a premonition of speedy relief. That night Basiliscus, the martyr, appeared to him and said, "Courage, my brother John, to-morrow we shall be together." In the morning he begged not to be moved, but was forced to go on by the guard. After going four miles he was so evidently dying that they took him back to the church. There he put on white robes, received the holy communion, offered his last prayer and thanksgiving which were his last words, "Glory to God for all things, amen," stretched out his feet and expired, September 14, 407.

7766. DEATH, Comfortless. Mr. Job Throgmorton, a Puritan divine, who was described by his contemporaries as being "as holy and as choice a preacher as any in England," is said to have lived thirty-seven years without any comfortable assurance as to his spiritual condition. When dying, he addressed the venerable Mr. Dod in the following words: "What will you say of him who is going out of the world, and can find no comfort?" "What will you say of him," replied Mr. Dod, "who, when he was going out of the world, found no comfort, but cried, 'My God, my God, why hast thou forsaken me?'" This prompt reply administered consolation to the troubled spirit of the dying friend, who departed an hour after, rejoicing in the Lord. *Anon.*

7767. DEATH, Condition of an Easy. The Princess Charlotte, of England, collected various opinions on the question, "What can make a death-bed easy?" Had she seen the martyrs triumphing in torture, and the trusting shouting victory through the blood of the Lamb in the midst of great pain, she would have sought no further answer than the Bible gives. Christians die well. He dies easily who feels that Christ died for him.

7768. DEATH, Confidence in. "I have no hope in what I have been or done," said Dr. Doddridge, on his dying-bed, "yet I am full of confidence; and this is my confidence, there is a hope set before me. I have fled—I still fly for refuge to that hope. In him I trust, in him I have strong consolation; and shall assuredly be accepted in this beloved of my soul."

7769. DEATH, Contrast in. When Joseph Sutcliff was near his last hour, he said, "I have been thinking of the difference between the death of Paul and of Byron. Paul said, 'The time of my departure is at hand; but there is laid up for me a crown.' Byron said,

> "'My days are in the yellow leaf,
> The flower, the fruit of life are gone;
> The worm, the canker, and the grief
> Are mine alone.'"

7770. DEATH, A Converted Heathen's. Rev. Mr. Arsmond gives the following account of the death of Vara, a blood-thirsty chief of Aimeo, who offered his own brother in sacrifice to his heathen gods before his conversion. "On seeing that the end of the venerable chief was fast approaching, I said to him, 'Are you sorry that you cast away your lying gods by which you used to gain so much property?' He was roused from his lethargy, and, with tears of pleasure sparkling in his eyes, he exclaimed. 'Oh, no no, no. What! can I be sorry for casting away death for life? Jesus is my rock, the fortification in which my soul takes shelter.' I said, 'Tell me on what you found your hopes of future blessedness.' He replied, 'I have been very wicked, but a great King from the other side of the skies sent his ambassadors with terms of peace. We could not tell for many years what these ambassadors wanted. At length Pomare obtained a victory, and invited all his subjects to come and take refuge under the wing of Jesus, and I was one of the first to do so. The blood of Jesus is my foundation. I grieve that all my children do not love him. Had they known the misery we endured under the reign of the devil, they would gladly take the gospel in exchange for their follies. Jesus is the best King; he gives a pillow without thorns!' A little time after, I asked him if he was afraid to die, when, with almost youthful energy, he replied, 'No, no. The canoe is in the sea, the sails are spread, she is ready for the gale. I have a good Pilot to guide me. My outside man and my inside man differ. Let the one rot till the trumpet shall sound, but let my soul wing her way to the throne of Jesus.' Soon afterwards Vara passed away to be forever with the Lord."

7771. DEATH, Conviction from. My first convictions on the subject of religion were confirmed by observing that really religious persons had some solid happiness among them, which I felt the vanities of the world could not give. I shall never forget standing by the bedside of my sick mother. "Are not you afraid to die?" I asked. "No." "No! Why does the uncertainty of another state give you no concern?" "Because God has said, 'Fear not; when thou passest through the waters, I will be with thee; and through the rivers, they shall not overflow thee.' 'Let me die the death of the righteous.'"   *Cecil.*

7772. DEATH, Cordial in. The Rev. James Hervey died on Christmas-day, December 25, 1758. When dying he thanked the physicians for their visits, and with great solemnity and sweetness in his countenance exclaimed, "Lord, now lettest thou thy servant depart in peace according to thy most holy and comfortable word, for mine eyes have seen thy precious salvation. Here, doctor, is my cordial! What are all the cordials given to support the dying,

in comparison of that which arises from the promises of salvation by Christ? This, this now supports me." About three o'clock he said, "The great conflict is over—now all is done;" after which he scarcely spoke except twice or thrice, "Precious salvation!" and then, leaning his head against the side of his chair, he closed his eyes to earth to open them in heaven.

7773. DEATH, Courage at. Leonard Vecchel, one of the Catholic martyrs of Gorkum, sighed at the thought of the effect his tragic death would have upon his mother. Another of those, Godfrey Dumas said to him as he mounted the scaffold, "Courage, master Leonard, this day we shall assist at the marriage supper of the Lamb."

7774. DEATH, Cowards or Fools at. Some old doctor or other said quaintly that patients were very apt to be fools and cowards. But a great many of the clergyman's patients are not only fools and cowards, but also liars. If you think I have used rather strong language, I shall have to read something to you out of the book of this keen and witty scholar—the great Erasmus—who "laid the egg of the Reformation which Luther hatched." Oh, you never read his *Naufragium,* or "Shipwreck," did you? Of course not; for if you had, I don't think you would have given me credit—or discredit—for entire originality in that speech of mine. That men are cowards in the contemplation of futurity he illustrates by the extraordinary antics of many on board the sinking vessel; that they are fools, by their praying to the sea, and making promises to bits of wood from the true cross, and all manner of similar nonsense; that they are fools, cowards, and liars all at once, by this story: I will put it into rough English for you: "I couldn't help laughing to hear one fellow brawling out, so that he might be sure to be heard, a promise to Saint Christopher of Paris—the monstrous statue in the great church there—that he would give him a wax-taper as big as himself. 'Mind what you promise,' said an acquaintance that stood near him, poking him with his elbow, 'you couldn't pay for it, if you sold all your things at auction.' 'Hold your tongue, you donkey!' said the fellow—but softly, so that Saint Christopher should not hear him—'do you think I'm in earnest? If once I get my foot on dry ground, catch me giving him so much as a tallow candle!'"   *Holmes.*

7775. DEATH Disarmed. Death is a dragon, the grave its den; a place of dread and terror; but Christ goes into its den, there grapples with it, and forever overcomes it, disarms it of all its terror; and not only makes it cease to be inimical, but to become the greatest blessing to the saints; a bed of rest, and a perfumed bed; they do but go into Christ's bed, where he lay before them, 1 Cor. 15: 15.
                    John Flavel

7776. DEATH, Diversities in. You have been in a ship when it entered the harbor, and you have noticed the different looks of the passengers as they turned their eyes ashore. There was one who, that he might not lose a moment's time, had got everything ready for landing long ago; and now he smiles and beckons to yonder party on the pier, who in their turn, are so eager to meet him, that they almost press over the margin of the quay; and no sooner is the gangway thrown across, than he has hold of the arm of one, and another is triumphant on his shoulder, and all the rest are leaping before and after him on their homeward way. But there is another, who showed no alacrity. He gazed with pensive eye on the nearer coast and seemed to grudge that the trip was over. He was a stranger going amongst strangers, and though sometimes during the voyage he had a momentary hope that something unexpected might occur, and that some friendly face might recognize him in regions where he was going an alien and an adventurer, no such welcoming face is there, and with reluctant steps he quits the vessel, and commits himself to the unknown country. And now that every one else has disembarked, who is this unhappy man whom they have brought on deck, and whom, groaning in his heavy chains, they are conducting to the dreaded shore? Alas! he is a felon and a runaway, whom they are bringing back to take his trial there; and no wonder he is loath to land. Now, dear brethren, our ship is sailing fast. We shall soon hear the raspings of the shallows, and the commotion overhead, which bespeak the port in view. When it comes to that, how shall you feel? Are you a stranger, or a convict, or are you going home? Can you say, "I know whom I have believed?" Have you a Friend within the vail? And however much you may enjoy the voyage, and however much you may like your fellow passengers, does your heart sometimes leap up at the prospect of seeing Jesus as he is, and so being ever with the Lord?   *Dr. J. Hamilton.*

7777. DEATH, Diversities of. On May 5th, 1821, Napoleon Bonaparte, in the delirium of his last sickness, cried, "*Tête d'armee*"—head of the army. They were the last words of a great but defeated and exiled general at St. Helena, whose ruling passion was strong in death. In the cabin of a ship at anchor in the port of the same island, twenty-four years later, lay the devoted Mrs. Judson turning homeward from her finished work. About to pass the same ordeal, she declared, "I ever love the Lord Jesus Christ," kissed her husband in token of her affection for him, and fell into a quiet slumber of an hour, when she awoke amid the angels. The Emperor was honored by a grand funeral and magnificent tomb. The missionary burial was unhonored and unsung. A simple slab marked her grave, bearing her name and age and the date of her death, and the verse,

"She sleeps sweetly here on this rock of the
   ocean,
Away from the home of her youth,
And far from the land where with heartfelt devo-
   tion,
She scattered the bright beams of truth."

7778. DEATH, Dread of. A Jewish record says, When Rabbi Jochanan, the son of Sachai, was ill and on his death-bed his disciples came to visit him. When he saw them he began to weep. "Light of Israel," said they to him "main pillar of the right, thou strong hammer, why dost thou weep?" He answered, "Were I led forth to judgment before a mortal king, who is here to-day and in his grave to-morrow; whose anger, were it excited against me, would not be lasting; whose fetters, were he to chain me, could not confine the body; whose infliction of death, were he to kill me, would not be eternal; whom I could mollify with words or bribe with gifts—even then I would weep How much greater is my cause for tears, now that I am to be led before the King of kings, the Holy One! Blessed be he who liveth and reigneth for ever! whose wrath, were it excited against me, is everlasting; whose fetters, were he to chain me, know no end; whose infliction of death, were he to kill me, would be eternal; whom I can neither mollify with words, nor bribe with gifts. Moreover, there are two paths open before me—the one leading to bliss, the other to torments; and I know not which of them it will be my doom to take. Then how can I abstain from weeping?" His disciples then said, "Our rabbi, give us thy blessing." He answered, "May the fear of the Deity be as strong on you as the fear of man!" One of them said, "What! no stronger?" He answered, "Oh that it were as strong! for you know that he that is about committing a sin says within himself, 'I must take care that no man seeth me.'"

7779. DEATH, Early. Youth is as fickle as old age. The young man may find graves enough of his length in burial places. As green wood and old logs meet in one fire, so young sinners and old sinners meet in one hell and burn together. When the young man is in his spring and prime, then he is cut off and dies: "One dying in his full strength (or in the strength of his perfection, as the Hebrews have it) being wholly at ease and quiet, his breasts are full of milk, and his bones are moistened with marrow," Job 21: 23, 24. David's children died when young, so did Job's and Jeroboam's, etc. Every day's experience tells us, that the young man's life is as much a vapor as the old man's is. I have read of an Italian poet, who brings in a proper young man, rich and potent, discoursing with Death in the habit of a mower, with his scythe in his hand, cutting down the life of man, "For all flesh is grass," Isa. 40: 6. "And wilt thou not spare any man's person," saith the young man? "I spare none," saith Death. Man's life is but a day, a short day, a winter's day. Ofttimes the sun goes down upon a man before it be well up. Your day is short, your work is great, your journey long, and, therefore, you should rise early, and set forward towards heaven betimes, as that man doth that hath a long journey to go in a winter's day.   *Brooks.*

7780. DEATH, Empty Hands in. I remember an Eastern legend which I have always thought furnished a remarkable though unconscious tommentary on the words of the Psalmist. Alexander the Great, we are there told, being upon his death-bed, commanded that when he was carried forth to the grave his hands should not be wrapped as was usual in the cere-cloths, but should be left outside the bier, so that all might see them, and might see that they were empty, that there was nothing in them; that he, born to one empire, and the conqueror of another, the possessor while he lived of two worlds—of the East and of the West—and of the treasures of both, yet now when he was dead could retain no smallest portion of these treasures; that in this matter the poorest beggar and he were at length upon equal terms.

Trench.

7781. DEATH, The Entrance to Happiness. The City of Rhegium was taken by Dionysius, the elder, after a long siege. The obstinate defense of Phyton, a most worthy man, aroused the captor's wrath, and he resolved to avenge himself. He ordered Phyton to execution and told him that he had on the previous day drowned his son and all his kindred. He answered, "They are by one day happier than I!"

7782. DEATH Everywhere. Death meets us everywhere, and is procured by every instrument and in all chances, and enters in at many doors—by violence and secret influence, by the aspect of a star and the stink of a mist, by the emissions of a cloud and the meeting of a vapor, by the fall of a chariot and the stumbling at a stone, by a full meal or an empty stomach, by watching at the wine or by watching at prayers, by the sun or the moon, by a heat or a cold, by sleepless nights or sleeping days, by water frozen into the hardness and sharpness of a dagger, or water thawed into the floods of a river, by a hair or a razor, by violent motion or sitting still, by severity or dissolution, by God's mercy or God's anger, by everything in Providence and everything in manners, by everything in nature and everything in chance: we take pains to heap up things useful to our life, and get our death in the purchase; and the person is snatched away and the goods remain. And all this is the law and constitution of nature; it is a punishment to our sins, the unalterable event of Providence, and the decree of heaven; the chains that confine us to this condition are as strong as destiny, and immutable as the eternal laws of God. *Jeremy Taylor.*

7783. DEATH, Evidences in. Rev. Leigh Richmond, in dying said, "Brother, brother, strong evidences, nothing but strong evidences will do in such an hour as this. I have looked here and looked there for them, and all have failed me; and so I cast myself on the sovereign, free, and full grace of God in the covenant by Jesus Christ; and there, brother, there, I have found peace." Even so; the free grace of the promise is our only hope.

7784. DEATH, Expectation of. Persons in health have died from the expectation of dying. It was once common for those who perished by violence to summon their destroyers to appear, within a stated time, before the tribunal of their God: and we have many perfectly attested instances in which, through fear and remorse, the perpetrators withered under the curse, and died. Pestilence does not kill with the rapidity of terror. The profligate abbess of a convent, the Princess Gonzaga, of Cleves, and Guize, the profligate Archbisop of Rheims, took it into their heads, for a jest, to visit one of the nuns by night, and exhort her as a person who was visibly dying. While in the performance of their heartless scheme they whispered to each other, "She is just departing," she departed in earnest. Her vigor, instead of detecting the trick, sank beneath the alarm; and the profane pair discovered, in the midst of their sport, that they were making merry with a corpse. *Wakley.*

7785. DEATH, Exposure to. Tasso and his friend Manso, with Scipio Belprato, were one day in a summer-house which commanded a full prospect of the sea, agitated at the time by a furious storm. Belprato observed "that he was astonished at the rashness and folly of men who would expose themselves to the rage of so merciless an element, where such numbers had suffered shipwreck." "And yet," said Tasso, "we every night go without fear to bed, where so many die every hour. Believe me, death will find us in all parts: and those places that appear the least exposed are not always the most secure from his attacks."

7786. DEATH, Faithful till. It was on January 4, 1869, that the Triumph was in the Bay of Biscay, on a voyage from Liverpool to Spain. The storm raged, the sea ran mountains high, and the ship dashed to and fro, when the captain gave orders to stow the maintop-gallant sail; but no one would venture. Then Jack called out, "I will venture my life to save the ship and crew, and if I die I will die at my duty." With a smile on his face, he quickly climbed the mast. He was a true missionary, with a single object in view, and that object was to save the lives of others even if he lost his own. He clung hard to the ropes, stowed the maintop-gallant sail, when suddenly to the horror of the crew, a sea came and washed the mainmast overboard, with poor Jack upon it! They heard him cry, "O my God!" and then they saw him no more. He had sacrificed himself for them.

Missionary News

7787. DEATH, Farewell in. An Indiana soldier lay dying in the hospital at Chattanooga. He was happy in Christ. He had his rings taken from his fingers to be sent to his sister, with the message that they were taken off when his hands were growing cold. He had three pictures which were held up before him by the chaplain. He took that of his mother first in his hand, kissed it fondly, and said, "Dear mother, good bye; I wish I could see you, but I am going to die in Georgia." With many sobs he repeated, "Good bye, good bye." Then he kissed his sister's picture, saying, "Dear sister; don't fret for me; I'll see you again; only be faithful; good bye, dear sister, good bye." Next he took and gazed upon the picture of a nameless friend and kissed it in silence. The patients of the ward,—such as could move, gathered around; others lifted themselves on elbow, to witness the scene. An opening life was cheerfully laid down. He said, "I was glad when I enlisted, and I am glad now. I am willing to die for my country."

7788. DEATH, Fearless of. Sir William Forbes, the biographer of Beatti, uttered this: "Tell those," said he, "that are drawing down to the bed of death, from my experience that it has no terrors; that in the hour when it is most wanted, there is mercy with the most high; and that some change takes place which fits the soul to meet its God." When the Earl of Derby came to his execution, although he had said in previous times, that he could die in fight, but knew not how it might be on the scaffold, he now said he could lay his head on the block as cheerfully as on his pillow. "Let my people know," said the pious Archdeacon Aylmer, "that their pastor died undaunted, and not afraid of death. I bless my God that I have no fear, no reluctance, but an assured confidence in the sin-overcoming merits of Jesus Christ."

7789. DEATH, Fear of. A little girl of eight years was on her dying bed, and weeping friends were gathered about her to watch the outgoing of her young life. She had reached the margin of the river of death. She became much agitated at what seemed to her a broad and impassable flood. After a little she grew calm, a smile of confidence lit up her face and saying, "O it is only a little brook," she passed joyously to the shining shore.

7790. DEATH, Feelings at. When Rev. Dr. James W. Alexander, for many years pastor of the Fifth Avenue Presbyterian church (a man of precious memory in the church of God), lay dying, he was approached by a friend who asked him how he felt, and said to him, "Suppose you were now to go to the judgment seat, what would be your feelings?" He was then within twenty hours of his decease, and he knew he was dying. "What would be my feelings," said he in reply, "if the curtain should drop now, and I at this moment were ushered into the presence of God? They would be these: first, I would prostrate myself in an unutterable sense of my nothingness and guilt; but, secondly, I would look upon my Redeemer with an inexpressible assurance of faith and love. A passage of Scripture which explains my present feeling is this: 'I know *whom* (with great emphasis) I have believed, and am persuaded that he is able to keep that which I have committed unto him against that day.' Some persons read it 'In whom I have believed,' but there is no preposition. Christ himself was the direct object of the Apostle's faith. 'I know whom I have believed;' that is, I am acquainted with him; I know him;" and relying on that only, he died, as millions of others have done, and as God grant we may, in the holy triumphs of the Gospel. *C. D. Foss.*

7791. DEATH a Ferry-Boat. Death to God's people is but a ferry-boat. Every day and every hour the boat pushes off with some of the saints, and returns for more.

S. S. Treasury.

7791. DEATH, The First. Those who are in Christ shall never taste of the second death; but, as to the first death, how art thou freed? I answer, thou art freed from the curse and from the sting of death; so thou mayest step on the back of death and go into endless glory. Therefore this first death is no death to those who art in Christ, but rather an entry, or passage, or port to eternal life. But if thou wouldst be sure to be freed from death, ther thou must first be freed from sin, by the law of the Spirit of life: and thou must know who it is that brings this freedom to thee, to wit, the Lord Jesus only. *John Welsh.*

7792. DEATH, Fletcher's. Rev. John Fletcher, of Madeley, returned home from his parish duties on a midsummer day, exhausted and feverish with cold. On the ensuing Sunday, resisting, after two days' confinement, the admonitions of his friends, he went to his church; it was the last day of his ministrations there. Before he had read far in the service, his countenance changed, he was seized with faintness, and could scarcely proceed. The congregation was alarmed and in tears; his wife pressed through the crowd, and entreated the dying man to desist; but he seemed to know it "was the last time," and persisted. The windows were opened, and afforded him relief; his sermon surprised his hearers by its more than usual pathos and power, and "an awful concern was awakened through the whole assembly." Descending from the pulpit, he walked up to the communion table, saying as he went, "I am going to throw myself under the wings of the cherubim, before the mercy-seat." Several times did he sink exhausted on the sacramental table, while the congregation wept and sobbed aloud at the sight. Having struggled through a service of four hours' duration, he was supported, while uttering benedictions on his people, to his chamber, where he fell in a swoon, and never again went out, but when borne to the grave. For several days he suffered much, but with continual praise upon his lips. "God is love! shout aloud! I want a gust of praise to go to the ends of the earth!" cried the sinking man. A visitor asked him if he thought God would not raise him up. "Raise me up in the resur——," he gasped. On the next Sunday a supplicatory hymn was sung for him in the church. A brother clergyman, who officiated on the occasion, says that there can be no description of the scene: the burst of sorrow that attended the supplication; the sadness, and even consternation, that prevailed through the village which had been consecrated so long by his holy life; the running to and fro of messengers with reports of his condition. "The members of every family sat together in silence that day, awaiting with trembling expectation the issue of every hour." The poor who came from a distance to attend the service, and who were usually entertained at his house, begged to see him once more. They were allowed to pass along the gallery, and to take, through the opened door of his chamber, their final look at his beloved face. He died that night. "I know thy soul," said his wife as she bent over him, when he could no longer speak; "I know thy soul; but for the sake of others, if Jesus be present with thee, lift up thy right hand." Immediately it was raised. "If the prospects of glory sweetly open before thee, repeat the sign." He instantly raised it again, and in half a minute a second time. He then threw it up, as if he would reach the top of the bed. After this his hands moved no more. Breathing like a person in common sleep, he died August 14, 1785, in the fifty-sixth year of his age. "Many exemplary men," said Wesley, "have I known, holy in heart and life, within four-score years; but one equal to him I have not known; one so inwardly and outwardly devoted to God, so unblamable a character in every respect, I have not found either in Europe or America, nor do I expect to find another such on this side of eternity." Weeping and lamenting thousands bore the remains of Fletcher to the grave, singing on the way:

"With heavenly weapons he has fought
  The battles of his Lord,
Finished his course, and kept the faith,
  And gained the great reward."
Stevens.

7793. DEATH, Forewarned of. It is noteworthy that in the three cases where the exact length of life was revealed, no practical good seems to have followed. *Hezekiah* was promised fifteen years of longer life, Isa. 38:5. Yet the very next chapter (written probably soon after) contains the record of his pride. *Hananiah* was forewarned that he should die the same year, Jer. 28:16. But no record is added of his repenting and preparing for death. *The rich fool* was allowed only a few hours, Luke 12:20. Yet there is no reason to think there was any softening result produced. *Bowes.*

7794. DEATH, Friends in. Severus, bishop of Ravenna, prepared a tomb for himself in his church. In it he placed the bodies of his wife, Vincentia, and of his daughter, Innocentia. After some years he was premonished that his time to die had come. He held service with the people, dismissed them, and closed the cathedral doors. Then, clothed in his episcopal robes, with one attendant, he went to the sepulchre of his family. They raised the stone from the tomb, and Severus, looking in, said: "My dear one, with whom I lived in love so long, make room for me, for this is my grave, and in death we shall not be divided." Immediately he descended into the tomb, laid himself down between his wife and daughter, crossed his hands upon his breast, looked up to heaven in prayer, gave one sigh and fell asleep, A. D. 390.

7795. DEATH, Gain of. "I am no longer disposed," says a Jew in writing to another, "to laugh at religion, or to plead that Christianity has no comforts in death. I witnessed the last moments of my worthy gardener, and wish I may die his death: and, if there is happiness in another life, this disciple of Jesus is assuredly happy. When the physician told him he was in extreme danger: 'How,' said he, 'can that be, when God is my Father, Jesus my Redeemer, heaven my country, and death the messenger of peace? The greatest risk I run is to die, but to die is to enter into complete and endless bliss.' His last words were, 'I die, but what needs that trouble me? My Jesus is the true God, and eternal life.'"

7796. DEATH, General Interest in. There is nothing in history which is so improving to the reader as those accounts which we meet with of the deaths of eminent persons, and of their behavior in that dreadful season. I may also add, that there are no parts in history which affect and please the reader in so sensible a manner. The reason I take to be this, because there is no other single circumstance in the story of any person which can possibly be the case of every one who reads it. A battle or a triumph are conjunctures in which not one man in a million is likely to be engaged; but when we see a person at the point of death, we cannot forbear being attentive to everything he says or does, because we are sure that, some time or other, we shall ourselves be in the same melancholy circumstances. The general, the statesman, or the philosopher, are, perhaps, characters which we may never act in; but the dying man is one whom, sooner or later, we shall certainly resemble. *Addison.*

7797. DEATH, Gentle. A Scotch minister upon his deathbed said, "I see Christ standing over Death's head, saying, 'Deal warily with my servant; loose thou this pin and that pin; for this tabernacle must be set up again.'"

7798. DEATH, Glorious. I have stood beside the dying soldier, when it has seemed as if a bridge of golden sheen was let down from heaven, a highway for the ransomed of the Lord. And that way cast up of God, has glowed with the steps of the angels, come to bear the soldier, who had made his last charge and fought his last battle, home. And up that shining path with angel convoy, the spirit has gone,—away from the clang of arms and the din of strife and the groans of the wounded — away, away to the very gates of pearl, to the peace like a river and the rest of God.
Herrick Johnson.

7799. DEATH, Habit in. After John Wesley's death a small tract was published, giving an account of it. One was put into the hands of a learned and philosophical man, who seemed to have a real respect for religion. After reading the tract, he said to the person who gave it to him, "Well, this is the most astonishing instance of the power of habit! Here is a man who had been threescore years praying, preaching, and singing psalms, and, behold, he thinks of nothing else when he is dying!"

7800. DEATH, Happiness after. She is gone! No longer shrinking from the winter wind, or lifting her calm pure forehead to the summer's kiss; no longer gazing with her blue and glorious eyes into a far-off sky; no longer yearning with a holy heart for heaven; no longer toiling painfully along the path, upward and upward, to the everlasting rock on which are based the walls of the city of the Most High; no longer here; she is there; gazing, seeing, knowing, loving, as the blessed only see, and know, and love. Earth has one angel less, and heaven one more, since yesterday. Already, kneeling at the throne, she has received her welcome, and is resting on the bosom of her Saviour. If human love hath power to penetrate the veil (and hath it not?), then there are yet living here a few who have the blessedness of knowing that an angel loves them.

Hawthorn.

7801. DEATH, Happy. Rev. John Janeway, when on his death-bed, was employed chiefly in praise. "Oh," said he to his friends, "help me to praise God; I have now nothing else to do. I have done with prayer and all other ordinances. Before a few hours are over I shall be in eternity, singing the song of Moses and the Lamb. I shall presently stand upon Mount Zion, with an innumerable company of angels, and spirits of just men made perfect, and with Jesus, the Mediator of the new covenant. I shall hear the voice of much people, and with them shall cry, hallelujah, glory, salvation, honor and power, unto the Lord our God! And again we shall say, hallelujah!" In this triumphant manner he expired, in the twenty-second year of his age.

7802. DEATH, Heathen View of. Sophocles, the most renowned of the Grecian poets, almost equally distinguished as dramatist, statesman, and philosopher, closed a career of eighty years, which the world has called brilliant, five centuries before the birth of our Saviour. But unenlightened by Christianity, there was no happy paradise of God opening before him. As he sank into the rayless grave he left behind him the following pathetic testimony:

Man's happiest lot is not to be;
And when we tread life's thorny steep,
Most blest are they who, earliest free,
Descend to death's eternal sleep.

J. S. C. Abbott.

7803. DEATH, Honorable. When Pelopidas, as the result of his valor in marching against the enemy of his city, was slain, those who were engaged in the contest with him would not put off their armor, unbridle their horses, or bind up their wounds until they had piled round his body the spoils of their enemy, and in token of the genuineness of their grief cut off the manes of their horses and the hair of their own heads. Throughout the camp there prevailed a melancholy silence, as though they had been defeated instead of being victorious. This was indeed to die with honor. So dies the Christian warrior, who has gathered around him a band of valiant men and inspired them with his own holy courage. None weep so sincerely over his grave as those who have been associated with him in conflict and in triumph.

7804. DEATH, Hopeless. "I have nothing to expect, sir, but condemnation; nothing to expect but condemnation." The speaker articulated with difficulty. He was a large man, massive of feature and muscular of limb. The awful pallor of the face was increased by the masses of thick black hair, that lay in confusion about the pillow, brushed off from the dead whiteness of his forehead. Struck down suddenly from full, hearty life to the bed of death, he made there and then an agonizing confession, such as racks the ear of the listner at unhappy death-beds. A meek woman sat near the nurse, who was striving quietly to alleviate the suffering he endured. "Oh, don't talk to me of pain!" he cried bitterly. "It is the mind, woman—the mind;" and agony overclouded his face. He continued slowly and deliberately: "There is a demon whispering in my ear for ever, 'You knew it at the time, and at every time; you knew it.' Knew what? Why, that a penalty must follow a broken law. Mark me—I have not opened a Bible for years—I have not entered a church; yet the very recollection that my mother taught me to pray (and she died when I was only six), has passed judgment upon all my sins. I have done wrong, knowing it was wrong, first with a few qualms, then brushing aside conscience, and at last with the coolness of a fiend. Sir, in one minute of all my life I have not lived for heaven; no, not one minute." "But Christ died for sinners, even the worst." "Oh, yes; Christ died for sinners; but my intellect is clear, sir; clearer than ever before. I tell you"—his voice sharpened, almost whistled, it was so shrill and concentrated—"I can see almost into eternity. I can feel that unless Christ is desired, sought after, longed for—that unless guilt is repented of, his death can do no good. Do I not repent? I am only savage at myself to think—to think, sir!" he lifted his right hand impressively, "that I have so cursed myself. Is that repentance? Do not try to console me; save your sympathy for those who will bear it, for I cannot. Thank you, nurse;" this as she wiped his brow, and moistened his parched lips. "I am not dead to kindness, if I am to hope. I thank you, sir, for your Christian offices, though they do me no good. If we sow thorns, you know, we cannot reap flowers; and corn will not grow from the seed of thistles. Heaven was made for the holy; 'without, are dogs, whoremongers, and adulterers.' There's a distinction; it's all right." After that, till eleven o'clock, his mind wandered: then he slept a few moments. Presently, roused by the striking of the clock, he looked around dreamily, and caught the eye of the nurse, and of his friend. "It's awful dark here," he whispered: "My feet stand on the slippery edge of a great gulf. Oh, for some foundation!" He stretched his hand out as if feeling for the way. "Christ is the only help—'I am the way, the truth, and the life,'" whispered the man of God. "Not for me!" and pen cannot describe the immeasurable woe in that answer. "I shall fall—I am falling!" he half shrieked in an instant after; he shuddered and all was over.   *Am. Messenger.*

7805. DEATH, Horrible. "I once attended on his dying bed," says the author of "Damascus," "a man whose early history had given promise of better things, but whose goodness was as the morning cloud and the early dew. As I entered the room, he fixed his eyes upon me with a fearful expression of countenance, and in the spirit, almost in the very language, of the Gadarene demoniac, exclaimed, 'Why are you come to torment me?' I replied, 'I am not come to torment you: I am come to tell you that there is mercy, mercy yet, and mercy even for you.' He raised his arm with vehemence, and said, 'No mercy for me! no mercy for me! no mercy for me! I have sinned through all: I have despised all. I am dying, and I am damned!' His arm fell, and he apparently ceased to breathe. I thought him dead, but was mistaken: there still was life, there was even consciousness. Fetching a long-drawn breath, as if for some desperate effort, and covering his face with the evident intention of concealing the agony which was written there, he uttered the most awful groan I ever heard, and then expired."

7806. DEATH, Humility in. Vincent de Paul died in Paris 1660, aged eighty-five. He was lowly born, a cowherd's son, but attained to great honor and usefulness as a preacher, and as an organizer of charitable institutions. The sisters of charity were first organized by him to care for the sick and the orphaned in his hospitals. His good works were numerous and his praise was on the lips of all. Near the close of his long and truly noble life, he was compelled to ride about in a carriage, which was then regarded as the privilege of the noble and wealthy only. He mourned the necessity and exclaimed, " I, a poor cowherd's son, to ride like a prince!" When near death he said, " One of these days the body of this old sinner will be laid in the dust, and be trodden under foot. Alas! my Lord! my sins multiply on me, and I never seem to amend." At last the stupor of the last sleep came upon him, but if the name of Jesus was whispered in his ear he gave signs of consciousness and pleasure.

7807. DEATH, Ignorance of the Time of. From the notion which some held of St. Columba, that he was able to foretell future events, a man asked him one day how long he had to live. " If your curiosity on that head could be satisfied," said the saint, " it could be of no use to you. But it is only God, who appoints the days of man, that knows when they are to terminate. Our business is to do our duty, not to pry into our destiny, God in mercy hath concealed from man the knowledge of his end. If he knew it was near, he would be disqualified for the duties of life; and if he knew it were distant, he would delay his preparation. You should, therefore, be satisfied with knowing that it is certain; and the safest way is to believe that it may be also near, and to make no delay in getting ready, lest it overtake you unprepared."

7808. DEATH, Individual. One may live as a conqueror, or a king, or a magistrate, but he must die a man. The bed of death brings every human being to his pure individuality, to the intense contemplation of that deepest and most solemn of all relations, the relation between the creature and his Creator.
Webster.

7809. DEATH, Inevitable. A California stage-driver, after having been engaged in that business for many years, was dying in San Francisco, and in his last moment he put his foot out of the bed and swung it back and forth Some one said to him: " Why do you make that motion with your foot?" He replied: " I am on the down grade, and I cannot get my foot on the brake." When our last moment comes, we cannot stop. Our going will be inevitable, and we shall not be able to get our foot on the brake.

7810. DEATH, Influence of. A devoted Christian mother had a reckless son. She spared no effort to reclaim him from the habits of drunkenness and debauch into which he had fallen, but all was vain. Her prayers to God to rescue her imperiled boy were incessant. At last she sank, heart-broken, into an untimely grave. The son come to look upon the face of his dead mother. His heart was rent as he thought of the ruin he had wrought. He charged himself with his mother's death, and cried out in agony, "Mother, what your life could not accomplish your death shall." That son is now a minister of the gospel.

7811. DEATH, Instantaneous. Jerome Cardan relates that eight reapers, who were eating their dinner under an oak-tree, were all struck by the same flash of lightning, the explosion of which was heard far away. When some people passing by approached to see what had happened, they found the reapers to all appearance continuing their repast; one still held his glass in his hand, another was in the act of putting a piece of bread in his mouth, a third had his hand in the dish. Death had come upon them suddenly whilst in these positions, when the thunderbolt fell. Azrael had seized upon them with so much violence that he had impressed upon the entire surface of their bodies the mournful tint of his black wings. One might have taken them for statues sculptured out of black marble! The catastrophe was so rapid that the faces of the victims had not had time to take any expression of pain; life was suppressed so instantaneously that the muscles remained unmoved. The eyes and the mouths were open, as in life; and had not the color of the skin been so much changed the illusion would have been complete.
Fouviell.

7812. DEATH, Joy at. Mrs. Rowe, when her acquaintance expressed to her the joy they felt at seeing her look so well, and possessed so much health as promised many years to come, was wont to reply, "that it was the same as telling a slave his fetters were like to be lasting, or complimenting him on the strength of the walls of his dungeon." Dr. Maclaine was fifty years minister of the English church at the Hague; but by the revolution in Holland in 1796, he took refuge in this country, where he died in peace and comfort. When informed that his disorder must be fatal, he replied, "You remember Socrates, the wisest and best of heathens, in this state could only express a hope mingled with anxiety and doubt; but, blessed be God, though a grievous sinner, in retiring to that bed from which I shall rise no more, I know in whom I have believed. Death cannot separate me from the love of Christ, and in him to die is gain." If a heathen philosopher rejoiced that he should die because he believed he should see Homer, Hesiod, and other eminent persons, how much more do I rejoice, said a pious old minister, who am sure to see Christ my Saviour, besides so many wise, holy, and renowned patriarchs, prophets and apostles.   *Buck.*

7813. DEATH, Joy in. A dying Hottentot girl, who had been instructed by the missionaries, emphasized her experience by repetition after the fashion of her tribe, "Jesus receiveth sinners, sinners, sinners! joy, joy, joy!"

7814. DEATH, Joyous. A soldier dying on a battlefield, while the blood was spurting from his wounds, thus addressed his Christian comrade: "Ah! comrade, the joys of my soul are greater than all the pains of my body; yes, indeed, Christ is precious, and I now prove that, having loved his own, he loveth them to the very end. Adieu, comrade, I am now going to be with Jesus;" and then waving his hand, and gazing around him, he cried out with a peculiar tone of voice, "Farewell, marches and trenches; farewell, fatigue-parties, and midnight revelings of drunken comrades; farewell, fields of battle, and blood, and slaughter; and farewell sun, and moon, and stars, and—" He paused, almost exhausted with his feelings, but soon said, "Farewell, beloved comrade in Christ Jesus; meet me in glory, for oh, in a few minutes more, my soul must depart, and then, yes,

"'Then I'll march up the heavenly street,
    And ground my arms at Jesus' feet!'"

He sank in death, and his soul sped on its expected march up the heavenly street.

7815. DEATH, Kneeling in. Alexander Cruden, well known as the author of that invaluable help to Bible study, the Concordance, was very poor. What little profit came from his book he gave away. When about seventy years of age he was found at his humble lodgings, kneeling by his chair, his Bible open before him, his face calm and peaceful, but his spirit gone to God. David Livingstone, the great explorer, when very ill of his last sickness, was left for a little time alone in his tent. Upon the return of his men he was found upon his knees. They paused a moment, but he moved not; then they entered, and touched him, but he was dead. A medical student in New York was recently missing at the breakfast table. He was sought in his room, and was found, the bed undisturbed, but he kneeling at its side, cold in death.   *Ch. Press.*

7816. DEATH, Knell of. I don't believe there is a man or woman that ever lived who is not afraid of death unless they knew that Jesus Christ would overcome death. Before I knew the son of God as my Saviour death was a ter-

rible enemy to me. Now up in that little New England village where I came from, in that little village it was the custom to toll out the bell whenever any one died, and to toll one stroke for every year. Sometimes they would toll out seventy strokes for a man of 70, or forty strokes for a man of 40. I used to think when they died at 70, and sometimes 80, well, that is a good ways off. But sometimes it would be a child at my age, and then it used to be very solemn. Sometimes I could not bear to sleep in a room alone. Death used to trouble me, but, thanks to God, it don't trouble me now. If he should send his messenger and the messenger should come up here on this platform and say to me, "Mr. Moody, your hour is come, I have got to take you away," it would be joyful news for me; for though I should be absent from the body, I should be present with the Lord. Through the world I can shout, "O death, where is thy sting?"   *Moody.*

7817. DEATH of Knox. Step into this room, where the greatest Scotchman lies a-dying, and see an example more striking, warning, alarming still. From the iron grasp of kings and princes, John Knox has wrung the rights of Scotland. Ready to contend even unto the death, he had bearded proud nobles, and yet prouder churchmen; he had stood under the fire of battle; he had been chained to the galley's oar; he had held the pulpit with a papist's carbine leveled at his fearless head; to plant God's truth, and that tree of civil and religious liberty which has struck its roots deep into our soil, and under whose broad shadow we are this day sitting, he had fought many a hard-won battle; but his hardest of all was fought in the darkness of the night and amid the solitude of a dying chamber. One morning his friends enter his apartment. They find him faint, pallid, wearing the look of one who has passed a troubled night. So he had. He had been fighting, not sleeping; wrestling, not resting; and it required all God's grace to bring him off a conqueror. Till daybreak, Jacob wrestled with the Angel of the Covenant; but Knox had passed that long night wrestling with the Prince of Darkness. Like Bunyan's pilgrim, he had encountered Apollyon in the valley, and their swords struck fire within the shadow of death. Into that room the enemy had come. He stands by the dying man's side He reminds him that he had been a standard bearer of the truth, a reformer, the most thorough of all the reformers; a bold confessor; a distinguished sufferer; the very foremost man of his time and country; and so attempts to persuade him, that surely such rare merits deserve the crown. The Christian conquered; but hard put to it, only conquered through him that loved him. His shield was the truth of my text. He had been lost, wrecked at the mouth of the very harbor, had he lost sight of this beacon, "I do not this for your sake, but for mine holy name's sake."   *Dr. Guthrie.*

7818. DEATH, Lamenting. A gigantic Spartan soldier was wounded in battle by an arrow. He was ambitious to do much execution against the enemy, and chagrined that he was compelled to die before he had drawn his sword. The young Christian soldier has no need of regrets when called to lay down his armor, however bright. He is called to be a member of the staff of Christ in heaven.

7819. DEATH, Land of. Owen, on his dying bed, dictated a short letter to a friend. The amanuensis had written, "I am yet in the land of the living," when Owen at once arrested him. "Stop, alter that; write 'I am yet in the land of the dying, but I hope soon to be in the land of the living.'"

7820. DEATH, Legend of. The following is from the sacred books of the Buddhists: Among the immediate followers of Buddha was a young girl named Koshagautami. She was a simple, artless, creature, married to an Indian youth like herself; and the pair dwelt together in a woodland country near the city of the famous Oriental teacher. They had a little child, of which Koshagautami was passionately fond, as is the wont of Eastern mothers. But it happened that the little one sickened and died, much to the astonishment of the young and ignorant parents, who had been brought up in a life so solitary that they knew nothing whatever about death. The mother was especially grieved to find that her child looked so still and pale, and felt so cold, although she pressed it constantly to her bosom, and tempted it with delicate food. She rocked and shook it to make it speak once more—she would have been glad to hear it cry, although in pain; for the silence and deadly heaviness of the little body filled her with a vague misery. She went about the woods with the baby upon her hip, as Indian women always carry their children, asking everybody whom she met to tell her what would be good for the baby, and why it was so quiet and so chill. The people whom she met looked very strangely at the tiny corpse, and shook their heads, saying that no medicine would do it good any more. This disappointed the mother so much, that she determined to seek out Buddha and to ask him, who was never at a loss, for something that would bring back the warmth and laughter to the small cheeks. The Master was seated under a banyan tree with his disciples, and, when the young mother came near with the child, beseeching him to say if he knew what would make it well again, he looked at her weeping countenance with great pity, and answered that he did. "Go," he said, "and bring me hither a handful of mustard-seed from a house where nobody has ever died, and then I will heal your son." Koshagautami repaired to the town with the child; and asked at the first house for a little mustard-seed; which was readily given, because of her gentle and sorrowful look. "Friend," said she to the goodman, "did ever any die in this household?—for then the seed would not do." The housekeeper shook his head mournfully, and replied that his eldest son had died there during the last moon. She went to the next residence, and to the next, and so on right through the town; but,

to her surprise, she found that into every house had entered the same disease of which her little one was sick—even DEATH. Ashamed to have been so passionate and importunate, when all the rest of the world suffered and submitted, she dared not take the child back to Buddha, but buried it tenderly in the forest, under the shade of an asoka-tree, and then returned to the spot where the Master was still teaching. "There was no one," she moaned, "who had mustard-seed to give me, of the kind you bade me bring." "No, Koshagautami; it does not grow in this world of pain and illusion! The living are very few; the dead are very many, my daughter!"

7821. DEATH, Liberty by. Rev. Wm. Jenkyn, one of the ejected Ministers in England, being imprisoned in Newgate, presented a petition to King Charles II. for a release, which was backed by an assurance from his physician, that his life was in danger from his close imprisonment. The answer returned was, "Jenkyn shall be a prisoner as long as he lives." A nobleman having sometime after heard of his death, said to the King, "May it please your Majesty, Jenkyn has got his liberty." Upon which he asked, with eagerness, "Ay! who gave it him?" The nobleman replied, "A greater than your Majesty—the King of kings."

7822. DEATH, Light at. A lady, while she was full of life, shrank from the thought of the night with dismay, because she could not see beyond it the dawn of the morning. When the end was near, her brother told me, she was the sunniest spirit in the house. She would talk of her going as of a dim passage into another room, of those who were waiting to see her, and of those she should wait to see, and so she passed away. Now what makes this difference between the living and the dying? Just this, as I look at it: that we have all been interpreting Paul's great word, "Death is swallowed up in victory," as if it read, Life is swallowed up in victory. We have wanted in this, as in so many other ways, to push the hands forward and bring in the revelation before it is ripe; to bear the image of the earthly and the heavenly together, and put on immortality while we are cabled about and almost lost in the mortal. "When will the Minot light strike out?" I inquired this summer when we were down at the sea; "The moment the sun goes down," my friend said, "now let us watch." We were standing on high land watching the long shadows steal over the waters, and so it was that the moment the sun went down the light flashed out, and came out clearer as the shadows deepened, until it seemed to brood over the bay like a benediction. But here is our trouble. We want to see the light on the forelands of heaven, in the glare of high noon, and are dismayed because it is not there. Then we stand beside our dying when their sun goes down, and lo! as we watch them they tell us of the light we can not see, making the dark waters radiant, and filling them with a great peace and sense of the impending morning and the home. *Robert Collyer*

7823. DEATH of Little Nell. She was dead. There, upon her little bed, she lay at rest. The solemn stillness was no marvel now. She was dead. No sleep so beautiful and calm, so free from trace of pain, so fair to look upon. She seemed a creature fresh from the hand of God, and waiting for the breath of life; not one who had lived and suffered death. Her couch was dressed with here and there some winter berries and green leaves, gathered in a spot she had been used to favor. "When I die, put near me something that has loved the light, and had the sky above it always." She was dead. Dear, gentle, patient, noble Nell, was dead. Her little bird—a poor slight thing the pressure of a finger would have crushed—was stirring nimbly in its cage; and the strong heart of its child-mistress was mute and motionless for ever. Where were the traces of her early cares, her sufferings, and fatigues? All gone. Sorrow was dead indeed in her, but peace and perfect happiness were born; imaged in her tranquil beauty and profound repose. And still her former self lay there, unaltered in this change. Yes. The old fireside had smiled upon that same sweet face: it had passed, like a dream, through haunts of misery and care; at the door of the poor schoolmaster on the summer evening, before the furnace-fire upon the cold wet night, at the still bedside of the dying boy, there had been the same mild, lovely look. So shall we know the angels in their majesty, after death. *Dickens.*

7824. DEATH of Little Paul. "Now lay me down," he said; "and Floy, come close to me, and let me see you!" Sister and brother wound their arms around each other, and the golden light came streaming in, and fell upon them, locked together. "How fast the river runs between its green banks and the rushes, Floy! But it's very near the sea. I hear the waves! They always said so!" Presently he told her that the motion of the boat upon the stream was lulling him to rest. How green the banks were now, how bright the flowers growing on them, and how tall the rushes! Now the boat was out at sea, but gliding smoothly on. And now there was a shore before him. Who stood on the bank? He put his hands together, as he had been used to do, at his prayers. He did not remove his arms to do it; but they saw him fold them so, behind her neck. "Mamma is like you, Floy. I know her by the face! But tell them that the print upon the stairs at school is not divine enough. The light about the head is shining on me as I go!" The golden ripple on the wall came back again, and nothing else stirred in the room. The old, old fashion! The fashion that came in with our first garments, and will last unchanged until our race has run its course, and the wide firmament is rolled up like a scroll. The old, old fashion—Death! Oh thank God, all who see it, for that older fashion yet, of immortality! And look upon us, angels of young children, with regards not quite estranged, when the swift river bears us to the ocean! *Dickens.*

7825. DEATH, Longing for. Why may not I as passionately wish to see an end of life, as a slave in a hot day gasps for the refreshment of the shade; or as the laborer longs for the evening, when he may rest, and be paid for his pains. *Bishop Patrick.*

7826. DEATH, Looking to Christ in. "I am going to him," said Dr. Owen, "whom my soul loved, or rather who has loved me with an everlasting love, which is the sole ground of all my consolation." When Mr. Payne said to him, "I have just been putting your book, on 'The Glory of Christ,' to the press," he answered, "I am glad to hear it; but, oh! brother Payne, the long looked-for day is come at last, in which I shall see that glory in another manner than I have ever done yet, or was capable of doing in this world." What a death was that, which was only a going forth to meet one whom the soul loved! "I desire to depart and to be with Christ, which is far better," said the Rev. John Brown, of Haddington; "and though I have lived sixty years very comfortably in the world, yet I would turn my back upon you all to be with Christ. Oh, commend Jesus! there is none like Christ, none like Christ! I have been looking at him these many years, and never yet could find a fault in him, but was of my own making, though he has seen ten thousand faults in me. Many a comely person have I seen, but none so comely as Christ. I am weak, but it is delightful to feel one's self in the everlasting arms. Oh! what must he be in himself, when it is he that sweetens heaven, sweetens scriptures, sweetens ordinances, sweetens earth, sweetens trial?" And when Rowland Hill was dying, all his thoughts were centered on beholding the person of his Lord, and being where he was. "I do believe," said the dying man, "that for the first ten thousand years after we enter the kingdom of glory it will be all surprise." "But will this surprise never end?" "Never, while we behold the person of our Lord." "You are going to be with Jesus, and to see him as he is," said a friend. "Yes!" replied Mr. Hill with emphasis, "and I shall be like him: that is the crowning point." *Power*

7827. DEATH, The Lot of All. Death is a mighty leveler. He spares none, he waits for none, and stands on no ceremony. He will not tarry till you are ready. He will not be kept out by moats, and doors, and bars, and bolts. The Englishman boasts that his home is his castle; but with all his boasting, he cannot exclude death. An Austrian nobleman forbade death and the small-pox to be named in his presence. But, named or not named, it matters little, in God's appointed hour death will come. One man rolls easily along the road in the easiest and handsomest carriage that money can procure. Another toils wearily along the path on foot. Yet both are sure to meet at last in the same home. One man like Absalom, has fifty servants to wait upon him and to do his bidding. Another has none to lift a finger to do him a service. But both are traveling to a place where they must lie down alone. One man is the owner of hundreds of thousands.

Another has scarce a shilling that he can call his own property. Yet neither one nor the other can carry one farthing with him into the unseen world. One man is the possessor of half a country. Another has not so much as a garden of herbs. And yet two paces of the vilest earth will be amply sufficient for either of them at the last. One man pampers his body with every possible delicacy, and clothes it in the richest and softest apparel. Another has scarcely enough to eat, and seldom enough to put on. Yet both alike are hurrying on to a day when "ashes to ashes, dust to dust," shall be proclaimed over them, and fifty years hence none shall be able to say, "This was the rich man's bone and this was the bone of the poor."　　　　　　　　　　　　　　*Ryle.*

7828. DEATH, Marks of. The change of countenance which sometimes precedes death was observed in Mr. George Moir, and was reported to him by his wife. He called for a mirror and could but notice his own changed appearance. He exclaimed, "Death has set his mark on my body, but Christ has set his mark upon my soul."

7829. DEATH, Meditating on. Robert Boyle returning from Rotterdam to Gravesend by ship was chased by a vessel supposed to be a pirate. He took a glass and looked at it. From it he drew the following lesson: "This glass does, indeed, cause the distrusted vessel to approach; but it causes her to approach only to our eyes, not to our ship. If she be not making up to us, this harmless instrument will prove no loadstone to draw her towards us: and if she be, it will put us in better readiness to receive her. Such an instrument, in relation to death, is the meditation of it, by mortals so much and so causelessly abhorred. For though most men studiously shun all thoughts of death, as if, like a nice acquaintance, he would forbear to visit where he knows he is never thought of; or as if we would exempt ourselves from being mortal, by forgetting that we are so; yet meditation on this subject brings the awful reality nearer to our view, without at all lessening the real distance betwixt us and death. If our last enemy be not approaching us, this innocent meditation will no more quicken his pace than direct his steps; and if he be, it will, without hastening his arrival, prepare us for his reception."

7830. DEATH, Melanchthon's. Melanchthon's mind was clear to the last, and the passion of expounding Scripture was strong upon him. He was very tender, and spoke to each—even to the little children. His consolation was "Christ is made unto us wisdom, righteousness, sanctification, and redemption." Having done all possible for his comfort, his son-in-law asked if he would have anything else. *"Aliud nihil, nisi cœlum."*—Nothing else but heaven, he answered. He fell into quiet and rested forever from his labors.

7831. DEATH, Mental Enlargement in. The ancients noticed increased powers of mind in dying people. Plutarch says, "It is not probable that in death the soul gains new powers which it was not before possessed of, when the mind was confined in the chains of the body; but it is much more probable that these powers were always in being, though dimmed and clogged by the body; and the soul is only then able to practice them when the corporeal bonds are loosened, and the drooping limbs and stagnant juices no longer oppress it."

7832. DEATH, Mindful of. When Bernard Gilpin was privately informed that his enemies had caused thirty-two articles to be drawn up against him in the strongest manner, and presented to Bonner, bishop of London, he said to his favorite domestic, "At length they have prevailed against me. I am accused to the bishop of London, from whom there will be no escaping. God forgive their malice, and grant me strength to undergo the trial." He then ordered his servant to provide a long garment for him, in which he might go decently to the stake, and desired it might be got ready with all expedition. "For I know not," says he, "how soon I may have occasion for it." As soon as this garment was provided, it is said, he used to put it on every day, till the bishop's messengers apprehended him. It were well if we all thus realized to ourselves the hour of our departure. We ought by anticipation to sleep in our shrouds, and go to bed in our sepulchres. To put on our cerements now is wisdom.　　　　　　　　　　　*Spurgeon.*

7833. DEATH, Mountains of. A mother thought her little sick boy was safe in the arms of Jesus. She thought he was trusting sweetly in Christ; but one day, as he drew towards the chambers of death, she came into his room, and he said, as she was looking out of the window, "Mother, what are those mountains that I see yonder?" The mother said, "Eddie, there is no mountain in sight of the house." "Don't you see them, mother?" said he; "they're so high and so dark. Eddie has got to cross those mountains. Won't you take him in your arms and carry him over those mountains?" The mother said, "Eddie, I would if I could, but I cannot." The mother then said, "Eddie, you must take your eyes off your mother. You must have your eyes upon Jesus. He will help you." The mother again prayed with him, and tried to get his little mind off from the dark mountain. All at once he said, "Mother, hark! don't you hear them call?" "Hear who, Eddie?" "Don't you see the angels just on the other side of the mountain? They are calling for me. Take me, mother, and carry me over the mountain." The mother said again, "Why, my boy, I cannot go with you; but Christ will be with you. He will take you safe over the mountains, if you trust him." Again the mother prayed for her little boy, for she could not bear to have him die in that state of mind, so troubled about the mountain. At length he closed his eyes, and he prayed, "Lord Jesus, be with me, and take me over the mountains." Then he opened his little eyes, and said, "Good-bye, mamma: Jesus is coming to carry me over the mountains;" and the little sufferer was gone. Sinner, Christ has come to-night to carry you over the mountains. *Moody.*

7834. DEATH, No Delaying. A physician was called to attend a woman who had been stabbed in a drunken brawl. When he came she exclaimed, "Doctor, can I live?" He examined the wound, and pronounced it mortal. "O doctor," she said, "do save my life for a month, that I may pray to God to pardon my sins!" "I never deceive my patients," he replied, "and I would not for the world deceive you. My opinion is, that you cannot live an hour." "O, for half an hour then, doctor! half an hour! half an hour!" She breathed her last uttering this cry.

7835. DEATH, No Escape from. In reading the epitaphs, and surveying the monuments of others, we should reflect on our own mortality. And not only reflect, but also prepare for the last scene, so that when it arrives we may meet it without dismay. The ancient Egyptians are said to have placed a skull upon the table at their most splendid banquets, in order to remind the guests of their mortality. Socrates disregarded the intercession of his friends, and when it was in his power to make his escape out of prison, he refused, and asked with his usual pleasantry, where he could escape death. "Where," says he to Crito, who had bribed the gaoler, and made his escape certain, "Where shall I fly to avoid this irrevocable doom passed on all mankind?" Reader, remember this, whatever you escape, where will you go to avoid death? How necessary, then, to seek the favor of him who alone can support in that moment, and grace alone can prepare for the awful event. *Buck.*

7836. DEATH Not Desired. Burckhardt relates, that when the plague visited Medina the Mohammedans, strict predestinarians, fled to the desert, excusing their conduct by saying that although the disease was a messenger sent to call them to heaven, yet they felt their own unworthiness to be so great that they thought it advisable to decline this special favor at present and leave the town. Men call for death, but when it comes it is usually unwelcome.

7837. DEATH, Not Ready for. A minister said to an emaciated soldier in hospital, "How are you to-day, my soldier friend?" "Poorly, sir; very poorly; a few days more, only a few." "You are all ready, I trust?" "I am going—there is no help for it; if you call that ready, I am ready." "I mean are you prepared to die? Is this exchange of worlds going to be pleasant to you?" "Pleasant! It is awful, sir; horrible beyond all account! But I have got to come to it!" The minister spoke to him of the offer of mercy through Christ. He replied, "I know it all, have heard it a thousand times, but it is not for me now." The minister urged him to come to Christ at once, and said it was a pity he had not done so before. "Pity! It's my ruin, sir. I cannot come. I will not. You come a little too late! It's getting dark now." Unconsciousness was fast settling upon him. In this attitude of despair he passed into eternity. "No, no—a boy again, a boy again," were his last words. His boyhood, innocent and full of good opportunities, was lost, and would not return at his call. The thought filled his soul with agony.

7838. DEATH, Occupation and. When the sensibility to outward impressions is lost or disordered, and the mind is delirious, the dying dream of their habitual occupations, and construct an imaginary present from the past. Dr. Armstrong departed delivering medical precepts. Napoleon fought some battles o'er again, and the last words he muttered were *tête d'armée.* Lord Tenderden, who passed straight from the judgment-seat to his death-bed, fancied himself still presiding at a trial, and expired with, "Gentlemen of the jury, you will now consider of your verdict." Dr. Adam, the author of the "Roman Antiquities," imagined himself in school, distributing praise and censure among his pupils: "But it grows dark," he said; "the boys may dismiss;" and instantly died. The physician, soldier, judge, schoolmaster, each had their thoughts on their several professions, and believed themselves engaged in the business of life when life itself was issuing out through their lips. *Fontenelle.*

7839. DEATH, Paine's. Before his death, Thomas Paine seems to have feared that some influence would be brought to bear upon him by which he should be lead to renounce the atheistic views advanced in his "Age of Reason." He then called upon Mr. Jarvis, a man of the same opinions, to witness, saying, "Now I am in health, and in perfect soundness of mind, is the time to express my opinion." He then solemnly affirmed his belief in the truth of his books. The reports of his friends put him in the most hostile attitude towards Christianity. Rev. Mr. Milledollar, a Presbyterian, and Rev. Mr. Cunningham called upon him as neighbors, and the latter warned him, "You have now a full view of death; you cannot live long, and whosoever does not believe in Christ will certainly be damned." Mr. Paine replied, "Let me have none of your popish stuff! Get away with you! Good morning!" He would hear nothing from Mr. Milledollar. When they had gone, he ordered his housekeeper, "Don't let 'em come here again; they trouble me." A Methodist minister gained admission to his sick-room, and warned him of the necessity of repentance. Mr. Paine was very angry, and sick as he was, rose up in his bed and declared if he was able, he would put him out of his room. An old disciple of Mr. Paine's called upon him, and narrated his conversion to Christianity. He was abruptly and angrily dismissed. His associates clustered about him constantly, asking him if he had any doubts on the subject of his teachings, and he as constantly affirming that he had none. His last words were, in answer to the question of Dr. Manly, his physician, "Do you wish to believe that Jesus is the Son of God?" He answered, "I have no wish to believe on that subject." Thus passed from earth Thomas Paine, an irascible, penurious, and unhappy old man. See vol. i., 1374.

7840. DEATH, Parting at. A minister called upon another, then upon his dying bed. As they shook hands at parting, the latter said, "Brother, we part at the footstool, we shall meet at the throne."

7841. DEATH, Patriotic. Rev. J. H. Knowles was called to see a wounded soldier. He had been brought in on a stretcher, and placed under the shade of a green tree. He was shot through the mouth; his tongue was cut, and he could not speak. As the chaplain approached him he made signs for pencil and paper, and wrote, "I am a Christian, prepared to die;" then looking around upon the soldiers near, he added another line, "Rally round the flag, boys, rally round the flag." Mr. Knowles took the paper, and read it aloud to his comrades. As he read, the dying man, speaking only with his animated face, raised his bloody hand over his head, and waved it as Marmion shook his sword, with all the enthusiasm of the charge; and then quietly, while every eye brimmed with tears, went away out of the midst of the company into the City of Peace.

7842. DEATH, Pause Before. A commander of Charles V. of Spain, requested a discharge from public service. The king required a reason. The officer replied, "There ought to be a pause between the tumult of life and the day of death."

7843. DEATH, Peaceful. Remember the happy, peaceful death of the righteous man can only be obtained or hoped for by those who have lived the life of the righteous. Remember that every guilty compliance with the humors of the world, every sinful indulgence of our own passions, is laying up cares and fears for the hour of darkness, and that the remembrance of ill-spent time will strew our sick bed with thorns and rack our sinking spirits with despair. *Heber.*

7844. DEATH, Peace in. Pastor Emille Cook, in returning to France from the Evangelical Alliance of 1873, suffered shipwreck. He was picked up and carried to the Loch Earn in a fainting state, almost naked, and suffering with cold. The Loch Earn was slowly sinking, but while others were taken off, he remained for six days to care for a wounded friend and encourage the crew. All were rescued from the sinking vessel, but excitement brought on a violent fever and nervous prostration. His hope was to live, to work for his native land, but God ordered otherwise. His physical struggles were great, and the last day of his life was one of intense agony. The last hour came. He made sign to have the Bible read. A friend read the sixth psalm. "Admirable! admirable!" said he. His wife told him "God will help you, my dear; he will give you his peace." He replied in almost a reproachful tone, "But I have it—peace; I have it." Then he fell into a half sleep. He uttered three sighs, and all was over.

7845. DEATH, Personification of. The personification of death in the act of executing the Divine commands is variously represented by different nations. The meanest is the common monkish one of a skeleton with dart and hour glass; while one of the most terrible is that of the Scandinavian poets, who represent him as mounted on horse-back, riding with inconceivable rapidity in pursuit of his prey, meagre and wan, and the horse possessing the same character as his rider. Yet this passage from the Apocalypse is in sublimity and terror superior to the most energetic specimens of Runic poetry: "And I looked, and behold a pale horse : and his name that sat on him was Death, and hell followed with him. And power was given unto them over the fourth part of the earth, to kill with sword, and with hunger and with death, and with the beasts of the earth." The word translated "pale" is peculiarly expressive in the original: it might be more adequately rendered "ghastly," meaning that wan and exanimate hue exhibited in certain diseases. *Mason Good*

7846. DEATH, Physical. Death does not strike all the organs of the body at the same time. Some may be said to survive others, and the lungs are among the last to give up the performance of their function and die. As death approaches, they become gradually more and more oppressed, the air-cells are loaded with an increased quantity of the fluid which naturally lubricates their surfaces; the atmosphere can now no longer come in contact with the minute blood-vessels spread over the air-cells, without first permeating this viscid fluid; hence the rattle. Nor is the contact sufficiently perfect to change the black venous into the red arterial blood. An unprepared fluid consequently issues from the lungs into the heart, and is thence transmitted to every other organ of the body. The brain receives it, and its energies appear to be lulled thereby into sleep—generally tranquil sleep, filled with dreams which impel the dying lip to murmur out the names of friends and the occupations and recollections of a past life; the peasant "babbles o' green fields;" and Napoleon expires amid visions of battle. *Sir H. Halford*

7847. DEATH, Picture of. The hour of death may be fitly likened to that celebrated picture in the National Gallery, of Perseus holding up the head of Medusa. That head turned all persons into stone who looked upon it. There is a warrior represented with a dart in his hand; he stands stiffened, turned into stone, with the javelin even in his fist. There is another with a poignard beneath his robe, about to stab; he is now the statue of an assassin, motionless and cold. Another is creeping along stealthily, like a man in ambuscade, and there he stands a consolidated rock; he has looked only upon that head, and he is frozen into stone. Such is death. What I am when death is held before me, that I must be forever. When my spirit departs, if God finds me hymning his praise, I shall hymn it in heaven; if he finds me breathing out oaths, I shall follow up those oaths in hell. *Spurgeon.*

7848. DEATH, Power of Habit in. An hour before Malherbe's death, says Bayle, after he had been two hours in an agony, he awakened on a sudden to reprove his landlady, who waited upon him, for using a word that was not good French; and when his confessor reprimanded him for it he told him he could not help it, and that he would defend the purity of the French language until death. When his confessor painted the joys of paradise with extraordinary eloquence, and asked him if he did not feel a vehement desire to enjoy such bliss, Malherbe, who had been more attentive to the holy man's manner than to his matter, captiously replied, "Speak no more of it; your bad style disgusts me." He was critical to the last gasp. Poor Sheridan, like Rabelais, in the midst of all his miseries preserved his pleasantry, and his perception of the ridiculous almost as long as life lasted. When lying on his death-bed, the solicitor, a gentleman who had been much favored in wills, waited on him; after the general legatee had left the room another friend came in, to whom the author of the "School for Scandal" said, "My friends have been very kind in calling upon me and offering their services in their respective ways; Dick W. has been here with his will-making face." *Physic and Physicians.*

7849. DEATH, Premonition of. The first symptom of approaching death with some is the strong presentiment that they are about to die. Ozanam, the mathematician, while in apparent health, rejected pupils, from the feeling that he was on the eve of resting from his labors; and he expired soon after, of an apoplectic stroke. Foote, prior to his departure for the continent, stood contemplating the picture of a brother author, and exclaimed, his eyes full of tears, "Poor Weston!" In the same dejected tone he added, after a pause: "Soon others shall say, 'Poor Foote!'" and, to the surprise of his friends, a few days proved the justice of his prognostication. The expectation of the event had a share in producing it; for a slight shock completes the destruction of prostrate energies. The case of Wolsey was singular. The morning before he died he asked Cavendish the hour, and was answered "Past eight." "Eight of the clock!" replied Wolsey, "that cannot be; eight of the clock, nay, nay, it cannot be eight of the clock, for by eight of the clock shall you lose your master." The day he miscalculated, the hour came true. On the following morning, as the clock struck eight, his troubled spirit passed from life. Cavendish and the bystanders thought he must have had a revelation of the time of his death; and from the way in which the fact had taken possession of his mind, we suspect that he had relied on astrological prediction, which had the credit of a revelation in his own esteem. *T. Wakley.*

7850. DEATH, Preparation for. Religion, indeed, is like the stone Chrysolapis, which will shine brightest in the dark of death. The truly religious may launch into the ocean of eternity, and sail to their everlasting harbor, as the Alexandrian ship came into the Roman haven, with top and top-gallant, with true comfort and undaunted courage: let death come

when it will, he can bid it welcome. Death is never sudden to a saint; no guest comes unawares to him who keepeth a constant table; but as when the day dawns to us in Europe, the shadows of the evening are stretched on Asia, so the day of their redemption will be a long night of destruction to thee. That jailer who knocketh off their fetters, and setteth them at that perfect liberty, will bind thee in chains of darkness, and haul thee to the dungeon of horror, whence thou shalt never come forth.
Swinnock.

7851. DEATH, Preparing for. The Observer relates that, in a recent prayer-meeting in Fulton street, New York, a gentleman from London stated that on his passage homeward they encountered a terrible storm. The shaft of the steamship was broken, one wheel was disabled, and they expected every moment to go down. On board they had in one cabin several Catholic priests, and as many nuns, or Sisters of Charity. They had also a very pious Methodist man. In the midst of the storm the priests were about to administer extreme unction, the last rite of the church, by which all sin is supposed to be washed away. This Methodist had been with them, and to him one of the priests said,—"I feel it my duty to tell you that we are about to administer extreme unction for the cleansing away of all sin. I must tell you that you are out of the true church, and that if you die as you are, you will be lost forever—you will be damned. Will you allow me to administer to you extreme unction, and thus save your soul?" "Sir," said the Methodist, "I have been down to my state-room for some time alone, with the High Priest of my profession. I have made a full and unreserved confession of all my sins. He has pronounced absolution from all my guilt. He has administered to me extreme unction. He has assured me that he is ready to receive me. He is mighty to save, and he tells me he can save, to the uttermost, all who come unto God through him. He has prepared me for death. I know that my Redeemer liveth. I am ready to have this vessel go down. I ask you if you really believe I need any preparation at your hands?" The priest said no more. *W. Jones.*

7852. DEATH, The Purifier. Under the ceremonial law, if earthen vessels were polluted, there was no way but to break them; so there is no way of purifying our sinful bodies but by breaking them by death. *Bp. Hopkins.*

7853. DEATH, Putting off the Thought of. Is it not then, think you, a great folly that men are so unwilling to think of death? Questionless it is. We see the mariner with joy thinks of the haven: the laborer is glad to see the evening: the soldier is not sorry when his warfare is accomplished: and shall we be grieved when the days of sin are ended? It seemeth by this which you have said that this life of ours is very troublesome; for we are mariners, our haven is happiness: travelers, our journey is to Paradise: laborers, our hire is heaven: and soldiers, our conquest is at death. Is, then, our life both miserable and changeable? Yea verily, for it is compared to a pilgrimage, in which is uncertainty: a flower, in which is mutability: a smoke, in which is vanity: a house of clay, in which is misery: a weaver's shuttle, in which is volubility: a shepherd's tent, in which is variety: a ship on the sea, in which is celerity: a mariner, who sitting, standing, sleeping, or waking, ever saileth on: a shadow, which is nothing to the body: to a thought, whereof we have thousands in one day: to a dream, whereof we have millions in one night: to vanity, which is nothing in itself; and to nothing, which hath no being in the world (Psalm 39: 5). If all this be true, as it must needs be, because God hath said it, the hour of death is far better than the day of our birth.	*Hill.*

7854. DEATH, Question of. Rev. Dr. Kidd, was an eccentric Scotch minister of some prominence. One of his parishioners says: "I was busy in my shop, when, in the midst of my work, in stepped the doctor. 'Did you expect me?' was his abrupt inquiry, without even waiting for a salutation. 'No,' was my reply. 'What if I had been Death?' he asked, when at once he stepped out as abruptly as he came, and was gone almost before I knew it."

7855. DEATH, Questions of. Rev. John Newton one day mentioned in company the death of a lady. A young woman who sat opposite immediately said, "O sir, how did she die?" The clergyman replied, "There is a more important question than that, my dear, which you should have asked first." "Sir," said she, "what question can be more important than 'How did she die?'" "How did she live?" was Mr. Newton's answer.

7856. DEATH, Quiet in. Sometimes the quiet death of a very bad man proceeds from stupidity, and want of a just sense of the danger of his condition, and this from a want of discipline and instruction in the nature and principles of religion. This temper looks like courage, because it is fearless of danger; but this fearlessness is founded in great ignorance and want of apprehension; whereas a true courage discerns the danger, and yet thinks it fit and reasonable to venture upon it. Now this stupidity of dying men, who have lived very ill, is commonly the case of such as have been brought up in ignorance, and have lived in great sensuality, by which means their spirits are immersed, and even stifled in carnality and sense; and no wonder, if they who live like beasts die in the same manner.	*Tillotson.*

7857. DEATH, Regret in. Salmasius, one of the most profound scholars of his time, saw cause to exclaim bitterly against himself. "Oh!" said he, shortly before his death, "I have lost a world of time—time, the most precious thing in the world! Had I but one year more, it should be spent in perusing David's Psalms and Paul's Epistles. Oh! sirs," said he, addressing those about him, "mind the world less and God more."

7858. DEATH, Rejoice at. Rejoice that it is the gracious pleasure of thy God, thou shalt not always inhabit a dungeon, nor lie amidst so impure and disconsolate darkness; that he will shortly exchange thy filthy garments for those of salvation and praise. The end approaches. As you turn over these leaves, so are your days turned over. And as you are now arrived at the end of this book, God will shortly write "finis" to the book of your life on earth, and show you your names written in heaven, in the book of that life which shall never end.	*Howe.*

7859. DEATH, Release by. God's house is a hospital at one end and a palace at the other. In the hospital end are Christ's members upon earth suffering with various diseases, and confined to a strict regimen of his appointing. What sort of a patient must he be who would be sorry to know that the hour is come for his dismission from the hospital, and to see the doors thrown wide open for his admission into the King's presence.	*Adams.*

7860. DEATH, Review at. When Pambo, the hermit, was dying, he said, "I thank God that not a day of my life has been spent in idleness. Never have I eaten bread that I have not earned with the sweat of my brow. I do not recall any bitter speech I have made, for which I ought to repent now." This is the man who learned to "offend not with his tongue." No. 5739.

7861. DEATH a Reward. Biton and Cleobis, two young men of Argos, their mother being the priestess of Juno, and the time being come that she was to go up to the temple to perform the rites of the goddess, and those whose office it was to draw her chariot tarrying longer than usual, these two young men harnessed themselves and took it up, and so carried their mother to the temple. She, being extremely taken with the piety of her sons, petitioned the goddess that she would bestow upon them the best present that could be given to men; accordingly she cast them into that deep sleep out of which they never awoke, taking this way to recompense their filial zeal with death. Pindar writes of Agamedes and Trophonius, that after they had built a temple at Delphi, they requested of Apollo a reward for their work. It was answered them that they should have it within seven days, but in the meanwhile they were commanded to live freely and indulge their genius; accordingly they obeyed the dictate, and the seventh night they died in their beds.	*Plutarch.*

7862. DEATH, Royalty at. Prince Albert when upon his dying bed said, "I have had wealth, rank and power. But if this were all I had, how wretched I should be now.

"'Rock of ages, cleft for me,
Let me hide myself in Thee.'"

7863. DEATH, Ruling Passion in. An old farmer, up to all methods for making a bargain, was very ill, and friends were expecting an early demise. His nephew and a man hired for the occasion butchered a steer that had been fattened, and when the job was completed the nephew entered the sick-room, where a few friends where assembled, when, to the astonishment of all, the old man opened his eyes and, turning his head slightly, said, in a full voice, drawling out the words: "What have you been doing?" "Killing the steer," was the reply. "What did you do with the hide?" "Left it in the barn; going to sell it by and by." "Let the boys drag it around the barn a couple of times; it will make it weigh heavier." And the good old man was gathered unto his fathers.   *Anon.*

7864. DEATH, Sayings in. Rev. Matthew Henry said to his old and intimate friend Mr. Illidge, on his death-bed, "You have been used to take notice of the sayings of dying men. This is mine. That a life spent in the service of God, and communion with him, is the most comfortable and pleasant life that any one can live in this world."

7865. DEATH, Sermon on. A man may read a sermon, the best and most passionate that ever man preached, if he shall but enter into the sepulchres of kings. In the same Escurial where the Spanish princes live in greatness and power, and decree war or peace, they have wisely placed a cemetery, where their ashes and their glory shall sleep till time shall be no more; and where our kings have been crowned their ancestors lie interred, and they must walk over their grandsire's head to take his crown. There is an acre sown with royal seed, the copy of the greatest change, from rich to naked, from ceiled roofs to arched coffins, from living like gods to dying like men. There is enough to cool the flames of lust, to abate the heights of pride, to appease the itch of covetous desires, to sully and dash out the dissembling colors of a lustful, artificial, and imaginary beauty. There the warlike and the peaceful, the fortunate and the miserable, the beloved and the despised princes, mingle their dust, and lay down their symbol of mortality, and tell all the world that, when we die, our ashes shall be equal to kings', and our accounts easier, and our pains for our crowns shall be less.   *Jeremy Taylor.*

7866. DEATH, Shrinkage by. Pope Leo IX. approached death with great calmness. He ordered his coffin to be placed in St. Peter's, and had his couch placed beside it. Rising up he looked into his coffin and said, "Behold, my brethren, the mutability of human things! The cell which was my dwelling when a monk expanded into yonder spacious palace; it shrinks again into this narrow coffin." He died before the altar of St. Peter's at Rome, A. D. 1054.

7867. DEATH, Simplicity in. Dr. Guthrie asked his friends to sing. They asked him, "What shall we sing for you?" He said, "Give me a bairn's hymn." They sang "Jesus, tender Shepherd, hear me," and "There is a happy land, far, far away." His faith was the faith of a little child. When asked, "Have you that Saviour now?" he answered, "Yes; I have none else." Then he was heard to murmur to himself, "Over on the other side," and kept ejaculating the words, "Happy, happy, happy!" And so he fell asleep in Jesus.

7868. DEATH, Solemnity of. Death is too se-

rious a subject for trifling or vaunting. A minister says, "I once knew an 'old disciple' who had no patience with Christians that were afraid to die: it was bringing, he said, such a reproach upon religion! For his own part, as he expressed it, he was always looking out for the holidays, and wondering why his father was so long in sending to take him home. But when the message came, he was filled with consternation. During the illness which brought him to the grave, he clung to earthly existence, with a tenacity which was perfectly distressing. On the announcement of his decease, a neighbor remarked concerning him, 'Poor old man! in life he would have given the world to die; and in death he would have given the world to live.'"

7869. DEATH, Spiritual. When at sea, it is the practice to attach heavy weights to a corpse, and it is then lowered into the deep waters. But the corpse, though carried downwards into the deep unfathomable gulf, is utterly unconscious of its sinking state, though it continues to descend till it meets the bottom. So the soul which is spiritually dead is continually thrust down and overwhelmed with the burden of its sins. Unconscious of its destination, it is irresistibly carried onwards. Its path is the downward path of destruction. It has a weight and a burden which it can no more cast off, than the corpse can disengage itself from its iron weights. Unconscious of ruin, it continues to fall until it is swallowed up in the depths of perdition. Nothing but the mighty hand of God can arrest it while plunging downwards in the gulfs of ruin.   *Salter.*

7870. DEATH, Sudden. Death does not always give warning beforehand; sometimes he gives the mortal blow suddenly; he comes behind with his dart, and strikes a man at the heart, before he saith, 'Have I found thee, O mine enemy?' (Kings 21: 30). Eutychus fell down dead suddenly (Acts 20: 9); death suddenly arrested David's sons and Job's sons; Augustus died in a compliment, Galba with a sentence, Vespasian with a jest; Zeuxis died laughing at the picture of an old woman which he drew with his own hand; Sophocles was choked with the stone in a grape; Diodorus the logician died for shame that he could not answer a joculary question propounded at the table by Stilpo; Johannes Measius, preaching upon the raising of the woman of Nain's son from the dead, within three hours after died himself.   *Brooks.*

7871. DEATH, Sunset. I sympathize with the sentiment of Rev. Dr. Few, of Georgia, when he lay a-dying. A brother sang for him that hymn which has this refrain, "I hope to die shouting, The Lord will provide." Said he, "I don't ask to die that way—but peacefully, like the sun goes down." So died Dr. A. L. P. Green. We had the privilege of more than one prayerful interview with him. He believed he was nearing the end when others had hope. "Doctor, you have done a great deal of preaching; how does it appear now, as you look back on it?" There was no remark of self-depreciation, as that he might have done it better, or more of it: but this was the deliberate reply, "I am impressed with its truth. What I have been preaching is true."

Bp. M' Tyere.

7872. DEATH, Temptations in. Rev. Joseph Alleine, in a sore conflict with Satan just before his death, said, "Away, thou foul fiend, thou enemy of mankind, thou subtle sophister! Art thou come now to molest me, now I am just going—now I am so weak, and death upon me! Trouble me not, for I am none of thine; I am the Lord's; Christ is mine, and I am his; his by covenant. I have sworn myself to be the Lord's, and his I will be;—therefore begone!" These last words he often repeated, "which," says Mrs. Alleine, "I took much notice of, that his covenanting with God was the means he used to expel the devil and all his temptations."

7873. DEATH, Terrors in. Bunyan shows his sagacity in representing his hero as beset with terrors and demoniacal mockeries before his final triumph; for the characters of neither good nor bad men can be inferred from their dying words. It pleases God usually to comfort exceedingly his children in the solemn crisis of death; and even the phantasies of the struggling and disordered mind generally then take their character from the habitually pious or godless course of the preceding life: but it is sometimes otherwise; disease and drugs have much effect on the shattered sensibilities; and Christian biography teaches that surviving friends should attach but little significance, whether saddening or consoling, to the last expressions of the dead; life, not death, reveals the probable fate of the soul. Thomas Walsh once heard Fletcher, of Madeley, preach in Wesley's chapel, in London, on the dying trials of good men. Fletcher supposed that some comparatively weak believers might die most cheerfully; and that some strong ones, for the further purification of their faith, or for inscrutable reasons, might have severe conflicts. At the subsequent meeting of the bands, Walsh opposed this opinion, and said he thought it bore hard against God's justice, faithfulness, and covenant love to his servants. Fletcher modestly observed that God's wisdom was sovereign and unsearchable; and though he was sorry he had given offence, yet he could not with a good conscience retract what he had said. With some degree of warmth Walsh replied, "Be it done unto you according to your faith, and be it done unto me according to mine!" and here the matter rested. Two years afterward Walsh needed in death the consolatory opinion of Fletcher. During some months he struggled with what were doubtless the agonies of a disordered nervous system. He was brought almost to the extremity of mental anguish, if not despair of his salvation. To his Christian brethren it was a mysterious spectacle, and public prayers were offered up for him in Dublin, London, and other places. "His great soul," says his biographer, "lay thus, as it were, in ruins for some considerable time, and poured out many a heavy groan and speechless tear from an oppressed heart and dying body. He sadly bewailed the absence of him whose wonted presence had so often given him the victory over the manifold contradictions and troubles which he endured for his name's sake." But as sometimes the clouds, thick on the whole heavens, are rent at the horizon the moment the sun seems to pause there before setting, and his last rays stream in and flood with effulgence and joy the whole sky, so was the darkness lifted from the last hour of this good man. After prayers had been offered in his chamber by a group of sympathizing friends, he requested to be left alone a few minutes that he might "meditate a litt'e." They withdrew, and he remained in profound prayer and self-recollection for some time. At length he broke out with the rapturous exclamation, "He is come! he is come! my Beloved is mine, and I am his; his forever!" and died. *Stevens.*

7874. DEATH, Time of. An eminent author suggests a motive which we may, with humble reverence, conceive as inducing the Father of mercies to choose the precise moment which he does for calling each of his children out of this world. He read an account of an accidental fire by which a house in the neighborhood of London was consumed. The father and mother escaped from the flames, bearing, as they first supposed, all their treasures with them. But on reckoning them up, the father discovered that the youngest child, then an infant, had in the confusion of the moment been left behind in an upper chamber. He instantly rushed back in the midst of the conflagration, ascended the stairs, and was seen by the assembled crowd of anxious spectators to enter the apartment, now illuminated by the flames. He flew to the bed—seized the child—enfolded him in his arms—and, just as he was on the point of bearing him off in triumph the floor gave way, and both were precipitated into the devouring element. Upon reading this, he could scarcely describe his feelings. In much weakness he was disposed to wonder why a merciful Providence should thus require an act of such heroic tenderness. But after a moment's pause, the following reflection came to his relief. If the saying of the wise may be applicable here, "where the tree falleth there it shall lie;" if precisely as our state is at the instant of death, so will our character be fixed for ever—how could this person have been summoned at a more auspicious moment? To mortal eyes, indeed, no sight could have been more agonizing, than that of a man perishing in so generous a struggle for the deliverance of his child. Such is the dark side of the picture which we see. But how glorious the reverse, presented to the assembly of invisible spectators! Amidst what joyful acclamations might these two have ascended from the flames into the regions of the blessed! How might the angels have rejoiced—with what transport might the spirits of the just be filled when this parent entered the gates of heaven with his infant in his arms;

the one to live for ever amongst the band of innocents, the other to take his station with those who "lost their life in this world, that they might keep it unto life eternal!"

Woodward.

7875. DEATH, Timidity at. Mrs. Sarah Wesley, the wife of Charles, was very timid at the approach of death. She asked all to pray fervently for her deliverance. She repeated "By thy precious death and passion, good Lord, deliver us;" and in struggle of soul pleaded "Open the gates! Open the gates!" Peace came to her before death. She passed through the gates to her rest without a groan.

7876. DEATH by Torture. In the persecution of Valerian in 258, Laurence, a deacon at Rome, was condemned to be tortured to death. A huge gridiron was made ready, the fire was kindled, and Laurence was stripped and laid upon it. The day was beautiful. The sun shone upon the face of the martyr and his countenance was radiant as the face of an angel. Not a murmur escaped him. He said, with a smile, to his tormentors, "Turn me, I am roasted on one side." He died without a cry or moan of pain, as calmly as if lying on a bed of down. Jesus can make even tortures pleasures, and pains joys.

7877. DEATH, Trifling in. A fatal malady seized on Cardinal Mazarin, whilst engaged in conferences about a treaty, and worn by mental fatigue, he consulted Guenaud, the physician, who told him he had but two months to live. Some days afterwards, Brienne perceived the cardinal in his night-cap and dressing-gown tottering along his gallery, pointing to his pictures, and exclaiming, "Must I quit all these?" He saw Brienne, and seized him. "Look at that Correggio! this Venus of Titian! that incomparable Deluge of Caracci! Ah! my friend, I must quit all these. Farewell, dear pictures, that I love so dearly, and that cost me so much!" A few days before his death he caused himself to be dressed, shaved, rouged and painted. In this state he was carried in his chair to the promenade, where the envious courtiers paid him ironical compliments on his appearance. Cards were the amusement of his deathbed, his hands being held by others; and they were only interrupted by the Papal Nuncio, who came to give the cardinal plenary indulgence.

Percy.

7878. DEATH, Two Pictures of. In a scantily-furnished chamber lies an old Scotch minister with thin, gray hair, and wrinkled skin. But his brow is high and broad; his deep-set eyes are bright and piercing; a smile plays round his lips; and though feeble and dying, he looks calm and happy. Let us speak to him and say: "Do you think yourself dying, dear sir?" He fixes his eye calmly upon you, and slowly he replies: "Really, friend, I am not anxious whether I am or not; for if I die, I shall be with God; if I live, he will be with me." Now let us step into yonder mansion. Entering a richly-furnished chamber, we find a dignified personage enfolded in warm robes, and seated in a large easy chair. He, too, is feeble and dying; but the light in his eyes is unsteady, and he looks like a man ill at ease with himself. Let us also ask him a question: "Mr Gibbon, how does the world appear to you now?" The eloquent historian of the Roman empire (for he it is) closes his eyes a moment, then opens them again, and with a deep sigh he replies: "All things are fleeting. When I look back, I see they have been fleeting; when I look forward, all is dark and doubtful."

Protestant Churchman.

7879. DEATH, Type of. Jordan is the type of death, dividing the wilderness, this world, from the land of promise, heaven. Israel passes through Jordan without feeling its waters, and comes with Joshua into the promised land. When he passes Jordan all Israel passes. And thus it was in Christ. The Church is dead with him, buried with him, risen with him.

A. Jukes.

7880. DEATH, Unexpected. At a banquet of Roman nobles, the discourse was upon what was the best sort of death. Cæsar said, "That which is unexpected." He had his wish gratified, dying in the fullness of his manhood and at the height of renown.

7881. DEATH, Unlooked for. "It has always appeared to me," says Dr. Johnson, " as one of the most striking passages in the visions of Quevedo, that which stigmatizes those as fools who complain that they failed of happiness by sudden death. Quevedo asks, 'How can death be sudden to a being who always knew that he must die, and that the time of his death was uncertain?'"

7882. DEATH, Unpleasing. Fuller, having pondered on all the modes of destruction, arrived at the short and decisive conclusion, "None please me." "But away," the good man adds, "with these thoughts; the mark must not choose what arrow shall be shot against it." The choice is not ours to make, and if it were the privilege would be an embarrassment. But there is consolation in the teaching of physiology. Of the innumerable weapons with which death is armed, the worst is less intolerable than imagination presents it; his visage is more terrible than his dart.

Fontanelle.

7883. DEATH, Unselfishness in. A private of the 11th Maine was mortally wounded in a charge. As his companions started to carry him to the rear, he looked up to his regimental commander, and said, in generous thoughtfulness of others, "Don't trouble the boys to carry me back, Colonel; it will only tire them. I can live but a few minutes, and can just as well die here."

7884. DEATH Vanquished. Through the Redeemer's sacrifice, death becomes to the Christian as one in a various catalogue of things which must work together for his good. So complete, indeed, is the atonement which has been made for human guilt, that the Father might cause our spirits to be enlightened and sanctified at once, and our bodies to pass at once into heaven, without tasting of death, were such his pleasure. But the wisdom which has determined that our victory over spiritual death should be by means of a various and protracted warfare, has arranged that victory over natural death should be through the passage of the grave. Thus a new character attaches to this event, when viewed in connection with the second Adam, instead of being regarded merely in its relation to the first. From the one, this enemy derives all that power which has rendered him the king of terrors; by the other, the foe has been deprived of his main strength, and rendered comparatively and ultimately harmless. *Vaughan.*

7885. DEATH, Vicarious. A sailing ship started from England loaded with passengers, who were seeking a home in America. Among them were two brothers: one was married: his wife and two children were already in America, and expecting his arrival; the other was single. The ship sprung a leak near the Banks, and had to be abandoned; the ship's boats were sufficient to take two-thirds of the passengers, and no more. It was determined by lot who should go into the boats, and who should stay on the sinking ship. In casting the lot, the single brother was chosen to go, and the married one elected to stay on the ship. They looked at each other, but did not speak; after a few breathless moments the single man stepped out of line and beckoned the brother to take his place. Said he, "You have a wife and two children depending upon you; I have none to care for but mother, and I never expect to see her." The married brother hesitated, and the other as much insisted on his going, until the time had arrived for one or the other to go. The married man jumped into the boat, and in a few minutes all was over with those that remained. He met his wife and children: their hearts were made glad together. The joy of that meeting, with new scenes, banished for a while the lost brother from the husband's memory, until his wife asked where James was (meaning the single brother). Then the scene on shipboard flashed before his mind, and, overwhelmed with grief, he wept, but did not speak. When he did speak, does any one suppose he said, I remember James as I do a bird I once had, or as the flowers that grew in our garden, or as I do a summer's day? No, hardly. He spoke, and it was this: "James gave his life for my life and yours;" then the whole story was told. The wife wept; they both wept and prayed together; and ever after, the mention of that brother's name brought tears to the eyes of those parents. *W. Gray.*

7886. DEATH, Victory over. A man having always been greatly troubled with the fear of death, told a friend that if he was aware of its approach, it would take three or four men to hold him. His friend encouraged him to believe that "as his day so should his strength be." After a long illness, the dying hour came. Satan whispered that he had been a deceiver and should die a hypocrite. Prayer was offered that these unreasonable fears might be dispelled, when he cried out, "The Lord

has come! Praise God! praise God!" Raising his hands, with holy exultation, he several times repeated, "Victory, Victory, Victory through the blood of the Lamb," and died with the words of triumph on his lips.

7887. DEATH, Views at. Rev. J. Hervey while on his death bed, dictated the following letter to a friend: "Now I apprehend myself near the close of life, and stand, as it were, on the brink of the grave, with eternity full in my view, perhaps my dear friend would be willing to know my sentiments in this awful situation. At such a juncture the mind is most unprejudiced, and the judgment not so liable to be dazzled by the glitter of worldly objects. I have been too fond of reading everything valuable and elegant that has been penned in our own language, and been peculiarly charmed with the historians, orators and poets of antiquity; but were I to renew my studies, I would take leave of these accomplished trifles; I would resign the delights of modern wits, amusements, and eloquence, and devote my attention to the Scriptures of truth. I would sit with much greater assiduity at my Divine Master's feet, and desire to know nothing but Jesus Christ and him crucified."

7888. DEATH, Voice from. Death, says Seneca, falls heavy upon him who is too much known to others, and too little to himself; and Pontanus, a man celebrated among the early restorers of literature, thought the study of our own hearts of so much importance, that he has recommended it from his tomb. "I am Pontanus, beloved by the powers of literature, admired by men of worth, and dignified by the monarchs of the world. Thou knowest now who I am, or more properly, who I was. For thee, stranger, I who am in darkness cannot know thee, but I entreat thee to know thyself." *Johnson.*

7889. DEATH, Vow at. Louis IX. of France was an honest man, a devout Christian, and a good king. In the eighteenth year of his reign A. D. 1244, he had a severe sickness, during which he made a vow that if spared he would head a crusade for the redemption of the Holy Land from the infidels. He had arranged all his affairs for his death, and fell into unconsciousness. Presently he gasped and revived. He said, "The day-spring from on high hath visited me by the grace of God, and hath called me back from death." He sent for the Bishop of Paris and directed him: "My Lord Bishop, put, I pray thee, on my shoulder the cross of voyage beyond the sea," which he reluctantly did. His mother and the entire court opposed his scheme, but in vain. He tenaciously held to his purpose and sailed with a large army in 1249, landing at Damietta. He met with disaster from the start. Sickness, death, and his own incompetency reduced his army to a wreck. A few only returned to France. Louis, though much humiliated, never forgot his vow, and in 1270 led another expedition toward Jerusalem, which fared as ill as the first. The remnant gladly returned to France bearing the body of King Louis. In his sickness he murmured, "We will go to Jerusalem," but it was the heavenly Jerusalem.

7890. DEATH, Warning of. St. Cyprian, bishop of Carthage, was warned in a vision of his approaching death. The manner of his condemnation, and method of his execution were shown him. He was first arrested and sent into exile with many other Christians. They lived in constant expectation of the arrival of the executioner at Curubis to send them to their crowns. It was a glorious company of the faithful, encouraging each other to hold out to the end that they might sooner enter the society of the blessed. An order came requiring Cyprian's return to Carthage. He answered to his name to the proconsul, and confessed his hostility to the heathen religion. The proconsul recited his orders from the Emperor Valerian. "Obey your orders," said Cyprian. The proconsul wrote, "I will that Thascius Cyprian be beheaded." "Blessed be God for it," said the saint. He was executed A. D. 258.

7891. DEATH, Willingness for. Of the great number to whom it has been my painful professional duty to have administered in the last hour of their lives, I have sometimes felt surprised that so few have appeared reluctant to go to the undiscovered country "from whose bourne no traveler returns." Many, we may easily suppose, have manifested this willingness to die from an impatience of suffering, or from that passive indifference which is sometimes the result of debility and bodily exhaustion. But I have seen those who have arrived at a fearless contemplation of the future from faith in the doctrine which our religion teaches. Such men were not only calm and supported, but cheerful in the hour of death; and I never quitted such a sick chamber without a hope that my last end might be like theirs.
Sir Henry Halford.

7892. DEATH, Worldling's View of. A dying worldling said: "My physician tells me I must die, and I feel that he tells me the truth. In my best hours, and in my worst, death has been perpetually upon my mind: it has covered me like a dread presence, weighed me down like an ocean, blinded me like a horrid vision, imprisoned my faculties as with bars and gates of iron. Often and often, when in saloons alive with mirth and splendor I have seemed the gayest of the inmates, this thought and fear of death have shot through my mind, and I have turned away sick and shuddering. What is it then to approach the reality? to feel it very near—very close at hand? stealing on, and on, and on, like the tide upon the shore, not to be driven back till it has engulfed its prey? What is it to apprehend the approach of the time when you must be a naked, guilty, trembling spirit, all memory, and all consciousness, never again for a single moment to sleep, or know oblivion from the crushing burden of the deeds done in the body! The dying may indeed be in a place of torment —in hell—before the time; and the remembrance of past life, stripped of all its deceptions, shriveled into insignificance, may appear, in connexion with eternity, but as a tiny shell tossed on the broad black surface of an ocean; then, again, the intense importance of that very insignificant fragment of time, and the intense remembrance of all that occupied it— its schemes, and dreams, and sins, and vanities, sweeping across the mind, in solemn order, like a procession of grim shadows, with death waiting to embosom all. O, well may I smite upon my breast, and cry, with all but despair, Woe is me for the past! woe, woe, for the past! Every dream is dissolved—every refuge of lies is plucked from me—every human consolation totters beneath me, like a bowing wall; and all the kingdoms of the world, and all the glory of them, could not bribe from my soul the remembrance of a single sin. Ambition, pleasure, fame, friendship, lie around like wrecks, and my soul is helpless in the midst of them, like the mariner on his wave-worn rock."

7893. DEATH-BED, Revelations of the. It is a fearful thing to wait and watch for the approach of death; to know that hope is gone, and recovery impossible; and to sit and count the dreary hours through long, long nights— such nights as only watchers by the bed of sickness know. It chills the blood to hear the dearest secrets of the heart—the pent-up, hidden secrets of many years—poured forth by the unconscious, helpless being before you; and to think how little the reserve and cunning of a whole life will avail when fever and delirium tear off the mask at last. Strange tales have been told in the wanderings of dying men; tales so full of guilt and crime, that those who stood by the sick person's couch have fled in horror and affright, lest they should be scared to madness by what they heard and saw; and many a wretch has died alone, raving of deeds the very name of which has driven the boldest man away.
Dickens.

7894. DEATH OF CHRIST, Biblical Types and Figures of. *Abel's sacrifice*, Gen. 4: 4; Heb. 11: 4. *Abraham's ram*, Gen. 22: 13. The *Jewish sacrifices* and offerings, varying in costliness and number, but all typical of the one great sacrifice and offering. The *paschal lamb*, Exod. 12: 3-7; John 19: 36; 1 Cor. 5: 7. The *smitten rock*, Exod. 17: 6; 1 Cor. 10: 4. The *scapegoat*, Lev. 16: 20-22. The *brazen serpent*, Num. 21: 9; John 3: 14, 15. The *leper's offering*—the bird killed, Lev. 14: 45. The *red heifer*, Num. 19: 2-6; Heb. 9: 13, 14. *Jonah* in the whale's belly, Jonah 1: 17; Matt. 12: 40. The roasting, slaying, drying, etc., of the different sacrifices and offerings; animals slain, consumed in whole or in part upon the altar; corn ground and baked; olives bruised, etc., all spoke of the sufferings of the one great Victim.
Bowes.

7895. DEATH OF CHRIST, Demand of the. A minister in one of our large cities prepared and preached, as he supposed, a most convincing sermon for the benefit of an influential member of his congregation, who was known to be of an infidel turn of mind. The sinner listened unmoved to the well-turned sentences and the earnest appeals; his heart was unaffected. On his return from church, he saw a tear trembling in the eye of his daughter, whom he tenderly loved; and he inquired the cause. The child informed him that she was thinking of what her Sunday-school teacher had told her of Jesus Christ. "And what did she tell you of Jesus Christ, my child?" he asked. "Why, she said he came down from heaven and died for poor me!" and in a moment the tears gushed from the eyes which had looked upon the beauties of only seven summers, as in the simplicity of childhood, she added, "Father, should I not love one who has loved me?" The proud heart of the infidel was touched. What the eloquent plea of his minister could not accomplish, the tender sentence of his child had done, and he retired to give vent to his own feelings in a silent but penitent prayer. That evening found him at the praying circle, where, with brokenness of spirit, he asked the prayers of God's people. In giving an account of his Christian experience, he remarked, "Under God I owe my conversion to a little child, who first convinced me by her artless simplicity that I ought to love one who has so loved me." *W. F. Crafts.*

7896. DEBT, Exemption from. The goddess Diana, in the city of Ephesus, gives to such debtors as can fly into her temple freedom and protection against their creditors; but the sanctuary of economy and moderation in expenses, into which no usurer can enter to pluck thence, and carry away any debtor prisoner, is always open for the prudent, and affords them a long and large space of joyful and honorable repose. *Plutarch.*

7897. DEBT, Payment of the. There was a man converted in Europe several years ago, and he liked the Gospel so well, he thought he would like to go and publish it. Great crowds came to hear him out of curiosity. The man was not much of a speaker, so the next night there wasn't many there, and the third night the man didn't get a hearer. But he was anxious to publish the Gospel, and so he got some great placards and posted them all over the town, that if there was any man in that town that was in debt, to come to his office between certain hours on a certain day with the proof of their indebtedness, and he would pay the debt. Well, of course, it went all over the town, but the people didn't believe him. One man said to his neighbor, "John, do you believe this man will pay our debts?" "Oh, of course not; that is a great sell; that is a hoax." The day came, and instead of there being a great rush, there didn't anybody come. Now, it is a great wonder that there isn't a great rush of men into the kingdom of God to have their debts paid when a man can be saved for nothing. About 10 o'clock there was a man walking in front of the office; he looked this way and that to see if there was anybody looking, and by and by he was satisfied there wasn't anybody looking, and he slipped in, and he said, "I saw a notice around town if any one would call here at a certain hour you would pay their debt. Is there any truth in it?" "Yes," says

the man, "it is quite true. Did you bring around the necessary papers?" "Yes." And after the man had paid the debt he said, "Sit down, I want to talk to you," and he kept him there until 12 o'clock. And before 12 o'clock had passed there were two more came and had their debts paid. At 12 o'clock he let them all out, when they found some other men standing around the door, and they said, "Well, you found he was willing to pay your debts, didn't you?" Yes, they said, it was quite true that he had paid their debts. "O, if this is so, we are going in to get our debts paid." And they went in, but it was too late. The man said if they had called within a certain hour he would have paid their debts. To every one of you that is a bankrupt sinner—and you never saw a sinner in the world but that he was a bankrupt sinner—Christ comes and he says, "I will pay the debt." And that is just what he wants to do to-night. Bear in mind that the Son of God came into the world to save sinners, and he has got the power to forgive sin. And he has not only got the power, but he is willing to save, and he is anxious to save; and so, my friends, if you will accept Christ's offer you can get out of this hall to-night cleansed of all sin. *Moody.*

7898. DEBT, Providential Relief From. A poor widow supported herself, in a seaport town, by the sale of small articles. She was much pressed for the payment of a bill, but had no money to meet it. She prayed God to send her relief. Just before the time when her goods would have been seized, she heard what she supposed to be the footsteps of her creditor. Instead, a company of sailors came, and bought articles to the exact value of the demanded debt.

7899. DEBT, The Unpaid. A gentleman, an essential part of whose religion was to pay his debts, dreamed that he had paid them all. He mentioned the fact with considerable satisfaction, when a personage replied as if he held some unsatisfied demand, "There is one debt you have not paid." "What is it?" said the man, with some anxiety. "You have not paid the debt of nature." It is true of all living, and payment may be demanded at any moment.

7900. DEBTOR, Lamentation of a. Well did an English author represent a poor debtor in the Fleet Prison answering a person who spoke to him of friends: "Friends!" exclaimed the man; "if I lay dead at the bottom of the deepest mine in the world, I could not be more forgotten or unheeded than I am here. I am a dead man;—dead to society, without the pity they bestow on those whose souls have passed away! Friends to see me! My God! I have shrunk from the prime of life into old age in this place; and there is not one to raise his hand above my bed, when I lay dead upon it, and say, 'It is a blessing he is gone!'" *G. W. Montgomery.*

7901. DEBTS, Payment of. Paying of debts is, next to the grace of God, the best means in the world to deliver you from a thousand temptations to sin and vanity. Pay your debts, and you will not have wherewithal to buy a costly toy or a pernicious pleasure. Pay your debts, and you will not have what to lose to a gamester. In short, pay your debts, and you will of necessity abstain from many indulgences that war against the spirit, and bring you into captivity to sin, and cannot fail to end in your utter destruction, both of soul and body.

Delany.

7902. DECAY, Example of. Empires, states, and kingdoms have, by the doom of the Supreme Providence, their fatal periods; great cities lie sadly buried in their dust; arts and sciences have not only their eclipses, but their wanings and deaths. The ghastly wonders of the world, raised by the ambition of ages, are overthrown and trampled. Some lights above, not idly entitled stars, are lost, and never more seen of us. The excellent fabric of this universe itself shall one day suffer ruin, or a change like a ruin; and should poor earthlings thus to be handled complain? *W. Drummond.*

7903. DECAY, Law of. No organized substance, no part of any plant or animal, after the extinction of the vital principle, is capable of resisting the chemical action of air and moisture; for all that power of resistance which they temporarily possessed as the bearers of life, the media of the vital manifestations, completely ceases with the death of the organism; their elements fall again under the unlimited dominion of the chemical forces.

Liebig.

7904. DECEIT, Detection of. An ass having put on a lion's skin, roamed about frightening all the silly animals he met with, and seeing a fox, he tried to frighten him also. But Reynard, having heard his voice, said, "Well, to be sure! and I should have been frightened too, if I had not heard you bray." They who assume a character that does not belong to them, generally betray themselves by overacting it. *Æsop.*

7905. DECEIT, Emblems of. The dank mossy sward is deceitful: its fresh and glossy carpet invites the traveler to leave the rough moorland tract; and, at the first step, horse and rider are buried in the morass. The sea in deceitful; what rage, what stormy passions sleep in that placid bosom! and how often, as vice serves her used-up victims, does she cast the bark that she received into her arms with sunny smiles a wreck upon the shore. The morning is oft deceitful; with bright promise of a brilliant day, it lures us from home; the sky ere noon begins to thicken; the sun looks sickly; the sluggish, heavily-laden clouds gather upon the hill-tops; the landscape closes in all around; the lark drops songless into her nest; the wind rises, moaning and chill; and at length, like adversities gathering round the gray head of age, tempest, storm, and rain, thicken on the dying day. The desert is deceitful; it mocks the traveler with its mirage. How life kindles in his drooping eye, as he sees the playful waves chase each other to the shore, and the plumes of the palm waving in the watery mirror! Faint, weary, parched,

perishing with thirst, he turns to bathe and drink; and exhausting what little strength remains in pursuit of a phantom, unhappy man! he has turned to die. Deceitful above sward or sea, sky or enchanting desert, is the heart of man; nor do I know a more marked or melancholy proof of this than that afforded by our light treatment of such weighty matters as sin and judgment. There is no exaggeration in the prophet's language, "The heart is deceitful above all things, and desperately wicked."

Dr. Guthrie.

7906. DECEIT, Fable of. The cat having a long time preyed upon the mice, the poor creatures at last, for their safety, contained themselves within their holes; but the cat finding his prey to cease, as being known to the mice that he was indeed their enemy and a cat, deviseth this course, following, namely, changeth his hue, getting on a religious habit, shaveth his crown, walks gravely by their holes; and yet perceiving that the mice kept their holes and looking out, suspected the worst, he formally and father-like, said unto them, "*Quod fueram non sum, frater, caput aspice tonsum.*" ("O brother, I am not as you take me for; I am no more a cat; see my habit and shaven crown.") Hereupon some of the more credulous and bold among them were again, by this deceit, snatched up; and therefore when afterwards he came, as before, to entice them forth, they would come out no more, but answered, "Talk what you can, we will never believe you; you bear still a cat's heart within you." And so here the Jesuits; yea, and priests too, for they are all joined in the tails like Samson's foxes: Ephraim against Manasseh, and Manasseh against Ephraim, and both against Judah.

E. Coke.

7907. DECEPTION, Fatal. Many years ago, when the Egyptian troops first conquered Nubia, a regiment was crossing a desert. The heat was oppressive, almost beyond endurance; the supply of water nearly exhausted. Far in the horizon they seemed to see a beautiful lake bordered with palm-trees. The Arab guide, who well understood the desert wastes, told the soldiers there was no lake there, that what they saw was only a mirage, a floating delusion on the sky. But the thirsty soldiers saw something which they believed to be water, and were determined to trust their sight rather than his words. They insisted upon their guide leading them to the water. He protested, and resisted even to death. When they had killed him, the whole regiment, wild with excitement and eager for the cooling waters, leave the course indicated by their guide and start for the lake. On and on they press over the burning sands; hour after hour they endure the heat, hoping to gain the refreshing waters of the lake, but that object flees before them like a phantom. Self-deceived, exhausted by the heat, and overcome with fatigue, they begin to fall upon the burning sands and die. They all perished. Long after, the Arabs in search found the body of the guide, a martyr to his faithfulness, while the bodies of the sol diers were found far out upon the wild wastes, where they fell in their vain search to find water where there was none. Their sincerity did not save them from death. *Sir S. W. Baker.*

7908. DECEPTION, Pleasure of Self. Many a man has a kind of a kaleidoscope, where the bits of broken glass are his own merits and fortunes, and they fall into harmonious arrangements, and delight him, often most mischievously and to his ultimate detriment; but they are a present pleasure. *Helps.*

7909. DECISION, Christian. That rich and blessed virgin in Basil, who was, for Christianity, condemned to the fire, and was offered if she would worship idols, to have her life and estate safe restored unto her, was obstinate in her resolution: "*Valeat vita, pereat pecunia;*" "I shall have more life in Christ, than in myself; all the emperors, all the physicians in the world, cannot make my life, which I have in myself, so long to-morrow as it is to-day; but in Christ, my life is not only an abiding, but an abounding life: I shall have more of that by losing mine own; my life in him is a hidden life; free from all injuries and persecutions of men: I shall have more riches in him than in myself, even unsearchable riches, which can never be stolen away, because they can never be exhausted. It is as possible for thieves to draw out the mines of India, or to steal away the sun out of his orb, as for any human violence to take away Christ from a man." Alike honorable was the answer of Frederic, the elector of Saxony, who, being prisoner to Charles V., was promised enlargement and restitution of dignity, if he would come to mass. "*Summum in terris dominum agnosco Cæsarem, in cœlis Deum,*"—"In all civil accommodations I am ready to yield unto Cæsar, but for heavenly things, I have but one master, and therefore I dare not serve two; Christ is more welcome to me in bonds, than the honors of Cæsar without Christ." Such acceptation hath the Gospel found amongst the renowned worthies heretofore: and the like entertainment should we all give unto it, even prefer it above our greatest glory: and as the Thessalonians did receive it with joy in the midst of afflictions, abide with Christ in his temptations; esteem his Gospel glorious, as the stars are in the darkness of the night, or as a torch, which blazeth most when it is most shaken.
Bp. Reynolds.

7910. DECISION, Circle for. Pompilius was sent to Antiochus with a letter from the senate, commanding him to withdraw his army out of Egypt, and to renounce the protection of that kingdom during the minority of Ptolemy's children. When he came towards him in his camp, Antiochus kindly saluted him at a distance, but without returning his salutation he delivered his letter; which being read, the king answered that he would consider and give his answer. Whereupon with his wand he made a circle around him, saying, "Consider and answer before you go out of this place." Then Antiochus answered he would give the Romans satisfaction. Man is called upon to decide the

question whether he will accept and serve Christ or not. The circle is drawn about each, and the time fixed within which he must answer.

7911. DECISION, Confiding. A little girl was awakened at a meeting where the story of the leper was told. The leper came to Jesus and worshiped him, saying, "Lord, if thou wilt, thou canst make me clean. And Jesus put forth his hand and touched him, saying, I will; be thou clean; and immediately his leprosy was cleansed." This little girl said, "I noticed that there was an 'if' in what the man said, but there was no 'if' in what Jesus said; so I went home and took out the 'if,' and I knelt down, and I said, 'Lord Jesus, thou canst, thou wilt make me clean; I give myself to thee.'" She was saved.

7912. DECISION, Examples of. Julius Palmer in Queen Mary's days, had life and preferment offered him if he would recant his faith in Christ. His answer was, that he had resigned his living in two places for the sake of the Gospel, and was now ready to yield his life on account of Christ. William Hunter, when urged by Bonner to recant, replied, he could only be moved by the Scriptures, for he reckoned the things of earth but dross for Christ; and, when the sheriff offered him a pardon at the stake if he would renounce his faith, he firmly rejected it. Antonius Riceto, a Venetian, was offered his life and considerable wealth if he would concede but a little, and when his son, with weeping, entreated him to do so, he answered that he was resolved to lose both children and estate for Christ. *Bibl. Treas.*

7913. DECISION, Importance of. Some years ago, while spending a pleasant holiday at Thun in Switzerland, four ministers of the gospel, of whom I was one, went into a boat for a row on the broad and rapid Aar, which flows past that city. When we had got to the middle of the stream, a most unseemly and ill-timed discussion arose among us, as to the point for which we should make. In our eager debate we lay upon our oars, and had much to say for and against different proposals; but meanwhile the swiftly flowing current was settling the question for us, and was hurrying us down to a very dangerous rapid, which we only escaped by long and arduous exertion. Thus it is often in the graver and more momentous interests of life. We imagine that no harm comes of our indecision, while in fact the undertow of fashion, or interest, or inclination, is bearing us away with it; and when we awake to our danger, it may be too late to ensure our safety. Hence, no matter how apparently trifling the thing may be that is put before us, if it involve a principle in it, we ought to settle at once what our duty in the case is, and do that promptly and with all our might.
W. M. Taylor.

7914. DECISION, Missionary. "Brothers, in a few days we shall be scattered, never perhaps to meet on earth again. We may soon lose sight of each other in widely-separated fields of ministerial labor. Though my field may be unknown to you, while I live you may always know Carlos R. Martin is somewhere tremendously determined to do good." These words were uttered at a farewell meeting of students of the Concord Biblical Institute. Bishop Baker on the day following asked Mr. Martin if he was willing to go as a missionary to China. He consented, on condition that the lady who was soon to be his bride approved. Speedily the mail brought the message from her, "Carlos, go where your duty calls you, and I will go with you, even to the ends of the earth." Years after, this devoted man, dying of cholera in the midst of life and usefulness, sent back to America this message: "I find it pays to be a Christian."

Charles E. Little.

7915. DECISION, Noble. Five boys, pupils in the boarding-school, were in the room. Four of them, contrary to the express rules, engaged in a game of cards. The fifth was not standing and looking on to see how the game would go, but engaged in some work of his own. One of the players was called out. "Come," said the others to their companion, "it is too bad to have the game stop in the middle. Come and take his place." "I do not know one card from another." "That makes no difference. We will teach you. Come, do not let our sport be spoiled." The boy perceived that this was the decisive moment. Ah, just such are the critical points—sometimes the turning-points of life. His resolution was instantly taken. He made no excuse, but at once planted himself squarely upon principle. "My father does not wish me to play cards, and I shall not act contrary to his wishes." This ended the matter. It did more. It established his position among his companions. It compelled their respect and preserved him from temptation in the future. Such a boy inspires confidence. The incident may seem small in itself, but it gives promise of the future better than thousands of gold. Three sterling qualities are manifested: A conscientious regard for the wishes of parents, superiority to the fear of the ridicule of his companions, and decision. These qualities form a shield and buckler to all temptation. Years have passed. That boy has become a man. Various and trying have been the scenes through which he has been called. Severe have been the temptations to which he has been exposed. But he has come forth as gold. No parent weeps, no friend blushes for him.

Am. Messenger.

7916. DECISION Overcome. While Mr. Wilson was teaching the people of Raiatea, South Sea Islands, an old man stood up, and exclaimed, "My forefathers worshiped Oro, the god of war, and so have I; nor shall anything you can say persuade me to forsake this way. And," said he, addressing the missionary, "what do you want more than you have already? Have you not won over such a chief, and such a chief?—ay, and you have Pomare herself! What want you more?" "All—all the people of Raiatea, and you yourself I want!" replied Mr. Wilson. "No, no," cried the old man: "me!—you shall never have me, I will do as my fathers have done: I will worship Oro. You shall never have me, I assure you." Yet, within six months from that time, this staunch adherent of the bloody superstition of Oro, the Moloch of the Pacific, became a worshiper of the true God. Such is the power of the Holy Spirit.

7917. DECISION, Promptitude in. Captain Oldrey, commanding the Hyacinth sloop of war, was working up for Barbadoes August 10, 1831, when the hurricane came on. He had been upon the deck during the finest weather ever witnessed in that climate, and had just been admiring the beauty of the evening. The atmosphere of the horizon was perfectly clear, not a cloud obscuring the sky; nor was there the least probability of a change, as far as could be judged from any appearance observable in the heavens or on the ocean. Going below to his cabin, the captain flung himself upon a sofa, and a minute or two afterwards, chancing to cast his eyes upon a barometer suspended near, he observed that the mercury was falling. It was a moment when he would not have thought of consulting the instrument for any purpose, and so strange did he think the circumstance that he rubbed his eyes, imagining he was deceived. Still the mercury fell; he got off the sofa, and, approaching the instrument, discovered that the quicksilver was falling with a perceptible motion. He went on deck, but the weather was as lovely as before; he descended again, shook the instrument, and still the descent was certain and continued. A fall so rapid and remarkable, of which he had never seen nor heard of a parallel instance, convinced him that something was about to happen. He called the first lieutenant and master, and stated what he had seen. These officers alleged that there could be no storm likely, the sea and sky were then so clear and beautiful. The captain was not of their opinion; and as the ordinary falling of the barometer indicated a storm, he resolved to prepare for one with a speed and energy proportioned to the singular rapidity of the indication. He ordered everything to be instantly made snug, the topmasts to be struck, and all to be got down and secured upon deck. The officers and ship's company were surprised and still incredulous. One man said to another, "The captain is determined to sweat us." By an activity urged on by the union of command and entreaty, all was lowered and secured. The officers of the ship, except the captain, were still of their previous opinion, and well they might be: so far, none of the appearances then existed that usually precede storms and hurricanes in that latitude. The evening had closed in by the time operations on board the ship were nearly completed. Captain Oldrey relaxed nothing in the way of preparation to the last, and saw it finished to his satisfaction. An hour or two had gone by afterwards, during which his mind had become composed with the reflection that he had prepared for the worst, when he had proof of the value of the instrumental warning: a storm did come on, and reached its fury almost at once, so that a rag of sail could not be kept up; the wind blew with a fury so great that the sea could not rise into waves, but became one vast plain of foam, on which the ship lay driving furiously along. Fortunately, there was ample sea-room. There is a delicacy of perception in a truly wise man which gives him warnings as decisive, respecting the coming storm of Divine vengeance, but which are as unappreciable by others as the indications of Captain Oldrey's barometer.   *F. F. Trench.*

7918. DECISION, Reward of. When William Lloyd Garrison commenced the publication of the "Liberator" he began with these memorable words: "I am in earnest—I will not equivocate—I will not excuse—I will not retreat a single inch—and I will be heard." He was heard—and the chains have fallen from the three millions of bondmen to whose service he consecrated his life.

7919. DECISION, Success of. When Mohammed began to proclaim himself God's prophet, some of his relations laughed at him, others became hostile to him, and so unpromising was his cause that his uncle, Abu Taleb, in whom he confided most, advised him to desist. He replied, resolutely, "Though they set the sun against me on my right hand, and the moon on my left, yet will I not give up this enterprise." His unfailing resolution carried him through persecution, opposition and flight, to the most signal success any impostor ever attained.

7920. DECISION, Symbol of. On a recent most instructive visit to the Assay Office in Wall street, I was shown a balance concerning which the courteous superintendent said: "The distinctive feature of this balance is its combination of sensitiveness with decision. It will be turned by the smallest fraction of a grain, and, whenever it is turned, it moves right on; we had one formerly which was extremely sensitive, but it lacked decision, so that it went quivering from one side to another for a long time before it settled; and, frequently, we wasted fifteen minutes in getting a result, which we can obtain from this one in a moment." As I listened to this admirable explanation, I could not help saying within myself: "How like that wavering balance many men are! They are abundantly sensitive, but they lack decisiveness; they take so long to settle what is to be done, that the opportunity of doing anything is sometimes gone before they are ready to begin!"   *Dr. Wm. M. Taylor.*

7921. DECREES, Disputing about the. A professor of religion, of dubious character, much given to disputation, came down to death with his ruling passion still predominant. A good Christian, at his bedside, said, "This is the decree you have now to do with. 'He that believeth shall be saved; he that believeth not shall be damned.'"

7922. DECREES, Mystery of the. Hillel, the holy, wished to explore and to explain the mystery of the divine decrees, and in order to prepare himself for such deep meditation he spent two days in fasting and prayer. On the third he ascended to the top of Carmel, and sat down beneath the shade of a juniper tree Here his mind collected its force, to cast its thoughts toward heaven and hell, eternity and infinity. But these thoughts recoiled on his own breast, like stones from the top of Gerizim. Hillel, at length tired of his fruitless contemplation, by chance turned his eyes toward a spot of earth not far distant, where something seemed to be moving. It was a mole, which in his darksome abode had perceived there was such a thing as light, and forgetting the weakness of his organs, desired to contemplate the sun at mid-day. But no sooner had he left his home than, blinded by the splendor of meridian beams, he wished himself again in his subterranean lodging. But ere he could accomplish his retreat, an eagle snatched him away, and flew off with him towards the valley of the son of Hinnom. "Blessed be God," said Hillel, "who hath conveyed instruction to the mind of his servant, and warned him of the danger of prying into that knowledge, the difficulty of which seems to imply that it is forbidden."   *Robert Philip.*

7923. DEDICATION, Biblical. The word "*Enoch*" means dedicated; and it is singular to observe how early the name was given, both in Cain's line, and in the line of Seth, Gen. 4: 17; 5: 24. *Lemuel,* Prov. 31: 1, means also devoted to God. The word *saints* has properly the same signification—sanctified, set apart for sacred purposes. To *consecrate.* The marginal translation of the Hebrew word is generally to "*fill the hand.*" See Exod. 28: 41; 32: 29; 1 Chron. 29: 5. To "*yield to God*"—in the Hebrew is to *give the hand.* Under the law. There were very numerous examples and illustrations of dedication and consecration of persons and things. The several *sacrifices and offerings,* especially the burnt-offering, which was to be wholly consumed, and which represents the entire dedication of the offerer to God. The *first-born of men,* Exod. 13: 2–12 (after 12, Israel's redemption); 22: 29. *The firstling of cattle,* Exod. 13: 12; 22: 30. *The first ripe fruits and corn,*—the first produce of oil, and wine, and fleece, Exod. 22: 29; Num. 18: 12. The fruit of trees in the fourth year, Lev. 19: 24. A *sheaf* was presented at harvest time as a wave offering, Lev. 23: 10–14; two wave loaves at Pentecost, Lev. 23: 17; dough, as a heave offering, Num. 15: 20. These were to be brought to God's house, Exod. 22: 29; 23: 19; with confession and thanksgiving, Deut. 26: 3–10. *Nazarites,* dedication of, Num. 6: 1–8. The house of the Lord. It is striking how largely the house of the Lord was enriched by dedicated things. The *tabernacle* was richly adorned from the spoils of Egypt; the gold and silver, and fine linen, and various things required. The Lord so ordered it, not only as intimating favor to the Gentiles, but as representing the use which God often makes of the

abilities and substance of strangers, in supporting and promoting true religion.—*Scott*, on
Exod. 25: 1-7. *The laver of brass* was made
of the looking-glasses of the women, Exod. 38:
8. *The temple of Solomon* was raised largely
by the dedicated things David gathered, 2 Sam.
8: 7, 8, 11; 1 Kings 7: 51; 1 Chron. 18: 7-11.
Large offerings were often voluntarily made,
which were devoted to holy purposes. See the
offerings of the officers and captains, after the
victory over Midian, Num. 31: 48-54, amounting to about £37,856; and the treasures of
dedicated things, set apart to maintain the
house of the Lord, from the days of Samuel,
by Samuel, Saul, Abner, Joab, &c., 1 Chron.
26: 26-28; and the superabundant treasures
of dedicated gifts in Hezekiah's time, 2 Chron.
31: 5-12. The WALL OF JERUSALEM,—the rebuilding of, was a noble example of difficult
work done in a pious spirit,—first "sanctified,"
Neh. 3: 1; then "dedicated," 12: 17. GIVEN
TO THE LORD. What large views St. Paul had
of the entire consecration of the believer to
God! See 1 Cor. 6: 19, 20; Rom. 12: 1; see
also Phil. 2: 17, where he speaks of himself as
willing to be "offered," "poured forth" (marg.),
like the libations or drink offerings of ancient
sacrifices, with cheerful surrender and sanctified joy. Note the beautiful expression in the
post-communion service of the Church of England—"And here we offer and present unto
thee, O Lord, ourselves, our souls and bodies,
to be a reasonable, holy, and lively sacrifice
unto thee." THE RIGHTFUL ORDER.—First the
person, then the gift; the heart, and then the
offering; see 2 Cor. 8: 5; Luke 11: 41; Heb.
11: 4.   *Bowes.*

7924. DEFEAT, Providential. History says
that Sapores, the King of Persia, besieged the
city of Nisibis, with every prospect of success.
St. James, the holy bishop of the city, prayed
God, most earnestly, to confound the enemy.
In answer there came an infinite number of
gnats, who so preyed upon the horses and their
riders as to throw the army into great confusion. This insignificant insect caused Sapores
to raise the siege, and, under God, saved the
city. The weakest things with God for their
ally, are stronger than the mightiest armies
contending against the right. "If God be for
us who shall be against us?" Rom. 8: 31.

7925. DEFECTS, Boasting of. Said a young
mole to her mother, "Mother, I can see." So,
in order to try her, her mother put a lump of
frankincense before her, and asked her what it
was. "A stone," said the young one. "O,
my child!" said the mother, "not only do you
not see, but you cannot even smell."
                           Æsop.

7926. DEFENCE, Hedge of. Roberts tells us
that in India it is said of a man who cannot
be injured, "Why attempt to hurt him? is
there not a hedge about him?" "You cannot
get at the fellow; he has a strong hedge about
him."

7927. DEFENCE, Instinct of. Brasidas, the
Lacedæmonian captain, by chance caught a
mouse among some dry figs; and, being bit by
her, let her go with this exclamation, "By
Hercules! there is no creature so little or so
weak that it cannot preserve its life if it dares
but defend it."

7928. DEFENCE, The Lord Our. In the early
part of the reign of Alexander I., Bible reading and habits of piety and devotion were held
in contempt among the upper classes in Russia; and when Prince Galitzin, in utter ignorance of religion, became a magnate of
the church by imperial appointment, he was
obliged to purchase a Bible secretly, that he
might acquaint himself with the first principles
of Christianity. His stolen study of the Holy
Book soon influenced the character and manners of the once haughty noble, so that all who
dared to do so sneered at him. In course of
time Napoleon invaded Russia, and all St.
Petersburg prepared either to fight or flee.
Galitzin alone remained unmoved. His palace was undergoing extensive repairs, and he
continued to superintend them as composedly
as if his country was in the midst of the profoundest peace. The Czar was astonished at
the apparent unconcern of his favorite prince,
and before putting himself at the head of his
armies he called on him, half fearing for the
soundness of Galitzin's patriotism. "What
does it mean," said he, "that you go on building when every one else prepares to flee?"
"The Lord is my defence, sire," answered Galitzin: "I am as safe here as anywhere."
Alexander demanded to know where he had
found this new confidence, and the prince
showed him his Bible. Strange as it may seem,
it was the first Bible the Czar had ever seen.
The first place which he opened was at the
ninety-first Psalm: "He that dwelleth in the
secret place of the Most High shall abide under the shadow of the Almighty," etc., and
Galitzin read to him the whole of that sweet,
grand Scripture. Profoundly impressed, the
Czar repaired to the cathedral for public worship preparatory to departing on his campaign.
The priest who conducted the service chose,
by a singular coincidence, the ninety-first
Psalm, to read: "He that dwelleth in the secret place of the Most High shall abide under
the shadow of the Almighty." "Did Galitzin
tell you to select that?" asked Alexander.
"I have not seen Galitzin," said the priest.
"I only prayed the Lord to be guided in my
choice." The Czar went a day's march with
his army, and in the evening, feeling anxious
and serious, he ordered his chaplain to read to
him in his tent. The chaplain began to read,
"He that dwelleth in the secret place of the
Most High shall abide under the shadow of
the Almighty." "Hold," cried Alexander;
"did Galitzin tell you to read that to me?"
"Assuredly not, sire," said the chaplain; "I
asked God to direct me to a passage, and then
I felt constrained to select this Psalm." From
that time Alexander secretly got access to a
Bible every day, and read it with wonder and
delight. And when Divine Providence scattered the great army of Napoleon, and drove
it out of Russia with a loss of 450,000 men

the Czar returned to his capital, borrowed Galitzin's Bible, and applied himself eagerly to the study of its precious pages until the Holy Spirit taught him to make it the rule of his life. Some years afterward two missionaries, who were preaching and teaching the Scriptures in St. Petersburg, learned this story from the mouth of Prince Galitzin, and heard the Czar himself confirm it during an impressive and memorable interview which he granted them at the palace. One of those missionaries was Stephen Grellet, a Quaker, who recorded the facts in his journal.

Youth's Companion.

7929. DEFENCE, Useless. The Chinese have been for at least two or three thousand years a wall-making people. It would bankrupt New York or Paris to build the walls of the city of Peking. The great wall of China is the wall of the world. It is forty feet high. The lower thirty feet is of hewn limestone or granite. Two modern carriages may pass each other upon the summit. It has a parapet throughout its whole length, with convenient staircases, buttress and garrison houses at every quarter of a mile, and it runs, not by cutting down hills and raising valleys, but over the uneven crests of the mountains and down through their gorges, a distance of a thousand miles. Admiral Rodgers and I calculated that it would cost more now to build the great wall of China, through its extent of one thousand miles, than it has cost to build the fifty-five thousand miles of railroad in the United States. What a commentary it is upon the splendid range of the human intellect to see this great utilitarian enterprise, so necessary and effective two thousand years ago, now not merely useless, but an incumbrance and an obstruction. *Wm. H. Seward.*

7930. DEFENCE, Wall of. On a certain occasion an embassador from Epirus, on a diplomatic mission, was shown by the king over his capital. The embassador knew of the monarch's fame—knew that though only nominally king of Sparta, he was ruler of Greece—and he had looked to see massive walls rearing aloft their embattled towers for the defense of the town; but he found nothing of the kind. He marveled much at this, and spoke of it to the king. "Sir," he said, "I have visited most of the principal towns, and I find no walls reared for defense. Why is this?" "Indeed, Sir Embassador," said Agesilaus, "thou canst not have looked carefully. Come with me to-morrow morning, and I will show you the walls of Sparta." Accordingly, on the following morning, the king led his great guest out upon the plains where his army was drawn up in full battle array, and, pointing proudly to the serried hosts, he said: "Thou beholdest the walls of Sparta—ten thousand men, and every man a brick!" *School Journal.*

7931. DEFILEMENT, Biblical. Figures of are *dogs,* generally wild in the East, prowling about the street, and feeding on garbage, Ps. 59: 6; Matt. 7: 6. *Swine,* delighting in filthiness, 2 Pet. 2: 22. *A cage of unclean birds,*

Jer. 5: 27; Rev. 18: 2. *Defiled garments,* Is. 64: 6; Rev. 3: 14. *Sepulchres* full of dead men's bones, and all uncleanness, Matt. 23: 27. *The leprosy,* the special type of sin, Lev. 13th and 14th chapters. The melancholy picture of corruption, loathsomeness, and decay; affecting persons, garments, houses; beginning insidiously, and spreading with a relentless progress, until complete destruction left nothing more to do; and besides incurable. The rites enjoined in the case of the leper all denoted, in the most humbling manner, the mournful effects of sin; see Lev. 13: 45, 46; the rent clothes, bare head, covered lip, and the leper's pitiable cry, if any one came near, "Unclean, unclean," and the separation from society, without the camp. Some of these signs are the same as those appointed in mourning for the dead. *Regulations about social life*—Child-bearing, Lev. 12: 2-8; food, Lev. 11; disease, Lev. 15; contact with uncleanness, Lev. 5: 2, 3; 11: 24, 25; 22: 5, 6. *Regulations about death*—Touching a dead body, or carcase of a beast, or a grave, Num. 19: 11-22; Lev. 17: 15, 16; 5: 2-13; even entering the tent where the dead lay, Num. 19: 14; the priests mourning for the dead, Lev. 21: 1-3. *Regulations about sacred duties*—Even taking part in these, in some cases, made men liable to ceremonial uncleanness. Burning the sin offering, *e.g.,* on the day of atonement, Lev. 16: 28; leading the scape-goat into the wilderness, Lev. 16: 26, etc. THE RED HEIFER was a striking illustration of the imputation of defilement, Num. 19: 1-10. (1) The heifer itself, as bearing the uncleanness of the people, was to be carried without the camp. (2) Eleazar was to offer it, not Aaron, that the high priest might not be defiled. (3) Eleazar, the priest, the man who burnt the heifer, and even the clean man that gathered the ashes, were all rendered ceremonially unclean by the performance of these duties. THE MORAL LEPROSY—It would be difficult to describe to the full the awful extent of the spreading taint of sin. Trace in Conc. under the head of *defiled,* and see how "sin" is inscribed on men's mind and conscience—body—hands—feet—flesh—garments—house—land, etc.; under *filthy*—"filthiness of the flesh and spirit"—"filthy communications"—"filthy lucre" (five times)—"all filthiness and superfluity of naughtiness"—"even our righteousnesses are as filthy rags," and man is "abominable and filthy"—"altogether filthy." Zech. 3—The high priest Zechariah represented Israel appearing before the Lord—first, clothed with filthy garments; then clothed with change of raiment, adorned and crowned with personal and official dignity. Haggai 2: 11-13. How much more easily is uncleanness communicated than purity! One drop of ink will stain a glass of water, but one drop of water cannot purify a glassful of ink. Isa. 52: 11—"Touch no unclean thing." One of the great lessons God would teach his Church. It was the charge given to Israel on their entering Canaan—"Defile not yourselves," see Conc.; on their leaving Babylon

Isa. 52: 11; applied to the Church of Christ in her separation from the world, 2 Cor. 6: 14.
Bowes.

7932. DEGENERATION, Human. I have read of a painter, who being warmly reprehended by a cardinal for putting too much red in the faces of St. Paul and St. Peter, answered, "It is to show how much they blush at the conduct of many who style themselves their successors." Were Abraham, the father of the faithful, now on earth, how would he disclaim all relation to many who call themselves his offspring! Though there was less grace discovered to the saints of old, yet there was more grace discovered by them. They knew little and did much; we know much and do little. *Secker.*

7933. DEGRADATION, Pagan. Rev. Mr. Kicherer, a German missionary, who labored for many years as a missionary in Southern Africa, gives the following account of the lowest and most degraded tribe of the Hottentot race called Bushmen: "Their manner of life is extremely wretched and disgusting. They delight to besmear their bodies with the fat of animals, mingled with ochre, and sometimes with grime. They are utter strangers to cleanliness, as they never wash their bodies, but suffer the dirt to accumulate, so that it will hang a considerable length from the elbows. Their huts are formed by digging a hole in the earth, about three feet deep, and then making a roof of reeds, which is, however, insufficient to keep off the rains. Here they lie close together like pigs in a sty. They are extremely lazy, so that nothing will rouse them to action but excessive hunger. They will continue several days together without food, rather than be at the pains of procuring it. When compelled to sally forth for prey, they are dexterous at destroying the various beasts which abound in the country; and they can run almost as well as a horse. They are total strangers to domestic happiness. The men have several wives; but conjugal affection is little known. They take no great care of their children, and never correct them except in a fit of rage, when they almost kill them by severe usage. In a quarrel between father and mother, or the several wives of the husband, the defeated party wreaks his or her vengeance on the child of the conqueror, which in general loses its life. Tame Hottentots seldom destroy their children, except in a fit of passion; but the Bushmen will kill their children without remorse, on various occasions; as when they are ill-shaped, when they are in want of food, when the father of the child has forsaken its mother, or when obliged to flee from the farmers or others; in which case they will strangle them, smother them, cast them away in the desert, or bury them alive. There are instances of parents throwing their offspring to the hungry lion, who stands roaring before their cavern, refusing to depart till some peace-offering be made to him. In general their children cease to be objects of a mother's care as soon as they are able to crawl about in the field. In some few instances, however, we have met with a spark of natural affection which places them on a level with the brute creation."

7934. DEGRADED, Renovation of the. The paper manufacturer is not nice in the choice of his materials. He does not reject a torn or a filthy piece as unfit for his purpose. All come alike to him. The clean and glancing cloth from the table of the rich and the filthy rags from a beggar's back are equally welcome. The clean cannot be serviceable without passing through the manufacturer's process, and the unclean can be made serviceable with it. He throws both into the same machine, puts both through the same process, and brings out both new creatures. The Pharisees were scandalized on observing that publicans and sinners came in streams to Christ, and were all accepted. "This man receiveth sinners," they complained. Yea, receiveth them; sinners are taken in between the wheels, at the commencement of this process; but at the end of it, saints in white clothing are thrown out, fit for the kingdom of heaven. Christ does not find any pure on earth; he makes them. Those that stand round the throne in white clothing were gathered from the mire. They were once darkness, though they be now light in the Lord. *Arnot.*

7935. DEGRADED, Transformation of the. In the manufacture of coal gas a large quantity of coal tar is left in the retorts. It is a black substance constantly giving off foul odors, and was for a time regarded as worthless. From this vile stuff more than forty different articles have been produced which promote health, gratify the most refined taste, and add to our comfort. Such is the transformation wrought by the gospel upon polluted, vicious and degraded men, and they become bright jewels in the Saviour's crown.

7936. DEGREES, History of. Irnerius, the celebrated jurist, is said to have introduced the degree of Doctor into the universities. The first ceremony of this kind was performed at Bologna, on the person of Bulgarus, in the year 1130, who began to profess the Roman law, and on that occasion was promoted to the doctorate. The custom was soon transferred from the faculty of law to that of theology; and Peter Lombard is the first doctor in sacred theology upon record in the university of Paris. Ancient English writers hold the venerable Bede to have been the first doctor of Cambridge, and John de Beverley at Oxford; the latter died in 712. But Spelman thinks there was no title or degree in England till about the year 1207. John Hambois is supposed to be the first musician who was honored with the title of doctor in England. Holinshed, in his "Chronicles," tells us—"John Hambois was an excellent musician, and for his notable cunning therein he was made a doctor of music."
Loaring.

7937. DEGREES, Mercenary. Luther relates, that Carolastad was promoted Doctor of Divinity eight years before he had read any of the Bible. Afterwards Luther conferred the degree of Doctor on one at Wittemberg, and made this speech: "Here I stand and do promote this man; and I know I do not rightly therein, and that thereby I do commit a mortal sin; but I do it for the gain of two gilders, which I get by him."

7938. DEITY, Footsteps of. There is no creature in the world, wherein we may not see enough to wonder at; for there is no worm of the earth, no spire of grass, no leaf, no twig, wherein we see not the footsteps of a Deity. The best visible creature is man. Now, what man is he that can make but an hair, or a straw, much less any sensitive creature, so as no less than an infinite power is seen in every object that presents itself to our eyes: if, therefore, we look only on the outside of these bodily substances, and we do not see God in every thing, we are no better than brutish; make use merely of our sense, without the least improvement of our faith or our reason. Contrary, then, to the opinion of those men who hold that a wise man should admire nothing, I say that a truly wise and good man should admire everything, or rather that infiniteness of wisdom and omnipotence which shows itself in every visible object.
Bishop Hall.

7939. DEITY, Omnipresence of. The unfathomable ether, that emblem of Omnipresent Deity, which, everywhere enfolding and supporting man, yet baffles his senses and is unperceived, except when he looks upwards and contemplates it above him. *Hare.*

7940. DEITY, World without a. What would the world be without a Deity, without love, justice, freedom, retribution? A gigantic corpse, from which the soul has fled; an unconscious play of things, in which there is no place for the highest and best—for virtue, love, perfection, but only for their names. A miserable, unmeaning, unsolvable, never-ending riddle; and the most wretched of beings in it —man, with the claims of his reason and the sentiments of his heart! *Zschokke.*

7941. DELAY, Beware of. When the Shunammite went to the prophet on behalf of her dead child, she made great haste to get to him, and said to her servant, "Drive and go forward, slack not thy pace;" but thou hast a business of greater concernment to go to Christ about than this woman had to go to the prophet. She had a dead son, and thou hast a soul dead in trespasses and sins; therefore make haste, go forward, slack not thy pace till thou hast gotten to Christ, and Christ hath given thee life. *Stockton.*

7942. DELAY, Fatal. During a violent storm, a trading vessel was wrecked on the west coast of England. Many of the crew perished, but the captain and his wife were providentially enabled to reach a rock, and, climbing up, escaped from the waves. But the danger was not over. The tide was rising, the cold intense; and it soon became evident that unless assistance was quickly rendered, they must perish. Happily, they were seen from the neighboring shore, and a boat was sent to attempt their rescue. As the boat could not possibly come close to the rock, the only alternative was to project a rope from the shore by a rocket, and then to haul them through the surf within reach of the boat. After many fruitless attempts this succeeded, and then the only way of deliverance was by springing into the wave at the moment of its highest swell, and being borne over the danger and pulled into the boat. The wife was the first to make the attempt, and was told what to do. All was ready. The big wave swelled full at her feet. "Now, now," shouted the crew, "spring into the wave!" Alas! she trembled, hesitated, delayed only a moment—but that moment was fatal. She leaped towards the receding wave, fell upon the rugged rocks beneath, and the next moment was dragged on board, a mangled, lifeless corpse. The captain, ignorant of her hapless fate, followed, and, taking the wave in the swell, was saved. *Anon.*

7943. DELAY, Folly of. More wise was the poor peasant in the fable, who is represented as coming and sitting by the side of a swiftly-flowing river, and who, because it flowed so swiftly, fancied that it must soon run dry, and therefore sat upon the brink and watched and waited; but still it flowed on. So it is with the man who waits for a more convenient season; the river of corruption, of obstacle, of impediment, runs on, and broadens, and deepens as it goes. *Hugh Stowell.*

7944. DELAY, A Little. During the closing services one Sabbath, my eyes rested on a lovely youth. I approached him, and exhorted him to repentance and faith on the Lord Jesus Christ. He replied, "I am not ready now, but in two weeks I am resolved to seek the salvation of my soul." A few days after, this minister was summoned to visit him upon a bed of sickness. He said to the minister, "I was invited to the Saviour at the meeting on the Sabbath, but replied that I was not ready then, and now I am not ready to die." On a subsequent visit, the dying youth exclaimed, "I was not ready to seek God at the meeting; I was not ready to die when the message came; and now I am not ready to lie down in hell! My two weeks have not yet elapsed when I hoped to have made my peace with God, and sickness, death, and hell have overtaken me, and I am forever lost." *E. P. Hill.*

7945. DELAY, Propensity to. Why will men put off this repentance until to-morrow, and day after day, in the way they do? Is it because they love sin so much? Is it because they want to have their own way? Why, it is very much like Pharaoh when he had the plague of the frogs. He could not take a step but that he put his foot down on a frog. There were frogs in his bed-room, in his sitting-room. They got into his kneading-troughs. Cut a loaf of bread and a frog would be found in it. It was frog, frog, frog. At last it annoyed him so he was compelled to send for Moses. And Moses said to him, When shall I ask the Lord to take them away? I remember well the first time I read that. I, of course, thought that Pharaoh, in answer to that question, would have said, "Now, now," with all his might, and with all the earnestness of which he was capable. Did he say that? Why, no; he said "To-morrow." He wanted the frogs all night. You laugh at that. Yet you want to hold on to your sins just as long as you are able. Well, are these sins so sweet, that you like them so? Like them, then, if you want to, but you hear what God says. He commands you to repent and leave them. *Moody.*

7946. DELAY, Risking. A young lady at church, in North Carolina, gave heed to a powerful and awakening sermon, the preacher urging an immediate acceptance of Christ, and warning of the dangers of delay and putting off for a more convenient season. A few days after the young lady was dangerously ill, and sent for the preacher to come and see her. He went and found her at death's door, and yet she told him she neither wished him to pray with or talk to her; that she had heard his sermon the Sunday before, and at the time had written with her pencil a certain sentence in her hymn-book, and ever since then all had been darkness and her heart as hard as stone. The preacher took the hymn-book, and read on the fly-leaf in the back of the book the following fatal sentence: "I'll run the risk." A few hours more, and the young woman died in the darkness of despair. She had run the risk. *Darnall.*

7947. DELAY, Too Long. A minister stroked the head of a young soldier as he lay upon his cot in the hospital, and said, "You are almost through with this world." "Am I?" "Yes, and I hope you are ready for the next." "No, I am not—not ready, not ready!" "Well, Jesus is all ready, and waiting right here. Shall I pray?" "Oh, no, no; it is too late! I ought to have been a Christian long ago." There was a time when he was deeply convicted. In memory of it he now cried, "That was the time; I might have come to Christ then, why didn't I? why didn't I?" He drew the blanket over his head, saying, "Don't talk to me any more; it's too late, I can't hear it." The next morning on the delegate's return death had done its work and his cot was empty.

7948. DELAY, Youthful. A young man who had been putting off the subject of religion was one day thrown from his horse and carried into the nearest house, and being told that he could not live an hour he cried out, "Must I go into eternity in an hour? Must I stand before my Judge in one short hour? God knows I have made no preparation for this event! I have heard of impenitent young men thus suddenly cut off, but it never occurred to me that I should be one! O tell me, tell me what I must do to be saved!" He was told that he must repent of his sins, and look to Jesus Christ for pardon. "But I do not know how to repent. The whole work of my life time is crowded into this hour of agony. O! what shall I do to be saved?" he continued to cry, with an eye glaring with desperation. But death would not wait, and, crying out for aid

and instruction, he sank back upon his pillow, and in a moment was in eternity.

7949. DELIBERATION, Rule for. Athenodorus. the philosopher, gave Augustus, the Roman Emperor, the following advice, viz.: "Before he did or said anything of unusual importance to repeat to himself the twenty-four letters of the Greek alphabet." The old philosopher hoped thereby to prevent hasty resolutions and precipitate action, which are soon followed by vain repentance.

7950. DELIVERANCE, Improvement of. A fashionable lady was driving along the road between Margate and Ramsgate. The road is situated upon the chalk cliffs which overhang the sea, and sometimes very near its edge. One day her horse took fright and backed the carriage so that she was thrown over the precipice. Some men who had seen the accident thought she must certainly be dashed in pieces on the rocks below. They were surprised to find that she was caught part way down by a projecting rock. They lowered themselves to where she lay and found her insensible, but they restored her to consciousness. She was not seriously injured, and soon pursued her course of life as thoughtless as usual. Some years after she heard a sermon, "Who redeemeth thy life from destruction," Ps. 103: 4, and saw and felt how ungrateful and thoughtless she had been, not to give her heart to that God who had so signally preserved her life. Then she made a consecration of herself to her Preserver and Redeemer.

7951. DELIVERANCE, Memento of. To commemorate the deliverance of England from the formidable Spanish Armada, Queen Elizabeth commanded a medal to be struck, representing the Armada scattered and sinking in the background, and in the front the British fleet riding triumphant, with the following passage as a motto round the medal: "Thou didst blow with thy wind, and the sea covered them."

7952. DELIVERANCE, Signal of. The original suggestion of the famous revival song, "Hold the Fort," was an incident of the late war. After the fall of Atlanta, when Gen. Hood started on his march north, the fort and base of supplies which Sherman had established at Altoona, were threatened, and Sherman started in hot haste to reinforce the garrison. Hood was attacking the fort with overwhelming forces, and the defenders were about to succumb when they saw Sherman's signal flag waving from a mountain top in the distance. The words of the signal were, "Hold the fort for I am coming." They were encouraged, and held the fortress till deliverance came.

7953. DELIVERANCE, Strange. A sailor named Campbell felt one evening, when near the African shore, a disposition to bathe. His companions would have dissuaded him from it, as they had recently seen several sharks; but being partly intoxicated, he would not listen to their persuasions. Nearly as soon as he was in the water, his companions saw an alligator directing its course towards him, and considered his escape from death impossible.

They fired at the alligator, but in vain. Campbell became aware of his danger, and immediately made for the shore. On approaching within a very short distance of some canes and shrubs that covered the bank, and while closely pursued by the alligator, a ferocious tiger sprang towards him at the very instant he was about being devoured by his first enemy. At this moment he was preserved. The eager tiger overleaped nim, fell into the grasp of the alligator, and, after a long struggle, was killed by him. Campbell was conveyed to his vessel, returned thanks to Providence which had preserved him, and from that period was a changed man.   *Anon.*

7954. DELIVERANCE, Transport of. Open the iron-bound door of the condemned cell, and by the dim light that struggles through its bars read the sovereign's free pardon to the felon, stretched, pale and emaciated, upon his pallet of straw; and the radiance you have kindled in that gloomy dungeon, and the transport you have created in that felon's heart, is a present realization. You have given him back a present life; you have touched a thousand chords in his bosom which awake a present harmony; and where, just previous, reigned sullen, grim despair, now reigns the sunlight joyousness of a present hope.   *Dr. O. Winslow.*

7955. DELUGE, Description of the. The waters rise till rivers swell into lakes, and lakes become seas, and the sea stretches out her arms along fertile plains to seize their flying population. Still the waters rise; and now mingled with beasts that terror has tamed, men climb to the mountain tops, with the flood roaring at their heels. Still the waters rise; and now each summit stands above them like a separate and sea-girt isle. Still the waters rise; and, crowding closer on the narrow spaces of lessening rill-tops, men and beasts fight for standing-room. Still the thunders roar, and the lightnings flash, and the rains descend, and the waters rise till the last survivor of the shrieking crowd is washed off, and the head of the highest Alp goes down beneath the wave. Now the waters rise no more. God's servant has done his work. He rests from his labors, and, all land drowned, all life destroyed, an awful silence reigning and a shoreless ocean rolling, Death for once has nothing to do but ride in triumph on the top of some giant billow, which, meeting no coast, no continent, no Alp, no Andes against which to break, sweeps round and round the world.   *Dr. Guthrie.*

7956. DELUSIONS, Destructive. There are many false lights in the world, there is but one true light. 'Tis our nature to be drawn forth and dazzled by those false lights, by worldly ambition, carnal pleasures, uncertain riches. We seek the sparkling but fatal deceit, we encircle it, hover nearer and nearer. Warnings there are to stop us in our deluded course. A kind hand would often stop us, often it is thrust between us and the scorching glare, too often with too many in vain. They reach the object of their desire, but it becomes their destruction. The true light, the source of life, and cheerful-

ness, and peace, has shined in vain for them; has been shunned as if it were some horrible and pestilential meteor. Would you see the parable of this in nature's volume? See the moth drawn forth by the glare of a mean and rank-smelling candle. Its red and glowing flame proves only too attractive; the insect hovers nearer and nearer, and the hand of the observer is often thrust before the treacherous light; how very often is the warning offered in vain,—the flame is reached, but with it death! For the same insect, the bright and glorious sun, the source of life and health, has shined in vain; the moth hath shunned it; we seldom see it on the wing till the bright and beautiful sun has come to its setting. *Salter.*

7957. DELUSION, The Sinner's. Be not like the foolish drunkard, who, staggering home one night, saw his candle lit for him. "Two candles!" said he, for his drunkenness made him see double, "I will blow out one," and as he blew it out, in a moment he was in the dark. Many a man sees double through the drunkenness of sin; he has one life to sow his wild oats in, and then he half expects another in which to turn to God; so, like a fool, he blows out the only candle that he has, and in the dark he will have to lie down forever. *Spurgeon.*

7958. DEMAND, Supply and. Had there been no monsters to subdue there had been no Hercules.   *T. Parker.*

7959. DEMONIAC, Healing a. If I were an artist, I would like to draw a picture, and hang it up on yonder wall, that you might see it; that is of the father that came to Christ with his beloved boy. He had been up on the mountain with Peter, James and John, and there he met Elias, the prophet, and Moses, the law-giver. Heaven and earth had come together, and there he had met his Father, and he had spoken to him that memorable night on the mountain. In the morning, when he came down, a crowd of people gathered round him, and some were laughing and talking; they had been trying to cast the evil spirit out of this boy, and told his pitiful story. No one knows but a father how much that man loved that boy; his heart was wrapped up in that child; but the boy was not only deaf and dumb, but he was possessed with a devil, and sometimes this devil would throw him into the fire and sometimes into the water; and when the father came to Jesus, he said to him, "Bring him unto me." And when he was coming, the devil cast him down to the ground. So every man on his way to Christ must first be cast down. There he lay foaming, wallowing, and Jesus only said, "How long has this been?" "From his birth," was the answer; "oh, you do not know how much I have suffered with this boy! When a child he was grievously tormented; he has broken my heart." Some of you here perhaps have children who are suffering from some terrible disease, and who are breaking your hearts—you can sympathize with that father. How that father wept when he brought that poor boy! And when Jesus saw that pitiful scene his heart was moved with compassion.

and with a word he cast out the devil. I can see the boy coming home with his father, leaping, and singing, and praying. Let us learn a lesson. Mother, father, have you got a son that the devil has taken possession of? Bring him to Jesus. He delights to save; he delights to bless. All we have to do is to take him in the arms of our faith, and bring him to Jesus. I want to call your attention to a difference between the father we read of in the 9th chapter of Mark and the poor leper in the 1st chapter. The leper says: "If thou wilt, thou canst make me whole." There was the "if" in the right place. The other said, "If thou canst, have compassion." He put the "if" in the wrong place. The Lord said, "If thou canst believe, all things are possible." Let us believe that the Son of God can save our sons and our daughters. Oh, have you got a poor drunken son? Have you a poor brother who is a slave to strong drink? Come; bring him to the meeting here to-morrow night and let your cry be, "Lord, have compassion on my darling boy and save him." *Moody.*

7960. DEMONS, Habitation of. It is said that St. Parthenius was casting a devil out of a man who had been a long time possessed, when the evil spirit asked for a habitation. Being promised one he said, "Thou wilt cast me out and bid me enter into a swine." "Nay, verily," said the saint, "I will offer thee a man to dwell in." Then the devil came out of the man and the saint said, "Come now, thou foul spirit, I am the man. Enter into me if thou canst." Then the devil cried out that he could not abide in so holy a tabernacle and so fled away. This is a legend of the fourth century.

7961. DENIALS, God's. Israel besought Moses to pray for the removal of the fiery serpents. The Lord did not remove the serpents, but gave them an effectual remedy for their bite, Num. 21:7-9. *Moses.*—His earnest request to enter the promised land was rejected, but God favored him with a miraculous view of Canaan before he died, and called him gently to himself in peace and honor, Deut. 3: 23-27; 34: 1-7. *David* very naturally prayed that his child might live. The Lord refused the request, but gave him another child, honorably born and rarely endowed, and "the Lord loved him," 2 Sam. 12:16-25. His desire to build the house of the Lord was also denied, but he was allowed to gather the materials for the work, 1 Chron. 28, 29. The *healed demoniac* wished to be with Christ. The Lord was pleased rather to send him forth as a missionary to his own home and country; and not improbably, the kinder reception our Lord met with when he came into those parts again, was greatly the result of this man's testimony, Mark 5: 19, 20; 7: 31-37; Matt. 15: 29-31. *St. Paul.*—What a singular link in the chain of God's providence is the narrative in Acts 16: 6-34. The apostle's desire to go into Bithynia was thwarted without any reason apparently being given; but the result proved the opening of the gospel to Philippi, and the founding of the first Christian church in Europe! So, similarly, the apostle's thrice repeated prayer for the removal of the "thorn in the flesh," was answered by the assurance of strength to endure the trial, 2 Cor. 12: 9. How many have cause to bless God for thwarted wishes! The LORD JESUS himself prayed that his bitter cup of suffering might be taken away, and "he was heard," Heb. 5: 7, but in being strengthened to bear the conflict. Luke 22: 42, 43. *Bowes.*

7962. DENOMINATIONS, Abolition of. I wish all names among the saints of God were swallowed up in that one of Christian. I long for professors to leave off placing religion in any saying, "I am a Churchman," "I am a Dissenter." My language to such is, "Are you of Christ? If so, I love you with all my heart." *Whitefield.*

7963. DENOMINATIONS, Traits of. Bishop Chase, an Episcopalian bishop of Ohio, met an old school-mate of whom he had been long ignorant, and finding him a judge of good standing, congratulated him upon their success in life, and the honorable position in which they found each other, concluding, "And, better than all, judge, I find you are a member of our church." "Well," said the judge, "that's more a matter of chance than anything else. You see, when I was getting established in my profession, wife and I thought we ought to join some church; 'twas more respectable. So, after mature deliberation, we settled down with the Baptists, and got on very well for a time; but they kept harping on 'faith,' 'faith,' till we pretty soon discovered that they required more 'faith' than we had; so it became necessary to make a change. We turned the matter over considerably, and at last, from various reasons, made up our minds to join the Methodists. Here we found the demand was, 'work,' 'work,' incessantly; and it was presently apparent that they demanded more 'work,' than we were able to perform. It was with great reluctance that we concluded that we must change again, and cast about with much caution, that this move might be final. At last we decided to connect ourselves with your church, bishop, and have got along famously ever since, without either faith or works."

7964. DENOMINATIONS Unknown in Heaven. A pious person once affirmed to me that on the previous night he had the following dream: He thought that he had died, and arrived at the gates of heaven. When he applied to the holy watchmen to admit him within the sacred walls, they inquired, "Whom do you want?" He replied that he belonged to the Independents, and wished to join them in that place. "There are no such people here!" was the answer that he got. "Well," said he, "I have had some connection with the Baptists; may I join them?" "We don't know any of that name," replied the heavenly watchman. It was in vain that he asked for Churchmen— they had never heard of such a term; there were not even any Wesleyans there. He was just going away in despair, when, as a last resource, he said, "But I am a Christian." At this word the gate of bliss flew open, and he was received as a welcome guest. *H. Townley*

7965. DENOMINATIONS, War among. Melanchthon mourned the divisions among Protestants, and sought to bring them together by the parable of the war between the wolves and the dogs. The wolves were somewhat afraid, for the dogs were many and strong, and they sent out a spy to observe them. On his return, the scout said, "It is true the dogs are many, but there are not many mastiffs among them. There are dogs of so many sorts one can hardly count them; and as for the worst of them," said he, "they are little dogs, which bark loudly, but cannot bite. However, this did not cheer me so much," said the wolf, "as this, that as they came marching on, I observed they were all snapping right and left at one another, and I could see clearly that though they all hate the wolf, yet each dog hates every other dog with all his heart." *Spurgeon.*

7966. DEPENDENCE, Benefit of. The joint dependence of human beings has led to the most beneficial results, inasmuch as long experience, has shown the inadequacy of unaided exertion. By so much as the highly cultivated individual is superior to the houseless savage, by so much is man in society, and assisted by his fellows raised above those who dwell in isolation and estrangement. Thus, human wants promote the cultivation of human energies, and evils at first sight irremediable, become the source of intelligence and refinement. The solitary wanderer may have few vices, but he can have no virtues; for the qualities that ennoble the heart of man, and send his intellect careering through the boundless fields of science and art, are to be ascribed to the influence of association with his fellows, on his mental, moral, and physical capabilities. The errors of society must be rectified by society itself; the breaking up of intercourse might diminish, but could not increase human excellence.
M'Cormac.

7967. DEPENDENCE, Support in. In an arch, each single stone, which, if severed from the rest, would be perhaps defenceless, is sufficiently secured by the solidity and entireness of the whole fabric of which it is a part.
Robert Boyle.

7968. DEPENDENCE, Universal. There is none made so great, but he may both need the help and service, and stand in fear of the power and unkindness, even of the meanest of mortals.
Seneca.

7969. DEPORTMENT, Rule for. Be reserved, but not sour; grave, but not formal; bold, but not rash; humble, but not servile; patient, but not insensible; constant, but not obstinate; cheerful, but not light. Rather be sweet-tempered than familiar; familiar, rather than intimate; and intimate with very few, and with those few upon good grounds. *Penn.*

7970. DEPRAVITY, Admission of. Rev. Dr. Waugh, of the Methodist Episcopal Mission in India, states that the Hindus and Mohammedans almost universally concede the depravity of the race. Among illustrative examples he give this from one of the chief men in Lucknow: "The sinfulness of man," said he, "is

easy enough understood when we remember that in disposing of a good thing—for instance milk—we have to carry it to men's doors; and when we wish to furnish that which is evil—that is, sell rum—we have but to open a shop, and they come to us. That is," continued the man, "we will make sacrifices to destroy ourselves, but none to help ourselves."

7971. DEPRAVITY, Corruption of. I have read of an English painter, who, after only meeting any stranger in the streets, could go home and paint that person's picture to the life. Let us suppose that one whose likeness is taken in this manner should happen to see unexpectedly his own picture. It would startle him. The exact similitude of air, shape, features and complexion, would convince him that the representation was designed for himself, though his own name be not affixed to it, and he is conscious that he never sat for the piece. In the scriptures of truth we have a striking delineation of human depravity through original sin. Though we have not sat to the inspired writers, the likeness suits us all. When the Spirit of God holds up the mirror and shows us to ourselves, we see, we feel, we deplore, our apostasy from, and our inability to recover the image of his rectitude. Experience proves the horrid likeness true; and we need no arguments to convince us, that in and of ourselves we are spiritually "wretched, and miserable, and poor, and blind, and naked." *Salter.*

7972. DEPRAVITY, Course of. We fall not from virtue, like Vulcan from heaven, in a day. Bad dispositions require some time to grow into bad habits; bad habits must undermine good, and oft-repeated acts make us habitually evil; so that by gradual depravations, and while we are but staggeringly evil, we are not left without parentheses of consideration, thoughtful rebukes, and merciful interventions, to recall us to ourselves. *Brown.*

7973. DEPRAVITY, Evidences of. As it is said of Crete, we may by great chance discover one single region of the world that never afforded any dens and coverts for wild beasts. But through the long succession of ages, even to this time, there scarce ever was a state or kingdom that hath not suffered under envy, hatred, emulation, the love of strife, fierce and unruly passions, of all others the most productive of enmity and ill-will among men. Nay, if nothing else will bring it to pass, familiarity will at last breed contempt, and the very friendship of men doth frequently draw them into quarrels, that prove sharp and sometimes implacable. *Plutarch.*

7974. DEPRAVITY, Heathen Testimony to. The fox in Æsop, disputing with the panther for the superiority in beautiful variety, when the latter had shown his body, and his superficies curiously stained and spotted, whereas the fox's tawny skin was ill-favored and unpleasant to the sight, said thus: "But if you, sir judge, will look within me, you will find me much fuller of variety than this leopard;" manifesting the nimble subtlety of his natural disposition, frequently changing as occasions require

Let us then say also to ourselves: "Thy body, O man, naturally of itself breeds many diseases and passions, and many it receives befalling it from without; but if thou shalt open thy interior, thou will find a certain various and abundantly furnished storehouse and (as Democritus says) treasury of evils, not flowing into it from abroad, but having as it were their inbred and original springs, which vice, exceedingly affluent and rich in passions, causes to break forth. *Plutarch.*

7975. DEPRAVITY, Infantile. A child of three years became enraged at her mother. She screamed and raved in her uncontrolled rage, and fell suddenly dead in the midst of her violent passion.

7976. DEPRAVITY, Parable of. Adam Sibbald, in a book called Orfie Sibbald and his Difficulties, thus illustrates depravity: "He opened the clock-case which stood in the corner, and cautiously extracted the pendulum. Instantly, and with loud whirr, the wheels of the clock flew round with prodigious speed, and the hands coursed rapidly over the dial-plate. After a few seconds of this, Adam inserted the pendulum, readjusted the hands, and returned to his seat. "Now, Orfie," he said, "let that parable speak. The wheels of the clock were every one of them there, and every one of them in working order. And yet, from the single want of the pendulum, the whole machine was perfectly useless for its only purpose of correctly measuring time; nay, it was in actual danger of breaking itself to pieces by its unregulated speed. But the moment that the pendulum was replaced, the same wheels in the same condition began to move with regularity, answering the chief end of the machine, and that with safety to themselves. And my parable applies to the case in hand, if you do not press it too far. The same man who, when left to himself, runs only to ruin, and is quite useless so far as glorifying God by his life is concerned, becomes now, when the fear and love of God are inserted into his heart as its regulating principle, a new man. The sinful disorder is checked; the ruinous waste is corrected; and, as in the case of the clock, the whole is effected by the mere insertion of the pendulum."

7977. DEPRAVITY, Question of. A caviler once asked Dr. Nettleton, "How came I by my wicked heart?" "That," he replied, "is a question which does not concern you so much as another, namely, How you shall get rid of it. You have a wicked heart, which renders you entirely unfit for the kingdom of God; and you must have a new heart, or you cannot be saved; and the question which now most deeply concerns you is, How shall you obtain it?" "But," says the man, "I wish you to tell me how I came by my wicked heart." "I shall not," replied Dr. Nettleton, "do that at present; for if I could do it to your entire satisfaction, it would not in the least help you toward obtaining a new heart. The great thing for which I am solicitous is, that you should become a new creature, and be prepared for heaven." As the man mani-

fested no disposition to hear anything on that subject, but still pressed the question how he came by his wicked heart, Dr. Nettleton told him that his condition resembled that of a man who is drowning, while his friends are attempting to save his life. As he rises to the surface of the water, he exclaims, "How came I here?" "That question," says one of his friends, "does not concern you now. Take hold of this rope." "But how came I here?" he asks again. "I shall not stop to answer that question now," replies his friend. "Then I'll drown," says the infatuated man; and spurning all proffered aid, sinks to the bottom.

7978. DESERTION, Spiritual. Vessels at sea, that are richly fraught with jewels and spices, may be in the dark and tossed in the storm; so a soul enriched with the treasures of grace, may yet be in the dark of desertion, and so tossed as to think it shall be cast away in the storm. *T. Watson.*

7979. DESIGNER, Omnipotent. In the mechanics' hall of the Centennial Exhibition was gathered the largest and most wonderful collection of machinery of all kinds that the world has ever seen. Here automatic machines were producing articles of various kinds. Every machine gave evidence of adaptation for its peculiar work. The looms produced sheetings or ribbons or cloths after their kind. No one saw such a prodigy as a thresher producing boots and shoes, or a printing press threshing grain. All this vast quantity of machinery, which did any work, was connected with a great centre of power, the Corliss engine. Upon this all depended. How small is this wonderful display compared with the wonders of creation! We serve the God who is the author both of the wisdom and the power here displayed.

7980. DESIRES, Government of the. Since, of desires, some are natural and necessary; others natural, but not necessary; and others neither natural nor necessary, but the offspring of a wrong judgment: it must be the office of temperance to gratify the first class, as far as nature requires; to restrain the second within the bounds of moderation; and as to the third resolutely to oppose, and if possible, entirely repress them. *History of Philosophy.*

7981. DESIRES, Gratification of. It is a most miserable state for a man to have everything according to his desire, and quietly to enjoy the pleasures of life. There needs no more to expose him to eternal misery. *Bishop Wilson.*

7982. DESIRES, Selfish: A Fable. An active young seal, after an excursion to the sunny South, returned and gave a glowing account of what he had seen to the icebergs of the Arctic. A silly young iceberg who thought himself adapted to shine in other society, became more dissatisfied than ever with his chilly surroundings, and resolved to make the same trip on his own account. He would not listen to the advice of his seniors, but broke recklessly away, and sailed, with all his ribs beating with joy, towards the glorious South

"Now I shall be of use in the world," he thought. But alas, for his good intentions! His first act was to smash and run down a boat in the dark, and he heard plenty of abuse from the sailors in the ship to which it was fastened by a rope. "Ah," he sighed, "I am clumsy, I am in the way;" and when knocked about by waves and winds, "Would I were back in the North! Ah," said he, "I did not know what a peaceful home I had till I lost it, and by my own wilfulness too;" and the poor iceberg sighed and melted in tears of distress and anxiety. He tried to return, but in vain. Alas! it is usually so with those who take a downward path. And the sun looked down on him and lighted up his crests and pinnacles, and the refraction of the light illuminated his crevices, and the soft waves curled round him and laved his base; but the poor iceberg wept the more. The treacherous sun, while beautifying him, only shone on him to melt his peaks one by one, until at last with a gurgling groan he disappeared in the lonely sea, an example to all who leave the station in which they are placed by a loving Father, for a pathway chosen by themselves, and which is certain to end in waste and ruin.

Sunday at Home.

7983. DESPAIR Arrested. Some hares, driven desperate by the enemies that compassed them about on every side, came to the sad resolution that there was nothing left for them but to make away with themselves, one and all. Off they scudded to a lake hard by, determined to drown themselves as the most miserable of creatures. A shoal of frogs seated upon the bank, frightened at the approach of the hares, leaped in the greatest alarm and confusion into the water. "Nay, then, my friends," said a hare that was foremost, "our case is not so desperate yet; for here are other poor creatures more faint-hearted than ourselves."

Æsop.

7984. DESPAIR, Crime of. There is a possibility of salvation to any yet living. While there is life there is hope. Out of the hell of despair there is redemption; though out of the despair of hell there is no redemption. I have read of one in despair whom Satan persuaded it was in vain to pray or serve God, for he must certainly go to hell, who yet went to prayer, and begged of God that if he must go to hell when he died, yet he would please to give him leave to serve him while he lived, upon which his terrors vanished; being clearly convinced none could pray that prayer that had sinned the sin against the Holy Ghost. Still again let me say to thee, as Tamar to Ammon in another case. This later evil in turning mercy out of doors is worse than the former abusing it, and forcing it to serve thy lusts. Both are naught (*i. e.*, wicked), this worse. The sin of Cain despairing was worse than the killing of his brother. There he wronged justice, here mercy; thereby he violated the law, hereby he disparaged the Gospel; thereby he set light by the blood of his brother, hereby of the blood of a Saviour,

which crieth louder for better things than the blood of Abel for vengeance. We say the like of Judas's despair; it was a greater sin than the betraying of his master. *Sheffield.*

7985. DESPAIR, Cure for. It is impossible for that man to despair who remembers that his helper is Omnipotent. *Jeremy Taylor.*

7986. DESPAIR Dishonors God. He that despairs degrades the Deity, and seems to intimate that he is insufficient, or unfaithful to his word, and in vain hath read the Scriptures, the world and man. *Feltham.*

7987. DESPAIR, Evils of. Despair makes a despicable figure, and is descended from a mean original. It is the offspring of fear, laziness, and impatience. It argues a defect of spirit and resolution, and ofttimes of honesty too. After all the exercise of this passion is so troublesome, that nothing but dint of evidence and demonstration should force it upon us. I would not despair unless I knew the irrevocable decree was passed; saw my misfortune recorded in the book of fate, and signed and sealed by necessity. *Jeremy Collier.*

7988. DESPAIR, Never. The New Hampshire troops went forth to engage in the siege of Louisburg, a French stronghold deemed impregnable, called "The Gibraltar of America," in the spirit of Crusaders, with the motto, "*Nil desperandum Christo subduce,*" inscribed upon their banners—Never despair with Christ for leader. Whitfield gave them this sentiment on leaving their native State. To them it was a constant inspiration, and a prophecy of victory from one of God's servants in whom they confided. The surrender of the fortress to the English was regarded as little less than miraculous. This event occurred in what is known as "King George's War," in 1745. The motto is appropriate to every Christian worker.

7989. DESPAIR Overcome. Once when Pelopidas was retreating with the Theban army, they came suddenly upon a much larger force of the Lacedemonians. A soldier ran and told him, "We are fallen into the hands of the enemy." Pelopidas answered, "And why not they into ours?" His skill as a general and the courage of his soldiers made it so. Faith, courage and fidelity will conquer.

7990. DESPONDENCY, Deliverance from. Rev. Robert Johnson gives a case of extreme despondency, resulting from physical debility. The lady overcame by looking to Jesus, and triumphed most gloriously during sickness and in death.

7991. DESPONDENCY, Genius and. The greatest geniuses seem to be subjects of despondency. Such was Shakspeare, who, at such times, thought himself no poet, and Raphael, who doubted his own right to be esteemed a painter. One great preacher hid himself for shame in a grave-yard, and others have wished that they could do so. More make the opposite mistake, and imagine themselves to be what they are not.

7992. DESPONDENCY, Lesson for. Rev. Thos. Collins, in visiting one of his parishioners, found her in a very depressed condition. She had her infant in her arms. Mr. Collins said, "Drop that little one upon the floor." With an air of wonder at such a request, she refused. "Well," said he, "for what price would you do it?" "Not for as many sovereigns as there are stars." "You would not?" "No, I would not." "And do you really think that you love your feeble children more than the Lord does his?" Her face brightened, and, aided by that lesson from her own maternal love, faith grew strong.

7993. DESTRUCTION Easy. The work of destruction is always easier than the work of reparation. It is an easy matter to swallow a bit of poisoned food; it is not so easy to undo the dire effects of it. It is easy to kindle a great conflagration; it is a work of toil and trouble to subdue the flames. It is an easy thing to sin, but its effects are dreadful.

T. Alexander.

7994. DETECTION Certain. A man committed a foul murder in a Scotch castle upon a young bridegroom, at whose marriage festivities he had hypocritically assisted. The assassin took a horse in the dead of night, and fled for his life through wood and winding path. When the sun dawned, he slackened his pace, and behold! he was emerging from a thicket in front of the very castle whence he had fled, and to which, by tortuous paths, he had returned. Horror seized him; he was discovered, and condemned to death. However far and swift we may fly, we shall find ourselves, when light returns, ever in the presence of our sin and of our Judge.

Anon.

7995. DETECTION, Example of. Dr. Donne, afterwards the celebrated Dean of St. Paul's, when he took possession of the first living to which he was inducted, walked into the yard of the church where he was to officiate. It happened that as he sauntered along the sexton was digging a grave, and the doctor stood for a moment to observe his operations. As the man was at work he threw up a skull which in some way or other engaged the doctor's attention. While he examined it he perceived a headless nail which perforated the temple, and which convinced him that some dreadful deed must have been perpetrated. Taking up the skull, he demanded of the grave-digger to whom it had belonged. The man instantly said that he knew very well, that it had belonged to a man who was accustomed to excess in the use of liquor, and who, one night having been guilty of his usual intemperance, had been found dead in his bed in the morning. Dr. Donne then asked, "Had he a wife?" The answer was in the affirmative, "What character does she bear?" The sexton said a very good one, only she was reflected upon for marrying immediately after the death of her husband. This was enough for the doctor, who, upon pretence of visiting all his parishioners, soon called upon the woman in question; and in course of conversation he inquired of what sickness her husband had died. She gave him precisely the same account as the sexton had

given before her. But the doctor produced the skull, and pointing to the place said, "Woman, do you know this nail?" The unhappy criminal was struck with horror at the demand and the sight, and instantly owned that she had been the perpetrator of the deed which had hurried her husband, in a state of intoxication, into the eternal world.

Providence of God Illustrated.

7996. DETECTION Sure. A gentleman owned a flute with one broken note, and the tunes played on it always missed that note. The flute was stolen, and no traces of it could be found for sometime. One day, in another part of the country, he heard a piping bullfinch whistling some tunes, but always dropping a note. This aroused his curiosity, and he found that the man that had taught the bird to sing was the one that had stolen the flute.

7997. DETERMINATION, Example of. There is one man known to history, and long illustrious among his fellow-men, who in his own meditations had reached the conviction that there was a new world far across the sea, and no disappointment or vexing delay could expel that conviction from his earnest mind. Neither the frowns nor the neglect of monarchs, neither hope deferred, nor the terrors of the deep, nor mutiny, nor tempest, nor death, could turn Columbus from his resolute purpose. On he pressed in spite of them all—serene amid the tempest—full of hope when all around seemed to tell only of despair; and he stood at last on the shores of a lovely island in the ocean— the discoverer of lands whose discovery has changed the history of the world. *Tweedie.*

7998. DETRACTION, Effect of. A piece of plate may become battered and scratched, so that its beauty is hopelessly gone, but it loses not its real worth; put it into the scale, and its weight and not its fashion shall be the estimate of its preciousness; throw it into the melting-pot and its purity will show its actual value. So there are many outward circumstances which may spoil the public repute in which a Christian is held, but his essential preciousness remains unchanged. God values him at as high a rate as ever. His unerring balance and crucible are not guided by appearances. How content may we be to be vile in the sight of men if we are accepted of the Lord. *Spurgeon.*

7999. DETRACTION, Harvest of. The detractor, though he sows but words, oftentimes reaps fewer requitals, or at least a plentiful harvest of his own grain. For he shall be sure to hear as much evil as he speaks, and howsoever he puts his faults behind himself, yet they hang before on the shoulder of another. *Anon.*

8000. DETRACTION, Honor of. Pope wrote to Addison, "I congratulate you upon having your share in that which all the great men and all the good men that ever lived have had their share of—envy and calumny. 'To be uncensured and to be obscure is the same thing.'"

8001. DEVELOPMENT, Animal. Empedocles thought that the first of all animals were trees, and they sprang from the earth before the sun in its glory enriched the world, and before day and night were distinguished.

8002. DEVELOPMENT, Law of. What could be more trivial than the heaving of the lid of a tea-kettle? Yet, in that motion lay the germ of ocean steamers, railways, and mills. Development dilates the small into the great. By that law sparks flame into conflagrations, fountains flow into streams, and the minute swell into the magnificent. The seeds of many a world-famed change were dropped in silence —night dews watered them when no eyes looked on; but at length they bore fruit in the hearts of millions; and the harvest of them waved over all the breadth of a continent.
S. Coley.

8003. DEVIL, Complaints of the. When people came to Poemen complaining of being tormented by the devil with discouraging thoughts, he used to say, "Ah! Isidore of Scete used to say under these circumstances, 'Well, devil, suppose I am lost? you will always be below me.'" At other times he said "Devils! devils! it is always devils that are complained of. I say self-will, self-will."

8004. DEVIL, Image of the. The devil has had his worshipers in Calcutta. A temple was erected, in the midst of it a throne, and a brazen statue placed upon it. A diadem was about his head, like the pontifical mitre amongst the Romans, from underneath which projected four prominent horns. He was represented with a very large mouth, a crooked nose, threatening eyes, cruel countenance and deformed hands and feet, altogether forming a very horrible image.

8005. DEVIL, Kiss of the. There was an Arab once who had the devil for his servant. When his term of service had expired, the devil begged as his reward to kiss the shoulders of his master. This request was granted, but out of the spots where the devil's lips had touched sprang serpents, which ever darted their fangs into the breast of the unhappy man. He strove to tear them away, but could not for the agony.
Philips Brooks.

8006. DEVIL Overcome. A monk came to Luther's house, and with great violence, knocked for admittance. On presenting himself to Luther, he told him that there were some Papistical errors about which he desired a conference, and he desired to propound some syllogisms. Luther solved some with ease, and others not so easily. Luther becoming wearied, angrily told the monk he gave him a great deal of trouble. Perceiving that the monk's hands were like birds' claws, he exclaimed, "Art thou he, then? listen to the sentence pronounced against thee, 'The seed of the woman shall bruise the serpent's head,'" and then added, "Nor shalt thou devour them all." The devil, overcome with this saying, angry and murmuring to himself, departed.

8007. DEVIL, Resist the. The race that shortens its weapons lengthens its boundaries. *Corollary.*—It was the Polish lance that left Poland at last with nothing of her own to bound. What business had Sarmatia to be fighting for liberty with a fifteen-foot pole between her and the breasts of her enemies? If she had but clutched the old Roman and young American weapon, and come to close quarters, there might have been a chance for her; but it would have spoiled the best passage in "The Pleasures of Hope."
Holmes.

8008. DEVIL, Silencing the. Datius, archbishop of Milan, arriving at Corinth with his companions, sought a house in which to lodge. He saw a mansion unoccupied. He was told that the place was haunted, and that no man could spend a night there. Datius replied, "Ghost and devil will not scare a servant of God." So himself and company lodged there. At midnight all were aroused by a hideous noise, described as "the braying of asses, the grunting of swine, the squeaking of rats, and the hissing of serpents." Datius, rising in his bed, shouted, "Oh, Satan! thou who saidst in thine heart, 'I will ascend into heaven; I will exalt my throne above the stars of God; I will be like the Most High!' (Isa. 14: 13, 14.) Well done, I say, Satan! Thou, who wouldst be like God, art reduced to bray like a jackass and grunt like a hog." Instantly there was silence, and the noises were heard no more.

8009. DEVIL Transformed. To a saint who was praying the evil spirit showed himself radiant with royal robes, and crowned with a jeweled diadem, and said, "I am Christ—I am descended on the earth—and I desired first to manifest myself to thee." The saint kept silent, and looked, and then said, "I will not believe that Christ has come, save in that state and form in which he suffered, save with the marks of the wounds of the cross." And the false apparition vanished. The application is this: Christ comes not in pride of intellect, or reputation for ability. These are the glittering robes in which Satan is now arrayed. Many spirits are abroad, more are issuing from the pit; the credentials which they display are the precious gifts of mind, beauty, richness, depth, originality. Christian, look hard at them with the saint in silence, and ask them for the print of the nails.
Dr. Howson.

8010. DEVIL, Works of the. The devil is the author of evil, the fountain of wickedness, the adversary of the truth, the corrupter of the world, man's perpetual enemy; he planteth snares, diggeth ditches, spurreth bodies; he goadeth souls, he suggesteth thoughts, belcheth anger, exposeth virtues to hatred, maketh vices beloved, soweth error, nourisheth contention, disturbeth peace, and scattereth affliction.
Quarles.

8011. DEVIL, Worship of the. All the worship or homage paid to anything by the natives of Western Africa is that of fear and dread, and not of love and respect. Hence, with this feeling they worship the devil, and offer sacrifices to him to cultivate his friendship and turn aside his anger, that he may do them no harm. About seventy miles from the mouth of the Gambia there is a sharp elbow-turn from left to right: the left bank is rather hilly, and is covered with trees. This is called the "Devil's

Point." The river is here about two miles wide; and, in passing this place, the natives are in the habit of consigning to the deep some small portions of the ship's cargo, or eatables, in honor of his Satanic Majesty, and to ensure a safe passage up and down the river. The first time I sailed up this splendid stream, I was requested to give something to the devil at this place, which, of course, I declined; but it is still practiced by the superstitious natives and sailors, for the Prince of Darkness is said to have his residence under that point of land, and to stretch out his long arms beneath the water, in order to receive the offerings presented by his worshipers.　　　　　*Fox.*

8012. DEVILS, Guard of. A man dreamt he was traveling, and came to a little church, and on the cupola of that church there was a devil fast asleep. He went along further, and came to a log cabin, and it was surrounded by devils all wide awake. He asked one of them what it meant; said the devil, "I will tell you. The fact is, that whole church is asleep and one devil can take care of all the people; but here are a man and woman who pray, and they have more power than the whole church."

8013. DEVOTION, Advantage of. Alexander the Great, when a child, was checked by his governor, Leonidas, for being over-profuse in spending perfumes; because on a day, being to sacrifice to the gods, he took both his hands full of frankincense and cast it into the fire; but afterwards, being a man, he conquered the country of Judea, (the fountain whence such spices did flow,) and sent Leonidas a present of five hundred talents' weight of frankincense, to show him how his former prodigality made him thrive the better in success, and to advise him to be no more niggardly in divine service. Thus they that sow plentifully shall reap plentifully. I see there is no such way to have a large harvest as to have a large heart. The free giving of the branches of our present estate to God is the readiest means to have the root increased for the future.　　　*Spencer.*

8014. DEVOTION, Benefit of. The man who lives under an habitual sense of the divine presence keeps up a perpetual cheerfulness of temper, and enjoys every moment the satisfaction of thinking himself in company with his dearest and best of friends. The time never lies heavy upon him: it is impossible for him to be alone. His thoughts and passions are the most busied at such hours when those of other men are the most inactive. He no sooner steps out of the world but his heart burns with devotion, swells with hope, and triumphs in the consciousness of that presence which everywhere surrounds him; or, on the contrary, pours out its fears, its sorrows, its apprehensions, to the great Supporter of its existence.　　　　　*Addison.*

8015. DEVOTION, Enemies to. St. Macrius once saw in a vision devils distracting monks in their devotions, closing the eyes of some in drowsiness, and filling the minds of others with wandering thoughts. Some repelled their approach by secret supernatural power; others dallied with their suggestions. The saint burst into tears, and at the end of the prayers admonished every one of his distraction, warned them of the snares of the enemy, and exhorted them to be watchful against his unseen attacks.

8016. DEVOTION, Examples of. Rev. William Bramwell was the honored instrument of many conversions among the Wesleyans of England. "Perhaps," observes Rev. William Dawson, in his funeral sermon, "it will not be asserting too much, if it be said, that, upon an average, he employed six hours out of the twenty-four in prayer and other exercises of the closet." "This is nothing like an exaggeration," add the members of his family, in their memoir, recently published. "On the contrary, it is probably much within the real truth, though it still embraces only a part of his devotional duties. There were, in addition, the supplications of the pulpit, in the prayer-meetings, in his pastoral visits;"—"and besides this," continues Mr. Dawson, "through the whole of the day he was darting the feelings of his heart to God by perpetual ejaculations; and when in company with his friends, he was continually leading them into the holiest by the blood of Jesus, and offering the sacrifices of prayer and praise." "Here, then," add his biographers, "was an amount of devotion which recalls the feats of some of the Puritan or Covenanting divines. Take the case of Mr. Welsh, of Ayr, the son-in-law of John Knox. Out of every twenty-four hours, eight were consumed in private prayer. Like his Wesleyan brother, he would wake in the middle of the night, throw a plaid around him, and renew his supplications without regard to the lapse of time."

8017. DEVOTION, Fire of. When night fell on Jerusalem, and the tide and hum of business had ceased, and one after another the lights were extinguished, and all fires quenched in the sleeping city, one was kept alive—the fire that burned on God's holy altar. "It shall not be put out," said the Lord; "the fire shall ever be burning on the altar; it shall never go out." Fed by such logs as blazed on the hearths and roared in the chimneys of olden times, yet this had not been kindled by man's hands, or blown into flame by his breath. Like God's love on a lost world, or his wrath on the head of his dying Son, it had descended from the skies. "There came," it is said, when Aaron and his sons were offering their first sacrifice, "fire out from before the Lord, and consumed the burnt-offering and the fat, which, when the people saw, they shouted and fell on their faces." Whether slumbering in its ashes or flaming with the fat of sacrifices, this fire burned by night and day on the altar; nor was it till after the lapse of nearly a thousand years that it went out—quenched hissing in the blood of priests who fell in defense of the temple at the first captivity. Now in that old altar on which the sacred fire was always burning, but where sacrifices were not always offering, we see the heart of a devout believer. He is not always praying; but within his bosom there is a heaven-kindled love, fires of desire, fervent longings, which make him always ready to pray and often engage him in prayer. And thus he who engages in devout meditations, and holds communion with God through his word and also through his works, may, in respect of his habitual, prevailing frame of mind, as well as of his frequent prayers, be said to "pray without ceasing," "always to pray;" he is like an Æolian harp, on whose strings, by night or day, the wind has but to breathe to wake up sweet and plaintive music.   *Anon.*

8018. DEVOTION, Glory of. The great antique heart: how like a child's in its simplicity, like a man's in its earnest solemnity and depth! Heaven lies over him wheresoever he goes or stands on the earth; making all the earth a mystic temple to him, the earth's business all a kind of worship. Glimpses of bright creatures flash in the common sunlight; angels yet hover, doing God's messages among men: that rainbow was set in the clouds by the hand of God! Wonder, miracle, encompass the man; he lives in an element of miracle; heaven's splendor over his head, hell's darkness under his feet; a great law of duty, high as these two infinitudes, dwarfing all else, annihilating all else—it was a reality, and it is one: the garment only of it is dead; the essence of it lives through all times and all eternity!   *Carlyle.*

8019. DEVOTION, Impaired. A boy who had been remarkable for the perfection of his lessons, and the teacher's weekly reports of whom showed the highest grade, was gradually reported to have deteriorated fifty per cent. His father expostulated with him. The boy could give no excuse. The father had a bushel of apples placed in the room and a bushel basket half filled with shavings. He directed the son to put all the apples into the basket on top of the shavings. The boy filled the basket, but the apples were only half gathered up when he called his father's attention to the fact that he could not get the apples all into the basket. "This," said the father, "will teach you why you have not mastered your lessons of late. You have occupied your time and half filled your mind with novels and play so that there was no room for other lessons." This pertinently teaches its religious lesson. How can there be entire or partial devotion when the heart is preoccupied with the world?

8020. DEVOTION, Interruption of. St. Frances, of Rome, was a faithful wife, as well as a devout Christian. One day she was reciting her prayers, when her husband called for her. Instantly she obeyed the call, did the desired service, and then returned to her prayers. Four times in succession was she thus interrupted, cheerfully answered the calls, and returned to her devotions without a shadow of annoyance. On resuming her missal, after her last interruption, she was greatly surprised to find the antiphon which she had four times begun and four times called to leave unfinished, written in letters of gold. The legend says that others saw the gilded letters, and that they remained in the book till the day of her death.

8021. DEVOTION, Model of. Bishop Janes, who grew to such majestic stature, gave undivided attention to his work. Having a little place out in the country, he visited it half a day each year for a settlement with his tenant, and that was all of the Church's time he gave to it. This scrupulous devotion exalted him into great usefulness—doubtless, the greatest usefulness of any man of this or the last generation—and, consequently, into the most substantial greatness. This we take to be a model life.   *Dr. Fowler.*

8022. DEVOTION, Neglect of. Eugippius relates that a poor man in Vienna left his prayers and spent the day in trying to keep the locusts off from his little patch of corn when he should have been at church. To his great surprise he found, when the next morning dawned, that his field had been stripped bare, while his neighbor's crops were untouched.

8023. DEVOTION, Personal. I have just put my soul as a blank into the hands of Jesus, my Redeemer, and desired him to write on it what he pleases: I know it will be his image.   *Whitefield.*

8024. DEVOTION, Prayer of. Grant, O Lord, that the sweet violence of thy most ardent love may disengage and separate me from every thing that is under heaven, and entirely consume me, that I may die for the love of thy infinite love. This I beg by thyself, O Son of God, who diedst for love of me. My God and my all! who art thou, O sweetest Lord? and who am I thy servant and a base worm? I desire to love thee, most holy Lord. I have consecrated to thee my soul and body, with all that I am. Did I know what to do more perfectly to glorify thee, that would I most ardently do.   *St. Francis of Assisi.*

8025. DEVOTION, Private. A man may pray with others from a variety of motives; but he will never love praying by himself until he feels his constant need of the Divine care, and views God as the chief good. Some professors are very deficient in this duty, in which they ought to abound. They are known by a sickly languor in other duties, and are proofs that none relish public ordinances so well as those who keep up a constant correspondence with heaven in private. Remissness in duty is always attended by a deficiency of comfort. We can only climb the mount of communion on the knee of prayers.   *Herrick.*

8026. DEVOTION, Propensity to. It has been observed by some writers, that man is more distinguished from the animal world by devotion than by reason, as several brute creatures discover in their actions something like a faint glimmering of reason, though they betray in no single circumstance of their behavior anything that bears the least affinity to devotion. It is certain, the propensity of the mind to religious worship, the natural tendency of the soul to fly to some superior being for succor in dangers and distresses, the gratitude to an invisible superintendent which arises in us upon receiving any extraordinary and unexpected good fortune, the acts of love and admiration with which the thoughts of men are so wonderfully transported in meditating upon the divine perfections, and the universal concurrence of all the nations under heaven in the great article of adoration, plainly show that devotion or religious worship must be the effect of tradition from some first founder of mankind, or that it is conformable to the natural light of reason, or that it proceeds from an instinct implanted in the soul itself. For my own part, I look upon all these to be the concurrent causes; but whichever of them shall be assigned as the principle of divine worship, it manifestly points to a Supreme Being as the first author of it.   *Addison.*

8027. DEVOTION, Result of. One asked Scipio the Elder in Sicily, on what confidence he presumed to pass with his navy against Carthage. He showed him three hundred disciplined men in armor, and pointed to a high tower on shore. "There is not one of these," said he, "that would not at my command go to the top of that tower and cast himself down headlong." Over he went, landed, and burnt the enemy's camp, and the Carthaginians sent to him, and covenanted to surrender their ships, elephants, and a sum of money.

8028. DEVOTION, Reward of. During the cholera season of 1832, Father Matthew administered the last rites of religion to a young man in whom he had a special interest, when he was called to go to another ward. He remained away but a short time, but when he returned he found the bed was unoccupied; the young man had been carried to the dead-house. Father Matthew could not believe that he was dead, and started to find him. An awful spectacle met his sight—piles of miserable coffins, bodies on tables, and on the floor, many wrapped like mummies in the sheets in which they had been snatched from the bed in which they died, these liberally coated with pitch or tar to prevent contagion. Amid this scene of horrors Father Matthew sought the young man. There lay the body, while near by stood two men preparing the tarred sheet in which they were to wrap it. "Stop," said Father Matthew, "that young man can't be dead. I was speaking to him a few moments ago. No, no, I can't believe it; he is not dead." There was a suspension of the loathsome work for a time, while Father Matthew knelt down beside the body and pressed his hand lightly on the region of the heart. A moment of suspense followed, while the devoted priest listened for the heart to tell its throbs. Suddenly he exclaimed, "Thank God! he is alive; I feel his heart beat; thank God, thank God!" He was removed back to the hospital, restoratives were applied, and in a few days he was able to pour forth his gratitude to his preserver, for had another minute passed he would have been lost to the world forever.

8029. DEVOTION, Secret. Secret devotions resemble the rivers which run under the earth; they steal from the eyes of the world to seek the eyes of God; and it often happens that those of whom we speak least on earth, are best known in heaven.   *Caussin.*

8030. DIAMOND, Peculiarity of the. The distinguishing peculiarity and most valuable characteristic of the diamond is the power it possesses of refracting and reflecting the prismatic colors: this property it is that gives fire, life, and brilliancy to it. Other stones reflect the light as they receive it—bright in proportion to their own transparency, but always colorless; and the ray comes out as it went in.   *Colton.*

8031. DIAMOND, Value of the. The diamond, the most costly of all substances, has intrinsic beauties of its own. It has a limpidity, a brilliancy, a fire appertaining to itself, but, above all, an absolute indestructibility far surpassing that of any known product, which gives the additional reason for its enhanced value. The first diamond taken from the bed of the Indian torrent, cut centuries ago, has not lost an atom of its weight, nor has a spark of its brilliant fire been dimmed. Though it has passed through millions of hands, it shows no trace of wear; it has been subjected to all temperatures and climates, and its shining lustre has never paled. This indestructibility has, then, made it inestimable as a standard of value. A thousand years ago it had its price, and a thousand years to come it must remain unchanged in form and lustre, and ever have intrinsic value.   *Anon.*

8032. DIE, Why will you? It is alleged by travelers that the ostrich, when hard pressed by the hunters, will thrust its head into a bush, and, without further attempt either at flight or resistance, quietly submit to the stroke of death. Men say that, having thus succeeded in shutting the pursuers out of its own sight, the bird is stupid enough to fancy that it has shut itself out of theirs, and that the danger which it has ceased to see, has ceased to exist. We doubt that. God makes no mistakes; and, guided as the lower animals are in all their instincts by infinite Wisdom, I fancy that a more correct knowledge of that creature would show that whatever stupidity there may be in the matter, lies not in the poor bird, but in man's rash conclusion regarding it. Man trusts to hopes which fail him, the spider never; she commits her weight to no thread which she has spun, till she has pulled on it with her arms, and proved its strength. Misfortune overtakes man unprovided and unprepared for it; not winter the active bee. Amid the blaze of Gospel light, man misses his road to heaven: but in the starless night, the swallows cleave their way through the pathless air, returning to the window nook where they were nestled; and through the darkest depths of ocean the fish steer their course back to the river where they were spawned. Would ye find folly, Solomon tells us where to seek it:— "Folly," says the wise man, "is bound in the heart of a child;" and what is folded up there like leaves in their bud, blows out in the deeds and habits of men. This poor bird, who has thrust its head into the bush, and stands quietly to receive the shot, has been hunted to death. For hours the cry of staunch pursuers has rung in its startled ear; for hours their feet have been on its weary track; it has exhausted strength, and breath, and craft, and cunning, to escape; and even yet, give it time to breathe, grant it but another chance, and it is away with the wind; with wings outspread and rapid feet it spurns the burning sand. It is because escape is hopeless and death is certain, that it has buried its head in that bush, and closed its eyes to a fate which it cannot avert. To man belongs the folly of closing his eyes to a fate which he can avert. He thrusts his head into the bush while escape is possible; and, because he can put death, and judgment, and eternity, out of mind, lives as if time had no bed of death, and eternity no bar of judgment. *Dr. Guthrie.*

8033. DIFFICULTIES, Biblical. *Great mountains,* Zech. 4:7; Matt. 17:20; 1 Cor. 13:2. *A lion in the way,* Prov. 22:13; 26:13. *A thorn hedge,* Prov. 15:19. *Thorns and briers,* Ezek. 2:6. *Gates of brass,* Ps. 107:16; Isa. 45:2. *Rough roads,* Ps. 18:33; Eph. 6:15. Eccles. 11:4.—"He that observeth the wind shall not sow," etc. THE HISTORY OF ISRAEL at different times may furnish a good illustration of the difficulties that attend the Christian warfare. On leaving Egypt, what could apparently seem more embarrassing than their position? and before entering the promised land, when the difficulty of conquest was enhanced by their unbelieving fears, and the report of the spies? See Num. 13:26-33. So in later times, as in the days of Hezekiah, Isa. 36:37; of Asa, 2 Chron. 14:9-15; of Jehoshaphat, 2 Chron. 20:1-30, and others. THE HISTORY of many eminent *saints* similarly shows that it is "no strange thing" to be dismayed by real or imagined difficulty. How many have shrunk back at first when called to undertake some important mission, like Moses, Gideon, Elijah, Jeremiah, Ezekiel? AFRAID OF SHADOWS. Our greatest fears often arise from imagined difficulties; which, when we go forward in the strength of the Lord, prove to be only shadows! It is to be noted, that the Anakims—the great giants—at the thought of whom Israel trembled, gave them really little opposition when they entered Canaan! HOW TO MEET DIFFICULTIES. Take two examples—Num. 13:26-33; 14:1-10. Copy the noble spirit of Caleb and Joshua, when the other spies would have disheartened the people. See especially 13:30; 14:8, 9. Nehemiah 3:4; 12:27.—The building of the wall of Jerusalem amidst the greatest opposition. FEAR NOT. See in Conc. the precious "Fear nots" of Scripture. They are generally found as the preparation and antidote for apprehended difficulty, or felt discouragement. 1 Cor. 16:8, 9.—"And there are many adversaries." Difficulties dishearten the weak and timid. They bring out the spirit of the brave. Difficulties make the man. QUESTIONS. Zech. 4:7.—"Who art thou, O great mountain?" Gen. 18:14; Jer. 32:17.—"Is anything too hard for the Lord?" Num. 11:23.—"Is the Lord's hand waxed short?" Isa. 50:2. Luke

1:34.—How shall this be? ANSWER. Luke 1:37.—"With God nothing shall be impossible." Isa. 59:1.—"Behold, the Lord's hand is not shortened that it cannot save." *Bowes*

8034. DIFFICULTIES, Surmounting. It is weak to be scared at difficulties, seeing that they generally diminish as they are approached, and oftentimes even entirely vanish. No man can tell what he can do till he tries. It is impossible to calculate the extent of human powers; it can only be ascertained by experiment. What has been accomplished by parties and by solitary individuals in the torrid and frozen regions, under circumstances the most difficult and appalling, should teach us that, when we ought to attempt, we should never despair. The reason why men oftener succeed in overcoming uncommon difficulties than ordinary ones, is, that in the first case they call into action the whole of their resources, and that in the last they act upon calculation, and generally undercalculate. Where there is no retreat, and the whole energy is forward, the chances are in favor of success: but a backward look is full of danger. Confidence of success is almost success; and obstacles often fall of themselves before a determination to overcome them. There is something in resolution which has an influence beyond itself, and it marches on like a mighty lord among its slaves; all is prostration where it appears. When bent on good, it is almost the noblest attribute of man; when on evil, the most dangerous. It is by habitual resolution that men succeed to any great extent; impulses are not sufficient. What is done at one moment is undone the next; and a step forward is nothing gained unless it is followed up. Resolution depends mainly on the state of the digestion, which St. Paul remarkably illustrates when he says, "Every man that striveth for the mastery is temperate in all things." *Moir.*

8035. DIFFICULTY, Benefit of. Difficulty is a severe instructor, set over us by the supreme ordinance of a parental guardian and legislator, who knows us better than we know ourselves; and he loves us better too. He that wrestles with us strengthens our nerves, and sharpens our skill. Our antagonist is our helper. This amicable conflict with difficulty obliges us to an intimate acquaintance with our object, and compels us to consider it in all its relations. It will not suffer us to be superficial. *Burke.*

8036. DIFFICULTY, Miracles of. It is difficulties which give birth to miracles. It is not every calamity that is a curse; and early adversity is often a blessing. Perhaps Madame de Maintenon would never have mounted a throne had not her cradle been rocked in a prison. Surmounted obstacles not only teach, but hearten us in our future struggles; for virtue must be learnt, though, unfortunately, some of the vices come as it were by inspiration. The austerities of our northern climate are thought to be the cause of our abundant comforts, as our wintry nights and our stormy seas have given us a race of seamen perhaps unequaled, and certainly not surpassed, by any in the world.   *Sharpe.*

8037. DILIGENCE, Blessing upon. A divine benediction is always invisibly breathed on painful and lawful diligence. Thus, the servant employed in making and blowing of the fire, though sent away thence as soon as it burneth clear, ofttimes getteth by his pains a more kindly and continuing heat than the master himself, who sitteth down by the same; and thus persons industriously occupying themselves thrive better on a little of their own honest getting than lazy heirs on the large revenues left unto them.   *Fuller.*

8038. DILIGENCE, Evil. Take a heretic, a rebel, a person that hath an ill cause to manage. What he is deficient in the strength of his cause, he makes up with diligence; while he that hath right on his side is cold, indiligent, lazy, inactive, trusting that the goodness of his cause will not fail to prevail without assistance. So wrong prevails, while evil persons are zealous and the good remiss.
                                  Jeremy Taylor.

8039. DILIGENCE, Lesson of. Select a large box and place in it as many cannon-balls as it will hold; it is after a fashion full, but it will hold more if smaller matters be found. Bring a quantity of marbles, very many of these may be packed in the spaces between the larger globes; the box is full now, but only in a sense; it will contain more yet. There are interstices in abundance, into which you may shake a considerable quantity of small shot; and now the chest is filled beyond all question, but yet there is room. You cannot put in another shot or marble, much less another cannon-ball, but you will find that several pounds of sand will slide down between the larger materials, and even then between the granules of sand, if you empty yonder jug, there will be space for all the water, and for the same quantity several times repeated. When there is no space for the great, there may be room for the little; where the little cannot enter, the less can make its way; and where the less is shut out, the least of all may find ample room and verge enough. Now, the diligent preacher may not be able to preach more sermons; his engagement book is crowded. He may not be able to offer more public prayers, or to search the word of God more constantly; there is as much time occupied with these things as could well be given to them. Still there must be stray moments, occasional intervals and snatches, which might hold a vast amount of little usefulnesses in the course of months and years. What a wealth of minor good, as we may think it to be, might be shaken down into the interstices of ten years' work, which might prove to be as precious in result, by the grace of God, as the greater works of the same period.
                                  Spurgeon.

8040. DILIGENCE, Missionary. Elliot, the apostle to the Indians, was easily moved to undertake their conversion by the seal of the Massachusetts colony, which had on it an Indian, with a label from his mouth, on which was the inscription, "Come over and help us." In the prosecution of his efforts to evangelize the Indians, he endured many hardships. In a letter to a friend, he says, "I have not been dry night nor day, from the third day of the week to the sixth, but so traveled; and at night pulled off my boots, wrung my stockings, and on with them again, and so continue. But God steps in and helps." After having formed, with the greatest difficulty, a grammar of the Indian language, he wrote, in a letter to a friend, "Prayers and pains, through faith in Christ Jesus, will do anything." Such was the diligence of Elliot in his great work that on the day of his death, in his eightieth year, the "Apostle of the Indians" was found teaching the alphabet to an Indian child at his bedside. "Why not rest from your labors now?" asked a friend. "Because," said the venerable man, "I have prayed to God to render me useful in my sphere; and now that I can no longer preach, he leaves me strength enough to teach this poor child his alphabet."

8041. DILIGENCE, Strength for. Perhaps thou findest the duty of thy calling too heavy for thy weak shoulders. Make bold by faith to lay the heaviest end of thy burden on God's shoulder, which is thine, if a believer, as sure as God can make it by promise. When at any time thou art sick of thy work, and ready to think with Jonas to run from it, encourage thyself with that of God to Gideon, whom he called from the flail to thresh the mountains. Go in this thy might. Hath not God called thee? Fall to the work God sets thee about, and thou engagest his strength for thee. "The way of the Lord is strength." Run from thy work, and thou engagest God's strength against thee; he will send some storm or other after thee to bring home his runaway servant. How oft hath the coward been killed in a ditch, or under some hedge, when the valiant soldier that stood his ground and kept his place got off with safety and honor!   *Gurnall.*

8042. DISAGREEMENTS, Advantage of. There was one Melanthius, who (whether in jest or earnest he said it, it matters not much) affirmed that the city of Athens owed its preservation to the dissensions and factions that were among the orators, giving withal this reason for his assertion, that thereby they were kept from inclining all of them to one side, so that by means of the differences among those statesmen there were always some that drew the saw the right way for the defeating of destructive counsels.   *Plutarch.*

8043. DISAGREEMENTS, Cause of. Many contentions arise out of sheer misunderstanding. Disputants often become metaphysical according to the explanation given by the Scotchman, who said: "Why, ye see, metaphysics is when twa men are talking thegither, and the ane of them dinna ken what he is talking aboot, and the ither canna understand him." Drs. Chalmers and Stuart must have been a "wee bit" metaphysical that day they got into a controversy about the nature of faith. Chalmers, compelled at length to leave his friend, said: "I nave time to say no more; but you will find my views fully and well put in a recent tract, called Difficulties in the way of Believing." "Why," exclaimed the astonished Dr. Stuart, "that is my own tract! I published it myself!" That man was surely wise who prefaced every debate with, "Gentlemen, define your terms." During the Peninsular war an officer of artillery had just served a gun with admirable precision against a body of men posted in a wood to his left. When the duke rode up, after turning his glass for a moment in that direction of the shot, he said, in his cool way, "Well aimed, Captain; but no more; they are our own 39th!" This sad blunder has been repeated too often in the armies of Jesus. With what fatal frequency have great guns of the church, which might have battered down citadels of Satan, been misdirected against Christian brethren! There are surely deviltries enough in the world to shoot at, without firing into each other.   *S. Coley.*

8044. DISBELIEF, Ignorance and. Absolute disbelief implies knowledge: it is the knowledge that such or such a thing is not true. If the mind admit a proposition without any desire for knowledge concerning it, this is credulity. If it is open to receive the proposition, but feels ignorance concerning it, this is doubt. In proportion as knowledge increases, doubt diminishes, and belief or disbelief strengthens. No one ought to profess to disbelieve any proposition, unless he is sure that he perfectly understands the subject to which it relates. To do so is the most absurd presumption. Those who profess to doubt the truth of important propositions thereby acknowledge their ignorance; they ought, therefore, not to rest till they have sought information by every possible means.   *Anon.*

8045. DISAPPOINTMENT, Fable of. A fox, just at the time of the vintage, stole into a vineyard where the ripe sunny grapes were trellised up on high in most tempting show. He made many a spring and jump after the luscious prize; but failing in all his attempts, he muttered as he retreated, "Well, what does it matter? the grapes are sour!"   *Æsop.*

8046. DISAPPOINTMENT, Providential. Two literary societies were formed by the students of a village academy during the absence of the principal, which held their meetings in a vacant house. The principal, on being informed of this, issued an order positively forbidding the meetings. There was great excitement among the students over this despotic order, but it was obeyed. They knew the kindness of the master, and judged that he had some reason for his action of which they were ignorant. On his return they asked for an explanation. He said: "A few days before I left you, three men, having been secretly lodged in the house where your meetings were held, died of the small-pox. Are you satisfied?" This was reason enough. Our kind Father often deals with his children in the same way. Our idols are broken, and our own purposes defeated, because he designs some better things for us.

8047. DISAPPOINTMENT, Sad. That which has died within us is often the saddest portion of what death has taken away—and to all, and above measure, to those in whom no higher life has been awakened. The heavy thought is the thought of what we were, of what we hoped and proposed to have been, of what we ought to have been, of what but for ourselves we might have been—set by the side of what we are, as though we are haunted by the side of our own youth. This is a thought the crushing weight of which nothing but a strength above our own can lighten.   *Hare.*

8048. DISCIPLINE, Analogy of. When in the city of Amsterdam, in Holland, I was very much interested in a visit we made to a place there famous for polishing diamonds. We saw the men as they were engaged in this work. When a diamond is first found, it has a rough, dark outside, and looks just like a common pebble. The outside must be ground off and the diamond be polished before it is fit for use. It takes a long time to do this, and it is very hard work. The diamond has to be fixed very firmly in the end of a piece of hard wood or metal. Then it is held close to the surface of a large metal wheel which is kept going round. Fine diamond dust is put on this wheel, because nothing else is hard enough to polish the diamond. And this work is kept on for days, and weeks, and months, and sometimes for several years, before it is finished. And if a diamond is intended to be used in the crown of a king, then longer time and greater pains are spent upon it, so as to make it look as brilliant and beautiful as can be. Now, Jesus calls his people his jewels. He intends them to shine like jewels in the crown he will wear in heaven. To fit them for this they must be polished like the diamond. And God makes use of the troubles he sends on his people in this world to polish his jewels. And when we get to heaven and see how beautiful they look, we shall see that it was indeed good for them that they were troubled. It has fitted them for greater happiness there.   *Dr. R. Newton.*

8049. DISCIPLINE, Example of. A once earnest and devoted Christian lost his spirituality through the usual influence of great worldly prosperity. The Lord would not give him up to apostasy and ruin. He took his wife from him by death, then a loved son; still no amendment. Then misfortune blighted his plans, but did not cure his worldliness. A loathsome and incurable disease fastened upon him, and while imprisoned by it, his house took fire. As he was carried from the burning building he exclaimed, "Blessed be God; I am cured at last," and shortly after died in the assurance of faith.

8050. DISCIPLINE, Intention of. "As an eagle stirreth up her nest." This illustration is one of the most beautiful and appropriate that could be conceived. It is taken from the habits of the eagle, which, when her young ones are well-fledged and would prefer to linger in downy ease, disturbs their nest, that they may be taught how to fly. Look at that parent bird picking at the nest which she hath built for her tender offspring: see how she breaks off one twig after another, exciting her brood to leave their nest and soar on high amid the sunshine of heaven. And if they will not leave it, she will break it further and further, until it is utterly broken up, and they are forced to fly or fall. Thus God deals with us. He knows our tendency to make this earth our rest, and he disturbs our nest to teach us to rise on the wings of faith towards the enduring realities of heaven. How often does God take away our earthly comforts when he sees that we cling too fondly to them! How often, in this world of vicissitude and change, do riches make themselves wings and fly away! By some unfortunate speculation, or in some way we know not how, lands and possessions are swept away at a stroke, and stranger feet now tread that abode which was once the home of competence and ease. The hopes of a rising family are blighted, and those who were fostered in the downy softness of luxury are turned out into a cold and pitiless world to work for their daily bread. Perhaps something upon which we placed the utmost reliance, upon which seemed to rest our only stay, is suddenly and mysteriously taken from us, and when we attempt to grasp it we find it gone. A gale at sea may destroy the hopes of the merchant; depression in trade may bring want to your door; the bankruptcy of some large mercantile firm, or the failure of a bank, may involve numbers in ruin, and plunge many families in misery hitherto unknown. How many have had occasion, from these and similar causes, and how many more will yet have occasion, to mourn over altered circumstances! Marvel not if it be thus with you; it is God stirring up your nest to teach you to wing your flight to heaven. All these things have a voice if ye will but hear, and seem to say, "Arise ye, and depart; for this is not your rest," Micah 2 : 10.   *Brock.*

8051. DISCIPLINE, Military. The leading idea of military discipline is to reduce the common men, in many respects, to the nature of machines; that they may have no volition of their own, but be actuated solely by that of their officers; that they may have such a superlative dread of those officers as annihilates all fear of the enemies; that they may move forwards when ordered without deeper reasoning or more concern than the firelocks they carry along with them.   *Sir J. Moore.*

8052. DISCIPLINE, Personal. It would seem, indeed, to be God's usual method to prepare men for extensive usefulness by the personal discipline of trial. Hence, when we see Bunyan encompassed by terrible temptations, and immured in bondage; Luther, in the fortress on the Wartburg, pining in sore sickness, and battling, in fancy, with embodied evil; Wesley wandering to Georgia and back, led through doubt and darkness to the long-deferred moment which ended his "legal years," and then welcomed on his evangelistic journeys with ovations of misrepresentation and mud;—we remember that this protracted suffering is but

the curriculum of heavenly discipline by which learning of him who is lowly, they are shriven of self and pride, and which superadds to the fortitude which bears all, and to the courage which dares all, the meekness and gentleness of Christ.   *Punshon.*

8053. DISCIPLINE, Reason for. We sometimes wonder, with regard to some of God's dealings with the elect, that he should cast them again and again into the crucible of trial. It seems to us as though they were already refined gold. But he sees that in them which we do not see, a further fineness which is possible; and he will not give over till that be obtained. It is just as in a portrait by some cunning artist, which is now drawing near to its completion. Men look at it, and count it perfect, and are well-nigh impatient that the artist does not now withhold his hand and declare it is finished, while he, knowing better, touches and retouches, returns again and again to his work. And why? Because there floats before him an ideal of possible excellence at which he has not yet arrived, but which he will not rest nor be contented till he has embodied in his work. It is thus with God and some of his elect servants.   *Trench.*

8054. DISCIPLINE, Results of. The law of habit when enlisted on the side of righteousness, not only strengthens and makes sure our resistance to vice, but facilitates the most arduous performances of virtue. The man whose thoughts, with the purposes and doings to which they lead, are at the bidding of conscience, will, by frequent repetition, at length describe the same track almost spontaneously—even as in physical education, things, laboriously learnt at the first, come to be done at last without the feeling of an effort. And so, in moral education, every new achievement of principle smooths the way to future achievements of the same kind; and the precious fruit or purchase of each moral virtue is to set us on higher and firmer vantage-ground for the conquests of principle in all time coming. He who resolutely bids away the suggestions of avarice, when they come in conflict with the incumbent generosity; or the suggestions of voluptuousness, when they come into conflict with the incumbent self-denial; or the suggestions of anger, when they come into conflict with the incumbent act of magnanimity and forbearance —will at length obtain, not a respite only, but a final deliverance from their intrusion. Conscience, the longer it has made way over the obstacles of selfishness and passion, the less will it give way to these adverse forces, themselves weakened by the repeated defeats which they have sustained in the warfare of moral discipline ; or, in other words, the oftener that conscience makes good the supremacy which she claims, the greater would be the work of violence, and less the strength for its accomplishment, to cast her down from that station of practical guidance and command, which of right belongs to her. It is just, because, in virtue of the law of suggestion, those trains of thought and feeling, which connect her first biddings with their final execution, are the less exposed at every new instance to be disturbed, and the more likely to be repeated over again, that every good principle is more strengthened by its exercise, and every good affection is more strengthened by its indulgence, than before. The acts of virtue ripen into habits; and the goodly and permanent result is, the formation or establishment of a virtuous character.   *Chalmers.*

8055. DISCIPLINE a Test. When Scoresby was selecting his men to accompany him in his Arctic explorations, he needed sailors that could stand the severest exposures, and who had nerve to bear the worst trials. So every man who applied to accompany the expedition was made to stand barefooted on a great block of ice while the surgeon examined his body, and Scoresby inquired into his past history. Scores were rejected at once, as they had not nerve to endure the test. The men who stood the trial made up a band of the most glorious heroes. So sometimes God tries us when he has in store for us some great undertaking. Many faint and excuse themselves from the start. Some endure, and make the heroes and leaders of the church.   *A. D. Vail.*

8056. DISCIPLINE, Work of. A mother endured a prolonged and painful illness with great patience. The evidence of her suffering often caused her attendants to weep with sympathy. The heroic sufferer replied to her attentive daughter, whose tears fell upon her mother's face, "Patience, darling; it is only the chiseling." She had learned the secret of philosophy and true Christian faith.

8057. DISCONTENT, Absurd. Anaxarchus told Alexander that there was an infinite number of worlds. At this he wept, and when asked if any accident had befallen him, he replied, "Do you not think it a matter of lamentation, that, when there is such a vast multitude of worlds, we have not conquered one?"

8058. DISCONTENT, Constant. A child about three years old was crying because his mother had shut the parlor door. "Poor thing," said a neighbor, "you have shut the child out." "It's all the same to him," said the mother; "he would cry if I called him in and then shut the door. It is a peculiarity of that boy, that if he is left rather suddenly on either side of a door, he considers himself shut out, and rebels accordingly." Many older people bear a remarkable resemblance to this child.

8059. DISCONTENT, Cure for. Beg of God a meek and quiet spirit, which is of so great price in the sight of God; and watch after your prayers, not only how the Lord answers, but how you endeavor. He that prays against discontent, binds himself to watch and strive against it, or else his prayers are sin. Beg an humble heart of God; the humble man is seldom discontented; he thinks that the least of mercies is good enough for the chief of sinners. Here is a poor house, coarse fare, hard lodgings, unkind usage; but it is good enough for me: any thing short of hell is mercy; if I have but bread to eat, and raiment to put on, it is

good fare for such an one as I. And then beg a mortified heart to all that is in the world When the heart is dead to the world, worldly troubles do not trouble. He that is dead to the world will save his bones whole: when crosses, straits, and troubles come upon him, it may be said of such an one, "Yonder man is dead already to the world, his heart is crucified to it; he feels nothing so as to be distempered by it." When we strip dead men they struggle not; we may take all, they are not troubled at it. Oh, beg such a heart, that God may do what he will with thee, that his will may be done; and this prayer will procure patience and help against discontent.   *Steele.*

8060. DISCONTENT, Delusion of The happiest of mankind, overlooking those solid blessings which they already have, set their hearts upon somewhat which they want; some untried pleasure, which if they could but taste, they should then be completely blest.   *Atterbury.*

8061. DISCONTENT, Emblem of. It is like ink poured into water, which fills the whole fountain full of blackness. It casts a cloud over the mind, and renders it more occupied about the evil which disquiets it, than about the means of removing it.   *Feltham.*

8062. DISCONTENT, Error of. The great error of our nature is, not to know where to stop, not to be satisfied with any reasonable acquirement; not to compound with our condition; but to lose all we have gained by an insatiable pursuit after more.   *Burke.*

8063. DISCONTENT, Incurable. An ass, belonging to a gardener, having little to eat and much to do, besought Jupiter to release him from the gardener's service, and give him another master. Jupiter, angry at his discontent, made him over to a potter. He had now heavier burdens to carry than before, and again appealed to Jupiter to relieve him, who accordingly contrived that he should be sold to a tanner. The ass having now fallen into worse hands than ever, and daily observing how his master was employed, exclaimed with a groan, "Alas, wretch that I am! it had been better for me to have remained content with my former masters, for now I see that my present owner not only works me harder while living, but will not even spare my hide when I am dead!"   *Æsop.*

8064. DISCONTENT, Misery of. The discontented is ever restless and uneasy, dissatisfied with his station in life, his connexions, and almost every circumstance that happens to him. He is continually peevish and fretful, impatient of every injury he receives, and unduly impressed with every disappointment he suffers. He considers most other persons as happier than himself, and enjoys hardly any of the blessings of Providence with a calm and grateful mind. He forms to himself a thousand distressing fears concerning futurity, and makes his present condition unhappy, by anticipating the misery he may endure in years to come.   *Stennett.*

8065. DISCONTENT, Reproof of. To reprove discontent, the ancients feigned that in hel' stood a man twisting a rope of hay; and stil he twisted on, suffering an ass to eat up all that was finished.　　*Jeremy Taylor.*

8066. DISCORD, Effect of. If one note in the organ be out of key, or harsh of tone, it mars the whole tune. All the other reeds may be in harmony; but the one defective reed destroys the sweetness of all the rest. In every tune it makes discord somewhere. Its noise jars out into every other note. And so one sin destroys the harmony of a whole life. A boy or girl may be obedient, filial, industrious, and honest; but ill-temper is a jarring reed that touches every grace with chill and discord. Let every affection, and every thought, and every word, and every action, be right: then there is music in the life.　　*Anon.*

8067. DISCORD, Forgetting. The Athenians struck from their calendar the second day of their month Bœdromion, because they had a story, that on that day their gods Neptune and Minerva quarreled. It is well to cancel from memory those disagreeable things that only afflict the soul and cast a black shadow over life.

8068. DISCORD, Rebuke of. Demaratus coming from Corinth into Macedonia when Philip and his queen and son were at odds, after a gracious reception was asked by the king, "What good understanding there was among the Grecians?" He replied, "Aye, by all means, sir, it highly becomes your majesty to enquire about the concord betwixt the Athenians and Peloponnesians, when you suffer your own family to be the scene of so much discord and contention."

8069. DISCOVERIES, Accidental. Newton was wont to speak of himself as "a child gathering pebbles on the seashore," and if there was any mental endowment in which he excelled the generality of men it was that of patience in the examination of the facts and phenomena of his subjects. A fall of an apple was but an insignificant affair, and had been witnessed by thousands, without any recognition of the principle that governed its fall. But Newton in his twenty-third year, decided that the attraction of gravitation caused it to fall. It was during the plague in London, and he had retreated into the country. He was lying under an apple tree, and an apple fell; he reflected if the attraction of gravitation did that it must be the same principle that keeps the sun in the centre of the solar system, the planets in their orbits, as they revolve around him, and their satellites in their order around them. Galileo standing one day in the church at Pisa noticed the movements of a suspended lamp, which some accidental disturbance had caused to vibrate. The invention of the pendulum was the result, the principle of the most perfect measure of time extant. This occurred when Galileo was not yet twenty years of age. In later years he heard a report while residing in Venice that an instrument had been presented to Count Maurice of Nassau that would make distant objects appear near. This was enough for Galileo; he set himself to work, and soon found that by a certain arrangement

of spherical glasses he could produce the same effect. To him, therefore, are we indebted for the discovery of the telescope. Prince Rupert noticed one morning a soldier rubbing the rust off his gun-barrel, occasioned by the dew of the night before, and that it left on the surface of the steel minute holes resembling a dark engraving. The mezzotinto was thus suggested to him, and its invention the result of his experiments. The waving of a linen shirt before the fire suggested to Stephen Mongolfier the invention of the air-balloon.

8070. DISCOVERY, Joy of. Such was the joy of Pythagoras at the completion of a certain geometric diagram that he sacrificed an ox in gratitude to the gods. Hiero, king of Syracuse, ordered a massive crown of gold to be prepared to be offered to the gods, as a tribute for success in war. It was suspected that the goldsmith had used silver in its construction. Archimedes was called in, and required to test it without marring the crown. While studying the problem he went to his bath. As he immersed his body the water ran over, and suggested to him the solution of the king's question. Forgetting himself, he ran home naked as he was, crying, as he went, "Eureka! Eureka!" He fixed the relative weight of water, gold and silver, and therefrom determined the proportion of gold and silver in the crown.

8071. DISCRETION, Advantage of. There is no talent so useful towards rising in the world, or which puts men more out of the power of fortune, than that quality generally possessed by the dullest sort of men, and in common speech called "discretion,"—a species of lower prudence, by the assistance of which people of the meanest intellectuals pass through the world in great tranquillity, neither giving nor taking offence. For want of a reasonable infusion of this everything fails. Had Windham possessed discretion in debate, or Sheridan in conduct, they might have ruled their age. *Swift.*

8072. DISCUSSION, Advantage of. Unless a variety of opinions are laid before us, we have no opportunity of selection, but are bound of necessity to adopt the particular view which may have been brought forward. The purity of gold cannot be ascertained by a single specimen, but when we have carefully compared it with others, we are able to fix upon the finest ore.　　*Herodotus.*

8073. DISCUSSION, Rule for. It is an excellent rule to be observed in all disputes, that men should give soft words and hard arguments; that they should not so much strive to vex, as to convince an opponent. *Bp. Wilkins.*

8074. DISEASE, The Cause of. I tell you honestly what I think is the cause of the complicated maladies of the human race:—it is their gormandizing and stuffing, and stimulating their digestive organs to an excess, thereby producing nervous disorders and irritations. The state of their minds is another grand cause: —the fidgeting and discontenting themselves about what cannot be helped; passions of all kinds—malignant passions pressing upon the mind, disturb the cerebral action, and do much harm.   *Dr. Abernethy.*

8075. DISHEARTENERS, Guilt of. It is cheap and easy to destroy. There is not a joyful boy or innocent girl, buoyant with fine purposes of duty, in all the street full of eager and rosy faces, but a cynic can chill and dishearten with a single word. Despondency comes readily enough to the most sanguine people. The cynic has only to follow the hint with his bitter confirmation, and they go home with heavier step and premature age. They will themselves quickly enough give the hint he wants to the cold wretch. Which of them has not failed to please where they most wished to please? or blundered where they were most ambitious of success? found themselves awkward, or tedious, or incapable of study, thought, or heroism, and only hoped by good sense and fidelity to do what they could, and pass unblamed? And this wicked malefactor makes their little hope less with satire and scepticism, and slackens the springs of endeavor. Yes, this is easy; but to help the young soul, add energy, inspire hopes, and blow the coals into a useful flame; to redeem defeat by new thought, by firm action, that is not easy—that is the work of divine men.   *Emerson.*

8076. DISHONESTY, Greed of. So grasping is dishonesty that it is no respecter of persons; it will cheat friends as well as foes; and were it possible even God himself.   *Bancroft.*

8077. DISHONESTY, Penalty of. John Eyre, whose name is recorded in the annals of crime as possessing £30,000, and yet being sentenced to transportation for stealing eleven quires of writing-paper, had an uncle, a gentleman of considerable property, who made his will in favor of a clergyman, his intimate friend, and committed it, unknown to the rest of the family, to the custody of the divine. However, not long before his death, having altered his mind with regard to the disposal of his wealth, he made another will, in which he left the clergyman only £500, bequeathing the bulk of his large property to his nephew and heir-at-law, Mr. Eyre. Soon after the old gentleman's death, Mr. Eyre, rummaging over his drawers, found this last will, and perceiving the legacy of £500 in it for the clergyman, without any hesitation or scruple of conscience, he put it into the fire, and took possession of the whole effects, in consequence of his uncle being supposed to die intestate. The clergyman coming to town soon after, and inquiring into the circumstances of his old friend's death, asked if he had made a will before he died. On being answered by Mr. Eyre in the negative, the clergyman very coolly put his hand in his pocket and pulled out the former will, which had been committed to his care, in which Mr. Eyre, sen., had bequeathed him the whole of his fortune, amounting to several thousand pounds, excepting a legacy of £200 to his nephew.   *Percy.*

8078. DISHONESTY, Revelation of. There is a Mohammedan tradition, that every man who has cheated or defrauded another, will appear at the day of judgment with whatever he has fraudulently obtained attached to his neck. What a spectacle will that be!

8079. DISHONESTY, Reward of. A wolf had seized a sheep from a fold, and was carrying it home to his own den, when he met a lion, who straightway laid hold of the sheep and bore it away. The wolf standing at a distance, cried out, that it was a great shame, and that the lion had robbed him of his own. The lion laughed, and said, "I suppose, then, that it was your good friend, the shepherd, who gave it to you."   *Æsop*

8080. DISINTERESTEDNESS, Heathen. Coleridge somewhere relates a story to this effect:—Alexander, during his march into Africa, came to a people dwelling in peaceful huts, who neither knew war nor conquest, and gold being offered to him, he refused it, saying, that his sole object was to learn the manners and customs of the inhabitants. "Stay with us," said the chief, "as long as it pleaseth thee." During the interview with the African chief, two of his subjects brought a case before him for judgment. The dispute was this: the one had bought of the other a piece of ground, which after the purchase was found to contain a treasure, for which he felt bound to pay. The other refused to receive anything, stating that when he sold the ground he sold it with all the advantages apparent or concealed which it might be found to afford. Said the chief, looking at the one, "You have a son;" and to the other, "you have a daughter—let them be married, and the treasure be given to them as a dowry." Alexander was astonished. "And what," said the chief, "would have been the decision in your country?" "We should have dismissed the parties," said Alexander, "and seized the treasure for the king's use." "And does the sun shine on your country?" said the chief, "does the rain fall there? are there any cattle there which feed upon the herbs and grass?" "Certainly," said Alexander. "Ah," said the chief, "it is for these innocent cattle that the Great Being permits the sun to shine, the rain to fall, and the grass to grow in your country." *F. F. Trench.*

8081. DISINTERESTEDNESS, Luther's. Luther's poverty did not arise from wanting the means of acquiring riches, for few men have had it in their power more easily to obtain them. The Elector of Saxony offered him the produce of a mine at Sneberg; but he nobly refused it, "lest," said he, "I should tempt the devil, who is lord of these subterraneous treasures, to tempt me." The enemies of Luther were no strangers to his contempt for gold. A poor student once telling him of his poverty, he desired his wife to give him a sum of money; and when she informed him they had none left, he immediately seized a cup of some value, which accidentally stood within his reach, and, giving it to the poor man, bade him go and sell it, and keep the money to supply his wants. In one of his epistles Luther says: "I have received one hundred guilders from Taubereim, and Schartts has given me fifty; so that I begin to fear lest God should reward me in this life. But I will not be satisfied with it. What have I to do with so much money? I gave half of it to P. Priorious and made the man glad."

8082. DISOBEDIENCE, Correction of. Dean Swift, though a good master, was very rigid with his servants. The task of hiring them was always entrusted to his housekeeper, but the only two positive commands he had for them he generally delivered himself. These were, to shut the door whenever they came into, or went out of, a room. One of his maid-servants one day asked permission to go to her sister's wedding, at a place about ten miles distant. Swift not only consented, but lent her one of his own horses, and ordered his servant to ride before her. The girl, in the ardor of her joy for this favor, forgot to shut the door after her when she left the room. In about a quarter of an hour afterwards the Dean sent a servant after her, to order her immediate return. The poor girl complied, and entering his presence, begged to know in what she offended or what her master wished. "Only shut the door," said the Dean, "and then resume your journey."   *Percy.*

8083. DISOBEDIENCE, Filial. Dr. Adam Clarke, when a little boy, one day disobeyed his mother, and the disobedience was accompanied with some look or gesture that indicated an undervaluing of her authority. This was a high affront; she immediately took up the Bible, and opened on these words, Prov. 30: 17, which she read and commented on in a most solemn manner: "The eye that mocketh at his father, and despiseth to obey his mother, the ravens of the valley shall pick it out, and the young eagles shall eat it." The poor culprit was cut to the heart, believing the words had been sent immediately from heaven; he went out into the fields with a troubled spirit, and was musing on this terrible denunciation of Divine displeasure, when the hoarse croak of a raven sounded to his conscience an alarm more dreadful than the cry of fire at midnight. He looked up, and soon perceived this most ominous bird, and actually supposing it to be the raven of which the text spoke, coming to pick out his eyes, he clapped his hands on them, and with the utmost speed and trepidation ran towards the house, as fast as his alarm and perturbation would admit, that he might escape the impending vengeance.   *Ethridge.*

8084. DISOBEDIENCE, Overcome. I have a little nephew who took a Bible he saw lying on the table and threw it on the floor. His mother said to him, "Go and pick up uncle's Bible." He said he didn't want to. His mother said, "I didn't ask you whether you wanted to or not; go and pick it up." Then the little fellow said, "I won't." His mother said, "Why, Charlie, who taught you that naughty word?" when she found out that he not only knew what it meant, but he meant every word he said. The mother says, "Charlie, I never heard you talk so before. If you don't go and pick up uncle's Bible, I shall punish you." And the little fellow says, "I won't do it." She told him again if he didn't pick up the Bible she would punish him, and he would have to pick it up too. Then he said he couldn't. I suppose he thought he couldn't; he didn't want to. That is the trouble with men, they don't want to come. Christ says, "Ye will not come unto me that ye might have life." It is not because men can't come to God; it is because they won't. The little fellow looked at it as though he would like to do it, but he couldn't. At last he just got down on the floor and got both his arms around the book, and tried and said he couldn't. Now the mother says, "Charlie, do you pick up that book or I shall punish you, and you will have to pick it up too." I felt very much interested for I knew if she didn't break his will he would break her heart eventually. At last she broke that little fellow's will, and the minute his will was broken, he picked up that book just as easy as that.   *Moody.*

8085. DISOBLIGING, Punishment of the. A man who kept a horse and an ass was wont in his journeys to spare the horse, and put all the burden upon the ass's back. The ass, who had been some while ailing, besought the horse one day to relieve him of part of his load; "For, if," said he, "you would take a fair portion, I shall soon get well again; but if you refuse to help me, this weight will kill me." The horse, however, bade the ass get on, and not trouble him with his complaints. The ass jogged on in silence, but presently, overcome with the weight of his burden, dropped down dead, as he had foretold. Upon this, the master coming up, unloosed the load from the dead ass, and putting it upon the horse's back made him carry the ass's carcass in addition. "Alas, for my ill-nature!" said the horse; "by refusing to bear my just portion of the load, I have now to carry the whole of it, with a dead weight into the bargain."   *Æsop.*

8086. DISPATCH, Kinds of. False dispatch is one of the most dangerous things to business that can be. It is like that which the physicians call pre-digestion, or hasty digestion, which is sure to fill the body full of crudities, and secret seeds of diseases. I knew a wise man had it for a by-word, "Stay a little, that we may make an end the sooner." On the other side, true dispatch is a rich thing; for time is the measure of business, as money is of wares; and business is bought at a dear hand when there is small dispatch.   *Bacon.*

8087. DISPOSITION, Amiable. A tender-hearted and compassionate disposition, which inclines men to pity and feel the misfortunes of others, and which is, even for its own sake, incapable of involving any man in ruin and misery, is of all tempers of mind the most amiable; and though it seldom receives much honor, is worthy of the highest.   *Fielding.*

8088. DISPOSITION, Good. A good disposition is more valuable than gold; for the latter is the gift of fortune, but the former is the dower of nature.   *Addison.*

8089. DISPOSITION, Unhappy. Philagrus, a Silician, a sophist, and a scholar of Sollianus, was of a very passionate temper, so much so that he gave one of his scholars a blow upon the face when he was asleep. When asked why he did not marry, he replied, "Because I am never pleased; no, not with myself."

8090. DISPOSITION, Varieties of. It is observed, that gold is both the fairest and the most solid of all metals, yet it.is the soonest melted with the fire; others, as they are coarser, so more churlish, and hard to be wrought on by a dissolution. Thus a sound and good heart is easily melted into fear and sorrow for sin, by the sense of God's judgments, whereas the carnal mind is stubborn and remorseless. All metals are but earth, yet some are of a finer quality than others; all hearts are but flesh, yet some are, through the power of grace, more capable of spiritual apprehensions than others. *Bp. Hall.*

8091. DISPUTATION, Patience in. My spirit felt composed after the dispute with a mocking moonshee, by simply looking to God, as one who had engaged to support his own cause; and I saw it to be my part to pursue my way through the wilderness of this world, looking only to that redemption which daily draweth nigh. The same thoughts continued through the evening. I reflected, while looking at the stream gliding by, the smooth current of which showed its motion only by the moon shining upon it, that all are alike carried down the stream of time, that in a few years there will be another race of Hindoos, Mussulmans, and English in this country, and we are now but just speaking to each other as we are passing along. How should this consideration quell the tumult of anger and impatience when I cannot convince men? Oh how feeble an instrument must a creature so short-sighted be! How necessary is it that God should be continually raising up instruments; and how easily can he do it; "the government is upon his shoulder," Jesus is able to bear the weight of it; we need not be oppressed with care and fear. *Henry Martyn.*

8092. DISPUTATION, Self-control in. Great care must be taken lest your debates break in upon your passions and awaken them to take part in the controversy. When the opponent pushes hard, and gives just and mortal wounds to our own opinion, our passions are very apt to feel the strokes, and to rise in resentment and defence. Self is so mingled with the sentiments which we have chosen, and has such a tender feeling of all the opposition which is made to them, that personal brawls are very ready to come in as seconds to succeed and finish the dispute of opinions. Then noise, and clamor, and folly appear in all their shapes, and chase reason and truth out of sight. *Dr. Watts.*

8093. DISPUTATIOUSNESS, Youthful. I never object to a certain degree of disputatiousness in a young man, from the age of seventeen to that of four or five and twenty, providing I find him always arguing on one side of the question. *Coleridge.*

8094. DISPUTES, Ecclesiastical. A gentleman, in company with Mr. John Newton, of London, lamented the violent disputes that often take place among Christians respecting the non-essentials of Christianity, and particularly church government. "Many," he said, "seem to give their chief attention to such topics, and take more pleasure in talking on these disputable points than on spiritual religion, the love of Christ, and the privileges of his people." "Sir," said the venerable old man, "did you ever see a whale-ship? I am told that when the fish is struck with the harpoon, and feels the smart of the wound, it sometimes makes for the boat, and would probably dash it to pieces. To prevent this, they throw a cask overboard; and when it is staved to pieces, they throw over another. Now, sir," added Mr. Newton, "church government is the tub which Satan has thrown over to the people of whom you speak."

8095. DISPUTES, Settlement of. In the Canton of Schwyz, a man named Frantz went one evening to Gaspard, who was working in his field, and said to him, "Friend, it is now mowing time; we have a difference about a meadow, you know, and I have got the judges to meet at Schwyz to determine the cause, since we cannot do it for ourselves; so you must come with me before them to-morrow." "You see, Frantz," replied Gaspard, "that I have mown all this field; I must get in this hay to-morrow; I cannot possibly leave it." "And," rejoined Frantz, "I cannot send away the judges now; they have fixed the day, and, besides, one ought to know whom the field belongs to before it is mown." They disputed the matter some time; at length Gaspard said to Frantz, "I will tell you how it shall be: go to-morrow to Schwyz, tell the judges both your reasons and mine, and then there will be no need for me to go." "Well," said the other, "if you choose to trust your cause to me, I will manage it as if it were my own." Matters thus settled, Frantz went to Schwyz, and pleaded before the judges his own and Gaspard's cause as well as he could. When the decision was given, Frantz reported it. "Gaspard," said he, "the field is yours. I congratulate you, neighbor. The judges have decided in your favor, and I am glad the affair is finished." They were firm friends ever after. *Percy.*

8096. DISSATISFACTION, Cause of. A little girl was one day working at her worsted. A stranger came into the parlor, and as he looked at her, said, with an apparent sneer: "My dear, what is that you are doing? I see nothing but tangled webs and confused knots." She looked up archly into his face, and replied, "You are looking on the wrong side;" and she turned it over, and there it was, a beautiful figure. Oh! my friends, how confused we are, just looking on the wrong side! *H. B. Ridgeway.*

8097. DISSATISFACTION, Confession of. Of all the multiplied men who lived in me, to a certain degree—the man of sentiment, the man of poetry, the man of oratory—nothing remains in me but the literary man. The literary man himself is far from being happy. Years do not yet bear me down. I bear more heavily the weight of my heart than the weight of my years. These years, like Macbeth's phantoms, pass their hands over my shoulder, and point out to me, not crowns, but a sepulchre: would to God I was now asleep in it! I have nothing in me wherewith to smile to the future of the past. I am growing old, without children, in my desolate house, surrounded by the tombs of all those I loved. All that remains to me of life is concentrated in a few hearts and in a modest inheritance. And even these hearts suffer because of me, and I am not sure that I shall not be dispossessed of that inheritance to-morrow, and go and die upon some stranger's road, as Dante says. The hearth on which my father placed his feet, and where I now place mine, is a borrowed hearth, which may be torn up at any hour; it may be sold and resold at any caprice of the auctioneer; and so may my mother's bed; so may the dog which licks my hand in pity when he sees my brow in agony as I look at him. The children of the Samians insulted Homer, because, they said, Homer obstructed the highways of the islands by singing poetry before the houses. I am not Homer; but my critics are more severe than the Samians. Upon these pages where they reproach me for heaping piles of vanity, it is not ink you read; no, believe me, it is not; but the sweat of my brow. It is not my name I seek to magnify, but the pledge of those who have no estate and no existence save that name. My name!—oh, I know as well as you do what that name is worth, and what will be its fate! I would with all my heart (God is my witness) that name had never been uttered. I would give all that may yet remain to me of life, if it were entirely buried, with him who bears it, in the silence of the tomb—noiselessly borne to the graveyard there, forgotten here. Life to me now is nothing worth. What have I now, I pray, to regret in life? Have not I seen all my thoughts perish before me? Do I design again to sing in life, with an extinguished voice, strophes which would end in sobs? Have I taste for returning into those political struggles which, were they even opened again, would no longer recognize my posthumous accents? Have I any firm hope in those forms of government which the people abandon with as much fickleness as they adopted them? Am I so insane as to believe that I shall cast, or that I shall sculpture—I alone—in bronze or marble, a colossal statue of the human race, when God has given wherewith to do so but sand and clay to the greatest of sculptors? Of what use is life when one can contemplate nothing but the ruins of those things which are recorded in his mind! Happy the men who die at their work, struck down by the revolutions in which they were engaged. Death is their punishment—aye, but it is their refuge! *M. de Lamartine.*

8098. DISSATISFACTION, Cured. A poor lame boy was converted, whose home surroundings were very unfriendly. He said, when relating his experience, "Once everything went wrong at our house; father was wrong, and mother was wrong, and sister was wrong; but now that Jesus is mine, it is all right, and I know why everything went wrong before; I was all wrong myself."

8099. DISSATISFACTION, Example of. "All these things are against me." Mrs. Wear always said that Jacob had taken the word out of her mouth. Why the affliction came to her house she never could fully understand; and why the minister should have preached from "Curse ye Meroz," when he knew that she was in a weak, nervous state, and would have preferred "Jesus wept," was a mystery greatly to the disadvantage of Providence; and why the postman should always begin to give out letters at the other end of the row was just a bit of spite on his part, and nothing better could be expected of such vermin. When the doctor told Mrs. Wear that he could do nothing more for her, she said she had always wondered what doctors were for. Her end was peace—to her family. *Dr. Joseph Parker.*

8100. DISSATISFACTION, Influence of. The traveler who comes to a country whose inhabitants are inhospitable, where the food is bad and difficult to be obtained, where the climate is unhealthy, where he encounters dangers from wild beasts, obnoxious serpents and irritating insects, will not delay his journey, but hasten on to a better country. Men in this world are travelers in such a country. They should hasten towards the land of "milk and honey," counting themselves "strangers and pilgrims" till they shall gain Heaven.

8101. DISSATISFACTION, Rebuke of. If you entered the workshop of a blacksmith, you would not dare to find fault with his bellows, anvils, and hammers. If you had not the skill of a workman, but the consideration of a man, what would you say? "It is not without cause the bellows are placed here; the artificer knew, though I do not know, the reason." You would not dare to find fault with the blacksmith in his shop, and do you dare to find fault with God in the world? *St. Bernard.*

8102. DISSATISFACTION, Wail of. Theodore Parker, the self-appointed reformer of Protestanism, did not attain the success which he expected, and relieves himself by writing in his journal, "Boston is the metropolis of snobs." "To me it seems as if my life was a failure. 1. Domestically. 'Tis mainly so: for I have no children. 2. Socially. It is completely a failure. Here I am as much an outcast from society as if I were a convicted pirate. I mean from all that calls itself 'decent society,' respectable society, in Boston. 3. Professionally. I stand all alone, not a minister with me. I see no young men rising up to take ground with me or in advance of me. I think that with a solitary exception, my professional influence has not been felt in a single young minister's soul." It seems not to have occurred to him that there was any other cause for his failure than the soil and the climate. He had forgotten the motto on Luther's monument.

8103. DISSIPATION, Study and. It is the commonly received notion that hard study is the unhealthy element of a college life; but from the tables of Harvard University, collected by Prof. Pierce from the last triennial catalogue, it is clearly demonstrated that the excess of death for the first ten years after graduation is found in that portion of each class of inferior scholarship. Every one who has seen the curriculum knows that where Æschylus and political economy injure one, late hours and rumpunches use up a dozen, and that their two little fingers are heavier than the loins of Euclid. Dissipation is a sure destroyer, and every young man who follows it is as the early flower exposed to untimely frost. Those who have been inveigled in the path of vice are named Legion. A few hours' sleep each night, high living, and plenty of "smashes," make war upon every function of the body—the brain, the heart, the lungs, the liver, the spine, the limbs, the bones, the flesh, every part and faculty overtasked and weakened by the terrific energy of passion loosened from restraint, until, like a dilapidated mansion, the "earthly house of this tabernacle" falls into ruinous decay. *Scientific American.*

8104. DISSIPATION, Tyranny of. I expect absolutely nothing of the man upon whom I see marks of dissipation. Five years ago I remember to have made the acquaintance of a young man who had a pew in my church, and after I had known him a little while I used to wish I could say something, but I hardly knew how. He was distant. His breath was not the most repelling thing to me. You know how it comes; you have seen it; a little fullness—getting a little full around the face, and a little full in the eyes; then a reddish appearance; then a florid aspect; then he passes from the reddish appearance into the florid, and from the florid into the purple—we have seen men who are purple. This young man is there now; he is in the purple stage. The next stage is—death! The enemy has got the mastery of him. I never knew the man to whip. A great many have attacked this enemy in the firm conviction that "I have seen him slay others, but I will be his master." Oh, how many are conquered! I know them and mark them. I see such young men almost every week, and converse with them about this matter of liquor-drinking, and nine times out of ten they think they are safe. I point out men, who twenty, fifteen or ten years ago, were moderate drinkers; but now liquor drinking has become their master. And you say, "I should think men would have more respect for themselves." So should I. But I simply prophesy, that if the habit is continued it will beat you; it always has. That is its business. You are doing a thousand other things; but liquor has just one purpose; it is always on the guard; it slumbers not, and sleeps not. It is like the coming of the snow-flake, or the pointing of the sculptor's chisel; it grows and multiplies, and multiplies and grows. It is like sleep coming upon a man; a man never knows just the moment when he goes to sleep; and a man never knows just the day when liquor is his master. After a while he comes to acknowledge, like the miser, "I am a slave."

Robert Laird Collier.

8105. DISTANCE, Effects of. As some travelers were making their way along the seashore, they came to a high cliff, and, looking out upon the sea, saw a faggot floating at a distance, which they thought at first must be a large ship; so they waited, expecting to see it come into harbor. As the faggot drifted nearer to the shore, they thought it no longer to be a ship, but a boat. But when it was at length thrown on the beach, they saw that it was nothing but a faggot after all. Dangers seem greatest at a distance; and coming events are magnified according to the interest or inclination of the beholder. *Æsop.*

8106. DISTINCTION, Danger of. The mice and the weasels had long been at war with each other, and the mice being always worsted in battle, at length agreed at a meeting, solemnly called for the occasion, that their defeat was attributable to nothing but their want of discipline, and they determined accordingly to elect regular commanders for the time to come. So they chose those whose valor and prowess most recommended them to the important post. The new commanders, proud of their position, and desirous of being as conspicuous as possible, bound horns upon their foreheads as a sort of crest and mark of distinction. Not long after a battle ensued. The mice, as before, were soon put to flight; the common herd escaped into their holes; but the commanders, not being able to get in from the length of their horns, were every one caught and devoured. *Æsop.*

8107. DISTRUST, Rebuke of. A correspondent of the New York *Evangelist* says: "Last year, coming from Pittsburgh east in a sleeping-car, my apartment was next to that occupied by a gentleman, his wife, and their little daughter, perhaps four years old, The lady was excessively timid—terribly nervous. The Horseshoe Curve seemed to be her especial terror, and my sleep, and I presume that of others, was disturbed by her talking to her husband of the peril. The engineer might be asleep, or the switch tender might be asleep, and then the train would certainly be plunged down the abyss. But it was worth while to be awake, when I heard the sweet rebuke, not intended, but real, of the little one: 'Ma, God takes care of us, and does God sleep?' Was not this the ordaining strength out of the mouth of babes? Happy for the mother if it proved strength to her faith!"

8108. DIVINE LOVE, Permanence of. There is nothing in the world so real and substantial as the love of God. One act of divine love is a more finished thing than a statue of Phidias or Praxiteles. It is more firm than the foundations of the Alps. It is more enduring than the round world which God hath made so strong. All things are bubbles to it. They have nothing in them. They mean little. They soon pass away. An act of love is a complete work, and has greater power and greater consequences than any other act. The mere act of dying is not equal to it. And yet this act of love can be made by a mental glance, quick as lightning, and piercing heaven. Such acts can be multiplied at will beyond our power of reckoning, and in the midst of apparently the most distracting occupations. So far from being weakened by repetition, they only grow more intense and more powerful. Yet they require no effort. To elicit them is even a pleasure to us. But when we put these facts alongside of our practice, it looks as if there must be a fallacy somewhere. All this can hardly be true, and yet we remain as we are. How incredible is the hardness of our own hearts! It is a fair match for the excess of God's love. Oh welcome then that beautiful spirit of reparation to the majesty of God, which so many of the saints have had! It is like making sweet honey out of bitter flowers. The little love we have for God thus, by this dear right of reparation, furnishes us with another means of loving him still more. Who will say that all things are not contrived for love?   *F. W. Faber.*

8109. DIVINE UNION, Blessedness of. Each moment of time is one of the successive and separate letters of the alphabet, which go to make up the great book of eternity. And eternity being the sum of all moments, and therefore the residence or locality of God in the higher sense, we are thus learning the letters of that book in which will be written out all truths and destinies for ourselves. To lose a moment by being out of harmony with the facts and requisitions of the moment is to lose a letter out of the great book, and thus to lose something of its infinite and eternal meanings. It was thus that God taught me while I was in the spiritual wilderness. I was thus enabled to see, and perhaps more clearly than others will be likely to do who have not passed through the same inward history, why he shut the old gateways and vistas of spiritual knowledge, which were suited to the beginnings of inward experience, and required me to meet with him and to dwell with him in the Eternal Now. It was one of the lessons of the desert; but the desert, I mean the spiritual desert, is one of the school-houses of the soul. And as soon as I had learned the lesson, which it seems to have been the object of the school of the desert to teach, the cloud was gradually lifted; the sunshine came down upon the rocks, the sands and pebbles grew up into flowers. I found the shepherd sitting beside the still waters, and I came up out of the entanglements of the wilderness into a firmer position and a clearer light than I had ever known before.
Dr. Thos. C. Upham.

8110. DIVINITY OF CHRIST, Argument for the. The following words of Napoleon were addressed to one of his generals, who appeared to consider Christ merely in the light of a great genius: "The triumph of love is, without dispute, the greatest of the miracles of Christ. He, and he only, has succeeded in raising the heart of man above visible things, even to the sacrifice of time; he alone, by establishing such an immolation, has established a link between heaven and earth. All those who sincerely believe in him experience this admirable, supernatural, all-powerful love, which is an inexplicable phenomenon, and cannot be attained by the reason and strength of man; it is a sacred fire which has been given to earth by this new Prometheus, and of which time, that great destroyer of all things, can neither waste the strength nor limit the duration. I, Napoleon, admire this fact more than any other, because I have often reflected upon it, and it affords me complete proof of the divinity of Christ! I have fascinated multitudes who would have died for me. God forbid that I should form any comparison between the enthusiasm of my soldiers and Christian charity, which are as different from one another as their causes! But, in fine, it was by my presence, by the electricity of my glance, by one single word, that I lighted the sacred fire in all hearts. Certainly I possess the secret of that magic power which carries the mind of man along with it: but I could not communicate it to any one; not one of my generals has received or imbibed it from me; neither have I the secret of causing my name and my love forever to remain enshrined in the heart of man, and of working wonders therein, unassisted by matter. Now that I am at St. Helena, now that I am fastened down alone upon this rock, who fights my battles and conquers empires for me? Where are the courtiers of my misfortunes? Do men think of me? Who exerts himself for me in Europe? Who has remained faithful to my cause? Where are my friends? Yes, two or three, immortalized by their fidelity, partake and console my exile! Such is the fate of great men! such is the fate of Cæsar and Alexander; and then we are forgotten! and the name of a conqueror, as well as that of an emperor, is nothing more than the subject of a college theme! Our exploits are at the mercy of any pedant who chooses to praise or insult us! How many and various judgments are passed on the great Louis XIV.! Scarcely was he dead when the great king himself was left alone in the solitude of his bed room at Versailles, neglected by his courtiers and perhaps their laughing-stock! He was no longer their master, but a corpse, the tenant of a coffin and a grave, and an object of horror from the fear of that decomposition which had already begun! Such is the approaching fate of the great Napoleon! What an abyss is there between the depths of my misery and the eternal reign of Christ, who is preached, praised, loved, adored, and living throughout the universe! Can that be called death? Is it not rather life? Behold the death of Christ! behold the death of a God!"

8111. DIVINITY OF CHRIST, Proof of the. When Ulysses returned with fond anticipations to his home in Ithaca, his family did not recognize him. Even the wife of his bosom denied her husband, so changed was he by an absence of twenty years, and the hardships of a long protracted war. It was thus true of the vexed and astonished Greek, as of a nobler king, that he came unto his own, and his own received him not. In this painful position of affairs he called for a bow which he had left at home, when, embarking for the siege of Troy, he bade farewell to the orange groves and vine-clad hills of Ithaca. With characteristic sagacity, he saw how a bow so stout and tough that none but himself could draw it might be made to bear witness on his behalf. He seized it. To their surprise and joy, like a green wand lopped from a willow tree, it yields to his arms; it bends, till the bow-string touches his ear. The wife, now sure that he is her long lost and long lamented husband, throws herself into his fond embraces, and his household confess him the true Ulysses. If I may compare small things with great, our Lord gave such proof of his divinity when he, too, stood a stranger in his own home, despised and rejected of men, a man of sorrows, and acquainted with grief. He bent the stubborn laws of nature to his will, and proved himself Creator by his mastery over creation. *Dr. Guthrie.*

8112. DIVISIONS, Danger of. Three bulls fed in a field together in the greatest peace and amity. A lion had long watched them in the hope of making prize of them, but found that there was little chance for him so long as they kept all together. He therefore began secretly to spread evil and slanderous reports of one against the other, till he had fomented a jealousy and distrust amongst them. No sooner did the lion see that they avoided one another, and fed each by himself apart, than he fell upon them singly, and so made an easy prey of them all. *Æsop.*

8113. DIVISIONS, Unity and. The narrow-minded and cold-hearted bigot, not content to find in the church substantial agreement amidst circumstantial variety, would reduce all to one single point of his own vision; and thus the faith of the Gospel vanishes under this rude and violent process. In matters connected with religion there may be difference without opposition, variety without discord, shades of difference without real diversity of sentiment. It could never be intended that the people of God should all hold the same opinions; if so, how could the apostle Paul say in reference to minor points of belief, "Let every man be fully persuaded in his own mind." *Godkin.*

8114. DIVORCE, Prevention of. Milton had not lived long with his first wife before a difference arose, which ended in a separation; the lady returned to the house of her father, and Milton published his work on the doctrine and discipline of divorces, with the intention, it is said, of marrying another wife. At the house of a friend his wife appeared suddenly before him, threw herself upon her knees and begged his pardon. Reconciliation followed, and the happiness of their after married life was uninterrupted. Their reconciliation, it is said, suggested Eve's address to Adam in "Paradise Lost."

" He from her turn'd : but Eve,
Not so repuls'd, with tears that ceas'd not flow-
ing.
And tresses all disorder'd, at his feet
Fell humble; and embracing them besought
His peace, and thus proceeded in her plaint:
'Forsake me not thus, Adam! witness heav'n
What love sincere, and reverence in my heart,
I bear thee, and unweeting have offended
Unhappily deceiv'd! Thy suppliant
I beg, and clasp thy knees: bereave me not
(Whereon I live!) thy gentle looks, thy aid,
Thy counsel, in this uttermost distress,
My only strength and stay! Forlorn of thee,
Whither shall I betake me—where subsist ?
While yet we live (scarce one short hour per-
haps),
Between us two let there be peace.' "

8115. DOCTRINE Doctored. "Babbage's Economy of Manufactures," says that "some years since, a mode of preparing old clover and trefoil seeds, by a process called 'doctoring,' became so prevalent as to attract the attention of the House of Commons. By this process old and worthless seed was rendered in appearance equal to the best. One witness tried some doctored seed, and found that not above one grain in a hundred grew." Crude notions, dogmatically propounded by beardless youths, is the doctored seed of our day. The harvest can only be thistles and tares, material for the flames.

8116. DOCTRINE, False. They which have been patrons of it before, should do like the father and mother of an idolater; that is, lay the first hand upon him to shorten his life.
Henry Smith.

8117. DOCTRINE, Heathen View of. A chief of the Bechuanas, after having listened to the Gospel from Rev. R. Moffat, calling thirty of his men about him, he addressed them, pointing to him, "There is Ra-Mary (Mr. Moffat) who tells me that the heavens were made, the earth also, by a beginner whom he calls Morimo. Have you ever heard anything to be compared with this? He says that the sun rises and sets by the power of Morimo; as also that Morimo causes winter to follow summer, the winds to blow, the rain to fall, the grass to grow, and the trees to bud;" and, casting his arm above and around him, added, "God works in everything you see and hear! Did you ever hear such words?" Seeing them ready to burst into laughter, he said, "Wait, I shall tell you more. Ra-Mary tells me that we have spirits in us which will never die; and that our bodies, though dead and buried, will rise and live again. Open your eyes to-day; did you ever hear fables like these?" This was followed by a burst of deafening laughter; and on its partially subsiding, the chief man begged him to say no more on such trifles, lest the people should think him mad.

8118. DOCTRINE, Importance of. When the peace and purity of our mind, the rectitude and happiness of our lives, and the blessedness of eternity, has so close and necessary a dependence upon the doctrines we imbibe, that we hereby either secure or forfeit them; who sees not, unless he be stupid and infatuated, that greater care and solicitude is necessary here, than in any matter whatever, because there is no other of equal moment? Bad money, or bad wares instead of good; an ill title or conveyance instead of a firm and clear one, may impoverish us: bad drugs instead of good may infect the body, and destroy the health: but what is all this to the dismal consequences of error and heresy, which impoverishes and infects the mind, perverts the life, and damns the man to all eternity? We must admit nothing hastily, assent to nothing without examining the grounds on which it stands. Credality, precipitation, and confidence are irreconcilable enemies to knowledge and wisdom. *Lucas.*

8119. DOCTRINE, Mixed. There is need of great caution in the trial and examination of doctrines. The devil sows his tares among the wheat. Errors, and these too, fatal and destructive ones, are frequently obtruded upon the world for the revelations of God; and every party, nay, every single author, lays the stress of salvation on their peculiar and distinguishing opinions. *Lucas.*

8120. DOCTRINE, Systems of. While the trees and flowers that clothe the fields of nature are thus dispersed over the wide surface of the earth, there are mountain regions lying within the tropics, where, in the course of a single day, the traveler finds every vegetable form peculiar to every line of latitude between the equator and the poles. These all laid out in regular arrangement. Leaving the palms which cover the mountain's feet, he ascends into the region of the olive; from thence he arises to a more temperate climate, where vines festoon the trees, or trail their limbs along the naked rock; still mounting, he reaches a belt of oaks and chestnuts; from that he passes to rugged heights, shaggy with the hardy pine; by and by, the trees are dwarfed into bushes; rising higher, his foot presses a soft carpet of lowly mosses; till, climbing the rocks where only lichens live, he leaves all life below; and now, shivering in the cold, panting in the thin air for breath, he stands on those dreary elevations where eternal winter sits on a throne of snow, and, waving her icy sceptre, says to vegetation, "Hitherto shalt thou come, but no further." Like some such lofty mountain of the tropics, there are portions of the divine word, where, in a space also of limited extent, within the short compass of a chapter, or even part of it, the more prominent doctrines of salvation are brought into juxtaposition, and arranged side by side, almost in systematic order. *Dr. Guthrie.*

8121. DOCTRINE, Unity of. Granite boulders lie scattered along through Vermont, New Hampshire, and out into the Atlantic ocean in a southeasterly direction. The geologist will look in vain for their native beds in the sections where they are found. Prof. Agassiz tells us that they came down from the north borne by the great ice waves of the glacier period. These stones are as mysterious as the various doctrines scattered through the Bible. We see them as men do the scattered boulders, but they are parts of one grand whole.

8122. DOGMATISM, Despotism of. Scientific knowledge, even in the most modest persons, has mingled with it a something which partakes of insolence. Absolute, peremptory facts are bullies, and those who keep company with them are apt to get a bullying habit of mind; not of manners, perhaps; they may be soft and smooth, but the smile they carry has a quiet assertion in it, such as the champion of the heavy weights, commonly the best natured, but not the most diffident of men, wears upon what he very inelegantly calls his "mug." Take the man for instance, who deals in the mathematical sciences. There is no elasticity in a mathematical fact; if you bring up against it, it never yields a hair's breadth, everything must go to pieces that comes in collision with it. What the mathematician knows, being absolute, unconditional, incapable of suffering question, it should tend, in the nature of things, to breed a despotic way of thinking. So of those who deal with the palpable and often unmistakable facts of external nature; only in a less degree. Every probability (and most of our common working beliefs are probabilities) is provided with buffers at both ends, which break the force of opposite opinions clashing against it; but scientific certainty has no spring in it, no courtesy, no possibility of yielding. All this must react on the minds that handle these forms of truth. *Holmes.*

8123. DOGMATISM, Spirit of. A dogmatical spirit inclines a man to be censorious of his neighbors. Every one of his opinions appears to him written, as it were, with sunbeams, and he grows angry that his neighbors do not see it in the same light. He is tempted to disdain his correspondents as men of low and dark understandings, because they do not believe what he does. *Watts.*

8124. DOGMATIST Defined. He who is certain, or presumes to say he knows, is, whether he be mistaken or in the right, a dogmatist. *Fleming.*

8125. DOING GOOD, Aim at. An English Lord congratulated Handel on the success of his new oratorio of the "Messiah," and thanked him for the entertainment he had furnished the people. Handel replied, "My lord, I should be sorry if I only entertained them; I wish to make them better." That preacher mistakes who does not in every sermon, prayer, conversation, visit, and all other work of his ministry aim to make people better. This will have a wider application, extending to all Christians.

8126. DOING GOOD, Effect of. I have read of one Pachomius, a soldier under Constantine the Emperor, how that his army being almost starved for want of necessary provision, he came to a city of Christians, and they of their own charity relieved them speedily and freely. He, wondering at their free and noble charity, inquired what kind of people they were whom he saw so bountiful. It was answered that they were Christians, whose profession it is to hurt no man, and do good to every man. Hereupon Pachomius, convinced of the excellence of this religion, threw away his arms and became a Christian, a saint. *Brooks.*

8127. DOING GOOD, Efforts at. For his way of living, if we are fallen into a generation wherein men will cry (*Sotah!*) "He is a fool" that practices it, as the rabbins foretell it will be in the generation wherein the Messiah comes; yet there will be a wiser generation, and "wisdom will be justified of her children." Among the Jews there has been an Ezra, whose head they called "the throne of wisdom;" among the Greeks there has been a Democritus, who was called "*Sophia*" in the abstract; the later ages knew a Gildas, who wore the surname of *Sapiens:* but it is the man whose temper and interest it is "to do good" that is the wise man after all. And, indeed, had a man the hands of a Briareus, they would all be too few to do good; he might find occasions to call for more than all of them. The English nation had once a sect of men called "*Bons hommes*," or "Good men." The ambition of this book is to revive and enlarge a sect that may claim that name; yea, to solicit that it may extend beyond the bounds of a sect, by the coming of all men into it. Of all the trees in the garden of God, which is there which envies not the palm-tree, out of which alone, as Plutarch informs us, the Babylonians derived more than three hundred commodities? or the cocoa-tree, so beneficial to man that a vessel may be built, and rigged, and freighted, and victualed, from that alone? To plant such trees of righteousness, and prune them, is the object of the book now before us. The men who devise good will now give me leave to remind them of a few things, by which they may be a little fortified for their grand intention; for, sirs, you are to pass between "*Bozeh*" (or dirty) and "*Seneh*" (or thorny), and encounter a host of things worse than Philistines, in your undertaking.

Cotton Mather's Essays.

8128. DOING GOOD, Example of. Dr. Cotton Mather, at the age of sixteen, adopted the maxim, "An opportunity to do good implies the positive duty to do it," and made it his rule in every relation of a long and well spent life. After he had attained to man's estate, he imposed on himself a rule never to enter any company where it was proper for him to speak without endeavoring to be useful in it; dropping, as opportunities might offer, some instructive hint or admonition. By way of improving every moment of his time, he avoided paying or receiving unnecessary visits. No day passed without some contrivance on his part "to do good," nor without his being able to say at the close of it, that some part of his income had been distributed for purposes of charity.

8129. DOING GOOD, Heathen Ideas of.

"I plough the spacious Berecynthian fields,
　Full six days' journey wide,

says one boastingly in the poet; the same man, if he were as much a lover of mankind as of husbandry, would much rather bestow his pains on such a farm, the fruits of which would serve a great number, than to be always dressing the olive-yard of some cynical malcontent, which,

when all was done, would scarce yield oil enough to dress a salad or to supply his lamp during the long winter evenings. Epicurus himself, who places happiness in the profoundest quiet and sluggish inactivity, as the only secure harbor from the storms of the troublesome world, could not but confess that it is both more noble and delightful to do than to receive a kindness; for there is nothing which produces so humane and genuine a sort of pleasure as that of doing good. He who gave the names to the three graces well understood this, for they all signify delectation and joy, and these surely are far greater and purer in him who does the good turn. This is so evidently true, that we all receive good turns blushing and in some confusion, but we are always gay and well pleased when we are conferring them. *Plutarch.*

8130. DOING GOOD, Influence of. The Christian commission treated Federal and Confederate soldiers alike. The effect upon the latter was remarkable. A delegate says, "As we have ministered to their wants and addressed words of kindness to them, tears have started from eyes unaccustomed to weeping. They fairly overwhelm us with their thankful expressions. 'This is what I call living Christianity,' one would say. 'This is the religion for me,' another would add. 'I can't stand this,' said a rough, hard-looking fellow, badly wounded in the foot, but able to hobble along on crutches, 'I can't stand this, boys; it overcomes me. I give in,' and as he came towards us his whole frame shook with emotion, and the big tears fell from his sunburnt face, tears which he awkwardly and vainly tried to hide from his comrades and us. 'You know,' he continued, 'I am no coward. I can face the enemy and not wink; but this kindness kills me; it breaks one all to pieces. I tell you, boys, this is no humbug. It's a big thing. It's the Gospel for body and soul—just what we all need.'"

8131. DOING GOOD, Power of. A Baptist lady, with a kind, Christian, motherly heart, talked familiarly with her Catholic servant-girl, telling what religion had done for her, and how happy it made her under life's burdens; and she showed by her sweet temper and kind spirit that she was all that she claimed. Bridget was affected, because she saw that that was just what she needed, but had not. She was sour, irritable, timid, and sometimes ugly; while her mistress was pleasant and patient under all circumstances, and never afraid to die. The good woman told the girl, too, how she obtained this grace, and where, and that every one might have it who would come to Jesus; that many Catholics had sought and found it, etc., which only deepened her impressions. At length she invited her to go to church, which she did, and sat with her in her fine-cushioned pew, like any other lady—not in a free seat in the gallery. This was repeated, and further appropriate conversations were had, until that girl accepted an invitation, went to the altar for prayers, and found the pearl of great price, to her unutterable joy.

The effect on her life was remarkable. The lady's husband, a venerable gentleman of the Unitarian persuasion, speaking to the writer of the case, soon after said he never saw such a change in a human being in his life, and that they had taken her from the kitchen and brought her to their table and fellowship as a daughter. *Dr. James Porter.*

8132. DOING GOOD, Prescription of. Lady Holland, a victim of ennui, complained that she did not know how to pass the time. The poet Rogers prescribed for her something new, viz: "To try to do a little good."

8133. DOING GOOD, Requirement of. The Gymnosophists were greatly opposed to idleness, and required of every pupil that he should tell of some good he had done or devised, every day before he was permitted to sit down to dinner.

8134. DOING GOOD, Result of. An accomplished and wealthy Christian lady of Richmond, Va., was out riding one day, when she came upon a well dressed young man who lay in the hot sun by the road side, dead drunk. The lady alighted, dipped her handkerchief in a stream near by, and spread it over his beautiful face, then returned to the city and reported his case to the police. Shortly afterward a stranger called upon the lady and said "I am ashamed to look you in the face. I am the man you so kindly cared for the other day. The name on the handkerchief with which you covered my face revealed my benefactress. I have come to thank you for your kindness. I have signed the pledge. With my hand on my mother's Bible, I have sworn, God being my helper, that I will never taste another drop of intoxicating liquor." He kept his pledge. His rescuer became his wife. His brilliant talents won for him a high place in the service of his country. This man was William Wirt.

8135. DOING WELL, Benefit of. The enterprising son of a widow sought work that he might help his mother. He could find employment in liquor-shops, but was too high-principled for that. At last he asked a prominent merchant, who sat reading his paper, the oft-repeated question, "Do you want a boy, sir?" The merchant looked at him, and said, "What can you do?" "I can do anything that will give me an honest living." "Well, take these boots down stairs and black them." In this he succeeded. The merchant said, "Why, my boy, you have done those very well." "Mother told me always to do well whatever I did." His engagement with the merchant was consummated. He became an honorable man, successful merchant, and bank president. The key to his success was "doing well," whether blacking boots or managing finance.

8136. DOOMSDAY, Every Day. One of the illusions is that the present hour is not the critical, decisive hour. Write it on your heart that every day is the best day in the year. No man has learned anything rightly until he knows that every day is Doomsday. *Emerson.*

8137. DOOR, Closed. In a town in the north of Scotland some boys were in the habit of meeting together for prayer. A little girl was passing, and heard them sing. She stopped to listen, and thinking it was just an ordinary prayer-meeting, she felt anxious to get in. Putting up her hand, she pulled the latch, but it would not open; it was fastened inside. She became very uneasy, and the thought arose in her mind, "What, if this were the door of heaven, and me outside?" She went home, but could not sleep. Day after day she became more troubled at the thought of being shut out of heaven. She went from one prayer-meeting to another, still finding no rest. At length, one day reading the tenth chapter of John, she came to the words, "I am the door." She paused, and read the verse again and again. Here was the very door she was seeking. She entered in and found peace.

8138. DOOR, Knock at the. Not many sounds in life (and I include all urban and all rural sounds) exceed in interest a knock at the door. It "gives a very echo to the throne where hope is seated." But its issues seldom answer to this oracle within;—it is so seldom that just the person we want to see comes. *Lamb.*

8139. DOOR, The Other. Mr. Whitefield was preaching on the text "And the door was shut." Two young men full of hilarity and glee remarked to one another, "What if one door be shut? another will open." Whitefield had not proceeded far in his discourse when he said, "It is possible there may be some careless, trifling persons here to-day who may ward off the force of this impressive subject by lightly thinking, 'What if the door be shut? another will open.' This repetition of their remark by the preacher came upon them like a sudden flash of lightning. It put an effectual stop to their trifling. The young men were sorely troubled under his pointed appeals. Whitefield went on to say with the utmost solemnity, "Yes, another door will open, and I will tell you what door it will be: it will be the door of the bottomless pit! the door of hell! the door that conceals from the eyes of angels the horrors of damnation!"

8140. DOOR, Sermon about the. A little boy is said to have preached the following on the text "I am the door:" "The first word is 'I.' That has only one letter in it. This means the Lord Jesus, the good Saviour, who loves little children. The second word is 'am.' That has two letters in it. When Jesus says 'I am the door,' of course he doesn't mean that he is a door like that you shut just now; but this little sermon is to show you how he is like a door. The third word is 'the,' which has three letters. Jesus says *the* door, because there is only one door into the kingdom of heaven. The fourth word is 'door,' which has four letters in it. A door lets people into the house; and if there was no door they could not get in. So the Lord Jesus lets his people into the kingdom of heaven; and if it was not for him they could not get in at all. A door keeps out the rain, and the dogs, and the thieves; and so Jesus keeps away all evil and hurtful things out of his beautiful heaven. Now when you want to go into a house, you go straight to the door; and so if we want to go into the kingdom of heaven, we must go to Jesus, and ask him to let us in."

8141. DOUBLE-MINDEDNESS, Biblical. Is LIKE a man with a *double heart*, Ps. 12:2 ("a heart and a heart," marg.—with truth on the surface and deception underneath); 1 Chron. 12:33 compared with ver. 38, men "of double heart" contrasted with "perfect" and "one" (united) heart. "Ungodly professors," says Cocceius, "have two hearts, two lords, two ways, two ends." But of the godly man it is said, "his heart is fixed," Ps. 112:1; yea, David says it twice, "My heart is fixed, O God, my heart is fixed," Ps. 57:7; see Hosea 10:2. Is LIKE "a *cake not turned*"—half baked, half dough, Hosea 7:8; as Israel mixed idolatry with the worship of God. Is LIKE a *speckled bird*, Jer. 12:9. Is LIKE a *kingdom, city, or house divided against itself*, that cannot stand, Matt. 12:25. ILLUSTRATIVE TEXTS. Lev. 19:19. "The original prohibition of mingling divers things may not inaptly be regarded, as implying a command of 'simplicity and godly sincerity' in all things. It may fairly be accommodated to the case of those who endeavor to reconcile the service of God and mammon, or the pleasures of the world with those of religion; to unite works and grace in the matter of justification, and to many other heterogeneous and unnatural commixtures."—*Scott.*— 1 Kings 18:21.—"How long halt ye between two opinions?" The idea is taken from a bird hopping recklessly about from bough to bough, not knowing on which to settle (*Dr. A. Clarke*); or, according to others, from the unequal walk of a lame person.—(*Scott.*) Ps. 119:113.—"I hate vain thoughts." The word "vain" is not in the original, and the meaning might be expressed, "I hate *other* thoughts—thoughts which are at variance with the one law I follow." Prov. 28:18.—"He that is perverse in his ways shall fall at once." The Hebrew word for "ways," is in the dual form, and means, properly, *in two ways.* "He that endeavors to preserve himelf by fraud and deceit, though he can wind and turn, and hath several shifts he thinks to save himself by, yet in one or other of them he shall perish."—*Bishop Patrick.*——Jer. 3: 10.—"And yet for all this her treacherous sister Judah hath not turned unto me with her whole heart, but feignedly, saith the Lord." Like Jehu, who "took no heed to walk in the law of the Lord his God with all his heart, for (he, too, was treacherous) he departed not from the sins of Jeroboam, who made Israel to sin," 2 Kings 10:31; or, like Amaziah, "who did that which was right in the sight of the Lord, but not with a perfect heart," 2 Chron. 25:2. Matt. 6:24.—"No man can serve two masters." True, a servant may follow two masters while they walk together, and strangers cannot judge which of the two he is engaged to serve; but if their roads part, it is then seen to which of the two he belongs.

                                 Bowes.

8142. DOUBLE-MINDEDNESS, Parable of. A ship's

crew rose in mutiny against the captain soon after they had lost sight of home. Then they said, "Who shall steer us safe to some foreign land?" So they appointed as pilot one of the mutineers, who said he knew the way. But the crew were divided among themselves; some thought the captain knew the way, others believed in the new pilot. At one time the captain's side got the upper hand, and then they used to unbind the captain and set him at the helm; then presently the other side would prevail, and they would push away the captain and put the mutineer in the captain's place. The consequence was that the vessel used to sail at one time in one way and at another time in quite the opposite way, so that they made no progress at all. At last, one evening as the sun was setting, one of the oldest and most experienced sailors said, "Look yonder; there is the Black Rock, on which hundreds of fine ships have been wrecked, and we are drifting toward it. Night is coming on, and the current is taking us fast to the rock. This comes of having more than one pilot."   *Arnot.*

8143. DOUBT, Biblical. Matt. 14: 31.— "Wherefore didst thou doubt?" ἐδίστασας.— "a figurative word, taken either from a person standing where two ways meet, not knowing which to choose; or from the tremulous motion of a balance when the weights on each side are nearly equal."—(*Parkhurst.*) The same word occurs Matt. 28. 17. Acts 10: 20; Rom. 4:20; James 1:6. Three texts, where the same Greek word is rendered by three different English words:—doubting—staggering—wavering. Luke 12: 29.—"Be not of doubtful mind." Or, as in the margin, "Live not in careful suspense." A figure derived from "floating in the air." (*Robinson.*) Or, as others take it, from a ship tossed in a storm upon the rising and falling waves, in continued unrest and perturbation.   *Bowes.*

8144. DOUBTING, Pains of. David Hume, after witnessing in the family of the venerable La Roche those consolations which the gospel only can impart, confessed with a sigh that "there were moments when, amidst all the pleasures of philosophical discovery, and the pride of literary fame, he wished that he had never doubted."

8145. DOUBTS, Preach Not. Do not preach your doubts. You are sure of enough in the book to preach about for a life-time. When you preach personal experience you come to Christ's formula, "Verily, verily, *I* say unto you." When you preach doubts or hearsay it is not "I," but somebody else, that preaches, and so is not evidence that is accepted by the court of the judgment. If you have only doubts, quit preaching. Only convictions generate convictions.   *Dr. Fowler.*

8146. DOUBTS, Ridicule of. A woman of the doubting kind went to her pastor and said, "Oh, I am dead, dead, twice dead, and plucked up by the root." He replied, "Sitting in my study the other day, I heard a sudden scream, 'John's in the well! John's fallen into the well!' Before I could reach the spot I heard the sad cry, 'John's dead—poor little Johnny's dead.' Leaning over the curb, I called out, 'John, are you dead?' 'Yes, grandfather, I'm dead,' replied John." The preacher remarked, "I was glad to hear it from his own mouth." Dead men do not report themselves.

8147. DOVES, Flight of. In the environs of the city, to the westward, near the Zainderood, are many pigeon-houses, erected at a distance from habitations, for the sole purpose of collecting pigeons' dung for manure. They are large round towers, rather broader at the bottom than the top, and crowned by conical spiracles, through which the pigeons descend. Their interior resembles a honey-comb, pierced with a thousand holes, each of which forms a snug retreat for a nest. More care appears to have been bestowed upon their outside than upon that of the generality of the dwelling-houses, for they are painted and ornamented. The extraordinary flights of pigeons which I have seen alight upon one of these buildings afford, perhaps, a good illustration for the passage in Isaiah, "Who are these that fly as a cloud, and as the doves to their windows?" Their great numbers, and the compactness of their mass, literally look like a cloud at a distance, and obscure the sun in their passage.
Morier.

8148. DREAM, Conviction Through a. Rev. Herbert Mendes ascribed his religious impressions to a dream. He thought he was called to the judgment, and heard the Judge say of his father and mother, "Well done." He heard his own name distinctly called, and appeared before the Judge, overwhelmed with conviction and in full expectation of punishment. He fell down at the feet of the Judge, and implored. "Lord, spare me yet a little longer, and when thou shalt call me again, I hope to be ready." The Judge, with a benignant smile, said, "Go then, and improve the time given thee." His after life showed the abiding results of a flitting dream.

8149. DREAM, Fulfillment of a. A lady placed a bouquet of tuberoses upon the table at the Fulton St. Prayer meeting, which Mr. Lanphier carried home with him. He was followed by a foreigner, who could not speak a word of English. By his gestures he called attention to the bouquet, and by means of an interpreter explained that he had a dream on his way to America in which he was directed to speak to a man whom he should see carrying white flowers. When the German saw the missionary with the white flowers in his hand, he thought of his dream, and tried to speak to him who carried it. In his dream the German received a German Bible from the man, and was instructed in the way of salvation. All this was literally fulfilled, and the man who had the dream is now an earnest missionary among his own countrymen.

8150. DREAM, A Warning. A lady related her dream as follows:—"In my sleep, I thought that I was in my dining room, with a large party of friends, when a most frightful figure appeared at the window, and seemed as if he wanted to get in. I asked what it was, and being told it was death, I was exceedingly alarmed, and begged they would keep him out but in spite of all their efforts, he forced his way in, and pointed his dart at me. I prayed earnestly that he would go away and not hurt me; on which he said, 'That he would leave me for the present, but in nine days he would return and take no denial.' After this, I thought I was carried to a beautiful place, where I saw an immense company of people, who appeared to be exceedingly happy. I understood it was heaven, and felt greatly disappointed and astonished that I did not find myself happy. I was not able to join in their employments, nor could I understand the cause of their joy. While I was musing on all this, one came to me, whom I supposed to be an angel. I asked him if this was heaven? He answered, 'Yes.' 'How does it happen then,' said I, 'that I am not happy?' 'Because,' he replied, 'it is not your place.' He then asked how I came there? I told him I did not know. On saying this, he conducted me to a door, which opening, I was instantly precipitated towards a most dreadful place, from which issued such doleful groans and piercing shrieks, as awoke me from my sleep." Having given this account of her dream, her visitor spoke to her very seriously, and advised her to consider it as a warning from God to attend to her best interests, and to prepare for death and eternity. At this the lady was offended and turned the conversation to other subjects. But the dream was verified. She died on the day indicated, and there seems to have been no change in the fashionable and worldly woman to indicate that the whole was not fulfilled.

8151. DREAMS, Conscience in. God strikes terror into the hearts of the wicked by dreams: as a *malus genius* is said to have appeared to Brutus the night before his death; or as the face of Hector was presented to Andromache —Virgil records the dream; or as that bloody tyrant, Richard the Third, in a dream the night before the battle of Bosworth Field, thought that all the devils in hell were hauling and tugging him in pieces, and all those he had murdered crying and shrieking out vengeance against him—though he thinks this was more than a dream. *Id credo non fuisse somnium sed conscientiam scelerum.* He judged it not so much a dream as the guilty conscience of his own wickedness. So to Robert Winter, one of the powder traitors, in a dream appeared the ghastly figures and distracted visages of his chief friends and confederates in that treason; not unlike the very same manner wherein they after stood on the pinnacles of the Parliament house. *Adams.*

8152. DREAMS, Felicity of. If we can sleep without dreaming, it is well that painful dreams are avoided. If, while we sleep, we can have any pleasing dreams, it is, as the French say, *tant gagné,* so much added to the pleasure of life. *Franklin.*

8153. DREAMS, Peculiarities of. A very remark

able circumstance, and an important point of analogy, is to be found in the extreme rapidity with which the mental operations are performed, or rather with which the material changes on which the ideas depend are excited in the hemispherial ganglia. It would appear as if a whole series of acts, that would really occupy a long lapse of time, pass ideally through the mind in one instant. We have in dreams no true perception of the lapse of time —a strange property of mind! for if such be also its property when entered into the eternal disembodied state, time will appear to us eternity. The relations of space, as well as of time, are also annihilated; so that while almost an eternity is compressed into a moment, infinite space is traversed more swiftly than by real thought. *Dr. Forbes Winslow.*

8154. DREAMS, Supernatural. The records of history, both sacred and profane, abound in instances of dreams which it is impossible to account for on any other hypothesis than that of a supernatural interposition. *Brande.*

8155. DREAMS, Views of. Luther objected to all reliance upon dreams, because many are deluded by them. He prayed God not to send him any, but to give him a sound understanding of his revealed will. An old author thought the ruling passion or trait of a man's mind would come out in dreams. "What is said of the ancient Persian kings that were seldom seen in the day, but came to view in the night, is true of a man's special or ruling sin. Good men have had clearer sight of their graces in the dreams of the night than in the duties of the day."

8156. DRESS, Beneficence and. What a remarkable woman Mrs. Fletcher was! In many things how Christ-like? What exemplary self-denial! What love of the poor! It is recorded of one year, than in it she spent, upon dress, but nineteen shillings, while she distributed to the necessitous £180. O that women of our time would follow in this track of simplicity and charity. *T. Collins.*

8157. DRESS, Cost of. A minister writes from Saratoga: "The belle of the season wears a dress valued at the amount of my salary for two years, and a set of diamonds equal in value to the cost of a comfortable mission church, with infant-room attached, gas-fixtures and cabinet organ included."

8158. DRESS, Game of. It is not the cheapest of games. I saw a brooch in a jeweler's in Bond Street, not an inch wide, and without any singular jewel in it, yet worth £3,000. And I wish I could tell you what this "play" costs altogether, in England, France, and Russia annually. But it is a pretty game, and on certain terms I like it; nay, I don't see it played quite as much as I would fain have it. You ladies like to lead the fashion—by all means lead it thoroughly, lead it far enough. Dress yourselves nicely, and dress everybody else nicely. Lead the fashions for the poor first; make them look well, and you yourselves will look, in ways of which you have now no conception, all the better. The fashions you have set for some time among your peasantry are not pretty ones; their doublets are too irregularly slashed, and the wind blows too frankly through them. *Ruskin.*

8159. DRESS, Idolatry in. Let the Christian dress so that Christian manhood shall not be overlaid, disguised, or misinterpreted. Let Christians so dress as to show that their hearts are not on these things, but heavenly. Whatever goes to indicate that dress is a supreme object in life, and whatever implies this, is just so far both wrong and unchristian. There is no better definition of an idol than that it steals the heart away from God; and when dress does this it is as much an idol as ever Moloch was; and it is fast coming to be seen that it is a worship no less cruel and bloody. *Rev. Dr. Buddington.*

8160. DRESS, Importance of. A stranger of tolerable sense, dressed like a gentleman, will be better received by those of quality above him, than one of much better parts whose dress is regulated by the rigid notions of frugality. A man's appearance falls within the censure of every one that sees him; his parts and learning very few are judges of; and even upon these few they cannot at first be well intruded; for policy and good breeding will counsel him to be reserved among strangers, and to support himself only by the common spirit of conversation. *Steele.*

8161. DRESS an Index of the Mind. As the index tells us the contents of stories, and directs to the particular chapter, even so does the outward habit and superficial order of garments (in man or woman) give us a taste of the spirit, and demonstratively point (as it were a manual note from the margin) all the internal quality of the soul: and there cannot be a more evident, palpable, gross manifestation of poor, degenerate, dunghilly blood and breeding, than a rude, unpolished, disordered, and slovenly outside. *Massinger.*

8162. DRESS, Preaching against. A young minister, addressing a fashionable audience, attacked their pride and extravagance, as displayed by their dresses, ribands, ruffles, chains and jewels. In the afternoon, an old minister preached powerfully on the corruption of human nature, the enmity of the soul towards God, and necessity for a new heart. In the evening, as they sat together in private, the young minister said, "Sir, why do you not preach against the vanity and pride of the people for dressing so extravagantly?" "Ah, my son," replied the venerable man, "while you are trimming off the top branches of the tree, I am endavoring to cut it up by the roots, and then the whole top must die!"

8163. DRESS, Pride in. He that is proud of the rustling of his silks, like a madman, laughs at the rattling of his fetters. For, indeed, clothes ought to be our remembrancers of our lost innocency; besides, why should any brag of what is but borrowed? Should the ostrich snatch off the gallant's feather, the beaver his hat, the goat his gloves, the sheep his suit, the silkworm his stockings, the neat his shoes (to strip him no further than modesty will give leave), he would be left in a cold condition. And yet it is more pardonable to be proud, even of cleanly rags, than (as many are) of affected slovenness. The one is proud of a molehill, the other of a dunghill. *Fuller.*

8164. DRESS, Rules for. Let women paint their eyes with tints of chastity, insert into their ears the word of God, tie the yoke of Christ around their necks, and adorn their whole persons with the silk of sanctity and the damask of devotion: let them adopt that chaste and simple, that neat and elegant style of dress, which so advantageously displays the charms of real beauty, instead of those preposterous fashions and fantastical draperies of dress which, while they conceal some few defects of person, expose so many defects of mind, and sacrifice to ostentatious finery all those mild, amiable, and modest virtues, by which the female character is so pleasingly adorned.
Tertullian.

8165. DRESS, Wealth and. The person whose clothes are extremely fine, I am too apt to consider as not being possessed of any superiority of fortune, but resembling those Indians who are found to wear all the gold they have in the world in a bob at the nose. *Goldsmith.*

8166. DRINKING, Progress of. The social glass leads on to the glass suggestive or the glass inspiring, and the glass restorative leads on to the glass strength-giving, and that again to glasses fast and frequent—glasses care-drowning, conscience-coaxing, grief-dispelling—till, gasping and dying, the hulk is towed ashore and pierced through with many sins; weak, wasted, worthless, the victim gives up the ghost, leaving in the tainted air a disastrous memory. *Dr. J. Hamilton.*

8167. DRUNKARD, Chain for the. Billy Dawson, the celebrated Wesleyan preacher, once appealed to the drunkard in the following language: "Suppose yourself to be a servant, and your master were to come in the morning and order you to make a strong chain; on the following morning he came again, and urged you to get on with it; and thus, day by day, you were ordered by your master to the same job. Suppose again, that while you were working, a person came in and asked if you knew what it was for; and that you answered in the negative, adding that you did not care so long as you got your wages. But this person tells you, that he knows it to be a fact that it is your master's intention to bind you with it in perpetual bondage; would you, I ask, add another link to it?" The man answered, "No; and all the money in the world would not hire me to it." Mr. Dawson then told him that the habits of drunkenness are the devil's chain, in which he keeps poor sinners in perpetual bondage, and that when they have added the last link, he chains them in hell forever. These words so impressed the mind of the man, that his conscience continued to remind him, "I am making another link for my chain!" until he relinquished his wicked course of life.

8168. DRUNKARD, Conversion of a. A talented young lawyer ran rapidly down the drunkard's road to ruin. Many attempts at reform were made, but uniformly failed. He was taken to a prayer-meeting where he was known, and fervent prayer was offered for him. Deeply moved, he went and knelt at the altar rail while mingled prayers went up for him. A change came over him, which he arose and publicly declared. His reformation was effectual. He soon obtained a large practice, and is now an eminent and successful lawyer.

8169. DRUNKARD, Portion of the. A well-known drunkard appeared at a religious meeting and declared that he was afraid of the drunkard's doom. Said he, "One of the lessons of my childhood was the text 'No drunkard shall inherit the kingdom of God.' It has followed me more than you would suppose. I have heard it in the night-watches and above the revels of a drunken carousal. It seemed to burn on the walls of the rum-shop in letters of fire. I have resolved to escape that doom. Will you give me a helping hand?" The hand of help was given, and the drunkard reformed. A notable "brand plucked from the burning."

8170. DRUNKARD, Salvation for the. In a great meeting in Lancashire, my home, where it was the custom to invite sinners to what we called the "penitent form," for prayer, there was a poor, wretched drunkard. As he was going out, some one asked him to remain. "You don't think I can be a Christian?" said the poor drunkard. "I do," was the answer, "if you are a sinner." "But I'm not going to sign the pledge any more," said he. "I've signed it twenty times, and never will again." "No matter; go and kneel with the others there, and we will pray for you." So he went, and good people knelt beside him and prayed. As he was kneeling there, the chapel door opened, and a poor little girl put her pale face inside. She had on no bonnet; her clothes were in tatters, and the rain dripped from them in little pools at her feet. She was afraid at first to come into the light and warmth out of the storm, but the man at the door drew her in. "What do you want, little girl?" "Please, sir, I heard as my father was coming in here, and I came to see if it was true. Why, that's my father," she said, pointing to the kneeling drunkard. "Tell me, please, sir, what he is doing." Then, permission being given, patter, patter went the little bare feet up the aisle to the penitent form. She knelt down by her father, and put her arms about his neck, and said, "Father, what are ye doing here?" "I'm asking God to forgive me for my badness." "And if he forgives you, shall we be happy then?" "Yes." "Shall we have bread then?" "Yes." "Will you never strike us again?" "No." "And will you stay here till I bring mother?" "Yes." Out she went into the storm, and soon came back with a wretched-looking woman, who had a tattered shawl over her head, and this poor wife went and knelt down by her husband's side, and prayed: "O God! save me, too. O God! save me, too!" And God heard and saved them all. Just as I was leaving England a friend came to me to say good-by. "I have been," said he, "to the home of that drunkard's family to take tea. You would not know them. There is plenty to eat, plenty to wear. Their home is a little heaven." *H. Morehouse.*

8171. DRUNKARD, Wail of a. The brilliant Charles Lamb wrote, "The waters have gone over me, but out of the black depths, could I be heard, I would cry out to all those who have set a foot in the perilous flood. Could the youth to whom the flavor of the first wine is delicious as the opening scenes of life, or the entering upon some newly-discovered paradise, look into my desolation, and be made to understand what a dreary thing it is when he shall feel himself going down a precipice with open eyes and passive will—to see all godliness emptied out of him, and yet not be able to forget a time when it was otherwise—to bear about the piteous spectacle of his own ruin; could he see my feverish eye, feverish with last night's drinking, and feverish looking for to-night's repetition of the folly; could he but feel the body of death out of which I cry hourly with feebler outcry to be delivered, it were enough to make him dash the sparkling beverage to the earth, in all the pride of its mantling temptation."

8172. DRUNKARDS, Responsibility of. It is a maxim in legal practice, that those who presume to commit crimes when drunk must submit to punishment when sober. This state of the law is not peculiar to modern times. In ancient Greece, it was decreed by Pittacus, that he who committed a crime when intoxicated should receive a double punishment—viz., one for the crime itself, and the other for the ebriety which prompted him to commit it. The Athenians not only punished offences done in drunkenness with increased severity, but, by an enactment of Solon, inebriation in a magistrate was made capital. In our own country, at the present time, acts of violence committed under its influence are held to be aggravated, rather than otherwise; nor can the person bring it forward as an extenuation of any folly or misdemeanor which he may chance to commit. A bond signed in intoxication holds in law, and is perfectly binding, unless it can be shown that the person who signed it was inebriated by the collusion or contrivance of those to whom the bond was given. *Anatomy of Drunkenness.*

8173. DRUNKENNESS, Breaking off. Webb, the celebrated English walker, who was remarkable for vigor both of body and mind, drank nothing but water. He was one day recommending his regimen to a friend who loved wine, and urging him with great earnestness to quit a course of luxury by which his health and intellects would be equally destroyed. The gentleman appeared convinced, and told him that he would conform to his counsel, though he thought he could not change his course of life at once, but would leave off strong liquors by degrees. "By degrees!" exclaimed Webb: "if you should unhappily fall into the fire, would you caution your servants to pull you out only by degrees?"
Anon.

8174. DRUNKENNESS, Brutality of. When this vice has taken fast hold of a man, farewell industry, farewell emulation, farewell attention to things worthy of attention, farewell love of virtuous society, farewell decency of manners, and farewell, too, even an attention to person; everything is sunk by this predominant and brutal appetite. In how many instances do we see men who have begun life with the brightest prospects before them, and who have closed it without one ray of comfort and consolation. Young men, with good fortunes, good talents, good tempers, good hearts, and sound constitutions, only by being drawn into the vortex of the drunkard, have become by degrees the most loathsome and despicable of mankind. In the house of the drunkard there is no happiness for any one. All is uncertainty and anxiety. He is not the same man for any one day at a time. No one knows of his outgoings or his incomings. When he will rise, or when he will lie down to rest, is wholly a matter of chance. That which he swallows for what he calls pleasure brings pain, as surely as the night brings the morning. Poverty and misery are in the train. To avoid these results, we are called upon to make no sacrifice. Abstinence requires no aid to accomplish it. Our own will is all that is requisite; and if we have not the will to avoid contempt, disgrace, and misery, we deserve neither relief nor compassion. *Cobbett.*

8175. DRUNKENNESS, Effects of. Now, amongst the rest, drunkenness seems to me to be a gross and brutish vice. The soul has the greatest interest in all the rest, and there are some vices that have something, if a man may so say, of generous in them. There are vices wherein there is a mixture of knowledge, diligence, valor, prudence, dexterity, and cunning; this is totally corporal and earthly, and the thickest-skulled nation this day in Europe is that where it is the most in fashion: other vices discompose the understanding; this totally overthrows it, and renders the body stupid. *Montaigne.*

8176. DRUNKENNESS, Fatal. An old sea-captain relates the following fact, of which he was an eye-witness:—"A collier brig was stranded on the Yorkshire coast, and I had occasion to assist in the distressing service of rescuing a part of the crew by drawing them up a vertical cliff, two or three hundred feet in altitude, by means of a very small rope, the only material at hand. The first two men who caught hold of the rope were hauled safely up to the top; but the next, after being drawn to a considerable height, slipped his hold and fell; and with the fourth and last who ventured upon this only chance of life, the rope gave way, and he also was plunged into the foaming breakers beneath. Immediately afterwards the vessel broke up, and the remnant of the ill-fated crew perished before our eyes. What now was the cause of this heart-rending event? Was stress of weather, or a contrary wind, or unavoidable accident? No such thing. It was the entire want of moral conduct in the crew. Every sailor, to a man, was in a state of intoxication! The helm was intrusted to a boy ignorant of the coast. He ran the vessel upon the rock at Whitby, and one-half of the miserable dissipated crew awoke to consciousness in eternity."

8177. DRUNKENNESS, Resolute. Theotymus, on being told by his physician that except he did abstain from drunkenness and excess, he was like to lose his eyes, his heart was so desperately set upon his sin, that he said—" *Vale lumen amicum;* Farewell sweet light, then, I must have my pleasure in that sin; I must drink, though I drink out my eyes; then farewell eyes, and farewell light and all!"

St. Ambrose.

8178. DRUNKENNESS, Supernatural. It is gravely related of the Irish St. Molua that his father became grossly drunk for seven hours. He assured his wife that he had not taken a drop of anything, but only inhaled the breath of his sleeping babe, the aforesaid saint, as he stooped down to kiss him. It is set down by his biographer as showing the miraculous power of the infant saint. No thought of any other cause seems to have occurred to them. This credulity is certainly a miracle.

8179. DRUNKENNESS, Tempt Not to. Col. John Trumbull, of Connecticut, used to relate the following of himself: An old Mohegan king named Zachary, used to dine annually with his father, then governor of the State. This Indian king had been a great drunkard, but was thoroughly reformed. John, one of the Governor's boys, knowing old Zachary's story, thought he would test him. At the table, he said to the old chief: "Zachary, this beer is excellent: will you taste it?" The old man dropped his knife, his black eye sparkling with indignation, as he said: "John, do you know what you are doing? You are serving the devil. I tell you that I am an Indian; and that if I should but taste the beer, I could not stop until I got to ruin, and became again the drunken, contemptible wretch your father remembers me to have been. John, while you live, never tempt a man to break a good resolution."

8180. DRUNKENNESS, Warning against. A Roman is represented, when he wished to excite the public indignation against the assassins of his friend, as having conveyed the pale, bloody and bleeding body to the public streets, and (lifting up the mantle that was thrown over it, and pointing to the wounds that covered it) as having then and there called for vengeance on the heads of the pitiless assassins. And if anything could make the drunkard hate his crime, or the sober shun it, it might be the dead body that in this church preached better against the crime of drunkenness than a hundred sermons. If there be such a sinner here to-day, I would rather have had him here some days ago. I can now only tell him what drunkenness will do, but I would then have shown

him. He has often had the warning of the living; he would then have had the warning of the dead. *Guthrie.*

8181. DRUNKENNESS, Woes of. It is not so much the money that drunkenness wastes as the misery it produces—the domestic, temporal, and eternal misery—which most of all appals us. As to the expense of this vice, great as it is, that we least deplore; for the loss of money, we hate it least. On the contrary, we should be content were the money and the vice to perish together. We should be content to pay that hundred million as yearly tribute, would this enemy to God and man, this foe to our peace and piety, leave these shores. We wish to keep, and, were it possible, to get back, something far more precious than money. Give that mother back her son, as he was on the day when he returned from his father's grave, and in all the affection of his uncorrupted boyhood, walked to the house of God with a widowed weeping woman leaning on his arm. Give that grieved man back his brother, as innocent and happy as in those days when the boys, twined in each other's arms, returned from school, bent over the same Bible, slept in the same bed, and never thought that the day would come when brother should blush for brother. Give this weeping wife, who sits before us wringing her hands in agony, the tears dripping through her jeweled fingers, and the lines of sorrow prematurely drawn on her beautiful brow, give her back the man she loved, such as he was when her young heart was won, when they stood side by side on the nuptial day, and receiving her from a fond father's hands, he promised his love to one whose heart he has broken, and whose once graceful form now bends with sorrow to the ground. Give me back, as a man, the friends of my youthful days, whose wrecks now lie thick on this wreck-strewn shore. Relieve us of the fears that lie heavy on our hearts for the character and the souls of some who hold parley with the devil by this forbidden tree, and are floating on the outer edge of that great gulf-stream, which sweeps its victims onwards to most woeful ruin. Could this be done, we would not talk of money. The hundred millions which drink costs this land is not to be weighed or even mentioned with this. Hearts are broken which no money can heal. Rachel is "weeping for her children," refusing to be comforted. *Guthrie.*

8182. DUELIST, The Remorse of a. For many years, there was in the lunatic asylum at Philadelphia, an intelligent and accomplished man, who, through his own untoward act, had made himself the victim of despair. He had killed his antagonist in a duel; but no sooner did he learn that his shot had taken fatal effect, than he abandoned himself to the horrors of remorse. Most pitiable it was to see him measure off the paces, stand and give the word—"Fire," then wring his hands and shriek—"He is dead! he is dead!" then pace again, and fire, and renew his self-upbraiding. In that fatal moment when his victim fell, conscience took up her iron sceptre, and smote down reason, and hope, and peace. So conscience "doth make cowards of us all." *Dr. Thompson.*

8183. DULLNESS, Failures of. The attempts, however, of dullness are constantly repeated, and as constantly fail. For the misfortune is, that the head of dullness, unlike the tail of the torpedo, loses nothing of her benumbing and lethargizing influence by reiterated discharges: horses may ride over her, and mules and asses may trample upon her, but, with an exhaustless and patient perversity, she continues her narcotic operations even to the end. *Colton.*

8184. DUPLICITY, Emblem of. A man and a satyr having struck up an acquaintance, sat down together to eat. The day being wintry and cold, the man put his fingers to his mouth and blew upon them. "What's that for, my friend?" asked the satyr. "My hands are so cold," said the man; "I do it to warm them." In a little while some hot food was placed before them, and the man, raising the dish to his mouth, again blew upon it. "And what's the meaning of that, now?" said the satyr. "Oh," replied the man, "my porridge is so hot, I do it to cool it." "Nay, then," said the satyr, "from this moment I renounce your friendship, for I will have nothing to do with one who blows hot and cold with the same mouth." *Æsop.*

8185. DURATION, Eternal. There is a great difference between the light of a taper, and that of a flambeau; but expose both to the light of the sun, and their difference will be imperceptible. In like manner eternal duration is so great an object, that it causes everything to disappear that can be compared with it. *Saurin.*

8186. DUTIES, Importance of. Never judge by appearances as to the relative importance of duties. What seems the least important may be all important. Had the widow not given her mite the day she did to the treasury, but delayed it a week, how much would she herself, and the whole Christian Church, have lost by the delay! *Macleod.*

8187. DUTIES, Practice of. There is a difference, and a wide one, between practicing moral duties and being a Christian. Christianity is a religion of motives. It substitutes an eternal motive for an earthly one: it substitutes the love of God for the love of the world or the love of self. There may be, and are, many persons who practice temperance and other virtues which Christianity inculcates, but who never think of doing so because they are so inculcated. It would be as absurd to ascribe a knowledge of mechanics to savages because they employ the lever, or of the principles of astronomy to brutes because in walking they preserve the centre of gravity, as it is to call such persons Christians. A Christian is one whose motives are Christian faith and Christian hope, and who is, moreover, able to give a reason for the hope that is in him. *Whately.*

8188. DUTIES, Presentation of. Boyd says, in his "Art of Putting Things," "What little child would have heart to begin the alphabet, if, before he did so, you put clearly before him all the school and college work of which it is the beginning? The poor little thing would knock up at once, wearied out by your want of skill in putting things. And so it is that Providence, kindly and gradually putting things, wiles us onward, still keeping hope and heart through the trials and cares of life. Ah! if we had had it put to us at the outset, how much we should have to go through to reach even our present stage of life, we should have been ready to think it the best plan to sit down and die at once; but, in compassion for human weakness, the great Director and Shower of events practices the art of putting things."

8189. DUTIES, Religious. The Christian ought to examine what operation, what influence his religious performances have upon him. Prayer, hearing, reading, and such-like duties, do naturally tend to enlighten the mind, purify the heart, increase our love, strengthen our faith, and confirm our hope: and therefore where this is not the effect of them, we may conclude that they are not discharged in that manner, and with that sincerity they ought. *Lucas.*

8190. DUTIES, Voluntary. Good duties must not be pressed nor beaten out of us, as the waters came out of the rock when Moses smote it with his rod; but must freely drop from us, as myrrh from the tree, or honey from the comb. If a willing mind be wanting, there wants that flower which should perfume our obedience, and make it a sweet smelling savor to God. *T. Watson.*

8191. DUTY, Adaptation of. Latimer was trained by his father to use the cross-bow. At first he was provided with a small bow adapted to his strength, and as he grew larger and stronger bigger bows were given him, till he was able to wield a man's weapon. The scholar is trained by an adjustment of lessons to his capacity, till he reads a thousand lines of Latin more easily than he did one line at the beginning. God has adjusted our duties in the same way. All are not laid upon us at once. First the little, then the great. Having done the little duties of the Christian life faithfully, we shall be prepared for the great ones.

8192. DUTY, Alternative of. On the occasion of a regiment of cavalry being ordered unexpectedly to the Cape of Good Hope, one of the officers, not very remarkable for his zeal in the performance of his duty, applied for leave to remain at home. The Duke's answer was very laconic—"Sail or sell." *Life of Wellington*

8193. DUTY, Benefit of. No man has a right to say he can do nothing for the benefit of mankind, who are less benefited by ambitious projects than by the sober fulfillment of each man's proper duties. By doing the proper duty in the proper place, a man may make the world his debtor. The results of "patient continuance in well-doing," are never to be measured by the weakness of the instrument, but by the omnipotence of him who blesseth the sincere efforts of obedient faith alike in the prince and in the cottage. *H. Thompson.*

8194. DUTY, Biblical. "Duties are ours, results are God's." see Exod. 23 : 24, 25 ; 2 Sam. 10 : 12 ; 1 Chron. 19 : 13. "The path of duty is the path of safety." "Never expect God's blessing out of God's way." See Gen. 31. 3 :— "Return . . . . I will be with thee," followed by 32. Oh, how happy are they who go on God's errands. 1 Kings 13—The "man of God" that came to Bethel;—*in* the way of duty, he had no fear, even to face the king, and the Lord protected him. *Out* of the path of obedience, how soon was he overtaken by God's judgment! *Flying* from the place and way of duty brings chastening and sorrow:— *Abraham—Hagar—David—Elijah—Jonah.* Matt. 10, is Christ's ordination charge to the Twelve. In chap. 11: 1 we read, "He made an end of *commanding.*" Christ's commissions are Christ's commands. *Duty* goes side by side with *privilege.* It runs throughout the whole Scripture, see 2 Cor. 6: 16, 17; 7: 1; Prov. 3: 5, 6; Col. 2: 6, 7; 3: 1; Heb. 12: 11, 12. *Bowes.*

8195. DUTY, Burden of. The Princess Elizabeth carried the crown for her sister in the procession at Mary's coronation, and complained to Noailles of its great weight. "Be patient," was the adroit answer, "it will seem lighter when on your own head." The outward forms of godliness are as burdensome to an unregenerate man as was the crown to the princess; but let him be born again and so made a possessor of the good things of divine grace, and they will sit easily enough upon his head, as his glory and delight. *Spurgeon.*

8196. DUTY, Conviction of. That we ought to do an action, is of itself a sufficient and ultimate answer to the questions, why we should do it?—how we are obliged to do it? The conviction of duty implies the soundest reason, the strongest obligation, of which our nature is susceptible. *Whewell.*

8197. DUTY, Fidelity to. During one of the civil wars of England, Dr. John Hacket, of London, was using the liturgy in his church, contrary to the law of Parliament, when armed soldiers rushed in and ordered him to desist. He went on reading the service with steady voice. A soldier aimed a pistol at his head, and threatened him with instant death if he did not stop. The undaunted minister replied, "Soldier, I am doing my duty; do you do yours," and went on reading the service. The soldiers, overmatched in courage, went away, leaving him victor at the post of duty.

8198. DUTY, The First. A young student who subsequently became a missionary, said, "When I was a child I was one day full of bright anticipations as to what I should do, and what I should be, when I became a man. My ideas, both with regard to business and the honors of life, were very glowing. My dear mother listened to my boyish prattle very patiently. When I ceased she paused a few moments, and then, drawing me gently to her side, with an affectionate and solemn tone she said, 'Seek first the kingdom of heaven.' That word 'first' was never forgotten by me. It made an impression on my mind which time never erased, and, by God's mercy, it led me to seek an interest in Jesus ; and now I can give up 'all for Christ.'"

8199. DUTY, Happiness in. Without recurring to any effects produced upon the general system, every individual in every stage, and under every circumstance of existence, has a post to maintain, in which he is placed by the Sovereign Disposer of the universe: on a diligent attention to the duties arising from that situation, whatever it be, and not from a desertion of it, must all our happiness depend. *Mrs. Carter.*

8200. DUTY, Help in. The area of duty, which is committed to the superintendence of each of us by the sublime code of evangelical morals, is confessedly larger than our scanty powers can occupy. In this state of original helplessness, accordingly, one resource only remains open to us,—to throw ourselves, with all our infirmities, on the Divine help. *Bishop Shuttleworth.*

8201. DUTY, Home. God took especial care, that the bird sitting over the eggs in her nest should not be hurt (Deut. 22: 6); but we find nothing to secure her if found abroad. In doing the duty of our place, we have heaven's word for our security; but on our own peril be it if we wander; then are we, like Shimei, out of its precincts, and lay ourselves open to some judgment or another: it is alike dangerous to do what we are not called to, and to neglect and leave undone the duty of our place. *Salter.*

8202. DUTY, Ideal of. Suppose the case of a young man entering upon life, with the cause of duty beginning to form in him, or at least working itself clear and firm in his mind, how directly must all his views of the near and the present be affected by his thought of the Supreme and the future? It may not be that he has any distinct consciousness of moulding his views of the one by the other. But not the less surely will the "life that now is" to him be moulded by the character of the life that he believes to be above him and before him. The lower will take its color from the higher—the "near" from the "heavenly horizon." There will be a light or a darkness shed around his present path in proportion as his faith opens a steady or a hesitating—a comprehensive or a partial—gaze into the future and unseen. *Dr. Tulloch.*

8203. DUTY, Imperfection and. A sculptor was at work forming a figure out of a faulty block of marble. A neighbor of his told him that it was absolutely impossible to make a perfect figure out of such imperfect materials. "All this is very true," replied the sculptor; "but this block of marble, such as it is, was sent to me to be formed into a statue; and as I cannot make it better, I must content myself in forming the best figure out of it that I can." A nurseryman about to transplant a number of young trees, some straight and others crooked thus reasoned with himself:—"These straight saplings will no doubt grow up to be fine trees without much attention on my part; but I will see if, by proper training, I cannot make something of the crooked ones also. There will be more trouble with them, no doubt, than with others, but for that very reason I shall be the better satisfied should I succeed."

8204. DUTY, Impression of. It is said that Lady Huntingdon was on her way to a brilliant assembly, when suddenly there darted into her soul these words, "Man's chief end is to glorify God and enjoy him forever," which she had long since committed to memory without feeling their mighty import. From that hour her life revolved around a new centre. She soon found peace and rest, and consecrated herself, her wealth, and her influence to God and humanity.

8205. DUTY, Inspiration from. England not long since lost her greatest hero. Full of years and honors, Wellington went down to his grave. A nation mourned him. They mourned him because he had done so much and done it so bravely and well for his country. He had faced perils by sea and by land. He had borne summer heat, and winter cold. He had stood in the "imminent deadly breach," and lifted up an unshrinking front when the air was blackened with fiery shot and bursting shell. He had trodden down his country's foes, and driven her would-be invader into dreary exile. He had maintained her cause against foreign treachery and domestic anarchy. Well, what was it that upheld this man through his wondrous career? What mighty motive lay at the root of his stern, but unimpeachable fidelity? Why that same cold and uninviting thing—as you deem it—a sense of duty. Duty was his watchword; duty to a human master— to a king. He never boasted higher motive —perhaps never thought of it. *Merry.*

8206. DUTY, Most Important. Archbishop Usher was preaching in the church in Covent Garden, when a messenger from the court announced that the King wished to see him immediately. The Archbishop told the messenger that he was engaged in God's business, and as soon as he had done he would attend upon the King, and then continued his sermon.

8207. DUTY, Neglect of. Thousands of men pass off the stage of life, and are heard of no more. Why? they do not partake of good in the world, and none were blessed by them; none could point to them as the means of their redemption; not a line they wrote, not a word they spake, could be recalled; and so they perished: their light went out in darkness, and they were not remembered more than insects of yesterday. Will you thus live and die, O man immortal? Live for something. Do good, and leave behind you a monument of virtue that the storm of time can never destroy. Write your name in kindness, love, and mercy, on the hearts of thousands you come in contact with year by year: you will never be forgotten. No! your name, your deeds, will be as legible on the hearts you leave behind you as the stars on the brow of evening. Good deeds will shine as the stars of heaven. *Chalmers.*

8208. DUTY, Path of. A young man went one evening to consult his minister respecting the situation which he filled in a large drapery establishment. His master required him to tell falsehoods about the goods, and to cheat the customers whenever he could do so; and his conscience told him that this was wrong. His minister advised him to refuse to act thus dishonestly. "I shall lose my place," said the young man. "Then lose your place; don't hesitate a moment." "I engaged for a year, and my year is not out." "No matter; you are ready to fulfill your engagement. But what was your engagement? Did you engage to deceive, to cheat and lie?" "Oh no, not at all." "Then certainly you need have no hesitation through fear of forfeiting your place. If he sends you away because you will not do such things for him, you will know him to be a bad man, from whom you may be glad to be separated." "I have no place to go to, and he knows it." "I would go anywhere, do anything, dig potatoes, black boots, sweep the streets for a living, sooner than yield to such temptations." "I don't think I can stay there; but I don't know what to do or where to look." "Look to God first, and trust in him. Do you think he will let you suffer, because, out of regard to his commandments, you have lost your place? Never. Such is not his way. Ask him to guide you." The young man acted upon the advice given. He was dismissed from his situation, but he found another, where he established a character for integrity and promptness, and entered afterwards into business for himself. He prospered, and is now a man of extensive property and high respectability.
Sunday Teacher's Treasury.

8209. DUTY, Refreshment by. A man shall carry a bucket of water on his head and be very tired with the burden; but that same man when he dives into the sea shall have a thousand buckets on his head without perceiving their weight, because he is in the element and it entirely surrounds him. The duties of holiness are very irksome to men who are not in the element of holiness; but when once those men are cast into the element of grace, then they bear ten times more, and feel no weight, but are refreshed thereby with joy unspeakable. *Spurgeon.*

8210. DUTY, Reward of. No man's spirits were ever hurt by doing his duty: on the contrary, one good action, one temptation resisted and overcome, one sacrifice of desire or interest, purely for conscience sake, will prove a cordial for weak and low spirits, far beyond what either indulgence, or diversion, or company, can do for them. *Paley.*

8211. DUTY, Routine of. Perhaps an apter simile cannot be formed to illustrate social life than that presented by the planets encircling the sun; while they harmoniously perform their daily revolutions and their annual circuits, and while they act upon the moons which subordinately revolve around them, the whole orderly system obeys each impulse of attraction received from the central orb; to him they turn for light and warmth; and the face of each planet, while beholding his brilliant glory, reflects his bright image, and becomes itself a luminary. Had man preserved entire his original likeness to his Creator, he would have displayed the divine likeness, not only in his soul—not only in his bodily glory and endowments—but likewise in his every minutest relation with other beings and things. Another very remarkable, and, I believe, designed coincidence, may be traced between the planetary and the social system: the one and the other are maintained in action and in order by an exactly similar principle, called attraction in the spheres and love in the hearts of mankind; and by this attraction or love, not only are the planets in the sky, and Christians upon earth, drawn mutually towards each other, but also drawn simultaneously towards their central source of life, and light, and happiness. *Lady's Magazine.*

8212. DUTY, Sacrifice for. In our late war a little drummer boy, after describing the hardships of the winter campaign, the cold, the biting, the pitiless wind, the hunger and the nakedness which they had to endure, concluded his letter to his mother with the simple and touching words, " But, mother, it is our duty, and for our duty we will die."

8213. DUTY, The Sense of. There is no evil that we cannot either face or fly from, but the consciousness of duty disregarded. A sense of duty pursues us ever. It is omnipresent, like the deity. If we take to ourselves the wings of the morning, and dwell in the uttermost parts of the sea, duty performed or duty violated is still with us, for our happiness or our misery. If we say, the darkness shall cover us —in the darkness, as in the light, our obligations are yet with us. We cannot escape their power, nor fly from their presence. They are with us in this life, will be with us at its close; and in that scene of inconceivable solemnity which yet lies further onward, we shall still find ourselves surrounded by the consciousness of duty, to pain us wherever it has been violated, and to console us so far as God may have given us grace to perform it. *Webster.*

8214. DUTY, Self–Sacrifice of. It is an impressive truth that, sometimes in the very lowest forms of duty, less than which would rank a man as a villain, there is, nevertheless, the sublimest ascent of self-sacrifice. To do less would class you as an object of eternal scorn; to do so much presumes the grandeur of heroism. *De Quincey.*

8215. DUTY, Triumphs of. There are few things more beautiful than the calm and resolute progress of an earnest spirit. The triumphs of genius may be more dazzling; the chances of good fortune may be more exciting; but neither are at all so interesting or so worthy as the achievements of a steady, faithful, and fervent energy. The moral elements give an infinitely higher value to the latter, while, at the same time, they bring it comparatively within the reach of all. Genius can be the lot of only a few; good fortune may come to any, but it would be the part of a fool to wait for it; whereas all may work with heartiness and might in the work to which they have given themselves. It is their simple duty to do this. It may seem but a small thing to do. No one certainly is entitled to any credit for doing it. Yet just because it is a duty, it will be found bearing a rich reward. The labor of the faithful is never in vain. The fruits will be found gathered into his hand, while the hasty garlands of genius are fading away, and the prizes of the merely fortunate are turned into vanity. *Dr. Tulloch.*

8216. DYING, Bliss of. The pain of dying must be distinguished from the pain of the previous disease, for when life ebbs sensibility declines. As death is the final extinction of corporal feeling, so numbness increases as death comes on. The prostration of disease, like healthful fatigue, engenders a growing stupor —a sensation of subsiding softly into a coveted repose. The transition resembles what may be seen in those lofty mountains, whose sides exhibit every climate in regular gradation: vegetation luxuriates at their base, and dwindles in the approach to the regions of snow till its feeblest manifestation is repressed by the cold. The so-called agony can never be more formidable than when the brain is the last to go, and the mind preserves to the end a rational cognizance of the state of the body; yet persons thus situated commonly attest that there are few things in life less painful than the close. "If I had strength enough to hold a pen," said William Hunter, "I would write how easy and delightful it is to die." "If this be dying," said the niece of Newton of Olney, "it is a pleasant thing to die;" "the very expression," adds her uncle, "which another friend of mine made use of on her death-bed, a few years ago." The same words have so often been uttered under similar circumstances, that we could fill pages with instances which are only varied by the name of the speaker. "If this be dying," said Lady Glenorchy, "it is the easiest thing imaginable." "I thought that dying had been more difficult," said Louis XIV. "I did not suppose it was so sweet to die," said Francis Suarez, the Spanish theologian. An agreeable surprise was the prevailing sentiment with them all; they expected the stream to terminate in the dash of the torrent, and they found it was losing itself in the gentlest current. The whole of the faculties seem sometimes concentrated on the placid enjoyment. Nor does the calm partake of the sensitiveness of sickness. There was a swell in the sea the day Collingwood breathed his last upon the element which had been the scene of his glory. Capt. Thomas expressed a fear that he was disturbed by the tossing of the ship: "No, Thomas," he replied, "I am now in a state in which nothing in this world can disturb me more. I am dying; and I am sure it must be consolatory to you, and all who love me, to see how comfortably I am coming to my end." *Fontenelle.*

8217. DYING, Contrast in. "Fool! fool! fool!" were the last words of one on his dying bed, who, it is to be feared, had procrastinated his repentance too long and too fearfully; while the humble Christian, sensible of a thousand failings and imperfections, still looks with the eye of faith on his Redeemer; and his soul, like the flight of an eagle towards the heavens, soars to the regions of everlasting happiness. *Jesse.*

8218. DYING, Experience in. Gert Links, a converted Hottentot of South Africa, noted for his excellence of character, having lived to good old age, said, when about to die, "I have at this moment a particular impression of the immortality of the soul, for my body is already half-dead; I have lost the use of both legs and one arm, and if my soul were not immortal, it would be half-dead also; but instead of that, I am constantly thinking of God and heaven, and I can think with great ease and freedom. I have also a special conviction that the Bible is God's book, and its blessed truths are constantly running through my mind, and afford me great comfort in my affliction. I wish to say further that I now see more clearly than ever that the missionaries are not common men, but servants of God sent to declare to us his Holy Word." He looked round upon the many friends who had assembled to hear his last words, and addressing them he said, "Pay great attention to the word of your teachers, and remember that they speak to you in the name of the Lord." Being faint, he said, "I have done." An hour afterward he was dead.

8219. DYING, Gate Open to the. A dying woman whom Mother Munroe of Boston led to Christ, said to her, "I will open the gates wide for you." When Mrs. Munroe came to death she repeated, "I shall go sweeping through the gates, washed in the blood of the Lamb." Who shall say her forerunner had not kept her word?

8220. DYING, Glorious. Glorious visions open to the dying saints of God. "The celestial city," says Payson, "is full in my view." "This is heaven begun," said Thomas Scott. "I breathe the air of heaven," said Stephen Gano. "I have been," said Walker of Truro, "upon the wings of the cherubim." "Christ—angels—beautiful—delightful!" were the last words of Dr. Hope. "I see things that are unutterable," said Rev. Mr. Holland. "I see the New Jerusalem," said Norman Smith. "They praise him! They praise him! What glory! the angels are waiting for me!" said Dr. Bateman. "Do you see," said Edmund Auger, "that blessed assembly who await my arrival? Do you hear that sweet music with which holy men invite me, that I may henceforth be a partaker of their happiness! How delightful it is to be in the society of blessed spirits! Let us go! We must go! Let me go!"

8221. DYING, Happy. Rev. A. M. French said, "I am going through the valley of the shadow

—who has any anxiety? I shall soon be with Jesus. How sweet to die in the will of the Lord! O my wife, my dear daughter, how sweet to die in the will of the Lord! the sweet will of the Lord!" Four times he repeated, "How sweet to die! How sweet to die!" and added: "Luxurious! luxurious! O that I could tell you how sweet!" At one of his latest rallyings, looking smilingly around, and speaking like a guest who had been making a short call in the room, he said, "Well, I guess I must go!"

8222. DYING, Invitation of the. An unconverted young woman stands by the bedside of a dying Christian. They have loved each other like two sisters. Unable to articulate, the dying one speaks through her eye. Catching the eye of her friend, and looking upward, she silently but significantly says to her, "Meet me up there." A single tear slid out from under the eyelid and paused on her pallid cheek, and remained there after her spirit had fled. To the survivor that crystal sermon was the most effective sermon ever addressed to her. No rest could she find, though she struggled for months, till she opened the door and let Christ in. For twenty-five years that individual has been the companion and helper of a minister of Jesus. *Christian Era.*

8223. DYING, Message of the. I went down the Tennessee river in war time with a boat-load of wounded men, after the battle of Shiloh. Many were mortally wounded; they had taken the worst cases first. I said to those who were with me, "We must not let these men die without telling them of heaven." One young man was unconscious, and they said he could not live. I asked the physician if he could not restore him long enough to get a message for his mother, and he gave me brandy and water, which I fed to him. He was a most beautiful boy. After a while he opened his eyes and looked around a little wild, and I placed my hand upon his brow and said, "My boy, do you know where you are?" At last he said, "I am on my way home to mother." "Yes." I said, "you are, but the doctor tells me you cannot live." I asked him for a message to his mother. He said, "Tell my mother that I die trusting in Christ." He did not know me, whether I was a friend or an enemy. He added, "Tell my mother and sisters to be sure to meet me in heaven," and in a few minutes he was unconscious, and in a few hours he died. They will meet in the morning—it is only a little while—for he died trusting in Christ. *Moody.*

8224. DYING, Simplicity in. A dying soldier boy in Stoneman Hospital called the ward master to him, put his arms around his neck and kissed him, and said, "I love everybody." Then he folded his arms upon his breast and slowly repeated his childhood's prayer, "Now I lay me down to sleep, I pray the Lord my soul to keep; if I should die before I wake, I pray the Lord my soul to take." The soldier boy and the great Dr. Nott died with the same prayer on their lips.

8225. DYING, Triumphant. A friend said to Dr. Simpson, of Hoxton Academy, near the last, "You will soon enter upon an eternal Sabbath." He answered, "I shall, it dawns." Just before he breathed his last, he apostrophized Death as if he saw him approaching: "Now have at thee, Death; have at thee, Death! What art thou? I am not afraid of thee! Thou art a vanquished enemy by the blood of the cross! Thou art only a skeleton—a mere phantom!" And repeating "Have at thee, Death," he "grappled in close combat with the king of terrors, and having like a mighty champion defied his utmost rage, Death at last confessed him conqueror, and wreathed around his brow the garland of immortal victory."

8226. DYING, Visions in. Timothy, a reader of the Church in the Thebaid, was requested to deliver up the sacred books of the Christians. He refused; and red-hot irons were applied to his ears, his eyelids were cut off, and he was tortured upon a wheel to induce him to yield. Then the governor sent Maura, the young wife of Timothy, who had been but twenty days married to him, to persuade him to yield. She chose rather to suffer with him. The hair was torn from her head in handfuls. At last both were nailed to a wall, and while stretched in mortal agony, they beheld a glorious vision of angels beckoning them to thrones in heaven by the side of the King of Glory, for whom they died.

8227. DYING TESTIMONIES, Christians'. An educated and converted Kaffir said, "Weep not for me, for I am leaning with my whole strength on Jesus Christ." Miss Fannie I. Mann said, "In that house of many mansions there will be one for me." Mrs. Phœbe Palmer said over the weeping friends who surrounded her bed, "The grace of our Lord Jesus Christ be with you all. Amen." Bishop Janes, resting on the Rock of Ages, exclaimed, "I am not disappointed."

8228. DYING TESTIMONIES, Ministers'. Henry Furlong said to his children: "Aim at high attainments in religion, and let your characters shine through your lives. Give my love to the brethren, and tell them I die on the Rock." The veteran Henry Slicer said, "My ministry counts for nothing now; my trust is only in the Mediator." In the dreams of a sick-bed the voice of the devoted Eddy rang out with the old missionary fervor, "We must, we can, we will conquer! Forward, is the word; sing and pray, eternity dawns!" Milton Hysore exclaimed, in the midst of a sermon, "Jesus saves me; saves me now!" and fell in the pulpit, never to speak again. J. R. West's last words were, "A band of angels waits to waft my spirit home: hallelujah!" Robert Kemp, "Now I lie down to sleep in Jesus!" William Grace, "O, the glory that shines around me!" J. A. Little, "These are the happiest moments of my life!" Stephen D. Brown, "I have been preparing for this hour for many years!" E. L. Janes, the bishop's twin brother, "It is all bright to me; how could I doubt?" John Trippett, "I have no fear of death; for fifty-four years I have not lost my peace with God." Alonzo Wood's last intelligible words, "Almost to Jesus!" George Jenkins, "Not a cloud overshadows my spiritual skies: all is well." A. A. Farr, "I have tried for a long time to be ready for two things, to preach and to die; I am ready to go home." John Hanlon, "Eternity is near: eternity, eternity! it is sweet to die in Jesus." John S. George, "I never thought I could draw near to death and feel so calm." James M'Millan, "O, the preciousness of Jesus." To his wife he said, "We have been very dear to each other, but Jesus is dearer than all." John Klien, "I am so inexpressibly happy now that I have given all into the hands of God! glorious, all glorious!" Daniel De Motte, "All is well! blessed Jesus!" Joseph White, "Come, Jesus; take me." John Blanpied, "The Lord is letting me down gently; happy in the Lord." J. W. Yokom, "Hark! I hear them! I see them!" Douglas Reagh went repeating the dying words of John Wesley, "The best of all is, God is with us." Micah Purkheiser, "The wires are laid and the poles are all up from 'Stony Point' to headquarters!" Tremillius, a converted Jew, cried the opposite to one of the Jewish rabble "Not Barabbas, but Jesus!"

8229. EAGLES, Flight of. I once saw a very interesting sight above one of the crags of Ben Nevis, as I was going, on the 20th of August, in the pursuit of black game. Two parent eagles were teaching their offspring, two young birds, the maneuvers of flight. They began by rising from the top of a mountain in the eye of the sun. It was about mid-day, and bright for this climate. They at first made small circles, and the young birds imitated them. They paused on their wings, waiting till they had made their first flight, and then took a second and larger gyration, always rising towards the sun, and enlarging their circle of flight, so as to make a gradually extending spiral. The young ones still slowly followed, apparently flying better as they mounted; and they continued this sublime kind of exercise, always rising, till they became mere points in the air, and the young ones were lost, and afterwards their parents, to our aching sight.

Sir Humphrey Davy.

8230. EAR, Mechanism of the. What in ordinary language we call the ear, is only the outer porch or entrance vestibule of a curious series of intricate, winding passages, which, like the lobbies of a great building, lead from the outer air into the inner chambers. Certain of these passages are full of air; others are full of liquid; and thin membranes are stretched like parchment curtains across the corridors at different places, and can be thrown into vibration, or made to tremble, as the head of a drum or the surface of a tambourine does when struck with a stick or the fingers. Between two of those parchment-like curtains, a chain of very small bones extends, which serves to tighten or relax these membranes, and to communicate vibrations to them. In the innermost place of all, rows of fine threads, called nerves, stretch like the strings of a piano from the last points to which the tremblings of thrillings reach, and pass inwards to the brain. If these threads or nerves are destroyed, the power of hearing as infallibly departs, as the power to give out sound is lost by a piano or violin when its strings are broken.   *Prof. Wilson.*

8231. EARLY DEATH, Parable of. To what is this like? It is like a king who, walking in his garden, saw some roses which were yet buds, breathing an ineffable sweetness. He thought, if these shed such sweetness while yet buds, what will they do when they are fully blown? After a while the king entered the garden anew, thinking to find the roses now blown, and to delight himself with their fragrance, but arriving at the place, he found them pale and withered, and yielding no smell. He exclaimed with regret, "Had I gathered them while yet tender and young, and while they gave forth their sweetness, I might have delighted myself with them, but now I have no pleasure in them." The next year the king walked in his garden, and finding rosebuds scattering fragrance, he commanded his servants, "Gather them, that I may enjoy them, before they wither, as they did last year."
R. C. Trench.

8232. EARLY PIETY, Examples of. Hannah Whitall Smith, of Philadelphia, when one of her daughters was yet but two years old, and was quite ill, says she took the child from her crib and told her plainly and tenderly of the Saviour and of his work for her. The child heard and believed. At once the little one showed trust in Jesus—a trust that thenceforward grew and strengthened with her advancing age until the sweet fruits of the Holy Spirit were manifest richly in her daily life. "That child is naughty sometimes. So are grown Christians." But all the evidence of Christian character which is found in the older disciples is given by the child. A young son of the same mother was a quick-tempered and troublesome boy. "He would say, 'I won't,' and get angry, and throw scissors, and do other naughty things." The other children of the family said they were going to ask Jesus to make Logan a Christian. He was four years old. They took him into a room by themselves, and all kneeled together. One prayed, saying, "Please, Jesus, make Logan a Christian." Another said, "I pray so, too, Jesus." Then they had Logan pray in the same way for himself. Rising from their knees, they said in child-like faith, "Now, Logan, Jesus says that he will give us what we ask of him. Thee must believe that he makes thee a Christian, because he says he will." Logan said, "I do believe it." "And from that time," said the mother, "the change in Logan was absolute and most remarkable. He was so good a boy that I was really afraid he wouldn't live." Again, the little daughter of one of her friends, on being told that Jesus could give her power over all temptation, went to him in trust, and found him as good as his word. So happy was she in his sustaining grace in her daily strug-gles with sin, that she would say to her mother, cheerily, "Mamma, isn't thee glad Jesus is making me good?" Then she would add, in hope of new attainments in the divine life, "But he's going to make me a great deal gooder than this."

8233. EARLY REST and Early Rising. The studious are noted for their disregard of "the regular hours of rest." The solemn stillness of night, inviting to those pursuits which require a fixed attention, and a connected series of thought and reasoning, leads them first into the habit; which is subsequently strengthened by the circumstance of intense application of the mind uninterrupted by sufficient and appropriate exercise, producing a state of nervous irritability inimical to sleep. Hence the student fears to leave his midnight lamp for a couch, which he can only occupy in a state of restlessness. Let him, however, relinquish his nocturnal studies, and seek, during the natural period, that repose which his mind and body alike demand—appropriating "the hours of early morn" to study, and the residue of the forenoon to exercise, and we are well persuaded that while his progress in the pursuit of knowledge would be in no degree retarded, he will be the gainer, not merely in the enjoyment of more perfect health, but in the increased clearness and vigor of the intellectual faculties. It has been very correctly remarked, that the atmosphere of the night is always more vitiated, and consequently less fit for respiration, than that of the day; and as we respire a greater portion of air when awake than in a sleeping state, it follows that from these, independent of other causes, the system is more liable to injury in the former than in the latter state. Early rising is equally important to the health of the system as early rest. On no account should any one permit himself again to slumber, after the moment of his first awakening in the morning, whether this happen at the early dawn or before the sun has risen; even though from accident or unavoidable causes he may not have enjoyed his six or eight hours of repose. It is much better to make up the deficiency, if necessary, at some other time, than to attempt taking another nap. Whoever shall accustom himself thus to rise, will enjoy more undisturbed sleep during the night, and awake far more refreshed, than those who indolently slumber all the morning. Even this second nap is, however, by no means so injurious to health as the practice of continuing in bed of a morning, long after waking; nothing tends, especially in children, and young persons generally, more effectually to unbrace the solids, exhaust the spirits, and thus to undermine the vigor, activity, and health of the system.
Dr. Hall.

8234. EARLY RISERS, Famous. Napoleon devoted only four hours to sleep; Lord Brougham spent the same time in bed when he was the most celebrated man in England. Dr. Parkhurst, the philologist, rose at five; Gibbon was in his study every morning, winter and summer, at six o'clock.

8235. EARLY RISING, Conclusion from. Apollonius being very early at Vespasian's gate, and finding him already up and at work, from thence conjectured that he was worthy to govern an empire, and said to his companion, "This man surely will be emperor, he is so early." The prophecy was fulfilled.

8236. EARLY RISING, Examples of. Sir Thomas More says that he wrote the "Utopia," by stealing time from his sleep and meals. He made it his invariable practice to rise at four. When Bp. Burnet was in college, his father aroused him to his studies every morning at four o'clock, and he continued to rise at that hour during the remainder of his life. Bishop Jewell rose regularly at four; the learned lawyer and pious Christian, Sir Matthew Hale, studied sixteen hours every day, and was an early riser. Dr. Parkhurst, the philologist, rose regularly at five in summer and six in the winter, and, in the latter season, he made his own fire. "I spent," says Dr. Paley, when giving an account of the early part of his life at college, "the first two years of my undergraduateship happily, but unprofitably. I was constantly in society, where we were not immoral, but idle and expensive. At the commencement of the third year, after having left the usual party at a late hour, I was awakened at five in the morning by one of my companions, who stood at my bedside and said, 'Paley, I have been thinking what a fool you are. I could do nothing, probably, if I were to try, and I could afford the indolent life you lead. You could do everything, and cannot afford it. I have had no sleep during the whole night on account of these reflections, and am now come solemnly to inform you that if you persist in your indolence I must renounce your society.' I was so struck," says Paley, "with the visit and the visitor, that I lay in bed great part of the day and formed my plan. I ordered my bedmaker to lay my fire every evening, in order that it might be lighted by myself. I arose at five, read during the whole day, took supper at nine, went to bed, and continued the practice up to this hour."

8237. EARLY RISING, Gain by. The difference between rising at five and seven o'clock in the morning, for the space of forty years, supposing a man to go to bed at the same hour at night, is equivalent to the addition of ten years to a man's life.   *Doddridge.*

8238. EARLY TRAINING Coerced. Teach a child there is harm in everything, however innocent, and so soon as it discovers the cheat, it will see no sin in anything. That's the reason deacons' sons seldom turn out well, and preachers' daughters are married through a window. Innocence is the sweetest thing in the world, and there is more of it than folks generally imagine. If you want some to transplant, don't seek it in the inclosures of cant, for it has only counterfeit ones; but go to the gardens of truth and sense. Coerced innocence is like an imprisoned lark—open the door, and it's off forever. The bird that roams through the sky and the groves unrestrained knows how to dodge the hawk and protect itself; but the caged one, the moment it leaves its bars and bolts behind, is pounced upon by the fowler or the vulture.   *Haliburton.*

8239. EARLY TRAINING, Power of. I, too, acknowledge the all but omnipotence of early culture and nurture. Hereby we have either a doddered dwarf bush, or a high-towering, wide-shadowing tree—either a sick, yellow cabbage, or an edible, luxuriant green one. Of a truth, it is the duty of all men, especially of all philosophers, to note down with accuracy the characteristic circumstances of their education—what furthered it, what hindered, what in any way modified it.   *Carlyle.*

8240. EARLY TRAINING, Responsibility for. A boy in Æsop's time stole a horn-book, and took it to his mother. She praised him for it. From that time he pursued a course of crime till he was detected, and sentenced to execution. At the last he called his mother to him and bit off her ear. The crowd upbraided him for his unnatural cruelty. He replied, "It is she who is the cause of my ruin; for if, when I stole my school-fellow's horn-book, and brought it to her, she had given me a sound flogging, I should never have so grown in wickedness as to come to this untimely end."

8241. EARNESTNESS, Christian. Matt. 11 : 12—"The kingdom of heaven suffereth violence, and the violent take it by force." How startling these words! Do violence to God? Storm the kingdom of heaven? He that forbids us to touch another's goods rejoices to have his own invaded; he that condemns the violence of avarice praises the violence of faith.   *Paulinus.*

8242. EARNESTNESS, Ministerial. Mr. Betterton, the actor, being one day at dinner at the Archbishop of Canterbury's, the latter expressed his astonishment that the representation of fables in their pieces should make more impression upon the mind than that of truth in the sermons of the clergy: upon which Mr. Betterton, explaining the reason of it, said, "May it please your Grace, it is because the clergy, in reading their sermons, pronounce them as if they were reading fables; but we, in acting our parts, and using them in a proper gesture, represent them as matters of fact."

8243. EARNESTNESS, Power of. It is not to be calculated how much a single man may effect who throws his whole powers into a thing. Who, for instance, can estimate the influence of Voltaire? He shed an influence of a peculiar sort over Europe. His powers were those of a gay buffoon, far different from those of Hume, and others of his class; but he threw himself wholly into them.   *Cecil.*

8244. EARNESTNESS, Result of. Have something to say, and burn to say it! It will be logic on fire! Bread may be so solid as to be good for nothing at all; so yeast is not good to live on. Have the real meal, and yeast enough to leaven it up. Put heart, soul and warmth in your sermons. An infidel once made this criticism of the Methodists: "If they were but panoplied in the literary armor of some other sects, in five years they would conquer the world for Jesus Christ." *Dr. H. C. Fish.*

8245. EARNESTNESS, Stimulated. Let none of my friends cry out to such a sluggish, luke-warm, unprofitable worm, "Spare thyself!" Rather spur me up, I pray you, with an "Awake thou that sleepest," and begin to do something for thy God! *Whitefield.*

8246. EARNESTNESS, Victorious. I am aware that many object to the severity of my language; but is there not cause for severity? I will be as harsh as truth, as uncompromising as justice. On this subject I do not wish to think, or speak, or write with moderation. No, no! Tell a man whose house is on fire to give a moderate alarm; tell him moderately to rescue his wife from the hands of the ravisher; tell the mother gradually to extricate her babe from the fire into which it has fallen; but urge me not to use moderation in a cause like the present. I am in earnest—I will not equivocate—I will not excuse—I will not retreat a single inch—AND I WILL BE HEARD. The apathy of the people is enough to make every statue leap from its pedestal, and to hasten the resurrection of the dead. *Wm. Lloyd Garrison.*

8247. EARTH Adapted to Man. The earth on which we tread, was evidently intended by the Creator to support man and other animals, along with their habitations, and to furnish those vegetable productions which are necessary for their subsistence; and, accordingly, he has given it that exact degree of consistency which is requisite for these purposes. Were it much harder than it now is; were it, for example, as dense as a rock, it would be incapable of cultivation, and vegetables could not be produced from its surface. Were it softer, it would be insufficient to support us, and we should sink at every step, like a person walking in a quagmire. The exact adjustment of the solid parts of our globe, to the nature and necessities of the beings which inhabit it, is an instance of Divine wisdom. *Dick.*

8248. EARTH, Attachment to the. A boy had the charge of a horse. He tied the end of the halter around his own arm, and lay down on the grass to sleep. The horse ran off, and the boy's arm was torn from his body. If he had held it loosely in his hand, the animal might have escaped, but the boy would have received no harm. It is thus that men foolishly bind, not their arms, but their very souls to some possession of the earth, and having made it fast, lie down to rest. When that possession falls away, as it often does, the man's heart is torn; if he had held it loosely he might have lost his treasure, but he would have retained possession of himself.

8249. EARTH, Destruction of the. What this change is to be, we dare not even conjecture; but we see in the heavens themselves some traces of destructive elements, and some indications of their power. The fragments of broken planets—the descent of meteoric stones upon our globe—the wheeling comets welding their loose materials at the solar furnace—the volcanic eruptions of our own satellite—the appearance of new stars, and the disappearance of others—are all foreshadows of that impending convulsion to which the system of the world is doomed. Thus placed on a planet which is to be burnt up, and under heavens which are to pass away; thus treading, as it were, on the cemeteries, and dwelling in the mausoleums of former worlds—let us learn the lesson of humility and wisdom, if we have not already been taught it in the school of revelation. *Timbs.*

8250. EARTH, End of the. Is it not probable, it may be asked, that the time will come when the globe itself will come to an end? And if it be so, can science detect the provision that is possibly made for this consummation of all things? We have seen that the atmosphere has for long been undergoing a change; that at a very early period it was charged with carbonic acid, the carbon of which now forms part of animal and vegetable structures. We saw, also, that at first it contained no ammonia; but since vegetation and decomposition began, the nitrogen that existed in the nitrates of the earth and some of the nitrogen of the atmosphere have been gradually entering into new combinations, and forming ammonia; and the quantity of ammonia, a substance at first non-existent, has gradually increased, and as it is volatile, the atmosphere now always contains some of it. The quantity has now become so great in it that it can always be detected by chemical analysis. There is an evident tendency of it to increase in the atmosphere. Now supposing it to go on increasing up to a certain point, it forms with air a mixture that, upon the application of fire, is violently explosive. An atmosphere charged with ammonia is liable to explode whenever a flash of lightning passes through it. And such an explosion would doubtless destroy, perhaps without leaving traces of, the present order of things. *Dr. Lindley Kemp.*

8251. EARTH, Glory of the. It was the glory of the earth that Christ trod upon its turf. It was the glory of the ocean that he sailed upon its bosom. It was the glory of the sun that it beamed upon his head. It was the glory of the air that it fanned his brow. It was the glory of the waters that they quenched his thirst. It was the glory of the flowers that they perfumed his path. What planet has been so honored as this? What world so visited, so distinguished, so blest? *Winslow.*

8252. EARTH, Motion of the. It is said that a farmer, about two hundred miles from New York, told his neighbors that he didn't believe any such foolishness as that about the world turning over every day; and he said that he would prove that he was right. So he placed a pumpkin on a stump, and sat on the fence watching it for twenty-four hours, and his neighbors sat there watching it with him. Sure enough, the pumpkin did not roll off, and the whole party went home convinced that the rotation business was a humbug.

8253. EARTH, Voice of the. The earth, from

her deep foundations, unites with the celestial orbs that roll throughout boundless space, to declare the glory and show forth the praise of their common Author and Preserver; and the voice of natural religion accords harmoniously with the testimonies of revelation, in ascribing the origin of the universe to the will of one eternal and dominant intelligence—the Almighty Lord and Supreme First Cause of all things that subsist.   *Buckland.*

8254. EARTHLY GLORY, Brevity of. William of Malmesbury tells the following curious story of the conversion of Ina, king of Wessex, A. D 726. The king made a great feast in one of his palaces, and invited his nobles and great men. The house was richly adorned, and the table laid with gold and silver service. The next day Ina set forth with his queen Ethelburga, to take up his abode in another house which he had. The house he had occupied was stripped of its fine ornaments, rich curtains, and gold and silver vessels, and by the queen's order was strewn with dung and filled with rubbish, and a sow with her pigs were put into the king's and queen's bed. When the royal train had gone forth some distance, the queen suggested to the king that they should return to the abandoned house, which they did. Then they discovered what a change had been wrought in a few hours. And Ethelburga said to the king, "Seest thou, O king, how the pomp of this world passeth away? Where are all thy goodly things? How foul is now the house which but yesterday was thy royal abode. Are not all the things of this life as a breath, yea, as a smoke, and as a wind that passeth away?" Then the old king resolved to spend the rest of his days in caring for his soul.

8255. EARTHLY GLORY, Uncertainty of. Sesostris, King of Egypt, having subdued many nations, ordered himself a chariot befitting so great a conqueror. A chariot of gold was made, and richly set with precious stones. Four kings were then yoked together, and made to draw the chariot, as often as the monarch required. One day it was drawn to a great festival, and Sesostris observed that one of the kings kept his eye fixed upon the wheel nearest him. He desired to know why he did so, and he told him he was simply "wondering at the unstable motion of the wheel that rolled up and down: first one part, and then another was uppermost, and the highest immediately became the lowest." This caused Sesostris to think of the frailty and uncertainty of human affairs, and he would no more be drawn in that proud manner.

8256. EARTHLY GLORY, Vanity of. Gilimex, King of the Vandals, being led in triumph by Belisarius, cried out, "Vanity of vanities, all is vanity." Charles V., Emperor of Germany, whom of all men the world judged most happy, cried out in reference to whatever is generally considered good and great, "Get you hence; let me hear no more of you."

8257. EARTHQUAKE, Effect of an. One of the most terrible earthquakes on record is that which happened at Lisbon on November 1, 1755. The morning was fine, and there was no apparent indication of the coming destruction. About nine o'clock a low, subterraneous rumbling was heard, which gradually increased, and culminated at last in a violent shock of earthquake, which leveled to the ground many of the principal buildings of the place. Three other shocks followed each other in rapid succession, and continued the work of destruction. Scarcely had the ill-fated inhabitants begun to realize the enormity of the disaster which had come upon them, when they were surprised by another visitation of a different, but not less destructive, character. The sea began to rush with great violence into the Tagus, which rose at once as much as forty feet above high-water mark. The water swept over a great part of the city, and many of the inhabitants fled from its approach to take refuge on a strong marble quay lately erected. They had collected there to the number of three thousand, when the quay was suddenly hurled bottom upwards, and every soul on it perished. There was another shock in the evening, which split the walls of several houses; but when it passed away, the rents closed up again so firmly that no trace of them could be seen. What the earthquake and flood had spared were consumed by fire. The 1st of November being All-Saints' Day, was kept as a high festival, and all the churches were brilliantly illuminated with candles. These falling, with the shock of the earthquake, against the timbers and curtains, set fire to them, and as there was no means of checking it, the conflagration spread rapidly. It is stated that by the combined effect of these disasters no less than sixty thousand persons perished.
                    Wonders of the World.

8258. EARTHQUAKE, Moral of an. He lay off Lisbon on this fatal first of November, preparing to hoist sail for England. He looked towards the city in the morning, which gave the promise of a fine day, and saw that proud metropolis rise above the waves in wealth and plenty, and founded on a rock that promised a poet's eternity, at least, to its grandeur. He looked an hour after, and saw the city involved in flames, and sinking in thunder. A sight more awful mortal eyes could not behold on this side the day of doom. And yet does not human pride make us miscalculate? A drunken beggar shall work as horrid a desolation with a kick of his foot against an ant-hill, as subterraneous air and fermented minerals to a populous city. And if we take in the universe of things rather than with a philosophical than a religious eye, where is the difference in point of real importance between them? A difference there is, and a very sensible one, in the merits of the two societies. The little Troglodytes amass neither superfluous nor imaginary wealth; and, consequently, have neither drones nor rogues among them.   *Warburton.*

8259. EASE, Buried in. Varia Servilius, descended of a Praetorian family, was remarkable for his idleness. As people passed by his house they would say, "Here lies Varia," speaking of him as a person that was not only dead, but buried.

8260. EASE, Seeking. The Sybarites banished from their city all sorts of artificers, and craftsmen that made any noise, that they might not be disturbed in their enjoyment of rest and repose.

8261. EAST, Regard for the. The east, in Scriptural language, was symbolically considered the more immediate residence of the Almighty, and has been emphatically alluded to in every age, although turning to the east savors, in some degree, of Catholicism, and even in the present day is one of the rites of that form of religion. The sun rises in the east, and the prophets of old always turned their faces in that direction when engaged in their devotions. A brilliant star appeared in the east at the birth of the Messiah. Baalam, Cyrus, and the Magi came from the east. It may be considered merely a sort of devotional piety commanded to be observed by the canon law. The Christian churches were anciently built due east and west; and in the early period of Christianity it was usual in Poland, Lithuania, and many other countries, when the creeds were read, for the nobility to rise up and stand facing the east, with their swords drawn, thereby intimating that they were ready, if necessary, to seal the truth of their belief with their blood and life. *Loaring.*

8262. EATING, Art of. To eat, in the true idea of the act, requires a far more scientific use of the mouth than is the case with mere feeding. Epicurism is no mere invention of low sensuality: they who practice it do but carry to an unworthy extreme one of the most excellent and characteristic powers of human nature. No man is wise who is not an epicure within the legitimate limits; none are more foolish and unkind to themselves than those who regard only quantity and speed. So with the mental palate. If we be not deliberate epicures in our reading, half our advantages and privileges are thrown away, and we are only like quadrupeds unintelligently munching grass. Not that we ought to pick out Apician morsels. *Grindon.*

8263. EATING, Condition of. A certain monk went to the convent at Mount Sinai, and finding all the inmates at work, shook his head, and said to the abbot, "Labor not for the meat which perisheth." "Very well," said the abbot, and ordered the good brother to a cell, and gave him a book to read. The monk retired, and sat hour after hour all day alone, wondering much that nobody called him to dinner or offered him any refreshment. Hungry and wearied out, the night at length arrived. He left his solitary cell, and repaired to the apartment of the abbot. "Father," says he, "do not the brethren eat to-day?" "Oh, yes," replied the abbot, "they have eaten plentifully." "Then how is it, Father," said the monk, "that you did not call me to partake with them?" "Because, brother," replied the abbot, "you are a spiritual man, and have no need of carnal food. For our part, we are

obliged to eat, and on that account we work; but you, brother, are above the want of the meat that perisheth." "Pardon me, Father," said the monk, "I perceive my mistake."

8264. EATING Sparingly. By a sparingness in diet, and eating as much as may be what is light and easy of digestion, I shall, doubtless, be able to think more clearly, and shall gain time. First, by lengthening out my life. Secondly, I shall need less time for digestion after meals. Thirdly, I shall be able to study more closely, without injury to my health. Fourthly, I shall need less time for sleep. Fifthly, I shall more seldom be troubled with the headache. *President Edwards.*

8265. ECCENTRICITY, Genius and. The great examples of Bacon, of Milton, of Newton, of Locke, and of others, happen to be directly against the popular inference, that a certain wildness of eccentricity and thoughtlessness of conduct are the necessary accompaniments of talent, and the sure indications of genius. Because some have united these extravagancies with great demonstrations of talent, as a Rousseau, a Chatterton, a Savage, a Burns, or a Byron; others, finding it less difficult to be eccentric than to be brilliant, have, therefore, adopted the one, in the hope that the world would give them credit for the other. But the greatest genius is never so great as when it is chastised and subdued by the highest reason: it is from such a combination, like that of Bucephalus, reined in by Alexander, that the most powerful efforts have been produced. And be it remembered, that minds of the very highest order, who have given an unrestrained course to their caprice, or to their passions, would have been so much higher by subduing them. *Colton.*

8266. ECONOMY, Advantages of. All to whom want is terrible, upon whatever principle, ought to think themselves obliged to learn the sage maxims of our parsimonious ancestors, and attain the salutary arts of contracting expense; for without economy none can be rich, and with it few can be poor. The mere power of saving what is already in our hands must be of easy acquisition to every mind; and as the example of Lord Bacon may show that the highest intellect cannot safely neglect it, a thousand instances every day prove that the humblest may practice it with success.

Johnson

8267. ECONOMY, Brevities. Beware of little expenses: a small leak will sink a great ship —*Franklin.*——He that is taught to live upon little, owes more to his father's wisdom, than he that has a great deal left him, does to his father's care.—*Penn.*——I had rather see my courtiers laugh at my avarice, than my people weep at my extravagance.—*Louis XII.* ——No man is rich whose expenditure exceeds his means; and no one is poor, whose incomings exceed his outgoings. *Haliburton.*

8268. ECONOMY Defined. We have warped the word "economy" in our English language into a meaning which it has no business whatever to bear. In our use of it, it constantly signifies merely sparing or saving; economy of money means saving money—economy of time, sparing time, and so on. But this is a wholly barbarous use of the word—barbarous in a double sense; for it is not English, and it is bad Greek. Economy no more means saving money than it means spending money. It means—the administration of a house; its stewardship; spending or saving, that is, whether money or time, or anything else, to the best possible advantage. In the simplest and clearest definition of it, economy, whether public or private, means the wise management of labor; and it means this mainly in three senses;—namely, first, applying your labor rationally; secondly, preserving its produce carefully; lastly, distributing its produce carefully.   *Ruskin.*

8269. ECONOMY, Industry and. Let honesty and industry be thy constant companions, and spend one penny daily less than thy gains: then shall thy hide-bound pocket soon begin to thrive, and will never again cry with the empty belly-ache; neither will creditors insult thee, nor want oppress, nor hunger bite, nor nakedness freeze thee. The whole hemisphere will shine brighter, and pleasure spring up in every corner of thy heart. Now, therefore, embrace these rules and be happy. Banish the bleak winds of sorrow from thy mind, and live independent. Then shalt thou be a man, and not hide thy face at the approach of the rich, nor suffer the pain of feeling little when the sons of fortune walk at thy right hand; for independency, whether with little or much, is good fortune, and places thee on even ground with the proudest of the golden fleece. Oh, then, be wise, and let industry walk with thee in the morning, and attend thee until thou reachest the evening hour for rest. Let honesty be as the breath of thy soul, and never forget to have a penny, when all thy expenses are enumerated and paid: then shalt thou reach the point of happiness, and independence shall be thy shield and buckler, thy helmet and crown; then shall thy soul walk upright, nor stoop to the silken wretch because he hath riches, nor pocket an abuse because the hand which offers it wears a ring set with diamonds.   *Franklin.*

8270. ECONOMY, Results of Trifling. Lafitte in boyhood applied to the rich banker M. Perregaux in Paris, in 1778, for a situation, and was informed that there would be no opening for a considerable time. As he passed from the office he stooped, picked up a pin, and placed it in the lapel of his coat. The banker from a window observed the action, and considered it the best kind of a recommendation for the young man. In the evening of the same day, M. Lafitte received the following note from M. Perregaux: "A place is made for you in my office, which you may take possession of to-morrow morning." From simple clerk he soon rose to be cashier—then partner—then head of the first banking-house in Paris; and, afterwards, in rapid succession, a deputy and president of the Council of Ministers, the highest point which a citizen could then attain.

8271. ECONOMY, Worthy. Let us learn the meaning of economy. Economy is a high, humane office; a sacrament, when its aim is grand; when it is the prudence of simple tastes; when it is practised for freedom, or love, or devotion. Much of the economy which we see in houses is of a base origin, and is best kept out of sight. Parched corn eaten to-day, that I may have roast fowl to my dinner to-morrow, is a baseness; but parched corn and a house with one apartment, that I may be free of all perturbations of mind; that I may be serene and docile to what the gods shall speak, and girt and road-ready for the lowest mission of knowledge or good will, is frugality for gods and heroes.   *Emerson.*

8272. EDUCATION, Agent of. There have been periods when the country heard with dismay that "The soldier was abroad." That is not the case now. Let the soldier be abroad: in the present age he can do nothing. There is another person abroad—a less important person in the eyes of some, an insignificant person, whose labors have tended to produce this state of things. The school-master is abroad! And I trust more to him, armed with his primer, than I do the soldier in full military array, for upholding and extending the liberties of his country.   *Lord Brougham.*

8273. EDUCATION, Aim of. It seemeth to me that the true idea of education is contained in the word itself, which signifies the act of drawing out, or educing; and being applied in a general sense to man, must signify the drawing forth or bringing out those powers which are implanted in him by the hand of his Maker. This, therefore, we must adopt as the rudimental idea of education: that it aims to do for man that which the agriculturist does for the fruits of the earth, and the gardener for the more choice and beautiful productions thereof: what the forester does for the trees of the forest, and the tamer and breaker-in of animals does for the several kinds of wild creatures.   *E. Irving.*

8274. EDUCATION, Barbarism and. The Goths despised education. An instance of this is the opposition they raised to the purpose of Amalasunta, who was eager to give the advantage of a liberal education to her son Alaric. "No, no," said the assembled warriors, " the idleness of study is unworthy of a Goth; high thoughts of glory are not fed by books, but by deeds of valor; he is to be a king whom all should dread. Shall he be compelled to dread his instructors? No."

8275. EDUCATION, Beginning of. Begin the education of the heart, not with the cultivation of noble propensities, but with the cutting away of those that are evil. When once the noxious herbs are withered and rooted out, then the more noble plants, strong in themselves, will shoot upwards. The virtuous heart, like the body, becomes strong and healthy more by labor than by nourishment.   *Richter.*

8276. EDUCATION, Benefits from. Education gives fecundity of thought, copiousness of illustration, quickness, vigor, fancy, words, images, and illustrations; it decorates every common thing, and gives the power of trifling without being undignified and absurd.
S. Smith.

8277. EDUCATION, Business of. The business of education is not to perfect a learner in all, or any of the sciences, but to give his mind that freedom, that disposition, and those habits, that may enable him to obtain any part of knowledge he shall apply himself to, or stand in need of, in the future course of his life.
Locke.

8278. EDUCATION, Christian. The great work of Christian education is not the direct and certain fruit of building schools and engaging schoolmasters, but something far beyond, to be compassed only by the joint efforts of all the whole church and nation, by the schoolmaster and the parent, by the schoolfellow at school, and by the brothers and sisters at home, by the clergyman in his calling, by the landlord in his calling, by the farmer and the tradesman, by the laborer and the professional man, and the man of independent income, whether large or small, in theirs; by the queen and her ministers, by the great council of the nation in parliament; by each and all of these laboring to remove temptations to evil, to make good easier and more honored, to confirm faith and holiness in others by their own example; in a word, to make men love and glorify their God and Saviour when they see the blessed fruits of his kingdom even here on earth.
Dr. Arnold.

8279. EDUCATION, Dual. Every man has two educations—that which is given to him, and the other that which he gives to himself. Of the two kinds, the latter is by far the most valuable. Indeed, all that is most worthy in a man, he must work out and conquer for himself. It is this that constitutes our real and best nourishment. What we are merely taught, seldom nourishes the mind like that which we teach ourselves.
Tynman.

8280. EDUCATION, Early. I think we may assert that in a hundred men, there more than ninety who are what they are, good or bad, useful or pernicious to society, from the instruction they have received. It is on education that depends the great difference observable among them. The least and most imperceptible impressions received in our infancy, have consequences very important, and of a long duration. It is with these first impressions as with a river, whose waters we can easily turn, by different canals, in quite opposite courses; so that from the insensible direction the stream receives at its source, it takes different directions; and at last arrives at places far distant from each other; and with the same facility we may, I think, turn the minds of children to what direction we please.
Locke.

8281. EDUCATION, Forgotten. It is said of the learned Castell, author of the "Lexicon Heptaglotton," that he so completely devoted himself to Oriental studies that he totally forgot his own language.

8282. EDUCATION, Inheritance of. We are, if we know how to use our advantages, inheritors of the wealth of all the richest times; strong in the power of the giants of all ages; placed on the summit of an edifice which thirty centuries have been employed in building.
Whewell.

8283. EDUCATION, A Liberal. He that makes his son worthy of esteem by giving him a liberal education, has a far better title to his obedience and duty than he that gives a large estate without it.
Socrates

8284. EDUCATION, Light of. Were it not better for a man in a fair room to set up one great light, or branching candlestick of lights, than to go about with a rushlight into every dark corner?
Bacon.

8285. EDUCATION, Lustre of. Virtue and talents, though allowed their due consideration, yet are not enough to procure a man a welcome wherever he comes. Nobody contents himself with rough diamonds, or wears them so. When polished and set, then they give a lustre.
Locke.

8286. EDUCATION, Mission of. I consider a human soul without education like marble in the quarry, which shows none of its inherent beauties until the skill of the polisher fetches out the colors, makes the surface shine, and discovers every ornamental cloud, spot, and vein that runs through the body of it. Education, after the same manner, when it works upon a noble mind, draws out to view every latent virtue and perfection, which without such helps are never able to make their appearance. If my reader will give me leave to change the allusion so soon upon him, I shall make use of the same instance to illustrate the force of education, which Aristotle has brought to explain his doctrine of substantial forms, when he tells us that a statue lies hid in a block of marble, and that the art of the statuary only clears away the superfluous matter and removes the rubbish. The figure is in the stone, the sculptor only finds it. What sculpture is to a block of marble, education is to a human soul. The philosopher, the saint, or the hero, the wise, the good, or the great man, very often lie hid and concealed in a plebeian, which a proper education might have disinterred, and have brought to light.
Addison.

8287. EDUCATION, Mistakes of. All of us, who are worth anything, spend our manhood in unlearning the follies, or expiating the mistakes, of our youth.
Shelley.

8288. EDUCATION, Neglect of Moral. A father inquires whether his boy can construe Homer, if he understands Horace, and can taste Virgil; but how seldom does he ask, or examine, or think whether he can restrain his passions; whether he is grateful, generous, humane, compassionate, just, and benevolent.
Lady Hervey.

8289. EDUCATION, Personal. Costly apparatus and splendid cabinets have no magical power to make scholars. As a man is in all circumstances, under God, the master of his own fortune, so he is the maker of his own mind. The Creator has so constituted the human intellect, that it can only grow by its own action: it will certainly and necessarily grow. Every man must, therefore, educate himself. His books and teacher are but helps; the work is his. A man is not educated until he has the ability to summon, in an emergency, his mental powers in vigorous exercise to effect the proposed object. It is not the man who has seen the most, or read the most, who can do this. Such an one is in danger of being borne down, like a beast of burden, by an overloaded mass of men's thoughts. Nor is it the man who can boast merely of native vigor and capacity. The greatest of all warriors, who went to the siege of Troy, had not the pre-eminence, because nature had given him strength and he carried the largest bow, but because self-discipline had taught him how to bend it. *Webster.*

8290. EDUCATION, Primary. Having learned our letters, and some small syllables printed on a fly-sheet of the Shorter Catechism, we were at once passed into the Book of Proverbs. In the olden time this was the universal custom in all the common schools in Scotland—a custom that should never have been abandoned. That book is without a rival for beginners, containing quite a repertory of monosyllables and pure Saxon—"English undefiled." Take this passage, for example, where, with one exception, every word is formed of a single syllable, and belongs to the Saxon tongue: "Train up a child in the way he should go: and when he is old, he will not depart from it." What a contrast to the silly trash of modern school-books for beginners, with such sentences as, "Tom has a dog," "The cat is good," "The cow has a calf!" *Dr. Guthrie.*

8291. EDUCATION, Profit of. All but ten of the signers of the Declaration of Independence were trained in universities and colleges. More than one-fourth of the members of the National Congress from the beginning to this day have been graduates of colleges. This fact, taking the ratio of population and graduates, shows that the colleges have given their graduates more than thirty chances to one. Were Cicero, and Pitt, and Sumner, less effective in their oratory because of the affluence of their culture? *Dr. Foss.*

8292. EDUCATION, Public or Private. At a great school there is all the splendor and illumination of many minds; the radiance of all is concentrated in each, or at least reflected upon each. But we must own that neither a dull boy, nor an idle boy, will do so well at a great school as at a private one. For, at a great school there are always boys enough to do well easily, who are sufficient to keep up the credit of the school; and the dull or idle boys are left at the end of the class, having the appearance of going through the course, but learning nothing at all. Such boys may do good at a private school, where constant attention is paid to them, and they are watched. So that the question of public or private education is not properly a general one; but whether one or the other is best for my son. *Dr. Johnson.*

8293. EDUCATION, Religion in. In America the college is the child of the church. The seal of Harvard University, the oldest on the continent, bears the legend, "*Christo et Ecclesiae.*" One of the hymns sung at the inauguration at Harvard is Luther's grand old lyric, beginning, "A strong tower is our God." Yale began in the gifts of a few Connecticut clergymen, who, bringing each a few books from their library, said, "I give these for the founding of a college." A late report of the commissioner of education shows that of the 368 colleges it enumerates, thirty only are known to be secular in their origin and management, while 261 are known to be under the care of different churches. *Dr. Foss*

8294. EDUCATION, Religious. There is no object of study which ought not to be studied in relation to Christianity. Must we not stand rebuked before the heathen, when we remember the most universal infusion of their idolatry into all the various occupations of life? Referring to the religion of ancient Rome, Mr. Gibbon tells us, "It was, moreover, interwoven with every circumstance of business or pleasure, of public or private life, with all the offices and amusements of society." And how interesting the reply of the Chickasaw Indian to Mr. Wesley, when he asked him if his tribe often thought and talked of their gods. "We think of them always," said the Indian; "wherever we are, we talk of them and to them, at home and abroad, in peace and in war, before and after the fight, and, indeed, whenever and wherever we meet together." *Anon.*

8295. EDUCATION, Self. Chevalier Ramsay gives the following account of Stone: "Born a son of the gardener of the Duke of Argyll, he arrived at eight years of age before he learned to read. By chance, a servant having taught young Stone the letters of the alphabet, there seemed nothing more to discover and expand his genius. He applied himself to study, and he arrived at the knowledge of the most sublime geometry and analysis, without a master, without a conductor, without any other guide than pure genius. At eighteen years of age he had made these considerable advances without being known, and without knowing himself the prodigiousness of his acquisitions. The Duke of Argyll, who joined to his military talents a general knowledge of every science that adorns the mind of a man of his rank, walking one day in his garden, saw lying on the grass a Latin copy of Sir Isaac Newton's celebrated 'Principia.' He called some one to him to take it and carry it back to his library. Our young gardener told him that the book belonged to him. 'To you!' replied the Duke; 'do you understand geometry, Latin, Newton?' 'I know a little of them,' replied the young man, with an air of simplicity, arising from a profound ignorance of his own knowledge and talents. The Duke was surprised, and having a taste for the sciences, he entered into conversation with the young mathematician; he asked him several questions, and was astonished at the force, the accuracy, and the candor of his answers. 'But how,' said the Duke, ' came you by the knowledge of all these things?' Stone replied, 'A servant taught me ten years since; does any one need to know anything more than the twenty-four letters, in order to learn everything else that one wishes?' The Duke's curiosity was redoubled; he sat down upon a bench, and requested a detail of his proceedings in becoming so learned. 'I first learned to read,' said Stone; 'the masons were then at work upon your house; I went near them one day, and saw the architect used a rule and compasses, and that he made calculations. I inquired what might be the meaning and use of these things, and I was informed that there was a science called arithmetic; I purchased a book of arithmetic, and I learned it. I was told there was another science called geometry; I bought the books, and I learned geometry. By reading, I found that there were good books of these sciences in Latin. I bought a dictionary, and I learned Latin; I understood, likewise, that there were good books of the same kind in French. I bought a dictionary, and I learned French. And this, my lord, is what I have done; it seems to me that we may learn everything when we know the twenty-four letters of the alphabet.' This account charmed the Duke. He drew this wonderful genius out of his obscurity, and provided him with an employment which left him plenty of time to cultivate the sciences. He discovered in him, also the same genius for music, for painting, for architecture, for all the sciences which depend on calculations and proportions." He distinguished himself especially as a mathematician, and was the author of Stone's "Mathematical Dictionary."

8296. EDUCATION, Sphere of. The effects of philosophy are different according to the difference of inclinations in men. If indeed it lights on one who loves a dull and inactive sort of life, that makes himself the centre and the little conveniences of life the circumference of all his thoughts, such a one does contract the sphere of her activity, so that only having made easy and comfortable the life of a single person, it fails and dies with him; but when it finds a man of ruling genius, one fitted for conversation and able to grapple with the difficulties of public business, if it once possess him with principles of honesty, honor, and religion, it takes a compendious method, by doing good to one, to oblige a great part of mankind. Such was the effect of the conversation of Anaxagoras with Pericles, of Plato with Dion, and of Pythagoras with the principal statesmen of Italy. *Plutarch.*

8297. EDUCATION, Superficial. Real education is the formation and training of the mind. To train the mind, requires hard, patient, and independent thinking and work; the mere crude teaching a youth a bundle of facts, which he acquires with no labor, and, only retaining,

neither digests nor assimilates, is no training at all; they no way nourish his mind, but deposited there, are utterly as raw and undigested as he swallowed them. He may be a full man, but it is the fullness of a bottle, which will pour out what has been previously poured in, whether vinegar or claret; he may be a convenient depository of other men's thoughts—he may have sufficient capacity for holding them;—but to call such a man educated is a misuse of terms. *Cayley.*

8298. EDUCATION, Unconscious. Every man is to himself what Plato calls the Great Year. He has his sowing time and his growing time, his weeding, his irrigating, and his harvest. The principles and ideas he puts into his mind in youth lie there, it may be, for many years, apparently unprolific. But nothing dies. There is a process going on unseen, and by the touch of circumstances the man springs forth into strength, he knows not how, as if by a miracle. But after all, he only reaps as he had sown.
J. A. St. John.

8299. EFFECTS, Abiding. The earth is a vast whispering gallery, and the centuries are but telegraphic wires which convey the thoughts of one age to another. The nineteenth century sits at one end of the telegraphic wire, and the first century at the other end, and the former hears transmitted to it lessons from the latter, that mould and shape it for heaven, for happiness, or woe. Nothing that is said is ever extinguished, nothing that is done ever ceases its influence. It goes out from us, and is never arrested or put an end to. The pebble that I drop into the sea will send out its undulations for ever and ever. The blow that I strike upon the earth will transmit its vibrations for ever and ever. The act I thought no eye followed, that deed which I fancied was done and annihilated forever, are each still sounding in successive vibrations and repetitions in the atmosphere, and throughout the earth, and at the judgment-seat God has but to make man's ear more sensitive, man's eye more susceptible, and all he said and did will come back to him, the good in sweet music, the evil in crashes and reverberations of woe and agony, that shall never, never cease. Science can demonstrate, with absolute precision, that a blow once struck, carries on its vibrations to the end, that a word once said is repeating itself in the air till the judgment-day; and Scripture leads us to infer that it will at that day meet us again, a memorial of the good or the evil we have done. *Cumming.*

8300. EFFECTS, Judging by. A dervish was journeying alone in the desert, when two merchants suddenly met him. "You have lost a camel," said he to the merchants. "Indeed we have," they replied. "Was he not blind in his right eye, and lame in his left leg?" said the dervish. "He was," replied the merchants. "Had he lost a front tooth?" said the dervish. "He had," rejoined the merchants. "And was he not loaded with honey on one side, and wheat on the other?" "Most certainly he was," they replied; "and as you have seen him so lately, and marked him so particularly, you can in all probability conduct us unto him." "My friends," said the dervish, "I have never seen your camel, nor ever heard of him, but from you." "A pretty story, truly!" said the merchants, "but where are the jewels, which formed part of his cargo?" "I have neither seen your camel nor your jewels," repeated the dervish. On this they seized his person, and forthwith hurried him before the cadi, where, on the strictest search, nothing could be found upon him, nor could any evidence whatever be adduced to convict him either of falsehood or of theft. They were then about to proceed against him as a sorcerer, when the dervish with great calmness thus addressed the court: "I have been much amused with your surprise, and own there has been some ground for your suspicions; but I have lived long, and alone, and I can find ample scope for observation, even in a desert. I knew that I had crossed the track of a camel that had strayed from its owner, because I saw no mark of any human footstep on the same route; I knew that the animal was blind in one eye, because it had cropped the herbage only on one side of its path; and I perceived that it was lame in one leg, from the faint impression which that particular foot had produced upon the sand: I concluded that the animal had lost one tooth, because wherever it had grazed a small tuft of herbage was left uninjured in the centre of its bite. As to that which formed the burden of the beast, the busy ants informed me that it was corn on the one side, and the clustering flies that it was honey on the other."

8301. EFFEMINACY, Example of. Sinyndirides the Sybarite excelled in effeminacy. At one time he cast himself upon a bed, prepared from the leaves of roses, and after taking a sleep complained that there were pustules upon his body, from lying upon so hard a bed. It is also said that when going to a distant country he was such an epicure, that he took with him a thousand cooks, a thousand fowlers, and as many fishermen.

8302. EFFEMINACY, Royal. Sardanapalus, king of Assyria, was of such an effeminate disposition that he adopted the fashion and dress of women, and practiced all their arts. Upon his sepulchre he caused a statue to be cut, attired like a woman, and under it was engraven "Sardanapalus, the son of Anacyndaraxes, hath built Anchiala and Tarsus in one day. Eat, drink and be merry; the rest is not worth the fillip of a finger." Cicero says that Aristotle, lighting upon this tomb and inscription, exclaimed, "It should have been upon the grave of a beast, not upon a tomb of a king."

8303. EFFORT, Daily. A Boston merchant resolved to let no day pass without personally persuading some one to come to Christ. This of course, led him to look out for opportunities. But on retiring one night it occurred to him that he had said nothing to any one on the subject during that day. At first he saw no chance to redeem himself, but remembering that a grocer near by generally kept open late, he arose, dressed, and went to the store, and found the man in good condition for conversation—alone and at leisure. That visit was the means of bringing the old gentleman to God and the church, with several of his family.

Dr. James Porter.

8304. EFFORT, Individual. It is said that an American declared he could fight the whole British army, and when he was asked how, he said, "Why, this is what I would do: I know I am the best swordsman in the world, so I would go and challenge one Britisher, and kill him; then take another, and kill him. Thus, I only want time enough, and I would kill the whole British army." It was a foolish boast, but illustrates the principle on which the world is to be conquered. One by one, and one per year by every Christian, and the race will be saved in ten years.

8305. EFFORT and Intercession. Mrs. Palmer tells of an invalid boy of eleven years, who asked his pastor, "Can you tell me anything I can do for Jesus?" The pastor directed him to pray for his most intimate friend, and to invite him to the class-meeting. He did so, and his friend was converted. He then began to pray for his unsaved father, and told him of his earnest desire for his conversion, and he became a Christian. Next he prayed for his own brother, with like result. From this time he continued to intercede for his friends and acquaintances. Too ill to attend the revival services in the church, he longed for his father's report of the meetings. One night he asked, "Father! was Samuel Coleman saved to-night?" "No, Samuel Coleman was not saved to-night, but he was forward kneeling at the form, crying for mercy," said his father. "Thank God!" The next night, on his father's return from meeting, he repeated the question, and, receiving an affirmative reply, said, "Thank God! then I can die happy," as though his life-work was finished, and soon after expired. Among his papers was found a list of fifty-five names, every one of which had with him been a subject of special prayer and effort, and all of whom had professed religion. The last name on the list was Samuel Coleman.

8306. EFFORT, Nature of Christian. He who in the regeneration has been made partaker of Christ, gives forth in his life Christ-like actions. There is a good deal of artificial charity agoing. People can tie oranges to the sprigs of a fir-tree in a parlor, and the show will gratify children on a winter evening. But true Christian beneficence is a fruit that grows, and is not tied on. It swells up from sap which the tree of righteousness draws out of that infinite love in which it is rooted. He who is in Christ cannot stand still, any more than the water in those iron tubes which traverse our streets in connection with the great reservoir; on it must flow, wherever there is an opening, by reason of the pressure from above. Hear the exclamation of that ancient Christian in explanation of his wonderful self-sacrifice and energetic labor for the good of men: "The love of Christ

constraineth me." Efforts burst impetuous from his bosom whenever an opening was made, because he was in union with the Fountain-head on high. As fruit is sweet and profitable, so are the efforts of Christians for the good of the world. And like the abundance with which good trees bear, is the abundance of a true disciple's labors. The fecundity of nature is a standing wonder with all who possess sufficient intelligence to observe it. The faculty of production in the vegetable creation is beyond all calculation or expression great. Through adverse seasons and other causes, the actual quantity of fruit brought to perfection is greatly limited; but the tendency and willingness and capability of plants to produce their fruit in inconceivable quantities may be seen everywhere in the teeming, flowering spring. Such is the tendency of a renewed heart.
Wm. Arnot.

8307. EFFORT, Special. A worthy Methodist, burning with a desire to do good and save souls, seeing a man on the road before him, hastened to make up to him, that he might deal with him about his soul. Ignorant of these good intentions, the other, taking him for a footpad, did all he could to throw him out, but in vain. At length the Methodist runs him down, confirming his worst fears—as they now stood face to face—with the startling question, "Are you prepared to die?" At this awful question, down goes the poor man on his knees, to offer the other all his money if he will but spare his life, happy, as the supposed footpad raised him, to find out his mistake.
Guthrie.

8308. EFFORT, Union of. A certain traveler, when rossing a bleak and precipitous mountain, reached a place where a great stone had rolled down from the heights above, and lodged in the path, completely filling it, so that it was impossible to pass. Night came on, and he sat down in sorrow, complaining bitterly of his desolate and helpless circumstances. At length, another traveler arrived, tried to remove the stone, and also sat down in despair. In the course of time a few more joined them, and sat down discouraged. One of them said, "Let us pray to God;" after which he arose, saying, "Let us all take hold of it together." They did so, and, by their united strength, rolled it over the precipice, and continued their journey.
Anon.

8309. EGOTISM, Avoiding. Lord Chesterfield in a letter to his son says, "The only sure way of avoiding these evils is never to speak of yourself at all. But when, historically, you are obliged to mention yourself, take care not to drop one single word that can directly or indirectly be construed as fishing for applause. Be your character what it will, it will be known; and nobody will take it upon your own word. Never imagine that anything you can say yourself will varnish your defects or add lustre to your perfections; but, on the contrary, it may, and nine times in ten will, make the former more glaring and the latter obscure. If you are silent upon your own subject,

neither envy, indignation, nor ridicule will obstruct or allay the applause which you may really deserve; but if you publish your own panegyric, upon any occasion, or in any shape whatsoever, and however artfully dressed or disguised, they will all conspire against you, and you will be disappointed of the very end you aim at."

8310. EGOTISM, Bravery and. After the remarkable campaign in which Xerxes was driven and frightened out of Greece by Themistocles, the Grecian officers undertook to decide by vote who had done the best service. Every ballot bore first the name of the voter, and second the name of Themistocles. It is always best to do our best, but not best to make proclamation of it.

8311. EGOTISM, Effect of. There can be no doubt that this remarkable man (Lord Byron) owed the vast influence which he exercised over his contemporaries at least as much to his gloomy egotism as to the real power of his poetry. We never could very clearly understand how it is that egotism, so unpopular in conversation, should be so popular in writing; or how it is that men who affect in their compositions qualities and feelings which they have not, impose so much more easily on their contemporaries than on posterity. *Lord Macaulay.*

8312. EGOTIST, Weakness of the. Only by the supernatural is a man strong—only by confiding in the Divinity which stirs within us. Nothing is so weak as an egotist—nothing is mightier than we, when we are vehicles of a truth before which the state and the individual are alike ephemeral.
Emerson.

8313. ELECTION, Doctrine of. This opinion is not believed by thee, but is only pretended, as a cloak for thy wickedness and idleness; for if thou dost believe that, if God hath elected, he will save thee however thou livest, why are not thy practices answerable to such principles? Why dost thou not leave thy ground unsowed, and thy calling unfollowed, and say, If God hath decreed me a crop of corn, I shall have it, whether I sow my ground or no; and if God hath decreed me an estate, I shall have it though I never mind my calling? Why dost thou not neglect and refuse eating, and drinking, and sleeping, and say, If God hath decreed that I shall live longer, I shall do it, though I never eat, or drink, or sleep? For God hath decreed these things concerning thy ground, estate, and natural life, as well as concerning thine eternal condition in the other world.
Spurgeon.

8314. ELECTION, Evidence of. There is no way for men to discern their names written in the book of life but by reading the work of sanctification in their own hearts. I desire no miraculous voice from heaven, no extraordinary signs, or unscriptural notices and informations in this matter. Lord, let me but find my heart obeying thy calls; my will obediently submitting to thy commands; sin my burden, and Christ my desire: I never crave a fairer or surer evidence of thy electing love to my soul: and if I had an oracle from heaven, an extraordinary messenger from the other world, to tell me thou lovest me, I have no reason to credit such a voice, whilst I find my heart wholly sensual, averse to God, and indisposed to all that is spiritual.   *Flavel.*

8315. ELECTION, General. One day the news came into the prison that there was a boat up from City Point, and there were over 900 men in the prison rejoicing at once. They expected to get good news. Then came the news that there was only one man in that whole number that was to be let go, and they all began to say, "Who is it?" It was some one who had some influential friend at Washington that had persuaded the Government to take an interest in him and get him out. The whole prison was excited. At last an officer came and shouted at the top of his voice, "Henry Clay Trumbull!" The chaplain told me his name never sounded so sweet to him as it did that day. That was election: but you can't find any Henry Clay Trumbull in the Bible. There is no special case in the Bible. God's proclamations are to all sinners. Everybody can get out of prison that wants to. The trouble is they don't want to go. They had rather be captives to some darling sin like lust, appetite, covetousness, than to be liberated. You need not be stumbling over election. The proclamation is, "Whosoever will, let him come and drink of the water of life freely."   *Moody.*

8316. ELECTION, Knowledge of. Now whosoever thou art that desirest to know whose names are written in heaven, who is elected to life eternal, it shall not be told thee this or that individual person; but generally thus, men so qualified, faithful in Christ and to Christ, obedient to the truth and for the truth; that have subjected their own affections, and resigned themselves to the guidance of the heavenly will. These men have made noble conquests, and shall have princely crowns. Find but in thyself this sanctimony, and thou art sure of thy election. In Rome the *patres conscripti* were distinguished by their robes, as the liveries of London from the rest of the company. So thy name is enrolled in the legend of God's saints, if thy livery witness it, that thy "conversation is in heaven" (1 John 3: 16).   *T. Adams.*

8317. ELECTION, Links in the Chain of. Archbishop Leighton uses the figure of a chain, which he describes as having its first and last link —election and final salvation—up in heaven in God's own hands; the middle one, which he says is effectual calling, being let down to earth into the hearts of his children; and they laying hold on it have sure hold on the other two, for no power can sever them. Then the events that lead to that calling, and those that follow it even to the final consummation and bliss of God's people in heaven may be so many connected and connecting links, not one of which but bears evidence of the Master's hand. How often does Satan exert all the skill of his infernal mechanism to hammer out an additional fetter for his blind and hopeless captive, already fast bound in misery and iron,

which is laid hold on by the divine alchemist, and changed into a golden link in the wondrous chain of providential mercies, destined to form an everlasting song of praise in the mouth of that ransomed sinner! We can say it of every dispensation towards us, that God has wrought it into a link in that precious chain; and such indeed is the retrospect of bygone days, when thus enlightened by the beams of covenant mercy.   *Anon.*

8318. ELECTION, True. It is not by the rapture of feelings, and by the luxuriance of thought, and by the warmth of those desires which descriptions of heaven may stir up within us, that I can prove myself predestined to a glorious inheritance. If I would find out what is hidden, I must follow what is revealed. The way to heaven is disclosed; am I walking in that way? It would be a poor proof that I were on my voyage to India; that, with glowing eloquence and thrilling poetry, I could discourse on the palm-groves and spice-isles of the East. Am I on the waters? is the sail hoisted to the wind? and does the land of my birth look blue and faint in the distance? The doctrine of election may have done harm to many; but only because they have fancied themselves elected to the end, and have forgotten that those whom Scripture calls elected are elected to the means. The Bible never speaks of men as elected to be saved from the shipwreck, but only as elected to tighten the ropes, and hoist the sails, and stand to the rudder. Let a man search faithfully; let him see that when Scripture describes Christians as elected, it is as elected to faith, as elected to sanctification, as elected to obedience; and the doctrine of election will be nothing but a stimulus to effort. It cannot act as a soporific. I shall cut away the boat, and let drive all human devices, and gird myself, amid the fierceness of the tempest, to steer the shattered vessel into port. *Melvill.*

8319. ELEVATION, True. True elevation does not consist in the elevation of nature, in the material or exterior hierarchy of beings. True elevation, an elevation essential and eternal, is one of merit, one of virtue. Birth, fortune, genius, are nothing before God. For what is birth before God who was never born? What is fortune before God who made the world? What is genius before God who is an infinite mind, and from whom we derive that little flame which we honor by so fine a name? Evidently nothing. That which is something before God, which approaches him, is personal elevation, due to an effort of virtue, which, in whatever rank of nature we are placed, reproduces in the soul an actual image of the Deity.   *Lacordaire.*

8320. ELIJAH, Character of. The Power which came upon him cut, by its fierce coming, all the ties which bound him to his kind, tore him from the plough, or from the pastoral solitude, and hurried him to the desert, and thence to the foot of the throne, or to the wheel of the triumphal chariot. And how startling his coming to crowned or conquering guilt! Wild from the wilderness, bearded like its lion-lord the fury of God glaring in his eye; his mantle heaving to his heaving breast; his words stern, swelling, tinged on their edges with a terrible poetry; his attitude dignity; his gesture power—how did he burst upon the astonished gaze! how swift and solemn his entrance! how short and spirit-like his stay! how dream-like, yet distinctly dreadful, the impression made by his words long after they had ceased to tingle on the ears! and how mysterious the solitude into which he seemed to melt away! Poet, nay prophet, were a feeble name for such a being. He was a momentary incarnation— a meteor kindled at the eye, and blown on the breath, of the Eternal. God testified him to be the greatest of the family of the prophets, by raising him to heaven. *G. Gilfillan.*

8321. ELISHA, Qualities of. Elisha was, in the strictest sense, a great and a good man; and in his goodness consisted his greatness. His life is a living sermon. He was to be found in season and out of season—in every occasion of need. Never do we find him lacking in moral courage. Wherever his word and presence were required to rebuke sin, this righteous man was "bold as a lion!" He seems to grudge no time, no labor, if only his great work be advanced. We find him in royal palaces, in martial camps, in weeping households. At one time, hurling the awful malediction over impenitence and wrong-doing; at another mingling his tears over "the loved and lost," and then his songs of joy over the lost, raised to be loved again. Poor and unostentatious in dress, in mien, in dwelling, he had been again and again the saviour of his country, and exercised what was equivalent to regal sway in court and city—by the throne and by the altar. He had fostered, with loving heart, the schools of the prophets—training, with holy fidelity, those on whom the mantle of his office and example was afterwards to fall. In fine, he was the John of the prophetic period, the Barnabas of the Old Testament. *Macduff.*

8322. ELOCUTION, Importance of. On being asked what was the first and chiefest among the precepts of rhetoric, Demosthenes answered—"Elocution;" what the second, he answered—"Elocution;" what the third, he answered still—"Elocution." *St. Augustine.*

8323. ELOQUENCE, Adaptation of. If our eloquence be directed above the heads of our hearers we shall do no execution. By pointing our arguments low, we stand a chance of hitting their hearts, as well as their heads. In addressing angels, we could hardly raise our eloquence too high; but we must remember that men are not angels. Would we warm them by our eloquence, unlike Mahomet's mountain, it must come down to them, since they cannot raise themselves to it. It must come home to their wants and their wishes, to their hopes and their fears, to their families and their fire-sides. The moon gives a far greater light than all the fixed stars put together, although she is much smaller than any of them; the reason is, that the stars are su-

perior and remote, but the moon is inferior and contiguous. *Colton.*

8324. ELOQUENCE, Finished. Phavorinus used to say of Plato and Lysias, "Take or change any word in an oration of Plato's, and you take from the eloquence; and the like will you do if you take or change a word in any sentence of Lysias."

8325. ELOQUENCE, God of. In Greek mythology Mercury was accounted the god of Eloquence. The most important item of his outfit was a rod or wand, by virtue of which he had the power of conducting some souls to hell, and freeing others from it. By this they signify that the power of eloquence frees from death such as the hangman waited for, and as often exposes innocence to the utmost severity of the law.

8326. ELOQUENCE, Power of. In whom does it not enkindle passion? Its matchless excellence is applicable everywhere, in all classes of life. The rich and the poor experience the effects of its magic influence. It excites the soldier to the charge and animates him to the conflict. The miser it teaches to weep over his error, and to despise the degrading betrayer of his peace. It convicts the infidel of his depravity, dispels the cloud that obscures his mind, and leaves it pure and elevated. The guilty are living monuments of its exertion, and the innocent hail it as the vindicator of its violated rights and the preserver of its sacred reputation. How often in the courts of justice does the criminal behold his arms unshackled, his character freed from suspicion, and his future left open before him with all its hopes of honors, station and dignity! And how often, in the halls of legislation, does eloquence unmask corruption, expose intrigue, and overthrow tyranny! In the cause of mercy it is omnipotent. It is bold in the consciousness of its superiority—fearless and unyielding in the purity of its motives. All opposition it destroys: all power it defies. *Melvill.*

8327. ELOQUENCE, Prayer and. Pericles the Athenian was said to thunder and lighten, and to carry a dreadful thunderbolt in his tongue by reason of his eloquence. Whenever he was to make an oration, he applied himself studiously to it, and always prayed first to the gods, that no single word might fall from his lips which was not agreeable to the matter in hand.

8328. ELOQUENCE, True. Oliver Cromwell was one day engaged in a warm argument with a lady upon the subject of oratory, in which she maintained that eloquence could only be acquired by those who made it their study in early youth, and their practice afterwards. The Lord Protector, on the contrary, maintained that there was no eloquence but that which sprang from the heart; since, when that was deeply interested in the attainment of any object, it never failed to supply a fluency and richness of expression which would in the comparison render vapid the studied speeches of the most celebrated orators. This argument ended, as most arguments do, in the lady's tenaciously adhering to her side of the question, and in the Protector's saying he had no doubt he should one day make her a convert to his opinion. Some days after, the lady was thrown into a state bordering on distraction by the unexpected arrest and imprisonment of her husband, who was conducted to the Tower as a traitor to the Government. The agonized wife flew to the Lord Protector, rushed through his guards, threw herself at his feet, and, with the most pathetic eloquence, pleaded for the life and innocence of her husband. Cromwell maintained a severe brow, till the petitioner, overpowered by the excess of her feelings and the energy with which she had expressed them, paused. His stern countenance then relaxed into a smile, and, extending to her an immediate liberation of her husband, he said, "I think all who have witnessed this scene will vote on my side of the question, in the dispute between us the other day, that the eloquence of the heart in power certainly surpasses all other eloquence." *Anon.*

8329. ELYSIUM Preferred. If I were now disengaged from my cumbrous body, and on my way to Elysium, and some superior being should meet me in my flight, and make the offer of returning, and remaining in my body, I should, without hesitation, reject the offer, so much should I prefer going to Elysium to be with Socrates, and Plato, and all the ancient worthies, and to spend my time in converse with them. *Cicero.*

8330. EMANCIPATION, Universal. I speak in the spirit of the British law, which makes liberty commensurate with and inseparable from British soil; which proclaims even to the stranger and sojourner, the moment he sets his foot upon British earth, that the ground on which he treads is holy, and consecrated by the genius of universal emancipation. No matter in what language his doom may have been pronounced; no matter what complexion, incompatible with freedom, an Indian or an African sun may have burnt upon him; no matter in what disastrous battle his liberty may have been cloven down; no matter with what solemnities he may have been devoted upon the altar of slavery; the first moment he touches the sacred soil of Britain, the altar and the god sink together in the dust; his soul walks abroad in her own majesty; his body swells beyond the measure of his chains that burst from around him; and he stands redeemed, regenerated, disenthralled, by the irresistible genius of universal emancipation! *Curran.*

8331. EMINENCE, Road to. I do not hesitate to say that the road to eminence and power from an obscure condition ought not to be made too easy, nor a thing too much of course. If rare merit be the rarest of all things, it ought to pass through some sort of probation. The temple of Honor ought to be seated on an eminence. If it be open through virtue, let it be remembered too, that virtue is never tried but by some difficulty, and some struggle. *Burke.*

8332. EMPLOYMENT, Advantage of. Assure yourself, that employment is one of the best remedies for the disappointments of life. Let even your calamity have the liberal effect of occupying you in some active virtue, so shall you in a manner remember others, till you forget yourself. *Pratt.*

8333. EMPLOYMENT, Amusements and. Employment does not mean no amusement; the workers, or those who use their time instead of wasting it, have more holidays than any one else, for every change is a going out to play. When rational and unsophisticated, play, commonly so-called, is still work; at all events, no man ever played genially and heartily without gaining something by it, and thus gathering from it a fruition of work. Play, moreover, is perfectly compatible with work: let no one suppose that art and science disallow it, or that they render play uninteresting and distasteful. Pastime and fun are as great a need as occupation, and as great a luxury. He who refuses to play is but a stately fool; to sport and gambol with children is one of the sweetest lyric-songs of life: grown people, however, should remember that, as the end of all exertions, even the slightest, should be profit, play should always be based upon an intelligent idea. People may be mirthful without being silly, just as they may be grave without being gloomy; a mind in right order can descend into frolics as readily as it can soar into magnificent ideas; for it is the characteristic of well-disciplined intelligence, and of purity and earnestness of the affections, that they are universal in their capacity. It is this which makes the philosopher, the true idea of whom is that of an amiable and pious man—who, with the profound and scientific, combines the lively and the droll. *Grindon.*

8334. EMPLOYMENT, Fixed. The Jews compared a man with a fixed employment to "a vineyard fenced." A good comparison. A man's activities, within his proper calling, are not like trees scattered up and down the wayside, or over the wilderness, when much of the fruit is lost; but like well-planted and well-trained vines in a garden, where the most is made of them, and they are all husbanded and preserved. *Stoughton.*

8335. EMPLOYMENT, Honorable. It is related of Sir Thomas More, by his daughter, that His Grace of Norfolk coming to dine with him, finds him in the church choir, singing, with a surplice on. "What!" cries the Duke as they walk home together, "my Lord Chancellor playing the parish-clerk! sure, you dishonor the King and his office." "Nay," says father, smiling, "your Grace must not deem that the King, your master and mine, will be offended at my honoring his Master." *F. F. Trench.*

8336. EMPLOYMENT, Most Useful. Suppose a man to have a talent at finding out springs and contriving of aqueducts (a piece of skill for which Hercules and other of the ancients are much celebrated in history), surely he could not so satisfactorily employ himself in sinking a well or driving water to some prirate seat or contemptible cottage, as in supplying conduits to some fair and populous city, in relieving an army just perishing from thirst, or in refreshing and adorning with fountains and cool streams the beautiful gardens of some glorious monarch. *Plutarch.*

8337. EMPLOYMENT Necessary for Man. With the exception of one extraordinary man, I have never known an individual—least of all, a man of genius—healthy and happy without a profession; that is, some regular employment, which does not depend on the will of the moment, and which can be carried on so far mechanically, that an average quantum only of health, spirits, and intellectual exertion are requisite to its faithful discharge. Three hours of leisure unannoyed by any alien anxiety, and looked forward to with delight as a change and recreation, will suffice to realize, in literature, a larger product of what is truly genial, than weeks of compulsion. *Coleridge.*

8338. EMPLOYMENT, Seek. Exert your talents and distinguish yourself, and don't think of retiring from the world until the world will be sorry that you retire. I hate a fellow whom pride, or cowardice, or laziness, drives into a corner, and who does nothing when he is there but sit and growl. Let him come out as I do, and bark. *Dr. S. Johnson.*

8339. EMPHASIS, Improper. The following story is told of a theological student at Andover, who had an excellent opinion of his own talents. On one occasion he asked the professor who taught elocution at the time: "What do I especially need to learn in this department?" "You ought first to learn to read," said the professor. "Oh, I can read now!" replied the student. The professor handed the young man a Testament, and pointed to the twenty-fifth verse of the twenty-fourth chapter of Luke's Gospel; he asked him to read that. The student read: "Then he said unto them, O fools, and slow of heart *to believe* all that, the prophets have spoken." "Ah," said the professor, "they were fools for believing the prophets, were they?" Of course that was not right, and so the young man tried again: "O fools, and slow of heart to believe *all* that the prophets have spoken." "The prophets, then, were sometimes liars?" asked the professor. "No. 'O fools, and slow of heart to believe all that the *prophets* have spoken." "According to this reading," the professor suggested, "the prophets were notorious liars." This was not a satisfactory conclusion, and so another trial was made: "O fools, and slow of heart to believe all that the prophets have *spoken*." "I see now," said the professor, "the prophets wrote the truth, but they spoke lies." This last criticism discouraged the student, and he acknowledged that he did not know how to read. "The difficulty lies in the fact that the words 'of heart to believe' apply to the whole of the latter part of the sentence, and emphasis on any particular word entirely destroys the meaning."

8340. ENCOURAGEMENT, Angelic. Ruffinus and Valerius suffered martyrdom about 287, at Vidola in Gaul. They were tortured upon the little horse and beaten with leaded whips till their bodies were a mass of mangled flesh. But just alive, they were cast into prison. In the night an angel stood before them holding a crown of dazzling brightness in either hand, and saying, "Be of good cheer, valiant soldiers of Jesus Christ. A little more of battle, and then these crowns are yours." In the morning they were ordered to execution, and went to receive their crowns.

8341. ENCOURAGEMENT from Small Things. Diogenes, once on a feast day, when very despondent and tempted to give up his philosophic life, received a lesson from a little mouse which came and nibbled the mouldy crusts in his pouch. Addressing himself he said, "What is the matter with thee, Diogenes? Thou seest this tiny mouse lives well, and is very glad of thy scraps; but thou, who must needs be a person of quality, forsooth art extremely sorry and out of humor, because thou dost not feast upon down-beds, and canst not have the genteel privilege at this merry time to be drunk as well as others."

8342. END, Consider the. It is said that as an ancient king of Tartary was riding with his officers of state, they met a dervis crying aloud, "To him that will give me a hundred dinars I will give a piece of good advice." The king, attracted by this strange declaration, stopped, and said to the dervis: "What advice is this that you offer for a hundred dinars?" "Sire," replied the dervis, "I shall be most thankful to tell you as soon as you order the money to be paid me." The king, expecting to hear something extraordinary, ordered the dervis to be paid at once; so he said: "Begin nothing without considering what the end may be." The officers of state, smiling at what they thought ridiculous advice, looked at the king, who they expected would be so enraged at this insult as to order the dervis to be severely punished. But the king said: "I see nothing to laugh at in this advice; on the contrary, I am persuaded that if it were more frequently practiced, men would escape many evils. Indeed, so convinced am I of the wisdom of this maxim, that I shall have it engraved on my plate, and written on the walls of my palace, so that it may be ever before me." Some time after this occurrence, one of the nobles of the court resolved to destroy the king, and place himself on the throne. In order to accomplish his purpose, he secured the confidence of one of the king's surgeons, to whom he gave a poisoned lancet, saying: "If you will bleed the king with this lancet I will give you ten thousand pieces of gold, and when I ascend the throne you shall be my vizier." This surgeon, dazzled by such brilliant prospects, wickedly assented to the proposal. Soon the king sent for this man to bleed him. He put the poisoned lancet into a side pocket, and hastened into the king's presence. The arm was tied, when suddenly the surgeon's eye read at the bottom of the basin: "Begin nothing without considering what the end may be." He thought within himself: "If I bleed the king with this lancet he will die, and I shall be seized and put to a cruel death. Then of what use will all the gold in the world be to me?" Then, returning the lancet to his pocket, he drew forth another. The king, observing this, and perceiving that he was much embarrassed, asked why he changed his lancet so suddenly. He stated that the point was broken; but the king, doubting his statement, commanded him to show it. This so agitated him that the king felt assured all was not right. He said: "Tell me instantly what you mean, or your head shall be severed from your body!" The surgeon, trembling with fear, promised to relate all to the king, if he would only pardon him The king consented, and the surgeon related the whole matter, acknowledging that had it not been for the words in the basin, he should have used the fatal lancet. The king summoned his court, and ordered the traitor to be executed. Then, turning to his officers, he said: "You now see that the advice of the dervis, at which you laughed, is most valuable; it has saved my life. Search out this dervis, that I may amply reward him for his wise maxim."

8343. END, Enduring to the. Among the different games and races at Athens, there was one in which they carried a burning torch in their hand. If they arrived to the end without its being extinguished, they obtained the prize. Thus, they only shall be saved, says the Saviour, who endure to the end. It is not the man who makes a splendid profession for a season—it is not the man who appears to carry the torch of truth only a part of the way, that shall be crowned—but he who perseveres, and whose lamp is trimmed, and who holds fast his confidence, and the rejoicing of his hope unto the end. Yet, alas! how many seem to bid fair for a season, but in time of temptation fall away. Epictetus tells us of a gentleman returning from banishment, who in his journey towards home, called at his house, told a sad story of an imprudent life; the greater part of which being now spent, he was resolved for the future to live philosophically—to engage in no business, to be candidate for no employment —not to go to court, nor to salute Cæsar with ambitious attendances: but to study, and worship the gods and die willingly, when nature or necessity called him. Just, however, as he was entering his door, letters from Cæsar met him, and invited him to court: where, alas! he forgot all his promises, which were warm upon his lips; grew pompous, secular, and ambitious; and gave the gods thanks for his preferment. Thus many form resolutions in their own strength, make for a season some pretensions to seriousness, but are like the children of Ephraim, who, though armed and carrying bows, yet turned back in the day of battle.
Buck.

8344. END, Question of the. A young shopman once took up a leaf of the Bible, and was about to tear it in pieces, and use it for packing up some small parcel, when a pious friend said, "Do not tear that: it contains the word of eternal life." The young man, though he did not relish the reproof, olded up the leaf, and put it in his pocket. Shortly after this, he said within himself, "Now I will see what kind of life it is of which this leaf speaks" On unfolding the leaf, the first words that caught his eye were the last in the book of Daniel: "But go thou thy way till the end be: for thou shalt rest, and stand in thy lot at the end of the days." He began immediately to inquire what his lot would be at the end of the days, and was led to a religious life.

8345. END OF THE WORLD, Expected. There was an almost universal idea, in the tenth century, that the end of the world was approaching. Many charters began with these words: "As the world is now drawing to its close." An army marching under the Emperor Otho I. was so terrified by an eclipse of the sun, which it conceived to announce this consummation, as to disperse hastily on all sides. This notion seems to have been founded on some confused theory of the Millennium, and died away with the dawn of the eleventh century.

8346. ENDURANCE, Sublimity of. I cannot help thinking that the severe and rigid economy of a man in distress has something in it very sublime, especially if it be endured for any length of time serenely and in silence. I remember a very striking instance of it in a young man, since dead; he was the son of a country curate, who had got him a berth on board a man-of-war, as a midshipman. The poor curate made a great effort for his son; fitted him out well with clothes, and gave him fifty pounds in money. The first week, the poor boy lost his chest, clothes, money, and everything he had in the world. The ship sailed for a foreign station; and his loss was without remedy. He immediately quitted his mess, ceased to associate with the other midshipmen, who were the sons of gentlemen; and for five years, without mentioning it to his parents—who he knew could not assist him—or without borrowing a farthing from any human being, without a single murmur or complaint, did that poor lad endure the most abject and degrading poverty, at a period of life when the feelings are most alive to ridicule, and the appetites most prone to indulgence. Now, I confess I am a mighty advocate for the sublimity of such long and patient endurance. If you can make the world stare and look on, there you have vanity, or compassion, to support you; but to bury all your wretchedness in your own mind—to resolve that you will have no man's pity, while you have one effort left to procure his respect—to harbor no mean thought in the midst of abject poverty, but, at the very time you are surrounded by circumstances of humility and depression, to found a spirit of modest independence upon the consciousness of having always acted well;—this is conduct, which, though found in the shade and retirement of life, ought to be held up to the praises of men, and to be looked upon as a noble model for imitation.
S. Smith.

8347. ENDURANCE, Uncomplaining. The orchardist takes much care of his trees, using saw and knife upon them, as well as spade and hoe about them. They do not cry out at the loss of their branches, or at being dug about, for this will do them nothing but good, causing a better growth, and more perfect fruit.

8348. ENDURANCE, Utility of. A sore-eyed Spartan enlisted as a soldier. One said to him, "Poor man, in thy condition what wilt thou do in a fight?" He answered, "If I can do nothing else I shall blunt the enemies' swords."

8349. ENEMIES, Kindness to. "Is this for me?" said a wounded Confederate colonel, a prisoner to whom a cup of coffee and a slice of buttered bread was handed. "Yes, sir. Will you please drink it?" "Well, this beats me. We don't treat our prisoners so." "We make no distinction," was the answer. The colonel drank his coffee and ate his bread in silence, but with tears in his eyes, which showed that his heart was touched.

8350. ENEMIES, Lessons from. Now, our enemy (to gratify his ill-will towards us) doth acquaint himself with the infirmities, both of our bodies and minds, with the debts we have contracted, and with all the differences that arise in our families, all which he knows as well, if not better than ourselves. He sticks fast to our faults, and chiefly makes his invidious remarks upon them. Nay, our most depraved affections, that are the worst distempers of our minds, are always the subject of his inquiry, just as vultures pursue putrid flesh, noisome and corrupted carcases, because they have no perception of those that are sound and are in health. So our enemies catch at our failings, and then they spread them abroad by uncharitable and ill-natured reports. Hence, we are taught this useful lesson for the direction and management of our conversations in the world, nat we be circumspect and wary in everything we speak or do, as if our enemy always stood at our elbow and overlooked every action. Hence, we learn to live blameless and inoffensive lives. *Plutarch.*

8351. ENEMIES, Love to. A few years since, a young man in the vicinity of Philadelphia was one evening stopped in a grove, with the demand, "Your money or your life!" The robber then presented a pistol to his breast. The young man, having a large sum of money, proceeded leisurely and calmly to hand it over to his enemy, at the same time setting before him the wickedness of his career. The rebuke of the young man cut the robber to the heart. He became enraged, cocked his pistol, held it to the young man's head, and with an oath, said, "Stop that preaching, or I will blow your brains out." The young man calmly replied, "Friend, to save my money I would not risk my life; but to save you from your evil course I am willing to die: I shall not cease pleading with you." He then urged the truth more earnestly and kindly. Soon the pistol fell to the ground, the tears began to flow, and the robber was overcome. He handed the money all

back, with the remark, "I cannot rob a man of such principles!" *Bibl. Treasury.*

8352. ENEMIES, Power Over. If strong and mighty enemies should come upon thee, assault and besiege thee, and thou hadst on thy side one whom thou knewest certainly to be lord, and to have power over all thine enemies, thou mightest lawfully be bold and without fear. Now have we, through faith, Christ on our side, which is Lord over all lords, which hath full power over all fortune and misfortune, prosperity and adversity. *Coverdale.*

8353. ENEMIES, Repugnance to. A cat, according to Æsop, in affected kindness asked a sick hen how she did. The hen replied with spirit, "The better if you were further off."

8354. ENEMIES, Surrender to. A venerable negro in Iowa was on trial for an offense against the State. When the case was announced in court, "The State of Iowa versus Sampson Cæsar," the aged African exclaimed: "What! de whole State of Iowa agin dis chile Den I surrenders."

8355. ENEMIES, Utilizing. The best experienced gardener cannot so change the nature of every tree, that it shall yield pleasant and well-tasting fruit; neither can the craftiest huntsman tame every beast. One therefore makes the best use he can of his trees, the other of his beast; although the first are barren and dry, the latter wild and ungovernable. So sea water is unwholesome, and not to be drunk; yet it affords nourishment to all sorts of fish, and serves as it were for a chariot to convey those who visit foreign countries. The Satyr would have kissed and embraced the fire the first time he saw it; but Prometheus bade him take heed, else he might have cause to lament the loss of his beard, if he came too near that which burns all it touches. Yet this very fire is a most beneficial thing to mankind; it bestows upon us both the blessings of light and heat, and serves those who know how to use it for the most excellent instrument of mechanical arts. Directed by these examples, we may be able to take right measures of our enemies, considering that by one handle or other we may lay hold of them for the use and benefit of our lives; though otherwise they may appear very untractable and hurtful to us. *Plutarch.*

8356. ENEMY, Giving Drink to an. At Hanover C. H., two wounded soldiers lay near each other. One of them, a Confederate from North Carolina, suffered much from thirst, and cried, "Water! water!" The other, a Federal, managed to crawl to a stream, fill his canteen, and returning with it, held it to the lips of the dying man. He in return gave the other his Testament, the thing he most prized, and in a few moments entered the land whose inhabitants thirst no more.

8357. ENEMY, His Own. "No one's enemy but his own," happens generally to be the enemy of everybody with whom he is in relation. The leading quality that goes to make this character is a reckless imprudence and a selfish pursuit of selfish enjoyments, independent of all consequences. "No one's enemy but his own," runs rapidly through his means; calls in a friendly way on his friends for bonds, bail, and securities; involves his nearest kin, leaves his wife a beggar, and quarters his orphans upon the public; and after enjoying himself to his last guinea, entails a life of dependence upon his progeny, and dies in the ill-understood reputation of a harmless folly, which is more injurious to society than some positive crimes. *Mrs. Jameson.*

8358. ENEMY, Punishing an. There is a Persian story of Gobryas, who contended with Darius against the Magi. Gobryas was pursued by one of them into a dark room, where a severe conflict went on. Darius entered to help his friend, but dared not attack with his sword, lest he should slay his friend; whereupon Gobryas bade him run both through together rather than fail.

8359. ENEMY, Rescuing an. In the year 1567, King Philip II. of Spain sent the Duke of Alva as Governor of the Low Countries. Alva was notorious for his bitter persecution of all who embraced the Reformed religion. So many people were put to death during the term of his government that it was called "The Reign of Terror," and his Council received the name of the "Blood Council." Amongst the persecuted people was a poor Protestant named Dirk Willemzoon, who was condemned to death for his opinions. Dirk made his escape from his persecutors, and fled for his life, pursued by an officer of justice. A frozen lake lay in his way. It was early in the year, and the ice had become unsafe; he ventured upon it; it cracked and shook beneath his steps as he ran, but he ran for his life; a horrible death would be his portion if he was caught. The shore lay before him; so on he ran over the trembling ice till at last he set foot on the firm shore. But a cry of terror came from behind: he looked back and saw the officer sinking through the broken ice into the waters of the lake. No one was near to help him but the poor fugitive, Dirk Willemzoon. He might have left the officer to perish, and escaped himself; but Dirk went back over the cracking ice, putting his own life in danger, and succeeded in reaching and saving his pursuer. *Anon.*

8360. ENEMY, Revenge upon an. Diogenes, to one that asked him how he might be revenged of his enemy, said, "The only way to gall and fret him effectually is for yourself to appear a good and honest man."

8361. ENEMY, Robbing an. Tasso was told that he had an opportunity of taking advantage of a bitter enemy. He replied, "I wish not to plunder him; but there are things I wish to take from him;—not his honor, his wealth, or his life—but his malice and ill-will."

8362. ENEMY, Trusting an. Some pigeons had long lived in fear of a kite, but by being always on the alert, and keeping near their dovecote, they had contrived hitherto to escape the attacks of the enemy. Finding his sallies unsuccessful, the kite betook himself to craft:

"Why," said he, "do you prefer this life of anxiety when, if you would only make me your king, I would secure you from every attack that could be made upon you?" The pigeons, trusting to his professions, called him to the throne; but no sooner was he established there than he exercised his prerogative by devouring a pigeon a day. Whereupon one that yet waited his turn said, "It serves us right." *Æsop.*

8363. ENEMY, Watching the. When in the immediate presence of the enemy Washington used to give the order, "Put only Americans on picket to-night."

8364. ENERGY, Effect of. It is idleness that creates impossibilities; and where men care not to do a thing they shelter themselves under a persuasion that it cannot be done. The shortest and surest way to prove a work possible, is strenuously to set about it; and no wonder if that proves it possible that for the most part makes it so. *South*

8365. ENERGY, Ministerial. Thaddeus Conolly of Ireland, says, "I went one Sabbath into a church to which a new incumbent had been lately appointed. The congregation did not exceed half a dozen, but the preacher delivered himself with as much energy and affection as if he were addressing a crowded audience. After the service, I expressed to the clergyman my wonder that he should preach so fervently to such a small number of people. 'Were there but one,' said he, 'my anxiety for his improvement would make me equally energetic.'" The following year Conolly went into the same church: the congregation was multiplied twenty-fold. The third year he found the church full.

8366. ENERGY, Power of. He who would do some great thing in this short life must apply himself to the work with such a concentration of his forces as to idle spectators, who live only to amuse themselves, looks like insanity. *John Foster.*

8367. ENERGY, Sphere of. I know it is common for men to say that such and such things are perfectly right, very desirable, but that, unfortunately, they are not practicable. Oh, no, sir! no! Those things which are not practicable are not desirable. There is nothing in the world really beneficial that does not lie within reach of an informed understanding and a well-directed pursuit. There is nothing that God has judged good for us that He has not given us the means to accomplish, both in the natural and the moral world. If we cry, like children, for the moon, like children we must cry on. *Burke.*

8368. ENGAGEMENTS, Keeping. Sextus Pompeius had seized upon Sicilia and Sardinia, and made war upon the triumvirate and people of Rome; having pressed them with want and scarcity, they sued for peace. Octavianus Cæsar and Antonius met Sextus, and terms of peace were agreed upon, and they mutually entertained one another. While the captains were with Sextus, on board his vessel, Menas, the Admiral of the Navy, asked him "If he should not cut the cables, put off the ship, and make him lord, not only of Sicily and Sardinia, but of the whole world itself?" It would have been a very easy thing to do, but Sextus regarded his honor too much for that. He replied, "Menas might have done it unknown to me; but since they are here let us think no more about it, for perjury is none of my property."

8369. ENGLAND, Blessings of. Oh, England! abode of comfort, and cleanliness, and decorum! Oh, blessed asylum of all that is worth having upon earth! Oh, sanctuary of religion and of liberty for the whole civilized world! It is only in viewing the state of other countries, that thy advantages can be duly estimated! May thy sons, who have "fought the good fight," but know and guard what they possess in thee! Oh, land of happy firesides, and cleanly hearths, and domestic peace; of filial piety, and parental love, and connubial joy; "the cradle of heroes, the school of sages, the temple of law, the altar of faith, the asylum of innocence," the bulwark of private security and of public honor. *Clarke.*

8370. ENJOYMENT, Capacity for. It is something to look upon enjoyment, so that it be free and wild, and in the face of nature, though it is but the enjoyment of an idiot. It is something to know that heaven has left the capacity of gladness in such a creature's breast; it is something to be assured that, however lightly men may crush that faculty in their fellows, the great Creator of mankind imparts it even to his despised and slighted work. Who would not rather see a poor idiot happy in the sunlight, than a wise man pining in a darkened jail? Ye men of gloom and austerity, who paint the face of Infinite Benevolence with an eternal frown, read in the everlasting book, wide open to your view, the lesson it would teach. Its pictures are not in black and sombre hues, but bright and glowing tints; its music—save when ye drown it—is not in sighs and groans, but songs and cheerful sounds. Listen to the million voices in the summer air, and find one dismal as your own. Remember, if ye can, the sense of hope and pleasure which every glad return of day awakens in the breast of all your kind who have not changed their nature, and learn some wisdom even from the witless, when their hearts are lifted up they know not why, by all the mirth and happiness it brings. *Dickens.*

8371. ENJOYMENT, Limited. Providence has fixed the limits of human enjoyment by immovable boundaries, and has set different gratifications at such a distance from each other, that no art or power can bring them together. This great law it is the business of every rational being to understand, that life may not pass away in an attempt to make contradictions consistent, to combine opposite qualities, and to unite things which the nature of their being must always keep asunder. *Johnson.*

8372. ENJOYMENT, Man's Power of. Let us look at the sky over our heads. What a lovely pros-

pect have we even there! Had God chosen, he might have made the sky of a dull and leaden hue. If the atmosphere were duly supplied with oxygen, we could live under a leaden sky as well as under one of the most gorgeous tints. There is no absolute necessity for the beauty, and oftentimes the splendor, which meets our eye when we look up. At one hour we see the sky a deep liquid blue, without a cloud or spot; then we have presented to us pillared masses of resplendent cloud, reminding us of the great white throne which shall be set; and then the scene changes again, and the pillared cloud is removed, and smaller clouds, all glittering in the sunshine, with swift yet stately motion, traverse that field of blue, and we think of the armies of heaven which follow Jesus on white horses. Oh! that sky is a grand and noble object of contemplation, and if only God teach us by his own handiwork, our hearts may be elevated, indeed, by looking at its glories. There go the pall-like clouds with their golden fringes, and their silver linings, telling us that there is wealth attached even to our darkest sorrows; there lie scattered all over the heavens the dappled masses of silver and gold, as though the Lord of glory had himself passed by that way, and it had been strewn for his feet by adoring angels' hands; yonder the heavens are overspread with a burnished sheet, as though the sun would remind us as he set of what shall be the portion of the Lord's people after their life's sunsetting, even the city of gold. Times there are when the jasper, the sapphire, the chalcedony, the emerald, the sardonyx, the sardius, the chrysolite, the beryl, the topaz, the chrysoprasus, the jacynth, and the amethyst, seem all flung in wild confusion abroad upon that sky; or when, amid its ever-changing hues, they seem to melt into, or give place to one another; and if we look at this sky as it is, and as it might have been, is there not cause for praise, even as we look up? But it is impossible to sum up man's daily powers of enjoyment. *Power.*

8373. ENJOYMENT, Natural. All real and wholesome enjoyments possible to man, have been just as possible to him since first he was made of the earth as they are now; and they are possible to him chiefly in peace. To watch the corn grow and the blossom set, to draw hard breath over plough-share and spade, to read, to think, to love, to hope, to pray—these are the things to make man happy; they have always had the power of doing these—they never will have power to do more. *Ruskin.*

8374. ENJOYMENT, Pursuit of. All solitary enjoyments quickly pall, or become painful, so that, perhaps, no more insufferable misery can be conceived than that which must follow incommunicable privileges. Only imagine a human being condemned to perpetual youth while all around him decay and die. Oh! how sincerely would he call upon death for deliverance! What, then, is to be done? Are we to struggle against all our desires? Luckily, we should strive in vain, or, could we succeed, we should be fools for our pains. To strangle a natural feeling is a partial suicide; but there is no need to extinguish the fertility of the soil lest the harvest should be unwholesome. Is it not better far to root up the weeds, and to plant fruits and flowers instead? Were but a tithe of the time and thought usually spent in learning the commonest accomplishments bestowed upon regulating our lives, how many evils would be avoided or lessened! how many pleasures would be created or increased!

Sharpe.

8375. ENJOYMENT, Religious. They might generally tell where a man's heart was by his joy. Some people went to religion for consolation. A member of the Rev. Rowland Hill's congregation had the habit of going to the theatre. Mr. Hill went to him and said, "This will never do—a member of my church in the habit of attending a theatre!" Mr. So-and-so replied that it surely must be a mistake, as he was not in the habit of going there, although it was true he did go now and then, for a treat. "Oh!" said Rowland Hill, "then you are a worse hypocrite than ever, sir. Suppose any one spread the report that I ate carrion, and I answered, "Well, there is no wrong in that; I don't eat carrion every day in the week; but I have a dish now and then for a treat! 'Why,' you would say, 'What a nasty, foul and filthy appetite Rowland Hill has to have to go to carrion for a treat.'" Religion was the Christian's truest treat, Christ was his enjoyment—he went to the house of God because there his heart leaped with holy mirth. Where their joy was, there would their heart be also. Was Jesus Christ the fountain of their joy? if not, he was none of theirs. Some Christians, like Peter, followed Christ afar off. Let them mend their pace—if they would be happy let them take Mary's place, Martha's, or John's. Let them have fellowship with Jesus.

Spurgeon.

8376. ENJOYMENT, Secret of. Life is made up of minutes, and its happiness of corresponding little pleasures: the wise man secures the atoms as they flit past him, and thus becomes owner of the aggregate. Making every circumstance of life—sensuous, moral, and intellectual—and every day and hour, contribute a little something, he finds that though a brilliant and memorable pleasure may come but twice or thrice, the secret of a happy life is nevertheless his own. That fine secret is not so much to lay plans for acquiring happy days, as to pluck our enjoyment on the spot; in other words, to spend that time in being happy, which so many lose in deliberating and scheming how to become so.

Grindon.

8377. ENJOYMENTS, Temporary. Every comfortable enjoyment, whether it be in relations, estate, health, or friends, is a candle lighted by Providence for our comfort in this world: and they are but candles, which will not always last: and those that last longest will at length be consumed and wasted. But oftentimes it falls out with them as with candles—they are blown out before they are half consumed.

Flavel.

8378. ENJOYMENTS, Uncertainty of. You would never think of detaining the birds which come in their season, and fill the air with their melody. Pet them and feed them as you may, they use their wings and fly away from you to a warmer clime. The flowers which adorn your grounds to-day will fade and die to-morrow. Such winged and vanishing things are all earthly enjoyments. One fountain only sends forth perpetual streams of joy—the fountain of life.

8379. ENLIGHTENMENT, Spiritual. "I remember once being present," says Captain Basil Hall, "at the Geological Society, when a bottle was produced which was said to contain certain Zoophytes (delicate water-animals, having the form of plants). It was handed round in the first instance among the initiated on the foremost benches, who commented freely with one another on the forms of the animals in the fluid; but when it came to our hands, we could discover nothing in the bottle but the most limpid fluid, without any trace, so far as our eyes could make out, of animals dead or alive, the whole appearing absolutely transparent. The surprise of the ignorant, at seeing nothing, was only equal to that of the learned, who saw so much to admire. Nor was it till we were specifically instructed what it was we were to look for, and the shape, size, and general aspect of the zoophytes pointed out, that our understanding began to co-operate with our sight in peopling the fluid which, up to that moment, had seemed perfectly uninhabited. The wonder then was, how we could possibly have omitted seeing objects now so palpable." How many are the things which appear to the illuminated Christians to be palpably revealed, which the unconverted cannot discover to have any place in the Scriptures of truth; and how much surprised does he feel that he could ever have overlooked them!

F. F. Trench.

8380. ENMITY to God. It profits nothing to be peaceful towards all men, if we be at war with God; it is no good to us if all men approve, and the Lord be offended; neither is there any danger, though all shun and hate us, if with God we find acceptance and love.

St. Chrysostom.

8381. ENNUI, The Evils Produced by. Ennui perhaps has made more gamblers than avarice, more drunkards than thirst, and perhaps as many suicides as despair.

Colton.

8382. ENTHUSIASM, Apostolic. There are some who, proscribing the exercise of the affections entirely in religion, would reduce Christianity to a mere rule of life; but, as such persons betray an extreme ignorance of human nature as well as of the Scriptures, I shall content myself with remarking that the apostles, had they lived in the days of these men would have been as little exempt from their ridicule as any other itinerants. If the supreme love of God, a solicitude to advance his honor, ardent desires after happiness, together with a comparative deadness to the present state, be enthusiasm, it is that enthusiasm which animated the Saviour and breathes throughout the Scriptures.

Robert Hall

8383. ENTHUSIASM, Demand for. We want enthusiasm in God's work. We find it in the world. Men are desperately in earnest in business circles. Hell is in earnest. Why should not we? We talk about infidelity, and all the isms that are creeping over the world. I am more afraid of cold formalism than anything else. Let the children of God but see eye to eye, and Christianity will overcome all the hosts of hell and death. There is as much power in the gospel to-day as ever. Man has been as bad as he can be. He was bad in Eden, he was bad for two thousand years under the law, and he has been bad these eighteen centuries under grace; but, my friends, there is power in the gospel to save. When men are willing to give their lives to work for God, then he takes these men and uses them. One thing I admire about Garibaldi—his enthusiasm. In 1867, when he was on his way to Rome, he was told that if he got there he would be imprisoned. Said he, "If fifty Garibaldis are imprisoned, let Rome be free." And when the cause of Christ is buried so deep in our hearts, that we do not think of ourselves, but are willing to die, then we will reach our fellow-men. *Moody.*

8384. ENTHUSIASM, Example of. Five years ago I went to Edinburgh, and stopped a week to hear one man speak—Dr. Duff, the returned missionary. A friend told me a few things about him, and I went to light my torch with his burning words. My friend told me that the year before he had spoken for some time, and fainted in the midst of his speech. When he recovered, he said, "I was speaking for India, was I not?" And they said he was. "Take me back, that I may finish my speech." And notwithstanding the entreaties of those around, he insisted on returning, and they brought him back. He then said, "Is it true that we have been sending appeal after appeal for young men to go to India, and none of our sons have gone? Is it true, Mr. Moderator, that Scotland has no more sons to give to the Lord Jesus? If it is true, although I have spent twenty-five years there, and lost my constitution—if it is true that Scotland has no more sons to give, I will be off to-morrow, and go to the shores of the Ganges, and there be a witness for Christ." That is what we want. A little more, a good deal more, of that enthusiasm, and Christianity will begin to move, and go through the world, and will reach men by thousands. *Moody.*

8385. ENTHUSIASM, Noble. Whitefield was ever busily engaged in his Master's work. He heard a voice constantly ringing in his ear the command, "Occupy till I come!" expecting soon to hear the same voice say, "Give an account of thy stewardship, for thou shalt be no longer steward." His motto was, "No nestling on this side eternity." At one time he writes, "Lord, when thou seest me in danger of nestling, in tender pity put a thorn into my nest to prevent my doing it;" and again, "I am determined to go on till I drop; to die fighting, though it be on my stumps."
Dr. J. B. Wakeley.

8386. ENTHUSIASM, Power of. Nothing is so contagious as enthusiasm; it is the real allegory of the lute of Orpheus; it moves stones, it charms brutes. Enthusiasm is the genius of sincerity, and truth accomplishes no victories without it. *Lord Lytton.*

8387. ENTHUSIASM, Religious. Souls are gravely warned, without regard to time, or place, or person, or condition, to be detached from the gifts of God, and to eschew sweet feelings, and gushing fervors, when the danger is rather in their attachment to their carriages and horses, their carpets and their old china, the parks and the opera, and the dear bright world. Why, if the poor Belgravians could get a little attachment, were it only to an image or a holy water-stoup, and I care not how inordinate, it would be a welcome miracle of grace, considering all they have to keep them far from God, for they move in a sphere which seems to be outside his omnipresence. No! no! the warnings of St. Theresa to barefooted Carmelites are hardly fit for such as those. Oh, better far to flutter like a moth round the candles of a gay benediction than lie without love in the proprieties of sensual ease and worldly comfort, which seem, but perhaps are not (and you cannot tell), without actual sin. *F. W. Faber.*

8388. ENTHUSIASM, Work Under. The great artist, Michael Angelo, was a man of eager ardent temperament, and when he came to work on marble he destroyed many a block of beautiful stone by his haste to get out his imprisoned idea; and it is said that some parts of some of his great statues are out of proportion, the marble having been cut away too much in the beginning to allow of their being finished in perfection. But just as they are, they are among the finest and grandest in the world. So many of our inspirations to goodness and usefulness are better wrought out in heat and haste than to never attempt them at all. The world needs the great soul of goodness and truth as well as the cold, correct, and faultless forms. *A. D. Vail.*

8389. ENVY, Avoid. Let age, not envy, draw wrinkles on thy cheeks; be content to be envied, but envy not. Emulation may be plausible, and indignation allowable, but admit no treaty with that passion which no circumstance can make good. A displacency at the good of others because they enjoy it, though not unworthy of it, is an absurd depravity, sticking fast unto corrupted nature, and often too hard for humility and charity, the great suppressors of envy. This surely is a lion not to be strangled but by Hercules himself, or the highest stress of our minds, and an atom of that power which subdueth all things unto itself. *Browne.*

8390. ENVY, Biblical. Is *"as rottenness in the bones,"* Prov. 14: 30. What rust is to iron, and mildew is to corn, and the moth is to the cloth it breeds in, that is envy to the unhappy heart in which it dwells. It is "the deadly nightshade," which produces nothing but rank poison; "the poisonful herb," which spreads nothing but death. See what an apostle says, James 3: 16. *A fire,* Ps. 37: 1

Heb., "*inflame* not thyself." *The evil eye*, Prov. 23 : 6; 28 : 22; Matt. 6 : 23; 20 : 15. "Envy is the devil's evil eye, as hypocrisy is the devil's cloven foot;" see 1 Sam. 18 : 9, "Saul eyed David." *How soon* envy rose in the world. "The first instances that we have of sin are Adam's pride and Cain's envy. The first man was undone by pride, and the second debauched by envy. The whole world, though otherwise empty of men, could not contain two brothers, when one was envied. Pride gave us the first *merit* of death, and envy the first *instance* of it: the one was the mother, the other the midwife, of human ruin."—*Manton*.——The *folly* of envy, see 1 Cor. 12 : 15–23. The foot envying the hand, or the ear envying the eye. *Freedom from envy*. It is beautiful to observe how some eminent saints have been marked by freedom from envy, as *Moses*, Num. 11 : 27–29; *Samuel*, 1 Sam. 15 : 11, 35; *Jonathan*, 1 Sam. 23 : 17, 18; *John the Baptist*, John 3 : 30; *Peter*, 2 Pet. 3 : 15; *Paul*, Phil. 1 : 15–18.   *Bowes*.

8391. ENVY, Cure of. We may cure envy in ourselves, either by considering how useless or how ill these things were for which we envy our neighbor, or else how we possess as much or as good things. If I envy his greatness, I consider that he wants my quiet; as also I consider that he possibly envies me as much as I do him; and that when I begun to examine exactly his perfections, and to balance them with my own, I found myself as happy as he was. And though many envy others, yet very few would change their condition even with those whom they envy, all being considered.
Mackenzie.

8392. ENVY, Dwelling of. There is no guard to be kept against envy, because no man knows where it dwells, and generous and innocent men are seldom jealous and suspicious till they feel the wound, or discern some notorious effect of it. It shelters itself for the most part in dark and melancholy constitutions, yet sometimes gets into less suspected lodgings, but never owns to be within when it is asked for.
Lord Clarendon.

8393. ENVY, Literary. Plato and Xenophon were cotemporaries; both were conversant with Socratic wisdom, and eminent persons in their times. Though they were well known to one another, and both voluminous writers, yet neither one mentioned the other in their writings.

8394. ENVY, Malignity of. Plutarch compares envious persons to cupping glasses, which ever draw the worst humors of the body to them; they are like flies, which resort only to the raw and corrupt parts of the body, or, if they light on a sound part, never leave blowing upon it till they have disposed it to putrefaction. When Momus could find no fault in the face of the picture of Venus, he picked a quarrel with her slipper.

8395. ENVY, Object of. Envy opposes him who is a beginner on the very steps of the tribune, hindering his access, but she meekly bears an accustomed and familiar glory, and not churlishly or difficultly. Wherefore, some resemble envy to smoke, for it arises thick at first, when the fire begins to burn; but when the flame grows clear, it vanishes away.
Plutarch.

8396. ENVY, Occasion of. Themistocles, while he was yet young, said that he had done nothing gallant, for he was not yet envied. And we know that as the cantharis is most busy with ripe fruits and roses in their beauty, so envy is most employed about the eminently good and those who are glorious in their places and esteem.   *Plutarch*.

8397. ENVY, Poison of. Quintilian tells of a rich man who poisoned the flowers in his garden, that his neighbor's bees might get no more honey there.

8398. ENVY, Self-destructive. A French officer, General Cherin, was once conducting a detachment through a deep and dangerous glen. Seeing that his men flagged, he encouraged them to bear the fatigues of the march patiently. A soldier near him muttered angrily, "It is all very well for you to talk of patience —you who are mounted on a fine horse; but for us poor wretches it is a different matter." The quick ear of the General heard the words. He felt that it was unjust that his men should think he would not willingly share all their dangers. He reined in his horse at once, and, dismounting, said to the murmuring soldier, "Here, take my place awhile." Scarcely had the latter mounted, his face covered with confusion, when a shot from the adjacent heights struck the poor fellow, and he fell badly wounded. The General turned to his troop and said, as some were told off to carry their comrade: "You see, my men, that the most elevated place is not the least dangerous."

8399. ENVY, Spirit of. Caligula, the emperor, deprived the noblest personages of Rome of their badges of honor, simply because he was envious of them. From Torquatus, the chain or collar; from Cincinnatus, the curled lock of hair, and from Pompeius, the surname of Great, belonging to his family. After he had entertained King Ptolomæus, he ordered him to be slain, because the people admired his purple robe.

8400. EPHESUS, Desolation of. Arundell says, "Once it had an idolatrous temple, celebrated for its magnificence as one of the wonders of the world, and the mountains of Corissus and and Prion re-echoed, with the shouts of ten thousand tongues, 'Great is Diana of the Ephesians!' Once it had Christian temples almost rivaling the Pagan in splendor, wherein the image that fell down from Jupiter lay prostrate before the cross, and many tongues, moved by the Holy Ghost, made public avowal that 'Great is the Lord Jesus!' Once it had a bishop, the angel of the church, Timothy, the beloved disciple of St. John; and tradition relates that it was honored with the last days of both these great men, and of the mother of our Lord. Some centuries passed on, and the altars of Jesus were again thrown down to make way for the delusions of Mahomet; the cross is removed from the dome of the church, and the crescent glitters in its stead. Now, a few unintelligible heaps of stones, with some mud cottages, untenanted, are all the remains of the great city of the Ephesians! The busy hum of a mighty population is silent in death; 'thy riches and thy fairs, thy merchandise, thy mariners and thy pilots, thy caulkers, and the occupiers of thy merchandise, and all thy men of war' are fallen (Ezek. 27: 27). Even the sea has retired from the scene of desolation, and a pestiential morass, covered with mud and rushes, has succeeded to the waters which brought up the ships laden with merchandise from every country." Dr. Eadie remarks: "While thousands over the world read the Epistle to the Ephesians, no one reads it in the place to which it was originally addressed. The lamp has been extinguished, and the sanctuary desolated. The threatened blight has fallen on Ephesus."

8401. EPICURE, Example of an. Mr. Rogerson, the son of a gentleman of large fortune in Gloucestershire, after receiving an excellent education, was sent abroad to make the grand tour. In this journey young Rogerson attended to nothing but the various modes of cookery and the methods of eating and drinking luxuriously. Before his return his father died, when he entered into the possession of a very large fortune, and a small landed estate. He was now able to look over his notes of epicurism, and to discover where the most exquisite dishes were to be had, and the best cooks to be procured. He had no other servants in his house but men cooks, for his footman, butler, housekeeper, coachman, and grooms, were all cooks. Amongst those that were more professionally so were three cooks from Italy, one from Florence, another from Siena, and another from Viterbo, who was employed for the special purpose of dressing one particular dish only, the *docce picante* of Florence. He had also a German cook for dressing the livers of turkeys, and the rest were all French. Mr. Rogerson had a messenger constantly traveling between Brittany and London, to bring him the eggs of a certain sort of plover near St. Malo; and so extravagant was he that he once ate a single dinner which, though consisting of two dishes only, cost him upwards of fifty guineas. He counted the minutes between his meals, and was wholly absorbed in devising means to indulge his appetite. In the course of nine years he found his table dreadfully abridged by the ruin of his fortune, and he was verging fast to poverty. When he had spent a fortune of a hundred and fifty thousand pounds, and was totally ruined, a friend gave him a guinea to keep him from starving; but a short time after he was found dressing an ortolan for himself. A few days afterwards he died by his own hand.   *Anon.*

8402. EPICURE, Portrait of an. Mr. Guthrie resided in a pension in Paris with a strange character, whom he called Boots, of whom he writes: "Boots would wade through fire and water for a full dinner. There is nothing on earth would pursuade him to march up to the cannon's mouth, but roast beef and plum pudding. But, place inside the breach a full smoking dish, sufficiently visible through the fire and dust and smoke of the deadly conflict, and Boots would fearlessly dash on, sword in hand, for the reeking prize!"

8403. EPIGRAMS, American. *Franklin.*—"He has paid dear for his whistle."——*Washington*—"To be prepared for war is the most effectual means of preserving peace."——*John Dickinson*, 1768—"By uniting we stand, by dividing we fall."——*Patrick Henry*—"Give me liberty or give me death," and, "If this be treason make the most of it."——*Thomas Paine*—"Rose like a rocket, fell like a stick!" "Times that try men's souls;" "One step from the sublime to the ridiculous."——*Jefferson* —"Few die and none resign."——*Josiah Quincy, Jr.*—"Wheresoever or howsoever we shall be called on to make our exit, we will die freemen."——*Henry Lee* gave Washington his immortal title, "First in war, first in peace, and first in the hearts of his countrymen."—— *Charles Cotesworth Pinckney* said "Millions for defense, but not one cent for tribute."—— *Josiah Quincy*, 1811—"Peaceably if we can, forcibly if we must."——*Daniel Webster*— "Live or die, survive or perish, I'm for the Constitution."——*Davy Crockett*—"Be sure you are right, then go ahead."——*Andrew Jackson*—"The Union—it must be preserved." ——*Commodore Perry's* announcement of the victory at the battle of Lake Erie, was, "We have met the enemy, and they are ours."—— *Gen. Taylor's* battle order—"A little more grape, Captain Bragg."——*General Grant*— "Let us have peace."——*Abraham Lincoln*— "With charity to all and malice toward none."

8404. EQUANIMITY Preserved. The equanimity which a few persons preserve through the diversities of prosperous and adverse life reminds me of certain aquatic plants which spread their tops on the surface of the water, and with a wonderful elasticity keep the surface still, if the water swells, or if it falls.   *J. Foster.*

8405. EQUITY, Fidelity to. Agesilaus, being bidden by his own father to give sentence contrary to law, replied, "I have been always taught by you to be observant of the laws, and I shall endeavor to obey you at this time by doing nothing contrary to them." And Themistocles, when Simonides tempted him to commit a piece of injustice, said, "You would be no good poet should you break the laws of verse; and should I judge against the law, I would make no better magistrate." *Plutarch.*

8406. EQUITY, Uncertainty of. Equity is a roguish thing. For law we have a measure; we know what to trust to. Equity is according to the conscience of him that is chancellor, and as that is larger or narrower, so is equity. It is all one as if they should make the standard for the measure we call a foot, a chancellor's foot. What an uncertain measure would this be! One has a long, another a short, a third an indifferent foot. It is the same thing in the chancellor's conscience.   *Selden.*

8407. EQUIVOCATION, Crime of. A sudden lie may be sometimes only manslaughter upon truth; but by a carefully constructed equivocation, truth always is with malice aforethought deliberately murdered. *Morley.*

8408. ERRING, Duty to the. Here are men of our own flesh and blood, with hearts that ache and yearn like ours, with souls just as precious as ours; and can we regard them with unfeeling eyes and stony hearts, as if their welfare in time and eternity were nothing to us? And can we, selfishly seeking our own good, be insensible to the iniquity and misery which daily meet our eyes, or forget the weak, the fallen, the deluded among us, and neglect to give them the helping hand and speak the warning word? All that is Christian and human in us bids us feel for our fellow-men as for ourselves, and stretch forth our hands to grasp and lead back every straying brother. *Dr. Fowler.*

8409. ERROR, Career of. Once upon the inclined road of error, and there is no swiftness so tremendous as that with which we dash adown the plane, no insensibility so obstinate as that which fastens on us through the quick descent. The start once made, and there is neither stopping nor waking until the last and lowest depth is sounded. Our natural fears and promptings become hushed with the first impetus, and we are lost to everything but the delusive tones of sin, which only cheat the senses and make our misery harmonious. Farewell all opportunities of escape—the strivings of conscience—the faithful whisperings of shame, which served us even when we stood trembling at the fatal point! Farewell the holy power of virtue, which made foul things look hideous, and good things lovely, and kept a guard about our hearts to welcome beauty and frighten off deformity! Farewell integrity—joy—rest—and happiness. *Melvill.*

8410. ERROR, Causes of. None sooner topple over into error than such who have not an honest heart to a nimble head. The richest soil, without culture, is most tainted with such weeds. *Anon.*

8411. ERROR, Effects of. If those alone who "sowed the wind did reap the whirlwind," it would be well. But the mischief is—that the blindness of bigotry, the madness of ambition, and the miscalculations of diplomacy, seek their victims principally amongst the innocent and the unoffending. The cottage is sure to suffer for every error of the court, the cabinet, or the camp. When error sits in the seat of power and of authority, and is generated in high places, it may be compared to that torrent which originates indeed in the mountain, but commits its devastation in the vale. *Colton.*

8412. ERROR, Encouragement of. Before we permit our severity to break loose upon any fault or error, we ought surely to consider how much we have countenanced or promoted it. *Johnson.*

8413. ERROR, Warnings of. It is a melancholy fact, verified by every day's observation, that the experience of the past is totally lost both upon individuals and nations. A few persons, indeed, who have attended to the history of former errors, are aware of the consequences to which they invariably lead, and lament the progress of national violence in the same way as they do the career of individual intemperance. But, upon the great mass of mankind—the young, the active, and the ambitious—such examples are wholly thrown away. Each successive generation plunges into the abyss of passion, without the slightest regard to the fatal effects which such conduct has produced upon their predecessors, and lament, when too late, the rashness with which they slighted the advice of experience, and stifled the voice of reason. *Steele.*

8414. ESCAPE, Only Means of. One April night, a mammoth ocean-steamer went crashing upon the coast of Nova Scotia. There was all the confusion of a wreck at sea, the hopeless cries of men, women, and children, the hurrying to and fro, the frantic shouts of the officers, and, added to all, came the hoarse cries of the tempest, the surging of the billows, the roar of the breakers. Between the rock, where the vessel struck, and the shore, was a passage-way a hundred yards wide. A rope was swung across this chasm of death, and by this line many of the dark group of survivors, one after another, successfully struggled to the shore. Dear friend, had you been there, would you not have pressed aside all possibilities of harm, and cried, "Let me grasp it!" The waves of death must overtake unpardoned sin. The one rope to save you is the help of the Lord Jesus Christ. Over the dark chasm between earth and heaven is swung this only hope of safety. Cling to it for your eternal life. *Am. Messenger.*

8415. ESTEEM, Reputation and. The consideration we are held in is owing to the effect which our personal qualities have on others. If these be great and exalted, they excite admiration; if amiable and endearing, they create friendship. We enjoy esteem much more than we do reputation; the one affects us nearly, the other lies more at a distance; and, though greater, we are less sensible of it, as it seldom comes close enough to become a real possession. We acquire the love of people, who being in our proximity, are presumed to know us; and we receive reputation (or celebrity) from such as are not personally acquainted with us. Merit secures to us the regard of our honest neighbors, and good fortune that of the public. Esteem is the harvest of a whole life spent in usefulness; but reputation is often bestowed upon a chance action, and depends most on success. *Sala.*

8416. ETERNITY, Belief in. There is, I know not how, in the minds of men, a certain presage, as it were, of a future existence; and this takes the deepest root, and is most discoverable, in the greatest geniuses and most exalted souls. *Cicero.*

8417. ETERNITY, Choice for. The following question is started by one of the schoolmen: Supposing the whole body of the earth were a great ball or mass of the finest sand, and that

a single grain or particle of this sand should be annihilated every thousand years: Supposing then that you had it in your choice to be happy all the while this prodigious mass of sand was consuming by this slow method until there was not a grain of it left, on condition you were to be miserable forever after! Or, supposing that you might be happy forever after, on condition that you would be miserable until the whole mass of sand were thus annihilated at the rate of one sand in a thousand years: which of these two cases would you make your choice? . . . Reason therefore tells us, without any manner of hesitation, which would be the better part in this choice. . . . But when the choice we actually have before us is this, whether we will choose to be happy for the space of only threescore and ten, nay, perhaps of only twenty or ten years, I might say of only a day or an hour, and miserable to all eternity, or, on the contrary, miserable for this short term of years, and happy for a whole eternity; what words are sufficient to express that folly and want of consideration which in such a case makes a wrong choice? I here put the case even at the worst, by supposing, what seldom happens, that a course of virtue makes us miserable in this life; but if we suppose, as it generally happens, that virtue would make us more happy even in this life than a contrary course of vice, how can we but wonder at the stupidity or madness of those persons who are capable of making so absurd a choice?
Addison.

8418. ETERNITY, Conceptions of. O eternity! eternity! How are our boldest, our strongest thoughts lost and overwhelmed in thee! Who can set landmarks to limit thy dimensions; or find plummets to fathom thy depths! Arithmeticians have figures to compute all the progressions of time; astronomers have instruments to calculate the distance of the planets; but what number can state, what lines can gauge, the lengths and breadths of eternity? It is higher than heaven, what canst thou do? deeper than hell, what canst thou know? The measure thereof is longer than the earth, broader than the sea. Mysterious, mighty existence! A sum not to be lessened by the largest deductions. An extent not to be contracted by all possible diminutions. None can truly say, after the most prodigious waste of ages, "that so much of eternity is gone." For, when millions of centuries are elapsed, it is but just commencing; and when millions more have run their ample round, it will be no nearer ending. Yea, when ages numerous as the bloom of spring, increased by the herbage of summer, both augmented by the leaves of autumn, and all multiplied by the drops of rain which drown the winter—when these, and ten thousand times ten thousand more—more than can be represented by any similitude, or imagined by any conception, are all revolved, eternity, vast, boundless, amazing eternity, will only be beginning, or rather, only beginning to begin. What a pleasant yet awful thought is this! Full of delight and full of dread. *Hervey.*

8419. ETERNITY, God and. A Christian, traveling in a steam-boat, distributed tracts. A gentleman took one, and folding it up, cut it with his pen-knife into small pieces; then holding it up in derision, threw it away. One piece adhered to his coat; he picked it off, and looking at it, saw only the word "God." He turned it over; on the other side, "Eternity." They stood out as living words before him. "God"—"Eternity!" He went to the bar, called for brandy to drink to drive them away; but in vain. Then to the gambling-table; to social intercourse and conversation; but those solemn words haunted him wherever he went, until he was brought a penitent to the feet of Jesus.

8420. ETERNITY, Home in. I heard of a man that was dying some time ago, a man of great wealth, and when the doctor told him he could not live, the lawyer was sent for to come and make out his will, and the dying man's little girl, only about four years old, did not understand what death meant, and when the mother told her that her papa was going away, the little child went to the bedside and looked into her father's eyes and asked, "Papa, have you got a home in that land you are going to?" And the question sunk down deep into his soul. He had spent all his time and all his energy in the accumulation of great wealth. He had a grand home and had now got to leave it; and how that question came home to him! *Moody.*

8421. ETERNITY, Import of. "Ever," a little word, but of immense significance! a child may speak it; but neither man nor angel can understand it. Oh, who can take the dimensions of eternity? The whole space between the creation of the world, and the dissolution of it, would not make a day in eternity; yea, so many years as there be days in that space, would not fill up an hour in eternity. Eternity is one entire circle, beginning and ending in itself. This present world, which is measured out by such divisions and distinctions of time, is therefore mortal, and will have an end.—2 Cor. 4: 18. If eternity did consist of finite times, though ever so large and vast, it would not be eternity, but a longer tract of time only; that which is made up of finite is finite. Eternity is but one immense, indivisible point, wherein there is neither first nor last, beginning nor ending, succession nor alteration, but is like God Himself, one and the same for ever. *Case.*

8422. ETERNITY Incomprehensible. None can comprehend eternity but the eternal God. Eternity is an ocean whereof we shall never see the shore; it is a deep where we can find no bottom; a labyrinth whence we cannot extricate ourselves, and where we shall ever lose the door. *Boston.*

8423. ETERNITY, Preaching for. The favorite maxim of Whitefield was to "preach as Apelles painted—for eternity." He was first struck with this maxim when a young man at the table of Archbishop Boulter in Ireland, where the great Doctor Delany said to him, "I wish.

whenever I go into a pulpit, to look upon it as the last time I shall ever preach, or the last time the people may hear me." Whitefield never forgot this remark. He often said, "Would ministers preach for eternity, they would then act the part of true Christian orators, and not only calmly and coolly inform the understanding, but, by persuasive, pathetic address, endeavor to move the affections and warm the heart. To act otherwise bespeaks a sad ignorance of human nature, and such an inexcusable indolence and indifference in the preacher as must constrain the hearers to suspect, whether they so will or not, that the preacher, let him be who he will, only deals in the false commerce of unfelt truth."

Dr. J. B. Wakeley.

8424. ETERNITY, Prepare for. Were any other event of far superior moment ascertained by evidence which made but a distant approach to that which attests the certainty of a life to come—had we equal assurance that after a very limited though uncertain period we should be called to migrate into a distant land whence we were never to return—the intelligence would fill every breast with solicitude; it would become the theme of every tongue; and we should avail ourselves with the utmost eagerness of all the means of information respecting the prospects which awaited us in that unknown country. Much of our attention would be occupied in preparing for our departure; we should cease to regard the place we now inhabit as our home, and nothing would be considered of moment but as it bore upon our future destination. How strange is it then that, with the certainty we all possess of shortly entering into another world, we avert our eyes as much as possible from the prospect; that we seldom permit it to penetrate us; and that the moment the recollection recurs we hasten to dismiss it as an unwelcome intrusion! Is it not surprising that the volume we profess to recognize as the record of immortality, and the sole depository of whatever information it is possible to obtain respecting the portion which awaits us, should be consigned to neglect, and rarely if ever consulted with the serious intention of ascertaining our future condition. *Robert Hall.*

8425. ETERNITY, Promises of. All great natures delight in stability; all great men find eternity affirmed in the very promises of their faculties. *Emerson.*

8426. ETERNITY, Prospect of. The prospect of a future state is the secret comfort and refreshment of my soul; it is that which makes nature look gay about me; it doubles all my pleasures, and supports me under all my afflictions. I can look at disappointments and misfortunes, pain and sickness, death itself, and, what is worse than death, the loss of those who are dearest to me, with indifference, so long as I keep in view the pleasures of eternity, and the state of being in which there will be no fears nor apprehensions, pains nor sorrows, sickness nor separation. Why will any man be so impertinently officious as to tell me all this is fancy

and delusion? Is there any merit in being the messenger of ill news? If it is a dream, let me enjoy it, since it makes me both the happier and better man. *Addison.*

8427. ETERNITY, Rewards of. He that will allow exquisite and endless happiness to be but the possible consequence of a good life here, and the contrary state the possible reward of a bad one, must own himself to judge very much amiss, if he does not conclude that a virtuous life, with the certain expectation of everlasting bliss which may come, is to be preferred to a vicious one, with the fear of that dreadful state of misery which it is very possible may overtake the guilty, or at best the terrible, uncertain hope of annihilation. This is evidently so, though the virtuous life here had nothing but pain, and the vicious, continual pleasure; which yet is for the most part quite otherwise, and wicked men have not much the odds to brag of, even in their present possession: nay, all things rightly considered, have I think, the worse part here. But when infinite happiness is put in one scale, against infinite misery in the other, if the worst that comes to the pious man if he mistakes, be the best that the wicked attain to if he be in the right, who can without madness run the venture? Who in his wits would choose to come within a possibility of infinite misery, which if he miss there is yet nothing to be got by that hazard? whereas, on the other side, the sober man ventures nothing against infinite happiness to be got, if his expectation comes to pass. If the good man be in the right, he is eternally happy; if he mistakes, he is not miserable, he feels nothing. On the other side, if the wicked be in the right, he is not happy; if he mistakes, he is infinitely miserable. *Locke.*

8428. ETERNITY, Time and. Eternity hath neither beginning nor end. Time hath both. Eternity comprehends in itself all years, all ages, all periods of ages, and differs from time as the sea and the rivers; the sea never changes place, and is always one water, but the rivers glide along and are swallowed up in the sea; so is time by eternity, *Charnock.*

8429. ETERNITY, Troubled at. I heard a few years ago of a scene that took place in London. A French nobleman went to consult Dr. Forbes Winslow. He felt he was going to lose his reason. Dr. Winslow wanted to find out what had brought this young man into this terrible state of mind. The young nobleman said he didn't know of anything in particular. "Have you lost any friends?" said the doctor. No, he didn't know as he had lost any friends. "Any property?" No, he didn't know as there was anything of that kind troubling him. "But," said the doctor, "there is something driving you into this state of mind." At last the young man confessed that he was an infidel, and said he: "My father was an infidel and my grandfather was an infidel; but, sir, for the last two years, this question has haunted me day and night, 'Eternity, and where shall I spend it?'" "Well," says the doctor, "I can't help you; you have come to the wrong physician." Says the young man, "Is there no help for me?" Have I got to be troubled with this forever? I cannot sleep more than an hour or two at night; I cannot rest; the question comes home to me, 'Eternity, and where shall I spend it?'" The doctor took him to the 53d chapter of Isaiah, and read that whole chapter through. "He was wounded for our transgressions, he was bruised for our iniquities." "Well," said the young man, "do you really believe that Jesus Christ was the Son of God, and voluntarily gave up his life, and came down into this world and suffered and died that we might live?" "Yes," said the doctor, "that is just what I believe. I was at one time an infidel myself. Settle that, and that question won't trouble you any more." And the light of eternity at last broke on this man, and he went back to Paris; and, just before Dr. Forbes Winslow died, he said that that nobleman had corresponded with him ever since like a Christain, and often mentioned where he settled the question where he would spend eternity. *Moody.*

8430. ETERNITY, Turning to. It is not in the heyday of health and enjoyment, it is not in the morning sunshine of his vernal day, that man can be expected feelingly to remember his latter end, and to fix his heart upon eternity. But in after-life many causes operate to wean us from the world: grief softens the heart, sickness searches it, the blossoms of hope are shed, death cuts down the flowers of the affections. The disappointed man turns his thoughts toward a state of existence where his wiser desires may be fixed with the certainty of faith; the successful man feels that the objects which he has ardently pursued fail to satisfy the cravings of an immortal spirit; the wicked man turneth away from his wickedness, that he may save his soul alive. *Southey.*

8431. ETERNITY, Voyage to. This world, in its course through space, is like a ship at sea. Every port is a landing place for eternity. On it goes, ever receiving and as often landing mortals on the eternal shores. Some make an early port, others a longer voyage, but the destination is the same. Swiftly speeds the ship; its passengers are constantly changing. Soon the voyage will be over, and the port of bliss or woe be gained.

8432. ETERNITY, Weight of. Upon laying a weight in one of the scales, inscribed eternity, though I threw in that of time, prosperity, affliction, wealth and poverty, which seemed very ponderous, they were not able to stir the opposite balance. *Addison.*

8433. ETERNITY, Window into. The Bible is a window in this prison of hope, through which we look into eternity. *Dwight.*

8434. ETIQUETTE, Undue Regard to. Philip the Third was gravely seated by the fireside; the fire-maker of the court had kindled so great a quantity of wood that the monarch was nearly suffocated with heat, and his grandeur would not suffer him to rise from the chair; the domestics could not presume to enter the apartment, because it was against the etiquette. At length the Marquis de Pota appeared, and

the king ordered him to damp the fires; but he excused himself, alleging that he was forbidden by the etiquette to perform such a function, for which the Duke d'Usseda ought to be called upon, as it was his business. The duke was gone out; the fire burned fiercer, and the king endured it rather than derogate from his dignity; but his blood was heated to such a degree that an erysipelas of the head appeared the next day, which, succeeded by a violent fever, carried him off in 1621, in the twenty-fourth year of his age. The palace was once on fire; a soldier, who knew the king's sister was in her apartment, and must inevitably have been consumed in a few moments by the flames, at the risk of his life rushed in, and brought her highness safe out in his arms; but the Spanish etiquette was here wofully broken into! The loyal soldier was brought to trial, and as it was impossible to deny that he had entered her apartment, the judges condemned him to die! The Spanish princess, however, condescended, in consideration of the circumstances, to pardon the soldier, and very benevolently saved his life! *Anon.*

8435. EVENING, Pleasures of the. There are two periods in the life of man in which the evening hour is peculiarly interesting—in youth and in old age. In youth, we love it for its mellow moonlight, its million of stars, its thin, rich and shooting shades, its still serenity; amid those who can commune with our loves, or twine the wreaths of friendship, while there is none to bear us witness but the heaven and the spirits that hold their endless Sabbath there,—or look into the deep bosom of creation, spread abroad like a canopy above us, and look and listen till we can almost see and hear the waving wings and melting songs of other worlds. To youth, evening is delightful: it accords with the flow of his light spirits, the fervor of his fancy, and the softness of his heart. Evening is also the delight of virtuous age: it seems an emblem of the tranquil close of busy life,—serene, placid, and mild, with the impress of its great Creator stamped upon it, it spreads its quiet wings over the grave, and seems to promise that all shall be peace beyond it. *Lord Lytton.*

8436. EVENTS, Extraordinary. Man reconciles himself to almost any event, however trying, if it happens in the ordinary course of nature. It is the extraordinary alone that he rebels against. There is a moral idea associated with this feeling; for the extraordinary appears to be something like an injustice of heaven. *Humboldt.*

8437. EVIDENCE, Chain of. In Captain Head's amusing and vivid description of his journey across the Pampas of South America occurs this anecdote. His guide one day suddenly stopped him, and pointing high into the air, cried out, "A lion!" Surprised at such an exclamation, accompanied with such an act, he turned up his eyes, and with difficulty perceived, at an immeasurable height, a flight of condors soaring in circles in a particular spot. Beneath that spot, far out of sight of himself or guide, lay the carcass, and over that carcass stood (as the guide well knew) the lion, whom the condors were eying with envy from their airy height. The signal of the birds was to him what the sight of the lion alone could have been to the traveler, a full assurance of its existence. *Herschel.*

8438. EVIDENCE, Circumstantial. At a table-d'hote at Ludwigsburg, one of the company was showing a very rare gold coin, which passed round the table on a plate, and gave rise to many suppositions as to its age, country, value, etc. The conversation then gradually branched off to other subjects, till the coin was forgotten, and on the owner asking for it back, to the surprise of all, it was not to be found. A gentleman sitting at the foot of the table was observed to be in much agitation; and as his embarrassment seemed to increase with the continuance of the search, the company were about to propose a very disagreeable measure, when suddenly a waiter entered the room, saying, "Here is the coin; the cook has just found it in one of the finger glasses." The relief to all was manifest; and now the suspected stranger for the first time spoke as follows: "Gentlemen, none of you can rejoice more than myself at the recovery of the coin; for picture to yourselves my painful situation! By a singular coincidence I have a duplicate of the very same coin in my purse! (here showing it to the company.) The idea that on the personal search which would probably be proposed, I would be taken for the purloiner of the coin, added to the fact that I am a stranger here, with no one to vouch for my integrity, had almost driven me distracted. The honesty of the cook, and lucky accident, has saved my honor." The friendly congratulations of the company soon effaced the remembrance of their unjust suspicions.

Deutsche Schnell Post.

8439. EVIL, Abhorring. A monk spoke to Poemen of a hermit who held all evil in abhorrence. "What do you mean by that expression?" he asked. The monk spoke in generalities. "Do not talk so vaguely. Say that he hates all the bad habits, bad tempers, bad thoughts which he finds in himself, and then I can understand you. I do not like the idea of monks learning about evil in order to acquire an abhorrence of it," said Poemen.

8440. EVIL, Avoid. To pray against temptations, and yet to rush into occasions, is to thrust your fingers into the fire, and then pray that they may not be burnt. The fable saith, "That the butterfly inquired of the owl, how she should do with the candle which had singed her wings; the owl counseled her, not so much as to behold the smoke." If you hold the stirrup, no wonder Satan gets into the saddle. *Secker.*

8441. EVIL, Dispersion of. Hesiod, the Greek poet, has the fancy that all evils were shut up in a box, and that Pandora, opening it, scattered all sorts of mischiefs over land and sea through the whole earth. Since that, diseases with silent feet creep over the earth and torment mankind.

8442. EVIL, Extinction of. It is certain that all the evils in society arise from want of faith in God, and of obedience to his laws; and it is no less certain, that by the prevalence of a lively and efficient belief, they would all be cured. If Christians in any country, yea, if any collected body of them, were what they might, and ought, and are commanded to be, the universal reception of the Gospel would follow as a natural and a promised result. And in a world of Christians, the extinction of physical evil might be looked for, if moral evil, that is, in Christian language, sin, were removed. *Southey.*

8443. EVIL, Forgiving. When the traveler Bruce was in Abyssinia, the governor, according to the custom, sent him horses for his own use. The groom urged Bruce to mount one of them, assuring him falsely that it was safe. Bruce was skilled in horsemanship, and completely conquered the animal. The governor was surprised at his success, and declared the groom should be put to death. "Sir," said the traveler, "as this man has attempted my life, according to the laws of the country, it is I that should name the punishment." "It is very true," replied the governor, "take him and cut him in a thousand pieces if thou wilt." "Then" said Bruce, "I am a Christian; I desire you to set this man at liberty, and give him the position he had before." Every one was pleased with him for returning good for evil, and the governor remarked, "A man who behaves as that man does, may go through any country."

8444. EVIL, Hiding from. At an explosion in a coal mine, one boy of about twelve was missing, several men were injured for life, and some were burnt to death on the spot. Search was made for the boy, and his name was called along the roads in the pit. At length they came to the place where he was last seen. The ass he was driving lay dead, and the boy was alive and well in a hole. He said, "I was driving the ass, when I saw a blue blaze coming along the road; and thinking all was not right, I crept into this hole, and here I am, quite safe."

8445. EVIL, Inherited. If a father indulges in drunkenness, what is the effect? His children inherit his weakness, his wife is covered with rags, his home is desolate. Is it not very cruel that by the father's drunken habits his poor sober wife, and his innocent children, should be doomed to suffer? But it is a fact. Does not the tyranny of an autocrat tell upon the comfort of his subjects? Turn back to 1715 and to 1745; certain noblemen stood by Prince Charles, believing him to be the legitimate successor to the throne. They lost the day. What was the consequence? That their descendants to this day are stripped of their noble rank, and they are in the eye of the law, and according to the usages of society, commoners. *Dr. Cumming.*

8446. EVIL, No Co-operation with. A master cooper called upon a colored man in Ohio, and wished to purchase some stave-timber

He inquired for what purpose he wanted it, and received for answer: "I have contracted for fifty whisky-barrels." "Well, sir," was the prompt reply, "I have the timber for sale, and want money; but no man shall purchase a stave from me for that purpose." Mr. Cooper was indignant to meet such stern reproach from a black, and called him a nigger. "That is very true," replied the other; "it is my misfortune to be a negro; I can't help that. But I can help selling my timber to make whisky-barrels, and I mean to help it."

8447. EVIL Not a Necessity. As surely as God is good, so surely there is no such thing as necessary evil. For by the religious mind, sickness, and pain, and death, are not to be accounted evils. Moral evils are of your own making; and undoubtedly, the greater part of them may be prevented. Deformities of mind, as of body, will sometimes occur. Some voluntary cast-aways there will always be, whom no fostering kindness and no parental care can preserve from self-destruction: but if any are lost for want of care and culture, there is a sin of omission in the society to which they belong. *Southey.*

8448. EVIL, Question of. If revelation speaks on the subject of the origin of evil, it speaks only to discourage dogmatism and temerity. In the most ancient, the most beautiful, and the most profound of all works on the subject, the book of Job, both the sufferer who complains of the divine government, and the injudicious advisers who attempt to defend it on wrong principles, are silenced by the voice of supreme wisdom, and reminded that the question is beyond the reach of the human intellect. St. Paul silences the supposed objector who strives to force him into controversy in the same manner. The church has been ever since the apostolic times agitated by this question, and by a question which is inseparable from it, the question of fate and free-will. The greatest theologians and philosophers have acknowledged that these things were too high for them, and have contented themselves with hinting at what seemed to be the most probable solution. What says Johnson? "All our effort ends in belief that for the evils of life there is some good reason, and in confession that the reason cannot be found." What says Paley? "Of the origin of evil no universal solution has been discovered; I mean, no solution which reaches to all cases of complaint. The consideration of general laws, although it may concern the question of the origin of evil very nearly, which I think it does, rests in views disproportionate to our faculties, and in a knowledge which we do not possess. It serves rather to account for the obscurity of the subject than to supply us with distinct answers to our difficulties." *Macaulay.*

8449. EVIL, Recompense of. During the revolutionary war lived Peter Miller, the leading member of an humble community of Baptists, located in the state of Pennsylvania. In this community lived a man who distinguished himself for very base conduct towards the society to which Mr. Miller belonged, and treason to his country. On the latter charge he was sentenced to death. No sooner was the sentence pronounced than Peter Miller set out on foot to visit General Washington, at Philadelphia, to intercede for the man's life. But he was told his prayer could not be granted "for his unfortunate friend." "My friend!" exclaimed Miller, "I have not a worse enemy living than that same man." "What," rejoined Washington, "you have walked sixty miles to save the life of your enemy? that in my judgment puts the matter in a different light; I will grant you his pardon." The pardon was made out, and, without a moment's delay, Miller proceeded on foot to a place fifteen miles distant, where the execution was to take place on the afternoon of the same day. He arrived just as the man was being conducted to the scaffold, who, seeing Miller in the crowd, remarked, "There is old Peter Miller; he has walked all the way from Ephrata to have his revenge gratified to-day by seeing me hung." These words had scarcely been spoken when he was made acquainted with the very different nature of Miller's visit, and that his life was spared. *Family Treasury.*

8450. EVIL, Seeds of. A man was once walking with a farmer through a beautiful field, when he happened to see a tall thistle on the other side of the fence. In a second, over the fence he jumped, and cut it off close to the ground. "Is that your field?" asked his companion. "O, no!" said the farmer, "bad weeds do not care much for fences, and if I should leave that thistle to blossom in my neighbor's field I should soon have plenty of my own." In some of our Western states the law requires the farmers and road-masters to destroy all weeds on their farms and in the highways.

8451. EVILS, Enduring. Pain and sickness, shame and reproach, poverty and old age, nay, death itself, considering the shortness of their duration, and the advantage we may reap from them, do not deserve the name of evils. A good mind may bear up under them with fortitude, and with cheerfulness of heart. The tossing of a tempest does not discompose him who is sure it will bring him to a joyful harbor. *Addison.*

8452. EVILS, Self-Imposed. As to those two hogsheads, my friend, which Homer says lie in heaven full, the one of good, the other of ill fates of men—it is not Jupiter that sits to draw out and transmit to some a moderate share of evils mixed with good, but to others only unqualified streams of evil; but it is ourselves who do it. Those of us that are wise, drawing out the good to temper with our evils, make our lives pleasant and potable; but the greater part (which are fools) are like sieves which let the best pass through, but the worst and the very dregs of misfortune stick to them and remain behind. *Plutarch.*

8453. EVIL SPEAKING, Caution to. Speak not ill of a great enemy, but rather give him good words, that he may use you the better if you chance to fall into his hands. The Spaniard did this when he was dying: his confessor told him, to work him to repentance, how the devil tormented the wicked that went to hell; the Spaniard, replying, called the devil "My lord: I hope my lord the devil is not so cruel." His confessor reproved him. "Excuse me," said the Don, "for calling him so: I know not into what hands I may fall; and if I happen into his, I hope he will use me the better for giving him good words." *Selden.*

8454. EVIL SPEAKING Rebuked. The following anecdote is related of the late Joseph John Gurney, of Norwich, England, by one who was often one of his family circle:—One night—I remember it well—I received a severe lesson on the sin of evil speaking. Severe I thought it then, and my heart rose in childish anger against him who gave it; but I had not lived long enough in this world to know how much mischief a child's thoughtless talk may do, and how often it happens that talkers run off the straight line of truth. S—— did not stand very high in my esteem, and I was about to speak further of her failings of temper. In a few moments my eye caught a look of such calm and steady displeasure, that I stopped short. There was no mistaking the meaning of that dark, speaking eye. It brought the color to my face, and confusion and shame to my heart. I was silent for a few moments, when Joseph John Gurney asked, very gravely, "Dost thou know any good thing to tell us of her?" I did not answer: and the question was more seriously asked: "Think; is there nothing good thou canst tell us of her?" "Oh yes; I know some good things, but——" "Would it not have been better, then, to relate those good things, than to have told us that which would lower her in our esteem? Since there is good to relate, would it not be kinder to be silent on the evil? for 'Charity rejoiceth not in iniquity.'"

8455. EVOLUTION Not Proved. His (Professor Huxley's) conclusion is an hypothesis evolved from an hypothesis. To see that this is indeed the case, let us put his argument in syllogistic form. It is as follows: Wherever we have an ascending series of animals with modifications of structure rising one above another, the later forms must have evolved themselves from the earlier. In the case of these fossil horses we have such a series, therefore the theory of evolution is established universally for all organized and animal life. Now, even if we admit his premises, every one must see that the conclusion is far too sweeping. It ought to have been confined to the horses of which he was treating. But passing that, let us ask where is the proof of the major premise? Indeed, that premise is suppressed altogether, and he nowhere attempts to show that the existence of an ascending series of animals, with modifications of structure ascending one above another, is an infallible indication that the higher members of the series evolved themselves out of the lower. The existence of a series does not necessarily involve the evolution of the higher members of it from the lower. The steps of a stair rise up one above another, but we cannot reason that therefore the whole staircase has developed itself out of the lowest step. It may be possible to arrange all the different modifications of the steam engine, from its first and crudest form up to its latest and most complete organized structure, in regular gradation; but that would not prove that the last grew out of the first. No doubt in such a case there has been progress—no doubt there has been development too—but it was progress guided and development directed by a presiding and intervening mind. All present experience is against this major premise which Huxley has so quietly taken for granted. It is a pure conjecture. I will go so far as to say that even if he should find in the geologic records all the intervening forms he desires, these will not furnish evidence that the higher members of the series rose out of the lower by a process of evolution. The existence of a graduated series is one thing; the growth of the series out of its lowest member is quite another. *Dr. W. M. Taylor.*

8456. EXACTNESS, Advantages of. What makes the scholar? Exactness. What is most likely to secure success in the learned professions? Exactness. What raises men of various callings to the highest position attainable by persons in their occupations? Exactness. What makes a man's word pass current as gold? His known exactness. What, above all things, is essential in the laboratory? Exactness. *S. Martin.*

8457. EXAGGERATION, Slander and. Being in the company of Mr. ——, I found he spoke with much fluency and propriety, and particularly about religion. My attention was excited by his conversation; for he appeared to have more enlarged views of men and things than most I had met with. He spoke in terms so high of some particular characters, as induced me to think their value was not sufficiently known. But soon after I was rather confounded by a sentiment he dropped concerning another character, which was as remarkable for its detraction as the other expressions were for their approbation. While I remained with him, he pursued the same method in his discourse, and I saw plainly he fell into the sin of exaggeration; for he could scarcely find words to express his encomiums on some, he again appeared at a loss to represent in a manner sufficiently horrid the faults of others. *Anon.*

8458. EXALTATION, Danger of. When I think on the eagle's carrying up of the shell-fish into the air, only to the end he may break him by his fall, it puts me in mind of the devil's costly courtesies, who out of the bounty of his subtility, is still ready to advance us to destruction. Thus more than once he dealt with my Redeemer; no sooner had he raised him to the top of an high pinnacle, but straight follows, "Cast thyself down." Having placed him on a high mountain, let him fall down, and he shall be largely rewarded with his own. If advancement be so dangerous, I will take heed of being ambitious. Any estate shall give me content: I am high enough if I can stand upright.

Warwick.

8459. EXALTATION, Punishment of. A noble chamber had Pope John XXI., writes Dr. Milman, "and when he was contemplating with too great pride the work of his own hands and burst out into laughter, at that moment the avenging roof came down upon his head." The catastrophe was held at the time to be a special judgment on a reprobate pontiff—Nebuchadnezzar's boast, and worse than Nebuchadnezzar's doom. The historian of Mexico tells us of Montezuma, while exacting from his people the homage of an adulation worthy of an oriental despot, and the profuse expenditure of whose court was a standing marvel, that, "while the empire seemed towering in its most palmy and prosperous state, the canker had eaten deepest into its heart." Ruin was at hand. The hour was come, and the man; and that man was Fernando Cortes. *F. Jacox.*

8460. EXAMPLE, Best. In the discharge of thy place, set before thee the best examples, for imitation is a globe of precepts; and after a time set before thee thine own example; and examine thyself strictly whether thou didst not best at first. Neglect not also the examples of those that have carried themselves ill in the same place; not to set off thyself by taxing their memory, but to direct thyself what to avoid. *Lord Bacon.*

8461. EXAMPLE, Choice of. Be sure you set your pattern right. Take not the most noisy and airy Christians, who glory in talk and censures. Take not one who hath an affectation of being religious after a new mode and fashion. Take not one who seeks to raise a fame for piety only by decrying or condemning this or that form of profession; and who, if there were no differences among us, would lose very much of his reputation for sanctity: for these are only torrents, that run with a violent stream; but they are shallow, and we know not how soon they may grow dry. . . . But propound those to yourselves for examples, who are of fixed principles and sober practices; who are grave and solid, and, in all the duties that belong to a Christian conversation, labor to do them substantially rather than ostentatiously; that live within God and themselves; that have deep thoughts and solid expressions of them, and whose actions are suitable and correspondent to both. Such a one is the Christian indeed; and such, for some such there are, I recommend to you for your imitation. And yet there is no man that walks so uprightly, but that sometimes he steps awry. And therefore be not led by a blind and implicit adherence to them, but continually eye the rule; and whereinsoever they forsake that, be they Apostles, yea, or if it were possible, even angels themselves, therein forsake them. *Hopkins.*

8462. EXAMPLE of Christ. Those that have searched into the monuments of Jerusalem write that our Lord was crucified with his face to the west; which, however spitefully meant of the Jews (as not allowing him worthy to look on the holy city and temple), yet was not without a mystery. "His eyes looked to the Gentiles," etc., saith the Psalmist. As Christ, therefore, on his cross, looked towards us, sinners of the Gentiles, so let us look up to him.

Bishop Hall.

8463. EXAMPLE Contagious. Nothing is so contagious as example. Never was there any considerable good or ill done that does not produce its like. We imitate good actions through emulation, and bad ones through a malignity in our nature, which shame conceals and example sets at liberty. *La Rochefoucauld.*

8464. EXAMPLE, Conversion by. A young lady very rich in earthly gifts had youth, beauty, wealth; but she had not the best gift, the "peace" that Jesus gives. She was not in the habit of visiting the poor, but one day she went with a friend to see an old woman who had been confined to bed for thirty years, suffering from a painful complaint, and was apparently near death. While the young lady stood pitying by, she was struck by hearing no word of repining or impatience. The aged Christian spoke of happiness and peace, the mercies she had experienced, the joys she was so soon to know. The contrast was great between these two—the one in the flush of youth, health, prosperity; the other so different! But the young lady turned to her friend, and said, "I would gladly change places with that poor creature to have her peace." The saint went to her rest, but the lesson was not lost; the young lady sought for peace in Jesus, and found it and became a consistent Christian.

8465. EXAMPLE, Dangerous. At a "Union Temperance Conference" in England, one of the speakers, Rev. C. Garrett, urged that, even if an occasional glass did not harm some who took it, the example might prove exceedingly harmful to others. He (Mr. Garrett) was fond of climbing. He had pretty strong limbs and a cool head. A few months ago he was climbing a precipice—he thought he could hold on with safety. When at a dangerous point he heard a voice which almost paralyzed him; it was the voice of his own boy, who had caught sight of him, and who was following not far behind. The voice said, "Papa, take the safe path, for I am following you." He stopped in a moment. He did not say, "I am not responsible for my example." He thought if his Fred should perish through his example, his heart would break; he therefore stopped in a moment. In like manner he would say to all his friends, "Take the safe path, because of those who are following you." He charged this upon the ministers especially, for the sake of the little ones that were coming up; in the name of the feeble ones, in the name of the reclaimed, in the name of all who were trying to rise, "Take the safe path!"

8466. EXAMPLE, Fatal. "I wish I was dead," said a little boy one day to his mother. "Why?" asked his kind mother. "Why, the boys all pester me so about father, and I don't want to go again, in the night, to the store after him." His mother talked to him, but thought he did not feel in earnest about it. But one day, when she had returned from a visit, she inquired for the children, and found all but this boy. She looked, she called, but no answer. She went to the barn as it was just growing dark. She opened the door, and there, in one corner, was her little sensitive boy hanging by the neck. She burst into tears. "Oh my son, my son, is it you?" She felt his cold hands, and he was dead. And at the funeral, his father promised to drink no more rum: "I have for ever done." A long time he kept his promise. One day, however, Deacon P. was in the store; and Deacon P. was a good man—he drank but little. He asked for some brandy. And while he drank it, he saw that same man who had been a drunkard looking at him; and he saw, too, that he was very uneasy; he walked about; he sat down. Again he would go to the door as if going away. He was in silent thought. At length he went to the counter and asked for a little brandy: "I may drink a little as well as Deacon P." He did drink, and became a confirmed drunkard again. *Vermont Chronicle.*

8467. EXAMPLE, Following Bad. Tinder is not apter to take fire, nor wax the impression of the seal, nor paper the ink, than youth is to follow ill examples. *Brooks.*

8468. EXAMPLE, Good. If the present lecturer has a right to consider himself a real Christian—if he has been of any service to his fellow creatures, and has attained to any usefulness in the church of Christ—he owes it, in the way of means and instrumentality, to the sight of a companion, who slept in the same room with him, bending his knees in prayer, on retiring to rest. That scene, so unostentatious, and yet so unconcealed, roused my slumbering conscience, and sent an arrow to my heart; for, though I had been religiously educated, I had restrained prayer, and cast off the fear of God. My conversion to God followed, and soon after my entrance upon college studies for the work of the ministry. Nearly half a century has rolled away since then, with all its multitudinous events; but that little chamber, that humble couch, that praying youth, are still present to my imagination, and will never be forgotten, even amidst the splendor of heaven, and through the ages of eternity. *J. A. James.*

8469. EXAMPLE, Imitating. Gallus Vibius, an eloquent Roman, imitated madmen till he became himself mad. Tully laughed at Hircus, a very ridiculous man, till he confessed, "While I laugh at him, I have almost become the same kind of person." The small feet of Chinese ladies are produced in imitation of a queen who had deformed feet.

8470. EXAMPLE, Inconsistent. Though "the words of the wise be as nails fastened by the masters of the assemblies," yet sure their examples are the hammer to drive them in to take the deeper hold. A father that whipt his son for swearing, and swore himself whilst he whipt him, did more harm by his example than good by his correction. *Dr. Fuller.*

8471. EXAMPLE, Influence of. The ancient Hungarian king, being benighted with his followers, who were weary by reason of the way, and wished to lay themselves down to rest on the snow-covered ground, knowing that if they slept their sleep would be the sleep of death, resorted to the device of commanding each man to tread in the foot-prints that he himself should make. Weary as they were, they felt that what their king could do they ought to do, and they followed him. Their freezing blood was warmed into a new life, and they were saved! And if we follow Christ, though it be a great way off, we shall be strengthened by his life, and day by day draw nearer to him. *J. G. Pilkington.*

8472. EXAMPLE, Jesus our. It is our comfort that we have always One to look to. Ours is no interminable road, no lonely, solitary path. Jesus, if we can only see aright, is never very far ahead. And this is great encouragement to us. The soldier whose officer says, not "Go on," but "Come on," has tenfold the spirit for entering the battle. The mowers who mow in line have much more heart during the burden and heat of the day when their scythes sweep through the grass keeping time to the stroke of their fellow-workmen in front. Even walking along the road ourselves, we know that we can walk better and continue longer if we be following some one that is a little way ahead. We have One always to look to, and we can most go out of ourselves when most we look at him. *Power.*

8473. EXAMPLE, License of. Ernest, Prince of Lunenburg, complained to Luther of the immeasurable drinking there was at court. Luther replied, "That Princes ought to look thereto." "Ah, sir," said the Prince, "We do so ourselves, otherwise it would long since have been done." "When the abbot throws the dice, the whole convent will play."

8474. EXAMPLE, Ministerial. One of my parishioners said to me, "I have something which I wish to say to you; but I am afraid you may be offended." "I answered," says Mr. Scott, "that I could not promise, but I hoped I should not." She then said, "You know A— B—; he has lately appeared attentive to religion, and has spoken to me concerning the sacrament; but last night he, with C— D—, and others, met to keep Christmas; and they played at cards, drank too much, and in the end quarrelled, and raised a sort of riot. And when I remonstrated with him on his conduct, as inconsistent with his professed attention to religion, his answer was, 'There is no harm in cards— Mr. Scott plays at cards.' This smote me to the heart. I saw that if I played at cards, however soberly and quietly, the people would be encouraged by my example to go farther; and if St. Paul would eat no flesh while the world stood, rather than cause his weak brother to offend, it would be inexcusable in me to throw such a stumbling-block in the way of my parishioners, in a matter certainly neither useful nor expedient. So far from being offended at the hint thus given me, I felt very thankful

to my faithful monitor, and promised her that she should never have occasion to repeat the admonition. That very evening I related the whole matter to the company, and declared my fixed resolution never to play at cards again. I expected I should be harassed with solicitations, but I was never asked to play afterwards.
Thomas Scott.

8475. EXAMPLE, Motive of. The efficacy of good examples in the formation of public opinion is incalculable. Though men justify their conduct by reasons, and sometimes bring the very rules of virtue to the touchstone of abstraction. yet they principally act from example. Metaphysical reasons have, in reality, as little to do in the formation of the principles of morals, as rules of grammar in the original structure of language, or those of criticism in the formation of orators and poets.
Robert Hall.

8476. EXAMPLE, Noble. Since the worst of times afford imitable examples of virtue; since no deluge of vice is like to be so general but more than eight will escape; eye well those heroes who have held their heads above water, who have touched pitch and not been defiled, and in the common contagion have remained uncorrupted.
Browne.

8477. EXAMPLE, Paternal. A man was walking through the deep snow when he heard the voice of his oldest son saying: "I'll step in father's tracks." He was trying to do it, and two younger brothers were at the same thing. The father went to the house of prayer to seek God that evening, thinking, "If I lead my sons thus, I'll make tracks for heaven."
Sunday-School Times.

8478. EXAMPLE, Power of. In a town of Bavaria there was a little tumble-down church building, where the duke, as often as he came that way, used to go in and pray. If, on coming out of the chapel, he happened to meet any one of the peasants in the field, he loved to converse with them in a friendly way. One day he met an old man with whom he fell into conversation on various things; and, taking a liking to the man, he asked him, in parting, whether he could do anything for him. The peasant replied, "Noble sir, you cannot do anything better for me than what you have done already." "How so?" answered he. "I do not know that I have done anything for you." "But I know it," said the old man; "for how can I ever forget that you saved my son? He traveled so long in the ways of sin that for a long time he would have nothing to do with the church or prayer, and sank every day deeper in wickedness. Sôme time ago he was here, and saw you, noble sir, enter the chapel. 'I should like to see what he does there,' said the young man scornfully, to himself, and he glided in after you. But when he saw you pray so devoutly, he was so deeply impressed that he also began to pray; and from that moment he became a new man. I thank you for it. And that is why I said you can never do me a greater favor than you have done me already.'
Anon.

8479. EXAMPLE, Preaching by. A pious man. who lived some six miles from the house of worship, complained to his pastor of the distance he had to go to attend public worship. "Never mind," said the minister, "remember every Sabbath you have the privilege of preaching a sermon six miles long—you preach the gospel to all the residents and people you pass."

8480. EXAMPLE, Silent. St. Claude, a man of eminent piety, was unjustly imprisoned in the Bastile. At the same time there was a man confined of so ferocious and brutal a disposition that no one dared to approach him. He seldom spoke without a volley of oaths and blasphemies, and struck every one who approached him with the utmost violence. Every expedient to humanize this monster had proved in vain, when the governor entreated Claude to undertake the work. His humility would have induced him to decline, but persuasion prevailed. Accordingly, the humble Christian was shut up with this human brute, who exhausted his ferocity in revilings, blows, and yet more savage tokens of the barbarity of his disposition. Whilst this treatment continued, silence, patience, and mildness, were the only reply of the man of God. His prayers achieved the rest. The monster at length looked on the face of his companion, suddenly threw himself at his feet, and embracing them, burst into a flood of tears, entreated his forgiveness, and besought him to give him instructions in the religion which thus influenced his conduct. He became entirely changed; and, even when his liberty was given him, he could scarcely be prevailed on to leave his Christian friend.
Anon.

8481. EXAMPLE, Stimulus of. Nestor's relation of his own achievements inflamed Patroclus and nine others with a vehement desire of single combat; and we know the counsel that brings persuasive deeds as well as words, a lively exemplar, and an immediate familiar incentive, insouls a man with courage—moves, yea, vehemently spurs him up to such a resolution of mind as cannot doubt the possibility and success of the attempt. *Plutarch.*

8482. EXAMPLE, Teaching and. It is the duty of every man to take care lest he should hinder the efficacy of his own instructions. When he desires to gain the belief of others, he should show that he believes himself; and when he teaches the fitness of virtue by his reasonings, he should, by his example, prove its possibility: thus much at least may be required of him, that he shall not act worse than others because he writes better, nor imagine that, by the merit of his genius, he may claim indulgence beyond mortals of the lower classes, and be excused for want of prudence or neglect of virtue.
Dr. S. Johnson.

8483. EXAMPLE, Teaching by. The novelist presents us with a scene in a prison, which is likely enough to have its counterpart in real life: "Mr. Eden, the gaol chaplain, had a great collection of photographs. His plan with Carter, a half-witted prisoner, was to tell him, by means of a photograph, some fact or anecdote. First, he would put under his eye a cruel or unjust action. He would point out the signs of suffering in one of the figures. Carter would understand this, because he saw it. Then Mr. Eden would excite his sympathy. 'Poor so-and-so,' he would say. Afterwards he would produce a picture of more moderate injustice, and so raise a shadow of a difficulty, and thus draw upon Carter's understanding as well as his sympathy. Then would come pictures of charity, of benevolence, of other good actions. Thus the chaplain got at this man's little bit of mind through the medium of the senses. Honor to all the great arts! The limit of their beauty and their usefulness has never yet been reached. Painting was the golden key which this thinking man held to the Bramah lock of an imbecile's understanding."

Papers on Preaching.

8484. EXCELLENCE, Cost of. It is certain that if every one could early enough be made to feel how full the world is already of excellence, and how much must be done to produce anything worthy of being placed beside what has already been produced; of a hundred youths who are now poetizing, scarcely one would feel enough courage, perseverance, and talent to work quietly for the attainment of a similar mastery. Many young painters would never have taken their pencils in hand, if they could have felt, known, and understood, early enough, what really produced a master like Raphael.

Goethe.

8485. EXCELLENCE, Human. Parted from God, human excellence is like the fabled flower which, according to the Rabbins, Eve plucked when passing out of Paradise—severed from its native root, it is only the touching memorial of a lost Eden; sad, while charming—beautiful, but dead. *Charles Stanford.*

8486. EXCELLENCE, Price of. Excellence is never granted to man, but as the reward of labor. It argues, indeed, no small strength of mind to persevere in the habits of industry, without the pleasure of perceiving those advantages which, like the hands of a clock, whilst they make hourly approaches to their front, yet proceed so slowly as to escape observation.

Sir Joshua Reynolds.

8487. EXCELSIOR, Import of. The individual who wishes to improve himself never finds a halting-place on earth. His career is upward, in one sense, whatever it may appear to be. His very degradations are means of increased ennoblement, because of incessant compurgation and purity. And in one respect the human almost surpasses the angelic lot; because the one, being perfect in its kind, does not, perhaps, admit of progress, and the other does indefinitely. The yearning to fulfill this progressive lot engenders a noble discontent, and that discontent is expressed by the word Excelsior. Observe, it is not Excelsius: it is therefore entirely interior; whereas Excelsius would refer to the circumstances, rather than to him who was in them. *M. G. Keon.*

8488. EXCESS, Evils of. Too much noise deafens us; too much light blinds us; too great a distance or too much of proximity equally prevents us from being able to see; too long and too short a discourse obscures our knowledge of a subject; too much of truth stuns us.

Pascal.

8489. EXCESS, Reaction of. Excess generally causes reaction, and produces a change in the opposite direction, whether it be in the seasons, or in individuals, or in governments. *Plato.*

8490. EXCITEMENT, Occasions for. Tell the mother, as she watches the dying agonies of her only babe, to beware of excitement; she has a husband left, and for his sake it behooves her to cling to life, and hope to be happy. Tell the widower, as he tears himself from the coffin of his best earthly treasure, to beware of excitement; his children are spared, and for their sakes he must return to the cares of life again. Tell the man whose house is burning over his head, to beware of excitement; for calmness and self-possession may facilitate his rescue. But never tell the sinner who bewails his transgressions, who apprehends the terrors of the Lord, who trembles at the thought of judgment to come; who is uncertain whether the next moment of his life will not find him in hell,—never tell that man to beware of excitement: (for what can you set before him to countervail his anxiety?) but caution him against a spirit of slumber; caution him against a return to indifference; tell him that the struggle is for immortality; and that the alternative is death,—certain, remediless, and eternal. *Anon.*

8491. EXCUSE, Absurd. One asks, "Was there ever an invalid so senseless as to say, When I am somewhat better, when the fever burns less fierce, I will repair to the hospital or to the physician?" Only sick souls are guilty of this folly.

8492. EXCUSE, False. A young man was brought to the hospital, City Point, shot in the neck and completely paralyzed. I spoke to him of preparation for death. "I might as well own up," he said, "I'm not prepared; I've lived a bad life, and been a great trouble to my mother. I've got no religion, and I don't want any. I won't burn out my candle now, and throw the snuff in God Almighty's face. I'll die as I've lived. It's honester." I argued with him, plead the promises, entreated him, but all to no purpose. "I deserve no mercy, I don't ask for any. I've never prayed, I'm not going to do so now."

Chas. Cutler.

8493. EXCUSE: No Time for Religion. An earnest minister called on a lady and found her too busy, as she said, to talk with him. He repeated the visits with no better success. At the last call she said, "Oh, be sure and not be long in coming back again, for I do wish to see you." In a few days he called. "I'm sorry," she said, the moment she opened the door, "I have no time to receive you to-day; I've a friend come from London, and I've to go out with him." "Well, you will have time to die, whether you're prepared or not. So you've no time just now?" "No, not to-day." "Well, let me say this to you, in case you and I never meet again, 'Behold, now is the accepted time, now is the day of salvation.'" She thanked him, and he went away. That night she and her brother went to the theatre. She was taken ill while there, went home, grew worse, and was in eternity by five o'clock the next morning. "The thing" said Mr. Paterson, "so impressed me, that I resolved, if God spared me, to labor by his grace more dili gently than ever."

8494. EXCUSE, Others' Sins an. A man on entering a stage-coach said, "My head aches dreadfully; I was very drunk last night." A gentleman affecting surprise, replied, "Drunk! sir. What! do you get drunk?" "Yes," said he, "and so does every one at times, I believe. I have no doubt but you do." "No, sir," he replied, "I do not." "What! never?" "No, never; and amongst other reasons I have for it, one is, I never find, being sober, that I have too much sense, and I am loth to lose what little I have."

8495. EXCUSES Always Easy. As a wolf was lapping at the head of a running brook, he spied a stray lamb paddling at some distance down the stream. Having made up his mind to seize her, he bethought himself how he might justify his violence. "Villain!" said he, running up to her, "how dare you muddle the water that I am drinking?" "Indeed," said the lamb humbly, "I do not see how I can disturb the water, since it runs from you to me, not from me to you." "Be that as it may," replied the wolf, "it was but a year ago that you called me many ill names." "Oh, sir!" said the lamb, trembling, "a year ago I was not born." "Well," replied the wolf, "if it was not you, it was your father, and that is all the same; but it is no use trying to argue me out of my supper;" and without another word he fell upon the poor helpless lamb, and tore her to pieces. *Æsop.*

8496. EXCUSES, Indian. The Catholic missionaries among the Hurons found them ready to receive instruction, assenting to the truth of every doctrine, and they seemed likely to become easy converts. But whenever the matter was brought to a point, and they were urged to accept the faith, they uniformly replied, "It is good for the French, but we are another people, with different customs." The spirit of this excuse was not confined to the red men.

8497. EXCUSES, Lies. I will not go on enumerating the possible and frequent excuses that men and women give—not that I have exhausted them; no. If I had exhausted all this afternoon, you would have as many more manufactured by to-morrow, or even before I got through the sermon. If you drive a man from behind one excuse, he takes immediate refuge behind another. If you drive him from that, he gets behind another like a flash. You cannot exhaust excuses. They are more numerous than the hairs upon your head. I will tell you what you can do with them. You can take them up and bind them in one bundle, and mark it "Lies, lies, lies," in great big letters. God will sweep away those refuges of lies. It is only a question of time. By and by you will be left without an excuse. He that believeth not will be without God, without hope, without excuse. Do not think of giving excuses here. If you have any excuse that you call good, if you have any excuse that you think will stand the light of eternity and of the judgment day, if you think you have any excuse that God will accept, do not give it up for anything I have said. Take it into the grave with you. Let it be buried with you, and when you come before him tell it out. If not, then give your excuses to us here to-day. It is easy to excuse yourself into hell, but you cannot excuse yourself out of it. It is easy to take a seat here, and to make light of everything you hear, and go away laughing and scoffing at the whole thing, but ah! it will be terrible to stand before God without an excuse. *Moody.*

8498. EXCUSES, Ready. A traveler in Venezuela returning to his lodging drunk, had hard work to find his hammock. He made many efforts to get his boots off, but was too drunk to accomplish it, and crawled into his hammock with them on. He was overheard to soliloquize, "Well, I have traveled all the world over; I lived five years in Cuba, four in Jamaica, five in Brazil; I have traveled through Spain and Portugal, and been in Africa, but I never before was in such an abominable country as this, where a man is obliged to go to bed with his boots on."

8499. EXCUSES, Useless. There was once a master who sent his servant with a letter: "Go," said he, "to such and such a town with it." He started, but he soon came back with the letter and said, "Master, I could not deliver it." "How was that?" said the master. "Sir, there is a deep river, and I cannot get across." Now, that looked very much like an excuse, didn't it, and like a very good excuse too? But the master knew better, and he said, "There was a ferry-boat across—did you call for the ferryman?" "No, sir, I did not." "Very well, then," said he, "the blame lies with you." Now, it is true you cannot save yourselves, most true, but there is One who can. Did you ever call to him to help you? If you did not, then surely the mischief, the fault, the blame, the ruin, must lie at your own door. Did you ever pray? Soul, did you ever cry out for the Ferryman? Did you ever say, when you found you could not get across the river—"Lord Jesus, save or I perish?" Why, if you had ever prayed that from your heart, he would have heard you. "Oh," saith one, "but I do not think he could hear me even if I called." I stood at Bangor, some time ago, and there is a ferry there across to Anglesea. You cannot be heard on the other side of the bank with your simple voice; but there is a speaking trumpet, and if you just speak through that you may say, "Hoy!" and it is heard all across the straits, and the boatman will come and meet you. Well now, prayer is God's great speaking trumpet, and if you come to God in prayer, pleading the name of Jesus, it is certain that he will hear you and deliver you. Away with your excuses, we pray you, away with your excuses, or else your excuses will but make fuel for your burning in hell!

Spurgeon.

8500. EXECUTION, Faulty. A wretched painter showed Apelles a picture, remarking that he had spent but little time upon it. Apelles answered, "If thou hadst not told me so, I see cause enough to believe it was a hasty draught; but I wonder that in that space of time thou hast not painted many more such pictures."

8501. EXERCISE, Importance of. Two friends are in a canoe in the Mozambique channel. A flaw of wind upsets the boat. Before they right her she fills with water, and sinks; and the two men are swimming for their lives. "Ah, well!" says one of them to the other, "it is a long pull to the shore, but the water is warm, and we are strong. We will hold by each other, and all will be well." "No," says his friend. "I have lost my breath already; each wave that strikes us knocks it from my body. If you reach the shore—and God grant you may!—tell my wife I remembered her as I died. Good-by, God bless you!" and he is gone. There is nothing his companion can do for him. For himself, all he can do is to swim, and then float and rest himself, and breathe; to swim again, and then float and rest again—hour after hour, to swim and float, swim and float, with that steady, calm determination that he will go home; that no blinding spray shall stifle him, and no despair weaken him—hour after hour, till at last the palm-trees show distinct upon the shore, and then the tall reeds, and then the figures of animals. Will one never feel bottom? Yes, at last his foot touches the coral, and with that touch he is safe. That story that man told me. Now, what is the difference between those two men? Why does one give up the contest at once, and resign himself to what people call his fate, while the other fights the circumstances for hours, and wins the battle? On shipboard one was as strong as the other. He was as brave. He was as prudent as the other. "What if he was?" you say. Strength and bravery and prudence were all needed in the crisis; but something else was needed also. The man had never trained himself to swim, if knowing a method were of much use, where one has not trained himself to the habit. But that training he had never given. Take that as a precise illustration, where nobody questions the answer, of the difference wrought in two men merely by exercise, or the steadiness of training. In matters like this, of pure bodily exercise, everybody sees and owns its work and its result.

E. E. Hale.

8502. EXERCISE, Power of. Æschylus chanced to be a spectator at the Isthmian games, where some were engaged at a sword play; seeing one of the combatants wounded, and observing that the theatre immediately made a great shouting upon it, he jogged one Ion, who sat next to him, and whispered to him, "Do you see what exercise can do? He that is wounded holds his peace, and the spectators cry out."

8503. EXERTION, Delightful. All exertion is in itself delightful, and active amusements seldom tire us. Helvetius owns that he could hardly listen to a concert for two hours, though he could play on an instrument all day long. The chase, we know, has always been the favorite amusement of kings and nobles. Not only fame and fortune, but pleasure is to be earned.

Abp. Sharp.

8504. EXERTIONS, Demand for. God has created man imperfect, and left him with many wants, as it were to stimulate each to individual exertion, and to make all feel that it is only by united exertions and combined action that these imperfections can be supplied, and these wants satisfied. This pre-supposes self-reliance and confidence in each other. *Prince Albert.*

8505. EXHORTATION, Appropriate. The profligate Duke of Warton recounted to Swift several extravagances he had run through. Swift observed to him, "You have had your frolics, my lord; let me recommend one more to you. Take a frolic to be virtuous; take my word for it, that one will do you more honor than all the other frolics of your whole life."

8506. EXHORTATION, Tender. An old divine says, "He that will take the bird, must not scare it. A froward, peevish messenger, is no friend to him that sends him. Sinners are not pelted into Christ with stones of hard-knocking language, but wooed into Christ by heart-melting exhortations."

8507. EXISTENCE, Animated. I would rather be a fly than a sublime mountain—than even Ætna. *J. Foster.*

8508. EXISTENCE Immeasurable. Existence is not to be measured by mere duration. An oak lives for centuries, generation after generation of mortals the meanwhile passing away; but who would exchange for the life of a plant, though protracted for ages, a single day of the existence of a living, conscious, thinking man? *Caird.*

8509. EXPECTATION: Proverb. You talk about your hopes of some coming good: what say the ancients? "Expectation is the midday dream of life."

8510. EXPEDIENCY, Carnal. It should well be considered, how often we find carnal expedients followed with disastrous results, especially in the histories of godly persons. *Abraham* twice tried to induce Sarah to equivocate Gen. 12: 10–13; 20: 5; and brought upon himself thereby the rebuke of a heathen king, and might, but for the Lord's intervention, have been involved in serious disaster. *Sarah* tried to hasten the fulfillment of the promise of a child, by persuading Abraham to take Hagar, Gen. 16: 2. It brought upon her Hagar's contempt, and ultimately led to Hagar's flight, besides bringing trouble between herself and her husband. *Rebekah and Jacob,* Gen. 27 How cunning was the plot Rebekah laid to obtain the blessing for Jacob, by deceit, to which Jacob consented! Her deceit ended in the hatred of Esau, in Jacob's being an exile for twenty years; and Rebekah never saw her favorite son again, after he left his father's house. *Ahab's* attempt, by disguising himself, to escape the judgment threatened by Micaiah, only exposed Jehoshaphat's life to danger, and failed to preserve his own, 1 Kings 22: 30–37. *Jeroboam.* God promised, when He raised Jeroboam to the throne, to make his throne as secure as David's, on condition of Jeroboam's obedience, 1 Kings 11: 38. But Jeroboam, not trusting God, thought he would secure it better by his own crafty policy. Thus "wise to do evil, but to do good having no knowledge," he and his family were soon cut off, 1 Kings 15: 29, and his name branded with perpetual infamy, 2 Kings 10: 31; 13: 6; 14: 24; 17: 22. *Jehoshaphat.* By marrying his son Jehoram to Athaliah, daughter of Ahab, it seems likely Jehoshaphat hoped to unite the two kingdoms of Israel and Judah, or, at least, make a durable peace. The expedient failed, 2 Kings 8: 16–18. *Jezebel's* plot to secure Naboth's vineyard by his death, brought the just retribution of her own death, 1 Kings 21: 23; 2 Kings 9: 36. *Hezekiah's* paying a bribe to the king of Assyria only impoverished himself, and was of no avail, 2 Kings 18: 14–17. *Caiaphas*, in condemning our Lord, sacrificed justice to expediency. His hope was, by this stroke of policy, to turn aside the ruin of his country by the Romans, John 11: 49, 50. The result was to bring the very ruin he sought to avert. *Pilate*, by scourging Christ, hoped to pacify the Jews, and wash his hands from the blood of an innocent man, John 19: 1. *Bowes.*

8511. EXPEDIENCY, Political. "These, fellow citizens, are my sentiments," said a western candidate for office, "as I'm a politician and an honest man! But if they do not suit you, fellow citizens, I can change them till they do."

8512. EXPEDIENCY, Tyranny of. It is easy to see how this moral discipline must fare under the doctrine of expediency—a doctrine which teaches man to be looking continually abroad—a doctrine which not only justifies but enjoins a distrust of the suggestions of the inward monitor; which will not permit the best feelings of the heart, its clearest dictates, its finest emotions, to have the smallest influence over the conduct; and, instead of yielding any thing to their direction, cites them at its bar. *Robert Hall.*

8513. EXPERIENCE, The Believer's. It is expressed in various ways: *Trying.*—The *Lord Jesus* is the foundation stone, precious and "*tried*"—tried by the experience of the saints of all ages, Isa. 28: 16. "The *words* of the Lord are pure words," like "silver tried" in the crucible, "purified seven times," Ps. 12: 6. The *gospel* of God's grace is like "gold tried in the fire," Rev. 3: 18. The saints find God's promises always true, and God's judgments alway right. *Proving*, by personal realization and heart experiences, Eccles. 7: 23. *Seeing*—a step beyond "the hearing of

the ear," Job. 42: 5. *Tasting*—the relish and sweet savor of spiritual blessings, Ps. 34: 8. *Exercised in discerning*, Heb. 5: 4; 12: 11 *Learning*—Phil. 4: 11, "I have learned" (literally, being initiated, as certain persons were, anciently, into the secrets of the heathen mysteries). *Knowing*—"I know"—"we know," etc., the emphatic utterance of assured belief, which occurs frequently, Job. 19: 25. The *Book of Psalms* owes to this much of its spiritual value. It is a record of the heart experiences of many tried saints, who themselves learnt wisdom from their deep trials of faith and patience. Mark, on reading the Psalms, how at times the psalmists pass from what the Lord does for men in general, to what he has done for them personally, See Ps. 4: 3.—"The Lord hath set apart the godly for himself: the Lord will hear when *I* call unto him." Ps. 37.—A psalm of experience—the testimony of an old man's faith. John 4: 39–42.—*Samaritan testimony.* "Come—see," was the woman's testimony, when she had herself seen and heard. "Now we believe," was the neighbors' testimony, on the same ground of their own experience. Rom. 5: 4.—"Patience worketh experience;" rather, the grateful approval of our faith and trust. Heb. 5: 13.—"Unskillful"—"hath no experience." (Marg.) There is generally a close connexion between these two; where there is little or no experience, we look in vain for much skillfulness in the word of righteousness. *St. Paul's* frequent references to his conversion and previous life are a standing testimony to the depth of his convictions; whilst the tone and style of his epistles show how deeply he had learnt by experience in himself to comfort and counsel others, 2 Cor. 1: 3–6; Acts 22: 1–21; 26: 9–23; 1 Cor. 15: 8, 9; Gal. 1: 13–24; Phil. 3: 4–11; 1 Tim. 1: 2–16. *St. Peter's Epistles* derive an additional force and beauty if received as the remembrance of Peter's history. 2 Pet. 2: 1, and 3: 17. *Bowes.*

8514. EXPERIENCE, Christian. Every man that goes to heaven by Christ will have a Christian experience; but I know some people who seem to me to be trusting in their experience. If I ask a man "What is the ground of your faith?" and he says, "I have felt this, and felt that;" then I say that ground of his faith is a rotten one; and he that rests on his feelings will be as much deceived as he that rests on his works. "Not of a man, neither by man," is true in this case. Because I have had an experience of my deep depravity, and been shaken over hell's mouth, am I to trust in this to be saved by it? No, no, beloved. The blood saves—not my sense of guilt; not my depravity; nor all my knowledge and understanding of it—but the blood, the blood alone. And so I may have had high and wrapt communion, and deep fellowship with Christ; but if I rest in my communion, I am as much deceived as he that rests on the Romish priests—for there is nothing in anything I can do, or be, or ever could be, that can save me; it is all in Christ from first to last; and, putting his pierced hand on all your doing, believing, seeing, feeling, experiences, he covers them all up, and says, "I am the way," and none of these. I like the way Wilcox puts this in his "Precious Drop of Honey." "All that is of nature's spinning," says he, "must be unraveled," and I like to know also, that even if I put the Spirit's work in the place of Christ, I make that work to be an anti-Christ.   *Spurgeon.*

8515. EXPERIENCE, Comparing. Mr. Turner, a missionary, related his experience of conversion. Joel Bulu, a South Sea Island pagan, heard it, and says, "My heart burned within me while I listened to his word; for in speaking of himself he told all I had felt, and I said to myself, 'We are like two canoes, sailing bow and bow, neither being swifter nor slower than the other.' Thus it was with me when he told of his repentance; but when he went on to speak of his faith in Christ, the forgiveness of his sins, and the peace and joy which he found in believing, then said I, 'My mast is broken, my sail is blown away; he is gone clean out of my sight, and I am left here drifting helplessly over the waves.' But while I listened eagerly to his words, telling of the love of Christ to him, my eyes were opened. I saw the way, and I, even I, also believed and lived. I was like a man fleeing for his life from an enemy behind him, and groping along the wall of a house in the dark to find the door, that he may enter in and escape, when lo! a door is suddenly opened before his face, and straightway, with one bound, he leaps within. Thus it was with me as I listened to the words of Mr. Turner: my heart was full of joy and love." Bulu became a very useful helper to the missionary.

8516. EXPERIENCE, Dearness of. Experience keeps a dear school, but fools will learn in no other, and scarcely in that; for it is true, we may give advice, but we cannot give conduct. Remember this: They that will not be counseled cannot be helped. If you do not hear reason, she will rap your knuckles. *Franklin.*

8517. EXPERIENCE, Deep. Shallow waters are easily muddied. After a night of storm the waters of the bay, along the beach, stirred by the winds, are foul and black with the mire and dirt. But look beyond, out into the deep water, how blue and clear it is! The white caps on the surface show the violence of the wind, but the water is too deep for the storms that sweep its surface to stir up the earth at the bottom. So is Christian experience. A shallow experience is easily disturbed; the merest trifles becloud and darken the soul whose piety is superficial; while the most furious storm of life fails to darken or disturb the soul which has attained a deep experience of the things of God. The agitation may produce a sparkle on the surface, but in the calm depths of such a spirit reigns eternal tranquillity, the peace of God that passeth all understanding.   *Beecher.*

8518. EXPERIENCE, Defective. We find persons acquainted with the fundamental doctrines of religion, and we are glad. But a year afterwards, we converse with them again, and find them just the same. Two years elapse, and we come into contact with them again, but still no progress can be perceived, till at length the sight of them reminds us of a piece of wood-work carved in the form of a tree, rather than a living production of nature; for there are no fresh shoots, nor any new foliage to be seen: on the contrary, the very same modes of speech, the same views and sentiments upon every point, and the same limited sphere of spiritual conception; no enlarged expansion of the inward horizon; not a single addition to the treasury of Christian knowledge.   *Salter.*

8519. EXPERIENCE, Dependence on. He hazardeth much who depends for his learning on experience. An unhappy master, he that is only made wise by many shipwrecks; a miserable merchant, that is neither rich nor wise till he has been bankrupt. By experience we find out a short way by a long wandering.   *Ascham.*

8520. EXPERIENCE, Depth of. In my house there is a well of extraordinary depth, which reminds me of something better than the boasted deep experience of certain censorious professors, who teach that to feel sin within is the main thing, but to be delivered from it of small consequence. When this well was commenced, the owner of the place resolved to have water, cost what it might. The well-sinkers dug through mud, and clay, and stone, but found no water; here was the deep experience of the corruptionist, all earth and no living spring, the filth revealed but not removed, the leper discovered but not healed. Another hundred feet of hard digging deep in the dark, but no water—still deeper experience. Then a third hundred feet, and still dirt, but no crystal—the very finest grade of your deeply experimental professor, who ridicules the joys of faith, as being of the flesh and presumptuous. Still on, on, on went the workers, till one day leaving their tools to go to dinner, upon their return they found that the water was rising fast, and their tools were drowned. Be this last my experience—to go so deep as to reach the springs of everlasting love, and find all my poor doings and efforts totally submerged, because the blessed fountains of grace have broken in upon me, covering all the mire, and rock, and earth, of my poor, naturally evil heart.   *Spurgeon.*

8521. EXPERIENCE, Disregarding. In the early days of American history, the Indians mounted upon swift horses, and, armed with bows and arrows, hunted the buffalo. They sought to secure their prey by driving them upon some high bluff, having a steep precipice on one side. Cutting off their retreat in the rear, and sending panic among the animals by hot pursuit and wild yells, they drove their victims to leap the cliff to their own destruction. Man, the reasoning animal, lured on by his own appetites, passions, and conceits, rushes through all barriers, disregards all experience, closes his ears to all warnings, and leaps the cliff of eternal ruin. It is the common course of folly. Every year, and in every community, this case s paralleled and repeated. "A prudent man foreseeth the evil, and hideth himself; but the simple pass on and are punished." (Prov. 22 : 3.)

8522. EXPERIENCE of Faith. Orthodoxy can be learned from others'; living faith must be a matter of personal experience. The Lord sent out his disciples, saying, "Ye shall testify of me, because ye have been with me from the beginning." He only is a witness who speaks of what he has seen with his own eyes, heard with his own ears, and handled with his own hands. Orthodoxy is merely another form of rationalism, if it be learned from without.
                                                    Buchsel.

8523. EXPERIENCE, Judging. Rev. John Wesley was asked by a young gentleman "if he had seen Whitefield's Journals." He replied he had. "And what do you think of them?" said he; "Don't you think they are cant, enthusiasm from end to end? I think so." Wesley inquired, "Why do you think so?" He replied, "Why, he talks so much of joy and stuff, and inward feelings. As I hope to be saved, I cannot tell what to make of it." Wesley asked, "Did you ever feel the love of God in your heart? If not, how should you tell what to make of it? Whatever is spoken of the religion of the heart, and of the inward workings of the Spirit of God, must appear enthusiasm to those who have not felt them; that is, if they take upon them to judge of the things of which they own they know nothing."

8524. EXPERIENCE, New Light in. A soldier after evening prayers came and asked the chaplain to pray with him. He said, "I have navigated every channel to perdition, but now I want to lead a different life." He was pointed to Jesus. He looked and lived. "Oh," said he, the next day, "how easy it is to be a Christian! I did not suppose it was so easy. I thought it was a long and very troublesome way; I just asked with all my heart, and I hadn't to wait for the answer; I just prayed to God, and light came in at once. How glorious everything is! Even this Virginia mud now seems to have become beautiful."

8525. EXPERIENCE, Ordeal of. A skeptical young man having heard several relations of religious experience in which a great change of disposition and enjoyment was affirmed, resolved to test it for himself. Without the sense of conviction for sin, he formed a plan of duty, viz., to forsake all sin, and to do every duty as long as life lasted, and announced his decision to his companions. He kept his purpose for some weeks without any change of feeling. He looked for a burden of conviction, but instead lost all feeling. He went on as usual in the way of Christian duty, when at length joy filled his soul. A great transformation had come over him. He felt it in every faculty, and knew the truth of religion to his entire satisfaction.

8526. EXPERIENCE of Solomon. Solomon went through a peculiar experience of his own, and God, who in nature gives sweet fruit to men through the root sap of a sour crab, when a new nature has been engrafted on the upper stem, did not disdain to bring forth fruits of righteousness through those parts of the king's experience that cleaved most closely to the dust. None of all the prophets could have written the Proverbs or the Preacher; for God is not wont, even in his miraculous interpositions, to make a fig-tree bear olive-berries, or a vine figs: every creature acts after its kind. When Solomon delineated the eager efforts of men in search of happiness, and the disappointment which ensued, he could say, like Bunyan, of that fierce and fruitless war, "I was there." The heights of human prosperity he had reached: the paths of human learning he had trodden, further than any of his day; the pleasures of wealth and power and pomp he had tasted, in all their variety. No spring of earthly delight could be named, of whose waters he had not deeply drunk. This is the man whom God hath chosen as the schoolmaster to teach us the vanity of the world when it is made the portion of the soul, and he hath done all things well. The man who has drained the cup of pleasure can best tell the taste of its dregs.   *Arnot.*

8527. EXPERIENCE, Thankful. I shall go to the gates of heaven as a poor, wretched, ruined sinner saved by grace. But when I begin to tell my tale of his wondrous love to me, methinks all the harps of heaven will be silent, and the angels, still as statues, will listen to my ascriptions.   *Dr. Robert Simpson.*

8528. EXTORTION, Reward of. An old New York merchant was noted for demanding the utmost farthing. He had conspicuously posted in sight of all, "No compromise." If a bankrupt debtor approached him and said, "How much will you accept and cancel my debt?" he would reply, "One hundred cents on the dollar, sir." Many who knew of his extortions, prophesied his downfall. At length retribution overtook him. His overthrow was sudden, complete and irretrievable.

8529. EXTRAVAGANCE, Beginning of. A young husband, whose business speculations were unsuccessful, said: "My wife's silver tea-set, the bridal gift of a rich uncle, doomed me to financial ruin. It involved a hundred unexpected expenses, which, in trying to meet, have made me the bankrupt that I am." His is the experience of many others, who, less wise, do not know what is the goblin of the house, working its destruction. A sagacious father of great wealth exceedingly mortified his daughter by ordering to be printed on her wedding cards, "No presents, except those adapted to an income of $1,000." Said he, "You must not expect to begin life in the style I am able, by many years of labor, to indulge; and I know nothing which will tempt you to try, more than the well-intentioned but pernicious gifts of rich friends." Such advice is timely. If other parents would follow the same plan, many young men would be spared years of incessant toil and anxiety; they would not find themselves on the downward road because their wives had worn all of their salary, or expended it on the appointment of the house.

The fate of the poor man who found a linch-pin and felt obliged to make a carriage to fit it, is the fate of the husband who finds his bride in possession of gold and silver valuables, and no large income to support the owner's gold and silver style.   *Anon.*

8530. EXTRAVAGANCE: Brevities. The injury of prodigality leads to this, that he that will not economize will have to agonize.—*Confucius.*——He that is extravagant will quickly become poor; and poverty will enforce dependence and invite corruption.—*Dr. Johnson.*——A miser grows rich by seeming poor; an extravagant man grows poor by seeming rich.—*Shenstone*——An extravagant man, who has nothing else to recommend him but a false generosity, is often more beloved than a person of a much more finished character, who is defective in this particular.   *Addison.*

8531. EXTRAVAGANCE, Fruits of. Extravagance does not pay. A piece of lace, fine as film and costly as diamonds, was offered for sale lately in Europe. Queens declined to purchase at the enormous price. The wives of great bankers passed by on the other side. An American lady heard of it and sent a check for the amount. This was a year or so ago. Last week the estate of the husband of this American lady passed into the hands of trustees, and some savings banks, with moneys of the poor and the industrious in their possession, were closed up. The moral every one may draw.   *Presbyterian.*

8532. EXTREMITY, Deliverance in. *Abraham.*—God spared Abraham from actually offering up his treasured child; but to what an extremity was he first brought. The knife was uplifted, and one moment more would have been too late! But that moment was enough! Gen. 22: 10–12; Rom. 4: 18. *Israel.*—How often were they delivered in times of extremity? *In Egypt,* when Pharaoh's cruel edict against the male children was well-nigh executed; when they were oppressed and crushed to the lowest point before they left the house of bondage. *In the wilderness,* when at times they suffered from thirst or other trials; when they were bitten by fiery serpents; smitten by the plague; it was generally in the extremity of distress that deliverance came; frequently it was not till then that they cried to the Lord. See Ps. 78: 34; 107: 6, 13, 19, 28. *In Canaan,* many times, as under Hezekiah, when the Lord interposed in the hour of danger, Isa. 37: 36. *In Babylon.*—The very last year of the predicted seventy came before any signs of deliverance appeared, Dan. 9: 1, 2; and meantime the crafty design of Haman had almost extirpated the whole nation. The gallows was erected for pious Mordecai before the Lord interposed to break the snare. Christ often saved when all other means failed. Luke 8: 43–50; 7: 12–15; Matt. 14: 25   *Bowes.*

8533. EYE, Chamber of the. The eye-chamber is small; but it is large enough. A single tent sufficed to lodge Napoleon; and Nelson guided the fleets of England from one little cabin. And so it is with the eye; it is set apart for the reception of one guest, whose name is Light, but also Legion; and as the privileged entrant counsels, the great arms and limbs of the body are set in motion.   *G. Wilson.*

8534. EYE, Education of the. The eye was intended by its Maker to be educated, and to be educated slowly; but if educated fully, its powers are almost boundless. It is assuredly then a thing to be profoundly regretted, that not one man in a thousand developes the hidden capacities of his organ of vision, either as regards its utilitarian or its æsthetic applications. The great majority of mankind do not and cannot see one fraction of what they were intended to see. The proverb, that "None are so blind as those who will not see," is as true of physical as of moral vision. By neglect and carelessness we have made ourselves unable to discern hundreds of things which are before us to be seen. Thomas Carlyle has summed up this in one pregnant sentence—"The eye sees what it brings the power to see." How true this is! The sailor on the lookout can see a ship where the landsman can see nothing; the Esquimaux can discover a white fox amid the white snow; the American backwoodsman will fire a rifle-ball so as to strike a nut out of the mouth of a squirrel without hurting it; the Red Indian boys hold their hands up as marks to each other, certain that the unerring arrow will be shot between the spread-out fingers; the astronomer can see a star in the sky, where to others the blue expanse is unbroken; the shepherd can distinguish the face of every sheep in the flock; the mosaic worker can detect distinctions of color, where others see none; and multitudes of additional examples might be given of what education does for the eye. It is not to be denied, that some eyes can be educated to a much greater extent than others; that, however, can be no excuse for neglecting to educate the eye. The worse it is, the more it needs education; the better it is, the more it will repay it.   *G. Wilson.*

8535. EYE, The Jaundiced. It may be said, that objects take a color from the eyes that look at them. That is true. The very sun, as well as sky, and sea, and mountains, appear yellow to the jaundiced eye; the brightest prospect wears an air of gloom to a gloomy mind; a sunny temper gilds the edges of life's blackest cloud, and flings a path of light across its stormies* sea; contentment sits down to a crust of bread and a cup of water, and gives God thanks; and the plainest face looks beautiful in the eyes of fond affection.   *Dr. Guthrie.*

8536. EYES, Ignorant. It is said that a countryman, who noticed that old people when they wanted to read put on a pair of spectacles, went into the city to a spectacle-maker to buy a pair. The spectacle-maker put a pair on the man's nose and gave him a book, which he took and looked at, but in a moment said: "These spectacles are not good." The dealer then put upon his nose the best glasses he had in the shop, but the countryman, after trying them, declared that they were no better than the others. At last the spectacle-maker said to him: "Friend, perhaps you don't know how to read." "Even so," said the countryman. "If I knew how to read without glasses, I shouldn't want to buy a pair to help me!"

8537. EYES, Importance of the. What is the world, says one, without the sun but a dark melancholy dungeon? What is a man without eyes, but monstrous and deformed. The two eyes are two luminaries, that God hath set up in the microcosm, man's little world. When God would express his tender love unto his people, he calls them the apple of his eye. "He that toucheth you, toucheth the apple of his eye." And the like phrase St. Paul makes use of, when he speaks of the love of the Galatians unto himself: "I bear you record, that if it had been possible, ye would have plucked out your eyes, and have given them to me." The Emperor Adrian with an arrow, by accident, put out one of his servant's eyes; he commanded him to be brought to him, and bade him ask what he might make him amends. The poor man was silent; he pressed him again, when he said he would ask nothing, but he wished he had the eye which he had lost; intimating that an emperor was not able to make satisfaction for the loss of an eye. So the light of divine truth is infinitely more valuable than all other blessings. If we come short of this, there can be no substitute found. If the soul should be lost, the whole world can afford us no relief. The Latin verses Adrian addressed to his soul, and translated by Pope ("Vital spark," etc.), are well known. *Buck.*

8538. EYES, Mechanism of the. The eye infinitely surpasses all the works of the industry of man. Its formation is the most astonishing thing the human understanding has been able to acquire a perfect knowledge of. The most skillful artist could imagine no machine of that kind which would not be much inferior to what we observe in the eye. Whatever sagacity or industry he might have, he could execute nothing which would not have the imperfections necessarily belonging to all the works of man. We cannot, it is true, perceive clearly the whole art of Divine Wisdom in the formation of this fine organ; but the little we do know is sufficient to convince us of the infinite knowledge, goodness, and power of our Creator. The most essential point is for us to make use of this knowledge, weak as it is, to magnify the name of the Most High. In the first place, the disposition of the external parts of the eye is admirable. With what intrenchment, what defence, the Creator has provided our eyes! They are placed in the head at a certain depth, and surrounded with hard and solid bones, that they may not easily be hurt. The eye-brows contribute also very much to the safety and preservation of this organ. Those hairs which form an arch over the eyes prevent drops of sweat, dust, or such things, falling from the forehead into them. The eye-lids are another security; and also, by closing in our sleep, they prevent the light from disturbing our rest.

The eye-lashes still add to the perfection of the eyes. They save us from a too strong light which might offend us; and they guard us from the smallest dust, which might otherwise hurt the sight. The internal make of the eye is still more admirable. The whole eye is composed of coats, of humors, of muscles and veins. The tunica, or exterior membrane, which is called cornea, is transparent, and so hard, that it can resist the roughest touch. Behind that there is another within which they call uvea, and which is circular and colored. In the middle of it there is an opening, which in called the pupil, and which appears black. Behind this opening is the crystal, which is very perfectly transparent, of a lenticular figure, and composed of several little flakes very thin, and arranged one over another. Underneath the crystal there is a moist and transparent substance, which they call the glassy humor, because it resembles melted glass. The cavity, or the hinder chamber, between the cornea and crystal, contains a moist humor, and liquid as water, for that reason called the watery humor. It can recruit itself when it has run out from a wound of the cornea. Six muscles, admirably well placed, move the eye on all sides, raise it, lower it, turn it to the right or left, obliquely, or round about, as occasion requires. What is the most admirable is the retina, a membrane which lines the inside bottom of the eye. It is nothing but a web of little fibres extremely fine, fastened to a nerve or sinew, which comes from the brain, and is called the optic nerve. It is in the retina that the vision is formed, because the objects paint themselves at the bottom of the eye on that tunica. And, though the images of exterior objects are painted upside down on the retina, they are still seen in their true position. Now, in order to form an idea of the extreme minuteness of this picture, we need only consider, that the space of half a mile—that is to say, of more than eleven hundred yards—when it is represented in the bottom of the eye, makes but the tenth part of an inch. *Sturm.*

8539. EYES, Power of the. Martin Luther was noted for his piercing eyes. A ruffian called upon him under pretence of a private conference, but with the real purpose of assassinating him. He was so confounded by the power of Luther's eyes that he left him unhurt. It is said that there were in Scythia women having two sights in each eye, and that they killed by their look whoever they looked upon when they were thoroughly angry.

8540. EYES, The Use of the. These are the windows which God hath placed in the top of the building, that man from thence may contemplate God's works, and take a prospect of heaven, the place of our eternal residence. *Manton.*

8541. EZEKIEL, Portrait of. Ezekiel was a priest as well as a prophet, and alludes more frequently than any of the prophets to the ceremonial institutes of the temple. He was every inch a Jew; and none of the prophets possessed more attachment to their country, more zeal for their law, and more hatred to its foes. We know little of his history; but we cannot check our fancy, as she seeks to represent to us the face and figure of this our favorite prophet. We see him young, slender, longlocked, stooping, as if under the burden of the Lord—with a visible fire in his eye and cheek, and an invisible fire about his motions and gestures, earnest purpose pursuing him like a ghost, a wild beauty hanging around him, like the silver on the blue cones of the pine, and the air of early death adding a supernatural age and dignity to his youthful aspect. We see him as he moved through the land, followed by looks of admiration, wonder, and fear; and, like the hero of "Excelsior," untouched by the love of maidens, unterrified by the counsel of elders, undismayed by danger or by death, climbing straight to his object. Such a being was Ezekiel—among men, but not of them—detained in the company of flesh, his feet on earth, his soul floating amid the cherubim. *G. Gilfillan.*

8542. FABLE, Influence of. Men are the subjects of it. Human actions, projects, thoughts, follies, and virtues, are delineated under the vail and emblems of animals endowed with the faculties of speech and reason. Thus human motives are dissected, human infirmities exposed, and human conduct described, in a method recommending itself to the conscience more forcibly than would the adoption of any definite reproof or any direct condemnation, and thereby saving the self-love of those to whom the counsel conveyed is applicable.
G. H. Townshend.

8543. FABLES, Advantage of. Among all the different ways of giving counsel, I think the finest, and that which pleases the most universally, is fable, in whatsoever shape it appears. If we consider this way of instructing or giving advice, it excels all others, because it is the least shocking, and the least subject to exceptions. This will appear to us if we reflect, in the first place, that upon the reading of a fable we are made to believe we advise ourselves. We peruse the author for the sake of the story, and consider the precepts rather as our own conclusions than his instructions. The moral insinuates itself imperceptibly; we are taught by surprise, and become wiser and better unawares. In short, by this method a man is so far overreached as to think he is directing himself, while he is following the dictates of another, and consequently is not sensible of that which is the most unpleasing circumstance in advice.
Addison.

8544. FABLES, Popularity of. As fables took their birth in the very infancy of learning, they never flourished more than when learning was at its greatest height. To justify this assertion, I shall put my reader in mind of Horace, the greatest wit and critic in the Augustan age, and of Boileau, the most correct poet among the moderns; not to mention La Fontaine, who by this way of writing is come more into vogue than any other author of our times.
Addison.

8545. FABLES, Teaching by. I have been always wonderfuly delighted with fables, allegories, and the like inventions, which the politest and the best instructors of mankind have always made use of. They take off from the severity of instruction, and enforce it at the same time that they conceal it.   *Addison.*

8546. FACETIOUSNESS, Diversion of. Facetiousness is not unseemly when it serves the purposes of wholesome diversion or pleasant conversation; nor is it contrary to the spirit and genius of Christianity, if it be kept within the bounds of prudence and charity.   *Wilson.*

8547. FACTS, Corruption of. Every day of my life makes me feel more and more how seldom a fact is accurately stated; how almost invariably when a story has passed through the mind of a third person it becomes, so far as regards the impression that it makes in further repetitions, little better than a falsehood; and this, too, though the narrator be the most truth-seeking person in existence.
Hawthorne.

8548. FACTS Mental Food. Facts are to the mind the same thing as food to the body. On the due digestion of facts depends the strength and wisdom of the one, just as vigor and health depend on the other. The wisest in council, the ablest in debate, and the most agreeable companion in the commerce of human life, is that man who has assimilated to his understanding the greatest number of facts.
Burke.

8549. FACULTIES, Development of the. We are born with faculties and powers capable almost of anything—such at least as would carry us further than can easily be imagined; but it is only the exercise of those powers which gives us ability and skill in anything, and leads us towards perfection.   *Locke.*

8550. FAILURE, Benefits from. Albeit failure in any cause produces a correspondent misery in the soul, yet it is, in a sense, the highway to success, inasmuch as every discovery of what is false leads us to seek earnestly after what is true, and every fresh experience points out some form of error which we shall afterward carefully eschew.   *Keats.*

8551. FAILURE, Philosophic Endurance of. A little child was chasing a butterfly. Whenever it alighted near her she tried to seize it with her tiny hand, but it always arose triumphantly and fluttered over her head as if to mock her feeble effort. Wearied at last, she threw herself upon the ground, and with a look of sweet resignation, exclaimed: "Well, no matter; it might have stung me."

8552. FAILURE, Substitute for. If you nave failed for this life, do not fail for the other, too. There is very much that may yet be done, even in the afternoon and twilight of men's lives, if they are hopeful and active. When one of my Norway spruces died from the rude handling of last winter, instead of rooting it up and throwing it away, I let the ampelopsis take possession of it, and it grew up rapidly through all the branches of the tree, and covered its top with leaves. And in the autumn, these

eaves, which had been green before, were all changed to a brilliant crimson; and the tree in its own life was not half so beautiful as it was when covered by this vine, clad with all the colors of the setting sun. Are you like an old tree that is dead, and has dropped all its foliage, and stands with its trunk and branches bare? Let faith and love cover you over, and you will be more comely and more useful standing clothed in such garniture than you were clad in all your former strength. Be patient, old man. Be patient, mother. Be patient, widow. Be patient, you that are impoverished. Be patient, men that are scarcely thought of, and are treading lower and lower. God thinks of you.
Beecher.

8553. FAILURE, Useful. It is far from being true, in the progress of knowledge, that after every failure we must recommence from the beginning. Every failure is a step to success; every detection of what is false directs us towards what is true; every trial exhausts some tempting form of error. Not only so; but scarcely any attempt is entirely a failure.
Whewell.

8554. FAITH, Absence of. When men cease to be faithful to their God, he who expects to find them so to each other, will be much disappointed. The primitive sincerity will accompany the primitive piety in her flight from the earth, and then interest will succeed conscience in the regulation of human conduct, till one man cannot trust another further than he holds him by that tie; hence, by the way, it is, that although many are infidels themselves, yet few choose to have their families and dependents such; as judging—and rightly judging—that true Christians are the only persons to be depended on for the exact discharge of their social duties.
Bishop Horne.

8555. FAITH, Aid to. Rev. Newman Hall aided a timid young disciple, who was a telegraph operator, by the following: "Suppose a man wrote a message, and having asked if it was all right, he went away, perfectly satisfied. Suppose there also came to your office an old lady, who never before had sent a telegram, and was full of doubts and fears about everything. She wrote her message, and said, 'Are you sure it will go?'—'O yes.' 'How long will it take?' 'Not more than an hour.' 'What, go two hundred miles in an hour? Are you sure?' 'Quite sure.' 'But will it go just as I send it?' 'Yes.' 'Are you sure they'll understand it.' 'Quite sure.' After many such questions she went away; and again came back to ask. Now, would a message be any slower in going, and would it be delivered with less accuracy, than the message of the man, who had no fear at all?"

8556. FAITH, Analogy of. There is the analogy of faith; it is a master-key, which not only opens particular doors, but carries you through the whole house. But an attachment to a rigid system is dangerous; Luther once turned out the Epistle of St. James because it disturbed his system. I shall preach, perhaps very usefully upon two opposite texts, while

kept apart; but, if I attempt nicely to reconcile them, it is ten to one if I do not begin to bungle.
Salter.

8557. FAITH, Answer to. A Christian friend came one day to Rev. Mr. Henke, who unhesitatingly invited him to dine with him, although he knew not what he could set before him. When the bell rang at noon, the servant passed through the room with an anxious countenance, in order unobservedly to beckon her master out. Henke, however, was not aware of her meaning, and only reminded her, at last, that it was time to lay the cloth. The servant was perplexed, and requested her master to step out to her for a minute. "Sir," she began in a mournful voice, "you wish me to lay the cloth; but don't you know that we have scarcely a piece of dry bread in the house, and you sent your last penny to a sick person this very day?" "Ah!" answered Henke with a smile, "is that all you have to say to me? Do but lay the cloth as usual; it will be time enough for the meat, when we sit down to table." The maid, not a little astonished, did as she was told. "Let us take our seats," said the friendly host, with a cheerful countenance. They sat down to the empty table, and the worthy childlike man offered up a prayer. On his saying "Amen!" the door-bell rang and there was a basket with abundance of food, which a neighbor had felt constrained to send him. Calmly, as if nothing particular had happened, Henke ordered all the dishes to be filled; and then looking smilingly at the astonished servant, he said: "Well, have you still anything to object to our kind entertainer?" These are valuable facts; but such things cannot be imitated. It is certainly easy to order the cloth to be laid; but nothing is accomplished by that. However, if you possess anything of Henke's faith, then do not hesitate to order the cloth to be laid. A Royal Host will provide the feast.
Krummacher.

8558. FAITH, Attendants of. Faith is a noble duchess; she ever hath her gentleman usher going before her, the confessing of sins; she hath a train after her, the fruits of good works, the walking in the commandments of God. He that believeth will not be idle; he will walk, he will do his business. Have ever the gentleman usher with you. So if you will try Faith, remember this rule, consider whether the train is waiting upon her.
Latimer.

8559. FAITH, Beautiful. A poor family in great need were being relieved by some Christian ladies; among other necessaries sent was a large basket filled with children's clothing. Little Ettie, a bright, curly-haired child of four years, stood looking on, asking questions, and wondering, "Who could be so good?" and "Who sent them, mamma?" till her mother replied, through her tears, "The Lord sent them, my dear. We must thank the Lord for all things." After the last garment was handed out, and she saw there was nothing suitable for her little baby-brother, she looked up sorrowfully to her mamma, and said, "I des de Lord fordot ee had a itty baby." So, going up to him, she placed her arm around his little neck, and kissed him, saying, "Don't feel bad, Dordy· de Lord will ememby oo some time." Not many days after this there was a parcel sent in, directed "To Baby B——." No sooner was it read than the little one clapped her hands, and shouted, " I knew de Lord ood tend baby tunfin pretty toon!" With impatience she waited the undoing of the bundle, and the first thing that she spied was a soft, white flannel blanket, which she quickly caught, and folded around him; then, taking the little dresses and other articles as fast as she could get them, laid them one by one in his lap. Then, with more than childish reverence, she said, "Now ess all fank de Lord; tause Dordy tant peak." Turning to the little fellow, she added, "Oo tut up oo eyes, baby." Then, "Don't ty, mamma. Dod ill tate dood tare of baby; I know he 'ill."   *Christian Era.*

8560. FAITH, Biblical. The *Greek* word for faith is derived from the verb meaning to persuade; passive, to be persuaded—to believe. It is called a *shield*, Eph. 6: 16; a *breastplate*, 1 Thess. 5: 8; a *grain of mustard seed*, Matt. 17: 20; one of the smallest of seeds, but containing the germ of a full-sized tree, see Matt. 13: 32. The true nature and office of faith are clearly illustrated by the many *expressions* which are used as synonyms. Faith is repeatedly spoken of as *believing*, especially by St. John, in whose gospel it occurs about eighty times; as receiving testimony—being persuaded—fully persuaded—seeing—looking—coming — apprehending — comprehending — taking hold—embracing—feeding—resting—trusting.—See Conc. under these and similar words. Heb. 11: 1—one of the few definitions given in Scripture—"Now faith is the confidence of things hoped for, the evidence of things not seen." (*Alford.*) "The confident expectation—the powerful conviction." (*Doddridge.*) The Greek word for "substance" properly means a foundation—a prop on which something can stand and be supported. Rom. 10: 10.—Faith is the *belief* of "the *heart.*" Matt. 16: 8; Mark 8: 17.—Faith is the *trust* of the heart, more than the mere intellectual apprehension.   *Bowes.*

8561. FAITH, Calmness of. An old divine says, "Faith may live in a storm, but it will not suffer a storm to live in it. As faith rises, so the blustering wind of discontented troublesome thoughts goes down. In the same proportion that there is faith in the heart, there is peace also: they are joined together. 'In returning and rest shall ye be saved; in quietness and confidence shall be your strength.'"

8562. FAITH, Chemistry of. It is the chemistry of faith (let me use that word) to turn all things into good and precious ore. It is Abraham's country, in a strange land; Jacob's wages, when Laban defrauded him; Moses' honor, when he refused to be called the son of Pharaoh's daughter; Rahab's security, when all Jericho besides did perish: David's rescue, when there was but a step between him and death: the power of the apostles, to be able to cast out devils: Mary Magdalene's sweet ointment, to take away the ill-savor of her sins. Plead, therefore, with the oratory of faith, and say, " Lord, I have no life but in thee, I have no joy but in thee, no salvation bt t in thee: but I have all these in thee; and how can my soul refuse to be comforted?"
        Bishop Hacket.

8563. FAITH, Childish. A boy aged four years heard his grandmother say, "My flowers will all be burnt up, and we shall have no strawberries." A few minutes afterward he was seen kneeling in one corner of the room, with his hands to his face, and was overheard praying thus: "O Lord! send down rain, so that grandma's flowers shan't be burnt up, and so we shall have plenty of strawberries." He then went to his grandmother, saying, "Your flowers won't burn up, grandma. We are going to have rain." "How do you know?" "Oh!" said he, "I have been praying for it, and it will come." He seemed to have no doubt about it. The next morning he came downstairs and went to the back door to see if it rained. According to his prediction, the rain was falling upon the thirsty flowers and the perishing berries. As soon as he saw it, he joyously shouted: "It's come, it's come, I knowed it would! I prayed for it."

8564. FAITH, Childlike. The first summer the war broke out I heard in the fall of that same year something that touched my heart. A poor woman had been made a widow by the war. In mid-winter time she heard that her husband had been cut down. She had two little children, and she did not know what would become of her; her health was not very good, and she had no money. A few days after the landlord came around for his rent. He was a poor, heartless wretch, and when she told him her husband was dead and she could not pay her rent, he said, with an oath, that he would not have any one in his house who could not pay. After he had gone she threw herself in the rocking-chair and wept; her little girl came to her and said: "Mamma, does not God answer prayer?" "Yes, my child." And the child wanted to put in practice what she had heard her mother preach. She said: "Then won't he take care of us if we ask him?" "I suppose he will." "Then may I go and ask him to take care of us?" "Yes, my child, you may if you want to." The lady told me of it the next day, and she said the child never looked so sweet to her as when she went into the room where her mother had taught her to pray. The door was open a little way, and she could see her; she put up her hands and her curls lay back from her face and she said, "Oh, Father! you came and took away my dear papa; he was killed in the war; my mamma has no money to pay the landlord the rent, and he is going to turn us out doors. We will sit on the door-step and catch cold and die unless you lend us a little house to live in." Then she went to her mother and said, "Jesus will take care of us, because I have asked him." There is faith for you! They did not have to pay any rent, a house was soon provided, and that widow and her children were taken care of.   *Moody.*

8565. FAITH, A Child's. Little Willie, whose father was a drunkard, went to his mother, saying, "Mother, can't I have some new boots? My toes are all out of these; the snow gets in, and I am so cold." Tearfully the mother replied, "Soon, Willie, I hope to give them to you." After waiting some days he sobbed, "O mother, it is too hard! Can't I get some boots anywhere?" He stood a moment, in deep thought, and then said, "Oh, I know! God will give them to me, of course. Why didn't I think of that before? I'll go right off and ask him." He walked out of the parlor into his mother's room, knelt down, and covering his face with his hand, prayed: "O God! father drinks; mother has no money; my feet get cold and wet. I want some boots. Please send me a pair, for Jesus' sake. Amen." He often repeated this petition, and expected an answer to his prayer. "They'll come, mother!" he would often say, encouragingly; "they'll come when God gets them ready." Within a week, a lady who loved the child came to take him out walking. He hesitated for a few moments, but soon determined to go, and away they started. At length the lady noticed his stockings peeping out at the toes of his boots, when she exclaimed, "Why, Willie, look at your feet! They will freeze. Why didn't you put on better boots?" "These are all I have, ma'am." "All you have! But why don't you have a new pair?" she inquired. "I will just as soon as God sends them," he replied. Tears filled the lady's eyes as she led him into a shoe-shop near by, saying, "There, child, select any pair you please." On his return he went to his mother, and showing his boots, said, "Look, mother! God has sent my boots! Mrs. Gray's money bought them, but God heard me ask for them, and I suppose he told Mrs. Gray to buy them for me." Then, kneeling at his mother's feet, he said, "Jesus, I thank you for my new boots. Please make me a good boy, and take care of mother. Amen."

8566. FAITH, Comfort of. The practice of this virtue administers great comfort to the mind of man in times of poverty and affliction, but most of all in the hour of death. When the soul is hovering in the last moments of its separation, when it is just entering on another state of existence, to converse with scenes and objects and companions that are altogether new—what can support her under such tremblings of thought, such fears, such anxiety, such apprehensions, but the casting of all her cares upon him who first gave her being, who has conducted her through one stage of it, and will be always with her to guide and comfort her in her progress through eternity?   *Addison.*

8567. FAITH, Commercial. Men of trade rely on the unseen. They freight their ships to China, and they bring back their cargoes, though they have never seen that land. Commerce, trade, exchange, are based upon this

faith. You place your money in your bank here and draw for it in London, though you have never been there; and you cross the ocean with the certainty that you will have the money in London when you get there. It is the same thing as to draw from the merits of Christ, and know you have the treasure when you cross the ocean and get into glory—the same principle precisely. Here is a man of means in your city, and I want money from the bank. I cannot get it on my own name, but I draw up a note and take it to him and he endorses it, and I go to the bank knowing I will get it. They don't know me, don't care for me; they would not trust me; but they know that man and his influence and power, and they trust him, and I go to the bank with perfect confidence that I will get the money, for I have the name of that millionaire. Jesus says, "Whatsoever ye ask in my name, the Father will give it you." There is a name that has power in heaven—all power, all wealth—and I ask in the name of Jesus, and I receive. And when I learn to go with the same confidence to the bank of glory in the name of Christ that I can go to the bank in your city in the name of one of your millionaires, then I have the things that I ask of God.   *Bp. Simpson.*

8568. FAITH, Cultivating. The faith to which the Scriptures attach such momentous consequences, and ascribe such glorious exploits, is a practical habit, which, like every other, is strengthened and increased by continual exercise. It is nourished by meditation, by prayer, and the devout perusal of the Scriptures; and the light which it diffuses becomes stronger and clearer by an uninterrupted converse with its object and a faithful compliance with its dictates; as on the contrary it is weakened and obscured by whatever wounds the conscience or impairs the purity and spirituality of the mind.   *Robert Hall.*

8569. FAITH in the Dark. Look at a railway train—all the carriages crowded with passengers. They fly over high bridges, and through dark tunnels, and the least mistake or fault of the engine-driver would produce a terrible accident. Do they see that man to whose care they have entrusted their lives? No. How, then, are they so calm and secure? Because they trust him.   *Bibl. Treas.*

8570. FAITH, Encouragement for. It may be thou art a poor, trembling soul; thy faith is weak, and thy assaults from Satan strong; thy corruptions great, and thy strength little; yea, thou art apt to dread that thou shalt one day be cast as a wreck on the shore of the infernal world. And yet to this day thy grace lives. Thou art still longing, panting, desiring, wishing, and groaning for God. Is it not worth while to turn and see this strange sight? A broken ship, with masts and hull rent and torn, full of leaks, yet towed along by the Almighty power through a tempestuous sea; nor tempestuous only, but thick set with armadas of sins, afflictions, doubts and temptations, safely into God's harbor! To see the poor smoking flax in the face of the boisterous winds, and liable to the frequent dashes of quenching waves, yet not blown out! In a word, to see a weak stripling in grace held up in God's arms until all enemies are under his feet! "This is the Lord's doing, and it is marvelous in our eyes."   *Salter.*

8571. FAITH, Faculty of. Faith is that strange faculty by which man feels the presence of the invisible, exactly as some animals have the power of seeing in the dark. That is the difference between the Christian and the world.

8572. FAITH, Flower of. In ascending the Alps, the traveler passes through different regions of vegetation. First comes the vine, then the fruit-trees, then magnificent forest-trees; higher up the stunted pines; higher again, dwarf-trees and mosses; at last, the regions of eternal snow. But far up, almost on the very top of the mountain, a tiny, sweet flower peeps through the snow. It has often drawn tears from the eyes of the manliest traveler. It blooms away there, cheerfully, sweetly. And thus, in the soul, you pass on through the regions of knowledge, emotion, will; and on the summit, despite the cold atmosphere of moral depravity and continual alienation—if you are a child of God—the flower of faith, true faith, ever blooms and cheers.   *Teachers' Treasury.*

8573. FAITH in God's Promises. Faith in God's promises may be compared to a bank-note; full and felt possession of the blessings promised is like ready cash. The man who has bank-notes to any given value looks upon himself as possessed of so much money, though in reality it is only so much paper. Thus faith is as satisfied, and rests with as great complacency in the promises of Jehovah, as if it had all the blessings of grace and glory in hand. In faith's estimation God's note is current coin.   *Salter.*

8574. FAITH, Golden Thread of. Each of the gospels might be read with profit, as affording illustrations of faith; perhaps St. John's especially (see John 6), where the office and work of faith are set forth by so many figures: coming to Christ—seeing—feeding—eating his flesh and drinking his blood, etc.—all synonymous with believing on him. An old writer (Adams) says, St. John treats in his Gospel especially of faith; in his Epistles of love; and in the Revelation of hope. Faith is the golden thread that runs through the many-linked chain of Christian graces. The Christian's life is the "life of faith," as it is written, "The just shall live by faith," Rom. 1: 17; Gal. 3: 11; Heb. 10: 38. We "stand"—we "walk—we "fight"—we "resist"—we "overcome," by faith. The duties and privileges of the Christian's life derive their energy and vigor from the energy of faith; hence we read of "the prayer of faith;" "the hearing of faith;" "the obedience of faith;" "the work of faith;" "the unity of the faith;" "the joy of faith;" the "profession of faith;" the "measure and proportion of faith;" "the righteousness of faith;" the "assurance of faith."   *Bowes.*

8575. FAITH and the Graces. Faith finds all the graces with work. As the rich tradesman gives out his wool, some to this man, and some to that, who all spin and work off the stock he gives them out, so that when he ceaseth to trade, they must also, because they have no stock but what he affords them; thus faith gives out to every grace what they act upon. If faith trades not, neither can they.   *Anon.*

8576. FAITH, Help to. The teacher of an infant school having directed a little fellow to move a stool, but so as not to be himself seen, thus endeavored to instruct his infant charge: "You cannot see any one moving the stool—is it not alive?" "Oh, no, it's not alive, never was alive; some one must be moving it." "But, my little fellow, you cannot see anybody; perhaps it moves itself?" "Oh, no, sir; though we do not see anybody, that does not make any odds: it does not move itself." He then told them of the sun, and the moon, and stars, and that although we did not see any one move them, yet it was certain they were moved, and no other could do so but God himself, but we could not see him. "Yes, it must be God." "But then, my little folks, you cannot see him?" "Please, sir, we must believe it." "Well, then, you believe it?" "Yes." "This then is faith."

8577. FAITH Honors God. When the late Elector of Hanover was declared by the Parliament of Great Britain successor to the vacant throne, several persons of distinction waited upon his highness, in order to make timely application for the most valuable preferments. Several requests of this nature were granted, and each was confirmed by a kind of promissory note. One gentleman, particularly, solicited for the Mastership of the Rolls. Being indulged in his desire, he was offered the same confirmation which had been vouchsafed to other successful petitioners; upon which he seemed to be under a pang of graceful confusion and surprise, begged that he might not put the royal donor to such unnecessary trouble, at the same time protesting that he looked upon his Highness's word as the very best ratification of his suit. With this conduct and this compliment the Elector was not a little pleased. "This is the gentleman," he said, "who does me a real honor—treats me like a king; and, whoever is disappointed, he shall certainly be gratified." So we are assured by the testimony of revelation that the patriarch who staggered not through unbelief gave—and in the most signal, the most acceptable manner—glory to God. (Rom. 4: 20.)   *Hervey.*

8578. FAITH, Hope and Charity. Justinian erected a church in Constantinople, which he consecrated to Eternal Wisdom, *Aiona Sophia.* In course of time the legend grew that St. Sophia was a great female soul, and that she was the mother of three fair daughters, Faith, Hope and Charity. Another addition made those daughters virgins and then martyrs. Then the grim joke that Faith, Hope and Charity were dead, originated. The relics of these saints are shown in the church of St

Peter and St. Sylvester at Rome. All this shows the danger of a literal translation of figures of speech.

8579. FAITH, Increase of. As a man beginning life without sixpence has made a fortune of tens of thousands, so he who at first has little faith may become like Abraham, or the woman of Canaan. Coal beds may be exhausted; gold and silver mines abandoned as not worth working any longer; but faith is a mine that cannot be exhausted.   *Griffith.*

8580. FAITH in the Invisible. Some believe the better for seeing Christ's sepulchre; and when they have seen the Red Sea, doubt not of the miracle. Now, contrarily, I bless myself, and am thankful, that I live not in the days of miracles, that I never saw Christ nor his disciples; I would not have been one of those Israelites that passed the Red Sea, nor one of Christ's patients on whom he wrought his wonders; then had my faith been thrust upon me; nor should I enjoy that greater blessing pronounced to all that believe and saw not. 'Tis an easy and necessary belief to credit what our eye and sense hath examined; I believe he was dead and buried, and rose again; and desire to see him in his glory, rather than to contemplate him in his cenotaph or sepulchre.   *T. Browne.*

8581. FAITH a Link. Faith brings us into contact with Christ. You have seen a chain in two pieces, and a link connecting them that looks like the letter S. Faith is that link; on the one side it takes hold of the Saviour, on the other it takes hold of the sinner.
   Thomas Jones.

8582. FAITH, Living by. "We live by faith," says the apostle, "and not by sight, or by sense." They are as two buckets—the life of faith, and the life of sense; when one goes up, the other goes down; the higher faith rises, the lower sense and reason; and the higher sense and reason, the lower faith. That is true of the schools. Reason going before faith weakens and diminishes it; but reason following upon faith, increases and strengthens it. Luther says well, "If you would believe, you must crucify that question, why?" God would not have us so full of wherefores. And if you would believe, you must go blindfold into God's command. Abraham subscribes to a blank when the Lord calls him out of his own country.   *Bridge.*

8583. FAITH, Means and. He that believes God for the event, believes him for the means also. If the patient dare trust the physician for his cure, he dare also follow his prescription in order to do it, and therefore, Christian, sit not still and say thy sins shall fall, but put thyself in array against them.   *Anon.*

8584. FAITH, Obedient. A minister wishing to teach a child the nature of faith took a chair and placed it at some distance from him, and told him to stand on it and fall forward, and he would catch him. The boy immediately got on to the chair, but did not fall forward. He wished to obey, but was afraid he would not catch him. He put, however, one hand upon the mantel-piece, thinking to save himself if he did not catch him; but the minister told him that would not do; he must trust to him alone. The minister then told him he would surely catch him if he would fall forward. The boy at last summoned all his courage and fell, and he caught him. The minister then told him that that was faith, and that he wished him to go with the same confidence to Jesus Christ.

8585. FAITH, Obscuration of. Let this thought, that God cannot lie, keep in conscious safety the heart of every one who looketh to Jesus. They who look shall be saved. The sun in the firmament is often faintly seen through a cloud; but the spectator may be no less looking at him than when he is seen in full and undiminished effulgence. It is not to him who sees Christ brightly that the promises are made, but to him who looks to Christ. A bright view may minister comfort; but it is the looking which ministers safety.   *Chalmers.*

8586. FAITH, Penetration of. God cannot be seen but covered under something. See his mercy in his anger. In what appears bringing us to hell, faith sees him bringing us to heaven; in darkness, it beholds brightness; in hiding his face from us, it beholds his cheering countenance. How did Job see God, but as you would say under Satan's cloak? For who cast the fire from heaven upon his goods? Who overthrew his house and stirred up men to take away his cattle, but Satan? And yet Job pierced through all these, and saw God's work, saying, "The Lord hath given, the Lord hath taken away; blessed be the name of the Lord."
   Bradford.

8587. FAITH a Pilgrim-grace. Faith is a right pilgrim-grace; it travels with us to heaven, and when it sees us safe got within our Father's doors (heaven I mean) it takes leave of us. Now the promise is this pilgrim's staff with which it sets forth, though (like Jacob on his way to Padan-Aram) it hath nothing else with it; "Remember thy word unto thy servant," saith David, "upon which thou hast caused me to hope."   *Anon.*

8588. FAITH, Pillars of. I remember an old experimental Christian speaking about the great pillars of our faith; he was a sailor; we were then on board ship, and there were sundry huge posts on the shore to which the ships were usually fastened by throwing a cable over them. After I had told him a great many promises, he said, "I know they are good, strong promises, but I cannot get near enough to shore to throw my cable around them; that is the difficulty." Now, it often happens that God's past mercies and loving-kindnesses would be good sure posts to hold on to, but we have not got faith enough to throw our cable round them, and so we go slipping down the stream of unbelief, because we cannot stay ourselves by our former mercies. I will, however, give you something that I think you can throw your cable over. If God has never been kind to you, one thing you surely know, and that is, he has been kind to others.   *Spurgeon*

8589. FAITH and Prayer. Faith builds in the dungeon and the lazar-house its sublimest shrines; and up through roofs of stone, that shut out the eye of heaven, ascends the ladder where the angels glide to and fro—Prayer.
Lytton.

8590. FAITH, Preserve Your. "In the Grecian courts the warrior who lost his sword or spear in battle was acquitted, but he who threw away his shield was severely punished, because by doing so he either displayed an unworthy cowardice or a contempt of danger or a despair which ill became a soldier. Nothing was to be preserved with such care as the shield. Like the modern standard, it was to be fought for to the death; and it was regarded as a great honor for a warrior to be borne back dead upon the shield that was braced to his arm when he went forth to fight." So faith must be preserved at all hazards.

8591. FAITH and Reason. An old writer compares Faith and Reason to two travelers: Faith is like a man in full health, who can walk his twenty or thirty miles at a time without suffering; Reason is like a little child, who can only with difficulty accomplish three or four miles. Well, says this old writer, on a given day Reason says to Faith, "O good Faith, let me walk with thee." Faith replies, "O Reason, thou canst never walk with me." Well, they set out together; when they come to a deep river, Reason says, "I can never ford this." When they reach a lofty mountain, there is the same exclamation of despair; and in such cases Faith, in order not to leave Reason behind, is obliged to carry him on his back; and, adds the writer, "Oh, what a luggage is Reason to Faith!"

8592. FAITH and Repentance. Faith and repentance are the whole duty of a Christian. Faith is a sacrifice of the understanding to God; repentance sacrifices the whole will; that gives the knowing, this gives up all the desiring faculties: that makes us disciples, this makes us servants of the holy Jesus, Nothing else was preached by the Apostles, nothing else was enjoined as the duty of man, nothing else did build up the body of Christian religion. So that as faith contains all that knowledge which is necessary to salvation, so repentance comprehends in all the whole practice and working duty of a returning Christian. *Bishop Taylor.*

8593. FAITH, Saving. An inquirer, anxious about his soul, went to a converted sailor and said, "I believe the Bible to be true, and every word of it from God. I know that I can be saved only by the redemption of Jesus Christ. I feel my misery as a sinner. I believe everything; but how am I to believe so as to be saved? I want faith; and how am I to get it?" He answered, "I did not once know what faith was, or how to obtain it; but I know now what it is, and believe I possess it. But I do not know that I can tell you what it is, or how to get it. I can tell you what it is not. It is not knocking off swearing, and drinking, and such like; and it is not reading the Bible, nor praying, nor being good. It is none of these; for, even if they would answer for the time to come, there is the old score still, and how are you to get clear of that? It is not anything you have done, or can do; it is only believing and trusting to what Christ has done. It is forsaking your sins, and looking for their pardon, and the salvation of your soul, because he died, and shed his blood for sin; and it is nothing else."

8594. FAITH, Security of. Cajetan organized the order of regular clerks, in 1524, called also Theatines, which had for its object the reformation of morals, then notoriously bad both among priests and people. The principle of the order was that it was to have no property, and also its members were never to beg. To live without either property or begging was a new idea, and the cardinals hesitated about sanctioning it. Its members considered Providence the best endowment. Cajetan opened a house at Naples, and the Count of Oppido wished to endow it with lands. Cajetan would not accept it. "But, my father," said the Count, "what security have you got that you will be able to obtain daily sustenance?" "What security have you, my lord?" "Oh, as for me," said the Count, "I trust that my farmers will pay their rents." "But if the crops fail they will not be able to do so." "We must trust God to give the seasons." "So, so," said Cajetan, "it comes to trust in God as the root of all security." "But," urged the Count, "your mode of living is all well enough in Venice, a large and opulent city; but Naples is small and poor." "The God of Venice is the God also of Naples," answered Cajetan.

8595. FAITH, Shield of. Chabuas, the Athenian general, ordered his soldiers to put one knee on the ground, and firmly to rest their spear on the other, and cover themselves with their shields, by which means he daunted the enemy. He had a statue raised to his honor in that same posture. Myrillus' shield, it is said, secured him in the field, and saved him when shipwrecked at sea, by wafting him to the shore. But how much more serviceable is the shield of faith. By this the Christian overcomes his spiritual enemies, and is enabled to triumph even in the midst of difficulties. Such at last will have to say, "I have fought a good fight, for I have kept the faith. Henceforth there is laid up for me a crown of righteousness, and not to me only, but to all them who love his appearing." *Buck.*

8596. FAITH, Temporary. What comfort is there of temporary faith, which giveth over when there is most need of it? What use of that illumination that leaveth us in darkness at the last? What were the foolish virgins better for that oil and light which failed them before they came to the wedding chamber?
Thomas Taylor.

8597. FAITH, Trial of. Is like the testing of *silver* in the fining pot, Prov. 17 : 3. *Gold* in the furnace, 1 Pet. 1 : 7. A beautiful image; only in one point there is a most important difference—gold, though the purest of metals, is not increased in the furnace; but faith, by being tried, "groweth exceedingly." EXAMPLES. *Noah* commanded to build an ark. A strange work, which had never been done before; a work of immense difficulty, toil, and patience; exposed to the ridicule of that unrighteous age; and then, when the ark was finished, he was told to enter it, when there was no sign of the threatened flood; nor was he told how long it might be before he was released from his confinement. What a test of "the obedience of faith!" *Abraham*, of all the early saints, was perhaps, tried the most—so many times, and so severely. (1) In the charge to leave his native land and kindred, and go to a land which the Lord would show him (it was not said at *first*, "which I will give thee") Gen. 12: 1. No place was named—no distance mentioned—no time of his prospective sojourn intimated. He was to go forth, "not knowing whither he went," Heb. 11: 8; and he had no inheritance in it, and no child, Acts 7: 5. (2) In the promise given of a "seed" which should inherit the land, when the Canaanite was then in full possession, Gen. 12: 6; 13: 15; and he had no heir (16: 1) for more than twenty years; and both he and Sarah were advanced in years when the promise was more definitely renewed, Gen. 18: 10–14; Rom. 4: 18–21. (3) In the strange command, when the promised seed was given at last, and had grown, to offer him for a burnt offering in the land of Moriah, Gen. 22: 1, 2; a command apparently contrary to all known laws of affection, reason, revelation, and against God's own promise of the seed's inheriting the land. What trial could well be greater? *Abraham, Isaac, and Jacob.*—It is not a little remarkable that there was a famine in the days of each of the honored three, Gen. 12:10; 26:1; 41:54; 43: 1. Thus were they not only called to wander in a strange land, but almost driven from it by want of sustenance. *Israel*, tried by their hard bondage in Egypt, and their wanderings in the wilderness, and at their entrance into Canaan; see Deut. 8: 2, 3. What a strange command it seemed, Exod. 14: 15, "Go forward!" "as if there had been a fleet of transport ships ready for them to embark in!" So the Lord tried their faith by leading them about, at times to places like Rephidim, where there was no water, Exod. 17: 1. *Job*, the patriarch, pre-eminent for unparalleled accumulation of trials, met with almost unexampled fortitude; see Job 1: 6–22; 2: 10; 13: 15. *Elijah*, the subject of many severe trials of faith. During the time of famine sent to Cherith (which means drought, as if it dried up sooner than other brooks), and when that was dried, ordered to go to Zarephath, a Gentile city, nearly a hundred miles off, in the very region where Jezebel came from, and find support there from a widow woman, whose name and residence were not foretold him. So, afterwards, through his life. *Bowes.*

8598. FAITH, True. Faith is the first stone of the building, but it is not the foundation. It is the act of cleaving to Christ, but all its value depends upon the worth of the Christ to whom you cleave. A man may have faith —real, ardent, energetic faith—in saints and images, and priests and relics; yet his faith does not save him. A drowning man puts forth his hand and seizes with more than natural energy a bit of froth that dances on the crest of a wave; his hand cleaves it like air, and he sinks helpless in the deep. He is lost, not for want of precision in his aim, or of energy in his grasp, but for want of truth and power in the phantom to which he fled.

Arnot.

8599. FAITH in the Unseen. Now there is a fact in nature, I cannot explain it, nor can you, that a piece of steel touched with a magnet trembles as it varies; suspend it on a pivot and it becomes a needle and it turns toward the pole. Why it turns I cannot tell. I say it is magnetism; it is influenced by the magnetic current. What makes that current, how it is developed and constituted I know not. Some of its facts I can see, and yet, I will risk my life, and the life of my friends, and all I have, on the certainty that everywhere, and under all circumstances, when left free from other influences, that needle will turn toward the pole. I go on the sea and the mariner may guide the ship by the sun and stars when visible; but there comes a time when the stars are invisible and the sun is not seen for days. There is a wild waste of billows all around and the tempests howl, and yet in the midst of that darkness and storm and threatened danger, the eye is kept on that needle, and believing that it points northward, and that there is a North, though I cannot see it, and while there may be rocks on the one hand and destruction on the other, I go safely through because I trust in the unseen. Great journeys are accomplished and great deeds are performed in the same manner. *Bishop Simpson.*

8600. FAITH, Vision of. Astronomy affords us an illustration of the relation of faith to sight. Those stars that are scattered like silver-dust over the firmament of heaven, but are only disclosed by the powerful glasses of the scientific inquirer, are to us objects of faith. Many stars we see, but these we see not. We believe that they exist on the evidence of others, who have had their vision enlarged by the appliances of science. What to us is an object of faith is to them one of sight. And there is a heavenly world far beyond all that the assisted sight of man has ever reached, which is not within the bounds of human experiment, and of which we can only learn through the revelation of God in Christ. The things of this world are received by the eye of faith, for "faith is the evidence of things not seen." Faith, in short, has the same relation to the things of heaven as sight has to the things of the world in which we live. *Pilkington.*

8601. FAITH, Walking by. The difference between walking by faith and by sight is wonderful! It is as great as that of our walking in a clear, shining morning, when the sky in summer is without a cloud, while the sun sheds his enlivening beams, or our going out in one of our November fogs, when the sky is overcast, and the heavy-clouded atmosphere looks gloom and sadness, and all nature is dreary and cheerless.   *Salter.*

8602. FAITH, What is. Mr. Wesley was once engaged in a very important conference with some of his leading associates. The subject of discussion was faith. No one was able to furnish a definition satisfactory to himself or to any one present. In the midst of their perplexity, Mr. Wesley said, "Let us call in Mrs. ——," naming an individual of strong good sense and of very deep piety. "She," continued Mr. Wesley, "can tell us just what faith is, because she has consciously exercised it." When asked to tell what faith is, her reply was this, "It is taking God at his word." "That will do," exclaimed Mr. Wesley. And that will do for us all.

8603. FAITH and Works. "Mamma," said a little girl in Philadelphia—when she was looking for a lost treasure, "I think God will help us find it if we ask him. So I'll pray, and you hunt."

8604. FAITH—not Works. Some years ago two men, a bargeman and a collier, were in a boat above the rapids of a cataract, and found themselves, unable to manage it, being carried so swiftly down the current that they must both inevitably be borne down and dashed to pieces. At last, however, one man was saved by floating a rope to him, which he grasped. The same instant that the rope came into his hand a log floated by the other man. The thoughtless and confused bargeman, instead of seizing the rope, laid hold on the log. It was a fatal mistake; they were both in imminent peril; but the one was drawn to shore, because he had a connection with the people on the land, while the other, clinging to the loose, floating log, was borne irresistibly along, and never heard of afterwards. Faith has a saving connection with Christ. Christ is on the shore, holding the rope, and, as we lay hold of it with the hand of our confidence, he pulls us to the shore; but our good works, having no connection with Christ, are drifted along down to the gulf of fell despair. Grapple our virtues as tightly as we may, even with hooks of steel, they cannot avail us in the least degree; they are the disconnected log which has no hold-fast on the heavenly shore.   *Spurgeon.*

8605. FAITH, Works and. Cromwell said to his soldiers on the field of battle, "Trust in the Lord, and rely on your pikes."

8606. FAITHFULNESS, Conjugal. A Shawnee Indian woman made this reply to a man whom she met in the woods, and who implored her to love and look on him: "Oulman, my husband, who is forever before my eyes, hinders me from seeing you or any other person."

8607. FAITHFULNESS, Divine. EMBLEMS. A *rock*, the representation of stability and endurance, Deut. 32:4. *A shield* or *buckler*, Ps. 91:4; 18:30. *The rainbow*, the "faithful witness in heaven," Ps. 89:37. Very

blessed assurances are given us of the Divine faithfulness. It is, firmer than the *strong mountains*, Isa. 54:10; more fixed than the *sun and moon* and ordinances of heaven, Jer. 31:35, 36; of *day and night*, 33; 20, 21, 25, 26; than the very existence of the heaven above and earth beneath, with them that dwell therein, Isa. 51:6: Matt. 5; 18; ... more certain than any *earthly parent's love*, Isa. 49:15, 16; *reaching to the clouds*, Ps. 57:10; 1 Kings 7:21. The two pillars in Solomon's temple—Boaz (in him is strength), and Jachin (he will establish) were probably meant as symbols, that the counsels and purposes of God are faithfulness and truth. Ps. 119:89, "Forever, O Lord, thy word is settled in heaven." Luther had this text written in charcoal upon the walls of his chamber and embroidered on the dresses of his servants. Ps. 119:160, "Thy word is true from the beginning." Dr. A. Clarke would translate this, "true from the first word." 2 Tim 2:19, "Nevertheless, the foundation of God standeth sure." Amidst all the upheavings of a restless world, and all the errors of a distracted Church, the rock of truth remains steadfast forever. The notions of men are constantly changing; the founders of systems pass away; but "the foundation of God standeth sure." The truth, the word, the promises, the covenant, of an unchanging God, are as sure as he is faithful.   *Bowes.*

8608. FAITHFULNESS, Evidence of. Mohammed, king of Khoozistan, was an exceedingly effeminate prince. Good fortune had given him a good minister, who was a sincere lover of justice, of his master, and of the country confided to his government. He made no enemies but such as he offended by a thorough disdain of all parasites; an integrity which neither blandishments nor money could shake. A conspiracy hatched against him drove him at length from the counsels of his prince. He neither offered to justify himself, nor to solicit his restoration; he simply wrote to the prince, "That as it was always his desire to be useful, he requested of his highness to grant him some barren lands, which he promised to cultivate, and which would be sufficient for his subsistence." Mohammed, who could not but esteem a man that had served him with fidelity, gave orders to search for some uncultivated estates in his dominions. None such, however, were to be found. All the lands were fertile; commerce and agriculture, equally encouraged, furnished the inhabitants with plenty; and throughout the whole land of Khoozistan there was neither an indigent person nor a barren territory to be found. The monarch, to whom this report was made by persons who were ignorant of the inferences to be necessarily drawn from it, sent a message to the discarded Vizier, stating that he had no barren lands to give him, but that he might make choice of any portion of cultivated territory which he pleased. "I desire nothing more," replied this great minister, "as a recompense for all my services, than the happiness which this answer gives me. I was willing my master should know the condition in which I have left his kingdom. Nothing remains for me but to wish that my successors may follow my example." The king was awakened by this answer to a just sense of the value of the man whom he had inconsiderately discarded from his service, and immediately reinstated him. *Anon.*

8609. FAITHFULNESS, Example of. Two Hanoverian horses assisted in drawing the same gun during the whole Peninsular war, in the German brigade of artillery. One of them met his death in an engagement; after which the survivor was picketed as usual, and his food was brought to him. He refused to eat, and kept constantly turning his head round to look for his companion, and sometimes calling him by a neigh. Every care was taken, and all means that could be thought of were adopted, to make him eat, but without effect. Other horses surrounded him on all sides, but he paid no attention to them; his whole demeanor indicated the deepest sorrow, and he died from hunger, not having eaten anything from the time his companion fell.

8610. FAITHFULNESS, God's. The family of a persecuted minister of the seventeenth century was several times reduced to great straits. Once, when they had breakfasted, and had nothing left for another meal, his wife exclaimed, "What shall I do with my poor children?" He persuaded her to walk abroad with him, and, seeing a little bird, he said, "Take notice how that little bird sits and chirps, though we cannot tell whether it has been to breakfast; and if it has, it knows not whither to go for dinner. Therefore be of good cheer, and do not distrust the providence of God; for are we not better than many sparrows?" Before dinner-time plenty of provisions were brought them.

8611. FAITHFULNESS, Import of. There is an intimate connection between the words "faith" and "faithfulness." The word "faith" as is obvious at once to the ear and to the eye, is part and parcel of the word "faithfulness." Faith is in faithfulness, because faithfulness is supposed to be the quality of a person's character who is faithful—that is, faithful, or full of faith. *Morrison.*

8612. FAITHFULNESS, Logic of. A Christian lady was engaged in marriage to a gentleman who respected, but did not confess, religion. Thinking that it might please him to attend a ball and mingle in the dance, she proposed that they both go to the ball. To her astonishment he declined, for he was greatly surprised that one who professed to follow Christ "in the narrow way" should offer to enter with him through that wide gate into "the broad way which leadeth to destruction." In a few minutes he withdrew for the evening. When he next called, he asked that their engagement of matrimony might be broken off. Mortified at the request of her affianced husband, she requested an explanation of his unlooked-for demand. He replied, "You have solemnly vowed to Christ to be his, yet you propose to turn your back on him and mingle with sinners in the dance. Your relation to Christ is more sacred than your relation to me could be if we were married. If you are untrue to God—in your offer to forsake him—what reason have I to believe you would not be untrue to me, and forsake me? The greater always includes the less." Severe as his conclusion was, she could not say it was unjust. *Ebenezer Arnold.*

8613. FAITHFULNESS, Required. When the battle of Corioli was being won through the stimulus given to the soldiers by the impassioned vigor of Caius Marcius, they mourned to see their leader covered with wounds and blood. They begged him to retire to the camp, but with characteristic bravery he exclaimed, "It is not for conquerors to be tired!" and joined them in prosecuting the victory to its brilliant end. Such language might well become the Christian warrior. He is tempted to lie down and rest before the conquest is complete and the triumph thoroughly achieved. But his conquests should but stir him with a holy zeal and fire him with a sublime courage, that he may be faithful unto death, and then receive a crown of life. *Anon.*

8614. FAITHFULNESS, Wayside. In 1854, Rev. T. H. Pearne and Bp. Simpson started on a canoe voyage up the Columbia river in Oregon. Their companions were some Indians and two drunken white men, who sought by profanity and obscenity to annoy the clerical passengers. One of the whites at length became stupid, and the other silent. The bishop asked the latter if his mother was still living. He said she was. "Is your mother a praying woman?" "O yes." "Do you think she prays for you every day?" He answered with feeling, "I have no doubt of it." "Do you suppose your mother knows the kind of life you are leading?" With tears and sobs the young man answered, "I would not have her know it for the world." The bishop's conversation continued with evident good effect. In 1864 Mr. Pearne met a well-dressed gentleman while traveling in a fine steamer on the same river. He said he was the man who passed up the river in a canoe with himself and the bishop ten years before. He informed Mr. Pearne that he was a religious man, and dated his reform from the bishop's conversation. He was married, had acquired a competence, and a respectable position in society. He ascribed all to the bishop's faithfulness.

8615. FALL, Children after the. In my travels through Syria, on a mountainous ridge, my attention was suddenly arrested by a magnificent grove of trees of the cedar species. They were evidently the growth of many ages, and had obtained the perfection of beauty and grandeur. As I descended into the vale I beheld a number of other trees stunted in their growth, and as remarkable for their meanness as the former were for their magnificence. The guide assured me that they were of the same species. I thought it impossible. Not a trace of resemblance could I find in them: but he assured me that they had been planted by the agency of the winds, and had fallen upon that spot. We had not proceeded very far before another group presented itself. These had been planted by the hand of man, and carefully attended to as they grew up. And on examining them I had no difficulty in discovering the family likeness to the first grove of trees; they were giving promise of great beauty, and seemed to say that, if ages were allowed for them to grow up, they would prove no insignificant rivals of their parent stock. This appears to be a remarkable emblem of the children of fallen Adam. They were "planted a noble vine, but how they are turned into the degenerate plant of a strange vine!" Like the scattered trees in the vale, they are stunted in their growth, mean, despicable and useless, having lost all resemblance to their parent stock. Instead of the image of God, they have the likeness of him whose children they are, and, like those trees where there is no friendly hand to cultivate them, they will continue forever in their degenerate and ruined state. But there is also another class, like the newly planted grove, who are brought under cultivation, and under the care and watchfulness of the good husbandman, their heavenly Father. These, though immeasurably inferior to the noble stock from which they were originally taken, are yet again bearing evident marks of their parentage, their high and heavenly original. Every year the family likeness appears more evident and conspicuous, and as "trees of the Lord," "the planting of his right hand," they have the promise that "they shall cast forth their roots as Lebanon; their branches shall spread, and their beauty shall be as the olive tree, and their smell as Lebanon." *Salter.*

8616. FALL, Consciousness of the. The degenerate plant has no consciousness of its own degradation, nor could it, when reduced to the character of a weed or a wild-flower, recognize in the fair and delicate garden-plant the type of its former self. The tamed and domesticated animal, stunted in size, and subjugated in spirit, could not feel any sense of humiliation when confronted with its wild brother of the desert, fierce, strong and free, as if discerning in that spectacle the noble type from which itself had fallen. But it is different with a conscious moral being. Reduce such an one ever so low, yet you cannot obliterate in his inner nature the consciousness of falling beneath himself; you cannot blot out from his mind the latent reminiscence of a nobler and better self which he might have been, and which to have lost is guilt and wretchedness. *Caird.*

8617. FALL, Traditions of the. Traditions of the fall in ancient history and mythology are very numerous. Thus on an ancient bas-relief there are two groups that offer, as it were, a biblical key to the whole scene. On the one hand are a man and a woman standing naked under a tree; the man with one hand raised to the tree, and the other directed towards the woman. It is such a picture that a child would

at once say, "That is Adam and Eve!" At the other extremity is a sedate and august figure, seated upon a rock, and strangling the serpent with his outstretched hand. Again Apollo is represented as the son of the supreme God: out of love to mankind he destroyed the serpent Python; after his victory the conqueror underwent a lustration in the vale of Tempe; here also he was crowned with laurel, and according to some, with that mysterious fruit the gathering of which had proved the source of all evil, and occasioned the necessity for the defeat of the serpent. So of the garden of the Hesperides, we read that, being situated at the extreme limit of the then known Africa, it was said to have been shut in by Atlas on every side by lofty mountains, on account of an ancient oracle that a son of the deity would at a certain time arrive, open a way of access thither, and carry off the golden apples which hung on a mysterious tree in the midst of the garden. Having procured access to the garden, and having destroyed the watchful serpent that kept the tree, the hero gathered the apples. In engraving from gems and other ancient remains, many representations of this event may be found. In all of them the Python is a serpent; and in all of them he is wreathed around a fruit-laden tree, exactly as modern painters represent him in their pictures of Eve's temptation. *Kitto.*

8618. FALL, Type of the. In all the sacrifices, from Adam to Christ, this was still preached to the world, that there was a fearful breach between God and man, and, therefore, that justice required that our blood should be shed. And the fire flaming upon the altar, which wholly burnt up the sacrifice, was a lively emblem of that fiery indignation that should devour the adversaries. But, above all, when Christ, the true and the great Sacrifice, was offered up to God, the clearest mirror was set before us in which to see our sin and misery by the fall. *John Flavel.*

8619. FALLING, Dishonor of. Lusts ever bring inconstancy with them, and make the soul, like weary and distempered bodies, never well in any posture or position. Wicked men flee like bees from one flower to another, from one vanity to another, can never find enough in any to satiate the endless intemperancy of unnatural desires. Only the gospel, being spiritually apprehended, hath treasures enough for the soul to rest in, and to seek no farther. And, therefore, falling away from the truth, power, or purity of the gospel, is said to expose Christ to shame, and to crucify him again. For as, in baptism, when we renounce sin, and betake ourselves to Christ, we do, as it were, expose sin unto public infamy, and nail it on the cross of Christ; so when we revolt from Christ unto sin again, and in our hearts turn back unto Egypt, and thrust him from us, we do then put him to shame again, as if he were either in his power deficient, or unfaithful in those promises which before we pretended to rely upon. If Israel, as they consulted, should likewise actually have rebelled against Moses, and returned in their body as well as in heart into Egypt again, what a scorn would it have wrought in that proud nation, that their vassals should voluntarily resume their thralldom, after so many boasts and appearances of deliverance! If a man should relinquish the service of some noble person, and apply himself unto some sordid master for subsistence, would not the mouths of men be quickly open or their minds jealous to suspect that however such a man carries a high name, and there be great expectations from attending on him, yet, in truth, he is but a dry master, whom his own servants do so publicly dishonor? So, when any men turn apostates from the power and profession of the gospel of Christ, presently wicked men are apt to blaspheme, and to conceive desperate prejudices against our high and holy calling.　　　　　*Bp. Reynolds.*

8620. **FALLING, Kept from.** If it is glory to him to rescue us when we sink, it is surely greater glory to keep us from sinking. Said one traveler to another, "I have great cause to be thankful; my horse stumbled, but did not fall." Said his companion, "I have greater cause to be thankful, for my horse did not even stumble at all." Nothing but constant confidence and trust in the Lord can keep us afloat; and, mark you, Jesus did not say to Peter that it was to be expected that he should doubt and begin to sink, but he said, "Wherefore didst thou doubt?"　　　　　*M. Monod.*

8621. **FALLING, Security Against.** One of the old Puritans, to remind him of his dependence upon God, used to keep a wine-glass with the foot broken off, and with this inscription upon it: "Hold thou me up and I shall be safe."

8622. **FALSEHOOD, Acting.** Robert Hall was spending an evening at the house of a friend. A lady who was there on a visit retired, that her little girl of four years old might go to bed. She returned in about half an hour, and said, "She is gone to sleep; I put on my nightcap and lay down by her, and she soon dropped off." Mr. Hall said, "Excuse me, madame, do you wish your child to grow up a liar?" Oh dear, no, sir; I should be shocked at such thing." "Then bear with me while I say you must never act a lie before her. Children are very quick observers, and soon learn that that which assumes to be what it is not is a lie, whether acted or spoken." This was uttered with a kindness which precluded offence, yet with a seriousness that could not be forgotten.

8623. **FALSEHOOD, Faith in.** The most absurd and injurious adage that has ever gained currency among mankind, is, that "it is no difference what a man believes, if he only be sincere." Now, the truth is, that the more sincerely a man believes falsehood, the more destructive it is to all his interests, for time and eternity. This statement can be confirmed in every mind beyond the reach of doubt. A gentleman of property and the highest respectability, in the course of his business transactions, became acquainted with an individual who, as the event showed, was a man destitute in a great degree of a conscientious regard of truth. The per-

suasions and false representations of this man led the gentleman referred to, to embark almost his entire fortune with him in speculations in which he was at that time engaged. While this matter was in progress, the friends of the gentleman called upon him, and stated their doubts of the individual's integrity who solicited his confidence, and likewise of the success of the enterprises in which he was solicited to engage. The advice of his friends was rejected —he placed confidence in the false statements of the individual referred to—he acted upon those statements, and was consequently involved in pecuniary distress. In this case the gentleman not only sincerely believed the falsehood to be the truth, but he had good motives in relation to the object which he desired to accomplish. He was a benevolent man. He had expended considerable sums for charitable and religious uses, and his desire was, by the increase of his property, to be enabled to accomplish greater good. In this case he was injured likewise by believing what others did not believe. The individual who seduced him into the speculation, had endeavored to lead others to take the same views and to act in the same way; they did not believe the falsehood, and were consequently, saved; he believed, and was consequently ruined. *Power.*

8624. **FALSEHOOD, Scars of.** To tell a falsehood is like the cut of a sabre, for, though the wound may heal, the scar will remain. *Saadi.*

8625. **FAME, Anxiety for.** Pausanias, an attendant of Philip, King of Macedon, asked Hermocles, "How may a man suddenly become famous?" He replied, "By killing some illustrious person; for thereby the glory of that man shall pass over to himself." Pausanias thereupon slew King Philip, and became as infamous for his crime, as the king had been famous for his virtue.

8626. **FAME, Brevity of.** There is no antidote against the opium of time, which temporally considereth all things: our fathers find their graves in our short memories, and sadly tell us how we may be buried in our survivors'. Gravestones tell truth scarce forty years. Generations pass while some trees stand, and old families last not three oaks.　　　　　*Browne.*

8627. **FAME, Efforts to Secure.** When Alexander the Great had demolished the walls of Thebes, Phrine, a beautiful and rich courtesan, went to the Thebans and offered to rebuild the walls at her own expense, provided she might be permitted to engrave on them these words, "Alexander overthrew Thebes, and Phrine did in this manner restore it."

8628. **FAME, Emptiness of.** We have a striking illustration of the emptiness of the rewards of fame, in the Memoirs of Henry Martyn. He tells, that after a severe contest with many distinguished competitors, for the prize of being Senior Wrangler, the highest mathematical honor which the University of Cambridge can bestow upon its students, the palm was awarded to him; and having received it, he exclaims, "I was astonished to find what a shadow I had grasped." Perhaps there never yet was a candidate for fame, whatever was the particular object for which he contended, who did not feel the same disappointment. The reward of fame may be compared to the garlands in the Olympic games, which began to wither the moment they were grasped by the hand, or worn upon the brow of the victor.   *Anon.*

8629. FAME, Favorites of. In Fame's temple there is always a niche to be found for rich dunces, importunate scoundrels, or successful butchers of the human race.   *Zimmerman.*

8630. FAME, Fickleness of. Among the writers of all ages, some deserve fame, and have it; others neither have nor deserve it; some have it, not deserving, others, though deserving, yet totally miss it, or have it not equal to their deserts.   *Milton.*

8631. FAME, The Hope of. My consolation for the sacrifices which I am called upon to make I must find in that hope of honorable fame which is to be acquired only by those who, according to the best of their judgment, fallible at the best, pursue the course which leads to the public good.   *Wellington.*

8632. FAME, Infamous. Erostratus, desirous of fame, set fire to the Temple of Diana at Ephesus. He confessed that his only reason for doing so, was that he might be remembered for it in aftertimes. So indignant were the Ephesians, that they made a severe decree that his name should never be mentioned.

8633. FAME, Limit of. An old woman in a village in the west of England was told one day that the king of Prussia was dead, such a report having arrived when the great Frederick was in the noon-day of his glory. Old Mary lifted up her great slow eyes at the news, and fixing them in the fullness of vacancy upon her informant, replied, "Is a? is a? The Lord ha' mercy! well, well! The king of Prussia—and who's he?" The who's he? of this old woman might serve as a text for a notable sermon upon ambition. "Who's he?" may now be asked of men greater than Frederick or Wellington, greater as discoverers than Sir Isaac or Sir Humphrey. Who built the pyramids? Who ate the first oyster? But the perception of the evanescence of the great names need not wait until forced upon the mind by associations like these. No; a few years only have to pass away, and a dark, mythological gloom comes down like the certain march of night, over names and performances exciting the most lively admiration and interest.   *Southey.*

8634. FAME, Perpetuating. Trajan, the Emperor, caused his name to be inscribed on everything he did, whether repairing old work or building anything new. So constantly did he demand this, he was scoffingly called the "Wall Flower, or Pellitory on the Wall."

8635. FAME, Representations of. The poets make fame a monster: they describe her in part finely and elegantly, and in part gravely and sententiously: they say, Look how many feathers she hath! so many eyes she hath underneath! so many tongues! so many voices! she pricks up so many ears! This is a flourish: there follow excellent parables: as that she gathereth strength in going; that she goeth upon the ground, and yet hideth her head in the clouds; that in the daytime she sitteth in a watch-tower, and flieth most by night; that she mingleth things done with things not done; and that she is a terror to great cities.   *Lord Bacon.*

8636. FAME, Silencing. Fame may be compared to a scold; the best way to silence her is to let her alone, and she will at last be out of breath in blowing her own trumpet. *Fuller.*

8637. FAME, Solicitude about. A boy's being flogged is not so severe as a man's having the hiss of the world against him. Men have a solicitude about fame; and the greater share they have of it, the more afraid they are of losing it.   *Dr. Johnson.*

8638. FAMILIARITY Breeds Contempt. A fox who had never seen a lion, when by chance he met him for the first time, was so terrified that he almost died of fright. When he met him the second time, he was still afraid, but managed to disguise his fear. When he saw him the third time, he was so much emboldened that he went up to him and asked him how he did.   *Æsop.*

8639. FAMILY, Death in a. A death in the family!—who at one period or another of his life has not been compelled to pass through that most dreadful of ordeals? Fortunate is he who has only once experienced the series of sensations implied by the words. How the same phenomena re-appear! There is the painful tension of mind, just lit up by feeble flashes of hope—then despair—and at last the end. The house which was the dwelling-place of the living becomes, for certain days, the abode of the dead. The mourners refuse to be comforted; the intrusive sun is excluded from the room; people move about with cautious step, and speak to each other with bated breath. Then again, in a few days, the house is restored to its living tenants. Gradually, and with a sense of strangeness at first, the "family" begin to run in the old grooves, the old occupations are resumed, strangers are re-admitted, and in a brief space things are as before.   *W. Irving.*

8640. FAMILY, Gatherings of the. There are some gatherings in this world which are largely alloyed with pain. Christmas or some birthday season comes round, inviting the members of a scattered family. The circle is again formed; but, like that of men who have been standing under fire, and closing up their ranks, how is it contracted from former years! There are well-remembered faces, and voices, and forms, that are missing here; and the family group, which looks down from the picture, is larger than the living company met at table. Some are dead and gone—"Joseph is not, and Simeon is not;" and a dark cloud hangs on a mother's brow, for on the cheek of yet another her anxious eye, quick to see, discovers an ominous spot that threatens to "take Benjamin away."   *Dr Guthrie*

8641. FAMILY, Honor of a. It was considered a great honor to a Roman family to have three of its members in succession attain to high office or position. The family of the Fabii was an example, the founder of which was President of the Roman Senate. His son also attained to that dignity, and his son after him. The same law holds in modern times. The families who attained dignity early in our national history, and have proved themselves worthy, like the Adamses, are held especially esteemed. In the religious world a similar succession is alike honorable, happy, and to be desired. The highest ambition of the parents should be satisfied with such a succession. The noblest aspirations of the children should be to have their names written in the Book of Life, and their family history a continuous record of devotion to Christ. Abraham was especially honored by God. He gives the reason: "Abraham shall surely become a great and mighty nation, and all the nations of the earth shall be blessed in him; for I know him that he will command his children and his household after him, and they shall keep the way of the Lord. Gen. 18: 18. Church history multiplies instances of family succession, both among ministers and laymen. Praying families, all over the land, may be traced back to pious homes. God honors family piety.

8642. FAMILY, Importance of the. Without the permanent union of the sexes there can be no permanent families: the dissolution of nuptial ties involves the dissolution of domestic society. But domestic society is the seminary of social affections, the cradle of sensibility, where the first elements are acquired of that tenderness and humanity which cement mankind together; and were they entirely extinguished the whole fabric of social institutions would be dissolved. Families are so many centres of attraction, which preserve mankind from being scattered and dissipated by the repulsive powers of selfishness. The order of nature is ever from particulars to generals. As in the operations of intellect we proceed from the contemplation of individuals to the formation of general abstractions, so in the development of the passions, in like manner, we advance from private to public affections; from the love of parents, brothers, and sisters, to those more expanded regards which embrace the immense society of human kind.   *Robert Hall.*

8643. FAMILY, a Little World. A family is a little world within doors; the miniature resemblance of the great world without.
     J. A. James.

8644. FAMILY, Manners of a. The manners of a family depend upon those of the master. His principles and practices soon diffuse themselves through the house, and the piety or profaneness, the sobriety or intemperance, the sloth or diligence of servants, discover to the world the nature of that fountain from which they flow.   *Bp. Horne.*

8645. FAMILY, The Religious Man in His. The religious man may be considered in his family as the keystone to the arch of a building, which binds and holds all the parts of the edifice together. If this keystone be removed, the fabric will tumble to the ground, and all the parts be separated from each other. Or he is to his family as the good shepherd under whose protection and care the flock may go in and out and find pasture; but when the shepherd is smitten, the sheep will be scattered.
     Salter

8646. FAMILY, Renunciation of. Irenæus, bishop of Birmich, Pannonia, was arrested by the order of Probus, the governor, and brought before him. His mother, wife and children surrounded him at the trial. His little children clung to his knees and implored him not to leave them. His wife wept upon his neck and besought him to comply with the emperor's edict and sacrifice to the gods, and save himself for the sake of his innocent children. The governor united his plea with theirs. Irenæus replied, "Our Lord Jesus Christ hath declared that the man who loveth father, or mother, wife or children, more than him, is not worthy of him; so that I forget that I am a father, a husband and a son." He was beheaded and his body cast into the sea, A. D. 304.

8647. FAMILY, Separation of a. A pious father said, "Once I dreamed that the day of judgment was come. I saw the Judge on his great white throne, and all nations were gathered before him. My wife and I were on the right hand; but I could not see my children. I went to the left hand of the Judge, and there found them all standing in the utmost despair. As soon as they saw me, they caught hold of me, and cried, 'O Father, we will never part.' I said, 'My dear children, I am come to try, if possible, to get you out of this awful situation.' So I took them all with me. But when we came near the Judge, I thought he cast an angry look, and said, 'What do thy children with thee now? They would not take thy warning when on earth, and they shall not share with thee the crown in heaven. Depart, ye cursed.' At a suitable time he told this to his children, which resulted in the awakening of all, and the conversion of five of them.

8648. FAMILY PRAYER, Duty of. Justice McLean, of Ohio, heard a minister preach. He had been a sceptic, and the minister spoke to him in such a way as convinced him of the truth of the Christian religion. He was led to see how Christ had died for him, and was born again. He went home. He had hardly got there before he said, 'We are going to have family prayer; let us go to the drawing-room and pray together." "But," said his wife, "there are four lawyers in; they have come to attend court. We don't want to go there; let us go to the kitchen to have prayers." Judge McLean, afterward Chief Justice of the United States, replied, "It's the first time I ever invited the Lord to my house, and I don't propose to invite him to the kitchen, by any means. If I am a Christian, I am to have family prayer." Fathers, remember that he went in to those lawyers, and said, "My friends, I have just been convinced of the truth of Christianity. I have found out Jesus died on the cross for me. I have given myself to him, and now I propose to invite him to my house. You may do as you please; stay or go. But I am now to make my first prayer in my own house." They said they would like very much to stay, and did stay. From that day Judge McLean lived a consistent Christian life, and died a Christian death."   *E. P. Hammond.*

8649. FAMILY PRAYER, Fidelity in. Rowland Hill once put up at a village inn. Bedtime came, and he said to the waiter who came out to say it was time the lights were out, "I have been waiting a long time, expecting to be called to family prayer." "Family prayer! we never have such things here." "Indeed! tell your master I cannot go to bed till we have prayer." The waiter told his master, who came and said, "Sir, I wish you would go to bed. I cannot go till I have seen the lights all out, I am so afraid of fire." "So am I; but I have been expecting to be summoned to family prayer." "It cannot be done at an inn." "Then get me my horses; I cannot sleep in a house where there is no family prayer." "I have no objection to have a prayer; but I do not know how." "Well, then, call your people." In a few minutes the family were upon their knees, and the landlord was called upon to pray. "Sir, I never prayed in all my life; I don't know how." "Then ask God to teach you." "God, teach us how to pray," said the landlord. "That is prayer; go on." "I'm sure I don't know what to say now, sir." "God has taught you to pray; thank him for it. Thank God Almighty for letting us pray to him." "I do." "Amen, amen!" said Mr. Hill, and then prayed himself. A chapel and a school were soon founded in that village as the result of this prayer.

8650. FAMILY PRAYER, General. The Rev. Joseph Dare from Australia, addressing the Wesleyan Conference held at Camborne in 1874, gave the following incident as illustrative of the prevalence of family prayer among the converts in Fiji: "I was taking tea with your missionary and his wife in the lone island of Kandavu, in the midst of 10,000 Fijians. As we were at tea the bell rang: the missionary said 'That is the signal for family worship. Now listen. You will hear the drum beat.' And immediately they began to echo to each other around the shores of that southern sea. The missionary said, 'There are 10,000 people on these islands, and I do not know of a single house in which there will not be family worship in the course of half an hour from this time.'" What a rebuke to older Christians.

8651. FAMILY PRAYER, Love for. A little boy, who did not like to go to bed before the evening prayer in the family, being very tired, went to his mother and asked that prayer might be had. His mother answered, "Wait a little while, I am busy now. As soon as my letter is done we will have prayers." "Don't you think, mamma, that prayer is more precious than writing letters; and can't that wait?" he asked. His mother was convinced, kissed her four-

year old boy and fulfilled his desire, satisfied that anything else had better wait than prayer.

8652. FAMILY PRAYER, Neglect of. An avaricious Ohio farmer, pressed with business, decided to forego family prayer. His wife expostulated, to no purpose. The men went to work one morning before breakfast, but no horn called them at the usual time. Angrily the husband went to the house, and saw his wife knitting, but no signs of breakfast. "What does this mean?" he said; "why are not the men called?" "I thought you had no time to eat?" "Do you think we can live without eating?" "As well as without praying," she said. "Well; get breakfast, and we will have prayers every morning." *Chas. E. Little.*

8653. FAMILY WORSHIP, Influence of. A Christian boy about fourteen years of age became impressed with the importance of family religion. As all the family were irreligious and illiterate but himself, he felt called to do the duty. He read the Scriptures and then prayed, the family looking curiously on. For some time he continued service in this manner. At length, one after another, they bowed beside him, till the whole group—father, mother and children—united in the hallowed exercise.

8654. FAMINE, Incident of. During the siege of Jerusalem, the extremity of the famine was such, that a Jewess of noble family, urged by the intolerant cravings of hunger, slew her infant child, and prepared it for a meal. She had actually eaten one-half of it, when the soldiers, allured by the smell of food, threatened her with instant death, if she refused to discover it. Intimidated by this menace, she immediately produced the remains of her son, which struck them with horror. At the recital of this melancholy and affecting occurrence, the whole city stood aghast, congratulating those whom death had hurried away from such heart-rending scenes.   *Whitecross.*

8655. FANATICISM, Credulity of. During the Irish rebellion, a Roman Catholic priest of the name of Roche told the soldiers that he would catch the bullets in his hand, and actually exhibited some which he pretended to have got in that manner. The imposture was by no means new. The demagogue Muncer, who, adding the fanaticism of religion to the extremest enthusiasm of republicanism, by his harangues to the populace of Mulhausen soon found himself at the head of forty thousand troops, thus addressed them: "Everything must yield to the Most High, who has placed me at the head of you. In vain the enemy's artillery shall thunder against you; in vain, indeed, for I will receive in the sleeve of my gown every bullet that shall be shot against you, and that alone shall be an impregnable rampart against all the efforts of the enemy." Muncer, however, was not so good as his word, for the Landgrave of Hesse and many of the nobility marching against him, his troops were defeated, himself taken prisoner, and carried to Mulhausen, where he perished upon a scaffold in 1525.   *Percy*

8656. FANATICISM, Example of. Eon de l'Etoile, a Frenchman of the XIIth century, conceived the insane idea that he was "judge of the quick and the dead," and that he shared the government with the Almighty. A crotched stick was his sceptre. When he turned its prongs upward he thereby gave God the government of two-thirds of the world; when he turned them down he assumed it. He had many followers, and was condemned by the Council of Rheims in 1148.

8657. FASHION, Appearance of. A beautiful envelope for mortality, presenting a glittering and polished exterior, the appearance of which gives no certain indication of the real value of what is contained therein. *Mrs. Balfour.*

8658. FASHION, Caprice of. Fashion always begins and ends in two things it abhors most —singularity and vulgarity. It is the perpetual setting up and disowning a certain standard of taste, elegance and refinement, which has no other formation or authority than that it is the prevailing distraction of the moment, which was yesterday ridiculous from its being new, and to-morrow will be odious from its being common. It is one of the most slight and insignificant of all things. It cannot be lasting, for it depends on the constant change and shifting of its own harlequin disguises; it cannot be sterling, for if it were it could not depend on the breath of caprice: it must be superficial, to produce its immediate effect on the gaping crowd; and frivolous, to admit of its being assumed at pleasure by the number of those who appear to be in the fashion, to be distinguished from the rest of the world. It is not anything in itself, nor the sign of anything but the folly and vanity of those who rely upon it as their greatest pride. Fashion is haughty, trifling, affected, servile, despotic, mean and ambitious, precise and fantastical, all in a breath—tied to no rule, and bound to conform to every rule of the minute. *Hazlitt.*

8659. FASHION, Evils of. Fashion makes people sit up at night when they ought to be in bed, and keeps them in bed in the morning when they ought to be up and doing. She makes her votaries visit when they would rather stay at home, eat when they are not hungry, and drink when they are not thirsty. She invades their pleasures, and interrupts their business; she compels them to dress gaily, either upon their own property or that of others; she makes them through life seek rest on a couch of anxiety, and leaves them, in the hour of desolation, on a bed of thorns. *Mrs. Balfour.*

8660. FASHION, Government of. Fashion is the great governor of this world. It presides not only in matters of dress and amusement, but in law, physic, politics, religion, and all other things of the gravest kind. Indeed the wisest of men would be puzzled to give any better reason why particular forms in all these have been at certain times universally received, and at other times universally rejected, than that they were in or out of fashion. *Fielding.*

8661. FASHIONS, Origin of. In the court of Alexander the Great, every one affected to carry his head awry because the mighty hero had a twist in his neck, which made it with him a grace of necessity. Dionysius was extremely short-sighted; and his flatterers, as Montaigne tells us, "ran against one another in his presence, stumbled at and overturned whatever was under foot to show that they were as purblind as their sovereign." Don John of Austria, son of Charles V., had a large patch of hair on one side of his head, which grew upright like bristles; and to conceal the peculiarity, he used to comb back the whole of the hair from his forehead. When he went as Governor into the Low Countries, all the people of fashion there immediately fell into the same mode, and from them it would seem to have descended to our own times. Ruffs, once so fashionable in England that even bishops and judges condescended to adopt them, and were the last to lay them aside, are said to have been introduced by Queen Anne, wife of James I., who wore them to conceal a wen in her neck. But what are all these instances to that of the Ethiopians, as recorded by Diodorus Siculus? "It was a custom among them," says he, "that when they had a lame or one-eyed sovereign, they would voluntarily break a limb, or pluck out an eye; for they thought it exceedingly uncomely in them to walk upright, when their prince was forced to halt; or to see with two eyes, when their gracious master could see only with one." *Anon.*

8662. FASTIDIOUSNESS, Selfishness of. Like other things spurious, fastidiousness is often inconsistent with itself: the coarsest things are done, the cruelest things said, by the most fastidious people. Horace Walpole was a proverb of epicurean particularity of taste; yet none of the vulgarians whom he vilified had a keener relish for a coarse allusion or a malicious falsehood. Beckford, of Fonthill, demanded that life should be thrice winnowed for his use; but what was his life? Louis XIV. was "insolently nice" in some things; what was he in others? If we observe a person proud of a reputation for fastidiousness, we shall always find that the egotism which is its life will at times lead him to say or do something disgusting. We need expect from such people no delicate, silent self-sacrifice, no tender watching for others' tastes or needs, no graceful yielding up of privileges in unconsidered trifles, on which wait no "flowing thanks." They may be kind and obliging to a certain extent, but when the service required involves anything disagreeable, anything offensive to the taste on which they pride themselves, we must apply elsewhere. Their fineness of nature sifts common duties, selecting for practice only those which will pass the test; and conscience is not hurt, for unsuspected pride has given her a bribe. *Mrs. Kirkland.*

8663. FASTING, Benefit of. Fasting, too much neglected and decried among us, is a good and beautiful institution. It gives a more tangible form to ideas that should habitually dominate us,—those of our unworthiness and our dependence. It restores to mind what it takes away from matter, and by relieving, in a manner, the soul that is generally oppressed with the burden of the flesh, it facilitates its soaring up towards the objects of the invisible world. Finally, by the voluntary privations it imposes, it increases our compassions for the involuntary privations of so many of our brethren, whose life, alas! is one perpetual fast. *Dr. Vinet.*

8664. FASTING, Need of. There are Christians whose "flesh," whether by its quantity or natural temperament, renders them sluggish, slothful, wavering, and physically by far too fond of the "good things" of the table and the wine-cellar. I don't like your rosy-faced, jowled, mobile-lipped connoisseurs of "cooking and vintage." That sort of Christian pressingly needs fasting, ay, thorough fasting. Brave, large-fleshed Martin Luther nobly confessed his need, and nobly acted it out, not without strife and "lusting." Of fasting as a whole and as applying to all, it may be said that while it has been perverted into a pestilent superstition, yet in the words of good Bishop Andrewes, "There is more fear of a pottingerful of gluttony than of a spoonful of superstition." *Grosart.*

8665. FASTING, Protracted. The question was asked, "Is it possible that any man can fast forty days and forty nights?" To which Rabbi Meir answered, "When thou takest up thy abode in any particular city, thou must live according to its customs. Moses ascended to heaven, where they neither eat nor drink; therefore he became assimilated to them. We are accustomed to eat and drink; and when angels descend to us they eat and drink also."

8666. FATALISM, Absurdity of. The absurdity of fatalism is well illustrated by an anecdote of a minister, living on the frontier of Missouri, who was in the habit of saying to his family and his church: "Friends, you need not take any unusual care about your lives; the moment of your death was 'writ' before the foundation of the world, and you cannot alter it." His wife observed, when he left on Saturday to meet one of his frontier missionary engagements, that he dressed the flint of his rifle with unusual care, put in dry powder, fresh tow, and took every pains to make sure that the gun should go off in case he came upon an Indian. It struck her one day as she saw him in his saddle, with his rifle on his shoulder, that his conduct contradicted his teachings, and she said to him: "My dear, why do you take this rifle with you? If it was 'writ' before the foundation of the world that you were to be killed during this trip by an Indian, that rifle won't prevent it; and if you are not to be killed, of course the rifle is unnecessary; so why take it with you at all?" "Yes," he replied, "to be sure, my dear, of course you are all very right, and that is a very proper view; but, see here, my dear—now—really—but then—you see, my dear—to be sure—but then —suppose I should meet an Indian while I am gone, and his time had come, and I hadn't my rifle with me, what would he do? Yes, my

dear, we must all contribute our part toward the fulfillment of the decrees of Providence." *Harper's Magazine.*

8667. FATALISM, Baseness of. It is beneath the dignity of a soul, that has but a grain of sense, to make chance, and winds, and waves the arbitrary disposers of his happiness; or, what is worse, to depend upon some mushroom upstart, which a chance smile raised out of his turf and rottenness, to a condition to which his mean soul is so unequal, that he himself fears and wonders at his own height. *Lucas*

8668. FATE: Brevities. All things are in fate, yet all things are not decreed by fate.—*Plato.* ——God over-rules all mutinous accidents, brings them under his laws of fate, and makes them all serviceable to his purpose.—*Antoninus.*——What must be, shall be; and that which is a necessity to him that struggles, is little more than choice to him that is willing. —*Seneca.*——We should consider, that though we are tied to the chains of fate, there are none but rational creatures have the privilege of moving freely, and making necessity a choice; all other things are forced onward, and dragged along to their doom.—*Antoninus.*

8669. FATE, Storm of. The Koran represents the destruction of Sodom as accomplished by a storm of stones of baked clay, each bearing its mark. The Mohammedan commentators say that this peculiar mark was the name of the person who was fated to be killed by the stone.

8670. FATHER, Counsel of a. The natural advisor of the child is the father. Archilochus, desiring to counsel Lycambes, whose father was dead, put the pen in the father's hand, that his advice might have the greater influence. So, Cicero desiring to instruct Clodia, raises up her father from the grave, and in his name gives his counsel to the daughter.

8671. FATHER, A Faithful. There was a man living in New York City, as elder in one of the Presbyterian churches. His little boy had been sick some time, but he had not considered him dangerous. He came home one day, and his wife was in great trouble. When he came into the house he found her weeping. "What is troubling you?" he said. "Why," she said, "there has been a great change in our boy since you left this morning. I am afraid he is dying. I wish you would go and see him, and if he is, tell him so." The father went in and took his seat at the head of the bed; he placed his hand on the forehead of the little boy, and he could see that death was stealing over him. He said to his boy, "My son, do you know you are dying?" and the little fellow looked surprised, and he said, "Am I, father? Is this death that I feel?" "Yes, my son, you are dying." "Shall I die to-day?" "Yes, you cannot live until night." And the little boy smiled, and said, "I will be with Jesus to-night, won't I?" "Yes, my son, you will be with the Saviour to-night," and the father turned away to conceal a tear; and when the little fellow saw the tears rolling down his father's cheeks, he said, "Don't weep for me, father; when I get to heaven, I will go straight to Jesus, and tell him that ever since I could remember, you tried to lead me to him." *Moody.*

8672. FATHER, God a. When we are full of this view of God, not a day goes by without our detecting something fatherly in him, which we never observed before. Everything about us alters by degrees. Duties grow into privileges; pains soften the heart with a delicious humility, and sorrows are heavenly presences. Work becomes rest, and weariness of limb and brain almost touches on the sweet languor of contemplation. It is as if earth were making itself into heaven; and at the commonest sights and sounds something tingles in our hearts as if God were just on the point of speaking or appearing. What another being is life when we have found out our Father; and if we work, it is beneath his eye, and if we play, it is in the light and encouragement of his smile. Earth's sunshine is heaven's radiance, and the stars of night as if the beginnings of the beatific vision; so soft, so sweet, so gentle, so reposeful, so almost infinite have all things become, because we have found our Father in our God. *F. W. Faber.*

8673. FATHER, God our Heavenly. God bears not in vain the name of a Father: he fills it up to the full. It is a name of indulgence, of hope, of provision—a name of protection. It argues the mitigation of punishment; a little is enough for a father. In all temptations, oh, let us by prayer fly to the arms of our heavenly Father! and expect from him all that a father should do for his child. But yet we must remember the name of a father is a word of relation; duty is expected from us; we must reverence him as a father with fear and love. He is a great God, we ought to fear him; he is merciful, yea, hath bowels of mercy, we ought to love him; if we tremble before him, we forget that he is loving; and if over-bold, we also forget that he is a great and holy God. Therefore we should always go to the throne of grace with reverence, holy love, and confidence in the name of Jesus. *Sibbes.*

8674. FATHER, God the. The full meaning of God's fatherhood was not brought out in Old Testament times as we understand it now, though it was known and recognized by pious saints. See 1 Chron. 29: 10; Ps. 103: 13; Isa. 63: 16—rather nationally than personally. THE GOSPEL OF ST. JOHN is the Gospel which speaks most of God as the "Father." It contains about one hundred references, with many varieties of expression. Eph. 3: 15—"Of whom the whole family in heaven and earth is named." Some refer this to Christ, but more generally it is referred to the Father. God's ownership over the Church is involved in its being named from him. To give a name to a person or a place denotes lordship over it, or interest in it; as a father gives his own name to a child; a husband to a wife; a conqueror to a conquered city. *Bowes.*

8675. FATHER, Prayerless. A father lived out in the Western country on the banks of the Mississippi river. The world called him rich, but how poor he was! Thank God! he is rich now. One day his oldest son was brought home to him unconscious; a terrible accident had happened, and the family physician was hurriedly called in. As he came in, the father said, "Doctor, do you think my son will recover?" "No," said the doctor, "he is dying, and cannot recover." "Well," says the father, "only bring him to that we may tell him. I don't want him to die without knowing that he is dying." The doctor said he would try, but that the boy was fast dying. After a while the boy did become conscious for a moment, and the father cried, "My boy, the doctor tells me you are dying, and cannot live. I could not let you die without letting you know it." The young man looked up to his father, and said, "Father, do you tell me I am going to die right away?" "Yes, my boy," said the agonized father, "you will be gone in a little while." "Oh, father, won't you pray for my lost soul?" Said the speechless father, "I cannot pray, my son." The boy grew unconscious, and after a little while was gone; and the father said when he buried that boy that if he could have called him back by prayer he would have given all he was worth. He had been with that boy all those years, and had never prayed once for him. *Moody.*

8676. FATHER, Riches of a. At the time of the burning of the Epworth rectory, in 1709, the Wesley family had a narrow escape. They were aroused only to find themselves enveloped in smoke and flame. They seized the children and waded through the fire, and thought all were safe. Then a cry from the nursery revealed the fact that one had been left. The father sprang for the stairway, but found it impassable. The child, John, went to the window for air, and the neighbors, climbing upon each other's shoulders, rescued him just as the roof fell in. The family wealth was all consumed. Seeing his children all safe, the father said, "Come neighbors, let us kneel down, let us give thanks unto God! He has given me all my eight children. Let the house go; I am rich enough." From this time the mother looked upon John as preserved by Providence for some great work. Both Samuel and Susanna Wesley seem to have had a strong presentiment that God had a great work for their children to do. How much the work surpassed the father's thought, when with the foresight of death upon him, he said, "Do not be concerned at my death; God will then begin to manifest himself to my family." This father said that God had assured him he should have all his nineteen children around him in heaven.

8677. FATHER, An Unfaithful. A father who had a son in college requested a minister, who was going through the town where he was, to call on him and converse with him in reference to the salvation of his soul. The minister complied. He alluded to the request of the father, who wished him by all means to attend first to the salvation of his soul. The young man replied, "Did my father send such word as that?"

"He did," was the reply. "Then," said the young man, "my father is a dishonest man." "But why do you say he is dishonest?" said the minister. "Because," replied the student, "he has often advised me, in regard to the course he would have me pursue in life, how to gain the riches, honors, and pleasures of the world; but he is not the man that has ever manifested any interest in regard to the salvation of my soul, any more than if I had no soul!"

8678. FATHER, Wealth of a. Call not that man wretched, who, whatever else he suffers as to pain inflicted, pleasure denied, has a child for whom he hopes, and on whom he dotes. Poverty may grind him to the dust, obscurity may cast its darkest mantle over him, the song of the gay may be far from his own dwelling, his face may be unknown to his neighbors, and his voice may be unheeded by those among whom he dwells—even pain may rack his joints, and sleep flee from his pillow; but he has a gem with which he would not part for wealth defying computation, for fame filling a world's ear, for the luxury of the highest health, or for the sweetest sleep that ever sat upon a mortal's eye.   *Coleridge.*

8679. FATHER, A Worldly. A father, whose accomplished and beautiful daughter became awakened and forsook her usual fashionable pleasures, used every means to divert her from religion. Novels, pleasure excursions, and gay amusements were tried, but rejected. He then plied her with promises and threatenings. She yielded. He decked her with the fillets of death, and led her to the sacrifice like a follower of Moloch. Her pastor says, "The end was accomplished: all thoughts of piety, and all concern for the future, vanished together. But, in less than a year, the gaudy deception was completely exploded! The fascinating and gay young lady was prostrated by a fever that bade defiance to medical skill. The approach of death was unequivocal; and the countenance of every attendant fell, as if they had heard the flight of his arrow. I see, even now, that look, directed to the father, by the dying martyr of folly. The glazing eye was dim in hopelessness; and yet there seemed a something in its expiring gaze that told reproof, and tenderness, and terror, in the same glance. And that voice—(its tone was decided, but sepulchral still,)—'My father! last year I would have sought the Redeemer. Father, your child is——.'" The desolate father in the presence of his dead, saw the awful result of his folly. Her lost soul cried out against him.

8680. FAULT-FINDER, Fate of the. Jupiter, Neptune, and Minerva, as the story goes, once contended which of them should make the most perfect thing. Jupiter made a man; Minerva made a house, and Neptune made a bull; and Momus—for he had not yet been turned out of Olympus—was chosen judge to decide which production had the greatest merit. He began by finding fault with the bull, because his horns were not below his eyes, so that he might see when he butted with them. Next he found fault with the man, because there was no window in his breast that all might see his inward thoughts and feelings. And lastly he found fault with the house, because it had no wheels to enable its inhabitants to remove from bad neighbors. But Jupiter forthwith drove the critic out of heaven, telling him that a fault-finder could never be pleased, and that it was time to criticise the works of others when he had done some good thing himself.   *Æsop.*

8681. FAULTS, Exposure of. If the best man's faults were written on his forehead, it would make him pull his hat over his eyes.
                Gaelic Proverb.

8682. FAULTS, Forgetting Our Own. "Why beholdest thou the mote that is in thy brother's eye, but considerest not the beam that is in thine own eye." There is a cutting question very similar to this of our Lord, proposed by a heathen.—"When you can so readily overlook your own wickedness, why are you more clear-sighted than the eagle or serpent of Epidaurus in spying out the failings of your friends?" This propensity of man to forget his own faults, and to look with the most critical accuracy into those of his neighbor, which he often magnifies, distorts, and caricatures, is not only reprehended in the sacred Scriptures, but also by many of the Greek and Roman writers.   *Harmer.*

8683. FAULTS, Judging. When a scar cannot be taken away, the next office is to hide it. Love is never so blind, as when it is to spy faults. It is like the painter, who about to draw the picture of a friend having a blemish in one eye, would picture only the other side of his face. It is a noble and great thing to cover the blemishes and to excuse the failings of a friend, to draw a curtain before his stains, and to display his perfections; to bury his weaknesses in silence, but to proclaim his virtue upon the house-top. It is an imitation of the charities of heaven, which, when the creature lies prostrate in the weakness of sleep and weariness, spreads the covering of night and darkness over it, to conceal it in that condition; but as soon as our spirits are refreshed, and nature returns to its morning vigor, God then bids the sun rise and the day shine upon us both to advance and to show that activity. It is the ennobling office of the understanding to correct the fallacious and mistaken reports of sense, and to assure us that the staff in the water is straight, though our eye would tell us it is crooked. So it is the excellency of friendship to rectify, or at least to qualify, the malignity of those surmises that would reprehend a friend, and traduce him to our thoughts. A friend will be sure to act the part of an advocate, before he will that of judge. *Dr. South.*

8684. FAULTS, Masked. We are willing enough to keep at ever so great a distance from the faults to which we have little or no inclination and often affect to make our zeal in that respect remarkable; but then, perhaps, more favorite vices have easy entrance into our breasts and take firm possession of them. We are shocked, for instance, and with much cause, at the monstrous and ruinous eagerness for pleasure, the profligate and unprecedented contempt of religion that prevails in the world; our behavior, on those heads, is unblamable, exemplary, and we value ourselves upon it beyond bounds. Yet possibly we indulge ourselves all the while to the full another way— are unjust and fraudulent, or selfish and unreasonable, or penurious and hard-hearted, or censorious and unforgiving, or peevish and ill-tempered; make every one about us uneasy, and those chiefly whose happiness ought to be our first care. This is applauding ourselves for being fortified, where the enemy is not likely to make an attack; and leaving the places that are most exposed, quite undefended.

Secker.

8685. FAULTS, Our Neighbors'. A man walking through the street had a wallet or sack on his shoulders, with a sort of pocket at each end; one part hung down before and the other behind him; some little boys ran after him and slily put feathers and rags into the hind pocket, but the man was not aware of the matter. Now, thought I, if he were to turn the wallet he would see what sort of stuff he was carrying, and how ridiculous his appearance. This, then, is just what the world does; we carry a wallet: in the pocket before we put our neighbors' faults, which are continually before our eyes, and in the hind pocket we put our own faults, and therefore know not how they are laughed at. Could we turn the wallet, we should be silent. When, therefore, you find yourself talking of others, turn the wallet.

Salter.

8686. FAULTS, No Room for. Lamachus, a Grecian general, chided a captain for a fault, He replied that he would do so no more. He answered, "Sir, in war there is no room for a second miscarriage."

8687. FAULTS, Ours and Others'. St. Pior once appeared at a conference with a large sack of sand on his back, and before him a basket containing more of the same base article. By this he symbolized our treatment of our own and others' faults. Our own, however heavy or numerous, we cast behind our backs, and seldom see; others', we carry as in a basket, and have them constantly before us.

8688. FAULTS, Overcoming. It is not so much the being exempt from faults, as the having overcome them, that is an advantage to us; it being with the follies of the mind, as with the weeds of a field, which, if destroyed and consumed upon the place where they grow, enrich and improve it more than if none had ever sprung there. *Swift.*

8689. FAULTS, Parable of. A hermit went to Poemen, the abbot, and asked him to expel a monk from his monastery for a fault which he did. The expelled monk cast himself into a ditch and wept there, refusing food or comfort. This was told the abbot, and he ordered him to be brought back to his cell, and sent also for the monk on whose advice he had been cast out. When he came Poemen said to him, "Two persons had each a dead man in his house, and yet one had the compassion to leave his and come to his neighbor's to bewail with him over his corpse." The hermit applied the parable to himself. "Poemen is high as heaven; I am base as the earth."

8690. FAULTS, Parading. They are fittest to find fault in whom there is no fault to be found. There is no removing blots from the paper, by laying upon them a blurred finger. Reader, what do you get by throwing stones at your enemy's windows, while your own children look out at the casements? He that blows into a heap of dust, is in danger of putting out his own eyes. *Secker.*

8691. FEAR, Bloody Sweat from. Maldonatus tells of a criminal in Paris, who receiving the sentence of death, was so frightened that he sweat drops of blood from several parts of his body. There is on record also the case of a young man of Belgium, condemned to be burnt, who through extreme fear sweat blood.

8692. FEAR, Bondage of. But of all fears, nothing so dazes and confounds as that of superstition. He fears not the sea that never goes to sea; nor a battle that follows not the camp; nor robbers that stirs not abroad; nor malicious informers that is a poor man; nor emulation that leads a private life; nor earthquakes that dwells in Gaul; nor thunderbolts that dwells in Ethiopia; but he that dreads divine powers dreads everything—the land, the sea, the air the dark, the light, a sound, a silence, a dream. —*Plutarch.*——They who are awake have a world in common amongst them; but they who are asleep are retired, each to his own private world. But the frightful visionary hath ne'er a world at all, either in common with others, or in private to himself; for neither can he use his reason when awake, nor be free from his fears when asleep; but he hath his reason always asleep, and his fears always awake; nor hath he either a hiding-place or refuge.

Heraclitus.

8693. FEAR, Cure for. At the wedding in a wealthy family the bride received $15,000 worth of presents. But after having received them, they were unhappy, fearing they would be robbed; so the only thing they could do was to take them to the safe deposit, where they still remain; and they are happy now, because they have deposited all where they have faith to believe it will be safe. We put some jewels into the hands of the Saviour, and some into the world, and then are uneasy. Let us give our all to Jesus. *F. Remington.*

8694. FEAR, Effects of. There is a virtuous fear, which is the effect of faith; and there is a vicious fear, which is the product of doubt. The former leads to hope as relying on God, in whom we believe: the latter inclines to despair, as not relying on God, in whom we do not believe. Persons of the one character fear to lose God; persons of the other character fear to find him. *Pascal.*

8695. FEAR, Fable of. A mouse that dwelt near the abode of a magician was kept in such constant distress by its fear of a cat that the magician, taking pity on it, turned it into a cat itself. Immediately it began to suffer from fear of a dog, so that the magician turned it into a dog. Then it began to suffer from fear of a tiger, and the magician, in disgust, said: "Be a mouse again. As you have only the heart of a mouse, it is impossible to help you by giving you the body of a noble animal." *Æson.*

8696. FEAR of God. A candle wakes some men as well as a noise; the eye of the Lord works upon a good soul as well as his hand; and a godly man is as much afflicted with the consideration, "Thou God seest me," as with "The Lord strikes me." *Dr. Donne.*

8697. FEAR, Godly. The fear peculiar to a Christian is not of that nature which is servile and tends to despair. It is not that of a slave, but of a son. They who are influenced by too great a degree of fear, may at last become subject to such despondency as to give up all hope, and relax in their diligence in the use of all the means. When Dionysius the tyrant, says Bp. Taylor, imposed intolerable tributes upon his Sicilian subjects, it amazed them, and they petitioned and cried for help, and flattered him, and feared, and obeyed him carefully; but he imposed still new ones, and greater, and at last left them poor as the valley of Vesuvius, or the top of Ætna; but then all being gone, the people grew idle and careless, and walked in the markets and public places, cursing the tyrant, and bitterly scoffing his person and vices; which when Dionysius heard, he caused the publicans and committees to withdraw their impost; "for now," says he, "they are dangerous, because they are desperate." When men have nothing, says the same author, they will despise their rulers. So it is in religion. If our fears be unreasonable, our diligence is none at all, and from whom we hope for nothing, neither benefit nor indemnity, we despise his command, and break his yoke, and trample it under our most miserable feet. Let our confidence be allayed with fear, and our fear be sharpened with the intertextures of a holy hope, and the active powers of our souls will be furnished with feet and wings, with eyes and hands, with consideration and diligence, with reason and encouragement. But despair is part of the punishment that is in hell, and the devils still do evil things, because they never hope to receive a good nor find a pardon. *Buck.*

8698. FEAR, Habit and. Habit diminishes fear when it raises up contrary associations, and increases it when it confirms the first associations. A man works in a gunpowder-mill every day of his life, with the utmost *sang froid*, which you would not be very much pleased to enter for half an hour. You have associated with the manufactory nothing but the accidents you have heard it is exposed to; he has associated with it the numberless days he has passed there in perfect security. For the same reason, a sailor-boy stands unconcerned upon the mast, a mason upon a ladder,

and a miner descends by his single rope. Their associations are altered by experience; therefore, in estimating the degree in which human creatures are under the influence of this passion, we must always remember their previous habits. *S. Smith.*

8699. FEAR, Labors of. In the first pitched battle the Romans fought against Hannibal, under the Consul Sempronius, a body of twenty thousand foot that had taken flight, seeing no other escape for their cowardice, threw themselves headlong upon the battalion of their enemies, with such wonderful fury, that they routed them with a very great slaughter. People work harder through fear than they would to gain a glorious victory.

8700. FEAR of the Lord. The terrors of the Lord are great, but they do not exercise supreme sway in a human heart, and lead all its affections whithersoever they will. His anger is not a ruling, leading, drawing power. It is mighty, but not to save. It is a force that casts the wicked into hell; but not a force that can win any son of man near in willing obedience. It is not a force in that direction. The stream of the Mississippi is a great power; it floats loaded ships or fallen forests downward with great velocity to the sea; but it cannot impel one tiny boat upward to the fertile regions near its source. This is done by another and an opposite power: a breath from heaven in the sail will carry the vessel up against the stream. So with the manifested terror of the Lord against all unrighteousness of men; its power is great—greater than we can know—who knoweth the power of thine anger? but it does not lead any one any way in the path of righteousness. *Arnott.*

8701. FEAR and Love. Fear produceth unwilling, servile performances, as those fruits that grow in winter or in cold countries, are sour, unsavory and unconcocted; but those which grow in summer or in hotter countries, by the warmth and influence of the sun, are sweet and wholesome. Such is the difference between those fruits of obedience which fear and love produceth. *Bishop Reynolds.*

8702. FEAR, Occasion of. I once met a little boy in Wales, crying bitterly at his father's door, afraid to go in. I asked him what was the matter. He told me that his mother had sent him out clean in the morning, but that he had got into the water, and made his clothes dirty. So he feared to go in, because his father would punish him. We have soiled our characters by sin, and therefore is it that we fear death—dread the meeting with our Father. *Thomas Jones.*

8703. FEAR, Only Object of. To fear the censure of men, when God is your judge; to fear their evil, when God is your defence; to fear death, when he is the entrance to life and felicity, is unreasonable and pernicious: but if you will turn your passion into duty, and joy, and security; fear to offend God, to enter voluntarily into temptation; fear the alluring face of lust, and the smooth entertainments of intemperance; fear the anger of God, when you have deserved it; and, when you have recovered from the snare, then infinitely fear to return into that condition, in which whosoever dwells, is the heir of fear and eternal sorrow. *Jeremy Taylor.*

8704. FEAR Removed. "Do you know," said a poor boy in a hospital in India to a lady who daily visited him, "what I've been thinking of all the morning?" "Of how soon you will see Jesus?" replied the lady. "Yes," he answered; "I've been thinking that I began this Sunday a poor sick boy in the hospital, surrounded by wicked men and sinful talk; and I think I shall be at home before night. I think I've begun a Sunday that will never end. I don't think I shall ever have another weekday." In the evening she visited him again, and found him lying with his eyes closed, sinking rapidly, but calmly. Stooping over him, she whispered, "'Yea, though I walk through the valley of the shadow of death, I will fear no evil; for thou art with me; thy rod and thy staff they comfort me.' Dear Willie, is Jesus with you?" "Oh yes." "Have you any fear?" "No, none; I have been wondering why they call it a dark valley. I have found the light growing much brighter every day since I first believed; and now it's so bright I must shut my eyes." After praying, he said, "That is my last prayer; now it shall be only praise for ever and ever."

8705. FEAR, Results of. Don Diogo Ossorious, a brave Spaniard of noble family, was so affected by being sentenced to death that his hair turned completely white. The king on hearing this, considered that he had suffered enough, and remitted his sentence. A boy lay upon his sick bed, and heard the physicians despairing of his life. Watching for and fearing death, his hair turned white in a single night. A young man, who was condemned to die, turned gray-headed in one night, through fear of death, and was thereupon pardoned.

8706. FEAR, Security from. What can that man fear who takes care to please a Being that is able to crush all his adversaries? *Addison.*

8707. FEAR, Slavish, Biblical. *Faintheartedness*, Lev. 26:36; as in Gideon's troops, Judges 7:3; cf. Deut. 20:8; a trembling heart, Deut. 28:65; like Saul, 1 Sam. 28:5; Felix, Acts 24:25; a melting heart, Joshua 5:1, 7:5. *Terrified* at the *sound of a shaken leaf*, Lev. 26:36; as with "a dreadful sound" in the ears, Job 15:21 ("a sound of fears," marg.); "as the trees of the wood are moved with the wind," Isa. 7:2. *Flying*, as from the sword, Lev. 26:36; when no man pursueth, Prov. 28:1; Lev. 26:17, 36. *Turning pale* with terror, as the word "perish" means literally, Acts 13:41. *The spirit of slaves*—of bondage and fear, Rom. 8:15; the fear that "hath torment," 1 John 4:18. *Adam*, Gen. 3:10: "I was afraid"—one of the first results of the fall. *Magor-missabib*, Jer. 20:3, 4. "Fear round about" (margin). The fear with which Pashur thought to alarm Jeremiah, recoiling upon himself. *Death*—"the king of terrors," Job 18: 14.   *Bowes.*

8708. FEAR, Well-grounded. A lady professor of religion, whose daily practice was not in harmony with it, once said to Rev. R. Hill, "Oh! I am afraid lest after all I should not be saved." He replied, "I am glad to hear it, for I have long been afraid for you, I assure you." The lady retired suddenly.

8709. FEAST, Demoralization of a. When Seneca describes the spare diet of some, he says, "The prisoner keeps a better table, and he that is to kill the criminal to-morrow morning gives him a better supper over night." When the heathens feasted their gods, they gave nothing but a fat ox, a ram, or a kid: they poured a little wine upon the altar, and burnt a handful of gum; but when they feasted themselves they had many vessels filled with Campanian wine, turtles from Liguria, Sicilian beeves, and wheat from Egypt, wild boars from Thyrium, and Grecian sheep; variety, and load, and curiosity, and cost; and so do we. It is so little we spend in religion, and so very much upon ourselves; so little to the poor, and so much without measure to make ourselves sick, that we seem to be in love with our own mischief, and so passionate for necessity and want, that we strive all the ways we can to make ourselves need more than nature intended. And what wisdom can be expected from them whose soul dwells in clouds of meat, and floats up and down in wine. It is a perfect shipwreck of a man; the pilot is intoxicated, the helm dashed in pieces, and the ship first reels, and by swallowing too much, itself is swallowed up at last. And therefore the madness of the young fellows of Agrigentum, who being drunk fancied themselves in a storm, and the house the ship, was more than the wild fancy of their cups, it was really so; they were all castaways, they were broken in pieces by the foul disorder of the storm. So have I seen the eye of the world looking down upon a fenny bottom, and drinking up two free draughts of moisture, gathered them into a cloud, and that cloud crept about his face, and made him first look red, and then covered him with darkness and an artificial night; so is our reason at a feast."   *Buck.*

8710. FEAST, A Frugal. Timotheus was in the habit of giving and attending great feasts and sumptuous suppers. Plato was desirous of drawing him from such entertainments, so invited him to a supper in the academy. No viands were provided that would fever the brain, or excite the imagination. Timotheus, the next day, perceiving the difference between these suppers and those he had been in the habit of taking, said, "That they who supped with Plato over night, found the pleasure and comfort thereof the next day."

8711. FEAST, The Gospel. Biblical. *Bread*—The Lord Jesus is "the bread of God"—"the true bread"—"the bread of life"—"the bread from heaven," John 6:32, 33, 35, 48, 50, 51, 58. Born at Bethlehem (which means "the house of bread"); like the good corn, bruised and broken; and "fine flour," baked, he gave his flesh for the life of the world. An old writer well says, of our need of him, "Without bread there is no feast; with bread, there need be no famine." *Water* "and wine," fresh and free —fructifying and reviving—a figure of the sweet ordinances of spiritual blessing, Ps. 23: 2; and of Christ himself and his spirit, John 4: 10, 14. *Wine*—"that maketh glad the heart of man," Ps. 104: 15—is symbolically used by Christ for the blessings of his kingdom, Cant. 5: 1; cf. Christ's first miracle, John 2: 8–10; and his last supper, Matt. 26: 27–29. Christ is the true vine, John 15: 1. *Milk*— The simplest food for babes, Heb. 5: 12; yet the token of wealth and rich abundance, Isa. 55: 1; 60: 16; the emblem of the sweet nourishment of the Divine Word, 1 Pet. 2: 3. *Honey*—The emblem of sweetness, Judges 14: 18; Isa. 55: 1; Ps. 19: 10; 119: 103. *Marrow and fatness*, Ps. 36: 8; 63: 5; Isa. 25: 6. *Fruit*—Representing the sweetness and variety of gospel blessings through Christ, see Cant. throughout. THE GOSPEL FEAST—"The wedding banquet"—the " great supper," Matt. 22: 1–14; Luke 14: 16–24. See Wisdom's feast, Prov. 9: 1–5; the bridegroom's call, Cant. 5: 1; the Lord's supper—the feast of commemoration, communion, and love, 1 Cor. 10: 16, 17; 11: 23–26. It is also represented figuratively how believers RECEIVE these gospel blessings. They *eat and drink* of Christ's bounty, Isa. 55: 1, 2; John 6: 48–58. They *taste* the Lord's goodness, Ps. 34: 8; 1 Pet. 2: 3. They *feed* (Christ's sheep) in the peaceful pastures, Ps. 23: 2; Isa. 40: 11. They sit down as Christ's guests in his banqueting house, Cant. 2: 4. They are "satisfied," "abundantly satisfied," with the fatness of the Lord's house, while they "drink of the river of his pleasure," Ps. 36: 8; 63: 5.   *Bowes.*

8712. FEATURES, Diversity of.   That men should vary in their features we might naturally expect from general analogy. There is nothing in nature that preserves an invariable uniformity. Two stones cannot be picked up on the seashore, nor two leaves from the densest forest, in every respect alike. Wherever we look, we find varieties of the same species distinguished by some striking change of aspect.   *Dr. Brewer.*

8713. FEATURES, Inherited.   A peculiar thickness of the under lip has been hereditary in the Imperial House of Hapsburgh ever since the marriage, some centuries ago, with the Polish family of Jagellon, whence it came. In our own royal family a certain fullness of the lower and lateral parts of the face is conspicuous in the portraits of the whole series of sovereigns from George I. to Victoria, and has been equally marked in other members of the family. The females of the ducal house of Gordon have long been remarkable for a peculiar elegant conformation of the neck. The Clackmannanshire Bruces, who are descended from a common stock with the famous Robert Bruce of Scotland, are said to have that strongly-marked form of the cheek-bones and jaws which appears on the coins of that heroic monarch, as it did in his actual face

when his bones were disinterred at Dunfermline, about thirty years ago. The prevalent tallness of the inhabitants of Potsdam, many of whom are descended from the guards of Frederick I.; the Spanish features observable in the people of the county of Galway, in which, some centuries ago, several Spanish settlements were made; and the hereditary beauty of the women of Prague—are well-known facts which have frequently attracted the attention of chronologists. The burgesses of Rome (the most invariable portion of every population) exhibit at the present day precisely the same type of face and form as their ancestors, whose busts may be seen carved in relief on the ancient sarcophagi; and the Jewish physiognomies portrayed upon the sepulchral monuments of Egypt are identical with those which may be observed among modern Jews in the streets of any of our great cities.   *Mantell.*

8714. FEELING, Apprehension of.   The sun is commonly said to rise and set. This, however, is spoken merely in complaisance to appearances. The truth is, that when the horizon of earth gets below the sun, we then perceive its beams, and when the horizon gets above it, we lose sight of them. Here remember, as before, that in all our varying frames of soul, the variations are not in God, but in ourselves. Remember, too, that you must lie low at his feet, if you would bask in the shinings of his face. Get above his word and ordinances, and no wonder if the horror of a great darkness falls upon you.   *Salter.*

8715. FEELING, Caprice of.   A quarter of an hour since how romantic, how enchanted with the favorite idea, how anticipative of pleasure from an expected meeting! I have advanced within two hundred yards of the place; the current of sentiment is changed, and I feel as if I could wish to slink away into deep and eternal solitude.   *J. Foster.*

8716. FEELING, Holy Spirit in.   Where the Spirit is, there is feeling. For the Spirit maketh us feel all things. Where the Spirit is not, there is no feeling, but a vain opinion or imagination. A physician serveth but for sick men, and that for such sick men as feel their sicknesses, and mourn, therefore, and long for health. Christ likewise serveth, but for such sinners only as feel their sin; and that for such sinners as sorrow and mourn in their hearts for health.   *Tindal.*

8717. FEELING, Judging from.   The industrious peasant, sitting in his easy chair, sees his children gathering round him, and courting his affections by a hundred little winning ways; he looks, and smiles, and loves. The next day he returns to his labor, and cheerfully bears the burden of the day, to provide for these, his little ones, and promote their interest. During his day's labor, he may not feel his love operate in such sensible emotions as he did the evening before. Nay, he may be so attentive to other things, as not immediately to have them in his thoughts. What then? He loves his children. Indeed, he gives proof of it, by cheerfully enduring the toils of labor, and willingly denying himself many a·comfort, that they might share their part; and were he to hear of their being injured or afflicted, he would quickly feel the returns of glowing affection in as strong or perhaps stronger motions than ever. Thus the believer may have real love to God in exercise, only it does not work in the same way as at some other times.

A. Fuller.

8718. FEELING, Over–Sensibility of. To feel is amiable; but to feel too keenly is injurious both to mind and body; and a habit of giving way to sensibility, which we should endeavor to regulate, though not to eradicate, may end in a morbid weakness of mind, which may appear to romantic persons very gentle and very interesting, but will undoubtedly render its victims very useless in society Our feelings were given us to excite to action, and when they end in themselves, they are impressed to no one good purpose that I know of.

Bishop Sandford.

8719. FEELING, Past. A man of fashion lived in dissipation and committed grave crimes, of which he was convicted, and for which he was sentenced to be hung. Dr. Leifchild visited him in Newgate prison, and endeavored to induce him to repent and prepare to meet his future judge. The condemned man listened impatiently and answered, "Sir, I appreciate your motive. I am not ignorant of the truths you have been stating. I could unfold to you depths of iniquity which would make you stand aghast. But I am not now about to become the pusillanimous creature that calls for pity and mercy, when I know it cannot be shown me. I cannot feel and I will not pray. You see that stone,"· pointing to the pavement, "it is an image of the insensibility of my heart to all the impressions you are striving to make." Repeated visits, though courteously received, were followed by no better results. He said near the last with great emphasis, "I told you it would be all in vain; I am past feeling." Thus he continued indifferent or defiant, counting the time, upon his watch, and announcing that in so many hours he should be in hell. In this hardened state he went out of the world.

8720. FEELING, Unsatisfactory. It is astonishing how whimsical people are about the way they will be saved! When God saves a man by thunder and lightning, he never likes it; he wishes he had been brought to God in the sunshine; and when a man is brought to God in the sunshine, he never likes it, but wishes it had been in the storm. Poor John Bunyan, in his deep experience, wished he had been brought in a gentler way to God; and many think they cannot be children of God, because they have not had so deep an experience as he had.

Spurgeon.

8721. FEELINGS, Influence of the. There are, certainly, moments in life when, though we may wish, may labor, to be common-place in our sensations, and matter-of-fact in our conduct, we cannot succeed. A tide of feeling will rush upon us, too powerful for the dikes and mounds raised up by reason and philosophy. Our minds sink under the flood of weakness, if it be so, which flows warmly over, impregnating, and probably purifying, every thought; for these moments may surely be considered as our best, the true intervals of enjoyment, when we throw off the thraldom of social restrictions, and revel alone in a boundless realm of freedom and romance. It is at such times that the imagination fixes on some object with an interest more than real—an exaggerated intensity, creating an atmosphere around, and giving to the meanest things within its influence a character not properly their own, as the fragrance of the rose envelopes, and might seem to breathe from, the veriest weed that crawls beneath it. *Grattan.*

8722. FEELINGS, Training the. As a gladiator trained the body, so must we train the mind, to self-sacrifice "to endure all things," to meet and overcome difficulty and danger. We must take the rough and thorny road as well as the smooth and pleasant; and a portion, at least, of our daily duty must be hard and disagreeable; for the mind cannot be kept strong and healthy in perpetual sunshine only, and the most dangerous of all states is that of constantly-recurring pleasure, ease, and prosperity. Most persons will find difficulties and hardships enough without seeking them; let them not repine, but take them as a part of that educational discipline necessary to fit the mind to arrive at its highest good. *Charles Bray.*

8723. FEELINGS, Variety of. Pleasure is in its nature a relative thing, and so imparts a peculiar relation and correspondence to the state and condition of the person to whom it is a pleasure. For of those who discourse of atoms, affirm that there are atoms of all forms, some round, some triangular, some square, and the like; all which are continually in motion, and never settle till they fall into a fit circumspection or place of the same figure; so there are the like great diversities of minds and objects. Whence it is that this object, striking upon a mind thus or thus disposed, flies off, and rebounds without making any impression; but the same luckily happening upon another, of a disposition, as it were, framed for it, is presently snatched at, and greedily clasped into the nearest unions and embraces. *South.*

8724. FEET, Sliding of the. During my journey in the Himalayas,　was often reminded of passages of scripture. The mountain roads are very narrow. They are not often wide enough for more than two men to walk together, and we generally find it easier to follow in single file. I never saw the men who carry loads walking two abreast. There are ascents and descents so steep as to require the traveler to plant his foot firmly and carefully, in order to prevent his falling—sliding—down the hill. In some places the roads lead around the side of a mountain, or along the bank of a torrent, with a precipice, either perpendicular, or nearly so, immediately on one side of it, of hundreds of feet in height. Sometimes the sharp ascent or descent is combined with the precipice on one side, and a further complication of the difficulty is made by both a slope of road toward its outer edge, and a chalky or friable kind of stone in the pathway, affording no safe hold to the feet. In many of these places the traveler looks down a giddy slope of a hundred, a thousand, or two thousand feet, on which no foothold could be found, with the consciousness that a false step, or a breaking of the bank under his foot, would precipitate him into the ravine filled with stones. I came to a place where the bank above the road had slipped and filled the pathway, excepting about eight inches at the outer edge. As the ravine was not very deep, and therefore did not look very fearful, I rode around the heap, and my horse's hind foot broke down the remainder of the pathway. He carried me safely over, however; but I could not help quoting to myself the words of the Psalmist, "My steps had well nigh slipped."   *J. Warren.*

8725. FEET, Washing the. I never understood the full meaning of our Lord's words in John 13: 10, until I beheld the better sort of East Indian natives return home after performing their customary ablutions. The passage reads thus, "He that is washed needeth not save to wash his feet, but is clean every whit." Thus as they return to their habitations barefoot, they necessarily contract in their progress some portion of dirt on their feet; and this is universally the case, however nigh their dwellings may be to the river side. When, therefore, they return, the first thing they do is to mount a low stool, and pour a small vessel of water to cleanse them from the soil which they may have contracted on their journey homewards; if they are of the higher class of society, a servant performs it for them, and then they are "clean every whit." Does not this in a figure represent to us the defilement which a Christian contracts, although he may have been cleansed by faith in a crucified Saviour; and the necessity of a continual application of the precious blood of atonement, in order that the soul may be "clean every whit?"   *Statham.*

8726. FELLOWSHIP, Human. God has created mankind for fellowship, and not for solitariness, which is clearly proved by this strong argument:—God, in creation of the world, created man and woman, to the end that the man in the woman should have a fellow.   *Luther.*

8727. FELLOWSHIP, Instinct of. The craving for fellowship shows itself at first in the youngest and most innocent childhood, and is the last feeling that dies out in humanity. None are so criminal as to have no power of love to others, and everything proves the value of fellowship, the great result being that "the great multitude which no man can number" will be bound together in one common unity. *Barry.*

8728. FETISH, African. The fetish of the pagans in Western Africa differs but little in its nature and object from the greegree of the Mohammedan, only it is not so generally worn on the person. Fetish may be made of a few pieces of colored rags, string, feathers, egg shells, the head of a snake, the claws of wild animals or certain birds, or a lock of a white man's hair. These and various other articles are fancifully combined and consecrated by the pagan priest, sometimes sprinkled with the blood of a sacrificed animal, put into a calabash and hung from a tree to keep off thieves disease or other misfortune. Sometimes it is used with the soil from a grave added, to curse or kill an enemy.

8729. FETISHES, Ashantee. The Ashantees have the most surprising confidence in the fetishes, which they purchase at an extravagant rate from the Moors, believing that they make them invulnerable and invincible in war, paralyze the hand of the enemy, shiver their weapons, divert the course of balls, and avert all evils but sickness (which they can only assuage) and natural death. The king gave to the king of Dagwumba, for the fetish or war-coat of Apokoo, the value of thirty slaves; for Odumata's, twenty; for Addo Quamina's, thirteen; for Akimpon's, twelve; for Akimponteä's, nine; and for those of greater captains in proportion. The generals being always in the rear of the army are pretty sure to escape, a circumstance much in favor of the Moors. Mr. Bowditch relates that several of the Ashantee captains offered seriously to let him fire at them; in short, their confidence in these fetishes is almost as incredible as the despondency and panic imposed on their southern and western enemies by the recollection of them; they impel the Ashantees, fearless and headlong, to the most daring enterprises; they dispirit their adversaries almost to the neglect of an interposition of fortune in their favor. The Ashantees believe that the constant prayers of the Moors, who have persuaded them that they converse with the Deity, invigorate themselves and gradually waste the spirit and strength of their enemies. This faith is not less impulsive, persistent, and overwhelming than that which achieved the Arabian conquests.   *Moister.*

8730. FICTION, Truth of. We must remember, that fiction is not falsehood. If a writer puts abstract virtues into book-clothing, and sends them upon stilts into the world, he is a bad writer; if he classifies men, and attributes all virtue to one class and all vice to another, he is a false writer. Then, again, if his ideal is so poor that he fancies man's welfare to consist in immediate happiness; if he means to paint a great man and paints only a greedy one, he is a mischievous writer; and not the less so, although by lamp-light and among a juvenile audience his coarse scene-painting should be thought very grand. He may be true to his own fancy, but he is false to nature. A writer of course cannot get beyond his own ideal; but at least he should see that he works up to it; and if it is a poor one, he had better write histories of the utmost concentration of dullness, than amuse us with unjust and untrue imaginings.   *Helps.*

8731. FIDELITY, Classic. Though many of

the followers of Ulysses were dragged and haled by Polyphemus, and had their heads dashed against the ground, they would not confess a word concerning their lord and master Ulysses, nor discover the long piece of wood that was put in the fire and prepared to put out his eye; but rather suffered themselves to be devoured raw than to disclose any one of their master's secrets; which was an example of fidelity and reservedness not to be paralleled.   *Plutarch.*

8732. FIDELITY, Duty of. The duty of a sailor is not to take to the boat, pull ashore, and leave the shrieking passengers to perish; but to stick by the ship as long as there is a hope of saving her. And the duty of a Christian is not to desert his post in the world, but to stay by it, to keep the ship afloat, and the world from perishing.

8733. FIDELITY, Examples of. Tarachus, at one time a Roman soldier, during the Diolcetian persecution in 303, was accused of being a Christian, and taken before the governors of the province for examination. He declared himself a Christian and an enemy to all idols. He defied torture and endured it with joy. To his tormentors he said: "I am strengthened by your blows, and my confidence in God and in Jesus Christ is increased." After this, being bidden to sacrifice he answered, "I am sixty-five years old; thus have I been brought up and I cannot forsake the truth now." He was then remanded to prison and loaded with chains to await death with his brethren. Probus next came before the judge. He was asked to renounce Christianity and promised honor and advancement. He answered "I want nothing of that kind. Formerly I owned considerable estate, but relinquished it to serve the living God through Jesus Christ." He was beaten till his blood flowed in streams and his tormentors asked, "Is thy obstinate folly incurable?" With every stroke they asked him, "Where is thy helper?" He answered, "He helps me and will help me; so that I do not obey you." "Look, wretch, upon thy mangled body." "The more my body suffers for Jesus Christ the more is my soul refreshed." Then he was cast into prison heavily ironed. Andronicus, a young nobleman, next stood before the governor. He confessed his rank and his faith in Christ with much boldness. The judge said, "Youth makes you insolent; I have my torments ready." Andronicus answered, "I am prepared for whatever may happen." He was exhorted to sacrifice before his body was mangled and he put to a cruel death. He replied, "I have never sacrificed to demons from my infancy and I will not now begin." He was tortured upon the rack, scraped with broken tiles, and salt was rubbed into his wounds, but remaining immovable was ordered to prison like the others. Three several times were these undaunted martyrs tortured. Each time with every conceivable cruelty, but with seared and scarred flesh, members cut off, teeth smashed in and tongues cut out, they maintained their fidelity to Christ to the end. At last they were thrown to the wild beasts in the amphitheatre of Anazarbus. They refused to touch them, and by the order of Maximus they were executed with the sword.

8734. FIDELITY, Military. An instance of the discipline in the Russian army occurred at a fire in the town of Bardosek. A sentinel on duty, having been forgotten, remained at his post. His watch-box was consumed, and his clothes were on fire, when a corporal arrived to relieve him. The Emperor hearing of the circumstance, sent the man fifty roubles, decorated him with the order of St. Anne, and gave instructions for him to be made a non-commissioned officer.

8735. FIDELITY, Result of. A large drug firm in the city of New York, advertised for a boy. Next day the store was thronged with applicants, and among them came a queer-looking little fellow, who had been abandoned by his parents, attended by his aunt. Looking at him, the merchant promptly said, "Can't take him; places all full. Besides, he is too small." "I know he is small," said the woman, "but he is very willing and faithful." Something about the boy made the merchant think again. His partner remarked that he did not see what they wanted of such a boy. But after consultation, the boy was set to work. A few days later a call was made on the boys in the store for some one to stay all night. The prompt response of the little fellow contrasted well with the reluctance of others. In the middle of the night the merchant looked in to see if all was right in the store, and discovered his youthful protege busy scissoring labels. "What are you doing there? I did not tell you to work at night." "I know that you did not tell me to, but I thought I might as well be doing something." In the morning the cashier had orders to double the boy's wages. Only a few weeks elapsed before a show of wild beasts passed through the streets, and, very naturally, all hands in the store rushed to witness the spectacle. A thief saw this opportunity, and entered in the rear to seize something, but in a twinkling found himself seized by the diminutive clerk aforesaid, and after a struggle he was captured. Not only was a robbery prevented, but valuable articles which had been taken from other stores were recovered. When questioned by the merchant why he stayed behind to watch, when all the others had quit work, the reply was "You told me never to leave the store when all the others were absent, and I thought I'd stay." Orders were given once more to double his salary. In 1860 he was receiving a salary of $2,500, and afterwards became a partner in the establishment.

8736. FIDELITY, Uncompromising. Anastasius, a zealous Christian, greatly coveted and often prayed for the martyr's crown. In Cesarea he openly rebuked a company of magicians. He confessed that he had once been one such, but renounced the practice and became a follower of Christ. Upon this he was thrown into a dungeon. After three days he was brought out, chained by the foot to another prisoner. His neck and one foot were drawn and fastened near together by a chain, and in this way he was compelled to carry stones. He was upbraided, his beard was plucked out, he was kicked and beaten. Called again before the governor, and urged to pronounce the Magian incantation, he would only reply, "I am a Christian." He was then disrobed and beaten with knotty clubs, without being bound, which he endured without moving or flinching. After this he was offered choice of office in the king's service if he would only privately renounce Christ in words. If he would only do this little thing he might adhere to him in his heart. Anastasius replied that he would never even seem to dissemble. He was then sent to king Chosroes, of Persia, by whom liberal offers were repeated, and when rejected, were followed by threats and reproaches. The martyr said to the king's messenger, "Do not give yourself so much trouble about me; by the grace of Christ, I am not to be moved." He was inhumanly beaten day after day, with bitter reproaches for having rejected the honors and bounties of the king. Heavy weights were laid upon his limbs, cutting to the bone. His endurance, patience and tranquillity was so great that it was reported to the king. One more attempt was made to overcome him. He was hung up by one hand for two hours, with heavy weights attached to his feet. Seeing that his will could not be overcome, preparations were made to strangle him. He rejoiced and thanked God for so happy a conclusion to his life. He was strangled A. D. 628.

8737. FIDELITY, Vows of. Christ came to possess the land, to garrison it, to occupy the field, to set it round with sacred sentinels, and to bring all his host in military order to serve him in fighting his battles. Accordingly he commissioned his apostles, when they thus went forth to their work, to commence it by the sacramental vow—"baptizing them"—placing them under the most solemn oaths to high heaven who were engaged in the work of the redemption of our fallen world. And as it is a work which engages the fullness of Father, Son, and Holy Ghost, the sacred vow of consecration was to be in that name, the names of the Persons of the Trinity, who unitedly engage in this work of man's redemption. It is a common usage, we believe, in the formation of armies, that each individual soldier, when mustered in, shall take a solemn oath of fealty to the power that he serves. *Dr. Curry.*

8738. FIGHTING till Death. Pietro Candiano, one of the dukes of Venice, died fighting against the Nauratines with the weapons in his hands. So a saint lives fighting and dies fighting, he stands fighting and falls fighting, with his spiritual weapons in his hands. *Brooks.*

8739. FIGHTING, Hard. After Commodore McDonough's great victory over the British fleet on Lake Champlain, the commander of the British land forces, Sir George Provost, sent to him to inquire the secret of his success.

He replied, writing on the sheet which contained the inquiry, "Hard fighting." He pushed on the battle, though his ship, the Saratoga, was riddled with shot, twice on fire, and in a sinking condition. He was twice knocked down, and reported killed, but revived and returned to the gun, which he sighted till victory was gained.

8740. FIGURES, Natural. "Nothing," says M. De Bretville, "is so easy or so natural as a figure. It has often given me pleasure to listen to peasants using in their talk figures so varied, so animated, and so free from vulgarity, that our artificial rhetoricians were quite outdone; and when I have heard this rhetoric of nature, I have been ashamed of myself for having made eloquence a study so long and to so little purpose." To which Du Marsais adds: "I am convinced that more figures are made in a single day at the market than in many days' sessions of the academy." The language of barbarous nations abounds in figures. Mr. Henry Rogers observed, "The old Scandinavians forbid trespass on the unfenced field, inasmuch as it has 'heaven for its roof,' and is 'under God's lock.'" Sir Philip Sidney "found the whisperings and disputations of the common people of his day to taste of a poetic vein."

8741. FIRE, Legend of Kindling. St. Kentigern lived in Scotland in the sixth century. While a boy at school with an old monk he was a great favorite with the master, which excited the jealousy of the other boys. In those times there was no ready means of rekindling fires, and it was the custom to keep them constantly burning. The boys were required at night in turn to rise and mend the fire. When Kentigern's turn came the boys extinguished the fire to injure him. Going to the fire place he found the fire entirely out. He took a few sticks and laid them on the cold hearth and blew upon them, invoking the name of the Trinity. The flame kindled at once, and with this miraculous fire the church candles were lighted.

8742. FIRE, Nature of. It is now known that fire is neither a distinct substance nor essence, as supposed by the ancients. It is a phenomenon consisting of the sudden and abundant evolution of heat and light produced when certain class of bodies, called combustibles, enter into chemical combination with the oxygen gas, which constitutes one of the constituents of the atmosphere. The term combustion, in the modern nomenclature of physics, has been adopted to express this phenomenon. *Dr. Lardner.*

8743. FIRE, Ordeal of. Nebuchadnezzar, King of Babylon, set up a great golden idol in the plain of Dura, and called together his nobles and officers from all parts of his realm to attend its dedication. They were gathered before the massive image, when a herald announced that all men were required to fall down and worship at the sound of the instruments, and whoever refused, or failed to do this, was to be cast into a burning furnace. After the act of adoration, certain persons ap proached the king, and accused three high officials, Shadrach, Meshach, and Abednego, with defying his authority. The enraged king ordered the offenders before him, and recited his unalterable mandate to them. They replied, "O, Nebuchadnezzar, we are not careful to answer thee in this matter. If it be so, the God whom we serve is able to deliver us from the burning, fiery furnace, and he will deliver us out of thine hand, O, King! but if not, be it known unto thee that we will not serve thy gods, nor worship the golden image which thou hast set up." The great king, so heroically defied, waxed furious, and ordered the furnace heated seven times hotter than usual. The rebels were tightly bound, and cast into the raging furnace, whose flames slew the executioners. The king looked into the furnace, and saw the three worthies walking, unbound and unharmed, and with them a fourth person, like the Son of God. The astonished king, calling the Hebrews by name, confessed that they were servants of the most high God. At his command they came forth, with no mark of fire upon them, or even a hair singed. Then Nebuchadnezzar issued a decree to all people prohibiting any utterance against the God of these worthies, "because there is no other god who can deliver after this sort." (Dan. 3.)

8744. FIRE, Symbols of. Several eminent critics believe the lamp of fire was an emblem of the Divine presence, and that it ratified the covenant with Abraham. It is an interesting fact that the burning lamp or fire is still used in the East in confirmation of a covenant. Should a person in the evening make a solemn promise to perform something for another, and should the latter doubt his word, the former will say, pointing to the flame of the lamp, "That is the witness." On occasions of greater importance, when two or more join in a covenant, should the fidelity of any be questioned, they will say, "We invoke the lamp of the Temple," as a witness. When an agreement of this kind has been broken, it will be said, "Who would have thought this? for the lamp of the Temple was invoked." That fire was a symbol of the Divine presence, no one acquainted with the sacred Scriptures can deny; and in the literature and customs of the East, the same thing is still asserted. In the ancient writings, where the marriages of the gods and demi-gods are described, it is always said the ceremony was performed in the presence of the God of fire. He was the witness. But it is also a general practice, at the celebration of respectable marriages at this day, to have a fire as a witness of the transaction. It is made of the wood of the mango-tree, or the Aal or Arasu, or Panne or Patàsu. The fire being kindled in the centre of the room, the young couple sit on stools; but when the Brahmin begins to repeat the incantations, they arise, and the bridegroom puts the little finger of his left hand round the little finger of the right hand of the bride, and they walk round the fire three times from left to right. "Fire is the witness of their covenant; and if they break it, fire

will be their destruction." In the Scanda Puràna, the father of the virgin who was to be married to the son of the Rishi, said to him, "Call your son, that I may give him to my daughter in the presence of the god of fire, that he may be the witness;" that being done. "Usteyàr gave his daughter Verunte in marriage, the fire being the witness." *Roberts.*

8745. FIRMNESS, Christian. In Galen's time it was a proverbial expression when any one would show the impossibility of a thing, "You may as soon turn a Christian from Christ as do it." There is an obstinancy of spirit which is our sin. But this is our glory. "In the matters of God," said Luther, "I assume this title, ' *Cedo nulli*,' I yield to none." *Flavel.*

8746. FIRMNESS, Duty of. Mere softness will not do. The down bed needs the solid wall of masonry behind it. A glove of velvet should cover the hand of iron, but an iron hand should be within the velvet glove. In railway trains there is a contrivance to prevent the collision of carriage against carriage. On the outer extremities, where likely to strike each other, there is a soft, spongy covering. Within, and at the very centre, is a spring, strong but yielding, yielding but strong. We ought ever to "speak the truth in love," and "be ready always to give an answer," to every man that asketh.
W. Arnot.

8747. FIRMNESS, Memento of. During the battle of Manassas, about 11 o'clock a. m., when that gallant and meritorious officer, Brig. Gen. Bernard E. Bee, was endeavoring to rally his troops in the small valley in rear of the Robinson house, he noticed Jackson's brigade, which had just arrived and taken position a little in rear of him, in a copse of small pines bordering the edge of the plateau where was about to be fought the first great battle of the war. Bee, finding that his appeal was unheeded by his brave but disorganized troops, then said to them, "Rally, men, rally! See Jackson's brigade standing there like a stone wall." Those words gave the appellation to that brigade, and thence to its heroic commander.
Beauregard.

8748. FIRMNESS, Symbol of. Stones still in the quarry are said to be living, like plants, connected with and nourished by their roots. The epithet means the firmness of that thing signified by the name of a stone, for nothing is firmer than stones growing in a quarry, as cleaving fast to a rock by the root. *Burder.*

8749. FLAG, Devotion to His. On seeing a young Prussian soldier who was pressing his flag to his bosom in the agonies of death, Napoleon said to his officers: "Gentlemen, you see that a soldier has a sentiment approaching idolatry for his flag. Render funereal honors at once to this young man. I regret that I do not know his name, that I might write to his family. Do not take away his flag; its silken folds will be an honorable shroud for him."
Bourrienne.

8750. FLAG, Preserving the. The passion of a French soldier for his flag is vividly revealed in a story of Sedan. At the moment of capit ulation, a captain, a lieutenant of Zouaves, and a brave sergeant, resolved that the flag which had been left in their keeping should not fall into the hands of the Prussians. So they took the emblem of France to pieces, one concealing the banner under his uniform, the other putting the balls into his pocket, and the third keeping the eagle. After the capitulation, it was agreed that all the relics should be confided to the care of the sergeant, who, being an Alsacian, could speak German. The brave sergeant then managed to escape from his captors, to don the guise of a peasant, and to obtain a basket, in which he placed the memorials of French glory. He then covered the precious relics with a mass of tobacco, which he gathered from the peasants, and, thus guarded against detection, he managed to pass through all the German lines, and to reach Paris.

8751. FLAG, Protected by the. A man came from Europe to this country, and went to Cuba in 1867. He was arrested for a spy, court-martialed, and condemned to be shot. He sent for the American and English consuls, and proved to them that he was no spy. They went to one of the Spanish officers and said, "This man you have condemned to be shot is an innocent man." The Spanish officer said, "The man has been legally tried by our laws and condemned, and the law must take its course and the man must die." The next morning the man was led out; the grave was already dug for him, and the black cap was put on him, and the soldiers were there ready to receive the order, "Fire," and in a few moments the man would be shot and be put in that grave. Then the American consul took the American flag and wrapped it around him, and the English consul took the English flag and wrapped it around him, and they said to those soldiers, "Fire on those flags if you dare!" Not a man dared; there were two great governments behind those flags. So Christ calls us to take shelter from our sins and all our enemies under the shadow of his cross.

8752. FLATTERER, Beware of a. Beware of him who flatters you, and commends you to your face, or to one he thinks will tell you of it; most probably he has either deceived and abused you, or means to do so. Remember the fable of the fox commending the singing of the crow, who had something in her mouth which the fox wanted. Be careful that you do not commend yourselves.   *Sir M. Hale.*

8753. FLATTERERS, Beware of. Take care thou be not made a fool by flatterers, for even the wisest men are abused by these. Know, therefore, that flatterers are the worst kind of traitors; for they will strengthen thy imperfections, encourage thee in all evils, correct thee in nothing, but so shadow and paint all thy vices and follies, as thou shalt never, by their will, discern evil from good, or vice from virtue: and because all men are apt to flatter themselves, to entertain the addition of other men's praises is most perilous. Do not, therefore, praise thyself, except thou wilt be counted a vainglorious fool: neither take delight in the praise of other men, except thou deserve it, and receive it from such as are worthy and honest, and will withal warn thee of thy faults; for flatterers have never any virtue; they are ever base, creeping, cowardly persons. A flatterer is said to be a beast that biteth smiling. But it is hard to know them from friends, they are so obsequious and full of protestation; for as a wolf resembles a dog, so doth a flatterer a friend. A flatterer is compared to an ape, who, because she cannot defend the house like a dog, labor as an ox, or bear burdens as a horse, doth therefore yet play tricks and provoke laughter.   *Raleigh.*

8754. FLATTERY, Love of. When Alexander had bestowed some considerable reward upon a jester, Agis, the Argive, through mere envy and vexation, cried out upon it as a most absurd action; which the king overhearing, he turned him about in great indignation at the insolence, saying, "What's that you prate, sirrah?" "Why truly," replied the man, "I must confess, I am not a little troubled to observe, that all you great men who are descended from Jupiter take a strange delight in flatterers and buffoons; for as Hercules had his Cercopians and Bacchus his Silenians about him, so, I see your majesty is pleased to have regard for such pleasant fellows, too."   *Plutarch.*

8755. FLATTERY, Poison of. He was justly accounted a skillful poisoner who destroyed his victims by bouquets of lovely and fragrant flowers. The art has not been lost; nay, is practiced every day by the world.   *Latimer.*

8756. FLATTERY Rebuked. Leo the emperor used to say, " *Occulti inimici pessimi,*" a close enemy is far worse than an open. When a court parasite praised Sigismund the emperor above measure, the emperor gave him a sound box on the ear. When Aristobulus the historian presented to Alexander the great book that he had written of his glorious acts, wherein he had flatteringly made him greater than he was, Alexander, after he had read the book, threw it into the river Hydaspes, and said to the author, "It were a good deed to throw thee after it." When the flatterers flattered Antigonus, he cried out, " *Mentiris, mentiris in gutture, hæ virtutes non latent in me,*" thou liest in thy throat; these virtues that thou speakest of I have not in me, but I am like a leopard, that have ten black spots to one white. Augustus Cæsar and Tiberius Cæsar were deadly enemies to flatterers, insomuch that they would not be called lords by their own children. A good symbol is attributed to Trebonianus Gallus, viz.: " *Nemo amicus idem et adulator,*" no flatterer can be a good friend. Aristippus, the philosopher, washing herbs for his dinner, said, "If Diogenes knew how to make use of kings, he need not live upon raw herbs, as he doth;" to which Diogenes replied, "that if Aristippus could content himself with herbs, he need not to turn spaniel, or flatter king Dionysius for a meal's meat." Flatterers are the very worst of sinners. The flatterers told Cæsar, that his freckles in his face were like the stars in the firmament; they bought and sold Aurelius the emperor at pleasure. And Augustus complained, when Barrus was dead, that he had none now left that would deal plainly and faithfully with him. *Brooks.*

8757. FLATTERY, Ruin by. When vice is extolled by the name of virtue, so that man is induced to sin not only without regret but with joy and triumph, and is hardened beyond the modesty of a blush for his enormities, this sort of flattery, I say, has been fatal even to whole kingdoms. It was this that ruined Sicily, by styling the tyranny of Dionysius and Plalaris nothing but justice and a hatred of villainous practices. It was this that overthrew Egypt, by palliating the king's effeminacy, his yellings, his enthusiastic rants, and his beating of drums, with the more plausible names of true religion and the worship of the gods. It was this that very nigh ruined the staunch Roman temper, by extenuating the voluptuousness, the luxury, the sumptuous shows and public profuseness of Antony, into the softer terms of humanity, good nature, and the generosity of a gentleman who knew how to use the greatness of his fortune. What but the charms of flattery made Ptolemy turn piper and fiddler? What else put on Nero's buskins and brought him on the stage? Have we not known several princes, if they sung a tolerable treble, termed Apollos; when they drank stoutly, styled Bacchuses; and upon wrestling, fencing, or the like, immediately dubbed by the name of Hercules, and hurried on by those empty titles to the commission of those acts which were infinitely beneath the dignity of their character? *Plutarch,*

8758. FLESH, Infirmities of the. If I cannot take pleasure in infirmities, I can sometimes feel the profit of them. I can conceive a king to pardon a rebel and take him into his family, and then say, "I appoint you for a season to wear a fetter. At a certain season I will send a messenger to knock it off. In the meantime, this fetter will serve to remind you of your state; it may humble you, and restrain you from rambling." *Newton.*

8759. FLESH, Weakness of the. And how sad it is to think, that the inferior part of our nature is true to its instincts and passions, and the superior has lost its power and fails of its vocation! Just as you sometimes see, in ancient mansions, the portion once devoted to divine service laid in ruins, while that which was designed for the good cheer of men is whole and in full repair; so it is with man; if we may so speak, the church of humanity is in a state of miserable decay and dilapidation, but the hall of entertainment is sound and furnished well. The principles and affections that belong to the lowest range and sphere of our being remain to grace and gladden life and fellowship, but the spirit which alone can consecrate and sanctify them is gone. As to religion, we are in woful plight, but our sensuous nature is quick and vigorous. How sorrowful to think that what we have in common with animals

should be strong and prosperous, and what allies us to the Deity should be weak and morbid. *Morris.*

8760. FLOODS, Eastern. The rains and floods and winds of an Eastern monsoon afford a striking illustration of this passage (Matt. 7: 27). When people in those regions speak of the strength of a house it is not by affirming, "It will last so many years;" but, "It will outstand the rains: it will not be injured by the floods." Houses built of the best materials, and having deep foundations, often in a few years yield to the rains of a monsoon. At first a small crack appears in some angle, which gradually becomes larger, till the whole building lumbers to the ground. And who can wonder at this, when he considers the state of the earth? For several months there is not a drop of rain, and the burning sun has loosened the ground on which the edifice stands; then all at once the torrents begin to descend, the chapped earth suddenly swells, and the change injures the foundations. Only the house founded upon a rock can outstand the rains and floods of a wet monsoon. *Roberts.*

8761. FLOWERS, Benefit by. I could tell you many stories of persons who by considering the flowers have got good. You remember how Mungo Park was traveling in the desert, and as he thought to lie there and die, how he caught sight of a little flower springing up in the sand by his side, and he thought—if God cares for the flower in the wilderness he will care for me. You remember Picciola and his prison flower—how, when despairing in his dungeon, the flower came up through a niche in the floor, and how it taught him many a useful lesson, and kept him from despair. When John Bunyan went to the house of the interpreter and was led into his room, the interpreter showed him all the beautiful symbols, and said to him, "Consider the lilies how they grow." It was a clod, now it hath come forth out of the black earth; God hath fashioned it. And as thou lookest on that remember all thy beauty is God-given. What a clod he finds thee, and how beautiful he is making thee. Consider the lily; it was not so always; it drinketh up continually out of the cup into which the water is poured, and so, if thou wilt continually receive the water which God will give thee, thou wilt grow in beauty and in purity. Consider the lily. Seest thou how earth feeds it, and air fans it, and heaven sends dews upon it; how earth and air and heaven combine to bless it? So all kinds of auxiliaries and agencies go to help thee. Consider the lily, how it grows; see from what it springs, and to what beauty it attains, and for what uses it blooms; and as thou considerest, learn the lesson. It is well to go into the interpreter's room. *S. Coley.*

8762. FLOWERS, Blessing of. How the universal heart of man blesses flowers! They are wreathed round the cradle, the marriage-altar, and the tomb. The Persian in the far East delights in their perfume, and writes his love in nosegays; while the Indian child of the far West claps his hands with glee as he gathers the abundant blossoms—the illuminated scriptures of the prairies. The Cupid of the ancient Hindoos tipped his arrows with flowers; and orange-flowers are a bridal crown with us—a nation of yesterday. Flowers garlanded the Grecian altar, and hung in votive wreath before the Christian shrine. All these are appropriate uses. Flowers should deck the brow of the youthful bride, for they are in themselves a lovely type of marriage. They should twine round the tomb, for their perpetually renewed beauty is a symbol of the resurrection. They should festoon the altar, for their fragrance and their beauty ascend in perpetual worship before the Most High. *Mrs. L. M. Child.*

8763. FLOWERS, Devotion to. Luther always kept a flower in a glass on his writing-table; and when he was waging his great public controversy with Eckius, he kept a flower in his hand. Lord Bacon has a beautiful passage about flowers. As to Shakespeare, he is a perfect Alpine valley—he is full of flowers; they spring, and blossom, and wave in every cleft of his mind. Even Milton, cold, serene, and stately as he is, breaks forth into exquisite gushes of tenderness and fancy when he marshals the flowers. *Mrs. Stowe.*

8764. FLOWERS, Influence of. A society has been formed in London, under Lord Shaftesbury's influence, which gives a box, tastily shaped for the window, and choice flower seeds and slips, to the very poor, who will promise to cultivate them. The result has been surprising. The flowers in the windows have brought decency and taste into the rooms, and saved the father from the ale-house in thousands of instances.

8765. FLOWERS, Lesson of. Flowers, of all created things, the most innocently simple and most superbly complex, playthings for childhood, ornaments of the grave, and companions of the cold corpse in the coffin! Flowers, beloved by the wandering idiot, and studied by the deep-thinking man of science! Flowers, that of perishing things are the most heavenly. Flowers, that unceasingly expand to heaven their grateful, and to man their cheerful, looks; partners of human joy, soothers of human sorrow; fit emblems of the victor's triumphs, of the young bride's blushes: welcome to the crowded halls, and graceful upon solitary graves. Flowers are, in the volume of nature, what the expression, "God is love," is in the volume of revelation. What a desolate place would be a world without a flower! It would be a face without a smile; a feast without a welcome. Are not flowers the stars of the earth, and are not our stars the flowers of heaven? One cannot look closely at the structure of a flower without loving it. They are emblems and manifestations of God's love to the creation, and they are the means and ministrations of man's love to his fellow-creatures; for they first awaken in his mind a sense of the beautiful and good. The very inutility of flowers is their elegance and great beauty; for they lead us to thoughts of generosity and moral beauty, detached from and superior to all selfishness; so that they are pretty lessons to nature's book of instruction, teaching man that he liveth not by bread or from bread alone, but that he hath another than an animal life. *Mrs. Balfour.*

8766. FLOWERS, Love for. Flowers seem intended for the solace of ordinary humanity: children love them; quiet, tender, contented ordinary people love them as they grow; luxurious and disorderly people rejoice in them gathered. They are the cottager's treasure; and in the crowded town, mark, as with a little broken fragment of rainbow, the windows of the workers in whose heart rests the covenant of peace. Passionate or religious minds contemplate them with fond, feverish intensity; the affection is seen severely calm in the works of many old religious painters, and mixed with more open and true country sentiment in those of our pre-Raphaelites. *Ruskin.*

8767. FLOWERS, Pleasure in. A gentleman, who was invited to view a grand building, holding in his hand a flower at the time, said he "wished to be excused; for I see more of God in this flower than in all the beautiful edifices in the world."

8768. FOLLOWING CHRIST in Earnest. Many follow God as Samson did his parents, till he lighted upon a honeycomb; or as a dog doth his master, till he meet with carrion; and then turn him up. Demas forsook God, and, embracing this present world, became afterwards a priest in an idol temple. *Trapp.*

8769. FOLLOWING CHRIST Fully. That flower that follows the sun, doth so even in cloudy days; when it doth not shine forth, yet it follows the hidden course and motion of it; so the soul that moves after God keeps that course when he hides his face; is content, yea, is glad at his will in all estates, or conditions, or wants. *Salter.*

8770. FOLLY, Biblical Presentation of. The root of folly is represented as in the heart, Ps. 14: 1; Prov. 12: 23; proceeding from within, Mark 7: 21, 22. "There is more folly in the heart of man than in the head. Foolishness stands first in the dark catalogues of evil," Rom. 1: 21; Titus 3: 3. Examples of folly are the foolish builder, Matt. 7: 26; the foolish virgins, Matt. 25: 3; the rich fool, Luke 12: 16.

8771. FOLLY, Royal. The emperor Caligula had a horse called Swift, with which he was infatuated. He had the horse sup with him. He set before him provender in a dish of gold, and gave him wine to drink in goblets of gold. He made this horse his colleague in the supreme pontificate, and would have made him a consul had he lived. The horse was allowed a house, family servants and household stuff. His stable was marble, his manger ivory, and his harness purple, adorned with precious stones.

8772. FOLLY, The Sinner's. Think what folly it is to dig for dross with mattocks of gold; to bestow the precious affections of our souls on white and yellow clay. How monstrous it is to see a man with his head and heart where his feet should be! to see the world in the heart and on the throne, and Christ at the footstool; to see the world possessing God's room both week-day and Sabbath-day, and getting the service which is due to him alone! How many are they who, on the Sabbath-day, worship the trinity of this world, mentioned 1 John 2: 16, more than the Trinity of heaven. *Boston.*

8773. FOOD, Forfeiture of. For what is food given? To enable us to carry on the necessary business of life, and that our support may be such as our work requires. This is the use of food. Man eats and drinks that he may work; therefore, the idle man forfeits his right to his daily bread.   *Jones of Nayland.*

8774. FOOD, God's Provision of. We are apt to think of the fields and the orchards as feeding us; but who makes the flax grow for the linen, and the wheat for the bread, and the wool on the sheep's back? Oh! I wish we could see through every grain-field, by every sheep-fold, under the trees of every orchard, the King's wagons! They drive up three times a day—morning, noon, and night. They bring furs from the Arctic, they bring fruits from the tropic, they bring bread from the temperate zone. The King looks out and he says, "There are twelve hundred millions of people to be fed and clothed. So many pounds of meat, so many barrels of flour, so many yards of cloth and linen and flannel, so many hats, so many socks, so many shoes;" enough for all, save that we who are greedy get more shoes than belong to us, and others go barefooted. None but a God could feed and clothe the world. None but a king's corn-crib could appease the world's famine. None but a king could tell how many wagons to send and how heavily to load them, and when they are to start. They are coming over the frozen ground to-day. Do you not hear their rumbling? They will stop at noon at your table. Oh! if for a little while they should cease. hunger would come into the nations, as to Utica when Hamilcar besieged it, and as in Jerusalem when Vespasian surrounded it; and the nations would be hollow-eyed, and fall upon each other in universal cannibalism; and skeleton would drop upon skeleton; and there would be no one to bury the dead; and the earth would be a field of bleached skeletons; and the birds of prey would fall dead, flock after flock, without any carcasses to devour; and the earth in silence would wheel around, one great black hearse! All life stopped because the King's wagons are stopped. Oh! thank God for bread—for bread!   *Talmage.*

8775. FOOD, Miraculous. A legend says that Abraham, in a time of famine, sent his servants to a friend in Egypt for corn. The friend refused it, saying it was only wanted to use in hospitalities or to be given to the poor. The chagrined servants, to conceal their ill-success, filled their sacks with fine white sand. Abraham learning this, was much troubled, and fell into a deep sleep. Sarah, not knowing the servants' failure, went to the sacks and found good flour, and baked bread. Abraham awaking asked her where she had obtained the flour.

"From your friend in Egypt," said she. "Nay," said the Patriarch, "it could have come from no other than my friend God Almighty."

8776. FOOD, Necessity for. Food is fuel. We require food frequently for just the same reason that a fire requires coals frequently, and a lamp oil—because we are burning away. The air that we breathe in our lungs contains oxygen, and this oxygen combines with or burns the muscles and other organs of our bodies, just as it does the coals in a fire. The heat produced in a man's body in the course of a day is considerable in quantity, though not very intense in quality. Taking the average, it is enough to raise five and a half gallons of water from freezing point to boiling point, and this is about the heat that would be given off during the burning of a pound of coals. All this heat comes from the slow wasting or burning of the substance of the body, so that it is evident that if we did not make up for this constant loss by eating food, our organs would soon be wasted away and consumed. A moment's thought will show how closely this agrees with well-known facts. Why does an animal become so thin during the slow and painful process of starvation? Because the slow fire in his body is not fed with the fuel of food.   *Anon.*

8777. FOOD, Providential. Rev. R. Moffat in his missionary explorations in South Africa, found his wants miraculously met. At one time, having been a night and a day without food, while pursuing his journey near evening, greatly exhausted and with no prospect of any relief, he saw in the distance a line of dust coming with the fleetness of an ostrich. It came within two hundred yards of him, and proved to be caused by a spring-bok chased by a wild dog. The dog overtook and killed his game at that place, and the missionary and his party received it with thankfulness, as food from God. It was a dog, this time, that brought his servants meat.

8778. FOOD, Signal for. A poor woman whose husband had been drafted into the Confederate army, was left in want with four little children dependent upon her. Among these was one child whose simple trust in a Heavenly Father's care seemed never to fail. As "the barrel of meal wasted," the mother's heart would fail; but the child noticed that the store was no sooner exhausted, than through the charity of kind friends, it was replenished again. One day he sat and thought over this until an idea seemed to flash through his mind, and he exclaimed, "Mother, I think God hears when we scrape the bottom of the barrel."

8779. FOOD, Spiritual. Matter is for mind. Souls grow as plants grow, by appropriating things ab extra to their use; and all things ab extra, even the most distant star that skirts the outer line of space, are for souls. But how is this appropriation to be made? How is this outward universe to promote the growth of our souls? Not without our willing and earnest effort. Put the acorn into a congenial soil, and external nature, by a necessity, will draw all the elements of vitality from its "milky veins," and elaborate them into majestic forests. The seed has no resisting force; it is passive in the plastic hand of nature. But it is not so with mind; it has a choice in the matter. No outward force, however mighty, can either injure or benefit, stunt or develop, the soul, without its consent. The outward universe, though organized for its service, may become its ruin. In many instances, instead of souls using it to their own growth and grandeur, it "uses them up;" deadens their sensibilities, benumbs their energies, moves them as mere wheels in its triumphal car. That men are, in numerous instances, "the creatures of circumstances," is a fact; that they are so by necessity is a falsehood. *Dr. Thomas.*

8780. FOOD, Thanks for. Gratitude for the common blessings of Providence is one of the most manifest duties of those who enjoy them, and is very properly expressed by giving thanks on their reception. Such a practice prevailed equally amongst heathen, Jews, and Christians. Athenæus says that in the famous regulation made by Amphictyon, King of Athens, with respect to the use of wine, he required that the name of Jupiter, the Sustainer, should be decently and reverently pronounced. The same author quotes Hermeias, an author extant in his time, who mentions a people in Egypt, inhabitants of the city of Naucrates, whose custom it was on certain occasions, after they had placed themselves in the usual posture of eating at table, to rise again and kneel; the priest then chanted a grace, according to a stated form among them, after which they joined in the meal. Clement of Alexandria also informs us that when the ancient Greeks met together to refresh themselves with the juice of the grape, they sang a piece of music which they called a scholion. Livy, too, speaks of it as a settled custom among the old Romans to offer sacrifice and prayer to the gods at their meals. Trigantius, a Jesuit, in his narrative of the expedition of the Jesuit missionaries into China, says of the Chinese, that "before they place themselves for partaking of an entertainment, the person who makes it sets a vessel, either of gold, or silver, or marble, or some such valuable material in a charger, full of wine, which he holds with both his hands, and then makes a low bow to the person of chief quality or character at the table. Then from the hall or dining-room he goes into the porch or entry, where he again makes a very low bow, and, turning his face to the south, pours out this wine upon the ground as a thankful oblation to the Lord of heaven. After thus repeating his reverential observance, he returns into the hall." As to the sentiments and behavior of the Jews on this point, Josephus, detailing the customs of the Essenes, says that the priest begs a blessing before they presume to take any nourishment: and it is looked upon as a great sin to take or taste before. And when the meal is over, the priest prays again, and the company with him bless and praise God as their preserver, and the donor of their life and nourishment. From the Hebrew ritual it would appear that the Jews had their psalms of thanksgiving, not only after eating their passover, but on a variety of other occasions, at and after meals, and even between their several courses and dishes; as when the best of their wine was brought upon the table, or the fruit of the garden. To this day the Jews are said to have their *zemiroth*, verses or songs of thanksgiving. The continuance of the custom among the Christians is founded in the high example of our Saviour himself. The primitive converts appear to have universally observed it. We read that St. Paul, "when he had spoken, took bread, and gave thanks to God in the presence of them all; and when he had broken it, began to eat" (Acts 27: 35). In the days immediately following the Apostles, we find abundant traces of this practice in the writings of the Fathers, particularly in the Clementine Constitution, in Chrysostom, and in Origen.

Anon.

8781. FOOL, An Elect. Pyoterius, a hermit of the Nile, was directed by an angel, "Go to the convent at Tabenna, and there shalt thou find an elect vessel full of the grace of God, and thou shalt know her by the crown that shines above her head." He tarried not till he reached the convent, and had the sisters pass in order before him. As each passed, he said, "The Lord hath not chosen thee." Then he asked, "Are there yet any more?" The abbess replied, "All are here save one, a half-witted creature, who is the kitchen drudge." "Bring her to me," said the hermit. When she came in, she was dressed in soiled garments, and had an old cloth on her head, but the hermit saw there the shining crown, and, falling at her feet, besought her blessing. They were all astonished. She had been the butt of all. The sisters in faultless habits swept by her proudly, or stopped only to pull her nose or slap her face. She bore her lot cheerfully, and was now indicated as the Lord's chosen. This is the legend of St. Isidora, illustrating how "fools shall not err."

8782. FOOLS: Angry with. Were I to be angry at men being fools, I could here find ample room for declamation; but, alas! I have been a fool myself; and why should I be angry with them for being something so natural to every child of humanity? *Goldsmith.*

8783. FOOLS: Brevities. People have no right to make fools of themselves, unless they have no relations to blush for them.—*Haliburton.*
——Of all thieves fools are the worst; they rob you of time and temper. *Goethe.*

8784. FOOTSTEPS, Tracing. The Arab who has applied himself diligently to this study, for it is only to be acquired by long practice, can generally ascertain, from inspecting the impression: 1. Whether the footsteps belong to his own or to some neighboring tribe, and consequently whether friend or foe has passed; 2. He knows, from the slightness or depth of the impression, whether the man who made it carried a load or not; 3. From the strength or faintness of the trace, whether he passed on the same day or one or two days before; and 4. From a certain regularity of intervals between the steps, a Bedouin judges whether the man is fatigued or not, and hence he can calculate the chance of overtaking him. This faculty of distinguishing footsteps on the ground extends to beasts (horses and camels) as well as men, and, in the exercise of it, the same observations will lead to the same results. *Robinson.*

8785. FOP: Brevities. A fop, who admires his person in a glass, soon enters into a resolution of making his fortune by it, not questioning but every woman that falls in his way will do him as much justice as himself.—*Hughes.* ——Nature has sometimes made a fool; but a coxcomb is always of a man's own making.— *Addison.*——Foppery is never cured; it is the bad stamina of the mind, which, like those of the body, are never rectified; once a coxcomb, and always a coxcomb. *Johnson.*

8786. FORBEARANCE, Example of. Of Mr. John Henderson it is observed, that the oldest of his friends never beheld him otherwise than calm and collected. It was a state of mind he retained under all circumstances. During his residence at Oxford, a student of the neighboring college, proud of his logical acquirements, was solicitous of a private disputation with the renowned Henderson. Some mutual friends introduced him, and having chosen his subject, they conversed for some time with equal candor and moderation; but Henderson's antagonist, perceiving his confutation inevitable (forgetting the character of a gentleman, and with a resentment engendered by his former arrogance), threw a full glass of wine in his face. Henderson, without altering his features, or changing his position, gently wiped his face, and then coolly replied, "This, sir, is a digression; now for the argument." *Buck.*

8787. FORBEARANCE, Love of. The apostle to the Indians, Rev. John Elliot, was characterized by his great love of peace. His advice to one in difficulty was, "Brother, compass them; learn the meaning of those three little words—bear, forbear, and forgive."

8788. FORBEARANCE, Pagan. The Emperor Antoninus said, "It becomes a man to love even those that offend him." Epictetus said, "A man hurts himself by injuring me: what, then, shall I therefore hurt myself by injuring him?" Seneca observed, "In benefits, it is a disgrace to be outdone; in injuries, to get the better."

8789. FOREBODING, Mistaken. John Condor was born in Cambridgeshire, England, June 3, 1714. His grandfather, Richard Condor, kissed him, and, with tears in his eyes, said, "Who knows what sad days these little eyes are likely to see?" Things wore at that time a threatening aspect, relative to Dissenters. Dr. Condor remarked upon mentioning the circumstance, "These eyes have, for more than sixty years seen nothing but goodness and mercy follow me and the churches of Christ, even to this day." Many a grim foreboding has heralded the greatest blessings.

8790. FOREBODING, Natural. We expect that nature will execute the chastisements of the spiritual world. Hence all nature becomes to the imagination leagued against the transgressor. The stars in their courses fight against Sisera. The wall of Siloam falls on guilty men. The sea will not carry the criminal, nor the plank bear him. The viper stings—everything is a minister of wrath. On this conviction nations constructed their trial by ordeal. The guilty man's sword would fail in the duel; and the foot would strike and be burnt by the hot ploughshare. Some idea of this sort lurks in all our minds. We picture to ourselves the spectres of the past haunting the nightly bed of the tyrant. We take for granted there is an avenger making life miserable.
F. W. Robertson.

8791. FORESIGHT, Divine. It has been adduced as a striking illustration of the Divine foresight, that the season of the birth of the young of certain animals should be adjusted to the season of the year, and to the period of the food most conducive to its well-being; the preparation for the birth of the animal, and the preparation for the birth of its food (say the larvæ of insects), dating from very different points of time. *McCosh.*

8792. FORGETFULNESS, A Drunkard's. John Clerk of Edinburgh, had been dipping into the convivial bowl, and had stayed out until early in the morning. Trying to go home he lost his way. Seeing some one coming towards him, he stopped the person with the question—"Do ye ken where John Clerk bides?" "I'm thinking," was the reply, "ye're Mr. John Clerk yoursel'." "Ay, ay!" answered he, "I ken that vary weel, my man; I ken I'm John Clerk, but I dinna ken where I live."

8793. FORGETFULNESS, Question of. A preacher in Germany was one day assailed by some opponents, and one person remarked that the Bible was full of fables. The objector referred to Paul having forgotten his mantle. The preacher said, "That is a passage quite suitable for me, perhaps also for you. I am very forgetful. I see here that the great apostle could forget, and this comforts me, and admonishes me also, that I should endeavor to make good what I forget. I thought once like you, and forgot the one thing needful; but I now endeavor not to forget the goodness of God. Have you, brother, forgotten this?"

8794. FORGIVENESS, Bravery of. The brave only know how to forgive; it is the most refined and generous pitch of virtue human nature can arrive at. Cowards have done good and kind actions; cowards have even fought, nay, sometimes conquered; but a coward never forgave—it is not in his nature. The power of doing it flows only from a strength and greatness of soul conscious of its own force and security, and above all the little temptations of resenting every fruitless attempt to interrupt its happiness. *Sterne.*

8795. FORGIVENESS, Christ-like. Sir Thomas More, Lord Chancellor of England, after having been tried at Westminster and condemned to death without any just cause, said to his judges, "As St. Paul held the clothes of those who stoned Stephen to death, and as they are both now saints in heaven, and shall continue there friends for ever; so I verily trust, and shall, therefore, most heartily pray, that though your lordships have now here on earth been judges to my condemnation, we may nevertheless hereafter cheerfully meet in heaven in everlasting salvation."

8796. FORGIVENESS, Conditioned. A Sunday-school teacher improving upon the day's lesson on the subject of forgiveness, asked a boy whether, in view of what he had been studying, he could forgive those who had insulted or struck him. "Ye-e-s, sir," replied the lad slowly, "I guess I could;" but he added in a much more rapid manner, "I could if he were bigger than I am."

8797. FORGIVENESS, Difficult. It is more easy to forgive the weak who have injured us, than the powerful whom we have injured. That conduct will be continued by our fears which commenced in our resentment. He that has gone so far as to cut the claws of the lion, will not feel himself quite secure until he has also drawn his teeth. *Colton.*

8798. FORGIVENESS, Divine. An English criminal, notorious for his crimes, was sentenced to be executed. While in prison he became thoroughly convicted of the enormity of his sins and truly penitent. He found pardon, and his heart was so filled with the love of God, that he cried out continually, "He is a great forgiver! He is a great forgiver."

8799. FORGIVENESS, Duty of. The duty of Christian forgiveness does not require you, nor are you allowed, to look on injustice, or any other fault, with indifference, as if it were nothing wrong at all, merely because it is you that have been wronged. But even where we cannot but censure, in a moral point of view, the conduct of those who have injured us, we should remember that such treatment as may be very fitting for them to receive may be very unfitting for us to give. To cherish, or to gratify, haughty resentment, is a departure from the pattern left us by him who "endured such contradiction of sinners against himself," not to be justified by any offence that can be committed against us. And it is this recollection of him who, faultless himself, designed to leave us an example of meekness and long-suffering, that is the true principle and motive of Christian forgiveness. We shall best fortify our patience under injuries by remembering how much we ourselves have to be forgiven, and that it was "while we were yet sinners, Christ died for us." Let the Christian therefore accustom himself to say of any one who has greatly wronged him, "That man owes me an hundred pence." *Whately.*

8800. FORGIVENESS, Freeness of. The first thing I remember is the death of my own father; I was four years of age. My mother was soon taken sick, and my eldest brother ran away from home about the same time. Troubles never come singly. Day after day mother would send us one and a half miles to the post office for letters from my runaway brother. She would often say: "Oh, could I hear that he was dead, it would be such a relief to me." It seemed as if she loved him more than the rest of us. I remember hearing her pray past midnight, "Oh God, bring back my boy. Bring him back, wherever he is." She used to leave a vacant chair at the table for him. I can remember how her hair turned gray. Before I was a Christian I used to pray, "Send back that boy." One day a stranger was seen coming up the hill. He came and stood on the porch outside the window, with arms folded, looking at mother. She said, "Oh, my son, is it possible you have come home? Come in." "No, mother," he said, "not until you forgive me." She rushed to his arms and forgave him! But my friends, this forgiveness is nothing to the sin that your heavenly Father wants you to confess to him. Oh, may you be wise to come to him now while God is willing. *Moody.*

8801. FORGIVENESS, God-like. A high official in England once went to Sir Eardley Wilmot in great wrath, and narrated the story of a great insult which he had received. He closed by asking him if he did not think it would be manly to resent it? "Yes," said the judge, "it will be manly to resent it; but it will be God-like to forgive it." The effect was to change the purpose and cool the anger of the insulted man.

8802. FORGIVENESS, God's. Let me go and saw off a branch from one of the trees that is now budding in my garden, and all summer long there will be an ugly scar where the gash has been made; but by next autumn it will be perfectly covered over by the growing; and by the following autumn it will be hidden out of sight; and in four or five years there will be but a slight scar to show where it has been; and in ten or twenty years you would never suspect that there had been an amputation. Now trees know how to overgrow their injuries and hide them; and love does not wait so long as trees do. It knows how to throw out all divine and beneficent juices, as it were, and hide from sight the wrongs done. And God says he forgives in the same way. He will never again make mention, as he declares in Ezekiel to his people, of their sins. He will never taunt them with them. *Beecher.*

8803. FORGIVENESS, Hope of. The young monk, Martin Luther, lay in his cell at Erfurt, stricken with severe sickness, and his soul riven with a deep sense of personal guilt. There he had prayed and fasted, and, like many other votaries of the Romish faith, had inflicted painful penances upon himself, but all in vain: a wound had been made which nothing but the grace of God could cure. His concern about his state had added strength to the fever that was wasting his frame, and brought his life to the verge of the grave. A venerable inmate of the monastery entered his cell. The old monk manifested the deepest sympathy for the poor sufferer, and attempted his best to com fort him. He slowly and gravely repeated the words of the "Apostles' Creed," "I believe in the forgiveness of sins." And, like cold water to a thirsty soul, or the first streak of the dawn to the lost and benighted wayfarer, the words of the old man brought light to the eyes and sent a thrill of joy to the heart of the seeker after peace and righteousness. The forgiveness of sins! The words stuck to him. And although he could not yet see how pardon was to be obtained, or on what ground it could be offered, yet the mere thought of its possibility filled him with hope and comfort and encouragement. "There is forgiveness with God, then," he said to himself. "There is a way of salvation, then. There is a door of hope. No matter how easy or how difficult to enter this gate. No matter how long or how short a time I take to find it. No matter how many or how few are seeking admission besides myself. It is enough for me to know that there is a chance, a possibility of obtaining salvation, and that my sins, which are many, may be forgiven."

8804. FORGIVENESS, Law of. A boy who had done a wrong, and confessed it, was sentenced by his father to live for three days upon bread and water as a punishment. For two days the plate of dry bread and cup of cold water was set before him, instead of his usual fare. On the morning of the third day, his father asked him how he liked his fare? The child answered, "I can eat it very well, papa, but I don't much like it;" and, after standing in silence for a few minutes, looked up, and said, "Can't you forgive me, papa?" "No, sir, I cannot; my word has passed, and you must take your three days, as I told you." The question was repeated, "But can't you really forgive me, papa?" "No," was the answer, "I cannot break my word." The boy said, "Then, papa, how could you say the Lord's Prayer this morning?" The father was struck with the child's reproof, ordered the bread and water to be removed, and said, with evident pleasure, "My boy, you have preached me a better sermon than ever I preached in my life."

8805. FORGIVENESS, Nobility of. Hath any wronged thee? Be bravely revenged; slight it, and the work is begun; forgive it, and it is finished. He is below himself that is not above an injury. *Quarles.*

8806. FORGIVENESS, Power for. Two wheels protrude from a factory, and are seen in motion on the outer wall by every passenger. They move into each other. The upper wheel is large, the under small. From without and at a distance you cannot tell whether the upper is impelling the under, or the under moving the upper. This question, however, might be settled by an inspection of the interior. By such an inspection it would be found that the larger and higher wheel communicates motion to the lower and smaller. If the upper wheel, which communicates the motion, should stand still, so also would the lower; but more than this: if the lower wheel, which receives the motion, should by some impediment be stopped,

the upper wheel would also stand still. It is in some such way that God's goodness in forgiving freely for Christ's sake our sins impels us to forgive from the heart those that have trespassed against us. The power is all from above; yet, though we by our goodness do not set the beneficent machinery in motion, we may see our badness cause it all to stand still. *Arnot.*

8807. FORGIVENESS, Profession of. "I asked a little gentleman at St. Just," says Wesley, "what objection there was to Edward Greenfield, a pious tinner, on whom the constables had seized." He said, "Why the man is well enough in other things, but his impudence the gentleman cannot bear. Why, sir, he says his sins are forgiven!"

8808. FORGIVENESS, Refusal of. There dwelt in Antioch, in the third century, a priest named Sapricius and a layman named Nicephorus, between whom a strong friendship existed. At length they became estranged, and would not speak to each other. After a time Nicephorus became convicted of the great sin of hatred, and sought reconciliation in various ways, without success. At last Nicephorus rushed into his presence, and with confession and tears begged pardon for Christ's sake. Sapricius, hardening his heart against his brother, refused to be reconciled. The Valerian persecution then breaking out, Sapricius was arrested, bore an unflinching testimony to Christ under the most exhausting tortures, and received joyfully his sentence that he should be beheaded for being a Christian. On his way to execution, Nicephorus cast himself before him, saying, "Martyr of Jesus Christ, forgive me my offense." He received no answer. This he repeated at the place of execution, and pleaded in view of his glorious confession and approaching martyrdom. The soldiers called him a fool for seeking pardon of a man about to be executed. Sapricius could not be moved to forgiveness. He was ordered to kneel that his head might be cut off. "Stop!" he cried, "do not put me to death; I will do what you desire; I am ready to make the sacrifice." Nicephorus, dismayed at his apostasy, cried, "Brother, what are you doing? Renounce not Jesus Christ. Forfeit not the crown you have already won by tortures and sufferings." But the spirit which enables men to endure martyrdom was withdrawn from him, because he would not forgive his brother, and he basely denied his Lord and Master. Then Nicephorus, filled with agony at Sapricius' fall, said to the executioners, "I am a Christian and believe in Jesus Christ, whom this wretch has renounced; behold me here ready to die in his stead." All were astonished. The officers knew not what to do, but reporting the case to the governor received the order, "If this man persists in refusing to sacrifice to the immortal gods, let him die by the sword." His refusal was not to be overcome, and he was executed and received the bright crown of martyrdom.

8809. FORGIVENESS Required. **Rev. Mr. Taylor** arranged a gathering of all those who had been brought to the knowledge of Christ by the means of his ministry. Service was held in the church, which was filled by hundreds of the New Zealanders, and after the service was over the administration of the Lord's Supper began. The first rail was filled, when Mr. Taylor saw a man kneeling at one end, suddenly get up and walk down the whole length of the church and take his seat; and before he could recover from his surprise, the man returned and knelt at the same spot and received the communion. Mr. Taylor was so struck with the man's manner that he afterward questioned him reproachfully why he had thus disturbed the congregation, when he received for an answer: "Mr. Taylor, when I went up to the table, I did not know by whom I should kneel; and when I found myself kneeling side by side with a man who, a few years ago, murdered my father, and drank his blood, and whom I swore that I would murder the first moment that I set eyes upon him, you may imagine what I felt. It overpowered me; I could not stand it; and I got up and walked back to my seat, and as I did so I saw that upper room and the supper, and I thought I heard a voice say, 'By this shall all men know that ye are my disciples, if ye have love one to another.' That did not overcome me. I sat down in my seat, and at once I thought I saw another sight—I thought I saw a cross and a man nailed upon it, and I heard him say, 'Father, forgive them, for they know not what they do;' and so I went back."

Missionary Advocate.

8810. FORGIVENESS, Seeking. A Christian said recently, "One day last week, as I had just seated myself at dinner, I was told that a boy outside on horseback wished to see me. I went out and found it was a neighbor's boy. I invited him in, but he declined, saying that he had something weighing very heavily upon his mind, and that he could not rest until he told it to me. 'I have,' said the boy, with tears in his eyes, 'trespassed a number of times on your property, stolen your fruit, etc., and I could not rest until I had asked your forgiveness.' I told him taking my fruit was no injury to me; that if God had forgiven his sins, it was all right with me. He rode off, thanking me, and seemed much relieved. Now, that boy displayed a very different spirit from a certain brother with whom I had a conversation the other day. I told him he should be willing to ask forgiveness of a friend whom he had offended, and that he should forgive his brother. 'O no! said he, 'I can't do that; it lies too deep in my heart.' And yet that man desires God and the Church to forgive him. But Jesus says, 'If ye forgive not men their trespasses, neither will your heavenly Father forgive your trespasses.'"

8811. FORGIVENESS a Settlement. A minister to whom one of his parishioners told his tale of sorrow, reproved him thus: "Deacon, I remember your son stoutly rebelled against your authority some time ago, but afterward felt sorry and repented of his sin, and humbly asked your forgiveness. Did you forgive him?' "Of course I did." "What did you forgive him for?" "Because I could not help it, when I saw how sorry he was." "And does he still ask forgiveness?" "No—no! Nothing is said about it. It is all settled forever." "Now, do you believe that you can be better to your son than God is to you? He pardons like a God"

8812. FORGIVENESS Sought. An old legend represents on the one hand the arrival before the throne of God of the penitent souls whom his pity admits into heaven; on the other, Satan, who says, "These souls have offended against thee a thousand times—I only once." "Hast thou ever asked forgiveness?" replies the eternal.

8813. FORGOTTEN, Fear of Being. Are not all things born to be forgotten? In truth it was a sore vexation to me when I saw, as the wise man saw of old, that whatever I could hope to perform must necessarily be of very temporary duration; and if so, why do it? Let me see! What have I done already? I have learned Welsh, and have translated the songs of Ab Gwilym; I have also rendered the old book of Danish ballads into English metre. Good! Have I done enough to secure myself a reputation of a thousand years? Well, but what's a thousand years after all, or twice a thousand years? Woe is me! I may just as well sit still. *Barrow.*

8814. FORMALISM, Avoid. Do not the "work of God negligently" (Jer. 48, 10.), let not thy heart be upon the world, when thy hand is lifted up in prayer; and be sure to prefer an action of religion in its place and proper season before all worldly pleasure, letting secular things, that may be dispensed with in themselves, in these circumstances wait upon the other; not like the patriarch who ran from the altar in St. Sophia to his stables in all his pontificals, and in the midst of his office, to see a colt newly fallen from his beloved and much valued mare Phorbante. More prudent and severe was that of Sir Thomas More, who being sent for by the king when he was at his prayers in public, returned answer he would attend him when he had first performed his service to the King of kings. And it did honor to Rusticus, that when letters from Cæsar were given him, he refused to open them till the philosopher had done his lecture. In honoring God and doing his work, put forth all thy strength; for of that time only thou mayest be most confident that it is gained which is prudently and zealously spent in God's service. *Jeremy Taylor.*

8815. FORMALISM, Churchly. Posture and imposture, flections and genuflections, bowing to right and curtsying to the left, and an immense amount of man-millinery. *Sydney Smith.*

8816. FORMALISM, Delusion of. If this hypocrisy, this resting in outward performances were so odious to God under the law, a religion full of shadows and ceremonies, certainly it will be much more odious to do so under the gospel, a religion of much more simplicity

and exacting so much the greater sincerity of the heart, even because it disburdens the outward man of the performance of legal rights and observances. And therefore, if we now under the gospel shall think to delude God Almighty, as Michael did Saul, with an idol handsomely dressed instead of the true David, we shall one day find that we have not mocked God, but ourselves; and that our portion among hypocrites shall be greater than theirs.
Chillingworth.

8817. FORMALISM, Fatal Delusion of. An English lady, a strong partisan of the Church of England, suddenly sickened, and with eternity before her, said to a clergyman who visited her: "It is kind of you to come to me, but it is in vain. It is too late to do anything for me now. Mine has been a Christless Christianity, and I must abide by the consequences. I have been a good church woman, and have passed for a good Christian. I have been diligent in my attendance at church, and have cared for an excellent ministry. I have never willingly passed by an opportunity of partaking of the holy communion. I have given largely to religious and charitable causes. I have admired Christianity, and have tried to bring its precepts into my practice. But I have never cared to know a living Saviour, to make a personal acquaintance with him, nor to know from him that my sins are forgiven. It is too late to seek it now. I have had the form of godliness without the power of it. I am lost—lost forever." She is one of thousands of staunch defenders and formal adherents of the church, but unsaved.

8818. FORMALIST, The Inconsistent. There are some if you would see their goodness, and be acquainted with their godliness, you must hit the right time, or else you will find none, like some flowers that are seen but some months in the year. This may be in the morning: you may take the hypocrite on his knees in a saint's posture; but when that fit is over, you shall see little of God in all its course, till night brings him again, of course, to the like duty. The watch is naught that goes only at first winding up, and stands all the day after; and so is that heart, that desires not always to keep in spiritual motion. *Anon.*

8819. FORMALISTS Enemies to Christ. I find no such enemies to the cross of Christ as those who keep the form of religion, and are orthodox in their notions, but at the same time are ignorant of an experimental acquaintance with Jesus. *Whitefield.*

8820. FORMS, Argument for. When we simulate the natural language of any feeling, we are apt to be affected by it almost, if not quite, to the same extent as when we contemplate it in another. If we strut along, brandishing a weapon, we feel somewhat like a hero for the moment. All unequivocally great actors have, while upon the stage, felt the emotions which they represented, and even for some time before and after. It is, for example, related of Mrs. Siddons, that, from the moment of her going into her carriage to proceed to the the-

atre, where she had to act a part, till her return home afterwards, she felt entirely as the person whom she was to represent, and could not without pain admit any other feeling into her mind. The celebrated French tragedian, Barron, who was naturally timid, always felt as a hero for several days after he had performed any of the principal characters of Corneille's plays. The semblance has been, to use a homely but expressive phrase, a shoeing-horn to the reality; and something has been created, and that a good something, out of nothing. The forms so universally used in worship are to be defended on the same grounds. Religious feeling has its natural language; submission is expressed by kneeling; solemnity by a composure of the countenance; imploration by the folding or clasping of the hands; the nondependence on self, which is one of the first dictates of religion, finds a proper external expression in a lowly attitude and a downcast look. When these expressions of feelings are simulated, the actual feeling itself, if it be not present already, is apt to be induced, and the object is, of course, far better gained than it would be if looks and gestures, expressive of indifference or of the opposite feelings, were maintained. *F. F. Trench.*

8821. FORMS, Value of. They are valuable in their own place, and for their own purposes; frames, as they are, to set the picture in; caskets for truth's jewels; dead poles, no doubt, yet useful to support living plants, and very beautiful when the bare stem is festooned with green leaves, and crowned with a head of flowers.
Dr. Guthrie.

8822. FORMULAS, Realities of. Formulas, too, as we call them, have a reality in human life. They are real as the very skin and muscular tissue of a man's life, and a most blessed, indispensable thing, so long as they have vitality withal, and are a living skin and tissue to him! No man, or man's life, can go abroad and do business in the world without skin and tissues. No; first of all, these have to fashion themselves, as indeed they spontaneously and inevitably do. Foam itself—and this is worth thinking of—can harden into oyster shell: all living objects do by necessity form to themselves a skin. *Carlyle.*

8823. FORMULAS, Utility of. What we call formulas are not in their origin bad; they are indispensably good. Formula is method, habitude, found wherever man is found. Formulas fashion themselves as paths do, as beaten highways, leading towards some sacred or high object, whither many men are bent. Consider it. One man, full of heartfelt, earnest impulse, finds out a way of doing somewhat, were it of uttering his soul's reverence for the Highest, were it but of fitly saluting his fellow-man. An inventor was needed to do that—a poet; he has articulated the dim struggling thought that dwelt in his own and many hearts. This is his way of doing that; these are his footsteps, the beginning of "a path." And now see: the second man travels naturally in the footsteps of his foregoer: it is the easiest

method. In the footsteps of his foregoer; yet with improvements, changes, where such seem good; at all events with enlargements, the path ever widening itself as more travel it, till at last there is a broad highway, whereon the whole world may travel and drive. Formulas all begin by being full of substance; you may call them the skin, the articulation into shape, into limbs and skin, of a substance that is already there; they had not been there otherwise. Idols, as we said, are not idolatrous till they become doubtful, empty for the worshiper's heart. Much as we talk against formulas, I hope no one of us is ignorant withal of the high significance of true formulas; that they were, and will ever be, the indispensablest furniture of our habitation in this world.
Carlyle.

8824. FORTITUDE, Christian. Peter Balsam was apprehended in the persecution of Maximus. Being brought before Severus, the governor, he was asked his name. Peter answered, " Balsam is the name of my family; but I received that of Peter in baptism." "Of what family, and of what country are you?" "I am a Christian." "What is your employ?" "What employ can I have more honorable, or what better thing can I do in the world, than to live a Christian." "Do you know the imperial edicts?" "I know the laws of God, the sovereign of the universe." "You shall quickly know that there is an edict of the most clement emperors, commanding all to sacrifice to the gods or be put to death." Peter answered, "You will also know one day that there is a law of the eternal King, proclaiming that every one shall perish who offers sacrifice to devils; which you do counsel me to obey, and which do you think should be my option: to die by your sword, or to be condemned to everlasting misery by the sentence of the great King and true God?" Severus said, "Seeing you ask my advice, it is then that you obey the edict, and sacrifice to the gods." "I can never be prevailed upon to sacrifice to gods of wood and stone, as those are which you adore." "I would have you know, that it is in my power to revenge these affronts by your death." "I had no intention to affront you. I only expressed what is written in the divine law," "Have compassion on yourself, and sacrifice." "If I am truly compassionate to myself, I ought not to sacrifice." "My desire is to use lenity; therefore, still do allow you time to consider with yourself, that you may save your life." "This delay will be to no purpose, for I shall not alter my mind; do now what you will be obliged to do soon, and complete the work which the devil, your father, has begun; for I will never do what Jesus Christ forbids me." Then Severus ordered him to be tortured upon the rack. " What say ye now, Peter," he cried, "do you begin to know what the rack is? are you yet willing to sacrifice?" He answered, "Tear me with iron hooks, and talk not of sacrificing to your devils; I have already told you that I will sacrifice to that God alone for whom I suffer." At this the gover-

nor commanded his tortures to be redoubled. The martyr sang aloud with great joy, "One thing I have desired of the Lord; this will I seek after: that I may dwell in the house of the Lord all the days of my life." The executioners became weary and others were ordered to take their place. The martyr's blood ran down in streams, and the pitying crowd cried out, "Obey the emperors; sacrifice and rescue yourself from these torments." "Do you call these torments?" replied Peter; "I, for my part, feel no pain; but this I know, that if I am not faithful to my God, I must expect real pains, such as cannot be conceived." Severus urged, "Sacrifice, Peter Balsam! or you will repent it." "Neither will I sacrifice nor shall I repent it." "I am just ready to pronounce sentence." Peter answered, "It is what I most earnestly desire." Then the governor thus sentenced him, "It is our order, that Peter Balsam, for having refused to obey the edicts of the invincible emperors, and having condemned our commands, after obstinately defending the law of a man crucified, be himself nailed to a cross." Thus the saint was crucified like his Master, A. D. 311.

8825. FORTITUDE, Demand for. None can aspire to act greatly, but those who are of force greatly to suffer. They who make the arrangements in the first run of misadventure, and in a temper of mind the common fruit of disappointment and dismay, put a seal on their calamities. To their power they take a security against any favors which they might hope from the usual inconstancy of fortune.   *Burke.*

8826. FORTITUDE, Emblem of. There is a mother-idea in each particular kind of tree, which, if well marked, is probably embodied in the poetry of every language. Take the oak, for instance, and we always find it standing as a type of strength and endurance. I wonder if you ever thought of the single mark of supremacy which distinguishes this tree from all our other forest trees? All the rest of them shirk the work of resisting gravity; the oak alone defies it. It chooses the horizontal direction for its limbs, so that their whole weight may tell,—and then stretches them out fifty or sixty feet, so that the strain may be mighty enough to be worth resisting. You will find that, in passing from the extreme downward droop of the branches of the weeping willow to the extreme upward inclination of those of the poplar, they sweep nearly half a circle. At 90° the oak stops short; to slant upward another degree would mark infirmity of purpose; to bend downwards, weakness of organization. The American elm betrays something of both, yet sometimes, as we shall see, puts on a certain resemblance to its sturdier neighbor.
Holmes.

8827. FORTUNE, Best. A Greek maiden, being asked what fortune she would bring her husband, replied, "I will bring him what gold cannot purchase, a heart unspotted, and virtue without a stain; the inheritance from parents who had these, and nothing else to leave me."
Mrs. Balfour.

8828. FORTUNE: Brevities. Good fortune that comes seldom, comes more welcome.—*Dryden.*——Receive the gifts of fortune without pride, and part with them without reluctance.—*Antoninus.*——Let Fortune do her worst, whatever she makes us lose, as long as she never makes us lose our honesty and our independence.—*Pope.*——Fortune gives too much to many, but to none enough.—*Martial.*——The wheel of fortune turns incessantly round, and who can say within himself, I shall to-day be uppermost!—*Confucius.*——We are sure to get the better of fortune, if we do but grapple with her.—*Seneca.*——There is some help for all the defects of fortune, for if a man cannot attain to the length of his wishes, he may have his remedy by cutting of them shorter.—*Cowley.*——The power of fortune is confessed only by the miserable; the happy impute all their success to prudence or merit.—*Swift.*——Fortune's wings are made of Time's feathers, which stay not whilst one may measure them. *Lilly.*

8829. FORTUNE, Defiance of. We ought likewise with an invincible spirit, and a bold security as regards futurity, to answer Fortune in those words which Socrates retorted upon his judges, "Anytus and Meletus may kill, but they cannot hurt me." So she can afflict me with disease, can spoil me of my riches, disgrace me with my prince, and bring me under a popular odium; but she cannot make a good man wicked, or the brave man a mean and degenerate coward; she cannot cast envy upon a generous temper, or destroy any of those habits of the mind which are useful to us in the conduct of our lives. *Plutarch.*

8830. FORTUNE, Encountering. Vice asks Fortune how she will make a man unhappy. "Fortune, dost thou threaten poverty? Metrocles laughs at thee, who, sleeping in the winter amongst the sheep, and in the summer in the porches of the temples, challenging the kings of the Persians, that wintered in Babylon and passed the summer in Media, to vie with him for happiness. Dost thou bring on servitude, bonds, and the being sold for a slave? Diogenes contemns thee, who being exposed to sale by pirates, cried out, 'Who will buy a master?' Dost thou brew a cup of poison? Didst thou not offer such a one to Socrates? And yet he mildly and meekly, without trembling or changing either color or countenance, drank it briskly up; whilst those who survived esteemed him happy." *Plutarch.*

8831. FORTUNE, Example of. Appius, a Roman, was proscribed by the triumvirate. Becoming aware of the fact, he divided his wealth among his servants, and with them set sail for Sicily. But a fearful storm arose, and his servants placed him in a small boat, assuring him he would be safer. In the meantime they sailed away with the ship and all his riches. The ship in which they sailed was cast away, and they lost all, while the winds wafted the little boat in safety to the desired haven.

8832. FORTUNE, Favorite of. Fortune always seemed to favor Timotheus, an Athenian general, and in every war he had an easy and assured victory. His rivals, envying his prosperity, painted Fortune casting cities and towns in his lap as he lay sleeping. Timotheus, seeing this emblem, said, "If I take cities while I sleep, what think you I shall do when I am awake?"

8833. FORTUNE, Not Blind. The Europeans are themselves blind who describe Fortune without sight. No first-rate beauty ever had finer eyes, or saw more clearly: they who have no other trade but seeking their fortune need never hope to find her; coquet-like, she flies from her close pursuers, and at last fixes on the plodding mechanic, who stays at home and minds his business. I am amazed how men can call her blind, when by the company she keeps she seems so very discerning. Wherever you see a gaming-table, be very sure Fortune is not there; when you see a man whose pocket-holes are laced with gold, be satisfied Fortune is not there; wherever you see a beautiful woman good-natured and obliging, be convinced Fortune is never there. In short, she is ever seen accompanying industry, and as often trundling a wheel-barrow as lolling in a coach-and-six. *Goldsmith.*

8834. FORTUNE, Symbols of. Alexander, who carved out his fortune with the sword, caused that emblem to be painted upon a table within the compass of a wheel. He showed thereby that what he had won by the sword was liable to be turned from him by the wheel of fortune. There is nothing more certain under the sun than the law of change. The victor of to-day will be conquered to-morrow, the rich will be poor, and the reverse. It requires all the fullness of grace, and all the power of philosophy, to stand like Daniel, steadfast through all to "the end of the days."

8835. FORTUNE, Too Late. Among the Sierra Nevada Mountains, I was walking with some of the passengers to relieve the overladen stage, and one of them gave me his history. He said, "With my wife I came to California twenty years ago. We suffered every hardship. I went to the mines, but had no luck. I afterward worked at a trade, but had no luck. Then I went to farming, but had no luck. We suffered almost starvation. Everything seemed to go against us. While we were in complete poverty, my wife died. After her death, I went again to the mines. I struck a vein of gold which yielded me forty thousand dollars. I am now on my way to San Francisco to transfer the mine, for which I am to receive one hundred thousand dollars." "Then," said I, "you are worth one hundred and forty thousand dollars." He said, "Yes; but it comes too late. My wife is gone. The money is nothing to me now." *Talmage.*

8836. FOUNDATION, Importance of the. The people of the goodly city of St. Louis look forward to the time when the ponderous engine, followed by its heavily freighted train, shall roll on the iron track that is to span their great river. To sustain the burden on their projected bridge, they are constructing founda tions of solid masonry, eighty feet in length and sixty feet in breadth, which are to be sunk seventy feet below the bed of the river, even down to the underlying rock formation, so useless do they deem it to raise supports for the great pressure of commerce on the basis of yielding water or of treacherous sand. Beloved, the immense burden which must come rolling on upon the next generation of living men demands of us that we build not slightly. Compute, if you can, the weight of interests with which the next hundred years will be freighted, and learn from your computation what moral masonry will be adequate to support that weight. Beneath all that man can build must lie the divine, the immovable Rock, which is the Son of God and the Saviour of men, and we, as builders, must go down to the rock and start from it with the foundations we lay. To do this, we must penetrate the accumulated débris of ages. It is said that an English builder, a few years since, determined to build a house within the walls of the old Jerusalem, and having resolved to lay its foundation on the rock of David's time, he found it necessary to excavate through fifty feet of accumulated rubbish. These Christian centuries have been prolific in religious rubbish, and whoever now will build with the Son of David must dig down through superstition, and priestcraft, and tradition, and prejudiced interpretations, until he find the "Word of the living God." *Dr. Hodge.*

8837. FOUNDATION, Sandy. A sudden but violent storm arose, and loud thunder echoed through the mountains. "The brow of the hill whereon their city (Nazareth) was built, was every moment gleaming as the lightning flashed. The rain fell in torrents; and in the course of an hour, a river flowed past the convent door, along what lately was a dry and quiet street. In the darkness of the night we heard loud shrieks for help. The flood carried away baskets, logs of wood, tables, and fruitstands. At length, a general alarm was given. Two houses, built on the sand, were undermined by the water, and both fell together, while the people in them escaped with difficulty. It was impossible not to pity these poor houseless creatures, and, at the same time, to thank God we were in a secure building. *A Sunday at Nazareth.*

8838. FOUNDATION, Sure. Shortly after the destruction of the Ocean Monarch in the English Channel, one of the largest vessels that ever sailed from our shores, and built by Capt. McKay, of East Boston, a vessel was sailing in the vicinity, when the sailors thought they heard the voice of singing; they immediately lowered a boat, and starting in the direction from whence the sound came, they discovered a speck on the wave, which proved to be a Christian woman, sitting on a single plank, singing this hymn:

"Jesus, lover of my soul,
  Let me to thy bosom fly,
While the nearer waters roll,
  While the tempest still is high," etc.

Those sailors who rescued her, might have supposed that the plank was all the support she had; but thank God, she was resting on the "foundation of the prophets and apostles, Jesus Christ being the chief corner-stone." This noble Christian woman was taken on board the ship, and brought to Boston, where she lived a few years. Then she removed I think to Warren, Mass., and from thence departed to be with Christ forever. *T. J. Abbott.*

8839. FOUNDATION, Without a. A strong-minded man, stricken with the pains of death, cried out in agony. His nurse tried to solace him. "Oh, don't talk to me of pain!" he cried, bitterly. "It is the mind, woman—the mind." Slowly and deliberately he said, "I knew it at the time—every time. I knew it —I knew that a penalty must follow sin; yet I have done wrong, knowing that it was wrong; first with a few qualms, then brushing aside conscience, and at last with the coolness of a fiend. For one minute of my life I have not lived for heaven, for God, for Christ; no, not one minute. Oh, yes, Christ died for sinners; but my intellect is clear—clearer than ever before, I tell you. I can see almost into eternity; I can feel that unless Christ is believed on, his death can do me no good." Soon after, he said, "I have been following up the natural laws, and I see an affinity between them and the great laws of God's universe. Heaven is for the holy: without are dogs and whoremongers. There's the distinction—it's all right, all right." At death he whispered, "It is awfully dark here; my feet stand on the slippery edge of a great gulf! Oh for some foundation!" He stretched his hand out, as if feeling for a way. "Christ," gently whispered his friend. "Not for me!" was his awful answer.

8840. FOUNTAIN OF LIFE, A Beggar at the. Here I see a beggar going along the turnpike road. He is worn out with disease. He is stiff in the joints. He is ulcered all over. He has rheum in his eyes. He is sick and wasted. He is in rags. Every time he puts down his swollen feet, he cries: "Oh! the pain!" He sees a fountain by the roadside under a tree, and he crawls up to that fountain and says: "I must wash. Here I may cool my ulcers. Here I may get rested." He stoops down, and scoops up on the palm of his hands enough water to slake his thirst; and that is all gone. Then he stoops down, and begins to wash his eyes; and the rheum is all gone. Then he puts in his swollen feet, and the swelling is gone. Then, willing no longer to be only half-cured, he plunges in, and his whole body is laved in the stream, and he gets upon the bark well. Meantime the owner of the mansion up yonder comes down, walking through the ravine with his only son, and he sees the bundle of rags, and asks: "Whose rags are these?" A voice from the fountain says: "Those are my rags." Then says the master to his son: "Go up to the house, and get the best new suit you can find and bring it down." And he brings down the clothes, and the beggar is clothed in them, and he looks around and says: "I was filthy, but now I am clean. I was ragged, but now I am robed. I was blind but now I see. Glory be to the owner of that mansion; and glory be that son who brought me that new suit of clothes; and glory be to this fountain, where I have washed, and where all who will may wash and be clean." *Talmage.*

8841. FRAILTY, Emblem of. It was in the bleak season of a cold autumn, by the side of a large moor, that I one day saw a shepherd's tent. It was composed of straw and fern, and secured under the warmer side of a hedge, with a few briers and stakes. Thither, for about a week, he took shelter until the herbage failed his flock, and he removed I know not whither. His tent was, however, left behind. A few days after, I rode that way, and looked for the shepherd's tent, but it was gone. The stormy winds had scattered its frail materials. *R. Marks.*

8842. FRAILTY, Reminders of. The Lamae or priests of Thibet, when ready to celebrate prayers, summoned the people with pipes made from dead men's bones. Their rosaries were made from the same, while they drank out of a skull. On being asked the reason for using these things, one of their chief priests replied, "They did it, *ad fatorum memoriam.*" They piped with the bones of the dead that the sad whispers might warn the people of the approach of death. The beads they wore put them in mind of the frail estate of their bodies; and drinking from a skull mortified their affections, repressed their pleasures, imbittered their tastes, lest they should relish too much the delights of life.

8843. FRAILTY, Type of. There is cultivated at Paris a species of serpentine aloe, whose large and beautiful flower does not blow till towards the month of July, and about five o'clock in the evening. It then opens its petals, expands them, fades, and dies. By ten o'clock it has withered in the presence of a crowd assembled to see it. A striking emblem of the life of man. *Bibl. Treasury.*

8844. FRAUD, Prevalence of. From the great houses in the City of London to the village grocer, the commercial life of England has been saturated with fraud. So deep has it gone that a strictly honest tradesman can hardly hold his ground against competition. You can no longer trust that any article that you buy is the thing which it pretends to be. We have false weights, false measures, cheating, and shoddy everywhere. Yet the clergy have seen all this grow up in absolute indifference; and the great question at this moment agitating the Church of England is the color of the ecclesiastical petticoats! Many hundred sermons have I heard in England; many a dissertation on the mysteries of the faith, on the divine mission of the clergy, on apostolical succession, on bishops, and justification, and the theory of good works, and verbal inspiration, and the efficacy of the sacraments; but never during these thirty wonderful years, never once that I can recollect on common honesty, or those primitive commandments—"Thou shalt not lie, and thou shalt not steal." *Froude.*

8845. FREEDOM, Claim your. A captive eagle was tethered to a stick by a chain ten feet long. He marched round in a circle till a deep track was worn, and years of practice confirmed the habit. At length its owner took off his chain and set him free. Still he pursued his usual circle, not claiming his freedom till some one pushed him from the beaten track. As if astonished, he looked around, flapped his wings, then, fixing his eye on the sun, soared upward, and was free.

8846. FREEDOM, Cost of. Hegesippus instigated the Athenians against Philip, when one of the assembly cried out, "You would not persuade us to a war?" "Yes, indeed, would I, and to mourning clothes and to public funerals and to funeral speeches, if we intend to live free, and not submit to the pleasures of the Macedonians."

8847. FREEDOM, Decree of. The emperor of Russia had a plan by which he was to liberate the serfs of that country. There were 40,000,000 of them. Of some of them, their whole time was sold; of others, only a part. The Emperor called around him his council, and wanted to have them devise some way to set the slaves at liberty. After they had conferred about it for six months, one night the Council sent in their decision, sealed, that they thought it was not expedient. The Emperor went down to the Greek church that night and partook of the Lord's Supper, and he set his house in order, and the next morning you could hear the tramp of soldiers in the streets of St. Petersburg. The Emperor summoned his guard, and before noon 65,000 men were surrounding that palace. Just at midnight there came out a proclamation that every slave in Russia was forever set free. If one man can liberate 40,000,000, has not God the power to liberate every captive in New York? If there is a poor slave here, if there is a child of earth here to-day who wants to be liberated, I have come to show that Christ came to bring liberty to the captive. *Moody.*

8848. FREEDOM, Ignorance of. Miss Smiley said that after the war, when she went down South, she was in a hotel, and the room she was to occupy was so dirty that she said to the old colored woman that had charge of the room, "Auntie, you know I cannot live in such dirt as this, and you know, now, that we Northern people set you colored people free. I am from the North, and I want you to show your love for the North by cleaning up this room." She then went away for a short time, and when she came back in about half an hour the room looked as if a half a day's work had been spent on it. And the old colored woman came up to her and said: "There! now be's I free or beant I?" "Why, what makes you ask that question?" said the lady. "Oh," says she, "my old massa says I beant free at all, no one has a right to make me free at all, and he hasn't given me my freedom; and when go out and see the colored people, they tell me I am free: and now be's I free or beant I?" And there the poor colored woman had been free for months, and didn't know it. That is what the devil is doing with a great many. They are free, and don't know it. Now perhaps the colored woman could not read the proclamation, and find out. If you cannot read it, you can get some of your friends to read it. The truth shall make you free. The truth shall snap every fetter, set at liberty every captive. *Moody.*

8849. FREEDOM, Jubilee of. We had been at Richmond but a few hours before I heard that the colored people were going to have a jubilee-meeting down in the great African church that night, and I thought to myself, although I am a white man, I will get in there somehow. I had a hard fight to get in, but I did succeed at last. It was probably the largest church in the South. There were supposed to be 3,000 or 4,000 black people there, and they had some chaplains of our Northern regiments for their orators on the occasion. Talk about eloquence. I never heard better. It seemed as if they were raised for the occasion. I remember one of them, as he stood there on the platform, pointed down to the mothers and said, "Mothers, you rejoice to-day that you are forever free, all your posterity is free, that little child has been taken from your bosom and sold off to some distant State for the last time." And some of those women shouted right out in meeting, "Glory to God!" They could not keep the good news to themselves. They believed they were delivered. They believed the good news. Then this man turned to the young men and said, "Young men, rejoice to-day. It is a day of jubilee, a day of glad-tidings. We come to proclaim to you that you are free. You have heard the crack of the slave-trader's whip for the last time." And they shouted and clapped their hands and said, "Glory to God!" Then he turned to the young ladies and said, "Rejoice to-day! you have been on the auction block and sold to captivity for the last time." And then the young maidens clapped their hands and shouted for joy. It was a jubilee. What made them so glad? They believed they were liberated, and that is what made them so joyful. People want to know why Christians are so joyful. It is because they have been delivered from Satan. Some of those slaves had good masters, and slavery was not hard for them, but some of them had unkind and cruel masters; but I will tell you no slave in all the Southern States ever had so mean a master as you have, and you have more reason to rejoice that Christ has come to set you free than any prisoner in our Southern States, and every one of you ought to rejoice that you hear the good news that Christ has come to proclaim liberty to the captive, to recover sight to the blind, to set at liberty those that are bound. Jesus has come to open the prison doors and let out the captive. *Moody.*

8850. FREEDOM, Land of. Before the war we had three millions of slaves. If a negro escaped from the South and got as far as Mason and Dixon's line, he was not safe even then. There was a Fugitive Slave Law which would have surrendered back that negro even if he had crossed that boundary. But there was a line over which should he go he would be free, and that line was the Canada boundary line. If he could cross that he would be forever a free man. Now for my illustration. A poor negro escapes from Kentucky, and has succeeded, after many a weary day, in crossing the Ohio river. Though he has placed this barrier between him and his pursuers, still he knows he is not absolutely free; he knows they can take him back out of that State should they come up with him. He has not yet come under any law that will protect him; he is still under our own flag, and the flag of our country cannot protect him. He must go further. He knows he must reach Canada before the dreaded apprehension of being consigned back to his chains and tortures and stripes can be dismissed from his thoughts. He says, "If I can only get under that flag I am a free man—no slave can breathe under that flag." So the poor man makes his way toward this haven of rest. You can see him running. Yet a little while and he hears the bloodhounds behind him; he knows his old master is on his track; they have fleet horses and they will soon catch him. He is but a short distance from the line now, but his pursuers are in sight. Can he reach it in time? He is right on the boundary now; he makes one more effort and he is safe. Here you see him one moment a slave; now he has crossed the line and is free. Before he had reached the line he was subject to be taken back by his old master, and he and his posterity would have been slaves. Yet he has now crossed that line, and they cannot touch him. All at once he goes over the line and is free. One minute he is a slave; the next minute he is a citizen. Once a slave; now a free man. Will you not also leave the devil's territory, my friends? The banner floats from Calvary, and when you come under its folds you are safe. *Moody.*

8851. FREEDOM, Repression of. When I was at Naples, I went with Signor Manso, a gentleman of excellent parts and breeding, who had been the familiar friend of that famous poet, Torquato Tasso, to see the burning mountain Vesuvius. I wondered how the peasants could venture to dwell so fearlessly and cheerfully on its sides, when the lava was flowing from its summit; but Manso smiled, and told me that when the fire descends freely they retreat before it without haste or fear. They can tell how fast it will move, and how far; and they know, moreover, that, though it may work some little damage, it will soon cover the fields over which it hath passed with rich vineyards and sweet flowers. But, when the flames are pent up in the mountain, then it is that they have reason to fear; then it is that the earth sinks and the sea swells; then cities are swallowed up, and their place knoweth them no more. So it is in politics: where the people

are most closely restrained, there it gives the greatest shocks to peace and order; therefore would I say to all kings, Let your demagogues lead crowds, lest they lead armies; let them bluster, lest they massacre: a little turbulence is, as it were, the rainbow of the state; it shows, indeed, that there is a passing shower; but it is a pledge that there shall be no deluge.
Milton.

8852. FREE GRACE, Duty and. Industry on our part is not superseded by the greatness and freeness of Divine grace; as when a schoolmaster teaches a boy gratis, the youth cannot attain his learning without some application of his own; and yet it doth not, therefore, cease to be free on the teacher's part, because attention is needful in the learner. So it is here. *Arrowsmith.*

8853. FREE GRACE, Experience of. Bunyan, in his Holy War, portrays the triumphs of grace in the treatment of the rebels in the town of Mansoul after their submission to Prince Emmanuel. The Prince ordered a delegation of prisoners to be sent from the town of Mansoul under the guard of Captain Boanerges and Captain Conviction. They were brought into the presence of the Prince in mourning robes, with ropes around their necks, smiting upon their breasts, and "durst not so much as lift their eyes up to heaven." Nor could they hold their peace, but they cried, "O wretched men of Mansoul! O unhappy men!" Then they fell prostrate upon their faces before the Prince. He ascended the throne and ordered the representatives to stand up before him. He asked them, "If they were servants of Shaddai, or had they suffered themselves to be corrupted and defiled by the abominable Diabolus? Would they have been content to have lived under such slavery and tyranny forever? And even when he came himself, against the town of Mansoul, did they not wish that he might gain a victory over them?" To all these questions they replied, "Yes, we have done worse, we deserve punishment, and even death, we have nothing to say, Lord; thou art just, for we have sinned." "Then the Prince commanded that an herald should be called, and he should go throughout the camp of Emmanuel and proclaim, with the sound of a trumpet, that the Prince had, in his Father's name and for his Father's glory, gotten a perfect conquest and victory over Mansoul, and that the prisoners should follow and say Amen." Then there was great rejoicing everywhere among the soldiers and captains of Prince Emmanuel's army, but in the hearts of the men of Mansoul this great joy was wanting. But the Prince called them to him again, and said to them, "The sins, trespasses, iniquities, that you, with the whole town of Mansoul, have from time to time committed against my Father and me, I have power and commandment from my Father to forgive to the town of Mansoul, and do forgive you accordingly." Having said this, he gave them a written parchment, and sealed with several seals, a large and general pardon, to be proclaimed through the whole town of Mansoul at the rising of the sun the next day. The mourning weeds were stripped from them, and he gave them "beauty for ashes. the oil of joy for mourning, and the garments of praise for the spirit of heaviness." He gave to them each jewels of gold and precious stones, and took away their ropes, and put chains of gold about their necks, and earrings in their ears. Then were their fetters broken to pieces before their faces, and cast into the air. So overjoyed were they, their pardon being so sudden and glorious, they almost fainted; but the Prince put his everlasting arms under them, embraced them and kissed them, and bade them be of good cheer. Then he sent them away to their homes with pipe and tabor. Joyful was the meeting of those that had gone down prisoners, with friends on their return. And when they heard the wonderful news of the wisdom and grace of Prince Emmanuel their joy knew no bounds. There was pardon for every one in Mansoul, each one was mentioned by name. Emmanuel came with royal retinue, and took up his abode in the town. He made them a great feast at the palace. He gave them luxuries from his Father's court. Man did eat angels' food, and had honey given him out of the rock.

8854. FREE GRACE, Memorial of. At the centennial year of British Methodism (1839), a commemorative medal was struck. On one side, in *alto relievo*, were the busts of John and Charles Wesley. From all the sermons and writings of John Wesley and the other founders of Methodism, they selected the following stanza from one of Charles Wesley's hymns, as best expressing the mission of that church:

> "O, for a trumpet voice
> On all the world to call;
> To bid their hearts rejoice
> In him who died for all;
> For all my Lord was crucified,
> For all, for all, my Saviour died !"

8855. FREE GRACE, Objections to. Bunyan represents the power of grace, as shown by its first offer to, and success with, the Jerusalem sinners, the murderers of Christ. Thus: "Repent, every one of you; be baptized, every one of you, in his name, for the remission of sins, and you shall, every one of you, receive the Holy Ghost. *Objection.* But I was one of those who plotted to take away his life. **May** I be saved by him? *Peter.* Every one of you. *Objection.* But I was one of them that bore false witness against him. Is there grace for me? *Peter.* For every one of you. *Objection.* But I was one of them that cried out, Crucify him! crucify him! and that desired that Barabbas, the murderer, might live, rather than him. What will become of me, think you? I am to preach repentance and remission of sins to every one of you, says Peter. *Objection.* But I was one of them who did spit in his face when he stood before his accusers; I also was one that mocked him when, in anguish, he hanged bleeding on the tree. Is there room for me? For every one of you, says Peter. *Objection.* But I was one of them that, in his extremity, said, Give him gall and vinegar to drink! Why may I not expect the same when anguish and guilt is upon me? *Peter.* Repent of these, your wickednesses, and here is remission of sins for every one of you. *Objection.* But I railed on him; I reviled him; I hated him; I rejoiced to see him mocked at by others. Can there be hopes for me? *Peter.* There is for every one of you. Oh, what a blessed Every-one-of-you is here! How willing was Peter, and the Lord Jesus, by his ministry, to catch these murderers with the word of the Gospel, that they might be monuments of the grace of God!"

8856. FREE GRACE, Power of. I was preaching one Sunday in a church where there was a fashionable audience, and after I got through the sermon, I said, "If there are any that would like to tarry a little while and would like to stay and talk, I would be glad to talk with you." They all got up, turned around, and went out. I felt as though I was abandoned. When I was going out, I saw a man getting behind the furnace. He hadn't any coat on, and he was weeping bitterly. I said, "My friend, what is the trouble?" He said, "You told me to-night that I could be saved; that the grace of God would reach me. You told me that there wasn't a man so far gone but the grace of God could reach him." He said, "I am an exile from my family; I have drunk up $20,000 within the last few months; I have drunk up the coat off my back, and if there is hope for a poor sinner like me I should like to be saved." It was just like a cup of refreshment to talk to that man. I didn't dare give him money for fear that he would drink it up; but I got him a place to stay that night, took an interest in him, and got him a coat, and six months after that, when I left Chicago for Europe—four months after—that man was one of the most earnest Christian men I knew. The Lord has blessed him wonderfully. He was an active, capable man. The grace of God can save just such if they will only repent. I don't care how low he has become, the grace of God can purge him of all his sin, and place him among the blessed. In proportion as man is a sinner, much more does the grace of God abound. There isn't a man but that the grace of God will give him the victory if he will only accept it.   *Moody.*

8857. FREE GRACE, Trophies of. Christ has put himself under the term of physician; consequently he desireth that his fame as to the salvation of sinners may spread abroad, that the world may see what he can do. And to this end he has not only commanded that the biggest sinners should have the first offer of his mercy; but has, as the physicians do, put out his bills, and published his doings, that things may be read and talked of. Yea, he has moreover, in these his blessed bills, the Holy Scriptures I mean, inserted the very names of persons, the places of their abode, and the great cures that by the means of his salvation he has wrought upon them to this very end. Here is, item, Such a one by my grace and redeeming blood, was made a monument of everlasting life; and such a one, by

my perfect obedience, became an heir of glory. And then he produceth their names. Item. saved Lot from the guilt and damnation that he had procured to himself by his incest. Item. I saved David from the vengeance that belonged to him for committing adultery and murder. Here also is Solomon, Manasseh, Peter, Magdalen, and many others made mention of in this book. Yea, here are their names, their sins, and their salvation recorded together, that you may read and know what a Saviour he is, and do him honor in the world.   *Bunyan.*

8858. FREE-THINKER, Simile of a. A visitor contemplating the grandeur of St. Paul's cathedral, London, says, "In the midst of my contemplations, I beheld a fly upon one of the pillars: and it straightway came into my head, that the same fly was a free-thinker; for it required some comprehension in the eyes of a spectator, to take in at one view the various parts of the building in order to observe their symmetry and design. But to the fly, whose whole prospect was confined to a little part of one of the stones of a single pillar, the joint beauty of the whole, or the distinction of its parts, were inconspicuous; and nothing could appear but small inequalities on the surface of the hewn stone, which, in the view of that insect, must have seemed so many deformed rocks and precipices."

8859. FREE-WILL, Dignity of. Rev. J. Bosworth gives the following conversation between King Alfred and Boethius. "I am sometimes very much disturbed," quoth Alfred. "At what?" I answered. "It is at this which thou sayest, that God gives to every one freedom to do evil as well as good, whichsoever he will; and thou sayest also, that God knoweth everything before it happens." "Then," quoth he, "I may very easily answer this remark. How would it look to you, if there were any very powerful King, and he had no freedmen in all his kingdom, but that all were slaves?" "Then," said I, "It would not seem to me right, nor reasonable, if servile men only should attend upon him." "Then," quoth he, "what would be more unnatural than if God, in all his kingdom, had no free creatures under his power? He, therefore, made two rational creatures free—angels and men. He gave them the great gift of freedom. Hence they could do evil as well as good, whichsoever they would. He gave this very fixed gift, and a very fixed law with that gift, to every man unto this end:—the freedom is, that man may do what he will; and the law is, that he will render to every man according to his works, either in this world or the future one—good or evil, whichsoever he doeth."

8860. FREE-WILL, Endowment of. It is a contradiction to let man be free, and force him to do right. God has performed this marvel of creating a being with free-will, independent, so to speak, of himself—a real cause in his universe. To say that he has created such a one, is to say that he has given him the power to fail. Without free-will there could be no human goodness. It is wise, therefore, and good in God to give birth to free-will. But once acknowledge free-will in man, and the origin of evil does not lie in God.

F. W. Robertson.

8861. FRETFULNESS, Argument Against. The argument used against fretfulness by the Psalmist deserves to be well fixed in our minds; and, indeed, if it were so, we should need no other argument: "Fret not thyself against the ungodly," etc., "for they shall soon be cut down like the grass," etc. (Ps. xxxvii.) Who could envy a flower, though ever so gay and beautiful in its colors, when he saw that the next stroke of the mower would sweep it away forever. *Bishop Horne.*

8862. FRETFULNESS, Folly of. It is not wise to fret under our trials: the high-mettled horse that is restive in the yoke only galls his shoulder—the poor bird that dashes itself against the bars of the cage only ruffles her feathers, and aggravates the suffering of captivity. *Teachers' Treasury.*

8863. FRETTING, Injurious. The rubbing of the eyes doth not fetch out the mote, but makes them more red and angry; no more doth the distraction and fretting of the mind discharge it of any ill humors, but rather makes them more abound to vex us. *Bishop Patrick.*

8864. FRETTING, Sin of. "I dare no more fret," said John Wesley, "than to curse and swear." One who knew him well said that he never saw him low-spirited or fretful in his life. He says, "To have persons at my ears murmuring and fretting at everything is like tearing the flesh from my bones. By the grace of God I am discontented at nothing. I see God sitting on the throne, and ruling all things."

8865. FRIEND, A Pretended. A wolf hung round a flock of sheep doing them no harm so long that the shepherd began to regard him as a friend rather than an enemy. Having need to leave the sheep for a day, he put the wolf in charge of the flock. The wolf saw his opportunity and began at once to devour the sheep. The shepherd on his return beholding the destruction of his flock, exclaimed, "Fool that I am! yet I deserve no less for trusting my sheep with a wolf."

8866. FRIENDS, Character of. Antisthenes used to wonder at those who were curious, in buying but an earthen dish, to see that it had no cracks or inconveniences, and yet would be careless in the choice of friends—to take them with the flaws of vice. *Feltham.*

8867. FRIENDS, Choice of. We ought always to make choice of persons of such worth and honor for our friends, that, if they should ever cease to be so, they will not abuse our confidence, nor give us cause to fear them as enemies. *Addison.*

8868. FRIENDS, Counsel of. A long life may be passed without finding a friend in whose understanding and virtue we can equally confide, and whose opinion we can value at once for its justness and sincerity. A weak man, however honest, is not qualified to judge. A man of the world, however penetrating, is not fit to counsel. Friends are often chosen for similitude of manners, and therefore each palliates the other's failings because they are his own. Friends are tender, and unwilling to give pain; or they are interested, and fearful to offend. *Johnson.*

8869. FRIENDS, Courtesy of. Don't flatter yourself that friendship authorizes you to say disagreeable things to your intimates. On the contrary, the nearer you come into relation with a person the more necessary do tact and courtesy become. Except in cases of necessity, which are rare, leave your friend to learn unpleasant truths from his enemies; they are ready enough to tell them. Good-breeding never forgets that *amour propre* is universal. When you read the story of the Archbishop and Gil Blas, you may laugh if you will, at the poor old man's delusion; but don't forget that the youth was the greater fool of the two, and that his master served such a booby rightly in turning him out of doors. *Holmes.*

8870. FRIENDS, Danger of. What the oracle foretold Timesias, concerning his planting a colony, that an hive of bees should be changed into a nest of wasps, may not impertinently be applied to those who seek after a hive of friends, but light before they know it upon a wasp-nest of enemies. *Plutarch.*

8871. FRIENDS, House Full of. When Socrates was building a house for himself at Athens, being asked by a person who observed the smallness of the design, why a man so eminent should not have an abode more suitable to his dignity; he replied, that he should think himself sufficiently accommodated if he should see that narrow habitation filled with real friends.

8872. FRIENDS, Making. It is better to decide a difference between our enemies, than our friends; for one of our friends will most likely become our enemy; but on the other hand, one of our enemies will probably become our friend. *Bias.*

8873. FRIENDS, Quarrels of. I have observed universally that the quarrels of friends, in the latter part of life, are never truly reconciled. A wound in the friendship of young persons, as in the bark of young trees, may be so grown over as to leave no scar. The case is very different in regard to old persons and timber. The reason of this may be accountable from the decline of the social passions, and the prevalence of spleen, suspicion, and rancor, towards the latter part of life. *Shenstone.*

8874. FRIENDS, Securing. Scipio Junior, a most estimable Roman, kept the precept of Polybius, and endeavored never to retire from the forum till by some means he had engaged some one to be his friend or companion.

8875. FRIENDS, Test of. Namertes was on an embassy, when one told him he was a happy man in having so many friends, and asked him if he knew any certain way to try whether a man had many real friends or not. Namertes replied, "Adversity."

8876. FRIENDS, Three Sorts of. There be three sorts of friends: the first is like a torch we meet in a dark street; the second is like a candle in a lanthorn that we overtake; the third is like a link that offers itself to the stumbling passenger. The met torch is the sweet-lipped friend, which lends us a flash of compliment for the time, but quickly leaves us to our former darkness. The overtaken lanthorn is the true friend, which, though it promise but a faint light, yet it goes along with us as far as it can to our journey's end. The offered link is the mercenary friend, which, though it be ready enough to do us service, yet that service hath a servile relation to our bounty.

Quarles.

8877. FRIENDSHIP: Brevities. Friendship improves happiness, and abates misery, by the doubling of our joy, and the dividing of our grief.—*Cicero.*——Friendship contracted with the wicked decreases from hour to hour, like the early shadow of the morning; but friendship formed with the virtuous will increase like the shadow of evening, till the sun of life shall set.—*Herder.*——He that doth a base thing in zeal for his friend, burns the golden thread that ties their hearts together. *Jeremy Taylor.*

8878. FRIENDSHIP, Devotion of. The friendship of Epaminondas and Pelopidas is celebrated in Grecian history. At the battle of Mantinea, they locked their shields together and fought, repulsing all enemies, till Pelopidas fell upon a heap of dead, bleeding from many wounds. Epaminondas resolved to die rather than leave the body of his friend, whom he supposed to be dead. Badly wounded himself, he fought till rescue came, and both were saved. From that day their friendship became proverbial. They were made generals of the Theban army, of equal authority, and no envy or rivalry ever existed between them while they lived.

8879. FRIENDSHIP, Example of. There is a remarkable example of friendship told of such as never heard of him who is the friend of sinners. It is so remarkable indeed that it procured divine honors to Orestes and Pylades from the Scythians—a race so bloody, rude and savage, that they are said to have fed on human flesh, and made drinking-cups of their enemies' skulls. Engaged in an arduous enterprise, Orestes and Pylades, two sworn friends, landed on the shores of the Chersonesus to find themselves in the dominions and power of a king whose practice was to seize on all strangers, and sacrifice them at the shrine of Diana. The travelers were arrested. They were carried before the tyrant; and, doomed to death, were delivered over to Iphigenia, who, as priestess of Diana's temple, had to immolate the victims. Her knife is buried in their bosoms but that she learns before the blow is struck that they are Greeks—natives of her own native country. Anxious to open up a communication with the land of her birth, she offers to spare one of the two, on condition that the survivor will become her messenger, and carry a letter to her friends in Greece. But which shall live, and which shall die? That is the question. The friendship which had endured for years, in travels, and courts,

and battle-fields, is now put to a strain it never bore before. And nobly it bears it! Neither will accept the office of messenger, leaving his fellow to the stroke of death. Each implores the priestess to select him for the sacrifice, and let the other go. While they contend for the pleasure and honor of dying, Iphigenia discovers in one of them her own brother! She embraces him; and, sparing both, flees with them from that cruel shore. Both are saved; and the story, borne on the wings of fame, flies abroad, fills the world with wonder, and, carried to distant regions, excited such admiration among the barbarous Scythians, that they paid divine honors to Orestes and Pylades, and, deifying these heroes, erected temples to their worship.

Dr. Guthrie.

8880. FRIENDSHIP, False. False friendship, like the ivy, decays and ruins the walls it embraces; but true friendship gives new life and animation to the object it supports. *Burton.*

8881. FRIENDSHIP, Flawed. Friendship is a vase which, when it is flawed by heat, or violence, or accident, may as well be broken at once; it can never be trusted after. The more graceful and ornamental it was, the more clearly do we discern the hopelessness of restoring it to its former state. Coarse stones, if they are fractured, may be cemented again; precious stones—never. *Landor.*

8882. FRIENDSHIP, Immortal. The friendship of high and sanctified spirits loses nothing by death but its alloy; failings disappear, and the virtues of those, whose "faces we shall behold no more," appear greater and more sacred when beheld through the shades of the sepulchre. *Robert Hall.*

8883. FRIENDSHIP, Importance of. When a man, blind from his birth, was asked what he thought the sun to be like, he replied, "Like friendship." He could not conceive of anything more fitting as a similitude for what he had been taught to regard as the most glorious of material objects, and whose quickening and exhilarating influences he had rejoiced to feel. And truly friendship is a sun, if not *the* sun, of life. All feel it ought to be so. It would be common-place to dwell upon its delights and advantages. The theme of poets and moralists in all ages and countries, what can be said upon it has been said so often as to make repetition stale, so well as to make improvement impossible. How friendship is a pearl of greatest price; how it is often more deep and steadfast than natural affection, "a friend" sometimes "sticketh closer than a brother:" how it is as useful as lovely, "strength and beauty;" how it lessens grief and increases pleasure; all this is familiar as the lessons of childhood, and true as the elementary principles of our nature. *Morris.*

8884. FRIENDSHIP, Intercourse of. The world would be more happy, if persons gave up more time to an intercourse of friendship. But money engrosses all our deference; and we scarce enjoy a social hour, because we think it unjustly stolen from the main business of life.

Shenstone.

8885. FRIENDSHIP, Lasting. Zeuxis replied to some who blamed the slowness of his pencil, that he therefore spent a long time in painting, because he designed his work should last for a long eternity. So he that would secure a lasting friendship and acquaintance must first deliberately judge and thoroughly try its worth before he settles it.   *Plutarch.*

8886. FRIENDSHIP, Love Kills. At the best, love is fatal to friendship. The most that friendship can do is to listen to love's talk of itself, and be the confidante of its rapturous joys, its transports of despair. The lover fancies himself all the fonder of his friend because of his passion for his mistress, but in reality he has no longer any need of the old comrade. They cannot talk sanely and frankly together any more; there is something now that they cannot share. Even if the lover desired to maintain the old affectionate relation, the mistress could not suffer it. The spectre of friendship is sometimes invited to haunt the home of the lovers after marriage: but when their happiness is flaunted in its face, when it has been shown the new house, the new china, the new carpets, the new garden, it is tacitly exorcised, and is not always called back again, except to be shown the new baby. The young spouses are willing to have the poor ghost remain; the wife learns whether it takes two or three lumps of sugar in its tea; the husband bids it smoke anywhere it likes, and the wife smiles a menacing acquiescence; but all the same they turn it out of doors. They praise it when it is gone, and they feel so much more comfortable to be alone.   *D. W. Howells.*

8887. FRIENDSHIP, Obligations of. Whoever employs many assistants in his affairs must in gratitude repay his service to as many when they need it; and as Briareus, who, with his hundred hands, was daily obliged for his bare subsistence to feed fifty stomachs, could thrive no better than ourselves, who supply a single one with two hands, so a man of many friends cannot boast any other privilege but that of being a slave to many, and of sharing in all the business cares and disquiet that may befall them.   *Plutarch.*

8888. FRIENDSHIP, Occasions of. There is such a natural principle of attraction in man towards man, that having trod the same tract of land, having breathed in the same climate, barely having been born in the same artificial district or division, becomes the occasion of contracting acquaintances and familiarities many years after: for any thing may serve the purpose. Thus, relations merely nominal are sought and invented, not by governors, but by the lowest of the people, which are found sufficient to hold mankind together in little fraternities and copartnerships; weak ties, indeed, and what may afford fund enough for ridicule, if they are absurdly considered as the *real principles* of that union; but they are, in truth, merely the *occasions*, as anything may be, of any thing to which our nature carries us on, according to its own previous bent and bias; which occasion, therefore, would be nothing at all, were there not this prior bias or disposition of nature.   *Butler*

8889. FRIENDSHIP Personified. The ancients pictured friendship as a young man, very fair, bareheaded, and meanly attired. On the outside of his garment was written, " *Vivere et mori*" (To live and die), and on his forehead, "*Æstate et Hieme*" (In summer and winter). His breast was open so that his heart might be seen. With his finger he pointed to his heart, upon which was written, " *Prope, Longe*" (Far and near").

8890. FRIENDSHIP, Sympathy of. Friendship is one of the greatest boons God can bestow on man. It is a union of our finest feelings; an uninterested binding of hearts, and a sympathy between two souls. It is an indefinable trust we repose in one another, a constant communication between two minds, and an unremitting anxiety for each other's souls. What, then, is the root, the cause, of friendship? Sympathy. Sympathy conceives friendship; friendship, love. Love is friendship. The tree that bears love, bears also friendship. Where friendship exists between two persons, there is also, always, hope; in adversity there is always a support, a refuge, a knowledge of there still remaining some succor; and as a babe cries for its mother for nourishment, so do we in adversity run to friendship for advice, fully relying on some means by which it may release us from the troubles of the world. And in true friendship there is cultivated such a love of God, such a devotion for the Creator of the world, that the chains become adamant. Friendship having thus a righteous appreciation of the Almighty's goodness and power, and a knowledge of his injunctions to the righteous, and the reward they may expect hereafter, it spreads around, everywhere, joy and happiness, causing not only fresh unions, but, with praiseworthy Christian exertion and love, rendering them inflexible.   *J. Hill.*

8891. FRIENDSHIP, Visit of. To a lady who called on Dr. Watts, he said, "Madam, your ladyship is come to see me on a very remarkable day." "Why is this day so remarkable?" asked she. "This very day thirty years," replied the doctor, "I came to the house of my good friend Sir Thomas Abney, intending to spend but one single week under his friendly roof, and I have extended my visit to his family to the length of exactly thirty years." Lady Abney, who was present, immediately said to the doctor, "Sir, what you term a long thirty years' visit, I consider as the best visit my family ever received."

8892. FRIENDSHIP, Worldly. When I see leaves drop from their trees in the beginning of autumn, just such, think I, is the friendship of the world. Whilst the sap of maintenance lasts, my friends swarm in abundance; but in the winter of my need they leave me naked. He is a happy man that hath a true friend at his need; but he is more truly happy that hath no need of his friend.   *Warwick.*

8893. FRUGALITY, Necessity of. It appears evident that frugality is necessary even to complete the pleasure of expense; for it may be generally remarked of those who squander what they know their fortune not sufficient to allow, that in their most jovial expense there always breaks out some proof of discontent and impatience; they either scatter with a kind of wild desperation and affected lavishness, as criminals brave the gallows when they cannot escape it, or pay their money with a peevish anxiety, and endeavor at once to spend idly and to save meanly: having neither firmness to deny their passions, nor courage to gratify them, they murmur at their own enjoyments, and poison the bowl of pleasure by reflection on the cost. *Johnson.*

8894. FRUGALITY, Pedigree of. Frugality may be termed the daughter of prudence, the sister of temperance, and the parent of liberty. He that is extravagant will quickly become poor, and poverty will enforce dependence, and invite corruption. *Johnson.*

8895. FRUGALITY, Roman. Marcus Cato, the Elder, never wore a garment that cost him more than an hundred pence. During his Praetor and Consulship, he drank the same wine his laborers did, and if he treated himself he brought his supper from market that cost him not more than thirty half-pence. A Babylonic garment that he inherited he disposed of. He used to say, "Nothing which is superfluous can be had at a small rate, and for my part I account that dear at a half-penny, of which I have no need."

8896. FRUGALITY, Royal. Cyrus, king of Persia, accepted the invitation of one of his friends to dine with him, and was desired to name the viands and where he would have the table spread. Cyrus replied, "It is my pleasure that you prepare this banquet on the side of the river, and that one loaf of bread be the only dish."

8897. FRUITFULNESS, Biblical Types of. *A vineyard.*—The Church is compared to a vineyard, where both the vineyard and the vine are types of fruitfulness, Ps. 80: 15; Isa. 5: 1–7; Hosea 14: 7; John 15: 1–8. *A garden,* Cant. 4: 12–15; Isa. 58: 11.—"A garden enclosed"—"a little spot enclosed by grace"—the emblem of beauty—fragrance—fruitfulness. *Trees of righteousness.* Believers are compared to fruitful trees :—The *apple* (or citron) for beauty and variety, Cant. 2: 3; the *vine* for luxuriance and richness of fruit, Ps. 80: 8–11; Cant. 2: 15; Jer. 2: 21; Hosea 14: 7; the *fig* for sweetness, Cant. 2: 13; Luke 13: 6; the *olive* for fatness, Hosea 14: 6; Rom. 11: 24; the *palm* for usefulness, Ps. 92: 12. *Fruits in their season.*—It is interesting to mark in the Canticles, how the rich variety of the Church's fruitfulness is set forth by the trees of the garden, each ripe in its own season. Here are "tender grapes" for the spring, 2: 13; spices and pleasant fruits for summer, 4: 13, 14; and nuts for autumn, 6: 11. The fruits Christians bear are not in every case, and at all times, the same. The plant of prosperity stands in the garden, and yields the rich fruit of thankfulness, whilst adversity brings forth sweet patience—suspense gently blossoms into hope—and service gradually ripens happiness. But every kind is beautiful in its season. *Bowes*

8898. FRUITFULNESS, Christian. A New England chemist has learned the art of planting grape vines in his laboratory, out of sight of the passing observer, and applying chemicals to their roots, which make the vines luxuriant and the fruit prolific in its season. The root is concealed, but the vines climb out and the fruit spreads itself before men. Emblem of the Christian life. The Christian is "rooted and built up in Christ," out of sight of the world's gaze, but his fruit will reveal him.

8899. FRUITFULNESS, False and True. Among the cocoa groves of Ceylon the traveler will find old trees one hundred feet high, with perhaps a hundred cocoa nuts far up among its top branches. He will find others, four in a place, planted one in each corner of a square covered with foliage and loaded with nuts. The stranger will prefer these trees for their apparent thriftiness, fruitfulness and accessibility, being not more than one-fourth as tall as the other trees. They mark the grave of a dead man, and their fruit and foliage are all false, put on as a religious service for the dead. Their similars are the moralist or legalist and the true Christian. In one case they are a natural growth; in the other, are put on, and there is a dead man beneath them.

8900. FUNERAL, A Hypocritical. A few days ago we were at the funeral of a dissolute creature, who, after fifty years' soaking in the wine-cask, had at last oozed away. The chancel was a floral exhibition ; the coffin hidden under harps and crowns; and above the whole rose a colossal anchor of camellias, the emblem of the hope that maketh not ashamed, safely fixed beyond the vail! What a mockery of Christian faith! What a contrast as the solemn services went forward, the Lesson answering, "Be not deceived," to the Epicurean proverb, "Let us eat and drink;" and the Collect praying that we may "rise from the death of sin to the life of righteousness!" Yet this is only one among many instances Nothing is fairer than such decoration in itself. Bring white flowers for the dead child, or for the pure of heart, lying in the white garments of a holy life; but when the emblem is so changed to an elaborate, gross, painful sham, it is an affront to the truth. *The Churchman.*

8901. FUNERALS, Impressiveness of. Few pageants can be more stately and frigid than an English funeral in town. It is made up of show and gloomy parade—mourning carriages mourning horses, mourning plumes, and hireling mourners, who make a mockery of grief. "There is a grave digged," says Jeremy Taylor, "and a solemn mourning, and a great talk in the neighborhood, and when the rites are finished, they shall be, and they shall be remembered no more." The associate in the gay and crowded city is soon forgotten ; the hurrying succession of new inmates and new pleasures effaces him from our minds, and the very scenes and circles in which he moved are incessantly fluctuating. But funerals in the country are solemnly impressive. The stroke of death makes a wider space in the village circle, and is an awful event in the tranquil uniformity of rural life. The passing bell tolls its knell in every ear; it steals with its pervading melancholy over hill and vale, and saddens all the landscape.   *W. Irving.*

8902. FUNERALS, Lessons of. It would not, indeed, be reasonable to expect, did we not know the inattention and perverseness of mankind, that any one who had followed a funeral could fail to return home with new resolutions of a holy life; for who can see the final period of all human schemes and undertakings without conviction of the vanity of all that terminates in the present state? For who can see the wise, the brave, the powerful, or the beauteous, carried to the grave, without reflection on the emptiness of all those distinctions which set us here in opposition to each other? And who, when he sees the vanity of all terrestrial advantages, can forbear to wish for a more permanent and certain happiness? Such wishes, perhaps, often arise, and such resolutions are often formed; but, before the resolution can be exerted—before the wish can regulate the conduct—new prospects open before us, new impressions are received; the temptations of the world solicit, the passions of the heart are put into commotion; we plunge again into the tumult, engage again in the contest, and forget that what we gain cannot be kept, and that the life for which we are thus busy to provide must be quickly at an end.   *Johnson.*

8903. FUTURE, Anxiety about the. The soul of man can never divest itself wholly of anxiety about its fate hereafter: there are hours when, even to the prosperous, in the midst of their pleasures, eternity is an awful thought; but how much more when those pleasures, one after another, begin to withdraw; when life alters its forms, and becomes dark and cheerless— when its changes warn the most inconsiderate that what is so mutable will soon pass entirely away. Then with pungent earnestness comes home that question to the heart, "Into what world are we next to go?" How miserable the man who, under the distractions of calamity, hangs doubtful about an event which so nearly concerns him; who, in the midst of doubts and anxieties, approaching to that awful boundary which separates this world from the next, shudders at the dark prospect before him, wishing to exist after death, and yet afraid of that existence; catching at every feeble hope which superstition can afford him, and trembling in the same moment from reflection upon his crimes!   *Blair.*

8904. FUTURE, Consideration of the. Planters of trees ought to encourage themselves, by considering all future time as present; indeed, such consideration would be a useful principle to all men in their conduct of life, as it respects both this world and the next.   *Bp. Watson.*

8905. FUTURE, Course of the. The future does not come from before to meet us, but comes up from behind over our heads.   *Rahel.*

8906. FUTURE, Description of the. The future, the last evangel, which has included all others. Its cathedral the dome of immensity—hast thou seen it? Coped with the star-galaxies; paved with the green mosaic of land and ocean; and for altar, verily, the star-throne of the eternal! Its litany and psalmody, the noble arts, the heroic work and suffering, and true heart-utterance of all the valiant of the sons of men. Its choir-music, the ancient winds and oceans, and deep-toned, inarticulate, but most speaking voices of destiny and history, supernal ever as of old, between two great Silences: "Stars silent rest o'er us, graves under us silent."   *Carlyle.*

8907. FUTURE, Hidden. God will not suffer man to have the knowledge of things to come: for if he had prescience of his prosperity, he would be careless: and understanding of his adversity, he would be senseless. *Augustine.*

8908. FUTURE, Judgment of the. Cicero was about to be offered a mission to Egypt by his political opponents, but self-respect would not allow him to accept it. He knew it would be regarded by the public as a bribe. Concerning this decision he wrote to his friend Atticus, "What will history say of me six hundred years hence? That is a judgment which I reverence much more than the small talk of such men as are now alive."

8909. FUTURE, Prospects of the. Interesting as has been the past history of our race, engrossing as must ever be the present—the future, more exciting still, mingles itself with every thought and sentiment, and casts its beams of hope, or its shadows of fear, over the stage both of active and contemplative life. In youth, we scarcely descry it in the distance. To the stripling and the man, it appears and disappears like a variable star, showing in painful succession its spots of light and of shade. In age, it looms gigantic to the eye, full of chastened hope and glorious anticipation; and at the great transition, when the outward eye is dim, the image of the future is the last picture which is effaced from the retina of the mind.   *Sir David Brewster.*

8910. FUTURE, Question of the. There is one question which combines with the interest of speculation and curiosity an interest incomparably greater, nearer, more affecting, more solemn. It is the simple question—"What shall we be?" How soon it is spoken! but who shall reply? Think how profoundly this question, this mystery, concerns us—and in comparison with this, what are to us all questions of all sciences? What to us all researches into the constitution and laws of material nature? What—all investigations into the history of past ages? What to us—the future career of events in the progress of states and empires? What to us—what shall become of this globe itself, or all the mundane system? What we shall be, we ourselves, is the matter of surpassing interest.   *John Foster.*

8911. FUTURE, Unalterableness of the. Our life is like the wax melting in the flame. Death puts his stamp on it, and then it cools, and the impress never can be changed. Or like the burning metal, running forth from the cauldron into the mould. Death cools us in that mould, and we are cast into that shape throughout eternity.   *Spurgeon.*

8912. FUTURITY, Compensation of. Futurity is the greatness of man, and that hereafter is the grand scene for the attainment of the fullness of his existence. When depressed and mortified by a conscious littleness of being, yet feeling emotions and intimations which seem to signify that he should not be little, he may look to futurity and exclaim—"I shall be great yonder!" When feeling how little belongs to him, how diminutive and poor his sphere of possession here, he may say, "The immense futurity is mine! I may be content to be poor awhile in the prospect of that!" If here obscure, and even despised, he may reflect, "Well, it is not here that I expect or want to verify my importance!" If forcibly admonished of the brevity of life, the thought may arise—"Well, the sooner my entrance on a life that shall have no end."   *John Foster.*

8913. FUTURITY, Prospects of. I must confess, I take a particular delight in these prospects of futurity, whether grounded upon the probable suggestions of a fine imagination, or the more severe conclusions of philosophy; as a man loves to hear all the discoveries or conjectures relating to a foreign country which he is at some time to inhabit. Prospects of this nature lighten the burden of any present evil, and refresh us under the worst and lowest circumstances of mortality. They extinguish in us both the fear and envy of human grandeur. Insolence shrinks its head, power disappears; pain, poverty, and death fly before them. In short, the mind that is habituated to the lively sense of an hereafter can hope for what is the most terrifying to the generality of mankind, and rejoice in what is the most afflicting.   *Addison.*

8914. GAIN, Dishonest. Such gain is a hoard of sorrows, a heap of miseries, a mass of corruption, a consuming rust and canker, a devouring fire, a condemning witness; and if this be not enough, a treasure of wrath.   *Clarkson.*

8915. GAIN, Immortal. Philip inquired of Demosthenes, whether he was afraid to lose his head. He answered, "No; for if I do lose it, the Athenians will bestow an immortal one upon me."

8916. GAMBLING, Evil Effects of. No passion can lead to such extremities, nor involve a man in such a complicated train of crimes and vices, and ruin whole families so completely, as the baneful rage for gambling. It produces and nourishes all imaginable disgraceful sensations; it is the most fertile nursery of covetousness, envy, rage, malice, dissimulation, falsehood, and foolish reliance on blind fortune; it frequently leads to fraud, quarrels, murder, forgery, meanness, and despair; and robs us in the most unpardonable manner of the greatest and most irrecoverable treasure—time.   *Knigge.*

8917. GAMBLING, Inhumanity of. Dr. Nott said, "The finished gambler has no heart; he would play at his brother's funeral; he would gamble upon his mother's coffin." Horace Walpole tells of a man having dropped dead at the door of White's club house, in London, into which he was carried. The members of the club immediately made bets whether he was dead or not; and, upon its being proposed to bleed him, the wagerers for his death objected, that it would affect the fairness of the bet.

8918. GAMBLING, Prevalence of. In Southern Germany men have been known to stake their all upon the turn of a single card, who, one month previously, had been worth not less than half a million florins. Not less reckless have been men in Hamburg and Lombardy. In Mexico, ventures of from twenty-five to one hundred thousand doubloons have been lost at only three different sittings at the same table. In France, the game of courting the smiles of fortune has often cost the player 5,000 francs an hour—a risk of $950 per hour. In Rome, that most ancient of all cities, men have ventured and lost, during one or two nights, not less than 10,000 ten-scudi gold pieces—a sum equal to about $100,000. In Spain, from the days of Columbus to the present time, many a don is recorded to have lost within twenty-four hours 800,000 doubloons—that is, $12,000,000 of our American gold coin. In England, where the spirit of gambling is not so conspicuous as in more southern countries, £10,000 is sometimes considered low play with certain aristocrats, but then it ranges upward occasionally to the round number of £50,000. In the United States, in one city alone, it is estimated from $50,000 to $500,000 will change hands through gambling means during one day and night. But, then, even these enumerations only apply to a certain class denominated the "bon ton, or aristocracy," of the world—hence do not take into consideration the class of gamblers lower down in the scale of life—yet, making a rough estimate from instances cited, we can honestly assert that the average gambling exchange of money throughout Christendom during but twenty-four hours may exceed, though it is not less than $80,000,000, or somewhere about $123,100,000,000 worth of specie in a year of 365 days.   *The Globe.*

8919. GAMBLING, Results of. In our large cities there is a sort of gambling which does not look particularly repulsive; for it is not carried on in "hells," and it pleads the sanction of titled names; and yet its results are hanging like a mill-stone round the neck of many a promising young man, and numbers of its victims must be sought in the Portland hulks or Dartmoor prison.   *Dr. J. Hamilton.*

8920. GAMESTER, A Female. Could we look into the mind of a female gamester, we should see it full of nothing but trumps and matadores. Her slumbers are haunted with kings, queens, and knaves. The day lies heavy upon her till the play-season returns, when for half a dozen hours together all her faculties are employed in shuffling, cutting, dealing, and sorting out a pack of cards, and no ideas to be discovered in a soul which calls itself rational, excepting little square figures of painted and spotted paper. *Guardian.*

8921. GARMENT, Import of the Wedding. The wedding garment is righteousness in its largest sense, the whole adornment of the new and spiritual man—including the faith without which it is impossible to please God, and the holiness without which no man shall see him, or, like the speechless guest, shall only see him to perish at his presence:—it is the faith which is the root of all graces, the mother of all virtues, and it is likewise those virtues and those graces themselves. *R. C. Trench.*

8922. GARMENT, Wedding. At the royal marriage of the Sultan Mahmoud, a few years ago, every guest was presented with a wedding garment. They were prepared by royal command, and paid for from the Sultan's exchequer. All were expected to array themselves in the garments provided. If any should neglect or refuse to do this it would be considered an insult to the Sultan. This custom was formerly general in the east.

8923. GARMENTS, Provisions of. Olearius gives an account of himself, with the ambassadors whom he accompanied, being invited to the table of the Persian king. He goes on to say, " It was told us by the mehmandar, that we, according to their usage, must hang the splendid vestments that were sent us from the king over our dresses, and so appear in his presence. The ambassadors at first refused; but the mehmandar urged it so earnestly, alleging, as also did others, that the omission would greatly displease the king, since all other envoys observed such a custom, that at last they consented, and hanged, as did we also, the splendid vests over their shoulders, and so the cavalcade proceeded."

8924. GARMENTS, Rending. The Jews mingled a great deal of ceremony with the tearing of garments, when any misfortune befell them. Sometimes they made the rent from the top downwards; sometimes from the skirt upwards. The requisite length was a hand's breadth. When made on the occasion of the death of parents, it was not sewed up again; when for the loss of other persons, it was sewed up at the end of thirty days. It is in reference to this practice that Solomon has said, there is " a time to rend, and a time to sew;" that is to say, a time to be afflicted, and a time to admit of consolation.—*Constable.*———They take a knife, and, holding the blade downwards, do give the upper garment a cut on the right side, and then rend it an hand's breadth. This is done for the five following relations, brother, sister, son, daughter, or wife; but for father or mother, the rent is on the left side, and in all the garments, as coat, waistcoat, etc. *Levi.*

8925. GATE, Entering the Strait. A missionary to the Hindus at Benares, said: " I spoke on the words, 'Enter ye in at the strait gate.' I explained to them the signification of the strait gate, and what they must do in order to get through. First, I represented, according to Hindu ideas, a worldly-minded person, who cares nothing about religion, and who hopes, nevertheless, at the end, to get to heaven. 'There,' I said, 'is one coming along, riding on an elephant; he appears in grand style; he cares nothing for God and eternity; he wants to enjoy the world; and yet he hopes to get to heaven in the end. Thus he is riding on towards the strait gate, hoping he may get through.' While speaking thus, one of my hearers called out, 'He must come down from his elephant, or he will never get through.' 'You are right,' I replied; 'yes, he must forsake his worldly mind, and descend from his height, and humble himself, or else he will never enter heaven.' Then I described another character, belonging to those of whom our Saviour said, 'Ye cannot serve God and mammon.' 'Here, my friends,' said I, ' comes a man who appears desirous to go to heaven; he has his eyes fixed on the strait gate, and is walking up to it; but on his back he carries a large bundle of various things: see how he groans under it! Will he succeed?' 'No,' said another man, 'he must leave his bundle behind, or else he will never get through.' 'You are perfectly right: if we wish to get through the strait gate into heaven the heart must be wholly given up to it: a divided heart God will not accept; he will either drive sin out of the heart of man, or sin will drive him out.' The people understood this very well, and applauded. The third class I wished to represent were the proud and self-righteous. Here I had nothing to do but to allude to a certain class of people who are constantly seen at Benares,—I mean the haughty Mohammedans. Without mentioning names, however, I continued, 'There comes another! You see he gives himself the air of a great and holy man. He says, I do no man any wrong; I repeat my prayers daily; I fast often; and give every one his due. Thus, conscious of his righteousness, he lifts up his head, and with firm step you see him walking up to the gate.' A man called out, 'He must stoop down, he must bow down, or else he will break his head,' I replied, 'Do you understand what you say?' 'Yes,' said he: 'he must leave his pride behind, and come as a poor sinner. Stooping signifies humility; and if he is not humbling himself, he will never enter through the strait gate.'"

8926. GATE, Vision of the Strait. I saw as if they were on the sunny side of some high mountain, there refreshing themselves with the pleasant beams of the sun, while I was shivering and shrinking in the cold, afflicted with frost, snow and dark clouds. Methought also betwixt me and them I saw a wall that did compass about this mountain. Now through this wall my soul did greatly desire to pass; concluding that if could, I would even go into the very midst of them, and there also comfort myself with the heat of their sun. About this wall I thought myself to go again and again, still prying as I went, to see if I could find some gap or passage to enter therein. But none could I find for some time. After much turning and moving about, at the last I saw, as it were, a narrow gap like a doorway in the wall through which I attempted to pass. Now, the passage being very strait and narrow, I made many offers to get in, but all in vain, even until I was well-nigh beat out by striving to get in. At last, with great striving, methought I at first did get in my head, and after that, by a sideling motion, my shoulders and my whole body. Then I was exceeding glad, went and sat down in the midst of them, and so was comforted with the light and heat of their sun. Now, this mountain and wall were thus made out to me. The mountain signified the Church of the living God; the sun that shone thereon, the comfortable shining of his merciful face on them that were therein; the wall, I thought was the world, that did make separation between the Christians and the world; and the gap that was in the wall, I thought, was Jesus Christ, who is the way to God the Father. But forasmuch as the passage was wonderful narrow, even so narrow that I could not but with great difficulty enter in thereat, it showed me that none could enter into life but those that were in downright earnest, and unless they left that wicked world behind them; for here was only room for body and soul, and not for body and soul and sin. *Bunyan.*

8927. GAYETY, Motives to. All assemblies of gayety are brought together by motives of the same kind. The theatre is not filled with those that know or regard the skill of the actor, nor the ball-room by those who dance, or attend to the dancers. To all places of general resort, where the standard of pleasure is erected, we run with equal eagerness, or appearance of eagerness, for very different reasons. One goes that he may say he has been there; another, because he never misses. This man goes to try what he can find, and that to discover what others find. Whatever diversion is costly will be frequented by those who desire to be thought rich; and whatever has, by any accident, become fashionable, easily continues its reputation, because every one is ashamed of not partaking it. *Johnson.*

8928. GENEROSITY, Arabian. Three men were disputing in the court of Caaba, who was the most liberal person among the Arabs. One gave the preference to Abdallah, the son of Jaafan, the uncle of Mohammed; another to Kais Ebn Saad Obâdah; and the third to Arâbah, of the tribe of Aros. After much debate, one that was present, to end the dispute, proposed that each of them should go to his friend, and ask his assistance; that they might see what every one gave, and form a judgment accordingly. This was agreed to; and Abdallah's friend going to him, found him with his foot in the stirrup, just mounting his camel for a journey, and thus accosted him; "Son of the uncle of the apostle of God, I am traveling, and in necessity." Upon which Abdallah alighted and bid him take the camel with all that was upon her; but desired him not to part with a sword, which happened to be fixed in the saddle, because it belonged to Ali, the son of Abutaleb. So he took the camel, and found on her some vests of silk, and 4,000 pieces of gold; but the thing of greatest value was the sword. The second went to Kais Ebn Saad, whose servant told him that his master was asleep, and desired to know his business. The friend answered that he came to ask Kais's assistance, being in want on the road. Whereupon the servant said that he had rather supply his necessity than wake his master; and gave him a purse of 7000 pieces of gold, assuring him that it was all the money then in the house. He also directed him to go to those who had the charge of the camels, with a certain token, and take a camel, and a slave, and return home with them. When Kais awoke, and his servant informed him what he had done, he gave him his freedom, and asked him why he did not call him, "for," said he, "I would have given him more." The third man went to Arâbah, and met him coming out of his house, in order to go to prayers, and leaning on two slaves, because his eyesight failed him. The friend no sooner made known his case than Arâbah let go the slaves, and, clapping his hands together, loudly lamented his misfortune in having no money, but desired him to take the two slaves, which the man refused to do, till Arâbah protested that, if he would not accept them, he gave them their liberty, and, leaving the slaves, groped his way along by the wall. On the return of the adventurers, judgment was unanimously, and with great justness, given by all who were present, that Arâbah was the most generous of the three. *George Sale.*

8929. GENEROSITY, Emblem of. Alexander Von Humboldt says of the cow-tree: "On the barren flank of a rock grows a tree with coriaceous and dry leaves. Its large woody roots can scarcely penetrate into the stone. For several months of the year not a single shower moistens its foliage. Its branches appear dead and dried; but when the trunk is pierced there flows from it a sweet and nourishing milk. It is at the rising of the sun that this vegetable fountain is most abundant. The negroes and natives are then seen hastening from all quarters, furnished with large bowls to receive the milk, which grows yellow, and thickens at its surface. Some empty their bowls under the tree itself, others carry the juice home to their children."

8930. GENEROSITY, Example. Turner, the painter, was one of the hanging committee of the Royal Academy, London. The walls were full when his attention was attracted by a picture sent in by an unknown provincial artist by the name of Bird. "A good picture," he exclaimed. "It must be hung up and exhibited." "Impossible," responded the other committee. "The arrangement cannot be disturbed. Quite impossible!" "A good picture," he repeated, "it must be hung up." They were obstinate and he resolute. He took down one of his own pictures and hung Bird's in its place. Moral: Do not imagine that you monopolize excellence. Give others a chance.

8931. GENEROSITY, Miracle of. Peter Damiani tells of a man confined in a monastery, whose eyes had been treacherously put out. Here he devoted himself to offices of charity, as far as his feeble body would permit. The man who had so cruelly put out his eyes, was brought in one day with a languishing malady. His conscience made him fear the man whom he had treated so, dreading that in revenge he might also put out his. But the blind man plead that he might be his nurse, and there devoted himself to him, giving him all the consideration and affection as was due a brother. Though blind, it was said he was all eyes, all arms, all hands, all heart to attend on him who had been so great an enemy.

8932. GENEROSITY Rewarded. During the siege of the Protestant city of Rochelle, some charitable individuals, who had previously formed secret magazines, relieved their starving brethren without blazoning their good deed. The relict of a merchant, named Prosni, who was left in charge of four orphan children, had liberally distributed her stores, while anything remained, among her less fortunate neighbors; and whenever she was reproached with profusion and want of foresight, she was in the habit of replying, "The Lord will provide for us." At length, when her stock of food was utterly exhausted, and she was spurned with taunts from the door of a relative, she returned home destitute, broken-hearted, and prepared to die, together with her children. But there was still a barrel and a cruse in reserve for the widow, who, humbly confident in the bounty of heaven, had shared her last morsel with her fellow-sufferers. Her little ones met her at the threshold with cries of joy. During her short absence, a stranger, visiting the house, had deposited in it a sack of flour; and the single bushel which it contained was so husbanded as to preserve their lives till the close of the siege. *Percy.*

8933. GENIUS, Alchemy of. The alchemy of genius can convert the commonest paths of life, the most commonplace and vulgar regions of society, into a perfect kingdom of romance. *Dufferin.*

8934. GENIUS, Fruitfulness of. Almost all poets of a first-rate excellence, dramatic poets above all, have been nearly as remarkable for the quantity as the quality of their compositions, nor has the first injuriously affected the second. Witness the seventy dramas of Æschylus, the more than ninety of Euripides, the hundred and thirteen of Sophocles. And if we consider the few years during which Shakspeare wrote, his fruitfulness is not less extraordinary. The vein has been a large and a copious one, and has flowed freely forth, keeping itself free and clear by the very act of its constant ebullition. And the fact is very explicable; it is not so much they that have spoken, as their nation that has spoken by them. *Trench.*

8935. GENIUS, Industry and. We would say of legal education, as we would say of all other education—that perseverance and a habit of attention are of more value than that sort of natural talent which consists in quick-ness of apprehension. A celebrated ambassador of the last age, when told what a clever boy his son was, exclaimed, "I would rather you had told me how industrious he was." Sir Henry Wotton, the famous provost of Eton College, we are told by Aubrey, could not abide wits. When any young scholar was commended to him as a wit, he would say, "Out upon him! I will have nothing to do with him; give me the plodding student: if I would look for wits I would go to Newgate for them; there be the wits." Something similar was the opinion of Hogarth: "I know of no such thing as genius," said he to Mr. Gilbert Cooper; "genius is nothing but labor and diligence." The well-known Judge Doddridge declares that he found by experience that "among a number of quick wits in youth, few are found in the end very fortunate for themselves, or very profitable to the commonwealth." *Law and Lawyers.*

8936. GENIUS, Influence of. It is the prerogative of genius to confer a measure of itself upon inferior intelligences. In reading the works of Milton, Bacon, and Newton, thoughts greater than the growth of our own minds are transplanted into them; and feelings more profound, sublime, or comprehensive, are insinuated amidst our ordinary train; while, in the eloquence with which they are clothed, we learn a new language, worthy of the new ideas created in us. By habitual communion with superior spirits, we are not only enabled to think their thoughts, speak their dialect, feel their emotions, but our own thoughts are refined, our scanty language is enriched, our common feelings are elevated; and though we may never attain their standard, yet by keeping company with them, we shall rise above our own; as trees growing in the society of a forest are said to draw each other up into shapely and stately proportion, while field and hedge-row stragglers, exposed to all weathers, never reach their full stature, luxuriance, or beauty. *James Montgomery.*

8937. GENIUS, Labor and. The greatest genius of his time, Alexander Hamilton, once said, "Men give me credit for genius. All the genius I have lies just in this: when I have a subject in hand, I study it profoundly. Day and night it is before me. I explore it in all its bearings. My mind becomes pervaded with it. Then the effect which I make, the people are pleased to call the fruit of genius. It is the fruit of labor and thought." Dr. Bethune said, respecting his own oratorical reputation, "People say it is genius. But I tell you it is hard sweat! That is the secret."

8938. GENIUS, Rarity of. The proportion of genius to the vulgar, is like one to a million; but genius without tyranny, without pretension, that judges the weak with equity, the superior with humanity, and equals with justice, is like one to ten millions. *Lavater.*

8939. GENIUS to be Respected. Genius, strictly speaking, is only entitled to respect when it promotes the peace and improves the happiness of mankind. What should we think of the gardener who planted his flower-bed with henbane and deadly night-shade? What should we think of the general who, being intrusted with an army and a plentiful supply of military stores, applied these powers to degrading and enslaving his own country? He would be visited with scorn, and punished as a traitor. And why should the man who directs the artillery of his genius, delegated to him for high and holy purposes, to shaking those foundations on which the happiness of his species rests, and who applies the divine spark within him to the kindling of low and debasing passions, be allowed to hear his plaudits swelled in proportion as his powers of doing mischief become apparent. Talent is always accompanied with the responsibility of using it rightly; and the neglect or pity of the virtuous is the penalty which the child of genius pays, or ought to pay, for its abuse. However splendid talents may compel our admiration, they have no right to claim the general esteem of mankind when their possessor exercises them without regard of what is due to the well-being of society and himself.   *Lit. Gazette.*

8940. GENIUS, Unknown. A man's genius is always, in the beginning of life, as much unknown to himself as to others; and it is only after frequent trials, attended with success, that he dares think himself equal to those undertakings in which those who have succeded have fixed the admiration of mankind. *Hume.*

8941. GENIUS, Wife of a. Oftentimes as I have lain swinging on the water, in the swell of the Chelsea ferryboats, in that long, sharp-pointed black cradle in which I love to let the great mother rock me, I have seen a tall ship glide by against the tide, as if drawn by some invisible tow-line, with a hundred strong arms pulling it. Her sails hung unfilled, her streamers were drooping, she had neither side-wheel nor stern-wheel; still she moved on, stately, in serene triumph, as if with her own life. But I knew that on the other side of the ship, hidden beneath the great bulk that swam so majestically, there was a little toiling steam tug, with heart of fire and arms of iron, that was hugging it close, and dragging it bravely on; and I knew that if the little steam tug untwined her arms and left the tall ship, it would wallow and roll about and drift hither and thither, and go off with the refluent tide, no man knows whither. And so I have known more than one genius, high-decked, full-freighted, wide-sailed, gay-pennoned, that, but for the bare toiling arms, and brave, warm, beating heart of the faithful little wife that nestled close in his shadow, and clung to him, so that no wind nor wave could part them, and dragged him on against all the tide of circumstance, would soon have gone down the stream and been heard of no more.   *Holmes.*

8942. GENTILES, Biblical. EMBLEMS. *Dogs,* Phil. 3: 2; Matt. 15: 26. *Wild olive trees,* Rom. 11: 24. *Christ's "other sheep, not of this fold,"* John 10: 16. *Aliens and strangers,* Eph. 2: 12. RECEPTION into the Church. Illustrated by—(*a*) Many of our Lord's para-

bles, as the transfer of the *Jewish vineyard,* Mark 12: 9. (*b*) *Peter's vision,* Acts 10: 10-16, 28. (*c*) "*The middle wall of partition*" broken down, Eph. 2: 14, referring probably to the partition wall in the Jewish temple, on which notices were put up forbidding Gentiles to enter; which parting-wall is done away in Christ. THE ABRAHAMIC COVENANT was designed to include all true believers, from the very first, especially as enlarged to Jacob, Gen. 35: 11; Rom. 4: 11, 12, 16, 17. THE TABERNACLE AND TEMPLE—It is well worthy of note how the materals of the tabernacle and temple were obtained from Gentile sources—the gold and silver and fine linen from Egypt; the cedars of Lebanon from Hiram; the brass from Syria, etc. THE LORD JESUS—The Lord's favor towards the Gentiles, and his tender dealings with them, were marked in many ways—(1) Some of Christ's most expressive titles exhibit this—"The light of the *world*" ("not of the Jews only"), Luke 2: 32; John 8: 12; cf. Isa. 42: 6, 7; so also the title of "the corner-stone," Eph. 2: 20; "the desire (or *desideratum*) of all nations," Haggai 2: 7. (2) Some of Christ's miracles—Matt. 8: 5-13 (the centurion's servant); Matt. 15: 21-28 (the Syrophœnician's daughter); Mark 5: 1-20 (the Gadarene—most probably a Gentile). (3) Some of Christ's parables. (4) His commendation of the faith of a Gentile, Matt. 8: 10; and of the good Samaritan, Luke 10: 30-37. Christ was honored at his birth by Gentiles from the East, Matt. 2: 1-11; and, near his death, by Gentiles from the West, John 12: 20-21. The first acknowledgment of the righteousness of Christ at his death was made, not by a priest nor by a Jew, but by a Gentile and a soldier, Mark 15: 39. THE GOSPELS of St. Mark and St. Luke were written especially for Gentile Christians. FOUR PRECIOUS WORDS, properly Jewish, have gained a common usage alike by Jew and Gentile—Abba—Hosanna—Hallelujah—Amen.   *Bowes.*

8943. GENTILES, Manifestation of Christ to the. A festival called the Epiphany, which signifies "an appearance of light, a manifestation," is kept on the 6th of January, to celebrate the manifestation of Christ to the Gentiles, and especially to the magi. His Majesty offers annually by proxy at the Chapel Royal, St. James', gold, frankincense and myrrh. In the eastern nations, when they did homage to their kings, they made them a present. Thus the subjection of the kings of Sheba to Christ is spoken of (Psalm 72: 10). What the wise men presented, were intended by Providence as a seasonable relief to Joseph and Mary in their poor condition. "These," says Mr. Henry, "were the products of their own country." What God favors us with, we must honor him with.   *Buck.*

8944. GENTLEMAN, Qualities of a. What is it to be a gentleman? It is to be honest, to be gentle, to be generous, to be brave, to be wise, and, possessing all these qualities, to exercise them in the most graceful outward manner. Ought a gentleman to be a loyal son, a true husband, an honest father? Ought his life to be decent, his bills to be paid, his tastes to be high and elegant, his aims in life lofty and noble?   *Thackeray.*

8945. GENTLEMAN, The True. The true gentleman is one whose nature has been fashioned after the highest models. It is a grand old name, that of gentleman, and has been recognized as a rank and power in all stages of society. To possess this character is a dignity of itself, commanding the instinctive homage of every generous mind, and those who will not bow to titular rank, will yet do homage to the gentleman. His qualities depend not upon fashion or manners, but upon moral worth—not on personal possessions, but on personal qualities. The Psalmist briefly describes him as one "that walketh uprightly, and worketh righteousness, and speaketh the truth in his heart."   *Smiles.*

8946. GENTLEMAN, True Basis of the. Religion is the most gentlemanly thing of the world. It alone will gentilize, if unmixed with cant.   *Coleridge.*

8947. GENTLEMEN, Rarity of. Perhaps a gentleman is a rarer man than some of us think for. Which of us can point out many such in his circle—men whose aims are generous, whose truth is constant, and not only constant in its kind, but elevated in its degree; whose want of meanness makes them simple, who can look the world honestly in the face, with an equal manly sympathy for the great and small? We all know a hundred whose coats are very well made, and a score who have excellent manners, and one or two happy beings who are what they call in the inner circles, and have shot into the very centre and bull's-eye of fashion; but of gentlemen, how many? Let us take a little scrap of paper, and each make out his list.   *Thackeray.*

8948. GENTLENESS, Advised. "I cannot forbear pointing out to you, my dearest child," said Lord Collingwood to his daughter, "the great advantage that will result from a temperate conduct and sweetness of manner to all people on all occasions. Never forget that you are a gentlewoman, and all your words and actions should make you gentle. I never heard your mother—your dear, good mother—say a harsh or hasty thing to any person in my life. Endeavor to imitate her. I am quick and hasty in my temper; but, my darling, it is a misfortune which, not having been sufficiently restrained in my youth, has caused me inexpressible pain. It has given me more trouble to subdue this impetuosity . than anything I ever undertook."

8949. GENTLENESS, Definition of. Gentleness, which belongs to virtue, is to be carefully distinguished from the mean spirit of cowards, and the fawning assent of sycophants. It removes no just right from fear; it gives up no important truth from flattery; it is, indeed, not only consistent with a firm mind, but it necessarily requires a manly spirit and a fixed principle, in order to give it any real value. *Blair.*

8950. GEOLOGY, Facts of. So long as phenomena are simply recorded, and only the natural and obvious causes drawn from them there can be no fear that the results of the study may prove hostile to religion. How much wiser was the counsel of Gamaliel, and how applicable to those who impugned these pursuits—"Refrain from these men and let them alone; for if the work be of men it will fall to nothing; but if of God ye are not able to destroy it." If the representations they have given of nature are the fictions of men, they cannot stand against the progress of science; if they truly picture the works of God, they must be easily reconcilable with his revealed manifestations. *Cardinal Wiseman.*

8951. GETTING ON, The Goddess of. Speaking of the real, active, continual, national worship, that by which men act while they live; not that which they talk of when they die. Now, we have indeed a nominal religion, to which we pay tithes of property and sevenths of time; but we have also a practical and earnest religion, to which we devote nine-tenths of our property and six-sevenths of our time; and we dispute a great deal about the nominal religion; but we are all unanimous about this practical one, of which I think you will admit that the ruling goddess may be best generally described as the "Goddess of Getting-on," or, "Britannia of the Market." The Athenians had an "Athena Agoraia," or Minerva of the market; but she was a subordinate type of their goddess, while our Britannia Agoraia is the principal type of ours. And all your great architectural works are, of course, built to her. It is long since you built a great cathedral; and how you would laugh at me, if I proposed building a cathedral on the top of one of those hills of yours, taking it for an Acropolis! But your railroad mounds—prolonged masses of Acropolis; your railroad stations—vaster than the Parthenon and innumerable; your chimneys—how much more mighty and costly than cathedral spires! your harbor piers; your warehouses; your exchanges!—all these are built to your great goddess of "Getting-on;" and she has formed, and will continue to form your architecture, as long as you worship her; and it is quite vain to ask me to tell you how to build to her; you know far better than I.   *Ruskin.*

8952. GHOSTS, Belief in. Our forefathers looked upon nature with more reverence and horror, before the world was enlightened by learning and philosophy; and loved to astonish themselves with the apprehensions of witchcraft, prodigies, charms and enchantments. There was not a village in England that had not a ghost in it; the church-yards were all haunted; every large common had a circle of fairies belonging to it; and there was not a shepherd to be met with who had not seen a spirit.   *Addison.*

8953. GIFT, Graceful. Arcesilaus visited Apelles in his sickness, and finding him extremely poor, repeated his visit with twenty drachms in his pocket. Sitting by his bedside, he said, "You have got nothing here but Em pedocles's elements, fire, water, earth, and the surrounding air; neither, methinks, do you lie easily." And stirring up his pillow, he put the money privately under his head. When the good old woman, his nurse, found it, and, in great wonder, acquainted Apelles with it, "Aye," said he, smiling, "this is a piece of Arcesilaus's thievery."

8954. GIFT of Tongues. The gift of tongues, and other supernatural faculties, were signs and seals of the spiritual power which had now visited the church, audible and visible attestations to the world of the divine energy which was now working in men's souls; these outward manifestations were intended to draw attention to the inward gift, to arouse carnal natures to the sense of what eye could not see and ear could not hear; but they were only as the thunder and lightning of the new spiritual world, occasional and impressive incidents and powers and processes, whose constant silent operation is the very life of men; were only, to quote Foster's expressive words, as "the ringing of the great bell of the universe," intimating that "the sermon to follow must be extraordinary." *Morris.*

8955. GIFTS, All Have. Every one hath some excellency or other in him, can we but find and improve it. God hath dispensed his gifts diversely, for the common benefit. And as, in the same pasture, the ox can find fodder, the hound a hare, the stork a lizard, the fair maid flowers: so there is none so worthless, but something may be made of him; some good extracted out of the unlikeliest. Yea, wisdom is such an elixir, as by contact (if there be any disposition of goodness in the same metal) it will render it of the property. *Trapp.*

8956. GIFTS, Angry. One day a native brought a hog to Hautia, the treasurer of the South Sea Islands Missionary Association, and throwing down the animal at his feet, said, in an angry tone, "Here's a pig for your Society." "Take it back again," replied Hautia, calmly; "God does not accept angry pigs." He then explained to the man the objects of missionary institutions, and the necessity of those who supported them doing so from right motives, especially enforcing the Scripture words, "The Lord loveth a cheerful giver." The man, exceedingly chagrined, was obliged to take his hog home again.

8957. GIFTS, Best. The best thing to give to your enemy is forgiveness; to an opponent, tolerance; to a friend, your heart; to your child, a good example; to a father, deference; to your mother, conduct that will make her proud of you; to yourself, respect; to all men, charity. *Mrs. Balfour.*

8958. GIFTS, Biblical. Luke 10: 17–20—The abundance of gifts, however great, can never be compared with the blessedness of saving grace. 1 Cor. 12: 4–11. (1) All our gifts are bestowed by God. (2) Our gifts are various—the blessed Spirit "dividing to every man severally as he will." (3) All are given for "profit," and not for pride. 1 Cor. 12: 31; 13—The greatest gifts are nothing in compar-

ison with love. Eph. 4: 7. (1) Every one has some gifts; therefore all should be useful. (2) No one has all gifts; therefore none should be proud. (3) Every one has his gifts, according to the gift of Christ; therefore all should be content. (4) Every one's gift is for the general good; therefore we should seek the union of the Church. (5) All gifts are out of Christ's fullness (ver. 8); therefore all should seek close union and fellowship with him.
Bowes.

8959. GIFTS, Diversity of. In the Christian church the gifts and graces of men differ widely: some are adapted to adorn one station of life, and some another; these to flourish best in the humble valley of life, and others to bear the rough blasts of the mountain. The soil of poverty is best suited to unfold the qualities of some, and others flourish well amidst the strong sunshine of prosperity and the fertile soil in which their lot has been planted. All, however, are alike nourished by the same general means of grace, though the Spirit "divideth to every man severally as he will;" but prayer, the breath of heaven, is the atmosphere in which all must live. All must be baptized and watered by the same Spirit, and be fed with a due portion of the wholesome food of God's word. Thus nurtured and strengthened, every member of the church, in his proper season and place, like the flowers of the garden, adorns the situation which he fills, becomes a bright and beautiful example of godliness in his particular sphere of duty, and abundantly proclaims the wisdom and goodness of him who transplanted him from the wilderness of this world, to a place where he may adorn and magnify the riches of divine grace. *Salter.*

8960. GIFTS, Estimate of. Artexerxes, King of Persia, received a gift from a country laborer of two handfuls of water from the river. He prized it highly, because the poor man had nothing else to give, and gave it with evident affection.

8961. GIFTS, Grace Preferable to. The meanest grace is above the highest intellectual parts, as the smile of a sunbeam is more powerful to chase away the grim darkness of the night than the sparkling of a diamond. *S. T. Treasury.*

8962. GIFTS without Hearts. It is said of the Lacedæmonians, who were a poor and homely people, that they offered lean sacrifices to their gods; and that the Athenians, who were a wise and wealthy people, offered fat and costly sacrifices; and yet in their wars the former had always mastery over the latter. Whereupon they went to the oracle to know the reason why those should speed worst who gave most. The oracle returned this answer to them: "The Lacedæmonians are a people who give their hearts to their gods, but the Athenians only give their gifts to their gods." Thus, hearts without gifts are better than gifts without hearts. *W. Secker.*

8963. GIFTS, Unacceptable. On the occasion of a missionary collection taken in native products, in Tahiti, a person brought a quantity of cocoa-nut oil to Pomare in a bad spirit, exclaim ing, "Here are five bamboos of oil; take them for your society." "No," said the King, "I will not mix your angry bamboos with the missionary oil; take them away."

8964. GIVING, Beauty of. The moon is a great giver, and she owes all her beauty to this habit of giving. Suppose the moon should swallow up, and keep to itself all the rays of light which the sun gives it, and should refuse to give them to us, what would the effect be? It would stop shining. And the moment it stopped shining it would lose all its beauty. All the beauty of the brilliancy of the diamond is owing to its reflecting, or giving away, the light which it receives from the sun. And this is the way with the moon. If it should stop shining, or giving away the light it gets from the sun, it would hang up in the sky a great black, ugly-looking ball. All its brightness and beauty would be gone. *Dr. Newton.*

8965. GIVING our Best to God. An illustration may be taken from some of the old sacred buildings. You will find them "finished with the most circumstantial elegance and minuteness in those concealed portions which are excluded from public view, and which can only be inspected by laborious climbing or groping," a fact explained by saying, "that the whole carving and execution was considered as an act of solemn worship and adoration, in which the artist offered up his best faculties to the praise of the Creator." These men of the "dark ages," as we love in the pride of our compassion to call them, had in this a true and grand idea: what would they say of our veneered and gilded modern life, in which everything is for show and nothing from reality, everything for a purpose and nothing from a principle? As these men builded, so David sacrificed. They builded not for man, and hence the secret and distant parts of the work were just as accurately conceived and finely finished as those exposed to the public gaze; their object was not to do something as cheaply and easily as possible, but something as well as possible; they wished to raise structures worthy of the Lord; they had a zeal for his glory and the glory of his worship which spurned meanness and imperfection, however hidden; and the same spirit in David rendered needful to him what was needless in itself, and made it "more blessed to give" an offering of his own, than one received from Araunah. (2 Sam. 24:24.) *Morris.*

8966. GIVING, Cheerful. As the Giver of all things, so each receiver loveth a cheerful giver. For a bargain is valued by the worth of the thing bought, but a gift by the party giving, which made the widow's mite of more worth than the riches of superfluity. I see then he gives not best that gives most, but he gives most that gives best. If then I cannot give bountifully, yet I will give freely, and what I want in my hand supply by my heart. He gives well that gives willingly. *Warwick.*

8967. GIVING to God. Behold, "I am a great King," saith God (Mal. 1:8, 14). He stands upon his seniority, and looks to be honored with the best of our substance. Mary that loved much, thought nothing too much for her Saviour. She brought an alabaster box of ointment of great price, and poured it upon him, and he defends her in it against those that held it waste (John 12:7). Among the Papists, their Lady of Loretto hath her churches so stuffed with vowed presents of the best, as they are fain to hang their cloisters and churchyards with them. Shall not their superstition rise up and condemn our irreligion, our slumbering service, and dough-baked duties? The Turks build their private houses low and homely, but their mosques or temples stately and magnificent. *Trapp.*

8968. GIVING, Means of. "A few days ago," says Dr. Schwartz, the editor of the *Scattered Nation*, and founder of a Christian Jewish home, "I received a letter, and on the inside of the envelope, which contained six penny stamps and nothing else, these words were written: 'Fasted a meal to give a meal.'"

8969. GIVING, Necessity for. Said a good man to me when I asked him, "How do you manage to give so much?" "The Lord is all the time shoveling it on me, and I would be overwhelmed if I did not give." God shovels wealth upon us, and if we do not shovel it back, we will be buried beneath it as by an avalanche of ruin. *Dr. Dashiell.*

8970. GIVING, the Only Saving. A gentleman of wealth in the city of New York once gave $25,000 for the erection of a church, where the congregation were too poor to build themselves. It became a church noted for the piety and evangelical character of its pastor and people. In a few years its liberal patron lost all his earthly fortune, and being approached by a friend, who has eyes only for this world, who said to him, "Now if you had the money you gave to —— church, it would set you up in business." "Sir," said he, "that is the only money I have saved; if it had not been there it would have gone with the other; as it is, I have it yielding me an interest which will only cease to accumulate when the knell of time is sounded, and during the ages of eternity will be poured into my bosom, in the blessed consolation that hundreds have bowed at the altar erected with that money, and acknowledged their Saviour."

8971. GIVING, Parsimonious. We give God the worst of all things, that hath given us the best. We cull out the bad sheep for his tithe, the sleepiest hours for his prayers, the clippings of our wealth for his poor, a corner of the heart for his ark, when Dagon sits uppermost in his temple. We give God measure for measure, but after an ill sort. For his blessings heapen, and shaken, and thrust together, iniquities pressed down and yet running over. He hath bowels of brass and a heart of iron, that cannot mourn at this our requital. *Adams.*

8972. GIVING, Receiving and. There is nothing made for itself—nothing whose powers and influences are entirely circumscribed to self. Whatever a creature receives it gives out, with the modification and increase of its own force. The clouds borrow water of the ocean but they pour it forth again in refreshing showers upon the thirsty hills, which in their turn send them amongst the valleys. Planets borrow light of their centres, and forthwith fling their rays abroad upon the dark regions of space through which they roll. The tree borrows from every part of the world in order to build up itself; but it gives out, in return, beauty, fragrance, and fruit. Thus, all things give what they appropriate. The material is but the emblem of the spiritual; and thus all nature typifies man's distributive function. Truly, he who appropriates and gives not is an anomaly in the universe. A miser is a monster that no heart can love. *Dr. Thomas.*

8973. GIVING, Rule for. Before a collection in Surrey Chapel, a gentleman on the platform said, "I hope every one will give a little." Upon this Rowland Hill arose and exclaimed in a loud voice, "I hope every one will give a deal."

8974. GIVING, the Tenth. Jay Cooke, of Philadelphia, early in his life read "Gold and the Gospel," and resolved to take Jacob's pledge, "Of all that thou shalt give me, I will surely give the tenth unto thee." He directed his clerk to open an account with O. P. J. (Old Patriarch Jacob), and to credit to it one-tenth of all the commissions that came into the office. Some of the largest financial transactions of the country were trusted to the firm of which he was a member, and its success was one of the wonders of the land. O. P. J. account amounted to a sum that would take the figures of five places to express. When asked how he could afford to give such large contributions, he said, "It don't cost me anything; it's the Lord's money I give."

8975. GLORY, Dawn of. Some years ago, in the city of Brooklyn, it was my great privilege to pay frequent pastoral visits to a saint on the eve of her translation. Her room was always an open gate of heaven. One day I received a message from her that she was in trouble, and wished to see me. Wondering what final art the arch enemy might be using against her, I hastened to her bedside. She said, "I cannot pray any more. As soon as I begin, my prayers are all turned into hallelujahs. I would have esteemed it a privilege if God would have permitted me to spend my remaining days in supplications for my friends; but as soon as I open my mouth, it is all glory, glory, glory!" I congratulated her on being drafted into the employment of the celestial choir before the time. She lived for two weeks in a gust of praise, and so she died. It seemed as though the "light which no man can approach unto" had streamed out over the walls of jasper, and come down to earth to linger about that humble cot. "Let me die the death of the righteous." *Dr. Foss.*

8976. GLORY, Death in Spite of. Constantine showed all the glories of Rome to a Persian king. The Persian said, "These are wonderful things, but yet I see that men die at Rome as well as in Persia."

8977. GLORY, Degrees of. Though the angels and saints have different degrees of glory, yet every one is perfectly happy and pleased. As the strings of an instrument differ in the size and sound; some are sharp and high, some grave and deep, others a mean, so that if every string had judgment and election, it would choose to be what it is: so from the different degrees of glory in heaven, the most amiable and equal order appears that satisfies every one. *Dr. Bates.*

8978. GLORY, Divine. God's glory is seen when he works by means; it is more seen when he works without means; it is seen, above all, when he works contrary to means. It was a great work to open the eyes of the blind; it was a greater still to do it by applying clay and spittle. He sent a horror of great darkness on Abraham, when he was preparing to give him the best light. He touched the hollow of Jacob's thigh, and lamed him, when he was going to bless him. He smote Paul with blindness, when he was intending to open the eyes of his mind. He refused the request of the woman of Canaan for a while, but afterwards she obtained her desire. See, therefore, that all the paths of the Lord are mercy, and that all things work together for good to them that love him. *Daniel Rowlands.*

8979. GLORY, End of. Cyrus the Great, after all his conquests and renown, ordered the following inscription to be engraved upon his tomb: "O man! whatsoever thou art, and whencesoever thou comest, I know that thou wilt come to the same condition in which I now am. I am Cyrus, who brought empire to the Persians. Do not envy me, I beseech thee, this little piece of ground which covereth my body."

8980. GLORY, Fickleness of. Heliogabalus sometimes had his courtiers tied fast to a great wheel, and then had it revolved swiftly, partly in the water. Sometimes they were in the air and sometimes deeply plunged in the water. Ambitious men are daily acting the same play. One of the Kings of France, seeing his likeness on a piece of money, and representing him upon the uppermost part of fortune's wheel, said to his Chancellor, "You would do well to pin it fast there, lest the wheel should turn again."

8981. GLORY, Foretaste and Consummation of. If there be so much delight in believing, oh, how much more is there in beholding! What is the wooing day to the wedding day? What is the sealing of the conveyance, to the enjoyment of the inheritance? or the foretaste of glory to the fullness of glory? The good things of that life are so great, as not to be measured; so many, as not to be enumerated; and so precious as not to be estimated. If the picture of holiness be so comely in its rough drafts, how lovely a piece will it be in all its perfections! Every grace which is here seen in its minority, shall be seen there in its maturity. *Secker.*

8982. GLORY, Heavenly. All that awaits us is glorious. There is "a rest," a Sabbath-keeping in store for us, Heb. 4: 6; and this "rest shall be glorious." Isa. 11: 10. The kingdom that we claim is a glorious kingdom, the crown which we are to wear is a glorious crown. The city of our habitation is a glorious city. The garments which shall clothe us are garments "for glory and beauty." Our bodies shall be glorious bodies, fashioned after the likeness of Christ's "glorious body." Phil. 3, 21. Our society shall be that of the glorified. Our songs shall be songs of glory. And of the region which we are to inhabit it is said, the glory of God doth lighten it, and the Lamb is the light thereof. Rev. 21: 23. "That they may behold my glory," the Lord pleaded for his own. This is the sum of all. Other glories there will be, as we shall see; but this is the sum of all. It is the very utmost that even "the Lord of glory" could ask for them.   *H. Bonar.*

8983. GLORY, Greed of. Darius sought to rescue his family from Alexander, and save a part of his kingdom, by offering him his daughter for his wife, and the largest part of his empire for her dower, and ten thousand talents. Alexander answered that he would not receive what he could command. Darius renewed his previous offer, only adding more gold. Alexander replied, "As the world would not endure two suns, neither could the earth endure two sovereign Emperors, without permutation of the state of all things. Yield today, or prepare for war to-morrow."

8984. GLORY, Passion for. One of the strongest incitements to excel in such arts and accomplishments as are in the highest esteem among men, is the natural passion which the mind of man has for glory; which though it may be faulty in the excess of it, ought by no means to be discouraged. Perhaps some moralists are too severe in beating down this principle, which seems to be a spring implanted by nature to give motion to all the latent powers of the soul, and is always observed to exert itself with the greatest force in the most generous dispositions. The men whose characters shone brightest among the ancient Romans were strongly animated by this passion.   *Hughes.*

8985. GLORY, Preservation of. As those workmen on whom was incumbent the charge of keeping in repair the Delian ship, by supplying and putting into the place of the decayed planks and timber others that were new and sound, seem to have preserved it from ancient times, as if it were eternal and incorruptible; so the preserving and upholding of one's glory is as the keeping in of a fire, a work of no difficulty, requiring only to be supplied with a little fuel; but when either of them is wholly extinct and suppressed, one cannot without labor rekindle it again. Lampis, the sea commander, being asked how he got his wealth, answered, "My greatest estate I gained easily enough, but the smaller slowly and with much labor."   *Plutarch.*

8986. GLORY, Road to. The road to glory would cease to be arduous, if it were trite and trodden; and great minds must be ready not only to take opportunities, but to make them. Alexander dragged the Pythian priestess to the temple on a forbidden day. She exclaimed "My son, thou art invincible!" which was oracle enough for him. On a second occasion he cut the Gordian knot, which others had in vain attempted to untie. Those who start for human glory, like the mettled hounds of Actæon, must pursue the game not only where there is a path, but where there is none. They must be able to simulate and dissimulate, to leap and to creep; to conquer the earth like Cæsar, or to fall down and kiss it like Brutus; to throw their sword like Brennus into the trembling scale; or, like Nelson, to snatch the laurels from the doubtful hand of victory, while she is hesitating where to bestow them. That policy that can strike only while the iron is hot, will be overcome by that perseverance which, like Cromwell's, can make the iron hot by striking; and he that can only rule the storm must yield to him who can both raise and rule it.   *Colton.*

8987. GLORY, Universal Desire for. Pliny finding fire everywhere, in every house, in the pebbles under his feet, in fiery meteors, and subterranean passages, and considering what a destructive element it is, marveled that the whole world was not consumed. Wanley applies this simile to a universal desire for earthly glory, and expresses his wonder that it has done no more harm than it has. Tacitus says that it is the last garment a man strips himself of.

8988. GLORY, Vision of. Thomas Aquinas, the Angelical doctor, the most famous preacher and extensive writer of his time, was engaged upon his Summa Theologiæ. He left off to celebrate the sacrament, when he was overwhelmed with glory and filled with a marvelous rapture. After this he could not be induced to sit down to his writing desk, nor would he dictate anything. His attendant, Rainald, urged him to finish the "Summa," then nearly completed. He replied "I cannot, for everything that I have written seems to me worthless compared with what I have seen, and what has been revealed to me." This occurred not long before his death. In its effulgence he finished his course, March 7th, 1274.

8989. GOD, Access to. During the war, President Lincoln was so besieged with applicants on various errands that he could not give audience to all, and men of influence could not see him when they wished. Many went away from the White House disappointed, unable to see the President. But there was a loved son of the President, little "Tad," who came and went when he pleased. Such is the privilege of the sons of God.

8990. GOD, Activity of. He works every moment in every part of this vast whole; moves every atom, expands every leaf, finishes every blade of grass, erects every tree, conducts every particle of vapor, every drop of rain, and every flake of snow; guides every ray of light, breathes in every wind, thunders in every storm, wings the lightning, pours the streams and rivers, empties the volcano, heaves the ocean, and shakes the globe. In the universe of minds, he formed, he preserves, he animates, and he directs, all the mysterious and wonderful powers of knowledge, virtue, and moral action, which fill up the infinite extent of his immense and eternal empire.   *Dr. Dwight.*

8991. GOD, All for. The Rev. John Leggoe, writing from Lakemba, on the Fiji Islands, gives an account of a missionary meeting held there in March, 1871. Each tribe came singing, led by their chiefs to the chapel, and passed up to the table, whereon they laid their gifts. "An old chief was leading his tribe to the chapel; and as soon as he reached the door, he was deeply moved and greatly excited, and with the tears streaming from his eyes, he cried out, 'What shall I give unto the Lord? Oh! that I had something to give him in return for all he has given me. Oh! that I were rich, that I had gold or land to give. I have only this mite (holding up a sovereign). No! this is not all. I will give myself—my body, my soul, my all.' Who can doubt, that the Lord accepted the offering?"

8992. GOD, All-Seeing. When spiders stretched their webs across the eyelids of Jupiter, notwithstanding all the efforts that Greek sculpture had put forth to make the image awful, the human worshiper would hide, without scruple, in his heart, the thoughts which he did not wish his deity to know. It was even an express tenet of the heathen superstitions that the authority of the gods was partial and local. One who was dreadful on the hills might be safely despised in the valleys. In this feature, as in all others, the popish idolatry, imitative rather than inventive, follows the rut in which the ancient current ran. A god or a saint that should really cast the glance of a pure eye into the conscience of the worshiper would not long be held in repute. The grass would grow again round that idol's shrine. A seeing god would not do: the idolater wants a blind god. The first cause of idolatry is a desire in an impure heart to escape from the look of the living God, and none but a dead image would serve the turn.   *Arnot.*

8993. GOD Always with us. Old Rome had (as every city amongst the heathen had) certain gods which they called their tutelar gods, gods that were affected to the preservation of that place; but they durst never call upon those gods by their proper names, for fear of losing them; lest if their names should be known by their enemies, their enemies should win away their gods from them, by bestowing more cost, or more devotion towards them than they themselves used. So also it is said of them, that when they had brought to Rome a foreign god, which they had taken in a conquered place, Victory, they cut the wings of their new god Victory, lest he should fly from them again. This was a misery, that they were not sure of their gods when they had them. We are; if he once come to us, he never goes from us, out of any variableness in himself, but in us only; that promise reaches to the whole church, and to every particular soul, "'Thy teacher shall not be removed into a corner any more, but thine eye shall see thy teachers," which in the original (as is applicable to our present purpose, noted by Rabbi Moses) is, *Non erunt doctores tui alati,* "Thy teachers shall have no wings, they shall never fly from thee; and so the great translation reads it, *non avolabunt."* As their great god Victory could not fly from Rome, so after this victory which God hath given his church in the Reformation, none of her teachers should fly to, or towards Rome. Every way that God comes to us, he comes with a purpose to stay, and would imprint in us an assurance that he doth so, and that impression is this compassing of thy soul "with songs of deliverance," in the signification of which word, we shall in one word conclude all.   *Dr. Donne.*

8994. GOD, Angry with. Montaigne tells of a neighboring king, who having received a blow from the hand of God, swore he would be revenged. In order to do so, he made a proclamation, that for ten years to come no one should pray to God, or so much as mention him throughout his dominions.

8995. GOD, Argument for. He who can imagine the universe fortuitous or self-created is not a subject for argument, provided he has the power of thinking, or even the faculty of seeing. He who sees no design cannot claim the character of a philosopher; for philosophy traces means and ends. He who traces no causes must not assume to be a metaphysician; and if he does trace them, he must arrive at a first cause. And he who perceives no final causes is equally deficient in metaphysics and in natural philosophy; since, without this, he cannot generalize—can discover no plan where there is no purpose. But if he who can see a creation without seeing a creator has made small advances in knowledge, so he who can philosophize on it, and not feel the eternal presence of its Great Author, is little to be envied, even as a mere philosopher; since he deprives the universe of all its grandeur, and himself of the pleasures springing from those exalted views which soar beyond the details of tangible forms and common events. And if with that presence around him he can be evil, he is an object of compassion; for he will be rejected by him whom he opposes or rejects.   *Dr. Macculloch.*

8996. GOD Armed. The Spartans always represented their gods in statues or images as fully armed. Charillus was asked the reason of this, and answered, "That those reproaches we cast upon men for their cowardice may not reflect upon the gods, and that our youths may not supplicate the deities unarmed."

8997. GOD, Assistance of. God and one man constitute a majority.—*Anon.*——God is multitudinous above all the nations of the earth.—*Beecher.*—— "A penny and Theresa are nothing, but a penny and God are everything," was St. Theresa's motto on founding a grand monastery.

8998. GOD, Benevolence of. The benevolence of our Great Creator is chanted even by things unpleasant to the ear. "The nuptial song of reptiles," says Kirby, "is not, like that of birds, the delight of every heart; but it is rather calculated to disturb and horrify than to still the soul. The hiss of serpents, the croakings of frogs and toads, the moanings of turtles, the bellowing of crocodiles and alligators, form their gamut of discords." Here, also, we may read beneficent design. Birds are the companions of man in the lawn and forest, in his solitary walks, amidst his rural labors, and around the home of his domestic enjoyments. They are, therefore, framed beautiful to the eye, and pleasing to the ear; but of the reptile tribes, some are his formidable enemies, and none were ever intended to be his associates. They shun cultivation, and inhabit unfrequented marshes or gloomy wilds. Their harsh notes and ungainly or disgusting forms, serve, therefore, to warn him of danger, or to turn his steps to places more fit for his habitation.   *H. Duncan.*

8999. GOD, Blessing or Curse of. A little, with the blessing of God upon it, is better than a great deal, with the encumbrance of his curse; his blessing can multiply a mite into a talent, but his curse will shrink a talent into a mite; by him the arms of the wicked are broken, and by him the righteous are upholden: so that the great question is, whether he be with or against us, and the great misfortune is, that this question is seldom asked. The favor of God is to them that obtain it a better and enduring substance, which, like the widow's barrel of oil, wasted not in the evil days of famine, nor will fail.   *Bp. Horne.*

9000. GOD, Care of. God is a perpetual refuge and security to his people. His providence is not confined to one generation; it is not one age only that tastes of his bounty and compassion. His eye never yet slept, nor hath he suffered the little ship of his church to be swallowed up, though it hath been tossed upon the waves; he hath always been a haven to preserve us, a house to secure us; he hath always had compassion to pity us, and power to protect us; he hath had a face to shine, when the world hath had an angry countenance to frown. He brought Enoch home by an extraordinary translation from a brutish world; and when he was resolved to reckon with men for their brutish lives, he lodged Noah, the phoenix of the world, in an ark, and kept him alive as a spark in the midst of many waters, whereby to rekindle a church in the world; in all generations he is a dwelling-place to secure his people here or entertain them above.   *Charnock.*

9001. GOD the Christian's Banker. We will suppose that some opulent person makes the tour of Europe. If his money fall short, he comforts himself with reflecting that he has a sufficient stock in the bank, which he can draw out at any time by writing to his cashiers. This is just the case, spiritually, with God's elect. They are travelers in a foreign land, remote from home. Their treasure is in heaven, and God himself is their banker: when their graces seem to be almost spent and exhausted, when the barrel of meal and cruse of oil appear to be failing, they need but draw upon God by prayer and faith, and humble waiting. The Holy Spirit will honor their bill at sight; and issue to them, from time to time, sufficient remittances to carry them to their journey's end.   *Salter.*

9002. GOD, Conception of. How mean and paltry are any words of ours to convey any idea of him who made this mighty world out of nothing, and with whom one day is as a thousand years, and a thousand years as one day! How weak and inadequate are our poor, feeble intellects to conceive of him who is perfect in all his works—perfect in the greatest as well as in the smallest; perfect in appointing the days and hours in which Jupiter, with all its satellites, shall travel round the sun; perfect in forming the smallest insect that creeps over a few feet of our little globe! How little can our busy helplessness comprehend a Being who is ever ordering all things in heaven and earth by universal Providence—ordering the rise and fall of nations and dynasties, like Nineveh and Carthage; ordering the exact length to which men like Alexander, and Tamerlane, and Napoleon shall extend their conquests, ordering the least step in the life of the humblest believer among his people, all at the same time, all unceasingly, all perfectly, all for his own glory! The blind man is no judge of the paintings of Rubens or Titian. The deaf man is insensible to the beauty of Handel's music. The Greenlander can have but a faint notion of the climate of the tropics. The Australian savage can form but a remote conception of a locomotive engine, however well you may describe it. There is no place in their minds to take in these things. They have no set of thoughts which can comprehend them. They have no mental fingers which can grasp them. And just in the same way the best and brightest ideas that man can form of God, compared to the reality which we shall see one day, are weak and faint indeed.   *Ryle.*

9003. GOD, Conscience and. The accusations of conscience evidence the omniscience and the holiness of God; the terrors of conscience, the justice of God; the approbations of conscience, the goodness of God. All the order in the world owes itself, next to the providence of God, to conscience; without it the world would be a Golgotha. As the creatures witness there was a first cause that produced them, so this principle in man evidenceth itself to be set by the same hand for the good of that which it had so framed. There could be no conscience if there was no God, and man could not be a rational creature if there were no conscience.   *Charnock.*

9004. GOD, Creation Glorifies. Every created thing glorifies God in its place, by fulfilling his will, and the great purpose of his providence: but man alone can give tongue to every creature, and pronounce for all a general doxology.   *Kirby.*

9005. GOD, Denial of. I question whether there ever was, or can be in the world, an uninterrupted and internal denial of the being of

God, or that men (unless we can suppose conscience utterly dead) can arrive to such a degree of impiety; for before they can stifle such sentiments in them (whatsoever they may assert) they must be utter strangers to the common conceptions of reason, and despoil themselves of their own humanity. He that dares to deny a God with his lips, yet sets up something or other as a God in his heart. Is it not lamentable that this sacred truth, consented to by all nations, which is the band of civil societies, the source of all order in the world, should be denied with a bare face, and disputed against, in companies, and the glory of a wise Creator ascribed to an unintelligent nature, to blind chance? Are not such worse than heathens?   *Charnock.*

9006. GOD, Derivation of. The very name God is a wonderful treasure-house, full of most precious love-thoughts, when we understand its meaning and history. When the old Anglo-Saxons were converted to Christianity, they sought for some word in their own language which would express the character of the divine Being as revealed to them in the Bible. They thought of his kindness, his mercy, his forgiveness, his patience, his love, and asked, "What name will best express these attributes?" And so they called him Good; and that is the origin of the name we use to-day. It is simply good shortened into God. What a wondrous treasure-mine it is!   *Anon.*

9007. GOD, Difference between Man and. A missionary in India was catechising the children of one of the schools. A Brahmin interrupted him, saying that the spirit of man and the spirit of God were one. The missionary called on the boys to refute it, by stating the difference between the spirit of man and God. They gave the following answers: "The spirit of man is created—God is its creator; the spirit of man is full of sin—God is a pure spirit; the spirit of man is subject to grief—God is infinitely blessed, and incapable of suffering. These two spirits can never be one."

9008. GOD, Disregard to. Is God a being less to be regarded than man, and more worthy of contempt than a creature? It would be strange if a benefactor should live in the same town, in the same house, with us, and we never exchange a word with him; yet this is our case, who have the works of God in our eyes, the goodness of God in our being, the mercy of God in our daily food, yet think so little of him, converse so little with him, serve everything before him, and prefer everything above him. Whence have we our mercies but from his hand? Who, beside him, maintains our breath at this moment? Would he call for our spirits this moment, they must depart from us to attend to his command. There is not a moment wherein our unworthy carriage is not aggravated, because there is not a moment wherein he is not our guardian and gives us not tastes of a fresh bounty.   *Charnock.*

9009. GOD, Enjoying. The devil told Bonaventura that he was a reprobate and should, therefore, seek to enjoy the pleasures of this world. The saint answered, "No, not so, Satan; if I must not enjoy God after this life, let me enjoy him as much as I can in it."

9010. GOD, Eternity of. When creation began, we know not. There were angels and there was a place of angelic habitation, before the creation of man, and of the world destined for his residence; and even among these pure, spiritual essences, there had been a rebellion and fall. How long these spirits had existed, and how many other orders of things besides, it is vain to conjecture; for conjecture could lead to nothing surer than itself. But of one thing we are certain; that how far back soever we suppose the commencement of creation carried, led it be not only beyond the actual range (if a definite range it may be said to have,) of the human imagination, but even beyond the greatest amount of ages and figures, in any way combined, could be made to express; still there was an eternity preceding, an eternity from which this unimaginable and incomputable duration has not made the minutest deduction; for it is the property of eternity, that it can be neither lengthened by additions, nor shortened by subtraction of the longest possible periods of time. Before the commencement of creation, therefore, before the fiat of Omnipotence, which gave being to the first dependent existence and dated the beginning of time, in infinite and incomprehensible solitude, yet in the boundless self-sufficiency of his blessed nature, feeling no want and no dreariness, Jehovah had, from eternity, existed alone. There is something awfully sublime in this conception of Deity. Our minds are overwhelmed when we attempt to think of infinite space, even as it is replenished with its millions of suns and systems of inhabited worlds; but still more are they baffled and put to a stand when we try to form a conception of immensity before sun or star existed, before any creature had a being, of immensity filled with nothing but the pure, etherial essence of the great uncreated Spirit. When we think of the millions of worlds, with all their interminable varieties of spiritual and material, animate and inanimate, brute and intelligent, tribes of beings, there is unavoidably in our minds the conception of deity, as having, in the superintendence of all his works of power, wisdom, and goodness, both incessant occupation and exhaustless sources of enjoyment.   *Dr. Wardlaw.*

9011. GOD, Eternity of, Defined. A mute was asked to give his idea of the eternity of God, and replied, "It is duration without beginning or end; existence without bound or dimension; present without past or future. His eternity is youth without infancy or old age; life without birth or death; to-day without yesterday or to-morrow."

9012. GOD, Evidence of a. "In the corner of a little garden," said Dr. Beattie of Aberdeen, "without informing any one of the circumstance, I wrote in the mould with my finger the three initial letters of my son's name, and sowed garden-cress in the furrows, covered up the seed, and smoothed the ground. Ten days after this he came running up to me, and with astonishment in his countenance told me his name was growing in the garden. I laughed at the report, and seemed to disregard it, but he insisted on my going to see what had happened. 'Yes,' said I carelessly, 'I see it is so, but what is there in this worth notice? Is it not mere chance?' 'It cannot be so,' he said; 'somebody must have contrived matters so as to produce it.' 'Look at yourself,' I replied, 'and consider your hands and fingers, your legs and feet; came you hither by chance?' 'No,' he answered, 'something must have made me.' 'And who is that something?' I asked. He said, 'I don't know.' I told him the name of that Great Being who had made him and all the world. This lesson affected him greatly, and he never forgot either it or the circumstance that introduced it."

9013. GOD, Existence of. The existence of God is the foundation of all religion. The whole building totters if the foundation be out of course: if we have not deliberate and right notions of it, we shall perform no worship, no service, yield no affection to him. If there be not a God, it is impossible there can be one; eternity is essential to the notion of a God; so all religion would be vain and unreasonable, to pay homage to that which is not in being, nor ever can be.   *Charnock.*

9014. GOD, Eye of. When we perceive that a vast number of objects enter in at our eye by a very small passage, and yet are so little jumbled in that crowd, that they open themselves regularly, though there is no great space for that either; and that they give us a distinct apprehension of many objects that lie before us, some even at a vast distance from us, both of their nature, color, and size; and by a secret geometry, from the angles that they make in our eye, we judge of the distance of all objects, both from us and from one another; if to this we add the vast number of figures that we receive and retain long and with great order in our brains, which we easily fetch up either in our thoughts or in our discourses, we shall find it less difficult to apprehend how an infinite mind should have the universal view of all things ever present before it.   *Bp. Burnet.*

9015. GOD, Faithfulness of. We ask Nature to say—whether her God, who is our God, is true to his word? whether he ever says, and fails to do? By the voices of the sun, the stars, the hills, the valleys, the streams, the cataracts, the rolling thunders, and the roaring sea, she returns a majestic answer. Spring comes with infant Nature waking in her arms; Summer comes bedecked with a robe of flowers; Autumn comes with her swarthy brow, crowned with vines, and on her back the sheaves of corn; Old Winter comes with his shivering limbs, and frozen locks, and hoary head; and these four witnesses—each laying one hand on the broad table of Nature, and lifting the other to heaven—swear by him that liveth for ever and ever, that all which God hath said, God shall do.   *Dr. Guthrie.*

9016. GOD our Father. A peasant in Switzerland was at work in his garden very early in the spring. A lady passing, said, "I fear the plants which have come forward rapidly will yet be destroyed by frost." "God has been our Father a great while," the confiding peasant replied.

9017. GOD, Favor of. It was the saying of a wise Roman, "I had rather have the esteem of the Emperor Augustus than his gifts:" for he was an understanding prince, and his favor very honorable. When Cyrus gave one of his friends a kiss, and another a wedge of gold, he that had the gold envied him that had the kiss as a greater expression of his favor. So the true Christian prefers the privilege of acceptance with God to the possession of any earthly comfort, for in the light of his countenance is life, and his favor is as the cloud of the latter rain.   *Buck.*

9018. GOD, General Worship of. Kircher lays it down as a certain principle, that there never was any people so rude which did not acknowledge and worship one supreme Deity. *Stillingfleet.*

9019. GOD, Geometrizing. A magazine writer tells of a gentleman who had the misfortune to be an unbeliever. One day he was walking in the woods reading the writings of Plato. He came to where the great writer uses the phrase "geometrizing." He thought to himself, "If I could see a plan and order in God's works, I could be a believer." Just then he saw a little "Texas star" at his feet. He picked it up, and thoughtlessly began to count its petals. He found there were five. He counted the stamens, and there were five of them. He counted the divisions at the base of the flower; there were five of them. He then set about multiplying these three fives to see how many chances there were of a flower being brought into existence without the aid of mind, and having in it these three fives. The chances against it were one hundred and twenty-five to one. He thought that was very strange. He examined another flower, and found it the same. He multiplied one hundred and twenty-five by itself to see how many chances there were against there being two flowers, each having these exact relations of numbers. He found the chances against it were fifteen thousand six hundred and twenty-five to one. But all around him were multitudes of these little flowers; they had been growing and blooming there for years. He thought this showed the order of intelligence, and that the mind that ordained it was God. And so he shut up his book, and picked up the little flower, and kissed it, and exclaimed, "Bloom on, little flower; sing on, little birds; you have a God, and I have a God; that God that made these little flowers made me."

9020. GOD, Glorifying. The battle of Pavia, in Italy, was fought between the French and the Imperialists, when the former were defeated, and their king, Francis I., taken prisoner. The unfortunate monarch wrote to his mother the melancholy news of his captivity, couched in these dignified and expressive terms,

"Tout est perdu, Madam ; hormis l'honneur."
All is lost but our honor. Let us sanctify this
idea by applying it to the Christian. He is
ever to remember that whatever loss he sus-
tains, it is incumbent on him to keep up the
dignity of his character. Even trifling things,
as they are called by some, he must watch
against; what may be winked at in others will
not be suffered to pass in him.   *Buck.*

9021. GOD, Government without. The being of
a God is the guard of the world; the sense of
a God is the foundation of civil order; without
this there is no tie upon the consciences of
men. What force would there be in oaths for
the decision of controversies, what right could
there be in appeals made to one that had no
being? A city of atheists would be a heap of
confusion; there could be no ground of any
commerce, when all the sacred bonds of it in
the consciences of men were snapt asunder,
which are torn to pieces and utterly destroyed
by denying the existence of God. What magistrate could be secure in his standing? What
private person could be secure in his right?
Can that, then, be a truth that is destructive
of all public good?   *Charnock.*

9022. GOD, Gratitude Due to. Manlius successfully defended the Capitol of Rome against assault and thereby won the gratitude of the
citizens. Afterward he was condemned to
death for some misdemeanor. The people remembered the favor which he had done them
in saving their Capitol, and would not allow
him to be slain anywhere in sight of it. They
found a place in a grove by the river side,
where no spire of the Capitol reminded them
of their ingratitude, and there they executed
him. Men who can find no place where God's
mercy reaches not, do not scruple to crucify
his Son afresh.

9023. GOD, Greatness of. And you, ye storms
howl out his greatness? Let your thunders
roll like drums in the march of God's armies!
Let your lightnings write his name in fire on
the midnight darkness; let the illimitable void
of space become one mouth for song; and let
the unnavigated ether, through its shoreless
depths, bear through the infinite remote, the
name of him whose goodness endureth forever!
    Spurgeon.

9024. GOD, Heathen Ideas of. A converted
Greenlander, said, "It is true, we were ignorant heathens, and knew nothing of God or a
Saviour; and, indeed, who should tell us of
him till you came? but thou must not imagine
that no Greenlander thinks about these things.
I myself have often thought a boat, with all
its tackle and implements, does not grow into
existence of itself, but must be made by the
labor and ingenuity of man; and one that does
not understand it would directly spoil it. Now
the meanest bird has far more skill displayed
in its structure than the best boat; and no
man can make a bird. But there is still a far
greater art shown in the formation of a man
than of any other creature. Who was it that
made him? I bethought me that he proceeded from his parents, and they from their

parents; but some must have been the first
parents; whence did they come? Common
report informs me they grew out of the earth;
but if so, why does it not still happen that
men grow out of the earth? And from whence
did this same earth itself, the sea, the sun, the
moon, the stars, arise into existence? Certainly there must be some being who made all
these things; a being that always was, and can
never cease to be. He must be inexpressibly
more mighty, knowing, and wise, than the
wisest man. He must be very good, too; because everything that he has made is good,
useful, and necessary for us."

9025. GOD, Heathen Notions of. Sir John Franklin, in his account of his second visit to the
Polar seas, gives the following as the ideas
of the elderly Esquimaux concerning God:
"'We believe that there is a Great Spirit, who
created everything, both us and the world for
our use. We suppose that he dwells in the
land from whence the white people come, that
he is kind to the inhabitants of those lands;
and that there are people who never die; and the
winds that blow from that quarter (the south)
are always warm. He does not know of the
wicked state of our country, nor the pitiful
condition in which we are.' To the question,
'Whom do your medicine-men address when
they conjure?' they answered, 'We do not
think they speak to the master of life; for if
they did, we should fare better than we do,
and should not die. He does not inhabit our
lands'"

9026. GOD, Humility before. A friend made
some remarks upon Rev. Chas. Simeon's
habit of giving expression to his religious
feeling in sighs and groans, "as if it indicated
that all was not right in his experience." He
drew up a paper in which occurred the following passage: "With this sweet hope of ultimate acceptance with God, I have always
enjoyed much cheerfulness before man; but I
have at the same time labored incessantly to
cultivate the deepest humility before God. I
have never thought that the circumstances
of God's having forgiven me, was any reason
why I should forgive myself; on the contrary
I have always judged it better to loathe myself the more, in proportion as I was assured
that God was pacified towards me. There are
but two objects that I have desired for these
forty years to behold; the one is, my own vileness; and the other is, the glory of God in the
face of Jesus Christ; and I have always
thought that they should be viewed together,
just as Aaron confessed all the sins of all
Israel whilst he put them on the head of the
scapegoat. The disease did not keep him from
applying to the remedy, nor did the remedy
keep him from feeling the disease."
    F. F. Trench.

9027. GOD, Ideas of. In 1853 Sir David Brewster was in Paris, and was taken to see the
astronomer Arago, who was then in deep suffering, and was soon to die. He thus describes
the interview: "We conversed upon the marvels of creation, and the name of God was in-

troduced. This led Arago to complain of the difficulties which his reason experienced in understanding God. 'But,' said I, 'it is still more difficult not to comprehend God.' He did not deny it. 'Only,' added he, 'in this case I abstain, for it is impossible for me to understand the God of you philosophers.' 'It is not with them we are dealing,' replied I, 'although I believe that true philosophy necessarily conducts us to belief in God : it is of the God of the Christian that I wish to speak.' 'Ah !' he exclaimed, 'he was the God of my mother, before whom she always experienced so much comfort in kneeling.' 'Doubtless,' I answered. He said no more ; his heart had spoken ; this he had understood."

9028. GOD, Immutability of. What encouragement could there be to lift up our eyes to one that were of one mind this day and of another mind to-morrow? Who would put up a petition to an earthly prince that were so mutable as to grant a petition one day and deny it another, and change his own act? But if a prince promise this or that thing upon such or such a condition, and you know his promise to be as unchangeable as the laws of the Medes and Persians, would any man reason thus: Because it is unchangeable we will not seek to him, we will not perform the condition upon which the fruit of the proclamation is to be enjoyed. Who would not count such an inference ridiculous? What blessings hath not God promised upon the condition of seeking him? *Charnock.*

9029. GOD, Incomprehensible. " Canst thou by searching find out God?" There is an unfathomable depth in all his decrees, in all his works; we cannot comprehend the reason of his works, much less that of his decrees, much less that in his nature; because his wisdom, being infinite as well as his power, can no more act to the highest pitch than his power. As his power is not terminated by what he hath wrought, but he could give further testimonies of it, so neither is his wisdom, but he could furnish us with infinite expressions and pieces of his skill. As in regard of his immensity he is not bounded by the limits of place; in regard of his eternity, not measured by the minutes of time; in regard of his power, not terminated with this or that number of objects; so, in regard of his wisdom, he is not confined to this or that particular mode of working; so that in regard of the reason of his actions as well as the glory and majesty of his nature, he dwells in unapproachable light, 1 Tim. 6 : 16; and whatsoever we understand of his wisdom in creation and providence is infinitely less than what is in himself and his own unbounded nature. *Charnock.*

9030. GOD, Indwelling of. You go past the dwelling of your neighbor. The door is closed that is wont hospitably to be opened. The windows are all shut. The curtains are down. There is no sound of pleasure in the yard. There is no coming or going of industrious feet. And you say, "The master is gone." Did you see him go? You did not. Have you searched the house ? You have not. But there were certain tokens when he was present by which you judged he was there. To-morrow you go past the same dwelling again, and the door stands open, the windows are no longer closed, the curtains are rolled up, there are merry sounds ringing in the house and in the yard, and there is smoke rising from the chimney. Now there is quite a different state of things; and you say, "Ah! the father has got home ?" Because there are so many things that indicate it. These effects are evidences to you that he is present. Now, the same thing is true of the chamber, the dwelling of a man's soul. When God is present, certain things bear witness, and the witnessing of these things is evidence of God present with us, and it is to be taken as a manifestation of that presence. *Beecher.*

9031. GOD, Inexhaustible. I have read of a Spanish ambassador that, coming to see the treasury of St. Mark, in Venice, that is so much cried up in the world, he fell a groping at the bottom of the chests and trunks to see whether they had any bottom, and being asked the reason why he did so, answered, "My master's treasure differs from yours, and excels yours, in that his hath no bottom as yours have," alluding to the mines in Mexico, Peru, and other parts of the Western India. All men's mints, bags, purses, and coffers may be quickly exhausted and drawn dry; but God is such an inexhaustible portion that he can never be drawn dry. All God's treasures are bottomless, and all his mints are bottomless, and all his bags are bottomless. Millions of thousands in heaven and earth feed every day upon him, and yet he feels it not; he is still giving away, and yet his purse is never empty; he is still filling all the court of heaven, and all the creatures on the earth, and yet he is a fountain that still overflows. *Brooks.*

9032. GOD, Invisible. A poor dumb boy, in whom I was interested, and whom I had been seeking to impress with the fact of the being of a God, told me that he had been looking everywhere for God, but could not find him; "there was God—no." I seized a pair of bellows, and blew a puff at his hand, which was red with cold on a winter's day. He showed signs of displeasure; told me it made his hands cold, while I, looking at the pipe of the bellows, told him I could see nothing; "there was wind—no!" He opened his eyes very wide, stared at me, and panted; a deep crimson suffused his whole face, and a soul, a real soul, shone in his strangely altered countenance, while he triumphantly repeated— "God like wind! God like wind!" *C. Elizabeth.*

9033. GOD, The Knowledge of. What must be the knowledge of him, from whom all created minds have derived both their power of knowing, and the innumerable objects of their knowledge! What must be the wisdom of him, from whom all beings derive their wisdom; from whom the emmet, the bee, and the stork, receive the skill to provide, without an error, their food, habitation, and safety; and the prophet and the seraph imbibe their exalted views of the innumerable, vast, and sublime wonders of creation, and of creating glory and greatness! *Dr. Dwight.*

9034. GOD, Letter to. Recently a letter came to the New York Post-office directed simply to "God." When opened it was found to be from a little girl, and ran thus: "Dear God, we are very poor. My brother needs a new coat very much. Won't you please to send him one, and then I shall worry no more about it." The letter was put into the hands of certain good ladies, who sent to the town in Massachusetts whence the letter came, and found the case genuine. The little girl's prayer was answered in due time.

9035. GOD is Light. Suppose the case of a cripple who had spent his life in a room where the sun was never seen. He has heard of its existence, he believes in it, and indeed, has seen enough of its light to give him high ideas of its glory. Wishing to see the sun, he is taken out at night into the streets of an illuminated city. At first he is delighted, dazzled; out after he has had time to reflect, he finds darkness spread amid the lights, and he asks, "Is this the sun?" He is taken out under the starry sky, and he is enraptured; but, on reflection, finds that night covers the earth, and again asks, "Is this the sun?" He is carried out some bright day at noontide, and no sooner does his eye open on the sky than all question is at an end. There is but one sun. His eye is content: it has seen its highest object, and feels there is nothing brighter. So with the soul: it enjoys all lights, yet amid those of art and nature, is still enquiring for something greater. But when it is led by the reconciling Christ into the presence of the Father, and he lifts up upon it the light of his countenance, all thought of anything greater disappears. As there is but one sun, so there is but one God. The soul which once discerns and knows him, feels that greater or brighter there is none, and that the only possibility of ever beholding more glory is by drawing nearer. *Dr. W. Arthur.*

9036. GOD, Likeness to. An old fable says, that a hungry harpy, a gigantic bird having a human face, seized a man, killed and devoured him, and afterward went to the water to drink. Therein she saw her own face reflected, and that it was like the man whom she had killed. Overcome with grief, she fell down and died. God made man in his own image. A discovery of this likeness should lead us to repentance and love.

9037. GOD, Living without. The high and the low, the young and the old, the busy and the idle, alike shun acquaintance with God, as if his very name brought uneasiness, and disturbed our comfort and repose. If we mention God to the young, we too often seem to be troubling them with what they had rather forget in such early days; while the aged dislike to be reminded of their misfortune, that their time on earth is drawing near to an end. If we mention God to the gay and happy, we ap-

pear to be interfering with their pleasures. If we mention him to the great and to the learned, they will intimate that such subjects belong rather to a humbler class and station. But the poor and laborious, on their part, refer us to those who have more information and more leisure. Thus, a large portion of mankind, in all classes, strive to keep God out of their thoughts, and to live, so far as in them lies, without him in the world. Yes, without him, who, as the Apostle says, "is not far from any one of us; for in him we live, and move, and have our being." Why should they act so strangely and unreasonably, if they believed that acquaintance with God would give them peace. *Bishop Sumner.*

9038. GOD, Love for. A little boy had a canary bird which he loved very much. His mother was taken ill, and the singing of the bird gave her great annoyance. The boy was told by the mother that his little bird gave her pain by its singing. He went at once and gave the bird away to his cousin, and then came home and told his mother that the canary would not disturb her any more, for he had given it to his cousin. "But did you not love it very much?" said the mother to him; "how could you part with it?" "It is true, I loved the bird, mother," he replied, "but I love you much more. I could not really love anything that gave you pain." We must love God as this boy loved his mother, more than we love anything else, and also everything that grieves him we must give up, however much we may like it. "You love me," said a mother to her little child, as she leaned over her in bed, "don't you?" "Yes," said the half-asleep child, "but I love God much more."

9039. GOD is Love. It is God's true name Why not indeed change the name of our Deity? Why not teach children to say, when asked— Who made you?—Love, the Father. Who redeems you?—Love, the Son. Who sanctifies you?—Love, the Holy Ghost. Why is this dear name not sown in our gardens in living green, hung on the walls of nurseries and on the portals of churches? Surely on some day of balm did this golden word pass across the mind of the Apostle, when, perhaps, pondering on the character of Jesus, and feeling his own heart burning within him, he spread out the spark in his bosom, till it became a flame, encompassing the universe, and the great generalization leaped from his lips—"God is Love." Complete as an epic, and immortal as complete, stands this poem-sentence, insulated in its own mild glory, and the cross of Jesus is below. *G. Gilfillan.*

9040. GOD, Love of. It breaks our hearts to behold our children struggling in the pangs of death; but the Lord beheld his Son struggling under agonies that never any felt before him. He saw him falling to the ground, groveling in the dust, sweating blood, and amidst those agonies, turning himself to his Father, and, with a heart-rending cry, beseeching him, "Father, if it be possible, let this cup pass." Luke 22: 42. That love must needs want a name, which made the Father of mercies deliver this only Son to such miseries for us.

John Flavel.

9041. GOD, Manifestations of. There is a beautiful story in ancient poetry. A great warrior, the hero of Troy, clad in fierce armor, stretches out his arms to embrace his child before he goes to the field of battle. The child is afraid of the dazzling helmet and nodding crest, and stern, warlike aspect of his father, and shrinks back in terror and alarm. But there is a loving, tender heart beating within that panoply of steel. The father unbinds his glittering helmet, lays aside his fierce armor, and comes to his child with outstretched arms and tender words of love. And the child shrinks from him no longer, but runs to his arms, pillows its head upon his bosom, and receives his parting embrace and kiss. So men are afraid of God when he appears in his majesty and terribleness. They think of his omnipotence, his glory, the awfulness of his throne, the terrors of his justice, and shrink back from him. But as this father laid aside his fierce armor and came to his child in all the tenderness of paternal affection, so God vails his glory and splendor and awfulness, and reveals himself to his children in the sweetest aspect of love. *Anon.*

9042. GOD, Manifested in Christ. A traveler writes, "I saw a flaming globe of fire, magnificent indeed, but too terrible for the eye to rest upon, if its beams had been naked and exposed; but it was suspended in a vase of crystal so transparent that while it softened the intensity of its rays, it shrouded nothing of its beauty. On the contrary, that which before would have been a mass of undistinguishable light, now emitted through the vase many beautiful and various colored rays, which riveted the beholder with wonder and astonishment." Such is God manifested in Christ. Out of Christ he meets the affrighted sinner's eye as a "consuming fire." *Salter.*

9043. GOD, Man Trying to Forget. Apart from clear acts of great and grievous sin, how is God forgotten, clean forgotten, by the greatest part of mankind. They live as if there were no God. It is not as if they openly rebelled against him. They pass him over and ignore him. He is an inconvenience in his own world, an impertinence in his own creation. So he has been quietly set on one side, as if he were an idol out of fashion, and in the way. Men of science, and politicians, have agreed on this, and men of business and wealth think it altogether the most decent thing to be silent about God; for it is difficult to speak of him, or have a view of him, without allowing too much to him.

F. W. Faber.

9044. GOD, Name of. Josephus relates that Alexander the Great, while engaged at the siege of Tyre, sent a demand for tribute and auxiliaries to the High Priest at Jerusalem. He refused because he was under treaty obligations to Darius. At this Alexander was enraged and vowed vengeance upon the Jews. After the reduction of Gaza, Alexander, with his army thirsting for plunder, hastened to Jerusalem. As they drew near the city they met a great procession of the people in white robes, headed by the priests in fine linen, and lead by the high priest in purple and scarlet clothing, his mitre on his head, and on his breast the golden breast-plate, upon which the name of God was engraved. Alexander, alone, in advance of his army, adored that name and saluted the high priest. The great captain's friends were astonished at him, and supposed he had become insane. A more effectual victory had been gained than if the city had withstood a siege. Years before, Alexander had a dream in which he saw the high-priest in this very dress. Now he recognized the hand of God. The high-priest, himself, was instructed in a dream how to receive him.

9045. GOD, Nature of. We are not to consider the world as the body of God: he is an uniform being, void of organs, members, or parts; and they are his creatures, subordinate to him, and subservient to his will. *Sir Isaac Newton.*

9046. GOD, Obscuration of. When the sun shines bright and warm, all the flowers of the field open and display their leaves, to receive him into their bosoms; but, when night comes, they fold together, and shut up all their glories: and, though they were like so many little suns shining here below, able, one would think, to force a day for themselves; yet, when the sun withdraws his beams, they droop, and hang the head, and stand neglected, dull and obscure things. So hath it fared with us: while God hath shone upon us with warm and cherishing influences, we opened, and spread, and flourished into a great pomp and glory; but he only hides his face, draws in his beams, and all our beautiful leaves shut up or fall to the ground, and leave us a bare stalk, poor and contemptible. *Bp. Hopkins.*

9047. GOD, Omnipotence of. One of the early Christians was much perplexed over the passage which represents the earth as founded upon the waters. Then he thought upon the omnipotence of God, and said, "I forgot God when I said, How can this be?" Many doubts are silenced in the same way. The power of God makes the yielding waters firm as adamant, or the airy nothing, upon which he is said to hang the world, stronger than pillars of brass.

9048. GOD, Omnipresence of. A teacher asked, "Where is God?" One boy replied, "In heaven;" another, "Everywhere," and another, "God is here."

9049. GOD, Omniscience of. There is a recent application of electricity by which, under the influence of its powerful light, the body can be illuminated so that the workings beneath the surface of the skin can be seen. Lift up the hand, and it will appear almost translucent, the bones and veins clearly appearing. It is so in some sort with God's introspection of the human heart. His eye, which shines brighter than the sun, searches us and discovers all our weakness and infirmity. *Pilkington.*

9050. GOD, Omniscient. There is not a city, there is not a village, not a house, on which the eye of God is not fixed. He notices the actions, words, and thoughts of every member of every family, in this and in every place. He observes every family in which no prayer is offered, and marks that as a house on which his blessing cannot rest. If they acknowledge not God, neither can God acknowledge them as his: for "them that honor me," saith God, "I will honor; and they that despise me shall be lightly esteemed." He sees the knavery and dishonesty which are practiced in some houses, and which the inhabitants of the houses think to shut in with the walls which enclose them. He notices the vain and unprofitable conversation of many who forget that for "every idle word that men shall speak, they shall give account thereof in the day of judgment;" and the wicked thoughts and desires which are indulged in privacy, by some who would blush to think that their imaginations were exposed to any human eye. He knows all the hypocrisy which sometimes lurks under fair words and specious performances. He knows and observes all and forgets nothing. He records all in his book of remembrance. Let the consideration that all things are naked and opened unto the eyes of him with whom we have to do, have its proper influence upon us. *Preston.*

9051. GOD, Oversight of. A man in the full strength of his years, but most helpless, being very deaf and almost totally blind, is an occasional visitor at our house. We take turns in talking to him, for the talk must be carried on in a key that soon tires ordinary lungs. The other day I was "the relief," and as I talked with the poor man I learned a lesson myself, for the man has wonderful faith. He cannot work, though willing enough, and he will not beg, but from day to day God feeds him. "Have you no fears in going about as you do," I said to him, "in cars and boats, and on the crowded streets?" "I used to have," he said, in the soft, low voice, which contrasts with the way people must shout at him, "but I never have now. God sees to me. I am always taken care of. Somebody finds me a seat, or helps me in and out, and I get along." "Do you ever hear anything in church?" is another question. "Well, not much; but I always go. I like to be there, and I find a blessing." *Christian Weekly.*

9052. GOD, Portion in. He that hath God for his portion shall have all other things cast into his store, as paper and packthread is cast into the bargain, or as a handful of corn is cast into the corn you try, or as hucksters cast in an over-cast among the fruit you try, or as an inch of measure is given unto an ell of cloth. Matt. 6: 25, 31–33. O sirs, how can that man be poor, how can that man want, that hath the Lord of heaven and earth for his portion? Surely he cannot want light that enjoys the sun, nor he cannot want bread that hath all sorts of grain in his barns, nor he cannot want water that hath the fountain at his door; no more can he want anything that hath God for his portion, who is everything,

and who will be everything to every gracious soul. O sirs! the thought, the tongue, the desire, the wish, the conception, all fall short of God, and of that great goodness that he hath laid up for them that fear him, and why then should they be afraid of wants? *Brooks.*

9053. GOD, Power of. The power which gave existence, is power which can know no limits. But to all beings, in heaven, and earth, and hell, he gave existence, and is therefore seen to possess powers which transcend every bound. The power which upholds, moves, and rules the universe, is also clearly illimitable. The power which is necessary to move a single world transcends all finite understanding. No definite number of finite beings possess sufficient power to move a single world a hair's breath; yet God moves the great world which we inhabit sixty-eight thousand miles in an hour; two hundred and sixty times faster than the swiftest motion of a cannon ball. Nor does he move this world only, but the whole system, of which it is a part; and all the worlds which replenish the immense stellary system, formed of suns innumerable, and of the planets which surround them. All these he has also moved from the beginning to the present moment; and yet "He fainteth not, neither is weary!" *Dr. Dwight.*

9054. GOD, Protection of. Luther, when making his way into the presence of Cardinal Cajetan, who had summoned him to answer for his heretical opinions at Augsburg, was asked by one of the Cardinal's minions where he should find a shelter if his patron, the Elector of Saxony, should desert him. "Under the shield of heaven!" was his reply.

9055. GOD, Providence of. Must not the conduct of a parent seem very unaccountable to a child when its inclinations are thwarted; when it is put to learn letters; when it is obliged to swallow bitter physic; to part with what it likes, and to suffer and do, and see many things done, contrary to its own judgment? Will it not, therefore, follow from hence, by a parity of reason, that the little child man, when it takes upon itself to judge of parental providence—a thing of yesterday to criticise the economy of the Ancient of Days—will it not follow, I say, that such a judge of such matters must be apt to make very erroneous judgments, esteeming those things in themselves unaccountable which he cannot account for; and concluding of some things, from an appearance of arbitrary carriage towards him, which is suited to his infancy and ignorance, that they are in themselves capricious or absurd, and cannot proceed from a wise, just, and benevolent God? *Berkeley.*

9056. GOD, Recognizing. A woman who had an idiotic child said she would be satisfied if she could only get one look of recognition. And so it is with God. He wants us to look to him; yet there are some Christians who never look up even so much as to say "Thank you." *Moody.*

9057. GOD, Recognition of. In the opening sentence of the Declaration of Independence there is a recognition of God. It closes with the sentence "And for the support of this declaration, with a firm reliance on the protection of Divine Providence, we mutually pledge," etc. In Article 13 of the Articles of Confederation can be found the following: "And whereas it hath pleased the Great Governor of the world to incline the hearts of the Legislatures," etc. And the articles end with the words, "Done at," etc., "in the year of our Lord," etc. The Treaty between the United States and Great Britain, 1783, begins with, "It having pleased the Divine Providence to dispose the hearts," etc. Finally the views of the President of the Convention which framed the Constitution: "Of all the dispositions and habits which lead to political prosperity, religion and morality are indispensable supports. In vain would that man claim the tribute of patriotism who should labor to subvert these great pillars of human happiness, these firmest props of the duties of men and citizens. And let us with caution indulge the supposition that morality can be maintained without religion. Whatever may be conceded to the influence of refined education on minds of peculiar structure, reason and experience forbid us to expect that national morality can prevail in exclusion of religious principle." *Washington's Farewell Address.*

9058. GOD, a Refuge. Travelers tell us that they who are at the top of the Alps can see great showers of rain fall under them, but not one drop of it falls on them. They who have God for their portion are in a high tower, and thereby safe from all troubles and showers. A drift-rain of evil will beat in at the creature's windows, be they never so well pointed; all the garments this world can make up cannot keep them that travel in such weather from being wet to the skin. No creature is able to bear the weight of its fellow-creature, but as reeds, break under, and as thorns, run into the sides that lean on them. The bow drawn beyond its compass breaks in sunder, and the string wound above its strength snaps in pieces. Such are outward helps to all that trust to them in hardships. *Swinnock.*

9059. GOD, Resemblance to. Resemblance to God results from our intimacy with him. "Evil communications corrupt good manners." But while a "companion of fools shall be destroyed, he that walketh with wise men shall be wise." We soon assume the manners of those with whom we are familiar, especially if the individual be a distinguished personage, and we preeminently revere and love him. Upon this principle, the more we have to do with God the more we shall grow into his likeness and "be followers of him as dear children." *Jay.*

9060. GOD, Resisting. As God is incapable of changing his resolves, because of his infinite wisdom, so he is incapable of being forced to any change, because of his infinite power. Being almighty, he can be no more changed from power to weakness, than, being all-wise, he can be changed from wisdom to folly, or, being omniscient, from knowledge to ignorance. He cannot be altered in his purposes,

because of his wisdom; nor in the manner and method of his actions, because of his infinite strength. Men, indeed, when their designs are laid deepest and their purposes stand firmest, yet are forced to stand still, or change the manner of the execution of their resolves, by reason of some outward accidents that obstruct them in their course: for, having not wisdom to foresee future hindrances, they have not power to prevent them, or strength to remove them, when they unexpectedly interpose themselves between their desire and performance; but no created power has strengh enough to be a bar against God. By the same act of his will that he resolves a thing, he can puff away any impediments that seem to rise up against him. He that wants no means to effect his purposes cannot be checked by anything that riseth up to stand in his way; heaven, earth, sea, the deepest places are too weak to resist his will. *Charnock.*

9061. GOD, Robbing. The Arabians offered sacrifices and other offerings to idols as well as to God, who was also often put off with the least portion, as Mohammed upbraids them. Thus when they planted fruit trees, or sowed a field, they divided it by a line into two parts, setting one apart for their idols, and the other for God; if any of the fruits happened to fall from the idol's into God's, they made restitution; but if from God's part into the idol's, they made no restitution. So when they watered the idol's grounds, if the water broke over the channels made for that purpose, and run on God's part, they dammed it up again; but if the contrary, they let it run on, saying, they wanted what was God's, but he wanted nothing. In the same manner, if the offering designed for God happened to be better than that designed for the idol, they made an exchange, but not otherwise. *George Sale.*

9062. GOD, Serving. When the son of Fluvius was found in the conspiracy of Catiline, the displeased father reprehended him sharply, saying, *Non ego te Catilini genui, sed patriæ* —"I did not beget you for Catiline, but for your country." This is the language of God to his children: I gave you not bodies and souls to serve sin with, but to serve me with. Our bodies were not formed to be instruments of unrighteous action, nor our souls the gloomy abodes of foul spirits. *Secker.*

9063. GOD, Strife with. It is observable how God's goodness strives with man's refractoriness. Man would sit down at this world, God bids him sell it and purchase a better; just as a father, who hath in his hand an apple and a piece of gold under it: the child comes, and with pulling gets the apple out of his father's hand; his father bids him throw it away, and he will give him the gold for it, which the child utterly refusing, eats it and is troubled with worms; so is the carnal and wilful man with the worm of the grave in this world, and the worm of conscience in the next. *Herbert.*

9064. GOD, Talking with. Never shall we be lonely, never have to complain of want of companionship, if we acquire this blessed habit of talking with God. There was an old Scotchman sitting by his humble fire, and a visitor asked him if he was not lonesome sitting there all day, and he said, "Nae, nae, I just sit here clacking wi' Jesus." When we say that "clacking" is with the Scotch the word for friendly talking, our readers will not suppose there was irreverence in the old man's words; perhaps they may see something to be envied as well as admired. *Power.*

9065. GOD, Taking Hold of. It makes a good deal of difference whether you take hold of God or whether he takes hold of you. My little girl to-day refused to let me take hold of her hand when we were walking together. She thought she could go alone. But when we came to a place that was slippery, she took hold, first of my little finger, and then, as it grew more icy, of my whole hand. As we went on, and it was growing worse, she let go entirely, and said, "Papa, take hold of me." She knew I was strong, and that she could not fall unless I fell. "Now," said he, "I have been slipping, slipping, for the last eleven years, and the reason is, that I have not put my hand into the hand of God. I have been trying to take hold of him, but not asking him to take hold of me. As long as he has hold of my hand I can't fall. He would have to be disenthroned first. If our hands are placed in his, whose throne is in heaven, we never can fall down into hell." *Moody.*

9066. GOD a Thief. The Sanhedrim Talmud gives the following legend: A prince once said to Rabbi Gamaliel, Your God is a thief; he surprised Adam in his sleep and stole a rib from him. The Rabbi's daughter overheard this speech, and whispered a word or two in her father's ear, asking his permission to answer this singular opinion of herself. He gave his consent. The girl stepped forward, and, feigning terror and dismay, threw her hands aloft in supplication, and cried out, "My liege, my liege, justice! revenge!" "What has happened?" asked the prince. "A wicked theft has taken place," she replied. "A robber has crept secretly into our house, carried away a silver goblet, and left a golden one in its stead." "What an upright thief!" exclaimed the prince; "would that such robbers were of more frequent occurrence!" "Behold, then, sire, the kind of thief our Creator was; he stole a rib from Adam, and gave him a beautiful wife instead." "Well said!" replied the prince.

9067. GOD, Threatening. Rev. G. S. Owen, missionary in China, says: "The wife of a man living at Chuen-sha, a city near Shanghai, had a severe attack of madness. At night she became especially wild, foaming and raging terribly. The husband went at once to the temple of the city god, presented various sacrifices and made vows; but his wife remained mad as ever. He went again and again; but to no purpose, the woman grew worse. The man got furious; he had half beggared himself by making offerings to the city god, yet his wife was no better. He would have his revenge. Away he went to the temple, and thus addressed the city god—'You call yourself the city god, while in reality you are an evil, money-loving, unjust demon. It was my ancestors who built you this fine temple, and I have been most regular and devout in my worship; in return you have made my wife mad, and refuse to cure her. Well, now mark what I say: if she is not better within three days, I will pull you down from that pedestal, and throw you into the first ditch I can find, and there you shall rot.' The woman got better within the prescribed time, and thus the god escaped the threatened punishment." Others than heathen first attempt to bribe and then to terrify their God into compliance with their schemes.

9068. GOD, Title of. Nothing is easier than to say the word universe, and yet it would take us millions of millions of years to bestow one hasty glance upon the surface of that small portion of it which lies within the range of our glasses. But what are all suns, comets, earths, moons, atmospheres, seas, rivers, mountains, valleys, plains, woods, cattle, wild beasts, fish, fowl, grasses, plants, shrubs, minerals, and metals, compared with the meaning of the one name—God! *Pulsford.*

9069. GOD, Trust in. William Rufus, having seen the coast of Ireland from some rocks in North Wales, said, "I will summon hither all the ships of my realm, and with them make a bridge to attack that country." This threatening being reported to Murchard, Prince of Leinster, he paused a moment, and then said, "Did the king add to this mighty threat, if God please?" On being assured he made no mention of God in his speech, he replied, "Sure that man puts his trust in human, not in divine power, I fear not his coming." *Buck.*

9070. GOD, Truth of. There is no truth which a man may more evidently make out to himself than the existence of a God; yet he that shall content himself with things as they minister to our pleasures and passions, and not make enquiry a little further into their causes and ends, may live long without any notion of such a being. *Locke.*

9071. GOD Unchangeable. There are many Christians, like young sailors, who think the shore and the whole land moves, when the ship and they themselves are moved; just so, not a few imagine that God is moved, and changes places, because their souls are subject to alteration; but the foundation of the Lord abideth sure.

9072. GOD, Unity of. Rev. W. Arthur narrates an interview with an aged Hindoo. The latter said, "Some time ago one of our people went to your house, you took him into your room and said a great deal of sense to him, and gave him a book. It was the first that had ever been in our town. We assembled and read it together. It certainly was a very wise book, but had one fault that very much surprised us all." What this grave fault was he refused to tell till he had been repeatedly urged to do so. He at length said, "The fault was this: it would not allow of any God but one!

Now what do you say to that?" He had rightly apprehended the unity of the God of the Bible. It leaves no place for his polytheistic faith.

9073. GOD Unsearchable. What is man? It seems an easy thing to answer that question; yet I am not sure that, even at this day, we have any correct definition which, distinguishing him on the one hand from the angelic race, and on the other hand from the higher orders of inferior creatures, is at once brief and comprehensive. Now, if we have such difficulty in defining even ourselves, or those objects that being patent to the senses may be made the subject of searching and long experiment, is it wonderful that when we rise above his works to their maker, from things finite to things infinite, it should be found much easier to ask than to answer the question, What is God? The telescope by which we hold converse with the stars, the microscope which unveils the secrets of nature, the crucible of the chemist, the knife of the anatomist, the reflective faculties of the philosopher, all the common instruments of science, avail not there. On the threshold of that impenetrable mystery, a voice arrests our steps. From out the clouds and darkness that are round about God's throne, the question comes, Who can by searching find out God, who can find out the Almighty to perfection? *Dr. Guthrie.*

9074. GOD, Veneration of. While earthly objects are exhausted by familiarity, the thought of God becomes to the devout man continually brighter, richer, vaster; derives fresh lustre from all that he observes of nature and Providence, and attracts to itself all the glories of the universe. The devout man, especially in moments of strong religious sensibility, feels distinctly that he has found the true happiness of man. He has found a being for his veneration and love, whose character is inexhaustible, who, after ages shall have passed, will still be uncomprehended in the extent of his perfections, and will still communicate to the pure mind stronger proofs of his excellence, and more intimate signs of his approval. *Channing.*

9075. GOD, Wealth in. You cannot call God father till communion with Christ be enjoyed; and when this is enjoyed your privileges become wonderful. Now you may look on God and say, "Thou art my portion." Now you may go to God and say, "Thou art my Father." Now you may behold the love of God and say, "This is my treasure;" and the covenant of God, and say, "This is my storehouse;" and the providence of God, and say, "This is my shield." Now you may look on Christ and say, "This is my Redeemer; he is mine and I am his; he lives in me, and I live in him; he dwells with me, and I dwell with him; he sups with me, and I feed on him; his blood is my refuge, and my heart is his mansion. He doth graciously traffic in my heart by his Spirit, and I can as freely traffic with heaven by his intercession." *Sedgwick.*

9076. GOD, Will of. He hath willed every-thing that may be for our good, if we perform the condition he hath required; and hath put it upon record, that we may know it and regulate our desires and supplications according to it. If we will not seek him, his immutability cannot be a bar, but our own folly is the cause, and by our neglect we despoil him of this perfection as to us, and either imply that he is not sincere, and means not as he speaks; or that he is as changeable as the wind, sometimes this thing, sometimes that, and not at all to be confided in. If we ask according to his revealed will, the unchangeableness of his nature will assure us of the grant; and what a presumption would it be in a creature dependent upon his sovereign, to ask that which he knows he has declared his will against; since there is no good we can want, but he hath promised to give, upon our sincere and ardent desire for it. *Charnock.*

9077. GOD, Workmanship of. What an immense workman is God in miniature as well as in the great! With the one hand, perhaps, he is making a ring of one hundred thousand miles in diameter, to revolve round a planet like Saturn, and with the other is forming a tooth in the ray of the feather of a humming bird, or a point in the claw of the foot of a microscopic insect. When he works in miniature, everything is gilded, polished and perfect; but whatever is made by human art, as a needle, etc., when viewed by a microscope appears rough, and coarse, and bungling. *Bishop Law.*

9078. GODLINESS, Advantage of. I think I could make it very plain, that even for the present life piety is the truest policy and the best possession. I believe, for instance, that the pious apprentice, who is prayerful and painstaking, will become a more accomplished artisan than his more infidel neighbor, who has nothing but self-interest to stimulate, and nothing but his own cleverness to help him. And when that Christian apprentice becomes a journeyman, however bitter the world's prejudice against piety may be, I have no fear but that his Master in heaven will find for his servant employment on earth. The king of Babylon had no liking to Daniel's religion, but he could not rule his 127 provinces without Daniel's help. And the king of Egypt would have been glad to have Joseph's finance and Joseph's forethought, without his piety; but, as he could not get the one without the other, he put up with the piety for the sake of the skillful policy. And so, sooner or later, the Christian workman will make himself indispensable. If he won't do a job on Sunday, neither will he be tipsy or stupefied with the previous day's debauch all Monday. If he will not tell a lie for his master, neither will he tell one to him; and, surely, that trade is bad where honesty is a bar to promotion. *Dr. Hamilton.*

9079. GODLINESS, Basis of. True faith and a godly life cannot be separated one from another, any more than the foundation can be separated from the building, or the root from the branches, the fire from the heat, the water from the moisture, the sun from the light. In a word, they are as two twins, who are born together, live together, and die together. Howsoever, in the hour and power of darkness, and in the vehemency of temptation, we may and do fail very often. Therefore, where true faith is not, there can be no godly life.

Richard Roger.

9080. GODLINESS, Biblical. What is godliness? Conformity to the mind and will of God,—having the heart and eye turned towards God. See such expressions as, "a good conscience towards God," 1 Pet. 3: 21; "faith to God-ward," 1 Thess. 1: 8; "trust through Christ to God-ward," 2 Cor. 3: 4; "alive unto God," Rom. 6: 11. See how reference to God is interwoven with holy things. We read of "godly sorrow"—"godly fear"—"godly sincerity"—"godly zeal"—"godly men"—"godly edifying"—"the doctrine according to godliness"—"the godly seed"—"godly jealousy," etc. In the New Testament the word "godliness" is used very frequently by St. Paul, and by him chiefly in 1 and 2 Timothy,—ten times in ten chapters. Was this because they were (with the Epistle to Titus) probably the last he wrote? as if the nearer he came to the end of his course, the more he viewed things with reference to God and godliness? *Bowes.*

9081. GODLINESS, Blessedness of. "O blessed be God that I was born," said the pious Halyburton when dying. "I have a father and ten brethren and sisters in heaven, and I shall be the eleventh. O blessed be the day that I was ever born! O that I were where he is! And yet were God to withdraw from me, I should be weak as water. All that I enjoy, though it be miracle on miracle, would not support me without fresh supplies from God. The thing I rejoice in is this, that God is altogether full; and that in the Mediator Christ Jesus is all the fullness of the God-head, and it will never run out. Study the power of religion. 'Tis the power of religion, and not a name, that will give the comfort I find. There is telling in this providence, and I shall be telling it to eternity. If there be such a glory in his conduct towards me now, what will it be to see the Lamb in the midst of the throne? My peace hath been like a river." Soon after, one of those about him having said, "You are now putting your seal to that truth, that great is the gain of godliness," he replied, "Yes, indeed." Soon after he entered into the possession of eternal gain.

9082. GODLINESS for Gain. Worldlings, instead of looking upon godliness as their greatest gain, will look upon gain as their greatest godliness. They love religion, not for the beauty existing in it, but for the dowry annexed to it. They are like the fox, that follows the lion for the prey that is falling from him. If there be no honey in the pot, such wasps will hover no longer about it. *Secker.*

9083. GODLINESS, Inspiration of. It is related of Lord Nelson, that at a critical moment a sudden glow of patriotism was kindled within him, and that from that time a radiant orb was suspended in his mind's eye which urged him onwards to renown. But what is this in comparison with the object which fills the eye of the believer's soul, when by faith he beholds the Saviour as the glory of the Lord, and follows on like the Israelites in the path of the fiery cloud pillar? *Salter.*

9084. GODLINESS, No Excess in. Every created thing has its bounds; but grace has none. In true godliness there is no excess. Those wells which are of God's digging can never be too full of water. He delights to see the trees of righteousness laden with the fruits of righteousness. *W. Secker.*

9085. GODLINESS, Power of. The power of godliness, among other things, hath these three advantages. It makes a man do everything strongly and mightily; and whatever might take a man off from duty, or distract or disturb him in it, all falls to nothing before this power. It makes a man inflexible in the ways of God, that he shall neither turn to the right hand nor to the left, but take straight steps towards the mark set before him. It makes a man invincible from all evils and enemies, because all the power against him is but the power of the creature, but the power in him is the power of God. And the power of God easily overcomes the mightiest power of the creature, but is never overcome by it. To conclude: the power of godliness is the doer of every duty in God's kingdom, the subduer of every sin, the conqueror of each tribulation and temptation, the life of every performance, the glory of each grace, the beauty and stability of a Christian's life. *W. Dell.*

9086. GODLINESS, Sincere. The watch is naught that goes only at first winding up, and stands all the day after; and so is that heart that desires not always to keep in spiritual motion. I confess there may be a great difference in the standing of two watches; one from the very watch itself, because it hath not the right make, and this will ever do so till altered; another possibly is true work, only some dust clogs the wheels, or a fall hath a little battered it, which removed, it will go well again. And there is as great difference between the sincere soul and hypocrite in this case; the sincere soul may be interrupted in its spiritual motion and Christian course, but it is from some temptation that at present clogs him; but he hath a new nature which inclines to a constant motion in holiness, and doth, upon removing the present impediment, return to its natural exercise of godliness; but the hypocrite fails in the very constitution and frame of his spirit; he hath not a principle of grace in him to keep him moving. Like an ill-made watch, he must first be taken all to pieces. *Salter.*

9087. GOLD, Danger of. A friend came to me one day who was about to start on a voyage during the troublous times of the war, with a large amount of gold belted around his waist. As I bade him good-by, I remarked, "Suppose the ship goes down, how about that gold around your waist? It will be very apt to interfere with the life-preserver and drag you to the bottom." O brethren! it is well enough to have gold, but sometimes it weighs heavier than the life-preserver. It sometimes is a mighty weight that crushes us down to hell. Hence, I say, we may covet large wealth and we may be glad when we find the church growing rich, but let us remember that with every dollar that comes into our pocket there comes a new responsibility for which we must give an account at God's judgment seat. *Dr. Dashiell.*

9088. GOLD, Death by. Tarpeia, the daughter of the governor of the fortress situated on the Capitoline Hill in Rome, was captivated with the golden bracelets of the Sabine soldiers, and stipulated to let them into the fortress if they would give her what they wore upon their left arms. The contract was made; the Sabines kept their promise. Tatius, their commander, was the first to deliver his bracelets and shield. The coveted treasures were thrown upon the traitress by each of the soldiers, till she sank beneath their weight and expired. Gold in quantities, won by treason, plunder, or even in honest ways, is commonly fatal to its possessors.

9089. GOLD, Disregard for. It became apparent that the "Central America" must go down. The storm did not abate, and the water gained upon the pumps. Several hundred miners were on board, returning to their early homes and friends. They had made their fortunes, and expected much happiness in enjoying them. In the first of the horror gold lost its attraction to them. The miners took off their treasure-belts and threw them aside. Carpet bags full of shining gold-dust were emptied on the floor of the cabin. One of these poured out one hundred thousand dollars worth in the cabin and bade any one take it who would. Greed was over-mastered, and the gold found no takers. They had endured great labors and hardships to acquire it, and now saw that the more they carried of it the quicker they would sink to the ocean's bottom. "Skin for skin, yea, all that a man hath will he give for his life." Job 2 : 4.

9090. GOLD, Encumbrance of. "When Cortez entered Mexico, he believed the conquest of the city easy. But on the night of July 7, 1620, he found it much too hot for him. A forced escape, sword in hand, through a narrow path, beset on either side by great numbers of infuriated natives, was the only one possible. Immense treasures, for which he had ventured into his perilous condition, lay about him. Notwithstanding the midnight trial of nimble feet and skillful sword-arms, some of his followers began to load themselves with gold and silver. 'He travels safest who travels lightest!' exclaimed the commander. But the Spaniards, being willing, as the majority of men of every age have been, to run great risks for gold, went forth to the conflict with the fatal encumbrance. About half of them perished by the way. Those who reached in safety the open country had at last been obliged to strip themselves for the flight." They who

were most heavily laden with treasure were most fiercely attacked, and suffered most. Dangers and trials increase with riches. Some have been thankful when the burden was removed.

9091. GOLD, Load of. There were two brothers; one, rich in the love of a good wife and children, but sick and poor in this world's goods; the other, Franz, was rich in money, which he loved better than anything else. Franz lived all alone. One bitter cold night, the wife of the sick brother came to the miser Franz, and begged for help, but he refused her, and she went away saying, "I pray God that the gold which has so hardened your heart may never weigh so heavy on your soul, that you cannot mount to glory." This frightened Franz. By and by a fairy came to him, shaking bags of gold, and said, "Lie down, put your strong box on your chest, and I will give you gold so long as you can bear its weight; but take care you don't get too much, for though I can give, I cannot take away." So Franz lay down, but he was so greedy of the gold that he kept wanting more, till at last he was so weighed down he could not move. And there he lay for years and years. At last a bright light shone, and a crowd of people gathered around him. He remembered his neighbors, his brother with the wife and children, but he couldn't go near them, for he was weighed down by this pile of gold. "O, take it off! take it off!" he cried, "and let me go." Then came a voice, "Any of you, his family, his neighbors, or servants, any one whom he has helped, may remove the awful load that binds him down." But no one stirred, and a cry burst from Franz as his eye went from face to face, and only the memory of unkind and selfish words and actions came up before him. He saw in his sister's face that same sad look, as on that stormy night long, long ago, when he drove her from his door cold, hungry, and sorrowful. Then a wail was heard with these words, "The gold that hardened his heart, has bound him to the earth; he can never rise to glory." *From the German.*

9092. GOLD No Cure. Rev. Jeremiah Burroughs mentions a rich man, who on his sick bed, called for his bags of money; and having laid a bag of gold to his heart, after a little he bade them take it away, saying, "It will not do! it will not do!"

9093. GOLD, Overladed with. At the time of the wreck of the Central America, when gold was thrown away as worse than useless, and millions worth could have been had by taking it, an old colored stewardess took her opportunity and ran the risk. She selected the heaviest belt she could find, and attached it to her person. An attempt was made to lower her into the boats with the other women, but she fell into the sea and was nearly drowned. At length she was drawn into the boat, but when she reached the Marine, the rescuing ship, she was too far gone to be resuscitated. Her precious lading had dragged her down and proved her ruin. She was the only woman lost, though others fell into the sea. A father handed his little daughter a purse full of gold, but she handed it back saying, "It is too heavy." She was right. It has drowned many in luxury and perdition.

9094. GOLD, Place for. Andrew Fuller was taken to the bank, when one of the clerks, to whom he had occasion to speak, showed him some ingots of gold. Thoughtfully eying the gold, he said, as he laid it down, "How much better is it to have this in the hand than in the heart!"

9095. GOLD, Root of. When an ambassador of Spain was brought into the treasury of Venice, and shown great quantities of gold, he began to dig to the bottom of the gold, and being asked why he did so, answered, "I do it to see whether this golden treasure hath any root." Industry and charity are the roots of gold. The diligent hand maketh rich. "There is that scattereth yet increaseth."

9096. GOLD, Temptation of. To turn Antony the hermit from a religious life, the devil cast gold along his path in great profusion. He would not stop to pick it up, but ran on in haste. A great silver plate was also thrown in his way. He said, "This is a trick of the devil. Devil, thou shalt not hinder my determination by this. Thy silver go with thee to perdition." Such is the legend.

9097. GOLD, Tomb of. Under hills of gold many a spiritual giant lies buried.

9098. GOLD, Unsatisfying. Pythes, a king of Greece, cotemporary with Xerxes, discovered a gold mine in his dominions, and set his subjects digging it, to the neglect of all other labor. The wives of the citizens began to petition the wife of Pythes. She undertook their case, and bade them be of good cheer. She required the goldsmiths to imitate in gold all sorts of loaves, junkets, fruits, and all sorts of fish and meats, which were favorites with Pythes. Returning hungry from a journey, the queen set before him a golden supper. Pythes was delighted with the workmanship, but soon began to call in earnest for something to eat. She brought on more golden viands. He cried in anger, "I am hungry!" She replied, "Thou hast made no other provisions for us; every skillful science and art being laid aside, no man works in husbandry; but neglecting sowing, planting, and tilling the ground, we delve and search for useless things, neglecting ourselves and subjects." Thereafter he divided his subjects, and set a part of them to till the soil, and engage in manufactures. In spite of his gold, Pythes grew despondent, and desired death. He built himself a tomb, and lived in it alone till his death, having resigned the government to his wife.

9099. GOLD, Unused. An old miser stored large treasures of gold in several bags, which he guarded with the greatest care. A cunning thief came and stole his gold, but took care to refill the bags with pebbles. The miser was as happy as before, for he knew nothing of his loss, and the pebbles served to satisfy his greed as well as the gold

9100. GOLD, Votaries of. Gold is the only power which receives universal homage. It is worshiped in all lands without a single temple, and by all classes without a single hypocrite; and often has it been able to boast of having armies for its priesthood, and hecatombs of human victims for its sacrifices. Where war has slain its thousands, gain has slaughtered its millions; for while the former operates only with the local and fitful terrors of an earthquake, the destructive influence of the latter is universal and increasing. Indeed, war itself —what has it often been but the art of gain practiced on a larger scale? the covetousness of a nation resolved on gain, impatient of delay, and leading on its subjects to deeds of rapine and blood? Its history is the history of slavery and oppression in all ages. For centuries, Africa, one quarter of the globe, has been set apart to supply the monster with victims, thousands at a meal. And, at this moment, what a populous and gigantic empire can it boast! the mine, with its unnatural drudgery; the manufactory, with its swarms of squalid misery; the plantation, with its inbruted gangs; and the market and the exchange, with their furrowed and care-worn countenances; these are only specimens of its more menial offices and subjects. Titles and honors are among its rewards, and thrones at its disposal. Among its counselors are kings, and many of the great and mighty of the earth enrolled among its subjects. Where are the waters not ploughed by its navies? What imperial element is not yoked to its car? Philosophy itself has become a mercenary in its pay; and Science, a votary at its shrine, brings all its noblest discoveries, as offerings, to its feet. What part of the globe's surface is not rapidly yielding up its lost stores of hidden treasure to the spirit of gain? Scorning the dream of the philosopher's stone, it aspires to turn the globe itself into gold. *Harris.*

9101. GOOD: Brevities. Ariston said, that neither a bath nor an oration doth any good, unless it purify, the one the skin, the other the heart. That is good which doth good.— *Venning.*——How indestructibly the good grows, and propagates itself, even among the weedy entanglements of evil!—*Carlyle.*—— A very small page will serve for the number of our good works, when vast volumes will not contain our evil deeds. *Bishop Wilson.*

9102. GOOD BREEDING, Civility and. Civility and good-breeding are generally thought, and often used as, synonymous terms, but are by no means so. Good-breeding necessarily implies civility; but civility does not reciprocally imply good-breeding. The former has its intrinsic weight and value, which the latter always adorns and often doubles by its workmanship. To sacrifice one's own self-love to other people's is a short, but, I believe, a true, definition of civility; to do it with ease, propriety, and grace, is good-breeding. The one is the result of good-nature; the other, of good sense, joined to experience, observation, and attention. *Lord Chesterfield*

9103. GOOD DEEDS, Harvest from. A good deed is never lost: he who sows courtesy reaps friendship, and he who plants kindness gathers love: pleasure bestowed upon a grateful mind was never sterile, but generally gratitude begets reward. *Basil.*

9104. GOOD DEEDS, Height of. He is good that does good to others. If he suffers for the good he does, he is better still; and if he suffers from them to whom he did good, he is arrived to that height of goodness, that nothing but an increase of his sufferings can add to it; if it proves his death, his virtue is at its summit—it is heroism complete. *La Bruyere.*

9105. GOOD DEEDS, Memory of. Some men live in their good deeds, and, like a beautiful insect, or a delicate moss preserved in a mass of golden aromatic amber, they seem to lie embalmed in the memory of their worth. *Teachers' Treasury.*

9106. GOOD DEEDS, Neglect of. That which is good to be done cannot be done too soon; and if it is neglected to be done early, it will frequently happen that it will not be done at all. *Bishop Mant.*

9107. GOOD DEEDS, Passion for. He who diffuses the most happiness and mitigates the most distress within his own circle is undoubtedly the best friend to his country and the world, since nothing more is necessary than for all men to imitate his conduct, to make the greatest part of the misery of the world cease in a moment. While the passion, then, of some is to shine, of some to govern, and of others to accumulate, let one great passion alone influence our breasts, the passion which reason ratifies, which conscience approves, which heaven inspires,—that of being and doing good. *Robert Hall.*

9108. GOOD DEEDS, Prolificness of. As the acorn, because God has given it "a forming form," and life after its kind, bears within it, not only the builder's oak, but shade for many a herd, food for countless animals, and at last, the gallant ship itself, and the materials of every use to which nature or art can put it and its descendants after it throughout all time; so does every good deed contain within itself endless and unexpected possibilities of other good, which may and will grow and multiply forever, in the genial light of him whose eternal mind conceived it, and whose eternal Spirit will forever quicken it, with that life of which he is the Giver and the Lord. *Charles Kingsley.*

9109. GOOD DEEDS, Relying on Our. As the phœnix in Arabia gathers sweet, odoriferous sticks together, and then blows them with her wings, and burns herself with them, so many a carnal professor burns himself with his own good works—that is, by his expecting and trusting to receive that by his works that is only to be received and expected from Jesus Christ. Though all that man can do towards the meriting of heaven is no more than the lifting up of a straw towards the meriting of a kingdom, yet such a proud piece man is, that he is ready enough to say, with proud Vega, *Cœlum gratis non accipiam,* "I will not have heaven of free cost." A proud heart would fain have that of debt which is merely of grace, and desires that to be of purchase which God hath intended to be of free mercy; which made one to say, that he would swim through a sea of brimstone that he might come to heaven at last; but he that swims not thither through the sea of Christ's blood, shall never come there. Man must swim thither, not through brimstone, but through blood, or he miscarries forever. *Brooks.*

9110. GOOD NAME, Loss of a. Be wondrous wary of your first comportment. Get a good name, and be very tender of it afterwards, for it is like the Venice glass, quickly cracked, never to be mended, though patched it may be. Take along with you this fable: Fire, Water, and Fame went to travel together. They consulted that, if they lost one another, how they might meet again. Fire said, "Where you see smoke, there you will find me." Water said, "When you see marsh and low ground, there you shall find me." Fame said, "Take heed how you lose me; for, if you do, you will run a great hazard never to meet me again; there is no retrieving of me." *Howell.*

9111. GOOD NAME, Value of a. A youth was apprenticed to a Quaker to learn the tanner's trade. The condition of service expressed by the Quaker was "Thee shall do as well by me as I do by thee." The boy won his employer's confidence, was honest, good-natured and industrious. Before the expiration of his time, the Quaker said to him, "Henry, I think of making thee a nice present when thy time is out. I cannot tell thee what the present is to be but it shall be worth more than a hundred pounds." Great expectations and many questions in regard to the present were kindled in the young man's mind. When the time arrived, the Quaker took him to his father, saying, "I will give thy present to thy father." On meeting the father the Quaker said, "Thy son is the best boy I ever had." Then looking at the young man he said, "This is thy present, Henry—A good name." Henry's golden visions vanished, but his father answered, "I would rather hear you say that of my son than to see you give him all the money you are worth, for 'a good name is rather to be chosen than great riches.'"

9112. GOOD-NATURE, Advantages of. Good nature is more agreeable in conversation than wit, and gives a certain air to the countenance which is more amiable than beauty. It shows virtue in the fairest light, takes off in some measure from the deformity of vice, and makes even folly and impertinence supportable. There is no society or conversation to be kept up in the world without good-nature, or something which must bear its appearance and supply its place. For this reason mankind have been forced to invent a kind of artificial humanity, which is what we express by the word good-breeding. For if we examine thoroughly the idea of what we call so, we shall find it to be nothing else but an imitation and mimicry of good-nature, or, in other terms, affability, complaisance, and easiness of temper reduced into an art. These exterior shows and appearances of humanity render a man wonderfully popular and beloved, when they are founded upon a real good-nature; but without it, are like hypocrisy in religion, or a bare form of holiness, which, when it is discovered, makes a man more detestable than professed impiety. Good-nature is generally born with us; health, prosperity, and kind treatment from the world are great cherishers of it where they find it; but nothing is capable of forcing it up where it does not grow of itself. It is one of the blessings of a happy constitution, which education may improve, but not produce. *Addison*.

9113. GOOD-NATURE, Virtue of. An attribute so precious, that, in my consideration, it becomes a virtue, is a gentle and constant equality of temper. To sustain it, not only exacts a pure mind, but a vigor of understanding which resists the petty vexations and fleeting contrarieties which a multitude of objects and events are continually bringing. What an unutterable charm does it give to the society of the man who possesses it! How is it possible to avoid loving him whom we are certain always to find with serenity on his brow, and a smile on his countenance? *Bp. E. Stanley*.

9114. GOODNESS, Blessedness of. Who can estimate the blessedness of a pious soul? Can the state of that soul be unhappy that is full of the Holy Ghost; full of love, joy, peace, long-suffering, gentleness, goodness, faith, meekness, temperance, those blessed fruits of that blessed Spirit? Blessedness is connaturalized unto this soul: everything doth its part, and all conspire to make it happy. This soul is a temple, a habitation of holiness. Here dwells a Deity in his glory. It is a paradise; a garden of God: here he walks and converses daily, delighted with its fragrant fruitfulness. He that hath those things, and aboundeth, is not barren or unfruitful in the knowledge of our Lord and Saviour Jesus: he is the Sun; and the knowledge of him, the quickening beams that cherish and ripen these fruits. But the soul that lacketh these things is a desert—a habitation of devils. *Howe*.

9115. GOODNESS, Emblem of. Goodness is a fountain whose stream flows forth in all seasons, spreading life along all its banks. It has no summer when its source is dried up, and no winter when its streams are congealed. It hastens to fulfill its work of beneficence, giving drink to the thirsty traveler here, turning the wheel of the miller there, and anon spreading itself through the meadows to bring forth corn for the farmer. It overcomes all obstructions, either finding some underground course, or accumulating force by which it removes and overleaps barriers. It pours its blessings alike upon the thoughtless and the thoughtful, upon the thankless and the thankful, scorning not the foot that tramples it, and blasting not the hand that smites it. It embraces "whatsoever things are true, honest, just, pure. lovely, and of good report." This fountain is God, and the good are its streams.

9116. GOODNESS, Festival of. Diogenes, seeing a man arranging himself to attend a great entertainment, asked him if every day was not a festival to a good man.

9117. GOODNESS, Hatred of. I happened once to be present in the room where a dying man could not leave the world until he lamented to a minister (whom he had sent for on his account), the unjust calumnies and injuries which he had often cast upon him. The minister asked the poor penitent what was the occasion of this abusive conduct; whether he had been imposed upon by any false report. The man made this answer, "No, sir, it was merely this I thought you were a good man, and that you did much good in the world, and therefore I hated you. Is it possible," he added, "for such a wretch to find pardon?" *Cotton Mather*.

9118. GOODNESS, Immortality of. "The evil men do lives after them, the good is oft interred with their bones." This trite quotation enshrines a specious falsehood. Goodness does not die. It cannot be drowned in the depths of ocean. It cannot be consumed by fire. It cannot be buried, though mountains were heaped upon it. It lives among the decay of the body, survives crucifixion like the Master, and like him must have an everlasting and an ever-widening influence. Like the self-sowing seed, one harvest shall follow another. This seed thou art scattering for eternity with a careful or a careless hand.

9119. GOODNESS, Import of. Goodness, as that which makes men prefer their duty and their promise before their passions or their interest, and is properly the object of trust, in our language goes rather by the name of honesty, though what we call an honest man the Romans called a good man, and honesty, in their language, as well as in French, rather signifies a composition of those qualities which generally acquire honor and esteem. *Temple*.

9120. GOODNESS, Majesty of. Henry II., of France, was so daunted by the heavenly majesty of a poor tailor, who was burnt before him, that he went home sad, and vowed that he would never be present at the death of such men any more. When Valens, the emperor, came in person to apprehend Basil, he saw such majesty in his very countenance that he reeled at the sight, and would have fallen backward to the ground had not his servants supported him.

9121. GOODNESS, Manifestation of Divine. Divine goodness was in all ages sending letters of advice and counsel from heaven, till the canon of Scripture was closed. It was goodness that revealed anything of his will after the fall; it was a further degree of goodness that he would add more cubits to its stature; and before he would lay aside his pencil, it grew up into that bulk wherein we have it; and his goodness is further seen in its preservation. He hath triumphed over the powers that opposed it. He hath maintained it against the blasts of hell, and spread it in all languages against the obstruction of men and devils. *Charnock*.

9122. GOODNESS, Measure of. He has more

goodness in his little finger than you have in your whole body. *Dean Swift.*

9123. GOODNESS, Monument to. Thousands of men breathe, move, and live, pass off the stage of life, and are heard of no more—Why? they do not partake of good in the world, and none were blessed by them; none could point to them as the means of their redemption; not a line they wrote, not a word they spoke, could be recalled; and so they perished; their light went out in darkness, and they were not remembered more than insects of yesterday. Will you thus live and die, O man immortal! Live for something. Do good, and leave behind you a monument of virtue that the storm of time can never destroy. Write your name, in kindness, love and mercy, on the hearts of the thousands you come in contact with year by year: you will never be forgotten. No, your name, your deeds, will be as legible on the hearts you leave behind as the stars on the brow of evening. Good deeds will shine as the stars of heaven. *Chalmers.*

9124. GOOD WORKS, Lesson of. Theodulus, a prefect of Constantinople under Theodosius the Great, like Solon, early tested the pleasures of the world and found them all vanities. He resigned his office, and informed his beautiful young wife, to whom he had been two years married, of his resolution to renounce all, even her, and live for God alone. She pleaded her faithfulness and love, and implored him not to leave her. He repulsed her, and next morning she was found cold and dead from a broken heart, with the tears still on her cheeks. He went to Edessa, found a pillar, upon which he lived winter and summer, night and day, for forty-eight years, fasting, praying and watching. At the end of that time, he thought of the sacrifices he had made of wealth, office and wife, and what austerities he had borne for so many years, and concluding that he must be near perfection, asked the Lord to show him who, if any, should be his equal in heavenly glory. The Lord answered him in a dream saying, "Cornelius the Clown." Then the hermit descended from his pillar and went in quest of this man of superior sanctity, inquiring everywhere for "Cornelius the Clown." He came after a while upon a masked piper, who was greatly amusing the crowd. The hermit plucked him by the sleeve, and taking him aside asked in amazement, "What good thing hast thou done to inherit eternal life? I have given up house and land and a dear wife. I have spent forty-eight years on a pillar, exposed to the glaring sun by day and to the numbing frosts by night. I have worn out my body with fasting. I have eaten but a crust and a raw olive in the day. What hast thou done? I have become stiff in my joints, my feet are sore and swollen with long standing. I have prayed night and day some hundred prayers daily, and I have watched by night as the stars wheeled above me. What hast thou done?" "I have done nothing," answered the piper; "I cannot compare with thee." The hermit persisted. "Thou hast done something.

I know that thou will be accounted great in heaven. Tell me what thou hast done?" "I am as vile as dirt. I have not even served God purely and honestly," said he. "Bethink thee what good thing thou hast done," urged the hermit. Then the piper recalled a kindness which he did not think worth mentioning. "Some time ago there was a virtuous young wife in this town, who had been married only two years, when her husband was cast into the debtor's prison. She was compelled to beg for food to keep him and herself alive. She was very fair and modest, and feared lest she should attract rude eyes, and when she begged held out both hands and hung down her face, murmuring only inarticulate words. I saw her one day and was grieved, for I had piped and danced in the court of her house for a few coppers not long before. Then I went to her and asked how much her husband owed, and she said, 'Four hundred pieces of silver.' I ran home and turned out my money box and found therein two hundred and thirty pieces. Then I took a pair of gold bracelets and some brooches which had belonged to my dead wife, and they were worth seventy pieces of silver. That was not enough, so I got together some of my silk theatrical dresses, and rolled them all up in a piece of linen and took it to the woman, and I said to her, 'There, take all and release your husband from jail.' And then I ran away. This I believe is the only good thing I have ever done." Then the hermit saw how this man had sacrificed himself for a stranger, whereas he had cast away his own wife and broken her heart, seeking only self. The hermit blessed the piper and thanked God for the lesson, and went back to his pillar a wiser man.

9125. GOOD WORKS, No Confidence in. Martin Boos, a Catholic, visiting a sick woman, said to her, "I doubt not but you will die calm and happy." "Wherefore?" asked the sick woman. "Because your life has all been made up of a series of good works." She sighed and said, "If I die confiding in the good works which you call to my recollection, I know for certain that I shall be condemned; but what renders me calm at this solemn hour is, that I trust solely in Jesus Christ my Saviour." "These few words," said Boos, "from the mouth of a dying woman who was reputed a saint, opened my eyes for the first time. I learned what that was—'Christ for us.'"

9126. GOOD WORKS, Rejected Notwithstanding. Mohammed pronounced his imprecation upon his uncle, Al Abbas, because he trusted in good works, done to the Moslems, without accepting their religion. To Mohammed's nephew, Ali, he said, "You rip up our ill actions, but take no notice of our good ones. We visit the temple at Mecca and adorn the Caaba with hangings, and give drink to the pilgrims and free captives." Mohammed allowed him no part in Paradise.

9127. GOOD WORKS, Trusting to. Martin Luther says, "You think you will go to heaven for good works; you might as well try to sail to America in a paper boat. You will be swamped on the voyage, if you attempt it. Your works will never carry you safely; overboard with them!"

9128. GOSPEL, Appreciating the. Rev. J. M. Ormsond overheard some converted Polynesian chiefs talking together thus: "But for our teachers, our grass on the hill, our fences and houses, would have been ashes long ago." "But for the gospel we should now have been on the mountains, squeezing moss for a drop of water, and smothering the cries of our children by filling their mouths with grass, dirt, or cloth." "Under the reign of Messiah we stretch out our feet at ease, eat our food, keep our pig by the house." "We did not know more than our ancestors, our kings, and our parents, and were all blind, till the birds flew across the great expanse with good seeds in their mouths, and planted them among us. We now gather fruit, and have continual harvest. It was God who put it into the hearts of those strangers to come to us. We have nothing to give them. They are a people who seek our good; but we are a people of thorny hands, of pointed tongues, and we have no thoughts." "If God were to take our teachers from us, we should soon be savages again." "Our hearts delight in war; but our teachers love peace, and we now have peace."

9129. GOSPEL, Change by the. The change in Savage Island is thus described: Fifteen years ago the natives lived in the bush like brutes; now villages and neat plastered cottages evidence the progress of civilization. Fifteen years ago anarchy, war, and bloodshed prevailed throughout the island; now law, order, and peace. Fifteen years ago the people were all dark and degraded, strangers to prayer and praise; now, clothed and in their right mind, they surround their family altars night and morning to bow down to the God of heaven, while the air is vocal with their songs of praise. Fifteen years ago they had no written language; now they have the Gospels and other books, with two thousand readers. Fifteen years ago they were all, before God, dead in sin; now there are 360 in church fellowship, living to his glory, besides many who, we have reason to hope, are new creatures in Christ Jesus. *W. G. Lawes.*

9130. GOSPEL, Delay of the. At Raiatea, one of the Society Islands, six hundred children were assembled at a feast. They marched through the settlement in procession, dressed in European garments, with little hats and bonnets made by those very parents who would have destroyed them, as was their cruel custom, had not the Gospel come to their rescue. They and their parents occupied the chapel. The appearance of the parents was most affecting. The eyes of some were beaming with delight, as the father said to the mother, "What a mercy it is that we spared our dear girl!" Bitter tears rolling down the saddened countenances of others, told the painful tale that all their children were destroyed. A venerable chief, gray with age, could bear the scene no longer; he arose, and, with an impassioned look and manner, exclaimed, "Let me speak; I must speak. Oh, that I had known that the Gospel was coming! my children would have been among this happy group; but, alas! I destroyed them all. I have not one left. I shall die childless, though I have been the father of nineteen children." Sitting down, he gave vent to his agonized feelings in a flood of tears. *Moister.*

9131. GOSPEL, Divinity of the. It is remarkable that infidels themselves have been obligated to give their testimony in its favor. Cæsar Vaninus, a sworn enemy to the Christian religion, and one who was industrious in searching out objections against it, owned that he could find nothing in it that savored of a carnal and worldly design. What says Bolingbroke? "No religion has ever appeared in the world of which the natural tendency is so much directed as the Christian, to promote the peace and happiness of mankind; and the gospel is one continued lesson of the strictest morality of justice, charity, and universal benevolence." The testimony of Gibbon is remarkable: "While the Roman empire," says he, "was invaded by open violence, or undermined by slow decay, a pure and humble religion greatly insinuated itself into the minds of men, grew up in silence and sobriety, derived new vigor from opposition, and finally erected the banner of the cross on the ruins of the capital." Again he says, "The Christian religion is a religion which diffuses among the people a pure, benevolent, and universal system of ethics, adapted to every condition of life, and recommended as the will and reason of the Supreme Deity, and enforced by the sanction of eternal rewards and punishments." Such are the testimonies of infidels, and true it is, that this noble system allows of no evil, but promotes the greatest good. *Buck.*

9132. GOSPEL, Duty towards the. Every Christian hath his talent given him, his service enjoined him. The gospel is a *depositum*, a public treasure, committed to the keeping of every Christian; each man having, as it were, a several key of the church, a several trust for the honor of this kingdom delivered unto him. As, in the solemn coronation of the prince, every peer of the realm hath his station about the throne, and with the touch of his hand upon the royal crown, declareth the personal duty of that honor which he is called unto, namely, to hold the crown on the head of his sovereign; to make it the main end of his greatness, to study, and by all means endeavor the establishment of his prince's throne; so every Christian, as soon as he hath the honor to be called unto the kingdom, and presence of Christ, hath immediately no meaner a *depositum* committed to his care, than the very throne and crown of his Saviour, than the public honor, peace, victory and stability of his Master's kingdom. *Bp. Reynolds.*

9133. GOSPEL, Faith in the. Paganism was never accepted as truth by the wise men of Greece, neither by Socrates, Pythagoras, Plato, Auaxagoras, nor Pericles. But, on the other side, the loftiest intellects, since the advent of Christianity have had faith, a living faith, a practical faith, in the mysteries and doctrines of the gospel. *Napoleon I.*

9134. GOSPEL, Glories of the. France has caused pictures to be made of all the great events of her military history, by famous painters, and has gathered these battle scenes into the great halls of the palace of Versailles, on which is the inscription, "To all the glories of France." It is a place of great interest, but it commemorates earthly glory. There are other battles and victories than these, in which God's people have been engaged all through the ages. These may be delineated with absolute truthfulness and in all their minutiæ upon the walls of the palace of God in the heavens. The pictures are daily made up and not to be revised. They will show Abraham, Peter, Luther, Wesley and all their subordinates, and portray their glorious victories. What a gallery of glorious mementos.

9135. GOSPEL, Go with the. If St. Paul had ever preached from "Go ye into all the world, and preach the Gospel to every creature," he would have laid great stress on the word "go." On your peril, do not substitute another word for "go." Preach is a good word. Direct is a good word. Collect is a good word. Give is a good word. They are all important in their places, and cannot be dispensed with. The Lord bless and prosper those who are so engaged; but still lay the stress on the word "go," for "how shall they hear without a preacher? and how shall they preach, except they be sent?" Six hundred millions of the human race are perishing; and there are perhaps thirty among all the Christians in Britain who are at this moment preparing to "go." Alas! my hand shakes and my heart trembles, "Is this thy kindness to thy friend!" *Knill.*

9136. GOSPEL, Great Plan of the. It is said that the architect of the great Strasbourg minster, who died before his work was done, left his plans so that everybody could see on paper what his general design was. It was clear to many that he wished the building to go up a certain height, and the spires to be in certain places; but after the man's hand was still in death, and his lips were no more active to reveal the magnitude of his plan, nobody could understand it. His daughter looked at the papers and rolled them over and over again, and tried to enter into her father's wonderful undertaking; and though she did superintend the work for years after his death, and was supposed to be the only one who could approach him, yet she died without comprehending his plan, and the magnificent minster to-day has great architectural deformities. No one was found who could conceive and understand the plan which the great architect had in his mind. So in this great plan of Jesus to save the world from its bondage, to break its fetters, to give sunlight to the soul, in that wonderful undertaking nobody could understand its magnitude,

and Christ stood alone. So it was all along that they were unable to conceive the wonderful character of his great mission, which was to save the world from its sins and redeem it from its bondage. *Dr. J. F. Hurst.*

9137. GOSPEL, Hero of the. A speaker said in a missionary address, "It is nearly two generations since a boat's crew left their ship to reach the Hervey Islands. One of the passengers upon that boat desired to land, but the boat's crew feared to do so, as the cannibals were gathered together on the shore. Holding up the Bible in his hand, he said, 'Live or die, put me ashore.' They would not go near the land; he plunged into the surf, and held high the book. He reached the land. The cannibals did not kill him, but he won their favor and lived among them, and for aught I know he died among them. Thirty years afterwards another ship reached the same Hervey Islands, bringing literally a cargo of Bibles. They were all wanted, and were taken with the greatest eagerness and paid for by these people. This was the result of the labors of that heroic young man who said, 'Live or die, put me ashore.'"

9138. GOSPEL, Hindrances to the. What has prevented the gospel from fulfilling its promise, and completely taking effect? what has hindered it from filling every heart, every province, the whole world, the entire mass of humanity, with the one spirit of Divine benevolence? Why, on the contrary, has the gospel, the great instrument of Divine love, been threatened, age after age, with failure? Owing solely to the treachery of those who have had the administration of it; owing entirely to the selfishness of the church. No element essential to success has been left out of its arrangements; all these elements have always been in the possession of the church: no new form of evil has arisen in the world; no antagonist has appeared there which the gospel did not encounter and subdue in its first onset: yet at this advanced stage of its existence, when it ought to be reposing from the conquest of the world, the church listens to an account of its early triumphs, as if they were meant only for wonder, and not for imitation; as if they partook too much of the romance of benevolence to be again attempted; now, when it ought to be holding the world in fee, it is barely occupying a few scattered provinces as if by sufferance, and has to begin its conflicts again. And, we repeat, the only adequate explanation of this appalling fact is, that selfishness, the sin of the world, has become the prevailing sin of the church. *Dr. J. Harris.*

9139. GOSPEL, Honoring the. We honor the gospel, when, in our greatest distress we make it our altar of refuge, our door of escape, the ground of all our hope and comfort, the only anchor to stay our souls in any spiritual tempest, the only staff to lean upon in our greatest darkness. *Bp. Reynolds.*

9140. GOSPEL, Humanity of the. Its coming found the heathen world without a single house of mercy. Search the Byzantine Chronicles and the pages of Publius Victor; and though the one describes all the public edifices of ancient Constantinople, and the other of ancient Rome, not a word is to be found in either of a charitable institution. Search the ancient marbles in your museums; descend and ransack the graves of Herculaneum and Pompeii; and question the many travelers who have visited the ruined cities of Greece and Rome; and see if amid all the splendid remains of statues and amphitheatres, baths, and granaries, temples, aqueducts, and palaces, mausoleums, columns and triumphal arches, a single fragment or inscription can be found telling us that it belonged to a refuge for human want or for the alleviation of human misery.

Dr. John Harris.

9141. GOSPEL, Importance of the. The gospel is not only wonderful, but all-important. It is the gospel of our salvation. It is the bread, the water of life. For dying souls it is the only remedy. It has done more already for the public welfare of nations than all the civil institutions of men; and by this alone will the wilderness and solitary place be made glad, and the desert rejoice and blossom as the rose. *Jay.*

9142. GOSPEL, Improving the. In the South Sea Islands, on the Sunday morning, the natives meet together in classes of ten or twelve families each, and distribute among themselves the respective portions of the sermon each individual should bring away; one saying, "Mine shall be the text, and all that is said in immediate connection with it;" another, "I will take care of the first division;" and a third, "I will bring home the particulars under that head;" thus the sermon is appropriated before it is delivered. In some of the more advanced stations, where the New Testament is in the hands of the people, the missionaries are in the habit of naming passages of Scripture which are illustrative of the particulars under discussion. For instance, if the missionary is preaching upon the love of Christ, his first division may be to describe the nature and properties of that love, and under this head, if he refer to its greatness, after having illustrated his point, he will desire his hearers, without specifying the verse or verses, to read with attention the third chapter of St. Paul's Epistle to the Ephesians, where they will find some sentiments applicable to that part of the subject. Opening their Testaments, the converted natives will find the chapter referred to, and make a mark against it. A second division may be the unchangeable nature of the Saviour's love; and the preacher having concluded his observations on this, he will desire the congregation to read carefully the eighth chapter of St. Paul's Epistle to the Romans, where they will find some passages illustrative of that particular. Again opening their Testaments, the chapter is sought and marked as before. Thus they proceed through the entire discourse. At a convenient time, the respective classes meet, and after commencing their social service with singing and prayer, one of the most intelligent of the members, as leader,

begins to inquire, "With whom is the text?" and proposes a variety of questions upon it. After this he asks for the divisions of the discourse; and when one has been given, he will say, "To what portion of Scripture were we referred?" The chapter having been named, they proceed to read it carefully over, and the verses thought to be most applicable are selected for observation. This is found to be a most excellent method of proceeding, as it not only induces the people to pay great attention to the sermon, but to search the Scriptures with interest, and also to exercise their minds on the meaning and application of what they hear and read. *Moister.*

9143. GOSPEL, Law and. An old writer says, "The law showeth us our sin, the gospel showeth us a remedy for it. The law showeth us our condemnation, the gospel showeth us our redemption. The law causeth wrath, the gospel is the word of grace. The law is the word of despair, the gospel is the word of comfort. The law says, Pay thy debt; the gospel says, Christ hath paid it. The law saith, Thou art a sinner, despair and thou shalt be damned; the gospel says, Thy sins are forgiven thee; be of good comfort, thou shalt be saved. The law saith, Make amends for thy sin; the gospel saith, Christ hath made it for thee. The law saith, Thy Father in heaven is angry with thee; the gospel saith, Christ hath pacified him with his blood. The law asks, Where is thy righteousness, goodness and satisfaction? The gospel saith, Christ is my righteousness, goodness, and satisfaction. The law saith, Thou art bound and indebted to me; the gospel saith, Christ hath delivered thee from them all. He that believeth not God's word believeth not God himself. The gospel is God's word; therefore he that believeth not the gospel believeth not God himself."

9144. GOSPEL, Living the. Martin Luther pronounced an expressive eulogy upon Nicholas Hausmann, pastor at Zwickau, in 1522, thus, "What we preach, he lives."

9145. GOSPEL, Message of the. A London city missionary whose success among fallen women had been remarkable, after a visit to the country, was returning through Yorkshire. He stopped at the inn, and after tea the matron went to a drawer and taking out the daguerreotype of a beautiful girl, handed it the missionary, saying, "It is my daughter, gone, lost, and yet—O sir, take with you this last memento of the one we loved so well, and if ever in your great city you see her face, go to her and tell her that her old home still waits for her, and her mother's heart still yearns for her." This is the message which is sent by Christ to every lost sinner.

9146. GOSPEL, Nature of the. The Gospel is the fulfillment of all hopes, the perfection of all philosophy, the interpretation of all revelations, the key to all the seeming contradictions of the physical and moral world.

Prof. Max Müller.

9147. GOSPEL, Need of a Plain. A sick Tennessee soldier signaled to a hospital visitor

Having gained his attention he said, "Stranger, the man that lay on that cot was taken out this morning, and I have got the same sickness. I don't know how soon my turn may come. I want you to tell me what I ought to do." The preacher began to explain the way of salvation. "Stranger," said the earnest soldier, "couldn't you make it very plain to a poor feller that never got no schooling." This brought the preacher to the plainest words and simple illustrations. Speaking to him of prayer, he quoted the 51st Psalm, 1–3. "That's it, preacher," said he, "my head is full of fever and I can't mind it. If it was writ down, now, and I was to read it, don't you think the Lord would hear me? I could spell it out, preacher, if you think he'd hear me." The preacher sought for a Bible that he might read it out of that, but could find none in camp. The anxious soldier being told of this, and promised a Bible on the morrow, asked, "What's to become of a poor feller if I should die to-night?"

9148. GOSPEL, Net of the. The draw-net was of immense length. On the coast of Cornwall, where it is now used, and bears the same name, seine or sean, it is sometimes half a mile in length, and scarcely could have been much smaller among the ancients, since it is spoken of as nearly taking in the compass of an entire bay. It is leaded below, that it may sweep the bottom of the sea, and supported with corks above, and, having been carried out so as to inclose a large space of sea, the ends are then brought together, and it is drawn up upon the beach with all that it contains. *R. C. Trench.*

9149. GOSPEL, Novelty of the. When Le Tourneau preached the last sermon at St. Benoit, at Paris, Louis XIV. inquired of Boileau, "If he knew anything of a preacher called Le Tourneau, whom everybody was running after?" "Sire," replied the poet, "your Majesty knows that people always run after novelties; this man preaches the Gospel." A Flemish preacher, in a sermon delivered before an audience wholly of the clergy, said, "We are worse than Judas; he sold and delivered his Master—we sell him, too, but deliver him not."

9150. GOSPEL, Objection to the. The first sermon preached by the Rev. Robert Hall at Cambridge, after he had become pastor of the congregation there, was on the doctrine of the Atonement. One of the congregation said to him, "Mr. Hall, this preaching won't do for us; it will only suit a congregation of old women." "Do you mean my sermon, sir, or the doctrine?" "Your doctrine." "Why is it that the doctrine is fit only for old women?" "Because it may suit the musings of people tottering upon the brink of the grave, and who are eagerly seeking comfort." "Thank you, sir, for your concession. The doctrine will not suit people of any age, unless it be true, and if it be true, it is not fitted for old women alone, but is equally important at every age."

9151. GOSPEL, Pardon and Holiness in the. The gospel runs in two golden streams—freedom from sin, purity of walking: they run undividedly all along, in one channel, yet without confusion one with another, as it is reported of some great rivers that run together between the same banks, and yet retain distinct colors and natures all the way, till they part. But these "streams that glad the city of God" never part from one another; the cleansing blood and the purifying light, these are the entire and perfect sum of the gospel; purification from sin, the guilt of sin, and the purity of walking in the light, flowing from that, make up the full complexion of Christianity, which are so nearly conjoined together, that if they be divided they cease to be, and cannot any of them subsist save in man's deluded imagination. *Salter.*

9152. GOSPEL, Philosophy of the. "Oh, Topsy, poor child, I love you," said Eva, with a sudden burst of feeling. "I love you because you haven't any father or mother or friends—because you have been a poor abused child! I love you, and I so want you to be good!" The keen round eyes of the black child were overcast with tears, large bright drops rolled heavily down one by one, and fell on the little white hand. In that moment, a ray of real belief, a ray of heavenly love, had penetrated the darkness of her heathen soul.
Mrs. H. B. Stowe.

9153. GOSPEL, Preaching the. Elliot, the Apostle to the Indians, once successfully preached the gospel to a solitary Indian woman. She came fifteen miles one day to hear him preach, but arrived just as the sermon closed. Seeing her disappointment and knowing her purpose, he approached her as she sat at the root of a tree, and with the aid of interpreters gave her the Gospel message, "that Christ Jesus came into the world to save sinners." It resulted in her conversion, and through her in the conversion of many of her tribe.

9154. GOSPEL, Proclaiming the. The bee-hunter of the frontier, where wild bees make their homes in hollow trees, takes a box in which is a quantity of honey, and goes to a field where he is likely to find bees gathering their store. He places the box where the bees will find the honey it contains. When a bee has discovered it he will load himself, then go to his hive and tell his companions of the treasures he has found. Some of them will return with him, and help gather the honey. The hunter watches their course, for bees usually travel in straight lines, and traces them home. Having tasted the gospel honey, the redeemed soul hastens to tell that it has found more than golden store, and others are led to seek a like supply.

9155. GOSPEL, Progress of the. A returned missionary says: "It is demonstrable that the success of the gospel in the last hundred years is greater than that which it has achieved in any preceding hundred years. We look back on the first ages of Christianity, and sigh for the gift of tongues, and for Pentecostal blessing; and yet in the last century more has been done to give the Bible to the world, than was done in the first ten centuries of our era. Twenty versions at most were made in the first one thousand years; in the last one hundred years a hundred and twenty have been made—in languages spoken by more than half the globe. There are more conversions in heathen countries in the present day, in proportion to the number of preachers employed, than there are at home. Even when Constantine proclaimed Christianity as the religion of the Roman Empire, the nominal Christians did not exceed one-hundredth part of the population of the entire globe. Nominal Christians now form one-fifth. Each new generation of the modern world consists of 30,000,000 of children, and they have to be Christianized one by one. Of these thirty millions 6,000,000 (one-fifth) become nominally Christians, and a considerable portion of them really Christians."

9156. GOSPEL, Providence and the. Soon after the missionaries began their work in Raiatea, an event occurred which deeply impressed the natives, and led many to accept the Gospel. Four men, two idolaters and two Christians, in a canoe were upset. The Christians began to pray earnestly. The idolaters said, "Why did you not pray sooner? It is of no use now, that we are in the water." Prayer continued, and all clung to the canoe, till a shark seized one of the idolaters. After a time the tide cast them upon a reef. Just as they struck it, a shark seized the only surviving idolater. The signal deliverance of the two who prayed, and death of the two who did not, strongly recommended the religion of prayer.

9157. GOSPEL, Receiving the. All human learning is of no avail. Reason must be put out of the question. I reasoned and debated and investigated, but I found no peace till I came to the gospel as a little child, till I received it as a babe. Then such a light was shed abroad in my heart, that I saw the whole scheme at once, and I found pleasure the most indescribable. I saw there was no good deed in myself. Though I had spent hours in examining my conduct, I found nothing I had done would give me real satisfaction. It was always mixed up with something selfish. But when I came to the gospel as a child, the Holy Spirit seemed to fill my heart. I then saw my selfishness in all its vivid deformity, and I found there was no acceptance with God, and no happiness, except through the blessed Redeemer. I stripped off all my own deeds—threw them aside—went to him naked—he received me as he promised he would, and presented me to the Father—then I felt joy unspeakable, and all fear of death at once vanished. *Dr. Gordon.*

9158. GOSPEL, Release of the. I used to be a good deal troubled with my sins, and I thought of the day of judgment, when all the sins that I had committed in secret should blaze out before the assembled universe. But when a man comes to Christ the gospel tells him they are all gone, and in Jesus Christ he is a new creature. All I know is that out of the love which my Lord has for me he has taken all my sins and cast them behind his back. That is, behind God's back. How is Satan to get at it? If God has forgiven our sins, they won't be mentioned. In Ezekiel we are told not one of them shall be mentioned. Isn't it a glorious thing to have all our sins blotted out? And there is another thought, and that is the judgment. You know if a man has committed some great crime, when he is to be brought into judgment how he dreads it! How he dreads that day when he is to be brought into court, when he is put into a box and witnesses are to come up and testify against him, and he is there to be judged! But, my friends, the gospel tells us that if we come to Christ, we shall never come into judgment. Why? Because Christ was judged for us. He was wounded for our transgressions. If he has been wounded for us, we haven't got to be wounded. "Verily, verily,"—which means truly, truly—"I say unto you"—now just put your name in there—"He that heareth my words, and believeth on him that sent me, hath"—h-a-t-h, hath. It don't say you shall have when you die. It says, hath—"He that heareth my words and believeth on him that sent me hath everlasting life, and shall not come into condemnation." That means into judgment. He shan't come into judgment, but is passed "from death into life." There is judgment out of the way. He shall never come into judgment. Why? Because God has forgiven us and given us eternal life. That is the gospel of Jesus Christ. *Moody.*

9159. GOSPEL, Seeds of the. I have seen a waste of stones with scarcely anything of soil amongst them; yet even there were one or two solitary flowers in blossom. The wind had scattered there the seeds, the dews of heaven had fallen upon them, the little germs within had found something wherein to strike root, and the plants had sprung up and flowered unobserved. Those plants shall wither there, and decay, form a vegetable mould, the fit receptacle of other seeds that shall spring up into other flowers, till the stony waste be covered with soil, and the soil with verdure and bloom. Thus are the seeds of the gospel carried abroad into heathen lands; thus are they fostered by the blessed Spirit of God; thus do they find in one or two happy hearts a soil wherein to strike; and thus do they spring up into the beautiful flower of a holy life. *Salter.*

9160. GOSPEL, Spreading the. Rev. Mr. Shaw, a missionary in Africa, was greatly surprised on finding an old slave Christian one hundred and sixty miles from any station, and it was thus explained to him: "My master, some time ago, hired one of your Namaquas to take care of the sheep. When he came amongst us we knew nothing of God or prayer, but he commenced singing hymns and praying with us every evening. He then read out of the Book and told us of Jesus Christ. The words which he preached were so good for me that I longed to read them for myself. He was willing to teach me, and gave me his books; but the hymn-book is old and shattered, so that I can scarcely read it. I long for another. Our teacher has gone away from us to the station, yet we still sing and pray together with our fellow-slaves every evening; and, whilst I am watching the sheep in the day, I try to improve myself. Others of the slaves have begun to pray, and long to be taught."

9161. GOSPEL, Tenderness of the. What then is the nature of this so marvelous transforming message of the gospel? It is a story, a simple story, such as a child will feel and weep over; such as a sage of seventy winters cannot fathom. It tells of a law holy as that eternal heart from which it springs; it paints the portrait of the righteousness consummate which images that law in the life; it celebrates the triumph of the moral conquest that makes the enfranchised conscience sovereign of man. Yet this were no more than others could in their measure rival. But, oh! a tale more touching than all this solemn strain is its exclusive privilege to unfold. It speaks,—it alone can speak of one whose purity, too perfect to brook one unatoned sin in the vast universe of his creation, was accompanied by a love too tender to endure that one pang should continue to exist for which his own high wisdom could not provide a remedy; of a love which drew the living Author of the law from his transcendent abode into our narrow nature, that he might quench the lightnings of his own avenging justice in streams of his own human blood. It tells of that inexpressible attachment of which all human relationships (for it names them all) are too weak to be the faintest shadows of a Creator who is father, and brother, and husband of his redeemed; and by all the insults of his humiliated life: by his despised poverty and his accumulated wrongs, by a sight which made the angels tremble and weep, though — mystery of unfathomed ingratitude!—men, its objects, can slumber as they listen, or wake to scoff. By the groans of Gethsemane and its bloody sweat, by the nails and the thorns of Calvary, by the last dark tortures of an expiring God, it prays us to love him in return! This may fail to move, but it is certain that this appeal to the grateful affections is the legitimate path to the great object of a renovation, that it is a justifiable path, that it is a practicable path, that if it fail, no other that men have ever devised can offer a chance of success. *Butler.*

9162. GOSPEL, Victories of the. Had it been published by a voice from heaven, that twelve poor men, taken out of boats and creeks, without any help of learning, should conquer the world to the cross, it might have been thought an illusion against all the reason of men; yet we know it was undertaken and accomplished by them. They published this doctrine in Jerusa.em, and quickly spread it over the greatest part of the world. Folly outwitted wisdom, and weakness overpowered strength. The conquest of the East by Alexander was not so admirable as the enterprise of these poor men. *Charnock.*

9163. GOSSIP, Classic. Ulysses, going into the region of departed souls, would not exchange so much as one word with his mother there till he had first obtained an answer from the oracle, and despatched the business he came about; and then, turning to her, he afforded some small time for a few impertinent questions about the other women upon the place, asking which was Tyro, and which was the fair Chloris, and concerning the unfortunate Epicasta. *Plutarch.*

9164. GOSSIP, Malicious. There are a set of malicious, prating, prudent gossips, both male and female, who murder character to kill time, and will rob a young fellow of his good name before he has years to know the value of it. *Sheridan.*

9165. GOVERNMENT, Best. The government which takes in the consent of the greatest number of people may justly be said to have the broadest bottom; and if it be terminated in the authority of one single person, it may be said to have the narrowest top, and so makes the firmest pyramid. *Temple.*

9166. GOVERNMENT, Family. The eldest son of President Edwards congratulated a friend on having a family of sons, and said to him, "Remember, there is but one mode of family government. I have brought up and educated fourteen boys, two of whom I brought up, or suffered to grow up, without the rod. One of these was my youngest brother, and the other, Aaron Burr, my sister's only son, both of whom had lost their parents in their childhood; and from both my observation and experience, I tell you, sir, a maple-sugar government will never answer. Beware how you let the first act of disobedience in your little boys go unnoticed, and unless evidence of repentance be manifest, unpunished."

9167. GOVERNMENT, God's. How magnificent is this idea of God's government! That he inspects the whole and every part of his universe every moment, and orders it according to the counsels of his infinite wisdom and goodness, by his omnipotent will, whose thought is power, and his acts ten thousand times quicker than the light, unconfused in a multiplicity exceeding number, and unwearied through eternity! *Dr. Ogden.*

9168. GOVERNMENT, Opinions on. With regard to the Greek sages, Solon was of opinion that the best government was that in which the collective body of citizens takes a part, when an injury is offered to the individual. Bion thought that was preferable in which good laws were despotic; Thales, that in which equality of property prevailed; Cleobulus, that in which fear of disgrace is stronger than the law. According to Chilo, that is the best in which the law speaks instead of the lawyer; and according to Periander, that in which power is confided to a small number of enlightened, disinterested and humane men. *Fitz-Raymond.*

9169. GOVERNMENT, Reason for. The reason for which government exists is, that one man, if stronger than another, will take from him whatever that other possesses and he desires. But if one man will do this, so will several. And if powers are put into the hands of a comparatively small number, called an aristocracy—powers which make them stronger than the rest of the community—they will take from the rest of the community as much as they please of the objects of desire. They will thus defeat the very end for which government was instituted. The unfitness, therefore, of an aristocracy to be entrusted with the powers of government rests on demonstration. *James Mill.*

9170. GOVERNMENT, Religion in. It seems to me a great truth, that human things cannot stand on selfishness, mechanical utilities, economics, and law courts; that if there be not a religious element in the relations of men, such relations are miserable, and doomed to ruin. *Carlyle.*

9171. GOVERNOR, A Good. Peter the Great frequently surprised the magistrates by his unexpected presence in the cities of the empire. Having arrived, without previous notice, at Olonez, he went first to the regency, and inquired of the governor how many suits there were depending in the court of chancery. "None, Sire," replied the governor. "None! how happens that?" "Why," replied the governor, "I endeavor to prevent law-suits, and, by conciliating the parties, I act in such a manner that no traces of difference remain in the archives. If I am wrong, your indulgence will excuse me." "I wish," replied the czar, "that all governors would act upon the same principles. Go on; God and your sovereign are equally satisfied." *Buck.*

9172. GRACE, Abounding. A debauchee recently found himself in extreme want in the city of St. Louis. His father, a gentleman of wealth, made every effort to save him from the demon of drink. He was well married, but those thus related to him felt themselves disgraced, and tried to secure a separation. His wife's father assured her that every want should be supplied if she would leave her drunken husband forever. Her heart clung to him, and her hope and faith longed and looked for his reformation. In St. Louis he went to the city prison to seek food, and a night's lodging. He was committed as a vagrant, and slept in the cells as a common prisoner. Here he began to come to himself. The next morning in rags and filth he went and told a minister his story. He said his father was a banker and a Methodist in Indianapolis, where his wife also lived, and that he himself had been educated a Methodist. The minister said, "You are the meanest specimen of a Methodist I ever saw." The minister telegraphed to his father, his name and condition, and received the reply, "He is my poor boy; send him home." He called to himself the aids of religion, the demon was bound and cast out. His father now rejoices in a dutiful son, and his wife in an affectionate husband. Behold a living parable of another prodigal son, showing how grace abounds.

9173. GRACE, Accepting. At Basle I was the guest of a dear Christian, who had inherited a

large house, at the entrance of which was a porter's lodge; but the owner did not go into that lodge and say it would be presumption to take possession of the house. When he received the title-deeds, he at once entered and occupied the whole mansion. There had been glorious things given to them in the name of Jesus Christ, and many had just gone into the porter's lodge, thinking that it would be presumption to enter further upon the wonderful gifts of God. This was wrong; the true humility was to acknowledge their own helplessness and take the place God gave them. *Smith.*

9174. GRACE, Adaptation of. Whenever the Lord sets his servants to do extraordinary work, he always gives them extraordinary strength; or if he puts them to unusual suffering, he gives them unusual patience. When we enter upon war with some petty New Zealand chief, our troops expect to have their charges defrayed, and accordingly we pay them gold by thousands, as their expenses may require; but when an army marches against a grim monarch, in an unknown country, who has insulted the British flag, we pay, as we know to our cost, not by thousands but by millions. And thus, if God calls us to common and ordinary trials, he will defray the charges of our warfare by thousands; but if he commands us to an unusual struggle with some tremendous foe, he will discharge the liabilities of our war by millions, according to the riches of his grace in which he has abounded towards us through Christ Jesus. *Spurgeon.*

9175. GRACE, Agents of. God is never tied to the use of means and instruments in dispensing his grace. He can work by little or by great means, by few or by many. He hath not limited himself to one way, or time, or manner of speaking, lest we should ascribe the glory to the means, to the tools, rather than to the blessed Workman and Author. Therefore he is pleased ever and anon to change the means, to break his tools, as it were, and throw them away, and make new ones. Hence, if men begin to think that a temple at Jerusalem hath any salvation in it, he will burn it up, and be worshiped in spirit and truth in every cottage. *Samuel Mather.*

9176. GRACE, Dishonoring. What would you think of one who was allowed to light his dwelling at night as brilliantly as he would, without cost, who should only kindle a solitary jet amid the darkness of his home, and sit down content in that somber twilight? Or of one who should have free access to a spacious garden filled with bloom, with leave to pluck and gather what he chose, who should only put one foot inside the gate, and take away a single flower? Or of one made welcome to draw from a bank account of millions, who should fill his check for only enough to keep him from absolute starvation? Would these men be any wiser, would they honor their benefactors more than we, to whom Jesus opens all his stores of grace, and who yet keep so faint a spark of spiritual life, and who experience so little of comfort and strength? *Dr. A. L. Stone*

9177. GRACE, Dying. Mosheh, the paramount chief of the Basuto tribe, was awakened and converted in his old age. He found a refuge from his sins in the passage, "Blessed is the man whose transgressions are forgiven." In his last sickness visions of the heavenly mansions filled him with inexpressible joy. At the last he called, "Help me that I may fly! help me that I may fly!" His sick room was filled with holy influence. What a wonder that such a bloody and vile sinner as he had been should triumph so! They go into the kingdom before us.

9178. GRACE, Experience of. A lady met an aged female groping her way along the street. The lady said "My friend, you seem to be aged and infirm, is your soul at peace with God." "Yes, I am old; next month I shall be ninety-two; but who asks about my soul? You are the first person who ever spoke to me about it." The lady thought she would not lose the opportunity of doing her good, and so accompanied her to her miserable home. She found her an inmate of a low, wretched family, who boarded her for the rent of the hovel they occupied, which belonged to a son in an adjacent city. She had been a wayward youth, with an ungovernable temper that had driven husband and children from her; she had led a life of infamy for twenty-five years, followed by wretchedness and poverty. Discarded by friends, and disowned by her own son, she was reaping the bitter wages of sin. She had retained her mind wonderfully for one so aged, and the instructions in childhood, of the blessed precepts of the Bible, were not altogether lost. Daily was she visited and labored with until God saw fit to bless her by sending the Holy Ghost to enlighten her darkened mind, and break the bondage of sin. A year from that time friends were called around her death-bed. Her last words were, "I am a great, great sinner, but Jesus is a great, great Saviour; glory be to his name."

9179. GRACE, Fountain of. All who ever have received grace have received it from the fullness of Jesus Christ. This is the common well of salvation, out of which all believers draw the water of life: there is no access to God but by him. Believers under the law received grace from this fountain, as well as those under the gospel: though the measure was different, yet the fountain was the same; as it is the same face which is veiled and at another time unveiled, as it is the same sum written in figures and at full length in plain words, so Christ and his grace was the same under the Old Testament and under the New. There is no difference in the substance of the promise and covenant of grace then and now. Christ is yesterday and to-day the same, the difference is only in circumstances—the manifestation under the Gospel is clearer, and the propagation of the Gospel is now of a larger extent to all nations.
Colvill.

9180. GRACE, Fullness of. The soul is the fullness of the body, actuating each part; God is the fullness of the soul; raising it, that there be nothing low; filling it up, that there be no painful want; filling it out, that there be no ugly wrinkles. The sea-plants lie flat, flabby and formless when the tide is out; but when that returns, they rise and stand, and beautifully wave themselves amid the vitalizing element; every stem full, every leaf full, every pore and vessel full. Thus it is with believers when flowed around and flowed into by the fullness of God. A heart enriched with this plenitude does more than occasionally advert to God, or draw near to him at times, as a duty or a necessity; God is its atmosphere, its abode. The apprehension of him is abiding; the reference to him habitual; the help from him unceasing. Into that soul Jehovah brings the court and kingdom of heaven, and makes it the wonder and admiration of the very angels." *Thomas Collins.*

9181. GRACE, Gifts versus. There is many a learned head in hell. Gifts are the gold that beautifies the temple; but grace is as the temple which sanctifies the gold. One tear, one groan, one breathing of an upright heart is more than the tongues of angels. *John Flavel.*

9182. GRACE and Glory. Inherent grace below resembles silver in the ore, which, though genuine silver, is mingled with much earth and dross: glory above resembles silver refined to its proper standard, and wrought into vessels of the most exquisite workmanship. *Salter.*

9183. GRACE, God of All. Men talk about grace, but they don't know much about it. These bankers, they talk about grace. If you want to borrow a thousand dollars, if you can give good security, they will let you have it and take your note, and you give your note and say, "So many months after date I promise to pay a thousand dollars." Then they give you what they call three days' grace, but they make you pay interest for those three days. That ain't grace. Then when your note comes due, if you can't pay but $950, they would sell everything you have got and make you pay the $50. Grace is giving the interest, principal and all. I tell you, if you want to get any grace, you must know God. He is the God of all grace. He wants to deal in grace; he wants to deal with that unmerited mercy, undeserved favor, unmerited love; and if God don't love man until he is worthy of his love, he won't have time for very much love for him. *Moody.*

9184. GRACE, Growth of. The growth of grace in the heart may be compared to the process of polishing metals. First, you have a dark opaque substance, neither possessing nor reflecting light. Presently, as the polisher plies his work, you will see here and there a spark darting out, then a strong light, till, by-and-by, it sends back a perfect image of the sun which shines upon it. So the work of grace, if begun in our hearts, must be gradually and continually going on; and it will not be completed till the image of God can be perfectly reflected in us. *Salter.*

9185. GRACE, Increase of. So much of the

spirit of grace and truth as we have here, is but the earnest and handsel of a greater sum, the seed and first fruits of a fuller harvest. Therefore the apostle mentions "a growing change from glory to glory by the Spirit of God." We must not expect a fulless till "the time of the restitution of all things," till that day of redemption and adoption, wherein the light which is here but sown for the righteous, shall grow up into a full harvest of holiness and of glory. *Bp. Reynolds.*

9186. GRACE, Living with. Mr. Whitefield found it impossible to live peaceably with a person whom he admittted to be a Christian. Concerning this he said, "Grace can live where I cannot."

9187. GRACE, Maturity in. Maturity in grace makes us willing to part with worldly goods; the green apple needs a sharp twist to separate it from the bough; but the ripe fruit parts readily from the wood. Maturity in grace makes it easier to part with life itself; the unripe pear is scarcely beaten down with much labor, while its mellow companion drops readily into the hand with the slightest shake. Rest assured that love to the things of this life, and cleaving to this present state, are sure indications of immaturity in the divine life. *Spurgeon.*

9188. GRACE, More. Rowland Hill tells a story of a rich man and a poor man of his congregation. The rich man came to Mr. Hill with a sum of money which he wished to give to the poor man, and asked Mr. Hill to give it to him as he thought best, either all at once or in small amounts. He sent the poor man a five pound note, with the indorsement— "More to follow." Every few months came the remittance with the same message—"More to follow." So it is with grace.

9189. GRACE, Moment by Moment. God does not give a reserve stock of grace which you can look at and say, "That is mine." He just gives you minute by minute, and moment by moment, what is needed. It is like this: suppose a man says to his friend, "I will give you an empty purse, and in it you shall find any money you want the very minute you want it. I shall never give you any to keep in your pocket, but you may go to your purse for anything." Would that man be a very rich man, or a very poor man? I think he would be both. If he wanted a penny to buy a newspaper, he must call on his friend, and go to his purse for it; if he wanted a shilling, he could go for that; if he wanted a hundred pounds, he could go for that; he could get anything he wanted, but there would be something he could not do—he could not put money on the table, and look at it and say, "What a rich man I am." He would get up with an empty purse, and go to bed with an empty purse, and yet he would have all he needed. That is the way God gives us his grace, never more than we need for the very minute—always quite enough. *A. Monod.*

9190. GRACE, Mutiny against. It is true, indeed, grace, wherever it is, hath a principle in itself that makes it desire and endeavor to preserve itself according to its strength, but, being overpowered, must perish, except assisted by God, as fire in green wood (which deadens and damps the part kindled) will in time go out, except blown up, or more fire be put to that little; so will grace in the heart. God brings his grace into the heart by conquest. Now, as in a conquered city, though some yield and become true subjects to the conqueror, yet others plot how they may shake off this yoke, and therefore it requires the same power to keep as to win it at first. The Christian hath an unregenerate part, that is discontented at this new change in the heart, and disdains as much to come under the sweet government of Christ's sceptre as the Sodomites that Lot should judge them—"What! this fellow, a stranger, control us?"—and Satan heads this mutinous rout against Christians: so that if God should not continually reinforce this his new planted colony in the heart, the very natives—I mean, corruptions that are left— would come out of their dens and holes where they lie lurking, and eat up the little grace the holiest on earth hath: it would be as bread to these devourers. *Gurnall.*

9191. GRACE, Necessity of. It is a remark, I think, of Archbishop Whateley, that in all European languages the words which express forgiveness imply a free gift. Wickliffe used quaintly to pray, "Lord save us gratis;" and until we truly recognize that, we are "justified freely by his grace" we shall be shooting with arrows that are pointless and unfeathered, and cannot hope to receive the fruit of our labor. It was this doctrine that brought comfort to Luther's troubled heart when the poor simple monk, who had not the ability to solve his doubts, and to whom he turned in his wretchedness and despair, repeated to him his own ground of hope, "I believe in the forgiveness of sins." *Pilkington.*

9192. GRACE, Oil of. Then I saw in my dream that the Interpreter took Christian by the hand, and led him into a place where was a fire burning against a wall, and one standing by it, always casting much water upon it, to quench it; yet did the fire burn higher and hotter. "Then," said Christian, "what means this?" The Interpreter answered, "This fire is the work of grace that is wrought in the heart; he that casts water upon it, to extinguish and put it out, is the devil; but, in that thou seest the fire, notwithstanding, burns higher and hotter, thou shalt also see the reason of that." So he had him about to the back side of the wall, where he saw a Man with a vessel of oil in his hand, of which he did also continually cast, but secretly, into the fire. "Then," said Christian, "what means this?" The Interpreter answered, "This is Christ, who continually, with the oil of his grace, maintains the work already begun in the heart; by means of which, notwithstanding what the devil can do, the souls of his people prove gracious still. And in that thou sawest that the Man stood behind the wall to maintain the fire, this is to teach thee that it is hard for the tempted to see how this work of grace is maintained in the soul." *Bunyan.*

9193. GRACE, Parable of. A friend of mine gave me this illustration of grace. Suppose, said he, that a man had a beautiful farm on the side of a mountain. Everything was in an enclosure. He had a great wall all around it. Everything within the walls was bright and green, while everything outside was hot and dried up. One day there came a messenger to the man that had the beautiful farm, and he said to him: "Sir, you have a beautiful, flourishing farm, but I want to make it better. I will increase its fertility; I will make it a thousand times better than it now is." "No," says the farmer, "my farm is good enough; you can do nothing to better it;" and drove him away. He wouldn't have his farm made better, and he built his walls still higher to keep all men out. Up in the mountain near the house was a fountain. Its stream was used to irrigate and beautify the farm, and from it the crystal waters came to the garden. And the man that sent to him said to himself, "This man won't let me make his garden more beautiful; he won't accept my kindness. I will build up a wall and cut the stream off." When the wall arose around the fountain's head the waters ceased to flow to the farm; the flowers began to fade and wither, and soon every thing presented the appearance of desolation and ruin. So the Lord of glory comes and wants to give us his grace, but we spurn it, refuse to accept his blessing, and we perish. Why, Christ had the hardest work of his ministration to teach this subject even to his apostles. When they were offered grace they wouldn't have it. They couldn't keep grace in the country. They built up a wall of unbelief, the stream of grace ceased to flow to them, and what was the result? The garden that once was there is now the only dried up and withered spot on the whole mountain round about. Grace has flowed out to the Gentiles and to all the nations, and what a blessing it has been! It was just because they built a wall of unbelief. That is just what the sinner is doing now. But if you'll only let the grace flow, nothing can hinder you from getting a blessing.
Moody.

9194. GRACE, Perquisites of. When the great bargain is concluded between God and the soul of man, God throws in the good and needful things of this life, as unworthy of mention in so great a transaction. Like the farmer who sells a large and valuable farm, he throws in certain second-hand implements of husbandry, or, like the importing merchant, who, in selling one of his ships, throws in any cordage or other shipstores that may be lying about the vessel; while he who seeks to get "all these things" without securing the kingdom of God, will be like the sailor, who, with ship-stores, finds when too late he has not the ship. In securing the greater, we get the less; but if we look only for the less, we shall fail to possess the greater, or enjoy the less. *Hopkins.*

9195. GRACE, Power of. Fifty years ago, a young school-master in Georgia, commenced a prayer-meeting, with such success as to arouse a blatant infidel, who boasted that he would be present at the next meeting and show that all Christians were "fools and liars." The school-master was dismayed. The circuit preacher was sick, but God sent Rev. John O. Andrew there that night, and he led the meeting. The infidel took a seat at the place where the leader must stand, and by him stood the preacher. The hymn over, the preacher requested all to kneel. The skeptic knelt with the others, after the Southern custom, and was greatly surprised when the minister asked him to pray. He thought it better to brave it than back down, and began, not as he had intended, "Lord, thou knowest I never did pray; thou knowest I cannot pray." "That's right, brother," said the minister, "tell him the truth, and he will help you." A few more efforts by the sceptic to say something, and the spirit of conviction come upon him, and he began to cry, "O Lord, have mercy on me." The room resounded with sobs and responses to his prayer. This continued for a half hour, when the skeptic found himself wonderfully changed, and magnified the grace of God. He became as strong for God as he had been for Satan, and was faithful to the end. Many have found Christ who sought him not.

9196. GRACE, Prayer for. A poor man in England before eating asked a blessing in these words, which were found written on a slip of paper, "Lord, give me grace to feel my need of grace: and give me grace to ask for grace: and give me grace to receive grace: and, O Lord, when grace is given, give me grace to use it. Amen."

9197. GRACE, Preservation of. How shall a wooden vessel be kept water-tight, so that the precious supply of the household may not ooze through its joints into the ground? Keep it always full of water. It is by a similar method that grace may be preserved in the heart of a Christian. Keep the vessel full, and it will not leak. *Anon.*

9198. GRACE, Receiving. When Dr. Arnold was in this country I heard him use in a sermon an illustration that impressed me. He said: "Haven't you ever been in a home where the family were at dinner, and haven't you seen the old family dog standing near and watching his master, and looking at every morsel of food as if he wished he had it? If his master drops a crumb he at once licks it up and devours it. but if he should set the dish of roast beef down and say, 'Come, come,' he wouldn't touch it —it's too much for him. So with God's children; they are willing to take a crumb, but refuse when God wants them to go for the platter." God wants you to come right to the throne of grace, and to come boldly. A while ago I learned from the Chicago papers that there had been a run on the banks there, and many of them were broken. What a good thing it would be to get up a run on the Bank of Heaven! What a glorious thing to get up a run on the throne of grace! God is able to help thee and deliver thee if you will only come to him. That's what grace is for. I want you to turn to the 8th verse of the 9th chapter of 2 Corinthians. I want you to mark that verse. If you have got your Bibles with you, draw a black mark right around that verse. Many want to know why Christians fail. It's because they don't come to God for grace. It's not because he hasn't got the ability. Men fail because they try to do too large a business on too small a capital. So with Christians; but God has got grace enough and capital enough. What would you think of a man who had $1,000,000 in the bank and only drew out a penny a day? That's you and I, and the sinner is blinder than we are. The throne of grace is established, and there we are to get all the grace we need. Sin is not so strong as the arm of God. He will help and deliver you if you will come and get the grace you need. *Moody.*

9199. GRACE, Reign of: Rom. 5 : 21. The apostle represents grace as a mighty monarch triumphing over a cruel usurper. Sin and grace both have their kingdoms; but the grand and final victory must belong to grace. St. Paul has been, not without impropriety, called "the apostle of grace." No New Testament writer so exalts and dwells upon "the riches"—"the exceeding riches" of grace. How he magnifies it—in his own experience, 1 Cor. 15 : 10; 1 Tim. 1 : 12–16; Gal. 1 : 15, 16; and in the calling of the Gentiles, Eph. 3 : 2, 7, 8, where he multiplies words to make the strongest superlatives—"the *gift* of the *grace given!*" All his fourteen epistles close with the prayer for grace. It seems to have been his sign-manual, which no other apostle used during his life-time, though St. John used it after his death. The word χαρις, so common to St. Paul and to St. Luke, is seldom or never used by St. Matthew or St. Mark. Gen. 3 : 15.—The first promise. It is a fact which should never be forgotten, how entirely the first promise speaks of grace. Our first parents sinned, but they showed no signs of repentance; they sought no pardon; they made no confession; they prayed no prayer; they fled from the Creator, and hid themselves amongst the trees of the garden! Truly, it was all of grace that the Lord came to them; it was his own free thought of love that gave the first acorn promise of redemption! Rev. 22 : 17, 21.' The last words of Revelation still speak of grace; the echo lingers. Despite all the accumulated guilt of man from Adam's days, and the attempts of thousands to poison the sweet waters, the river of the water of life still flows fresh and bright and full. As the first promise came by grace, so the last offer of a free salvation speaks of the same: only the river flows in a wider, broader channel. *Bowes.*

9200. GRACE Seeking the Sinner. Abraham, of Mesopotamia, having sought in vain for happiness in the field of honor, wealth, and love, abandoned all —riches, friends, and wife—for a hermitage in the desert. While there, an orphan-girl, seven years of age, named Mary was brought to him, as his next of kin, to educate and care for. He had a cell built for her near his own, and loved her as a father. At the age of twenty she became enamored of a young man, who led her away from her uncle, and then abandoned her. She fell into the degradation of reckless women. Her uncle grieved greatly over her sad fate, and sent out inquiries in all directions that he might discover her whereabouts. He learned that she was at Assos, a city of the Troad. Then he broke down the door of his cell, cast off his sackcloth garment, and, disguising himself as a soldier, he went forth to recover his fallen niece. He hired a lodging next door to her house, but could get no opportunity to speak to her. Then he went to her house, ordered supper, and bade that Mary should eat with him. She came to the supper adorned with jewels and trinkets, and wantonly dressed, talking lightly and laughing loudly. Her uncle knew her, and was so overcome with grief that he could hardly restrain his emotions. Seeing this, the girl looked closely in his face, and discovered something which recalled other days. Her eyes met the tearful eyes of her uncle, and she cried, "Oh, God! would that I had died three years ago! This man recalls to me my dear old uncle, and days of innocence and joy." Then he threw back his hood, and caught her by the hands, saying, "Mary, my child!" She recognized him, and swooned away. He moaned over her, and said, "My dearest child, what has befallen thee? O, why didst thou not reveal to me thy first temptation, and I would have besieged heaven with tears and prayers to save thee? Why didst thou desert me, and bring this intolerable anguish upon me?" She was speechless before him. "My own Mary, wilt thou not speak to me?" he pleaded. His whole frame was shaken, and his tears flowed in streams. "Upon me be thy sin, my child," he said. "I will answer for it at the Judgment-day of God. I will suffer in expiation of thy crime. Only return, my child." Full of contrition, she answered, "I cannot look thee in the face, uncle, and how can I call on God, whom I have so outraged?" "I will bear the burden of thy sin. Let it weigh on me, Mary. Only return to the old place, and I will pray instantly for thee. Come, child, follow!" She fell at his feet, sobbing, kissed them, and said, "I will follow thee, uncle." He caught her up, and bade her fly at once. She desired to gather up her rich dresses and jewelry, but he said, "Leave them, leave them; they scent of evil." Then, says the legend, he took her on his back, as a shepherd carries his strayed sheep, and returned to his solitary life. She was truly reclaimed, and is commemorated in the calendar on March 16.

9201. GRACE, Sin and. These two, grace and sin, are like two buckets of a well; when one is up, the other is down. They are like the two laurels at Rome; when one flourishes, the other withers. The more grace thrives in the soul, the more sin dies in the soul. From naught they grow to be very naught, and from very naught to be stalk naught. Lactant said of Lucian, *Nec Diis, nec hominibus pepercit,* he spareth neither God nor man.   *Brooks.*

9202. GRACE, Sovereign. Oh, how sovereign! Oh, how sovereign! Grace is the only thing that can make us like God. I might be dragged through heaven, earth, and hell, and I should be still the same sinful, polluted wretch, unless God himself should renew and cleanse me.   *Dying words of Payson.*

9203. GRACE, Symbol of. "As thy day so shall thy strength be." The woman who had lost her husband went to Elisha with a story that would move the heart of Elisha or any one else. Her husband had died a bankrupt and they would sell her boys into slavery. She came to Elisha and told her story. He asked her what she had to pay. She replied a pot of oil. Elisha told her to go home, "borrow vessels, not a few, take oil and pour into the empty vessels." Men in these times wouldn't believe in this. They would say, "What, take a pot of oil and pour into all these vessels—what good will that do?" Not so with this poor widow. She has faith and does as she is told. She goes to her neighbors and asks for vessels; they can lend her a few. She takes all they have and goes on. She clears out the next house, and the next, and the next. "Borrow," says the prophet, and she goes on until her house is filled with vessels. "Now close the doors," she says to her sons. And she pours oil into the first vessel and fills it full, and the next, and the next, and the next, in the same way. She pours it in, and pours it in, and the boys run and get more vessels, until the house is full of oil. Then she goes to Elisha and asks what she shall do. He tells her "Go sell the oil and pay the debt." Now, Christ pays the debt and gives us enough to live on besides. He doesn't merely pay our debt—he gives us enough to live on. He gives according to our need.   *Moody.*

9204. GRACE, Throne of. There is no court in all God's dominions that a sinner can come to and find any mercy or grace but only at a throne of grace. If you talk of law, or justice, or equity, these are all frightful courts to sensible sinners. They know their cause and their case is bad, and that if they come to any bar but that of the throne of grace they must be cast. But at this throne of grace they that have nothing may get all things, they that deserve nothing may get everything, they that deserve wrath may obtain mercy, they that are cast and condemned at the court of justice may be acquitted and freed from all sentences, and be adjudged to eternal life by the grace of God in Christ Jesus. All that is needful to salvation is dispensed at this throne. Yet all that is given is old in the purpose of grace from eternity—old in the everlasting covenant, old in the purchase of Jesus Christ; only it is newly given according to the sinner's necessity.   *Robert Traill.*

9205. GRACE, Tide of. There are seasons more favorable and full of grace than others. In this there is nothing surprising, but much that is in harmony with the common dispensations of Providence. Does not the success of the farmer, seaman, merchant—of men in many other circumstances—chiefly depend on their seizing opportunities which come and go like showers; which flow and ebb like the tides of the ocean? The sea is not always full. Twice a day she deserts her shores, and leaves the vessels high and dry upon the beach; so that they who would sail must wait and watch, and take the tide; and larger ships can only get afloat, or, if afloat, get across the bar and into harbor, when, through a favorable conjunction of celestial influences, the sea swells in stream or spring tides beyond her common bounds. The seaman has his spring-tides; the husbandman has his spring-time; and those showers, and soft winds, and sunny hours, on the prompt and diligent improvement of which the state of the barn and granary depends.   *Guthrie.*

9206. GRACE, Time for. An artist solicited permission to paint a portrait of the Queen. The favor was granted, and the favor was great, for it would make the fortune of the man. A place was fixed, and a time. At the fixed place and time the Queen appeared; but the artist was not there—he was not ready yet. When he did arrive, a message was communicated to him that her Majesty had departed and would not return. Such is the tale. The King eternal consented to meet man. He fixed in his covenant, and promised in his word, the object, place, and time of the meeting: it is for salvation; it is in Christ; it is now. He has been true to his own appointment, but how often is it otherwise with man!   *Arnot.*

9207. GRACEFULNESS, Traits of. Gracefulness is an idea not very different from beauty: it consists in much the same things. Gracefulness is an idea belonging to posture and motion. In both these, to be graceful, it is requisite that there be no appearance of difficulty; there is required a small inflexion of the body, and a composure of the parts in such a manner as not to encumber each other, not to appear divided by sharp and sudden angles. In this ease, this roundness, this delicacy of attitude and motion, it is that all the magic of grace consists, and what is called its *je ne sais quoi,* as will be obvious to any observer who considers attentively the Venus de Medicis, the Antinous, or any statue generally allowed to be graceful in a high degree. *Burke.*

9208. GRACES, Chain of. It is most certain there is a chain of graces linked together, and they who have one have all in some good measure. They who have a lively hope have fervent love to God; and they who love God love their neighbors; and they who love God and neighbor hate sin; and they who hate sin sorrow for it; and they who sorrow for sin will avoid the occasion of it; and they that are thus watchful will pray fervently; and they who pray will meditate; and they who pray and meditate at home will join seriously in the public worship of God. Thus graces are combined and holy duties linked together, and no grace is alone.　　　　　　*N. Parkhurst.*

9209. GRACES, Development of the. Every man that has cultivated fruit knows that no tree can bear very richly the first year. The first year a tree bears, the fruit is of the lowest quality; the second year it is a little better; the third year it is still better; the fourth year it is better yet; and it continues to improve every year until the tenth; and then you begin to know what is the best thing that tree can do. Trees have to go through a maturing process of ten years' duration before they can bear fruit of the highest flavors. So it is with the Christian.　　　　　　*Beecher.*

9210. GRACES, Production of the. We go to God and say, "Lord, give me humility," and we should be glad if God would drop it right down to us. We ask him for faith, patience, and for spiritual joy and insight; we ask for willingness to live or to die; we ask for these higher developments. But, my friends, these are tropical plants; they never grow in any other climate than a climate as hot as love. You must have this fundamental quality, and you have to carry it to a high degree of development before it is possible to have these Christian graces. Suppose a man should plant orange and lemon trees in Canada, and pray that God would give him heavy crops. People would say, the climate of Canada is not able to produce oranges and lemons. If a man goes down to the southern part of Florida he need not pray much to have a large crop of oranges and lemons; but if he plants them in Kamtschatka, he would not get them by all the prayers he might offer. We cannot have right virtues without right conditions. Here are men who are selfish and worldly, full of bartering and trafficking affections—men who live in a low and chilled state, and yet praying for these higher graces, thinking that if they could once get those graces they would rise into a warmer state; but they must get into a warmer state where these graces will grow, before they can have them. Change the climate of the soul, and these will become spontaneous and fruitful. As selfishness is the bane and the curse of life, so this love that is disinterested, and that serves, is the bounty and the divinity of life.　　　　　　*Beecher.*

9211. GRACES, Queen of the. Love is the diamond among the jewels of the believer's breastplate. The other graces shine like the precious stones of nature, with their own peculiar lustre and various hues, but the diamond is white. Now, in white all the other colors are united; so, in love is centred every other Christian grace and virtue; "love is the fulfilling of the law." It is the only source of true obedience to the commands of God. If we love God, we must necessarily love that holy law which is a transcript of his divine mind and will.　　　　　　*Salter.*

9212. GRAFTING, New Process of. If you should go over one of our large nurseries in the month of August, and look down through the long even rows of young trees, you would see in front of every row perhaps one man, perhaps several, sitting on the ground doing something to the trees. If you should go close up to one of them, you would see that he takes in his fingers a tiny bud, not so big as the end of your finger, makes a little slit with a sharp knife in the bark of the young tree, and slips in the bud. If it lives and grows, the tree will bear just such fruit as that one from which the bud was taken. But why does he not let the young trees alone? Some are apple-trees, some pears, some peaches. Why does he not let them grow up to bear just such fruit as they naturally would? Because, in most cases, the natural fruit would be worthless. The owner and master of the nursery wants his trees to bear the very best fruit; so he puts in buds of the very best kind, and the tree is changed, and bears different fruit from its own natural product. If you go into a Sunday-school, you will see exactly the same process going on.　　　　　　*Anon.*

9213. GRAFTING, Practice of. "Can the fig-tree, my brethren, bear olive berries?" This metaphor is one which the Roman gardeners endeavored to realize. Pliny says, "After that the fig-tree hath gotten some strength, and is grown to a sufficient highness to bear a graft, the branch or bough of the olive being well cleansed and made neat, and the head end thereof thwited (*sic*) and shaped sharp, howbeit not yet cut from the mother stock, must be set fast in the shank of the fig-tree, where it must be kept well and surely tied with bands. For the space of three years it is suffered to grow indifferently between two mothers, or rather by the means thereof two mother stocks are grown and united together; but in the fourth year it is cut wholly from the own mother, and is become altogether an adopted child to the fig-tree wherein it is incorporate. A pretty device, I assure you, to make a fig-tree bear olives, the secret whereof is not known to every man."

9214. GRAIL, Legend of the Holy. The Holy Grail, according to some legends of the middle ages, was the cup used by our Saviour in dispensing the wine at the last supper; and according to others, the platter on which the paschal lamb was served at the last Passover observed by our Lord. By some it was said to have been preserved by Joseph of Arimathea, who received into it the blood which flowed from the Redeemer's wounds as he hung on the cross. By others it was said to have been brought down from heaven by angels, and committed to the charge of a body of knights, who guarded it on the top of a lofty mountain. This cup, according to the legend if approached by any one but a perfectly pure and holy person, would be borne away and vanish from their sight. This led to the quest of the Holy Grail, which was to be sought for on every side by a knight who was perfectly chaste in thought, word, and act.　　　　　　*Webster.*

9215. GRATITUDE, Christian. Gratitude is a

temper of mind which denotes a desire of acknowledging the receipt of a benefit. The mind which does not so feel is not as it ought to be. When the apostle Paul says of the heathen, "Neither were they thankful," he seems to stamp the sin of ingratitude as peculiarly odious. But, like every other grace which is required of us, virtuous gratitude depends, in part, on right views. A right view of benefits received, of the source from whence they flow, and of our own demerit, has a direct tendency to excite gratitude; and while the mind is influenced by sovereign grace, this will be the pleasing effect. The devout Christian surveys the sovereign benevolence of the Creator in every person, in every object, in every quality, and in every event. Sovereign benevolence forces itself on every sense, and pervades his grateful heart. And then, when he extends his views to a future state, and contemplates the operations of grace—sovereign, distinguishing efficacious grace—he is melted into reverential awe and grateful praise, and exclaims, "Why me, Lord?" Glory, everlasting glory to him that sitteth on the throne, and to the Lamb of God that was slain, who hath redeemed us to God by his blood, and hath given us the earnest of his own inheritance.　　*E. Williams.*

9216. GRATITUDE, Effect of. A gentleman of fortune, but a stranger to personal religion, one evening took a solitary walk through part of his grounds. He happened to come near a mean hut, where a poor man lived with a numerous family, who earned their bread by daily labor. He heard a continued and pretty loud voice. Not knowing what it was, curiosity prompted him to listen. The man happened to be at prayer with his family. So soon as he could distinguish the words, he heard him giving thanks to God, for the goodness of his providence, in giving them food to eat and raiment to put on, and in supplying them with what was necessary and comfortable in the present life. He was immediately struck with astonishment and confusion, and said to himself, "Does this poor man, who has nothing but the meanest fare, and that purchased by severe labor, give thanks to God for his goodness to himself and family; and I, who enjoy ease and honor, and everything that is pleasant and desirable, have hardly ever bent my knee, or made any acknowledgment to my Maker and Preserver!" This occurrence was the means of bringing him to a real sense of religion.

9217. GRATITUDE, Example of. A ship was sailing in a very rough sea, when the cry was heard, "Man overboard." Volunteers only would be expected to attempt a rescue in such a sea. The mate and two sailors were lowered and rowed for the man. As they rose upon a mountain wave they saw the man in the distance and shouted "coming." After a heroic and perilous struggle they reached him as he was ready to sink. They then thought of their frightful distance from the ship, and struggled for life to regain it. They reached the vessel, and were drawn safely upon the deck. The mate says, "We were all exhausted, but the rescued man could neither speak nor walk; yet he had a full sense of his condition. He clasped our feet, and began to kiss them. We disengaged ourselves from his embrace. He then crawled after us, and, as we stepped back to avoid him, he followed us, looking up at one moment with smiles and tears, and then patting our wet foot-prints with his hand, he kissed them with an eager fondness. I never witnessed such a scene in my life. If he had been our greatest enemy, he would have been perfectly subdued by our kindness. The man was a passenger. During the whole remaining part of the voyage he showed the deepest gratitude, and when we reached the port he loaded us with presents." Christ did more than this for the soul of man. What a debt we owe him?

9218. GRATITUDE, Flow of. "The currents of grace run in circles as well as those of nature. The electric current does not go along the wire unless it comes back through the earth to complete the circle. A picture of it is seen in a well-known apparatus for ventilation. Two tubes joined together, stretch from the interior of a building through the roof into the air. The air flows up through one lobe of the tube out of the building, and down through the other lobe into the building. When the process is set agoing it continues. But if you stop the ascending current, you thereby also make the descending current to cease; and if you stop the descending current, the ascending one is arrested too." So, when the soul is united to God, it receives blessings and completes the circuit by constant returns of gratitude and thanksgiving.

9219. GRATITUDE, Humble. Two cardinals saw a shepherd in the field weeping, asked the cause, and endeavored to console him. At first he refused to tell, but finally acknowledged that it was gratitude to God, for making man so comely a creature, instead of so deformed as the little toad. The cardinals thought of the advantages they had over this poor man, and cried out, "O, St. Austin! how truly didst thou say, 'the unlearned rise and take heaven by force, and we, with all our learning, wallow in flesh and blood!'"

9220. GRATITUDE, Immoderate. Darius, before he was king, was on an expedition to Egypt. Here he saw Syloson walking in the marketplace in a glittering cloak. Darius went to him and desired to buy the cloak, but Syloson told him "he would not sell it, but would give it him on the condition, that he would never part with it." Darius received it and in process of time became king. Syloson then came to Susa the palace, saying he was one that deserved well of the king, and sought an audience. Darius seeing him exclaimed, "O thou most generous among men, art thou he, who, when I had no power, gavest me that cloak, which though small in itself, was yet as acceptable then as greater things would be to me now? I will reward thee with silver and gold."

But Syloson said, "Give me neither silver or gold, but give me the kingdom of my dead brother, which is now ruled over by a servant." And Darius rewarded him with a kingdom for a cloak.

9221. GRATITUDE, Lesson of. A well-to-do farmer who ridiculed Christianity, and never attended church, was led there by the fame of the preacher. He heard a sermon from the text: "The ox knoweth his owner," etc. At the time he was disgusted with all he saw and heard. Not long after, in a very irritable mood, he undertook to plough a field. One of his oxen stepped over the chain. He flew at it in a rage, and beat it mercilessly. After this, while passing in front of the abused ox, he looked up in his master's face and licked his arm. The text above came to his mind with power. He felt his own baseness, unyoked his oxen and gave up work, that he might get out of his trouble. He was led to a profession of Christianity, and over the stall of the abused ox, now his favorite, he placed the motto: "The ox knoweth his owner."

9222. GRATITUDE, Unchanging. When the Caliph Haroun al Raschid had put to death his Vizier, Jaffier Bermekee, he ordered that none should speak in praise of the latter under pain of death. One old Arab continued to declare the merits of the late minister. He was summoned into the monarch's presence, and asked how he dared to transgress. "I should have been a monster of ingratitude had I not," said the Arab, and then proceeded to relate how Jaffier had taken notice of him, and at length raised him from poverty and obscurity to position and affluence, "I owe all to him," he continued; "and was it possible for me to be deterred by death itself from doing justice to his memory?" Struck with the courage and fidelity of the man, the Caliph sought to gain his admiration by more splendid generosity than that of the Vizier, and presented him with his golden sceptre, studded with precious jewels. "I take it," cried the grateful but undaunted Arab; "but this also, Commander of the Faithful, is from Bermekee!"

9223. GRAVE, Distance to the. As a tract of country narrowed in the distance, expands itself when we approach, thus the way to our near grave appears to us as long as it did formerly when we were far off.   *Richter.*

9224. GRAVE, Meditation at the. The grave of those we loved, what a place for meditation! There it is that we call up in long review the whole history of virtue and gentleness, and the thousand endearments, lavished upon us, almost unheeded, in the daily intercourse of intimacy; there it is that we dwell upon the tenderness, the solemn, awful tenderness, of the parting scene. The bed of death, with all its stifled griefs, its noiseless attendance, its mute, watchful assiduities; the last testimonies of expiring love! the feeble, fluttering, thrilling, oh, how thrilling, pressure of the hand; the last fond look of the glazing eye, turning upon us, even from the threshold of existence! the faint, faltering accents, struggling in death to give one more assurance of affection!
    W. Irving

9225. GRAVE, No Work in the. In the Peruvian collection at the Centennial Exhibition were mummies and relics of the Incas, supposed to be three thousand years old. These people had not heard the word, "There is no work, nor device, nor knowledge in the grave." They buried the warrior and his bows and arrows together, beside the workman his tools were placed, and with the housewife long wooden needles and coarse yarn were laid, that she might go on with her work. Hunger and thirst were expected and provided for. In the hand of a baby mummy was found an ear of corn. Treasures were buried with their owners. Immense wardrobes are found encased with the body of some princess of fashion. The arms, the food, the ready material, the rich toilets, the wealth have remained unused since the day of burial. "Vanity of vanities."

9226. GRAVE, Peaceful Associations of the. It buries every error, covers every defect, extinguishes every resentment. From its peaceful bosom spring none but fond regrets and tender recollections. Who can look down upon the grave of an enemy, and not feel a compunctious throb that he should have warred with the poor handful of dust that lies mouldering before him?   *W. Irving.*

9227. GRAVE, Perfumed by Christ. If I wear a rose in my bosom, it scents my whole person. Has the Saviour a place in my breast, he communicates the fragrance of his merits to my soul, and his spirit fills the atmosphere through which I move, as it were with the breath of heaven. Even in death the rose is sweet, passing sweet, and sweetens every place where it lies. Thus the rose of Sharon has given the fragrance of life to the very chambers of death and the grave, and to that wardrobe of the saints where their material garments are to be laid up till the morning of the resurrection, then to be brought forth beautiful and fresh, fit for the court of heaven.   *East.*

9228. GREAT, Exposure of the. Trees growing upon the tops of lofty mountains are constantly exposed to the winds and storms which are almost incessant there, while peace and calm reign in the vale below. Such is the condition of men high in office—always disturbed, and soon overthrown. One of the English kings had for his coat of arms, a crown upon a bed of thorns.

9229. GREAT, Fear of the. When Lord Brook lay on his death-bed, Rev. Samuel Hardy went to him and said, "My Lord, you of the nobility are the most unhappy men in the world: nobody dares to come near to you to tell you of your faults, or put you in the right way to heaven."

9230. GREAT, Impotence of the. There is none made so great but he may both need the help and service, and stand in fear of the power and unkindness, even of the meanest of mortals.
    Seneca.

9231. GREAT, Pretensions of the. I look upon

the great as a set of good-natured misguided people, who are indebted to us, and not to themselves, for all the happiness they enjoy. For our pleasure, and not their own, they sweat under a cumbrous heap of finery; for our pleasure the lackeyed train, the slow parading pageant, with all the gravity of grandeur, moves in review; a single coat, or a single footman, answers all the purposes of the most indolent refinement as well; and those who have twenty may be said to keep one for their own pleasure and the other nineteen merely for ours. So true is the observation of Confucius, that we take greater pains to persuade others that we are happy, than in endeavoring to think so ourselves. *Goldsmith.*

9232. GREAT, Salvation of the. Luther said of Elizabeth, a pious queen of Denmark, "Christ will sometimes carry a queen to heaven." The rich and great are so rarely seen at Christ's altars as to occasion the remark, "Rich men are choice dishes at God's table." Not many great, not many wise, not many noble hath God called.

9233. GREAT MEN, Classes of. Were we to distinguish the ranks of men by their genius and capacity, more than by their virtue and usefulness to the public, great philosophers would certainly challenge the first rank, and must be placed at the top of mankind. So rare is this character, that perhaps there have not as yet been above two in the world who can lay a just claim to it. At least Galileo and Newton seem to me so far to excel all the rest, that I cannot admit any other into the same place with them. Great poets may challenge the second place; and this species of genius, though rare, is yet much more frequent than the former. Of the Greek poets that remain, Homer alone seems to merit this character; of the Romans, Virgil, Horace, and Lucretius; of the English, Milton and Pope; Corneille, Racine, Boileau, and Voltaire of the French; Tasso and Ariosto of the Italians. *David Hume.*

9234. GREAT MEN, Early Training of. The discourses and rules of philosophy, being once deeply stamped and imprinted on the minds of great personages, will stick so close, that the prince shall seem no other than justice incarnate and animated law. This was the design of Plato's voyage into Sicily—he hoped that the lectures of his philosophy would serve for laws to Dionysius, and bring his affairs into a good posture. But the soul of that unfortunate prince was like paper scribbled all over with the characters of vice; its piercing and corroding quality had stained quite through, and sunk into the very substance of his soul. Whereas, if such persons are to profit by sage lessons, they must be taken when they are at full speed. *Plutarch.*

9235. GREAT MEN, Fewness of. In the development of any principle or cause, there is a tendency to having fewer conspicuously great men, because it tends to make all men great. One Columbus goes before, but a thousand follow after. One Faust develops printing, but ten thousand better printers live in every land.

One Washington draws his sword for liberty, but an army arises whose devotion, no privation can diminish, and whose ardor no winter can chill. So one Abraham pioneers in the realm of faith, and an army of occupation follows. So one Luther, Wesley, Asbury, explores the realms of power in spiritual life, and is followed, or ought to be, by ten thousand times ten thousand, and thousands of thousands as heroic in devotion, as sublime in faith, as rich in experience, and in victories as grand.

　　　　　　　Dr. H. W. Warren.

9236. GREAT MEN, Idea of. An old lady said that her idea of a great man was "a man who was keerful of his clothes, didn't drink spirits, kin read the Bible without spelling the words, and kin eat a cold dinner on wash-day, to save the wimmin folks the trouble of cooking."

9237. GREAT MEN, Influencing. How are their hearts dilated with joy who are benefactors to whole cities, provinces, and kingdoms! And such benefactors are they who instill good principles into those upon whom so many millions do depend. On the other hand, those who debauch the minds of great men—as sycophants, false informers, and flatterers, worse than both, manifestly do—are the centre of all the curses of a nation, as men who do not only infuse deadly poison into the cistern of a private house, but into the public springs of which so many thousands are to drink. He who instructs an ordinary man makes him to pass his life decently and with comfort; but he who instructs a prince, by correcting his errors and clearing his understanding, is a philosopher for the public, by rectifying the very mould and model by which whole nations are formed and regulated. *Plutarch.*

9238. GREAT MEN, Spirit of. A great man is affable in his converse, generous in his temper, and immovable in what he has maturely resolved upon; and as prosperity does not make him haughty and imperious, so neither does adversity sink him into meanness and dejection; for if ever he shows more spirit than ordinary, it is when he is ill-used and the world frowns upon him; in short, he is equally removed from the extremes of servility and pride, and scorns either to trample upon a worm or sneak to an emperor. *Jeremy Collier.*

9239. GREAT MEN, Superiority of. Society indeed has its great men and its little men, as the earth has its mountains and its valleys. But the inequalities of intellect, like the inequalities of the surface of our globe, bear so small a proportion to the mass that in calculating its great revolutions they may safely be neglected. The sun illuminates the hills whilst it is still below the horizon, and truth is discovered by the highest minds a little before it becomes manifest to the multitude. This is the extent of their superiority. They are the first to catch and reflect a light which, without their assistance, must in a short time be visible to those who lie far beneath them. The same remark will apply equally to the fine arts. The laws on which depend the progress and decline of poetry, painting, and sculpture, operate with little less certainty than those which regulate the periodical returns of heat and cold, of fertility and barrenness. Those who seem to lead the public taste are, in general, merely outrunning it in the direction which it is spontaneously pursuing. *Lord Macaulay.*

9240. GREAT MEN, Weakness of. The first Napoleon had a cowardly dread of satire, and could endure any hardship rather than be made to appear ridiculous. This accounts for his enmity to the witty Madame De Stael, whose merciless tongue spared no one. He shrunk from her with morbid apprehension, and wrote autograph notes to Fouche, calling his attention to the placards and verses of the street corners. There is something more than ludicrous in the spectacle of this rude soldier with a million armed men under his command, and half Europe at his feet, sitting down in rage and afright to order Fouche to send a little woman over the frontiers lest she should say something about him for the drawing-rooms of Paris to laugh at. Yet history votes this man a hero. *Anon.*

9241. GREATNESS: Brevities. Greatness is nothing, unless it be lasting.—*Napoleon I.*——The less you speak of your greatness, the more I shall think of it.—*Lord Bacon.*——Some men are born great, some achieve greatness, and some have greatness thrust upon them.—*Shakespeare.*——All men, without exception, have something to learn; whatever may be the distinguished rank which they hold in society, they can never be truly great but by personal merit. *Zimmerman.*

9242. GREATNESS, Death and. The reign of Louis XV. of France was that of an oriental monarch. His power was unlimited, and his court presented a scene of luxurious splendor such as never was witnessed in any Christian land. He was depraved and sensual, and had but little regard for his subjects, or sympathy with mankind. The Bastile frowned on France, and the nation lay enchained at the feet of the king. Who that saw this powerful monarch in the glittering saloons of the Palace of Versailles ever dreamed that, in the trying hour of death, he would be left utterly alone? In the spring of 1774 he fell a victim to an infectious disease, contracted by his vices, that made him a spectacle terrible to behold. The sickness proved fatal. He was for a time deceived by court intrigue in respect to his danger, and his mind was filled with terror when he became conscious of his approaching end. "I would fain die as a Christian, and not as an infidel," he gloomily said to one of his profligate companions, as he began to fear for his life. He caused his repentance for his past scandals to be publicly proclaimed; his brain was haunted by the sins of the past, and his remorse in view of eternity was extreme. His courtiers, seeing no hope of his recovery, deserted him, and his guilty and conscience-smitten paramour fled. One domestic only was left to attend him, and she awaited his commands in an outer room. And thus, with no hope to dissipate the clouds that hung over the future, and with no one to soothe his pillow, the unhappy monarch approached his dissolution. It is the night of the 10th of May. He is dying. A lamp has been placed in the window of his chamber, and the domestic has been charged to extinguish the flame as soon as he shall expire; the courtiers flock together in a distant part of the palace, awaiting the signal of his demise. Are those the once smiling eyes that watched him in his revels, that now so eagerly watch for the light to be extinguished? Yes, those impatient watchers are the flatterers of old. So it is ever with the friendship won by the glitter of wealth and power. The old clock of Versailles announces the slow-paced hours. Still the light glimmers and burns. It is midnight. The old clock slowly tolls the hour of twelve. The light is extinguished, and the light-hearted and excited courtiers hurry away to announce to Louis XVI. that he is the king of France. So perishes worldly pomp, and to such an humiliating end comes wickedness in high places. The humblest peasant that dies in the arms of Jesus is more favored than such a king. *Anon.*

9243. GREATNESS, Empty. Charles V., Emperor of Germany, King of Spain and Lord of the Netherlands, was born at Ghent, in the year 1500. He fought sixty battles, in most of which he was victorious; obtained six triumphs, conquered four kingdoms, and added eight principalities to his dominions; an a.most unparalleled instance of worldly prosperity and the greatness of human glory. But all these fruits of his ambition, and all the honors that attended him, could not yield him true and solid satisfaction. Reflecting on the evils and miseries which he had occasioned, and convinced of the emptiness of earthly magnificence, he became disgusted with all the splendor that surrounded him, and spent the rest of his days in retirement. *Bib. Treasury.*

9244. GREATNESS, Human. We cannot look, however imperfectly, upon a great man, without gaining something by him. He is the living light-fountain, which it is good and pleasant to be near; the light which enlightens, which has enlightened, the darkness of the world; and this, not as a kindled lamp only, but rather a natural luminary, shining by the gift of heaven; a flowing light-fountain, as I say, of native original insight, of manhood and heroic nobleness, in whose radiance all souls feel that it is well with them. *Carlyle.*

9245. GREATNESS, Humility of. Samuel Drew. the shoemaker and philosopher, who wrote a valuable work on the immortality of the soul, long after he had become celebrated as a writer, used to be seen sweeping the street before his door, or helping an apprentice to carry in the winter's coals. Some one told him that he compromised his dignity by so doing. He replied, "The man who is ashamed to carry in his own coals deserves to sit all the winter by an empty grate."

9246. GREATNESS, Immunities of. What right had Alexander over the great number of nations, which did not know even the name of

Greece, and had never done him the least injury? The Scythian Ambassador spoke very judiciously when he addressed him in these words: "What have we to do with thee? We never once set our feet in thy country. Are not those who live in woods allowed to be ignorant of thee, and the place from whence thou comest? Thou boastest that the only design of thy marching is to extirpate robbers; thou thyself art the greatest robber in the world." This is Alexander's exact character, in which there is nothing to be rejected. A pirate spoke to him to the same effect, and in stronger terms. Alexander asked him, "What right he had to infest the seas?" "The same that thou hast," replied the pirate, with a generous liberty, "to infest the world; but because I do this in a small ship, I am called a robber, and because thou actest the same part with a great fleet, thou art styled a conqueror." *Rollin.*

9247. GREATNESS, Meanness of. Alexander the Great both envied and hated Perdiccas, because he was warlike; Lysimachus, because he was skillful in the arts of a general; and Seleucus, because he was of great courage. He was offended with the liberality of Antigonus, the imperial dignity and authority of Attalus, and the prosperous felicity and good fortune of Ptolemæus.

9248. GREATNESS, Mental. Greatness is not a teachable or gainable thing, but the expression of the mind of a God-made great man. Teach, or preach, or labor as you will, everlasting difference is set between one man's capacity and another's; and this God-given supremacy is the priceless thing, always just as rare in the world at one time as another. What you can manufacture or communicate, you can lower the price of, but this mental supremacy is incommunicable; you will never multiply its quantity, nor lower its price; and nearly the best thing that men can generally do is to set themselves, not to the attainment, but the discovery of this; learning to know gold, when we see it, from iron-glance, and diamond from flint-sand, being for most of us a more profitable employment than trying to make diamonds out of our own charcoal. *Ruskin.*

9249. GREATNESS, Price of. There is but one method, and that is hard labor; and a man who will not pay that price for greatness, had better at once dedicate himself to the pursuit of the fox, or sport with the tangles of Neæra's hair, or talk of bullocks, and glory in the goad! *S. Smith.*

9250. GREATNESS, Religious. The greatness of all actions is measured by the worthiness of the subject from which they proceed, and the object whereabout they are conversant. We must of necessity, in both respects, acknowledge that this present world affordeth not anything comparable unto the duties of religion. *Hooker.*

9251. GREATNESS, Simplicity of. The Rev. J. Wesley once preached at Lincoln from Luke 10 : 42 : "One thing is needful." When the congregation were retiring from the church, a lady exclaimed, in a tone of great surprise, "Is this the great Mr. Wesley, of whom we hear so much in the present day? Why, the poorest might have understood him." The gentleman to whom this remark was made, replied, "In this, madam, he displays his greatness; that, while the poorest can understand him, the most learned are edified, and cannot be offended."

9252. GREATNESS, Title to. He alone is worthy of the appellation who does great things, or teaches how they may be done, or describes them with a suitable majesty when they have been done; but those only are great things which tend to render life more happy, which **increase the innocent enjoyments and comforts of existence, or which pave the way to a state of future bliss more permanent and more pure.** *Milton.*

9253. GREATNESS, True. Greatness lies not in being strong, but in the right using of strength; and strength is not used rightly when it only serves to carry a man above his fellows for his own solitary glory. He is greatest whose strength carries up the most hearts by the attraction of his own. *Beecher.*

9254. GREATNESS, Worth of. The great high-road of human welfare lies along the highway of steadfast well-doing; and they who are the most persistent, and work in the truest spirt, will invariably be the most successful: success treads on the heels of every right effort. *Smiles.*

9255. GREED, Fable of. A man in the mint was told that he might take away one pocketful of gold, if he would run right straight home with it and not stop by the way nor touch his pocket. So he filled his largest pocket full of gold and started for home. But as he was running down a little hill the gold hung heavy, tore off his pocket, and fell down in the road When he had got home, and found his gold and his pocket gone together, "Alas!" said he, "had I taken less I should have more." *T. K. Beecher.*

9256. GREEDINESS, Fatal. A certain man had the good fortune to possess a goose that laid him a golden egg every day. But dissatisfied with so slow an income, and thinking to seize the whole treasure at once, he killed the goose; and cutting her open, found her—just what any other goose would be! Much wants more and loses all. *Æsop.*

9257. GREEGREE, Mohammedan. The Mohammedans of Western Africa wear amulets called *greegrees* for protection from danger, and as ornaments. One wears it as a protection from drowning, another as a shield from a musket shot, and so on. They consist of scraps of the Koran, in Arabic, encased in leather or colored cloth, and are variously worn upon the person. They are also hung up in their shops and houses. The greegrees are prepared by the priests and sold to the deluded people.

9258. GRIEF, Beneficial. Grief, like night, is salutary. It cools down the soul, by putting out its feverish fires; and if it oppresses her, it also compresses her energies. The load once gone, she will go forth with greater buoyancy to new pleasures.   *Pulsford.*

9259. GRIEF, Brevity of. All grief for what cannot in the course of nature be helped, soon wears away; in some sooner indeed, in some later; but it never continues very long, unless where there is madness, such as will make a man have pride so fixed in his mind as to imagine himself a king; or any other passion in an unreasonable way: for all unnecessary grief is unwise, and therefore will not long be retained by a sound mind. If indeed, the cause of our grief is occasioned by our own misconduct, if grief is mingled with remorse of conscience, it should be lasting.   *Dr. Johnson.*

9260. GRIEF, Consolation for. A steamer was sinking with hundreds of persons on board. Only one boat load was saved. As a man was leaping into the boat, a girl who could not be taken into the boat, and who knew that she must soon be drowned, handed him a note, saying, "Give this to my mother!" The man was saved; the girl, with hundreds of other persons, was drowned. The mother received the note, in which was written, "Dear mother, you must not grieve for me. I am going to Jesus."

9261. GRIEF, Effect of. Uvipertus was elected Bishop, and went to Rome to receive confirmation from the Pope. But he rejected him on account of his youthful appearance. From grief, the next night his hair turned entirely gray, and the Pope could do nothing else but confirm him.

9262. GRIEF, Excessive. A mother whose child God had taken to himself, locked herself in her room, grieved over her loss, and in her blindness charged God foolishly. After a time her husband induced her to walk with him in the garden. She stooped to pluck a flower but her husband interposed. "What! deny me a flower!" said she. He answered, "You have denied God your flower; and you ought not to think it hard in me to deny you mine." The lady felt and profited by the appropriate reproof.

9263. GRIEF, Healer of. Time heals all griefs, even the bitterest, and it is well that it should be so. A long-indulged sorrow for the dead, or for any other hopeless loss, would deaden our sympathies for those still left, and thus make a sinful apathy steal over the soul, absorbing all its powers, and causing the many blessings of life to be felt as curses. As the bosom of earth blooms again and again, having buried out of sight the dead leaves of autumn, and loosed the frosty bands of winter; so does the heart (in spite of all that melancholy poets write) feel many renewed springs and summers. It is a beautiful and a blessed world we live in, and whilst that life lasts, to lose the enjoyment of it is a sin.   *Chambers.*

9264. GRIEF, Heathen View of. They say that an ancient philosopher came to Queen Arsinoe, who was then sorrowful for the death of her son, and discoursed to her after this manner: "At the time that Jupiter distributed honor amongst the under deities, it happened that Grief was absent; but he came at last when all

dignities were disposed of, and then desired that he might have some share in the promotions. Jupiter, having no better vacancies left, bestowed upon him sorrow and funeral tears." He made this inference from the story: "Therefore," saith he, "as other demons love and frequent those who give them hospitable receptions, so sadness will never come near you, if you do not give it encouragement; but if you caress it with those particular honors which it challengeth as its due, which are sighs and tears, it will have an unlucky affection for you, and will always supply you with fresh occasion that the observance may be continued." This speech had its desired effect.   *Plutarch.*

9265. GRIEF, Improper. Ebenezer Adams, an eminent member of the Society of Friends, on visiting a lady of rank, whom he found, six months after the death of her husband, on a sofa, covered with black cloth, and in all the dignity of woe, approached her with great solemnity, and, gently taking her by the hand, thus addressed her: "So, friend, I see, then, thou hast not yet forgiven God Almighty." This reproof had so great an effect on the lady, that she immediately laid aside her violent grief, and again entered on the discharge of the duties of life.   *J. G. Wilson*

9266. GRIEF, Need of Relief for. It was said that Hippocrates drove away maladies, and almost snatched bodies out of the hands of death. Antiphon, of Greece, envious of Hippocrates' glory, promised to do for the soul what he did for the body, and proposed the "Art of curing grief." Wanley says "All ages are abundant in misery, and they should likewise produce great comforts to sweeten the acerbities of human life. Another Helena were needful to mingle the divine drug of Nepenthe in the meat of so many afflicted persons as the world affords."

9267. GRIEF Personified. We have often dreamed of grief. She had the beauty of all truly great things—the sublimity of the infinite; she was an abyss, but the ocean too has abysses which reflect, while softening them, the azure and the smile of the sky. Grief advanced like a tragic queen; she held a dagger; tears were in her eyes; her melancholy form spoke of despair; and yet what majesty in her bearing, what an austere beauty in that face, all-indifferent to the impression it made! Grief walked with royal steps; the very folds of her robe fell with a stern grace; her voice, even through its sobs, raised noble emotions; and our spirit, thirsting and sighing after immensity, opened out with a thrill to receive the divine guest.   *Gasparin.*

9268. GRIEF, Yielding to. When we suffer grief, like a canker, to eat into the soul, and, like a fire in the bones, to consume the marrow and drink up the spirits, we are accessory to the wrong done both to our bodies and souls; we waste our own candle, and put out our own light.   *Sibbes*

9269. GROWTH, Demand for. There is a generation of Christians in this age who grieve me to the heart. They make my blood run cold. I cannot understand them. For anything that man's eye can see, they make no progress. They never seem to get on. Years roll on, and they are just the same,—the same besetting sins, the same infirmities of disposition, the same weakness in trial, the same chilliness of heart, the same apathy, the same faint resemblance to Christ—but no new knowledge, no increased interest in the kingdom, no freshness, no new strength, no new fruits, as if they grew. Are they not forgetting that growth is a proof of life—that even the yew tree grows, and the snail and the sloth move? Are they not forgetting how awfully far a man may go, and yet not be a true Christian? He may be like a waxwork figure, the very image of a believer, and yet not have within him the breath of God: he may have a name to live, and be dead after all. We ought to have looked on this world as an inn, and we have settled down in it as if it were our home: it ought to have been counted our school of training for eternity, and we have been at ease in it as if it were our continuing city, or trifled away time in it, as if we were meant to play and not to learn. We ought to have been careful for nothing, and we have been careful and troubled about many things —we have allowed the affairs of this life to eat out the heart of our spirituality, and have been cumbered with much serving.   *Ryle.*

9270. GROWTH, Fruitful. When he comes, he will turn up your leaves; and look that, like the tree of life (Rev. 22: 21), we bear fruit every month: or that we be like the lemon-tree, which ever and anon sendeth forth new lemons as soon as the former are fallen down with ripeness: or the Egyptian fig-tree, which, saith Solinus, beareth fruit seven times a year; pull off a fig, and another breaks forth in the place shortly after. Now if we be found like the barren fig-tree (Luke 13), that had leaves only; or the cypress-tree, which is said to be fair and tall, but altogether fruitless; or the cyparit-tree, of which Pliny affirmeth, that is *natu morosa, fructu supervacanea, baccis parva, foliis amara, odore violenta, ac ne umbrâ quidem gratiosa;* what can we expect, but that he should set down his basket, and taking up his axe, hew us down as fuel for the fire of hell? Spain is said to have nothing barren in it, or not some way useful; *In Hispani nihil ignavum, nihil sterile.* And why should Christ's orchard, the Church? He pares and prunes his leaves and luxuriances; yea, cuts and slashes where need requires; and all that we may bear more fruit.   *Trapp.*

9271. GROWTH, Mementos of. We have the likenesses of our boys taken on every birthday, and twelve of the annual portraits are now framed in one picture, so that we see them at a glace from their babyhood to their youth. Suppose such photographic memorials of our own spiritual life had been taken and preserved, would there be a regular advance, as in these boys, or should we still have been exhibited in the perambulator? Have not some grown awhile, and then suddenly dwarfed? Have not others gone back to babyhood? Here is a wide field for reflection.   *Spurgeon.*

9272. GROWTH, Plant. The creation of vegetables is placed by Moses subsequent to the production of light and of the atmosphere, immediately after the waters had receded from the land, and just before the creation and arrangement of the solar system. This position of vegetables in the series of creation exactly answers the demands of our present knowledge. Instead of requiring the sun's light to germinate, seeds and plants, in order to do so, must be sowed and placed in darkness before they begin to vegetate. A small heat and moisture first cause their living principle to begin its operations, but they cannot flower and fruit until they receive the solar beams; nor could they grow without light, air, and moisture. A portion of oxygen air is essential to vegetation. Hence the previous atmosphere, which contains in its composition that portion, was indispensable, as was also some water on the soil where they were to grow. This exact placing of the vegetable formation and first germination is another test of the authenticity of the Hebrew cosmogony, which random fiction could not have stood.   *Sharon Turner.*

9273. GROWTH, Religious. The law of growth is to be considered; and that law contemplates a regular series of unfoldings, the last and best of which cannot take place until after the intermediate ones have taken place. When a plant comes up, you may, as much as you please, try to force it instantly to its blossom and fruit; but it will be of no avail. That which you seek is the ideal of the plant; that is the state to which it is to come; but it can not come to that state except by going through a great many intermediate ones, one after another. From the lowest state it constantly ascends to the highest. Imagine a tree, sprung from the ground, and grown a year, and then having in itself the conception of an oak-tree, and wishing, longing, and condemning itself because it is not an oak tree the first year. It tries to stretch out its branches and become an oak tree, and mourns because there are no acorns on its boughs. It can attain the proportions of the oak tree; but it will take time. Men living among Christians who are broad, large, free, well-developed in their religious life, form an ideal conception of what are the fruits of the higher forms, the later developments of Christian experience; and they enter upon a Christian life, and join the church; and they want to be, in intensity, in breadth, in scope, in fruitfulness, that which has been held up before them as an ideal. They will come to it by growth, but they will not come to it in any other way. There is no efficiency of the Spirit that works miracles, and that precedes those steady laws of the mind by which the mind progresses from stage to stage.   *Beecher.*

9274. GROWTH, Spiritual. Unless the gastric juice be healthy, the best food cannot nourish

That wonderful solvent which God has provided, must melt, separate, and dissolve the food, or else it will not assimilate; it will not be digested—"carried through" the system—repairing its waters, supply fresh elements of combination for its various parts; feeding the blood; keeping that current of life full, and so by it pouring into the furthest creeks of this wonderful body of ours, the tide of health. Faith is to the soul what that wonderful solvent is to the body; without faith, "the Word preached will not profit;" unless mixed with "faith in them that hear," it will be "the savor of death unto death," killing instead of nourishing. Without faith there is no assimilation of divine truth; it never passes into the system, never becomes part of the man, so as to "nourish him up by the words of sound doctrine." Without faith he is the sickly patient starving in sight of food, and lean and thin in the midst of plenty. *Champney.*

9275. GROWTH, True Christian. There are religious writers and speakers who represent the progress of man as consisting in the growth of something added to his nature, rather than in the development of his nature itself. Hence we have books on the subject whose very title propounds this notion; such, for example, as "The Rise and Progress of Religion in the Soul," as if the soul were a flower-bed, and religion some precious seed deposited in its soil. The transposition would be the true idea—namely, The rise and progress of the soul in religion; that is, in all that is true, benevolent, and God-like. The Scripture speaks of the progress of a holy soul as the progress of "the shining light." It appears on the horizon, gradually ascends to the meridian, "shining brighter and brighter" in every stage. They speak of it as the progress of the racer pressing towards the mark. Every power of the man is brought into play. And they speak of it as the progress of the human body in passing from infancy to manhood. The whole body—every fibre, muscle, bone, limb, and organ, advances at the same time. *Dr. Thomas.*

9276. GRUMBLERS, Fable of. A heavy wagon was being dragged along a country lane by a team of oxen. The axle-tree groaned and creaked terribly, when the oxen turning round, thus addressed the wheels: "Halloa, there! why do you make so much noise? we bear all the labor, and we, not you, ought to cry out!" Those complain first in our churches who have least to do. The gift of grumbling is largely dispensed among those who have no other talents, or who keep what they have wrapped up in a napkin. *Spurgeon.*

9277. GUIDANCE, Lesson of. The patter of little feet on my office floor and a glad voice exclaiming, "Papa, I'se come to 'scort you home!" made known to me the presence of my little six-year old darling, who often came at that hour "to take me home," as she said. Soon we were going hand in hand on the homeward way. "Now, papa, let's play I was a poor little blind girl, and you must let me hold your hand tight, and you lead me along and tell me where to step and how to go." So the merry blue eyes were shut tight and we began: Now step up, now step down, here we go round the corner, and so on, till we were safely arrived at home, and the darling was nestling in my arms, saying, "Wasn't it nice, papa? I never peeked once!" "But," said mamma, "didn't you feel afraid you would fall, dear?" With a look of trusting love came the answer: "Oh, no, mamma! I had a tight hold of papa's hand, and I knew he would take me safely over the hard places." Dear trusting childhood! What a lesson to our doubting, troubled hearts! Oh, that we might with just this loving trust clasp the heavenly Father's hand! up and down the steep paths, round the sharp corners, and over all the rough places of this troublous, changeful life, never letting go and never open our eyes to wonder or doubt as to his way—knowing that it will at last bring us, when the weary walk is done, to rest in his loving arms forever more. *S. S. Teacher.*

9278. GUIDES, Safe. A Christian, in all his ways, must have three guides—Truth, Charity, Wisdom: Truth to go before him, Charity and Wisdom on either hand. If any of the three be absent, he walks amiss. I have seen some do hurt, by following a truth uncharitably; and others, while they would salve up an error with love, have failed in their wisdom, and offended against justice. *Bishop Hall.*

9279. GUILT, Contrasts of. While I was occupying the Fulton-street pulpit in New York, the governor of the City Tombs prison said he would like to have me go down and talk to the prisoners. After the prisoners were all brought in I found there was no chapel in connection with that prison, and I had to talk to them in their cells. I talked from a little iron bridge running across the narrow passage-way, to some three or four hundred prisoners, and could not see a man. After I had done, I thought I would like to see who I had been talking to, and how they had received the gospel. I went to the first door and looked in the little window of a cell where the inmates could have best heard me. There were some men playing at cards. No doubt they had been playing all the while I had been preaching. They did not want to hear. I said, "My friends, what is your trouble?" "Well, stranger, false witnesses appeared against us. We are innocent." I said to myself, "Christ cannot save anybody here; there is nobody guilty." I went to the occupiers of the next cell, and asked why they were there. They said, "We got into bad company, and the man who did the deed got clear, and we got caught." I said, "Christ cannot save anybody here." I went to the next cell and asked how it was with them. They said, "False witnesses went into court and swore falsely." I said, "Christ cannot save anybody here." I went to the next cell and said, "How is it with you?" The reply was, "The fact is the man who did the deed is very much like me. I am perfectly innocent." I never found so many innocent men in a prison in my life. It seemed that the magistrates who sent them there were the only guilty ones. I began to get discouraged, but when I had got almost through I found one man with his elbows on his knees and two streams of tears running down his cheeks. I looked in at the little window, and I said, "My friend, what is the trouble?" He looked up with despair and remorse on his face, and said, "My sins are more than I can bear." I said, "Thank God for that." "Ain't you the man that has been talking to us? I thought you said you was a friend: and you say you are glad my sins are more than I can bear." "Yes." "I don't understand your friendship if you are glad my sins are more than I can bear." "I will explain it to you. If your sins are more than you can bear, you will cast them on one that will bear them for you." "Who is that?" "It is the Lord Jesus," and I stood there at that prison door and preached Christ, and held up Christ for that poor wounded man, who was believed to be the worst man in the whole prison of the city of New York. After telling him of Christ, I got down and prayed. After I prayed, I said, "Now you pray." He said he could not pray; it would be blasphemy. But the man put his head on the pavement, and, like the publican, without even lifting his eyes towards heaven, he cried, "God be merciful to me a sinner!" After prayer, when he got up, I took his hand, and he gave me a warm grasp of the hand; a hot tear fell on my hand, which burned down into my soul. I got so interested in the man that before I started for the hotel I said, "I will pray for you to-night, and I would have you join me in prayer at the same time." That night while I was praying in my hotel, as I told him I should pray for him at a certain hour, it seemed as if I knew that God was answering my prayer. I could not leave New York and go back to Chicago until I had seen that man. No sooner did I fix my eye on the man's countenance, than I saw that a great change had taken place. Remorse and gloom had fled away, and the face of the man was streaming with celestial light. He seized my hand, and tears of joy trickled over his cheeks. I said, "Tell me all about it;" and he said, "Last night, when in my cell praying—I do not know the exact time, because when I came to prison they took away my watch; but I think it was about midnight—the Lord Jesus took away the burden, and set me entirely free, and since then I am the happiest man in the whole city of New York."   *D. L. Moody.*

9280. GUILT, Degrees of. It is base to filch a purse, daring to embezzle a million, but it is great beyond measure to steal a crown. The sin lessens, in human estimation only, as the guilt increases.   *Schiller.*

9281. GUILT, Detection of. A rich pearl merchant, in ancient times, visited a distant country with a valuable stock of diamonds, taking with him his son and a young slave. He had made his intended sale to great profit, and was ready to return, when he died suddenly. The slave at once declared himself to be the merchant's son and heir, and took possession of his property. In vain the son declared the truth: the slave being the most intelligent and prepossessing, and proof being absent. The case went into a court of law, and was thrown out for want of proof on either side. The case coming to the king's notice, he ordered both claimants to present their arguments to him, each to put his head through an opening in a curtain into the king's presence and tell his story, with the understanding that the head was to be cut off from the guilty one. An officer present stood ready for the execution. After each had spoken, furnishing still no decisive grounds for decision, the judge cried, "Enough, strike off the villain's head." The executioner sprang towards the witnesses with drawn scimitar. The true son stood firm in conscious innocence. The slave drew back his head in guilty fear. The decision was given for the son, and the slave suffered the threatened punishment for his crime.

9282. GUILT, Discovery of. A man called upon a minister and demanded to be shown a letter which he was satisfied some calumniator must have written to him before he prepared the sermon which he heard him preach on the day previous. No such letter, nor any other information, had been received by the preacher; but the Holy Spirit had so applied his words as to awaken the man's conscience, and he saw his own sins so clearly that he thought the preacher must have been informed all about them. He conceived the words, "Be sure your sin will find you out," addressed to himself, personally. The minister said, "Can you look me in the face as you must your Judge in the great day, and declare that you are innocent of the sin laid to your charge?" The man turned pale with rage and fear, and declared that he would make no man his confessor. The minister then showed him how God had given him a view of himself, that he intended by alarming him to save his soul from hell. The man left in tears, saying, "I never met anything like this. I am guilty, and hope this conversation will be of advantage to me."

9283. GUILT, Proclivity of. When once a man has involved himself deeply in guilt, he has no safe ground to stand upon. Every thing is unsound and rotten under his feet. The crimes he has already committed may have an unseen connection with others, of which he has not the slightest suspicion; and he may be hurried, when he least intends it, into enormities of which he once thought himself utterly incapable.   *Bishop Porteus.*

9284. GUILT, Self-Punishment of. Nothing is more common than for great thieves to ride in triumph when small ones are punished. But let wickedness escape as it may at the law, it never fails of doing itself justice; for every guilty person is his own hangman.   *Seneca.*

9285. GUILT in Sickness. Sickness and suffering come with double force upon guilt; anguish of mind lessens the strength, as well as increases the smart; 'tis like a wound in the sword hand, the man is disabled in that which should defend him; he drops his guard, and his heart lies open to the next pass. We ought to summon in all our force upon this occasion, and to fortify ourselves with recollection and good practice, to animate our courage from the topics of honor and interest, from all the weighty considerations of this world and the next, to take in the auxiliaries of religion, and implore the assistance of heaven, that pain may never force us to outlive our patience or our honesty, that we may stand firm against the last assault, of what kind soever, and meet death with resolution, as it lies in the order of Providence; in short, that we may die without being conquered, carry a good conscience along with us, and leave a useful precedent behind us. *Jeremy Collier.*

9286. GUILT, Slavery of. The slave who digs in the mine or labors at the oar, can rejoice at the prospect of laying down his burden together with his life; but to the slave of guilt there arises no hope from death. On the contrary, he is obliged to look forward with constant terror to this most certain of all events, as the conclusion of all his hopes, and the commencement of his greatest miseries. *Blair.*

9287. GUILT, Torment of. Think not that guilt requires the burning torches of the furies to agitate and torment it. Frauds, crimes, remembrances of the past, terrors of the future —these are the domestic furies that are ever present to the mind of the impious. *Cicero.*

9288. GUILT, Transfer of. For a long time before the conversion of the Rev. C. Simeon, he had been in the deepest distress, envying even the dogs that passed under his window. In Passion-week he met with the expression in "Bishop Wilson on the Lord's Supper," "that the Jews knew what they did when they transferred their sins to the head of their offering." "The thought rushed into my mind," says he, "What! may I transfer all my guilt to another? Has God provided an offering for me, that I may lay my sins on his head? Then, God willing, I will not bear them one moment longer. Accordingly, I sought to lay my sins upon the sacred head of Jesus, and on the Wednesday began to have a hope of mercy; on the Thursday that hope increased, and on Friday and Saturday it became more strong; and on the Sunday morning (Easter Day) I awoke early, with these words upon my heart and lips:

'Jesus Christ is risen to-day!
Hallelujah! Hallelujah!'"

From that hour he had peace.

9289. GUILT, Unhappiness of. Guilt, though it may attain temporal splendor, can never confer real happiness. The evident consequences of our crimes long survive their commission, and, like the ghosts of the murdered, forever haunt the steps of the malefactor. The paths of virtue, though seldom those of worldly greatness, are always those of pleasantness and peace. *Sir Walter Scott.*

9290. HABIT, Beware of a Bad. Beware of a bad habit. It makes its first appearance as a tiny fay, and is so innocent, so playful, so minute, that none save a precisian would denounce it, and it seems hardly worth while to whisk it away. The trick is a good joke, the lie is white, the glass is harmless, the theft is only a few apples, the bet is only sixpence, the debt is only half a crown. But the tiny fay is capable of becoming a tremendous giant; and if you connive and harbor him, he will nourish himself at your expense, and then, springing on you as an armed man, will drag you down to destruction. *Dr. J. Hamilton.*

9291. HABIT, Chains of. It is important to keep in mind that—as is evident from what is seen daily about us—habits are formed, not at one stroke, but gradually and insensibly; so that, unless vigilant care be employed, a great change may come over the character without our being conscious of any. For, as Dr. Johnson has well expressed it, "The diminutive chains of habit are seldom heavy enough to be felt, till they are too strong to be broken." *Whately.*

9292. HABIT, Danger of. It is mentioned of a friend of Charles I. in the civil war of the Parliament, that he had made up his mind to take horse and join the royal party, but for one circumstance, that he could not reconcile himself to the thought of being an hour or two less in bed than he had been accustomed in his own quiet home; and he therefore, after duly reflecting on the impossibility of being both a good subject and a good sleeper, contented himself with remaining to enjoy his repose. Absurd as such an anecdote may seem, it states only what passes innumerable times through the silent hearts of those who are enslaved by their habits. In similar comparisons of the most important duties with the most paltry but habitual pleasures, how many more virtuous actions would have been performed on earth, if the performance of them had not been inconsistent with enjoyments, as insignificant in themselves as an hour of unnecessary and perhaps hurtful slumber! *Salter.*

9293. HABIT, Destructive. I remember once riding from Buffalo to the Niagara Falls. I said to a gentleman, "What river is that, sir?" "That," said he, "is Niagara river." "Well, it is a beautiful stream," said I; "bright, and fair, and glassy. How far are the rapids?" "Only a mile or two," was the reply. "Is it possible that only a mile from us we shall find the water in the turbulence which it must show near the falls?" "You will find it so, sir." And so I found it; and the first sight of Niagara I shall never forget. Now launch your bark on that Niagara river; it is bright, smooth, beautiful and glassy. There is a ripple at the bow; the silver wake you leave behind adds to your enjoyment. Down the stream you glide, oars, sails and helm in proper trim, and you set out on your pleasure excursion. Suddenly some one cries out from the bank, "Young men, ahoy!" "What is it?" "The rapids are below you!" "Ha! ha! we have heard of the rapids; but we are not such fools as to get there. If we go too fast, then we shall up with the helm, and steer to the shore; we will set the mast in the socket, hoist the sail, and speed to the land. Then on, boys; don't be alarmed, there is no danger." "Young men, ahoy there!" "What is it?" "The rapids are below you." "Ha! ha! we laugh and quaff; all things delight us. What care we for the future! No man ever saw it. 'Sufficient unto the day is the evil thereof.' We will enjoy life while we may, will catch pleasure as it flies. This is enjoyment; time enough to steer out of danger when we are sailing swiftly with the current." "Young men, ahoy!" "What is it?" "Beware! beware! The rapids are below you!" "Now you see the water foaming all around. See how fast you pass that point! Up with the helm! Now turn! Pull hard! Quick! quick! quick! Pull for your lives! Pull till the blood starts from your nostrils, and the veins stand like whip-cords upon your brow! Set the mast in the socket! hoist the sail! Ah! ah! it is too late! Shrieking, howling, blaspheming, over they go." Thousands go over the rapids of intemperance every year through the power of habit, crying all the while, "When I find out that it is injuring me, I will give it up!" *J. B. Gough.*

9294. HABIT, Fundamental Law of. Habit is the deepest law of human nature. It is our supreme strength, if also, in certain circumstances, our miserablest weakness. Let me go once, scanning my way with any earnestness of outlook, and successfully arriving, my footsteps are an invitation to me a second time to go by the same way; it is easier than any other way. Habit is our primal fundamental law; habit and imitation: there is nothing more perennial in us than these two. They are the source of all working and all apprenticeship, of all practice and all learning in this world. *Carlyle.*

9295. HABIT, Groove of. In the old cities that have been exhumed, road-beds have been found in a great state of preservation, though they have been covered up two thousand years. Tracks of chariots, six inches deep, are there, worn in the solid stones. So evil habits cut their deep grooves into the human soul, which cannot be erased by the hand of death or the lapse of years.

9296. HABIT, Hardening Power of. The ploughman frequently comes upon a tough place, through which it is very difficult to drive the plough. He finds that it is an old road-bed, or hard-trodden path. Habitual sins make such tough spots in our natures. Ordinary influences will not break them up. The pick and crowbar must be applied. Extra spiritual aid must be sought that these hard places do not ruin the crop of grace.

9297. HABIT, Interrupted. Scott, in his autobiography, tells this story of himself. One boy was always above him in his class; do what he would he could not pass him, till, observing him always fumbling at a lower button of his waistcoat as he answered a question, it occurred to him to cut it off on the sly. He

watched with some anxiety for the result. The ruse answered only too well. When the boy was again questioned, his fingers sought for the button; missing it, in his distress he looked down for it in vain. "He stood confounded," says the penitent aggressor. "I took his place, nor did he ever recover it, or suspect the author of his wrong." This story tells two ways. Doubtless some bodily habits establish associations favorable to the memory, and quieting to irritability; the mischief is, that the mind becomes dependent, and is stranded when cut off from the old moorings.

9298. HABIT, Prevalence of. Habit hath so vast a prevalence over the human mind that there is scarce anything too strange or too strong to be asserted of it. The story of the miser, who from long accustoming to cheat others, came at last to cheat himself, and with great delight and triumph picked his own pocket of a guinea to convey to his hoard, is not impossible or improbable. *Fielding.*

9299. HABIT, Religious. Mr. and Mrs. Loveless would have me live with them, but they charged me very little for my board, whereby I was enabled, with my salary, to support seven native schools. These were so situated that I could visit them all in one day. My horse and gig were seen constantly on the rounds; and my horse at last knew where to stop as well as I did. This nearly cost a Bengal officer his life. Captain Page, a godly man, who was staying with us until a ship was ready to take him to the Cape, one morning requested me to lend him my horse and gig to take him to the city. The captain was driving officer-like, when the horse stopped suddenly, and nearly threw him out. He inquired, "What place is this?" The answer was, "It's the Sailor's Hospital." They started again, and soon the horse stopped suddenly, and the captain was nearly out as before. "What's this?"—"A school, sir," was the reply. At last he finished his business, and resolved to return another way. By doing this he came near my schools, and again and again the horse stopped. When he got home, he said, "I am glad that I have returned without broken bones, but never will I drive a religious horse again." *Richard Knill.*

9300. HABIT, Struggle against. A Moravian missionary, entering his hut in Guiana, South America, was attacked by a boa-constrictor. The huge serpent lowered itself from the rafters and coiled about him, as its method is to strangle its victims. He felt the increasing pressure of its tightening folds, and gave himself up in despair. Fearing that his death would be attributed to the treachery of the Indians, he took a piece of chalk and wrote upon the table, "A serpent has killed me." He was mistaken; he was not dead, but only despairing. Then the promise of Christ to his disciples, that they should have power to tread on serpents and scorpions and not be hurt thereby, come into his mind and renewed his courage and strength. He redoubled his exertions to free himself from the terrible coil, and succeeded. But it was a supreme effort, such as a man can make only in some great crisis of his life. This fact enshrines a vivid symbol of evil habit. The boa-constrictor is the contracting coil of evil habit, ever tightening, which will result inevitably in death. The power of Christ is the only means of deliverance. There is in this hope, for those who have written themselves dead. While there is life there is receptive power, and Christ will supply strength to overcome.

9301. HABITS, Accumulation of. Like flakes of snow, that fall unperceived upon the earth, the seemingly unimportant events of life succeed one another. As the snow gathers together, so are our habits formed. No single flake that is added to the pile produces a sensible change; no single action creates, however it may exhibit, a man's character; but as the tempest hurls the avalanche down the mountain, and overwhelms the inhabitant and his habitation, so passion, acting upon the elements of mischief which pernicious habits have brought together by imperceptible accumulation, may overthrow the edifice of truth and virtue.   *Bentham.*

9302. HABITS, Alteration of. A physical habit is like a tree that has grown crooked. You cannot go to the orchard, and take hold of a tree that has grown thus, and straighten it, and say, "Now keep straight!" and have it obey you. What can you do? You can drive down a stake, and bind it to the tree, bending it back a little, and scarifying the bark on one side. And if, after that, you bend it back a little more every month, keeping it taut through the season, and from season to season, at last you will succeed in making it permanently straight. You can straighten it, but you cannot do it immediately; you must take one or two years for it.   *Beecher.*

9303. HABITS, Cure for Bad. A minister said, "Suppose some cold morning you should go into a neighbor's house, and find him busy at work on his windows, scratching away, and should ask what he was up to, and he should reply, 'Why, I am trying to remove the frost; but as fast as I get it off one square, it comes on another,' would you not say, 'Why, man, let your windows alone, and kindle your fire, and the frost will soon come off?' And have you not seen people who try to break off their bad habits one after another without avail? Well, they are like the man who tried to scratch the frost from his windows. Let the fire of love to God and man, kindled at the altar of prayer, burn in their hearts, and the bad habits will soon melt away."

9304. HABITS, Destructive Power of Bad. The surgeon of a regiment in India relates the following incident: "A soldier rushed into the tent to inform me that one of his comrades was drowning in a pond close by, and nobody could attempt to save him in consequence of the dense weeds which covered the surface. On repairing to the spot, we found the poor fellow in his last struggle, manfully attempting to extricate himself from the meshes of rope-like grass that encircled his body; but, to all ap-pearance, the more he labored to escape, the more firmly they became coiled round his limbs. At last he sank, and the floating plants closed in, and left not a trace of the disaster. After some delay, a raft was made, and we put off to the spot, and sinking a pole some twelve feet, a native dived, holding on by the stake, and brought the body to the surface. I shall never forget the expression of the dead man's face—the clenched teeth, and fearful distortion of the countenance, while coils of long trailing weeds clung round his body and limbs, the muscles of which stood out stiff and rigid, whilst his hands grasped thick masses, showing how bravely he had struggled for life."

9305. HABITS, Incurable. An old man showed his deformed fingers and said, "In these crooked fingers there is a good text for a talk to children. For over fifty years I used to drive a stage, and these bent fingers show the effect of holding the reins for so many years."

9306. HABITS, Legends of Good and Evil. When you look upon that familiar figure of Laocoön and his sons, bound every limb by the folds of the serpent, and hand, foot, head, all, you will see what the ancients mean by this dragon; you will see what was the conception of human sin to the most ancient people of this world. The power of a vice, the power of a habit, to bind and bind every faculty and every power, is shown in that dragon which the ancients called Archae, afterward Ahmas, the Sanskrit for sin, afterward the Latin word *anguis,* a serpent, and afterward our "anguish." This great legend of the binding serpent, with which the dragon stories begin, has been reproduced again and again in manifold forms, and it is turned into many little stories that the Germans tell their children; and on the confines of Austria, in Minor Russia, in parts of Poland, every child will tell them to you. There is the story, for instance, of a little boy and little girl who go about gathering strawberries, and after they have gathered a number of strawberries, they meet an old woman who asks for some berries. The little girl gives her freely, but the boy says he doesn't gather strawberries for old women. After the children pass on, the old woman calls them back, and gives to each of them a little box. The little girl opens her box and finds two little snow-white caterpillars, which, while she looks upon them, turn to butterflies, and then they grow and grow until they become angels, and bear her away to Paradise. The little boy opens his box and finds two tiny little black bugs, which swell until they become serpents, and bind all his limbs, and take him to a forest where he is wandering to this day. This is the story that the fathers and mothers tell their children, as showing the gradual growth of good and evil habits and principles, from the smallest to the largest forces, until they uplift the whole being, or bind it in all the powers of evil.   *Conway.*

9307. HAND, Legend of a. An early English legend relates that a Cornish nobleman cut off the foot and hand of his nephew and heir, and seut him thus maimed to a convent. A brazen foot and silver hand were provided him. When about fourteen years old the abbot took him out with him to gather nuts. There the boy used his silver hand to clasp the branches or pick the nuts as if it had been a living member, as the abbot saw to his great amazement. Christ can restore the withered hand, or make life animate the artificial hand.

9308. HAND, Mechanism of the. From the shoulder to the tips of the fingers there are thirty-two distinct bones, curiously articulated one with another, which could not be imitated with any expectation of success, viz.: one shoulder blade, one collar-bone, one arm-bone, two in the fore-arm, eight in the carpus or wrist, five in the palm of the hand, two in the thumb, and twelve in the fingers. Next, to move those thirty-two bones in all the directions they were designed to act, there is a perfect labyrinth of delicate cordage, which, when separated and distinctly displayed, shows that there are forty-six muscles—and some anatomists make more—to extend, bend, turn, clench, unclench, nip, squeeze, and make all the movements which we can give the arm and hand by simply willing to do so. But in order that the mind may hold positive control over those thirty differently formed bones by the forty-six muscles, of which no two are alike, there are long nerves running like telegraphic wires from the arm-pit to the smallest fibre of every muscle. From the plexus in the axilla, or arm-pit, the nerves hold communication, through the intervention of other nerve-threads, with the brain. One set of nerves, or rather telegraph cords, convey messages to the fingers, and another set send back word to the brain of the reception of the order, and how business is transpiring. Beside all these complications, to nourish and keep the several parts vitalized, there are arteries, veins, lymphatics, absorbents, exhalent tubes, and tissues almost beyond enumeration, to keep the whole in working order. And when in good condition what power it exerts! It conveys an ineffable language, which even brute animals understand. It menaces, invites, repels, or gives character and grandeur to the expressions of an orator. It is a hammer, a vice, a punch, wrench, a lever, a pry, a force, and a mighty power by which the pyramids were reared, cathedrals called into being from the hardest quarries; and all that is amazing, surprising, delicate or calculated to advance civilization in art, literature and science, is accomplished by those wonderful instruments—human hands.   *Anon.*

9309. HAND, The Offending A young man, named Clitus, stirred up sedition in the city of Tiberias against Flavius Josephus, the governor. Being delivered over to punishment, Josephus sentenced him to have both his hands cut off. The young man pleaded to have one of them spared. To that Josephus consented. The young man then courageously took his sword and cut off his own left hand. This kind of punishment was common in those days, and explains Christ's reference to the offending hand.

9310. HAND, Power of the. The lion has powerful fangs and claws; the hare has swiftness of foot, but in other points is defenceless. But to man, the only animal that partakes of divine intelligence, the Creator has given, in lieu of every other natural weapon, or organ of defence, that instrument—the hand; an instrument applicable to every art and occasion, as well of peace as of war. Man, therefore, wants not a hoof, or horn, or any other natural weapon; inasmuch as he is able with his hand to grasp a much more effective weapon—the sword or spear. Besides which, natural weapons can be employed only in close conflict, while some of the weapons employed by man, as javelins or arrows, are even more effectual at a distance. And again, though man may be inferior to the lion in swiftness, yet, by his dexterity and skill, he breaks into his use a still swifter animal—the horse; mounted on whose back, he can escape from or pursue the lion, or attack him at every advantage. He is enabled, moreover, by means of this instrument, to clothe himself with armor of various kinds, or to intrench himself within camps or fenced cities. Whereas, were his hands encumbered with any natural armor, he would be unable to employ them for the fabrication of those instruments and means which give him such a decided advantage over all the other animals of creation. Nor have we yet enumerated the most important of those privileges which the hand imparts to man. With this he weaves the garment that protects him from the summer's heat or winter's cold; with this he forms the various furniture of nets and snares, which give him a dominion over the inhabitants as well of the water as of the air and earth; with his hand he constructs the lyre and lute, and the numerous instruments employed in the several arts of life; with his hand he erects altars and shrines to immortal gods; and lastly, by means of the same instrument, he bequeaths to posterity, in writings, the intellectual treasures of his own divine imagination.   *Galen.*

9311. HAND, Shakes of the. There is nothing more characteristic than shakes of the hand. I have classified them. There is the high official,—the body erect, and a rapid, short shake, near the chin. There is the mortmain,—the flat hand introduced into your palm, and hardly conscious of its contiguity. The digital,—one finger held out, much used by the high clergy. There is the shakus rusticus, where your hand is siezed in an iron grasp, betokening rude health, warm heart, and distance from the metropolis, but producing a strong sense of relief on your part when you find your hand released and your fingers unbroken. The next to this is the retentive shake,—one which, beginning with vigor, pauses, as it were to take breath, but without relinquishing its prey, and before you are aware begins again, till you feel anxious as to the result, and have no shake left in you. There are other varieties, but this is enough for one lesson.   *S. Smith.*

9312. HAND, Superiority of the. The organs of all other senses, even in their greatest perfection, are beholden to the hand for the enhancement and the exaltation of their powers. It constructs for the eye a copy of itself, and thus gives it a telescope with which to range among the stars; and by another copy, on a slightly different plan, furnishes it with a microscope, and introduces it into a new world of wonders. It constructs for the ear the instruments by which it is educated, and sounds them in its hearing till its powers are trained to the full. It plucks for the nostril the flower which it longs to smell, and distils for it the fragrance which it covets. As for the tongue, if it had not the hand to serve it, it might abdicate its throne as the lord of taste. In short, the organ of touch is the minister of its sister senses, and, without any play of words, is the handmaid of them all.   *Prof. Wilson.*

9313. HANDS, Joining. The joining of hands has, amongst Eastern nations, long been the method of binding an engagement, and has had all the force of an oath. The circumstance is alluded to by Mr. Bruce: "I was so enraged at the traitorous part which Hassan had acted, that at parting I could not help saying to Ibrahim, 'Now, sheikh, I have done everything you have desired without ever expecting fee or reward; the only thing I now ask you, and it is probably the last, is that you will avenge me upon this Hassan, who is every day in your power.' Upon this, he gave me his hand, saying, 'He shall not die in his bed, or I shall never see old age.'" The joining of hands naturally signifies contracting a friendship and making a covenant, 2 Kings 10: 15; Prov. 11: 21. The right hand was esteemed so sacred that Cicero calls it the witness of our faith.
       Bib. Treasury.

9314. HANDS, Kissing. This custom is very ancient, and was once universal. The Greeks adored their gods by the simple compliment of kissing their hands; and the Romans were treated as atheists, if they would not perform the same act when they entered a temple. This custom, however, as a religious ceremony, declined with Paganism; but was continued as a salutation by inferiors to their superiors, or as a token of esteem among friends. At present, it is only practiced as a mark of obedience from the subject to the sovereign, and by lovers who are solicitous to preserve this ancient usage in its full power.   *I. Disraeli.*

9315. HAPPINESS, Child's Idea of. A little girl was asked what was the meaning of the word happy. Her beautiful answer was, "It is to feel as if you wanted to give all your things to your little sister."

9316. HAPPINESS, Christian. An old colored woman went to a Delegate of the Christian Commission at Vicksburg, who was very ill with fever and much depressed in spirit, and said, "Massa, does ye see de bright side dis mornin'?" "No, Nanny," said I, "it isn't so bright as I wish it was." "Well, massa, I allus sees de bright side." "You do?" said I; "maybe you havn't had much trouble?"

"Maybe not," she said; and then went on to tell me in her simple, broken way, of her life in Virginia, of the selling of her children one by one, of the auction sale of her husband, and then of herself. She was alone now in camp, without having heard from one of her kindred for years: "Maybe I ain't seen no trouble, massa?" "But, Nanny," said I, "have you seen the bright side all the time?" "Allus, massa, allus." "Well, how did you do it?" "Dis is de way, massa. When I see de brack cloud comin' over"—and she waved her dark hand inside the tent, as though one might be settling down there—"an' 'pears like it's comin' crushin' down on me, den I jist whips aroun' on de oder side, and I find de Lord Jesus dar; an' den it's all bright an' cl'ar. De bright side's allus whar Jesus is, massa." "Well, Nanny," said I, "if you can do that, I think I ought to." "'Pears like you ought to, massa, an' you's a preacher of de word of Jesus." She went away; I turned myself on my blanket and said in my heart, "'The Lord is my Shepherd.' It is all right and well. Now, come fever or health, come death or life, come burial on the Yazoo Bluff or in the churchyard at home—the Lord is my Shepherd." With this sweet peace of rest, God's care and love became very precious to me. I fell asleep. When I woke I was in a perspiration; my fever was broken. "Old Nanny's" faith had made me whole.   *E. P. Smith.*

9317. HAPPINESS, Coming of. President Nott, in his wise old age, once took a newly-married pair aside, and said: "I want to give you this advice, my children—don't try to be happy. Happiness is a shy nymph, and if you chase her you will never catch her. But just go quietly on and do your duty, and she will come to you."

9318. HAPPINESS, Desire for. If we ascend the thrones of princes, if we enter the palaces of the great, if we walk through the mansions of courtiers and statesmen, if we pry into the abodes of poverty and indigence, if we mingle with poets or philosophers, with manufacturers, merchants, mechanics, peasants, or beggars; if we survey the busy, bustling scene of a large city, the sequestered village, or the cot which stands in the lonely desert—we shall find in every situation, and among every class, beings animated with desires of happiness, which no present enjoyment can gratify, and which no object within the limits of time can fully satiate.   *Dr. T. Dick.*

9319. HAPPINESS, Diffusers of. Some men move through life as a band of music moves down the street, flinging out pleasures on every side through the air to every one, far and near, who can listen. Some men fill the air with their presence and sweetness, as orchards, in October days, fill the air with the perfume of ripe fruit. Some women cling to their own houses like the honeysuckle over the door, yet, like it, fill all the region with the subtle fragrance of their goodness. How great a bounty and a blessing is it so to hold the royal gifts of the soul that they shall be music to some, and fragrance to others, and life to all! It would be no unworthy thing to live for, to make the power which we have within us the breath of other men's joy: to fill the atmosphere which they must stand in with a brightness which they cannot create for themselves. *Beecher.*

9320. HAPPINESS, Disturbances of. In the constitution both of our mind and of our body everything must go on right, and harmonize well together, to make us happy; but should one thing go wrong, that is quite enough to make us miserable; and although the joys of this world are vain and short, yet its sorrows are real and lasting: for I will show you a ton of perfect pain with greater ease than one ounce of perfect pleasure; and he knows little of himself or of the world, who does not think it sufficient happiness to be free from sorrow: therefore, give a wise man health, and he will give himself every other thing. I say, give him health; for it often happens that the most ignorant empiric can do us the greatest harm, although the most skillful physician knows not how to do us the slightest good. *Colton.*

9321. HAPPINESS, Domestic. Think of this, my good friend, and as you have kind affections to make some good girl happy, settle yourself in life while you are young, and lay up, by so doing, a stock of domestic happiness against age or bodily decay. There are many good things in life, whatever satirists and misanthropes may say to the contrary; but probably the best of all, next to a conscience void of offence, (without which, by the bye, they can hardly exist,) are the quiet exercise and enjoyment of social feelings, in which we are at once happy ourselves, and the cause of happiness to those who are dearest to us. *Sir W. Scott.*

9322. HAPPINESS, Empty. If you were to see a man endeavoring all his life to satisfy his thirst by holding up an empty cup to his lips, you would certainly despise his ignorance; but if you should see others of brighter parts, and finer understanding, ridicule the dull satisfaction of one cup and think to satisfy their own thirst by a variety of golden and gilt empty cups, would you think that these were the wiser or happier, or better employed for their parts? Now this is all the difference you can see in the happiness of this life. The dull and heavy soul may be content with one empty appearance of happiness. But then let the wit, the great scholar, the fine genius, the great statesmen, the polite gentleman, lay all their heads together, and they can only show you more and various empty appearances of happiness; give them all the world into their hands, let them cut and carve as they please. they can only make a greater variety of empty cups· for search as deep and look as far as you will, there is nothing here to be found that is nobler and greater than high eating and drinking, than rich dress and applause, and vanity; unless you look for it in the wisdom and laws of religion. *Salter.*

9323. Happiness, Enduring. No man thinks himself miserable till he hath lost his happiness. A godly man is blessed when afflicted and buffeted, because God is the proper orb in which he doth fix, and he hath his God still. (Job 5 : 17.) When a few leaves blow off, his comfort is, he hath the fruit and the tree still. As a man worth millions, he can rejoice though he lose some mites. In the Salentine country there is mention made of a lake brimful; put in never so much, it runneth not over; draw out what you can, it is still full. Such is the condition of a Christian—he hath never too much; and take away what you will, having God, is still full. *Swinnock.*

9324. HAPPINESS, False. Reader let no man ever delude you into supposing that you can be happy in this world without repentance. Oh! no! You may laugh and dance, and go upon Sundays in excursion trains, and crack good jokes, and sing good songs, and say, "Cheer, boys, cheer!" and "There's a good time coming;"—but all this is no proof that you are happy. So long as you do not quarrel with sin, you will never be a truly happy man. Thousands go on for a time in this way, and seem merry before the eyes of men, and yet in their heart carry about a lurking sorrow. *Ryle.*

9325. HAPPINESS, Foundation of. The foundation of domestic happiness is faith in the virtue of woman; the foundation of political happiness is confidence in the integrity of man; the foundation of all happiness, temporal and eternal, is reliance on the goodness of God. *Landor.*

9326. HAPPINESS, Humility and. I fear I have not learned the secret of true happiness, a poor and contrite spirit.—*Henry Martyn.*— Truth and happiness inhabit a palace, into which none can enter but humble, sincere, and constant lovers. *Lucas.*

9327. HAPPINESS, Key to. A little boy went to his mother and said, "I tried to make little sister happy. I couldn't make her happy no how I could fix it; but I made myself happy trying to make her happy."

9328. HAPPINESS, Land of. The French have an ideal happy land, called Cocaigne. It is full of men and women who are always happy. It is always day there; and there are no storms of rain or snow; no extreme of heat or cold; no dangers from lightning or whirlwind; no quarreling or war; no sickness or death. There is a fair abbey with white monks and gray nuns. The cloister is built of gems and spices. All about are birds merrily singing, ready roasted, flying into the hungry mouths, among them buttered larks. All down the streets go roasted geese. There is a river of wine. The ladies are all fair; every month one has new clothes. There bubbles up the fountain of perpetual youth, which will restore to bloom and vigor all who bathe in it, be they ever so ugly or old.

9329. HAPPINESS, National. An Oriental story says that a prince asked two of his wisest counselors, how he might make his people most happy; and allowed them two months to prepare their reply. At the required time, the two wise men stood before their master—

the one bending beneath a great roll of papy-rus-leaves containing two hundred written rules, the other walking empty-handed. The reading of the two hundred rules sadly wea-ried the prince, who then called upon the other counselor to produce his reply, which was given in two words: "Love God." "How?" said the prince. "Did I not require to know how I might render my people most happy? And thou only directest me to love God." "True," replied the wise man; "but thou canst not love God without loving thy people also."

9330. HAPPINESS, Negative. What is happi-ness? It ain't bein' idle, that's a fact—no idle man or woman ever was happy since the world began. Employment gives both appe-tite and digestion. Duty makes pleasure doubly sweet by contrast. When the harness is off, if the work ain't too hard, a critter likes to kick up his heels. When pleasure is the business of life, it ceases to be pleasure; and when it's all labor, and no play, work, like an unstuffed saddle, cuts into the very bone. Neither labor nor idleness has a road that leads to happiness—one has no room for the heart, and the other corrupts it. Hard work is the best of the two, for that has, at all events, sound sleep—the other has restless pillows and unrefreshing sleep; one is a misfortune, the other is a curse; and money ain't happiness, that's as clear as mud. *Haliburton.*

9331. HAPPINESS, Non-essential. Happiness is not what we are to look for. Let us do right, and then, whether happiness comes or unhap-piness, it is no very mighty matter. If it come, life will be sweet; if it do not come, life will be bitter—bitter, not sweet, and yet to be borne. *Froude.*

9332. HAPPINESS, Promoting. Sydney Smith cut the following from a newspaper, and pre-served it: "When you rise in the morning, form a resolution to make the day a happy one to a fellow-creature. It is easily done; a left-off garment to the man who needs it, a kind word to the sorrowful, an encouraging expression to the striving—trifles in themselves light as air—will do it at least for the twenty-four hours. And if you are young, depend upon it, it will tell when you are old; and if you are old, rest assured, it will send you gently and happily down the stream of time to eternity. By the most simple arithmetical sum, look at the result. If you send one per-son, only one, happily through each day, that is three hundred and sixty-five in the course of the year. And supposing you live forty years only after you commence that course of medicine, you have made 14,600 beings happy, at all events for a time."

9333. HAPPINESS, Pursuing. 'Tis to be happy that we run after pleasures. But we, alas! mis-take our happiness, and foolishly seek it where it is not to be found; as silly children think to catch the sun, when they see it setting at so near a distance. They travel on and tire themselves in vain; for the thing they seek is in another world. *Bishop Hickes.*

9334. HAPPINESS, Quest of. When man was made in the image of God, Happiness, one of the attendant angels which stand before the throne of God, was deputed to wait upon man and be his constant companion. But when sin marred his beautiful image, and he lost his high nobility, Happiness, who could no longer be-hold her heavenly Father's image upon earth, sighed to return, and quitting man, ascended to her bright abode in heaven. Man, now wearied and distressed at the loss of his angelic compan-ion, wandered about in quest of a friend to sup-ply her place. He looked out anxiously on Nature, and saw her gay and cheerful; but Nature assured him in awful accents, she knew no bliss for man. He questioned Love, who appeared so bright and joyous in hope; but she timidly shrank from the inquiry, while her eyes dropped fast with tears. He sought of Friendship, but she sighed and answered, "Caprice, anxiety, and the fear of change are ever with me." He followed after Vice, who boasted loudly and promised great things; but before she left him the borrowed roses fell from her withered brow. He thought at last he should succeed if he found Virtue; but she as-sured him with tender sorrow that penitence was her rightful and proper name, and that the bliss he sought for was not in her power to bestow. Disappointed and wearied, he now in despair applied to Death, who, relaxing his forbidding aspect, smiled upon him and said, "No longer upon earth can Happiness be found: I am a friend of man and a guide to Happiness. Let the voice of him who died on Calvary bring man to me; and I am commis-sioned to conduct him into the presence of Happiness, who shall never leave nor forsake him through the countless ages of eternity." *Salter.*

9335. HAPPINESS, Reciprocal. A poor man entered a merchant's office, and seeing large sums of money, exclaimed, "How happy a lit-tle of that money would make me!" The mer-chant heard him, and asked, "how much it would take to make him happy." He told the merchant how destitute his family were, and added that he thought five pounds would make them comfortable. The merchant ordered that sum to be paid him. At the close of the day, the clerk asked the merchant to what account he should charge the money given the poor man. He replied, "For making a poor man happy, five pounds."

9336. HAPPINESS, Risking Eternal. As to the eternal reward of grace, its distance is so short and uncertain, that if men were not infatuated, it is a wonder that it is not constantly observ-ant to their minds, and that its glorious bright-ness does not dazzle their eyes. A good man is never sure that heaven is at an hour's dis-tance from him. It looks like a choosing of misery when one takes the course that leads to it, though he is sure eternity is not far off, at the furthest he can possibly expect; when he knows not but the next moment may land him on that unknown shore, and plunge him in an abyss of wretchedness; when he runs that risk for pleasures which he is not sure whether he shall ever attain to, and which he is sure will vanish away like shadows.

Maclaurin.

9337. HAPPINESS, Sources of. God made the beasts looking down towards the earth to shew that their satisfaction might be brought from thence, and accordingly it does afford them what is suited to their appetite; but the erect figure of man's body, which looketh upward, shewed him that his happiness lay above him —in God—and that he was to expect it from heaven, and not from earth. *Thomas Boston.*

9338. HAPPINESS, True. Happiness consists in loving and being loved. There is enough to love in the world; but to be loved we must deserve it. We may be admired for our beauty or talent, courted for our influence or wealth, but we can only be loved as we are good. Therefore happiness consists in goodness. *Anon.*

9339. HAPPINESS, True Way to. A young gentleman was descanting upon the pleasures of the chase as practiced in England, in a promiscuous company. A minister present could not see the fun of being unhorsed and bruised or immersed in a quagmire. He exclaimed, " Is this the way to happiness ? Do you call this pleasure ? I feel grateful I have discovered another way to happiness than the one you have mentioned." The young sportsman expressed a wish to know a better way. "I have," answered the minister, "a map in my pocket which will describe the way, and the only true way to bliss." Having raised his curiosity, and the company appearing as anxious as this youth, he took out a small pocket Testament, and pointing to these words, "I am the Way, the Truth and the Life," put the book into his hands. This broke up the conversation. Most people want happiness in some other way than through Christ.

9340. HAPPINESS, Trying to Work out. There are those that would hammer out their own happiness, like the spider climbing up by the thread of her own weaving. Of all the parts and abilities that be in you, you may well say as the young man did of his hatchet, "Alas, master! it was but borrowed." (2 Kings, 6 : 6.)

Brooks.

9341. HAPPINESS, Where is. If the Scriptures are a delusion, where will we seek our happiness ? In wealth ? It is a splendid incumbrance. In honor ? It is a glittering bubble. In the pleasures of the world ? They are like the brine of the ocean to a thirsty palate, will irritate rather than satisfy. In gay entertaining company ? This is only a temporary opiate, not a lasting cure. But in the precious promises of the Gospel, and its renewing energy on our hearts; in the discoveries of God's love to poor sinners; in the displays of God's infinitely rich grace; and in the hope of his everlasting glory ; in these grand specifics, for preparing and dispensing which revelation has the patent—true health, ease, and felicity are to be found. *Hervey.*

9342. HAPPINESS, Within. This truth ought to be deeply printed in minds studious of wisdom and their own content, that they bear their happiness or unhappiness within their own breast ; and that all outward things have a right and a wrong handle. He that takes them by the right handle finds them good; he that takes them by the wrong indiscreetly, finds them evil. Take a knife by the haft, it will serve you; take it by the edge, it will cut you. There is no good thing but is mingled with evil; there is no evil but some good enters into the composition. The same truth holds in all persons, actions, and events. Out of the worst, a well composed mind, endowed with the grace of God, may extract good, with no other chemistry than piety, wisdom and serenity. It lieth in us as we incline our minds to be pleased or displeased with most things in the world. One that hath fed his eyes with the rich prospect of delicate countries, as Lombardy, Anjou, where all the beauties and dainties of nature assembled, will another time take no less delight in a wild and rugged prospect of high bare mountains, and fifty stories of steep rocks, as about the Grande Chartreuse and the bottom of Ardennes, where the very horror contributes to the delectation. If I have been delighted to see the trees of my orchard, in the spring blossomed, in the summer shady, in autumn hung with fruit; I will delight again after the fall of the leaf, to see through my trees new prospects which the bushy boughs hid before; and will be pleased with the sight of the snow candied about the branches, as the flowers of the season.

Du Moulin.

9343. HAPPINESS, The World's. Oromazes had an enchanted egg, in which he boasted that he had enclosed all the happiness of the world. When the egg was broken it was found to contain nothing but wind.

9344. HARDNESS OF HEART, Biblical. *A heart of stone.* Ezek. 11 : 19. *A face harder than a rock,* Jer. 5 : 3. *Stiff of forehead and hard of heart,* Ezek. 3 : 7. *Hard as an adamant stone,* probably a diamond. *Torpid and benumbed,* Rom. 11 : 7, 8 (quoting Isa. 29 : 10), according to the view of Hammond and others, is taken from the figure of one benumbed, through the stupefying draught given to condemned criminals before execution. *Seared, cauterized,* or *branded,* "as with a hot iron," 1 Tim. 4 : 2; made callous; a terrible mark of the apostasy of " the latter times." " *Past feeling,* because of the blindness (marg., hardness) of their heart," Eph. 4 : 18, 19. Isa. 6 : 9, 10—It is a noteworthy fact that this solemn passage is quoted most frequently in the New Testament, of any Old Testament text. EXAMPLES. *Pharaoh*—the Old Testament type of incorrigible hardness of heart, defiant alike of mercy and of judgment. It is remarkable that Pharaoh " seems to have been more emboldened to sin, by those miracles of mercy which removed the plagues, than by those of judgment which inflicted them."—(*Nicholls.*) The *Canaanites* in the time of Joshua were a striking example of those who have had many warnings, and yet refuse all thought of submission. They had heard of the flood; of the destruction of Sodom and Gomorrah, and the cities of the plain; the plagues of Egypt; the destruction of Pharaoh; the destruction of their neighbors the Amorites; the miraculous passage of the Jordan; the miraculous overthrow of Jericho; the faith and preservation of Rahab and her family; and yet they hardened their hearts against fear, and were justly destroyed, Joshua 10: 40. *Jeroboam*, the son of Nebat, though so solemnly warned by what happened to him and to the prophet of Judah, was in no degree softened, 1 Kings 13: 4, 24, 33. *Ahaziah's* hardened impenitence, even upon his death-bed, 2 Kings 1: 4. *Herod* hardened his heart by putting his reprover into prison, and allowing a just man to be wantonly put to death, Mark 6: 17, 27.   *Bowes.*

9345. HARLOT, Conversion of a. The story of Eudocia, a beautiful woman of Heliopolis, though doubtless largely fable, illustrates the power of grace. She was in her own richly-furnished house at midnight, awakened by the voice of a priest in the next house discoursing of the coming of Christ to judgment. She became alarmed, and in the morning sent for the monk. He told her what she must do to be saved. She closed her house, put off her rich array, fasted for seven days, and felt deeply her sins. To a priest she said, "O, sir, I am a grievous sinner—a sea of guilt!" "Be of good cheer," he replied. "The sea of guilt may be changed into a port of salvation, and the waves tossing with passion sink into ineffable calm." After fasting, in her exhaustion, she fell into a trance. She says, "Lo! an angel took me by the hand, and led me into heaven, where was unspeakable light, and there I saw the blessed ones in white. All their countenances lit up as I approached, and they came running towards me, and greeted me, even me, as a sister. Then there came up a shadow horrible and black, and it shrieked, saying, 'This woman is mine. I have used her to destroy many, and shall she be saved? I, for one little disobedience, was cast out of heaven, and here is this beast, steeped from head to foot in pollution, admitted to the company of the elect. Take them all; scrape all the rascals and harlots on earth together, and admit them into your society. I will off to my hell, and grovel there in fire forever.' Then I heard a voice answer, 'God willeth not the death of a sinner, but rather that he should be converted and live.' After that the angel took me by the hand, and led me home again, saying, 'There is joy in heaven over one sinner that repenteth,' and the vision vanished." She had great wealth, but gave it all away, devoted herself to the monastic life, resisted all temptation, and finally suffered martyrdom.

9346. HARLOTS, Labor for. In the seventh century there came to the city of Alexandria an old man of sixty in a monk's garb. He first secured the names of all the abandoned women of the city. He obtained work for himself, and at night, taking the wages of the day, went to one of these women, and after supping with her, gave her his day's earnings saying, "I give thee this that thou mayest spend one night without sin." Then he passed the night praying for the woman with many tears. Going forth he exacted the promise that his visit should not be revealed while he lived. Much scandal soon grew out of these visits. The monk refused to give any account of it saying, "There is one Judge and one day of judgment, wherein every man shall give account of his own works." He bore the reproach and suspicion without murmuring neither letting his benevolent work be known, lest the houses of ill-fame should be closed against him, nor desisting from it. At last, coming one morning from a harlot's door, a man saw him and struck him, saying, "How, rascal, do you outrage Christ by not mending your wicked ways?" The monk went to his chamber to die, and the man entered the harlot's house, and there learned of his noble work. He was struck with contrition and went into the streets proclaiming how he and the people had wronged the monk. A crowd followed the man as he went to beg the monk's pardon. They found him kneeling with hands clasped cold in death. Before him lay the text in writing, "Judge nothing before the time until the Lord come, who both will bring to light the hidden things of darkness, and will make manifest the counsels of the heart." (1 Cor. 4: 5.) At his funeral great numbers who had been reformed by him, walked in procession before his body, bearing lamps and candles crying, "We have lost our deliverer and instructor," and narrating their rescue through his prayers and zeal for their souls. Thus was manifest how great a work he had done. This is the authentic story of St. Vitalis.

9347. HARMONY, Fable of. There was a feud; red and blue and yellow stood in open defiance, each of the other two. "Acknowledge me chief," said red, "I am ever the emblem of charity. All that is warm and redolent of comfort and kindness is arrayed in my tints. I rest on this rose and claim precedence." "Acknowledge me chief," said blue, "I am the emblem of truth. All that is high and pure and just wears my hue. I rise and shine from yonder sky, and claim precedence." "Acknowledge me chief," said yellow, "I am the emblem of light and glory. Kings are crowned, palaces glitter, with my lustrious color. Receive me, O sun: to thee I call, and claim precedence." "Ah! my children," said the sun, "the very heavens weep at your disunion. Be reconciled, I pray, and show your strength of beauty where it must ever lie—in harmony" And they arose at the entreaty, and embraced in tearful clouds; and the sun shone out on them, and glorious in loveliness was the rainbow they made.   *S. T. Treasury.*

9348. HARVEST, Rejoicing for the. On seeing the caravan, one of the laborers ran from his companions, and approaching us, stood on his hands, with his feet aloft in the air, and gave other demonstrations of joy, when he presented us with an ear of corn and a flower, as an offering of the first-fruits of the year. Another remnant also of another very ancient usage, in the wave offering of the sheaf and the ear of corn, commanded to the Israelites by Moses. We returned them for a handful of paras, or small tin coin, and answered the shout of joy which echoed from the field by acclamations from the caravan. *Buckingham.*

9349. HASTE and Dispatch. I knew a wise man that had it for a by-word, when he saw men hasten to a conclusion, "Stay a little, that we may make an end the sooner." On the other side, true dispatch is a rich thing; for time is the measure of business, as money is of wares; and business is bought at a dear hand where there is small dispatch. The Spartans and Spaniards have been noted to be of small dispatch. *Mi venga la muerte de Spagna;—* "Let my death come from Spain," for then it will be sure to be long in coming. *Bacon.*

9350. HASTE, Sin of. Haste is the besetting sin of America. We do not run "with patience" the race that is set before us. There is not a day that goes by that we do not see in manuscript, book or paper, signs of the hurry that is the curse of American literature. Our artists are in a hurry; and good ideals are half drawn because they have not time to study their subject. Our engravers are in a hurry; and good blocks are spoilt by skillful workmen who have not time to be careful. Our editors are in a hurry; and their crude thoughts are embodied in editorials written at a dash, brilliant, but ineffective, because not matured. Our writers are in a hurry; and American books are slovenly in scholarship, and careless in execution, and marred by rhetorical and sometimes even grammatical blunders, that would disgrace a college composition. Our merchants are in a hurry; and they launch out in wild speculations that bring ninety-three out of every hundred into bankruptcy. Our ministers are in a hurry; and they sacrifice themselves without serving their parishes, by working under an unnatural excitement. We hear on every side exhortations to activity, industry, energy. We would fain exhort to calmness, sobriety. moderation, leisurely industry. *Christian Weekly.*

9351. HATRED, Envy and. Hatred proceeds from an opinion that the person we hate is evil; if not generally so, at least in particular to us. For they who think themselves injured are apt to hate the author of their wrong; yea, even those who are reputed injurious or malicious to others than ourselves we usually nauseate and abhor. But envy has only one sort of object, the felicity of others. Whence it becomes infinite, and like an evil or diseased eye, is offended with everything that is bright. *Plutarch.*

9352. HATRED, Prevalence of. There is no faculty of the human soul so persistent and universal as that of hatred. There are hatreds of race; hatreds of sect; social and personal hatreds. If thoughts of hatred were thunder and lightning, there would be a storm over the whole earth all the year round. Twenty people cannot be together, but some one suffers from their conversation. Let a man come into the company who from some cause is obnoxious to them, and no sooner does he depart than the ill-smelling flowers of hatred swell their buds, and give forth their malign influences through the room. *Beecher.*

9353. HATRED, Romish. The name of Calvin was an odious one to the Papists. In the Spanish expurgatorial index they gave directions that his name should be suppressed; while proselytes to the Romish faith would change the offensive name, if they possessed it.

9354. HEAD, The Human. The head has the most beautiful appearance, as well as the highest station, in a human figure. Nature has laid out all her art in beautifying the face; she has touched it with vermilion, planted in it a double row of ivory, made it the seat of smiles and blushes, lighted it up and enlivened it with the brightness of the eyes, hung it on each side with curious organs of sense, given it airs and graces that cannot be described, and surrounded it with such a flowing shade of hair as sets all its beauties in the most agreeable light. In short, she seems to have designed the head as the cupola to the most glorious of her works. *Addison.*

9355. HEALING, Miracles of. Christ cured diseased minds and chronic or temporary diseases with equal success. A late writer says, "We find Christ curing natural defects, which no physician of the highest modern skill would hope to succeed with. Blindness was then, as now, common in the East; many were blind from birth, and others were afflicted with ophthalmia and other painful diseases of these organs. The deaf, and therefore either dumb, or capable only of imperfect utterance, become as others when Christ speaks. The lame or halt, suddenly acquiring the use of those limbs which had long been apparently dead, rejoice and can scarcely control themselves under the emotions of astonishment which they feel at the newly-found power."

9356. HEALTH, Benefit of. Health is the soul that animates all enjoyments of life, which fade, and are tasteless, if not dead, without it. A man starves at the best and the greatest tables, makes faces at the noblest and most delicate wines, is poor and wretched in the midst of the greatest treasures and fortunes, with common diseases; strength grows decrepit, youth loses all vigor. and beauty all charms; music grows harsh, and conversation disagreeable; palaces are prisons, or of equal confinement; riches are useless, honor and attendance are cumbersome, and crowns themselves are a burden: but if diseases are painful and violent, they equal all conditions of life, make no difference between a prince and a beggar; and a fit of the stone or the colic puts a king on the rack, and makes him as miserable as he can the meanest, the worst and most criminal of his subjects. *Temple.*

9357. HEALTH, Lost. Among the manifold misfortunes that may befall humanity, the loss of health is one of the severest. All the joys that life can give cannot outweigh the sufferings of the sick. Give the sick man everything, and leave him his sufferings, and he will feel that half the world is lost to him. Lay him on a soft silken ~ouch, he will nevertheless groan sleepless unde the pressure of his sufferings; while the mist..able beggar, blessed with health, sleeps sweetly on the hard ground. Spread his table with dainty meats and choice drinks, and he will thrust back the hand that proffers them, and envy the poor man who thoroughly enjoys his dry crust. Surround him with the pomp of kings; let his chair be a throne, and his crutch a world-swaying sceptre; he will look with contemptuous eye on marble, on gold, and on purple, and would deem himself happy could he enjoy, even were it under a thatched roof, the health of the meanest of his servants. *Zschokke.*

9358. HEALTH, Restoration of. Who would not be covetous, and with reason, if health could be purchased with gold? Who not ambitious, if it were at the command of power, or restored by honor? But, alas! a white staff will not help gouty feet to walk better than a common cane; nor a blue ribbon bind up a wound so well as a fillet; the glitter of gold or diamonds will but hurt sore eyes, instead of curing them; and an aching head will be no more eased by wearing a crown instead of a common night-cap. *Temple.*

9359. HEALTH, Value of. He that loses his conscience has nothing left that is worth keeping. Therefore, be sure you look to that. And in the next place look to your health; and if you have it, praise God, and value it next to a good conscience; for health is the second blessing that we mortals are capable of, a blessing that money cannot buy; therefore value it, and be thankful for it.
Izaak Walton.

9360. HEARERS, Choice of. John Wesley always preferred the middling and lower classes to the wealthy. He said, "If I might choose, I should still, as I have done hitherto, preach the gospel to the poor." Preaching in Monktown church, a large, old, ruinous building, he says, "I suppose it has scarce had such a congregation during this century. Many of them were gay, genteel people, so I spoke on the first elements of the gospel, but I was still out of their depth. Oh, how hard it is to be shallow enough for a polite audience!"
Dr. J. B. Wakeley.

9361. HEARERS, Forgetful. Some hearers have bad memories. Their memories are like leaky vessels: all the precious wine of holy doctrine that is poured in runs out presently. Ministers cannot by study find a truth so fast as others lose it. If a truth delivered doth not stay in the memory, we can never be nourished up in the word of truth. If thieves steal away people's money, they tell every one, and make their complaints that they have been robbed; but there is a worse thief they are not aware of. How many sermons hath the devil stolen from them! How many truths have they been robbed of, which might have been so many death-bed cordials! *T. Watson.*

9362. HEARERS Only. It pleaseth men to hear of speculative doctrines, and to be entertained with a luscious preaching of the gospel, made up all of promises, and these wholly unconditional. It gratifies them to hear what is done without them, rather than what is done within them, and the necessity of sincere and entire obedience to our Saviour's precepts urged upon them. *Dr. Worthington.*

9363. HEARERS, Opinionated. Persons sitting under a stated ministry attach themselves to a particular pastor, and are so entirely absorbed in him and attached to his habits of thought and modes of illustration as not to be able to endure anything else, much less to profit by it. Like as a tree sheltered from some winds, and only exposed to one from a particular point of the compass, becomes bent in that direction, so the mind of these parties leans, bows, and only yields to the common current. These mental slaves seem to have lost the use of a part of their capacity—taste and feeling. Bring them to listen to a ministry at once plain, clear, and evangelical, but the idioms, tones, topics, and gestures of which are not in the mould of their own "dear minister," and they do not even understand it. The poor man cannot pronounce their "shibboleth," and that is quite enough; he is put down as a very dunce, and often as no gospel minister. It is a great misfortune for the soul not to have room for growth, to be pent up in some miserably narrow enclosure, or to be twisted out of the course of nature to one particular point of fanatical folly. This is proof, as clear as light, that they have been resting on the mannerism of the instrument, instead of the truth delivered. *Dr. Dixon.*

9364. HEARERS, Sleepy. Rev. Mr. Fuller, of Kettering, perceived some of his hearers to be drowsy, as soon as he had read his text. He struck the Bible three times against the side of the pulpit, calling out, "What! asleep already! I am often afraid I should preach you asleep: but the fault cannot be mine to-day, for I have not yet begun!"

9365. HEARERS, Test of. I marked a house standing on the soft sandy cliff, on which the sea is continually making inroads. Already vast portions of the headlands, with the buildings that were upon them, have been washed away; and it is plain that the remaining mansion, however stately and strongly built, must soon follow. How much labor has been spent in vain! How unwise was the builder who raised so costly a structure on so unsafe a site. How grievous that what is so fair in appearance should be so insecure in reality! You may have often seen a far poorer structure set upon some rocky crag, that beats back upon the surges which break themselves upon it, and where it has for ages defied "the stormy wind and tempest." The builder knew what he was doing, when he built on a rock. He wanted it to last for ages, and to stand the utmost violence of the elements; and he chose a foundation which no force of wind and waves could undermine. As years pass by, the building seems only to become more like the rock on which it stands. A day is coming which will assuredly prove on what foundation we have built our house; in other words, whether we have been hearers only, or doers as well as hearers of the word; whether we have been truly or only seemingly religious. Our deeds are at best imperfect; but if done with a sincere and faithful heart, God will accept them, through the mediation of our blessed Saviour; and the flood that will sweep away the hypocrite and the formal professor, will leave us uninjured, and monuments forever of his saving mercy.   *Bp. Trower.*

9366. HEARERS, Too Generous. A colored preacher was descanting on the different ways in which men lose their souls. Under one head he said that men often lose their souls through excessive generosity. "What!" he exclaimed, "you tell me you never heard of that before? You say, ministers often tell us we lose our souls for our stinginess, and for being covetous—but who ever heard of a man that hurt himself by going too far t'other way? I tell you how they do it. They sit down under the sermon, and when the preacher touch upon this sin or that sin, they no take it to themselves, but give this part of the sermon to one brother, and that part to another brother. And so they give away the whole sermon, and it do them no good. And that's the way they lose their souls by being too generous."

9367. HEARERS, Various. 1. The inattentive hearer, that taketh very little heed to what he heareth. 2. The inconsiderate hearer, that never ponders what he hears, nor compares one thing with another. 3. The injudicious hearer, that never makes any judgment, whether it be true or false. 4. The unapprehensive hearer, who hears all his days, but is never the wiser. 5. The stupid, unaffected hearer, that is as a rock and a stone under the word. 6. There are your prejudiced, disaffected hearers, who hear with dislike, especially those things which relate to practice. 7. Your fantastical, voluptuous hearers, that hear only to please their fancy or imaginations. They come on purpose to try if they can hear a pretty sentence, any fine jingle, any flashes of wit. 8. Your notional hearers, that are of somewhat a higher form and sect than the others. They always come to learn some kind of novelty. 9. Those talkative persons, who only come to hear, that they may furnish themselves with notions for the sake of discourse. 10. The censorious and critical hearers, who come on purpose not as doers of the law, but as judges. 11. Malicious hearers, that come on purpose to seek an advantage against those they come to hear, particularly from what they preach. Thus you see the characters of those who are "Hearers only," which are various and manifold. *Howe.*

9368. HEARING, Attentive. Aruleus Rusticus was listening to a lecture by Plutarch, when a soldier entered and delivered him a letter from the emperor. The lecturer stopped to give him time to read the letter, but he would not allow it, postponing the letter of the prince for the lecture of a philosopher.

9369. HEARING, Biblical. *Aaron and his sons.*—At their consecration, the blood of the ram was to be put partly upon the tip of the right ear, Exod. 29 : 20; not only as one of the three extremities of the body, but probably also with a symbolical meaning—that they should be ever ready to hear the Divine commands. *The leper.*—At the cleansing of the leper in like manner some of the blood of the trespass-offering, and some of the holy oil, was to be put upon the tip of the right ear, Lev. 14 : 14, 17. *The faithful servant*, whose ear was to be bored through at his master's door, was a beautiful token of willingness, cheerfully to hear and obey a master's wishes, Exod. 21 : 6. How *many kinds of ears and hearing* are spoken of in Scripture! Dull, heavy, itching, uncircumcised, opened, obedient ears.—See Conc.; and also Ezekiel's hearers, Ezek. 33 : 30–33; Athenian hearers, Acts 17 : 21; the parable of the sower, Mark 4 : 14–20. How MANY PRECEPTS urge the duty of attentive hearing!—See Conc. under give ear—hearken—diligently—incline the ear (the figure of one stooping down to catch the faintest whisper)—"swift to hear." "Hear this word" (the beginning of three consecutive chapters of Amos, 3, 4, 5,); "Hear, all ye people;" "Hear, I pray you, . . ye princes;" "Hear ye now what the Lord saith,"—the three sections of the prophecy of Micah (1 : 2; 3 : 1, 9; 6 : 1, 2,); "He that hath ears to hear, let him hear." No precept, perhaps, was so frequently repeated by Christ as this, Matt. 11 : 15; 13 : 9, 43; Mark 4 : 9, 23; 7 : 16; Luke 14 : 35. Even from the throne above, he addressed the same charge to each of the seven churches, "He that hath an ear, let him hear what the Spirit saith unto the churches," Rev. 2 : 7, 11, 17, 29; 3 : 6, 13, 22; also Christ's miracles of healing the deaf, Matt. 11 : 11; Mark 7 : 37; 9 : 25, with their symbolical and spiritual meaning.   *Bowes.*

9370. HEARING, Defending the. There are many organs and other parts of the body which serve as avenues and inlets for the soul to give admission to vice; there is but one passage of virtue into young minds, and that is by the ears. For this reason Xenocrates was of opinion that children ought to have a defence fitted to their ears rather than fencers or prize-players, because the ears only of the latter suffered by the blows, but the morals of the former were hurt and maimed by words.   *Plutarch.*

9371. HEARING, Different Results of. At Basle, Switzerland, we crossed the river Rhine by a curious ferry. The current of the river propels the boat from side to side in either direction as you wish. The same influence carries passengers in opposite directions. Thus it is with the ordinances of the church, the hearing of the word, and other means of grace. By them one is carried heavenward and another hellward, according to the direction each attendant is pursuing. The best influences improved give life, rejected death. Alas, that many are sweeping at a swifter rate towards ruin because of the current of good influences which they are in!

9372. HEARING, Duty of. This is not a fair-weather duty. Has not the business of eternity as urgent claims as the business of time? Then it is not too high to let one rule govern decisions in both cases. The preacher is sent to be heard. He comes to tell the good news. He will be pretty certain to tell the best news he has. Joy bubbles up in the heart and ripples out over the lips, while sorrow settles, like life's sediment, in the bottom of the heart, to clog its throbbings. His best may not suit you. Remember that there are only a few model preachers. We have read of only one perfect Model, and he was crucified many centuries ago.   *Dr. C. H. Fowler.*

9373. HEARING, Figure of. Plutarch compares hearing to filling one vessel from another, in which care is taken to place the vessel to be filled so that the contents of the other may be poured into it without spilling. To fill one vessel from another there must be something in it besides wind. The moral of this will suggest itself to every hearer and speaker.

9374. HEARING, Formal. "Well, Master Jackson," said his minister, walking homewards after service with an industrious laborer, who was a constant attendant: "well, Master Jackson, Sunday must be a blessed day of rest for you, who work so hard all the week! And you make a good use of the day, for you are always to be seen at church!" "Ay, sir," replied Jackson, "it is indeed a blessed day; I works hard enough all the week, and then I comes to church o' Sundays, and sets me down, and lays my legs up, and thinks o' nothing."
                                                    Southey.

9375. HEARING, Motives to. A lady once heard Rev. Ebenezer Erskine preach without knowing who he was, and was much profited by his discourse. Having learned his name, she resolved to hear him the next Sabbath in his own church, which she did, but without the influences she felt on the first occasion. Wondering at this, she stated the case to Mr. Erskine, and asked what might be the reason of such a difference in her feeling. He replied, "Madame, the reason is this: last Sabbath you went to hear Jesus Christ preached, but to-day you have come to hear Ebenezer Erskine preach."

9376. HEARING, Neglect of. To a person who excused his non-attendance at public worship by pleading the disagreeable appearance and manner of the minister, the Bishop of Alet said, "Let us look more at our Saviour, and less at the instruments. Elijah was as well nourished when the bread from heaven was brought by a raven, as Ishmael when the spring of water was revealed to him by an angel. Whether, then, we are fed immediately from God, as the Israelites, with manna in the wilderness, or by the glorious instrumentality of those who may seem to us as angels, or by the base one of those who seem to us contemptible,

let us be content and thankful if they are appointed of God, and if the bread and water of life they bring."

9377. HEARING, Peculiar. Naturalists affirm that there are tiny creatures with auricular organs so constructed that they cannot hear the thunder of heaven or the speech of men. The only sounds that strike their tympanum are the hum of bees, the grasshopper's call, and such like feeble pipings.   *S. Coley*

9378. HEARING, Pre-occupied. A man who had been a faithful attendant at church for fourteen years was taken sick and was visited by the preacher. He was unconverted; and when urged to seek for pardon, and not to rest until he knew his sins forgiven, he expressed great surprise. He did not know that it was possible! "Have you not attended ——— church?" "Yes," was the reply; "but I do not know that I ever heard a sermon." "What do you mean? You have regularly sat there for some fourteen years, and not heard a sermon? How can that be?" "Why," said he, "the truth is this: as soon as the preacher took his text I began to think of my business; and I had acquired such a habit of abstraction that while the preacher was preaching, I could trace out on the panel of the seat before me all the work of the past week; and, having reviewed that, could lay all my plans for the week to come. And the consequence is, that I do not know that I ever heard a sermon."

9379. HEART, Argument from the. An anatomist, as Dr. Paley observes, who understood the structure of the heart, might say beforehand that it would play; but he would expect, I think, from the complexity of its mechanism, and the delicacy of many of its parts, that it should always be liable to derangement, or that it would soon work itself out. Yet shall this wonderful machine go night and day, for eighty years together, at the rate of a hundred thousand strokes every twenty-four hours, having at every stroke a great resistance to overcome; and shall continue this action for this length of time, without disorder and without weariness. Each ventricle will at least contain one ounce of blood. The heart contracts four thousand times in one hour, from which it follows, that there passes through the heart every hour four thousand ounces or three hundred and fifty pounds of blood. Now the whole mass of blood is said to be about twenty-five pounds, so that a quantity of blood, equal to the whole mass of blood, passes through the heart fourteen times in one hour; which is about once every four minutes. When we reflect also upon the number of muscles, not fewer than four hundred and forty-six in the human body, known and named; how contiguous they lie to each other, as it were, over one another; crossing one another; sometimes embedding in one another; sometimes perforating one another; an arrangement which leaves to each its liberty, and its full play; this must necessarily require meditation and counsel, Dr. Nienentyt, in the Leipsic Transaction, reckons up a hundred muscles that are em ployed every time we breathe; yet we take in or let out our breath without reflecting what a work is hereby performed—what an apparatus is laid in of instruments for the service, and how many such contribute their assistance to the effect. Breathing with ease is a blessing of every moment; yet of all others, it is that which we possess with the least consciousness. A man in an asthma is the only man who knows how to esteem it. *Buck.*

9380. HEART, A Bad. A little Kansas boy, well up in theology, watched the servant as she prepared the potatoes for dinner. She took up a large and fine one, cut it in two and found it hollow and black inside with dry rot. Willie exclaimed, "Why, Maggie, that potato isn't a Christian." "What do you mean?' asked Maggie. "Don't you see it has a bad heart ?'" was Willie's reply.

9381. HEART, Beginning at the. It is observed of the spider that in the morning, before she seeks her prey, she mends her broken web, and in doing this she always begins in the middle. And shall those who call themselves Christians rise and pursue the callings and profits of the world, and yet be unconcerned about the broken webs of their lives, and especially of their hearts? Those who would have the cocks run with wholesome water should look well to the springs that supply them. The heart is the presence-chamber where the King of glory takes up his residence. That which is most worthy in us should be resigned to him who is most worthy of us. *Secker.*

9382. HEART, The Bolted. Christ comes to bless us, but we bolt our hearts against him. In Glasgow they were telling me of a scene that occurred when Dr. Arnot was preaching there. A woman was in great distress about her rent. She could not pay it, and so he took some money, and going to the house, went to the door and knocked. He listened, and thought he heard the footsteps of some one inside, and so he knocked louder. No one came, and he knocked still louder, but after waiting some time he went away disappointed. A few days afterward he met this lady on the street at Glasgow and told her that he heard she had been in great distress and he went around to help her, and the woman threw up both hands and said, "Why, Doctor, that was not you, was it? I was in the house all the time, and I thought it was the landlord coming around to get the rent, and I kept the door bolted." *Moody.*

9383. HEART, Care of the. The heart may be engaged in a little business, as much, if thou watch it not, as in many and great affairs. A man may drown in a little brook or pool, as well as in a great river, if he lie down and plunge himself into it, and put his head under water. Some care thou must have, that thou mayest not care. Those things that are thorns indeed, thou must make a hedge of them, to keep out those temptations that accompany sloth, and extreme want that waits on it; but let them be the hedge, suffer them not to grow within the garden. *Coleridge.*

9384. HEART, Carnal or Spiritual. In the heart of a carnal man all things lie in a confused order, heaven below, and earth at top; earth seems to him to be vast and infinite, but heaven a little inconsiderable spot. But in the heart of a child of God everything keeps its natural posture. There earth sinks, as being the dregs of his thoughts and cares, but heaven shines above, very bright and glorious; earth seems to him to be but a little spot, as indeed it is, which is seldom seen or noted by him, but heaven is an infinite boundless sea of mercy, which he is still looking into and admiring. *Hopkins.*

9385. HEART, Closet of the. Let me step into your heart, sir, and peep upon its furniture. My hands are pretty honest; you may trust me; and nothing will be found, I fear, to tempt a man to be a thief. Well, to be sure, what a filthy closet is here! Never swept, for certain, since you were christened. And what a fat idol stands skulking in the corner! A sweet heart-sin, I warrant it. How it simpers, and seems as pleasant as a right eye! Can you find a will to part with it, or strength to pluck it out? And supposing you a match for this self-denial, can you so command your heart as to hate the sin you do forsake? This is certainly required. Truth is called for in the inward parts. God will have sin not only cast aside, but cast away with abhorrence. So he speaks, "Ye that love the Lord hate evil." *John Berridge.*

9386. HEART, Color of the. If a bowl of dye be crimson, whatever you draw out of it will be red; if a coat be black, each thread you pull from it will be black. So, if our hearts are sinful, whatever issues from them will be more or less sinful. *Bolton.*

9387. HEART, Discipline of the. As smiths, better to work their iron, put it back frequently into the furnace, to be softened by the fire; and gardeners, to preserve a fine row of cedars and myrtles, frequently cut off the superfluous leaves and blossoms; so to preserve a soul in the fervor of virtue, it must often replace itself in the furnace of the exercises, and there, enlightened by God on its defects, divest itself of them and amend. *Ignatius.*

9388. HEART, Double. Rev. William Johnston, missionary in Africa, gives the following account: "One woman was much distressed and wept, and said that she had two hearts, which troubled her so much that she did not know what to do. One was the new heart, that told her all things that she had ever been doing. The same heart told her that she must go to Jesus Christ, and tell him all her sins, as she had heard at church; but her old heart told her, 'Never mind, God no save black man, but white man. How know he died for black man?' Her new heart said, 'Go, cry to him, and ask.' 'Old heart tell me, do my work first: fetch water, make fire, wash, and then go pray. When work done, then me forget to pray. I don't know what I do.' I read to her the seventh chapter of Romans, and showed that the Apostle Paul felt the same things, and spoke of two principles in man. When I came to the verse, 'O wretched man that I am! who shall deliver me from the body of this death?' she said, 'Ah, Massa, that me: me no know what to do.' I added the words of St. Paul, 'I thank God, through Jesus Christ;' and explained to her the love of Christ, how he died for sinners like her. She burst into tears; and has continued ever since, so far as I know, to follow her Saviour."

9389. HEART, Figures of the. Old Humphrey compares the heart to a lamp which must be filled and trimmed. To a ship whose hull and rigging must be cared for. "Have an eye to the crew, and take especial care what merchandise you put aboard; mind that you have plenty of ballast, and that you carry not too much sail. Mind you have a heavenly Pilot at the helm. Be prepared for storms, for you will have them, whether you are prepared for them or not. Encourage the hope of a fair voyage and a happy arrival at a heavenly haven. A besieged city, liable to attacks on all sides. Go round about it; tell the towers thereof, and mark well the bulwarks; while you defend one part, keep a good look-out on the other; while you build up the bastion here, let not the gateway be left defenceless there. Shells may be thrown over the walls, and sappers may mine a way under them. Be alive! be diligent! post your sentinels! have a watchword! take care whom you let in, and whom you allow to go out. Muster your troops, and see that there be no traitors among them. You have plenty to do, and plenty to attend to; keep, then, your heart with all diligence."

9390. HEART a Garden. Shall we compare the garden to the heart of man? the flowers to Christian virtues and graces, the weeds to corruptions? The weed springeth of itself, but the flower must be sown by the gardener, and tended by his care. Some flowers require more care than others; they are brought from countries afar off, from brighter skies and more genial soils, and require all the vigilance and tenderness of the gardener, lest they be blighted by our colder winds, or starved by our ungenial ground. *Salter.*

9391. HEART, Giving the. A little boy said to his mother, "What does it mean to give your heart to God?" The mother said, "Charlie, do you love anybody?" With a look of surprise the child answered, "I love you; I love my father, and my sister, and Henry." "Then you give your heart to your father, to Henry, to your sister, to me; and you show that love by doing all you can for us, and obeying our commands. And you ought," continued his mother, "to love God the best, because he gave you your father and mother, and he gave you his dear Son, Jesus Christ, who came from heaven to die that you may live forever."

9392. HEART, God in the. Naturalists tell us that the loadstone will not draw in the presence of the diamond. O sirs! whilst a man can eye God as his portion, all the pride, pomp, bravery, glory, and gallantry in the world will never be able to draw him from God. It is reported that when the tyrant Trajan commanded Ignatius to be ripped up and un boweled, they found Jesus Christ written upon his heart in characters of gold. Here was a heart worth gold indeed; Christ carried away his heart from all other things. *Brooks.*

9393. HEART, God's Temple. Be diligent. Sometimes speak to God, at other times hear him speak to you. Let him regulate your soul. Whom he hath made rich, none shall make poor. There can be no penury with him whose heart has once been enriched with celestial bounty. Roofs arched with gold, and palaces adorned with marble, are vile in comparison with that house which the Lord has chosen to be his temple, in which the Holy Ghost dwells. Illuminate this house with the light of righteousness. Its ornaments shall never fade, and it shall dwell hereafter in spotless beauty and eternal majesty. *St. Cyprian.*

9394. HEART, Greed of the. The heart of a man is a short word, a small substance, scarce enough to give a kite a meal; yet great in capacity, yea, so indefinite in desire that the round globe of the world cannot fill the three corners of it, when it desires more, and cries "Give, give!" I will set it over to the Infinite Good, where the more it hath it may desire more, and see more to be desired. *Bishop Hall.*

9395. HEART a Hive. Take your place beside a hive of bees in a summer day at noon, and watch the busy traffickers. The outward-bound brush quickly past the heavy-laden in comers in the narrow passage. They flow like two opposite streams of water in the same channel, without impeding each other's motions. Every one is in haste: none tarries for a neighbor. Such a hive is a human heart, and the swarm of winged thoughts which harbor there maintain an intercourse with all the world in constant circulation, while the man sits among the worshipers still, and upright and steady as a bee-hive upon its pedestal. The thoughts that issue from their home in that human heart, bold like robbers in the dark, overleap the fences of holiness, suck at will every flower that they reckon sweet, and return to deposit their gatherings in the owner's cup. The eyes of the Lord are there, beholding the evil. *Arnot.*

9396. HEART, Idolatry in the. A man may hang the Decalogue upon the walls of his home, and still be an idolater—even as many a one has the Lord's Prayer, for an ornament, on the walls of his chamber, who yet forgets to pray, both at evening and morning. The thing to be done is, to hang the Decalogue on the inner walls of the heart. *Chicago Pulpit.*

9397. HEART, Keeping the. "Keep thy heart with all diligence, for out of it are the issues of life." As good housekeeping is essential to domestic comfort, so good heart-keeping is essential to healthful and happy piety. *Cuyler.*

9398. HEART, Mechanism of the. With what wonderful and inimitable art is that musculous body constructed, which is situated in the cav lty of the breast, and is called the heart? Its form is something like an obtuse pyramid; and it is so placed that the point inclines a little to the left side. Its substance appears to be a series of fleshy fibres interwoven with infinite art, in such a manner that the external fibres extend from the left side of the heart towards the right, and the internal fibres from the right side towards the left. This intestine has within it two cavities, called ventricles, separated from one another by a fleshy partition. In that there is a vein which conducts the blood of the upper parts of the body into the right ventricle of the heart; another which brings back the blood from the lower parts into that same cavity; an artery which sends it from thence into the lungs; another vein through which it runs from the lungs into the left ventricle, from whence it is sent over the whole body through the great artery. On the one side of the right ventricle is a sort of musculous bag, which is called the auricle of the heart, and which receives the blood before it has entered the right ventricle. Another auricle, not less useful, hangs at the left ventricle, that the blood may stop there during a new contraction. All the blood passes through the heart. It continually goes in and out; and by the contraction of this intestine, it is sent into every part of the human body, and circulates through all the veins. When even all the other members of the body are at rest, the heart is in perpetual motion, from the first moment of life to the last. In a state of health, the heart contracts itself at least sixty times in a minute, and consequently 3,600 times in an hour; and at each beating of the pulse it throws out about two ounces of blood. The force it must use to do so is not small. For in order to throw out the blood, so that it should reach only as far as two feet in the great artery, the heart must resist a weight of 12,600 pounds; and consequently in twenty-four hours, a resistance of 224,000,000 pounds weight. All these things are equally admirable and incomprehensible. They lead us to cry out with wonder and astonishment, How great is our divine Creator! Who can describe his glory!   *Sturm.*

9399. HEART, Morals of the. Moral life is no creation of moral phrases. The words that are truly vital powers for good or evil are only those which, as Pindar says, "The tongue draws up from the deep heart."   *Whipple.*

9400. HEART, Parable of the. I held in my hand a little dry tree, an infant hemlock. Had it lived a century it might have towered up above all the forest, and held up its head in majesty. But it grew on a sort of bog, and a muskrat, digging his hole under it, bit off its roots, and it was dead. It was full of limbs and knots and gnarls, and I felt curious to know how it happened that it was so. "Poor fellow! If you had all these limbs and knots to support, I don't wonder you died." "And with my roots, which were my mouths with which to feed, all cut off, too." "Yes, but where do all these ugly limbs come from?"

said I. "Just where all ugly things come from," said he. "I am pretty much like you men. Find out where my limbs come from, and you will find where all human sins come from." "I'll take you at your word, sir." So I took out my knife, and peeled off all the bark. But the limbs and the knots were left. "You must go deeper than that, sir." So I began to split and take off layer of wood after layer. But all the knots were there. "Deeper still," said the dry stick. Then I split it all off, and, separating it, the heart was laid bare; it looked like a small rod about six feet long, and perhaps an inch through at the large ends. Ah! and I was now surprised to see that every limb and knot and gnarl started in the heart. Every one was there, and every one grew out of the heart. The germ or the starting-point of each one was the center of the heart.   *Anon.*

9401. HEART, Purged. The heart must be made a temple to God, wherein sacrifices do ascend; but, that they may be accepted, it must be purged of idols, nothing left in any corner, though never so secret, to stir the jealousy of our God, who sees through all. Oh, happy that heart that is, as Jacob's house, purged, in which no more idols are to be found, but the holy God dwelling there alone as in his holy temple!   *Leighton.*

9402. HEART, Purity of. A little girl who had been reading the beatitudes, was asked which she should desire most to possess. She replied, "I would rather be pure in heart." On being asked the reason of her preference, she answered to this effect: "Sir, if I could but obtain a pure heart, I should then possess all the other good qualities spoken of in this chapter."

9403. HEART, Purifying our Own. If a housewife wants her parlor to be thoroughly cleansed that the most critical visitor will find nothing but to approve, she opens all the blinds and lets the sunlight stream in. In this glare of light she sweeps, and dusts, and scrubs, and polishes. No speck of dust, no cobweb, no thread or scrap escapes her observation. If any nooks or hiding-places of dust remain unvisited, because her time or strength or courage fails, she at least knows of them, and purposes to attend to them at some future time. The light in which her visitors see the room, however strong, is less searching than that to which the housekeeper herself has already exposed it. However severe the judgments they pass, her own have been more intolerant. See, under this homely figure, the Christian purifying his heart in the sight of God. He floods, with the light of God's perfect law, the inner chambers of his life. Before his all-seeing Father he cleanses and purifies himself within.   *Salter.*

9404. HEART, Responsibility of the. It is reported that Apollodorus in a dream beheld himself flayed by the Scythians and then boiled, and that his heart, speaking to him out of the kettle, uttered these words, "I am the cause of thy suffering all this."

9405. HEART, Softening the. A Syrian anchor

ite went to Poemen, lamenting the hardness of his heart. "Read the word of God," said he, "the drop of a fountain pierces the stone, and the gentle word falling softly, day by day, on the dead, hard heart after awhile infallibly melts it."

9406. HEART, Spiritual Disease of the. Some malady which you do not understand troubles and alarms you. The physician is called. Thinking that the illness proceeds from a certain inflammatory process on a portion of your skin, you anxiously direct his attention to the spot. Silently, but sympathizingly, he looks at the place where you have bidden him look, and because you have bidden him look there, but soon he turns away. He is busy with an instrument on another part of your body. He presses his trumpet tube gently to your breast, and listens for the pulsations which faintly but distinctly pass through. He looks and listens there, and saddens as he looks. You again direct attention to the cutaneous eruption which annoys you. He sighs and sits silent. When you reiterate your request that something should be done for the external eruption, he gently shakes his head, and answers not a word. From this silence you would learn the truth at last; you would not miss its meaning long. O, miss not the meaning of the Lord when he points to the seat of the soul's disease: "Ye will not come." These, his enemies, dwell in your heart. *W. Arnot.*

9407. HEART, Stability of. If the world be in the middle of the heart, it will be often shaken, for all there is continual motion and change; but God in it keeps it stable. Labor, therefore, to get God into your hearts, residing in the midst of them; and then, in the midst of all conditions, they shall not move. *Leighton.*

9408. HEART, Stony. A little girl begged of her father to give her just three yards of ground; she wanted a little garden which should be her own, her very own. Well, he gave her just that little piece of ground; and O, how pleased she was! She raked it smooth and dropped in some seeds, and ere long they sprung up; but they soon withered away. She could not get them to grow. And she asked her father to come and look at her garden; and when he came, he knew it was like the stony ground in the scripture parable—that there was no depth of earth. Just under the soil was a stone slab which had somehow been covered over. Very much against her will he swept away all that superincumbent little bit of soil—flowers, roots, and every thing; and then he struck hard at the slab, broke it in pieces, and took it away, and then, after digging deeply into the soil, he made it smooth and straight. And then the seed was sown, and the seed took root. Ah! he had taken the stone out. Sometimes you want the garden of the heart to bring forth—but, alas! there are stones in it. You may try to plant the truth, but it won't grow; it cannot, till the great Father takes the stone out of the heart. Well, he can do it; and then the root will strike, and the flowers will bloom; and you

that want your children to be virtuous must teach them to ask, as you ask for them, that the Father may take the stone out of the heart. *S. Coley.*

9409. HEART, Testing the. Stanhurst draws a lesson from the method of determining the rightful owner of certain debatable lands between England and Ireland. Toads or snakes were put upon the disputed territory, and, if they lived, it was concluded the lands belonged to England; if they died, to Ireland. So, if venomous passions or lusts live in the heart, it belongs to Satan, and its city is hell; but if they die, so that there is no life in them, it belongs to Christ, and its inheritance shall be a mansion in heaven.

9410. HEART, Treasures of the. The devil knows that if there be any good treasure, it is in our hearts; and he would gladly have the key of these cabinets that he might rob us of our jewels. A heart which is sanctified is better than a tongue that is silvered. He that gives only the skin of worship to God receives only the shell of comfort from God. It is not the bare touching of the strings that makes an harmonious tune. A spiritual man may pray carnally, but a carnal man cannot pray spiritually. If God's mercies do not eat out the heart of our sins, our sins will soon eat out the heart of our duties. A work that is heartless is a work that is fruitless. God cares not for the crazy cabinet, but for the precious jewel. *Brooke.*

9411. HEART, Unfruitfulness of the. There are some soils so shallow, and wanting in mould, and have so little depth, that while they are suited to bring forth flowers, bear but an imperfect crop of fruit. So there is much ground in the hearts of many, which, while it can bring forth the glittering leaves of a showy profession, yet bears no good fruit, or very sparingly. *Salter.*

9412. HEART, War in the. A man that is divided between piety and sin is like one that lives on the confines of two mighty contending states; his heart is a constant seat of war, and he is sometimes under the dominion of virtue, and sometimes under the tyranny of vice. *Jeremiah Seed.*

9413. HEARTS, Broken. I believe in broken hearts and the possibility of dying of disappointed love. I do not, however, consider it a malady often fatal to my own sex; but I firmly believe that it withers down many a lovely woman into an early grave. Man is the creature of interest and ambition. His nature leads him forth into the struggle and bustle of the world. Love is but the embellishment of his early life, or a song piped in the intervals of the acts. He seeks for fame, for fortune, for space in the world's thought, and dominion over his fellow-men. But a woman's whole life is a history of the affections. The heart is her world: it is there her ambition strives for empire; it is there her avarice seeks for hidden treasures. She sends forth her sympathies on adventure; she embarks her whole soul in the traffic of affection; and if shipwrecked, her case is hopeless—for it is a bankruptcy of the heart.   *W. Irving.*

9414. HEAT, Effects of. The application of heat to the various branches of the mechanical and chemical arts has, within a few years, effected a greater change in the condition of man than had been accomplished in any equal period of his existence. Armed by the expansion and condensation of fluids, with a power equal to that of the lightning itself, conquering time and space, he flies over plains, and travels on paths cut by human industry even through mountains, with a velocity and smoothness more like planetary than terrestrial motion; he crosses the deep in opposition to wind and tide; he makes the elements of air and water the carriers of warmth, not only to banish winter from his home, but to adorn it, even during the snow-storm, with the blossoms of spring; and, like a magician, he raises from the gloomy and deep abyss of the mine the spirit of light, to dispel the midnight darkness.   *Somerville.*

9415. HEATHEN, Exposure of the. Suppose a precipice, at the foot of which the deep ocean is foaming; and suppose a procession, consisting of men, women and children, moving on, night and day, two abreast, and at the rate of two miles a hour; and suppose that when they reached the precipice, they threw themselves over, and were engulfed in the devouring waters; and suppose that you inhabited a cottage near the precipice, and heard the ceaseless scream, and shriek, and loud agony of those perishing amid the billows—could you dwell in that house? Would it be possible to remain quiet? Would you not rush forth and endeavor to arouse the neighborhood to prevent those deluded persons from destroying themselves?   *Dr. Somerville.*

9416. HEATHENISM, Bloody Rites of. Divi, as the Hindus believe, is the goddess who thirsts for blood; and hence at her annual *mela* much profit is supposed to be gained by making her blood-offerings. The whole process of worship and sacrifice is disgusting in the extreme; and as we have looked upon it during the past fortnight, our hearts have been greatly moved, and we have longed for the power to vividly portray the scene before the church at home. Sheep, goats, lambs, pigs and even chickens are brought and slaughtered to propitiate the goddess. The deluded devotee brings his offering, and after washing it and himself in a pool of dirty water, he presents himself before the temple, where stand two butchers (priests they can hardly be called), with bloody hands and knives. A rope is slipped over the head of the struggling victim, the butcher's knife suddenly descends, and in an instant the head is off, and falls to the ground. The man who brings the offering quickly gathers up the bleeding head, and rushes with it into the temple, to sprinkle with blood the image of the goddess. A relative or friend takes up the quivering body and carries it away, to be eaten by the family. Other members of the family buy cocoanuts, sweet-

meats, flowers, etc., and present these before the goddess. Others bring young pigs, and holding them by the hind legs, they dash out their brains on a certain stone, and then smear with the blood another idol near at hand This horrible work is accompanied by the beating of drums, ringing of bells, and singing, and continues with great enthusiasm from sunrise to sunset.   *B. H. Badley.*

9417. HEATHENISM, Cruelty of. Bernier relates some incidents of the barbarous custom in India, (now prohibited), of widows immolating themselves on the funeral pile of their husbands. He says, "I have seen some of these victims who, at the sight of the fire and the pile, would have gone back when it was unhappily too late; those demons, the attendant Brahmins, with their great sticks, astound them, and sometimes even thrust them into the fire, as I once saw them act to a young woman who retreated five or six paces from the pile; perceiving her much disturbed, they absolutely forced her into the flames. For my own part, I have often been so enraged at these Brahmins, that if I dared I could have strangled them. I remember, among other occasions, that at Lahore I once saw a very handsome and very young woman burnt, not more, I believe, than twelve years of age. This poor, unhappy creature appeared more dead than alive when she came near the pile, and shook and wept bitterly; upon which three or four of these executioners, the Brahmins, together with an old hag who held her under the arm, pushed her forward, and made her sit down upon the wood; and lest she should run away, they tied her hands and legs, and so burnt her alive."

9418. HEAVEN, Adjustment in. An aged Christian paused to rest himself from a heavy load on a warm summer day. An acquaintance accosted him as a splendid carriage rolled past, in which a haughty man rode, whose whole appearance bespoke a life of luxurious ease. "What do you think of the providence of which you sometimes speak?" said the acquaintance. "You know that that is a wicked man; yet he spreads himself like a green bay-tree. His eyes stand out with fatness; he is not plagued as other men; while you, believing that all the silver and gold is the Lord's, serving him and trusting in his providence, and toiling and sweating in your old age, get little more than bread and water. How can you reconcile this with a just providence?" The aged man looked at the questioner with amazement, and, with the greatest earnestness, replied: "Couple heaven with it! couple heaven with it, and then?"

9419. HEAVEN, Admittance to. At heaven's gate there stands an angel, with charge to admit none but those who in their countenances bear the same features as the Lord of the place. Here comes a monarch with a crown upon his head. The angel pays him no respect, but reminds him that the diadems of earth have no value in heaven. A company of eminent men advance dressed in robes of state, and others

adorned with the gowns of learning, but to these no deference is rendered, for their faces are very unlike the Crucified. A maiden comes forward, fair and comely, but the celestial watcher sees not in that sparkling eye and ruddy cheek the beauty for which he is looking. A man of renown cometh up heralded by fame, and preceded by the admiring clamor of mankind; but the angel saith, "Such applause may please the sons of men, but thou hast no right to enter here." But free admittance is always given to those who in holiness are made like their Lord. Poor they may have been; illiterate they may have been; but the angel as he looks at them smiles a welcome as he says, "It is Christ again; a transcript of the holy child Jesus. Come in, come in; eternal glory thou shalt win. Thou shalt sit in heaven with Christ, for thou art like him."
Spurgeon.

9420. HEAVEN, All White in. A minister asked a colored boy, aged eleven years, "Do you really believe that there are any black children in heaven?" He reflected a moment, then answered, "No, Massa, I 'specs dey isn't." "Well, then, you can't go there, can you?" "Reckon I kin, massa." "But how can you go there when there are no black children there?" "'Kase dey is all white." "But how's that?" "Oh, dey is all washed white in de blood of de Lamb!" It was a child's faith, true to fact, whatever may be thought of its form.

9421. HEAVEN, Biblical Figures of. *A paradise restored,* 2 Cor. 12: 2, 4; Rev. 2: 7; where there will be more than Eden's beauty and Eden's peace, and no serpent creeping in to steal away sweet happiness. *A city,* Heb. 11: 16; 13: 14; a "city of God," without griefs or graves, or sins or sorrows; whose inhabitants no census has ever numbered; whose walls are salvation, and whose gates are praise. *A country*—a "better country—that is, an heavenly" (literally, a Fatherland), Heb. 11: 16; the meeting-place of those who were redeemed from among men unto God, and who worship him with holy angels in sinless happiness. *A temple,* Rev. 3: 12; 7: 15; bright with the Divine glory, filled with the Divine presence. *A garner,* Matt. 3: 12. *A kingdom*—"the kingdom of Christ and of God," Eph. 5: 5; "the everlasting kingdom of our Lord and Saviour Jesus Christ," 2 Pet. 1: 11. *An inheritance* "incorruptible, undefiled, and that fadeth not away," 1 Pet. 1: 4; "the inheritance of the saints in light," Col. 1: 12. *"The rest* that remaineth for the people of God," Heb. 4: 9 ("the keeping of a Sabbath," marg.); the rest from care and sin and sorrow, from labor and trouble, weakness and want. *God's dwelling-place,* 1 Kings 8: 30; Matt. 6: 9. *God's throne,* Isa. 66: 1; 1 Kings 8: 27; Acts 17: 24. The *"Father's house"* of "many mansions," prepared for the redeemed by Christ, John 14: 2. *Bowes.*

9422. HEAVEN: Brevities. Heaven's gates are wide enough to admit of many sinners, but too narrow to admit of any sin.—*Howels.*——

The earth is our workhouse, but heaven is our storehouse. This is a place to run in, and that is a place to rest in.—*Secker.*——The gates of heaven are shut upon workers and open to believers; shut to those who come with money in their hands, but open to those who are content to enter without paying anything for their entrance.—*J. Simpson.*——It is impossible to have a lively hope in another life, and yet be deeply immersed in the enjoyments of this.
Atterbury.

9423. HEAVEN, Care for. Anaxagoras being accused of not studying politics for his country's good replied, "I have a great care of my country," pointing up to heaven. So a Christian looks upon heaven as his country, and considers himself as a stranger and a pilgrim here on earth; nor will his heavenly-mindedness detract from his patriotism; for he is the best friend to order and happiness on earth, whose affections are most set on things in heaven. *Anon.*

9424. HEAVEN, Child's Thought of. A mother overheard her little four-year-old boy soliloquizing thus about getting to heaven: "Heaven is a great way off. I wonder how I can get there. Oh, I know how! I will get a ladder, and put it on the top of a great big tree. Then I'll climb up and knock at the door of heaven. Then God will open the door and say, 'Who is there?' And I'll say, 'It's me, little Frankie.' Then God will open the door and say, 'Come in, little Frankie.'"
S. T. Treasury.

9425. HEAVEN, Christians in. I have read of Ingo, an ancient king of the Draves, who making a stately feast, appointed his nobles, at that time pagans, to sit in the hall below, and commanded certain poor Christians to be brought up into his presence-chamber, to sit with him at his table, to eat and drink of his kingly cheer; at which many wondering, he said, "He accounted Christians, though never so poor, a greater ornament to his table, and more worthy of his company, than the greatest peers unconverted to the Christian faith; for when these might be thrust down to hell, those might be his consorts and fellow-princes in heaven." "Who hath raised us up," saith the apostle, "and made us sit together in heavenly places in Christ Jesus." *Brooks.*

9426. HEAVEN, Climbing up to. The Mohammedans say that Nimrod built a tower in Babel to the height of about ten thousand feet, nearly one-third of a mile, purposing to ascend to heaven and wage war upon its inhabitants. God defeated the plan by sending a whirlwind and an earthquake, which utterly overthrew the tower. Others say he built the tower that he might visit Abraham's God in heaven, whom, for a time, he professed to serve. When the tower was overthrown, his desire to scale heaven continuing, he entered a chest, and was borne by four monstrous birds through the air till they wearied, and dropped him upon the top of a mountain. So fail all plans to gain heaven, except through Christ.

9427. HEAVEN, Company of. If the mere con

ception of the reunion of good men in a future state infused a momentary rapture into the mind of Tully—if an airy speculation, for there is reason to fear it had little hold on his convictions, could inspire him with such delight—what may we be expected to feel who are assured of such an event by the true sayings of God! How should we rejoice in the prospect, the certainty rather, of spending a blissful eternity with those whom we loved on earth; of seeing them emerge from the ruins of the tomb and the deeper ruins of the fall, not only uninjured, but refined and perfected, "with every tear wiped from their eyes," standing before the throne of God and the Lamb in white robes, and palms in their hands, crying with a loud voice, Salvation to God that sitteth upon the throne, and to the Lamb forever and ever! What delight will it afford to renew the sweet counsel we have taken together, to recount the toils of combat and the labor of the way, and to approach, not the house, but the throne, of God in company, in order to join in the symphonies of heavenly voices, and lose ourselves amid the splendor and fruitions of the beatific vision!
Robert Hall.

9428. HEAVEN, Compensations of. Think how completely all the griefs of this mortal life will be compensated by one age, for instance, of the felicities beyond the grave; and then think that one age multiplied ten thousand times is not so much to eternity as one grain of sand is to the whole material universe. Think what a state it will be to be growing happier and happier still as ages pass away, and yet leave something still happier to come!
John Foster.

9429. HEAVEN, Completeness in. There are many graces for which we may not cease hourly to sue, graces which are in bestowing always, but never come to be fully had in this present life; and therefore, when all things here have an end, endless thanks must have their beginning in a state which bringeth the full and final satisfaction of all such perpetual desires.
Hooker.

9430. HEAVEN, Contending for. The real business in hand for Christians is not heaven, but holiness. The issue may be left in the Leader's hands: the duty of the soldiers is to stand where they are placed, and strike as long as they see a foe. Until the trumpet shall sound, calling the weary to rest, our part is to fight. Woe to the deceiver who fraternizes with the enemy, or strikes with half his force a feeble blow! The kingdom of heaven is within you; within you, therefore, its battles must be fought and its victories won. Strike, and spare not for their crying. It is not a languid expectation of an easy heaven; it is a battle that is before us to-day. He is the best soldier in the warfare who hates most his Sovereign's enemy and his own. Polluting lust is the spark that kindles hell: there is no other way of being saved from that burning than by stamping out the embers of sin that lie hidden in the ashes of your own heart.

"The God of peace shall bruise Satan under your feet shortly." God will subdue the adversary; but he will subdue him under your own feet.
Arnot.

9431. HEAVEN, Denominations in. A young convert dreamed that he was translated to heaven. He thought Jesus Christ questioned each one as to their ecclesiastical position when on earth. One was an Episcopalian, another a Baptist, another a Presbyterian. Places were assigned to each denominationally. At last a poor Indian came trembling; not knowing the theological differences of his brethren, he was afraid there was no place assigned for him. When asked what he was, he replied, "I am a Christian, and love the Lord Jesus with all my heart." "Then," said the Saviour, "you may walk all about heaven, hither and thither, just as you please."

9432. HEAVEN, Despised. As a man that comes into America, and sees the natives regard more a piece of glass, or an old knife, than a piece of gold, may think, Surely these people never heard of the worth of gold, or else they would not exchange it for toys; so a man that looked only upon the lives of most men, and did not hear their contrary confessions, would think either these men never heard of heaven, or else they never heard of its excellency and glory. As the Indians who live among the golden mines do little regard it, but are weary of the daily toil of getting it, when other nations will compass the world, and venture their lives, and sail through storms and waves to get it; so we that live where the gospel groweth, where heaven is urged upon us at our doors, and the manna falls upon our tents, do little regard it, and wish these mines of gold were further from us, that we might not be put upon the toil of getting it, when some that want it would be glad of it upon harder terms.
Salter.

9433. HEAVEN, Discoveries of. A man on the summit of a lofty mountain commands a wider landscape, and sees things that on the plains below would have been quite invisible. So many things unknown, incomprehensible to us on the plains of earth, will be all visible on the mount of heaven.
Dr. Guthrie.

9434. HEAVEN Disregarded. There in a room was a man that could look no way but downward, with a muck-rake in his hand. There stood also One over his head with a crown in his hand, and proffered him that crown for his muck-rake; but the man did neither look up nor regard, but raked to himself the straws, the small sticks, and dust of the floor. It is to show that heaven is but a fable to some, and that things here are counted the only things substantial.
Bunyan.

9435. HEAVEN, Distance to. Approaching a village far up on the side of the Alps, our party saw its buildings with remarkable distinctness, and were able to count the panes of glass in a window of the church. We thought the distance very short, and expected to reach it in a quarter of an hour at most. We walked on without getting perceptibly nearer, realizing more and more how we had misjudged the distance. The atmosphere was clearer and more rarefied than we were accustomed to. We gained it at last by perseverance, and found sweet rest after our toil. So sometimes we dwell in high altitudes of grace; heaven seems very near, and the hills of Beulah are in full view. At other times the clouds and fogs, through suffering and temptation, cut off our vision. We are just as near heaven in the one experience as the other, and just as sure of gaining it, if our feet are in the path of life.

9436. HEAVEN, Doing Business for. Heaven is one of our offices, and there is much business to be despatched in its beautiful courts; business for the interests of Jesus, business which he has at heart, and, therefore, which it behoves us to have in hand.   *F. W. Faber.*

9437. HEAVEN, Earth and. What is an earthly manor compared to an heavenly mansion? As carnal things seem small to a spiritual man, so spiritual things appear small to a carnal man. There is no moving after things beyond the sphere of our own knowledge. Heaven is to the worldling as a mine of gold covered with earth and rubbish; or as a bed of pearl enclosed in a heap of sand. But if he had the eyes of an eagle to see it, he would wish for the wings of an eagle to soar unto it. There is no more comparison to be made between heaven and earth, than there is between a piece of rusty iron and refined gold. It is the expectation of a future glorious heritage, which is the Jacob's staff of saints, with which they walk through this dark pilgrimage.
Secker.

9438. HEAVEN, Emblems of. As opposed to sin, and its bitter, baleful consequences, heaven is set forth in the Bible through the emblems of everything we cherish as most dear and long for as most desirable. It is painted in colors that glow upon the canvas. Raise your eyes to the new Jerusalem. Gold paves its streets, and around its secure and blissful homes rise walls of jasper. Earth holds no such city; the depths of ocean no such pearls as form its gates. No storms sweep its glassy sea; no winter strips its trees; no thunders shake its serene and cloudless sky. Day there never darkens into night. Harps and palms are in the hands, while crowns of glory flash and blaze upon the heads of its sinless and white-robed inhabitants. From this distant and stormy orb, as the dove eyed the ark, faith gazes on the glorious vision, and weary of the strife, longing to be gone, cries, "O that I had wings like a dove! for then would I fly away and be at rest."   *Guthrie.*

9439. HEAVEN, Enduring for. I have always been peculiarly subject to sea-sickness. When I was going abroad, and all the wonders of the continent were dazzling my imagination, I used to lie in my berth scarcely able to stir, wilted and worthless. I knew there were ten days between New York and Liverpool; and I used to say to myself: "Well, are you willing to take these ten days of nausea and universal disgust for the sake of three months of exqui-

site joy which you are going to have on the continent?" I said: "This is about as bad as anything can well be in this world; but for the sake of that which is beyond it, I will take even this." Returning, we had a passage of seventeen days. We came with a water-logged steamship. She was loaded down deeper by many feet than she should have been. It was stormy from shore to shore, without a single fair day. But the place to which we were going was my home; there was my family; there was my church; there were my friends, who were as dear to me as my own life. And I lay perfectly happy in the midst of sickness and nausea. All that the boat could do to me could not keep down the exultation and joy which rose up in me. For every single hour was carrying me nearer and nearer to the spot where was all that I loved in the world. It was deep, dark midnight when we ran into Halifax. I could see nothing. Yet the moment we came into still water, I rose from my berth and got upon deck. And as I sat near the smoke stack, while they were unloading the cargo upon the wharf, I saw the shadow of a person apparently going backward and forward near me. At last the thought occurred to me, "Am I watched?" Just then the person addressed me, saying: "Is this Mr. Beecher?" "It is," I replied. "I have a telegram for you from your wife." I had not realized that I had struck the continent where my family were. There in the middle of the night and in darkness, the intelligence that I had a telegram from home—I cannot tell you what thrill it sent through me. We are all sailing home; and by and by, when we are not thinking of it, some shadowy thing (men call it death), at midnight, will pass by, and will call us by name, and will say: "I have a message for you from home. God waits for you." It is but a hand-breadth. And on the stormy sea there are men who stop and think of discomforts when home and heart are calling for them. Are they worthy of anything but pity who are not able to bear the hardships of the voyage when they are going home? It will not be long before you, and I, and every one of us, will hear the messenger sent to bring us back to heaven.   *Beecher.*

9440. HEAVEN, Excellence of. If earth that is provided for mortality, and is possessed by the Maker's enemies, has so much pleasure in it, that worldings think it worth the account of their heaven, what must heaven needs be that is provided for God himself and his friends? How can it be less in weight than God is above his creatures, and God's friends are better than his enemies?   *Bp. Hall.*

9441. HEAVEN, Foretaste of. If we really live under the hope of future happiness, we shall taste it by way of anticipation and forethought; an image of it will meet our minds often, and stay there, as all pleasing expectations do.
Atterbury.

9442. HEAVEN, Gate Open to. The death of the Rev. Thomas Collins' mother, was beautifully tranquil. He says, "Nearly the last thing she did was to repeat the Hundreth Psalm, a favorite with her. Her cough compelled a pause at the words, 'O go your way into his gates with thanksgiving.' She never finished the recitation, and was only able to add:—'His gates—his gates.—Go into them;—yes, I may, for they are open—wide open to me; and have been for some time.' And so, without another word, speedily and peacefully she passed those heavenly portals which her faith had gazed upon."

9443. HEAVEN, a Glorious Change. Palmer, of Reading, England, being condemned to die, in Queen Mary's time, was exhorted to recant, and among other things a friend said to him, "Take pity on thy golden years and pleasant flowers of youth, before it be too late." His reply was, "Sir, I long for those springing flowers which shall never fade away." When he was in the midst of the flames he exhorted his companions to constancy, saying, "We shall not end our lives in the fire, but make a change for a better life; yea, for coals we shall receive pearls."

9444. HEAVEN, Glory in. Fulgentius visited Rome, and observed the glory of the Roman nobility, the triumphant pomp of King Theodoric, and the universal splendor and gayety of that city. It raised his thoughts to heavenly joys, and he said to some of his friends that accompanied him, "How beautiful must the celestial Jerusalem be, since terrestrial Rome is so glittering! If such honor be given to lovers of vanity, what glory shall be imparted to the saints, who are lovers and followers of truth!"

9445. HEAVEN, Glory of. To the eye of man the sun appears a pure light, a mass of unmingled glory. Were we to ascend with a continual flight towards this luminary, and could we, like the eagle, gaze upon this lustre, we should in our progress behold its splendor become every moment more intense. As we rose through the heavens, we should see a little orb changing gradually unto a great world; and as we advanced nearer and nearer, should behold it expanding every way, until all that was before us became an universe of excessive and immeasurable glory. Thus the heavenly inhabitant will, at the commencement of his happy existence, see the divine system filled with magnificence and splendor and arrayed in beauty; and, as he advances onwards through the successive periods of duration, will behold all things more and more luminous, transporting, and sun-like for ever.　　　　　*Dr. Dwight.*

9446. HEAVEN, No Graves in. A little child filled the heart of a grieving mourner with joy, by saying as she pointed to heaven, "There are no graves there."

9447. HEAVEN, God's House. This glorious world is "the house of God," or the peculiar and favorite place of his residence; the place where those manifestations of himself are seen, which he is pleased to make, as the most special displays of his presence and character. Present in all other places, he is peculiarly present here. It is also "the throne of God," the seat of universal and endless dominion; where the Divine authority is peculiarly exercised and made known, and the splendor of the Divine government exhibited with singular effulgence and glory. It is the residence of his most favored creatures; of the saints, who are redeemed by the blood of his Son; and of the angels, who, innumerable in multitude, "stand round about his throne." It is the everlasting seat of consummate holiness or virtue; where that Divine principle shines without alloy, flourishes in immortal youth, and reigns and triumphs with eternal glory. It is the place in which are seen all the finishings of Divine workmanship, and in which the beauty and greatness of the Infinite Mind, and the endless diversities of omniscient skill, appear in all their most exquisite forms, and in the last degrees of refinement and perfection. It is the centre of all Divine communication; the city, in which all the paths of Providence terminate; the ocean, from which all the streams of Infinite Wisdom and Goodness proceed, and into which they return, to flow again and forever. It is the theatre in which an eternal providence of progressive knowledge, power, and love, rendered daily more and more beautiful and amiable, wonderful and majestic, is begun and carried on through ages, which will never approach towards an end. It is the place where all the works of God are studied and understood, through an eternal progress of knowledge; where all the diversities of virtuous intelligence, all the forms and hues of moral beauty, brighten in an unceasing gradation; and where gratitude, love, enjoyment, and praise, resound day and night in a more and more perfect harmony throughout the immensity of duration.　　　　　*Dwight.*

9448. HEAVEN, Going to. A gentleman said to an old negro slave, "You are an old man; will you not die soon?" "Yes, massa." "Well, where are you going?" "To the good land." "What makes you think so?" "Well, massa, I can't 'zactly 'splain; but somehow, as I comes nearer to death, Jesus and I get nearer and nearer together."

9449. HEAVEN, Happiness in. What matters it if thou art not happy on earth, provided thou art so in heaven? Heaven may have happiness as utterly unknown to us as the gift of vision would be to a man born blind. If we consider the inlets of pleasure from five senses only, we may be sure that the same Being who created us could have given us five hundred if he pleased. Mutual love, pure and exalted, founded on charms both mental and corporeal, as it constitutes the highest happiness on earth, may, for anything we know to the contrary, also form the lowest happiness of heaven. And it would appear consonant with the administration of Providence in other matters that there should be a link between heaven and earth; for in all cases a chasm seems to be purposely avoided; "*prudento Deo.*" Thus the material world has its links, by which it is made to shake hands, as it were, with the veg etable—the vegetable with the animal, the animal with the intellectual, and the intellectual with what we may be allowed to hope of the angelic. *Colton.*

9450. HEAVEN, Hell and. That which makes hell so full of horror, is, that it is below all hopes; and that which makes heaven so full of splendor, is, that it is above all fears. The one is a night without the return of day; the other is a day free from the approach of night. *Secker.*

9451. HEAVEN, Holiness our Qualification for. From justification arises our title to heaven; from sanctification arises our meetness for it. A king's son is heir-apparent to his father's crown. We will suppose the young prince to be educated with all the advantages, and to be possessor of all the attainments, that are necessary to constitute a complete monarch. His accomplishments, however great, do not entitle him to the kingdom; they only qualify him for it: so the holiness and obedience of the saints are no part of that right on which their claim to glory is founded, or for which it is given; but a part of that spiritual education, whereby they are fitted and made meet to inherit "the kingdom prepared for them from the foundation of the world." Though the mariner see not the pole-star, yet the needle of the compass that points to it tells him which way he sails. Thus the heart that is touched with the loadstone of divine love, trembling with godly fear, and yet still looking towards God by fixed believing, points at the love of election, and tells the soul that its course is heavenward, towards the haven of eternal rest. *Salter.*

9452. HEAVEN, Honors of. From the Bible I take it that the redeemed of earth will somehow get a little nearer to the great white throne than any other inhabitants of that country. It seems to me our relationship is a little different, in the wonderful mercy of God. I think the time will come when the redeemed who have been steadfast, and maintained their fealty to God and to the great Captain of their salvation, rising from their dusty graves, and called up into that eternal world, will hear him say to Gabriel, Michael, and all the host of heaven, "Fall back! fall back!" And he that sitteth upon the throne, and is King of kings and Lord of lords, will exclaim, "Come, ye blessed of my father, inherit the kingdom prepared for you from the foundation of the world." It seems to me we shall get a little nearer; that there will be a kind of relationship which angels will not know anything about; that there will be a feeling of love, gratitude, and adoration in the redeemed host that those who kept their first estate will not feel as we do. How we honor those who have stood up like men when it required men to stand! Some of us older ones can remember having met, in other days, the remnant of the grand old army of '76. I have seen a few of them. Rude, poor, uncultivated men they were; but how we honored them, and loved to do them reverence! How even the little bright-eyed boys and girls would look slyly up out of the corners of their eyes amidst their curls when an old Revolutionary soldier passed, and whispered to each other, "He is an old Revolutionary soldier." I like that; I think it is right, and I think God likes it. *Bp. Ames.*

9453. HEAVEN, Hope of. Not only is there comfort for the breaking up of our relationships on earth by death, but I declare to you that after having, by reason of my profession, pondered this subject to comfort mourners all my life long, during the thirty-five years of my ministry, I am more and more personally satisfied every single year that if for this life only we have hope, we are of all men most miserable. And I tell you truly that if I were to be convinced to-morrow that this is all a fiction, that there is no existence beyond the grave, I would seal my mouth with the seven seals of the Apocalypse, which no man could break open, before I would whisper that guilty disclosure. In this world of sin, he who takes away the hope of heaven takes away the consolation of those that sorrow. There is nothing else that can comfort a heart crushed by bereavement and losses. It is but for a moment. Out of my tree the bird has flown, and sings there no more. But it sits in the tree of life and sings, and I shall hear it again. I am alone; I have no counselor; I am without a companion; I am heart-sick and life-sick—but what then? I shall find again all that I have lost, and more, and more blessedly. Sorrows, as storms, bring down the clouds close to the earth; sorrows bring heaven down close; and they are instruments of cleansing and purifying. *Beecher.*

9454. HEAVEN, Incitement to Seek. The Jesuit Fathers tried to move a sick Huron by the misery of life, the joys of heaven, and the pains of hell. He said, "I wish to go where my ancestors have gone." One asked him, "Do they hunt the caribou in heaven?" "Oh, no," replied the missionary. "Then I will not go there. Idleness is bad everywhere," responded the Indian. The fear of starvation in the regions of the blessed, was a great obstacle to their conversion, and the fathers had to assure them that the stock of game was there unlimited. Others feared that there would not be a supply of tobacco in heaven, and felt that they could not be happy there without it.

9455. HEAVEN Inconceivable. The joys of heaven are without example, above experience, and beyond imagination; for which the whole creation wants a comparison; we, an apprehension; and even the word of God, a revelation. *Norris.*

9456. HEAVEN Indescribable. It is not for any mortal creature to make a map of that Canaan which lies above; it is, to all of us who live here on the hither side of death, an unknown country and an undiscovered land. It may be that some heavenly pilgrim, who, with his holy thoughts and holy desires, is continually traveling thitherward, arrives sometimes near the borders of the promised land and the suburbs of the new Jerusalem and gets upon the top of Pisgah, and there has the perfect prospect of a fair country, which lies a far way off; but he cannot tell how to describe it. *Bp. Rust.*

9457. HEAVEN, Infamy of Losing. The infamy of losing heaven we may in some sort declare, under the example of a mighty king, who, having no heir to succeed him in his kingdom, took up a beautiful boy at the church door, and nourished him as his son, and in his testament commanded, that if at ripe years his conditions were virtuous and suitable to his calling, he should be received as a lawful king, and seated on his royal throne; but if he proved vicious and unfit for government, they should punish him with infamy, and send him to the galleys. The kingdom obeyed his command, provided him excellent tutors; but he became so untoward and ill-inclined, that he would learn nothing, flung away his books, spent his time amongst other boys in making houses of clay and other fooleries; for which his governors chastised him, and advised him of what was fitting and most imported him; but all did no good, only when they reprehended him he would weep—not because he repented, but because they hindered his sport; and the next day he did the same. The more he grew in age, the worse he became; and although they informed him of the king's testament, and what behoved him, all was to no purpose; until at last all being weary of his ill-conditions, declared him unworthy to reign, despoiled him of his royal ornaments, and condemned him with infamy unto the galleys. What greater ignominy can there be than this, to lose a kingdom, and to be made a galley-slave? A more ignominious, and a more lamentable tragedy is that of a Christian condemned after his probation; who was taken by God from the gates of death, with the condition, that if he kept his commandments, he should reign in heaven, and if not, he should be condemned: but he, forgetting those obligations, without respect of his tutors, or ministers, who exhorted him, both by their doctrine and example, what was fitting for a child of God; yet he, neither moved by their advice, nor the chastisements of heaven, by which God overthrew his vain intentions, and thwarted his unlawful pleasures, only lamented his temporal losses, and not his offenses, and the time of his death, was sentenced to be deprived of the kingdom of heaven and precipitated into hell. *Salter.*

9458. HEAVEN, Knowledge in. An infant, standing on the top of a mountain, may see much further than a giant at its base; and even so the lisping babe, whom Jesus has taken from a mother's bosom to his own, excels in knowledge the profoundest of philosophers and greatest of divines. *Dr. Guthrie.*

9459. HEAVEN at Last. After the fever of life—after wearinesses, sicknesses, fightings and despondings, languor and fretfulness, struggling and failing—struggling and succeeding—after all the changes and chances of this troubled and unhealthy state, at length comes death—at length the white throne of God—at length the beatific vision. *Newman.*

9460. HEAVEN, Locality of. Where is heaven? I cannot tell. Even to the eye of faith, heaven looks much like a star to the eye of flesh. Set there on the brow of night, it shines most bright—most beautiful; but it is separated from us by so great a distance as to be raised almost as high above our investigations as above the storms and clouds of earth. A shining object, we see it gleaming in the fields of space; but we see nothing more, even when our eyes are assisted by the most powerful telescope. Nor does the matter cost us the least anxiety. If God spared not his own Son, heaven shall want nothing to make us supremely and eternally happy. *Dr. Guthrie.*

9461. HEAVEN, Longing for. O, Jerusalem, Jerusalem, the only place that can ease us of this misery! the place where the beloved of my soul dwelleth, the vision of peace, the seat of true tranquillity and repose, how fain would I have the satisfaction of being in the sure way to thy felicity! This is all the peace I wish for in the world. No other happiness do I thirst after, as everything can testify that hath been privy to my thoughts. There is never a room in my house but hath been filled with the noise of my sighs and groans after thee, O, Jerusalem! Every tree that grows in my ground hath thy sweet name engraven upon it. The birds of the air, if they can understand, are witnesses how incessantly my soul pants and longs to fly unto thee, O, Jerusalem! What charitable hand will guide me in the way to thy treasures? Who will bring me unto that strong city, the retreat of my wearied mind, the refuge to recruit my tired spirits, the only place of my security, my joy, my life itself? Wilt not thou, O God, who hast led me to the knowledge of it, who hast filled me with these desires, and hast brought me into a disesteem and contempt of all other things? *Patrick.*

9462. HEAVEN, Manners of. It would not do to wear furs and speak the tongue of the Greenlanders out in Dahomey or Old Calabar. So I must get the language of heaven, and have its habits learned, to be fit to go there. *Edmond.*

9463. HEAVEN, Meeting in. A few years ago a man of means, with a large heart, and genial manners, and loving convival companions, was engaged to be married to a very worthy and estimable young lady. He had a present fortune and a home in the future. All at once that lady died. He bent over her lifeless form, and nearly died of a broken heart. What to do he did not know. He had no friend near to guide him, and instead of yielding himself to the providence of God, he turned his back upon him, and cursed heaven and earth, and rushed into the commotions of a daily life, where he found companions who were willing to lead him into many expenditures and vices. But one day he met a friend, who had been yoked with him in his gay living, in the counting house. He opened his safe, and by one of those strange fatalities he took out a little box. He saw a little silver key and a lock of golden hair. The key belonged to his wife's casket, and the lock of hair he had cut from her head. He looked at these two mementos, and then thought of the awful distance now between him and her. It struck him so forcibly that turning to his friend he said, "Ed, do you think I will ever see her again?" His friend being an honest man, answered, "I don't believe you ever will." "What! not see her again: why?" "No, George, because you and I have not been living the kind of life to take us where she has gone. But you can meet her there:" and George turned to his friend and said, "I am going to meet that girl there." Ed joined my church some months ago, and George joined it yesterday, and he said to me, "I would not take millions for my hope." *Dr. Hepworth.*

9464. HEAVEN, A Minister's Welcome to. A Wesleyan missionary in Ashantee, visited his first convert there, who was then on his dying bed. The convert said: "I hear you preached last night about heaven. I could not be there, but I am going to heaven itself; and when I get there I will go to my Saviour and throw myself at his feet, and thank him for his mercy in sending a missionary to this land to tell me of the truth. Then I will come back to the gate and sit down till you come, and then I will take you to my Saviour's throne and say: You are the man who first told me of the cross of Christ."

9465. HEAVEN, Morning in. A traveler arriving at the city of Basle, Switzerland, by night drew this lesson: "We are now in a strange city : the entire place is shrouded in darkness. All is silent as the grave, or the far-off sky. How ignorant we are of the appearance of the city, or the surrounding landscape! But when the morning comes, the dim outlines which we have obscurely seen through the gloom of night, will be perceived with certainty and clearness. And thus it is, I have been thinking, with dying persons. Though quite on the verge of eternal scenes, yet the things revealed in the Bible as belonging to eternity can only be realized by faith: 'clouds and darkness' rest upon them; but, just as the morning light shall make us familiar with this fine old city, so with our departing this life—the night of death shall be succeeded by the daylight of eternity, when all those realities which were but matters of faith shall be clearly revealed to the astonished soul."

9466. HEAVEN, Music in. He that at midnight, when the very laborer sleeps securely, should hear, as I have often done, the sweet descants, the natural rising and falling, the doubling and redoubling of the nightingale's voice, might well be lifted above earth, and say, Lord, what music hast thou provided for the saints in heaven, when thou affordest bad men such music upon earth! *Izaak Walton.*

9467. HEAVEN, Music of. Our knowledge of the kind of delight afforded by the experience of earthly music may enable us to form a conception of the higher degree. The conception may be inadequate, and yet, so far as it can reach, it may be an approximation to the reality. And so, in like manner, with the beautiful in scenery. It would be folly to attempt to describe the details of heavenly scenery, but the general idea stands sufficiently out to justify belief. The most glorious bursts of harmony that ever thrilled and quivered through the brain of Handel, the pealing triumphs of "Hallelujah Chorus," the glowing snatches of Mozart, the gorgeous sonatas of Beethoven, the almost speaking melodies of Mendelssohn, and all the exquisite conceptions of the most gifted masters, may be only faint and far-off echoes of the grander performances above; yet as echoes they bring down something of heavenly music to the conceptions of men on earth, and make us yearn and bend before the thought, "If these be echoes, what must the realities be?" *Eternal Homes.*

9468. HEAVEN, Negative. Of the positive joys of heaven we can form no conception; but its negative delights form a sufficiently attractive picture—no pain; no thirst; no hunger; no horror of the past; no fear of the future: no failure of mental capacity; no intellectual deficiency; no morbid imaginations; no follies; no stupidities: but, above all, no insulted feelings; no wounded affections; no despised love or unrequited regard; no hate, envy, jealousy, or indignation of or at others; no falsehood, dishonesty, dissimulation, hypocrisy, grief, or remorse. In a word, to end where I began, no sin and no suffering. *Prof. Wilson.*

9469. HEAVEN, No Night in. Upon the tombstone of a girl, blind from her birth, is this inscription, "There is no night there."

9470. HEAVEN, No Other Way to. I heard of a man some time ago that was going to get into heaven in his own way. He did not believe in the Bible or the love of God, but was going to get in on account of his good deeds. He was very liberal, gave a great deal of money, and he thought the more he gave the better it would be in the other world. I don't as a general thing believe in dreams, but sometimes they teach good lessons. This man dreamed one night that he was building a ladder to heaven, and he dreamed that every good deed he did it put him one round higher on this ladder, and when he did an extra good deed it put him up a good many rounds; and in his dream he kept going, going up, until at last he got out of sight, and he went on and on doing his good deeds, and the ladder went up higher and higher, until at last he thought he saw it run up to the very throne of God. Then in his dream he died, and a mighty Voice came rolling down from above, "He that climbeth up some other way, the same is a thief and a robber," and down came his ladder and he woke from his sleep and thought, "If I go to heaven I must go some other way." *Moody.*

9471. HEAVEN, No Treasure in. Mr. Jacob Strawn, the largest farmer in the State of Illinois, took Chaplain McCabe and myself to the top of his house, to show us his splendid farms lying along the country in every direc tion far as the eye could reach. I asked him how many acres he owned. "Forty thousand, all under cultivation." "How much is the land worth an acre?" "Not less than $50, sir." "Then you are worth $2,000,000?" "Yes, and I made it all myself: when I started I hadn't fifty cents." I turned to him. A look of pride flushed his face, while his eyes swept the country in every direction. "Mr. Strawn, you have asked me to look north and south, east and west, and view your possessions; and you say I cannot see the end. Now, may I ask you to look up yonder. How much do you own up there?" "Ah," said he, the tears filling up his eyes, "I'm afraid I am poor up there." Mr. Strawn died suddenly about one year afterwards. *Wm. Reynolds.*

9472. HEAVEN, One Gate to. The ancient city of Troy had but one gate. Go round and round the city, you would have found no other. If you wanted to get in, there was but one way. So to the golden city of heaven there is but one gate. Christ says, "I am the door." *Anon.*

9473. HEAVEN Ours. I once heard a father tell that when he removed his family to a new residence, where the accommodation was much more ample, and the substance much more rich and varied than that to which they had previously been accustomed, his youngest son, yet a lisping infant, ran around every room, and scanned every article with ecstasy, calling out in childish wonder at every new sight, "Is this ours, father, and is this ours?" The child did not say "yours," and I observed that the father, while he told the story, was not offended with the freedom. You could read in his glistening eye that the infant's confidence in appropriating as his own all that his father had was an important element in his satisfaction. Such, I suppose, will be the surprise and joy, and appropriating confidence, with which the child of our Father's family will count all his own when he is removed from the comparatively mean condition of things present, and enters the infinite of things to come. When the glories of heaven burst upon his view, he does not stand at a distance, like a stranger, saying, "O God, these are thine." He bounds forward to touch and taste every provision which these blessed mansions contain, exclaiming, as he looks in the Father's face, "Father, this and this is ours!" The dear child is glad of all the Father's riches, and the Father is gladder of his dear child. *Arnot.*

9474. HEAVEN, Pointing to. A disconsolate deaf old woman was passing her days in the almshouse of Paris. The chaplain came by, and, seeing her despairing look, simply pointed upward. The action told her to look up. The clouds were scattered. After poverty, sickness, and death, comes heaven.

9475. HEAVEN, Preparation for. Let us consider we are, professedly, going to heaven, that region of light and life, and purity and love. It well indeed becomes them that are upon the way thither modestly to inquire after truth.

Humble, serious, diligent endeavors to increase in divine knowledge are very suitable to our present state of darkness and imperfection. The product of such inquiries we shall carry to heaven with us, with whatsoever is most akin thereto (besides their usefulness in the way thither). We shall carry truth and the knowledge of God to heaven with us; we shall carry purity thither, devotedness of soul to God and our Redeemer, divine love and joy, if we have their beginnings here, with whatsoever else of real permanent excellency that hath a settled fixed seat and place in our souls now; and shall there have them in perfection. But do we think we shall carry strife to heaven? Shall we carry anger to heaven? Envyings, heart-burnings, animosities, enmities, hatred of our brethren and fellow-Christians—shall we carry these to heaven with us? Let us labor to divest ourselves, and strike off from our spirits everything that shall not go with us to heaven, or is equally unsuitable to our end and way, that there may be nothing to obstruct and hinder our abundant entrance at length into the everlasting kingdom. *Howe.*

9476. HEAVEN Present. A boy walking with his mother, looked up to the sky and said, "O, mother, heaven is so far off I'm afraid I shall never get there." "My dear," said his mother, "heaven must come to us before we can go to it."

9477. HEAVEN, Presenting. Aristotle writes of a parcel of ground in Sicily, that sendeth such a strong smell of fragrant flowers to all the fields and leaves thereabouts, that no hound can hunt there: the scent is so confounded by the sweet smell of those flowers. Labor we so to present heavenly sweetness; so to savor the things above, that we may have no mind to hunt after earthly vanities. *Trappe.*

9478. HEAVEN, Qualification for. The last use which I shall make of this remarkable property in human nature of being delighted with those actions to which it is accustomed, is to show how absolutely necessary it is for us to gain habits of virtue in this life, if we would enjoy the pleasures of the next. The state of bliss we call heaven will not be capable of affecting those minds which are not thus qualified for it. We must in this world gain a relish of truth and virtue, if we would be able to taste that knowledge and perfection which are to make us happy in the next. The seeds of those spiritual joys and raptures which are to rise up and flourish in the soul to all eternity must be planted in her during this her present state of probation. In short, heaven is not to be looked upon only as the reward, but as the natural effect, of a religious life. *Addison.*

9479. HEAVEN, Question About. A little girl was going to bed. Her sister used to sleep on the pillow beside her. "Mamma," asked she, "who do you think Fannie sleeps with now in heaven?" "There is no night there," answered her mother. "Mamma," asked the little girl, "does a soul have eyes to see with? Will Fanny know us when we come?" "The Bible tells us that we shall see as we are seen and know as we are known," replied mother. "We shall see then," said the little girl; "but our eyes will not be crying eyes, will they, mamma?" "No, my child. God will wipe away all tears," said her mother. As she spoke, a small tear stood in her own eye, but it quickly went away. Little Jane saw it, and said within herself, "God wipes away mamma's tears now." "There will be nothing to hurt in heaven, and no dark; will there be?" asked the little one. "No, my child, for the glory of God lightens it, and the Lamb is the light thereof." "And what dress shall we wear?" "Jesus has a dress for all his little ones," said mamma; "the beautiful garments of righteousness. They are white and shining." "And I must keep it so nice, mamma?" "Yes, my child; an unkind word will spot it; a sinful thought will stain it; but there is no sin in heaven; and it is the beauty of heaven that we shall not want to do or to think a wrong thing." "And we shall not keep wanting things," said little Jane, thinking, perhaps, of the rocking-horse and the candy, and the big doll of Emma's which she could not have. "No, my darling," said her mother, taking her little girl in her arms; "for we shall be satisfied when we awake in his likeness."

9480. HEAVEN, Raptures of. If one could but look awhile through the chinks of heaven's door, and see the beauty and bliss of Paradise; if he could but lay his ear to heaven, and hear the ravishing music of those seraphic spirits. and the anthems of praise which they sing; how would his soul be exhilarated and transported with joy! *T. Watson.*

9481. HEAVEN, Recognition in. I must confess, as the experience of my own soul, that the expectation of loving my friends in heaven principally kindles my love to them while on earth. If I thought I should never know, and consequently never love them after this life, I should number them with temporal things, and love them as such; but I now delightfully converse with my pious friends, in a firm persuasion that I shall converse with them for ever; and I take comfort in those that are dead or absent, believing that I shall shortly meet them in heaven, and love them with a heavenly love. *Baxter.*

9482. HEAVEN, Registered in. Christmas Evans was addressing a Bible Society meeting over which the Marquis of Anglesea presided, when he turned, and personally addressed the marquis, "I imagine, my lord, that you have died, and that the angel of death has taken your soul to the portals of the holy city. Only a few are admitted into Paradise; the entrance is narrow and jealously watched. 'Open!' shouts the angel of death as he presses forward to secure a place in heaven worthy of your lordship. 'Who to?' asks the guardian of Paradise with an authoritative voice. 'To the Honorable the Marquis of Anglesea.' 'Who is he?' 'An old officer in the army of the Duke of Wellington.' 'In that capacity,' says Peter, 'he is not on my list.'

'But he has filled the office of high master of the ordnance.' 'That may be possible, but we know him not.' 'He has been several times lord-lieutenant of Ireland.' 'I say nothing to the contrary, but he is to us a total stranger.' 'He was the leader of the Horse Guards at the battle of Waterloo.' 'I repeat that we know nothing of him.' 'Besides that, he was for many years President of the Bible Society.' 'Ha!' shouts Peter; 'that alters the case. He can enter in; indeed, I see his name recorded among the blessed on the books of my Father.'"

9483. HEAVEN, Review in. Our past lives will, when we attain the perfection of our being, be present to us again. There are close analogies between the laws of duration and of space. And these may help us to illustrate the manner in which the several stages of our former existence may reappear. A traveler who sets out upon a line of road sees a given object before him; as he advances, he comes up with that object, and it is present; he proceeds, and passes it and sees it no more. But let the traveler be elevated into the air, or ascend a mountain, and the whole line of progress which, as he journeyed, was measured out in gradual succession, becomes all at once present to him again. So with respect to the passenger through time. While here below, he reached and passed his several stages one by one: but when ascended to his eternal state, he may look down and see the whole path of life before him. *Woodward.*

9484. HEAVEN, Ripe for. Let the mantle of worldly enjoyments hang loose about you, that it may be easily dropped when death comes to carry you into another world. When the corn is forsaking the ground it is ready for the sickle; when the fruit is ripe, it falls off the tree easily. So when a Christian's heart is truly weaned from the world, he is prepared for death, and it will be the more easy to him. A heart disengaged from the world is a heavenly one, and then we are ready for heaven when our heart is there before us. *Boston.*

9485. HEAVEN, Road to. Didst thou never know of any that were in a journey, and, coming to some deep dirty lane, they thought to avoid it, and broke over the hedge into the field? But when they had rode round and round, they could find no way out, but were forced to go out where they got in; and then, notwithstanding their unwillingness, to go through that miry lane, or else not to go that journey—truly so it is in the journey to heaven. Thou art now come to this deep lane of humiliation, through which all must go that will reach that city whose "builder and maker is God." *Swinnock.*

9486. HEAVEN, Roll Call in. The hospital tents had been filling up as fast as the wounded men had been brought to the rear. Among the number was a young man mortally wounded and not able to speak. It was near midnight and many a loved one lay sleeping on the battle-field—that sleep that knows no wakening until Jesus shall call for them. The surgeons had been on their rounds of duty, and for a moment all was quiet. Suddenly this young man, before speechless, calls in a clear voice, "Here." The surgeon hastened to his side, and asked what he wished. "Nothing," he said; "they are calling the roll in heaven, and I was answering to my name." He turned his head and was gone—gone to join the great army whose uniform is washed white in the blood of the Lamb, and to answer to his name at the roll call in heaven.

9487. HEAVEN, Securing. "Thou shalt guide me with thy counsel, and afterward receive me to glory." The glory is a thing future and invisible; but the hope of it in a believer's heart is present and felt. The only link by which we can connect ourselves with the glory to be revealed, is present reconciliation to God through his grace. The full form of this is, "Christ in you, the hope of glory." It is not, I shall make my way in; but, "Thou shalt receive me." It does not imply any preternatural knowledge of heaven, but a spiritual cummunion with the Friend of sinners, who is already there. God with us, is in heaven God for us. "Lord, Lord, open to us!" But will he receive me then? That question must be answered by another,—Do you receive him now? If Christ knocks in vain at the door of your heart, you will knock in vain at the door of his heaven. Unless the kingdom of God be within you here, you shall not be within the kingdom of God yonder. *Arnot.*

9488. HEAVEN, Shut Out of. An old minister related the following incident: "He had preached the Word for many a year in a wood hard by a beautiful village in the Inverness-shire Highlands, and it was his invariable custom, on dismissing his own congregation, to repair to the Baptist Chapel in this village to partake of the Lord's Supper with his people assembled there. It was then usual to shut the gates during this service, in order that communicants might not be exposed to any disturbance through persons going out or coming in. On one occasion the burden of the Lord pressed upon his servant with more than ordinary severity, and anxious to deliver it and clear his soul, he detained his hearers a little beyond the time, and consequently had to hurry to the chapel. As he drew near he noticed the door-keeper retire from the outer gate, after having shut it. He called to him, quickening his pace at the same time, but his cry was not heard, the attendant retreated inside and the minister came up 'just in time' to see the door put to, and hear it fastened from within. He walked round the chapel looking up at the windows, but could gain no admittance; there was only one door, and that door was shut. He listened and heard the singing, and thought how happy God's people were inside, while he himself was shut out. The circumstance made an impression upon him at the time which he could never afterwards forget, and he was led to ask himself the question, 'Shall it be so at the last? Shall I come up

to the gate of heaven only in time to be too late, to find the last ransomed one admitted, and the door everlastingly shut?'"

9489. HEAVEN, Signs in. The eclipse of the moon is occasioned by a diametrical opposition of the earth between it and the sun, and can only happen when the moon is at the full. The Jews, not being acquainted with the physical cause of eclipses, looked upon them, whether of sun or moon, as signs of the divine displeasure. The Athenian army, under Niceas, when they were about to withdraw secretly from Sicily, seeing the moon suddenly eclipsed, refused to embark, which proved fatal to them, as they were all shortly afterwards slain or taken prisoners. *Buck.*

9490. HEAVEN, Straight Road to. A clergyman preached on the doctrine of future punishment. He was followed home by a man who told him that he did not believe the doctrine he had been preaching, and desired him to prove it. The clergyman said he had proved it from the Bible. But said the unbeliever, "I do not find anything in my Bible to prove that the sinner is eternally damned. I believe that mankind will be judged for the sins done in the body, and those that deserve punishment will be sent to hell and will remain there until the debt is paid." "I have but one word to say to you," said the minister, "and that is, Christ died for you, and there is a straight road to heaven; but if you prefer to go round through hell to get there, I cannot help it." These words, "There is a straight road to heaven," rang in his ears, and he was soon brought to believe in Jesus.

9491. HEAVEN, Suggestions of. The belief in the existence of the Happy Isles in the west, seems to have arisen from the discoveries of foreign and strange objects washed up by the ocean, and left upon the shore. Tree branches, fruits and nuts, all unknown, were demonstrations of the reality of these islands. Carved fragments of wood, and an abandoned canoe, sent Columbus to search for the undiscovered land. The shores of this earth are strewn with branches, fruits, and fragments floated hither from another world. Branches of the tree of life are here. Its fruits, love, joy, peace are found. They show the land from which they come, to be one of the fullness of joy and everlasting pleasure. It is the truest wisdom to begin at once the voyage to the Happy Isles.

9492. HEAVEN, Superiority of. To one firmly persuaded of the reality of heavenly happiness, and earnestly desirous of obtaining it, all earthly satisfactions must needs look little, and grow flat and unsavory. *Atterbury.*

9493. HEAVEN, Unity in. I have seen a field here, and a field there, stand thick with corn —a hedge or two has separated them. At the proper season the reapers entered; soon the earth was disburdened, and the grain was conveyed to its destined resting-place, where, blended together in the barn or in the stack, it could not be known that a hedge had ever separated this corn from that. Thus it is with the church. Here it grows, as it were, in different fields, and even, it may be, by different hedges. By and by, when the harvest is come, all God's wheat shall be gathered into the garner, without one single mark to distinguish that once they differed in outward circumstantials of form and order. *Toplady.*

9494. HEAVEN, Wonder in. I imagine when Christ calls home his old, scattered, battered veterans of the cross, who have stood up against sin, hell and the devil, and wicked men—stood as the anvil to the stroke—when God lets them in through the gates into that city, the angels will say to each other, "Look! there is the travail of his soul; there is the purchase of his blood; there are human beings from the dusty battle-fields of earth—from that land of sin; there are those who stood up for God—who counted not their lives, fortunes, or anything else dear to them, that they might win Christ." I don't know about this, but some of us will know before long. We shall be introduced to those who have gone home before. We shall not be ashamed of Christ, but rejoice in that he counted us worthy to suffer for his name's sake. I think when that time comes, every redeemed soul from earth will be a sort of walking wonder in the golden streets, to be gazed at and admired of all who love the Lord Jesus Christ. Then we shall near the finale of the whole matter, "Well done!" Brother, did you ever think what that meant when God Almighty speaks it? That "well done" means heaven, glory, immortality, eternal life! When God says, "Well done," there are no temptations, trials, or dangers after that. *Bishop Ames.*

9495. HEAVENLY-MINDEDNESS, Quiet of. Seneca says it is the higher heavens that are more tranquil, where there are neither clouds nor winds, storms nor tempests, and it is the inferior heavens that lighten and thunder, and the nearer the earth the more tempestuous and unquiet. So the sublime and heavenly-minded is placed in a calm and quiet station. *Flavel.*

9496. HEAVENS, The Arctic. The intense beauty of the arctic firmament can hardly be imagined. It looked close above our heads, with its stars magnified in glory, and the very planets twinkling so much as to baffle the observations of our astronomer. I am afraid to speak of some of these night scenes. I have trodden the deck and the floes when the life of earth seemed suspended—its movements, its sounds, its coloring, its companionships; and as I looked on the radiant hemisphere circling above me, as if rendering worship to the unseen Centre of Light, I have ejaculated, in humility of spirit, "Lord, what is man, that thou art mindful of him?" *Kane.*

9497. HELL, Bridge over. Mohammedans hold that those who are to be admitted into paradise will take the right-hand way, and those who are destined to hell-fire will take the left; but both of them must first pass the bridge called, in Arabic, Al Sirât, which they say is laid over the midst of hell, and describe to be finer than a hair and sharper than the edge of a sword; so that it seems very difficult to conceive how any one shall be able to stand upon it. The bridge is beset on each side with briars and hooked thorns; which will, however, be no impediment to the good, for they shall pass with wonderful ease and swiftness, like lightning or the wind, Mohammed and his Moslems leading the way; whereas the wicked, with the slipperiness and extreme narrowness of the pass, the entangling of the thorns, and the extinction of the light which directed the former to paradise, will soon miss their footing and fall down headlong into hell, which is gaping beneath them. *George Sale.*

9498. HELL, Choosing. Whitefield says a minister in Scotland related to him the following story, which he knew to be true: "A woman who was dying was asked by the minister, 'Where do you hope to go when you die?' She answered, 'I don't care where I go.' 'What?' said he; 'don't care whether you go to heaven or hell?' 'No,' said she, 'I don't care whither I go.' 'But,' said he, 'if you had your choice, where would you go?' 'To hell,' she replied. 'Are you mad? will you go to hell?' 'Yes,' said she, 'I will.' 'Why so?' he asked. 'Why,' said she, 'because all my relations are there.' The preacher in attending her funeral related this sad story, which produced quite a shuddering among the people.'

9499. HELL, Considering. Three men visited Sisoes, the hermit. One said, "My father, I think of the fires of hell, and they fill me with horror. How shall I escape them?" The second said, "My father, I think of the gnashing of teeth, and the never-dying worm, and am haunted by that thought. What shall I do?" The third said, "And I, O father, have ever before me the awful outer darkness, and the unspeakable horror thereof oppresses me." To each of these he gave no answer; but, after a pause, stated his own experience on these questions: "I have never given them a thought. I think how good my God is, and I know he will have pity on me." Thus men are diversely incited to the religious life. The love of God casts out all fear. "Alas!" he added, "I should have been a better man had I thought like you."

9500. HELL, Disbelief in. To disbelieve it is not to destroy the fact. Even in Scotland, the narrow end of an island nowhere very broad, I have met with persons well advanced in life, of good common education, and good common sense, who had never seen the sea. Suppose that these persons should have cause greatly to dread the sea, and should therefore ardently desire that there were no such thing in existence. Suppose further that, in the common way of the world. the wish should become father to the thought, and that they at last should firmly believe that there is not a sea. Would their sentiments change the state of the fact? Sinners, to whom the name and nature of a place of punishment are disagreeable, have no more power to annihilate the object of their aversion than the shepherds of the Cheviots to wipe out the sea by a wish

The sea is near these men, though they have never seen it; and if they were cast into it, they would perish, notwithstanding their opinion. *Arnot.*

9501. HELL, Dispute About. A young man called on a preacher whom he had heard preach on future punishment, and said, " I believe there is a small dispute between you and me, sir; and I thought I would call this morning, and try to settle it." "Ah," said he, "what is it?" "Why," replied he, "you say that the wicked will go into everlasting punishment; and I do not think that they will." "O, if that is all," answered the minister, "there is no dispute between you and me. If you turn to Matthew 24: 46, you will find that the dispute is between you and the Lord Jesus Christ; and I advise you to go immediately and settle it with him."

9502. HELL, Doubting a. For a man to doubt whether there be any hell, and thereupon to live as if absolutely there were none, but when he dies to find himself confuted in the flames, this must be the height of woe and disappointment, and a bitter conviction of an irrational venture and absurd choice. *South.*

9503. HELL, Dread of. Col. Richardson, an orthodox Christian, and two Universalists, were in a boat on the Niagara river, some distance above the falls. The Universalists began to rally the colonel on his belief of future punishment, and expressed their astonishment that a man of his powers of mind should be so far misled as to believe the horrid dogma. The colonel defended his opinions, and the result was a controversy, which was carried on so long and earnestly that when they, after some time, looked round, they found that the boat was hurrying, with great rapidity, towards the falls. The Universalists at once dropped the oars, and began to cry to God to have mercy on them. Richardson laid hold of the oars, exerted all his strength, and, by God's mercy, they reached the shore. When they had landed, he addressed his companions: "Gentlemen, it is not long since you were railing at me for believing in future punishment. Your opinion is, that when a man dies, the first thing of which he is conscious is being in heaven: now, I want to know why you were so terribly frightened when you thought that in five minutes more you'd be over the falls in glory?" The Universalists were silent for some time: at length one of them said, "I'll tell you what, Colonel Richardson, Universalism does very well in smooth water, but it will never do to go over the Falls of Niagara!"

9504. HELL, Existence of. Verily, it is well for our own sakes to think sometimes of that horrid place! As truly as fair France lies across the Channel, as truly as the sun is shining on the white walls, and gay bridges, and bright gardens, and many-storied palaces of its beautiful capital, as truly as that thousands of men and women there are living real lives and fulfilling various destinies, so truly is there such a place as hell, all alive this hour with the multitudinous life of countless agon-ies, and innumerable gradations of despair. Save the blessed in heaven, none live so keen or conscious a life as those millions of ruined souls. It is not impossible that we may go there too. It is not impossible that we may have sent some there already. When we pass along the streets, we must often see those who will inhabit there forever. There are some there now who were not there an hour ago. There are some now in the green fields, or in the busy towns, on comfortable beds, or on the sunshiny seas, who, in another hour, perhaps, will have gone there. This is a dreadfully real truth. *F. W. Faber.*

9505. HELL, Extemporized. An old colored minister, in a sermon on hell, pictured it as a region of ice and snow, where the damned froze throughout eternity. When privately asked his purpose in representing Gehenna in this way, he said: "I don't dare to tell dem people nuffin else. Why, if I were to say dat hell was warm, some o'dem old rheumatic niggas would be wanting to start down dar de very fust frost!" This story originated, if we are not mistaken, with Dr. Johnson. He tells it of a Scotch minister at the Hebrides, who otherwise as orthodox as the very "Catecheese," gave the above description of the place of torments, and afterwards, to the doctor, reasons similar to the above for so unusual a representation. *Anon.*

9506. HELL, Fear of. The fear of hell may indeed in some desperate cases, like the *moxa*, give the first rouse from a moral lethargy, like the green venom of copper, by evacuating poison or a dead load from the inner man, prepare it for nobler ministrations and medicines from the realm of light and life, that nourish while they stimulate. *Coleridge.*

9507. HELL, Fire of. The sentence of the damned includes hell-fire; a tremendous penalty which we dare not explain away, and whose literal import no man has authority to deny. But hell-fire is not the sum of their penal sufferings: there is also the worm that dieth not; the self-consuming, everlasting anguish of a bad mind,—the grim, comfortless, unutterable, destitute despair of a desolate and abominable spirit, tormented with unavailing yet inevitable reflection on the interminable miseries of the wrath to come. The sum of these things is the loss of the soul; that is, the loss of its eternal happiness, and its condemnation to perpetual misery. *I. Keeling.*

9508. HELL, Glimpses of. Its locality is untold, its creation and date are left in obscurity, its names are various; but all rather veils the discoveries of what seems elaborately concealed. It is hell, the hidden or sunken place; it is Gehenna, Tophet; it is a smoke ascending, as if to darken the universe; it is a lake burning with fire and brimstone, but of which the interior is unseen; it is a pit bottomless, a fire unquenchable, a worm undying, a death—the second and the last; it is "without," yet not unvisited or unseen; they shall be tormented in the presence of the Lamb and the holy angels; they shall go forth and look on the carcasses of them that were slain, whose worm dieth not. This is all, or nearly all, we know of it. And yet how unspeakably tremendous! Like the disappointed words upon the wall (in Coleridge's "*Dream*") taken singly each word is a riddle—put them together, and what a lesson of horrid terror do they combine to teach!   *Gilfillan.*

9509. HELL, Immunity from. The superstition of the scapular is one of the absurdities of Romanism. According to the authentic record, the Virgin Mary appeared to St. Simon Stock, having in her hand a scapular, a little brown woolen habit, to cover the shoulders, chest and back, and informed him that whosoever wore a similar article received from a Carmelite, should escape the flames of hell. This invention received the sanction of Pope Clement X. Pope John XXII., in his bull "Sabbathine," proclaimed that all who wore the scapular in life would be delivered from the flames of purgatory on the Saturday following the day of their death. Pope Clement VII. confirmed this in 1528. This secured the Carmelites a large business at the expense of souls who confided in it.

9510. HELL, Memory in. If it be one end of future punishment to make wicked men sensible of their folly and ingratitude and of the mercy and favors they have abused, it is probable that, in that future world or region to which they shall be confined, everything will be so arranged as to bring to their recollection the comforts they had abused and the Divine goodness they had despised, and to make them feel sensations opposite to those which were produced by the benevolent arrangements which exist in the present state.   *Dr. T. Dick.*

9511. HELL, Mohammedan. The Mohammedans are taught that hell is divided into seven stories, or apartments, one below another, designed for the reception of as many distinct classes of the damned. The first, which they call Jehennam, they say, will be the receptacle of those who acknowledged one God; that is, the wicked Mohammedans, who, after having there been punished according to their demerits, will at length be released. The second, named Ladhâ, they assigned to the Jews; the third, named al Hotama, to the Christians; the fourth, named al Säîr, to the Sabians; the fifth, named Sakar, to the Magians; the sixth, named al Jahîm, to the idolaters; and the seventh, which is the lowest and worst of all, and is called al Hâwiyat, to the hypocrites, or those who outwardly professed some religion, but in their hearts were of none.   *George Sale.*

9512. HELL, Personal. The heart of man is the place the devil dwells in: I feel sometimes a hell within myself: Lucifer keeps his court in my breast. Legion is revived in me. There are as many hells as Anaxarchus conceited worlds: there was more than one hell in Magdalene, when there were seven devils, for every devil is an hell unto himself; he holds enough of torture in his own *ubi*, and needs not the misery of circumference to afflict him; and thus a distracted conscience here is a shadow or introduction unto hell hereafter.   *Browne.*

9513. HELL, Sinner's Own Way to. Whitefield reproved a young man for swearing, and requested him not to do so again. He replied "Doctor, it is very hard that you will not let a man go to hell his own way."

9514. HELL, Society of. In hell thou shalt have none but a company of damned souls, with an innumerable company of devils, to keep company with thee. While thou art in this world, the very thought of the devils appearing to thee, makes thy flesh to tremble, and thine hair ready to stand upright on thy head. But, oh, what wilt thou do when not only the supposition of the devils appearing, but the real society of all the devils of hell will be with thee, howling, roaring and screeching in such a hideous manner that thou wilt be even at thy wits' end, and be ready to run stark mad again for anguish and torments. If after ten thousand years, an end should come, there would be comfort. But here is thy misery, here thou must be forever. When thou seest what an innumerable company of howling devils thou art amongst, thou shalt think this again, This is my portion forever. When thou hast been in hell so many thousand years as there are stars in the firmament, or drops in the sea, or sands on the sea-shore, yet thou hast to lie there forever. Oh, this one word ever, how will it torment thy soul!   *Bunyan.*

9515. HELL, Torments of. They who believe not shall have garments of fire fitted unto them; boiling water shall be poured on their heads; their bowels shall be dissolved thereby, and also their skins; and they shall be beaten with maces of iron. So often as they shall endeavor to get out of hell, because of the anguish of their torments, they shall be dragged back into the same, and their tormentors shall say unto them, "Taste ye the pain of burning."
                               Koran.

9516. HELL, Working Hard for. Many might go to heaven with half the labor they go to hell, if they would venture their industry the right way.   *Ben Jonson.*

9517. HELP, Condition of Heavenly. As a countryman was carelessly driving his wagon along a miry lane, his wheels stuck so deep in the clay that the horses came to a stand-still. Upon this the man, without making the least effort of his own, began to call upon Hercules to come and help him out of his trouble. But Hercules bade him lay his shoulder to the wheel, assuring him that heaven only aided those who endeavored to help themselves. It is in vain to expect our prayers to be heard, if we do not strive as well as pray.   *Æsop.*

9518. HELP, Divine : Biblical. *Ebenezer*—"the *stone of help*"—1 Sam. 7: 12 (marg.); the pious memorial, set up in remembrance of God's past mercies. The help of *God's countenance*, Ps. 42: 5. An expression implying omniscient care, unfailing sympathy, and fatherly readiness to help. David's believing expectation of this, kept him from sinking; nay, it kept him from drooping! His harp was a palliative to Saul's melancholy, but his hope was an effectual cure for his own. The help of *God's hand*, see Job 8: 20—"He will not take the ungodly by the hand," is the marginal reading, where the text is "neither will he help the evil doers;" see Ps. 119: 173. The help of *God's shield*, Deut. 33: 29; Ps. 115: 9–11 (three times). THE BOOK OF PSALMS contains about fifty references to help. Two thoughts seem to be clearly brought out by them—Vain is the help of *man*, see Ps. 60: 11, etc. Sufficient is the help of *God*, Ps. 46: 1; 22: 19. The earnest cry for *speedy* help should be noted. "Make haste to help me;" "Make no tarrying;" see Ps. 46: 5—"God shall help her, and that right early"—margin, "when the morning appeareth," as Ps. 30: 5. 1 Chron. 15: 26—"God helped the Levites." It might scarcely seem as if they required Divine help in this case; but perhaps they were afraid after the breach upon Uzzah. In any case, it is well to acknowledge our dependence upon God's help in everything, especially in our religious duties, Ps. 94: 17. 2 Chron. 32: 7, 8 —Hezekiah's noble confidence. Acts 26: 22— St. Paul's testimony, after well nigh thirty years of Christian warfare. THE LORD JESUS. The "mighty One" chosen to be our Helper, Ps. 89: 19; "able to succor," Heb. 2: 18; to help them that have "no helper," Ps. 72: 12; just as he so graciously helped the impotent man at the pool, John 5: 7, 8; the blessed Mediator, through whom we may "come boldly to the throne of grace" for "help," Heb. 4: 16; the Son "made perfect through sufferings," who himself has felt the succor of the Father's help, Isa. 50: 7–9.　　　　*Bowes.*

9519. HELP, Mutual. An ant went to a fountain to quench his thirst, and tumbling in, was almost drowned. But a dove that happened to be sitting on a neighboring tree, saw the ant's danger, and plucking off a leaf, let it drop into the water before him, and the ant mounting upon it, was presently wafted safe ashore. Just at that time, a fowler was spreading his net, and was in the act of ensnaring the dove, when the ant perceiving his object, bit his heel. The start which the man gave made him drop his net; and the dove, aroused to a sense of her danger, flew safe away.
　　　　　　　　　　　　Æsop.

9520. HELP, Providential. A Russian fable tells of a man who wished to accomplish a journey over the snow and ice, through an inhospitable region infested with ravenous wolves. The distance was so great that it could only be traversed in a day by the strongest and swiftest horse to be found. Thus furnished, the traveler set forth to cross the steppe. When well on his way a huge wolf sprang upon the horse and devoured him. The wolf then became entangled in the harness and sped forth at a rapid rate, and soon drew the traveler to the very place he sought. Rev. Wm. Taylor says the devil has often attacked him in this way, and the result has only been to take him the quicker over the rough roads to the place desired. The devil himself becomes the Lord's servant to save and help his people.

9521. HELP, Reciprocal. In 1864, the steamship Askalon, bound from Liverpool to Port-au-Prince, was lost. She was overtaken by a storm, which she was unable to withstand. Hard effort of the crew kept her afloat till the Dutch barque Almonde discovered her distress, and rescued the crew, thirty-seven in number. It was soon after discovered that the rescuing ship had sprung a leak. The work of all hands at the pumps was required to save the ship. Without the aid of the rescued sailors, they must have been lost. In saving others, they saved themselves.

9522. HELP, Reward of. When I dig a man out of trouble, the hole that he leaves behind him is the grave where I bury my own trouble.
　　　　　　　　　S. T. Treasury.

9523. HELP, Swift. I had a friend who stood by the rail-track at Carlisle, Pa., when the ammunition had given out at Antietam; and he saw the train from Harrisburg, freighted with shot and shell, as it went thundering down toward the battle-field. He said that it stopped not for any crossing. They put down the brakes for no grade. They held up for no peril. The wheels were on fire with the speed as they dashed past. If the train did not come up in time with the ammunition, it might as well not come at all. So, my friends, there are times in our lives when we must have help immediately or perish. The grace that comes too late is no grace at all. O! is it not blessed to think that God is always in such quick pursuit of his dear children?　　*Talmage.*

9524. HERESY, Odor of. The Jesuit P. Francisco de Fonseca says: "I will relate another prodigy that occurred in Vienna, and which will serve not a little to confirm us in the faith with which we devoutly reverence these things. The Count of Harrach, who was greatly favored by the Duke of Saxony, besought him that he would be pleased to bestow upon him some of the very many relics in his treasury, which he preserved rather for curiosity than for devotion. The duke with much benignity ordered that various glasses should be given him, full of precious relics of Christ, of the most holy Virgin, the apostles, the innocents, and other various saints, and desired two Lutheran ministers to pack them with all decency in a valuable box, which the duke himself locked and sealed with his own seal, to prevent any fraud, and then sent it to Vienna. The box arrived at Vienna, and was deposited in the count's chapel, which is in Preiner Street; the count sent word to the bishop, that he might come to see, open, and authenticate the relics. The bishop came, and upon his opening the box there issued out a stench so abominable that it was not to be borne, and the whole chapel was infected with it. The bishop ordered that the reliquaries should be taken out, in order that he might carefully examine the cause of so strange an accident. This was done, and they soon discovered the mystery, for they found a case from which this pestilential odor proceeded: there was in it a piece of cloth with this inscription, 'Relics of Martin Luther's

Breeches,' which the Lutheran preachers, in mockery of our piety, had placed among the sacred relics. These abominable remains of the heresiarch were burnt by command of the bishop, and then not only did the stink cease, but there issued from the sacred relics a most sweet perfume, which filled the whole chapel."

9525. HERESY, Trifling. Say they, all heresies and all heretics are not equal; some, comparatively, are "little" to be regarded, and it's cruelty to meddle with these that seem to profess fair. "No," saith he, "take them all, even the 'little foxes;' for though they be little, yet they are foxes, though they be not of the grossest kind." As all scandals in facts are not alike, yet none is to be dispensed with, "so they are," saith he, "'foxes,' and corrupt others." For a "little leaven will leaven the whole lump." Often small-like schisms or heresies, such as the Novatians and Donatists, etc., have been exceedingly defacing to the beauty of the Church. "Therefore," saith he, "hunt and take them all." *Durham.*

9526. HERMITS, First Principles of. A rule among the hermits of Scete was never to teach others what they had not themselves first practiced. In their novitiate they learned to master themselves after the method of the philosophers of Greece. How to overcome pride, anger, lust and every manifestation of self, was their constant study. They treated the body as the stronghold of the enemy, which was to be conquered. St. John, the hermit, says, "If a general would take a city, he begins the siege by cutting off its supplies of water and provisions; so by sobriety, fasting and maceration of the flesh, are our affections and passions to be reduced and our domestic enemy weakened." By this practice of perfect self-denial they expected to secure the death of self and all vicious inclinations. Defects of virtue arise from unvanquished self. Alms, fasts and devotions profit nothing where self is not dead. These are the first principles of the hermit life.

9527. HERO, A Brave. In August, 1864, Commodore Farragut resolved to pass the obstructions and forts in Mobile bay. He intended to lead the line of battle with his flagship, the Hartford, but yielded to the unanimous request of his commanders. He protested that exposure was one of the penalties of rank, and that the flagship would be the main target of the enemy. The movement was very hazardous. The channel was known to be planted with torpedoes, and above the fort the powerful ram Tennessee waited to run them down. The Brooklyn led the line, but faltered at a perilous moment. Hesitation now would ensure defeat. The Commodore had lashed himself to the mast, where he overlooked the battle. He at once ordered his own ship to the front and led the fleet to victory.

9528. HERO, Definition of a. A hero is a man of high achievement, who performs famous exploits, who does things that are heroical, and in all his actions and demeanor is a hero indeed. *H. Brooke.*

9529. HEROISM, Christian. The mission ship sent a delegation on to the shore of Raratonga at night-fall, who were barbarously treated and all would have been slain but for a Raratonga woman, whom they brought along with them. The company on their return to the ship decided against attempting to plant a mission there. At this juncture a converted Tahitian, named Papehia, came forward, and offered to be left to attempt the work of evangelizing the people alone. "Whether the savages spare me or kill me," said the intrepid teacher, "I will land among them. 'The Lord is my shepherd, I am in his hand.'" Clothing himself in a shirt and a few yards of calico as a wrapper, and tying in a handkerchief Tahitian portions of the Holy Scriptures, he committed himself to the waves. On the reef there stood a number of warriors. They looked with proud distain on the humble servant of Christ as he approached, and seemed ready to strike him with their spears. God was his shield, and Raratonga redeemed his reward.

9530. HEROISM, Medal for. The examination was being held in an English Academy. Many ladies and gentlemen were present. James Hartley had taken the prize as best scholar, and was again called forward by the principal, who said he was about to confer a rare medal seldom merited. "Not long since some of the scholars belonging to this academy were flying a kite, just as a poor boy on horseback rode by. The horse took fright, threw the boy off, and injured him so badly that for weeks he was confined to the house. Only one of the scholars went to inquire after the boy who was hurt. He found that the boy was the grandson of a poor widow, whose only support consisted in selling milk. When she saw the wounded boy, she said, "Now there is no one to take care of the cow." The pupil volunteered to take care of the cow; and when he found that money was wanted for medicine, he gave the money he had saved to buy boots. The poor old woman, seeing how much he needed shoes, insisted that he wear a pair belonging to her poor Henry. The scholar bought the boots, clumsy as they were, and has worn them up to this time. Abuse and ridicule have been heaped upon him for driving a cow, selling milk, and wearing clumsy shoes; but he has fulfilled this self-imposed duty cheerfully. These facts were only learned by accident yesterday." Young Hartley meekly received the medal, which he richly deserved.

9531. HEROISM, Military. In the war of La Vendée, General Kléber, with four thousand men, was completely surrounded by an overwhelming force of the enemy, and saw no other way of saving his little band, except by stopping for a short time the passage of the Vendeans through a narrow ravine, which was all that was between the two armies. He called an officer to him, for whom he had a particular friendship and esteem. "Take," said he to him, "a company of grenadiers; stop the enemy before that ravine; you will be killed but you will save your comrades." "General

I shall do it," replied the officer, who received the order to immolate himself with as much calmness as if it had been a simple military evolution. The prediction of Kléber was but too fatally verified. The brave officer arrested the enemy's progress, but perished in the achievement.　　　　*Percy.*

9532. HEROISM, Remarkable. In September, 1857, a steamer bringing five hundred miners from the rich diggings of California to New York, encountered a fearful storm soon after leaving Havana. The vessel became disabled, and was kept afloat only by the herculean efforts of the crew and passengers in bailing out the water. For eighteen hours they labored, hoping that some passing ship would come to the rescue. Their vessel could not be kept afloat much longer, and despair began to settle down upon them. The brig Marine discovered their signal of distress, and stood off to await the steamer's boats with their loads of passengers. There was room only for the women and children. Not a male passenger attempted to enter the boats, and all were launched safely. These miners had with them ten millions of gold and gold dust, which they had labored very hard to accumulate, and with this they had delighted in the thought of surprising their friends on reaching home. The four hundred men counted it all, and their own lives also, less than that of the helpless women and children. They were frigidly calm with death staring them in the face. To this noble courage many owed their lives. Before the boats could return their vessel went down, and nearly all of this band of heroes were engulfed in the greedy sea.

9533. HEROISM, Unconscious. In the Gayoso Hospital, at Memphis, was a soldier who had lost an arm and leg in the assault at Vicksburg. Some cordial was given him, and he was made as comfortable as possible by Mr. F. G. Ensign, one of the agents of the Christian Commission. "Who are you? Where did you get these things?" asked the soldier. Mr. Ensign told him they came from Northern homes; they were sent by people who loved him. Tears came into his eyes as he lay quiet for a moment, and then he said, "Why, I haven't done anything to be remembered so." "You have given your leg and arm," was the reply, but this fact did not strike him as at all important; he only reiterated, "I haven't done anything." He was offered a Bible. "Well," said he, when his eye rested on the page without pain, "this is best of all. I have been here for weeks, and I did want to read the Bible so. This is just what I want. Who sent it?" And when told, the unselfish heart found utterance, "Why, I haven't done anything."

9534. HESITATION, Weakness of. Hesitation is a sign of weakness, for inasmuch as the comparative good and evil of the different modes of action about which we hesitate are seldom equally balanced, a strong mind should perceive the slightest inclination of the beam with the glance of an eagle, particularly as there are cases where the preponderance will be very minute, even although there should be life in one scale, and death in the other. *Colton.*

9535. HIDING PLACES, Oriental. We see in the case of David, and in that of many other good men, that they had to conceal themselves often in caves, mountains, and desert places, from the pursuit of their enemies. In countries like these, where the police is imperfect, where population is much scattered, and where it is very easy to sustain life, it can be no wonder that offenders and injured men often conceal themselves for months and years from the vigilance of their pursuers. It is an every-day occurrence to hear of men thus hiding themselves. Has a person to account for his conduct, or to appear in a court of justice? He packs up his valuables and makes a start into the jungle, or to some distant country. Perhaps he prowls about the skirts of a forest, and occasionally visits his family in the night. See him on his way; he walks so softly that the most delicate-eared animal cannot detect him; he looks in every direction; puts his ear near the ground, and listens for any sound; again he proceeds, sometimes crawling, sometimes walking, till he has reached his hiding-place. But the natives themselves are famous for assisting each other to elude the search of their pursuers, and often as did Jonathan and Ahimaaz, they conceal themselves in the well. Sometimes an offender will run to a man of rank who is at enmity with his foe, and exclaim, "My lord, you must be my hiding-place against that wicked man, who has committed so many crimes against you." "Ah, the good man! he was my hiding-place." *Roberts.*

9536. HIGHER LIFE, Attaining. I have known men who have been up in balloons, and they have told me that when they want to rise higher they just throw out some of the sand with which they ballast the balloon. Now, I believe one reason why so many people are earthly-minded and have so little of the spirit of heaven is that they have got too much ballast in the shape of love for earthly joys and gains; and what you want is to throw out some of the sand, and you will rise higher. *Moody.*

9537. HIGHWAY, God's. In the early times, if a man traveling in the king's highway between sun and sun, was robbed, he could recover all damages from the government of the country; but if he traveled in any other place and in any other time, it was at his own hazard and peril. So with God's highway, cast up for the redeemed to walk in. If we walk in God's highway we shall have God's protection. But wo be to us if we try any other route or method than he marks out.

9538. HISTORY, Burden of. History is but a kind of Newgate Calendar, a register of the crimes and miseries that man has inflicted on his fellow-man. It is a huge libel on human nature, to which we industriously add page after page, volume after volume, as if we were building up a monument to the honor rather than the infamy of our species. If we turn over the pages of these chronicles that man has written of himself, what are the characters dignified by the appellation of "great," and held up to the admiration of posterity? Tyrants, robbers, conquerors, renowned only for the magnitude of their misdeeds and the stupendous wrongs and miseries they have inflicted on mankind—warriors who have hired themselves to the trade of blood, not from motives of virtuous patriotism, or to protect the injured and defenceless, but merely to gain the vaunted glory of being successful in massacring their fellow-beings! What are the great events that constitute a glorious era? The fall of empires, the desolation of happy countries, splendid cities smoking in their ruins, the proudest works of art tumbled in the dust, the shrieks and groans of whole nations ascending unto heaven. *W. Irving.*

9539. HISTORY, Revelations of. Peter the Great, Emperor of Russia, was one day in a sailing-boat, when he became so angry with one of his companions that he seized him, with the intention of throwing him overboard. "You may drown me," said his subject, "but your history will tell of it." This reminder was effectual, and the emperor pardoned the man.

9540. HOBBY, A Medical. A certain doctor always treated his juvenile patients for "worms," whatever might happen to be their symptoms. One day, being called to a boy who was suffering severely, he felt the pulse, and, looking at the mother, with a solemn shake of the head, said, "Worms, madam! worms!" "Now, Doctor," said the mother, "it isn't worms at all, I tell ye; that boy fell down on the woodpile and broke his leg, and I want you to stop crying 'worms' and set it immediately." "Ah!" said the Doctor, determined not to be put down, "Worms in the wood, madam! worms in the wood!"

9541. HOLINESS, Ashamed of. What though the polite man count thy fashion a little odd, and too precise; it is because he knows nothing above that model of goodness which he hath set himself, and therefore approves of nothing beyond it; he knows not God, and therefore doth not discern and esteem what is most like him. When courtiers come down into the country, the common home-bred people possibly think their habit strange; but they care not for that—it is the fashion of court. What need, then, that Christians should be so tender-foreheaded as to be put out of countenance because the world looks upon holiness as a singularity? It is the only fashion in the highest court, yea, of the King of kings himself. *Coleridge.*

9542. HOLINESS, Aversion to. Man's nature, being contrary to holiness, hath an aversion to any act of homage to God, because holiness must at least be pretended. In every duty wherein we have a communion with God, holiness is requisite; now, as men are against the truth of holiness, because it is unsuitable to them, so they are not friends to those duties which require it, and for some space divert them from the thoughts of their beloved lusts. The word of the Lord is a yoke, prayer a drudgery, obedience a strange element. We are like fish that "drink up iniquity like water," and come not to the bank without the force of an angle; no more willing to do service for God, than a fish is of itself to do service for man. *Charnock.*

9543. HOLINESS, Beauty of. True holiness is a plain and an even thing, without falsehood, guile, perverseness of spirit, deceitfulness of heart, or starting aside. It hath one end, one rule, one way, one heart; whereas hypocrites are, in the Scripture, called "double-minded men," because they pretend to God, and follow the world:—and "crooked men," like the swelling of a wall, whose parts are not perpendicular, nor level to their foundation. Now rectitude, sincerity, and singleness of heart, are ever, both in the eyes of God and man, beautiful things. *Salter.*

9544. HOLINESS, Divine. In the temple, every "little" ornament even of the mighty structure that crowned the cliffs of Zion was "holy" to the Lord. Not the great courts and inner shrines and pillared halls merely, but all. Not a carven pomegranate, not a bell, silver or golden, but was "holy." The table and its lamps, with flowers of silver light, tent and staves, fluttering curtain and ascending incense, altar and sacrifice, breast-plate and ephod, mitre and gem-clasped girdle, wreathen chains and jeweled hangings—over all was inscribed holy; while within, in the innermost shrine, where God manifested himself above the mercy-seat, was the holiest. Thus the utter holiness of that God with whom they had to do was by every detail impressed upon the heart and conscience of ancient Israel. *Grosart.*

9545. HOLINESS, Emblems of. The laurel, firm, erect, and bold, expands its leaf of vivid green. In spite of the united, the repeated attacks of wind, and rain, and frost, it preserves an undismayed lively look, and maintains its post while withering millions fall around. Worthy, by vanquishing the rugged force of winter, worthy to adorn the triumphant conqueror's brow. The bay-tree scorns to be a mean pensioner on a few transient sunny gleams; or, with a servile obsequiousness, to vary its appearance in conformity to the changing seasons: by such indications of sterling worth, and staunch resolution, reading a lecture to the poet's genius, while it weaves the chaplet for his temples. These, and a few other plants, clad with native verdure, retain their comely aspect in the bleakest climes and in the coldest months. *Ruskin.*

9546. HOLINESS, Experience of. A Quaker lady of wealth, position and culture, was happily converted to God, and clearly taught the precious reality that Christ is the Lord our Righteousness. All doubt and fear as to her present acceptance and final salvation passed away, and she was happier than she had ever been before in her life. But one thing troubled her. She had her besetting sins, which she tried hard, but in vain, to conquer. She could suppress them, but she could not exterminate them. She could keep in the word, but she could not keep out the feeling. Another thing troubled her, too. Her service was more from duty than love, and her heart was not satisfied, neither was her conscience at rest in having it so. She wanted to have the well-spring of life in her as a fountain whence should flow forth rivers of living water. To attain this she made vigorous and persistent efforts, all however under a sense that the responsibility of the thing was upon her. Her efforts resulted only in deepening conviction and increasing her burden of heart. At last in a meeting she heard of the better way of faith in Jesus, and left herself, burden and all, in his hands. Light at once began to flow in upon her soul, and she became as happy as happy could be. When asked how it came about, "Oh," said she, "I just shifted the responsibility over upon Jesus." *W. E. Boardman.*

9547. HOLINESS, Instantaneous. The separation of sin from the soul is constantly preceded and followed by a gradual work: but is that separation in itself instantaneous, or is it not? In examining this, let us go on step by step. An instantaneous change has been wrought in some believers: none can deny this. Since that change, they enjoy perfect love. They feel this, and this alone. They "rejoice evermore, pray without ceasing, and in everything give thanks." Now this is all that I mean by perfection. Therefore, these are witnesses of the perfection which I preach. But in some, this change was not instantaneous. They did not perceive the instant when it was wrought. It is often difficult to perceive the instant when a man dies: yet there is an instant when life ceases. And, if ever sin ceases, there must be a last moment of its existence, and a first moment of our deliverance from it. *J. Wesley.*

9548. HOLINESS, Living. Lycurgus would allow none of his laws to be written. He would have the principles of government interwoven in the lives and manners of the people, as most conducive to their happiness. Their education would be such as to imprint these laws upon their minds, that they might remain perpetually before them. He will most faithfully abide by the king's commandment who has the word of God so engraven upon his heart that nothing can erase it. The multiplication of Bibles that stand upon book-shelves or lie upon tables is an easy matter; but to multiply copies of walking Scriptures, in the form of holy men who can say, "Thy word have I hid in my heart," is much more difficult. *Anon.*

9549. HOLINESS, a Preparation. The heathen had this notion: they would not permit any to come to their religious services unless they were prepared. That saying of Æneas in the poem, to his father, when he came from the war, is a clear proof; *Tu genitor*, etc. "Father, do you meddle with the sacrifices; but as for me it is a sinful thing to touch them, till I have washed myself in the fountain." This was an outward external rite amongst them for cleansing themselves. The very heathen saw they must not meddle with their holy things till

they were cleansed: therefore they had one who cried out to the people when they came to sacrifice: "All you that are unclean and profane, go far away from these sacrifices." Not only the word of God, but the very light of nature taught them not to meddle with holy things till they were sanctified. Take heed how you hear; not only hear, but take heed to prepare yourselves for hearing: "look to thy feet (it hath the same sense) when thou comest into the house of God:" prepare thyself, be not hasty, lest thine be counted but the "Sacrifice of Fools." *Caryl.*

9550. HOLINESS, Reasonableness of. For where is the absurdity of this doctrine? If the light of a candle, brought into a dark room, can instantly expel the darkness; and if, upon opening the shutters at noon, your gloomy apartment can be instantly filled with meridian light; why might not the instantaneous rending of the vail of unbelief, or the sudden and full opening of the eye of faith, instantly fill your soul with the light of truth and the fire of love, supposing the Sun of Righteousness arise upon you with healing in his wings? May not the Sanctifier descend upon your waiting soul as quickly as the Spirit descended upon your Lord at his baptism? Did it not descend as a dove; that is, with the soft motion of a dove, which swiftly shoots down, and instantly alights? A good man said once, "A mote is little when compared to the sun; but I am far less before God." Alluding to this comparison, I ask, if the sun could instantly kindle a mote; nay, if a burning-glass can in a moment calcine a bone, and turn a stone to lime; and if the dim flame of a candle can, in the twinkling of an eye, destroy the flying insect which comes within its sphere; how unscriptural and irrational is it to suppose, that when God fully baptizes a soul with his sanctifying Spirit, and with the celestial fire of his love, he cannot, in an instant, destroy the man of sin, burn up the chaff of corruption, melt the heart of stone into a heart of flesh, and kindle the believing soul into pure seraphic love. *John Fletcher.*

9551. HOLINESS, Receiving. It may be with the root of sin, as with its fruit: some souls parley many years before they can be persuaded to give up all their outward sins, and others part with them instantaneously. You may compare the former to those besieged towns which make a long resistance; while the latter resemble those fortresses which are surprised and taken by storm. Travelers inform us that vegetation is so quick and powerful in some warm climates, that the seeds of some vegetables yield a salad in less than twenty-four hours. Should a northern philosopher say, "Impossible!" and should an English gardener exclaim against such mushroom-salad, they would only expose their prejudices, as do those who decry instantaneous justification, or mock at the possibility of the instantaneous destruction of indwelling sin. *John Fletcher.*

9552. HOLY OF HOLIES, Penalty of Entering the

It was death for any one except the high-priest to enter the holy of holies. So carefully was this observed and provided for, that to prevent it being necessary for any one to enter to bring out the body of the high-priest in case he should die there, before the Lord, on the great day of expiation, a cord was fastened to his foot, the end of which was left beyond the veil, that he might be drawn out by it, if such a circumstance occurred. It should be observed that the Jews were always in dread lest the high-priest should perish in performing the services of that great day.   *Kitto.*

9553. HOLY SPIRIT, Agency of the. Unconverted men often say, "If these things are so, if they are so clear and great, why cannot we see them?" And there is no answer to be given but this, "Ye are blind." "But we want to see them. If they are real, they are our concern as well as yours. Oh, that some preacher would come who had power to make us see them!" Poor souls, there is no such preacher, and you need not wait for him. Let him gather God's light as he will, he can but pour it on blind eyes. A burning glass will condense sunbeams into a focus of brightness; and if a blind eye be put there, not a whit will it see, though it be consumed. Light is the remedy for darkness, not blindness. Neither will strong powers of understanding on your part serve. The great Earl of Chatham once went with a pious friend to hear Mr. Cecil. The sermon was on the Spirit's agency in the hearts of believers. As they were coming from the church, the mighty statesman confessed that he could not understand it all, and asked his friend if he supposed that any one in the house could. "Why yes," said he, "there were many plain, unlettered women, and some children there, who understood every word of it, and heard it with joy." *Dr. Hoge.*

9554. HOLY SPIRIT, Biblical. The Gift of the Spirit is frequently described by words expressive of abundance and continuance. Thus the Holy Ghost is spoken of as—*Coming*, as a mighty and powerful impulse, as in the case of Othniel, Jephthah, Samson, etc., personally, and upon the Church collectively. *Poured out*, Ps. 1: 23; Isa. 44: 3; Joel 2: 28, 29; Zech. 12: 10; Acts 2: 17, 18. *Shed* abundantly, Titus 3: 6. *Clothing*, Judges 6: 34; 1 Chron. 12: 18, margins; so Luke 24: 49—"endued," or invested with the Spirit. *Dwelling*, Ps. 68: 18; John 14: 17; Rom. 6: 9; 1 Cor. 3: 16, and also 6: 19. *Abiding*, John 14: 16. *Supplying* the wants of the Church, Phil. 1: 19. The Greek word here (Phil. 1: 19), is taken from the office of the Choregus, whose place it was to supply the chorus, at his own expense, with ornaments and all other necessaries. So the Holy Spirit supplies the wants of the Church. St. Luke's Gospel contains the most frequent references to the Holy Ghost of all the gospels. In the first four chapters, we read of Zacharias and Elizabeth, John the Baptist, Mary, Simeon, and our Lord himself, being filled with, or moved by, the Holy Ghost. A striking con-

trast. Thomas, though one of our Lord's chosen apostles, who had been with him during his ministry, and heard him so often foretell his own resurrection, yet refused to believe the resurrection, until compelled by sight to say, "My Lord," John 20: 18. Elizabeth—less favored—when Mary came to see her before he was born, at once acknowledged her as "the mother of my Lord," Luke 1: 43. "Elizabeth," we read, "was filled with the Holy Ghost," ver. 44. Filled with the Spirit—Full of the Holy Ghost. How often these pregnant expressions occur; denoting the energizing, ennobling power of the Spirit in the heart of God's saints. They are generally marked by some special result following. Take, *e. g.*, the following cases: *Bezaleel*—Exod. 31: 3; 35: 30, 31—"filled with the spirit of God;" to prepare the materials for the tabernacle. *Zacharias and Elizabeth*—Luke 1: 41, 67—inspired with the spirit of prophecy. *John Baptist*, Luke 1: 15, 16. (See the beautiful connection.) The *disciples* at Pentecost, and afterwards—Acts 2: 4; 13: 52—endued with the ordinary and extraordinary gifts of the Spirit. *The seven deacons*—Acts 6—qualified for their important offices; filled with wisdom, ver. 3; faith, ver. 5; and power, ver. 8. *Peter*—Acts 4: 8; 13: 19, 20—emboldened to confess Jesus Christ without fear. *Stephen*—Acts 6: 5—witnessing a good confession; rejoicing in the midst of danger, 6: 15; calm in the hour of death, 7: 55. *St. Paul*—Acts 9: 17; 13: 9—even from the commencement of his ministerial course, was filled with the Holy Ghost.   *Bowes.*

9555. HOLY SPIRIT, Descent of the. July 23d, 1839, whilst the Rev. William Burns, jun., was preaching in his father's church, "he clasped his hands, lifted his eyes to heaven, and, in an agony for the Holy Ghost to descend upon the people, exclaimed, 'O come! come!' and being strengthened in his faith, 'He is coming! He is coming!' Suddenly a voice was heard from among the congregation, 'He is come! He is come! Hallelujah! Hallelujah! Glory be to God!' This ran like electricity through the whole assembly of fifteen hundred persons: and the scene which succeeded will not admit of description. Here was the formalist of fifty years' standing in the church, shaking from head to foot, and crying aloud for mercy. Then the cry was heard, 'What must I do to be saved?' while others were in exultation, exclaiming, 'Behold, God is become my salvation!' An elder, who was endeavoring to direct and comfort his aged mother, was seized by the convincing power of the Spirit; and with a voice which, had it not been heard whence it came, could scarcely have been believed to be human, cried out, 'O Christ, have mercy on my soul! O, break this hard heart!' Presently one ran to the manse with tidings of what had taken place in the church—when one of the ministers ascended the pulpit, gave a few words of advice, sung, prayed, and dismissed the congregation. But although the people left the church, many of them would not and did not go home till God had blessed them. The vestry was filled with penitents; other places in the town were opened for them; and scenes were witnessed that day in Kilsyth, the like of which had not been known within the memory of any then living. Numbers felt the gospel to be the power of God to salvation."

9556. HOLY SPIRIT, Earnest of the. In the early times, when land was sold, the owner cut a turf from the greensward and cast it into the cap of the purchaser as a token that it was his; or he tore off the branch of a tree and put it into the new owner's hand to show that he was entitled to all the products of the soil; and when the purchaser of a house received seizin or possession, the key of the door, or a bundle of thatch plucked from the roof, signified that the building was yielded up to him. The God of all grace has given to his people all the perfections of heaven to be their heritage for ever, and the earnest of his Spirit is to them the blessed token that all things are theirs. The Spirit's work of comfort and sanctification is a part of heaven's covenant blessings, a turf from the soil of Canaan, a twig from the tree of life, the key to mansions in the skies. Possessing the earnest of the Spirit, we have received *seizin* of heaven. *Spurgeon.*

9557. HOLY SPIRIT, Effects of the. Mark the rain that falls from above, and the same shower that droppeth out of one cloud increaseth sundry plants in a garden, and severally, according to the condition of every plant; in one stalk it makes a rose, in another a violet, divers in a third, and sweetening all. So the Spirit works its multiform effects in several complexions, and all according to the increase of God. Is thy habit and inclination choleric? Why, try thyself if thou be very apt to be zealous in a good cause, and it turns thy natural infirmity into a holy heat. Is melancholy predominant? The grace of God will turn that sad humor into devotion, prayer, and mortifying thy pleasures to die unto the world. Is thy temperature sanguine and cheerful? The goodness of God will allow it unto thee in thy civil life, in a good mean; but over and above, it will make thee bountiful, easy to pardon injuries, glad of reconciliations, comfortable to the distressed, always rejoicing in the Lord. Is a man fearful? If this freezing disease, which is in thee from thy mother's womb, be not absolutely cured, yet the Holy Ghost will work upon it, to make thy conscience tender, wary to give no offence, to make thee pitiful, penitent, contrite, ready to weep for thy transgressions. *F. F. Trench.*

9558. HOLY SPIRIT, Energy of the. At a revival meeting in a Southern State, a notoriously wicked infidel appeared, and stood outside while the meeting was going on in the church. A young girl arose, and gave a simple experience of love and faith. Her words were as the pebbles which David hurled at the giant. The wicked man heard, and fell, like Goliath, to the earth. The preacher and others took him up, and carried him inside.

He was converted, and became eminent for piety and usefulness. At a love-feast held in a barn in Vermont, from which the songs and experiences were heard by the crowd outside, the Holy Ghost came down upon them, and many were converted.

9559. HOLY SPIRIT, Gentleness of. It is curious to remark, that wherever the Holy Ghost is spoken of in the Bible, he is spoken of in terms of gentleness and love. We often read of "the wrath of God" the Father, as Rom. 1 : 18; and we read of the wrath of God the Son, as Ps. 2 : 12; but we nowhere read of the wrath of God the Holy Ghost. *M'Cheyne.*

9560. HOLY SPIRIT Grieved. A chaplain in passing through one of the wards of a hospital thought he saw a familiar face. He recognized the youth as one of his Sabbath school boys, his father a deacon in the Congregationalist church, and his mother a praying woman. It was understood that he could not live, and the chaplain was anxious to know if he was ready to exchange worlds. He met a clear intellectual response to all that was said of Christ as a Saviour, but insisted upon saying that "he knew he was going to perdition." He was told that there was hope in Christ, if he would but cast himself upon him. He responded, "I know that, but I don't want go to Christ. I don't have any interest in him." "But can't you pray, 'God be merciful to me a sinner?'" asked the chaplain. "Yes," he replied, "I can say the words, but I don't feel it. My time has passed. Last year I thought that I was a Christian, and my father wanted me to join the church. Then I made up my mind that I'd see a little more of the world before I bound myself down, and now it is too late." He continued in this state about three weeks and then died, begging the chaplain not to tell his mother the state of his mind, and desiring him to implore his younger brother to take warning by his awful end. Gentle and winning in all his ways, he lacked a preparation to meet his God.

9561. HOLY SPIRIT, Influence of the. A little girl was sitting with her uncle while he was casting up accounts. All was quiet for a time, when she heard him say, "There! I have quite a nice little sum laid up against a time of need." "What are you talking about?" asked the little girl. "About my treasures that I have laid up," said the uncle. "Up in heaven?" she asked; for she heard her father read at prayers that morning about laying up treasures in heaven. The response was, "No! my treasures are all on earth; some in banks, and some in other places." "But ain't you got any up in heaven?" persisted the little child. "Well, I don't believe I have," replied the man; "but you may leave me now, I'm going out." Impressed with the thought that he was not rich towards God, he began immediately to lay up treasure in heaven. The words of the child, impressed by the Holy Spirit, led him to an active Christian life.

9562. HOLY SPIRIT, Life by the. Correct opinions are in order to correct morals, but a man's opinions may be right, while his heart and life are wrong. Colton wrote more moral precepts than any man of his time, and violated them all. We can put truth into the mind of our fellow-man no farther than the understanding. We cannot reach the moral nature by light alone. When one changes the opinions of an erring brother on moral subjects, something is accomplished; but to give a disposition to love and obey truth is a different thing. The Holy Spirit alone sinks the truth through the intelligence into the conscience and the affections. Truth is light, but it is not life. Alone it is like the sun in winter; it shines but to enlighten a dead, cold earth. With the Spirit it is like the sun in summer; it shines with life in its light, vivifying nature and producing blade, flower and fruitage. So the light of divine truth shines in the darkness of the natural mind, and the darkness appreciates it not, until by the Spirit it becomes "spirit and life" to the soul. "In him was life, and that life was the light of men."   *Walker.*

9563. HOLY SPIRIT, Outpouring of the. The following marvelous account is fully authenticated: Rev. John Easter was holding a meeting in the forest; it was in the mid-day of his fame and power; hundreds and hundreds had gathered to hear the wonderful man. In the midst of his sermon, while all were hanging on his lips in breathless silence, suddenly a rushing sound as of a mighty wind smote the ears of the hearers. All eyes were instantly turned upward, but no storm had smitten the forest; not a twig, not a leaf stirred; still the awful sound swept over and around them. Instantly several hundred horses broke from their fastenings, and rushed wildly in all directions through the woods; hundreds of men and women fell flat upon their faces, stricken down by the mighty power of God. The cry of conviction that arose was appalling; even the holiest of Christians trembled in the presence of that mysterious sound. The work of conversion was as instantaneous as the work of conviction, and many were the witnesses for Christ that arose in the midst of the awe-stricken multitude. The effects of this display of divine power were great indeed on the part of the people far and near. The work spread like fire in dry stubble, and hundreds were added to the church.
Episcopal Methodist.

9564. HOLY SPIRIT, Power of the. During the persecution in 303, a timid deacon of Antioch, in Egypt, hired a piper and dancer to personate him before the governor, and bring him a certificate showing that Apollonius had sacrificed. Christians who did thus were called libellatics, but not apostates. The piper put on Apollonius' hood and cloak, and went before the judge. He said, "What art thou, fellow? A Christian perhaps, muffled thus, as if thou feardest to be seen." Then the Holy Spirit came mightily upon him, and he who came a heathen with fraudulent intent said, "Yes, my lord, I am a Christian." "Thou knowest the choice that is set before thee, torture or sacrifice," said the judge. "I will not sacrifice,"

said the piper. He now had courage to refuse the very work he came to do. The magistrate said, "Send for Philemon, the piper; perchance his sweet melodies will drive away the fancies of this fool, and allure him to the worship of our gods." The piper was sought, but could not be found. In his stead his brother was brought and questioned as to where this piper was. Pointing to the man in the hooded cloak he said, "That is he." They plucked off the cloak, and there stood the piper in his gay buskins with his reeds in his hands. The judge laughed heartily and pronounced it a rare joke. "We make no account of this, man," said he, "for to this thou wast born and bred, that thou shouldst shake our sides with laughter. Now sacrifice and end the farce." Philemon persistently refused, and the judge knew that no jest was meant. The piper broke his reeds, received baptism, and maintained a firm confession of Christ to the end.

9565. HOLY SPIRIT Quenched. A gentleman called his sons around his dying bed, and said, "When I was a youth, the Spirit strove with me, and seemed to say, 'Seek religion now;' but Satan suggested the necessity of waiting till I grew up, because it was incompatible with youthful amusement; so I resolved I would wait till I grew up to be a man. I did so, and was then reminded of my promise to seek religion; but Satan again advised me to wait till middle age, for business and a young family demanded all my attention. Yes, I said, I will do so—I will wait till middle age. I did so—my serious impressions left me for some years. They were again renewed; conscience reminded me of my promises; the Spirit said, 'Seek religion now;' but then I had less time than ever; Satan advised my waiting till I was old, then my children would be settled in business, and I should have nothing else to do; I could then give an undivided attention to it. I listened to his suggestion, and the Spirit ceased to strive with me. I have lived to be old, but now I have no desire as formerly to attend to the concerns of my soul; my heart is hardened. I have resisted and quenched the Spirit; now there is no hope; already I feel a hell within, the beginning of an eternal misery. I feel the gnawings of that worm that never dies. Take warning from my miserable end; seek religion now; let nothing tempt you to put off this important concern." Then in the greatest agonies he expired.

9566. HOLY SPIRIT, Resisting the. Take heed of resisting the Spirit when he makes his approach to thee in the Word. Sometimes he knocks, and, meeting a repulse, goes from the sinner's door. He that hath promised to come in if we open, hath not promised to come again if we unkindly send him away.   *Gurnall.*

9567. HOLY SPIRIT, Silent Working of the. Can I see the dew of heaven as it falls on a summer evening? I cannot. It comes down softly and gently, noiselessly and imperceptibly. But when I go forth in the morning after a cloudless night, and see every leaf sparkling with moisture, and feel every blade of grass damp and wet, I say at once, "There has been a dew." Just so it is with the presence of the Spirit in the soul.   *Ryle.*

9568. HOLY SPIRIT, Withdrawal of the. When God takes his Holy Spirit from the sinner, he is left to the hardness and obduracy of his own depraved nature; no godly grief can ever affect his heart, no tears of penitential sorrow furrow his cheek: he sins without any remorse; from conscience he receives no checks; judgments excite in him no alarm; the bounties of Divine Providence, scattered liberally around him, awaken no sensations of gratitude: with an understanding dark as hell can make it, he has a heart unfeeling as a stone, and hard as adamant: and whatever view we take of the Spirit of God, or whatever office he may be presented as sustaining, his final abandonment of us must be considered, in its results, too tremendously horrible to admit of any adequate description. Is he a comforter?—When he is withdrawn, we can have none to comfort our hearts; for to all others we may say, "Miserable comforters are ye all." Man can have no sources of consolation in himself: when God leaves him, misery becomes his inalienable inheritance. Is the Spirit of God a guide?—Without him we are left to "grope, as if we had no eyes," and to "stumble at noonday as in the night;" to wander heedlessly and blindly on, in the mazes of error and delusion, the remaining days of our vain life, which we spend as a shadow; or to be like mariners "with ship half-foundered and with compass lost," left to the mercy of the waves, in midnight darkness on a stormy sea. Is the Spirit of God a sanctifier? is his agency essential to our being made meet to be partakers of the inheritance of the saints in light? If, therefore, God take his Holy Spirit from us, the things that belong unto our peace will be hid from our eyes, and we must remain eternally unprepared for the heavenly world.   *Anon.*

9569. HOME, Advice for the. It is just as possible to keep a calm house as a clean house, a cheerful house, an orderly house, as a furnished house, if the heads set themselves to do so. Where is the difficulty of consulting each other's weakness, as well as each other's wants; each other's tempers, as well as each other's health; each other's comfort, as well as each other's character? Oh! it is by leaving the peace at home to chance, instead of pursuing it by system, that so many houses are unhappy. It deserves notice, also, that almost any one can be courteous and forbearing and patient in a neighbor's house. If anything go wrong, or be out of time, or disagreeable there, it is made the best of, not the worst; even efforts are made to excuse it, and to show that it is not felt; or, if felt, it is attributed to accident, not design; and this is not only easy, but natural, in the house of a friend. I will not, therefore, believe that what is so natural in the house of another is impossible at home; but maintain, without fear, that all the courtesies of social life may be upheld in domestic societies. A husband

as willing to be pleased at home, and as anxious to please as in his neighbor's house; and a wife as intent on making things comfortable every day to her family as on set days to her guests, could not fail to make their own home happy. Let us not evade the point of these remarks by recurring to the maxim about allowances for temper. It is worse than folly to refer to our temper, unless we could prove that we gained anything good by giving way to it. Fits of ill-humor punish us quite as much, if not more than those they are vented upon; and it actually requires more effort, and inflicts more pain to give them up, than would be requisite to avoid them.   *Phillip.*

9570. HOME, Almost. A poor widow had been long struggling with adversity. The husband of her youth had been torn from her embrace by the ruthless hand of death. Her children, one by one, had been consigned to the dark and gloomy grave, and she was left to plod in sorrow her weary journey alone. Eager to join her loved ones who were beckoning her from the skies, she exclaims, " Patience, my soul; it won't be long; I'm almost home!" A man of God who had "served his generation," and whose work was done, when bidding farewell to his weeping family and friends, exclaimed, "Before morning I shall be at home!"   *Epis. Methodist.*

9571. HOME, Ambition of All. To be happy at home, is the ultimate result of all ambition; the end to which every enterprise and labor tends, and of which every desire prompts the prosecution. It is indeed at home that every man must be known by those who would make a just estimate either of his virtue or felicity; for smiles and embroidery are alike occasional, and the mind is often dressed for show in painted honor and fictitious benevolence.   *Johnson.*

9572. HOME, Education in the. The fireside is a seminary of infinite importance. Few can receive the honors of a college, but all are graduates of the home. The learning of the university may fade from the recollection, its classic lore may moulder in the halls of memory; but the simple lessons of home, enameled upon the heart of childhood, defy the rust of years, and outlive the more mature but less vivid pictures of after years. So deep, so lasting, indeed, are the impressions of early life, that you often see a man in the imbecility of age holding fresh in his recollection the events of childhood, while all the wide space between that and the present hour is a blasted and forgotten waste. You have perchance seen an old and half-obliterated portrait, and in the attempt to have it cleaned and restored, you may have seen it fade away, while a brighter and more perfect picture, painted beneath, is revealed to view. This portrait, first drawn upon the canvas, is no inapt illustration of youth; and though it may be concealed by some after-design, still the original traits will shine through the outward picture, giving it tone while fresh, and surviving it in decay.   *Goodrich*

9573. HOME, Esteeming. It was the policy of the good old gentleman to make his children feel that home was the happiest place in the world; and I value this delicious home-feeling as one of the choicest gifts a parent can bestow. — *W. Irving.*

9574. HOME, A Godly. Are you not surprised to find how independent of money peace of conscience is, and how much happiness can be condensed in the humblest home? A cottage will not hold the bulky furniture and sumptuous accommodations of a mansion; but if God be there, a cottage will hold as much happiness as might stock a palace. — *Dr. J. Hamilton.*

9575. HOME, Gone. A dying soldier was asked for a last message for his father. He was silent a moment, a smile playing over his face, "Tell him I have gone home." "Have you any message for your wife?" "Tell her I have gone home." "Is there nothing more you want to say, no other message I can bear for you?" "No, that is enough. They will all understand it—I have gone home."

9576. HOME, Influence of. Those of you who are best acquainted with the world, or who have read most extensively the histories of men, will allow that, in the formation of character, the most telling influence is the early home. It is that home which often in boyhood has formed beforehand our most famous scholars, our most celebrated heroes, our most devoted missionaries; and even when men have grown up reckless and reprobate, and have broken all restraints, human and divine, the last anchor which has dragged, the last cable they have been able to snap, is the memory which moored them to a virtuous home. — *Dr. J. Hamilton.*

9577. HOME, Happy. Six of the seven wise men of Greece give their opinion of what constitutes a happy home as follows: Solon thought the house most happy where the estate was got without injustice, kept without distrust, and spent without repentance. Bias said, "That house is happy where the master does freely and voluntarily at home what the law compels him to do abroad." Thales held that house most happy where the master had most leisure and respite from business. Cleobulus said, "That in which the master is more beloved than feared." Pittacus said, "That is most happy where superfluities are not required and necessaries are not wanting." Chilo added, "That house is most happy where the master rules as a monarch in his kingdom." And he proceeded, "When a certain Lacedæmonian desired Lycurgus to establish a democracy in the city, 'Go you, friend,' replied he, 'and make the experiment first in your own house.'"

9578. HOME, Trifles Affect. The road to home happiness lies over small stepping-stones. Slight circumstances are the stumbling-blocks of families. The prick of a pin, says the proverb, is enough to make an empire insipid. The tenderer the feelings, the painfuller the wound. A cold, unkind word checks and withers the blossom of the dearest love, as the most delicate rings of the vine are troubled by the faintest breeze. The misery of a life is born of a chance observation. If the true history of quarrels, public and private, were honestly written, it would be silenced with an uproar of derision. — *E. Jesse.*

9579. HOME, Unhappy. A late writer says, "I am one of those whose lot in life has been to go out into an unfriendly world at an early age; and of nearly twenty families in which I made my home in the course of about nine years, there were only three that could be designated as happy families. The source of trouble was not so much the lack of love, as the lack of care to manifest it."

9580. HONESTY, Christian. The captain of a troop of German cavalry called at the door of a cottage, in a lonely valley, and was met by a venerable Moravian. "Father," said the officer, "show me a field where I can set my troops a-foraging." "Presently," replied he. The old man conducted them out of the valley. After a quarter of an hour's march, they found a fine field of barley. "There is the very thing we want," said the captain. "Have patience for a few minutes," replied his guide, "you shall be satisfied." They went on, and at the distance of about a quarter of a league further, they at length reached another field of barley. The troop immediately dismounted, cut and secured the grain, and remounted. The officer, upon this, said to his conductor, "Father, you have given yourself and us unnecessary trouble: the first field was much better than this." "Very true, Sir," replied the man; "but it was not mine."

9581. HONESTY, Commercial. A linen merchant in Coleraine offered the famous Dr. Adam Clarke, when a youth, a situation in his warehouse, which was accepted by him with the consent of his parents. He knew well that his clerk was religious, but he was not sensible of the extent of principle which actuated him. Some differences arose at times about the way of conducting the business, which were settled pretty amicably. But the time of the great Dublin market approached, and the merchant was busy preparing for it. The master and man were together in the folding-room, when one of the pieces was found short of the required number of yards. "Come," says the merchant, "it is but a trifle. We shall soon stretch it, and make out the yard. Come, Adam, take one end, and pull against me." Adam had neither ears nor heart for the proposal, and absolutely refused to do what he thought a dishonest thing. A long argument and expostulation followed, in which the usages of the trade were strongly and variously enforced; but all in vain. Adam kept to his purpose, resolving to suffer rather than sin. He was therefore obliged to call for one of his men less scrupulous, and Adam retired quietly to his desk. Soon after he informed his "young friend," as he always seemed proud to call him, that it was very clear he was not fit for worldly business, and wished him to look out for some employment more congenial to his own mind; and with what result is well known.

9582. HONESTY, Death or. Put it out of the power of truth to give you an ill character; and if anybody reports you not to be an honest man, let your practice give him the lie; and to make all sure, you should resolve to live no longer than you can live honestly; for it is better to be nothing than a knave.
Antoninus.

9583. HONESTY, Estimating. There is no ascertaining the quality of a tree but by its fruits. When the wheels of a clock move within, the hands on the dial will move without. When the heart of a man is sound in conversion, then the life will be fair in profession. When the conduit is walled in, how shall we judge of the spring but by the waters which run through the pipes? *Secker.*

9584. HONESTY, Fable of. A woodman was felling a tree on the bank of a river, and by chance let slip his axe into the water, when it immediately sunk to the bottom. Being thereupon in great distress, he sat down and lamented his loss bitterly. But Mercury, whose river it was, taking compassion on him, and hearing from him the cause of his sorrow, dived to the bottom of the river, and bringing up a golden axe, asked the woodman if that were his. Upon the man's denying it, Mercury dived a second time, and brought up one of silver. Again the man denied that it was his. So diving a third time, he produced the identical axe which he had lost. "That is mine!" said the woodman, delighted to have recovered his own; and so pleased was Mercury with the fellow's truth and honesty, that he at once made him a present of the other two. The man goes to his companions, and giving them an account of what had happened to him, one of them determined to try whether he might not have the like good fortune. So repairing to the same place, as if for the purpose of cutting wood, he let slip his axe on purpose into the river, and then sat down on the bank, and made a great show of weeping. Mercury appeared as before, and hearing from him that his tears were caused by the loss of his axe, dived once more into the stream; and bringing up a golden axe, asked him if that was the axe he had lost. "Aye, surely," said the man, eagerly; and he was about to grasp the treasure, when Mercury, to punish his impudence and lying, not only refused to give him that, but would not so much as restore him his own axe again. *Æsop.*

9585. HONESTY, Faith and. There are those who have received the Scriptures, unto whom if thou trust a talent they will restore it unto thee; and there are also of them, those unto whom if thou trust a dinar, they will not restore it unto thee, unless thou stand over them continually with great urgency. *Koran.*

9586. HONESTY, Language of. The Arabs, notorious for their robberies, do not say, when exhibiting their plunder, "I robbed a man of it," but, "I gained it." The thief has an honest tongue.

9587. HONESTY, Moral. They that cry down moral honesty cry down that which is a great part of religion—my duty towards God, and my duty towards man. What care I to see a man run after a sermon, if he cozen and cheat as soon as he comes home? On the other side, morality must not be without religion; for if so, it may change as I see convenient. Religion must govern it. He that has no religion to govern his morality is not better than my mastiff dog: so long as you stroke and please him, and do not pinch him, he will play with you as finely as may be: he is a very good moral mastiff; but if you hurt him he will fly in your face. *Selden.*

9588. HONESTY, Principle of. As a man can never be truly honest unless he be religious, so, on the other hand, whatever show of religion a man may make, he cannot be truly religious in God's judgment unless he is honest in his conversation towards his neighbor.
Bishop Mant.

9589. HONESTY, Rare. A poor widow at Lisbon, went several times to the ante-chamber of the Court, and though frequently ordered to retire, she as constantly returned the next day, saying she must speak to the king. At length she saw him passing by, and presented a casket to him, saying, "Sire, behold what I have discovered among the rubbish of some of the ruined edifices by the great earthquake of 1755. I am a poor widow, and have six children. That casket would relieve me from my present distresses; but I prefer my honor with a good conscience, to all the treasures in the world. I deliver this to your Majesty, as the most proper person to restore it to its lawful possessor, and to recompense me for the discovery." The king immediately ordered the casket to be opened, and was struck with the beauty of the jewels which it contained; after which he commended the widow's honesty and assured her of his protection, and ordered twenty thousand piastres to be given to her. He caused search to be made to discover the real proprietor; and ordered if their researches should prove fruitless, that the jewels should be sold, and the proceeds appropriated to the use of the widow and her children.

9590. HONESTY, Record of. The obituary of Mr. Martin recently appeared, remarkable for its rarity in these days of demoralization, both in public and private life: "At Plainfield, N. J. Henry A. H. Martin, locally known as 'the man whom everybody trusted,' died on Friday. He was town collector for fifteen years, and his accounts never varied a cent. No nominations were ever made against him at an election."

9591. HONESTY, Religion and. A West India planter would not allow the missionaries to preach to his slaves. Visiting a neighboring plantation, he was astonished to find fruits exposed, yet untouched: "How is this?" said he; "you negroes are always ready to take everything you can lay your hands on." "No, massa," replied a slave, "negroes who pray never thieve." He saw his error. "What have I been about, not to let the missionaries come to my estate?" he exclaimed. He at once sent a request to the missionaries to come and teach his slaves whenever they pleased.

9592. HONESTY, Result of. Charlie received the lesson of honesty at an early age from his widowed mother. He won the approval of his employer, who gratified his mother when he told her that her son could be trusted anywhere. But a dark day came upon them. They were poor; his work would be done in one day more. He expressed his anxieties to his trusting mother, who said God had taken care of them when he was not large enough to help, and he would not forsake them now. The next day his employer handed him a bill, saying, "Take this ten dollar bill, pay Jones and Young, and bring the change." Without looking at the bill, he put it into his pocket. On his way he looked at it, and found he had one hundred instead of ten dollars. He met an associate and told him the case, and was told that he was a fool to think of returning the money. He went to the bank, had his bill changed, and rolled up ninety dollars for his employer. On the way to pay the bills he met him much excited, and was told he must have given one hundred dollars to some men that were in his office. Charlie said, "You gave it to me, and here is the change." His employer said, "You are an honest boy, and I must see that you have another situation." He kept his word, and Charlie was installed in the bank which had changed his hundred-dollar bill, with some fear at seeing so small a boy have so much money. He prospered, and has placed the secret of his success over his private desk, "Honesty is the best policy."

9593. HONESTY, Success of. The fortune of the Rothschilds is traced to the honesty of Moses Rothschild, of Frankfort. During the French Revolution, a prince of Hesse-Cassel, fleeing through Frankfort, left his treasures with a small Jew banker there, who refused to give him a receipt for them. Afterwards the French plundered the Jew, robbing him of all but the prince's treasures, which were buried in his garden. These he dug up, and used in trade, and when the times of peace returned, he restored the money and jewels to the prince, though he had lost his own. The prince in gratitude recommended the honest banker to various sovereigns. His business prospered, and his house has exercised a greater influence in the affairs of Europe than any king. Strict honesty has been their principle. People found that they could be trusted, and unprecedented success is the result.

9594. HONESTY, Tested. The Prince of Conti, at the siege of Phillipsburg, in 1734, threw a purse to a brave grenadier, excusing the smallness of the sum it contained, as being too poor a reward for such courage as his. Next morning the grenadier went to the Prince with two diamond rings, and other jewels of value. "Sir," said he, "the gold I found in your purse, I suppose you intended for me; but these I bring back to you, having no claim to them."

"You have doubly deserved them by your bravery, and by your honesty," said the Prince, "therefore they are yours."

9595. HONESTY, Triumph of. A schoolboy went to a situation, and one Saturday his master gave him a sovereign by mistake for a shilling. The boy had a hard battle about that sovereign. "The sovereign must go back to your master," says conscience; "it is not yours." "Your master gave it you," says temptation; "keep it, Willie; perhaps it was not a mistake, and if it was, it will never be found out. "Don't listen to temptation, Willie," says conscience; "you know it was a mistake, and that you have no right to the sovereign." "You are very poor," says temptation; "look at your clothes, Willie, how old they are, and this will buy new ones." "You are wrong, Willie, to listen to what temptation is saying; listen to what the Bible says, Willie: 'Resist the devil, and he will flee from you,'" says conscience. "I say, Willie, you will be a blockhead," says temptation, "if you don't keep the sovereign." "It will be a curse to you as long as you live," says conscience, "if you do; and then there is another world, Willie; take it back at once." "Nay, wait till to-morrow," says temptation, "it will be time enough." "'Whatsoever thy hand findeth to do, do it with thy might,'" says conscience; "do it at once, and you will have a quiet Sunday." Poor Willie! It was a sad fight, but conscience had something more to say yet. "What did the teacher at the Sunday-school talk about last Sunday, Willie? What was the text? 'Thou God seest me.'" "Oh," cried Willie, "Thou God seest me!" In a few minutes he reached his master's house. The mistake was made known and the money returned. The master said little. Willie won the confidence of his employer, was promoted, and rose rapidly to a place of trust and to a condition of prosperity.

9596. HONESTY, Unpopular. Bishop Ames tells a story of a slave master in the olden time who said to his chattel, "Pompey, I hear you are a great preacher." "Yes, massa, de Lord do help me powerful sometimes." "Well, Pompey, don't you think the negroes steal little things on the plantation?" "I'se mighty 'fraid they does, massa." "Then, Pompey, I want you to preach a sermon to the negroes against stealing." After a brief reflection, Pompey replied, "You see, massa, dat wouldn't never do, 'cause 'twould trow such a col'ness over de meetin'."

9597. HONOR, Appeal to. James Harper left his father's house in boyhood, to learn the trade of printer in the city of New York. His parents were Methodists of the earnest sort. Family prayer, led by his mother, was the last service at parting. When seated in the wagon, his mother took him by the hand and said, "James, remember you have got good blood in you; don't disgrace it." He knew this counsel covered all of life, and related alike to business and religion. Industry, honesty and piety carried him safely through all temptations, and steadily to great success. He was the founder of the famous publishing house of Harper Brothers, and once mayor of New York. The old appeal to honor needs to be revived in these times.

9598. HONOR, Brief. All the officers of a company engaged on the Weldon Road had either been killed or wounded. The sergeant upon whom devolved the command was frightened, and the line began to waver. A corporal instantly snatched the colors, stepped to the front, and led the men to victory. A brigadier near by noticed the occurrence and sent for the corporal after the fight, to learn his name, much to the brave man's discomposure, for he was afraid he had somehow subjected himself to military discipline. The officer took him to the major-general commanding the corps, and related the circumstances, the poor corporal meanwhile wishing himself well out of the scrape. After a little private conference, the two generals came forward and pinned a captain's straps upon the corporal's shoulders, sending him back to command the company. Before night there was another charge upon the enemy's position; the newly-made captain, while gallantly leading his men, was shot through the heart. *E. F. Williams.*

9599. HONOR, Chasing. Honor, like the shadow, follows those that flee from it, but flies from those that pursue it. *Anon.*

9600. HONOR, Conferring. The Spartan king, Agesilaus the Great, was put in a dishonorable place at a heathen solemnity. He endured it, saying, "I'll show that it is not the places that grace men, but men the places." The Thasians, having received great benefits by him, made him a god, and erected temples to his honor. They sent ambassadors to announce the fact, and congratulate him. He asked them, "Can your country make men gods?" They assented, and he rejoined, "Go to, make yourselves all gods first, and then I will believe you can make me one."

9601. HONOR, Moderate. Anaxagoras, putting back the other honors that were given him, desired that on the day of his death the children might have leave to play and intermit their studies. The honor also which Pittacus received had something political; for being bid to take what portion he would of the land he had gotten for his citizens, he accepted as much as he could reach with the cast of his dart. So Cocles, the Roman, took as much as he himself, being lame, could plough in a day. For the honor should not be a recompense of the action, but an acknowledgment of gratitude, that it may continue also long, as those did which we have mentioned. But of the three hundred statues erected to Demetrius Phalereus, not one was eaten into rust or covered with filth, they being all pulled down whilst himself was yet alive, and those of Demades were melted into chamber-pots. *Plutarch.*

9602. HONOR, Pagan. The physician of Pyrrhus proposed to Fabricius to poison his master. The noble Roman general sent the traitor's letter to Pyrrhus, saying, "Prince, know better for the future how to choose both your friends and foes" To requite this act of generosity, Pyrrhus released all the Roman prisoners; but Fabricius would only receive them on condition that he would accept an equal number in exchange. Said he, "Do not believe, Pyrrhus, that I have discovered this treachery to you out of particular regard to your person, or for the hope of advantage; but because the Romans shun base stratagems, and will not triumph but with open force."

9603. HONOR Rejected. Genuine faith influences us to deny ourselves, to renounce the world, to cherish holiness, to bear reproach, and to look beyond the present scene to the world of light and eternal glory. Such an effect will be produced, more or less, on all who possess this divine grace. The Marquis of Vico, in Italy, when he was come to years, and to the knowledge of Jesus Christ, refused to be called the son and heir to a Marquis, a cup-bearer to an Emperor, and nephew to a Pope, and chose rather to suffer affliction, persecution, banishment, loss of lands, living, wife, children, honors, and preferments, than to enjoy the sinful pleasures of Italy for a season; esteeming the reproach of Christ greater riches than all the honors of the most brilliant connections, and all the enjoyments of the most ample fortune; for he had respect unto the recompense of the reward. *Biblical Treasury.*

9604. HONOR, Renunciation of. The Emperor Charles V., of Spain, became satiated with the emptiness of earthly grandeur, and tired of the burden of government, and disgusted with the fashions and dissipation of court life. He abdicated the throne by a legal document, which he signed at Zuytburg, Sept. 7, 1556, renouncing all his earthly offices, honors, and wealth. He retired to a monastery in Placentia, and endeavored, by devotional reading, meditation, and prayer, to prepare for death. He busied himself sometimes by working in his garden or making clocks. He had his funeral celebrated before his death, at which he assisted, that he might be the better prepared for its coming.

9605. HONOR, Resigned. Doris governed the commonwealth of Athens for thirty-six years with honor. Becoming wearied of public life, he sought a home on a farm in a village not far from Athens, where he spent his time in reading books of husbandry by night, and utilizing his new-found knowledge by day. Thus he spent fifteen years of his life. Over his door these words were engraved: "Fortune and hope, adieu to you both, seeing I have found the entrance to rest and contentment."

9606. HONOR, Roman. Fabius had agreed with Hannibal for the exchange of captives; and he that had the most in number, should receive money for the overplus. Fabius acquainted the Senate of this agreement, and that Hannibal, having two hundred and forty more captives, requested the money might be sent to ransom them. This the Senate refused, and said, "It was not for the honor of the republic to free those men whose coward ice had made them the prey of their enemies." Fabius took this rebuff patiently, and finding he had not the money, and not wishing to deceive Hannibal, he sent his son to Rome, commanding him to sell his lands, and return with the money to the camp. This was speedily accomplished. He sent the ransom money to Hannibal, and the prisoners were liberated.

9607. HONOR, Seat of. The hall in which a wealthy Chinese receives his guest, is open in front and has a screen in the back. Before this screen a square table is usually placed, which may either serve as an altar for the reception of offerings of meat and incense, or as a board for the entertainment of the host and his friends. A row of chairs runs from the bottom to the top of the room, corresponding with the ends of this table. A quadrangle is thus formed, at the top of which stands the table, on each side a line of seats with perpendicular backs, and at the bottom, which is left unoccupied, the party enters. The visitor bows as he advances within the ranges, and is forthwith invited to sit down, which he does, after some hesitation, by taking the lowest room, or the seat at the bottom of the line. He is scarcely seated before he is told, with a peremptory tone, a little softened by the melodious accent of kindness to "come up higher." As soon as he has consented to this new arrangement, the host sits down on the seat immediately below the stranger, and thus awards to him the higher or more honorable place. *S. S. Visitor.*

9608. HONOR, Source of. Virtue and honor are such inseparable companions that the heathens would admit no man into the temple of Honor who did not pass into it through the temple of Virtue. Princes, indeed, may confer honors, or rather titles and names of honor; but they are a man's or a woman's own actions which must make him or her truly honorable. And every man's life is the herald's office from which he must derive that which must blazon him to the world; honor being but the reflection of a man's own actions, shining bright in the face of all about him, and from thence rebounding on himself. It teaches a man not to avenge a contumelious or a reproachful word, but to be above it, and therefore it was greatly spoken by Caius Marcus. He said he valued not what men could say of him, for if they spoke true they must needs speak honorably of him: if otherwise, his life and his manners should be their confutation. *South.*

9609. HONOR, Worldly. How loosely do honors sit on men, when every disease shakes them off and lays them in the dust. How miserable is the condition of the glory of this world, which hardly holds out a life, but often dies before us, ravished away by a frown or forfeited by a fault. Or, if it do last as long as its owner, with the staff of office cracked and thrown into the grave, is there buried with the corpse. *King.*

9610. HONOR, Youthful. More worship the rising than the setting sun. *Pompey.*

9611. HONORING THE LORD. 1 Sam. 2: 30—

The great principle, "Them that honor me I will honor." It was a singular coincidence, that when the Rev. C. Simeon's funeral sermons were preached, two of the preachers, without any previous consultation, fixed upon this text- "What a testimony to a holy life!" At the end of the Franco-Prussian war in 1871, the Emperor of Prussia had a medal struck off of two different kinds, for combatants and non-combatants, both bearing the device—"God was with us, to him be the honor." God's honor is the first thing to be thought of. *Bowes.*

9612. HOPE, Basis of Christian. When he lay on an expected deathbed (though God spared him some years longer to the world and Church), his attendants asked John Wesley what were his hopes for eternity. And something like this was his reply: "For fifty years, amid scorn and hardship, I have been wandering up and down this world to preach Jesus Christ, and I have done what in me lay to serve my blessed Master." Now what he had done, how poor he lived, how hard he labored, with what holy fire his bosom burned, with what success he preached, how brilliantly he illustrated the character—"Dying, and behold we live; unknown, and yet well-known; poor, yet making many rich; having nothing, yet possessing all things"—these things his life and works attest. They are recorded in his church's history, and seen in the crown he wears in heaven, so bright with a blaze of jewels—the saved through his agency. Yet thus he spake, "My hope for eternity? My only hopes rest on Christ.

" 'I the chief of sinners am,
But Jesus died for me.' "
Guthrie.

9613. HOPE, Biblical. An *anchor*, Heb. 6: 19. A *harbor*, or "place of repair," Joel 3: 16, marg. A *helmet*, 1 Thess. 5: 8. A *door*, Hosea 2: 14, 15, like "*the valley of Achor*" (the scene of Israel's trouble, Joshua 7: 26, marg., and one of the first earnests of their future acquisitions in Canaan), for a "door of hope." Deep humblings of heart are often "the door of hope" to joy and victory. The hope of a *tree* cut down, Job 14: 7. The hope in the *ploughman's* expectation, 1 Cor. 9: 10; James 5: 7. The hope in a *parent's* chastening of a wayward child, Prov. 19: 18. Rom 8: 19.—"The earnest expectation of the creature waiteth;" properly, looking out with outstretched neck, as if in intense and eager expectation of some much longed-for object. 1 Cor. 13: 13.—Rendered by Macbride, Faith-Expectation—Love. The *encouragement* of hope, Ezra 10: 2. The *patience* of hope, 1 Thess. 1: 3; Rom. 8: 24; 15: 4; 5: 4; Lam 3: 26. The *joy* of hope, Ps. 12: 12; Prov 10: 28; Rom. 5. 2; Heb. 3: 6. The *strength* of hope, Ps. 31: 24; Joel 3: 15—(hope and strength.) The *persistency* of hope, Ps. 71 14; Rom. 4: 18–20. The *service* of hope Acts 26: 6, 7. The *reward* of hope, Prov 10: 28; 13: 12. The Psalms of David — It is worthy of note, that in the Psalms of

David, written in his deepest trouble, from the persecution of Saul, the rebellion of Absalom, etc., we always find some ray of hope. Hope to the end, 1 Pet. 1: 13. Weiss calls Peter the apostle of hope. In five chapters he has ten allusions to the future. *Bowes.*

9614. HOPE, Brevities. Hope is like the cork in the net, which keeps the soul from sinking in despair; and fear is like the lead to the net, which keeps it from floating in presumption. — *Watson.*——Hope is the element by which the afflicted live, the anchor of the soul in a storm, the bladder which keeps up a man from sinking when in deep waters, and upholds a man in life when death knocks at the door.
William Greenhill.

9615. HOPE, Cheering. The traveler, when taken in a storm, can stand patiently under a tree while it rains, because he hopes it is but a shower, and sees it clear up in one part of the heavens while it is dark in another. Providence is never so dark and cloudy, but hope can see fair weather coming. *Anon.*

9616. HOPE, Death Bed of. Richard Bacon, Jr., a young American poet of much promise, died in 1841, at the early age of twenty-four. He constructed the plan of a great poem to be entitled, "The Death Bed of Hope." In his sickness, and in great agony and despair, he exclaimed, "Strange! was it not strange that I should have thought of that subject? Now I see it all: I am without hope."

9617. HOPE, Drafts of. Hope is a prodigal young heir, and experience is his banker; but his drafts are seldom honored, since there is often a heavy balance against him, because he draws largely on a small capital, is not yet in possession, and if he were, would die. *Colton.*

9618. HOPE, Extent of. Hope is the tenant, not of a heart that was never broken, but of a heart that has been broken and healed again. A pure, bright star fixed high in heaven, it reaches with its rays the uplifted eye of the weary pilgrim; but stars shine not in the day; the darkness brings them out. So grief summons hope to the aid of the sufferer. When the ransomed rise from the sleep of the grave, and open their eyes on the dawning of an everlasting day, this gentle star, which had often soothed them in the night of their pilgrimage, will nowhere be found in all the upper firmament; for, in presence of the Sun of righteousness, hope, no longer needed, no more appears.
Arnot.

9619. HOPE, Faith and. Hope is not paid down in ready money (as we say, what we hope for), but we have a good bond by assurance. Hope has still something in hand, because that which faith lays hold of is actually its own. Hope is faith's rent-gatherer, and takes up that which faith claims upon the bargain which Christ has made for us. An earnest penny is more than nothing; and the ground of our work is the earnest which God gives us of our inheritance. Just as the blossoms of spring do not only promise, but are God's earnest to represent the fruits which will wax ripe in autumn. *Salter.*

9620. HOPE, False. Let thy hope of heaven moderate thy affections to earth. "Be sober and hope," saith the apostle (1 Peter 1: 13). You that look for so much in another world may very well be content with a little in this. Nothing more unbecomes a heavenly hope than an earthly heart. You would think it an unseemly thing to see some rich man, that hath a vast estate, among the poor gleaners in harvest-time, as busy to pick up the ears of corn that are left in the field as the most miserable beggar in the company. Oh, how all the world would cry shame of such a sordid-spirited man! Well, Christian, be not angry if I tell thee that thou dost a more shameful thing thyself by far, if thou that pretendest to hope for heaven beest as eager in the pursuit of this world's trash as the poor carnal wretch is who expects no portion but what God hath left him to pick up in the field of this world. Certainly thy hope is either false, or at best but very little. *Gurnall.*

9621. HOPE, Heathen. Aristippus, a Socratic philosopher, was wrecked upon the island of Rhodes, and lost his all. Walking along the shore, he saw geometrical figures traced upon the sand. Returning to his company he desired them to hope for the best, "for," said he, "even here I perceive the footsteps of men."

9622. HOPE, Living. The same Scripture that speaks of a living (lively) hope, reveals incidentally how we may reach it: "Begotten again into a living hope" (1 Pet. 1: 3). How has that strong nether ring got into the equally strong upper ring, so that they form one chain and safely bear their burden? In the fires. It was brought to a white heat ere it could be welded in. It is by a similar process that a soul's hope is admitted into living faith, and so becomes living too. A cold heart in contact with the dead letter of the truth will not suffice, although the two are fitted to each other with all the exactitude of a confession. There must be a melting heart. It is when the heart flows down like water under the glow of redeeming love, that hope is fixed on faith, and faith is fixed on Jesus, never to part again.
Arnot.

9623. HOPE, Loss of. The setting of a great hope is like the setting of the sun. The brightness of our life is gone, shadows of the evening fall around us, and the world seems but a dim reflection itself—a broader shadow. We look forward into the coming lonely night: the soul withdraws itself. Then stars arise, and the night is holy. *Longfellow.*

9624. HOPE, Power of. Hope keeps our hearts from bursting under the pressure of evils; and that flattering mirror gives us a prospect of greater good. Hence some call it the manna from heaven, that comforts us in all extremities. Others call it the pleasant and honest flatterer, that caresses the unhappy with expectation of happiness in the bosom of futurity. When all other things fail us, hope stands by us to the last. Hope gives freedom to the captive when chained to the oar; health to the sick, while death grins in his face: vio tory to the defeated; and wealth to the beggar, while he is craving an alms.   *Wanley.*

9625. HOPE, Promises of. Hope is necessary in every condition. The miseries of poverty, of sickness, of captivity, would, without this comfort, be insupportable; nor does it appear that the happiest lot of terrestrial existence can set us above the want of this general blessing; or that life, when the gifts of nature and of fortune are accumulated upon it, would not still be wretched, were it not elevated and delighted by the expectation of some new possession, of some enjoyment yet behind, by which the wish shall be at last satisfied, and the heart filled up to its utmost extent. Hope is, indeed, very fallacious, and promises what it seldom gives; but its promises are more valuable than the gifts of fortune, and it seldom frustrates us without assuring us of recompensing the delay by a greater bounty.
    Dr. S. Johnson.

9626. HOPE, Proper Use of. Used with due abstinence, hope acts as a healthful tonic; intemperately indulged, as an enervating opiate. The visions of future triumph, which at first animate exertion, if dwelt upon too intently, will usurp the place of the stern reality; and noble objects will be contemplated, not for their own inherent worth, but on account of the day-dreams they engender. Thus hope, aided by imagination, makes one man a hero, another a somnambulist, and a third a lunatic; while it renders them all enthusiasts.
    Sir J. Stephens.

9627. HOPE, Reservation of. When Alexander started on his expedition to Persia, he divided his patrimony among his Macedonian friends. To one he gave a field, to another a village, to a third a town, and to the fourth a port; and in this manner he disposed of all his revenues. Perdiccas said, "What have you reserved for yourself, O, king?" "My hopes," he replied. Then said Perdiccas, "Of those hopes, then, we who are your followers, will also be partakers." His followers then resigned what had previously been given to them, from the same consideration. So the Christian resigns all but his hope in Christ.

9628. HOPE, Spring of. The spring returns with the blossoms and flowers, its green foliage and blue sky. The voices of the singing birds are heard once more, and earth adorned as a bride looks forth rejoicing. The storms of winter have passed away, its coldness and desolation are felt no more. So the believer emerges out of all that was dark, and dreary, and chilling, with fears and apprehensions as to an eternal state of things, and a new world of light and gladness springs up to cheer and animate him. Hope in Christ is to the little world of the inner man what spring is to the external world of nature—an animating principle in perpetual operation, to soften the present if it be gloomy, and to gild the prospect before us with bright expectations of good things to come.   *Salter.*

9629. HOPE, Support of. If we would be in a fit posture for suffering, we must get a lively hope of eternal life. As our life is a sea, hope is compared to an anchor, which makes us stand steady in a storm; as our life is a warfare, hope is compared to an helmet, which covers the soul in times of danger; as the body liveth *spirando*, by breathing, so the soul liveth *spirando*, by hoping. A man cannot drown so long as his head is above water; hope lifts up the head, and looks up to the redemption and salvation which is to come in another world, in its fullness and perfection. Hope doth three things: it assures good things to come; it disposes us for them; it waits for them unto the end; each of which will be of singular use to fit us for pious sufferings.
    Polhill.

9630. HOPE, Survival of. A cruel tyrant cast one of his subjects into a cage, and there kept him as a wild beast. His hands were cut off, his nostrils slit, and his face sadly disfigured by wounds and bruises. He was advised in this his extremity to refrain from food, and thus shorten his sufferings. But he rejected their counsel with indignation, saying, "While a man is alive, all things are to be hoped for by him."

9631. HORSE, Prayer for a. On Wednesday morning, after spending the preceding night at Mr. Cunningham's, Mr. Rowland Hill and Mr. Haldane were about to proceed southward, when Mr. Hill's carriage being brought to the door, his horse was found to be dead lame. A farrier was sent for, who after a careful examination reported that the seat of the mischief was in the shoulder, that the disease was incurable, and that they might shoot the poor animal as soon as they pleased. To this proposal Mr. Hill was by no means prepared to accede. Indeed it seemed to Mr. Haldane as precipitate as the conduct of an Irish sailor on board the Monarch, who, on seeing another knocked down senseless by a splinter, and supposing his companion to be dead, went up to Captain Duncan on the quarter-deck, in the midst of the action with Languard off St. Vincent, and exclaimed, "Shall we jerk him overboard, sir?" On that occasion the sailor revived in a short time, and was even able to work at his gun. In the present instance the horse too recovered, and was able to carry his master on many a future errand of mercy. Meanwhile, however, the travelers availed themselves of Mr. Cunningham's hospitality, and remained for two days more at his place near Dunbar. In the evening Mr. Hill conducted family worship; and after supplications for the family, domestics and friends, added a fervent prayer for the restoration of the valuable animal which had carried him so many thousand miles, preaching the everlasting gospel to his fellow-sinners. Mr. Cunningham, who was remarkable for the staid and orderly, if not stiff, demeanor which characterized the Anti-burghers, was not only surprised but grieved, and even scandalized, at what he deemed so great an impropriety. He remonstrated with his guest. But Mr. Hill stoutly defended his conduct by an appeal to

Scripture, and the superintending watchfulness of him without whom a sparrow falls not to the ground. He persisted in his prayer. During the two days he continued at Dunbar, and although he left the horse in a hopeless state, to follow in charge of his servant by easy stages, he continued his prayer night and morning, till one day at an inn in Yorkshire, while the two travelers were sitting at breakfast, they heard a horse and chaise trot quickly into the yard, and in looking out saw that Mr. Hill's servant had arrived, bringing the horse perfectly restored. Mr. Hill did not fail to return thanks, and begged his fellow-traveler to consider whether the minuteness of his prayers had deserved the censure which had been directed against them. *Lives of the Haldanes.*

9632. HOSPITALITY, Biblical. Be not forgetful to entertain strangers, Heb. 13:2. It is observed by Gouge—"I find not this composition in any Greek author before the apostles' time; as it is probable they were the first authors thereof. St. Paul uses it four times. It is also used 1 Pet. 4:9. Rom. 12:13—"Given to hospitality." Literally, *pursuing* it—a strong word, intimating that we should not only embrace the opportunity, but even seek it—regard it as a privilege and an honor. The Christians in St. Paul's times were for the most part poor (see Heb. 10:38); yet the duty is pressed upon such no less than on the rich. Hospitality in the poor is often a test of godly character, 1 Kings 17:12. An abundant RECOMPENSE generally follows hospitality. Of this we have many examples: *Abraham* received the strangers who came to him, and "thereby entertained angels unawares;" nay more, he received the Lord of angels, Gen. 18; Heb. 13:2. *Lot* was delivered from Sodom by the angels he received. *Laban's* hospitality was rewarded by his finding a faithful servant for himself, and a good husband for his daughter, and the Lord's blessing on his house; see Gen. 30:27. *Rahab* received the spies, and afforded them protection. How abundantly she was repaid in the preservation of herself and of her kindred, Joshua 6:22, 23–25. *The widow of Zarephath* had indeed her faith and compassion put to a severe test in a time of famine. But she was more than repaid in the provision for herself and son, and the restoration of her dead son to life, 1 Kings 17:8–24. *The Shunammite* was rewarded in a similar manner for kindness to Elisha the man of God, 2 Kings 4:8–37. *Martha and Mary*, in giving the Master a welcome in their home at Bethany. How they were honored in his teaching, and in the stupendous miracle of raising their brother from the grave, Luke 10:38–42; John 11. *Zacchæus* received the Lord joyfully, and salvation came to his house, Luke 19:1–10. *Lydia—Justus—Gaius*, gave the apostles and the brethren shelter in those days of peril and persecution. "The household of Stephanas" is especially favored with honorable mention, 1 Cor. 16:15; Acts 16:15, 40; 18:7; Rom. 16:23; 3 John 5, 6. *Publius* and the people of Melita courteously entertained St. Paul, and Publius's father was miraculously healed of a dangerous illness, and after him many others also, Acts 28:1–10. The LORD JESUS himself honored hospitality in his first miracle at Cana; and, though he had no earthly home, he provided "a table in the wilderness" for those who followed him, and wrought two striking miracles to feed the hungry. *Bowes.*

9633. HOSPITALITY, Heathen. Mungo Park, when suffering under the pangs of hunger, rode up to the Dooty's house, in a Foulah village, but was denied admittance; nor could he even obtain a handful of corn either for himself or his horse. "Turning," says he, "from this inhospitable door, I rode slowly out of the town; and perceiving some low Scotland huts without the walls, I directed my steps towards them, knowing that in Africa, as well as in Europe, hospitality does not always prefer the highest dwellings. At the door of one of these huts, an old motherly-looking woman sat spinning cotton. I made signs to her that I was hungry, and inquired if she had any victuals with her in her hut. She immediately laid down her distaff, and desired me, in Arabic, to come in. When I had seated myself on the floor, she set before me a dish of kouskous that had been left the preceding night, of which I made a tolerable meal; and, in return for this kindness, I gave her one of my pocket handkerchiefs, begging, at the same time, a little corn for my horse, which she readily brought me. Overcome with joy at so unexpected a deliverance, I lifted up my eyes to heaven; and, whilst my heart swelled with gratitude, I returned thanks to that gracious and bountiful Being, whose power had supported me under so many dangers, and had now spread for me a table in the wilderness."

9634. HOSPITALITY, Mohammedan. I was beginning to make my meal upon the food we had with us, when in came nine people, each bearing a dish. A large tray was raised on the rim of a corn sieve placed on the ground, in the centre of which was placed a tureen of soup, with pieces of bread around it. The stranger, my servant, and a person who seemed to be the head man of the village, sat around the tray dipping their wooden spoons or fingers into each dish as it was placed in succession before them. Of the nine dishes I observed three were soups. I asked why this was, and who was to pay for the repast? and was informed it was the custom of the people, strictly enjoined by their religion, that as soon as a stranger appears, each peasant should bring his dish, he himself remaining to partake of it after the stranger—a sort of pic-nic, of which the stranger partakes without contributing. The hospitality extends to everything he requires: his horse is fed, and wood is brought for his fire, each inhabitant feeling honored by offering something. This custom accounts for the frequent occurring of the same dish, as no one knows what his neighbor will contribute. Towards a Turkish guest this practice is perfectly disinterested, but from a European they may possibly be led to expect a return, although to offer payment would be an insult. The whole of the contributors afterwards sat down and ate in another part of the room. *Fellows.*

9635. HOSPITALITY, Oriental. On two occasions we arrived at a camp late at night, and, halting before a tent, found the owner, with his wife and children, having arranged their carpets, etc., for the night, had just retired to rest; when it was astonishing to see the good humor with which they all arose again, and kindled a fire, the wife commencing to knead the dough, and prepare our supper, our Arabs making no apology, but taking all as a matter of course, though the nights were bitterly cold."
Irby and Mangles.

9636. HOSPITALITY, Outraged. Gedaliah, a man of great benevolence and integrity, was made governor of Judea by the Babylonian general, after his conquest of the Jews. He invited those who had fled to return and cultivate their lands, and promised them protection. Among those who came to him was one Ishmael, to whom he showed great hospitality. It was reported to Gedaliah that this man sought to kill him, but he could not be induced to believe that a guest of his, to whom he had shown such favor, could be guilty of such base treachery. His informer proposed to slay the suspected guest, but Gedaliah said it was better for himself to be slain than to destroy a man who had fled to him for refuge, and intrusted his safety to him. Soon after Gedaliah entertained Ishmael and his company at a splendid feast, and then the ingrate violated the sancity of hospitality by slaying his magnanimous host.

9637. HOSPITALITY, Selfish. A poor wandering woman, who had crossed the Border and traveled north into Scotland until she was belated and benighted, knocked at the door of a house where a light came streaming out of the window, and cast herself on the charity of its tenants, asking a morsel of bread and a night's lodging. This was her touching and simple appeal: "Is there no good Christian here who will have pity on me and take me in?" "Na, na," was the answer of a rough voice, as the door, which had been opened at her knocking, was rudely shut in her face, "there are nae Christians here; we are a' Johnstones and Jardines!" *Guthrie.*

9638. HOSPITALITY, Token of. The *tessera hospitalis*, the tally or token of hospitality, was employed by the ancients. At a time when houses of public entertainment were less common, private hospitality was the more necessary. When one person was received kindly by another, or a contract of friendship was entered into, the *tessera* was given. It was so named from its shape, being four-sided: it was sometimes of wood, sometimes of stone; it was divided in two by the contracting parties; each wrote his own name on half of the *tessera*; then they exchanged pieces, and therefore the name or device on the piece of the *tessera* which each received was the name the other person had written upon it, and

which no one else knew but him who received it. It was carefully prized, and entitled the bearer to protection and hospitality. Plautus, in one of his plays, refers to this custom. Hanno inquires of a stranger where he may find Agorastocles, and discovers to his surprise that he is addressing the object of his search. "If so," he says "compare, if you please, this hospitable *tessera*; here it is; I have it with me." Agorastocles replies, "It is the exact counterpart; I have the other part at home." Hanno responds, "O my friend, I rejoice to meet thee; thy father was my friend, my guest; I divided with him this hospitable *tessera.*" "Therefore," said Agorastocles, "thou shalt have a home with me, for I reverence hospitality." Beautiful illustration of gospel truth! The Saviour visits the sinner's heart, and being received as a guest, bestows the white stone, the token of his unchanging love. He enrols our name as among his friends. He makes an everlasting covenant with us, ordered in all things and sure. He promises never to leave nor forsake us. He tells us, "we shall never perish." He gives us the *tessera*, the white stone! *N. Hall.*

9639. HOSPITALS, Treasures in. The founder of a hospital for lepers and cripples near Alexandria, showing his visitors through the upper wards, occupied by women, used to say, "Behold my jacinths." Descending to the lower floors, occupied by men, "See my emeralds."

9640. HOURS, Flight of the. Hours have wings, and fly up to the Author of Time, and carry news of our usage: all our prayers cannot entreat one of them to return or slacken his pace. *Zimmerman.*

9641. HOURS, Lost. Lost, yesterday, somewhere between sunrise and sunset, two golden hours, each set with sixty diamond minutes. No reward is offered, for they have gone forever! *H. Mann.*

9642. HOUSEHOLD, Chinese God of the. Among the Chinese a very curious custom is observed on their New-Year's eve. They have a sort of mystical divinity among them called the Kitchen God, who has no temple or image, but is worshiped under the representation of an engraving, generally about a foot square, which is conspicuously pasted on the kitchen-range. This god is the household divinity of the Chinese. He is supposed to go once a year on a mission to the chief god to report to him the doings of the family during the past twelve months. A ceremonious feast is held in his honor on the night of his supposed departure, with the view of propitiating him to make a satisfactory report of the family. After the feast is ended, the picture is carefully removed and burned in the fire with great ceremony. On New-Year's day, a new picture is put up, and the kitchen god is invoked to resume his household supervision. *Anon.*

9643. HOUSEHOLD, Quarrels in a. The best have their domestic contentions; some household words will now and then pass betwixt them. We match not with angels, but men and women. Two flints may as soon smite together and not fire come forth, as two persons meet in marriage and not offences fall out. Publius Rubius Celer was held a happy man among the Romans, who commanded it to be engraven upon his grave-stone that he had lived three-and-forty years and eight months with C. Ennia, his wife, *sine querela*—without the least quarrel. Alphonsus, king of Aragon, was wont to say that, to procure a quiet life, the husband must be deaf and the wife blind. But they say better that advise to a mutual forbearance, that no offence be given on either side; or, if given, yet not taken. The second blow makes the fray, we say. But be not both incensed together. Let two fires meet, and it will be hard quenching them. A choleric couple being asked how they agreed so well, the husband made this answer: "When my wife's fit is on, I bear with her, as Abram did with Sarah; and when my fit is on me, she bears with me; and so we never chide together, but asunder." *Trapp.*

9644. HOUSE OF GOD, Everywhere. You have all got into the habit of calling the church the "house of God." I have seen over the doors of many churches, the legend actually carved, "This is the house of God, and this is the gate of heaven." Now, note where that legend comes from, and of what place it was first spoken. A boy leaves his father's house to go on a long journey on foot, to visit his uncle; he has to cross a wild hilly desert; just as if one of your own boys had to cross the wilds of Westmoreland, to visit an uncle at Carlisle. The second or third day your boy finds himself somewhere between Hawes and Brough, in the midst of the moors, at sunset. It is stony ground, and boggy; he cannot go one foot farther that night. Down he lies to sleep on Wharnside where best he may, gathering a few of the stones together to put under his head; so wild the place is, he cannot get anything but stones. And there, under the broad night, he has a dream; and he sees a ladder set up on the earth, and the top of it reaches to heaven, and the angels of God are ascending and descending upon it. And when he wakes out of his sleep, he says, "How dreadful is this place; surely, this is none other than the house of God, and this is the gate of heaven." This place, observe: not this church; not this city: not this stone even, which he puts up for a memorial—the piece of flint on which his head has lain: but this place; this windy slope of Wharnside; this moorland hollow, torrent-bitten, snow-blighted; this any place where God lets down the ladder. And how are you to know where that will be? or how are you to determine where it may be, but by being ready for it always? Do you know where the lightning is to fall next? You do know that, partly; you can guide the lightning: but you cannot guide the going forth of the Spirit, which is as the lightning when it shines from the east to the west. We call our churches temples. Now, you know, or ought to know, they are not temples. They have never had, never can have,

anything whatever to do with temples. They are "synagogues," "gathering-places," where you gather yourselves together as an assembly; and by not calling them so, you again miss the force of another mighty text—"Thou, when thou prayest, shalt not be as the hypocrites are; for they love to pray standing in the churches (we should translate it), that they may be seen of men—but thou, when thou prayest, enter into thy closet, and when thou hast shut thy door, pray to thy Father," "which is," not in chancel nor in aisle, but "in secret." Now you feel, as I say this to you—I know you feel—as if I were trying to take away the honor of your churches. Not so; I am trying to prove to you the honor of your houses and your hills; I am trying to show you, not that the church is not sacred, but that the whole earth is. I would have you feel what careless, what constant, what infectious sin there is in all modes of thought, whereby, in calling your churches only "holy," you call your hearths and homes profane; and have separated yourselves from the heathen, by casting all your household gods to the ground, instead of recognizing, in the places of their many and feeble lares, the presence of your One and Mighty Lord. *Ruskin.*

9645. HOUSES, Preferable. Houses are built to live in, and not to look on; therefore let use be preferred before uniformity, except where both may be had. Leave the goodly fabrics of houses for beauty only to the enchanted palaces of the poets, who build them with small cost. *Lord Bacon.*

9646. HUMANITY, Advantage of. It is related that when Agrippa was in a private station, he was accused by one of his servants of having spoken injuriously of Tiberius, and was condemned by the Emperor to be exposed in chains before the palace gate. The weather was very hot, and Agrippa became exceedingly thirsty. Seeing Thaumastus, a servant of Caligula, pass by with a pitcher of water, he called to him, and entreated leave to drink. The servant presented the pitcher with much courtesy, and Agrippa having allayed his thirst, said to him, "Assure thyself, Thaumastus, that if I get out of this captivity, I will one day pay thee well for this draught of water." Tiberius dying, his successor, Caligula. soon after not only set Agrippa at liberty, but made him King of Judæa. In this high situation Agrippa was not unmindful of the glass of water given to him when a captive. He immediately sent for Thaumastus, and made him comptroller of his household.

9647. HUMANITY, Lesson of. The night after the battle of Bassano, the moon rose cloudless and brilliant over the sanguinary scene. Napoleon, who seldom exhibited even exhilaration of spirits in the hour of victory, rode, accompanied by his staff, over the plain covered with the bodies of the dying and the dead, and, silent and thoughtful, seemed lost in painful reverie. It was midnight; the confusion and the uproar of the battle had passed away, and the deep silence of the calm starlight night was only disturbed by the moans of the wounded and dying. Suddenly a dog sprang from beneath the cloak of his dead master, and rushed to Napoleon as if frantically imploring his aid, and then rushed back again to the mangled corpse, licking the blood from its face and hands, and howling most piteously. Napoleon was deeply moved by the affecting scene, and turned to his officers, with his hand pointed towards the faithful dog, and said with evident emotion—"There, gentlemen, that dog teaches us a lesson of humanity." *Denton.*

9648. HUMANITY, Memory of. Pericles, the noble Athenian, lay dying. His friends thought that he was so far gone as not to understand them. They recounted his virtues, his riches, his eloquence, and his numerous victories. But he heard all that passed, and said, "I wonder that you celebrate those deeds of mine, in which fortune has challenged a part, and which are common to other leaders, and yet pass over in silence that which is the greatest and most excellent of them all—that none of my fellow citizens have ever put on mourning through my means." His clemency to his most bitter enemies was remarkable, none ever suffering from his hand, though he remained in power for years.

9649. HUMANITY, Model of. Sir Philip Sidney was Governor of Flushing, and General of the Horse, under his uncle, the Earl of Leicester. His valor, which was esteemed great, and not exceeded by any of his age, was at least equaled by his humanity. After he had received his death-wound at the battle of Zütphen, and was overcome with thirst from excessive bleeding, he called for drink, which was soon brought him. At the same time a poor soldier, dangerously wounded, was carried along, who fixed his eager eyes upon the bottle just as Sir Philip was lifting it to his mouth. Sir Philip immediately presented it to him, with the remark, "Thy necessity is greater than mine." *Percy.*

9650. HUMANITY, Official. The wife of a defaulting officer called upon Gen. Grant last December to implore the release of her husband from the Albany penitentiary. She told the President that crushing as the sorrow was to herself, she would try to bear it; but that every morning, without an exception, since her husband's incarceration, her four little children had come to her bedside with the tearful inquiry, "Will dear papa come home to-day?" "This plea of my children will, I know, ere long drive me into insanity. And now," said she, "my little ones have varied their agonizing questioning, with a pathos that is maddening, to 'Won't papa come home Christmas?'" "Madam, I will consult the Attorney-General and do whatever I can for your husband with his approval." "I know that will all be useless," said the grief-stricken wife. "His decision will only be adverse, and I may as well go home and tell my children at once their papa can't come home, and give up in despair." "Wait a moment," said the President, and sitting down, he hastily penned a note to Attorney-General Williams, and nervously handing it to her said, "Go and tell your children that their papa shall come Christmas!" Almost fainting, the woman was carried from the Executive office, with the open note in her hand. On examining it, it was found to be a peremptory order for the immediate release of the husband and father. But this was not all. All over the page were great blots of the President's fast-falling tears as he wrote. On the night before Christmas there was a house in Washington as joyous as it had been desolate, and other eyes dropped great tears as the recital was made of President Grant's tenderness and mercy in restoring their long-absent papa to the children of Paymaster Hodges. *Norwalk Gazette.*

9651. HUMANITY, Reward of. A poor man had been fishing all day to supply the wants of his large and needy family. Being unsuccessful, he was disheartened, and was about to give it up, when he threw out his line and drew in a human skull. His first impulse was to throw it back into the water. He decided, however, to bury it, thinking, as he did so, that it might be a portion of the body of some poor man, whose children were longing for food as his were. On digging the grave for it, he found a rich treasure hidden away. With such a prize, he returned to his home rejoicing. Thus the love we show to our brethren is often rewarded with a Heavenly Father's beneficence.

9652. HUMANITY, True. True humanity consists not in a squeamish ear; it consists not in starting or shrinking at tales of misery, but in a disposition of heart to relieve it. True humanity appertains rather to the mind than to the nerves, and prompts men to use real and active endeavors to execute the actions which it suggests. *C. J. Fox.*

9653. HUMAN NATURE, Characteristics of. Human nature is not so much depraved as to hinder us from respecting goodness in others, though we ourselves want it. This is the reason why we are so much charmed with the pretty prattle of children, and even the expressions of pleasure or uneasiness in some part of the creation. They are without artifice or malice; and we love truth too well to resist the charms of sincerity. *Steele.*

9654. HUMAN NATURE, Divineness of. With our sciences and our cyclopædias, we are apt to forget the divineness in those laboratories of ours. We ought not to forget it! That once well forgotten, I know not what else were worth remembering! Most sciences, I think, were then a very dead thing—withered, contentious, empty—a thistle in late autumn. The best science, without this, is but as the dead timber; it is not the growing tree and forest —which gives ever-new timber among other things! Man cannot know either, unless he can worship in some way. His knowledge is a pedantry and dead thistle, otherwise. *Carlyle.*

9655. HUMAN NATURE, Inconsistency of. The practice of men holds not an equal pace; yea, and often runs counter to their theory: we naturally know what is good, but naturally pursue what is evil; the rhetoric wherewith I persuade another cannot persuade myself: there is a depraved appetite in us that will with patience hear the learned instructions of reason, but yet perform no farther than agrees to its own irregular humor. In brief, we all are monsters, that is, a composition of man and beast, wherein we must endeavor to be as the poets fancy that wise man Chiron; that is, to have the region of man above that of beast, and sense to sit but at the feet of reason. Lastly, I do desire with God, that all, but yet affirm with men, that few shall know salvation: that the bridge is narrow, the passage straight unto life: yet those who do confine the church of God either to particular nations, churches, or families, have made it far narrower than our Saviour ever meant it.   *Browne.*

9656. HUMAN NATURE, Rebellion of. Did you ever, of a hot afternoon, witness the contest of innumerable worms over a carrion carcass? Did you ever notice the greediness, and selfishness, and quarrelsomeness displayed by the actors in a scene like that? And yet such a contest is decent, compared with the gigantic contest that has been carried on for thousands of years by the vermicular human race, and God has looked upon it, dwelt and pondered over it, and carried it in his heart; and all this time he has not ceased to pour out upon the world, in rich abundance, the blessings of his never-failing love!   *Beecher.*

9657. HUMILIATION Advised. A great monarch was accustomed on set occasions to entertain all the beggars of the city. Around him were placed his courtiers, all clothed in rich apparel; the beggars sat at the same table in their rags of poverty. Now it came to pass, that on a certain day one of the courtiers had spoiled his silken apparel, so that he dared not put it on, and he felt, "I cannot go to the king's feast to-day, for my robe is foul." He sat weeping till the thought struck him, "To-morrow, when the king holds his feast, some will come as courtiers, happily decked in their beautiful array; but others will come and be made quite as welcome who will be dressed in rags. Well, well," said he, "so long as I may see the king's face, and sit at the royal table, I will enter among the beggars." So without mourning because he had lost his silken habit, he put on the rags of a beggar, and he saw the king's face as well as if he had worn his scarlet and fine linen.   *Spurgeon.*

9658. HUMILIATION, Christ's. It is said that when the story of West India slavery was told to the Moravians, and it was told that it was impossible to reach the slave population because they were so separated from the ruling classes, two Moravian missionaries offered themselves, and said, "We will go and be slaves on the plantations, and work and toil, if need be, under the lash, to get right beside the poor slaves and instruct them." And they left their homes, went to the West Indies, went to work on the plantations as slaves, and by the side of slaves, to get close to the hearts of slaves; and the slaves heard them, and their hearts were touched, because they had humbled themselves to their condition. That was grand; it was glorious; and yet Christ's example was more glorious, for he stepped from heaven to earth to get by our side; he laid himself down beside us that we might feel the throbbings of his bosom, be encircled in the embrace of his loving arms, be drawn right up beside him, and feel him whisper to our ears, "God is love."   *Bp. Simpson.*

9659. HUMILITY, Advantage of. The high mountains are barren, but the low valleys are covered over with corn; and accordingly the showers of God's grace fall into lowly hearts and humble souls. The more poor in spirit, the more self-empty, the more earnestly we are desirous of spiritual things; and such shall be filled.   *Worthington.*

9660. HUMILITY, Affected. True and genuine humility does not lie in a person's affecting the meanest habit, or yet a singularity of dress, however mean, that he may not seem to be proud. I speak not this, however, to cloak the proud gaudiness of any. Excess in costly attire, following vain, strange, light, immodest fashions, is a great sin and shame of our times. Oh, how many are there that in this way glory in their shame! Were the "daughters of Zion" reproved and threatened for this sin by the prophet Isaiah (ch. iii.) ever more guilty than multitudes among us at this day? But yet I must tell you that a proud heart may be under vile raiment too. Some may be proud of an affected plainness—proud of their seeming free from pride, of their looking like humble, mortified men. And some there are whose pride lies not so much in gaudy dress and fine clothes, which one would think that none but children and fools would be taken with, as in a high conceit of themselves—their knowledge, light, and perfection.   *Barrett.*

9661. HUMILITY, Arguments for. All the world all that we are, and all that we have, our bodies and our souls, our actions and our sufferings, our conditions at home, our accidents abroad, our many sins and our seldom virtues, are as so many arguments to make our souls dwell low in the deep valley of humility.   *Jeremy Taylor.*

9662. HUMILITY, Biblical Examples of. *John the Baptist*—How beautiful it is to compare John's testimony of himself, and Christ's commendation of him! The Baptist himself never forgot his inferiority to Christ. "I am," he said, "the voice," John 1: 23; whilst Jesus was "the Word," John 1: 1; "the latchet of whose shoes," he said, "I am not worthy to stoop down and unloose," Mark 1: 7; "He must increase, but I must decrease," John 3: 30. Yet see what the Master said in exaltation of one so humble, Matt. 11: 21; John 5: 35. *Mary*—Three times we read of her in the same posture, sitting "at the feet of Jesus," Luke 10: 39; John 11: 32; 12: 3. The *Evangelists* are remarkable for so frequently omitting the points of history which might have thrown honor upon themselves; whilst they are careful to mention things which might tend to their own humiliation. *St. Matthew, e. g.,* records his own name as "the publican" (10: 3), and makes no mention of having *himself* made the great feast at his house (9: 10), nor of his having left all to follow Christ, Luke 5: 27–29—a circumstance which he carefully records about James and John, 4: 20–22. *St. Mark,* writing, as is supposed, under the direction of St. Peter, makes no mention of the keys, nor of his (Peter's) walking on the water, whilst he records most fully Peter's rebuke, 8: 33; and Peter's fall, and Peter's repentance, 14: 66–72. *St. John*—"That other disciple," who modestly conceals his own name.   *Bowes.*

9663. HUMILITY, Conquests of. The devil told St. Macarius, "I can surpass thee in watching, fasting and many other things; but humility conquers and disarms me."

9664. HUMILITY, Cultivation of. St. Francis Borgia, the Duke of Gandia, who had renounced all his wealth and honors for the monastic life, signed his letters, *Francis the Sinner.* This he declared to be his only title. For six years he rated himself at the feet of Judas. Then he recalled the fact that Christ washed the traitor's feet. From that time he looked upon himself as below all creatures. He said, "I consider in my morning meditation that hell is my due; and I think that all men, even children and dumb creatures, ought to cry out to me, 'Away; hell is thy place; thy soul ought to be in hell.'" From this standpoint of his own unworthiness he obtained enlarged views of the love and mercy of God. He chose the meanest cell and the poorest fare. A lady of rank said to him, "Your condition, Francis, is wretched, if after exchanging your riches for so great poverty, you should not gain heaven in the end." He replied, "I should be miserable indeed; but as for the exchange, I have been already a great gainer by it."

9665. HUMILITY, Derivation of. The whole Roman language, even with all the improvements of the Augustan age, does not afford so much as a name for humility (the word from whence we borrow this, as is well known, bearing in Latin a quite different meaning); no, nor was one found in all the copious language of the Greeks till it was made by the great Apostle.   *John Wesley.*

9666. HUMILITY, Effect of. The grandest edifices, the tallest towers, the loftiest spires, rest upon deep foundations. The very safety of eminent gifts and pre-eminent graces lies in their association with deep humility. They were dangerous without it. Great men do need to be good men. Look at this mighty ship, a leviathan on the deep. With her towering masts, and carrying a cloud of canvas, how she steadies herself on the waves, and walks erect upon the rolling waters, like a thing of inherent, self-regulating life. When the corn is waving, and trees are bending, and foaming billows roll before the blast and break in thunders on the beach, why is she not flung on her beam ends, sent down foundering into the deep? Why, because, unseen, beneath the surface, a vast well-ballasted hull gives her balance, and, taking hold of the water, keeps her steady under a press of sail, and on the bosom of a swelling sea. Even so, to preserve the saint upright, erect, and safe from falling, God gives him balance and ballast, bestowing on the man to whom he has given lofty endowments the attendant grace of a proportionate humility.   *Guthrie.*

9667. HUMILITY, Emblem of. Observe the peculiar characters of the grass, which adapt it especially for the service of man, are its apparent humility and cheerfulness. Its humility, in that it seems created only for lowest service, appointed to be trodden on and fed upon. Its cheerfulness, in that it seems to exult under all kinds of violence and suffering. You roll it, and it is stronger the next day; you mow it, and it multiplies its shoots, as if it were grateful; you tread upon it, and it only sends up richer perfume. Spring comes; and it rejoices with all the earth—glowing with variegated flame of flowers, waving in soft depth of fruitful strength. Winter comes; and though it will not mock its fellow-plants by growing then, it will not pine and mourn, and turn colorless and leafless as they. It is always green, and is only the brighter and gayer for the hoar frost.   *Ruskin.*

9668. HUMILITY Entrance to Honor. Prov. 15: 33, "Before honor is humility." In Caius College, Cambridge, there are three gateways in succession: "the first is called Humilitatis, the next Virtutis, the third (which opens towards the Senate House), Honoris. Not in vain did our forefathers make these emblems of an undergraduate's progress; and happy would it be if every youth entered by the gate of humility, to pass through the gate of Christian virtue, that he might come forth in the highest sense to that of honor."   *R. F. Walker.*

9669. HUMILITY, Examples of. The truly virtuous or valorous are no whit ashamed of their mean parentage, but rather glory in themselves, that their merit hath advanced them above so many thousands far better descended. Dr. Cox, almoner, and Sir John Cheek, tutor to King Edward VI., were men of mean "birth, but so well esteemed," saith the historian, "for virtue and bearing, that they might well be said to be born of themselves." So were Iphicrates, that brave Athenian, the son of a cobbler; Eumenes, one of Alexander's best captains, the son of a carter; Agathocles, king of Sicily, the son of a potter, etc. And these would many a time freely discourse of their beginning, and plainly relate their bringing up, and what their parents were.   *Trapp.*

9670. HUMILITY, Gain of. Many a poor man makes a bright Christian; God keep him humble that he may dwell in his heart, and that the beams of his grace may shine in his heart. See yon evening star, how bright it shines, how pure and steady are its rays; but look, it is lower in the heavens than those stars which sparkle with a restless twinkling in the higher region of the skies. God keep you low, that you may shine bright.   *Salter*

9671. HUMILITY, Grace of. It was well observed by Austin, "that they who will ascend to God must descend in self-abasement and humility." The farther from pride, the nearer to God. He that ascends in himself, descends and falls from God. Pride and vain glory are the prime elements of vain philosophy; whereas sacred and sound philosophy is found in humility. Ships that are heaviest laden sail lowest; so a mind laden with sound philosophy is most humble. *Gale.*

9672. HUMILITY, Flower of. 'Tis a fair and fragrant flower; in its appearance modest, in its situation low and hidden; it doth not flaunt its beauties to every vulgar eye, or throw its odors upon every passing gale; 'tis unknown to the earthly botanist, it discovers itself only to the spiritual searcher; neither does he find it among those gay and gaudy tribes of flowers with which the generalty are so easily captivated, but in some obscure and unfrequented spot, where the prints of human footsteps are rarely seen. But whenever he finds it, he is sure to behold its bosom opened to the Sun of Righteousness, receiving new sweets in perpetual succession from his exhaustless source. *Caspipini.*

9673. HUMILITY, Heathen. Epaminondas, that heathen captain, finding himself lifted up in the day of his public triumph, the next day went drooping and hanging down his head; but being asked what was the reason of his so great dejection, made answer: "Yesterday I felt myself transported with vain-glory, therefore I chastise myself for it to-day." *Plutarch.*

9674. HUMILITY, Intellectual. It is said that the young students of Athens, called themselves *sophoi*, wise men; having studied some time they thought it an honor to be termed *philosophoi*, lovers of wisdom; but at length, when they had made good progress in learning, they accounted themselves *moroi*, mere ignoramuses, that understood nothing at all. The more knowledge they had, the more they discovered their own ignorance.

9675. HUMILITY, Lesson of. Ruffinus, a friend of St. Francis of Assisi, asked the latter to tell him what he thought of himself. Francis answered, "I esteem myself the greatest sinner of any in the world, and that I serve God less than any other man." "How can that be," said Ruffinus, "seeing some are thieves, some murderers, some adulterers, and many most profane and wicked wretches, such as are in the very gall of bitterness, such as never think of God or goodness, and thou art not only free from these, but withal a man of much sanctity and holiness?" Francis replied, "No doubt, if God had been so merciful to them as he hath been to me, they would have showed themselves more thankful than I have been; and, besides, if God had forsaken me, I should have committed far greater sins than they have done." Examples of humility have now to be sought in the lives of the ancients. It is quite time for a revival of this old-fashioned virtue.

9676. HUMILITY, Model of. Christ voluntarily mourned, because mourning humiliates, and he would be humble; he daily suffered, because suffering subdues the pride of human hearts, and he would teach us to accomplish that conquest. It was the humiliation of a God to take our nature at all; it was the humiliation of a man to crucify that nature daily. He knew what sages had failed to see, that it was loftiest when lowest; that as it sank to humbleness it rose in glory. And thus, the model of all he taught, himself "the first-born from the dead," he soared to heaven with a spirit lowly as the grave he left; thus beats there, at the right hand of the Majesty on high, a human heart—the heart of an enthroned King—more softly subdued to mercy, more meekly patient, than ever sorrowed among the loneliest solitudes of earthly affliction. *W. A. Butler.*

9677. HUMILITY, Profit of. Dr. Morrison, missionary in China, sent home to ask for an assistant. Attention was called to a young man of Aberdeen, who wished to devote himself to missionary work. When he came before the committee his appearance was so unpromising that they said, "He will never do for a missionary; he is too rustic." Then they thought he might be good enough for a servant. One of the committee was requested to speak to the young man in private. He was told of the objection to his being a missionary, and also of the proposal to send him out as a servant. He was asked if he were willing. He replied, without any hesitation and with a bright smile, "Yes, sir, most certainly; I am willing to do anything, so that I am in the work. To be a 'hewer of wood and a drawer of water,' is too great an honor for me, when the Lord's house is building." That unpromising rustic became the famous Dr. Milne.

9678. HUMILITY, Promoting. It was said of St. Bernard that bright rays proceeded from his eyes, because of his great humility. If he saw a man in poor raiment, he would reason in this way: "This man bears his poverty with greater patience than you, Bernard;" and seeing one in costly apparel, he would say: "Perhaps, under those fine clothes, there is a better man than Bernard is in coarse garments." He was always esteeming others better than himself.

9679. HUMILITY, Royal. Trajan, the Roman Emperor, has set us an example of condescension and affability. He was equal, indeed, to the greatest generals of antiquity; but the sounding titles of Optimus and the Father of his Country did not elate him. All the oldest soldiers he knew by their own name; he conversed with them with the greatest familiarity, and never retired to his tent before he had visited the camps. He refused the statues which the flattery of friends wished to erect to him, and he ridiculed the follies of an enlightened nation that could pay adoration to cold inanimate pieces of marble. His public entry into Rome gained him the hearts of the people; he appeared on foot, and showed himself an enemy to parade and ostentatious equipage. His wish to listen to the just complaints of his subects, distinguished his palace by the inscription of "The Public Palace."   *Buck.*

9680. HUMILITY, Spiritual. The humble soul is like the violet, which grows low, hangs the head downwards, and hides itself with its own leaves; and were it not that the fragrant smell of his many graces discovered him to the world, he would choose to live and die in secrecy.
Teachers' Treasury.

9681. HUMILITY, Testing. A monk fasted excessively and offered long prayers. Pachomius, his abbott, suspecting that he was influenced more by self-esteem than true piety, bade him eat regularly, and not pray except at the usual service with the rest of the brethren. The monk refused to obey. Soon after, the abbot sent his disciple Theodore to his cell to see what he was about. He came back and reported that he found the rebellious monk praying. "Go and interrupt him several times," said the master. Theodore did so, till at length the devout monk could endure it no longer. He swore at his disturber and seizing a stick endeavored to chastise him. "Ah!" said Pachomius, "it is quite evident that he needs true conversion."

9682. HUMILITY, Test of. We learn from coins and inscriptions, that the couriers in the service of the Roman government had the privilege of traveling through the provinces free of expense, and of calling on the villagers to forward their carriages and baggage to the next town. Under a despotic government, this became a cruel grievance. Every Roman of high rank claimed the same privilege; the horses were unyoked from the plough to be harnessed to the rich man's carriage. It was the most galling injustice which the provinces suffered. We have an inscription on the frontier-town of Egypt and Nubia, mentioning its petition for a redress of this grievance; and a coin of Nerva's reign records its abolition in Italy. Our Lord could give no stronger exhortation to patient humility than by advising his Syrian hearers, instead of resenting the demand for one stage's "vehiculation," to go willingly a second time.   *Eclectic Review.*

9683. HUMILITY, True. When Matthew Prior was servant to King William's ambassador in France, A. D. 1698, he was shown by the French king's household at Versailles, picture stories of Louis XIV., painted by Le Brun; and being asked whether the actions of King William were likewise to be seen in his palace, Prior answered, "No; the monuments of my master's actions are to be seen everywhere but in his own house." So the good works of a true believer shine everywhere except in his own esteem.   *Salter.*

9684. HUNGER, Absence of. "Never," said a poor woman, "did I understand the sweetness of those blessed words, 'they shall hunger no more,' until I looked upon the pale, pinched face of my little child, who died upon my bosom for want of food."

9685. HUNGER, Influence of. Hunger is one of the beneficent and terrible instincts. It is, indeed, the very fire of life, underlying all impulses to labor, and moving man to noble activities by its imperious demands. Look where we may, we see it as the motive power which sets the vast array of human machinery in action. It is hunger which brings these stalwart navvies together in orderly gangs to cut paths through mountains, to throw bridges across rivers, to intersect the land with the great iron-ways which bring city into daily communication with city. Hunger is the overseer of those men erecting palaces, prison-houses, barracks, and villas. Hunger sits at the loom, which, with stealthy power, is weaving the wondrous fabrics of cotton and silk. Hunger labors at the furnace and the plough, coercing the native indolence of man into strenuous and incessant activity. Let food be abundant and easy of access, and civilization becomes impossible; for our higher efforts are dependent on our lower impulses in an indissoluble manner. Nothing but the necessities of food will force man to labor, which he hates, and will always avoid when possible. And although this seems obvious only when applied to the laboring classes, it is equally, though less obviously true, when applied to all other classes; for the money we all labor to gain is nothing but food, and the surplus of food, which will buy other men's labor. If in this sense hunger is seen to be a beneficent instinct, in another sense it is terrible; for when its progress is unchecked it becomes a devouring flame, destroying all that is noble in man, subjugating his humanity, and making the brute dominant in him, till finally life itself is extinguished. Beside the picture of the activities it inspires, we might also place a picture of the ferocities it evokes. Many an appalling story might be cited, from that of Ugolino in the famine-tower to those of wretched shipwrecked men and women who have been impelled by the madness of starvation to murder their companions that they might feed upon their flesh.   *Smiles.*

9686. HUSBAND, Devotion of a. Two snakes were found in the house of Titus Gracchus. The Augurs decided that one of them must die. If the male should be put to death, Cornelia would soon die; if the female, Titus Gracchus would die. "Dismiss, then, the female," said Gracchus, "so that Cornelia may survive me, for she is the younger of the two." Gracchus died soon after, leaving many sons, to whom Cornelia devoted her entire attention. Her husband's memory was so dear to her, that she refused a proffered marriage with Ptolemy, king of Egypt. The splendor of a diadem and the pomp of a rich kingdom was not sufficient to break her constancy to one who had sacrificed his life for her.

9687. HUSBANDS, Hen-pecked. Socrates, who is by all accounts the undoubted head of the sect of the hen-pecked, owned and acknowledged that he owed great part of his virtue to the exercise which his useful wife constantly gave it. There are several good instructions may be drawn from his wise answers to the people of less fortitude than himself on this subject. A friend, with indignation, asked nim how so good a man could live with so violent a creature? He observed to him, that they who learn to keep a good seat on horseback mount the least manageable they can get; and when they have mastered them, they are sure never to be discomposed on the backs of steeds less restive. At several times, to different persons, on the same subject, he has said, "My dear friend, you are beholden to Xantippe that I bear so well your flying out in a dispute." *Steele.*

9688. HUSBANDS, Ill-natured. Patricius was a pagan of most ungovernable temper, who poured out his violence upon his patient, Christian wife, Monica. At length he was softened by her exemplary conduct, and became a Christian. They were the parents of the famous Augustine. When Monica heard ladies complain of the ill nature and bad treatment which they received from their husbands, she asked, "Who are to blame? Are not we and our sharp tongues?" For herself, she never answered his sharp words, nor provoked him by her own complaints. It is said that many matrons followed her example with success. We recommend the experiment to any who are similarly troubled.

9689. HUSBAND AND WIFE, Reconciliation of. A man complained to St. Columba, that his wife had taken an aversion to him and abandoned him. The saint called her and reminded her of her duties. "I am ready to do everything," said the woman. "I will obey you in the hardest things you can command. I will go even, if it is desired, on pilgrimage to Jerusalem, or I will shut myself up in a nunnery; in short, I will do everything except live with that man." The saint told her there could be no question of a pilgrimage, or a convent, so long as her husband lived. "But," said he, "let us try to pray to God, all three fasting, you, your husband and myself." "Oh, I know that you can obtain what is impossible from God." Columba prayed all night. Next morning he said to the woman, "Tell me, to what convent are you bound after your yesterday's projects?" "To none," said she. "My heart has been changed to-night. I know not how I have passed from hate to love." From that till death, their married life was most happy.

9690. HUSBAND AND WIFE, Unity of. Husband and wife should be like two candles burning together, which make the house more lightsome; or like two fragrant flowers bound up in one nosegay, that augment its sweetness; or like two well-tuned instruments, which, sounding together, make the more melodious music. Husband and wife—what are they but as two springs meeting, and so joining their streams that they make but one current? *W. Secker.*

9691. HYPOCHONDRIAC, Cure of a. A young student at college became so deeply hypochondriac that he proclaimed himself dead, and ordered the college bell to be tolled on the occasion of his death. In this he was indulged; but the man employed to execute the task appeared to the student to perform it so imperfectly, that he arose from his bed, in a fury of passion, to toll the bell for his own departure. When he had finished, he retired to his bed in a state of profuse perspiration, and was from that moment alive and well. *Dr. Mead.*

9692. HYPOCRISY, Biblical Figures of. The Greek word properly refers to an actor, one who wears a mask and plays a part on the stage. It is compared to *leaven*, Luke 12: 1. *Whited sepulchres*, Matt. 23: 27–31; painted and garnished, but full of the decay of death. *A whited wall*, Acts 23: 3. *Graves overgrown* with grass, and concealed from the notice of those who walk over them, and are hurt or defiled by the unexpected contact, Luke 11: 44. *Potsherds*, covered with silver dross, Prov. 26: 23. *Tares*, Matt. 13: 38, remarkable for their resemblance to good wheat, especially in the early stages. *Wolves in sheep's clothing*, Matt. 7: 15. *Wells without water*, 2 Pet. 2: 17; Jude 12. *A cloak* to cover sin, 1 Thess. 2: 5; 1 Pet. 2: 16. *Deceitful kisses*, Prov. 27: 6 (Absalom, 2 Sam. 15: 5; Joab, 20: 9, 10; Judas, Luke 22: 47, 48). *The spider's web*, Job 8: 13, 14, a figure of the hypocrite's trust. *The rush without water*, and flag without mire, Job 8: 11–13, a figure of the hypocrite's hope. Matt. 26: 65.— "Rending the garments" was a sign of mourning amongst the Jews, but it was also a frequent evidence of their hypocrisy. It is said that many of them took good care to rend the garment on the seam, so that they might, without much trouble or loss, repair the rent. —(*Jacobi.*) Like the "hypocritical mockers in feasts," Ps. 35: 16; and the hired mourners and minstrels so customary in Eastern countries in the house of death, Matt. 9: 13; Mal. 3: 14 (see marg.). *Bowes.*

9693. HYPOCRISY, Common. The shops in the square of San Marco were all religiously closed, for the day was a high festival: we were much disappointed, for it was our last day, and we desired to take away with us some souvenirs of lovely Venice; but our regret soon vanished, for on looking at the shop we meant to patronize, we readily discovered signs of traffic within. We stepped to the side door, and found, when one or two other customers had been served, that we might purchase to our heart's content, saint or no saint. After this fashion too many keep the laws of God to the eye, but violate them in the heart. The shutters are up as if the man no more dealt with sin and Satan; but a brisk commerce is going on behind the scenes. *Spurgeon.*

9694. HYPOCRISY, Concealment of. Formality frequently takes its dwelling near the chambers of integrity, and so assumes its name; the soul not suspecting that hell should make so near an approach to heaven. A rotten post, though covered with gold, is more fit to be burned in the fire, than for the building of a fabric. Where there is a pure conscience, there will be a pure conversation. The dial of our faces does not infallibly show the time of day in our hearts; the humblest looks may enamel the former, while unbounded pride covers the latter. Unclean spirits may inhabit the chamber when they look not out at the window. A hypocrite may be both the fairest and the foulest creature in the world; he may be fairest outwardly in the eyes of man, and foulest inwardly in the sight of God. How commonly do such unclean swans cover their black flesh with their white feathers! Though such wear the mantle of Samuel, that should bear the name of Satan.   *Secker.*

9695. HYPOCRISY, Confession of. A reliable author says, "A young man, who held a confidential post in a large mercantile establishment, and who, as a church member and a Sabbath-school teacher, had for years maintained an unsuspected reputation, during an illness which elicited his real character, confessed that his whole life had been one course of concealed iniquity. The statement was ascertained to be perfectly correct; and he died in the agonies of despair."

9696. HYPOCRISY, Examples of. Julius Cæsar was a great dissembler. He would appear to be pleased with his friends, though he might through others be seeking their ruin. Cicero was in this manner banished from Rome. So also was Pompey rendered odious in the sight of the people, and when he fled into Egypt, Cæsar pursued him there. But when Pompey's head was brought to him, he shed tears and said, "It is the victory and not the revenge that pleases me." Charles the Ninth of France, a little before the massacre of St. Bartholomew's invited Admiral Coligni to his palace, desiring to receive counsel from, and promising to abide by his decisions, affirming that he revered him as a son should a father. Very shortly after he caused him to be ignominiously put to death.

9697. HYPOCRISY versus Honesty. Hypocrisy desires to seem good rather than to be so: honesty desires to be good rather than seem so. The worldlings purchase reputation by the sale of desert, wise men buy desert with the hazard of reputation. I would do much to hear well, more to deserve well, and rather lose opinion than merit. It shall more joy me that I know myself what I am, than it shall grieve me to hear what others report me. I had rather deserve well without praise, than do ill with commendation.   *Warwick.*

9698. HYPOCRISY, Religious. He that hath a false end in his profession, will soon come to an end of his profession, when he is pinched on that toe where his corn is: I mean, called to deny that his naughty heart aimed at all this while; now his heart fails him, he can go no farther. O, take heed of this squint-eye to our profit, pleasure, or anything beneath Christ and heaven; for they will take away your heart, as the prophet saith of wine and women; that is, our love; and if our love be taken away, there will be little courage left for Christ. Like some soldiers, when once they meet with a rich booty at the sacking of some town, are spoiled for fighting ever after.   *Gurnall.*

9699. HYPOCRISY, Speciousness of. While every vice is hid by hypocrisy, every virtue is suspected to be hypocrisy. This excuses the bad from imitating virtue, the ungenerous from rewarding it; and the suspicion is looked upon as wisdom, as if it was not as necessary a part of wisdom to know what to believe, as what to reject.   *Mrs. Montague.*

9700. HYPOCRITE, Assumption of the. Apes will be imitating men: spiders have their webs, and wasps their honeycombs. Hypocrites will needs to do something, that they may seem to be somebody; but, for want of an inward principle, they do nothing well; they amend one error with another, as Esau here (Gen. 28); and as Herod prevents perjury by murder. Thus, while they shun the sands, they rush upon the rocks; and while they keep off the shallows, they fall into the whirlpool.   *Trapp.*

9701. HYPOCRITE, Detection of a. Consider, hypocrisy lies close in the heart; if thou art not very careful, thou mayest easily pass a false judgment on thyself. They who went to search the cellar under the Parliament, at first saw nothing but coals and winter provisions; but upon a review, when they came to throw away that stuff, they found all but provision for the devil's kitchen; then the mystery of iniquity was uncased, and the barrels of powder appeared. How many are there that, from some duties of piety they perform, some seeming zeal they express in profession, presently cry, "Omnia bene," and are so kind to themselves as to vote themselves good Christians, who, did they but take the pains to throw those aside, they might find a foul hypocrite at the bottom of them all!   *Anon.*

9702. HYPOCRITE, Doom of a. N——— was a branch of a pious family, some of whose ancestors were martyrs. She was religiously educated by her pious parents; and her education, particularly her knowledge of history, was extensive. In her study of history the progress of religion had attracted her chief attention. Religious topics were her element; her remarks often evinced the correctness and vigor of her judgment; and she often delighted the social circle by her striking application of the current matters of conversation to the subject of religion. Like the rest of the pious family, she seemed devoted to all the duties of a Christian, with only one exception, and this they wondered at; that she did not attend with them at the Lord's table. All regarded her as an ornament of religion, and urged her to take part in this ordinance. In one year N——— lost both her pious parents, and she had just put off mourning when she was taken desperately ill. Having been on terms of intimacy with the family, I was sent for at her request to visit the dying sister. I certainly went prepared to see a Christian die: but what was my astonishment to behold those features, instead of smiling in death, as I expected, clothed in all the horrors of mental agony! Bidding me sit down, and ascertaining that there were no witnesses, she addressd me in nearly these terms: "I am glad you have come: I can not bear to go out of the world a deceiver, but I am unable to tell the sad secret of my heart to those about me; it would be too much for them to bear. I am not the character my friends have supposed. I am not religious—do not interrupt me—I have talked about religion, my passions have often felt the powers of the world to come, and my imagination roved at large among things unseen; I have amused myself with these matters, and regarded with the interest of an amateur their effects upon minds whom I reckoned of an inferior order, though ennobled by a birth from heaven. But amidst all, my own heart has never loved religion as a personal thing: indeed, I have never concerned myself about it for myself, and now I must die without any of its prospects, and be shut out forever from all its enjoyments." I paused a moment, and began to observe that "Life is the season of hope," and admitting all I heard to be correct, still the Saviour's saying, "Whosoever cometh unto me I will in no wise cast out," is equally entitled to credit. But she cut me short, observing, "The vigor of my youth and the strength of my intellect I have wasted in living to myself; I never cared for the divine approbation; and God is justly my adversary. Cast down as I am, I cannot go with a piteous tale of misery to petition for mercy for which I can plead no services, nor live to show any gratitude. I know already what you would say to these sentiments—you would hold out mercy as yet attainable; but my heart revolts at it. Heaven would be no heaven to me on the terms I can only enter it. I have been a worthless idler, and cannot endure to receive the reward of a faithful soldier." Surprised as I was, I endeavored to enforce the necessity of renouncing such sentiments, and was urging that a good confession, though late, would find acceptance, when she interrupted me with some energy: "No, sir, spare me, spare yourself; my character is finished; what I am, that shall I be forever. The tree is even now falling: it is too late to direct where its trunk shall be extended on the earth." The doctor coming in, I soon after took my leave, intending to renew my visit, but in the morning learned that N—— had expired in the night.

Pastoral Letters.

9703. HYPOCRITE, Emblems of the. Hypocrites resemble looking-glasses, which present the faces which are not in them. Oh, how desirous are men to put the fairest gloves upon the foulest hands, and the finest paint upon the rottenest posts! To counterfeit the coin of heaven is to commit treason against the King of heaven. Who would spread a curious cloth upon a dusty table? If a mariner set sail in an unsound bottom, he may reasonably expect to lose his voyage. No wise virgin would carry a lamp without light. O professor, either get the latter or part with the former. None are so black in the eyes of the Deity as those who paint spiritual beauty where there is no spirituality. *Secker.*

9704. HYPOCRITE, Exposure of the. A false friend is worse than an open enemy. A painted harlot is less dangerous than a painted hypo-

crite. A treacherous Judas is more abhorred of God than a bloody Pilate. Christians! remember the sheep's clothing will soon be stripped from the wolf's back. The velvet plaster of profession shall not always conceal the offensive ulcer of corruption. Neither the ship of formality nor hypocrisy will carry one person to the harbor of felicity. The blazing lamps of foolish virgins may light them to the bridegroom's gate, but not into his chamber. . . . . Oh, what vanity it is to lop off the boughs, and leave the roots which can send forth more; or to empty the cistern, and leave the fountain running which can soon fill it again! Such may swim in the water as the visible church; but when the net is drawn to shore, they must be thrown away as bad fishes. Though the tares and the wheat may grow in the field together, yet they will not be housed in the granary together. *Secker.*

9705. HYPOCRITE, Fate of the. A wolf, once upon a time, resolved to disguise himself, thinking that he should thus gain an easier livelihood. Having, therefore, clothed himself in a sheep's skin, he contrived to get among a flock of sheep, and fed along with them, so that even the shepherd was deceived. The wolf was shut up with the sheep, and the door made fast. But the shepherd, wanting something for his supper, and going in to fetch out a sheep, mistook the wolf for one of them and killed him on the spot. *Æsop.*

9706. HYPOCRITES, Carefulness of. Hypocrites make a great business about small matters, and in the mean time neglect weighty duties. They are careful to pay the tithe of mint, and omit the weightier matters. Like one who comes into a shop to make a very small purchase, and steals a costly article—a pennyworth to steal a pound's worth; or is punctual in paying a small debt, that he may get deeper into our books, and cheat us of a greater sum; comply in circumstances and terms, but make no conscience of greater. *Salter.*

9707. HYPOCRITES the Devil's Dupes. If the devil ever laughs, it must be at hypocrites; they are the greatest dupes he has. They serve him better than any others, and receive no wages; nay, what is still more extraordinary, they submit to greater mortifications to go to hell than the sincerest Christians to go to heaven. *Colton.*

9708. HYPOCRITES, Motives of. God is in the hypocrite's mouth, but the world is in his heart, which he expects to gain through his good reputation. I have read of one that offered his prince a great sum of money to have leave once or twice a day to come into his presence, and only say, "God save your Majesty!" The prince wondering at this large offer for so small a favor, asked him, "What advantage would this afford him?" "O sire," saith he, "this, though I have nothing else at your hands, will get me a name in the country for one who is a great favorite at court, and such an opinion will help me to more at the year's end, than it costs me for the purchase." Thus some, by the name they get for great saints, advance their worldly interests, which lie at the bottom of all their profession. *Gurnall.*

9709. HYPOCRITES, Schemes of. The abbot in Melanchthon lived strictly, and walked demurely, and looked humbly, so long as he was but a monk; but when, by his seeming extraordinary sanctity, he got to be abbot, he grew intolerable, proud, and insolent, and, being asked the reason of it, confessed "that his former lowly look was but to see if he could find the keys of the abbey." *Brooks.*

9710. IDEAL, Influence of an. Every man has at times in his mind the ideal of what he should be, but is not. This ideal may be high and complete, or it may be quite low and insufficient; yet, in all men that really seek to improve, it is better than the actual character. Perhaps no one is so satisfied with himself that he never wishes to be wiser, better, and more holy. Man never falls so low that he can see nothing higher than himself. This ideal man which we project, as it were, out of ourselves, and seek to make real—this wisdom, goodness, and holiness, which we aim to transfer from our thoughts to our life—has an action more or less powerful on each man, rendering him dissatisfied with present attainments, and restless unless he is becoming better. With some men it takes the rose out of the cheek, and forces them to wander a long pilgrimage of temptations before they reach the Delectable Mountains of tranquillity, and find "rest" under the tree of life. *T. Parker.*

9711. IDEAL, Unattainable. Alas! we know that ideals can never be completely embodied in practice. Ideals must ever lie a great way off, and we will thankfully content ourselves with any not intolerable approximation thereto! Let no man, as Schiller says, too querulously "measure by a scale of perfection the meagre product of reality" in this poor world of ours. We will esteem him no wise man; we will esteem him a sickly, discontented, foolish man. And yet, on the other hand, it is never to be forgotten that ideals do exist; that if they be not approximated to at all, the whole matter goes to wreck! Infallibly. No bricklayer builds a wall perpendicular; mathematically, this is not possible; a certain degree of perpendicularity suffices him, and he, like a good bricklayer, who must have done with his job, leaves it so. And yet, if he sway too much from the perpendicular, above all, if he throw plummet and level quite away from him, and pile brick on brick heedless, just as it comes to hand, such bricklayer, I think, is in a bad way. He has forgotten himself; but the law of gravitation does not forget to act on him; he and his wall rush down into a confused welter of ruins! *Carlyle.*

9712. IDEALISM, Value of. Precious beyond rubies is the idealism which can invest with celestial dignity the earthly avocation, and which, even when the hands are engaged in downright drudgery, can fill the mind with noble thoughts, and carry you through the daily task as a son or daughter of the king. *Dr. J. Hamilton.*

9713. IDIOSYNCRASY, Acquaintance with our. It is a very wise rule in the conduct of the understanding, to acquire early a correct notion of your own peculiar constitution of mind, and to become well acquainted, as a physician would say, with your idiosyncrasy! Are you an acute man, and see sharply for small distances? or are you a comprehensive man, and able to take in wide and extensive views into your mind? Does your mind turn its ideas into wit? or are you apt to take a common-sense view of the objects presented to you? Have you an exuberant imagination, or a correct judgment? Are you quick, or slow? accurate, or hasty? a great reader, or a great thinker? It is a prodigious point gained if any man can find out where his powers lie, and what are his deficiences—if he can contrive to ascertain what nature intended him for. *S. Smith.*

9714. IDIOSYNCRASY, General. The variety of distempers in men's minds is as great as of those in their bodies: some are epidemic, few escape them, and every one, too, if he would look into himself, would find some defect of his particular genius. There is scarcely any one without some idiosyncrasy that he suffers by. *Locke.*

9715. IDLENESS, Accounting for. Some one, in casting up his accounts, put down a very large sum per annum for his idleness. But there is another account more awful than that of our expenses, in which many will find that their idleness has mainly contributed to the balance against them. From its very inaction, idleness ultimately becomes the most active cause of evil; as a palsy is more to be dreaded than a fever. *Colton.*

9716. IDLENESS, Bane of. Idleness is the great corrupter of youth, and the bane and dishonor of middle age. He who, in the prime of life, finds time to hang heavy on his hands, may with much reason suspect that he has not consulted the duties which the consideration of his age imposed on him; assuredly he has not consulted his happiness. *Blair.*

9717. IDLENESS Considered. It is very great vanity in many professors to mind more other men's business than their own; from the society of such saints we must withdraw. No man is too noble to have a calling. If iron had reason, it would choose rather to be used in labor, than to grow rusty in a corner. By the law of Mohamet, the Grand Turk himself was to be of some trade. The hour of idleness is the hour of temptation. An idle person is the devil's tennis-ball, tossed by him at his pleasure. God ordained that the neck of the consecrated ass should be broken (Exodus xiii. 13), instead of sacrificing it; peradventure, because that animal hath ever been the hieroglyphic of sloth and laziness. Among the Egyptians idleness was a capital crime. Among the Locrians, he that lent money to an idle person was to lose it. Among the Corinthians, idle persons were delivered to the carnifex. By the laws of Solon, idle persons were to suffer death. The ancients call idleness the burial of a living man; and Seneca had rather be sick than idle. Now, shall nature do more than grace? Shall poor blind heathens be so severe against idle persons, and shall Christians embrace them? Should they not rather turn their backs upon them and have no intercourse with them who think themselves too great, or too good, to hold the plough?   *T. Brooks.*

9718. IDLENESS, Cure for. I apprehend there is not a more miserable, as well as a more worthless being, than a young man of fortune who has nothing to do but to find some new way of doing nothing. In a neighboring nation they endure no idleness among them. If any poor man turns idle, and admonition does him no good, they take the folllowing method to make him work: they confine him in a large cistern, into which the water runs so fast that unless he pumps it out with all his might for several hours, it will prevail over him and drown him.   *Sir W. Jones.*

9719. IDLENESS, Degradation of. Æleas, king of Scythia, said that when he was idle he considered himself no better than his horse-keeper.

9720. IDLENESS, Employment of. Domitian, while he held the empire, was so given up to sloth and idleness that he spent most of his time in pricking flies to death with the point of a needle. When it was asked, "Who is with the emperor," the answer would be, "Not so much as a fly."

9721. IDLENESS not Enjoyment. So far from complete inaction being perfect enjoyment, there are few sufferings greater than that which the total absence of occupation generally induces. Count Caylus, the celebrated French antiquary, spent much time in engraving the plates which illustrate his valuable works. When his friends asked him why he worked so hard at such an almost mechanical occupation, he replied, "*Je grave pour ne pas me pendre*"—I engrave lest I should hang myself. Nature has beneficently provided that if the greater proportion of her sons must earn their bread by the sweat of their brow, that bread is far sweeter from the previous effort than if it fell spontaneously into the hand of listless indolence. It is scarcely to be questioned, then, that labor is desirable for its own sake, as well as for the substantial results which it affords; and, consequently, that it by no means lessens, but rather adds to, the general chance of happiness, that nearly all the members of society should, in some shape or other, be placed under an obligation to labor for their support.   *Dr. Potter.*

9722. IDLENESS, Figure of. Hast thou looked on the potter's wheel, — one of the venerablest objects, old as the prophet Ezekiel, and far older? Rude lumps of clay, how they spin themselves up, by mere quick whirling, into beautiful circular dishes! And fancy the most assiduous potter, but without his wheel, reduced to make dishes by mere kneading and baking! Even such a potter were destiny with a human soul that would rest and lie at ease,—that would not work and spin! Of an idle, unrevolving man, the kindest destiny can bake and knead nothing other than a botch: let her spend on him what expensive coloring, or gilding and enameling she will, he is but a botch —a mere enameled vessel of dishonor. *Carlyle.*

9723. IDLENESS, Intellectual. It is no more possible for an idle man to keep together a certain stock of knowledge, than it is possible to keep together a stock of ice exposed to a meridian sun. Every day destroys a fact, a relation, or an influence; and the only method of preserving the bulk and value of the pile is by constantly adding to it.   *S. Smith.*

9724. IDLENESS, Mental. Dionysius the elder was asked if he was at leisure, and had no business at present. He replied, "The gods forbid that it ever should be so with me; for a bow, if it be over-bent, will break; but the mind breaks if it be over-slack."

9725. IDLENESS, Offense of. Herondas, hearing that an Athenian had been condemned for idleness, desired to be shown the man that had been convicted of so gentlemanly an offense.

9726. IDLENESS, Opposition to. The Romans set up in temples within the city the goddesses Agenotea, Stimula, and Strenua, to be worshiped. They would not receive Quies, or Rest, as a goddess in the city; but built a temple for her in the Lavicanian way, and thither they sent the idle people of the commonwealth with their sacrifices.

9727. IDLENESS, Penalty for. The Egyptian law declared that after a person was thrice convicted of idleness, he should be declared infamous. Draco punished idleness with death. Solon required the council of the Areopagus to investigate every man's means of living, and to chastise the idle.

9728. IDLENESS, A Philosopher of. Altades, the twelfth king of Babylon, an idle and slothful person, laid down two maxims, which he called his own. The first was, "That he was a vain and foolish man, who, with continual labor and misery, makes war to the destruction of himself and others." His other was, "He is the most fool of all that, with toil and labor, heaps up a treasure, not for himself, but his posterity." From this idle philosophy, he collected two things: "That no war was to be made because of the labor, and that we should enjoy the riches and glory that was got by the sweat and miseries of others." Altades' life was formed on this basis, and was most vicious and useless.

9729. IDLENESS, Sin of. I would have every one lay to heart, that a state of idleness is a state of damnable sin. Idleness is directly repugnant to the great ends of God, both in our creation and redemption. As to our creation: can we imagine that God, who created not any thing but for some excellent end, should create man for none, or for a silly one? The spirit within us is an active and vivacious principle: our rational faculties qualify us for doing good: this is the proper work of reason, the truest and most natural pleasure of a rational soul Who can think now, that our wise Creator lighted this candle within us, that we might oppress and stifle it by negligence and idleness?

that he contrived and destined such a mind to squander and fool away its talents in vanity and impertinence? As to our redemption, it is evident both what the design of it is, and how opposite idleness is to it. Christ gave himself for us, "to redeem us from all iniquity, and to purify to himself a peculiar people, zealous of good works." How little, then, can a useless and barren life answer the expectations of God? What a miserable return must it be to the blood of his Son; and how utterly must it disappoint all the purposes of his Word and Spirit! *Lucas.*

9730. IDLENESS and Trifling. An Athenian said to Nicander, "You Spartans are extremely idle." "You say true," he answered, "but we do not busy ourselves, like you, in every trifle."

9731. IDOLATRY, Conversion from. As Pontius, the little son of a Roman senator, was passing through a street in Rome, he heard many voices chanting the 115 Ps. He was impressed by the words, "As for our God, he is in heaven; he hath done whatsoever pleased him. Their idols are silver and gold; even the work of men's hands. They have mouths, but they speak not; eyes have they, but they see not. They have ears, and hear not; noses have they, and smell not. They have hands, and handle not; feet have they, and walk not; neither speak they through their throat." He went up to the door and knocked. The doorkeeper looked out, and reported to the bishop, "It is only a little fellow knocking at the door." "Well, open and let him in," said he, "for of such is the kingdom of heaven." Having been admitted, he went up to Pontianus, the bishop, and said, "Teach me that beautiful song I heard you sing. It is all so true. You sang that they had feet, and walk not. I know that they cannot move, and that people are afraid of their being blown over by the wind, or stolen, or knocked down by accident; and I have myself seen how they are fastened into their pedestals with melted lead." The bishop was astonished at the boy's perception, and saw that the Holy Spirit was enlightening him. He asked him about his parents. Learning that they were pagans, the bishop said, "God in his own good time may enlighten thy father as he is illumining thee." On his return home the boy was so full of this new religion that he could but tell his father all about it. The boy led his father to the bishop. Both became catechumens, and were baptized together. This boy Christian became a hero for Christ, and died a martyr, A. D. 257.

9732. IDOLATRY, Destroying. The Koran relates that Abraham endeavored to convert his father and neighbors from idolatry. In their absence, he went into the temple, where their idols stood, and broke them in pieces, except one large one. When they discovered the misfortune of their gods, they accused Abraham with destroying them. He answered, "Nay; but that big one has done it. Ask them, if they can speak." They said, "Thou knowest that these speak not." Abraham said, "Do ye, then worship that which cannot profit you at all, neither can it hurt you? Fie on you, and that which ye worship instead of God!" Then they cast him into a great fire to avenge their gods; but the fire did not burn him, for his God delivered him

9733. IDOLATRY, Ignorance and. A missionary at Sierra Leone called on a heathen widow, and was surprised at the evidences of heathen darkness which he saw. He writes: "She had in her room four gods—one for herself, one for her husband, and one for each of her two children. She had been rubbing *eggiddi* (a rich kind of food made of Indian corn, beaten fine in a mortar, and mixed with palm oil) on their mouths; but they ate not. I endeavored to show her the folly of such practices; but she was joined to her idols!"

9734. IDOLATRY, Local. The Romans deified their own city, and built a temple to her on Mt. Palatine, calling in the provinces to do her homage. This spirit is common to modern times.

9735. IDOLATRY, Motive of. The Romans worshiped some of their deities that they might do them good; but they worshiped the fever and ague that they might do them less harm.

9736. IDOLS, Accusations of. Mohammed was unsparing in his denunciations of idolatry. He hurls all his anathemas against it. His followers believe that, in the day of judgment, God, by his mighty power, will bring the idol gods to bear swift testimony against idolaters, that the idols will open their mouths in accusation against, instead of intercession for them. We may, with equal probability, extend the application to each improper object of human devotion.

9737. IDOLS, Classification of. I do find, therefore, in this enchanted glass, four idols, or false appearances, of several distinct sorts, every sort comprehending many divisions. The first sort I call idols of the nation or tribe; the second, idols of the den or cave; the third, idols of the forum; and the fourth, idols of the theatre. *Bacon.*

9738. IDOLS, Destruction of. King Olaf and his retinue came to a place where the Pagan farmers armed against him. A meeting was called, and the king exhorted them to accept the true God and put away their idols. Gudbrand, the chief of the place, answered, "We know nothing of him thou speakest about. Dost thou call him a God whom no one can see? We have a god that we should have brought unto the assembly to-day, but that it is so rainy; and the sight of him will make your blood run cold." It was arranged that if the morrow should be fair, the idol should be brought, and after a further explanation they would either do as the king desired or else fight him. This god was Thor the Thunderer. Every day five cakes were set before him, and as they disappeared, he was believed to have consumed them. The next day was favorable. The council gathered, the king with his bishop Grimkel and other attendants on one side of the plain, and the pagans on the other. A great **image**, gleaming with silver and gold and jewels, was brought in on the shoulders of the Pagans and set down in the midst of the field. The heathen chief stood up and said, ' Where now, O king, is thy God? I think he will be abashed before this glorious god of ours, whom I see you fear." Then King Olaf arose and answered, " Much hast thou talked, and greatly hast thou wondered, because thou canst not see our God; but we expect his arrival. Thou wouldst frighten us with thy blind and deaf god, who cannot move and must be borne upon your shoulders. But now," he cried aloud, "look to the east; behold, our God, is coming!" All looked that way, and at the instant Kolbing, a faithful servant of the king, smote the idol with a large club, as previously instructed. The fragments of the terrific god were scattered on all sides, and out came a great swarm of rats and mice. The Pagans fled in all directions. The king rose and said, " Ye see yourselves what your god can do— the idol ye adorned with gold and silver, and to which ye offered meat. Take now your gold and ornaments from the grass, and give them to your wives and daughters; but never hang them hereafter on stocks and stones." He then offered them the alternative of accepting Christianity or fighting his army. To fight was folly, and the Pagans sullenly submitted, and were baptized by the bishop. Thus was idolatry put away in the eleventh century.

9739. IF, The Danger of. The heathens have observed that, in rhetoric, it is a point of chiefest cunning, when you would outface a man, or importune him to do a thing, to press and urge him with that which he will not, or cannot, for shame, deny to be in himself; as, by saying, "If you have any wit, then you will do thus and thus; if you be an honest man, or a good fellow, do this." So here the devil, not being to learn any point of subtlety, comes to our Saviour, saying, " If thou be the Son of God," as it may be doubted. You being in this case, then " make these stones bread." No, no, it follows not; a man may be the Son of God, and not show it by any such art. So, when Pilate asked who accused Christ, they answered, " If he had not been a malefactor, we would not have brought him before thee." They were jolly, grave men; it was a flat flattery. This ought to put us in mind, when we are tempted in like manner, that we take heed that we be not outfaced.   *Andrewes.*

9740. IGNORANCE, Ancient. Archelaus, king of Macedon, was so ignorant of the things of nature, that upon the eclipse of the sun, amazed with fear, he caused the gates of the palace to be shut up, and the hair of his son to be cut off, as the custom was in solemn mournings. "Great men and learned," saith Pliny, " who know more in natural causes than others do, feared the extinction of the stars, or some mischief to befall them, in their eclipses. Pindarus and Stofichorus were subjects to this fear, attributing the failing of their lights to the power of witchcraft."   *Wanley.*

9741. IGNORANCE, Contentions from. I believe that it is from our ignorance that our contentions flow; we debate with strife and with wrath, with bickering and with hatred; but of the thing debated upon we remain in the profoundest ignorance. Like the laborers of Babel, while we endeavor in vain to express our meaning to each other, the fabric by which, for a common end, we would have ascended to heaven from the ills of earth, remains forever unadvanced and incomplete.   *Lytton.*

9742. IGNORANCE, Deformity of. As blindness is the deformity of the face, so is ignorance the deformity of the soul. As the want of fleshly eyes spoils the beauty of the face, so the want of spiritual eyes spoils the beauty of the soul. A man without knowledge is as a workman without his hands, as a painter without his eyes, as a traveler without his legs, or as a ship without sails, or a bird without wings, or like a body without soul.   *Brooks.*

9743. IGNORANCE, Deprecating. When the Duchess of Modena was complained to that her son had too many branches to learn at one time, and that his health was suffering from the excessive labor, she calmly replied : " It were better for me to have no son than to have an ignorant son."   *Hutchinson.*

9744. IGNORANCE, Fate of. I turned my head to look back, and saw Ignorance coming up to the river side; but he soon got over, and that without half the difficulty which the other two men met with. For it happened that there was then in that place one Vain Hope, a ferryman, that with his boat helped him over; so he, as the other I saw, did ascend the hill to come up to the gate, only he came alone; neither did any man meet him with the least encouragement. When he was coming up to the gate, he looked up to the writing that was above, and then began to knock, supposing that entrance should have been quickly administered to him; but he was asked by the men that looked over the top of the gate, " Whence come you, and what would you have?" He answered, "I have ate and drank in the presence of the King, and he has taught in our streets." Then they asked for his certificate, that they might go in and show it to the King · so he fumbled in his bosom for one, and found none. Then said they "You have none!" But the man answered never a word. So they told the King, but he would not come down to see him, but commanded the two shining ones that conducted Christian and Hopeful to the city to go out and take Ignorance, and bind him hand and foot, and have him away. Then they took him up and carried him through the air to the door that I saw on the side of the hill, and put him in there. Then I saw that there was a way to hell even from the gates of heaven, as well as from the City of Destruction.   *John Bunyan.*

9745. IGNORANCE, Guilt of. He that voluntarily continues ignorant, is guilty of all the crimes which ignorance produces: as to him that should extinguish the tapers of a lighthouse might justly be imputed the calamities of shipwrecks.   *Dr. Johnson.*

9746. IGNORANCE, Inexcusable. To write or talk concerning any subject, without having previously taken the pains to understand it, is a breach of the duty which we owe to ourselves, though it may be no offence against the laws of the land. The privilege of talking and even publishing nonsense is necessary in a free state; but the more sparingly we make use of it the better. *Coleridge.*

9747. IGNORANCE, Instinct and. As a cock was scratching up the straw in a farmyard, in search of food for the hens, he hit upon a jewel that by some chance had found its way there. "He!" said he, "you are a very fine thing, no doubt, to those who prize you; but give me a barley-corn before all the pearls in the world." The cock was a sensible cock; but there are many silly people who despise what is precious because they cannot understand it. *Æsop.*

9748. IGNORANCE, Unexpected. Samuel Wesley visited one of his parishioners as he was upon his dying bed—a man who had never missed going to church in forty years. Thomas, where do you think your soul will go?" "Soul! soul!" said Thomas. "Yes, sir," said Mr. Wesley, "do you not know what your soul is?" "Ay, surely," said Thomas; "why, it is a little bone in the back that lives longer than the body." "So much," says John Wesley, who related it on the authority of Dr. Lupton, who had it from his father. "had Thomas learned from hearing sermons, and exceedingly good sermons, for forty years." *Dr. J. B. Wakeley.*

9749. IGNORANCE, Violence of. There never was any party, faction, sect, or cabal whatsoever, in which the most ignorant were not the most violent: for a bee is not a busier animal than a blockhead. However, such instruments are necessary to politicians; and, perhaps, it may be with states as with clocks, which must have some lead weight hanging at them, to help and regulate the motion of the finer and more useful parts. *Pope.*

9750. ILLIBERALITY Cured. A little girl cured her fashionable mother of giving little when she should have given much, by saying, "I wonder if Mr. —— saw what you gave this morning? If he didn't, God did, and he knows how rich you are."

9751. ILLIBERALITY, Excuse for. A clergyman was endeavoring to get a subscription in aid of some charitable institution out of a close parishioner, who attempted to excuse himself on the ground that he already owed a great deal of money. "But, said the minister, "you owe God a larger debt than you do any one else." "That is so, parson; but then he ain't pushing like the balance of my creditors."

9752. ILLIBERALITY, Self-Condemned. A man being asked for five dollars for a worthy object of benevolence, replied, "O, I can't! I have had $100,000 lying in bank several months without drawing interest." He could not perceive that he had condemned himself.

9753. ILLS, Bear Present. The beeves, once on a time, determined to make an end of the butchers, whose whole art, they said, was conceived for their destruction. So they assembled together, and had already whetted their horns for the contest, when a very old ox, who had long worked at the plough, thus addressed them: "Have a care, my friends, what you do. These men, at least, kill us with decency and skill; but if we fall into the hands of botchers instead of butchers, we shall suffer a double death; for be well assured, men will not go without beef, even though they were without butchers." Better to bear with the ills we have than to fly to others that we know not of. *Æsop.*

9754. ILLS, No Remedies for. A rich slipper will not cure the gout, a diamond ring a whitlow, nor will an imperial diadem ease the headache. *Plutarch.*

9755. ILLS, Origin of. All ills spring from some vice, either in ourselves or others; and even many of our diseases proceed from the same origin. Remove the vices and the ills follow. You must only take care to remove all the vices. If you remove part, you may render the matter worse. By banishing vicious luxury, without curing sloth and an indifference to others, you only diminish industry in the State, and add nothing to men's charity or their generosity. *David Hume.*

9756. ILLUSTRATION, Advantage of. An illustration is a moral painting on which the imagination has been employed; and it has the advantage over the simple annunciation of a truth, that it appeals to both the faculties—the reason and imagination; like the painting on the canvas, which, while it charms the eye, also interests the mind—or like the incense which flamed on Jewish altars, which arrested the eye with its cloudy pillar, while it regaled the senses with its fragrance. *Salter.*

9757. ILLUSTRATION, Benefit of. Illustration includes everything which is employed to make an argument intelligible, attractive, or convincing; but in more recent times it has been restricted to such rhetorical figures as the metaphor, simile, allegory and parable. In this narrower sense I use it now, and in treating of it we must bear in mind, that illustrations ought not to form the staple of a sermon. There must be something to be illustrated. The beauty of a simile lies in its pertinence to the point you design to brighten by its light; but when illustrations are employed purely for the sake of the stories in which they consist, are a snare to the poverty of thought, they are a snare to the preacher and an offence to the hearer. We may paint a picture, but we must never do that simply for the sake of the picture. We must not construct ornament, but seek only to ornament construction. But, presuming that you have in your discourse a body of substantial thought or a closely-linked argumentative chain, what is the use of illustration? Various answers, all equally true and equally important, may be given. It helps to make the matter in hand more plain. It uses that which is known and acknowledged to be true in such a way as to lead the mind of the hearer to the acceptance of something else, of which hitherto he has been in doubt.

It employs the imagination for the assistance of the judgment, and brings the material to the aid of the spiritual, using the one as a diagram for the demonstration of the other. But there is more than an illuminating power in a good illustration. There is a force of proof as well. Wherever similes rest on the unity between God's world and man's nature, they are arguments, as well as illustrations. The "like" is intimately connected with the "likely." The similitude is a ground of probability; and, as the physical philosopher by analogy has been led to some of his finest discoveries, so the preacher by the use of illustration may lead his hearers to the discovery of new truths. There is a principle of unity running through revelation, nature and Providence, such that what is found in one has its "double" in the others. This is the principle that gives the Saviour's parables their power. They are not merely felicitous yet arbitrary illustrations. They are outward symbols of inward realities. And, though we may not claim the same force of argument for every analogy which we discover; yet in so far as the analogy is true, the illustration we use has a force of proof; and even when it may fall short of establishing a probability, it is invaluable, as Butler has shown in his immortal work, in answering objections. But the employment of telling illustrations is of great service in awakening the interest of an audience. The "like" leads to the "likely" and is that for which men have a "liking." Every one delights in a vivid and effective illustration. And just as the child reads the book to find out what the picture means, so a hearer will listen to learn what you are going to make of your analogy. While you are dealing with the story he is all attention, and it will be your own fault if, before his interest flags, you have not insinuated your lesson or pointed your application. Moreover, impressions thus produced are never forgotten. You may find difficulty in recalling an intricate argument; but that which has been fastened to an illustration fixes itself in your memory. Guthrie has put the whole thing into a nutshell when he says—his own words illustrating the very principle laid down: "By awakening and gratifying the imagination, the truth finds its way more readily to the heart and makes a deeper impression on the memory. The story, like a float, keeps it from sinking; like a nail, fastens it in the mind; like the feathers of an arrow, makes it strike; and, like the barb, makes it stick." *Dr. W. M. Taylor.*

9758. ILLUSTRATION, Blunder in. Coleridge tells the following story of Lord Kenyon. In one of his speeches his lordship said: "Above all, need I name to you the Emperor Julian, who was so celebrated for the practice of every Christian virtue that he was called Julian the Apostle!"

9759. ILLUSTRATION, Cautions Regarding. But a few cautions must be observed in the use of illustrations. For one thing, we must not attempt to illustrate that which is already perfectly plain. You cannot handle crystal without leaving on it the marks of your touch, and they will mar its transparency. Again, do not use too many illustrations for the same purpose. The effect of such a course will be to bewilder and dazzle, rather than to enlighten. One lamp is worth a million fire-flies. When, therefore, you have obtained a good illustration, leave it to do its work and go on. Still further, do not use as illustrations things which are in themselves recondite and obscure, needing to be explained. Take the familiar to brighten that which is strange; but, just because you are dealing in the familiar, take care that you have got it accurately; for if your hearers see that you cannot be depended on in describing things in their department, they will place no reliance on you when you are talking of matters in your own. Finally, be careful always that the full force of the illustration goes to illuminate the truth which you are expounding. The foot-lights are studiously veiled from the eyes of the spectators; but they throw a lustre on the actor's face. Like them, our illustrations must not draw attention to ourselves, but to the truth we have in hand. We must not turn them on ourselves, but on the Master and his work. It is as criminal to hide him beneath gorgeous illustrations as it is to ignore him altogether. We may and ought to cover our faces before him; but we must never put a veil, no matter how exquisite may be its texture, over his countenance. *Dr. W. M. Taylor.*

9760. ILLUSTRATION, Cultivating the Faculty of. But how are we to get illustrations? In answer, let me say, first, that no one should be discouraged here; for, judging from my own experience, there is no faculty more susceptible of development by culture than that of discovering analogies. We may paraphrase here the inscription on Wren's monument, and say, "*Si illustrationes quaeris circumspice.*" You will find them everywhere—in the talk of the children and the shouts of the schoolboys; on the street and in the store; on the ship and in the railroad car; in the field of Nature and on the page of literature. Only compel yourself for a time to look at everything with the question uppermost, "What use can I make of that in commending the truth of Christ to my fellow-men?" And by and by you will have so formed the habit that, unconsciously and without any effort on your part, the finest analogies will strike you. *Dr. W. M. Taylor.*

9761. ILLUSTRATION, Effect of. The effect of illustration is that which Wharton has remarked respecting the moral passages in Dyer's poetry—that "the unexpected insertion of such reflections imparts to us the same pleasure which we feel, when, in wandering through a wilderness or grove, we suddenly behold in the turning of the walk a statue of some virtue or muse."

9762. ILLUSTRATION, Example of. The philospher Knox refers to Hannah More's recommendation of this manner of instruction as follows: "I am ready to think he (John Wesley) came nearer your own most excellent idea than any other person whose writings I have seen. When you 'advise, instruct to be communicated, in a way that shall interest the feelings by lively images;' and when you observe that 'there seems to be no good reason why religion must be dry and uninteresting, while every other thing is to be made amusing;' and ask, 'why should not the most entertaining powers of the human mind be supremely consecrated to that subject which is most worthy of their full exercise?' I read that of which I must say, John Wesley gives me the most entire exemplification I have ever met with, except in the Bible." *Salter.*

9763. ILLUSTRATION, Facility of. Whitefield understood the power of illustration. He ever kept the volume of nature open before him, delighting to unfold its magnificent pages. The ocean, the thunder-storm, the bow encircling the heavens, furnished him with themes to illustrate his subject; or a trial, or a pilot-fish, or a furnace—in fact, anything and everything, whether magnificently grand or ever so insignificant, he made subservient to his oratorical powers. His eloquence reminded one of the ocean, adding, as it does, to its own boundlessness, contributions from every part of the universe. Well has it been said that Whitefield "ransacked creation for figures, time for facts, heaven for motives, hell for warnings, and eternity for arguments."
Philips.

9764. ILLUSTRATION, Notable Examples of. George Herbert says, "It is an ill mason that refuseth any stone; and there is no knowledge but, in a skillful hand, serves either positively as it is, or else to illustrate some other knowledge." In all ages they have been the greatest powers, both in the pulpit, in the class-room, and on the platform, who have kept this truth in mind. The fathers of the early church, who lived in days nearest to those of the Son of man—the Puritans, whose names are inspiration still—enrich their discourses with simile, metaphor and anecdote. These made all nature, all history, all the lives of men their treasury, out of which to bring the "new" things which were to embellish and enforce the "old." *Dr. W. M. Punshon.*

9765. ILLUSTRATION, Power of. If a man would use illustration as a power for good, he must cultivate a refinement of thought in his own mind. He must have a clear perception of the truth itself, and of the fitness and fulness of the analogy by which he means to illuminate it; and then he must learn to present it gracefully, that it may attract without startling, and be a "power of surprise" without awakening either repulsion or alarm. Above all, he must remember that the illustration is but the hand-maid in the palace, while truth is the queen upon the throne. And he will take care that truth be not hampered by too many handmaids, nor, like the Roman matron, hindered in her progress by the weight of her own jewels.
Dr. W. M. Punshon.

9766. ILLUSTRATIONS, Arrows. Talking of preaching, Dr. Guthrie said to me, "When I was in my first parish, I used to have a class of young pupils whom I questioned about my sermons. Thus I learned what parts were best remembered, and I found that they always remembered best the parts that had illustrations So I resolved never to shoot off an arrow without winging it." *Newman Hall*

9767. ILLUSTRATIONS, Books of. To a letter, inquiring as to the propriety of the use of Cyclopædias of Illustration, Dr. Curry replied in the *Christian Advocate:* "To us it seems that the worst thing a minister can do (leaving immoralities aside) is to preach poor sermons; and yet there is reason to suspect that there is a great amount of poor preaching. Whatever means, therefore, are not immoral, may be resorted to, to remedy this evil, and should be freely used, so as to make the sermons really good. One minister out of four may have the genius requisite to originate sermons in due supply for a regular course of church services. The other three-fourths must either draw on other men's productions, or else starve their hearers on weak and ill-prepared diet. There are enough ways in which any minister of fair intelligence and a modicum of common sense may avail himself of the helps offered him in the wide range of pulpit literature, so as to give both richness and variety to his ministrations; and he must be very unskillful who could not do this without making false pretenses to originality. It is sometimes thought that such a method would favor idleness in the preacher, but we think quite the contrary. Whoever shall attempt to wisely select and skillfully arrange the best thoughts of the great Christian thinkers, so as to present a proper unity in each discourse or arranged selection, will find that he has given himself no inconsiderable task. It certainly is not designed to find a way for preaching made easy; but, if possible, to replace the vapid common-places of very many of our prevailing spoken sermons by something better, because richer in thought and more forcible in illustration and application."

9768. ILLUSTRATIONS, Enticement of. Plato in his Symposium, where he disputed of the chief end of the chief good, and is altogether on subjects theological, doth not lay down strong and close demonstrations; he doth not prepare himself for the contest like a wrestler, that he may take the fastest hold of his adversary and be more sure of giving him the trip; but he draws men on by more soft and pliable attacks, by pleasant fictions and pat examples.
Plutarch.

9769. ILLUSTRATIONS, Memory of. George Herbert, in his "Country Parson," says: "Sometimes he tells them stories and sayings of others, according as his text invites him: for them also men heed, and remember better than exhortations which, though earnest, die with the sermon. But stories and sayings they will remember."

9770. ILLUSTRATIONS, Natural. The whole visible world is a large Bible full of parables, allegories, and doctrines. They were written before there were men to read them, that after man's creation he might immediately begin to learn and spell; as you have seen a schoolmaster write on the black-board before the children assemble, so as not to lose time, but to be able to begin his instructions at once.

Alban Stolz.

9771. ILLUSTRATIONS, Oriental. Molly says of his journey in the East:—Every day brought some new scene, which explained some passage of the Bible we had hardly understood, or gave force to some other one, which we had scarcely appreciated. One day we met a Bedouin, rich in herds, who was pursuing a single sheep, or camel, across the sandy wastes, tracking the animal by its footsteps; the next we might come on the ninety-and-nine left without their shepherd. We have felt the disappointment of arriving at a well and finding the waters bitter. And the cup of cold water cannot be fully appreciated except in a country like this, where the water, rare to get at any time, can hardly ever be obtained, even tepid, and generally has a taste of the skin it is kept in, which would disgust any but the most thirsty. Our Lord's command is still obeyed by these people, indeed, throughout the East, and you may always drink any quantity of water, whoever it may belong to. I was surprised once at seeing a Bedouin walk up to my camel and drink a whole bottle of water, my supply for the day; and I have often, when out shooting, gone into a hut or tent, and asked for water, which the poor people have had to carry a great distance. Not only have I never been refused, but my offer of a piastre or two was never accepted; they gave it to me, as a Nubian woman once beautifully expressed it, "for God's sake." One of our guides told us how he was ruined last year; for, entrusting his flocks to a "hireling," they were all eaten by a wolf (hyena), and scattered over the desert, while he was leading some merchants over the sandy plains. When, after a march of ten days over stony hills and arid plains of deep sand, we came suddenly upon the broad river, winding through the rich green of the durra-covered banks, we could exclaim with the Psalmist, "He maketh me to lie down in green pastures; he leadeth me beside still waters;" and, as a Bedouin in advance of us called his servant, who was walking before him with his sandals, that he might put them on before he reached the village, we remembered that John the Baptist did not deem himself worthy to unloose the latchet of our Saviour's shoes.

9772. ILLUSTRATIONS, Result of. There was a wild, dissolute, brilliant English youth, who distributed the drink at a public house. In the same town was a dissenting chapel whither a story-telling cobbler drew the people by the power of his illustrations. The youth said to his companions, "Come, let us go down and hear old Cole tell his stories." They went, and the result was the youth's conversion, followed by a ministry of remarkable power and eloquence in the life of George Whitefield.

9773. IMAGINATION, Chambers of the. The mind of man is a chamber of imagery. We have the power to conceive picturesque thoughts to conjure up scenes and circumstances from either experience or imagination, and thus to constitute the mind as a picture gallery, more or less furnished in proportion as we cultivate the study and taste for these things. It is thus that the "Pilgrim's Progress" has commanded a reputation beyond that of any other uninspired work. It is itself a gallery of pictures—states of mind described, abstract principles personified, and the whole inward experience of the soul expressed in the form of outward and familiar illustration. *R. Maguire.*

9774. IMAGINATION, Charm of. It is this talent of affecting the imagination that gives an embellishment to good sense, and makes one man's compositions more agreeable than another's. It sets off all writings in general, but is the very life and highest perfection of poetry, where it shines in an eminent degree. It has preserved several poems for many ages, that have nothing else to recommend them; and where all the other beauties are present, the work appears dry and insipid if this single one be wanting. It has something in it like creation. It bestows a kind of existence, and draws up to the reader's view several objects which are not to be found in being. It makes additions to nature, and gives a greater variety to God's works. In a word, it is able to beautify and adorn the most illustrious scenes in the universe, or to fill the mind with more glorious shows and apparitions than can be found in any part of it. *Addison.*

9775. IMAGINATION, Imposition of. A nobleman in Portugal became possessed with the idea that God would never pardon his sins. His agony was great, and he wasted away as if by disease. Every means was made use of that would divert his mind, but all to no purpose. At last it was decided to break the spell by artifice. Going into a room above him, about midnight, an opening was made in the ceiling, and an artificial angel, having a drawn sword in his right hand, and a lighted torch in his left, appeared to him. He rose up in his bed and adored the angel, and while he worshiped, the angel told him "all his sins had been forgiven." The torch was then extinguished, and the angel passed away. The man was overjoyed at the vision, and roused his family to tell them what had transpired. After that his health became good, and he was never troubled with the thought of unpardoned sin.

9776. IMAGINATION, Pleasures of the. A man of a polite imagination is let into a great many pleasures that the vulgar are not capable of receiving. He can converse with a picture, and find an agreeable companion in a statue. He meets with a secret refreshment in a description, and often feels a greater satisfaction in the prospect of fields and meadows than another does in the possession. It gives him, indeed, a kind of property in everything he sees, and makes the most rude, uncultivated parts of nature administer to his pleasures: so that he looks upon the world as it were in another light, and discovers in it a multitude of charms that conceal themselves from the generality of mankind.   *Addison.*

9777. IMAGINATION, Riches of. Thrasilaus, the son of Pythodorus, imagined that all the ships that came into the harbor belonged to him. He would number them and dismiss them, but took no account of those that were shipwrecked. Thus he was rich, while harmlessly but pleasantly passing his time. In after times, when cured of this malady, he affirmed that he never lived so happily as when indulging in his madness.

9778. IMITATION, Faulty. When a boy is learning to write, his master either gives him a copy-slip or else writes the first line in the page for him. Now, I have often seen a boy write the next line with some care, looking at the letters he had to copy. But when he came to the third line, instead of looking at his copy, he looked only at his own writing just above. And what came of that? Why, he copied all his faults, and made more too, so that every line down the page was worse than the one before it. He never tried to make each line more like his copy.   *Dr. J. M. Freeman.*

9779. IMITATION, Law of. Now, it is the nature of love, at least in reference to a superior, that it always inclines and disposes to imitation of him. A child's love to his father disposes him to imitate his father, and especially does the love of God's children dispose them to imitate their Heavenly Father.
    Dr. J. Edwards.

9780. IMITATION, Passion of. The second passion belonging to society is imitation, or, if you will, a desire of imitating, and consequently a pleasure in it. This passion arises from much the same cause with sympathy. For as sympathy makes us take a concern in whatever men feel, so this affection prompts us to copy whatever they do; and consequently we have a pleasure in imitating, and in whatever belongs to imitation merely as it is such, without any intervention of the reasoning faculty; but solely from our natural constitution, which Providence has framed in such a manner as to find either pleasure or delight, according to the nature of the object, in whatever regards the purposes of our being. It is by imitation far more than by precept that we learn everything; and what we learn thus, we acquire not only more effectually, but more pleasantly. This forms our manners, our opinions, our lives. It is one of the strongest links of society; it is a species of mutual compliance which all men yield to each other, without constraint to themselves, and which is extremely flattering to all. Herein it is that painting and many other agreeable arts have the principal foundations of their power.   *Burke.*

9781. IMMENSITY, Image of. I never passed the desert without experiencing very painful emotions. It was the image of immensity to my thoughts. It showed no limits. It had neither beginning nor end. It was an ocean for the foot of man!   *Napoleon I.*

9782. IMMORTALITY, Consideration of. The cast of mind which is natural to a discreet man makes him look forward into futurity, and consider what will be his condition millions of ages hence, as well as what it is at present. He knows that the misery or happiness which are reserved for him in another world lose nothing of their reality by being at so great distance from him. The objects do not appear little to him because they are remote. He considers that those pleasures and pains which lie hid in eternity approach nearer to him every moment, and will be present with him in their full weight and measure, as much as those pains and pleasures which he feels at this very instant. For this reason he is careful to secure to himself that which is the proper happiness of his nature and the ultimate design of his being. He carries his thoughts to the end of every action, and considers the most distant as well as the most immediate effects of it. He supersedes every little prospect of gain and advantage which offers itself here, if he does not find it consistent with his views of an hereafter. In a word, his hopes are full of immortality, his schemes are large and glorious, and his conduct suitable to one who knows his true interest, and how to pursue it by proper methods.   *Addison.*

9783. IMMORTALITY, Emblems of. An English nobleman was once exploring among the catacombs of Egypt. He came to one mummy case, which bore a date two thousand years before. On unwrapping the many folds of linen from the shriveled form, he found in the blackened hand a dahlia bulb. For all these ages the hand of death had held it. Could there be life in it still? The gentleman took it home, and placed it in a pot of warm moist soil. He tended it carefully for a few weeks; and what was his surprise and delight, to see the soil part, and the tender shoots of a strong, vigorous dahlia spring up. In due time it bore a beautiful blossom, which was looked upon with an interest deeper and stronger than ever greeted such a flower before. It seemed almost beyond belief that life could exist so long, shut out from all that nourishes life. Yet this is but a faint type of the immortality of that soul which once moved the lifeless hand which so long had grasped it.   *F. F. Trench.*

9784. IMMORTALITY, Faith in. Plato represents his admirable Socrates, after an unjust condemnation to death in the prison at Athens, encompassed with a noble circle of philosphers, discoursing of the soul's immortality; and that having finished his arguments for it, he drank the cup of poison with an undisturbed courage, as one that did not lose, but exchange this short and wretched life for a blessed and eternal. For thus he argued, that there are two ways of departing souls, leading to two contrary states, of felicity and of misery. Those who had defiled themselves with sensual vices, and given full scope to boundless lust in their private conversation, or who by frauds and violence had been injurious to the commonwealth, are dragged to a place of torment, and forever excluded from the joyful presence of the blessed society above. But those who had preserved themselves upright and chaste, at the greatest distance possible from the contagion of the flesh, and had during their union with human bodies imitated the divine life, by an easy and open way returned to God from whom they came. And this was not the sense only of the more virtuous heathens, but even some of those who had done the greatest force to human nature, yet could not so slacken their minds and corrupt their wills, but there remained in them stinging apprehensions of punishment hereafter. 　　　　　　　　　　　　*Buck.*

9785. IMMORTALITY, Forfeiture of. Before a court in the province of Pesth, Hungary, a suit was pending in which an aged Jew was to make a statement under oath. He was about to take the oath, when another Jew arose and protested against it. "This man dare not take an oath." "Why not?" asked the judge. "There exists a Hebrew prayer which contains the sentence that 'every Jew has a share in the life to come.' About twenty years ago, I was present when the man who is now about to take an oath sold his 'share in the life to come,' guaranteed to him in the prayer, to another Jew, a Mr. Y., who paid him a certain amount of money for it. As he, therefore, can not count any longer on a future existence, he has nothing to fear or hope for in the life to come; it must be certainly indifferent to him whether he swear to a truth or a falsehood." After examination the statement was found to be true, and the court granted the protest of the old man, and the party who sold his "share in the life to come" was declared incapable of taking an oath.

9786. IMMORTALITY, Heathen. If the soul be immortal, it requires to be cultivated with attention, not only for what we call the time of life, but for that which is to follow—I mean eternity; and the least neglect in this point may be attended with endless consequences. If death were the final dissolution of being, the wicked would be great gainers by it, by being delivered at once from their bodies, their souls, and their vices; but, as the soul is immortal, it has no other means of being freed from its evils, nor any safety for it, but in becoming very good and very wise; for it carries nothing with it but its bad or good deeds, its virtues and vices, which are commonly the consequences of the education it has received, and the causes of eternal happiness or misery. 　　　　　　　　　　　　*Socrates.*

9787. IMMORTALITY, Heathen Ideas of. Can we think that God so little considers his own actions, or is such a waster of his time in trifles, that, if we had nothing of divine within us, nothing that in the least resembled his perfections, nothing permanent and stable, but were only poor creatures that (according to Homer's expression) faded and dropped like withered leaves, and in a short time too, yet he should make so great account of us—like women that bestow their pains in making little gardens, no less delightful to them than the gardens of Adonis, in earthen pans and pots—as to create us souls to blossom and flourish only for a day in a soft and tender body of flesh, without any firm and solid root of life, and then to be blasted and extinguished in a moment upon every slight occasion? It is impious to declare that the human soul can die. There is one and the same reason to confirm the providence of God and the immortality of the soul; neither is it possible to admit the one if you deny the other. Now, then, the soul surviving after the decease of the body, the inference is the stronger that it partakes of punishment and reward. For during the mortal life the soul is in continual combat, like a wrestler; but after all those conflicts are at an end, she then receives according to her merits. What the punishments and what the rewards of past transgressions or just and laudable actions are to be while the soul is thus alone by itself, is nothing at all to us that are alive; for either they are altogether concealed from our knowledge, or else we give little credit to them. 　　　　　　　　*Plutarch.*

9788. IMMORTALITY, Importance of. The annunciation of life and immortality by the gospel, did it contain no other truth, were sufficient to cast all the discoveries of science into shade, and to reduce the highest improvements of reason to the comparative nothingness which the flight of a moment bears to eternity. By this discovery the prospects of human nature are infinitely widened, the creature of yesterday becomes the child of eternity; and as felicity is not the less valuable in the eye of reason because it is remote, nor the misery which is certain less to be deprecated because it is not immediately felt, the care of our future interests becomes our chief, and, properly speaking, our only concern. All besides will shortly become nothing; and, therefore, whenever it comes into competition with these, it is as the small dust of the balance. *Robert Hall.*

9789. IMMORTALITY, Legend of. A strong friendship existed between Michael Mercatus, the elder, and Marsilius Ficinus. They possessed an equal veneration for the doctrines of Plato, and discoursed together on the state of man after death. When their disputation and discourse had grown somewhat lengthy they mutually agreed: "That whichsoever of them two should first depart out of this life, he should inform the survivor of the state of the other life, and whether the soul be immortal or not." Some time after this agreement was made, Michael Mercatus was early at his study, when he heard the noise of a horse upon a gallop, and then stopping at his door. He heard Marsilius, his friend, crying to him: "O Michael, Michael! those things are true, they are true!" Michael wondering to hear his friend's voice, rose up, and opening the casement saw Marsilius riding away on a white horse. He called after him, and followed him with his eye, but he soon vanished out of sight. Amazed at this, he solicitously inquired if anything had happened to Marsilius, who then lived at Florence. Upon inquiry he found that he had died at the very time he had heard and seen him.

9790. IMMORTALITY, Opinions of. Plato and Pythagoras say that the soul is immortal; when it departs out of the body, it retreats to the Soul of the World, which is a being of the same nature with it. The Stoics—when the souls leave the bodies, they are carried to divers places; the souls of the unlearned and ignorant descend to the coagmentation of earthly things, but the learned and vigorous endure till the general fire. Epicurus and Democritus—the soul is mortal and perisheth with the body. Plato and Pythagoras—that part of the soul of man which is rational is eternal; for though it be not God, yet it is the product of an eternal Deity; but that part of the soul which is divested of reason dies.

Plutarch.

9791. IMMORTALITY, Pagan Faith in. When I consider the wonderful activity of the mind, so great a memory of what is past, and such a capacity of penetrating into the future; when I behold such a number of arts and sciences, and such a multitude of discoveries thence arising: I believe and am firmly persuaded that a nature which contains so many things within itself cannot be mortal . . . . But if I err in believing that the souls of men are immortal, I willingly err; nor while I live would I wish to have this delightful error extorted from me; and if after death I shall feel nothing, as some minute philosophers think, I am not afraid lest dead philosophers should laugh at me for the error. *Cicero.*

9792. IMMORTALITY, Question of. Upon this short question, "Is man immortal, or is he not?" depends all that is valuable in science, in morals, and in theology,—and all that is most interesting to man as a social being and as a rational and accountable intelligence. If he is destined to an eternal existence, an immense importance must attach to all his present affections, actions and pursuits; and it must be a matter of infinite moment that they be directed in such a channel as will tend to carry him forward in safety to the felicities of a future world. But if his whole existence be circumscribed within the circle of a few fleeting years, man appears an enigma, an inexplicable phenomenon in the universe, human life a mystery, the world a scene of confusion, virtue a mere phantom, the Creator a capricious being, and his plans and arrangements an inextricable maze. *Dr. Dick.*

9793. IMMORTALITY, Seekers after. As all people feel that they must die, each seeks immortality on earth, that he may be had in everlasting remembrance. Some great princes and kings seek it by raising great columns of stone, and high pyramids, great churches, costly and glorious palaces, castles, etc. Soldiers hunt after praise and honor, by obtaining famous victories. The learned seek an undying name by writing books. With these, and such like things, people think to be immortal. *Luther.*

9794. IMMUTABILITY, Divine. If God be immutable, it is sad news to those that are re-

solved in wickedness, or careless of returning to that duty he requires. Sinners must not expect that God will alter his will, make a breach upon his nature, and violate his own word, to gratify their lusts. No, it is not reasonable God should dishonor himself to secure them, and cease to be God, that they may continue to be wicked, by changing his own nature, that they may be unchanged in their vanity. God is the same; goodness is as amiable in his sight, and sin as abominable in his eyes, now, as it was at the beginning of the world. Being the same God, he is the same enemy to the wicked, as the same friend to the righteous. He is the same in knowledge, and cannot forget sinful acts. He is the same in will, and cannot approve of unrighteous practices. Goodness cannot but be alway the object of his love, and wickedness cannot but be alway the object of his hatred; and as his aversion to sin is alway the same, so as he hath been in his judgments upon sinners, the same he will be still; for the same perfection of immutability belongs to his justice for the punishment of sin, as to his holiness for his disaffection to sin. *Charnock.*

9795. IMPATIENCE, Aggravation of. "If God afflict thee, let not impatience add to the affliction." Impatience makes the wound more painful. Hannah More on her dying bed was asked, "Is there anything we can do for you?" She answered, "Nothing; but leave me and forgive me if I am impatient."

9796. IMPATIENCE, Biblical Examples of. *Esau,* Gen. 25: 29-31. "Behold I am at the point to die." Esau was then only about thirty-two, and in perfect health! "And what profit shall this birthright do to me?" Too impatient to wait, the craving a moment's gratification, made him blind to the value of the birthright he recklessly threw away! *Sarah,* Gen. 16, grown weary of waiting God's time, tried to hasten, by means of her own devising, the fulfillment of God's promise. *Rachel.*—"Give me children, or else I die," Gen. 30: 1. Oh, how hard it would go with us, if God gave us all our desires! Rachel had children given her, and died in child-bearing, Gen. 35: 16-20. "Enjoyments snatched out of God's hands, like fruit plucked before it is ripe, soon rot, and only injure. Like David's child, born in adultery, they die in the birth."—(*Gurnall.*)

Bowes.

9797. IMPATIENCE, Nature of. Impatience is a quality sudden, eager, and insatiable, which grasps at all, and admits of no delay: scorning to wait God's leisure, and attend humbly and dutifully upon the issues of his wise and just Providence. *South.*

9798. IMPATIENCE, Penalty of. A mother who was preparing some flour to bake into bread, left it for a few moments, when little Mary, with childish curiosity took hold of the dish, which fell to the floor, spilling the contents. The mother struck the child a severe blow, saying, with anger, that she was always in the way. Two weeks after the child sickened and died. On her death-bed, while delirious, she asked her mother if there would be room for her among the angels. "I was always in your way, mother—you had no room for little Mary! And will I be in the angels' way?" The broken-hearted mother saw her fault, and would have done anything to save her child or wipe the dark spot from her own or the child's memory. God often takes us at our word.

9799. IMPERFECTION, Human. In playing over a tune upon an instrument, a single string may jar and slip, and yet the main be musical. It would be folly, indeed, to think our fields had no corn in them, because there is chaff about the wheat; or that the ore had no gold in it, because there is dross among it. In heaven there is service alone without any sin; in hell there is sin alone without any service: but on earth there is sin and service in the same man, as there is light and shade in the same picture. *Secker.*

9800. IMPERFECTION, Marks of. A large and beautiful block of marble was brought from Paros, out of which it was designed to chisel a statue of the great Napoleon. The famous sculptor, Canova, surveyed it with critical eyes, before commencing work upon it, and discovered a slight red mark traversing the block. To the unskilled it was an insignificant matter, but Canova said, "I cannot work upon this; it has a flaw. It is not perfectly pure and white. I will not lay my chisel upon it." So he rejected it. What imperfections does the omniscient eye detect in the purest human characters? Yet he does not reject them on this account.

9801. IMPERFECTIONS, Universal. I have known several persons of great fame for wisdom in public affairs and councils, governed by foolish servants. I have known great ministers, distinguished for wit and learning, who preferred none but dunces. I have known men of valor cowards to their wives. I have known men of cunning perpetually cheated. I knew three ministers, who would exactly compute and settle the accounts of a kingdom, wholly ignorant of their own economy. *Walpole.*

9802. IMPIETY, Bold. Mahomet Effendi was a man well skilled in Oriental learning, but a vile blasphemer. One of his principal arguments against the being of God was, "That if there was a God, and he so wise and omnipotent as his priests declared him to be, he would never suffer him to live that was the greatest enemy and reproacher of the Deity in the world, but would strike him dead with lightning, or by some other dreadful punishment, and thus make him an example to others." He was at last condemned to die for his open blasphemy. He chose rather to die a martyr for his wicked principles than to obtain life by reformation, and so was executed.

9803. IMPIETY, Mohammedan. Mahomet Second made a furious assault upon the city of Scodra, but was repulsed by its inhabitants. In his rage, he wished he had never heard the name of Scodra, and most horribly blasphemed God, impiously, saying, "That it was enough for God to take care of heavenly things, and not to cross him in his worldly actions."

9804. IMPIETY, Papal. Pope Leo Tenth, looking at the pile of money he had accumulated through the sale of indulgences, said to Cardinal Bembo, "See what a deal of wealth we have gotten by this fable of Christ!" When he lay upon his death-bed, the cardinal repeated a passage of scripture to comfort him. He sneeringly replied, "Away with these baubles concerning Christ!"

9805. IMPIETY, Punishment of. The punishment for sacrilege among the Grecians was death. Philomelus, Onomarchus, and Phaillus, had despoiled the temple of Delphos, and their punishment was divinely allotted them. One was thrown from a steep place and killed; one was burnt alive, and the other was drowned.

9806. IMPOSSIBILITY, Conditions of. An orphan boy was left to the tender and loving authority of five old-maid aunts (the five wise virgins, as they thought). One said he might go anywhere, except out of doors—he must not be allowed to become a street-rat; another said he might go anywhere, except in the house; the third said he must not stand up; the fourth forbade his sitting down; and the fifth forbade his lying down. So the poor boy was reduced to a state of absolute impossibility. *Dr. Fowler.*

9807. IMPOSSIBILITY, Example of. The Egyptian hieroglyphics represent an impossibility by depicting a man walking on the sea.

9808. IMPRACTICABLE, Fable of the. Once upon a time the mice being sadly distressed by the persecution of the cat, resolved to call a meeting to decide upon the best means of getting rid of this continual annoyance. Many plans were discussed and rejected; at last a young mouse got up, and proposed that a bell should be hung round the cat's neck, that they might for the future always have notice of her coming, and so be enabled to escape. This proposition was hailed with the greatest applause, and was agreed to at once unanimously. Upon which an old mouse, who had sat silent all the while, got up and said that he considered the contrivance most ingenious, and that it would, no doubt, be quite successful; but he had only one short question to put, namely, which of them it was who would bell the cat? *Æsop.*

9809. IMPRECATIONS Answered. Some English soldiers in the time of Edward the Sixth, were shipwrecked on the French coast in a storm. In great distress they prayed they might be saved. One soldier instead of praying, cried out, "Gallows, claim thy due." When he did arrive home he met the fate for which he prayed. Another man was wont on every ordinary occasion to say, "If it be not so, I pray God I may rot before I die." His prayer was answered. A mother, who was very angry with her son, cried, "Go thy ways, God grant thou mayest never return alive again to me." The same day the young man was drowned.

9810. IMPRECATIONS Fulfilled. Narcissus, Bishop of Jerusalem, a man of faultless life, and faithful in reproving vice of every kind, was falsely accused. His first accuser said in closing his testimony, "If these things are not so, may I perish by fire." Another said, "If

I speak anything of falsehood, I pray God I may be consumed by some cruel disease." The third said, "If I accuse him falsely, I pray God that I may become blind." The accusations against the Bishop were not believed by such as knew the great integrity of the man, but from grief he left his bishopric and retired into private life. But his accusers escaped not the all-seeing justice of heaven. For the house of one of them took fire, and he and his family perished in the flames. The second languished away under a loathsome disease; and the other, seeing the terrible end of his companions, confessed their villainy, and wept over his crime so long that he utterly lost his sight.

9811. IMPRESSIONS, Distant. Any satisfaction we have recently enjoyed, and of which the memory is fresh and perfect, operates on the will with more violence than another of which the traces are decayed and obliterated. Contiguity in time and place has an amazing effect upon the passions. An enormous globe of fire, which fell at Pekin, would not excite half the interest which the most trifling phenomenon could give birth to nearer home. I am persuaded many men might be picked out of the streets, who, for a thousand guineas laid down, would consent to submit to a very cruel death in fifteen years from the time of receiving the money. *S. Smith.*

9812. IMPRESSIONS, False. Thomas Jackson, in his Life of the Rev. Richard Watson, relates, "that when traveling together, in passing by a churchyard, which is close by the Bath and Bristol road, Mr. Watson pointed to a gravestone, in a conspicuous situation, and said, 'The first time I traveled this way, that gravestone caught my eye; and especially the words, *who died, aged forty-two.* A very deep impression, for which I could not account, was immediately made upon my mind, that I should die precisely at the same age. The impression was both strong and sudden. I have already passed beyond that period; and this shows how little stress can be justly laid upon those sudden impulses and impressions of which some people make so much account.' This impression, it appears, had created considerable uneasiness in the family of Mr. Watson; but its precise effect upon his own mind it is not easy to determine."

9813. IMPRESSIONS Followed. John Bunyan was allowed by his jailer to often leave prison. An officer was sent by his persecutors to inquire into the matter. It so happened that Bunyan was out that night with his family; but he was so restless he could not sleep, and determined to return to the prison. The jailer blamed him for coming in at so unseasonable an hour. The next morning early the officer arrived, and asked, "Are all the prisoners safe?" "Yes." "Is John Bunyan safe?" "Yes." "Let me see him." He answered to the call, and all was well. The messenger left, and the jailer told Bunyan to go in and out when he pleased; "you know better when to return than I can tell you."

9814. IMPRESSIONS, Obeying. As Admiral Williams sailed near the Island of Ascension, a desolate and uninhabited place, he felt a strong impulse to call there. This course seemed absurd, but the impression grew upon him as he saw the dim outline of the island, and was sailing every moment so that it would be more difficult to call. He gave the order to "put about ship" and steer for Ascension, to which the second officer objected. The Admiral persisted. As they neared it, they caught sight of a signal of distress, and soon rescued sixteen shipwrecked men who were just at the point of starvation.

9815. IMPRISONMENT, Expenses of. If we estimate at a shilling a day what is lost by the inaction, and consumed in the support, of each man chained down to involuntary idleness by imprisonment, the public loss will rise in one year to three hundred thousand pounds; in ten years, to more than a sixth part of our circulating coin. *Johnson.*

9816. IMPRISONMENT, Glorying in. Guy de Brez, a French preacher, was imprisoned in the castle of Tournay. A lady who visited him said she wondered how he could eat, or drink, or sleep in quiet. "Madam," said he, "my chains do not terrify me, or break my sleep; on the contrary, I glory and take delight therein, esteeming them at an higher rate than chains and rings of gold, or jewels of any price whatever. The rattling of my chains is like the effect of an instrument of music in my ears: not that such an effect comes merely from my chains, but it is because I am bound therewith for maintaining the truth of the gospel."

9817. IMPROVEMENT, Discouraged in. Some men get early disgusted with the task of improvement, and the cultivation of the mind, from some excesses which they have committed, and mistakes into which they have been betrayed, at the beginning of life. They abuse the whole art of navigation because they have stuck upon a shoal; whereas, the business is—to refit, careen, and set out a second time The navigation is very difficult: few of us get through it at first without some rubs and losses, which the world is always ready to forgive, where they are honestly confessed, and diligently repaired. *S. Smith.*

9818. IMPROVEMENT, Moral. Infinite toil would not enable you to sweep away a mist; but by ascending a little, you may often look over it altogether. So it is with our moral improvement: we wrestle fiercely with a vicious habit, which could have no hold upon us if we ascended into a higher moral atmosphere. *Helps.*

9819. IMPROVEMENTS, Objectors to. Baron Humboldt, a traveler in South America, tells us that, upon a road being made over a part of the great chain of mountains called the Andes, the government was petitioned against the road by a body of men, who for centuries had gained a living by carrying travelers in baskets strapped upon their backs over the fearful rocks, which only three guides could cross. Which was the best course;—to make the road, and create the thousand employments

belonging to freedom of intercourse for these very carriers of travelers, and for all other men; or to leave the mountains without a road, that the poor guides might gain a premium for risking their lives in an unnecessary peril?
Charles Knight.

9820. IMPROVIDENCE, Characteristics of. It has always been more difficult for a man to keep than to get; for, in the one case, fortune aids, which often assists injustice; but in the other case, sense is required. Therefore, we often see a person deficient in cleverness rise to wealth; and then, from want of sense, roll head-over-heels to the bottom. *Basil.*

9821. IMPROVIDENCE, Fable of. On a cold frosty day an ant was dragging out some of the corn which he had laid up in summer time, to dry it. A grasshopper, half-perished with hunger, besought the ant to give him a morsel of it to preserve his life. "What were you doing," said the ant, "this last summer?" "Oh," said the grasshopper, "I was not idle. I kept singing all the summer long." Said the ant, laughing and shutting up his granary, "Since you could sing all summer, you may dance all winter." *Æsop.*

9822. IMPUDENCE Gratified. Philip Melanchthon had gathered together a great quantity of rare coin in gold and silver, and took delight in exhibiting them to his friends, to whom he would now and then give a choice piece. One day a foreigner was visiting him, to whom he showed his collection, and seeing he was pleased with them, bade him choose out one or two of the pieces that he desired the most. "I desire them all," replied the stranger. Melanchthon, though disgusted with his immodesty and impudence, gave them all, that he might satisfy his covetousness.

9823. IMPUDENCE, Refusal of. While Archelaus, King of Macedon, sat at supper, one of his guests asked as a gift, the cup of gold out of which the king himself drank. The king called a page, and commanded him to give the cup to Euripides, who sat at the table with him; then looking earnestly at the impudent person who craved it, said, "As for you, sir, you are worthy for your asking to go without, but Euripides deserveth to have, though he asketh not."

9824. IMPURITY, Detection of. Two of the early Christians, while in prison expecting martyrdom, became estranged. A dream which one of them had was received as an admonition, and resulted in reconciliation. In the dream they came into a very luminous place, where their garments became white, and their flesh whiter than their garments, and so wonderfully transparent that there was nothing in their hearts not clearly exposed to view. The dreamer saw in his own heart a dark spot, and decided that it was his coldness towards his Christian brother. Thereby they were reunited and prepared for their martyrdom, which followed only a few days later.

9825. IMPURITY, Passion of. A monk came to Poemen, whose mind was inflamed with impure imaginations. "What shall I do, my father,

my father?" he cried. The abbot led him out where the flat, glaring desert lay before him, and the mirage quivered above the sands. A hot blast, as from a furnace, blew upon them. "Open the breast of your habit," said Poemen. The wind struck the bared breast of the monk. "Fold your robe again," said Poemen. "And now tell me, have you enclosed the wind in your bosom?" "No." "So let passion sweep by like a hot breath, fanning you. You can not help that. Let it pass. Do not take it in and harbor it."

9826. INABILITY, Human, Biblical. May be illustrated by the case of *Leprosy*—the deep and foul stain, which was not only loathsome, but incurable, Lev. 13. *Silly sheep going astray*, Isa. 53: 6.—Proverbial for their proneness to wander, and their inability to find their way back. The *Ethiopian.*—"Can the Ethiopian change his skin, or the leopard his spots?" Jer. 13: 23. A picture of sin, inborn by nature, strengthened by education and confirmed by habit. The *bankrupt debtor*, who owed ten thousand talents, and had nothing to pay, Matt. 18: 24. A *corrupt tree*, that cannot bring good fruit, Matt. 7: 18. A *branch* severed from the parent stem, John 15: 5. We may also add the representations in *Christ's miracle* of man's natural impotence, which were no doubt designed to be symbolical. The man born blind, John 9; the man with a withered hand, to whom Christ said, "Stretch forth thine hand," Matt. 12: 13; the impotent man at Bethesda, "without strength," and "who had no helper," John 5: 7; the deaf, deformed, demoniacs, etc.; sad pictures of suffering humanity, but emblems of the sadder state of sin and spiritual helplessness. *Bowes.*

9827. INAPPROPRIATENESS, Case of. During the war a lady, distributing tracts in the wards of a hospital, was shocked to hear a soldier laughing at her, and turned to reprove him. "Why, look here, madam," said the soldier, "you have given me a tract on the sin of dancing, when I've both legs shot off."

9828. INCARNATION, Mystery of. For the sun to fall from its sphere, and be degraded into a wandering atom; for an angel to be turned out from heaven, and be converted into a fly or a worm, had not been such abasement; for they were but creatures before, and so they would abide still, though in an inferior rank. But for the infinite glorious Creator of all things to become a creature, is a mystery exceeding all human understanding.
John Flavel.

9829. INCLINATION, Mere. A mere inclination to a thing is not properly a willing of that thing; and yet in matters of duty men frequently reckon it for such; for otherwise how should they so often plead and rest in the honest and well-inclined dispositions of their minds, when they are justly charged with an actual non-performance of the law? *South.*

9830. INCONSISTENCY, Biblical Figures of. "The salt losing its savor;" of all things then most worthless; a figure used three times by our Lord in his teaching, Matt. 5: 13; Mark 9:

50; Luke 14: 34, 35. "*Spots* in your feasts of charity," Jude 12. The Greek word refers to dangerous rocks sunken under the sea. *Spots and blemishes,* 2 Pet. 2: 13. Rom. 2: 17-24.—The sins of teachers are the teachers of sins. Prov. 25: 26.—The inconsistencies and falls of professed believers before the wicked, are like "a troubled fountain, and a corrupt (or muddy) spring." Prov. 25: 28.— "He that hath no rule over his own spirit is like a city that is broken down, and without walls,"—lying open to the attacks of every enemy, who may enter without resistance the unguarded castle. Eccles. 10: 1.—"Dead flies" in the ointment are like "a little folly" to the reputation of one honored for wisdom and good character. John 18: 25.—"Art not thou also one of his disciples?" "Did not I see thee in the garden with him?" ver. 26. Peter was now not at the upper end of the hall, standing by his Master, ready to witness for him, but at the lower end, amongst his enemies, following Jesus "afar off." *Bowes.*

9831. INCONSISTENCY, Effects of. There is no favorite child of nature who may hold the fireball in the hollow of his hand and trifle with it without being burnt; there is no selected child of grace who can live an irregular life without unrest; or be proud, and at the same time have peace; or indolent, and receive fresh inspiration; or remain unloving and cold, and yet see, and hear, and feel the things which God hath prepared for them that love him. *F. W. Robertson.*

9832. INCONSISTENCY, Emblem of. A drunken man trying to walk on both sides of the same street at the same time is the emblem of inconsistency. It is a thing hard to do, but he does it. We account for it by saying, "O, he is drunk!" There is a fearful amount of moral drunkenness, professors going zig-zag in the way, and traveling the distance three times over, if they do not fall quite into the ditch. The moral drunkard shall not inherit the kingdom of heaven.

9833. INCONSISTENCY, Example of. A traveler in Russia says: "A lady, on leaving a private party in St. Petersburg at a rather advanced hour in the morning, called a droschky, and having given directions to the driver, the latter proceeded toward her home, as she thought, instead of which he drove her to a rather deserted part of the city, when he suddenly turned round and cut her throat, the sable-lined cloak in which she was enveloped having excited his cupidity. Having divested her of this, he dragged the body to the brink of the canal, and threw her into it. On his way back to the stand he was hailed by a gentleman, and however reluctant, obliged to take him as a fare. The gentleman not only noticed the cloak, but, touching it, found his fingers stained with blood. He said nothing till he reached a police station, where, having ordered the driver to stop, he gave him into custody on suspicion. The gentleman was the husband of the lady, and recognized the cloak as belonging to his wife. The tragedy happened during Lent, when meat is forbidden. The murdered lady had a little basket with her which contained a pie. Having been asked by the commissary why he had not eaten the pie, 'How could I think of eating the pie! replied the assassin, 'it may contain meat, and'—devoutly crossing himself—'I am, thank God, a good Christian!'"

9834. INCONSISTENCY, Ignorant. A lady was convinced that her colored cook had stolen a goose. The woman stoutly and angrily denied it. On the following Sunday morning the cook asked leave to go out for the day that she might attend the "'munion." Her mistress was quite willing that she should go, but wondered at her thinking of going to the communion. "You know you took that goose; how can you think of going to the ''munion?'" "Well, missus," said she, "if you will have it, I did take the goose; but if you suppose that for the matter of one goose I am going to renounce my Lord and Saviour, you're very much mistaken."

9835. INCONSISTENCY, Pagan. A missionary in Africa says: "One day a trader chief came to join my church with his two wives—one old and ugly, the other a handsome young negress. 'That will never do,' I cried; 'my religion allows a man but one wife Choose one for the partner of your joys and sorrows, and make suitable provision for the other.' They all went away looking very crest-fallen. A week or two afterward the old chief came back, leading the young and pretty one, both looking very happy. 'Me come back,' he said; 'me all ready now.' 'That is right,' said I; 'and, pray, how have you disposed of the other wife?' 'All right,' he said; 'me ate her up!'"

9836. INCONSISTENCY, Self-Condemnation for. How commonly doth the whole course of our lives displease ourselves as much as others; and yet we live on in contradiction to our reason, and sometimes to our inclinations too! How unlike are we in conversation, to ourselves in retirement! How unlike are we in the devotions of our closets, to ourselves in the employment of our several professions! How calm, sedate, wise, holy, and resolved in the one! How anxious and uneasy; how foolish, earthy, and inconstant in the other! But in nothing does our deviation from reason more evidently appear than in two things: first, in our proposing to ourselves false and irrational ends of life; secondly, in our insincerity in pursuing the true and rational one, that is, happiness. *Lucas.*

9837. INCONSTANCY, Artful. It is said of Alcibiades that he passed through more mutations than the chameleon has colors. Socrates, in his Ecclesiastical History, says of Ecebolius that he was a Christian under Constantine, a pagan under Julian, and a Christian again under Jovinian. A Scotch politician, named Lydington, became so famous for his variableness that he was called Chameleon Lydington. Caligula's attendants never knew what to expect from him, so inconstant was he.

9838. INCONSTANCY, Emblem of. In the country of the Troglodytæ it said that there is a ake, the water of which is bitter and salt thrice a day, then it returns to sweet again, and in the same manner it is in the night also; whereupon it hath gained the name of the mad water. Some men are no less unequal and inconstant in their manners than these waters are in their tastes; now courteous, and then rough; now prodigal, and straight sordid; one while extremely kind, and ere long vehemently hating where they passionately loved before.

Wanley.

9839. INCONSTANCY, Popular. As long as Marius, the younger, was successful in wars, he was called by the Romans the Son of Mars. But as soon as fortune began to frown upon him they called him the Son of Venus, and destroyed the statues that were erected in honor of his exploits. In like manner the Athenians had flattered Demetrius during his extensive victories, and had set up two hundred statues in his honor. But when they heard of his overthrow by Ptolemy, King of Egypt, and that he was coming to them for succor, they sent him word that he must not come near them, for they had made a decree that no king should come into Athens; and they took down the statues and broke them to pieces before the year was out.

9840. INCREDULITY, Faith and. Two children were standing at evening on the summit of a hill, watching the setting sun as it seemed slowly to roll along the bright horizon. "What a way," said the elder, "the sun has moved since we saw it coming from behind that tree!" "And yet you remember," said the little one, "we learned this morning's lesson with our father, that the sun never moves at all." "I know we did," replied the first; "but I do not believe it, because I see it is not so. I saw the sun rise there this morning, and I see it set there to-night. How can a thing get all that distance without moving? You know very well, that if we did not move, we should remain always just where we are upon the hill." "But our father," said the other, "told us it is the earth that moves." "That is impossible, too," replied the elder; "for you see it does not move: I am standing upon it now, and so are you, and it does not stir: how can you pretend to think it moves, while all the time it stands quietly under our feet?" These simple ones might divide mankind between them, and carry the banner of their parties through the world from first to last, from the gates of Paradise to the judgment-seat: there never has been, and there never will be, any other division, but they that take, and they that will not take, their Father's word.

A. Monod.

9841. INCREDULITY, Ignorant. A native of India, in England, said to his teacher, "O, sir, what wicked men these sailors are! What do you think they have been telling me? They say that, in England, sometimes the water gets so hard that men can stand upon it: but do you think that I believe them? No I don't." The missionary replied, "But it is so, my dear: and now you believe it, don't you?" "Yes,"

said she, "I believe it because you say so; but how can it be?"

9842. INDECISION, Emblems of. The expression, "How long halt ye between two opinions?" is rather an explanation than a literal rendering of the original, which to us has a significance that ought not to be lost. Literally the words may be translated, "How long leap ye upon two branches?"—a most beautiful poetical allusion to the restlessness of a bird, which remains not long in one posture, but is continually hopping from branch to branch. Some what less expressive, but still very significant, is the version which others extract from the original word,—"How long limp ye upon two hams?"—alluding to the alternate movements of the body—now on one side and then on the other—of a lame man in his walk. *Kitto.*

9843. INDECISION, Influence of. Indecision is that slatternly housewife by whose fault chiefly the moth and the rust are allowed to make such dull work of life; corrupting all the gleam and gloss of earth's perishable treasures.

Edith Clarel.

9844. INDIGESTION, Evils of. How many serious family quarrels, marriages out of spite, alterations of wills, and secessions to the Church of Rome, might have been prevented by a gentle dose of blue pill! What awful instances of chronic dyspepsia are presented to our view by the immortal bard in the characters of Hamlet and Othello! I look with awe on the digestion of such a man as the present King of Naples. Banish dyspepsia and spirituous liquors from society, and you would have no crime, or at least so little that you would not consider it worth mentioning. *Kingsley*

9845. INDISCRETION, Mischief of. An indiscreet man is more hurtful than an ill-natured one, for, as the latter will only attack his enemies, and those he wishes ill to, the other injures indifferently both friends and foes. *Addison.*

9846. INDOLENCE, Hereditary Sin of. If you ask me which is the real hereditary sin of human nature, do you imagine I shall answer, pride, or luxury, or ambition, or egotism? No: I shall say indolence. Who conquers indolence will conquer all the rest. Indeed, all good principles must stagnate without mental activity. *Zimmerman.*

9847. INDOLENCE, Remonstrance against. Since thou hast an alarm in thy breast, which tells thee thou hast a living spirit in thee above two thousand times in an hour, dull not away thy days in slothful supinity and the tediousness of doing nothing. To strenuous minds there is an inquietude in overquietness, and no laboriousness in labor; and to tread a mile after the slow pace of a snail, or the heavy measures of the lazy of Brazilia, were a most tiring penance, and worse than a race of some furlongs at the Olympics. The rapid courses of the heavenly bodies are rather imitable by our thoughts, than our corporeal motions: yet the solemn motions of our lives amount unto a greater measure than is commonly apprehended. Some few men have surrounded the globe of the earth; yet many in the set loco-motions and movements of their days have measured the circuit of it, and twenty thousand miles have been exceeded by them.

T. Browne.

9848. INDULGENCE, Danger of. The Syrian Semiramis was a poor wench, kept by one of Ninus' slaves, till Ninus meeting her and taking a fancy to her, at length doted upon her to that degree that she not only governed him as she pleased, but contemned him; so that, finding that she had got the absolute mastery over him, she became so bold as to desire him to do her the favor to see her sit but one day upon the throne, with the royal diadem upon her head, dispatching the public business. The king consented, and gave order to all his officers to yield her the same obedience as to himself. At first she was very moderate in her commands, only to make trial of the guards about her; but when she saw that they obeyed her without the least hesitation or murmuring, she commanded them first to lay hold of Ninus himself, then to bind him, at length to kill him. Which being done, she took the government upon herself, and reigned victoriously over all Asia.

Plutarch.

9849. INDULGENCES, Papal. A Saxon gentleman had heard Tetzel at Leipsic, and was much shocked by his impostures. He went to the monk and inquired if he was authorized to pardon sins in intention, or such as the applicant intended to commit? "Assuredly," answered Tetzel; "I have full power from the Pope to do so." "Well," returned the gentleman, "I want to take some slight revenge on one of my enemies without attempting his life. I will pay you ten crowns if you will give me a letter of indulgence that shall bear me harmless." Tetzel made some scruples; they struck their bargain for thirty crowns. Shortly after, the monk set out from Leipsic. The gentleman, attended by his servants, laid wait for him in a wood between Jüterboch and Treblin, fell upon him, gave him a beating, and carried off the rich chest of indulgence-money the inquisitor had with him. Tetzel clamored against this act of violence, and brought an action before the judges. But the gentleman showed the letter signed by Tetzel himself, which exempted him beforehand from all responsibility. Duke George, who had at first been much irritated at this action, upon seeing this writing, ordered that the accused should be acquitted.

D'Aubigne.

9850. INDUSTRY, Advantages of. There is no art or science that is too difficult for industry to attain to; it is the gift of tongues, and makes a man understood and valued in all countries, and by all nations. It is the philosopher's stone that turns all metals, and even stones, into gold, and suffers no want to break into its dwelling. It is the northwest passage, that brings the merchant's ships as soon to him as he can desire. In a word, it conquers all enemies, and makes fortune itself pay contribution.

Lord Clarendon.

9851. INDUSTRY, Bread of. The bread earned by the sweat of the brow is thrice blessed, and it is far sweeter than the tasteless loaf of idleness.

Crowquill.

9852. INDUSTRY, Capacity for. People may tell you of your being unfit for some peculiar occupations in life; but heed them not. Whatever employ you follow with perseverance and assiduity will be found fit for you; it will be your support in youth, and your comfort in age. In learning the useful part of any profession, very moderate abilities will suffice—great abilities are generally injurious to the possessors. Life has been compared to a race: but the allusion still improves by observing that the most swift are ever the most apt to stray from the course.

Goldsmith.

9853. INDUSTRY, Enforced. The court of the Areopagites was the most renowned in the city of Athens. It inquired into the manner of life of each Athenian, what was his income, and how he sustained his family. They were instructed to follow some honest course of life, knowing they were to give a public account thereof. If a man was convicted of idleness, a mark of infamy was set upon him, or he was ejected from the city, as an unprofitable person.

9854. INDUSTRY, God's Delight in Man's. I persuade myself that the bountiful and gracious Author of man's being and faculties, and all things else, delights in the beauty of his creation, and is well pleased with the industry of man in adorning the earth with beautiful cities and castles, with pleasant villages and country houses, with regular gardens and orchards, and plantations of all sorts of shrubs, and herbs, and fruits, for meat, medicine, or moderate delight; with shady woods and groves, and walks set with rows of elegant trees; with pastures clothed with flocks, and valleys covered over with corn, and meadows burthened with grass, and whatever else differenceth a civil and well-cultivated region from a barren and desolate wilderness.

Ray.

9855. INDUSTRY, Habits of. A man who gives his children habits of industry, provides for them better than by giving them a fortune.

Whateley.

9856. INDUSTRY, Honored. I spent no time in taverns, games, or frolics of any kind; and my industry in my business continued as indefatigable as it was necessary. I was indebted for my printing-house; I had a young family coming on to be educated; and I had two competitors to contend with for business, who were established in the place before me. My circumstances, however, grew daily easier. My original habits of frugality continuing, and my father having, among his instructions to me when a boy, frequently repeated a proverb of Solomon—"Seest thou a man diligent in his business? he shall stand before kings;" I thence considered industry as a means of obtaining wealth and distinction; which encouraged me, though I did not think that I should ever literally stand before kings; which, however, has since happened; for I have stood before five, and even had the honor of dining with one, the King of Denmark.

Franklin.

9857. INFANCY, Consecrating. Augustine has a strong saying, that "he tasted of the salt of God in his mother's womb;" a forcible utterance of the fact that he was by Monica pledged unto the Lord ere he saw the light, dedicated before he was born. The Rev. Thomas Collins was not wanting in this preconsecration. When he was first brought to his father, he took him, placed a Bible on his breast, and folded the left arm around it; then, after putting a pen in the tiny right hand, knelt down, and prayed that God would accept the lad; would make him a faithful witness of that saving word: would help him with tongue and pen, to bless his fellows. Historians tell that the infant Bernard, with equal form and at as early an opportunity was offered to Jesus, and thenceforth regarded as one separated unto, and to be disciplined for the most arduous service of the Great Master. Very likely the parents, both of the Methodist and of the mediæval saint, found real stimulus to faithful training in the memory of their voluntary pledge. *S. Coley.*

9858. INFANT BAPTISM, Abuse of. I say it is a farce, and with many of you who make no further use of the baptism of your children, it is a farce. That is to be the initiation of discipline. You remember how the father of Hannibal took his child to the altar of the gods, and swore that child to eternal enmity to Rome. Now, suppose he had never reminded him of the vows under which he was laid; I tell you they would as much have been forgotten, and would have had as much effect on the child's life, as some sorry game of childhood. But there was not a day after that that the father did not say, "My child, you are sworn to smite Rome." He was brought up to it, and it became a settled principle with him, till when he was a man he did smite Rome as Rome had never been smitten before. Now, I tell you, you have sworn your child to be a true soldier of Christ; you have sworn your child to enmity to the world, the flesh, and the devil. What are you doing? Not one single day should pass without the child being reminded of these things; not one single month should go by without your saying, "My child, are you true? You are sworn to Christ, and if you live not to him your life will be a burden. You are sworn to be true to him, and to withhold your life is one long felony." If you do that, the baptismal bond will not be a little thing, but your children will grow up in the nurture and admonition of the Lord, a generation to serve God; and they shall deal such blows to Satan and his kingdom as have never smitten them before. Baptism is the dedication of the child's life; it is the first act of that series of discipline which is to train up the child "in the nurture and admonition of the Lord." *S. Coley.*

9859. INFANT, Death of an. Those who have lost an infant are never, as it were, without an infant child. Their other children grow up to manhood and womanhood, and suffer all the changes of mortality; but this one alone is rendered an immortal child; for death has arrested it with his kindly harshness, and blessed it into an eternal image of youth and innocence. *Leigh Hunt.*

9860. INFANTS, Blessing. It was the custom of the Jews to bring their infant children, on the first anniversary of their birth, to be blessed by the Rabbi of their synagogue. *Dr. Holme.*

9861. INFANTS, Safety of. A minister had noticed that a Scotch grave-digger took particular pains in dressing and caring for the graves of infants, and he asked why he did so. John paused a moment at his work, and looking up to the sky, said, "Of such is the kingdom of heaven." "And is it on this account you tend and adorn them with so much care?" "Surely, sir," answered John, "I cannot make too fine the bed-covering of a little innocent sleeper that is waiting there until it is God's time to waken it, and cover it with a white robe, and waft it to glory. Where such grandeur is awaiting it yonder, it is fit that it should be decked out here. I think the Saviour will like to see white clover spread about it; do you not think so too, sir?" "But why not thus cover larger graves?" asked the minister; "the dust of all his saints is precious in the Saviour's sight." "Very true, sir," responded John, with great solemnity, "but I cannot be sure who are his saints and who are not. I hope there are many lying in the kirkyard; but it would be great presumption to mark them out. There are some I am quite sure about, and I keep their graves as neat as I can, and plant a bit of flower here and there as a sign of my hope, but dare not give them the white shirt," referring to the white clover. "It's clean different, though, with the bairns."

9862. INFIDEL, Christian Burial Denied to an. Whitefield visited an unbeliever during a lingering illness. At one time he asked him what was his religion. He answered, "Religion is of so many sects I know not which to choose." Another time he offered to pray with him, but he would not accept it, upon which he resolved to go to see him no more. But being told, two days before he died, that he had an inclination to see him, he went again, and after a little conversation, put the following questions to him: "Do you believe Jesus Christ to be God, and the one Mediator between God and man?" He said, "I believe Jesus Christ was a good man." "Do you believe the Holy Scriptures?" "I believe something of the Old Testament; the New I do not believe at all." "Do you believe, sir, in a judgment to come?" He turned himself about, and replied, "I know not what to say to that." "Alas, sir!" Whitefield said, "if all these things should be true, what?" These words gave him great concern, for he seemed afterward to be very uneasy, grew delirious, and in a day or two departed. The day after his decease he was carried to the ground, and Whitefield refused to read the service over him; but he went to the grave, and told the people what had passed between them, and warned them all against infidelity.

9863. INFIDEL, Death of an: Voltaire. In "Simp

son's Plea for Religion," published at the commencement of this century, are the following facts in regard to Voltaire: "When the first apprehensions for his life were entertained, D'Alembert, Diderot and Marmontel hastened to support his resolution, but they were only witnesses of their own ignominy. The long agony of the dying sceptic was characterized by rage, remorse, recantation, blasphemy and reproach. In the first days of his illness, in spite of all his associates, he showed signs of wishing to return unto the God he had so often blasphemed. He called for a priest. His danger increasing, he sent the following note to the Abbé Gaultier: "You had promised, sir, to come and hear me. I entreat you would take the trouble of calling on me as soon as possible. Signed, VOLTAIRE, Paris, 26th Feb., 1778." A few days after, he wrote the following declaration, in the presence of Abbé Gaultier, the Abbé Mignot, and the Marquis de Villevielile, copied from the minutes deposited with M. Mouet, Notary of Paris: "I, the underwritten, declare that, for these four days past, having been afflicted with a vomiting of blood, at the age of eighty-four, and not having been able to drag myself to the church, the Rev. the Rector of Sulpice having been pleased to add to his good works that of sending to me the Abbé Gaultier, I confessed to him, and if it please God to dispose of me, I die in the church in which I was born; hoping that the Divine mercy will deign to pardon all faults. Second March, 1778, signed in presence of Abbé Mignot, my nephew, and the Marquis de Villevielile, my friend." The Marquis de Villevielile was the individual to whom, eleven years before, Voltaire wrote: "Conceal your march from the enemy in your endeavors to crush the wretch!" A favorite motto, with which he closed his letters to his friends was, "Crush, then, do crush the Wretch," referring to Christ. Voltaire permitted the above declaration to be carried to the Rector of Sulpice and to the Archbishop of Paris, to know whether it would be sufficient. But when Abbé Gaultier returned with the answer, it was impossible for him to gain admittance to the patient. The conspirators strained every nerve to prevent their chief from consummating his recantation, and every avenue was closed against the priest whom Voltaire had sent for. Rage succeeded to fury, and fury to rage, during the remainder of his life. Sometimes he would turn upon his companions: "Retire! it is you that have brought me to my present state. Begone! I could have done without you all, but you could not exist without me. And what a wretched glory you have procured me." They could hear him, the prey of anguish and dread, alternately supplicating and blaspheming that God against whom he had conspired; and in plaintive accents he would cry, "O Christ! O Jesus Christ!" Then he would complain that he was abandoned by God and man. The hand that had traced in ancient writ the sentence of an impious and reviling king, seemed to trace before his eyes his own impious motto. "Crush, then, do crush the Wretch!" In vain he turned his head away; the time was coming apace when he was to appear before the tribunal of him whom he had blasphemed; and his physicians, particularly M. Tronchin, retired, declaring that the death of this impious man was terrible indeed. The pride of the conspirators would willingly have suppressed these declarations, but in vain. Mareschal de Richelieu fled from the bed-side, declaring it to be a sight too terrible to be endured: and M. Tronchin said that "the furies of Orestes could give but a faint idea of those of Voltaire." Could he say, then, at the last, "I have fought a good fight; I have kept the faith?" This account of the death of Voltaire was confirmed by a letter from M. de Luc, an eminent philosopher, and a man of the strictest honor and probity.   *D. Dorchester.*

9864. INFIDEL, Inconsistency of an. This miserable man had an only daughter lying upon a sick-bed; his wife, I may observe, who died, was in her life-time a devoted, spiritual-minded and praying Christian. When the daughter's death was very near and all hope of restoration was utterly dissipated, she called her father to her bed-side, and said: "My mother died a Christian some years ago, rejoicing in Jesus, and assured of heaven; you are a disbeliever in Christianity; I am going to make the last venture; am I to die in my mother's faith, or in yours? I beseech you to advise me," she said with earnestness and fervor, "whether I am to die in my mother's faith, or in yours." The father's struggle between affection to his only child and the pride of devotedness to his principles was tremendous; but at last, amid a burst of tears and in an agony of feeling, the hardened, yet melting infidel said: "Die in your mother's faith." And she died in her mother's faith. And yet the man who gave that advice lives to propagate infidelity in the world, and labors with all the energy he has to make men as contaminated as himself.   *Dr. Cumming.*

9865. INFIDEL, Judgment of an. An infidel who had publicly lauded the writings of Paine and Voltaire, as superior to the Bible, was asked: "Have you a family?" "Yes; a wife and children." "Which would you recommend to them, infidelity or Christianity?" Confounded at this home thrust, he answered, "I never heard that kind of argument before; I would rather give them the Bible than any infidel book."

9866. INFIDEL, Sealing an. An old minister in Massachusetts visited a dying infidel, and found him in despair, from which nothing could release him. Before leaving, the infidel made the following strange request: "I want to preach at my own funeral; and when you have closed the other parts of the service, I want you to come down from the pulpit and place your two fore-fingers on my lips, and say, 'This soul is sealed for hell!'" "You must spare me from such a commission. It will frighten the people," said the minister. "It is my dying request, and I feel that you must do it. Let others take warning by my death. I cannot excuse you." The minister complied. At his funeral, after he had finished the sermon, he came down from the pulpit, and, approaching the coffin, laid the tips of his fingers on those marble lips, and with tears streaming from his eyes, stated the man's dying request, and pronounced the words, "This soul is sealed for hell!"

9867. INFIDELITY, The Bible and. It is only in the creation that all our ideas and conceptions of a word of God can unite. The creation speaketh a universal language, independently of human speech or human language, multiplied and various as they be. It is an ever-existing original, which every man can read. It cannot be forged; it cannot be counterfeited; it cannot be lost; it cannot be altered; it cannot be suppressed. It does not depend upon the will of man whether it shall be published or not; it publishes itself from one end of the earth to the other. It preaches to all nations, and to all worlds; and this Word of God reveals to man all that is necessary to know of God. *Thomas Paine.*

9868. INFIDELITY, Credulity of. It is most important to keep in mind the self-evident, but often forgotten maxim, that disbelief is belief; only, they have reference to opposite conclusions—*e. g.*, to disbelieve the real existence of the city of Troy is to believe that it was feigned—and which conclusion implies the greater credulity is the question to be decided. To some it may appear more, to others less probable, that a Greek poet should have celebrated (with whatever exaggeration) some of the feats of arms in which his countrymen had actually been engaged, than that he should have passed by all these, and resorted to such as were wholly imaginary. So, also, though the terms "infidel" and "unbeliever" are commonly applied to one who rejects Christianity, it is plain that to disbelieve its divine origin is to believe its human origin: and which belief requires the more credulous mind is the very question at issue. A man who should doubt whether there is such a city as Rome would imply his belief in (what most would account a moral impossibility) the possibility of such multitudes of independent witnesses having concurred in a fabrication.
Illustrations of Truth.

9869. INFIDELITY, Effects of. Mr. Paine submitted the manuscript of an infidel article to his friend Dr. Franklin for his opinion. The doctor, though himself an infidel, replied, "I would advise you not to attempt to unchain the tiger, but to burn this piece before it is seen by any other person. If men are so wicked with religion, what would they be without it!"

9870. INFIDELITY and Faith. Infidelity and Faith look both through the same perspective glass, but at contrary ends. Infidelity looks through the wrong end of the glass; and, therefore, sees those objects near, which are afar off, and makes great things little,—diminishing the greatest spiritual blessings, and removing far from us threatened evils: Faith looks at the right end, and brings the blessings that are far off in time close to our eye, and multiplies God's mercies, which in the distance lost their greatness. *Bishop Hall.*

9871. INFIDELITY, French. Near the close of the eighteenth century, "infidelity had become the fashion of the public mind. Its evil influences, like the smoke from the abyss mentioned in the apocalypse, had ushered in an unnatural night upon the European continent, compared with which the gloom of the so-called dark ages was sunshine. Faith was dying out of men's hearts all over the land. Voltaire's Satanic gibes, the dismal rant of Jean Jacques Rousseau, Lessing's astute skepticism, the God-denying blasphemies of Holbach, and even the poetic rationalism of Herder,—together with the example of kings and queens, and the nobility generally, upon the minds of those who could not read,—were all telling upon various orders of minds, and tending to bring about the same disastrous consummation. The priest at the altar, the monarch on the throne, the doctor in the college chair, the dramatist on the stage, the wit in the *salon*, the soldier in the ranks, the trader in the shop, the peasant at the plough—blasphemed God, and renounced the hope of immortality." From this terrible seeding France has reaped a sad harvest of irreligion, debauch, bloody revolutions and communism.

9872. INFIDELITY, Hopeless. Mr. Owen visiting Alexander Campbell, at Bethany, they went to the family burying-ground. Mr. Owen, addressing himself to Mr. Campbell, said, "There is one advantage I have over the Christian—I am not afraid to die. Most Christians have fear in death; but if some few items of my business were settled, I should be perfectly willing to die at any moment." "Well," answered Mr. Campbell, "you say you have no fear in death; have you any hope in death?" After a solemn pause—"No," said Mr. Owen. "Then," rejoined Mr. Campbell, pointing to an ox standing near, "you are on a level with that brute. He has fed until he is satisfied, and stands in the shade, whisking off the flies, and has neither hope nor fear in death."

9873. INFIDELITY, Insincerity of. An infidel lecturer addressed an audience with great earnestness, denying God and immortality, and uttering the most horrid blasphemies. When he was done, a man of middle age arose, and said: "My friends, I have a word to speak to you to-night. I am not about to refute any of the arguments of the orator. I shall not criticise his style. I shall say nothing concerning what I believe to be the blasphemies he has uttered; but I shall simply relate to you a fact, and, after I have done that, you shall draw your own conclusions. Yesterday I walked by the side of yonder river; I saw on its floods a young man in a boat; the boat was unmanageable; it was going fast toward the rapids. He could not use the oars, and I saw that he was not capable of bringing the boat to the shore. I saw that young man wring his hands in agony. By and by he gave up the attempt to save his life, kneeled down and cried with desperate earnestness, "O God, save my soul. If my body cannot be saved, save my soul!' I heard him confess that he had been a blasphemer. I heard him vow that if his life were spared he would never be such again. I heard him implore the mercy of heaven for Jesus Christ's sake, and earnestly plead that he might be washed in his blood. These arms saved that young man from the flood. I plunged in, brought the boat to shore, and saved his life. That same young man has just now addressed you, and cursed his Maker. What say you to this, sirs?" The speaker sat down. A shudder ran through the young man himself, and the audience saw, that while it was a fine thing to act the bravado against Almighty God on dry land, when danger was distant, it was not the same near the verge of the grave.

9874. INFIDELITY, Propagating. Sheridan, the noted infidel, said in a speech on the French Revolution in the House of Commons: "Although no man can command his conviction, I have ever considered a deliberate disposition to make proselytes to infidelity as an unaccountable depravity. Whoever attempts to pluck the belief or the prejudice on this subject, style it which he will, from the bosom of one man, woman, or child, commits a brutal outrage, the motives for which I have never been able to trace or conceive."

9875. INFIDELITY, Results of. Thomas Paine tells us that he has passed through the forest of Christianity and hewn down every tree; and yet, in the language of a quaint writer, he did not bark the first sapling. They all stood firmer after Paine passed through with his hosts of satellites than before, and will forever stand beautiful and green with immortality.
Bp. Bowman.

9876. INFIDELITY Tested. A very wicked man affirmed that he did not believe there was either God or devil, heaven or hell. Not long after he was apprehended for a notorious crime, and condemned to be hung. A minister sought admittance to his cell, and told him he was desirous of knowing if his atheistical principles had changed any in view of approaching death. With many tears he bewailed his former life; he said, "That a prison, and the serious thoughts of death, had opened the eyes of his understanding, and that when he said there was no God, he had not heartily believed what he said; but leading such a wicked life as he had, he thought it necessary to blind his conscience, and outbrave the world, with a pretence that it was his principle."

9877. INFIDELITY, Thoughtlessness of. Boswell asked Dr. Johnson, the great lexicographer, if he did not think Foote, the famous tragedian, was an infidel. Johnson replied, "I do not know, sir, that the fellow is an infidel; but if he be an infidel, he is an infidel as a dog is an infidel: that is to say, he has never thought upon the subject." This being reported to Foote, he exclaimed indignantly, "What, sir, to talk thus of a man of liberal education; a man who for years was at the University of Oxford; a man who has added sixteen new characters to the literature of his country!" Foote's case is only too common. Men of little minds and partial culture condemn religion and reject God.

9878. INFIDELITY, Worthlessness of. Infidelity gives nothing in return for what it takes away. What, then, is it worth? Every thing to be valued has a compensating power. Not a blade of grass that withers, or the ugliest weed that is flung away to rot and die, but reproduces something. Nothing in nature is barren. Therefore, everything that is or seems opposed to nature cannot be true; it can only exist in the shape that a diseased man imparts to one of its coinages. Infidelity is one of these coinages—a mass of base money that won't pass current with any heart that loves truly, or any head that thinks correctly. And infidels are poor, sad creatures; they carry about them a load of dejection and desolation, not the less heavy that it is invisible. It is the fearful blindness of the soul. *Chalmers.*

9879. INFIDELS, Agreement of. There is but one thing in which infidels do agree, and that is, in their rejection of Christianity; though here, again, no two of them will agree as to their reasons for rejecting it. In this respect they remind us of the story of an Irishman who landed in New York on the crisis of an election, and—whether the process of naturalization was consummated on the spot, or Pat was required to personate some missing voter, we don't know—but he was challenged to give a vote for or against the Government. "Is there a Government?" was the single question Pat asked. "Yes," was the answer. "Then," cried he, with a flourish of his shillalah; "then I'm agin it!" "Is there religion?" asks your average Free-thinker; "Is there a revelation? Then I'm agin it!" *Dr. Curry.*

9880. INFIDELS, Effrontery of. Rousseau, who was first a Protestant, then a Romanist, then an infidel, is characterized by unmitigated conceit. After a life of crime and debauchery, in which he gloried, according to his autobiography, he wrote, "No man can come to the throne of God and say, I am a better man than Rousseau." His last-recorded utterance was: "Eternal Being, the soul that I am going to give thee back is as pure as it was when it proceeded from thee. Make it a partaker of thy felicity."

9881. INFIDELS, Ignorance of. The biographer of Thomas Paine, the author of "The Age of Reason," in order to excuse the blunder which Paine made in his criticisms on the Bible, says, that at "the time he wrote the first part of the work 'he was without a Bible, neither could he procure one.'"

9882. INFIDELS, Works of. "When an infidel comes forth from the grave," says Jallaloddin, "his works shall be represented to him under the ugliest form that ever he beheld, having a most deformed countenance, a filthy smell, and a disagreeable voice; so that he shall cry out,

God defend me from thee! What art thou? I never saw any thing more detestable.' To which the figures will answer, 'Why dost thou wonder at my ugliness? I am thy evil works; thou didst ride upon me while thou wast in the world, but now will I ride upon thee, and thou shalt carry me.' And immediately he shall get upon him; and whatever he shall meet shall terrify him, and say, 'Hail, thou enemy of God.'"

9883. INFINITY, Characteristics of. Infinity is the retirement in which perfect love and wisdom only dwell with God. In infinity and eternity the sceptic sees an abyss, in which all is lost. I see in them the residence of Almighty power, in which my reason and my wishes find equally a firm support. Here, holding by the pillars of heaven, I exist—I stand fast. *Miller.*

9884. INFIRMITIES, Benefit of. It is found in husbandry that the removal of the small stones which frequently encumber the fields does not increase the crop. In many soils they are an advantage, attracting the moisture, and radiating the heat. Around these stones you will find the largest berries. In an experiment made in England the result of removing the stones was so unfavorable to the crop that they were brought back and spread over the ground. We often cry out, like Paul, for the removal of some thorn in the flesh. After-experience teaches us it is better that it should remain. We may learn the sufficiency of grace, and glory even in our infirmities.

9885. INFIRMITY, Sins of. When Pompey could not prevail with a city to billet his army with them, he persuaded them to admit of a few weak, maimed soldiers; but those soon recovered their strength, and opened the gates to the whole army. And thus is it that the devil courts us only to lodge some small sin— a sin of infirmity or two—which, being admitted, soon gathers strength and sinews, and so subdues us. *Price.*

9886. INFLUENCE, Abiding. It was a striking remark of a dying man, whose life had been, alas! but poorly spent, "Oh that my influence could be gathered up, and buried with me!" It could not be. That man's influence survives him; it still lives, is still working on, and will live and work for centuries to come. He could not when he came to die, and perceived how sad and deleterious his influence had been—he could not put forth his dying hand and arrest that influence. It was too late; he had put in motion an agency which he was altogether powerless to arrest. His body could be enrouded, and coffined, and buried out of sight, but not his influence; for that, alas! corrupt and deadly as it is, there is no shroud, no burial. It walks the earth like a pestilence—like the angel of death, and will walk till the hand of God arrests and chains it. *Anon.*

9887. INFLUENCE, Biblical Figures of. *Ointment* that bewrayeth itself, Prov. 27:16; Eccles. 7:1. *Sound*, spreading far and wide, like the shrill blast of the trumpet, 1 Thess. 1:8. *Leaven*, gradually fermenting and working into the whole mass, for good, Matt. 13:

33; or for evil, Luke 12:1; 1 Cor. 5:7, 8 Gal. 5:9. *Salt*, preserving and seasoning Matt. 5:13. "*A root of bitterness,*" Heb. 12: 15; cf. Deut. 29:18, marg.—"a poisonful herb." See in Heb. 12:15, what may come from one root—"lest there be *any* root.... and thereby *many* be defiled." *A canker or gangrene*, 2 Tim. 2:17, *i. e.* a mortification in the flesh, which, unless stopped, is fatal. *Bewitching* or fascinating, Gal. 3:1. *A viper brood*, Ps. 58:4; 140:3; Matt. 3:7. *Tares*, choking the good wheat, Matt. 13:24–30. *Bowes.*

9888. INFLUENCE, Contagious. In the temple of Apollo, at Babylon, there was said to be a little cabinet of gold. A soldier passing it one day chanced to open it, whence there was breathed out such a pestilent air, that it first infected the Parthians, then the adjacent provinces, and crept over almost all the inhabited parts of the world. Such was the fury of that plague, that it destroyed almost the third part of mankind.

9889. INFLUENCE, Dangerous. Among the high Alps at certain seasons the traveler is told to proceed very quietly, for on the steep slopes overhead the snow hangs so evenly balanced that the sound of a voice or the report of a gun may destroy the equilibrium, and bring down an immense avalanche that will overwhelm everything in ruin in its downward path. And so about our way there may be a soul in the very crisis of its moral history, trembling between life and death, and a mere touch or shadow may determine its destiny. A young lady who was deeply impressed with the truth, and was ready, under a conviction of sin, to ask, "What must I do to be saved?" had all her solemn impressions dissipated by the unseemly jesting and laughter of a member of the church by her side as she passed out of the sanctuary. Her irreverent and worldly spirit cast a repellent shadow on that young lady not far from the kingdom of God. *T. Stork.*

9890. INFLUENCE, Female. If mankind had been perpetuated without their milder companions, a strong and iron race would have inhabited the earth. There is something in the active spirits and powers of the manly portion of our common species which loves difficulties, enterprise, exertion, dangers, and personal displays. These qualities and propensities would too often animate self-love and selfishness into continual strife, civil discord, and battle, if no softer and kinder companions were about such beings, to occupy some portion of their thoughts and attentions, to create and cherish milder and sweeter feelings, and to provide for them the more soothing happiness of a quiet home and a domestic life. Tenderness, sympathy, good humor, smiles, gentleness, benignity, and affection, can diffuse pleasures more grateful than those of irritation and contest, and awaken the sensibilities that most favor intellectual and moral cultivation. *S. Turner.*

9891. INFLUENCE, Maternal. The mother of the Rev. John Newton, a pious woman of the south of England, died when he was but seven years old, leaving him only the memory of her

¬eligious teaching and goodness. At an early age he became a dissipated sailor. The memory of his mother brought him to himself and started a stream of incalculable influence. Through him Claudius Buchanan was converted, who became a missionary to India. He wrote "The Star in the East," which made Adoniram Judson a missionary to India. Newton was also the means of converting Thomas Scott, the commentator. Through him Cowper was rescued from despondency and his harp tuned to the key of religion. His influence upon the career of Wilberforce is asserted, and also that the abolition of the slave trade was one of its remote results. Wilberforce wrote "A Practical View of Christianity," a useful book, the instrument of converting Leigh Richmond the author of "The Dairyman's Daughter," which has saved thousands. Back of it all stands the faithful mother of John Newton.

9892. INFLUENCE, Parental. We may see, with broad and distinct lines, in every land, how vast and extensive, how lengthened, how enduring is the influence of the conduct of the parent on the character and happiness of future ages! An infant born in New Zealand follows its cruel parents in barbarism and cannibalism: an infant in China inherits the deceitfulness and ungodliness of Chinese paganism; infants among Arabs, Hottentots, American Indians, are brought up in all the respective peculiarities, vices, and miseries of their various countries, and continue in them, unless God graciously interposes, with deepening darkness and misery. Yet the original ancestors of all these, thus sunk in error and wickedness, were the sons of one man, and had equal advantages in the beginning, till parents led the way in evil. Ham and his son Canaan departed from the good ways of Noah, and so all Africa became debased. In one branch of the family of Shem, chiefly through God's special interposition in the call of Abraham, the Church of God continued for 2,000 years; in other branches we see the issues of wickedness throughout the immense continent of Asia. What a blessing was Abraham's piety to his posterity!
E. Bickersteth.

9893. INFLUENCE, Posthumous. Theodore Parker lay on his dying bed in Florence, his great expectations unfulfilled. Hope still survived. He said, "There are two Theodore Parkers now: one is dying here in Italy, and the other I have planted in America." He died among strangers, and was buried in the Protestant Cemetery at Florence.

9894. INFLUENCE, Records of. Nothing takes place without leaving traces behind it; and these are in many cases so distinct and various, as to leave not a doubt of their cause. We all understand how, in the material world, events testify of themselves to future ages. Should we visit an unknown region, and behold masses of lava covered with soil of different degrees of thickness, and surrounding a blackened crater, we should have as firm a persuasion of the occurrence of remote and successive volcanic eruptions, as if we had lived through the ages in which they took place. The chasms of the earth would report how terribly it had been shaken, and the awful might of long extinguished fires would be written in desolations which ages had failed to efface. Now conquest, and civil and religious revolutions, leave equally their impressions on society, leave institutions, manners, and a variety of monuments, which are inexplicable without them, and which, taken together, admit not a doubt of their occurrence. *Channing.*

9895. INFLUENCE, Secret of. Henry III. of France inquired why it was that the Duke of Guise appeared to charm everybody. The answer was, "The Duke of Guise endeavors to do good to all people without exception, directly by himself, or indirectly by his recommendation. He is civil, courteous, liberal, has always something good to say of everybody, and never speaks ill of any. This is the reason he reigns in men's hearts as absolutely as your majesty does in your kingdom."

9896. INFLUENCE, Spiritual. McCheyne had in a rare and singular degree his "conversation in heaven," and the influence for good he left in every place which he visited was quite extraordinary. I remember Dr. Anderson, of Morpeth, telling me how, when he was minister of St. Fergus, which he left at the disruption, McCheyne had spent a day or two in his manse; and not only while he was there, but for a week or two after he had left, it seemed a heavenlier place than ever before. Associated with McCheyne's person, appearance and conservation, on the walls of the house and everything around seemed to be inscribed, "Holiness unto the Lord."
Dr. Guthrie.

9897. INFLUENCE, Sum Total of. No human being can come into this world without increasing or diminishing the sum total of human happiness, not only of the present, but of every subsequent age of humanity. No one can detach himself from this connection. There is no sequestered spot in the universe, no dark niche along the disc of non-existence, to which he can retreat from his relations to others, where he can withdraw the influence of his existence upon the moral destiny of the world; everywhere his presence or absence will be felt—everywhere he will have companions who will be better or worse for his influence. It is an old saying, and one of fearful and fathomless import, that we are forming characters for eternity. Forming characters! Whose? our own or others? Both; and in that momentous fact lies the peril and responsibility of our existence. Who is sufficient for the thought? Thousands of my fellow-beings will yearly enter eternity with characters differing from those they would have carried thither had I never lived. The sunlight of that world will reveal my finger-marks in their primary formations, and in their successive strata of thought and life. *Elihu Burritt.*

9898. INFLUENCE, Teacher's. Isocrates being once asked how he, who was not very elo quent himself, could make others so, he answered, "Just as a whetstone cannot cut, yet it will sharpen knives for that purpose."

9899. INFLUENCE, Wide. Sir Astley Cooper, while writing a "vade mecum" for surgeons, would accomplish more than if that time had all been spent in setting broken bones. It was worth while locking Paul up in the gaol to get his prison epistles out of him. The debility—then mourned—which gave John Wesley leisure to pen his "Notes," will yield larger harvest than strength through all those months to go "gospelling" twice a day could have reaped. They who direct an age's intellect are more potent, though to the eye less active, than those who do its deeds. He who could purge a fever-breathing atmosphere would well affect the national health more than the hardest-working parish doctor, though his case-book were filled with notices of typhoid patients successfully treated.   *S. Coley.*

9900. INGRATITUDE, Alexander's. Parmenio was a faithful general under Philip and Alexander. He opened the way for them into Asia, had depressed Attalus, the king's enemy, and always led the king's vanguard; a man beloved by all the men of war; and all the glory and fame Alexander possessed appeared to come through the counsel of Parmenio. He had sacrificed two of his sons in battle, Hector and Nicanor, and another on suspicion of treason for the good of his country. Alexander, however, determined to take his life, having become jealous of his popularity. Cleander and Polydamus, Parmenio's most trusted friends, were sent to slay him, without even giving him a reason for doing so, and while he was reading a letter from the king himself, in apparent security.

9901. INGRATITUDE, Blindness of. Some travelers on a hot day in summer, oppressed with the noontide sun, perceiving a plane-tree near at hand, made straight for it, and throwing themselves on the ground, rested under its shade. Looking up, as they lay, towards the tree, they said one to another, "What a useless tree to man is this barren plane!" But the plane-tree answered them, "Ungrateful creatures! at the very moment you are enjoying benefit from me, you rail at me as being good for nothing."   *Æsop.*

9902. INGRATITUDE, Example of. An Englishman, named Inkle, would have been slain by the bloody Caribs, but a girl of the tribe pitied, concealed and fed him, until such time as an English vessel visited the coast, when she helped him to escape. The Indian girl had become much interested in the man for whom she had done so much, and asked that she might go with him, which was granted. On reaching the Barbadoes, the heartless wretch sold the girl, to whom he owed his life, into hopeless slavery. This is the story of Inkle and Yarico.

9903. INGRATITUDE, Experience of. Do you know what is more hard to bear than the reverses of fortune? It is the baseness, the hideous ingratitude, of man. I turn my head in disgust from their cowardice and selfishness. I hold life in horror: death is repose—repose at last. What I have suffered for the last twenty days cannot be comprehended.   *Napoleon I.*

9904. INGRATITUDE, Fortune of. Humphrey Bannister was brought up and exalted to promotion by the Duke of Buckingham, then his master. The Duke by reason of the separation of his army, that he had raised against Richard the usurper, was driven to seek refuge with Bannister, with whom he had every reason to expect security. Upon the king offering one thousand pounds reward for the Duke, Bannister betrayed his benefactor. He was sent under strong guard to the king, in Salisbury, and there publicly beheaded. But the vengeance of God followed Bannister to his entire discomfiture. His eldest son became insane; his eldest daughter was suddenly stricken with leprosy, another son became seriously deformed, and another was drowned, and he was himself found guilty of murder, and spared only from death by the clemency of his persecutors; while through his perfidious action, in betraying his friend, the king would not allow him to receive the price of his master's blood, saying that "he who would be so untrue to so good a master must needs be false to all others."

9905. INGRATITUDE, Frequency of. As there are no laws extant against ingratitude, so it is utterly impossible to contrive any that in all circumstances shall reach it. If it were actionable, there would not be courts enough in the whole world to try the causes in. There can be no setting a day for the requiting of benefits as for the payment of money; nor any estimate upon the benefits themselves; but the whole matter rests in the conscience of both parties: and then there are so many degrees of it, that the same rule will never serve all.   *Seneca.*

9906. INGRATITUDE, Pride and. There neither is nor ever was any person remarkably ungrateful who was not also insufferably proud; for as snakes breed on dunghills, not singly, but in knots, so in such base hearts you always find pride and ingratitude twisted together. Ingratitude overlooks all kindness, but it is because pride makes it carry its head so high. In a word, ingratitude is too base to return a kindness, too proud to regard it, much like the tops of mountains, barren indeed, but yet lofty; they produce nothing; they feed nobody; they clothe nobody; yet are high and stately, and look down upon all the world.   *South.*

9907. INGRATITUDE, Punishment of. Lycurgus, being asked why in his laws he had set down no punishment for ingratitude, answered, "I have left it to the gods to punish."   *Abp. Sandys.*

9908. INGRATITUDE, Similes of. Ingratitude is a nail which, driven into the tree of courtesy, causes it to wither; it is a broken channel, by which the foundations of the affections are undermined; and a lump of soot, which, falling into the dish of friendship, destroys its scent and flavor.   *Basil.*

9909. INGRATITUDE, Spectacle of. When Tamerlane had overcome and taken prisoner Bajazet, the great Turk, he asked him, "Whether he had ever given God thanks for making him so great an emperor?" Bajazet confessed "that he had never so much as thought of such a thing." Tamerlane replied, "That it was no wonder that so ungrateful a man should be made a spectacle of misery, for you being blind in one eye, and I lame in one leg, what worth is there in us, that God should set us over two such mighty empires, when he could command men so much worthier than ourselves?"

9910. INHOSPITALITY Rebuked. A minister who had traveled far to preach, after the sermon waited some time, expecting some one of the brethren to invite him home to dinner. In this he was disappointed; one and another departed, until the house was almost empty. He walked up to an elderly-looking gentleman, and said: "Will you go home to dinner with me to-day, brother?" "Where do you live?" "About twenty miles from this, sir." "No," said the man, coloring, "but you must go with me." "Thank you, I will cheerfully." The minister was no more troubled about his dinner at that appointment.

9911. INJURIES, Benefits and. Aristotle was asked what grew old the soonest? He replied, "Benefits." What then grows old the latest?" and he answered "Injuries."

9912. INJURIES, Forgetting. A man who had done Sir Matthew Hale a great injury, went afterwards to him for his advice in the settlement of his estate. He gave it very frankly, but would accept no fee for it. When asked how he could use a man so kindly who had wronged him so much, he answered: "I thank God I have learned to forget injuries."

9913. INJURIES, Forgetting and Forgiving. How many are there who profess to forgive, but cannot forget an injury. Such are like persons who sweep the chamber, but leave the dust behind the door. Whenever we grant our offending brethren a discharge, our hearts also should set their hands to the acquittance. *Secker.*

9914. INJURY, Damaging. Plato says that it is worse to do than to suffer injury, and that a man injures himself more when he hurts another, than he would be injured if he were the sufferer.

9915. INJUSTICE, Criticising. The Mohammedan commentators relate that Moses thought too highly of himself, and God sent him to learn wisdom of the prophet Al Khedr. According to the Koran, Moses went to him and was accepted as his disciple, with the condition that he should ask nothing concerning anything which he should see. They went together in a ship, and the prophet took an axe and made a hole in its bottom. Moses could not keep silence at this injustice, and said, "Hast thou made a hole therein that thou mightest drown those who are on board? Now hast thou done a strange thing." They left the ship and met a youth, whom the prophet slew.

Moses said, "Hast thou slain an innocent person? Now hast thou committed an unjust action." The prophet said, "Did I not tell thee thou couldst not bear with me?" Moses promised silence, and they went together to a city whose inhabitants refused to give them food. Finding a piece of wall ready to tumble down, the prophet built it up again. Moses' spirit chafed at this doing good to those who had refused them food, and he broke the condition again. Before they separated the prophet made the following explanation: "The vessel belonged to certain poor men who did business in the sea, and I was minded to render it unserviceable, because there was a king behind them who took every sound ship by force. As to the youth, his parents were true believers, and we feared lest he, being an unbeliever, should oblige them to suffer his perverseness and ingratitude. The wall belonged to two orphan youths in the city, and under it was a treasure hidden which belonged to them; and their father was a righteous man, the Lord was pleased that they should attain their full age, and take forth their treasure. I did not what thou hast seen of mine own will, but by God's direction. This is the explanation of that which thou couldst not bear with patience."

9916. INJUSTICE, Rebuke of. A Moorish king desired to purchase a piece of ground of a woman, but she preferred not to part with the inheritance of her fathers. The field was therefore siezed, and a pavilion erected. The poor woman complained to the Cadi of the injustice, and he promised to do all in his power to make it right. One day, while the king was in the field, the Cadi came with an empty sack and asked permission to fill it with the earth on which he was treading. He obtained leave, and when the sack was filled, he requested the king to complete his kindness by helping him load his ass with it. The monarch laughed, and tried to lift it, but soon let it drop, complaining of its great weight. "It is, however," said the Cadi, "only a small part of the ground thou hast wrested from one of thy subjects; how then wilt thou bear the weight of the whole field, when thou shalt appear before the great Judge laden with thine iniquity?" The king, thankful for the reproof, restored the field to its owner, together with the pavilion and the wealth which it contained.

9917. INJUSTICE, Treatment of. Any contumely, any outrage, is readily passed over by the indulgence which we all owe to sudden passion. These things are soon forgot upon occasions in which all men are so apt to forget themselves. Deliberate injuries, to a degree, must be remembered, because they require deliberate precautions to be secured against their return. *Burke.*

9918. INNOCENCE, Example of. Portius Cato the Elder was a man of great integrity. His honesty and severity made him a great many enemies, who were constantly troubling him. Fifty times he was accused, and as many times found innocent. At length, in his old age, he was accused, when he demanded that Tiberius Semphronius Gracchus, his bitterest enemy, should be appointed his judge. Even he acquitted him, and declared that he was innocent. After that he lived in honor and security.

9919. INNOCENCE, Memento of. Upon a tombstone in Rome is an inscription in these words, "Julia B. Prisca, *vixit Annos XXVI. Nihil unquam peccavit nisi quod mortua est.*" In this only she did amiss, that she died.

9920. INNOCENCE, Peace of. How many bitter thoughts does the innocent man avoid! Serenity and cheerfulness are his portion. Hope is continually pouring its balm into his soul. His heart is at rest, whilst others are goaded and tortured by the stings of a wounded conscience, the remonstrances and risings up of principles which they cannot forget; perpetually teased by returning temptations, perpetually lamenting defeated resolutions. *Paley.*

9921. INNOCENCE, Power of. What a power there is in innocence! whose very helplessness is its safeguard; in whose presence even Passion himself stands abashed, and turns worshiper at the very altar he came to despoil. *Moore.*

9922. INNOCENCE, Rare. Asclepiodorus journeyed from the city of Athens into Syria, stopping at the large cities on the way, that he might study the habits and customs of men. On his return he said he had not met with more than three men that "lived with modesty and according to the rules of honesty and justice." One was Ilapius, a philosopher in Antioch; the other Mares, of Laodicea, the most honest man of the age; the third, Dominus, a philosopher.

9923. INNOCENCY, Well-armed. A naked man with innocency, is better armed than Goliath in brass or iron. *Bp. Reynolds.*

9924. INNOCENT, Accusing the. Be careful how you hastily accuse, or even suspect persons of crime, or repair the mischiefs which often result from such a course. A story is told of a banker who missed a hundred-pound note from his safe. He had placed it there himself. No one had access to the safe but a confidential clerk. The clerk was charged with the theft, but declared his entire innocence. He had long served the banker; no suspicion had ever before attached to him. But the money was gone, and how else could it have been removed? He only could enter the safe, therefore he must have stolen it. Circumstances were against him, so he was dismissed. The charge clung to him. He could obtain no other situation, and finally died in disgrace and poverty. Years afterward the safe was overhauled for repairs, and there, behind the drawer from which it had slipped when placed by the owner, was the hundred-pound note. Yet every one at the time believed the clerk guilty, because no other reason could be found for the disappearance of the money. Similar experiences are constantly occurring. *Anon.*

9925. INNOCENT, Advantage of Being. It is far better to be innocent than penitent;—to prevent the malady than invent the remedy. *W. Secker.*

9926. INNOCENT, Evil Spoken of the. There is none so innocent as not to be evil spoken of; none so wicked as to want all commendation. There are too many who condemn the just, and not a few who justify the wicked. I often hear both envy and flattery speaking falsehoods of myself to myself: may not the like tongues perform the like task of others to others? I will know others by what they do themselves; but not learn myself by what hear of others I will be careful of mine own actions, not credulous of others' relations. *A. Warwick*

9927. INNOCENTS, Slaughter of. In 1641, Sir Phelim O'Neil, and other Papists, commenced a universal massacre of the Protestants in Ireland. "No age," says Hume, "no sex, no condition, was spared. The wife, weeping for her butchered husband, and embracing her helpless children, was pierced with them, and perished by the same stroke. In vain did flight save from the first assault. Destruction was everywhere let loose, and met the hunted victims at every turn. They were stripped of their very clothes, and turned out naked and defenceless in all the rigors of winter. The feeble age of children, the tender sex of women, soon sunk under the multiplied rigors of cold and hunger. Here the husband, bidding a final adieu to his expiring family, envied them that fate which he himself expected so soon to share! There the son, having long supported his aged parent, with reluctance obeyed his last command, and abandoning him in his utmost distress, reserved himself to the hopes of avenging that death which all his efforts could not prevent or delay." Forty thousand persons perished in these massacres!

9928. INQUISITION, Fear of the. A Spanish inquisitor desirous of eating some pears that grew in a poor man's orchard not far from him, sent for the man. The message caused such fright, that he was taken sick. On being informed that his pears were the only cause for sending for him, he caused his tree to be cut down, and carried with all the pears on it to the inquisitor's house. On being asked the reason for such a performance, he said "he would not keep that thing about him, which should give an occasion for their lordships to send any more for him."

9929. INSANITY, Varieties of. Burton, in his "Anatomy of Melancholy," gives the story of a physician in Milan who kept a house for the reception of lunatics, and by way of cure used to make his patients stand for a length of time in a pit of water, some up to the knees, some to the girdle, and others as high as the chin, *pro modo insaniæ*, according as they were more or less affected. An inmate of this establishment, who happened "by chance" to be pretty well recovered, was standing at the door of the house, and, seeing a gallant cavalier ride past with a hawk on his fist, and his spaniels after him, he must needs ask, "What do these preparations mean?" The cavalier answered, "To kill game." "What may the game be worth which you kill in the course of a year?" rejoined the patient. "About five or ten crowns." "And what may your horse, dogs, and hawks, stand you in?" "Four hundred crowns more." On hearing this, the patient, with great earnestness of manner, bade the cavalier instantly be gone, as he valued his life and welfare; "for," said he, "if our master come and find you here, he will put you into his pit up to the very chin."

9930. INSIGNIFICANCE, Advantage of. A fisherman was drawing up a net which he had cast into the sea, full of all sorts of fish. The little fish escaped through the meshes of the net, and got back into the deep, but the great fish were all caught and hauled into the ship. *Æsop.*

9931. INSPIRATION, Conviction of. A Chinese assistant instructed for some time in the New Testament by Bishop Boone, one day came into the room with an open Testament in his hand and exclaimed, "Whoever made this book made me. It knows all that is in my heart; it tells me what no one else except God can know about me. Whoever made me, wrote that book." This conviction was followed by conversion.

9932. INSPIRATION, The Style of. Some men ask, If the prophets spake as they were moved by the Holy Ghost, why did they not all speak in the same manner? why these varieties of style? I will answer that by asking you another question: Why do not all the pipes of that organ give one and the same sound? What awakens all the sounds but one and the same blast from the wind-chest? If there be a monoblast, why is there not a monotone? Because the pipes are of different shapes and different sizes: the awakening breath is one, the intonation varies with the shape and size of the pipe. The inspiration was one, but the style and manner varied with the disposition and character of the writer.   *Dean M'Neile.*

9933. INSTINCT, Argument from. All creatures have a natural affection to their young ones; all young ones, by a natural instinct, move to and receive the nourishment that is proper for them; some are their own physicians, as well as their own caterers, and naturally discern what preserves them in life, and what restores them when sick. The swallow flies to its celandine, and the toad hastens to its plantain. Can we behold the spider's nests, or silkworm's web, the bee's closets, or the ant's granaries, without acknowledging a higher being than a creature, who hath planted that genius in them?   *Charnock.*

9934. INSTINCT, Law of. Beasts, birds, and insects, even to the minutest and meanest of their kind, act with the unerring providence of instinct; man, the while, who possesses a higher faculty, abuses it, and therefore goes blundering on. They, by their unconscious and unhesitating obedience to the laws of nature, fulfill the end of their existence; he, in wilful neglect of the laws of God, loses sight of the end of his.   *Southey.*

9935. INSTINCT, Man's. Man's instincts are elevated, ennobled by the moral ends and purposes of his being, He is not destined to be the slave of blind impulses, a vessel purposeless, unmeant. He is constituted, by his moral and intelligent will, to be the first freed being, the masterwork and the end of nature; but this freedom and high office can only co-exist with fealty and devotion to the service of truth and virtue.   *Matthew Greene.*

9936. INSTINCT, Reason and. No sound philosopher will confound instinct with reason because an orang-outang has used a walking-stick, or a trained elephant a lever. Reason imparts powers that are progressive, and that, in many cases, without any assignable limit; instinct only measures out faculties that arrive at a certain point, and then invariably stand still. Five thousand years have added no improvement to the hive of the bee, nor to the house of the beaver; but look at the habitations and the achievements of man. *Colton.*

9937. INSTRUCTION, Frozen. Antiphanes said merrily, that in a certain city the cold was so intense that words were congealed as soon as spoken, but that after some time they thawed and became audible, so that the words spoken in winter were articulated next summer. Even so, the many excellent precepts of Plato, which he instilled into the tender ears of his scholars were scarce perceived and distinguished by many of them, till they grew men and attained the warm vigorous summer of their age.   *Plutarch.*

9938. INSTRUCTION, Repetition of. Repetition is the mother, not only of study, but also of education. Like the fresco-painter, the teacher lays colors on the wet plaster, which ever fade away, and which he must ever renew until they remain and brightly shine.   *Richter.*

9939. INSTRUMENTS, God's. What if a dozen pickaxes, standing together aside in the corner, after the day's work, should begin to talk among themselves, and say one to another: "We are getting so dull, and so used up, that I think we shall not be able to support these miners much longer." Suppose they should dream, because they were employed to pick in the mountain by the hand of intelligence and strength, that therefore on them the whole success of the miners depended. And yet, men, who are God's pickaxes, are afraid that the gold, and silver, and iron, and copper of truth will be lost in this world. But God is the miner. It is his thought and hand that use you. Not that the pickaxe is not a very good thing, and quite necessary for human industry; but after all, it is an instrument, and is subordinate to the might and power that are behind and above it.   *Beecher.*

9940. INSULT, Customary. A lion worn out with years lay stretched upon the ground, utterly helpless, and drawing his last breath. A boar came up, and to satisfy an ancient grudge, drove at him with his tusks. Next a bull, determined to be revenged on an old enemy, gored him with his horns. Upon this an ass, seeing that the old lion could thus be treated with impunity, thought that he would show his spite also, and came and threw his heels in the lion's face. Whereupon the dying beast exclaimed: "The insults of the powerful were bad enough, but those I could have managed to bear; but to be spurned by so base a creature as thou, the disgrace of nature, is to die a double death." *Æsop*.

9941. INSULT, Provocation of. People are generally very ready to put up with even intentional injury, when neither preceded nor followed by insult. I recollect a strong instance of this. A man applied to me for a warrant against another for knocking out one of his front teeth, which he held up before me. On my remarking upon his loss, he replied, "Oh! I should not have come for that, only he called me a thief." It is useful in going through life to bear in mind that courtesy to, and sympathy with, those we have accidentally injured, ordinarily diminish greatly the amount of reparation required, and sometimes even inspire as much good-will as a benefit conferred. *Moir*.

9942. INTEGRITY, Example of. The integrity of Biblius, the Roman, was such that he would not pick up any thing that was lost in the street, but would pass it by, saying, "It was kind of a blossom of injustice, to seize upon what was so found." The law of Stagira was, "Take not that up, which you never laid down."

9943. INTEGRITY, Preserve thy. Perish what may—gold, silver, houses, lands; let the winds of misfortune dash our vessel on the sunken rock; but let integrity be like the valued keepsake the sailor-boy lashed with the rope round his body, the only thing we care to save. *Macduff*.

9944. INTELLECT, Development of the. By the pursuit of the intellect the mind is always carried forward in search of something more excellent than it finds, and obtains its proper superiority over the common senses of life by learning to feel itself capable of higher aims and nobler enjoyments. In this gradual exaltation of human nature every art contributes its contingent towards the general supply of mental pleasure. *Sir. J. Reynolds*.

9945. INTELLECT, Employments of the. To perceive external objects, to conceive of them, to remember, to imagine, to compare, to judge, to abstract and to analyze, to connect thought with thought, according to the real relation between one notion and another;—these are the employments of the intellectual powers; and these occupations of the mind, though most often, if not always connected with, or preceded, or followed by desires or emotions, of some sort, are essentially different from loving, hating, fearing, hoping, etc. *I. Taylor*.

9946. INTELLECT, Pleasures of. The more any object is spiritualized, the more delightful it is. There is much delight in the tragical representation of those things which in reality would be sights full of amazement and horror. The ticklings of fancy are more delightful than the touches of sense. How does poetry insinuate and turn about the minds of men! Anacreon might take more delight in one of his odes than in one of his cups; Catullus might easily find more sweetness in one of his epigrams than in the lips of a Lesbia. Sappho might take more complacency in one of her verses than in her practices. The nearer any thing comes to mental joy, the purer and choicer it is. It is the observation not only of Aristotle, but of every one almost, "Some things delight merely because of their novelty;" and that surely upon this account, because the mind, which is the spring of joy, is more fixed and intense upon such things. The rosebud thus pleases more than the blown rose. *Lamb*.

9947. INTELLECT, Power of. Some men of a secluded and studious life have sent forth from their closet or their cloister, rays of intellectual light that have agitated courts, and revolutionized kingdoms; like the moon which, though far removed from the ocean, and shining upon it with a serene and sober light, is the chief cause of all those ebbings and flowings which incessantly disturb that restless world of waters. *Colton*.

9948. INTELLECT, Right Use of the. The powers of the intellect are not given to man merely for self; they are not intended to aid his own cunning, and craft, and intrigues, and conspiracies, and enrichment. They will do nothing for these base purposes. The instinct of a tiger, a vulture, or a fox will do better. Genius and abilities are given as lamps to the world, not to self. *Brydges*.

9949. INTELLECT, Unseen. There can be no doubt that there are many premature births in the mental world; and Gray is not far wrong when he thinks that many mute inglorious Miltons may have been buried in village obscurity. Nature, no doubt, in her boundless and untraceable prodigality, allows much of her noblest creation, the inventive and intelligent mind of man, to run to waste. The whole analogy of created things indicates this. The most powerful intellect just as it arrives at maturity sinks into the grave; and the baffled hopes of those who have watched the precocious promise of genius and wisdom, are surely not always fond illusions. But it should seem, on the other hand, that if we may so speak, there is always a vast floating capital of invention and intellect, which only requires to be directed into the proper channels to multiply a hundred fold. Great occasions seem always to call forth great minds; and that great mind which is best adapted to the necessities and to the character of the age, springs at once to the first rank. Whenever any important question has arisen, some bold intellect has arisen to grapple with it; and it is this happy coincidence between the character and powers of the commanding mind, and the intellectual or social necessities of the time, which brings to maturity all the noblest and the sempiternal works of human genius. *Quarterly Review*.

9950. INTEMPERANCE, Companions of. Intemperance is a hydra with a hundred heads. She never stalks abroad unaccompanied with impurity, anger, and the most infamous profligacies. *St. Chrysostom.*

9951. INTEMPERANCE Death's Prime Minister. Death, the king of terrors, was determined to choose a prime minister, and his pale courtiers, the ghastly train of diseases, were all summoned to attend, when each preferred his claim to the honor of this illustrious office. Fever urged the numbers he had destroyed; cold palsy set forth his pretensions by shaking all his limbs; gout hobbled up, and alleged his great power in racking every joint; and asthma's inability to speak was a strong, though silent, argument in favor of his claim. Stone and colic pleaded their violence; plague, his rapid progress in destruction; and consumption, though slow, insisted that he was sure. In the midst of this contention the court was disturbed with the noise of music, dancing, feasting, and revelry; when immediately entered a lady, with a bold lascivious air, and flushed jovial countenance. She was attended on one hand by a troop of bacchanals: and on the other, by a train of wanton youths and damsels, who danced half naked to the softest musical instruments; her name was Intemperance, she waved her hand, and thus addressed the crowd of diseases: "Give way, ye sickly band of pretenders, nor dare to vie with my superior merits in the service of this monarch! am I not your parent—the author of your being? Do ye not derive your power of shortening human life almost wholly from me? who then so fit as myself for this important office?" The grisly monarch grinned a smile of approbation, placed her at his right hand, and she immediately became his principal favorite and Prime Minister.
Illustrations of Truth.

9952. INTEMPERANCE, Hereditary Effect of. It is remarkable that all the diseases from drinking spirituous or fermented liquors are liable to become hereditary, even to the third generation; and gradually to increase, if the cause be continued, till the family becomes extinct.
Dr. E. Darwin.

9953. INTEMPERANCE, Personal Effects of. Wine heightens indifference into love, love into jealousy, and jealousy into madness. It often turns the good-natured man into an idiot, and the choleric into an assassin. It gives bitterness to resentment, it makes vanity insupportable, and displays every little spot of the soul in its utmost deformity. Nor does this vice only betray the hidden faults of a man, and show them in the most odious colors, but often occasions faults to which he is not naturally subject. There is more of turn than of truth in a saying of Seneca, that drunkenness does not produce but discover faults. Common experience teaches us the contrary. Wine throws a man out of himself, and infuses qualities into the mind which she is a stranger to in her sober moments. *Addison.*

9954. INTEMPERANCE, Preventing. Diogenes, the Athenian philosopher, met a young man who was on his way to a bacchanalian feast.

He stopped him and carried him back to his own friends, to keep him out of danger. Prevention is the work of the hour. Old inebriates will soon be all dead. If their ranks are not recruited, the sad procession of drunkards marching fantastically to their grave will be ended.

9955. INTEMPERANCE, Roman. In the first ages of Rome, no one was permitted to drink wine till thirty years of age. Later, when wealth had increased and the grape became abundant, they vied with each other in the quantity of wine they could drink. Of Cicero, the younger, Pliny says, "He drank as if he wished to deprive Antony, the murderer of his father, of the glory of being the greatest drunkard of the age." The Emperor Tiberius was always drunk, so that Seneca says of him, "He was never drunk but once: that was from the moment of his first intoxication to the day of his death." He appointed Pomponius Flaccus and Lucius Piso to high offices because they had passed two days and nights with him at table at a single drunken carousal, which fact he expressed in their patent of office.

9956. INTEMPERANCE, Suicide by. Those men who destroy a healthful constitution of body by intemperance and an irregular life, do as manifestly kill themselves as those who hang, or poison, or drown themselves. *Sherlock.*

9957. INTEMPERANCE, Trophies of. Like the skulls which a savage carries at his girdle, or sets up on poles in his palace-yard, and tells the traveler what a mighty warrior this or the other was till his axe or arrow laid him low; so, of all the sins, intemperance is the one which, reaped from the ranks of British genius, boasts the most crowded row of ghastly trophies. To say nothing of the many sorely wounded, amongst the actually slain in numbers, the musician and the artist, the philosopher and the poet, the physician and the lawyer, the statesman and the judge. *Dr. J. Hamilton.*

9958. INTEMPERANCE, Upsetting Sin of. President McCosh, of Princeton College, tells the story of a negro who prayed earnestly that he and his colored brethren might be preserved from what he called their "upsettin' sins." "Brudder," said one of his friends at the close of meeting, "you ain't got de hang ob dat ar word. It's 'besettin',' not 'upsettin'.'" "Brudder," replied the other, "if dat's so, it's so. But I was prayin' the Lord to save us from the sin of intoxication, and if dat ain't a upsettin' sin, I dunno what am."

9959. INTENTIONS, Biblical. The Lord discerns them, Heb. 4 : 12. The chief value of good deeds, lies in their right intentions. Abraham offered Isaac not in deed but in intention; and the intention was accepted, Heb. 11 : 17. *David* was commended because he desired to build the temple, 1 Kings, 8 : 18. *The widow's mite.* Mark 12 : 43. *Mary*—What a noble eulogy. "She hath done what she could." Mark 14 : 8. The *Macedonian's* liberality, 2 Cor. 8 : 2, 3, 12. Wickedness lies not in acts only, but in intentions. *Looking* may be *lusting*, Matt. 5 : 28. *Hatred is* accounted murder, 1 John 3 : 15 ; Jacob was a murderer when he wished to kill Esau, Gen. 22 : 41 ; Joseph's brethren, Gen. 37 : 20, 21 ; Saul wishing to kill David, 1 Sam. 18 : 25 ; Solomon wishing to kill Jeroboam, 1 Kings 11 : 40. *Good intentions* cannot justify wrong actions. *Gideon*, Judges 8 : 24–27. *Uzzah*, 2 Sam. 6 : 6, 7. *James and John*, Luke 9 : 54. *Peter*, John 18 : 10.   *Bowes.*

9960. INTENTIONS, Exposure of. I care not if there were a window in my heart for all mankind to see the uprightness of my intentions.   *Whitefield.*

9961. INTENTIONS, Transient. No sooner does the warm aspect of good fortune shine, than all the plans of virtue, raised like a beautiful frost-work in the winter season of adversity, thaw and disappear.   *Warburton.*

9962. INTERCESSION, Christ's. The bank-note without a signature at the bottom, is nothing but a worthless piece of paper. The stroke of a pen confers on it all its value. The prayer of a poor child of Adam is a feeble thing in itself, but once endorsed by the hand of the Lord Jesus, it availeth much. There was an officer in the city of Rome who was appointed to have his doors always open, in order to receive any Roman citizen who applied to him for help. Just so the ear of the Lord Jesus is ever open to the cry of all who want mercy and grace. It is his office to help them. Their prayer is his delight. Reader, think of this. Is not this encouragement?   *Ryle.*

9963. INTERCESSION, Effects of Christ's. We have an advocate, who stops whatever plea may be brought in against us by the devil, or the law, and answers all by his satisfaction : he gets out fresh pardons for new sins. And this advocate is "with the Father." He doth not say with his Father, though that had been a singular support in itself; nor yet with our Father, which is a sweet encouragement singly considered; but with *the* Father, which takes in both, to make the encouragement full. Remember, you that are cast down under the sense of sin, that Jesus, your friend in the court above, "is able to save to the uttermost." Which is, as one calls it, a reaching word, and extends itself so far that thou canst not look beyond it. "Let thy soul be set on the highest mount that any creature ever attained, and enlarged to take into view the most spacious prospect, both of sin and misery, and the difficulties of being saved, that ever yet oppressed any poor humble soul; yea, join to these all the hindrances and objections, that the heart of man can invent against itself and salvation: lift up thine eyes, and look to the utmost thou canst see—and Christ, by his intercession, is able to save thee beyond the horizon and largest compass of thy thoughts, even to the utmost."   *John Flavel.*

9964. INTERCESSION, Example of. About the year 1350 Edward III. of England invaded France with thirty thousand men, and at the battle of Crecy defeated Philip, who was at the head of the French army. After the battle Edward besieged the city of Calais, which, after an obstinate resistance of a year, was taken by the English king. He offered to spare the lives of the inhabitants on condition that six of their principal citizens should be delivered up to him, with halters round their necks, to be immediately executed. When these terms were announced in the city there was consternation on every countenance. The rulers of the town came together, and the question was publicly proposed, "Who will offer himself as an atonement for the city ?" There was silence in the assembly. The form in which the question was put suggested another, which, after the lapse of a few moments, fell from the same lips : "Who will imitate Christ, who gave himself for the salvation of men ?" Eustace St. Pierre, the commander of the town, immediately stepped forward and said, "I will lay down my life for your sakes. I do it freely—cheerfully. Who is the next one ?" "Your son," cried a young man, not yet arrived at manhood. "Who next ?" Another and another quickly offered, until the whole number was made up. They started for the English camp. Their families and fellow-citizens clung around them, groaning and weeping until the noise was heard in the opposite army. On reaching it they were received by the soldiers of Edward with every mark of commiseration and friendship. They appeared before the king. "Are these the principal inhabitants of Calais ?" he inquired sternly. "Of France, my lord," they replied. "Lead them to execution." At this moment a shout of triumph was heard in the camp. The queen had just arrived. She was immediately informed of the punishment about to be inflicted on the six victims. Hastening to the king, she pleaded for their pardon. At first he sternly refused to grant it, but her earnestness conquered, and the king yielded. Calling the captives before her, she said, "Natives of France, though you were ten-fold the enemies of our throne, yet we loose your chains. We snatch you from the scaffold. You are free." What a forcible emblem is this of the intercession of our Lord Jesus Christ! When we submit our hearts as captives to the Father, and feel that we are condemned and lost, we have an effectual Mediator who stays the hand of justice. The queen, by her relation to the victorious monarch, succeeded. Not another in his army could have done so. So Christ, by his relation to the Father—his Son, his only Son—can never plead in vain. But Jesus has done more than the queen of England ever did for the captives of Calais. He gave himself. He shed his blood to save us.   *Carter.*

9965. INTERCESSION, Import of. Intercession is a law term, borrowed from courts of judicature, and signifies the action of a proxy or attorney, either in suing out the rights of his client, or answering the cavils and objections brought against him by the plaintiff. This Christ doth for believers. Intercession is of three sorts. 1. Charitative intercession. Thus one man is bound to pray and intercede for another (1. Tim. 2: 1, 2). 2. **Adjutory inter-cession**. Thus the Holy Spirit makes intercession for believers (Rom. 8: 26, 27). 3. An official and authoritative intercession. And this properly belongs to Christ.   *Hopkins.*

9966. INTERCESSION, Romish. A poor Protestant tenant of the second Duke Gordon having fallen behind in his rent, in the Duke's absence, the farmer's stock was seized and advertised to be sold by auction on a fixed day. The Duke returned home in the interval, and the tenant went to him to supplicate for indulgence. "What is the matter, Donald?" said the Duke, as he saw him enter, and noted his sorrowful face. The tenant told his story of poverty so touchingly that the Duke was moved, and forgave him all the debt and restored him to favor. With a light heart he was retiring through the hall which was hung with portraits, and observing them he inquired who they were. "These," said the Duke, who was a Romanist, "are the saints who intercede with God for me." "My lord Duke," said Donald, "would it not be better to apply yourself direct to God? I went to muckle Sawney Gordon, and to little Sawney Gordon, but if I hadn't have come to your good Grace's self, I could not have got my discharge, and both I and my bairns had been turned out of house and home."

9967. INTERCESSOR, Appointing an. It was a custom in Vienna, in the sixth century to select some holy monk, and to wall him up in a cell where he would enjoy uninterrupted seclusion, and employ all his time in fasting and prayer for the blessing of God upon the people. St. Chef was chosen for this important work, and discharged it with great fervor. Every priest should be an intercessor, bringing down blessings upon the souls in his charge. Yea, every Christian stands between some soul and God.

9968. INTEREST, Influence of. Humboldt says that the copper-colored native of Central America, far more accustomed than the European traveler to the burning heat of the climate, yet complains more when upon a journey, because he is stimulated by no interest. The same Indian who would complain, when in botanizing he was loaded with a box full of plants, would row his canoe fourteen or fifteen hours together against the current without a murmur, because he wished to return to his family. Labors of love are light. Routine is a hard master. Love much, and you can do much. Impossibilities disappear when zeal is fervent.   *Spurgeon.*

9969. INTEREST, Power of. No blister draws sharper than interest does. Of all industries, none is comparable to that of interest. It works day and night, in fair weather or foul. It has no sound in its footsteps, but travels fast. It gnaws at a man's substance with invisible teeth. It binds industry with its film, as a fly is bound upon a spider's web.   *Beecher.*

9970. INTERMEDIATE STATE, Jewish Idea of the. The Jews say that the angel of death, coming and sitting on the grave, the soul immediately enters the body, and raises it on its feet; that

he then examines the departed person, and stripes him with a chain half of iron and half of fire; at the first blow all his limbs are loosened, at the second his bones are scattered, which are gathered together again by angels, and the third stroke reduces the body to dust and ashes, and it returns into the grave. This rack, or torture, they call Hibbut hakkeber, or the beating of the sepulchre, and pretend that all men in general must undergo it, except only those who die on the evening of the Sabbath, or have dwelt in the land of Israel.   *George Sale.*

9971. INTERMEDIATE STATE, Mohammedan Idea of the. When a corpse is laid in the grave, they say he is received by an angel who gives him notice of the coming of the two examiners, which are two black livid angels, of a terrible appearance, named Monker and Nakîr. These order the dead person to sit upright, and examine him concerning his faith as to the unity of God and the mission of Mohammed; if he answer rightly, they suffer the body to rest in peace, and it is refreshed by the air of Paradise; but if not, they beat him on the temples with iron maces, till he roars out for anguish so loud that he is heard by all from east to west, except men and genii. Then they press the earth on the corpse, which is gnawed and stung till the resurrection by ninety-nine dragons, with seven heads each; or, as others say, their sins will become venomous beasts, the grievous ones stinging like dragons, the smaller like scorpions, and the others like serpents; circumstances which some understand in a figurative sense.   *George Sale.*

9972. INVISIBLE, Love for the. Mr. Kilpin says of his son: "My boy said to me, before he was six years old, 'Tell me, papa, how is it that we can love persons when we have not seen them?' 'Ask yourself,' I replied, 'who gave you your beaver hat?' 'Grandpapa.' 'Do you love him?' 'Yes.' 'Have you seen him?' 'No.' 'Yet you love him. Why do you love him?' 'Because I have heard you say such a number of pretty things about him.' 'Did you believe that what I said of him was true?' 'Yes, to be sure I did.' 'Then you love him by faith, do you not?' 'Yes.' 'So then, having not seen, we love; and though now we see him not, yet believing, we rejoice with joy unspeakable and full of glory.'"

9973. INVITATION, Accepting the. In the courts of law if a man be called as a witness, no sooner is his name mentioned, though he may be at the end of the court, than he begins to force his way up to the witness box. Nobody says, "Why is this man pushing here?" or, if they should say, "Who are you?" it would be a sufficient answer to say, "My name was called." "But you are not rich, you have no gold ring upon your finger!" "No, but that is not my right of way: I was called." "Sir, you are not a man of repute, or rank, or character!" "It matters not, I was called. Make way." So make way, ye doubts and fears; make way, ye devils of the infernal lake; Christ calls the sinner. Sinner, come; for though thou hast naught to recommend thee, yet it is written, "Him that cometh unto me I will in no wise tast out."

Spurgeon.

9974. INVITATION, Discipline and. A farmer wished to take his sheep out of a barren field into a rich pasture. He set open the gate between the lots, and called the sheep. A part of them went in at once, but others disregarded the call, and seemed resolved to stay and starve in the old place. Then he cut some long sticks, and sent his men to drive them in. God's ways are herein symbolized. He invites sinners into his own rich pastures of grace, and sets open the gate. When they refuse he sends the rod of affliction upon them to drive them into the green fields on the banks of the river of life.

9975. INVITATION, Society for. A gentleman residing in one of our cities was deeply impressed and grieved by seeing multitudes who neglected public worship, and he determined to make the effort to induce some of the Sabbath-breakers to frequent the house of God. It required some little effort at first, but he overcame his timidity. The Lord's day evening he went forth with his holy purpose, and, meeting a young man who did not appear to be on his way to a place of worship, he respectfully addressed him, got into conversation with him, and persuaded the stranger to accompany him to worship, and as an inducement offered him a seat in his own pew. Succeeding in this, he was emboldened and encouraged to proceed in the line of Christian activity and usefulness. And now mark with what a blessed result. He was the means of leading one hundred young men to become stated attendants at the sanctuary, many of whom have been truly converted to God. A minister of the gospel mentioned this at one of his prayer-meetings, when the idea was caught up by some persons present, who at once said, "How admirable a plan this is for doing good!" A little association was immediately formed, called "The Invitation Society." In sixteen months two hundred persons were persuaded by eight or ten of its agents no longer to forsake the assembling of themselves together in the house of prayer. One of these agents, an earnest Christian in humble life, devoted himself to this work, and was the means of bringing forty to hear the word of life. *J. A. Adams.*

9976. IRASCIBILITY, Treatment of. This criminal habit is oftenest found in spoiled children, pampered old ladies and men in their dotage. The subjects of it are as sensitive as the snakes which are constantly darting out their tongues and glaring at you. Those who suffer most from them are their own friends, children, and servants, upon whom they pour out their wrath without stint. Outside they "may smile and smile," and seem saints. We either kill the snakes, or shut them up in a cage, and put a guard about them, and warn people to keep away. Every irascible person ought to be compelled to give warning to all comers, like the lepers of old. Avoid them. "With an angry man thou shalt not go." Beware of

cultivating it yourself. Conquer passion, or it will conquer you.

9977. IRREGULARITY, Scriptural. "What is your opinion of the Ranters?" was asked of Robert Hall. "Don't you think they ought to be put down?" "I don't know enough of their conduct to say that. What do they do? Do they inculcate antinomianism, or do they exhibit immorality in their lives?" "Not that I know of; but they fall into very irregular practices." "Indeed! What practices?" "Why, sir, when they enter a village they begin to sing hymns, and they go on singing until they collect a number of people about them, on the village green, or in some neighboring field, and then they preach." "Well: whether they may be prudent or expedient, or not, depends upon circumstances; but as yet I see no criminality." "But you must admit, Mr. Hall that it is very irregular." "And suppose I do admit that, what follows? Was not our Lord's rebuking the scribes and Pharisees, and driving the buyers and sellers out of the temple, very irregular? Was not almost all he did in his public ministry very irregular? Was not the course of the apostles, and of Stephen, and of many of the evangelists, very irregular? Were not the proceedings of Luther and Calvin and of their fellow-workers in the Reformation very irregular? a complete and shocking innovation upon all the quiescent doings of the papists? And were not the whole lives of Whitefield and Wesley very irregular lives, as you view such things? Yet how infinitely is the world indebted to all these! No, sir; there must be something widely different from mere irregularity before I can condemn."

Gregory.

9978. IRRESOLUTION, Evils of. In matters of great concern, and which must be done, there is no surer argument of a weak mind than irresolution; to be undetermined, where the case is so plain, and the necessity so urgent; to be always intending to live a new life, but never to find time to set about it: this is as if a man should put off eating, and drinking, and sleeping, from one day and night to another, till he is starved and destroyed. *Tillotson.*

9979. IRRESOLUTION, Misery of. I hope, when you know the worst, you will at once leap into the river, and swim through handsomely, and not, weather-beaten with the divers blasts of irresolution, stand shivering upon the brink.

Suckling.

9980. IRRESOLUTION, Vice of. Irresolution is a worse vice than rashness. He that shoots best may sometimes miss the mark; but he that shoots not at all, can never hit it. Irresolution loosens all the joints of a state; like an ague, it shakes not this or that limb, but all the body is at once in a fit. The irresolute man is lifted from one place to another, and hath no place left to rest on. He flecks from one egg to another; so hatcheth nothing, but addles all his actions. *Feltham.*

9981. IRREVERENCE, Beware of. We must take heed how we accustom ourselves to a slight and irreverent use of the name of God, and of the phrases and expressions of the Holy Bible, which ought not to be applied upon every slight occasion. *Tillotson.*

9982. IRREVERENCE, Crime of. To call God to witness truth, or a lie perhaps; or to appeal to him on every trivial occasion, in common discourse, customarily without consideration, is one of the highest indignities and affronts that can be offered him. *Ray.*

9983. ISAIAH, Character of. He was a prince amid a generation of princes, a Titan among a tribe of Titans; and of all the prophets who rose on aspiring pinion to meet the Sun of Righteousness, it was his, the Evangelical Eagle, to mount highest, and to catch on his wing the richest anticipation of his rising. It was his, too, to pierce most clearly down into the abyss of the future, and become an eyewitness of the great events which were enclosed in its womb. He is the most eloquent, the most dramatic, the most poetic, in one word, the most complete of the Bards of Israel. He has not the austere majesty of Moses, the gorgeous natural description of Job, Ezekiel's rough and rapid vehemence, like a red torrent from the hills seeking the Lake of Galilee in the day of storm, David's high gusts of lyric enthusiasm, dying away into the low wailings of penitential sorrow, Daniel's awful allegory, John's piled and enthroned thunders; his power is solemn, sustained and majestic; his step moves gracefully, at the same time that it shakes the wilderness. We have little doubt that many of his visions became objective, and actually painted themselves on the prophet's eye. Would we had witnessed that awful eye as it was piercing the depths of time, seeing the future glaring through the thin mist of the present! *G. Gilfillan.*

9984. JAMES, Martyrdom of St. James, "the Lord's Brother," so much resembled him that it is reported that it required the kiss of the traitor Judas, to point out the real Christ to the soldiers. He is said to have been the first bishop of Jerusalem. To him St. Paul was sent after his conversion. "Go show these things unto James and to the brethren." His success in establishing the church brought down the vengeance of the Jews upon him. The Scribes and Pharisees were set to entrap him. They flattered him as a just man, having the respect of the whole nation, and desired that he should correct the people in regard to Jesus on the approaching Paschal festival. They placed him on a wing of the temple where he could be seen and heard of all, and then called to him, "Tell us, O Justus, whom we have all the reason in the world to believe. Seeing the people are generally led away with the doctrine of Jesus that was crucified, tell us what is this institution of the crucified Jesus." The apostle spake so that the people heard, "Why do ye inquire of Jesus, the Son of man? He sitteth in heaven at the right hand of the Majesty on high, and will come again in the clouds of heaven." The people hearing this, blessed Jesus, and shouted "Hosanna to the Son of David!" The Scribes and Pharisees saw that they had made a mistake in relying upon flatterers to change the voice of James, for he had strengthened the cause of Jesus. They cried out that he had become an impostor, and pushed him off the temple. He was bruised but not killed by the fall, and began to pray for his persecutors. They cast stones upon him, and then one of them beat out his brains with a fuller's club. His martyrdom was accomplished at Jerusalem A. D. 62, in the ninety-sixth year of his age.

9985. JEALOUSY, Love without. Love may exist without jealousy, although this is rare; but jealousy may exist without love, and this is common; for jealousy can feed on that which is bitter, no less than on that which is sweet, and is sustained by pride as often as by affection. *Colton.*

9986. JEALOUSY, Poison of. Jealousy may be compared to Indian arrows, so envenomed, that if they prick the skin it is very dangerous; but if they draw blood, it is irrecoverably deadly. The first motions that arise from this root of bitterness have their evil effects; but where the disease progresses, it poisons all our comforts, and throws us headlong into the most tragical resolutions. *Wanley.*

9987. JEERING, Cruel. Scoff not at the natural defects of any which are not in their power to amend. Oh, it is cruel to beat a cripple with his own crutches! *Fuller.*

9988. JEERING, Unallowable. Jeer not others upon any occasion. If they be foolish, God hath denied them understanding; if they be vicious, you ought to pity, not revile them; if deformed, God framed their bodies, and will you scorn his workmanship? Are you wiser than your Creator? If poor, poverty was designed for a motive to charity, not to contempt; you cannot see what riches they have within. Especially despise not your aged parents, if they be come to their second childhood, and be not so wise as formerly; they are yet your parents; your duty is not diminished. *South.*

9989. JEHOVAH, The Name. Jehovah is a name of great power and efficacy; a name that hath in it three syllables, to signify the Trinity of Persons; the eternity of God, One in Three, and Three in One. A name of such dread and reverence among the Jews, that they tremble to name it, and, therefore, they used the name *Adonai*, Lord, in all their devotion. *Rayment.*

9990. JEREMIAH, Character of. The first quality exhibited in Jeremiah's character and history is shrinking timidity. His first words are, "Ah! Lord God, behold I cannot speak, for I am a child!" The storm of inspiration had seized on a sensitive plant or quivering aspen, instead of an oak or a pine. And yet this very weakness serves at length to attest the power and truth of the afflatus. Jeremiah with a less pronounced personality than his brethren, supplies a better image of an instrument in God's hand, of one moved, tuned, taught from behind and above. Strong in supernal strength, the child is made a "fenced city, an iron pillar, and a brazen wall." Traces, indeed, of his original feebleness and reluctance to undertake stern duties are found scattered throughout his prophecy. But he is reassured by remembering that the Lord is with him as a "mighty terrible One." His chief power, beside pathos, is impassioned exhortation. His prophecy is one long exhortation. He is urgent, vehement, to agony.

Gilfillan.

9991. JERUSALEM, Overthrow of. Our Saviour's words were literally fulfilled, even when royalty tried to prevent it. Titus was very desirous of preserving the temple; he had expressed the like desire of preserving the city too, and repeatedly sent Josephus, the historian, and other Jews, to persuade them to surrender. The Jews themselves set fire to the gates, through which the Romans were endeavoring to force an entrance, and one of the soldiers threw a burning brand into a window of the temple; the flames soon spread, and the people and soldiers rushed to the spot, shouting and fighting. Titus hastened to the place, calling to the soldiers to quench the fire, but they either could not hear or would not hear, and those behind encouraged those before them to set other parts on fire. Titus then, supposing that the interior might yet be saved, ordered the crowd of soldiers to be beaten back; but their anger and hatred of the Jews, and a certain vehement fury, overcame their reverence for their commander, and one of them threw the fire within, when the flame then burst forth, and thus the whole temple was burnt down, even contrary to the will of Cæsar: as if not one jot or tittle of our Lord's word should pass away until all should be fulfilled.

Dr. Cumming.

9992. JERUSALEM, People of. Jerusalem is one of the dullest places I ever entered, and if the traveler did not come here to converse with the dead, rather than the living, he would be much disappointed. It has no commerce, few manufactures, and when the pilgrims are absent, little intercourse with other people or cities. There are three descriptions of persons within its walls, all of whom have a rooted antipathy to each other. The Jew despises alike the Mussulman and Christian, and regards them both as intruders upon the soil given to his nation by God. The Mussulman, with a consciousness of greater political dignity, and with a supposed freedom from the degrading superstitions that the others practice, looks upon himself as far above the Israelite dog and the Nazarite kaffer, and he would not willingly allow them to tread the same earth or breathe the same air. The Christian, with equal pride, curses the hand of the Islam oppressor, under which he constantly writhes, and turns from the child of Abraham as from one who would defile his purity, or steal his purse.

Hardy.

9993. JERUSALEM, Warning to. There was one Jesus, son of Ananias, a countryman of mean birth, four years before the war against the Jews, at a time when all was in deep peace and tranquillity, who, coming up to the feast of tabernacles, according to the custom, began on a sudden to cry out, and say, "A voice from the east, a voice from the west, a voice from the four winds, a voice against Jerusalem and the temple, a voice against bridegrooms and brides, a voice against all the people." Thus he went about all the narrow lanes, crying night and day: and being apprehended and scourged, he still continued the same language under the blows without any other word. And they, upon this, supposing (as it was) that it was some divine motion, brought him to the Roman prefect: and by his appointment, being wounded by whips and the flesh torn to the bones, he neither entreated, nor shed a tear; but to every blow, in a most lamentable, mournful note, cried out, "Woe, woe to Jerusalem." This he continued to do till the time of the siege, seven years together; and, at last, to his extraordinary note of woe to the city, the people, the temple, adding "Woe also to me," a stone from the battlements fell down upon him and killed him.

Josephus.

9994. JESTING, Proper and Improper. A jest should be such—that all shall be able to join in the laugh which it occasions; but if it bears hard upon one of the company, like the crack of a string, it makes a stop in the music.

Feltham.

9995. JESTING, Lawful. Some men are of a very cheerful disposition, and God forbid that all such should be condemned for lightness. O let not any envious eye disinherit men of that which is their "portion in this life, comfortably to enjoy the blessings thereof!" Harmless mirth is the best cordial against the consumption of the spirit; wherefore, jesting is not unlawful, if it trespasseth not in quantity, quality, or season.

T. Fuller.

9996. JESUIT, Character of a. A Jesuit may be shortly described as an empty suit of clothes, with another person living in them, who acts for him, thinks for him, decides for him, whether he shall be a prince or a beggar, and moves him about wheresoever he pleases· who allows him to exhibit the external aspect of a man, but leaves him none of the privileges—no liberty, no property, no affections, not even the power to refuse obedience when ordered to commit the most atrocious of crimes; for, the more he outrages his own feelings, the greater his merits. Obedience to the Superior is his only idea of virtue, and in all other respects he is a mere image.

Southey.

9997. JESUITISM, Doings of. Ignatius's black militia, armed with this precious message of salvation, have now been campaigning over all the world for about three hundred years; and, openly or secretly, have done a mighty work! Who can count what a work! Where you meet a man believing in the salutary nature of falsehoods, or the divine authority of things doubtful, and fancying that to serve the good cause he must call the devil to his aid, there is a follower of Unsaint Ignatius. Not till the last of these men has vanished from earth will our account with Ignatius be quite settled, and his black militia have got their mittimus to chaos again. They have given a new substantive to modern languages. The word Jesuitism now, in all countries, expresses an idea for which there was in nature no prototype before. Not till these late centuries had the human soul generated that abomination, or needed to name it. Truly, they have achieved great things in the world; and a general result, which we may call stupendous. Not victory for Ignatius and the black militia —no, till the universe itself become a cunningly-devised fable, and God the Maker abdicates in favor of Beelzebub, I do not see how victory can fall on that side! But they have done such deadly execution on the general soul of man, and have wrought such havoc on the terrestrial and supernal interests of this world, as insure to Jesuitism a long memory in human annals.   *Carlyle.*

9998. JESUS, Blood of. Poets have loved the music of the mountain stream, as it tinkled down the hills amidst the stones, or murmured under leafy shades. Scripture speaks of the voice of God as the voice of many waters. So it is with the precious blood of Jesus: it has a voice which God hears, speaking better things than the blood of Abel, more than restoring to him again the lost music of his primeval creation.   *Faber.*

9999. JESUS, Companionship of. I went into a tent at the general hospital, and there lay a beautiful drummer boy, sixteen years old, burning up with fever. I asked him where his home was. "In Massachusetts, sir." "Are you not lonely here, far from father and mother, and friends, and so sick?" "Oh, no," was his answer; "how could I be lonely, when Jesus is here?" The smile that lit his deep blue eye, and played for a moment over his fevered lips as he uttered the words, will never cease to be the sweetest and freshest picture in my memory. My companion asked him, "How long is it since you loved Jesus?" "So long that I cannot remember when I did not love him."   *W. G. Taylor.*

10,000. JESUS, Esteem, not Love for. A Friend who, after listening to the eloquent praise bestowed by a gifted acquaintance upon the character and career of Christ, put the plain question, "Friend R., does thee love the Lord Jesus Christ?" The deliberate answer was, "No, sir, I am ashamed to say that I do not." The simple reply, "We wish thee did, Friend R.," was spoken with a tenderness, significance, and earnestness which could never be forgotten.

10,001. JESUS Found. A teacher in a Chinese Sunday-school in California, in talking with his class, ascertained that one of his pupils was a believing Christian, and asked him how he came to find Jesus. "Me no find Jesus," said the boy; "Jesus find me."

10,002. JESUS, Greatness of. His greatness transcends everything that is merely particular and individual. 'Tis not the greatness of the lawgiver, or of the hero,—the greatness of the thinker, or of the artist; nor is it the greatness in which the spirit of one single nation is

concentrated; no, it is a perfect mirror of humanity—the greatness of the true and universal human.   *Ullmann.*

10,003. JESUS, Help in the Name of. A great general who was about to undertake an expedition to rid his country of a ravaging enemy, dreamed the night before that Alexander the Great called him. He obeyed the call, and found the great hero very sick in bed, but he promised that he would immediately grant him help When asked how a sick man could help a warrior in the fight, he replied, "I will do it with my name."

10,004. JESUS, Leaning on. A little girl lay near death. "Does my little one feel sad at the thought of her death?" asked her papa, as he watched the look of pain on her face. "No, dear papa," said she, smiling, "my hand is all the while in the hand of Jesus, and he will not let it go." "Are you afraid, dear child?" asked her minister at another time. "No, I cannot fear while Jesus supports me," she replied. "But are you not weary with bearing pain?" She said, "I am leaning on Jesus, and don't mind the pain." And so she went to the fold above, leaning on the Good Shepherd who "gathers the lambs in his arms."

10,005. JESUS, Lessons of. The life of Jesus is not described to be like a picture in a chamber of pleasure, only for beauty and entertainment of the eye; but like the Egyptian hieroglyphics, whose every feature is a precept, and the images converse with men by sense and signification of excellent discourses.
                                    Bp. Taylor.

10,006. JESUS, Mission of. A city missionary was visiting one of the lowest and most degraded courts in London, when a woman said something like this to him: "You say you care for us, and are anxious about us; but it is a very easy thing for you to come from your clean quiet home just to visit us. Would you come and bring your family, and live in this court, expose yourself to all these evils day by day, in order to lift us up?" Jesus met this demand, took upon him our flesh, dwelt in our world, exposed himself to trial and death to save us.

10,007. JESUS, The Name of. This name Jesus is compared to "oil poured out;" oil being kept close, it sendeth not forth such a savor, as it doth being poured out; and oil hath these properties, it suppleth, it cherisheth, it maketh look cheerfully: so doth this name of Jesus; it suppleth the hardness of our hearts, it cherisheth the weakness of our faith, enlighteneth the darkness of our soul, and maketh man look with a cheerful countenance towards the throne of grace.   *Sutton.*

10,008. JESUS, Need of. A pastor related the following incident: "Some time since, in the place where I have been preaching, I called at his office to see the gentleman who had charge of the railroad shops—a strange-looking man, almost dwarfish in stature, but with such a head and features as might belong to a giant. We spoke of religion. He talked freely; as we separated, however, expressing himself in these terms: 'I am interested in church matters, and am always glad to see ministers when they call. But I have thought the subject over long and carefully, and have come to the deliberate decision that I have no need of Jesus.' A single week had not passed before that man was taken sick. His disease was accompanied with such inflammation of the throat as forbade his speaking at all. This enforced silence continued until the hour of death, when he was enabled to utter simply this one despairing whisper: 'Who shall carry me over the river?'"

10,009. JESUS, Our. A little three-year-old girl stood at the window one pleasant Sabbath "watching for papa," who was at church. Soon she spied him coming, and as he entered the door she raised her dark eyes to him, and said: "Papa, what did Mr. Roberts preach about this morning?" Her father replied: "He preached about Jesus." "Papa, was it our Jesus?" she asked. "Yes," said her father, "it was our Jesus." The dark eyes brightened at the thought that papa's minister knew her Jesus, and talked about him to his congregation. *Dr. Vincent.*

10,010. JESUS, Perfection of. One flaw or fault of temper, one symptom of moral impotence or of moral perversion, one hasty word, one ill-considered act, would have shattered the ideal for ever. *Liddon.*

10,011. JESUS, Presence of. Abydis, a Christian child, was struck by that terrible disease, the leprosy. A cell was constructed for her, where she must spend her days alone. As she entered it, a sense of her utter helplessness and desolation came over her, and she fell to the ground in great agony. She was conscious of being caught and held up. Shuddering, she opened her eyes and looked, and One was raising her up, upon whose brow was a wreath of thorns, and in whose hands and feet were nail-prints. "My child," said he, "I will never leave thee nor forsake thee." Her sufferings were very great. Her eyes grew dark, one after the other, but in her blindness she saw clearly her Guardian ever present. So had we spiritual vision, we should see Jesus constantly with us, as did the blind child of this legend.

10,012. JESUS, Sleep in. It is reported as a matter of great honor to the celebrated painter Leonardo da Vinci, that he expired in the arms of Francis I. who came to pay him a visit in his last illness. The eye which is enlightened by divine grace sees infinitely more glory in the last hours of a true Christian departing in a cottage with the triumphs of faith in his soul, than in all that could be derived from the most condescending attentions of the greatest princes in the world; these are mortal like all other men, and can yield no more than kind expressions of benevolence, even where they are sincere: but the believer in Jesus hath the God of heaven and earth bestowing real blessings while he lies upon his couch, and (to use the emphatic expression of the Psalmist) "making all his bed in his sickness."

He gloriously expires in the bosom of his Redeemer, and is carried to the blissful habitation of the saints in light. *Buck.*

10,013. JESUS, Visit of. An old gentleman much reduced in circumstances, and financially embarrassed, was visited by a friend, who said to him, "I hope Jesus visits you." "Visits me!" said the old man, "he lives with me all the time." *W. F. Sherwin.*

10,014. JESUS, The Word of. There was one lately who saw herself to be lost; who, when told that Jesus' own word was that he came to seek and to save the lost, and that he was there—willing to save her, because he had said it—exclaimed: "Then I take him at his word. He is mine!" *J. H. Wilson.*

10,015. JESUS, Work for. The teacher of an infant class one Sunday morning asked her scholars, "What have you done for the Saviour since last we met?" One said, "I have earned some money for the heathen by doing errands;" another, "I tend our sick baby;" another, "I fetch hunchback Billy to school." One after another told of the little activities and self-denials of the week, so pleasing to the teacher, and still more to him who said, "Suffer little children to come unto me." At last a little four-year-old hand was stretched up, and moved hastily to and fro to attract the teacher's attention. "Well, my dear, what are you doing to please Jesus?" The little eager face flushed with excitement as the unexpected reply came: "I scrubs, ma'am!"

10,016. JEWS, Biblical Figures of the. The *vine* and *vineyard*, Ps. 80 8: Is. 5: 1–7; Jer. 2: 21. *The barren fig-tree*, Luke 13: 6–9; Mark 11: 12–14, 20. *The olive* into which the Gentile Church was grafted, Rom. 11: 17–21. *The dry tree*, fit only for burning, Luke 23: 21. *The dry bones*, Ezek. 37: 1–14. *A vessel wherein is no pleasure*, Hos. 8: 8. *Corn sifted*, yet not lost, Amos 9: 9. *The Lord's peculiar treasure*, Ex. 12: 5; Ps. 135: 4. The Lord's portion, the lot of his inheritance, Deut. 32: 9. *Bowes.*

10,017. JEWS, Captivity of. What a mournful company! The sick, the bed-rid, the blind; old men tottering forth on the staff of age, and plucking their gray beards with grief; the skeleton infant hanging on a breast that famine and sorrow have dried; mothers with terror-stricken children clinging to their sides, or worse, with tender daughters imploring their protection from these rude and ruffian soldiers; a few gallant men, the brave survivors of the fight, wasted by famine, bleeding from unbandaged wounds, their arms bound, and anger flashing through the tears that stream from their eyes as they are turned on matrons and maidens shrieking, struggling, fainting, in the arms of brutal passion. How they strain at their bonds! how bitterly they envy their more fortunate compatriots who lie in the bloody breach, nor have survived to see the horrors of that day! The piety that abhors the sins of this people is not incompatible with the pity that sympathizes with their sorrows. We could sit down and weep with Jeremiah, as, resting on a broken pillar of God's temple, desolation around him, no sound in his ear but that long wild wail of the captive band, he wrings his hands, and, raising them to heaven, cries, "Oh that my head were waters, and mine eyes a fountain of tears, that I might weep day and night for the slain of the daughter of my people."   *Dr. Guthrie.*

10,018. JEWS, Christ and the. A learned Rabbi of the Jews, at Aleppo, being dangerously ill, called his friends together, and desired them seriously to consider the various former captivities endured by their nation, as a punishment for the hardness of their hearts, and their present captivity, which was continued sixteen hundred years, "the occasion of which," said he, "is doubtless our unbelief. We have long looked for the Messiah, and the Christians have believed in one Jesus, of our nation, who was of the seed of Abraham and David, and born in Bethlehem, and for aught we know, may be the true Messiah; and we may have suffered this long captivity because we have rejected him. Therefore my advice is, as my last words, that if the Messiah, which we expect, do not come at or about the year 1650, reckoning from the birth of their Christ, then you may know and believe that this Jesus is the Christ, and you shall have no other."
     Whitecross.

10,019. JEWS, Determined Blindness of the. At a solemn disputation which was held at Venice, in the seventeenth century, between a Jew and a Christian—the Christian strongly argued, from Daniel's prophecy of the seventy weeks, that Jesus was the Messiah whom the Jews had long expected from the predictions of their prophets: the learned Rabbi who presided at this disputation, was so forcibly struck by the argument, that he put an end to the business by saying, "Let us shut up our Bibles, for if we proceed in the examination of this prophecy, it will make us all become Christians."   *Bp. Watson.*

10,020. JEWS, Power of the. The Jews, although scattered over the face of the earth, yet maintain a secret and indissoluble bond of union and common interest. In every country they are, as it were, the servants; but the time may come when they will virtually be the masters in their turn. Even at the present time are they not, to a great extent, the arbiters of the fate of Europe? Maintaining, on the one hand, the bond between the different states, by the mysterious power of wealth which they possess; and on the other, loosening the ties of social life, and introducing or fostering ideas of change and revolution among various peoples? In the Jewish nation stirs the Nemesis of the destiny of Europe.
     Baron von Haxthausen.

10,021. JEWS, Wailing Place of the. The only point at which the Jews are permitted to approach their ancient temple is at a spot known as the Jews' wailing-place. There is a fragment of the old wall still left standing—a rood's length of cyclopean blocks piled stone upon stone—by whom? No one can tell, but certainly dating back to the time of Herod Once each week the devout Jews assemble before that wall, sit down humbly, take out their Hebrew Scriptures from their bosoms, and read the appropriate psalms and pray. It is pitiful indeed to witness that scene. Cast out, degraded, calling to remembrance their songs of ancient days, they sit and weep, and dream of the old times, when as yet the spoiler had not spoiled their sanctuary, nor laid waste their precious things. They sit and rock themselves in weeping, hoping still, hoping ever for better days. You see women, mere girls sometimes, sobbing out prayers into the very chinks of the old wall, as if thereby to wait them sooner entrance into the holy place. The hard stones are even polished with the touch of tender flesh that for ages has lovingly caressed them. Such earnestness of grief is affecting beyond measure to him who sees it. On this weekly day of wailing, I believe, the Jews here are unvexed in their devotions by Moslem intrusion. On other days, however, it is not so, for children straying into the place are hissed at and insulted. *Sunday at Home.*

10,022. JOKE, Fatal. Antigonus commanded Eutropion, his master-cook, to go to Theocritus and settle some accounts with him. When he had called frequently about the business, Theocritus said, "I know that thou hast a mind to dish me up raw to that Cyclops;" reproaching at once the king with the want of his eye, and the cook with his employment. Eutropion replied, "Then thou shalt lose thy head, as the penalty of thy loquacity and madness." He was as good as his word; for he departed and informed the king, who sent and put Theocritus to death.

10,023. JOKING, Caution Necessary in. Never risk a joke, even the least offensive in its nature, and the most common, with a person who is not well bred, and possessed of sense to comprehend it.   *La Bruyère.*

10,024. JOKING, Danger of. I have never forgotten what happened when Sydney Smith—who, as everybody knows, was an exceedingly sensible man, and a gentleman, every inch of him—ventured to preach a sermon on the duties of Royalty. The *Quarterly*, "so savage and tartarly," came down upon him in the most contemptuous style, as "a joker of jokes," a "diner-out of the first water," in one of his own phrases; sneering at him, insulting him, as nothing but a toady of a court, sneaking behind the anonymous, would ever have been mean enough to do to a man of his position and genius, or to any decent person even. If I were giving advice to a young fellow of talent, with two or three facets to his mind, I would tell him by all means to keep his wit in the background, until after he had made a reputation by his more solid qualities.
     Holmes.

10,025. JOSEPH as a Type. Joseph is the eldest son of Jacob's younger and best beloved wife. Here, again, we get the two wives, as in a former instance, bringing out the same truth, though with some additions. Leah, the elder wife, has all her children before Rachel, the younger, has any. The Jewish dispensation had all its children before the Christian dispensation had any. Christ, the first-born from the grave, was the first son of the Rachel dispensation. This son, the beloved of his father, is cast out by his brethren, the children of the elder wife, and cast into Egypt, the constant type of the Gentile world. There, after a season of suffering and shame, he is exalted to be head over the kingdom, his wife is given him from out of the Gentiles, and then his brethren, the children of the first wife, know him. This type, I think, needs no explanation; if explanation be needed, the eleventh of Romans will supply it. The sin of the Jews, the elder brethren, is made the riches of the Gentiles for a season, until the elder brethren in need are brought to know and worship their brother, and are reconciled to him. *A. Jukes.*

10,026. JOSHUA, Character of. Joshua was, in every sense of the word, a great character, a saintly hero—the man not only of his age, but of many ages. If his name do not shine so conspicuously mid the galaxy of patriarchs and ancient worthies, it is very much because, as has been said of him, "the man himself is eclipsed by the brilliancy of his deeds;" like the sun in a gorgeous western sky, when the pile of amber-clouds, the golden linings and drapery with which he is surrounded, pale the lustre of the great luminary. *Macduff.*

10,027. JOY, Believer's. There is more joy in the penitential mournings of a believer than in all the mirth of a wicked man. I appeal to you that have had melted hearts, whether you have not found a secret content and sweetness in your mourning? So far from wishing to be rid of your meltings, you rather fear the removal of them. *Crisp.*

10,028. JOY, Biblical Emblems of. *Light* from heaven, pure, cheering, diffusive, often eclipsed, sweetest after gloom and darkness. *Singing and music*, the natural expression of cheerfulness and joy, especially at times of festivity and rejoicing. God giveth his beloved "songs in the night;" Zion's pilgrims "sing in the way;" "the ransomed of the Lord shall . . . . come to Zion . . . . with songs." *Dancing, leaping, shouting* for joy, Jer. 31: 13; Ps. 30: 11; Isa. 35: 6; Ezra 3: 12; Luke 6: 23; Acts 3: 8. *Seed* sown in the earth, awhile hidden, but, by its nature, in due time bursting into beauty, Ps. 97: 11. *The gladness of nature* in her times of joy. *The singing of birds* in early spring, Cant. 2: 12. *A desert land* blooming with beautiful and fragrant flowers, Is. 35: 1, 2. *A watered garden*, Jer. 31: 12. *The joy of festivity,—wine*, Ps. 104: 15; Cant. 1: 2; Isa. 25: 6; Zech. 10: 7. Christ's first miracle had a symbolical reference, doubtless, to the joy of his kingdom, John 2: 10. *Oil*—"the oil of gladness," Ps. 45: 7; "the oil of joy for mourning," Is. 61: 3; the festive anointing, Ps. 23: 5. *White garments*, Eccles. 9: 8; Rev. 3: 5. *The joy of the bride and bridegroom*, Isa. 61: 10; 62: 5; Jer. 33: 11. Rev. 21: 2. *The joy of harvest*, Isa. 9: 3;

Deut. 12: 7; Ps. 126: 5, 6, rejoicing in a finished work; joy natural, grateful, social. *The joy of victory*, "when men divide the spoil," Isa. 9: 3; Ps. 119: 162; 1 Sam. 30: 16. *The joy of a treasure found*, Matt. 13: 44. *A father's joy* in receiving home a long-lost son, Luke 15: 22–24; the joy of reconciliation. *Bowes.*

10,029. JOY Cometh in the Morning. Just as a man who has traveled in the dark, looks back at break of day from some lofty eminence on the way that he has gone, and admires the beauty and magnificence of objects that he passed, aware only of their existence and not their claims, or even deeming them objects of fear and not of delight, so the disciples, when enlightened from above, recalled the scenes and events of their Master's life, and rejoiced in much which at the time they had not understood, or which had even perplexed and grieved them. Thus was it especially with the death and departure of Christ. They were to his followers like the fabled statue of Memnon, which sent forth sounds, mournful in the night, but melodious at the rising of the sun: when God's morning light arose, how sweet the notes those facts, once only sad, emitted! *Morris.*

10,030. JOY, Cured by. Pope Julius II. was very ill of a fever, but on receiving a message that auxiliary forces were coming to him from the king of Spain, to help in an emergency, he was entirely cured.

10,031. JOY, Death from. We have the examples of the Roman lady who died for joy to see her son safe returned from the defeat of Cannæ; and of Sophocles, and Dionysius the tyrant, who died of joy; and of Talva, who died in Corsica, reading news of the honors the Roman senate had decreed in his favor. We have moreover one, in the time of Pope Leo the Tenth, who upon the news of the taking of Milan, a thing he had so ardently and passionately desired, was wrapt with so sudden an excess of joy that he immediately fell into a fever and died. *Montaigne.*

10,032. JOY of Discovery. New discoveries of science have been followed by overpowering joy. Columbus was thrilled with rapture as indications of land began to appear in the Saragassa sea. Sea-weeds came drifting across the track of the ships; land birds of beautiful plumage circled around the masts; the air became mild and fragrant; "it wanted but the song of the nightingale to make it like the month of April in Andalusia." All the October night before the shadows lifted on the new world, the pulses of the Spaniards throbbed with expectant joy. In the gold of the sunrise Columbus fell upon the earth and kissed it. Tears of joy streamed from his eyes when the banner of Castile was unrolled in the breeze. *Te Deums* rose with the morning songs of the birds. A new world had rewarded the prayers and toils and struggles of a great adventurer. *Morning Star.*

10,033. JOY, Ecstasy of. Mithridates, king of Asia, became interested in an old musician who had performed at a feast for him. One morning on awaking, the old man saw the tables in his house covered with vessels of silver and gold, a number of servants around him, who offered him rich garments, and a horse standing at the door, as it was usual among the king's friends. He was astonished, and would fain have fled out of the house. But the servants detained him; and told him that the inheritance of a rich man had been conferred upon him by the king, and that these were but the first-fruits of his fortune. At last, believing the reports, he put on the purple robe, mounted the horse, and as he rode through the city, cried out, "All these are mine! All these are mine!" Greater treasures are the gift of Christ to every believer. Shall he not rejoice evermore?

10,034. JOY, Eternal. The sufferings of the just may well be likened to fleeting shadows or passing dreams. As soon as the bright morning of eternity begins to dawn, the shadows of mortality are forever dissipated; and they forget at once, in the glorious light of God's majesty, the tribulations which they have endured for his cause. The unspeakable joys of which they partake so absorb all their faculties, that there is no room left for sorrow or suffering. If, indeed, their past trials are remembered by them, it is but to swell with fresh rapture, and to tune their voices to louder anthems in the praise of him who has given them, in exchange for the cross, such an exceeding and eternal weight of glory.
Massillon.

10,035. JOY, Fatal. Diagoras, of Rhoades, had three sons, young men, who were all crowned victors in the Olympic games in one day. The sons came and embraced their aged father, and each placed their wreath upon his head. He was so overcome with excess of delight, that he fell into their arms and died.

10,036. JOY, Health from. Joy is one of the greatest panaceas of life. No joy is more healthful, or better calculated to prolong life, than that which is to be found in domestic happiness, in the company of cheerful and good men, and in contemplating with delight the beauties of nature. A day spent in the country, under a serene sky, amidst a circle of agreeable friends, is certainly a more positive means of prolonging life than all the vital elixirs in the world. *Hukeland.*

10,037. JOY in Religion. Some people are afraid of anything like joy in religion. They have none themselves, and they do not love to see it in others. Their religion is something like the stars, very high and very clear, but very cold. When they see tears of anxiety, or tears of joy, they cry out, Enthusiasm! enthusiasm! "I sat down under his shadow with great delight." Is this enthusiam? "May the God of hope fill you with all joy and peace in believing." If it be really in sitting under the shadow of Christ, let there be no bounds to our joy. Oh! if God would but open our eyes and give us simple childlike faith to look to Jesus, to sit under his shadow, then would songs of joy arise from all our dwellings.

"Rejoice in the Lord always, and again I say, Rejoice." *M'Cheyne.*

10,038. JOY, Spiritual. The Christian has a *fons perennies* within him. He is satisfied from himself. The men of the world borrow all their joy from without. Joy wholly from without is false, precarious, and short. From without it may be gathered, but like gathered flowers, though fair and sweet for a season, it must soon wither and become offensive. Joy from within is like smelling the rose on the tree, it is more sweet and fair, and I must add, it is immortal. *Salter.*

10,039. JOY, Testimony of. Bapa Padmanji, one of the native converts in India, said in a private letter, "How I long for my bed! Not that I may sleep—I lie awake often and long! but to hold sweet communion with my God. What shall I render unto him for all his revelations and gifts to me? Were there no historical evidence of the truth of Christianity, were there no well-established miracles, still I should believe that the religion propagated by the fishermen of Galilee is divine. The holy joys it brings to me must be from heaven. Do I write this boastingly, brother? Nay, it is with tears of humble gratitude that I tell of the goodness of the Lord."

10,040. JUDGE, No Man His Own. One of the first motives to civil society, and which becomes one of its fundamental laws, is that no man should be judge in his own cause. By this each person has at once divested himself of the first fundamental right of uncovenanted man, that is to judge for himself and to assert his own cause. He abdicates all right to be his own governor. He inclusively in a great measure abandons the right of self-defence, the first law of nature. Men cannot enjoy the rights of an uncivil and a civil state together. That he may obtain justice, he gives up the right of determining what it is in points the most essential to him. That he may secure some liberty, he makes a surrender in trust of the whole of it. *Burke.*

10,041. JUDGMENT, Book of. It is possible that all thoughts are in themselves imperishable; and that if the intelligent faculty should be rendered more comprehensive, it would require only a different and duly proportioned organization—the body celestial instead of the body terrestial—to bring before every human soul the collective experience of its whole past existence. And this—this, perchance, is the dread Book of Judgment, in whose mysterious hieroglyphics every idle word is recorded. Yea, in the very nature of a living soul, it may be more possible that heaven and earth should pass away, than that a single act, a single thought, should be loosened or lost from that living chain of causes, to all whose links, conscious or unconscious, the free will, our only absolute self, is co-extensive and co-present.
Coleridge.

10,042. JUDGMENT, Excuses at the. I wish every man who argues against the Christian religion would take this one serious thought along with him, that he must one day, if he

believes that God will judge the world, argue the case once more at the judgment-seat of God; and let him try his reasons accordingly. Do you reject the gospel, because you will admit nothing that pretends to be a revelation? Consider well. Is it a reason that you will justify to the face of God? Will you tell him that you had resolved to receive no positive commands from him, nor to admit any of his declarations for law? If it will not be a good reason then, it is not a good reason now; and the stoutest heart will tremble to give such an impious reason to the Almighty, which is a plain defiance to his wisdom and authority.
Sherlock.

10,043. JUDGMENT, First in the. There is a tradition among the Mohammedans that the Jews will be the first to be judged—that God will reproach them before the assembled world, and condemn them, and order them to hell.

10,044. JUDGMENT, Indifference to the. When Channing was a boy of ten years, he heard Dr. Hopkins preach a forcible sermon on the reasonableness of a future judgment. He was deeply impressed, and expected his father, who was a deacon of the Congregational church, to speak to him about his soul's salvation. He did not utter a word in regard to the sermon, or his danger, but, on reaching home, sat down to read. Dr. Channing says, "I made up my mind that my father did not believe one word that he had heard. He was not alarmed, why should I be? and I dismissed the whole subject from my thoughts." His father's thoughtlessness drove him into the ranks of heterodoxy, and he became the champion of Unitarianism.

10,045. JUDGMENT, Legend of. Moses, a monk of Scete in Egypt, was called upon to judge a brother overtaken in a fault. He refused; but being again called, filled a basket with sand, and placing it upon his back, went to the court. They asked, "O Father! what art thou doing?" He answered, "My sons, all my sins are behind my back following me, and I see them not, and shall I judge this day the sins of another man?"

10,046. JUDGMENT, Lesson of the. A young man who graduated at West Point said, so intense was the feeling and anxiety felt with regard to the final examination at the close of the course, that the first scholar in his class fainted and fell at the first question asked him. He felt that his standing in the profession he had chosen was now at stake, that his future position depended upon the manner in which he acquitted himself. If the loss or gain of a little worldly distinction could so move a man, what must be the feeling of the soul as it stands alone at the bar of God? We shall be judged as individuals. West Point honors are but for the little moment of time here, but the results of this final examination are for eternity. The cadet keeps this examination constantly in view. He studies and drills with the wrestler's earnestness to attain a high standing at the close. How strange that we so lose sight of this solemn hour! There are often mistakes made in worldly judgment, but there will be no mistake there. *S. S. Times.*

10,047. JUDGMENT, Prejudice in. Nero thought no person chaste, because he was so unchaste himself. Such as are troubled with the jaundice see all things yellow. Those who are most religious, are least censorious. "Who art thou that judgest another man's servant!" Those who are fellow creatures with men, should not be fellow judges with God. *Secker.*

10,048. JUDGMENT, Question of the. "Will my case be called to-day?" said an eager client to his lawyer. "Are you sure that nothing is left undone? If judgment is pronounced against me, I am a ruined man." The lawyer was a Christian man, and he inquired, "What if my case come on to-day before the eternal judge, whose sentence there is no reversing! am I prepared?"

10,049. JUDGMENT, Reversal of. Philip, king of the Macedonians, fell asleep while hearing a case. Suddenly awakening, he gave an unjust sentence. The injured person cried out, "I appeal." The king, with indignation, asked, "To whom?" He replied, "From yourself sleeping to yourself waking." The king reheard the case and reversed the judgment.

10,050. JUDGMENT, The Sinner at the. At the day of judgment, the attention excited by the surrounding scene, the strange aspect of nature, the dissolution of the elements, and the last trump, will have no other effect than to cause the reflections of the sinner to return with a more overwhelming tide on his own character, his sentence, his unchanging destiny; and amidst the innumerable millions who surround him, he will mourn apart. It is thus the Christian minister should endeavor to prepare the tribunal of conscience, and turn the eyes of every one of his hearers on himself.
Robert Hall.

10,051. JUDGMENT, Slighting the. A man would be counted a fool to slight a judge before whom he is to have a trial of his whole estate. The trial we have before God is of otherwise importance; it concerns our eternal happiness or misery; and yet dare we affront him?
Bunyan.

10,052. JUDGMENT, Storm of. As that storm roars the loudest which has been the longest gathering, so God's reckoning day with sinners, by being long coming, will be the more terrible when it comes. *Guthrie.*

10,053. JUDGMENT, The Worldling at the. Chosroes, King of Persia, in conversation with two philosophers and his vizier, asked, "What situation of man is most to be deplored?" One of the philosophers maintained that it was old age, accompanied with extreme poverty; the other, that it was to have the body oppressed by infirmities, the mind worn out, and the heart broken by a heavy series of misfortunes. "I know a condition more to be pitied," said the vizier, "and it is that of him who has passed through life without doing good, and who, unexpectedly surprised by death, is sent to appear before the tribunal of the sovereign Judge." *Whitecross.*

10,054. JUDGMENT-DAY, Anticipating the. Philip the Third, of Spain, whose life was free from gross evils, professed, "that he would rather lose his kingdom than offend God willingly;" yet being in the agony of death, and considering more thoroughly of his account he was to give to God, fear struck into him, and these words brake from him: "Oh! would to God I had never reigned. Oh that those years that I have spent in my kingdom, I had lived a solitary life in the wilderness! Oh that I had lived a solitary life with God! How much more securely should I now have died! How much more confidently should I have gone to the throne of God! What doth all my glory profit me, but that I have so much the more torment in my death?" God keeps an exact account of every penny that is laid out on him and his, and that is laid out against him and his; and this in the day of account men shall know and feel, though now they wink and will not understand. The sleeping of vengeance causeth the overflowing of sin, and the overflowing of sin causeth the awakening of vengeance. Abused mercy will certainly turn into fury. God's forbearance is no quittance. The day is at hand when he will pay wicked men for the abuse of old and new mercies. If he seem to be slow, yet he is sure. He hath leaden heels, but iron hands. The farther he stretcheth his bow, or draweth his arrow, the deeper he will wound in the day of vengeance. Men's actions are all in print in heaven, and God will, in the day of account, read them aloud in the ears of all the world, that they may all say Amen to that righteous sentence that he shall pass upon all despisers and abusers of mercy. *Brooks.*

10,055. JUDGMENT-DAY, Appeal to the. I am content to wait till the judgment-day for the clearing up of my character; and, after I am dead, I desire no other epitaph than this, "Here lies George Whitefield." What sort of a man he was the great day will discover. *Whitefield.*

10,056. JUDGMENT-DAY, Certainty of the. The bringing into judgment is a thing which is known by reason, and is clear by the light of nature; wherefore, in Austria, one of the nobles dying, who had lived fourscore and thirteen years, and had spent all his life in pleasures and delights, never being troubled with any infirmity, and this being told to Frederick the emperor, "From hence," saith he, "we may conclude the soul's immortality; for if there be a God that ruleth this world, as divines and philosophers do teach, and that he is just no one denieth, surely there are other places to which souls after death do go, and do receive for their deeds either reward or punishment; for here we see that neither rewards are given to the good, nor punishment to the evil." *Brooks.*

10,057. JUDGMENT-DAY, Disclosures of the. The philosophic historian is expected not only to tell us that certain events occurred, but also to trace them to their origin, and tell how it was they were brought about; the skillful physician is expected not only to discern the marks of disease, but also to trace it to its source, and tell us what functions are deranged; but, in arguing from the seen and known to the unseen and the unknown, how often, how grievously do they err. A time, however, is coming when there shall be a great bringing together of causes and effects, of motives and actions, and when no mistake shall be made—that time is the judgment day; then it shall be seen not only what men did, but why they did it. *Power.*

10,058. JUDGMENT-DAY, Discoursing on the. When Jonathan Edwards preached at Enfield, there was "such a breathing of distress," that he was compelled to stop, and request the people to retain their composure. He discoursed on the judgment to come, as if he were standing on "the sides of eternity," and the people heard him as if they were listening to the sound of "the last trump," or to their own sentences of condemnation from the lips of the Son of God. *Turnbull.*

10,059. JUDGMENT-DAY, Impartiality of the. All the senates that ever were convened, and all the assemblies that ever met upon business or pleasure; all the armies that were ever conducted into the field, and all the generals who conducted them; in a word, all the men and women that shall have lived, from the first pair to their last born son and daughter, are to appear together, and to take their respective trials at the day of the great assize. High and low, rich and poor, learned and unlearned, will then be distinguished only by their virtues and their vices; so that the whole world shall perceive and acknowledge that "God is no respecter of persons." The injured virgin, the afflicted widow, and the oppressed orphan, shall then see those, face to face, who have spoiled them of their innocence, their reputation, or their substance. There men shall meet all those who seduced them, or whom they have seduced, into the ways of sin; and all those who have directed and encouraged them, or whom they have directed and encouraged, to proceed in the paths of righteousness. From the former they shall turn away with shame and fear; the latter they shall behold with joy and rejoicing. There they shall view the wisdom of religion in the persons of the righteous, and wonder why they did not see it before, and get themselves up to the study of it; there they shall clearly behold the folly of irreligion, in the persons of the wicked, and be astonished at their insensibility in following so hard after it. Amidst all this unimaginable multitude there shall not be one idle and unconcerned spectator; not one that shall have leisure to trouble himself with the affairs of his neighbor. Every man will have a cause to be heard, and how will he be straitened until it be determined! *Bishop Horne.*

10,060. JUDGMENT-DAY, Lessons of the. Methinks neither the voice of the archangel, nor the trump of God, nor the dissolution of the elements, nor the face of the Judge itself, from which the heavens will flee away, will he

so dismaying and terrible to these men as the sight of the poor members of Christ; whom, having spurned and rejected in the days of their humiliation, they will then behold with amazement united to their Lord, covered with his glory, and seated on his throne. How will they be astonished to see them surrounded with so much majesty! How will they cast down their eyes in their presence! How will they curse that gold which will then eat their flesh as with fire, and that avarice, that indolence, that voluptuousness, which will entitle them to so much misery! You will then learn that the imitation of Christ is the only wisdom: you will then be convinced it is better to be endeared to the cottage than admired in the palace; when to have wiped the tears of the afflicted, and inherited the prayers of the widow and the fatherless, shall be found a richer patrimony than the favor of princes.
Robert Hall.

10,061. JUDGMENT-DAY, Methods of the. Memory will answer the books which shall be opened at the Judgment, recording the deeds done in the body, as face answers face in a mirror. There will be a perfect correspondence between the subjective and the objective record. The finest lines, the most delicate light and shade, will be identical in each picture. God's omniscience treasures eternally, unchangeably, every lightest thought and intent of every created mind. There is an absolute record of all finite activity, outside the agent. We cannot conceive how it is kept, but we know that it is exact, infallible, exhaustive, because it is God's record. At the Judgment, the human soul, willing or unwilling, will take the witness-stand. Memory will identify every deed done in the body. The drowning recall everything. Lines written with invisible ink become legible when exposed to light. Earthly life will be read again, not a line or word erased. Conscience will acknowledge the perfect justice of God's law. Human reason will approve of the exact application of that law to the precise facts in the life of every individual. Sin will be compelled " to the teeth and forehead of its faults to give in evidence." Every knee shall bow, every mouth shall be stopped. The lustre of the great white throne will throw its beams to illuminate the remotest universe. In the response of memory to God's eternal record, the soul will walk down a hall of mirrors, where every act of its earthly life was not on one side, but on all sides, at every instant photographed, to be preserved forever. The transient shall be made permanent. Earthly life shall be the base, the pedestal on which the future eternal life shall rise. According to the foundation shall be the superstructure. Every pillar in the temple of God will remind us of earth. As it rises upward and upward, still it shall reveal the lines first sketched in time. The inconceivable future beyond Resurrection will ever refer back to the twofold but identical records, the memory of man, and the judgment books of God.
Dr. Boardman.

10,062. JUDGMENT-DAY, Separation at the. The Seer in the Shepherd of Hermas is shown a number of trees, all which, while it is winter, are alike without their leaves, and seeming, therefore, to him all alike dead; and he is told that as the dry and the green trees are not distinguishable from one another in the winter, while all alike are leafless and bare, so neither in the present age are the just from sinners. The second time he is shown the trees, but now some of them are putting forth leaves, while others are still remaining bare. Thus shall it be in the future age, which for the just shall be a summer, and they shall be declared openly, while their hidden life shall then manifest itself; but for the sinners it shall still be winter, and they, remaining without leaf or fruit, shall as dry wood be cut down for the burning. *R. C. Trench.*

10,063. JUDGMENTS, Divine. The whole design of men's preservation hath been beaten in pieces by some unforeseen circumstance, so that judgments have broken in upon them without control, and all their subtleties been outwitted: the strange crossing of some in their estates, though the most wise, industrious, and frugal persons, and that by strange and unexpected ways; and it is observable how often everything contributes to carry on a judgment intended, as if they rationally designed it: all these loudly proclaim a God in the world; if there were no God, there would be no sin; if no sin, there would be no punishment. *Charnock.*

10,064. JUDGMENTS, Uncharitable. We cannot be guilty of a greater act of uncharitableness than to interpret the afflictions which befall our neighbors as punishments and judgments. It aggravates the evil to him who suffers, when he looks upon himself as the mark of divine vengeance, and abates the compassion of those towards him who regard him in so dreadful a light. This humor of turning every misfortune into a judgment, proceeds from wrong notions of religion, which in its own nature produces good will towards men, and puts the mildest construction upon every accident that befalls them. In this case, therefore, it is not religion that sours a man's temper, but it is his temper that sours his religion. *Addison.*

10,065. JUSTICE, Advantage of. The surest and most pleasant path to universal esteem and true popularity is to be just; for all men esteem him most who secures most their private interest, and protects best their innocence. And all who have any notion of a Deity believe that justice is one of his chief a tributes; and that, therefore, whoever is just is next in nature to him, and the best picture of him, and to be reverenced and loved. *Mackenzie.*

10,066. JUSTICE, Appeal for. An imprisoned minister instructed a nobleman to make his appeal for justice as follows: "I desire you to make known my lamentable case to Her Majesty's honorable Privy Council, or to Her Majesty herself, that the cause of my imprisonment may be examined, and that I may be delivered from this hard usage. For I desire justice, and not mercy, being conscious of my own innocency. My old adversary, the archbishop (Whitgift), hath treated me more like a Turk or a dog, than a man, or a minister of Jesus Christ."

10,067. JUSTICE, Appeal from. King Canute, of Denmark, undertook to clear his realm of robbers and pirates. Of these last he had captured several, and when they were about to be executed one of them cried out that he was of royal blood, and related to Canute. The king replied that, to honor his extraction, he should be hung from the top of the highest mast of his ship, which was done.

10,068. JUSTICE, Definition of. Justice, as defined in the institutes of Justinian, nearly two thousand years ago, and as it is felt and understood by all who understand human relations and human rights is : *"Constans et perpetua voluntas, jus suum cuique tribuere"*—a constant and perpetual will to render to every one that which is his own.   *J. Q. Adams.*

10,069. JUSTICE, Doing. One hour in the execution of justice is worth seventy years of prayer.   *Mohammed.*

10,070. JUSTICE, Execution of. Spitigneus, Prince of Bohemia, was stopped while riding out by a woman who implored him to listen to her plea. He told her to await his return. She told him it would prove dangerous to her, for that she was to make her appearance in an hour or else forfeit her bond. The prince endeavored to refer the woman to other judges, but she cried out, "That he himself, and not others, was the judge whom God had appointed her." He alighted from his horse, and with great patience, for two hours, gave attention to the cause of the poor woman.

10,071. JUSTICE, First. When about to take a collection, Rowland Hill said: "From the great sympathy I have witnessed in your countenances, and the strict attention you have honored me with, there is only one thing I am afraid of, that some of you may feel inclined to give too much. Now it is my duty to inform you that justice, though not so pleasant, yet should always be a prior virtue to generosity; therefore, as you will all immediately be waited upon in your respective pews, I wish to have it thoroughly understood that no person will think of putting anything into the plate who cannot pay his debts."

10,072. JUSTICE, Hand of. Slow goes the hand of justice, like the shadow on the sun-dial; ever moving, yet creeping slowly on, with a motion all but imperceptible. Still stand in awe. The hand of justice has not stopped. Although imperceptible, it steadily advances; by and by it reaches the tenth, eleventh, and twelfth hour. And now the bell strikes. Then, unless you have fled to Christ, the blow, which was so slow to fall, shall descend over the head of impenitence with accumulated force.   *Dr. Guthrie.*

10,073. JUSTICE, Hatred of. When the Athenians were fully bent to banish Aristides by ostracism, an illiterate country-fellow came to him with his shell, and asked him to write in it the name of Aristides. "Friend," said he "do you know Aristides?" "Not I," said the fellow; "but I do not like his surname of Just." He said no more, but wrote his name in the shell and gave it him. Thus the truest man in Athens was banished from the city, because of the popular hatred of virtue.

10,074. JUSTICE, Inexorable. How astonishing was the rigid justice of Brutus the Elder, who, in spite of all the passions of a father, passed sentence of death upon his own sons, for conspiring against the liberty of their country! While the amiable youths stood trembling and weeping before him, and hoping their tears would be the most powerful defence with a father; while the senate whisper for the moderation of the punishment, and that they might escape with banishment; while his fellow-consul is silent; while the multitude tremble and expect the decision with horror;—the inexorable Brutus rises, in all the stern majesty of justice, and turning to the lictors, who were the executioners, says to them, "To you, lictors, I deliver them." In this sentence he persisted, inexorable, notwithstanding the weeping intercession of the multitude, and the cries of the young men, calling upon their father by the most endearing names. The lictors seized them, stripped them naked, bound their hands behind them, beat them with rods, and then struck off their heads; the inexorable Brutus looking on the bloody spectacle with unaltered countenance. Thus the father was lost in the judge; the love of justice overcame all the fondness of the parent; private interest was swallowed up in regard for the public good, and the honor and security of government. This, perhaps, is the most striking resemblance of the justice of Deity that can be found in the history of mankind. But how far short does it fall! How trifling were the sufferings of these youths, compared with those of the Son of God! They, too, were criminals—he was holy and free from sin. How insignificant the law and government for which they suffered, to that of the divine!
          Davies.

10,075. JUSTICE, Interest in, Solon, being asked what city was best modeled, replied. "That, where those who are not injured are no less ready to prosecute and punish offenders than those who are."

10,076. JUSTICE, Motto of. The Emperor Maximilian's motto was, *"Fiat justitia ruat cœlum;"* "Let justice be done, though the heavens fall."

10,077. JUSTICE, Mal-administration of. If they which employ their labor and travail about the public administration of justice, follow it only as a trade, with unquenchable thirst of gain, being not in heart persuaded that justice is God's own work, and themselves his agents in this business—the sentence of right, God's own verdict, and themselves his priests to deliver it; formalities of justice do but serve to smother right; and that which was necessarily ordained for the common good is, through shameful abuse, made the cause of common misery. *Hooker.*

10,078. JUSTICE, March of. God's justice on offenders goes not always in the same path nor the same pace; and he is not pardoned for the the fault who is for a while reprieved from the punishment. "Yea, sometimes the guest in the inn goes quietly to bed before the reckoning for his supper is brought to him to discharge." *Fuller.*

10,079. JUSTICE, Memorial of. Near Potsdam (Prussia), in the reign of Frederick King of Prussia, was a mill which interfered with a view from the windows of Sans Souci. Annoyed by this inconvenience to his favorite residence, the king sent to inquire the price for which the mill would be sold by the owner. "For no price," was the reply of the sturdy Prussian; and in a moment of anger, Frederick gave orders that the mill should be pulled down. "The king may do this," said the miller, quietly folding his arms, "but there are laws in Prussia;" and forthwith he commenced proceedings against the monarch, the result of which was, the court sentenced Frederick to rebuild the mill, and to pay besides a large sum of money as compensation for the injury which he had done. The king was mortified, but had the magnanimity to say, addressing himself to his courtiers, "I am glad to find that just laws and upright judges exist in my kingdom." A few years ago, the head of the honest miller's family, who had in due course of time succeeded to the hereditary possession of his little estate, finding himself, after a long struggle with losses occasioned by the war, which brought ruin into many a house besides his own, involved in pecuniary difficulties that had become insurmountable, wrote to the then king of Prussia, reminding him of the refusal experienced by Frederick the Great at the hands of his ancestors, and stating that if his majesty now entertained a similar desire to obtain possession of the property, it would be very agreeable to him, in his present embarrassed circumstances, to sell the mill. The king immediately wrote, with his own hand, the following reply: "My dear neighbor:—I cannot allow you to sell the mill; it must remain in your possession as long as one member of your family exists; for it belongs to the history of Prussia. I lament, however, to hear that you are in circumstances of embarrassment; and therefore send you 6000 dollars (about £1000 sterling) to arrange your affairs, in the hope that this sum will be sufficient for the purpose. Consider me always your affectionate neighbor, *Frederick William.*"

10,080. JUSTICE, Regard for. Mahomet II. executed his own son, Mustapha, for adultery. The emperor Otho the First caused the head of a man, who had committed a rape, to be cut off, though the woman had condoned the crime by marrying the man. The emperor said, "A collusion among yourselves cannot make void the law."

10,081. JUSTICE, Sacrifice for. Phocion would not so much as appear in behalf of his son-in-law, Charicles, when he was accused for having taken money of Harpalus; but having said, "Only for acts of justice have I made you my son-in-law," went his way. And Timoleon, the Corinthian, when he could not by admonitions or requests dissuade his brother from being a tyrant, confederated with his destroyers.
Plutarch.

10,082. JUSTICE in Sodom. When Eliezer, the servant of Abraham, came to to the city of Sodom, he saw an inhabitant of that city maltreating a stranger and robbing him of his clothes. "Why dost thou rob the poor stranger?" exclaimed Eliezer, enraged; "how darest thou commit such a crime?" "Art thou," asked the robber, "this man's brother, or our judge?" Eliezer made no reply, but went about to assist the stranger. Thereupon the robber picked up a stone, hurled it at Eliezer, and struck him on the forehead. The blood began instantly to flow from the painful wound, and Eliezer stood perplexed, unable to stop the streaming blood. He thought the villain would regret his rash misdeed, but the latter saucily cried, "How beautifully the blood is trickling down—how beautifully!" "Thou hast wounded," exclaimed Eliezer, "nay, thou hast almost killed me, and dost thou even deride me? I shall obtain justice! I am going directly to the court!" "That is just the place where I wish to go with thee," cried the audacious villain. A vast crowd of the inhabitants had in the meantime gathered around them; they seized the screaming Eliezer, and dragged him to the residence of the judge. "Stranger," exclaimed the latter, "why dost thou raise such a tumult in our peaceful city?" "I am a peaceable man," replied Eliezer; "I saw a stranger in thy city robbed, and when I wished to help him this man cast a stone at my forehead, mocked me, and in connection with his associates dragged me hither. Behold what a wound he has struck; see how the blood flows." "Then," said the judge gravely, "thou must pay him eight silver shekels, for this is the price which the surgeons of this city charge for blood-letting!" Such was the decision of the judge of Sodom. *Hood.*

10,083. JUSTICE, True. The Thebans represented true justice as having neither hands nor eyes, for the judge should neither receive bribes nor respect persons. The English for similar reasons picture her with a sword in one hand, scales in the other, and bandaged eyes. Whatever doubt there may be as to the justice of the earthly judge, there can be none as to that of the heavenly.

10,084. JUSTICE, Unspotted. The idea that the judicial officer is supposed to be vested with ermine, though fabulous and mythical, is yet more eloquent in its significance. We are told that the little creature called ermine is so sensitive to its own cleanliness that it becomes paralyzed and powerless at the slightest touch of defilement upon its snow-white fur. When the hunters are pursuing it, they spread with mire the pass leading to its haunts, to wards which they then draw it, knowing that it will submit to be captured rather than defile itself. And a like sensibility should belong to him who comes to exercise the august functions of judge.   *John S. T. Sneed.*

10,085. JUSTIFICATION, Attendant of. Justification regards something done for us; sanctification something done in us. The one is a change in our state, the other in our nature. The one is perfect, the other gradual. The one is derived from the obedience of the Saviour, the other from his spirit. The one gives us a title to heaven, the other a meetness for it. Suppose you had a son—you forbade him to enter a place of contagion on pain of losing all you could leave him. He goes, and is seized with the infection. He is guilty, for he has transgressed your command, but he is also diseased. Do you not perceive that your forgiving does not heal him? He wants not only the father's pardon, but the physician's aid. In vain is he freed from the forfeiture of his estate, if he be left under the force of the disorder.   *Jay.*

10,086. JUSTIFICATION, Constituents of. Justification consists of these two parts—remission and acceptance. Remission of sins takes away our liableness to death; acceptance of our persons gives us a title unto life. Now, to be free from our obnoxiousness to death, and instated in a right to eternal life, these two constitute a perfect justification. For, to be accepted of God in Christ, is no other than for God, through the righteousness and obedience of Christ imputed to us, to own and acknowledge us to have a right to heaven.   *Hopkins.*

10,087. JUSTIFICATION, Means of. "How do you think you are to be justified before God?" said an Irish clergyman to a man in his parish. "How, sir? By the righteousness of Christ, to be sure!" "Well, but I want you to inform me what you understand by the righteousness of Christ," rejoined the clergyman. The man hesitated for a moment, and then replied: "Suppose, sir, I want to go to Limerick. I go down to the railway station, and try to get into a carriage. A porter comes up to me and asks for my ticket. I am obliged to tell him I have none, and have no money to buy one. He pushes me back, and says I must not go. A kind, rich man is standing by; he says to me, 'I will purchase a ticket for you.' This he does, and hands it to me. I show it to the porter, who then allows me to get into a carriage, and away I go to Limerick. In the same way I want to go to heaven. I have no way of purchasing the title to it. Jesus sees my anxiety to go; he died to pay the debt of my sins; he gives me his righteousness; I show this to God; and as the railway ticket admitted me to the train, this gives me a title to heaven which of myself I did not possess, and by my own power I could never have obtained."

10,088. KEEPER, The Lord Our. A pious friend of the late Duncan Matheson, dying, ordered the following to be put on his tombstone: "J. McP——. Born,——. Died,——. Kept."

10,089. KINDNESS, Acts of. In the inte course of social life, it is by little acts of watchful kindness recurring daily and hourly—and the opportunities of doing kindnesses, if sought for are forever starting up,—it is by words, by tones, by gestures, by looks, that affection is won and preserved. He who neglects these trifles, yet boasts that, whenever a great sacrifice is called for, he shall be ready to make it, will rarely be loved. The likelihood is, he will not make it; and if he does, it will be much rather for his own sake than for his neighbor's. Many persons, indeed, are said to be penny-wise and pound-foolish! but they who are penny-foolish will hardly be pound-wise; although selfish vanity may now and then for a moment get the better of selfish indolence; for wisdom will always have a microscope in her hand.   *Sala*

10,090. KINDNESS, Biblical. *Rahab*—amply rewarded for preserving the life of the spies by the preservation of herself and family, Joshua 2: 18. *Jonathan's* kindness to David, which led to his children's preservation, 2 Sam. 9: 7; 21: 7. *The centurion's* anxiety for the welfare of his sick servant, was the cause of his own faith being confirmed. He built the Jews a synagogue, and they interceded for him to Christ, Luke 7: 2–10. *The good Samaritan*—an example of genuine kindness shown to a stranger, without regard to personal claim, race or religion, Luke 10: 30–37. *Cornelius*, Acts 10: 4. *The barbarous people of Melita*, very fully repaid for their kindness to the shipwrecked mariners, Acts 28: 1–10.   *Bowes.*

10,091. KINDNESS, Christ's Approval of. I shall never forget my own feelings when, distant once in the land of Palestine, I was ill, and knew not when I should return. In that distant land I received a letter from my family, and in that letter it was stated that a dear friend had given a token of regard to my youngest child, then a comparative infant, and my heart swelled more with affection for that friend than had he sent a token of affection to me. It was given to the smallest of my children, the little one, and he had done it unto me; and my heart, half across the globe, swelled with affection to a friend I could not see, because he had remembered a little one. So the great Father has his little ones scattered all over our land, in hovels, in cellars, in garrets, and abodes of affliction, and in scenes of poverty, and he sees when an act of kindness is done to one of the least of them, and in the heaven of heavens he says, "Inasmuch as ye have done it unto one of the least of these, ye have done it unto me."   *Bp. Simpson.*

10,092. KINDNESS, Duty of. The great duty of life is not to give pain; and the most acute reasoner cannot find an excuse for one who voluntarily wounds the heart of a fellow-creature. Even for their own sakes, people should show kindness and regard to their dependents. They are often better served in trifles, in proportion as they are rather feared than loved; but how small is this gain compared with the loss sustained in all the weightier affairs of life! Then the faithful servant shows himself at once as a friend, while one who serves from fear shows himself as an enemy.

Frederika Bremer.

10,093. KINDNESS, Greatest. I regard it as a singular kindness to man that he is selected to be the instrument of saving his fellow-men. The God of salvation, the Author and Finisher of our faith, might have arranged it otherwise. Who shall limit the Holy One of Israel? The field is the world. And as the husbandman ploughs his fields and sows his seed in spring by the same hands that bind the golden sheaves of autumn, God might have sent those angels to sow the gospel, who shall descend at the judgment to reap the harvest. But though these blessed and benevolent spirits, who are sent forth to minister for them who shall be heirs of salvation, take a lively interest in the work; though watching from on high the progress of a Redeemer's cause, they rejoice in each new jewel that adds lustre to his crown, and in every new province that is won for his kingdom; and though there be more joy even in heaven than on earth when man is saved, a higher joy among these angels over one sinner that repenteth than over ninety and nine just persons, yet theirs is little more than the pleasure of spectators. Theirs is the joy of the crowd who, occupying the shore, or clustered on its heights, with eager eyes and beating hearts follow the bold swimmer's movements, and watching his head as it rises and sinks among the waves, see him near the drowning child, and pluck from the billows their half-drowned prey; and, trembling lest strength should fail him, look on with anxious hearts, till, buffeting his way back, he reaches the strand, and amid their shouts and sympathies restores her boy to the arms of a fainting mother. *Dr. Guthrie.*

10,094. KINDNESS, Jewels of. Wandregisl was of noble blood, but desired to leave the court of king Dagobert, and become a monk. The king would not give his consent, and summoned him into his presence. The young man started for the palace and passed near the gate a poor man, struggling to right his cart, which had been upset in the mud. The courtiers passed by with no sympathy or proffer of aid, but with curses for encumbering the road. Wandregisl laid hold of the cart, righted it, set the poor man on his way, and became much soiled with mud in the good work. In this condition he went boldly into the presence of the king, and the courtiers greeted his appearance with derisive laughter. There, in answer to the king's question, he explained the reason of his soiled condition. The king was satisfied. The laughter of the courtiers ceased. To them the king said,

"Look and fix your gaze on the soiled raiment;
So the world its heroes pays with a sorry payment.   [royal,
But to me these mud-stains are jewels fair and
Sent by one who dwells afar, to his servant loyal."

So he won the king's permission to devote himself to the monastic life, and became the "patron saint of peasants."

10,095. KINDNESS, Mistaken. Once upon a time, there was a very kind-hearted little boy who owned a dog. He was deeply attached to the animal, and yet, notwithstanding his love, our little friend became convinced—such are the strange contradictions in human nature—that the dog's tail needed shortening. To be sure, the operation would occasion a deal of pain; but the tail was unsatisfactory (to the boy), and that was sufficient; it must come off. But here the tender-heartedness of the child rose beautifully to view. He felt that to cut it off all at once would occasion too much pain; and so, because he shrank from unnecessarily hurting the feelings of the dog, he concluded to cut it off an inch a day, till the desired length was "gradually" attained. Now I fearlessly affirm that if that dog's tail had to come off, it would have been far less exasperating to have it off at once, and not at the rate of an inch a day. *Verbum sap!*   *Evangelist.*

10,096. KINDNESS, Motive to. A man came to Poemen and said, "I have got a neighbor, and I am continually doing him little acts of kindness, yet I always find that there is self-satisfaction or some mean, unworthy motive mixed up with my interest. Shall I forbear?" Poemen answered, "There were two men who had fields. The one sowed corn and with it tares; the other sowed nothing, and his field was soon covered with weeds. He who had sowed corn and tares reaped a mixed crop, some good and some bad; but he saved the corn by sorting it from the tares. Which acted the best?" There could be but one answer.

10,097. KINDNESS Reciprocated. A lion was sleeping in his lair, when a mouse, not knowing where he was going, ran over the mighty beast's nose and awakened him. The lion clapped his paw upon the frightened little creature, and was about to make an end of him in a moment, when the mouse, in a pitiable tone, besought him to spare one who had so unconsciously offended, and not stain his honorable paw with so small a prey. The lion, smiling at his little prisoner's fright, generously let him go. Now it happened no long time after, that the lion, while ranging the woods for his prey, fell into the toils of the hunters: and finding himself entangled without hope of escape, set up a roar that filled the whole forest with its echo. The mouse, recognizing the voice of his former preserver, ran to the spot, and without more ado set to work to nibble the knot in the cord that bound the lion, and in a short time set the noble beast at liberty; thus convincing him that kindness is seldom thrown away, and that there is no creature so much below another but that he may have it in his power to return a good office. *Æsop.*

10,098. KINDNESS, Recompense of. The earnestness of a little girl in offering her chestnuts arrested the attention of a young man, and he gave her a shilling. She ran home with it to her sick mother. So small a gift made joy in the house. Years after a poor man called upon a rich bank director to ask for a position as messenger. The director's wife recognized him as he passed out as the donor of the shilling to her. She learned his business with her husband, and said, "Give him the situation." "Why?" said he. "Because I ask it as a favor, and you have promised me never to deny me a favor." He promised it, and that night sent a note to the applicant notifying him of his appointment. His wife explained the reason for her request to her husband, and he replied, "That is right, my little wife; never forget one who was kind to you in the days when you needed help most." The clerk received the note as he sat beside his sick wife. Opening it, he exclaimed, "Good news, wife! We shall not starve. Here is a promise of a situation." His wife called his attention to something which fell out upon the floor. It was a fifty-pound note, folded in a paper bearing the inscription, "In grateful remembrance of the silver shilling which a kind stranger bestowed on a little chestnut-girl twenty years ago."

10,099. KINDNESS, Record of. Mr. Cathcart kept a diary which was, "A memorial of acts of kindness, that as memory is liable to fail, and as the kindness and friendship of former times may be forgotten, the remembrance of friendly offices done to the writer or his family, or to his particular friends, might be preserved, in order that he may himself repay the debt in grateful acknowledgments while he lives, and that his family after him might know to whom their father owed obligations, and might feel every debt of gratitude due by him as an obligation on themselves."

10,100. KINDNESS, Requital of. There will come a time when three words uttered with charity and meekness, shall receive a far more blessed reward than three thousand volumes written with disdainful sharpness of wit. But the manner of men's writing must not alienate our hearts from the truth, if it appear they have the truth.　　*Hooker.*

10,101. KINDNESS, Self-Approbation of. Good and friendly conduct may meet with an unworthy, with an ungrateful, return; but the absence of gratitude on the part of the receiver cannot destroy the self-approbation which recompenses the giver: and we may scatter the seeds of courtesy and kindness around us at so little expense. Some of them will inevitably fall on good ground, and grow up into benevolence in the minds of others; and all of them will bear fruit of happiness in the bosom whence they spring. Once blest are all the virtues; twice blest sometimes.
Jeremy Bentham

10,102. KINDNESS, Testimonial to. There were a brother and sister who loved one another very much. He was the older, and was taken ill and died. They laid him out on his own little bed, and his mother took his little sister to look at him. She stood and looked at his sweet face, as white and cold as marble, and she wept very much. At last she said:

"Mother, may I take hold of his hand?" She placed it in hers, when the sister, lifting it up and stroking it gently, said: "This little hand never struck me!"

10,103. KINDNESS, Trifling. After Luther had returned from his trial before the emperor at Worms, much exhausted, to his hotel, the Roman Catholic Duke Eric, of Brunswick, sent him a glass of beer which he had first tasted. After drinking, Luther said, "As this day Duke Eric has remembered me, so may our Lord Jesus Christ remember him in the hour of his struggle." The servant reported the prayer to the Duke. When in old age the Duke came to die he ordered a servant to read the Bible to him. He opened and read, to the dying man's great comfort, "Whosoever shall give a cup of cold water to drink, in my name, verily I say unto you he shall not lose his reward."

10,104. KING, Exalted to be. After Alexander had deposed Strato, king of Sidon, he caused a new king to be appointed, and Abdalonimus, a remote descendant of the royal line, was fixed upon. The peculiarity of his case was his deep poverty, which was known to have been caused by his unswerving honesty. Alexander's agents found him weeding his garden. They saluted him king, and one of them, addressing him, said, "You must now change your tatters for the dress I have brought you. Put off the mean and contemptible habit in which you have grown old. Assume the garments of a prince; but when you are seated on the throne, continue to preserve the virtue which made you worthy of it. And when you shall have ascended it, and by that means become the supreme dispenser of life and death over all your citizens, be sure never to forget the condition in which, or rather for which, you were elected." Abdalonimus looked upon the whole as a dream, and, unable to guess the meaning of it, asked if they were not ashamed to ridicule him in that manner. He made a great resistance, but they themselves washed him, and threw over his shoulders a purple robe, richly embroidered with gold; then, after repeated oaths of their being in earnest, they conducted him to the palace. The news of this was immediately spread over the whole city. Most of the inhabitants were overjoyed at it, but some murmured, especially the rich, who, despising Abdalonimus's former abject state, could not forbear showing their resentment in the king's court. Alexander commanded the newly-elected prince to be sent for; and after surveying him attentively a long while, spoke thus: "Thy air and mien do not contradict what is related of thy extraction, but I should be glad to know with what frame of mind thou didst bear thy poverty?" "O king," replied he, "these hands have procured me all I desired; and whilst I possessed nothing, I wanted nothing." This answer gave Alexander a high idea of Abdalonimus's virtue; so that he presented him not only with all the rich furniture which had belonged to Strato, and part of the Persian plunder, but likewise annexed one of the neighboring provinces to his dominions.

10,105. KING, Parable of the Disguised. There was once a wise and powerful king, who, that he might the better acquaint himself with the actual condition of his people, determined to travel through his realm in disguise. So, laying aside his jeweled crown and his robes of state, and assuming the plain attire of a common peasant, he set out unobserved and unattended upon his journey. Of the many who met him day by day, few gave him more than a passing glance; for none suspected that beneath this ordinary and homely exterior was hid the form of their great sovereign, who had exchanged his crown for a cap, his scepter for a staff, and his palace for such chance lodging-places as he might find by the way. It happened that he stopped at a wayside inn for rest and food. On entering, he found that many other travelers had arrived before him, and among them he observed a knight whom he quickly recognized as a resident at his distant court. Scarcely any notice was taken of the disguised king, and at first not even the host himself seemed disposed to pay any attention to so humble a guest; until presently the king, advancing to the host as he sat the centre of a noisy knot of gossipers, made known his wants, when of a sudden the knight just mentioned, who had only momentarily glanced at the stranger to resume immediately the polishing of his scabbard, started at the sound, and springing to his feet, came forward with the exclamation, "Who is this?" "Only some beggarly peasant," replied the inkeeper, contemptuously eyeing the object of remark. For a moment the hum of voices hushed, and all eyes turned toward him whose appearance had provoked such a question and such an answer, while the knight drew still nearer to the mysterious stranger, as if to remove or confirm some suspicion that filled his mind. And before another word could be uttered the knight cried out, in tones which brought every one in the room to his feet: "This may be the dress of a peasant and of a beggar, but the voice is that of my lord the king!" *Krummacher.*

10,106. KINGDOM OF CHRIST, Belonging to the. The King of Prussia visited a village school, and was welcomed by the children. After their speaker had made a speech for them, he thanked them. Then taking an orange from a plate, he asked, "To what kingdom does this belong?" "The vegetable kingdom, sire," said a little girl. The king took a gold coin from his pocket, and, holding it up, asked, "And to what kingdom does this belong?" "To the mineral kingdom," said the little girl. "And to what kingdom do I belong, then?" asked the king. The little girl did not like to say "The animal kingdom." Just then it flashed into her mind that "God made man in his own image," and, looking up with a brightening eye, she said, "To God's kingdom, sire." The king was deeply moved. A tear stood in his eye. He placed his hand on the child's head, and said, most devoutly. "God grant that I may be accounted worthy of that kingdom." Thus did the words of a little child move the heart of a king. Little children, learn from this that even your words may do both good and harm. A pert word may wound the heart of a mother; a loving one may make it glad. My little children, let your words be kind, true, and right.

10,107. KINGDOM OF CHRIST, Feature of the. The Lord founded a kingdom, very unlike any other kingdom. He founded it without drum, or trumpet, or banner, or scepter, or throne, or crown. He founded it without geographical limits, without fortress, without fleets. He founded it as a kingdom whose foundations were laid in thought; as a kingdom whose wars were to be carried on in thought; as a kingdom whose instruments were those of thought; whose sword was not the sword in hand, but the sword that "proceedeth out of the mouth of God;" whose charter was the power of the Word; whose battle-field was only and ever the battle-field of thought. Into this world of thought Christ's kingdom came, to attack all who opposed; and in its own calm, searching, but irrepressible way, with a word, with a message, with an invitation, with an argument, with an exhortation, with an entreaty, with a continuous pointing upward, upward, as if it had a distinct connection with invisible powers, which it had; and "bringing into captivity every thought to the obedience of Christ;" thoughts high, thoughts deep, thoughts old, thoughts built upon the foundations, as men supposed, of everlasting principles; thoughts certainly reared up with all the elaborate beauty of human genius and of vast national toil; thoughts consolidated by the suffrage of ages, and thoughts adorned and enriched by the splendor of empires! What was the result? Of all other powers none has the hold upon human thought that Christ has at this moment, and there is none advancing year by year as in the kingdom of the Lord Christ. The world has been always talking of its feebleness and failure, but where is the power that will venture at this moment to say: "I will sweep Christ out of human thought."
                Dr. Wm. Arthur.

10,108. KINGDOM OF GOD, Preparation for the. Almost every one has been taught to pray daily, "Thy kingdom come." If you do not wish for his kingdom, don't pray for it. But, if you do, you must do more than pray for it; you must work for it. And to work for it, you must know what it is; we have all prayed for it many a day without thinking. Observe, it is a kingdom that is to come to us; we are not to go to it. Also, it is not to be a kingdom of the dead, but of the living. Also, it is not to come all at once, but quietly; nobody knows how. "The kingdom of God cometh not with observation." Also, it is not to come outside of us, but in the hearts of us: "The kingdom of God is within you." And being within us, it is not a thing to be seen, but to be felt; and though it brings all substance of good with it it does not consist in that: "The kingdom of

God is not meat and drink, but righteousness, peace, and joy in the Holy Ghost;" joy, that is to say, in the holy, healthful, and helpful spirit. Now, if we want to work for this kingdom, and to bring it and enter into it, there's just one condition to be first accepted. You must enter into it as children, or not at all: "Whosoever will not receive it as a little child, shall not enter therein."   *Ruskin.*

10,109. KINGDOM OF GRACE, Entering the. Major-General Burn relates that he had a dream shortly after the death of a brother, which changed the whole course of his life. He thought that they sat together on the old church-yard wall, when his brother asked him to go with him into the church. They started, passed through the porch, and the brother entered the door into the inner room, when it slid down, leaving the general out. He attempted to enter by stooping, but could not, as the door continued to slide down. Grieved at being left behind, he got down and tried to crawl through beneath the door with his clothes on, but failed. Then he threw off all his clothing but an embroidered silk waistcoat, bought in France, of which he was very proud, and tried to bore his way like a worm under the door, but could not get in. At last, in desperation, he drew off the waistcoat and forced his head under the door, and pressing his body so hardly upon the stones as to draw blood, he got safely through. He was at once clothed in white and surrounded by his brother and a goodly company of saints. With them he received the bread and wine in the Lord's Supper, and was filled with unspeakable ecstasy. He awoke singing the praises of God. From this dream he dates his conversion. The resolution and renunciation of all things necessary to salvation are herein illustrated.

10,110. KINGDOM OF HEAVEN, Closing the. A very high church clergyman of Brooklyn was recently called to attend a dying boy. He induced him to confess that he had attended a Methodist prayer-meeting, and to advise his irreligious father to be confirmed in the Episcopal church. After his death, this clergyman went about warning the children to keep away from the Methodist Sunday-school and prayer-meeting by the fate of this boy. "Ye neither enter yourselves nor suffer them that are entering to go in." Matt. 13: 13.

10,111. KINGDOM OF HEAVEN, Shutting the. A girl nine years old had attended a school, in which the children of Roman Catholics are taught by Protestants to read the Bible. She was taken very ill, and when there seemed no hope of her getting better, her parents sent for a popish priest. When he came, he said to her: "Child, you are in an awful state; you are just going to die. I beg you, before you depart, to make your dying request to your father and mother, that they will not send your brothers and sisters to the school that you went to." The little girl raised herself up in bed, and said, "My dear father and mother I make it my dying request, that you will send my brothers and sisters to that school; for there I was first taught that I was a sinner, and that I must depend alone upon Jesus Christ for salvation." She soon expired.

10,112. KING'S SON, Parable of the. There was once a king's son, who heard that the people in one of the king's countries a long way off used to be afraid of the king, and used to say that the king did not care for them. So he thought to himself, "I will go and teach them better." But he said, "If I go with my fine robes and crown, they will say, 'What do you know about a poor man's life? You do not know what it is to be cold and half naked and hungry.' I will put off my royal dress, and I will wear clothes like the poor people, and live and eat as they do." So he changed his clothes and left his palace, and went to that distant country, and there he lived among the poor, leading a harder life than any of them. And yet, though he was often hungry and cold, and sometimes did not know where to find a night's lodging, he never complained and never broke the laws. After he had lived in that country for some time, he went back to the king at home. It happened that soon afterward the people of the country sent messengers to the king to complain that the laws were too hard. The king's son then said to these messengers: "Believe me, the laws are all for the best, and the king loves you as though you were his own children." "Ah," said the messengers, "but you do not understand our way of life, how poor and miserable we are, and how hard it is to live." "You are wrong," said the prince; "I understand your life quite well, for I lived myself as a poor man among you for a long time. I know you have to suffer a good deal; every one of your troubles is known to me, for I have suffered the same things. Yet still I assure you that the king is very fond of you, and will make you perfectly happy in the end." Then the people, when they heard that the king's son had lived among them and knew all about their troubles, began to be more hopeful, for they said, "He knows what it is to suffer, and he will surely help us." The king's son is Jesus, who is the Son of God the Father. Jesus was, as we are, tempted to do wrong. He knew what it was to be poor and hungry and homeless; he felt the bitterness of death. More than this, he knew what it was to be persecuted by enemies, and to be misunderstood and deserted by his dearest friends.
                           Krummacher.

10,113. KNOCKING, Custom of. Orientals give warning of their approach at the outer gate or entrance, either by calling or knocking. To stand and call is a very respectful and common mode. Thus it was in Bible times, and to it there are many very interesting allusions. Moses commanded (Deut. 24: 10) the holder of a pledge to stand without, and call to the owners thereof to come forth; this was to avoid the insolent intrusion of cruel creditors. Peter stood knocking at the outer door, and so did the three men sent to Joppa by Cornelius.
                           Thomson

10,114. KNOT, The Gordian. According to ancient history, this knot was made in the harness of a chariot by Gordius, King of Phrygia, which knot was so intricate as to baffle every attempt to untie it, or even to find out where it began or ended. The oracle of the day having declared that he who succeeded in solving the complication should be the conqueror of the world, Alexander the Great determined to effect it if possible. Aware that if he failed his followers would be dispirited, he determined to separate it with his sword, and with one blow he cut the knot which was fraught with such interest to the whole world. The expression "cutting the Gordian knot," has consequently been used to signify eluding any difficulty or task by bold or unusual means. *Loaring.*

10,115. KNOWLEDGE, Advantage of. In England, a man of small fortune may cast his regards around him, and say, with truth and exultation, "I am lodged in a house that affords me conveniences and comforts which even a king could not command some centuries ago. There are ships crossing the seas in every direction to bring me what is useful to me from all parts of the earth. In China, men are gathering the tea-leaf for me; in America, they are planting cotton for me; in the West India Islands, they are preparing my sugar and coffee; in Italy, they are feeding silkworms for me; in Saxony, they are shearing the sheep to make me clothing; at home, powerful steam-engines are spinning and weaving for me, and making cutlery for me, and pumping the mines, that the materials useful for me may be procured. My patrimony was small, yet I have post-coaches running day and night, on all the roads, to carry my correspondence; I have roads, and canals, and bridges, to bear the coal for my winter fire; nay, I have protecting fleets and armies around my happy country to secure my enjoyments and repose. Then I have editors and printers, who daily send me an account of what is going on throughout the world among all these people who serve me. And in a corner of my house, I have books! the miracle of all my possessions, for they transport me instantly, not only to all places, but to all times. By my books, I can conjure up before me, to vivid existence, all the great and good men of antiquity; and for my individual satisfaction, I can make them act over again the most renowned of their exploits; the orators declaim for me; the historians recite; the poets sing; in a word, from the equator to the pole, and from the beginning of time until now, by my books, I can be where I please." *Dr. Arnott.*

10,116. KNOWLEDGE Alone. Naked knowledge will be as unserviceable to the soul in a dying day, as a painted fire would be to the frozen body in a cold day. As some articles are tanned by the same sun in which others are whitened; so are some professors hardened under the same gospel by which others are softened. As it is lost labor to smite the flint, if it progagate no sparks; so it is fruitless toil to furnish our heads with light, if it refine not our hearts. Satan may as well put out our eyes, that we should not see the truth; as cut off our feet, that we should not walk in the truth. Naked knowledge may make the head giddy; but it will never make the heart holy
Secker.

10,117. KNOWLEDGE, Benefit of. As the power of acquiring knowledge is to be ascribed to reason, so the attainment of it mightily strengthens and improves it, and thereby enables it to enrich itself with future acquisitions. Knowledge in general expands the mind, exalts the faculties, refines the taste of pleasure, and opens numerous sources of intellectual enjoyment. By means of it we become less dependent for satisfaction upon the sensitive appetites, the gross pleasures of sense are more easily despised, and we are made to feel the superiority of the spiritual to the material part of our nature. Instead of being continually solicited by the influence and irritation of sensible objects, the mind can retire within herself and expatiate in the cool and quiet walks of contemplation. *Robert Hall.*

10,118. KNOWLEDGE, Christian. If any man's head or tongue should grow apace, and all the rest of his body not grow, it would certainly make him a monster; and they are no other that are knowing and talkative Christians, and grow daily in these respects, but not at all in holiness of heart and life, which is the proper growth of the children of God. *Salter.*

10,119. KNOWLEDGE, Concealment of. "Whoever concealeth the knowledge which God shall give him," says Mohammed, "God shall put on him a bridle of fire on the day of resurrection."

10,120. KNOWLEDGE, Cultivation of. I make not my head a grave, but a treasury of knowledge; I intend no monopoly, but a community in learning; I study not for my own sake only, but for theirs that study not for themselves; I envy no man that knows more than myself, but pity them that know less. I instruct no man as an exercise of my knowledge, or with an intent rather to nourish and keep it alive in mine own head, than beget and propagate it in his; and, in the midst of all my endeavors, there is but one thought that dejects me—that my acquired parts must perish with myself, nor can be legacied among my honored friends.
Browne.

10,121. KNOWLEDGE, Desire for. The desire of knowledge, like the thirst of riches, increases ever with the acquisition of it.—*Sterne.*——Knowledge always desires increase: it is like fire, which must be first kindled by some external agent, but which will afterwards propagate itself. *Johnson.*

10,122. KNOWLEDGE, Discolored. Knowledge indeed is as necessary as light, and in this coming age most fairly promises to be as common as water, and as free as air. But as it has been wisely ordained that light should have no color, water no taste, and air no odor, so knowledge also should be equally pure, and without admixture. If it comes to us through the medium of prejudice, it will be discolored; through the channels of custom, it will be adulterated; through the Gothic walls of the college, or of the cloister, it will smell of the lamp.   *Colton.*

10,123. KNOWLEDGE, Divine and Human. An old preacher compares the divine knowledge to a sheet almanac upon which all the days and weeks of a year past or to come, can be seen, *uno intuito*, at one view. Could this be extended to cover all the years of time and eternity, and be made to embrace the records of all worlds, and all beings, it would represent the extent of the divine knowledge. Man's knowledge is represented by a book almanac, which has a leaf for a day, for it is only by the moment that we learn anything, and our knowledge is limited to a few things, and to the past and present.

10,124. KNOWLEDGE, Extent of. Strabo was entitled to be called a profound geographer eighteen hundred years ago. A geographer who had never heard of America would now be laughed at by the girls of a boarding-school. What would now be thought of the greatest chemist or geologist of 1746? The truth is that in all science mankind is constantly advancing. Every generation has its front and its rear rank; but the rear rank of a later occupies the ground which was occupied by the front rank of a former.   *Macaulay.*

10,125. KNOWLEDGE, Figures of. The *tree of knowledge*, Gen. 2: 9; 3: 6. Pleasant and promising. The test of man's obedience, and the occasion of man's fall. It was significant that our first parents longed more for the tree of knowledge than for the tree of life. "They would rather be learned than holy." (*Leighton.*) "The *key of knowledge*," Luke 11 : 52, to open or shut the cabinet of truth. A *crown*, Prov. 14: 18, encircling the brow of the prudent. A *sweet savor* or *perfume;* so the apostle compares the knowledge of Christ to the perfumes scattered in ancient triumphal processions, 2 Cor. 2: 14.   *Bowes.*

10,126. KNOWLEDGE, First Step to. A mouse that had lived all its life in a chest, says the fable, chanced one day to creep up to the edge, and, peeping out exclaimed with wonder, "I did not think the world was so large." The first step to knowledge is, to know that we are ignorant. It is a great point to know our place: for want of this, a man in private life, instead of attending to the affairs of his "chest," is ever peeping out, and then he becomes a philosopher! He must then know everything, and presumptuously pry into the deep and secret councils of God: not considering that man is finite, he has no faculties to comprehend and judge of the great scheme of things. We can form no other knowledge of spiritual things, except what God has taught us in his Word, and where he stops we must stop.   *Cecil.*

10,127. KNOWLEDGE, Glorying in. In 1201, Simon Tournay, after he had excelled all his contemporaries at Oxford, in learning, and became so eminent in Paris as to be made the chief doctor of the Sorbonne, grew so proud, that while he regarded Aristotle as superior to Moses and Christ, he considered him as but equal to himself! He became such an idiot at length, as not to know one letter in a book, or one thing he had ever done.   *Whitecross.*

10,128. KNOWLEDGE, How to Obtain. Properly, there is no other knowledge but that which is got by working; the rest is yet all a hypothesis of knowledge; a thing to be argued of in schools; a thing floating in the clouds, in endless logic-vortices, till we try and fix it.   *Carlyle.*

10,129. KNOWLEDGE, Importance of. Nothing is so costly as ignorance. You sow the wrong seed, you plant the wrong field, you build with the wrong timber, you buy the wrong ticket, you take the wrong train, you settle in the wrong locality, or you take the wrong medicine, and no money can make good your mistake.   *Dr. Fowler.*

10,130. KNOWLEDGE, Prayer and. Prayer is a proper means for the increase of knowledge. Prayer is the golden key that unlocks that treasure. When Daniel was to expound the secret contained in the king's dream, about which the Chaldean magicians had racked their brains to no purpose; what course did Daniel take? "He went to his house," Dan. 2: 17, 18, "and made the thing known to Hananiah, Michael, and Azariah, his companions; that they would desire mercies of the God of heaven concerning his secret." And then was the secret revealed to Daniel. Luther was wont to say, "Three things made a divine; meditation, temptation, and prayer." Holy Mr. Bradford was wont to study upon his knees. If Christ be our teacher it becomes all his saints to be at his feet.   *John Flavel.*

10,131. KNOWLEDGE, Pride of. The Apostle Paul says, "Knowledge puffeth up." I have seen boys and girls very proud over their lessons and examinations, who had not wisdom enough to mend their clothes, or make a fire, or sweep a carpet, or harness a horse, or live two days without help. Wisdom is useful; knowledge is the raw stuff out of which we make wisdom.   *Thomas K. Beecher.*

10,132. KNOWLEDGE, Profitable. There is no kind of knowledge which, in the hands of the diligent and skillful, will not turn to account. Honey exudes from all flowers, the bitter not excepted; and the bee knows how to extract it.   *Bishop Horne.*

10,133. KNOWLEDGE, Pursuit of. In the pursuit of knowledge, follow it wherever it is to be found; like fern, it is the produce of all climates, and like coin, its circulation is not restricted to any particular class. We are ignorant in youth from idleness, and we continue so in manhood from pride: for pride is less ashamed of being ignorant than of being instructed, and she looks too high to find that which very often lies beneath her. Mr. Locke was asked how he had contrived to accumulate a mine of knowledge so rich, yet so extensive and so deep: he replied that he attributed what little he knew, to the not being ashamed to ask for information; and to the rule he had laid down, of conversing with all descriptions of men of those topics chiefly that formed their own peculiar professions or pursuits.   *Colton.*

10,134. KNOWLEDGE, Safe. Even Indians never use poisoned arrows for killing their game. Christian parents ought to use as much discretion in the treatment of their children.   *Dr. Fowler.*

10,135. KNOWLEDGE, Safeguard of. "My child," said St. Columbian to Luanus, when he saw how ardently he devoted himself to learning, "Thou hast asked a perilous gift of God. Many, out of undue love of knowledge, have made shipwreck of their souls." "My father," replied the boy, "If I learn to know God, I shall never offend him, for they only offend him who know him not." "Go, my son," said the abbot, "remain firm in that faith, and true science shall conduct you on the road to heaven."

10,136. KNOWLEDGE, Sorrow of. A Brahmin, whose religion prohibited the use of anything which would destroy life, was shown a glass of water through the microscope. The water was alive with loathsome reptiles. He had destroyed hundred of lives at a single draught, and was filled with apprehension. He asked the missionary to let him take the wonderful instrument. After examining it, he asked, "Are there more in this country,?" "No, this is all," said the missionary. The Brahmin struck it upon a stone and broke it in pieces, saying, "You have destroyed my peace of mind. I shall never know joy any more, but you shall not harm my people. They will not believe what you say. They will cleave to their religion, and die in the comfort that it offers." He laid his sorrow to his increased knowledge, but received not the comforts of Christianity to repay his loss.

10,137. KNOWLEDGE, Summary of. The greater part of the sciences comprise but one single word—perhaps; and the whole history of mankind contains no more than three:—they are born, suffer, and die.   *Dabshelim.*

10,138. KNOWLEDGE, Superficial. When we talk of men of deep science, do we mean that they have got to the bottom or near the bottom of science? Do we mean that they know all that is capable of being known? Do we mean even that they know in their own especial department all that the smatterers of the next generation will know? Why, if we compare the little truth that we know with the infinite mass of truth which we do not know, we are all shallow together; and the greatest philosophers that ever lived would be the first to confess their shallowness.   *Lord Macaulay.*

10,139. KNOWLEDGE, Thirst for. The tree of knowledge cannot be ascended without considerable labor. The fruit, when gathered, though perhaps sweet at first, is not without its attendants, anxiety and care; nay, too often is it an occasion of pride and consequence. Prometheus, who according to fable, was the great inventor of arts and philosophy, is represented as having an eagle or vulture perpetu-

ally gnawing his liver, to denote those continual cares and anxieties of mind which knowing and inquisitive men are exposed to. *Buck.*

10,140. KNOWLEDGE. Tree of. The tree of knowledge is grafted upon the tree of life; and that fruit which brought the fear of death into the world, budding on an immortal stock, becomes the fruit of the promise of immortality.   *Sir H. Davy.*

10,141. KNOWLEDGE, True. When the worldly-wise have dived into the bottom of Nature's sea, they are able to bring up from thence, instead of these pearls of price, nothing but handsful of shells and gravel. Knowledge, indeed, and good parts managed by grace are like the rod in Moses' hand, wonder-workers, but turn to serpents when they are cast upon the ground, and employed in promoting earthly designs. Learning in religious hearts, like that gold in the Israelites' ear-rings, is a most precious ornament; but if men pervert it to base wicked ends, or begin to make an idol of it, as they did a golden calf of their ear-rings, it then becomes an abomination. *Arrowsmith.*

10,142. KNOWLEDGE, Useful. There is a fountain in London that is opened by a spring. A man wanted to drink, but no one could tell him how to open it. At last a little dirty bootblack steps up and touches the spring, and the water gushes out. He knew more than the Bishop of London about it.   *Moody.*

10,143. KNOWLEDGE, Use of. The whole body of knowledge tends, in consequence of the existence of difficulties, to the elucidation of Scripture; the cultivation even of the merely ornamental parts of learning, is requisite to the defence of revelation, and consequently, justifiable in a still larger extent than it would otherwise have been. The minutest branches of philosophy, and the most trivial recreations of the mind, thus become important in a religious point of view. We are evidently, therefore, deeply indebted to the difficulties of Scripture, because by making every species of knowledge subservient to the illustration and vindication of religious truth, they have dignified and sanctified, as it were, the scientific amusements of our leisure hours, and heightened the pleasure of studying the subordinate branches of literature, by teaching us that we may be usefully employed, even in our intellectual relaxations.   *Benson.*

10,144. KORAN, Reverence for the. The Koran is held in the greatest reverence and esteem among the Mohammedans. They dare not so much as touch it without being first washed or legally purified; which lest they should do by inadvertence, they write these words on the cover label, "Let none touch it but they who are clean." They read it with great care and respect, never holding it below their girdles. They swear by it, consult it on the weighty occasions, carry it with them to war, write sentences of it on their banners, adorn it with gold and precious stones, and knowingly suffer it not to be in the possession of any of a different persuasion.   *George Sale.*

10,145. LABOR, Blessings of. Labor, though

It was at first inflicted as a curse, seems to be the gentlest of all punishments, and is fruitful of a thousand blessings: the same Providence which permits diseases, produces remedies; when it sends sorrows, it often sends friends and supporters; if it gives a scanty income, it gives good sense, and knowledge, and contentment, which love to dwell under homely roofs; with sickness come humility, and repentance, and piety; and affliction and grace walk hand in hand.   *Jortin.*

10,146. LABOR, Eminence and. When we read the lives of distinguished men in any department, we find them almost always celebrated for the amount of labor they could perform. Demosthenes, Julius Cæsar, Henry of France, Lord Bacon, Sir Isaac Newton, Franklin, Washington, Napoleon, different as they were in their intellectual and moral qualities, were all renowned as hard workers. We read how many days they could support the fatigues of a march; how early they rose; how late they watched; how many hours they spent in the field, in the cabinet, in the court; how many secretaries they kept employed; in short, how hard they worked.   *Everett.*

10,147. LABOR, Faithful in. Bonaventura, the Seraphic Doctor, was general of the Franciscan Order, one of whose rules required a rotation of work among the members. Gregory X. sent him a cardinal's hat by two nuncios, who found him in the kitchen washing the plates after dinner. The nuncios were amazed. The Seraphic Doctor, without a blush, excused himself from attending to their business till he had finished his dishes. So the Cardinal's hat was hung on a dog-wood tree near the kitchen door, till the dishes were finished and the new Cardinal's hands were dried.

10,148. LABOR, Healthfulness of. There is a story in the Arabian Nights' Tales of a king who had long languished under an ill habit of body, and had taken abundance of remedies to no purpose. At length, a physician cured him by the following method: He took a hollow ball of wood, and filled it with several drugs; after which he closed it up so artificially that nothing appeared. He likewise took a mall, and after having hollowed the handle, and that part which strikes the ball, he closed in them several drugs after the same manner as in the ball itself. He then ordered the Sultan, who was his patient, to exercise himself early in the morning with these rightly prepared instruments till such time as he should sweat; when, as the story goes, the virtue of the medicaments perspiring through the wood had so good an influence on the Sultan's constitution, that they cured him of an indisposition which all the compositions he had taken inwardly had not been able to remove. This Eastern allegory is finely contrived to show us how beneficial bodily labor is to health, and that exercise is the most effectual physic. *Addison.*

10,149. LABOR, Honors to. Statues in every public place should record its wonders; oratorios should be composed in its honor; its insignia—the plough, the spade, and the loom—

should decorate state carriages, and ornament churches and public halls; while its successful votaries should wear the honored decoration of "The Order of Industry."   *J. Johnson*

10,150. LABOR, Incessancy of. The more we accomplish, the more we have to accomplish. All things are full of labor; and, therefore, the more we acquire, the more care and the more toil to secure our acquisitions. Good men can never retire from their works of benevolence; their fortune is never made. I never heard of an apostle, prophet, or public benefactor, retiring from their respective fields of labor. Moses, and Paul, and Peter, died with their harness on. So did Luther, and Calvin, and Wesley, and a thousand others as deserving, though not so well known to fame. We are inured to labor. It was first a duty; it is now a pleasure. Still there is such a thing as overworking man and beast, mind and body. The mainspring of a watch needs repose, and is the better for it. The muscles of an elephant, and the wings of a swift bird, are at length fatigued. Heaven gives rest to the earth because it needs it; and winter is more pregnant with blessings to the soil than summer with its flowers and fruits. But in the war for truth and against error, there is no discharge.   *A. Campbell.*

10,151. LABOR, Law of. There is nothing truly valuable which can be purchased without pains and labor. The gods have set a price upon every real and noble pleasure. If you would gain the favor of the Deity, you must be at the pains of worshiping him; if the friendship of good men, you must study to oblige them; if you would be honored by your country, you must take care to serve it. In short, if you would be eminent in war or peace, you must become master of all the qualifications that can make you so.   *Addison.*

10,152. LABOR, Life-character of. Labor is life: from the inmost heart of the worker rises his God-given force—the sacred celestial life-essence breathed into him by the Almighty God!   *Carlyle.*

10,153. LABOR, Need of. King Antigonus, when he had not for a long time seen Cleanthes, the philosopher, said to him, "Dost thou yet, O, Cleanthes, continue to grind?" "Yes, sir," replied Cleanthes, "I still grind, and that I do to gain my living, and not to depart from philosophy." How great and generous was the courage of this man, who, coming from the mill and the kneading-trough, did with the same hand which had been employed in turning the stone and moulding the dough, write of the nature of the gods, moon, stars, and sun.   *Plutarch*

10,154. LABOR, No Rest from. Miserable is he who slumbers on in idleness, miserable the workman who sleeps before the hour of his rest, or who sits down in the shadow while his brethren work in the sun. There is no rest from labor on earth. There are always duties to perform and functions to exercise, functions which are ever enlarging and extending in proportion to the growth of our moral and

mental station. Man is born to work, and he must work while it is day. "Have I not," said a great worker, "an eternity to rest in?"
Tynman.

10,155. LABOR, Place for. See the spider casting out her film to the gale, she feels persuaded that somewhere or other it will adhere and form the commencement of her web. She commits the slender filament to the breeze, believing that there is a place provided for it to fix itself. In this fashion, should we believingly cast forth our endeavors in this life, confident that God will find a place for us. He who bids us play and work will aid our efforts and guide us in his Providence in a right way. Sit not still in despair, O son of toil, but again cast out the floating thread of hopeful endeavor and the wind of love will bear it to its resting place. *Spurgeon.*

10,156. LABOR, Power for. Karamsin, the Russian traveler, having observed Lavater's diligence in study, visiting the sick, and relieving the poor, greatly surprised at his activity, said to him, "Whence have you so much strength of mind and power of endurance?" "My friend," replied he, "man rarely wants the power to work, when he possesses the will; the more I labor in the discharge of my duties, so much the more ability and inclination to labor do I constantly find within myself."

10,157. LABOR, Prayer and. Labor is of noble birth; but prayer is the daughter of heaven. Labor has a place near the throne, but prayer touches the golden sceptre. Labor, Martha-like, is busy with much serving; but prayer sits with Mary at the feet of Jesus. Labor climbs the mountain-peak with Moses; but prayer soars upward, with Elijah, in a chariot of fire. Labor has the raven's wing, yet sometimes goes forth in vain; but prayer has the pinions of the dove, and never returns but with the olive-leaf of blessing! *W. H. Groser.*

10,158. LABOR, Prayer with. Anthony the hermit, was sitting in his cell in the wilderness, grievously tempted with importunate thoughts, and fell into sadness and darkness. Then he prayed, "Lord, I desire to be saved, but my thoughts are a hindrance to me. What shall I do in my present affliction? How shall I be saved?" Soon after he went outside of his cell and saw a man sitting and working, then leaving his work to pray, afterwards sitting down to his work twisting a palm rope, and after a time engaging again in prayer. He concluded this to be an angel sent from God to instruct him in duty. Then the angel addressed him and said, "Do so, and thou shalt be saved." Thereafter the great hermit and all his followers were diligent in labor and in prayer.

10,159. LABOR, Value of. God is constantly teaching us that nothing valuable is ever obtained without labor; and that no labor can be honestly expended without our getting its value in return. He is not careful to make everything easy to man. The Bible itself is no light book; human duty no holiday engagement. The grammar of deep personal religion, and the grammar of real practical virtue, are not to be learned by any facile Hamiltonian methods. *Binney.*

10,160. LABORERS, Hiring. Morier, in the record of his second journey through Persia, mentions having noted in the market-place at Hamadan, a custom like that alluded to in the parable of the laborers. "Here we observed every morning before the sun rose, that a numerous band of peasants were collected with spades in their hands, waiting to be hired for the day, to work in the surrounding fields. This custom struck me as a most happy illustration of our Saviour's parable, particularly when, passing by the same place late in the day, we found others standing idle, and remembered his words, 'Why stand ye here all the day idle?' as most applicable to their situation, for on putting the very same question to them, they answered us, 'Because no man hath hired us.'" Josephus says that Ananus paid the workmen who were employed in the rebuilding or beautifying of the temple, a whole day's pay, even though they should have labored but a single hour.

10,161. LABORERS, Parable of the. Lightfoot quotes from the Talmud concerning a celebrated rabbi, who died at a very early age, as follows: "To what was R. Bon Bar Chaiza like? To a king who hired many laborers, among whom there was one hired who performed his task extraordinarily well. What did the king? He took him aside, and walked with him to and fro. When even was come, those laborers came that they might receive their hire, and he gave him a complete hire with the rest. And the laborers murmured, saying, 'We have labored hard all the day, and this man only two hours, yet he hath received as much wages as we.' The king said to them, 'He hath labored more in those two hours than you in the whole day.' So R. Bon plied the law more in eight and twenty years than another in a hundred years."

10,162. LADIES, Education of. Most ladies who have had what is considered as an education, have no idea of an education progressive through life. Having attained a certain measure of accomplishment, knowledge, manners, etc., they consider themselves as made up, and so take their station; they are pictures which, being quite finished, are put in a frame—a gilded one, if possible, and hung up in permanence of beauty!—permanence, that is to say, till Old Time, with his rude and dirty fingers, soil the charming colors. *J. Foster.*

10,163. LADIES, Influence of. Man is but a rough pebble without the attrition received from contact with the gentler sex: it is wonderful how the ladies pumice a man down into a smoothness which occasions him to roll over and over with the rest of his species, jostling but not wounding his neighbors, as the waves of circumstances bring him into collision with them. *Capt. Marryat.*

10,164. LAITY, Influence of. Leaders are not independent of the masses. Nay, we may make these masses lead us, and these leaders be obliged to become followers. After the storming of the heights of Spicheren, the commander of the Prussian battalion was arrested for having charged without orders, without having waited for artillery to clear his way and for reserves to cover his flank. His defense was this: "I had nothing to do with that attack, neither had my subordinate officers; but when we came to that attacking line, every one of my men rushed forward, and all we could do was to follow on, keep order, and hold the height they won."   *Anon.*

10,165. LAMBS, Carrying the. As I stood among the tombs in the suburbs of Jerusalem, there came a flock of sheep who made for the tomb; but, finding it occupied, turned into another one for shelter. Coming after the sheep was a little boy—a shepherd boy. He was clad in the garb the shepherd boys wore, and the only garment he had was a cotton one, folded around him, lapped over and fastened with a girdle. He was coming slowly, through the storm, and, as he drew near, I saw that his bosom was very full. And I looked, and as he got almost to me, I saw he had a little lamb, very young, that he had picked up, in one side of his bosom; and on further regarding him, I found that he had still another on the other side. They could not keep up with the flock in the storm, and to shelter them from the weather he had put them in his bosom. I had often thought of it before, but it never struck me so forcibly that my Saviour was carrying his lambs in his bosom. I was in very poor health, and did not know that I should ever see my home again, and I thought, at that moment, of my little ones whom I had left in the bosom of that home. And I looked through the storm on the hills of Judea, and thought of the Mediterranean Sea, and of the Atlantic Ocean, and of the eastern shore of my own country, and of the Alleghany Mountains; and away over those mountains I thought of my home and my little children I had left there— my little lambs. I said to myself, at that moment, "I trust to my Saviour. If I shall fail to pass over all this distance, and if I never shall see the loved ones of my home again, I shall meet them in heaven: for he will carry the lambs in his bosom, and I shall meet them in the day of eternity." Oh, what joy thrilled through my heart! And when I see a mother weeping and a father weeping for the little ones taken away, I think of Jesus—that he has taken them to his bosom, out of the storm and out of the tempests of this world—they are safe in the mansions of glory and of God. Oh, yes, we shall see our little ones and our loved ones, at last, angels of God! Are you, mothers, and you, fathers, and you, dear friends, prepared to meet them in glory? They are singing yonder, to-day! Listen to them! Are you prepared to sing there with them? They see the face of our Saviour! Can you look up and say, "I see his face?" Can you feel, to-day, that "before the throne your Saviour stands, your name is written on his hands?"

            Bp. Simpson.

10,166. LAMP, Foot. The streets of Jerusalem are very narrow, and no one is allowed to go out at night without a light. Throw open your lattice in the evening and look out, you will see what seem to be little stars twinkling on the pavement. You will hear the clatter of sandals, as the late traveler rattles along. As the party approaches, you will see that he has a little lamp fastened to his foot, to make his step a safe one. In an instant the verse comes to your memory, written in that same city three thousand years ago, "Thy Word is a lamp to my feet, and a light to my path."

            Anon.

10,167. LAMP, Lesson from a. One so anxious about his soul that he could not rest, took a lamp and went to see his pastor, in order to gain instruction and help. He started to return home in much the same state of mind as when he went. All was so dark ahead that his way was closed up. Said the minister, "Why do you carry that lamp?" "To light the way," he replied. "But as you stand there can you see all the way home?" asked the minister. "O no; it looks very dark a little before me," he replied. "Of what use then is it?" persisted the questioner. "Why, I'll take it with me, and it will light my path all the way," answered the man. As he did so, the illustration helped him to see at what he stumbled. There in the street he believed to the saving of his soul, and went on his way rejoicing, walking in the light which dispelled the darkness.

            G. R. Snyder.

10,168. LANGUAGE, Feebleness of. If a poet were to come into the world endowed with a genius, suppose ten times more sublime than Milton's, must he not abandon the attempt at composition in despair, from finding that language, like a feeble tool, breaks in his hand— from finding that when he attempts to pour any of his mental fluid into the vessel of language, that vessel in a moment melts or bursts; from finding that, though he is Hercules every inch, he is armed but with a distaff, and cannot give his mighty strength its proportional effect without his club?

            John Foster.

10,169. LAUGHTER, The Advantages of. Laughter is a most healthful exertion; it is one of the greatest helps to digestion with which I am acquainted; and the custom prevalent among our forefathers of exciting it at table by jesters and buffoons, was founded on true medical principles.   *Dr. Hufeland.*

10,170. LAUGHTER, Death from. Philemon, a comic poet, when an old man, saw an ass eating up some figs that a boy had laid down. When the boy returned, he said to him, "Go and fetch the ass some drink." He was so pleased with his own jest that he died laughing. Zeuxis Heracleotes, the most excellent painter of his age, painted an old woman. She was represented as a short, dry, toothless, bloodless thing, with hollow eyes, hanging cheeks, chin pointing out, her mouth bending inward, her nose fallen and bowing; altogether, it was so ridiculous a picture that he was seized with a fit of laughter, and he died upon the spot.

10,171. LAUGHTER, The Power of. By means of laughter absolute monarchs have been controlled upon their thrones, demagogues have been checked in their career, and even Demos himself has been made to laugh at his own follies, till he was almost shamed into good sense. *Neaves.*

10,172. LAW, Definition of. Law, in its most general and comprehensive sense, signifies a rule of action; and is applied indiscriminately to all kinds of action, whether animate or inanimate, rational or irrational. Thus, we say, the laws of motion, of gravitation, of optics, or mechanics, as well as the laws of nature and of nations. And it is that rule of action which is prescribed by some superior, and which the inferior is bound to obey. *Blackstone.*

10,173. LAW, Dignity of. Of law there can be no less acknowledged than that her seat is the bosom of God, her voice the harmony of the world; all things do her homage, the very least as feeling her care, and the greatest as not exempted from her power; both angels and men, and creatures of what condition soever, though each in different sort and manner, yet all with uniform consent, admiring her as the mother of their peace and joy. *Hooker.*

10,174. LAW, Execution of. Diocles made a law that no man should come armed into a public assembly. Through inadvertency he chanced to break the law himself, and it was said, "He has broken a law he has made himself." He turned to his accuser and said with a loud voice, "No the law shall have its sanction," and drawing his sword killed himself.

10,175. LAW, Expedients of. An old barrister was giving advice to his son, who was just entering upon the practice of his father's profession. "My son," said the counselor, "if you have a case where the law is plainly on your side, but justice seems to be clearly against you, urge upon the jury the vast importance of sustaining the law. If, on the other hand, you are in doubt about the law, but your client's case is founded on justice, insist on the necessity of doing justice, though the heavens fall." "But," asked the son, "how shall I manage a case where law and justice are dead against me?" "In that case," replied the old man, "talk round it."

10,176. LAW, Folly of Going to. To go to law, is for two persons to kindle a fire at their own cost to warm others, and singe themselves to cinders; and because they cannot agree as to what is truth and equity, they will both agree to unplume themselves, that others may be decorated with their feathers. *Feltham.*

10,177. LAW and Gospel. The doctrine of the gospel is the revelation of the Son of God. This is a doctrine quite contrary to the law, which revealeth not the Son of God, but showeth forth sin—it revealeth death, the wrath and judgment of God, and hell. The gospel, therefore, is such a doctrine as admitteth no law; yea, it must be as separate from the law as there is distance between heaven and earth. The gospel teacheth me, not what I ought to do—for that is the proper office of the law—but what Jesus Christ the Son of God hath done for me. *Luther.*

10,178. LAW, Higher. I know no human being exempt from the law. The law is the security of the people; it is the security of every person that is governed, and of every person that governs. There is but one law for all, namely, that law which governs all law, the law of our Creator, the law of humanity, justice, equity—the Law of Nature and of Nations. So far as any laws fortify this primeval law, and give it more precision, more energy, more effect by their declarations, such laws enter into the sanctuary, and participate in the sacredness of its character. *Burke.*

10,179. LAW, Obligation of the Moral. 1 Cor. 9 : 21.—The moral law is still a rule of life to us. Those that think they have done with the law shall find that the law has not done with them. It is a striking fact, that while infidels have presumed to mock the Lawgiver, and him who has redeemed us from the curse of the law, they have never attempted to touch the law itself. The perfection of the Ten Commandments stands before the civilized world unimpeached, as a perfect rule of right and wrong. *Bowes*

10,180. LAW, Observance of. A deacon of good repute kept a grocery store in old times. He sold rum by the quart, but was prohibited by the law from selling it in smaller quantities. A man entered and wanted a pint of rum. The deacon refused to sell a pint. The man asked his reason. He said, "Because it is contrary to the law." Looking the deacon squarely in the eye, the man said, "Deacon Bartlett, if you are no better than the law makes you, you will go to hell sure." *Dr. Holme.*

10,181. LAW, Obstructions to. Suppose into a piece of complicated machinery an obstruction is thrown. The whole force of the propelling power will be directed to the obstruction, and one of two things will occur—either the obstruction will be removed or crushed, or the machinery will break down. If I tie a band closely around my arm the whole force of the system of circulation will be directed to the band, and either it will be broken or the system of circulation will be so far destroyed. Now, mark, not only one of the two results will follow, but the whole propelling power will be directed to the obstruction, and the system breaks down only through inherent weakness or insufficiency of power to remove the obstruction. But when this is applied to the divine government, natural or moral, it can never fail through lack of executive power or inherent weakness. *Dr. J. A. M. Chapman.*

10,182. LAW, Quarrels of. A lion and a bear found the carcass of a fawn, and had a long fight for it. The contest was so hard and even, that, at last, both of them, half-blinded and half-dead, lay panting on the ground, without strength to touch the prize which was stretched between them. A fox coming by at the time, and seeing their helpless condition, stepped between the combatants and carried off the booty. "Poor creatures that we are," cried they, "who have been exhausting all our strength and injuring one another, merely to give a rogue a dinner!" *Æsop.*

10,183. LAW, Requisites for Going to. Wisely has it been said that he who would go to law must have a good cause, a good purse, a good attorney, a good advocate, good evidence, and a good judge and jury—and having all these goods, unless he has also good luck, he will stand but a bad chance of success. *Trusler.*

10,184. LAW, Spiritual. To preach up justification by the law, as a covenant, is legal; and makes void the death and merits of Jesus Christ; but to preach obedience to the law, as a rule, is evangelical: and it savors as much of a New-Testament-spirit, as they phrase it, to urge the commands of the law, as to display the promise of the gospel. *Hopkins.*

10,185. LAW, The Sword and the. In all governments, there must of necessity be both the law and the sword: laws without arms would give us not liberty, but licentiousness; and arms without laws would produce not subjection, but slavery. The law, therefore, should be unto the sword what the handle is to the hatchet; it should direct the stroke, and temper the force. *Colton.*

10,186. LAW, Violation of. The violation of law tends to the ruin of the violator or law by action or reaction. There are general laws governing the material world, the violation of which would be followed by the most disastrous consequences. But as their subjects are not moral agents, they are exempt from such a possibility; yet this alters not the fact. If the sun, in violation of law, should withhold its light and heat; if the evaporation of water should cease, and there be no former and latter rain; if the gases of the atmosphere should combine in different proportions; if a planet should deviate a single inch from its orbit, or lag behind a single minute, what ruinous results would follow! This is true also in regard to the laws of our physical nature. If I thrust my hand into the burning embers, or leap from a house-top and dislocate a joint; if I refrain from eating and drinking; if I violate any law of health and life, the penalty follows more or less quickly upon the heels of the violation. The same principle is illustrated in civil government. If a law is violated, and the penalty is not inflicted, it in so far breaks down the government; if the penalty is inflicted, it is so far ruinous to the violator. One or the other of these results must inevitably follow. If there be power and soundness enough in the government, the law will be executed; if not, it breaks down at that point. *Dr. J. A. M. Chapman.*

10,187. LAWS, Divine. Laws, written, if not on stone tables, yet on the azure of infinitude, in the inner heart of God's creation, certain as life, certain as death! I say, the laws are there, and thou shalt not disobey them. It were better for thee not. Better a hundred deaths than yes! Terrible "penalties" withal, if thou still need penalties, are there for disobeying! *Carlyle.*

10,188. LEADER, Christ our. The Lord Jesus leads his people, as the *pillar of cloud and of fire* went before Israel for guidance and protection, Exod. 13: 21, 22; 40: 36-38; Neh. 9: 12, 19. The *ark* led them over Jordan, Joshua 3. A *shepherd* leads his flock, Ps. 23: 2, 3; Isa. 40: 11; John 10: 3, 4. A *standard-bearer* among the Church's hosts, Cant. 5: 10 (marg.); see Isa. 11: 10; cf. the type, 2 Sam. 18: 3. A *forerunner*, Heb. 6: 20. *Joshua* led the children of Israel into Canaan, Deut. 1: 38. Isa. 55: 4.—"A leader and commander." Not every commander is a leader, but the Lord Jesus heartens his soldiers by going before. "He is commander by his precept, and a leader by his example; our business is to obey and follow him." *Bowes.*

10,189. LEAF, Fading. Already the tints of autumn are stealing upon the forest. Here and there we see a falling leaf; and in many which are yet on their branches, the full green of summer is passing into a paler hue. How gradually does the change come on! We scarcely perceive a difference from day to day, but after the interval of a week it is distinctly seen; and then the breeze of autumn snaps the link by which the shred was joined to its branch, and wafts it to its resting place under the parent tree. And such is the strength of man. "We all do fade as a leaf." The freshness of youth soon passes into the maturity of manhood; and thus by gradual but rapid steps, the feebleness of age comes on. Thus is our strength but labor and sorrow, so soon passeth it away, and we are gone. Let it not steal on us unawares; nor let it be said of us, "Gray hairs are on him here and there, yet he knoweth it not." In youth and health let us think on our common frailty, and put away from us "the pride of life;" remembering that we must soon return to the dust from whence we came. The leaves with which the earth is strewn will know no second spring. Our great Redeemer has won for us a resurrection from the grave. So live, that your hope at last may be full of immortality. *Bp. Trower*

10,190. LEARNING, Advancement of. I have ever observed it to have been the office of a wise patriot, among the greatest affairs of the state, to take care of the commonwealth of learning. For schools they are the seminaries of state, and nothing is worthier the study of a statesman than that part of the republic which we call the advancement of letters. *Ben Jonson.*

10,191. LEARNING, Always. Cardinal Farnese discovered the great genius Michael Angelo walking alone amid the ruins of the Coliseum. He expressed his surprise at finding him so occupied. The modest artist answered, "I go to school that I may continue to learn." The growing men and the greatest men are always at school.

10,192. LEARNING, Intention of. Every artificer and profession endeavors to make the thing fit and to answer the end for which it is ntended. Those that till the ground, or that break in horses, or train dogs, their business is to make the most of things, and drive them up to the top of their kind; and what other view has learning and education but to improve the faculties, and to set them the right way to work. *Antoninus.*

10,193. LEARNING Little by Little. The story is told of St. Isadore, of Seville, that he found it so hard to learn, and study such drudgery that he ran away from school. In the heat of the day he sat down to rest beside a little spring that trickled over a rock. He noticed that the water fell in drops and only one drop at a time, yet they had worn away a large stone. It recalled him to his lessons. Diligent application overcame his dullness and made him one of the first scholars of his time. God's messengers to him were little drops of water. "Those drops," says his biographer, "gave to Spain an historian and to the Church a doctor."

10,194. LEARNING, Men of. Dante was, perhaps, more than any man of his age skilled in the learning of his times. He sustained at the University of Paris, an argument against fourteen disputants. He was conqueror in all. Michael Angelo was the architect of St. Peter's; he also painted the roof of the Sistine Chapel; his sculptured monuments are amongst the greatest efforts of genius; and as a poet and philosopher he was excelled by none of his time. We are told some extraordinary things relative to the acquirements of James Crichton —surnamed the Admirable Crichton. Before his twentieth year he had run through the whole circle of the sciences; could speak and write ten languages; was distinguished for his skill in singing and playing upon all sorts of instruments. In Paris he disputed in Hebrew, Syriac, Arabic, Greek, Latin, Spanish, French, Italian, English, Dutch, Flemish, and Sclavonic; and, what is still more extraordinary, in either prose or verse. Biography tells us of Sir William Jones, who died comparatively young, and yet acquired a critical knowledge of eight languages—English, Latin, French, Italian, Greek, Arabic, Persian, and Sanscrit; he also knew eight others less perfectly, but was able to read them with the occasional use of a dictionary—Spanish, Portuguese, German, Runic, Hebrew, Bengalee, Hindostanee, Turkish; and he knew so much of twelve other tongues, that they were easily attainable by him, had life and leisure permitted his application to them—Tibetian, Pâli, Phalavi, Deri, Russian, Syriac, Ethiopic, Coptic, Welsh, Swedish, Dutch, and Chinese. *J. Johnson.*

10,195. LEARNING without Religion. Without religion, learning is only a lamp on the outside of a palace. It may serve to throw a gleam of light on those that are without, while the inhabitant sits in darkness. *Salter.*

10,196. LEARNING, Time for. It matters not what sea a ship is to sail. Its keel must be securely laid, its masts firmly set, its rigging of the toughest fibre, in order to sail any sea in safety. One hour's tussle with the tempest will test the fiber of its timbers, which were toughened by a hundred years' wrestle with Norwegian blasts. The student whose special work in life is yet unchosen should be made to feel that in some work he will have need of the completest possible discipline of all his powers and the largest attainable acquirements. Now is the time to get ready. When the storm bursts, there will be no time to set the mast or hang the rudder. *President Foss.*

10,197. LEGENDS, Irish. The Lives of the Saints abound in incidents, both marvelous and amusing. Judging from these the Irish must have been from the first the greatest liars in the world. Not one of their saints but is characterized by the most absurd marvels. A thief stole and eat up one of St. Patrick's pet goats. The saint going out into the fields called the pet, when it sent forth its answering bleat from the stomach of the thief. There came up out of the sea thirty sea-green horses, and galloped to Lamora, where the abbot, Ruadan, presented them to king Dermot, and the king won a race with one of them. After a while these marvelous sea-horses returned to the sea. A woman visits a battle-field in search of her husband. She finds his head only. She pronounces the name of the Holy Trinity and the headless trunk of her husband walks up to her. She places the head upon the body and it instantly adheres so perfectly that no scar remains. The man comes to life and survives many years. In dealing with the Irish their credulity and superstition has been largely operated upon.

10,198. LEISURE, Compulsory. A gentleman called upon a merchant to engage him in Christian work. He excused himself, saying he was too busy. He really was a very busy man. He allowed his business to engross all his time and talents. Sickness next looked into that merchant's counting-room, and found him too busy to be sick. A little exercise of his power, and the merchant closed up his ledgers, laid down his pen, and called an assistant to help him home. Then in spite of the pressure of business, death laid his cold hand on his brow and said, "Go with me." Sickness and death do not wait our leisure. Religion and its duties are postponed at our eternal peril.

10,199. LEPERS, Description of. Never can we forget a company of miserable lepers sitting in a row by the wayside as we entered the Jaffa gate. More disgusting objects in human flesh can hardly be imagined. The hair and eyebrows had fallen off; the faces were livid, bloated, and covered with festering ulcers; and the eyes bloodshot or blind. The nose of one was half eaten off, the upper lip of another entirely gone. The hands of one were fingerless, the arms of another handless. As we passed them, they extended their diseased hands towards us, and in a dry, husky, gasping voice, cried, "Howadji, Allah, backsheesh;" that is, Traveler, in the name of God, money. O, how vividly did those pitiable objects bring to mind the expression, "The leprosy of sin;" and what an illustration were they of the power of that Jesus who could say to a leper

"I will; be thou clean!" This malady is beyond the reach of medical skill. Some years ago a French physician, supposing he had found a cure, went to Jerusalem to try the value of his discovery; but instead of helping the lepers, he became a victim of the dreadful disease, and died within three months. It is not, however, generally considered contagious, but is transmitted from parent to child, It is common to see a frightfully diseased mother with a bright healthy child in her arms; but the little one inherits the curse, and in a few years is sure to be a leper. Strange that marriages among them are not prohibited.

S. W. Brown.

10,200. LETTER, An Ill-tempered. An ill-tempered letter, once sent, will embitter a life-time. We once saw an old gentleman, with a wise, fine head, calm face, and most benevolent look, but evidently thin-skinned and irascible, beg of a post-master to return him a letter which he had dropped into the box. To do so, as everybody knows, is illegal; but won over by the old gentleman's importunity, the post-master complied, upon full proof, in comparing the writing, etc., being given. Then, with a beaming face, the old gentleman tore the letter into fragments, and scattering them to the wind, exclaimed, "Ah! I've preserved my friend." The fact is, he had written a letter in a state of irritation, which was probably unjust and hurtful, but which he had wisely recalled. "Written words remain," is not only a proverb, but a very grave caution; and hence the advice—never to write in anger, or at any rate, to keep your letter till you are cool.

Friswell.

10,201. LIARS, Evil of. Epametus said that liars were the cause of all the villainies and injustice in the world.

10,202. LIARS, Fate of. In the general post-office sorting room there is a hole in the wall, darkened by a grating, through which a frequent watch is kept upon the letter-sorters. Notwithstanding this, deceit often goes undetected by man, but never undetected by the eye of God. A confirmed liar is like a crooked, knotty tree, fit only for the fire. We despise and discard a watch that never tells the true time, a ruler that will not enable you to rule a straight line, a portrait that is not faithful; so God will, at the Judgment-day, dismiss from his presence "all liars." *Dr. J. H. Vincent.*

10,203. LIARS, Punishment of. I am charmed with many points of the Turkish law, particularly the punishment of the convicted. They are burnt on the forehead with a hot iron when they are proved the authors of any notorious falsehood. *Lady Montague.*

10,204. LIBERALITY, Christian. You will say, here is a marvelous doctrine, which commandeth nothing but give, give: if I should follow this doctrine, I should give so much, that at the length I shall have nothing left for myself. These be the words of infidelity: he that speaketh such words is a faithless man. And I pray you tell me, have ye heard of any man that came to poverty because he gave unto the poor? have you heard tell of such a one! No, I am sure you have not. And I dare lay my head to pledge for it, that no man living hath come, or shall hereafter come to poverty, because he hath been liberal in helping the poor. For God is a true God, and no liar: he promiseth us in his word that we shall have the more by giving to the needy. Therefore the way to get is to scatter that you have. Give, and you shall gain. If you ask me how I shall get riches, I make thee this answer—scatter that thou hast; for giving is gaining. But you must take heed and scatter it according unto God's will and pleasure: that is, to relieve the poor withal, to scatter it amongst the flock of Christ; whosoever giveth so shall surely gain, for Christ saith, "give and it shall be given unto you." It shall be given unto you—this is a sweet word, we can not well away with that; but how shall we come by it?—Give.

Bishop Latimer.

10,205. LIBERTY, False Application of. The word liberty has been falsely used by persons who, being degenerately profligate in private life, and mischievous in public, had no hope left but in fomenting discord. *Tacitus.*

10,206. LIBERTY, Joy of. When all Greece had assembled to behold the Isthmian games, silence was ordered by the sound of a trumpet, when the crier proclaimed, "The senate and people of Rome, and Titus Quinctius Flaminius, their general, do give liberty and immunity to all the cities of Greece that were under the jurisdiction of King Philip." At first there was a deep silence, as if the people heard nothing, and the crier repeated the same words. At this, there went up such a strong and universal shout of joy that the birds that flew above their heads fell down as if amazed among them. Livy said that "the joy was greater than the minds of men were able to comprehend, so that they scarce believed what they heard; they gazed upon one another as if they thought themselves deluded by a dream."

10,207. LIBERTY, News of. When Wilberforce was trying to get a bill through Parliament to liberate all the slaves under the British flag, away off in the islands subject to the British rule there was great excitement. They were anxious to get their liberty. When they were expecting the vessel which would bring the news that the bill had failed or succeeded, thousands of people went down to the shore to get the first news. The captain of the coming vessel knew how anxious they were to get it. As soon as the vessel was in sight, and he saw the multitude on the shore watching for him, he shouted the words, "Free! free! free!" and they all took up the cry, and it spread through the island.

10,208. LIBERTY, Sacrifice for. The burning of Moscow at the approach of Napoleon, is accounted the greatest sacrifice for patriotism which modern history records. But what is this devotion of wealth, or the destruction of a city, to the thousands of lives that have been laid cheerfully down in defence of liberty, of which history makes no personal mention.

Not a few families know best their own sacrifices.

10,209. LIBERTY, Transformation of. Ariosto tells a pretty story of a fairy, who, by some mysterious law of her nature, was condemned to appear at certain seasons in the form of a foul and poisonous snake. Those who injured her during the period of her disguise were forever excluded from participation in the blessings which she bestowed. But to those who, in spite of her loathsome aspect, pitied and protected her, she afterwards revealed herself in the beautiful and celestial form which was natural to her, accompanied their steps, granted all their wishes, filled their houses with wealth, made them happy in love and victorious in war. Such a spirit is liberty. At times she takes the form of a hateful reptile. She grovels, she hisses, she stings. But woe to those who in disgust shall venture to crush her! And happy are those who, having dared to receive her in her degraded and frightful shape, shall at length be rewarded by her in the time of her beauty and her glory! *Macaulay.*

10,210. LIBERTY, Waiting for. When a prisoner first leaves his cell, he cannot bear the light of day; he is unable to discriminate colors or recognize faces. But the remedy is, not to remand him into his dungeon, but to accustom him to the rays of the sun. The blaze of truth and liberty may at first dazzle and bewilder nations which have become half blind in the house of bondage. But let them gaze on, and they will soon be able to bear it. In a few years men learn to reason. The extreme violence of opinion subsides. Hostile theories correct each other. The scattered elements of truth cease to contend, and begin to coalesce. And at length a system of justice and order is educed out of the chaos. If men are to wait for liberty till they become wise and good in slavery, they may, indeed, wait forever. *Macaulay.*

10,211. LIBERTY, Working for. In 1813, the plague raged fearfully in Malta. There were not enough well persons to bury the dead and care for the sick. In the emergency, they had recourse to a number of French and Italian prisoners, promising them their liberty, when the plague should subside, for their services. They gladly accepted the offer, and labored most faithfully in their perilous work, and seemed to be under the special protection of Providence while so engaged, and won their freedom.

10,212. LIBRARY, Miracle of a. What a happiness is it, that without all offence of necromancy, I may here call up any of the ancient worthies of learning, whether human or divine, and confer with them of all my doubts! that I can, at pleasure, summon whole synods of reverend fathers and acute doctors from all the coasts of the earth, to give their well-studied judgments in all points of question which I propose! Neither can I cast my eye casually upon any of these silent masters but I must learn somewhat. It is wantonness to complain of choice. No law binds us to read

all; but the more we can take in and digest, the better-liking must the mind needs be. Blessed be God, that hath set up so many clear lamps in his Church! Now, none but the wilfully blind can plead darkness. And blessed be the memory of those his faithful servants that have left their blood, their spirits, their lives, in these precious books; and have willingly wasted themselves into these during monuments, to give light unto others. *Bishop Hall.*

10,213. LIE, Erasure of a. A little boy told a lie. His mother was grieved, and told him how much she was distressed; and, what was far more important, that God was displeased with him, that God kept a big book, and his name was written in that book, and over against the name of Alexander McPheeters there was a big black mark, for the story he had told. She noticed that the little fellow seemed serious and thoughtful all the afternoon, and that night when he was about to go to bed, he got down on his knees, and before saying his usual prayer, with great earnestness he exclaimed, "O Lord! please lub it out." That big black mark had been troubling him all day, and he wanted it rubbed out.

10,214. LIE, Fatal. A little boy, for a trick, pointed with his finger to the wrong road when a man asked which way the doctor went. As a result, the man missed the doctor, and his little boy died, because the doctor came too late to take a fish-bone from his throat. At the funeral, the minister said that the boy was killed by a lie, which another boy told with his finger. *Anon.*

10,215. LIES, Avoiding. I saw a singular specimen of earnest Hindooism in church this morning—a religious mendicant, or fakir, who never speaks, having embraced the singular idea that by remaining silent at all times he would never lie, and consequently become very holy. *J. D. Brown.*

10,216. LIES, Half. Satan rarely tries to do mischief by a pure, unvarnished, palpable lie; for, fallen as humanity is, a lie manifestly so is not palatable: an alloy needs to be amalgamated with some gold—the great lie requires a sprinkling of a great truth—Satan's brass must have stuck upon it the stamp and superscription of Jesus, before it can have currency or circulation among mankind. *Dr. Cumming.*

10,217. LIFE, Arithmetic of. Do you remember the inexorable logic of that remarkable arithmetical speech which Thomas De Quincey made to himself and to some imaginary friend, when standing precisely where you are standing to-day, at the beginning of his work of life? "My friend, you make very free with your days; pray, how many do you expect to have? What is your rental as regards the total harvest of days which this life is likely to yield? Let us consider." Then follows his arithmetic, which I give without his language. Seventy years of life yield 25,550 days. Remember, now, that twenty years have gone before beginning—before having attained any skill or system, or any definite purpose in the

distribution of time. Deduction No. 1, for twenty years before beginning, 7,300 days; remainder, 18,250 days. Out of this remainder you have to deduct one third at a blow for one item, sleep. Deduction No. 2, 6,080 days, leaving remainder No. 2, 12,170 days. Once more De Quincey says, on account of illness, of recreation, and the serious occupations spread over the surface of life, it will be little enough to deduct another third. In the case of the minister it will be more, rather than less; for, as I understand him, the time occupied in public speaking comes in here—but call it one-third. Deduction No. 3, 4,060 days, leaves remainder No. 3, 8,110 days. Finally, he says for the single item which the Roman armies grouped under the phrase "*corpus curare,*" attendance upon the animal necessities—eating, drinking, washing, bathing and exercise —deduct the smallest proper amount from the last remainder of 8,110 days, and you will have less than 4,000 days in a long life left for the direct development of all that is most august in the nature of man. After that comes the night, when no man can work. Four thousand days—one solid mass of time, amounting to eleven and a half continuous years. This, brethren, is your intellectual and spiritual working life to-day. Does it look small? It is priceless. Its value is incomputable. To what could I compare it? To the sparkling crown jewels of the Tower of London? To the glittering treasures of the Saxon Green Vault? To the massive jewelry of the walls, even of the Apocalyptic City? They cannot represent its value. Nothing can so well picture its worth as the Master's own Parable of the Pounds. This is the glorious inheritance which, in the name of that Master, I commit to your hands to-day, with his own great charge, "Occupy till I come."
Dr. Henry Smith.

10,218. LIFE, Boundary of. I compare life to a little wilderness, surrounded by a high dead wall. Within this space we muse and walk in quest of the new and happy, forgetting the insuperable limit, till, with surprise, we find ourselves stopped by the dead wall: we turn away, and muse and walk again, till, on another side, we find ourselves close against the dead wall. Whichever way we turn—still the same.
John Foster.

10,219. LIFE, Brevity of. We need no reed, no pole, no measuring line, wherewith to take the dimensions of our days; nor any skill in arithmetic, wherewith to compute the number of them. No; we have the standard of them at our fingers' ends; and there is no multiplication of it; it is but one hand-breath in all.
Henry.

10,220. LIFE, Brief. And surely, if we deduct all those days of our life which we might wish unlived, and which abate the comfort of those we now live, if we reckon up only those days which God hath accepted of our lives, a life of good years will hardly be a span long; the son in this sense may outlive the father, and none climacterically old.
Browne.

10,221. LIFE, Christian. It is by going on to new problems that the mathematician perfects himself in science; it is by copying new scenes that the artist perfects himself in art; it is by practising new pieces that the musician perfects himself in song; and it is by new manifestations of Jesus that the believer also makes his advances.
Power.

10,222. LIFE, Circle of. Vice-President Wilson is reported as saying a few months before his death: "Our lives, after all, are a great deal like a circle, which commences at our birth, and as the circle draws nearer to its close we, in our mind's eye, can see clearer our childhood and our earlier life, with its triumphs, its hardships, its pleasures, its sorrows, and its lost opportunities. I don't know, however, as I would wish to live my life over, for everything has been ordered by a good Providence. Oh, yes—our lives are just like a circle."

10,223. LIFE, Close of. Life's evening, we may rest assured, will take its character from the day which has preceded it; and if we would close our career in the comfort of religious hope, we must prepare for it by early and continuous religious habit.
Shuttleworth.

10,224. LIFE, Darkened. The mass of Christians make a little dark world of their own, and live there. They build the walls of their houses out of their troubles and sorrows. They put stained glass in their windows. They keep the doors locked. It is all dark about them. No sunshine comes into their chambers, and no fire burns on the hearth. They have no pictures on their walls but the pictures of their dead joys. And there they live, from year to year, in gloom and sadness, because they will not let God's sunshine in. I meet many persons who can talk for hours of their troubles, sorrows and cares, who seem to forget that God ever made a flower, or a star, or a sunbeam, or did a single kind, tender thing for them.
J. R. Miller.

10,225. LIFE, Desire of. We are naturally desirous to live; and though we prize life above all earthly things, yet we are ashamed to profess that we desire it for its own sake, but pretend some other subordinate reason to affect it. One would live to finish his building or clear his purchase; another to breed his children and see them well matched: one would fain outlive his trial at law; another wishes to outwear an emulous co-rival; one would fain outlast a lease that holds him off from his long-expected possessions; another would live to see the times amend, and a re-establishment of a public peace. Thus we would seem to wish life for anything but itself.
Bishop Hall.

10,226. LIFE, Dissatisfied with. The godly have oft a satiety of life: as willing they are to leave the world, as men are wont to be to rise from the board when they have eaten their fill. They feign that when Tithonus might have been made immortal, he would not, because of the miseries of life. This made Plotinus the Platonist account mortality a mercy, and Cato protest that if any god would grant him if old to be made young again, he would seriously refuse it. "As for me," said Queen Elizabeth, in a certain speech, "I see no such great cause why I should be fond to live, or afraid to die." While I call to mind things past, behold things present, and expect things to come, I hold him happiest that goeth hence soonest. *Trapp.*

10,227. LIFE, Division of. I highly approve the end and intent of Pythagoras's injunction; which is, to dedicate the first part of life more to hear and learn, in order to collect materials out of which to form opinions founded on proper lights, and well-examined sound principles, than to be presuming, prompt, and flippant in hazarding one's own slight crude notions of things, and thus exposing the nakedness and emptiness of the mind, like a house opened to company before it is fitted either with necessities or any ornament for their reception and entertainment. *Earl of Chatham.*

10,228. LIFE, Doubling. A good man doubles the length of his existence; to have lived so as to look back with pleasure on our past existence is to live twice. *Martial.*

10,229. LIFE, Effort to Prolong. Amestes, the wife of the great monarch Xerxes, buried alive in the ground twelve persons, as an offering to Pluto, for the prolonging of her own life.

10,230. LIFE, Embroidering. Life is like a roll of costly material passing swiftly through our hands, and we must embroider our pattern on it as it goes. We cannot wait to pick up a false stich, or pause too long before we set another. Only, if we keep our eye ever on our great Exemplar, we shall find, when he finishes off our work, and smooths out its rumples, and cuts away its frayed ends, then even its spots and mistakes fall into a purpose in its plan. *Edward Garrett.*

10,231. LIFE, Ending. Augustus, a few minutes before his death, asked his friends who stood about him, if they thought he had acted his part well; and upon receiving such an answer as was due to his extraordinary merit, "Let me, then," says he, "go off the stage with your applause;" using the expression with which the Roman actors made their exit at the conclusion of a dramatic piece. I could wish that men, while they are in health, would consider well the nature of the part they are engaged in, and what figure it will make in the minds they leave behind them; whether it was worth coming into the world for; whether it be suitable to a reasonable being; in short, whether it appears graceful in this life, or will turn to advantage in the next. *Addison.*

10,232. LIFE, Estimate of. There appears to exist a greater desire to live long than to live well! Measure by man's desires, he cannot live long enough; measure by his good deeds, and he has not lived long enough, measure by his evil deeds, and he has lived too long. *Zimmerman.*

10,233. LIFE, Eternity and. Think of "living!" Thy life, wert thou the "pitifullest of all the sons of earth," is no idle dream, but a solemn reality. It is thy own; it is all thou hast to front eternity with. Work, then, even as he has done, and does, "like a star, unhasting, yet unresting." *Carlyle*

10,234. LIFE, Evanescent. Children frequently write their names in the white sand by the sea shore, only to see them washed out again by the incoming wave; or in the snow, from which they quickly disappear before the rays of the sun. Where have you written? on the face of the transient earth, or on the tablets of the immortal soul? It is well to test our work by this question.

10,235. LIFE, Examples of. It is the greatest and first use of history to show us the sublime in morals, and to tell us what great men have done in perilous seasons. Such beings, and such actions, dignify our nature, and breathe into us a virtuous pride which is the parent of every good. Wherever you meet with them in the page of history, read them, mark them, and learn from them how to live and how to die; for the object of common men is only to live. The object of such men as I have spoken of, was to live grandly, and in favor with their own difficult spirits; to live, if in war, gloriously; if in peace, usefully, justly and freely! *S. Smith.*

10,236. LIFE, Exercise in. Too often neglected and allowed to lapse into wickedness, trained and exercised, life will quicken into grandeur. "It is better to wear out than rust out," says a homely proverb, with more meaning than people commonly suppose. Rust consumes faster than use. To "wear out," implies life and its pleasures; to "rust," the stagnation of death. *Grindon.*

10,237. LIFE, Failure in. Many men fail in life from the want, as they are too ready to suppose, of those great occasions wherein they might have shown their trustworthiness and their integrity. But all such persons should remember, that in order to try whether a vessel be leaky, we first prove it with water before we trust it with wine. The more minute, trivial, and we might say vernacular opportunities of being just and upright, are constantly occurring to every one; and it is an unimpeachable character in these lesser things that almost invariably prepares and produces those opportunities of greater advancement, and of higher confidence, which turn out so rich a harvest, but which those alone are permitted to reap who have previously sown. *Colton.*

10,238. LIFE, Frailty of. My life is a frail life; a corruptible life: a life, which the more it increaseth, the more it decreaseth: the farther it goeth, the nearer it cometh to death. A deceitful life, and like a shadow, full of the snares of death: now I rejoice, now I languish; now I flourish, now infirm; now I live, and straight I die; now I seem happy, always miserable; now I laugh, now I weep: thus all things are subject to mutability, that nothing continueth an hour in one estate: oh, joy above joy, exceeding all joy, without which there is no joy, when shall I enter into thee, that I may see my God that dwelleth in thee! *St. Augustine*

10,239. LIFE, Glory of. A medical student went to Fasle, in the sixteenth century, to obtain the degree of M. D. When his studies were nearly completed he was stricken with mortal sickness. The prize he sought was constantly before his mind. He could not die easily without it. So, in his bed, and on the verge of eternity, he was made a doctor, to his great satisfaction; and then died like any plebeian.

10,240. LIFE, Guarded. Our passage through life is like that of the children of Israel through the Red Sea. Doubt and darkness are before us, unless God enlighten our path: the enemy presseth upon us behind, unless God check his pursuit: the waters stand in heaps on each hand of us; if they open a path to us, it is through the word of his power, which were he to recall, the water-flood stands ready to overflow us, the deep to swallow us up, the pit to shut her mouth upon us. Amidst perils, which thus encompass us round on every side, what continual need have we to look up to the Almighty for aid and support! *Townson.*

10,241. LIFE, Happiest Period of. Probably the happiest period in life most frequently is in middle age, when the eager passions of youth are cooled, and the infirmities of age not yet begun; as we see that the shadows which are at morning and evening so large, almost entirely disappear at mid-day. *Dr. T. Arnold.*

10,242. LIFE, Hidden. A great preacher compares the hidden life of the Christian to the telegraph wires, from which the wailing of the winds is often heard, while at the same time it may be some messages of love or peace are passing through them. Sorrow may range without, but the child of God is receiving grace, strength and hope, unseen by the keenest observer.

10,243. LIFE, Human. This life is a season of probation, assigned to us for the purpose of making our choice between everlasting happiness or misery. This life, considered as it is in itself, is an object of contempt. We may say of it, with the sacred writer, that it is a shadow that passeth away; a vanity which has nothing real or solid; a flower which fadeth; grass which withereth and is cut down; a vapor which dissolves into air; a dream which leaves no trace after the sleep is gone; a thought which presents itself to the mind, but abideth not; an apparition; a nothing before God. But when we contemplate this life in its relation to the great end which God proposes to himself in bestowing it upon us, let us form exalted ideas of it; let us carefully compute all its subdivisions; let us husband with scrupulous attention all the instants of it, even the most minute and imperceptible; let us regret the precious moments which we have irrecoverably lost. For this shadow which passeth, this vanity which hath nothing real or solid, this flower which fadeth, this grass which is cut down and withereth, this vapor which melteth into air, this forgotten dream, this transient thought, this apparition destitute of body and substance, this nothing, this span of life so vile and contemptible,—is time which we must redeem, a time of visitation which we must know, a time accepted; a day of salvation which we must improve, a period of forbearance and long-suffering which we must embrace, a time beyond which there shall be time no longer, because, after life is finished, tears are unavailing, sighs impotent, prayers are disregarded, and repentance is ineffectual. *Saurin.*

10,244. LIFE, An Infidel's. I now found myself, in the decline of life, a prey to tormenting maladies, and believing myself at the close of my career without having once tasted the sublime pleasures after which my heart panted. Why was it that, with a soul naturally expansive, whose very existence was benevolence, I have never found one single friend with feelings like my own? A prey to the cravings of a heart which have never been satisfied, I perceived myself arrived at the confines of old age, and dying ere I had begun to live. I considered destiny as in my debt for promises which she had never realized. Why was I created with faculties so refined, yet which were never intended to be adequately employed? I felt my own value, and revenged myself of my fate by recollecting and shedding tears for its injustice. *J. J. Rousseau.*

10,245. LIFE, Joy and Sorrow in. Ha is the interjection of laughter; ah is the interjection of sorrow. The difference betwixt them very small, as consisting only in the transposition of what is no substantial letter, but a bare aspiration. How quickly, in the age of a minute, in the very turning of a breath, is our mirth changed into mourning! *T. Fuller.*

10,246. LIFE, Lengthening. Mycerinus, son of Cleops, king of Egypt, caused the temples of the gods to be re-opened, which his father had ordered closed, and gave liberty to the oppressed of his people. But the oracle sent him word from the city of Buti, that he should live but six years, and die in the seventh. Indignant at the idea, he determined to deceive the oracle if possible, by causing many lamps to be made and lighted at night. By these he indulged his genius, and kept in constant action night and day, intending in this way to lengthen his six years to twelve.

10,247. LIFE, Living. "In my opinion, he only may be truly said to live, and enjoy his being, who is engaged in some laudable pursuit, and acquires a name by some illustrious action or useful art." Thus the heathen Sallust places life in activity. Rousseau, the infidel, could find no reason for his existence, and felt himself mocked by destiny. The philosopher Locke declared that there is no satisfaction, except in doing well, and the hopes of a future life.

10,248. LIFE, a Loan. Some men make a womanish complaint that it is a great misfortune to die before our time. I would ask, What time? Is it that of nature? But she, indeed, has lent us life, as we do a sum of money, only no certain day is fixed for payment. What reason, then, to complain if she demands it at pleasure, since it was on this condition you received it?　　　*Cicero.*

10,249. LIFE, Measure of. They report that about Pontus, there are some creatures of such an extempore being that the whole time of their life is confined within the space of a day; for they are brought forth in the morning, are in the prime of their existence at noon, grow old at night, and then die. Dost thou not think that if these had the soul and reason of a man, that they would be so affected, and that things would happen to them after the same manner as to us?—that those who died before the meridian would be lamented with tears and groans—and that we should call them happy who lived their day out? For the measure of a man's life is the well spending of it, and not the length.　　　*Plutarch.*

10,250. LIFE, Mingled. The web of our life is of a mingled yarn, good and ill together: our virtues would be proud, if our faults whipped them not; and our crimes would despair, if they were not cherished by our virtues.　　　*Shakspeare.*

10,251. LIFE, Nearing the End of. "We are traveling," says John Newton, in writing to a friend, "in the coach of time; every day and hour brings us nearer home, and the coach wheels whirl round apace when we are upon the road; we seldom think the carriage goes too fast; we are pleased to pass the milestones; I call new-year's day, or my birth-day, a milestone. I have now almost reached my seventy-third year by mile-stones; what dangers have I escaped or been brought through? If my heart would jump to be within three miles of you, why does it not jump from morning till night, to think that I am probably within three years of seeing the Lamb upon the throne, and joining in the praises of the blessed spirits of the redeemed, who behold him without a veil or a cloud, and are filled with his glory and love!"

10,252. LIFE, Object of. There are almost as many interests in the world as there are men. Every one you meet in the streets is going after something. You see it in his face, his quick eye, and his rapid walk. Either it is political, or literary, or mercantile, or scientific, or fashionable, or simply ambitious, or dishonest. Still, whatever it is, every man has wedded the interest of his choice, and is doing his duty to it. He works hard for it all day; he goes to bed with the thought of it, and he wakes with it in the morning. Even on Sunday, it is rather his hand that is resting than his head or his heart; they are full of his interests. Look what men will do, singly or banded, to put down slavery, or to get free trade, or to compete for a large order, or to carry the mails, or to make new railroads. It is plain men have interests enough in the world, that they love them dearly, and work for them manfully. Oh, that it were all for God—the good, the merciful, the eternal God.　*F. W. Faber.*

10,253. LIFE, Parable of. A parable says that there was a great king who employed his people to weave for him. The silk, and woof,

and patterns were al given by the king, and he looked for diligent working people. He was very indulgent, and told them when any difficulty arose to send to him, and he would help them; and never to fear troubling him, but to ask for help and instruction. Among many men and women busy at their looms was one little child whom the king did not think too young to work. Often alone at her work, cheerfully and patiently she labored. One day, when the men and women were distressed at the sight of their failures—the silks were tangled, and the weaving unlike the pattern—they gathered round the child and said, "Tell us how it is that you are so happy in your work. We are always in difficulties." "Then why do you not send to the king?" said the little weaver; "he told us that we might do so." "So we do, night and morning." "Ah," said the child, "but I send as often as I have a little tangle."

10,254. LIFE, Passing through. When men travel in stage coaches in grand mountain countries, some ride in the inside with the curtains fastened down. They see nothing of the beauty of the scenes through which they pass. Others ride outside, and see every grand thing by the way. This illustrates the way different persons go through God's world. Many pass through shut up inside a dark, dismal coach, with all the curtains drawn tight, themselves shut in, and all of God's joy and beauty shut out; others ride outside, and catch a glimpse of every fair and lovely thing by the way. They breathe the fresh air, hear the joyous songs of the birds, see the fields, brooks, rivers, mountains and skies, and quaff delight everywhere,　　　　*J. R. Miller.*

10,255. LIFE, Pendulum of. At every swing of the pendulum a spirit goes into eternity. Between the rising and the setting of every sun, 43,000 souls are summoned before their Creator. Death is ever busy, night and day, at all seasons, and in all climes. He is supplied with a boundless variety of darts and arrows, with which he accomplishes his work. Could all the forms in which death comes to man be written together, what a long and fearful catalogue would it make! Think of the innumerable number of diseases, all at the command of death. And, as though these were not sufficient, see how man is exposed to fatal accidents on every hand, and at every moment. Flavel said, that "the smallest pore in the body is a door large enough to let in death. The least gnat in the air may choke one, as it did Adrian, a pope of Rome. A little hair in milk may strangle one, as it did a councillor in Rome. A little skin of a raisin may stop one's breath, as it did the lyric poet, Anacreon."　　*Teachers' Treasury.*

10,256. LIFE, Phases of. At twenty years of age, the will reigns; at thirty, the wit; and at forty, the judgment.　　　*Gratian.*

10,257. LIFE, Pivots in. Biography is full of illustrations of the turning of the tide of men's lives by the most insignificant (yet mightily significant) occurrences. The current of John

Fletcher's life was turned by the spilling of a pot of coffee.   *Dr. Foss.*

10,258. LIFE, Portraits of. By the discoveries of modern science, the rays of the sun are made to form the exact portrait of him on whom they shine. We are all living in the sunlight of eternity, which is transferring to plates more enduring than brass, the exact portrait of the soul in every successive act, with all its attendant circumstances. Interesting to the antiquary is the moment when he drags out from the sands of Egypt some obelisk on which the "pen of iron, and the point of a diamond," have graven the portraits, the attitudes, the dresses, and the pursuits of men who lived and died three thousand years ago. But none can utter the interest of that moment, when from the silence of eternity shall be brought out tablets thick set with the sculptured history of a sinful soul, and men and angels, with the sinner himself, shall gaze appalled on the faithful portraiture of a life of sin.   *Wm. Jones.*

10,259. LIFE, Prolonging. The philosopher Descartes suggested to Sir Kenelm Digby that he would employ himself better in seeking to discover some means of prolonging human life, than in philosophical speculations. Descartes assured him that he had reflected long upon the subject, and though he dared not promise immortality, he was certain he had the power of enabling men to attain the age of the patriarchs. This conceit of his was well known in Holland. His pupil, Abbe Picot, believing this, discredited the report of his death.

10,260. LIFE, Purpose of. I have read of an author, who, whilst he was writing a book he was about to publish, would every now and then look back to the title to see if his work corresponded thereto, and if it answered the expectation raised thereby. Now, the use I would make hereof, and would recommend to you, is for thee, O sinner, to look back every now and then, and consider for what thou wast created; and for thee, O saint, to look back every now and then, and consider for what thou wast redeemed.   *Ashburner.*

10,261. LIFE, Race for. A hound, having started a hare from a bush, chased her for some distance, but the hare had the best of it, and got off. A goatherd, who was coming by, jeered at the hound, saying that puss was the better runner of the two. "You forget," replied the hound, "that it is one thing to be running for your dinner, and another for your life."   *Æsop.*

10,262. LIFE, Record of. According to the Koran, the angel AL SIGIL keeps a complete record of every man's life, embracing thoughts and deeds, good and bad. At a man's death, the scroll is rolled up and preserved, to be reproduced at the resurrection.

10,263. LIFE, Register of. One of the Rev. John Fletcher's parishioners in Madeley, says that when a young man, he was married by Mr. Fletcher, who said to him, as soon as the service was concluded, and he was about to make the accustomed entry, "Well, William, you have had your name entered into our reg-ister once before this." "Yes, sir, at my baptism." "And now your name will be entered a second time; you have no doubt thought much about your present step, and made proper preparations for it in a great many different ways." "Yes, sir." "Recollect, however, that a third entry of your name—the register of your burial—will sooner or later take place. Think, then, about death, and make preparation for that also, lest it overtake you as a thief in the night."

10,264. LIFE, Re-Lived. The little boy—son of Lady Duncan—beautifully dressed in the Highland dress, was carried to Vicky, and gave her a basket with fruit and flowers. I said to Albert I could hardly believe that our child was traveling with us; it put me so in mind of myself when I was the "little Princess." Albert observed that it was always said that parents lived their lives over again in their children, which is a very pleasant feeling.   *Queen Victoria.*

10,265. LIFE, Re-Living. Though I think no man can live well once but he that could live well twice, yet for my own part I would not live over my hours past, or begin again the thread of my days: not upon Cicero's ground, because I have lived them well, but for fear I should live them worse.   *Sir T. Browne.*

10,266. LIFE, Results of a. It was the boast of Augustus that he found the city of Rome built of brick, and that he left it built of marble.

10,267. LIFE, Riddle of. How true is that old fable of the sphinx who sat by the wayside, propounding her riddle to the passengers, which if they could not answer, she destroyed them! Such a sphinx is this life of ours to all men and societies of men. Nature, like the sphinx, is of womanly celestial loveliness and tenderness; the face and bosom of a goddess, but ending in claws and the body of a lioness. There is in her a celestial beauty, which means celestial order, pliancy to wisdom; but there is also a darkness, a ferocity, a fatality, which are infernal. She is a goddess, but one not yet disimprisoned; one still half imprisoned,—the inarticulate, lovely, still encased in the inarticulate, chaotic. How true! And does she not propound her riddles to us? Of each man she asks daily, in mild voice, yet with a terrible significance, "Knowest thou the meaning of this day? What thou canst do to-day, wisely attempt to do." Nature, universe, destiny, existence, howsoever we name this great unnameable fact in the midst of which we live and struggle, is as a heavenly bride and conquest to the wise and brave, to those who can discern her behests and do them; a destroying fiend to those who cannot. Answer her riddle, it is well with thee. Answer it not, pass on regarding it not, it will answer itself: the solution of it is a thing of teeth and claws. Nature is a dumb lioness, deaf to thy pleadings, fiercely devouring.   *Carlyle.*

10,268. LIFE, Rule of. While Thomas Paine resided in Bordentown, N. J., he met the Rev. Dr. Staughton. After some remarks of a general character, Paine observed, "Mr. Staughton, what a pity it is that man has not some comprehensive and perfect rule for the government of his life!" The doctor replied, "Mr. Paine, there is such a rule." "What is that?" Paine inquired. Dr. S. repeated the passage, "Thou shalt love the Lord thy God with all thy heart, and thy neighbor as thyself." Abashed and confused, Paine replied, "Oh, that's in your Bible," and immediately walked away.

10,269. LIFE, Serious. Inscriptions were common upon old-time English houses. One, still standing in Cheshire, has the following inscription: "*Fleres si scires unum tua tempora mensem; ridis cum non scis si sit forsitan una dies.*" You would weep if you knew that your life was limited to one month; yet you laugh when you know not but that it may be restricted to a day.

10,270. LIFE, a Sermon. Our every life is a sermon. Our birth is the text from which we start. Youth is the introduction to the discourse. During our manhood we lay down a few propositions and prove them. Some of the passages are dull, and some are sprightly. Then come inferences and applications. At seventy years we say, "Fifthly and lastly." The doxology is sung. The benediction is pronounced. The book is closed. It is getting cold. Frost on the window-pane. Audidience gone. Shut up the church. Sexton goes home with the key on his shoulder.
Talmage.

10,271. LIFE, Shortness of. "A man is a bubble," said the Greek proverb, which Lucian represents to this purpose, saying, "All the world is a storm, and men rise up in their several generations like bubbles descending from God, and the dew of heaven, and some of these instantly sink into the deluge of their first parent, and are hidden in a sheet of water, having had no other business in the world but to be born, that they may be able to die; others float up and down two or three turns, and suddenly disappear, and give their place to others: and they that live longest upon the face of the waters are in perpetual motion, restless and uneasy, and being crushed with a great drop of the cloud, sink into flatness and a froth; the change not being great, it being hardly possible it should be more a nothing than it was before." Homer calls a man "a leaf," the smallest, the weakest piece of a short-lived, unsteady plant. Pindar calls him "the dream of a shadow;" another, "the dream of the shadow of smoke."
Jeremy Taylor.

10,272. LIFE, Stream of. Beneath me flows the Rhine, and, like the stream of time, it flows amid the ruins of the past. I see myself therein, and know that I am old. Thou, too, shalt be old. Be wise in season. Like the stream of thy life runs the stream beneath us. Down from the distant Alps, out into the wide world, it bursts away, like a youth from the house of his fathers. Broad-breasted and strong, and with earnest endeavors, like manhood, it makes itself a way through these difficult mountain-passes. And at length, in old age, it falters, and its steps are weary and slow, and it sinks into the sand, and through its grave passes into the great ocean, which is its eternity. Thus shall it be with thee. *Longfellow.*

10,273. LIFE Too Short. Themistocles, a renowned Grecian general, lived to the advanced age of one hundred and seven. Seeing that his end was hastening, he grieved that he must die, saying, "It is but now chiefly that I began to grow wise."

10,274. LIFE, Tragedy of. Act. 1.—Young man starting from home. Parents and sisters weeping to see him go. Wagon passing over the hill. Farewell kiss thrown back. Ring the bell and let the curtain drop. Act 2.—Marriage altar. Bright lights. Full organ. White vail trailing through the aisle. Prayer and congratulations, and exclamations of "How well she looks!" Ring the bell and let the curtain drop. Act 3.—Midnight. Woman waiting for staggering steps. Old garments stuck into broken window panes. Many marks of hardship on the face. Biting the nails of bloodless fingers. Neglect, cruelty, disgrace. Ring the bell and let the curtain drop. Act 4.—Three graves in a very dark place. Grave of a child, who died from want of medicine; grave of a husband and father, who died of dissipation; grave of a wife and mother, who died of a broken heart. Plenty of weeds, but no flowers! Oh, what a blasted heath, with three graves! Ring the bell and let the curtain drop. Act 5.—A destroyed soul's eternity. No light; no music; no hope! Despair coiling around the heart with unutterable anguish. Blackness of darkness forever! Woe! woe! woe! I cannot bear longer to look. I close my eyes at this last act of the tragedy. Quick! quick! Ring the bell and let the curtain drop. *Talmage.*

10,275. LIFE, True. The mere lapse of years is not life. To eat, and drink, and sleep, to be exposed to darkness and the light, to pace round in the mill of habit, and turn thought into an implement of trade, this is not life. In all this but a poor fraction of the consciousness of humanity is awakened; and the sanctities will slumber which make it worth while to be. Knowledge, truth, love, beauty, goodness, faith, alone can give vitality to the mechanism of existence. The laugh of mirth that vibrates through the heart; the tears that freshen the dry wastes within; the music that brings childhood back; the prayer that calls the future near; the doubt which makes us meditate; the death which startles us with mystery; the hardship which forces us to struggle; the anxiety that ends in trust; are the true nourishment of our natural being.
James Martineau.

10,276. LIFE, Use of. You have seen the tiny blossom of the fruit-trees opening in early spring. After basking a few days in the sun, it fades and falls. A germ is left behind on the branch, but it is scarcely discernible among the leaves. It is a green speck that can hardly be felt between your fingers. If a hungry man should pluck and eat it, the morsel would not satisfy; the germ as to present use is a sapless, tasteless nothing. Grasped now as your object and end, it is the most worthless of all things; but left, and cherished as the germ of fruit, it is the most precious. This life is the bud of eternity; if plucked, and used as the portion of the soul, that soul will be empty now and empty forever. But, while thus abused it is worthless, rightly used it is beyond all price. Here is generated, cherished, ripened, the life that will never die.

Arnot.

10,277. LIFE, Wanted. The old Spartan, who tried to make a corpse stand upright, but found that it would fall, said, "Ah, it wants something inside!" Yes, it wanted life.

S. Coley.

10,278. LIFE, Way of. The way is good, says Chrysostom, if it be to a feast, though through a dark and miry lane; if to an execution, not good, though through the fairest street of the city. *Non qua sed quo.* Not the way, but the end, is to be mainly considered.

Anon.

10,279. LIFE, Work of. On the day before his death, Dr. Arnold, of Rugby, made the following entry in his journal: "The day after tomorrow is my birthday, if I am permitted to live to see it—my forty-seventh birthday since my birth. How large a portion of my life on earth is already passed! And then what is to follow this life? How visibly my outward work seems contracting and softening away into the gentler employments of old age. In one sense, how nearly can I now say '*Vixi;*' and I thank God that, as far as ambition is concerned, it is I trust fully mortified. I have no desire other than to step back from my present place in the world, and not to rise to a higher. Still there are works which, with God's permission, I would do before the night cometh; especially that great work, if I might be permitted to take part in it. But, above all, let me mind my own personal work, to keep myself pure and zealous and believing, laboring to do God's will, yet not anxious that it should be done by me rather than by others, if God disapproves of my doing it." He woke next morning, between five and six, in pain. At eight o'clock he was dead!

10,280. LIGHT, Divine. "God is light." 1 John 1:5. Clothed with light as with a garment, Ps. 104:2; dwelling in light inaccessible to mortal frames, 1 Tim. 6:16; "the Father of lights," James 1:17; "the light dwelleth with him," Dan. 2:22. CHRIST is "the light of the world," John 8:12; 12:46; "the true light," 1:9; "the light of men," 1:4; "a light to lighten the Gentiles," Luke 2:32; the light of the holy Jerusalem, Rev. 21:23; "the bright and morning star," Rev. 22:16; "the Sun of righteousness," Mal. 4:2; typified by the pillar of fire in the wilderness, and the golden candlestick in the Tabernacle and Temple.

Bowes.

10,281. LIGHT, Guiding. A fisherman off the coast of Scotland was overtaken by a storm before which he drifted at the mercy of the winds. He would have made for the harbor whence he came, but dense darkness came on, and there was no light by which he could shape his course. His frail fishing-smack began to leak badly, and could not long stand the storm, if she was not quickly driven upon the rocks. The fisherman prayed silently for deliverance. Soon after his son cried, "Father, I see a light." It was even so. The father saw it, shaped his course by it, and gained in safety the very harbor he desired to reach. The light which saved him was in his own house, and was lighted by one of his boys, and set by accident in the window. The fisherman during the rest of his life kept a light in that window, which was succeeded after his death by the Rocky Shore Island Light. "Let your light so shine."

10,282. LIGHT, Mental and Moral. Science and art may invent splendid modes of illuminating the apartments of the opulent; but these are all poor and worthless compared with the light which the sun sends into our windows,—which he pours freely, impartially, over hill and valley, which kindles daily the eastern and western sky; and so the common lights of reason, and conscience and love, are of more worth and dignity than the rare endowments which give celebrity to a few.

Dr. Channing.

10,283. LIGHT, More. When one of the Reformers had acquitted himself in a public disputation with great credit to his Master's cause, a friend begged to see the notes which he had been observed to write, supposing that he had taken down the arguments of his opponents, and sketched the substance of his own reply. He was greatly surprised to find that his notes consisted of these ejaculatory petitions, "More light, Lord,—more light, more light!"

10,284. LIGHT, Omniscience and. What an emblem is light of omniscience! We question it of the atom and the distant world, and it answers us with its full revelations. God says his eyes are on the ways of men, and he seeth all their doings; there is no darkness nor shadow of death where the workers of iniquity may hide themselves. The figure is, that God uses light as the means of his omniscience.

Dr. H. W. Warren.

10,285. LIGHT, Reflection of. If the sun shines on a dull brick or stone, they reflect none of its beams, there is nothing in them capable of this, nor is there in an ungodly man any natural power of reflecting the light of God. But let the sun shine upon a diamond, and see what rays of sparkling beauty it emits. Just so the Christian who has the graces of the Spirit. When God shines on his soul, beams of celestial loveliness are reflected by him on the world.

Rowland Hill.

10,286. LIGHT, Rekindled. St. Gudula was accustomed just before daybreak to visit an oratory about two miles from her father's castle to pray. One wild night, says the legend, the Prince of the power of the air extinguished the light which a servant maid carried before her. She was on a desolate heath, and the darkness was so dense that she could not find the path. She knelt and prayed to God for help, and the light in her lantern was rekindled, to her great relief and joy. Paintings of this saint represent her as carrying a lantern. She lived in Brabant in the seventh century.

10,287. LIGHT, Shining. The sun's rays go alike above, below, on all sides, and in all directions. It looks every way, and in every way sends forth what it has received. A candle, too, sends its light equally into all corners of the room; wherever you stand, its light comes to you alike. So, from a Christian, light should go forth in all directions, and at all times, naturally, not by impulsive emissions, but by regular irradiations. *Morse.*

10,288. LIGHT, Shunning the. Some people retire to conceal their defects. Too much light discovers the wrinkles, which makes them choose to sit out of the sun. *Collier.*

10,289. LIGHT, A Small. A man said, "I have no more influence than a farthing rushlight." "Well," was the reply, "a farthing rushlight can do a good deal; it can set a haystack on fire; it can burn down a house—yea, more, it will enable a poor creature to read a chapter in God's book. Go your way, friend; let your farthing rushlight so shine before men, that others, seeing your good works, may glorify your Father which is in heaven."

10,290. LIGHTS, The Lower. A vessel was coming into Cleveland harbor on a stormy night. The pilot saw the upper lights on the bluff burning, but not the lower, and asked the captain if he had better put out into the lake again. The captain was afraid of the storm on the lake, and thought they had better try to make the harbor. They did so, but were wrecked, and many lives lost, all because the lower lights had been put out by the storm. The upper lights of heaven are burning as brightly as ever, but the lower lights are out or dimly burning. God wants us to keep them burning, so as to keep people from stumbling over us, or being lost because our light is out. *Moody.*

10,291. LIGHTNING, Effect of. Arago found it related somewhere that lightning, which fell one day into the shop of a Suabian cobbler, respected the person of the artisan himself, but had the singular effect of magnetizing all his tools. The fantastic book in which the learned secretary of the academy found this account represents the cobbler in great dismay. His hammer, his pincers, his awl, attracted all the nails and needles of the establishment, and caused them to adhere firmly to the tools. The poor fellow thought everything in his shop had been bedeviled, or that he was dreaming. *Fonvielle.*

10,292. LIKENESS, Necessary to Liking. A collier, who had more room in his house than he wanted for himself, proposed to a fuller to come and take up his quarters with him. "Thank you," said the fuller, "but I must decline your offer; for I fear that as fast as I whiten my goods you will blacken them again."

10,293. LILIES, Oriental. "Our camels," says a traveler in Palestine, "were scattered on the mountain slopes in search of food. On these heights the lilies abounded, with grass and low shrubs between. I noticed that the camels did not touch the lilies at all, but cropped what lay between. It reminded me of the words, 'He feedeth among the lilies'—among, but not on the lilies; for, while the lily furnishes no acceptable food for flocks and herds, it seems, by the shade of its high, broad leaves, to retain the moisture, and so to nourish herbage wherever it grows. The place of lilies would thus be the place of the richest pasture, as Solomon evidently indicates, when, again using the figure, he speaks of the 'young roes which feed among the lilies.'" In the course of his travels in the East, Dr. Bonar informs us that he came to immense beds of lilies and hyacinths of various kinds. They grew thickly together, and covered miles of sand. "They grow," he tells us, "in almost incredible numbers and luxuriance—often where nothing else flourishes—reminding one of the prophet's allusion, 'He shall grow as the lily.'"

10,294. LITERATURE, Divine Protection of. The first national library founded in Egypt seemed to have been placed under the protection of the divinities, for their statues magnificently adorned this temple, dedicated at once to religion and to literature. It was still further embellished by a well-known inscription, forever grateful to the votary of literature; on the front was engraven "The nourishment of the soul;" or, according to Diodorus, "The medicine of the mind." *I. Disraeli.*

10,295. LITERATURE, Pleasures of. How I pity those who have no love of reading, of study, or of the fine arts! I have passed my youth amidst amusements and in the most brilliant society; but I can assert with perfect truth, that I have never tasted pleasures so true as those I have found in the study of books, in writing, or in music. The days that succeed brilliant entertainments are always melancholy, but those which follow days of study are delicious; we have gained something; we have acquired some new knowledge, and we recall the past day not only without disgust and without regret, but with consummate satisfaction. *Madame de Genlis.*

10,296. LITTLE FOXES, Danger from. I remember that when I was shown one, it was with the greatest difficulty I could persuade myself that the little, very little creature—not larger than a jerboa, or our common kitten—playing with deft foot-fall and kindly-intelligent eye about its cage, really was the destructive spoiler represented. It so happened, however, that the keeper of the gardens where it was, on coming round to arrange its crib, made a discovery that satisfied me of the character, or no character, of the very "little" deceiver before me. Lifting up the floor straw, he discovered a deep-burrowed hole that went right beneath the separating wall of the adjoining den—a tiger's; and with a start, examining it, the keeper found that another hour of secret working would have overthrown the wall, and let loose the fierce beast of prey. The whole had been done within a few hours. Those "little," grayish-white feet, licked pure and clean of all betraying soil, and that "little" sharp nose, so innocent and "pitiful" looking, had done their stealthy work: and apalling might have been the issue. I remember well how, as the littered, concealing straw was raised, the consciously guilty "little" hypocrite slunk back with drooped brush into the corner. *Grosart.*

10,297. LITTLE SINS, Fable of. A watch, of which better things were expected, behaved badly and was taken to the watchmaker for correction. He examined it with a powerful glass, and discovered a single little grain of sand. As he was about to remove it, it cried out, "Let me alone! I am but a small thing, and take up so little room. I cannot possibly injure the watch. Twenty or thirty might do harm, but I cannot; so let me alone." The watchmaker replied, "You must come out, for you spoil my work; and all the more so that you are so small, and but a few people can see you." Little sins ruin the most promising characters, and taint the best efforts.

10,298. LITTLE SINS, Growth of. "In the gardens of Hampton Court you will see many trees entirely vanquished and well nigh strangled by huge coils of ivy, which are wound about them like the snakes around the unhappy Laocoon: there is no untwisting the folds, they are too giant-like, and fast fixed, and every hour the rootlets of the climber are sucking the life out of the unhappy tree. Yet there was a day when the ivy was a tiny aspirant, only asking a little aid in climbing; had it been denied then, the tree had never become its victim; but by degrees the humble weakling grew in strength and arrogance, and at last it assumed the mastery, and the tall tree became the prey of the creeping, insinuating destroyer." Vice, intemperance, lust, avarice, anger, like the vines twine about a man, extract the life from him, and leave him a wreck.

10,299. LITTLE SINS, Treachery of. A vessel will sink, whether filled with heavy stones or with sand. Fine grains of sand will bury travelers in the desert. Fine flakes of snow, so light that they seem to hang in the air and scarce to fall, will, if they gather over the sleepy wayfarer, extinguish life; if they drift, they will bury whole houses and their dwellers. Fine, delicate sins, as people think them, will chill the soul and take away its life.
Dr. Pusey.

10,300. LITTLE THINGS, Damage of. A single pin fell upon a web of cloth as it was being passed over a drum. It cut a hole in the cloth with every revolution of the drum, and damaged it to the extent of three hundred dollars. Little sins, exaggerations, lies, dishonesty, are pins on the drum, that damage the web of character beyond computation.

10,301. LITTLE THINGS, Importance of. Let us not neglect little duties—let us not allow ourselves in little faults. Whatever we may like to think, nothing is really of small importance that affects the soul. All diseases are small at the beginning. Many a death-bed begins with a "little cold." Nothing that can grow is large all at once—the greatest sin must have a beginning. Nothing that is great comes to perfection in a day—characters and habits are all the result of little actions. Little strokes made that ark which saved Noah. Little pins held firm that tabernacle which was the glory of Israel. We too are traveling through a wilderness—let us be like the family of Merari, and be careful not to leave the pins behind. (Numbers 4: 32.) *Ryle.*

10,302. LITTLE THINGS, Influence of. A vessel passing through the English Channel was driven ashore at Beachy-head, by a storm, and the whole crew were washed overboard; four only being saved from immediate death, by being thrown on the rocks by which the vessel struck. A terrible fate seemed to await them; for although not under water, the waves appeared to be rapidly gaining on them. The darkness of the night, and the violence of the storm, prevented any help coming to them; and they sat waiting to be engulfed as their shipmates had been. In this terrible moment one of the sufferers, grasping a reed to hold himself more firmly to the rock, at once recognized it as the samphire; and knowing that the samphire is never submerged by the sea, he felt assured that he could say to the waves, "Hitherto shalt thou come, but no farther.". Encouraged by this, the poor fellows remained stationary until the morning. They were not deceived. The sea gradually retired; light broke on the shipwrecked seamen, and they were rescued from their perilous position.

10,303. LOGIC, Mathematical. A widow woman kept a hen that laid an egg every morning. Thought the woman to herself, "If I double my hen's allowance of barley she will lay twice a day." So she tried her plan, and the hen became so fat and sleek that she left off laying altogether. *Æsop.*

10,304. LONELINESS, Relief for. An orphan drummer-boy entered the office of the Christian Commission, and said that he had no friends, and had not received a letter in two years. "Would you like to have a letter?" asked the agent. "Oh yes, indeed I would." "Well, my son, I think I have one for you." He went to a bag, and taking out a letter written by a Sunday-school scholar for some lonely soldier, handed it to him. He took it and wept for joy, because he was remembered by somebody.

10,305. LONGING, Emblem of. A young man wanted to be a missionary; but his wealthy and worldly father thought he was too good for that, so he made a merchant of him. The young man went sadly about his daily tasks. Like the statue of Columbus at Genoa, which is made ever to look longingly westward, the heart of the disappointed young man would look longingly toward the ministry--toward the sublime services of that Prince of missionaries, the Lord Jesus Christ. 　　*Anon.*

10,306. LOOKING BACK: Oriental Custom. When men or women leave their house, they never look back, as "it would be very unfortunate." Should a husband have left anything which his wife knows he will require, she will not call on him to turn or look back; but will either take the article herself, or send it by another. Should a man, on some great emergency, have to look back, he will not then proceed on the business he was about to transact. When a person goes along the road (especially in the evening), he will take great care not to look back, "because the evil spirits would assuredly seize him." When they go on a journey, they will not look behind, though the palankeen or bandy would be close upon them; they step a little on one side, and then look at you. Should a person have to leave the house of a friend after sunset, he will be advised in going home not to look back: "As much as possible keep your eyes closed; fear not." Has a person made an offering to the evil spirits? he must take particular care, when he leaves the place, not to look back. A female known to me is believed to have got her crooked neck by looking back. Such observations as the following may be often heard in private conversation: "Have you heard that Comáran is very ill?" "No; what is the matter with him?" "Matter! why, he has looked back, and the evil spirit has caught him." *Roberts.*

10,307. LOQUACITY, Repenting of. Simonides said that he had often repented of talking, but never of being silent.

10,308. LOQUACITY, Restraining. The tongue ought to be environed with reason as with a rampart perpetually lying before it, like a mound, to stop the overflowing and slippery exuberance of impertinent talk; that we may not seem to be more silly than geese, which, when they take their flight out of Cilicia over the mountain Taurus, which abounds with eagles, are reported to carry every one a good big stone in their bills, instead of a bridle or barricade, to restrain their goggling. By which means they cross those hideous forests in the night time undiscovered. 　*Plutarch.*

10,309. LORD'S SUPPER, Import of the. A Malay youth, who was being educated in Scotland, as he came out of church one Sunday, was asked, "What have you seen in church to-day?" He answered, "I see people take bread and wine." "And what does that mean?" "The body and blood of Jesus Christ." "Is it really the body and blood of Jesus Christ?" "O, no," said he, "not all same: it keep in mind—keep in mind his body and blood—he die for sinners."

10,310. LORD'S SUPPER, a Memorial. The Lord's supper comes to us like a ring plucked off from Christ's finger, or a bracelet from his arm; or rather like his picture from his breast, delivered to us with such words as these, "As oft as you look on this, remember me."
　　　　John Flavel.

10,311. LORD'S SUPPER, Real Presence in the. Rev. Dr. Cumming, of London, says that in the Highlands of Scotland he once met a lady of noble birth, who asked him if he believed in the "real presence." "Certainly I do," he said, "I am very glad," she replied, "but you are the first Protestant clergyman I ever met with who did." "We attach different meanings to the same words," said Dr. Cumming. "I believe in the real presence of our Lord wherever two or three are gathered together in his name. I cannot believe as you do about the real presence, when I consider the words 'In remembrance of me.' Memory has to do with the past, with an absent friend. To eat and drink in remembrance of one who is actually present before one's eyes is an absurdity." A lady who accompanied her was silent; but a few months ago, Dr. Cumming received a letter from her father, saying that when his daughter went to Scotland she was on the verge of Romanism, owing to the influence of this noble friend, and that the words of Dr. Cumming on "In remembrance of me," were blessed by God in preventing her from becoming a Romanist, and that she was converted, and had just died rejoicing in Christ.

10,312. LORD'S SUPPER, Title in the. The Lord's supper being an evident proof that the New Testament is in full force, (it being the cup of the New Testament in his blood, Matt. 26:28,) it tends much to our satisfaction, as the legal execution of the deed by which we hold and enjoy our estate. So that when he saith, "Take, eat," it is as much as if God should stand before you at the table with Christ, with all the promises in his hand; and say, "I deliver this to thee as my deed." *John Flavel.*

10,313. LORD'S SUPPER, Unfit Array for the. To the table of the Lord many come with garlanded brow to commemorate him whose crown was of thorns; and, unfitly, stretch forth a jeweled hand to receive his sign whose hands the nails did tear. 　　　　*T. Collins.*

10,314. LOSSES, Lessons Derived from. A man seems never to know what anything means till he has lost it; and this, I suppose, is the reason why losses, vanishing away of things, are among the teachings of this world of shadows. The substance, indeed, teacheth, but the vacuity, whence it has disappeared, yet more. The full significancy of those words, property, ease, health—the wealth of meaning that lies in the fond epithets, parent, child, friend—we never know till they are taken away; till, in place of the bright, visible being, comes the awful and desolate shadow, where nothing is, where we stretch our hands in vain, and strain our eyes upon dark and dismal vacuity. Still, in that vacuity, we do not lose the object that we loved; it only becomes more real to us. Thus do blessings not only brighten when they depart, but are fixed in enduring reality; and friendship itself receives its everlasting seal beneath the cold impress of death. 　　*Dewey.*

10,315. LOSSES, Philosophic Endurance of. Aristippus lost a very fine farm, at which a feigned friend expressed great sympathy, and complained loudly. Aristippus replied, "Thou hast but one piece of land, but have I not three farms yet remaining? Why, then, should I not rather lament your misfortune, since it is the raving only of a madman to be concerned at what is lost, and not rejoice at what is left?"

10,316. LOSSES, Providence in. A traveler had lost himself in one of those hot, sandy deserts, where it is possible to journey for weeks without seeing a human dwelling. Almost famished by hunger and thirst, he at length reached a shady palm-tree and a spring of fresh water. Near the spring lay a small bag. "God be praised," said the man, when he felt the bag; "perhaps these are peas, which may save me from dying of hunger." He opened the bag eagerly, and was much disappointed when he found that it contained pearls, which, though valuable in themselves, are of no use to a man at the point of death from starvation. However, he took courage, and prayed fervently to God; and presently he saw a Moor riding quickly toward him on a camel, who took pity on him, and gave him bread and fruit. This Moor was seeking his bag of pearls, which he had lost, and upon receiving them from the traveler, he said, "How wonderful are the ways of Providence! I thought it a great misfortune to lose the pearls, and this same loss has afforded me the happiness of saving your life." *S. S. Visitor.*

10,317. LOSSES, Riches with. Dr. Poisal tells of an aged friend who had been very rich, but was suddenly reduced to poverty. His wife was anxious lest this reverse should unsettle her husband's faith. She watched him closely for a few days, to see its effect. His patient composure surprised her, and she told him of the fears she had felt for him, and expressed joy at his cheerfulness. With tearful eyes he said, "Wife, I have not lost everything." "Has thee not?" said she, "I thought all was lost." "Nay," said he, "I have yet one old bond left." Desiring to be sure, she asked to see the bond. "Get me the Bible," said he. She began to have visions of treasures hidden among its leaves in more prosperous days. "Open it and read the 13th chapter of Hebrews, fifth verse." She read, "I will never leave thee nor forsake thee." "Now, husband, I understand thee: God's promise is thy old bond." "Yes," said he. He is rich who has God for his banker, though his name would secure no earthly credit.

10,318. LOSSES, Selfishness in. The little son of a clergyman had two five-cent pieces given him, and was asked what he would do with them. Putting his finger upon one, the boy said: "This one I am going to give to the heathen, and the other I am going to keep myself." After playing with them awhile, one of them was lost, and he could not find it. "Well, my boy," said the father, "which one have you lost?" "Oh," said he, "I have lost the one I was going to give to the heathen."

10,319. LOST, Cry of the. A boy was sent on an errand during a severe snow-storm, and missing his way, wandered about till he was ready to perish. About midnight a gentleman heard a piteous voice crying, "Lost! lost! lost!" He sent out men to search for the lost person, and they soon found and saved the boy. But for his own fear and cry, he must have perished. This symbolizes the case of every sinner.

10,320. LOST, Hunting for the. A lady, observing the loss from her ring of a small but valuable stone, told her servant, who immediately said she would look for it, and left the room; she quickly returned with a lighted oil lamp, a dust-pan and brush. Putting the former on the floor by her side, she commenced sweeping the room all over most diligently; and looking by the light of the lamp carefully through the dust, she soon produced the tiny but precious stone. The eyes of the poor woman brightened when she discovered and restored it; and then, going into the verandah, she told the rest of the servants how she had found the stone which had been lost. *Anon.*

10,321. LOST, Searching for the. In wild countries, for children, or even men, to lose themselves, in the forests or on the prairies, is not an unfrequent occurrence. Then the alarm is given, "Lost! lost! a child lost, or a man lost," is the cry. The search begins. Man is lost. Christ is searching for him. So are all true Christians.

10,322. LOST, Sympathy for the. A theological student at the Biblical Institute, Concord, N. H., visited a lady who lay upon her dying bed despairing of salvation. No message of his could drive away this awful conviction. She said, "Ten years ago I might have been saved; but now I am lost, lost, lost." The student left her and returned to his books, but could not concentrate his mind upon his studies while that despairing cry, "Lost, lost," ran through his soul. "What business have I with books," he said to himself, "while a soul is perishing?" Again he visited the dying woman only to hear the same cry, "I am lost, lost, lost." The Spirit gave him the word, "Thank God for that, for now I know that you are one that Christ came to save."

10,323. LOVE, Appreciation of. During the chaplaincy of Rev. J. B. Finley at the Ohio penitentiary, a remarkable work of grace occurred in that institution. On visiting one of the happy converts, the chaplain found that in the overflow of his new-found love he had written with a piece of chalk all over the walls of his cell, " God is love! God is love!" O that all eyes might be opened to this heavenly vision.

10,324. LOVE, Baptism of. Frequently at the great Roman games, the emperors, in order to gratify the citizens of Rome, caused sweet perfumes to be rained down upon them through the awning which covered the amphitheatre. Behold the vases, the huge vessels of perfume! But there is naught here to delight you so long as the jars are sealed; but let the vases be opened, and the vessels be poured out, and let the drops of perfumed rain begin to descend, and every one is refreshed and gratified thereby. Such is the love of God. There is a richness and a fulness in it, but it is not per ceived till the Spirit of God pours it out like the rain of fragrance over the heads and hearts of all the living children of God. See, then, the need of having the love of God shed abroad in the heart by the Holy Ghost! *Spurgeon.*

10,325. LOVE, Blindness of. Hiero was upbraided by an enemy on account of his offensive breath, and having returned home demanded of his wife why she had not informed him of it. The innocent woman answered, "I thought all men's breath had that smell." *Plutarch.*

10,326. LOVE, Christ's. It is like *a magnificent temple*, Eph. 3: 16–18, whose breadth and length, and depth and height, are symbols of the abounding extent of the love of Christ! The breadth may represent Christ's world-wide love; the length its extent throughout all ages; the depth represents the wisdom; the height its being beyond the reach of any foe— or perhaps, the Saviour's love raising the sinner from the depth of misery to the height of happiness. *Bowes.*

10,327. LOVE, Climax of. A colored soldier said in a religious meeting, "I love my Saviour, I love the church of Christ, I love the world, I love everybody, I love them that don't love me."

10,328. LOVE Commanded. Deut. 6: 5; 11: 13; Matt. 22: 36–38. "Thou shalt love the Lord thy God with all thy heart, and with all thy soul, and with all thy mind." As if he would not leave out the least sinew or string of the heart; the least faculty or power of the soul; the least organ or action of strength. So Bernard: "'With all my heart,' that is, affectionately; 'with all my soul,' that is, wisely; 'with all my strength,' that is, constantly. Let the zeal of thy heart inflame thy love to God; let the wisdom of thy soul guide it; let the strength of thy might confirm it." (*Adams*). "If any man love not the Lord Jesus Christ, let him be *Anathema Maranatha.*" 1 Cor. 16: 22.

10,329. LOVE, Conception of. Rowland Hill was endeavoring to convey to his hearers, by a variety of illustrations, some idea of his conceptions of the Divine love; but suddenly casting his eyes towards heaven, he exclaimed, "But I am unable to reach the lofty theme!— yet I do not think that the smallest fish that swims in the boundless ocean ever complains of the immeasurable vastness of the deep. So it is with me: I can plunge, with my puny capacity, into a subject the immensity of which I shall never be able fully to comprehend!"

10,330. LOVE, Demands of. There is no more terrible inquisition than that of affection; for we all belong to it; its treasure is in our heart, and to deprive it of that is to defraud it of its due. Those who love us insist upon reading us. Indifference may be diverted, love cannot; love demands the reason of a sigh—of a pale cheek; and at the same time that it makes our happiness obligatory, it insists upon full confession as equally a duty. Love, like the sun, absorbs all clouds; to suffer in its presence is almost to do it wrong; at least it is to own that it is powerless to fill the heart—unskilled to heal it. There is occasionally a reproach,

—there is almost always some concealment, in the sadness of a beloved being. *Gasparin.*

10,331. LOVE, Demonstration of. The three sons of an eastern queen tried to show their love for their mother, by gifts laid upon her grave. The spectators most applauded one, who made a libation of his own blood. The offering of a few drops in honor of his mother, was counted a great virtue; but Christ poured out his blood for his enemies.

10,332. LOVE, Descent of. Love, it has been said, descends more abundantly than it ascends. The love of parents for their children has always been far more powerful than that of children for their parents; and who among the sons of men ever loved God with a thousandth part of the love which God has manifested to us? *J. C. Hare.*

10,333. LOVE, Devoted. Leander, a young man of Abydos, was deeply in love with Hero, a beautiful virgin of Sestos. The narrow sea of the Hellespont lay between the two towns. Leander swam across in the night, guided by Hero's torch, which she held from one of the tower windows. One night on endeavoring to cross, when the waves ran high, he was drowned and his dead body was cast up on the shore at Sestos, where Hero from her tower beheld it. Not able to outlive her great loss, she cast herself headlong from the tower into the sea, and perished.

10,334. LOVE, Efforts of. In Cromwell's time a soldier was condemned to be executed " at the ringing of the curfew." He was engaged to be married to a beautiful lady. This lady pleaded with the judge and with Cromwell for pardon, but in vain. All preparations for the execution were made, and all awaited the signal bell. The sexton, old and deaf, threw himself upon the rope, as was his custom, but no sound. The young lady climbed the belfry stair, caught and held the tongue of the bell at the risk of her own life. At length the bell ceased to swing. The deaf old sexton supposed he had rung the curfew. The brave lady descended, wounded and bleeding. Cromwell came to demand why the bell was silent. She met him, and

At his feet she told her story, showed her hands
  all bruised and torn ;
And her sweet young face, still haggard with the
  anguish it had worn,
Touched his heart with sudden pity, lit his eyes
  with misty light:
" Go, your lover lives," cried Cromwell: "curfew
  shall not ring to-night."

10,335. LOVE, Foolishness of. It happened in days of old that a lion fell in love with a woodman's daughter, and had the folly to ask her of her father in marriage. The woodman was not much pleased with the offer, and declined the honor of so dangerous an alliance. But upon the lion threatening him with his royal displeasure, the poor man, seeing that so formidable a creature was not to be denied, hit at length upon this expedient: "I feel greatly flattered," said he, "with your proposal; but, noble sir, what great teeth you have got! and what great claws you have got! where is the damsel that would not be frightened at such weapons as these? You must have your teeth drawn and your claws pared before you can be a suitable bridegroom for my daughter." The lion straightway submitted (for what will not a body do for love?) and then called upon the father to accept him as a son-in-law. But the woodman, no longer afraid of the tamed and disarmed bully, seized a stout cudgel and drove the unreasonable suitor from his door. *Æsop.*

10,336. LOVE, Generosity of. Love trades not for home returns; it amply pays itself in serving its beloved. It is reported of one who, being asked for who he labored most, answered, " For my friends." And being asked for whom he labored least, he answered, " For my friends." Love doth most, and yet thinks least of what it does. *Secker.*

10,337. LOVE, Incredible. Mr. Nott, missionary in the South Sea Islands, was reading a portion of the Gospel of John to a number of the natives. One who had listened to the words, interrupted him, and said, " What words were those you read? What sounds were those I heard? Let me hear those words again." Mr. Nott again read the verse, " God so loved the world," etc., when the native rose from his seat, and said, " Is that true? Can that be true? God loved the world, when the world not love him. God so loved the world, as to give his Son to die, that man might not die. Can that be true?" Mr. Nott again read the verse, and said it was true, and that it was the message God had sent to them; and that whosoever believed in him would not perish, but be happy after death. This incredible love won the native's heart.

10,338. LOVE, Indestructible. Asbestos is the most extraordinary of all fossils. It is of the nature of alabaster, but it may be drawn out into fine silken threads of a grayish or silver color. It is indissolvable in water, and remains unconsumed in fire. A handkerchief, made of this material, many years ago, and presented to the Royal Society of England, was thrown into an intensly hot fire, and lost but two drachms of its weight, and when thus heated was laid upon white paper, and did not burn it. Connubial love is like the asbestos. Neither fire nor water can destroy it; for it can neither be dissolved nor consumed. The waves of sorrow will not wash it away; the scorching flames of tribulation will not burn it up. If this be true concerning genuine connubial love, how beautifully does it illustrate the indissolvable love between Christ and his church, which is called " The bride, the Lamb's wife!" (Rev. 21: 9). *Dr. Stryker.*

10,339. LOVE, Infinite. If an angel were to fly swiftly over the earth on a summer morning while the pearly dew of heaven rested on the flowers; and go into every garden, the king's, the rich man's, the peasant's, the child's, and were to bring from each one the choicest, loveliest, sweetest flower that blooms in each, and gather them all into one cluster in his radiant hands, what a beautiful bouquet it would be! And if an angel were to fly swiftly all over the earth, into every sweet and holy home, into every spot where one heart yearns over another, and were to take out of every father's heart, and every mother's heart, and out of every heart that loves, its holiest flower of affection, and gather all into one cluster, what a blessed love-garland would his eyes behold! What a holy love would this aggregation of all earth's loves be! Yet infinitely sweeter and holier than this grouping of all earth's holiest affections, is the love that fills the heart of our Father in heaven. *J. R. Miller.*

10,340. LOVE, Legend of. A legend of St. John the apostle says that when a feeble old man, too weak to walk to the assemblies of the church, he was borne there by his disciples; and addressing the people as he spread abroad his hands, repeated again and again, " Love one another:" and when asked why he said ever the same thing, replied, " Because there is nothing else: attain that, and you have enough."

10,341. LOVE, Longing for. Frank Bragg, a boy of fifteen, one of the bravest of Birges' sharpshooters, was dying in Paducah hospital. As the dew of death gathered on his brow he said, " O, I am going to die, and there is no one to love me. If my sisters were only here! but I have no friends near me now." The nurse told him he had many friends, and greatest of all, God would be his friend. The last thought cheered him. He said his mother taught him to pray when a child, and that he always prayed every day. He said, " I am not afraid to die, but I want some one to love me." His nurse said, " Frankie, I love you. Poor boy, you shall not be left alone." She kissed his pale forehead lovingly. " Kiss me again," he said, " that was given so like my sister." Then, speaking to another nurse, he said, " Mrs. S., won't you kiss me, too? I don't think it will be so hard to die if you will both love me." With his face nestled against his nurses, he fell quietly into his last sleep.

10,342. LOVE, Measureless. Blessed sunshine covers the earth on the sweet summer day. It fills the valleys, spreads over the waters, bathes the fields, paints the flowers. And all this sunshine is from one sun, and the sun himself is greater than all his beams. If all his light could be gathered from the mountains, from the valleys, from the waters, from the forests; and if all that he has poured out in past ages could be gathered up again, the sun himself is immeasurably greater than all this vast ocean of gathered beams. So earth's loves are but beams from God's heart. He made us in his image. Our affections are all kindled at his heart. Father, mother, child, sister, brother, wife, husband, friend, all are but cups which God's own love has filled. And so of all human hearts in the past. And God's heart is immeasurably greater than all its outflowings and creations. If, then, all the love that has ever throbbed in human hearts from Adam's down through all the ages, and all that lives to-day on earth, could be poured into one great ocean heart, God's love is infinitely more than all. *J. R. Miller.*

10,343. LOVE, Measure of Christ's. What an excellent, lovely One is Christ! Put the beauty of ten thousand paradises like the garden of Eden into one; put all trees, all flowers, all smells, all colors, all tastes, all joys, all sweetness, all loveliness in one,—oh, what a fair and excellent thing it would be! And yet it should be less, to that fair and dearest, well-beloved Christ, than one drop of rain to the whole seas, rivers, lakes, and fountains of ten thousand earths. Now, for God to bestow the mercy of mercies, the most precious thing in heaven or earth, upon poor sinners, what manner of love is this! *John Flavel.*

10,344. LOVE, Measure of God's. Pliny declares that Cicero once saw the Iliad of Homer written in so small a character that it could be contained in a nutshell. Peter Bales, a celebrated caligrapher, in the days of Queen Elizabeth, wrote the whole Bible so that it was shut up in a common walnut as its casket. In these days of advanced mechanism even greater marvels in miniature have been achieved, but never has so much meaning been compressed into so small a space as in that famous little word "So," in the text which tells us that "God so loved the world, that he gave his only-begotten Son, that whosoever believeth in him should not perish, but have everlasting life." *Spurgeon.*

10,345. LOVE, Mother's. In a spring freshet a river rent away a bough whereon a bird had built a cottage for her summer home. Down the white and whirling stream drifted the green branch, with its wicker cup of unfledged song, and fluttering beside it went the mother-bird. Unheeding the roaring river, on she went, her cries of agony and fear piercing the pauses in the storm. How like the love of an old-fashioned mother, who followed the child she had plucked from her heart all over the world. Swept away by passion that child might be, it mattered not; though he was bearing away with him the fragrance of the shattered roof-tree, yet that mother was with him, a Ruth through all his life, and a Rachel at his death. *Lamartine.*

10,346. LOVE, Ocean of. When one who has never sailed out upon the ocean stands on its shore and watches the trembling waves as they surge and break upon the sands, how little does he know of the majesty and grandeur of the great deep, of its storms, of its power, of its secrets, of its unfathomable chambers, of its unweighed treasures? He sees only the little silver edge that breaks at his feet. So we stand but where the Spirit of God breaks upon the shore of our world. We see its silver edge. We feel the plash of its waves upon our hearts. But of its infinite reaches and outgoings beyond our shores we know almost nothing. Yet blessed are they who even stand by the shore and lave their hearts in even the shallowest eddies of this divine ocean. *J. R. Miller.*

10,347. LOVE, Parental. A German mother, who often resorted to the graveyard to weep over the graves of her eleven dead children, had yet a living son, whose misconduct was the greatest sorrow of her life. One day he ran away from home: the mother's heart followed him in his prodigal flight. She sent a messenger to search for him. To him she said, "If you find my boy sick, or in prison, or in any want, do all that you can for him, and I will repay you." She charged him to search through the streets and alleys of a great city till he should find him. If parents, "being evil," are so moved, how much more God, who is all love?

10,348. LOVE, Paternal. A steamer was wrecked on Lake Pontchartrain, on which were a father, mother, and their six children. The father was a stalwart man and good swimmer, and resolved to get them all safely to land or perish in the attempt. He told his children not to be afraid, that he would come for them. He then jumped overboard, and his wife after him. Taking her by the hair, he drew her along through the breakers, and landed her safely on shore. Then he plunged into the mad waves, and went back to the ship for his children. One by one he brought them to the shore. Only one remained upon the vessel. The devoted father had not strength to stand up when the last was brought in. Friends expostulated with him against the farther exposure of his valuable life. He said, "Jimmie's aboard, and I promised to come for him." Then he floated back to the ship, and just as it was about to go down, he called to Jimmie to jump into the water. He had strength only to seize his boy, fold his arms about him, and press him to his bosom, and, thus enfolded, they sank together, to rise no more. Such is the love of a father. "As the Father hath loved me, even so have I loved you."

10,349. LOVE, Sacrifice for. Pyramus, a young man of Babylon, was deeply in love with Thisbe, the daughter of one that lived next neighbor. The parents looked upon this with disfavor, and they were not suffered so much as to meet. At last, through a chink in the wall, they appointed a place of meeting outside the city, under a mulberry tree. Thisbe arrived first at the place designated; but being terrified by seeing a lion passing by, she fled into a cave In her flight she had dropped her veil, which the lioness tossed about with her bloody mouth, and so left it. Soon after Pyramus came, and seeing the veil Thisbe wore all bloody, he rashly concluded that she had been torn to pieces by some wild beast; and, therefore, slew himself. Thisbe came out of the cave when she thought the lioness had gone, with great desire to meet her lover; but finding him slain, she was so overcome with grief, that she threw herself upon his sword, and died with him.

10,350. LOVE, Sameness of. The game of love is the same, whether the player be clad in velvet or in hodden gray. Beneath the gilded ceilings of a palace, or the lowly rafters of a cabin, there are the same hopes and fears, the same jealousies, and distrusts, and despondings; the wiles and stratagems are all alike;

for, after all, the stake is human happiness, whether he who risks it be a peer or a peasant.

Lever.

10,351. LOVE, Seeking and Following. Professor Tholuck, of the University of Halle, was so devoted to the moral interests of his students, and sought after the erring with so much tenderness and care, that he was called the student-professor. He not only sought, but followed up his seeking. There was a student brought near his heart by a godly mother. He was led away into evil; contrition and return followed; then came another fall. "When he could be found at home at no other time, I sought him more than once at six o'clock in the morning. I visited him in prison, that I might remind him of what he well knew, but always forgot." He now promised again to abandon his associates, and enter upon a new life. Four or five days after, late in the evening, came a card from him: "Tholuck sighs, Tholuck prays, but we will have our drunk out." Still the student-professor perseveres in the love that seeks and follows. And that youth is now a preacher of the gospel of Jesus in the imperial city of Berlin. Hundreds and thousands of youthful hearts have thus been won by this man of God; won from rationalism and infidelity to Christ and the church. How much has this good man been enabled to do by his teaching, his preaching, and his written works! His praise is in all the churches! Hear him as he says, "What I have done in this way is known to the world; but all this I value less than that I have been permitted, though in weakness and imperfection, to exercise that love which seeks and follows. This is a work of which the world knows little, but of which the Lord God knows much." *G. Draper.*

10,352. LOVE, Trial of. Sozomon tells of a merchant, whose two sons being taken captives and condemned to die, he offered himself to die for them; and withal promised to give the soldiers all the gold he had. They pitied the poor man, and accepted him for one of his sons, but could not let them both escape, because such a number must be put to death. The man, looking upon and lamenting for both his sons, could not find in his heart to make choice of either, and stood deliberating till they were both slain.

10,353. LOVE, True. True love, like fire, burns hottest when the weather is coldest. Histories make mention of one Ursinus, a physician, that being to die for the gospel, and beginning to waver, Vitalis, a godly man, stepped to him, and though he knew it would cost him his life, encouraged him, saying, "What! have you been so industrious heretofore, to preserve men's bodies, and will you now shrink at the saving of your own soul? Be courageous!" For which faithful counsel he was condemned, and suffered accordingly.

Swinnock.

10,354. LOVE, Unlimited. A gentleman was visiting at a house some time ago. He noticed that the mother seemed agitated and was all the while going out and coming in. He went to her and asked what troubled her. She took him out into another room and introduced him to her boy. There he was, a poor wretched boy, all mangled and bruised with the fall of sin. She said, "I have much more trouble with him than with all the rest. He has wandered far, but he is my boy yet."

10,355. LOVE, Woman's. Oh, the love of woman! the love of woman! How high will it not rise! and to what lowly depths will it not stoop! How many injuries will it not forgive! What obstacle will it not overcome, and what sacrifices will it not make, rather than give up the being upon which it has been once wholly and truthfully fixed! Perennial of life, which grows up under every climate, how small would the sum of man's happiness be without thee! No coldness, no neglect, no harshness, no cruelty, can extinguish thee! Like the fabled lamp in the sepulchre, thou sheddest thy pure light in the human heart, when everything around thee there is dead forever! *Carleton.*

10,356. LOVER, Hope of a. A lover's hope resembles the bean in the nursery tale; let it once take root, and it will grow so rapidly, that, in the course of a few hours, the giant Imagination builds a castle on the top, and by-and-by comes Disappointment with the curtal-axe, and hews down both the plant and the superstructure. *Sir Walter Scott.*

10,357. LUCK, Good and Bad. I may here, as well as anywhere, impart the secret of what is called good and bad luck. There are men who, supposing Providence to have an implacable spite against them, bemoan in the poverty of a wretched old age the misfortunes of their lives. Luck for ever runs against them, and for others. One, with a good profession, lost his luck in the river, where he idled away his time a-fishing, when he should have been in the office. Another, with a good trade, perpetually burnt up his luck by his hot temper, which provoked all his employers to leave him. Another, with a lucrative business, lost his luck by amazing diligence at everything but his business. Another, who steadily followed his trade, as steadily followed his bottle. Another who was honest and constant to his work, erred by his perpetual misjudgments—he lacked discretion. Hundreds lose their luck by indorsing, by sanguine speculations, by trusting fraudulent men, and by dishonest gains. A man never has good luck who has a bad wife. I never knew an early-rising, hard-working, prudent man, careful of his earnings, and strictly honest, who complained of bad luck. A good character, good habits, and iron industry, are impregnable to the assaults of all the ill-luck that fools ever dreamed of. But when I see a tatterdemalion creeping out of a grocery late in the forenoon, with his hands stuck into his pockets, the rim of his hat turned up, and the crown knocked in, I know he has had bad luck—for the worst of all luck is to be a sluggard, a knave, or a tippler. *Addison.*

10,358. LUCK, Knowledge and. There is a

man in Berkshire, England, who was in Australia when the first discoveries of gold were made. The miners brought in their nuggets, and took them to the local banks. The bankers were a little nervous about the business, uncertain about the quality of the gold, and waited to see its character established. This man had a taste for natural sciences, and knew something about metallurgy. He tried each test, solid and fluid, satisfied himself of the quality of the gold, and then, with all the money he had or could borrow, he bought as much gold as might be, and showed as profit a hundred thousand pounds in the course of a day or two. His "luck" was observation and knowledge, and a happy tact in applying them. *F. Arnold.*

10,359. LUCK, Labor and. Luck is waiting for something to turn up. Labor, with keen eyes and strong will, will turn up something. Luck lies in bed, and wishes the postman would bring him news of a legacy. Labor turns out at six o'clock, and, with busy pen or ringing hammer, lays the foundation of a competence. Luck whines. Labor whistles. Luck relies on chances. Labor depends on character. Luck slips down to indigence. Labor strides upward to independence. *Cobden.*

10,360. LUCK, Superstition of. Giacomo, in Venice or the Romagna, a man of many murders, but pious, will cross himself nine times before taking to the road and inserting his stiletto in the first traveler he meets. A young English lady, or an old one, will examine her coffee-cups, throw spilt salt over her left shoulder, and shriek when knives are placed crossways on the dinner-table. Paddy in Connemara will load his old gun with a blessed bullet, before taking aim from behind a hedge at a bailiff. An old nurse in the midland counties will throw a shoe after her daughter when she goes to service or to market. Why do all these do such funny things? Why did Cæsar, tumbling on his nose as he landed nineteen hundred years ago on these shores, tell a lie to persuade his soldiers that is was no bad omen, but an intentional worshiping of the gods? Why do certain pious Christians travel to Loretto or Rome, Mussulmans to Mecca, Hindoos to the Ganges? Why do Pierre and Wilhelm give a larger price for the odd numbers, the 7, 13, 21, and others in a lottery, than for the even? Why did good old Dr. Johnson touch the tops of the posts as he went along Fleet Street, and preserve his orange-pips with a sacred devotion? There is but one answer to all these questions, and to as many more as would fill this page. Because one and all believed in Fortune, Chance, Luck, call it what you will—blind goddess, capricious jade, or discerning deity: Fate, if you wish it, superior to Jupiter, Queen of the gods themselves, stronger far than wisdom, skill, or strength. *The Gentle Life.*

10,361. LUKEWARMNESS, Prevention of. An earnest minister drew a lesson from the text, "Stir up the gift which is in thee." "See, this fire needs the poker; if we do not take the poker and stir, it would quickly go out. Although there are all the materials for a good fire there, I must stir the fire to make it burn brightly, and I must take care how to stir it. Mental materials are not only necessary, but activity, to give them life and ventilation. We all have gifts and fires within us; but they all need stirring, or they will never burn. Little heathen boys have minds; little beggar boys have minds; but they have no friends to help them to stir them, and cannot themselves do it. Anna, what gift does God bestow on his people?" "The gift of the Holy Ghost." "Yes; God giveth his Holy Spirit to them that ask and seek him. There is a text which says, 'the spirit of the prophets is subject to the prophets.' God's gift does not move and propel us as that steam carriage is moved by the fire and the steam, without our knowing anything about it. We can resist God's gift. We can quench God's gift. If Christians are cold, it is because they do not stir up the gift that is in them. If preachers are cold, it is because they do not stir up the fire in them. God answers by fire to his people; and if we cannot impart fire to others, it is a proof that we have not stirred up our own fire. Don't forget you all have a fire in you, but it will only burn as you stir it."

10,362. LUST, Apostrophe to. O lust, thou infernal fire! whose fuel is gluttony; whose flame is pride; whose sparkles are wanton words; whose smoke is infamy; whose ashes are uncleanness; whose end is hell. *Quarles.*

10,363. LUST, Fascination of. Lusts (as to the actings, I mean) are like agues; the fit is not always on, and yet the man not rid of his disease; and some men's lusts, like some agues, have not such quick returns as others. The river doth not move always one way; now 'tis coming anon falling water; and though it doth not rise when it falls, yet it hath not lost its other motion. Now the tide of lust is up, anon 'tis down, and a man recoils, and seems to run from it, but it returns again upon him. Who would have thought to have seen Pharaoh in his mad fit again, that should have been with him in his good mood, when he bid Moses and the people go? But, alas! the man was not altered. Thus, may be when a strong occasion comes, this (like an easterly wind to some of our ports) will bring in the tide of thy lusts so strongly that thy soul, that seemed as clear of thy lust as the naked sands are of water, will be in a few moments covered and as deep under their waves as ever. But the longer the banks have held the better; yet shouldst thou never more satisfy thy lust, yet this is not enough to clear thee from being a hypocrite. *Salter.*

10,364. LUSTS Must be Overcome. A Christian hath no such enemies without him as unruly and undisciplined lusts and passions within him: and it is a vain thing to think of overcoming the world without us, until this world within us be brought into subjection; for without the lusts and corruptions within, the world, and the evil men of the world, and the evil one of the world, could not hurt us. *Sir M. Hale*

10,365. LUXURY, Evils of. Luxury makes a man so soft, that it is hard to please him, and easy to trouble him; so that his pleasures at last become his burden. Whereas the frugal and temperate man can, by fasting till a convenient time, make any food pleasant. The luxurious must at last owe to this temperance that health and ease which his false pleasures have robbed him of; he must abstain from his wines, feastings, and fruits, until temperance has cured him. And I have known many who, after they have been tortured by the tyranny of luxury, whilst they had riches in abundance to feed it, become very healthful and strong, when they fall into that poverty which they had so abhorred. *Dr. Ferguson.*

10,366. LUXURY, Proud. It is said that Nero would not fish but with nets of gold attached to purple cords, and that he delighted to dig the earth with a golden spade.

10,367. LYING, Crime of. I really know nothing more criminal, more mean, and more ridiculous, than lying. It is the production either of malice, cowardice, or vanity; and generally misses of its aim in every one of these views; for lies are always detected, sooner or later. If I tell a malicious lie, in order to affect any man's fortune or character, I may indeed injure him for some time; but I shall be sure to be the greatest sufferer myself at last; for as soon as ever I am detected (and detected I most certainly shall be) I am blasted for the infamous attempt; and whatever is said afterwards to the disadvantage of that person, however true, passes for calumny. If I lie, or equivocate— for it is the same thing—in order to excuse myself for something that I have said or done, and to avoid the danger or the shame that I apprehend from it, I discover at once my fear, as well as my falsehood; and only increase, instead of avoiding, the danger and the shame: I show myself to be the lowest and the meanest of mankind, and am sure to be always treated as such. *Lord Chesterfield.*

10,368. LYING, Gain of. The gain of lying is nothing else but not to be trusted of any, nor to be believed when we say the truth.
Sir Walter Raleigh.

10,369. LYING, Habit of. Lying supplies those who are addicted to it with a plausible apology for every crime, and with a supposed shelter from every punishment. It tempts them to run into danger from the mere expectation of impunity, and when practiced with frequent success it teaches them to confound the gradations of guilt, from the effects of which there is, in their imaginations at least, one sure and common protection. It corrupts the early simplicity of youth; it blasts the fairest blossoms of genius; and will most assuredly counteract every effort by which we may hope to improve the talents and mature the virtues of those whom it infects. *Dr. Parr.*

10,370. LYING, Hatred of. One of the fathers has carried this point so high as to declare he would not tell a lie though he were sure to gain heaven by it. However extravagant such a protestation may appear, every one will own that a man may say, very reasonably, he would not tell a lie if he were sure to gain hell by it; or, if you have a mind to soften the expression, that he would not tell a lie to gain any temporal reward by it, when he should run the hazard of losing much more than it was possible for him to gain. *Addison.*

10,371. LYING, Improvement in. Although the devil be the father of lies, he seems, like other great inventors, to have lost much of his reputation by the continual improvements which have been made upon him. *Swift.*

10,372. LYING, Resolved against. A little orphan boy having loitered on an errand, recollected himself and ran back to his uncle's workshop with all speed. "What are you running yourself out of breath for?" asked one of the men; "tell your uncle that the people kept you waiting." "Why, that would be a lie." "To be sure it would; but what's the odds?" "I a liar! I tell a lie!" cried the boy indignantly; "no, not to escape a beating every day. My mother always told me that lying was the first step to ruin, and my Bible says that a liar shall not enter heaven."

10,373. LYING, Treatment of. A lie should be trampled on and extinguished wherever found: I am for fumigating the atmosphere when I suspect that falsehood, like pestilence, breathes around me. *Carlyle.*

10,374. MAGIC, Notion of. Magic! And what is magic? When the traveler beholds in Persia the ruins of palaces and temples, the ignorant inhabitants inform him they were the work of magicians! What is beyond their own power, the vulgar cannot comprehend to be lawfully in the power of others. But if by magic you mean a perpetual research amongst all that is more latent and obscure in nature, I answer, I profess that magic, and that he who does so, comes but nearer to the fountain of all belief. Knowest thou not that magic was taught in the schools of old? But how, and by whom? as the last and most solemn lesson, by the priests who ministered to the temple. *E. B. Lytton.*

10,375. MALACHI, Character of. The word means—"My angel or messenger." Hence some have contended that there was no such person as Malachi, but that Ezra was the author of the book bearing his name. Origen even maintains that the author was an incarnate angel. The general opinion, however, is, that he was a real personage, who flourished about four hundred years before Christ. It was meet that the ancient dispensation should close amid such cloudy uncertainties. It had been all along the "religion of the veil." There was a veil, verily, upon more than the face of Moses. Everything from Sinai—its centre, down to the last bell or pomegranate —wore a veil. Over Malachi's face, form, and fortunes, it hangs dark and impenetrable. A masked actor, his tread and his voice are terrible. The last pages of the Old Testament seem to stir as in a furious wind, and the word "curse," echoing down to the very roots of Calvary, closes the record. *G. Gilfillan.*

10,376. MALEVOLENCE, Bitterness of. Malevolence is, in point of fact, a real colocynth juice; for, if it once infect the heart, nothing in a neighbor any longer pleases. If he walk, his gait is proud and haughty; if he laugh, he is derisive; if he weep, he is hypocritical; if he look grave, he is insolent. Every fault swells into magnitude, and every virtue shrinks into littleness. *Gothold.*

10,377. MAMMON, Delusions of. Do not believe the impotent idol. His golden mountains are but the ocean's foam; his paradises deceptive phantoms. *Krummacher.*

10,378. MAN, Apostrophe to. The great Pan of old, who was clothed in a leopard skin to signify the beautiful variety of things, and the firmament his coat of stars, was but the representative of thee, O rich and various man! thou palace of sight and sound, carrying in thy senses the morning and the night, and the unfathomable galaxy; in thy brain, the geometry of the city of God; in thy heart, the power of love and the realms of right and wrong!
Emerson.

10,379. MAN like a Book. Man is like a book; his birth is the title-page to the book; his baptisme is the epistle dedicatory; his groans and crying are the epistle to the reader; his infancy and childhood are the argument, or contents of the whole ensuing treatise; his life and actions are the subject or matter of the book; his sins and errors of his life are the errata or faults escaped in the printing; and his repentance is the correction of them. Now amongst books (we know) some are large volumes, in *Folio;* some little ones, in *Decimo sexto;* and some are of other sizes, in *Octavo* or *Quarto.* Again, some of these are fairer bound, some in a plainer manner; some are bound in strong velame, or leather, and some in thin paper. Some again have piety for their subject, and treat of godlinesse; others are prophane pamphlets, full of wantonnesse and folly; but in the last page of every one of them, there stands a word, which is FINIS, implying the end of all. *Richard Gove,* 1652.

10,380. MAN, A Brainless. A fox had stolen into the house of an actor, and in rummaging among his various properties, laid hold of a highly-finished mask. "A fine looking head, indeed!" cried he; "what a pity it is that it wants brains!" *Æsop.*

10,381. MAN, Christ's Power over. There is a legend in Iceland which says that when Jesus was a boy, playing with his comrades one Sabbath-day, he made birds of clay; and as these birds of clay were standing upon the ground, an old Sadducee came along, and he was disgusted at the sport, and dashed the birds to pieces; but the legend says that Jesus waved his hand above the broken birds, and they took wing, and went singing heavenward. Of course, that is a fable among the Icelanders; but it is not a fable that we are dust, and that the hand of Divine grace waved over us once, we go singing toward the skies. *Talmage.*

10,382. MAN, Dependence of. For the continuance of life a thousand provisions are made. If the vital actions of a man's frame were directed by his will, they are necessarily so minute and complicated, that they would immediately fall into confusion. He cannot draw a breath without the exercise of sensibilities as well-ordered as those of the eye or ear. A tracery of nervous cords unites many organs in sympathy, of which, if one filament were broken, pain, and spasm, and suffocation would ensue. The action of the heart, and the circulation of his blood, and all the vital functions, are governed through means and by laws which are not dependent on his will, and to which the powers of his mind are altogether inadequate. For, had they been under the influence of his will, a doubt, a moment's pause of irresolution, a forgetfulness of a single action at its appointed time, would have terminated his existence. *Bell.*

10,383. MAN, Enthusiasm of. It is not to taste sweet things, but to do noble and true things, and vindicate himself under God's heaven as a God-made man, that the poorest son of Adam dimly longs. Show him the way of doing that, the dullest day-drudge kindles into a hero. They wrong man greatly who say he is to be seduced by ease. Difficulty, abnegation, martyrdom, death are the allurements that act on the heart of man. Kindle the inner genial life of him, you have a flame that burns up all lower considerations. Not happiness, but something higher: one sees this even in the frivolous classes, with their "point of honor" and the like. Not by flattering our appetites; no, by awakening the heroic that slumbers in every heart, can any religion gain followers. *Carlyle.*

10,384. MAN, Fallen. In some respects manifestly made for a sphere higher than he fills, he appears to us like a creature of the air which a cruel hand has stripped of its silken wings. How painfully he resembles this hapless object which has just fallen on the pages of a book that we read by the candle on an autumn evening! It retains the wish, but has lost the power to fly. Allured by the taper's glare, it has brushed the flame, and, drooping with a heavy fall, now crawls wingless across the leaf, and seeks the finger of mercy to end its misery. Compare man with any of the other creatures, and how directly we come to the conclusion that he is not, nor can be, the same creature with which God crowned the glorious work of creation! *Dr. Guthrie.*

10,385. MAN, Glorified. The dynasty of the future is to have glorified man for its inhabitant; but it is to be the dynasty—"the kingdom"—not of glorified man made in the image of God, but of God himself in the form of man. Creation and the Creator meet at one point, and in one person. The long ascending line from dead matter to man has been a progress Godwards—not an asymptotical progress, but destined from the beginning to furnish a point of union; and, occupying that point as true God and true Man—as Creator and created—we recognize the adorable Monarch of all the future! *H. Miller.*

10,386. MAN a Heavenly Plant. Man is not an earthly and unmovable, but a heavenly plant, the head raising the body erect as from a root, and directed upwards toward heaven.
Plato.

10,387. MAN, Idiosyncrasies of. Men often remind me of pears in their way of coming to maturity. Some are ripe at twenty, like human jargonelles, and must be made the most of, for their day is soon over. Some come into their perfect condition late, like the autumn kinds, and they last better than the summer fruit. And some fruit that like the winter-nelis, have been hard and uninviting until all the rest have had their season, get their glow and perfume long after the frost and snow have done their worst with the orchards. Beware of rash criticisms; the rough and astringent fruit you condemn may be an autumn or a winter pear, and that which you picked up beneath the same bough in August may have been only its worm-eaten wind-falls. *Holmes.*

10,388. MAN, Immortality of. Canst thou think it worth the while, that the Maker of the universe should create a soul, and send it down into the world, on purpose to superintend these trivial affairs—to keep alive a silly piece of well-figured earth while it eats and drinks, to move it to and fro in chase of shadows, to hold it up while others bow the knee and do it homage—as if it had not some higher work to mind in reference to another state? Art thou contented to live long in the world to such purposes? What low, worthless spirit is this that had rather be so employed, than in the visions of his Maker's face; that chooses thus to entertain itself on earth rather than partake the effusions of the Divine glory above; that had rather creep with worms than soar with angels; associate with brutes than with the spirits of just men made perfect? Who can solve the phenomena, or give a rational account why there should be such a creature as man upon the earth, aside from the hopes of another world? *Howe.*

10,389. MAN, Infelicity of. Our life is painful and full of difficulties; and if it doth not labor with them in its own nature, yet we ourselves have infected it with that corruption. For the inconstancy of Fortune joined us at the beginning of our journey, and hath accompanied us ever since; so that it can produce nothing sound or comfortable unto us; and the bitter potion was mingled for us as soon as we were born. For the principles of our nature being mortal is the cause that our judgment is depraved, that diseases, cares, and all those fatal inconveniences afflict mankind. *Crantor.*

10,390. MAN, Inference of. You see a beautiful capital still bearing some of the flowers and some vestiges of the foliage which the sculptor's chisel had carved upon the marble. It lies on the ground, half-buried under rank weeds and nettles, while beside it the headless shaft of a noble column springs from its pedestal. Would you not at once conclude that its present condition, so base and mean, was not its original position? You say the lightning bolt must have struck it down; or an earthquake had shaken its foundations; or some ignorant barbarian had climbed the shaft, and with rude hand hurled it to the ground. Well, we look at man, and arrive at a similar conclusion. *Guthrie.*

10,391. MAN, The Last. A strange story is related respecting the great earthquake of 1747. It is said that all the inhabitants of Callao, except one man, lost their lives during this earthquake. This man was standing on the fort which overlooked the harbor, when he saw the sea retire to a great distance, and then come sweeping back like a vast mountain of water. A cry of "Miserere!" arose from all parts of the town, "and then in a moment all was silent"—where the town had once flourished there was a wide expanse of sea. But the same green wave which destroyed the town swept towards him a small boat, into which he leaped, and so escaped. *W. Brock.*

10,392. MAN, Life in. Rowland Hill once conversed with a celebrated sculptor, who had been hewing out a block of marble to represent that great patriot, Lord Chatham. "There," said the sculptor, "is not that a fine form?" "Now, sir," said Mr. Hill, "can you put life into it? else, with all its beauty, it is still but a block of marble." God put life into his creation, and man became a living soul. Christ puts new life into dead men.

10,393. MAN, The Melancholy. He is one that keeps the worst company in the world, that is, his own; and though he be always falling out and quarreling with himself, yet he has not the power to endure any other conversation. His head is haunted like a house, with evil spirits and apparitions, that terrify and fright him out of himself, till he stands empty and forsaken. *S. Butler.*

10,394. MAN a Miracle. The essence of our being, the mystery in us that calls itself "I," —ah, what words have we for such things?— is a breath of heaven; the Highest Being reveals himself in man. This body, these faculties, this life of ours, is it not all as a vesture for that Unnamed? "There is but one temple in the universe," says the devout Novalis, "and that is the body of man. Nothing is holier than that high form. Bending before men is a reverence done to this revelation in the flesh. We touch heaven when we lay our hand on a human body!" This sounds much like a mere flourish of rhetoric; but it is not so. If well meditated, it will turn out to be a scientific fact; the expression, in such words as can be had, of the actual truth of the thing. We are the miracle of miracles—the great inscrutable mystery of God. We cannot understand it, we know not how to speak of it; but we may feel and know, if we like, that it is verily so. *Carlyle.*

10,395. MAN, Nobility of. Man is but a reed, the feeblest thing in nature, but he is a reed that thinks. It needs not that the universe arm itself to crush him. An exhalation, a drop of water, suffices to destroy him. But were the universe to crush him, man is yet nobler than the universe, for he knows that he dies; and the universe, even in prevailing against him, knows not its power. *Pascal.*

10,396. MAN, An Obstinate. He is resolved to understand no man's reason but his own, because he finds no man can understand his but himself. His wits are like a sack, which the French proverb says is tied faster before it is full than when it is; and his opinions are like plants that grow upon rocks, that stick fast, though they have no rooting. His understanding is hardened like Pharaoh's heart, and is proof against all sorts of judgments whatsoever. *Bp. Butler.*

10,397. MAN, A Passionate. He has his type in the rapid river, to whose raging current no precious freight can ever be trusted. It hurls whatever it grasps upon the rocks, and strews the fragments along its banks.

10,398. MAN, Preservation of. That which hath power to give itself being cannot want power to preserve that being. Preservation is not more difficult than creation. If the first man made himself, why did he not preserve himself? He is not now among the living in the world. How came he to be so feeble as to sink into the grave? Why did he not inspire himself with new heat and moisture, and fill his languishing limbs and declining body with new strength? *Charnock.*

10,399. MAN, Race of. The human race may be compared to an immense temple ruined, but now rebuilding, the numerous compartments of which represent the several nations of the earth. True, the different portions of the edifice present great anomalies; but yet the foundation and the corner-stone are the same. All spring from the same level, and all should be directed to the same end. The walls of the building have been thrown down, and the stones scattered by a great earthquake; yet a mighty Architect has appeared, and his powerful hand is gradually raising the temple-walls. The only difference between one side of the edifice and the other is, that here the restoration is somewhat further advanced, while there it is less forward. Alas! some places are still overgrown with thorns, where not a single stone appears. Yet the great Architect may one day look down on these desolate spots, and there the building may suddenly and rapidly spring up, reaching the summit long before those lofty walls which seem to have outgrown the others, but which are still standing half-raised and incomplete. "The last shall be first." *Merle D'Aubigné.*

10,400. MAN, Repairing. When Alexander, the crown prince of Russia, was in England, he ordered a watch made. So intricate was its mechanism and peculiar its combinations that when injured not a man in Russia could repair it; and it necessarily had to be returned to its maker for repairs. Howell says, "When Adam was called into existence, angels must have beheld him with delightful surprise. By the attacks of sin and Satan, the image of God was lost, the spirituality of the creature was annihilated. Who can repair the human mechanism? He only who first taught the machine to move in his own image, who is acquainted with all the springs and principles of human action. Pretenders have tried it again and again, but to no purpose. When we open the volume of inspiration, we behold the machine once more in the hands of the Maker. He can repair it; and, not only so, it will be so improved by him as eventually to comprise many glories to which the angels must be strangers forever."

10,401. MAN, Signs of a Wise. These are the signs of a wise man: to reprove nobody, to praise nobody, to blame nobody, nor ever to speak of himself as an uncommon man. *Epictetus.*

10,402. MAN, Six Species of. According to Linnæus and Buffon, there are six different species among mankind. The first comprehends the Laplanders, the Esquimaux Indians, the Samoied Tartars, the inhabitants of Nova Zembla, Borandians, Greenlanders, and the people of Kamtschatka. The second is the Tartar race, comprehending the Chinese and the Japanese. The third are the southern Asiatics, or the inhabitants of India. The negroes of Africa constitute the fourth striking variety in the human species. The natives of America are the fifth race of men. And the Europeans may be considered as the sixth and last variety of the human kind. *Buck.*

10,403. MAN, Unreliability of a Bad. During the course of my life, I have acquired some knowledge of men and manners, in active life, and amidst occupations the most various. From that knowledge, and from all my experience, I now protest that I never knew a man that was bad fit for any service that was good. There was always some disqualifying ingredient mixing with the compound and spoiling it. The man seems paralytic on that side: his muscles there have lost their tone and natural properties; they cannot move. In short, the accomplishment of anything good is a physical impossibility in such a man. He could not if he would, and it is not more certain than that he would not if he could, do a good or a virtuous action. *Burke.*

10,404. MAN Well-armed. The bark of a tree contains an oily juice, which, when it is in greater plenty than can be exhaled by the sun, renders the plant evergreen. Such is the state of the man whose virtue is proof against the scorching heats of temptation and persecution: he is "like a green olive tree" in the courts of the temple, "his leaf shall not wither." *Bishop Horne.*

10,405. MANHOOD, Degradation of. Whatever profession a young man may choose, let him take heed lest he merge his profession of a man in his profession of law, or medicine, or journalism, or whatever it be. A man's profession should always be incidental and subordinate to himself, never the chief thing to be said about him. There was once a cynical Frenchman who, recognizing that he had made the mistake we have warned against, had engraved upon his tomb by way of epitaph: "Born a man; died a grocer." Don't let it be said of you that, born a man, you died a tradesman, no matter what the trade may be, liberal or mechanical.   *Springfield Union.*

10,406. MANNA, Typology of. That wonderful food, "spiritual meat," 1 Cor. 10:3; "angels' food," Ps. 78, 25; which God rained down from heaven, Ex. 16:4—a striking type of the inexhaustible store of grace and mercy which comes through Christ. It is computed that to supply the vast camp of Israel with food would require 15,000,000 pounds of manna every week. But this God gave for forty years and it never failed! Oh! the fullness of Christ! He that sent the manna is the manna that he sent—the hidden manna, Rev. 2:17.   *Bowes.*

10,407. MANNERS, Importance of. Manners are of more importance than laws. Upon them, in a great measure, the laws depend. The law touches us but here and there, now and then. Manners are what vex or soothe, corrupt or purify, exalt or debase, barbarize or refine us, by a constant, steady, uniform, insensible operation, like that of the air we breathe in. They give their whole form and color to our lives. According to their quality, they aid morals, they supply them, or they totally destroy them.   *Burke.*

10,408. MANNERS, Influence of. Almost every man can recall scores of cases within his knowledge where pleasing manners have made the fortune of lawyers, doctors, divines, merchants and in short, men in every walk of life. Polished manners have often made scoundrels successful, while the best of men by their hardness and coldness have done themselves incalculable injury—the shell being so rough that the world could not believe there was a precious kernel within. Civility is to a man what beauty is to a woman. It creates an instantaneous impression in his behalf, while the opposite quality excites as quick a prejudice against him. It is a real ornament—the most beautiful dress that man or woman can wear—and worth more as a means of winning favor than the finest clothes and jewels ever worn. The gruffest man loves to be appreciated; and it is oftener the sweet smile of a woman, which we think intended for us alone, than a pair of Juno-like eyes, or "lips that seem on roses fed," that bewitches our heart, and lays us low at the feet of her whom we afterward marry.   *Prof. Mathews.*

10,409. MANNERS, Neglected. The manners, which are neglected as small things, are often those which decide men for or against you. A slight attention to them would have prevented their ill judgments. There is scarcely anything required to be believed proud, uncivil, scornful, disobliging—and still less to be esteemed quite the reverse of all this.   *La Bruyère.*

10,410. MANNERS, Striking. Some questions were asked Robert Hall as to Mrs. More's conversation: He said "So far as I can judge, she talks but little on ordinary occasions; and

when she speaks, it is generally to utter some sententious remark." A lady present inquired if there was anything particularly striking in Mrs. More's manners. "Nothing striking, ma'am, certainly not. Her manners are too perfectly proper to be striking. Striking manners are bad manners you know, ma'am. She is a perfect lady, and studiously avoids those peculiarities and eccentricities which constitute striking manners."   *Gregory.*

10,411. MANNERS, Vulgarity of. A vulgar man is captious and jealous; eager and impetuous about trifles. He suspects himself to be slighted, thinks everything that is said meant at him; if the company happens to laugh, he is persuaded they laugh at him; he grows angry and testy, says something very impertinent, and draws himself into a scrape, by showing what he calls a proper spirit, and asserting himself.   *Chesterfield.*

10,412. MARRIAGE, Advantages of. Marriage has in it less of beauty, but more of safety, than the single life; it hath not more ease, but less danger; it is more merry and more sad; it is fuller of sorrows and fuller of joys; it lies under more burdens, but is supported by all the strengths of love and charity; and those burdens are delightful. Marriage is the mother of the world, and preserves kingdoms, and fills cities and churches, and heaven itself. Celibacy, like the fly in the heart of an apple, dwells in perpetual sweetness, but sits alone, and is confined and dies in singularity; but marriage, like the useful bee, builds a house, and gathers sweetness from every flower, and labors and unites into societies and republics, and sends out colonies, and feeds the world with delicacies, and obeys the king, and keeps order, and exercises many virtues, and promotes the interest of mankind, and is that state of good to which God hath designed the present constitution of the world.   *Jeremy Taylor.*

10,413. MARRIAGE, Advice Concerning. Rev. Philip Henry used to say, both to his children and others, in reference to marriage, "Keep within the bounds of profession; look at suitableness in age, quality, education, temper," etc. He used to observe, from Gen. 2:18 "I will make him a help-meet for him," that where there is not meetness, there will not be much help. He commonly said to his children, with reference to their choice in marriage, "Please God, and please yourselves, and you shall never displease me;" and greatly blamed those parents who conclude matches for their children without their consent. He sometimes mentioned the saying of a pious woman, who had many daughters, "The care of most people is how to get good husbands for their daughters; but my care is to fit my daughters to be good wives, and then let God provide for them."

10,414. MARRIAGE, Ceremony at. From the animals offered at the nuptual sacrifices to Juno, the goddess of wedlock, the gall was taken away and cast behind the altar, to signify that betwixt the young couple there should be nothing of bitterness or discontent, but that in their stead, sweetness and love should fill up the whole space of their lives.

10,415. MARRIAGE, Childless. Marriage without children is the world without the sun!
Luther.

10,416. MARRIAGE, Circumspection in. When it shall please God to bring thee to man's estate, use great providence and circumspection in choosing thy wife: for from thence will spring all thy future good or evil. And it is an action of life like unto a stratagem of war—wherein a man can err but once. If thy estate be good, match near home and at leisure; if weak, far off and quickly. Inquire diligently of her disposition, and how her parents have been inclined in their youth. Let her not be poor, how noble soever; for a man can buy nothing in the market with gentility. Nor choose a base and uncomely creature altogether for wealth; for it will cause contempt in others, and loathing in thee. Neither make choice of a dwarf or a fool; for, by the one thou shalt beget a race of pigmies; the other will be thy continual disgrace, and it will *yirke* thee to hear her talk. For thou shalt find it, to thy great grief, that there is nothing more fulsome than a she-fool. *Lord Burleigh.*

10,417. MARRIAGE, Counsels for. Many a marriage has commenced, like the morning, red, and perished like a mushroom. Wherefore? Because the married pair neglected to be as agreeable to each other after their union as they were before it. Seek always to please each other, my children, but in doing so keep heaven in mind. Lavish not your love to-day, remembering that marriage has a morrow and again a morrow. Bethink ye, my daughters, what the word house-wife expresses. The married woman is her husband's domestic trust. On her he ought to be able to place his reliance in house and family; to her he should confide the key of his heart and the lock of his store-room. His honor and his home are under her protection, his welfare in her hands. Ponder this! And you, my sons, be true men of honor, and good fathers of your families. Act in such wise that your wives respect and love you. And what more shall I say to you, my children? Peruse diligently the word of God; that will guide you out of storm and dead calm, and bring you safe into port. And as for the rest—do your best!
Frederika Bremer.

10,418. MARRIAGE, Death at the. During the siege of Charleston, Lieutenant de Rochelle, of the Confederate army, was about to be united in marriage to Miss Anna Pickens, the daughter of Ex-Governor Pickens, at the house of Gen. Bonham. As the clergyman was asking the bride if she was ready, a shell fell upon the roof of the house, penetrated to the room where the company were assembled, burst and wounded nine persons, and among the rest, the bride. When order was restored the bride lay motionless upon the carpet. Her betrothed, kneeling and bending over her was weeping bitterly, and trying to staunch the blood that welled from a terrible wound under her left breast. A surgeon came and declared that Miss Pickens had not more than two hours to live. When informed of this the heroic bride said she would die worthy of her intended soldier-husband. He proposed that the ceremony should proceed. She lay upon a sofa, her bridal robes soiled with her own blood, her hair dishevelled, yet very beautiful. The clergyman asked the questions, to which she assented, while the groom held her hand. Another had even now come for her. The foam was upon her lips as the service ended. Within an hour the bridal chamber was the place of mourning, and death had claimed her for his own bride.

10,419. MARRIAGE, Effect of. An idol may be undefied by many accidental causes. Marriage in particular is a kind of counter-apotheosis, or deification inverted. When a man becomes familiar with his goddess, she quickly sinks into a woman. *Addison.*

10,420. MARRIAGE, Ill-assorted. Helen was covetous, Paris luxurious. On the other side, Ulysses was prudent, Penelope chaste. Happy, therefore, was the match between the latter; but the nuptials of the former brought an Iliad of miseries as well upon the Greeks as barbarians. *Plutarch.*

10,421. MARRIAGE, Love and. Sir Walter Farquhar calling one day on Mr. Pitt, the Premier observed him to be unusually ruffled, and inquired what was the matter. "Why, to tell you the truth," replied Sir Walter, "I am extremely angry with my daughter. She has permitted herself to form an attachment to a young gentleman by no means qualified in point of rank or fortune to be my son-in-law." "Now, let me say one word in the young lady's behalf," returned the minister. "Is the young man you mention of a respectable family?" "He is." "Is he respectable in himself?" "He is." "Has he the manners and education of a gentleman?" "He has." "Has he an estimable character?" "He has." "Why, then, my dear Sir Walter, hesitate no longer. You and I are well acquainted with the delusions of life. Let your daughter follow her own inclinations, since they appear to be virtuous. You have had more opportunities than I have of knowing the value of affection, and ought to respect it. Let the union take place, and I will not be unmindful that I had the pleasure of recommending it." The father consented, the lovers were united, and no one had any cause to regret the event.

10,422. MARRIAGE, Love in. In wedlock to love is a far greater blessing than to be beloved, since it preserves and keeps people from falling into many errors—nay, all those that corrupt and ruin matrimony. *Plutarch*

10,423. MARRIAGE, Pre-determined. A woman went to the Rev. S. Kilpin, of Exeter, to obtain his opinion on the important subject of marriage. She told her tale, and sought advice. Mr. Kilpin guessed how matters stood, and asked if the day for her marriage was not fixed for Tuesday? "O no, sir, not till Thursday," she replied. This is the usual way. People ask others' advice to get an approval of that which they have pre-determined. They treat God in the same way.

10,424. MARRIAGE, Prevention of. A young lady came from England to marry a young man to whom she had been long engaged. Soon after her arrival she learned that he had formed the habit of drinking to excess. She told him she could not marry him. He protested his love and promised to reform. She answered nobly and firmly, "No, I dare not trust my future happiness to a man who has formed such a habit. I came three thousand miles to marry the man I loved, but rather than marry a drunkard I will travel three thousand back again." She kept her word, and saved herself from a lifelong association with a loathsome drunkard.

10,425. MARRIAGE, Proposal of. One day Deacon Marvin, of Puritan fame, mounted his gray horse and rode to the house where Sarah and Betty Lee lived. Without dismounting he called Betty to him, and told her that the Lord had sent him there to marry her. With equal scripturalness she replied, "The Lord's will be done."

10,426. MARRIAGE, Religion in. Eliza Ambert, a young Parisian lady, discarded a gentleman to whom she was to have been married, because he ridiculed religion Having given him a gentle reproof, he replied, "A man of the world can not be so old-fashioned as to regard God and religion." She replied, "From this moment, sir, when I discover that you do not regard religion, I cease to be yours. He who does not love and honor God can never love his wife constantly and sincerely." And she adhered to her decision.

10,427. MARRIAGE, Responsibility of. Oh! surely marriage is a great and sacred responsibility. It is a bark in which two souls venture out on life's stormy sea, with no aid but their own to help them; the well-doing of their frail vessel must in future solely rest upon themselves; no one can take part either to mar or make their bliss or misery.   *J. Hamilton.*

10,428. MARRIAGE, Solemnity of. A canny Scotch girl approached her father on the subject of her marriage. He answered "Janet, it is a solemn thing to be married." "Yes, father," said she, "but it is more solemn not to be."

10,429. MARRIAGE, Stimulus of. To tell the truth, however, family and poverty have done more to support me than I have to support them. They have compelled me to make exertions that I hardly thought myself capable of; and often, when on the eve of despairing, they have forced me, like a coward in a corner, to fight like a hero, not for myself, but for my wife and little ones.   *Power.*

10,430. MARRIAGE, Uncomfortable. A Roman, who had divorced his wife, to the surprise of everybody—a lady sober, chaste, beautiful and rich—was asked the reason of his conduct. Lifting his foot and showing his buskin, he answered, "Is not this a new, handsome, perfect shoe? Yet no man but myself knows where it pinches me."

10,431. MARRIAGE, Unity of. Two persons who have chosen each other out of all the species, with design to be each other's mutual comfort and entertainment, have in that action bound themselves to be good-humored, affable, discreet, forgiving, patient, and joyful, with respect to each other's frailties and perfections, to the end of their lives. The wiser of the two (and it always happens one of them is such) will, for her or his own sake, keep things from outrage with the utmost sanctity. When this union is thus preserved, the most indifferent circumstance administers delight. Their condition is an endless source of new gratifications.   *Sir R. Steele*

10,432. MARRIAGE, Unsuitable. Marriages are styled matches; yet amongst those many that are married, how few are there that are matched! Husbands and wives are like locks and keys, that rather break than open, except the wards be answerable.   *W. Secker.*

10,433. MARTYR, Qualities of a. It is not every suffering that makes a martyr; but suffering for the word of God after a right manner; that is, not only for righteousness, but for righteousness sake; not only for truth, but out of love to truth; not only for God's word, but according to it; to wit: in that holy, humble, meek manner, as the word of God requireth.   *Bunyan.*

10,434. MARTYRDOM, Joy at. A Dutch martyr, feeling the flames, said, "Ah, what a small pain is this compared with the glory to come!" John Noyes took up a fagot at the fire, and kissing it, said, "Blessed be the time that ever I was born to come to this preferment."

10,435. MARTYRDOM, Novel. Restituta, an African virgin, in the reign of Valerian, was arrested as a Christian at Carthage, and condemned by a judge named Proculus, to be placed in an old boat filled with pitch and other combustibles, and sent adrift. She was bound fast in the boat, the pitch was lighted, the wind blew off shore, and the martyr sped swiftly in her fiery bark, Elijah-like, toward the sea of eternity.

10,436. MARTYRDOM, Passion for. Eulalia was the daughter of a Christian farmer near Barcelona. She was possessed by the spirit of the times, which coveted martyrdom. When she heard that the persecutions were renewed, she cried: "Thanks do I render thee, Lord Jesus Christ, and glory to thy holy name; for now I behold that which I have desired, and believe that with thy help all my desire shall be accomplished." The next night a frail young girl presented herself before the persecutor, defying him and his gods. He ordered her to be whipped, thinking that her ardor would cool, under the suffering. She rejoiced while the lash lacerated her tender flesh. She was stretched upon the little horse, and her sides were torn with hooks and burned with torches. In great agony, but still resolute, she prayed, "Lord Jesus Christ hear my prayer, perfect thy work in me and bid me be numbered among thine elect in the rest of life eternal." Immediately her soul sped to the paradise of God as a dove to its nest. It was ordered that her body should hang upon the rack to be devoured by the birds, A. D. 303.

10,437. MARTYRS, Decision of. In one of the persecutions of the Protestants in Scotland, Margaret Wilson, a girl of eighteen, and a widow of sixty-three, were sentenced to death by drowning. Stakes were driven into the beach sand while the tide was out, and they were fastened to them and left to perish.

10,438. MARTYRS, Endurance of. When three irons were brought for the purpose of fastening Hooper to the stake, he said, "Trouble not yourselves; I doubt not God will give strength sufficient to abide the fire without these bands; notwithstanding, suspecting the weakness of the flesh, although I have assured confidence in God's strength, do as ye think good." In the fire Hooper stood praying, "O Jesus, son of David, have mercy upon me, and receive my soul." And when the fire was spent, he wiped his eyes with his hands, and mildly, but earnestly, entreated that more fire might be brought. After suffering inexpressible torments for three-quarters of an hour, the martyr, bowing forwards, yielded up the spirit, dying as quietly as a child in his bed. The account of Latimer at the stake shows us how the bowed-down frame can be strengthened for its terrible conflict. We are told that "his mortal frame becoming invigorated at the prospect of the near approach of his journey's end, he no longer appeared a withered, crooked old man, his body crazed and bending under the weight of years, but he stood upright, as comely a father as one would desire to behold."
Power.

10,439. MARTYRS, Number of the. According to the calculation of some, about two hundred thousand suffered death in seven years under Pope Julian; no less than a hundred thousand were massacred by the French in the space of three months; the Waldenses who perished amounted to one million; within thirty years, the Jesuits destroyed nine hundred thousand; under the Duke of Alva, thirty-six thousand were executed by the common hangman; a hundred and fifty thousand perished in the Inquisition, and a hundred and fifty thousand by the Irish massacre; besides the vast multitude of whom the world could never be particularly informed, who were proscribed, banished, burned, starved, buried alive, smothered, suffocated, drowned, assassinated, chained to the galleys for life, or immured within the horrid walls of the Bastile, or others of their church or state prisons. According to some, the whole number of persons massacred since the last few centuries amounts to fifty millions!
Arvine.

10,440. MARTYRS, Record of. It was a custom of the churches as early as 150, to keep a record of such of their members as had suffered martyrdom, though only catechumens of the lowest rank. This record covered the main events of their lives, their conversion, their distinguishing virtues, the miracles they had wrought, and the death they suffered. These lives were called "Acts of the Martyrs." A collection of them was made by Eusebius, the father of ecclesiastical history. Their influence was great, attesting the divinity of the Christian religion and leading many to covet the martyr's crown. It was an early custom for the local churches to celebrate the day on which any of its members suffered martyrdom. It was accounted the birth-day of the martyr, on which he entered upon eternal glory. The book containing the record of these days was called the Calendar. From these early records of the different churches the calendar of the Romish church is made up. It is a field rich in illustrative material of a kind that will gain the attention, though not always historically reliable.

10,441. MARTYRS of Vice. The martyrs to vice far exceed the martyrs to virtue, both in endurance and in number. So blinded are we by our passions that we suffer more to be damned than to be saved! *Colton.*

10,442. MARTYRS, Victory of the. During the Diocletian persecution, Firmus and Rusticus were thrown into prison for being Christians. Proculus, the bishop, embraced them, and said, "Be strong in the Lord Jesus, and receive me, my brethren, as your fellow in death." They said, "So be it;" and he took his place with them. When the officer came to bring the martyrs before the judge, he found him there, and said, "What does that old man want among these condemned criminals?" Proculus answered, "They are not condemned criminals, but crowned victors of the Lord; and would that I might share their glory." He held up his hands, and was bound and led before the magistrate with Firmus and Rusticus. His application was explained to the judge. He refused him the honor of martyrdom, and ordered that he should be unbound and sent off.

10,443. MASSES, Discouragement with the. A zealous London clergyman went to preach to the neglected around the Seven Dials. He carried his overcoat on his arm and his gold-headed cane in his hand. A crowd was soon gathered of the roughest kind. One said, "May I hold your reverence's cane?" another, his coat; a third, his hat; which offers were accepted. The preaching done, he looked for his property, but it had all disappeared, never to return. He was indignant, and said, "I come here at great personal inconvenience to do you good. One of you has stolen my hat, another my cane, and a third my overcoat. You are a set of ingrates. I wash my hands of all of you. You may die in your sins if you will. I will have no more to do with you."

10,444. MASTER, Ascertaining the. When you see a dog following two men, you know not to which of them he belongs while they walk together; but let them come to a parting road, and one go one way, and the other another way, then you will know which is the dog's master. So at times will you and the world go hand in hand. While a man may have the

world, and a religious profession too, we cannot tell which is the man's master, God or the world : but stay till the man comes to a parting road ; God calls him this way, and the world calls him that way. Well, if God be his master, he follows religion, and lets the world go ; but if the world be his master, then he follows the world and the lusts thereof, and lets God, and conscience, and religion go.
R. Erskine.

10,445. MASTERS, Duty of. As masters must not be fierce, so neither familiar with their servants. Cato was in both the extremes ; one while he would eat and drink, and work naked with them ; and when he had worn them out with work, sell them like horses in a market. So the Romans in general, at their feast called Saturnalia, did wait on their servants ; the servants sat at the table, and the masters served them : yet possibly, before the year was expired, would kill them as dogs. *Swinnock.*

10,446. MATURITY, Marks of. Some time after Mr. Newton had published his Omicron's letters, and described the three stages of growth in religion—from the blade, the ear, and the full corn in the ear—distinguishing them by the letters A, B, and C, a conceited young minister wrote to Mr. N., telling him that he read his own character accurately drawn in that of C; Mr. N. wrote in reply, that in drawing the character of C, or full maturity, he had forgotten to add, till now, one prominent feature of C's character, namely— that C never knew his own face. *Whitecross.*

10,447. MATURITY, Signs of. 1. When the corn is near ripe, it bows the head and stoops lower than when it was green. When the people of God are near ripe for heaven, they grow more humble and self-denying than in the days of their first profession. The longer a saint grows in this world, the better he is still acquainted with his own heart and his obligations to God—both which are very humbling things. Paul had one foot in heaven when he called himself the chiefest of sinners and least of saints. 2. When harvest is nigh, the grain is more solid and pithy than ever it was before ; green corn is soft and spongy, but ripe corn is substantial and weighty : so it is with Christians ; the affections of a young Christian, perhaps, are more fervent and sprightly, but those of a grown Christian are more judicious and solid : their love to Christ abounds more and more in all judgment (Phil. 1; 9). The limbs of a child are more active and pliable ; but as he grows up to a perfect state, the parts are more consolidated and firmly knit. The fingers of the old musician are not so nimble, but he hath a more judicious ear in music than in his youth. 3. When corn is dead ripe, it's apt to fall of its own accord to the ground, and there shed ; whereby it doth, as it were, anticipate the harvestman, and call upon him to put in the sickle. Not unlike to which are the lookings and longings, the groanings, hastenings of ready Christians to their expected glory : they hasten to the coming of the Lord ; or as Montanus more fitly

renders it, they hasten the coming of the Lord, *i. e.* they are urgent and instant in their desires and cries to hasten his coming ; their desires sally forth to meet the Lord, they willingly take death by the hand : as the corn bends to the earth, so do these souls to heaven. This shows harvest to be near.   *Flavel.*

10,448. MEANNESS, Height of. About as mean a position as any man can put himself into, is to work all the time for the devil, and look all the time to the Lord for his pay. *Clemmens.*

10,449. MEANS, Conduct Respecting. I would neither have you be idle in the means, nor make an idol of the means. Though it be the mariner's duty to weigh his anchor, and spread his sails ; yet he cannot make his voyage until the winds blow. The pipes will yield no conveyance, unless the springs yield their concurrence.   *W. Secker.*

10,450. MEANS, Endeavors and. There can be no end without means : and God furnishes no means that exempt us from the task and duty of joining our own best endeavors. The original stock, or wild olive-tree of our natural powers, was not given us to be burnt or blighted, but to be grafted on.   *Coleridge.*

10,451. MEANS, Use of. In vain do the inhabitants of London go to their conduits for supply, unless the man who has the master-key turns the water on. And in vain do we think to quench our thirst at ordinances, unless God communicates the living water of his Spirit.   *Salter.*

10,452. MEANS OF GRACE, Interruptions of the. Long interruptions in the use of our religious duties will hinder the fruits of them ; when there are gaps and strides between the performance of duties, we lose the benefit of them. As it is with our bodies, if a man make a free and a liberal meal, this will not maintain his body to-morrow and the day after ; but he must have constant food, else nature languishes and decays ; so if you are delighted to-day, but should neglect to be so for many days after, you will lose the benefit of it, and the soul decays and languishes. If the bird leaves her nest for a long space, the eggs chill, and are not fit for production ; but when there's a constant incubation, then they bring forth ; so, when we leave religious duties for a long space, our affections chill, and grow cold, and are not fit to produce holiness and comfort to our souls ; but when we are constant in this work then shall we find the advantage of it. *Slater.*

10,453. MEANS OF GRACE, Neglecting the. A man went to live in a town where he built a house for himself and his family. He next provided a cistern for the reception of the water which he knew he must have for the comfort of his household. Day after day he looked anxiously into the cistern, but no water was there, because he had laid no pipes to carry the water from the reservoir to his house. "What a stupid man !" you say, "surely no one ever acted so unwisely." Perhaps Nathan's announcement to David, "Thou art the man;" may be used to you.

10,454. MEAT-OFFERING, Import of the. The

meat-offering consisted of flour, oil, and frankincense. In the burnt-offering the life was offered; in the meat-offering, the fruits. The life God claimed, but the fruits were given to man. Life represents what all owe to God; the fruits of the earth what we owe to man. "In the burnt-offering, the surrender of life represents the fulfillment of man's duty to God; in the meat-offering, the gift of corn and oil represents the fulfillment of man's duty to his neighbor. The burnt-offering is the perfect fulfillment of the laws of the first table; the meat-offering, the perfect fulfillment of the second." The latter was joined with the former; as, "the burnt-offering and its meat-offering." Both were necessary for completeness of symbol. The fine flour of the meat-offering symbolizes Christ, the true "Bread of Life," bruised for us. The oil of the meat-offering poured upon the flour is a type of the Holy Ghost poured upon man. "The bruised corn and the oil are always together." The frankincense of the meat-offering, when burned, sent forth a delightful perfume, and is a type of the abiding fragrance of the sacrifice of Christ. The salt required to season the meat-offering represents the incorruptibility, perpetuity, and saving power of Christ.

10,455. MEDDLESOMENESS Punished. I saw two men fighting together till a third, casually passing by, interposed himself to part them; the blows of one fell on his face, of the other on his back, of both on his body, being the screen betwixt the fiery anger of the two fighters. Some of the beholders laughed at him as well enough served for meddling with matters which belonged not to him.
Thomas Fuller.

10,456. MEDDLING, Danger of. A monkey was sitting up in a high tree, when, seeing some fishermen laying their nets in a river, he watched what they were doing. The men had no sooner set their nets, and retired a short distance to their dinner, than the monkey came down from the tree, thinking that he would try his hand at the same sport. But in attempting to lay the nets, he got so entangled in them that, being well nigh choked, he was forced to exclaim, "This serves me right; for what business had I, who know nothing of fishing, to meddle with such tackle as this."
Æsop.

10,457. MEDIATION, Analogy of. The whole analogy of nature removes all imagined presumption against the notion of a "Mediator between God and man." For we find all living creatures are brought into the world, and their life in infancy is preserved by the instrumentality of others; and every satisfaction of it, some way or other, is bestowed by the like means.
Butler.

10,458. MEDIATION, Conditions of. A bridge flung across the river must touch both shores, or it could not be a medium of passage; and it seems but the language of fair analogy to say that a Mediator between God and man must, in the mystery of his being, touch both natures, or he could not be the medium of in-

tercourse. The yearnings of sinful but penitent humanity find voice in the ancient cry, "O that there were a daysman between us, to lay his hands on both!" We need an intervening person who can reach up to heaven and down to earth; lay a hand of divinity on God, and a hand of humanity on man; for how could he who is only God mediate between God and man; and how could he who is only man mediate between man and God?
C. Stanford.

10,459. MEDIATION, Successful. Rev. Thomas Collins possessed a strong sympathy for the little children. One little fellow, the son of his host, had fallen under the displeasure of his parents, and had been sent to bed. Mr. C. says he went away and prayed for him, and then asked permission of his parents to go and visit him in his room. The request was granted. He told the lad of his sin, and of the sorrow it caused him. That it not only separated him from his friends, but also from God. The little fellow wept much, and wanted his parents called that he might ask their pardon. The mediation was accepted, and he was restored to favor. Some hours after, when no eye could see, he clasped Mr. Collins' hand, and pressed it to his lips. Mr. Collins says, "I felt his meaning, and it moved my heart much. There rose within me memory of the woman who came behind the Lord, and wept upon his feet."

10,460. MEDIATOR: Examples. *Joseph's brethren* tried to make their brother's steward their friend, to come between him and them, Gen. 43: 19–24. *Israel* desiring Moses to speak for them with God, Exod. 20: 18–21. *Moses* standing in the breach, Ps. 106: 23. *Aaron* standing "between the dead and the living," to turn away the plague, Num. 16: 48; see also the design of the Levitical service, "that there be no wrath any more upon the children of Israel," Num. 18: 5. *Jonathan* coming between Saul, his father, and David, his friend, 1 Sam. 19: 4–7. *Abigail* intercepting the wrath of David from coming upon Nabal, 1 Sam. 25: 14–35. *Joab*, by his skillful policy, restoring Absalom to his father's favor, 2 Sam. 14. *Blastus*, the king's chamberlain, interceding between Herod and the men of Tyre and Sidon, Acts 12: 20.
Bowes.

10,461. MEDIATOR, Royal. Sometimes there were more kings than one at Sparta, who governed by joint authority. A king was occasionally sent to some neighboring state in character of a Spartan ambassador. Did he, when so sent, cease to be a king of Sparta because he was an ambassador? No, he did not divest himself of his regal dignity, but only added to it that of public deputation. So Christ, in becoming man, did not cease to be God; but, though he ever was, and still continued to be, King of the whole creation, acted as the voluntary Servant and Messenger of the Father.
Illus. of Truth.

10,462. MEDITATION, Advantage of. Scripture truth becomes more profitable by meditation The promises are flowers, growing in the paradise of scripture; meditation, like the bee, sucks out the sweetness of them. The promises are of no use or comfort to us till they are meditated upon. For as the roses hanging in the garden may give a fragrant perfume, yet their sweet water is distilled only by the fire, so the promises are sweet in reading over, but the water of these roses—the spirit and quintessence of the promises—is distilled into the soul only by meditation. The incense, when it is pounded and beaten, smells sweetest. Meditating on a promise, like the beating of the incense, makes it most odoriferous and pleasant. The promises may be compared to a golden mine, which then only enricheth when the gold is dug out. By holy meditation we dig out that spiritual gold which lies hid in the mine of the promise, and so we come to be enriched. Cardan saith, "There is no precious stone but hath some hidden virtue in it." They are called "precious promises." (2 Peter 1 : 4.) When they are applied by meditation, then their virtue appears, and they become precious indeed. *T. Watson.*

10,463. MEDITATION, Benefits of. By meditation we ransack our deep and false hearts, find out our secret enemies, buckle with them, expel them, arm ourselves against their re-entrance. By this we make use of all good means, fit ourselves to all good duties; by this we descry our weaknesses, obtain redress, prevent temptations, cheer up our solitariness, temper our occasions of delight, get more light into our knowledge, more heat to our affections, more life to our devotion. By this we see our Saviour with Stephen, we talk with God as Moses did, and by this we are ravished with blessed Paul into Paradise, and see that heaven we are loath to leave, but cannot utter. *Bp. Hall.*

10,464. MEDITATION, Excellency of. Meditation is a soul-fattening duty; it is a grace-strengthening duty, it is a duty-crowning duty. Gerson calls meditation the nurse of prayer; Jerome calls it his paradise; Basil calls it the treasury where all the graces are locked up; Theophylact calls it the very gate and portal by which we enter into glory; and Aristotle, though a heathen, placeth felicity in the contemplation of the mind. You may read much and hear much, yet without meditation you will never be excellent, you will never be eminent Christians. *Brooks.*

10,465. MEDITATION, Use of. An old divine says, "Meditation is to the sermon what the harrow is to the seed—it covers those truths which else might have been picked or washed away."

10,466. MEEKNESS, Biblical. There are many kinds of meekness, all commended as marks of a Christian spirit: The meekness of *love,* 1 Cor. 13 : 5, 7. The meekness of *wisdom,* James 2 : 13. The meekness of *teaching,* 2 Tim. 2 : 25. The meekness of *self-restraint,* Exod. 23 : 4–9; Prov. 6 : 32; 19 : 11. The meekness of *long-forbearing,* Prov. 28 : 15. Examples of meekness are Joseph, Moses, David, and Christ who when reviled returned it not, and when crucified prayed for his murderers. Rev. 5 : 8.—"A Lamb, as it had been

slain;" ἀρνίον, a little or delicate lamb. It is singular to find this word, except in John 21, peculiar to the Apocalypse, in which it refers twenty-eight times to the Lamb of God; why does not seem certain, unless to put forward more prominently his meek and gentle nature. *Bowes.*

10,467. MEEKNESS, Christian. By the universal voice of his army, Godfrey of Bouillon was saluted king of Jerusalem, upon taking it from the Saracens at the end of the first crusade. A crown of gold was also brought him, sparkling with jewels. He set it aside, saying, "It is most unfit for me, who am a mortal man, a servant and a sinner, to be crowned with gems and gold, where Christ, the Son of God, who made heaven and earth, was crowned with thorns."

10,468. MEEKNESS, Importance of. Meekness is one of the rarest of virtues. It is more rare than pearls, or than opals, or than diamonds. The gold of Ophir is not to be mentioned by the side of it. Meekness is like the sum of all the rays of light which shine upon the earth, and give to things the qualities which they possess in our sight. It is the substance of the faculties of a man raised up in sweetness and power, and shining out as the sun shines in summer days, with such gentleness as to nourish, and not to singe, the tenderest flowers. *Beecher.*

10,469. MELANCHOLY Cured. A young man conceived himself to be dead, and desired to be buried before his flesh became offensive. His funeral was held; and on the way to the grave some fellows met the train, and inquired who they were burying. Being told, they said his friends were well rid of him, for if he had lived he would surely have come to the gallows. The listening corpse, now indignant, answered, "You do me great wrong." They only reviled him the more. The corpse, now lively enough, sprang forth, clad in his shroud, resolved to punish his maligners. In the chase which ensued, his delusion vanished, and he returned home a cured man.

10,470. MEMORIAL, Lasting. Sir Bernard Burke says: "In 1850, a pedigree research led me to pay a visit to the village of Finderne. I sought for the ancient hall; not a stone remained to tell where it had stood. I entered the church; not a single record of a Finderne was there! I accosted a villager, hoping to glean some stray traditions of the Findernes. 'Findernes!' said he, 'we have no Findernes here; but we have something that once belonged to them, we have Findernes' flowers.' 'Show them me,' I replied; and the old man led me into a field which still retained faint traces of terraces and foundations. 'There,' said he, pointing to a bank of 'garden flowers grown wild,' 'there are the Findernes' flowers, brought by Sir Geoffrey from the Holy Land; and do what we will, they will never die!'"

10,471. MEMORY, Acquisitive. The power of acquisition is usually strongest in early life, is materially diminished in middle age, and is still less in old age. Theodore Parker in youth could repeat a hymn from once hearing it read. He could recite several hundred lines of a poem at once. In mature years, his biographer says, he acquired one hundred and fifty lines of blank verse by a single reading, so as to be able to repeat it. His ease of acquisition seems to have been confined to poetical compositions, and is an exception to the above law.

10,472. MEMORY, Activity of. Joseph Scaliger committed to memory in twenty-one days the whole of Homer's works, the Iliads, containing thirty-one thousand six hundred and seventy verses, and the Odysseys about the same.

10,473. MEMORY, Bad. A gentlemen had so bad a memory, and so circumscribed, that he scarce knew what he read. A friend knowing this, lent him the same book to read seven times over; and being asked afterwards how he liked it, replied, "I think it is an admirable production; but the author sometimes repeats the same things." *Thiébault.*

10,474. MEMORY, Definition of. Memory is the cabinet of imagination, the treasury of reason, the registry of conscience, and the council-chamber of thought.—*Basile.*——It is the treasure-house of the mind, wherein the monuments thereof are kept and preserved. *Fuller.*

10,475. MEMORY, Exact. Carneades, a Grecian, had such a retentive memory, that he was able to repeat the entire contents of a library with as much ease as if he was reading out of the books themselves.

10,476. MEMORY, Good. I could repeat two thousand names in the same order as they were spoken, and when as many as were scholars to my master brought each of them several verses to him, so that the number of them amounted to more than two hundred, beginning at the last I could recite them orderly unto the first; nor was my memory only apt to receive such things as I would commit to it, but was also a faithful preserver of all that I had entrusted it with. *Seneca.*

10,477. MEMORY, Method with. Memory is like a purse; if it be overfull, that it cannot be shut, all will drop out of it. Marshal thy notions into handsome method. A man will carry twice more weight, trussed and packed up in bundles, than when it lies untowardly flapping and hanging about his shoulders. *Fuller.*

10,478. MEMORY, Pictures of. A painter, famous for his delineations of natural scenery, domestic life and battle scenes, was compelled, by ill-health, to give over his work and seek rest in the country. There he grew worse, and in his delirium he described the several scenes and groups he had studied and portrayed. His room became a chamber of imagery on whose walls all the studies and paintings of his life re-appeared. What he had contemplated, conceived and forgotten, reappeared under the influence of disease. What pictures of earthly scenes will the day of judgment bring before the mind, which will justify the decision of the righteous Judge!

10,479. MEMORY, Pollution of. Almost twenty years since I heard a profane jest, and still remember it. How many pious passages of far later date have I forgotten! It seems my soul is like a filthy pond wherein fish die soon and frogs live long. Lord, raze this profane jest out of my memory. Leave not a letter thereof behind, lest my corruption (an apt scholar) guess it out again; and be pleased to write some pious meditation in the place thereof. And grant, Lord, for the time to come, (because such bad guests are easier kept out), that I may be careful not to admit what I find so difficult to expel. *T. Fuller.*

10,480. MEMORY, Powerful. A young Corsican became noted for his power of memory. The judge proposed a test to which he instantly consented. He dictated Latin, Greek and all kinds of barbarous names, not any one of them having any dependence on the other. He became weary with dictating, and the boy tired writing them off. He then told the young man he would be satisfied if he could repeat half of what had been given. In a few seconds he began, and repeated the names in the very same order they were set down, without any hesitation. Then beginning at the last, he recited them all backward to the first. Then he named the first, third, fifth, and in that order repeated all. His memory was so retentive that he could repeat any thing entrusted to it a year after, with perfect accuracy.

10,481. MEMORY, Purifying the. A minister conversing with a woman who was washing wool in a sieve by dipping it in a stream, she said, "I hope I shall have reason to bless God for you to all eternity. I heard you preach at W——, some years back; and hope your sermon was the means of doing me great good." "Indeed, I rejoice to hear it; pray what was the subject?" said he. "Ah, sir, I can't recollect that; mine is such a bad head." "How then can it have done you good, if you don't even remember it?" "Sir, my poor mind is like this sieve; the sieve doesn't hold the water, but it runs through and cleanses the wool: my memory does not keep the words, but, blessed be God, he made them touch the heart: and now I don't love sin; I go whenever I can to hear of Jesus Christ; and I beg him every day to wash me in his own blood."

10,482. MEMORY, Retentive. Porson, when a boy at Eton school, going up for a lesson one day, was accosted by a boy in the same form, "Porson, what have you got there?" "Horace." "Let me look at it." Porson handed the book to the boy, who, pretending to return it, dexterously substituted another in its place, with which Porson proceeded. Being called on by the master, he read and construed Carm. i. x. very regularly. Observing the class to laugh, the master said, "Porson, you seem to me to be reading on one side of the page while I am looking at the other; pray whose edition have you?" Porson hesitated. "Let me see it," rejoined the master; who, to his great surprise, found it to be an English Ovid. Porson was ordered to go on, which he did easily, correctly, and promptly to the end of the ode.

10,483. MEMORY, Sanctified When Alexander the Great had overthrown Darius, king of Persia, he took among the spoils a most rich cabinet full of the choicest jewels that were in all the world; upon which there rose a dispute before him, to what use he should put the cabinet; and every one having spent his judgment according to his fancy, the king himself concluded that he would keep the cabinet, to be a treasury to lay up the books of Homer in, which were his greatest joy and delight. A sanctified memory is a rich cabinet full of the choicest thoughts of God; it is that rich treasury wherein a Christian is still a-laying up more and more precious thoughts of God, and more and more high and holy thoughts of God, and more and more honorable and noble thoughts of God, and more and more awful and reverent thoughts of God, and more and more sweet and comfortable thoughts of God, and more and more tender and compassionate thoughts of God, etc.   *Brooks.*

10,484. MEMORY, Test of. Voltaire was to read to Frederick of Prussia a poem of considerable length which he had just composed. After he had finished reading, the king remarked only, "That poem is stolen; I have heard it before." "That is impossible," said the poet. Frederick said he could prove it, and he sent for a man who, to the great confusion of Voltaire, repeated the poem word for word. The person had been placed behind a screen, and from once hearing the poem was able to repeat it correctly.   *Dr. McCosh.*

10,485. MEMORY, Utilizing the. The best way to remember a thing is thoroughly to understand it, and often to recall it to mind. By reading continually with great attention, and never passing a passage without understanding and considering it well, the memory will be stored with knowledge; and things will occur at times when we want them, though we can never recollect the passages or from whence we draw our ideas.   *Trusler.*

10,486. MEMORY Well Used. It is said of Rev. Thomas Fuller, that he could dictate to five several writers at the same time on as many different subjects. When in the company of a committee of commissioners, they praised him for his great memory. He said it was true that fame had given him a good memory, and he would like to give them an example of it. The committee were delighted, laid aside their business, and asked him to begin. "Gentlemen," he said, "your worships have thought fit to sequester a poor but honest parson, my neighbor, from his living, and have committed him to prison. He has a large family of children, his circumstances are indifferent; if you will please to release him out of prison, and restore him to his living, I will never forget the kindness as long as I live." The jest was received with applause, and the parson restored to his living.

10,487. MEN, Christ's Image in. We all know by a recent discovery—the calotype and the daguerreotype—that light writes itself; that the light reflected from an object writes that object by a mysterious power upon the susceptible page that is exposed to it. So we, looking to Christ, and receiving from him, as he is revealed in the Bible, the glorious beams that are radiated from his character, shall have impressed upon our living selves the very likeness of Christ, till men can see Christ in us, and Christ on us, and that we are, indeed, what we should be,—followers of him.
    Dr. Cumming.

10,488. MEN, Classes of. It is with men as with animals—you may divide them into two classes, vertebrated and invertebrated. Animals remarkable for dignity, and elevation in the scale of existence, are vertebrated or backboned; their backbones give them eminence and place: all animals to which we apply the term "inferior" want this backbone, and they can only crawl or creep, because they are invertebrated. We have often thought, when looking among men, that this is the great distinction we notice between them—the successful and the unsuccessful, the principled and the unprincipled, the true and the false. We recoil instinctively from the touch of the spider and the wasp, the leech and the slug; and we recoil as instinctively from that large class of persons of whom these little creatures are a sort of moral analogy, because they have no backbone. They can sting sometimes; they can weave a brittle web sometimes; they leave here and there a slimy trail; they can draw blood; and the instincts of society and humanity recoil from them. They have no backbone.   *Paxton Hood.*

10,489. MEN, Insane. Every man is a divinity in disguise, a god playing the fool. It seems as if heaven had sent its insane angels into our world as to an asylum. And here they will break out into their native music, and utter at intervals the words they have heard in heaven; then the mad fit returns, and they mope and wallow like dogs!   *Emerson.*

10,490. MEN, Rarity of Good. If man alone is a wonder, the good and virtuous man must certainly be a double one. He is such a rarity that Diogenes thought the sun at noon scarce a sufficient light to make his discovery by, when he went up and down in quest of such a one, whimsically carrying a candle and a lamp to assist his discovery. "A good man is neither quickly made nor easily understood; for like the Phoenix of Arabia, there is possibly one of them born in the space of five hundred years."   *Wanley.*

10,491. MEN, Reliable. Napoleon, in his confidential conversations with me, drew a distinction between a man of honor and a conscientious man, giving his preference to the former; because, he said, we know what to expect from a man who is bound simply and purely by his words and his engagements, while in the other case we depend on his opinions and feelings, which may vary. "He does that which he thinks he ought to do, or which he supposes is best. Thus," he added, "my father-in-law, the Emperor of Austria, has done that which he believes conducive to the inter est of his people. He is an honest man, a conscientious man, but not a man of honor. You, for example, if the enemy had invaded France and stood upon the heights of Montmartre, you believe, perhaps with reason, that the welfare of your country commands you to desert me, and you do it; you may be a good Frenchman, a brave man, a conscientious man, but you are not a man of honor." *Marmont.*

10,492. MEN, Three Classes of. There are but three classes of men: the retrograde, the stationary, and the progressive. *Lavater.*

10,493. MEN Thrown Away. Kings who affect to be familiar with their companions make use of men as they do of oranges; they take oranges to extract their juice, and when they are well-sucked they throw them away. Take care the king does not do the same to you; be careful that he does not read all your thoughts; otherwise he will throw you aside to the back of his chest, as a book of which he has read enough. *Alva.*

10,494. MEN, Underground. There was never a ray of starlight in the Mammoth Cave of Kentucky: only the red glare of torches ever lights its walls. So there are many men whose minds are all underground, and unlighted save by the torches of selfishness and passion. *Teachers' Treasury.*

10,495. MEN, Variation among. When King Antiochus was coming upon Greece with great forces, and all men trembled at the report of his numbers and equipage, T. Quinctius told the Achaians this story: "Once I dined with a friend at Chalcis; and when I wondered at the variety of the dishes, said my host, 'All these are pork; only in dressing and sauces they differ.' And, therefore, be not you amazed at the king's forces when you hear talk of spearmen, and men-at arms, and choice footmen, and horse-archers, for all these are but Syrians, with some little difference in their weapons."

10,496. MERCIES, Acknowledgment of. What would a blind man give to see the pleasant rivers, and meadows, and flowers, and fountains, that we have met with! I have been told, that if a man that was born blind, could obtain to have his sight for but only one hour during his whole life, and should, at the first opening of his eyes, fix his sight upon the sun when it was in its full glory, either at the rising or setting of it, he would be so transported and amazed, and so admire the glory of it, that he would not willingly turn his eyes from that first ravishing object, to behold all the other various beauties this world could present to him. And this, and many other like blessings, we enjoy daily; and for most of them, because they be so common, most men forget to pay their praises; but let not us, because it is a sacrifice so pleasing to him that made the sun, and us, and still protects us, and gives us flowers, and showers, and meat, and content. *Izaak Walton.*

10,497. MERCIES, Computation of. An old divine compares man to a merchant's agent, who has a great store of goods and money in his hands, but is so busy that he can get no time to settle with his principal. The Christian must consider his mercies, and will soon feel that he can never pay the debt of gratitude due to God.

10,498. MERCIES, Continuous. It is by no means pleasant when reading an interesting article in your magazine to find yourself pulled up short with the ominous words, "to be continued." Yet they are words of good cheer if applied to other matters. What a comfort to remember that the Lord's mercy and loving-kindness is to be continued! Much as we have experienced in the long years of our pilgrimage, we have by no means outlived eternal love. Providential goodness is an endless chain, a stream which follows the pilgrim, a wheel perpetually revolving, a star for ever shining, and leading us to the place where he is who was once a babe in Bethlehem. All the volumes which record the doings of divine grace are but part of a series to be continued. *Spurgeon.*

10,499. MERCIES, God's. The air is not so full of motes, of atoms, as the church is of mercies; and as we can suck in no part of air but we take in those motes, those atoms; so here, in the congregation, we cannot suck in a word from the preacher, we cannot speak, we cannot sigh a prayer to God, but that whole breath is made of mercy. *Dr. Donne.*

10,500. MERCIES Remembered. Bishop Hutton was traveling between Wensleydale and Ingleton, when he dismounted and retired to a particular spot, where he knelt down and continued some time in prayer. On his return, one of his attendants inquired his reason for this act. The bishop informed him, that when he was a poor boy, he traveled over that cold and bleak mountain without shoes or stockings, and that he remembered disturbing a cow on the identical spot where he prayed, that he might warm his feet and legs on the place where she had lain. His feelings of gratitude would not allow him to pass the place without presenting his thanksgivings to God for his mercies to him.

10,501. MERCIES, Yearly. An English preacher takes a hungry man into a hall with plates laid for 1,460 persons. Here are supplies of all kinds in bountiful profusion. The man would like to sit down at one of these plates. "Ah!" says his guide, "would you be thankful? then you shall have your breakfast, something quite as good as anything here; only just wait until I tell you something. You can't have these, for they are the ghosts of what you have already had. They are the 365 breakfasts, the 365 dinners, the 365 teas, and the 365 suppers you had last year. They make 1,460 in all." "You don't mean to say I had all those?" "Yes; and many baskets full of odds and ends beside." And now, we will dismiss our friend to eat his meal, we trust with some new feelings dawning upon him of what heaps of mercies he has had even in this one matter of food. *Buck.*

10,502. MERCY, Abuse of. It is said of the

original Indians of Florida, that when they could not pay their debts, they took a short method of settling the account, by knocking their creditors on the head. Sinners in a state of unregeneracy, though partly sensible that they do not keep the law of God, yet think to knock God's justice on the head, by pleading absolute mercy. *Salter.*

10,503. MERCY, Door of. The door of mercy has hinges, and it may be shut, and then locked with the adamantine key of justice.

Dr. Raleigh.

10,504. MERCY, Emblems of Divine. *The rainbow,* Gen. 9:13; Ezek. 1:28; Rev. 4:3; 10:1; the divinely appointed token of the covenant of mercy, beautiful in its simplicity, blessed in its perpetuity, the bright bow formed on the dark cloud. *The mercy-seat* or propitiatory, Exod. 25:17–22; the lid of the ark, made of pure gold, of one piece with the cherubim; the appointed meeting-place of Jehovah with his people. *A beautiful temple,* "built up forever," Ps. 89:2; rising, in spite of opposition, stone by stone, to perfection and completion. *A father's pity,* Ps. 103:13. *A pioneer or harbinger,* Ps. 89:16; going before to mark out the way. *A girdle* that compasses the righteous man on every side, Ps. 32:10. *A prop or support,* Ps. 94:18. *Bowes.*

10,505. MERCY, God's. We must tell concerning God's mercy as we do concerning God himself, that he is that great Fountain of which we all drink, and the great Rock of which we all eat, and on which we all dwell, and under whose shadow we all are refreshed. God's mercy is all this; and we can only draw the great lines of it, and reckon the constellations of our hemisphere, instead of telling the number of the stars. We only reckon what we feel and what we live by; and though there be, in every one of these lines of life, enough to engage us forever to do God service, and to give him praises, yet it is certain there are very many mercies of God on us, and towards us, and concerning us, which we neither feel nor see nor understand as yet; but yet we are blessed by them, and are preserved and secure; and we shall know them when we come to give God thanks in the festivities of an eternal Sabbath. *Jeremy Taylor.*

10,506. MERCY, Instinctive Cry for. In the battle of Bull Run, a wounded soldier, as he fell, cried, "God have mercy on my soul." The cry became contagious. One after another took it up till the chorus became general in that section, "God have mercy upon my soul." Irreligious men repeated it, and dated their religious experience from it. O, that this cry might sweep the land!

10,507. MERCY, Limitless. The freshness of grace is set forth by the expressions used, as, Isa. 55:1; 52:3, buying "without money and without price;" redeemed when "without strength," Rom. 5:6 (the very word used in Greek for the "impotent folk" and "the impotent man," John 5:3, 7); without limit on God's part, to "whosoever will call on the name of the Lord," Joel 2:32; "whosoever will take of the water of life freely," Rev. 22, 18. Richard Baxter used to say, "I conceive there could be no word so strong as the "whosoever" in the gospel offer. If God had put my own name in his word, and made it an express revelation that Richard Baxter might be saved, it would not have been half so strong, because there might have been many Richard Baxters, and how could I be certified that it was for me especially the word was meant? But when he has said *'whosoever* will,' then I can have no doubt. The word is so inclusive, that none need fear exclusion; so gracious that none need apprehend rejection." *Bowes.*

10,508. MERCY, Question of. A South Sea Islander of the baser sort went to the missionary with a most important question. With much emotion he said, "You know I am a wicked man. Shame covers my face, and holds me back. To-day I have broke through all fear. I want to know, is there room for me? Can I expect mercy?" When asked how such thoughts came into his mind, he replied, "I was at work putting up my garden fence. Greatly wearied, I sat down on a little bank to rest, and said within myself. All this garden, and death for my soul; all this great property, and death forever! Oh, what shall I do?" He was instructed more perfectly, and God answered his question with the assurance of salvation.

10,509. MERCY, Rejection of. It is horrible pride for a beggar to starve rather than to take alms at a rich man's hands—a malefactor rather to choose a halter than a pardon from his gracious prince; but here is one infinitely surpassing both—a soul pining and perishing in sin, and yet rejecting the mercy of God and the helping hand of Christ to save him.

Gurnall.

10,510. MERCY, Shoreless Ocean of. O this mercy of God! I am told it is an ocean. Then I place on it four swift sailing craft, with compass, and charts, and choice rigging, and skillful navigators; and I tell them to launch away, and discover for me the extent of this ocean. That craft puts out in one direction, and sails to the north; this to the south; this to the east; this to the west. They crowd on all their canvass, and sail ten thousand years, and one day come up the harbor of heaven; and I shout to them from the beach, "Have you found the shore?" and they answer, "No shore to God's mercy!" Swift angels, dispatched from the throne, attempt to go across it. For a million years they fly and fly; but then they come back and fold their wings at the foot of the throne, and cry, "No shore; no shore to God's mercy!" Mercy! Mercy! Mercy! I sing it. I preach it. I pray it. Here I find a man bound hand and foot to the devil; but with one stroke of the hammer of God's truth the chains fall off, and he is free forever. Mercy! Mercy! Mercy! There is no depth it cannot fathom. There is no height it cannot scale. There is no infinity it cannot compass. *Talmage.*

10,511. MERCY, Stores of. God hath stores

of mercy lying by him; his exchequer is never empty; he keeps mercy for thousands (Exod. 34: 7), in a readiness to deal it upon thousand millions of sins, as well as millions of persons. Abraham, Isaac and Jacob, and all that were before, have not wasted it; and if God were to proclaim his name again, it is the same still, for his name as well as his essence is unchangeable. *Charnock.*

10,512. MERCY, Yielding to. I heard once a story from a soldier, who, with his company, had laid siege against a fort, that so long as the besieged were persuaded their foes would show them no favor, they fought like madmen; but when they saw one of their fellows taken and received to favor, they all came tumbling down from their fortress and delivered themselves into their enemies' hands. I am persuaded, did men believe that there is grace and willingness in the heart of Christ to save sinners, as the word imports there is, they would come tumbling into his arms; but Satan has blinded their minds that they cannot see this thing. *Bunyan.*

10,513. MERIT, Absence of all. We must be emptied of self before we can be filled with grace; we must be stripped of our rags before we can be clothed with righteousness; we must be unclothed that we may be clothed; wounded, that we may be healed; killed, that we may be made alive; buried in disgrace, that we may rise in holy glory. These words, "sown in corruption, that we may be raised in incorruption; sown in dishonor, that we may be raised in glory; sown in weakness, that we may be raised in power," are as true of the soul as the body. To borrow an illustration from the surgeon's art, the bone that is set wrong must be broken again, in order that it may be set aright. I press this truth on your attention. It is certain, that a soul filled with self has no room for God; and, like the inn of Bethlehem, given to lodge, crowded with meaner guests, a heart pre-occupied by pride and her godless train has no chamber within which Christ may be born "in us the hope of glory." *Dr. Guthrie.*

10,514. MERIT, Assumption of. Was ever invalid so bereft of sense as to say, "When I am somewhat better, when this fever burns less fierce, this pulse beats more calm, this running ulcer has a less loathsome and offensive discharge, I will repair to the hospital?" But such is their folly who intend, when they are holier, to go to Jesus. Go to him as you are; just as you are. The worse your case, the higher in a sense may be your assurance of an immediate salvation. Yours is the hope of the maimed and bleeding soldier, whom kind comrades bear from the deadly trench. He knows that the worse his wound the more confidently he can reckon on the surgeon's earliest care; and that from the very couch, where noblest birth or highest rank lies stretched under some less serious injury, that man of humanity, image of the great Physician, will turn to kneel by the pallet of a poor orphan boy, the meanest private, a mutilated

enemy, to tie the severed vessel, and stem the tide that pours his life's blood upon the ground. *Dr. Guthrie.*

10,515. MERIT, Baseless. A ship bound for Australia sprung a leak in a storm. On board was a very nervous man, who, the captain feared, would communicate panic to the other passengers. As he came to inquire if their condition was so alarming, the captain confirmed his fears, but told him to say nothing of what he knew, and asked him to help save the ship by holding a rope till he should be released. He stood faithfully at his post, holding the rope tightly, though much wearied, till the storm was over, and he was discharged. He expected to receive the public thanks of passengers and crew for saving the ship, and hinted as much to the captain. He answered, "What, sir, do you think you saved the vessel? I gave you that rope to hold to keep you engaged, that you might not be in such a feverish state of alarm." Men vastly over-estimate their works. They are too insignificant to merit mention, and generally serve only to keep us out of mischief. Whatever we do, we can never merit heaven or save ourselves.

10,516. MERIT, Rewards of. I know not why we should delay our tokens of respect to those who deserve them, until the heart that our sympathy could have gladdened has ceased to beat. As men cannot read the epitaphs inscribed upon the marble that covers them, so the tombs that we erect to virtue often only prove our repentance, that we neglected it when with us. *Bulwer-Lytton.*

10,517. METHOD, Importance of. From the cotter's hearth, or the workshop of the artisan, to the palace or the arsenal, the first merit, that which admits neither substitute nor equivalent, is that everything is in its place. Where this charm is wanting, every other merit either loses its name, or becomes an additional ground of accusation and regret. Of one by whom it is eminently possessed, we say proverbially, he is like clockwork. The resemblance extends beyond the point of regularity, and yet falls short of the truth. Both do, indeed, at once divide and announce the silent and otherwise indistinguishable lapse of time. But the man of methodical industry and honorable pursuits does more: he realizes its ideal divisions, and gives a character and individuality to its moments. If the idle are described as killing time, he may be justly said to call it into life and moral being while he makes it the distinct object not only of the consciousness, but of the conscience. He organizes the hours, and gives them a soul; and that, the very essence of which is to fleet away, and evermore to have been, he takes up into his own permanence and communicates to it the imperishableness of a spiritual nature. *Coleridge.*

10,518. METHOD, Slaves to. Of method this may be said—if we make it our slave, it is well; but it is bad if we are slaves to method. A gentleman once told me, that he made it a regular rule to read fifty pages every day of some author or other, and on no account to fall short of that number, nor to exceed it. I silently set him down for a man who might have taste to read something worth writing, but who never could have genius himself to write anything worth reading.   *Colton.*

10,519. METHOD, Want of. Irregularity and want of method are only supportable in men of great learning or genius, who are often too full to be exact, and therefore choose to throw down their pearls in heaps before the reader, rather than be at the pains of stringing them.   *Addison.*

10,520. METHODISM, Influence of. After the establishment of the American Republic, the institution of Methodism is the greatest event of the eighteenth century, and of all the men who lived in that century there is no one whose influence upon after ages equals that of John Wesley. Of the seventy-five millions who speak the English tongue, about three and a half millions are members of the Methodist Church; four millions more are pupils in their Sunday-schools; and the regular attendants upon Methodist worship cannot be less than as many more—fifteen millions in all. Thus, one-fifth of all who speak our language are directly moulded, for this life and the life to come, by Methodism. We doubt if any other Protestant communion really numbers as many. The established churches of England and Germany indeed nominally include more; but in counting their numbers all who do not formally belong to other communions are put down as Episcopalians or Lutherans. Fully two-thirds of the Methodists are in the United States. To Methodism more than to any other one thing it is owing that our Western States grew up into civilization without passing through a period of semi-barbarism. Southey expressed no more than the bare truth when he said, "I consider Wesley as the most influential mind of the last century—the man who will have produced the greatest effects centuries or perhaps millenniums hence, if the present race of men shall continue so long." This judgment is coming to be acknowledged. Within a few months past a site has been appropriated in Westminster Abbey for a monument to John Wesley. Of all the great Englishmen there commemorated there is no one more worthy of a place.   *Dr. A. H. Guernsey.*

10,521. METHODISM, Preservation of. I asked the Rev. John Wesley, in 1783, what must be done to keep Methodism alive when he was dead, to which he immediately answered: "The Methodists must take heed to their doctrine, their experience, their practice, and their discipline. If they attend to their doctrines only, they will make the people Antinomians; if to the experimental part of religion only, they will make them enthusiasts; if to the practical part only, they will make them Pharisees; and if they do not attend to their discipline, they will be like persons who bestow much pains in cultivating their garden, and put no fence round it, to save it from the wild boar of the forest."   *Robert Miller.*

10,522. METHODISTS, Two Kinds of. A plain Christian, on being called by a profligate worldling, "a Methodist," replied, "Sir, whether you are aware of it or not, you are equally a Methodist with myself." "How? how?" asked the scoffer, with many oaths. "Pray be calm," said the other: "there are but two methods—the method of salvation, and the method of damnation: in one of these you certainly are; in which, I leave you to decide."

10,523. MIND, Abstraction of. An astronomer used to walk out every night to gaze upon the stars. It happened one night that, as he was wandering in the outskirts of the city, with his whole thoughts rapt up in the skies, he fell into a well. On his hallooing and calling out, one who heard his cries ran up to him, and when he had listened to his story, said, "My good man, while you are trying to pry into the mysteries of heaven, you overlook the common objects that are under your feet."   *Æsop.*

10,524. MIND, Classes of. All fact-collectors, who have no aim beyond their facts, are one-story men. Two-story men compare, reason, generalize, using the labors of the fact-collectors as well as their own. Three-story men idealize, imagine, predict; their best illumination comes from above, through the skylight. There are minds with large ground-floors that can store an infinite amount of knowledge; some librarians, for instance, who know enough of books to help other people without being able to make much other use of their knowledge, have intellects of this class. Your great working lawyer has two spacious stories; his mind is clear, because his mental floors are large, and he has room to arrange his thoughts so that he can get at them—facts below, principles above, and all in ordered series. Poets are often narrow below, incapable of clear statement, and with small power of consecutive reasoning, but full of light, if sometimes rather bare of furniture in the attics.   *Holmes.*

10,525. MIND, Failure of the. The failure of the mind in old age is often less the result of natural decay than of disuse. Ambition has ceased to operate; contentment brings indolence; indolence, decay of mental power, *ennui*, and sometimes death. Men have been known to die, literally speaking, of disease induced by intellectual vacancy.   *Sir Benjamin Brodie.*

10,526. MIND, Immortality of. Our thoughts, our reminiscences, our intellectual acquirements, die with us to this world; but to this world only. If they are what they ought to be, they are treasures which we lay up for heaven. That which is of the earth, earthly, perishes with rank, honors, authority, and other earthly and perishable things; but nothing that is worth retaining can be lost. Affections, well-placed and dutifully cherished; friendships, happily formed and faithfully maintained; knowledge, acquired with worthy intent; and intellectual powers that have been diligently improved, are the talents which our Lord and Master has committed to our keeping; these will accompany us into another

state of existence, as surely as the soul in that state retains its identity and its consciousness.
Southey.

10,527. MIND, Infancy of. In infancy the mind is peculiarly ductile. We bring into the world with us nothing that deserves the name of habit: are neither virtuous nor vicious, active nor idle, inattentive nor curious. The infant comes into our hands a subject capable of certain impressions, and of being led on to a certain degree of improvement. His mind is like his body; what at first was cartilage, gradually becomes bone. Just so the mind acquires its solidity; and what might originally have been bent in a thousand directions, becomes stiff, unmanageable and unimpressible. *Godwin.*

10,528. MIND, Intolerance to Defects of. Whence comes it to pass that we have so much patience with those who are maimed in body, and so little with those who are defective in mind? It is because the cripple acknowledges that we have the use of our legs; whereas the fool obstinately maintains that we are the persons who halt in understanding. Without this difference in the case, neither object would move our resentment, but both our compassion.
Pascal.

10,529. MIND, Irregularity of. A gentleman put into the hands of a watchmaker an exquisite watch, which went irregularly. It was as perfect a piece of work as ever was made. He took it to pieces and put it together again twenty times; no matter of defect was to be discovered, and yet the watch went intolerably. At last, it struck him that possibly the balance-wheel might have been near a magnet. On applying a needle to it, he found his suspicions true; here was all the mischief. The steel works in the other parts of the watch had a perpetual influence on its motions; and the watch went as well as possible with a new wheel. If the soundest mind be magnetized by any predilection, it must act irregularly.
Cecil.

10,530. MIND, Kingdom of. Reason, as the princess, dwells in the highest and inwardest room; the senses are the guard and attendants on the court, without whose aid nothing is admitted into the presence; the supreme faculties are the Peers; the outward parts and inward affections are the Commons. *Bp. Hall.*

10,531. MIND in Old Age. The age of a cultivated mind is even more complacent, and even more luxurious, than the youth. It is the reward of the due use of the endowments bestowed by nature; while they who in youth have made no provision for age, are left like an unsheltered tree, stripped of its leaves and its branches, shaking and withering before the cold blasts of winter. In truth, nothing is so happy to itself, and so attractive to others, as a genuine and refined imagination, that knows its own powers, and throws forth its treasures with frankness and fearlessness. *Southey.*

10,532. MIND, Triumph of. It is interesting to notice how some minds seem almost to create themselves, springing up under every disadvantage, and working their solitary but irresistible way through a thousand obstacles. Nature seems to delight in disappointing the assiduities of art, with which it would rear dullness to maturity; and to glory in the vigor and luxuriance of her chance productions. She scatters the seeds of genius to the winds, and though some may perish among the stony places of the world, and some may be choked by the thorns and brambles of early adversity, yet others will now and then strike root even in the clefts of the rock, struggle bravely up into sunshine, and spread over their sterile birth-place all the beauties of vegetation.
Washington Irving.

10,533. MIND, Writing on. Dr. Payson sent a message to the young men who were studying for the ministry in one of the colleges, as follows: "What if God should place in your hand a diamond, and tell you to inscribe on it a sentence which should be read at the last day, and shown there as an index of your thoughts and feelings. What care and caution would you exercise in the selection? Now this is what God has done. He has placed before you immortal minds, more imperishable than the diamond, on which you are about to inscribe, every day and every hour, by your instructions, by your spirit, or by your example, something which will remain, and be exhibited for or against you at the judgment-day."

10,534. MINDS, Great and Little. Great minds mould things to thoughts; little minds mould thoughts to things. *Theo. Parker.*

10,535. MINISTER, Faith of a. The salary of a certain minister was insufficient for the support of his family. But his trust was in God; and he was accustomed to say, "If the Lord sees that the people have crowded me into too short a pasture, he will send some one to throw me a fork-full of fodder over the wall."

10,536. MINISTER, Friendly. In an age when men choose their doctrines by the men that preach them, his credentials as a pastor will be most readily accepted, who shows himself the follower of one who turned and said to his disciples, "But I have called you friends." This should not be forgotten; it is of more value than many rubrics. The proverb says that more flies are caught with sugar than vinegar. *Papers on Preaching*

10,537. MINISTER, Helping the. "I am past usefulness," said an old lady to her minister; "the Lord spares my days, but I do no good now." "You are doing a great deal of good," said the minister; "you help me to preach every Sabbath." She was very much surprised. Help her minister to preach! "Why, how?" "In the first place," said he, "you are always in your seat at church, and that helps me. In the second place, you are always wide-awake, looking right up into my face, and that helps me. In the third place, I often see tears running down your cheeks, and that helps me very much."

10,538. MINISTER, Legacy of the. Lying on his death-bed, he bequeaths to each of his parishioners his precepts and example for a leg acy. And they in requital erect every one a monument for him in their hearts. He is so far from that base jealousy that his memory should be outshined by a brighter successor, and from that wicked desire that his people may find his worth by the worthlessness of him that succeeds, that he doth heartily pray to God to provide them a better pastor after his decease. As for outward estate, he commonly lives in too bare pasture to die fat. It is well if he hath gathered any flesh, being more in blessing than bulk. *Fuller.*

10,539. MINISTER, Life of the. Oh, study not only to preach exactly, but to live exactly! Let the misplacing of one action in your lives trouble you more than the misplacing of words in your discourses. This is the way to succeed in your embassy, and give up your account with joy. *Flavel.*

10,540. MINISTER, Prayers of a. A minister's prayers may be compared to the powder, by firing which, the cannon ball is sent upon its errand; without the prayers, his sermons will be little better than a heap of cannon-balls without powder. There must be prayer from a heart on fire. Some sermons are like a bright artillery-piece for a model; all finished, burnished, shining; everybody says, what a splendid piece of ordnance! People stand and look in its mouth, and measure its breech, and lift the ball it can carry, and admire it without fear, for there is no powder in it. It is not meant to shoot any person, but to attract admiration as a finished piece of ordnance. An elaborate model sermon, without prayer, is a gun that a man might put his ear to the muzzle without fear. And some sermons are like the artillery-pieces that are wheeled into line in a sham fight, and fired with blank cartridges. There must be both powder and ball, if execution is to be done. Above all things, there must be prayer. There must be prayer on fire. *N. Y. Evangelist.*

10,541. MINISTER, Praying for the. A person called on his minister to tell him he could not enjoy his preaching as much as he once did. "Well, my brother," said the minister, "before you tell me what you have to find fault with in me, let us pray together; will you kneel down and pray for me?" They knelt down and prayed, and when they arose, the minister said, "Now, dear brother, sit down and tell me what fault you have to find." The man said, "I am ashamed of myself. I have no fault to find at all." "Why, how is that, my brother?" "Why, sir, since you have asked me to pray for you I cannot find fault with you; I believe now, sir, that the fault is in myself; I never prayed for you before, but now I will."

10,542. MINISTERS, Curse upon Idle. Rev. Thomas Shephard, an excellent preacher, took great pains in his preparations for the pulpit. He used to say, "God will curse that man's labor who goes idly up and down all the week, and then goes into his study on a Saturday afternoon. God knows that we have not too much time to pray in, and weep in, and get our hearts into a fit frame for the duties of the Sabbath."

10,543. MINISTERS, Divine Mission of. Men of God have always, from time to time, walked among men, and made their commission felt in the heart and soul of the commonest hearer. *Emerson.*

10,544. MINISTERS: Fishers of Men. There are many special fitnesses in this image. The fisher casts in his net, not knowing whether he shall gather—whether many or few, or whether any at all shall reward his labors. Nor is it for nothing that the promise clothes itself in language drawn from the occupation of the fisher rather than from the nearly allied pursuits of the hunter. The fisher does more often take his prey alive; he draws it to him, does not drive it from him—and not merely to himself, but draws all he has taken to one another. The work of the fisher is rather a work of art and skill than of force and violence. And there is indeed an aspect in which the death of the fish which follows on its being drawn out of the waters, has its analogy in the higher spirit world. The man drawn forth from the gospel nets—from the worldly, sinful element in which before he lived and moved—does die to sin, die to the world, but only that out of this death he may rise to a higher life in Christ. *Trench.*

10,545. MINISTERS, Godless. It is true that a man may impart light to others who does not himself see the light. It is true that, like a concave speculum, cut from a block of ice, which by its power of concentrating the rays of the sun, kindles touch-wood or explodes gunpowder, a preacher may set others on fire, when his own heart is cold as frost. It is true that he may stand like a lifeless finger-post, pointing the way on a road where he neither leads nor follows. *Dr. Guthrie.*

10,546. MINISTERS to be Honored. As Lord Lieutenant of Hampshire, the late Duke of Wellington always made a point of receiving and entertaining the Judges when they arrived in the county on circuit. He felt that the Judges represented the Sovereign; and no claims of society, no call even of duty, was strong enough to hinder him from paying the same marks of respect which his loyalty would have induced him to pay to the Sovereign had she been personally present. *Biblical Treasury.*

10,547. MINISTERS, Humbug. A clerical humbug, I conceive, is a minister who expects from his profession what he could not gain from his character as an individual. *Dr. Hodge.*

10,548. MINISTERS, Imperfection of. To expect perfection in ministers is to expect against the wisdom of God. In a pipe which conveys water into a house there may be such a flaw as will sometimes admit some dust or earth to mix itself with the water; will you therefore reject the water itself, and say, that if you may not have it just as it ariseth in the fountain, you will not regard it, when you live far from the fountain itself, and can have no water but what is conveyed in pipes liable to such defects? *Salter.*

10,549. MINISTERS, Judgment of. An old divine

preaching before the clergy, anticipated their final examination with much effect. He represented the Judge asking, "What did you preach for?" "I preached, Lord, that I might keep a good living that was left me by my father; which, if I had not entered the ministry, would have been wholly lost to me and my family." Christ addresses him, "Stand by, thou hast thy reward." The question is put to another, "And what did you preach for?" "Lord, 1 was applauded as a learned man; and I preached to keep up the reputation of an excellent orator, and an ingenious preacher." The answer of Christ to him also is, "Stand by, thou hast had thy reward." The Judge puts the question to a third, "And what did you preach for?" "Lord," saith he, "I neither aimed at the great things of this world, though I was thankful for the conveniences of life which thou gavest me; nor did I preach that I might gain the character of a wit, or of a man of parts, or of a fine scholar; but I preached in compassion to souls, and to please and honor thee: my design, Lord, in preaching, was that I might win souls to thy blessed Majesty." The Judge was now described as calling out, "Room, men! room, angels! let this man come and sit with me on my throne: he has owned and honored me on earth, and I will own and honor him through all the ages of eternity."

10,550. MINISTERS, Objections to. John Ploughman once said, "I never knew a good horse which had not some odd habit or other, and I never yet saw a minister worth his salt who had not some crotchet or oddity. Now, these are bits of cheese that cavilers smell out and nibble at: the first is too flowery, and the second is too dull. Dear me, if all God's creatures were judged in this way, we should wring the dove's neck for being too tame, shoot the robins for eating spiders, kill the crows for swinging their tails, and the hens for not giving us milk. When a man wants to beat a dog he can soon find a stick, and at this rate any fool may have something to say against the best minister in England." *Spurgeon.*

10,551. MINISTERS, Office of. That a man stand and speak of spiritual things to men. It is beautiful;—even in its great obscuration and decadence, it is among the beautifullest, most touching objects one sees on the earth. This speaking man has indeed, in these times, wandered terribly from the point; has, alas, as it were, totally lost sight of the point; yet, at bottom, whom have we to compare with him? Of all public functionaries boarded and lodged on the industry of modern Europe, is there one worthier of the board he has? A man ever professing, and never so languidly making still some endeavor, to save the souls of men: contrast him with a man professing to do little but shoot the partridges of men! I wish he could find the point again, this speaking one; and stick to it with tenacity, with deadly energy; for there is need of him yet! The speaking function—this of truth coming to us with a living voice, nay in a living shape, and as a concrete practical exemplar: this, with all our writing and printing functions, has a perennial place. Could he but find the point again—take the old spectacles off his nose, and looking up discover, almost in contact with him, what the real Satan, and soul-devouring, world-devouring devil, now is. *Carlyle.*

10,552. MINISTERS, Perseverance of. Away with those nice novelists that can abide to hear nothing but what is new minted. Ministers meet with many that are slow of heart and dull of hearing; these must have "precept upon precept, line upon line," etc.; many also of brawny breasts and horny heart-strings; that, as ducklings stoop and dive at any little stone thrown by a man at them yet shrink not at the heaven's great thunder, etc. Here a minister must beat and inculcate; turn himself into all fashions of spirits and speech, to win and work upon his hearers. "He must so long pursue and stand upon one and the same point," saith Austin, "till, by the gesture and countenance of his auditors, he perceives they understand and assent to it." *Trapp.*

10,553. MINISTERS, Responsibility of. The medical attendant of my brother has just been expressing his surprise to see how much I am worn within this last half-year; I am very sensible of it myself; and expect that I shall be much more worn, if my people continue in such a grievous state. I would that my eyes "were a fountain of tears, to run down day and night." I have been used to read the scriptures to get from them rich discoveries of the power and grace of Christ; to learn how to minister to a loving and obedient people; I am now reading them really and literally to know how to minister to a conceited, contentious, and rebellious people. Two qualities, I am sure, are requisite, meekness and patience, yet, in some cases, I shall be constrained to rebuke with authority; I have been used to sail in the Pacific; I am now learning to navigate the Red Sea, that is full of shoals and rocks, with a very intricate passage. I trust the Lord will carry me safely through; but my former trials have been nothing to this. *Simeon.*

10,554. MINISTERS, Right Choice of. For if no prince will send a mechanic from his loom or his shears, in an honorable embassage to some other foreign prince, shall we think that the Lord will send forth stupid and unprepared instruments about so great a work as the perfecting of the saints and edification of the church? It is registered for the perpetual dishonor of that wicked king Jeroboam, who made no other use of any religion but as a secondary bye-thing, to be the supplement of policy, that "he made of the lowest of the people," those who were really such as the apostles were falsely esteemed to be, the scum and off-scouring of men, "to be priests unto the Lord." *Bp. Reynolds.*

10,555. MINISTRY, Emblem of the. Upon the pulpit of a church in a Tyrolese village, is an emblem of what the ministry should be. It is an extended arm, carved from wood, holding up the cross in the sight of all. Christ crucified must be held up, as the only atonement for sin, and hope for the sinner.

10,556. MINISTRY, Support of the. A missionary traveling over the island of Hayti, found himself preceded by a report which threatened seriously to interfere with his comfort. One of the most intelligent natives said to him: "Minister, they tell me a strange thing about you: they tell me you never eat." Having started early, without breakfast, and traveled far, he had internal evidence of the contrary, and he stoutly denied the statement, demanding that the test should be made. A plain meal was set before him, and lo! he ate like other men, greatly to the surprise of the natives. How near this legend comes to being general, many a minister's lean larder will testify.

10,557. MINISTRY, Thrust into the. A minister advised a young man thus: "The word translated 'send laborers into his harvest,' signifies thrust; and, if God intends you to be a minister of his, he will thrust you out, though earth and hell should oppose; but, if God does not send you, it will be much better to work at any calling than to go into the ministry yourself."

10,558. MINISTRY, Trifling in the. I hope my younger brethren in the ministry will pardon me if I entreat their particular attention to this admonition—not to give the main part of their time to the curiosities of learning, and only a few fragments of it to their great work, the cure of souls, lest they see cause in their last moments to adopt the words of dying Grotius, perhaps with much more propriety than he could use them—"I have lost a life in busy trifling." *Dr. Doddridge.*

10,559. MIRACLES, Constant. An Eastern fable says, that a boy challenged his teacher to prove to him the existence of a God by working a miracle. The teacher, who was a priest, procured a large vessel filled with earth, in which he deposited a kernel in the boy's presence, and bade him pay attention. In the place where the kernel was put, a green shoot soon appeared, the shoot became a stem, the stem put forth leaves and branches, which soon spread over the whole apartment. It then budded with blossoms, which dropping off left golden fruit in their place, and in the short space of an hour there appeared a noble tree in the place of the little seed. The youth, overcome with amazement, exclaimed, "Now I know there is a God, for I have seen his power!" The priest smiled at him, and said, "Simple child, do you only now believe? Does not what you have just seen take place in innumerable instances, year after year, only by a slower process? But is it the less marvelous on that account?"

10,560. MIRACLES, Continuation of. God has been working miracles all along the line of Christian history. The day of miracles is not past. It is a great miracle, I know, to open the eye of the blind man, but it is a greater miracle to open the eye of the blind soul and make it see. It is a great miracle to unstop the ear of one that is deaf, so that the vibrations of the atmosphere will produce sound; it is a greater miracle to open the hidden ear of the soul and bid it hear the voice that speaks in the language of the Spirit. It is a great miracle to bring to life one who is dead and had been laid in the grave; it is a greater miracle to bring the soul from spiritual death to a life of righteousness. *Dr. Kynett.*

10,561. MIRACLES, Denying. Denying the possibility of miracles seems to me quite as unjustifiable as speculative Atheism.
Prof. Huxley.

10,562. MIRACLES, Legend of. The recovery of lost articles through a fish is a common miracle of hagiology. The wife of king Roderick gave her bridal ring to a knight of the court. The king recovered it from the knight, but cast it into the Clyde. He then went to the Queen and demanded the ring. As she could not produce it, she was cast into prison and ordered to be executed in a few days. St. Kintigern, greatly moved by her case, prayed to God to rescue her. A salmon was caught in the Clyde, and in it the ring was found, which was given to the saint, and by him to the Queen, who thereby was able to meet the king's demand and save her own life. In commemoration of this St. Kintegern is represented in art, holding the episcopal cross in one hand and a salmon with a ring in its month in the other.

10,563. MIRACLES, Modern. The daughter of a missionary in Kansas had a shrunken limb; two inches too short, out of joint at the thigh, stiff at the knee; and according to the best medical opinion she was a hopeless cripple. She was twelve years of age, and simple enough to believe the scripture, "The prayer of faith shall save the sick." She told her faith to her mother, and asked her to unite with her in prayer for her cure. The mother reasoned with the girl that this was her cross, and that she ought to have grace to bear it. Her answer was, "Mother, I have faith, and if you have, there will be two of us, and I can be cured." She pressed the case with her mother day after day, saying, "Mother, I want you to pray now to Jesus to cure me." The mother prayed, and became unconscious of all surroundings, till she was aroused by the cry of her little girl, "Mother, wake up! Jesus has cured me! Oh, I am well! I am all well!!" The limb is perfect, like the other. The mother says her child has been whole from that hour. The little girl's answer to all is, "The Saviour has cured me."

10,564. MIRACLES, Necessity of. It cannot be questioned that miracles were necessary to moral progress in the time of Christ. No truth, as from God, could have been received without them. All men believed that their divinities granted power to their votaries to work miracles. Either the new religion must be introduced by miracles, or God must, by miracle, destroy the conviction in all minds that miracles could be wrought. *Walker.*

10,565. MIRACLES, Papist. In the monas

tery at Isenach stands an image which I have seen. When a wealthy person came hither to pray to it (it was Mary with her child), the child turned away his face from the sinner to the mother; but if the sinner gave liberally to that monastery, then the child turned to him again; and if he promised to give more, then the child showed itself very friendly and loving, and stretched out its arms over him in the form of a cross. But this picture and image was made hollow within, and prepared with locks, lines, and screws; and behind it stood a knave to move them—and so were the people mocked and deceived, who took it to be a miracle wrought by Divine Providence! *Luther.*

10,566. MIRACLES, Reception of. A legend says that the prophet Sâleh tried to reclaim the tribe of Thamud from idolatry. The people demanded a miracle to prove his divine commission, and one, pointing to a large rock, asked him to bring a camel big with young out of it. They promised to accept his religion if he did so. Instantly the rock began to heave, its side opened and out of it came a camel meeting the demand in every particular. All were surprised, but very few believed. Instead of this, the people cut the hamstrings of the camel and killed her. God was so much displeased at this conduct that he destroyed the town and its inhabitants three days after by an earthquake, the archangel Gabriel crying aloud, "Die all of you." Mohammed refers to this fable and warns unbelievers by it.

10,567. MIRACLES, Working. A person may be endowed with the gift of miracles, yet may lose his soul. Miracles insure not salvation; they may indeed secure esteem and applause, but what will it avail a man to be esteemed on earth and afterwards be delivered up to hell torments? *Fulgentius, 533.*

10,568. MIRTH, Cheerfulness and. I have always preferred cheerfulness to mirth. The latter I consider as an act, the former as a habit of the mind. Mirth is short and transient, cheerfulness fixed and permanent. Those are often raised into the greatest transports of mirth who are subject to the greatest depressions of melancholy. On the contrary, cheerfulness, though it does not give the mind such an exquisite gladness, prevents us from falling into any depths of sorrow. Mirth is like a flash of lightning, that breaks through a gloom of clouds, and glitters for a moment; cheerfulness keeps up a kind of daylight in the mind, and fills it with a steady and perpetual serenity. *Addison.*

10,569. MIRTH, Devotion of. Mirth is the sweet wine of human life. It should be offered sparkling with zestful life unto God. He desires no emasculated or murdered offerings. *Beecher.*

10,570. MIRTH, Madness of. I think the men of this world, like children in a dangerous storm in the sea, that play and make sport with the white foam of the waves thereof coming in to sink and drown them; so are men making fool's sport with the white pleasures of a stormy world that will sink them. But, alas! what have we to do with their sports

which they make? If Solomon said of laughter that it was madness, what may we say of this world's laughing and sporting themselves with gold and silver, and honors, and court, and broad large conquests, but that they are poor souls, in the height and rage of a fever gone mad? Then a straw, a fig, for all created sports and rejoicing out of Christ.
Rutherford.

10,571. MISANTHROPE, Description of the. He is a man who avoids society only to free himself from the trouble of being useful to it. He is a man who considers his neighbors only on the side of their defects, not knowing the art of combining their virtues with their vices, and of rendering the imperfections of other people tolerable by reflecting on his own. He is a man more employed in finding out and inflicting punishments on the guilty, than in devising means to reform them. He is a man who talks of nothing but banishing and executing; and who, because he thinks his talents are not sufficiently valued and employed by his fellow-citizens, or rather because they know his foibles, and do not choose to be subject to his caprice, talks of quitting cities, towns and societies, and of living in dens or deserts.
Saurin.

10,572. MISANTHROPE, Heathen. Timon, the Athenian, was nicknamed the Man-hater. He was once possessed of great wealth, but through too great liberality he lost it all, and was reduced to extreme poverty. In this condition he experienced the malice and ingratitude of those whom he had served. He thereupon became a great hater of mankind, was glad of their misfortunes, and worked the ruin of all he could, with safety to himself. He built him a house in the fields that he might avoid the society of men; allowing only one, Apemantus, a person much like himself, to disturb his solitude. Apemantus said to Timon, "Is not this a fine supper?" He answered, "It would be much better if thou wert absent." Timon gave orders that his sepulchre should be set behind a dunghill, and this epitaph to be written, "Here now I lie, after my wretched fall; ask not my name, the gods destroy you all."

10,573. MISER, Beneficent. Mr. Taylor, a London stock-jobber, who died worth a hundred thousand pounds, Consols, was so penurious that he scarcely allowed himself the necessaries of life. A few days before his decease, the officers of the parish in which he resided waited upon him at his request. They found the old man on a wretched bed in a garret, making his dinner on a thin rasher of bacon and a potato. He informed the overseers of the poor that he had left by his will £1,000 sterling for their relief, and inquired if they would not allow him discount for prompt payment. They assented, and he, much delighted, immediately gave them a check on his banker for £950, and soon after breathed his last.

10,574. MISER, The Rich. He has a heart that will serve him to hear a thousand lectures about charity without the least damage to his

pocket. As for the pleasure of doing good, he understands it not; he has no notion of the matter: nor will the spectacles with which he tells his money help him to see Jesus Christ in a poor man. As for being rewarded in another world, and lending to God to be hereafter repaid with interest, he is not for this spiritual sort of usury, but looks upon what is lent to God as little better than a desperate debt. The plain truth of it is, he does not like his security, but thinks a mortgage is better.
Norris.

10,575. MISERY, Causes of. Misery is caused for the most part, not by a heavy crush of disaster, but by the corrosion of less visible evils, which canker enjoyment, and undermine security. The visit of an invader is necessarily rare, but domestic animosities allow no cessaion. *Johnson.*

10,576. MISERY, Happiness and. The misery of human life is made up of large masses, each separated from the other by certain intervals. One year, the death of a child; years after, a failure in trade; after another longer or shorter interval, a daughter may have married unhappily; in all but the singularly unfortunate, the integral parts that compose the sum total of the unhappiness of a man's life are easily counted and distinctly remembered. The happiness of life, on the contrary, is made up of minute fractions; the little soon-forgotten charities of a kiss, a smile, a kind look, a heartfelt compliment in the disguise of playful raillery, and the countless other infinitesimals of pleasurable thought and genial feeling. *Coleridge.*

10,577. MISERY, Influence of. Did you ever happen to see that most soft-spoken and velvet-handed steam-engine at the mint? The smooth piston slides backward and forward as a lady might slip her delicate finger in and out of a ring. The engine lays one of its fingers calmly, but firmly, upon a bit of metal; it is a coin now, and will remember that touch, and tell a new race about it, when the date upon it is crusted over with twenty centuries. So it is that a great, silent-moving misery puts a new stamp on us in an hour or a moment—as sharp an impression as if it had taken half a life-time to engrave it. *Holmes.*

10,578. MISFORTUNE, Good Fortune. Zeno, who became renowned as one of the seven wise men of Greece, heard that his last ship, with a rich cargo, had been lost in a tempest, and exclaimed, "Fortune, I applaud thy contrivance, who, by this means, hast reduced me to a threadbare cloak and the piazza of the Stoics."

10,579. MISFORTUNE, Overcoming. If a man loses his property at thirty or forty years of age, it is only a sharp discipline generally, by which later he comes to larger success. It is all folly for a man to sit down in mid-life discouraged. The marshals of Napoleon came to their commander, and said, "We have lost the battle, and we are being cut to pieces." Napoleon took his watch from his pocket, and said, "It is only two o'clock in the afternoon. You have lost the battle, but we have time

enough to win another. Charge upon the foe!" Though the meridian of life has passed with you, and you have been routed in many a conflict, give not up in discouragement. There are victories yet for you to gain. *Anon.*

10,580. MISFORTUNE, Test of. A servant of Cæsar censured him for bestowing his gifts on those who had an abundance already, rather than on him who had nothing. Cæsar said that gifts were not for those who deserved well, but for those that were destined by fate. He commanded two boxes to be made of the same size, form, and weight; in the one he put gold, and in the other lead. He then called his faithful servant, and told him to choose between them. He took them up, poised them in his hands, and decided to take the one which contained the lead. The emperor opened the box, and said, "Thou canst plainly see that not my good-will has been wanting, but thy ill-fortune, that hitherto thou hast had no reward from me."

10,581. MISFORTUNES, Conduct in. If misfortunes have befallen you by your own misconduct, live and be wiser for the future. If they have befallen you by the fault of others, live; you have nothing wherewith to reproach yourself. If your character be unjustly attacked, live; time will remove the aspersion. If you have spiteful enemies, live; and disappoint their malevolence. If you have kind and faithful friends (and kindred), live; to bless and protect them. If you hope for immortality, live; and prepare to enjoy it. *John Herries.*

10,582. MISFORTUNES, Opinions concerning. When misfortunes happen to such as dissent from us in matters of religion, we call them judgments; when to those of our own sect, we call them trials; when to persons neither way distinguished, we are content to impute them to the settled course of things. *Shenstone.*

10,583. MISFORTUNES, Preference for. If all the misfortunes of mankind were cast into a public stock, in order to be equally distributed among the whole species, those who now think themselves the most unhappy would prefer the share they are already possessed of, before that which would fall to them by such a division. *Socrates.*

10,584. MISFORTUNES, Unavoidable. As daily experience makes it evident that misfortunes are unavoidably incident to human life, that calamity will neither be repelled by fortitude, nor escaped by flight; neither awed by greatness, nor eluded by obscurity; philosophers have endeavored to reconcile us to that condition which they cannot teach us to merit, by persuading us that most of our evils are made afflictive only by ignorance or perverseness, and that nature has annexed to every vicissitude of external circumstances some advantage sufficient to over-balance all its inconveniences. *Johnson.*

10,585. MISSED or Not. When an oak, or any noble and useful tree, is uprooted, his removal creates a blank. For years after, when you look to the place which once knew him, you see that something is missing. The branches of adjacent trees have not yet supplied the void. They still hesitate to supply the place formerly filled by their powerful neighbor; and there is still a deep chasm in the ground—a ragged pit—which shows how far his giant roots once spread. But when a leafless pole, a wooden pin, is plucked up, it comes easy and clean away. There is no rending of the turf, no marring of the landscape, no vacuity created, no regret. It leaves no memento, and is never missed. Brethren, which are you?

Dr. Hamilton.

10,586. MISSIONARIES, Haste for. A heathen woman went to a missionary in India on the occasion of an anniversary of the mission children, and said, "Why did you not come sooner, that my little boy might have been here?" She explained that she once had a little boy, whom she took into the jungle and slew before the missionaries came. She represents millions who say, "Why did you not come sooner?"

10,587. MISSIONARY, Zeal of a. Winfrid, or Boniface, having laid the axe at the roots of the trees, literally, in Germany, cutting down the oaks sacred to Thor, planting churches and making converts with remarkable success, longed for new fields and fresh conquests. When over seventy-five years of age, he set forth (so strong was his ruling passion) to win pagan Friesland to Christ. He appointed a bishop to succeed him at Mainz, and left everything, as if he did not expect to return. He took with him his shroud and St. Ambrose's treatise on the "Advantage of Death." With a company of eight, he entered upon his work, and met with good success. Many had been baptized. The pagans became alarmed, and went against him with an armed band. Boniface knew too well their bloody intent. He exhorted his followers not to resist, but to await the crown of martyrdom. He himself took a volume of the gospel for a pillow, and, stretching his neck upon it for the blow, received his release in 755. Few are the names of missionary heroes more illustrious than his.

10,588. MISSIONS, Basis for. The Baptist Missionary Society of England owes its existence and success to the unflagging zeal of the shoemaker, school-master and preacher, William Carey, of Nottingham. He preached a powerful sermon from Is. 54: 23, of which the two leading divisions were, "Expect great things from God"—"Attempt great things for God." Under its influence a mission to the heathen was resolved upon. Mr. Carey became its first missionary, sailing for India in 1793. His expectations were not disappointed.

10,589. MISSIONS, Consecrated to. "Is it not a great trial to you to part with your eldest son?" said a missionary secretary to a gentleman who had come to London to take leave of his son, who was to embark the next day for a foreign land. "Yes," was the answer, "it is a great trial, but I have been expecting it for a long time. The day my son was born," he continued, "I attended a missionary meeting, and was greatly impressed with what I heard; when I went home, I took the babe out of bed, and holding it in my arms, I said to my wife, 'Will you give this boy to the missions?' 'Yes,' she replied, 'I will.' From that time I have been expecting he would go, though he never knew the circumstance till he offered himself for a missionary."

10,590. MISSIONS, Era of. It was not until Christians became inflamed with the zeal of Wesley, who said, "The world is my parish," and Whitefield, who saw in every man a brother, that missions assumed any importance among Protestants. To this epoch the great societies of England, date their origin. "The Society for the Propagation of the Gospel in Foreign Parts," the oldest of all, was organized in 1701. "Church Missionary Society," in 1799. "Scotch Missionary Society" in 1796. "London Missionary Society" in 1794. "Baptist Missionary Society" in 1792. "Wesleyan Missionary Society" in 1769. The foregoing are all in Great Britain. "The American Board of Foreign Missions" was organized in 1810. "The American Baptist Missionary Society" in 1814. "The Methodist Episcopal Missionary Society" in 1819. "The Episcopal Board of Missions" in 1820. Various minor societies exist, of later origin. The obstacles attending the beginning of new mission enterprises have been overcome. The great harvest of the heathen world is being rapidly gathered. Soon the inhabitants of heaven will shout, "The kingdoms of this world are become the kingdoms of our Lord and of his Christ." Rev. 11: 17.

10,591. MISSIONS, Field of. Dr. Guthrie was looking down upon the degraded people of the Cowgate, Edinburgh, where he went to try the power of the gospel on the heathen at home, when he suddenly met Dr. Chalmers who exclaimed, "A beautiful field, sir; a very fine field of operation." Comparing it with his country charge, Guthrie says, "It is the change from the green fields and woods and the light of nature to the darkness and blackness of a coal pit."

10,592. MISSIONS, Gifts to. Rev. John Williams proposed to his Raitean converts that each family should set apart a pig to be sold for the missionary cause. They gladly accepted the proposal, and the next morning the squealing of pigs was heard as they received the mark in the ear which indicated their designation to this service. The result was a money contribution of £103. An Englishman sent half a pint of beans to a missionary meeting with the request that some one would plant them for three years and give the result to missions. Two farmers took them with this result: first year eleven pints, second year nine bushels, third year two hundred and seventy-six bushels, which netted £81, 14s., 9d. Missionary hens are another device—the setting apart of a hen or more, whose entire products shall be devoted to missions. Bullocks, cows, sheep, ducks, bees, fish-pots, cocoa-nut, cherry and other fruit-trees have been set apart for the same purpose.

10,593. MISSIONS, Gold for. John Sunday, the converted Indian chief of Upper Canada, addressing a missionary meeting in England, in his appeal to the benevolence of the people, previous to collection, said, "There is a gentleman, I suppose, now in this house; he is a very fine gentleman, but he is very modest. He does not like to show himself. I do not know how long it is since I saw him, he comes out so little. I am very much afraid he sleeps a great deal of his time, when he ought to be going about doing good. His name is Mr. Gold. Mr. Gold, are you here to-night? or are you sleeping in your iron chest? Come out, Mr. Gold; come out, and help us to do this great work, to send the gospel to every creature. Ah, Mr. Gold, you ought to be ashamed of yourself, to sleep so much in your iron chest! Look at your white brother, Mr. Silver, he does a great deal of good in the world, while you are sleeping. Come out, Mr. Gold! Look, too, at your brown brother, Mr. Copper, he is everywhere! See him running about doing all the good he can. Why don't you come out, Mr. Gold? Well, if you won't come out and give us yourself, send us your shirt, that is a bank note, and we will excuse you this time."

10,594. MISSIONS, Love for. A late writer says, "Why was Christ's long journey from heaven? Why his long sojourn amidst poverty and scorn? Why his toilsome ministry in Galilee and Judæa? Why the journey to Jerusalem, and the known betrayal, rejection and cruel death there? Ah, "the Son of man came to seek and to save that which was lost." With the Spirit of the Master upon them, thousands have gone forth upon the same errand.

10,595. MISSIONS, Martyrs of. The missionaries' torch has been lighted in every land. Their bones scattered everywhere are the seed of a bountiful harvest, to be gathered when the earth shall be fully ripe. Some fell by the malaria of an inhospitable climate, like Melville B. Cox in Africa. Thousands of true martyrs have thus died for their faith. Rev. William Thielfall was martyred in Namaqualand, in 1825; Rev. J. S. Thomas in Kaffirland, in 1856; Rev. John Williams in Erromanga, in 1838; Rev. J. G. Gordon in the same place, in 1872; Rev. Thomas Baker in Fiji in 1867; Bishop Patterson and Rev. Mr. Atkin, in Malanesia in 1871. The only wonder is, considering the ignorance, superstition and cruelty of the heathen, that so few have been called to shed their blood for Christ.

10,596. MISSIONS, Official Tribute to. The English blue-book, published in 1875, after a summary of missions in India, about half of which are American enterprises, closes with the following tribute: "The government in India cannot but acknowledge the great obligation under which it is laid by these six hundred missionaries, whose blameless example and self-denying labors are infusing new vigor into the stereotyped life of the great population placed under English rule, and are preparing them to be in every way better citizens of the great empire in which they dwell."

10597. MISSIONS, Providence and. Rev. John Thomas, founder of the Friendly Islands Mission, applied to the London Missionary Society for permission to extend his work to the island of Haabai, whose chief desired his coming. He waited with some anxiety for a reply. About that time a box was washed ashore, and carried to one of the missionaries, containing a letter from the society authorizing the establishment of the mission. Neither the vessel to which the letter was entrusted, the crew, nor any of the freight, except the box containing the letter authorizing a new effort for the salvation of the heathen, which came to the right place at the right time, was ever heard from.

10,598. MISSIONS, Result of Love for. A poor Christian mechanic was much chagrined that he could give so little for missions when the subscription was passed among the workmen in the factory. He told his wife of it, and she was inspired to try to earn something for the cause of missions. She secured some silk-twist and a few button-moulds, and began the manufacture of silk buttons. She sent a sample to a New York merchant, saying that, if they would sell, the money was to be her husband's contribution for missions. She received answer, "Make as many as you choose; I can sell a hundred dozen." The wife made her venture unknown to her husband; but now he was let into the secret. Success crowned her efforts. Machinery supplanted hand labor. A large manufactory, extensive business, and ample fortune grew up from and rewarded their love and labor for missions.

10,599. MISSIONS, Societies for. The different missionary societies have been compared to ships, which, though sometimes crowded while in harbor together, will have room enough when they go forth into the broad sea. Now, sir, all I mean to say is, that the Methodist missionary ship is one, among others, of the great fleet, by which it is intended to carry to the ends of the earth the blessings of the gospel; that this ship, like the rest, must be manned, freighted, and provisioned for the voyage; and that our most strenuous efforts, and those of our friends, are necessary to fit it for the sea, and to prepare it for the service on which it is destined to proceed. Other denominations are concerned for their own respective ships, and we must particularly care for ours. But our sincere and ardent prayer is, that God may send them all a safe and prosperous voyage.   *Dr. Bunting.*

10,600. MISSIONS, Spirit of. When Francis Xavier, the Jesuit, called "The Apostle of the Indies," proposed his mission, his friends tried by every possible representation of the dangers and hardships involved, to deter him from going. He replied, "The most tractable and opulent nations will not want preachers; but this is for me, because others will not undertake it. If the country abounded in odoriferous woods and mines of gold, all dangers would be braved in order to procure them. Should merchants, then, be more intrepid than missionaries? Shall these unfortunate people be excluded from the blessings of redemption? It is true they are very barbarous and brutal, but even were they more so, he who can convert even stones into children of Abraham, cannot he soften their hearts? Should I be instrumental in the salvation of but one of them, I should think myself well recompensed for all the labors and dangers by which you endeavor to affright me."

10,601. MISSIONS, Supplies for. In 1871 the Berlin Missionary Society found itself in debt 10,000 thalers. In 1857 it had received a donation of three square miles land on Vaal River, South Africa. The land was worthless, out diamonds were discovered upon it at this juncture, and enough was realized by a percentage paid by the miners to extinguish the debt.

10,602. MISSIONS, Supporting. The now famous missionary, Carey, when bidding farewell to his friends, in 1793, to go to India, said, "I'll go down into the pit if you'll hold the rope."

10,603. MISSIONS, Support of. One of the Secretaries of the Methodist Missionary Society says that the last words Bishop Janes said to him, a little before his death, were, "The Church of the Lord Jesus Christ must sustain the work of the Lord Jesus Christ!"

10,604. MISSIONS, Temporal Advantage of. Protestant missions have everywhere carried our civilization with them and created a demand for our products of art and manufacture. England estimates that for every pound sterling she has expended in foreign missions she has received back ten. They are thus shown to be a good investment for a people whose only idea is to make money. A thousand per cent. profit ought to attract capitalists. But that is only a trifle of the award to be distributed when the final account shall be made up. Many a man has lived to say, "The most satisfactory investment I ever made is what I gave away."

10,605. MISSIONS, Trophy of. Robert Moffat, the great African missionary, regarded Africaner, the notorious Hottentot chief, as the greatest trophy of his mission work. He was the scourge and terror of that country. The people did not believe it possible that he could be converted, and after he became a Christian they required the ocular demonstration of seeing him in company with the missionary. A more bloody man never tested the power of Christ to save. He went with Mr. Moffat to Cape Town. On the way he mentioned the fact of Africaner's conversion, when a Dutch farmer answered, "I can believe almost anything you say, but that I cannot credit. There are seven wonders in the world; that would be the eighth." Mr. Moffat assured the farmer that the desperado had become a changed man. "Well," said he, "if what you say is true, I have only one wish, and that is to see Africaner before I die; and when you return, as sure as the sun is over our heads, I will go with you to see him, though he killed my own

uncle." At this the missionary conducting the farmer to the wagon, pointed to the chief, and said, "This is Africaner." The farmer was astounded. Starting back, he said, "Are you Africaner?" The chief doffed his hat, made a respectful bow, and said, "I am;" at the same time testifying to the truth of the missionary's statement respecting his conversion. Then exclaimed the farmer, "O, God, what a miracle of Thy power. What cannot Thy grace accomplish?" He was much attached to the missionaries, and was a remarkable example of the power of grace.

10,606. MISSIONS, Twenty-fold Return for Gifts to. An English society were endeavoring to bring their gifts up to their usual standard. One of the leaders said, "Let us make another collection. I will give another shilling." George Leal, a farm-laborer, responded, "And so would I, if I had one with me" "I'll lend you a shilling, George," said the leader, as he handed him one to drop into the plate. "Well done, George Leal!" exclaimed the minister, "the Lord will reward you tenfold." This stimulated others; the plate went round a second time, and the deficiency was more than made up. When the meeting was over, the minister greeted George Leal with unusual warmth, remarking, "Remember what I said, George; the Lord will reward you tenfold." The next day, when Leal went into the field to his ploughing, he had not gone many yards when the ploughshare turned up a sovereign. George called to his master, and asked if he knew who had lost a sovereign, quite willing to give it up. "Nay, George," said the farmer, "it must have been in the ground many years. It is thy own good luck, keep it." Thus quickly and twenty-fold did the Lord reward his gift.

10,607. MISTAKES, Important. A Roman army was thrown into a disastrous rout by the inclination of a standard, as was the custom in case of submission. Rome itself was once conquered by Arnulphus, through the boisterous chase of a hare by his soldiers, which was mistaken for a fierce assault by the Romans. Arnulphus, perceiving his advantage, made a successful attack. A mistaken command has lost a battle; a mistaken movement has lost an Empire.

10,608. MISTAKES, No Exemption from. Exemption from mistake is not the privilege of mortals; but when our mistakes are involuntary, we owe each other every candid consideration; and the man who, on discovering his errors, acknowledges and corrects them, is scarcely less entitled to our esteem than if he had not erred.   *Dr. Pye Smith.*

10,609. MISTRUST, Prevalence of. The world is an old woman, that mistakes any gilt farthing for a gold coin; whereby, being often cheated, she will henceforth trust nothing but the common copper.   *Carlyle.*

10,610. MITES, Our Two. Our two mites, a vile body and a sinful soul, are all that he requires, and shall he not have those?
      Whitefield

10,611. MODERATION, Importance of. Intemperance is a perfect destruction of wisdom, "a full-gorged belly never produced a sprightly mind," and, therefore, this kind of men are called γαστέρες ἀργαί, "slow-bellies," so St. Paul, concerning the intemperate Cretans, out of their own poet: they are like the tigers of Brazil, which when they are empty are bold and swift, and full of sagacity; but being full, sneak away from the barking of a village dog. So are these men, wise in the morning, quick and fit for business; but when the sun gives the sign to spread the tables, and intemperance brings in the messes, and drunkenness fills the bowl, then the man falls away, and leaves a beast in his room. A full meal is like Sisera's banquet, at the end of which there is a nail struck into a man's head; so Porphyry, "It knocks a man down and nails his soul to the sensual mixtures of the body."
Jeremy Taylor.

10,612. MODERATION, Submissive. He therefore hath cast up his accounts the best, who, confining himself within due bounds, hath such ascendant over his temper, as to bear prosperous and adverse fortune with the same equality, whichsoever it is that happens to him in this life. He puts on those resolutions as if he were in a popular government where magistracy is decided by lot; if it luckily fall to his share, he obeys his fortune; but if it passeth him, he doth not repine at it. So we must submit to the dispensation of human affairs, without being uneasy and querulous.
Plutarch.

10,613. MODESTY, Absence of. Nothing can atone for the want of modesty, without which beauty is ungraceful and wit detestable.
Addison.

10,614. MODESTY, Abuse of. I have observed that under the notion of modesty men have indulged themselves in a spiritless sheepishness, and been forever lost to themselves, their families, their friends, and their country. When a man has taken care to pretend to nothing but what he may justly aim at, and can execute as well as any other, without injustice to any other, it is ever want of breeding, or courage, to be brow-beaten, or elbowed out of his honest ambition. I have said often, modesty must be an act of the will, and yet it always implies self-denial: for if a man has an ardent desire to do what is laudable for him to perform, and from an unmanly bashfulness shrinks away, and lets his merit languish in silence, he ought not to be angry at the world that a more unskillful actor succeeds in his part, because he has not confidence to come upon the stage himself. *Steele.*

10,615. MODESTY, Instinct of. The spirit of suicide became epidemic among the girls of Milesia. Neither prayers nor tears of friends availed anything, and they died daily by their own hands. At last a council sent forth an edict that every girl that laid violent hands on herself should, dead as she was, be carried naked along the market place. The edict had its desired effect. Those that trembled not at death would not endure a wrong to their modesty.

10,616. MODESTY, Test of. A company of Milesians agreed with some Coos fishermen for their draught, whatever it should prove to be. They drew up a table of gold, and a strife commenced between the fishermen and the buyers; terminating in a war between the cities in favor of their citizens. At last it was resolved to consult the oracle Apollo, and he told them to send the table to the man they considered wisest. It was therefore sent to Thales, the Milesian. Thales sent it to Bias, saying, "He was wiser than himself." Bias sent it to another wiser than he, and so it passed from one to another till it returned to Thales again; he sent it at last to Thebes, to be consecrated to the Ismenian Apollo. Thus it passed in turn to seven men, who, thereafter, received the name of the "Seven wise men of Greece."

10,617. MOHAMMED, Religion of. From his earliest youth Mohammed was addicted to religious contemplation: each year, during the month of Ramadan, he withdrew from the world and from the arms of Cadijah : in the cave of Hera, three miles from Mecca, he consulted the spirit of fraud or enthusiasm, whose abode is not in the heavens, but in the mind of the prophet. The faith which, under the name of Islam, he preached to his family and nation, is compounded of an eternal truth, and a necessary fiction—that there is only one God, and that Mohammed is the apostle of God. *Gibbon.*

10,618. MOHAMMEDANISM, Dogmas of. The religious dogmas of this strange sect are few and simple, but their superstitious ceremonies are numerous and diversified. The first article in their creed, "There is one God, and Mohammed is his prophet," is perpetually on their lips, and the knowledge of many of their votaries seems to go no further than this. They abstain from wine and strong drink, which appears to be the best feature in their system; they practice polygamy, believe in a sensual paradise after death, and propagate their religious tenets by the power of the sword. They are extremely superstitious, and wear amulets on their persons formed of small portions of the Koran, believing that these will preserve them from danger and promote their well-being. *Moister.*

10,619. MOHAMMEDANISM, Secret of the Success of. Mohammed's creed we call a kind of Christianity. The truth of it is imbedded in portentous error and falsehood; but the truth of it makes it be believed, not the falsehood: it succeeded by its truth. A bastard kind of Christianity, but a living kind, with a heart-life in it; not dead, chopping, barren logic merely! Out of all that rubbish of Arab idolatries, argumentative theologies, traditions, subtleties, rumors and hypotheses of Greeks and Jews, with their idle wire-drawings, this wild man of the desert, with his wild sincere heart, earnest as death and life, with his great flashing natural eyesight, had seen into the kernel of the matter. Idolatry is nothing: "These wooden idols of yours, ye rub them with oil and wax, and the flies stick on them; these are wood I tell you! They can do nothing for you; they are an impotent blasphemous pretence: a horror and abomination, if ye knew them. God alone is; God alone has power; he made us, he can kill us and keep us alive; 'Allah akbar.' God is great. Understand that his will is the best for you; that howsoever sore to flesh and blood, you will find it the wisest, best; you are bound to take it so; in this world and in the next, you have no other thing that you can do!" And now, if the wild idolatrous men did believe this, and with their fiery hearts laid hold of it to do it, in what form soever it came to them, I say it is well worthy of being believed. *Carlyle.*

10,620. MOMENT, Importance of the Present. There is no moment like the present; not only so, but, moreover, there is no moment at all, that is, no instant force and energy, but in the present. The man who will not execute his resolutions when they are fresh upon him, can have no hope from them afterwards; they will be dissipated, lost, and perish in the hurry and skurry of the world, or sunk in the slough of indolence. *Miss Edgeworth.*

10,621. MONEY, Benefits of. By doing good with his money, a man, as it were, stamps the image of God upon it, and makes it pass current for the merchandise of heaven. *Rutledge.*

10,622. MONEY, Buried with His. It is related that a certain monk, an anchoret in Nitria, had accumulated one hundred crowns by weaving cloth. After his death his brethren met to decide what should be done with the money. Some proposed to give it to the poor, others to the church. The decision of the leaders, Macarius, Pambo, and Isidore, was that it should be cast into the grave of the deceased, and be buried with him, while the words were pronounced, "May thy money perish with thee." It struck such terror into the monks that none dared lay up any more money.

10,623. MONEY, How to Get. To get money, study and act out the Book of Proverbs. *S. Martin.*

10,624. MONEY, Laughter over. A blind fiddler was laughed at, and the boy that led him cried, "Father, let us be gone; they do nothing but laugh at you." "Hold thy peace, boy," said the fiddler; "we shall have their money presently, and then we will laugh at them."

10,625. MONEY, Making. The first of all English games is making money. That is an all-absorbing game; and we knock each other down oftener in playing at that than at football, or any other roughest sport; and it is absolutely without purpose: no one who engages hear,ily in that game ever knows why. Ask a great money-maker what he wants to do with his money—he never knows. He doesn't make it to do anything with it. He gets it only that he may get it. "What will you make of what you have got?" you ask. "Well, I'll get more," he says. Just as, at cricket, you get more runs. There is no use in the runs, but to get more of them than other people is the game. So all that great foul city of London there—rattling, growling, smoking, stinking,—a ghastly heap of fermented brickwork, pouring out poison at every pore—you fancy it is a city of work? Not a street of it! It is a great city of play; very nasty play, and very hard play, but still play. It is only Lord's cricket-ground without the turf; a huge billiard-table without the cloth, and with pockets as deep as the bottomless pit; but mainly a billiard-table after all. *Ruskin.*

10,626. MONEY, Necessity for. Pelopidas, the Theban general, neglecting his business affairs, and spending his estate, was admonished that money was a very necessary thing. Pointing to a man who was both lame and blind, he said, "So it is for Nicomedas there."

10,627. MONEY, Profitless. An English merchant, who had accumulated three millions of money, for a long time before he died had a notion that he should die in the work-house. He used to work in his own garden, and one of his own men paid him 18s. a week for his labor.

10,628. MONEY, Rules for. John Wesley says, "Get all you can, save all you can, give all you can. Permit me to speak of myself as freely as I would of any other man. I gain all I can without hurting my body or soul. I save all I can; not wasting anything, not a sheet of paper, nor a cup of water. I do not lay out anything, not a shilling, unless a sacrifice for God; yet, by giving all I can, I am effectually secured from laying up treasures upon earth. Yea, and that I do this, I call upon both friends and foes to testify."

10,629. MONEY, Temptations of. Anaxander, the son of Eurycrates, to one asking him why the Spartans laid up no money in the exchequer, replied, that the keepers of it might not be tempted to be knaves. *Plutarch.*

10,630. MONEY, Test of. Here is the test, with every man, of whether money is the principal object with him or not. If in mid-life he could pause and say, "Now, have I enough to live upon, I'll live upon it; and having well-earned it, I will also well spend it, and go out of the world poor as I came into it;" then money is not principal with him; but if, having enough to live upon in the manner befitting his character and rank, he still wants to make more, and to die rich, then money is the principal object with him, and it becomes a curse to himself, and generally to those who spend it after him. For you know it must be spent some day; the only question is whether the man who makes it shall spend it, or some one else. And generally it is better for the maker to spend it, for he will know best its value and use. This is the true law of life. *Ruskin.*

10,631. MONEY, Worship of. Your god, your great Bel, your fish-tailed Dagon, rises before me as a demon. You, and such as you, have raised him to a throne, put on him a crown, given him a sceptre. Behold how hideously he governs! See him busied at the work he likes best—making marriages. He binds the young to the old, the strong to the imbecile. He stretches out the arm of Mezentius, and fetters the dead to the living. In his realm there is hatred—secret hatred: there is disgust—unspoken disgust: there is treachery—family treachery: there is vice—deep, deadly, domestic vice. In his dominions, children grow unloving between parents who have never loved; infants are nursed in deception from their very birth; they are reared in an atmosphere corrupt with lies. *Charlotte Brontë.*

10,632. MONITORS, Employment of. Persons of the greatest eminence have anciently had their monitors. Agathocles, a Sicilian prince, has his earthen plate set before him, to remind him that he had been a potter. The Roman triumvirs, in the meridian of their splendor, had a servant behind them, crying to each—" *Memento te esse hominem*," that is—Remember that you are only a man.   *W. Secker.*

10,633. MONOMANIAC, The Cure of a. Some people are paralyzed for life by some monomania. They remind us of an invalid who was afflicted by the delusion that he was made of pipe-clay, and if violently struck against any object, he would snap into fragments! He was only cured by a friend, who drove him into a meadow, and managed to upset the vehicle in the right place. The poor monomaniac shrieked frightfully as the carriage went over; but he rose from the ground sound in mind as well as in body.   *Cuyler.*

10,634. MONUMENT, Honorable Deeds a. When King Agesilaus was dying, he gave orders that there should be no fiction or counterfeit, as he called statues, made of him, adding, "For if I have done any honorable exploit, that is my monument; but if I have done none at all, your statues will signify nothing."

10,635. MONUMENT, Want of a. Cato the elder said, "I would rather men should ask why Cato had no statue than why he had one." It was his protest against the rage for statues, then the highest ambition of many worthless men.

10,636. MORALIST, Not Christian. A Christian is one who is positive. A Christian is a fruit-bearer. A moral man is a vine that does not bear fruit. But then it bears everything else—good leaves, a good strong stem, a healthy root, everything that is good and nice in it except the fruit. A Christian man is one that developes graces into positivity. He acts out of himself and upon others. A moral man is one that simply defends himself from the action of evil. A moral man is like an empty bottle, well corked, so that no defilement can get into it—so that it may be kept pure within. Pure? And what is the use of a bottle that is pure, if it is empty and corked up? A moral man, I repeat, is a negative. He does not swear, he does not steal, and he does not murder, and he does not get drunk, and his whole life is not. His language is, "Thou shalt not," and "Thou shalt not," and "Thou shalt not." He is not all over, and nothing more! He is not positive.   *Beecher.*

10,637. MORALITY, Averaging. An irreligious man used to average his morality thus: "I am doing pretty well on the whole. I sometimes get mad and swear, but then I am strictly honest. I work on Sunday when I am particularly busy, but I give a good deal to the poor, and I never was drunk in my life." He hired a Scotchman to build a fence around his pasture lot, and gave him special instructions to make it strong. In the evening, he said to his man, "Well, Jock, is the fence built, and is it tight and strong?" "I canna say that it is all tight and strong," he replied, "but it's a good average fence, anyhow. If some parts of it are a little weak, other parts are extra strong. I don't know but I may have left a gap here and there a yard wide or so; but then I made up for it by doubling the number of rails on each side of the gap. I dare say, the cattle will find it a good fence on the whole, and will like it, though I canna just say that it is perfect in every part." "What!" cried the man, "Do you tell me that you have built a fence around my lot with weak places in it, and gaps in it? Why, you might as well build no fence at all. If there is one opening, or a place where an opening can be made, the cattle will be sure to find it, and all go through. Don't you know, man, that a fence must be perfect, or it is worthless?" "I used to think so," said the Scotchman; "but I hear you talk so much about averaging matters with the Lord, it seemed to me that we might try it with the cattle. If an average fence won't do for them, I am afraid that an average character won't do in the day of judgment."

10,638. MORALITY, Insufficiency of. The Rev. Father Taylor, of the Boston Sailors' Home, on one occasion preaching of the insufficiency of the moral principles without religious feelings, exclaimed, "Go heat your ovens with snow-balls! What! shall I send you to heaven with such an icicle in your pocket? I might as well put a millstone round your neck to teach you to swim!"   *Mrs. Jameson.*

10,639. MORALS, Christian. The sages of antiquity perceived and announced many moral truths of the highest value, some of them synonymous with those of the New Testament. But what care men for moral truth when it is uttered only by one whom men esteem as a fellow-mortal equal with themselves, one who has no authority to prescribe duty, or to command obedience? Of what avail, in a moral estimate, was the wisdom of Plato, or the morals of Socrates, Seneca, or Tully! The moral precepts of Seneca were given to the Romans at the same time with those of Christ. In an age when the highest intelligence co-existed in the empire with the greatest profligacy, Seneca's morals had no more influence upon the character of those who received and believed them, than they had upon the statues in the Pantheon. Seneca himself was accused of profligacy; and he was both the instructor and the victim of the worst of the Romans. The people believed his precepts and grew worse, while those who believed the teaching of the gospel in the same ages grew better. This is the vital point.   *Walker.*

10,640. MORALS, Old. Live by old ethics and the classical rules of honesty. Put no new names or notions upon authentic virtues and vices. Think not that morality is ambulatory; that vices in one age are not vices in another; or that virtues which are under the everlasting seal of right reason may be stamped by opinion! And therefore, though vicious times invert the opinions of things, and set up new ethics against virtue, yet hold thou unto old morality; and rather than follow a multitude to do evil, stand like Pompey's pillar conspicuous by thyself, and single in integrity. *Browne.*

10,641. MORALS, Standards of. Before Socrates, it was said, "Let us do good to those who love us, and evil to those who hate us." Socrates changed the precept, and said, "Let us do good to our friends, and let us do no evil to enemies." Jesus Christ says, "Bless them that curse you." "Love your enemies."

10,642. MORNING, Duty of the. A king was once going out for a morning ride. Waiting a few moments for Lord Dartmouth, one of his party rebuked him for his tardiness. He answered, "I have learned to wait upon the King of kings before I wait upon my earthly sovereign."

10,643. MORNING, Joy of the. When we rise fresh and vigorous in the morning, the world seems fresh too, and we think we shall never be tired of business or pleasure; but by that time the evening is come, we find ourselves heartily so; we quit all its enjoyments readily and gladly; we retire willingly into a little cell; we lie down in darkness, and resign ourselves to the arms of sleep with perfect satisfaction and complacency. Apply this to youth and old age—life and death. *Bishop Horne.*

10,644. MORNING, Prayer in the. On the first of May in the olden times, according to annual custom, many inhabitants of London went into the fields to bathe their faces with the early dew upon the grass, under the idea that it would render them beautiful. Some writers call the custom superstitious; it may have been so, but this we know, that to bathe one's face every morning in the dew of heaven by prayer and communion, is the sure way to obtain true beauty of life and character.   *Spurgeon.*

10,645. MOROSENESS, Cure for. Plato, observing the morose and sour humor of Xenocrates, otherwise a person of great virtue and worth, admonished him to sacrifice to the Graces. In like manner, I am of opinion that it behooves a woman of moderation to crave the assistance of the Graces in her behavior towards her husband, thereby (according to the saying of Metroporus) to render their society mutually harmonious to each other.   *Plutarch.*

10,646. MORTALITY, All Shrouded in. All human divinity will soon be shrouded in mortality. Death levels the highest mountains with the lowest valleys. He mows down the fairest lilies as well as the foulest thistles. The robes of illustrious princes, and the rags of homely peasants, are both laid aside in the wardrobe of the grave.   *W. Secker.*

10,647. MORTALITY, Emblem of. The human race resemble the withering foliage of a wide forest. While the air is calm, we perceive single leaves scattering here and there from the branches; but sometimes a tempest or a whirlwind precipitates thousands in a moment. It is a moderate computation which supposes a hundred thousand millions to have died since the exit of righteous Abel.   *John Foster.*

10,648. MOSES, The Character of. He undoubtedly was the Homer, as well as the Solon of his country. We can never separate his genius from his character, so meek, yet stern; from his appearance, so gravely commanding, so spiritually severe; from his law, girt with dark thunder and embroidered fires; and from certain incidents in his history—his figure in the ark, when, at the sight of the strange, richly-attired lady, "behold the babe wept"—his attitude beside the bush that burned in the wilderness—his sudden entrance into the presence of Pharaoh—his lifting up, with that sinewy, swarthy hand, the rod over the Red Sea—his ascent up the black precipices of Sinai—his death on Pisgah, with the Promised Land full in view—his mystic burial in a secret vale by the hand of the Eternal—his position as the leader of the great Exodus of the tribes, and the founder of a strict, complicated and magnificent polity—all this has given a supplemental and extraordinary interest to the writings of Moses. He is the sternest of all the scripture writers, and the most laconic. His writings may be called hieroglyphics of the strangest and greatest events in the early part of the world's history.   *G. Gilfillan.*

10,649. MOTHER, Influence of a. My mother asked me never to use tobacco; I have never touched it from that time to the present day. She asked me not to gamble, and I have never gambled, and I cannot tell who is losing in games that are being played. She admonished me, too, against hard drinking; and whatever capacity for endurance I have at present, and whatever usefulness I may have attained in life, I have attributed to having complied with her pious and correct wishes. When I was seven years of age she asked me not to drink, and then I made a resolution of total abstinence; and that I have adhered to it through all time, I owe to my mother. *Thos. H. Benton.*

10,650. MOTHER Instructed. A noble lady told me that, when she was crying on account of the death of one of her children, and refusing to be comforted because the child was not, her little daughter came innocently to her one day, and said, "Mamma, is God Almighty dead, that makes you cry so?" The mother, startled by this inquiry, blushed, and answered, "No, my child, the Lord is not dead." Said the little girl, "Mamma, will you lend me your glove?" "Yes, my child." Soon after the mother asked for it again. Then the little girl said, "Now you have taken away the glove from me, shall I cry because you have taken away your own glove? And did not the Lord give you my sister. and will you cry because the Lord has taken her away?" The mother was instructed from the lips of her little one; she kissed the rod and the hand that appointed it, and said with great submission, "The Lord gave, and the Lord hath taken away, and blessed be the name of the Lord." *Whitefield.*

10,651. MOTHER, Love for. Pomponius Atticus, a Roman, pronounced a funeral oration on the death of his mother, and asserted that though he had resided with her sixty-seven years, he was never once reconciled to her, because there never happened the least discord between them, and consequently there was no need of reconciliation.

10,652. MOTHER, Memory of. One of Massachusetts' sons lay in the hospital-tent dying. I spoke to the dying boy of mother, of Jesus, of home, of heaven. I believe it to be a great characteristic of the American heart, that it clings to home and mother. I remember passing over a battle-field, and seeing a man just dying. His mind was wandering. His spirit was no longer on that bloody field; it was at his home far away. A smile passed over his face—a smile, oh, of such sweetness, as, looking up, he said, "Oh, mother! O, mother! I'm so glad you have come!" And it seemed as if she was there by his side. By-and-by he said again, "It's cold! it's cold! Won't you pull the blanket over me?" I stooped down, and pulled the poor fellow's ragged blanket closer to his shivering form. And he smiled again, "That will do, mother; that will do!" And so, turning over, he passed sweetly into rest, and was borne up to the presence of God on the wings of a pious mother's prayers.
Geo. J. Mingins.

10,653. MOTHER, A Missionary. When John Wesley was about deciding to go as a missionary to Georgia, he asked the consent of his noble mother, Mrs. Susanna Wesley. She replied, "Had I a hundred sons, I should be glad to see them all engaged in such a blessed work, although I might see them no more in this world."

10,654. MOTHERS, Noble Work of. A mother took alone the burden of life when her husband laid it down; without much property, out of her penury, by her planning and industry night and day, by her wilfulness of love, by her fidelity, brings up her children; and life has six men, all of whom are like pillars in the temple of God. And O, do not read to me of the campaigns of Cæsar; tell me nothing about Napoleon's wonderful exploits; I tell you that, as God and the angels look down upon the silent history of that woman's administration, and upon those men-building processes which went on in her heart and mind through a score of years, nothing exterior, no outward development of kingdoms, no empire-building, can compare with what she has done. Nothing can compare in beauty, and wonder, and admirableness, and divinity itself, to the silent work in obscure dwellings of faithful women bringing their children to honor and virtue and piety. I tell you, the inside is larger than the outside. The loom is more than the fabric. The thinker is more than thought. The builder is more than the building. *Beecher*

10,655. MOTHERS, Religious. Hooker used to say, "If I had no other reason and motive for being religious, I would earnestly strive to be so for the sake of my aged mother, that I might requite her care of me, and cause the widow's heart to sing for joy." Mrs. Doddridge, when her son was quite a little boy, used to teach him scripture history from the Dutch tiles of the fire-place, on which there were pictures of subjects taken from the Bible. He never forgot those early instructions, and probably to them, under God, his future character and usefulness may be traced. Dr. Johnson said he distinctly remembered the time and place where his mother first taught him of "heaven, a place where good people go, and of hell, a place where bad people go." Out of one hundred and twenty candidates for the ministry it was found that more than one hundred attributed their religious experience to the example and prayers of their mothers.

10,656. MOTIVES, Reward of. Plato, who was out of favor with Dionysius, King of Sicily, having gained audience with him, said, "Sir, if you were informed there were a certain ruffian come into your island with a design upon your majesty's person, but, for want of an opportunity, could not execute the villainy, would you suffer him to go off unpunished?" "No, by no means," replied the king; "for we ought to detest and revenge not only the overt acts, but the malicious intentions of our enemies." "Well, then, on the other hand," said Plato, "if there should come a person to court, out of pure kindness and ambition, to serve your majesty, and you would not give him an opportunity of expressing it, were it reasonable to dismiss him with scorn and disrespect?" The king saw the application, and restored both Plato and another philosopher, Æschines, to favor, and treated them with great honor.

10,657. MOURNING, Oriental. LeBrun describes the custom of Syrian women going to the tombs of deceased relatives at set times to weep there, as follows: "While I was at Ramah, I saw a very great company of these weeping women going out of the town. I followed them, and, after having observed the place they visited, adjacent to their sepulchres, in order to make their usual lamentations, I placed myself on an elevated spot. They first went and seated themselves on the sepulchres, and wept there; where, after having remained about half an hour, some of them rose up, and formed a ring, holding each other by the hand. Quickly two of them quitted the others, and placed themselves in the centre of the circle, where they made so much noise by screaming, and clapping their hands, as, together with their various contortions, might have subjected themselves to the suspicion of madness. After that they returned, and seated themselves to weep again, till they gradually withdrew to their homes. The dresses they wore were such as they generally used, white, or any other color; but when they rose up to form a circle together, they put on a black veil over the upper parts of their persons."

10,658. MURDER a Part of Worship. In India there is a class called Thugs, who fancy they shall get an addition to their happiness hereafter for every human being they murder; so that murder is not only their trade, but is actually part and parcel of their daily worship! *Cumming.*

10,659. MURDER, Steps to. A man who was condemned to be hung for murder, and awaited execution in prison, drew upon the walls of his cell the sketch of a man upon the gallows with five steps leading to the platform on which it stood. On the first step he wrote, "Disobedience to parents;" on the second step, "Sabbath breaking;" on the third step, "Gambling and drunkenness;" on the fourth step, "Murder;" on the fifth, "The Fatal Platform." It was doubtless a true sketch of his own progress in sin to disgrace and the murderer's doom.

10,660. MURDERER, Detection of a. A murder had been committed, and many persons were brought before the judge, but they all pleaded innocence. He bade them all bare their breasts, and then he laid his hand upon their hearts. Finding one whose heart beat harder than the rest, he said, "Thou art the author of this murder." Conscious of his guilt, his tell-tale heart betrayed him. He confessed the crime and was punished.

10,661. MURDERER, Good Character of a. Burke, a man who had committed sixteen murders, was considered a very respectable man, correct in his habits, affable and affectionate in his family. "A man may smile, and smile, and be a villain."

10,662. MURDERER, Horrors of a. Coleridge tells of an Italian who assassinated a nobleman in Rome, and fled to Hamburg for safety. He had not passed many weeks before, one day, in the crowded street, he heard his name called by a voice familiar to him: he turned short round, and saw the face of his victim looking at him with a fixed eye. From that moment he had no peace: at all hours, in all places, and amidst all companies, however engaged he might be, he heard the voice, and could never help looking around; and whenever he so looked round he always encountered the same face, staring close upon him. The Italian said he had struggled long, but life was a burden which he could now no longer bear; and he was resolved to return to Rome, to surrender himself to justice, and expiate his crime on the scaffold.

10,663. MURMURING, Fight Against. As the King of Syria said to his captains, "Fight neither with small nor great, but with the King of Israel;" so say I, fight not so much against this sin or that, but fight against your murmuring, which is a mother-sin; make use of all your Christian armor, make use of all the ammunition of heaven (Eph. 6: 10, 11), to destroy the mother; and in destroying of her you will destroy the daughters. When Goliath was slain, the Philistines fled; when a general in any army is cut off, the common soldiers are easily and quickly routed and destroyed. So destroy but murmuring, and you will quickly destroy disobedience, ingratitude, impatience, distrust, etc. O kill this mother-sin, that this may never kill thy soul! I have read of Sennacherib, that after his army was destroyed by an angel, and he returned home to his own country, he inquired of one about him what he thought the reason might be why God so favored the Jews. He answered that there was one Abraham their father that was willing to sacrifice his son to death at the command of God, and that ever since that time God favored that people. "Well," said Sennacherib, "if that be so, I have two sons, and I will sacrifice them both to death, if that will procure their God to favor me;" which when his two sons heard, they (as the story goeth) slew their father (Isa. 37: 38), choosing rather to kill than to be killed. So do thou choose rather to kill this mother-sin than to be killed by it. *Brooks.*

10,664. MUSIC, Fable of. Maurice Connor, the blind Irish piper, could play an air which would set everything, alive or dead, capering. At the very first note of that tune the brogues began shaking upon the feet of all who heard it, old or young; then the feet began going, going from under them, and at last up and away with them, dancing like mad, whisking here, there and everywhere, like a straw in a storm—there was no halting while the music lasted. One day Maurice piped his tune on the sea-shore, and at once every inch of it was covered with all manner of fish, jumping and plunging about to the music; and every moment more and more would tumble out of the water, charmed by the wonderful tune. Crabs of monstrous size spun round and round on one claw with the nimbleness of a dancing master, and twirled and tossed their other claws about.

10,665. MUSIC, Heaven's Sweet. There are various sounds in nature all plaintive and sad: the voice of winds, the chime of waves, and the song of birds, are all in minor keys, as if all creation groaned, and travailed in pain, waiting for deliverance, that grand deliverance which is the burden of prophecy, when the great Composer shall transpose all her strains from the minor into the major, and the wild wail of nature shall give way to the glad harmony of the everlasting jubilee, the joyous strain of which shall reverberate from heaven to earth, and the wide universe be as a whispering gallery, ever repeating its sweet music. *Dr. Cumming.*

10,666. MUSIC, Indulgence in. Music is the only sensual gratification which mankind may indulge in to excess without injury to their moral or religious feelings. *Addison.*

10,667. MUSIC, Influence of. The meaning of song goes deep. Who is there that, in logical words, can express the effect music has on us?

A kind of inarticulate, unfathomable speech, which leads us to the edge of the infinite, and lets us for moments gaze into that! *Carlyle.*

10,668. MUSIC, Mystery of. The greatest mystery of all art, perhaps, is music; the soul that leaps from the mere material chords and pipes, and, whilst it emanates from, plays upon the spirit of man: think of the harp, or—if you prefer the more common thing—the piano, the organ; what wonderful writing it is! Words, poems, paintings, marbles are quite coarse in comparison. The artist who performs upon the keys may, perhaps, be a mechanician, little more, and have very little apprehension of the inner spirit which created the wonderful relation of those notes and bars; but think what it was! The great musician himself cannot understand the mystery by which the inner hidden numbers came to represent unimaginable, and except in this way, inexpressible emotions and desires. The instrument is to the soul, perverse piece of wood, or wire, or brass, that it is, what the body of man is to his mind. *Hood.*

10,669. MUSIC, Spell of. Dr. Worgan has so touched the organ at St. John's, that I have been turning backward and forward over the prayer-book for the first lesson in Isaiah, and wondered that I could not find Isaiah there. The musician and the orator fall short of the full power of their science, if the hearer is left in possession of himself. *R. Cecil.*

10,670. MUSIC, Undying. Music, once admitted to the soul, becomes a sort of spirit, and never dies. It wanders perturbedly through the halls and galleries of the memory, and is often heard again, distinct and living as when it first displaced the wavelets of the air.
E. B. Lytton.

10,671. MUSIC, Universal. Music forms the universal language which, when all other languages were confounded, the confusion of Babel left unconfounded. The white man and the black man, the red man and the yellow man, can sing together, however difficult they may find it to be to talk to each other: and both sexes and all ages may thus express their emotions simultaneously. *Prof. G. Wilson.*

10,672. MYSTERIES, Confession of. It is not given to man to discover all the works and ways of God. Perhaps these, notwithstanding all our boasted discoveries and the pride of science, lie as unknown to us as the wide forest to the microscopic insect, whose life is a day, and whose world is a leaf—that narrow territory the scene of its most distant journeys, its country, its cradle, and its grave. With what modesty, then, should the highest intellect bear itself in presence of the Creator! These are sentiments which the great Laplace, unbeliever though he was, echoed in this, one of his last and not least memorable utterances "It is the little that we know; it is the great that remains unknown." *Guthrie.*

10,673. MYSTERIES, Divine. In the meditation of Divine mysteries, keep thy heart humble and thy thoughts holy: let philosophy not be ashamed to be confuted, nor logic blush to be confounded: what thou canst not prove approve; what thou canst not comprehend, believe; and what thou canst believe, admire; so shall thy ignorance be satisfied in thy faith, and thy doubts swallowed up with wonders. The best way to see daylight is to put out thy candle. *Quarles.*

10,674. MYSTERY, Key to. A French artisan questioned much the dispensations of Providence in the government of the world. One day, in visiting a ribbon manufactory, his attention was attracted by an extraordinary piece of machinery. Countless wheels and thousands of threads were twirling in all directions; he could understand nothing of its movements. He was informed however, that all this motion was connected with the center, where there was a chest which was kept shut. Anxious to understand the principle of the machine, he asked permission to see the interior, "The master has the key," was the reply. The words were like a flash of light. Here was the answer to all his perplexed thoughts. Yes; the Master has the key. He governs and directs all. It is enough.

10,675. MYSTERY, Reason for. An intelligent sceptic caviled much over the mysteries of Christianity. At length he was soundly converted. A friend asked him, "Well, my dear sir, and what do you think now of the doctrine of the resurrection?" "O, sir," he replied, "two words from Paul conquered me: 'Thou fool!' Do you see this Bible?" (taking up a beautiful copy of the scriptures, fastened with a silver clasp;) "and will you read the words upon the clasp that shuts it?" His friend read, engraven on the silver clasp, "Thou fool!" "There," said he, "are the words that conquered me. It was no argument, no reasoning, no satisfying my objections; but God convincing me that I was a fool: and thenceforward I determined I would have my Bible clasped with those words, 'Thou fool!' and never again would come to the consideration of its sacred mysteries, but through their medium. I will remember that I am a fool, and God only is wise."

10,676. NAKED, Clothing the. It is said that a Russian soldier, one very cold night, kept duty between one sentry-box and another. A poor workingman, moved with pity, took off his coat and lent it to the soldier to keep him warm; adding, that he should soon reach home, while the soldier would be exposed out of doors for the night. The cold was so intense that the soldier was found dead in the morning. Sometime afterwards the poor man was laid on his death-bed, and in a dream saw Jesus appear to him. "You have got my coat on," said the man. "Yes, it is the coat you lent to me that cold night when I was on duty and you passed by. I was naked, and you clothed me."

10,677. NAME, A Bad. A good Quaker, who was especially averse to violence and bloodshedding, had a dog that he wished to be rid of, and so he pushed him out into the street, saying as he did so, "I will not kill thee, but

1 will give thee a bad name;" and then he shouted aloud, "Mad dog! mad dog!" and so set the whole town upon his track to destroy him. Afterwards, when it was ascertained that the dog was not mad, it was too late to reverse the wrong done.   *Dr. Curry.*

10,678. NAME, A Good. Consider that the invisible thing called a good name is made up of the breath of numbers that speak well of you; so that, if by a disobliging word you silence the meanest, the gale will be less strong which is to bear up your esteem. And though nothing is so vain as the eager pursuit of empty applause, yet to be well thought of, and to be kindly used by the world, is like a glory about a woman's head; it is a perfume she carries about with her, and leaveth wherever she goeth; it is a charm against ill will. Malice may empty her quiver, but cannot wound; the dirt will not stick, the jests will not take; without the consent of the world, a scandal doth not go deep; it is only a slight stroke upon the injured party, and returneth with the greater force upon those that gave it.   *Saville.*

10,679. NAME, Inappropriate. Dr. Guthrie reports having read of one Rev. Mr. Scamp, who was, in a sense, always a scamp, yet was much esteemed while he lived, and died greatly lamented.

10,680. NAME, The Mighty. In the days of miracles, the name of Jesus carried with it the idea of his authority and the efficacy of his power. Uttered by the lips of faith, it was a word of resistless might. It healed disease, shed light on the darkness of the blind, and breathed warm life into the cold form of death. It mastered devils, controlled the powers of hell, and commanded the wildest elements of nature into instant obedience. Like Pharaoh's signet on Joseph's hand, he who used that name in faith, was endowed for the time with sovereign power. Powerful as was this sign when used by faith, yet on unbelieving lips no name was more useless. Like a residuum from which the ethereal spirit has been evaporated, or a body bereft of life, it possessed no virtue or power whatever. In mere name there was no charm either to pour light on a blind man's eye-ball, or restore vigor to a withered limb.   *Dr. Guthrie.*

10,681. NAMES, Importance of. There is much, nay almost all, in names. The name is the earliest garment you wrap round the earth, to which it thenceforth cleaves more tenaciously (for there are names that have lasted nigh thirty centuries) than the very skin. And now from without, what mystic influences does it not send inwards, even to the centre, especially in those plastic first-times, when the whole soul is yet infantine, soft; and the invisible seed-grain will grow to be an all-over-shadowing tree! Names? Could I unfold the influence of names, which are the most important of all clothings, I were a second great Trismegistus. Not only all common speech, but science—poetry itself—is no other, if thou consider it, than a right naming. Adam's first task was giving names to natural appearances. What is ours still but a continuation of the same, be the appearance exotic, vegetable, organic, mechanic, stars, or starry movements (as in science); or (as in poetry) passions, virtues, calamities, God, attributes, gods!   *Carlyle.*

10,682. NAMES, Need of. He that has complex ideas, without particular names for them would be in no better case than a bookseller who had volumes that lay unbound and without title, which he could make known to others only by showing the loose sheets.   *Locke.*

10,683. NATION, Prayer for the. During the Revolutionary war, General Washington's army was reduced at one time to great straits, and the people were greatly dispirited. One of them who left his home with an anxious heart, one day, as he was passing the edge of a wood near the camp, heard the sound of a voice. He stopped to listen, and looking between the trunks of the large trees, he saw General Washington engaged in prayer. He passed quietly on, that he might not disturb him; and on returning home, told his family, "America will prevail," and then related what he had heard and seen.

10,684. NATIONS, Crises of. There are brief crisis in which the drift of individual and natural history is determined, sometimes unexpectedly; critical moments on which great decisions hang; days which, like a mountain in a plain, lift themselves above the dead level of common days into everlasting eminence. Our Day of Independence was such a day; so was the day of Marathon, and the day of Waterloo. Napoleon admitted that the Austrians fought grandly on the field of Rivoli, and said, "They failed because they do not understand the value of minutes." Humboldt refers the discovery of America to "a wonderful concatenation of trivial circumstances," including a flight of parrots.   *Dr. Foss.*

10,685. NATURAL MAN, Door to the. The abbot Timothy, told Poemen, of a woman in a neighboring town, who was a sinner; "Yet," said he, "the woman has elements of good in her. She is spoken of as very charitable to the poor." Poemen answered, "If there is a rent in the clouds the sun will shine through." Still later he was informed that the woman was going on in the same way. He said, "Do not be afraid; she will serve God in the end." At last the sinning woman come herself to visit Poemen. His gentleness and boundless charity won her heart. She become thoroughly penitent, poured out floods of tears, and resolved to abandon sin and live to God alone. She afterwards lived a holy live.

10,686. NATURAL MAN, Evidence from the. You might as well try to write with pen and ink on the rubbish from which paper is manufactured as expect legible evidence for the truth of the gospel in the life and spirit of one who has not gotten a "clean heart," who has not been born again.   *Arnot.*

10,687. NATURAL MAN, Impotence of the. If the ship launched, rigged, and with her sails spread cannot stir, till the wind come fair, and fills them; much less can the timber, that lies in the carpenter's yard, hew and frame itself into a ship. If the living tree cannot grow, except the root communicates its sap, much less can a dead rotten stake in the hedge, which hath no root, live of its own accord. In a word, if a Christian, that hath his spiritual life of grace, cannot exercise this life without strength from above, then surely one void of this new life, dead in sin and trespasses, can never be able to beget this in himself, or concur to the production of it. The state of unregeneracy is a state of impotency. "When we were without strength, in due time Christ died for the ungodly" (Rom. 5 : 6). And as Christ found the lump of mankind covered with the ruins of their lapsed estate (no more able to raise themselves from under the weight of God's wrath, which lay upon them, than one buried under the rubbish of a fallen house, is to free himself of that weight without help), so the Spirit finds sinners in as helpless a condition, as unable to repent or believe on Christ for salvation, as they were of themselves to purchase it.   *Gurnall.*

10,688. NATURAL MAN, Inability of the. In his lapsed and sinful state, man is not capable, of and by himself, either to think, to will, or to do, that which is really good; but it is necessary for him to be regenerated and renewed in his intellect, affections, or will, and in all his powers, by God in Christ through the Holy Spirit, that he may be qualified rightly to understand, esteem, consider, will, and perform whatever is truly good. I ascribe to divine grace the commencement, the continuance, and the consummation of all good; and to such an extent do I carry its influence, that a man, though already regenerate, can neither conceive, will, nor do any good at all, nor resist any evil temptation, without this preventing and exciting, this following and co-operating grace.   *Arminius.*

10,689. NATURAL MAN, Spots of the. Every man hath a double spot on him, the heart spot and the life spot; the spot of original, and the spots of actual sins. But Christ was without either. 1 Pet. 1 : 19.   *John Flavel.*

10,690. NATURE, Admiration for. A pious acquaintance, remarkable for the quaint shrewdness of his observations, one day, when walking in a garden, having pulled a flower of exquisite loveliness, after expressing, in his own characteristic way, his admiration of its various beauties, took up a clod of the soil in his other hand, and naïvely, but emphatically, exclaimed, "What but Almighty power could extract that from this?"   *Duncan.*

10,691. NATURE alone Antique. It struck me much, as I sat by the Kuhbach one silent noontide, and watched it flowing, gurgling, to think how this same streamlet had flowed and gurgled through all changes of weather and of fortune, from beyond the earliest date of history. Yes, probably on the morning when Joshua forded Jordan; even as at the mid-day when Cæsar, doubtless with difficulty, swam

the Nile, yet kept his Commentaries dry—this little Kuhbach, assiduous as Tiber, Eurotas, or Siloa, was murmuring on across the wilderness, as yet unnamed, unseen : here, too, as in the Euphrates and the Ganges, is a vein or veinlet of the grand world-circulation of waters, which, with its atmospheric arteries, has lasted and lasts, simply with the world. Thou fool! Nature alone is antique, and the oldest art a mushroom; that idle crag thou sittest on is six thousand years of age.   *Carlyle.*

10,692. NATURE, Beauty of. The various productions of nature were not made for us to tread upon, nor only to feed our eyes with their grateful variety, or to bring a sweet odor to us; but there is a more internal beauty in them for our minds to prey upon, did we but penetrate beyond the surface of these things into their hidden properties.   *Bp. Patrick.*

10,693. NATURE, Blot in. Ruskin says:— "The Savoyard's cottage, standing in the midst of an inconceivable, inexpressible beauty, set on some sloping bank of golden sward, with clear fountains flowing beside it, and wild flowers, and noble trees, and goodly rocks, gathered round into a perfection as of Paradise, is itself a dark and plague-like stain in the midst of the gentle landscape. Within a certain distance of its threshold the ground is foul and cattle-trampled; its timbers are black with smoke, its garden choked with weeds and nameless refuse, its chambers empty and joyless, the light and wind gleaming and filtering through the crannies of their stones." Man is the blot on the landscape, the discord in the harmony of nature, the stranger and alien, who walks blindly amid God's glorious works.

10,694. NATURE, Calm of. Surely, there is something in the unruffled calm of nature that overawes our little anxieties and doubts: the sight of the deep-blue sky, and the clustering stars above, seems to impart a quiet to the mind.   *Edwards.*

10,695. NATURE, Cause of. How often might a man, after he had jumbled a set of letters in a bag, fling them upon the ground before they would fall into an exact poem, yea, or so much as make a good discourse in prose! And may not a little book be as easily made by chance as this great volume of the world? How long might a man be in sprinkling colors upon a canvas with a careless hand before they could happen to make the exact picture of a man? And is a man easier made by chance than his picture? How long might twenty thousand blind men, which should be sent out from the several remote parts of England, wander up and down before they would all meet in Salisbury Plains, and fall into rank and file in the exact order of an army? And yet this is much more easy to be imagined than how the innumerable blind parts of matter should rendezvous themselves into a world.   *Tillotson.*

10,696. NATURE, Confidence from. It is truly a most Christian exercise to extract a sentiment of piety from the works and appearances of nature. Our Saviour expatiates on a flower, and draws from it the delightful argument of confidence in God. He gives us to see that taste may be combined with piety, and that the same heart may be occupied with all that is serious in the contemplations of religion, and be, at the same time, alive to the charms and loveliness of nature. *Chalmers.*

10,697. NATURE, Considering. Nothing can be more ungrateful than to pass over the works of God without consideration. To study them is among the highest gratifications the human mind can enjoy, provided the study is conducted upon religious principles. The book of Nature is open to all. "On every leaf, 'Creator, God,' is written." *Mrs. Trimmer.*

10,698. NATURE, Delight in. Better for a man never to have seen them, or to see them with the eyes of a brute, stupid and unconscious of what he beholds, than not to be able to say: "The Maker of all these wonders is my friend!" Their eyes have never been opened to see that they are trifles; mine have been, and will be till they are closed forever. They think a fine estate, a large conservatory, a hot-house rich as a West-Indian garden, things of consequence; visit them with pleasure, and muse upon them with ten times more. I am pleased with a frame of four lights, doubtful whether the few panes it contains will ever be worth a farthing; amuse myself with a green-house, which Lord Bute's gardener could take upon his back and walk away with; and when I have paid it the accustomed visit, and watered it, and given it air, I say to myself,— "This is not mine; 'tis a plaything lent me for the present; I must leave it soon." *Cowper.*

10,699. NATURE, Economy of. In nature, all is managed for the best with perfect frugality and just reserve, profuse to none, but bountiful to all; never employing on one thing more than enough, but with exact economy retrenching the superfluous, and adding force to what is principal in everything. *Shaftesbury.*

10,700. NATURE, Exhaustless Beauty of. Nature has scattered around us, on every side, and for every sense, an inexhaustible profusion of beauty and sweetness, if we will but perceive it. The pleasures we derive from musical sounds, and the forms of trees, are surely not given us in vain; and if we are constantly alive to these, we can never be in want of subjects of agreeable contemplation, and must be habitually cheerful. *Basil Hall.*

10,701. NATURE, Force of. Nature always springs to the surface, and manages to show what she is. It is vain to stop or try to drive her back. She breaks through every obstacle, pushes forward, and at last makes for herself a way. *Boileau.*

10,702. NATURE, Imitation of. Nature imitates herself. A grain thrown into good ground brings forth fruit; a principle thrown into a good mind brings forth fruit. Everything is created and conducted by the same Master: the root, the branch, the fruits; the principles, the consequences. *Pascal.*

10,703. NATURE, Intention of. Nature intends that, at fixed periods, men should succeed each other by the instrumentality of death. We

shall never outwit Nature; we shall die as usual. *Fontenelle.*

10,704. NATURE, Laws of. In the laws of nature we have not blind unintellectual fatalities, but expressions of divine volitions. Oersted never wrote a finer truth than that the conception of the universe is incomplete if not comprehended as a constant and continuous work of the Eternally-creating Spirit; nor Emerson, in relation to the same fact, "that it takes as much life to conserve as to create." Because of these great verities is it that to study the laws of nature is in reality to study the modes of God's action; that science is simply a "history of the divine operations in matter and mind; that the world, with all its antiquity, is every moment a new creation— the song of the morning stars unsuspended and unsuspendable to the ear that will listen for it,—a virgin to every wooer of the beautiful and the true. *Grindon.*

10,705. NATURE, Lesson from. Nothing surely can be better adapted to turn man's thoughts off his own self-sufficiency than the works of nature. Wherever he rests his attention, whether on matter organized, or unorganized; there he will discover convincing evidence of his own ignorance; and at the same time, the omnipotence of a first great cause will be impressed on his mind, and influence his understanding. *Maund.*

10,706. NATURE, Perfection of. The British Museum possessed in the Portland Vase one of the finest remains of ancient art; and it may be remembered how, some years ago, the world of taste was shocked to hear that this precious relic had been shattered by a maniac hand. Without disparaging classic taste or that exquisite example of it, I will venture to say, that there is not a poor worm which we tread upon, not a rare leaf, that, like a ruined but reckless man, dances merrily in its fallen state to the autumn winds, but has superior claims upon our study and our admiration. The child who plucks a rose to pieces, or crushes the fragile form of a fluttering insect, destroys a work which the highest art could not invent, nor man's best skilled hand construct. That champion of the truth dealt the atheist a crushing blow, who told him that the very feather with which he penned the words, "There is no God," refuted the audacious lie. *Dr. Guthrie.*

10,707. NATURE, Sacredness of. To those who believe in God, and try to see God in all things, the most minute natural phenomenon cannot be secular. It must be divine—deliberately divine; and I can use no less lofty word. The grain of dust can no more go from God's presence, or flee from God's Spirit, than you or I can. If it go up to the physical heaven, and float—as it actually often does— far above the clouds, in those higher strata of the atmosphere which the aeronaut has never visited, even there it will be obeying physical laws, which we term hastily laws of nature, but which are really laws of God; and if it go down into the abyss, if it be buried fathoms miles, below the surface, and become an atom of some rock in the process of consolidation, has it escaped from God, even in the bowels of the earth? Is it not there obeying the will and mind of God? *Kingsley.*

10,708. NATURE, Study of. It is to be lamented, that many who have made great discoveries, and been justly celebrated for their deep researches into the works of God our Creator, have extolled the work, but forgotten the hand who formed it. With pleasure, however, we can read an instance to the contrary in the great Linnæus. "The deeper he penetrated into the secrets of nature, the more he admired the wisdom of the Creator. He praised this wisdom in his works, recommended it by his speeches, and honored it in his actions. Wherever he found an opportunity of expatiating on the greatness, the providence, and omnipotence of God, which frequently happened in his lectures and botanical excursions, his heart glowed with a celestial fire, and his mouth poured forth torrents of admirable eloquence." This great man died on the 10th of January, 1778. *Buck.*

10,709. NATURE, Teachings of. When children meet with primroses, nuts, or apples in their way, I see those pleasures are ofttimes occasions to make them loiter in their errands, so that they are sure to have their parents' displeasure, and ofttimes their late return finds a barred entrance to their home; whereas those who meet with dangers in the way, make haste in their journey, and their speed makes them welcomed with commendation. Nature hath sent me abroad into the world, and I am every day traveling homeward. If I meet with store of miseries in my way, discretion shall teach me a religious haste in my journey. And if I meet with pleasures, they shall pleasure me only by putting me in mind of my pleasures at home, which shall teach me to scorn these as worse than trifles. I will never more reckon a troublesome life a curse, but a blessing. A pleasant journey is dear bought with the loss of home. *Warwick.*

10,710. NATURE, Unchangeable. A certain man bought a Blackamoor, and thinking that the color of his skin arose from the neglect of his former master, he no sooner brought him home than he procured all manner of scouring apparatus, scrubbing-brushes, soaps, and sand-paper, and set to work, with his servants, to wash him white again. They drenched and rubbed him for an hour, but all in vain; his skin remained as black as ever; while the poor wretch all but died from the cold he caught under the operation. No human means avail of themselves to change a nature originally evil. *Æsop.*

10,711. NATURE, Wrath and Love in. Wrath and threatening are invariably mingled with love, and in the utmost solitudes of nature the existence of hell seems to me as legibly declared by a thousand spiritual utterances as of heaven. It is well for us to dwell with thankfulness on the unfolding of the flower, and the falling of tne dew, and the sleep of the green fields in the sunshine; but the blasted trunk, the barren rock, the moaning of the bleak winds, the roar of the black, perilous whirlpools and the mountain streams, the solemn solitudes of moors and seas, the continual fading of all beauty into darkness, of all strength into dust—have these no language for us? We may seek to escape their teachings by reasonings touching the good which is wrought out of all evil, but it is vain sophistry. The good succeeds to the evil as the day succeeds to the night, but so also the evil to the good. Ebal and Gerizim, birth and death, light and darkness, heaven and hell, divide the existence of man and his futurity. *Ruskin.*

10,712. NECESSITIES, Small. We ought to be thankful to nature for having made those things which are necessary easy to be discovered; while other things that are difficult to be known, are not necessary. *Epicurus.*

10,713. NECESSITY, Abuse of. The word "necessary" is miserably applied. It disordereth families, and overturneth government, by being so abused. Remember that children and fools want everything because they want judgment to distinguish; and therefore there is no stronger evidence of a crazy understanding than the making too large a catalogue of things necessary. *Lord Halifax.*

10,714. NEGLECT, Atoning for. Arsenius was the tutor of Arcadius and Honorius, the sons of the Emperor Theodosius, having the responsibility of their education. He lived in great splendor at the court of the emperor in Constantinople, neglecting his great duty to the future emperors. Not a noble lesson did he impress upon his pupils. As emperor Arcadius was characterized by his utter incompetency, and weakness, and Honorius by his frivolity, devoting his attention to poultry breeding instead of governing his empire. Their tutor fled to the desert to escape, if possible, all reminders of his neglected duty. The hermits hailed him as the father of the emperors. It was the keenest sarcasm, but well deserved. He fled from them to seek entire solitude in the wildest waste. There in absolute silence and constant remorse, he spent the long years. Men visited his cave, but could never induce him to speak. He wept till the lashes were worn from his eyelids, hoping by his austerities to atone for his sins of omission which had degraded the Empire, through the faults and weakness of its rulers. Thus he continued till his death.

10,715. NEGLECT, Conduct under. When you meet with neglect, let it rouse you to exertion, instead of mortifying your pride. Set about lessening those defects which expose you to neglect, and improve those excellencies which command attention and respect. *S. Smith.*

10,716. NEGLECT, A Momentary. Rev. Mr. Ware said that in visiting the Insane Asylum, on Blackwell's Island, he saw a poor man who wrung his hands, and cried, "O, that I only had!" "O, that I only had!" When spoken to, he would always reply with the greatest agony expressed in every feature and this was all he was ever known to say month after month, "O, that I only had." Mr. Ware asked the keeper the cause of this self-accusation, and was informed that the man had been a watchman at one of the railroad bridges, and when the bridge was open it was his duty to throw up a signal light to warn any approaching train of danger. One dark night, when the bridge was open, the watchman failed to give the signal, and a whole train was wrecked and many lives were lost. When the authorities looked for him, they found a lunatic whose only cry was "O, that I only had." For a moment he failed to do that which was required of him, and that failure sent many to an untimely grave, and destroyed his own reason. On the other shore the corrupter of souls will see his ruinous work and will find occasion for the wail, "O that I only had."

10,717. NEGLECT, Parable of. A Jewish parable says, that a king invited his servants to a festival. Some of these prepared and adorned themselves, and waited at the door till he should pass in; others said there would be time enough for this, as the feast would be a long time in preparing, and so went about their ordinary business. The latter, when the king demanded suddenly the presence of his guests, had no time to change their apparel; but were obliged to appear before him in sordid garments as they were. He was displeased, and would not allow them to taste of his banquet, but made them stand by while the others feasted.

10,718. NEGLIGENCE, Evil Results of. The best ground untilled, soonest runs out into rank weeds. A man of knowledge that is either negligent or uncorrected, cannot but grow wild and godless. *Bishop Hall.*

10,719. NEIGHBOR, Good. Themistocles, according to Plutarch, had a farm for sale. He sent out a crier to proclaim its advantages, and particularly to declare that it had a good neighbor. The point was well made; all want good neighbors. To have such, we must be such. Christianity makes good neighborhood. "Thou shalt love thy neighbor as thyself." Then we shall have no bad neighbors.

10,720. NEIGHBOR, Hatred of. Uladislaus Locticus, King of Poland, went to view the dead on a field of battle. Florianus Sharus, a knight, lay wounded, his hands holding his bowels, to keep them from gushing out. "How great is the torment of this man!" said the king. Sharus replied that "There was a greater torment, and that was to dwell with an illdisposed neighbor, which," he said, "I can testify from experience." "Well," saith the king, "if thou recoverest from thy wound, I will ease thee of thy illneighbor." The man got well, and the king kept his promise, and not only turned out the person complained of, but gave the whole village to Sharus.

10,721. NEIGHBOR, Our. Our neighbor is man! wherever he may be found, whatever may be the color of his skin, into whatever pit of misery and degradation he may have fallen. Neither

principalities, nor powers, nor things present or to come, can ever break up that heaven-created relation. *Burritt.*

10,722. NEIGHBOR, Power over a. Sextus Marius invited his neighbor, with whom he was offended, to be his guest for two days. On the first of these two days he pulled down his neighbor's farm-house; the second, he had it rebuilt larger and better than before. This he did to show what good or ill he could do them at his pleasure.

10,723. NEIGHBOR, Who is my. Luke 10: 29. The heading of this chapter in our English Bible supplies a good answer: "Christ teacheth the lawyer how to take every one for his neighbor that needeth his mercy." An illustrative answer to the question may be found in the comparison of two Old Testament texts, Exod. 23: 45, with Deut. 22: 1-4; where the Jews were enjoined to pursue the same law of kindness towards an "enemy," one "that hateth thee," as to a brother, one of the same race and kindred. The sight of distress or helplessness is all that true kindness needs to find a neighbor! St. Paul, in Rom. 13: 8, 9, extends the love of our neighbor to the widest limit: "He that loveth *another* hath fulfilled the law," which he makes synonymous with "Thou shalt love thy *neighbor* as thyself." *Bowes.*

10,724. NERVES, Sympathy of the. When the nerves, from long habit, have been accustomed to transmit their messages from distinct parts, and are suddenly cut off from them, they still retain along their trunks the sympathetic or sensational actions. Thus, a man who has had a leg amputated will feel distinctly along the course of the trunk of the nerve sensations from toes which no longer exist. The mind also is influenced by this; and frequently this peculiar direct nervous action can only be allayed by that which is negative and reflex. A curious instance occurred within my own experience. An old sailor suffered much from this; he retained his diseased foot too long, but at last consented to amputation. I knew him only with a wooden leg. When he had his nervous pains, he always called for hot water, into which he put his wooden stump. If told of his folly in supposing that such a proceeding could do any good, he would become enraged, and his paroxysm of pain would increase; but if gratified he took things easy, and the process actually appeared to do him good, though all must know there could be no real benefit. Still, here is the effect of mind over matter. *Ridge.*

10,725. NERVOUSNESS, Influence of. He experiences that nervous agitation to which brave men as well as cowards are subject; with this difference, that the one sinks under it, like the vine under the hail-storm, and the other collects his energies to shake it off, as the cedar of Lebanon is said to elevate its boughs to disperse the snow which accumulates upon them. *Sir Walter Scott.*

10,726. NERVOUS SYSTEM, The. So delicate is the fine tracery of the nervous structure, that the damage of a single fibre or a set of fibres destroys the unity of the whole. It is like a grand orchestra, in which one instrument alone out of time or tune disturbs the harmony of the rest, and the finest musical composition in the world is entirely spoiled by its discord. And this serious evil is apparent, not only in old age, but even in the young, in whom the disastrous consequences of injury to the brain, etc., are far more important both to themselves and to the world.

Dr. Forbes Winslow.

10,727. NEUTRALITY, Picture of. When the papists were displeased with Erasmus, on account of his neutrality, they painted him as hanging between heaven and earth; indicating thereby that he belonged to neither, or rather, that he was as unfit to go to heaven as to live upon earth. *Wilson.*

10,728. NEW BIRTH. Alternative of the. One evening a pastor spoke to a very cultivated and moral young lady, saying, "Except a man be born again, he cannot enter the kingdom of heaven. And if not heaven, what then? There is but one other place, and that is hell!" She trusted in her morality and was offended. That night she dreamed that the day of judgment, had come and saw the Judge seated upon the clouds, and felt herself irresistibly drawn towards him. The words, "If not born again, not heaven; and if not heaven, hell," rang in her ears. She awoke in great terror and began to call on God for mercy. Her repentance was thorough, her conversion clear, and her death a few years after triumphant.

10,729. NEW BIRTH, Change by. To hew a block of marble from the quarry, and carve it into a noble statue—to break up a waste wilderness, and turn it into a garden of flowers—to melt a lump of iron-stone, and forge it into watch-springs; all these are mighty changes. Yet they all come short of the change which every child of Adam requires; for they are merely the same thing in a new form—the same substance in a new shape. But man requires the grafting in of that which he had not before. He needs a change as great as a resurrection from the dead. He must become a new creature. Old things must pass away, and all things must become new. He must be born again—born from above—born of God. The natural birth is not a whit more necessary to the life of the body than is the spiritual birth to the life of the soul. *Ryle.*

10,730. NEW BIRTH, Change in. Chrysostom ingeniously remarks that the animals which went out of Noah's ark went out the same as they came in. The crow went out a crow, the fox a fox, and the porcupine, all armed with its living arrows, was a porcupine still. But the church transforms the animals she receives into her bosom, not by any change in their substance, but by the extirpation of their sin. Like unto a crow that sinner entered the church, who, having hardened his heart by delaying repentance, ever croaked to the same tune, "To-morrow, to-morrow;" now, behold, he goes out mourning like a dove. Like unto a spiteful fox that swindler entered the church,

who built his house on the ruin of his competitors; and behold, he goes out more harmless than a lamb, willing to sacrifice his own interests for the welfare of others. And that impatient, quarrelsome man, who made every one smart who touched him, came here like unto a bristly porcupine; and behold, he goes away like a loving spaniel that is tractable and gentle to all. And what new creatures have we here? The magic viands of a Circe formerly metamorphosed men into brutes; but such is not the effect of our gracious food—it rather changes the brutes into true men.

Segneri.

10,731. NEW BIRTH, Death and. Those born once, die twice—they die a temporal and an eternal death. But those who are born twice, die only once; for over them the second death hath no power. *Anon.*

10,732. NEW BIRTH, Mystery of the. Rev. George Whitefield, having occasion to write to Dr. Franklin, in a letter, dated August 17, 1752, said, "I find you grow more and more famous in the learned world. As you have made a pretty considerable progress in the mysteries of electricity, I would now humbly recommend to your diligent, unprejudiced pursuit and study, the mystery of the new birth. It is a most important, interesting study; and when, mastered, will richly answer and repay you for all your pains. One, at whose bar we are shortly to appear, hath solemnly declared without it we cannot enter the kingdom of heaven. You will excuse this freedom. I must have something of Christ in all my letters."

10,733. NEW BIRTH, Necessity of the. A Hindoo said to a native priest, "I am sure that if I lead a good life, and do what is right, giving up my bad habits, God will be pleased with me, and receive me into heaven." He replied, "You know the Babool tree (a tree with long and sharp thorns). Now, suppose you break off from its branches a hundred or more of the nasty thorns that it has, will the tree on that account cease to be a Babool tree? Certainly not. Suppose you should apparently succeed in breaking off one or another, or even many of your evil ways and habits, you would yet remain an evil tree, *i. e.*, a naturally bad man. You must have an entire new nature; must become a new man, in order to please God; and only Christ can give you a new heart."

10,734. NEW BIRTH, Need for. It makes but little difference whether a man give up the kingdom of heaven altogether or attempt to enter it without being "born again." In either case he continues dead in trespasses and sins. The difference is that of a corpse with all the offensive accompaniment of death upon it, and that of a dead man embalmed and his nakedness covered with goodly clothing. In the one case he lies in acknowledged lifelessness—in the other, his cadaverous form is clothed in garments, and placed in the attitude of life, so as to exclude the idea of death; but stiffened limbs, and a countenance of death-like expression in the mummy, betray its case.

Salter.

10,735. NEW BIRTH, Nobility of the. Our new birth makes us more honorable than our natural birth, let our birth-right dignities be what they will. The children of nobles are, by nature, the children of wrath, even as others; *Omnis sanguis concolor*, all blood is of one color: it is all tainted in Adam, and mingled together in his posterity. "There is no king," saith Seneca, "which rose not from a servant; there is no servant which rose not from a king." *Flavel.*

10,736. NEW BIRTH, Objections to the, Overcome. Cyprian, of Carthage, was of noble family, and was surrounded with all the advantages of wealth and rank. He rode through the city splendidly attired and attended by a pompous retinue. Heathen as he was, he staggered at the doctrine of the new birth. He wrote to Donatus, "I could not conceive how a man could receive the principles of a new life, cease to be what he was before, and become quite a new person, though retaining the same bodily constitution. How can I leave off, suddenly, old and radical customs? How can one who remains in the midst of the objects which have so long charmed his senses, strip himself of his former inclinations and inveterate habits, closely riveted in the very frame of his being? How rarely does a man become content with plain apparel and unornamented dress, who has been used to sparkle in gold, and jewels, and embroidered garments!" From such thoughts as these Cyprian concluded that any considerable change was impossible to him, despaired of a cure, and hugged the chain of his vicious practices, which had become a part of himself. In spite of all this unbelief the change came. He says, "The Spirit of God descended upon me, and I became a new creature. All my difficulties were surprisingly cleared, my doubts were resolved, and all my former darkness was dispelled. Things appeared easy to me which before I had looked upon as difficult and discouraging. I was convinced that I was able to do and suffer all that which before had seemed impossible. I then saw that the earthly principle which I derived from my first birth exposed me to sin and death, but that the new principle which I had received from the Spirit of God in the new birth, gave me new ideas and inclinations, and directed all my views to God." This shows how strikingly similar is the conversion of a heathen of the third century to that of a sinner of the nineteenth. It was followed by a life of eminent piety and the martyr's death.

10,737. NEW BIRTH, Waiting for the. Rev. C. P. Hard gives an account of a man who, from ten years of age, was profane, intemperate, and unrestrained in sin. Years of dissipation brought on delirium tremens. He then saw his degradation, and prayed earnestly to God for deliverance. Incessantly he prayed. At noon he stood between two large stores in the village street with closed eyes. People said he was drunk or crazy. Some one asked him why he stood there. He answered, "I am waiting to be born again." He was called to dinner, but refused to go. At supper time he stood there still praying and waiting. The transformation had begun. He soon rejoiced as a new creature in Christ, and demonstrated the change by a new life.

10,738. NEW JERUSALEM, Parallel of the. In its general plan, the symbolical city presents a striking resemblance to the description of Ecbatana, furnished by the father of secular history. "Of this city, one wall encompassed another, and each rose by the height of its battlements above the one beyond it. The ground, which was a circular hill, favored this construction; but it owed still more to the labors bestowed upon the work. The orbicular walls were seven in number; within the last stood the royal palace and the treasuries. The largest of the walls nearly equaled the circumference of Athens. The battlements of this outer wall were white; those of the second, black; of the third, purple; of the fourth, blue; of the fifth, orange; all the battlements being thus covered with a pigment. Of the last two walls, the battlements of the one were plated with silver, those of the other with gold. Thus the Median city consisted of seven circular terraces, each distinguished by the color of its wall; whereas the Apocalyptic city is described as a quadrangle of twelve stages or foundations; but the points of coincidence are highly illustrative of the emblematic description. The precious stones of which the walls of the holy city appeared to consist, whatever mystical or symbolical significance may attach to them, are obviously intended to describe the color of each resplendent elevation; and although the colors do not occur in the precise prismatic order, the combination would have the general effect of a double rainbow. *Josiah Conder.*

10,739. NEWSPAPERS, Power of. They preach to the people daily, weekly; admonishing kings themselves; advising peace or war with an authority which only the first reformers and a long-past class of popes were possessed of, inflicting moral censure; imparting moral encouragement, consolation, edification; in all ways diligently "administering the discipline of the church." It may be said, too, that in private disposition the new preachers somewhat resemble the mendicant friars of old times; outwardly, full of holy zeal; inwardly, not without stratagem, and hunger for terrestrial things. *Carlyle.*

10,740. NEW YEAR, Beginning of the. There exists a very beautiful custom in Germany, which it would be well to imitate everywhere. On the first day of the New Year, whatever may have been the quarrels or estrangement between friends and relatives, mutual visits are interchanged, kindly greetings given and received—all is forgotten and forgiven. Let this custom begin with reconciliation to God, then friendship and fellowship may be found that shall be blessed and lasting.

10,741. NIGHT, Study at. There is a reason why students prefer the night to the day for their labors. Through the day their thoughts are diverted into a thousand streams; but at night they settle into pools which, deep and undisturbed, reflect the stars. But night labor, in time, will destroy the student; for it is marrow from his own bones with which he fills his lamp.   *Beecher.*

10,742. NIGHT, Tranquillity of. I cannot think without admiration and gratitude on the tender care of Providence to secure us repose at night. When the day closes, a calm is spread over all nature, which proclaims to every creature a rest from labor, and invites mankind to sleep. During the time destined for the repose of man, nature, in favor of him, suspends noise, dazzling light, and every lively impression. All animals whose activity might disturb our sleep have themselves occasion to sleep. The birds seek their nests; the horse, the ox, and our other domestic animals sleep around us. But this tranquillity in the night is not equally agreeable to everybody. Many, who from pain, sickness, and other accidents, pass restless nights, wish this calm, this melancholy silence interrupted. Their sufferings and their uneasiness seem to increase, whilst all are asleep around them. They reckon the hours, and are impatient for day, in the hope that society will be some relief to them. Many wicked people also, who pass the day in continual disorder and dissipation, find the tranquillity of the night painful and troublesome. It awakens their conscience, and the least noise frightens them. Health and peace of mind procure the sweetest sleep. God has disposed all things happily to give us a quiet repose.   *Sturm.*

10,743. NIGHT, Works of. The day is given us to work in; and, therefore, in the morning, as soon as we have our day before us, we should endeavor "to walk honestly." Night-works are commonly works of uncleanness, violence, dishonor; and, therefore, want a cover of darkness to hide them. Thieves use to come in the night. The eye of the adulterer waiteth for the twilight, saying, "No eye shall see me"—and disguiseth himself. In the twilight, in the evening, in the black and dark night, he goeth to the house of the strange woman. The oppressor diggeth through houses in the dark. For "the morning is to them as the shadow of death." "They that are drunken, are drunken in the night." Sins are of the nature of some sullen weeds, which will grow nowhere but in the side of wells, and of dark places. But works of Christianity are neither unclean, nor dishonorable; they are beautiful and royal works, they are exemplary, and, therefore, public works; they are themselves light! "Let your light so shine before men;" and, therefore, they ought to be done in the light.   *Bp. Reynolds.*

10,744. NO, Absence of. It was said of the people of Asia that they were all slaves to one man, because they could not pronounce the word "No."

10,745. NO, Advice on. Learn to say—No! and it will be of more use to you than to be able to read Latin.   *Spurgeon.*

10,746. NO Described. No is a surly, honest fellow, speaks his mind rough and round at once.   *Scott.*

10,747. NO, Importance of. The monosyllable No, one of the easiest learned by the child, but the most difficult to practice by the man, contains within it the import of a life, and the weal or woe of an eternity.   *J. Johnson.*

10,748. NOBILITY, Patriotic. Epaminondas, through jealousy, was not chosen general in a war that needed a most skillful leader. One was taken who was little skilled in military arts, and Epaminondas went as a private. Disaster followed the new general, and the army was brought into almost inextricable difficulty. All looked inquiringly for Epaminondas. Regardless of the injury or the repulse they had offered him, he came forth cheerfully and delivered the army from its peril, and conducted it in safety home again.

10,749. NOBILITY, Real. We must have kings we must have nobles; nature is always providing such in every society; only let us have the real instead of the titular. In every society, some are born to rule, and some to advise. The chief is the chief all the world over, only not his cap and plume. It is only this dislike of the pretender which makes men sometimes unjust to the true and finished man.   *Emerson.*

10,750. NOBODY, Deeds of. The power of Nobody is becoming so enormous in England, and he alone is responsible for so many proceedings, both in the way of commission and omission; he hath so much to answer for, and is so constantly called to account; that a few remarks upon him may not be ill-timed. The hand which this surprising person had in the late war is amazing to consider. It was he who left the tents behind, who left the baggage behind, who chose the worst possible ground for encampments, who provided no means of transport, who killed the horses, who paralyzed the commissariat, who knew nothing of the business he proposed to know and monopolized, who decimated the English army. It was Nobody who gave out the famous unroasted coffee; it was Nobody who made the hospitals more horrible than language can describe; it was Nobody who occasioned all the dire confusion of Balaklava harbor; it was even Nobody who ordered the fatal Balaklava cavalry charge. The non-relief of Kars was the work of Nobody, and Nobody has justly and severely suffered for that infamous transaction. It is difficult for the mind to span the career of Nobody. The sphere of action opened to this wonderful person so enlarges every day, that the limited faculties of anybody are too weak to compass it.   *Anon.*

10,751. NON-RESISTANCE, Example of. A Swiss Bible peddler entered the cot of a peasant, and offered his wares. The man became enraged and with much abuse struck the peddler a heavy blow upon the cheek. The latter laid down his pack, then uncovered his arm and exhibited remarkably developed muscles, saying, "Look at my hand, its furrows show that I have worked; feel my muscles, they show that I am fit for any work; look me straight in the face. Do I quail before you? Judge then, for yourself, if it is fear that makes me do what I am about to. In this book my Master says, 'When they shall smite you on the one cheek turn to them the other, also.' You have smitten me on one cheek, here is the other; smite!" The man was overcome, his rage subsided, and he bought the Bible which held the secret of such self-control.

10,752. NON-RESISTANCE, Power of. Robert Barclay, the celebrated apologist of the Quakers, was attacked by highwaymen, in England, adhered to his non-resistance principles, and signally triumphed. The pistol was leveled at Barclay, and a determined demand made for his purse. Calm and self-possessed, he looked the robber in the face with a firm but meek benignity, assured him he was his and every man's friend, that he was willing and ready to relieve his wants, that he was free from the fear of death through a divine hope in immortality, and therefore was not to be intimidated by a deadly weapon; and then appealed to him, whether he could have the heart to shed the blood of one who had no other feeling or purpose but to do him good. The robber was confounded; his eye melted, his brawny arm trembled, his pistol fell to his side, and he fled from the presence of the non-resistant hero, whom he could no longer confront.   *Percy.*

10,753. NOTHING, Doing. "Curse ye Meroz. By whose authority? The angel of the Lord's. What has Meroz done? Nothing. Why then is Meroz to be cursed? Because he did nothing. What ought Meroz to have done? Come to the help of the Lord. Could not the Lord do without Meroz? The Lord did do without Meroz. Did the Lord sustain, then, any loss? No, but Meroz did. Is Meroz then to be cursed? Yes, and that bitterly. Is it right that a man should be cursed for doing nothing? Yes, when he ought to do something. Who says so? The angel of the Lord. 'That servant which knew his Lord's will, and did it not, shall be beaten with many stripes.' (Luke 12: 47.)"   *Anon.*

10,754. NOVELS, Evils of. Girls learn from such books to think coarsely and boldly about lovers and marrying; their early modesty is effaced by the craving for admiration; their warm affections are silenced by the desire for selfish triumph; they lose the fresh and honest feelings of youth while they are yet scarcely developed; they pass with sad rapidity from their early visions of Tancred and Orlando to notions of good connections, establishments, excellent matches, etc.; and yet they think, and their mammas think, that they are only advancing in "prudence" and knowledge of the world—that bad, contaminating knowledge of the world, which I sometimes imagine must have been the very apple that Eve plucked from the forbidden tree. Alas! when once tasted, the garden of life is an innocent and happy Paradise no more.   *Sala.*

10,755. NOVELS, Injury by. It cannot but be injurious to the human mind never to be called into effort. The habit of receiving pleasure without any exertion of thought, by the mere excitement of curiosity and sensibility, may be justly ranked among the worst effects of habitual novel-reading. Like idle morning visitors, the brisk and breathless periods hurry in and hurry off in quick and profitless succession; each, indeed, for the moment of its stay, prevents the pain of vacancy, while it indulges the love of sloth; but altogether they leave the mistress of the house—the soul, I mean—flat and exhausted, incapable of attending to her own concerns, and unfitted for the conversation of more rational guests.   *Coleridge.*

10,756. NOVELTY, Charms of. Novelty has charms that our minds can hardly withstand. The most valuable things, if they have for a long while appeared among us, do not make any impression as they are good, but give us a distaste as they are old. But when the influence of this fantastical humor is over, the same men or things will come to be admired again, by a happy return of our good taste.   *Thackeray.*

10,757. NOVELTY, Seeking for. Before I translated the New Testament out of the Greek, all longed after it; when it was done, their longing lasted scarce four weeks. Then they desired the books of Moses; when I had translated these, they had enough thereof in a short time. After that, they would have the Psalms; of these they were soon weary, and desired other books. So it will be with the book of Ecclesiastes, which they now long for, and about which I have taken great pains. All is acceptable until our giddy brains be satisfied; afterwards we let things lie, and seek after new.   *Luther.*

10,758. NOW, Opinions about. One of our poets (Cowley) speaks of an "everlasting now." If such a condition of existence were offered to us in this world, and it were put to the vote whether we should accept the offer and fix all things immutably as they are, who are they whose voices would be given in the affirmative? Not those who are in pursuit of fortune, or of fame, or of knowledge, or of enjoyment, or of happiness; though with regard to all of these, as far as any of them are attainable, there is more pleasure in the pursuit than in the attainment. Not those who are at sea, or traveling in a stage coach. Not the man who is shaving himself. Not those who have the toothache, or who are having a tooth drawn. The fashionable beauty might; and the fashionable singer, and the fashionable opera dancer, and the actor who is in the height of his power and reputation. So might the alderman at a city feast. So would the heir who is squandering a large fortune faster than it was accumulated for him. And the thief who is not taken. And the convict who is not hanged; and the scoffer at religion, whose heart belies his tongue. Not the wise and the good. Not those who are in sickness or in sorrow. Not I.   *Southey*

10,759. NOW, Rejecting Christ. A pastor urged a young lady of his congregation and Sabbath-school to come to Jesus now. She impatiently answered, "You are always urging me now, now. I cannot see the need of such great hurry." "I have no authority to preach or teach any other gospel." "O, well, I'll risk it," she defiantly replied, as she started on a summer's pleasure trip. A tragic end in a burning steamer on the Hudson river closed the short chapter of her life.

10,760. OATH, Fidelity to an. John the First, King of France, was overthrown in battle, and made prisoner by Edward the Black Prince, afterwards taken into England. He remained a prisoner four years, and was then suffered to return to France upon certain conditions, which, if he could make his subjects agree to, he should be free; if otherwise, he promised by oath to return. He could not prevail upon them to accept the hard terms that were proffered, so he returned to England, and there died.

10,761. OATHS, Reliable. Louis, the French king, was taken prisoner by Meletisaka, the Sultan; and conditions of peace being concluded between them, for more assurance thereof, the Sultan offered to swear, if he failed in performance of anything, to renounce his Mohammed; requiring likewise of the king to swear, if he failed in anything that he had promised, to deny his Christ to be God: which profane oath the king detesting, and wishing rather to die than give the same, the Sultan, wondering at his constancy, took his word without any oath at all, and so published the league. *Trapp.*

10,762. OBEDIENCE, Advantage of. A poor man applied to Stephen Girard, saying that he was ready to do anything that would bring him an honest living. "I will give you a dollar a day," said Girard. "You take that pile of stones that you see in the end of the lot, and carry them to the other side and pile them up in the same manner that they are now." The man did the job and received his dollar. Next morning he reappeared and was sent by his strange employer to replace the stones as he first found them. So the laborer wrought faithfully every day for a week, carrying the stones from one place to another without a murmur or question. On Saturday night the eccentric banker said to him, "I like you, there is no nonsense about you; you do what you are told to do. Many men would have objected to doing the work over and over. You shall have work as long as I have anything for anybody to do." Such servants the Lord wants.

10,763. OBEDIENCE, Angelic. A teacher was explaining to her class the words concerning God's angels, "ministers of his who do his pleasure," and asked: "How do the angels carry out God's will?" Many answers followed. One said: "They do it directly." Another: "They do it with all their heart." A third: "They do it well." And after a pause a quiet little girl added: "They do it without asking any questions."

10,764. OBEDIENCE, Duty of. An officer who had received his orders from the Duke of Wellington, urged the impossibility of executing them. Wellington replied, "I did not ask your opinion; I gave you my orders, and expect them to be obeyed." Implicit obedience is required of every soldier of Christ.

> Ours not to reason why;
> Ours not to make reply;
> Ours but to do or die.

10,765. OBEDIENCE, Enforced. The little son of the commander of an American man-of-war lying in the Bay of Naples, one day climbed the rigging and stood upon the main truck, at the very top of the mast. The sailors looked at him in amazement. The father coming on deck discovered his peril. Should the boy fall upon deck his death was sure. His father seized a gun, and bringing it to his shoulder, shouted through his speaking trumpet, "Jump into the water, or I'll shoot you!" He obeyed, cleared the ship's side, and was soon rescued by the sailors. His father's apparent cruelty was the truest love, and his only salvation.

10,766. OBEDIENCE, Exceptions to. I hear much of "obedience;" how that the kindred virtues are prescribed and exemplified by Jesuitism; the truth of which, and the merit of which, far be it from me to deny. Obedience, a virtue universally forgotten in these days, will have to become universally known again. Obedience is good and indispensable; but if it be obedience to what is wrong and false, there is no name for such a depth of human cowardice and calamity, spurned everlastingly by the gods. Loyalty! Will you be loyal to Beelzebub? Will you make "a covenant with death and hell?" I will not be loyal to Beelzebub; I will become a nomadic Choctaw rather, a barricading *Sans culotte*, a Conciliation-hall repealer; anything and everything is venial to that. *Carlyle.*

10,767. OBEDIENCE, Fruit of. St. John, the dwarf, an anchoret of Scete, was ordered by his superior to plant a dry staff in the ground, and water it daily, till it should bring forth fruit. The river was at a far distance, and the way over the hot sand; but the dwarf obeyed the order implicitly, without a murmur, or speaking one word for three years, when the stick put forth leaves and blossoms, and bore fruit. The hermit who gave the order gathered the fruit, carried it to the church, and gave it to the brethren, saying, "Take and eat the fruit of obedience."

10,768. OBEDIENCE, Happiness of. It is foolish to strive with what we cannot avoid; we are born subjects, and to obey God is perfect liberty: he that does this, shall be free, safe, and quiet; all his actions shall succeed to his wishes. *Seneca.*

10,769. OBEDIENCE, Implicit. One of the attendants of the Emperor Tiberius was celebrated for his unfailing obedience to the wishes of his master. He was asked, if he had been ordered to burn the Capitol, whether he would have done it. He answered that Tiberius would never have given him the order; but if he had, he should have thought it right and should have obeyed it, for Tiberius would never have laid such a command on him if it had not been for the advantage of the Roman people. God is infallible, and his commands make right. Obedience to them must characterize his people.

10,770. OBEDIENCE, Light and. Jesus Christ intended, when he opened your eyes, that your eyes should direct your feet. Light is a special help to obedience, and obedience is a singular help to increase your light.　　*Flavel.*

10,771. OBEDIENCE, No Substitute for. Pachomius, abbot of the monastery of Tabenna, was informed that no salads or cooked vegetables had been served on the table for a long time, though the rules required it. He sought the cook and inquired, "What is there for dinner to-day?" "Bread and salt." "But the rule commands vegetables and soup." "My father, so many of the monks deny themselves any thing except bread, and it is such trouble preparing the vegetables and salads, and besides it is so disappointing to see them come from the table almost untouched, when I have spent so much time in getting them ready, that I thought I could employ my time more profitably in making mats." Having learned the time of this neglect the abbot said, "Bring all the mats thou hast made and show them to me." So the cook with much pride placed a great pile of them before the abbot. He seized a fire brand and set them all in a blaze, saying, "What! withdraw from some of the monks the opportunity of denying themselves, and those who are sickly the necessary delicacies, and from the young their needful support, because it gives thee a little trouble, and because thou thoughtest to do better by plaiting." To obey is better than sacrifice.

10,772. OBEDIENCE, Order of. There is one commandment that must go foremost, and make a way for all the rest; and this is his commandment, that ye should believe on his Son whom he has sent. To be reconciled unto God through the death of his Son, this is the one thing needful to all true obedience; and so especially this law of God, that in every thing we should pray to him and give thanks, cannot be put in practice by an alienated and suspicious heart.　　*Arnot.*

10,773. OBEDIENCE, Oriental. Zunchinius, Emperor of China, was determined to rid himself of Gueio, a high government official. He sent him to visit the tombs of his ancestors; but he had not gone far when he sent him a silver box with a silk halter folded neatly in it. Gueio understood by this that he was commanded to hang himself, which he did accordingly.

10,774. OBEDIENCE, Oriental Proverbs of. "Young man, talk not to me with infant wisdom what are the sayings of the ancients. You ought to obey your parents. Listen: 'The father and the mother are the first deities a child has to acknowledge.' Is it not said, 'Children who obey willingly are as ambrosia to the gods?'"

10,775. OBEDIENCE, Parable of. A fox, seeing the fish in great trouble, darting hither and thither, while the stream was being drawn with nets, proposed to them to leap on dry land. This is put in a Rabbi's mouth, who, when the Graeco-Syrian kings were threatening with death all who observe the law, was counseled by his friends to abandon it. He would say, "We, like the fish in the stream, are indeed in danger now; but yet, while we continue in obedience to God, we are in our element; but if, to escape the danger, we forsake that, then we inevitably perish."　　*R. C. Trench.*

10,776. OBEDIENCE, Sacrifice and. Deut. 27: 1–8. The memorial remembrance of the law. The connection is very striking of this ordinance. They were to write the law upon the stones on Ebal, and to build an altar close by, to signify that the law was to be kept before them; and no less that we cannot look upon the law with comfort apart from the altar, which represents sacrifice and atonement.　　*Bowes.*

10,777. OBEDIENCE, Trifling. Deut. 22: 6, 7.— The bird's nest. The Jews say that this is "the least commandment." It is striking that for so small a matter, so weighty a motive should be assigned! Is not this to teach us that the smallest matters should be regulated by the principles of the highest law? As in a map of small dimensions, the prick of a pin may represent the space of a hundred miles, so in the law of God, obedience or neglect of the least commandment may involve the smile or frown of God the Judge!　　*Bowes.*

10,778. OBEDIENCE, Unconditional. The Chasians among the Syrians were in the habit of obeying their superiors at the cost of their lives. At the first intimation from their king, they would throw themselves headlong from rocks and towers, leap into the waves, or throw themselves into the fire. When Henry Earl of Campania passed through their country, the Prince of the Chasians wished to show the Earl the strange obedience of his people. Seeing several persons standing on the top of a high tower, he called to one of them by name. At this he threw himself down in their presence, and immediately died. The prince desired to give other commands, but the earl, horrified, begged him to desist.

10,779. OBEDIENCE, Unquestioning. St. John, the dwarf, was the most noted for his unquestioning, uncomplaining and enduring obedience of any in the long roll of monastic worthies. He had a capricious director who laid upon him the most unreasonable tasks. On one occasion he ordered him to throw their dinner out of the window, which was obeyed. At another time the old monk wished to exhibit the docility of his disciple, and commanded John to roll a huge rock up to his door, an impossible task. Without a question John ran to it, put his shoulder against it, and did his best to perform the work, till recalled by his master. This discipline only served to perfect his self-subjugation.

10,780. OBLIGATION, Biblical Figures of. *Servants,* entrusted with a master's property,

Matt. 25: 14–30; Luke 19: 12–27; Mark 13: 34–36. *Stewards*, Luke 12: 42; 1 Cor. 4: 1, 2; 1 Pet. 4: 10. *Husbandmen* in charge of the vineyard, Mark 12: 1–9. *Debtors*, Rom. 1: 14; 8: 12; Gal. 5: 3 (marg). *Wives*, bound during the husband's lifetime, Rom. 7: 2. *Teachers*, who must expect a stricter judgment, and if unfaithful, look for a heavier condemnation than other men, James 3: 1 (Greek). *Ministers*, under shepherds, responsible to the great Master and Head, 1 Cor. 4: 1; Matt. 23: 8; 1 Pet. 5: 4.   *Bowes.*

10,781. OBLIVION, Human. Oblivion is not to be hired: the greatest part must be content to be as though they had not been; to be found in the register of God, not in the record of man. Twenty-seven names make up the first story before the flood; and the recorded names ever since contain not one living century. The number of the dead long exceedeth all that shall live. The night of time far surpasseth the day, and who knows when was the equinox? Every hour adds unto that current arithmetic which scarce stands one moment. And since death must be the Lucina of life— and even Pagans could doubt whether thus to live were to die—since our longest sun sets at right descensions, and makes but winter arches, and therefore it cannot be long before we lie down in darkness, and have our light in ashes —since the brother of death daily haunts us with dying mementos, and time, that grows old in itself, bids us hope no long duration, diuturnity is a dream, and folly of expectation.   *Browne.*

10,782. OBSCURITY, Ministerial. Queen Caroline, consort of George II., in conversation one day with Archbishop Blackburn, asked him if Mr. Butler, the famous author of the "Analogy," while yet a country rector, was dead. "No madam," was the reply. Mr. Butler is not dead, but he is buried!"—alluding to his close retirement in the country parish of Stanhope.

10,783. OBSERVATION, The Pleasures of. What a large volume of adventures may be grasped within this little span of life, by him who interests his heart in everything; and who, having eyes to see what time and chance are perpetually holding out to him as he journeyeth on his way, misses nothing he can fairly lay his hands on! I pity the man who can travel from Dan to Beersheba, and cry—"'Tis all barren." And so it is; and so is all the world to him who will not cultivate the fruit it offers. "I declare," said I, clapping my hands cheerily together, "that were I in a desert, I would find out wherewith in it to call forth my affections. If I could do no better, I would fasten them upon some sweet myrtle, or seek some melancholy cypress to connect myself to. I would court their shade, and greet them kindly for their protection. I would cut my name upon them, and swear they were the loveliest trees throughout the desert; if their leaves withered, I would teach myself to mourn; and when they rejoiced, I would rejoice along with them."   *Sterne*

10,784. OBSERVATIONS, General. General observations drawn from particulars are the jewels of knowledge, comprehending great store in a little room; but they are therefore to be made with the greater care and caution, lest, if we take counterfeit for true, our loss and shame be the greater when our stock comes to a severe scrutiny.   *Locke.*

10,785. OBSERVERS, Superficial. There are some persons that never arrive at any deep, solid, or valuable knowledge in any science, or any business of life, because they are perpetually fluttering over the surface of things, in a curious or wandering search of infinite variety; ever hearing, reading, or asking after something new, but impatient of any labor to lay up and preserve the ideas they have gained: their souls may be compared to a looking-glass, that wheresoever you turn it, it receives the images of all objects, but retains none.   *Dr. Watts.*

10,786. OBSTINACY, Folly of. The American turkey is a silly bird; and the French call a person a *dindon* (a turkey) whom we, with less propriety, call a goose, that being very far from a silly bird. In America they are said to entrap the wild turkey through their silliness. On a slope, at the edge, of a wood a kind of pen is made with sticks and covered over. At the lowest part an opening is left, sufficient to admit a turkey; and corn is strewn within and without the pen to entice them in. When they have entered, they might escape by simply descending to the entrance, and walking out the way they walked in. But, instead of this, they vainly beat against the sides of the pen till the trapper comes and dispatches them. Many featherless bipeds are like these turkeys. When it is plainly proved that you have formed a rash judgment, or taken an unwise step, the right course manifestly is to confess this, and retract and retrace your steps. But most men are too much of turkeys to do this. Usually, when a man finds himself in a pen, and there is no thoroughfare, rather than descend so far as to own a mistake, and walk out of the error the same way he had walked into it, he will resort to every kind of shuffle. He will insist on it that he was quite right all along, but that there has been a change in some of the people or in the circumstances. Or perhaps he will flatly deny that he ever said so and so, or maintain that he was misunderstood—anything rather than retract and acknowledge an error. And yet a man who does this frankly will usually obtain great applause for his candor and good sense; even more perhaps than he would have had if he had avoided the error from the first. Yet even this will not tempt most men to take the ingenuous and wise course. They are too much like the turkeys.   *F. F. Trench.*

10,787. OBSTINACY, Human. When the dove was weary she recollected the ark, and flew into Noah's hand at once: there are weary souls who know the ark, but will not fly to it. When an Israelite had slain, inadvertently, his fellow, he knew the city of refuge, he feared the avenger of blood, and he fled along the road to the place of safety; but multitudes know the refuge, and every Sabbath we set up the sigr-posts along the road, but yet they come not to find salvation. The destitute waifs and strays of the streets of London find out the night refuge and ask for shelter; they cluster round our workhouse doors like sparrows under the eaves of a building on a rainy day; they piteously crave for lodging and a crust of bread; yet crowds of poor benighted spirits, when the house of mercy is lighted up, and the invitation is plainly written in bold letters, "Whosoever will, let him turn in hither," will not come.   *Spurgeon.*

10,788. OBSTRUCTION, Example of. In Scotland two sailors who had been drinking heavily, took their boat to pull off to the ship; but after rowing some time, as they made no progress, each accused the other of want of effort. Again they tried, but with no better success. Finally after an hour's work, when they had become a little sobered, one of them happened to look over the side, and discovered the difficulty. "Why, Sandy," said he, "we haven't pulled the anchor up!" So here, the sins of many seem to hold them fast; but if they will break off their sins by repentance, they can pull off in safety.

10,789. OBSTRUCTIONIST, A Model. A dog made his bed in a manger, and lay snarling and growling to keep the oxen from their provender. "See," said one of them, "what a miserable cur! who can neither eat hay himself, nor will allow those to eat who can."   *Æsop.*

10,790. OCCUPATION, Adaptation to. Patrick Henry, after a vagrant boyhood, passed in fishing and hunting, was established in a country store by his father. At the end of the first year he failed. He married at the age of eighteen, and the parents of the young couple gave them a farm. Two years of farming showed his failure as a farmer. Another trial of merchandising proved another failure. He then read law for six weeks, and after an examination before John Randolph, was admitted to the bar. For four years he was a briefless barrister. The case of the "People against the Parsons," brought out his powers, and he rose at once to the first place. He had at last found his vocation. From that time to be eloquent as "Patrick against the Parsons," was the highest compliment that could be paid to an orator. The moral of all this is, "If at first you don't succeed," try something else.

10,791. OCCUPATION, Bias of. There was a city in expectation of being besieged, and a council was called accordingly to discuss the best means of fortifying it. A bricklayer gave his opinion that no material was so good as brick for the purpose. A carpenter begged leave to suggest that timber would be far preferable. Upon which a currier started up, and said, "Sirs, when you have said all that can be said, there is nothing in the world like leather."   *Æsop.*

10,792. OCCUPATION, Blindness of. An under-

taker visited the Centennial Exhibition, which contained a vast collection of the treasures of art and industry, and reported that he saw nothing there but one fine hearse and some nice coffins.

10,793. OCCUPATION, Happiness of. Occupation was one of the pleasures of Paradise, and we cannot be happy without it. *Mrs. Jameson.*

10,794. OCCUPATION, Idolatry of. A blacksmith, who had been employed one day on the Mission premises in India, took away his tools next morning for the purpose of worshiping them, it being the day on which the Hindoos pay divine honors to the implements of their various trades; the files and hammers of the smiths, the chisels and saws of the carpenter, the diamond of the glazier, the crucible of the goldsmith, etc., etc., all become idols on this anniversary.   *Whitecross.*

10,795. OCEAN, Descriptions of the. A lady, on seeing the sea at Brighton for the first time, exclaimed, "What a beautiful field!" She had never seen such a beautiful green, moving, sparkling, grassy prairie. Mr. Leigh Hunt lavished a page of admiration in *The Liberal* upon a line of Ariosto's describing the waves as "Neptune's white herds lowing o'er the deep." Anacreon exclaims, in language appropriate to calm seas and smooth sand-beaches, "How the waves of the sea kiss the shore!" Saint-Lambert, in his Saisons, has four lines descriptive of the waves of a stormy sea dashing upon the beach, which have been much admired by writers upon imitative harmony. "Neptune has raised up his turbulent plains, the sea falls and leaps upon the trembling shores. She remounts, groans, and with redoubled blows makes the abyss and the shaken mountains resound."   *Household Words.*

10,796. OFFENCE, Cherishing. Dogs bark at all persons indifferently; so if thou persecutest everybody that offends thee, thou wilt bring the matter to this pass by thy imprudence, that all things will flow down into this imbecility of thy mind, as a place void and capable of receiving them, and at last thou wilt be filled with nothing but other men's miscarriages.   *Plutarch.*

10,797. OFFENCE, Common. Dr. Richie, divinity professor in the University of Edinburgh, was thus addressed by one of his hearers, "Sir, you have insulted me to-day in the church. I have been three times in church lately, and on every one of them you have been holding me up to the derision of the audience; so I tell you, sir, I shall never more enter the church of Tarbolton again, unless you give me your solemn promise, that you will abstain from such topics in future, as I am resolved I shall no more furnish you with the theme of your discourse." The faithful preacher often finds his words so applied as to make the hearer think he has learned of his secret sins.

10,798. OFFERING, Savor of the. Christ's offering was "a sweet-smelling savor" unto God. The meaning is, that as men are offended with a nauseous smell, and on the contrary delighted with sweet odors and fragrance, so the blessed

God, speaking after the manner of men, is offended, and filled with loathing and abhorrence by our sins; but infinitely pleased and delighted in the offering of Christ for them, which came up as an odor of sweet-smelling savor to him, whereof the costly perfumes under the laws were types and shadows. Isa. 53: 10.

John Flavel.

10,799. OFFERINGS, Christ in the. Christ is the offering, Christ is the priest, Christ is the offerer. He comes as offerer, but we cannot see the offerer without the offering, and the offerer is himself the offering, and he who is both offerer and offering is also the priest. As man under the law, our substitute, Christ, stood for us toward God as offerer. He took "the body prepared for him" as his offering, that in it and by it he might reconcile us to God. Thus when sacrifice and offering had wholly failed, when at man's hand God would no more accept them, then said he, "Lo, I come." Thus his body was his offering; he willingly offered it; and then, as priest, he took the blood into the holiest. As offerer, we see him man under the law, standing our substitute, for us to fulfill all righteousness. As priest, we have him presented as the mediator, God's messenger between himself and Israel. While as the offering he is seen the innocent victim, a sweet savor to God, yet bearing the sin and dying for it. Thus in the self-same type the offerer sets forth Christ in his person, as the one who became man to meet God's requirements; the offering presents him in his character and work, as the victim by which the atonement was ratified; while the priest gives us a third picture of him, in his official relation, as the appointed mediator and intercessor. Accordingly, when we have a type in which the offering is most prominent, the leading thought will be Christ the victim. On the other hand, when the offerer or priest predominates, it will respectively be Christ as man or Christ as mediator. *A. Jukes.*

10,800. OFFERINGS, Sin in Our. Leaven is mixed with the choicest offerings of the most devoted Christians. But our God has foreseen and provided for it. Thus at the offering at Pentecost, and the oblation with the Peace-offering (appointed emblems of the church's offering), leavened cakes were offered to the Lord; but though accepted, they could not be burnt as a sweet savor. No measure of oil, that is, the Spirit, could counteract the effect of leaven. A cake might be anointed again and again, but if there had been leaven in its composition, it could not be put upon the altar. What a lesson for those who are looking for the Spirit in them rather than to Christ for them as the ground of acceptance. *A. Jukes.*

10,801. OFFICE, Disappointed Seeker of. Paedaretus, when he was not chosen among the three hundred, (which was the highest office and honor in the city), went away cheerfully and smiling, saying he was glad if the city had three hundred better citizens than himself.

Plutarch.

10,802. OFFICE, Love of. Profligacy in taking office is so extreme, that we have no doubt public men may be found, who for half a century would postpone all remedies for a pestilence, if the preservation of their places depended upon the propagation of the virus.

S. Smith.

10,803. OFFICE-SEEKERS, Hungry. A fox, while crossing a river, was driven by the stream into a narrow gorge, and lay there for a long time, unable to get out, covered with myriads of horse-flies that had fastened themselves upon him. A hedgehog, who was wandering in that direction, saw him; and, taking compassion on him, asked him if he should drive away the flies that were so tormenting him. But the fox begged him to do nothing of the sort. "Why not?" asked the hedgehog. "Because," replied the fox, "these flies that are upon me now, are already full, and draw but little blood; but should you remove them, a swarm of fresh and hungry ones will come, who will not leave a drop of blood in my body."

Æsop.

10,804. OLD, Fear of Growing. Among the various follies by which we increase the natural and unavoidable miseries of life, is the dread of approaching age. The sight of a gray hair has often caused a severer pang than the loss of a child or a husband. After a certain age, every returning birth-day is saluted with silent sorrow, and we conceal the number of our years with as much solicitude as the consciousness of an atrocious crime. *Dr. Knox.*

10,805. OLD AGE, Decay in. An old man of three-score and ten was cutting down a decayed tree, and was deeply impressed that it represented himself. Body and soul were decayed. The conviction led him to prayer, to Christ and to a good hope of immortal life.

10,806. OLD AGE, Need of Christ in. Mr. Edward Riddell, an aged Christian in Hull, England, remarked, a few days before his death, "Some may suppose that a person at my time of life, and after so long making a profession of religion, has nothing to do but to die and go to heaven; but I find that I have as much need to go to God, through Christ, as a sinner, at the last hour as at the beginning. The blood of Christ, the death of Christ, his victory and fullness, are my only ground of faith, hope and confidence; there is the same need of him to be the Finisher of my faith as there was to be the Author of it." *Whitecross.*

10,807. OLD AGE, Redemption of Time in. A sibyl came to Tarquinius Superbus, King of Rome, and brought nine volumes of a book, demanding a high price for them. Thinking it too much, he refused, and she immediately burned three, demanding for the six the price of the nine. He still declined to give it, and she burned three more, asking the full sum for the remaining three. He, thinking there must be something extraordinary in the books, and fearing to lose them all, gave for the three the price he had refused for nine. So time, as it dwindles, grows more valuable. There are three divisions of man's life—youth, manhood, and old age; and ministers advise men to redeem all this time—youth, manhood, and old age; but in youth men conceive the price they are required to pay in self-denial too great, and they spend it in folly. In manhood they are again advised to redeem the remainder, but they still think the price too great. And then, perhaps, when it comes to the last stage of their lives, they are glad enough to redeem what remains; but here the case is different. The sibyl still demanded but the same price for the remaining three which she had asked for all the nine; but the old, if they are induced to redeem the time at all, which is very unlikely, will have to pay more for the last volumes than they were asked for the whole number at the first; the habit of sinning so greatly increases the difficulty of turning to God. *F. F. Trench.*

10,808. OLD AGE, Reward in. A military gentleman visiting the Rev. John Martin, who had long been in ill-heath, remarked, "If I had power over the pension list, I would put you on half pay for your long and faithful services." Mr. M. replied, "Your master may put you off with half pay in your old age, but my Master will not serve me so meanly. He will give me full pay. Through grace I expect a full reward."

10,809. OLD AGE, Spiritual Growth in. Pliny writes of the crocodile, that she grows to her last day. (Hosea 14: 5-7.) So aged saints; they grow rich in spiritual experiences to the last. An old Christian, being once asked if he grew in goodness, answered, "Yea, doubtless I do; for God hath said, 'The righteous shall flourish like the palm tree.'" (Ps. 92: 12-14.) "Now, the palm tree never loseth his leaf or fruit," saith Pliny; "he shall grow like a cedar in Lebanon." "They shall still bring forth fruit in old age; they shall be fat and flourishing." *Brooks.*

10,810. OLD AGE, Temptations in. An old man said, "I am eighty-two years of age, and God has graciously given me, among many mercies, the mercy of being made sensible of his goodness. I remember, in my boyhood, hearing an aged minister declare from the pulpit, that when he was forty years old he considered himself so good, that he believed the temptations of Satan had no power over him; but when he was three-score and ten, he was obliged to confess that Satan had a bait for old birds still. I am eighty-two; and, as the minister found at three-score years and ten, so I find at eighty-two, that I am a poor, weak, worthless creature, totally dependent on God's goodness and grace, feeling every day of my life that Satan has a bait for old birds still."

10,811. OMNIPOTENCE, Divine. Power is that glorious attribute of God Almighty which furnishes the rest of his perfections. 'Tis his omnipotence that makes his wisdom and goodness effectual, and succeed to the length of his will. Thus his decrees are immutable, and his counsels stand; this secures his prerogative, and guards the sovereignty of his being; 'twas his power which made his ideas fruitful, and struck the world out of his thought. 'Twas this which answered the model of the creation, gave birth to time and nature, and brought them forth at his first call; thus, he spake the word, and they were made; he commanded, and they were created. 'Tis the Divine power which is the basis of all things, which continues the vigor of the second causes, and keeps the sun and moon in repair. This holds everything constant to appointment, and true to the first plan; thus, the revolutions of the seasons, the support of animals, the perpetuity of species, is carried on and maintained. Without this, things would soon run riot, and ramble out of distinction; the succors of life would be cut off, and nature drop into decay. Omniscience and goodness without a correspondent power would be strangely short of satisfaction; to know everything, without being able to supply defects and remedy disorders, must prove an unpleasant speculation; to see so many noble schemes languish in the mind and prove abortive, to see the most consummate wisdom, the most generous temper, fettered and disarmed, must be a grievance; but when omnipotence comes into the notion, the grandeur is perfect and the pleasure entire. *Jeremy Collier.*

10,812. OMNIPOTENCE, Resisting. If you would shrink from resisting the authority of a sovereign, who has judges, and officers, and armies, and navies, in his control, then, how can you ever dare, how can you ever wish to dare to confront the power and majesty of the Eternal One;—of that One who can enwrap the heavens with his thunder clouds, and make you the mark of all their volleyed lightnings; who can array his volcanoes in battalions, and bury you beneath their molten lavas; who can sink you in the earth's central fires, to lie without consuming in that seething cauldron, or imprison you in the eternal solitudes of polar ice; or—unspeakably more terrible than all this—can turn your own soul inward in retrospection upon its past life, to read its own history of voluntary wrong, in its self-recorded Book of Judgment? Nor can you find refuge in non-existence. You may call upon the seas to drown you, but there is not water enough in all the seas. You may call upon the fires to consume you, but the fires will say, we cannot consume remorse. You may call upon arctic frost to congeal the currents of life, but they will say, we have no power over the currents of thought, or the pulses of immortal life. You may call upon the universe to annihilate you, but the universe will respond, "God alone can annihilate; and God will say, live forever." *Horace Mann.*

10,813. OMNIPOTENCE, Using. The order of nature is not that we should do things, but that we should make one thing do another. Direct lifting is displeasing to the Supreme intelligence. He furnishes all forces; he has no conceivable poverty of power. All drafts upon Omnipotence leave it undiminished. So he simply wishes us to seize and use his forces. We are not doers, but causers. We are combiners. We are to touch levers, work keys open valves, harness energies. This is our work in the world.   *Dr. Fowler.*

10,814. OMNIPRESENCE, Divine. God is everywhere present by his power. He rolls the orbs of heaven with his hand; he fixes the earth with his foot, he guides all the creatures with his eye, and refreshes them with his influence; he makes the powers of hell to shake with his terrors, and binds the devils with his word, and throws them out with his command; and sends the angels on embassies with his decrees; he hardens the joints of infants, and confirms the bones when they are fashioned secretly in the earth; he it is that assists at the numerous production of fishes, and there is not one hollowness in the bottom of the sea but he shows himself to be the Lord of it, by sustaining there the creatures that come to dwell in it; and in the wilderness, the vulture and the stork, the dragon and the satyr, the unicorn and the elk, live upon his provisions, and revere his power, and feel the force of his almightiness. Let everything represent to your spirit the presence, the excellency, and the power of God.   *Jeremy Taylor.*

10,815. OMNIPRESENCE, Elevation by. There is something in the thought of being surrounded, even upon earth, by the Majesty on high, that gives a peculiar elevation and serenity of soul. To be assured in the loneliest hour of unknown or neglected sorrow, that every sigh ascends to the eternal Throne, and every secret prayer can be heard in heaven; to feel that, in every act of conscious rectitude, the heart can appeal, amidst all the contradictions of sinners, to One who seeth not as man seeth, produces a peace which the world can never give. Feeling itself, like Enoch walking with God, the heart perceives a spirituality and purity in every joy, a mercy and a balm in every sorrow, and, exalted above the intrusions of an intermeddling world, has its "conversation in heaven."   *Mathew.*

10,816. OMNIPRESENCE, Escape from. A very little girl was warned of the danger of lying by her mother, and told the fate of Ananias and Sapphira. She thought it easy enough to escape, and said, " I would run up the street." Many larger people act on this foolish idea. Men ask in vain, "Whither shall I flee from thy presence?" They may get beyond the jurisdiction of the laws of states and nations for punishment or extradition, but they cannot cross the boundary of God's empire, or escape for a moment the presence of his Spirit.

10,817. OMNIPRESENCE, Praying to. To God belongeth the east and the west, therefore whithersoever ye turn yourselves to pray, there is the face of God; for God is omnipresent and omniscient.   *From the Koran.*

10,818. OMNISCIENCE, Emblem of. What would you say, if wherever you turned, whatever you were doing, whatever thinking, whether in public or private, with a confidential friend telling your secrets, or alone planning them—if, I say, you saw an eye constantly fixed on you, from whose watching, though you strove ever so much, you could never escape;

and even if you closed your own eye to avoid, you still fancied that to get rid of was impossible, that it could perceive your every thought? The supposition is awful enough. There is such an eye, though the business and struggles of the world too often prevent us from considering this awful truth. In crowds we are too much interrupted, in the pursuit of self-interest we are too much perverted, in camps we are struggling for life and death, in courts we see none but the eye of a human sovereign; nevertheless, the Divine eye is always upon us, and when we least think of it, is noting all, and, whatever we may think of it, will remember all.   *De Vere.*

10,819. OMNISCIENCE, Forgotten. Cato was so grave and so good a man, that none would behave unseemly in his presence: whence it grew to a proverbial caveat, "Take heed what you do, for Cato sees you!" How reproachful it is to us, that the eyes of a man should have more effect upon our manners, than the penetrating eyes of God!   *Secker.*

10,820. OMNISCIENCE, Infinitude of. Momus, one of the heathen gods, is said to have complained of Vulcan, that he had not set a grate at every man's breast. God hath a glazed window in the darkest houses of clay: he sees what is done in them, when none other can. To God's omnipotence there is nothing impossible; and to God's omniscience there is nothing invisible. I never look for those persons to swallow gnats, who will easily and greedily swallow camels.   *Secker.*

10,821. OMNISCIENCE, Records of. As it was said of the Doomsday Book prepared by the Norman king, that *nec lacus, nec lucus, nec locus*— neither lake, nor grove, nor spot of earth— in all the realm of England, was omitted from the inventory, so he who " knows our thoughts long before" will have in his remembrance every act of our lives, every secret and forgotten sin, and at the last day they will be trumpeted forth from the highest battlement of heaven.   *Pilkington.*

10,822. OMNISCIENCE, Restraint of. Hans Christian Andersen, the popular Danish writer, when a boy, was out with his mother gleaning, in the fields of a man who was said to be very cruel. They saw him coming, and all started to run away. But Hans's clumsy wooden shoes came off; the stubble, or short stumps of the grain-stalk which had been left by the reapers, hurt his tender feet, so that he could not keep up with the others; and he found that he must be caught. The rough owner of the field was very near, and could now almost reach him with his heavy whip; when Hans, whose hopeless case now suddenly filled him with new courage, stopped and turned, and looking into the man's face said, " How dare you strike me, when God can see you?" The anger of the man was subdued, and instead of striking the boy, he gently stroked his cheeks and gave him some money.

10,823. OMNISCIENCE, Symbol of. Plato says that the king of Lydia had a ring with which, when he turned its head to the palm of his hand, he could see every person, and yet he himself remain invisible. Though we cannot see God while we live, yet he can see how we live. For his eyes are upon the ways of man; and he seeth all his goings. Man may gild over the leaves of a blurred life with the profession of holiness; but God can unmask the painted Jezebel of hypocrisy, and lay her naked to her own shame. *Secker.*

10,824. OPINION, Force of. Whenever a painful duty comes before us, we must not think what the world will say, but we must set our faces as a flint, and go through with it. Human respect has been the ruin of many souls. It is the close connection of moral cowardice, that fruitful source of everything that is base and wicked. And it must be remarked that this is especially the sin of civilization. In earlier times, when every man's hand is openly against his neighbor, he cares less what that neighbor thinks of him; but as peace prevails, credit is generated, character assumes a new value, a corporate public opinion begins to act; and then the temptation is to refer things to an enlightened public opinion, rather than to the law of God. *Bishop Forbes.*

10,825. OPINIONS, Arbitrary. It is too much stiffness to stand ever on the height, and to give no quarter in matter of opinion; like those peremptory Egyptians, who in several cities would either profess to abhor the crocodile or to deify him. There is a mean, if we could hit on it, in all save fundamental quarrels, worthy to be the scope of all our charitable desires; which, if we could attain and rest in, we and the church of God should be peaceful and happy. *Bishop Hall.*

10,826. OPINIONS, Non-Criminality of. Opinions, so far from being under the power of other men's will, are not under a man's own; they are the offspring of his reason, whether he be well or ill-informed. Opinions, therefore, cannot be justly imputed to any man as crimes. *Dr. J. Moore.*

10,827. OPINIONS, Vassalage of. There is no greater vassalage than that of being enslaved to opinions. The dogmatist is pent up in his prison, and sees no light but what comes in at those grates. He hath no liberty of thoughts, no prospect of various objects: while the considerate and modest inquirer hath a large sphere of motion, and the satisfaction of more open light; he sees far, and enjoys the pleasure of surveying the divers images of the mind. But the opiniator hath a poor shriveled soul, that will but just hold his little set of thoughts. His appetite after knowledge is satisfied with his few mushrooms. *Glanvill.*

10,828. OPPORTUNITY, Emblems of. *Morning and evening,* Eccles. 11 : 6, the time for work. *The day-time,* John 11 : 9, 10; 12 : 35, 36, contrasted with the time of night and darkness. *To-day,* Ps. 95 : 7; Heb. 3 : 7–15, contrasted with the future. *Summer and harvest,* Prov. 6 : 6–8; 10 : 5; Matt. 9 : 38. *The day of visitation,* Luke 19 : 44. *The day of salvation,* Isa. 49 : 8; 2 Cor. 6 : 2. *The acceptable time,* Isa. 49 : 8; Ps. 69 : 13. *A time*

when seeking may expect to find, Isa. 55 : 6 Ps. 32 : 8, marg. *Space to repent,* Rev. 2 : 22. *An open door,* Acts 14 : 27; 1 Cor. 16 : 9; 2 Cor. 2 : 12; Col. 4 : 3; Rev. 3 : 8. *Dumb creatures* may teach man knowledge. They know their "appointed times;" as the ant, Prov. 6 : 6–9; the stork, the crane and the swallow, Jer. 8 : 7. *Bowes.*

10,829. OPPORTUNITY, Importance of. Opportunity is in respect to time, in some sense, as time is in respect to eternity: it is the small moment, the exact point, the critical minute, on which every good work so much depends. *Sprat.*

10,830. OPPORTUNITY, Improvement of. You do well to improve your opportunity; to speak in the rural phrase, this is your sowing time, and the sheaves you look for can never be yours, unless you make that use of it. The color of our whole life is generally such as the three or four first years in which we are our own masters, make it. Then it is that we may be said to shape our destiny, and to treasure up for ourselves a series of future successes or disappointments. *Cowper.*

10,831. OPPORTUNITY, Irrecoverable. At the wreck of the London, a young lady was invited to take a place in a boat on the point of leaving the ship. She looked at the stormy sea, and the distance to be jumped, although small, appeared a very great one in her eyes. She hesitated. While she waited, the danger became imminent. "Jump," cried those in the boat; "we must be off. Jump, or you will be too late!" Again she looked, but again she hesitated, and now it was too late, for the boat was moving off; the distance was now really too great. "Stay! come back!" she cried, as a sense of her dreadful situation came to her; "oh, come back!" This was now impossible, and she was lost.

10,832. OPPORTUNITY, Lost. Many solemn and familiar texts stand as beacon lights to warn of this peril: "The door was shut"—"The night cometh when no man can work"—"The kingdom of God shall be taken from you"—"I will remove thy candlestick out of his place." See the doom pronounced upon Jerusalem, because the Jews knew not the time of their visitation; therefore, the things offered for their peace were justly "hid." So upon Chorazin, Bethsaida, etc. Napoleon used to say, "There is a crisis in every battle: ten or fifteen minutes, on which the issue of the battle depends; to gain this is victory; to lose it is defeat." *Bowes.*

10,833. OPPORTUNITY, Preciousness of. Opportunity is a golden word, and is itself more precious than rubies. *J. A. James.*

10,834. OPPORTUNITY, Trifling with. A very rich man, who owned many houses and broad acres, and besides had much gold stored up in banks, having heard of a single diamond worth all his property, resolved to purchase it. Having converted his real estate into money, he set sail for the land where the wonderful stone was, bought the precious jewel, and started homeward. Day after day he walked the deck of the ship, carrying the diamond in his hand, and frequently, in childish glee, throwing it into the air and catching it. The captain and passengers advised him to be more careful, lest by accident he lose the stone, and nothing but poverty and sorrow await him on his arrival home. But he paid no heed to their cautions, and every day he became more determined in his foolishness. Higher and higher he cast his diamond, laughing as he caught it falling. At last his beloved country was visible, and a few hours more, and he would be on shore. For the last time he cast the stone into the air, and, rasher than ever, alas! threw it far out of his reach, and saw all his future happiness and wealth sink beneath the waves as the ship touched the shore. Thus it is that many people trifle with the precious privileges they possess, until at last they are gone forever.   *Anon.*

10,835. OPPOSER, A Habitual. The oracle declared that there was one man in Athens of a contrary opinion to all the rest. Search was made for this man, and Phocion was found. He confessed, saying, "I, Phocion, am the man. I, alone, am pleased with nothing the common people say or do." He once gave an opinion which was approved by the people, and said to a friend, "Have I not unawares spoken some mischievous thing or other?"

10,836. OPPOSITION, Effects of. The effects of opposition are wonderful. There are men who rise refreshed on hearing of a threat; men to whom a crisis which intimidates and paralyses the majority—demanding, not the faculties of prudence and thrift, but comprehension, immovableness, the readiness of sacrifice—comes graceful and beloved as a bride!   *Emerson.*

10,837. OPPOSITION Overcome. A young man was converted, which aroused the wrath of his irreligious father, and he threatened to turn him from home if he continued, and gave him till the morrow to decide. When it arrived he told his father, "I cannot violate my conscience, I cannot forsake my God." "Leave immediately," said the father. Upon the threshold, he asked the father for one favor. As the last it was promised. He asked his father and mother to kneel with him in prayer. They knelt, and the son prayed earnestly. The good Spirit touched the father's heart, and when they rose up he said, "You need not go, John. Come in and stay." All were converted and became members of the church.

10,838. OPPRESSION, Egyptian. While staying at Alexandria, we passed a public building in course of erection. A great number of women and children of both sexes were carrying away the earth excavated for the foundation. Some laborers had loosened the soil, and the poor creatures then scraped it with their hands into circular baskets, which they bore away on their backs; they were barefooted, and very slenderly covered with rags. Several task-masters, who have not ceased out of Egypt since the time of the Pharaohs, stood at intervals holding a scourge of cords, which was not spared if any

of the people, as they passed by crouching under their burdens, seemed to slacken in their work. They had all been pressed into the service by the pasha's officers, and were paid the miserable sum of half a piastre a day.
        Boat and Caravan.

10,839. OPPRESSION, Resistance to. The poorest being that crawls on earth, contending to save itself from injustice and oppression, is an object respectable in the eyes of God and man.   *Burke.*

10,840. OPPRESSORS, Everywhere. There are sharks in the ocean, and wolves in the forest, and eagles in the air, and tyrants on thrones, and tormentors in cottages. *Dr. J. Hamilton.*

10,841. ORATOR, The Pulpit. Whitefield's preeminence as a pulpit orator is universally acknowledged. He stands alone, without a superior, without an equal; like Saul of old, towering head and shoulders above his fellows; occupying a similar place among pulpit orators to that which Luther does among reformers, Shakspeare and Milton among poets, Michael Angelo among sculptors, Raphael among painters, Haydn and Handel in music, and Newton in astronomy. He rises above other pulpit orators like the lofty tower above some noble edifice. To leave out George Whitefield from among pulpit orators would be like a performance of the tragedy of Hamlet with the character of the Prince of Denmark omitted; like leaving out the name of Washington from our Revolutionary history, or obliterating the sun from the solar system.   *J. B. Wakeley.*

10,842. ORATOR, Treasures of the. A public speaker should lay under tribute all knowledge. Let him, like the Roman general, try to gather spoils and trophies from all nations and from every age, to deck the triumphs of his cause. Nothing which in all his researches he gathers should he despise. What seems useless to-day may prove of greatest value to-morrow. What seems a dull pebble may flash when held up to the light with the brilliancy of the diamond. More than one public speaker has done what the old alchemists failed to do —taken materials which seemed base and insignificant, and by genius and skill transmuted them into gold.   *Anon.*

10,843. ORATORY, Bid for. Garrick once said, "I would give a hundred guineas if I could only say 'O!' like Mr. Whitefield."

10,844. ORATORY, Effects of. When the Roman people had listened to the diffuse and polished discourses of Cicero, they departed, saying one to another, "What a splendid speech our orator has made!" But when the Athenians heard Demosthenes, he so filled them with the subject-matter of his oration, that they quite forgot the orator, and left him at the finish of his harangue, breathing revenge, and exclaiming, "Let us go and fight against Philip!"   *Colton.*

10,845. ORATORY, Price of. Demosthenes was very desirous to learn oratory, and because he could not give the full price, which was a thousand drachms, he offered Isocrates two hundred, the fifth part, if he would teach him but the fifth part of his art. Isocrates answered, "We do not use, Demosthenes, to impart our skill by halves; but as men sell good fish whole or altogether, so if thou hast a desire to learn, we will teach thee our full art, and not a piece of it."

10,846. ORATORY, Restraints of. Caius Gracchus, the orator, had naturally a harsh voice and violent delivery. He practised his voice with a flute, used by the teachers of the time for the purpose. When he pleaded at the bar one of his servants stood in hearing, and recalled him from his loud vociferation by sounding the proper note.

10,847. ORDEAL, Decision by. Constantine summoned a council of the bishops to meet in Constantinople, in 680, to settle the Monothelite controversy. The majority favored the view of two wills in Christ. Polychronius, one of the minority, vehemently challenged the Council to settle the matter by miracle. Said he, "Let me lay my testimony on the breast of a dead man, and it will revive him." It was agreed to; a corpse was brought into the assembly, and the testimony of Polychronius, sealed up, was laid on its breast. The bishops sat in grave expectancy. Hours passed, but the corpse was lifeless still. The doctrine was declared false by the chosen test. Its originator asked for more time. It was refused, and Monothelite doctrine was declared a heresy, and those who held it were anathematized.

10,848. ORDER, Argument from. Order is an effect of reason and counsel; this reason and counsel must have its residence in some being before this order was fixed: the things ordered are always distinct from that reason and counsel whereby they are ordered, and also after it, as the effect is after the cause. No man begins a piece of work but he hath the model of it in his own mind; no man builds a house, or makes a watch, but he hath the idea or copy of it in his own head. This beautiful world bespeaks an idea of it, or a model: since there is such a magnificent wisdom in the make of each creature, and the proportion of one creature to another, this model must be before the world, as the pattern is always before the thing that is wrought by it. This, therefore, must be in some intelligent and wise agent, and this is God. *Charnock.*

10,849. ORDER, Interruption of. If nature should intermit her course, and leave altogether, though it were but for awhile, the observation of her own laws; if those principal and mother elements of the world, whereof all things in this lower world are made, should lose the qalities which now they have; if the frame of that heavenly arch erected over our heads should loosen and dissolve itself; if the prince of the lights of heaven, which now as a giant doth run his unwearied course, should, as it were, through a languishing faintness, begin to stand and to rest himself; if the moon should wander from her beaten way, the times and seasons of the year blend themselves by disordered and confused mixtures, the winds breathe out their last gasp, the clouds yield

no rain, the earth be defeated of heavenly influence, the fruits of the earth pine as children at the breasts of their mother no longer able to yield them relief: what would become of man himself, whom these things do now all serve? See we not plainly that obedience of creatures unto the law of nature is the stay of the whole world? *Hooker.*

10,850. ORDER, Wise. When Bishop Andrews first became bishop of Winton, a distant relation, a blacksmith, applied to him to be ordained, and provided with a benefice. "No" said his lordship, "you shall have the best forge in the country; but every man in his own order and station."

10,851. ORDINANCES, Benefit of. The ordinances are like the pool of Bethesda, John 5: 4. At a certain time an angel came down and troubled the waters, and then they had a healing virtue in them. So the Spirit comes down at certain times in the Word and opens the heart, and then it becomes the power of God to salvation. So that when you see souls daily sitting under excellent means of grace, and still remaining dead, you may say as Martha did to Christ of her brother Lazarus, " Lord, if thou hadst been here," they had not remained dead. If thou hadst been in this sermon, it had not been so ineffectual to them.
John Flavel.

10,852. ORGANIZATION, Benefit of. "Well, John," said Mr. Whitefield to one of Mr. Wesley's itinerant preachers, "are you still a Wesleyan?" "Yes, sir," replied John, "and I thank God that I have the privilege of being in connection with Mr. Wesley, and one of his preachers." "John," said Mr. Whitefield, "thou art in the right place. My brother Wesley acted wisely. The souls that were awakened under his ministry he joined in class, and thus preserved the fruits of his labor. This I neglected, and my people are a rope of sand."

10,853. ORIGINALITY, Meaning of. People are always talking about originality; but what do they mean? As soon as we are born, the world begins to work upon us; and this goes on to the end. And after all, what can we call our own, except energy, strength, and will? If I could give an account of all that I owe to great predecessors and contemporaries, there would be but a small balance in my favor. *Goethe.*

10,854. ORIGINALITY Uncommon. Millions of people are provided with their thoughts as with their clothes; authors, printers, booksellers, and newsmen stand, in relation to their minds, simply as shoemakers and tailors stand, to their bodies. Certain ideas come up, and are adopted, as long-tailed great coats or skeleton petticoats are adopted. No doubt, if we all thought—each man only a little—of the spirit and meaning of each act of life, the business of life would be done with an earnestness quite frightful to be told about; though glorious to think about, if one were by chance to think. *Anon.*

10,855. ORNAMENT, Guide to. Nature is the true guide in our application of ornament.

She delights in it, but ever in subserviency to use. Men generally pursue an opposite course, and adorn only to encumber. With the refined few, simplicity is the feature of greatest merit in ornament. The trifling, the vulgarminded, and the ignorant, prize only what is striking and costly,—something showy in contrast, and difficult to be obtained. *Moir.*

10,856. ORNAMENTS, New Use of. The Rev. Thos. Collins both hated and dreaded worldly conformity. It seemed to him the moth and rust of the church. His exhortations upon this subject inclined many to lay aside jewels and flowers for the Lord's sake. Not a few brought to him the garlands that had decked their brows. They became the ornaments of a missionary May-pole, six feet high, and tastefully wreathed from top to bottom; though it could not be proud, it was exceedingly pretty. A missionary box formed the base of this trophy of crucified vanity. *S. Coley.*

10,857. ORNAMENTS, Spiritual. Jewels from heaven, set deep within your souls, and glancing at every turn through the transparency of an unaffected life, will do more to make your persons attractive than all the diamonds that ever decked a queen. *Teachers' Treasury.*

10,858. ORPHANS, Work for. The most remarkable work of any age is that of George Müller, of Bristol, England. He was early employed as a Church missionary in Bristol, but his partiality for neglected orphans made him unpopular, and his support was withdrawn. Then he took six orphans to care for, with no one but God to look to for help, and God adopted his work. His establishment has from this small beginning grown to immense proportions, embracing seven large buildings, each having accommodations for 500 children —3,500 in all. For more than thirty years he has carried on his great work without a patron or a banker save his God. When he needs anything he prays for the article—food, clothes, or money—never resorting to personal appeal. He prays for men by name. The orphans are his nobility. To a lord who applied for admittance out of the usual visiting hours, the keeper replied, "Dukes and lords are of no account; orphans take rank here."

10,859. OSTENTATION, Puffed up with. As you see in a pair of bellows, there is a forced breath without life, so in those that are puffed up with the wind of ostentation, there may be charitable words without works. *Bp. Hall.*

10,860. OSTENTATION, Rebuke of. When George Faulkner, the printer, returned from London, where he had been soliciting subscriptions for his edition of Dean Swift's works, he went to pay his respects to him, dressed in a lace waistcoat, a bag wig and other fopperies. Swift received him with the same ceremonies as if he had been a stranger. "And pray, sir," said he, "what are your commands with me?" "I thought it was my duty, sir," replied George, "to wait on you immediately on my arrival from London." "Pray, sir, who are you?" "George Faulkner, the printer, sir." "You George Faulkner the printer! why, you are the most impudent, barefaced scoundrel of an impostor I have ever met with! George Faulkner is a plain, sober citizen, and would never trick himself out in lace and other fopperies. Get you gone, you rascal, or I will immediately send you to the house of correction." Away went George as fast as he could, and having changed his dress he returned to the deanery, where he was received with the greatest cordiality. "My friend George," says the Dean, "I am glad to see you returned safe from London. Why, here has been an impudent fellow with me just now, dressed in lace waistcoat, and he would fain pass himself off for you, but I soon sent him away with a flea in his ear."

10,861. OTHERS, Preferring. At an accident in a coal mine a rope broke and precipitated several men to the bottom of the shaft. Two boys caught hold of a stationary chain, and held on till relief came. A man was let down by a rope to rescue them. He first came to Daniel Harding, who cried, "Don't mind me. I can hold on a little longer. Save Joseph Brauer first, who is a little lower down, and nearly exhausted." The rescuer obeyed this instruction, and after twenty minutes returned and saved the boy who risked his own life for another.

10,862. OTHERS, Rewarding. A spelling contest was held in a school, and the prize for the victor was an elegant Bible. The contestants were reduced to two, Lizzie, the daughter of a poor, hard-working widow, and Susie, the daughter of a well-to-do-farmer. The sympathy of the school was with the poor girl. Susie misspelled a word, and Lizzie won the coveted prize. Going home the mother said, "Susie, could not you have spelt that word?" "Yes, ma." "Then why did you not do it?" "Lizzie, you know, is a poor little girl, and she has not many presents. She wanted the Bible very much, and she tried so hard for it, I thought I'd let her have it." "What made you do that, Susie?" "My Sunday-school lesson, mother, which said, 'in honor preferring one another.' So I thought I'd try it, and I'm glad I did." A few days after Susie received as a birth-day present a beautiful Bible, and on the fly-leaf was written the text, "In honor preferring one another," the observance of which had made her so happy.

10,863. PAIN, Yielding to. In the middle ages, those who had studied the arts of torture knew well that the man who could face the lion in the amphitheatre, or sit boldly on the heated iron-seat, would be overcome by the simple dropping of water, day by day, on the same place, like the firm rock corroded by the waves of ages. So our own strength must yield to pain. *F. W. Robertson.*

10,864. PAINTERS, Industry of. When we read the lives of the most eminent painters, every page informs us that no part of their time was spent in dissipation. Even an increase of fame served only to augment their industry. To be convinced with what persevering assiduity they pursued their studies, we need only reflect on their method of proceeding in their most celebrated works. When they conceived a subject, they first made a variety of sketches, then a finished drawing of the whole; after that a more correct drawing of every separate part—heads, hands, feet, and pieces of drapery; they then painted the picture, and after all re-touched it from the life. The pictures thus wrought with such pains, now appear as the effect of enchantment, as if some mighty genius had struck them off at a blow.

Sir J. Reynolds.

10,865. PALM-TREE, Use of the. The palm-tree, from its erect and noble growth and its heavenward direction, is used in Psalm 92: 12, as an illustration of the righteous. Its branches are also used as emblems of victory or triumph. In the heavenly Jerusalem, the great multitude who stood before the throne and before the Lamb, are represented as " clothed with white robes, and palms in their hands."

Prof. Balfour.

10,866. PANTHEISM, Caution against. It is not theism I fear so much in the present time as pantheism. It is not the system which says nothing is true, so much as the system which says everything is true. It is not the system which says there is no Saviour, so much as the system which says there are many Saviours, and many ways to peace. It is the system which is so liberal, that it dares not say anything is false. It is the system which is so charitable, that it will allow everything to be true. It is the system which seems ready to allow honor to others, as well as our Lord Jesus Christ—to hope well of all men, however contradictory their religious opinions may be. Confucius and Zoroaster, Socrates and Mahomet, the Indian Brahmins and the African devil-worshipers, Arius and Pelagius, Ignatius Loyola and Socinus, all are to be treated respectfully, none are to be condemned. It is the system which bids us smile complacently on all creeds and systems of religion, the Bible and the Koran, the Hindoo Vedas and the Persian 'Zendavesta, the old wives' fables of Rabbinical writers, and the rubbish of Patristic traditions, the Racovian Catechism and the Thirty-nine Articles, the Revelations of Emanuel Swedenborg and the Book of Mormon of Joseph Smith; all are to be listened to; none are to be denounced as lies. It is the system which is so scrupulous about the feelings of others that we are never to say they are wrong. It is the system which is so liberal that it calls a man a bigot if he dares to say, " I know my views are right." This is the system, which is the tone of feeling which I fear in this day. This is the system which I desire emphatically to testify against and denounce. *Ryle.*

10,867. PANTHEISM, System of. Pantheism is a system which confounds the infinite and the finite, and which makes God the sum of all things. God, it teaches, is brutal in brute matter, mighty in the forces of nature, feeling in the animal, thinking and conscious only in man. This system is, in its first aspect, more noble than material atheism, but in truth it is not less fatal to all that is noble and good. It indeed makes man, nay, the beasts that perish, nay, the very dung on the earth—divine; but it also makes God human, animal, material. It degrades what is high by exalting what is low. Better to deny God than to debase him! Pantheism is, if possible, a worse atheism.

Bp. Jeune.

10,868. PARABLES, Nature's. The world is a great storehouse of parables of moral truths. The scriptures give us a key to these. David says, "They compassed me about as bees." Isaiah, speaking for God, says, "The ox knoweth his owner and the ass his master's crib: but Israel doth not know, my people doth not consider." In short, everything about us is a picture lesson to enlightened eyes, and every voice of nature is the voice of God to hearing ears. A late writer says, "The most fundamental truths of the Bible are put in the form of visions, allegories, parables. It is as a grand symbolic history in many of its parts, in which every character and scene is a shadow-picture addressed to the imagination, revealing, as all such shadows do, the celestial light streaming from the sky windows above. In the words of Christ this kind of teaching is especially prominent. Nature speaks, as it were, with articulate voice. The birds of the air talk of his providence. The lilies of the field blossom with his beauty."

10,869. PARABLES, Old Testament. The prophets made use of parables to give a stronger impression to prince and people of the threatenings or of the promises they made to them. Nathan reproved David under the parable of a rich man that had taken away and killed the lamb of a poor man (2 Sam. 12: 2, 3). The woman of Tekoah, that was hired by Joab to reconcile the mind of the same prince towards his son Absalom, proposed to him the parable of her two sons, that fought together in the field, and one of whom having killed the other, they were going to put the murderer to death, and so to deprive her of both her sons at once (2 Sam. 14: 2, 3). Jotham, son of Gideon, proposed to the men of Shechem the parable of the bramble, whom the trees had a mind to choose for their king (Judges 9: 7, 8). The prophets often reprove the infidelity of Jerusalem under the parable of an adulterous wife. They describe the violence of such princes as are enemies to the people of God under the representation of lions, eagles, bears, etc. *Cruden.*

10,870. PARABLES, Scripture. The word " parable" is sometimes used in Scripture in a large and general sense, and applied to short sententious sayings, maxims, or aphorisms, expressed in a figurative, proverbial, or even poetical manner. But in its strict and appropriate meaning, especially as applied to our Saviour's parables, it signifies a short narrative of some event or fact, real or fictitious, in which a continued comparison is carried on between sensible and spiritual objects, and under this similitude some important doctrine, moral or religious, is conveyed and enforced.

Porteus.

10,871. PARABLES, Use of. A man may be so situated that though his life is in imminent danger, he cannot perceive the danger, and consequently makes no effort to escape. Further, his mind may be so prejudiced that he still counts the beam on which he stands secure, although a neighbor has faithfully given warning that it is about to fall; it may be that because he stands on it he cannot see its frailty. Let some friend who knows his danger, but wishes him well, approach the spot and hold a mirror in such a position that the infatuated man shall see reflected in it the under and ailing side of the beam that lies between him and the abyss. The work is done: the object is gained: the confident fool, made wise at length, leaps for life upon the solid ground. *Arnot.*

10,872. PARADISE, Adamic. Its trees and fruits, its fields arrayed in verdure and adorned in flowers, the life which breathed in its winds and flowed in its rivers, the serenity of its sky and the splendor of its sunshine, together with the immortality which gilded and burnished all its beautiful scenes, have filled the heart with rapture, and awakened the most romantic visions of the imagination. The poets of the West, and still more those of the East, have, down to the present hour, kindled at the thought of this scene of beauty and fragrance; and the very name of Eden has met the eye as a gem in the verse which it adorned. *Dr. Dwight.*

10,873. PARADISE, Heavenly and Earthly. But where is this paradise? what is this paradise? We can say, in answer to these questions, that with this heavenly paradise into which the redeemed at death do enter, the ancient, the earthly paradise is not fit to be compared. In the one, the direct intercourse with God was but occasional; in the other it shall be constant. In the one, the Deity was known only as he revealed Himself in the works of creation and in the ways of his providence; in the other, it will be as the God of our redemption, the God and Father of our Lord and Saviour Jesus, that he will be recognized, adored, obeyed—all the higher moral attributes of his nature shining forth in harmonious and illustrious display. Into the earthly paradise the tempter entered; from the heavenly he will be shut out. From the earthly paradise sad exiles once were driven; from the heavenly we shall go no more out for ever. Still, however, after all such imperfect and unsatisfying comparisons, the questions return upon us—Where and what is the paradise of the redeemed? Our simplest and our best answers to those questions perhaps are these—Where is paradise? wherever Jesus is. What is paradise? to be forever with, and to be fully like our Lord. *Hanna.*

10,874. PARADISE, Individual. Every man has a paradise around him till he sins, and the angel of an accusing conscience drives him from his Eden. And even then there are holy hours, when this angel sleeps, and man comes back, and with the innocent eyes of a child

looks into his lost paradise again—into the broad gates and rural solitudes of nature.
Longfellow.

10,875. PARADISE, Legend of Journeying to. St. Gertrude is the popular patron saint of travelers. She established many large hospices for the entertainment of travelers, and it became a custom to drink to her honor before starting on a journey. After her death it came at length to be a popular superstition that she gave entertainment to souls on the way to paradise. This journey was supposed to occupy three days. The first night the fleeting soul lodged with St. Gertrude, the second with St. Gabriel, and on the third entered paradise. St. Gertrude is regarded by Romanists as the patroness of departed souls.

10,876. PARADISE, Location of. A manuscript in the British Museum says that "Paradise is neither in heaven nor on earth. Noah's flood was forty fathoms high, over the highest hills that are on earth; and paradise is forty fathoms higher than Noah's flood was, and it hangeth between heaven and earth wonderfully, as the ruler of all things made it. And it is perfectly level, both in length and breadth. There is neither hollow nor hill; nor is there frost nor snow, hail nor rain; but there is *fons vitæ*, that is, the well of life. When the calends of January commence, then floweth the well so beautifully, and so gently, and no deeper than man may wet his finger on the front, over all that land. And so likewise each month; once when the month comes in the well begins to flow. And there is the copse of wood, which is called Radion Saltus, where each tree is as straight as an arrow, and so high that no earthly man ever saw so high, or can say of what kind they are. And there never falleth a leaf off, for they are evergreen, beautiful and pleasant, full of happiness. Paradise is upright on the eastern part of the world. There is neither heat nor hunger, nor is there ever night, but always day. The sun there shineth seven times brighter than on this earth. Therein dwell innumerable angels of God with the holy souls till doomsday. Therein dwelleth a beautiful bird called Phoenix; he is large and grand, as the Mighty One formed him; he is the lord over all birds."

10,877. PARADISE, Luxuries of. Says Mohammed, "The very meanest in paradise will have eighty thousand servants, seventy-two wives of the girls of paradise, beside the wives he had in this world, and a tent erected for him of pearls, jacinths, and emeralds, of a very large extent." According to another tradition, he will be waited on by three hundred attendants while he eats, will be served in dishes of gold, whereof three hundred shall be set before him at once, containing each a different kind of food, the last morsel of which will be as grateful as the first; and will also be supplied with as many sorts of liquors in vessels of the same metal; and, to complete the entertainment, there will be no want of wine, which will not inebriate. *George Sale.*

10,878. PARADISE, Mohammedan. They say it

is situate above the seven heavens, (or in the seventh heaven,) and next under the throne of God; and to express the amenity of the place, tell us that the earth of it is of the finest wheat flour, or of the purest musk, or, as others will have it, of saffron; that its stones are pearls and jacinths, the walls of its buildings enriched with gold and silver, and that the trunks of all its trees are of gold; among which the most remarkable is the tree called Tûba, or the tree of happiness. Concerning this tree they fable that it stands in the palace of Mohammed, though a branch of it will reach to the house of every true believer; that it will be laden with pomegranates, grapes, dates, and other fruits of surprising bigness, and of tastes unknown to mortals. So that if a man desire to eat of any particular fruit, it will immediately be presented him; or, if he choose flesh, birds ready dressed will be set before him, according to his wish. They add, that the boughs of this tree will spontaneously bend down to the hand of the person who would gather of its fruits, and that it will supply the blessed not only with food, but also with silken garments, and beasts to ride on, ready saddled and bridled, and adorned with rich trappings, which will burst forth from its fruits; and that this tree is so large, that a person mounted on the fleetest horse would not be able to gallop from one end of its shade to the other in a hundred years.   *George Sale.*

10,879. PARADISE, Music of. Mohammedans believe that the ravishing songs of the angel Israfil, who has the most melodious voice of all God's creatures, and of the daughters of paradise, and even the trees themselves, will celebrate the divine praises with a harmony exceeding whatever mortals have heard; to which will be joined the sound of bells hanging on the trees, which will be put in motion by the wind proceeding from the throne of God, so oft as the blessed wish for music; nay, the very clashing of the golden-bodied trees, whose fruits are pearls and emeralds, will surpass human imagination.   *Geo. Sale.*

10,880. PARADISE, Search after the. Paludanus relates that Alexander the Great was full of longing desire to behold the earthly paradise, and that he undertook his wars in the East for the express purpose of reaching it. He states that on his nearing Eden, an old man was captured in a ravine by some of Alexander's soldiers, and they were about to conduct him to their monarch, when the venerable man said, "Go and announce to Alexander that it is in vain he seeks paradise; his efforts will be perfectly fruitless, for the way to paradise is the way of humility, a way of which he knows nothing. Take this stone, and give it to Alexander, and say to him 'From this stone learn what you must know of yourself.'" Now, this stone was of great value, and excessively heavy, outweighing and excelling in value all other gems, but when reduced to powder it was as light as a tuft of hay, and as worthless; by which token the mysterious old man meant that Alexander alive was the

39

greatest of monarchs, but Alexander dead would be a thing of naught. *Barring-Gould.*

10,881. PARADISE, Traditions of. There was a general belief among the ancients in the existence in the West of a great continent called Atlantis. (Vol. I., 2984.) Here Kronos, time, lay asleep, guarded by hundred-handed Briareus. The land was thought to possess every sensuous attraction—a land of groves, flowers, fruits, delightful airs, fountains and streams. It resembled the paradise of Jews and Christians. The fathers tried to drive the heathen fable from the minds of the people, but could not. Christopher Columbus was doubtless stimulated to turn the prows of his ships westward by the same tradition. He thought he had found the Atlantis of the ancients and the paradise of the Christians when he discovered the new world. He wrote, "The saintly theologians and philosophers were right when they fixed the site of the terrestrial paradise in the extreme Orient, because it is a most temperate clime; and the lands which I have just discovered are the limits of the Orient." In 1498, he wrote, "I am convinced that there is the terrestrial paradise."

10,882. PARDON, Appeal for. Some old soldiers, sentenced to be shot, passing by Marshal Turenne on their way to execution, pointed to their many visible scars. This mute appeal had the desired effect. The Marshal prevented the execution by giving them a free pardon. The condemned sinner, on the way to execution, if he point penitently, not to his own scars, but the wounds and blood of Christ, shall have pardon and everlasting life.

10,883. PARDON Detained. In the Isle of Man, as I was one day walking on the seashore, I remember contemplating with thrilling interest an old, gray, ruined tower, covered with ivy. There was a remarkable history connected with the spot. In that tower was formerly hanged one of the best governors the island ever possessed. He had been accused of treachery to the king during the time of the civil wars, and received sentence of death. Intercession was made on his behalf, and a pardon was sent; but that fell into the hands of his bitter enemy, who kept it locked up, and the governor was hanged. His name is still honored by many, and you may often hear a pathetic ballad sung to his memory to the music of the spinning wheel. We must feel horror-struck at the turpitude of that man who, having the pardon for his fellow-creature in his possession, could keep it back, and let him die the death of a traitor. But let us restrain our indignation till we ask ourselves whether God might not point his finger to most of us, and say, Thou art the man. Thou hast a pardon in thine hands to save thy fellow-creature, not from temporal, but from eternal death. Thou hast a pardon suited to all, designed for all. Thou hast enjoyed it thyself, but hast thou not kept it back from thy brother, instead of sending it to the ends of the earth?   *Hugh Stowell.*

10,884. PARDON, Forfeited. Clark Fairbanks

of Massachussetts, was convicted of arson, and sentenced to State Prison for life. After a time of good behavior on the part of the prisoner, and the discovery of some mitigating circumstances of his guilt, a petition was sent to Gov. Claflin for his pardon. This was granted on condition that if he was ever again guilty of a crime he should return and serve out his original sentence. For a while he conducted himself well, but eventually was committed to the House of Correction for assault and battery. On the expiration of this period, the warden of the State Prison claimed him to serve out the sentence, the pardon of which he had forfeited. So it is with pardoned sinners who return again to sin.

10,885. PARDON a Free Gift. A minister, trying to instruct an old man how to get pardon, said, "Now, suppose I were to go to a shop and buy something for you, and pay for it, and tell you to go and fetch it, need you take any money with you?" "No," said the old man, "it would be paid for." "Need you make any promise to pay at some future time?" he then asked. "No," he replied, "I should have it for nothing." "So," he continued, "is it with forgiveness of sins; the Lord Jesus has paid the full price for it. He has had the groans, the sighs, the tears, the wrath, the pain, the punishment; yea, all that sin deserved! He bore it all! He paid the whole! Yes, bought forgiveness with his precious blood, and now he gives it as a gift to all who bring their sins to him." Said the old man, as his eyes filled with tears, "I see it now; it is pardon for nothing! pardon for nothing! Christ has bought it, and he will give it to me!"

10,886. PARDON, Haste for. Among the company awaiting in the ante-room of the White House to see Mr. Lincoln, Gen. Fisk saw an old man, whose sorrowful looks won his pity. From him he learned that he had been there four days, seeking an interview with the President to obtain from him a pardon for his son, who was in Nashville under sentence of death. Gen. Fisk outlined the case on a card, and sent it to Mr. Lincoln with the request that he would see the man. Instantly the order came, and past senators, governors, and generals, the old man was ushered into Mr. Lincoln's presence. He showed his papers, which the President took, and said he would give his answer next day. The father, in agony of fear for the fate of his son, cried aloud, "To-morrow may be too late. My son is under sentence of death. The decision must be made right off." The President took the papers up again, and wrote on them the word "Pardoned." The old man received them amid tears of joy over the salvation of his son.

10,887. PARDON, No Substitute for. If a friend should come to a malefactor on his way to the gallows, put a bouquet into his hands, and bid him be of good cheer, smell on that. Alas! this would bring little joy with it to the poor man's heart, who sees the place of execution before him. But if one comes from the prince with a pardon, which he puts into his hand, and bids him be of good cheer, this, and this only, will reach the poor man's heart, and overcome it with a sudden ravishment of joy. Truly anything short of pardoning mercy is as inconsiderable to a troubled conscience, towards any relieving or pacifying it, as that posy in a dying prisoner's hand would be. *Gurnall.*

10,888. PARDON, Settlement by. James, the brother of Henry Erskine, remarked, "We all need to settle our accounts with God betimes." Henry replied, "I know no way, dear brother, of settling my accounts, but by receiving a free pardon from my Redeemer."

10,889. PARDON, Unexpected. A soldier in the West Indies, condemned by a court-martial, was led out to be shot. His coffin was placed before him, upon which he was requested to kneel; and the regiment to which he belonged was drawn up to witness the affecting scene. A bandage was placed over the eyes of the unhappy culprit, and the chaplain, after commending his soul to God, had left him, when the commanding officer cried, in a solemn but firm tone, "Make ready! Present!" and then, instead of commanding the soldiers to fire, as the unfortunate man expected, he stepped up to him, and said, "The governor pardons you." The soldier, on hearing this, fell from his coffin, and swooned; but on coming to himself, he clapped his hands for joy, and loudly exclaimed, "God bless the governor! He has saved my life! He has saved my life!"   *Dr. Robert Young.*

10,890. PARENT, A Cruel. It was said that Herod, in slaying the infants of Bethlehem, caused the death of his own son. Augustus Cæsar, on hearing this at Rome, said, "It was better to be Herod's pig than his son." This was an allusion to the custom of the Jews, who, not being permitted to eat any swine's flesh, that animal was left to die a natural death.

10,891. PARENT, A Severe. The youngest son of a Mardonian peasant became a libertine. The father did all he could to have him change his course, and as a last resource brought him before King Artaxerxes, and desired his death. The king, amazed at his course, said, "How can you, my friend, endure to see your son die before your face?" He being a gardener by trade, replied, "As willingly as I would pull away leaves from a rank lettuce, and not hurt the root." The king threatened the son with death if he did not do better, and raised the father to the dignity of a judge.

10,892. PARENT, An Unnatural. Pausanias, a Spartan captain, was convicted by the Ephori of a conspiracy with the Persians, against his country. He fled to the temple of Minerva for sanctuary. It being unlawful to force him from thence, the magistrate gave an order to build a wall about him that he might be guarded until he starved to death. His mother brought the first stone that would make her only son a prisoner till death.

10,893. PARENTS, Influence of. The opinions, the spirit, the conversation, the manners of the parent, influence the child. Whatever

sort of man he is, such, in a great degree, will be the child; unless constitution or accident give him another turn. If the parent is a fantastic man; if he is a genealogist, knows nothing but who married such an one, and who married such an one; if he is a sensualist, a low wretch, his children will usually catch these tastes. If he is a literary man, his very girls will talk learnedly. If he is a griping, hard, miserly man, such will be his children. This I speak of as generally the case. It may happen that the parent's disposition may have no ground to work on in that of the child. It may happen that the child may be driven into disgust: the miser, for instance, often implants disgust, and his son becomes a spendthrift.
Cecil.

10,894. PARENTS, Memory of. A prison chaplain, after extensive observation, concludes: "The last thing forgotten in all the recklessness of dissolute profligacy, is the prayer or hymn taught by a mother's lips, or uttered at a father's knee; and where there seems to have been any pains bestowed even by one parent to train up a child aright, there is in general more than ordinary ground for hope."

10,895. PARENTS, Responsibility of. And what will parents be able to say to God at the day of judgment, for all their neglect of their children, in matter of instruction and example, and restraint from evil? How will it make your ears tingle when God shall arise terribly to judgment, and say to you, "Behold the children which I have given you; they were ignorant, and you instructed them not; they made themselves vile and you restrained them not. Why did you not have them instructed and trained up in piety and devotion? You have neglected this duty, and now your children, whose souls you have ruined by your neglect, will follow you to hell, to be an addition to your torments there!" Will not your children themselves challenge you at that day and say to you, one by one, "Had you been as careful to teach me the good knowledge of the Lord as I was capable of learning it—had you been as forward to instruct me in my duty as I was ready to have hearkened to it—it had not been with me as it is this day; I had not now stood here trembling, in fearful expectation of the eternal doom which is just ready to be passed upon me?"
Tillotson.

10,896. PARENTS, Rewards of. He that plants a vine in the vernal equinox gathers grapes upon it in the autumnal. He that sows wheat at the setting of the Pleiades reaps it at their rising. Man's education is laborious, his increase slow, his virtue lies at a distance; so that most parents die before their children show their virtue. Neocles never saw Themistocles' victory at Salamis, nor Miltiades the valor of Cimon at Eurymedon; Xanthippus never heard Pericles pleading; nor Aristo Plato philosophizing; nor did the fathers of Euripides and Sophocles know the victories their sons won, though they heard them stammering and learning to talk. *Plutarch.*

10,897. PARENTS, Slighting. To such as have parents I commend the consideration of **Prov.** 30: 17, which should be to them as the handwriting that appeared upon the wall to Belshazzar. "The eye that mocketh at his father, and despiseth to obey his mother, the raven of the valley shall pick it out, and the young eagles shall eat it." That is, they shall be brought to an untimely end, and the birds of the air shall eat that eye that, but for the parent it despised, had never seen the light. It may be you are vigorous and young, they decayed and wrinkled with age; but saith the Holy Ghost, "Despise not thy mother when she is old." Prov. 23: 22. It may be you are rich, they are poor; own and honor them in their poverty, and despise them not. God will requite it if you do. *Flavel.*

10,898. PARENTS, Support of. It is a saying frequent among the Jews, "A child should rather labor at the mill than suffer his parents to want." And to the same effect is that other saying, "Your parents must be supplied by you if you have it; if not you ought to beg for them, rather than see them perish." *Flavel.*

10,899. PARTING, Pangs of. We cannot part with our friends. We cannot let our angels go. We do not see that they only go out that archangels may come in. We are idolaters of the old. We do not believe in the richness of the soul, in its proper eternity and omnipresence. We do not believe there is any force in to-day to rival or re-create that beautiful yesterday. We linger in the ruins of the old tent, where once we had bread, and shelter, and organs, nor believe that the spirit can feed, cover, and nerve us again. We cannot again find aught so dear, so sweet, so graceful, but we sit and weep in vain. The voice of the Almighty saith, "Up and onward for evermore!" We cannot stay amid the ruins. Neither will we rely on the new; and so we walk ever with reverted eyes, like those monsters who look backwards. *Emerson.*

10,900. PARTNER, A Stupid. A man or woman with a stupid or perverse partner, but still hoping to see this partner become all that is desired, is like a man with a wooden leg wishing it might become a vital one, and sometimes for a moment fancying this almost possible! *John Foster.*

10,901. PARTNERSHIP, Useless. A lion was roaming on the sea-shore, when seeing a dolphin basking on the surface of the water, he invited him to form an alliance with him, "for," said he, "as I am the king of the beasts, and you are the king of the fishes, we ought to be the greatest friends and allies possible." The dolphin gladly assented; and the lion, not long after, having a fight with a wild bull, called upon the dolphin for his promised support. But when he, though ready to assist him, found himself unable to come out of the sea for the purpose, the lion accused him of having betrayed him. "Do not blame me," said the dolphin in reply, "but blame my nature, which, however powerful at sea, is altogether helpless on land." *Æsop.*

10,902. PASSION, Allurements of. The legend of

Tannhauser is that he was riding through Hoesel Vale, on his way to Wartburg, when, as he was passing a cliff in the Hörselloch, he saw a female figure of unearthly beauty, whom he recognized as Venus. She spoke to him enchanting words, strains of sweetest music meanwhile filling the air, a roseate light glowing around and charming nymphs scattering roses at her feet. He left his horse and followed the charmer, at the tread of whose feet flowers sprang up, till he entered a mountain cave and found himself in the palace of Venus. Here he passed seven years in revelry and debauch, surrounded by all the pleasure and magnificence of the heathen goddess' home. He was filled with satiety and loathing, and longed for the blue sky and fresh breezes of the outside world. In vain he besought from Venus permission to depart. In his despondency he called upon the Virgin Mary, and a passage opened to him, and he stood once more upon the earth. He delighted in all the beauties of rural nature around him. Then the tones of the church bell fell upon his ear so long used only to Bacchanal songs, and he hastened to make his confession. The priest was horror-struck at the recital of his foul crimes, and refused him absolution. He went from one to another to seek relief till he came to the pope himself. Urban IV. listened to his confession of appalling guilt and earnest prayer for absolution. He thrust the penitent indignantly away, exclaiming, "Guilt such as thine can never, never, be remitted. Sooner shall this staff in my hand grow green and blossom, than that God should pardon thee." Tannhauser, disheartened, started to return to the only asylum that would receive him. Three days after his departure Urban discovered that his staff had burst into leaves and flowers. He hastened to send messengers after the penitent with his blessing. They could only discover that a weary man had just entered the Hörselloch.

10,903. PASSIONS, Disappointment of. It is folly to pretend that one ever wholly recovers from a disappointed passion. Such wounds always leave a scar. There are faces I can never look upon without emotion; there are names I can never hear spoken without almost starting.
Longfellow.

10,904. PASSIONS, Dominance of the. There is a fable which represents that the tail of the snake obtained authority over the head and led the way, head following. The tail being altogether blind, dashed against a stone at one moment, and the next against a tree, and at last drowned both itself and the head in the river of death. The moral is, beware of allowing your passions and animal instincts to control your moral and intellectual nature. To disregard this is to rush upon disaster and final ruin.

10,905. PASSIONS, Obstructions of the. How perfectly sweet and gentle that little brook is that runs through the meadow! Put an obstruction six inches high across it, and see how it will complain day and night. Every min-

ute it murmurs its complaint. Build the obstruction higher, and see how its voice increases! Build it still higher, and see how it pours itself, complaining incessantly and loudly. It is not until you lay an obstruction across the passions of men that you know the force of that stream which you are checking. *Beecher.*

10,906. PASSIONS, Tyranny of the. We say of a man who has no will-mastery, "He is ruled by his passions;" they govern him. not he them. Centuries ago an Arab wrote, "Passion is a tyrant which slays those whom it governs." It is like fire, which, once thoroughly kindled, can scarcely be quenched; or like the torrent, which, when it is swollen, can no longer be restrained with its banks. Call not him a prisoner who has been put in fetters by his enemy, but rather him whose own passions overpowered him to destruction. *J. Johnson.*

10,907. PASSOVER, Import of the. The elect family, with shoes on their feet, and their loins girt ready for flight from Egypt, are standing by night within the house whose door-posts are sprinkled with blood, while the destroying angel is abroad in judgment, in the death of their first-born, judging the pride of Egypt. And this is the one great truth in Egypt—the sprinkled blood, and its value, and its value as delivering from judgment. In Egypt it is much to know that Israel is redeemed, and that there is safety in the blood of sprinkling. But the blood of Jesus has much more connected with it than mere deliverance from Egypt or salvation; yet this is the only use of it which is known by Israel in the house of bondage. For Israel in Egypt, for the Christian in the world, the one great truth is the Passover, redemption through the blood of the Lamb, salvation, not for our righteousness' sake, but because the blood is on the door-post.
A. Jukes.

10,908. PAST, Clinging to the. How very apt we are to outlive in our attitude or energies what has passed. We cling to the shell—to the husk—to the garments—after the kernel, the essence, the life has gone. If only we are looking heavenwards, in the right direction, we do not see that we may be merely "gazing," and nothing more. We are not apt to see how much of emptiness there is in what appears so right in itself. We cling to places, long after those who peopled them are gone—to forms, long after their spirit has died out—to positions, which we ourselves once rightly occupied, when circumstances have been so changed that it is meaningless to stand in that position any more.
Power.

10,909. PAST, Future and. The world has arrived at a period which renders it the part of fashion to pay homage to the prospective precedents of the future, in preference to those of the past. The past is dead, and has no resurrection; but the future is endowed with such a life, that it lives to us even in anticipation. The past is, in many things, the foe of mankind; the future is, in all things, our friend. For the past has no hope; the future is both hope and fruition. The past is the text-book of tyrants; the future the Bible of the free. Those who are solely governed by the past, stand, like Lot's wife, crystallized in the act of looking backward, and forever incapable of looking forward. 　　　　　　　　　*Marryat.*

10,910. PASTOR, An Enemy to His. When Homer had spent many lines in dispraising the body of Thyrsites, he briefly describes his mind thus: that he was an enemy to Ulysses, a wise and eloquent man. And there can be no more said of a bad man than this: that he is an enemy to his pastor. That is enough to brand him. 　　　　　　　　　*Skinner.*

10,911. PASTOR, A Faithful. Poemen, the hermit, heard of an old man dwelling at a long distance, who was much troubled in conscience. He made a weary journey over the desert to see him, and had framed three arguments, which he hoped would bring peace to his mind. When he reached him he had forgotten one of his consolations. Returning home, the third point came back to him just as he was about laying his hand on the lock of the door. Without entering his house, he retraced his journey to pour his third consolation into the old man's ear. The man was moved at his solicitude for souls, and said, "Thou art, indeed, a Poemen— a shepherd of the flock of Jesus."

10,912. PASTOR, Perseverance of a. Rev. S. Thornton called to see an irreligious parishioner in his sickness. The old man recognizing his voice, called out from his room, "I don't want you here; you may go away." The next day Mr. Thornton again presented himself, with inquiries after him, and an expressed desire to see him; calling out from the stairs, "Well, my friend, may I come up to you to-day?" Again he was answered, "I don't want you here." Twenty-one days successively did the patient clergyman call with the same request, and on the twenty-second obtained admittance to the bed-side of the sick man. Ever after he was permitted to read God's Word to him, and pray with him. The aged man was converted, recovered, and became a faithful Christian.

10,913. PASTOR, Work of the. A late writer says, "It is written in the annals of art, that sculptors have spent months in wandering from quarry to quarry in search of a block fleckless and crystalline, to worthily embody their ideal; and then have given months and years to the slow shaping of the crudeness of the stone into the grace of outline and loveliness of feature, that reproduced in the imperishable whiteness of the marble the dream of beauty which filled their thought. And surely the work of shaping souls into the symmetry of Christ-likeness has its greater inspirations."

10,914. PASTORS, Advantage of New. When Scipio Junior was appointed to command the Roman army and fight the Numantines, he found it enervated, demoralized, and beaten. He reorganized it and infused his own indomitable spirit into it, and then engaged and routed the enemy. The officers of the foe rebuked their soldiers, and asked why they fled from those they had pursued so often. A Numantine soldier answered, "The sheep are the same still, but they have another shepherd."

10,915. PATIENCE, Need of. Progress of the best kind is comparatively slow. Great results cannot be achieved at once; and we must be satisfied to advance in life as we walk, step by step. De Maistre says, "To know how to wait is the great secret of success." We must sow before we can reap, and often have to wait long, content, meanwhile, to look patiently forward in hope; the fruit best worth waiting for often ripening the slowest. It is always a mark of short-sightedness and of weakness to be impatient of results. Thus true growth is often baffled; like little children who plant seeds in their garden, and grub them up to see how they grow, and so kill them through their impatience. 　　*Smiles.*

10,916. PATIENCE, Offices of. The offices of patience are as varied as the ills of this life. We have need of it with ourselves and with others; with those below and those above us, and with our own equals; with those who love us, and those who love us not; for the greatest things, and for the least; against sudden inroads of trouble, and under our daily burdens; disappointments as to the weather, or the breaking of the heart; in the weariness of the body, or the wearing of the soul; in our own failure of duty, or others' failure to us; in every-day wants, or in the aching of sickness, or the decay of age; in disappointment, bereavement, losses, injuries, reproaches; in heaviness of the heart, or its sickness amid delayed hopes. 　　　　　　　*Dr. Pusey.*

10,917. PATIENCE Prescribed. If thou intendest to vanquish the greatest, the most abominable and wickedest enemy, who is able to do thee mischief both in body and soul, and against whom thou preparest all sorts of weapons, but cannot overcome, then know that there is a sweet and loving physical herb to serve thee, named *Patientia.* 　*Luther.*

10,918. PATIENCE, Result of. An emperor of China, once passing through his dominions, was entertained in a house in which the master, with his wife, children, daughter-in-law, grand-children, and servants, all lived together in perfect harmony. The emperor, struck with admiration at the spectacle, requested the head of the family to inform him what means he used to preserve quiet among such a number and variety of persons. The old man, taking out his pencil, wrote these three words: "Patience—Patience—Patience."

10,919. PATRIOTISM, Passion of. John Burns, of Gettysburg, in his seventieth year, offered himself to General Wister, commander of what was known as the "Iron Brigade." He was dressed in Continental coat, vest and corduroys which he had worn in the war of 1812. He told the General that he had fought for his country in 1812, and he wanted to fight for it again. The officer looked at him, and seeing that he was in earnest, said, "God bless the old soldier, he shall have a chance." He joined the 7th Wisconsin, and performed a brave man's duty, until the close of the first day's battle, when he was hit four times, and fell into the enemy's hands. His escape from death was marvelous. A pair of old-fashioned spectacles averted the first blow; a truss he wore, the second; the third ball passed through his leg, and the fourth through his arm, but broke no bones. He lay on the field all night, and through a neighbor's kindness was taken to his own house in town. Here a rebel officer visited him, and inquired what part he had taken in the fight, but he made no reply. Shortly after the officer left another ball came through the window, grazed the wounded man's breast and buried itself in the wall. He had just turned over. If he had not, the minie ball would have passed through him.

10,920. PATRIOTISM, Pleasure of. Neither Montaigne in writing his essays, nor Descartes in building new worlds, nor Burnet in framing an antediluvian earth, no, nor Newton in discovering and establishing the true laws of nature on experiment and a sublime geometry, felt more intellectual joys than he feels who is a real patriot, who bends all the force of his understanding, and directs all his thoughts and actions, to the good of his country.
Bolingbroke.

10,921. PATTERNS, Highest. There is no manner of inconvenience in having a pattern propounded to us of so great perfection as is above our reach to attain to, and there may be great advantages in it. The way to excel in any kind is to propose the brightest and most perfect examples to our imitation. No man can write after too perfect and good a copy; and though he can never reach the perfection of it, yet he is like to learn more than by one less perfect. He that aims at the heavens, which yet he is sure to come short of, is like to shoot higher than he that aims at a mark within his reach.
Tillotson.

10,922. PEACE, Christ's. A chaplain related the story of a little girl, who when told that her father had gone to heaven, asked her mother, "If she had not better begin to pack up too, and get ready to go?" A soldier heard it and said, "I am glad you told us that story about packing up, it made the thing so plain to me. I haven't much learning, and I haven't tried to understand these things much; but now I see through it all. I want you to help me pack up. Pray with me, chaplain." While prayer was being offered, the earnest heart cried out, "Oh do Lord, help me! help me!" The Holy Spirit was there. This poor man cried, and the Lord heard him, and he said, "I am happy now; I have found Jesus," with a face radiant with joy. "What of your body?" one asked, "are you suffering now?" He had been shot through the right shoulder and left leg, and had an arm taken off. "Oh," said he, "my wounds are nothing now. I can bear them all. I have peace within."

10,923. PEACE, Ecclesiastical. Constantine, finding that there were many differences existing between the fathers of the church, convened the Nicene Council. He desired them to bring in writing all their accusations and complaints. After he had received all that were proffered, he bound them in a bundle, and saying that he had not so much as looked at them, burnt them before the Council. Constantine then exhorted them to peace and cordial agreement among themselves.

10,924. PEACE, Fable of. Once on a time, the wolves sent an embassy to the sheep, desiring that there might be peace between them for the time to come. "Why," said they, "should we be forever waging this deadly strife? Those wicked dogs are the cause of all; they are incessantly barking at us, and provoking us. Send them away, and there will be no longer any obstacle to our eternal friendship and peace." The silly sheep listened, the dogs were dismissed, and the flock, thus deprived of their best protectors, became an easy prey to their treacherous enemy.
Æsop.

10,925. PEACE, Making. It would be very desirable to follow the example of the excellent Dr. Cotton Mather, who formed a society of peacemakers, whose professed business it was to compose differences, and prevent lawsuits. It was his laudable ambition to be able to say, "He did not know of any person in the world who had done him any ill office but he had done him a good one for it. The Greeks had their αμνηστω, whereby they took an order that all wrongs and injuries should be buried and forgotten amongst them. The primitive Christians had their αγαπαι, their love-feasts, for the like purpose. In this let us set like good examples.
Buck.

10,926. PEACE, Possible. Is there, in fact, such a thing as an attainable habit of mind that can remain at peace no matter what external circumstances may be? No matter what worries—no matter what perplexities, what thwartings, what cares, what dangers; no matter what slanders, what revilings, what persecutions—is it possible to keep an immovable peace? When suddenly called to die, or to face sorrows worse than death, is it possible to be still at peace? Yes, it is.
Mrs. H. B. Stowe.

10,927. PEACE, Prosperity and. Those that are versed in the keeping and breeding of bees look on that hive to be healthiest and in best condition where there is most humming, and which is fullest of bustle and noise; but he to whom God has committed the care of the rational and political hive will perceive the felicity of the people to consist chiefly in quietness and tranquillity.
Plutarch.

10,928. PEACE, Silence and. Heraclitus was asked to speak on the subject of peace, unity, and concord. Ascending the rostrum, he called for a cup of clear water, upon which he sprinkled some bran or meal, with a little glacon or herb, and then supped it off. This done, without speaking one word, departed: leaving the people to wonder what he meant. He desired to teach them that they must cease from immoderate expenses, and be happy with things cheap and easy to be had; this being a certain way to promote peace and harmony.

10,929. PEACE, Source of. It is the religion

of Jesus alone that can give peace to man: it unites him with his Saviour; it subdues his passions, it controls his desires, it consoles him with the love of Christ; it gives him joy even in sorrow; and this is a joy that cannot be taken away.   *Fenelon.*

10,930. PEARLS, Buying. A gentleman purchased a string of imitation pearls in Paris, for which he paid ninety cents. This necklace he gave to his daughter for one of her dolls. A jeweler called one evening while the child was amusing herself with her new toy. "How foolish you are to let a child have so valuable an object to play with," remarked the jeweler to the father. "Valuable!" responded the latter. "I gave four francs and a half for it the other day." The jeweler took the necklace from the little girl, and examined it minutely. "I do not care what you paid for it," said he; "but this much I do know, the pearls are real!" Further examination proved that the necklace was worth at least two thousand dollars. He who buys virtue gets the priceless pearls, and he who buys pleasure has a wax or glass imitation of no value.

10,931. PEDANTRY Defined. Pedantry consists in the use of words unsuitable to the time, place, and company.   *Coleridge.*

10,932. PEEVISHNESS, Canker of. Peevishness may be considered the canker of life, that destroys its vigor, and checks its improvement; that creeps on with hourly depredations, and taints and vitiates what it cannot consume.
                    Johnson.

10,933. PEN, Office of the. The pen is the tongue of the hand—a silent utterer of words for the eye—the unmusical substitute of the literal tongue, which is the soul's prophet, the heart's minister, and the interpreter of the understanding.   *Beecher.*

10,934. PENANCE, Revolting. According to Cæsarius of Heisterbach, a usurer of Cologne was greatly troubled on account of his sins, and confessed to a priest. For penance the priest bade him fill a large chest with bread for the church of St. Gereon. Next day the loaves were found to have been changed into frogs and toads. The priest recalled him to look at his offering. "Behold," said he, "the value of your offering in the sight of God!" The terrified usurer cried out, "Lord, what shall I do?" The priest said to him, "If you wish to be saved, lie this night naked amid the reptiles." Nature could but revolt from the loathsome bed; but so great was the man's contrition, that he consented, choosing rather a bed among worms which perish, than with those which are eternal. He laid down in the chest, and the priest closed it upon him and departed. The next day he returned and opened the chest, but found nothing save the bones of the man. This man chose such a bed to save his soul. The debauchee has a like bed forever.

10,935. PENANCE, Violent. In the eleventh century a voluntary penance was introduced, consisting of violent self-flagellation. The infliction of three thousand stripes, while the

votary recited ten psalms, constituted one year of ecclesiastical penance. The recitation of the whole Psalter and the infliction of fifteen thousand lashes, was esteemed equivalent to one hundred years. With this course of discipline was usually combined great abstemiousness, and the usual features of the life of an anchoret. One of these flagellants, St. Dominic, cried with tears, "I am become a sensual man." His explanation was that he had eaten a little raw fennel with his dry bread on Sundays and Thursdays, on account of feeble health.

10,936. PENITENCE versus Penance. A hermit came to the abbot Poemen and said, "My father, I have committed a grievous fault, and must do penance for it for three years." "Three years!" answered Poemen, "that is a very long penance." "What! is that too long? At least for a year, then." "Too long, too long," said Poemen. One present inquired, "How long would you have him punish himself for his fault—forty days?" "This is too much," said the abbot; "a broken and a contrite heart God will not despise with only three days of penance."

10,937. PENTECOST, First Christian. Next to the day of Christ's death, the day of Pentecost was the greatest day that ever dawned on our world. It was the first day of the last and best dispensation of revealed religion. It was, as it has been well called, "the birthday" of the Christian Church. It was the first day of the new creation, in which the elements which had previously existed in a state of chaotic confusion began to be fashioned and arranged by the plastic power of the Spirit of glory and of God.   *Morris.*

10,938. PENURIOUSNESS, Fable of. A certain boy put his hand into a pitcher where great plenty of figs and filberts were deposited; he grasped as many as his fist could possibly hold, but when he endeavored to pull it out, the narrowness of the neck prevented him. Unwilling to lose any of them, but unable to draw out his hand, he burst into tears, and bitterly bemoaned his hard fortune. An honest fellow who stood by, gave him this wise and reasonable advice: "Grasp only half the quantity, and you will easily succeed."   *Æsop.*

10,939. PEOPLE, Power of the. Let no man slight the scorn and hate of the people. When it is unjust, it is a wolf; but when it is just, a dragon. Though the tyrant, seated high, does think he may contemn their malice; yet he ought to remember that they have many hands, while he hath one neck only. If he, being single, be dangerous to many, those many will to him alone be dangerous in their hate. The sands of Africa, though they be but barren dust and lightness, yet, angered by the winds, they bury both the horse and traveler alive.
                    Feltham.

10,940. PERFECTION, Aiming for. A Wesleyan once asked Rev. Mr. Dunn, of Portsea, whether he thought a state of sinless perfection attainable in this life? Mr. D. replied, "Let us, my friend, seek after it as eagerly as if it were attainable."

10,941. PERFECTION, Boasting of. He who boasts of being perfect is perfect in folly. I never saw a perfect man. Every rose has its thorns, and every day its night. Even the sun shows spots, and the skies are darkened with clouds. And faults of some kind nestle in every bosom.   *Spurgeon.*

10,942. PERFECTION Emblem of Human. Pliny informs us that Zeuxis once painted a boy holding a dish full of grapes so well that the birds were deceived, and flew to the grapes to peck at them. Zeuxis, notwithstanding, was dissatisfied with the picture. "For," said he, "had I painted the boy as well as he ought to have been painted, the birds would have been afraid to touch them." Thus does the Christian dwell more on his shortcomings than on his attainments.   *F. F. Trench.*

10,943. PERFECTION, Estimating. Two brothers, Spaniards, spent their lives and fortunes in different ways. One lived in the desert practicing the austerities and charities of an eremite; the other built hospitals and monasteries. When both were dead, the question arose among the monks as to which of them was the most perfect. They appealed to their abbot, Pambo, and he said, "Both were perfect before God; there are many roads to perfection beside that which leads through the desert cell."

10,944. PERFECTION, Example of. It is said in classic history that a statuary, who resolved to cut out of the Parian marble a female figure the most beautiful and graceful the world ever saw or the poet ever dreamed of, induced all the beauties of Greece to come to him in succession, while he selected from each the feature that was in the highest perfection, and transferred it to the marble on which he was working; and when this beautiful thing was finished, it became the admiration of Greece and of the utmost bound of Europe. In order to form a perfect character, we need copy none but Christ.   *F. F. Trench.*

10,945. PERFECTION, Excelling in. God revealed to Macarius, the anchoret of Scete, far-famed for his austerities, devotions and sanctity, that there were two married women in a neighboring town of greater perfection than himself. He left the desert, staff in hand, in search of them. He found them unknown to fame, unmarked by beauty or fortune, practicing the plain virtues of humility, patience, charity, self-denial and resignation, doing their duty in their domestic relation with cheerfulness, and maintaining a devotional spirit by ejaculatory prayer and frequent consecrations of soul and body to God.

10,946. PERFECTION, Motto of. I once observed the following motto attached to a coat-of-arms on a gentleman's carriage, *Tout bien, ou rien,* "Everything well, or nothing," and it struck me as being peculiarly expressive of what ought to be the Christian's feeling.   *F. F. Trench.*

10,947. PERFECTION, Objection to. A young man in conversation with the late Alexander Patrick of Airdrie, Scotland, attempted to discredit the doctrine of Christian perfection, as taught by the Wesleyans, and rested his whole objection upon a fact in his own experience, declaring that he was daily tormented with bad thoughts, and could not be free from them. "My bairn," said Mr. P., "ye maunna judge o' others by yoursel'. And, ye ken, a bad neebour is no ane o' the family. If ye would just da wi' your ill thoughts as ye da to an ill neebour, that is, dinna gie 'em a stool to sit doun on, ye'll no be sae muckle troubled as ye hae been. It is no impossible, mon, to affront 'em all."   *J. G. Wilson.*

10,948. PERFUMES, Oriental Use of. The Egyptians, Persians, Greeks, Hebrews, and in a word all the ancient nations who had attained to civilization, were addicted to the use of perfumes to an extent to which no European people at the present day affords any parallel. But it was not merely as contributing to the luxury of the body that they were prized. Perfumes were largely employed at the solemn rites which were celebrated at the burial of the dead, and lavishly expended at the public religious services. Take the Hebrews, and observe how great was the importance attached by them to the sacred employment of fragrant substances. The altar of incense stood in a most conspicuous part of the temple, and sweet incense was burned upon it every day. The high priest was forbidden to enter "the holiest of all" unless bearing in his hand the censer from which clouds of perfumed smoke rose before the mercy seat. A portion of frankincense, consisting of many sweet-smelling substances, was added to the sacrifices; and a richly perfumed oil was employed to anoint the altars and other equipments of the temple, and the priests themselves, as a mark of their appointment to the service of God.   *Prof. G. Wilson.*

10,949. PERIL, Unseen. A stranger traveling on foot one intensely dark night, in the Isle of Man, was compelled to feel his way. He came to what seemed a low wall, concluded he had lost his way, and thought to find the road on the other side. He sprang upon the wall and let himself down the length of his arms, but finding no footing drew himself up and returned to the side he had left. He regained the road and reached his destination. The next day he revisited the place where he hung over the wall, and was filled with horror at the awful peril he had escaped. Had he let go, he must have been dashed to pieces on the rocks at the bottom of an awful precipice.

10,950. PERISHING, Rescue the. A neglected soldier shot through the cheeks and roots of his tongue lay in a niche of the fence upon the field of Antietam. A gentleman from Philadelphia discovered him by the light of his lantern, had his wound dressed, and, by special care, saved his life. His gratitude was great. The rescuer was afterwards introduced to the wife of the heroic soldier by her husband, who said, while tears of gratitude filled his eyes, "The man who picked me up at midnight, and dressed my wound, when I had given myself up to die." Souls are wounded, and lie around us waiting for relief, which we can give, and save a soul from death.

10,951. PERJURY, Memento of. Ludovicus, King of Burgundy, was taken prisoner, but was given his liberty upon promising not to make war again. Upon receiving his freedom, he raised a stronger army than before. He was again overcome, and lost all. His eyes were plucked out, and these words were branded upon his forehead: "This man was saved by clemency, and lost by perjury."

10,952. PERJURY, Punishment of. In 1444, Uladislaus, King of Poland, fought against Amurath the Turkish king, and defeated him. A treaty of peace was made, and mutually sworn to by both kings, one swearing upon the Evangelists, and the other on the Koran. But through the influence of the pope, Cardinal Julian was sent to break the league, and absolve Uladislaus from his oath. This renewed the war, and the Turks were being beaten with great slaughter. Amurath seeing the crucifix displayed on the ensigns of the Christians, tore the late treaty from his bosom, and holding it up in his hand, looked up to heaven, exclaiming, "Behold thou crucified Christ, this is the league, thy Christians, in thy name, made with me, which they have without cause violated. Now if thou be God, as they say thou art, revenge the wrong now done unto thy name and me, and show thy power upon thy perjured people, who in their deeds deny thee, their God." The tide of battle turned. Uladislaus was slain, and his head was borne on the end of a lance. The legate, who had instigated the war, was also slain, and his body was treated with great indignity by the Turks.

10,953. PERSECUTION of Bunyan. The bill of indictment preferred against John Bunyan ran thus:—"John Bunyan hath devilishly and perniciously abstained from coming to church to hear divine service, and is a common upholder of several unlawful meetings and conventicles, to the disturbance and distraction of the good subjects of this kingdom, contrary to the laws of our sovereign lord the king." He was convicted, and imprisoned twelve years and six months.

10,954. PERSECUTION, Continuation of. Cain's club is still carried up and down, crimsoned with the blood of Abel. *Buckholtzer.*

10,955. PERSECUTION, Figures of. The *darkness* that fell upon Abram when the burning lamp passed between the divided sacrifice, Gen. 15: 9–21. The *burning bush*, Exod. 3: 1, 2 The *wicked husbandmen* in the vineyard, Matt. 21: 33–35. The *wild boar* rooting up the vine, Ps. 80: 12, 13. The *bulls of Bashan* —fierce *dogs*, Ps. 22: 12, 13, 16, 20; the *lion* 2 Tim. 4: 17; grievous *wolves*, Acts 20: 29. *Archers*, Gen. 49: 23. A *great fight of afflictions*, Heb. 10: 32. *Bowes.*

10,956. PERSECUTION, No Religion in. I love to see a man zealous in a good matter, and especially when his zeal shows itself for advancing morality and promoting the happiness of mankind. But when I find the instruments he works with are racks and gibbets, galleys and dungeons: when he imprisons men's persons, confiscates their estates, ruins their families, and burns the body to save the soul, I cannot stick to pronounce of such a one that (whatever he may think of his faith and religion) his faith is vain and his religion unprofitable.
Addison.

10,957. PERSECUTION Overruled. An Irish girl renounced Romanism, and by order of the priest was turned out of her father's house. A Protestant neighbor took her in, but the priest, jealous of her good fortune, ordered her recall to her father's house, and that an attempt should be made to change her by kindness. This new experiment having been tried in vain, it was resolved to send her to her brother in America, a most bigoted Catholic and violent man. When she met him she resolved to tell him at once of her change of religion. She expected nothing less than the most cruel treatment, and was greatly astonished when he responded by embracing her, and saying, "Mary, it is but three weeks since I too have renounced Romanism, and have peace in coming directly to Jesus Christ, our Lord and Saviour."

10,958. PERSECUTION, Popular. Before the times of Galileo and Harvey, the world believed in the diurnal immovability of the earth, and the stagnation of the blood; and for denying these, the one was persecuted and the other ridiculed. The intelligence and virtue of Socrates were punished with death. Anaxagoras, when he attempted to propagate a just notion of the Supreme Being, was dragged to prison. Aristotle, after a long series of persecutions, swallowed poison. The great geometricians and chemists, as Gerbert, Roger Bacon, and others, were abhorred as magicians. Virgilius, bishop of Saltzburg, having asserted that there existed antipodes, the Archbishop of Mentz declared him an heretic, and consigned him to the flames; and the Abbot Trithemius, who was fond of improving stenography, or the art of secret writing, having published some curious works on that subject, they were condemned, as works full of diabolical mysteries. Galileo was condemned at Rome publicly to disavow his sentiments regarding the motion of the earth, the truth of which must have been abundantly manifest: he was imprisoned in the Inquisition, and visited by Milton, who tells us he was then poor and old. *Disraeli.*

10,959. PERSECUTION, Riches of. A certain person, on seeing a Christian woman go cheerfully to prison, said to her, "O you have not yet tasted of the bitterness of death." She as cheerfully answered, "No, nor never shall; for Christ hath promised that those who keep his sayings shall never see death." *Secker.*

10,960. PERSECUTION, Safety in. As long as the waters of persecution are on the earth, so long we dwell in the ark; but where the land is dry, the dove itself will be tempted to a wandering course of life, and never return to the house of her safety. *Jeremy Taylor.*

10,961. PERSECUTION, Support in. In the time of persecution a judge, in the days of Charles II., said to a good old saint who was persecuted, "I will banish you to America." "Very well," said she; "judge, you cannot send me out of my Father's country."
Whitefield.

10,962. PERSECUTION, Surviving. There were ten persecutions in the first hundred years of the Church, during which hundreds of thousands of Christians were destroyed, and the enemies often thought they had crushed out the new religion. Diocletian had a medal struck with the false boast, "The Christian religion is destroyed, and the worship of the gods is restored." Behold! the stone from the mountain so often smitten fills the whole earth.

10,963. PERSECUTION, Useless. The history of persecution is a history of endeavors to cheat nature; to make water run up hill, to twist a rope of sand. It makes no difference whether the actors be many or one, a tyrant or a mob. *Emerson.*

10,964. PERSEVERANCE, Christian. It is with Christian work just as with all other work, the chief desideratum is persistent application. Arago says, in his autobiography, that his greatest master in mathematics was a word or two of advice, which he found in the binding of one of his text-books, the words of D'Alembert to a discouraged student: "Go on, sir, go on." Those two little words made Arago the greatest astronomical mathematician of his age. And those two words have made many a life a poem which shall sing forever. Christ abbreviated them into one, and his almighty "Go" (spoken when he stood on the extreme verge of this world, only one step from his throne), drove Paul restlessly around Asia and Europe with the message of mercy, and has been sounding in the ear of the Church ever since as its unrepealed and unrepealable marching order. *Dr. Foss.*

10,965. PERSEVERANCE, Effect of. A very little girl undertook to carry a ton of coal, a shovelful at a time, from the sidewalk to a bin in the cellar. An observer asked her, "Do you expect to get all that coal in with that little shovel?" She answered, "Yes sir, if I work long enough." Trifling efforts persisted in will accomplish more than spasmodic endeavors of greater pretensions.

10,966. PERSEVERANCE of Faith. An unbelieving heart may have some flash of spirit and resolution, but it wants free mettle and will be sure to jade in a long journey. Faith will throw in the net of prayer again and again, as long as God commands and the promise encourageth. The greyhound hunts by sight; when he cannot see his game, he gives over running: but the true hound by scent; he hunts over hedge and ditch; though he sees not the hare, he pursues all the day long. Thus an unbelieving heart, may be drawn out upon some visible probabilities and sensible hopes of a coming mercy to pray and exercise a little faith; but when they are out of sight, his heart fails him; but faith keeps the scent of the promise, and gives not over the chase. *Salter.*

10,967. PERSEVERANCE, Final. When Diogenes had spent the greater part of his life in observing the most extreme and scrupulous self-denial, and was fast verging on ninety years of age, one of his friends recommended him to indulge himself a little. "What!" exclaimed he; "would you have me quit the race close by the goal?"

10,968. PERSEVERANCE, Lesson of. The Chinese tell of one of their countrymen, a student, who, disheartened by the difficulties in his way, threw down his book in despair; when, seeing a woman rubbing a crowbar on a stone, he inquired the reason, and was told that she wanted a needle, and thought she would rub down the crowbar till she got it small enough. Provoked by this example of patience to "try again," he resumed his studies, and became one of the three foremost scholars in the empire.
Matthews.

10,969. PERSEVERANCE, Path of. "Search the Scriptures." There are treasures in them more precious than silver and gold; but they do not lie upon the surface: they must be sought with the miner's perseverance, and the miner's toil. And what is the miner's toil? what is the miner's perseverance? Take as an illustration the touching story told of one lying in the churchyard among the mountains, in Wordsworth's "Excursion." He describes one of a band of miners, who, when others were foiled and gave up—

"Alone,
Urged unremittingly the stubborn work,
Unseconded, uncountenanced; then, as time
Passed on, while still his lonely efforts found
No recompense, derided;"

but still he dug on, unmoved by derision, and unshaken by failure, till at length, after twenty years, he came upon the long-sought prize. The joy of his success was too much for him: his mind gave way under it. But the point for us to notice is the patient, persevering toil with which, "hoping against hope," he labored on till he succeeded. And of this, the poet tells us there is left a record on the rock:

"Conspicuous to this day
The path remains that linked his cottage door
To the mine's mouth; a long and slanting tract
Upon the rugged mountain's stony side,
Worn by his daily visits to and from
The darksome centre of a constant hope. . .
And it is named, in memory of the event,
THE PATH OF PERSEVERANCE."
Morse.

10,970. PERSEVERANCE, Power of. Perpetual pushing and assurance put a difficulty out of countenance, and make a seeming impossibility give way.—*Jeremy Collier.*——That policy that can strike only while the iron is hot, will be overcome by that perseverance which, like Cromwell's, can make the iron hot by striking; and he that can only rule the storm must yield to him who can both raise and rule it. *Colton.*

10,971. PERSEVERANCE, Resistless. All the performances of human art at which we look with praise or wonder are instances of the resistless force of perseverance. It is by this that the quarry becomes a pyramid, and that distant countries are united by canals. If a man was to compare the effect of a single stroke of a pickaxe, or of one impression of the spade, with the general design and last result, he would be overwhelmed by the sense of their disproportion; yet those petty operations, incessantly continued, in time surmount the greatest difficulties, and mountains are leveled and oceans bounded by the slender force of human beings. *Johnson.*

10,972. PERSEVERANCE, Satanic. The Hebrew writers note that the devil's name, Beelzebub, signifieth a great flesh-fly or a master-fly: flee him away never so often, he will still fly thither again. So the devil will never cease molesting us, till the "smoking flax" be quite quenched, and the "bruised reed" clean broken.
Bp. Andrews.

10,973. PERSEVERANCE, Successful. Kepler undertook to solve the laws of the planetary system. The Ptolemaic theory of axles and cranks, long and short, by which the planets were strung together and kept in motion, was absurd. No wonder King Alfonso, of Castile, said of it, "If I had been consulted at the creation, I could have done the thing better than that!" Then came the developments of Copernicus, which considered the sun as the centre of the planetary system, and the earth as revolving upon its own axis once in twenty-four hours. It was found that circular orbits did not conform to the observations. Tycho Brahé studied the heavens, and his secrets furnished Kepler a basis of computation. Comparing his own tables of observations of the planet Mars with those of Brahé, he found a difference of eight minutes of a degree. Then he exclaimed, "Out of these eight minutes we will construct a new theory that will explain the movements of all planets." For eight years he tried to hunt down the secret. He tried nineteen hypotheses in vain, and then the ellipse suggested itself as a possible solution. Seventeen years of unflagging toil won a glorious success. In the enthusiasm of victory hard-earned, he exclaimed, "Nothing holds me. The die is cast. The book is written, to be read now or by posterity, I care not which. It may well wait a century for a reader, since God has waited six thousand years for an observer." Kepler's three laws are a memento of perseverance.

10,974. PERSEVERANCE, Useless. Rev. Wm. Davy, of Lustleigh, England, finished "a system of divinity," embracing twenty-six volumes, after twelve years of unremitting toil. He set up the types, of which he had enough for two pages, and printed forty copies of the first three hundred pages, and fourteen of the remainder of the work. The record of perseverance only remains, which resulted in aggravated poverty and disappointment.

10,975. PERSONAL EFFORT, Lesson of. Rev. F. G. Clark went into the orchard where the workmen were busy picking apples, climbing tall ladders placed against the trees, and plucking off the reluctant fruit. A strong wind the day before had shaken off half the fruit, and it lay on the ground ungathered, apparently perfect. "Look here," said he, "why not put in these apples? They are perfectly sound." "No," said the farmer, "not one of these will answer for winter use. They will show a bruise in thirty days, and will begin to perish. Don't put an apple into the barrel which is not hand-picked. Those are the only ones you can rely upon." In this the doctor saw a sermon for soul-savers. They mistake who wait for some mighty rushing wind to shake down the fruit which they are sent to gather carefully by hand. Fruit for winter must all be hand-picked.

10,976. PERSONAL EFFORT, Unpromising. A minister preached a searching sermon on this subject, and at its close assigned some work to each member of his church, except one servant girl, who he did not expect could do anything. She went to the minister after the service and reminded him that he had not assigned any work for her. "Well, Mary," said he, "I don't know what work to set apart for you, unless you try to convert the family with whom you are living; but the difference in your social stations would, I fear, render it difficult." She began at once to pray for her master and mistress, and spent most of that Sunday night in the attic in that service. That same night the mistress awoke in agony of soul, and desired her husband to send for the minister. He wished to call a doctor. She said she was not sick, but lost. They then thought of their pious servant, and as he went to call her, he heard her praying, "God save master and mistress." Her prayer was heard, and both were converted. Great results in saving souls often follow the most unpromising agents.

10,977. PETER, Martyrdom of St. · According to tradition St. Peter was imprisoned in Rome in the time of Nero, and sentenced to suffer death as a Christian. As the day approached, the Christians of Rome besought him with great earnestness to escape. Moved by their tears he started to flee. Escaped from the prison, he was approaching the gate of the city when he met the blessed Master, bearing his cross. "Lord, whither goest thou?" exclaimed the astonished apostle. "I go to be crucified in Rome afresh." Peter at once returned, and gave himself up to his keepers. He is supposed to have been scourged before execution, according to the Roman custom. He was condemned to crucifixion, the most ignominious mode of punishment known to the Romans. He besought his executioners that he might suffer with his head downwards, pleading his unworthiness to die in the same posture as his Lord, which was granted, A. D. 65.

10,978. PHILANTHROPY, Law of. Plato once gave a charity to a degraded wretch, at which his followers greatly wondered. Plato replied, "I show mercy to the man, not as he is wicked, but because he is a man of my own nature." If the philosophic heathen appreherded this law, how much more ought they who recognize the leadership of him who made "all one in Christ Jesus."

10,979. PHILOSOPHY, Death and. The fear of death is so strong, that by it men are kept in bondage all their days. It is an enemy that threatens none whom it does not strike, and there is none but it threatens. Certainly that spectre which Cæsar had not courage to look in the face is very affrighting. Alexander himself, that so often despised it in the field, when passion that transported him cast a vail over his eyes—yet when he was struck with a mortal disease in Babylon, and had death in his view, his palace was filled with priests and diviners, and no superstition was so sottish but he used to preserve himself. And although the philosophers seemed to contemn death, yet the great preparations they made to encounter it argue a secret fear in their breasts. Many discourses, reasonings, and arguments are employed to sweeten the necessity, that cruel necessity, but they are all ineffectual.
Dr. Bates.

10,980. PHILOSOPHY, Impotence of. The heathen philosophers professing themselves to be wise in their speculations, became fools in practice, and were confounded with all their philosophy when they should have made use of it. Some killed themselves from the apprehension of sufferings. Their death was not the effect of courage, but cowardice, the remedy of their fear. Others, impatient of disappointment in their great designs, refused to live. I will instance two of the most eminent among them, Cato and Brutus: they were both philosophers of the manly sect, and virtue never appeared with a brighter lustre among the heathens than when joined with a stoical resolution. And they were not imperfect proficients, but masters in philosophy. Seneca employs all the ornaments of his eloquence to make Cato's eulogy. He represents him as the consummate exemplar of wisdom; as one that realized the sublime idea of virtue described in their writings. And Brutus was esteemed equal to Cato. Yet these, with all the power of their philosophy, were not able to bear the shocks of adversity. Like raw fencers, one thrust put them into such disorders that they forget all their instructions in the place of trial. For, being unsuccessful in their endeavors to restore Rome to its liberty, overcome with discontent and despair, they laid violent hands upon themselves. Cato, being prevented in his first attempt, afterwards tore open his wounds with fierceness and rage. And Brutus, ready to plunge his sword into his breast, complained that virtue was but a vain name. So insufficient are the best precepts of mere rational reason to relieve us in distress. As torrents that are dried up in the heat of summer, when there is most need of them; so all comforts fail in the extremity, that are not derived from the fountain of life.
Dr. Bates.

10,981. PHILOSOPHY, Influence of. The true philosophy is a spring and principle of motion wherever it comes; it makes man active and industrious, it sets every wheel and faculty a-going, it stores our minds with axioms and rules by which to make a sound judgment; it determines the will to the choice of what is honorable and just; and it wings all our faculties to the swiftest prosecution of it. It is accompanied with an elevation and nobleness of mind, joined with a coolness and sweetness of behavior, and backed with a becoming assurance and inflexible resolution.
Plutarch.

10,982. PHILOSOPHY, Road to. The road to true philosophy is precisely the same with that which leads to true religion; and from both one and the other, unless we would enter in as little children, we must expect to be totally excluded.
Lord Bacon.

10,983. PHILOSOPHY, True. Rest not in the high-stained paradoxes of old philosophy, supported by naked reason and the reward of mortal felicity; but labor in the ethics of faith, built upon heavenly assistance, and the happiness of both beings. Understand the rules, but swear not unto the doctrines, of Zeno or Epicurus. Look beyond Antoninus, and terminate not thy morals in Seneca or Epictetus. Let not the twelve, but the two tables be thy law; let Pythagoras be thy remembrancer, not thy textuary and final instructor; and learn the vanity of the world rather from Solomon than Phocylides. Sleep not in the dogmas of the Peripatus, Academy, or Porticus. Be a moralist of the Mount, an Epictetus in the faith, and Christianize thy notions. *T. Browne.*

10,984. PHILOSOPHY, Unused. In the Academy the philosophers made a great many excellent discourses, and asked Panthroidas how he liked them. He answered, "Indeed I think them very good; but of no profit at all, since you yourselves do not use them."

10,985. PHOTOGRAPHY, Nature's. We do not know but it may imprint upon the world our features as they are modified by various passions, and thus fill nature with daguerreotype impressions of all our actions that are performed in daylight. It may be, too, that there are tests by which nature, more skillfully than any human photographist, can bring out and fix those portraits, so that acuter senses than ours shall see them, as on a great canvas, spread over the material universe. Perhaps, too, they may never fade from that canvas, but become specimens in the great picture-gallery of eternity.
Prof. Hitchcock.

10,986. PHYLACTERIES, Jewish. Phylacteries—the common Greek word for amulets—were worn very generally by the Jews at the commencement of the Christian era. They consist of a narrow strip of parchment, about eighteen inches long, on which are carefully written in voweled Hebrew four passages from the Old Testament (Exod. 13: 2–17; Deut. 6: 4–9, 13–22). The strip is rolled up, and placed in a little leathern box, one inch and a half square, which is then bound to the left elbow by cowhide straps half an inch wide, and long enough to be wound spirally about the arm down to the base of the middle finger. There is a smaller phylactery for the forehead, the

box for which is scarcely an inch square. It has also a leathern fillet, which is tied at the back of the head, and then brought around to the breast. When Christ reproved the Pharisees for making broad their phylacteries (Matt. 23: 5), he doubtless alluded to their custom of increasing this smaller box, so as to make its diameter three or four inches, and conspicuously wearing it over their eyes to attract the attention of the multitude. Except by the Pharisees, who paraded them on all occasions, they were worn only at times of prayer. Subsequently they were put on for charms, like the Koran among the modern Mohammedans, and were supposed to drive away the devil, ward off temptation, and insure long life.
Prof. Hitchcock.

10,987. PIETY, Beauty of Early. No music could ever equal the heaven-born cries of new-born babes. When the snowdrops of youth appear in the garden of the church, it evinces that there is a glorious summer approaching.
Secker.

10,988. PIETY, Confidence in. A Southern Methodist bishop said there was in his neighborhood a slaveholder of fortune, a gay man, who gave himself much to field sports and other amusements. He used often to invite his pastor to dinner and to accompany him in his pleasure-seeking excursions of various kinds. The minister cheerfully accepted his invitations, and a friendship grew up between the pastor and his parishioner, that grew into an intimacy, which continued till the last sickness of this gay man. When his wife was apprised that her husband could live but a short time, she was much alarmed for his soul, and inquired if she should not call in their minister. He replied: "No, my dear; he is not the man for me to see now. He was my companion, as you know, in worldly sports and pleasure-seeking; he loved good dinners and a jolly time. I then enjoyed his society and found him a pleasant companion. But I see now that I never had any real confidence in his piety, and have now no confidence in the efficacy of his prayers. I am now a dying man, and need the instruction and prayers of somebody that can prevail with God. We have been much together; but our pastor has never been in serious earnest with me about the salvation of my soul, and he is not the man to help me now." The wife was greatly affected, and said, "What shall I do, then?" He replied, "My coachman, Tom, is a pious man. I have confidence in his prayers. I have often overheard him pray when about the barn or stables, and his prayers have always struck me as being quite sincere and earnest. I never heard any foolishness from him. He has always been honest and earnest as a Christian-man. Call him." Tom was called, and came within the door, dropping his hat and looking tenderly and compassionately at his dying master. The dying man put forth his hand, saying, "Come here, Tom. Take my hand. Tom, can you pray for your dying master?" The slave poured out his soul in earnest prayer.

10,989. PIETY, Effect of Early. Rev. T. Reader, when a child, was deeply impressed with divine truth. A stranger visiting the family, observed that he did not fail to shut himself up alone for prayer. He was powerfully struck with a sense of his own negligence, and said, "Shall a little child be so anxious for a place of retirement to pray, and I never prayed in my life!" From that time he began to be serious, and not only became a Christian, but a very valuable minister of Christ. "I myself," says Mr. Thornton, "have known parents growing gray in the drudgery of sin and Satan, who have been brought, through the pious and affectionate endeavors of their own children, to enjoy the glorious liberty of Christ." *Buck*

10,990. PIETY, Motives to. We are surrounded by motives to piety and devotion, if we would but mind them. The poor are designed to excite our liberality; the miserable, our pity; the sick, our assistance; the ignorant, our instruction; those that are fallen, our helping hand. In those who are vain, we see the vanity of the world; in those who are wicked, our own frailty. When we see good men rewarded, it confirms our hope; and when evil men are punished, it excites our fear. *Bishop Wilson.*

10,991. PIETY, Order of. True piety is a principle of order in the soul—a beautiful and strong axis by which it is ever borne up, and on which it turns in harmony with the music of the spheres. It is like the great law of attraction, maintaining the soul's activity, and keeping the soul in its place; wheeling it in quiet but rapid motion, and ever keeping it in a measured circle round the throne of God, its centre and its sun. *Stoughton.*

10,992. PITY, A Father's. A gray-headed and pious father had a very wicked son. The old man had often wrestled with God on his behalf. But he became worse and worse. Never did the father close his doors against him. One of the father's neighbors said to him, "Why harbor that reprobate son of yours? Why don't you turn him out of doors, and banish him from your house?" "Ay, ay," said the aged saint, "you can all turn him out of doors but his own father."

10,993. PITY, Self-sacrificing. A runaway from the galleys of Toulouse, seeking safety in the country, came upon a cottage whose inmates were in great distress. He learned that they were that day to be turned out of doors for non-payment of rent, and that they had no means of obtaining food or shelter. The galley-slave proposed to the peasant that he should take him back to the galleys and obtain the reward of fifty francs, given for the return of an escaped prisoner. The peasant, astonished, refused the offer. The convict said he would go and give himself up if he did not accept. He yielded, and having returned the prisoner, received his fifty francs reward. He then went to the mayor and told him the whole story, which secured an examination of the prisoner's case. It resulted in his being pardoned.

10,994. PITY, Verbal. Be ye warmed. and

be ye filled, is the furthest most professors go. Words are cheap, and cost nothing, and therefore, many can say they pity, and that extremely too, when at the same time their practice shows it is only verbal, and not a real compassion.   *Whitefield.*

10,995. PLACE, Suitable. A monk asked Poeman, the hermit, "Where shall I settle down? What place will be most suitable for me?" He replied, "Any will be suitable where you do not cause annoyance to other people." Had I better live in community or in solitude?" asked another. "Wherever you find yourself humble-minded, there you may dwell with security. But if you have a great opinion of yourself, nowhere is fit for you," he answered.

10,996. PLAGIARISTS, Fate of. There is a very pretty Eastern tale, of which the fate of plagiarists often reminds us. The slave of a magician saw his master wave his wand, and heard him give orders to the spirits, who arose at the summons. The slave stole the wand, and waved it himself in the air; but he had not observed that his master used his left hand for that purpose. The spirits thus irregularly summoned, tore the thief to pieces instead of obeying his orders.   *Macaulay.*

10,997. PLAINNESS, Demand for. Think of that railway excursion train as it hurries onwards with impetuous speed! A rapid impulse bears forward the whole; one single bystander directs and controls it all. In an unexpected moment a shock, as of a thunderbolt, crushes them together; in the twinkling of an eye the elements of destruction are let loose; each hapless one becomes an instrument of injury or death to his neighbor. What pen can paint the terror, the agony, the anguish of such a scene! They will be remembered for long, long years in mutilated forms, in shaken nerves, in bereaved or orphaned homes; the records will make multitudes shudder by their firesides, or will haunt them in their slumbers. Such have been the effects of one false or mistaken signal! Let us who are ministers of the gospel remember what interests we hold, and by how much the soul is more precious than the body. Let us beware! We are the signalmen!   *J. G. Miall.*

10,998. PLANS, Interrupted. In the heathery turf you will often find a plant chiefly remarkable for its peculiar roots; from the main stem down to the minutest fibre, you will find them all abruptly terminate, as if shorn or bitten off, and the quaint superstition of the country people alleges that once on a time it was a plant of singular potency for healing all sorts of maladies, and therefore the great enemy of man in his malignity bit off the roots, in which its virtues resided. The plant with this odd history, is a very good emblem of many well-meaning but little-effecting people. They might be defined as *radicibus præmorsis,* or rather *inceptis succisis.* The efficacy of every good work lies in its completion, and all their good works terminate abruptly, and are left off unfinished. The devil frustrates their effi-

cacy by cutting off their ends; their unprofitable history is made up of plans and projects schemes of usefulness that were never gone about, and magnificent undertakings that were never carried forward; societies that were set agoing, then left to shift for themselves, and forlorn beings who for a time were taken up and instructed, and just when they were beginning to show symptoms of improvement were cast on the world again. *Dr. J. Hamilton.*

10,999. PLANS, Unsuccessful. Siramnes, a Persian, was much wondered at because he spoke like a wise man, but failed in all his plans. In extenuation he said, "I myself am master of my words, but the king and fortune have power over my actions."

11,000. PLEASURE, Billows of. I have sat upon the shore, and waited for the gradual approach of the sea, and have seen its dancing waves and white surf, and admired that he who measured it with his hand had given to it such life and motion; and I have lingered till its gentle waters grew into mighty billows, and had well-nigh swept me from my firmest footing. So have I seen a heedless youth gazing with a too curious spirit upon the sweet motions and gentle approaches of an inviting pleasure, till it has detained his eye and imprisoned his feet, and swelled upon his soul, and swept him to a swift destruction.

         Mrs. Montague.

11,001. PLEASURE, Costly. A pot of honey having been upset in a grocer's shop, the flies came around it in swarms to eat it up, nor would they move from the spot while there was a drop left. At length their feet became so clogged that they could not fly away, and, stifled in the luscious sweets, they exclaimed, "Miserable creatures that we are, who, for the sake of an hour's pleasure, have thrown away our lives!"   *Æsop.*

11,002. PLEASURE, Cost of. An English gentleman was blamed by his business partner for giving so much money for religious objects. He replied, "Your fox-hounds cost more in one year than my religion ever cost me in two."

11,003. PLEASURE, Effects of. It is said that Valentinian II. was fond of pleasures, but he showed, notwithstanding, a noble contempt of them. When his people complained of his too great attachment to them, he ordered all the festivals of the circus to be abolished, and all the wild beasts that were kept for the entertainment of the people to be slain. And what great value should we set upon the pleasures of the world? They pass away as soon as they have wearied out the body, and leave it as a bunch of grapes whose juice hath been pressed out; which made one to say, "I see no greater pleasure in this world than the contempt of pleasure." Julian, though an apostate, yet professed that the pleasures of the body were far below a great spirit. And Tully saith, "He is not worthy of the name of a man that would entirely spend one whole day in pleasures." Voluptas, the goddess of sensual pleasures, was worshiped at Rome, where she had a temple. She was represented as a young and beautiful woman, well dressed, and elegantly adorned, seated on a throne, and having virtue under her feet. This representation is just enough; the love of pleasure is too often attended with the sacrifice of virtue.

Buck.

11,004. PLEASURE, Epochs of. No enjoyment, however inconsiderable, is confined to the present moment. A man is the happier for life from having made once an agreeable tour, or lived for any length of time with pleasant people, or enjoyed any considerable interval of innocent pleasure. *Sydney Smith.*

11,005. PLEASURE, Lure of. The town of Hamelin, according to a medieval fable, was fearfully infested with rats in 1284. The people were worried by night and by day. The cook in the kitchen, the babe in the cradle, and the people at church were all disturbed by them. A piper, dressed in a suit of many colors, came to the town, and proposed to rid it of vermin for a consideration. His terms were accepted. Thereupon the piper began to play, and the rats began to come forth from their holes and dens, and to follow the piper. He led them to the river Weser, into which they all plunged, and were drowned. The piper returned, and claimed the stipulated reward; but the townsfolk, being no longer in fear of the rats, refused payment, and justified their refusal by accusing the rat charmer of sorcery. Behold his retribution! On a day in June, the pied piper re-appeared in the streets of Hamelin town. He put the magic pipe to his lips, and before he sounded three notes all the little boys and girls of the town came skipping to meet him. He led them forth, a merry procession of laughing and dancing children, to the Koppenberg, a mountain outside the town. Its side opened to the piper, and the strange procession passed in, and was seen no more. Two only—one blind, the other dumb—were left to point out the place where the children vanished. Thus perished one hundred and twenty children. Many have been lured to living tombs, a worse fate, by the charmer Pleasure.

11,006. PLEASURE, Mental. When the lovers of the art of painting are so enamored with the charmingness of their own performances, that Nicias, as he was drawing the Evocation of Ghosts in Homer, often asked his servants whether he had dined or no; and when King Ptolemy had sent him three-score talents for his piece, after it was finished, he would neither accept the money nor part with his work; what and how great satisfaction may we then suppose to have been reaped from geometry and astronomy by Euclid when he wrote his dioptrics; by Philippus when he had perfected his demonstration of the figure of the moon; by Archimedes when, with the help of a certain angle, he had found the sun's diameter to make the same part of the largest circle that that angle made of four right angles.

Plutarch.

11,007. PLEASURE, Modification of. Age and maturity pass a real and a marvelous change upon the diet and recreations of the same person; so that no man at the years and vigor of thirty is either fond of sugar-plums or rattles: in like manner, when reason, by the assistance of grace, has prevailed over and outgrown the encroachments of sense, the delights of sensuality are to such an one but as a hobby-horse would be to a counselor of state, or as tasteless as a bundle of hay to a hungry lion. Every alteration of a man's condition infallibly infers an alteration of his pleasures.

South.

11,008. PLEASURE, Palace of. The palace of pleasure has a gorgeous street entrance, adorned with statuary and brilliant with variegated lights, and the passer is lured in by strains of music. The exit is a dark, narrow, concealed rear way, which leads into the fields where swine are kept. They are soon reached, and the votaries of pleasure are glad to feed with the brutish herd.

11,009. PLEASURE, Pursuit of. Pleasures are Junos in the pursuit, and but clouds in the enjoyment. Pleasure is a beautiful harlot sitting in her chariot, whose four wheels are pride, gluttony, lust, and idleness. The two horses are prosperity and abundance; the two drivers are idleness and security; her attendants and followers are guilt, grief, late repentance, if any, and oft death and ruin. Many great men, and many strong men, and many rich men, and many hopeful men, and many young men, have come to their ends by her; but never any enjoyed full satisfaction and content in her. *Brooks.*

11,010. PLEASURES, Unsubstantial. Pleasures are not of such a solid nature that we can dive into them; we must merely skim over them: they resemble those boggy lands over which we must run lightly, without stopping to put down our feet. *Fontenelle.*

11,011. POETRY, The Best of. The best kind of poetry is ever in alliance with real uncorrupted Christianity; and with the degeneracy of the one always comes the decline of the other; for it is to Christianity that we owe the fullest inspirations of the celestial spirit of poetry. *J. A. St. John.*

11,012. POETRY, Elevating Qualities of. Poetry has been to me "its own exceeding great reward;" it has soothed my afflictions; it has multiplied and refined my enjoyments; it has endeared solitude; and it has given me the habit of wishing to discover the good and the beautiful in all that meets and surrounds me.

Coleridge.

11,013. POETRY, Emotions of. There are so many tender and holy emotions flying about in our inward world, which, like angels, can never assume the body of an outward act; so many rich and lovely flowers spring up which bear no seed, that it is a happiness poetry was invented, which receives into its limbus all these incorporeal spirits, and the perfume of all these flowers. *Richter.*

11,014. POETRY, Pleasure in. A true reader of poetry partakes of a more than ordinary portion of the poetic nature; and no one can be completely such, who does not love, or take an interest in everything that interests the poet, from the firmament to the daisy—from the highest heart of man to the most pitiable of the low.   *Hunt.*

11,015. POLICY, Advantage of. Pliny tells of a dolphin attacking a crocodile, and finding his hard scales impenetrable, he dove under him and struck from below, and killed him by penetrating this unprotected spot. Spencer says, "What instinct taught the creature, reason teaches man—to strike the enemy in the weakest part, and leave things impossible unattempted."

11,016. POLITENESS, Advantage of. It is said that a gentlemen on a battle-field, happening to bow to an officer who addressed him, a cannon-ball just then went through his hair, and took off the head of the one behind him. The officer, when he saw the marvelous escape, observed that no man ever lost by politeness.

11,017. POLITENESS, Instinctive. Dr. Whewell was one day walking with his little dog, when, by accident, he trod on his tail. Quite instinctively he turned around, made a bow, raised his hat, and gravely said, "I beg your pardon."

11,018. POLITENESS, True. I believe it is best to be known by description, definition not being able to comprise it. I would, however, venture to call it benevolence in trifles, or the preference of others to ourselves, in little daily occurrences in the commerce of life. A better place, a more commodious seat, priority in being helped at table; what is it but sacrificing ourselves in such trifles to the convenience and pleasure of others? And this constitutes true politeness. It is a perpetual attention (by habit it grows easy and natural to us) to the little wants of those we are with, by which we either prevent or remove them. Bowing, ceremonies, formal compliments, stiff civilities, will never be politeness; that must be easy, natural, unstudied, manly, noble. And what will give this but a mind benevolent, and perpetually attentive to exert that amiable disposition in trifles towards all you converse and live with?   *Chesterfield.*

11,019. POLITENESS, Unusual. Politeness should be a constant habit. A lady, expecting to have some company, tried to improve her children's neglected manners. She drilled them very carefully in what they were to say, and when the time arrived, placed them in a row in the parlor. The children sat very still until all the company were assembled, when they all jumped up together and repeated, like a lesson, "Yes, ma'am," "No, ma'am," "Yes, sir," "No, sir," "Thank you, ma'am," "Thank you, sir," and then ran off.

11,020. POOR, Advantage of the. Mohammed declares that the poor will enter paradise five hundred years before the rich, and that he had a view of paradise, in which he saw that a majority of its inhabitants were the poor people of this world.

11,021. POOR, Neglect of the. I fancy in some sad abode of this city, some invisible pallet of straw, a man, a Christian man, pining, perishing, without an attendant, looking his last upon nakedness and misery, feeling his last in the pangs of hunger and thirst. The righteous spirit of the man being disembodied, I fancy it to myself, rising to heaven, encircled by an attendance of celestial spirits, daughters of mercy, who waited upon his soul when mankind deserted his body. The attended spirit I fancy rising to the habitation of God, and reporting in the righteous ear of the Governor of the earth, how it fared with him amid all the extravagance and outlay of this city. And saith the indignant Governor of men, "They had not a morsel of bread nor a drop of water to bestow upon my saint. Who of my angels will go for me where I will send? Go, thou angel of famine; break the growing ear with thy wing, and let mildew feed upon their meal. Go, thou angel of plague, and shake thy wings once more over the devoted city. Go, thou angel of fire, and consume all the neighborhood where my saint suffered unheeded and unpitied. Burn it, and let its flame not quench till their pavilions are a heap of smouldering ashes."   *Edward Irving.*

11,022. POOR, Pillaging the. The nets which we use against the poor are just those worldly embarrassments which either their ignorance or their improvidence are almost certain at some time or other to bring them into; then, just at the time when we ought to hasten to help them, and teach them how to manage better in future, we rush forward to pillage them, and force all we can out of them in their adversity. For, to take one instance only, remember this is literally and simply what we do whenever we buy, or try to buy, cheap goods —goods offered at a price which we know cannot be remunerative for the labor involved in them. Whenever we buy such goods, we are stealing somebody's labor.   *Ruskin.*

11,023. POOR, Sympathy with the. St. Yoo, of Kermartin, was a lawyer in early life, and was called "the advocate of the poor." As a lawyer he always endeavored to prevent rather than promote quarrels. As a judge he was just and incorruptible. For the poor he felt special interest, and from them would take no fees. One morning a poor, half-naked beggar was found upon his doorstep, who had passed the night there shivering with the cold. The next night he made the beggar sleep in his own bed, and he himself lay upon the doorstep, that he might learn from experience what the sufferings of the poor are, and have always a true sympathy for them.

11,024. POOR, Will of the. What will become of my family? is often an anxious question to the poor. They can do no better than to follow Luther's example, and give them to God. In his last will and testament occurs the following remarkable passage: "Lord God, I thank thee, for that thou hast been pleased to make me a poor and indigent man upon earth. I have neither house, nor land, nor money to leave behind me. Thou hast given me wife and children, whom I now restore to thee. Lord, nourish, teach, and preserve them, as thou hast me."

11,025. POPE, Adoring the. Think of an intelligent person crossing himself before the picture of the pope as devoutly as before a crucifix. Yet it is the custom of Romanists in this day in this land. A traveler found a degraded Japanese worshiping the picture of Napoleon. Which is the greatest idolater?

11,026. POPE, Worshiping the. On the first occasion when a new pope appears in public after his election to the pontificate, he is elevated into an object of adoration in the temple of God. The new pope, wearing his mitre, is lifted up by cardinals, and is placed by them on the high altar of the principal church at Rome—St. Peter's. He is seated there upon the altar of God; and while he there sits, the Roman hierarchy bow down before him, and kiss those feet which tread on the altar of God. This ceremony of adoration is prescribed by the official book of Roman ceremonies, entitled *Cæremoniale Romanum;* it may be seen described in Lib. iii., sect. 1, of the edition of 1572; and it has been performed on the election of every pope for many centuries in succession. It was performed to the present pope on Wednesday, June 17, 1846. This ceremony is called oy Roman writers the *Adoratio Pontificis*, and it is represented in the Roman coinage with the following remarkable inscription: *"Quem creant, adorant"*—"whom they create they adore." Whom the Roman hierarchy make by their own votes to be pope, him they adore when made; they worship the work of their own hand. They make an image, and then worship it.   *Wordsworth.*

11,027. POPERY, Absurdity of. Inquisitive and restless spirits frequently take refuge from their own skepticism in the bosom of a church which pretends to infallibility, and, after questioning the existence of a Deity, bring themselves to worship a wafer.   *Macaulay.*

11,028. POPERY, Decay of. Popery can build new chapels—welcome to do so, to all lengths. Popery cannot come back, any more than Paganism can, which also still lingers in some countries. But, indeed, it is with these things as with the ebbing of the sea: you look at the waves oscillating hither, thither, on the beach; for minutes you cannot tell how it is going; look in half an hour where it is—look in half a century where your popehood is! Alas, would there were no greater danger to our Europe than the poor old pope's revival! Thor may as soon try to revive.   *Carlyle.*

11,029. POPULARITY, A Desirable. I do not affect to scorn the opinion of mankind. I wish earnestly for popularity; I will seek, and I will have popularity; that popularity which follows, and not that which is run after.   *Mansfield.*

11,030. POPULARITY, Test of. Antigonus had taken upon him the name and dignity of King of Macedon. He was told that the people were dis-

contented with this assumption. So he laid down his crown and sceptre, advised them of his conquests, and openly admonished them that, "If they knew any man more worthy of the kingdom than himself, they should, at their pleasure, dispose of the crown and sceptre to that person." The people were so much moved by his address that they besought him to re-assume the reins of government, which he utterly refused to do until the authors of the sedition were punished.

11,031. POPULARITY, Unsatisfactory. It is not the applause of a day, it is not the huzzas of thousands, that can give a moment's satisfaction to a rational being: that man's mind must, indeed, be a weak one, and his ambition of a most depraved sort, who can be captivated by such wretched allurements, or satisfied with such momentary gratification.   *Mansfield.*

11,032. PORTION, God our. Propriety makes every comfort a pleasurable comfort, a delightful comfort. When a man walks in a fair meadow, and can write mine upon it, and into a pleasant garden, and can write mine upon it, and into a fruitful corn-field, and can write mine upon it, and into a stately habitation, and can write mine upon it, and into a rich mine, and can write mine upon it, oh, how doth it please him? how doth it delight him? how doth it joy and rejoice him? Of all words, this word *meum* is the sweetest and the comfortablest. Ah! when a man can look upon God, and write *meum;* when he can look upon God, and say, This God is my portion; when he can look upon God, and say with Thomas, "My Lord and my God" (John 20: 28), how will all the springs of joy rise in his soul! Oh, who can but joy to be owner of that God that fills heaven and earth with his fulness? who can but rejoice to have him for his portion, in having whom he hath all things, in having whom he can want nothing? The serious thoughts of our propriety in God will add much to all our sweets, yea, it will make every bitter sweet.   *Brooks.*

11,033. POSSESSION, Importance of. An angler who gained his livelihood by fishing, after a long day's toil, caught nothing but one little fish. "Spare me," said the little creature, "I beseech you; so small as I am, I shall make you but a sorry meal. I am not come to my full size yet; throw me back into the river for the present, and then, when I am grown bigger and worth eating, you may come here and catch me again." "No, no," said the man; "I have got you now, but if you once get back into the water, your tune will be, 'Catch me if you can.'" A bird in the hand is worth two in the bush.   *Æsop.*

11,034. POSSESSION, Value of. One's own—what a charm there is in the words! how long it takes boy and man to find out their worth! how fast most of us hold on to them! faster and more jealously, the nearer we are to the general home, into which we can take nothing, but must go naked as we came into the world. When shall we learn that he who multiplieth

possessions multiplieth troubles, and that the one single use of things which we call our own, is that they may be his who hath need of them?
Hughes.

11,035. POTTAGE, Oriental. The people of the East are exceedingly fond of pottage, which they call kool. It is something like gruel, and is made of various kinds of grain, which are first beaten in a mortar. The red pottage is made of kurakan and other grains, but is not superior to the other. For such a contemptible mess, then, did Esau sell his birthright. When a man has sold his fields or gardens for an insignificant sum, the people say, "The fellow has sold his land for pottage." Does a father give his daughter in marriage to a low-caste man? it is observed, "He has given her for pottage." Does a person by base means seek for some paltry enjoyment? it is said, "For one leaf (namely, leaf-full) of pottage he will do nine days' work." Has a learned man stooped to anything which was not expected from him? it is said, "The learned one has fallen into the pottage-pot." Has he given instruction or advice to others? "The lizard which gave warning to the people has fallen into the pottage-pot." Of a man in great poverty it is remarked, "Alas! he cannot get pottage." A beggar asks, "Sir, will you give me a little pottage?" Does a man seek to acquire great things by small means? "He is trying to procure rubies by pottage." When a person greatly flatters another, it is common to say, "He praises him only for his pottage." Does a king greatly oppress his subjects? it is said, "He only governs for his pottage." Has an individual lost much money by trade? "The speculation has broken his pottage-pot." Does a rich man threaten to ruin a poor man? the latter asks, "Will the lightning strike my pottage-pot?"
Roberts.

11,036. POTTER, Figure of the. An Oriental traveler says: "I have been out on the shore again, examining a native manufactory of pottery, and was delighted to find the whole biblical apparatus complete, and in full operation. There was the potter sitting at his 'frame,' and turning the 'wheel' with his foot. He had a heap of the prepared clay near him, and a pan of water by his side. Taking a lump in his hand, he placed it on the top of the wheel (which revolves horizontally), and smoothed it into a low cone, like the upper end of a sugar-loaf; then thrusting his thumb into the top of it, he opened a hole down through the centre, and this he constantly widened, by pressing the edges of the revolving cone between his hands. As it enlarged and became thinner, he gave it whatever shape he pleased with the utmost ease and expedition. This, I suppose, is the exact point of those biblical comparisons between the human and the divine potter: 'O house of Israel, cannot I do with you as this potter? saith the Lord. Behold, as the clay is in the potter's hands, so are ye in my hand, saith the Lord,' Jer. 18: 6. When Jeremiah was watching the potter, the vessel was marred in his hand, and 'so he made

it again another vessel, as seemed good to the potter to make it,' Jer. 18: 4. I had to wait a long time for that, but it happened at last. From some defect in the clay, or because he had taken too little, the potter suddenly changed his mind, crushed his growing jar instantly into a shapeless mass of mud, and beginning anew, fashioned it into a totally different vessel. It is evident, from numerous expressions in the Bible, that the potter's vessel was the synonym of utter fragility; and to say that the wicked should be broken to pieces as a potter's vessel, was to threaten the most ruinous destruction. In this day of strong stone pottery, we should hardly have adopted this language."

11,037. POVERTY, Choice of. St. Francis of Assisi chose a life of poverty. He was a partner with his father in the mercantile business, and besides was the prospective heir of considerable wealth. At the age of twenty-five he went to the bishop of the place, with his father, to make a legal renunciation of his inheritance. He stripped off the robes he wore and gave them to his father, that his renunciation of earthly goods might be complete, saying, "Hitherto I have called you father on earth; but now I say with more confidence, Our Father who art in heaven, in whom I place all my hope and treasure." He wore no shoes or girdle, but contented himself with one poor coat, girt with a cord. He was led to hold poverty in high esteem, because Christ possessed no earthly goods, was born in a stable, subsisted by charity, had no place to lay his head, and died naked upon a cross. He says, "Poverty is the way of salvation, the nurse of humility, and the root of perfection." It was the basis upon which his order of monks was founded. He called poverty his spouse, his queen, his mother, and desired it for his portion.

11,038. POVERTY, Virtuous. St. Guy, known as "The Poor Man of Anderlech," was the child of poor but pious parents, who gave their son the maxim, "We shall be rich enough if we fear God." He considered the lot of poverty as one of great advantage, exempt from many of the temptations of the rich, and especially honored in being chosen by our Saviour on earth. St. Augustine reckoned among the reprobate: first, those who had their comforts on earth; second, those who grieved and murmured because they were deprived of them. He was very benevolent, often fasting himself that he might be able to relieve others. He was once induced to join a merchant in a commercial venture by the prospect of acquiring more for charitable use. The Lord showed him the folly of looking to his own prudence rather than relying upon him. The ship of whose cargo he was part owner, was wrecked in passing out of the harbor of Laken. He considered it a punishment for his rashness in being lured by a specious motive, A. D. 1033

11,039. POWER, Abstract. Power in itself is an abstraction. We can never see it, we cannot hear it, we cannot feel it, we cannot taste it, we cannot smell it. We witness its results everywhere. I see now the train moving; it is not power itself, but an evidence of it. I heard the thunder roaring; it was not power in itself, but the consequence of it. I am thrown down by some force; it is the result of some invisible power. The mind may influence, through various mediums, the objects of its operations into tears, laughter, joy or misery: all this is the result of power. All forms of power in themselves are equally invisible; power is alone known in its agents and results. *T. Hughes.*

11,040. POWER, Concentration of. The weakest living creature, by concentrating his powers on a single object, can accomplish something. The strongest, by dispersing his over many, may fail to accomplish anything. The drop, by continually falling, bores its passage through the hardest rock. The hasty torrent rushes over it with hideous uproar, and leaves no trace behind. *Carlyle.*

11,041. POWER, Conditions of. In driving piles, a machine is used by which a huge weight is lifted up and then made to fall upon the head of the pile. Of course the higher the weight is lifted the more powerful is the blow which it gives when it descends. Now, if we would tell upon our age and come down upon society with ponderous blows, we must see to it that we are uplifted as near to God as possible. All our power will depend upon the elevation of our spirits. Prayer, meditation, devotion, communion, are like a windlass to wind us up aloft: it is not lost time which we spend in such sacred exercises, for we are thus accumulating force, so that when we come down to our actual labor for God, we shall descend with an energy unknown to those to whom communion is unknown. *Spurgeon.*

11,042. POWER, Converting. A soldier rose in meeting, during the war, and said, "My friends, I left home an infidel, but I left a praying wife. A week ago I received a letter from her, in which she expressed anxiety for the welfare of my soul, and desired to know if I still held to my old views. I wrote an answer, and in bitter words defended my old position. As I was about to seal the letter, it seemed to me I could not send it. I wrote another, softened down considerably from the first, but when that was done I could not send it. I began another, but such was the power of the Spirit upon my heart that I fell upon my knees and begged for forgiveness before God. I could not finish the letter, until I could say to my dear wife that Christ had forgiven my sins. I have been permitted to write to her that I am to-night rejoicing in her Saviour."

11,043. POWER, Gentle. If we aim a blow with a poker at a fly that perches on the forehead, we run a great risk of knocking out the brains. Coarse dealings with spiritual deficiencies are productive of incalculable ill; they were never adopted by our Lord. *Power.*

11,044. POWER, Holy Spirit's. At Everton, when the Rev. Mr. Berridge was preaching, Sabbath, May 20, 1759, from, "Having a form of godliness, but denying the power thereof," an eye-witness thus describes the effect: "When the power of religion began to be spoken of, the presence of God really filled the place; and whilst poor sinners felt the sentence of death in their souls, what sounds of distress did I hear! The greatest number of those who cried, or fell, were men; but some women, and several children, felt the power of the same Almighty Spirit, and seemed just sinking into hell. This occasioned a mixture of various sounds—some shrieking and some roaring aloud. The most general was a loud breathing, like that of persons half strangled, gasping for life." Most of the cries were like men dying in anguish. Many wept silently, others fell down as dead, others in violent agitation. Strong and healthy young men fell in convulsions.

11,045. POWER, Individual. Examples might easily be multiplied of the great power one person may exercise, for good or for evil. "One sinner destroyeth much good," Eccles. 9: 18; one traitor within the camp may counteract the valor of thousands of brave men; one evil-disposed child may kindle a fire which twenty strong men cannot quench, and twenty years cannot repair. What power Moses had, single-handed, to face the whole multitude of Israel's hosts! Exod. 32: 26; and Elijah, to confront Ahab and the eight hundred and fifty priests, and the people of Israel, 1 Kings 18: 22, 40: see similarly the examples of Shamgar, slaying with his ox-goad six hundred men, Judges 3: 31; Samson, a thousand men, Judges 15: 15; David becoming the chapion of his nation, 1 Sam. 17; the poor wise man who delivered a city by his wisdom, Eccles. 9: 14, 15. *Bowes.*

11,046. POWER, Reception of. Mr. Moody attributes his success as an evangelist to the baptism of the Holy Ghost upon his own soul. He had been converted for twenty-one years, and had been teaching a mission-school in Chicago. He felt that he needed power. He says, "My desire was that I might have a fresh anointing. I preached and preached; but it was beating against the air. I requested a good woman and a few others to come and pray with me every Friday at four o'clock. Oh! how piteously I prayed to God that he might fill the empty vessel! After the fire in Chicago I was in New York City, and going into a bank on Wall street it seemed as if I felt a strange and mighty power coming over me. I went up to the hotel, and there in my room I wept before God. I cried: 'Oh, my God, stay thy hand.' He gave me such a fulness, that it seemed more than I could contain. May God forgive me if I should speak in a boastful way, but I do not know a sermon that I have preached since but that God has given me some soul."

11,047. POWER, Spiritual. Electricity has been known for years to be an attracting substance, but its power who estimated? We know, to-day, that electric fluid is in us—in inanimate substances too, as well as animate; that electric fluid penetrates everywhere; and yet we never feel it, save when the equilibrium is disturbed, and we are made to perceive the sudden passage. It is about us, in us, connected with our breath, with the beating of our hearts, the circulation of our blood; it runs along the course of our nerves; to some extent we feel by it—I had almost said, to some extent we think by it; and yet how little is known of its power! That same something in us and around us—call it electricity, magnetism, or what you will—by which we navigate the ocean, drive machinery, apply inventions to the arts, is becoming an immense power; yet who can tell what it is, where it is, where it springs from? God has wrapped it up in everything around us. Put me on that stand, isolated, brought into contact with the electrical machine, and though not aware of its presence, I am full of it, and it comes out of me in all directions; yet I have no consciousness of its tangibility. May it not be an illustration of how spiritual influences may come down and be with us; that they may have great power, which, if properly applied, might transform our natures? *Bp. Simpson.*

11,048. PRACTICE, Inconsistent. A wolf looking into a hut and seeing some shepherds comfortably regaling themselves on a joint of mutton—"A pretty row," said he, "would these men have made if they had caught me at such a supper!" *Æsop.*

11,049. PRACTICE, Lesson of. A neighbor near my study persists in practicing upon the flute. He bores my ears as with an auger, and renders it almost an impossibility to think. Up and down his scale he runs remorselessly, until even the calamity of temporary deafness would almost be welcome to me. Yet he teaches me that I must practice if I would be perfect; must exercise myself unto godliness if I would be skilful; must, in fact, make myself familiar with the word of God, with holy living, and saintly dying. Such practice, moreover, will be as charming as my neighbor's flute is intolerable. *Spurgeon.*

11,050. PRACTICE, Need of. He who hears the law, and does not practice it, is like a man who ploughs and sows, but never reaps. *Jewish Proverb.*

11,051. PRACTICE, Precept and. He that gives proper precepts, and then sets improper examples, resembles that foolish person who labors hard to kindle a fire, and when he has done it throws cold water upon it to quench it. Though such a physician may administer the reviving cordial to some fainting disciple, yet he is in danger himself of dying in a swoon. I may say of such professors as was once said of a certain preacher, that when he was in the pulpit it was a pity he should ever leave it, he was so excellent an instructor; but when he was out of it, it was a pity he should ever ascend it again, he was so wretched a liver. *Secker.*

11,052. PRAISE, Chorus of. There was a beautiful tradition among the Jews which

Lancisius quotes from Philo. It is to this effect: When God had created the world, he asked the angels what they thought of this work of his hands. One of them replied that it was so vast and so perfect that only one thing was wanting to it, namely, that there should be created a clear, mighty, and harmonious voice, which should fill all the quarters of the world incessantly with its sweet sound, thus day and night to offer thanksgiving to its Maker for his incomparable blessings. Thus our thanksgiving should not be an exercise of devotion practiced now and then. It should be incessant, the voice of a love which is ever living and fresh in our hearts. *F. W. Faber.*

11,053. PRAISE, Effects of. Praise has different effects, according to the mind it meets with; it makes a wise man modest, but a fool more arrogant. *Feltham.*

11,054. PRAISE, Encouragement of. Praise is the greatest encouragement we chameleons can pretend to, or rather the manna that keeps soul and body together; we devour it as if it were angels' food, and vainly think we grow immortal. There is nothing transports a poet, next to love, like commending in the right place. *D. K. Lee.*

11,055. PRAISE, Eternal. Rev. John Janeway, on his death-bed, said, "Come, help me with praises; all is too little: come, help me, O ye glorious and mighty angels, who are so well skilled in this heavenly work of praise. Praise him, all ye creatures upon the earth; let everything that hath being help me to praise him. Hallelujah, hallelujah, hallelujah! Praise is now my work, and I shall be engaged in that sweet employment forever."

11,056. PRAISE, God not Affected by. Not that praise can add to God's glory, nor blasphemies detract from it. The blessing tongue cannot make him better, nor the cursing worse—as the sun is neither bettered by birds singing, nor battered by dogs barking. He is so infinitely great, and constantly good, that his glory admits neither addition nor diminution. *Adams.*

11,057. PRAISE, Grateful. A converted sailor, in the gladness of his first love, was heard to exclaim, "To save such a sinner as I am! He shall never hear the end of it."

11,058. PRAISE in the Heart. Lord, my voice by nature is harsh and untunable, and it is vain to lavish any art to better it. Can my singing of psalms be pleasing to thy ears, which is unpleasant to my own? Yet, though I cannot chant with the nightingale, or chirp with the blackbird, I had rather chatter with the swallow, yea, rather croak with the raven, than be altogether silent. Hadst thou given me a better voice, I would have praised thee with a better voice; now what my music wants in sweetness let it have in sense—singing praises with my understanding. Yea, Lord, create in me a new heart, therein to make melody, and I will be contented with my old voice until, in thy due time, being admitted unto the choir of heaven, I have another, more harmonious, bestowed on me. *T. Fuller.*

11,059. PRAISE, Loud. Noise is what the Hindoos best understand, and he that sings the loudest is considered to sing the best. There are also English congregations that would be puzzled to give as pertinent a reason for their silence as these Hindoo Christians for the opposite. I have occasionally remonstrated with them on the subject, but the reply I once received silenced me forever after. "Sing softly, brother," I said to one of the principal members. "Sing softly," he replied; "is it you, our father, who tells us to sing softly? Did you ever hear us sing the praises of our Hindoo gods? how we threw our heads backward, and with all our might shouted out the praises of those who are no gods! And now do you tell us to whisper the praises of Jesus? No, sir, we cannot—we must express in loud tones our gratitude to him who loved and died for us." *Gorgerly.*

11,060. PRAISE, Supernatural. The Talmudists teach, that when David became fatigued by singing psalms, he called the sun, moon, stars, dragons, fire, hail, snow, rain, wind, mountains, hills, trees, beasts, cattle, reptiles, birds and men, and they relieved him in chanting the Creator's praise. This results from a literal interpretaion of Ps. 148. It is a beautiful fancy.

11,061. PRAYER, Access in. However early in the morning you seek the gate of access, you find it already open, and however deep the midnight moment when you find yourself in the sudden arms of death, the winged prayer can bring an instant Saviour; and this wherever you are. It needs not that you ascend some special Pisgah or Moriah. It needs not that you should enter some awful shrine, or pull off your shoes on some holy ground. Could a memento be reared on every spot from which an acceptable prayer has passed away, and on which a prompt answer has come down, we should find *Jehovah Shammah,* "the Lord hath been here," inscribed on many a cottage hearth, and many a dungeon floor. We should find it not only in Jerusalem's proud temple and David's cedar galleries, but in the fisherman's cottage by the brink of the Gennesaret, and in the upper chamber where Pentecost began. And whether it be the field where Isaac went down to meditate, or the rocky knoll where Israel wrestled, or the den where Daniel gazed on the hungry lions, and the lions gazed on him, or the hill-side where the Man of Sorrows prayed all night, we should still discern the ladder's feet let down from heaven—the landing place of mercies, because the starting place of prayer. *Dr. J. Hamilton.*

11,062. PRAYER, Agency of. Prayer can obtain everything; can open the windows of heaven and shut the gates of hell; can put a holy constraint upon God, and detain an angel till he leaves a blessing; can open the treasures of rain, and soften the iron ribs of rocks till they melt into a flowing river; can arrest the sun in his course, and send the winds upon our errands. *Jeremy Taylor.*

11,063. PRAYER, Answer to A minister related the case of a little boy with a sore hand, which had become so bad that the physician decided it must be amputated to save the boy's life. The day was fixed for the operation. On hearing this, the boy went to a retired spot, fell on his knees, and begged God, for Jesus' sake, to save his poor hand. The next day the physician came and examined the hand, when, to the astonishment of all, it was found to be so much better that amputation was unnecessary. The hand got quite well again, the little boy grew up to be a man, "and," continued the minister, holding up his right hand, "this unworthy hand can now be shown to you as a monument of prayer answered through Divine mercy."

11,064. PRAYER, Appropriate. A poor man broke his limb, and could earn nothing for the support of his family. Some good people appointed a prayer meeting at his house at which it was prayed that the misfortune might be overruled to the afflicted man's eternal good. A young man interrupted the meeting by announcing that the squire, a person well known by that designation, had sent his prayers to the meeting in a cart, and asked for help to bring them in. Family supplies, in large store, were soon laid upon the before-empty shelves of the poor man's larder. The meeting ended in a general diffusion of the spirit of this material prayer, many following the example of the thoughtful and liberal squire.

11,065. PRAYER, Ashamed of. I was attending a dying man, who had been a sergeant in the 7th Dragoon Guards. He had ruined his health by drinking spirits. He had been a careless, thoughtless man about his soul. He told me upon his death-bed that when he first began to pray, he was so ashamed of his wife knowing it, that when he went upstairs to pray, he would take his shoes off, and creep up in his stockings. Verily, I am afraid there are many like him! Do not you be one of them. Whatever you are ashamed of, never be ashamed of seeking God. *Ryle.*

11,066. PRAYER, Beginning of. In every building the first stone must be laid, and the first blow must be struck. The ark was one hundred and twenty years in building; yet there was a day when Noah laid his axe to the first tree he cut down to form it. The temple of Solomon was a glorious building, but there was a day when the first huge stone was laid at the foot of Mount Moriah. When does the building of the Spirit really begin to appear in a man's heart? It begins, so far as we can judge, when he first pours out his heart to God in prayer. *Ryle.*

11,067. PRAYER, Believing. Prayer brings the mind to the immediate contemplation of God's character, and holds it there, till by comparison and aspiration the believer's soul is properly impressed, and his wants properly felt. The more subtle physical processes and affinities become, the better are the analogies which they furnish of processes in the spiritual world. The influence of believing prayer has a good analogy in the recently discovered daguerreotype. By means of this process the features of natural objects are thrown upon a sensitive sheet through a lens, and leave their impression upon that sheet. So when the character of God is, by means of prayer, brought to bear upon the mind of the believer—that mind being rendered sensitive by the Holy Spirit—it impresses there the Divine image. In this manner the image of Christ is formed in the soul, the existence of which the scriptures represent as inspiring the believer with the hope of glory. *Walker.*

11,068. PRAYER: Brevities. When thou prayest rather let thy heart be without words, than thy words without heart. Prayer will make a man cease from sin, or sin will entice a man to cease from prayer. The spirit of prayer is more precious than treasures of gold and silver. Pray often; for prayer is a shield to the soul, a sacrifice to God, and a scourge for Satan. *Bunyan.*

11,069. PRAYER, Business and. The greater thy business is, by so much the more thou hast need to pray for God's good-speed and blessing upon it, seeing it is certain nothing can prosper without his blessing. The time spent in prayer never hinders, but furthers and prospers, a man's journey and business; therefore, though thy haste be never so much, or thy business never so great, yet go not about it, nor out of thy doors, till thou hast prayed. *Bishop Bayley.*

11,070. PRAYER, Children's. Children's prayers are heard. Let us enlist them for our work. The great Melanchthon did not despise them. Cast down and disheartened once, we read, that taking an evening walk he heard the voices of children at prayer, and he at once brightened up, and exclaimed to some friends, "Brethren, take courage; the children are praying for us." *H. C. Trumbull.*

11,071. PRAYER, Concentrated. Not long since I met with a young Christian lady who was compelled against her will to be present at the opera, a place wholly unfit for a child of God, and I suppose in the opinion of most, a very unsuitable one for prayer; but the testimony of that person was, that she never felt herself nearer to God in her life. She was there against her will, and God knew it, and he gave her power wholly to abstract herself from the sights and sounds around, and speak with him. *Power.*

11,072. PRAYER, Continue in. Sir Walter Raleigh asked a favor of Queen Elizabeth, which he frequently did; to which she replied, "Raleigh, when will you leave off begging?" "When your Majesty leaves off giving," he replied. So long must we continue praying.

11,073. PRAYER, Definiteness in. A Christian lawyer lost some legal papers of great value at a critical time, as they were required in a case at nine o'clock next morning. He hunted the office through in vain. He then resorted to prayer, and asked God to relieve him before the appointed hour. He was at his office early, and a quarter before nine a stranger entered and handed him a parcel, which was found to contain the missing papers.

11,074. PRAYER, Differences of. Mental prayer, when our spirits wander, is like a watch standing still, because the spring is down, wind it up again, and it goes on regularly. But in vocal prayer, if the words run on and the spirit wanders, the clock strikes false, the hand points not the right hour, because something is in disorder, and the striking is nothing but noise. In mental prayer we confess God's omniscience, in vocal prayer we call angels to witness. In the first our spirits rejoice in God, in the second the angels rejoice in us. Mental prayer is the best remedy against the lightness and indifference of affections, but vocal prayer is the aptest instrument of communion. *Jeremy Taylor.*

11,075. PRAYER, Direction of. We must come to God in the name of Christ, then he will be our bondsman, surety, indorser, intercessor with the Father. He will present our petition, and plead his own merits in our behalf; and he never pleads in vain. As the high-priest, under the Levitical dispensation, entered the Holy of Holies once a year, bearing the names of the chosen tribes on his breast-plate, so the great High-Priest of our profession now stands in the holiest of all, bearing the name of every follower and friend on his heart. When you send up your prayers, be sure to direct them to the care of the Redeemer, and then they will never miscarry. *M. Henry.*

11,076. PRAYER, Discoveries of. A man bought a house and lot for one hundred pounds, which he was to pay by installments. During his life he paid all but ten pounds. His widow managed to raise this balance, and went with it to redeem the estate. She was then informed that she must produce the receipts, or the property would be sold to pay the debt. The distressed widow searched her house through for them, but in vain. Her little son suggested that Jesus could help them in their trouble. So they prayed to him about it. As they rose from prayer a brilliant firefly darted into the window, wheeled around the room, and then settled down under an old chest of drawers. The boy had it pulled out a little, that he might catch the insect, and as it moved out fell the lost receipts. An angel from heaven could not have revealed the receipts more successfully or opportunely than did the straying firefly.

11,077. PRAYER, Diversion in. If a man brought a request to an earthly monarch, but instead of making it, were to turn aside and talk with his neighbor, might not the king be justly displeased? *Trench.*

11,078. PRAYER. Earnest. Mr. Zeller, who kept a school at Benggen, used to illustrate what a life of prayer is by giving a child the end of a thread, and taking the other into another room. When the thread was pulled tight, the slightest check could be felt; when it was slack, not even the hardest.

11,079. PRAYER, Ease of. Look at the incredible ease of prayer. Every time, place, posture, is fitting; for there is no time, place, or posture, in and by which we cannot reverently confess the presence of God. Talent is not needed. Eloquence is out of place. Dignity is no recommendation. Our want is our eloquence, our misery our recommendation. Thought is quick as lightning, and quick as lightning can it multiply effectual prayer. Actions can pray; sufferings can pray. There need no ceremonies; there are no rubrics to keep. The whole function is expressed in a word; it is simply this—the child at his father's knee, his words stumbling over each other from very earnestness, and his wistful face pleading better than his hardly intelligible prayer.   *F. W. Faber.*

11,080. PRAYER, Family. In Greenland, when a stranger knocks at the door, he asks, "Is God in this house?" and if they answer, "Yes," he enters. Reader, this little messenger knocks at your door with the Greenland salutation, Is God in this house? Were you, like Abraham, entertaining an angel unawares, what would be the report he would take back to heaven? Would he find you commanding your children and your household, and teaching them the way of the Lord? Would he find an altar in your dwelling? Do you worship God with your children? If not, then God is not in your house. A prayerless family is a godless family.   *Dr. J. Hamilton.*

11,081. PRAYER, Fidelity in. Of all the ministers with whom I have ever been associated, from the commencement of my ministry to this hour, and with whom I have been thrown in most intimate relations, Bishop Janes spent most time in private prayer; and I think those who have enjoyed, intimately, his society, and have been thrown where he was, have felt the same thing. He pleaded earnestly, not only for himself and his family, but for the whole Church; and the first year I was associated with him he told me he made it a point of duty to take a list of all the presiding elders he had appointed during the year, and every day to offer for them and their success, personal supplication to Almighty God, and, in addition to all this, as many of the ministers whose peculiar situation and circumstances had commended them specially to his care. And thus he lingered on his knees, while most others would rise, still pleading for the blessing of God upon his brethren and upon the Church.   *Bp. Simpson.*

11,082. PRAYER, Formality in. We may insensibly get into the habit of using the fittest possible words, and offering the most scriptural petitions, and yet do it all by rote without feeling it, and walk daily round an old beaten path, like a horse in a mill. I desire to touch this point with caution and delicacy. I know that there are certain great things we daily want, and that there is nothing necessarily formal in asking for these things in the same words. The world, the devil, and our hearts, are daily the same. Of necessity, we must daily go over old ground. But this I say, we must be very careful on this point. If the skeleton and outline of our prayers be by habit almost a form, let us strive that the clothing and filling up of our prayers be as far as possible of the Spirit. As to praying out of a book, it is a habit I cannot praise. If we can tell our doctors the state of our bodies without a book, we ought to be able to tell the state of our souls to God. I have no objection to a man using crutches, when he is first recovering from a broken limb. It is better to use crutches than not to walk at all. But if I saw him all his life on crutches, I should not think it matter for congratulation. I should like to see him strong enough to throw his crutches away.   *Ryle.*

11,083. PRAYER, God in. It appeared to me a wonder that God should regard the prayers of such polluted worms until I discovered in the light of this text, "the Spirit helpeth our infirmities," etc., that it was the Holy Ghost that prayed. I could not help exclaiming, No wonder God hears prayer when it is the Holy Ghost that prays. What an awful place is the Christian's closet! The whole Trinity is about it when he kneels. There is the Spirit praying to the Father through the Son.   *Dr. Griffin.*

11,084. PRAYER, Honor of. A monarch vested in gorgeous habiliments is far less illustrious than a kneeling suppliant ennobled and adorned by communion with his God. Consider how august a privilege it is, when angels are present, and archangels throng around; when cherubim and seraphim encircle in their blaze the throne; that a mortal may approach with unrestrained confidence, and converse with heaven's dread Sovereign! O, what honor was ever conferred like this!   *Chrysostom.*

11,085. PRAYER, Incentive to. The worldling plies his prayers as sailors do their pumps when the ship leaks and the storm rages, from fear of the loss of the ship and cargo.

11,086. PRAYER, Memory of a Mother's. A converted gambler said, in a Fulton street meeting, "I have been a very wicked man, and have lived a rough life. My Sabbaths have been chiefly spent in cock-fighting, dog-fighting, and gambling. My companions have been the vilest; yet there has not been a day for ten years that I have not remembered my mother's prayers which she offered for me at the side of my bed. They have followed me, not only reformed me, but made me a Christian."

11,087. PRAYER, Mohammedan. Mohammed called prayer the pillar of religion and the key of paradise. He required his followers to pray five times every twenty-four hours. 1. Before sunrise. 2. A little past noon. 3. Before sunset. 4. After sunset. 5. After dark. At these times the Muezzim cry from the steeples of the mosques, "To prayer, O ye faithful!" Every votary prays towards the temple of Mecca. If clad in costly robes, and adorned with rich jewels, they lay them off before prayer, lest they should seem proud in addressing God. He enjoined the cultivation of the true spirit of prayer, as well as the faithful observance of the form.

11,088. PRAYER, Mother's. Augustine inherited the impetuous nature of his pagan father rather than the gentle traits of his beautiful, Christian mother. His rejection of Christianity and open immorality of life caused his mother great sorrow. For years she had tried to train him in the right way, and had prayed unceasingly for his soul. She went to the bishop with her sorrow. "Wait," said he, "your son's heart is not now disposed to receive the truth. Wait the Lord's good time." And then, to keep her heart from breaking, and keep her instant in prayer, he said, "Go on praying; the child of so many prayers cannot perish." He ran away from home that he might have greater license. She followed him by her prayers, and finally sought him in the distant land, and there saw him converted. Monica died in 387.

11,089. PRAYER, Mother's. The son of a widow, living at a whaling port in New England, shipped on a whaler for a three years' cruise. His mother waited, prayed and watched for his safe return. At last a ship was seen entering the offing, and was soon discovered to be the one on which her son had sailed. Before the ship entered the harbor a fearful storm arose, which drove it upon the rocks and scattered the broken wreck along the beach. All night long the mother prayed for the safety of her boy. At early dawn a knock was heard at her door. On opening it her son rushed into her arms, saying, "Mother, I knew you would pray me home." There are many sons that must be prayed home to heaven.

11,090. PRAYER, No Unanswered. There is no such thing in the long history of God's kingdom as an unanswered prayer. Every true desire from a child's heart finds some true answer in the heart of God. Most certain it is that the prayer of the Church of God since creation has not been the cry of orphans in an empty home, without a father to hear or answer. Jesus Christ did not pray in vain, or to an unknown God, nor has he spoken in ignorance of God or of his brethren, when he says, "Ask and receive, that your joy may be full."   *Norman Macleod.*

11,091. PRAYER, Power of. At the close of a prayer-meeting, the pastor observed a little girl about twelve years of age remaining upon her knees when most of the congregation had retired. Thinking the child had fallen asleep, he touched her, and told her it was time to return home. To his surprise, he found that she was engaged in prayer, and he said, "All things whatsoever ye shall ask in prayer, believing, ye shall receive." She looked at her pastor earnestly, and inquired, "Is it so? Does God say that?" He took up a Bible and read the passage aloud. She immediately commenced praying, "Lord, send my father to the church. Lord, send my father here?" Thus she continued for about half an hour, attracting by her earnest cry the attention of persons who had lingered about the door. At last, a man rushed into the church, ran up the aisle, and sank upon his knees by the side of his child, exclaiming, "What do you want of me?" She threw her arms about his neck, and began to pray, "O Lord, convert my father!" Soon the man's heart was melted, and he began to pray for himself. The child's father was three miles from the church when she commenced praying for him. He was packing goods in a wagon, and he felt an irresistible impulse to return home. Driving rapidly to his house, he left the goods in the wagon, and hastened to the church, where he found his daughter crying mightily to God in his behalf, and he was there led to the Saviour.

11,092. PRAYER, Practice in. A youth who had been reared a Roman Catholic was converted in a revival. He was soon called upon to take part in public prayer, in which he proved to be very proficient. His old companions were amazed, and went to the meeting for the purpose of hearing him. At last an idea struck one of them. "I know," he said, "how it is that he prays so well; he practices in private!"

11,093. PRAYER, Presenting. Nehemiah obtained a commission from King Xerxes to rebuild the city and temple of Jerusalem, and also requisitions for aid of all kinds upon Adeus, governor of Syria, and others. Nehemiah took these letters up to Jerusalem with him, there presented them to the Lord, and then sent them on their way. When Sennacherib sent his letter of defiance of the living God to Hezekiah, he spread it out before the Lord, and the Lord answered him by a letter by the hand of Isaiah. It was a literal reply to his petition, and assured his heart. It was followed by the signal overthrow of Sennacherib's host. That night the angel of the Lord passed through the camp of the Assyrians and slew one hundred and eighty-five thousand of them. Nehemiah lays his epistles of encouragement before the Lord when he goes to rebuild the walls of Jerusalem, and the Lord gives him success. Hezekiah lays open the proud and boastful Assyrian's letter of insult to the living God, and pleads for vengeance and the preservation of the city, and the Lord sends Sennacherib the most signal defeat in all the annals of war. 2 Kings, 19. (See Cyclopædia of Poetical Illustrations. No. 2934.)

11,094. PRAYER, Relief by. The cashier of a New York bank could not make his account balance by many thousands of dollars. He alone had charge of the books. He had never used a dollar of the bank's funds, nor could he detect any error in the accounts. It was in the era of embezzlements and defalcations On the morrow the bank examiner would examine his accounts and declare him a defaulter As the account now stood the result was inevitable. On the following morning in agony of spirit he entered the directors' room, and for one hour upon his knees, urged his case before God. Calm came to his troubled heart. As if led by an invisible hand he went from his knees to the safe, and took out a blotter long unused. It opened upon pages of accounts which had evidently not been copied. This providential discovery made the account balance, vindicated the cashier, and showed the faithfulness of God who has said, "Call upon me in the day of trouble and I will answer thee."

11,095. PRAYER, Silent. At the opening of the Anderson School of Natural History, on Penikese Island, Prof. Agassiz, after alluding to their peculiar surroundings, proposed the observance of "a moment of silence" for asking the divine blessing. Acting upon this suggestion, the students reverently bowed their heads, and the Professor, with devout mien, stood uncovered before them, all united in silent supplication. One says, "We know of few finer pictures than that one on the island of Penikese, when our acknowledged modern king of science, with bared head and reverent mien, amid the scattered stones, and sea-gull's nests, and the rude gatherings of his projected work, stood with his forty pupils, waiting on the Almighty Creator."

11,096. PRAYER, Specific. A lady lay upon her bed suffering violent pain in the head, and while thus suffering, she said to a friend, who was watching by her side, "If only I could get ten minutes' sleep, I should feel better." The friend said nothing, but offered up a silent prayer to God to grant the ten minutes' sleep. True! the petition was feeble, and the faith feeble, but the Lord, who is very tender, did not despise either the feebleness of the faith, or the smallness of the subject of the request. The patient immediately slept, and described her sleep as most delicious.　　*Power.*

10,097. PRAYER, Subjects of. Is everything to be a subject of prayer? Certainly. So thought Fowell Buxton even of those amusements with which, in holiday times, he was wont to brace up mind and body for noble labors in the cause of God and his country. So thought that Corsican patriot who never went down to battle till he had gone down on his knees, nor ever leveled a rifle that never missed without praying for the soul he was about to send into eternity. And so speaks Paul, when, linking peace and prayer together, he writes, "Be careful for nothing; but in everything by prayer and supplication, with thanksgiving, let your request be made known unto God; and the peace of God, which passeth all understanding, shall keep your hearts and minds, through Jesus Christ."
　　　　　　　　　　Dr. Guthrie.

11,098. PRAYER, Submission in. The wife of St. Francis Borgia, duke of Gandia, was suffering under a protracted and severe illness, which threatened her death. The duke, a very pious man, fasted and prayed much for her recovery. One day, while praying in his closet, he heard a voice distinctly say, "If thou wouldst have the life of the duchess prolonged, it shall be granted, but it is not expedient for thee." With an overwhelming sense of the Divine condescension and love, he hastened to free himself from

this responsibility, saying, 'O God, leave not this which is only in thy power to my will! I am bound in all things to conform my will to thine. Thou alone knowest what is best, and what is for my good. Let not my will be done, but thine with my wife, my children, myself, and all things thou hast given me."

11,099. PRAYER, Substitute for. It is said the Japanese, instead of spending their time in listening to a long sermon, march decorously to the temple wherein their priests are performing service, throw in a printed prayer and a little money, and go about their business with a satisfied conscience.

11,100. PRAYER, Urging. The celebrated John Foster, in a sermon to young people, said, "My dear young friends, I conjure each one of you not to sleep this night without prayer. If you can't pray at least say, Lord Jesus, save my soul! Lord Jesus, save my soul. Let that simple prayer be perseveringly offered, with the desire accompanying the words, and you cannot pray in vain, you cannot fail to receive a glorious answer." Sometime after he received a letter from a young man who heard the sermon, acted upon the counsel, and found it true to the saving of his soul.

11,101. PRAYER, Utility of. Prayer is not a sentiment or a theory; it is a working instrument, which is to do certain things, just as a pen is to write, or a knife to cut.

11,102. PRAYER, Weeping and. As music upon the water sounds further and more harmoniously than upon the land, so prayers joined with tears. These if they proceed from faith, are showers quenching the devil's cannon-shot; a second baptism of the soul, wherein it is rinsed anew, nay, perfectly anew, as the tears of vines cure the leprosy, as the lame were healed in the troubled waters.　　*Trapp.*

11,103. PRAYER, What is? A little deaf and dumb girl was once asked by a lady, who wrote the question on a slate: "What is prayer?" The little girl took the pencil and wrote the reply: "Prayer is the wish of the heart."

11,104. PRAYER, Wonders of. Abraham's servant prays, Rebekah appears. Jacob wrestles and prays, and prevails with Christ; Esau's mind is wonderfully turned from the revengeful purpose he had harbored for twenty years. Moses prays, Amalek is discomfited. Joshua prays, Acham is discovered. Hannah prays, Samuel is born. David prays, Ahithophel hangs himself. Asa prays, a victory is gained. Jehoshaphat cries to God, God turns away his foes. Isaiah and Hezekiah pray, 185,000 Assyrians are dead in twelve hours. Daniel prays, the lions are muzzled. Daniel prays, the seventy weeks are revealed. Mordecai and Esther fast, Haman is hanged on his own gallows in three days. Ezra prays at Ahava, God answers. Nehemiah darts a prayer, the king's heart is softened in a minute. Elijah prays, a drought of three years succeeds. Elijah prays, rain descends apace. Elisha prays, Jordan is divided. Elisha prays, a child's soul comes back; for prayer reaches eternity. The Church prays ardently, Peter is delivered by an angel.   *J. Ryland.*

11,105. PRAYERS, Work and. A Roman general attributed his victory to the fact that the gods favored him because he begged for success with his drawn sword in his hand, and fought while he cried to heaven for help.

11,106. PRAYERLESSNESS Rebuked. A little boy said his prayers preparatory to retiring for the night, while his prayerless father stood by. Rising from his knees, he said, "Now, father, I have said my prayers; have you said yours? Are you too big to pray?"

11,107. PRAYER-MEETING, Drawing Lots in. A traveler reports attending a prayer-meeting in Stuttgart, Germany. He says, "At the beginning of the meeting each person took a piece of paper from the table. On inquiry, I found it was drawing of lots as to the order of prayers. The papers were numbered. Number one prayed first, and was followed by number two, and by others, according to the numbers they had drawn. The object is to prevent embarrassment and a painful waiting one for another. There are many such gatherings found here. They form what is called the inner circles. The sexes do not meet, but women's prayer-meetings are also held."

11,108. PRAYER-MEETINGS, Objection to. Rev. William Dawson was accosted by an individual, who said he had been present at a certain meeting; that he liked the preaching very well indeed, but was much dissatisfied with the prayer-meeting; adding, that he usually lost all the good he had received during the sermon by remaining in these noisy meetings. Mr. D. replied, that he should have united with the people of God in the prayer-meeting, if he desired to retain or obtain good. "O," said the gentleman, "I went into the gallery, where I leaned over the front, and saw the whole; but I could get no good: I lost, indeed, all the benefit I had received during the sermon." "It is easy to account for that," rejoined Mr. Dawson. "How so?" inquired the other. "You mounted to the top of the house, and, on looking down your neighbor's chimney to see what kind of a fire he kept, you got your eyes filled with smoke. Had you entered by the door, gone into the room, and mingled with the family around the household hearth, you would have enjoyed the benefit of the fire as well as they. Sir, you have got the smoke in your eyes!"

11,109. PREACHER, Blunder of a. A doctor of divinity went to preach in Glenisla, and thought, that being a pastoral parish, the twenty-third Psalm would form a peculiarly suitable subject; and from that, as he was very capable of doing, he delivered an admirable discourse. But there was a "dead fly" in the apothecary's ointment that marred the sermon and lowered the man. Ignorant of the fact that sheep in our moist climate, and amid the dew-covered and green, succulent herbage, are independent of streams, and, indeed, seldom drink water but when sick, he expatiated, as he spoke of "the still waters,"

on the importance of water to the flocks—a blunder and display of ignorance the stupidest discovered; and as they lingered to light their pipes by the church door, he had the mortification on retiring to hear himself and his sermon treated with contempt; one shepherd saying to another, "Puir bodie! Heard ye ever the like o' yon aboot the sheep drinkin'?"
        Guthrie.

11,110. PREACHER, The Distracted. Daniel Webster told the following of old Father Searl, the minister of his boyhood. It was customary then to wear buckskin breeches in cool weather. One Sunday morning, in the autumn, Father Searl brought his down from the garret; but the wasps had taken possession of them during the summer and were having a nice time in them. By dint of effort, he got out the intruders, as he supposed, and dressed for meeting. But while reading the Scriptures to the congregation, he felt a dagger from one of the small-waisted fellows, and jumped about the pulpit slapping his thighs. But the more he slapped around and danced the more he was stung. The people thought him crazy, and were in commotion what to do. He explained the matter by exclaiming, "Brethren don't be alarmed. The word of the Lord is in my mouth, but the devil is in my breeches."

11,111. PREACHER, The Earnest. However highly gifted he may otherwise be, it is a valid objection to a preacher, that he does not feel what he says; that spoils more than his oratory. Once on a time an obscure man rose up to address the French Convention. At the close of his oration, Mirabeau, the giant genius of the Revolution, turned round to his neighbor, and eagerly asked, "Who is that?" The other, who had been in no way interested by the address, wondered at Mirabeau's curiosity. Whereupon the latter said, "That man will yet act a great part;" and added, on being asked for an explanation, "He speaks as one who believes every word he says." Much of pulpit power under God depends on that; admits of that explanation, or of one allied to it. They make others feel who feel themselves.
        Dr. Guthrie.

11,112. PREACHER, Industrious. The Rev. Mr. Duchal, an eminent Irish Non-conformist divine, of the beginning of the eighteenth century, was noted for his careful and persevering sermon making. In the last twenty years of his life, he composed over seven hundred sermons of superior excellence.

11,113. PREACHER, Lesson of a. A minister recovering from a dangerous illness, was thus addressed by one of his friends: "Though God seems to be bringing you up from the gates of death, yet it will be a long time before you will sufficiently retrieve your strength, and regain vigor enough of mind to preach as usual." The convalescent answered: "You are mistaken, my friend; for this six weeks illness has taught me more divinity than all my past studies and all my ten years' ministry put together."

11,114. PREACHER, A Pedantic. In the town of

Goslar, in the Hartz mountain, there is in the principal square a fountain evidently of mediæval date, but the peculiarity of its construction is that no one can reach the water so as to fill a bucket or even get a drink to quench his thirst. Both the jets, and the basin into which they fall, are above the reach of any man of ordinary stature; yet the fountain was intended to supply the public with water, and it fulfills its design by a method which we never saw in use before; every person brings a spout or trough with him long enough to reach the top of the fountain and bring the water down into his pitcher. Sixpennyworth of mason's work with a chisel would have made the crystal stream available to all; but no, every one must bring a trough or go away unsupplied. When the preachers of the gospel talk in so lofty a style that each hearer needs to bring a dictionary, they remind us of the absurd fountain of Goslar. *Spurgeon.*

11,115. PREACHER and People. The tree is known by its fruit—the preacher by his people; for whenever I have found it difficult to awaken and arrest the attention of an audience lolling at their ease, and wearing in their faces an air of dull indifference, I did not need any one to tell me that their usual Sabbaths were a weariness—their minister a poor, uninteresting preacher. And much have they to answer for, who, devoting too little time and labor to their sermons, indulge their taste, some for literature, and others for laziness, at the expense of their people's souls.
Dr. Guthrie.

11,116. PREACHER, A Soul-Saving. Michael Angelo, when painting an altar-piece in the conventual church, in Florence, in order that the figures might be as death-like as possible, obtained permission of the prior to have the coffins of the newly-buried opened and placed beside him during the night; an appalling expedient, but successful in enabling him to reproduce with terrible effect, not the mortal pallor only, but the very anatomy of death. If we would preach well to the souls of men we must acquaint ourselves with their ruined state, must have their case always on our hearts both by night and day, must know the terrors of the Lord and the value of the soul, and feel a sacred sympathy with perishing sinners. *Spurgeon.*

11,117. PREACHING, Attraction of. The power of the magnet gains nothing from the gilder's or the graver's art; its attraction lies in itself, and is diminished by foreign accretions. So it is with the greatest of all magnets of which Christ spake when he said: "And I, if I be lifted up, will draw all men unto me." We may draw men to ourselves by genius, eloquence, eccentricity, but we can draw men to Christ only by the attraction of the Cross.
J. A. James.

11,118. PREACHING, Attractive. Fishermen throw over the food which the fish like best, and attract them to their nets by thousands. A person with grain or bread crumbs may gather hundreds of sparrows about him in the parks of the city of New York, but if he does not feed them well they will not stay long. Take the lesson, O ye that are appointed to "feed the flock of God." Distribute bountifully the true bread, and hungry souls will gather about you and be satisfied.

11,119. PREACHING, Beginning of. It would be well, if some who have taken upon themselves the ministry of the gospel, would first preach to themselves, then afterwards to others. *Cardinal Pole.*

11,120. PREACHING, Best Manner of. You know how you would feel and speak in a parlor concerning a friend who was in imminent danger of his life, and with what energetic pathos of diction and countenance you would enforce the observance of that which you really thought would be for his preservation. You could not think of playing the orator, of studying your emphasis, cadences and gestures; you would be yourself, and the interesting nature of your subject, impressing your heart, would furnish you with the most natural tone of voice, the most proper language, the most engaging features, and the most suitable and graceful gestures. What you would thus be in the parlor, be in the pulpit, and you will not fail to please, to affect, and to profit. *Garrick.*

11,121. PREACHING Christ. When we speak of preaching the gospel, we do not mean reiterating certain truths to the exclusion of all others; our duty is to present, as in a great historical picture, the whole of God's word, every figure in its place and proportion; ever bearing in mind that the great center figure of the group, on which the whole depends, is the Lord Jesus Christ. *Stowell.*

11,122. PREACHING, Christ's Company in. Robert Bruce, a Scotch minister, failed to appear at the time of worship. The bell ceased and the people waited, but still he did not come. The beadle was sent to learn the cause of delay. He found the preacher's house closed, but heard him say repeatedly, "I protest, I will not go except thou go with me." He supposed he was trying to induce some visitor to accompany him to church. Mr. Bruce soon appeared, and the people knew that he prevailed, for his word was, "In demonstration of the Spirit, and with power."

11,123. PREACHING, Difference in. Vincent Ferrier, the eloquent preaching friar of the fifteenth century, used to prepare his sermons kneeling before a crucifix, looking constantly at the wounds represented. He was called to preach before a high dignitary of state, and took great care to prepare his sermon according to the rules of oratory. It was a signal failure. Next day he preached in his usual style, and electrified his hearers. The prince, who had heard him on both occasions, asked him how he could account for so great a difference in the sermons. He answered, "Yesterday Vincent Ferrier preached, to-day Jesus Christ." He is sometimes represented in art with the name of Jesus written on his breast.

11,124. PREACHING, Dull. Aimless, lifeless, monotonous sermons often suggest Sydney Smith's sarcastic inquiry, "Is sin to be taken from men, as Eve was from Adam, by casting them into a deep slumber?"

11,125. PREACHING, Earnestness in. Professor Lawson, a theological teacher in England, tells of one of his pupils, Andrew Fletcher, who, after completing his theological studies, passed the first two years of his ministry in a colleagueship with his father, a clergyman of Perthshire, Scotland. When the father preached, the listeners were few; when the son discoursed, the house was flooded. The father's sermons elicited no praises, the son's were loudly applauded; whereat the former became jealous and irritable. At length the son borrowed one of his father's sermons, and on the following Sunday preached it from memory with great emphasis and animation. The hearers were louder than ever in praise of the youthful orator, and one worthy remarked, "The old man never in his life preached a sermon equal to that!" So, too, when a friend of Mirabeau complained that the Assembly would not listen to him, that fiery leader asked for his speech, and the next day electrified the Assembly by uttering as his own the words they had refused to hear from another. In either case it was the manner that made all the difference. *Talmage.*

11,126. PREACHING, Educational Influence of. Sermons certainly are equal in their literary character and in their delivery, taken as a whole, to the discourses which are given to our students in our schools; and if so, why not have the corresponding effect? That boy who begins to attend church at the age of fourteen, when he is capable of understanding these discourses, and is regularly in the house of God on the Sabbath listening to them, when he becomes twenty-one, has spent a whole year in this school; when he is twenty-eight he has spent two years; when he is thirty-five he has spent three years; when he is forty-two he has spent four years—as much time as is employed by a student in going through college; and he has been under as good tuition, his mind has been employed on as interesting questions, his mental exercises have been as strong, as grand, and as consecutive as those which are employed in college. *Bp. Janes.*

11,127. PREACHING, Energetic. The thin-skinned preacher will bleed at every scratch; and yet, for my part, I have always found those men most respected, and even most followed, who have not paid respect to any person, who have said what they thought, and nailed their colors to the mast. Even the world honors consistency and courage, and the plainest speaker will have, in general, the most hearers. The only part by which a bull can be safely taken is the horns. *Power.*

11,128. PREACHING, Exchange of. Rev. Dr. Love exchanged pulpits with Dr. Chalmers when the popularity of the latter was attracting great crowds to his church in Glasgow. The audience manifested their displeasure at his appearance by turning away from the church doors, or rising to leave. Dr. Love arose and said, "We will not begin the public worship of God till the chaff blows off." The cure was effectual for that time at least.

11,129. PREACHING, Extempore. When John Wesley first began to preach, he went to a church but had forgotten his sermon. A woman noticed that he was deeply agitated, and inquired, "Pray, sir, what is the matter with you?" He replied, "I have not brought a sermon with me." Putting her hand upon his shoulder, she said, "Is that all? Cannot you trust God for a sermon?" That question had such an effect upon him that he ascended the pulpit and preached extempore, with great freedom to himself and acceptance to the people, and he never afterwards took a written sermon into the pulpit. On visiting the same church years after he mentioned this fact.

11,130. PREACHING, Fanciful. Bp. Reynolds says that Praxiteles made the silly people worship the image of his strumpet, under the title and pretence of Venus. He applied this to those preachers who impose upon weak and incautious hearers the visions of their own fancy, the crude and unnourishing vapors of empty wit for the indubiate truth of God.

11,131. PREACHING, Fidelity in. Bishop Jewell, that blessed minister of the Church of England, on being asked by a gentleman who met his lordship going on foot to preach to a few people, why he, weak as he was, should thus expose himself, received the reply, "It becomes a bishop to die preaching." *Whitefield.*

11,132. PREACHING, Harmless. Chinese gymnasts exhibit remarkable skill in throwing knives at a person to see how near they can come and not hit. To hit would show great want of skill. To stick the knives in the wall all around and within a hair's breadth of the person is their aim. It has been affirmed that there are preachers who are experts in this art. Their audiences are perfectly safe. However sharp the words they utter, they are so aimed as to be sure not to hit. If any sinner should be pricked in his heart, and go to such a minister for instruction, he would recommend him to travel and shake off his morbid mood.

11,133. PREACHING, Holy Violence in. A holy violence in preachers is but a true zeal for the souls of men, and if they do you violence it is no more than if they pull your arm out of joint, when to save you from drowning, they pull you out of a river; and if you complain, it is no more to be regarded than the outcries of children against their rulers, or sick men against their physicians. *Salter.*

11,134. PREACHING, Incomprehensible. A young minister preaching for an old one, asked his opinion of his discourse. Said he, "Many of the words you used were beyond the comprehension of your hearers: thus, for instance, the word 'inference,' perhaps not half of my parishioners understand its meaning." "Inference, inference!" exclaimed the other, "why every one must understand that." "I think you will find it not so; there is my clerk now, he prides himself upon his learning, and in truth is very intelligent. We will try him: Zechariah, come hither. My brother here wishes you to draw an inference; can you do it?" "Why I am pretty strong; but John the coachman, is stronger than I, I'll ask him." Zechariah sought the coachman, and returning reported: "John says he has never tried to draw an inference, sir; but he reckons that his horses will draw anything the traces will hold!"

11,135. PREACHING, Insensibility to. A nobleman skilled in music, who had often observed the Rev. Mr. Cadogan's inattention to his performance, said to him one day, "Come, I am determined to make you feel the force of music; pay particular attention to this piece." It accordingly was played. "Well, what do you say now?" "Why, just what I said before." "What! can you hear this and not be charmed? Well, I am quite surprised at your insensibility. Where are your ears?" "Bear with me, my lord," replied Mr. Cadogan, "Since I too have had my surprise. I have often from the pulpit set before you the most striking and affecting truths; I have sounded notes that might have raised the dead; I have said, 'Surely he will feel now;' but you never seemed to be charmed with my music, though infinitely more interesting than yours. I too have been ready to say, with astonishment, 'Where are his ears?'"

11,136. PREACHING, Logical. Sir William Hamilton said to me one day quietly, "Your friend, Dr. Guthrie, is the best preacher I ever heard." I answered I did not wonder at the opinion, but I was surprised to hear it expressed by so great a logician of one not specially possessed of large logical power. He replied, with great emphasis, "Sir, he has the best of all logic; there is but one step between his premise and conclusion." *Dr. McCosh.*

11,137. PREACHING, Loud. "Were you ever a fisherman?" said an aged man to a student of divinity. "Yes, I have fished with the rod," was his reply. "O, but I mean with the net?" "No, I never did." "Well, you need to learn it. And do you know that when there is thunder the fish go to the bottom of the sea?" "Yes, I know that to be a fact." Many ministers forget that.

11,138. PREACHING, Non-Effective. What excellent preachers were Isaiah and Jeremiah to the Jews! The former spake of Christ more like an evangelist of the New than a prophet of the Old Testament; the latter was a most convincing and pathetical preacher; yet the one complains. "Who hath believed our report? and to whom is the arm of the Lord revealed?" Isa. 53: 1. The other laments the ill-success of his ministry: "The bellows are burnt, the lead is consumed of the fire, the founder melteth in vain." Jer. 6: 29. Under the New Testament, what people ever enjoyed such choice helps and means as those that lived under the ministry of Christ and the apostles? Yet how many remained still in darkness! "We have piped to you, but ye have not danced; we have mourned unto you, but ye have not lamented." Matt. 11: 17. Neither the delightful airs of mercy, nor the doleful tones of judgment, could affect or move their hearts.   *John Flavel.*

11,139. PREACHING, Original. One of Mr. Bramwell's hearers once asked another, "How is it that Mr. Bramwell always has something new to tell us when he preaches?" The other answered, "Why you see Brother Bramwell lives so near the gates of heaven that he hears a great many things that we don't get near enough to hear anything about."

11,140. PREACHING, Plain. Who expects to find "Bradshaw" full of Latin quotations? You get it as a guide; and you want it to be as plain as possible. You have lost your "way" among some mountains one night, and are overtaken by some classic—who says, "I will tell you 'the way' to get home in sixteen different languages," none of which you comprehend. I think you would reply, "I would rather be told it, sir, in one that I could understand." Or, if some profound professor should inform you that he could explain the geological strata and formation of the soil on which you were standing—I think you would say, "If you could point me to my own abode, I should be more grateful." And I think if some poor ragged girl, or shepherd boy, could tell you of a "way" by which you could escape that wood or yonder precipice, and reach an hospitable shelter, such information would undoubtedly be more profitable to you. *Spurgeon.*

11,141. PREACHING, Powerful. An irreligious and worldly farmer grumbled because his neighbors wasted their time in attending a protracted meeting. He was ploughing a field near the church and could hear the singing, and occasionally distinguish a word of the sermon. The preacher frequently repeated the text, "Turn ye to the stronghold," Zech. 9: 12. The ploughman understood it. It rang in his ears and sank into his heart. The good Spirit was outside as well as inside the church. The text seemed a personal address to himself. "Turn ye, turn ye." He unyoked his oxen, and in his working clothes presented himself as a seeker with the others at the end of the service. He was saved, and no longer depreciates protracted meetings. "Turn ye to the stronghold" has become the golden text of his family.

11,142. PREACHING, Prayerful. Pray without ceasing. On the old men-of-war the gunners sighted their pieces on their knees. This is true in the divine navy.   *Dr. C. H. Fowler.*

11,143. PREACHING, Seasonable. The bishop sent for John Berridge to reprove him for preaching at all hours and on all days. "My Lord," said he modestly, "I preach only at two times." "Which are they, Mr. Berridge?" "In season and out of season, my lord."

11,144. PREACHING, Searching. Cotton Mather says of the apostle to the Indians, John Eliot, when he began to preach in the Colonies in 1632, "When he preached, he spoke as many thunderbolts as words. He would sound the trump of God against all vice with a most penetrating liveliness, and make his pulpit another Mount Sinai."

11,145. PREACHING, Secret of Successful. Dr. Finney tells of a pastor who enjoyed a revival every year for twelve years, and could not account for it, till one evening, at a prayer-meeting, a brother confessed that for a number of years past he had been in the habit of "spending every Saturday night, until midnight, in prayer for his pastor the next day."

11,146. PREACHING, Test of. I have heard some persons, when leaving a place of worship, admiring the minister, and exclaiming, "What splendid language!" May they rather say, after hearing me, "What sinners we are! What a glorious Christ we have! What a blessed salvation!"   *Rowland Hill.*

11,147. PREACHING, Truthful. The pious wife of a preacher said to her husband, "Sir, your preaching would starve all the Christians in the world." "Starve all the Christians in the world!" said the astonished preacher; "why, do I not speak the truth?" "Yes," replied she, "and so you would were you to stand in the desk all day, and say my name is Mary. But, sir, there is something beside the letter in the truth of the gospel." The result was, a very important change in the ministerial efforts of the clergyman. This hint should be given to all ministers.

11,148. PREACHING, Verbal. The Lacedæmonian in Plutarch said, when he heard how sweetly the nightingale sang, "O, that I had this bird; surely it is a rare dish;" and after a while, when he had taken it, and ate it, and found but a little picking meat, he concluded with that proverbial saying, *Vox et prœterea nihil,* "Now I see thou art mere voice, and nothing else." And such are they that go up into the pulpit with stentorian voices, that have big words, but small matter, so that the people may be said to hear a sound, but know not what it means.   *Fenner.*

11,149. PREACHING, Wandering. Wm. Bramwell was preaching in a little village, on one occasion, and the German minister, Trubner, went to hear him. Trubner was a very cultivated scholar, and a profound critic; and when some of Bramwell's friends saw him there, they said, "Alas! alas! for poor Bramwell; how Trubner will criticise him!" He preached the everlasting gospel of Jesus Christ with great power; and when Trubner went out of church, one of his friends said to him, "How did you like him? Don't you think he wanders a good deal in his preaching?" "Oh, yes," said the old Lutheran, "he do wander most delightfully from the subject to be of heart."

11,150. PREDESTINATION, Mohammedan. The Mohammedans are taught by the Koran to believe in God's absolute decree and predestination, both of good and evil. For the orthodox doctrine is, that whatever hath, or shall come to pass in the world, whether it be good, or whether it be bad, proceedeth entirely from the divine will, and is irrevocably fixed and recorded from all eternity in the preserved table; God having secretly predetermined not only the adverse and prosperous fortune of every person in this world, in the most minute particulars, but also his faith or infidelity, his obedience or disobedience, and consequently his everlasting happiness or misery after death; which fate or predestination it is not possible by any foresight or wisdom to avoid.   *George Sale.*

11,151. PREDESTINATION, Restraint of. Give me a village, give me a hamlet, give me a few scattered houses, where the people are in anxiety about their soul's salvation, and I would rather send among them a Wesleyan Methodist, with all his Arminianism, than I would send a sturdy, square-built Calvinist, who is so straight-laced in the rigidity of his system that he cannot present a free gospel to every creature.   *Dr. Chalmers.*

11,152. PREFACE, Matter for Our. Why are not more gems from our great authors scattered over the country? Great books are not in everybody's reach; and though it is better to know them thoroughly than to know them only here and there, yet it is a good work to give a little to those who have neither time nor means to get more. Let every book-worm, when in any fragrant scarce old tome he discovers a sentence, a story, an illustration, that does his heart good, hasten to give it.   *Coleridge.*

11,153. PREFACE, Use of a. A good preface is as essential to put the reader into good humor, as a good prologue is to a play, or a fine symphony is to an opera, containing something analogous to the work itself; so that we may feel its want as a desire not elsewhere to be gratified. The Italians call the preface—*La salsa del libro*—the sauce of the book; and, if well-seasoned, it creates an appetite in the reader to devour the book itself.   *I. Disraeli.*

11,154. PREJUDICE, Offending. We must take sides in the wrangle of prejudices, and consequently be antagonized by many good and earnest people. It is always right to advocate our side; but never right to advocate the other. People pray the old hunter's prayer: "Lord, help me against the bear; but if you can't help me, don't help the bear."   *Dr. Fowler.*

11,155. PREPARATION, Advantage of. It is as much our interest as it is our duty to be seasonably awakened out of our pleasant but most pernicious drowsiness. This was exemplified to us by holy Mr. Bradford, the martyr, when the keeper's wife came running into his chamber, saying, "O Mr. Bradford, I bring you heavy tidings, for to-morrow you must be burned, your chain is now buying, and presently you must go to Newgate." He put off his hat, and looking up to heaven, said, "O Lord, I thank thee for it; I have looked for this a long time; it comes not suddenly to me, the Lord make me worthy of it." See in this example the singular advantage of a prepared and ready soul.   *Flavel.*

11,156. PREPARATION, Providential. An English town-missionary called upon a very fierce man, and asked the privilege of reading the Bible and praying with his family. It was granted on condition of his answering the question correctly, "Is the word girl in any part of the Bible? if so, where is to be found, and how often?" "Well, sir; the word girl is in the Bible only once, and may be found in Joel 3: 3. The words are, 'And sold a girl for wine, that they might drink.'" "Well," replied the man. "I am dead beat; I durst have bet five pounds you could not have told." "And I could not have told yesterday," said the visitor. "For several days I have been praying that the Lord would open me a way into this house, and this very morning, when reading the Scriptures in my family, I was surprised to find the word girl, and got the Concordance to see if it occurred again, and found it did not. And now, sir, I believe that God did know, and does know, what will come to pass; and surely his hand is in this for my protection and your good." The incident led to the conversion of the man, his wife, and two of the lodgers.

11,157. PREPARATION, Thorough. Sir Joshua Reynolds once executed a small sketch, and offered it for sale at fifty guineas. "So much as that, Sir Joshua! Why it was the work of only a few hours." "Not so," was his reply, "it cost me forty years of hard labor." He meant that every stroke of his pencil was done with the skill which forty years imparted.

11,158. PREPARATION, Urged. Be fit for the wall; square, polish, prepare thyself for it; do not limit thyself to the bare acquisition of such knowledge as is absolutely necessary for thy present position: but rather learn languages, acquire useful information, stretch thyself out this way and that, cherishing whatever aptitudes thou findest in thyself; and it is certain thy turn will come. Thou wilt not be left in the way; sooner or later the builders will be glad of thee; the wall will need thee to fill a place in it, quite as much as thou needest a place to occupy in the wall. *F. F. Trench.*

11,159. PREPARATION, Want of. It is reported that two as famous orators as ever lived, Demosthenes and Alcibiades, were somewhat weak and faulty in this point. The timorousness of the former is known by every school-boy; and as for Alcibiades, though he was as sagacious and happy in his thoughts as any man whatever, yet for want of a little assurance in speaking a thing, he very often miserably lost himself in his pleadings, for he would falter and make pauses in the very middle of his orations, purely for want of a single word or some neat expression that he had in his papers, but could not presently remember. To give you another instance of the prince of poets, Homer: he was so blinded with an over-confidence of his abilities in poetry, that he has slipped a false quantity, and left it on record, in the very first verse of his Iliads. Seeing, then, the learnedest men and greatest artists have failed, and may fail, for want of caution or confidence, it ought more nearly to concern those that earnestly follow virtue, not to slip the least opportunity of improvement.
Plutarch.

11,160. PRESENT, Importance of the. Be every minute, **man, a full life to thee! Despise** anxiety and wishing, the future and the past! If the second-pointer can be no road-pointer, with an Eden for thy soul, the month-pointer will still less be so, for thou livest not from month to month, but from second to second! Enjoy thy existence more than thy manner of existence, and let the dearest object of thy consciousness be this consciousness itself! Make not the present a means of thy future; for this future is nothing but a coming present; and the present, which thou despisest
Richter

11,161. PRESENT, Work for the. If your dwelling were on fire, and you stood quiet, unconcerned, men would think that you were insane! But, ah! the souls of men are on fire, and they are quiet, and think nothing of it. It is a time of great seriousness with many. It is a time for recalling the truths of God which were taught in the days of your purity and innocence. It is a time for remembering God, from whom you have wandered away. It is a time for measuring yourself and seeing how far down you have gone. It is a time for sounding to see whether there is not consumption in the soul. It is a time for examining to see if the heart is right. It is a time to look at the spine and see whether you are not decaying there. It is a time for searching inside. It is a time for self-examination. It is a time for casting off insincerity and hypocrisy, and honestly and earnestly, in a manly way, living a new life.
Beecher.

11,162. PRESENTIMENT, Evil of, Alas! there are times when foreshadowings of evil, vaporous and undefined, rise up over the soul, like the night mists over the meadow-land, obscuring not only the landmarks of earth, but dimming even the star-guides of heaven. At such periods we find our only safety in solitude and prayer.
A. B. Edwards.

11,163. PRESENTIMENT Fulfilled. On the afternoon of the day on which the President was shot, there was a Cabinet Council, at which he presided. While they were waiting for Mr. Stanton, Mr. Lincoln said, with his chin down on his breast, "Gentlemen, something very extraordinary is going to happen, and that very soon." To which the Attorney-General had observed, "Something good, sir, I hope," when the President answered, very gravely, "I don't know, I don't know, but it will happen, and shortly, too." As they were all impressed by his manner, the Attorney-General took him up again. "Have you received any information, sir, not yet disclosed to us?" "No," answered the President; "but I have had a dream, and I have now had the same dream three times—once on the night preceding the battle of Bull Run; once on the night preceding such another (naming a battle also not favorable to the North)." His chin sunk on his breast again, and he sat reflecting. "Might one ask the nature of this dream, sir?" said the Attorney-General. "Well," replied the President, without lifting his head or changing his attitude, "I am on a great, broad, rolling river, and I am in a boat—and I drift and I drift—but this is not business," suddenly raising his face and looking round the table as Mr. Stanton entered, "Let us proceed to business, gentlemen." Mr. Stanton and the Attorney-General said it would be curious to notice whether anything ensued on this; and they agreed to notice. He was shot that sight.   *Forster.*

11,164. PRESUMPTION, Advance of. Every presumption is properly an encroachment, and all encroachment carries in it still a further and a further invasion upon the person encroached upon. It enters into the soul as a gangrene does into the body, which spreads as well as infects, and with a running progress carries a venom and a contagion over all the members. Presumption never stops in its first attempt. If Cæsar comes once to pass the Rubicon, he will be sure to march further on, even till he enters the very bowels of Rome, and break open the Capitol itself. He that wades so far as to wet and foul himself, cares not how much he trashes further. *Dr. South.*

11,165. PRESUMPTION, Danger of. A scientific gentleman was examining the scene of a fatal explosion. He was accompanied by the under-viewer of the colliery, and as they were inspecting the edges of a goaf (a region of foul air), it was observed that the "Davies" which they carried were "a-fire." "I suppose," said the inspector, "that there is a good deal of fire-damp hereabouts?" "Thousands and thousands of cubic feet all through the goaf!" coolly replied his companion. "Why," exclaimed the official, "do you mean to say that there is nothing but that shred of wire-gauze between us and eternity?" "Nothing at all," said the under-viewer, very composedly. "There's nothing here, where we stand, but that gauze-wire to keep the whole mine from being blown into the air!" The precipitate retreat of the government official was instantaneous. And thus should it be with the sinner: his retreat from the ways of sin, those goafs of poisonous air, should be instantaneous.   *F. F. Trench.*

11,166. PRESUMPTION, Fable of. The pomegranate and the apple had a contest on the score of beauty. When words ran high, and the strife waxed dangerous, a bramble, thrusting his head from a neighboring bush, cried out, "We have disputed long enough; let there be no more rivalry betwixt us." The most insignificant are generally the most presuming.   *Æsop.*

11,167. PRESUMPTION, Folly of. In the strait between Johor and Rhio, there is a small white rock, called the "White Stone," very little elevated above the water, and so exactly in the centre of the passage, that many vessels, unacquainted with it, have been wrecked upon it. A Portuguese merchant passing this strait, in a vessel of his own, richly laden with gold and other valuable commodities, asked the pilot when this rock would be passed; but each moment appearing to him

long until he was secure from the danger, he repeated his question so often, that the pilot impatiently told him the rock was passed. The merchant, transported with joy, impiously exclaimed, that "God could not now make him poor." But in a little while, the vessel struck on the White Stone, and all his wealth was engulfed in the abyss: life alone remained to make him feel his misery and his punishment.   *Whitecross.*

11,168. PRESUMPTION, Pagan. Caligula used to talk to the statue of Jupiter Capitolinus as to a living person, sometimes in censure, and again in praise. Being angry because his banquet was disturbed by the thunder and lightning, he challenged the Thunder, Jupiter, to fight with him.

11,169. PRIDE, Answer to. Notker Balbulus was remarkable for his musical ability and knowledge of theology. He became a favorite of Charles the Fat, much to the chagrin of his jealous and proud chaplain. This man thought to humble Notker publicly. So he approached that composer as he was playing on his psaltery, saying to the company, "We will put a puzzling question to this most sapient and profound theologian." Then to Notker, "Master, solve us a point in divinity, we pray, What is God Almighty doing now?" "God Almighty is doing now what he has been doing in past ages, and will do as long as the world lasts: he is casting down the proud and is exalting the humble."

11,170. PRIDE, Baseless. The proud fly, sitting upon the chariot-wheel, which, hurried with violence, huffed up the sand, gave out that it was she which made all that glorious dust. The ass, carrying the Egyptian goddess, swelled with an opinion that all those crouches, cringes, and obeisances were made to him. But it is the case, not the carcase, they gape for. So may the chased stag boast how many hounds he hath attending him. They attend, indeed, as ravens a dying beast. Actæon found the kind truth of their attendance.   *Adams.*

11,171. PRIDE, Checks to. What is the man proud of? Money? It will not procure for him one night's sleep. It will not buy back a lost friend. It will not bribe off approaching death. Land? A very little bit of it will serve him soon. Learning? If he be equal to Newton, he has gathered one little pebble on the ocean's shore, and even that one he must soon lay down again. *Teachers' Treasury*

11,172. PRIDE, Compensation of. Some women are proud of their fine clothes, and when they have less wit and sense than the rest of their neighbors, comfort themselves that they have more lace. Some ladies put so much weight upon ornaments that, if one could see into their hearts, it would be found that even the thought of death was made less heavy to them by the contemplation of their being laid out in state, and honorably attended to the grave.   *Anon.*

11,173. PRIDE, Consequences of. Nature teaches us, that those trees bend the most freely, which bear the most fully. As a proud heart loves none but itself; so it is beloved by none but itself. Who would attempt to gain those pinnacles, that none have ascended without fears or descended without falls? It is recorded of Timotheus the Athenian, that when he was giving an account of his government and successes to the state, he frequently asserted with a vaunting air, "In this fortune had no hand." After this he never prospered, was quickly after disgraced and died in exile.   *Secker.*

11,174. PRIDE, Contemptuous. Demetrius, one of Alexander's successors, was so proud and disdainful, as not to allow those who transacted business with him liberty of speech; or else he treated them with so much rudeness, as obliged them to quit his presence in disgust. He suffered the Athenian ambassadors to wait two whole years before he gave them audience; and by the haughtiness of his behaviour, at last provoked his subjects to revolt from his authority, and expel him from his throne.
                                Whitecross.

11,175. PRIDE, Fall of. A tortoise, dissatisfied with his lowly life, when he beheld so many of the birds, his neighbors, disporting themselves in the clouds, and thinking that, if he could but once get up into the air, he could soar with the best of them, called one day upon an eagle, and offered him all the treasures of ocean if he could only teach him to fly The eagle would have declined the task, assuring him that the thing was not only absurd but impossible; but being further pressed by the entreaties and promises of the tortoise, he at length consented to do for him the best he could. So taking him up to a great height in the air and loosing his hold upon him, "Now, then!" cried the eagle; but the tortoise, before he could answer him a word, fell plump upon a rock, and was dashed to pieces. *Æsop.*

11,176. PRIDE, How to Humble. You may strip man bare of every earthly possession; you may leave him like a leafless trunk, or a dismantled wreck; you may bereave him of all that is held dear. Affectio may weep over him; authority may command; agony may lacerate; poverty may press him to the dust. To all these the law of God may add its terrors; and the dread of an undone eternity, of a lost soul, or a forfeited heaven, may complete the climax of woe; but all will not suffice to humble man. To Christ he must come at last to learn to be meek and lowly.
                                Tweedie.

11,177. PRIDE, Judicious Use of. In beginning the world, if you don't wish to get chafed at every turn, fold up your pride carefully, put it under lock and key, and only let it out to air on grand occasions. Pride is a garment all stiff brocade outside, all grating sackcloth on the side next to the skin. Even kings do not wear the dalmaticum except at a coronation.   *Lytton.*

11,178. PRIDE, Offset to. Take some quiet, sober moment of life, and add together the two ideas of price and man; behold him, creature of a span high, stalking through infinite space in all the grandeur of littleness. Perched on a speck of the universe, every wind of heaven strikes into his blood the coldness of death; his soul floats from his body like melody from the string; day and night, as dust on the wheel, he is rolled along the heavens, through a labyrinth of worlds, and all the creations of God are flaming above and beneath. Is this a creature to make for himself a crown of glory, to deny his own flesh, to mock at his fellow, sprung from that dust to which both will soon return? Does the proud man not err? Does he not suffer? Does he not die? When he reasons, is he never stopped by difficulties? When he acts, is he never tempted by pleasure? When he lives, is he free from pain? When he dies, can he escape the common grave? Pride is not the heritage of man; humility should dwell with frailty, and atone for ignorance, error, and imperfection.
                                Sydney Smith.

11,179. PRIDE, Removal of. When you pour water into bottles or any other vessels, the air that was in them before presently flies out and gives place to the more substantial body. Even so it is with those that have had many good precepts instilled into them, and their minds replenished with solid truths. They presently find that all empty vanity flies off; that the imposthume of pride breaks; that they do not value themselves for beard and gown only, but bend their actions and endeavors to the bettering of their rational faculties.
                                Plutarch.

11,180. PRIDE, Resisting. St. Macarious, the anchoret, who become famous for his abstemiousness and many mortifications of the body, was greatly tempted to leave his cave in the desert and go to Rome to serve the sick in the hospitals. He decided that this tempter was none other than spiritual pride and vain glory. Being much pressed with this tempter, he said, throwing himself upon the ground in his cell, "Drag me hence, if you can by force, for I will not stir." While he lay thus the tempter was disarmed. When he arose, the temptation was renewed. The saint then filled two large baskets with sand, and putting one on either shoulder, started forth into the wilderness. Meeting an acquaintance, he was asked what it meant. The saint's reply was, "I am tormenting my tormenter." The record says his temptation soon left him.

11,181. PRIDE, Retort upon. After the battle at Chaeronea, Philip sent Archidamus a haughty letter. The latter returned this answer, "If you measure your shadow, you will find it is no greater than before the victory."

11,182. PRIDE, Roman. Metellus, a Roman general, was so proud of a victory gained over Sertorius in battle that he desired to be called Imperator. He required the people to set up altars and offer sacrifices to him in every city he entered. He wore garlands of flowers upon his head, and a triumphal robe wrapped about him. At banquets, the image of Victory was made to go up and down the room moved by machinery, carrying trophies of gold, and crowns, and garlands; while a number of beautiful boys and girls followed, singing songs composed in praise of Metellus.

11,183. PRIDE, Temptation to. A godly man offered up a prayer without one wandering thought; and afterwards described it as the worst which he had ever offered, because, as he said, the devil made him proud of it. So was it also with the minister, who, upon being told by one more ready to praise the preacher than profit by his sermon, that he had delivered all excellent discourse, replied, "You need not tell me that; Satan told me so before I left the pulpit."   *Dr. Guthrie.*

11,184. PRIDE, Tower of. The Babel-tower of sin is a tower which a man builds in pride, and when its top reaches to heaven, then it is suddenly thrown down.   *Wordsworth.*

11,185. PRIDE, Universal. A lady, laboring among the degraded residents of the Five Points, says that there is pride even there. One refused to associate with another because she had only one chair in her room, while she had two.

11,186. PRIDE, Vagaries of. Pride is an evil that puts men upon all manner of evil. Accius the poet, though he were a dwarf, yet would be pictured tall of stature. Psaphon, a proud Lybian, would needs be a god, and, having caught some birds, he taught them to say "The great god Psaphon." Proud Simon in Lucian, having got a little wealth, changed his name from Simon to Simonides, for that there were so many beggars of his kin, and set the house on fire wherein he was born because nobody should point at it.   *Brooks.*

11,187. PRIDE, Vice of. Pride is so unsociable a vice, and does all things with so ill a grace, that there is no closing with it. A proud man will be sure to challenge more than belongs to him; you must expect him stiff in his conversation, fulsome in commending himself, and bitter in his reproofs.   *J. Collier.*

11,188. PRIDE, Vicious. A bad dog had a pillet of wood attached to his neck to prevent his harming his neighbors. Of this he was very proud, and ran through the market place to display his ornament, shaking his clog to attract attention. A wise friend whispered to him, "The less noise you make the better; your mark of distinction is no reward of merit, but a badge of disgrace." Beware of glorying in your shame.

11,189. PRINCIPLE, True to. In the town where I was born, a little way out of Boston, there was a boy by the name of Henry. When I was twelve years old my father took me to an academy, more than fifty miles from home. But Henry learned a trade. The prospect was that he would be a mechanic, and I should be a scholar. Henry worked well; he talked well; he read and studied evenings; he went to political meetings. A mutual friend of ours encouraged him to speak at these meetings, but with a sob in his heart he said. "How can I ever be anything when my father is a drinking man?" He solemnly signed the pledge of total abstinence; he began to make short speeches; the young men said: "Let us send him to the Legislature." At every step he did his best. Finally Massachusetts sent a petition by him to Congress. John Quincy Adams, from Massachusetts, invited him to dinner. While at dinner, Mr. Adams filled his glass, and, turning to the young mechanic, said, "Will you drink a glass of wine with me?" He hated to refuse; there was the ex-President of the United States; there was a company of great men. All eyes were upon him. And so he hesitated and grew red in the face, and finally stammered out, "Excuse me, sir, I never drink wine." The next day this anecdote was published in a Washington paper. It was copied all over Massachusetts, and the people said, "Here is a man that stands by his principles. He can be trusted. Let us promote him." And so he went up higher. He was made a Congressman, then a Senator, and finally Vice-President of the United States. That boy was Henry Wilson.   *Dr. Newell.*

11,190. PRINTING, Accuracy of. Every royal octavo page of this book contains seven thousand distinct pieces of type metal, from the size of a comma to a capital M. The entire book will require the handling of five million six hundred thousand types. The misplacing of any one of them would cause a blunder. Mechanical perfection has not yet been attained in the art, and the wonder to the initiated will be that so high a degree of accuracy has been secured.

11,191. PRISON, Deliverance from. During the persecutions of the third century, Felix, a priest of Nola in Campania, was cast into a dark dungeon, heavily ironed. One night an angel stood by him and bade him go forth on a mission of mercy. The chains fell from his neck and hands, his feet were disengaged, and the dungeon glowed with a brilliant light. The doors of the prison opened by themselves, and Felix followed his angelic attendant, who showed him the work appointed him. Such deliverance has every saved soul.

11,192. PRIVILEGES, Reminders of Misused. Metawatwees, an Indian chief, related to Zeisberger that he had been thirteen Sundays to Lichtenau, the Moravian settlement, to hear the truth, and that as he had returned, he had cut thirteen notches in the bark of the trees. Now when he passed the trees with his warriors, these notches met his eye at every turn and he paused and wept to think how often he had heard of Christ in vain.   *J. G. Wilson.*

11,193. PROBATION, Dignity of. Considered as a state of probation, our present condition loses all its inherent meanness; it derives a moral grandeur even from the shortness of its duration, when viewed as a contest for an immortal crown, in which the candidates are exhibited on a theatre, a spectacle to beings of the highest order, who conscious of the tremendous importance of the issue, of the magnitude of the interest at stake, survey the combatants from on high with benevolent and trembling solicitude.   *Robert Hall.*

11,194. PROBATION, Foreknowledge and. Among

other controversies, that of Fatum is also crept in, and to tie things to come, and even our own wills to a certain and inevitable necessity, we are yet upon this argument of time past: "Since God foresees that all things shall so fall out, as doubtless he does, it must then necessarily follow that they must so fall out." To which our masters reply, "That the seeing anything come to pass, as we do, and as God himself does (for all things being present with him, he rather sees, than foresees) is not to compel an event: that is, we see because things do fall out, but things do not fall out because we see. Events cause knowledge, but knowledge does not cause events. That which we see happen does happen; but it might have happened otherwise: and God, in the catalogue of the cause of events which he has in his prescience, has also those which we call accidental and unvoluntary, which depend upon the liberty he has given our free will, and knows that we do amiss because we would do so." *Montaigne.*

11,195. PROBATION, Improvement of. Man has but one state of probation, and that of an exceeding short continuance; and, therefore, since he cannot serve God long, he should serve him much; employ every minute of his life to the best advantage; thicken his devotions; hallow every day in his calendar by religious exercises, and every action in his life by holy reference and designments; for let him make what haste he can to be wise, time will outrun him. *J. Norris.*

11,196. PROBATION, Predestination and. Either predestination admits the existence of free will, or it rejects it. If it admits it, what kind of predetermined result can that be which a simple determination, a stop, a word, may alter or modify, *ad infinitum?* If predestination, on the contrary, rejects the existence of free will, it is quite another question: in that case a child need only be thrown into its cradle as soon as it is born; there is no necessity for bestowing the least care upon it; for if it be irrevocably determined that it is to live, it will grow though no food should be given to it. You see that such a doctrine cannot be maintained; predestination is a word without meaning. *Napoleon.*

11,197. PROCRASTINATION, Continuation of. Uncle Toby, in Tristram Shandy, threatened to oil the latch every day for forty years. Its squeaking every morning appealed to his heart, but he died without doing it. *Dr. Holme.*

11,198. PROCRASTINATION, Danger of. A young man in Pennsylvania, who had been deeply convicted during the progress of a revival, was asked by his pastor to come to Christ. He answered, "Not to-night; perhaps I will to-morrow night." The next day the pastor went out into the country, and while on his way perceived at a distance persons gathering in the street, and when he reached the place, he at once saw that this young man to whom he had spoken the previous evening was nearly killed by being thrown from a horse. They carried him into a neighbor's house, where he lived but a few minutes. His last words were, "Lost! lost! and forever lost!" The call of mercy is often followed closely by the summons to judgment.

11,199. PROCRASTINATION, Fatal. A young man in Chicago, to the crime of drunkenness added another for which he was sent to prison, and having served his time resolved to reform. He told a philanthropic gentleman his history, and through him secured a situation. This man exhorted him to seek Christ. He said, "I will when I have built up a character with my employers." In this he succeeded. He was again exhorted to seek Christ, but replied, "The time is not quite come yet." Two days after, the man was suddenly prostrated, and the man who had befriended him was sent for. He whispered, "Your soul, is it safe?" He could only shake his head. The time of death had come to him, and the time for repentance was past forever.

11,200. PROCRASTINATION, Habit of. A bright boy heard and was deeply impressed by the text, "My son, give me thine heart." Satan whispered, "Time enough yet," and he put it off. Ten years later a brilliant young collegian heard the same text under circumstances which seemed to make that the time of his salvation. Again the tempter whispered, "Time enough yet." Twenty years later a statesman of no mean renown listened to the same text from an aged bishop, and felt it to be a message to himself. This time the tempter said, "Visit foreign countries before you give God your heart." A traveler in Paris was stricken with cholera. His greatest suffering was agony of soul because he was not prepared to die, and had not now time to get ready. His last words were, "Too late." The boy, the collegian, the statesman, and the traveler were one. Procrastination is Satan's best game.

11,201. PROCRASTINATION, Lesson of. A pastor drew the following lesson from the fate of a white dove, which got into his chimney and perished in the fire burning in the grate below. "I believe it is no uncommon experience of lost souls, that efforts to 'save themselves' are too late, and that if half the anxiety to escape 'the damnation of hell,' which is felt at the end of their downward course, were felt at the beginning of it, multitudes of souls might be saved. I think there can be no doubt that when this dove first got into the chimney, a few vigorous strokes of its long pinions would have immediately extricated it, and carried it triumphantly into the outer air; and there is still less doubt that if sinners would, on the first perception of their danger, make a vigorous effort to overcome the surrounding obstacles which prevent their going to Christ, they would soon be safe; but their indecision, and their good intentions not being followed up by 'the performance of the same,' like the lazy flapping of the pigeon's wings, only sinks them deeper into sin, while the force of habit increases the difficulty of their ever 'ceasing to do evil and learning to do well.' And thus 't goes on with them, until perhaps in the stinging of a guilty conscience they may (like the pigeon near the bottom of the chimney), be said to feel the very flames of hell before they actually drop into it. Now, dear brethren, there may be some of you who are, compared with others, just at the commencement of the downward course, and I advise you to get out of it at once, let the effort to do so cost you what it may, for most assuredly it can never cost you less than it would now; and take the word of a minister who speaks to you from an open Bible, what you yourselves know to be the truth of God, that as surely as ever the shaft f that chimney led from the cool air above to the fire below, so surely does the way of sin and worldliness lead to hell; and as certainly as that poor little bird, in spite of all its efforts, was conducted from light and liberty above, through the filth and darkness of the chimney, into a blazing fire at the bottom, so surely— unless God should interpose in a manner which you have reason to believe he will not do—so surely may you, before your course is actually terminated, find yourselves irretrievably ruined. If you doubt it, read Proverbs 1: 24–31."

11,202. PROCRASTINATION, Pagan View of. A Pagan moralist hath represented the folly of an attachment to this world almost as strongly as a Christian could express it. "Thou art a passenger," says he, "and thy ship hath put into harbor for a few hours. The tide and the wind serve, and the pilot calls thee to depart, and thou art amusing thyself, and gathering shells and pebbles on the shore, till they set sail without thee." So is every Christian who, being on his voyage to a happy eternity, delays and loiters, and thinks and acts as if he were to dwell here forever. *Jortin.*

11,203. PRODIGAL, Desperation of the. When the dreams of greatness are over, and the riot of pleasure has ceased, the change to want and degradation is often too sudden, and always too great, to be borne with equanimity. In the earlier moments of desperation, it is not uncommon to see the prodigal betake himself for refuge from the load of humiliation and despair, to poison, the pistol, or the halter. Among those who become suicides, in the possession of their reason, a more numerous list is nowhere found than that which is composed of ruined prodigals. *Dr. Dwight.*

11,204. PRODIGAL, Hope of the. A painter in London was engaged upon a picture of the Prodigal Son. He had sketched his design, thrown in the accessories, but still wanted a model for his central figure. He went out into the lowest quarters of the city to search for the embodiment of his ideal of the prodigal. At length he met a man with all the marks of dissipation, crime, and poverty upon him. His face was pinched with hunger, his eyes bloodshot, his garments foul and tattered. The painter said to him, "Will you come to me to-morrow? I'll give you a guinea if you will." The engagement was made. At the time and place indicated the vagabond appeared. He had washed himself, and put on better robes. On seeing him, the artist cried, "Go away! I don't want you; I want the man I saw yesterday." So the sinner wants to make himself better, but God wants the prodigal in all his vileness and rags. He proposes to put royal robes on returning prodigals.

11,205. PRODIGAL, Love for the. A lady came to Liverpool to see me. She said she had a boy nineteen years of age, who had left her. She showed me his photograph, and asked me to put it in my pocket. "You stand before many and large assemblies, Mr. Moody. My boy may be in London now. Oh, look at the audiences to whom you will preach; look earnestly. You may see my dear boy before you. If you do see him, tell him to come back to me. Oh, implore him to come to his sorrowing mother, to his deserted home. He may be in trouble; he may be suffering; tell him for his loving mother that all is forgiven and forgotten, and he will find comfort and peace at home." On the back of this photograph she had written his full name and ad dress; she had noted his complexion, the color of his eyes and hair; why he had left home. "When you preach, Mr. Moody, look for my poor boy," were the parting words of that mother. That young man may be in this hall to-night. If he is, I want to tell him that your mother loves you still. I will read out his name, and if any of you ever hear of that young man, just tell him that his mother is waiting with a loving heart and a tender embrace for him. His name is Arthur P. Oxley, of Manchester, England. Such a message God sends to every one of his wandering children. *Moody.*

11,206. PRODIGAL, Parable of the. I asked a young woman upon the street, "What portion of the scripture did you the most good?" She replied, "That which does all men good, the parable of the Prodigal Son. It is so pleasant, so plain! There stands the father with outstretched arms. It is wonderful, the love of Jesus Christ for the sinner!" *Ralph Wells.*

11,207. PRODIGAL, Rescue of a. At a camp meeting a young man was seen leaning against a tree, looking sorrowful and forlorn. His clothes were ragged, his feet bare. A minister went to him and asked him if he did not wish to come to Christ. He replied, "I have been thinking about it; I wish I could, but I am ashamed to go and kneel there, people will look at my bare feet." The minister said, "Come just as you are: I remember a young man with tattered robes and bare feet, who was poor and sad as you are, but he thought of his father's house where there was enough and to spare." "Oh," interrupted the young man, "that's in the Bible." "Yes, it's the prodigal coming home to his father, like you, with bare feet and poor clothes." "I'll go to my father," he said going to the altar. In a few moments there was a light in his face at which you might have kindled a star.

11,208. PRODIGALITY, Roman. Heliogabalus was very lavish in his expenditures. His fishponds he filled with rose water. His lamps were supplied with precious balsam, distilled from trees in Arabia. His dining room was strewed with saffron, and his porticoes with the dust of gold. Upon his shoes were pearls and precious stones, and he was never known to wear a garment a second time, though made of the richest material.

11,209. PRODIGALITY, Royal. Paschisyrus, King of Crete, after spending all he had, or could raise, as a last resource sold his kingdom, and retired to private life. He died a miserable death in the city of Amathunta, in Cyprus.

11,210. PROFANITY, Beware of. A very estimable man of sixty was prostrated with brain fever, and in his delirium shocked his friends by his blasphemous profanity. After his recovery he was told of it, and confessed that in youth he was terribly profane. "It is forty years since I uttered a profane word. I supposed the habit was gone from me; but the leprosy is still in my blood. The tiger is chained, but he is alive." Daily grace is the only cure. Beware of profanity in youth.

11,211. PROFANITY, Correcting. A tradesman commencing business was very much distressed at the profanity of many of his customers. He made an effort to stop it, by hanging above his counter, "Friend, don't swear." If an oath was uttered, he kindly showed the party the fearful consequences of breaking the third commandment. Swearing was not only abolished from the store, but also, from many of the homes and manufactories of the place.

11,212. PROFANITY, Correction of. A man said to a dreadful swearer, who was cursing himself in a fearful manner, "Friend, do you not know what Amen means?" "To be sure I do," said he: "it means, So be it." "Then," said he, "how angry you would be if any one should say Amen to the curses you have pronounced against your poor eyes and precious limbs. If God should happen to say Amen, what will become of you?" This rebuke led to his conversion.

11,213. PROFANITY, Covenant against. At a service held in Benton Barracks, St. Louis, with the 33d Missouri Regement, Dr. Nelson proposed that the soldiers should enter into a covenant to allow Colonel, afterward General, Clinton B. Fisk, to do all the swearing for the regiment. This was unanimously agreed to, the whole regiment rising to their feet to ratify it. At headquarters a card was posted, with the inscription, "Swear not at all. Attention is called to the 3d commandment, and 3d article of war." For months not an oath was heard in this command; but one day the colonel heard hard swearing, and perceived that it was by a teamster of his own regiment, whose mules had run his heavy laden wagon against a stump and broken the pole. Soon after, General Fisk accosted the driver, "John did I not hear some one swearing most dreadfully an hour ago down on the bottom?" "I think you did, General." "Do you know who it was?" "Yes, sir; it was me, General." "Do you not remember the covenant entered into at Benton Barracks, St. Louis, with Rev. Dr. Nelson, that I should do all the swearing for my old regiment?" "To be sure I do, General," said John; "but then you were not there to do it, and it had to be done right off."

11,214. PROFANITY, Reproof of. Dr. Annesley, while dining at a coffee-house, ordered a glass of water to be sent to the gentleman in the next box, whose profane oaths were very annoying. He was surprised, and said he had given no such order. The doctor said, gravely "I thought to cool your tongue after the fiery language you have been using." The man was offended and challenged him, but he excused himself on account of his cloth. Some years after he met the man, who apologized and thanked him for his reproof, which had cured him of a wicked habit.

11,215. PROFANITY, Saved from. A man of large wealth lived in Illinois, and had everything to make life pleasant to him, but he was a very profane, godless man. He would curse everything and everybody. Even the wife of his bosom had curses showered down upon her, and his children used to be witnesses of his frightful oaths. One day I set out to go to see him. I was near his house when he stepped out of the front door. I stepped up— "This is Mr. P., I believe?" "Yes, sir," in a gruff, unwelcome voice, "that is my name; what do you want?" He knew very well who I was; he mistrusted what I wanted. "I would like to ask you a question," I replied, "Well, what is it?" "I am told," I said, "that you are very wealthy, that God has blessed you with great wealth, that you have a beautiful wife and lovely children, and I just want to know why you treat God in the way you do." The tears came out of his eyes and he said, "Come in, come in." So I entered and he told me that he had tried a thousand times to stop swearing, but he couldn't. I told him to trust to Jesus and he would stop it for him—that's what he came into the world to do; and the result was that he let Christ take the burden. He confessed his sin, had the prayers of all the Christians round about, and in a year he became one of the elders of the church. *Moody.*

11,216. PROFESSION, Abuse of. He that abuses his own profession will not patiently bear with any one else who does so. And this is one of our most subtle operations of self love; for when we abuse our own profession we tacitly except ourselves; but when another abuses it, we are far from being certain that this is the case. *Colton.*

11,217. PROFESSION, Exceptions to. Many people are offended with the profession of religion, because all are not religious who make a profession. A little consideration will correct this error. Does the sheep despise its fleece because the wolf has worn it? Who blames a crystal river because some melancholy men have drowned themselves in its streams? The best drugs have their adulterants. And will you refuse an opiate, because some have wantonly poisoned themselves with it? Though you have been cozened with false colors, yet you should not disesteem that which is dyed in grain. He is a bad economist who, having a spot in his garment, cuts off the cloth, instead of rubbing off the dirt. God rejects all religion but his own.   *Secker.*

11,218. PROFESSION, Holding Fast Our. When tempted to desert the truth, or to renounce the cause of Christ, "we may," says Andrew Fuller, "imagine that the martyrs in heaven are calling to us. One may say, 'Hold it fast; I died in a dungeon rather than forego it.' 'Hold it fast,' says another; 'I bled for it.' 'Hold it fast,' says a third; 'I burned for it.'" A dying English girl said, "I cleave to Jesus as the limpets to the rocks."

11,219. PROFESSION, Making no. Some excuse their evil ways by saying, like a certain young lady, "I make no profession; if I did, the case would be different." She seemed to think that fact exempted her from obligation. An irreligious man said, "Thank God, I am not a hypocrite." A Christian answered, appropriately, "He might have said with equal propriety, 'Thank God, I am wicked enough to make no secret of my sin.'" When you have heard of some scandalous professor who has brought reproach on religion, you have secretly thought, "How much better am I!" How much, think you? I own that you are more consistent, but your consistency avails you nothing: it is only consistency in sin; it is only the consistency of being bad altogether, without pretending to be otherwise; and nothing but blindness and self-deception the most determined can lead you to imagine yourself in a fairer way to heaven, than are those who have openly forsaken the path of righteousness.   *Anon.*

11,220. PROFESSOR, The Mere. The mere professor reminds me of a sow that I saw luxuriating in her sty when almost over head and heels in the mire. Now suppose any of you were to take Bess (the sow), and wash her; and suppose, after having dressed her in a silk gown, and put a smart cap on her head, you were to take her into any of your parlors, and were to set her down to tea in company; she might look very demure for a time, and might not even give a single grunt; but you would observe that she occasionally gave a sly look towards the door, which showed that she felt herself in an uncomfortable position; and the moment she perceived that the door was open, she would give you another proof of the fact by running out of the room as fast as she could. Follow the sow, with her silk gown and her fancy cap, and in a few seconds you will find that she has returned to her sty and is again wallowing in the mire. Just so it is with the unrenewed man: sin is his element; and though he may be induced, from a variety of motives, to put on at times a show of religion, you will easily perceive that he feels himself to be under unpleasant restraints, and that he will return again to his sins wherever an opportunity of doing so, unknown to his acquaintances, presents itself to him.   *Rowland Hill.*

11,221. PROFIT, Pleasure and. The two common shrines to which most men offer up the application of their thoughts and their lives, are profit and pleasure; and by their devotions to either of these, they are vulgarly distinguished into two sects, and are called busy or idle men; whether these words differ in meaning, or only in sound, I know very well may be disputed, and with appearance enough; since the covetous man takes as much pleasure in his gains as the voluptuous in his luxury, and would not pursue his business unless he were pleased with it, upon the last account of what he most wishes and desires; nor would care for the increase of his fortunes, unless he thereby proposed that of his pleasures too, in one kind or other; so that pleasure may be said to be his end, whether he will allow to find it in his pursuit or no.   *Temple.*

11,222. PROFIT, Seeking for. All that we see men so very serious and industrious about, which we call business; that which they trudge for in the streets, which they work or wait for in the shops, which they meet and crowd for in the exchange, which they sue for in the hall and solicit for at the court, which they plow and dig for, which they march and fight for in the field, which they travel for on land, and sail for among rocks and storms on the sea, which they plod for in the closet and dispute for in the schools (yea, may we not add, which they frequently pray for and preach for in the church!), what is it but profit? *Dr. Barrow.*

11,223. PROGRESS, Evidence of. History is full of the signs of this natural progress of society. We see in almost every part of the annals of mankind how the industry of individuals, struggling up against wars, taxes, famines, conflagrations, mischievous prohibitions, and more mischievous protections, creates faster than governments can squander, and repairs whatever invaders can destroy. We see the wealth of nations increasing, and all the arts of life approaching nearer and nearer to perfection, in spite of the grossest corruption and the wildest profusion on the part of rulers.   *Macaulay.*

11,224. PROGRESS, Example of. A boy twelve years old once stopped at a country tavern, and paid for his lodging and breakfast by sawing wood, instead of asking it as a gift. Fifty years later, the same person passed the same inn as George Peabody, the banker.

11,225. PROGRESS, March of. Agesilaus the Great, marching with his army through Thrace, used to inquire whether he passed through the country of an enemy or a friend. He sent the same questions to the King of Macedon; who replied that he would consider it. Hearing this, Agesilaus said, "Let him consider; we will be marching on." The King of Macedon, overawed at this, could do nothing else, and so sent word that he admitted him as a friend.

11,226. PROGRESS, Political. The history of England is the history of progress; and, when we take a comprehensive view of it, it is so. But when examined in small separate portions, it may, with more propriety, be called a his tory of actions and reactions. We have often thought that the motion of the public mind in our country resembles that of the sea when the tide is rising. Each successive wave rushes forward, breaks, and rolls back; but the great flood is steadily coming in. A person who looked on the waters only for a moment might fancy that they were retiring. A person who looked on them only for five minutes might fancy that they were rushing capriciously to and fro. But when he keeps his eye on them for a quarter of an hour, and sees one sea-mark disappear after another, it is impossible for him to doubt of the general direction in which the ocean is moved. Just such has been the course of events in England. In the history of the national mind, which is, in truth, the history of the nation, we must carefully distinguish between that recoil which regularly follows every advance, and a great general ebb. If we take centuries, if, for example, we compare 1794 with 1660 or with 1685, we cannot doubt in which direction society is proceeding. *Macaulay.*

11,227. PROGRESS, Safety in. Flying birds are never taken in a fowler's snare. *Secker.*

11,228. PROGRESS, Spiritual. I find the great thing in this world is not so much where we stand, as in what direction we are moving. To reach the port of heaven, we must sail sometimes with the wind and sometimes against it—but we must sail, and not drift, nor lie at anchor. *Holmes.*

11,229. PROGRESS, Striving after. I will take heed of quenching the spark, and strive to kindle a fire. He ne'er was so good as he should be, that doth not strive to be better than he is; he never will be better than he is, that doth not fear to be worse than he was. *Warwick.*

11,230. PROHIBITION, Need of. The old Romans twisted hay around the horns of dangerous cattle to warn the people to run for their lives; but, although we have been for years hanging warnings, and arguments, and persuasions on the arms of the demon intemperance, men do not fly from it, and hence the need of Prohibition. *Edwin Holmes.*

11,231. PROMISES, Biblical. A man in London had all the promises of God printed together in a little book, and some time after some one in the country sent up for a copy. He received the answer that the "Promises of God" were out of print. At one time in Chicago, when the meetings grew a little dull, I told them we would go through the Bible and look for all the promises given us; and from that time there were no more dull meetings. We had never realized before what promises God has made to those who believe in Jesus Christ. *Moody.*

11,232. PROMISES, Comforts of the. The comforts of the promises are universal, such as agree with every estate, and suit every malady; they are the strong man's meat, and the sick man's cordial, the condemned sinner's pardon, and the justified person's evidence; but the best of the world's comforts are only

applicable to some particular conditions, and serve as salve for some few sores. Riches are a remedy against the pressing evils of want and poverty, but this cannot purchase ease to the pained. Armor of proof is a defence against the sword and bullet, but can no way serve to keep off the stings of piercing care; oils and balsams are useful for bruises and broken bones, but they are needless to a hungry man that seeks not after medicines but food. But the comforts of the promises are in their operations and efficacy of an unlimited extent; they flow immediately from the Father of mercies and God of all comfort, and are, therefore, sent to revive and establish, how disconsolate in any kind whatever the condition of a believer is. *Spurgeon.*

11,233. PROMISES, Date of the. God's promises are dated, but with a mysterious character; and, for want of skill in God's chronology, we are prone to think God forgets us, when, indeed, we forget ourselves in being so bold to set God a time of our own, and in being angry that he comes not just then to us. *Gurnall.*

11,234. PROMISES, Faith and the. Faith melts promises into arguments as the soldier doth lead into bullets, and then helps the Christian to send them with a force to heaven in fervent prayer; whereas a promise in an unbeliever's mouth is like a shot in a gun's mouth without any fire to put to it. *Gurnall.*

11,235. PROMISES, Light of the. The railway train, like some vast serpent, hissing as it moves swiftly along, plunges underground. The bright sun is suddenly lost, but the traveler's eye observes, for the first time, perhaps, the railway carriage lamp; and though it was there all the while, yet because the sun made its light needless, it was not observed. God's promises are like that railway light. The Christian traveler has them with him always, though when the sun is shining, and prosperity beaming upon him, he does not remark them. But let trouble come, let his course lie through the darkness of sorrow or trial, and the blessed promise shines out like the railway lamp, to cheer him, and shed its gentle and welcome light most brightly when the gloom is thickest. *Champneys.*

11,236. PROMISES, Profuse in. The man who is wantonly profuse of his promises, ought to sink his credit as much as a tradesman would by uttering a great number of promissory notes, payable at a distant day. The truest conclusion in both cases is, that neither intend, or will be able to pay. And as the latter most probably intends to cheat you of your money, so the former at least designs to cheat you of your thanks. *Fielding.*

11,237. PROMISES, Satan's. Alexander, who grew fond of frequent carousals, once invited his friends and officers to supper. He promised a crown to the man who could drink the most wine. One of his guests consumed such an immense quantity that three days after winning the diadem he died. So Satan outwits those to whom he makes promise of rewards and honors. *Anon.*

11,238. PROMISES. Special Claim to the. A pious son, whose father had died in his absence, returning to his weeping friends said, "Mother, we have a new claim on God to-day. You, my dear mother, have a claim on him for a husband, and my sisters, brother, and myself, have a claim on him for a father."

11,239. PROMISES, Unclaimed. An aged and ragged Indian wandered into one of our western settlements, begging for food to keep him from starving. A bright-colored ribbon, from which was suspended a small, dirty pouch, was seen around his neck. On being questioned, he said it was a charm given him in his younger days; and opening it, displayed a faded, greasy paper, which he handed to the interrogator for inspection. It proved to be a regular discharge from the Federal army, entitling him to a pension for life, and signed by General Washington himself! Here was a name which would be honored almost anywhere, and which, if presented in the right place, would have insured him support and plenty for the remainder of his days; and yet he wandered about hungry, helpless, and forlorn, begging of the charitable bread to keep him from famishing. What a picture of men with all the promises of Jesus in their hands—and of Christians, too, with the charter of their inheritance in full possession—yet starving in the wilderness ! *Anon.*

11,240. PROMPTNESS, Ministerial. A prompt minister succeeded a very tardy and irregular one. The people were like the priest, and instead of arriving at church at eleven o'clock, assembled about twelve. The new minister began service promptly at eleven, and many of his parishioners found the sermon nearly over on their arrival, to their surprise and chagrin. Others arrived after the benediction. He asked if they wished to change the hour of service, and assured them of his readiness to be present promptly at any time fixed by them. His congregation came to be as prompt as himself. A minister usually has only himself to blame for a tardy congregation.

11,241. PROPERTY, Passsion for. Property communicates a charm to whatever is the object of it. It is the first of our abstract ideas: it cleaves to us the closest and the longest. It endears to the child its plaything, to the peasant his cottage, to the landholder his estate. It supplies the place of prospect and scenery. Instead of coveting the beauty of distant situations, it teaches every man to find it in his own. It gives boldness and grandeur to plains and fens, tinge and coloring to clays and fallows. *Paley.*

11,242. PROPHECY, Evidence of. Some of the Prince of Conde's friends tried often to disturb his faith in Christianity. He always replied, 'You give yourselves a good deal of unnecessary trouble; the dispersion of the Jews will always be an undeniable proof to me of the truth of our holy religion."

11,243. PROPHECY, Fanciful Interpretation of. Interpreters of prophecy during the last few centuries have been most of them led by their fancy. One of them sees in the sublimities of the Revelation the form of Louis Napoleon where two or three hundred years ago half Christendom saw the pope, and the other half Martin Luther. The other day one of the seers saw Sebastopol in the prophecies, and now another detects the Suez Canal, and we feel pretty sure that the Council at Rome will soon be spied out in Daniel or Ezekiel. The fact is, when fancy is their guide men wander as in a maze. Spiritualistic interpreters see, like children gazing into the fire, not what is really before them, but what is in their own heads. *Spurgeon.*

11,244. PROPHECY, Profitless. Cassandra's gift of prophecy was of no advantage to the citizens of Troy, who would not believe her. *Plutarch.*

11,245. PROPHECY and Providence. Josephus draws an argument against the Epicurians, who deny a divine providence from the fulfillment of Daniel's prophecy foretelling the taking away of the daily sacrifice from the temple, which happened accordingly, many years after, under Antiochus Epiphanes. The same deduction may be drawn from all prophecy. "Hence we discover that the world is not carried along of its own accord, without a ruler and a curator, like ships without pilots, which we see drowned by the winds, or like chariots without drivers, which are overturned; so would the world be dashed to pieces by its being carried without a Providence, and so perish and come to naught."

11,246. PROPOSAL, Graceful. A celebrated doctor of divinity, after a few hours' conversation with a lady, wrote to her thus: "My dear Madam—In a few hours you have obtained a place in my heart, which I could not have expected in as many weeks: indeed, so fully have you possessed yourself that unless you consent to become a tenant for life, not only will our parting be exceedingly troublesome, but I fear that many terms will elapse before I can prepare the premises for another occupant." It is needless to say that the lady came to terms. *Hood*

11,247. PROSPERITY, Arrogance of. Plato being desired by the Cyrenians to prescribe to them good laws, and to settle their government, refused to do it, saying that it was a hard matter to give them any law whilst they enjoyed so much prosperity, since nothing is so fierce, arrogant, and untamable, as a man that thinks himself to be in a happy condition.

11,248. PROSPERITY, Caution in. God's checks are but symptoms of his mercy, but his silence is the harbinger of judgment. Be circumspect and provident. Hast thou a fair summer? Provide for a hard winter. The world's river ebbs alone; it flows not. He that goes merrily with the stream must bale up. Flatter thyself no longer in thy prosperous sin, but be truly sensible of thy own presumption. Look seriously into thy approaching danger, and humble thyself with contrition. If thou procure sour herbs, God will provide his passover *Quarles.*

11,249. PROSPERITY, Danger of. "There are seeds," says Saurin, "of some passions, which remain, as it were, buried during the first years of life, and which vegetate only in mature age." Valerian, the emperor, was at first distinguished for his temperance, moderation, and many virtues, which fixed the uninfluenced choice of all Rome upon him; but when he was invested with the purple, he displayed inability, meanness, cowardice, and seldom acted with any prudence. So dangerous is prosperity! *Buck.*

11,250. PROSPERITY, Discomfort in. I have seen a young and healthful person warm and ruddy under a poor and thin garment, when at the same time an old rich person hath been cold and paralytic under a load of sables and the skins of foxes. It is the body that makes the clothes warm, and not the clothes the body; and the spirit of a man makes felicity and content, not any spoils of a rich fortune wrapped about a sickly and uneasy soul. Apollodorus was a traitor and a tyrant, and the world wondered to see a bad man have so good a fortune, but knew not that he nourished scorpions in his breast, and that his liver and his heart were eaten up with spectres and images of death. Does he not drink more sweetly that takes his beverage in an earthen vessel than he that looks and searches into his golden chalices for fear of poison, and looks pale at every sudden noise, and sleeps in armor, and trusts nobody, and does not trust God for his safety, but does greater wickedness only to escape awhile unpunished for his former crimes? *Jeremy Taylor.*

11,251. PROSPERITY, Exposure of. I once received in the pulpit the following note: "The prayers of this congregation are earnestly desired for a man who is prospering in his worldly concerns." *Wm. Jay.*

11,252. PROSPERITY, Insecurity of. Prosperity is not to be deemed the greatest security. The lofty unbending cedar is more exposed to the injurious blast than the lowly shrub. The little pinnace rides safely along the shore, while the gallant ship advancing is wrecked. Those sheep which have the most wool, are generally the soonest fleeced. Poverty is its own defence against robbery. A fawning world is worse than a frowning world. Who would shake those trees upon which there is no fruit? *Secker.*

11,253. PROSPERITY, Misery with. It was a good speech of an emperor, "You," said he, "gaze upon my purple robe and golden crown; but did you know what cares are under it, you would not take it up from the ground to have it." It was a true saying of Augustine on the twenty-sixth Psalm, "Many are miserable by loving hurtful things, but they are more miserable by having them." *Brooks.*

11,254. PROSPERITY, Trial of. When fire is put to green wood, there comes out abundance of watery stuff that before appeared not; when the pond is empty, the mud, filth and toads come to light. The snow covers many a dunghill, so doth prosperity many a rotten heart. It is easy to wade in a warm bath, and every bird can sing in a sunshiny day, etc. Hard weather tries what health we have, afflictions try what sap we have, what grace we have. Withered leaves soon fall off in windy weather, rotten boughs quickly break with heavy weights. *Brooks.*

11,255. PROSPERITY, Wicked. There are some people that differ little or nothing from children who, many times beholding malefactors upon the stage in their gilded vestments and short purple cloaks, dancing with crowns upon their heads, admire and look upon them as the most happy persons in the world, till they see them gored, and lashed, and flames of fire curling from underneath their sumptuous and gaudy garments. Thus, there are many wicked men, surrounded with numerous families, splendid in the pomp of magistracy, and illustrious for the greatness of their power, whose punishments never display themselves till those glorious persons come to be the public spectacles of the people, either slain and lying weltering in their blood, or else standing on the top of a rock, ready to be tumbled headlong down the precipice. *Plutarch.*

11,256. PROTECTION, Divine. Three hundred Christian converts, in the army of the King of Madagascar, refused to bow down before the national idol. Their service against the enemy was required, so the commander resolved not to kill them, but to place them where they would be sure to be slain in battle. They met the enemy in a deep ravine, and led the attack. At the close of a hard battle, in which many pagans were slain or wounded, it was found that not a Christian soldier was missing. Because of this signal deliverance, many pagans renounced idolatry from that day.

11,257. PROTECTION, Legend of. St. Comgall, the monk, was forced to bear arms, much against his will. It was winter, and the soldiers were encamped upon a bleak moor. Many sheltered themselves from the drifting snow and biting cold by erecting temporary huts. Comgall made no such provision, and it was noticed that no snow fell upon him, and in the morning a wall of snow was found encompassing him, which protected him from the northern blast. The Lord can be a wall of fire or of snow round about his people as they need.

11,258. PROTESTANT, Origin of the Word. The name of Protestant took its rise 1529. At this time a few of the electors and princes of Germany, joined by the inhabitants of Strasburg, Nuremberg, Ulm, Constance, Hailbron, and several other cities, published a protestation against a decree of the Diet (the assembly of the States of the German Empire), and petitioned the emperor to have it revoked. Hence the name of Protestants was at that period given to the reformers of religion in Germany: and it has since become the general denomination of sects of every description, who, continuing to profess Christianity, abjure the errors of popery, whose adherents are called Romanists, Catholics, Roman Catholics, or more properly Papists, because of their sub-jection to the pope, whom the greater part of them receive and honor as Christ's vicar and universal bishop.   *Buck.*

11,259. PROTESTANT, Responsibilities of a. As a Protestant, every mature man, the humblest and poorest, has the same dignified right over his own opinions and profession of faith that he has over his own hearth. But his hearth can rarely be abused; whereas his religious system, being a vast kingdom, opening by im-measurable gates upon worlds of light and worlds of darkness, now brings him within a new amenability—called upon to answer new impeachments, and to seek for new assistances. Formerly another was answerable for his be-lief. Now he has new rights; but these have burdened him with new obligations; he is crowned with the glory and the palms of an intellectual creature; but he is alarmed by the certainty of corresponding struggles. Prot-estantism it is that has created him into this child and heir of liberty; Protestantism it is that has invested him with these unbounded privileges of private judgment, giving him in one moment the sublime powers of an autocrat within one solitary conscience; but Protest-antism it is that has introduced him to the most dreadful of responsibilities.
T. de Quincey.

11,260. PROVERBS, Wisdom of. Like those concentrated essences of food which are so much used by travelers in our day, the proverb may not present to the eye the appearance of the wisdom that it was originally made of; but a great quantity of the raw material has been used up in making one, and that one, when skill-fully dissolved, will spread out to its original dimensions. Much matter is pressed into little room, that it may keep and carry. Wisdom in this portable form, acts an important part in human life. The character of a people gives shape to their proverbs; and again, the proverbs go to mould the character of the people who use them. These well-worn words are precious, as being real gold, and convenient as being a portable, stamped and recognized currency. As a general rule, proverbs spring from the people at large, as herbage springs spontaneously from the soil, and the parentage of the individual remains forever unknown. Very few proverbs are attached, even tradi-tionally, to the name of any man as their au-thor. From time to time collections of these products are made, and catalogued by the curious; and the stock is continually increas-ing as the active life of a nation gives them off.
Arnot.

11,261. PROVIDENCE, Adaptations of. Suppose the mole should cry, "How I could have hon-ored the Creator had I been allowed to fly!" it would be very foolish, for a mole flying would be a most ridiculous object; while a mole fashioning its tunnels and casting up its castles is viewed with admiring wonder by the naturalist, who perceives its remarkable suit-ability to its sphere. The fish of the sea might say, "How could I display the wisdom

of God if I could sing, or mount a tree, like a bird!" but a dolphin in a tree would be a very grotesque affair, and there would be no wisdom of God to admire in trouts singing in the groves; but when the fish cuts the wave with agile fin, all who have observed it say how wonderfully it is adapted to its habitat, how exactly its every bone is fitted for its mode of life. Brother, it is just so with you. If you begin to say, "I cannot glorify God where I am, and as I am," I answer, neither could you anywhere if not where you are.
Spurgeon.

11,262. PROVIDENCE, Ahead of. Luther was very importunate at the throne of grace to know the mind of God in a certain matter; and it seemed to him as if he heard God speak to his heart thus: "I am not to be traced." One adds, "If he is not to be traced, he may be trusted; and that religion is of little value which will not enable a man to trust God where he can neither trace nor see him. But there is a time for everything beneath the sun; and the Almighty has his 'times and seasons.' It has been frequently with my hopes and de-sires, in regard to Providence, as with my watch and the sun. My watch has often been ahead of true time: I have gone faster than Providence, and have been forced to stand still and wait, or I have been set back pain-fully. Flavel says, 'Some providences, like Hebrew letters, must be read backwards.'"
J. G. Wilson.

11,263. PROVIDENCE, Balance of. Divine Prov-idence tempers his blessings to secure their bet-ter effect. He keeps our joys and our fears on an even balance, that we may neither presume nor despair. By such compositions God is pleased to make our crosses more tolerable, and our enjoyments more wholesome and safe.
Wogan.

11,264. PROVIDENCE, Dependence on. We are too apt to forget our actual dependence on Providence for the circumstances of every in-stant. The most trivial events may determine our state in the world. Turning up one street instead of another may bring us in company with a person whom we should not otherwise have met; and this may lead to a train of other events which may determine the happiness or misery of our lives.   *Cecil.*

11,265. PROVIDENCE, Firm Trust in. When worthy Mr. Hern lay upon his death bed, his wife, with great concern, asked him what was to become of her and her very large family! He answered, "Peace, sweetheart! that God who feeds the ravens will not starve the Herns."   *W. Secker.*

11,266. PROVIDENCE, Harmonies of. In the baptistery of the cathedral at Pisa is a wonder-ful dome. Spacious, symmetrical; composed of the choicest marble, it is a delight to stand beneath, and gaze upon its beauties. Thus I stood, one sunny April day, when suddenly the air became instinct with melody. The great dome seemed full of harmony. The waves of music vibrated to and fro, loudly beating against the walls, swelling into full chords like the roll of a grand organ, and then dying away into soft, long-drawn, far-receding echoes, melting in the distance into silence. It was only my guide, who, lingering behind me a moment, had softly murmured a triple chord. But beneath that magic roof every sound resolved into a symphony. No discord can reach the summit of that dome and live. Every noise made in the building, the slamming of seats, the tramping of feet, all the murmur and bustle of the crowd, are caught up, softened, harmonized, blended and echoed back in music. So it seems to me that over our life hangs the great dome of God's providence. Standing, as we do, beneath it, no act in the divine administration toward us, no affliction, no grief, no loss which our heavenly Father sends, however hard to bear it may be, but will come back at last, softened and blended into harmony, within the over-arching dome of his wisdom, mercy and power, till to our corrected sense it shall be the sweetest music of heaven.　　　*J. Dorman Steele.*

11,267. PROVIDENCE, Incidents of. St. Felix escaped arrest and martyrdom by crawling through a small hole in an old stone wall, which was instantly closed by spiders' webs. His pursuers saw the place, but the spiders' webs satisfied them that no one had recently passed through it.

11,268. PROVIDENCE, Links of. If I had not met a certain person, I should not have changed my profession; if I had not known a certain lady, I should not probably have met this person; if that lady had not had a delicate daughter who was disturbed by the barking of my dog, I should not have known her; if my dog had not barked that night, I should now have been in the Dragoons, or fertilizing the soil of India. Who can say that these things were not ordered, and that, apparently, the merest trifles do not produce failure and a marred existence?　　　*F. W. Robertson.*

11,269. PROVIDENCE, Minister of. A missionary in Jamaica was benighted in a very dangerous part of his way, which lay along a steep precipice. A misstep in the dark would send him into eternity. A little insect called the candle-fly, came to his relief, hovering about the missionary, and lighting him over the rough places till the danger was past. Providence has innumerable unexpected agents to relieve or to overwhelm.

11,270. PROVIDENCE, Omnipresence of. I asked a hermit once, in Italy, how he could venture to live alone in a single cottage, on the top of a mountain, a mile from any habitation? He replied that Providence was his very next door neighbor.　　　*Sterne.*

11,271. PROVIDENCE, Preparations of. An old Jewish legend assures us concerning the cloud that conducted Israel through the wilderness, that it did not only show them the way, but also prepared it; that it did not only lead them in the way which they must go, but also fitted the way for them to go upon it; that it cleared all the mountains and smoothed all the rocks; that it cleared all the bushes and

removed all the trees. Whether fact or fancy with the Jews, it is true of God's providence toward his people.

11,272. PROVIDENCE, Preserved by. A godly man, as he was going to take ship for France, broke his leg; and the ship that he would have gone in was cast away, and not a man saved. Brooks says, "By breaking a bone his life was saved. So the Lord many times breaks our bones, but it is in order to the saving of our lives and our souls forever."

11,273. PROVIDENCE, Rescue of. The poet Cowper, in his insane melancholy, resolved to drown himself in the Thames. He ordered a coachman, who was well acquainted with London, to drive him to Blackfriars Bridge. Strangely enough, the man drove all over London, but could not find the bridge. At this Cowper's mood changed, and he directed the driver to take him home. When he reached his room, he composed that beautiful hymn,

"God moves in a mysterious way
His wonders to perform."

11,274. PROVIDENCE, Restraints of. Julian had two great designs before him; one was to conquer the Persians, the other to root out the Galileans, as he, by way of contempt, called the Christians; but he would begin with the Persians, and then make a sacrifice of all the Christians to his idols. He did so, and perished in the first attempt.　　　*John Flavel.*

11,275. PROVIDENCE, Revelations of. A boy was lost by his drunken father in this great city, and he could get no tidings from his mother. Many years had passed, and he became anxious to discover his parents. He went to the Fulton-street meeting, and asked for prayers that he might find his parents. His mother chanced to be present, and revealed herself to the great astonishment of all. In the same meeting, at another time, a young man rose up, and said, "I have been an infidel for fourteen years; I had the prayers of a pious mother, but I spurned them. I have not seen her for fifteen years; I suppose she has given me up as lost. I don't know where to find her; but I would like to tell her what the Lord has done for me in answer to her earnest prayers." Just then his mother, who was present, recognized him, and cried out, "O my son! my son!"

11,276. PROVIDENCE, Seasonable. Everything comes in its own season. The fruits for man are so ordered that every month shall yield its unfailing supply. The markets of the metropolis receive the products of every clime. Out of season many things are rare and dear, or not to be had at any price. It is no use to worry about them. The fruits of the earth will come to the farmer in their due season. The lesson is, the blessings of Providence have their season, as well as the fruits and the flowers.

11,277. PROVIDENCE, Seeing God in. A person in company with Mr. Newton of London, remarked, that the East India Company had overset the college at Calcutta. "What a pity!" said a gentleman present. "No," said

Mr. N., "no pity—it must do good. If you had a plan in view, and could hinder opposition, would you not prevent it?" "Yes, sir." "Well, God can hinder all opposition to his plans: he has permitted that to take place, but he will carry on his own plan. I am learning to see God in all things; I believe not a person knocks at my door but is sent by God."

11,278. PROVIDENCE, Special. During the gale of December 5th, 1871, the Rev. Samuel Harris, of New Haven, who delivered the course of lectures before the Boston Theological Seminary that week, was sitting in his own room, No. 99 Marlborough Hotel, Boston, writing. Being at a loss for a word, he clasped his hands over the top of his head, and tilted back his chair to meditate. Scarcely had he done so, when a chimney was thrown over, and a mass of brick and mortar came through the roof and the ceiling, crushing the table on which he had been writing. But for the position he was in he would have been instantly killed. The hole made in the roof was at least ten by fourteen feet. *Zion's Herald.*

11,279. PROVIDENCE, Upborne by. God is said to have brought the Israelites out of Egypt on eagles' wings. Now, eagles, when removing their young ones, have a different posture from other fowl, proper to themselves (fit it is that there should be a distinction betwixt sovereigns and subjects), carrying their prey in their talons, but young ones on their backs, so interposing their whole bodies betwixt them and harm. The old eagle's body is the young eagle's shield, and must be shot through before her young ones can be hurt. Thus God, in saving the Jews, put himself betwixt them and danger. Surely, God, so loving under the law, is no less gracious in the gospel: our souls are better secured, not only above his wings, but in his body: your life is hid with Christ in God. No fear then of harm: God first must be pierced before we can be prejudiced. *T. Fuller.*

11,280. PROVIDENCE, Warnings of. Pharaoh, Sennacherib, both the Julians, and innumerable more, are the lasting monuments of his righteous retribution. It is true, a sinner may do evil a hundred times, and his days be prolonged; but ofttimes God hangs up some eminent sinners in chains, as spectacles and warnings to others. Many a heavy blow hath Providence given to the enemies of God, from which they were never able to recover. Christ rules, and that with a rod of iron, in the midst of his enemies. Psalm 110: 2. *John Flavel.*

11,281. PROVOCATION, Avoid. Pythagoras's direction was, "Dig not up fire with a sword;" that is, "Provoke not a person already swollen with anger by petulant and evil speeches."

11,282. PROVOCATION, Enduring. A man saw a Christian bear ill manners and intentional insult with great equanimity. He said to himself, "There must be something more in this man's religion than I have suspected." This led to his conversion. The indulgence of resentment has had the opposite effect.

11,283. PRUDENCE, Christian. King Josiah, one of the most lovely darlings of God's favor among all the kings in Judah, fell under the sword for pressing further against his enemies than the word of the Lord did permit him. The ancient Eliberitan Council enacted, that all those who plucked down the idols or temples of the heathen should not be accounted martyrs, though they died for the faith of Christ, because they plucked persecution upon themselves, and provoked their own martyrdom. *Bp. Hacket.*

11,284. PRUDENCE, Judgment and. A ship may be well equipped both as to sails and as to guns, but if she be destitute both of ballast and of rudder, she can neither fight with effect nor fly with adroitness, and she must strike to a vessel less strong, but more manageable: and so it is with men; they may have the gifts both of talent and of wit, but unless they have also prudence and judgment to dictate the when, the where, and the how those gifts are to be exerted, the possessors of them will be doomed to conquer only where nothing is to be gained, but to be defeated where everything is to be lost; they will be out-done by men of less brilliant, but more convertible qualifications, and whose strength, in one point, is not counterbalanced by any disproportion in another. *Colton.*

11,285. PRUDENCE, Rules of. The rules of prudence in general, like the laws of the stone tables, are, for the most part, prohibitive. Thou shalt not, is their characteristic formula; and it is an especial part of Christian prudence that it should be so. *Coleridge.*

11,286. PRUDENCE, Value of. Those who, in the confidence of superior capacities or attainments, neglect the common maxims of life, should be reminded that nothing will supply the want of prudence; but that negligence and irregularity, long continued, will make knowledge useless, wit ridiculous, and genius contemptible. *Johnson.*

11,287. PUBLICITY, Newspaper. There is a report of a famous battle called Aliwal, which gained its fame not by anything remarkable in itself, but by the exaggeration of an enthusiastic reporter. Of it an officer wrote "Aliwal was the battle of the dispatch, for none of us knew that we had fought a battle until the particulars appeared in a document, which did more than justice to every one concerned." Revivalists, Evangelists, and even pastors have been gazetted in this foolish fashion of the day. It always reacts disastrously upon all concerned.

11,288. PUGNACITY, Resistless. A pertinent story says that an Irishman, entering the fair at Ballinagone, saw the well-defined form of a large round head bulging out the canvas of a tent. The temptation was irresistible; up went his shillelagh, down went the man. Forth rushed from the tent a host of angry fellows to avenge the onslaught. Judge of their astonishment when they found the assailant to be one of their own faction. "Och, Nicholas!" said they, "and did ye not know that it was Brady O'Brien ye hit?" "Truth, did I uot," says he; "bad luck to me for that same; but shure, if my own father had been there, and his head looking so nice and convenient, I could not have helped myself!"

11,289. PULPIT, Deceit in the. Alas for that man who consents to think one thing in his closet, and preach another in his pulpit! God shall judge him in his mercy, not man in his wrath. But over his study, and over his pulpit might be writ, "EMPTINESS;" on his canonical robes, on his forehead and right hand, "DECEIT, *Deceit.*"	*Theodore Parker.*

11,290. PULPIT, Power of the. Clemens Brentano, a literary acquaintance of Dr. Krummacher, and a Catholic, once said to the doctor, "Till you Protestants pull down the chatter-box," ("Plapperkasten,") he meant the pulpit, "or, at least, throw it into the corner, where it ought to be, there is no hope of you." I could only reply to him, "It is true indeed, that our 'Plapperkasten' stands greatly in the way of you Catholics." The pulpit is the Thermopylæ of Protestantism, the tower of the flock, the palladium of the Church of God. Well might Paul magnify his office, for not only Glasgow but the city of our God "flourishes by the preaching of the word."	*Spurgeon.*

11,291. PUNCTUALITY, Exact. John Quincy Adams, who filled a greater number of important offices, political and civil, than has any other American, was pre-eminently punctual. He was an economist of moments, and was never known to be behind time. His reputation in this respect was such that when in his old age he was a member of the House of Representatives at Washington, and a gentleman observed that it was time to call the House to order, another replied, "No, Mr. Adams is not in his seat." The clock, it was found, was actually three minutes too fast; and before three minutes had elapsed Mr. Adams was at his post.	*Mathews.*

11,292. PUNCTUALITY, Example of. Lord Nelson was about leaving London for his last successful expedition. It was necessary for some cabin furniture to be sent on board his ship, and the upholsterer called to say that everything would be in readiness, and would leave at six in the morning. Nelson said, "And you will go and see them off, Mr. A." "I shall my lord; I shall be there punctually at six." "A quarter before six," said Mr. Nelson; "be there a quarter before six. To that quarter of an hour I owe everything in life."

11,293. PUNCTUALITY, Importance of. Punctuality is important, because it subserves the peace and good temper of a family; the want of it not only infringes on necessary duty, but sometimes excludes this duty. Punctuality is important, as it gains time; it is like packing things in a box; a good packer will get in half as much more as a bad one. The calmness of mind which it produces is another advantage of punctuality; a disorderly man is always in a hurry, he has no time to speak with you, because he is going elsewhere; and when he gets there, he is too late for his busi-

ness, or he must hurry away to another before he can finish it. It was a wise maxim of the Duke of Newcastle—"I do one thing at a time." Punctuality gives weight to character. "Such a man has made an appointment; then I know he will keep it." And this generates punctuality in you; for, like other virtues it propagates itself.	*Cecil.*

11,294. PUNISHMENT, Awaiting. It was the custom in Persia to have an iron seat placed in front of the king's palace. This was the only sanctuary great criminals had, and here at the Tripod of the king they would sit for days, awaiting with fearful expectation, their sentence, and it was only ended by the taking of life. Such is the perilous condition of every guilty sinner before God.

11,295. PUNISHMENT, Delayed. Bias said once to a notorious reprobate: "It is not that I doubt thou wilt suffer the just reward of thy wickedness, but I fear that I myself shall not live to see it. For what did the punishment of Aristocrates avail the Messenians who were killed before it came to pass? He, having betrayed them at the battle of Taphrus, yet remained undetected for above twenty years together, and all that while reigned king of the Arcadians, till at length, discovered and apprehended, he received the merited recompense of his treachery. But alas! they whom he betrayed were all dead at the same time."

11,296. PUNISHMENT, Exemplary. Plutarch tells of his preceptor, Ammonius, who corrected his pupils by punishing his own son. The pupils had over-indulged their appetites at dinner. At his after dinner lecture, the philosopher ordered his freedman to whip the lecturer's son in presence of all, because he required sauce with his food, indicating that it was an example of punishment from which all were to take warning. This was the nearest to corporeal punishment he could inflict, as the Greek law allowed only the parent to whip a pupil.

11,297. PUNISHMENT, Future. There is no pain like that of burning. Put your finger in the candle for a moment if you doubt this, and try. Fire is the most destructive and devouring of all elements. Look in the mouth of a blast furnace, and think what it would be to be there. Fire is of all elements most opposed to life. Creatures can live in air, and earth, and water; but nothing can live in fire. Yet fire is the portion to which the Christless and unbelieving will come. Christ will "burn up the chaff with fire."	*Ryle.*

11,298. PUNISHMENT, No Proxy. St. Bernard being consulted by one of his followers, whether he might accept of two benefices, replied, "And how will you be able to serve them both?" "I intend," answered the priest, "to officiate in one of them by a deputy." "Will your deputy suffer eternal punishment for you, too?" asked St. Bernard. "Believe me, you may serve your cure by proxy, but you must suffer the penalty in person."

11,299. PUNISHMENT, Release from. When Rev. H. M. Gallaher was a little school-boy in Ireland, playing with his companions on grounds belonging to an Earl, they were climbing a tree, and broke a limb. The Earl, hearing the crash, hurried to the spot to catch the offenders; but the boys all fled except himself, a little fellow in the top of the tree. "Come down," called the Earl's stern voice, and he came down trembling with fear. "Here," calling a man-servant, "take this boy to the guard-house," and the servant grabbed his coat collar, and was marching him off, when the Earl said, "What's your name?" "Henry M. Gallaher." "Are you a relative of James Gallaher?" Straightening up, the little fellow replied, "I am his eldest son." The Earl waved his hand to the servant, saying, "Let the lad go; I know his father." Henry went home, and told his mother what had happened, and how he was released. Taking him on her knee, she said, "Now, my son, I want you to remember that that is just what Jesus is to you. When you are called, at the last day, to answer for your sins and follies, God will say, "Let Henry Gallaher go; I know his Redeemer."

11,300. PUNISHMENT, Substitute for. In Edinburgh, I saw a sight I never shall forget, a man hanged. For many sins? No, for one. He stole a parcel from a stage-coach, and he was led out to die before the crowd. Did any friend come and loose the rope, and say, " Put it round my neck, I will die instead?" No, none. At one point he broke the law, and died for it. I saw another sight; I saw myself undone, deserving hell, a lost sinner, for many, many sins, to suffer stripes forever. But I looked up and saw my Substitute, Jesus, hanging on the cross. I looked and was forgiven. *Sir James Simpson.*

11,301. PURITANISM, Achievements of. Historians have loved to eulogize the manners and virtues, the glory and the benefits of chivalry. Puritanism accomplished far more. If it had the sectarian crime of intolerance, chivalry had the vices of dissoluteness. The knights were brave from gallantry of spirit; the puritans from the fear of God. The knights were proud of loyalty; the puritans of liberty. The knights did homage to monarchs, in whose smile they beheld honor, whose rebuke was the wound of disgrace; the puritans, disdaining ceremony, would not bow at the name of Jesus, nor bend the knee to the King of kings. Chivalry delighted in outward show, favored pleasure, multiplied amusements, and degraded the human race by an exclusive respect for the privileged classes; puritanism bridled the passions, commanded the virtues of self-denial, and rescued the name of man from dishonor. The former valued courtesy; the latter justice. The former adorned society by graceful refinements; the latter founded national grandeur on universal education. The institutions of chivalry were subverted by the gradually increasing weight, and knowledge, and opulence of the industrial classes; the puritans, relying upon those classes, planted in their hearts the undying principles of liberty. *Bancroft.*

11,302. PURITANISM, Doings of. We may censure puritanism us we please; and no one of us, I suppose, but would find it a very rough, defective thing. But we, and all men, may understand that it was a genuine thing; for nature has adopted it, and it has grown and grows. I say sometimes, that all goes by wager of battle in this world; that strength, well understood, is the measure of all worth. Give a thing time; if it can succeed it is the right thing. Look now at American-Saxondom; and at that little fact of the sailing of the Mayflower, two hundred years ago, from Delft Haven, in Holland! Were we of large sense as the Greeks were, we had found a poem here,—one of nature's own poems, such as she writes in broad facts over great continents: for it was properly the beginning of America. There were straggling settlers in America before; some material as of a body was there; but the soul of it was first this. *Carlyle*

11,303. PURITY, Emblem of. Dr. J. P. Newman held up two bottles of Jordan water, one of them pure and transparent, the other discolored and roily, especially when shaken up. Shake the first as much as you would, it was always clear. It was originally the same muddy water as the other, but had been purified by filtration through charcoal. To these Dr. Newman compared the pure and impure heart.

11,304. PURITY, Token of. The household of Jacob had strange gods among them; and he ordered them to put them away, and to make themselves clean, and to change their garments, in token of their purity. When people have been to an unholy place, on returning they always wash their persons and change their garments. No man can go to the temple wearing a dirty cloth; he must either put on a clean one, or go himself to a tank and wash it if it be soiled, or he must put on one which is quite new. Near the temples men may be often seen washing their clothes, in order to prepare themselves for some religious ceremony. See also Exod. 19: 10.
Biblical Treasury.

11,305. PURPOSE, Dominant. Peter the Hermit visited Palestine in the latter part of the eleventh century, and was so enraged at the Turks for their cruel treatment of Christians, that he resolved to rescue the holy soil. Returning he went through the towns of France and Italy, bareheaded and barefooted, bearing a heavy crucifix, and picturing with extreme eloquence and enthusiasm, the sufferings of the pilgrims to the holy places. He soon gathered an army of 60,000, which he led toward Jerusalem.

11,306. QUARRELS, Ancient. The Mohammedans keep a feast called Arafat, which is accounted for by the following legend: Eve was one day admiring a beautiful figure which was reflected from a looking-glass as she stood before it when Satan made his appearance, and assured her that Adam, her husband, loved the lady she saw in the glass more than he loved her. On hearing this, Eve was offended and ran away from Adam, and wandered about in the world for several years. At length she met Adam on the top of a mountain called Arafat, near Mecca, where they become reconciled. This is the first trace of a long succession of domestic discords not always so happily ended.

11,307. QUARRELS, Avoid. Francis I. of France, was in counsel with his Generals, as to the way they should take to lead the army to the invasion of Italy. Amaril, a fool, who unseen, had heard their propositions, sprang up and advised them rather "to consider which way they should bring the army back, out of Italy again; for it is easy to engage in quarrels, but hard to be disengaged from them."

11,308. QUARRELS, Fatal. The remark of one of two brothers, "Would that I had as many oxen as I see stars in the sky," grew into a quarrel, in which the brothers slew each other with the sword. The death of two brothers, one of them a cardinal, was the result of a dispute as to whose dog first laid hold of a hare. A quarrel between two sisters-in-law resulted in the death of the husband of each, and the loss of the crown of England to one of the families. The boxing of a boy on the ear in Italy originated the factions of the "Black and the White," and caused much bloodshed.

11,309. QUARRELS, How to Avoid. A young fox asked his father if he could not teach him some trick to defeat the dogs, if he should fall in with them. The father had grown gray in a long life of depredation and danger, and his scars bore witness to his narrow escapes in the chase, or his less honorable encounters with the faithful guardians of the hen-roost. He replied with a sigh, "After all my experience, I am forced to confess that the best trick is, to keep out of their way." *Persian Fable.*

11,310. QUARRELS, Parties to. In most quarrels there is a fault on both sides. A quarrel may be compared to a spark, which cannot be produced without a flint as well as a steel; either of them may hammer on wood forever, no fire will follow. *South.*

11,311. QUARRELS, Rejecting. I commend his discretion and valor who, walking in London streets, met a gallant, who cried to him a pretty distance beforehand, "I will have the wall!" "Yea," answered he, "and take the house too, if you can but agree with the landlord." *Fuller.*

11,312. QUARRELS, Seeking. Cælius, the orator, was a most passionate person. Asking a client one day many questions, and he agreeing with him in all things, in anger Cælius cried out in open court, "Say something contrary to me, that so we may quarrel."

11,313. QUARRELS, Subduing. Two boys having heard of Dr. Franklin's experiment of stilling the waves with oil, were impatient to repeat it. A brisk wind proving favorable to the trial, they hastened to a sheet of water and scattered the oil upon the pool. It spread itself instantly on all sides, calming the whole surface of the water. The youths inquired the cause of such a wonderful result. They were informed that the wind, blowing upon water which is covered with a coat of oil, slides over the surface of it, and produces no friction that can raise a wave. "This curious philosophical fact suggests a most important moral reflection. When you suffer yourselves to be ruffled by passion, your minds resemble the puddle in a storm. But reason, if you hearken to her voice, will then, like oil poured upon the water, calm the turbulence within you and restore you to serenity and peace."

11,314. QUARRELSOME, Banishment of the. Two quarrelsome persons brought their case before king Philip, of Macedon. He adjudicated in this summary manner. To the first, he said, "I command you immediately to run out of Macedon." To the other, he said, "See that you make all imaginable haste after him."

11,315. QUICKNESS, Fascination of. There is something extremely fascinating in quickness; and most men are desirous of appearing quick. The great rule for becoming so, is—by not attempting to appear quicker than you really are; by resolving to understand yourself and others, and to know what you mean, and what they mean, before you speak or answer. *S. Smith.*

11,316. QUIETNESS, Advantage of. The dew which so bountifully baptizes the flowers and grass, on quiet summer evenings, does not distil in wind and storm. So the dews of grace come down on calm and trustful souls. If we would receive the Holy Spirit of which the dew is an emblem, we must abide in patience and prayer, down low, as the grass waits for the dew.

11,317. QUIETNESS, Christian. In the year 1666, an opinion ran through the nation that the end of the world would come that year. Sir Matthew Hale, going that year to the Western Circuit, as he was on the bench at the assizes, a most terrible storm fell out very unexpectedly, accompanied with such flashes of lightning and crashings of thunder, that the like will hardly fall out in an age; upon which a rumor ran through the crowd "that now was the end of the world, and the day of judgment was begun!" At this there followed a general consternation in the assembly, and all men forgot the business they were met about, and betook themselves to their prayers. This, added to the horror raised by the storm, looked very dismal; but the judge was not a bit affected, and was going on with the business of the court in his ordinary manner! *Bp. Burnet.*

11,318. QUIETNESS, Example of. Dr. Sanderson has so conquered all repining and ambitious thoughts, and with them all other unruly passions, that if the accidents of the day proved to his danger or damage, yet he both began and ended it with an even and undisturbed quietness; always praising God that he had not withdrawn food and raiment from him and his poor family; nor suffered him to violate his conscience for his safety, or to support himself or them in a more splendid or plentiful condition; and that he therefore resolved with David, "that his praise should be always in his mouth."   *Izaak Walton.*

11,319. QUOTATION, Advantages of. A well-read writer, with good taste, is one who has the command of the wit of other men; he searches where knowledge is to be found; and though he may not himself excel in invention, his ingenuity may compose one of those agreeable books, the *deliciæ* of literature, that will outlast the fading meteors of his day. Epicurus is said to have borrowed from no writer in his three hundred inspired volumes, while Plutarch, Seneca, and the elder Pliny made such free use of their libraries; and it has happened that Epicurus, with his unsubstantial nothingness, has "melted into thin air," while the solid treasures have buoyed themselves up amidst the wrecks of nations.   *Disraeli.*

11,320. QUOTATIONS, How to Use. If we steal thoughts from the moderns, it will be cried down as plagiarism; if from the ancients, it will be cried up as erudition. But in this respect every author is a Spartan, being more ashamed of the discovery than of the depredation. I have somewhere seen it observed that we should make the same use of a book that the bee does of a flower; she steals sweets from it, but does not injure it; and those sweets she herself improves and concocts into honey.
       Colton.

11,321. QUOTATIONS, Poetical. If the grain were separated from the chaff which fills the works of our national poets, what is truly valuable would be to what is useless in the proportion of a mole-hill to a mountain. *Burke.*

11 322. QUOTATIONS, Reading for. Dr. Richard Bentley, finding his son reading a novel, said to him, "Why read a book which you cannot quote?"

11,323. QUOTATIONS, Use of. Whatever is felicitously expressed risks being worse expressed: it is a wretched taste to be gratified with mediocrity when the excellent lies before us. We quote, to save proving what has been demonstrated. We quote, to screen ourselves from the odium of doubtful opinions, which the world would not willingly accept from ourselves; and we may quote from the curiosity which only a quotation itself can give, when in our own words it would be divested of that tint of ancient phrase, that detail of narrative, and that *naiveté*, which we have forever lost, and which we like to recollect once had an existence. The ancients, who in these matters were not perhaps such blockheads as some may conceive, considered poetical quotation as one of the requisite ornaments of oratory. Cicero, even in his philosophical works, is as little sparing of quotations as Plutarch. Old Montaigne is so stuffed with them, that he owns, if they were taken out of him, little of himself would remain; and yet this never injured that original turn which the old Gascon has given to his thoughts. I suspect that Addison hardly ever composed a Spectator which was not founded on some quotation, noted in those three folio manuscript volumes which he pre-

viously collected; and Addison lasts, while Steele, who always wrote from first impressions and to the times, with perhaps no inferior genius, has passed away, insomuch that Beattie once considered that he was obliging the world by collecting Addison's papers, and carefully omitting Steele's.   *Disraeli.*

11,324. RAINBOW, Worship of the. Homer, with remarkable conformity to Scripture, speaks of the rainbow which Jove hath set in the cloud a token to men. Iris, or the rainbow, was worshiped not only by the Greeks and Romans, but also by the Peruvians in South America.   *L'Abbé Lambert.*

11,325. RATIONALIST, Description of a. The rationalist is distinguished from the atheist by his theoretical belief of a Supreme Power, and he is distinguished from the pantheist by his denial of an ever-present and all-pervading divine energy. The pantheist says, "God is at hand;" the rationalist says, "God is afar off." Pantheism sees the Divine Being in all things, and confounds the Creator with his creation; whereas rationalism, though distinguishing him from his works, banishes him into a distant solitude. Its distinctive characteristic, as a form of infidelity, is, that while admitting the world to have been originally created by God, it as it were extrudes him from that world by reducing it to a self-sustained mechanism, and by resolving what are generally understood by the works of Providence into a regularly successive series of necessary developments. The seed, having the vegetative power in itself, is cast by the husbandman into the soil, and there, aided merely by natural agencies, is left to develop itself into the full-grown plant or tree. The watch, complete in its wheels and mainspring, is wound up, and continues to move, though ever so far distant from the maker. The shipbuilder having finished and launched the ship, leaves it entirely to the care of the sailors. Such are specimens of some of the analogies by which men would exclude God from his own world, and make the universe, if not independent of his creative power, altogether independent of his presence and control.
       T. Pearson.

11,326. READER, Great. William King, the poet, was, at eighteen years of age, elected to Christ Church, where he is said to have prosecuted his studies with so much intenseness and activity, that, before he was eight years standing, he had read over and made remarks upon considerably more than twenty thousand books and manuscripts!   *Buck.*

11,327. READING, Directions for. If the books which you read are your own, mark with a pen or pencil the most considerable things in them which you desire to remember. Thus you may read that book the second time over with half the trouble, by your eye running over the paragraphs which your pencil has noted. It is but a very weak objection against this practice to say, "I shall spoil my book;" for I persuade myself that you did not buy it as a bookseller, to sell it again for gain, but as a scholar to improve your mind by it; and if the mind be improved, your advantage is abundant, though your book yields less money to your executors.   *Watts.*

11,328. READING, Historic. All books are properly the record of the history of past men. What thoughts past men had in them; what actions past men did; the summary of all books whatsoever lies there. It is on this ground that the class of books specifically named history can be safely recommended as the basis of all study of books; the preliminary to all right and full understanding of anything we can expect to find in books. Past history, and especially the past history of one's own native country—everybody may be advised to begin with that. Let him study that faithfully, innumerable inquiries, with due indications, will branch out from it; he has a broad beaten highway from which all the country is more or less visible—there traveling, let him choose where he will dwell.   *Carlyle.*

11,329. READING, Instruction for. Whenever you read the writings or hear the orations of the philosophers, attend alway to things more than words, and be not taken with what is curious and of a delicate thread and contexture, more than that which is strong, nervous, and beneficial. So in perusing poems or histories, be sure that nothing escapes you that is appositely said, in relation to the cultivation of manners or the calming of turbulent, immoderate passions; but always give it a note, and make it surely your own. Simonides said that a student in philosophy should be like a bee. That laborious creature, when it is amongst flowers, makes it a business industriously to extract the yellow honey out of them all; whilst others care and seek for nothing else except smell and color.   *Plutarch.*

11,330. READING, Possibility of. There is hardly any man of business who could not find time for at least ten pages a day in some solid book of history, science, art or religion; and so read as to master it. Let him actually do this, and at the end of the year what has he accomplished? He has made himself the master of thirty-six hundred and fifty pages. Continuing to do this a few years, he has not only acquired a habit of method and of economy of time which is invaluable, but has qualified himself to stand alongside with intelligent men. He is prepared to make an honorable and useful mark in the world. President Porter tells us of a lady who spent fifteen months of leisure, snatched by fragments from onerous family cares and brilliant social engagements, in reading the history of Greece as written by a great variety of authors, and illustrated by many accessories of art. The hint is a good one to follow. One spot of knowledge thus securely gained, may prove at once a starting point from which to push out in whatever direction may be chosen.
                              H. M. Grout.

11,331. READING, St. Jerome's. St. Jerome was thoroughly versed in the polite literature of his day, and a master of rhetoric and oratory.

The eloquence of Cicero, the stateliness of Fronto, and the smoothness of Pliny were his delight. For his devotion to these he considered himself reproved by a dream which he had. He thought he was arraigned before the judgment seat of Christ, and was asked what his profession was. He answered, "I am a Christian." "Thou liest," said the judge, " Thou art a Ciceronian, for the works of that author possess thy heart.". The judge ordered him to be severely scourged by angels. The memory of his chastisement and his fault, though only dream, never left him. "From that time," he says, "I gave myself to the reading of divine things with greater diligence and attention than I had ever read the other authors."

11,332. REASON, Influence of. "Child," said my father to me, when I was young, "you think to carry everything by dint of argument. But you will find, by and by, how very little is ever done in the world by clear reason." Very little, indeed! It is true of almost all men, except so far as we are taught of God, passion and prejudice govern the world; only under the name of reason. It is our part, by religion and reason joined, to counteract them all we can.   *John Wesley.*

11,333. REASON, Presumption of. What surprises me, what stumbles me, what frightens me, is to see a diminutive creature, a little ray of light glimmering through a few feeble organs, controvert a point with the Supreme Being; oppose the intelligence that sitteth at the helm of the world; question what he affirms, dispute what he determines, appeal from his decisions, and, even after God has given evidence, reject all doctrines that are beyond his capacity! Enter into thy nothingness, mortal creature! What madness animates thee? How darest thou pretend, thou who art but a point, thou whose essence is but an atom, to measure thyself with the Supreme Being—with him whom the heaven of heavens could not contain?   *Saurin.*

11,334. REBELLION, Human. A robin happened to fly into the room, and in its efforts to escape again, dashed itself madly against the walls and ceiling, until its poor little head and wings were sore and bleeding. On my attempting to catch and set it free it only redoubled its frantic efforts, and when in my hand struggled so violently as only to hurt its bruised sides more. Ah, I thought, thus it is with that poor widow, with us all, when the Lord straitens us with trouble. We dash and wound our poor hearts against the firm wall of his will; we think of nothing but escape, and struggle madly against the kind and most gentle Hand that only holds us with its " wholesome strength," whose " end" and aim are but to restore us to the bright open air of his mercies that we may sun our hearts with his presence, and wing our way more freely towards himself.   *Anon.*

11,335. REBUKE, Effectual. A preacher was much annoyed by persons talking and laughing during his sermon. He paused, looked at the disturbers, and said, "I am always afraid to reprove those who misbehave in church. In the early part of my ministry I made a great mistake. As I was preaching, a young man who sat just before me was laughing, talking, and making uncouth grimaces. I paused and administrated a severe rebuke. After the close of the service, one of the official members came and said tc me, 'Brother, you made a great mistake. That young man whom you reproved is an idiot.' Since then I have always been afraid to reprove those who misbehave in church, lest I should repeat that mistake and reprove another idiot." After that there was good order.

11,336. RECIPROCITY, Example of. Pior, a hermit, visited another hermit, named Pambo, and when meal-time arrived, took from his pilgrim's wallet a piece of bread. "Why have you brought your food with you?" asked Pambo. "I did not wish to be a charge to your hospitality," answered Pior. Soon after the case was reversed. Pambo visiting Pior drew forth at meal-time his bread and water. "Why have you brought water and bread, my brother?" asked Pior. "I did not wish to be a charge to your hospitality," he answered.

11,337. RECOGNITION, Basis of. That identity of persons, and recognition after death are indeed facts, may be clearly comprehended also from the definite and distinctive position of man in the sight of God. "Fear not, I have redeemed thee, I have called thee by thy name" (Isa. 43: 1). "I will not blot out his name out of the book of life, but I will confess his name before my Father and before his angels" (Rev. 3: 5). St. Paul speaks of those whose names are in the book of life; and St. James of those whose names are not in the book of life. And numerous other passages might be quoted to show that the Christian especially will stand before God in heaven as personally and as individually known and distinguishable from his fellow-beings as he now stands before God and man on earth. The deduction is obvious; where individuality exists, recognition is a necessary consequence. If, with our present limited faculties, men know each other after long absence, and change from youth to age, is it possible that redeemed men, with the enlarged perceptions of a higher existence, can fail to recognize the earthly friends who were the faithful solace of their life's pilgrimage? *W. Merry.*

11,338. RECONCILIATION, Example of. An eldest son in England was ejected from his father's house with high words. The father hardened his heart against him, but the mother longed for her boy's return. The son in his pride refused to return till his father should send for him. The mother pined and sickened, and when on the verge of death made her last request to her husband to recall their son, which he granted. The first train brought him. The unreconciled father and son stood in the presence of the dying woman. She took the hand of each and strove to bring about a reconciliation. But neither would speak. With her

last strength she placed the hand of the son in the hand of the father, and sank down into the arms of death. The father looked at the wife and then at the boy; he caught his eye; they fell upon each other's necks, and there stood weeping by the bed of the departed.

11,339. RECONCILIATION, Necessity for. A pastor was stationed where two leading officials were at variance, making everything unpleasant about them, and hindering the work. All efforts to adjust the matter had proved unavailing, and how to meet the case without doing more hurt than good, was still a question. At a church meeting one evening, the pastor, who was full of expedients for good, invited the whole church to gather around the altar for singing and prayer. They did so, the unfriendly officials occupying a prominent place as usual. "Now," said the pastor, "let us be united, and to test ourselves, we will rise and repeat the Lord's Prayer together." So they arose and commenced, "Our Father, which art in heaven," and proceeded as far as "forgive us our debts as we," when there was a manifest break, the contending parties dropping out. Noticing their embarrassment, the minister proposed that they should try it again. They did so, and reached the point requiring forgiveness, when they faltered as before. "What!" said the pastor, "can't we go through with this? let us try it once more, and put our whole hearts into it." So they began again, and as they neared the point of difficulty, the eyes of the two officials met, when they approached and embraced each other, and went through the whole prayer squarely, saying, "forgive us our debts as we forgive our debtors." This was an affecting scene, and, amid tears and rejoicings, the war of years was terminated forever. *Dr. J. Porter.*

11,340. RECORD, Life's. There is an invisible pen always writing over our heads, and making an exact register of all the transactions of our life. Not our public conduct only, and what we reckon the momentous parts of our life, but the indulgence of our private pleasures, the amusement of our secret thoughts and idle hours, shall be brought into account. *Blair.*

11,341. RECREATION, Benefits of. Recreation is intended to the mind, as whetting is to the scythe, to sharpen the edge of it, which otherwise would grow dull and blunt. He, therefore, that spends his whole time in recreation, is ever whetting, never mowing; his grass may grow and his steed starve: as, contrarily, he that always toils and never recreates, is ever mowing, never whetting; laboring much to little purpose. As good no scythe as no edge. Then only doth the work go forward, when the scythe is so seasonably and moderately whetted, that it may cut, and so cut that it may have the help of sharpening. *Bishop Hall.*

11,342. RECREATION, Royal. Pope Leo the Tenth spent so much time at the chase, that his business was neglected, bulls and pardons were left unsigned, and serious losses were often incurred. Hartabus, king of Hircania spent his time in catching moles; Bias, king of Lydia, in stabbing frogs; Eropus, king of the Macedonians, in making little table lanterns, and the king of Parthia in sharpening the points of arrows and javelins. Mahomet, who subverted the empire of Greece, carved out wooden spoons, even when giving audience to ambassadors.

11,343. REDEMPTION, Experience of. A negro on the coast of Africa, became distressed about his soul. One day an English sailor heard his lamentations, and told him that he must go to England, and there he would hear of the Christian's God, who paid the debt. The negro resolved to follow this advice. After a long search to find a ship, he obtained leave to work his passage to England. On board the ship, and in the streets of London, he inquired in vain for the object of his search. The negro, asking "for the Christian's God dat pay de debt," was ridiculed as a fool, or pitied as a lunatic. One day a gentleman overheard him, and stopping to speak to him, told him if he would go to a certain place that evening, he would hear about the Christian's God. He went, and found that the gentleman who had spoken to him was himself the preacher. There he heard of the debt of sin; how Jesus had paid that debt, and, having paid it, invites poor, helpless sinners to come to him and find peace and rest. Before the sermon was finished, the poor negro started up in his seat, with clasped hands, and tears streaming down his sable cheeks, and those near him could hear him whisper, "Me have found him! Me have found him! the Christian's God dat pay de debt!"

11,344. REDEMPTION, Joy of. A minister, preaching from the text, "If our transgressions and our sins be upon us, and we pine away in them, how should we then live?" said, "I knew a poor widow who had got into a little debt that was a burden upon her, which she could not remove, just as a sin is a debt or burden upon the conscience, which no man is able to cast off. Her language to herself was, 'How can I live with this burden? My little furniture, my all will be sold! I must go to the workhouse, where I must mix with bad people, who know not my Saviour, and who take his name in vain!' A benevolent individual, hearing of her distress, sent to the creditor, desiring him to bring a receipt in full, and he should have his money. He took the receipt and gave it to the widow. 'O,' said she, 'now I shall live! I shall live!'"

11,345. REDEMPTION, Light of. Suppose you are standing over against some palace, and it is near midnight. Forth from that palace gate there comes a procession: the prince has come forth, attended by many of his train. He has not gone far, however, before you hear that he has dropped a beautiful gem. He is anxious about that gem, not simply for its intrinsic value, but it was the gift of one he loved. He calls for lights. You never saw the prince in your life, and in that dim darkness you have not been able to see much, ex-

cept a very imperfect outline of him. But now a lamp has come, and the prince, in his anxiety to find his gem, takes the lamp in his own hand, and there he is looking for the lost gem. Now the light which falls on the road where that gem is lying goes up into the face of the prince; and while he finds the gem, you see him as you never would have seen him but for that loss. Now it is like that with the revelation of God. When he came forth from the retirement of eternity for the salvation of souls, there was light which, while it was thrown on the poor lost sinner, that he might be found, was thrown upon the face of God, who came to seek him and to save him. *Coley.*

11,346. REDEMPTION Prefigured. Nature is full of indications of divine attributes. Natural law, through all time, and round the world, conveys hints and germs of heaven, of hell, of vicarious suffering, and of remedial mercy. It teaches these four things. Disobey and suffer, obey and enjoy; these are its first and fundamental lessons, which are the rude seed-forms of those higher truths; purity and heaven, impurity and hell. Then throughout the world we see illustrations of the fact that one man can suffer for another. In the mother's suffering, and in the father's watch and care, the child grows out of impurity and rudeness into purity and gentleness. Vicarious suffering is a law of the household and of society. Remedial mercy is also a truth which nature hints. It is one of the eternal truths of God's nature. In the natural world, within certain bounds, a man's wrong-doing may be repaired, if he turn from his transgression and repent. There is provision for every bone to knit together again when fractured, for every muscle to heal when lacerated, and for every nerve when shattered and diseased to return again to health. Thus in nature we see prefigured the great scheme of redemption. Purity gives heaven; impurity eternal wail and woe. But there is vicarious suffering to bring men from the one to the other. If through Christ there be repentance and turning from evil, there is also health and restoration. And these things are indicated in nature—when we know how to see them there—but are authoritatively taught only in the New Testament. In nature they are as twilight, while in the gospel they glow with noonday brightness. *Beecher.*

11,347. REDEMPTION, Ownership by. A benevolent gentleman went South some years ago and purchased a slave. When he returned to the North, he said to the man, "You are now free, you can go where you please." "But," said the slave, "I will stay with you." Supposing he was not understood, he again said, "You are free to go wherever you please." The man replied, "I will stay with you; you bought me, and paid the price with your money, and I shall stay and serve you: I do not wish to go anywhere else." So it is with me; I have been bought at a great price, and I do not wish to serve any one but Jesus. *Wm. McAlister.*

11,348. REDEMPTION, Wonder of. O my soul.

a wonder above wonders—an incomprehensibility above all admiration—a depth past finding out! Under this shadow, O my soul, refresh thyself! If thy sins fear the hand of justice, behold thy Sanctuary; if thy offences tremble before the Judge, behold thy Advocate; if thy creditor threaten a prison, behold thy bail; behold the Lamb of God, that hath taken thy sins from thee; behold of heaven and earth, that hath prepared a kingdom for thee. Be ravished, O my soul! O bless the name of Elohim! O bless the name of our Emmanuel with praises and eternal hallelujahs! *Quarles.*

11,349. REFLECTION, Art of. Reader! you have been bred in a land abounding with men able in arts, learning, and knowledges manifold: this man in one, this in another; few in many, none in all. But there is one art of which every man should be a master—the art of reflection. If you are not a thinking man, to what purpose are you a man at all? In like manner, there is one knowledge which it is every man's duty and interest to acquire—namely, self-knowledge. Or to what end was man alone, of all animals, endued by the Creator with the faculty of self-consciousness? *Coleridge.*

11,350. REFLECTION, Spiritual. When St. Athanasius sent for St. Pambo to leave the desert and come to Alexandria, the holy abbot saw a gaily-dressed actress in the streets; whereupon he began to weep. When he was asked why he did so, he answered, "Two things move me; one is the damnation of that woman; and another is, that I do not take as much pains to please God as she does to please wicked men." You see even sinful things were steps to God for him. *F. W. Faber.*

11,351. REFORM, Abhorrence of. So it is and must be always, my dear boys. If the angel Gabriel were to come down from heaven and head a successful rise against the most abominable and unrighteous vested interest which this poor old world groans under, he would most certainly lose his character for many years, probably for centuries, not only with upholders of the said vested interest, but with the respectable mass of the people he had delivered. They wouldn't ask him to dinner, or let their names appear with his in the papers; they would be careful how they spoke of him in the palaver or at their clubs. *Hughes.*

11,352. REFORM, Beginning of. Reform, like charity, must begin at home. Once well at home, how will it radiate outwards, irrepressible, into all that we touch and handle, speak and work; kindling ever new light by incalculable contagion, spreading, in geometric ratio, far and wide, doing good only wherever it spreads, and not evil. *Carlyle.*

11,353. REFORM, Need of. Educate the people; enlighten, elevate the people; lift the people to the plane of your reform; prove to them that it is desirable and important, and it is secured. Reform! O, how much we need it! not on the banners of political parties, but in the hearts and consciences of the people;

not on the lips, but in the lives, of politicians, not in promised legislation, but in present political action; not simply the management of government when obtained; but in the means and methods by which that management is sought. *Dr. J. A. M. Chapman.*

11,354. REFORM, Religion and. A man of good parts and considerable culture fell under the influence of drink. A missionary found him friendless and desolate, rescued him from his degradation, and secured him a situation. After a little he fell into his former habits and lost his place. This experience was repeated many times during ten years, the missionary holding on to him, feeding and clothing him in need, and getting new places for him whenever he would reform for a short time. At length the inebriate began to feel deeply troubled about his sins. He had tried to reform, and failed so often and for such a long time, that he felt there was no hope for him. Then he turned to God for help, and was saved. From that hour his demon was cast out. He became a devoted and honored Christian man, prospered in business, and is a conspicuous example of the power of the religion of Christ to save the drunkard.

11,355. REFORMATION, Crisis of the. Luther's appearance at the Diet of Worms, on the 17th of April, 1521, may be considered as the greatest scene in modern European history; the point, indeed, from which the whole subsequent history of civilization takes its rise. The world's pomp and power sits there on this hand: on that stands up for God's truth one man, Hans Luther, the poor miner's son. It is, as we say, the greatest moment in the modern history of man. English Puritanism, England and its Parliaments, America's vast work these two centuries, French revolution, Europe and its work everywhere at present—the germ of it all lay there; had Luther in that moment done other, it had all been otherwise. *Carlyle.*

11,356. REFORMATION, External. The custom prevails in Paris of giving old buildings a new appearance, by recutting the stones of the walls. By this means the church of St. Genevieve has recently been modernized and beautified. It is so identified with the bloody massacre of St. Bartholomew's, that no renovation can obliterate its foul blot; its stains will not out, nor its vile memories die. Old sinners seek to quiet their consciences in the same way. They recast and polish the outside with remarkable success, but the deep stains of guilt will not depart, except by the application of the blood of Christ. Beware of confounding reformation with conversion! Bloody memories cluster about the church of St. Genevieve, and bleaching bones fill its vaults, in spite of its external renovation.

11,357. REFUGE, Christ a. I remember a story in Alexander's wars, that when he came to besiege the Sogdians, a people who dwelt upon a rock, or had the literal munition of rocks for their defence, they jeered him and asked him whether his soldiers had wings or no. "Unless your soldiers can fly in the air we fear you not." It is a most certain truth, when God exalts a people, he can set them upon a rock so high that, unless their adversaries have wings, and those more than eagles' wings, to soar higher than God himself, they are beyond annoyance. He carries his own upon eagles' wings; what wings, then, must they have who get above his people. *Caryl.*

11,358. REFUGE, Heathen. Among the first temples built after the founding of Rome was one to the God of Refuge, which they called the Temple of the Asylæn God. This was always open to all who came. Here the slave was free from his master, the debtor from his creditor, and the murderer from the avenger of blood, or the magistrate. This asylum was preserved from all violation by direction of the oracle of Apollo.

11,359. REFUGE, Refusing. Often the trembling fugitive mistakes the fortress for a prison, and refuses to enter in. A single soldier in an enemy's country is crossing a plain in haste, and making towards a castle whose battlements appear in relief on the distant sky. A man, who appears a native of the place, joins him from a by-path, and asks with apparent kindness whither he is going. "To yonder fortress," says the soldier, "where my sovereign's army lies in strength." The stranger, under pretence of friendship, endeavors to persuade him that it is a prison. He is an emissary of the enemy, sent to detain the fugitive until it be too late, and then cut him off. In this way many are turned back from the place of refuge; the agents of the enemy under various disguises join themselves to them, and insinuate that to be seriously religious is to throw their liberty away.   *Wm. Arnot.*

11,360. REFUGE, Where is? Many a criminal has fled over seas into inhospitable wilds or into other countries, to escape the just penalty for his crimes. The weakness of civil government has been his safety. But where shall he flee for refuge who has sinned against God, whose empire is the universe, and who, from his perfect nature, must recognize and punish the sin? Christ is the only appointed refuge.

11,361. REGENERATION, Effect of. Give me a man of passionate, abusive, headstrong temper, and with only a few of the words of God, I will make him as gentle as a lamb. Give me a greedy, covetous, selfish wretch, and I will teach him to distribute his riches with a liberal, unsparing hand. Give me a cruel bloodthirsty monster, and all his rage will be changed into love. Give me a man guilty of injustice, full of ignorance, and lost in wickedness, he shall soon become just, prudent and holy: in the single laver of regeneration he shall be cleansed from all his malignity.
Lactantius.

11,362. REGENERATION, Feigned. A man's conversation may be civilized, when his heart is not evangelized. There is as much difference between nature restrained and nature renewed as between the glimmering of a glowworm and the splendor of the noonday sun.

A bad man is certainly worse when he is seemingly best. We must not account every one a soldier who swaggers with the sword. A rusty scimitar may frequently be found in a highly-trimmed scabbard. What is it to have our hands as white as snow, if our hearts be as black as the bottomless pit? Such professors resemble curious bubbles, smooth and clear without, yet only filled with air. *Secker.*

11,363. REGENERATION, Need of. A countryman carried his gun to a gunsmith for repairs. The latter examined it, and, finding it too far gone for repairing, said, "Your gun is in a very worn-out, ruinous, good-for-nothing condition; what sort of repairing do you want for it?" "Well," said the countryman, "I don't see as I can do with anything short of a new stock, lock, and barrel; that ought to set it up again." "Why," said the smith, "you had better have a new gun altogether." "Ah!" was the reply, "I never thought of that; and it strikes me that is just what I do want. A new stock, lock, and barrel! Why, that's about equal to a new gun altogether, and that's what I'll have." Man finds himself in similar condition, and needs to be made new.

11,364. REGRETS, Fruitless. "I would give a thousand worlds, if I had them," said a reformed man at a temperance meeting; "if I could only blot out the consequences of my past conduct."

11,365. RELIGION, Argument for. My religion is very simple. I look at this universe, so vast, so complex, so magnificent, and I say to myself that it cannot be the result of chance, but the work, however intended, of an unknown omnipotent Being, as superior to man as the universe is superior to the finest machines of human invention. Search the philosophers, and you will not find a stronger or more decisive argument. *Napoleon I.*

11,366. RELIGION, Asylum of. It not unfrequently happens that men are found ready to reject religion in time of health and peace, who fly to it in times of sickness and peril. Eutropius, a high official in Constantinople, in the time of Chrysostom, caused a law to be passed denying the right of asylum to the altars of the churches, or those who fled to them for safety. By a revolution in the government he was soon after compelled to clasp the altar to save his life. Upon this Chrysostom said, "The altar is more powerful than ever, now that it holds the lion chained."

11,367. RELIGION, Bequeathing. The will of Patrick Henry closed with the following testimony to the value of the Christian religion: "I have now disposed of all my property to my family. There is one more thing I wish I could give them, and that is the Christian religion. If they had that, and I had not given them one shilling, they would be rich; and if they had not that, and I had given them all the world, they would be poor."

11,368. RELIGION, Business Advantage of. A young countryman, with strong marks of rusticity upon him, came to New York to engage in business. The first Sabbath he went down to the old Wall-street church, and was invited by Robert Lenox, afterwards president of the Bible Society, to a seat in his pew. The next morning he started with letters of introduction, which he brought with him to buy leather to start shoemaking. He asked for credit, and was in return asked for references. He thought he could furnish them, as his father had some acquaintances in the city. The merchant asked: "Did I not see you yesterday in Mr. Lenox's pew?" "I don't know, sir. I was at church, and a kind gentleman asked me to sit in his pew." "Yes, young man, that was Robert Lenox. I'll trust any one that Mr. Lenox invites into his pew. You need not trouble yourself about references; when the goods are gone come and get more." The young man became a prominent and successful merchant, and always attributed his success to his attending church on his first Sunday in New York.

11,369. RELIGION, Defaming. How common it is for men first to throw dirt in the face of religion, and then persuade themselves it is its natural complexion! They represent it to themselves in a shape least pleasing to them, and then bring that as a plea why they give it no better entertainment.   *Stillingfleet.*

11,370. RELIGION, Devotees of. God does not look for the chief confession of his name from beneath the cathedral's fretted roof, but from the commonest paths and homes of life; not from surpliced ministers or chanting choirs, but from men in their coats, their hosen, and their hats. Sublimer deeds of heroism have been done in coat, and hosen, and hat, than in the warrior's mail; and the histories of heaven are fuller of what has been done in the common walks of life, than of what has been done in the battle-field.   *Power.*

11,371. RELIGION, Difficulties of. Difficulty is a relative thing. The subject that is difficult to one mind is mere rudiment to another. The A B C of Newton are inscrutable enigmas to the mass, and that which stretched beyond the grasp of the great astronomer, may be the simplest elements in the knowledge of an angel. What is mystery to an angel is alphabet to God. Yes, and even to the same mind, subjects once most difficult become most plain. That which overtasked our energies at school is too easy for effort now. Interminable ages of progression are before us. The present intellectual mountains will dwindle into particles as we advance—particles of light streaming a radiance on our future steps.   *Dr. Thomas.*

11,372. RELIGION, Effects of. Oh, the wonders it will accomplish! It wipes guilt from the conscience, rolls the world out of the heart, and darkness from the mind. It will brighten the most gloomy scene, smooth the most rugged path, and cheer the most despairing mind. It will put honey into the bitterest cup, and health into the most diseased soul. It will give hope to the heart, health to the face, oil to the head, light to the eye, strength to the hand, and swiftness to the foot. It will make life pleasant, labor sweet, and death triumph-

ant. It gives faith to the fearful, courage to the timid, and strength to the weak. It robs the grave of its terrors, and death of its sting. It subdues sin, severs from self, makes faith strong, love active, hope lively, and zeal invincible. It gives sonship for slavery, robes for rags, makes the cross light, and reproach pleasant; it will transform a dungeon into a palace, and make the fires of martyrdom as refreshing as the cool breeze of summer. It snaps legal bonds, loosens the soul, clarifies the mind, purifies the affections, and often lifts the saint to the very gates of heaven. . . No man can deserve it; money cannot buy it, or good deeds procure it; grace reigns here!   *Balfern.*

11,373. RELIGION, Espousing. Wolf relates that a knight was engaged in a game of ball, and desiring to relieve himself of his ring, he placed it upon the finger of a statue of the Virgin. On returning for it he found the hand of the image firmly clasped, and the ring immovable. He interpreted the marvel as a call to the religious life. He considered himself espoused to the Virgin, renounced the world and entered a monastery.

11,374. RELIGION, Force of. You have seen a noble vessel going forth from the docks. The tide was in her favor, and away she went, sailing gallantly along, the admiration of all. She was, however, dependent upon outward influences. But you have seen a steamer, starting perhaps from the same place; if the tide was in her favor, so much the better, but whether or not, on she went, for she had a moving power, a "kingdom within;" and religion is just such an influence.   *Dr. Jenkyn.*

11,375. RELIGION, Gifts for. The similitude of those who lay out their substance for advancing the religion of God, is as a grain of corn which produceth seven ears, and every ear a hundred grains.   *Koran.*

11,376. RELIGION, Half Way. It is this half way religion that undoes the professing world. The heart can never be at unity with itself till it is wholly centered in God.   *Whitefield.*

11,377. RELIGION, Honorary. Vespasian determined upon the restoration of the sacred buildings, and the temple of Jupiter Capitolinus. He carried timber upon his own back, wrought in the foundations with his own hands, and thought it not dishonoring to work on anything that concerned the worship of the gods.

11,378. RELIGION, Importance of. Religion, the final centre of repose; the goal to which all things tend, which gives to time all its importance, to eternity all its glory; apart from which man is a shadow, his very existence a riddle, and the stupendous scenes which surround him as incoherent and unmeaning as the leaves which the sibyl scattered in the wind.   *Robert Hall.*

11,379. RELIGION, Man without. Man without religion is like a leaky vessel without hands on the tempestuous ocean. Sin has already made a destructive inroad in his nature, and the tide of corruption is daily flowing into and filling his soul; he is tossed about without aid on the boisterous ocean of the world, till at last he breaks to pieces, and sinks to rise no more. He is a ship without a pilot—a vessel without a rudder. *Salter.*

11,880. RELIGION, **Method in.** There is a great difference betwixt the sight of the several parts of a clock or watch, as they are disjointed and scattered abroad, and the seeing of them conjointed, and in use and motion. To see here a pin and there a wheel, and not know how to set them altogether, nor even see them in their due places, will give but little satisfaction. It is the frame and design of holy doctrine that must be known, and every part should be discerned as it hath its particular use to that design, and as it is connected with the other parts. *Flavel.*

11,381. RELIGION, **Mixture of.** The use of silk is prohibited to Mohammedans by law, it being considered an excrement. They avoid the interdict by mixing the least possible quantity of cotton with it. Religion is fashionable in these times, but it is taken only in the smallest quantities. A very thin coating will satisfy the worldly and fashionable heart, and the thinner the more satisfaction. A little religion seems enough in many minds to sanctify falsehood, pride, dishonesty, and general unreliability, and a large profession of religion seems enough to cover every conceivable offence.

11,382. RELIGION, Price of. Whitefield, preaching in Philadelphia, cried out in the midst of the sermon, "I am going to turn merchant today. I have valuable commodities to offer for sale, but I say not, as your merchants do, If you will come up to my price, I'll sell to you; but, If you will come down to my price; for if you have a farthing to bring you cannot be a purchaser." They were urged to "buy the truth;" to "buy wine and milk without money and without price."

11,383. RELIGION, Rekindled. The sacred fire among the Greeks was kept constantly burning in the temples at Athens and in Delphi. Provision was made that if by any cause it should be extinguished, as when the temple was burned, or as when in Rome, the very altar was overturned in war, it should be rekindled only by the flame drawn from the pure rays of the sun. Religion in the soul must be kindled by rays from the sun of righteousness, and rekindled in the same way.

11,384. RELIGION, Riches and. Religion brings forth riches, but the daughter devours the mother. *Anon.*

11,385. RELIGION, Romish. During all the ages of papal domination in Europe a religious person "did not mean any one who felt and allowed the bonds that bound him to God and his fellow men, but one who had taken peculiar vows upon him, a member of one of the monkish orders; a 'religious house' did not mean, nor does it now mean in the Church of Rome, a Christian household, ordered in the fear of God, but a house in which those persons were gathered together according to the rule of some man, Benedict or Dominic, or some other. A

'religion' meant not a service of God, but an order of monkery; and taking the monastic vows was termed going into a 'religion.' Now what an awful light does this one word so used throw on the entire state of mind and habits of thought in those ages! That then was 'religion,' and nothing else was deserving of the name! And 'religious was a title which might not be given to parents and children, husbands and wives, men and women fulfilling faithfully and holily in the world the several duties of their stations, but only to those who had devised self-chosen service for themselves.'" *Trench.*

11,386. RELIGION, Sunday. To many of us, alas! our religion is like a stop in an organ which we can pull out "and shut off" at our own will. On Sunday mornings we pull it out, "and for a time it discourses excellent music;" but we push it in on Sunday evenings, and use it no more till the week has run out. Religion is only the Sunday stop in the organ of our life. *S. Cox.*

11,387. RELIGION, Testing. In the ninth century an enthusiastic Scandinavian chief named Herringar was converted, and proposed to put the boasted power of the gods of his heathen neighbors to the proof. He said, "Lo, the rainy season is at hand; call ye upon your gods that the rain may be restrained from falling upon you, and I will call on my God, Jesus Christ, that no drop fall on me; and the god that answereth our prayers let him be god." They agreed to this. Herringar and a little child took one side of a field, and his heathen neighbors the other. In a few moments rain fell in torrents upon the heathen, while on Herringar not a drop fell. He then exhorted them to accept Christ thus shown to be the true God.

11,388. RELIGION, Transformation by. A degraded man, idle, ragged, and barefoot, who spent his Sabbaths in hunting and fishing, had a family of similar character, the disgrace of the neighborhood. A change came over all. The father became a Christian and a respectable man. His family could not be recognized, so great was the change. His house and home was entirely transformed. This miracle has religion wrought in thousands of instances.

11,389. RELIGION, True. Claude, the celebrated French minister, said on his death-bed, "I have carefully examined all religions. No one appears to me worthy of the wisdom of God, and capable of leading men to happiness, but the Christian religion. I have diligently studied Popery and Protestanism. The Protestant is, I think, the only good religion. It is all founded on the Holy Scriptures, the word of God. From this, as from a fountain, all religion must be drawn. Scripture is the root, the Protestant religion is the trunk and branches of the tree. It becomes you all to keep steady to it."

11,390. REMEMBRANCE, Proper Use of. What man should learn is, to reject all that is useless in remembrance, and to retain with cheerfulness all that can profit and amend. **Forget**

not thy sins, that thou mayest sorrow and repent; remember death, that thou mayest sin no more; remember the judgment of God, that thou mayest justly fear; and never forget his mercy, that thou mayest never be led to despair.   *Petrarch.*

11,391. REMORSE, Beginning of. Sin and hedgehogs are born without spikes, but how they prick and wound after their birth we all know. The most unhappy being is he who feels remorse before the (sinful) deed, and brings forth a sin already furnished with teeth in its birth, the bite of which is soon prolonged into an incurable wound of the conscience.
Richter.

11,392. REMORSE in Death. Behold all the gloomy apartments opening, in which the wicked have died; contemplate first the triumphs of iniquity, and here behold their close; witness the terrific faith, the too late repentance, the prayers suffocated by despair, and the mortal agonies! These once they would not believe; they refused to consider them; they could not allow that the career of crime and pleasure was to end. But now truth, like a blazing star, darts over the mind, and but shows the way to that "darkness visible" which no light can cheer. "Dying wretch!" we say in imagination to each of these, "is religion true? Do you believe in a God, and another life, and a retribution?" "Oh, yes!" he answers, and expires.   *John Foster.*

11,393. REMORSE, Described. Conscience is God's officer and vicegerent in man; set by him to be, as it were, thy angel, keeper, monitor, remembrancer, king, prophet, examiner, judge —yea, thy lower heaven. If thou slightest it, it will be an adversary, informer, accuser, witness, judge, jailer, tormentor, a worm, rack, dungeon, unto thee—yea, thy upper hell!
Dr. Fuller.

11,394. REMORSE, Horror of. Tiberius felt the remorse of conscience so violent, that he protested to the senate that he suffered death daily. Richard III., after the murder of his two innocent nephews, had fearful dreams and visions; insomuch that he did often leap out of his bed in the dark, and catching his sword, which, always naked, stuck by his side, he would go distractedly about the chamber, everywhere seeking to find out the cause of his own occasioned disquiet. It is as proper for sin to raise fears in the soul, as for rotten flesh and wood to breed worms. That worm that never dies is bred here in the froth of filthy lusts and flagitious courses, and lies gnawing and grubbing upon men's inwards, many times in the ruff of all their jollity. This makes Saul call for a minstrel, Belshazzar for his carousing cups, Cain for his workmen to build him a city, others for other of the devil's anodynes, to put by the pangs of their wounded spirits and throbbing consciences. Charles IX., after the massacre of France, could never endure to be awakened in the night without music, or some like diversion; he became as terrible to himself as formerly he had been to others.   *Trapp.*

11,395. REMORSE, Occasions for. A man can not spend all his life in frolic: age, or disease, or solitude, will bring some hours of serious consideration, and it will then afford no comfort to think that he has extended the dominion of vice; that he has loaded himself with the crimes of others, and can never know the extent of his own wickedness, or make reparation for the mischief that he has caused. There is not perhaps in all the stores of ideal anguish a thought more painful than the consciousness of having propagated corruption by vitiating principles; of having not only drawn others from the path of virtue, but blocked up the way by which they should return; of having blinded them to every beauty but the paint of pleasure, and deafened them to every call but the alluring voice of the syrens of destruction.   *Dr. S. Johnson.*

11,396. REMORSE, Power of. Rev. Benjamin Abbott, a very searching preacher of New Jersey, in the midst of a scathing indictment of crime, cried out, "For aught I know, there may be a murderer in this congregation." A large man in the audience rose and ran for the door, exclaiming, "I am the murderer; I killed a man fifteen years ago." At the door he thought himself met by two men with drawn swords, who were trying to stab him. He turned back and threw himself upon the floor, crying out in great agony.

11,397. REMORSE, Stings of. There is no man that is knowingly wicked but is guilty to himself; and there is no man that carries guilt about him, but he receives a sting into his soul.   *Tillotson.*

11,398. REMORSE, Unendurable. A man and his wife were executed at Augsburg for a murder committed twenty-one years before. Wincze, a lawyer, removed to Augsburg, where he became intimate in the family of M. Glegg, to whose daughter he paid his addresses; but the old gentleman not sanctioning his visits, he met the daughter privately and persuaded her, in order to remove the only obstacle to their union, to administer poison to her father. The horrid plan succeeded; no suspicions were entertained, and their union put him in possession of the old man's wealth. During a period of twenty-one years they lived externally happy, but in secret a prey to the greatest remorse. At length, unable to endure any longer the weight of guilt, the wife made confession of the particulars of the crime, and both were punished.

11,399. REPENTANCE, Analogy of. Suppose I am to go down to Boston to-night, and I go down to the Union depot and say to a man I see there, "Can you tell me, is this train going to Boston?" and the man says, "Yes," and I go and get on board the train, and Mr. Dodge comes along and says, "Where are you going?" I say, "I am going to Boston," and Mr. Dodge says, "Well, you are on the wrong train, that train is going to Albany." "But, Mr. Dodge, I am quite sure I am right; I asked a railroad man here, and he told me this was the train." And Mr. Dodge says, "Moody, I know all about these trains; I have lived here 40 years, and go up and down on these trains every day," and at last Mr. Dodge convinces me I am on the wrong train. That is conviction, not conversion. But if I don't remain on that train, but just get into the other train, that is repentance. Just to change trains—that is repentance. *Moody.*

11,400. REPENTANCE, Ceaseless. "Sir," said a young man to Philip Henry, "how long should a man go on repenting? How long, Mr. Henry, do you mean to go on repenting yourself?" He replied, "Sir, I hope to carry my repentance to the very gates of heaven. Every day I find I am a sinner, and every day I need to repent. I mean to carry my repentance, by God's help, up to the very gates of heaven." Reader, may this be our divinity, your divinity, my divinity; your theology, my theology! May repentance toward God and faith toward our Lord Jesus Christ be Jachin and Boaz—the two great pillars before the temple of our religion, the corner-stones in our system of Christianity! (2 Chron. 3 : 17.) *Ryle.*

11,401. REPENTANCE at Death. There is one case of death-bed repentance recorded—the penitent thief—that no one should despair; and only one, that no one should presume. *St. Augustine.*

11,402. REPENTANCE. Death-Bed. A minister of long experience and careful observation, visited more than two thousand persons apparently in a dying condition, who manifested such signs of penitence as to encourage hope of their salvation. These were restored to health, and nothing less than Christian lives could have been expected of them, but only two out of two thousand manifested a saving change. How unreliable are sick-bed manifestations!

11,403. REPENTANCE, Delaying. When men feel sickness arresting, then they fear death is approaching. But we begin to die as soon as ever we begin to live. Every man's passing-bell hangs in his own steeple. Take him in his four elements, of earth, air, fire, and water. In the earth, he is as fleeting dust; in the air, he is as disappearing vapor; in the water, he is as a breaking bubble; and in the fire, he is as consuming smoke. Many think not of living any holier, till they can live no longer; but one to-day is worth two to-morrows. Reader, you know not how soon the sails of your life may be rolled up, or how nigh you are to your eternal haven; and if you have not Jesus as your pilot within you, you will suffer an eternal shipwreck. *Secker.*

11,404. REPENTANCE, Early. The more we number our days, the fewer sins we shall have to number. As a copy is then safest from blotting when dust is put upon it, so are we from sinning when, in the time of our youth, we remember that we are but dust. The tears of young penitents do more scorch the devils than all the flames of hell; for hereby all their hopes are blasted, and the great underminer countermined and blown up. *Mane* is the devil's verb; he bids tarry, time enough to repent; but *mane* is God's adverb; he bids repent early, in the morning of thy youth, for then thy sins will be fewer and lesser. Well young men, remember this: he that will not at first hand buy good counsel cheap, shall at the second-hand buy repentance over dear. *Brooks.*

11,405. REPENTANCE, Exhortation to. Oh! that I did know what arguments would persuade you; and what words would work thy heart hereto. If I were sure it would prevail, I would come down from the pulpit, and go from man to man upon my knees, with the request and advice in the text: "Oh! kiss the Son, lest he be angry, and you perish." *Baxter.*

11,406. REPENTANCE, Fable of. A kite, who had been long very ill, said to his mother, "Don't cry, mother, but go and pray to the gods that I may recover from this dreadful disease and pain." "Alas! child," said the mother, "which of the gods can I entreat for one who has robbed all their altars?" A death-bed repentance is poor amends for the errors of a life-time. *Æsop.*

11,407. REPENTANCE, Faith and. Repentance is Faith's usher, and dews all her way with tears. Repentance reads the law and weeps; Faith reads the gospel and comforts. Repentance looks on the rigorous brow of Moses; Faith beholds the sweet countenance of Christ Jesus. *T. Adams.*

11,408. REPENTANCE, Forced. It is said by some that so soon as the soul of the sinner is separated from sense, and experiences in the next world the evil consequences of sin, those evil consequences will lead to repentance. We answer that repentance, in view of the experience of evil or the fear of evil, is repentance toward self, not toward God. The more men repent from an experience of evil consequences, the more they are damned. The thief always repents when the sheriff arrests him. Death forces many men to submit, others to repent. Such repentance is by necessity; or in view of consequences, not in view of God's goodness and of the evil of sin. Some weak people talk of repentance on the gallows. Dying sinners and murderers often repent, but it is a repentance forced in view of the termination of their moral agency. In this world, "repentance toward God" works by reformation; and faith in our Lord Jesus Christ works by love. In the world of doom, when moral probation is ended, repentance, by the necessity of the case, works by remorse; and faith by trembling. *Walker.*

11,409. REPENTANCE, Method of. You might pound a lump of ice with a pestle into a thousand fragments, but it would still continue ice. But bring it in beside your own bright and blazing fire, and soon, in that genial glow, the living waters flow. A man may try to make himself contrite. He may search out his sins, and dwell on all their enormity, and still feel no true repentance. But come to Jesus with his words of grace and truth. Let that frozen spirit bask in the beams of the sun of righteousness—then will it melt. *Dr. J. Hamilton.*

11,410. REPENTANCE, Peter's. Peter falls dreadfully, but rises by repentance sweetly; a look of love from Christ melts him into tears. He knew that repentance was the key to the kingdom of grace. As once his faith was so great that he leapt, as it were, into a sea of waters, to come to Christ; so now his repentance was so great that he leapt, as it were, into a sea of tears, for that he had gone from Christ. Some say that, after his sad fall, he was ever and anon weeping, and that his face was even furrowed with continual tears. He had no sooner taken in poison, but he vomited it up again, ere it got to the vitals; he had no sooner handled this serpent, but he turned it into a rod to scourge his soul with remorse for sinning against such clear light, and strong love, and sweet discoveries of the heart of Christ to him. Clement notes that Peter so repented, that all his life after, every night when he heard the cock crow, he would fall upon his knees, and, weeping bitterly, would beg pardon for his sin. Ah, souls, you can easily sin as the saints, but can you repent with the saints? *Brooks.*

11,411. REPENTANCE, Preaching. Rev. Philip Henry often preached on the doctrine of faith and repentance. He used to say that he had been told concerning the famous Mr. Dod, that some called him in scorn, faith and repentance; because he insisted so much in these two in all his preaching. "But," says he, "if this be to be vile, I will be yet more vile, for faith and repentance are all in all in Christianity. If I were to die in the pulpit, I would desire to die preaching repentance; or if I die out of the pulpit, I would desire to die practicing repentance."

11,412. REPENTANCE, Public. The Mohammedan account of the preaching of Jonah to the Ninevites says that he exhorted them to repentance, and threatened them with destruction in three days if they disregarded his call. They scorned him, and cast him out of the city. Near the end of the time, a great black cloud, charged with fire, which filled the air with smoke, hung over their city, and filled them with consternation. Then they went into the fields, put sackcloth upon themselves, their children and their cattle, and sincerely repenting, asked God to forgive them. God heard their prayer, and the storm passed over.

11,413. REPENTANCE, Self-Condemnation of. To repent is to accuse and condemn ourselves; to charge upon ourselves the desert of hell; to take part with God against ourselves, and to justify him in all that he does against us; to be ashamed and confounded for our sins; to have them ever in our eyes, and at all times upon our hearts, that we may be in daily sorrow for them; to part with our right hands and eyes, that is, with those pleasurable sins which have been as dear to us as our lives, so as never to have to do with them more, and to hate them, so as to destroy them as things which by nature we are wholly disinclined to. For we naturally love and think well of ourselves, hide our deformities, lessen and excuse our faults, indulge ourselves in the things that please us, are mad upon our lusts, and follow them, though to our own destruction. *Francis Fuller.*

11,414. REPENTANCE, True. Like Janus Bifrons, the Roman god looking two ways, a true repentance not only bemoans the past but takes heed to the future. Repentance, like the lights of a ship at her bow and her stern, not only looks to the track she has made, but to the path before her. A godly sorrow moves the Christian to weep over the failure of the past, but his eyes are not so blurred with tears but that he can look watchfully into the future, and profiting by the experience of former failures make straight paths for his feet. *Pilkington.*

11,415. REPENTANCE, Waiting for. He that waits for repentance waits for that which cannot be had as long as it is waited for. It is absurd for a man to wait for that which he himself has to do. *Nevins.*

11,416. REPETITION, Advantage of. A garment that is double-dyed, dipped again and again, will retain the color a great while. *Philip Henry.*

11,417. REPETITION, Use of. "He must be a poor creature," says Holmes, "that does not often repeat himself. Imagine the author of the excellent piece of advice, 'Know thyself,' never alluding to that sentiment again during the course of a protracted existence! Why, the truths a man carries about with him are his tools; and do you think a carpenter is bound to use the same plane but once to smooth a knotty board with, or to hang up his hammer after it has driven its first nail? I shall never repeat a conversation, but an idea often. I shall use the same types when I like, but not commonly the same stereotypes. A thought is often original, though you have uttered it a hundred times. It has come to you over a new route, and by a new and express train of associations."

11,418. REPRIEVE, Reception of a. Rev. J. Denham Smith, of England, obtained a reprieve from the Queen for a man who was sentenced to be hung. He was in the greatest haste to reach the man, and anxious as to how he should break the good news to him who was already dead in law, and who had, as he supposed, bidden his last farewell to his wife and children. Admitted to him he said, "My poor man, can you read?" "Yes," was the reply. Fearing to break the royal pardon to him too suddenly, he added, "Would you like your life?" "Sir," he responds, "do not trifle with me." "But life is sweet; is it not?" "Sir, I had rather you would not speak to me." "But would you not like me to procure your life?" "It is of no use, sir; I'm justly condemned. I'm a dead man." "But the Queen could give you your life." He looked inquiringly, but was silent. "Can you read this?" said Mr. Smith. When he learned of his reprieve he dropped down at the messenger's feet, and lay insensible. It was more than he could bear. Mr. Smith says: "What! when a man to whom a reprieve is announced, granting him a few more short years of natural life, falls down as dead, may not a sinner, who finds he is not to be lost, but that on believing he is saved; he has Christ, and heaven, and everlasting life; I say, may not he weep? Yea, cry? Cry for joy!"

11,419. REPROOF, Discretion in. Discretion in the choice of seasons for reproving, is no less necessary than zeal and faithfulness in reproving. Good mariners do not hoist up sail in every wind.   *Trapp.*

11,420. REPROOF, Misplaced. We ought not to discover the imperfections of an husband before his wife, nor of a father before his children, nor of a lover in company of his mistress, nor of masters in presence of their scholars, or the like; for it touches a man to the quick to be rebuked before those whom he would have think honorably of him. They who aim at the interest and reformation of their friends rather than ostentation and popularity, ought, among other things, to beware of exposing them too publicly.   *Plutarch.*

11,421. REPROOF, Penalty for. Aratus, a Sycionian, by his valor freed and restored his country to liberty; but King Philip caused him to be put to death by poison, because he had with too great freedom reprehended the king for his faults.

11,422. REPROOF, Where to Begin. Fredericus, a newly-consecrated ¨ishop of Utrecht, was at a feast given by the Emperor Ludovicus Pius. The emperor told the bishop "he must remember to deal justly as in the sight of God, in the way of his vocation, without respect of persons." "Your majesty gives me good advice," said he, "but will you please to tell me whether I had best to begin, with this fish upon my plate, at the head or the tail?" "At the head," said the emperor, "for that is the more noble part." "Then, sir," said the bishop, "I commence with you." He then administered a terrible rebuke, which was not only well received, but improved upon.

11,423. REPUBLIC, Elements of Permanence in a. The seven wise men of Greece being asked what are the elements of perpetuity in a republic, answered severally. Solon: "I hold that city or state happy, and most likely to remain democratic, in which those that are not personally injured are yet as forward to question and correct wrong-doers as is that person who is immediately wronged." Bias added: "Where all fear the law as they fear a tyrant." Thirdly, Thales said: "Where the citizens are neither too rich nor too poor." Fourthly, Anacharsis said: "Where, though in all other respects they are equals, yet virtuous men are advanced and vicious men degraded." Fifthly, Cleobulus said: "Where the rulers fear reproof, and shame more than the law." Sixthly, Pittacus said: "Where bad men are prohibited from ruling, and good men from not ruling." Chilo, pausing a little while, determined that the best and most durable state was where the subjects minded the aw most and the orators least.

11,424. REPUBLICS, Advantage of. In republics the advantages are—liberty, or exemption from needless restrictions, equal laws, regulations adapted to the wants and circumstances of the people, public spirit, frugality, averseness to war, the opportunities which democratic assemblies afford to men of every description of producing their abilities and counsels to public observation, and the exciting thereby and calling forth to the service of the commonwealth, the faculties of its best citizens.   *Adn. Paley.*

11,425. REPULSE, Bearing. Diogenes went to all the statues in the Ceramicus begging. When asked the import of his strange action, he said he was practising how to bear a repulse.

11,426. REPUTATION, Benefits of. Reputation is one of the prizes for which men contend; it is, as Mr. Burke calls it, "the cheap defence and ornament of nations, and the nurse of manly exertions;" it produces more labor and more talent than twice the wealth of a country could ever rear up. It is the coin of genius; and it is the imperious duty of every man to bestow it with the most scrupulous justice and the wisest economy.   *S. Smith.*

11,427. REPUTATION, Good. Your innocence, by God's grace, no one can take from you without your own consent; but the fruit of a fair reputation, so beautiful and fragrant, and in all respects so precious, this, alas! hangs exposed to the assault of every passenger; the lowest, as he goes along, can fling a stone upwards, and laugh to see the prize fall, though he cannot gather it. We have an account of a certain tribe of savages who are possessed of a persuasion, that whenever they have slain a man, they are immediately endowed with all his good qualities; which they think are transfused from the soul of the dead unto the person that has killed him. You will not wonder that murders are frequent in that country; and that it is very dangerous for a man of merit to be found unguarded among people of such principles.   *Ogden.*

11,428. REPUTATION, Symbol of. A Turk, it is said, took a piece of white cloth to a dyer to have it dyed black. He was so pleased with the result that after a time he went to him with a piece of black cloth, and asked to have it made white. But the dyer answered: "A piece of white cloth is like a man's reputation; it can be dyed black, but you cannot make it white again."

11,429. RESCUE, Remarkable. Rev. Richard Boardman, one of the first Wesleyan missionaries to America, before his coming here went to preach at Mould, in Flintshire, England. His way lay along the sands by the sea-shore, and was safe enough at low tide. The tide closed in upon him so that he could go neither forward nor backward, and high rocks cut of escape by land. He gave himself up for lost, and commended his soul to God. Two men came running down a hill across the water, and taking a boat rescued him, just as the water reached his knees as he sat in the sad dle. His horse swam to land by the side of the boat. While in the boat, one of the men said, "Surely, sir, God is with you." He answered, "I trust he is.' The man replied, "I know he is;" and then related the following circumstance. "Last night I dreamed that I must go to the top of such a hill. When I awoke, the dream made such an impression on my mind that I could not rest. I therefore went and called upon this man to accompany me. When we came to the place, we saw nothing more than usual. However, I begged him to go to another hill at a small distance; and there we saw your distressed situation." God had other work for Boardman, and preserved him for it.

11,430. RESCUE, A Sinner's. A shoemaker dug a well about twelve feet deep, near his house, which caved in before its completion, leaving an irregular hole with sloping sides. One day his son fell into it, and with all his efforts could not climb out. Filled with alarm he cried loudly to his father for help. His father heard him, and climbing down the sloping sides of the pit, reached down a strap to his boy, saying, "Take hold." He did so and was quickly lifted out. The sinner is in a pit and cannot extricate himself. If he but cry to the heavenly Father, he will reach down his promises, upon which he may take hold and be lifted to a place of safety.

11,431. RESIGNATION, Christian. Fenelon, gazing upon the remains of his illustrious pupil, the Duke of Burgundy, as he lay dead in his coffin, said, "There lies my beloved prince, for whom my affection was equal to the tenderest parent. Nor was my affection lost; he loved me in return with the ardor of a son. There he lies, and all my worldly happiness lies dead with him. But if the turning of a straw would call him back to life, I would not, for ten thousand worlds, be the turner of that straw, in opposition to the will of God."

11,432. RESIGNATION, Example of. An Indian, descending the Niagara river, was thrown into the rapids above the sublime cataract. The nursling of the desert rowed with an incredible vigor at first, in an intense struggle for life. Seeing his efforts useless, he dropped his oars, sung his death-song and floated in calmness down the abyss! His example is worthy of the imitation of all. While there is hope, let us nerve all our force to avail ourselves of all the chances it suggests. When hope ceases, and peril must be braved, wisdom counsels calm resignation. *Dion.*

11,433. RESIGNATION, Light of. True resignation, which always brings with it the confidence that unchangeable goodness will make even the disappointment of our hopes and the contradictions of life conducive to some benefit, casts a grave but tranquil light over the prospect of even a toilsome and troubled life. *Humboldt.*

11,434. RESIGNATION, Prayer and. A boy lost a valuable and much-prized ring, at which he was very much grieved. He prayed about it. His sister said, "What is the use of praying about a ring? will praying bring it back?" He replied, "No, sister, perhaps not, but it has done this for me; it has made me quite willing to do without the ring if it is God's will; and is not that almost as good as having it?"

11,435. RESOLUTION, Example of. Fulgentius was reared amid the luxuries of a senatorial family at Carthage, and lived about the end of the fourth century. He had wealth and office, but renounced all for a monastic life. The abbot to whom he applied repulsed him, saying, "Go and first learn to live in the world, abstracted from its pleasures. Who can suppose that you, relinquishing a life of softness and ease, can take up with our coarse diet and clothing, and inure yourself to our watchings and fastings." The young nobleman replied, "He who hath inspired me with the will to serve him can also furnish me with courage and strength." His resolute reply gained him admission to the monastery. His mother was greatly grieved, and presenting herself before the gates, cried out, "Faustus, restore to me my son, to the people their governor. The church always protects widows; why, then, do you rob me of my son?" This she repeated for many days, till she saw that her son's resolution was unalterable. He lived a devout life, and is reputed to have wrought many miracles, and holds a place in the saint's calendar for Jan. 1st.

11,436. RESOLUTION, Successful. Sheridan, the orator, believed in himself, and this self-confidence doubtless contributed to the failure of his first effort in Parliament, which was utter and apparently irretrievable. His friends considered him a hopeless failure, and advised him to seek some new field. He replied, "It is in me, and it shall come out." In the dark hour of defeat he resolved upon success, and won it.

11,437. RESPECT, Personal. Whenever we can bring a man to have a proper respect for himself, that moment we have secured him against the commission of any heinous crime. *Halliday.*

11,438. RESPECT, Preservation of. Not only study that those with whom you live should habitually respect you, but cultivate such manners as will secure the respect of persons with whom you occasionally converse. Keep up the habit of being respected, and do not attempt to be more amusing and agreeable than is consistent with the preservation of respect. *S. Smith.*

11,439. RESPIRATION, Process of. It appears that when respiration is performed naturally, there are about 18 respirations in one minute, 1,080 in the hour, and 25,920 in the 24 hours. By each inspiration a pint of air is sent to the lungs—that is, 18 pints in a minute; in the hour more than two hogsheads, and in the 24 hours more than 57 hogsheads. When the body is in a state of health, there will be 72 pulsations of the heart in one minute. Every pulsation sends to the lungs two ounces of blood. Thus, 146 ounces, about an imperial gallon, are sent to the lungs, for the purpose of arterialization, or purification, every minute. In one hour there are sent 450 pints, in 24 hours nearly 11,000 pints. The blood performs a complete circuit in the system in 110 seconds, and 540 circuits in 24 hours. There are three complete circulations of the blood in every eight minutes of time. The object of this beautiful arrangement is to ventilate the blood. A constant supply of fresh air is an absolute necessity of our nature. If we are deprived of it, we die at once; if the air is vitiated, we suffer langnor, which very often results in disease. *Dr. S. Smith.*

11,440. RESPONSIBILITY, Individual. Princes and kings—poor men and peasants, all alike must attend to the wants of their own bodies, and their own minds. No man can eat, drink, or sleep, by proxy. No man can get the alphabet learned for him by another. All these are things which everybody must do for himself, or they will not be done at all. Just as it is with the mind and body, so it is with the soul. There are certain things absolutely needful to the soul's health and well being. Each must attend to these things for himself. Each must repent for himself. Each must apply to Christ for himself. And for himself each must speak to God, and pray. You must do it for yourself, for by nobody else can it be done. *Ryle.*

11,441. RESPONSIBILITY, Moral. To be morally responsible, a man must be a free, rational, moral agent. First, he must be in present possession of his reason to distinguish truth from falsehood. Secondly, he must also have in exercise a moral sense to distinguish right from wrong. Thirdly, his will, in its volitions or executive acts, must be self-determined—that is, determined by its own spontaneous affections and desires. If any of these are wanting, the man is insane, and neither free nor responsible. *Prof. Hodge.*

11,442. RESPONSIBILITY, Necessity of. If the master takes no account of his servants, they will make small account of him, and care not what they spend, who are never brought to an audit. *Fuller.*

11,443. REST, Disturbance of. I know that even the big planet, while it sweeps on in its pathway of light, thrills with a disturbing tremor if any foreign object swims across its orbit; and similarly I know, place anything between the heart and Christ, there will be, not utter "falling" from "the way," but certain disturbance of the calm of the resting soul that hath found rest in him. *Grosart.*

11,444. REST, Emblem of. A ship's compass adjusted as to keep its level amidst all the heavings of the sea. Though forming part of a structure that feels every motion of the restless waves, it has an arrangement of its own that keeps it always in place, and in working order. Look at it when you will, it is pointing, trembling perhaps, but truly, to the pole. So each soul in this life needs an adjustment of its own, that amid the fluctuations of the " earthen vessel," it may be kept ever in a

position to feel the power of its great attraction in the skies. *Christi in Treasury.*

11,445. REST, Happiness in. All things have a propensity towards that in which they place their felicity. If a stone were laid in the the concave of the moon, though air, and fire, and water were between, yet it would break through all, and be restless till it come to the earth, its centre. A suitable and unchangeable rest is the only satisfaction of the rational creature. All the tossings and agitations of the soul are but so many wings to carry him hither and thither, that he may find out a place where to rest. Let this eagle once find out and fasten on the true carcase, he is contented; as the needle pointing to the north, though before in motion, yet now he is quiet. Therefore, the philosopher, though in one place he tells us that delight consisteth in motion, yet in another place tells us that it consisteth rather in rest. *Swinnock.*

11,446. REST, Industrious. The rest which a troubled soul finds in Christ is like the rest which the Pilgrim Fathers found on the American continent. When they stepped upon the shore free, feeling God's earth firm under their feet, and seeing God's sunlight bright above their heads, they said and sung, " This is our rest." But they meant not idleness. Each family reared a cabin in the bush, and forthwith waged war against the desert, until they had subdued it, and turned it into a fruitful field. Their resting-place was their working-place; and none the worse in their esteem was the rest because of the labor that accompanied it. Beyond the reach of the tyrant, and past the dangers of the sea, the rest they sought and found was a place to work in, and useful labor close at hand. *Arnot.*

11,447. REST, Motto of. The motto of Philip de Marnix, Lord Sainte-Aldegonde, one of the most efficient leaders in that great Netherlands revolt against despotism in the sixteenth century, was *Repos Ailleurs*, or "Rest elsewhere."

11,448. REST, Places of. In eastern countries, where the habit of hospitality is stronger than with us, the traveler is sometimes surprised and regaled by much-needed but unexpected wayside comforts. Yonder husbandman, who is now a-field at his work, was here in the early morning to leave by the wayside that pitcher of water that the passing traveler might drink. This clump of trees which makes a thick and welcome "shadow from the heat," was planted by one who expected neither fame nor money for his toil, and who now lies in a nameless grave. Hands now mouldering in dust scooped out this cool seat in the rock. Some "Father Jacob gave us this well after drinking thereof himself, and his children, and his cattle." Travelers from the west are much affected by such instances of pure humanity and unselfish kindness. And yet these are but feeble types, mere dim shadows of divine thoughtfulness and care. *Raleigh.*

11,449. REST, Pursuit of. Rest unto our souls! 'tis all we want, the end of all our wishes and pursuits: give us a prospect of this, we take the wings of the morning, and fly to the uttermost parts of the earth to have it in possession: we seek for it in titles, in riches, and pleasures, climb up after it by ambition, come down again, and stoop for it by avarice, try all extremes: still we are gone out of the way; nor is it till after many miserable experiments that we are convinced at last, but where there is a prospect of finding it; and that is within ourselves, in a meek and lowly disposition of heart.   *Sterne.*

11,450. REST, Safe. Years ago one of our fleets was terribly shattered by a violent gale. It was found that some of the ships were unaffected by its violence. They were in, what mariners call "the eye of the storm." While all around was desolation, they were safe. So it is with him who has the peace of God in his heart.   *Pilkington.*

11,451. RESTITUTION, Exemplary. A gentleman who had been the agent in the sale of oil stock, by which the purchasers lost their money, felt that this stood in the way of his religious progress. He resolved to make restitution if it impoverished him. His way was made practicable, and his heart was filled with joy.

11,452. RESTORATION, Glory of. Dr. Holme gives us an illustration by which Dr. Burchard used to enforce the necessity of the new birth. A very wicked man died, and his spirit entered the fires of purgation in the eternal world. After a thorough cleansing he was admitted to heaven. A new robe was put on him, a crown set on his head, and a harp was given to him, and he was required to sing. "What shall I sing?" said he. The angel said, "There is only one song sung here. Blessing and honor, and glory, and power be unto him that sitteth upon the throne, and to the Lamb forever and ever." But, said the man, "I can't sing that song." "Honor to whom honor is due, say I. If I sing, it will be glory and honor to the devil, who burnt me out like an old pipe and fitted me for heaven."

11,453. RESTRAINT, Type of. As the plough is the typical instrument of industry, so the fetter is the typical instrument of the restraint or subjection necessary in a nation—either literally for its evil-doers, or figuratively, in accepting laws, for its wise and good men. Wise laws and just restraints are to a noble nation not chains, but chain mail—strength and defence. Therefore the first power of a nation consists in knowing how to guide the plough, its second power consists in knowing how to wear the fetter.   *Ruskin.*

11,454. RESURRECTION, Biblical Figures of the. *A tree cut down revived* and sprouting, through the scent of water, Job 14: 7-15. *Herbs revived* by the moisture of dew, after the parching heat of the burning day, Isa. 26: 29. *Dry bones,* of all things most unlikely to be restored to life, Ezek. 37: 1-14. *Awaking* out of sleep, Ps. 17: 15; Dan. 12: 2; John 11: 11. *A corn of wheat,* or *seed sown,* dying to live, John 12: 24; 1 Cor. 15: 36-38.   *Bowes.*

11,455. RESURRECTION, Certain. "All that are in their graves shall hear his voice;" no grave may refuse to give up its dead. There have been some singular graves made in the world, and extraordinary pains taken to conceal them; but they, as well as the most ordinary receptacles of the dead, must give up their dead. Alaric, king of the Goths, had a curious grave. He had besieged, and levied an enormous tribute upon Rome, and was proceeding to Sicily, when he died suddenly. It is related that his victorious army caused their captives to turn aside the course of the river Busentinus, to make his grave in the bed of the river; and then, when they had buried him in it, and restored the waters to their former channel, they slew upon the spot all who had been engaged in the work, that none might tell the secret to the Romans. Neither will Attila's numerous coffins confine him in the grave. History tells us that he was buried in a wide plain, in a coffin enclosed in one of gold, another of silver, and a third of iron; that with his body was interred an immense amount of treasure; and that the spot might forever remain unknown, those who buried him were killed. But at the judgment-day, he will come forth from his grave, and give an account of all his bloody victories.   *F. F. Trench.*

11,456. RESURRECTION, Emblem of the. An army chaplain tells of having bivouacked with his brigade upon an open field, each soldier wrapped in his blanket, but with nothing over him but the cold, cloudy sky. On arising next morning all over that field were little mounds like new-made graves, each covered with a drapery of snow, which had fallen two or three inches deep during the night, and covered every sleeping soldier, as if in the winding-sheet of death. While he was gazing upon the strange spectacle, here and there a man began to stir, rise, shake himself, and stand forth in momentary amazement at the sight. It was a symbol of the resurrection, and failed not to make its impression upon the beholder.

11,457. RESURRECTION, First Fruits of the. There is a story that once a party of sailors on shore on some island of the sea, ate freely of some plant that threw them into a deep sleep. As they returned not, others came in search of their companions, and found them lying apparently dead. Anxiously they set to work to rouse the drugged sleepers, and the recovery of the first was a glad omen that the rest ere long would revive, as in time they did. So was the resurrection of Christ the pledge and proof of a like immortality assured to his followers.   *Bibl. Treasury.*

11,458. RESURRECTION, Identity in the. The divinely-chosen analogy of the seed and the plant is to me of all the most suggestive regarding our spiritual body as it shall be hereafter. For, take the bulb of a nyacinth, or of any other flower, submit it to the naturalist, and he will tell you by aid of the microscope what the perfected flower will be; yet who that did not know the mysteries of vegetation could believe that from that unpromising bulb would spring the gorgeous flower enveloped in its sheltering leaves? Yet such shall be our body then compared with our body now.

E. H. Bickersteth.

11,459. RESURRECTION, Memento of the. That is a beautiful thought of the Israelites of our days; when they enter their cemetery to deposit one of their number, it is said, they bow together three times to the ground; then seizing the grass of the tomb which they are about to enter, and casting it behind them, they utter in chorus these words of the prophet: "Thy bones shall flourish like the grass: O my brother, thy bones shall flourish like the grass!" My brethren, I come here to do something of a similar kind to-day. I take, as it were, handfuls of the grass and flowers with which the spring has covered our fields, and amidst the concerts of gratitude and joy heard everywhere around us at this season of miracles, I exclaim, "Resurrection! Resurrection!" I declare to you that your bones, though laid in the very dust, shall flourish like the grass, with the whole of nature, which lives again. I preach to you the resurrection of the just. *Gaussen.*

11,460. RESURRECTION, Method of the. The Koran represents Abraham as saying, "O Lord, show me how thou wilt raise the dead?" God said, "Dost thou not yet believe?" The patriarch answered, "Yea; but I ask this that my heart may rest at ease." Then God said, "Take four birds, and divide them, and lay a part of them on every mountain; then call them, and they shall come to thee." The legend says that he took an eagle, a peacock, a raven, and a cock, cut them in pieces, and mingled them together, and then scattered the parts upon several mountains, but retained the heads of the birds in his hands. He called each bird by name, and immediately the parts flew together from all quarters, and were joined to their several heads. This satisfied Abraham, who, seeing a dead body upon the sea-shore partly devoured by wild beasts, and birds, and fish, was troubled in spirit as to its resurrection.

11,461. RESURRECTION, No Deformities in the. There are no defects or deformities in the children of the resurrection. What members are now defective or deformed will then be restored to their perfect being and beauty; "for," as Tertullian says, "if the universal death of all parts be rescinded by the resurrection, how much more the partial death of any single member!" *John Flavel.*

11,462. RESURRECTION, None Forgotten in the. Lady Maxwell was at one time much troubled by the curious temptation that she was so insignificant, she would be liable to be passed over hereafter. But we may meet all such temptations as Monica, the mother of Augustine, met the surprise of her friends at Ostia, when they expressed their wonder that she did not fear to leave her body so far from her own country. "Nothing," said she, "is far from God, and I do not fear that he should not know where to find me at the resurrection."

The small, as well as the great, are remembered in the grand distribution of rewards. The four-and-twenty elders give thanks in Rev. 11, that the time of the dead has come that they should be judged; and that God should give reward unto his servants, the prophets, and to the saints, and to them that fear his name, both small and great. Whenever we are oppressed with a sense of our own insignificance we must fall back upon the comprehensiveness of God's thought; the wideness of its range, the minuteness of its detail.

Power.

11,463. RESURRECTION, Obstructing the. In Queen Mary's days, the body of Peter Martyr's wife was, by the charity of that time, taken out of the grave and buried in a dunghill, in detestation of that great scholar, her husband, sometime professor of divinity in the University of Oxford; but when the tide was once turned, and that Queen Elizabeth, of happy memory, swayed the scepter of this State, her bones were reduced to their place, and there mingled with the bones of St. Frideswide, to this intent, that if ever there should come an alteration of religion in England again, then they should not be able to discern the ashes of the one from the other. Thus death hath mixed and blended the bodies of men, women and children with the flesh of beasts, birds, and serpents; hath tossed, typed, and turned ashes both into air and water, to puzzle the God of heaven and earth to find them, but all in vain. *Anon.*

11,464. RESURRECTION, Possibility of. An apochryphal legend, referred to in the Koran, represents Ezra as riding by the ruins of Jerusalem, after its demolition by the Chaldeans, and doubting the ability of God to restore the city and its inhabitants. Then God slew Ezra. He lay where he fell for one hundred years, when God restored him to life. The bones of the ass, upon which he had ridden, lay scattered about. While the prophet looked on these came together, were clothed with flesh, the animal was reanimated, and began to bray. But during the whole hundred years the basket of figs and cruse of wine he had with him at the time of his death were perfectly preserved. Then Ezra said, "I know that God is able to do all these things."

11,465. RESURRECTION, Preventing the. A glorious company of martyrs, suffered death after enduring the most fearful tortures at Lyons, in A. D. 177, in the reign of Marcus Aurelius. Among them Pothinus, bishop of Lyons; Sanctus, a deacon; Maturus, a young convert; Blandina, a slave; Alexander, a physician, and Ponticus, a lad of fifteen. These all bore their sufferings cheerfully and heroically, and their very chains appeared more like the ornaments of a bride than the masks of malefactors. Their bodies were burned to ashes and the ashes were thrown into the Rhone. Their persecutors intended thereby to prevent their resurrection, hope of which they saw had animated the martyrs. "Let us see now," they said, "if they will return again to life, and whether their God can save them and deliver them out of our hands."

11,466. RESURRECTION, Promise of. One may occasionally see a plant which, through being under more favorable circumstances than its companions, appears with an early blade or leaves, while around it all others are torpid in the cold of winter. Such a plant is, as it were, the "first fruits of those that slept,"—the promise that the verdure of spring and the ripeness of summer will again cover the face of the earth. *Bib. Treas.*

11,467. RESURRECTION, Suggestions of the. Beside the principles of which we consist, and the actions which flow from us, the consideration of the things without us, and the natural course of variations in the creature, will render the resurrection yet more highly probable. Every space of twenty-four hours teacheth thus much, in which there is always a revolution amounting to a resurrection. The day dies into a night, and is buried in silence and in darkness; in the next morning it appeareth again and reviveth, opening the grave of darkness, rising from the dead of night; this is a diurnal resurrection. As the day dies into night, so doth the summer into winter: the sap is said to descend into the root, and there it lies buried in the ground; the earth is covered with snow, or crusted with frost, and becomes a general sepulchre; when the spring appeareth, all begin to rise; the plants and flowers peep out of their graves, revive, and grow, and flourish; this is the annual resurrection. *Dr. J. Pearson.*

11,468. RESURRECTION OF CHRIST, Emblem of the. We have contemplated Christ's humiliation: the Sun of Righteousness appeared as a setting sun gone out of sight. But as the sun, when to us it is set, begins a new day in another part of the world, so Christ, having finished his course in this world, rises again, and that to perform another glorious part of his work in the world above. *John Flavel.*

11,469. RESURRECTION OF CHRIST, Legend of the. After the resurrection of Christ, "he was seen of James." Jerome gives the following account of this appearance on the authority of the Hebrew Gospel of the Nazarenes. St. James had solemnly sworn, at the time he ate the last supper, that he would eat bread no more till he saw the Lord risen from the dead. After his resurrection our Lord went to James and ordered bread to be set before him, which he took, blessed, and brake, and gave to him, saying, "Eat thy bread, my brother, for the Son of man is truly risen from among them that sleep."

11,470. RESURRECTION OF CHRIST, Type of the. Christ is the "first-fruits of them that sleep." According to the Levitical law, before the harvest could be gathered, the sickle was to be put into the corn and the "sheaf of the first-fruits" was to be brought unto the priest who was to "wave the sheaf before the Lord." This sheaf was to be offered on the morrow after the Sabbath, that is, on the Lord's day —the day on which we celebrate the resurrec-

tion of Christ from the dead. What a wondrous figure of the resurrection of Christ! The waving is a sign of life, and he had life from the dead on the day after the Jewish Sabbath. The wave-sheaf too was an earnest that the whole field should be reaped, as well as a sample of the harvest. Christ therefore being raised, we shall all rise; and as Christ after his resurrection had the same moral character that he possessed before his death—loving his apostles spite of their forsaking him—so shall we be in the resurrection. *Pilkington.*

11,471. RETALIATION, Legal. MacDonald, a noted thief of Scotland, had committed many murders, and was unmercifully cruel. Once he nailed horseshoes to the feet of a poor widow, because, in her grief, she swore she would report him to the king. He was taken prisoner with twelve of his associates; and King James I. of Scotland caused them all in like manner to be shod and for three days they were driven about the city of Edinburgh a spectacle to the people, after which they were put to death.

11,472. RETALIATION, Synonym for. In one of the famous wars between Carthage and Rome, Hannibal, a Carthaginian leader, and one of the most wonderful men of antiquity, led his army into Italy, and for several years continued to threaten the city and lay waste the surrounding country. Scipio, a Roman general, saw the necessity of getting rid of Hannibal and his forces, and so determined to lead an army into Africa and threaten Carthage, and thus make it necessary for Hannibal to return home for its defence. This scheme had its intended effect; and in all after time this retaliating upon an enemy by adopting his own tactics, is called carrying the war into Africa. *Anon.*

11,473. RETREAT, Not Practiced in. A German story says that after the concert of the Prussian military in Paris, before the Emperor Napoleon III., he entered into conversation with Kapellmeister Parlow. In the course of the talk, the Emperor lifted one of the brass instruments, found it heavy, and asked: "Do your band-people wear their knapsacks in the field, as well as carry these things?" "Certainly, sire," answered Parlow. "But how," asked the emperor, "do they manage in retreat?" "Don't know, your Majesty; that's not practiced among our people." The subsequent German victories must have impressed the remark upon Napoleon.

11,474. RETRIBUTION, Call for. The Æqui made a league and swore fidelity to the Romans. They afterwards revolted, and began war. Ambassadors were sent to them demanding satisfaction, but they treated them with contempt, and bade them deliver their message to an oak that grew near by. Accordingly one of the ambassadors turned to the oak and said, "Thou hallowed oak, and whatever else belongs to the gods in this place, hear, and bear witness to this perfidiousness, and favor our just complaints, that by the assistance of the gods, we may be revenged of this perjury'

The Romans gave battle to the Æqui, and utterly destroyed the perjured nation.

11,475. RETRIBUTION, Emblem of. The war chariots of ancient times, armed with scythes and drawn by frantic steeds intended to mow down the ranks of the enemy, frequently returned upon their own friends and wrought the greatest havoc.

11,476. RETRIBUTION, Example of. Banishment was made a law by Celisthenes, an Athenian, and he was the first to suffer from it. Gryphus, king of Egypt, on coming in from the hunt, was offered by his mother a cup of poison. He had been forewarned, and insisted that she should drink of it first. He plainly told that he had heard of her intention, and in order to clear herself of such an accusation, there was no way for her but to drink it. The son stood by and saw the miserable queen take the poison, from the effects of which she soon after died.

11,477. RETRIBUTION, Fable of. A viper entering a smith's shop began looking about for something to eat. At length, seeing a file, he went up to it and commenced biting at it; but the file bade him to leave him alone, saying, "You are likely to get little from me, whose business it is to bite others." *Æsop.*

11,478. RETRIBUTION, Instrument of. Marius was a cutler by trade, and one of the Thirty Tyrants during the reign of Gallienus. He was chosen emperor one day, and reigned the next, and the third was slain by one of his soldiers, who, striking him, said, "This is with a sword which was made by thyself."

11,479. RETRIBUTION, Law of. An African slave trader received a pistol in exchange for a slave, whom he had stolen from his native freedom. He wore the pistol proudly in his belt. One day it was accidentally discharged, and the man-stealer was slain by the reward of his crime.

11,480. RETRIBUTION, Speedy. In the reign of Henry VII., Dr. Whittington, a bishop's chancellor, having condemned a pious woman to the flames at Ch'pping, Sodbury, went to that town to witness the courageous manner in which she set her seal to the truth of the gospel. On his return from that affecting scene, a furious bull passed through the crowd, none of whom suffered from him, gored the chancellor, and suddenly inflicted death in a most awful manner. *Whitecross.*

11,481. RETRIBUTION, Swift. A man in Germany sent a young girl with 200 florins, to a town among the mountains. She was overtaken by a person who offered to accompany her, and pretended to know a short cut to the town. He led her to the shaft of an unworked mine, intending to throw her into it and obtain her money. She gave him the money, and he ordered her to prepare for death. Just then his foot stumbled, and he fell to the bottom of the shaft, where he had expected to throw the poor girl. He was found there dead, with the money in his possession.

11,482. RETROSPECTION, Effect of. When I look upon the tombs of the great, every motion of envy dies; when I read the epitaphs of the beautiful, every inordinate desire forsakes me; when I meet with the grief of parents upon a tombstone, my heart melts with compassion; when I see the tombs of the parents themselves, I reflect how vain it is to grieve for those whom we must quickly follow; when I see kings lying beside those who deposed them, when I behold rival wits placed side by side, or the holy men who divided the world with their contests and disputes, I reflect with sorrow and astonishment on the frivolous competitions, factions, and debates of mankind. *Addison*

11,483. REUNION, Providential. At the time of the wreck of the Rothsay Castle, a father and child sought safety by climbing the mast, but the boy was not able to hold on, and was soon lost from the father. Next morning the father was rescued, and went reluctlantly ashore, thinking how he should meet his wife without the boy. The boy was picked up, taken ashore, and placed in the same bed with his father, unknown to each other or their rescuers, till they were clasped in each other's arms. It is easy for Omnipotence to reunite our scattered households in heaven.

11,484. REUNION, Unexpected. A commander of a British vessel of war, sailing from the Cape of Good Hope, was charged with the convoy of a little sloop to England, laden with an exceedingly valuable cargo. They were in mutual sight for many days, when a storm arose, and separated them so widely that, after the storm had passed, and the sea once more had become peaceful, they could not see each other. In vain the man-of-war searched the horizon to find her smaller and weaker consort. No trace of the sloop was to be found. With a heavy heart, the captain of the war ship pursued his course homeward, not expecting to see his little charge again. He entered the Channel, and anchored off Portsmouth, in a fog, saddened at the remembrance of the lost ship; but, when the thick fog lifted, what was his surprise at seeing the little lost craft anchored in peace directly by his side, having arrived at home before him! Each was ignorant of the course of the other, till they lay side by side at anchor in the harbor. So will it be with many who, by Providence, are separated from our families, our Sabbath-schools, our pastoral charges, to pursue the voyage of life without us, when we shall meet them at last in heaven, to go no more out forever Ignorance of their safety may distress us now, but when the darkness is passed, and the true light shineth, we shall welcome with delight those who may have reached the shining shore before us, or that shall come after. *Dr. S. H. Tyng.*

11,485. REVELATION, Need for. If Adam needed to hear his Father's voice, sounding amid the fair bowers and the unshaded glory of paradise, surely much more does this prodigal world, that has gone astray from him, need to hear a Father's voice asking after us, and the first intimations of a Father's desire that the lost may be found, and the dead at length become alive.   *Cumming.*

11,486. REVENGE, Bloody. Cyrus, the elder, by strategy defeated Spargapises, and he was brought bound before him. Cyrus ordered his fetters unloosed; and, in desperation, he slew himself. After this Cyrus was defeated, and Tamyris, mother of Spargapises, finding the dead body of Cyrus, caused his head to be cut off and to be thrown into a vessel filled with human blood, saying, "Satiate thyself with blood which thou hast so much thirsted after."

11,487. REVENGE, Characterized. Revenge is a cruel word; manhood, some call it; but it is rather doghood. The manlier any man is, the milder and more merciful.   *Trapp.*

11,488. REVENGE, Dearly Bought. A horse had the whole range of a meadow to himself; but a stag coming and damaging the pasture, the horse, anxious to have his revenge, asked a man if he could not assist him in punishing the stag. "Yes," said the man, "only let me put a bit in your mouth, and get upon your back, and I will find the weapons." The horse agreed, and the man mounted accordingly; but instead of getting his revenge, the horse has been from that time forward the slave of man.   *Æsop.*

11,489. REVENGE, Heathen. At the formation of the second Triumvirate, the sacrifice of that master of eloquence, Cicero, was agreed upon, and a large reward was offered for his head. He fled and might have escaped but for his own indecision. His murderers found him at his country villa, and severed his head from his body with the sword. They cut off his hands and carried them with his head to Antony. Forsyth says, "He was seated on a tribunal administering justice in the forum, when they made their way through the crowd with the ghastly relics in their hands. His eyes sparkled with joy, and he not only paid the promised reward, but added to it an enormous sum. What more precious gift could he present to his wife Fulvia than the head of their deadliest enemy? She took it, and placing it upon her lap, addressed it as if it were alive, in words of bitter insult. She dragged out the tongue, whose sarcasms she had often felt, and with feminine rage pierced it with her bodkin. It was then taken and nailed to the Rostra, to moulder there in mockery of his eloquence, of which that spot had so often been the scene. A sadder sight was never gazed upon in Rome."

11,490. REVENGE, Prevented. A Christian told Sisoes, the Theban, of his intention to revenge a wrong done him. He advised him against such a course, but to leave vengeance to God. "I will not; I cannot," said the man. Then they knelt together in prayer, and Sisoes prayed, "O God, take, we pray thee, no more concern about our affairs; be no longer our protector; we are going henceforth to manage for ourselves, avenge ourselves, and do all the rest that thou hast hitherto done for us!" The man became ashamed of himself, and abandoned his intention.

11,491. REVENGE, True. Diogenes being asked by what means a man might revenge himself upon his enemies, replied, "By becoming himself a good and honest man."

11,492. REVIVALS, Aim for. A pastor entering upon a new charge said to his people that his object in coming to them was to save sinners—that all his services would be aimed at that—and he wished the church to co-operate with him. This announcement was carried out for two years, and many hearts seemed to be centered upon that grand point. The people understood that their salvation was the object of every service. Some surrendered the first month, others the next, and so on during the whole term, and as they did so they fell into a line, and did what they could to save others. The result was over three hundred were added to the church, in monthly installments of from five to thirty, by the ordinary means of grace.   *Dr. James Porter.*

11,493. REVIVALS, Demand for. The churches need revivals. The constant tendency is to fall into routine and to run on in old ruts. The abiding need is of spontaneity. Solid forts are a necessity in war, so also are the light troops and the flying artillery. This need is most felt in old, well-established, and highly organized churches. When an iceberg breaks off in the far north, and floats southward in early summer, it cools the air and all water around. But when the Gulf Stream sends northward its southern waters, they carry to the shores of England and northern Europe something of a tropic summer. Those who come into a church in a revival come not as icebergs freighted with chills of death, but as the robins come, seemingly bringing the summer with them. New life is imparted to the church's activities, and the old members, like old trees in springtime, begin to bear fruit.   *Beecher.*

11,494. REVIVALS, Necessity of. My brethren, we must have revivals! It must rain faster, or we perish with drought! There is no such thing as a growing, progressive church without them; no such thing as a prosperous country without them. God has never multiplied his people, never built up his kingdom rapidly without them, and never will. This is the thought I would impress upon those who hear me—the indispensable necessity of revivals of religion to perpetuate the church and to convert the world. Revivals are necessary as a kind of substitute for miracles. God is the author of conversion; but not in the way of miracles—not without reference to and conformity with the laws of mind. Miracles cannot convert the soul. How many of those who witnessed the miracles of Christ, do you suppose, were converted by the prodigies that astounded them? Miracles had their use, but that use was not the conversion of the soul. But now their object is accomplished; the gospel is authenticated; the work is under motion. Hear the world roar as it rushes along; and see, as civilization advances, wealth accumulates, luxury abounds, and society rises higher and higher, how men dislike the humbling doctrines of the cross! Religion becomes offensive; the gospel is odious; and if they go on, they will scout it out of the world with their sneers and contempt. How are you to make head against all this accumulating hatred? By jogging along in the old orthodox way? No; men will go to hell by whole generations if something be not done. But go into a church filled with these gay, self-sufficient, contemptuous schemers, when the Spirit of God is abroad, and the atmosphere of revivals envelops the mass. Then see how they stir; what an arrest is put upon the current of their worldliness! The whole town is affected. Conviction spreads from heart to heart, like a fire in a dry forest. Everybody feels, and you cannot tell why. In Litchfield, during a great revival, I would hear of conversions taking place simultaneously ten miles apart, without any contact or intercommunion. The gospel then took hold. It was invested with a kind of almightiness. It is impossible for the truth to make such impression at any other time. We must have revivals, if the world is ever to be converted. To wait till the church is filled with the droppings of the sanctuary is to wait for ever.

Dr. Lyman Beecher.

11,495. REVIVALS, Renewal of. There was a heathen custom in Helvetia of celebrating the sun's return to heat and power, on what is now Easter eve. For some days previous all the fires were extinguished that they might be relighted from the sacred fires in the temple on Tara hill. The people waited for the appearance of this sacred flame, and hastened from it to rekindle the fires on their own cold hearths. On many a home altar the fire has gone out. These should all be rekindled from the sacred revival fires that blaze around us. If the sacred fire has gone out on the altar of our heart it is time to relight it.

11,496. REVIVALS, Secret of. A revival occurred in Orange county, New York, in the summer of 1828. The work began without any known cause. The inquiry was made, "Who is praying? This work must be in answer to somebody's prayers." If was afterwards learned that two old church members, who lived one mile apart, had made arrangements to meet half way between them in a piece of thick bushes every evening at sundown to pray God to revive his work. Their prayers were answered, and one hundred and fifty were added, during the months of July, August and September, to the church.

11,497. REVIVAL, Streams of. In the East the rivers in the dry seasons are little more than fleeting streams, and sometimes they are entirely evaporated by the powerful action of the sun's rays. The rainy season comes, and the beds of the ancient rivers begin to receive their annual tribute from the fruitful clouds; and the mountain torrent, rolling in its accustomed channel, causes the streams to return again, changing the sandy waste into a majestic river, raising the sower's hopes, replenish this parched land with the long-desired verdure, and man and beast again rejoice in the earth's abundance.   *W. Brown.*

11,498. REWARD, Expectation of. The Christian expects his reward, not as due to merit, but as connected, in a constitution of grace, with those acts which grace enables him to perform. The pilgrim who has been led to the gate of heaven will not knock there as worthy of being admitted; but the gate shall open to him, because he is brought thither. He who sows, even with tears, the precious seed of faith, hope, and love, shall "doubtless come again with joy and bring his sheaves with him," because it is in the very nature of that seed to yield, under the kindly influence secured to it, a joyful harvest.   *Cecil.*

11,499. REWARD, Greatness of God's. God's reward is exceeding great. He will also recompense our losses for his sake, as the king of Poland did his noble servant Zelilaus; having lost his hand in his wars, he sent him a golden hand for it; so Caius gave Agrippa, that had been imprisoned for his sake, a chain of gold as heavy as his chain of iron had been.

Trapp.

11,500. REWARD, Immediate. John Andrew Jones, a Baptist minister, whilst walking in Cheapside, London, was appealed to by some one he knew for help. He had but a shilling in the world, and questioned whether to give it or not. The distress of his friend prevailed, and the poor preacher gave away his last farthing. The promise come to his mind. "He that hath pity upon the poor lendeth to the Lord, and that which he hath given will he pay him again." He passed on a few yards only, before he met a gentleman who said, "Ah, Mr Jones, I am glad to see you. I have had this sovereign in my pocket this week past, for some poor minister, and you may as well have it." In relating the story, Mr. Jones usually added, "If I had not stopped to give relief, I should have missed the gentleman and the sovereign too."

11,501. REWARD, Penalty and. Cato, the elder, said he would rather not be rewarded for his good deeds than not punished for his evil deeds; and that at any time he could pardon all other offenders besides himself.

11,502. REWARD, Unexpected. A Paduca woman had been taken captive by the Pawnees and was to be put to death. She was fastened to the stake, and the wood was about to be set on fire, when the young chieftain of his tribe came to her rescue. He was mounted on a horse, and led another. To the astonishment of all, he rode up to the pile, freed her from the stake, placed her upon the other horse and carried her off in triumph. It was so unexpected that it was thought to be nothing less than the Great Spirit's ordering. The young chieftain took his captive to her home and friends, and returned to his tribe without censure. His conduct, though extraordinary, passed unnoticed by them, but a silver medal was awarded him by the pupils of a ladies' seminary in Washington, for having rescued one of their sex from so unnatural a fate. On receiving the medal he said, "I am glad my brothers and sisters have heard of the good act that I have done. I did it in ignorance, and did not know I did good; but by your giving me this medal I know it."

11,503. RICH, Poverty of the. A Boston five-millionaire refused to give a donation on the ground that he had many hundreds of thousands lying in the banks without interest. A New York twenty-millionaire will plead equal poverty. And the richest family in Mexico had several millions left them by their founder, and three millions more to the poor of Mexico, and appropriated it all to themselves as being the poor of Mexico. The only way is for every body to reckon himself rich, and to be liberal accordingly.   *Bp. Haven.*

11,504. RICHES, Biblical Figures of. *Thorns,* Matt. 13: 7; our Lord's figure of the two extremes which choke the word, "the care of this world, and the deceitfulness of riches." *Treasures* got with toil, kept with care, and always liable to be lost, Prov. 15: 16; 10: 2; Matt. 6: 19; Jer. 49: 4; James 5: 1, 2. *A strong city and high wall,* which the rich man in his "conceit" thinks to be "impregnable," Prov. 18: 11. *Thick clay,* Hab. 2: 6, with which covetous men load themselves, to their own sorrow and destruction. *A snare* or pit, 1 Tim. 6: 9, concealed in the ground, and covered over. *Deep and dangerous waters,* 1 Tim. 6: 9, where sailors are driven upon the rocks and shipwrecked. *The sweet morsel* quickly swallowed down, and as quickly cast up again, Job 20: 15. *Vanity* (Heb. a vapor), "tossed to and fro of them that seek death," Prov. 21: 6. *The partridge sitting on eggs, and hatching them not,* Jer. 17: 11. One of the large speculators in the railway mania many years ago becoming deeply involved, committed suicide, and left on his desk a paper, with written on it, Jer. 17: 11.   *Bowes.*

11,505. RICHES, Contented without. Upon the best observation I could ever make, I am induced to believe that it is much easier to be contented without riches than with them. It is so natural for a rich man to make his gold his god; for whatever a person loves most, that thing, be it what it will, he will certainly make his god. It is so difficult not to trust in it, not to depend upon it for support and happiness, that I do not know one rich man in the world with whom I would exchange conditions.   *Mrs. Wesley.*

11,506. RICHES, Despising. In St. Mark's church, Venice, will be found the tomb of Duke Sebastian Foscarinus. Upon it are inscribed these words, "Hear, O ye Venetians! and I will tell you which is the best thing in the world; it is to contemn and despise riches."

11,507. RICHES, Dissatisfied with. A gentleman of vast fortune sent for a friend to settle some affairs; and while they were together, he walked to the window, and observed a chimney-sweeper's boy with his sack passing by. His friend was surprised to see the tears burst from his eyes; and, clasping his hands, he exclaimed—"Now would I give every shilling I am worth in the world to change beings with that little sweep!"   *Buck.*

11,508. RICHES, Fleeting Na ure of. Solomon compares wealth to a wild fowl. Riches make themselves wings; they fly away as an eagle towards heaven; (Prov. 23: 5;) not some tame house-bird, or a hawk that may be fetched down with a lure, or found again by her bells; but an eagle, that violently cuts the air, and is gone past recalling. Wealth is like a bird; it hops all day from man to man, as that doth from tree to tree; and none can say where it will roost or rest at night. It is like a vagrant fellow, which because he is big-boned, and able to work, a man takes in a-doors, and cherisheth; and perhaps for a while he takes pains; but when he spies opportunity the fugitive servant is gone, and takes away more with him than all his service came to. The world may seem to stand thee in some stead for a reason, but at last irrevocably runs away, and carries with it thy joys; thy goods, as Rachel stole Laban's idols; thy peace and content of heart goes with it, and thou art left desperate.
Adams.

11,509. RICHES, Gathering and Scattering. An old woman, who showed the house and pictures at Towchester, England, said, "That is Sir Robert Farmer; he lived in the country, took care of his estate, built this house and paid for it; managed well, saved money and died rich: —This is his son. He was made a lord, took a place at court, spent his estate, and died a beggar!"

11,510. RICHES, Haste for. I see put up over business men's desks sometimes, "A penny saved is a penny earned," "Time is money," and a great many other whetstone maxims to make men sharp for this world. I have thought it might be well to put up some other things in business establishments for the benefit of the young men connected with them; and it would not hurt the principals to look at them. I would put up the picture of a gallows, of a poor-house, of a penitentiary, of the yard with its striped inmates, and of reeling drunkards; and above these I would have this motto: "The paradise of smart young men!" For cause produces effect; and they are constantly doing the things which lead to such a paradise. And when they have come to it they are in dismay, and they say, "How did this befall me?" It is as if a man should fall into the water, and then say, "Astonishing that I am wet!" Would it not be astonishing if he were not? It is as if a man should put his hand in the fire, and say, "Why, it burns!" Did fire ever do anything else? Young men set out to achieve success in forbidden ways, and they have only succeeded in cheating themselves; and they are amazed. They meant to have riches without earning them, and the result is that they are poverty-stricken through and through. They meant to take advantage of everybody's trust for their own benefit. By and by everybody loses confidence in them and when they are mildewed and blasted, and nobody will trust them, they think the world is hard and inhospitable. *Beecher.*

11,511. RICHES, Heavenly. O blinder than beetles! The merchant refuseth no adventure for hope of gain; the hunter shrinketh at no weather for love of game; the soldier declineth no danger for desire either of glory or spoil: and shall we frame to ourselves either an ease in not understanding, or an idleness in not using those things which will be a means to us not only to avoid intolerable and endless pains, but to attain both immeasurable and immortal glory, pleasure and gain? *Hayward.*

11,512. RICHES, Inconstancy of. A few years since those giants of the Stock Exchange, Drew and Vanderbilt, were contending for the control of the Erie Railroad. The wealth of either was counted by millions. The eyes of the nation and the world were upon them. Mr. Beecher looking on said, "Oh God, who are these men? With phosphoric light I see standing over their portals the Divine handwriting, ' Fool! fool!' And God says to them, ' In a year or two whose shall these things be?'" The first of these men *lost* his wealth; the second *left* his.

11,513. RICHES, Marrying for. It is better for a man to be chained with fetters of gold, as they bind their prisoners in Ethiopia, than to be tied to the riches of a wife.
Pisias in Plutarch.

11,514. RICHES, Passion for. The taste for real glory and real greatness declines more and more amongst us every day. New-raised families, intoxicated with their sudden increase of fortune, and whose extravagant expenses are insufficient to exhaust the immense treasures they have heaped up, lead us to look upon nothing as truly great and valuable but wealth, and that in abundance; so that not only poverty, but a moderate income, is considered as an insupportable shame; and all merit and honor are made to consist in the magnificence of our buildings, furniture, equipage, and tables. *Rollin.*

11,515. RICHES, Safe Growth of. If men were content to grow rich somewhat more slowly, they would grow rich much more surely. If they would use their capital within reasonable limits, and transact with it only so much business as it could fairly control, they would be far less liable to lose it. Excessive profits always involve the liability of great risks—as in a lottery, in which there are high prizes, there must be a great proportion of blanks.
Wayland.

11,516. RICHES, Snares of. Riches is compared to sharp stakes, or other piercing things, 1 Tim. 6: 10. The word περιεπειραν signifies to be transfixed in every part, and probably refers to one of the snares or pits spoken of, ver. 9, where a hole is dug in the earth, and filled with sharp stakes, then slightly covered over, so that whatever steps on it, falls in, and is "pierced through" with much pain and suffering. *Dr. A. Clarke.*

11,517. RICHES, Unhappy with. Stephen Girard, of Philadelphia, the infidel founder of Girard College, into which all clergymen are forbidden to enter, when surrounded by immense wealth, and supposed to be taking supreme delight in its accumulation, wrote thus to a friend: "As to myself, I live like a galley slave, constantly occupied, and often passing the night without sleeping. I am wrapped in a labyrinth of affairs, and worn out with care. I do not value fortune. The love of labor is my highest emotion. When I rise in the morning, my only effort is to labor so hard during the day that when night comes I may be enabled to sleep soundly."

11,518. RICHES, Use of. Let rich men therefore take heed how they handle their thorns; let them gird up the loins of their minds, lest their long garments hinder them in the way to heaven; let them see to it, that they be not tied to their abundance, as little Lentulus was said to have been to his long sword; that they be not held prisoners in those golden fetters, as the king of Armenia was by Antony, and so sent by him as a present to Cleopatra; lest at length they send their mammon of unrighteousness, as Crœsus did his fetters, for a present to the devil, who had deluded him with false hopes of victory. *Trapp.*

11,519. RICHES, Worshiping. There were those among the heathen that worshiped the emerald as the true deity. The sick made pilgrimages to worship it, and there offered their gifts. The descendants of the treasure-worshipers have spread over the whole earth.

11,520. RIGHT, Departure from. Men begin and say, "The right." It seems hard to forget themselves: so they say, "The right and I." That serves their turn, so they take another step, and say, "I and the right." That does a good deal better; and they end by saying, "I without the right or against it." Thus they go to the devil and nobody cares how soon. God honors him who says "The right."
Theodore Parker.

11,521. RIGHT is Might. A man is right and invincible, virtuous, and on the road towards sure conquest, precisely while he joins himself to the great deep law of the world, in spite of all superficial laws, temporary appearances, profit-and-loss calculation;—he is victorious while he co-operates with that great central law—not victorious otherwise; and surely his first chance of co-operating with it, or getting into the course of it, is to know with his own soul that it is—that it is good, and alone good. This is the soul of Islam; it is properly the soul of Christianity; for Islam is definable as a confused form of Christianity; had Christianity not been, neither had it been. Christianity also commands us, before all, to be resigned to God. We are to take no counsel with flesh and blood; give ear to no vain cavils, vain sorrows and wishes; to know that we know nothing; that the worst and cruelest to our eyes is not what it seems; that we have to receive whatsoever befalls us as sent from God above, and say, "It is good and wise—God is great! Though he slay me, yet will I trust in him." Islam means in its way denial of self—annihilation of self. This is yet the highest wisdom that heaven has revealed to our earth. *Carlyle.*

11,522. RIGHT, Universality of. In the army drinking and treating customs were general. One noble captain had the heroism to decline the often proffered treat. An observer asked him, "Do you always reject intoxicating liquor?" "Yes." "Do you not take it to correct this Yazoo water?" "Never." "You must have belonged to the cold water army in your boyhood." "Yes; but I learned something better than that; my mother taught me what is right is right, and coming to Mississippi don't make any difference. It would not be right for me to accept an invitation to drink at home; it is no more right here; therefore, I don't drink." This rule should be reduced to universal practice. The narrator of the above afterward met a mother who wanted to see some one who had met her boy, naming his office and regiment. He told her of the noble examples of piety which were found in the army, and related the case of the captain. She exclaimed, "That's beautiful! that's beautiful! his mother must be proud of him." "Yes," said he, "she is, and you are the proud mother." Amid grateful tears, she exclaimed, "Is that my boy?—is that my Will? It's just like him; I knew he would do so. He always was a good boy; he told me he always would be, and I knew he would." The mother and son were worthy of each other. We want a world full of such mothers and sons.

11,523. RIGHTEOUS, Death of the. In the article of death, the righteous have glorious prerogatives. The truth of this principle is generally admitted. We do not hear men exclaiming, "Let me die the death of the philosopher!" in whatever terms they express their admiration of his talents, his experiments and his discoveries; or, "Let me die the death of the warrior!" with whatever ardor they celebrate his martial virtues and his military achievements; or, "Let me die the death of the statesman!" whatever encomiums they may be disposed to pass on his political abilities. No, their language is, "Let me die the death of the righteous, and let my last end be like his." *James Dore.*

11,524. RIGHTEOUSNESS, Garment of. In feudal times, when bishops held their strong castles and had numerous fighting men, one of them fought at the head of his retainers against King Richard, and being taken prisoner, was confined in one of the king's castles. The pope hearing this, sent an ambassador to the king, saying, "Set my son free." One of the courtiers at the king's order brought forward the prelate's helmet and coat of mail, and the king, turning to the ambassador, said, "Go ask hy master is this thy son's coat or no?" The world requires that the servants of Christ should wear the garment of righteousness.

11,525. RIGHTEOUSNESS, Human. God pronounces our righteousness—observe, not our wickednesses, but our devotions, our charities, our costliest sacrifices, our most applauded services—to be filthy rags. Trust not, therefore, to them. What man in his senses would think of going to court in rags, in rags to wait upon a king? Nor think that the righteousness of the cross was wrought to patch up these, to supplement, as some say, what is either defective or altogether a-wanting in our personal merits; nor fancy, like some who would embrace a Saviour, and yet keep their sins, that you may wear these rags beneath his righteousness. Away with them; not as a dress, which one may lay aside, to be afterwards resumed; but cast them away, as the beggar who, having got better clothing, throws his rags into the nearest ditch, and leaves them there to rottenness and decay. You cannot otherwise be saved. *Dr. Guthrie.*

11,526. RIGHTEOUSNESS, Robe of. When our war was going on, men used to come to enlist, and the man who came with a fine suit of clothes on, and the hod-carrier in his dirty garments, would both have to take off their clothes and put on the uniform of the Government. And so, when men go into the kingdom of God, they have to put on the livery of heaven. You need not dress up for Christ, because he will strip you when you come, and put on you the robes of his righteousness. *Moody.*

11,527. RIGHTEOUSNESS, Sun of. Anaxagoras, the philosopher, being asked what he was born for, answered, "To see the heavens, the sun and the moon." Eudoxus, another philosopher, said, "He could be content to perish could he get so near the sun as to learn the nature of it." How much greater delight can the Christian enjoy in the beams of the Sun of Righteousness?—in the Creator of the world's luminary?

11,528. RITUALISM Unchristian. Some brethren cannot preach without the gown and the cassock, and some without the altar, and some without five thousand pieces of frippery. Any one who chooses to reason will say, "This cannot be the religion of Christ's open-air sermons on the mountain top; this cannot be the religion of the dozen poor fishermen who 'turned the world upside down;' this cannot be the religion of Paul, who preached the gospel of Christ, dressed in common garb, with no altar or tools to use, only his simple tongue, and won souls for his Master." *Spurgeon*

11,529. ROCK, Founded on. A young minister in Wales, going to a very exposed locality, slept at a farm house on the highest point of land in the country. He retired to rest, when the wind blew a tempest, the rain beat upon the house heavily, and he feared it must fall. He could not rest; he rose, sat by the fire and prepared for the worst. But it stood firm and unshaken. The morning came; the minister expressed his fears, and felt very timid, and wondered how the farmer could sleep so securely, exposed to such a storm. "Oh," said the farmer, "I had no fear of the house falling, and you need not to have feared either for it is founded upon a rock."

11,530. ROCK, Our. There was a certain nobleman who kept a deistical chaplain and his lady a Christian one. When he was dying he said to his chaplain, "I liked you very well when I was in health, but it is my lady's chaplain I must have when I am sick." How true "their rock is not as our rock, our enemies themselves being judges!" *Whitefield.*

11,531. ROCK OF AGES, Building on the. A soldier asked a delegate of the Christian Commission, "Won't you please tell me how I may build on the 'Rock'?' I was thinking of it while on guard, the other day." He told his story in brief: He was from New York City, had received his mother's dying blessing. Before she breathed her last, she sang this hymn and said, "George, my son, I would not feel so badly about your enlisting, if you were only built upon that 'Rock.'" These sacred memories were revived by the singing of the hymn, Rock of Ages; and as the delegate and soldier knelt on the dusty road-side, beneath the stars, the wanderer lost his weariness and thirst for sin, in the shadow of the "Rock of Ages." *G. Bringhurst.*

11,532. ROD, Kissing the. Tiribazus, a Persian nobleman, was approached by officers for the purpose of arresting him. He drew his sword to defend himself, but when he learned it was only desired to bring him into the presence of the king, he yielded with joy. Afflictions are God's messengers to bring us into his presence.

11,533. ROGUES, City of. King Philip built a city which he named Poneropolis or Roguetown, and in it he placed a colony of rogues and vagabonds. It is a symbol of the minds of the vicious full of wickedness of every kind and age.

11,534. ROMANISM, Conversion from. A Romanist, in California, was called upon to pray with a dying neighbor. He said he was a Catholic and could read a prayer if he had a book. This was not desired, a praying Methodist was sent for, who came, read the Scriptures, and prayed most fervently, to the great comfort of the dying man. The Romanist went home in thoughtful mood, and related the matter to his family. "This Methodist religion," said he, "in new. I would like to know more about it. This kind of praying has a wonderful effect." In a short time a Bible agent called, and the Romanist purchased a Bible and commenced "searching the Scriptures" with great earnestness. The Spirit wrought conviction in his heart, and his wife and grown-up daughter were equally earnest inquirers after the truth as it is taught in the Gospel. In a few weeks they were all happy in the love of the Saviour.

11,535. ROMANISM, Unscriptural. Papist missionaries went among the New Zealand converts and tried to lead them to worship the Virgin Mary, pray to the saints, and use images. They urged the authority of the Church of Rome, of the supremacy of the pope, of the antiquity of the Romish communion. The New Zealanders knew the Bible, and they heard all this calmly, and gave this memorable answer: "It cannot be true, because it is not in the Book." Ryle says, "All the learning in the world could never have supplied a better answer than that. Latimer, or Knox, or Owen, could never have made a more crushing reply."

11,536. RUBICON, Passing the. When Cæsar undertook the conquest of Italy, the act of crossing the river Rubicon was the first and significant step of the enterprise. Hence the phrase—"to pass the Rubicon"—signifies to take the decisive step by which one is committed to a hazardous or difficult enterprise. *Dr. Webster.*

11,537. RUDENESS, Folly of. Nothing is more silly than the pleasure some people take in "speaking their minds." A man of this make will say a rude thing for the mere pleasure of saying it, when an opposite behavior, full as innocent, might have preserved his friend, or made his fortune. *Steele.*

11,538. RUDENESS Prohibited. A man has no more right to say an uncivil thing than to act one; no more right to say a rude thing to another, than to knock him down. *Johnson.*

11,539. RUMORS, Spreading. The art of spreading rumors may be compared to the art of pin-making. There is usually some truth, which I call the wire; as this passes from hand to hand, one gives it a polish, another a point, others make and put on the head, and at last the pin is completed. *John Newton.*

11,540. RUM, Attendant of. At a railroad station recently an anxious inquirer came up to the door of the baggage-car and said: "Is there anything for me?" After some search among boxes and trunks, the baggage-master rolled out a keg of whiskey. "Anything more?" asked the grocer. "Yes," said the baggage-man, "there's a gravestone that goes with that liquor."

11,541. RUMSELLER, Criminality of the. Any young man found drunk should be imprisoned and his term increased for each offence. The man who sells intoxicating beverages is a greater criminal and with less excuse. He goes into the business with a perfect knowledge of the fact that he is going to earn his living by the ruin of his fellow-men. He is morally responsible for the crimes that men commit who are made criminals by him, and he ought to be penally responsible. Every day that he carries on the business is fraught with great evil, since it has nothing in it but the essence of crime and deviltry. His name should be written on the list of criminals high above that of murderers, robbers, ravishers, and thieves, as the greatest criminal of them all. *Bp. Foster.*

11,542. SABBATH, American. Agassiz was asked what impressed him most on his arrival in this country. He answered, "The quiet of an American Sabbath."

11,543. SABBATH, Conditions of Keeping the. Two ministers undertook to correct an indolent young man for Sabbath-breaking. The first spoke solemnly on the command, "Remember the Sabbath-day to keep it holy." The other said, "You have forgotten one-half of the commandment; 'Six days shalt thou labor, and do all thy work,' for if a man does not labor six days of the week, he is not likely to rest properly on the seventh."

11,544. SABBATH, Desecration of the. The importance of the religious observance of the Sabbath is seldom sufficiently estimated. The violation of this duty by the young is one of the most decided marks of incipient moral degeneracy. Religious restraint is fast losing its hold upon that young man, who, having been educated in the fear of God, begins to spend the Sabbath in idleness, or in amusement. And so also of communities. The desecration of the Sabbath is one of those evident indications of that criminal recklessness, that insane love of pleasure, and that subjection to the government of appetite and passion, which forebodes that the "beginning of the end" of social happiness, and of true national prosperity, has arrived. *Wayland.*

11,545. SABBATH, Emblem of the. The green oasis, the little grassy meadow in the wilderness, where, after the week-days' journey, the pilgrim halts for refreshment and repose; where he rests beneath the shade of the lofty palm-trees, and dips his vessel in the waters of the calm, clear stream, and recovers his strength to go forth again upon his pilgrimage in the desert with renewed vigor and cheerfulness. *Reade.*

11,546. SABBATH, The Last. When that last Sabbath comes—the Sabbath of all creation—the heart, wearied with its tumultuous beatings, shall have rest; the soul, fevered with its anxieties, shall enjoy peace. The Sun of that Sabbath will never set, or hide his splendors in a cloud. The flowers that grow in its light will never fade. Our earthly Sabbaths are but dim reflections of the heavenly Sabbath, cast down upon the earth, dimmed by the transit of their rays from so great a height and so distant a world. The fairest landscapes, or combinations of scenery upon earth, are but the outskirts of the paradise of God, foreearnests and intimations of that which lies beyond them; and the happiest Sabbath-heart, whose every pulse is a Sabbath-bell, hears but a very inadequate echo of the chimes and harmonies of that Sabbath, that rest, where we "rest not day and night," in which the song is ever new, and yet ever sung.
Dr. Cumming.

11,547. SABBATH-BREAKER, Fate of the. A worldly man, living on the shores of a beautiful lake, built a yacht for pleasure excursions. The minister called upon him, and expressed his fears that it would demoralize the young people, and prove a Sabbath-breaker. The man said, defiantly, "That is just what I'll name my boat. She shall be called the Sabbath-breaker." She was launched upon a Sunday, and her trial trip was made also on a Sunday. Many were invited to the excursion. Her ill-omened name floated on the flag, and caused many to refuse to go on board. A large company went, and mirth and music

made them forget their fears. Suddenly, a flaw of wind struck the boat. She capsized, and fifty of her passengers were drowned. Just above the water floated her name, "The Sabbath-breaker."

11,548. SABBATH-BREAKER, Heaven of the. There is a place in Paris, called the Champs-Elysées, or the plain of heaven, a beautiful public walk, with trees and gardens. It is the chief scene of their Sabbath desecration, and an awful scene it is! Oh, thought I, if this be the heaven the Parisian loves, he will never enjoy the pure heaven that is above. *M'Cheyne.*

11,549. SABBATH BREAKING, Effects of. In New Hampshire there were two neighborhoods —the one of six families, the other of five families. The six families disregarded the Sabbath. In time, five of these families were broken up by the separation of husbands and wives; the other by the father becoming a thief. Eight or nine of the parents became drunkards, one committed suicide, and all came to penury. Of some forty or fifty descendants, about twenty are known to be drunkards and gamblers and dissolute. Four or five have been in State prison. One fell in a duel. Some are in the almshouse. Only one became a Christian, and he after first having been outrageously dissipated. The other five families that regarded the Sabbath were all prospered. Eight or ten of the children are consistent members of the Church. Some of them became officers in the Church; one is a minister of the gospel; one is a missionary to China. No poverty among any of them. The homestead is now in the hands of the third generation. Those who have died, have died in the peace of the gospel. Oh! is there nothing in remembering God's holy day? *Talmage.*

11,550. SABBATH BREAKING, Excuse for. A Syrian convert to Christianity was ordered by his employer to work on Sunday, but he declined. "But," said the master, "does not the Master say that if a man has an ox or an ass that falls into a pit on the Sabbath day, he may pull him out?" "Yes," answered Hayop, "but if the ass has a habit of falling into the same pit every Sabbath day, then the man should either fill up the pit or sell that ass."

11,551. SABBATH-BREAKING, Legend of. A German legend says that ages ago an old man went into the forest one Sunday morning to cut wood. Having gathered a bundle of sticks he threw it over his shoulder and took his way homeward. He met a man in Sunday clothes, going towards the Church, who asked him. "Do you know that this is Sunday on earth, when all must rest from their labors?" "Sunday on earth or Monday in heaven, it is all the same to me," laughed the Sabbath-breaker. "Then bear your bundle for ever," answered the stranger; "and as you value not Sunday on earth, yours shall be a perpetual Monday in heaven; and you shall stand for eternity in the moon, a warning to all Sabbath-breakers." Thereupon the man was caught up into the moon, where he has stood with the bundle on his back ever since.

11,552. SACRAMENT, Reconciliation before the. George IV. desired the sacrament and sent for the Bishop of Winchester to administer it. He became angry with the messenger he sent, because of what he considered unnecessary delay. He reprimanded the servant, discharged him, and immediately requested the bishop to proceed. This the bishop refused while any anger remained in the king's mind toward any fellow-creature. The king, recollecting himself, said, "My lord, you are right." He then sent for the offending servant, became reconciled to him and restored him to his place, after which the sacrament was duly administered.

11,553. SACRIFICE, Beneficial. If thy foot or thy hand happen to be mortified, thou wilt give money to the chirurgeon to cut them off. Calypso presented Ulysses with a robe breathing forth the sweet-scented odor of an immortal body, which she put on him as a token of the love she had borne him. But when his ship was cast away and himself ready to sink to the bottom, not being able to keep above the water by reason of his wet robe which weighed him down, he put it off and threw it away. Afterwards he was safely landed, and wanted neither food nor raiment. *Plutarch.*

11,554. SACRIFICE, Loyal. Xerxes, in fleeing from Greece, took refuge in a boat. So many crowded upon its decks, there was danger of its sinking. Xerxes, seeing the danger, exclaimed, "Since upon you, O Persians, depends the safety of your king, let me know how far you take yourselves to be concerned therein." He had no sooner spoken, before most of them had jumped into the sea, and so insured the life of their king.

11,555. SACRIFICE, A Mother's. An Italian mother felt herself stricken with the plague, and, anxious lest her two boys should be infected, she locked the children into a room, and left the house. She denied herself the pleasure of a last embrace. Her eldest child saw her from the window. "Good-bye, mother," said he, wondering why his mother left him so strangely. "Good-bye, mother," repeated the youngest child, stretching his little hand out of the window. The mother paused: her heart was drawn toward her children, and she was on the point of returning: she struggled hard, while the tears rolled down her cheeks at the sight of her helpless babes. At length she turned from them. The children continued to cry, "Good-bye, mother." The sounds sent a thrill of anguish to her heart; but she pressed on to the pest house, where she died in two days.

11,556. SACRIFICE, Necessity for. Arnot represents Christ as a King's son, who offered himself as a hostage for certain rebellious subjects. He took their place and they were set free. Because they were freed he must bear the punishment due them.

11,557. SACRIFICE, Patriotic. It was told Codrus, the seventeenth king of Athens, that the oracle had promised his enemies, the Dorians and Heraclidæ, that they should gain a victory over him if his life should be spared. Thereupon, in the year 1068 B. C., he devoted himself to death to save his country.

11,558. SACRIFCE, Prevalence of. Its universal prevalence is an irrefragable evidence of one out of two facts. It is either a proof that the doctrine was taught by the common progenitor of mankind, to whom it was in some way supernaturally communicated; or that was an instinct implanted by the Author of our being, which, like all other instincts, must meet with its appropriate answer. *T. Ragg.*

11,559. SACRIFICE, Work not. Dr. Livingstone, in writing of the dangers he had to undergo in his missionary travels in South Africa, said, "I do not mention these privations as if I consider them to be 'sacrifices,' for I think that the word ought never to be applied to anything we can do for him who came down from heaven and died for us."

11,560. SACRILEGE, Punishment of. The spirit of God will not endure to have holy things profaned as if they were common or unclean. Belshazzar converted the consecrated vessels of the temple into instruments of luxury and intemperance; but the Lord tempered his wine with dregs, and made them prove unto him as cups of trembling and astonishment. Herod polluted the sepulchres of the saints with a sacrilegious search for treasures, presumed to have been there hidden, and God made fire rise out of the earth, to devour the over-busy searchers. Antiochus ransacked the temple of the Lord; Heliodorus emptied the treasures of their consecrated money; Pompey defiled the Sabbath and the sanctury; Crassus robbed the house of God of ten thousand talents. But enquire into the event of these insolences; and we shall find that true then, of which later ages have given many examples and are still likely to give more, that stolen bread hath gravel in it to choke those that devour it—that ruin is ever the child of sacrilege—that mischief setteth a period to the lives and designs of profane men.

Bp. Reynolds.

11,561. SAFETY, A Christian's. A British subject may be safe, although surrounded by enemies in a distant land—not that he hath strength to contend alone against armed thousands, but because he is a subject of our queen. A despot on his throne, a horde of savages in their desert, have permitted a helpless traveler to pass unharmed, like a lamb among lions—although like lions looking on a lamb, they thirsted for his blood—because they knew his sovereign's watchfulness, and feared his sovereign's power. The feeble stranger has a charmed life in the midst of his enemies, because a royal arm unseen encompasses him as with a shield. The power thus wielded by an earthly throne may suggest and symbolize the perfect protection of Omnipotence. A British subject's confidence in his queen may rebuke the feeble faith of a Christian. *Arnot.*

11,562. SAINTS, Company of the. These glorious citizens of the heavenly Jerusalem, he has chosen out of all the tribes of the children of Israel, and out of all nations, without any distinction of Greek or barbarian; persons of all ages, shewing there is no age which is not ripe or fit for heaven; and out of all states and conditions; in the throne, amidst the pomp of worldly grandeur; in the cottage, in the army, in trade, in the magistracy; clergymen, monks, virgins, married persons, widows, slaves, and freemen. In a word, what state is there that has not been honored with its saints? And they were all made saints by the very occupations of their states, and by the ordinary occurrences of life, prosperity and adversity; health and sickness, honor and contempt, riches and poverty—all which they made the means of their sanctification by the constant exercise of patience, humility, meekness, charity, resignation, and devotion. This is the manifold grace of God. He has employed all means; he has set all things at work to shew in ages to come the abundant riches of his grace. How do these happy souls, eternal monuments of God's infinite power and clemency, praise his goodness without ceasing! I will sing to the Lord, for he hath triumphed gloriously, etc. And casting their crowns before his throne, they give to him all the glory of their triumphs. *Alban Butler.*

11,563. SAINTS, Imitation of the. To animate and encourage ourselves in the vigorous pursuit of Christian perfection, and in advancing towards the glory of the saints, we ought often to lift up our eyes to heaven, and contemplate these glorious conquerors of the world, clothed with robes of immortality, and say to ourselves: "These were once mortal, weak men, subject to passions and miseries as we are now: and if we are faithful to our sacred engagements to God, we shall very shortly be made companions of their glory, and attain to the same bliss." But for this we must walk in their steps; that is to say, we must with them take up our cross, renounce the world and ourselves, and make our lives a course of labor, prayer, and penitence. We are lost if we seek any other path. We must either renounce the world and the flesh with the saints, or we renounce heaven with the wicked. *Alban Butler.*

11,564. SAINTS, Worship of the. Soon after the coronation of Henry II. of France, a tailor was apprehended for working on a saint's day; and, being asked why he gave such offence to religion, his reply was, "I am a poor man, and have nothing but my labor to depend upon; necessity requires that I should be industrious, and my conscience tells me there is no day but the Sabbath which I ought to keep sacred from labor." He was committed to prison, and being brought to trial, was condemned to be burnt.

11,565. SALVATION, Anxiety for. A vessel struck on the rocks. She had only one lifeboat. In that the passengers and the crew were going ashore. The vessel was sinking deeper and deeper. A little girl stood on the deck, waiting for her turn to get into the boat. The boat came and went repeatedly, but her turn did not seem to come. She could wait

no longer, and leaped on the taffrail, and then sprang into the sea, crying, "Save me next! Save me next!"

11,566. SALVATION, Condition of. A young lady, while crossing the ice, fell through. A gentleman, hearing her cry for help, hastened to the spot. He put out both hands, saying, "Clasp my hands tightly, and I will save you." She replied, "O, I cannot lift up both hands, one rests upon the ice; were I to raise it I should surely sink." He answered, "Let go your hold upon the ice; trust me, and I will save you; were I to take but one I could not draw you out." She obeyed and he drew her out rejoicing. So Christ waits to save imperiled sinners, but they must give him both hands, and trust him fully.

11,567. SALVATION, Co-operation in. A little girl fell into a cistern, and called loudly for help, when her mother hastened to her rescue. Telling how she was saved, she said, "I reached up as far as I could and mother did the rest." So Christ saves the sinner.

11,568. SALVATION, Earnestness for. A number of years ago a vessel was wrecked. The lifeboats were not enough to take all the passengers. A man who was swimming in the water swam up to one of the life-boats that were full and seized it with his hand. They tried to prevent him, but the man was terribly in earnest about saving his life, and one of the men in the boat just drew a sword and cut off his hand. But the man didn't give up; he reached out the other hand. He was terriby in earnest. He wanted to save his life. But the man in the boat took the sword and cut off his other hand. But the man did not give up. He swam up to the boat and he seized it with his teeth. Some of them said, "Let us not cut his head off," and they drew him in. That man was terribly in earnest. His earnestness saved him.   *Moody.*

11,569. SALVATION, False Ways of. They are climbing up a steep precipice of ice, toiling hard and yet slipping backwards as fast they climb. They are pouring water into a cask full of holes, laboring busily, and yet no nearer the end of their work than when they began. They are rowing a boat against a rapid stream, plying the oar diligently, and yet in reality losing ground every minute. They are trying to build up a wall of loose sand, wearing themselves out with fatigue, and yet seeing their work roll down on them as fast as they throw it up. They are trying to pump dry a sinking ship. The water gains on them and they will soon be drowned. Such is the experience, in every part of the world, of all who think to cleanse themselves from their sins.   *Ryle.*

11,570. SALVATION First. A boy was bathing in a river, and, getting out of his depth, was on the point of sinking, when he saw a wayfarer coming by, to whom he called out for help with all his might and main. The man began to read the boy a lecture for his fool-hardiness; but the urchin cried out, "O, save me now, sir! and read me the lecture afterwards."   *Æsop*

11,571. SALVATION, Interest in. As we prize any good, so we labor more or less to assure ourselves of it. If a prince should lose a pin from his sleeve or a penny out of his purse, and one should bring him news it is found, the things are so inconsiderable that he would not care whether it were true or not. But if his kingdom lay at stake in the field, and intelligence comes that his army hath got the day, and beaten the enemy, O how he would long to have his hope, that is now raised a little, confirmed more strongly by another post! Is heaven worth so little that you can be satisfied with a few probabilities and uncertainties? Thou basely despisest that blessed place, if thou be no more solicitous to know the truth of thy title to it. At the cost of all else secure that.   *Gurnall.*

11,572. SALVATION, Life-boat of. A man strolled out to a rock in the sea at ebb-tide, amused himself upon it till he was weary, and lying down to rest, fell asleep. When he awoke the tide returning had cut off his retreat to the shore, and the sea would soon cover the place on which he stood. He could not swim, and had no boat by which to escape. Death confronted him; he raised a signal of distress. It was seen from the shore, and a life-boat hastened to his rescue. He sprang into it, exclaiming, "Thank God, I am saved." This imperiled man represents the sinner; the life-boat is Christ. To yield all to him is to be saved.

11,573. SALVATION, Method of. A poor man, in crossing a heath in the dark, missed his way, and fell into a pit; but, although considerably injured, he was not killed. After being in the pit for some hours, his cries for help brought several persons to his assistance, who threw him the end of a rope, and promised to draw him from his wretched situation, if he would lay hold of it. He did so, and was saved. Now, that poor man, as soon as he saw the rope, believed there was deliverance for him: that was the faith of credence. But when he took hold of the rope, and was delivered, that was the faith of trust or appropriation. Your circumstances, in a spiritual sense, are very similar to those of that man; for you are said to be in "an horrible pit;" but, blessed be God, your Saviour appears at the mouth of the pit; and, calling to you, says, "Whosoever believeth in me shall not perish, but have everlasting life." This is the rope he throws down for your rescue; and there is no way of your escaping, but by taking hold of it. You are not merely to credit the promise of salvation thus given, but you must take hold of it; and instantly will your feet be placed upon a rock, and a new song be put into your mouth, even of thanksgiving to your great Deliverer. It is possible that when the unfortunate man saw the rope, he might feel some degree of timidity in trusting himself to it; but when he considered that it was the only way of escape, he would seize it at once, with eagerness of mind and effort becoming his situation. You must do likewise. Venture upon the rope your Saviour offers you; grasp the promise of salvation through the Redeemer's blood; or you will die in the pit, and be eternally lost, there being no other escape.   *Dr. Robert Young.*

11,574. SALVATION, Neglect of. The saddest road to hell is that which runs under the pulpit, past the Bible, and through the midst of warnings and invitations.   *Ryle.*

11,575. SALVATION, Only Way of. A traveler relates that among the Alps there is a narrow path along the precipitous slope of a summit, which is crossed by a deep and dark defile. When the guides, one before and another behind the traveler, reach this fearful seam, they pause upon the dizzy edge to reassure his mind; then the leader makes a swing from a projecting rock, and lands upon the opposite side. Immediately turning towards the man he has left, urged forward by his rear-guard, he kneels upon the margin of the abyss, extends his hand over it, and says, "Place your foot there, and trust my arm to bring you over safely." It is done, and in a moment the traveler stands on the solid path, leading into a sweet and smiling landscape among the mountains—"peace reposing in the bosom of strength." This is called "the terrible pass." How forcibly it represents the convicted sinner's transition from disloyalty to reconciliation! He reaches the limit of his own wisdom and strength in seeking peace. Then Jesus bridges the gulf of alienation and death with his scarred hand, and invites the sinner to step by faith thereon, trust his Saviour and be saved. How simple the act! How glorious the result! He is brought over the terrible, dreaded pass, into "a large place," and one full of fragrance and song. Refusing to advance, escape is cut off, and he falls into "the blackness of darkness forever."   *Herald of Mercy.*

11,576. SALVATION, Quest of. Two brothers visited Pambo, and one said, "Father, I fast twice a week and eat only two loaves; shall I save my soul?" The other said, "I pick two pods of beans and give them in alms daily; shall I save my soul?" He did not answer at once, but at the end of four days, as they were about to depart, he said, "Pambo fasts two days a week and eats only two loaves, and does this make a monk of him? Pambo picks two bean-pods and gives them in alms every-day; does that make a monk of him? By no means." After a pause he added, "Keep your conscience void of offence toward God and your neighbor, and so shall ye be saved."

11,577. SALVATION, Tidings of. It is said that after the first announcement of the loss of the steamer Central America, with her hundreds of passengers, a pilot-boat was seen coming up the bay with all sails set and colors flying, and on her deck was unusual excitement. Her captain ran out to the end of the bowsprit, and as the boat neared the dock cried, "Three more saved! Three more saved!" The crowd caught it up and passed it along till every street and avenue of New York echoed with the cry, "Three more saved!"

Who wonders at the joy in heaven over one repenting sinner? The surprise is that all men do not have as great an interest in the salvation of the souls as the bodies of men.

11,578. SALVATION, Unlimited. How rich are the terms Scripture applies to salvation through Jesus. He is able to save them to the uttermost that come to God by him. What can go further than uttermost? Dr. Clarke says, "He is able to save from the power, guilt, nature, and punishment of sin—to the uttermost—to all intents, degrees, and purposes; and always, and in and through all times, places and circumstances; for all this is implied in the original word." The Dutch Bible translates this word "perfectly," the German has it "forever," Dr. L. Van Ess translates it "complete," the Berlenburg Bible gives it "most perfectly," the Catholic Bible (German) "eternally," Dr. Stier renders it "most complete." The original word seems to combine the two ideas of continuity and utmost completeness. Hence Jesus saves forever, to the uttermost.   *Bp. Yeakel.*

11,579. SALVATION, Uttermost. A city missionary was called from his bed at midnight, to meet a half-clothed little girl, who said as she saw him, "Be you the man that preached last night, and said, that Christ could save to the uttermost?" "Yes." "Well, I was there, and I want you to come right down to my house and try to save my poor father?" "What's the matter with your father?" "He's a good father when he don't drink, but he's out of work now, and he drinks awfully. He's almost killed my poor mother; but if Jesus can save to the uttermost, he can save him." Her house, a miserable underground room, without fire, light or furniture of any kind, was soon reached. On a little filthy straw in a corner, lay the bleeding and moaning mother. Her story was the too common one of drink, poverty and hunger. When the drunken father come home and found no supper, he stabbed his wife, and she expected him to return and finish his bloody work. Just then he came in, brandishing his still bloody knife. The missionary began to talk kindly to him and he became subdued. The little girl went up to the missionary, "Don't talk to father; it won't do any good. If talking would have saved him, he would have been saved long ago. You must ask Jesus, who saves to the uttermost, to save my poor father." At this challenge to faith he knelt down and prayed with unwonted power. The murderous father was melted into consciousness and repentance. Mercy was revealed and grace triumphed. That night the demon was cast out; one of the vilest sinners was saved to the uttermost. A new era dawned on that family. The reformed father found work, the mother was made comfortable and recovered, and the little girl was happy in leading her father to the Sunday-school, where he could learn more about him who "saves to the uttermost."

11,580. SANCTIFICATION, Influence of. The strong castle of the soul being taken and sanc-

tified, the tower of the body commanded by it presently yieldeth. When Satan sat on the throne of the soul as king, the members of the body (which the Holy Ghost termed in unregenerate persons "weapons of unrighteousness," Rom. 6 : 13), were his militia, and employed to defend his unjust title, to execute his ungodly designs, to perform his hellish pleasure—the head to plot, the hand to act, the feet to run, the eyes to see, the ears to hear, the tongue to speak for him. But, as when an enemy is conquered and a magazine in war is taken, the general maketh use of those arms and the ammunition for his service, which before employed against him: so the strong man Satan, being beaten out of his strongholds by Christ, the stronger than he, the members of the body which before were "instruments of unrighteousness" unto sin, are now "instruments of righteousness unto God" (Rom. 6 : 13).
                                        Swinnock.

11,581. SANCTIFICATION, Instantaneous. We are to come to God for an instantaneous and complete purification from all sins, as for instantaneous pardon. In no part of the scriptures are we directed to seek remission of sins *seriatim*—one now, and another then, and so on. Neither, in any part, are we directed to seek holiness by gradation. Neither a gradation-pardon, nor a gradation-purification, exists in the Bible.   *Dr. A. Clark.*

11,582. SARDIS, Fate of. Sardis, the capital of Lydia, identified with the names of Croesus, and Cyrus, and Alexander, and covering the plain with her thousands of inhabitants and tens of thousands of men of war—great even in the days of Augustus—ruined by earthquakes, and restored to its importance by the munificence of Tiberius—Christian Sardis, offering her hymns of thanksgiving for deliverance from Pagan persecution in the magnificent temple of the virgin and apostle; Sardis again fallen under the yoke of a false religion, but still retaining her numerous population and powerful defence only five hundred years ago; what is Sardis now? "How doth the city sit solitary that was full of people?" Lam. 1 : 1. A few mud huts, inhabited by Turkish herdsmen, and a mill or two, contain all the present population of Sardis.   *Arundell.*

11,583. SATAN, Arts of. "Satan knows," says an old writer, "what orders thou keepest in thy house and closet; and, though he hath not a key to thy heart, yet he can stand in the next room to it and lightly hear what is whispered there. He hunts the Christian by the scent of his own feet, and, if once he doth smell which way thy heart inclines, he knows how to take the hint."

11,584. SATAN, Enmity of. I was once sailing on the broad Pacific. One day, when the sea was very calm, in looking out upon the water on the Mexican coast, I saw what seemed to be a long, sharp, pointed knife rising above the surface and cutting the water, while it kept along with the ship for an hour or more. On looking narrowly, I saw it was the fin of a shark rising from his back. This creature was following us, ready to catch any one who might fall overboard. It was very large, and had cold, murderous eyes. Thus it was gliding noiselessly along, watching for a chance to do some awful work of blood. So I thought that great enemy of souls, Satan, follows men, hoping to seize them in some unguarded moment, and drag them down to destruction. *Anon.*

11,585. SATAN, Give no Advantage to. Alexander of Macedon, having observed that in close fighting the beards of his soldiers gave an advantage to his enemies, ordered them to be cut off, that no handle might be given to the foe. So should Christians renounce even their delights and pleasures, much more their .usts and sins, lest Satan should get advantage of them. *Anon.*

11,586. SATAN, Statue of. The statue of the tempter at the side of one of the great doors of Strasburg Cathedral is in my opinion one of the most wonderful products of genius. Those thin, worn, wasted, sharpened features, the so palpable contractions of a once noble face, the compressed ascetic lips, the strange checked smile, the clutching hand seemingly going through the mantle, whose quivering folds thrill in their revelation of the dumb misery within, the twining snake's semi-show, the uneasy resting feet, no one who has looked at earnestly will soon forget. Copies are found elsewhere, *e. g.* in Basle, and indeed all over the museums of the continent, but they do not approach the profoundly conceived original. The tempter holds the plucked "apple," surely in itself a stroke of intellect. *Grosart.*

11,587. SATAN, Subtlety of. The tempter always flings over, at least on the ugliest side, some shred of an angel's garment. An enemy who desired to destroy you by your own deed, would not lead you straight to a yawning precipice, and bid you cast yourself down. He would rather lead you along a flowery path, until you should insensibly be drawn into a spot which would give way beneath you.
Teachers' Treasury.

11,588. SATAN, Ubiquity of. Satan goeth to and fro through the earth; he is an ubiquitary, he stays nowhere. It is the folly of popish votaries, that think to shut themselves up in walls from the temptations of Satan: cloisters are as open to Satan as the open field. Satan walketh to and fro through the earth. *Caryl.*

11,589. SATAN, Wiles of. There were some young cavaliers in Pompey's army who were exceedingly proud of the beauty of their appearance. Cæsar's generals, perceiving this, gave orders that, instead of aiming at their legs and thighs, the javelins should be directed at their faces, that so they might be deprived of sight. This was the very thing they wished to avoid. They could not bear the thought of returning to their homes with deformed features, and, when they saw the gleaming steel dazzling before their eyes, they covered their faces with their hands, turned away their heads, and fled in confusion and infamy from the field. Just that point where we least expect and can least afford to be attacked, and about which we manifest the most pride, Satan will try to reach, that he may not only wound us, but, if possible, also disfigure our character. *Anon.*

11,590. SATIETY, Confession of. A French gentleman of wealth and culture who had nothing to do but enjoy himself, sought pleasure in travel. He visited different countries, observing scenes, manners, and men till he became wearied of it. He read much. There was no hindrance to his tasting every source of pleasure, which he did with even better than usual results. After this he says, "I am at a loss what to do. I know not where to go or what to see that I am not already acquainted with. There is nothing new to sharpen my curiosity or stimulate me to exertion. I am sated. Life to me has exhausted its charms. The world has no new face for me, nor can it open any new prospect to my view."

11,591. SATIETY, Examples of. Who aspires to a loftier elevation of honor than that attained by Burke? And yet he says, he would not give one peck of refuse wheat for all that is called fame in this world. What is the declaration of Byron, after having drained the cup of earthly pleasure to its dregs? It is, that his life has been passed in wretchedness, and that he longs to rush into the thickest of the battle, that he may terminate his miserable existence by a sudden death.
H. Southgate.

11,592. SAVED First. "Sir," said an ungodly man to Rev. T. Collins, "I hope to be saved at last." "It would be better, friend," was the reply, "to be saved at first. Let us go down on our knees and seek the blessing now."

11,593. SAVIOUR, A Mother. A child was bitten by a poisonous serpent. Its mother, moved by her own deep love, placed her lips over the wound to suck out the poison. She succeeded, and saved the child's life, but, in so doing, received the poison into her own system through an abrasion of the skin of her lip, and lost her own life.

11,594. SAVIOUR, Omnipresence of the. The city of Ulm, with a garrison of forty thousand, opened its gates and surrendered to Napoleon without firing a gun. Such was the terror inspired by his name and presence. On the same day the naval battle of Trafalgar was fought, and his own navy was ground to pieces. When Napoleon heard of this disaster, he said petulantly, "I cannot be present everywhere at once." In this our leader is superior to all chieftains, for he is with his people in every place.

11,595. SAVIOUR, Praising the. Titus Flaminius freed the Grecians from the bondage with which they had long been oppressed. When the herald proclaimed the articles of peace, the Greeks so pressed upon him he was in danger of losing his life. Reading the agreement the second time to them, and they fully understanding its import, they shouted for joy crying, Σω: ηρ, Σωτηρ, "A Saviour, a Saviour," till the heavens rung with their acclamations. All night the Grecians surrounded Titus' tent, and, with songs of praise and instruments of music, extolled him as a god that had delivered them. Flavel says, in applying this, "Ye that have escaped the wrath of God, by the humiliation of his Son, extol your great Redeemer, and forever celebrate his praises."

11,596. SAVIOUR, Remembering the. When the memory of Rev. John Newton was nearly gone, he used to say, that whatever else he might forget, he still remembered two things: 1st. That he was a great sinner; 2d. That Jesus Christ was a great Saviour.

11,597. SCANDAL, Influence of. He that speaks ill of another, commonly before he is aware, makes himself such a one as he speaks against; for if he had civility or breeding, he would forbear such kind of language. *John Selden.*

11,598. SCANDAL, No Recalling. A woman who freely used her tongue to the scandal of others, made a confession to the priest of what she had done. He gave her a ripe thistle top, and told her to go out and scatter the seeds one by one. She obeyed, and then returned and told her confessor. To her amazement, he bade her go back and gather the scattered seeds; and when she objected that it would be impossible, he replied that it would be still more difficult to gather up and destroy all the evil reports which she had circulated about others.

11,599. SCANDAL, Thoroughfare of. That proverbial saying, "Ill news goes quick and far," was occasioned chiefly by busy, ill-natured men, who very unwillingly hear or talk of anything else. For their ears, like cupping-glasses that attract the most noxious humors in the body, are ever sucking in the most spiteful and malicious reports; and, as in some cities, there are certain ominous gates through which nothing passes but scavengers' carts or the sledges of malefactors, so nothing goes in at their ears or out of their mouths but obscene, tragical, and horrid relations. *Plutarch.*

11,600. SCAPE-GOAT, Custom of the. Moravian missionaries in Thibet mention this singular custom at Shassa: "Every year the Lama community provide a man of the lowest class, dress him up in goat skin, with the hair outside, and a singular head-dress, and then drive him out of the town to the river, where they lay on him the sins of the whole people. The man has then to cross the river, and live in a wilderness in solitude for some weeks, being abundantly supplied with food during this season. On his return he receives many presents from the people. The disgrace is so great, however, that no one is found voluntarily to go through the ceremony, except in very rare instances. It is a singular analogy to the scape-goat of the Old Testament."

11,601. SCARS, Honorable. I wish to have the honor to die fighting. I would have all my scars in my breast. Methinks I would not be wounded running away, or skulking into a hiding-place. Though I long to go to heaven to see my glorious Master, what a poor figure shall I make among the saints, confessors and martyrs that surround his throne, without some deeper signature of his divine impress, without more scars of Christian honor. I do not envy those who choose to sleep in a whole skin. *Whitefield.*

11,602. SCEPTICS, Controversies with. The old fable tells us of a boy who mounted a scavenger's cart with base intent to throw dirt at the moon; whereat another boy, with better intentions, but scarcely less folly, came running with a basin of water to wash the moon, and make its face clean again. Certain sceptics are forever inventing new infidelities with which they endeavor to defile the fair face of the gospel, and many ministers forsake the preaching of Christ crucified, to answer their endless quibbles: to both of these the ancient fable may be instructive. *Spurgeon.*

11,603. SCEPTICS, Reasons of. "It often happens that men who arraign religion have been arraigned by it;" and their defence of scepticism is to justify their own conduct.

11,604. SCHEMES, Advice Regarding. Some are prolific in schemes of usefulness, but are miserably poor in execution. Like some trees, they spend themselves in blossoms, and never yield fruit. A gentleman, last summer, showed me a fine tree in his grounds, which he said he had resolved to cut down; for although for years it had produced finer blossoms than any other tree in his orchard or garden, yet it never bore fruit. He mentioned this to a friend, who said, "The fact is, the tree spends itself in blossoms. I advise you to cut the rind off it, nearly half way round, and it will probably have less blossoms, but it will bear fruit." He did so, and the result was that it afterwards produced more and better fruit than any other tree in the garden. Let me, therefore, advise you to cut some of the rind from your schemes, that they may not spend themselves in blossoms, but may work out the fruits of usefulness. *J. Griffin.*

11,605. SCIENCE, Joy of. On the 3d of June, 1797, long before the first glimmering of day, there might have been seen in a little Pennsylvania village a young man at his telescope, in pensive silence and trembling anxiety, awaiting the breaking of dawn. The sunlight shoots up over the far, blue hills, clear and golden. The young man intently watches the brightening of day, his telescope poised, and his heart throbbing with emotion. He sees a celestial messenger approaching the sun; he sees a shadow creep slowly, faintly upon the edge of the flaming circle; he sees a dark spot on the limb of the great luminary, creeping slowly, slowly toward the centre. The form of the young man sways to and fro with exhilaration and delight; the deductions of astronomical science are proving true; the prophecies of Kepler are fulfilling. His face becomes as rigid as marble; his eyes grow dim; a sudden darkness sweeps across his brain; Rittenhouse sees Venus crowning the disk of the sun he sinks back unconscious. *Morning Star.*

11,606. SCOFFER, Judgment on a. The Rev. John Henley, when attempting to preach out of doors, was so persistently disturbed by a rude blasphemer, that he thought it wise to dismiss the congregation with a blessing, subsequently announcing the date upon which he would again be there. "Ay," cried the sot, "and I'll be here with you and put you down again." "God will not let you." "I'll try him," said the ribald. "God will not let you," was firmly repeated. The day came. Henley preached, and the congregation shuddered as ere the service was halfway through, they saw the coffined corpse of that shameless man borne past them to its unhonored grave.
T. Collins.

11,607. SCOFFER Rebuked. A lady once completely shut up a pretended freethinker, who had been repeating a number of absurdities to prove that men had no souls. The company seemed contented with staring at him, instead of replying. He addressed this lady, and asked her with an air of triumph, what she thought of his philosophy. "It appears to me, sir," she replied, "that you have been employing a good deal of talent to prove yourself a beast." *Power.*

11,608. SCOFFERS, Prophecy of. A little girl engaged in reading her Bible, was accosted by a sceptic with, "Child, you can't understand that book, and it is not true!" Looking at him, she said, "There is one thing in the Bible certainly true." "Pray, what is that?" "The Bible says, 'In the last days shall come scoffers,' and are you one of them?"

11,609. SCOLDING, Perpetuation of. Passionate chiding carries rough language with it, and the names that parents and preceptors give children, they will not be ashamed to bestow on others. *Locke.*

11,610. SCORPION, Poison of the. A scorpion was caught by some men in California, who tormented it until, in its rage, it struck itself on its back with its poisonous dart. It immediately grew quiet, and in less than ten minutes died from its own sting.

11,611. SCRIPTURE, Anachronisms in. In one of his finest poems, "Gertrude of Wyoming," Campbell commits a strange anachronism in respect of climate. Forgetting that the valley in which occurred the dark tragedy he celebrates is in the bleak and shaggy uplands of Pennsylvania, he introduces, if I err not, the condor wheeling over its blood-reddened cliff —the flamingo flaming with purple wings through the reeds—the crocodile laving its mailed length in the river—the palm tossing its plume in the glades; none of which by any possibility could be found beneath such an iron sky. Curiously enough, exactly similar slips occur in the writings of the world's greatest minds, as Shakspeare, Milton, Bacon, Sir Thomas Browne. There are no such slips, even the slightest, from beginning to end of the Word of God. *Grosart.*

11,612. SCRIPTURE, Comments on. It is something like good Mr. Mason's notes in Bunyan's "Pilgrim." He asked one of his parishioners once, "Have you ever read Bunyan's 'Pilgrim?'—and do you understand the volume?" "Oh yes!" was the reply, "I understand the book well enough; and I hope by the grace of God, one of these days, I shall be able to understand your explanations of it!" So I doubt not many of our hearers will say, "I understand the text, 'Believe on the Lord Jesus Christ, and thou shalt be saved,' and do not doubt one day I shall understand your explanation of it." *Spurgeon.*

11,613. SCRIPTURE, Frame Work of. The historical matters of Scripture, both narrative and prophecy, constitute the bones of its system; whereas the spiritual matters are its muscles, blood-vessels and nerves. As the bones are necessary to the human system, so Scripture must have its historical matters. The expositor who nullifies the historical ground-work of Scripture for the sake of finding only spiritual truths everywhere, brings death on all correct interpretation.
J. A. Bengel.

11,614. SCRIPTURE, Freshness of the. Mr. Geo. Müller, founder of the Orphan Home, England, says, "In forty-six years I have read my Bible through a hundred times; yet it is always fresh and new when I begin it again."

11,615. SCRIPTURE, Misuse of. Ireneus likens the Gnostics' dealing with Scripture, their violent transpositions of it—till it became altogether a different thing in their hands—to their fraud, who should break up some work of exquisite mosaic, wrought by a skillful artificer to present the effigy of a king, and should then recompose the pieces upon some wholly different plan, and make them to express some vile image of a fox or dog, hoping that, since they could point to the stones as being the same, they should be able to persuade the simple that this was the king's image still.
Trench.

11,616. SCRIPTURE, Treasures of. Place yourself in imagination by the side of an Australian gold-digging, and observe the earth that is drawn up from its bottom. It is likely that your unpractised eye will see nothing in that heap but rubbish, and dirt and stones. And yet that very heap of earth may prove, on washing, to be full of particles of the purest gold. It is just the same with the Bible. We shall find hereafter that every verse of it contained gold. *Ryle.*

11,617. SCRIPTURES, Power of the. A native African preacher said, "We know that rocks are very hard. Our cutlasses and hoes can do nothing against them, so we leave them alone. But white people have something that can break up and scatter any rock in Uwet or Umon. You will admit that something must be more powerful than rocks. So we all know what country, laws and customs are; we cannot change them, so we leave them alone. But a thing has come to Calabar, even God's word, and it has broken up and scattered customs that our fathers thought would remain forever! What must you say concerning that word but that it is more powerful than the customs of our country? You know how strong your hearts are. Hearts as strong as yours have been changed in our town, have been changed by this word; and what must you, therefore, say but that this word is more powerful than a Calabar heart? Bend your heads, then, before this word."

11,618. SEA, Authority over the. Thomas Mann, a waterman on the Thames, being once employed to row a party, one of the number proposed singing, "Rule Britannia." Mann remarked, that he had heard Mr. Newton say, "God rules the waves, not Britannia."

11,619. SEA-VOYAGE, Lesson from a. Save only that we were mercifully preserved from peril, we had in our eleven days' voyage a compression of the experience of all possible voyages. I could not help thinking that it set forth in similitude the history of many a Christian life. Calm at the start; broken and troubled water when the Atlantic surges met us; heavy gales, blowing furiously against our progress; a sea majestic in its wrath, now making the ship to shake with trembling, now drenching it with showers of spray; the presence of three large icebergs, beautiful, but dangerous neighbors; a shroud of fog, which wrapped the heavens from our sight for a day and a half, during which the dreary fog-horn groaned out its dirge-like sound; calmer water as we approached the land, and then a brilliant sun, and a sea of exquisite beauty, as we sailed through the Narrows, and anchored in the fair haven. Do you not think that there are in our voyage the elements of a perpetual sermon? What heart, which has any experience of the things of God, does not understand this vicissitude within itself? How often is the fair start for heaven clouded soon by opposition and difficulty; then the blasts of persecution are fierce, and the billows of passion are angry. Then the heart is frosted by the world's chill neighborhood, or darkened by the gathering doubts which heap their shadows round it. Oh, that the similitude may be carried on to the end! calm water coming with the latest sunrise, and an "abundant entrance" and a joyous welcome at last!   *Punshon.*

11,620. SEAL, Use of the. The 3d chapter of John and the 33d verse: "He that hath received his testimony hath set to his seal that God is true." "He that hath received his testimony—'his,' that is, God's testimony—hath set to his seal that God is true." In the old days men used to wear a ring, a signet ring, and instead of signing their names to a document, they used to take that ring and sign that document, and so Christ uses that as an illustration. Now, Christ says if you will set to your seal that God is true, he will believe it. You then set to your seal that God is true.   *Moody.*

11,621. SEASON, Word in. A traveler came suddenly upon a minister, who sat upon a seat on an eminence from which a beautiful landscape was to be seen. He expressed his surprise and admiration of the view, and branched off to speak of scenes in Switzerland, interlard-

ing his descriptions, with frequent oaths "That," said he, "is the place to make a man happy! It would make you happy, indeed, to be there." The minister answered, seriously, "I perceive, sir, it has not made you happy." The traveler wondered how this stranger should know anything about him, and asked to know the reason of his remark. The minister answered, "It is evident from the manner in which you alluded to God. How a human being, estranged from him, the only source of real happiness, can be happy, is a problem yet to be solved. Solve it if you can." It was an opportune word uttered by the ready Dr. J. Leifchild.

11,622. SECRETS, Undesirable. Philippides, the comedian, being asked by King Lysimachus, what he desired should be given to him, answered, "Anything but a secret."

11,623. SECTS: None in Heaven. Mr. Whitefield, on one occasion, was preaching earnestly in Philadelphia, from the balcony of the court-house, when suddenly he cried out, "Father Abraham, whom have you in heaven? Any Episcopalians?" "No." "Any Presbyterians?" "No." "Have you any Independents or Seceders?" "No." "Have you any Methodists there?" "No, no, no." "Whom have you there?" "We don't know those names here. All who are here are Christians —believers in Christ—men who have overcome by the blood of the Lamb and the word of his testimony." "O, is this the case?" said Whitefield; "then God help me, God help us all, to forget party names, and to become Christians in deed and in truth!"

11,624. SECURITY, False. Security has been the ruin of multitudes, both in temporal and spiritual things. Commerce, warfare, the lives of families and of nations are full of stories of the wreck and ruin which false security has caused. In the spiritual life, some of the greatest falls have come by it; some of the greatest successes have been missed by it; it is one of the most powerful weapons in Satan's hands when used at the proper time; and that time he accurately knows.   *Power.*

11,625. SECURITY, Vain. Why will God's children build Babels? Why will they flatter themselves that God owns and approves of them because he suffers them to build high? In mercy to them, such building must come down. Lay your foundation deep in the knowledge of yourself, and you cannot build too high.   *Whitefield.*

11,626. SEED, Fruitful. The botanist Ray tells us that he counted 2,000 grains of maize on a single plant of maize sprung from one seed, 4,000 seeds on one plant of sun-flower, 32,000 seeds on a single poppy plant, and 36,000 seeds on one plant of tobacco. Pliny tells us that a Roman governor in Africa sent to the Emperor Augustus a single plant of corn with 340 stems, bearing 340 ears; that is to say, at least 60,000 grains of corn, had been produced from a single seed. In modern times 12,780 grains have been produced by a single grain of the famous corn of Smyrna. In eight years as much corn might spring from one seed as to supply all mankind with bread for a year and a half. *Gaussen.*

11,627. SEED, A Random. Rev. Mr. Grinnell, a missionary among the early settlers of the state of New York, gave a boy, whose religious education had been neglected, a sixpence to read the third chapter and third verse of John over three times. Twenty years later, passing through a poor section of the same State, he met a man who told him his experience including the gift of the sixpence as above. The verse "Verily, verily, I say unto thee, except a man be born again he cannot see the kingdom of God," followed him for many years, and finally led him to Christ.

11,628. SEED, Scattering. Philip Henry said to the minister of Broad Oaks, on meeting him, "I have been making bold to throw a handful of seed into your ground." "Thank you, sir," said he; "God bless it, and may it make work enough for us both!"

11,629. SEED, Self-Sowing. The self-propagating power of herbs and plants, by means of their seeds, is an admirable provision of the Creator for the perpetuation of their species. If there were not a man upon the earth, they would still clothe it with verdure and adorn it with beauty. For not only is the seed produced in itself, but sown by itself, also. In countless ways, and in a diversity of operations, it is its own sower. Sometimes it is found on the summit of elastic spires, to be agitated by the winds, which, when it is fully prepared, carry it forth in currents of air even to other regions. Sometimes birds of the air and beasts of the field convey it in their systems to different places by a mysterious process, which prevents it, while administering to their nourishment, from being injured, and even helps to its being quickened in its vegetative powers. It even floats upon the water as well as upon the air, in which case it is provided with a covering which is insoluble, and operates not until it strikes against some hard substance and is broken, when it lets forth its contents, which adhere to the substance; and by this means the dry coral rocks are clothed with verdure, and the island raised above the surface of the ocean adorned with a living green. *Dr. Leifchild.*

11,630. SEED, Treatment of the. There are two ways of treating the seed. The botanist splits it up, and discourses on its curious characteristics: the simple husbandman eats and sows; sows and eats. Similarly there are two ways of treating the gospel. A critic dissects it, raises a mountain of debate about the structure of the whole, and relation of its parts; and when he is done with his argument, he is done; to him the letter is dead; he neither lives on it himself, nor spreads it for the good of his neighbors; he neither eats nor sows. The disciple of Jesus, hungering for righteousness, takes the seed whole; it is bread for to-day's hunger, and seed for to-morrow's supply. *W. Arnot.*

11,631. SEEKING THE LORD, Time for. A young man sentenced to death said, two days before his execution, "I am afraid that nothing but the fear of death and hell makes me seek the Saviour now, and that I cannot expect to find him. The words, 'Seek ye the Lord while he may be found,' trouble my mind very much, as they show me that there is a time when he may not be found."

11,632. SELF, Danger of. Do you want to know the man against whom you have most reason to guard yourself? Your looking-glass will give you a very fair likeness of his face. *Whately.*

11,633. SELF, Idolatry of. Oh if I could be master of that house-idol, myself, mine own wit, will, credit, and ease, how blessed were I? We have need to be redeemed from ourselves, as much as from the devil and the world. Learn to put out yourselves, and put in Christ for yourselves. I should make a good bargain, and give old for new, if I could turn out self, and substitute Christ my Lord in place of myself; to say, "Not I, but Christ; not my will, but Christ's; not my lusts, not my credit, but Christ, Christ." *John Flavel.*

11,634. SELF-CONCEIT, Example of. There is an account of one Chrysippus who was famous only for his conceit. A neighbor asked him to whom he should send his son for instruction. "To me," he said, "if I did but imagine that any person excelled myself, I would read philosophy under him."

11,635. SELF-CONTROL, Absence of. Peter the Great made a law that if any nobleman beat or ill-treated his slaves, he should be looked upon as insane, and a guardian appointed to take care of his person and of his estate. This great monarch once struck his gardener, who, being a man of keen sensibility, took to his bed, and died in a few days. Peter, hearing of this, exclaimed, with tears in his eyes, "Alas! I have civilized my own subjects, I have conquered other nations, yet I have not been able to conquer or civilize myself."

11,636. SELF-CONTROL, Philosophic. A young man desired to become the disciple of a philosopher and attend his lectures. "Go first," said he, "to the marble quarries and carry stones for three years, among the malefactors condemned to the mines." He did so and reported to the philosopher at the end of the time. He was sent back to repeat his experience, and to pay money to those who should most bitterly insult and revile him, but to make no answer. He obeyed, and after another three years reported to his tutor. He was told that he might now go to Athens and be initiated into the schools of the philosophers. At the city gate an old man sat, who made it his business to abuse all who passed. The young man said nothing, but laughed to hear himself so outrageously abused. The old man asked the reason for his conduct. He said, "I have given money these three years to all who have treated me as you do; and shall I not laugh now it costs me nothing to be reviled?" The old man answered, "Welcome to the schools of philosophy! You are worthy of a seat in them." He added, "Behold the gate of heaven. All the faithful servants of the Lord have entered into this joy by suffering injuries and humiliations with meekness and patience." It is related of many that they have so disciplined themselves as to be able to endure reviling opposition or slight without the least emotion of anger or resentment, by the power of philosophy alone.

11,637. SELF-ESTEEM, Rebuke to. The tombs about Alexandria contain the remains of once proud princes as well as the dust of plebeians. This has been taken out and sold as a fertilizer, and is known in the trade as "Egyptian guano." Four thousand years ago no pains or cost was spared to honor this dust now so dishonored.

11,638. SELF-EXAMINATION, Daily. Daily examination is an antidote against the temptations of the following day, and constant examination of ourselves after duty is a preservative against vain encroachments in following duties; and upon the finding them out, let us apply the blood of Christ by faith for our cure, and draw strength from the death of Christ for the conquest of them, and let us also be humbled. God lifts up the humble; when we are humbled for our carnal frames in one duty, we shall find ourselves by the grace of God more elevated in the next. *Charnock.*

11,639. SELF-EXAMINATION, Fearing. As it is an evidence that those tradesmen are embarrassed in their estates, who are afraid to look into their books; so it is plain that there is something wrong within, among all those who are afraid to look within. *Secker.*

11,640. SELF-EXAMINATION, Method of. To take a distinct and orderly survey of all duties, that of Xenophon will be good direction, who said that it was the manner of discreet housekeepers to place their weapons of war, utensils for the kitchen, instruments of husbandry, and furniture for religious services, each in several and proper repositories. So every man that would make an exact inquiry into, and take a just account of himself, should first make a particular search into the several mischiefs that proceed from each passion within him, whether it be envy or jealousy, covetousness or cowardice, or any other vicious inclinations; and then distribute and range them all (as it were) into distinct apartments. This done, make thy reviews upon them with the most accurate inspection, so that nothing may divert thee from the severest scrutiny. *Plutarch.*

11,641. SELF-EXAMINATION, Necessity of. The reason why there is so little self-condemnation, is because there is so little self-examination. For want of it many are like travelers skilled in other countries, but ignorant of their own.

11,642. SELF-EXAMINATION, Standard for. The conscience of the natural man is like a fraudulent man with false weights and measures, from whom we shall be sure to have no just weight. We must therefore take the golden balance of the sanctuary. Here, indeed, even our best services, when weighed with the law of God, will be found wanting; but the fullness

of the redemption in the blood of Jesus—the freeness of his promises to every repenting sinner—the merit of his sinless obedience—these, on which the believer builds his hopes, however nicely weighed in the balance of truth, will want nothing of that true weight which the justice of God will demand at our hands. *Salter*

11,643. SELF-EXAMINATION, Use of. A Highlander bought a barometer and afterwards complained that it made no improvement in the weather. Self-examination will be of no advantage unless it reveals our failures and deficiencies and incites us to improvement. The examination of symptoms without taking the doctor's remedy is useless.

11,644. SELF-IMPORTANCE, Rebuke of. William Penn and Thomas Story once took shelter beneath a house in Pennsylvania, from the rain. The owner came forth with great pomp of manner, and said, "How dare you take shelter here without my leave? Do you know who I am? I am the mayor of this place." "Pooh! pooh!" said Friend Story, "my friend here makes such things as thou art: he is the Governor of Pennsylvania."

11,645. SELFISHNESS, Common. How many are there who occupy public places with private spirits! While they pretended to undertake everything for the good of others; it has appeared, that they undertook nothing but for the good of themselves. Such suckers at the roots have drawn away the sap and nourishment from the tree. They have set kingdoms on fire, that they might roast their own venison at the flames. These drones stealing into the hive have fed upon the honey; while the laboring bees have been famished. Too many resemble ravenous birds, which at first seem to bewail the dying sheep; but at last, are found picking out their eyes. These people never want fire, so long as any yard affords fuel. They enrich their own sideboards with other men's plate. There is a proverb, but none of Solomon's, "Every man for himself, and God for us all." But where every man is for himself, the devil will have all. Whosoever is a seeker of himself, is not found of God. Though he may find himself in this life, he will lose himself in death. *Secker.*

11,646. SELFISHNESS Punished. Old Churchill was riding on horseback, when he met an old woman who had not so many of this world's good things as he. He handed her a quarter of a dollar and rode on. He had ridden only a short distance, when he soliloquized thus: "Now, shouldn't I have done better if I had kept my money and bought myself something?" Wheeling his horse, he rode back to the old lady and said: "Give me that money!" She handed it to him. Placing it in his wallet, and at the same time handing her a five-dollar bill, he exclaimed: "There, self, now I guess you'll wish you had kept still."

11,647. SELFISHNESS, Unhappiness of. It is curious to observe how people who are always thinking of their own pleasure or interest will often, if possessing considerable ability, make

others give way to them, and obtain everything they seek, except happiness. For, like a spoiled child, who at length cries for the moon, they are always dissatisfied. And the benevolent who are always thinking of others, and sacrificing their own personal gratifications, are usually the happiest of mankind.
Whately.

11,648. SELF-LOVE, Crime of. If self-denial be the greatest part of godliness, the great letter in the alphabet of religion, self-love is the great letter in the alphabet of practical atheism. Self is the great anti-Christ and anti-God in the world, that sets up itself above all that is called God; self-love is the captain of that black band (2 Tim. 3: 2): it sits in the temple of God, and would be adored as God. Self-love begins; but denying the power of godliness, which is the same with denying the ruling power of God, ends the list.
Charnock.

11,649. SELF-REFORMATION, Duty of. Though few men are likely to be called on to take part in the reformation of any public institutions, yet there is no one of us but what ought to engage in the important work of self-reformation, and according to the well-known proverb, "If each would sweep before his own door, we should have a clean street." Some may have more, and some less, of dust and other nuisances to sweep away; some of one kind, and some of another. But those who have the least to do have something to do; and they should feel it an encouragement to do it, that they can so easily remedy the beginnings of small evils before they have accumulated into a great one. Begin reforming, therefore, at once: proceed in reforming steadily and cautiously, and go on reforming forever.
Whately.

11,650. SELF-RESPECT, Importance of. I am fully persuaded that one of the best springs of generous and worthy actions is the having generous and worthy thoughts of ourselves. Whoever has a mean opinion of the dignity of his nature will act in no higher a rank than he has allotted himself in his own estimation. If he considers his being as circumscribed by the uncertain term of a few years, his designs will be contracted into the same narrow span he imagines is to bound his existence. How can he exalt his thoughts to anything great and noble, who only believes that, after a short turn on the stage of this world, he is to sink into oblivion, and to lose his consciousness forever?
Hughes.

11,651. SELF-RIGHTEOUSNESS, Ruined by. "A gentleman in our late civil wars," says Cowley, "when his quarters were beaten up by the enemy, was taken prisoner, and lost his life afterwards, only by staying to put on a band, and adjust his periwig: he would escape like a person of quality, or not at all, and died the noble martyr of ceremony and gentility." Poor fool, and yet he is as bad who waits till he is dressed in the rags of his own fitness before he will come to Jesus. He will die a martyr to pride and self-righteousness. *Spurgeon.*

11,652. SELF-SEEKERS, Reward of. A certain king had a minstrel whom he commanded to play before him. It was a day of high feasting; the cups were flowing and many great guests were assembled. The minstrel laid his fingers among the strings of his harp, and woke them all to the sweetest melody, but the hymn was to the glory of himself. It was a celebration of the exploits of song which the bard had himself performed, and told how he had excelled high-born Hoel's harp, and emulated soft Llewellyn's lay. In high-sounding strains he sang himself and all his glories. When the feast was over, the harper said to the monarch, "O king, give me thy guerdon; let the minstrel's mede be paid." Then the monarch replied, "Thou hast sung unto thyself, pay thyself; thine own praises were thy theme; be thyself the paymaster." The harper cried, "Did I not sing sweetly? O king, give me thy gold!" But the king answered, "So much the worse for thy pride, that thou shouldst lavish such sweetness upon thyself. Get thee gone, thou shalt not serve in my train." *Spurgeon.*

11,653. SENSE, Want of. The president of a Scotch college addressed a new class as follows, "Young men, you have come here seeking knowledge, and you may get that. And some of you are desiring religion. You can doubtless get that if you seek it. But if you lack common sense, no power in earth or heaven can give you that."

11,654. SEPARATION, Example of. Ko-sanlone, a converted Chinese, when in America on a visit, was deeply impressed with the little difference he saw between the style of living of many professing Christians and the men of the world. Adverting to the matter, he said, "When the disciples in my country come out from the world, they come clear out."

11,655. SERIOUSNESS, Reasons for. When Secretary Walsingham arrived at old age, he retired to the country to end his days in quiet. Some of his former companions came to see him, and rallied him for his melancholy. He answered, "No, I am not melancholy, but I am serious; and it is very proper that we should be so! Ah, my friends, while we laugh, everything is serious about us. God is serious, who exerciseth patience towards us; Christ is serious, who shed his atoning blood for us; the Holy Ghost is serious, who striveth against the obstinacy of our hearts; the Holy Scriptures are serious books; they present to our thoughts the most serious concerns in all the world; the holy sacraments represent very serious and awful matters; the whole creation is serious in serving God and us; all in heaven are serious; all who are in hell are serious. How then can we be gay and trifling?"

11,656. SERMONS, Brilliant. Sir Astley Cooper, visiting Paris, was asked by the surgeon *en chef* of the empire how many times he had performed a certain wonderful feat of surgery. He replied, "Thirteen times." "Ah, but, monsieur, I have done him one hundred and sixty times. How many times did you save his life?" continued the curious Frenchman after he had looked into the blank amazement of Sir Astley's face. "I," said the Englishman, "saved eleven out of the thirteen. How many did you save out of one hundred and sixty?" "Ah, monsieur, I lose dem all, but de operation was very brilliant." Such is the effect of many brilliant sermons.

11,657. SERMONS, Done. I remember our countryman, Bromeard, tells us of one who, meeting his neighbor coming out of the church, asked him, "What! is the sermon done?" "Done," said the other, "no: it is said, it is ended, but it is not so soon done." And surely so it is with us: we have good store of sermons said, but we have only a few that are done: and one sermon done is worth a thousand said and heard; for, "not the hearers of the law, but the doers of it are justified." And "if ye know these things, blessed are ye if ye do them." "Glory, honor, and peace to every man that worketh good!" *Bp. Hall.*

11,658. SERMONS, Effective. Joseph Benson preached a sermon in Cornwall, to a large congregation in the open air, through which five hundred people professed religion and joined the Wesleyans. Seventy-six persons attributed their conversion to a single sermon by a Canadian minister. Thirty-six souls were reported saved by another sermon, and twenty-eight by another. Eighty-four by another.

11,659. SERMONS, Fine. Samuel Wesley wrote to his curate: "I sincerely hate what some people call a fine sermon, with just nothing in it. I cannot help thinking that it is very much like our fashionable poetry—polite nothing." John Wesley says: "I could write as floridly as the admired Dr. South, but I dare not. I would no more preach a fine sermon than wear a fine coat."

11,660. SERMONS, Helps to. I think it were well for their congregations if some of our Scotch ministers, who are not specially gifted as preachers, though very good pastors, would, without being slavish copyists, draw to a large extent on the rich stores of the old or foreign divines, or Puritan Fathers. *Dr. Guthrie.*

11,661. SERMONS, Length of. There is much ado being made just now about the proper length of sermons. The rule seems to be, as deduced from a vast number of particular facts and opinions, that the length of a sermon should be equal to its breadth and depth. It should be, in fact, the square thing. It ought not to be measured by the linear foot, as men measure tape and ribbons, but by the cubic foot, as men measure wheat and other grain. If it has no depth, it ought to have no length. *Witness.*

11,662. SERMONS, Making. A young clergyman once visited Dr. Bellamy, and inquired, "What shall I do to supply myself with matter for my sermons?" The doctor quaintly replied: "Fill up the cask, fill up the cask, fill up the cask; and then, if you tap it anywhere, you will get a good stream. But if you put in but little, it will dribble, dribble, dribble, and you must tip, tip, tip, and then you get but little after all."

11,663. SERMONS, Materials for. A young man in one of our seminaries came to me and said, "I have been trying very hard to write a sermon, and I find it the most difficult thing in the world to do." I said to him, "My dear young friend, were you ever at a mill? Do you know what the hopper and bin are? Suppose the miller should rouse his hands, set the stones going, hang the bags on the hooks at the bin, and then stand wondering why he does not get any meal." Some one says to him, "Why, you have forgotten to put corn in the hopper!" My dear young man, you cannot get meal at the bin till you put corn in the hopper. *Dr. S. H. Tyng.*

11,664. SERMONS, Preparation of. I used the simplest, plainest terms, avoiding anything vulgar, but always, where possible, employing the Saxon tongue—the mother tongue of my hearers. I studied the style of the addresses which the ancient and inspired prophets delivered to the people of Israel, and saw how, differing from dry disquisition or a naked statement of truths, they abounded in metaphors, figures, and illustrations. I turned to the gospels, and found that he who knew what was in man, what could best illuminate a subject, win the attention, and move the heart, used parables or illustrations, stories, comparisons, drawn from the scene of nature and familiar life, to a large extent in his teachings in regard to which a woman—type of the masses—said, "The parts of the Bible I like best are the 'likes.'" Taught by such models, and encouraged in my resolution by such authorities, I resolved to follow, though it should be at a vast distance, these ancient masters of the art of preaching; being all the more ready to do so as it would be in harmony with the natural turn and bias of my own mind. I was careful to observe by the faces of my hearers, and also by the account the more intelligent of my Sunday class gave of my discourses, the style and character of those parts which had made the deepest impression, that I might cultivate it. After my discourse was written, I spent hours in correcting it; latterly always for that purpose keeping a blank page on my manuscript opposite a written one, cutting out dry bits, giving point to dull ones, making clear any obscurity, and narrative parts more graphic, throwing more pathos into appeals, and copying God in his works by adding the ornamental to the useful. The longer I have lived and composed, I have acted more and more according to the saying of Sir Joshua Reynolds in his lectures on "Paintings," that God does not give excellence to men but as the reward of labor. *Dr. Guthrie.*

11,665. SERMONS, Providential. Dr. Jamieson, of Edinburgh, sought for two days for a text, but failed to select one up to the time of opening his Bible to preach. As he did this his eyes rested on Ps. 32: 1, "Blessed is he whose transgression is forgiven, whose sin is covered." He spoke extemporaneously with great enlargement. Next morning a woman called on him, who said that she had doubted

God and the Bible, and that during the previous week she resolved to discard religion and burn her Bible unless the preacher preached from the before-mentioned text.

11,666. SERMONS, Reading. Norman McLeod was once preaching in a district where the reading of a sermon is regarded as the greatest fault of which the minister can be guilty. When the congregation dispersed, an old woman, overflowing with enthusiasm, addressed her neighbor: "Did ye ever hear ony thing eae gran'? Wasna that a sermon?" But all her expressions of admiration being met by a stolid glance, she shouted, "Speak, woman! wasna that a sermon?" "Oh, ay," replied her friend, sulkily, "but he read it." "Read it!" said the other, with indignant emphasis; "I wadna hae cared if he had whustled it."

11,667. SERMONS, Repeating. An old divine says, "The minister cannot be always preaching: two or three hours maybe in a week he spends among his people in the pulpit, holding the glass of the gospel before their faces; but the lives of professors, these preach all the week long; if they were but holy and exemplary, they would be as a repetition of the preacher's sermon to their families and neighbors among whom they converse, and keep the sound of his doctrine continually ringing in their ears. This would give Christians an amiable advantage in doing good to their carnal neighbors by counsel and reproof, which now is seldom done, and when done it proves to little purpose, because not backed with their own exemplary walking."

11,668. SERMONS, Successful. I once said to myself in the foolishness of my heart, "What sort of sermon must that have been which was preached by St. Peter, when three thousand souls were converted at once?" What sort of sermon?—such as other sermons: there is nothing to be found in it extraordinary. The effect was not produced by St. Peter's eloquence, but by the mighty power of God, present with his Word. *Cecil.*

11,669. SERVANT, A Devout. Isidore, the patron saint of Madrid, whose festival is held there on the 10th of May, attended by the ringing of bells, processions and joyous festivities, was only a common farm servant who did not forget the heavenly Master while serving the earthly. His fellow servants accused him to their master of being late at his work. When charged with this, he replied, "It may be true that I am later at my work than some of the other laborers, but I do my utmost to make up for the few minutes snatched for prayer. I pray you, compare my work with theirs, and if I have defrauded you in the least gladly will I make amends by paying you out of my private store." The master was silent, but not satisfied, and resolved to see for himself. Next morning he hid himself in the field to which the servant was assigned. He was later than the others in starting his plough, and the indignant master resolved to rate him soundly. He started to do this, but was

rested by a strange vision. In the clear sunlight he saw a pair of white oxen drawing a plough, held by an angel. Up the field and down the field quickly passed the strange team, turning a clean furrow. The master started to go to Isidore, whom he saw bowing over his plough, while his boy drove the oxen, when the vision vanished. The master asked him who his assistants were. The surprised ploughman answered, "Sir, I work alone, and know of none save God, to whom I look." This legend enshrines a grand truth—God helps those who honor him.

11,670. SERVICE, Ceaseless. The stream has been turning yonder mill-wheel for years without wearying or complaint. The brook has been going on for ages, spreading fertility and beauty over all its borders, and will "go on forever." So let thy Christian service be uncomplaining, beneficent, ceaseless.

11,671. SERVICE, Honor of. A victor at the Olympic games was asked, "Spartan, what will you get by this victory?" He answered, "I shall have the honor to fight foremost in the ranks of my prince." Hard service brings promotion, danger, responsibility, and requires increased effort.

11,672. SHADOW, Measuring Time by the. "The people of the East measure time by the length of their shadow. Hence if you ask a man what o'clock it is, he immediately goes in the sun, stands erect, then looks where his shadow terminates; he measures the length with his feet, and tells you nearly the time. Thus they earnestly desire the shadow, which indicates the time for leaving their work. A person wishing to leave his toil often cries out, 'How long my shadow is in coming!' When asked, 'Why did you not come sooner?' his answer is, 'Because I waited for my shadow.'" *Roberts.*

11,673. SHAME, Allegory of. Guilt and Shame (says the allegory) were at first companions, and in the beginning of their journey inseparably kept together. But their union was soon found to be disagreeable and inconvenient to both: Guilt gave Shame frequent uneasiness, and Shame often betrayed the secret conspiracies of Guilt. After a long disagreement, therefore, they at length consented to part forever. Guilt boldly walked forward alone, to overtake Fate, that went before in the shape of an executioner; but Shame, being naturally timorous, returned back to keep company with Virtue, which in the beginning of their journey they had left behind. Thus, after men have traveled through a few stages in vice, Shame forsakes them, and returns back to wait upon the few virtues they have still remaining. *Goldsmith.*

11,674. SHAMS, Popular. Empty chests, boxes and drawers painted brilliantly and lettered in gold, make a fine display on the shelves of the apothecary and the merchant. The bottles being transparent, can be easily filled with a little tinted water. Fruits, vegetables, and meats are so perfectly imitated that the sham does not appear to the casual observer. Sham are everywhere. There are business shams, political shams, society shams, literary shams and religious shams, worthless trash put up for exhibition. It is a losing business. The deception will soon be detected, and he who practices it be dishonored beyond retrieve.

11,675. SHEEP, The Lost. "As I came over, the heath, I noticed a solitary sheep, which had evidently wandered from its fold. It bleated piteously, and was scared at every sound, and every shadow. It seemed to be calling for its companions, and vainly trying to recover and retrace the path, by which it had so rashly strayed from its home. I went towards the poor wanderer; but it fled from a stranger; and would probably have perished in that solitude, had not the shepherd missed it from the fold, and come in time to seek it. As soon as he espied it from a distance, he hastened towards it; and the sheep, aware of his kindly purpose, suffered him to come near, and take it in his arms. He raised it on his shoulders, and bore it away rejoicing." It is a true emblem of the lost sinner.

11,676. SHEPHERD, Faithfulness of the. Many adventures with wild beasts still occur. There are wolves in abundance, and leopards and panthers exceeding fierce, prowl about those wild wadies in the region of Tyre. They not unfrequently attack the flock in the very presence of the shepherd, and he must be ready to do battle at a moment's warning. And when the thief and robber come (and come they do), the faithful shepherd has often to put his life in his hand to defend his flock. A poor, faithful fellow between Tiberius and Tabor, instead of fleeing, actually fought three Bedouin robbers, until he was hacked to pieces with their khanjars, and died among the sheep he was defending.   *Thomson.*

11,677. SHEPHERD, Voice of the. A traveler asserted to an eastern shepherd, that the sheep knew the dress of their master, not his voice. The shepherd to refute the point changed dresses with the traveler. He went among the sheep with the shepherd's dress, called the sheep, and tried to lead them, but they knew not his voice, and never moved. But when the shepherd called, though in a strange dress, they ran at once to him. "A stranger will they not follow."

11,678. SHOES: Oriental Custom. "Put off thy shoes from off thy feet, for the place whereon thou standest is holy ground." Exod. 3: 5. This putting off the shoes is an invariable custom in the East as an act of courtesy or reverence. The Mussulman on entering his mosque, the Copt in passing into his church, leaves his shoes at the door; it is, indeed, common to all Orientals in the act of worship; nor that alone, for it is done as a mark of respect on appearing before a superior.
Sunday at Home.

11,679. SICK, Exposure of the. In the most ancient times the custom was to exhibit the sick in public places that benevolent persons or others who had suffered from the same disease, or had labored for such, might commu-

nicate a remedy. In this way the science of medicine began. If people with moral infirmities would do the same, many a sick soul would be cured.

11,680. SICK, Healing the. When Myconius was very ill, apparently sick unto death, he wrote to Luther. On reception of the letter, Luther fell on his knees, and prayed, "O Lord, my God! no, thou must not take yet our brother Myconius to thyself; thy cause will not prosper without him. Amen." He then wrote to his sick friend, "There is no cause for fear, dear Myconius; the Lord will not let me hear that thou art dead. You shall not, and must not die. Amen." This letter aroused Myconius so that an ulcer upon his lungs discharged, and he was healed.

11,681. SICKNESS, Admonition of. Antigonus, successor to Alexander, after recovering from a severe illness, said, "It has done me no harm, for it has taught me not to be so proud by putting me in mind that I am but a mortal man."

11,682. SICKNESS, Chamber of. It may be said, that disease generally brings that equality which death completes. The distinctions which set one man so far above another, are very little preserved in the gloom of a sick-chamber, where it will be in vain to expect entertainment from the gay, or instruction from the wise; where all human glory is obliterated, the wit clouded, the reason perverted, and the hero subdued; where the highest and brightest of mortals find nothing left but consciousness and innocence.   *Addison.*

11,683. SICKNESS, Joy in. A sick man said, "Days, weeks, and months have rolled round during my affliction, and I have scarcely known the night from the day, nor the day from the night, so rapidly and joyfully have the hours escaped me; I have felt nothing but joy and love; not for a moment have I been impatient or weary, or wished it otherwise with me, so marvelously has God wrought in me. This is the hand of God. This never grew in nature's soil."

11,684. SICKNESS, Recovery from. I was near port, but have put out to sea again. O, that it may be to pilot in some more dear souls! May we at last enter port with a full gale! We are sure of getting safe at last into the harbor, for Jesus is our pilot.   *Whitefield.*

11,685. SIGHT, Danger of. There is a legend which represents St. Bridget as engaged in holy conversation as the sun went down with a devout, but blind nun called Dara. They talked of the love of Jesus and the joys of paradise, unconscious of the passing hours till the sun rose next morn and spread its golden light over a beautiful landscape. Then Bridget wished that Dara might see all this beauty. She prayed and touched Dara's eyes and they were healed. Dara looked up at the golden sun, at the trees and flowers adorned with dew drops that flashed like jewels, and out upon the joyous world. After a little while she said, "Close my eyes again, for when the world is so visible to the eyes, God appears less clearly to the soul." Then Bridget prayed again and Dara's blindness returned, A. D. 525.

11,686. SIGHT, Recovery of. A poor blind man, who had a wife and children whom he had never seen, sought a cure quite late in life, from a skillful physician. His opinion was that his sight might be restored, but with considerable suffering and risk. "I will submit to anything; I will endure anything, if I can only see," said the man. The operation was successfully performed. Gradually the light was admitted till his eyes were strong enough to look upon his wife and children. He called them to him, and required them to speak, that he might be assured of the reality of his newly-found faculty. He looked out upon the earth and up to the heavens, and his heart was filled with amazement and gladness. Then he said, "Bring me the doctor who has opened this glorious world to me; I love him better than all else." We are all blind. Christ can open our eyes and enable us to say, "Whereas I was blind, now I see."

11,687. SIGHT, Superiority of. Sight is the short road to knowledge, it is also the direct path to love; the eye is the first, the readiest, the surest of instructors. Why do we say "Example is better than precept?" The one appeals to the eye, the other to the ear, and the eye is quicker than the ear. *A. B. Evans.*

11,688. SILENCE, Bad. Silence is an excellent thing, but people who hold their tongues should not always account themselves silent. If their minds are occupied with their neighbor's short-comings, their silence is as bad as sensible chattering. *Poemen.*

11,689. SILENCE, Compulsory. Zeno, that he might not be compelled by the tortures of his body to betray, against his will, the secrets entrusted in his breast, bit off his tongue, and spit it in the tyrant's face. *Plutarch.*

11,690. SILENCE, Wisdom of. The lion called the sheep to ask her if his breath smelt; she said, "Ay;" he bit off her head for a fool. He called the wolf and asked him. He said "No;" he tore him in pieces for a flatterer. At last he called the fox, and asked him. Truly he had got a cold, and could not smell. *Æsop.*

11,691. SILENCE, Wise. In a certain assembly, when Demaratus was asked whether he held his tongue because he was a fool, or for want of words, replied, "A fool cannot hold his tongue." *Plutarch.*

11,692. SIN, Ashamed of. Mr. Perkins, afterwards a very excellent and useful minister, when a student at Cambridge, was much given to the indulgence of sin, from which he was reclaimed in a very remarkable manner. Passing along one of the streets of that town, he overheard a woman say to her peevish child, "Hold your tongue, or I will give you to drunken Perkins yonder." This led him to resolve on reformation, and was the occasion of his conversion.

11,693. SIN, Beginnings of. Thieves, when they go to rob a house, if they cannot force the doors, or the wall is so strong that they cannot break through, then they bring little boys along with them, and these they put in at the windows; who are no sooner in but they unbolt the doors, and let in the whole company of thieves. And thus Satan, when by greater sins he cannot tell how to enter the soul, then he puts on and makes way by lesser, which insensibly having got entrance, set open the doors of the eyes and the doors of the ears; then comes in the whole rabble. There they take up their quarters; there, like unruly soldiers, they rule, domineer, and do what they list, to the ruin of the soul so possessed. *Alsop*

11,694. SIN, Burden of. As when a current of electricity is passed through filings of silver, the tiny pieces of metal are melted into one mass, so, under the influence of the Holy Spirit, do all our sins seem welded together into one fearful burden which weighs us down to perdition. *Pilkington.*

11,695. SIN, Contagion of. Men carefully avoid those who have any infectious disease. The sign of small-pox on a house is a greater protection than lock and key. The danger is only physical. But when sin is uncovered men gaze upon it with morbid curiosity. It is spread from mouth to mouth, and published in the Gazette. The first shock is overcome by familiarity. It communicates some of its virus to every one who sees, hears or tells of it. Sin and sinners are inseparable. They are not fit companions for yourself or children. Remember your liability to take this deadly infection, and avoid the locality as far as possible.

11,696. SIN, Cutting off the Hand of. The red hand of Ireland. This motto of the ancient line of O'Neil was obtained in a remarkable way. Some adventurers of the very olden time were bent upon an expedition from somewhere or other, perhaps Germany, Denmark, or Britain; and their leader, who was a daring captain of, it is to be feared, the "bold buccaneer" type, gave out that whoever first touched land should possess the territory they were making for. One of the band was named O'Neil, and he (from whom descended the princes of Ulster) determined to have the territory, rowed mightily towards the shore. But, lo! a rival boat pressed him hard, gained upon him, at last outstripped him. What was to be done? Have the land he would; that he had from the first settled with himself! But how? Why thus. With a grim look of mingled wrath and triumph at the rival boat, this strong-nerved, iron-minded O'Neil dropped the oars, seized a battle-axe, cut off one of the hands that had so lately plied them, and threw it upon the shore he determined to possess. And now "the bloody hand" is the badge of baronetcy in general, not the motto, but the badge; the motto is the O'Neil's, the badge signifies baronetcy. Now if this ready sacrifice and painful loss was endured in order to gain an earthly inheritance, what sacrifices and what losses can be counted too great for obtaining a heavenly inheritance? "If thy hand or thy foot offend thee, cut them off, and cast them from thee: it is better for thee to enter into life halt or maimed, rather than having two hands or two feet to be cast into everlasting fire." *Dr. Guthrie.*

11,697. SIN, Danger of. Those who would not fall into the river, should beware how they approach too near to its banks. He that crushes the egg, need not fear the flight of the bird. He who would not drink of the wine of wrath, let him not touch the cup of pleasure. He who would not hear the passing-bell of eternal death, should not finger the rope of sin. A person who carries gun-powder about him, can never stand too far from the fire. If we accompany sin one mile, it will compel us to go twain. It swells like Elijah's cloud, from the size of a man's hand to such an expansion as to cover the whole sky. *Secker.*

11,698. SIN, Defending. A lawyer undertook the defense of a robber on the promise of a thousand crowns reward. He won his case, and his client brought him the coveted money. The night being stormy, the lawyer invited him to lodge in his house. At midnight the robber arose, gagged his legal defender, retook the thousand crowns, and gathering all the treasure he could find, bade his helpless host good-bye. Such is the deceit of sin, and the reward of iniquity.

11,699. SIN, Description of. Look now at sin. Pluck off that painted mask, and turn upon her face the lamp of God's Word. We start —it reveals a death's head. I stay not to quote texts descriptive of sin. It is a debt, a burden, a thief, a sickness, a leprosy, a plague, a poison, a serpent, a sting : everything that man hates it is ; a load of curses, and calamities beneath whose crushing, most intolerable pressure, the whole creation groaneth. Name me the evil that springs not from this root— the crime that I may not lay at its door. Who is the hoary sexton that digs man a grave? Who is the painted temptress that steals his virtue? Who is the murderess that destroys his life? Who is this sorceress that first deceives, and then damns his soul?—Sin. Who with icy breath, blights the fair blossoms of youth? Who breaks the hearts of parents? Who brings old men's gray hairs with sorrow to the grave?—Sin. Who, by a more hideous metamorphosis than Ovid even fancied, changes gentle children into vipers, tender mothers into monsters, and their fathers into worse than Herods, the murderers of their own innocents? —Sin. Who casts the apple of discord on household hearts? Who lights the torch of war, and bears it blazing over trembling lands? Who by divisions in the church, rends Christ's seamless robe?—Sin. Who is this Delilah that sings the Nazarite asleep, and delivers up the strength of God into the hands of the uncircumcised? Who, winning smiles on her face, honeyed flattery on her tongue, stands in the door to offer the sacred rites of hospitality, and when suspicion sleeps, treacherously pierces our temples with a nail? What fair Siren is this, who, seated on a rock by the deadly pool, smiles to deceive, sings to lure, kisses to betray, and flings her arm around our neck, to leap with us into perdition?—Sin. Who turns the soft and gentlest heart to stone? Who hurls reason from her lofty throne, and impels sinners, mad as Gadarene swine, down the precipice, into a lake of fire?—Sin. *Dr. Guthrie.*

11,700. SIN, Fear of. Eudocia angrily threatened St. Chrysostom with banishment. He calmly replied : " Go tell her, I fear nothing but sin."

11,701. SIN, Grooves of. The solid rock summits of our mountains are often found to be scarred and grooved, sometimes to the depth of several inches. A mighty force coming down from the northwest, when these tall hilltops were just rising above the water, thrust its ploughshares into and left its ineffaceable furrows. Temptation and sin will sweep down with fearful force upon the human soul, and leave it scarred and furrowed. Some times one crime cuts a deep groove into the soul, which no good deeds can ever fill up. At other times it is accomplished by repeated sins which constitute a habit. In either case only divine power can restore the soul.

11,702. SIN, Growth of. Austin, writing upon John, tells a story of a certain man, that was of an opinion that the devil did make the fly and not God. Saith one to him, " If the devil made flies, then the devil made worms, and God did not make them, for they are living creatures as well as flies." " True," said he, " the devil did make worms." " But," said the other, " if the devil did make worms, then he made birds, beasts, and man." He granted all. " Thus," saith Austin, " by denying God in the fly he came to deny God in man, and to deny the whole creation." *Brooks.*

11,703. SIN, Hardening Effects of. Dr. Preston tells us of a professor who on one occasion was found drunk, and when much depressed on account of his folly, the devil said to him, by way of temptation, " Do it again, do it again; for," said he, " the grief you feel about it now you will never feel any more if you commit the sin again." Dr. Preston says that the man yielded to the temptation, and from that time he never did feel the slightest regret at his drunkenness, and lived and died a confirmed sot, though formerly he had been a very high professor. *Spurgeon.*

11,704. SIN, Hatred of. An Arminian controverting with a Calvinist, said, " If I believed your doctrine and was sure that I was a converted man, I would take my fill of sin." The Calvinist replied, " How much sin do you think it would take to fill a true Christian to his own satisfaction?" He hit a striking fact, though no answer. The Christian loathes sin, the sinner loves it.

11,705. SIN, Increase of. One danger of secret sin is that a man cannot commit it without being by-and-by betrayed into a public sin. If a man commit one sin, it is like the melting of the lower glacier upon the Alps, the others must follow in time. As certainly as you heap one stone upon the cairn to-day, the next day you will cast another, until the heap reared stone by stone shall become a very pyramid. See the coral insect at work you cannot decree where it shall stay its pile. It will not build its rock as high as you please; it will not stay until an island shall be created. Sin cannot be held in with bit and bridle; it must be mortified.   *Spurgeon.*

11,706. SIN, Insidiousness of. Sin is like the little serpent aspis, which stings men, whereby they fall into a pleasant sleep, and in that sleep die.   *Swinnock.*

11,707. SIN, Origin of. Dr. Emmons, of Northampton, boldly taught that God was the author of sin. The discussion of this subject raged with great fury. One of his opponents retorted upon him with a vision. He said he was traveling in the west of England, when he saw a great black cloud, out of which gradually developed a figure, much like a man. He asked him who he was, and received answer that he was the devil. Again he was asked what he was doing, and where he was going. The devil flew into a great rage, and said that every mean crime, great or small, committed in that country was charged upon him; that he was about to take up his abode in Northampton, America, where such transactions were charged directly to the Almighty.   *Dr. Holme.*

11,708. SIN, Overcoming. Sin is to be overcome, not so much by maintaining a direct opposition to it, as by cultivating opposite principles. Would you kill the weeds in your garden, plant it with good seed: if the ground be well occupied, there will be less need of the labor of the hoe. If a man wished to quench fire, he might fight it with his hands till he was burnt to death; the only way is to apply an opposite element. *Andrew Fuller.*

11,709. SIN, Poison of. A man who wished to buy a handsome ring, went into a jeweler's in Paris. The jeweler showed him a very ancient gold ring, remarkably fine, and curious on this account, that on the inside of it were two little lion's claws. The buyer, while looking at the others, was playing with this; at last he purchased another, and went away. But he had scarcely reached home, when first his hand, then his side, then his whole body became numb and without feeling, as if he had a stroke of palsy; and it grew worse and worse, till the physician, who came in haste, thought him dying. "You must somehow have taken poison," he said. The sick man protested that he had not. At length some one remembered this ring; and it was then discovered to be what used to be called a death-ring, and which was often employed in those wicked Italian states three or four hundred years ago. If a man hated another, and desired to murder him, he would present him with one of them. In the inside was a drop of deadly poison, and a very small hole, out of which it would not make its way except it was squeezed. When the poor man was wearing it, the murderer would come and shake his hand violently, the lion's claw would give his finger a little scratch, and in a few hours he was a dead man. Now, see why I told you this story. For four hundred years this ring had kept its poison, and at the end of that time it was strong enough almost to kill the man who had unintentionally scratched his finger with the claw; for he was only saved by great skill on the part of the physician, and by the strongest medicines. I thought, when I read that story, how like this poison was to sin. You may commit a sin now, and for the present forget it; and perhaps ten or twelve years hence the wound you then, so to speak, gave yourself, may break out again, and that more dangerously than ever. And the greatest danger of all is, lest the thoughts of sins we have committed, and the pleasure we had in committing them, should come back upon us in the hour of death. *Dr. J. M. Neale.*

11,710. SIN, Pollution of. How deep is the pollution of sin, that nothing but the blood of Christ can cleanse it! All the tears of a penitent sinner, should he shed as many as there have fallen drops of rain since the creation, cannot wash away one sin. The everlasting burnings in hell cannot purify the flaming conscience from the least sin.   *John Flavel.*

11,711. SIN by Proxy. According to an old writer, no Capuchin among the papists may take or touch silver. This metal is as great an anathema to them as the wedge of gold to Achan, at the offer whereof they start back as Moses from the serpent; yet the monk has a boy behind him who will receive and carry home any quantity, and neither complain of metal or measure. Such are those who are great sticklers themselves for outward observance in religion, but at the same time compel their servants to sin on their account. They who sin by substitute shall be damned in person.   *Spurgeon.*

11,712. SIN, Punishment of. What a diabolical invention was the "Virgin's kiss," once used by the fathers of the Inquisition! The victim was pushed forward to kiss the image, when, lo, its arms enclosed him in a deadly embrace, piercing his body with a hundred hidden knives. The tempting pleasures of sin offer to the unwary just such a virgin's kiss. The sinful joys of the flesh lead, even in this world, to results most terrible, while in the world to come the daggers of remorse and despair will cut and wound beyond all remedy.   *Spurgeon.*

11,713. SIN, Rebuke of. An old English woman, hearing some gentlemen engaged in improper conversation, said, "Sirs, you are making work for repentance." It is an important thought that should check every sinful action.

11,714. SIN, Relief from. A converted Hindoo came to be baptized. He said he had been for years searching for a way of happiness in Poojahs (holy places in the river, etc.), but all in vain; but when he heard the word of Christ he could not rest. He sat up a whole night in distress of mind. He had great fears about his sins. When asked how he lost them, he said, "They went away in thinking of Christ." We shall never get rid of our fear in any other way.

11,715. SIN, Revelation of. Coals of fire cannot be concealed beneath the most sumptuous apparel, they will betray themselves with smoke and flame; nor can darling sins be long hidden beneath the most ostentatious profession, they will sooner or later discover themselves, and burn sad holes in a man's reputation. Sin needs quenching in the Saviour's blood, not concealing under the garb of religion. *Spurgeon.*

11,716. SIN, Review of. A dying miner, lying on a bed of boughs, said to his comrades, "I have now reached a point at which the whole scene of my life seems to lie visibly before me. Every action that I have committed, every sin, every crime that I have perpetrated before God, seems to stare me right in the face. I can see my way clear back to my youth, and, as I look, the scenes of iniquity and guilt in which I have been engaged pass one another before me in terrible review." They sang with him, and prayed with him, and endeavored to console him and point him to Jesus; but, said he, "It's all over now; all over! I have rejected Christ, and there is no salvation for me." He died soon after.

11,717. SIN, Snares of. I read an account of a man who saw a very curious spectacle—that of a black snake more than a foot long suspended in the air in a perfect sack of spider's web. And the spider was not a large one. It was one of those small spiders. It bore no proportion to its victim, nor could he by any biting hurt him. But there he had him imprisoned. He had drawn him, little by little, into the air, and the snake could not help himself. Probably the serpent was torpid, or the enemy was so small that he did not know that he was upon him. And the spider spun out of his bowels a little film, not a third part as large as the smallest silk thread that a woman uses withal, and he dipped down and touched the snake with it, and it stuck. He took another little film and touched him with that, and it stuck. He went on industriously, and as the snake lay quiet, he put another and another film upon him; and as there was time enough, he added another and another, till there were a hundred, a thousand, ten thousand of them. And by-and-by these little weak strands, no one of which was strong enough to hold a gnat, when multiplied became strong enough to encase the victim. A million times stronger the snake was than that miserable little spider, and yet the spider caught him; he webbed him round and round, until when he tried to move he was held fast. The web had grown strong out of its weakness. By putting one strand here and another there, and drawing on this, that, and the other, the spider at last lifted the burden, and it hung suspended in the air. I have seen men webbed by offences in that same way, and no one of the offences was much larger than the film of a spider's web, and at last they were imprisoned and destroyed. *Anon.*

11,718. SIN, Stain of. Look, as one drop of ink coloreth a whole glass of water, so one gross sin, one shameful action, one hour's compliance with anything of antichrist, will color and stain all the great things that ever you have suffered, and all the good things that ever you have performed; it will stain and color all the good prayers that ever you have made, and all the good sermons that ever you have heard, and all the good books that ever you have read, and all the good words that ever you have spoke, and all the good works that ever you have done, and therefore, whatever you do keep off from sin, and keep off from all sinful compliances, as you would keep off from hell itself. *Brooks.*

11,719. SIN, Torture of. It is reported that the cantharis fly, by a certain kind of contrariety, carries within itself the cure of the wound which it inflicts. On the other side wickedness, at the same time it is committed, engendering its own vexation and torment not at last, but at the very instant of the injury offered, suffers the reward of the injustice it has done. And as every malefactor who suffers in his body bears his own cross to the place of execution, so are all the various torments of various wicked actions prepared by wickedness herself. *Plutarch.*

11,720. SIN, Unpardonable. Aretius, a godly and eminent author, speaking of the sin against the Holy Ghost, said: "I saw and knew the man myself, and it is no feigned story. There was a merchant in Strasburg, whose whole life was abominable for whoredom, usury, drunkenness, contempt of God's word; he spent his life in gaming and whoring to his old age. At last he came to reflect on himself, and be sensible of the dreadful judgments of God hanging over his head. Then did his conscience so affright, and the devil accuse and terrify him, that he fell into open and downright desperation. He confessed and yielded himself to the devil as being his. He said, the mercy and grace of God could not be so great as to pardon sins so great as his. Then what horror was upon him, gnashing of teeth, weeping, wailing; yea, he would challenge Satan, and wish the devil would fetch him away to his destined torments. He threw himself all along upon the ground; refused both meat and drink. Had you seen him, you would never have forgot him while you had lived; you had seen the fullest pattern of a despairing person. Yet, after the many pains of godly and learned men who came to him, watched with him, reasoned with him, laid open the word and will of God, and after many prayers, public and private, put up for him, at length he recovered and became truly penitent; and having lived piously for certain years after, he died peaceably." He concluded, it is not an easy matter to determine of any man sinning against the Holy Ghost, and incapable of mercy, so long as he live. *Sheffield.*

11,721. SIN, Vengeance upon. After Julius Cæsar was murdered, Antonius brought forth his coat, all bloody and cut, and laid it before the people, saying, "Look, here you have the Emperor's coat thus bloody and torn;" whereupon the people were presently in an uproar and cried out to slay those murderers; and they took their tables and stools that were in the place, and set them on fire, and ran to the houses of them that had slain Cæsar, and burnt them. So that when we consider that sin hath slain our Lord Jesus, ah, how should it provoke our hearts to be revenged on sin, that hath murdered the Lord of glory, and hath done that mischief that all the devils in hell could never have done? *Brooks.*

11,722. SIN, War upon. Men hunt the lion, tiger, wolf, or other beast of prey till they are exterminated. Bounties are offered by the government for the heads of such. If it is discovered that one has visited a certain place the alarm is given, and men turn out for miles around, and organize for a bear or wolf hunt. The beast may have taken a pig from the sty, or a sheep from the flock. There is a beast loose in the land which is a man destroyer. No cannibal was ever so voracious of human flesh. He is found destroying even in our cities and villages. Sound the alarm. Gather the people and hunt him from your midst. It is the raging wild beast rum.

11,723. SIN Washed Away. A woman went to a minister carrying a heavy bundle of wet sand. "Do you see what this is, sir?" said she. "Yes," was the reply," "it is wet sand.' "But, do you know what it means?" "I do not know exactly what you mean by it; what is it?" "Ah, sir," she said, "that's me, and the number of my sins they cannot be counted." And then she exclaimed, "O wretched creature that I am! how can such a wretch as I ever be saved?" "Where did you get the sand?" asked the minister. "At the Beacon." "Go back then to the Beacon; take a spade with you; dig, dig, and raise a great mound; shovel it up as high as ever you can, then leave it there; take your stand by the seashore, and watch the effect of the waves upon the heap of sand." "Ah, sir," she exclaimed, "I see what you mean—the blood, the blood, the blood of Christ; it would wash it all away."

11,724. SIN, Whirlpool of. Mr. Ogden was descending the Columbia river in one of the boats of the United States Exploring Expedition, with ten Canadian voyagers, all well experienced in their duties. On arriving at the Dalles, they deemed it practicable to run them, in order to save the portage. Mr. Ogden determined, however, that he would pass the portage on foot, believing, nevertheless, the river was in such a state that it was quite safe for the boat to pass down. He was accordingly landed, ascended the rocks, from which he had a full view of the water beneath, and of the boat in its passage. At first she seemed to skim over the waters like the flight of a bird; but he soon perceived her stop, and the struggle of the oarsmen, together with the anxious shout of the bowman, soon told him that they had encountered the whirl. Strongly they plied their oars, and deep anxiety, if not fear, was expressed in their movements. They began to move, not forward, but onward with the whirl. Round they swept with increasing velocity, still struggling to avoid the now evident fate that awaited them. A few more turns, each more rapid than the last, until they reached the centre, when in an instant the boat, with all her crew, disappeared. So short had been the struggle, that it was with difficulty Mr. Ogden could realize that all had perished. Only one body out of the ten was afterward found at the bottom of the Dalles, torn and mangled by the strife it had gone through. *Anon.*

11,725. SIN, Wounds of. In the heart of the old elm, which has been the pride and ornament of Boston Common for a century, but which like all earthly things came to its end, was found a flattened bullet which it had concealed for two hundred years, as was shown by the number of rings enclosing it. The wood had closed over it, but could not throw off the wound, or conceal it always. Men, have carried bullets in various members of their bodies, even in the brain, sometimes for years, unconsciously. So it is with the soul. A wound in youth may be carried till old age and death, almost forgotten, or it may be an open wound that will not heal. It will have its effect and be revealed at last. The wounds of sin can be cured only by the great physician.

11,726. SINCERITY Defined. Sincerity is to speak as we think, to do as we pretend and profess, to perform and make good what we promise, and really to be what we would seem and appear to be. *Tillotson.*

11,727. SINCERITY, Importance of. True wisdom and greatness of mind raise a man above the need of using little tricks and devices. Sincerity and honesty carries one through many difficulties which all the arts he can invent would never help him through. For nothing doth a man more real mischief in the world than to be suspected of too much craft; because every one stands upon his guard against him, and suspects plots and designs where there are none intended: insomuch that though he speaks with all the sincerity that is possible, yet nothing he saith can be believed. *Stillingfleet.*

11,728. SINGING, Benefits of. There is nothing like singing to keep your spirits alive. When we have been in trouble, we have often thought ourselves to be well-nigh overwhelmed with difficulty; and we have said, "Let us have a song." We have begun to sing; and Martin Luther says, "The devil cannot bear singing." That is about the truth; he does not like music. It was so in Saul's days: an evil spirit rested on Saul, but when David played on his harp, the evil spirit went from him. This is usually the case; if we can begin to sing, we shall remove our fears. *Spurgeon.*

11,729. SINNER, Address to the. O sinner, what a condition wilt thou fall into when thou departest this world, if thou depart unconverted! Thou hadst better have been smothered the first hour thou wast born; thou hadst better been plucked one limb from another, thou hadst better been made a dog, a toad, a serpent, than to die unconverted; and this thou wilt find true if thou repent not.

Bunyan.

11,730. SINNER, Contrast to the. The godless person is like the ferret, which hath its name in Hebrew from squeaking and crying, because he squeaketh sadly if taken from his prey. When the godly man (as Paulinus Molanus, when his city was plundered by the barbarians) though he be robbed of his earthly riches, hath a treasure in heaven, and may say, "Lord, why should I be disquieted for my silver and gold? for thou to me art all things." "Having nothing, yet he possesseth all things." *Swinnock.*

11,731. SINNERS, Blindness of. A gentleman after attending church one day, said, "Here is gratitude for you; here I and my family have shown this man the greatest kindness, and the return he makes when he gets into the pulpit, is to tell us that we are great sinners unless we repent. He preaches that our good works go for nothing before God. This sermon will do very well for a penitentiary; but before a genteel and respectable audience, to tell them that they are sinners, is the most extraordinary conduct that I ever met with."

11,732. SINNERS, Exposure of. Last night, when I was thinking upon this subject, I had a half-waking dream, and I thought I stood out along the Hudson River Railroad track, and I saw a man sitting on that track. I went up to him and said, "My friend, don't you know you are in peril? The Chicago express will be along in a few moments." I found he was deaf and did not hear. I tried to pull him away from that peril, and he resisted me, and said, "What do you mean by bothering me? I am doing nothing. Am I disturbing you? I am doing nothing at all. I am just sitting here." At that moment I heard in the distance the thunder of the express train. A moment afterwards I saw the headlight of the locomotive flash around the corner. I held fast to the rocks that I might not be caught in the rush of the train. Like a horizontal thunderbolt it hurled past. When the flagman came, five minutes after, with his lantern, there was not so much as a vestige left to show that a man had perished there. What had the victim been doing there? Nothing at all. He was only sitting still—sitting still to die. So I find men in my audience to-night. I tell them the peril of living without God and without hope in the world. They say, "I am not doing anything. I don't lie. I don't swear. I don't steal. I don't break the Sabbath-day. I am sitting here to-night in my indifference, and what you say has no effect upon my soul at all. I am just sitting here." Meanwhile the long train of eternal disaster is nearing the crossing, and the bridges groan, and the cinders fly, and the brakes clank, and the driving wheel speeds on, and there is a blinding rush, and in the twinkling of an eye they "perish from the way when God's wrath is kindled but a little." *Talmage.*

11,733. SINNERS, Following. A minister was awakened at midnight by a message from a sick young lady who wished to see him. As he entered the room, he noticed a younger sister of the dying girl, who was evidently fast following her into eternity. He asked the sick girl of her prospects, and as he did so, the younger sister arose and abruptly left the room. He was rejoiced to find that the dying girl was leaning on the strong arm of Christ. And so she died—in hope. Only a few weeks from her death, he was again sent for; this time to visit the younger sister, who was following the elder to the grave. As he went to her bedside, she looked up with great anxiety, and asked, "Mr. M——, do you remember, when you were here before, and began to talk to my sister about death, I left the room?" "Yes; why did you do so?" "Because I did not wish to hear what you would say; and now see where I am. Oh, Mr. M——, why did you not follow me, and make me hear?" There was agony, even despair in her tones, as she said it; and then she added, "Oh, it is a dreadful—dreadful thing to die." And before many hours she died—in despair.

11,734. SINNERS, Hope for. A woman who did not consider herself bad, was anxious about her soul. She went to a church where she heard the minister preach that the ungodly would be saved. That day she took a place with the ungodly and was saved. Christ came to save sinners, not the righteous.

11,735. SIN-OFFERING, Christ Our. The sin-offering was burnt without the camp. The other offerings were, without exception, burnt on the altar in the Tabernacle. Here "the skin of the bullock, and all his flesh, with his head, and with his legs, his inwards, etc., even the whole bullock shall he carry without the camp, and burn him on the wood with fire." It testified how completely the offering was identified with the sin it suffered for; so completely identified that it was itself looked at as sin, and as such cast out of the camp into the wilderness. A part indeed, "the fat," was burnt on the altar, to show that the offering though made a sin-bearer, was itself perfect. But the body of the victim, "even the whole bullock," was cast forth without the camp. "Wherefore Jesus also, that he might sanctify the people with his own blood, suffered without the gate." He was cast out as one who was unfit for Jerusalem, as unworthy a place in the city of God. *A. Jukes.*

11,736. SINS, Danger of Small. Little sins arm God's terrible power and vengeance against you. As the page carries the sword of a great warrior after him, so your little sins bear the sword of God's justice, and put it into his hands against you. *Hopkins.*

11,737. SINS, Forgotten. There is nothing that happens, you know, which must not inevitably, and which does not actually, photograph itself in every conceivable aspect and in all dimensions. The infinite galleries of the past await but one brief process, and all their pictures will be called out and fixed forever. We had a curious illustration of the great fact on a very humble scale. When a certain bookcase, long standing in one place, for which it was built, was removed, there was the exact image on the wall of the whole, and of many of its portions. But in the midst of this picture was another—the precise outline of a map which had hung on the wall before the bookcase was built. We had all forgotten everything about the map, until we saw its photograph on the wall. Then we remembered it, as some day or other we may remember a sin which has been built over and covered up, when this lower universe is pulled away from before the wall of infinity, where the wrongdoing stands self-recorded. *Holmes.*

11,738. SINS, Magnitude of. No sin against God can be little; because it is against the great God of heaven and earth; but if the sinner can find out a little god, it may be easy to find out little sins. *Bunyan.*

11,739. SINS, Progress of Little. The least sin is rather to be avoided and prevented than the greatest sufferings; if this cockatrice be not crushed in the egg, it will soon become a serpent; the very thought of sin, if but thought on, will break out into action, action into custom, custom into habit, and then both body and soul are lost irrecoverably to all eternity. The least sin is very dangerous. Cæsar was stabbed with bodkins; Herod was eaten up of lice; Pope Adrian was choked with a gnat; a mouse is but little, yet killeth an elephant if he gets up into his trunk; a scorpion is little, yet able to sting a lion to death; though the leopard be great, yet he is poisoned with a head of garlic; the least spark may consume the greatest house, and the least leak sink the greatest ship; a little postern opened may betray the greatest city; a dram of poison diffuseth itself to all parts, till it strangle the vital spirits, and turn out the soul from the body. If the serpent can but wriggle in his tail by an evil thought, he will soon make a surprisal of the soul, as you see in that great instance of Adam and Eve. *Brooks.*

11,740. SINS, Secret. The ichneumon-fly lays its eggs in the body of the caterpillar. When the egg is hatched the larva begins to feed at once on the body of the poor worm. It avoids, by a remarkable instinct, the vital parts, and the caterpillar creeps on his way feeding as unconsciously as if he were in no danger. So many a soul is lost by some secret sin. The friends of a young man were shocked by finding him suddenly transformed into a drunkard. Before they suspected him he was lost to all shame or self-respect. He had been for years drinking in secret before this exposure, and the last stages were very rapid. There is a little weed which sometimes creeps into our canals and rivers, which seems very insignificant at first; but if left to itself it grows so fast, and its rope-like stems become so matted, that it seriously hinders navigation. Just such a multiplying evil is one little secret sin suffered to take root in the heart. Let us offer every day the prayer, "Cleanse thou me from secret faults." *Am. Messenger.*

11,741. SLANDER, How to Endure. It was reported to the poet Tasso that a malicious enemy spoke ill of him to all the world. "Let him persevere," said Tasso. "his rancor gives me no pain. How much better is it that he should speak ill of me to all the world, than that all the world should speak ill of me to him."

11,742. SLANDER, Punishment of. In early times, in the city of New York, slander was esteemed a rank offence. One Jan Adamzen, for slandering certain respectable persons, was condemned to be "stuck through the tongue with a red-hot iron, and banished from the province."

11,743. SLANDER, Sharpness of. Thearidas, the Spartan, was whetting his sword, when one asked him, "Is it sharp, Thearidas?" He replied, "Yes, sharper than slander."

11,744. SLANDER, Symbol of. There is in the museum at Venice, a machine by which some forgotten Italian tyrant used to shoot poisoned needles at the objects of his hatred. If merely used against our enemies, how much better than the tongues of back-biters and slanderers, who hurl poisoned words indiscriminately.

11,745. SLAVERY, Abolition of. In the Declaration of Independence the doors of the Temple of Liberty were thrown wide open; but the nation could not take slavery into it, and so they were closed, and it remained eighty-five years in the vestibule, cramped, embarrassed and agitated by a declaration of principles opposed by the constitutional law of the land, until Abraham Lincoln, our second Washington, issued his immortal Proclamation of General Emancipation; and then the doors of the Temple of Liberty swung once more upon their golden hinges, and the whole nation entered—the meanest slave beside the haughtiest aristocrat, endowed with the same inalienable rights of life, liberty, and the pursuit of happiness. *Dr. J. A. M. Chapman.*

11,746. SLEEP, Boon of. Sleep; what a rich boon it is to frail and weary men! It is one of God's purest acts of beneficence. He gives what he never needs, what he never takes. He sheds a sweet oblivion round and round the world, himself keeping watch, while man, and beast, and bird, and even, in a measure, bud, and leaf, and blossom, take their rest. Sleep; it comes to the wet sea-boy in the rudest hour, to the poor slave in the intervals of his hopeless toil, to the traveler in the forest or on the mountains, and—marvel of mercy! —to the sinner under the heavy load of his sin! *Raleigh.*

11,747. SLEEP, Characteristic. Even sleep is characteristic. How charming are children in their lovely innocence! how angel-like their blooming hue! How painful and anxious is the sleep and expression in the countenance of the guilty! *Humboldt.*

11,748. SLEEP, Tradition of. A tradition, related by Rabbi Jachonnan in the Talmud, is that one Onias, who lived seventy years before Christ, was meditating on the text, "When the Lord turned the captivity of Zion, then vere we like unto them that dream." He thought "seventy years of captivity. How could that pass as a dream?" Then he saw a man planting a carob-tree, and he asked him, "How long before that tree will bear fruit?" "Seventy years." "Fool! think you that you will live to eat of the fruit of the tree you plant?" "Rabbi, my father planted a carob-tree, of which I eat now. I plant this that my son may eat thereof." The day being hot, Onias entered a cave, and fell asleep. When he awoke, he saw a man gathering the fruit of a carob-tree. "Did you plant the tree?" he asked. "No, Rabbi, my grandfather planted it seventy years ago." Then Onias returned to his house, and found it occupied by his grandson, and knew that he had slept seventy years.

11,749. SLOTH, Spiritual. A man who is under the dominion of spiritual sloth is like one who has a journey to take, but who has fetters on his legs; like a soldier who must stand up in a battle, but without armor or weapons of offence; or like a mariner who sits inactive in his boat, and leaves it to the mercy of the waves. Do you imagine that all that is necessary for you to do is to step into the boat, and lie down and sleep, and leave it to pursue its own course? This is enough if you are to sail with the stream, and only to be stopped when you reach the gulf of perdition below. But if you are to sail against the stream, and avoid having your bark dashed upon some neighboring rock, there must be watchfulness, and strength, and exertion, or you will never reach the fountain of life. *Salter.*

11,750. SMALL SINS, Effect of. In the fortification of a city or town all the ramparts are not castles and strongholds; but between fort and fort there is a line drawn that joins all together and makes the place impregnable. So it is in the fortification of the soul by sin. All sins are not strongholds of Satan: they are greater and grosser sins: but between these is drawn a line of smaller sins so close that you cannot find a breach in it, and by these the heart is fenced against God. *Secker.*

11,751. SMALL THINGS, Perfection by. How frequently are small things those which perfect anything! For instance: it is the bloom of the plum which perfects it, the scent in the flower, the cut of the nostril, or the dimples in a countenance, the short strings in a harp, the delicate finishing touches in a picture. What perfects a fireside but the children links? what perfects a cathedral choir but the children's notes? and what perfects God's praise but the "mouth of babes and sucklings?" *W. J. Bolton.*

11,752. SMILE, Effect of a. A minister said to me, "I want you to notice that family in one of the front seats, and when we go home I want to tell you their story." When we got home I asked him for the story, and he said, "All that family were won by a smile." "Why," said I, "how's that?" "Well," said he, "as I was walking down a street one day I saw a

child at a window; it smiled, and I smiled, and we bowed. So it was the second time; I bowed, she bowed. It was not long before there was another child, and I had got in a habit of looking and bowing, and pretty soon the group grew, and at last, as I went by, a lady was with them. I didn't know what to do. I didn't want to bow to her, but I knew the children expected it, and so I bowed to them all. And the mother saw I was a minister, because I carried a Bible every Sunday morning. So the children followed me the next Sunday and found I was a minister. And they thought I was the greatest preacher, and their parents must hear me. A minister who is kind to a child and gives him a pat on the head, why the children will think he is the greatest preacher in the world. Kindness goes a great way. And the father and mother and five children were converted, and have joined the church." *Moody.*

11,753. SMOKING, Abandoning. When the use of tobacco was fashionable even among the genteel, in walking through a village, I passed a store where I knew there were some very fine cigars. I was immediately seized with the hankering so well known to habitual smokers. The determination arose to lay out a few shillings in purchasing some. As I had been endeavoring to accustom myself to regard my money as the Lord's and myself as the steward, I tried the rule in that case. I found myself unwilling to charge such an item on my account book. A faithful steward would make no such expenditure, thought I. The money which had been taken out was dropped again into my pocket, and I passed on. I have ever found it difficult to smoke cigars since that time. The cure which I propose is, to ask the blessing of God on all expenditures, and try to be faithful stewards of the Lord's money. *Ohio Observer.*

11,754. SNARES, Escaping from. St. Antony saw in a vision the earth covered so thickly with snares that it seemed impossible to put down a foot without being caught in them. Then he cried out, "Who, O Lord, shall escape them all?" A voice replied, "Humility, O, Antony!"

11,755. SNEERING, Import of. The most insignificant people are the most apt to sneer at others. They are safe from reprisals, and have no hope of rising in their own esteem but by lowering their neighbors. The severest critics are always those who have either never attempted, or who have failed in original composition. *Hazlitt.*

11,756. SNOW, Voice of the. The Rev. R. M. M'Cheyne was observed looking out of his window one clear frosty winter's day, during his sickness. The sun shone, and the snow glittered with whiteness. He looked upon it with glowing eyes and was heard to say to himself, "Whiter than snow! whiter than snow!" Evidently re-calling Isaiah's word from the Lord, "Though your sins be as scarlet they shall be as white as snow." Is. 1: 18.

11,757. SOCIETY, Changes of. Society undergoes continual changes: it is barbarous, it is civilized, it is Christianized, it is rich, it is scientific: but this change is not amelioration. For everything that is given, something is taken. Society acquires new arts, and loses old instincts. The civilized man has built a coach, but has lost the use of his feet: he has a fine Geneva watch, but cannot tell the hour by the sun. *Emerson.*

11,758. SOCIETY, Restraints of. Anub and his six brothers were hermits, and lived together in a deserted pagan temple at Terenuth in the fifth century. At first Anub, the eldest of the brothers, every morning threw stones at the face of one of the idols, and at night he bowed before it, and apologized for the insult of the morning. He continued this strange conduct for seven days, when his brothers asked him what he meant. He answered, "I threw stones at the face of the image. Did it scowl, or look sulky, or utter words of anger?" "No." "And when I bowed the knee to it, and showed it profound respect, did it look pleased?" "No." Then said Anub, "Here are we seven brothers. If we purpose in our hearts to be like that image, unmoved by what we may say or do to one another, then, by all means, let us dwell here together. But if we are going to resent wrongs, or utter bitter speeches, or covet flattery, here are four doors, and let us separate." The lesson seems to have been effectual. They abode together in peace, till death separated them, under the rule of Anub—sitting at a common table, none of them saying, "Give me something else; I cannot eat this."

11,759. SOLDIER, Face of the. I well remember reading of a soldier tall and strong, who had a wondrous cuirass of gold, curiously-wrought; but it was buckled behind by straps that had seen much service. They were weather-stained and worn, and men said they were altogether unbecoming so gorgeous a breast-plate. His comrades said, however, that it mattered not, that his enemies never saw anything unseemly, for he never turned his back to them. And we truly should ever stand, presenting a bold front to our spiritual enemies. Our safety is in fighting, not in flight. *Pilkington.*

11,760. SOLDIERS, Christ's. The birthday of the Emperor Maximian was celebrated by the army with great pomp, and many sacrifices to the gods, in which all were requested to participate. Marcellus, a Christian, was a captain in the legion of Trajan. He refused to participate in the idolatrous ceremonies, cast off his military belt, threw down his arms, and the vine branch which he carried as insignia of office, and declared himself a soldier of Jesus Christ. For this he was taken before the prefect of the legion, and said in answer to the charge of desertion and impiety, "When you celebrated the emperor's festival, I said aloud that I was a Christian, and could serve no other than Jesus Christ, the Son of God." At a further hearing he maintained firmly his previous decision, and was led forthwith to execution. He laid down his life A. D. 298, at Tangiers, Africa, sooner than participate, even in a general way, in the pagan festivities.

11,761. SOLDIERS, Reliable. During the war in India, the British army were nearly surprised by the enemy. The commander-in-chief sent in great haste to order a particular corps to occupy at once a prescribed post. The order was to no purpose, for the men of that corps were so many of them intoxicated that they were unfit for duty. The danger would presently have become serious. The general knew this well, and he knew, too, how it could best be met. "Then," said he, when told that his former order was unavailing, "call out Havelock's saints; they are never drunk, and Havelock is always ready." They were immediately unders arm, and the enemy were repulsed.

11,762. SOLDIERS, Religious. The strict temperance and religious devotion of Havelock's corps of the British army in India, secured for it the contemptuous epithet, "Havelock's Saints." It was reported in England that the general had turned preacher, and a committee of investigation was appointed. It was found that he had prayers with his troops both morning and evening; that on Sunday he formed them in a hollow square and preached to them. Their religion did not make them worse, but better soldiers. The report said: "No troops in India are as well drilled, as well equipped, as efficient. In time of trouble, the cry is, 'Bring out the saints.' They are never drunk. Havelock never blunders. Should trouble arise in India, Havelock's Corps will be the main reliance of the government." And so it proved on the outbreak of the Sepoy rebellion.

11,763. SOLITUDE, Disadvantages of. In complete solitude, the eye wants objects, the heart wants attachments, the understanding wants reciprocation. The character loses its tenderness when it has nothing to love, its firmness when it has none to strengthen it, its sweetness when it has nothing to soothe it, its patience when it meets no contradiction, its humility when it is surrounded by dependants, and its delicacy in the conversations of the uninformed. *Hannah More.*

11,764. SOLITUDE, Happiness in. Solitude is not always desolation. How solitary, yet how glad is the mathematician, among his silent ratios and quiet trains of reasoning! How solitary, yet serene, the astronomer on his watch-tower, under the twinkling of the midnight stars! How solitary the student amongst his books, and yet who more blest than he? How solitary the poet, whilst his images are either slowly arising around or swiftly sweeping across his soul, and he is tempted to say, "This is the gate of heaven!" To make solitude happy, two elements are required: first, that the mind be at ease and satisfied with itself; and secondly, that it be employed also in some object out of itself. If a mind is not self-satisfied, solitude is solitude no more, "but peopled with the furies." If a mind be not occupied with some subject out of itself, its solitude may be luxurious, but is selfish, and will by-and-by become miserable.   *G. Gilfillan.*

11,765. SOLITUDE, Sins of. More and greater sins are committed when men are alone than when they keep themselves in fellowship. When Eve in paradise walked alone, then came the evil one and deceived her. Whoever is amongst honest men and in honest company, is ashamed to sin; or, at least, he has no place or opportunity to do so. When King David was alone and idle, and went not out into the wars, he fell into adultery and murder; and I have myself found, that I have never fallen into more sin than when I was alone. Solitariness inviteth to melancholy; and a person alone hath often some heavy and evil thoughts; so hath he strange thoughts, and construeth everything in the worst sense. Melancholy is an instrument of the devil, by which he accomplishes his wicked purposes. The deeper a person is plunged into that state, the more power the devil hath over him. To live in an open, public state, is the safest. Openly, and amongst other persons, a man must live civilly and honestly—must appear to fear God, and do his duty towards men.
     Luther.

11,766. SOLOMON, King. Full of sublime devotion, equally full of practical sagacity; the extemporizer of the loftiest litany in existence, withal the author of the pungent Proverbs; able to mount up on Rapture's ethereal pinion to the region of the seraphim, and keenly alive to all the details of business, and shrewd in his human intercourse; zealous in collecting gold, yet lavish in expending it; sumptuous in his tastes, and splendid in costume; and—except in so far as intellectual vastitude necessitated a certain catholicity—the patriot intense, the Israelite indeed: like a Colossus on a mountain-top, his sunward side was the glory toward which one millennium of his nation had all along been climbing—his darker side, with its overlapping beams, is still the mightiest object in that nation's memory.
     Dr. J. Hamilton.

11,767. SORROW, Benefit of. God sees that they are very good for us; for, as seeds that are deepest covered with snow in winter flourish most in spring; or as the wind by beating down the flame raiseth it higher and hotter; and as when we would have fires flame the more, we sprinkle water upon them; even so, when the Lord would increase our joy and thankfulness, he allays it with tears of affliction.   *Salter.*

11,768. SORROW, Chariot of. There is no suffering, no sorrow, no human experience, that you have not the power to rise above, to subdue—nay, to harness to you, and make carry you. For sufferings, rightly understood, are, as it were, God's coursers harnessed to your chariot to bear you up. Horses and a chariot of fire did the prophet have to take him to heaven; but he is not the only one that went to heaven in a chariot of fire. Thousands are riding in chariots of fire. Sorrow is the fire, and troubles are those coursers by which

myriads of men are being drawn, in that flaming chariot, heavenward.   *Beecher.*

11,769. SORROW, Flowers of. There is a tree near Bombay called "The Sorrowful Tree." It blooms only in the night. So soon as the sun declines the flowers burst out. We may, like that tree, bring forth flowers of grace in the night of sorrow.

11,770. SORROW for Sins of Others. St. Lawrence Justinian, the Patriarch of Venice, says, "He cannot help sorrowing for other people's sins, who sorrows truly for his own. A healthy limb on the body, that helps not the others when they are sick, occupies its place in vain. These members likewise of the church, who see their brethren's sin and do not weep over it, or compassionate the ruin of their souls, are useless members. When our Redeemer wept over the city that was to perish, he considered it the more to be deplored as it knew not itself its deplorable condition. As many, therefore, as are set on fire by the torch of love, weep over other men's sins as if they were their own. Yet no one worthily deplores the sins of others, who by voluntary falls neglects his own. We must at least cease to sin wilfully, if we desire to mourn over the falls of others." St. Augustine says, "We mourn over the sins of others, we suffer violence, we are tormented in our minds." St. Chrysostom says that Moses was raised above the people because he habitually deplored the sins of others. "He," says the same holy Doctor, "who sorrows for other men's sins, has the tenderness of an apostle, and is an imitator of that blessed One, who said, 'Who is weak and I am not weak? who is offended, and I burn not?'"   *F. W. Faber.*

11,771. SORROWS, Entertainment of. That which the French proverb hath of sickness is true to all evils, that they come on horseback and go away on foot. We have often seen a sudden fall, or one meal's surfeit hath stuck by many to their graves; whereas pleasures come like oxen, slow and heavily, and go away like post-horses, upon the spur. Sorrows, because they are lingering guests, I will entertain but moderately, knowing that the more they are made of, the longer they will continue; and for pleasures, because they stay not. and do but call to drink at my door, I will use them as passengers, with slight respect. He is his own best friend that makes least of both of them.   *Bishop Hall.*

11,772. SOUL, Auction of a. Rev. Rowland Hill was preaching in the open air in the Moorfields, London. His text was taken from the Song of Solomon 1: 5, "I am black, but comely." The text he regarded as having application to the Church, which, in the estimation of the world, was black—"black as the tents of Kedar"—but, in the estimation of her glorified Head, comely, comely, "as the curtains of Solomon." While discussing these themes, Lady Anne Erskine passed that way. Seeing the immense multitude, she asked one of her attendants the cause of this assemblage, and learned that Rowland Hill was preaching to the people. She had often wished to hear nim, and resolved to avail herself of the present opportunity to gratify that cherished desire. She requested her driver to place her carriage as near to the preacher's stand as possible, so that she might hear every word that he uttered. In a few moments she found herself immediately in the rear of the temporary pulpit from which the speaker addressed the listening throng, that being the only unoccupied position within reach of his voice. The splendor of her equipage turned the attention of many of the people away from the sermon. Rowland Hill detected the diversion, and hastened to remedy it. Elevating his voice beyond its usual pitch, he exclaimed, "My brethren, I am now going to hold an auction or vendue, and I bespeak your attention for a few moments. I have here a lady and her equipage to expose to public sale; but the lady is the principal and the only object, indeed, that I wish to dispose of at present, and there are already three earnest bidders in the field. The first is the World. Well, and what will you give for her? 'I will give riches, honor, pleasure.' That will not do. She is worth more than that; for she will live when the riches, honors, and pleasures of the world have passed away like a snow-wreath beneath a vernal shower. You cannot have her. The next bidder is the devil. Well, and what will you give for her? 'I will give all the kingdoms of the earth and the glory of them.' That will not do; for she will continue to exist when the kingdoms of the earth and the glory of them have vanished like the shadows of the night before the orient beams. You cannot have her. But list, I hear the voice of another bidder, and who is that? Why, the Lord Jesus Christ! Well, what will you give for her? 'I will give grace here and glory hereafter; an inheritance incorruptible, undefiled, and that fadeth not away.' Well, well," said the preacher, "blessed Jesus, it is just as I expected; just the noble generosity which thou are wont to display. I will place her at your disposal. She is 'black, but comely,' and you shall be the purchaser. Let heaven and earth authenticate this transaction." And then, turning to Lady Anne, who had listened with emotions of wonder and alarm, the speaker, exclaimed, "Madam! madam! do you object to this bargain? Remember you are Jesus Christ's property from this time henceforth and for evermore. Heaven and earth have attested the solemn and irreversible contract! Remember, you are the property of the Son of God. He died for your rescue and your purchase. Can you, will you, dare you object?" The appeal was blessed to her conversion, and she became identified with Lady Huntingdon, in earnest Christian work.

11,773. SOUL, A Blind. Judge what a sad and dangerous state a blind soul is in; just like a fiery, high-mettled horse, whose eyes are out, furiously carrying his rider upon rocks, pits, and precipices. I remember Chrysostom, speaking of the loss of a soul, says if a man lose an eye, ear, hand, or foot, there is another to supply its want: "God hath given us those members double; but he hath not given us two souls," that if one be lost, yet the other may be saved. Surely it were better for thee to have every member of thy body made the subject of the most exquisite racking torments than for spiritual blindness to befall thy soul.
John Flavel.

11,774. SOUL, Computing the Value of the. An earnest minister said to a young college graduate, "I have heard you are celebrated for your mathematical skill; I have a problem which I wish you to solve." "What is it?" The clergyman answered, "What shall it profit a man if he should gain the whole world, and lose his own soul?" The young man thought over the problem, and endeavored to shake off the impression; but in vain. Everywhere the question returned to him, "What if I gain the whole world, and lose my own soul?" It resulted in his conversion, and he become a preacher of the gospel.

11,775. SOUL, Death and the. A little English girl, about seven years of age, went, accompanied by a brother younger than herself, to see an aunt who lay dead. On their return home, the little boy expressed his surprise that he had seen her, saying, "I always thought when people were dead, that they went to heaven; but my aunt did not, for I saw her." His sister replied, "I fear you do not understand it: it is not the body that goes to heaven; it is the *think* that goes to heaven: the body remains, and it is put into the grave, where it sleeps till God shall raise it up again."

11,776. SOUL, Description of a. Laura Bridgman was an exceedingly interesting young girl who was not only deaf and dumb, but blind. Her instructor, endeavoring to show the difference between the material and immaterial, used the word soul? "What is soul?" she asked, "That which thinks, feels, hopes, loves," "And aches," she responded eagerly.

11,777. SOUL, Existence of the. All philosophers, a few epicureans and Pyrrhonists excepted, have acknowledged the existence of the soul as one of the first and most unexceptionable principles of human science. Now, whence could a notion so universal arise? Let us examine our own minds, and we shall find it could arise from nothing but consciousness, a certain irresistible persuasion that we have a soul distinct from the body. The evidence of this notion is instructive; it is the evidence of internal sense. Reasoning can neither prove nor disprove it. Descartes and his disciple Malebranche, acknowledge that the existence of the human soul must be believed by all men, even by those who can bring themselves to doubt of everything else. *Buck.*

11,778. SOUL, Growth of the. The progress of the soul is something unique. It is not like the progress of planets—they run in circles; their course is an eternal careering through the same scenes and circumstances. When they have once swept their spheric pathways, though they move for ever, their age of novelty is over; henceforth, on them the same ether will breathe, and the same suns will shine. But the soul, in every stage of growth, rises into a new sphere of conscious being. In each original thought it soars to a new orbit and rolls through a new and brighter firmament; in every fresh resolve it feels an outbirth into another and a higher world. Nor is the progress of the soul exactly like that of the tree. The tree exhausts itself in growing; its growth is but a progress to decay and destruction; though it flourish for a thousand years it has an end: death will seize it, root and branch, and crumble it to dust. But the soul contains inexhaustible germs, and when it is under the influence of godliness, it is placed amidst inexhaustible elements of nutrition; it is rooted beside the eternal river of infinite truth and love. Its progress indeed is more like the progress of the little stone in the prophet's dream, than aught else which I can think of. That stone moved by its own force, and grew as it moved; it swelled in every revolution, it expanded to a mountain, it penetrated the clouds, it filled the world. It stopped in its growth because its motion ceased; it ceased in its motion because it had filled its sphere. It is even so with a holy soul; it moves by its own force; it expands as it moves, and it will move for ever, if it have space: and space it will have, for its sphere is the illimitable. Here we have touched the margin of the profoundest poetry of our being; and if our imagination cross the line, and enter the mystic realm, we shall sit mute in wonder. The idea of infinitude seals the lips, and stops the pen. *Dr. Thomas.*

11,779. SOUL, Inscrutability of the. The first philosophers, whether Chaldeans or Egyptians, said there must be something within us which produces our thoughts. That something must be very subtle: it is a breath; it is fire; it is ether; it is a quintessence; it is a slender likeness; it is an intelechia; it is a number; it is harmony; lastly, according to the divine Plato, it is a compound of the same and the other! It is atoms which think in us, said Epicurus, after Democritus. But, my friend, how does an atom think? Acknowledge that thou knowest nothing of the matter. *Voltaire.*

11,780. SOUL, Killing the. A vindictive Italian captured his enemy and required him first to renounce all hope in Christ or suffer instant death. The timid man complied. His enemy then stabbed him to the heart, exclaiming, "I have sweet revenge, for I have killed soul and body both."

11,781. SOUL, Longing of the. The human soul is like a bird that is born in a cage. Nothing can deprive it of its natural longings, or obliterate the mysterious remembrance of its heritage. *Epes Sargent.*

11,782. SOUL, Martyr's Care for his. When one of the martyrs was going to the stake, a nobleman besought him to take care of his soul. "So I will," he replied, "for I give my body to be burnt, rather than have my soul defiled."

11,783. SOUL, Music in the. "The following experiment, described by Prof. Tyndall, shows how music may be transmitted by an ordinary wooden rod. In a room two floors beneath his lecture-room there was a piano upon which an artist was playing, but the audience could not hear it. A rod of deal, with its lower end resting upon the sounding-board of the piano, extended upward through the two floors, its upper end being exposed before the lecture-table. But still no sound was heard. A violin was then placed upon the end of the rod, which was thrown into resonance by the ascending thrills, and instantly the music of the piano was given out in the lecture-room. A guitar and a harp were substituted for the violin, and with the same result. The vibrations of the pianostrings were communicated to the soundingboard, they traversed the long rod, were reproduced by the resonant bodies above, the air was carved into waves, and the whole musical composition was delivered to the listening audience." This represents our unmusical hearts, but when they are tuned by the Spirit and connected with Christ, the soul of harmony, by faith, they will give forth melody to the observing world.

11,784. SOUL, Nakedness of the. Consider your deplorable state who are wholly naked and unarmed. Can you pity the beggar at your door, (when you see such in a winter-day, shivering with naked back, exposed to the fury of the cold) and not pity your own far more dismal soul-nakedness, by which thou liest open to heaven's wrath, and hell's malice? Shall their nakedness cover them with shame, fill them with fear of perishing, which makes them with pitiful moans knock and cry for relief, as it is reported of Russia, where their poor (through extreme necessity) have this desperate manner of begging in the streets: Give me, and cut me; give me, and kill me! And canst thou let Satan come and cut thy throat in thy bed of sloth, rather than accept of clothes to cover, yea, armor to defend thee? *Gurnall.*

11,785. SOUL, Preservation of the. Every traveler has something very precious in his custody, his own soul. You will lose it pilgrim, if you go off the way. The miners in the goldfields of Australia, when they have gathered a large quantity of the dust, make for the city with the treasure. The mine is far in the interior, the country is wild, the bush is infested by robbers; the miners keep the road and the daylight. They march in company, and close by the guard sent to protect them. They do not stray from the path among the woods, for they carry with them a treasure which they value, and they are determined to run no risks. *Arnot.*

11,786. SOUL, Question of the. "What shall it profit a man if he gain the whole world and lose his own soul?" A lady riding in a carriage saw something in the street which she supposed of value, and caused her coachman to get it. It was a Sunday-school card with the above text upon it. It arrested her attention and led her to Christ. The history of this one text would fill a volume.

11,787. SOUL, Responsibility for. Restore to the Lord the spirit entire, as thou hast received it; for if thou gavest to a fuller a garment which was entire, and desirest so to receive it again; but the fuller restored it to thee rent, wouldst thou receive it? Wouldst thou not say in anger, "I delivered to thee my garment entire, wherefore hast thou torn it, and made it useless? It is now, on account of the rent which thou hast made in it, of no more service to me." If thou then grievest for thy garment, and complainest because thou receivest it not entire again, how, thinkest thou, will the Lord deal with thee, who gave thee a perfect spirit; but which spirit thou hast marred, so that it can be of no more service to the Lord? for it became useless when corrupted by thee. *Anon.*

11,788. SOUL, Return of the. A legend says that the body of Melonius, a holy man, bishop of Rennes in Brittany, who died while on a journey through his diocese, was placed in a boat and returned to Rennes without oars or sails, against the current of the stream. However it may be with the body, there is no doubt that the soul finds its way at death to its home, either the ready mansions of the saints or the dark abodes of the lost.

11,789. SOUL, Sadness of. Cardinal Richelieu, who had given law to Europe for many years, acknowledged the unhappy state of his mind to P. du Moulin. Being asked why he was so sad, the Cardinal replied, "The soul is a serious thing; it must either be sad here or be sad forever."

11,790. SOUL, Sin in the. Many people can mourn over a body from which a soul is departed, but they cannot mourn over a soul whom God has deserted: alas! what is the bite of a fly, to the stinging of a scorpion; or a spot in the face to a stab in the heart? Inward diseases are least visible, and yet most fatal. A man may die of the plague, although his spots never appear. Sin in the soul is like Jonah in the ship; it turns the smoothest water into a troubled ocean. We must mourn for sin on earth, or burn for sin in hell. It is the coldness of our hearts which kindles the fire of God's anger. *Secker.*

11,791. SOUL, Spoliation of the. When the impious king Antiochus entered the temple of Jerusalem to lay it waste, his first act was to remove the golden altar, and the candlestick, which was also of gold. The devil acts in the same manner when he intends to deprive of spiritual good that soul which is the temple of the living God: he takes from it the altar —that is, fervor of mind; he removes from it the candlestick—that is, the light which makes known the eternal maxims. The devil cannot take from the soul the light of faith: he, however, removes the light of consideration; so that the soul may not reflect on what it believes. And as it is of no avail to open the eyes in the dark, so, says St. Augustine, "it is of no advantage to be near the light if the eyes are closed." The eternal maxims, considered in the light of faith, are most clear; yet, if we do not open the eyes of the mind by meditating on them, we live as if we were perfectly blind: and so precipitate ourselves into every vice. *Ignatius.*

11,792. SOUL, Voice of the. After all, let a man take what pains he may to hush it down, a human soul is an awful, ghostly, unquiet possession for a bad man to have. Who knows the metes and bounds of it? Who knows all its awful perhapses—those shudderings and tremblings, which it can no more live down than it can outlive its own eternity! What a fool is he who locks his door to keep out spirits, who has in his own bosom a spirit he dares not meet alone; whose voice, smothered far down, and piled over with mountains of earthliness, is yet like the forewarning trumpet of doom! *Mrs. Stowe.*

11,793. SOUL, Voyage of the. Baring-Gould gives, on the authority of Macpherson, the following legend: One day a famous Druid of Skerr sat upon the rocks by the sea shore musing. A storm arose, the waves dashed high and the winds howled. Out of it a boat, with white sails and gleaming oars, emerged. In it were no sailors; the boat seemed to live and move of itself. A voice called to the Druid, "Arise, and see the Green Isle of those who have passed away!" He entered the boat; the wind shifted at once, and amid clouds and spray he sailed forth. Seven days gleamed on him through the mist; on the eighth the waves rolled violently, the vessel pitched and darkness thickened around him, when suddenly he heard a cry, "The Isle! the Isle!" The clouds parted before him, the wave abated, the wind died away, and the vessel rushed into dazzling light. Before his eyes lay the isle of the departed, basking in golden light. Its hills sloped green and tufted with beauteous trees to the shore; the mountain tops were enveloped in bright and transparent clouds, from which gushed limpid streams, which, wandering down the steep hill-sides with pleasant harp-like murmur, emptied themselves into the twinkling blue bays; the valleys were open and free to the ocean; trees loaded with leaves, which scarcely waved to the light breeze, were scattered on the green declivities and rising ground; all was calm and bright, the pure sun of autumn shone from his blue sky on the fields; he hastened not to the west for repose, nor was he seen to rise in the east, but hung as a golden lamp, ever illuminating the Fortunate. There in radiant halls, dwelt the spirits of the departed, ever blooming and beautiful, ever laughing and gay.

11,794. SOUL, Weeding the. King Charles the Fat sent a messenger to Notker, the monk, to ask what he should do for his soul, who found him in his garden weeding it and watering the plants. "Tell the king to do what I am doing now," was all the answer he made. When this was reported to the king, he said, "Yes, that is the sum of all. Away with the weeds of vice, and water the plants of grace."

11,795. SOUL AND BODY, Reunion of the. Even the glorified soul in heaven has a natural desire of union with its own body. We are all sensible of the soul's affection to the body now, its sympathy with it, and unwillingness to be separated from it. It is said to be "at home in the body." 2 Cor. 5: 6. This inclination remains in heaven; it reckons not itself completely happy till its older dear companion and partner be with it. Now, when this inclination to its own body, its longings after it, are gratified with the sight and enjoyment of it again, what a joyful meeting will this be! especially if we consider the excellent temper and state in which they shall meet each other. For as the body shall be raised with all the improvements and endowments imaginable which may render it every way desirable, so the soul comes down immediately from God out of heaven, shining in its holiness and glory. And thus it re-enters its body, and animates it again.   *John Flavel.*

11,796. SOULS, Converting. I have passed through many places of honor and trust, both in church and state, more than any of my order in England these seventy years back; yet were I but assured that by my preaching I had but converted one soul to God, I should take therein more spiritual joy and comfort, than in all the honors and offices which have been bestowed upon me.   *Archbishop Williams.*

11,797. SOULS, Earnestness for. A little while ago, a clegyman said to a young man who never thought of his soul, "My dear young friend, I think you are going to lose your soul! You are putting off the day of salvation—neglecting all these solemn matters; going on heedlessly, I fear, to the day of your death." The young man looked up with surprise, and said, "I don't think so! And you must really pardon me, but I have my doubts whether you really think so, or your church thinks so." The minister was astonished. He never suspected the young man of scepticism. "How so?" he asked. "Why, my mother belongs to your church. Don't they all think as you do." "Yes, they do." "Well, then, don't my mother love me? And do you think she would never have told me, if she thought I was going straight to perdition? And there's my sister; don't she believe as you do?" "Yes." "Now, then, I know my sister loves me. Dont, don't, don't you think she would warn me if she thought I was going to perdition?"   *J. W. Smith.*

11,798. SOULS, Labor for. A minister whose pastorate of twenty years had not been crowned with many souls, was waited upon by a committee of his congregation to request him to resign on account of his unfruitful ministry. Incidentally the committee stated that he had been the means of converting only one soul in twenty years. "Do you say that? Do you know that one soul has been converted? Then here goes for another twenty years' work for another soul." The serious question would be how many more might and would have been saved through a more efficient preacher? How many were lost in that time? Our ministry should save souls, or give place to one that will.

11,799. SOULS, Perseverance for. A missionary from India, addressing an assembly, said he had been obliged to wait twelve years before God had rescued by his instrumentality one soul from the darkness of heathenism. But if he were asked whether he would have gone to the heathen, if he had been told thirty years before how little fruit of his labors he would have seen, he now answered most cheerfully, "Yes, indeed, I would have gone!"

11,800. SOULS, Price of. All they who wrong others to enrich themselves; all that rob upon the highway, pick pockets, or break open houses; all that forge deeds, forswear themselves, or suborn others to do so in law-suits; all that willingly cheat, defraud or overreach their neighbors, in buying or selling their goods; all that pilfer and steal, or so much as withhold and conceal what they know belongs to another; all that are able, yet will not pay what they owe, but lie in prison, or hide themselves, or at least pretend they cannot do it; all that smuggle the king's customs, or corrupt his officers, and by that means keep to themselves what the law hath made due to him; all that refuse or neglect to relieve those of their relations or others, which are really in need, and so withhold from them the maintenance which God hath appointed for them; all that oppress and gripe poor workmen in their prices, or servants in the wages which are due to them; all that work upon people's necessities, and extort from them more than the laws of the land allow of; all that follow such unlawful trades as tend to the corrupting of youth, and to the nourishing of vice and wickedness in the world; all that by false weights or measures, by lying, over-reckoning, or by any trick, impose on those they deal with; and all that are conscious to themselves that, by these and such like unlawful ways, they have got other men's money, goods or estate in their hands, and yet will not restore them again to their right owners as far as they are able,—these all as plainly lose their souls for this world as if they should make a solemn contract or bargain with the devil that, upon condition, they may have such and such things at present, he shall have their souls forever; for so he will, and leave them in the lurch, too: he will serve them in their own kind; as they cheated others, he will cheat them, and put them off with nothing but dreams and fancies, instead of the great profit and advantage they expected.   *Bishop Beveridge.*

11,801. SOULS, Unwelcome Effort for. A man had been repeatedly urged to seek Christ, and did not fail to show his displeasure. His friends were in earnest, and would not let him alone. At last, yielding to their persistence, he went to the altar of prayer. He was converted, and said to those who had pressed him, "God bless you for persevering, for if you had not I might have been lost. I am so thankful that you did not let me alone."

11,802. SOULS, Watching for. I visit and examine every district of my large congregation every year. My father did so; and though the increasing population of the country has enlarged the congregation considerably, I follow his example. Though urged by my friends to lessen my labor, I still go on; and my vigorous health fits me for a toil that would be oppressive to others. Old Mr. Shirra, of Kirkaldy, said to his brethren, when urging them to hard service, "It will not look the worse at the day of judgment." *Dr. H. Belfrage.*

11,803. SOUL-SAVING, Co-operation in. I don't know of anything that would make a man get up quicker than to have four people combining to try to bring him to Christ. Suppose one man calls upon him after breakfast; he doesn't think much about it; he has had some one invite him to Christ before. Suppose before dinner the second man comes and says, "I want to lead you to Christ. I want to introduce you to the Son of God." The man is quite aroused now; perhaps he has never had the subject presented to him by two different men in one day. But the third man has come, and the man has become thoroughly aroused by this time, and he says to himself, "Why, I never thought so much about my soul as I have to-day." But before the man gets to bed at night the fourth man has come, and I will guarantee that he won't sleep much that night—four men trying to bring him to Christ. If we can't bring our friends to Christ, let us get others to help us. If four men won't do it, let us add the fifth, and the Lord will see our faith, and the Lord will honor our faith, and we shall see them saved. *Moody.*

11,804. SOUL-SAVING, Estimate of. A cotemporary writer says, "If we were to suppose the present population of our globe to be sixteen hundred millions, which is probably an overestimate, and that in all that vast number there was but one true Christian, and that he should be instrumental in the hands of the blessed Sprit, during the coming year, of the conversion of two others to Christ, and that each of these new converts should instrumentally lead two others to Christ during the first year of their spiritual life, and that the work should thus continue—each new convert leading two others to Christ within a year of his conversion, how long would it take at this rate for the whole sixteen hundred millions to be brought to Christ? The answer will doubtless startle many of our readers; but if we may rely upon figures, the whole world would be converted in a little less than thirty years and a half, or within less than a single generation! Is such a work too mighty for God's Spirit to accomplish, or for the church to strive to achieve? But let us vary somewhat the conditions. Instead of supposing, as above, that there was but one true Christian in all the world, let us, with a nearer approximation to the truth, suppose the number to be at least twenty millions. This is probably much below the truth. If each one of these should bring to Christ instrumentally a single soul within the coming year, the whole number would be doubled before the close of 1877. If similar blessed results should follow prayer and effort

in 1878, and be continued year after year—each true Christian becoming instrumental by prayer and personal effort in the salvation of only one soul each year—long before the year 1883 would have come to a close, the grand chorus would be heard in heaven: 'The kingdoms of this world have become the kingdoms of our Lord and his Christ, and he shall reign for ever and ever.' By each true Christian bringing instrumentally one soul to Christ each year, in less than seven years the world would be regenerated!"

11,805. SOUL-SAVING, Reward of. A young minister lodging in Margate, England, was aroused from slumber by hearing the cry, "Ramsgate, Ramsgate." He endeavored to find its source, but could not. Again he slumbered and was aroused by the same cry, "Ramsgate, Ramsgate." He concluded that the voice called him thither, and in the morning, obedient to the impulse, he set forth. Arrived there, he met an old friend who invited him to dine at his house, which was situated on an eminence fronting the sea. After dinner he strolled along the beach, where several youths were bathing. To one venturesome swimmer his attention was particularly drawn. He saw him suddenly disappear, and watched in vain for his reappearance. He noted the spot, called for the most expert swimmer of the boys, and encouraged him to rescue his friend. The brave youth dived at the place indicated, found the body and brought it ashore apparently lifeless. The man at once set about using all the usual appliances for resorting suspended animation. Constant friction and artificial breathing were resorted to for a long time with no success. The bystanders said further efforts were useless, and refused to help longer. The minister felt that his work in Ramsgate was to save this youth, and he persevered in his efforts. At last slight signs of life were manifested. Slowly animation returned. The youth was placed in a warm bed in the house where the minister had dined, and fell into a quiet sleep, closely watched by his rescuer. After a time he awoke and inquired how he came there. He was told of his narrow escape, and filled with gratitude threw himself at the feet his rescuer, exclaiming, "My more than father!" He felt himself fully repaid for his labors. He was invited to be present at the meeting of the Royal Humane Society for that year. His philanthropic deed had become well known. At the meeting, side doors were thrown open suddenly, when a procession of rescued men filed slowly through the hall, every one of whom had been snatched from a watery grave by the efforts of some one. In the procession was the rescued youth, scanning every face as he passed till he recognized his deliverer. He broke from the lines, and ran to embrace him, and the whole assembly was moved by the spectacle. He was summoned to the chair, and received the honors, thanks and medal of the society. If such is the reward of saving a life, what shall be the honor bestowed upon him who rescues a soul from death in the presence of saints, angels and God?

11,806. SOUL-SAVING, Skill in. A little girl found a fragment of a paper, on which was a picture. She carried it to her father, a poor inebriate, and expressed her delight with the beautiful picture, but the father could see no beauty in it. "O, yes, papa," said she, "it is a beautiful picture." It represented a father, mother, and little girl at prayer. "Just think, papa, if this man praying was you, and this woman was mamma, and this little girl was me, what a happy home we should have!" She had her idea of a happy home from an uncle's where she had visited, and, in memory of it, she appealed to her father. The father's heart melted, the picture prophecy became reality, and all the characters in it are now members of the Free-Will Baptist Church in Candia, N. H.

11,807. SOUL-SAVING, Successful. The wife of a pastor requested twelve of the leading unconverted men of the parish to meet her at the parsonage on a specified evening. They all came and had a brief conversation on the subject of personal religion. While they were together the pastor was in another room praying for them. The lady wrestled all night in prayer for these men, and prevailed. Nine of the twelve men were converted within three weeks from that time.

11,808. SOWING, Daily. A gentleman visiting at the house of a farmer, saw him scattering grain broadcast upon his field and asked, "What are you sowing." "Wheat," was the answer. "And what do you expect to reap from it?" "Why wheat, of course," said the farmer. The same day some little thing provoked the farmer, and he flew into a violent passion, and, forgetting, in his excitement, the presence of his guest, swore most profanely. The gentleman said, "And what are you sowing now?" A new light at once flashed upon the farmer from the question of the morning. "What!" he said, in a subdued and thoughtful tone, "do you take such serious views of life as that, such serious views of every mood, and word and action?" "Yes," was the reply; "for every mood helps to form the permanent temper; and for every word we must give account; and every act but aids to form a habit; and habits are to the soul what the veins and arteries are to the blood—the courses in which it moves, and will move for ever. By all these little things we are forming character, and that character will go with us to eternity, and according to it will be our destiny forever."

11,809. SOWING, Picture of. I was at the Paris Exhibition in 1867, and noticed there a little oil painting, only about a foot square, and the face was the most hideous I have ever seen. On the paper attached to the painting were the words "Sowing the tares," and the face looked more like a demon's than a man's. As he sowed these tares, up came serpents and reptiles, and they were crawling up on his body, and all around were woods with wolves and animals prowling in them. I have seen that picture many times since. Ah! the reaping time is coming.   *Moody.*

11,810. SPARROWS, Lesson from the. The sparrows which flutter and twitter about dilapidated buildings at Jerusalem, and crevices of the city walls, are very numerous. In some of the more lonely streets they are so noisy as almost to overpower every other sound. A person who resided in the country told me that these birds are sometimes brought to market in order to be sold as food. Being so small and abundant, their value singly must, of course, be trifling; and hence, as the custom of selling them was an ancient one, we see how pertinent was the Saviour's illustration for showing how minutely God watches over all events, and how entirely his people may rely on his care and goodness. *Biblical Treasury.*

11,811. SPEAKING, Good. Archbishop Whately says, that, while the true object of oratory is to carry one's point, "many a wandering discourse one hears in which the preacher aims at nothing and hits it." As a contrast to this kind of oratory, we have the remark made as to the speeches of Bishop Blomfield, that they were "those of one who had something to say, not of one who had to say something."

11,812. SPEECH, Silence and. Plato says, that for a word, which is the lightest of all things, both gods and men inflict the heaviest penalties. But silence, which can never be called to an account, doth not only, as Hippocrates hath observed, extinguished thirst, but it bears up against all manner of slanders, with the constancy of Socrates and the courage of Hercules, who were no more concerned than a fly at what others said or did.   *Plutarch.*

11,813. SPENDTHRIFTS, Punishment of. It is said that in Padua there was a stone called the Stone of Turpitude. It was situated near the Senate-house, and to it all spendthrifts and debtors were brought and condemned to sit nude upon the stone. Thus publicly disgraced they were less likely to indulge in excessive prodigality in the future. Such a stone at the present time might find numerous occupants.

11,814. SPIRIT, Return of the. The Rabbis have delivered what follows, on Eccl. 12:7, where it is written, "The spirit shall return unto God who gave it." He gave it to thee unspotted, see that thou restore it unspotted to him again. It is like a mortal king, who distributed royal vestments to his servants. Then those that were wise, folded them carefully up, and laid them by in the wardrobe; but those that were foolish went their way, and, clothed in these garments, engaged in their ordinary work. After awhile the king was well pleased with the wise, and said, "Let the vestments be laid up in the wardrobe, and let these depart in peace." But he was angry with the foolish servants, and said, "Let the vestments be given to be washed, and those servants be cast into prison." So will the Lord do with the bodies of the righteous, as it is written, Isaiah 57:2; with their souls, 1 Sam. 35:29;

but with the bodies of the wicked, Isaiah 48: 22; 57: 21; and with their souls, 1 Sam. 25: 29.

11,815. SPIRIT, Wounds of the. The strokes of the "Sword of the Spirit" alight only on the conscience, and its edge is anointed with a balm to heal every wound it may inflict.

Dr. J. Harris.

11,816. SPIRITUALITY, Promotion of. It is said of St. Francis of Assisi, whatever he did, or wherever he was, his soul was always raised to heaven, and he seemed continually to dwell with angels. He consulted God before everything he did, and he taught his brethren to set a high value upon, and by humility, self-denial, and assiduous recollection, to endeavor to obtain the most perfect spirit of prayer, which is the source of all spiritual blessings, and without which a soul can do very little good. The practice of mental prayer was the favorite exercise which he strongly recommended. Persons who labored under any interior weight of sadness, or spiritual dryness, he vehemently exhorted to have resort to fervent prayer, and to keep themselves as much as possible in the presence of their Heavenly Father, till he should restore to them the joy of salvation. Otherwise, said he, a disposition of sadness, which comes from Babylon, that is, from the world, will gain ground, and produce a great rust in the affections of the soul.

Alban Butler.

11,817. SPRING, Contemplation of. There is no way in which the young can better learn the sentiments of devotion, or the old preserve them, than by cultivating those habits of thought and observation which convert the scenes of nature into the temple of God; which make us see the Deity in every appearance we behold, and change the world, in which the ignorant and the thoughtless see only the reign of time and chance, into the kingdom of the living and ever-present God of the universe. Reflections of this kind arise very naturally amidst the scenes we at present behold. In the beautiful language of the wise man, "The winter is over and gone, the flowers appear on the earth, and the time of the singing of birds is come." In these moments we are witnessing the most beautiful and astonishing spectacle that nature ever presents to our view. The earth, as by an annual miracle, arises, as it were, from her grave into life and beauty. It is in a peculiar manner the season of happiness. The vegetable world is spreading beauty and fragrance amidst the dwellings of men. The animal creation is rising into life; millions of seen, and myriads of unseen beings are enjoying their new-born existence, and hailing with inarticulate voice the Power which gave them birth. Is there a time when we can better learn the goodness of the universal God? Is it not wise to go abroad into nature, and associate his name with everything which at this season delights the eye and gratifies the heart?

Alison.

11,818. SPRING, Resurrection of. Beautiful is the season of awakening nature and spring—beautiful is the dawning day of summer; there is new life in the garden, the forest, and the field—beautiful! the hard reign of the winter is over, the birds have come back to us, the flowers appear on the earth—nature is awake again, is alive again, after her long sleep; the morning and the evening twilights are sacred to all sacred thoughts—spring is here. In the May boughs, in the lengthening twilight, in the note of the bird, in the gentle dew, in the fragrance of the flowers, in the echoing woods and hills, choral with the ring of waterfalls and rivulets rushing on their way, there is the glad voice—spring is here. Nature has been in her coffin long enough; God has touched the bier, and said, "Damsel, I say unto thee, arise," and she that was dead has heard the voice, and has come forth. The heart acknowledges the sway of the new life; so ever life lies deeper than death; the grave of death is only the urn, the sacred depository of life.

Hood.

11,819. SPRING, Spiritual. When our Lord spoke those great words, "God is a spirit, and they that worship him must worship him in spirit and in truth," words so fatal to priestcraft and to mere sacerdotalism; it was the spring-time of the world none the less because the beams had not struck down into the whole darkness. Spring is none the less here because there are clefts of the mountains where the snows as yet is unmelted, and rivers where the ice is yet unlocked. I step from the coffin of nature to the coffin of a dispensation. In the day of our Lord it was all-expiring; it was the advent of the spiritual—"That was not first which is spiritual, but that which is natural, and afterward that which is spiritual." The empire of the world's winter-day was dying, nor was there a word spoken by our Lord which was not seed for a new vernal empire of perpetual beauty. Judaism lay a dead root in a dry ground in the world's history, in a few years to be consigned to the lumber-room of the world's antiquities: but there was a seed in it; God, whose fingers touch the roots of trees and flowers, was at its heart in the germinating principle of life, grafting a new spirituality into it.

Hood.

11,820. SPRING, Symbology of. There is another symbol of spring; I refer to the singular preservation of the numberless germs which come to light, at this glad season, in all parts of the earth, the air, and the waters. The seed is to the plant what the egg is to the insect, or the bud to that which proceeds from it. In each egg there is a germ, containing the lineaments of a little animal, which needs only heat to develop it. In each seed also is a germ from which the plant issues. And as no vegetable is produced without a seed, to which it owes its first existence, no animal can come to the light which has not been prepared in an egg. But science has already numbered upon the globe ten thousand different species of plants, each of which proceeds from a germ peculiar to itself. And yet, my brethren, it is surprising that all these seeds of plants and eggs of insects, scattered everywhere, by millions upon millions, are never mistaken by the spring in its innumerable resurrections; the cochineal never arising where we expected the ant, or the tamarind in the place of the sycamore, or the mint and the cummin in the place of the hyssop or the mustard. But it is especially surprising how all these germs can, previous to their renewal, brave the power of the elements, the moisture of the night, the rigor of the winter, frequently long years, and sometimes also ages, without losing anything of their germinating virtue, or of that mysterious life which lies concealed in their interior. You have doubtless heard the tradition that the Greek missionaries, thirteen hundred years ago, secretly conveyed from China to Europe in the hollow of a pilgrim's staff, the first eggs of those marvelous worms which at this day supply us with silk, and which by their labors year after year enrich so many countries. You know also how in European markets people trade in these germs under the name of seed, as you would do with the seed of poppies or wheat. Our countryman, the illustrious Bonnet, mentions some little animals whose germs sustain, without perishing, the heat of boiling water; while others, still more remarkable, those for example, of the eels in rickety corn, or of polypi in rain-water, are preserved dry, and in a state of apparent death for many years, the one in the corn and the other in the dust. Corn has been discovered both in Europe and in Africa, which had been buried for several ages in cavities, or subterranean hollows, whose germs came to light as soon as one of our springs shed upon them its quickening breath. And to mention still one thing more, have you not heard of those Celtic tombs, and of the skeletons and seeds, lately discovered near Bergerac, in France? Under the head of each of these skeletons, buried, it is said, two thousand years ago, the superstition of the Druid priests had placed a block, and under each of these blocks in a little circular cavity covered with cement, a small quantity of seeds. Well, these seeds of two thousands years' duration, being collected and sown with particular care, have rapidly germinated; and the heliotrope, the trefoil, and the blue-bell have been seen springing in resurrection of life, after twenty centuries of a burial; so that last year you might have beheld, with your own eyes, those marvelous plants blossoming in beauty, under the light of our own spring, after their germs had slept two thousand years under the heads of the dead and in the dust of the tombs. O, my beloved brethren, my companions in the journey to the tomb, what may we not anticipate? Are not these sublime and imposing symbols; and am I not right in saying that they are rich in instruction and consolation? Do they not justify us in affirming that those very dead, whose dried skulls preserved the germs of the sunflower, the blue-bell, and the clover, shall also rise from their own dust in the last great day; that their germs shall be preserved, in spite

of all the powers of the elements and the duration of ages; that then Jesus will come in the clouds of heaven; that there will be a resurrection of the just and of the unjust; that all the dead that are in their graves shall hear his voice, and that he will quicken their bodies by his Spirit that dwelleth in them? *Gaussen.*

11,821. SPRINKLING, Custom of. In the East, when a prince or a great man gives a grand entertainment, there are servants who sprinkle with perfumed liquids (as rose water, etc.) the several guests as they enter. This sprinkling is understood to fit them for the presence of the entertainer, to declare them his guests, and, as such, to place them under his favor and protection. *Dr. Kitto.*

11,822. STABILITY, Condition of. A bronze figure of Luther, with gown and bands and the Bible in his arms, stands upon a pedestal of polished granite under a Gothic canopy at Wittenberg. Upon the base of the monument is the inscription, "Ist's Gottes Werk, so wirds bestehen. Ist's Menchen Werk wirds untergehen." If it is God's work it will stand, but if it is man's work it will perish. The ever spreading religion called Protestantism is Luther's noblest monument.

11,823. STEALING Arrested. The Rev. J. Smith, of Bathurst, South Africa, reports the following case, showing the power of conscience: "A fine, tall, athletic young man, a Caffre, addicted to all the debasing and demoralizing customs of his nation, one night resolved to go into the colony for the purpose of stealing a horse, which is a common practice with them. He immediately left his home, came into the colony, and watched for an opportunity of accomplishing his purpose, which soon presented itself. He found two horses grazing in a sheltered situation near a bush, and he instantly seized one of them, and made off with it as fast as he could. Elated with his success, and rejoicing in the prospect of securing his prize without being detected, he proceeded homewards, when all at once, the thought struck him, 'Thou shalt not steal.' He could go no further; he immediately drew up the horse, and said to himself; 'What is this? I have frequently heard these words before in the church; but I never felt as I do now. This must be the word of God.' He dismounted, and held the bridle in his hand, hesitating whether to go forward with the horse, or to return back with it, and restore it to its owner. In this position he continued for upwards of an hour. At last he resolved to take the horse back again, which he accordingly did, and returned home a true penitent, determined to serve God. When he reached his dwelling, he could not rest; sleep had departed from him; the arrows of conviction stuck fast in his conscience, and he could not shake them off. The next day he took an ox out of his *kraal* (or cattle place), and went to the nearest village to sell it, in order that he might buy European clothing with the money, and attend the house of God like a Christian. When he returned with his clothes, he went to the minister's house, told him all that had taken place, and requested to be admitted on trial as a church member. The minister, cheered with his statement, gladly received him; and, after keeping him on trial the appointed time, and finding him consistent in his conduct, a short time ago baptized him; and he is now a full member of the Christian church, and adorning his Christian profession."

11,824. STEALING, Conversion from. A highway robber, who had taken a gentleman's watch, money, and what he supposed to be valuable papers, found among them a sermon on the text, "Thou shalt not steal." The coincidence struck his attention, and the sermon alarmed him as he read it. He restored the stolen valuables to the minister, and became a reformed man.

11,825. STEWARDS, Oriental. Nearly all respectable families in the East have a steward, whose name in Tamul is Kanikapulle. He is sometimes one who has been master himself, or he is a relation, or has been selected on account of former services. His pay is often a mere trifle, and sometimes he has not any stipulated salary, but derives perquisites according to the extent of his master's dealings. Should there be money to give out on loan, he always demands from the borrower a certain percentage, and the least demur will cause him to say, "You cannot have the money; I have many other applicants." Is the produce of the land to be disposed of, he again squeezes something out of the purchaser, and if possible out of his master into the bargain. Has he anything to buy for the house, he grinds the face of the dealer, and demands a handsome present for the custom. Does he pay the servants or laborers, they must each dole out a trifle for their monthly or daily stipend; he never gives out goods or money without taking a bond or a "bill," which is sometimes written by the debtor, and always has his signature. Sometimes he brings false bonds and counterfeit jewels, and gives out large sums of money: and when his accomplices have decamped, he pretends to be, of all men, the most astonished at their villainy! When detected, he has generally a good store of his own filthy lucre, but should he not have succeeded, he would sooner starve than work, for the latter would be a mortal disgrace to a man of his rank! Even common beggars sometimes remind us of the passage, "I cannot dig." Religious mendicants swarm in every part of the East, and when you advise them to work, they cast upon you a contemptuous scowl, and walk off in great dudgeon, exclaiming, "We work! We have never done such a thing; we are not able. You are joking, my lord!" *Roberts.*

11,826. STONES, Sermons in. There are no natural objects out of which more can be learned than out of stones. They seem to have been created especially to reward a patient observer. Nearly all other objects in nature can be seen, to some extent, without patience, and are pleasant even in being half seen.

Trees, clouds and rivers are enjoyable, even by the careless; but the stone under his foot has for carelessness nothing in it but stumbling; no pleasure is languidly to be had out of it, nor food, nor good of any kind; nothing but symbolism of the hard heart and the unfatherly gift. And yet, do but give it some reverence and watchfulness, and there is bread of thought in it, more than in any other lowly feature of all the landscape; for a stone when it is examined will be found a mountain in miniature. The fineness of nature's work is so great, that, into a single block, a foot or two in diameter, she can compress as many changes of form and structure, on a small scale, as she needs for her mountains on a large one; and taking moss for forests, and grains of crystal for crags, the surface of a stone, in by far the plurality of instances, is more interesting than the surface of an ordinary hill; more fantastic in form, and incomparably richer in color.
Ruskin.

11,827. STONING, Death by. A crier marched before the man who was to die, proclaiming his offence and the names of the witnesses on whose testimony he had been convicted. This was for the humane purpose of enabling any one possessing knowledge of the parties and circumstances to come forward and arrest the execution, until his further evidence had been heard and considered. Hence, usually the tribunal which had sentenced the prisoner remained sitting to hear such evidence as might be thus produced, and did not rise until the execution had taken place. Arrived at the place, the convict was divested of his clothing, except a small covering about the loins; and, his hands being bound, he was taken to the top of some eminence not less than twice a man's height. When the top was reached, the witnesses laid their hands upon him, and then cast off their upper clothing that they might be the more ready for the active exertion their position imposed. To prevent their clothes from being lost, they were consigned to the care of some friend. All being ready, one of the witnesses cast the condemned down from that high place with great violence, endeavoring to do it so that he should fall upon a large stone which was designedly placed below. The fall usually rendered him insensible, if it did not kill him; but, if he was not dead, those below turned him upon his back, and then the other witnesses remaining above cast down a large stone aimed at his chest. This stroke was generally mortal; but, if not, the people below hastened to cast stones at him till no life remained. Thus the execution was quickly over, and was attended by fewer revolting circumstances than must have ensued from that indiscriminate pelting by the people which is commonly supposed to have constituted the stoning to death. It would seem that Stephen rose from his fall to his knees, and in that posture prayed for the forgiveness of his murderers—a circumstance which imparts an additional touching emphasis to his prayer.
Kitto.

11,828. STORMS, Facing. The ship that is anchored is sensitive to every change of wind or tide, and ever turns sharply around to meet and resist the stream, from what direction soever it may flow. A ship is safest with her head to the sea and the tempest. In great storms the safety of all often depends on the skill with which the sailors can keep her head to the rolling breakers. Life and death have sometimes hung for a day and a night in the balance, whether the weary steersman could keep her head to the storm until the storm should cease. Even a single wave allowed to strike her on the broadside might send all to the bottom. But to keep the ship in the attitude of safety, there is no effort and no art equal to the anchor. As soon as the anchor feels the ground, the vessel that had been drifting broadside, is brought up, and turns to the waves a sharp prow that cleaves them in two and sends them harmless along the sides. Watch from a height any group of ships that may be lying in an open roadstead. At night when you retire they all point westward; in the morning they are all looking to the east. Each ship has infalliby felt the first veering of the wind or water, and instantly veered in the requisite direction, so that neither wind nor wave has ever been able to strike her on the broadside. Thereby hangs the safety of the ship. Ships not at anchor do not turn and face the foe. The ship that is left loose will be caught by a gust on her side, and easily thrown over. As with ships, so with souls. *Arnot.*

11,829. STRIFE, Agent of. A trumpeter being taken prisoner in a battle, begged hard for quarter. "Spare me, good sirs, I beseech you," said he, " and put me not to death without cause, for I have killed no one myself, nor have I any arms but this trumpet only." "For that very reason," said they who had seized him, "shall you sooner die, for without the spirit to fight, yourself, you stir up others to warfare and bloodshed." *Æsop.*

11,830. STRIFE, Portents of. There is something irritating and belligerent in the sluggish atmosphere that precedes a storm. Even before the clouds gather along the horizon with portentous shade and mysterious muttering, the herds are in disorder, and some of the stoutest within the fold engaged in actual combat, trampling the pasture under foot in wanton strife. It is said of bees, that when they stir and strive among themselves, it is an indication that they are about to lose their queen. The commotion is a sign of trouble in the hive. The buzzing and darting of bees in every direction, all readier to sting than to work, is an outward manifestation of an internal disturbance. *Alexander Clark.*

11,831. STUDY, Methods of. It would have been well if Bacon had added some hints as to the mode of study: how books are to be chewed, and swallowed, and digested. For, besides inattentive readers, who measure their proficiency by the pages they have gone over, it is quite possible, and not uncommon, to read most laboriously, even so as to get by heart the words of a book, without really studying it at all; that is, without employing the thoughts on the subject. *Whately.*

11,832. STUDY, Subjects of. I received a most useful hint from Dr. Bacon, then father of the University, when I was at college. I used to frequently visit him at his living, near Oxford. He would frequently say to me, "What are you doing? What are your studies?" "I am reading so and so." "You are quite wrong. When I was young, I could turn any piece of Hebrew into Greek verse with ease. But when I came into this parish, and had to teach ignorant people, I was wholly at a loss. I had no furniture. They thought me a great man, but that was their ignorance; for I knew as little as they did of what it was most important for them to know. Study chiefly what you can turn to good account in your future life." *R. Cecil.*

11,833. STUPIDITY, Cause for. A facetious Irish minister remarked upon one of his stupid brethren, "Head! he has no head; what you call a head is only a top-knot that his maker put there to keep him from raveling out."

11,834. STUPIDITY, Reason of. Gough tells of a man who in attending lectures always left at a certain time. He was not a doctor, nor a man who was seeking to make himself conspicuous, and this eccentricity occasioned considerable remark among his neighbors. The reason of his action was not understood until after death, when a *post mortem* examination was held, when it was found that his skull had thickened, and kept thickening until there was no space left for his brain, and so he got filled up early and left to avoid an explosion.

11,835. STUPIDITY, Unconquerable. For of a truth stupidity is strong—most strong, as the poet Schiller sings, "Against stupidity the very gods fight unvictorious." There is in it a placid inexhaustibility—a calm viscous infinitude—which will baffle even the gods—which will say calmly, "Try all your lightnings here: see whether I cannot quench them." *Carlyle.*

11,836. STYLE, Attention to. Cicero was accustomed to construct his orations with the greatest care, and even to labor to bring his sentences to the highest polish. On one occasion he had not satisfied himself and the appointed time for his address was at hand. At this point one of his slaves brought him word that the assembly was postponed for a day. Cicero was so rejoiced at this announcement, because of the time it would give him for preparation, that he gave the slave his liberty.

11,837. STYLE, Power of. In nothing is the creative power of a gifted writer seen more than in his style; true, his words may be found in the dictionary, but there they lie disjointed and dead. What a wonderful life does he breathe into them, by compacting them into his sentences. Perhaps he uses no term which has not been hackneyed by ordinary writers; and yet with these vulgar materials what miracles does he achieve! What a world of

thought does he condense into a phrase! By new combinations of common words, what delicate hues or what a blaze of light does he pour over his subject! Power of style depends very little on the structure or copiousness of the language which the writer of genius employs, but chiefly, if not wholly, on his own mind. The words arranged in his dictionary, are no more fitted to depict his thoughts, than the block of marble in the sculptor's shop to show forth the conceptions which are dawning in his mind. Both are inert materials. The power which pervades them comes from the soul; and the same creative energy is manifested in the production of a noble style, as in extracting beautiful forms from lifeless stone.
Dr. Channing.

11,838. STYLE, Verbose. Plutarch had rather we should applaud his judgment than commend his knowledge, and had rather leave us with an appetite to read more, than glutted with that we have already read. He knew very well that a man may say too much even upon the best subjects, and that Alexandrides did justly reproach him who made very eloquent, but too long, speeches to the Ephori, when he said, "O stranger! thou speakest the things thou oughtest to speak, but not after the manner that thou shouldst speak them." Such as have lean and spare bodies stuff themselves out with clothes; so they who are defective in matter endeavor to make amends with words. *Montaigne.*

11,839. SUBMISSION, Acceptable. The inhabitants of a Carthagenian city rebelled against their king, and he sent out his proclamation of intention to destroy the city. For this purpose he marched his army toward the doomed place. At his approach the great men of the city went out to meet him barefooted, and with ropes on their necks in token of unconditional submission, and gave him the keys. Taking the keys, he said, "Live, O my children, for I love you still." The rebellious soul is safe when it throws itself thus upon the mercy of Christ.

11,840. SUBMISSION, Demand for. During the Revolutionary war, Dr. Franklin, then ambassador of the new republic to the court of France, applied to the ambassador of King George III., asking him to treat for an exchange of prisoners. He received the spirited reply, "The king's ambassador receives no application from rebels unless they come to implore his majesty's mercy." The like submission is necessary in appealing to the Supreme Ruler. There can be no compromise with him. To contend against the Almighty is the most glaring folly.

11,841. SUBMISSION, Necessity for. Three years ago two friends of mine, good swimmers, by the name of Wells and Baker, went out into the lake to swim. Wells was taken with cramps, and was drowning. Baker swam to him, when Wells seized hold of both of his arms, and they went down together. Baker succeeded in releasing himself, and when they came to the surface he called to Wells, "I can save you, Wells, but you must let me get hold of you by the hair, and not hold my hands." Wells promised to do so if he would only try it again. He went to him again, and the second time he seized him, and both went down under the water again. Under the water there was a terrible struggle, but at last Baker got away and swam out a few rods, and turned around and saw his friend drowning. He heard his piercing cry for help, but he could not save him. If he had only stopped trying! So the Lord will save every sinner who stops trying and only trusts him. *Moody.*

11,842. SUBMISSION, Reason for. I have watched an insect making its way with some earnest purpose along the highway, so long that I have become much interested in the success of its errand. When a loaded cart was coming up, whose wheel would have crushed the creature in an instant, I have laid a twig across its path, and compelled it to turn aside. Oh, how it stormed and fretted against my interference: if it could communicate with its kind, it would have a tale of hardship to recount that night, of some unknown and adverse power that stopped its progress and overturned its plans. Conceive, now, that intelligence should be communicated to that tiny being, and it should discover that another being, immeasurably raised above its comprehension, had in compassion saved it from death! Such will be the discoveries made in the light of heaven of the deliverances God wrought for his people. Oh, that will be joyful, to find out more and more of that incomprehensible thing. *Arnot.*

11,843. SUBMISSION, Wise. The Tusculani, a people of Italy, having offended the Romans, whose power was infinitely superior to theirs, Camillus, at the head of a considerable army, was on his march to subdue them. Conscious of their inability to cope with such an enemy, they took the following method to appease him: They declined all thoughts of resistance, set open their gates, and every man applied himself to his proper business, resolving to submit where they knew it was in vain to contend. Camillus entering their city, was struck with the wisdom and candor of their conduct, and addressed himself to them in these words: "You only, of all people, have found out the true method of abating the Roman fury, and your submission has proved your best defence. Upon these terms, we can no more find in our heart to injure you than upon other terms you could have found power to oppose us." The chief magistrate replied, "We have so sincerely repented of our former folly, that in confidence of that satisfaction to a generous enemy, we are not afraid to acknowledge our fault." Thus he who confesseth and forsaketh his sins, shall find mercy.
Buck.

11,844. SUBSTITUTE, Christ Our. A visitor said to a sick soldier, "You have a 'Substitute;' have you, brother? You see there is a last great 'Draft' coming, for which every man on earth is enrolled. I was in Ohio a few weeks ago, and some who didn't go to war tried very hard to get exempted, and if they could not, they took great trouble to find a substitute, paying large sums to get others to take their chance, as they call it, of death. Now against that last grand draft there is a substitute provided, who has already taken our place, even unto death, and he is offered 'without money and without price.'"

11,845. SUCCESS, Ministerial. The greatest success of the period has doubtless been gained by Rev. Chas. H. Spurgeon, of London. His commencement was discouraging; his work has been essentially missionary. The masses, for whom he longed, neglected him. He resolved to be heard, and said, "You shall hear me! If you will not hear me in a black coat, I will make you hear me in a red one." He was jeered at by the mob, caricatured by *Punch*, and written down by the *The Times.* He has a fine voice, earnest piety, and genuine love for souls. His personal influence is very great; his good sense is apparent in all his work. His individuality and vitality are very great. He is supreme in his church, and is never trammeled by boards of deacons, elders, or trustees; his wish is law among them. He built his great Metropolitan Tabernacle, personally collecting the funds for it. The same is true of his college and orphanage. He has written many books, edits a magazine, besides publishing more sermons than any living preacher, which are scattered in palace and cottage. It may encourage some of us to hear this wonderful man say, "The bane of my life is to keep myself steady at work. I often get discouraged, and think I should have done better at something else."

11,846. SUCCESS, Secret of. The lives of public men in America are so often dramatic and full of sudden and great changes that they attract little notice, and few of us trouble ourselves to deduce any signification touching our own work or aims from them. A man dies who has reached the second highest rank in the Government, and we hear without surprise the story of the excessive poverty and hard straits of his childhood. From the day of his birth until he was twenty-one he tells us that he had not had in all one dollar to spend. After that he had worked at shoemaking, making $5 a week, of which $2 went for board. His family and himself were abjectly ignorant, as well as poor. Yet, when we hear that in this strait he "made up his mind to go to school" and to succeed, and that he did it, and died Vice-President of the United States, we take it quite as a matter of course, and expend no wonder on the case. So, too, with the history of the elder Astor, recalled by the death of his son. A butcher boy sets out with his bundle on his shoulder for America, having made up his mind to be honest, to work, and to make money. We are not startled at all to know that when he died he bequeathed to his son $20,000,000. Every one of us can reckon in our own experience instances of success, not as extreme, but quite as remarkable as these. Men start in the race of life handicapped with every weight of poverty, disease, and inability, but they "make up their minds" to reach this or that point, and they reach it. Nor is success so easy in this country that we should receive it without surprise. The road is not broad but narrow, and the multitude are all in it. Where one achieves the prize, thousands sink discouraged, and among the thousands there are men more brilliant, shrewder, more richly endowed with wit, culture, and even judgment, than the winners. Why were they winners, then? Their aims were not always the best, but they conquered them, and surely it is worth our while to know how they did it; what was the secret of their power over other men and circumstances. The secret we believe to lie in their thorough earnestness and sincerity. They "made up their minds" as to what they wanted. They never altered them. There was no sham or faltering about Henry Wilson, John Jacob Astor, Franklin, Girard. You may call them a bull-dog race of men; but it is the bull-dog, after all, that brings down the prey, not the graceful spaniel. "Here stand I," says Luther, "and if all the tiles in Worms were devils, I could do no otherwise."   *N. Y. Tribune.*

11,847. SUCCESS, True Basis of. Admiral Farragut gave the following account of his start in life: "My father was sent down to New Orleans, with the little navy we then had, to look after the treason of Burr. I accompanied him as cabin-boy, and was ten years of age. I had some qualities which I thought made a man of me. I could swear like an old salt; could drink a stiff glass of grog as if I had doubled Cape Horn, and could smoke like a locomotive. I was great at cards, and fond of gaming in every shape. At the close of the dinner, one day, my father turned every body out of the cabin, locked the door, and said to me, 'David what do you mean to be?' 'I mean to follow the sea.' 'Follow the sea! Yes, be a poor, miserable, drunken sailor before the mast, kicked and cuffed about the world, and die in some fever hospital in a foreign clime.' 'No,' I said, 'I'll tread the quarter-deck and command, as you do.' 'No, David; no boy ever trod the quarter-deck with such principles as you have, and such habits as you exhibit. You'll have to change your whole course of life if you ever become a man.' My father left me and went on deck. I was stunned by the rebuke and overwhelmed with mortification. 'A poor, miserable, drunken sailor before the mast, kicked and cuffed about the world, and to die in some fever hospital! That's my fate, is it? I'll change my life, and change it at once. I will never utter another oath; I will never drink another drop of intoxicating liquor; I will never gamble.' And as God is my witness, I have kept those three vows to this hour. Shortly after, I became a Christian. That act settled my destiny for time and eternity."

11,848. SUFFERING, Avenues of. Suffering comes to us through and from our whole nature. It cannot be winked out of sight. It

cannot be thrust into a subordinate place in the picture of human life. It is the chief burden of history. It is the solemn theme of one of the highest departments of literature— the tragic drama. It gives to fictions their deep interest: it wails through much of our poetry. A large part of human vocations are intended to shut up some of its avenues. It has left traces on every human countenance over which years have passed. It is to not a few the most vivid recollection of life.
Dr. Channing.

11,849. SUFFERING, Biblical. May we not safely say, there is *no book* of the Bible which has not some reference to trial, whilst many parts are full of reference to the subject. In the Book of Psalms, *e. g.*, out of one hundred and fifty Psalms, it is reckoned that in ninety some allusion is made to suffering! There is no *saint* in the Bible, of whose history we have any lengthened record, who was not called to endure trouble in some form; and very frequently the most eminent saints were most tried. Those who were called to important services, were generally trained in the school of affliction. *Bowes.*

11,850. SUFFERING, Satisfaction in. Payson, in the midst of great suffering, being asked if he saw any special reason for the visitation, replied, "No, but I am as well satisfied as if I should see ten thousand; God's will is the very perfection of all reasons."

11,851. SUFFERING, Shrinking from. It is a memorable tribute that is paid to the martyrs in the Epistle to the Hebrews (11: 35): "Others were tortured, not accepting deliverance." May we not accuse ourselves that we are too apt to accept deliverance, any kind of deliverance, and from any quarter, if only it be deliverance. Infinitely better, my brother, my sister, cry for grace to "endure unto the end." *Grosart.*

11,852. SUICIDE, Argument from. Suicide itself, that fearful abuse of the dominion of the soul over the body, is a strong proof of the distinction of their destinies. Can the power that kills be the same that is killed? Must it not necessarily be something superior and surviving? The act of the soul, which in that fatal instant is in one sense so great an act of power, can it at the same time be the act of its own annihilation? The will kills the body; but who kills the will? *Nicolas.*

11,853. SUICIDE, Temptation to. Have you ever had the awful spectre of suicide raised up before your mind? It is very dreadful. But says good Thomas White: "Thou mayest be a child of God for all this, for our Saviour was tempted to 'cast himself down.'" *Grosart.*

11,854. SUN, Lesson from the. More joyful eyes look at the setting than at the rising sun. Burdens are laid down by the poor, whom the sun consoles more than the rich. No star and no moon announce the rising sun; and does not the setting sun, like a lover, leave behind his image in the moon! I yearn towards him when he sets, not when he rises. He is more nearly of kin to us in his setting, and he is

more gentle to the evening star, which, in rising, he, warrior-like, annihilates. The moon and star of love glimmer after he has gone. He dies and goes under the earth, in order to make us blessed, and when I die, may he set half an hour later than I. I should like to take my leave of earth with the sun; but he should stay and look upon it a little time longer than I. *Richter.*

11,855. SUN, Symbology of the. The sun is the fountain of light to this lower world. Day by day it rises on us with its gladdening beams: and with the return of light is connected the sense of reviving power in ourselves; invigorated health and cheerfulness; renewed and willing application to appointed duties. God himself has made it the ruler over the day. All nature seems to own its influence. The flowers that drooped, or closed their leaves during the night, expand themselves again when the sun ariseth. The gorgeous colors with which the clouds that were lately dark are now illuminated, bespeak the return of the absent king; and the clouds themselves are scattered at his approach. The loathsome or savage creatures that love darkness, now "get them away together, and lay down in their dens. Man goeth forth to his work and to his labor until the evening." Christ is to the moral world what the sun is to the natural world; the Source of life, and health, and motion. He is the "Sun of righteousness;" because the robe of righteousness in which his people "shine" is the light from him which they reflect, and on this account his church is said to be "clothed with the sun." And the inward righteousness also, in which they are created anew after the image of God, is derived from his illuminating presence in their hearts. And he rises on us "with healing in his wings;" because he brings with him, day by day, spiritual health to those who are diseased in soul, comfort to those who mourn, rest to the weary and heavy laden. The world has long lain in darkness and the shadow of death, waiting with "earnest expectation" for the first tokens of the "dayspring from on high;" even as travelers in a starless night, or as they that watch in loneliness and weariness, wait with eager longing for the burst of morning. At length the Sun of righteousness arose: when he who was with the Father from all eternity was born at Bethlehem; and took our nature upon him. And as the light from the morning sun travels with inconceivable speed to the remotest corners of the earth, and penetrates into the darkest recesses, so did the light from the Sun of righteousness penetrate "the dark places of the earth." It scattered the mists of ignorance and sin, and called forth from the garden of God's church those fruits and flowers which it could never otherwise have borne. Nor is his power to heal and comfort diminished by the lapse of years. *Bp. Trower.*

11,856. SUNBEAMS, Resurrection of. Nothing in this vast creation is ever lost. Individuals may be losers through carelessness; but to the world at large no created substance can be lost. One combination of things is often changed into another, but no ingredient is ever utterly destroyed; for at this moment the created universe does not contain one particle of matter more, nor one particle less, than belonged to it that day it came fresh from the creating hand of him who made all things very good. Never did a sunbeam shine in vain, and therefore no sunbeam that ever streaked this world with light could be finally lost. Yet the sunbeam, lovely as it is, has had its grave, and there sometimes for unnumbered ages it has slept in undisturbed repose. What is coal but latent sunbeams, which need only to be ignited to start again into active life? The sun, when many thousand years younger than he is now, cast forth his radiant beams on the surface of the world, and noble trees of ferns and other acrogens started at his bidding into vigorous life; they lived, died, and underwent changes which made them coal— yes, coal—and the old sun, he did it all. These sunbeams have long been burned in the form of coal; and though by ignition their resurrection-life is but a dim shadow of their early brightness, they are yet sunbeams. We have nothing but sunlight in summer or in winter, think or talk as we may. The fire on our hearths, the gas in our tubes, the oil in our lamps, and the candles on our tables, are all products of the sunbeam. We kindle them, and in the very act raise the sunbeam from its grave, and send it forth to run perchance a long cycle of changes ere again it rests in such a peace as that we have dragged it from.

Brooke.

11,857. SUNDAY, Carrying. I had a friend, in Syracuse, who lived to be one hundred years of age. He said to me, in his ninety-ninth year, "I went across the mountains in the early history of this country. Sabbath morning came. We were beyond the reach of civilization. My comrades were all going out for an excursion. I said, 'No, I won't go, it is Sunday.' Why, they laughed. They said, 'We haven't any Sunday here.' 'Oh! yes.' I said, 'you have. I brought it with me over the mountains.' "

Talmage.

11,858. SUNDAY, Typology of. The eighth day is always typical of resurrection. The eighth day, the day after the seventh or Sabbath, answers to the first day of the week on which Christ rose; it is, however, the first day in reference to seven having gone before. Seven days include the periods proper to the first creation. The eighth day, as it takes us beyond and out of these—that is, beyond the limits of the old creation—brings us in type into a new order of things and times—into the new creation or resurrection.

A. Jukes.

11,859. SUNDAY, Using. Make the Lord's day the market for thy soul; let the whole day be spent in prayer, repetitions, or meditations. Lay aside the affairs of the other parts of the week; let the sermon thou hast heard be converted into prayer. Shall God allow thee six days, and wilt not thou afford him one?

Bunyan.

11,860. SUNDAY-SCHOOL, Faithful to the. James Kershaw, of England, once a poor boy, but afterward a member of Parliament, revisited the Sabbath-school of his early days, and looked over the old class-books. He was gratified to see that for seven years while a scholar, and fourteen years while a teacher, he had not been once absent. He then expressed his conviction that his attachment to the Sabbath-school and his deep regard for the Sabbath, were the foundation of all his blessings, temporal and spiritual.

11,861. SUNDAY-SCHOOL, Recommendation of the. A wholesale liquor dealer one day accosted Moses F. Odell, the well-known superintendent of Sand St. M. E. S. S., Brooklyn: "I want you to send me a first-rate clerk—one that you can recommend. He must be prompt, smart, and reliable. In short, he must be a first-class Sunday-school boy." "Why do you want a clerk out of my Sunday-school? You're not a Christian; you don't attend church; your children are not in the Sunday-school." "O, that's all very well," replied the German free-thinker, "I can take care of myself; but I won't have anybody in my store that I can't trust. I know these Sunday-school boys, and they'll do to tie to. They won't drink my liquor, nor rob my till." It must be said that Sunday-school boys do not do the foul work of liquor dealers, but the indorsement is good.

11,862. SUNDAY-SCHOOLS, Advantage of. A little boy said to his irreligious mother, as she smoothed his dying pillow, "Oh, mother, you have never taught me anything about Jesus; and had it not been for the Sabbath-school teachers, I should now be dying without a hope in him, and must have been lost forever.'

11,863. SUNDAY-SCHOOLS, Mission of. A new and beautiful flower has recently been discovered in the State of Texas. It is called the compass flower, because all its petals point to the north. In sunshine and in storm, by day and by night, the little flower points northward, and though the traveler may perchance be lost in the Texan wilds, yet, if he can only find one of these little compass flowers, he may, by looking at it, find his bearings and ascertain the true, the right way. Now, the mission of the Sabbath-school is to sow the seeds of truth in the heart of the little ones; those seeds will spring up as the seeds of flowers, and the blossoms will appear, beautiful and lovely in the sight of heaven, and as this compass flower points toward the north, they will point toward Christ. And, gazing upon these compass flowers of truth, planted by the instrumentality of some humble Sunday-school teacher, many a poor wanderer may be brought back to the way of peace and righteousness

Anon.

11,864. SUNSET, Beauties of. I see the sun standing amid roses in the western sky, into which he has thrown his ray-brush, wherewith he has to-day been painting the earth; and when I look round a little in our picture-exhibition, his enameling is still hot on the mountains, on the moist chalk of the moist earth, the flowers, full of sap-colors, are laid out to dry, and the forget-me-not with miniature colors; under the varnish of the streams the skyey painter has penciled his own eye; and the clouds, like a decoration painter, he has touched off with wild outlines and single tints; and so he stands at the border of the earth. *Richter.*

11,865. SUPERINTENDENCE, Importance of. Superintending is the most costly and the most valuable work done in the world. Every business pays for superintending. A major-general is allowed sixteen rations, and more than a hundred salaries of the common soldiers. Bank management, presidents or cashiers, whichever happens to do the thinking, are paid enormous salaries. Bank directors know too much to commit their money to cheap men. Railroad superintendents are paid for their nerve power. Secretaries of insurance companies receive from $8,000 to $40,000 per year. Great factories employ superintendents at advanced wages. Great mercantile houses employ a good force of walking men, to look after the clerks and the customers. One single government building in this country cost the government millions on account of poor superintending. *Dr. C. H. Fowler.*

11,866. SUPERSTITION, African. In case of sickness or death in the family of a Kaffir, of South Africa, the witch has been at work they think, and they ask, "Who is the witch?" A witch doctor is sent for, and he accuses a person of wealth, as whatever he has is given up to confiscation. The chief commands the accused to appear, and the mob proceed to "smell out" the culprit. The trial is by ordeal, and sometimes by enforced confession. The accused may be bound tightly, smeared with grease, and seated upon an anthill to be stung by ants. Again hot stones are applied to the body, or death by strangulation, or burning at the stake, is the fate of the victim. A witch doctor is also a rain-maker, who by incantations, sacrifices of cattle, and various ceremonies, tries to prolong his rites till rain comes, when he claims success.

11,867. SUPERSTITION, Fatal. Nicias, an Athenian general, filled with fear at a lunar eclipse sat still and was made prisoner, and his entire army of forty thousand men were slain or captured.

11,868. SUPERSTITION, Victims of. The Jews once sat quietly, it being their Sabbath-day, and suffered their enemies to rear their scaling ladders, and make themselves masters of their walls, and so lay still until they were caught like so many trout in the drag-net of their own superstition. *Plutarch.*

11,869. SUPERSTITIONS, Common. Why is it that sailors cling to port on a Friday, and loose their ships and weigh anchor on Sunday? Why did the ancients build a temple to Fortune, consult oracles, and venerate white stones rather than black stones? Why did our grandmothers dislike the assemblage of nine rooks, turn back when they met a dog crossing their path, and show an antipathy to black cats? Why does a Fijian, to propitiate his ugly wooden god, offer him a *bakolo*, the dead body of his brother? Why was it improper to eat beans and the seeds of the lupine? What magic makes the third time never like the rest? At the wicked little German towns where small grand-dukes improve their revenues licensing gaming tables, you will find old gamblers begging the youngest in the company, often an English boy who has come to look about him, to take for them the first throw of the dice. Why so? Why is a fresh hand more likely to throw the three sixes than an old one? *The Gentle Life.*

11,870. SUPPORT, Divine. I have read of famous Mr. Dod, who is doubtless now high in heaven, who intended to marry, was much troubled with fears and cares how he should live in that condition, his incomes being so small that they would but maintain him in a single condition; and looking out at a window, and seeing a hen scraping for food for her numerous brood about her, thought thus with himself: This hen did but live before it had these chickens, and now she lives with all her little ones; upon which he added this thought also: I see the fowls of the air neither sow nor reap, nor gather into barns, but yet my heavenly Father feeds them, Matt. 6: 25; and thus he overcame his fears of wanting. O Christians! you have such a Father for your portion, as will as soon cease to be, as he will cease to supply you with all things necessary for your good. *Brooks.*

11,871. SUPPORT, Miraculous. The legend of Nicholas von der Flue is that for twenty years he lived without partaking of food of any kind. He lived the life of a hermit, and spent his time in prayer and meditation, meditating much on the passion of Jesus Christ, and therein he said he found supernatural food and received miraculous strength. It is written "Man shall not live by bread alone."

11,872. SUPPORT, Prayer and Trust for. Stilling, a celebrated German writer, in early life was very poor He wished to study medicine. He had a firm faith in God. He reasoned thus: "God begins nothing without terminating it gloriously. He alone has ordered my present circumstances, and everything regarding me he will bring about in his own way." His friends were as poor as himself, and they wondered where he would get the money he needed for his education. After raising all he could for his long journey to Strasburg, where he was to spend the winter, he started on his way, but when he reached Frankfort, which was three days' ride from Strasburg, he had only one dollar left. He said nothing, but he prayed much. While walking the streets he met a merchant belonging to his native place, who said: "Stilling, what brought you here?" "I am going to Strasburg to study medicine." "Where do you get your money to study with?" "I have a rich father in heaven." "How much money have you on hand?" "One dollar," said Stilling. "So!" said the merchant. "Well, I'm one of your father's stewards," and he handed him thirty-three dollars. His money was soon reduced to one dollar. One morning his room-mate said to him, "Stilling, I believe you did not bring much money with you," and gave him thirty dollars in gold. In a few months after this he had no money to pay his college dues. The lecturer's fee must be paid by six o'clock on Thursday evening, or he would be obliged to leave college. Five o'clock came, and still he had no money. Then, while he was in great grief, and praying to God for help, a gentleman came in and gave him forty dollars in gold.

11,873. SURETY, Christ our. Abu Kabus Al Nooman, King of Hira, had two days, one of which he called the fortunate and the other the unfortunate day. Whoever met him on the former day he sent away in safety, loaded with gifts; but whoever met him on the latter day he caused to be slain. On this day an Arab, who had befriended him, came before him. The king could not discharge him on account of his law, and to execute him would be to violate the law of hospitality. So he devised a respite for a year on condition that he should provide a surety that at the end of a year he would return and suffer death. A prince of the king's court pitied the man, and became his surety, and he was discharged. The last day of his respite having arrived, and the principal not having arrived, the king ordered the surety to prepare for death. Before the day had passed, the man himself appeared and relieved the surety. The king was surprised at the man's generosity and fidelity, and asked him why he did not let his surety suffer. He replied that he was a Christian, and only did what his religion taught. The king thereupon pardoned the man, and was himself baptized in the name of Christ. We are represented by the condemned man. Christ became our surety to God, and actually died for us; but he has risen. He has ascended to heaven, and is there our surety still.

11,874. SURETYSHIP, Oriental. The Hindoo proverb says, "He who stands before may have to pay." This is the idea of a surety. He stands before the debtor, and covenants with the creditor for the payment of the money; he who stands before, is literally betwixt the contending parties. In this respect " was Jesus made a surety" for us; he stood before and between, and thus became our Mesites, or "Mediator." This practice of suretyship, however, is also common in the most trifling affairs of life: *Pare-ellutha-vonum,* that is, "Sign your name," is a request preferred by every one who is desirous of obtaining additional security to a petty agreement. In every legal court or magistrate's office may be seen, now and then, a trio entering, thus to become responsible for the engagements of another. The cause of all this suretyship probably is the bad faith which so commonly prevails amongst the heathen.   *Roberts.*

11,875. SURPRISE, Provision against. Iphecrates once pitched his camp in the territory of his allies, yet he fortified it as carefully as if he had been in an enemy's country. He was asked, "What are you afraid of ?" He answered, "Of all speeches for a general none is so dishonorable as 'I should not have thought it.'"

11,876. SURRENDER, Complete. When Henry VIII. had determined to make himself head of the English Church, he insisted that the convocation should accept his headship without limiting and modifying clauses. He refused to entertain any compromises, and vowed that "he would have no *tantums,*" as he called them. Thus when a sinner parleys with his Saviour he would fain have a little of the honor of his salvation, he would save alive some favorite sin, he would fain amend the humbling terms of grace—but there is no help for it, Jesus will be all in all, and the sinner must be nothing at all. The surrender must be complete, there must be no *tantums,* but the heart must without reserve submit to the sovereignty of the Redeemer.   *Spurgeon.*

11,877. SURRENDER, Full. When General Lee surrendered with his army, every other army of the Confederate States at once gave up: and there are certain pitched battles with Satan and with the flesh which we have to take part in, but when we conquer in them, a thousand other things which had been worrying us are gone too.   *R. P. Smith.*

11,878. SURRENDER, No. Some are in the habit of shouting "No surrender;" but I say we should all surrender; we should surrender our passions, and our prejudices, and our uncharitableness towards others. We should seek to win as much as we can from the common humanity of our adversaries. The good and the wise will pursue this course, and they will succeed; whilst the treacherous, the arrogant, and the intolerant, will dwindle far behind in the march, and will perish of self-contention, instead of coming up to win the laurels.   *Bamford.*

11,879. SURRENDER, A Wise. A commander who held a rock fortress in India, which was thought to be impregnable, surrendered himself and his stronghold, to Alexander. He made him governor of it and the surrounding country, saying, "I take this for a wise man who chose rather to commit himself to a good man than to a strong place." The encomium is appropriate to every man who delivers up the stronghold of self to God's irresistible Son Jesus Christ.

11,880. SUSPENSE, Anguish of. Of all the conditions to which the heart is subject, suspense is one that most gnaws and cankers into the frame. One little month of that suspense when it involves death, we are told by an eye witness, in "Wakefield on the punishment of death," is sufficient to plough fixed lines and furrows in a convict of five-and-twenty—sufficient to dash the brown hair with gray, and to bleach the gray to white.   *Bulwer-Lytton.*

11,881. SUSPICION, Demoralization of. Suspicion is not less an enemy to virtue than to happiness; he that is already corrupt is naturally suspicious, and he that becomes suspicious will quickly be corrupt. It is too common for us to learn the frauds by which ourselves have suffered; men who are once persuaded that deceit will be employed against them, sometimes think the same arts justified by the necessity of defence. Even they whose virtue is too well established to give way to example, or be shaken by sophistry, must yet feel their love of mankind diminished with their esteem, and grow less zealous for the happiness of those by whom they imagine their own happiness endangered. *Johnson.*

11,882. SWEARER Rebuked. Mr. Meikle, a surgeon at Carnwath, in Scotland, was once called to attend a gentleman who had been stung in the face by a wasp or bee, and found him very impatient, and swearing, on account of his pain, in great wrath. "O, doctor," said he, "I am in great torment; can you any way help?" "Do not fear," replied Mr. M., "all will be over in a little while." Still, however, the gentleman continued to swear, and at length his attendant determined to reprove him. "I see nothing the matter," said he, "only it might have been in a better place." "Where might it have been?" asked the sufferer. "Why, on the tip of your tongue."

11,883. SWEARING, Degradation of. It is no mark of a gentleman to swear. The most worthless and vile, the refuse of mankind, the drunkard and the prostitute, swear as well as the best dressed and educated gentleman. No particular endowments are requisite to give a finish to the art of cursing. The basest and meanest of mankind swear with as much tact and skill as the most refined; and he that wishes to degrade himself to the very lowest level of pollution and shame, should learn to be a common swearer. Any man has talents enough to learn to curse God, and imprecate perdition on himself and his fellow-men. Profane swearing never did any man any good. No man is the richer, or wiser, or happier for it. It helps no one's education or manners. It commends no one to any society. It is disgusting to the refined, abominable to the good; insulting to those with whom we associate; degrading to the mind; unprofitable, needless and injurious to society; and wantonly to profane his name, to call his vengeance down, to curse him, and to invoke his vengeance, is perhaps of all offences the most awful in the sight of God. *Louth.*

11,884. SWORD, Pen and. Men in the olden time won glory by the steel that flashed in their hands amid the smoke and din of battle. Men in the present day control nations and win battles by the steel they handle in their libraries; the former was the sword of steel, the latter the steel pen. *Mrs. Balfour.*

11,885. SYMPATHY, Condition of. A minister, noted for intellectual strength, was felt to be out of place in the house of affliction. Sickness and death had never touched him or his. A loathsome disease finally entered his family, rendered his wife helpless, and carried off his darling child, for whom he prayed, like David, that he might be spared. The pastor came forth from that furnace a changed man, as remarkable for his sympathy and consolation as he had previously been for his stoicism.

11,886. SYMPATHY, Duty of. Sympathy is a debt we owe to sufferers. For Christians to be rejoicing when their brethren are weeping, is like putting silver-lace upon a mourning-suit. Our own particular losses and distresses resemble the extinguishing of a candle, which only occasions darkness in one room: but the general distresses of the church are like the eclipsing of the sun, which overshadows the whole hemisphere. Sympathy renders a doleful state more joyful. Alexander refused water in a time of great scarcity, because there was not enough for his whole army! It should be among Christians, as among lute-strings, when one is touched the others tremble. Believers should be neither proud flesh, nor dead flesh. Jeremiah suffered not in his person, being under the protection of the Divine Being: but though he dwelt securely from the hand of mortality, yet he was filled with the bowels of sympathy. Though he wrote of the Jews' desolations, yet he named them Jeremiah's Lamentations. *Secker.*

11,887. SYMPATHY, Effect of. Mr. Mingins, of New York, said a lady came into the office of the City Mission and wanted a few tracts. She didn't feel as if she could do very much of active work for the Lord, but felt like giving away a few tracts. One day she saw a policeman taking a poor drunken woman to jail, a miserable object, ragged, dirty, with hair disordered, but the lady's heart went out in sympathy toward her. She found the woman after she came out of jail, and just went and folded her arms around her, and kissed her. The woman exclaimed, "My God, what did you do that for?" and she replied, "I don't know, but I think Jesus sent me to do it." The woman said, "Oh, don't kiss me any more, you'll break my heart. Why, nobody hasn't kissed me since my mother died." But that kiss brought the woman to the feet of the Saviour, and for the last three years she has been living a godly Christian life, won to God by a kiss.

11,888. SYMPATHY, Experience and. An English Chief Justice of the Common Pleas, passing by the village stocks, desired to be shut in, that he might know what the punishment was, which was done. The friend passed on and forgot him till he became wearied. He called to a person passing to let him out, who replied, "No, no, old gentleman, you was not set there for nothing." He was compelled to wait till his friend sent a servant to release him. Sometime after a case came before him for false imprisonment and setting in the stocks. The attorney for the defense ridiculed the charge as no punishment. The Chief Justice whispered, "Brother, have you ever been in the stocks?" The attorney answered, "Really, my lord, never." The Judge replied, "Then I have, and I assure you it is no such trifle as you represent."

11,889. SYMPATHY, Law of. Human Nature is fallen, and I am not in the habit of unduly exalting it; yet regarded from this point of view, it presents some vestiges of a departed glory—the last lights of sunset. Let me illustrate this by an example, over which I can fancy the angels bending with admiration:—A boat of castaways lay on the lone sea, drifting on a shoreless ocean; bread they had none; water they had none; no ship, no sail hove in sight. Among the dead and dying, a boy lay clasped in his mother's arms; with looks—for his lips were black and speechless—that seemed to cry, "Mother, mother, give me bread!" A rough sailor, who had kept and concealed a shell-fish for his own last extremity, looked on the child and tears started to his eye; he raised his rough hand to wipe them from his cheek; and then drawing out his prized last morsel, put it to lips of the dying boy. I don't know where he sailed from; I know neither his name nor his creed; but I know this—that I would rather my soul were bound up in the same bundle with his, than with the souls of those who go to church, and, having no bowels of mercy, heap up money, while other men are dying of starvation. Till she has sunk into the lowest depth of selfishness and sin, Human Nature could not enjoy the banquet when hungry faces were staring in at the window, and not the music of the tabret and viol filled the air, but the low moanings of manly suffering and the weeping of mothers whose children cry for bread and they have none to give them. The gospel of Jesus Christ directs us to love even our enemies—if they hunger, to feed them; if they thirst, to give them drink; and though Human Nature may not be great enough to forgive an enemy, she is kind enough to pity a sufferer, and to sympathize with suffering. Give her way, then! Yield to her generous impulses! *Dr. Guthrie.*

11,890. SYMPATHY, Need of. A gentleman one day came to my office for the purpose of getting me interested in a young man who had just got out of the penitentiary. "He says," said the gentleman, "he don't want to go to the office, but I want your permission to bring him in and introduce him." I said, "Bring him in." The gentleman brought him in and introduced him, and I took him by the hand and told him I was glad to see him. I invited him to my house, and when I took him into my family I introduced him as my friend. When my little daughter came into the room, I said, "Emma, this is papa's friend." And she went up and kissed him, and the man sobbed aloud. After the child left the room, I said, "What is the matter?" "O, sir," he said "I have not had a kiss for years. The last kiss I had was from my mother, and she was dying. I thought I would never have another one again." His heart was broken.
Moody.

11,891. TABERNACLE, Frailty of the. A tabernacle is a frail, temporary dwelling, generally of cloth, which men make for shelter by night, when they expect to be so short a time in the place that it is not worth while to erect a more substantial edifice. The Hebrews in the wilderness dwelt in tents, shifting their encampment from day to day. Travelers and soldiers use them still. A few posts, a few cords, and a few pieces of cloth constitute the dwelling. It is easily set up, and easily taken down again. The body is frequently compared to a tent. It is very beautiful but very frail. Here we come abreast of an unfathomable mystery. Seeing it is made so perfect, why is it made so feeble? All the skill of the world could not make even a tolerable imitation of its mechanism; and yet the prick of a pin will turn it into dust.   *Arnot.*

11,892. TACITURNITY, Military. Metellus, a Roman commander, was asked by a centurion, "What new design he had in hand?" He curtly replied, "If I thought my shirt was privy to any part of my counsel, I would immediately pluck it off and burn it."

11,893. TACITURNITY, Philosophic. The ambassadors of the king of Persia, when at Athens, were invited to a feast, at which many philosophers were present. All had offered some sentiment except Zeno; who unlike the others, continued silent throughout the entertainment. When asked what word they should take to the king, he remarked, "Nothing further than this, that you saw at Athens an old man, who knew how to hold his tongue."

11,894. TALENTS, Accounting for. Slaves in antiquity were often artisans, or men allowed otherwise to engage freely in business, paying, as it was frequently arranged, a fixed yearly sum to their master; or they had money committed to them wherewith to trade on his account, or with which to enlarge their business, and to bring in to him a share of their profits.
Trench.

11,895. TALENTS, Concentrated. The work of the Church, like the work of the world, is done by the average men. Five talents trained on a single point are far better than ten talents trained on ten points. Farragut won his great victory, and achieved unfading fame, by converting his fleet into a grindstone that rubbed on the opposing fort, and ground it out, with a loss so small as not to be perceived when distributed over the circle of his fleet. What the Church wants is average men, concentrated into greatness.   *Dr. Fowler.*

11,896. TALENTS, Parable of the. The Romans used to let a Jewish prince reign, with the title of king, and with some of the power of king. Archelaus, son of Herod, reigned in this way. He had gone to Rome to get his claim to king established by the Roman government. This was well known to the disciples, as happening in their own country but a few years before. Our Lord likened himself to this prince. He was going into a far country, to receive a kingdom, and to return. He was about to go to heaven; hence he would return, and then his kingdom would be fully set up upon earth, and he would reign as a king indeed. But this was not to be yet; he was not even then gone. Now he has been gone for above eighteen hundred years, but he has not yet returned. It seems likely that our Lord in the parable alludes to this. As the Jews had refused Archelaus as their temporal king, because he was cruel, so would they refuse Christ as their Spiritual King and Saviour, because of his goodness.   *Trench.*

11,897. TALENTS, Two. "What talents have I?" asked a desponding lady. "Well, at all events, two; leisure and God's word—time and truth. Let them be well used, and your crown will be bright."   *T. Collins.*

11,898. TALENTS, Unused. A penalty is affixed to the non-use of our faculties and abilities, both in nature and grace. The man who, like the Fakir in India, refuses to use his arm, will lose ability to use it. The man who refuses to use his moral faculties in the service of God, will lose moral strength in the faculty which is not exercised. All our faculties gain strength by exercise, and lose strength by non-use.   *Walker.*

11,899. TALKER, A Habitual. His measure of talk is till his wind is spent, and then he is not silenced, but becalmed. His ears have catched the itch of his tongue; and though he scratch them, like a beast with his hoof, he finds a pleasure in it. He shakes a man by the ear as a dog does a pig, and never loosens his hold till he has tired himself as well as his patient. He is a walking pillory, and punishes more ears than a dozen standing ones. He will hold any argument rather than his tongue, and maintain both sides at his own charge; for he will tell you what you will say, though perhaps he does not intend to give you leave. His tongue is always in motion, though very seldom to the purpose: like a barber's scissors, which are kept snipping as well when they do not cut, as when they do. He is so full of words that they run over, and are thrown away to no purpose; and so empty of things, or sense, that his dryness has made his leaks so wide, whatsoever is put in him runs out immediately. He is so long delivering himself, that those that hear him desire to be delivered too, or despatched out of their pain. *S. Butler.*

11,900. TARES, Scattering. It is said that "The country of Ill Will" is the by-name of a district hard by St. Arnaud, in the north of France. There, tenants, when ejected by a landlord, or when they have ended their tenancy on uncomfortable terms, have been in the habit of spoiling the crop to come by vindictively sowing tares, and other coarse strangling weeds, among the wheat, whence has been derived the sinister name in question. The practice has been made penal; and any man proved to have tampered with another man's harvest will be dealt with as a criminal.

11,901. TARES, Sowing. Roberts says, "See that lurking villain watching for the time when his neighbor shall plow his field; he carefully marks the period when the work has been finished, and goes the night following and casts in what the natives call pandinella, *i. e.* pig-pandy; this being of rapid growth, springs up before the good seed, and scatters itself before the other can be reaped, so that the poor owner of the field will be years

before he can get rid of the troublesome weed. But there is another noisome plant which these wretches cast into the ground of those they hate, called *perum-pirandi*, which is more destructive to vegetation than any other plant. Has a man purchased a field out of the hands of another, the offended person says, 'I will plant the *perum-pirandi* in his grounds.'" Commenting on this note of Roberts', Archbishop Trench says, "A friend who has occupied a judicial station in India confirms this account;" and he adds, "we are not now without this form of malice nearer home. Thus, in Ireland, I have known an out-going tenant, in spite at his ejection, to sow wild oats in the fields which he was leaving. These, like the plant mentioned above, ripening and seeding themselves before the crops in which they were mingled, it became next to impossible to get rid of them."

11,902. TASTE, Morality of. Taste is not only a part and an index of morality—it is the only morality. The first, and last, and closest trial question to any living creature is, "What do you like?" Tell me what you like, and I'll tell you what you are. Go out into the street, and ask the first man or woman you meet, what their "taste" is; and if they answer candidly, you know them, body and soul. "You, my friend in the rags, with the unsteady gait, what do you like?" "A pipe, and a quartern of gin." I know you. "You, good woman, with the quick step and tidy bonnet, what do you like?" "A swept hearth and a clean tea-table; and my husband opposite me, and a baby at my breast." Good, I know you also. "You, little girl, with the golden hair and the soft eyes, what do you like?" "My canary, and a run among the wood hyacinths." "You little boy, with the dirty hands and the low forehead, what do you like?" "A shy at the sparrows, and a game at pitch-farthing." Good; we know them all now. What more need we ask? "Nay," perhaps you answer, "We need rather to ask what these people and children do, than what they like. If they do right, it is no matter that they like what is wrong; and if they do wrong it is no matter that they like what is right. Doing is the great thing; and it does not matter that the man likes drinking, so that he does not drink; nor that the little girl likes to be kind to her canary, if she will not learn her lessons; nor that the little boy likes throwing stones at the sparrows, if he goes to the Sunday-school." Indeed, for a short time, and in a provisional sense, this is true. For if, resolutely, people do what is right, in time they come to like doing it. But they only are in a right moral state when they have come to like doing it; and as long as they don't like it they are still in a vicious state. The man is not in health of body who is always thirsting for the bottle in the cupboard, though he bravely bears his thirst; but the man who heartily enjoys water in the morn, and wine in the even; each in its proper quantity and time. And the entire object of true education is to make people not merely do the right things, but enjoy the right things—not merely industrious, but to love industry—not merely learned, but to love knowledge—not merely pure, but to love purity—not merely just, but to hunger and thirst after justice.

Ruskin.

11,903. TAXES, Self-Imposed. "Friends," says he, "the taxes are indeed very heavy; and, if those laid on by the government were the only ones we had to pay, we might more easily discharge them; but we have many others, and much more grievous to some of us. We are taxed twice as much by our idleness, three times as much by our pride, and four times as much by our folly; and from these taxes the commissioners cannot ease or deliver us by allowing an abatement." *Dr. Franklin.*

11,904. TEACHER, Bible-Class. There is in Troy, N. Y., a teacher who has instructed a Bible-class for twenty-two years. The original class numbered sixteen. The sum of all her scholars is 500. Of these 300 became members of the church. They are mostly poor, yet her class supports a native missionary in Burmah, a theological student in the South, and aids a poor church in Iowa. The secret of her success is, 1. Piety. 2. Personal devotion to her scholars. 3. Social influence. Her scholars are her friends and associates, and she is their spiritual guide.

11,905. TEACHER, Blaming the. Diogenes saw a youth devouring his food very greedily. He gave the boy's tutor a box on the ear, holding him to be responsible for the boy's faults, and not the boy who had not learned better manners.

11,906. TEACHER, Interesting. A Lacedæmonian tutor, being asked what good he did to the children whom he had in charge, answered, "I make good and honest things pleasant to children."

11,907. TEACHER, Persevering. The salvation of the famous Dr. Morrison, the first Protestant missionary to China was the result of the persevering efforts of a timid Sunday-school teacher. A young lady in an English school undertook to gather a class from the ragged boys of the town. Morrison was one of them. He was given a suit of clothes by the superintendent. After this he absented himself from class till his clothes were worn out. The teacher sought him and promised him another suit if he would come to her class. The second trial resulted like the first. The third time she went for him and promised him a third suit of clothes. After this she went for him for three Sabbaths. The fourth and ever after he came of his own accord. He became pious and useful. His great work was the translation of the Bible into Chinese.

11,908. TEACHER, Preparation of a. An old Waterloo guide spent eight months in studying the ground plans of battle, reports, despatches, histories, narratives and whatever he could get to throw light upon that renowned field of blood. Then he offered himself as guide to visitors. The work of the teacher of religious truth to the young is far more responsible, and demands more care, preparation and prayer.

11,909. TEACHING, Motto of. Tyndale, the translator of the English Bible, had for his motto. "Banish me to the poorest corner of the world if you please, but let me teach the little children and preach the gospel."

11,910. TEARS, Vale of. "Good men weep easily," says the Greek poet; and the better any are, the more inclined to weeping, especially under affliction. As you may see in David, whose tears, instead of gems, were the ornaments of his bed; in Jonathan, Job, Ezra, Daniel, etc. "How," says one, "shall God wipe away my tears in heaven if I shed none on earth? And how shall I reap in joy if I sow not in tears? I was born with tears, and I shall die with tears; and why then should I live without them in this valley of tears?"

Brooks.

11,911. TELEGRAPH, Conversion through the. A young telegraph operator in Ohio was told that a friend of his in another office had been converted. Doubting the statement, he sat down to the instrument, and inquired, "Was there a conversion in your office yesterday?" He received the reply, "Yes; it was me. Seek ye the Lord while he may be found." He asked again, "Will you pray for me that I may find the Saviour?" The reply came, "I will; pray for yourself." In a few days the young men were received into the Christian Church on the confession of their faith.

11,912. TELEGRAPH, Story of the. After making his wonderful discovery, Prof. Morse sought aid from Congress, to establish a line between Washington and Baltimore, at its session in 1843. A bill for this purpose passed the Senate, but in the House it had not been reached up to its last session, and the pressure of bills was so great that it seemed impossible that it should be acted upon. Prof. Morse went away disheartened. The next morning Miss Annie Ellsworth, daughter of the first commissioner of patents, called and congratulated him on the passage of his bill. He could hardly believe it. For this service he gave her the privilege of sending the first message. When the line was completed, Prof. Morse sent to her for it. She wrote, "What hath God wrought!" A despairing inventor received the news of his unexpected success from his friend's daughter, and made her a promise, which he kept, and thus linked her name with his own in one of the greatest of modern inventions.

11,913. TEMERITY, Foolish. Otho was advised by his friend, when pressed in battle by Vitellius, to protract the fight as long as possible, because the enemy was suffering for provisions. But heedless of advice, he threw his whole army into the conflict, and lost both his army and his empire. He killed himself, and was laid in an unhonored grave. Had he avoided an engagement, hunger would have routed his enemy.

11,914. TEMPER, Aggravation of. A man can scarcely keep in tune who unstrings his nerves by lying late in bed in the morning, or who indulges in absinthe, and other extremely cogent beverages, or who neglects healthy exercise; his tuning-up will not be the bracing of a wholesome system, but the straining of strings which will become attenuated, and at length give way. Only fancy a man taking a violin with worn strings to the maker, and saying, "Kindly tune up this instrument." The answer would be, "The strings are pretty well done for, sir." And yet that is exactly what some people expect their doctors to do, viz: to tune them up when their nerve-strings are pretty nearly done for. *Statham.*

11,915. TEMPER, Christian. The right temper of a Christian is—to run always cross to the corrupt stream of the world and human iniquity; and to be willingly carried along with the stream of Divine Providence, and not at all to stir a hand, no, nor a thought to row against that mighty current; and not only is he carried with it upon necessity, because there is no steering against it, but cheerfully and voluntarily—not because he must, but because he would. *Leighton.*

11,916. TEMPER, Conquest of. A lady of Boston, was of a peculiarly irritable temper, and it caused her, as a professed Christian, the deepest grief. She struggled, prayed and resolved against it in vain. Every purpose was swept away in the first excitement of even a slight temptation. She was urged at a meeting to confide, by simple faith, in the power of Christ to keep her, and to make a full-hearted surrender of her entire being to him for that purpose. There she consciously laid her soul in the hands of Jesus. Her peculiar trials and temptations were at home, and these she had always declared to be so many that it was impossible for her to rise above them. Opening the front door, she saw a domestic violating one of her most explicit rules by carrying a slop-pail down the front stairs; and, to make the matter worse, the domestic was so alarmed at the sight of her mistress that she dropped the pail, and the water flowed down the stairs and over the carpet into the hall! The lady uttered not a word, but whispered over and over, "Jesus, help me! Jesus, help me!" and gained the victory. With entire composure she went in, and from that moment, she says, she found no difficulty in controlling her before ungovernable temper.

11,917. TEMPERANCE, Rewards of. Temperance puts wood on the fire, meal in the barrel, flour in the tub, money in the purse, credit in the country, contentment in the house, clothes on the back, and vigor in the body.
Dr. Franklin.

11,918. TEMPERANCE, Want of. Rev. J. J. Talbott, who recently died drunk in Elkhart, Ind., said: "I had position high and holy. The demon tore from around me the robes of my sacred office, and sent me forth churchless and godless, a very hissing and by-word among men. Afterward my voice was heard in the courts. But the dust gathered on my open books, and no footfall crossed the threshold of the drunkard's office. I had money ample for all necessities, but it went to feed the coffers of the devils who possessed me. I had a home adorned with all that wealth and the most exquisite taste could suggest. The devil crossed its threshold, and the light faded from its chambers; and thus I stand, a clergyman without a church, a barrister without a brief, a man with scarcely a friend, and a soul without hope—all swallowed up in the maelstrom of drink."

11,919. TEMPLE, Desecration of the. The mosque at the time of our passing through it was full of people, though these were not worshipers, nor was it at either of the usual hours of public prayers. Some of the parties were assembled to smoke, others to play at chess, and some apparently to drive bargains of trade, but certainly none to pray. It was indeed a living picture of what we might believe the temple at Jerusalem to have been, when those who sold oxen and sheep and doves, and the changers of money sitting there, were driven out by Jesus with a scourge of cords and their tables overturned. It was, in short, a place of public resort and thoroughfare, a house of merchandise, as the temple of the Jews had become in the days of the Messiah.
Buckingham.

11,920. TEMPLE, Living Pillars of the. The Samoans believed that their chiefs, in a future state would be sent to a place called Pulotu. There they would be the supporting pillars of the temple of the king of the place. Death brought promotion to a nobler service, as they immediately became columns of living men usefully adorning the mansion of the king of Pulotu. We are forcibly reminded of the words of the Revelator, "Him that overcometh will I make a pillar in the temple of my God."

11,921. TEMPLE, Stones in Christ's. A man dreamed that he was trying to build for himself a temple to commemorate his name. He wanted a whole temple to himself, and an angel came to show him one that was a model of beauty. But there was one stone missing from its peak, and the man asked the angel where it was. "There has never been one there," replied the angel. "We intended to place you there, but you say that you want a whole temple to yourself, and so the place will be filled by some one else. But you will never have your special temple." Then the man, aroused by his fears, started up from his sleep, crying, "O, God, put me in your temple. Put me in, even though I can be but a chink stone. Put me in!"

11,922. TEMPTATION, Avoiding. It is an all too common sin to repeat the sin of the man in the iron cage in Bunyan's peerless allegory, who said, "I have tempted the devil, and he is come to me;" or as dear old Thomas Fuller puts it, "to holloa in the ear of a sleeping temptation." O, my brethren, beloved, may you and I be saved from that! May we be "led" ever by the Spirit. *Grosart.*

11,923. TEMPTATION, Disguised. When I see the fisher bait his hook, I think on Satan's subtle malice, who sugars over his poisoned hooks with seeming pleasures. Thus Eve's apple was candied with divine knowledge, "Ye shall be as Gods, knowing good and evil." When I see the fish fast hanged, I think upon the covetous worldling, who leaps at the profit without considering the danger. Thus Achan takes the gold and the garment, and never considers that his life must answer it. If Satan be such a fisher of men, it is good to look before we leap. Honey may be eaten, so that we take heed of the sting: I will honestly enjoy my delights, but not buy them with danger. *Warwick.*

11,924. TEMPTATION, Fleeing from. St. Martian, a monk of Cesarea, was greatly tempted to commit vile sin. When just at the point to yield he thrust his limbs into the fire, saying, "O, Martian, how feels this fire to thee now? Yet it is not comparable to that which will consume the sinner." Thus he conquered. Afterward he resolved to find a place where temptation could not so readily reach him. He found an island off the coast, on which was a cave. Here he lived with all the advantages of solitude, for six years. Then temptation came to him again, and he fled to escape it. Fruitless task. The only refuge from it is in the grave.

11,925. TEMPTATION, Liable to. Jovinian, the heretic, whom St. Jerome opposed, would needs think, or at least say, that after baptism no man was tempted of the devil; not only not overcome, but not tempted. But our baptism does not drown the devil. "Few wrestlers that never took fall; none that may not, since we are all at best but wrestlers." "*Vita hominis piraterium,*" says St. Ambrose. Others read it, "Man's life is a warfare; and that is labor enough and danger enough. But to be still upon so inconstant an element as the water, and still pursued by pirates, or consorted with pirates, is more; and *vita piraterium,* says he, man's life, every man's life, is spent among pirates, pursued by them, or consorted with them. The devil hath not a more subtle temptation to ensnare me with than to bring me to think myself temptation proof, above temptation. *Dr. Donne.*

11,926. TEMPTATION, Occasions of. No sooner was Christ out of the water of baptism than in the fire of temptation. So David, after his anointing, was hunted "as a partridge upon the mountains." Israel is no sooner out of Egypt than Pharaoh pursues them. Hezekiah no sooner had left that solemn passover than Sennacherib comes up against him. St. Paul is assaulted with vile temptations after the "abundance of his revelations;" and Christ teacheth us, after forgiveness of sins, to look for temptation, and to pray against them. While Jacob would be Laban's drudge and packhorse, all was well; but when once he began to flee, he makes after him with all his might. All was jolly quiet at Ephesus before St. Paul came thither; but then "there arose no small stir about that way." All the while our Saviour lay in his father's shop, and med-

dled only with carpenter's chips, the devil troubled him not; but now that he is to enter more publicly upon his office of mediatorship, the tempter pierceth his tender soul with many sorrows by solicitation to sin. And dealt he so with the green tree, what will he do with the dry? *Trapp.*

11,927. TEMPTATION, Outward and Inward. Our temptations are chiefly inward, because they find good entertainment in us (our disposition being like a mutinous city that is not only besieged with strong enemies without, but with false traitors within, ready to betray it), contrarily Christ's temptations, if not only, yet chiefly are external, presented by outward voices and objects to his outward senses; but presently, by the perfect light of his mind and unchangeable holiness of his will, discerned and repelled, that they could not get within him, and much less to be moved and affected with them. *Taylor.*

11,928. TEMPTATION, Providential. Nor could he here (Matt. 4:1) attempt anything against Christ until the Spirit had "led" him "to be tempted" of him, and had, as it were, committed him to his hands. Neither over the body or goods of righteous Job, until the Lord had said to him, "Lo, he (Job 1:12) and all that he hath is in thy hands, only save his life" (2:6). Neither over the unclean swine of the faithless Gergesenes, until it was said unto him "go;" yea, and that albeit they were "a legion of devils" (Mark 5:9, 13). That therefore we are tempted, it absolutely cometh not of the power of the devil, but from the providence of the Lord himself, who also hath "led" us by his Spirit "to be tempted." So saith Tertullian (*Lib. de Persecutione*): *Persecutiones veniunt aliquando per diabolum non autem a diabolo*—persecutions come sometimes by the devil, but not of the devil; that is by him as the instrument and not of him as the author. We are in the hands of God, not in the hands of the devil. *Colfe.*

11,929. TEMPTATION, Reality of Christ's. We must approach the temptation not from the side of the Lord's supreme divinity, but from the side of the incarnation. I believe the incarnation constituted the Eternal Son of God as really a man as I myself am a man. I believe that being so constituted a man, he was in all respects "temptable," and that he was actually "tempted" according to the manner of human temptations. Those who wonder to very bewilderment over this fact forget that, in the fall of the angels who "kept not their estate," and in the fall of Adam and Eve, we have examples of sinless creatures being successfully tempted. There must, therefore, have been *media* whereby sin could and did penetrate those sinless spirits. And while, as matter of fact, the Lord Jesus stood, while, as matter of fact, the Lord Jesus gave no response to sin, while, as matter of fact, there was awful shadow, but no stain, yet equally, as matter of fact, is it told us that the temptation was no slight thing, no unreal or mask-conflict, but an awful reality; as real as Gethsemane and

Calvary, and that emphatically "he suffered being tempted" (Heb. 2: 18), having overcome "without sin," but not without agonizing conflict with sin.   *Grosart.*

11,930. TEMPTATION Resisted. The junior class of a Southern college had assembled in a student's room to spend the night in riot and debauch. Amid the crowd was one who had never recited a bad lesson since his matriculation. In his studies he was head and shoulders above the class. That day he had failed. A shade of the deepest gloom came over him and he was melancholy. But wine and jest passed round while he felt like Lucifer in Eden, where all was joy and gladness around him. Said a classmate: "Come, Bob, quaff this bumper, and it will make you feel bright as a hermit's lamp." The tempter whispered in his ear. "Drink once and forget the past." A powerful struggle seemed to be going on in his mind for a moment; but at last he silently shook his head, and retiring from the room, gave vent to a flood of tears. That boy never drank—not even once. He took the valedictory, and is now president of a college. *Anon.*

11,931. TEMPTATION, Rules for Escaping. Fly from all occasions of temptation. If still tempted, fly further still. If there is no escape possible, then have done with running away. Show a bold face, and take the two-edged sword of the Spirit. Some temptations must be taken by the throat, as David killed the lion. Others must be stifled, as David hugged the bear to death. Some you had better keep to yourselves, and don't give them air. Shut them up as scorpions in a bottle. Scorpions in such confinement soon die; but, if allowed out for a crawl, and then put back into the bottles and corked down, they will live a long while, and give trouble. Keep the cork down on some temptations, and they die of themselves.   *Poemen, A. D. 450.*

11,932. TEMPTATION, Running from. Augustine, one of the Christian fathers, before his conversion, lived with an ill woman, and some time after she accosted him as usual. He ran away with all his might, and she ran after him, crying, "Wherefore runnest thou away? It is I." He answered, "I run away because I am not I. I am a new man."

11,933. TEMPTATION, Seeking. A drunken student, trying to excuse his intoxication, said, "I don't know how it is that I am here in this condition, but now that I am in for it, I mean to go the whole figure. One might as well be killed for a sheep as for a lamb. I had no idea of getting into such a spree. I cannot tell what brought it about. I suppose Satan tempted me." "Poh!" said another, " he didn't do any such thing. Do you want to know how it happened with me. I went up to my room and read awhile, I smoked a cigar and then grew restless, and wanted some exciting pleasures, and after waiting for Satan to come to me, I came out in search of him, and here I am. The devil is very easily found by those who seek him, and it is a mean, cowardly piece of business to lay the blame where it

does not belong, and say that he tempts us, when we run to put ourselves in the way of temptation."

11,934. TEMPTATION, Similes of. Temptations resemble the rocks which rest their jagged sides above the waves when it is low water. No vessel dares come near them. But after a while the tide comes sweeping into the bay, and buries the rocks under a flood of water, so that the largest ships may ride in safety above their teeth of death together with the lightest skiff. In our unbelief we often ask, How can I hope to resist the many enemies who constantly seem to be seeking my destruction? But before long the influence of the Holy Spirit will come, bearing us in safety like a rising tide over the rocks of temptation.
                Bower.

11,935. TEMPTATION, Subduing. St. Benedict sought an increase of grace and exemption from temptation by wearing a rough hair shirt, and living, as he did for three years, in a desolate cave, beyond the reach of man. His scanty food was let down to him at the end of a cord. Even there temptations beset him. The memory of a beautiful woman he had met haunted him continually, and so impressed him, that he was on the point of leaving his seclusion to follow her. Near his grotto was a clump of thorns and briers. Having undressed, he threw himself among them and rolled about till his nude body was covered with bleeding wounds. This he continued till the infernal fire was extinguished forever. Others have prostrated themselves before the thicket of thorns which was the bed of triumph to this spiritual hero.

11,936. TEMPTATION, Subtlety of. Satan will lie in wait for the Christian in his time of weakness, even as the wild beasts do at the water side for the cattle coming to drink. Nay, when having resisted manfully, the Christian has driven off the enemy, he should look well that he be not wounded by the vanquished foe, who often makes a Parthian retreat.   *Pilkington.*

11,937. TEMPTATION, Sudden. Some, indeed, plead their natural proneness to sin, excusing themselves on that ground; or on this, that the temptation before which they fell, struck them with the suddenness and vehemence of a hurricane. The command, however, to watch and pray leaves you without excuse. You were fully warned. You should have been on the outlook for the white squall. The sentinel is righteously shot, who is caught asleep upon his post.   *Dr. Guthrie.*

11,938. TEMPTATION, Uses of. Some errors and offences do rub salt upon a good man's integrity, that it may not putrefy with presumption.   *St. Ambrose.*

11,939. TENDERNESS, Power of. God is not only energetic, but tender also in action; he is the God of the dewdrops, as well as the God of the thunder-showers; the God of the tender grass blade, as much as of the mountain oak. We read of great machines which are able to crush iron bars, and yet they can touch so

gently as not to break the shell of the smallest egg; as it is with them, so is it with the hand of the Most High: he can crush a world, and yet bind up a wound. And great need have we of tenderness in our low estate; a little thing would crush us: we have such bruised and feeble souls, that unless we had One who would deal tenderly with us, we must soon be destroyed. There are many soul diseases, to which a tender hand alone can minister; just as there are many states of body which need tender and patient nursing, and which cannot otherwise be successfully dealt with, even by any amount of skill. This tenderness we see continually in action in woman's ministrations in ordinary life. Her voice has notes more sweet and soft than can be distilled from any instrument of music; her hand has a touch more delicate and fine than even the breath of any summer's breeze; it is to her man carries the stories of his sorrows; it is she that has to follow his aching, heavy head; well as he thinks he can do without her in the more exciting scenes of life, he finds that he is not independent when the time comes for suffering and grief. And what makes woman equal to sustaining the heavy burden thus cast upon her? How comes the ivy to be able to sustain the oak, around which it used to cling, ornamenting it, while it owned its lordship and strength! She does all in the power of the tenderness of her nature; rugged and uncouth would life indeed be if such tenderness were withdrawn. But pass away to divine things—from woman, to him that was born of woman—and what do we find, but tenderness of action in him? That tenderness, which in any of mankind is but as a spark from the fire, is perfect in his bosom; its fullness is there; and it is continually being shown to them.
Power.

11,940. TERROR, Cause of. In a sea-fight between Antiochus and the Romans, the former was made victorious by an adroit device of Hannibal. He caused a great number of serpents to be gathered and placed in earthen pots, and thrown into the Roman vessels during the thickest of the fight. These unlooked-for enemies gliding everywhere produced such dismay that the Romans soon betook themselves to flight.

11,941. TERROR, Use of. Terror is subservient to love. As a skillful painter fills the background of his picture with his darker colors, so God introduces the smoke of torment and the black thunder-clouds of Sinai to give brighter prominence to Jesus, the Cross of Calvary, and his love to the chief of sinners.
Dr. Guthrie.

11,942. TESTAMENT, The New. All the genius and learning of the heathen world, all the penetration of Pythagoras, Socrates and Aristotle, had never been able to produce such a system of moral duty, and so rational an account of Providence and of man, and is to be found in the New Testament. *Beattie.*

11,943. TESTAMENT, The Old and New. Though the New Testament is not to be interpreted by the Old, but rather the Old Testament by the New, yet when the light of the latter dispensation is thrown upon the elder one, it is often reflected back as in a mirror, so as to cast additional lustre upon itself. Like that secret writing, which is invisible to the reader till, held before the flame, it gives forth the precious truth for which the soul was longing, so are there myriads of bright and holy thoughts within that volume, which conceal themselves from such as are cold in their affections towards its Author, but which are brought out by the warmth of heavenly desires, giving sweet assurances of mercy and rich promises of blessing, when held before a glowing and a grateful heart. *Stainforth.*

11,944. TESTAMENTS, Character of the. The Old Testament is chiefly a law-book, teaching what we should do or not do, and showing examples and acts how such laws were observed and transgressed. But the New Testament is a book wherein is written the Gospel of God's promises, and the acts of those that believed, and those that believed not. *Luther.*

11,945. THANKFULNESS, Biblical. Our English word *thankful* is allied, from its Anglo-Saxon derivation, to *thinkful.* To be thankful is to be thoughtful or mindful of a benefit received. The various feasts of the Jewish economy were designed to teach the spirit of thankfulness and praise, especially after harvest and vintage, and after special mercies. The Feast of Weeks—of Tabernacles—the Peace offering of thanksgiving, Lev. 7: 11–15 —the Drink offering, and others—all had this meaning. It is to be observed that there was special provision made in Solomon's temple and in the second temple for the service of thanksgiving, see 1 Chron. 16: 4–6; 23: 30; 2 Chron. 5: 12, 13; and for the second temple, Neh. 11: 17; 12: 8, 27, 31. A transient thought is too mean for a standing mercy. How many beautiful examples have we of the memorials the saints of old preserved of God's goodness: like Jacob's pillar, Gen. 35: 14; Joshua's twelve stones at Gilgal, Joshua 4; the golden pot of manna and Aaron's rod laid up in the ark, Exod. 16: 33; Num. 17: 10; Heb. 9: 4; the stone Ebenezer, 1 Sam. 7: 12; David's sword, 1 Sam. 21: 9. *Bowes.*

11,946. THANKFULNESS, Christian. Rev. T. Collins writes of an invalid thankful for intervals of ease, but doubtful of God's mighty mercy in Jesus. He said to him, "Thomas, suppose I plunged into the Severn to save you from drowning, got you out, led you home, and at parting on your door step gave you a lozenge. What would rise to your mind ever after when you thought of me? The lozenge? the lozenge?" "O no, sir! the rescue!" "Well, let it be so concerning Jesus. You tell me of just one of his little gifts. Speak as Paul did of his dying love. Say, 'He loved me, and gave himself for me.' Think of that till it sets your soul on fire; think of that till a passion for him swells within you."

11,947. THANKFULNESS, Effect of. St. Felix of Cantalice, cultivated the thankful spirit.

He was employed begging food and money for his monastery, and when given anything, replied, *Deo gratias*, "Thanks be to God." This ejaculation was constantly on his lips. He came upon two gentlemen one day engaged in fighting a duel. He rushed between them, grasped their swords and held them firmly, crying, "Say *Deo gratias*, my brethren; say *Deo gratias*, each of you." Turned aside from their intention, they repeated the mighty words. "Now your battle is done," said the monk. He listened to the grievance of each, reconciled them, and they parted friends. He come at length to be called Bro. Deo Gratias. The little children along the street would surround him, crying, "*Deo gratias*, Brother Felix, *Deo gratias*." He would reply with great pleasure, "My dear children, *Deo gratias!* God bless you all." Happy would all be if *Deo gratias* were written on their hearts and constantly felt in all the vicissitudes of life.

11,948. THANKFULNESS, Emblem of. The circulations of the ocean constitute a plain and permanent picture of these relations between a human soul and a redeeming God. The sea is always drawing what it needs down to itself, and also always sending up of its abundance into the heavens. It is always getting, and always giving. So, when in the covenant the true relation has been constituted, the redeemed one gets and gives, gives and gets; draws from God a stream of benefits, sends up to God the incense of praise.   *Arnot.*

11,949. THANKSGIVING, Blessing of. Therefore look up to heaven, and give thanks, as the little birds do when they sip a drop of water. If thou obeyest the Lord, thou shalt be blessed in the city and blessed in the field. As the fable is that the unicorn dips his horn into the river, and makes it wholesome for all the beasts to drink, so the mercy of the Lord shall breathe on all thy sustenance and sanctify it for cheerfulness and health, and thy bones shall be filled with marrow and fatness. But though we take our meat from God, yet through infidelity it seems to me we will not take his word, that he will concoct it to vivify and strengthen us.   *Bp. Hacket.*

11,950. THANKSGIVING, Duty of. Our whole life should speak forth our thankfulness; every condition and place we are in should be a witness of our thankfulness: this will make the time and places we live in the better for us. When we ourselves are monuments of God's mercy, it is fit we should be patterns of his praises, and leave monuments to others. We should think life is given to us to do something better than to live in: we live not to live; our life is not the end of itself, but the praise of the Giver. God hath joined his glory and our happiness together: it is fit that we should refer all that is good to his glory, who hath joined his glory to our best good in being glorified in our salvation (Ps. 50: 14; 116: 17). Praise is a just and due tribute for all God's blessings; for what else do the best favors of God especially call for at our hands? How do all creatures praise God but by our mouths?

It is a debt always owing, and always paying, and the more we pay, the more we shall owe; upon the due discharge of this debt, the soul will find much peace. A thankful heart to God for his blessings is the greatest blessing of all. Were it not for a few gracious souls, what honor would God have of the rest of the unthankful world? which should stir us up the more to be trumpets of God's praises in the midst of his enemies; because this, in some sort, hath a prerogative above our praising God 'in heaven: for there God hath no enemies to dishonor him (Ps. 145: 10-12; 148; 150).   *Sibbs.*

11,951. THANKSGIVING, Reason for. When our national independence had been triumphantly achieved, the colonies held general jubilee. King George, who had been sadly worsted in the conflict, thinking himself quite as pious as his disloyal subjects, and not to be outdone in godliness by such rebels against the divine right, appointed also a day of thanksgiving for the restoration of peace to his long-disturbed empire. In the vicinity of the monarch's residence, then Windsor Castle, dwelt a most estimable member of the Church, who shared his sovereign's intimacy, and conversed with him freely. On this occasion the worthy divine ventured to say, "Your Majesty has sent out a proclamation for a day of thanksgiving. For what are we to give thanks? Is it because your Majesty has lost thirteen of the fairest jewels from your crown?" "No, no," replied the monarch, "not for that." "Well, then, shall we give thanks because so many millions of treasure have been spent in this war, and so many millions added to the public debt?" "No, no," again replied the King, "not for that." "Shall we, then, give thanks that so many thousands of our fellowmen have poured out their life-blood in this unhappy and unnatural struggle between those of the same race and religion?" "No, no," exclaimed the king for the third time, "not that." "For what, then, may it please your Majesty, are we to give thanks?" asked the pious divine. "Thank God!" cried the King, most energetically, "thank God it is not any worse." Yes, and here is a reason for thankfulness in all circumstances, since it is never so bad with us as it might be; and even if God be pouring out the vials of his anger, yet, blessed be his name, he never empties them to the uttermost!   *Dr. Charles Wadsworth.*

11,952. THEATRE, Attending the. Dr. Rush told a friend that he was once in conversation with a lady, a professor of religion, who was speaking of the pleasure she anticipated at the theatre in the evening. "What, madam!" said he, "do you go to the theatre?" "Yes," was the reply, "and don't you go, doctor?" "No, madam," said he, "I never go to such places." "Why, sir, do you not go? Do you think it sinful?" said she. He replied, "I never will publish to the world that I think Jesus Christ a bad Master, and religion an unsatisfying portion, which I should do, if I went on the devil's ground in quest of happiness."

11,953. THEATRE, Teachings of the. The toleration of improper sentiments as well as language in our public places of amusements, forms a great objection to them. The indignation which Solon expressed on seeing the tragical representations of Thespis is well known; and he sternly observed, that if falsehood and fiction were tolerated on the stage, they would soon find their way among the common occupations of men. Even Addison's Cato contains poison, and is, as one observes, so much the more dangerous, because the destructive ingredient is concealed by the delightful admixtures of sound taste and fine sentiment. But how does Cato die? and what was the effect of the exhibition on the mind of the unhappy Mr. Budgell, who, on retiring, as it is supposed, from the theatre, plunged into the Thames, and was found with this defence on his person:

> What Cato did, and Addison approved,
> Must needs be right.
>
> *Buck.*

11,954. THEATRE, Warnings against the. The great tragedian, Macready, would never allow his daughter to enter the theatre. A recent memoir of an actor of brilliant genius, written by his daughter, states that his children during their childhood were carefully kept from everything connected with his profession. A son of this actor, on being recently consulted by a soldier's orphan daughter in reference to going upon the stage, earnestly entreated her to abandon the idea, on account of the immorality of such a life. Another eminent actor, George Vanderhoff, on quitting the profession for the bar, gave the following gratuitous advice to any "ingenious youth" thinking of becoming an actor: "Go to sea; go to law; go to church; go to Italy, and strike a blow for liberty; go to any thing or anywhere that will give you an honest and decent livelihood, rather than go upon the stage. To any young lady with a similiar proclivity, I would say, Buy a sewing machine and take in plain work first; so shall you save much sorrow, bitter disappointment, secret tears." *Anon.*

11,955. THEATRE, Way of the. A young man entering a theatre heard an usher call out, "This way to the pit." The thought was at once forced upon him, "This place leads to the bottomless pit." He found pleasure in the theatre no longer, and afterwards became both a Christian and a minister.

11,956. THEFT, Punishment of. The Mohammedan law required that the hand of the thief should be cut off.

11,957. THEOLOGY, Court of. Theology is the empress of the world; mysteries are her privy council; religion is her clergy; the arts her nobility; philosophy her secretary; the graces her maids of honor; the moral virtues the ladies of her bed-chamber; peace is her chamberlain; true joy and endless pleasure are her courtiers; plenty her treasurer; poverty her exchequer; the temple is her court; if thou desire access to this great majesty, the way is by her courtiers, if thou hast no power there,

the common way to the sovereign is the secretary. *Quarles*

11,958. THEOLOGY, Summary of. Dr. Archibald Alexander, of Princeton, was a preacher of Christ for sixty years, and a professor of divinity for forty. He died on the 22d October, 1851. On his death-bed, he was heard to say to a friend, "All my theology is reduced to this narrow compass—Jesus Christ came into the world to save sinners."

11,959. THINGS, Estimate of. To prize every thing according to its real use, ought to be the aim of a rational being. There are few things which can much conduce to happiness, and, therefore, few things to be ardently desired. He that looks upon the business and bustle of the world with the philosophy with which Socrates surveyed the fair at Athens, will turn away at last with his exclamation: "How many things are here which I do not want." *Johnson.*

11,960. THINKERS, Rarity of. Rev. Caleb C. Colton wrote more quotable thoughts on moral subjects than any modern writer. He says in the preface of his work, "Lacon," "I have addressed this volume to those who think, and some may accuse me of an ostentatious independence, in presuming to inscribe a book to so small a minority. But a volume addressed to those who think is in fact addressed to all the world; for although the proportion of those who do think be extremely small, yet every individual flatters himself that he is one of the number."

11,961. THINKERS, Scarcity of. Thinkers are scarce as gold; but he whose thoughts embrace all his subject, and who pursues it uninterruptedly and fearless of consequences, is a diamond of enormous size. *Lavater.*

11,962. THIRST, Martyrdom by. Ten Christians were enclosed in a walled space, open at the top, and exposed to the broiling, mid-summer sun of Egypt. Water was set where they could easily reach it, and this was made the test of their fidelity to God. If they drank, it was a sign of yielding to the demands of the heathen; if not, they must suffer the result. They sang hymns till their throats were parched and their voices failed. Their thirst was intense, but not one of them would touch the adjuring water, which, at best, could give them but brief relief, while fidelity to Christ soon secured them eternal supplies from the river of life in paradise.

11,963. THOROUGHNESS, Example of. Dr. Wayland, the late President of Brown University, Providence, R. I., threw the whole force of his being into whatever he was engaged in, and thought nothing he did well done so long as it might be done better. His own hard study and complete preparation for the classes he held must have been a greater incentive than any maxims he could have given upon the subject, although his advice to his students was after this wise: "Be thoroughly master of your studies. Do not think 'This will do' if you can possibly do it better." Even in gardening, which was his "recreation," and took the place of social relaxation, nothing satisfied him short of perfection. He liked to have the earliest and best fruits, flowers, or vegetables. When he assumed the presidential chair of Brown, so high was his ideal, that after the work in his own department was done, if any deficiency occurred in the duties of others he would perform them rather than have the college fall below the standard to which he aspired to raise it. *Christian Weekly.*

11,964. THOUGHT, Food for. He who has thought for himself, depends not exclusively on others; and yet neither will he depend exclusively upon himself. He deals with raw materials of thought, and knows processes of preparation; but he does not manufacture for all his needs. He buys at the market of wisdom; but when he buys, he judges well and carefully of worth, and can detect adulteration. He can look around the world, and discern uses in things that other men will despise. He can scheme, invent, and combine for himself. Having thoughts of his own, he will speak of truth and opinion generally, as one who has seen and examined, not merely has heard the report of other men. The reflective man will see in his very pathway illustrations, opportunities, and phenomena, for which it might once have seemed necessary to go far and to search widely. It is a fault in life as great as obvious that we see not, or heed not, how principles that we honor and profess to obey may be, and are, applied or violated in our common conduct. He who meditates will be able to see this, and to show it. Accustoming himself to think, he will soon find shining within him, as central suns, certain great fixed principles. In their light will he see the things of his life, and of the world; his whole being will almost unconsciously become orderly and vivified, changed and glorious, under the influence of these suns. *Trinal.*

11,965. THOUGHT, Fruitfulness of. Some may know the story of the first weeping willow, introduced into England by the poet Pope, who found one twig in a Turkish basket of figs that had been given him, putting out a bud. He planted it in his garden, and reared it to a tree, whence all those beautiful trees in this country have been propagated. The weeping willow of Twickenham is no more; but its graceful offspring, bending over many a stream, live far and wide. So many a thought, slight in the outset, conveyed or sprung up by seeming chance, has led to inventions the most important, endeavors the most valuable, or has had other influence most extensive. *Sheppard.*

11,966. THOUGHT, Immortality of a. Beautiful it is to understand and know that a thought did never yet die; that, as thou, the originator thereof, hast gathered it, and created it from the whole past, so thou wilt transmit it to the whole future. It is thus that the heroic heart, the seeing eye of the first times, still feels and sees in us of the latest, that the wise man stands ever encompassed and spiritually embraced by a cloud of witnesses and brothers;

and there is a living literal communion of saints, wide as the world itself, and as the history of the world. *Carlyle.*

11,967. THOUGHT, Man Made for. Man is evidently made for thinking: this is the only excellence that he can boast. To think aright is the sum of human duty; and the true art of thinking is to begin with ourselves, our Author, and our end. And yet what is it that engrosses the thoughts of the world? Not any of these objects; but pleasure, wealth, honor, and esteem; in fine, the making ourselves kings without reflecting what it is to be a king, or to be a man. *Pascal*

11,968. THOUGHT, Productiveness of. Thought engenders thought. Place one idea on paper, another will follow it, and still another, until you have written a page; you cannot fathom your mind. There is a well of thought there which has no bottom; the more you draw from it, the more clear and fruitful it will be. If you neglect to think for yourself, and use other people's thoughts, giving them utterance only you will never know what you are capable of At first your ideas may come out in lumps homely and shapeless; but no matter, time and perseverance will arrange and refine them. Learn to think, and you will learn to write; the more you think, the better you express your ideas. *Sala*

11,969. THOUGHT, Repetition of. It is good to repeat old thoughts in the newest books, because the old works in which they stand are not read. New translations of many truths, as of foreign standard works, must be given forth every half century. *Richter*

11,970. THOUGHT, Value of a. I look upon every true thought as a valuable acquisition to society, which cannot possibly hurt or obstruct the good effect of any other truth whatsoever; for they all partake of one common essence, and necessarily coincide with each other; and, like the drops of rain which fall separately into the river, mix themselves at once with the stream, and strengthen the general current. *Middleton.*

11,971. THOUGHTS, Escape from Evil. John, the dwarf, used to say that as a man climbs a tree when he sees a wild beast or a serpent coming towards him, so a person who sees any evil thoughts coming upon him, must ascend up to God by earnest prayer. He was greatly charmed by heavenly contemplation and desired to enjoy it constantly. He said one day to his elder brother, "I wish to live without distraction or earthly concern like the angels, that, I may be able to serve and praise God without interruption." So saying, he left all, and went into the unfrequented wilderness. There a few days of solitude, silence and hunger, subdued him, and he returned, and knocked at the door of his brother's cell. His brother asked his name. He answered, "I am your brother John." "How can that be?" said he, "my brother John has become an angel, and lives no more among men." The youthful hermit was satisfied that angelic attainments were not for him, even in solitude.

11,972. THOUGHTS, First. In matters of expediency and prudence wait for the afterthoughts; but in matters of conscious and present duty, take the first thoughts that arise, for they are the divinest. *Dr. Raleigh.*

11,973. THOUGHTS, Good. Good thoughts are blessed guests, and should be heartily welcomed, well fed, and much sought after. Like rose leaves, they give out a sweet smell if laid up in the jar of memory. *Spurgeon.*

11,974. THOUGHTS, Power over. A certain wise man replied to one who said, "Such and such thoughts have come into my mind," by saying, "Let them go again." And another wise oracle said, "Thou canst not prevent the birds from flying above thy head, but thou canst prevent their building their nests in thy hair." *Luther.*

11,975. THOUGHTS, Sinful. A monk came to Poemen and asked, "Father what am I to do? I have impure thoughts arising in my mind." "Don't think of them," he answered. "And ill-natured thoughts of others rise up." "Don't think of them." "Temptations are like an axe," says Sisoes; "they cut down your hopes of salvation and lop off your virtues, but they can do nothing against you unless you take them up by an act of will, and give consent to them."

11,976. THOUGHTS, Temptation in. St. Catharine of Sienna, was horribly tempted with vile thoughts and impure images of the imagination. She suffered great agony in wrestling against them. After such a season she was conscious of the presence of the Lord Jesus, and cried, "O, my Saviour, my Lord, why didst thou forsake me?" "My child," he answered, "I have been with thee through all." "What, my Lord! in the midst of these vile thoughts and foul imaginations?" "My child yes, I was in thy heart all the while, for thy will did not consent to the thoughts and images presented to thee."

11,977. THREATS, Abstaining from. I consider it a mark of great prudence in a man to abstain from threats or any contemptuous expressions; for neither of these weaken the enemy, but threats make him more cautious, and the other excites his hatred and a desire to revenge himself. *Machiavelli.*

11,978. THRESHING, Oriental. The threshing-floors of Migdol were near our tents. We went over to them in the gray twilight. They are simply circles of smooth ground, fifteen or twenty yards in diameter. Each had on it a heap of newly reaped grain; and round the outer edges of the heaps were broad flattened belts, where the "instruments" had already been at work. Labor had ceased for the night, and the oxen were feeding freely on the half-trodden grain, as if their master was resolved to obey to the letter the Scripture command, 'Thou shalt not muzzle the ox when he treadeth out the corn" (Deut. 24:4). The "thresh-iag-instruments" are flat, heavy, wooden slabs, some five feet long by three wide, slightly turned up in front. The under surface is thickly studded with knobs of hard stone or iron. A massive prison door with its rows of projecting nail-heads will give the best idea of a *mowrej*, as the instrument is now called. Each is drawn by a yoke of oxen. The driver stands on the mowrej, and the goad with which he urges on and directs the movements of his team, is a formidable weapon. It is sometimes ten feet long, and has a sharp iron point. We could now see that the feat of Shamgar, who "slew of the Philistines six hundred men with an ox goad," was not so very wonderful as some have been accustomed to think (Jud 3:31). The oxen advanced in front, "treading out" the grain, and the mowrej follows, crushing and cutting the straw with its "teeth," till it is reduced almost to dust. (2 Kings 13:7.) *Dr. Porter.*

11,979. TIME, Accounting for. Cato and other heathens held that account must be given not only of our labor, but also of our leisure. At the great day it will appear that they that have spent their time in mourning have done better than they that have spent their time in dancing, and they that have spent many days in humiliation than they that have spent many days in idle recreations. I have read of a devout man who, when he heard a clock strike, would say, "Here is one hour past that I have to answer for." As time is very precious, so it is very short. Time is very swift; it is suddenly gone. *Brooks.*

11,980. TIME, Benediction of. Father Time is not always a hard parent, and, though he tarries for none of his children, often lays his hand lightly upon those who have used him well, making them old men and women inexorably enough, but leaving their hearts and spirits young and in full vigor. With such people the gray head is but the impression of the old fellow's hand in giving them his blessing, and every wrinkle but a notch in the quiet calendar of a well-spent life. *Dickens.*

11,981. TIME Cast Away. Coming hastily into a chamber, I had almost thrown down a crystal hour-glass: fear lest I had, made me grieve as if I had broken it. But, alas! how much more precious time have I cast away without any regret? The hour-glass was but crystal, each hour a pearl: that, but like to be broken—this, lost outright: that, but casually—this, done willfully. A better hour-glass might be bought; but time once lost is lost forever. Thus we grieve more for toys than for treasures. Lord, give me an hour-glass, not to be by me, but in me. Teach me the number of my days—an hour-glass to turn me —that I may apply my heart unto wisdom. *Fuller.*

11,982. TIME, Consecration of. David was hid in the cave of Adullam, when the Philistines were encamped at Rephaim, and at the end of the plain. David had nothing to drink for twenty-four hours, and as he lay panting in the cave, with his men of arms about him, he said, "O that one would give me drink of the water of the well of Bethlehem that is at the gate!" It was an ejaculation which fierce thirst wrung from him. There were three brave men who at once determined to gratify his wish, and they went over the plain, where the arrows were raining down on them; but through the midst of these hurtling arrows and flying javelins they went to the well of Bethlehem, got the water, and brought a gourd full of it to the king to slake his thirst. I know nothing richer or grander in the Old Testament, nor in the history of man, than David's conduct then. He would not drink of it, but poured it out as a libation to the Lord; and why? "My God forbid it me, that I should do this thing: shall I drink the blood of these men that have put their lives in jeopardy? for with the jeopardy of their lives they brought it!" Do you see the application I would make of this? Every hour of your human life and mine; every drop of this precious time, which God gives us in drops, was purchased with a dearer blood and more fearful peril of sacrifice than this. It was not merely through the arrows hurled from the towers of Bethlehem: it was not merely breasting the javelins of the Philistines, that Christ our Saviour purchased for us the gift of this precious time allowed to us in this life. Oh, no! He received into his divine breast all the arrows of hell; he poured out his most precious blood in sorrow and agony, to buy this time for you and me. Shall we drink up these hours that Christ has purchased, and waste them as they come? Oh, no! Say rather, I will pour them out to the Lord; I will glorify him with this time that he has purchased for me. *Dr. John McClintock.*

11,983. TIME, Conviction from. A young man attended a ball and was highly delighted with the diversion. In the midst of their enjoyment the clock struck one. That striking passage of Dr. Young instantly rushed upon his mind:

" The bell strikes one—we take no note of time,
　But from its loss:—to give it then a tongue
　Is wise in man. As if an angel spoke,
　I feel the solemn sound; if heard aright,
　It is the knell of my departed hours."

Conviction seized the youth. He left the ball room, retired to his closet and gave himself to Christ.

11,984. TIME, Curative Influence of. Time cures every wound, and though the scar may remain and occasionally ache, yet the earliest agony of its recent infliction is felt no more. *Scott.*

11,985. TIME, Definition of. Plato says that time is a movable image of eternity, or the interval of the world's motion.

11,986. TIME, Economy with. Many people take no care of their money till they have come nearly to the end of it, and others do just the same with their time. Their best days they throw away, let them run like sand through their fingers, as long as they think they have an almost countless number of them to spend; but when they find their days flowing rapidly away, so that at last they have very few left, then they will at once make a very wise use of them; but unluckily, they have by that time no notion how to do it. *Gotthelf.*

11,987. TIME, Flight of. Let good fellows sit in a tavern from sun to sun, and they think the day very short, confessing (though insensible of their loss) that time is a light-headed runner. Bind them to the church for two hours, and you put an ache into their bones—the seats be too hard. Now time is a creeper, and many a weary look is cast up to the glass. It is a man's mind that renders any work troublesome or pleasant. *Adams.*

11,988. TIME, Fragments of. Philip of Macedon was one day drinking deep with some of his courtiers, when he began to discourse about the odes and tragedies of Dionysius the elder, disputing the likelihood of his having found leisure to write them. The son of the deceased poet exclaimed, "They were written in the time which you and I and other happy fellows spent over the bowl." If we could trace the history of the productions of the greatest men, the number of whose achievements amaze and astonish us, we should find that the hours spent by their fellows in trifling and sin were the precious seasons which, husbanded by them with care, brought forth such grand results. Fragments of time should be gathered as carefully as fragments of gems from the lapidary's floor, or dust of gold from amid the shavings of the gold-beater's room. *Anon.*

11,989. TIME, Making up. Lord Wilmington observed of the Duke of Newcastle, the prime minister, "He loses half an hour every morning, and runs after it during all the day, without being able to overtake it." *Selwyn.*

11,990. TIME, Mystery of. That great mystery of Time, were there no other—the illimitable, silent, never-resting thing called Time, rolling, rushing on, swift, silent, like an all-embracing ocean-tide, on which we and all the universe swim like exhalations, like apparitions which are and then are not—this is forever very literally a miracle—a thing to strike us dumb; for we have no word to speak about it. *Carlyle.*

11,991. TIME, Opportunity and. Great is the worth and excellency of time, all the treasures of the world cannot protract, stop, or call back one minute of time. O what is man, that the heavenly bodies should be wheeled about by Almighty Power in constant revolutions, to beget time for him! (Psalm 8:3.) More precious are the seasons and opportunities that are in time for our souls; those are the golden spots of time, like the pearl in the oyster-shell, of much more value than the shell that contains it. There is much time in a short opportunity. There is a day on which our eternal happiness depends (Luke 19:41, 42; Heb. 4:7). Lost opportunity is never to be recovered by the soul any more (Ezek. 24:13; Rev. 22:11). To come before the opportunity, is to come before the bird is hatched; and to come after it, is to come when the bird is flown. There is no calling back time, when it is once past. See this in the examples you find (Luke 13:26; Eccles. 9:10). It is wholly uncertain to every soul, whether the present day may not determine his leave in this tabernacle, and a writ of ejection be served by debts upon his soul to-morrow (James 4: 13; Luke 12: 20). As soon as ever time shall end, eternity takes place. The stream of time delivers souls daily into the boundless ocean of vast eternity. *Ad hoc momento pendet œternitas.* We are now measured by time, hereafter by eternity.   *Flavel.*

11,992. TIME, Redeeming. That time ought to be redeemed, is a lesson that hath been taught by the very heathens themselves. It was the saying of Pittacus, one of the seven wise men, "Know time, lose not a minute." And so Seneca: "Time is the only thing," saith he, "that we can innocently be covetous of, and yet there is nothing of which we are more lavishly and profusely prodigal." And Chrestus, a sophister of Byzantium in the time of Hadrianus the emperor, was much given to wine; yet he always counted time so precious, that when he had misspent his time all the day, he would redeem it at night. Chilo, one of the seven sages, being asked what was the hardest thing in the world to be done, answered, "To use and employ a man's time well." Cato held, that an account must be given, not only of our labor, but also of our leisure. And Ælian gives this testimony of the Lacedæmonians, "They were hugely covetous of their time, spending it all about necessary things, and suffering no citizen either to be idle or play." "And," saith another, "we trifle with that which is most precious, and throw away that which is our greatest interest to redeem." Certainly, these heathens will rise in judgment, not only against Domitian, the Roman emperor, who spent much of his time in killing of flies; nor only against Archimedes, who spent his time in drawing lines on the ground when Syracuse was taken; nor only against Artaxerxes, who spent his time in making hafts for knives; nor only against Solyman the great Turk, who spent his time in making notches of horn for bows; nor only against Eropas, a Macedonian king, who spent his time in making of lanterns; nor only against Hyrcanus the king of Parthia, who spent his time in catching of moles; but also against many professors who, instead of redeeming of precious time, do trifle and fool away much of their precious time at the glass, the comb, the lute, the viol, the pipe, or at vain sports and foolish pastimes, or by idle jestings, immoderate sleeping, and superfluous feasting. *Brooks.*

11,993. TIME, Ripening Influence of. It is an old and trite saying, "How rapidly time urges his flight; sometimes as a relentless, unsparing destroyer; but oftener as a swift-winged, and beautiful angel; changing, yet not taking away this world's blessings: making our past sorrows look dim in the distance; opening many flowers of pleasure on our way, and gradually ripening our souls for the great and glorious harvest of eternity. *William Chambers.*

11,994. TIME, Stealing. Whether a man steals from me a dollar or the half hour in which I can earn that sum is to me a matter of indifference. The former crime may be the more demoralizing to the offender; but my loss

is as great in one case as in the other. It has been justly said that there is as much injustice and cruelty in destroying a man's comfort during the five minutes you keep him waiting as in giving him an actual blow. But suppose ten or twenty men are kept waiting for one man. By an utterly inexcusable negligence he causes an utter perdition of capital and labor to that amount, more, perhaps, to say nothing of the vexation he has caused, unfitting twenty men for their duties for all the rest of the day.   *Mathews.*

11,995. TIME, Uncertainty of. A minister requested a lady to engage in a charitable work to which he thought her adapted. She declined, saying, "My stay here will be probably too short to be of use. I do not know that I shall be here three months." He answered her, "I do not know that I shall be here one." She felt his reproof and accepted the proffered duty.

11,996. TIME, Wasting. If a person were so foolish as to throw away a valuable piece of money into a pit, or in the sea, he would not literally throw away anything but the metal; but virtually he would throw away whatever best thing it would have purchased, as bread, clothing, refreshments, medicine for the sick, instructive books, etc. Even so, a person wasting time throws away, not the time itself only, but the opportunities and the privileges which that time presents.   *John Foster.*

11,997. TIME, Well Disposed. When Drexelius was asked by his friend Faustinus how he could do so much as he had done, he answered, "The year has three hundred and sixty-five days, or eight thousand four hundred and sixty hours: in so many hours great things may be done; the slow tortoise made a long journey by losing no time."   *Bp. Horne.*

11,998. TITHES, Custom of. That tithes were not confined to the Jewish priesthood, we learn from the fact of their having been very generally copied from the patriarchs by Gentile nations. Among the Greeks and Romans tenths were frequently dedicated out of a man's substance to their gods, sometimes as a lasting obligation, sometimes only on particular occasions; but it was customary to dedicate the tenth of the spoils of war to Jupiter Praedator, to Mars, and to Hercules. A tenth part of private possessions was also in some places dedicated to Diana. The Carthaginians sent a tenth of their profits to the Hercules of Tyre, of which city they were a colony. The Persians gave to their gods the tenth of war spoils. The Pelasgians paid tithes to the oracle of Apollo at Delphi.   *Mrs. Mackesy.*

11,999. TOBACCO, Cost of. Bishop Thompson stated in one of his addresses that the "church spends more money for tobacco than would support her ministry at home and her missions abroad."

12,000. TOBACCO, Saved from. A prominent member and official in a New York church had been addicted to the constant use of tobacco for forty years, until its daily use had become seemingly necessary to health, if not to life. He had made many efforts to rid himself of the doubtful practice, but always failed because of the inward gnawing which its long-continued use had created, and which forced him to begin the practice again. At last, on a certain occasion, in the presence of the writer, he said, "I have long been seeking a deeper work of grace; tobacco appears to hinder me; but I had not supposed it possible to be saved from the dreadful power of this habit until now. Never before have I trusted Jesus to save me from the appetite as well as the use of it, but now I do;" and, suiting the action to the word, he threw far away from him the tobacco he held in his hand. He still lives, and for several years has reiterated this testimony: "From that hour all desire left me, and I have ever since hated what I once so fondly loved." *W. H. Boole.*

12,001. TO-DAY, Battle of. You remember how Leonidas, the Spartan, kept back the Persian hosts. He stood in the narrow pass of Thermopylæ, and as the foe came up, one by one, each man was able to push back his enemy, and they might have kept Greece thus for many a day. But suppose Leonidas and his handful of men had gone out into the wide open plain, and attacked the Persians—why, they must have died at once, though they should have fought like lions. Christian, stand you in the narrow pass of to-day, and as your troubles come, one by one, by faith you shall find out that your strength is sufficient for you; but if you go out into the vast plain of time, and think to meet all the troubles that shall ever come at once, it must be too much for you. Will you please not to borrow misery, for you will have enough of your own. "Sufficient unto the day is the evil thereof."
Spurgeon.

12,002. TO-DAY, Duties of. Enjoy the blessings of this day, if God sends them, and the evils of it bear patiently and sweetly; for this day only is ours; we are dead to yesterday, and we are not yet born to the morrow.
Bp. Taylor.

12,003. TO-DAY, Proper use of. Now, is it safe, think you, to pass this day? A hard heart is a provoking heart; and, as long as it continues hard, continues provoking God and despising the Holy Ghost. To-day, therefore, hear his voice; that is, this present day. But which is that day? It is this very time wherein you stand before God, and in which you hear me. If you embrace the opportunity, happy are you; if not, you shall give as dear an account as for anything you ever heard in your life. There is no dallying with God; take his proffer, take him at his word in a matter of salvation. He calls thee "to-day;" peradventure he will speak no more!
Archbishop Usher.

12,004. TOMBS, Human. How many are so entombed by the riches, the honors, the pleasures and the sins of the world, as only to be taken out of them to be buried in the earth.
Marsh.

12,005. TO-MORROW, A Delusion. Say not, "I will do it to-morrow! Some other time." To-morrow may not be yours. To-morrow is a delusive phantom, ever beckoning the traveler toward the brink of a precipice. To-morrow is a courteous traitor, a smiling assassin, "Satan's chief recruiting-sergeant, paving with good intentions the road to hell!" *Anon.*

12,006. TONGUE, Admonition to the. Some are of opinion that nature hath shut up the tongue with a double portcullis of lips and teeth on purpose that man, by their manner of disposition, might have a constant and silent kind of admonition, that he should not be over-hasty to speak. *Wanley.*

12,007. TONGUE: Brevities. "There are some persons so full of nothings, that, like the strait sea of Pontus, they perpetually empty themselves by their mouths, making every company or single person they fasten on to be their Propontis." "The talking man makes himself artificially deaf, being like a man in the steeple when the bells ring." "Great knowledge, if it be without vanity, is the most severe bridle of the tongue. For so have I heard that all the noises and pratings of the pool, the croaking of frogs and toads, is hushed and appeased upon the instant of bringing upon them the light of a candle or torch. Every beam of reason and ray of knowledge checks the dissoluteness of the tongue."

12,008. TONGUE, Good and Bad. A certain person sent Bias, one of the seven wise men of Greece, a beast for sacrifice, with the request that he should return to him the best and worst part of its flesh. Bias returned the tongue of the animal to the donor. This act did much to gain for him a recognition as one of the wise men.

12,009. TONGUE, Good or Evil. Than a good tongue, there is nothing better; than an evil, nothing worse. It hath no mean; it is either exceedingly good or excessively evil. It knows nothing but extremes; and is if good, best of all; if bad, worst of all. If it be good, it is a walking garden that scatters in every place a sweet flower, an herb of grace to the hearers. If it be evil, it is a wild bedlam full of goading and maddening mischiefs. So the tongue is every man's best or worst movable. *Adams.*

12,010. TONGUE, Punishing the. St. Clara, of Rimini, practiced great austerities, sleeping on a hard board and wearing iron rings around her neck and wrists, to punish herself for extravagance in jewelry when young. She once spoke intemperately of some one who annoyed her, and afterwards punished herself by pinching her tongue with a pair of pincers, so that she could not speak for two or three days.

12,011. TONGUE, Servitude of the. The tongue is the slave of the body as well as of the soul. The heart says—"Make love for me," and the tongue makes love for the heart; the brain says—"Discourse for me," and the tongue discourses for the brain; the soul says—"Pray for me, sing for me, curse for me, tell lies for me," and the tongue prays, sings, curses, and tells lies for the soul. *Prof. G. Wilson.*

12,012. TONGUE, Wounds by the. A wound

from a tongue is worse than a wound from a sword; the latter affects only the body,—the former the soul, the spirit.   *Pythagoras.*

12,013. TONGUES, Gift of. The apostles, speaking on the day of Pentecost to the people, in their respective languages, was to us a plain intimation of the mind and will of God, that the sacred records should be preserved by all nations in their own tongue; that the Scriptures should be read, and public worship performed in the vulgar languages of the nations.   *M. Henry.*

12,014. TONGUES, Unconverted. There are many persons who think they are Christians because they have had experience; but they do not feel it to be their Christian duty to use their tongues according to the laws of kindness. Nor do they think, in the confession of their sins, to confess that, day in and day out, they are making somebody unhappy by the manner in which they use that member.   *Beecher.*

12,015. TOO LATE, Almost. After Sir Colin Campbell's silent retreat from Lucknow, in the war in India, there was one man left behind. "Captain Waterman," says Mr. Rees, in his personal narrative of the siege, "having gone to his bed in a retired corner of the brigade mess-house, overslept himself. He had been forgotten. At two o'clock in the morning he got up, and found to his horror that we had already left. He hoped against hope, and visited every outpost. All was deserted and silent. To be the only man in an open intrenchment, and fifty thousand furious barbarians outside! It was horrible to contemplate. His situation frightened him. He took to his heels, and he ran till he could scarcely breathe. Still the same silence, the same stillness, interrupted only by the occasional report of the enemy's gun or musketry. At last he came up with the retiring rear-guard, mad with excitement and breathless with fatigue."

12,016. TOO LATE, Effects of Being. A railroad train was running along at unusually quick speed. A curve was just ahead, and the train was late, very late; still the conductor hoped to pass the curve safely. Suddenly a locomotive dashed into sight. In an instant there was a collision, a shriek, a shock, and fifty persons were killed, and all because an engineer had been behind time.   *Anon.*

12,017. TOO LATE: Examples. "Too late!" Oh! word of terror, which has often fallen like the thunder of God upon many a heart of man. See that father as he hastens from the burning house, and thinks that he has taken all the children with him! He counts; one dear head is missing; he hastens back. "Too late!" is the hollow sound that strikes his ear. The stone wall tumbles under the roaring torrent of flame. He swoons, and sinks to the ground. Who is that hastening through the darkness of the night on the winged courser? It is the son who has been wandering in the ways of sin, and now at last longs to hear from the lips of his dying father the words, "I have forgiven you!" Soon he is at his journey's end. In the twinkling of an eye he is at the door. "Too late!" shrieks forth the mother's voice; "that mouth is closed forever!" and he sinks, fainting, into her arms. See that victim for the scaffold, and the executioner whetting the steel of death! The multitude stand shivering and dumb. Who is that heaving in sight on yonder distant hill, beckoning with signs of joy? It is the king's express; he brings a pardon! Nearer and nearer come the steps. Pardon! resounds through the crowd; softly at first, and then louder, and yet louder. "Too late!" The guilty head has fallen! Yea, since the world began the heart of many a man has been fearfully pierced through with the cutting words, "Too late!" But, oh! who will describe to me the lamentation that will arise when, at the boundary line which parts time from eternity, the voice of the righteous Judge will say, "Too late!" Long have the wide gates of heaven and its messengers cried at one time and another, "To-day, if ye will hear his voice!" Man! man! how then will it be with you when once those gates, with appalling sound, shall be shut for eternity?   *Tholuck.*

12,018. TOO LATE, Result of Being. At the wreck of the steamer London, in January, 1866, the announcement was made that there was no hope of saving the ship, by Rev. D. J. Draper, who said at the same time that there was hope for all who would flee to Christ. He had an attentive audience, who were more than willing to hear about salvation in Christ. The only remaining boat was launched, the second engineer taking command. The heroic captain said to him, "There is not much chance for the boat. There is none for the ship. Your duty is done; mine is to remain here. Get in and take charge of the few it will hold." As they dropped into the boat, the engineer urged the captain to join them. "No," said the brave Englishman, "I will go down with the passengers; but I wish you God-speed and safe to land!" He threw them a compass, and gave them their course, saying, "East-north-east to Brest, ninety miles." At that instant, a lady, bare-headed, with disheveled hair, and with "livid horror on her face," shrieked aloud amidst the wind, "A thousand guineas for a place in that boat!" The doctor's assistant offered five hundred pounds for a seat in it, and pleaded his official relation to the crew. It was too late. The small boat, with nineteen persons, was pulled away, and within five minutes afterwards the steamship, the London, with her living cargo of more than two hundred and twenty immortal men, women and children—was seen to settle stern foremost, throw up her bows in the air, and then plunge headlong down through the dark whelming waters into the deep grave of the ocean. The boat's company were rescued next day.

12,019. TORMENT, Smoke of. A coal pit took fire, a dense volume of smoke was rising from its mouth, while below were the poor miners being suffocated or consumed. The smoke of their torment did not ascend forever, for ere that had ceased, their sufferings had ended in death. But there is a torment that is enduring, a smoke " that ascendeth forever and ever."

12,020. TORTURE, Example of. King Sapor, of Persia, required the Christians in his realm to adore the sun and fire. Jonas and Barachisius refused to obey. The executioners poured melted lead into the nostrils of Jonas, placed red-hot iron plates under his arms, and hung him up by one foot, till he fainted. They then cut off his hands and feet, tore out his tongue, and afterward crushed him to death in a grape press. They thrust sharp splinters into the body of Barachisius till he resembled a porcupine, and then rolled him on the ground to drive them in.

12,021. TRACT, Influence of a. The mate of a vessel received Dr. Payson's tract "Address to Seamen." The question, "Whither are you bound?" arrested his attention, led him to reflection, fastened conviction upon him, and led him to resolve upon reform. He delayed the fulfillment of his promise till severely wounded and shipwrecked, and in utter helplessness he fell into the arms of Christ.

12,022. TRACT, Name of. A minister gave a negro in his congregation a tract, and some time afterwards asked what he thought of it. "Oh, massa," said he, "it do me soul good. I never knew before why dey call 'em tracks, but when I read dat little book it track me dis way, and it track me dat way; it track me all day, and it track me all night. When I go out in de barn, it track me dare; when I go out in de woods, it track me dare; when I came in de house, it track me dare; it track me eberywhere I go. Den I know why dey call 'em tracks." He became a sincere Christian.

12,023. TRADITION, Unreliable. Would persons as readily believe the correctness of a report transmitted by word of mouth in popular rumors from one end of the kingdom to another, as if it came in a letter passed from one person to another over the same space? Would they think that because they could trust most servants to deliver a letter however long or important, therefore they could trust the same man to deliver the contents of a long and important letter, in a message by word of mouth? Let us put a familiar case: a footman brings you a letter from a friend upon whose word you can perfectly rely, giving an account of something that has happened to himself, and the exact account of which it concerned you to know. While you are reading and answering the letter, the footman goes into the kitchen and there gives your cook an account of the same thing, which he says he overheard the upper servants at home talking over as related to them by the valet, who said he had it from your friend's son's own lips; the cook relates the story to your groom, and he in turn tells you. Would you judge of that story by the letter, or the letter by the story?
Illustrations of Truth.

12,024. TRAITOR Punished. When the Emperor Aurelian came to the city of Thyana,

and found the gates of the city shut against him, he swore he would make such a slaughter that he would not leave a dog alive. Heracleon, fearing to perish in the city, betrayed it into Aurelian's hands. Aurelian caused all the dogs in the city to be slain; but gave all the citizens a free pardon, except Heracleon, whom he caused to be slain, saying, "He would never prove faithful to him who had been the betrayer of his own country."

12,025. TRANSFORMATION, Legend of. The North American Indians, giving the origin of their maize, say that a beautiful girl, pursued by a river god, took refuge among the reeds, twining them about her to hide herself, upon which her slender form was changed into a graceful stalk, her teeth into milk-white kernels, and her lovely floating hair into silk; and, in place of reeds and maiden, there stood only a tall, bending stalk of Indian corn; so that ever after, in the rustle of a waving cornfield, the red man could hear the stirring of a company of timid girls. *Appleton's Journal*

12,026. TRANSFORMATION, Sudden. Euripides's Iolaus, a feeble, superannuated old man, by means of a certain prayer, became, on a sudden, youthful and strong for battle; but the Stoics' wise man was, yesterday, most detestable and the worst of villains; but to-day is changed on a sudden into a state of virtue.
Plutarch.

12,027. TRANSGRESSOR, Hard Way of the. Go down to the Tombs. I am told that that little bridge over the prison yard, over which the prisoners are led, has written on one side the words, "The way of the transgressor is hard." If that is not true, how do they dare put it on there? They ought to take it off. There is not a man in all New York but knows as he goes down deep in his heart that the way of the transgressor is hard. On the other side of that bridge it is written, "The Bridge of Sighs;" and over that the young men pass every day, and every one of them will testify that that portion of the Bible is true where it says the way of the transgressor is hard. So don't give that as an excuse. *Moody.*

12,028. TRANSMIGRATION, Pagan. Many of the heathen priests in India teach their followers that the soul, after it has worn out one body, passes into another. They say if a person has not attended to the worship of the gods, or neglected the priests, then the soul at death will go into a deformed and afflicted body; or, if he has given much money to the idol-temples, then he shall be again born into the world in a beautiful form, and shall be rich and happy. A soul, they say, may pass into the body of a bird, beast, or insect, and be punished in its new state for the sins of a previous one; so that it may dwell in a buffalo or a butterfly, a fierce tiger or a gentle dove, according to its character in this life. And after many millions of changes, the highest state of perfection will be when it passes into the body of a white elephant. A Hindoo was lying upon his bed, expecting soon to die. A priest came to see him, when the dying man ex claimed, "What will become of me?" "Oh," said the priest, "you will inhabit another body." "And where," said he, "shall I go then?" "Into another; and so on through thousands of millions." The mind of the poor sufferer darted across the whole period of changes as though it were only an instant, and cried, "Where shall I go then?" The priest could not reply, and the unhappy idolater died in the dark as to his final destiny. *Moister.*

12,029. TREASURE, Heavenly. The old Grecians that had fed altogether on acorns before, after that bread came in amongst them, made no reckoning of their mast any more, but kept it only for their swine. And leathern and iron money began to grow out of request amongst the Lacedæmonians, after that gold and silver came in use. So when a man hath once found the favor of God in his heart, and the love of God in Christ hath once lighted on it, and got assurance of it, he ceaseth then to be greedy of this world's trash. *Gataker.*

12,030. TREASURE, Hidden. A writer on Oriental literature and customs mentions that in the East, on account of the frequent changes of dynasties, and the revolutions which accompany them, many rich men divide their goods into three parts: one they employ in commerce, or for their necessary support; one they turn into jewels, which should it prove needful to fly, could be easily carried with them: a third part they bury. But while they trust no one with the place where the treasure is buried, so is the same, should they not return to the spot before their death, as good as lost to the living (Jer. 41: 8), until by chance a lucky peasant, while he is digging his field, lights upon it. And thus, when we read in Eastern tales how a man has found a buried treasure, and in a moment risen from poverty to great riches, this is, in fact, an occurrence that not unfrequently happens, and is a natural consequence of the customs of these people. Modern books of travel continually bear witness to the universal belief in the existence of such hid treasures. Often, too, a man abandoning the regular pursuits of industry, will devote himself to treasure-seeking, in the hope of growing rich of a sudden. *Trench.*

12,031. TREASURE, Indestructible. Rev. John Newton one day called to visit a family that had suffered the loss of all they possessed by fire. He found the pious mistress, and saluted her with, "I give you joy, madam." Surprised, and ready to be offended, she exclaimed, "What! joy that all my property is consumed?" "Oh no," he answered, "but joy that you have so much property that fire cannot touch." This allusion to her real treasures checked her grief; and she wiped away her tears.

12,032. TREASURE, Search for. After Mardonius had been conquered at Plataea, a report existed that he had left great treasures buried within the circuit where his tent had stood; Polycrates, a Theban, buying the ground, sought long for the treasure, but not finding it, inquired at Delphi, and was told "to turn every stone," which doing he found it. Such the proverb collectors give as the origin of the proverb, πάντα λίθον ἴνει. *Trench.*

12,033. TREASURE, Testing. Praxitiles told Phryne, that she might choose from his studio any statue that she pleased. Not knowing which was the most valuable, she caused some one to come in as if in haste and tell the artist that his studio was on fire. He, startled at the news, cried out, "Are the Cupid and the Satyr safe?" By this statagem she saw what he prized the most, and chose the Cupid.

12,034. TREASURES, Imperishable. Stilpon, the philosopher, when his city was burned, and his wife and children in it, and he alone escaped, was asked whether he had lost anything. He replied, "All my treasures are with me—justice, virtue, temperance, prudence, and this inviolable principle, not to esteem anything as my proper good that can be taken from me."

12,035. TREE, Lesson from a Fallen. The sound of the woodman's axe gives note that some giant of the forest is about to fall: and now the crashing boughs tell plainly that the work is done, and the pride of the summer foliage is brought down to the ground. See what a gap is made in the screen of wood, and how the eye can now wander over the soft meadows, and the distant village, that were hid before! Let us go towards the opening that is so apparent, and consider what solemn or useful reflections may be suggested by a sight of the fallen tree. It lies in the direction in which it fell. While it still flourished in its pride and glory, the direction as well as the period of its fall was uncertain. It was possible that it might fall towards the north or towards the south: nor was there any reason why it should not enjoy the sunshine, and the rain, through many a verdant summer. But the word was given that the axe should be laid into its root, and now the direction in which it should fall is no more a question. It is a fixed and unalterable fact. The period during which one or the other direction could have been given to its fall is past and gone forever. Surely a thought of unspeakable importance is thus suggested to us. The stroke of death fixes the direction and the character of our future and eternal state of being. *Bp. Trower.*

12,036. TREE, Quality of a. There is no ascertaining the quality of a tree, but by its fruits. When the wheels of a clock move within, the hands on the dial will move without. When the heart of a man is sound in conversion, then the life will be fair in profession. When the conduit is walled in, how shall we judge of the spring, but by the waters which run through the pipes? *Secker.*

12,037. TREE OF LIFE, Import of the. The Tree of Life was a token of the Creator's preserving care and a memento of the creature's dependence. What it was like we do not know, but it possessed a marvelous efficacy. As long as man ate of it he could not die: and it has been ingeniously suggested that the protracted lives of the antediluvians were owing to the power of this paradisaic antidote lingering for ages in the human constitution. But however this may be, the Tree was a type of the one great source of immortality. It taught the creature that he was not his own preserver. It reminded him that the "Fountain of Life" was external to himself, and that the only security for his own life's prolongation was the constant command of this soul-gladdening and life-confirming sustenance. And most likely every time that he partook of it, he was conscious of an intenser immortality. Possibly the consummation of each day's lightsome labor, and coincident with those visits of his heavenly Father, which made so welcome the cool of the day, we can imagine him resorting to the spot where stood the sacramental symbol—its very continuance a sign that on either side the covenant continued still inviolate—devoutly stretching forth his hand to the laden bough, and whilst he and his partner ate the mystic fruit, which filled all their being with celestial joy and raised them nearer to the angels, overhearing from above the voice of God, answering with their evening hymn, and then sinking into hallowed slumber beneath the sacred shadow. But there is still a Tree of Life. Instead of abandoning our guilty race to self-entailed destruction, in his unspeakable mercy, God has interposed, and in the mission and atonement of his own dear Son has provided a salvation for sinners of mankind. And throughout the inspired records, the Saviour and his work are repeatedly introduced under the vail of this most ancient emblem.

Dr. J. Hamilton.

12,038. TREE OF LIFE, Typology of the. A beautiful figure, found in several of the dispensations, originally in the sacramental tree in Eden, Gen. 2 : 9, and 3 : 22; ultimately in paradise restored, Rev. 22 : 2 ; Ezekiel's (chap. 47 : 12) are probably also symbolical, the fruit for meat, and the leaf for medicine, representing the full provision of God's love. *Bowes.*

12,039. TREES, Souls in. Plato and Empedocles believe that plants are animals, and are endowed with souls; of this there are clear arguments, for they have tossing and shaking, and their branches are extended; when the woodmen bend them they yield, but they return to their former straightness and strength again when they are let loose, and even draw up weights that are laid upon them. *Plutarch.*

12,040. TRESPASS Defined. If a man wronged God, that was trespass; if he wronged or robbed his neighbor, that was trespass. We read: "If a soul commit a trespass, and sin through ignorance in the holy things of the Lord, then he shall make amends for the harm that he hath done." Again, "If a soul sin, and commit a trespass against the Lord, and lie unto his neighbor, in that which was delivered him to keep, or in fellowship, or in a thing taken away by violence, or hath deceived his neighbor; or have found that which was lost, and lieth concerning it, and sweareth falsely; in any of all these that a man doeth, sinning

therein, then it shall be, because he hath sinned, and is guilty, that he shall restore that which he took violently away, or the thing which he hath deceitfully gotten, or that which was delivered to him to keep, or the lost thing which he found." Here trespass is a wrong done to God, or wrong done to a neighbor: we read of "violently taking," "deceitfully getting," and "swearing falsely about that which is found." In every case of trespass, wrong was done; there was an act of evil by which another was injured. And the offering for this act, the trespass-offering (in this a contrast to the sin-offering) was offered by the offerer, not because he was, but because he had done evil. *A. Jukes.*

12,041. TRIAL, Succor in. At the battle of Cressy, where Edward the Black Prince, then a youth of eighteen years of age, led the van, the king, his father, drew up a strong party on a rising ground, and there beheld the conflict in readiness to send relief where it should be wanted. The young prince being sharply charged, and in some danger, sent to his father for succor; and as the king delayed to send it, another messenger was sent to crave immediate assistance. To him the king replied, "Go, tell my son that I am not so inexperienced a commander as not to know when succor is wanted, nor so careless a father as not to send it." He intended the honor of the day should be his son's, and therefore let him with courage stand to it, assured that help should be had when it might conduce most to his renown. God draws forth his servants to fight in the pitched field against Satan and his wicked instruments. But they, poor hearts, when the charge is sharp, are ready to despond, and cry with Peter, "Save, Lord, we perish;" but God is too watchful to overlook their exigencies, and too much a father to neglect their succor. If help, however, be delayed, it is that the victory may be more glorious by the difficulty of overcoming. *Spurgeon.*

12,042. TRIAL, Test of. A virtuous and well disposed person is like good metal—the more he is fired the more he is refined; the more he is opposed the more he is approved. Wrongs may well try him, and touch him; but they cannot imprint on him any false stamp.

Richelieu.

12,043. TRIALS, Benefits of. Of a truth there is a paradise within this thorn-hedge. Many a time the people of God are in bonds which are never loosed till they be bound with cords of affliction. God takes them and throws them into a fiery furnace that burns off their bonds; and then, like the three children (Dan. 3 : 25), they are loose, walking in the midst of the fire. God gives his children a portion, with one bitter ingredient; if that will not work upon them, he will put in a second, and so on, as there is need, that they may work together for their good. With cross winds he hastens them to their harbor. Worldly things are often such a load to the Christian that he moves but very slowly heavenward. God sends a wind of trouble that blows the burden off his back, and then he walks more speedily on his way, after God hath drawn some gilded earth from him that was drawing his heart away from God. *Boston.*

12,044. TRIALS, Fiery. I have observed, that towns which have been casually burnt, have been built again more beautiful than before; mud walls afterwards made of stone; and roofs formerly but thatched, after advanced to be tiled. The apostle tells me that I must not think strange concerning the fiery trial which is to happen unto me. May I likewise prove improved by it. Let my renewed soul, which grows out of the ashes of the old man, be a more firm fabric, and a stronger structure: so shall affliction be my advantage. *Fuller.*

12,045. TRIALS, Ordeal of. When a founder has cast his bell, he does not at once put it into the steeple, but tries it with the hammer, and beats it on every side, to see if there be a flaw. So when Christ converts a man he does not at once convey him to heaven, but suffers him first to be beaten upon by many temptations and afflictions, and then exalts him to his crown. As snow is of itself cold, yet warms and refreshes the earth, so afflictions, though in themselves grievous, keep the Christian's soul warm and make it fruitful. *Mason.*

12,046. TRIALS, Similitude of. In a foundry-yard great piles of iron, ready for melting, were gathered. I noticed one heap of columns, broken, bent, split, shattered. I went into the foundry. They were "tapping" the furnace, and the molten metal flowed out in one stream of fire, sending up a sputter of sparks whiter than the stars. A row of men, on whose swarthy faces fell the strange glare of the fire, stood a little way from the furnace to catch the iron in ladles and carry it off to be run in the moulds. I knew those broken columns would some day be cast into the furnace, softened, melted, to run out in a stream of fire, and be moulded again in tall, shapely pillars. In no other way could they be of use. They must be melted. That very afternoon I saw a mother all bent and broken by affliction. She had parted with an only child. Just the Sabbath before had the earth been broken for that child's grave. I pitied that mother. How keenly her Saviour felt for her! And yet, perhaps, the only way to reach some elements in that mother's character, and change them, was through affliction. The character was not worthless; far from it. It only needed melting. Oh, the pain of that furnace of suffering, its smart, its agony! But in just this way is character sometimes formed, its qualities shaped into the strong, stately pillars sustaining the interests of the Redeemer's kingdom. *Anon.*

11,047. TRIALS, Tests. The storm tries the buildings, and discovers which is built upon a rock, and which upon the sands. The storm tries the pilot. The touchstone tries the metal whether it be gold or copper. The furnace tries the gold whether it be pure or dross. So afflictions and persecutions try the Christian.

Paint will rub off with washing, but true beauty by washing will appear more beautiful. *Francis Roberts.*

12,048. TRIALS, Visitation of. All trials are sent for two ends, that we may be better acquainted with the Lord Jesus, and with our own wicked hearts. Luther said that he never undertook any fresh work, but he was visited either with a fit of sickness or some powerful temptation. *Whitefield.*

12,049. TRIBULATION, Benefits of. A consideration of the benefit of afflictions should teach us to bear them patiently when they fall to our lot, and to be thankful to heaven for having planted such barriers around us, to restrain the exuberance of our follies and our crimes. Let the sacred fences be removed; exempt the ambitious from disappointment and the guilty from remorse; let luxury go unattended with disease, and indiscretion lead into no embarrassments or distresses; our vices would range without control, and the impetuosity of our passions have no bounds; every family would be filled with strife, every nation with carnage, and a deluge of calamities would break in upon us which would produce more misery in a year than is inflicted by the hand of Providence in a lapse of ages. *Robert Hall.*

12,050. TRIFLES, Delaying for. Bede says that Theodore, being appointed a bishop, delayed four months for his hair to grow, that it might be cut in the shape of a crown, before departing for his bishopric in Britain.

12,051. TRIFLES, Importance of. If we had eyes adapted to the sight, we should see, on looking into the smallest seed, the future flower or tree enclosed in it. God will look into our feelings and motives as into seeds; by those embryos of action he will infallibly determine what we are, and will show what we should have been had there been scope and stage for their development and maturity. Nothing will be made light of. The very dust of the balances shall be taken into account. It is in the moral world as it is in the natural, where every substance weighs something; though we speak of imponderable bodies, yet nature knows nothing of positive levity: and were men possessed of the necessary scales, the requisite instrument, we should find the same holds true in the moral world. Nothing is insignificant on which sin has breathed the breath of hell: everything is important in which holiness has impressed itself in the painted characters. And accordingly "there is nothing covered that shall not be revealed; and hid that shall not be known." However unimportant now in the estimation of men, yet, when placed in the light of the divine countenance, like the atom in the sun's rays, it shall be deserving attention; and as the minutest molecule of matter contains all the primordial elements of a world, so the least atom of that mind shall be found to include in it the essential elements of heaven. *Harris.*

12,052. TRINITY, Derivation of. The word "Trinity," in its Latin form *Trinitas*, is derived from the adjective *trinus*, "threefold."

or "three in one." It is nowhere employed in Holy Scripture, but was a term invented and used as early as the second century, to express the doctrine by a single word, for the sake of brevity and convenience. *Bp. Hall.*

12,053. TRINITY, Glory to the. That holy man, St. Francis, of Assissi, found appropriate expression of the ardent devotions of his soul in the constant repetition of the doxology, "Glory be to the Father, and to the Son, and to the Holy Ghost; as it was in the beginning, is now, and ever shall be, world without end. Amen." He recommended the same exercise to others, who found it very helpful to spirituality.

12,054. TRINITY, Incomprehensibility of the. An infidel was scoffing at the doctrine of the Trinity. He turned to a gentleman, and said, "Do you believe such nonsense?" "Tell me how that candle burns," said the other. "Why, the tallow, the cotton, and the atmospheric air produces light," said the infidel. "Then they make one light, do they not?" "Yes." "Will you tell me how they are three, and yet but one light?" "No, I cannot." "But you believe it?" The scoffer was put to shame.

12,055. TRINITY, Names of. The two principal names which are applied to deity in the Old Testament are Jehovah and God (in Hebrew, *Elohim*). The former is God's proper name, and clearly applies to the divine essence. This name is always singular, and may be rendered, "He who exists." The other name, *Aleim* or *Elohim*, is plural. And the question occurs, Why is the name Jehovah, which refers to his essence, always singular? Plainly, to express the unity of the divine essence. Why is the other, *Elohim*, plural? As clearly to denote a plurality of persons in the Godhead. *Field.*

12,056. TRINITY, Symbol of the. This symbol, light, is composed of three parts, one visible and two invisible: first, illuminative rays, which affect our vision, and by their Fraunhofer lines bring to us a knowledge of the substance of the suns from which they spring; second, chemical rays, which cause growth, and give the results of photography; and, third, the principle called heat, separate from either. So is God revealed—three persons in one God. No man hath seen the Father, or the Holy Ghost: but the Son has been seen of men. Each of these component parts is capable of separate and independent action. Each can be sundered from the other, and still retain its full efficiency. The illuminative rays still stream with their incredible swiftness, still bloom with incomprehensible color, and still bear their records of other worlds, after the other two component parts have been turned to other work. There could be no other so happy illustration of the incomprehensible triune nature of God. *Dr. H. W. Warren.*

12,057. TRINITY, Understanding the. He who goes about to speak of the mystery of the Trinity, and does it by words, and names of man's invention, talking of essence and existences, hypostases and personalities, priority in co-equality, and unity in pluralities, may amuse himself and build a tabernacle in his head, and talk something—he knows not what; but the renewed man, that feels the power of the Father, to whom the Son is become wisdom, sanctification and redemption, in whose heart the love of the Spirit of God is shed abroad—this man, though he understand nothing of what is unintelligible, yet he alone truly understands the Christian doctrine of the Trinity. *Jeremy Taylor.*

12,058. TRINITY, Unity of the. A converted Indian gave the following reason for his belief in the Trinity: "We go down to the river in winter, and we see it covered with snow; we dig through the snow, and we come to the ice; we chop through the ice, and we come to the water; snow is water, ice is water, water is water; therefore the three are one."

12,059. TRIUMPH, Celebration of. In September, 61 B. C., the most magnificent triumph ever seen in Rome was given to Pompey. For two days the grand procession of trophies from every land moved along the Via Sacra, amid the applause of the admiring Romans. At the head of the procession were carried brazen tablets on which were engraven the the names of the conquered nations, Pontus, Armenia, Cappadocia, Paphlagonia, Media, Colchis, Iberia, Albania, Syria, Cilicia, Mesopotamia, Phœnecia, Palestine, Judea and Arabia, including a thousand castles and nine hundred cities. The tablets declared that he had increased the revenues of the empire by thirty-five million drachmas, beside gold and silver vessels which he placed in the treasury, valued at twenty thousand talents, having also divided great spoils among his soldiers, not less than fifteen hundred drachmas to any. A long retinue of captives followed his triumphal chariot, including the son of Tigranes, king of Armenia, with his wife and daughter, Zosima, the wife of Tigranes, Aristobulus, king of Judea, and hostages of various nations. As many trophies were carried in procession as Pompey had gained victories either by himself or his officers. The remarkable circumstance of this celebration was that it declared him conqueror of the whole world. He first conquered Africa and received a triumph for it; next he overran Europe, and was again honored with a triumph; lastly he subdued Asia, and brought its spoils to Rome. Another captain has girded on his sword and gone forth to conquer the world. He has already subdued many nations, made innumerable captives, and enriched his followers with great spoil. Not long hence his universal triumph will be celebrated. Pompey's honor can give but a dim hint of the glorious triumph which awaits the King of Zion when he shall enter the New Jerusalem attended by captives from every land and nation and tongue under heaven.

12,060. TRIUMPH, Christian. The highest honor which the Romans bestowed upon their greatest captains was to grant them a day of triumph, and, in that, permission to wear a crown of grass or leaves, which withered the day following; but the triumph of the just shall be eternal, and their never-fading crown is God himself. O, most happy diadem! O, most precious garland of the saints, which is of as great worth and value as is God himself! Sapores, King of the Persians, was most ambitious of honor, and would, therefore, be called "The Brother of the Sun and Moon, and Friend to the Planets." This vain prince erected a most glorious throne, which he placed on high, and thereon sat in great majesty, having under his feet a globe of glass, whereon were artificially represented the motions of the sun, the moon, and the stars; and to sit crowned above this fantastical heaven he esteemed as a great honor. What shall be, then, the honor of the just, who shall truly and really sit above the sun, the moon, and the firmament, crowned by the hand of God himself, and that with a crown of gold, graven with the seal of holiness and the glory of honor? And this honor arrives at that height that Christ himself tells us, "He who shall overcome, I will give him to sit with me in my throne; even as I have overcome, and have sat with the Father in his throne."

Jeremy Taylor.

12,061. TRIUMPH, Importance of. The one important thing about every good enterprise is that it should be successful. Every laborer is entitled to his reward, and triumph is the most satisfactory part of his recompense. Triumph crowns only completed endeavors. "Triumphant" should characterize our lives and deaths, and be an appropriate inscription on our tombstones. All the rhetoric of the historian cannot express so much honor as the simple record, "Triumphant through the blood of the Lamb!"

12,062. TROUBLE, Escape from. There are many coal-pits in Wales. There are men down there who hardly have a gleam of sunlight. How are they to get up? There is a string at the bottom, they pull it, a bell up at the top rings, a rope, worked by a steam engine, is let down, and in this way they ascend to the top. A man gets down into the pit of trouble; he cannot get up himself, he must ring the bell of prayer, and God will hear it, and send down the rope that is to lift him out of it.

Thomas Jones.

12,063. TROUBLE, No Preventing. In the palace of the Constantines was a luxurious chamber called the purple—where all the princes and princesses first saw the light—the emperor thinking by this means to abolish the acerbities attending their existence. The favored children, however, saluted life with tears and groans, as well as others; and many of them were so overwhelmed with disasters, both in their own persons and families, that he who was of the meanest birth in all their empire, would have been very loth to have exchanged conditions with them.

12,064. TROUBLE, Rise above. When birds are flying over, and the fowler lies in wait for them, if they fly low some are wounded, and some, swerving sideways, plunge into the thicket and hide themselves. But you will find that immediately after the first discharge of the gun the flock rise and fly higher. And at the next discharge they rise again, and fly still higher. And not many times has the plunging shot thinned their number before they take so high a level that it is vain that the fowler aims at them, because they are above the reach of his shot. When troubles come upon you, fly higher. And if they still strike you, fly still higher. And by and by you will rise so high in the spiritual life, that your affections will be set on things so entirely above that these troubles shall not be able to touch you.

Beecher.

12,065. TROUBLE, Support in. When I first amused myself with going out to sea, when the winds arose, and the waves become a little rough, I found a difficulty to keep my legs on the deck, but I tumbled and tossed about like a porpoise on the water. At last I caught hold of a rope that was floating about, and then I was enabled to stand upright. So when, in prayer, a multitude of troublous thoughts invade your peace, or when the winds and waves of temptation arise, look out for the rope, lay hold of it, and stay yourself on the faithfulness of God in his covenant with his people and in his promises. Hold fast by that rope, and you shall stand.

Salter.

12,066. TROUBLES, Beneficial. It is to a Christian consideration one of God's greatest mercies that this world is full of troubles; for if we so much court her now she is foul, what would we do if she were beautiful? if we take such pains to gather thorns and thistles, what would we do for figs and grapes?

Lord Capel.

12,067. TROUBLES, Little. Let us not try to manage our little troubles by ourselves, lest greater ones spring out of them. Little troubles are like little seeds, they are small enough in themselves, but they are capable of producing great and important results. The oak is the produce of the acorn, the tangled brier comes from a seed on which no thorn can be seen; the Christian who will manage his little troubles by himself, will soon find that he must manage much greater ones than he bargained for at first.

Power.

12,068. TRUMPET, Call of the. At a village of the Hartz Mountains, it is the custom to usher in the Sabbath by the blowing of trumpets. Their call awakes the people and invites them to the special duties and joys of a new Sabbath. So may the last trumpet's sound awaken us to the joys of God's eternal Sabbath day.

12,069. TRUST, False Objects of. King George III. was one day looking at the plate which had been brought from Hanover and observing one of the articles with the arms of the electorate engraved upon it, he said to the domestic who attended him, "This belonged to King George II.; I know it by the Latin inscription," which he read, adding, "In English it is, 'I trust in my sword.' This," said he, "I always disliked; for had I nothing to trust in but my sword, I well know what would be the result; therefore, when I came to the crown, I altered it. My motto is—'I trust in the truth of the Christian religion.'" He then said, "Which of the two inscriptions do you like best?" The attendant replied, "Your Majesty's is infinitely preferable to the other." He said, "I have ever thought so, and ever shall think so; for therein is my trust and confidence. Think you, is it possible for any one to be happy and comfortable within himself, who has not that trust and confidence? I know there are those who affect to be at ease while living in a state of infidelity; but it is all affectation; it is only the semblance of happiness—the thing itself is impossible."

12,070. TRUST not in Man. The bankrupt who asks a bankrupt to set him up in business again is only losing time. The pauper who travels off to a neighbor pauper, and begs him to help him out of difficulties, is only troubling himself in vain. The prisoner does not beg his fellow prisoner to set him free. The shipwrecked sailor does not call on his shipwrecked comrade to place him safe ashore. Help in all these cases must come from some other quarter. Relief in all these cases must be sought from some other hand. Reader, it is just the same in the matter of cleansing away your sins. So long as you seek it from man, whether man ordained or man not ordained, you seek it where it cannot be found. *Ryle.*

12,071. TRUST, Misplaced. It is like *a spider's web*, Job 8: 14. *A broken tooth and foot out of joint*, Prov. 25: 19. *Parched heath* in the desert, Jer. 17: 5, 6. *A lie*, Jer. 28: 15; 29: 31; Hosea 10: 13. *Leaning upon the Lord*, when living in sin, Micah 3: 11; Isa. 48: 2; Jer. 7: 4. *Trusting in Egypt.* Always the great snare of Israel from the first, though they were specially warned against it, Deut. 17: 16. It is compared to trusting in a shadow, Isa. 30: 2, 3; to leaning upon the staff of a bruised reed, 36: 6; Ezek. 29: 6, 7; see Isa. 50: 1-7; 31: 1. *Bowes.*

12,072. TRUST IN GOD, Figures of. *To cling* is the original meaning of one of the Hebrew words used for trust. It is the word used for a child clinging to its mother's breast. *To run for shelter*, the original meaning of another Hebrew word; see Ruth 2: 12. *To lean upon*, another Hebrew word, from which the word Amen is derived. Two FIGURES are given of holy trust. The *stability of Mount Zion*, Ps. 125 : 1. The *luxuriant growth of a tree* by the waters, Jer. 17: 7, 8. *Bowes.*

12,073. TRUST IN GOD, Power of. What was the vain boast of philosophers—that by the power of reason they could make all accidents to contribute to their happiness—is the real privilege we obtain by a regular trust in God, who directs and orders all events that happen for the everlasting good of his servants. *Bates.*

12,074. TRUST IN GOD, Safety of. A traveler in the Alps had been climbing a precipice which gradually became more and more steep. But he was lured onward by the pleasure of the exercise and the purpose of reaching the top, till he found he could go no further.

Now, looking back he saw he could not return. To attempt to descend would be certain destruction. He was in great peril. He had but an inch or two of footing, which might at any moment give way, and his strength was beginning to fail. He had been watched by a friend, who saw his peril, and by another route reached the summit of the rock and lowered a rope. What must he do? Believe! He hesitated. The rope might break, his friend's arm might fail, but the path was crumbling, his own strength was going; so he believed: that is, he trusted his friend and obeyed his directions, and so was drawn up to safety. So let us believe and be saved. Let us take Christ at his word. Let us accept his mercy and obey his commands. Then shall we be saved—saved from guilt and condemnation; saved from death and judgment; saved now from wretchedness and ruin. We shall be saved, and so able to fulfill our high vocation to live for God and serve him. *Newman Hall.*

12,075. TRUSTING, Trying Versus. "The eternal God is my Refuge, and underneath are the everlasting arms." In preaching upon this subject on a certain occasion, the Rev. T. Collins said, "One Sabbath I entered the cottage of a good man, and said, 'Well, James, is your soul joying in God to-day?' 'Indeed,' said he, 'no. My mind is clouded, my prayer feeble, and my heart cold. I can, however, still conscientiously say that I hate sin, and, though with many fears that it will master me, strive against it.' I replied, 'You want perfect love, James.' 'I do, I feel I do,' he said. 'Have it then,' I answered. 'Is not that what I wish? Is not that what I am trying for?' 'Yes, James, you have tried too much, and trusted too little. Here, read this :

'Round thee, and beneath are spread
The everlasting arms.

Whose arms?' 'God's.' 'Where spread?' 'Around my soul and underneath.' 'Why, man, say you so? Sink down upon them then, and rest.' 'I will try,' said the man. 'James! James! there you are again; trying instead of trusting. Suppose you placed your child in the cradle, and said, "Now, dear one, rest," would you expect the little creature to set itself shaking the cradle, and to say, "I am trying?" would he rest so?' 'No, sir, he must be still to rest.' 'And so must you, James. Tell God, "Thou art mine, and I am thine :" cast thyself on his fidelity; sink down upon him, and, on an arm firmer than rock, tenderer than a mother's, thou shalt rest.'" *S. Coley.*

12,076. TRUTH, Advantages of. Truth has all the advantages of appearance, and many more; and, upon every account, sincerity is true wisdom. As to the affairs of this world, integrity hath many advantages over all the arts of dissimulation and deceit. It is much the plainer and easier, much the safer and more secure way; it hath less of trouble and difficulty, of entanglement and perplexity, of danger and hazard; it is the shortest and nearest way to our end, carrying us thither in a straight line and will hold out and last, when deceit and cunning, which continually grow weaker and less effectual, will finally fail us. *Tillotson.*

12,077. TRUTH, Denying. When the majestic form of truth approaches, it is easier for a disingenuous mind to start aside into a thicket till she is past, and then reappearing say, "It was not Truth," than to meet her, and bow, and obey.   *John Foster.*

12,078. TRUTH, Derivation of. Truth, in Hebrew, signifies firmness; in Greek, that which cannot be hid, or that which is unconcealed; open, in opposition to falsehood, which lurks in the darkness. Such an instance serves to remind us of our Lord's words, "He that doeth truth cometh to the light." "Truth," says the Greek derivation, "is that which cannot be hid; it may be suppressed for a time—it may seem to be buried forever—but its very nature secures its ultimate revival and resurrection." The Hebrew derivation again reminds us of its indestructible firmness. The everlasting hills may tremble, the solid rocks may be shattered to atoms, the "heaven and earth may pass (Matt. 5: 18), but truth remains immovable."   *Henry Craik.*

12,079. TRUTH, Domain of. There can be no treaty dividing the domain of truth. Every one truth is connected with every other truth in this great universe of God. The connection may be one of infinite subtlety and apparent distance—running, as it were, under ground for a long way, but always asserting itself at last somewhere and at some time. No bargaining, no fencing off the ground, no form of process will avail to bar this right of way. Blessed right, enforced by blessed power!   *Argyll.*

12,080. TRUTH, Enlivening the. All experience teaches that truth, separate from a sense of the authority of God, does not become life in man's moral nature. It has no efficacy to quicken the conscience or to purify the heart. There is no moral efficacy, even in inspired truth, unless the soul recognizes in it the will and heart of God in regard to man. The words of Jesus had not the same efficacy before the advent of the Spirit as afterwards. Jesus taught, as we have noticed, why this was so. The God-sense was not connected with them in the mind of others until after the resurrection of Christ, and the advent of the Spirit; but when the Holy Ghost came, "He convinced men of sin, righteousness, and judgment," because he attached the authority and will of God to the life and teaching of Jesus. While they viewed Christ as a man like themselves, they felt less sense of obligation.   *Walker.*

12,081. TRUTH, Fidelity of. If I had promised you an acorn next first of October, and all the oaks in England had been blighted, it would become my duty to send to Spain for one, but not for the value of the acorn. Did you ever hear of Ruy Diaz el Campeador, who in order to arm his men for a campaign against the Moors, had borrowed money upon some chests of stones, which the Jews of Burgos who lent it, imagined to be plate? He redeemed the pledge, and when his generals, on seeing the chests opened, wondered at his doing so (honesty does not seem to have been the Spaniard's forte in those days), he said, " Do you not know that there were in those chests a treasure far more precious than anything you can see? they contained *el oro de mi verdad*—the gold of my truth." Far more than meets the eye is implied in the keeping or not keeping of a trifling rubric; it is not the thing itself, but it is the compromise of principle—it is the difference between truth and falsehood—between honesty and dishonesty.   *Newland.*

12,082. TRUTH, Fragments of. Where are divers opinions, they may be all false; there can be but one true: and that one truth ofttimes must be fetched by piecemeal out of divers branches of contrary opinions. For, it falls out not seldom, that truth is through ignorance or rash vehemence scattered into sundry parts; and like to a little silver melted among ruins of a burnt house, must be tried out from heaps of much superfluous ashes. There is much pains in the search of it, much skill in finding it; the value of it once found, requites the cost of both.   *Bishop Hall.*

12,083. TRUTH, God and. God and truth are always on the same side.   *Theodore Parker.*

12,084. TRUTH, Martyrs for the. To die for the truth is not to die for one's country, but to die for the world. Truth, like the *Venus de Medicis*, will pass down in thirty fragments to posterity; but posterity will collect and recompose them into a goddess. Then also thy temple, O eternal truth, that now stands half below the earth, made hollow by the sepulchres of its witnesses, will raise itself in the total majesty of proportions, and will stand in monumental granite; and every pillar on which it rests will be fixed in the grave of a martyr.   *Richter.*

12,085. TRUTH, Mistaking. The house of error stands close alongside the house of truth. The door of one is so like the door of the other that there is continual risk of mistakes. *Ryle.*

12,086. TRUTH, Path of. The path of truth is a plain and safe path; that of falsehood is a perplexing maze. After the first departure from sincerity, it is not in your power to stop. One artifice unavoidably leads on to another, till, as the intricacy of the labyrinth increases, you are left entangled in your own snare.   *Blair.*

12,087. TRUTH, Penalty of Violating. There was a law among the Persians and Indians, that if any person was three times convicted of falsehood, they should, upon the pain of incurring the penalty of death, never speak a word again as long as they lived.

12,088. TRUTH, Rarity of. Augustus Caesar, after a long search through his realm, found but one man who was said never to have told a lie. He was considered worthy to be the chief sacrificer in the Temple of Truth.

12,089. TRUTH, Rejecters of. It is something notable how the errorists talk about truth. It is the prominent word on the lips of Theodore Parker. He considered himself the apostle of truth. When he deliberately took his position against the inspiration, facts and miracles of the Bible, he thought himself launching out into the open and broad sea of truth. On his visit to Europe, in 1840, he walked up and down in front of the church in Wittemberg, to which Luther nailed his theses of defiance to the pope, feeling himself called to a like important mission. He says, "I felt the spirit of the great reformer. Three centuries and a quarter and what a change! Three centuries and a quarter more and it will be said, 'The Protestant Reformation did little in comparison with what has since been done.' Well if THIS work be of God." Such was the vision of the Boston reformer. Alas! for the reality.

12,090. TRUTH, Self-manifesting Power of. As light opens the close-shut flower-bud to receive light, or as the sunbeam, playing on a sleeper's eyes, by its gentle irritation opens them to see its own brightness; so the truth of God, shining on the soul, quickens and stirs into activity the faculty by which that very truth is perceived. It matters little which of the two operations, in logical or in natural order, be first; practically they may be regarded as simultaneous. The perception rouses the faculty, and yet the faculty is implied in the perception. The truth awakens the mind, and yet the mind must be in activity ere the truth can reach it. And the same two-fold process is carried on in the whole subsequent progress of the soul. Light and the organ of vision, knowledge and the understanding, divine truth and the spiritual reason, grow and expand together. They act and react. They are reciprocally helpful. They are, each by turn, cause and effect. *Caird.*

12,091. TRUTH, Stand for. The Guthrie family motto was "*Sto pro veritate*"—Stand for the truth.

12,092. TRUTH, Support of. It is not wrangling disputes, and syllogistical reasonings that are the mighty pillars which underprop truth in the world : if we would but underset it with the holiness of our hearts and lives, it should never fail. Truth is a prevailing and conquering thing, and would quickly overcome the world, did not the earthiness of our dispositions and the darkness of our false hearts hinder it. *Cudworth.*

12,093. TRUTH, Throwing Away. We must never throw away a bushel of truth because it happens to contain a few grains of chaff; on the contrary, we may sometimes profitably receive a bushel of chaff for the few grains of truth it may contain. *Dean Stanley.*

12,094. TRUTH, Virtue and. The study of truth is perpetually joined with the love of virtue; for there is no virtue which derives not its original from truth, as, on the contrary, there is no vice which has not its beginning in a lie. Truth is the foundation of all knowledge, and the cement of all societies. *Casuerba.*

12,095. TRUTH, What is? Fulgentio was preaching on Pilate's question, and told his hearers that after long searching he had at last found it: "Here it is," said he, drawing a New Testament from his pocket.

12,096. TRUTH, Wisdom of. It will be found that all frauds, like the "wall daubed with untempered mortar," with which men think to buttress up an edifice, tend to the decay of that which they are devised to support. This truth, however, will never be steadily acted on by those who have no moral detestation of falsehood. It is not given to those who do not prize straightforwardness for its own sake to perceive that it is the wisest course. *Whately.*

12,097. TRUTHFULNESS, Credit for. The philosopher Xenocrates, being summoned to give evidence in a civil case, and advancing to take the witness' stand, was informed that his word was sufficient. Petrarch, before an ecclesiastical tribunal, where an oath had been required of others, was told by the presiding cardinal. "As for you, Petrarch, your word is sufficient."

12,098. TRUTHFULNESS, Reputation for. A young volunteer was expecting daily to be ordered to the seat of war. One day his mother gave him an unpaid bill with money and asked him to pay it. When he returned home that night she said, "Did you pay the bill?" "Yes," he answered. In a few days the bill was sent in a second time. "I thought," said she to her son, "that you paid this." "I really don't remember, mother; you know I've had so very many things on my mind." "But you said you did." "Well," he answered, "if I said I did, I did." He went away, and the mother took the bill herself to the store. The young man had been known in town all his life, and what opinion was held of him this will show. "I am quite sure," she said, "that my son paid this some days ago; he has been very busy since, and has quite forgotten about it; but he told me that day he had, and says if he said then that he had, he is quite sure that he did." "Well," said the man, "I forgot about it; but if he ever said he did, he did."

12,099. TYPES, Christ in the. An old writer says, "God in the types of the last dispensation, was teaching his children their letters. In this dispensation he is teaching them to put these letters together, and they find that the letters, arrange them as we will, spell Christ, and nothing but Christ."

12,100. TYPES of the Pentateuch. The types of Genesis foreshadow God's great dispensational purposes respecting man's development, shewing in mystery his secret will and way, respecting the different successive dispensations. The types of Exodus—I speak, of course, generally—bring out, as their characteristic, redemption and its consequences; a chosen people are here redeemed out of bondage, and brought into a place of nearness to God. Leviticus again differs from each of these, dealing, I think I may say solely, in types connected with access to God. Numbers and Joshua are again perfectly different, the one giving us types connected with our pilgrimage as in the wilderness; the other, types of our place as over Jordan, that is, as dead and risen with Christ. *A. Jukes.*

12,101. TYPES, Scripture. In the Old Testament there are typical persons, things, times, and actions arranged by God himself, under different classes, each one distinct from the other, and each having something characteristic. The books of the Old Testament are God's divisions; each of them may be called one of God's chapters; and in each of these books we find something different as respects the character of the types they contain. Christ is indeed the key to them all. He is the key of the types, and the key to the Bible. Of him God has given us more than sketches; the word from end to end is full of him. In the word we have a whole Christ presented to us: Christ in his offices, in his character; in his person; Christ in his relations to God and man; Christ in his body to the church; Christ as giving to God all that God required from man; Christ as bringing to man all that man required from God; Christ as seen in this dispensation in suffering; Christ as seen in the next dispensation in glory; Christ as the first and the last; as "all and in all" to his people. *A. Jukes.*

12,102. UNBELIEF, Barrenness of. There is but one thing without honor; smitten with eternal barrenness, inability to do or to be: insincerity, unbelief. He who believes no thing, who believes only the shows of things, is not in relation with nature and fact at all. *Carlyle.*

12,103. UNBELIEF, God Dishonored by. A very tender parent had a son, who from his earliest years proved headstrong and dissolute. Conscious of the extent of his demerits, he dreaded and hated his parent. Meanwhile every means was used to disarm him of these suspicions, so unworthy of the tenderness and love which yearned in his father's bosom, and of all the kindness and forbearance which were lavished upon him. Eventually the means appeared to be successful, and confidence, in a great degree, took the place of his ungenerous suspicions. Entertained in the family as one who had never trespassed, he now left his home to embark in mercantile affairs, and was assured that if in any extremity he would apply to his parent, he should find his application kindly received. In the course of years it fell out that he was reduced to extremity; but instead of communicating his case to his parent, his base suspicion and disbelief of his tenderness and care again occupied him, and he neglected to apply to him. Who can tell how deeply that father's heart was rent at such depravity of feeling? Yet this is the case of the believer, who, pardoned and accepted, and made partaker of a Father's love and covenant promises, when under distress refuses to trust his heavenly and almighty Parent, throws away his filial confidence, and with his old suspicions stands aloof in sullen distrust. *Salter.*

12,104. UNBELIEF, Obstinacy of. Galileo invented the telescope with which he observed the satellites of Jupiter, and invited a man who was opposed to him to look through it that he might observe Jupiter's moons. The man refused, saying, "If I should see them, how could I maintain my opinions, which I have advanced against your philosophy?"

12,105. UNBELIEF Refuted. It is said of the great Galileo—who had been accused of infidelity because he asserted that the earth went round the sun, in apparent contradiction to the language of Scripture—that, when questioned by the Roman Inquisition as to his belief in the Supreme Being, he pointed to a straw lying on the floor of his dungeon, saying to his accusers that, from the structure of that trifling object, he would infer with certainty the existence of an intelligent Creator. And this is the welcome conclusion to which an attentive examination of the grass of the field inevitably leads. *Macmillan.*

12,106. UNBELIEF, Works of. Unbelief is the occasion of all sin, and the very bond of iniquity. It does nothing but darken and destroy. It makes the world a moral desert, where no divine footsteps are heard, where no angels ascend and descend, where no living hand adorns the fields, feeds the fowls of heaven or regulates events. Thus it makes nature, the garden of God, a mere automaton, and the history of Providence a fortuitous succession of events; a man, a creature of accidents, and prayer a useless ceremony. It annihilates even the vestiges of heaven that still remain upon the earth, and stops the way to every higher region. *Krummacher.*

12,107. UNDERSTANDING, Exercise of the. Nobody knows what strength of parts he has till he has tried them. And of the understanding one may most truly say, that its force is greater generally than it thinks, till it is put to it. And, therefore, the proper remedy here is but to set the mind to work, and apply the thoughts vigorously to the business; for it holds in the struggles of the mind as in those of war, *dum putant se vincere, vicere.* A persuasion that we shall overcome any difficulties that we meet with in the sciences, seldom fails to carry us through them. Nobody knows the strength of his mind, and the force of steady and regular application, till he has tried. This is certain; he that sets out upon weak legs will not only go further, but grow stronger too, than one who, with a vigorous constitution and firm limbs, only sits still. *Locke.*

12,108. UNDERSTANDING, Unreliable. A thing may be very useful, which we must not lean upon, lest it should break and let us fall; a reed from an osier bed is very useful to make baskets, but you would not lean upon it. So our understandings are very useful, but the best of them are not sufficiently strong to lean upon. *J. Curwen.*

12,109. UNFAITHFULNESS, Curse upon. The least unfaithfulness may bring a curse upon us, as the foot of the chamois on the snowy mountains, or the breath of a traveler who sings or shouts on his snowy road, may cause an avalanche which shall entomb the village now full of life and gayety at the mountain's base. *S. Martin.*

12,110. UNFAITHFULNESS, Inexcusable. An officer of Alexander's army was directed to lay in provisions for his master's coming, but instead of doing so, he collected three thousand talents in money but no food. Alexander pointed to his horses, and bade him offer the gold to them, but they refused it, and he ordered the lieutenant into custody for his folly in providing money rather than bread.

12,111. UNFAITHFULNESS, Penalty of. A great captain thought he gave that soldier but his due whom he ran through with his sword because he found him asleep when he should have stood sentinel, excusing his severity with this, that he left him as he found him—*Mortuum inveni, et mortuum reliqui*—"I found him dead in sleep, and left him but asleep in death." 　　　　　　*Gurnall.*

12,112. UNHAPPINESS, Human. Herbert, the great thinker, philosophized about himself, philosophized about this world, philosophized about everything, then in his dying moment asked that only one word might be cut upon his tombstone, and that word "*Infelicissimus*," —most unhappy—descriptive of the state of the lives and of the deaths of those who take their case out of the hand of God. The only appropriate inscription for their banqueting hall and their equipage and their grave, and the wall of their eternal prison-house— "*Infelicissimus.*" In drooling, moral idiocy they are scrabbling at the door of their happiness, which never opens: miserably playing the fool. 　　　　　　*Talmage.*

12,113. UNION, Basis of. A portly Quaker taking Mr. Whitefield by the hand, said: "Friend George, I am as thou art; I am for bringing all to the life and power of the everliving God, and therefore if thou wilt not quarrel with me about my hat, I will not quarrel with thee about thy gown."

12,114. UNION, Biblical Figures of. The *body*, which having many members—feeble and strong—less and more honorable—is still "fitly framed" and "compacted together," Rom. 12:4; 1 Cor. 12:12–27; Eph. 4:13–16. The *family* of the redeemed, militant and glorified, Eph. 3:15. A *loaf*—the emblem alike of Christ's natural body, broken for us, and of the united members of Christ's mystical body —many, but united, 1 Cor. 10:17. A *temple* formed of living stones, built up upon the "living stone," Eph. 2:21; 1 Pet. 2:4, 5. A *flock*, with many folds, under the great and good Shepherd's care, John 10:16. The *curtains of the tabernacle*, linked together by golden taches, that it might be "one tabernacle," Exod. 26:1–11; 36:18. The *annual feasts of Israel* helped largely to foster the spirit of union. The *camp of Israel*, gathered round the central tabernacle, Num. 2. The *one stick*, which was the sign of the brotherhood of Ephraim and Judah, Ezek. 37:19. *Christ's coat*, "without seam, woven from the top throughout," John 19:23, 24. 　　*Bowes.*

12,115. UNION, Christian. I do not want the walls of separation between different orders of Christians to be destroyed, but only lowered, that we may shake hands a little easier over them. 　　　　　　*Rowland Hill.*

12,116. UNION, Importance of. Scilurus, on his death-bed, being about to leave four-score surviving children, offered a bundle of darts to each of them, and bade them break them. When all refused, drawing out one by one, he easily broke them; thus teaching them, that if they held together they would continue strong; but if they fell out, and were divided, they would become weak. 　　*Plutarch.*

12,117. UNION, Military. The Macedonian phalanx is said to have been like a solid union of shields that were locked together, while each soldier kept his place in the moving mass. But, if one of them fell out of the ranks, the square being broken, an advantage was gained by the foe which not unfrequently terminated in a severe slaughter of the otherwise invincible army. The strength of each individual lay in the compactness of the body of which he formed but an inconsiderable but necessary part. Individual influence may be powerless when it stands alone, but Christians in union and under their great Captain have irresistible force to attack sin, whereby they can overcome it, and locked hearts are better than locked shields in the holy war. 　　*Anon.*

12,118. UNION, Strength in. If you consider how it is that a hempen twine is made strong enough to draw a loaded wagon, or to bear the strain of a ship as she rides at anchor, you will see a significancy that perhaps did not occur to you before, in the use which Holy Scripture make of this work of human art as an emblem. It is formed of many threads, twisted together into one cord, and these cords are again combined into one cable. Each thread in itself is so weak, that a child could break, or the slightest weight would burst it; but when the threads are twined into one rope, their united strength is such as would have seemed incredible. "A threefold cord is not quickly broken." The truth is just brought before us that union is strength. They who are weak and helpless singly, are able to produce a vast result when they combine their powers. It was in order to restrain his sinful creatures from doing what they had imagined to do, that God scattered them over the face of the earth; and he gathers together again his elect people in one body in Christ, that by uniting their various energies in one work, and for one end, they may strengthen each other's hands, and effectually "bruise under foot" the powers of darkness. 　　*Bp. Trower.*

12,119. UNION, Strength of. In the Centennial Exhibition was a powerful magnet, that would lift a weight of eighteen hundred pounds. It was formed of a hundred thin plates, no one of them of much magnetic power, but together holding the weight, an illustration of the proverb, "Union is strength, dissension weakness."

12,120. UNION, Unnatural. I remember it is noted in our English history as a very remarkable thing, that when the Severn overflowed part of Somersetshire, it was observed that dogs and hares, cats and rats, to avoid the common destruction, would swim to the next rising ground, and abide quietly together in that common danger, without the least discovery of their natural antipathy. 　　*Flavel.*

12,121. UNITY, Dream of. We thought we were at sea, saw a great commotion, and heard voices high and loud. It was a conference of the waves. Listening, we heard one wave say, "See that city yonder with her marble mansions and many spires, that is New York, the metropolis of the United States. Let us inundate that city, and we inundate the States; say, shall it be done?" and there followed a big swell which we interpreted as saying, "It shall be done!" But a lull succeeded, and in its quiet we heard a modest voice say, "Under present circumstances the thing is impracticable. Along the coast, at the base of that city, there are millions of little sands, tiny and weak apart, but massive and strong when united, as they now are, and while that remains, the thing is not only impracticable, but, let me add, impossible; divide them, and your work is done." Blue with anger, foaming in passion, the leader leaped on the back of the tide, while the winds gave martial music, and with a voice like that of thunder, cried, "We revenge the insult. On! and the thing is done! Talk no more of sands. We defy; we conquer! On! on!!" And on they went, and as we saw it in our dream, the march was grand. Nothing daunted, the sands kept close, compact, united. The waves dashed on, and bore down in their fury, but only to dash themselves into fragments and spray—an ignominious defeat. In our delight we shouted, "A city saved! Victory! In union there is strength," and thus awoke ourselves, and our dream was over. *J. Johns.*

12,122. UNIVERSE, Extent of the. According to a German poet God called man into the vestibule of heaven, saying, "Come up higher, and I will show thee the glory of my house." And to his angels, who stood about his throne, he said, "Take him, strip him of his robes of flesh; cleanse his affections; put a new breath into his nostrils; but touch not his human heart—the heart that fears and hopes and trembles." A moment, and it was done, and the man stood ready for his unknown voyage. Under the guidance of a mighty angel, with sound of flying pinions, they sped away from the battlements of heaven. Sometimes on the mighty angel's wings they fled through Saharas of darkness, wildernesses of death. At length, from a distance not counted, save in the arithmetic of heaven, light beamed upon them—a sleepy flame, as seen through a hazy cloud. They sped on in their terrible speed to meet the light; the light with lesser speed came to meet them. In a moment the wheeling of planets; then came long eternities of twilight; then again, on the right hand and on the left, appeared more constellations. At last the man sunk down, crying, "Angel, I can go no further; let me down into the grave and hide me from the infinitude of the universe, for end there is none." "End there is none?" demanded the angel. And from the glittering stars that shone around, there came a choral shout, "End there is none!" "End there is none?" demanded the angel again; "and is it this that

awes thy soul? I answer, End there is none to the universe of God! Lo, also, of him who made it there is no beginning!" *Prof. Mitchell.*

12,123. UNIVERSE, Order in the. If the atoms have by chance formed so many sorts of figures, why did it never fall out that they made a house or a shoe? Why at the same rate should we not believe that an infinite number of Greek letters strowed all over a certain place might possibly fall into the contexture of the Iliad? *Montaigne.*

12,124. UNKINDNESS, Effect of. More hearts pine away in secret anguish for unkindness from those who should be their comforters, than for any other calamity in life. *Dr. E. Young.*

12,125. UNSEEN, Care for the. A pagan sculptor was engaged to erect a statue in one of the Grecian temples, which was to be set in the wall. He wrought the back of the statue, which would be concealed, with the same care as the front. He was asked why he did this, and answered, "The gods see everywhere."

12,126. UNSELFISHNESS, Maternal. It is reported of Agrippina, the mother of Nero, who being told, "That if ever her son came to be an emperor, he would be her murderer," she made this reply, "I am content to perish if he may be emperor." What she expressed vaingloriously, that we should do religiously: "Let us perish, so our neighbors, our relations, and our country be bettered." *Secker.*

12,127. UNTHANKFULNESS, Crime of. If it be a fault to be matched even with murder not to requite man with thankfulness, what a crime is it to deal unthankfully with God!
Ambrose.

12,128. UPRIGHTNESS, Emblem of. The pine, placed nearly always among scenes disordered and desolate, brings into them all possible elements of order and precision. Lowland trees may lean to this side and that, though it is but a meadow breeze that bends them, or a bank of cowslips from which their trunks lean aslope. But let storm and avalanche do their worst, and let the pine find only a ledge of vertical precipice to cling to, it will nevertheless grow straight. Thrust a rod from its last shoot down the stem, it shall point to the centre of the earth as long as the tree lives. *Anon.*

12,129. USEFULNESS, Absence of. In the school of Pythagoras it was a point of discipline, that if among the *akoustikoi*, or probationers, there were any who grew weary of studying to be useful, and returned to an idle life, they were to regard them as dead; and, upon their departing, to perform their obsequies, and raise them tombs with inscriptions, to warn others of the like mortality, and quicken them to refine their souls above that wretched state. *Addison.*

12,130. USEFULNESS, Advantages of. It is a great satisfaction, at the close of life, to be able to look back on the years that are past, and to feel that you have lived, not for yourself alone, but that you have been useful to others. You may be assured, also, that the same feeling is a source of comfort and happiness at any period of life. Nothing in this world is so good as usefulness. It binds your fellow-creatures to you, and you to them; it tends to the improvement of your own character; and it gives you a real importance in society, much beyond what any artificial station can bestow. *Brodie.*

12,131. USEFULNESS, Inevitable. Knowest thou not that thou canst not move a step on this earth without finding some duty to be done, and that every man is useful to his kind, by the very fact of his existence? *Carlyle.*

12,132. USEFULNESS, Opportunities of. How often do we sigh for opportunities of doing good, whilst we neglect the openings of providence in little things, which would frequently lead to the accomplishment of most important usefulness! Dr. Johnson used to say, "He who waits to do a great deal of good at once will never do any." Good is done by degrees. However small in proportion the benefit which follows individual attempts to do good, a great deal may thus be accomplished by perseverance, even in the midst of discouragements and disappointments. *Crabb.*

12,133. USEFULNESS, Posthumous. Bunyan is dead, but his bright spirit still walks the earth in his Pilgrim's Progress. Baxter is dead, but souls are still quickened by the Saints' Rest. Cowper is dead, but the "golden apples" are still as fresh as when newly gathered in the "silver basket" of the Olney Hymns. Eliot is dead, but the missionary enterprise is young. Henry Martyn is dead, but who can count the apostolic spirits who, phœnix-like, have started from his funeral pile? Howard is dead, but modern philanthropy is only commencing its career. Raikes is dead, but the Sabbath-schools go on. Wilberforce is dead, but the negro will find for ages a protector in his memory. *Dr. J. Hamilton.*

12,134. UTILITY before Ornament. A stag one summer's day came to a pool to quench his thrist, and as he stood drinking he saw his form reflected in the water. "What beauty and strength," said he, "are in these horns of mine; but how unseemly are these weak and slender feet!" While he was thus criticising, after his own fancies, the form which Nature had given him, the huntsmen and hounds drew that way. The feet, with which he had found so much fault, soon carried him out of the reach of his pursuers; but the horns, of which he was so vain, becoming entangled in a thicket, held him till the hunters again came up to him, and proved the cause of his death. *Æsop.*

12,135. VALOR, Modern. General Fisk tells of a colored color-bearer, who, when the captain of his company gave the order for the men to fall back, thinking their exposure too serious, kept on alone in advance. He was personally ordered to fall back, lest the colors should be lost. He shouted to his captain, "Dese colors never fall back! You jess bring up de men to them, and dey won't be lost."

12,136. VALOR, Seat of. The estimate and valor of a man consists in the heart and in the will; there his true honor lies. Valor is sta-

bility, not of arms and of legs; but of courage and the soul: it does not lie in the valor of our horse, nor of our arms, but in ourselves. He that falls obstinately in his courage, if his legs fail him, fights upon his knees. *Montaigne.*

12,137. VANITY, Biblical Figures of. *Fading flowers,* Isa. 28:1. *Hasty fruit* of summer, Isa. 28:1; no sooner discovered than gathered and eaten. *Broken cisterns* that can retain no water, Jer. 2:23. *Perishing gourds,* like Jonah's, 4:6-10. *Reeds,* easily bruised and broken, a vain support to lean upon, Isa. 36:6. *Brooks in summer* vanishing in the heat, dried up when most needed, Job 6:15-17. *Cockatrice* (marg., adders') eggs, Isa. 59:5. *Spiders' webs,* Isa. 59:5, 6. *Vapor* or *breath,* James 4:14. *The mirage* of the desert, Isa. 35:7; the waters that fail and cheat the traveler, Jer. 15:18. *Wind,* Prov. 11:29, inheriting; Eccles. 5:16, laboring for; Hosea 8:7, sowing. *Feeding on ashes,* Isa. 44:20; on husks, Luke 15:16; on wind, Hosea 12:1. *Putting wages* into a bag with holes, Haggai 1:6. *Laboring in the very fire,* Hab. 2:13. *Rejoicing in a thing of naught,* Amos 6:13. *Physicians of no value,* Job 13:4. *Bowes.*

12,138. VANITY, Check to. When you are disposed to be vain of your mental acquirements, look up to those who are more accomplished than yourself, that you may be fired with emulation; but when you feel dissatisfied with your circumstances, look down on those beneath you, that you may learn contentment. *Dr. J. Moore.*

12,139. VANITY, Emblems of. Honor must put off its robes when the play is done; make it never so glorious a show on this world's stage, it hath but a short part to act. A great name of worldly glory is but like a peal rung on the bells; the common people are the clappers; the rope that moves them is popularity; if you once let go your hold and leave pulling, the clapper lies still, and farewell honor. Strength, though like Jeroboam it put forth the arm of oppression, shall soon fall down withered. (1 Kings 13:4.) Beauty is like an almanac: if it last a year it is well. Pleasure like lightning: *oritur moritur;* sweet, but short; a flash, and away. All vanities are but butterflies, which wanton children greedily catch for; and sometimes they fly beside them, sometimes before them, sometimes behind them, sometimes close by them; yea, through their fingers, and yet they miss them; and when they have them, they are but butterflies; they have painted wings, but are crude and squalid worms. Such are the things of this world, vanities, butterflies. *Vel sequendo labimur, vel assequendo lædimur.* The world itself is not unlike an artichoke; nine parts of it are unprofitable leaves, scarce the tithe is good: about it there is a little picking meat, nothing so wholesome as dainty: in the midst of it there is a core, which is enough to choke them that devour it. *Adams.*

12,140. VANITY, Force of. O, Vanity, how little is thy force acknowledged, or thy operations discerned! How wantonly dost thou deceive mankind, under different disguises! Sometimes thou dost wear the face of pity; sometimes of generosity; nay, thou hast the assurance to put on those glorious ornaments which belong only to heroic virtue. *Fielding.*

12,141. VANITY, Memento of. There once stood at one end of the Library in Dublin a globe of the world, and at the other a skeleton of a man. Suppose the skeleton to represent Alexander, and his conquests to have been universal, what does it profit him now? Suppose it is all that remains of the gold-clasping Rothschild; what will his millions profit him now? Skeletons hold no sceptres, wield no swords, drive no pens, grasp no gold, court no favor, hear no censure and regard no praise. They cannot be endured in the palaces where once they reigned. This is the end of all. The flesh to the worms, and the skeleton—a powerless thing—mocks our pride by only a little slower decay.

12,142. VANITY, Personal. Most persons are like Themistocles, who never found himself so much contented as when he found himself praised. I will not say a gracious heart never lifts up itself; but I will say, that grace in the heart never lifts it up. *Secker.*

12,143. VANITY, Real. Philip the Good attended a royal wedding in Flanders. For days feasting and hilarity was kept up. Walking out one evening he saw a man dead drunk snoring by the road-side. He caused his followers to take him to the palace, where he was stripped of his old clothes and dressed in full court costume. When he awoke he found every one ready to wait upon him. The poor fellow wondered how he came there, surrounded by so much splendor. All day long they caused him to think himself some great duke, and when night came, he heard music and saw all the pleasures of a full court. But late at night, when well drunk, and fast asleep, the old clothes were put upon him, and he was taken back to his place in the street. The man ever after insisted that he had seen a vision.

12,144. VANITY, Universal. Hardly shall you meet with man or woman so aged or ill-favored but if you will commend them for comeliness, nay, and for youth too, shall take it well. *South.*

12,145. VANITY, Vices of. Vanity is the foundation of the most ridiculous and contemptible vices—the vices of affectation and common lying. *Adam Smith.*

12,146. VANITY, Weeds of. How much I regret to see so generally abandoned to the weeds of vanity that fertile and vigorous space of life in which might be planted the oaks and fruit-trees of enlightened principle and virtuous habit, which, growing up, would yield to old age an enjoyment, a glory, and a shade! *John Foster.*

12,147. VARIETY, Nature's. Ruskin says, "Break off an elm bough three feet long, in full leaf, and lay it on the table before you, and try to draw it, leaf for leaf. It is ten to one if on the whole bough (provided you do not twist it about as you work) you find one form of a leaf exactly like another; perhaps you will not even have one complete. Every leaf will be oblique, or foreshortened, or curled, or crossed by another, or shaded by another, or have something or other the matter with it; and though the whole bough will look graceful and symmetrical, you will scarcely be able to tell how or why it does so, since there is not one line of it like another." What variety then must we expect in life and experience!

12,148. VAUNTING, Folly of. A lion and an ass made an agreement to go out hunting together. By-and-by they came to a cave where many wild goats abode. The lion took up his station at the mouth of the cave, and the ass, going within, kicked and brayed and made a mighty fuss to frighten them out. When the lion had caught very many of them, the ass came out and asked him if he had not made a noble fight, and routed the goats properly. "Yes, indeed," said the lion; "and I assure you, you would have frightened me too, if I had not known you to be an ass." *Æsop.*

12,149. VENGEANCE, Expectation of. Joseph Upcheer, a colored Christian soldier, said, "Some say dar's no God is dis war. But I puts my trust in de Lord, an' balls don't scare me. De han' ob de Lord is in de war." One asked, "What do you think is the cause of it, Joseph?" He revolved the question a moment and then said earnestly, "So much unfair work am de cause of the war. My old uncle, who died twenty years ago, put his han' on my head once, and says he, 'Young dog, make haste and grow. Bimby you'll have a gun and fight.' Wese been 'pecting dis war, sah, dere's been so much unfair work." *G. N. Marden.*

12,150. VENGEANCE, Goddess of. The old Greeks personated conscience and called the goddess Nemesis. First she is the personification of moral reverence for law, and last she becomes the angel of vengeance, overtaking with fullest retribution the reckless transgressor. I shall never forget a picture seen in my boyhood. A prodigal fleeing for his life, a thousand sins stirring his soul like a tempest, his eyes starting from their sockets: behind him the swiftly-flying Nemesis with the flashing weapon uplifted, ready to strike him down. The poor wretch cannot escape the blow. Thus is every sinner relentlessly pursued by the avenging deity whose sword is sharp, and swift, and sure. *Dr. Geo. H. Whitney.*

12,151. VERACITY, Importance of. When the materials of a building are solid blocks of stone, very rude architecture will suffice; but a structure of rotten materials needs the most careful adjustment in order to make it stand. *Whately.*

12,152. VESSEL, Fil'ing the. Methought I looked and saw the Master standing, and at his feet lay an earthen vessel. It was not broken, not unfitted for service, yet there it lay, powerless and useless, until he took it up. He held it awhile, and I saw that he was filling it, and anon, I beheld him walking in his garden, whither he had "gone down to gather lilies." The earthen vessel was yet again in his hand, and with it he watered his beauteous plants, and caused their odors to be shed forth yet more abundantly. Then I said to myself, "Sorrowing Christian, hush! hush! peace, be, still! thou art this earthen vessel; powerless, it is true, yet not broken, still fit for the Master's use. Sometimes thou mayst be laid aside altogether from active service, and the question may arise, what is the Master doing with me now? Then may a voice speak to thine inmost heart, 'he is filling the vessel, yes, only filling it ready for use.' Dost thou ask in what manner? Nay, be silent. Is it not all too great an honor for thee to be used by him at all? Be content, whether thou art employed in watering the lilies, or in washing the feet of the saints." Truly, it is a matter of small moment. Enough, surely enough, for an earthen vessel, to be in the Master's hands, and employed in the Master's service. *Anon.*

12,153. VICE, Allies of. I think you will find it true, that, before any vice can fasten on a man, body, mind, or moral nature must be debilitated. The mosses and fungi gather on sickly trees, not thriving ones: and the odious parasites which fasten on the human frame choose that which is already enfeebled. Mr. Walker, the hygeian humorist, declared that he had such a healthy skin it was impossible for any impurity to stick to it, and maintained that it was an absurdity to wash a face which was of necessity always clean. I don't know how much fancy there was in this; but there is no fancy in saying that the lassitude of tired-out operatives, and the languor of imaginative natures in their periods of collapse, and the vacuity of minds untrained to labor and discipline, fit the soul and body for the germination of the seeds of intemperance. *Holmes.*

12,154. VICE, Escape from. He that is deeply engaged in vice is like a man laid fast in a bog, who by a faint and lazy struggling to get out does but spend his strength to no purpose, and sinks the deeper into it: the only way is, by a resolute and vigorous effort to spring out, if possible, at once. When men are sorely urged and pressed, they find a power in themselves which they thought they had not. *Tillotson.*

12,155. VICE, Infelicity of. So absolutely does vice dispose of all men, being such a self-sufficient worker of infelicity, that it has no need either of instruments or servants. Other tyrants, endeavoring to render those men miserable whom they punish, maintain executioners and tormentors, devise searing-irons and racks to plague the reasonless soul. But vice, without any preparation of engines, as soon as it enters into the soul, torments and dejects it, filling a man with grief, lamentations, sorrow and repentance. *Plutarch.*

12,156. VICE, Unhappiness of. The greatest miracle that the Almighty could perform would be to make a bad man happy, even in heaven: he must unparadise that blessed place to accomplish it. In its primary signification all vice, that is, all excess, brings its own punishment even here. By certain fixed, settled and established laws of him who is the God of

Nature, excess of every kind destroys that constitution that temperance would preserve. The debauchee, therefore, offers up his body a "living sacrifice" to sin. *Colton.*

12,157. VICISSITUDE, Design of. As pleasant and as much desired as fair weather is wont to be, and as much as we become discontented at a lowering and dropping sky, yet the one is no less necessary or useful in its season than the other. For too interrupted a course of heat and sunshine would make the season fruitful in nothing but in caterpillars, or such kind of vermin, and in diseases; and is far more proper to fill graves than barns. Whereas seasonable vicissitudes of clouds, and cloudy weather, make both the ground fruitful, and the season healthful. Thus in our outward condition, too long and constant a prosperity is wont to make the soul barren of all but such wantonness as 'tis ill to be fruitful of; and the interposition of seasonable afflictions is as necessary and advantageous, as it can be unwelcome. *R. Boyle.*

12,158. VICTORY, Biblical Emblems of. *Palm branches,* Rev. 7: 9. *Crowns. Riding in triumph,* as ancient victors were wont to do, leading their captives in chains, and scattering incense and precious gift in their triumphant progress, 2 Cor. 2: 14. *Putting the feet upon the necks of vanquished foes,* as Josh. 10: 24. *Treading under foot,* as ashes, Mal. 4: 3; as the mire of the streets, Micah 7: 10. *Sitting on thrones,* Matt. 19: 28; Rev. 20: 4. *Bowes.*

12,159. VICTORY, Cheap. Victories that are cheap, are cheap. Those only are worth having which come as the result of hard fighting. *Beecher.*

12,160. VICTORY, Faith in. Agesilaus, while in Egypt with a very few soldiers, had to encounter a host of two hundred thousand men. He wrote the word Victory in the palm of his left hand. When the priest cut up a bird for an augury Agesilaus took its liver and pressing it in his marked hand, printed upon it the word he had written there. He then showed the wonder to the soldiers, telling them that the gods had given them this certain omen of victory. Believing the victory certain they went bravely into battle, resolved upon victory, and won it. The church has for her confidence the more "sure word of prophecy." Resolutely let the battle be pushed till victory is universal.

12,161. VICTORY, God of. A large army of Suevi and Alemanni swept down upon Gaul for the purpose of plunder. Clovis, a pagan, gathered his force, and met them not far from Cologne. His Christian wife, Clotildis, said to him before his departure, "My lord, you are going to conquer; but, in order to be victorious, you must invoke the God of the Christians. He is the sole Lord of the universe, and is called the God of Armies. If you call upon him in faith, nothing can resist you. Though your enemies were a hundred against one, you would triumph over them." The shock of the enemy was terrible. Clovis's cavalry was routed, the battle was evidently going against him, and his best efforts failed to rally his troops. Then he thought of the words of his queen, and, in his great extremity, lifted his eyes to heaven, and prayed, "O, Christ, whom Clotildis invokes as the Son of the living God, I implore thy succor; I have called upon my gods, and find they have no power; I, therefore, invoke thee; I believe in thee; deliver me from mine enemies, and I will be baptized in thy name." The fortunes of the day began to change immediately. The enemies were routed and reduced to tributaries. This victory is set down as miraculous, and from it Clovis dates his conversion to Christianity, A. D. 496.

12,162. VICTORY, A Martyr's. James Renwick, who was martyred at the age of twenty-six, in Scotland, before his execution, exclaimed, "O Lord, thou hast brought me within two hours of eternity; and this is no matter of terror to me more than if I were to lie down on a bed of roses: nay, through grace, to thy praise I may say, I never had the fear of death since I came to this prison; but from the place whence I was taken I could have gone very composedly to the scaffold. O, how can I contain this, to be within two hours of the crown of glory?" On hearing the drums beat for the guards to turn out, he exclaimed, "Yonder is the welcome warning to my marriage: the bridegroom is coming: I am ready, I am ready!"

12,163. VICTORY Not to Numbers. Lucullus, with an army of ten thousand foot and one thousand horse, fought Tigranes in Armenia, who led an army of one hundred and fifty thousand men. The Roman general gained a remarkable victory, slaying more than one hundred thousand of the enemy, and losing but five of his own men.

12,164. VICTORY Proclamation of. After Commodore Perry's decisive victory in the war of 1812, on Lake Erie, he announced the result to the government thus: "We have met the enemy and they are ours." So it may be said of Christ and soon will be said by the church.

12,165. VIGILANCE, Duty of. Never in all the admonitions which fell from those holy lips did Christ impress upon the mind of man a more solemn duty than when he proclaimed, "What I say unto you, I say unto all, Watch!" Not in the series of parables wherewith he engraved his thoughts by illustration and simile upon his hearers did he ever insist upon any duty which is more completely a guide to our path, a light upon our way, a warning against danger, and source of internal confidence in pursuit of the discovery of another and a better world, than is vigilance. *Bellew.*

12,166. VIRGINS, Parable of the. A sailor once listened to the reading of the parable of the ten virgins, at a cottage meeting. Sometime after he went again, and said, "I have not forgotten the parable of the ten virgins, and all that was then said. I was far away at sea when the words were brought home to me." It had been part of his employment to light the lamps at sea; and one evening he discovered that the supply of oil was getting low, and

would scarcely last till they arrived in port. "I knew," he said, "that the captain would be very angry, and that I should in all probability lose my situation. Then came to my mind the parable of the virgins, and I said to myself, I am in danger of offending an earthly master, and of being shut out from my employment on board his ship; but oh, what is that to not being ready when my heavenly. Master calls me, and to being shut out of heaven?" The poor man with tears added, "I prayed then most earnestly that God would give me his grace, and save me in Jesus Christ." His lamp was filled with the oil of grace.

12,167. VIRTUE, Practicing. Eudaemonidas saw Xenocrates when he was very old, in the academy reading philosophy to his scholars. He was told that he was in quest of virtue. He inquired, "When does he intend to practice it?" The aged need to use great diligence as well as the young.

12,168. VIRTUE, Religion and. Religion or virtue, in a large sense, includes duty to God and our neighbor; but in a proper sense, virtue signifies duty towards men, and religion duty to God. *Dr. I. Watts.*

12,169. VIRTUE, Value of. Plato, who was a competent judge, was of opinion that virtue was a more valuable treasure than all the riches above the earth or all the mines beneath it. *Plutarch.*

12,170. VISITATION, Divine. Put your ear to the rail track and you can hear the train coming miles away: so I to-day put my ear to the ground, and I heard the thundering on of the lightning train of God's mercies and judgments. The mercy of God is first to be tried upon this nation. It will be preached in the pulpits, in theatres, on the streets, everywhere. People will be invited to accept the mercy of the gospel, and the story and the song and the prayer will be "mercy." But suppose they do not accept the offer of mercy—what then? Then God will come with his judgments, and the grasshoppers will eat the crops, and the freshets will devastate the valleys, and the defalcations will swallow the money markets, and the fires will burn cities into ashes, and the earth will quake from pole to pole. Year of mercies and of judgments. Year of invitation and of warning. Year of jubilee and of woe. Which side are you going to be on? *Talmage.*

12,171. VISITATION, Tract. Harlan Page superintended thirty tract distributers in the city of New York, and he observed that in the course of three or four years, though the district had been regularly gone through by the visitors, yet only four conversions had occurred which could be traced to their agency. Aware of the cause of such limited success, he called his distributers together, and laid before them the return. He told them, "The fault lies with yourselves: you are not doing the work right. Have you not," he said, "one or more individuals in your district for the salvation of whose souls you can labor, either by prayer or by speaking to them?"

The result was, that the distributors singled out eighty-four cases for their special labor; and in the course of eight months, thirty-four hopeful conversions were reported; all but four of whom had been converted by direct conversation and prayer.

12,172. VISITING, Encouragement to. Do not be afraid of venturing a few visits for the Lord. There was in a certain minister's district a public house, in which neither the landlord nor his wife were professors of religion. It was quite a resort for the thoughtless and profane, and he dreaded visiting the place; but conceiving it to be his duty he nerved himself up to the task. He was respectfully received and invited into the sitting room, where he found the tavern keeper and his wife alone. He conversed with, or rather talked to them about the interests of their immortal souls; endeavoring to show them the responsibility of their station; and urged them to give immediate attention to the things which belonged to their peace; but could get no other answer than a promise from the landlord that he would think of it. He left the house with a heavy heart, feeling that he had done no good. They soon left the place, and the minister, ten years after, received a very kind note from the man, informing him that the conversation which seemed to be so little regarded, had resulted in the conversion of both himself and his wife. *Power.*

12,173. VOLITION, Influence of. A man with a half-volition goes backwards and forwards, and makes no way on the smoothest road; a man with a whole volition advances on the roughest, and will reach his purpose, if there be even a little wisdom in it. *Carlyle.*

12,174. VOW, Reminded of a. A sea-captain related his misfortunes: the wreck of his ship, and his own escape after floating several days on a plank. A gentleman who heard it asked him privately if he did not in that hour of peril vow to serve the Lord if he would deliver him. The captain became angry, and replied: "It is none of your business." His questioner treated him very kindly, while he was ill at ease. The next day the captain called on him and said: "Sir, I have not slept a wink since I saw you; I abused you yesterday; I am now come to ask your pardon. I *did*, while on that plank, vow to God, that I would live differently from what I ever had done; and, by God's help, from this time forward, I am determined to do so."

12,175. VOWS, Avaricious. A rich heathen, in a storm at sea, vowed to Jupiter if he would save him and his vessel, he would sacrifice a hundred oxen. When the storm abated, he thought an offering of seven oxen sufficient. And so after each storm his sacrifice decreased. From seven oxen to one, and then to a sheep; and when at last safe on shore, a few dates were regarded as enough. But these dates were eaten up while on his way to the altar, and the shells alone left for an offering to Jupiter. The human heart has been the same selfish thing in all ages.

12,176. WAITING, The Christian. Conceive the case of a man who, having been cast upon a dreary inhospitable island, awaits the time for a vessel to come and bear him away. He paces its barren and desert sands, and looks up at the overcast sky, anxiously waiting for the arrival of the vessel to carry him to a land of light and fertility. So the Christian, like the exile on a rock, feels that he is far from his natural home, and is looking for and hasting unto the day of our Lord Jesus Christ. He knows that the vessel is prepared, and the convoy ready, which are to bear him hence from a barren wilderness to a happy land flowing with milk and honey. *Salter.*

12,177. WAITING, Examples of. You remember that strange half-involuntary "forty years" of Moses in the "wilderness" of Midian, when he had fled from Egypt. You remember, too, the almost equally strange years of retirement in "Arabia," by Paul, when, if ever, humanly speaking, instant action was needed. And preeminently you remember the amazing charge of the ascending Lord to the disciples, "Tarry at Jerusalem." Speaking after the manner of men, one could not have wondered if out-spoken Peter, or fervid James, had said: "Tarry, Lord! How long?" "Tarry, Lord! is there not a perishing world, groaning for the 'good news?'" "Tarry! did we hear thee aright, Lord? Was the word not haste?" Nay; "Being assembled together with them, He commanded them that they should not depart from Jerusalem, but wait for the promise of the Father." (Acts 1:4.) *Grosart.*

12,178. WANTS, Book of. On a tradesman's table I noticed a book labeled *Want Book*. What a practical suggestion for a man of prayer! He should put down all his needs on the tablets of his heart, and then present his want book to his God. If we knew all our need, what a large want book we should require! How comforting to know that Jesus has a supply book, which exactly meets our want book! Promises, providences, and divine visitations combine to meet the necessities of all the faithful. *Spurgeon.*

12,179. WANTS, Imaginary. A great number of our wants are simply special wants of the imagination; we want them because we think that we want them; they give us no enjoyment when we obtain them. *Fichte.*

12,180. WANTS, Ruinous. We are ruined, not by what we really want, but by what we think we do; therefore, never go abroad in search of your wants; if they be real wants, they will come home in search of you; for he that buys what he does not want, will soon want what he cannot buy. *Colton.*

12,181. WAR, Absurdity of. "What are you thinking, my man?" said Lord Hill, as he approached a soldier who was leaning in a gloomy mood upon his firelock, while around him lay mangled thousands of French and English a few hours after the battle of Salamanca had been won by the British. The soldier started, and, after saluting his general, answered, "I was thinking, my lord, how many widows and orphans I have this day made for one shilling."

12,182. WAR, Contrast of. It is not known where he that invented the plough was born, nor where he died; yet he has effected more for the happiness of the world than the whole race of heroes and of conquerors, who have drenched it with tears, and manured it with blood, and whose birth, parentage, and education have been handed down to us with a precision proportionate to the mischief they have done. *Colton.*

12,183. WAR, Cost of. Give me the money that has been spent in war, and I will purchase every foot of land upon the globe. I will clothe every man, woman, and child in an attire of which kings and queens would be proud. I will build a school-house on every hill-side, and in every valley over the whole earth; I will build an academy in every town, and endow it; a college in every State, and fill it with able professors; I will crown every hill with a place of worship, consecrated to the promulgation of the gospel of peace; I will support in every pulpit an able teacher of righteousness, so that on every Sabbath morning the chime on one hill should answer to the chime on another round the earth's wide circumference; and the voice of prayer, and the song of praise, should ascend like a universal holocaust to heaven. *Stebbins.*

12,184. WAR, Destruction by. In 1756, Edmund Burke estimated the loss of human life by war, both directly and indirectly, at 35,000,000,000, about twenty-three times the present population of the globe, now estimated to be 1,425,000,000.

12,185. WAR, God of. The Alani have no temples or shrines; but with barbarous ceremonies they fix a naked sword in the ground. This they religiously worship as the god of the region of their abode.

12,186. WAR, Horror of. Take my word for it, if you had seen but one day of war, you would pray to almighty God that you might never see such a thing again. *Wellington.*

12,187. WAR, Preparation for. Suppose a gentleman, living in a suburban house, with his garden separated only by a fruit-wall from his next door neighbor's, and he had called me to consult with him on the furnishing of his drawing-room. I begin looking about me, I find the walls rather bare; I think such and such a paper might be desirable—perhaps a little fresco here and there on the ceiling—a damask curtain or so at the windows. "Ah," says my employer, "damask curtains, indeed! that's all very fine, but you know I can't afford that kind of thing just now!" "Yet the world credits you with a splendid income!" "Ah, yes," says my friend, "but do you know, at present I am obliged to spend it nearly all in steel-traps?" "Steel-traps! for whom?" "Why, for that fellow on the other side the wall, you know: we're very good friends, capital friends; but we are obliged to keep our traps set on both sides of the wall; we could not possibly keep on friendly terms without them and our spring guns. The worst of it is, we are both clever fellows enough; and there's never a day passes that we don't find out a new trap, or a new gun barrel, or something; we spend about fifteen millions a year each in our traps, take it all together; and I don't see how we're to do with less?" A highly comic state of life for two private gentlemen! but for two nations, it seems to me, not wholly comic. Bedlam would be comic, perhaps, if there were only one madman in it; and your Christmas pantomime is comic when there is only one clown in it; but when the whole world turns clowns, and paints itself red with its own heart's blood instead of vermilion, it is something else than comic, I think. *Ruskin.*

12,188. WAR, Weapons of. Cannon and fire arms are cruel and damnable machines; I believe them to have been the direct suggestion of the devil. Against the flying ball no valor avails; the soldier is dead ere he sees the means of his destruction. If Adam had seen in a vision the horrible instruments his children were to invent, he would have died of grief. *Luther.*

12,189. WARFARE, Christian. At one time a detachment of English soldiers under Sir Philip Sydney was called to meet a much more numerous force of the enemy. Their commander sent them word that if they would each fight an enemy he would take care of all the rest. Christ proposes to do better than this. He gives us strength to fight all our battles, retrieves our reverses, and gains the victory beyond a peradventure. (Matt. 28: 20.)

12,190. WARFARE, Constant. When the warriors in the old heroic days had no human enemies with whom to fight, they employed their time in fighting with wild beasts. Thus Theseus, desiring to keep himself in action, went forth against the Marathonian bull, which had wrought immense mischief to the inhabitants of Tetrapeus. We should keep our armor bright by constant fighting. *Anon.*

12,191. WARFARE, Life's. Our life is a warfare: and we ought not, while passing through it, to sleep without a sentinel, or march without a scout. He who neglects either of these precautions exposes himself to surprise, and to become a prey to the diligence and perseverance of his adversary. *Feltham.*

12,192. WARNING, Angry at a. A pilot guiding a steamer down the Cumberland saw a light, apparently from a small craft, in the middle of the narrow channel. His impulse was to disregard the signal and run down the boat. As he came near, a voice shouted. "Keep off, keep off." In great anger he cursed what he supposed to be a boatman in his way. On arriving at his next landing he learned that a huge rock had fallen from the mountain into the bed of the stream, and that a signal was placed there to warn the coming boats of the unknown danger. Alas! many regard God's warnings in the same way, and are angry with any who tell them of the rocks in their course. They will understand better at the end.

12,193. WARNING, Disregard of. The night before Cæsar's death his wife dreamed that their house had fallen and wounded her husband, and that he sought refuge in her arms. The armor of Mars, then Cæsar's by virtue of office, rattled upon the wall, and the door of his sleeping-room opened of itself. The omens from the feeding of poultry were unfavorable, and he resolved to stay in doors that day. The senate met, among them the conspirators, with concealed daggers, waiting for Cæsar. A messenger from them announced the readiness of the senate to receive him, but he still lingered. Decemus Brutus then went to Cæsar, and persuaded him to accompany him to the senate-house. On the way, a paper was put into his hands, which revealed the plot for his assassination, which he thrust into the folds of his robe unread. He passed a soothsayer, who had warned him to beware of the Ides of March, and said, "You see the day you feared has come, and I am still alive." He answered, "Yes, it has come, but it has not yet passed." As he passed his own statue, which stood at the entrance of the senate-house, it fell, and was broken into fragments. As he entered, the senators rose, received him with honor, and welcomed him; but it was to the banquet of death! At a signal, the conspirators gathered about him. Casca struck the first blow. Then dagger after dagger was plunged into Cæsar's body. Seeing Brutus, whom he much loved, ready to strike, he cried, "You, too, Brutus, my son?" and submitted to his fate. Had he kept his resolution, and stayed at home; had he read the paper, or regarded the warning of the soothsayer, he would have escaped. How many warnings the sinner disregards in rushing upon his doom!

12,194. WARNING, Kindness of. That father who sees his son tottering toward the brink of a precipice, and, as he sees him, cries out sharply, "Stop, stop!"—does not that father love his son? That tender mother who sees her infant on the point of eating some poisonous berry, and cries out sharply, "Stop, stop! put it down!"—does not that mother love that child? It is indifference that lets people alone, and allows them to go on every one in his own way. It is love, tender love, that warns and raises the cry of alarm. The cry of "Fire! fire!" at midnight may sometimes startle a man out of his sleep, rudely, harshly, unpleasantly. But who would complain if that cry was the means of saving his life? The words, "Except ye repent, ye shall perish," may seem at first sight stern and severe. But they are words of love, and may be the means of delivering precious souls from hell.
Ryle.

12,195. WARNING, Noah's. An Oriental legend says that God ordered Noah to make an instrument of wood, such as is used to this day in the East instead of bells, to call the people to church, and directed him to strike upon it three times every day to call the people together at the place where the ark was building, and to warn them of the impending deluge, from which they could escape only by repentance.

12,196. WARNING, Unheeded. A great fire was raging in one of our cities, in which Bishop Janes was passing the night. The continued alarms and lurid glare called him forth to the scene of the fire. On a housetop near the conflagration, were two men, extinguishing every spark that might alight. They had gained this by passing over other roofs, and there was no other means of escape but as they came. The flames made rapid progress. So busy were the two men as not to observe or think of their danger. The crowd below saw them and sent up a great cry of alarm. The imperiled men did not even now understand that they were being warned. A few minutes more and a roof fell, cutting off all retreat. The flames hastened in their destructive work, till the men bound in by fire sought in vain for escape. Oh, worldling! be warned in time, before you are encircled with inevitable doom.

12,197. WATCHFULNESS, Adaptation to. Man is a movable watch tower. His telescopes, placed upon the highest point, are easily made to sweep the whole horizon. Here man is given the strict order, "Watch." He cannot desert his post, but he may sleep in it. Foes may be expected from any quarter. Vigilance is his only safeguard.

12,198. WATCHFULNESS, Demand for. A friend was recently overtaken by night on a mountain ridge. The path behind was too perilous to be retraced in the darkness, and the way in front was stopped by a projecting rock, which in his exhausted state he could not scale. His only alternative was to wait for the morning. But his resting-place was a steep slope, ending in a sheer precipice. One careless movement might prove his destruction. As the darkness deepened, the danger was disguised. With a lessening sense of peril, there came on increasing drowsiness. What efforts were his during those long hours to drive off sleep! How he had to stir up his mind to a conviction of the necessity of unremitting vigilance! For, should he once be overpowered, he might unconsciously slide down his sloping couch, and be hurled into the valley below. Such is our position. If we would not fall down the precipice, let us watch lest during slumber we slip along the treacherous incline.
Newman Hall.

12,199. WATCHFULNESS, Examples of. When a flock of rooks light on a field, foraging, they often set one of their number on a tree or the fence, to watch when any one approaches, and caw alarm. At sea a sailor is sent to the mast-head to look out, and tell when the sail of another ship appears in sight, or distant land comes in view; especially at night and in storm, lest the vessel suddenly strike some other bark, or on a floating iceberg, or rush among the breakers. In these cases there is watching against evil.
Edmond.

12,200. WATCHFULNESS, Fable of. A doe that had but one eye used to graze near the sea, and that she might be the more secure from attack, kept her eye towards the land against the approach of the hunters, and her blind side towards the sea, whence she feared no danger. But some sailors rowing by in a boat and seeing her, aimed at her from the water and shot her. When at her last gasp, she sighed to herself, "Ill-fated creature that I am! I was safe on the land side, whence I expected to be attacked, but find an enemy in the sea, to which I most looked for protection."

Æsop.

12,201. WATCHFULNESS, Need of Prayerful. Watch, for your passions are strong. Deal by yourselves as men deal by themselves who carry dynamite to and fro. A man who is laden with explosive materials does not go into foundries and blacksmith shops. He does not resort to places where sparks are flying abroad. He seeks safe ways. He avoids places of peril. He is conscious all the time that he is carrying death about himself if he exposes it to the touch of fire. When they were storing that great cavern of Hell Gate with explosive tubes there were to be three thousand handled by two hundred or a hundred and fifty men; and they all knew that if any man dropped one the whole would explode in a moment and they would perish; and with what care and circumspection did every man of them labor! If it did not turn the hair of the superintendent gray it ought to have done it, to watch the work! Now, if men felt that they were bearing explosive materials within them, if they had a sense of the training that is needed in certain parts of their nature, and if they joined training to prayer, then they might hope to have some answer to their petitions.

Beecher.

12,202. WATCHFULNESS, Security of. Souls, you are no longer safe and secure than when you are upon your watch. While Antipater kept the watch, Alexander was safe; and while we keep a strict watch, we are safe. A watchful soul is a soul upon the wing, a soul out of gun-shot, a soul upon a rock, a soul in a castle, a soul above the clouds, a soul held fast in everlasting arms. *Brooks.*

12,203. WATCHING, Ceaseless. Alexander, founder of the Accœmeti, or Sleepless Ones, established his community of monks at Gomon on the Bosphorus, A. D. 430. They numbered three hundred, and were divided into six choirs, who sang alternately. Night and day ceaselessly their songs of praise ascended to Christ. They sang and watched continually for the coming of the Bridegroom. This ceaseless song and vigil was the characteristic of this order.

12,204. WATCHING, Neglect of. A ship was swept by a resistless storm upon a rocky coast. A passenger asked if there was any hope of safety, and being told that there was none, threw himself into his berth in despair. Just before the ship struck, it was lifted over a reef of rocks by a huge wave and left upon a sand-bar. On the instant the captain and crew escaped in safety to the shore. The passenger was lost because he did not watch.

12,205. WATER, Costly. It is related of Sous, an early Lacedæmonian king, that he and his army were cut off by his enemy from his water supply. He agreed to give up all his conquests, provided himself and all his army should drink of a certain spring. The conditions being accepted, he offered to give his kingdom to any one of his forces who would forbear drinking. Not one was willing to pay such a trifling price, even for a kingdom. The king himself went to the spring, sprinkled his face, but did not drink, and thus saved his kingdom.

12,206. WATER, Dying for. A party of men riding through a country where there was water for neither man nor beast, came suddenly into the neighborhood of a river. The jaded horses sprang forward with new life, and plunged into the stream. Not far away they found a woman and exhausted man overcome by thirst. When found, he could only whisper, "Water! water!" It was brought to him, and every care was taken to secure his recovery. All must have died but for the water. One was worse off than the others. This is a parable of the "living waters." All must have it; all may have it. Some must help others to get it.

12,207. WATER, Price of. Water in the Orient is scarce, and hard to be obtained. He who owns a fountain sells the water, and often asks an extortionous price. Quarrels arise, and wars have been waged for water. The poor might be unable to buy it, but Christ invites all to living water "without money and without price."

12,208. WEAK, Encouragement to the. The babes in a family are as much loved and thought of as the elder brothers and sisters. The tender seedlings in a garden are as diligently looked after as the old trees. The lambs in a flock are as carefully tended by the good shepherd as the old sheep. Oh! rest assured it is just the same in Christ's family, in Christ's garden, in Christ's flock. All are loved. All are tenderly thought of. All are cared for. And all shall be found in his garner at last. *Ryle.*

12,209. WEAKNESS, Biblical Figures of. *A bruised reed*—a thing at the best pliable—weak—powerless to resist; much more a reed when bruised and drooping, Isa. 42: 3; Matt. 12: 20. *Babes—little children,* 1 Cor. 3: 1; 13: 11; Heb. 5: 13; 1 Pet. 2: 2; 1 John 2: 13. *Lambs,* Isa. 40: 11; John 21: 15 (the word here means little delicate lambs). *Doves* —turtle doves, timid and trembling, Ps. 74: 19. *Worms,* Isa. 41: 14. "Jacob" in his low estate—"thou worm Jacob," feeble and trampled upon, yet acknowledged by God— "worms" but not vipers. God's "*little ones,*" so called twice in Zechariah and four times in St. Matthew. *Bowes.*

12,210. WEAKNESS, Strength in. Some living creatures maintain their hold by foot or body on flat surfaces, by a method that seems like magic, and with a tenacity that amazes the observer. A fly marches at ease with feet uppermost on a plastered ceiling, and a mollusc sticking to the smooth, water-worn surface of a basaltic rock, while the long swell of the Atlantic at every pulse sends a huge white billow, roaring and hissing, and cracking and crunching over it, are objects of wonder to the on-looker. That apparently super-natural solidity is the most natural thing in the world. It is emptiness that imparts so much strength to these feeble creatures. A vacuum, on the one side within a web-foot, and on the other within the shell, is the secret of their power. By dint of that emptiness in itself, the creature quietly and easily clings to the wall or the rock, so making all the strength of the wall or rock its own. By its emptiness it is held fast; the moment it becomes full it drops off. Ah, it is the self-emptiness of a humble, trustful soul, that makes the Redeemer's strength his own, and so keeps him safe in an evil world. *Arnot.*

12,211. WEAKNESS, Upheld by Grace. A noble vessel, in the year 1800, appeared off the Goodwin sands with signals of distress. She had been for some time making signals for a pilot, and having been observed on shore, a small skiff put off with an experienced one on board. But before it could reach her, she was driven on the sands, and became a wreck. The well-piloted little skiff escaped the dangers, and returned safely to port. So, weakness, upheld by almighty grace, is safe—while the strongest without it must fail. *Salter.*

12,212. WEALTH, Acquisition of. Wealth is not acquired, as many persons suppose, by fortunate speculations and splendid enterprises, but by the daily practice of industry, frugality and economy. He who relies upon these means will rarely be found destitute, and he who relies upon any other will generally become bankrupt. *Wayland.*

12,213. WEALTH, Covenant for. There are some who made a covenant with God, saying, "Verily, if he give us of his abundance we will give alms." It is said that Mohammed wrote this to cover the case of Thalaba Eben Hateb, who came to him desiring that he would pray God to bestow riches upon him. The people dissuaded him, telling him that wealth would only increase his temptations or induce covetousness. But Thalaba repeated his request, and made the most solemn promise that he would use his riches for charity and religion. His desire was granted, and in a short time Thalaba became very rich. Mohammed sent collectors to him to solicit his proportion of alms, but he found some excuse and sent them away empty. His greed led him to break his vow. It is the usual way. Mohammed says, "When he had given unto them of his abundance they became covetous thereof. They failed to perform unto God that which they had promised. God shall scoff at them, and they shall suffer a grievous punishment."

12,214. WEALTH without Heaven. A nobleman invited the neighboring minister one day to dine with him. Before dinner they walked into the garden, and after viewing the various productions and rarities with which it abound-

ed, the host exclaimed, 'Well, Mr. D——, you see I want for nothing; I have all that my heart can wish for." As the minister made no reply, but appeared thoughtful, his lordship asked him the reason. "Why, my lord," said the old man, "I have been thinking that a man may have all these things, and never see heaven after all." These words led to the conversion of the nobleman.

12,215. WEALTH, Imperishable. Aristippus having lost all his goods by shipwreck, found his knowledge adequate to supply his wants. He sent this counsel to his friends, "I advise you to procure such riches for your children as a tempest at sea has no power over."

12,216. WEALTH, Poverty of. Cornelius Vanderbilt, though not the rich possessor of a world, had acquired the largest fortune ever gained by an American: estimated at $100,-000,000. Around his dying bed his friends sang at his request, "Come, ye sinners, poor and needy, weak and wounded, sick and sore." He often repeated, "I am poor and needy." Thus the hundred-millionaire seeks true riches in Christ.

12,217. WEALTH, Uncertainty of. A storm at sea, a spark of fire, an unfaithful servant, a false oath, or a treacherous friend, may quickly bring a man to sit with Job upon a dunghill. Look, as the bird flies from tree to tree, and as the beggar goes from door to door, and as the pilgrim travels from place to place, and as the physician walks from patient to patient; so all the riches, honors, and glory of this world do either fly from man to man, or else walk from man to man. Now one is exalted, and anon he is debased; now one is full, and anon he is hungry; now one is clothed gloriously, and anon he is clothed with rags; now one is at liberty, and anon he is under restraint; now a man hath many friends, and anon he hath never a friend. There is nothing but vanity and uncertainty in all earthly portions. *Brooks.*

12,218. WEDDING, A Jewish Custom at a. The Jews had a custom at their wedding feasts for the married couple to drink out of the same glass together, and then to break it in pieces; teaching them, by that emblem, that whatever felicity they expected together, their lives, upon which it all depended, were frail and brittle as glass. No sooner joined, but they were warned to prepare for separation. *Buck.*

12,219. WELCOME, Custom of. In Pompeii the custom was to place a caged magpie in the vestibule of the houses, who was taught to salute the visitors with the word "χαιρε," "Hail." The Romans used to have the word "*Salve*," Hail, inscribed upon the titles of their entrance halls.

12,220. WICKED, Brief Life of the. "The wicked shall not live out half their days." The case of murders is almost a literal proof of the text. It is very seldom that a convicted murderer has reached the age of thirty-five, and they are almost always men of great vitality. We have collected a list, taking them as they came, from the newspapers of recent months

We noted fifty cases (taking no pains to get all), and not one of the fifty was over thirty-five.   *D. H. Wheeler.*

12,221. WICKED, Desires of the. They are mere flashes; as a sudden light, that rather blinds a man than shews him the way. So these enlightenings—they are not constant. Wicked men often have sudden motions and flashes and desires. "Oh, that I might die the death of the righteous." Oh, that I were in such a man's estate. But it is but a sudden flash and lightning. They are like a torrent, a strong sudden stream, that comes suddenly and makes a noise, but it hath no spring to feed it. The desires of God's children—they are fed with a spring, they are constant, they are streams, and not flashes.   *Sibbs.*

12,222. WICKED, Destruction of the. If the wicked flourish, and thou suffer, be not discouraged; they are fatted for destruction, thou art dieted for health.   *Fuller.*

12,223. WICKED, Envying the. "Their end was bitter as the smoke," said an aged teacher. "What meanest thou, O, master?" asked his young disciple. "I was thinking of the unrighteous," replied the old man, "and of how too often I, like the Psalmist, have been envious when they were in prosperity. Their lives have seemed so bright and glowing that I have thought they resembled the blaze of a cheerful fire on a winter night. But as I have watched them, they have suddenly vanished, like the flame that fades into black and bitter smoke, and I have ceased to envy them. Trust not, O, my scholar, only to that which appears brilliant, but watch also for its ending, lest thou be deceived."

12,224. WICKED, Prosperity of the. Prescott says, "One of the most important festivals was that in honor of the god Tezcathepola, whose rank was inferior only to the Supreme Being. He was called 'the soul of the world,' and supposed to have been its creator. He was depicted as a handsome man, endowed with perpetual youth. A year before the intended sacrifice, a captive, distinguished for his personal beauty, and without a blemish on his body, was selected to represent this deity. Certain tutors took charge of him, and instructed him how to perform his new part with becoming grace and dignity. He was arrayed in a splendid dress, regaled with incense, and with a profusion of sweet-scented flowers, of which the Mexicans were as fond as their descendants of the present day. When he went abroad he was attended by a train of the royal pages, and as he halted in the street to play some favorite melody, the crowd prostrated themselves before him, and did him homage as the representative of their good deity. In this way he led an easy, luxurious life, till within a month of his sacrifice. Four beautiful girls, bearing the names of the principal goddesses, were then selected; with them he lived in idle dalliance, and feasted at the banquets of the principal nobles, who paid him all the honor of a divinity. At length the fatal day of sacrifice arrived—the term of his short-lived glo-ries was at an end; he was stripped of his gaudy apparel, and bade adieu to the fair partners of his revelries. One of the royal barges transported him across the lake to a temple which rose on its margin: hither the inhabitants of the capital flocked to witness the consummation of the ceremony. As the sad procession wound up the sides of the pyramid, the unhappy victim threw away his gay chaplet of flowers, and broke in pieces the musical instruments with which he had solaced the hours of his captivity. On the summit he was received by six priests, whose long and matted locks flowed disorderly over their sable robes covered with hieroglyphic scrolls of mystic import. They led him to the sacrificial stone, a huge block of jasper, with its upper surface somewhat convex: on this the prisoner was stretched. Five priests secured his head and his limbs; while the sixth, clad in a scarlet mantle, emblematic of his bloody office, dexterously opened the breast of his wretched victim with a sharp razor, made of a volcanic substance, hard as flint—and inserting his hand in the wound, tore out the palpitating heart. The minister of death, first holding this up towards the sun, an object of worship through Anahuac, cast it at the feet of the deity to whom the temple was devoted, while the multitude below prostrated themselves in humble adoration. The tragic story of this prisoner was expounded by the priests as the type of human destiny, which, brilliant in its commencement, too often closes in sorrow and disaster." Thus far the historian—I rather view the tragedy as typical of the ungodly, who abounding in wealth, and, using it for the gratification of all their carnal appetites, are really only like oxen fattening for their slaughter.   *F. F. Trench.*

12,225. WICKED, Punishment of the. A wicked Austrian nobleman lived to the advanced age of ninety-three, and had not in all that time been visited with either grief or affliction. Frederick the Third on hearing of his death said, "This is what divines teach, that after death there is some place where we receive reward or punishment, since we see often in this world neither the just rewarded, nor the wicked punished."

12,226. WICKED, Restraining the. "My hook in thy nose!" What an expressive phrase is this. A bull with a hook in its nose can be led even by a little child. The ferocity of the animal is untamed, his might and strength remain as they were before, but he is powerless; the least plunge or struggle is restrained by the pain of the hook or ring. Thus the Lord often controls wicked men; He leaves them their ferocity of nature, but so puts them under restraint, and that by apparently unimportant means, that they cannot hurt his people. We must not so much look for the changing of the bull's nature, as for the putting the hook in his nose.   *Power.*

12,227. WICKED, Vain Expectations of the. Not many years ago a dissolute young man of large fortune made an attempt upon the life of an actress, and immediately destroyed his own life. In a letter written by him before the perpetration of these foul deeds, he signified his deliberate intention of thus committing a double murder, and that he and his intended victim might go to heaven together, and remarks that he was in a state of ecstatic joy at the prospect! Here was a debauchee, a frequenter of theatres, a murderer, a suicide, and yet anticipating the rewards of heaven! Nor does this wretched man's case afford as exaggerated a view as might be supposed, of the delusive hopes of heaven which are entertained by multitudes. In my own ministerial experience, I have known a case almost as gross; and what are the generality of men doing in places where the gospel is faithfully preached, but living in known sin, and still expecting to go to heaven at last?　　　*F. F. Trench.*

12,228. WIFE, Benefit of a Cross. Xanthippe, though she was a woman of a very troublesome spirit, could never move Socrates to a passion. Being accustomed to bear patiently this heavy burden at home, he was never in the least moved by the most scurrilous and abusive tongues he met with abroad.　　*Plutarch.*

12,229. WIFE, A Good. A good wife is heaven's last best gift to a man; his angel of mercy; minister of graces innumerable; his gem of many virtues; his casket of jewels; her voice, his sweetest music; her smiles, his brightest day; her kiss, the guardian of his innocence; her arms, the pale of his safety, the balm of his health, the balsam of his life; her industry, his surest wealth; her economy, his safest steward; her lips, his faithful counselors; her bosom, the softest pillow of his cares; and her prayers, the ablest advocates of heaven's blessing on his head.
　　　　　　　　　　Jeremy Taylor.

12,230. WIFE a Plague. Pittacus, celebrated for fortitude, wisdom, and justice, gave a banquet to several friends, when his wife entered in ill-humor and overturned the table. His guests were greatly surprised and annoyed; but he said, "Every one of you hath his particular plague, and my wife is mine, and he is very happy who hath this only."

12,231. WIFE, A Rich. As there is little or no use to be made of a mirror, though in a frame of gold, enchased with all the sparkling variety of the richest gems, unless it render back the true similitude of the image it receives; so is there nothing of profit in a wealthy dowry, unless the conditions, the temper, the humor of the wife be conformable to the natural dispositions and inclination of the husband, and he sees the virtues of his own mind exactly represented in hers.　*Plutarch.*

12,232. WILLFULNESS, Fate of. An ass that was being driven along the road by his master, started on ahead, and leaving the beaten track, made as fast as he could for the edge of a precipice. When he was just on the point of falling over, his master ran up, and seizing him by the tail, endeavored to pull him back; but the ass resisting and pulling the contrary way, the man let go his hold, saying, "Well,

Jack, if you will be master I cannot help it A willful beast must go his own way." *Æsop.*

12,233. WILL, Need of. In the schools of the wrestling master, when a boy falls he is bidden to get up again, and go on wrestling day by day till he has acquired strength; and we must do the same, and not be like those poor wretches who, after one failure, suffer themselves to be swept along as by a torrent. You need but will, and it is done; but if you relax your efforts, you will be ruined; for ruin and recovery are both from within.　　*Epictetus.*

12,234. WILL, Responsibility of. The inward principle to the outward act is as the kernel to the shell; but yet, in the first place, the shell is necessary for the kernel, and that by which it is commonly known; and in the next place, as the shell comes first, and the kernel grows gradually, and hardens within it, so it is with the moral principle in man. Legality precedes morality in every individual, even as the Jewish dispensation preceded the Christian in the education of the world at large. When may the will be taken for the deed? When the will is the obedience of the whole man; when the will is, in fact, the deed, that is, all the deed in our power. In every other case, it is bending the bow without shooting the arrow. The bird of paradise gleams on the lofty branch, and the man takes aim and draws the tough yew into a crescent with might and main! and lo! there is never an arrow on the string!　　　　　　*Coleridge.*

12,235. WISDOM, Counsel of. Delay hath undone many for the other world. Haste hath undone more for this. Time, well managed, saves all in both.　　　　　　　*Anon.*

12,236. WISDOM, Deliverance by. Anaximenes, met Alexander when he was marching to destroy Lampsacus. Alexander, suspecting that Anaximenes was coming to intercede for the safety of the city, immediately resolved to frustrate his purpose by taking an oath that he would not grant him anything that he should ask. "Then," said Anaximenes, "I request that you will destroy this city." Alexander was thus outwitted, but he respected his oath, and the city was spared. Thus it was the wisdom of one man which, by suddenly taking advantage of Alexander's oath, saved a noble city from destruction. Solomon could not, of course, have this instance in view, because he lived long before it occurred; but he might have others in view equally true. His design was to show that in this life virtue and wisdom may perform the most important services, and yet often be unrewarded; and hence the certainty of a future life, when God will render to every man according to his deeds.　　　　　　　*W. Cooke.*

12,237. WISDOM, Essentials of. Living in an age of extraordinary events and revolutions, I have learned from thence this truth, which I desire might thus be communicated to posterity:—that all is vanity which is not honest, and that there is no solid wisdom but in real piety.　*Evelyn's Epitaph, by himself.*

12,238. WISDOM, Particulars of. Perfect wisdom hath four parts, viz.: wisdom, the principle of doing things aright; justice, the principle of doing things equally in public and private; fortitude, the principle of not flying danger, but meeting it; and temperance, the principle of subduing desires, and living moderately.　　*Plato.*

12,239. WISDOM, Seeking. A gentleman who was afterwards for many years a clergyman of distinguished acceptance in the church of England, one day called upon Dr. James Foster to converse with him upon the skepticism which then oppressed his own mind. After the necessary introduction, he began to state his objections, when the doctor, with the benevolent gravity for which he was so distinguished, stopped him with this question, "Have you asked a solution of your difficulties from God this morning? Have you prayed to the Fountain of all light for information?" Upon receiving an answer in the negative, he rejoined, "Sir, you will excuse my gratifying your curiosity on the subject of the revelation, while you are chargeable with the breach of the first duties of natural religion."　　*Buck.*

12,240. WISDOM, Spouse of. Laurence Justinian, bishop of Venice in the fifteenth century, was called in a special manner to consecrate himself to the service of God. In his nineteenth year he saw in a vision eternal wisdom in the dress of a damsel of charming countenance. She addressed him, saying, "Why seekest thou rest to thy mind, out of thyself sometimes in this object and sometimes in that? What thou desirest is to be found only with me; behold, it is in my hands. Seek it in me who am the wisdom of God. By taking me for thy spouse thou shalt be possessed of inestimable treasure." That instant he was overcome by her attractions and resolved to possess her. He was of the best family in Venice, and honor and preferment lay before him. He placed on one side honors, riches, worldly pleasures, on the other hardships, poverty and self-denial. Then he said to his soul, "Hast thou courage, my soul, to despise these delights, and devote thyself to a life of cross-bearing and mortifications?" Casting himself upon Christ for strength, he espoused wisdom. On his dying bed he said, "Behold the spouse; let us go forth and meet him," and added, "Good Jesus: behold I come."

12,241. WISHES, Ignorance of our Own. I respect the man who knows distinctly what he wishes. The greater part of all the mischief in the world arises from the fact that men do not sufficiently understand their own aims. They have undertaken to build a tower, and spend no more labor on the foundation than would be necessary to erect a hut.　　*Goethe.*

12,242. WIT, Acquirement of. It is imagined that wit is a sort of inexplicable visitation, that it comes and goes with the rapidity of lightning, and that it is quite as unattainable as beauty or just proportion. I am so much of a contrary way of thinking, that I am convinced a man might sit down as systematically, and as successfully, to the study of wit, as he might to the study of mathematics: and I would answer for it, that by giving up only six hours a day to being witty, he should come on prodigiously before mid-summer, so that his friends should hardly know him again.
　　S. Smith.

12,243. WIT, Example of. Two cardinals upbraided Raphael Urbanus, for representing St. Peter and St. Paul with high color. He replied that he had not painted them in such a paleness and leanness in their faces as they had contracted while living, with their fastings and troubles; but that he had imitated that redness which came upon them now they were amongst the blessed, where they blushed at the manners and life of their successors."

12,244. WIT, Greek. "There, my lad," said an Athenian once to a little Hebrew boy, by the way of joke, "here is a pruta (a small coin, of less value than a farthing); bring me something for it, of which I may eat enough, leave some for my host, and carry some home to my family." The witty boy went and brought him salt. "Salt," exclaimed the Athenian; "I did not tell thee to bring salt!" "Nay," replied the boy, archly, "didst thou not say, 'Bring me of what I may eat, leave, and take some home?' Verily, of this thou mayest eat, leave some behind, and still have plenty to carry home."　　*Medrash Eoh.*

12,245. WIT, Shallowness of. Wonder why authors and actors are ashamed of being funny? Why, there are obvious reasons, and deep philosophical ones. The clown knows very well that the women are not in love with him, but with Hamlet, the fellow in the black coat and plumed hat. Passion never laughs. The wit knows that his place is at the tail of the procession. If you want the deep, underlying reason, I must take more time to tell it. There is a perfect consciousness in every form of wit—using that term in its general sense—that its essence consists in a partial and incomplete view of whatever it touches. It throws a single ray, separated from the rest—red, yellow, blue, or any intermediate shade—upon an object; never white light; that is the province of wisdom. We get beautiful effects from wit—all the prismatic colors—but never the object, as it is in fair daylight. A pun, which is a kind of wit, is a different and much shallower trick in mental optics; throwing the shadows of two objects so that one overlies the other. Poetry uses the rainbow tints for special effects, but always keeps its essential object in the purest white light of truth.
　　Holmes.

12,246. WITNESS, A Royal. Herodotus says that at the battle of Salamis Xerxes took his position on Mount Ægaleas, overlooking the fight. Whenever he saw any of his own men performing deeds of valor, he inquired who they were, and caused his scribes to write down their names and residences. On this record the reward would be bestowed in due time. We are a spectacle to men, angels and to God, and the record of our lives is being made up.

12,247. WITNESS, An Unexpected. A legend

of St. Severus of the fifth century states that a bath-house keeper brought suit against the widow of one of his deceased patrons for a large sum, which he affirmed her husband owed him at the time of his death. The judge approved the claim and ordered that the widow and her children should be sold to pay it. The widow fled to St. Severus and besought protection against this extortion. He asked her if the deceased owed the bath-keeper anything. She thought there might have been a trifling debt, but not so large a sum. The saint said, "The dead man himself shall give evidence." He took his staff and went to the tomb of the dead man and called upon him to answer him truly how much he owed the bath keeper. Then the corpse opened its eyes, and rose and said, "I owe but one egg," then fell back again as rigid as before. At the Almighty summons witnesses shall arise on the day of judgment against all sinners.

12,248. WITNESS OF THE SPIRIT, Doctrine of. Wilson condenses from Rev. C. Prest, some testimonies to this doctrine. Novatian, A.D. 250, in his work on the Trinity, speaks very distinctly of the Holy Ghost as the author of regeneration; the pledge of the promised inheritance, and, as it were, the handwriting of eternal salvation. Chrysostom, A. D. 398, teaches that the testimony declared Romans 8: 16, "is not the voice of the gift or grace which is conferred upon us, but of the comforting Spirit, inwardly assuring us that we are the sons of God." Bernard, A. D. 1115, in Sermon V., "That which lieth hid concerning us in the heart of the Father, may by his Spirit be revealed unto us; and the same Spirit, testifying unto us, may persuade our spirits that we are the sons of God." Calvin, A. D. 1539, on Romans 8: 16, says, "St. Paul means, that the Spirit of God gives such a testimony to us, that he being our guide and teacher, our spirit perceives our adoption of God to be certain. For our own mind, of itself, independent of the preceding testimony of the Spirit, could not produce this persuasion in us. For whilst the Spirit witnesses that we are the sons of God, he at the same time inspires this confidence in our minds."

12,249. WITNESS OF THE SPIRIT, Testimony to the. Owen, A. D. 1657, on communion with God; "The Spirit worketh joy in the hearts of believers immediately by himself, without the consideration of any other acts or works of his, or the interpositions of any reasonings, or deductions, or conclusions. This does not arise from our reflex consideration of the love of God, but rather gives occasion thereunto. He so sheds abroad the love of God in our hearts, and fills them with gladness by an immediate act and operation." And again: "The Comforter comes; and by a word of promise, or otherwise, overpowers the heart with a comfortable persuasion, (and bears down all objections,) that he is a child of God." Isaac Ambrose, A. D. 1652, in his "Middle Things:" "The Spirit gives a distinct witness of his own, which is his immediate work, and

is in a way of peculiarity and transcendency called, 'the witness of the Spirit.' And this evidence is solitary, without reference to inherent graces; yet, however, it excludes them not." In the confession of faith issued by the assembly of divines, under the article Assurance, in the third edition, 1688, we read: "This certainly is not a bare conjectural and probable persuasion, but an infallible assurance of faith, founded upon the testimony of the spirit of adoption witnessing with our spirit that we are the children of God."
C. Prest.

12,250. WIVES, Disciplining. It is not surprising that in the establishment of an African with several wives, there should sometimes occur "family jars." When these are so serious as to defy the authority of the master of the house, which is not unfrequently the case, recourse is had to an institution called Mumbo Jumbo. This is a person unknown, with a mask on his face, a staff in his hand, and robed in a singular dress made of the bark of a tree. When he is seen entering a village in the dusk of the evening, and approaching the *bentang*, where the people are assembling for their usual amusements, great is the curiosity excited as to the parties who may have occasioned the visit of the mysterious personage. There are many palpitations and heart-searchings among the ladies whose consciences tell them that they have not been remarkably loving, mild and pacific in their respective families. At length Mumbo Jumbo, with unerring aim, seizes upon the unfortunate vixen to be punished for her misconduct. He strips her naked, ties her to a post, and severely beats her with his rod till she cries for mercy, and promises not to offend again, whilst the bystanders of both sexes look on with derisive bursts of laughter, and shouts of savage joy, forgetting that their turn to be punished may soon come. This Mumbo Jumbo may be the husband of the lady thus chastised, or it may be his friend whose services have been engaged for the occasion. Having executed his office in perfect disguise, he retires in the darkness of the night, takes of his dress, and hangs it up in a tree near the village, where it remains suspended, *in terrorem*, as a standing warning to unruly wives. Some of the African ladies think there ought to be instituted a Mumbo Jumbo for naughty husbands as well as disobedient wives.
Moister.

12,251. WOMAN, Ornaments of. Crates said, "That is ornament which adorns; and that adorns a woman which renders her more comely and decent. This is an honor conferred upon her, not by the lustre of gold, the sparkling of emeralds and diamonds, nor splendor of the purple tincture, but by the real embellishments of gravity, discretion, humility and modesty."

12,252. WOMAN, Perfection of. A beautiful and chaste woman is the perfect workmanship of God, the true glory of angels, the rare miracle of earth, and the sole wonder of the world.
Hermes.

12,253. WOMAN, Right of. Kings say they

reign by divine right, and impiously stamp *Rex Dei gratia* upon innocent copper; but woman is the only sovereign who can justly use these words, and she may, "I am a woman by the grace of God." She alone rules by divine right.   *Theodore Parker.*

12,254. WOMAN, Sympathy of. A recent traveler says, "I have always remarked that women in all countries are civil, obliging, tender and humane. To a woman, whether civilized or savage, I never addressed myself in the language of decency and friendship without receiving a decent and friendly answer. With man it has often been otherwise. In wandering over the barren plains of inhospitable Denmark, through honest Sweden and frozen Lapland, rude and churlish Finland, unprincipled Russia, and the widespread regions of the wandering Tartar, if hungry, dry, cold, wet or sick, the women have ever been friendly to me, and uniformly so: and to add to this virtue (so worthy the appellation of benevolence), these actions have been performed in so free and kind a manner, that if I was dry, I drank the sweetest draught, and if hungry, I ate the coarsest morsel with a double relish."

12,255. WOMAN, Temptation of. Woman is often abused because Mother Eve did not throw the apple in the serpent's face, instead of being wheedled into eating it. But, if it had been offered to her precious spouse, he would not have stood there, Shall—I—shall I —ing? but would merely have said, "Apples, indeed! so early! Thank ye, Mister Snake!" and would have eaten it without thinking of conscience. Now, the sons of this biped pique themselves upon being men, not women.
                              Theodore Parker.

12,256. WOMEN, Heathen Hatred of. Cato the Censor had such a hatred for women that it was his common saying, "That if the world was without women, the conversation of men would not be exempt from the company of the gods." Hyppolitus said in Seneca that he hated, cursed, and detested them all. That water would dwell kindly with fire, or the morning light should brighten from the west, or wolves would lie down calmly with lambs, ere he would give over his hatred of the female sex.

12,257. WOMEN, Power of. Whatever may be the customs and laws of a country, the women of it decide the morals. Free or subjugated, they reign, because they hold possession of our passions. But their influence is more or less salutary, according to the degree of esteem which is granted them. Whether they are our idols or companions, courtesans or beasts of burthen, the reaction is complete, and they make us such as they are themselves. It seems as if Nature connected our intelligence with their dignity, as we connect our morality with their virtue. This, therefore, is a law of eternal justice: man cannot degrade woman without himself falling into degradation; he cannot raise them without himself becoming better. Let us cast our eyes over the globe, and observe those two great divi-

sions of the human race, the East and the West. One half of the ancient world remains without progress or thought, and under the load of a barbarous cultivation; women there are slaves. The other half advances toward freedom and light: the women are loved and honored.   *Martin.*

12,258. WOMEN, Resolute. The Thessalonians were marching upon the Phocians with the announced intention of slaying all the men, and selling all the women and children into slavery. Diaphantus proposed that the men should fight the Thessalonians, and the women and children be gathered in one place and surrounded with combustibles whereby they might be burned to ashes, sooner than fall into the enemy's hands. The vote was taken, and women and children agreed to sacrifice themselves. The Phocians, joining battle at Cleone, fought desperately, remembering their wives and children, and won the victory. This resolution of the Phocian women was honored with a festival for many years.

12,259. WOMEN, Strength of. 'Tis a powerful sex; they were too strong for the first, the strongest and the wisest man that was; they must needs be strong when one hair of a woman can draw more than a hundred pair of oxen!
                              Howell.

12,260. WOMEN, Unmarried. I speculate much on the existence of unmarried and never-to-be-married women nowadays; and I have already got to the point of considering that there is no more respectable character on this earth than an unmarried woman, who makes her own way through life quietly, perseveringly, without support of husband or brother; and who retains in her possession a well-regulated mind, a disposition to enjoy simple pleasures, and fortitude to support inevitable pains, sympathy with the sufferings of others, and willingness to relieve want as far as her means extend.   *Charlotte Bronté.*

12,261. WOMEN, Usefulness of. Women, so amiable in themselves, are never so amiable as when they are useful; and as for beauty, though men may fall in love with girls at play, there is nothing to make them stand to their love like seeing them at work. *Cobbett.*

12,262. WORD, The Divine. The divine person who has accomplished the salvation of mankind is called the Word, and the Word of God, Rev. 19: 13; not only because God at first created, and still governs all things, by him, but because, as men discover their sentiments and designs to one another by the intervention of words, speech, or discourse, so God by his Son discovers his gracious designs in the fullest and clearest manner to men.
                              Igdalia.

12,263. WORD, Influence of the. A tree which is fastened unto a wall, in which the heat of the sun is more permanent and united, will bring forth ripe fruit before the ordinary season: so a people upon whom the light of the gospel hath constantly shined, and which doth often drink in the rain which falleth upon it, must needs bring forth summer-fruit, sins speedily ripe, and, therefore, be so much nearer unto cursing. There is but a year between such a tree and the fire. *Bp. Reynolds.*

12,264. WORD, Power of the. Though men were as hard as rocks, the Word is a hammer which can break them; though as sharp as thorns and briers the Word is a fire which can devour and torment them; though as strong as kingdoms and nations, the Word is able to root them up, and to pull them down; though as fierce as dragons and lions, the Word is able to trample upon them and chain them up.
Bp. Reynolds.

12,265. WORD, Sharpness of God's. The Jewish priest required a strong and skillful hand to do the ordinary work of his holy calling. It needed both strength and skill to lay the victim on the altar, to guide the sharp two-edged sacrificial knife straight through the carcass, till the very back-bone was severed, the whole laid bare, and the very joints and marrow exposed and separated. For this reason (as well as because he was a type of him who is perfect), because such persons ordinarily are deficient in bodily strength, no deformed person could be high priest, he could not do the work required of him. There is a knife sharper than that two-edged sword, and a hand to guide its blade and apply its edges and point, stronger and surer than the Jewish priest's. That knife is the Word of God: it is a "living" word; it has a power to lay open hearts far greater than that sacrificial knife had to lay bare the bodies of the sacrifice; its edge is sharper than that of the two-edged sword; and, when driven home and directed by the hand of the almighty Spirit, "it pierces even to the dividing asunder of the joints and marrow, the soul and spirit," and lays bare "the thoughts and intents of the heart." *W. W. Champneys.*

12,266. WORDS, Choice of. I have first considered whether it be worth while to say a thing at all, before I have taken any trouble to say it well; knowing that words are but air, and that both are capable of much condensation. Words indeed are but the signs and counters of knowledge, and their currency should be strictly regulated by the capital which they represent. *Colton.*

12,267. WORDS, Good and Evil. Dost thou not see how God putteth forth a parable, representing a good word as a good tree, whose root is firmly fixed in the earth and whose branches reach unto heaven, which bringeth forth its fruit at all seasons by the will of its Lord? And the likeness of an evil word is an evil tree, which is torn up from the face of the earth, and hath no stability. *Koran.*

12,268. WORDS, Power of. Words, when well chosen, have so great a force in them, that a description often gives us more lively ideas than the sight of things themselves. The reader finds a scene drawn in stronger colors, and painted more to the life in his imagination, by the help of words, than by an actual survey of the scene which they describe.
Addison

12,269. WORDS, Seasonable. It is a special piece of wisdom to improve the season of sickness for the good of thy neighbor's soul. When the wax is softened, then we clap the seal upon it, lest it harden again, and be incapable of any impression. When the hand of God hath by sickness made the heart of thy wicked friend or brother soft and tender, then do thy utmost to stamp the image of God upon it. Paul would preach whilst a door was open, and there was likelihood of doing good. It is a great encouragement to work, when the subject upon which we bestow our pains seems capable of what we prosecute, and probable to answer our labor. We have some heart to strike a nail into a board, because there is hope it will enter; but no list to drive a nail into a flint, because we despair of effecting it. The smith strikes when the iron is hot; he knoweth, if he should stay till it is cold, his labor would be in vain. *Swinnock.*

12,270. WORDS Seeds. Cast forth thy act, thy word, into the ever-living, ever-working universe: it is a seed-grain that cannot die; unnoticed to-day, it will be found flourishing as a banyan grove, perhaps, also, as a hemlock forest, after a thousand years. *Carlyle.*

12,271. WORK, Adaptation to. Work is the key that has unlocked all the treasures throughout the centuries. Nature is a workshop. She carries on an infinite variety of activities. She has all tools. She has a bench and kit for every mortal, where the tools and the hands match. The misplacing of workmen and the mixing of tools are not her fault. To bring each to his own stall is no small part of the work to be done. Nature simply makes this possible by furnishing both the stalls and men.
Dr. C. H. Fowler.

12,272. WORK, Enthusiastic. The bulbous-headed fellows that steam well when they are at work, are the men that draw big audiences, and give us marrowy books and pictures. It is a good sign to have one's feet grow cold when he is writing. A great writer and speaker once told me that he often wrote with his feet in hot water; but for this, all his blood would have run into his head, as the mercury sometimes withdraws into the ball of a thermometer. *Browne.*

12,273. WORK, Gospel of. The latest gospel in this world is, know thy work and do it. "Know thyself;" long enough has that poor "self" of thine tormented thee; thou wilt never get to "know" it, I believe! Think it not thy business, this of knowing thyself: thou art an unknowable individual: know what thou canst work at, and work at it like a Hercules! That will be thy better plan.
Carlyle.

12,274. WORK, Happiness of. The only happiness a brave man ever troubled himself with asking much about was happiness enough to get his work done. Not "I can't eat!" but, "I can't work!"—that was the burden of all wise complaining among men. It is, after all, the one unhappiness of a man—that he cannot work; that he cannot get his destiny as a man fulfilled. Behold, the day is passing

swiftly over, our life is passing swiftly away, and the night cometh, wherein no man can work. The night once come, our happiness, our unhappiness,—it is all abolished, vanished, clean gone; a thing that has been: "not of the slightest consequence" whether we were happy as eupeptic Curtis, as the fattest pig of Epicurus, or unhappy as Job with pot-sherds, as musical Byron with Giaours and sensibilities of the heart; as the unmusical meat-jack with hard labor and rust! But our work!—behold, that is not abolished, that has not vanished: our work, behold, it remains, or the want of it remains—for endless times and eternities, remains; and that is now the sole question with us for evermore! Brief brawling day, with its noisy phantasms, its poor paper crowns tinsel-gilt, is gone, and divine everlasting night, with her star-diadems, with her silences and her veracities, is come!
Carlyle.

12,275. WORK, Honest. St. Tyllo, of Collogue, was educated as a goldsmith, and was noted for his skill, honesty, and piety. He wrought curious vessels, and set rare gems for the king. His motto was, "Whatsoever ye would that men should do unto you, do ye even so unto them." As he wrought he studied the Bible, which he always kept open before him. From the shop he was called to the office of an abbot. We want more saints in the workshops.

12,276. WORK, Incentive in. An ordinary mechanic, for instance a maker of musical instruments, would be much more attentive and pleased at his work if he knew that his harp would be touched by the famous Amphion, and in his hand serve for the builder of Thebes, or if that Thales had bespoke it, who was so great a master that by the force of his music he pacified a popular tumult amongst the Lacedæmonians. *Plutarch.*

12,277. WORK, Influence of. Sir S. Romilly refused to speak in popular assemblies, confining himself to the House of Commons, where a measure can be carried by a speech. The business of the House of Commons is conducted by a few persons, but these are hard-worked. Sir Robert Peel "knew the Blue Books by heart." His colleagues and rivals carry Hansard in their heads. The high civil and legal offices are not beds of ease, but posts which exact frightful amounts of mental labor. Many of the great leaders, like Pitt, Canning, Castlereagh, Romilly, are soon worked to death. They are excellent judges in England of a good worker, and when they find one, like Clarendon, Sir Philip Warwick, Sir William Coventry, Ashley, Burke, Thurlow, Mansfield, Pitt, Eldon, Peel, or Russell, there is nothing too good or too high for him. *Emerson.*

12,278. WORK, Library of. The vast sum of inventions is an immense library, whose every page is some crowded, agonizing life-record. Step by step, up from barbarism to beauty and power, is the toiling march. Every inch that has been gained and held has been secured by some unresting soul. The multiplicity of achievements, from reapers for our harvest to gas for our streets, from spindles for our factories to cables for our oceans, all have a history of toil. The cook, the dentist, the doctor, the shoemaker, the tailor, the engineer, prepare better nutriments, better securities, and more abundant vitality. Old veins are filled with new blood, and old nerves with new electricity; but all this represents fifty years of harvest and fifty centuries of seed-time, and both are work-days. *Dr. C. H. Fowler.*

12,279. WORK, Out-door. Perhaps there are some of my readers who do no out-of-door work for Christ, who neither plough the ground for him, nor feed his sheep. Ploughing is hard, and to our dainty notions, soiling work; and so we will not plough for Christ. It is hard work to lift one's foot in the heavy clay—to set it down often only to lift it up with greater difficulty still; nothing springs up immediately from the ploughing, the prospect of harvest gain must be remote, and so you plough not— and what, if neither shall you reap? Oh, if there were a speedy return for their toil, perhaps some of the Lord's people who now do nothing would undertake labor on his behalf. If, in the fields around us, as men turned up the furrow, the reaper overtook the sower, and the seed threw up its sprouts, beneath the ploughman's very steps, carpeting his feet with green; if, as they sweated in ploughing, the sprouts became headed with grain, and cooled the laborer's fevered brows with the breezes which undulated the waving corn, murmuring like the melodies of another world, amid the bending stalks, as slowly, and solemnly, and keeping time to the beat of some unseen hand, they sway to and fro—if this were the ploughman's lot, and ere the earth was reddened with the steel—man's toil on earth, it became gilded with the harvest—God's gift from heaven; daintier hands than any which now guide the plough would be engaged in the almost poetic toil; but such is not earthly ploughing, and such is not heavenly ploughing either; and because it is present labor with only a future profit, and present toil, and present offence to our fastidious tastes, some of the Lord's people are leaving his out-of-door work undone.
Power.

12,280. WORK, Physical. Dr. H. W. Warren says that a man doing his best work, shoveling sand, or pumping water, could do no more in his whole life time than could be accomplished by three tons of coal. His moral is that man had better go to the Allegheny mountains, dig out three tons of coal, and take his exit, if his only purpose is manual labor.

12,281. WORK, Test of. Work is the divine test of greatness. It is a quaint old law, as it stands in the New Testament, that the chiefest must serve most; but so it also stands in the order of the universe. We honor the men who serve most. In times of great national peril some man steps to the front and does a hero's work, and, whether he will or no, he must thereafter bear a hero's honors. Some man hews his way through all the walls of past ignorance, and discovers a new world or lays an ocean cable, and for his great service he must be rewarded. Serving most he becomes chiefest. How simple this makes all the questions of ambition and fame! The one thing that is always sure to be appreciated is work. Every man can afford to work, and take the consequences in due time.   *Dr. C. H. Fowler.*

12,282. WORK, Whose? You cannot serve two masters—you must serve one or other. If your work is first with you, and your fee second, work is your master, and the Lord of work, who is God. But if your fee is first with you, and your work second, fee is your master, and the lord of fee, who is the devil; and not only the devil, but the lowest of devils—"the least erected fiend that fell." So there you have it in brief terms—work first, you are God's servants; fee first, you are the fiend's. And it makes a difference, now and ever, believe me, whether you serve him who has on his vesture and thigh written, "King of kings," and whose service is perfect freedom; or him on whose vesture and thigh the name is written, "Slave of slaves," and whose service is perfect slavery.   *Ruskin.*

12,283. WORKS, Immortality by. William of Wickham was appointed by King Edward III. to build a stately church. It was a great success, and won him much fame. The architect wrote on one of the windows, "This work made William Wickham." Afterward the king charged him with assuming the honor of the work. He explained that he had only affirmed that the work made him; as he was before poor, but now in good credit; before unknown but now famous. Works make men, and are the test of men.

12,284. WORLD, Burning the. Chemistry says water will burn. Your firemen will tell you the same thing. Geology says that we live upon a cooled crust, and that the central parts of the earth are liquid fire. Let now one of those forces of the upheaval of continents, which geologists have at their command when they need them, break up the bed of the Pacific ocean, and let down the ocean of water upon the ocean of fire, and how long will it be before the old chaos will be upon us? Or, if we take the dynamic theory of heat, Tyndall tells us, that simply to stop the earth in its orbit, would generate heat enough to dissipate the whole of it into vapor. I suppose that is science, as much so, certainly, as the speculations of geologists. Add to this what is now known of the decomposing and rending power of all-pervasive imponderable agents, of which we can have no conception. Faraday says, that in a single drop of water there is latent electricity enough for an ordinary flash of lightning. Add this, and we shall see that science joins with the Bible in labeling the earth, "reserved unto fire."   *Hopkins.*

12,285. WORLD, Christian and the. The bird of paradise, which has such a dower of exquisitely beautiful feathers, cannot fly with the wind; if it attempts to do so, the current, being much swifter than its flight, so ruffles its plumage as to impede its progress, and finally to terminate it; it is, therefore, compelled to fly against the wind, which keeps its feathers in their place, and thus it gains the place where it would be. So the Christian must not attempt to go with the current of a sinful world; if he does, it will not only hinder, but end his religious progress; but he must go against it, and then every effort of his soul will surely be upward, Godward.   *Dr. Davies.*

12,286. WORLD, Deception of the. A lady being once told that the world in all its glory was but vanity, returned for answer, "True, I have heard that Solomon said so; but he tried it before he said it, and so will I." He that knocks at the creature's door for supplies, will find an empty house kept there. "All the rivers run into the sea, yet the sea is not full." Though all the rising streams of worldly profits may run into the hearts of men, yet they cannot fill up the hearts of men.   *Secker.*

12,287. WORLD, Hero of the. The hero of the world is the man that makes a bustle—the man that makes the road smoke under his chaise-and-four—the man that raises a dust about him—the man that manages or devastates empires!   *R. Cecil.*

12,288. WORLD, Offers of the. When Darius, king of Persia, offered Alexander all the country which lies at the west of the Euphrates, with his daughter Statira in marriage, and 10,000 talents of gold, Parmenio took occasion to observe, that he would without hesitation accept of these conditions, if he were Alexander. "So would I, were I Parmenio," replied the conqueror. Thus a Christian must not accept of any proposition made by the world beneath the dignity of his character, but must fight the good fight of faith.   *Buck.*

12,289. WORLD, Preferring this. It was the saying of a cardinal, "I prefer a part in the honors of Paris to a part in the happiness of paradise." What is the glimmering of a candle to the shining of the sun? or the value of brass compared with gold? Thoughtless children are taken up more with present counters than with future crowns. Thus, while the shadow is embraced, the substance is neglected; and short-sighted man courts the vail, when he should admire the face.   *Secker.*

12,290. WORLD, Reflective Character of the. We may be pretty certain that persons whom all the world treat ill deserve entirely the treatment they get. The world is a looking-glass, and gives back to every man the reflection of his own face. Frown at it, and it will in turn look sourly upon you; laugh at it and with it, and it is a jolly, kind companion; and so let all young persons take their choice. *Thackeray.*

12,291. WORLD, This and the Next. They say the sinner drags the harrow in this world, and the wagon in the world to come.   *Tauler.*

12,292. WORLD, Unreliable. Everything below is too base for the soul's nobility, and too brittle for the soul's stability. Who would set that vessel under the droppings of a cistern, which is able to contain all the waters of the ocean.   *Secker*

12,293. WORLDLINESS, Absorption of. Mrs. H. More, says her biographer, "after pointing out to us some of the many beautiful objects to be seen from the room in which we were sitting, conducted us into an adjoining apartment, which was her sleeping room; and pointing to an arm chair, 'that chair,' said she, 'I call my home. Here,' looking out of a window, 'is what I call my moral prospect. You see yonder distant hill which limits the prospect in that direction. You see this tree before my window directly in range of the hill. The tree, you observe from being near, appears higher than the hill which is distant; though the hill actually is much higher than the tree. Now this tree represents to my mind the objects of time; that hill, the objects of eternity. The former, like the tree, from being reviewed near at hand, appears great. The latter, like the distant hill, appears small.'"

12,294. WORLDLINESS, Effects of. Mithridates was overcome in battle by Lucullus, and sought safety in flight. Seeing his pursuers were gaining upon him, he caused great quantities of gold to be scattered in the way. The Romans stopped to pick up the treasure, and Mithridates escaped. Their avarice deprived them of the fruits of their victory.

12,295. WORLDLINESS, Diversion of. Martin de Golin, master of the Teutonic order, was taken prisoner by the Prussians, and delivered bound to be beheaded. But he persuaded his executioner first to take off his costly clothes, which otherwise would be spoiled with the sprinkling of the blood. Now the prisoner, being partially unbound to be unclothed, and finding his arms somewhat loosened, struck the executioner to the ground, killed him afterwards with his own sword, and so regained both his life and liberty. We are all Achans by nature, and the Babylonish garment is a bait for our covetousness; whilst therefore we ask to take the plunder of this wardrobe, we let go the mastery we had formerly of it. *T. Fuller.*

12,296. WORLDLINESS, End of. If riches have been your idol hoarded up in your coffers, or lavished out upon yourselves, they will, when the day of reckoning comes, be like the garment of pitch and brimstone, which is put on the criminal condemned to the flames. *Hervey.*

12,297. WORLDLINESS, Fate of. Tamerlane had great success as a warrior, and desired to make further conquests, but was afraid that the terror of his arms would precede him, and cause the people to hide their treasures. So he sent soldiers dressed in the habit of merchantmen, with camels laden with rich booty, into the richest cities of Asia. He commanded that the articles should be sold at very low prices, that the people might be induced to bring out their gold and silver and buy. Then before they could hide their treasures again, Tamerlane would sweep down upon them unawares, and plunder them of all they had.

12,298. WORLDLING, Dying Cry of a. The lamentable cry of poor Adrain, when he felt death approaching was, "Oh my poor wandering soul! alas! whither art thou going! where

must thou lodge this night? Thou shalt never jest more, never be merry more!" *Flavel.*

12,299. WORLDLING, Symbol of the. I have seen a poor blind worm on the top of a slender pole, stretching every ring of its fragile form, and groping all round in vacant space—tingling with impatience to climb higher, but doomed to stop there. It was a caterpillar, whom a rough wind had shaken from the green tree where it was quietly feeding. When it found itself on the hard ground, it wandered about "in dry places seeking rest and finding none," till it reached the bottom of this wall —the foot of this pole—and then it climbed. But you see it has made nothing of it. The green-painted pole is a very different thing from the leafy tree it used to live in. Poor creature!—it is hungry; and the reason why it runs along, and stretches upward so anxiously, is, if happily it may find the juicy foliage it once fed upon. It will never find it there. Up among the branches of the tree of life man once had his home, his resting-place—and there he fed sweetly; but a rough storm of temptation shook him down; and now he runs about among the "dry places seeking rest, and finding none." And you will sometimes find him —poor groveling worm! fallen man!—trying to better himself by climbing up some painted pole; and once he gains its top, you will see him exploring blindly round in emptiness; feeling for some higher object on which to rest —some green thing for his hungry soul to feed on; pivoting and balancing himself, and stretching outward and upward. But the tree of life is not there. Till it comes to live on God himself, the hungry soul of man never will be satisfied. *F. F. Trench.*

12,300. WORSHIP, Be Punctual at. Be in you place; battles are won not by the men on the muster-roll, but by the men in the engagement. As a rule, sermons are none too warm; an empty pew throws a bucket of cold water over the pulpit. We have seen very good preachers, like very good gophers, drowned out. Every seat in the prayer-meeting is occupied; when you are not in your seat there, some evil spirit occupies it, trying to represent you. *Dr. C. H. Fowler.*

12,301. WORSHIP, Devotion in. We have some instances in history which should shame us as Christians, and teach us to cultivate a spirit of attention and solemnity both in the closet and in the public worship of God. It is said when the troops had broken into the city of Jerusalem, the people fled some one way and some another, but the priests went on with their sacrifices and the holy rites of the temple, as if they heard nothing; though they rushed in with their swords, yet they preferred their duty to their safety. *Buck.*

12,302. WORSHIP, Dress for. The Mohammedans think it indecent to come into God's presence in a slovenly manner. So they imagine that they ought not to appear before him in habits too rich or sumptuous, and particularly in clothes adorned with gold or silver, lest they should seem proud. *George Sale.*

12,303. WORSHIP, Domestic. Every man ought to consider himself as the minister and steward of the church in his own house. And it is his own fault, and, let me add, his folly, if the church in his house be not a lively and genuine part of that branch of Christ's Holy Catholic Church to which he himself belongs. *Bishop Blomfield.*

12,304. WORSHIP, Heartless. Without the heart it is no worship; it is a stage play: an acting a part without being that person really which is acted by us: a hypocrite, in the notion of the world, is a stage-player. We may as well say a man may believe with his body, as worship God only with his body. Faith is a great ingredient in worship; and it is "with the heart man believes unto righteousness." We may be truly said to worship God, though we want perfection; but we cannot be said to worship him if we want sincerity; a statue upon a tomb, with eyes and hands lifted up, offers as good and true a service; it wants only a voice, the gestures and postures are the same; nay, the service is better; it is not a mockery; it represents all that it can be framed to; but to worship without our spirits, is a presenting God with a picture, an echo, voice, and nothing else; a compliment; a mere lie; a "compassing him about with lies." *Charnock.*

12,305. WORSHIP, Holiness of. The holiness of God's *worship* is stamped on the very name sanctuary, *i. e.*, a holy place. It was marked most prominently in every part of the tabernacle worship; in the "holy sanctuary," the unblemished sacrifices offered upon the "holy altar," by holy persons, in holy garments, with holy vessels, and in the observance of the holy Sabbath, and the presenting of holy gifts. Everything about the service of the Lord was to be holy—"holy water," "holy ointment," etc. When the altar of burnt-offering at the entrance of the tabernacle is declared to be most holy, the marginal reading is still more emphatic—"It shall be an altar *holiness of holinesses*," Exod. 40: 10. *Bowes.*

12,306. WORSHIP, Jewish. Hardy thus describes the worship in the largest synagogue in Jerusalem: "The women sat at the entrance and in the outer court. The service was chanted, in general by the whole assembly. Nearly all had books in their hands, and they moved their bodies to and fro continually, in conformity, as they say, to the words of David, 'All my bones shall praise thee.' It was mournful to see old men suddenly, with an expression near to agony, lifting up their long, thin, fleshless fingers toward heaven, and crying aloud, as if to say, 'Lord, how long?'"

12,307. WORSHIP, Selfish. "He had respect to the recompense of reward." This might be a good glass to look through, but it is a bad object to look to. The poets report, that many who at first paid their suits to the famous Penelope, were afterwards married to the maidens who attended her. The ass which carried the Egyptian goddess, had many bare heads and bended knees before it; but they were all to the burden, and none to the beast. Thus many are advocates for the enjoyment of happiness, and enemies to the employment of holiness. Demetrius cries up the goddess Diana; yet it was not her temple, but her silver shrines, he so much adored. He was more in love with her wealth, than with her worship. "Sirs, ye know that by this craft we have our wealth." *Secker.*

12,308. WORSHIP, Sensuous. It is indeed the fact that things sensuous in connection with the spiritual help those who are spiritual rather than those who are sensuous. The sensuous lose themselves in them, and in the feelings which they excite; the spiritual make them instruments of truth and holiness. The sensuous are like Jacob lying on the hard ground, dreamily looking at the ladder between heaven and earth, as a beauteous vision; the spiritual are like the angels of God which ascend and descend upon it. *Morris.*

12,309. WORSHIP, Spiritual. Our worship is spiritual when the door of the heart is shut against all intruders, as our Saviour commands in closet-duties. It was not his meaning to command the shutting the closet-door, and leave the heart-door open for every thought that would be apt to haunt us. Worldly affections are to be laid aside if we would have our worship spiritual; this was meant by the Jewish custom of wiping or washing off the dust of their feet before their entrance into the temple, and of not bringing money in their girdles. To be spiritual in worship, is to have our souls gathered and bound up wholly in themselves, and offered to God. *Charnock.*

12,310. WRATH to Come. A man listened to searching appeals to sinners from Mr. Whitfield, and remained unmoved. Then Whitfield, with uplifted hands, and in a flood of tears, cried out, "O, the wrath to come! the wrath to come!" These words entered his heart. Wherever he went the awful knell rang through his soul. He fled to Christ for safety.

12,311. WRATH, Divine. *Burning heat.*— "Hot anger," Judges 2: 14, 20; 3: 8; 10· 7; "hot displeasure," Deut. 9: 19; the anger and jealousy of the Lord smoking against sinners, Deut. 29: 20; "fiery indignation" (the terrible anger of insulted mercy). The *vintage-wine-press*—wine, used especially in the Book of Revelation. *Vials* "full of the wrath of God," Rev. 15: 7, 16; the concentration of Divine fury. The *cup* of fury—dregs of the cup of trembling, Jer. 25: 15, 17. "*Vessels of wrath*, fitted to destruction," Rom. 9: 22. "*Children of wrath*," Eph. 2: 8. "The *day of wrath*," Rom. 2: 5; Rev. 6: 17. Three times in Isaiah "the *day* of vengeance" is contrasted with "the *year* of the redeemed." "The *wrath of God*" revealed—coming— poured out—abiding—filled up in its awful fullness upon the ungodly. "The *wrath of the Lamb*."—One of the most awful words of Scripture! Christ, "the Lamb of God," "slain from the foundation of the world," so gentle—tender—meek; yet in the day of terror full of wrath and holy vengeance! "The wrath of the Lamb." The word must imply all the indignation of insulted mercy and rejected love! *Bowes.*

12,312. WRATH, Flee from. Antigonus dreamt that he saw Mithridates reaping a golden harvest. Thereupon he resolved to kill him. He told this to his son Demetrius, at the same time making him swear to conceal his intention. Demetrius took Mithridates to walk with him by the sea side. With the point of his spear he wrote the words, "Fly, Mithridates." He fled into Pontus where he reigned, by his flight saving his life, and gaining a kingdom. Sinner, fly to Christ and you shall save your soul from death and gain the kingdom of eternal glory.

12,313. WRATH, Reserved. I once took tea with a lady who was very particular about her china. The servant unfortunately broke the best bread-and-butter plate; but her mistress took very little notice of the circumstance at the time, only remarking, "Never mind, Mary, never mind, accidents cannot be prevented." "I shall have it by-and-by," said the servant, when she got out of the room; and so it turned out. The good woman's temper was corked up for a season, but it came out with terrible vengeance when the company retired. *Rowland Hill.*

12,314. WRATH, Treasuring up. Every man is treasuring up stores for eternity; the good are laying up treasures in heaven, where moth doth not corrupt; the evil and impenitent are "treasuring up wrath against the day of wrath." What an idea is this! Treasures of wrath! Whatever the impenitent man is doing, he is treasuring up wrath. He may be getting wealth; but he is treasuring up wrath. He may be getting fame; but he is treasuring up wrath. He may be forming pleasing connections; but he is also treasuring up wrath: every day adds something to the heap. Every oath the swearer utters, there is something gone to the heap of wrath. Every lie the liar tells, every licentious act the lewd man commits, adds something to the treasure of wrath. The sinner has a weightier treasure of wrath to-day than he had yesterday; he will have a weightier to-morrow than he has to-day. When he lies down at night, he is richer in vengeance than when he arose in the morning. He is continually deepening and darkening his eternal portion. Every neglected Sabbath increases his store of wrath; every forgotten sermon adds something to the weight of punishment. All the checks of conscience, all the remonstrances of friends, all the advice and prayers of parents, will be taken into the account; and all will tend to increase the treasures of wrath laid up against the day of wrath. *J. A. James.*

12,315. WRECK, Warnings of. Sailing down the Thames, one occasionally sees a green flag, inscribed with the word WRECK over a piece of mast, or the funnel of a steamer, which is just visible above the water. Alas, how many lives ought thus be marked, lest they prove ruinous to others! The debauched, the self-righteous, the spendthrift, the apostate, the drunken,—how appropriately might the flag be placed over them, for they each are a wreck! *Spurgeon.*

12,316. WRECKERS, Work of. "Lukewarm" professors are like the wreckers on the Florida reefs, who kindle false lights to lure the vessels to destruction. A ship is coming in after nightfall. The night is dark and stormy. The sea runs high. The ship labors. The tempest howls through the rigging. The great waves smite her. The master paces the quarter-deck, anxious and watchful. Oh! if he could see the harbor-light to guide him in the safe channel. He hails the "look-out" in the maintop: "Hallo, aloft!" "Ay, ay, sir." "Do you see the light?" "No light." And again keen eyes peer through the darkness. The vessel rushes blindly on her course. Ah! is that the combing of the breaker? "Hallo, aloft! do you see the light?" "No-o-o!" The storm increases. The vessel groans and strains in every timber. The sea rages. And now the shout comes down: "On deck, there! I see the light!" "Where away?" "Two points off the lee bow." "Steady, quartermaster; keep her full!" And on she ploughs her way, cheered by the guiding light. Ah! what is this? She is in the midst of breakers! And now she strikes on the reef, and the masts "go by the board," and the wreckers come tumbling in over her bulwarks, and their knives are red, and their hands filled with plunder. Their false light has cast away the ship. So a treacherous Christian says to the souls of his fellow-men: "Follow me. I am going into port. I will guide you safely." And following, they come upon the rocks of perdition—and he is a murderer of souls. *President Finney.*

12,317. YEAR, Wail of the Dying. "Listen to me, ye mortals! for I also am of the race of the ephemerals. I had my sturdy youth, when it seemed that my life would never end; and I dug, and ploughed, and planted, and enjoyed my jocund prime and my golden summer; and I decked myself in the garlands of May, and reaped the yellow harvest, and gathed the purple vintage of autumn; but scarcely had I attained the object of my desires, and secured the plenty for which I labored, than I found the shadows lengthening, and the days shortening, and my breath growing short with them, and decrepitude coming upon me, and the days at hand of which I said, 'I have no pleasure in them.' I have laid up riches, and know not who shall gather them; have planted trees which must shade far distant years, and stored the vintage of which other years must drink." *Prof. Rogers.*

12,318. YEARS, Biblical. Years of *weakness* and *sorrow*, Eccles. 12 : 1; years of *visitation* (severe judgments), Jer. 11 : 23; years of *recompenses*, Isa. 34 : 8; years of *rest*, Lev. 25 : 5; and of *release*, Deut. 15 : 1, 9; 31 : 10: the seventh year. Years of *jubilee*, Lev. 25

8–54; 27: 17, 18; the representation of rest —release—liberty—provision—restoration; probably the special type and shadow of millennial happiness; Isa. 61 : 2.—"The *Acceptable year of the Lord*" most probably alludes to this; the special *year of grace*, when debts were remitted, forfeited inheritances restored, servants set at liberty, and general rest and peace enjoyed. Year of *the Lord's redeemed*, Isa. 63 : 4. Years of *forbearance*, Luke 13 : 7. Years of *probation*, Luke 13 : 8. Years of *revival*, Hab. 3 : 2; Years of *death*, Jer. 28 : 16, 17.—"This year thou shalt die." *Bowes*.

12,319. YES and No. Man's first word is— Yes; his second—No; his third and last— Yes. Most stop short at the first; very few get to the last. *Attwell*.

12,320. YOUNG, Counsel to the. Might I give counsel to my young hearer, I would say, Try to frequent the company of your betters; in books and life that is the most wholesome society; learn to admire rightly—the great pleasure of life is that. Note what the great specially admire; they admire great things: narrow spirits admire basely, and worship meanly. *Thackeray*.

12,321. YOUNG MAN, Salvation of a. A young captain in the English army, found after the battle that his Bible had been struck by a musket-ball, which penetrated to the text, Ecclesiastes 11 : 9, "Rejoice, O young man, in thy youth; and let thy heart cheer thee in the days of thy youth, and walk in the ways of thine heart, and in the sight of thine eyes; but know thou, that for all these things God will bring thee into judgment." His Bible saved his life, and this providence was the means of awakening and saving his soul.

12,322. YOUNG MEN, Advice to. Taste not of fish that have black tails; that is, converse not with men that are smutted with vicious qualities. Stride not over the beam of the scales; wherein is taught us the regard we ought to have for justice, so as not to go beyond its measures. Sit not on a choenix; wherein sloth is forbidden and we are required to take care to provide ourselves with the necessaries of life. Do not strike hands with every man; this means we ought not to be over-hasty to make acquaintance or friendship with others. Wear not a tight ring; that is we are to labor after a free and independent way of living, and to submit to no fetters. Eat not thy heart; which forbids to afflict our souls, and waste them with vexatious cares. Abstain from beans; that is, keep out of public offices, for anciently the choice of the officers of state was made by beans. *Plutarch*.

12,323. YOUNG MEN Defined. I used to think that young men were men of 17, or 20, or possibly 25. When I was a lad, I thought if ever I reached 30 I should be a man of mature years; and should I ever arrive at 50 I should be an old man. But as I have passed from decade to decade, until I have gone over all these boundary lines, I feel that I have not got out of the sphere of young men. I find young men older than I am. I think of the words of the Apostle: "I write to you, young men, because you are strong." As long as a man is strong he is a young man. As long as a man is strong—be he 20 or be he 60—his heart is young. He may be a boy; he may be a grandfather; he is a young man. In trying to draw the line, I have thought that some are old at 20, and some are young at 300—or say, a thousand. The great trees of California, botanists say, have been growing since Noah's flood. They show very little signs of age yet. They are still strong, flourishing, beautiful, and I have come to the conclusion that men are very much like those trees. A tree is never to be counted old as long as its heart is sound, and it is able to bear fruit. Well, while a man's heart is sound and he is able to do good, I say he is to be classed among young men.

Bp. Simpson.

12,324. YOUNG MEN, Success of. The greatest captains of ancient and modern times, both conquered Italy at twenty-five. Youth, extreme youth, overthrew the Persian empire. Don John, of Austria, won Lepanto at twenty-five, the greatest battle of modern time; had it not been for the jealousy of Philip, the next year he would have been Emperor of Mauritania. Gaston de Foix was only twenty-two when he stood a victor on the plain of Ravenna. Every one remembers Condé and Roeroy at the same age. Gustavus Adolphus died at thirty-eight—look at his captains, that wonderful Duke of Wiemar, only thirty-six when he died. Bauèr himself, after all his miracles, died at forty-five. Cortes was little more than thirty when he gazed upon the golden cupolas of Mexico. When Maurice of Saxony died at thirty-two all Europe acknowledged the loss of the greatest captain and the profoundest statesman of the age. Then there is Nelson, Clive; but these are warriors, and, perhaps, you may think there are greater things than war; I do not. I worship the Lord of Hosts. But take the most illustrious achievements of civil prudence. Innocent III., the greatest of the popes, was the despot of Christendom at thirty-seven. John de Medici was a cardinal at fifteen, and, Guicciardini tells us, baffled with his craft Ferdinand of Aragon himself. He was pope, as Leo X., at thirty-seven. Luther robbed even him of his richest province at thirty-five. Take Ignatius Loyola and John Wesley; they worked with young brains. Ignatius was only thirty when he made his pilgrimage, and wrote the "Spiritual Exercises." Pascal wrote a great work at sixteen (the greatest of Frenchmen), and died at thirty-seven. Ah! that fatal thirty-seven! which reminds me of Byron, greater even as a man than a writer. Was it experience that guided the pencil of Raphael when he painted the palaces of Rome? He died at thirty-seven. Richelieu was secretary of state at thirty-one. Well, then, there are Bolingbroke and Pitt, both ministers before other men leave off cricket. Grotius was in practice at seventeen, and attorney-general at twenty-four. And Acquavivia was general of the Jesuits, ruled every cabinet in Europe, and colonized America before he was thirty-seven. What a career! the secret sway of Europe! that was indeed a position! But it is needless to multiply instances—the history of heroes is the history of youth.   *Disraeli.*

12,325. YOUNG MEN, Temptations of. Cæsarius of Heisterboch relates that Philip, a great necromancer, took a company of Swabian and Bavarian youths to a lonely place, and entertained them at their request, with his incantations. He drew a circle round them with his sword and warned them not to leave it on any account. By his first incantation he surrounded them with armed men who dared them to conflict, but none were lured forth. By his second enchantment he surrounded them with a company of beautiful dancing damsels, who tried every power of attraction upon them. A nymph, whose beauty exceeded all others, advanced to one of the young men and wrought such effect upon him, that he forgot the restriction and stretched forth his finger beyond the circle to receive the ring which she proffered. She at once seized him and drew him after her. It was not till after much trouble that the necromancer was able to recover him. This circle is the rule of right and virtue. The armed men are pride, ambition, passion. The charmers are intemperance, voluptuousness and sensuality. The only safety is within the circle. The first finger over the line and the whole body will follow to shame and ruin.

12,326. YOUTH, Counsel to. Vigor, energy, resolution, firmness of purpose,—these carry the day. Is there one whom difficulties dishearten—who bend to the storm? He will do little. Is there one who will conquer? That man never fails. Let it be your first study to teach the world that you are not wood and straw—some iron in you. Let men know that what you say you will do; that your decision, once made, is final—no wavering; that once resolved, you are not to be allured nor intimidated. Acquire and maintain that character.
                        T. F. Buxton.

12,327. YOUTH, Friendship Formed in. In young minds there is commonly a strong propensity to particular intimacies and friendships. Youth, indeed, is the season when friendships are sometimes formed, which not only continue through succeeding life, but which glow to the last with a tenderness unknown to the connections begun in cooler years. The propensity, therefore, is not to be discouraged, though, at the same time, it must be regulated with much circumspection and care.   *Blair.*

12,328. YOUTH, Importance of Turning to God in. Young reader, remember that your youthful sins lay a foundation for aged sorrows; you have but one arrow to shoot at the mark; and if that be shot at random, God may never put another into your bow.   *Secker.*

12,329. YOUTH, Impressions of. The late Dr. Spencer said, that when he was a lad his father gave him a little tree that had just been grafted. One day, in his father's absence, he let the colt into the garden, and the young animal broke off the graf. It was mended, however, on the following day, and continued to grow finely. Years passed, and young Spencer became a man, and a minister. Some time after he became a pastor he made a visit to the old homestead where he spent his boyhood. His little sapling had become a large tree, and was loaded with apples. During the night after his arrival at the homestead, there was a violent thunder-shower, and the wind blew fearfully. He rose early in the morning, and on going out found his tree lying prostrate upon the ground. The wind had twisted it off just where the colt had broken it when it was a sapling. Probably the storm would not have broken it at all, if it had not been broken when it was small. It will usually be found that those who are vicious in manhood dropped a seed of vice in the morning of life; that the fallen youth, who was religiously trained, and has become corrupt, broke off his connection with virtuous ways just where he did a wicked thing in boyhood. Here is a fact to be pondered.   *Teachers' Treasury.*

12,330. YOUTH, Precocious. It is remarkable that there is nothing less promising than, in early youth, a certain full-formed, settled, and as it may be called, adult character. A lad who has, to a degree that excites wonder and admiration, the character and demeanor of an intelligent man of mature age, will probably be that, and nothing more, all his life, and will cease accordingly to be anything remarkable, because it was his precocity alone that ever made him so. It is remarked by greyhound fanciers that a well-formed, compact-shaped puppy never makes a fleet dog. They see more promise in the loose-jointed, awkward, clumsy ones. And even so, there is a kind of crudity and unsettledness in the minds of those young persons who turn out ultimately the most eminent.   *Whately.*

12,331. YOUTH, Religion in. Oh, seek religion now, because this is the molding age. Now, because it is the freest part of your time. Now, because your life is immediately uncertain; you are not certain that you shall attain the years of your fathers; there are graves in the church-yard just of your length, and skulls of all sorts and sizes in Golgotha, as the Jew's proverb is. Now, because God will not spare you on account of your youth, if you die without an interest in Christ. Now, because your life will be the more eminently useful, serviceable to God, when you know him betimes, and early begin this service. Augustin repented, and so have many others since, that he began so late, and knew God no sooner. Now, because your whole life will be happier, if the morning of it is dedicated to the Lord. The first fruits sanctify the whole harvest; this will have a sweet influence upon all your days, whatever changes, straits, or troubles you may meet.   *John Flavel.*

12,332. YOUTH, Renewal of. Some of the South Sea Islanders have a tradition of a river in the world of spirits called the "Water of

Life." It was supposed that the aged, when they died, went and bathed there, and became young again, then returned to earth, to live life over again.

12,333. YOUTH, Season of. Youth is the spring of life; and by this will be determined the glory of summer, the abundance of autumn, the provision of winter. It is the morning of life; and if the Sun of Righteousness does not dispel the moral mists and fogs before noon, the whole day generally remains overspread and gloomy. It is the seed-time; and "what a man soweth, that shall he also reap." Everything of importance is affected by religion in this period of life.　　　　*W. Jay.*

12,334. YOUTH, Thoughtless. A youth thoughtless, when all the happiness of his home forever depends on the chances of an hour! A youth thoughtless, when the career of all his days depends on the opportunity of a moment! A youth thoughtless, when his every act is a foundation-stone of future conduct, and every imagination a fountain of life or death! Be thoughtless in any after years rather than now; though, indeed, there is only one place where a man may be nobly thoughtless—his death-bed. Nothing should ever be left to be done there.　　　　*Ruskin.*

12,335. ZEAL, Apostolic. The zeal of the Apostles was this—they preached publicly and privately; they prayed for all men; they wept to God for the hardness of men's hearts; they became all things to all men, that they might gain some; they traveled through deeps and deserts; they endured the heat of the Syrian star and the violence of Euroclydon, winds and tempests, seas and prisons, mockings and scourgings, fastings and poverty, labor and watching; they endured every man and wronged no man; they would do any good, and suffer any evil, if they had but hopes to prevail upon a soul; they persuaded men meekly, they entreated them humbly, they convinced them powerfully; they watched for their good, but meddled not with their interest: and this is the Christian zeal, the zeal of meekness, the zeal of charity, the zeal of patience.　　　　*Bp. Taylor.*

12,336. ZEAL, Attraction of. Humboldt, the great traveler, says: "It seems remarkable that in the hottest as well as the coldest climates people display the same predilection for heat. On the introduction of Christianity into Iceland, the inhabitants would be baptized only in the hot springs of Hecla; and in the torrid zone, in the plains as well as in the Cordilleras, the natives flock from all parts to the thermal waters." So with the preachers of the gospel. They must have the baptism of fire.

12,337. ZEAL, Christian. Weak in yourselves, but strong in God, go forth on this God-like enterprise; the motto on your banner, the prayer of your heart this wish of Brainerd, "O, that I were a flaming fire in the service of my God."　　　　*Dr. Guthrie.*

12,338. ZEAL, Cruel. King Olaf, of Norway, was the bloody foe of heathenism. He reigned twenty-five years, the scourge and terror of his own people, and never made a friend. Their maimed bodies, burned homes, plundered property, was a perpetual memorial of his merciless zeal. He called to his aid robbers and vagabonds, and enrolled them in his army, requiring only one condition, that they should be baptized in the name of Christ. He had white crosses painted on the shields and helmets of all his soldiers. He gave them for a battle cry, "Forward, Christian men! Crossmen!" With all this his last battle was a sad defeat, in which he was slain in 1030. He justified himself, and his horrible barbarities, by saying, "I had God's honor to defend."

12,339. ZEAL, Demands for Ministerial. Mr. Whitefield preached in Yorkshire, near Haworth; thousands gathered in the fields to hear him preach. A temporary pulpit had been erected, and Whitefield, on ascending it and surveying the vast multitude, who with upturned faces stood ready to hear the words about to fall from his lips, was pervaded with a peculiarly solemn feeling. With uplifted hands he offered a most impressive prayer, invoking the Divine presence and the Divine blessing. Then, in a manner peculiarly solemn, he announced his text, "It is appointed unto men once to die, and after this the judgment." After reading the text he paused for a moment before he proceeded, when suddenly a wild, terrifying shriek issued from the centre of the congregation. At once there was great alarm and confusion. Whitefield requested the people to remain quiet, until the cause could be ascertained. Mr. Grimshaw, leaving the pulpit where had been sitting during the sermon, hurried to the spot, and in a few moments was seen passing toward where Mr. Whitefield stood, exclaiming, "Brother Whitefield, you stand between the dead and the dying! An immortal soul has just passed into eternity; the destroying angel is passing over the congregation; cry aloud and spare not." The solemn event was announced to the awe-struck congregation. After a few moments Mr. Whitefield read his text again, and was about to proceed with his discourse, when another loud and piercing shriek proceeded from near the place where Lady Huntingdon and Lady Margaret Ingham were standing. It fell upon the multitude like the sound of the last trump when they ascertained the cause of this second alarm, that another person had fallen by the hand of death. When the consternation had somewhat subsided, Mr. Whitefield proceeded with his sermon amid the stillness of death and the solemnity of the grave.　　*Dr. J. B. Wakeley.*

12,340. ZEAL, Desire for. I want to see all in a flame of fire. You know what kind of fire I mean. I desire that none of my wild-fire may be mixed with the pure fire of holy zeal coming from God's altar.　　　　*Whitefield.*

12,341. ZEAL, Longing for. Oh that I had so much zeal as to steep it in its own liquor; to set it forth in its own colors; that the seraphim would touch my tongue with a live coal from the divine altar, that I might regain the decayed credit of it with the sons of men! It is good to be zealous in good things; and is it not best in the best? Or is there any better than God? or the kingdom of heaven? *S. Ward.*

12,342. ZEAL, Ministerial. Every Brahmin is required by the shastas to keep alive the fire which consumes the offering on the day of his investment to the day of his death. In the family of Krishna-Chundra Roy, such a fire has been kept burning for seventy years. It is a hard requirement for the poor priests. Christ requires of his ministers that the fire of love for God and souls shall never grow dim or go out.

12,343. ZEAL, Philanthropic. When I think, after the experience of one life, what I could and would do in an amended edition of it; what I could and would do, more and better than I have done, for the cause of humanity, of temperance, and of peace; for breaking the rod of the oppressor; for the higher education of the world, and especially for the higher education of the best part of it—woman: when I think of these things, I feel the Phœnix-spirit glowing within me; I pant, I yearn, for another warfare in behalf of right, in hostility to wrong, where, without furlough, and without going into winter-quarters, I would enlist for another fifty years' campaign, and fight it out for the glory of God and the welfare of man. *Horace Mann.*

12,344. ZEAL, Religious. No man is fervent and zealous as he ought, but he that prefers religion before business, charity before his own ease, the relief of his brother before money, heaven before secular regards, and God before his friend or interest. Which rule is not to be understood absolutely, and in particular instances, but always generally; and when it descends to particulars it must be in proportion to circumstances, and by their proper measures. *Jeremy Taylor.*

12,345. ZEAL, Sacrifice to. St. Almachus was so filled with sorrow at the thought of so many souls damned forever through the gladiatorial shows, that he visited Rome to stop them. He rushed into the amphitheatre where men were slaying each other for the amusement of others, remonstrated with them, and tried to prevent the worse than useless effusion of blood. He was struck down and torn asunder because of his benevolent attempt. The emperor Honorius made his death the occasion of the entire abolition of the gladiatorial shows. His death accomplished what his life failed to do. He died January 1st, 404.

12,346. ZEAL, Success of. Bishop Latimer was not such a deeply read scholar as Cranmer or Ridley. He could not quote fathers from memory as they did. He refused to be drawn into arguments about antiquity. He stuck to his Bible. Yet it is not too much to say that no English reformer made such a lasting impression on the nation as old Latimer did. And

what was the reason? His simple zeal. Baxter, the Puritan, was not equal to some of his contemporaries in intellectual gifts. It is no disparagement to say that he does not stand on a level with Manton or Owen. Yet few men probably exercised so wide an influence on the generation in which he lived. And what was the reason? His burning zeal. Whitefield, and Wesley, and Berridge, and Venn, were inferior in mental attainments to Bishops Butler and Watson. But they produced effects on the people in this country which fifty Butlers and Watsons would probably never have produced. They saved the Church of England from ruin. And what was one secret of their power? Their zeal. *Ryle.*

12,347. ZEAL, True. The true and godly zeal eateth and devoureth up the heart, even as the thing that is eaten is turned into the substance of him that eateth it; and as iron, while it is burning hot, is turned into the nature of the fire, so great and so just is the grief that they which have this zeal conceive when they see God's house spoiled or his holy name dishonored. *Bp. Jewell.*

12,348. ZION, Mount. Mount Zion was one of the heights on which Jerusalem was built. It stood near Mount Moriah, where Abraham offered up Isaac to the Lord, and witnessed that greatest triumph of human faith; and centuries afterwards, when the temple covered the summit of the former, it formed the heart and strength of the city. Situated at the southern extremity, it rose above every other part of Jerusalem, and came in time to stand for the city itself. At first it seems strange that Zion should have become a word filled with such endearing associations to the Jews. They could never let it go from them when speaking of their city. If her strength as a fortress was spoken of, the language was—"Walk about Zion, and go round about her; tell the towers thereof: mark ye well her bulwarks, and consider her palaces;" if her elevation, it was—"The holy hill of Zion." God's affection for it was thus expressed—"He loveth the gates of Zion;" "The Lord hath chosen Zion." Occupied by the son of Jesse, it became "The city of David," the representative of all that was dear and cherished in Israel. Thus everything conspired to render "Zion" the spell-word of the nation, and on its summit the heart of Israel seemed to lie and throb. But at length it was visited by misfortune and ruin, and the eagles of Cæsar took the place of the banner of David. Now the plough-share is driven over the top of Zion. Where its towers and palaces stood, grain waves in the passing wind, or ruins, overlying each other, attest the truth of the Word of God. The Arab spurs his steed along the forsaken streets, or scornfully stands on Mount Zion, and surveys the forsaken city of God. *Headley.*

TOPICAL INDEX.

Reference is always made to the illustrations by number. The numbers refer to synonymous or related general subjects, or to scattered illustrations of the topic in the Index. A dash between two numbers indicates that all between them are referred to. This volume begins with number 6276.

HARMONY, J347. 6887. 8066–8068. 11266. 12113–12?20.

HARSHNESS, 10095. 7668–7677. 11609.

HARVEST, 9348. 6636. 10217. 11809. 11900. 11901.

HASTE, 9349. 9350. 6919. 7074. 8086. 8100. 9795–9798. 10586. 10886. 12154.

HATRED, 9351–9353. 6942. 8358. 10376. 10720. 7256. 8380. 8085.

HEAD, 9354.

HEALING, 9355. 11680.

HEALTH, 9356–9359. 6886. 6990. 10148.

HEARERS, 9360–9367.

HEARING, 9368–9378. 9142. 9279. 6624. 6625.

HEART, 9379–9413. 6379. 6380. 7110. 7146. 7214. 7905. 8962. 9344. 9512. 10108.

HEAT, 9414. 8741–8744. 8776. 12342.

HEATHEN, 9415. 8117. 9731–9735.

HEATHENISM, 9416. 9417. 6375. 8274. 11866–11868. 9731–9738. 10586–10607.

HEAVEN, 9418–9496. 6600. 6601. 6759. 6760. 7128. 7309. 7466. 7830. 7964. 8372. 8981. 8982. 9561. 10738.

HELL, 9497–9516. 7739. 8139. 9450. 9503. 9866. 9970. 9971. 10041–10062. 12020.

HELP, 9517–9523. 8733. 10003. 10253. 11870–11872. 10089–10103.

HELPLESSNESS, 8200. 9826. 12208–12211.

HERESY, 9524. 9525. 6826.

HERITAGE, 7205. 7254. 8445. 8713. 9173. 10034. 11032. 8827. 10110. 10111.

HERMITS, 9526. 6777. 9124. 9526. 11763–11765.

HERO, 9527. 9528. 9246. 11522. 12287.

HEROISM, 9529–9533. 6918. 8214. 8346 9137. 10654.

HESITATION, 9534. 9842. 9843. 9978–9980. 8141. 8142. 9837–9839.

HIDING PLACES, 9535. 11531. 11357–11360.

HIGH PRIEST, 6573–6575. 9552. 12265. 6276.

HIGHER LIFE, 9536. 7724. 7224. 7408. 11816. 12064. 8013–8029.

HIGHWAY, 9537. 9470.

HISTORY, 9538. 9539. 7006. 8908. 10235. 11328.

HOBBY, 9540. 11040.

HOLINESS, 9541–9551. 6864–6873. 9401–9403. 9451. 9896. 11303. 11304. 11580. 11581.

HOLY OF HOLIES, 9552.

HOLY SPIRIT, 9553–9568. 6609. 7233. 7556–7569. 7916. 8716. 8954. 10937. 11042. 11083. 11720.

HOME, 9569–9579. 8201. 9642. 9643. 8639–8647. 10649–10655. 10890–10898.

HONESTY, 9580–9596. 6699. 6962. 9918–9926. 9942. 9943. 12237.

HONOR, 9597–9610. 6390. 6477. 6705. 7217. 7413. 7658–7663. 7936. 8331. 8625–8637. 9020. 9119. 9452. 9582. 9668. 10491. 11084.

HONORING THE LORD, 9611. 8368. 9176. 10546. 12103.

HOPE, 9612–9630. 6478–6482. 6665. 7290. 7648. 8509. 11465. 11734.

HOPELESSNESS, 7983–7990. 9453. 9703. 9872.

HORSE, 9631. 6515. 6518.

HOSPITALITY, 9632–9638. 7176. 9910.

HOSPITALS, 9639.

HOURS, 9640. 9641. 11979–11997.

HOUSEHOLD, 9642. 9643. 8641–8647. 9569–9579. 10890–10898.

HOUSE, 9644. 9645. 9569–9579.

HUMANITY, 9646–9652. 6945–6948. 7238. 9140 10379–10404. 10978. 11805.

HUMAN NATURE, 9653–9656. 10378–10404.

HUMBUG, 10547.

HUMILIATION, 9657. 9658. 8459. 10006. 10112. 9258–9268. 11767–11771.

HUMILITY, 9658–9683. 7806. 8059. 8925. 9026. 9245. 10466–10468. 11754.

HUNGER, 9684. 9685. 6926–6930. 7052. 8654. 11118. 11037. 11038.

HUSBAND, 9686–9690. 10412–10432. 12228–12231. 9642. 9643.

HYPOCHONDRIAC, 9691. 9775. 10469. 10633.

HYPOCRISY, 9692–9699. 7262. 7446. 7906. 8708. 10994. 11220. 11674.

HYPOCRITES, 9700–9709.

IDEA, 6932. 7314. 11964–11976.

IDEAL, 9710. 9711. 9136.

IDEALISM, 9712. 9773–9777.

IDIOSYNCRASY, 9713. 9714. 6988. 7068. 10387. 8265. 11040.

IDLENESS, 9715–9730. 9846. 9847. 10542. 10753. 8259, 8260. 11749.

IDOLATRY, 9731–9735. 6519. 7097. 9385. 9415–9417. 11633. 9128–9162.

IDOLS, 9736–9738.

IF, 9739. 8192. 7627–7631.

IGNORANCE, 9740–9749. 6787. 6788. 6789. 6824. 7308. 7528. 7724. 7727. 8536. 9733. 9915. 10127. 10672–10675.

ILLIBERALITY, 9750–9752. 6638–6654. 7055. 11646. 7595–7606.

ILLS, 9753–9755. 8450. 8451. 9911–9914. 11680–11684. 10578–10584.

ILLUSTRATIONS, 9756–9772. 6437. 6483–6486. 7135. 8542–8548. 8740. 10868–10871. 11260. 11664.

IMAGINATION, 9773–9777. 7088. 7784. 9712. 10724. 9710–9712.

IMITATION, 9778–9780. 7133. 8460–8483. 8661. 8820. 9692–9709. 10921. 8768. 8769.

IMMENSITY, 9781. 7617. 9883. 10510. 10795.

IMMORTALITY, 9782–9793. 6955. 7152. 8218. 8416–8433. 8903–8913. 9123. 9491. 10388 11772–11862.

IMMUTABILITY, 9794. 9028. 9071.

IMPATIENCE, 9795–9798. 10529. 6496–6514. 8680. 8861–8864. 9976.

IMPERFECTIONS, 9799–9802. 8203. 8793. 9711. 10548. 10607. 10608. 9884.

IMPIETY, 9803. 9805. 11560. 11606–11608.

IMPOSSIBILITY, 9806. 9807. 8364–8367.

IMPRACTICABLE, 9808. 9820. 10131. 11832.

IMPRECATIONS, 9809. 9810. 6613. 6840–6843 11210–11215. 7691–7696.

IMPRESSIONS, 9811–9814. 11162. 11163.

IMPRISONMENT, 9815. 9816. 7201. 7407. 7900. 11191.

IMPROVEMENT, 9817–9819. 11223–11229. 7678–7681.

IMPROVIDENCE, 9820. 9821. 8529–8531. 11208 11209. 11813. 11996.

IMPUDENCE, 9822. 9823. 6586–6589.

NOBODY, 10750.
NON-RESISTANCE, 10751. 10752.
NOTHING, 10753.
NOVELS, 10754-10755. 8019. 8730.
NOVELTY, 10756. 10757. 7022. 9149 10958. 7687-7690.
NOW, 10758. 10759. 10620. 11160-11163 12001-12003. 7627-7631.

OATHS, 10760. 10761. 9313. 10951. 10952. 11210-11215.
OBEDIENCE, 10762-10779. 6377. 6805. 7448. 8082-8084. 8584.
OBJECTIONS, 6771. 6795. 7170. 7236. 7977. 9819. 11108. 8491-8499.
OBLIGATION, 10780. 8186-8215. 8887. 11439-11441.
OBLIVION, 10781. 11364. 8792. 8793. 6284. 8067. 9043. 9361. 9912. 9913.
OBSCURITY, 10782. 9949. 9930.
OBSERVATIONS, 10783. 10784. 7234. 8105. 8300. 10254. 11817.
OBSERVERS, 10785. 8784. 11960. 11961.
OBSTINACY, 10786. 10787. 7463. 8745-8748. 10396. 12104. 12232. 12326.
OBSTRUCTION, 10788. 6281. 6850. 7173. 8033-8036. 9090. 9138. 11518. 10532.
OBSTRUCTIONIST, 10789. 7012. 7285. 10835.
OCCUPATION, 10790-10794. 6426. 6427. 6958-6973. 8332-8338. 9850-9856.
OCEAN, 10795. 11618. 11619.
OFFENSE, 10796. 10797. 11281. 11282. 7380. 7381.
OFFERINGS, 10798-10800. 6957. 10456. 10948. 11735. 11553-11559. 6444-6446.
OFFICE, 10801. 10802. 6454. 6632. 6633.
OFFICE SEEKERS, 10803. 6460. 8362.
OLD, 10804. 6413-6418.
OLD AGE, 10805-10810. 6413-6423. 6473. 7023. 7031. 7312. 9178. 10251. 10531. 11980.
OLD TESTAMENT, 12099-12101.
OMNIPOTENCE, 10811-10813. 9047. 9060.
OMNIPRESENCE, 10814-10817. 7112. 7174. 8993. 9048. 9644. 10011. 11594. 11976.
OMNISCIENCE, 10818-10823. 7126. 8992. 9014. 9049-9051. 8989-9077.
OPINIONS, 10824-10827. 6317. 10640.
OPPORTUNITY, 10828-10833. 7532. 7737. 7941-7948. 8128. 9205. 11996. 12001-12003.
OPPOSER, 10834. 10789.
OPPOSITION, 10835-10837. 6776. 6783. 10953-10963.
OPPRESSION, 10838. 10879. 8122-8124. 11745.
OPPRESSOR, 10840.
ORATOR, 10841. 10842.
ORATORY, 10843-10846. 8322-8328. 11811. 11836-11838. 11812.
ORDEAL, 10847. 8743. 8790. 11866. 6482. 6609. 7265. 12041-12049.
ORDER, 10848-10850. 6603. 10991. 11380. 10172-10187. 10517-10519.
ORDINANCES, 10851. 6683-6685. 10309-10313.
ORGANIZATION, 10852.
ORIGINALITY, 10853. 10854. 6904. 11139. 11660.
ORNAMENTS, 10855-10857. 6341-6343. 8162. 10094. 11188. 12134.
ORPHANS, 10858.
OSTENTATION, 10859. 10860. 8785. 10931.

OTHERS, 10861. 10862. 8494. 8687.
OWNERSHIP, 11032-11034. 6989. 9473.

PAIN, 10863. 11096. 11848-11851. 12020.
PAINE, THOMAS, 6304. 9865. 10268.
PAINTERS, 10864. 10478. 11006. 11157.
PALM TREE, 10865.
PANTHEISM, 10866. 10867.
PARABLES, 10868-10871. 9770.
PARADISE, 10872-10881. 6453. 8329.
PARDON, 10882-10889. 7122. 7393-7399 7954. 8794-8812. 9158. 9172-9206. 10085-10087. 11418.
PARENTS, 10890-10898. 6474-6477. 7097. 7732. 9892. 10774. 10649-10655.
PARKER, THEODORE, 7438. 9893. 10471. 12089.
PARSIMONY, 9750-9752. 10935.
PARTING, 10899. 8877. 8814.
PARTNER, 10900. 11105.
PARTNERSHIP, 10901. 8603.
PASSIONS, 10902-10906. 6496-6514. 9409. 9825. 9976. 11914-11916. 12201.
PASSOVER, 10907. 6871.
PAST, 10908. 10909. 11482.
PASTOR, 10910-10914. 10553. 11109. 12172.
PATIENCE, 10915-10918. 8056. 8824-8826. 8346-8348. 12176. 12177.
PATRIOTISM, 10919. 10920. 8212. 8348.
PATTERNS, 10921. 8460-8483. 9710. 9773-9780. 10230. 11048-11051.
PEACE, 10922-10929. 8464. 8561. 11316-11318. 11443-11450. 7376.
PEARLS, 10930. 8030. 8031.
PEDANTRY, 10931. 11114.
PEEVISHNESS, 10932. 11306-11314. 11914-11916. 9976. 8861-8864.
PEN, 10933. 9899. 10200. 11884.
PENALTY, 10777. 11294-11300.
PENANCE, 10934. 10935.
PENITENCE, 10936. 6674. 7488. 11399-11415. 6614. 11631.
PENTECOST, 10937. 11044. 12013. 9553-9568.
PENURIOUSNESS, 10938. 10573. 10574. 10448 10377. 6638-6654. 7595-7606.
PEOPLE, 10939. 10443.
PERFECTION, 10940-10947. 7026. 7231. 8484-8487. 8500. 9077. 11827.
PERFUMES, 10948. 10007. 10798. 11821.
PERIL, 10949. 7705-7725. 8201. 11165. 11724. 8414. 11592-12074.
PERISHING, 10950. 10319-10322. 11203-11207 11429. 11430. 11565-11579.
PERJURY, 10951. 10952. 11474.
PERSECUTION, 10953-10963. 6776. 6783. 7132. 7660. 9927. 10433-10442. 10837.
PERSEVERANCE, 10964-10974. 6951. 7576 8215. 8343. 9817-9819. 10912. 11799. 11801. 11846.
PERSONAL EFFORT, 10975. 10976. 6323. 7040 8125-8134. 8303-8308. 9975. 10964-10974 11796-11807. 12171.
PESTILENCE, 6568. 9888.
PETER, 10977. 11410. 11668.
PHILANTHROPY, 10978. 6945-6948. 7238 9140 9649-9652. 8865-8876.
PHILOSOPHY, 10979-10984. 11605.
PHOTOGRAPHY, 10985. 7033. 9134. 10487 11067. 11737.

SABBATH, 11542–11546. 11857–11859.
SABBATH-BREAKERS, 11547. 11548.
SABBATH-BREAKING, 11549–11551.
SACRAMENT, 11552. 7349–7352. 10309–10313.
SACRIFICE, 11553–11559. 6863–6873. 6957.
  8962. 10861. 10862. 10798–10800. 10993.
  11593. 12126.
SACRILEGE, 11560. 9802–9805. 10554. 11919.
  6840–6843. 11164–11168.
SAFETY, 11561. 6445. 6478–6482. 6984. 7226.
  11256. 11257. 7950–7954. 11624. 11625.
SAINTS, 11562–11564. 10423–10442. 8013–
  8029. 9441–9551. 11816.
SALVATION, 11565–11579. 6300. 6613–6622.
  6815. 7685. 7686. 11592. 11723. 31964–
  11976.
SANCTIFICATION, 11580. 71581. 6864–6873.
  7923. 9541–9551. 10085. 11303. 11304.
SARDIS, 11582.
SATAN, 11583–11589. 6534. 8003–8012. 9512.
  11237. 11922–11933. 12197–12203.
SATIETY, 11590. 11591. 6540. 8097–8102.
  8381. 9604. 8044–8046.
SATISFACTION, 7181. 7367. 7441–7485. 7860.
SAVED, 11592. 12074. 7546–7555.
SAVIOUR, 11593–11596. 8857. 9125.
SCANDAL, 11597–11599. 6974. 7998–8000.
  10307. 10308. 9163. 9164.
SCAPE-GOAT, 11600. 11844.
SCARS, 11601. 8624. 11701. 11725.
SCEPTICS, 11602. 11603. 11606–11608. 11702.
  10675. 12102–12106. 9862–9882.
SCHEMES, 11604. 10998. 10999.
SCHOOLS, 8292. 11653. 11904–11909.
SCIENCE, 11605. 7243. 8122. 8950. 10138.
  10979–10984. 11095. 10190–10196.
SCOFFERS, 11606–11608. 6603–6612. 9803–
  9805. 9862–9882.
SCOLDING, 11609. 8688. 8099. 7014. 9276.
  10541. 10550. 10642. 8861–8864.
SCORPION, 11610.
SCOURGING, 7183. 7187.
SCRIPTURES, 11611–11617. 6761–6826. 9931.
  9932. 11942–11944.
SEA, 11618.
SEAL, 11620.
SEASON, 11621. 11143. 11276. 11817–11821.
  12269. 10828–10833.
SEA VOYAGE, 11619.
SECRETS, 11622. 11689. 11740. 11892. 11893.
SECTS, 11623. 6827. 6828. 7962–7965. 9431.
SECURITY. 11624. 11625. 8594. 6468–6482.
  6984. 7950–7954. 11561.
SEED, 11626–11630. 8450. 9159. 12270.
SEEKING THE LORD, 11631. 6300. 7106–7109.
  7184. 7203. 7263. 7393–7399. 7505–7545.
  7911. 10001.
SELF, 11632. 11633. 6635. 7476. 7908. 8279.
  11634–11652. 8309–8312.
SELF-CONCEIT, 11634. 6549. 8309–8312. 6562–
  6565.
SELF-CONTROL, 11635. 11636. 6496–6514. 8092.
  8502. 8786. 8404.
SELF-ESTEEM, 11637. 12137–12146. 10513–
  10516.
SELF-EXAMINATION, 11638–11643. 6496. 11161.
SELF-IMPORTANCE, 11644. 8309–8312. 6586–
  6589.

SELFISHNESS, 11645–11647. 6565. 8085. 8662
  9061. 9138. 9637. 10318. 11648. 11652.
SELF-KNOWLEDGE, 7888. 12273.
SELF-LOVE, 11648. 9848.
SELF-REFORMATION, 11649. 6463. 11351–11356.
SELF-RESPECT, 11650. 10491. 11437.
SELF-RIGHTEOUSNESS, 11651. 9109. 9124–9127
  10513–10516. 11525. 10636.
SELF-SEEKING, 11652. 8310. 8768. 12307.
SENSE, 11653. 10724. 6278–6282. 6982–6988.
SENSIBILITY, 8714–8723. 8490.
SEPARATION, 11654. 7283. 7299. 8647. 10062.
  10899. 12285. 8112. 8113.
SERIOUSNESS, 11655. 10269. 11789.
SERMONS, 11656–11668. 8244. 8479. 9756–
  9772. 10536–10558. 11112–11117.
SERVANT, 11669. 6899. 10989. 12011. 12282.
SERVICE, 11670. 11671. 11765. 12271.
SHADOW, 11672.
SHAME, 11673. 6958. 7607. 11692.
SHAMS, 11674. 6586–6588. 8844. 9692–9709.
SHEEP, 11675. 10165. 11676. 11677.
SHEPHERD, 11676. 11677. 6799. 7549. 10165.
  10911. 11675.
SHIELD, 8595. 11256. 11257.
SHOES, 11678. 8724. 8725.
SICK, 11679. 11680. 9639. 8074.
SICKNESS, 11681–11684. 6399. 8074. 9285.
  9356–9359. 11113. 9753–9755.
SIGHT, 11685–11687. 6853–6861. 8533–8540.
  10280–10290.
SILENCE, 11688. 11689. 6513. 7709. 10215.
  10928. 11812. 11892. 11893.
SIMPLICITY, 9251. 9147. 10997. 11127. 11134.
SIN, 11692–11725. 6689. 6711. 6715. 6756.
  6757. 7409–7438. 7574–7578. 7623–7626.
  7728–7731. 7931. 7970–7977. 8439–8450.
  9035. 9201. 10296. 10299. 12153–12156.
  11729–11740.
SINCERITY, 11726. 11727. 7907. 8623. 11111.
SINGING, 11728. 6398. 6515. 7060. 7209. 10664–
  10671. 11052–11060.
SINNERS, 11729–11734. 6310. 7216. 8772.
  12220–12227. 7623–7626.
SIN-OFFERING, 11735. 6899. 7310. 9279–9289.
SINS, 11736–11740. 6578. 7652. 11750.
SLANDER, 11741–11744. 6309. 6534. 6660–
  6662. 6977–6982. 8454. 11597–11599. 12014.
SLAVERY, 11745. 6829. 6899. 6991. 8167.
  9286. 10906. 8330 8369. 8845–8848. 10205–
  10211.
SLEEP, 11746–11748. 8233. 8234.
SLOTH, 11749. 7223. 9715–9730. 7386. 9846.
  9847. 8259. 8260.
SMALL SINS, 11750. 8736. 9885. 10296. 10299.
SMALL THINGS, 11751. 7436. 8341. 9848. 12050.
  12051. 10611. 7046.
SMILE, 11752. 7060–7066.
SMOKING, 11753. 11999. 12000.
SNARES, 11754. 7324. 11589. 11717. 11583.
  11922–11938. 6440–6442.
SNEERING, 11755. 6297. 6298. 9987. 9988.
SNOW, 11756. 9420.
SOCIETY, 11757. 11758. 6579–6585. 6905. 6911.
  7353–7362. 8727. 8865–8892. 12320.
SOLDIERS, 11759–11762. 9494. 10919. 6561.
  6687. 6688. 12181–12188.
SOLITUDE, 11763–11765. 7225. 6577. 9526.

Solomon, 11766. 6540. 8526.

Sorrow, 11767–11771. 6353–6356. 6381–6412. 7486–7488. 8048–8056. 9258–9268. 11848–11851. 12062–12067.

Soul, 11772–11802. 6400. 6478–6482. 6884. 6893. 6955. 7440. 7717. 7869. 8779. 8903–8913. 9748. 9782–9793. 10523. 11100.

Soul Saving, 11803–11807. 6429. 7505–7545. 7744. 8028. 8147. 8303–8308. 9172–9206. 9973–9975. 10093. 10913. 10950. 10975. 10976. 11116. 11492–11496. 11796–11802.

Sowing, 11808. 11809. 9348. 11900. 11901.

Sparrows, 11810. 8610.

Speaking, 11811. 6932–6934. 9163. 9164. 8323–8328. 10841–10846.

Speech, 11812. 7493–7504. 12266–12270.

Spendthrifts, 11813. 11996. 8529–8531. 9820. 9821. 11208. 11209.

Spirit, 11814. 11815. 9007. 9032. 9560–9565. 9782–9793. 11772–11802.

Spirituality, 11816. 7145. 9046. 9423. 11971. 12309. 8013–8029. 9078–9086.

Spring, 11817–11820. 9628

Sprinkling, 11821.

Spurgeon, Charles H., 11845.

Stability, 11822. 7551. 11761. 11762. 7462. 7463. 8745–8748.

Stealing, 11823. 11824. 8076–8079. 8844. 9280. 9596. 11956. 11994.

Stewards, 11825. 11894.

Stones, 11826. 8748. 9408. 11921.

Stoning, 11827.

Storms, 11828. 8760.

Strife, 11829. 11830. 10922–10929. 11288. 7468–7470. 8738. 8739. 11306–11314.

Study, 11831. 11832. 6807. 6920. 8103. 8236. 8272–8298. 8937. 10115–10143. 10741.

Stupidity, 11833–11835. 6920. 7856. 8032. 8183. 10380. 9826. 8781–8783.

Style, 11836–11838. 7848. 12266. 12270.

Submission, 11839–11843. 6311. 7380. 7381. 7441–7447. 8221. 11098. 11431–11434. 11532. 11876–11879.

Substitute, 11844. 6618. 7138. 9158. 9288. 11300. 11600. 7885. 9686.

Success, 11845–11847. 6430. 6831. 6967. 7040. 8553. 8951. 9153. 9252–9254. 9593. 10357–10359. 10964–10974. 11247–11255. 12324.

Sudden Conversion, 7233. 7515–7540. 7545. 7586. 9195. 9558.

Suffering, 11848-11851. 6381–6412. 6529. 6896. 7639. 8347. 8824–8826.

Suicide, 11852. 11853. 8466. 10615.

Sun, 11854. 11855. 7297. 9445. 10281–10290. 11864. 8261. 11856.

Sunbeam, 11856.

Sunday, 11857–11859. 11542–11550.

Sunday-school, 11860–11863. 6917. 7086. 11904–11909.

Sunset, 11864. 8435.

Superintendence, 11865.

Superstition, 11866–11869. 7459. 7626. 8578. 8728. 8729. 9257. 9509. 10986.

Supplies, 8594. 12178. 8773–8780.

Support, 11870–11872. 6401. 6402. 6722. 7217. 7402. 8621. 9174. 9629. 12208–12211.

Surety, 11873. 7137. 11299 6613–6622. 11343–11348. 11844.

Suretyship, 11874.

Surprise, 11875. 7881. 11937. 12154.

Surrender, 11876–11879. 7206. 11839–11843. 11399–11415. 7441. 7448.

Suspense, 11880. 8136–8143. 9842. 9843.

Suspicion, 11881. 10610. 11250. 6309.

Swearer, 11882. 11883. 11210.–11215. 6840–6843.

Sword, 11884. 10185. 11743. 12181–12188.

Sympathy, 11885–11890. 6976. 7319. 7363–7366. 7487. 8408. 11023. 11939. 12254.

Tabernacle, 11891.

Taciturnity, 11892. 11893. 11688. 11689.

Talents, 11894–11899. 6986–6988. 7170. 8955–8962. 8549. 10523–10534.

Tares, 11900. 11901. 11809.

Taste, 11902. 6988.

Taxes, 11903. 11002. 12183.

Teacher, 11904–11908. 7191. 9237. 10714.

Teaching, 11909. 8483. 9937. 11416. 11417. 6624. 6625. 8272–8298.

Tears, 11910. 7366. 7778.

Telegraph, 11911. 11912. 10291.

Temerity, 11913. 11164–11168.

Temper, 11914–11916. 6496–6514. 8066–8068. 8087–8089. 9112. 9976. 10932.

Temperance, 11917. 11918. 6288–6293. 8166–8181. 9950–9958. 11230.

Temple, 11919–11921. 6892. 9393. 9644. 9991. 10399. 11791.

Temptation, 11922–11938. 6514. 7546. 7872. 9096. 10810. 11583–11589.

Tenderness, 11939. 10165. 12331. 7363–7366.

Terror, 11940. 11941. 7873. 8691–8707. 8839.

Testament, 11942–11944. 12099–12101. 12095.

Tests, 6482. 6609. 6817. 6971. 7059. 7231. 7247. 7248. 7265. 8055. 8940. 10847. 11902. 12041–12049.

Thankfulness, 11945–11948. 9215–9222.

Thanksgiving, 11949–11951. 7193. 8780. 11052–11060. 6398. 11728

Theatre, 11952–11955. 6468. 6472. 8375. 8927.

Theft, 11956. 8076–8079. 11823. 11824. 11994.

Theology, 11957. 11958. 8115–8121. 8989–9077. 9524. 9525.

Things, 11959. 6941. 7894. 9413. 8436. 8547. 8548. 6313–6322.

Thinkers, 11960. 11961. 8784. 9233–9240.

Thirst, 11962. 12205–12207.

Thoroughness, 11963. 6308. 8135. 8456.

Thoughtlessness, 12331. 6284. 6294.

Thoughts, 11964–11976. 6583. 6904–6912. 8937. 9395. 10107. 10395. 10783–10785. 10947. 11350. 11960. 11961.

Threats, 11977. 9067. 10765.

Threshing, 11978.

Time, 11979-11997. 7735–7738. 7834. 8037–8041. 8234–8237. 9263. 9640. 9641. 10217. 10807. 11672. 10568. 10569. 10621. 10684

Tithes, 11998. 7443.

Tobacco, 11999. 12000. 10649. 11753.